# A₂ ALTITUDE CORRECTION TABLES 10°–90°—SUN, STARS, PLANETS

## OCT.—MAR. SUN APR.—SEPT.

| App. Alt. | Lower Limb | Upper Limb | App. Alt. | Lower Limb | Upper Limb |
|---|---|---|---|---|---|
| ° ′ | ′ | ′ | ° ′ | ′ | ′ |
| 9 33 | +10·8 | −21·5 | 9 39 | +10·6 | −21·2 |
| 9 45 | +10·9 | −21·4 | 9 50 | +10·7 | −21·1 |
| 9 56 | +11·0 | −21·3 | 10 02 | +10·8 | −21·0 |
| 10 08 | +11·1 | −21·2 | 10 14 | +10·9 | −20·9 |
| 10 20 | +11·2 | −21·1 | 10 27 | +11·0 | −20·8 |
| 10 33 | +11·3 | −21·0 | 10 40 | +11·1 | −20·7 |
| 10 46 | +11·4 | −20·9 | 10 53 | +11·2 | −20·6 |
| 11 00 | +11·5 | −20·8 | 11 07 | +11·3 | −20·5 |
| 11 15 | +11·6 | −20·7 | 11 22 | +11·4 | −20·4 |
| 11 30 | +11·7 | −20·6 | 11 37 | +11·5 | −20·3 |
| 11 45 | +11·8 | −20·5 | 11 53 | +11·6 | −20·2 |
| 12 01 | +11·9 | −20·4 | 12 10 | +11·7 | −20·1 |
| 12 18 | +12·0 | −20·3 | 12 27 | +11·8 | −20·0 |
| 12 36 | +12·1 | −20·2 | 12 45 | +11·9 | −19·9 |
| 12 54 | +12·2 | −20·1 | 13 04 | +12·0 | −19·8 |
| 13 14 | +12·3 | −20·0 | 13 24 | +12·1 | −19·7 |
| 13 34 | +12·4 | −19·9 | 13 44 | +12·2 | −19·6 |
| 13 55 | +12·5 | −19·8 | 14 06 | +12·3 | −19·5 |
| 14 17 | +12·6 | −19·7 | 14 29 | +12·4 | −19·4 |
| 14 41 | +12·7 | −19·6 | 14 53 | +12·5 | −19·3 |
| 15 05 | +12·8 | −19·5 | 15 18 | +12·6 | −19·2 |
| 15 31 | +12·9 | −19·4 | 15 45 | +12·7 | −19·1 |
| 15 59 | +13·0 | −19·3 | 16 13 | +12·8 | −19·0 |
| 16 27 | +13·1 | −19·2 | 16 43 | +12·9 | −18·9 |
| 16 58 | +13·2 | −19·1 | 17 14 | +13·0 | −18·8 |
| 17 30 | +13·3 | −19·0 | 17 47 | +13·1 | −18·7 |
| 18 05 | +13·4 | −18·9 | 18 23 | +13·2 | −18·6 |
| 18 41 | +13·5 | −18·8 | 19 00 | +13·3 | −18·5 |
| 19 20 | +13·6 | −18·7 | 19 41 | +13·4 | −18·4 |
| 20 02 | +13·7 | −18·6 | 20 24 | +13·5 | −18·3 |
| 20 46 | +13·8 | −18·5 | 21 10 | +13·6 | −18·2 |
| 21 34 | +13·9 | −18·4 | 21 59 | +13·7 | −18·1 |
| 22 25 | +14·0 | −18·3 | 22 52 | +13·8 | −18·0 |
| 23 20 | +14·1 | −18·2 | 23 49 | +13·9 | −17·9 |
| 24 20 | +14·2 | −18·1 | 24 51 | +14·0 | −17·8 |
| 25 24 | +14·3 | −18·0 | 25 58 | +14·1 | −17·7 |
| 26 34 | +14·4 | −17·9 | 27 11 | +14·2 | −17·6 |
| 27 50 | +14·5 | −17·8 | 28 31 | +14·3 | −17·5 |
| 29 13 | +14·6 | −17·7 | 29 58 | +14·4 | −17·4 |
| 30 44 | +14·7 | −17·6 | 31 33 | +14·5 | −17·3 |
| 32 24 | +14·8 | −17·5 | 33 18 | +14·6 | −17·2 |
| 34 15 | +14·9 | −17·4 | 35 15 | +14·7 | −17·1 |
| 36 17 | +15·0 | −17·3 | 37 24 | +14·8 | −17·0 |
| 38 34 | +15·1 | −17·2 | 39 48 | +14·9 | −16·9 |
| 41 06 | +15·2 | −17·1 | 42 28 | +15·0 | −16·8 |
| 43 56 | +15·3 | −17·0 | 45 29 | +15·1 | −16·7 |
| 47 07 | +15·4 | −16·9 | 48 52 | +15·2 | −16·6 |
| 50 43 | +15·5 | −16·8 | 52 41 | +15·3 | −16·5 |
| 54 46 | +15·6 | −16·7 | 56 59 | +15·4 | −16·4 |
| 59 21 | +15·7 | −16·6 | 61 50 | +15·5 | −16·3 |
| 64 28 | +15·8 | −16·5 | 67 15 | +15·6 | −16·2 |
| 70 10 | +15·9 | −16·4 | 73 14 | +15·7 | −16·1 |
| 76 24 | +16·0 | −16·3 | 79 42 | +15·8 | −16·0 |
| 83 05 | +16·1 | −16·2 | 86 31 | +15·9 | −15·9 |
| 90 00 | | | 90 00 | | |

## STARS AND PLANETS

| App. Alt. | Corrⁿ |
|---|---|
| ° ′ | ′ |
| 9 55 | −5·3 |
| 10 07 | −5·2 |
| 10 20 | −5·1 |
| 10 32 | −5·0 |
| 10 46 | −4·9 |
| 10 59 | −4·8 |
| 11 14 | −4·7 |
| 11 29 | −4·6 |
| 11 44 | −4·5 |
| 12 00 | −4·4 |
| 12 17 | −4·3 |
| 12 35 | −4·2 |
| 12 53 | −4·1 |
| 13 12 | −4·0 |
| 13 32 | −3·9 |
| 13 53 | −3·8 |
| 14 16 | −3·7 |
| 14 39 | −3·6 |
| 15 03 | −3·5 |
| 15 29 | −3·4 |
| 15 56 | −3·3 |
| 16 25 | −3·2 |
| 16 55 | −3·1 |
| 17 27 | −3·0 |
| 18 01 | −2·9 |
| 18 37 | −2·8 |
| 19 16 | −2·7 |
| 19 56 | −2·6 |
| 20 40 | −2·5 |
| 21 27 | −2·4 |
| 22 17 | −2·3 |
| 23 11 | −2·2 |
| 24 09 | −2·1 |
| 25 12 | −2·0 |
| 26 20 | −1·9 |
| 27 34 | −1·8 |
| 28 54 | −1·7 |
| 30 22 | −1·6 |
| 31 58 | −1·5 |
| 33 43 | −1·4 |
| 35 38 | −1·3 |
| 37 45 | −1·2 |
| 40 06 | −1·1 |
| 42 42 | −1·0 |
| 45 34 | −0·9 |
| 48 45 | −0·8 |
| 52 16 | −0·7 |
| 56 09 | −0·6 |
| 60 26 | −0·5 |
| 65 06 | −0·4 |
| 70 09 | −0·3 |
| 75 32 | −0·2 |
| 81 12 | −0·1 |
| 87 03 | 0·0 |
| 90 00 | |

### App. Alt. — Additional Corrⁿ

**2022**

**VENUS**

Jan. 1–Jan. 6
Jan. 11–Jan. 29

| ° ′ | ′ |
|---|---|
| 0 | |
| 26 | +0·5 |
| 46 | +0·4 |
| 60 | +0·3 |
| 73 | +0·2 |
| 84 | +0·1 |

Jan. 7–Jan. 10

| ° ′ | ′ |
|---|---|
| 0 | |
| 24 | +0·6 |
| 41 | +0·5 |
| 54 | +0·4 |
| 65 | +0·3 |
| 76 | +0·2 |
| 85 | +0·1 |

Jan. 30–Feb. 13

| ° ′ | ′ |
|---|---|
| 0 | |
| 29 | +0·4 |
| 51 | +0·3 |
| 68 | +0·2 |
| 83 | +0·1 |

Feb. 14–Mar. 8

| ° ′ | ′ |
|---|---|
| 0 | |
| 34 | +0·3 |
| 60 | +0·2 |
| 80 | +0·1 |

Mar. 9–Apr. 28

| ° ′ | ′ |
|---|---|
| 0 | |
| 41 | +0·2 |
| 76 | +0·1 |

Apr. 29–Dec. 31

| ° ′ | ′ |
|---|---|
| 0 | |
| 60 | +0·1 |

**MARS**

Jan. 1–Aug. 28

| ° ′ | ′ |
|---|---|
| 0 | |
| 60 | +0·1 |

Aug. 29–Nov. 9
Dec. 22–Dec. 31

| ° ′ | ′ |
|---|---|
| 0 | |
| 41 | +0·2 |
| 76 | +0·1 |

Nov. 10–Dec. 21

| ° ′ | ′ |
|---|---|
| 0 | |
| 34 | +0·3 |
| 60 | +0·2 |
| 80 | +0·1 |

## DIP

| Ht. of Eye | Corrⁿ | Ht. of Eye | Ht. of Eye | Corrⁿ |
|---|---|---|---|---|
| m | ′ | ft. | m | ′ |
| 2·4 | −2·8 | 8·0 | 1·0 | − 1·8 |
| 2·6 | −2·9 | 8·6 | 1·5 | − 2·2 |
| 2·8 | | 9·2 | 2·0 | − 2·5 |
| 3·0 | −3·0 | 9·8 | 2·5 | − 2·8 |
| 3·2 | −3·1 | 10·5 | 3·0 | − 3·0 |
| 3·4 | −3·2 | 11·2 | | |
| 3·6 | −3·3 | 11·9 | See table |
| 3·8 | −3·4 | 12·6 | ← |
| 4·0 | −3·5 | 13·3 | m | ′ |
| 4·3 | −3·6 | 14·1 | 20 | − 7·9 |
| 4·5 | −3·7 | 14·9 | 22 | − 8·3 |
| 4·7 | −3·8 | 15·7 | 24 | − 8·6 |
| 5·0 | −3·9 | 16·5 | 26 | − 9·0 |
| 5·2 | −4·0 | 17·4 | 28 | − 9·3 |
| 5·5 | −4·1 | 18·3 | | |
| 5·8 | −4·2 | 19·1 | 30 | − 9·6 |
| 6·1 | −4·3 | 20·1 | 32 | −10·0 |
| 6·3 | −4·4 | 21·0 | 34 | −10·3 |
| 6·6 | −4·5 | 22·0 | 36 | −10·6 |
| 6·9 | −4·6 | 22·9 | 38 | −10·8 |
| 7·2 | −4·7 | 23·9 | | |
| 7·5 | −4·8 | 24·9 | 40 | −11·1 |
| 7·9 | −4·9 | 26·0 | 42 | −11·4 |
| 8·2 | −5·0 | 27·1 | 44 | −11·7 |
| 8·5 | −5·1 | 28·1 | 46 | −11·9 |
| 8·8 | −5·2 | 29·2 | 48 | −12·2 |
| 9·2 | −5·3 | 30·4 | ft. | |
| 9·5 | −5·4 | 31·5 | 2 | − 1·4 |
| 9·9 | −5·5 | 32·7 | 4 | − 1·9 |
| 10·3 | −5·6 | 33·9 | 6 | − 2·4 |
| 10·6 | −5·7 | 35·1 | 8 | − 2·7 |
| 11·0 | −5·8 | 36·3 | 10 | − 3·1 |
| 11·4 | −5·9 | 37·6 | | |
| 11·8 | −6·0 | 38·9 | See table |
| 12·2 | −6·1 | 40·1 | ← |
| 12·6 | −6·2 | 41·5 | ft. | ′ |
| 13·0 | −6·3 | 42·8 | 70 | − 8·1 |
| 13·4 | −6·4 | 44·2 | 75 | − 8·4 |
| 13·8 | −6·5 | 45·5 | 80 | − 8·7 |
| 14·2 | −6·6 | 46·9 | 85 | − 8·9 |
| 14·7 | −6·7 | 48·4 | 90 | − 9·2 |
| 15·1 | −6·8 | 49·8 | 95 | − 9·5 |
| 15·5 | −6·9 | 51·3 | 100 | − 9·7 |
| 16·0 | −7·0 | 52·8 | 105 | − 9·9 |
| 16·5 | −7·1 | 54·3 | 110 | −10·2 |
| 16·9 | −7·2 | 55·8 | 115 | −10·4 |
| 17·4 | −7·3 | 57·4 | 120 | −10·6 |
| 17·9 | −7·4 | 58·9 | 125 | −10·8 |
| 18·4 | −7·5 | 60·5 | | |
| 18·8 | −7·6 | 62·1 | 130 | −11·1 |
| 19·3 | −7·7 | 63·8 | 135 | −11·3 |
| 19·8 | −7·8 | 65·4 | 140 | −11·5 |
| 20·4 | −7·9 | 67·1 | 145 | −11·7 |
| 20·9 | −8·0 | 68·8 | 150 | −11·9 |
| 21·4 | −8·1 | 70·5 | 155 | −12·1 |

App. Alt. = Apparent altitude = Sextant altitude corrected for index error and dip.

# ALTITUDE CORRECTION TABLES 0°-10°—SUN, STARS, PLANETS A3

| App. Alt. | OCT.—MAR. SUN Lower Limb | Upper Limb | APR.—SEPT. Lower Limb | Upper Limb | STARS PLANETS | App. Alt. | OCT.—MAR. SUN Lower Limb | Upper Limb | APR.—SEPT. Lower Limb | Upper Limb | STARS PLANETS |
|---|---|---|---|---|---|---|---|---|---|---|---|
| ° ′ | ′ | ′ | ′ | ′ | ′ | ° ′ | ′ | ′ | ′ | ′ | ′ |
| 0 00 | − 17·5 | − 49·8 | − 17·8 | − 49·6 | − 33·8 | 3 30 | + 3·4 | − 28·9 | + 3·1 | − 28·7 | − 12·9 |
| 0 03 | 16·9 | 49·2 | 17·2 | 49·0 | 33·2 | 3 35 | 3·6 | 28·7 | 3·3 | 28·5 | 12·7 |
| 0 06 | 16·3 | 48·6 | 16·6 | 48·4 | 32·6 | 3 40 | 3·8 | 28·5 | 3·6 | 28·2 | 12·5 |
| 0 09 | 15·7 | 48·0 | 16·0 | 47·8 | 32·0 | 3 45 | 4·0 | 28·3 | 3·8 | 28·0 | 12·3 |
| 0 12 | 15·2 | 47·5 | 15·4 | 47·2 | 31·5 | 3 50 | 4·2 | 28·1 | 4·0 | 27·8 | 12·1 |
| 0 15 | 14·6 | 46·9 | 14·8 | 46·6 | 30·9 | 3 55 | 4·4 | 27·9 | 4·1 | 27·7 | 11·9 |
| 0 18 | − 14·1 | − 46·4 | − 14·3 | − 46·1 | − 30·4 | 4 00 | + 4·6 | − 27·7 | + 4·3 | − 27·5 | − 11·7 |
| 0 21 | 13·5 | 45·8 | 13·8 | 45·6 | 29·8 | 4 05 | 4·8 | 27·5 | 4·5 | 27·3 | 11·5 |
| 0 24 | 13·0 | 45·3 | 13·3 | 45·1 | 29·3 | 4 10 | 4·9 | 27·4 | 4·7 | 27·1 | 11·4 |
| 0 27 | 12·5 | 44·8 | 12·8 | 44·6 | 28·8 | 4 15 | 5·1 | 27·2 | 4·9 | 26·9 | 11·2 |
| 0 30 | 12·0 | 44·3 | 12·3 | 44·1 | 28·3 | 4 20 | 5·3 | 27·0 | 5·0 | 26·8 | 11·0 |
| 0 33 | 11·6 | 43·9 | 11·8 | 43·6 | 27·9 | 4 25 | 5·4 | 26·9 | 5·2 | 26·6 | 10·9 |
| 0 36 | − 11·1 | − 43·4 | − 11·3 | − 43·1 | − 27·4 | 4 30 | + 5·6 | − 26·7 | + 5·3 | − 26·5 | − 10·7 |
| 0 39 | 10·6 | 42·9 | 10·9 | 42·7 | 26·9 | 4 35 | 5·7 | 26·6 | 5·5 | 26·3 | 10·6 |
| 0 42 | 10·2 | 42·5 | 10·5 | 42·3 | 26·5 | 4 40 | 5·9 | 26·4 | 5·6 | 26·2 | 10·4 |
| 0 45 | 9·8 | 42·1 | 10·0 | 41·8 | 26·1 | 4 45 | 6·0 | 26·3 | 5·8 | 26·0 | 10·3 |
| 0 48 | 9·4 | 41·7 | 9·6 | 41·4 | 25·7 | 4 50 | 6·2 | 26·1 | 5·9 | 25·9 | 10·1 |
| 0 51 | 9·0 | 41·3 | 9·2 | 41·0 | 25·3 | 4 55 | 6·3 | 26·0 | 6·1 | 25·7 | 10·0 |
| 0 54 | − 8·6 | − 40·9 | − 8·8 | − 40·6 | − 24·9 | 5 00 | + 6·4 | − 25·9 | + 6·2 | − 25·6 | − 9·8 |
| 0 57 | 8·2 | 40·5 | 8·4 | 40·2 | 24·5 | 5 05 | 6·6 | 25·7 | 6·3 | 25·5 | 9·7 |
| 1 00 | 7·8 | 40·1 | 8·0 | 39·8 | 24·1 | 5 10 | 6·7 | 25·6 | 6·5 | 25·3 | 9·6 |
| 1 03 | 7·4 | 39·7 | 7·7 | 39·5 | 23·7 | 5 15 | 6·8 | 25·5 | 6·6 | 25·2 | 9·5 |
| 1 06 | 7·1 | 39·4 | 7·3 | 39·1 | 23·4 | 5 20 | 7·0 | 25·3 | 6·7 | 25·1 | 9·3 |
| 1 09 | 6·7 | 39·0 | 7·0 | 38·8 | 23·0 | 5 25 | 7·1 | 25·2 | 6·8 | 25·0 | 9·2 |
| 1 12 | − 6·4 | − 38·7 | − 6·6 | − 38·4 | − 22·7 | 5 30 | + 7·2 | − 25·1 | + 6·9 | − 24·9 | − 9·1 |
| 1 15 | 6·0 | 38·3 | 6·3 | 38·1 | 22·3 | 5 35 | 7·3 | 25·0 | 7·1 | 24·7 | 9·0 |
| 1 18 | 5·7 | 38·0 | 6·0 | 37·8 | 22·0 | 5 40 | 7·4 | 24·9 | 7·2 | 24·6 | 8·9 |
| 1 21 | 5·4 | 37·7 | 5·7 | 37·5 | 21·7 | 5 45 | 7·5 | 24·8 | 7·3 | 24·5 | 8·8 |
| 1 24 | 5·1 | 37·4 | 5·3 | 37·1 | 21·4 | 5 50 | 7·6 | 24·7 | 7·4 | 24·4 | 8·7 |
| 1 27 | 4·8 | 37·1 | 5·0 | 36·8 | 21·1 | 5 55 | 7·7 | 24·6 | 7·5 | 24·3 | 8·6 |
| 1 30 | − 4·5 | − 36·8 | − 4·7 | − 36·5 | − 20·8 | 6 00 | + 7·8 | − 24·5 | + 7·6 | − 24·2 | − 8·5 |
| 1 35 | 4·0 | 36·3 | 4·3 | 36·1 | 20·3 | 6 10 | 8·0 | 24·3 | 7·8 | 24·0 | 8·3 |
| 1 40 | 3·6 | 35·9 | 3·8 | 35·6 | 19·9 | 6 20 | 8·2 | 24·1 | 8·0 | 23·8 | 8·1 |
| 1 45 | 3·1 | 35·4 | 3·4 | 35·2 | 19·4 | 6 30 | 8·4 | 23·9 | 8·2 | 23·6 | 7·9 |
| 1 50 | 2·7 | 35·0 | 2·9 | 34·7 | 19·0 | 6 40 | 8·6 | 23·7 | 8·3 | 23·5 | 7·7 |
| 1 55 | 2·3 | 34·6 | 2·5 | 34·3 | 18·6 | 6 50 | 8·7 | 23·6 | 8·5 | 23·3 | 7·6 |
| 2 00 | − 1·9 | − 34·2 | − 2·1 | − 33·9 | − 18·2 | 7 00 | + 8·9 | − 23·4 | + 8·7 | − 23·1 | − 7·4 |
| 2 05 | 1·5 | 33·8 | 1·7 | 33·5 | 17·8 | 7 10 | 9·1 | 23·2 | 8·8 | 23·0 | 7·2 |
| 2 10 | 1·1 | 33·4 | 1·4 | 33·2 | 17·4 | 7 20 | 9·2 | 23·1 | 9·0 | 22·8 | 7·1 |
| 2 15 | 0·8 | 33·1 | 1·0 | 32·8 | 17·1 | 7 30 | 9·3 | 23·0 | 9·1 | 22·7 | 6·9 |
| 2 20 | 0·4 | 32·7 | 0·7 | 32·5 | 16·7 | 7 40 | 9·5 | 22·8 | 9·2 | 22·6 | 6·8 |
| 2 25 | − 0·1 | 32·4 | − 0·3 | 32·1 | 16·4 | 7 50 | 9·6 | 22·7 | 9·4 | 22·4 | 6·7 |
| 2 30 | + 0·2 | − 32·1 | 0·0 | − 31·8 | − 16·1 | 8 00 | + 9·7 | − 22·6 | + 9·5 | − 22·3 | − 6·6 |
| 2 35 | 0·5 | 31·8 | + 0·3 | 31·5 | 15·8 | 8 10 | 9·9 | 22·4 | 9·6 | 22·2 | 6·4 |
| 2 40 | 0·8 | 31·5 | 0·6 | 31·2 | 15·4 | 8 20 | 10·0 | 22·3 | 9·7 | 22·1 | 6·3 |
| 2 45 | 1·1 | 31·2 | 0·9 | 30·9 | 15·2 | 8 30 | 10·1 | 22·2 | 9·9 | 21·9 | 6·2 |
| 2 50 | 1·4 | 30·9 | 1·2 | 30·6 | 14·9 | 8 40 | 10·2 | 22·1 | 10·0 | 21·8 | 6·1 |
| 2 55 | 1·7 | 30·6 | 1·4 | 30·4 | 14·6 | 8 50 | 10·3 | 22·0 | 10·1 | 21·7 | 6·0 |
| 3 00 | + 2·0 | − 30·3 | + 1·7 | − 30·1 | − 14·3 | 9 00 | + 10·4 | − 21·9 | + 10·2 | − 21·6 | − 5·9 |
| 3 05 | 2·2 | 30·1 | 2·0 | 29·8 | 14·1 | 9 10 | 10·5 | 21·8 | 10·3 | 21·5 | 5·8 |
| 3 10 | 2·5 | 29·8 | 2·2 | 29·6 | 13·8 | 9 20 | 10·6 | 21·7 | 10·4 | 21·4 | 5·7 |
| 3 15 | 2·7 | 29·6 | 2·5 | 29·3 | 13·6 | 9 30 | 10·7 | 21·6 | 10·5 | 21·3 | 5·6 |
| 3 20 | 2·9 | 29·4 | 2·7 | 29·1 | 13·4 | 9 40 | 10·8 | 21·5 | 10·6 | 21·2 | 5·5 |
| 3 25 | 3·2 | 29·1 | 2·9 | 28·9 | 13·1 | 9 50 | 10·9 | 21·4 | 10·6 | 21·2 | 5·4 |
| 3 30 | + 3·4 | − 28·9 | + 3·1 | − 28·7 | − 12·9 | 10 00 | + 11·0 | − 21·3 | + 10·7 | − 21·1 | − 5·3 |

Additional corrections for temperature and pressure are given on the following page.

For bubble sextant observations ignore dip and use the star corrections for Sun, planets and stars.

# A4 ALTITUDE CORRECTION TABLES—ADDITIONAL CORRECTIONS

## ADDITIONAL REFRACTION CORRECTIONS FOR NON-STANDARD CONDITIONS

| App. Alt. | A | B | C | D | E | F | G | H | J | K | L | M | N | P | App. Alt. |
|---|---|---|---|---|---|---|---|---|---|---|---|---|---|---|---|
| ° ′ | ′ | ′ | ′ | ′ | ′ | ′ | ′ | ′ | ′ | ′ | ′ | ′ | ′ | ′ | ° ′ |
| 00 00 | −7·3 | −5·9 | −4·6 | −3·4 | −2·2 | −1·1 | 0·0 | +1·0 | +2·0 | +3·0 | +4·0 | +4·9 | +5·9 | +6·9 | 00 00 |
| 00 30 | 5·5 | 4·5 | 3·5 | 2·6 | 1·7 | 0·8 | 0·0 | 0·8 | 1·6 | 2·3 | 3·1 | 3·8 | 4·5 | 5·3 | 00 30 |
| 01 00 | 4·4 | 3·5 | 2·8 | 2·0 | 1·3 | 0·7 | 0·0 | 0·6 | 1·2 | 1·8 | 2·4 | 3·0 | 3·6 | 4·2 | 01 00 |
| 01 30 | 3·5 | 2·9 | 2·2 | 1·7 | 1·1 | 0·5 | 0·0 | 0·5 | 1·0 | 1·5 | 2·0 | 2·5 | 2·9 | 3·4 | 01 30 |
| 02 00 | 2·9 | 2·4 | 1·9 | 1·4 | 0·9 | 0·4 | 0·0 | 0·4 | 0·8 | 1·3 | 1·7 | 2·0 | 2·4 | 2·8 | 02 00 |
| 02 30 | −2·5 | −2·0 | −1·6 | −1·2 | −0·8 | −0·4 | 0·0 | +0·4 | +0·7 | +1·1 | +1·4 | +1·7 | +2·1 | +2·4 | 02 30 |
| 03 00 | 2·1 | 1·7 | 1·4 | 1·0 | 0·7 | 0·3 | 0·0 | 0·3 | 0·6 | 0·9 | 1·2 | 1·5 | 1·8 | 2·1 | 03 00 |
| 03 30 | 1·9 | 1·5 | 1·2 | 0·9 | 0·6 | 0·3 | 0·0 | 0·3 | 0·5 | 0·8 | 1·1 | 1·3 | 1·6 | 1·8 | 03 30 |
| 04 00 | 1·6 | 1·3 | 1·1 | 0·8 | 0·5 | 0·3 | 0·0 | 0·2 | 0·5 | 0·7 | 0·9 | 1·2 | 1·4 | 1·6 | 04 00 |
| 04 30 | 1·5 | 1·2 | 0·9 | 0·7 | 0·5 | 0·2 | 0·0 | 0·2 | 0·4 | 0·6 | 0·8 | 1·0 | 1·3 | 1·5 | 04 30 |
| 05 00 | −1·3 | −1·1 | −0·9 | −0·6 | −0·4 | −0·2 | 0·0 | +0·2 | +0·4 | +0·6 | +0·8 | +0·9 | +1·1 | +1·3 | 05 00 |
| 06 | 1·1 | 0·9 | 0·7 | 0·5 | 0·3 | 0·2 | 0·0 | 0·2 | 0·3 | 0·5 | 0·6 | 0·8 | 0·9 | 1·1 | 06 |
| 07 | 1·0 | 0·8 | 0·6 | 0·5 | 0·3 | 0·1 | 0·0 | 0·1 | 0·3 | 0·4 | 0·5 | 0·7 | 0·8 | 0·9 | 07 |
| 08 | 0·8 | 0·7 | 0·5 | 0·4 | 0·3 | 0·1 | 0·0 | 0·1 | 0·2 | 0·4 | 0·5 | 0·6 | 0·7 | 0·8 | 08 |
| 09 | 0·7 | 0·6 | 0·5 | 0·4 | 0·2 | 0·1 | 0·0 | 0·1 | 0·2 | 0·3 | 0·4 | 0·5 | 0·6 | 0·7 | 09 |
| 10 00 | −0·7 | −0·5 | −0·4 | −0·3 | −0·2 | −0·1 | 0·0 | +0·1 | +0·2 | +0·3 | +0·4 | +0·5 | +0·6 | +0·7 | 10 00 |
| 12 | 0·6 | 0·5 | 0·4 | 0·3 | 0·2 | 0·1 | 0·0 | 0·1 | 0·2 | 0·2 | 0·3 | 0·4 | 0·5 | 0·5 | 12 |
| 14 | 0·5 | 0·4 | 0·3 | 0·2 | 0·1 | 0·1 | 0·0 | 0·1 | 0·1 | 0·2 | 0·3 | 0·3 | 0·4 | 0·5 | 14 |
| 16 | 0·4 | 0·3 | 0·3 | 0·2 | 0·1 | 0·1 | 0·0 | 0·1 | 0·1 | 0·2 | 0·2 | 0·3 | 0·3 | 0·4 | 16 |
| 18 | 0·4 | 0·3 | 0·2 | 0·2 | 0·1 | −0·1 | 0·0 | +0·1 | 0·1 | 0·2 | 0·2 | 0·3 | 0·3 | 0·4 | 18 |
| 20 00 | −0·3 | −0·3 | −0·2 | −0·2 | −0·1 | 0·0 | 0·0 | 0·0 | +0·1 | +0·1 | +0·2 | +0·2 | +0·3 | +0·3 | 20 00 |
| 25 | 0·3 | 0·2 | 0·2 | 0·1 | 0·1 | 0·0 | 0·0 | 0·0 | 0·1 | 0·1 | 0·1 | 0·2 | 0·2 | 0·2 | 25 |
| 30 | 0·2 | 0·2 | 0·1 | 0·1 | 0·1 | 0·0 | 0·0 | 0·0 | +0·1 | 0·1 | 0·1 | 0·1 | 0·2 | 0·2 | 30 |
| 35 | 0·2 | 0·1 | 0·1 | 0·1 | −0·1 | 0·0 | 0·0 | 0·0 | 0·0 | 0·1 | 0·1 | 0·1 | 0·1 | 0·2 | 35 |
| 40 | 0·1 | 0·1 | 0·1 | −0·1 | 0·0 | 0·0 | 0·0 | 0·0 | 0·0 | +0·1 | 0·1 | 0·1 | 0·1 | 0·1 | 40 |
| 50 00 | −0·1 | −0·1 | −0·1 | 0·0 | 0·0 | 0·0 | 0·0 | 0·0 | 0·0 | 0·0 | +0·1 | +0·1 | +0·1 | +0·1 | 50 00 |

The graph is entered with arguments temperature and pressure to find a zone letter; using as arguments this zone letter and apparent altitude (sextant altitude corrected for index error and dip), a correction is taken from the table. This correction is to be applied to the sextant altitude in addition to the corrections for standard conditions (for the Sun, stars and planets from page A2-A3 and for the Moon from pages xxxiv and xxxv).

# 2022
# Nautical Almanac
## COMMERCIAL EDITION

## PUBLISHED BY:

Paradise Cay Publications, Inc.
PO Box 29
Arcata, CA 95518-0029
Tel: 1-707-822-9063
Fax: 1-707-822-9163
www.paracay.com

NOTE

Every care is taken to prevent errors in the production of this publication. As a final precaution it is recommended that the sequence of pages in this copy be examined on receipt. If faulty, it should be returned for replacement.

PREFACE

The first three sections of this book are a complete and accurate duplications from *The Nautical Almanac* produced jointly by Her Majesty's Nautical Almanac Office, United Kingdom Hydrographic Office, Admiralty Way, Taunton, Somerset, TA1 2DN, United Kingdom and the Nautical Almanac Office of the US Naval Observatory.

The following United States government work is excerpted from the above notice and no copyright is claimed for it in the United States: pages 6 and 7, and pages 286-317.

The UK Hydrographic Office makes the accompanying 2019 Nautical Almanac data available to Paradise Cay Publications Inc for use in accordance with Licence agreement GB CS-001-Paradise Cay Publications.

We gratefully acknowledge the United Kingdom Hydrographic Office and the United States Naval Observatory for permission to use the material contained in the almanac section of this publication.

CONDITIONS OF RELEASE

DISCLAIMER

Whilst the UK Hydrographic Office has endeavoured to ensure that the material supplied is suitable for the purpose, it accepts no liability (to the maximum extent permitted by law) for any damage or loss of any nature arising from its use. The material supplied is used entirely at the Recipient's own risk.

# THE NAUTICAL ALMANAC 2022

## LIST OF CONTENTS

## RELIGIOUS CALENDARS

| | | | | |
|---|---|---|---|---|
| Epiphany | Jan. 6 | Low Sunday | Apr. 24 |
| Septuagesima Sunday | Feb. 13 | Rogation Sunday | May 22 |
| Quinquagesima Sunday | Feb. 27 | Ascension Day—Holy Thursday | May 26 |
| Ash Wednesday | Mar. 2 | Whit Sunday—Pentecost | June 5 |
| Quadragesima Sunday | Mar. 6 | Trinity Sunday | June 12 |
| Palm Sunday | Apr. 10 | Corpus Christi | June 16 |
| Good Friday | Apr. 15 | First Sunday in Advent | Nov. 27 |
| Easter Day | Apr. 17 | Christmas Day (Sunday) | Dec. 25 |
| | | | |
| First Day of Passover (Pesach) | Apr. 16 | Day of Atonement (Yom Kippur) | Oct. 5 |
| Feast of Weeks (Shavuot) | June 5 | First day of Tabernacles (Succoth) | Oct. 10 |
| Jewish New Year 5783 (Rosh Hashanah) | Sept. 26 | | |
| | | | |
| Ramadân, First day of (tabular) | Apr. 3 | Islamic New Year (1444) | July 30 |

The Jewish and Islamic dates above are tabular dates, which begin at sunset on the previous evening and end at sunset on the date tabulated. In practice, the dates of Islamic fasts and festivals are determined by an actual sighting of the appropriate new moon.

## CIVIL CALENDAR—UNITED KINGDOM

| | | | |
|---|---|---|---|
| Accession of Queen Elizabeth II | Feb. 6 | Birthday of Prince Philip, Duke of Edinburgh | June 10 |
| St David (Wales) | Mar. 1 | The Queen's Official Birthday† | June 11 |
| Commonwealth Day | Mar. 14 | Remembrance Sunday | Nov. 13 |
| St Patrick (Ireland) | Mar. 17 | Birthday of the Prince of Wales | Nov. 14 |
| Birthday of Queen Elizabeth II | Apr. 21 | St Andrew (Scotland) | Nov. 30 |
| St George (England) | Apr. 23 | | |
| Coronation Day | June 2 | | |

## PUBLIC HOLIDAYS

England and Wales—Jan. 3†, Apr. 15, Apr. 18, May 2†, June 2, June 3, Aug. 29, Dec. 26, Dec. 27
Northern Ireland—Jan. 3†, Mar. 17, Apr. 15, Apr. 18, May 2†, June 2, June 3, July 12†, Aug. 29, Dec. 26, Dec. 27
Scotland—Jan. 3, Jan. 4, Apr. 15, May 2, June 2, June 3, Aug. 1, Dec. 26†, Dec. 27

## CIVIL CALENDAR—UNITED STATES OF AMERICA

| | | | |
|---|---|---|---|
| New Year's Day | Jan. 1 | Labor Day | Sept. 5 |
| Martin Luther King's Birthday | Jan. 17 | Columbus Day | Oct. 10 |
| Washington's Birthday | Feb. 21 | General Election Day | Nov. 8 |
| Memorial Day | May 30 | Veterans Day | Nov. 11 |
| Independence Day | July 4 | Thanksgiving Day | Nov. 24 |

†Dates subject to confirmation

## PHASES OF THE MOON

| New Moon | | | | First Quarter | | | | Full Moon | | | | Last Quarter | | | |
|---|---|---|---|---|---|---|---|---|---|---|---|---|---|---|---|
| | d | h | m | | d | h | m | | d | h | m | | d | h | m |
| Jan. | 2 | 18 | 33 | Jan. | 9 | 18 | 11 | Jan. | 17 | 23 | 48 | Jan. | 25 | 13 | 41 |
| Feb. | 1 | 05 | 46 | Feb. | 8 | 13 | 50 | Feb. | 16 | 16 | 57 | Feb. | 23 | 22 | 32 |
| Mar. | 2 | 17 | 35 | Mar. | 10 | 10 | 45 | Mar. | 18 | 07 | 18 | Mar. | 25 | 05 | 37 |
| Apr. | 1 | 06 | 24 | Apr. | 9 | 06 | 48 | Apr. | 16 | 18 | 55 | Apr. | 23 | 11 | 56 |
| Apr. | 30 | 20 | 28 | May | 9 | 00 | 21 | May | 16 | 04 | 14 | May | 22 | 18 | 43 |
| May | 30 | 11 | 30 | June | 7 | 14 | 49 | June | 14 | 11 | 52 | June | 21 | 03 | 11 |
| June | 29 | 02 | 52 | July | 7 | 02 | 14 | July | 13 | 18 | 38 | July | 20 | 14 | 19 |
| July | 28 | 17 | 55 | Aug. | 5 | 11 | 07 | Aug. | 12 | 01 | 36 | Aug. | 19 | 04 | 36 |
| Aug. | 27 | 08 | 17 | Sept. | 3 | 18 | 08 | Sept. | 10 | 09 | 59 | Sept. | 17 | 21 | 52 |
| Sept. | 25 | 21 | 55 | Oct. | 3 | 00 | 14 | Oct. | 9 | 20 | 55 | Oct. | 17 | 17 | 15 |
| Oct. | 25 | 10 | 49 | Nov. | 1 | 06 | 37 | Nov. | 8 | 11 | 02 | Nov. | 16 | 13 | 27 |
| Nov. | 23 | 22 | 57 | Nov. | 30 | 14 | 37 | Dec. | 8 | 04 | 08 | Dec. | 16 | 08 | 56 |
| Dec. | 23 | 10 | 17 | Dec. | 30 | 01 | 21 | | | | | | | | |

## DAYS OF THE WEEK AND DAYS OF THE YEAR

| Day | JAN. Wk Yr | FEB. Wk Yr | MAR. Wk Yr | APR. Wk Yr | MAY Wk Yr | JUNE Wk Yr | JULY Wk Yr | AUG. Wk Yr | SEPT. Wk Yr | OCT. Wk Yr | NOV. Wk Yr | DEC. Wk Yr |
|---|---|---|---|---|---|---|---|---|---|---|---|---|
| 1 | Sa. 1 | Tu. 32 | Tu. 60 | F. 91 | Su. 121 | W. 152 | F. 182 | M. 213 | Th. 244 | Sa. 274 | Tu. 305 | Th. 335 |
| 2 | Su. 2 | W. 33 | W. 61 | Sa. 92 | M. 122 | Th. 153 | Sa. 183 | Tu. 214 | F. 245 | Su. 275 | W. 306 | F. 336 |
| 3 | M. 3 | Th. 34 | Th. 62 | Su. 93 | Tu. 123 | F. 154 | Su. 184 | W. 215 | Sa. 246 | M. 276 | Th. 307 | Sa. 337 |
| 4 | Tu. 4 | F. 35 | F. 63 | M. 94 | W. 124 | Sa. 155 | M. 185 | Th. 216 | Su. 247 | Tu. 277 | F. 308 | Su. 338 |
| 5 | W. 5 | Sa. 36 | Sa. 64 | Tu. 95 | Th. 125 | Su. 156 | Tu. 186 | F. 217 | M. 248 | W. 278 | Sa. 309 | M. 339 |
| 6 | Th. 6 | Su. 37 | Su. 65 | W. 96 | F. 126 | M. 157 | W. 187 | Sa. 218 | Tu. 249 | Th. 279 | Su. 310 | Tu. 340 |
| 7 | F. 7 | M. 38 | M. 66 | Th. 97 | Sa. 127 | Tu. 158 | Th. 188 | Su. 219 | W. 250 | F. 280 | M. 311 | W. 341 |
| 8 | Sa. 8 | Tu. 39 | Tu. 67 | F. 98 | Su. 128 | W. 159 | F. 189 | M. 220 | Th. 251 | Sa. 281 | Tu. 312 | Th. 342 |
| 9 | Su. 9 | W. 40 | W. 68 | Sa. 99 | M. 129 | Th. 160 | Sa. 190 | Tu. 221 | F. 252 | Su. 282 | W. 313 | F. 343 |
| 10 | M. 10 | Th. 41 | Th. 69 | Su. 100 | Tu. 130 | F. 161 | Su. 191 | W. 222 | Sa. 253 | M. 283 | Th. 314 | Sa. 344 |
| 11 | Tu. 11 | F. 42 | F. 70 | M. 101 | W. 131 | Sa. 162 | M. 192 | Th. 223 | Su. 254 | Tu. 284 | F. 315 | Su. 345 |
| 12 | W. 12 | Sa. 43 | Sa. 71 | Tu. 102 | Th. 132 | Su. 163 | Tu. 193 | F. 224 | M. 255 | W. 285 | Sa. 316 | M. 346 |
| 13 | Th. 13 | Su. 44 | Su. 72 | W. 103 | F. 133 | M. 164 | W. 194 | Sa. 225 | Tu. 256 | Th. 286 | Su. 317 | Tu. 347 |
| 14 | F. 14 | M. 45 | M. 73 | Th. 104 | Sa. 134 | Tu. 165 | Th. 195 | Su. 226 | W. 257 | F. 287 | M. 318 | W. 348 |
| 15 | Sa. 15 | Tu. 46 | Tu. 74 | F. 105 | Su. 135 | W. 166 | F. 196 | M. 227 | Th. 258 | Sa. 288 | Tu. 319 | Th. 349 |
| 16 | Su. 16 | W. 47 | W. 75 | Sa. 106 | M. 136 | Th. 167 | Sa. 197 | Tu. 228 | F. 259 | Su. 289 | W. 320 | F. 350 |
| 17 | M. 17 | Th. 48 | Th. 76 | Su. 107 | Tu. 137 | F. 168 | Su. 198 | W. 229 | Sa. 260 | M. 290 | Th. 321 | Sa. 351 |
| 18 | Tu. 18 | F. 49 | F. 77 | M. 108 | W. 138 | Sa. 169 | M. 199 | Th. 230 | Su. 261 | Tu. 291 | F. 322 | Su. 352 |
| 19 | W. 19 | Sa. 50 | Sa. 78 | Tu. 109 | Th. 139 | Su. 170 | Tu. 200 | F. 231 | M. 262 | W. 292 | Sa. 323 | M. 353 |
| 20 | Th. 20 | Su. 51 | Su. 79 | W. 110 | F. 140 | M. 171 | W. 201 | Sa. 232 | Tu. 263 | Th. 293 | Su. 324 | Tu. 354 |
| 21 | F. 21 | M. 52 | M. 80 | Th. 111 | Sa. 141 | Tu. 172 | Th. 202 | Su. 233 | W. 264 | F. 294 | M. 325 | W. 355 |
| 22 | Sa. 22 | Tu. 53 | Tu. 81 | F. 112 | Su. 142 | W. 173 | F. 203 | M. 234 | Th. 265 | Sa. 295 | Tu. 326 | Th. 356 |
| 23 | Su. 23 | W. 54 | W. 82 | Sa. 113 | M. 143 | Th. 174 | Sa. 204 | Tu. 235 | F. 266 | Su. 296 | W. 327 | F. 357 |
| 24 | M. 24 | Th. 55 | Th. 83 | Su. 114 | Tu. 144 | F. 175 | Su. 205 | W. 236 | Sa. 267 | M. 297 | Th. 328 | Sa. 358 |
| 25 | Tu. 25 | F. 56 | F. 84 | M. 115 | W. 145 | Sa. 176 | M. 206 | Th. 237 | Su. 268 | Tu. 298 | F. 329 | Su. 359 |
| 26 | W. 26 | Sa. 57 | Sa. 85 | Tu. 116 | Th. 146 | Su. 177 | Tu. 207 | F. 238 | M. 269 | W. 299 | Sa. 330 | M. 360 |
| 27 | Th. 27 | Su. 58 | Su. 86 | W. 117 | F. 147 | M. 178 | W. 208 | Sa. 239 | Tu. 270 | Th. 300 | Su. 331 | Tu. 361 |
| 28 | F. 28 | M. 59 | M. 87 | Th. 118 | Sa. 148 | Tu. 179 | Th. 209 | Su. 240 | W. 271 | F. 301 | M. 332 | W. 362 |
| 29 | Sa. 29 | | Tu. 88 | F. 119 | Su. 149 | W. 180 | F. 210 | M. 241 | Th. 272 | Sa. 302 | Tu. 333 | Th. 363 |
| 30 | Su. 30 | | W. 89 | Sa. 120 | M. 150 | Th. 181 | Sa. 211 | Tu. 242 | F. 273 | Su. 303 | W. 334 | F. 364 |
| 31 | M. 31 | | Th. 90 | | Tu. 151 | | Su. 212 | W. 243 | | M. 304 | | Sa. 365 |

## ECLIPSES

There are two eclipses of the Sun.

1. *A partial eclipse of the Sun,* April 30. See map on page 6. The eclipse begins at $18^h 45^m$ and ends at $22^h 38^m$. The time of greatest eclipse is $20^h 41^m$ when 0.64 of the Sun's diameter is obscured.

2. *A total eclipse of the Moon,* May 16. The umbral eclipse begins at $02^h 28^m$ and ends at $05^h 55^m$. Totality lasts from $03^h 29^m$ to $04^h 54^m$. It is visible from most of Africa except the north-eastern part, western Europe, Iceland, the southern tip of Greenland, the Americas except north-western Canada and Alaska and most of Polynesia except the westernmost parts.

3. *A partial eclipse of the Sun,* October 25. See map on page 7. The eclipse begins at $08^h 58^m$ and ends at $13^h 02^m$. The time of greatest eclipse is $11^h 00^m$ when 0.86 of the Sun's diameter is obscured.

4. *A total eclipse of the Moon,* November 8. The umbral eclipse begins at $09^h 09^m$ and ends at $12^h 49^m$. Totality lasts from $10^h 16^m$ to $11^h 42^m$. It is visible from the north-western part of South America, North and Central America, the Pacific Ocean region, Australasia, south-east Asia, Japan, China and eastern and central Russia.

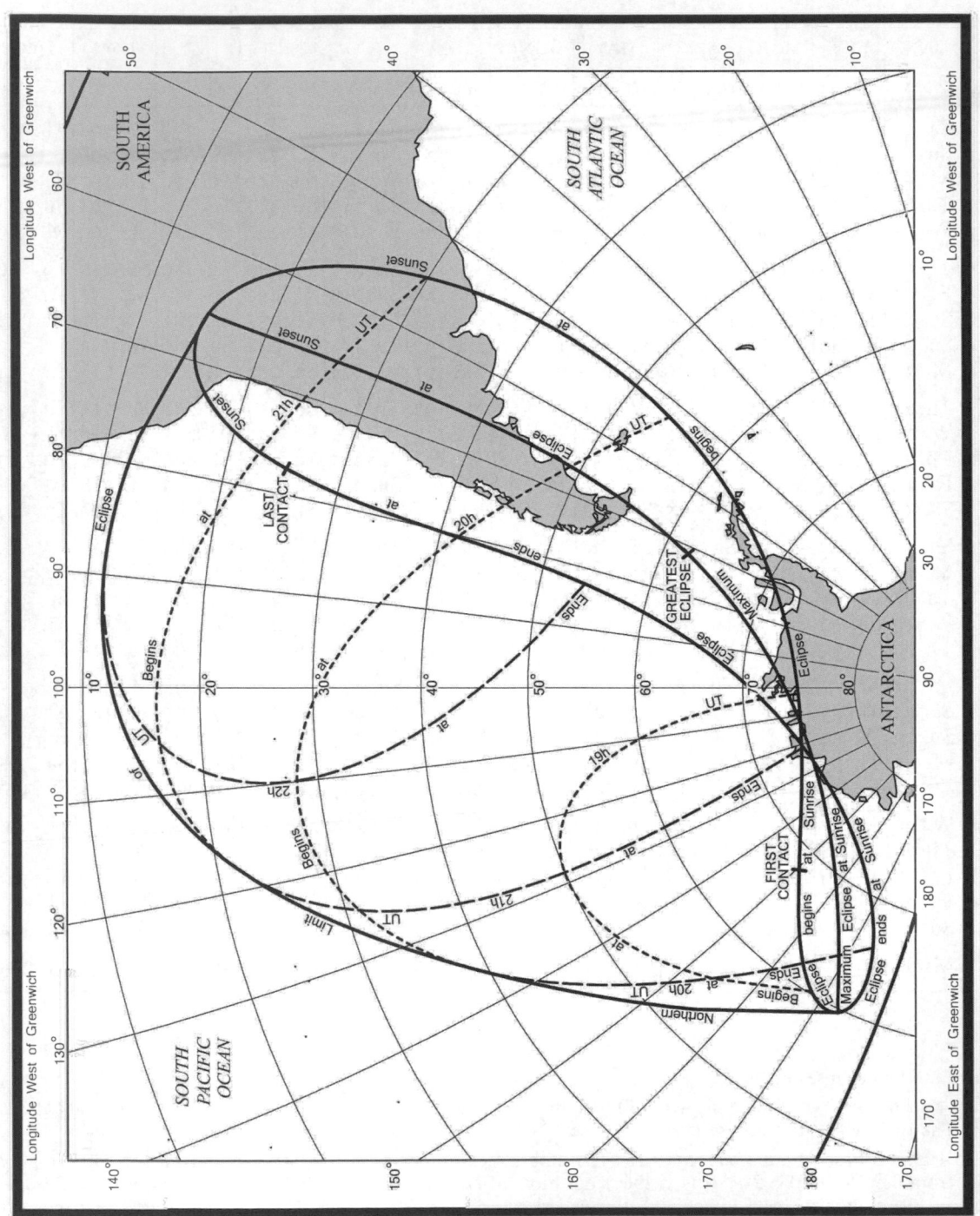

## SOLAR ECLIPSE DIAGRAMS

The principal features shown on the above diagrams are: the paths of total and annular eclipses; the northern and southern limits of partial eclipse; the sunrise and sunset curves; dashed lines which show the times of beginning and end of partial eclipse at hourly intervals.

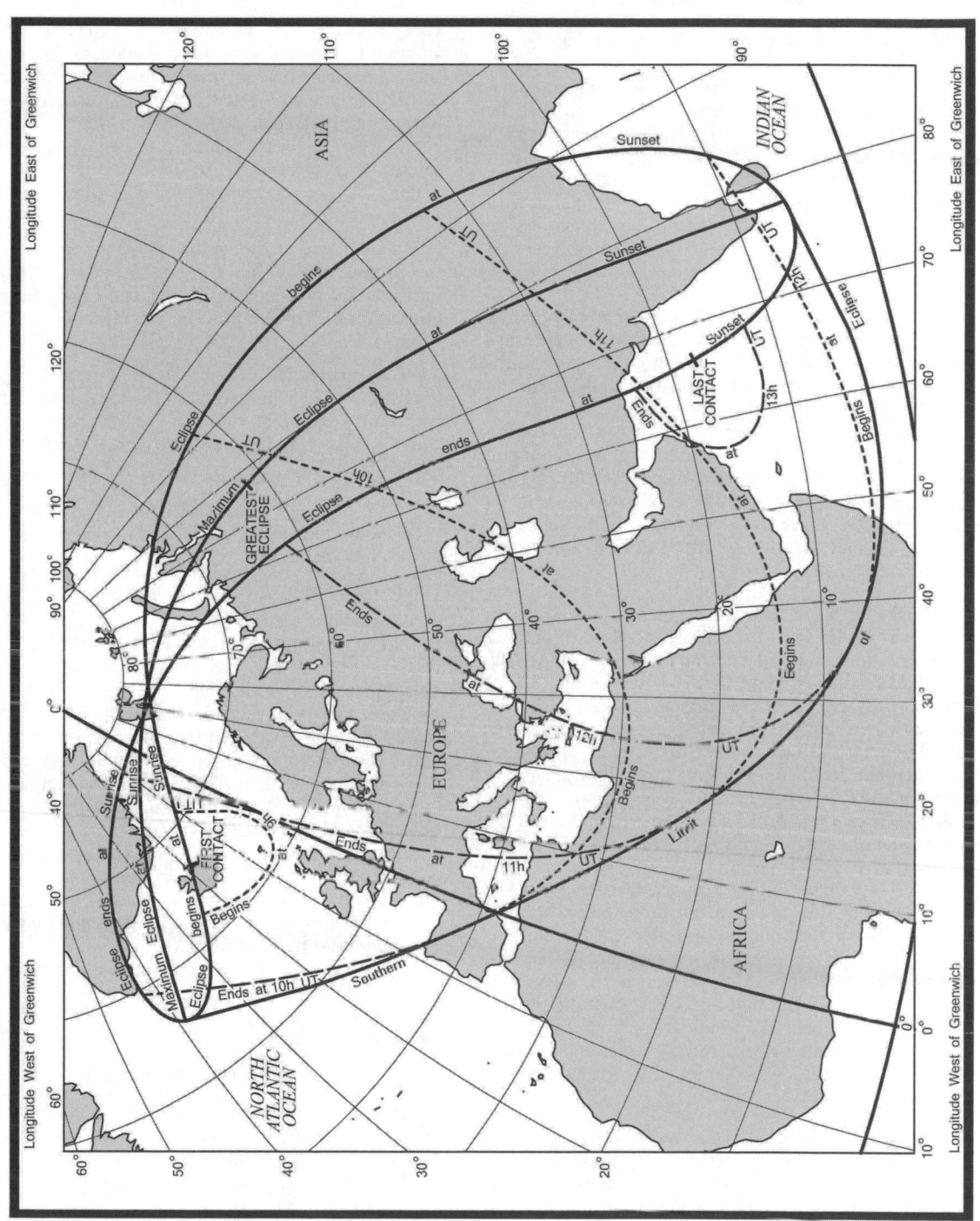

## SOLAR ECLIPSE DIAGRAMS

Further details of the paths and times of central eclipse are given in
*The Astronomical Almanac.*

## VISIBILITY OF PLANETS

VENUS is a brilliant object in the evening sky at the beginning of January, and then after a few days becomes too close to the Sun for observation until mid-January, when it reappears as a morning star. It can then be seen in the morning sky until mid-September when it again becomes too close to the Sun for observation; from early December until the end of the year it is visible in the evening sky. Venus is in conjunction with Mars on February 13 and March 12, with Saturn on March 29 and Jupiter on April 30 and with Mercury on December 29.

MARS can be seen in the morning sky from the beginning of the year as it passes through Ophiuchus, Sagittarius, Capricornus, Aquarius, Pisces, briefly into Cetus, returning to Pisces in mid-June then into Aries and Taurus. Its westward elongation gradually increases (passing 4° N of Aldebaran on September 9) until it is at opposition on December 8 when it is visible throughout the night. Its eastward elongation gradually decreases during the remainder of the year (passing 8° N of Aldebaran on December 22). Mars is in conjuction with Venus on February 13 and March 12, with Saturn on April 4 and with Jupiter on May 29.

JUPITER can be seen in the evening sky in Aquarius at the start of the year. It becomes too close to the Sun for observation after mid-February and reappears in the morning sky during mid-March. It moves into Pisces in mid-April and into Cetus in late June. Its westward elongation gradually increases and in early September moves into Pisces once more. Jupiter is at opposition on September 26 when it is visible throughout the night, and from late December it can be seen in the evening sky. Jupiter is in conjunction with Mercury on March 20, with Venus on April 30 and with Mars on May 29.

SATURN can be seen in the evening sky in Capricornus and reamins in this constellation throughout the year. In mid-January it becomes too close to the Sun for observation and reappears in the morning sky in late February. It is at opposition on August 14 when it is visible throughout the night. Its eastward elongation then gradually decreases and mid-November it can only be seen in the evening sky. Saturn is in conjunction with Mercury on March 2, with Venus on March 29 and with Mars on April 4.

MERCURY can only be seen low in the east before sunrise, or low in the west after sunset (about the time of beginning or end of civil twilight). It is visible in the mornings between the following approximate dates: January 29 (+2·2) to March 24 (−1·0), May 31 (+3·2) to July 9 (−1·4), and September 30 (+1·9) to October 26 (−1·1); the planet is brighter at the end of each period. It is visible in the evenings between the following approximate dates: January 1 (−0·7) to January 17 (+1·4), April 11 (−1·5) to May 12 (+2·9), July 25 (−1·2) to September 17 (+2·6) and November 25 (−0·7) to December 31 (+0·8); the planet is brighter at the beginning of each period. The figures in parentheses are the magnitudes.

## PLANET DIAGRAM

*General Description.* The diagram on the opposite page shows, in graphical form for any date during the year, the local mean time of meridian passage of the Sun, of the five planets Mercury, Venus, Mars, Jupiter, and Saturn, and of each 30° of SHA; intermediate lines corresponding to particular stars, may be drawn in by the user if desired. It is intended to provide a general picture of the availability of planets and stars for observation.

On each side of the line marking the time of meridian passage of the Sun a band, $45^m$ wide, is shaded to indicate that planets and most stars crossing the meridian within $45^m$ of the Sun are too close to the Sun for observation.

*Method of use and interpretation.* For any date, the diagram provides immediately the local mean times of meridian passage of the Sun, planets and stars, and thus the following information:

  (a) whether a planet or star is too close to the Sun for observation;

  (b) some indication of its position in the sky, especially during twilight;

  (c) the proximity of other planets.

When the meridian passage of an outer planet occurs at midnight, the body is in opposition to the Sun and is visible all night; a planet may then be observable during both morning and evening twilights. As the time of meridian passage decreases, the body eventually ceases to be observable in the morning, but its altitude above the eastern horizon at sunset gradually increases; this continues until the body is on the meridian during evening twilight. From then onwards, the body is observable above the western horizon and its altitude at sunset gradually decreases; eventually the body becomes too close to the Sun for observation. When the body again becomes visible it is seen low in the east during morning twilight; its altitude at sunrise increases until meridian passage occurs during morning twilight. Then, as the time of meridian passage decreases to $0^h$, the body is observable in the west during morning twilight with a gradually decreasing altitude, until it once again reaches opposition.

### DO NOT CONFUSE

Mercury with Saturn in mid-January and again from late February to early March; on both occasions Mercury is the brighter object.

Venus with Mars from early March to late in the same month, with Saturn from late March to early April, with Jupiter from late April to early May and with Mercury in early December and again in late December; on all occasions Venus is the brighter object.

Jupiter with Mercury in mid-March and with Mars from late May to early June; on both occasions Jupiter is the brighter object.

Mars with Saturn from late March until mid-April when Saturn is the brighter object.

# LOCAL MEAN TIME OF MERIDIAN PASSAGE

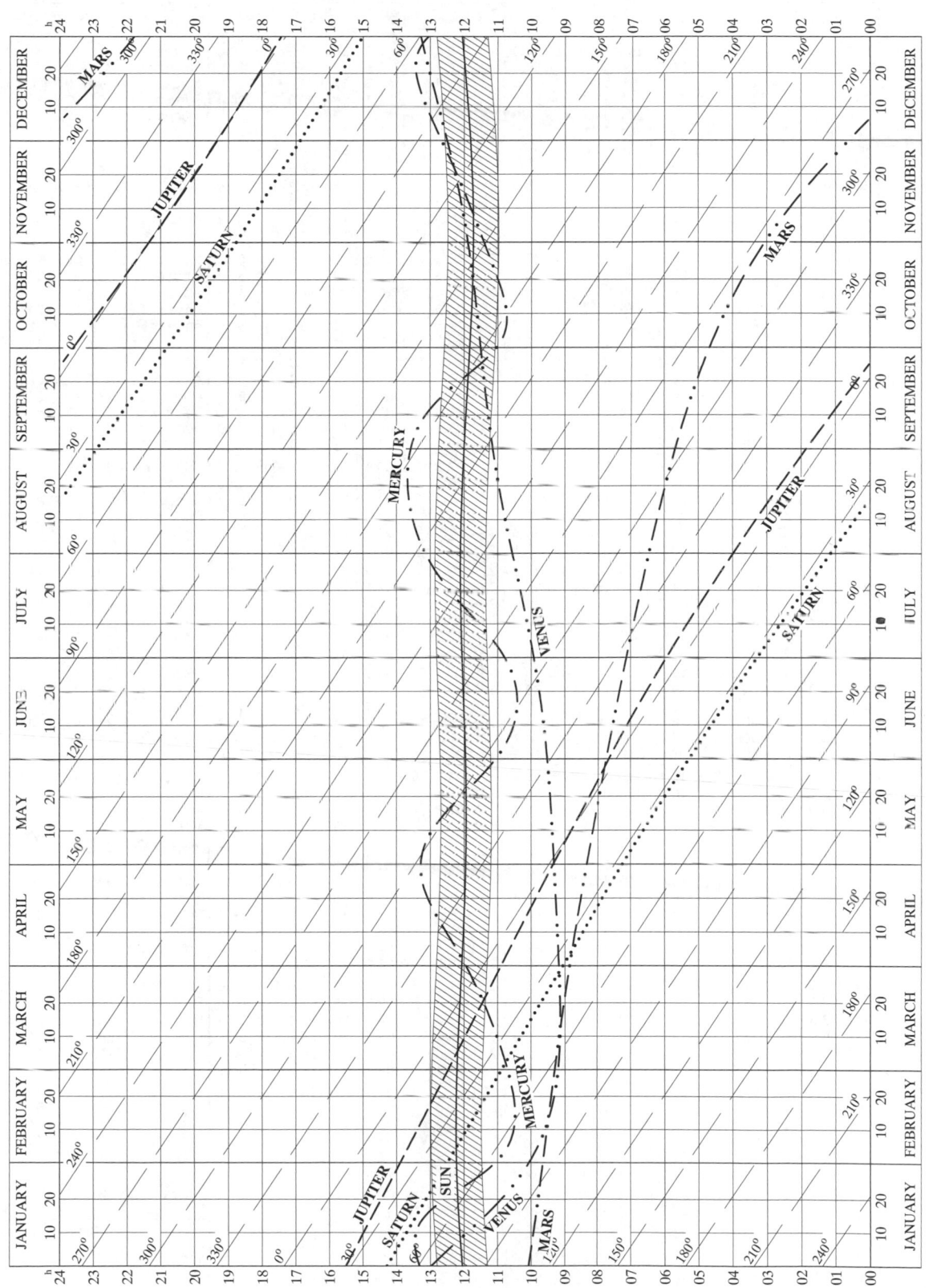

LOCAL MEAN TIME OF MERIDIAN PASSAGE

## 2022 JANUARY 1, 2, 3 (SAT., SUN., MON.)

| UT | ARIES GHA | VENUS −4·2 GHA | Dec | MARS +1·5 GHA | Dec | JUPITER −2·1 GHA | Dec | SATURN +0·7 GHA | Dec | STARS Name | SHA | Dec |
|---|---|---|---|---|---|---|---|---|---|---|---|---|
| **1** 00 | 100 37.6 | 166 00.5 | S18 35.2 | 208 58.0 | S22 30.0 | 127 39.4 | S12 12.7 | 146 01.3 | S18 00.6 | Acamar | 315 13.4 | S40 13.3 |
| 01 | 115 40.0 | 181 04.3 | 34.7 | 223 58.6 | 30.2 | 142 41.4 | 12.5 | 161 03.5 | 00.6 | Achernar | 335 22.0 | S57 07.9 |
| 02 | 130 42.5 | 196 08.1 | 34.3 | 238 59.1 | 30.5 | 157 43.4 | 12.3 | 176 05.7 | 00.5 | Acrux | 173 02.7 | S63 12.9 |
| 03 | 145 45.0 | 211 12.0 .. | 33.9 | 253 59.7 .. | 30.7 | 172 45.4 .. | 12.1 | 191 07.9 .. | 00.4 | Adhara | 255 07.4 | S29 00.1 |
| 04 | 160 47.4 | 226 15.8 | 33.4 | 269 00.3 | 31.0 | 187 47.3 | 12.0 | 206 10.1 | 00.3 | Aldebaran | 290 42.2 | N16 33.2 |
| 05 | 175 49.9 | 241 19.7 | 33.0 | 284 00.8 | 31.2 | 202 49.3 | 11.8 | 221 12.3 | 00.3 | | | |
| 06 | 190 52.4 | 256 23.6 | S18 32.5 | 299 01.4 | S22 31.5 | 217 51.3 | S12 11.6 | 236 14.5 | S18 00.2 | Alioth | 166 15.2 | N55 50.2 |
| 07 | 205 54.8 | 271 27.4 | 32.1 | 314 01.9 | 31.7 | 232 53.3 | 11.4 | 251 16.6 | 00.1 | Alkaid | 152 54.2 | N49 12.0 |
| 08 | 220 57.3 | 286 31.3 | 31.7 | 329 02.5 | 32.0 | 247 55.3 | 11.3 | 266 18.8 | 00.0 | Alnair | 27 36.4 | S46 51.5 |
| S 09 | 235 59.8 | 301 35.1 .. | 31.2 | 344 03.1 .. | 32.2 | 262 57.3 .. | 11.1 | 281 21.0 | 18 00.0 | Alnilam | 275 39.9 | S 1 11.3 |
| A 10 | 251 02.2 | 316 39.0 | 30.8 | 359 03.6 | 32.5 | 277 59.3 | 10.9 | 296 23.2 | 17 59.9 | Alphard | 217 49.9 | S 8 45.2 |
| T 11 | 266 04.7 | 331 42.9 | 30.4 | 14 04.2 | 32.7 | 293 01.3 | 10.7 | 311 25.4 | 59.8 | | | |
| U 12 | 281 07.2 | 346 46.8 | S18 29.9 | 29 04.7 | S22 33.0 | 308 03.3 | S12 10.5 | 326 27.6 | S17 59.7 | Alphecca | 126 06.1 | N26 38.4 |
| R 13 | 296 09.6 | 1 50.6 | 29.5 | 44 05.3 | 33.2 | 323 05.3 | 10.4 | 341 29.8 | 59.7 | Alpheratz | 357 37.4 | N29 12.8 |
| D 14 | 311 12.1 | 16 54.5 | 29.1 | 59 05.8 | 33.5 | 338 07.3 | 10.2 | 356 32.0 | 59.6 | Altair | 62 02.7 | N 8 55.6 |
| A 15 | 326 14.5 | 31 58.4 .. | 28.6 | 74 06.4 .. | 33.7 | 353 09.3 .. | 10.0 | 11 34.2 .. | 59.5 | Ankaa | 353 09.7 | S42 11.5 |
| Y 16 | 341 17.0 | 47 02.3 | 28.2 | 89 07.0 | 33.9 | 8 11.3 | 09.8 | 26 36.4 | 59.4 | Antares | 112 19.2 | S26 28.7 |
| 17 | 356 19.5 | 62 06.2 | 27.8 | 104 07.5 | 34.2 | 23 13.3 | 09.7 | 41 38.5 | 59.4 | | | |
| 18 | 11 21.9 | 77 10.1 | S18 27.3 | 119 08.1 | S22 34.4 | 38 15.3 | S12 09.5 | 56 40.7 | S17 59.3 | Arcturus | 145 50.3 | N19 04.0 |
| 19 | 26 24.4 | 92 14.0 | 26.9 | 134 08.6 | 34.7 | 53 17.3 | 09.3 | 71 42.9 | 59.2 | Atria | 107 16.1 | S69 03.8 |
| 20 | 41 26.9 | 107 17.9 | 26.5 | 149 09.2 | 34.9 | 68 19.3 | 09.1 | 86 45.1 | 59.1 | Avior | 234 15.1 | S59 34.6 |
| 21 | 56 29.3 | 122 21.8 .. | 26.0 | 164 09.7 .. | 35.2 | 83 21.3 .. | 09.0 | 101 47.3 .. | 59.1 | Bellatrix | 278 25.2 | N 6 22.1 |
| 22 | 71 31.8 | 137 25.7 | 25.6 | 179 10.3 | 35.4 | 98 23.3 | 08.8 | 116 49.5 | 59.0 | Betelgeuse | 270 54.4 | N 7 24.6 |
| 23 | 86 34.3 | 152 29.6 | 25.2 | 194 10.8 | 35.6 | 113 25.3 | 08.6 | 131 51.7 | 58.9 | | | |
| **2** 00 | 101 36.7 | 167 33.5 | S18 24.7 | 209 11.4 | S22 35.9 | 128 27.3 | S12 08.4 | 146 53.9 | S17 58.8 | Canopus | 263 52.9 | S52 42.5 |
| 01 | 116 39.2 | 182 37.4 | 24.3 | 224 12.0 | 36.1 | 143 29.3 | 08.2 | 161 56.1 | 58.8 | Capella | 280 25.1 | N46 01.2 |
| 02 | 131 41.7 | 197 41.3 | 23.9 | 239 12.5 | 36.4 | 158 31.3 | 08.1 | 176 58.3 | 58.7 | Deneb | 49 27.9 | N45 21.6 |
| 03 | 146 44.1 | 212 45.2 .. | 23.4 | 254 13.1 .. | 36.6 | 173 33.2 .. | 07.9 | 192 00.4 .. | 58.6 | Denebola | 182 43.8 | N14 26.9 |
| 04 | 161 46.6 | 227 49.1 | 23.0 | 269 13.6 | 36.8 | 188 35.2 | 07.7 | 207 02.6 | 58.5 | Diphda | 348 49.8 | S17 52.2 |
| 05 | 176 49.0 | 242 53.1 | 22.6 | 284 14.2 | 37.1 | 203 37.2 | 07.5 | 222 04.8 | 58.5 | | | |
| 06 | 191 51.5 | 257 57.0 | S18 22.2 | 299 14.7 | S22 37.3 | 218 39.2 | S12 07.4 | 237 07.0 | S17 58.4 | Dubhe | 193 43.8 | N61 37.7 |
| 07 | 206 54.0 | 273 00.9 | 21.7 | 314 15.3 | 37.6 | 233 41.2 | 07.2 | 252 09.2 | 58.3 | Elnath | 278 04.6 | N28 37.5 |
| 08 | 221 56.4 | 288 04.8 | 21.3 | 329 15.8 | 37.8 | 248 43.2 | 07.0 | 267 11.4 | 58.2 | Eltanin | 90 43.9 | N51 29.1 |
| S 09 | 236 58.9 | 303 08.8 .. | 20.9 | 344 16.4 .. | 38.0 | 263 45.2 .. | 06.8 | 282 13.6 .. | 58.2 | Enif | 33 41.5 | N 9 58.5 |
| U 10 | 252 01.4 | 318 12.7 | 20.5 | 359 16.9 | 38.3 | 278 47.2 | 06.6 | 297 15.8 | 58.1 | Fomalhaut | 15 17.4 | S29 30.6 |
| N 11 | 267 03.8 | 333 16.6 | 20.0 | 14 17.5 | 38.5 | 293 49.2 | 06.5 | 312 18.0 | 58.0 | | | |
| D 12 | 282 06.3 | 348 20.6 | S18 19.6 | 29 18.0 | S22 38.8 | 308 51.2 | S12 06.3 | 327 20.1 | S17 57.9 | Gacrux | 171 54.3 | S57 13.8 |
| A 13 | 297 08.8 | 3 24.5 | 19.2 | 44 18.6 | 39.0 | 323 53.2 | 06.1 | 342 22.3 | 57.9 | Gienah | 175 46.1 | S17 39.7 |
| Y 14 | 312 11.2 | 18 28.5 | 18.8 | 59 19.2 | 39.2 | 338 55.2 | 05.9 | 357 24.5 | 57.8 | Hadar | 148 39.7 | S60 28.4 |
| 15 | 327 13.7 | 33 32.4 .. | 18.3 | 74 19.7 .. | 39.5 | 353 57.2 .. | 05.7 | 12 26.7 .. | 57.7 | Hamal | 327 53.8 | N23 34.0 |
| 16 | 342 16.2 | 48 36.4 | 17.9 | 89 20.3 | 39.7 | 8 59.2 | 05.6 | 27 28.9 | 57.6 | Kaus Aust. | 83 36.2 | S34 22.4 |
| 17 | 357 18.6 | 63 40.3 | 17.5 | 104 20.8 | 39.9 | 24 01.2 | 05.4 | 42 31.1 | 57.6 | | | |
| 18 | 12 21.1 | 78 44.3 | S18 17.1 | 119 21.4 | S22 40.2 | 39 03.1 | S12 05.2 | 57 33.3 | S17 57.5 | Kochab | 137 20.5 | N74 03.7 |
| 19 | 27 23.5 | 93 48.2 | 16.7 | 134 21.9 | 40.4 | 54 05.1 | 05.0 | 72 35.5 | 57.4 | Markab | 13 32.5 | N15 19.4 |
| 20 | 42 26.0 | 108 52.2 | 16.2 | 149 22.5 | 40.6 | 69 07.1 | 04.9 | 87 37.6 | 57.3 | Menkar | 314 08.5 | N 4 10.5 |
| 21 | 57 28.5 | 123 56.1 .. | 15.8 | 164 23.0 .. | 40.9 | 84 09.1 .. | 04.7 | 102 39.8 .. | 57.3 | Menkent | 148 00.7 | S36 28.4 |
| 22 | 72 30.9 | 139 00.1 | 15.4 | 179 23.6 | 41.1 | 99 11.1 | 04.5 | 117 42.0 | 57.2 | Miaplacidus | 221 37.9 | S69 48.2 |
| 23 | 87 33.4 | 154 04.1 | 15.0 | 194 24.1 | 41.3 | 114 13.1 | 04.3 | 132 44.2 | 57.1 | | | |
| **3** 00 | 102 35.9 | 169 08.0 | S18 14.6 | 209 24.7 | S22 41.6 | 129 15.1 | S12 04.1 | 147 46.4 | S17 57.0 | Mirfak | 308 31.4 | N49 56.4 |
| 01 | 117 38.3 | 184 12.0 | 14.1 | 224 25.2 | 41.8 | 144 17.1 | 04.0 | 162 48.6 | 57.0 | Nunki | 75 51.2 | S26 16.2 |
| 02 | 132 40.8 | 199 16.0 | 13.7 | 239 25.8 | 42.0 | 159 19.1 | 03.8 | 177 50.8 | 56.9 | Peacock | 53 10.2 | S56 40.0 |
| 03 | 147 43.3 | 214 20.0 .. | 13.3 | 254 26.3 .. | 42.3 | 174 21.1 .. | 03.6 | 192 53.0 .. | 56.8 | Pollux | 243 20.0 | N27 58.3 |
| 04 | 162 45.7 | 229 23.9 | 12.9 | 269 26.9 | 42.5 | 189 23.1 | 03.4 | 207 55.1 | 56.7 | Procyon | 244 53.1 | N 5 10.1 |
| 05 | 177 48.2 | 244 27.9 | 12.5 | 284 27.4 | 42.7 | 204 25.0 | 03.2 | 222 57.3 | 56.7 | | | |
| 06 | 192 50.7 | 259 31.9 | S18 12.1 | 299 28.0 | S22 43.0 | 219 27.0 | S12 03.1 | 237 59.5 | S17 56.6 | Rasalhague | 96 01.2 | N12 32.6 |
| 07 | 207 53.1 | 274 35.9 | 11.6 | 314 28.5 | 43.2 | 234 29.0 | 02.9 | 253 01.7 | 56.5 | Regulus | 207 36.9 | N11 51.6 |
| 08 | 222 55.6 | 289 39.9 | 11.2 | 329 29.1 | 43.4 | 249 31.0 | 02.7 | 268 03.9 | 56.4 | Rigel | 281 05.9 | S 8 10.7 |
| M 09 | 237 58.0 | 304 43.9 .. | 10.8 | 344 29.6 .. | 43.6 | 264 33.0 .. | 02.5 | 283 06.1 .. | 56.4 | Rigil Kent. | 139 44.0 | S60 55.2 |
| O 10 | 253 00.5 | 319 47.9 | 10.4 | 359 30.2 | 43.9 | 279 35.0 | 02.3 | 298 08.3 | 56.3 | Sabik | 102 05.9 | S15 45.1 |
| N 11 | 268 03.0 | 334 51.8 | 10.0 | 14 30.7 | 44.1 | 294 37.0 | 02.2 | 313 10.5 | 56.2 | | | |
| D 12 | 283 05.4 | 349 55.8 | S18 09.6 | 29 31.3 | S22 44.3 | 309 39.0 | S12 02.0 | 328 12.6 | S17 56.1 | Schedar | 349 33.8 | N56 39.7 |
| A 13 | 298 07.9 | 4 59.8 | 09.2 | 44 31.8 | 44.6 | 324 41.0 | 01.8 | 343 14.8 | 56.1 | Shaula | 96 14.1 | S37 07.1 |
| Y 14 | 313 10.4 | 20 03.8 | 08.7 | 59 32.4 | 44.8 | 339 43.0 | 01.6 | 358 17.0 | 56.0 | Sirius | 258 28.1 | S16 44.8 |
| 15 | 328 12.8 | 35 07.8 .. | 08.3 | 74 32.9 .. | 45.0 | 354 44.9 .. | 01.4 | 13 19.2 .. | 55.9 | Spica | 158 25.0 | S11 16.4 |
| 16 | 343 15.3 | 50 11.8 | 07.9 | 89 33.5 | 45.2 | 9 46.9 | 01.3 | 28 21.4 | 55.8 | Suhail | 222 47.7 | S43 31.1 |
| 17 | 358 17.8 | 65 15.9 | 07.5 | 104 34.0 | 45.5 | 24 48.9 | 01.1 | 43 23.6 | 55.7 | | | |
| 18 | 13 20.2 | 80 19.9 | S18 07.1 | 119 34.6 | S22 45.7 | 39 50.9 | S12 00.9 | 58 25.8 | S17 55.7 | Vega | 80 35.3 | N38 48.2 |
| 19 | 28 22.7 | 95 23.9 | 06.7 | 134 35.1 | 45.9 | 54 52.9 | 00.7 | 73 27.9 | 55.6 | Zuben'ubi | 136 58.9 | S16 07.8 |
| 20 | 43 25.2 | 110 27.9 | 06.3 | 149 35.6 | 46.1 | 69 54.9 | 00.5 | 88 30.1 | 55.5 | | SHA | Mer. Pass. |
| 21 | 58 27.6 | 125 31.9 .. | 05.9 | 164 36.2 .. | 46.4 | 84 56.9 .. | 00.4 | 103 32.3 .. | 55.4 | Venus | 65 56.7 | 12 46 |
| 22 | 73 30.1 | 140 35.9 | 05.5 | 179 36.7 | 46.6 | 99 58.9 | 00.2 | 118 34.5 | 55.4 | Mars | 107 34.7 | 10 03 |
| 23 | 88 32.5 | 155 39.9 | 05.1 | 194 37.3 | 46.8 | 115 00.8 | 00.0 | 133 36.7 | 55.3 | Jupiter | 26 50.5 | 15 24 |
| Mer. Pass. | 17 10.7 | v 3.9 | d 0.4 | v 0.6 | d 0.2 | v 2.0 | d 0.2 | v 2.2 | d 0.1 | Saturn | 45 17.2 | 14 10 |

## SUN and MOON

| UT d h | SUN GHA | SUN Dec | MOON GHA | v | MOON Dec | d | HP |
|---|---|---|---|---|---|---|---|
| **1** 00 | 179 10.3 | S23 01.2 | 206 32.5 | 2.8 | S23 55.2 | 7.3 | 61.1 |
| 01 | 194 10.0 | 01.0 | 220 54.3 | 2.8 | 24 02.5 | 7.1 | 61.1 |
| 02 | 209 09.7 | 00.8 | 235 16.1 | 2.7 | 24 09.6 | 7.0 | 61.1 |
| 03 | 224 09.4 | .. 00.6 | 249 37.8 | 2.6 | 24 16.6 | 6.8 | 61.1 |
| 04 | 239 09.1 | 00.4 | 263 59.4 | 2.5 | 24 23.4 | 6.6 | 61.1 |
| 05 | 254 08.8 | 00.2 | 278 20.9 | 2.4 | 24 30.0 | 6.4 | 61.2 |
| 06 | 269 08.6 | S23 00.0 | 292 42.3 | 2.4 | S24 36.4 | 6.2 | 61.2 |
| 07 | 284 08.3 | 22 59.8 | 307 03.7 | 2.2 | 24 42.6 | 6.0 | 61.2 |
| S 08 | 299 08.0 | 59.6 | 321 24.9 | 2.2 | 24 48.6 | 5.9 | 61.2 |
| A 09 | 314 07.7 | .. 59.4 | 335 46.1 | 2.1 | 24 54.5 | 5.7 | 61.2 |
| T 10 | 329 07.4 | 59.2 | 350 07.2 | 2.1 | 25 00.2 | 5.4 | 61.2 |
| U 11 | 344 07.1 | 58.9 | 4 28.3 | 1.9 | 25 05.6 | 5.3 | 61.2 |
| R 12 | 359 06.8 | S22 58.7 | 18 49.2 | 1.9 | S25 10.9 | 5.1 | 61.2 |
| D 13 | 14 06.5 | 58.5 | 33 10.1 | 1.8 | 25 16.0 | 4.9 | 61.2 |
| A 14 | 29 06.2 | 58.3 | 47 30.9 | 1.8 | 25 20.9 | 4.7 | 61.2 |
| Y 15 | 44 05.9 | .. 58.1 | 61 51.7 | 1.7 | 25 25.6 | 4.6 | 61.2 |
| 16 | 59 05.6 | 57.9 | 76 12.4 | 1.6 | 25 30.2 | 4.3 | 61.2 |
| 17 | 74 05.3 | 57.7 | 90 33.0 | 1.6 | 25 34.5 | 4.1 | 61.2 |
| 18 | 89 05.0 | S22 57.5 | 104 53.6 | 1.5 | S25 38.6 | 3.9 | 61.2 |
| 19 | 104 04.7 | 57.2 | 119 14.1 | 1.5 | 25 42.5 | 3.7 | 61.2 |
| 20 | 119 04.4 | 57.0 | 133 34.6 | 1.4 | 25 46.2 | 3.5 | 61.2 |
| 21 | 134 04.1 | . 56.8 | 147 55.0 | 1.4 | 25 49.7 | 3.3 | 61.2 |
| 22 | 149 03.8 | 56.6 | 162 15.4 | 1.4 | 25 53.0 | 3.2 | 61.2 |
| 23 | 164 03.5 | 56.4 | 176 35.8 | 1.3 | 25 56.2 | 2.9 | 61.2 |
| **2** 00 | 179 03.2 | S22 56.1 | 190 56.1 | 1.3 | S25 59.1 | 2.7 | 61.2 |
| 01 | 194 03.0 | 55.9 | 205 16.4 | 1.2 | 26 01.8 | 2.5 | 61.2 |
| 02 | 209 02.7 | 55.7 | 219 36.6 | 1.2 | 26 04.3 | 2.3 | 61.2 |
| 03 | 224 02.4 | .. 55.5 | 233 56.8 | 1.2 | 26 06.6 | 2.1 | 61.2 |
| 04 | 239 02.1 | 55.3 | 248 17.0 | 1.2 | 26 08.7 | 1.8 | 61.2 |
| 05 | 254 01.8 | 55.0 | 262 37.2 | 1.2 | 26 10.5 | 1.7 | 61.2 |
| 06 | 269 01.5 | S22 54.8 | 276 57.4 | 1.1 | S26 12.2 | 1.5 | 61.2 |
| 07 | 284 01.2 | 54.6 | 291 17.5 | 1.2 | 26 13.7 | 1.2 | 61.2 |
| S 08 | 299 00.9 | 54.4 | 305 37.7 | 1.1 | 26 14.9 | 1.1 | 61.2 |
| U 09 | 314 00.6 | .. 54.1 | 319 57.8 | 1.1 | 26 16.0 | 0.8 | 61.2 |
| N 10 | 329 00.3 | 53.9 | 334 17.9 | 1.1 | 26 16.8 | 0.7 | 61.2 |
| D 11 | 344 00.0 | 53.7 | 348 38.0 | 1.2 | 26 17.5 | 0.4 | 61.2 |
| A 12 | 358 59.7 | S22 53.4 | 2 58.2 | 1.1 | S26 17.9 | 0.2 | 61.2 |
| Y 13 | 13 59.4 | 53.2 | 17 18.3 | 1.1 | 26 18.1 | 0.1 | 61.2 |
| 14 | 28 59.2 | 53.0 | 31 38.4 | 1.2 | 26 18.2 | 0.2 | 61.2 |
| 15 | 43 58.9 | .. 52.8 | 45 58.6 | 1.1 | 26 18.0 | 0.4 | 61.2 |
| 16 | 58 58.6 | 52.5 | 60 18.7 | 1.2 | 26 17.6 | 0.6 | 61.2 |
| 17 | 73 58.3 | 52.3 | 74 38.9 | 1.2 | 26 17.0 | 0.0 | 61.2 |
| 18 | 88 58.0 | S22 52.1 | 88 59.1 | 1.3 | S26 16.2 | 1.1 | 61.1 |
| 19 | 103 57.7 | 51.8 | 103 19.4 | 1.2 | 26 15.1 | 1.2 | 61.1 |
| 20 | 118 57.4 | 51.6 | 117 39.6 | 1.3 | 26 13.9 | 1.4 | 61.1 |
| 21 | 133 57.1 | .. 51.3 | 131 59.9 | 1.4 | 26 12.5 | 1.6 | 61.1 |
| 22 | 148 56.8 | 51.1 | 146 20.3 | 1.4 | 26 10.9 | 1.9 | 61.1 |
| 23 | 163 56.5 | 50.9 | 160 40.7 | 1.4 | 26 09.0 | 2.0 | 61.1 |
| **3** 00 | 178 56.2 | S22 50.6 | 175 01.1 | 1.4 | S26 07.0 | 2.3 | 61.1 |
| 01 | 193 56.0 | 50.4 | 189 21.5 | 1.5 | 26 04.7 | 2.4 | 61.1 |
| 02 | 208 55.7 | 50.2 | 203 42.0 | 1.6 | 26 02.3 | 2.6 | 61.0 |
| 03 | 223 55.4 | .. 49.9 | 218 02.6 | 1.6 | 25 59.7 | 2.9 | 61.0 |
| 04 | 238 55.1 | 49.7 | 232 23.2 | 1.7 | 25 56.8 | 3.0 | 61.0 |
| 05 | 253 54.8 | 49.4 | 246 43.9 | 1.7 | 25 53.8 | 3.3 | 61.0 |
| 06 | 268 54.5 | S22 49.2 | 261 04.6 | 1.8 | S25 50.5 | 3.4 | 61.0 |
| 07 | 283 54.2 | 48.9 | 275 25.4 | 1.9 | 25 47.1 | 3.6 | 61.0 |
| M 08 | 298 53.9 | 48.7 | 289 46.3 | 1.9 | 25 43.5 | 3.9 | 60.9 |
| O 09 | 313 53.6 | .. 48.4 | 304 07.2 | 2.0 | 25 39.6 | 4.0 | 60.9 |
| N 10 | 328 53.4 | 48.2 | 318 28.2 | 2.1 | 25 35.6 | 4.2 | 60.9 |
| D 11 | 343 53.1 | 48.0 | 332 49.3 | 2.2 | 25 31.4 | 4.4 | 60.9 |
| A 12 | 358 52.8 | S22 47.7 | 347 10.5 | 2.2 | S25 27.0 | 4.6 | 60.9 |
| Y 13 | 13 52.5 | 47.5 | 1 31.7 | 2.3 | 25 22.4 | 4.8 | 60.8 |
| 14 | 28 52.2 | 47.2 | 15 53.0 | 2.4 | 25 17.6 | 4.9 | 60.8 |
| 15 | 43 51.9 | .. 47.0 | 30 14.4 | 2.5 | 25 12.7 | 5.2 | 60.8 |
| 16 | 58 51.6 | 46.7 | 44 35.9 | 2.6 | 25 07.5 | 5.3 | 60.8 |
| 17 | 73 51.3 | 46.4 | 58 57.5 | 2.7 | 25 02.2 | 5.5 | 60.7 |
| 18 | 88 51.1 | S22 46.2 | 73 19.2 | 2.8 | S24 56.7 | 5.7 | 60.7 |
| 19 | 103 50.8 | 45.9 | 87 41.0 | 2.9 | 24 51.0 | 5.9 | 60.7 |
| 20 | 118 50.5 | 45.7 | 102 02.9 | 2.9 | 24 45.1 | 6.1 | 60.7 |
| 21 | 133 50.2 | .. 45.4 | 116 24.8 | 3.1 | 24 39.0 | 6.2 | 60.7 |
| 22 | 148 49.9 | 45.2 | 130 46.9 | 3.2 | 24 32.8 | 6.4 | 60.6 |
| 23 | 163 49.6 | 44.9 | 145 09.1 | 3.2 | S24 26.4 | 6.6 | 60.6 |
| | SD 16.3 | d 0.2 | SD 16.7 | | 16.7 | | 16.6 |

## Twilight — Sunrise — Moonrise

| Lat. | Naut. | Civil | Sunrise | Moonrise 1 | 2 | 3 | 4 |
|---|---|---|---|---|---|---|---|
| N 72 | 08 23 | 10 39 | ■■■ | ■■■ | ■■■ | ■■■ | ■■■ |
| N 70 | 08 04 | 09 48 | ■■■ | ■■■ | ■■■ | ■■■ | ■■■ |
| 68 | 07 49 | 09 16 | ■■■ | ■■■ | ■■■ | ■■■ | ■■■ |
| 66 | 07 37 | 08 52 | 10 26 | ■■■ | ■■■ | ■■■ | 12 39 |
| 64 | 07 26 | 08 34 | 09 48 | 09 35 | ■■■ | 12 09 | 11 53 |
| 62 | 07 17 | 08 18 | 09 22 | 08 42 | 10 21 | 11 08 | 11 23 |
| 60 | 07 09 | 08 05 | 09 02 | 08 10 | 09 40 | 10 34 | 11 00 |
| N 58 | 07 02 | 07 54 | 08 44 | 07 47 | 09 12 | 10 09 | 10 41 |
| 56 | 06 55 | 07 44 | 08 31 | 07 27 | 08 50 | 09 49 | 10 26 |
| 54 | 06 50 | 07 35 | 08 19 | 07 11 | 08 32 | 09 32 | 10 12 |
| 52 | 06 44 | 07 27 | 08 08 | 06 58 | 08 16 | 09 17 | 10 00 |
| 50 | 06 39 | 07 20 | 07 58 | 06 45 | 08 03 | 09 05 | 09 50 |
| 45 | 06 28 | 07 05 | 07 38 | 06 21 | 07 36 | 08 39 | 09 28 |
| N 40 | 06 18 | 06 52 | 07 22 | 06 01 | 07 14 | 08 18 | 09 10 |
| 35 | 06 09 | 06 40 | 07 08 | 05 44 | 06 56 | 08 01 | 08 55 |
| 30 | 06 00 | 06 30 | 06 56 | 05 30 | 06 41 | 07 46 | 08 42 |
| 20 | 05 44 | 06 11 | 06 35 | 05 06 | 06 15 | 07 21 | 08 19 |
| N 10 | 05 28 | 05 55 | 06 17 | 04 45 | 05 53 | 06 59 | 08 00 |
| 0 | 05 12 | 05 38 | 06 00 | 04 26 | 05 32 | 06 38 | 07 42 |
| S 10 | 04 53 | 05 20 | 05 43 | 04 07 | 05 11 | 06 18 | 07 23 |
| 20 | 04 31 | 05 00 | 05 25 | 03 46 | 04 49 | 05 56 | 07 04 |
| 30 | 04 03 | 04 36 | 05 03 | 03 23 | 04 23 | 05 30 | 06 41 |
| 35 | 03 44 | 04 21 | 04 50 | 03 09 | 04 08 | 05 15 | 06 28 |
| 40 | 03 22 | 04 03 | 04 36 | 02 53 | 03 50 | 04 58 | 06 12 |
| 45 | 02 52 | 03 41 | 04 18 | 02 35 | 03 29 | 04 37 | 05 54 |
| S 50 | 02 09 | 03 12 | 03 56 | 02 11 | 03 03 | 04 11 | 05 31 |
| 52 | 01 43 | 02 58 | 03 46 | 02 00 | 02 50 | 03 58 | 05 20 |
| 54 | 01 03 | 02 41 | 03 34 | 01 48 | 02 35 | 03 43 | 05 07 |
| 56 | //// | 02 19 | 03 21 | 01 33 | 02 18 | 03 26 | 04 53 |
| 58 | //// | 01 52 | 03 04 | 01 17 | 01 58 | 03 05 | 04 36 |
| S 60 | //// | 01 09 | 02 45 | 00 56 | 01 32 | 02 39 | 04 15 |

## Sunset — Twilight — Moonset

| Lat. | Sunset | Civil | Naut. | Moonset 1 | 2 | 3 | 4 |
|---|---|---|---|---|---|---|---|
| N 72 | ■■■ | 13 29 | 15 46 | ■■■ | ■■■ | ■■■ | ■■■ |
| N 70 | ■■■ | 14 21 | 16 04 | ■■■ | ■■■ | ■■■ | ■■■ |
| 68 | ■■■ | 14 53 | 16 19 | ■■■ | ■■■ | ■■■ | ■■■ |
| 66 | 13 42 | 15 16 | 16 32 | ■■■ | ■■■ | ■■■ | 15 27 |
| 64 | 14 20 | 15 35 | 16 42 | 11 40 | ■■■ | 13 45 | 16 12 |
| 62 | 14 46 | 15 50 | 16 51 | 12 33 | 13 13 | 14 45 | 16 41 |
| 60 | 15 07 | 16 03 | 16 59 | 13 05 | 13 55 | 15 19 | 17 03 |
| N 58 | 15 23 | 16 14 | 17 06 | 13 30 | 14 23 | 15 44 | 17 21 |
| 56 | 15 37 | 16 24 | 17 13 | 13 49 | 14 45 | 16 04 | 17 36 |
| 54 | 15 50 | 16 33 | 17 19 | 14 06 | 15 03 | 16 20 | 17 49 |
| 52 | 16 00 | 16 41 | 17 24 | 14 20 | 15 18 | 16 34 | 17 59 |
| 50 | 16 10 | 16 48 | 17 29 | 14 32 | 15 32 | 16 47 | 18 11 |
| 45 | 16 30 | 17 03 | 17 41 | 14 58 | 15 59 | 17 12 | 18 32 |
| N 40 | 16 46 | 17 17 | 17 51 | 15 18 | 16 21 | 17 32 | 18 48 |
| 35 | 17 00 | 17 28 | 18 01 | 15 35 | 16 38 | 17 49 | 19 03 |
| 30 | 17 12 | 17 38 | 18 08 | 15 50 | 16 54 | 18 04 | 19 15 |
| 20 | 17 33 | 17 57 | 18 24 | 16 15 | 17 20 | 18 28 | 19 36 |
| N 10 | 17 51 | 18 13 | 18 40 | 16 37 | 17 42 | 18 49 | 19 54 |
| 0 | 18 08 | 18 30 | 18 56 | 16 57 | 18 03 | 19 09 | 20 10 |
| S 10 | 18 25 | 18 48 | 19 15 | 17 17 | 18 24 | 19 28 | 20 27 |
| 20 | 18 43 | 19 08 | 19 37 | 17 39 | 18 47 | 19 49 | 20 45 |
| 30 | 19 05 | 19 32 | 20 05 | 18 04 | 19 12 | 20 13 | 21 05 |
| 35 | 19 17 | 19 47 | 20 23 | 18 19 | 19 28 | 20 27 | 21 16 |
| 40 | 19 32 | 20 05 | 20 46 | 18 36 | 19 45 | 20 43 | 21 30 |
| 45 | 19 50 | 20 27 | 21 15 | 18 57 | 20 06 | 21 03 | 21 45 |
| S 50 | 20 11 | 20 55 | 21 58 | 19 23 | 20 33 | 21 26 | 22 05 |
| 52 | 20 22 | 21 10 | 22 24 | 19 35 | 20 46 | 21 38 | 22 14 |
| 54 | 20 34 | 21 27 | 23 02 | 19 50 | 21 01 | 21 51 | 22 24 |
| 56 | 20 47 | 21 48 | //// | 20 07 | 21 18 | 22 06 | 22 35 |
| 58 | 21 03 | 22 15 | //// | 20 27 | 21 39 | 22 23 | 22 48 |
| S 60 | 21 23 | 22 56 | //// | 20 53 | 22 05 | 22 44 | 23 03 |

## SUN and MOON

| Day | Eqn. of Time 00h | 12h | Mer. Pass. | Mer. Pass. Upper | Lower | Age | Phase |
|---|---|---|---|---|---|---|---|
| d | m s | m s | h m | h m | h m | d | % |
| 1 | 03 18 | 03 32 | 12 04 | 10 41 | 23 14 | 28 | 2 |
| 2 | 03 46 | 04 00 | 12 04 | 11 48 | 24 21 | 29 | 0 |
| 3 | 04 14 | 04 28 | 12 04 | 12 54 | 00 21 | 01 | 1 |

| UT | ARIES GHA | VENUS −4.3 GHA | Dec | MARS +1.5 GHA | Dec | JUPITER −2.1 GHA | Dec | SATURN +0.7 GHA | Dec | STARS Name | SHA | Dec |
|---|---|---|---|---|---|---|---|---|---|---|---|---|
| **4** 00 | 103 35.0 | 170 44.0 | S18 04.7 | 209 37.8 | S22 47.0 | 130 02.8 | S11 59.8 | 148 38.9 | S17 55.2 | Acamar | 315 13.4 | S40 13.3 |
| 01 | 118 37.5 | 185 48.0 | 04.3 | 224 38.4 | 47.3 | 145 04.8 | 59.6 | 163 41.1 | 55.1 | Achernar | 335 22.0 | S57 07.9 |
| 02 | 133 39.9 | 200 52.0 | 03.8 | 239 38.9 | 47.5 | 160 06.8 | 59.5 | 178 43.3 | 55.1 | Acrux | 173 02.6 | S63 12.9 |
| 03 | 148 42.4 | 215 56.0 | .. 03.4 | 254 39.5 | .. 47.7 | 175 08.8 | .. 59.3 | 193 45.4 | .. 55.0 | Adhara | 255 07.4 | S29 00.1 |
| 04 | 163 44.9 | 231 00.1 | 03.0 | 269 40.0 | 47.9 | 190 10.8 | 59.1 | 208 47.6 | 54.9 | Aldebaran | 290 42.1 | N16 33.2 |
| 05 | 178 47.3 | 246 04.1 | 02.6 | 284 40.6 | 48.2 | 205 12.8 | 58.9 | 223 49.8 | 54.8 | | | |
| 06 | 193 49.8 | 261 08.1 | S18 02.2 | 299 41.1 | S22 48.4 | 220 14.8 | S11 58.7 | 238 52.0 | S17 54.8 | Alioth | 166 15.2 | N55 50.2 |
| 07 | 208 52.3 | 276 12.1 | 01.8 | 314 41.7 | 48.6 | 235 16.7 | 58.6 | 253 54.2 | 54.7 | Alkaid | 152 54.1 | N49 12.0 |
| 08 | 223 54.7 | 291 16.2 | 01.4 | 329 42.2 | 48.8 | 250 18.7 | 58.4 | 268 56.4 | 54.6 | Alnair | 27 36.4 | S46 51.5 |
| T 09 | 238 57.2 | 306 20.2 | .. 01.0 | 344 42.7 | .. 49.0 | 265 20.7 | .. 58.2 | 283 58.6 | .. 54.5 | Alnilam | 275 39.9 | S 1 11.3 |
| U 10 | 253 59.7 | 321 24.3 | 00.6 | 359 43.3 | 49.3 | 280 22.7 | 58.0 | 299 00.7 | 54.5 | Alphard | 217 49.9 | S 8 45.2 |
| E 11 | 269 02.1 | 336 28.3 | 18 00.2 | 14 43.8 | 49.5 | 295 24.7 | 57.8 | 314 02.9 | 54.4 | | | |
| S 12 | 284 04.6 | 351 32.3 | S17 59.8 | 29 44.4 | S22 49.7 | 310 26.7 | S11 57.6 | 329 05.1 | S17 54.3 | Alphecca | 126 06.1 | N26 38.3 |
| D 13 | 299 07.0 | 6 36.4 | 59.4 | 44 44.9 | 49.9 | 325 28.7 | 57.5 | 344 07.3 | 54.2 | Alpheratz | 357 37.4 | N29 12.8 |
| A 14 | 314 09.5 | 21 40.4 | 59.0 | 59 45.5 | 50.1 | 340 30.7 | 57.3 | 359 09.5 | 54.1 | Altair | 62 02.7 | N 8 55.5 |
| Y 15 | 329 12.0 | 36 44.5 | .. 58.6 | 74 46.0 | .. 50.4 | 355 32.6 | .. 57.1 | 14 11.7 | .. 54.1 | Ankaa | 353 09.7 | S42 11.5 |
| 16 | 344 14.4 | 51 48.5 | 58.2 | 89 46.6 | 50.6 | 10 34.6 | 56.9 | 29 13.8 | 54.0 | Antares | 112 19.2 | S26 28.7 |
| 17 | 359 16.9 | 66 52.6 | 57.8 | 104 47.1 | 50.8 | 25 36.6 | 56.7 | 44 16.0 | 53.9 | | | |
| 18 | 14 19.4 | 81 56.6 | S17 57.4 | 119 47.6 | S22 51.0 | 40 38.6 | S11 56.6 | 59 18.2 | S17 53.8 | Arcturus | 145 50.3 | N19 04.0 |
| 19 | 29 21.8 | 97 00.7 | 57.0 | 134 48.2 | 51.2 | 55 40.6 | 56.4 | 74 20.4 | 53.8 | Atria | 107 16.1 | S69 03.8 |
| 20 | 44 24.3 | 112 04.7 | 56.6 | 149 48.7 | 51.4 | 70 42.6 | 56.2 | 89 22.6 | 53.7 | Avior | 234 15.1 | S59 34.6 |
| 21 | 59 26.8 | 127 08.8 | .. 56.3 | 164 49.3 | .. 51.7 | 85 44.5 | .. 56.0 | 104 24.8 | .. 53.6 | Bellatrix | 278 25.2 | N 6 22.1 |
| 22 | 74 29.2 | 142 12.9 | 55.9 | 179 49.8 | 51.9 | 100 46.5 | 55.8 | 119 27.0 | 53.5 | Betelgeuse | 270 54.4 | N 7 24.6 |
| 23 | 89 31.7 | 157 16.9 | 55.5 | 194 50.4 | 52.1 | 115 48.5 | 55.6 | 134 29.1 | 53.5 | | | |
| **5** 00 | 104 34.1 | 172 21.0 | S17 55.1 | 209 50.9 | S22 52.3 | 130 50.5 | S11 55.5 | 149 31.3 | S17 53.4 | Canopus | 263 52.9 | S52 42.5 |
| 01 | 119 36.6 | 187 25.0 | 54.7 | 224 51.4 | 52.5 | 145 52.5 | 55.3 | 164 33.5 | 53.3 | Capella | 280 25.1 | N46 01.2 |
| 02 | 134 39.1 | 202 29.1 | 54.3 | 239 52.0 | 52.7 | 160 54.5 | 55.1 | 179 35.7 | 53.2 | Deneb | 49 27.9 | N45 21.6 |
| 03 | 149 41.5 | 217 33.2 | .. 53.9 | 254 52.5 | .. 52.9 | 175 56.5 | .. 54.9 | 194 37.9 | .. 53.2 | Denebola | 182 27.4 | N14 26.9 |
| 04 | 164 44.0 | 232 37.2 | 53.5 | 269 53.1 | 53.2 | 190 58.4 | 54.7 | 209 40.1 | 53.1 | Diphda | 348 49.8 | S17 52.2 |
| 05 | 179 46.5 | 247 41.3 | 53.1 | 284 53.6 | 53.4 | 206 00.4 | 54.6 | 224 42.3 | 53.0 | | | |
| 06 | 194 48.9 | 262 45.4 | S17 52.7 | 299 54.2 | S22 53.6 | 221 02.4 | S11 54.4 | 239 44.4 | S17 52.9 | Dubhe | 193 43.8 | N61 37.7 |
| W 07 | 209 51.4 | 277 49.5 | 52.3 | 314 54.7 | 53.8 | 236 04.4 | 54.2 | 254 46.6 | 52.8 | Elnath | 278 04.6 | N28 37.5 |
| E 08 | 224 53.9 | 292 53.5 | 51.9 | 329 55.2 | 54.0 | 251 06.4 | 54.0 | 269 48.8 | 52.8 | Eltanin | 90 43.9 | N51 29.1 |
| D 09 | 239 56.3 | 307 57.6 | .. 51.6 | 344 55.8 | .. 54.2 | 266 08.4 | .. 53.8 | 284 51.0 | .. 52.7 | Enif | 33 41.5 | N 9 58.5 |
| N 10 | 254 58.8 | 323 01.7 | 51.2 | 359 56.3 | 54.4 | 281 10.3 | 53.6 | 299 53.2 | 52.6 | Fomalhaut | 15 17.4 | S29 30.6 |
| E 11 | 270 01.3 | 338 05.8 | 50.8 | 14 56.9 | 54.6 | 296 12.3 | 53.5 | 314 55.4 | 52.5 | | | |
| S 12 | 285 03.7 | 353 09.8 | S17 50.4 | 29 57.4 | S22 54.9 | 311 14.3 | S11 53.3 | 329 57.5 | S17 52.5 | Gacrux | 171 54.3 | S57 13.8 |
| D 13 | 300 06.2 | 8 13.9 | 50.0 | 44 57.9 | 55.1 | 326 16.3 | 53.1 | 344 59.7 | 52.4 | Gienah | 175 46.1 | S17 39.7 |
| A 14 | 315 08.6 | 23 18.0 | 49.6 | 59 58.5 | 55.3 | 341 18.3 | 52.9 | 0 01.9 | 52.3 | Hadar | 148 39.7 | S60 28.4 |
| Y 15 | 330 11.1 | 38 22.1 | .. 49.2 | 74 59.0 | .. 55.5 | 356 20.3 | .. 52.7 | 15 04.1 | .. 52.2 | Hamal | 327 53.8 | N23 34.0 |
| 16 | 345 13.6 | 53 26.2 | 48.9 | 89 59.6 | 55.7 | 11 22.2 | 52.5 | 30 06.3 | 52.2 | Kaus Aust. | 83 36.2 | S34 22.4 |
| 17 | 0 16.0 | 68 30.2 | 48.5 | 105 00.1 | 55.9 | 26 24.2 | 52.4 | 45 08.5 | 52.1 | | | |
| 18 | 15 18.5 | 83 34.3 | S17 48.1 | 120 00.6 | S22 56.1 | 41 26.2 | S11 52.2 | 60 10.6 | S17 52.0 | Kochab | 137 20.5 | N74 03.6 |
| 19 | 30 21.0 | 98 38.4 | 47.7 | 135 01.2 | 56.3 | 56 28.2 | 52.0 | 75 12.8 | 51.9 | Markab | 13 32.5 | N15 19.4 |
| 20 | 45 23.4 | 113 42.5 | 47.3 | 150 01.7 | 56.5 | 71 30.2 | 51.8 | 90 15.0 | 51.8 | Menkar | 314 08.5 | N 4 10.5 |
| 21 | 60 25.9 | 128 46.6 | .. 46.9 | 165 02.3 | .. 56.7 | 86 32.1 | .. 51.6 | 105 17.2 | .. 51.8 | Menkent | 148 00.6 | S36 28.4 |
| 22 | 75 28.4 | 143 50.7 | 46.6 | 180 02.8 | 56.9 | 101 34.1 | 51.4 | 120 19.4 | 51.7 | Miaplacidus | 221 37.9 | S69 48.2 |
| 23 | 90 30.8 | 158 54.8 | 46.2 | 195 03.3 | 57.1 | 116 36.1 | 51.3 | 135 21.6 | 51.6 | | | |
| **6** 00 | 105 33.3 | 173 58.9 | S17 45.8 | 210 03.9 | S22 57.3 | 131 38.1 | S11 51.1 | 150 23.7 | S17 51.5 | Mirfak | 308 31.4 | N49 56.4 |
| 01 | 120 35.8 | 189 03.0 | 45.4 | 225 04.4 | 57.6 | 146 40.1 | 50.9 | 165 25.9 | 51.5 | Nunki | 75 51.2 | S26 16.2 |
| 02 | 135 38.2 | 204 07.1 | 45.1 | 240 04.9 | 57.8 | 161 42.1 | 50.7 | 180 28.1 | 51.4 | Peacock | 53 10.2 | S56 40.0 |
| 03 | 150 40.7 | 219 11.2 | .. 44.7 | 255 05.5 | .. 58.0 | 176 44.0 | .. 50.5 | 195 30.3 | .. 51.3 | Pollux | 243 20.0 | N27 58.3 |
| 04 | 165 43.1 | 234 15.2 | 44.3 | 270 06.0 | 58.2 | 191 46.0 | 50.3 | 210 32.5 | 51.2 | Procyon | 244 53.1 | N 5 10.1 |
| 05 | 180 45.6 | 249 19.3 | 43.9 | 285 06.6 | 58.4 | 206 48.0 | 50.2 | 225 34.7 | 51.2 | | | |
| 06 | 195 48.1 | 264 23.4 | S17 43.5 | 300 07.1 | S22 58.6 | 221 50.0 | S11 50.0 | 240 36.8 | S17 51.1 | Rasalhague | 96 01.2 | N12 32.6 |
| 07 | 210 50.5 | 279 27.5 | 43.2 | 315 07.6 | 58.8 | 236 52.0 | 49.8 | 255 39.0 | 51.0 | Regulus | 207 36.8 | N11 51.6 |
| T 08 | 225 53.0 | 294 31.6 | 42.8 | 330 08.2 | 59.0 | 251 53.9 | 49.6 | 270 41.2 | 50.9 | Rigel | 281 05.9 | S 8 10.7 |
| H 09 | 240 55.5 | 309 35.7 | .. 42.4 | 345 08.7 | .. 59.2 | 266 55.9 | .. 49.4 | 285 43.4 | .. 50.8 | Rigil Kent. | 139 45.3 | S60 55.2 |
| U 10 | 255 57.9 | 324 39.8 | 42.1 | 0 09.2 | 59.4 | 281 57.9 | 49.2 | 300 45.6 | 50.8 | Sabik | 102 05.9 | S15 45.1 |
| R 11 | 271 00.4 | 339 44.0 | 41.7 | 15 09.8 | 59.6 | 296 59.9 | 49.1 | 315 47.8 | 50.7 | | | |
| S 12 | 286 02.9 | 354 48.1 | S17 41.3 | 30 10.3 | S22 59.8 | 312 01.9 | S11 48.9 | 330 49.9 | S17 50.6 | Schedar | 349 33.8 | N56 39.7 |
| D 13 | 301 05.3 | 9 52.2 | 40.9 | 45 10.9 | 23 00.0 | 327 03.8 | 48.7 | 345 52.1 | 50.5 | Shaula | 96 14.1 | S37 07.1 |
| A 14 | 316 07.8 | 24 56.3 | 40.6 | 60 11.4 | 00.2 | 342 05.8 | 48.5 | 0 54.3 | 50.5 | Sirius | 258 28.1 | S16 44.8 |
| Y 15 | 331 10.3 | 40 00.4 | .. 40.2 | 75 11.9 | .. 00.4 | 357 07.8 | .. 48.3 | 15 56.5 | .. 50.4 | Spica | 158 24.9 | S11 16.4 |
| 16 | 346 12.7 | 55 04.5 | 39.8 | 90 12.5 | 00.6 | 12 09.8 | 48.1 | 30 58.7 | 50.3 | Suhail | 222 47.7 | S43 31.1 |
| 17 | 1 15.2 | 70 08.6 | 39.5 | 105 13.0 | 00.8 | 27 11.8 | 47.9 | 46 00.8 | 50.2 | | | |
| 18 | 16 17.6 | 85 12.7 | S17 39.1 | 120 13.5 | S23 01.0 | 42 13.7 | S11 47.8 | 61 03.0 | S17 50.1 | Vega | 80 35.3 | N38 48.2 |
| 19 | 31 20.1 | 100 16.8 | 38.7 | 135 14.1 | 01.2 | 57 15.7 | 47.6 | 76 05.2 | 50.1 | Zuben'ubi | 136 58.9 | S16 07.9 |
| 20 | 46 22.6 | 115 20.9 | 38.4 | 150 14.6 | 01.4 | 72 17.7 | 47.4 | 91 07.4 | 50.0 | | SHA | Mer. Pass. |
| 21 | 61 25.0 | 130 25.0 | .. 38.0 | 165 15.1 | .. 01.6 | 87 19.7 | .. 47.2 | 106 09.6 | .. 49.9 | Venus | 67 46.8 | 12 27 |
| 22 | 76 27.5 | 145 29.1 | 37.6 | 180 15.7 | 01.8 | 102 21.6 | 47.0 | 121 11.8 | 49.8 | Mars | 105 16.8 | 10 00 |
| 23 | 91 30.0 | 160 33.2 | 37.3 | 195 16.2 | 02.0 | 117 23.6 | 46.8 | 136 13.9 | 49.8 | Jupiter | 26 16.4 | 15 15 |
| Mer. Pass. 16 58.9 | | v 4.1 | d 0.4 | v 0.5 | d 0.2 | v 2.0 | d 0.2 | v 2.2 | d 0.1 | Saturn | 44 57.2 | 14 00 |

| UT | SUN GHA | Dec | MOON GHA | v | Dec | d | HP |
|---|---|---|---|---|---|---|---|
| d h | ° ′ | ° ′ | ° ′ | ′ | ° ′ | ′ | ′ |
| **4** 00 | 178 49.3 | S22 44.7 | 159 31.3 | 3.4 | S24 19.8 | 6.7 | 60.6 |
| 01 | 193 49.1 | 44.4 | 173 53.7 | 3.5 | 24 13.1 | 6.9 | 60.6 |
| 02 | 208 48.8 | 44.1 | 188 16.2 | 3.6 | 24 06.2 | 7.1 | 60.5 |
| 03 | 223 48.5 | .. 43.9 | 202 38.8 | 3.7 | 23 59.1 | 7.2 | 60.5 |
| 04 | 238 48.2 | 43.6 | 217 01.5 | 3.9 | 23 51.9 | 7.4 | 60.5 |
| 05 | 253 47.9 | 43.4 | 231 24.4 | 3.9 | 23 44.5 | 7.6 | 60.4 |
| 06 | 268 47.6 | S22 43.1 | 245 47.3 | 4.1 | S23 36.9 | 7.7 | 60.4 |
| 07 | 283 47.3 | 42.8 | 260 10.4 | 4.1 | 23 29.2 | 7.9 | 60.4 |
| T 08 | 298 47.1 | 42.6 | 274 33.5 | 4.3 | 23 21.3 | 8.1 | 60.4 |
| U 09 | 313 46.8 | .. 42.3 | 288 56.8 | 4.4 | 23 13.2 | 8.2 | 60.3 |
| E 10 | 328 46.5 | 42.0 | 303 20.2 | 4.6 | 23 05.0 | 8.3 | 60.3 |
| S 11 | 343 46.2 | 41.8 | 317 43.8 | 4.6 | 22 56.7 | 8.5 | 60.3 |
| D 12 | 358 45.9 | S22 41.5 | 332 07.4 | 4.8 | S22 48.2 | 8.6 | 60.2 |
| A 13 | 13 45.6 | 41.2 | 346 31.2 | 4.9 | 22 39.6 | 8.8 | 60.2 |
| Y 14 | 28 45.4 | 41.0 | 0 55.1 | 5.0 | 22 30.8 | 8.9 | 60.2 |
| 15 | 43 45.1 | .. 40.7 | 15 19.1 | 5.2 | 22 21.9 | 9.1 | 60.1 |
| 16 | 58 44.8 | 40.4 | 29 43.3 | 5.3 | 22 12.8 | 9.2 | 60.1 |
| 17 | 73 44.5 | 40.2 | 44 07.6 | 5.4 | 22 03.6 | 9.4 | 60.1 |
| 18 | 88 44.2 | S22 39.9 | 58 32.0 | 5.5 | S21 54.2 | 9.4 | 60.0 |
| 19 | 103 43.9 | 39.6 | 72 56.5 | 5.7 | 21 44.8 | 9.7 | 60.0 |
| 20 | 118 43.7 | 39.3 | 87 21.2 | 5.8 | 21 35.1 | 9.7 | 60.0 |
| 21 | 133 43.4 | .. 39.1 | 101 46.0 | 5.9 | 21 25.4 | 9.9 | 59.9 |
| 22 | 148 43.1 | 38.8 | 116 10.9 | 6.1 | 21 15.5 | 10.0 | 59.9 |
| 23 | 163 42.8 | 38.5 | 130 36.0 | 6.1 | 21 05.5 | 10.1 | 59.9 |
| **5** 00 | 178 42.5 | S22 38.2 | 145 01.1 | 6.4 | S20 55.4 | 10.2 | 59.8 |
| 01 | 193 42.3 | 38.0 | 159 26.5 | 6.4 | 20 45.2 | 10.4 | 59.8 |
| 02 | 208 42.0 | 37.7 | 173 51.9 | 6.6 | 20 34.8 | 10.5 | 59.8 |
| 03 | 223 41.7 | .. 37.4 | 188 17.5 | 6.7 | 20 24.3 | 10.6 | 59.7 |
| 04 | 238 41.4 | 37.1 | 202 43.2 | 6.8 | 20 13.7 | 10.7 | 59.7 |
| 05 | 253 41.1 | 36.8 | 217 09.0 | 7.0 | 20 03.0 | 10.8 | 59.7 |
| 06 | 268 40.9 | S22 36.6 | 231 35.0 | 7.1 | S19 52.2 | 10.9 | 59.6 |
| W 07 | 283 40.6 | 36.3 | 246 01.1 | 7.2 | 19 41.3 | 11.1 | 59.6 |
| E 08 | 298 40.3 | 36.0 | 260 27.3 | 7.3 | 19 30.2 | 11.1 | 59.6 |
| D 09 | 313 40.0 | .. 35.7 | 274 53.6 | 7.5 | 19 19.1 | 11.3 | 59.5 |
| N 10 | 328 39.7 | 35.4 | 289 20.1 | 7.6 | 19 07.8 | 11.3 | 59.5 |
| E 11 | 343 39.5 | 35.1 | 303 46.7 | 7.8 | 18 56.5 | 11.5 | 59.5 |
| S 12 | 358 39.2 | S22 34.9 | 318 13.5 | 7.9 | S18 45.0 | 11.5 | 59.4 |
| D 13 | 13 38.9 | 34.6 | 332 40.4 | 8.0 | 18 33.5 | 11.7 | 59.4 |
| A 14 | 28 38.6 | 34.3 | 347 07.4 | 8.1 | 18 21.8 | 11.7 | 59.3 |
| Y 15 | 43 38.3 | .. 34.0 | 1 34.5 | 8.3 | 18 10.1 | 11.8 | 59.3 |
| 16 | 58 38.1 | 33.7 | 16 01.8 | 8.3 | 17 58.3 | 11.9 | 59.3 |
| 17 | 73 37.8 | 33.4 | 30 29.1 | 8.5 | 17 46.4 | 12.0 | 59.2 |
| 18 | 88 37.5 | S22 33.1 | 44 56.6 | 8.7 | S17 34.4 | 12.1 | 59.2 |
| 19 | 103 37.2 | 32.8 | 59 24.3 | 8.7 | 17 22.3 | 12.2 | 59.1 |
| 20 | 118 37.0 | 32.5 | 73 52.0 | 8.9 | 17 10.1 | 12.3 | 59.1 |
| 21 | 133 36.7 | .. 32.3 | 88 19.9 | 9.0 | 16 57.8 | 12.3 | 59.1 |
| 22 | 148 36.4 | 32.0 | 102 47.9 | 9.2 | 16 45.5 | 12.4 | 59.0 |
| 23 | 163 36.1 | 31.7 | 117 16.1 | 9.2 | 16 33.1 | 12.5 | 59.0 |
| **6** 00 | 178 35.8 | S22 31.4 | 131 44.3 | 9.4 | S16 20.6 | 12.6 | 58.9 |
| 01 | 193 35.6 | 31.1 | 146 12.7 | 9.5 | 16 08.0 | 12.6 | 58.9 |
| 02 | 208 35.3 | 30.8 | 160 41.2 | 9.6 | 15 55.4 | 12.7 | 58.9 |
| 03 | 223 35.0 | .. 30.5 | 175 09.8 | 9.8 | 15 42.7 | 12.8 | 58.8 |
| 04 | 238 34.7 | 30.2 | 189 38.6 | 9.8 | 15 29.9 | 12.8 | 58.8 |
| 05 | 253 34.5 | 29.9 | 204 07.4 | 10.0 | 15 17.1 | 12.9 | 58.7 |
| 06 | 268 34.2 | S22 29.6 | 218 36.4 | 10.1 | S15 04.2 | 13.0 | 58.7 |
| 07 | 283 33.9 | 29.3 | 233 05.5 | 10.2 | 14 51.2 | 13.0 | 58.7 |
| T 08 | 298 33.6 | 29.0 | 247 34.7 | 10.3 | 14 38.2 | 13.1 | 58.6 |
| H 09 | 313 33.4 | .. 28.7 | 262 04.0 | 10.4 | 14 25.1 | 13.2 | 58.6 |
| U 10 | 328 33.1 | 28.4 | 276 33.4 | 10.6 | 14 11.9 | 13.2 | 58.5 |
| R 11 | 343 32.8 | 28.1 | 291 03.0 | 10.6 | 13 58.7 | 13.2 | 58.5 |
| S 12 | 358 32.5 | S22 27.8 | 305 32.6 | 10.8 | S13 45.5 | 13.3 | 58.5 |
| D 13 | 13 32.3 | 27.5 | 320 02.4 | 10.9 | 13 32.2 | 13.4 | 58.4 |
| A 14 | 28 32.0 | 27.2 | 334 32.3 | 10.9 | 13 18.8 | 13.4 | 58.4 |
| Y 15 | 43 31.7 | .. 26.8 | 349 02.2 | 11.1 | 13 05.4 | 13.5 | 58.3 |
| 16 | 58 31.5 | 26.5 | 3 32.3 | 11.2 | 12 51.9 | 13.5 | 58.3 |
| 17 | 73 31.2 | 26.2 | 18 02.5 | 11.3 | 12 38.4 | 13.5 | 58.3 |
| 18 | 88 30.9 | S22 25.9 | 32 32.8 | 11.4 | S12 24.9 | 13.6 | 58.2 |
| 19 | 103 30.6 | 25.6 | 47 03.2 | 11.5 | 12 11.3 | 13.6 | 58.2 |
| 20 | 118 30.4 | 25.3 | 61 33.7 | 11.6 | 11 57.7 | 13.7 | 58.1 |
| 21 | 133 30.1 | .. 25.0 | 76 04.3 | 11.7 | 11 44.0 | 13.7 | 58.1 |
| 22 | 148 29.8 | 24.7 | 90 35.0 | 11.8 | 11 30.3 | 13.8 | 58.1 |
| 23 | 163 29.5 | 24.4 | 105 05.8 | 11.9 | S11 16.5 | 13.8 | 58.0 |
| | SD 16.3 | d 0.3 | SD 16.4 | | 16.2 | | 15.9 |

| Lat. | Naut. | Civil | Sunrise | Moonrise 4 | 5 | 6 | 7 |
|---|---|---|---|---|---|---|---|
| ° | h m | h m | h m | h m | h m | h m | h m |
| N 72 | 08 19 | 10 30 | ■■■ | ■■■ | ■■■ | 12 54 | 12 12 |
| N 70 | 08 01 | 09 43 | ■■■ | ■■■ | 13 22 | 12 29 | 12 00 |
| 68 | 07 47 | 09 12 | 11 29 | ■■■ | 12 38 | 12 09 | 11 50 |
| 66 | 07 35 | 08 49 | 10 20 | 12 39 | 12 08 | 11 53 | 11 42 |
| 64 | 07 25 | 08 31 | 09 45 | 11 53 | 11 46 | 11 40 | 11 35 |
| 62 | 07 16 | 08 16 | 09 19 | 11 23 | 11 28 | 11 29 | 11 29 |
| 60 | 07 08 | 08 04 | 09 00 | 11 00 | 11 12 | 11 19 | 11 24 |
| N 58 | 07 01 | 07 53 | 08 43 | 10 41 | 11 00 | 11 11 | 11 19 |
| 56 | 06 55 | 07 43 | 08 30 | 10 26 | 10 48 | 11 04 | 11 15 |
| 54 | 06 49 | 07 35 | 08 18 | 10 12 | 10 39 | 10 57 | 11 11 |
| 52 | 06 44 | 07 27 | 08 07 | 10 00 | 10 30 | 10 51 | 11 07 |
| 50 | 06 39 | 07 20 | 07 58 | 09 50 | 10 22 | 10 46 | 11 04 |
| 45 | 06 28 | 07 05 | 07 38 | 09 28 | 10 05 | 10 34 | 10 58 |
| N 40 | 06 18 | 06 52 | 07 22 | 09 10 | 09 51 | 10 24 | 10 52 |
| 35 | 06 09 | 06 41 | 07 08 | 08 55 | 09 39 | 10 16 | 10 47 |
| 30 | 06 01 | 06 30 | 06 57 | 08 42 | 09 29 | 10 08 | 10 42 |
| 20 | 05 45 | 06 12 | 06 36 | 08 19 | 09 11 | 09 55 | 10 35 |
| N 10 | 05 30 | 05 56 | 06 18 | 08 00 | 08 55 | 09 44 | 10 28 |
| 0 | 05 13 | 05 39 | 06 02 | 07 42 | 08 40 | 09 33 | 10 22 |
| S 10 | 04 55 | 05 22 | 05 45 | 07 23 | 08 26 | 09 23 | 10 15 |
| 20 | 04 33 | 05 02 | 05 26 | 07 04 | 08 10 | 09 11 | 10 09 |
| 30 | 04 05 | 04 38 | 05 05 | 06 41 | 07 51 | 08 58 | 10 01 |
| 35 | 03 47 | 04 23 | 04 53 | 06 28 | 07 41 | 08 51 | 09 56 |
| 40 | 03 25 | 04 06 | 04 38 | 06 12 | 07 28 | 08 42 | 09 51 |
| 45 | 02 56 | 03 44 | 04 21 | 05 54 | 07 14 | 08 32 | 09 45 |
| S 50 | 02 14 | 03 16 | 04 00 | 05 31 | 06 56 | 08 19 | 09 38 |
| 52 | 01 49 | 03 02 | 03 49 | 05 20 | 06 47 | 08 13 | 09 35 |
| 54 | 01 13 | 02 45 | 03 38 | 05 07 | 06 38 | 08 07 | 09 31 |
| 56 | //// | 02 25 | 03 24 | 04 53 | 06 27 | 08 00 | 09 27 |
| 58 | //// | 01 58 | 03 09 | 04 36 | 06 15 | 07 52 | 09 23 |
| S 60 | //// | 01 19 | 02 50 | 04 15 | 06 00 | 07 42 | 09 18 |

| Lat. | Sunset | Civil | Naut. | Moonset 4 | 5 | 6 | 7 |
|---|---|---|---|---|---|---|---|
| ° | h m | h m | h m | h m | h m | h m | h m |
| N 72 | ■■■ | 13 42 | 15 52 | ■■■ | ■■■ | 19 03 | 21 24 |
| N 70 | ■■■ | 14 29 | 16 10 | ■■■ | 16 45 | 19 26 | 21 41 |
| 68 | 12 42 | 14 59 | 16 24 | ■■■ | 17 28 | 19 44 | 21 47 |
| 66 | 13 51 | 15 22 | 16 36 | 15 27 | 17 56 | 19 58 | 21 52 |
| 64 | 14 27 | 15 40 | 16 46 | 16 12 | 18 18 | 20 10 | 21 52 |
| 62 | 14 52 | 15 55 | 16 55 | 16 41 | 18 35 | 20 20 | 21 57 |
| 60 | 15 11 | 16 07 | 17 03 | 17 03 | 18 49 | 20 28 | 22 01 |
| N 58 | 15 28 | 16 18 | 17 10 | 17 21 | 19 01 | 20 35 | 22 04 |
| 56 | 15 41 | 16 28 | 17 16 | 17 36 | 19 11 | 20 42 | 22 07 |
| 54 | 15 53 | 16 36 | 17 22 | 17 49 | 19 20 | 20 48 | 22 10 |
| 52 | 16 04 | 16 44 | 17 27 | 18 01 | 19 28 | 20 53 | 22 12 |
| 50 | 16 13 | 16 51 | 17 32 | 18 11 | 19 36 | 20 57 | 22 14 |
| 45 | 16 33 | 17 06 | 17 43 | 18 32 | 19 51 | 21 07 | 22 19 |
| N 40 | 16 49 | 17 19 | 17 53 | 18 48 | 20 04 | 21 16 | 22 23 |
| 35 | 17 02 | 17 30 | 18 02 | 19 03 | 20 14 | 21 23 | 22 27 |
| 30 | 17 14 | 17 40 | 18 10 | 19 15 | 20 24 | 21 29 | 22 30 |
| 20 | 17 35 | 17 58 | 18 26 | 19 36 | 20 40 | 21 39 | 22 35 |
| N 10 | 17 52 | 18 15 | 18 41 | 19 54 | 20 53 | 21 48 | 22 39 |
| 0 | 18 09 | 18 31 | 18 58 | 20 10 | 21 06 | 21 57 | 22 44 |
| S 10 | 18 26 | 18 49 | 19 16 | 20 27 | 21 19 | 22 05 | 22 48 |
| 20 | 18 44 | 19 09 | 19 38 | 20 45 | 21 32 | 22 14 | 22 52 |
| 30 | 19 05 | 19 32 | 20 05 | 21 05 | 21 48 | 22 25 | 22 57 |
| 35 | 19 18 | 19 47 | 20 23 | 21 16 | 21 57 | 22 30 | 23 00 |
| 40 | 19 32 | 20 04 | 20 45 | 21 30 | 22 07 | 22 37 | 23 03 |
| 45 | 19 49 | 20 26 | 21 14 | 21 45 | 22 18 | 22 45 | 23 07 |
| S 50 | 20 11 | 20 54 | 21 56 | 22 05 | 22 32 | 22 54 | 23 11 |
| 52 | 20 21 | 21 08 | 22 20 | 22 14 | 22 39 | 22 58 | 23 13 |
| 54 | 20 32 | 21 25 | 22 56 | 22 24 | 22 46 | 23 02 | 23 15 |
| 56 | 20 46 | 21 45 | //// | 22 35 | 22 54 | 23 07 | 23 18 |
| 58 | 21 01 | 22 11 | //// | 22 48 | 23 03 | 23 13 | 23 20 |
| S 60 | 21 20 | 22 49 | //// | 23 03 | 23 13 | 23 19 | 23 23 |

| Day | SUN Eqn. of Time 00h | 12h | Mer. Pass. | MOON Mer. Pass. Upper | Lower | Age | Phase |
|---|---|---|---|---|---|---|---|
| d | m s | m s | h m | h m | h m | d | % |
| 4 | 04 42 | 04 56 | 12 05 | 13 56 | 01 25 | 02 | 5 |
| 5 | 05 09 | 05 23 | 12 05 | 14 53 | 02 26 | 03 | 11 |
| 6 | 05 36 | 05 49 | 12 06 | 15 45 | 03 20 | 04 | 19 |

| UT | ARIES GHA | VENUS −4.1 GHA | Dec | MARS +1.5 GHA | Dec | JUPITER −2.1 GHA | Dec | SATURN +0.7 GHA | Dec | STARS Name | SHA | Dec |
|---|---|---|---|---|---|---|---|---|---|---|---|---|
| 7 00 | 106 32.4 | 175 37.4 | S17 36.9 | 210 16.7 | S23 02.2 | 132 25.6 | S11 46.6 | 151 16.1 | S17 49.7 | Acamar | 315 13.5 | S40 13.3 |
| 01 | 121 34.9 | 190 41.5 | 36.5 | 225 17.3 | 02.4 | 147 27.6 | 46.5 | 166 18.3 | 49.6 | Achernar | 335 22.0 | S57 07.9 |
| 02 | 136 37.4 | 205 45.6 | 36.2 | 240 17.8 | 02.6 | 162 29.6 | 46.3 | 181 20.5 | 49.5 | Acrux | 173 02.6 | S63 12.9 |
| 03 | 151 39.8 | 220 49.7 .. | 35.8 | 255 18.4 .. | 02.8 | 177 31.5 .. | 46.1 | 196 22.7 .. | 49.5 | Adhara | 255 07.4 | S29 00.1 |
| 04 | 166 42.3 | 235 53.8 | 35.4 | 270 18.9 | 03.0 | 192 33.5 | 45.9 | 211 24.9 | 49.4 | Aldebaran | 290 42.2 | N16 33.2 |
| 05 | 181 44.7 | 250 57.9 | 35.1 | 285 19.4 | 03.2 | 207 35.5 | 45.7 | 226 27.0 | 49.3 | | | |
| 06 | 196 47.2 | 266 02.0 | S17 34.7 | 300 20.0 | S23 03.4 | 222 37.5 | S11 45.5 | 241 29.2 | S17 49.2 | Alioth | 166 15.2 | N55 50.2 |
| 07 | 211 49.7 | 281 06.2 | 34.4 | 315 20.5 | 03.5 | 237 39.4 | 45.4 | 256 31.4 | 49.1 | Alkaid | 152 54.1 | N49 12.0 |
| 08 | 226 52.1 | 296 10.3 | 34.0 | 330 21.0 | 03.7 | 252 41.4 | 45.2 | 271 33.6 | 49.1 | Alnair | 27 36.4 | S46 51.5 |
| F 09 | 241 54.6 | 311 14.4 .. | 33.6 | 345 21.6 .. | 03.9 | 267 43.4 .. | 45.0 | 286 35.8 .. | 49.0 | Alnilam | 275 39.9 | S 1 11.4 |
| R 10 | 256 57.1 | 326 18.5 | 33.3 | 0 22.1 | 04.1 | 282 45.4 | 44.8 | 301 37.9 | 48.9 | Alphard | 217 49.9 | S 8 45.2 |
| I 11 | 271 59.5 | 341 22.6 | 32.9 | 15 22.6 | 04.3 | 297 47.4 | 44.6 | 316 40.1 | 48.8 | | | |
| D 12 | 287 02.0 | 356 26.7 | S17 32.6 | 30 23.2 | S23 04.5 | 312 49.3 | S11 44.4 | 331 42.3 | S17 48.8 | Alphecca | 126 06.1 | N26 38.3 |
| A 13 | 302 04.5 | 11 30.9 | 32.2 | 45 23.7 | 04.7 | 327 51.3 | 44.2 | 346 44.5 | 48.7 | Alpheratz | 357 37.4 | N29 12.8 |
| Y 14 | 317 06.9 | 26 35.0 | 31.8 | 60 24.2 | 04.9 | 342 53.3 | 44.1 | 1 46.7 | 48.6 | Altair | 62 02.7 | N 8 55.5 |
| 15 | 332 09.4 | 41 39.1 .. | 31.5 | 75 24.8 .. | 05.1 | 357 55.3 .. | 43.9 | 16 48.8 .. | 48.5 | Ankaa | 353 09.7 | S42 11.5 |
| 16 | 347 11.9 | 56 43.2 | 31.1 | 90 25.3 | 05.3 | 12 57.2 | 43.7 | 31 51.0 | 48.4 | Antares | 112 19.1 | S26 28.7 |
| 17 | 2 14.3 | 71 47.3 | 30.8 | 105 25.8 | 05.5 | 27 59.2 | 43.5 | 46 53.2 | 48.4 | | | |
| 18 | 17 16.8 | 86 51.5 | S17 30.4 | 120 26.3 | S23 05.7 | 43 01.2 | S11 43.3 | 61 55.4 | S17 48.3 | Arcturus | 145 50.3 | N19 04.0 |
| 19 | 32 19.2 | 101 55.6 | 30.1 | 135 26.9 | 05.8 | 58 03.2 | 43.1 | 76 57.6 | 48.2 | Atria | 107 16.1 | S69 03.8 |
| 20 | 47 21.7 | 116 59.7 | 29.7 | 150 27.4 | 06.0 | 73 05.1 | 42.9 | 91 59.7 | 48.1 | Avior | 234 15.1 | S59 34.7 |
| 21 | 62 24.2 | 132 03.8 .. | 29.4 | 165 27.9 .. | 06.2 | 88 07.1 .. | 42.7 | 107 01.9 .. | 48.0 | Bellatrix | 278 25.2 | N 6 22.1 |
| 22 | 77 26.6 | 147 07.9 | 29.0 | 180 28.5 | 06.4 | 103 09.1 | 42.6 | 122 04.1 | 48.0 | Betelgeuse | 270 54.4 | N 7 24.6 |
| 23 | 92 29.1 | 162 12.1 | 28.7 | 195 29.0 | 06.6 | 118 11.1 | 42.4 | 137 06.3 | 47.9 | | | |
| 8 00 | 107 31.6 | 177 16.2 | S17 28.3 | 210 29.5 | S23 06.8 | 133 13.0 | S11 42.2 | 152 08.5 | S17 47.8 | Canopus | 263 52.9 | S52 42.5 |
| 01 | 122 34.0 | 192 20.3 | 28.0 | 225 30.1 | 07.0 | 148 15.0 | 42.0 | 167 10.7 | 47.7 | Capella | 280 25.1 | N46 01.2 |
| 02 | 137 36.5 | 207 24.4 | 27.6 | 240 30.6 | 07.2 | 163 17.0 | 41.8 | 182 12.8 | 47.7 | Deneb | 49 27.9 | N45 21.5 |
| 03 | 152 39.0 | 222 28.5 .. | 27.3 | 255 31.1 .. | 07.3 | 178 19.0 .. | 41.6 | 197 15.0 .. | 47.6 | Denebola | 182 27.4 | N14 26.9 |
| 04 | 167 41.4 | 237 32.7 | 26.9 | 270 31.7 | 07.5 | 193 20.9 | 41.4 | 212 17.2 | 47.5 | Diphda | 348 49.8 | S17 52.2 |
| 05 | 182 43.9 | 252 36.8 | 26.6 | 285 32.2 | 07.7 | 208 22.9 | 41.3 | 227 19.4 | 47.4 | | | |
| 06 | 197 46.4 | 267 40.9 | S17 26.2 | 300 32.7 | S23 07.9 | 223 24.9 | S11 41.1 | 242 21.6 | S17 47.3 | Dubhe | 193 43.7 | N61 37.7 |
| 07 | 212 48.8 | 282 45.0 | 25.9 | 315 33.2 | 08.1 | 238 26.9 | 40.9 | 257 23.7 | 47.3 | Elnath | 278 04.6 | N28 37.5 |
| S 08 | 227 51.3 | 297 49.2 | 25.5 | 330 33.8 | 08.3 | 253 28.8 | 40.7 | 272 25.9 | 47.2 | Eltanin | 90 48.3 | N51 29.0 |
| A 09 | 242 53.7 | 312 53.3 .. | 25.2 | 345 34.3 .. | 08.5 | 268 30.8 .. | 40.5 | 287 28.1 .. | 47.1 | Enif | 33 41.5 | N 9 58.5 |
| T 10 | 257 56.2 | 327 57.4 | 24.8 | 0 34.8 | 08.6 | 283 32.8 | 40.3 | 302 30.3 | 47.0 | Fomalhaut | 15 17.5 | S29 30.6 |
| U 11 | 272 58.7 | 343 01.5 | 24.5 | 15 35.4 | 08.8 | 298 34.8 | 40.1 | 317 32.5 | 47.0 | | | |
| R 12 | 288 01.1 | 358 05.6 | S17 24.2 | 30 35.9 | S23 09.0 | 313 36.7 | S11 39.9 | 332 34.6 | S17 46.9 | Gacrux | 171 54.2 | S57 13.8 |
| D 13 | 303 03.6 | 13 09.8 | 23.8 | 45 36.4 | 09.2 | 328 38.7 | 39.8 | 347 36.8 | 46.8 | Gienah | 175 46.0 | S17 39.7 |
| A 14 | 318 06.1 | 28 13.9 | 23.5 | 60 36.9 | 09.4 | 343 40.7 | 39.6 | 2 39.0 | 46.7 | Hadar | 148 39.6 | S60 28.4 |
| Y 15 | 333 08.5 | 43 18.0 .. | 23.1 | 75 37.5 .. | 09.6 | 358 42.7 .. | 39.4 | 17 41.2 .. | 46.6 | Hamal | 327 53.9 | N23 34.0 |
| 16 | 348 11.0 | 58 22.1 | 22.8 | 90 38.0 | 09.7 | 13 44.6 | 39.2 | 32 43.4 | 46.6 | Kaus Aust. | 83 36.2 | S34 22.4 |
| 17 | 3 13.5 | 73 26.2 | 22.5 | 105 38.5 | 09.9 | 28 46.6 | 39.0 | 47 45.5 | 46.5 | | | |
| 18 | 18 15.9 | 88 30.4 | S17 22.1 | 120 39.1 | S23 10.1 | 43 48.6 | S11 38.8 | 62 47.7 | S17 46.4 | Kochab | 137 20.4 | N74 03.6 |
| 19 | 33 18.4 | 103 34.5 | 21.8 | 135 39.6 | 10.3 | 58 50.5 | 38.6 | 77 49.9 | 46.3 | Markab | 13 32.5 | N15 19.4 |
| 20 | 48 20.8 | 118 38.6 | 21.4 | 150 40.1 | 10.5 | 73 52.5 | 38.4 | 92 52.1 | 46.2 | Menkar | 314 08.6 | N 4 10.5 |
| 21 | 63 23.3 | 133 42.7 .. | 21.1 | 165 40.6 .. | 10.6 | 88 54.5 .. | 38.3 | 107 54.3 .. | 46.2 | Menkent | 148 00.6 | S36 28.4 |
| 22 | 78 25.8 | 148 46.8 | 20.8 | 180 41.2 | 10.8 | 103 56.5 | 38.1 | 122 56.4 | 46.1 | Miaplacidus | 221 37.9 | S69 48.2 |
| 23 | 93 28.2 | 163 51.0 | 20.4 | 195 41.7 | 11.0 | 118 58.4 | 37.9 | 137 58.6 | 46.0 | | | |
| 9 00 | 108 30.7 | 178 55.1 | S17 20.1 | 210 42.2 | S23 11.2 | 134 00.4 | S11 37.7 | 153 00.8 | S17 45.9 | Mirfak | 308 31.4 | N49 56.5 |
| 01 | 123 33.2 | 193 59.2 | 19.7 | 225 42.8 | 11.4 | 149 02.4 | 37.5 | 168 03.0 | 45.9 | Nunki | 75 51.2 | S26 16.2 |
| 02 | 138 35.6 | 209 03.3 | 19.4 | 240 43.3 | 11.5 | 164 04.4 | 37.3 | 183 05.2 | 45.8 | Peacock | 53 10.2 | S56 40.0 |
| 03 | 153 38.1 | 224 07.4 .. | 19.1 | 255 43.8 .. | 11.7 | 179 06.3 .. | 37.1 | 198 07.3 .. | 45.7 | Pollux | 243 19.9 | N27 58.3 |
| 04 | 168 40.6 | 239 11.6 | 18.7 | 270 44.3 | 11.9 | 194 08.3 | 36.9 | 213 09.5 | 45.6 | Procyon | 244 53.1 | N 5 10.1 |
| 05 | 183 43.0 | 254 15.7 | 18.4 | 285 44.9 | 12.1 | 209 10.3 | 36.8 | 228 11.7 | 45.5 | | | |
| 06 | 198 45.5 | 269 19.8 | S17 18.1 | 300 45.4 | S23 12.2 | 224 12.2 | S11 36.6 | 243 13.9 | S17 45.5 | Rasalhague | 96 01.2 | N12 32.6 |
| 07 | 213 48.0 | 284 23.9 | 17.7 | 315 45.9 | 12.4 | 239 14.2 | 36.4 | 258 16.0 | 45.4 | Regulus | 207 36.8 | N11 51.5 |
| 08 | 228 50.4 | 299 28.0 | 17.4 | 330 46.4 | 12.6 | 254 16.2 | 36.2 | 273 18.2 | 45.3 | Rigel | 281 05.9 | S 8 10.7 |
| S 09 | 243 52.9 | 314 32.1 .. | 17.1 | 345 47.0 .. | 12.8 | 269 18.2 .. | 36.0 | 288 20.4 .. | 45.2 | Rigil Kent. | 139 43.9 | S60 55.2 |
| U 10 | 258 55.3 | 329 36.3 | 16.8 | 0 47.5 | 12.9 | 284 20.1 | 35.8 | 303 22.6 | 45.1 | Sabik | 102 05.9 | S15 45.1 |
| N 11 | 273 57.8 | 344 40.4 | 16.4 | 15 48.0 | 13.1 | 299 22.1 | 35.6 | 318 24.8 | 45.1 | | | |
| D 12 | 289 00.3 | 359 44.5 | S17 16.1 | 30 48.5 | S23 13.3 | 314 24.1 | S11 35.4 | 333 26.9 | S17 45.0 | Schedar | 349 33.8 | N56 39.7 |
| A 13 | 304 02.7 | 14 48.6 | 15.8 | 45 49.1 | 13.5 | 329 26.0 | 35.2 | 348 29.1 | 44.9 | Shaula | 96 14.1 | S37 07.1 |
| Y 14 | 319 05.2 | 29 52.7 | 15.4 | 60 49.6 | 13.6 | 344 28.0 | 35.1 | 3 31.3 | 44.8 | Sirius | 258 28.0 | S16 44.8 |
| 15 | 334 07.7 | 44 56.8 .. | 15.1 | 75 50.1 .. | 13.8 | 359 30.0 .. | 34.9 | 18 33.5 .. | 44.8 | Spica | 158 24.9 | S11 16.5 |
| 16 | 349 10.1 | 60 01.0 | 14.8 | 90 50.6 | 14.0 | 14 31.9 | 34.7 | 33 35.7 | 44.7 | Suhail | 222 47.7 | S43 31.1 |
| 17 | 4 12.6 | 75 05.1 | 14.5 | 105 51.2 | 14.2 | 29 33.9 | 34.5 | 48 37.8 | 44.6 | | | |
| 18 | 19 15.1 | 90 09.2 | S17 14.1 | 120 51.7 | S23 14.3 | 44 35.9 | S11 34.3 | 63 40.0 | S17 44.5 | Vega | 80 35.3 | N38 48.2 |
| 19 | 34 17.5 | 105 13.3 | 13.8 | 135 52.2 | 14.5 | 59 37.9 | 34.1 | 78 42.2 | 44.4 | Zuben'ubi | 136 58.9 | S16 07.9 |
| 20 | 49 20.0 | 120 17.4 | 13.5 | 150 52.7 | 14.7 | 74 39.8 | 33.9 | 93 44.4 | 44.4 | | SHA | Mer. Pass. |
| 21 | 64 22.4 | 135 21.5 .. | 13.2 | 165 53.3 .. | 14.8 | 89 41.8 .. | 33.7 | 108 46.5 .. | 44.3 | | ° ′ | h m |
| 22 | 79 24.9 | 150 25.6 | 12.8 | 180 53.8 | 15.0 | 104 43.8 | 33.5 | 123 48.7 | 44.2 | Venus | 69 44.6 | 12 08 |
| 23 | 94 27.4 | 165 29.7 | 12.5 | 195 54.3 | 15.2 | 119 45.7 | 33.4 | 138 50.9 | 44.1 | Mars | 102 58.0 | 9 58 |
| | h m | | | | | | | | | Jupiter | 25 41.5 | 15 05 |
| Mer. Pass. 16 47.1 | v 4.1 d 0.3 | v 0.5 | d 0.2 | v 2.0 | d 0.2 | v 2.2 | d 0.1 | | | Saturn | 44 36.9 | 13 49 |

## SUN and MOON

| UT | SUN GHA | SUN Dec | MOON GHA | v | MOON Dec | d | HP |
|---|---|---|---|---|---|---|---|
| d h | ° ′ | ° ′ | ° ′ | ′ | ° ′ | ′ | ′ |
| **7** 00 | 178 29.3 | S22 24.1 | 119 36.7 | 12.0 | S11 02.7 | 13.8 | 58.0 |
| 01 | 193 29.0 | 23.7 | 134 07.7 | 12.1 | 10 48.9 | 13.9 | 57.9 |
| 02 | 208 28.7 | 23.4 | 148 38.8 | 12.2 | 10 35.0 | 13.8 | 57.9 |
| 03 | 223 28.5 | .. 23.1 | 163 10.0 | 12.2 | 10 21.2 | 14.0 | 57.9 |
| 04 | 238 28.2 | 22.8 | 177 41.2 | 12.4 | 10 07.2 | 13.9 | 57.8 |
| 05 | 253 27.9 | 22.5 | 192 12.6 | 12.4 | 9 53.3 | 14.0 | 57.8 |
| 06 | 268 27.7 | S22 22.2 | 206 44.0 | 12.6 | S 9 39.3 | 14.0 | 57.7 |
| 07 | 283 27.4 | 21.8 | 221 15.6 | 12.6 | 9 25.3 | 14.0 | 57.7 |
| F 08 | 298 27.1 | 21.5 | 235 47.2 | 12.7 | 9 11.3 | 14.0 | 57.7 |
| R 09 | 313 26.8 | .. 21.2 | 250 18.9 | 12.8 | 8 57.3 | 14.1 | 57.6 |
| I 10 | 328 26.6 | 20.9 | 264 50.7 | 12.9 | 8 43.2 | 14.1 | 57.6 |
| D 11 | 343 26.3 | 20.6 | 279 22.6 | 13.0 | 8 29.1 | 14.1 | 57.5 |
| A 12 | 358 26.0 | S22 20.2 | 293 54.6 | 13.0 | S 8 15.0 | 14.1 | 57.5 |
| Y 13 | 13 25.8 | 19.9 | 308 26.6 | 13.1 | 8 00.9 | 14.2 | 57.5 |
| 14 | 28 25.5 | 19.6 | 322 58.7 | 13.2 | 7 46.7 | 14.1 | 57.4 |
| 15 | 43 25.2 | .. 19.3 | 337 30.9 | 13.3 | 7 32.6 | 14.2 | 57.4 |
| 16 | 58 25.0 | 18.9 | 352 03.2 | 13.4 | 7 18.4 | 14.2 | 57.3 |
| 17 | 73 24.7 | 18.6 | 6 35.6 | 13.4 | 7 04.2 | 14.2 | 57.3 |
| 18 | 88 24.4 | S22 18.3 | 21 08.0 | 13.5 | S 6 50.0 | 14.2 | 57.3 |
| 19 | 103 24.2 | 17.9 | 35 40.5 | 13.5 | 6 35.8 | 14.2 | 57.2 |
| 20 | 118 23.9 | 17.6 | 50 13.0 | 13.7 | 6 21.6 | 14.2 | 57.2 |
| 21 | 133 23.6 | .. 17.3 | 64 45.7 | 13.7 | 6 07.4 | 14.3 | 57.1 |
| 22 | 148 23.4 | 17.0 | 79 18.4 | 13.8 | 5 53.1 | 14.2 | 57.1 |
| 23 | 163 23.1 | 16.6 | 93 51.2 | 13.8 | 5 38.9 | 14.3 | 57.1 |
| **8** 00 | 178 22.8 | S22 16.3 | 108 24.0 | 13.9 | S 5 24.6 | 14.2 | 57.0 |
| 01 | 193 22.6 | 16.0 | 122 56.9 | 14.0 | 5 10.4 | 14.3 | 57.0 |
| 02 | 208 22.3 | 15.6 | 137 29.9 | 14.0 | 4 56.1 | 14.2 | 57.0 |
| 03 | 223 22.0 | .. 15.3 | 152 02.9 | 14.1 | 4 41.9 | 14.3 | 56.9 |
| 04 | 238 21.8 | 15.0 | 166 36.0 | 14.1 | 4 27.6 | 14.2 | 56.9 |
| 05 | 253 21.5 | 14.6 | 181 09.1 | 14.2 | 4 13.4 | 14.3 | 56.8 |
| 06 | 268 21.2 | S22 14.3 | 195 42.3 | 14.3 | S 3 59.1 | 14.2 | 56.8 |
| S 07 | 283 21.0 | 13.9 | 210 15.6 | 14.3 | 3 44.9 | 14.3 | 56.8 |
| A 08 | 298 20.7 | 13.6 | 224 48.9 | 14.4 | 3 30.6 | 14.2 | 56.7 |
| T 09 | 313 20.4 | .. 13.3 | 239 22.3 | 14.4 | 3 16.4 | 14.3 | 56.7 |
| U 10 | 328 20.2 | 12.9 | 253 55.7 | 14.5 | 3 02.1 | 14.2 | 56.7 |
| R 11 | 343 19.9 | 12.6 | 268 29.2 | 14.5 | 2 47.9 | 14.3 | 56.6 |
| D 12 | 358 19.7 | S22 12.3 | 283 02.7 | 14.6 | S 2 33.6 | 14.2 | 56.6 |
| A 13 | 13 19.4 | 11.9 | 297 36.3 | 14.6 | 2 19.4 | 14.2 | 56.5 |
| Y 14 | 28 19.1 | 11.6 | 312 09.9 | 14.7 | 2 05.2 | 14.2 | 56.5 |
| 15 | 43 18.9 | .. 11.2 | 326 43.6 | 14.7 | 1 51.0 | 14.2 | 56.5 |
| 16 | 58 18.6 | 10.9 | 341 17.3 | 14.7 | 1 36.8 | 14.2 | 56.4 |
| 17 | 73 18.3 | 10.5 | 355 51.0 | 14.8 | 1 22.6 | 14.1 | 56.4 |
| 18 | 88 18.1 | S22 10.2 | 10 24.8 | 14.9 | S 1 08.5 | 14.2 | 56.4 |
| 19 | 103 17.8 | 09.8 | 24 58.7 | 14.9 | 0 54.3 | 14.1 | 56.3 |
| 20 | 118 17.6 | 09.5 | 39 32.6 | 14.9 | 0 40.2 | 14.2 | 56.3 |
| 21 | 133 17.3 | .. 09.1 | 54 06.5 | 14.9 | 0 26.0 | 14.1 | 56.3 |
| 22 | 148 17.0 | 08.8 | 68 40.4 | 15.0 | S 0 11.9 | 14.1 | 56.2 |
| 23 | 163 16.7 | 08.4 | 83 14.4 | 15.1 | N 0 02.2 | 14.0 | 56.2 |
| **9** 00 | 178 16.5 | S22 08.1 | 97 48.5 | 15.0 | N 0 16.2 | 14.1 | 56.2 |
| 01 | 193 16.3 | 07.7 | 112 22.5 | 15.1 | 0 30.3 | 14.0 | 56.1 |
| 02 | 208 16.0 | 07.4 | 126 56.6 | 15.1 | 0 44.3 | 14.1 | 56.1 |
| 03 | 223 15.7 | .. 07.0 | 141 30.7 | 15.2 | 0 58.4 | 14.0 | 56.1 |
| 04 | 238 15.5 | 06.7 | 156 04.9 | 15.2 | 1 12.4 | 13.9 | 56.0 |
| 05 | 253 15.2 | 06.3 | 170 39.1 | 15.2 | 1 26.3 | 14.0 | 56.0 |
| 06 | 268 15.0 | S22 06.0 | 185 13.3 | 15.2 | N 1 40.3 | 13.9 | 56.0 |
| 07 | 283 14.7 | 05.6 | 199 47.5 | 15.3 | 1 54.2 | 13.9 | 55.9 |
| S 08 | 298 14.4 | 05.3 | 214 21.8 | 15.3 | 2 08.1 | 13.9 | 55.9 |
| U 09 | 313 14.2 | .. 04.9 | 228 56.1 | 15.3 | 2 22.0 | 13.9 | 55.9 |
| N 10 | 328 13.9 | 04.6 | 243 30.4 | 15.3 | 2 35.9 | 13.8 | 55.8 |
| D 11 | 343 13.7 | 04.2 | 258 04.7 | 15.4 | 2 49.7 | 13.8 | 55.8 |
| A 12 | 358 13.4 | S22 03.8 | 272 39.1 | 15.3 | N 3 03.5 | 13.8 | 55.8 |
| Y 13 | 13 13.1 | 03.5 | 287 13.4 | 15.4 | 3 17.3 | 13.7 | 55.7 |
| 14 | 28 12.9 | 03.1 | 301 47.8 | 15.4 | 3 31.0 | 13.8 | 55.7 |
| 15 | 43 12.6 | .. 02.8 | 316 22.2 | 15.4 | 3 44.8 | 13.6 | 55.7 |
| 16 | 58 12.4 | 02.4 | 330 56.6 | 15.5 | 3 58.4 | 13.7 | 55.7 |
| 17 | 73 12.1 | 02.0 | 345 31.1 | 15.4 | 4 12.1 | 13.6 | 55.6 |
| 18 | 88 11.9 | S22 01.7 | 0 05.5 | 15.5 | N 4 25.7 | 13.6 | 55.6 |
| 19 | 103 11.6 | 01.3 | 14 40.0 | 15.5 | 4 39.3 | 13.6 | 55.6 |
| 20 | 118 11.4 | 00.9 | 29 14.5 | 15.4 | 4 52.9 | 13.5 | 55.5 |
| 21 | 133 11.1 | .. 00.6 | 43 48.9 | 15.5 | 5 06.4 | 13.5 | 55.5 |
| 22 | 148 10.8 | 22 00.2 | 58 23.4 | 15.5 | 5 19.9 | 13.5 | 55.5 |
| 23 | 163 10.6 | S21 59.8 | 72 57.9 | 15.5 | N 5 33.4 | 13.4 | 55.5 |
| | SD 16.3 | d 0.3 | SD 15.7 | | 15.4 | | 15.2 |

## Twilight, Sunrise and Moonrise

| Lat. | Twilight Naut. | Twilight Civil | Sunrise | Moonrise 7 | 8 | 9 | 10 |
|---|---|---|---|---|---|---|---|
| ° | h m | h m | h m | h m | h m | h m | h m |
| N 72 | 08 15 | 10 19 | ■■■ | 12 12 | 11 41 | 11 14 | 10 45 |
| N 70 | 07 58 | 09 36 | ■■■ | 12 00 | 11 38 | 11 18 | 10 57 |
| 68 | 07 44 | 09 07 | 11 09 | 11 50 | 11 35 | 11 21 | 11 06 |
| 66 | 07 32 | 08 46 | 10 13 | 11 42 | 11 32 | 11 23 | 11 14 |
| 64 | 07 23 | 08 28 | 09 40 | 11 35 | 11 30 | 11 25 | 11 21 |
| 62 | 07 14 | 08 14 | 09 16 | 11 29 | 11 28 | 11 27 | 11 27 |
| 60 | 07 07 | 08 02 | 08 57 | 11 24 | 11 26 | 11 29 | 11 32 |
| N 58 | 07 00 | 07 51 | 08 41 | 11 19 | 11 25 | 11 30 | 11 36 |
| 56 | 06 54 | 07 42 | 08 28 | 11 15 | 11 24 | 11 32 | 11 40 |
| 54 | 06 48 | 07 34 | 08 16 | 11 11 | 11 22 | 11 33 | 11 44 |
| 52 | 06 43 | 07 26 | 08 06 | 11 07 | 11 21 | 11 34 | 11 47 |
| 50 | 06 38 | 07 19 | 07 57 | 11 04 | 11 20 | 11 35 | 11 50 |
| 45 | 06 28 | 07 04 | 07 38 | 10 58 | 11 18 | 11 37 | 11 57 |
| N 40 | 06 18 | 06 52 | 07 22 | 10 52 | 11 16 | 11 39 | 12 02 |
| 35 | 06 09 | 06 41 | 07 09 | 10 47 | 11 15 | 11 41 | 12 07 |
| 30 | 06 01 | 06 31 | 06 57 | 10 42 | 11 13 | 11 42 | 12 11 |
| 20 | 05 46 | 06 13 | 06 37 | 10 35 | 11 11 | 11 45 | 12 19 |
| N 10 | 05 31 | 05 57 | 06 19 | 10 28 | 11 09 | 11 47 | 12 25 |
| 0 | 05 15 | 05 41 | 06 03 | 10 22 | 11 07 | 11 50 | 12 32 |
| S 10 | 04 57 | 05 24 | 05 46 | 10 15 | 11 05 | 11 52 | 12 38 |
| 20 | 04 35 | 05 04 | 05 28 | 10 09 | 11 03 | 11 54 | 12 45 |
| 30 | 04 08 | 04 41 | 05 08 | 10 01 | 11 00 | 11 57 | 12 52 |
| 35 | 03 50 | 04 26 | 04 55 | 09 56 | 10 59 | 11 58 | 12 57 |
| 40 | 03 28 | 04 09 | 04 41 | 09 51 | 10 57 | 12 00 | 13 02 |
| 45 | 03 00 | 03 48 | 04 24 | 09 45 | 10 55 | 12 02 | 13 08 |
| S 50 | 02 19 | 03 20 | 04 03 | 09 38 | 10 53 | 12 05 | 13 15 |
| 52 | 01 56 | 03 06 | 03 53 | 09 35 | 10 52 | 12 06 | 13 18 |
| 54 | 01 22 | 02 50 | 03 42 | 09 31 | 10 51 | 12 07 | 13 22 |
| 56 | //// | 02 31 | 03 29 | 09 27 | 10 50 | 12 09 | 13 26 |
| 58 | //// | 02 06 | 03 14 | 09 23 | 10 48 | 12 10 | 13 31 |
| S 60 | //// | 01 30 | 02 56 | 09 18 | 10 47 | 12 12 | 13 36 |

## Sunset, Twilight and Moonset

| Lat. | Sunset | Twilight Civil | Twilight Naut. | Moonset 7 | 8 | 9 | 10 |
|---|---|---|---|---|---|---|---|
| ° | h m | h m | h m | h m | h m | h m | h m |
| N 72 | ■■■ | 13 55 | 15 59 | 21 24 | 23 28 | 25 28 | 01 28 |
| N 70 | ■■■ | 14 38 | 16 16 | 21 33 | 23 28 | 25 19 | 01 19 |
| 68 | 13 05 | 15 06 | 16 30 | 21 41 | 23 28 | 25 11 | 01 11 |
| 66 | 14 01 | 15 28 | 16 41 | 21 47 | 23 28 | 25 05 | 01 05 |
| 64 | 14 34 | 15 45 | 16 51 | 21 52 | 23 28 | 25 00 | 01 00 |
| 62 | 14 58 | 16 00 | 17 00 | 21 57 | 23 28 | 24 56 | 00 56 |
| 60 | 15 17 | 16 12 | 17 07 | 22 01 | 23 28 | 24 52 | 00 52 |
| N 58 | 15 33 | 16 22 | 17 14 | 22 04 | 23 28 | 24 49 | 00 49 |
| 56 | 15 46 | 16 32 | 17 20 | 22 07 | 23 28 | 24 46 | 00 46 |
| 54 | 15 58 | 16 40 | 17 26 | 22 10 | 23 28 | 24 43 | 00 43 |
| 52 | 16 08 | 16 48 | 17 31 | 22 12 | 23 28 | 24 41 | 00 41 |
| 50 | 16 17 | 16 54 | 17 35 | 22 14 | 23 28 | 24 39 | 00 39 |
| 45 | 16 36 | 17 09 | 17 46 | 22 19 | 23 28 | 24 34 | 00 34 |
| N 40 | 16 52 | 17 22 | 17 56 | 22 23 | 23 28 | 24 30 | 00 30 |
| 35 | 17 05 | 17 33 | 18 04 | 22 27 | 23 28 | 24 27 | 00 27 |
| 30 | 17 17 | 17 43 | 18 12 | 22 30 | 23 28 | 24 24 | 00 24 |
| 20 | 17 37 | 18 00 | 18 28 | 22 35 | 23 28 | 24 18 | 00 18 |
| N 10 | 17 54 | 18 17 | 18 43 | 22 39 | 23 27 | 24 14 | 00 14 |
| 0 | 18 10 | 18 33 | 18 59 | 22 44 | 23 27 | 24 10 | 00 10 |
| S 10 | 18 27 | 18 50 | 19 17 | 22 48 | 23 27 | 24 05 | 00 05 |
| 20 | 18 45 | 19 09 | 19 38 | 22 52 | 23 27 | 24 01 | 00 01 |
| 30 | 19 06 | 19 33 | 20 05 | 22 57 | 23 27 | 23 56 | 24 25 |
| 35 | 19 18 | 19 47 | 20 25 | 23 00 | 23 27 | 23 53 | 24 19 |
| 40 | 19 32 | 20 04 | 20 44 | 23 03 | 23 27 | 23 50 | 24 13 |
| 45 | 19 49 | 20 25 | 21 13 | 23 07 | 23 27 | 23 46 | 24 06 |
| S 50 | 20 09 | 20 52 | 21 53 | 23 11 | 23 26 | 23 41 | 23 57 |
| 52 | 20 19 | 21 06 | 22 16 | 23 13 | 23 26 | 23 39 | 23 53 |
| 54 | 20 31 | 21 22 | 22 48 | 23 15 | 23 26 | 23 37 | 23 48 |
| 56 | 20 44 | 21 41 | //// | 23 18 | 23 26 | 23 34 | 23 43 |
| 58 | 20 59 | 22 06 | //// | 23 20 | 23 26 | 23 32 | 23 38 |
| S 60 | 21 17 | 22 41 | //// | 23 23 | 23 26 | 23 29 | 23 31 |

### SUN and MOON

| Day | Eqn. of Time 00h | Eqn. of Time 12h | Mer. Pass. | Mer. Pass. Upper | Mer. Pass. Lower | Age | Phase |
|---|---|---|---|---|---|---|---|
| d | m s | m s | h m | h m | h m | d | % |
| 7 | 06 02 | 06 15 | 12 06 | 16 33 | 04 10 | 05 | 28 |
| 8 | 06 28 | 06 41 | 12 07 | 17 17 | 04 55 | 06 | 38 |
| 9 | 06 53 | 07 06 | 12 07 | 18 00 | 05 38 | 07 | 48 |

| UT | ARIES GHA | VENUS −4.3 GHA | Dec | MARS +1.5 GHA | Dec | JUPITER −2.1 GHA | Dec | SATURN +0.7 GHA | Dec | STARS Name | SHA | Dec |
|---|---|---|---|---|---|---|---|---|---|---|---|---|
| **10** 00 | 109 29.8 | 180 33.8 | S17 12.2 | 210 54.8 | S23 15.4 | 134 47.7 | S11 33.2 | 153 53.1 | S17 44.0 | Acamar | 315 13.5 | S40 13.3 |
| 01 | 124 32.3 | 195 38.0 | 11.9 | 225 55.4 | 15.5 | 149 49.7 | 33.0 | 168 55.3 | 44.0 | Achernar | 335 22.0 | S57 07.9 |
| 02 | 139 34.8 | 210 42.1 | 11.6 | 240 55.9 | 15.7 | 164 51.6 | 32.8 | 183 57.4 | 43.9 | Acrux | 173 02.6 | S63 12.9 |
| 03 | 154 37.2 | 225 46.2 .. | 11.2 | 255 56.4 .. | 15.9 | 179 53.6 .. | 32.6 | 198 59.6 .. | 43.8 | Adhara | 255 07.4 | S29 00.2 |
| 04 | 169 39.7 | 240 50.3 | 10.9 | 270 56.9 | 16.0 | 194 55.6 | 32.4 | 214 01.8 | 43.7 | Aldebaran | 290 42.2 | N16 33.2 |
| 05 | 184 42.2 | 255 54.4 | 10.6 | 285 57.4 | 16.2 | 209 57.6 | 32.2 | 229 04.0 | 43.6 | | | |
| 06 | 199 44.6 | 270 58.5 | S17 10.3 | 300 58.0 | S23 16.4 | 224 59.5 | S11 32.0 | 244 06.2 | S17 43.6 | Alioth | 166 15.1 | N55 50.2 |
| 07 | 214 47.1 | 286 02.6 | 10.0 | 315 58.5 | 16.5 | 240 01.5 | 31.8 | 259 08.3 | 43.5 | Alkaid | 152 54.1 | N49 12.0 |
| 08 | 229 49.6 | 301 06.7 | 09.7 | 330 59.0 | 16.7 | 255 03.5 | 31.6 | 274 10.5 | 43.4 | Alnair | 27 36.4 | S46 51.5 |
| M 09 | 244 52.0 | 316 10.8 .. | 09.3 | 345 59.5 .. | 16.9 | 270 05.4 .. | 31.5 | 289 12.7 .. | 43.3 | Alnilam | 275 39.9 | S 1 11.4 |
| O 10 | 259 54.5 | 331 14.9 | 09.0 | 1 00.1 | 17.0 | 285 07.4 | 31.3 | 304 14.9 | 43.2 | Alphard | 217 49.9 | S 8 45.2 |
| N 11 | 274 56.9 | 346 19.0 | 08.7 | 16 00.6 | 17.2 | 300 09.4 | 31.1 | 319 17.0 | 43.2 | | | |
| D 12 | 289 59.4 | 1 23.1 | S17 08.4 | 31 01.1 | S23 17.4 | 315 11.3 | S11 30.9 | 334 19.2 | S17 43.1 | Alphecca | 126 06.1 | N26 38.3 |
| A 13 | 305 01.9 | 16 27.2 | 08.1 | 46 01.6 | 17.5 | 330 13.3 | 30.7 | 349 21.4 | 43.0 | Alpheratz | 357 37.4 | N29 12.7 |
| Y 14 | 320 04.3 | 31 31.3 | 07.8 | 61 02.1 | 17.7 | 345 15.3 | 30.5 | 4 23.6 | 42.9 | Altair | 62 02.7 | N 8 55.5 |
| 15 | 335 06.8 | 46 35.4 .. | 07.5 | 76 02.7 .. | 17.8 | 0 17.2 .. | 30.3 | 19 25.7 .. | 42.9 | Ankaa | 353 09.7 | S42 11.5 |
| 16 | 350 09.3 | 61 39.5 | 07.2 | 91 03.2 | 18.0 | 15 19.2 | 30.1 | 34 27.9 | 42.8 | Antares | 112 19.1 | S26 28.7 |
| 17 | 5 11.7 | 76 43.6 | 06.9 | 106 03.7 | 18.2 | 30 21.2 | 29.9 | 49 30.1 | 42.7 | | | |
| 18 | 20 14.2 | 91 47.7 | S17 06.6 | 121 04.2 | S23 18.3 | 45 23.1 | S11 29.7 | 64 32.3 | S17 42.6 | Arcturus | 145 50.3 | N19 04.0 |
| 19 | 35 16.7 | 106 51.8 | 06.2 | 136 04.8 | 18.5 | 60 25.1 | 29.6 | 79 34.5 | 42.5 | Atria | 107 16.0 | S69 03.8 |
| 20 | 50 19.1 | 121 55.9 | 05.9 | 151 05.3 | 18.7 | 75 27.1 | 29.4 | 94 36.6 | 42.5 | Avior | 234 15.0 | S59 34.7 |
| 21 | 65 21.6 | 137 00.0 .. | 05.6 | 166 05.8 .. | 18.8 | 90 29.0 .. | 29.2 | 109 38.8 .. | 42.4 | Bellatrix | 278 25.2 | N 6 22.1 |
| 22 | 80 24.1 | 152 04.0 | 05.3 | 181 06.3 | 19.0 | 105 31.0 | 29.0 | 124 41.0 | 42.3 | Betelgeuse | 270 54.4 | N 7 24.6 |
| 23 | 95 26.5 | 167 08.1 | 05.0 | 196 06.8 | 19.1 | 120 33.0 | 28.8 | 139 43.2 | 42.2 | | | |
| **11** 00 | 110 29.0 | 182 12.2 | S17 04.7 | 211 07.4 | S23 19.3 | 135 34.9 | S11 28.6 | 154 45.3 | S17 42.1 | Canopus | 263 52.9 | S52 42.5 |
| 01 | 125 31.4 | 197 16.3 | 04.4 | 226 07.9 | 19.5 | 150 36.9 | 28.4 | 169 47.5 | 42.1 | Capella | 280 25.1 | N46 01.2 |
| 02 | 140 33.9 | 212 20.4 | 04.1 | 241 08.4 | 19.6 | 165 38.9 | 28.2 | 184 49.7 | 42.0 | Deneb | 49 27.9 | N45 21.5 |
| 03 | 155 36.4 | 227 24.5 .. | 03.8 | 256 08.9 .. | 19.8 | 180 40.8 .. | 28.0 | 199 51.9 .. | 41.9 | Denebola | 182 27.3 | N14 26.9 |
| 04 | 170 38.8 | 242 28.6 | 03.5 | 271 09.4 | 19.9 | 195 42.8 | 27.8 | 214 54.1 | 41.8 | Diphda | 348 49.8 | S17 52.2 |
| 05 | 185 41.3 | 257 32.6 | 03.2 | 286 10.0 | 20.1 | 210 44.8 | 27.6 | 229 56.2 | 41.7 | | | |
| 06 | 200 43.8 | 272 36.7 | S17 02.9 | 301 10.5 | S23 20.3 | 225 46.7 | S11 27.5 | 244 58.4 | S17 41.7 | Dubhe | 193 43.7 | N61 37.7 |
| 07 | 215 46.2 | 287 40.8 | 02.6 | 316 11.0 | 20.4 | 240 48.7 | 27.3 | 260 00.6 | 41.6 | Elnath | 278 04.6 | N28 37.5 |
| T 08 | 230 48.7 | 302 44.9 | 02.3 | 331 11.5 | 20.6 | 255 50.7 | 27.1 | 275 02.8 | 41.5 | Eltanin | 90 43.8 | N51 29.0 |
| U 09 | 245 51.2 | 317 49.0 .. | 02.0 | 346 12.0 .. | 20.7 | 270 52.6 .. | 26.9 | 290 04.9 .. | 41.4 | Enif | 33 41.5 | N 9 58.5 |
| E 10 | 260 53.6 | 332 53.0 | 01.7 | 1 12.5 | 20.9 | 285 54.6 | 26.7 | 305 07.1 | 41.3 | Fomalhaut | 15 17.5 | S29 30.6 |
| S 11 | 275 56.1 | 347 57.1 | 01.4 | 16 13.1 | 21.0 | 300 56.6 | 26.5 | 320 09.3 | 41.3 | | | |
| D 12 | 290 58.5 | 3 01.2 | S17 01.1 | 31 13.6 | S23 21.2 | 315 58.5 | S11 26.3 | 335 11.5 | S17 41.2 | Gacrux | 171 54.2 | S57 13.8 |
| A 13 | 306 01.0 | 18 05.3 | 00.8 | 46 14.1 | 21.3 | 331 00.5 | 26.1 | 350 13.6 | 41.1 | Gienah | 175 46.0 | S17 39.7 |
| Y 14 | 321 03.5 | 33 09.3 | 00.6 | 61 14.6 | 21.5 | 346 02.5 | 25.9 | 5 15.8 | 41.0 | Hadar | 148 39.6 | S60 28.4 |
| 15 | 336 05.9 | 48 13.4 .. | 00.3 | 76 15.1 .. | 21.7 | 1 04.4 .. | 25.7 | 20 18.0 .. | 40.9 | Hamal | 327 53.9 | N23 34.0 |
| 16 | 351 08.4 | 63 17.5 | 17 00.0 | 91 15.7 | 21.8 | 16 06.4 | 25.5 | 35 20.2 | 40.9 | Kaus Aust. | 83 36.2 | S34 22.4 |
| 17 | 6 10.9 | 78 21.5 | 16 59.7 | 106 16.2 | 22.0 | 31 08.3 | 25.3 | 50 22.3 | 40.8 | | | |
| 18 | 21 13.3 | 93 25.6 | S16 59.4 | 121 16.7 | S23 22.1 | 46 10.3 | S11 25.2 | 65 24.5 | S17 40.7 | Kochab | 137 20.3 | N74 03.6 |
| 19 | 36 15.8 | 108 29.7 | 59.1 | 136 17.2 | 22.3 | 61 12.3 | 25.0 | 80 26.7 | 40.6 | Markab | 13 32.5 | N15 19.4 |
| 20 | 51 18.3 | 123 33.7 | 58.8 | 151 17.7 | 22.4 | 76 14.2 | 24.8 | 95 28.9 | 40.5 | Menkar | 314 08.6 | N 4 10.5 |
| 21 | 66 20.7 | 138 37.8 .. | 58.5 | 166 18.2 .. | 22.6 | 91 16.2 .. | 24.6 | 110 31.1 .. | 40.5 | Menkent | 148 00.6 | S36 28.4 |
| 22 | 81 23.2 | 153 41.8 | 58.2 | 181 18.8 | 22.7 | 106 18.2 | 24.4 | 125 33.2 | 40.4 | Miaplacidus | 221 37.8 | S69 48.2 |
| 23 | 96 25.7 | 168 45.9 | 58.0 | 196 19.3 | 22.9 | 121 20.1 | 24.2 | 140 35.4 | 40.3 | | | |
| **12** 00 | 111 28.1 | 183 50.0 | S16 57.7 | 211 19.8 | S23 23.0 | 136 22.1 | S11 24.0 | 155 37.6 | S17 40.2 | Mirfak | 308 31.5 | N49 56.5 |
| 01 | 126 30.6 | 198 54.0 | 57.4 | 226 20.3 | 23.2 | 151 24.1 | 23.8 | 170 39.8 | 40.1 | Nunki | 75 51.2 | S26 16.2 |
| 02 | 141 33.0 | 213 58.1 | 57.1 | 241 20.8 | 23.3 | 166 26.0 | 23.6 | 185 41.9 | 40.1 | Peacock | 53 10.2 | S56 40.0 |
| 03 | 156 35.5 | 229 02.1 .. | 56.8 | 256 21.3 .. | 23.5 | 181 28.0 .. | 23.4 | 200 44.1 .. | 40.0 | Pollux | 243 19.9 | N27 58.3 |
| 04 | 171 38.0 | 244 06.2 | 56.5 | 271 21.9 | 23.6 | 196 30.0 | 23.2 | 215 46.3 | 39.9 | Procyon | 244 53.1 | N 5 10.1 |
| 05 | 186 40.4 | 259 10.2 | 56.3 | 286 22.4 | 23.8 | 211 31.9 | 23.0 | 230 48.5 | 39.8 | | | |
| 06 | 201 42.9 | 274 14.3 | S16 56.0 | 301 22.9 | S23 23.9 | 226 33.9 | S11 22.8 | 245 50.6 | S17 39.7 | Rasalhague | 96 01.1 | N12 32.6 |
| W 07 | 216 45.4 | 289 18.3 | 55.7 | 316 23.4 | 24.1 | 241 35.8 | 22.7 | 260 52.8 | 39.7 | Regulus | 207 36.8 | N11 51.5 |
| E 08 | 231 47.8 | 304 22.3 | 55.4 | 331 23.9 | 24.2 | 256 37.8 | 22.5 | 275 55.0 | 39.6 | Rigel | 281 05.9 | S 8 10.7 |
| D 09 | 246 50.3 | 319 26.4 .. | 55.2 | 346 24.4 .. | 24.4 | 271 39.8 .. | 22.3 | 290 57.2 .. | 39.5 | Rigil Kent. | 139 43.9 | S60 55.2 |
| N 10 | 261 52.8 | 334 30.4 | 54.9 | 1 24.9 | 24.5 | 286 41.7 | 22.1 | 305 59.3 | 39.4 | Sabik | 102 05.9 | S15 45.1 |
| E 11 | 276 55.2 | 349 34.5 | 54.6 | 16 25.5 | 24.7 | 301 43.7 | 21.9 | 321 01.5 | 39.3 | | | |
| S 12 | 291 57.7 | 4 38.5 | S16 54.3 | 31 26.0 | S23 24.8 | 316 45.7 | S11 21.7 | 336 03.7 | S17 39.3 | Schedar | 349 33.9 | N56 39.6 |
| D 13 | 307 00.2 | 19 42.5 | 54.1 | 46 26.5 | 25.0 | 331 47.6 | 21.5 | 351 05.9 | 39.2 | Shaula | 96 14.1 | S37 07.1 |
| A 14 | 322 02.6 | 34 46.6 | 53.8 | 61 27.0 | 25.1 | 346 49.6 | 21.3 | 6 08.0 | 39.1 | Sirius | 258 28.0 | S16 44.8 |
| Y 15 | 337 05.1 | 49 50.6 .. | 53.5 | 76 27.5 .. | 25.2 | 1 51.5 .. | 21.1 | 21 10.2 .. | 39.0 | Spica | 158 24.9 | S11 16.5 |
| 16 | 352 07.5 | 64 54.6 | 53.2 | 91 28.0 | 25.4 | 16 53.5 | 20.9 | 36 12.4 | 38.9 | Suhail | 222 47.7 | S43 31.1 |
| 17 | 7 10.0 | 79 58.6 | 53.0 | 106 28.6 | 25.5 | 31 55.5 | 20.7 | 51 14.6 | 38.9 | | | |
| 18 | 22 12.5 | 95 02.7 | S16 52.7 | 121 29.1 | S23 25.7 | 46 57.4 | S11 20.5 | 66 16.7 | S17 38.8 | Vega | 80 35.3 | N38 48.2 |
| 19 | 37 14.9 | 110 06.7 | 52.4 | 136 29.6 | 25.8 | 61 59.4 | 20.3 | 81 18.9 | 38.7 | Zuben'ubi | 136 58.9 | S16 07.9 |
| 20 | 52 17.4 | 125 10.7 | 52.2 | 151 30.1 | 26.0 | 77 01.4 | 20.1 | 96 21.1 | 38.6 | | SHA | Mer. Pass. |
| 21 | 67 19.9 | 140 14.7 .. | 51.9 | 166 30.6 .. | 26.1 | 92 03.3 .. | 20.0 | 111 23.3 .. | 38.5 | | ° ′ | h m |
| 22 | 82 22.3 | 155 18.7 | 51.6 | 181 31.1 | 26.2 | 107 05.3 | 19.8 | 126 25.4 | 38.5 | Venus | 71 43.2 | 11 48 |
| 23 | 97 24.8 | 170 22.8 | 51.4 | 196 31.6 | 26.4 | 122 07.2 | 19.6 | 141 27.6 | 38.4 | Mars | 100 38.4 | 9 55 |
| | h m | | | | | | | | | Jupiter | 25 06.0 | 14 56 |
| Mer. Pass. 16 35.3 | v 4.1 d 0.3 | | | v 0.5 d 0.2 | | v 2.0 d 0.2 | | v 2.2 d 0.1 | | Saturn | 44 16.4 | 13 39 |

| UT | SUN GHA | SUN Dec | MOON GHA | v | MOON Dec | d | HP |
|---|---|---|---|---|---|---|---|
| d h | ° ′ | ° ′ | ° ′ | ′ | ° ′ | ′ | ′ |
| **10** 00 | 178 10.3 | S21 59.5 | 87 32.4 | 15.5 | N 5 46.8 | 13.4 | 55.4 |
| 01 | 193 10.1 | 59.1 | 102 06.9 | 15.6 | 6 00.2 | 13.4 | 55.4 |
| 02 | 208 09.8 | 58.7 | 116 41.5 | 15.5 | 6 13.6 | 13.3 | 55.4 |
| 03 | 223 09.6 .. | 58.4 | 131 16.0 | 15.5 | 6 26.9 | 13.3 | 55.3 |
| 04 | 238 09.3 | 58.0 | 145 50.5 | 15.5 | 6 40.2 | 13.2 | 55.3 |
| 05 | 253 09.1 | 57.6 | 160 25.0 | 15.5 | 6 53.4 | 13.2 | 55.3 |
| 06 | 268 08.8 | S21 57.2 | 174 59.5 | 15.5 | N 7 06.6 | 13.2 | 55.3 |
| 07 | 283 08.6 | 56.9 | 189 34.0 | 15.6 | 7 19.8 | 13.1 | 55.2 |
| M 08 | 298 08.3 | 56.5 | 204 08.6 | 15.5 | 7 32.9 | 13.1 | 55.2 |
| O 09 | 313 08.1 .. | 56.1 | 218 43.1 | 15.5 | 7 46.0 | 13.0 | 55.2 |
| N 10 | 328 07.8 | 55.7 | 233 17.6 | 15.5 | 7 59.0 | 13.0 | 55.2 |
| D 11 | 343 07.6 | 55.4 | 247 52.1 | 15.5 | 8 12.0 | 13.0 | 55.1 |
| A 12 | 358 07.3 | S21 55.0 | 262 26.6 | 15.5 | N 8 25.0 | 12.9 | 55.1 |
| Y 13 | 13 07.0 | 54.6 | 277 01.1 | 15.5 | 8 37.9 | 12.8 | 55.1 |
| 14 | 28 06.8 | 54.2 | 291 35.6 | 15.4 | 8 50.7 | 12.8 | 55.1 |
| 15 | 43 06.5 .. | 53.9 | 306 10.0 | 15.5 | 9 03.5 | 12.8 | 55.0 |
| 16 | 58 06.3 | 53.5 | 320 44.5 | 15.5 | 9 16.3 | 12.7 | 55.0 |
| 17 | 73 06.0 | 53.1 | 335 19.0 | 15.4 | 9 29.0 | 12.7 | 55.0 |
| 18 | 88 05.8 | S21 52.7 | 349 53.4 | 15.4 | N 9 41.7 | 12.6 | 55.0 |
| 19 | 103 05.5 | 52.3 | 4 27.8 | 15.4 | 9 54.3 | 12.6 | 55.0 |
| 20 | 118 05.3 | 51.9 | 19 02.2 | 15.4 | 10 06.9 | 12.6 | 54.9 |
| 21 | 133 05.0 .. | 51.6 | 33 36.6 | 15.4 | 10 19.5 | 12.4 | 54.9 |
| 22 | 148 04.8 | 51.2 | 48 11.0 | 15.4 | 10 31.9 | 12.5 | 54.9 |
| 23 | 163 04.5 | 50.8 | 62 45.4 | 15.3 | 10 44.4 | 12.4 | 54.9 |
| **11** 00 | 178 04.3 | S21 50.4 | 77 19.7 | 15.4 | N10 56.8 | 12.3 | 54.8 |
| 01 | 193 04.1 | 50.0 | 91 54.1 | 15.3 | 11 09.1 | 12.3 | 54.8 |
| 02 | 208 03.8 | 49.6 | 106 28.4 | 15.3 | 11 21.4 | 12.2 | 54.8 |
| 03 | 223 03.6 .. | 49.2 | 121 02.7 | 15.2 | 11 33.6 | 12.1 | 54.8 |
| 04 | 238 03.3 | 48.9 | 135 36.9 | 15.3 | 11 45.7 | 12.2 | 54.8 |
| 05 | 253 03.1 | 48.5 | 150 11.2 | 15.2 | 11 57.9 | 12.0 | 54.7 |
| 06 | 268 02.8 | S21 48.1 | 164 45.4 | 15.2 | N12 09.9 | 12.0 | 54.7 |
| T 07 | 283 02.6 | 47.7 | 179 19.6 | 15.2 | 12 21.9 | 12.0 | 54.7 |
| U 08 | 298 02.3 | 47.3 | 193 53.8 | 15.1 | 12 33.9 | 11.9 | 54.7 |
| E 09 | 313 02.1 .. | 46.9 | 208 27.9 | 15.1 | 12 45.8 | 11.8 | 54.7 |
| S 10 | 328 01.8 | 46.5 | 223 02.0 | 15.1 | 12 57.6 | 11.8 | 54.7 |
| D 11 | 343 01.6 | 46.1 | 237 36.1 | 15.1 | 13 09.4 | 11.7 | 54.6 |
| A 12 | 358 01.3 | S21 45.7 | 252 10.2 | 15.0 | N13 21.1 | 11.6 | 54.6 |
| Y 13 | 13 01.1 | 45.3 | 266 44.2 | 15.0 | 13 32.7 | 11.6 | 54.6 |
| 14 | 28 00.9 | 44.9 | 281 18.2 | 15.0 | 13 44.3 | 11.6 | 54.6 |
| 15 | 43 00.6 .. | 44.5 | 295 52.2 | 14.9 | 13 55.9 | 11.4 | 54.6 |
| 16 | 58 00.4 | 44.1 | 310 26.1 | 14.9 | 14 07.3 | 11.4 | 54.5 |
| 17 | 73 00.1 | 43.7 | 325 00.0 | 14.9 | 14 18.7 | 11.4 | 54.5 |
| 18 | 87 59.9 | S21 43.3 | 339 33.9 | 14.8 | N14 30.1 | 11.3 | 54.5 |
| 19 | 102 59.6 | 42.9 | 354 07.7 | 14.8 | 14 41.4 | 11.2 | 54.5 |
| 20 | 117 59.4 | 42.5 | 8 41.5 | 14.8 | 14 52.6 | 11.1 | 54.5 |
| 21 | 132 59.1 .. | 42.1 | 23 15.3 | 14.8 | 15 03.7 | 11.1 | 54.5 |
| 22 | 147 58.9 | 41.7 | 37 49.1 | 14.7 | 15 14.8 | 11.0 | 54.5 |
| 23 | 162 58.7 | 41.3 | 52 22.8 | 14.6 | 15 25.8 | 11.0 | 54.4 |
| **12** 00 | 177 58.4 | S21 40.9 | 66 56.4 | 14.6 | N15 36.8 | 10.9 | 54.4 |
| 01 | 192 58.2 | 40.5 | 81 30.0 | 14.6 | 15 47.7 | 10.8 | 54.4 |
| 02 | 207 57.9 | 40.1 | 96 03.6 | 14.6 | 15 58.5 | 10.7 | 54.4 |
| 03 | 222 57.7 .. | 39.7 | 110 37.2 | 14.5 | 16 09.2 | 10.7 | 54.4 |
| 04 | 237 57.5 | 39.3 | 125 10.7 | 14.4 | 16 19.9 | 10.6 | 54.4 |
| 05 | 252 57.2 | 38.9 | 139 44.1 | 14.4 | 16 30.5 | 10.6 | 54.4 |
| 06 | 267 57.0 | S21 38.5 | 154 17.5 | 14.4 | N16 41.1 | 10.4 | 54.3 |
| W 07 | 282 56.7 | 38.1 | 168 50.9 | 14.4 | 16 51.5 | 10.4 | 54.3 |
| E 08 | 297 56.5 | 37.7 | 183 24.3 | 14.3 | 17 01.9 | 10.3 | 54.3 |
| D 09 | 312 56.3 .. | 37.3 | 197 57.6 | 14.2 | 17 12.2 | 10.3 | 54.3 |
| N 10 | 327 56.0 | 36.8 | 212 30.8 | 14.2 | 17 22.5 | 10.2 | 54.3 |
| E 11 | 342 55.8 | 36.4 | 227 04.0 | 14.2 | 17 32.7 | 10.1 | 54.3 |
| S 12 | 357 55.5 | S21 36.0 | 241 37.2 | 14.1 | N17 42.8 | 10.0 | 54.3 |
| D 13 | 12 55.3 | 35.6 | 256 10.3 | 14.1 | 17 52.8 | 9.9 | 54.3 |
| A 14 | 27 55.1 | 35.2 | 270 43.4 | 14.0 | 18 02.7 | 9.9 | 54.3 |
| Y 15 | 42 54.8 .. | 34.8 | 285 16.4 | 14.0 | 18 12.6 | 9.8 | 54.2 |
| 16 | 57 54.6 | 34.4 | 299 49.4 | 13.9 | 18 22.4 | 9.7 | 54.2 |
| 17 | 72 54.3 | 34.0 | 314 22.3 | 13.9 | 18 32.1 | 9.6 | 54.2 |
| 18 | 87 54.1 | S21 33.5 | 328 55.2 | 13.8 | N18 41.7 | 9.6 | 54.2 |
| 19 | 102 53.9 | 33.1 | 343 28.0 | 13.8 | 18 51.3 | 9.4 | 54.2 |
| 20 | 117 53.6 | 32.7 | 358 00.8 | 13.7 | 19 00.7 | 9.4 | 54.2 |
| 21 | 132 53.4 .. | 32.3 | 12 33.5 | 13.7 | 19 10.1 | 9.3 | 54.2 |
| 22 | 147 53.2 | 31.9 | 27 06.2 | 13.6 | 19 19.4 | 9.2 | 54.2 |
| 23 | 162 52.9 | 31.4 | 41 38.8 | 13.6 | N19 28.6 | 9.2 | 54.2 |
| | SD 16.3 | d 0.4 | SD 15.0 | | 14.9 | | 14.8 |

### Twilight / Moonrise

| Lat. | Naut. | Civil | Sunrise | Moonrise 10 | 11 | 12 | 13 |
|---|---|---|---|---|---|---|---|
| ° | h m | h m | h m | h m | h m | h m | h m |
| N 72 | 08 09 | 10 07 | ■■ | 10 45 | 10 09 | 09 02 | ▭ |
| N 70 | 07 53 | 09 29 | ■■ | 10 57 | 10 32 | 09 55 | ▭ |
| 68 | 07 40 | 09 02 | 10 53 | 11 06 | 10 50 | 10 28 | 09 48 |
| 66 | 07 29 | 08 41 | 10 05 | 11 14 | 11 04 | 10 52 | 10 35 |
| 64 | 07 20 | 08 25 | 09 34 | 11 21 | 11 16 | 11 11 | 11 06 |
| 62 | 07 12 | 08 11 | 09 11 | 11 27 | 11 26 | 11 27 | 11 29 |
| 60 | 07 04 | 07 59 | 08 53 | 11 32 | 11 35 | 11 40 | 11 48 |
| N 58 | 06 58 | 07 49 | 08 38 | 11 36 | 11 43 | 11 51 | 12 04 |
| 56 | 06 52 | 07 40 | 08 25 | 11 40 | 11 50 | 12 01 | 12 17 |
| 54 | 06 47 | 07 32 | 08 14 | 11 44 | 11 56 | 12 10 | 12 28 |
| 52 | 06 42 | 07 25 | 08 04 | 11 47 | 12 01 | 12 18 | 12 39 |
| 50 | 06 37 | 07 18 | 07 55 | 11 50 | 12 06 | 12 25 | 12 48 |
| 45 | 06 27 | 07 04 | 07 37 | 11 57 | 12 17 | 12 40 | 13 07 |
| N 40 | 06 18 | 06 51 | 07 21 | 12 02 | 12 26 | 12 53 | 13 23 |
| 35 | 06 09 | 06 41 | 07 08 | 12 07 | 12 34 | 13 04 | 13 37 |
| 30 | 06 01 | 06 31 | 06 57 | 12 11 | 12 41 | 13 13 | 13 48 |
| 20 | 05 47 | 06 14 | 06 37 | 12 19 | 12 53 | 13 30 | 14 09 |
| N 10 | 05 32 | 05 58 | 06 20 | 12 25 | 13 04 | 13 44 | 14 26 |
| 0 | 05 16 | 05 42 | 06 04 | 12 32 | 13 14 | 13 57 | 14 43 |
| S 10 | 04 58 | 05 25 | 05 48 | 12 38 | 13 24 | 14 11 | 15 00 |
| 20 | 04 37 | 05 06 | 05 30 | 12 45 | 13 35 | 14 26 | 15 17 |
| 30 | 04 10 | 04 43 | 05 10 | 12 52 | 13 47 | 14 43 | 15 38 |
| 35 | 03 53 | 04 29 | 04 58 | 12 57 | 13 54 | 14 52 | 15 50 |
| 40 | 03 32 | 04 12 | 04 44 | 13 02 | 14 03 | 15 04 | 16 04 |
| 45 | 03 04 | 03 52 | 04 28 | 13 08 | 14 13 | 15 17 | 16 21 |
| S 50 | 02 25 | 03 25 | 04 07 | 13 15 | 14 24 | 15 33 | 16 42 |
| 52 | 02 03 | 03 12 | 03 58 | 13 18 | 14 30 | 15 41 | 16 52 |
| 54 | 01 32 | 02 56 | 03 47 | 13 22 | 14 36 | 15 50 | 17 03 |
| 56 | 00 31 | 02 37 | 03 34 | 13 26 | 14 43 | 15 59 | 17 16 |
| 58 | //// | 02 13 | 03 19 | 13 31 | 14 50 | 16 11 | 17 30 |
| S 60 | //// | 01 41 | 03 02 | 13 36 | 14 59 | 16 23 | 17 48 |

### Sunset / Twilight / Moonset

| Lat. | Sunset | Civil | Naut. | Moonset 10 | 11 | 12 | 13 |
|---|---|---|---|---|---|---|---|
| ° | h m | h m | h m | h m | h m | h m | h m |
| N 72 | ■■ | 14 09 | 16 07 | 01 28 | 03 33 | 06 10 | ▭ |
| N 70 | ■■ | 14 48 | 16 23 | 01 19 | 03 12 | 05 19 | ▭ |
| 68 | 13 24 | 15 15 | 16 36 | 01 11 | 02 56 | 04 47 | 07 01 |
| 66 | 14 12 | 15 35 | 16 47 | 01 05 | 02 43 | 04 24 | 06 14 |
| 64 | 14 42 | 15 52 | 16 57 | 01 00 | 02 32 | 04 06 | 05 44 |
| 62 | 15 05 | 16 05 | 17 05 | 00 56 | 02 23 | 03 52 | 05 22 |
| 60 | 15 23 | 16 17 | 17 12 | 00 52 | 02 16 | 03 39 | 05 04 |
| N 58 | 15 38 | 16 27 | 17 18 | 00 49 | 02 09 | 03 29 | 04 49 |
| 56 | 15 51 | 16 36 | 17 24 | 00 46 | 02 03 | 03 19 | 04 36 |
| 54 | 16 02 | 16 44 | 17 29 | 00 43 | 01 57 | 03 11 | 04 25 |
| 52 | 16 12 | 16 52 | 17 34 | 00 41 | 01 53 | 03 04 | 04 15 |
| 50 | 16 21 | 16 58 | 17 39 | 00 39 | 01 48 | 02 58 | 04 06 |
| 45 | 16 40 | 17 13 | 17 49 | 00 34 | 01 39 | 02 44 | 03 48 |
| N 40 | 16 55 | 17 25 | 17 58 | 00 30 | 01 31 | 02 32 | 03 33 |
| 35 | 17 08 | 17 35 | 18 07 | 00 27 | 01 25 | 02 22 | 03 20 |
| 30 | 17 19 | 17 45 | 18 15 | 00 24 | 01 19 | 02 14 | 03 09 |
| 20 | 17 38 | 18 02 | 18 29 | 00 18 | 01 09 | 01 59 | 02 51 |
| N 10 | 17 56 | 18 18 | 18 44 | 00 14 | 01 00 | 01 47 | 02 34 |
| 0 | 18 12 | 18 34 | 19 00 | 00 10 | 00 52 | 01 35 | 02 19 |
| S 10 | 18 28 | 18 51 | 19 17 | 00 05 | 00 44 | 01 23 | 02 04 |
| 20 | 18 45 | 19 09 | 19 38 | 00 01 | 00 35 | 01 10 | 01 48 |
| 30 | 19 05 | 19 32 | 20 05 | 24 25 | 00 25 | 00 56 | 01 29 |
| 35 | 19 17 | 19 46 | 20 22 | 24 19 | 00 19 | 00 48 | 01 19 |
| 40 | 19 31 | 20 03 | 20 43 | 24 13 | 00 13 | 00 38 | 01 06 |
| 45 | 19 47 | 20 23 | 21 10 | 24 06 | 00 06 | 00 27 | 00 52 |
| S 50 | 20 08 | 20 50 | 21 49 | 23 57 | 24 14 | 00 14 | 00 34 |
| 52 | 20 17 | 21 03 | 22 11 | 23 53 | 24 08 | 00 08 | 00 26 |
| 54 | 20 28 | 21 19 | 22 41 | 23 48 | 24 01 | 00 01 | 00 17 |
| 56 | 20 41 | 21 37 | 23 35 | 23 43 | 23 54 | 24 07 | 00 07 |
| 58 | 20 55 | 22 00 | //// | 23 38 | 23 45 | 23 55 | 24 10 |
| S 60 | 21 12 | 22 32 | //// | 23 31 | 23 35 | 23 42 | 23 52 |

### SUN / MOON

| Day | Eqn. of Time 00ʰ | 12ʰ | Mer. Pass. | Mer. Pass. Upper | Lower | Age | Phase |
|---|---|---|---|---|---|---|---|
| d | m s | m s | h m | h m | h m | d | % |
| 10 | 07 18 | 07 30 | 12 08 | 18 42 | 06 21 | 08 | 57 |
| 11 | 07 42 | 07 54 | 12 08 | 19 24 | 07 03 | 09 | 67 |
| 12 | 08 06 | 08 17 | 12 08 | 20 08 | 07 46 | 10 | 75 |

| UT | ARIES GHA | VENUS −4.2 GHA | Dec | MARS +1.5 GHA | Dec | JUPITER −2.1 GHA | Dec | SATURN +0.7 GHA | Dec | STARS Name | SHA | Dec |
|---|---|---|---|---|---|---|---|---|---|---|---|---|
| **13** 00 | 112 27.3 | 185 26.8 | S16 51.1 | 211 32.1 | S23 26.5 | 137 09.2 | S11 19.4 | 156 29.8 | S17 38.3 | Acamar | 315 13.5 | S40 13.3 |
| 01 | 127 29.7 | 200 30.8 | 50.8 | 226 32.7 | 26.7 | 152 11.2 | 19.2 | 171 32.0 | 38.2 | Achernar | 335 22.0 | S57 07.9 |
| 02 | 142 32.2 | 215 34.8 | 50.6 | 241 33.2 | 26.8 | 167 13.1 | 19.0 | 186 34.1 | 38.1 | Acrux | 173 02.5 | S63 12.9 |
| 03 | 157 34.7 | 230 38.8 .. | 50.3 | 256 33.7 .. | 27.0 | 182 15.1 .. | 18.8 | 201 36.3 .. | 38.1 | Adhara | 255 07.4 | S29 00.2 |
| 04 | 172 37.1 | 245 42.8 | 50.0 | 271 34.2 | 27.1 | 197 17.0 | 18.6 | 216 38.5 | 38.0 | Aldebaran | 290 42.2 | N16 33.2 |
| 05 | 187 39.6 | 260 46.8 | 49.8 | 286 34.7 | 27.2 | 212 19.0 | 18.4 | 231 40.7 | 37.9 | | | |
| 06 | 202 42.0 | 275 50.8 | S16 49.5 | 301 35.2 | S23 27.4 | 227 21.0 | S11 18.2 | 246 42.8 | S17 37.8 | Alioth | 166 15.1 | N55 50.2 |
| 07 | 217 44.5 | 290 54.8 | 49.3 | 316 35.7 | 27.5 | 242 22.9 | 18.0 | 261 45.0 | 37.7 | Alkaid | 152 54.0 | N49 12.0 |
| T 08 | 232 47.0 | 305 58.8 | 49.0 | 331 36.2 | 27.6 | 257 24.9 | 17.8 | 276 47.2 | 37.6 | Alnair | 27 36.4 | S46 51.5 |
| H 09 | 247 49.4 | 321 02.8 .. | 48.7 | 346 36.8 .. | 27.8 | 272 26.8 .. | 17.6 | 291 49.4 .. | 37.6 | Alnilam | 275 39.9 | S 1 11.4 |
| U 10 | 262 51.9 | 336 06.8 | 48.5 | 1 37.3 | 27.9 | 287 28.8 | 17.4 | 306 51.5 | 37.5 | Alphard | 217 49.9 | S 8 45.2 |
| R 11 | 277 54.4 | 351 10.8 | 48.2 | 16 37.8 | 28.1 | 302 30.8 | 17.2 | 321 53.7 | 37.4 | | | |
| S 12 | 292 56.8 | 6 14.7 | S16 48.0 | 31 38.3 | S23 28.2 | 317 32.7 | S11 17.0 | 336 55.9 | S17 37.3 | Alphecca | 126 06.0 | N26 38.3 |
| D 13 | 307 59.3 | 21 18.7 | 47.7 | 46 38.8 | 28.3 | 332 34.7 | 16.8 | 351 58.1 | 37.2 | Alpheratz | 357 37.4 | N29 12.7 |
| A 14 | 323 01.8 | 36 22.7 | 47.5 | 61 39.3 | 28.5 | 347 36.6 | 16.7 | 7 00.2 | 37.2 | Altair | 62 02.7 | N 8 55.5 |
| Y 15 | 338 04.2 | 51 26.7 .. | 47.2 | 76 39.8 .. | 28.6 | 2 38.6 .. | 16.5 | 22 02.4 .. | 37.1 | Ankaa | 353 09.7 | S42 11.5 |
| 16 | 353 06.7 | 66 30.7 | 47.0 | 91 40.3 | 28.7 | 17 40.6 | 16.3 | 37 04.6 | 37.0 | Antares | 112 19.1 | S26 28.7 |
| 17 | 8 09.1 | 81 34.6 | 46.7 | 106 40.8 | 28.9 | 32 42.5 | 16.1 | 52 06.8 | 36.9 | | | |
| 18 | 23 11.6 | 96 38.6 | S16 46.5 | 121 41.4 | S23 29.0 | 47 44.5 | S11 15.9 | 67 08.9 | S17 36.8 | Arcturus | 145 50.2 | N19 04.0 |
| 19 | 38 14.1 | 111 42.6 | 46.2 | 136 41.9 | 29.1 | 62 46.4 | 15.7 | 82 11.1 | 36.8 | Atria | 107 16.0 | S69 03.8 |
| 20 | 53 16.5 | 126 46.6 | 46.0 | 151 42.4 | 29.3 | 77 48.4 | 15.5 | 97 13.3 | 36.7 | Avior | 234 15.0 | S59 34.7 |
| 21 | 68 19.0 | 141 50.5 .. | 45.7 | 166 42.9 .. | 29.4 | 92 50.4 .. | 15.3 | 112 15.5 .. | 36.6 | Bellatrix | 278 25.2 | N 6 22.1 |
| 22 | 83 21.5 | 156 54.5 | 45.5 | 181 43.4 | 29.5 | 107 52.3 | 15.1 | 127 17.6 | 36.5 | Betelgeuse | 270 54.4 | N 7 24.6 |
| 23 | 98 23.9 | 171 58.4 | 45.2 | 196 43.9 | 29.7 | 122 54.3 | 14.9 | 142 19.8 | 36.4 | | | |
| **14** 00 | 113 26.4 | 187 02.4 | S16 45.0 | 211 44.4 | S23 29.8 | 137 56.2 | S11 14.7 | 157 22.0 | S17 36.4 | Canopus | 263 52.9 | S52 42.5 |
| 01 | 128 28.9 | 202 06.4 | 44.7 | 226 44.9 | 29.9 | 152 58.2 | 14.5 | 172 24.2 | 36.3 | Capella | 280 25.1 | N46 01.2 |
| 02 | 143 31.3 | 217 10.3 | 44.5 | 241 45.4 | 30.1 | 168 00.1 | 14.3 | 187 26.3 | 36.2 | Deneb | 49 27.9 | N45 21.5 |
| 03 | 158 33.8 | 232 14.3 .. | 44.3 | 256 46.0 .. | 30.2 | 183 02.1 .. | 14.1 | 202 28.5 .. | 36.1 | Denebola | 182 27.3 | N14 26.9 |
| 04 | 173 36.3 | 247 18.2 | 44.0 | 271 46.5 | 30.3 | 198 04.1 | 13.9 | 217 30.7 | 36.0 | Diphda | 348 49.8 | S17 52.2 |
| 05 | 188 38.7 | 262 22.2 | 43.8 | 286 47.0 | 30.5 | 213 06.0 | 13.7 | 232 32.8 | 36.0 | | | |
| 06 | 203 41.2 | 277 26.1 | S16 43.5 | 301 47.5 | S23 30.6 | 228 08.0 | S11 13.5 | 247 35.0 | S17 35.9 | Dubhe | 193 43.7 | N61 37.7 |
| 07 | 218 43.6 | 292 30.0 | 43.3 | 316 48.0 | 30.7 | 243 09.9 | 13.3 | 262 37.2 | 35.8 | Elnath | 278 04.6 | N28 37.5 |
| F 08 | 233 46.1 | 307 34.0 | 43.1 | 331 48.5 | 30.9 | 258 11.9 | 13.1 | 277 39.4 | 35.7 | Eltanin | 90 43.8 | N51 29.0 |
| R 09 | 248 48.6 | 322 37.9 .. | 42.8 | 346 49.0 .. | 31.0 | 273 13.9 .. | 13.0 | 292 41.5 .. | 35.6 | Enif | 33 41.5 | N 9 58.5 |
| I 10 | 263 51.0 | 337 41.8 | 42.6 | 1 49.5 | 31.1 | 288 15.8 | 12.8 | 307 43.7 | 35.5 | Fomalhaut | 15 17.5 | S29 30.6 |
| D 11 | 278 53.5 | 352 45.8 | 42.3 | 16 50.0 | 31.2 | 303 17.8 | 12.6 | 322 45.9 | 35.5 | | | |
| A 12 | 293 56.0 | 7 49.7 | S16 42.1 | 31 50.5 | S23 31.4 | 318 19.7 | S11 12.4 | 337 48.1 | S17 35.4 | Gacrux | 171 54.2 | S57 13.9 |
| Y 13 | 308 58.4 | 22 53.6 | 41.9 | 46 51.0 | 31.5 | 333 21.7 | 12.2 | 352 50.2 | 35.3 | Gienah | 175 46.0 | S17 39.7 |
| 14 | 324 00.9 | 37 57.6 | 41.6 | 61 51.5 | 31.6 | 348 23.6 | 12.0 | 7 52.4 | 35.2 | Hadar | 148 39.5 | S60 28.4 |
| 15 | 339 03.4 | 53 01.5 .. | 41.4 | 76 52.1 .. | 31.7 | 3 25.6 .. | 11.8 | 22 54.6 .. | 35.1 | Hamal | 327 53.9 | N23 34.0 |
| 16 | 354 05.8 | 68 05.4 | 41.2 | 91 52.6 | 31.9 | 18 27.6 | 11.6 | 37 56.8 | 35.1 | Kaus Aust. | 83 36.2 | S34 22.4 |
| 17 | 9 08.3 | 83 09.3 | 41.0 | 106 53.1 | 32.0 | 33 29.5 | 11.4 | 52 58.9 | 35.0 | | | |
| 18 | 24 10.8 | 98 13.2 | S16 40.7 | 121 53.6 | S23 32.1 | 48 31.5 | S11 11.2 | 68 01.1 | S17 34.9 | Kochab | 137 20.3 | N74 03.6 |
| 19 | 39 13.2 | 113 17.1 | 40.5 | 136 54.1 | 32.2 | 63 33.4 | 11.0 | 83 03.3 | 34.8 | Markab | 13 32.5 | N15 19.4 |
| 20 | 54 15.7 | 128 21.0 | 40.3 | 151 54.6 | 32.4 | 78 35.4 | 10.8 | 98 05.4 | 34.7 | Menkar | 314 08.6 | N 4 10.5 |
| 21 | 69 18.1 | 143 24.9 .. | 40.0 | 166 55.1 .. | 32.5 | 93 37.3 .. | 10.6 | 113 07.6 .. | 34.7 | Menkent | 148 00.6 | S36 28.4 |
| 22 | 84 20.6 | 158 28.8 | 39.8 | 181 55.6 | 32.6 | 108 39.3 | 10.4 | 128 09.8 | 34.6 | Miaplacidus | 221 37.8 | S69 48.3 |
| 23 | 99 23.1 | 173 32.7 | 39.6 | 196 56.1 | 32.7 | 123 41.2 | 10.2 | 143 12.0 | 34.5 | | | |
| **15** 00 | 114 25.5 | 188 36.6 | S16 39.4 | 211 56.6 | S23 32.9 | 138 43.2 | S11 10.0 | 158 14.1 | S17 34.4 | Mirfak | 308 31.5 | N49 56.5 |
| 01 | 129 28.0 | 203 40.5 | 39.1 | 226 57.1 | 33.0 | 153 45.2 | 09.8 | 173 16.3 | 34.3 | Nunki | 75 51.2 | S26 16.2 |
| 02 | 144 30.5 | 218 44.4 | 38.9 | 241 57.6 | 33.1 | 168 47.1 | 09.6 | 188 18.5 | 34.2 | Peacock | 53 10.2 | S56 40.0 |
| 03 | 159 32.9 | 233 48.3 .. | 38.7 | 256 58.1 .. | 33.2 | 183 49.1 .. | 09.4 | 203 20.7 .. | 34.2 | Pollux | 243 19.9 | N27 58.3 |
| 04 | 174 35.4 | 248 52.2 | 38.5 | 271 58.6 | 33.3 | 198 51.0 | 09.2 | 218 22.8 | 34.1 | Procyon | 244 53.1 | N 5 10.1 |
| 05 | 189 37.9 | 263 56.1 | 38.3 | 286 59.2 | 33.5 | 213 53.0 | 09.0 | 233 25.0 | 34.0 | | | |
| 06 | 204 40.3 | 278 59.9 | S16 38.0 | 301 59.7 | S23 33.6 | 228 54.9 | S11 08.8 | 248 27.2 | S17 33.9 | Rasalhague | 96 01.1 | N12 32.6 |
| 07 | 219 42.8 | 294 03.8 | 37.8 | 317 00.2 | 33.7 | 243 56.9 | 08.6 | 263 29.3 | 33.8 | Regulus | 207 36.8 | N11 51.5 |
| S 08 | 234 45.3 | 309 07.7 | 37.6 | 332 00.7 | 33.8 | 258 58.8 | 08.4 | 278 31.5 | 33.8 | Rigel | 281 05.9 | S 8 10.7 |
| A 09 | 249 47.7 | 324 11.6 .. | 37.4 | 347 01.2 .. | 33.9 | 274 00.8 .. | 08.2 | 293 33.7 .. | 33.7 | Rigil Kent. | 139 43.8 | S60 55.2 |
| T 10 | 264 50.2 | 339 15.4 | 37.2 | 2 01.7 | 34.1 | 289 02.8 | 08.1 | 308 35.9 | 33.6 | Sabik | 102 05.9 | S15 45.1 |
| U 11 | 279 52.6 | 354 19.3 | 37.0 | 17 02.2 | 34.2 | 304 04.7 | 07.9 | 323 38.0 | 33.5 | | | |
| R 12 | 294 55.1 | 9 23.2 | S16 36.7 | 32 02.7 | S23 34.3 | 319 06.7 | S11 07.7 | 338 40.2 | S17 33.4 | Schedar | 349 33.9 | N56 39.6 |
| D 13 | 309 57.6 | 24 27.0 | 36.5 | 47 03.2 | 34.4 | 334 08.6 | 07.5 | 353 42.4 | 33.4 | Shaula | 96 14.1 | S37 07.1 |
| A 14 | 325 00.0 | 39 30.9 | 36.3 | 62 03.7 | 34.5 | 349 10.6 | 07.3 | 8 44.6 | 33.3 | Sirius | 258 28.0 | S16 44.9 |
| Y 15 | 340 02.5 | 54 34.7 .. | 36.1 | 77 04.2 .. | 34.6 | 4 12.5 .. | 07.1 | 23 46.7 .. | 33.2 | Spica | 158 24.9 | S11 16.5 |
| 16 | 355 05.0 | 69 38.6 | 35.9 | 92 04.7 | 34.8 | 19 14.5 | 06.9 | 38 48.9 | 33.1 | Suhail | 222 47.7 | S43 31.2 |
| 17 | 10 07.4 | 84 42.4 | 35.7 | 107 05.2 | 34.9 | 34 16.4 | 06.7 | 53 51.1 | 33.0 | | | |
| 18 | 25 09.9 | 99 46.3 | S16 35.5 | 122 05.7 | S23 35.0 | 49 18.4 | S11 06.5 | 68 53.2 | S17 32.9 | Vega | 80 35.3 | N38 48.1 |
| 19 | 40 12.4 | 114 50.1 | 35.3 | 137 06.2 | 35.1 | 64 20.3 | 06.3 | 83 55.4 | 32.9 | Zuben'ubi | 136 58.8 | S16 07.9 |
| 20 | 55 14.8 | 129 53.9 | 35.1 | 152 06.7 | 35.2 | 79 22.3 | 06.1 | 98 57.6 | 32.8 | | SHA | Mer.Pass. |
| 21 | 70 17.3 | 144 57.8 .. | 34.9 | 167 07.2 .. | 35.3 | 94 24.3 .. | 05.9 | 113 59.8 .. | 32.7 | Venus | 73 36.0 | 11 29 |
| 22 | 85 19.8 | 160 01.6 | 34.6 | 182 07.7 | 35.5 | 109 26.2 | 05.7 | 129 01.9 | 32.6 | Mars | 98 18.0 | 9 53 |
| 23 | 100 22.2 | 175 05.4 | 34.4 | 197 08.2 | 35.6 | 124 28.2 | 05.5 | 144 04.1 | 32.5 | Jupiter | 24 29.8 | 14 46 |
| Mer.Pass. 16 23.5 | | v 3.9 | d 0.2 | v 0.5 | d 0.1 | v 2.0 | d 0.2 | v 2.2 | d 0.1 | Saturn | 43 55.6 | 13 29 |

## SUN / MOON

| UT | SUN GHA | SUN Dec | MOON GHA | v | MOON Dec | d | HP |
|---|---|---|---|---|---|---|---|
| d h | ° ′ | ° ′ | ° ′ | ′ | ° ′ | ′ | ′ |
| 13 00 | 177 52.7 | S21 31.0 | 56 11.4 | 13.5 | N19 37.8 | 9.0 | 54.2 |
| 01 | 192 52.5 | 30.6 | 70 43.9 | 13.5 | 19 46.8 | 9.0 | 54.2 |
| 02 | 207 52.2 | 30.2 | 85 16.4 | 13.5 | 19 55.8 | 8.9 | 54.1 |
| 03 | 222 52.0 . . | 29.8 | 99 48.9 | 13.3 | 20 04.7 | 8.8 | 54.1 |
| 04 | 237 51.8 | 29.3 | 114 21.2 | 13.4 | 20 13.5 | 8.7 | 54.1 |
| 05 | 252 51.5 | 28.9 | 128 53.6 | 13.3 | 20 22.2 | 8.6 | 54.1 |
| 06 | 267 51.3 | S21 28.5 | 143 25.9 | 13.2 | N20 30.8 | 8.6 | 54.1 |
| 07 | 282 51.1 | 28.1 | 157 58.1 | 13.1 | 20 39.4 | 8.4 | 54.1 |
| T 08 | 297 50.8 | 27.6 | 172 30.2 | 13.2 | 20 47.8 | 8.3 | 54.1 |
| H 09 | 312 50.6 . . | 27.2 | 187 02.4 | 13.0 | 20 56.1 | 8.3 | 54.1 |
| U 10 | 327 50.4 | 26.8 | 201 34.4 | 13.1 | 21 04.4 | 8.2 | 54.1 |
| R 11 | 342 50.1 | 26.3 | 216 06.5 | 12.9 | 21 12.6 | 8.1 | 54.1 |
| S 12 | 357 49.9 | S21 25.9 | 230 38.4 | 12.9 | N21 20.7 | 7.9 | 54.1 |
| D 13 | 12 49.7 | 25.5 | 245 10.3 | 12.9 | 21 28.6 | 7.9 | 54.1 |
| A 14 | 27 49.4 | 25.1 | 259 42.2 | 12.8 | 21 36.5 | 7.8 | 54.1 |
| Y 15 | 42 49.2 . . | 24.6 | 274 14.0 | 12.7 | 21 44.3 | 7.7 | 54.1 |
| 16 | 57 49.0 | 24.2 | 288 45.7 | 12.7 | 21 52.0 | 7.7 | 54.1 |
| 17 | 72 48.7 | 23.8 | 303 17.4 | 12.7 | 21 59.7 | 7.5 | 54.1 |
| 18 | 87 48.5 | S21 23.3 | 317 49.1 | 12.5 | N22 07.2 | 7.4 | 54.1 |
| 19 | 102 48.3 | 22.9 | 332 20.6 | 12.6 | 22 14.6 | 7.3 | 54.1 |
| 20 | 117 48.0 | 22.5 | 346 52.2 | 12.5 | 22 21.9 | 7.2 | 54.1 |
| 21 | 132 47.8 . . | 22.0 | 1 23.7 | 12.4 | 22 29.1 | 7.1 | 54.1 |
| 22 | 147 47.6 | 21.6 | 15 55.1 | 12.4 | 22 36.2 | 7.1 | 54.0 |
| 23 | 162 47.4 | 21.1 | 30 26.5 | 12.3 | 22 43.3 | 6.9 | 54.0 |
| 14 00 | 177 47.1 | S21 20.7 | 44 57.8 | 12.3 | N22 50.2 | 6.8 | 54.0 |
| 01 | 192 46.9 | 20.3 | 59 29.1 | 12.2 | 22 57.0 | 6.7 | 54.0 |
| 02 | 207 46.7 | 19.8 | 74 00.3 | 12.1 | 23 03.7 | 6.6 | 54.0 |
| 03 | 222 46.4 . . | 19.4 | 88 31.4 | 12.1 | 23 10.3 | 6.5 | 54.0 |
| 04 | 237 46.2 | 18.9 | 103 02.5 | 12.1 | 23 16.8 | 6.4 | 54.0 |
| 05 | 252 46.0 | 18.5 | 117 33.6 | 12.0 | 23 23.2 | 6.3 | 54.0 |
| 06 | 267 45.8 | S21 18.1 | 132 04.6 | 12.0 | N23 29.5 | 6.2 | 54.0 |
| 07 | 282 45.5 | 17.6 | 146 35.6 | 11.9 | 23 35.7 | 6.1 | 54.0 |
| 08 | 297 45.3 | 17.2 | 161 06.5 | 11.8 | 23 41.8 | 6.0 | 54.0 |
| F 09 | 312 45.1 . . | 16.7 | 175 37.3 | 11.8 | 23 47.8 | 5.9 | 54.0 |
| R 10 | 327 44.9 | 16.3 | 190 08.1 | 11.8 | 23 53.7 | 5.7 | 54.0 |
| I 11 | 342 44.6 | 15.8 | 204 38.9 | 11.7 | 23 59.4 | 5.7 | 54.0 |
| D 12 | 357 44.4 | S21 15.4 | 219 09.6 | 11.6 | N24 05.1 | 5.6 | 54.0 |
| A 13 | 12 44.2 | 14.9 | 233 40.2 | 11.6 | 24 10.7 | 5.4 | 54.0 |
| Y 14 | 27 44.0 | 14.5 | 248 10.8 | 11.6 | 24 16.1 | 5.3 | 54.0 |
| 15 | 42 43.7 . . | 14.0 | 262 41.4 | 11.5 | 24 21.4 | 5.2 | 54.0 |
| 16 | 57 43.5 | 13.6 | 277 11.9 | 11.4 | 24 26.6 | 5.1 | 54.0 |
| 17 | 72 43.3 | 13.1 | 291 42.3 | 11.4 | 24 31.7 | 5.0 | 54.0 |
| 18 | 87 43.1 | S21 12.7 | 306 12.7 | 11.4 | N24 36.7 | 4.9 | 54.0 |
| 19 | 102 42.8 | 12.2 | 320 43.1 | 11.3 | 24 41.6 | 4.8 | 54.0 |
| 20 | 117 42.6 | 11.8 | 335 13.4 | 11.3 | 24 46.4 | 4.6 | 54.0 |
| 21 | 132 42.4 . . | 11.3 | 349 43.7 | 11.2 | 24 51.0 | 4.6 | 54.0 |
| 22 | 147 42.2 | 10.9 | 4 13.9 | 11.2 | 24 55.6 | 4.4 | 54.1 |
| 23 | 162 41.9 | 10.4 | 18 44.1 | 11.1 | 25 00.0 | 4.3 | 54.1 |
| 15 00 | 177 41.7 | S21 10.0 | 33 14.2 | 11.1 | N25 04.3 | 4.2 | 54.1 |
| 01 | 192 41.5 | 09.5 | 47 44.3 | 11.0 | 25 08.5 | 4.1 | 54.1 |
| 02 | 207 41.3 | 09.1 | 62 14.3 | 11.0 | 25 12.6 | 3.9 | 54.1 |
| 03 | 222 41.1 . . | 08.6 | 76 44.3 | 11.0 | 25 16.5 | 3.9 | 54.1 |
| 04 | 237 40.8 | 08.1 | 91 14.3 | 10.9 | 25 20.4 | 3.7 | 54.1 |
| 05 | 252 40.6 | 07.7 | 105 44.2 | 10.9 | 25 24.1 | 3.6 | 54.1 |
| 06 | 267 40.4 | S21 07.2 | 120 14.1 | 10.8 | N25 27.7 | 3.5 | 54.1 |
| 07 | 282 40.2 | 06.8 | 134 43.9 | 10.8 | 25 31.2 | 3.3 | 54.1 |
| S 08 | 297 40.0 | 06.3 | 149 13.7 | 10.8 | 25 34.5 | 3.3 | 54.1 |
| A 09 | 312 39.7 . . | 05.8 | 163 43.5 | 10.7 | 25 37.8 | 3.1 | 54.1 |
| T 10 | 327 39.5 | 05.4 | 178 13.2 | 10.7 | 25 40.9 | 3.0 | 54.1 |
| U 11 | 342 39.3 | 04.9 | 192 42.9 | 10.6 | 25 43.9 | 2.9 | 54.1 |
| R 12 | 357 39.1 | S21 04.5 | 207 12.5 | 10.5 | N25 46.8 | 2.7 | 54.1 |
| D 13 | 12 38.9 | 04.0 | 221 42.2 | 10.5 | 25 49.5 | 2.7 | 54.1 |
| A 14 | 27 38.7 | 03.5 | 236 11.7 | 10.6 | 25 52.2 | 2.5 | 54.1 |
| Y 15 | 42 38.4 . . | 03.1 | 250 41.3 | 10.5 | 25 54.7 | 2.4 | 54.1 |
| 16 | 57 38.2 | 02.6 | 265 10.8 | 10.5 | 25 57.1 | 2.2 | 54.1 |
| 17 | 72 38.0 | 02.1 | 279 40.3 | 10.5 | 25 59.3 | 2.2 | 54.1 |
| 18 | 87 37.8 | S21 01.7 | 294 09.8 | 10.4 | N26 01.5 | 2.0 | 54.1 |
| 19 | 102 37.6 | 01.2 | 308 39.2 | 10.4 | 26 03.5 | 1.9 | 54.1 |
| 20 | 117 37.4 | 00.7 | 323 08.6 | 10.4 | 26 05.4 | 1.7 | 54.2 |
| 21 | 132 37.1 | 21 00.3 | 337 38.0 | 10.3 | 26 07.1 | 1.7 | 54.2 |
| 22 | 147 36.9 | 20 59.8 | 352 07.3 | 10.3 | 26 08.8 | 1.5 | 54.2 |
| 23 | 162 36.7 | S20 59.3 | 6 36.6 | 10.3 | N26 10.3 | 1.3 | 54.2 |
| | SD 16.3 | d 0.4 | SD 14.7 | | 14.7 | | 14.7 |

## Twilight / Sunrise / Moonrise

| Lat. | Naut. | Civil | Sunrise | Moonrise 13 | 14 | 15 | 16 |
|---|---|---|---|---|---|---|---|
| ° | h m | h m | h m | h m | h m | h m | h m |
| N 72 | 08 03 | 09 56 | ■ | □ | □ | □ | □ |
| N 70 | 07 48 | 09 21 | ■ | □ | □ | □ | □ |
| 68 | 07 36 | 08 56 | 10 38 | 09 48 | □ | □ | □ |
| 66 | 07 25 | 08 36 | 09 56 | 10 35 | 09 51 | □ | □ |
| 64 | 07 16 | 08 20 | 09 28 | 11 06 | 11 00 | 10 50 | □ |
| 62 | 07 09 | 08 07 | 09 06 | 11 29 | 11 36 | 11 52 | 12 30 |
| 60 | 07 02 | 07 56 | 08 49 | 11 48 | 12 02 | 12 26 | 13 09 |
| N 58 | 06 56 | 07 46 | 08 35 | 12 04 | 12 22 | 12 51 | 13 36 |
| 56 | 06 50 | 07 38 | 08 22 | 12 17 | 12 39 | 13 11 | 13 57 |
| 54 | 06 45 | 07 30 | 08 12 | 12 28 | 12 53 | 13 28 | 14 14 |
| 52 | 06 40 | 07 23 | 08 02 | 12 39 | 13 06 | 13 42 | 14 29 |
| 50 | 06 36 | 07 16 | 07 53 | 12 48 | 13 17 | 13 55 | 14 42 |
| 45 | 06 26 | 07 02 | 07 35 | 13 07 | 13 40 | 14 20 | 15 09 |
| N 40 | 06 17 | 06 51 | 07 20 | 13 23 | 13 59 | 14 41 | 15 30 |
| 35 | 06 09 | 06 40 | 07 08 | 13 37 | 14 15 | 14 58 | 15 48 |
| 30 | 06 01 | 06 31 | 06 57 | 13 48 | 14 28 | 15 13 | 16 03 |
| 20 | 05 47 | 06 14 | 06 38 | 14 09 | 14 51 | 15 38 | 16 29 |
| N 10 | 05 33 | 05 59 | 06 21 | 14 26 | 15 12 | 16 00 | 16 51 |
| 0 | 05 17 | 05 43 | 06 05 | 14 43 | 15 31 | 16 20 | 17 11 |
| S 10 | 05 00 | 05 27 | 05 50 | 15 00 | 15 50 | 16 41 | 17 32 |
| 20 | 04 40 | 05 08 | 05 32 | 15 17 | 16 10 | 17 03 | 17 54 |
| 30 | 04 13 | 04 46 | 05 13 | 15 38 | 16 34 | 17 28 | 18 20 |
| 35 | 03 57 | 04 32 | 05 01 | 15 50 | 16 48 | 17 43 | 18 35 |
| 40 | 03 36 | 04 16 | 04 48 | 16 04 | 17 04 | 18 01 | 18 53 |
| 45 | 03 09 | 03 56 | 04 32 | 16 21 | 17 23 | 18 22 | 19 14 |
| S 50 | 02 32 | 03 30 | 04 12 | 16 42 | 17 48 | 18 48 | 19 41 |
| 52 | 02 11 | 03 17 | 04 02 | 16 52 | 17 59 | 19 01 | 19 54 |
| 54 | 01 43 | 03 02 | 03 52 | 17 03 | 18 13 | 19 16 | 20 09 |
| 56 | 00 57 | 02 44 | 03 40 | 17 16 | 18 29 | 19 34 | 20 26 |
| 58 | //// | 02 22 | 03 26 | 17 30 | 18 47 | 19 55 | 20 47 |
| S 60 | //// | 01 52 | 03 09 | 17 48 | 19 10 | 20 22 | 21 14 |

## Sunset / Twilight / Moonset

| Lat. | Sunset | Civil | Naut. | Moonset 13 | 14 | 15 | 16 |
|---|---|---|---|---|---|---|---|
| ° | h m | h m | h m | h m | h m | h m | h m |
| N 72 | ■ | 14 23 | 16 16 | □ | □ | □ | □ |
| N 70 | ■ | 14 58 | 16 31 | □ | □ | □ | □ |
| 68 | 13 41 | 15 23 | 16 43 | 07 01 | □ | □ | □ |
| 66 | 14 23 | 15 43 | 16 54 | 06 14 | 08 36 | □ | □ |
| 64 | 14 51 | 15 58 | 17 02 | 05 44 | 07 28 | 09 20 | □ |
| 62 | 15 12 | 16 11 | 17 10 | 05 22 | 06 53 | 08 19 | 09 26 |
| 60 | 15 29 | 16 23 | 17 17 | 05 04 | 06 27 | 07 45 | 08 40 |
| N 58 | 15 44 | 16 32 | 17 23 | 04 49 | 06 07 | 07 20 | 08 21 |
| 56 | 15 56 | 16 41 | 17 28 | 04 36 | 05 51 | 07 00 | 07 59 |
| 54 | 16 07 | 16 49 | 17 33 | 04 25 | 05 37 | 06 44 | 07 42 |
| 52 | 16 17 | 16 56 | 17 38 | 04 15 | 05 25 | 06 30 | 07 27 |
| 50 | 16 25 | 17 02 | 17 43 | 04 06 | 05 14 | 06 17 | 07 14 |
| 45 | 16 43 | 17 16 | 17 52 | 03 48 | 04 51 | 05 52 | 06 47 |
| N 40 | 16 58 | 17 28 | 18 01 | 03 33 | 04 33 | 05 32 | 06 26 |
| 35 | 17 11 | 17 38 | 18 09 | 03 20 | 04 18 | 05 15 | 06 09 |
| 30 | 17 22 | 17 47 | 18 17 | 03 09 | 04 05 | 05 00 | 05 53 |
| 20 | 17 40 | 18 04 | 18 31 | 02 51 | 03 43 | 04 36 | 05 28 |
| N 10 | 17 57 | 18 20 | 18 46 | 02 34 | 03 24 | 04 14 | 05 06 |
| 0 | 18 13 | 18 35 | 19 01 | 02 19 | 03 06 | 03 54 | 04 45 |
| S 10 | 18 28 | 18 51 | 19 18 | 02 04 | 02 48 | 03 35 | 04 24 |
| 20 | 18 45 | 19 10 | 19 38 | 01 48 | 02 29 | 03 13 | 04 02 |
| 30 | 19 05 | 19 32 | 20 04 | 01 29 | 02 07 | 02 49 | 03 36 |
| 35 | 19 17 | 19 46 | 20 21 | 01 19 | 01 54 | 02 35 | 03 21 |
| 40 | 19 30 | 20 02 | 20 41 | 01 06 | 01 39 | 02 18 | 03 04 |
| 45 | 19 46 | 20 22 | 21 08 | 00 52 | 01 22 | 01 58 | 02 42 |
| S 50 | 20 06 | 20 47 | 21 45 | 00 34 | 01 00 | 01 33 | 02 16 |
| 52 | 20 15 | 21 00 | 22 06 | 00 26 | 00 50 | 01 21 | 02 03 |
| 54 | 20 25 | 21 15 | 22 33 | 00 17 | 00 38 | 01 07 | 01 48 |
| 56 | 20 37 | 21 32 | 23 16 | 00 07 | 00 25 | 00 52 | 01 30 |
| 58 | 20 51 | 21 54 | //// | 24 10 | 00 10 | 00 33 | 01 09 |
| S 60 | 21 08 | 22 23 | //// | 23 52 | 24 09 | 00 09 | 00 41 |

## SUN / MOON

| Day | Eqn. of Time 00ʰ | 12ʰ | Mer. Pass. | Mer. Pass. Upper | Lower | Age | Phase |
|---|---|---|---|---|---|---|---|
| d | m s | m s | h m | h m | h m | d | % |
| 13 | 08 29 | 08 40 | 12 09 | 20 54 | 08 31 | 11 | 83 |
| 14 | 08 51 | 09 02 | 12 09 | 21 42 | 09 18 | 12 | 89 |
| 15 | 09 13 | 09 23 | 12 09 | 22 33 | 10 07 | 13 | 94 |

| UT (d h) | ARIES GHA | VENUS −4.3 GHA | Dec | MARS +1.5 GHA | Dec | JUPITER −2.1 GHA | Dec | SATURN +0.7 GHA | Dec | STARS Name | SHA | Dec |
|---|---|---|---|---|---|---|---|---|---|---|---|---|
| **16 00** | 115 24.7 | 190 09.2 | S16 34.2 | 212 08.7 | S23 35.7 | 139 30.1 | S11 05.3 | 159 06.3 | S17 32.5 | Acamar | 315 13.5 | S40 13.3 |
| 01 | 130 27.1 | 205 13.1 | 34.0 | 227 09.2 | 35.8 | 154 32.1 | 05.1 | 174 08.5 | 32.4 | Achernar | 335 22.1 | S57 07.9 |
| 02 | 145 29.6 | 220 16.9 | 33.8 | 242 09.8 | 35.9 | 169 34.0 | 04.9 | 189 10.6 | 32.3 | Acrux | 173 02.5 | S63 12.9 |
| 03 | 160 32.1 | 235 20.7 .. | 33.6 | 257 10.3 .. | 36.0 | 184 36.0 .. | 04.7 | 204 12.8 .. | 32.2 | Adhara | 255 07.4 | S29 00.2 |
| 04 | 175 34.5 | 250 24.5 | 33.4 | 272 10.8 | 36.1 | 199 37.9 | 04.5 | 219 15.0 | 32.1 | Aldebaran | 290 42.2 | N16 33.2 |
| 05 | 190 37.0 | 265 28.3 | 33.2 | 287 11.3 | 36.2 | 214 39.9 | 04.3 | 234 17.1 | 32.0 | | | |
| 06 | 205 39.5 | 280 32.1 | S16 33.0 | 302 11.8 | S23 36.4 | 229 41.8 | S11 04.1 | 249 19.3 | S17 32.0 | Alioth | 166 15.0 | N55 50.2 |
| 07 | 220 41.9 | 295 35.9 | 32.8 | 317 12.3 | 36.5 | 244 43.8 | 03.9 | 264 21.5 | 31.9 | Alkaid | 152 54.0 | N49 12.0 |
| 08 | 235 44.4 | 310 39.7 | 32.6 | 332 12.8 | 36.6 | 259 45.7 | 03.7 | 279 23.7 | 31.8 | Alnair | 27 36.4 | S46 51.5 |
| 09 | 250 46.9 | 325 43.5 .. | 32.4 | 347 13.3 .. | 36.7 | 274 47.7 .. | 03.5 | 294 25.8 .. | 31.7 | Alnilam | 275 39.9 | S 1 11.4 |
| 10 | 265 49.3 | 340 47.3 | 32.3 | 2 13.8 | 36.8 | 289 49.6 | 03.3 | 309 28.0 | 31.6 | Alphard | 217 49.8 | S 8 45.2 |
| 11 | 280 51.8 | 355 51.1 | 32.1 | 17 14.3 | 36.9 | 304 51.6 | 03.1 | 324 30.2 | 31.6 | | | |
| 12 | 295 54.2 | 10 54.9 | S16 31.9 | 32 14.8 | S23 37.0 | 319 53.6 | S11 02.9 | 339 32.3 | S17 31.5 | Alphecca | 126 06.0 | N26 38.3 |
| 13 | 310 56.7 | 25 58.7 | 31.7 | 47 15.3 | 37.1 | 334 55.5 | 02.7 | 354 34.5 | 31.4 | Alpheratz | 357 37.4 | N29 12.7 |
| 14 | 325 59.2 | 41 02.4 | 31.5 | 62 15.8 | 37.2 | 349 57.5 | 02.5 | 9 36.7 | 31.3 | Altair | 62 02.7 | N 8 55.5 |
| 15 | 341 01.6 | 56 06.2 .. | 31.3 | 77 16.3 .. | 37.3 | 4 59.4 .. | 02.3 | 24 38.9 .. | 31.2 | Ankaa | 353 09.7 | S42 11.5 |
| 16 | 356 04.1 | 71 10.0 | 31.1 | 92 16.8 | 37.4 | 20 01.4 | 02.1 | 39 41.0 | 31.1 | Antares | 112 19.1 | S26 28.7 |
| 17 | 11 06.6 | 86 13.8 | 30.9 | 107 17.3 | 37.5 | 35 03.3 | 01.9 | 54 43.2 | 31.1 | | | |
| 18 | 26 09.0 | 101 17.5 | S16 30.7 | 122 17.8 | S23 37.6 | 50 05.3 | S11 01.7 | 69 45.4 | S17 31.0 | Arcturus | 145 50.2 | N19 04.0 |
| 19 | 41 11.5 | 116 21.3 | 30.5 | 137 18.3 | 37.8 | 65 07.2 | 01.5 | 84 47.5 | 30.9 | Atria | 107 15.9 | S69 03.7 |
| 20 | 56 14.0 | 131 25.0 | 30.4 | 152 18.8 | 37.9 | 80 09.2 | 01.3 | 99 49.7 | 30.8 | Avior | 234 15.0 | S59 34.7 |
| 21 | 71 16.4 | 146 28.8 .. | 30.2 | 167 19.3 .. | 38.0 | 95 11.1 .. | 01.1 | 114 51.9 .. | 30.7 | Bellatrix | 278 25.2 | N 6 22.1 |
| 22 | 86 18.9 | 161 32.6 | 30.0 | 182 19.8 | 38.1 | 110 13.1 | 00.9 | 129 54.1 | 30.7 | Betelgeuse | 270 54.4 | N 7 24.6 |
| 23 | 101 21.4 | 176 36.3 | 29.8 | 197 20.3 | 38.2 | 125 15.0 | 00.7 | 144 56.2 | 30.6 | | | |
| **17 00** | 116 23.8 | 191 40.0 | S16 29.6 | 212 20.8 | S23 38.3 | 140 17.0 | S11 00.5 | 159 58.4 | S17 30.5 | Canopus | 263 52.9 | S52 42.6 |
| 01 | 131 26.3 | 206 43.8 | 29.4 | 227 21.3 | 38.4 | 155 18.9 | 00.3 | 175 00.6 | 30.4 | Capella | 280 25.1 | N46 01.2 |
| 02 | 146 28.7 | 221 47.5 | 29.3 | 242 21.8 | 38.5 | 170 20.9 | 11 00.1 | 190 02.7 | 30.3 | Deneb | 49 27.9 | N45 21.5 |
| 03 | 161 31.2 | 236 51.3 .. | 29.1 | 257 22.3 .. | 38.6 | 185 22.8 | 10 59.9 | 205 04.9 .. | 30.2 | Denebola | 182 27.3 | N14 26.9 |
| 04 | 176 33.7 | 251 55.0 | 28.9 | 272 22.8 | 38.7 | 200 24.8 | 59.7 | 220 07.1 | 30.2 | Diphda | 348 49.8 | S17 52.2 |
| 05 | 191 36.1 | 266 58.7 | 28.7 | 287 23.3 | 38.8 | 215 26.7 | 59.5 | 235 09.3 | 30.1 | | | |
| 06 | 206 38.6 | 282 02.4 | S16 28.5 | 302 23.8 | S23 38.9 | 230 28.7 | S10 59.3 | 250 11.4 | S17 30.0 | Dubhe | 193 43.6 | N61 37.7 |
| 07 | 221 41.1 | 297 06.2 | 28.4 | 317 24.3 | 39.0 | 245 30.6 | 59.1 | 265 13.6 | 29.9 | Elnath | 278 04.6 | N28 37.5 |
| 08 | 236 43.5 | 312 09.9 | 28.2 | 332 24.8 | 39.1 | 260 32.6 | 58.9 | 280 15.8 | 29.8 | Eltanin | 90 43.8 | N51 29.0 |
| 09 | 251 46.0 | 327 13.6 .. | 28.0 | 347 25.3 .. | 39.2 | 275 34.5 .. | 58.7 | 295 17.9 .. | 29.7 | Enif | 33 41.5 | N 9 58.5 |
| 10 | 266 48.5 | 342 17.3 | 27.8 | 2 25.8 | 39.3 | 290 36.5 | 58.5 | 310 20.1 | 29.7 | Fomalhaut | 15 17.5 | S29 30.6 |
| 11 | 281 50.9 | 357 21.0 | 27.7 | 17 26.3 | 39.4 | 305 38.4 | 58.3 | 325 22.3 | 29.6 | | | |
| 12 | 296 53.4 | 12 24.7 | S16 27.5 | 32 26.8 | S23 39.5 | 320 40.4 | S10 58.1 | 340 24.5 | S17 29.5 | Gacrux | 171 54.1 | S57 13.9 |
| 13 | 311 55.9 | 27 28.4 | 27.3 | 47 27.3 | 39.6 | 335 42.3 | 57.9 | 355 26.6 | 29.4 | Gienah | 175 46.0 | S17 39.7 |
| 14 | 326 58.3 | 42 32.1 | 27.2 | 62 27.8 | 39.7 | 350 44.3 | 57.7 | 10 28.8 | 29.3 | Hadar | 148 39.5 | S60 28.4 |
| 15 | 342 00.8 | 57 35.8 .. | 27.0 | 77 28.3 .. | 39.8 | 5 46.2 .. | 57.6 | 25 31.0 .. | 29.3 | Hamal | 327 53.9 | N23 34.0 |
| 16 | 357 03.2 | 72 39.5 | 26.8 | 92 28.8 | 39.9 | 20 48.2 | 57.4 | 40 33.1 | 29.2 | Kaus Aust. | 83 36.1 | S34 22.4 |
| 17 | 12 05.7 | 87 43.2 | 26.6 | 107 29.3 | 40.0 | 35 50.1 | 57.2 | 55 35.3 | 29.1 | | | |
| 18 | 27 08.2 | 102 46.8 | S16 26.5 | 122 29.8 | S23 40.1 | 50 52.1 | S10 57.0 | 70 37.5 | S17 29.0 | Kochab | 137 20.2 | N74 03.6 |
| 19 | 42 10.6 | 117 50.5 | 26.3 | 137 30.3 | 40.2 | 65 54.0 | 56.8 | 85 39.6 | 28.9 | Markab | 13 32.5 | N15 19.4 |
| 20 | 57 13.1 | 132 54.2 | 26.1 | 152 30.8 | 40.3 | 80 56.0 | 56.6 | 100 41.8 | 28.8 | Menkar | 314 08.6 | N 4 10.4 |
| 21 | 72 15.6 | 147 57.9 .. | 26.0 | 167 31.3 .. | 40.4 | 95 57.9 .. | 56.4 | 115 44.0 .. | 28.8 | Menkent | 148 00.5 | S36 28.5 |
| 22 | 87 18.0 | 163 01.5 | 25.8 | 182 31.8 | 40.4 | 110 59.9 | 56.2 | 130 46.2 | 28.7 | Miaplacidus | 221 37.8 | S69 48.3 |
| 23 | 102 20.5 | 178 05.2 | 25.7 | 197 32.3 | 40.5 | 126 01.8 | 56.0 | 145 48.3 | 28.6 | | | |
| **18 00** | 117 23.0 | 193 08.9 | S16 25.5 | 212 32.8 | S23 40.6 | 141 03.8 | S10 55.8 | 160 50.5 | S17 28.5 | Mirfak | 308 31.5 | N49 56.5 |
| 01 | 132 25.4 | 208 12.5 | 25.3 | 227 33.3 | 40.7 | 156 05.7 | 55.6 | 175 52.7 | 28.4 | Nunki | 75 51.1 | S26 16.2 |
| 02 | 147 27.9 | 223 16.2 | 25.2 | 242 33.8 | 40.8 | 171 07.7 | 55.4 | 190 54.8 | 28.3 | Peacock | 53 10.2 | S56 39.9 |
| 03 | 162 30.4 | 238 19.8 .. | 25.0 | 257 34.3 .. | 40.9 | 186 09.6 .. | 55.2 | 205 57.0 .. | 28.3 | Pollux | 243 19.9 | N27 58.3 |
| 04 | 177 32.8 | 253 23.5 | 24.9 | 272 34.8 | 41.0 | 201 11.6 | 55.0 | 220 59.2 | 28.2 | Procyon | 244 53.0 | N 5 10.1 |
| 05 | 192 35.3 | 268 27.1 | 24.7 | 287 35.3 | 41.1 | 216 13.5 | 54.8 | 236 01.4 | 28.1 | | | |
| 06 | 207 37.7 | 283 30.7 | S16 24.5 | 302 35.8 | S23 41.2 | 231 15.5 | S10 54.6 | 251 03.5 | S17 28.0 | Rasalhague | 96 01.1 | N12 32.6 |
| 07 | 222 40.2 | 298 34.4 | 24.4 | 317 36.3 | 41.3 | 246 17.4 | 54.4 | 266 05.7 | 27.9 | Regulus | 207 36.8 | N11 51.5 |
| 08 | 237 42.7 | 313 38.0 | 24.2 | 332 36.8 | 41.4 | 261 19.4 | 54.2 | 281 07.9 | 27.9 | Rigel | 281 05.9 | S 8 10.7 |
| 09 | 252 45.1 | 328 41.6 .. | 24.1 | 347 37.2 .. | 41.5 | 276 21.3 .. | 54.0 | 296 10.0 .. | 27.8 | Rigil Kent. | 139 43.8 | S60 55.2 |
| 10 | 267 47.6 | 343 45.2 | 23.9 | 2 37.7 | 41.6 | 291 23.3 | 53.8 | 311 12.2 | 27.7 | Sabik | 102 05.9 | S15 45.1 |
| 11 | 282 50.1 | 358 48.9 | 23.8 | 17 38.2 | 41.6 | 306 25.2 | 53.6 | 326 14.4 | 27.6 | | | |
| 12 | 297 52.5 | 13 52.5 | S16 23.6 | 32 38.7 | S23 41.7 | 321 27.1 | S10 53.3 | 341 16.5 | S17 27.5 | Schedar | 349 33.9 | N56 39.6 |
| 13 | 312 55.0 | 28 56.1 | 23.5 | 47 39.2 | 41.8 | 336 29.1 | 53.1 | 356 18.7 | 27.5 | Shaula | 96 14.0 | S37 07.1 |
| 14 | 327 57.5 | 43 59.7 | 23.3 | 62 39.7 | 41.9 | 351 31.0 | 52.9 | 11 20.9 | 27.4 | Sirius | 258 28.0 | S16 44.9 |
| 15 | 342 59.9 | 59 03.3 .. | 23.2 | 77 40.2 .. | 42.0 | 6 33.0 .. | 52.7 | 26 23.1 .. | 27.3 | Spica | 158 24.8 | S11 16.5 |
| 16 | 358 02.4 | 74 06.9 | 23.0 | 92 40.7 | 42.1 | 21 34.9 | 52.5 | 41 25.2 | 27.2 | Suhail | 222 47.6 | S43 31.2 |
| 17 | 13 04.9 | 89 10.5 | 22.9 | 107 41.2 | 42.2 | 36 36.9 | 52.3 | 56 27.4 | 27.1 | | | |
| 18 | 28 07.3 | 104 14.1 | S16 22.7 | 122 41.7 | S23 42.3 | 51 38.8 | S10 52.1 | 71 29.6 | S17 27.0 | Vega | 80 35.3 | N38 48.1 |
| 19 | 43 09.8 | 119 17.7 | 22.6 | 137 42.2 | 42.3 | 66 40.8 | 51.9 | 86 31.7 | 26.9 | Zuben'ubi | 136 58.8 | S16 07.9 |
| 20 | 58 12.2 | 134 21.2 | 22.4 | 152 42.7 | 42.4 | 81 42.7 | 51.7 | 101 33.9 | 26.9 | | SHA | Mer. Pass. |
| 21 | 73 14.7 | 149 24.8 .. | 22.3 | 167 43.2 .. | 42.5 | 96 44.7 .. | 51.5 | 116 36.1 .. | 26.8 | | ° ′ | h m |
| 22 | 88 17.2 | 164 28.4 | 22.2 | 182 43.7 | 42.6 | 111 46.6 | 51.3 | 131 38.2 | 26.7 | Venus | 75 16.2 | 11 11 |
| 23 | 103 19.6 | 179 32.0 | 22.0 | 197 44.2 | 42.7 | 126 48.6 | 51.1 | 146 40.4 | 26.6 | Mars | 95 57.0 | 9 50 |
| Mer. Pass. | 16 11.8 | v 3.7 | d 0.2 | v 0.5 | d 0.1 | v 1.9 | d 0.2 | v 2.2 | d 0.1 | Jupiter | 23 53.2 | 14 37 |
| | | | | | | | | | | Saturn | 43 34.6 | 13 18 |

| UT | SUN GHA | SUN Dec | MOON GHA | v | MOON Dec | d | HP |
|---|---|---|---|---|---|---|---|
| d h | ° ′ | ° ′ | ° ′ | ′ | ° ′ | ′ | ′ |
| **16** 00 | 177 36.5 | S20 58.8 | 21 05.9 | 10.3 | N26 11.6 | 1.3 | 54.2 |
| 01 | 192 36.3 | 58.4 | 35 35.2 | 10.3 | 26 12.9 | 1.1 | 54.2 |
| 02 | 207 36.1 | 57.9 | 50 04.4 | 10.3 | 26 14.0 | 1.0 | 54.2 |
| 03 | 222 35.9 | . . 57.4 | 64 33.7 | 10.2 | 26 15.0 | 0.9 | 54.2 |
| 04 | 237 35.6 | 56.9 | 79 02.9 | 10.2 | 26 15.9 | 0.8 | 54.2 |
| 05 | 252 35.4 | 56.5 | 93 32.1 | 10.1 | 26 16.7 | 0.6 | 54.2 |
| 06 | 267 35.2 | S20 56.0 | 108 01.2 | 10.2 | N26 17.3 | 0.5 | 54.2 |
| 07 | 282 35.0 | 55.5 | 122 30.4 | 10.1 | 26 17.8 | 0.3 | 54.2 |
| S 08 | 297 34.8 | 55.0 | 136 59.5 | 10.2 | 26 18.1 | 0.3 | 54.2 |
| U 09 | 312 34.6 | . . 54.6 | 151 28.7 | 10.1 | 26 18.4 | 0.1 | 54.2 |
| N 10 | 327 34.4 | 54.1 | 165 57.8 | 10.1 | 26 18.5 | 0.1 | 54.3 |
| D 11 | 342 34.2 | 53.6 | 180 26.9 | 10.1 | 26 18.4 | 0.1 | 54.3 |
| A 12 | 357 33.9 | S20 53.1 | 194 56.0 | 10.0 | N26 18.3 | 0.3 | 54.3 |
| Y 13 | 12 33.7 | 52.6 | 209 25.0 | 10.1 | 26 18.0 | 0.4 | 54.3 |
| 14 | 27 33.5 | 52.2 | 223 54.1 | 10.1 | 26 17.6 | 0.6 | 54.3 |
| 15 | 42 33.3 | . . 51.7 | 238 23.2 | 10.0 | 26 17.0 | 0.6 | 54.3 |
| 16 | 57 33.1 | 51.2 | 252 52.2 | 10.0 | 26 16.4 | 0.8 | 54.3 |
| 17 | 72 32.9 | 50.7 | 267 21.2 | 10.1 | 26 15.6 | 1.0 | 54.3 |
| 18 | 87 32.7 | S20 50.2 | 281 50.3 | 10.0 | N26 14.6 | 1.0 | 54.3 |
| 19 | 102 32.5 | 49.7 | 296 19.3 | 10.1 | 26 13.6 | 1.2 | 54.3 |
| 20 | 117 32.3 | 49.3 | 310 48.4 | 10.0 | 26 12.4 | 1.3 | 54.4 |
| 21 | 132 32.1 | . . 48.8 | 325 17.4 | 10.0 | 26 11.1 | 1.5 | 54.4 |
| 22 | 147 31.8 | 48.3 | 339 46.4 | 10.0 | 26 09.6 | 1.6 | 54.4 |
| 23 | 162 31.6 | 47.8 | 354 15.4 | 10.1 | 26 08.0 | 1.7 | 54.4 |
| **17** 00 | 177 31.4 | S20 47.3 | 8 44.5 | 10.0 | N26 06.3 | 1.8 | 54.4 |
| 01 | 192 31.2 | 46.8 | 23 13.5 | 10.1 | 26 04.5 | 2.0 | 54.4 |
| 02 | 207 31.0 | 46.3 | 37 42.6 | 10.0 | 26 02.5 | 2.1 | 54.4 |
| 03 | 222 30.8 | . . 45.8 | 52 11.6 | 10.0 | 26 00.4 | 2.2 | 54.4 |
| 04 | 237 30.6 | 45.3 | 66 40.6 | 10.1 | 25 58.2 | 2.4 | 54.4 |
| 05 | 252 30.4 | 44.9 | 81 09.7 | 10.1 | 25 55.8 | 2.5 | 54.4 |
| 06 | 267 30.2 | S20 44.4 | 95 38.8 | 10.0 | N25 53.3 | 2.6 | 54.5 |
| 07 | 282 30.0 | 43.9 | 110 07.8 | 10.1 | 25 50.7 | 2.7 | 54.5 |
| M 08 | 297 29.8 | 43.4 | 124 36.9 | 10.1 | 25 48.0 | 2.9 | 54.5 |
| O 09 | 312 29.6 | . . 42.9 | 139 06.0 | 10.1 | 25 45.1 | 3.0 | 54.5 |
| N 10 | 327 29.4 | 42.4 | 153 35.1 | 10.2 | 25 42.1 | 3.1 | 54.5 |
| D 11 | 342 29.2 | 41.9 | 168 04.3 | 10.1 | 25 39.0 | 3.3 | 54.5 |
| A 12 | 357 29.0 | S20 41.4 | 182 33.4 | 10.1 | N25 35.7 | 3.4 | 54.5 |
| Y 13 | 12 28.8 | 40.9 | 197 02.5 | 10.2 | 25 32.3 | 3.5 | 54.5 |
| 14 | 27 28.6 | 40.4 | 211 31.7 | 10.2 | 25 28.8 | 3.6 | 54.6 |
| 15 | 42 28.4 | . . 39.9 | 226 00.9 | 10.2 | 25 25.2 | 3.8 | 54.6 |
| 16 | 57 28.2 | 39.4 | 240 30.1 | 10.3 | 25 21.4 | 3.9 | 54.6 |
| 17 | 72 28.0 | 38.9 | 254 59.3 | 10.3 | 25 17.5 | 4.0 | 54.6 |
| 18 | 87 27.8 | S20 38.4 | 269 28.6 | 10.2 | N25 13.5 | 4.1 | 54.6 |
| 19 | 102 27.6 | 37.9 | 283 57.8 | 10.3 | 25 09.4 | 4.3 | 54.6 |
| 20 | 117 27.3 | 37.4 | 298 27.1 | 10.4 | 25 05.1 | 4.4 | 54.6 |
| 21 | 132 27.1 | . . 36.9 | 312 56.5 | 10.3 | 25 00.7 | 4.5 | 54.6 |
| 22 | 147 26.9 | 36.4 | 327 25.8 | 10.4 | 24 56.2 | 4.7 | 54.7 |
| 23 | 162 26.7 | 35.9 | 341 55.2 | 10.3 | 24 51.5 | 4.7 | 54.7 |
| **18** 00 | 177 26.5 | S20 35.4 | 356 24.5 | 10.5 | N24 46.8 | 4.9 | 54.7 |
| 01 | 192 26.3 | 34.9 | 10 54.0 | 10.4 | 24 41.9 | 5.0 | 54.7 |
| 02 | 207 26.1 | 34.4 | 25 23.4 | 10.5 | 24 36.9 | 5.2 | 54.7 |
| 03 | 222 25.9 | . . 33.9 | 39 52.9 | 10.5 | 24 31.7 | 5.2 | 54.7 |
| 04 | 237 25.7 | 33.4 | 54 22.4 | 10.5 | 24 26.5 | 5.4 | 54.7 |
| 05 | 252 25.6 | 32.8 | 68 51.9 | 10.6 | 24 21.1 | 5.5 | 54.7 |
| 06 | 267 25.4 | S20 32.3 | 83 21.5 | 10.6 | N24 15.6 | 5.7 | 54.8 |
| 07 | 282 25.2 | 31.8 | 97 51.1 | 10.6 | 24 09.9 | 5.7 | 54.8 |
| T 08 | 297 25.0 | 31.3 | 112 20.7 | 10.6 | 24 04.2 | 5.9 | 54.8 |
| U 09 | 312 24.8 | . . 30.8 | 126 50.3 | 10.7 | 23 58.3 | 6.0 | 54.8 |
| E 10 | 327 24.6 | 30.3 | 141 20.0 | 10.8 | 23 52.3 | 6.1 | 54.8 |
| S 11 | 342 24.4 | 29.8 | 155 49.8 | 10.7 | 23 46.2 | 6.2 | 54.8 |
| D 12 | 357 24.2 | S20 29.3 | 170 19.5 | 10.8 | N23 40.0 | 6.3 | 54.9 |
| A 13 | 12 24.0 | 28.8 | 184 49.3 | 10.9 | 23 33.7 | 6.5 | 54.9 |
| Y 14 | 27 23.8 | 28.2 | 199 19.2 | 10.8 | 23 27.2 | 6.6 | 54.9 |
| 15 | 42 23.6 | . . 27.7 | 213 49.0 | 10.9 | 23 20.6 | 6.7 | 54.9 |
| 16 | 57 23.4 | 27.2 | 228 18.9 | 11.0 | 23 13.9 | 6.8 | 54.9 |
| 17 | 72 23.2 | 26.7 | 242 48.9 | 11.0 | 23 07.1 | 6.9 | 54.9 |
| 18 | 87 23.0 | S20 26.2 | 257 18.9 | 11.0 | N23 00.2 | 7.0 | 54.9 |
| 19 | 102 22.8 | 25.7 | 271 48.9 | 11.1 | 22 53.2 | 7.2 | 55.0 |
| 20 | 117 22.6 | 25.1 | 286 19.0 | 11.1 | 22 46.0 | 7.3 | 55.0 |
| 21 | 132 22.4 | . . 24.6 | 300 49.1 | 11.1 | 22 38.7 | 7.3 | 55.0 |
| 22 | 147 22.2 | 24.1 | 315 19.2 | 11.2 | 22 31.4 | 7.5 | 55.0 |
| 23 | 162 22.0 | 23.6 | 329 49.4 | 11.2 | N22 23.9 | 7.6 | 55.0 |
| | SD 16.3 | d 0.5 | SD 14.8 | 14.9 | | | 14.9 |

| Lat. | Naut. | Civil | Sunrise | Moonrise 16 | 17 | 18 | 19 |
|---|---|---|---|---|---|---|---|
| ° | h m | h m | h m | h m | h m | h m | h m |
| N 72 | 07 56 | 09 43 | ■■ | □ | □ | □ | □ |
| N 70 | 07 42 | 09 12 | 11 42 | □ | □ | □ | |
| 68 | 07 30 | 08 49 | 10 24 | □ | □ | □ | 15 15 |
| 66 | 07 21 | 08 30 | 09 47 | □ | □ | 13 36 | 15 56 |
| 64 | 07 12 | 08 16 | 09 21 | □ | 12 41 | 14 36 | 16 24 |
| 62 | 07 05 | 08 03 | 09 01 | 12 30 | 13 40 | 15 10 | 16 45 |
| 60 | 06 59 | 07 52 | 08 44 | 13 09 | 14 14 | 15 34 | 17 02 |
| N 58 | 06 53 | 07 43 | 08 31 | 13 36 | 14 38 | 15 54 | 17 17 |
| 56 | 06 48 | 07 35 | 08 19 | 13 57 | 14 58 | 16 10 | 17 29 |
| 54 | 06 43 | 07 27 | 08 08 | 14 14 | 15 14 | 16 24 | 17 40 |
| 52 | 06 38 | 07 21 | 07 59 | 14 29 | 15 28 | 16 36 | 17 49 |
| 50 | 06 34 | 07 14 | 07 51 | 14 42 | 15 40 | 16 47 | 17 58 |
| 45 | 06 25 | 07 01 | 07 34 | 15 09 | 16 06 | 17 09 | 18 15 |
| N 40 | 06 16 | 06 50 | 07 19 | 15 30 | 16 26 | 17 26 | 18 30 |
| 35 | 06 09 | 06 40 | 07 07 | 15 48 | 16 43 | 17 41 | 18 42 |
| 30 | 06 01 | 06 31 | 06 56 | 16 03 | 16 57 | 17 54 | 18 53 |
| 20 | 05 47 | 06 14 | 06 38 | 16 29 | 17 22 | 18 16 | 19 11 |
| N 10 | 05 33 | 05 59 | 06 22 | 16 51 | 17 43 | 18 35 | 19 27 |
| 0 | 05 19 | 05 44 | 06 06 | 17 11 | 18 03 | 18 53 | 19 42 |
| S 10 | 05 02 | 05 28 | 05 51 | 17 32 | 18 22 | 19 11 | 19 56 |
| 20 | 04 42 | 05 10 | 05 34 | 17 54 | 18 43 | 19 29 | 20 12 |
| 30 | 04 16 | 04 49 | 05 15 | 18 20 | 19 08 | 19 51 | 20 30 |
| 35 | 04 00 | 04 35 | 05 04 | 18 35 | 19 22 | 20 04 | 20 40 |
| 40 | 03 40 | 04 19 | 04 51 | 18 53 | 19 39 | 20 18 | 20 52 |
| 45 | 03 14 | 04 00 | 04 35 | 19 14 | 19 58 | 20 35 | 21 06 |
| S 50 | 02 38 | 03 35 | 04 16 | 19 41 | 20 23 | 20 57 | 21 23 |
| 52 | 02 19 | 03 23 | 04 07 | 19 54 | 20 35 | 21 07 | 21 31 |
| 54 | 01 53 | 03 08 | 03 57 | 20 09 | 20 49 | 21 18 | 21 40 |
| 56 | 01 15 | 02 51 | 03 45 | 20 26 | 21 04 | 21 31 | 21 50 |
| 58 | //// | 02 30 | 03 32 | 20 47 | 21 23 | 21 46 | 22 01 |
| S 60 | //// | 02 03 | 03 16 | 21 14 | 21 46 | 22 04 | 22 14 |

| Lat. | Sunset | Twilight Civil | Naut. | Moonset 16 | 17 | 18 | 19 |
|---|---|---|---|---|---|---|---|
| ° | h m | h m | h m | h m | h m | h m | h m |
| N 72 | ■■ | 14 38 | 16 25 | □ | □ | □ | □ |
| N 70 | 12 39 | 15 09 | 16 39 | □ | □ | □ | |
| 68 | 13 57 | 15 32 | 16 51 | □ | □ | □ | 11 58 |
| 66 | 14 34 | 15 51 | 17 00 | □ | □ | 11 53 | 11 16 |
| 64 | 15 00 | 16 05 | 17 08 | □ | 11 02 | 10 53 | 10 47 |
| 62 | 15 20 | 16 18 | 17 16 | 09 26 | 10 03 | 10 18 | 10 25 |
| 60 | 15 36 | 16 28 | 17 22 | 00 18 | 09 29 | 09 53 | 10 07 |
| N 58 | 15 50 | 16 38 | 17 28 | 08 21 | 09 05 | 09 33 | 09 52 |
| 56 | 16 02 | 16 46 | 17 33 | 07 59 | 08 45 | 09 17 | 09 39 |
| 54 | 16 12 | 16 53 | 17 38 | 07 42 | 08 28 | 09 03 | 09 28 |
| 52 | 16 21 | 17 00 | 17 42 | 07 27 | 08 14 | 08 50 | 09 18 |
| 50 | 16 30 | 17 06 | 17 46 | 07 14 | 08 02 | 08 39 | 09 09 |
| 45 | 16 47 | 17 20 | 17 56 | 06 47 | 07 36 | 08 16 | 08 50 |
| N 40 | 17 01 | 17 31 | 18 04 | 06 26 | 07 15 | 07 58 | 08 35 |
| 35 | 17 13 | 17 41 | 18 12 | 06 09 | 06 58 | 07 42 | 08 21 |
| 30 | 17 24 | 17 50 | 18 19 | 05 53 | 06 43 | 07 29 | 08 10 |
| 20 | 17 42 | 18 06 | 18 33 | 05 28 | 06 18 | 07 06 | 07 50 |
| N 10 | 17 59 | 18 21 | 18 47 | 05 06 | 05 57 | 06 46 | 07 33 |
| 0 | 18 14 | 18 36 | 19 02 | 04 45 | 05 36 | 06 27 | 07 17 |
| S 10 | 18 29 | 18 52 | 19 18 | 04 24 | 05 16 | 06 08 | 07 00 |
| 20 | 18 45 | 19 09 | 19 38 | 04 02 | 04 54 | 05 48 | 06 43 |
| 30 | 19 05 | 19 31 | 20 03 | 03 36 | 04 29 | 05 24 | 06 22 |
| 35 | 19 16 | 19 44 | 20 19 | 03 21 | 04 13 | 05 11 | 06 10 |
| 40 | 19 29 | 20 00 | 20 39 | 03 04 | 03 56 | 04 54 | 05 57 |
| 45 | 19 44 | 20 19 | 21 05 | 02 42 | 03 35 | 04 35 | 05 40 |
| S 50 | 20 03 | 20 44 | 21 40 | 02 16 | 03 09 | 04 11 | 05 20 |
| 52 | 20 12 | 20 56 | 22 00 | 02 03 | 02 56 | 03 59 | 05 10 |
| 54 | 20 22 | 21 10 | 22 24 | 01 48 | 02 41 | 03 46 | 05 00 |
| 56 | 20 34 | 21 27 | 23 01 | 01 30 | 02 23 | 03 31 | 04 47 |
| 58 | 20 47 | 21 48 | //// | 01 09 | 02 02 | 03 12 | 04 33 |
| S 60 | 21 02 | 22 14 | //// | 00 41 | 01 35 | 02 50 | 04 16 |

| Day | SUN Eqn. of Time 00h | 12h | SUN Mer. Pass. | MOON Mer. Pass. Upper | Lower | Age | Phase |
|---|---|---|---|---|---|---|---|
| d | m s | m s | h m | h m | h m | d | % |
| 16 | 09 34 | 09 44 | 12 10 | 23 24 | 10 58 | 14 | 98 |
| 17 | 09 54 | 10 04 | 12 10 | 24 15 | 11 49 | 15 | 100 |
| 18 | 10 13 | 10 23 | 12 10 | 00 15 | 12 40 | 16 | 100 ○ |

| UT | ARIES GHA | VENUS −4.5 GHA | Dec | MARS +1.5 GHA | Dec | JUPITER −2.1 GHA | Dec | SATURN +0.7 GHA | Dec | STARS Name | SHA | Dec |
|---|---|---|---|---|---|---|---|---|---|---|---|---|
| **19** 00 | 118 22.1 | 194 35.5 | S16 21.9 | 212 44.7 | S23 42.8 | 141 50.5 | S10 50.9 | 161 42.6 | S17 26.5 | Acamar | 315 13.5 | S40 13.3 |
| 01 | 133 24.6 | 209 39.1 | 21.7 | 227 45.2 | 42.8 | 156 52.5 | 50.7 | 176 44.8 | 26.4 | Achernar | 335 22.1 | S57 07.9 |
| 02 | 148 27.0 | 224 42.6 .. | 21.6 | 242 45.7 | 42.9 | 171 54.4 | 50.5 | 191 46.9 | 26.4 | Acrux | 173 02.4 | S63 12.9 |
| 03 | 163 29.5 | 239 46.2 .. | 21.5 | 257 46.2 .. | 43.0 | 186 56.4 .. | 50.3 | 206 49.1 .. | 26.3 | Adhara | 255 07.4 | S29 00.2 |
| 04 | 178 32.0 | 254 49.8 | 21.3 | 272 46.7 | 43.1 | 201 58.3 | 50.1 | 221 51.3 | 26.2 | Aldebaran | 290 42.2 | N16 33.2 |
| 05 | 193 34.4 | 269 53.3 | 21.2 | 287 47.2 | 43.2 | 217 00.2 | 49.9 | 236 53.4 | 26.1 | | | |
| 06 | 208 36.9 | 284 56.8 | S16 21.1 | 302 47.7 | S23 43.3 | 232 02.2 | S10 49.7 | 251 55.6 | S17 26.0 | Alioth | 166 15.0 | N55 50.2 |
| W 07 | 223 39.3 | 300 00.4 | 20.9 | 317 48.1 | 43.3 | 247 04.1 | 49.5 | 266 57.8 | 26.0 | Alkaid | 152 54.0 | N49 12.0 |
| E 08 | 238 41.8 | 315 03.9 | 20.8 | 332 48.6 | 43.4 | 262 06.1 | 49.3 | 281 59.9 | 25.9 | Alnair | 27 36.4 | S46 51.5 |
| D 09 | 253 44.3 | 330 07.4 .. | 20.7 | 347 49.1 .. | 43.5 | 277 08.0 .. | 49.1 | 297 02.1 .. | 25.8 | Alnilam | 275 39.9 | S 1 11.4 |
| N 10 | 268 46.7 | 345 11.0 | 20.5 | 2 49.6 | 43.6 | 292 10.0 | 48.9 | 312 04.3 | 25.7 | Alphard | 217 49.8 | S 8 45.2 |
| E 11 | 283 49.2 | 0 14.5 | 20.4 | 17 50.1 | 43.7 | 307 11.9 | 48.7 | 327 06.4 | 25.6 | | | |
| S 12 | 298 51.7 | 15 18.0 | S16 20.3 | 32 50.6 | S23 43.7 | 322 13.9 | S10 48.5 | 342 08.6 | S17 25.5 | Alphecca | 126 06.0 | N26 38.3 |
| D 13 | 313 54.1 | 30 21.5 | 20.1 | 47 51.1 | 43.8 | 337 15.8 | 48.3 | 357 10.8 | 25.5 | Alpheratz | 357 37.4 | N29 12.7 |
| A 14 | 328 56.6 | 45 25.0 | 20.0 | 62 51.6 | 43.9 | 352 17.8 | 48.1 | 12 13.0 | 25.4 | Altair | 62 02.7 | N 8 55.5 |
| Y 15 | 343 59.1 | 60 28.5 .. | 19.9 | 77 52.1 .. | 44.0 | 7 19.7 .. | 47.9 | 27 15.1 .. | 25.3 | Ankaa | 353 09.7 | S42 11.5 |
| 16 | 359 01.5 | 75 32.1 | 19.7 | 92 52.6 | 44.1 | 22 21.6 | 47.7 | 42 17.3 | 25.2 | Antares | 112 19.0 | S26 28.7 |
| 17 | 14 04.0 | 90 35.5 | 19.6 | 107 53.1 | 44.1 | 37 23.6 | 47.5 | 57 19.5 | 25.1 | | | |
| 18 | 29 06.5 | 105 39.0 | S16 19.5 | 122 53.6 | S23 44.2 | 52 25.5 | S10 47.3 | 72 21.6 | S17 25.0 | Arcturus | 145 50.2 | N19 04.0 |
| 19 | 44 08.9 | 120 42.5 | 19.4 | 137 54.1 | 44.3 | 67 27.5 | 47.1 | 87 23.8 | 25.0 | Atria | 107 15.9 | S69 03.7 |
| 20 | 59 11.4 | 135 46.0 | 19.2 | 152 54.6 | 44.4 | 82 29.4 | 46.9 | 102 26.0 | 24.9 | Avior | 234 15.0 | S59 34.7 |
| 21 | 74 13.8 | 150 49.5 .. | 19.1 | 167 55.1 .. | 44.4 | 97 31.4 .. | 46.7 | 117 28.1 .. | 24.8 | Bellatrix | 278 25.2 | N 6 22.1 |
| 22 | 89 16.3 | 165 53.0 | 19.0 | 182 55.5 | 44.5 | 112 33.3 | 46.5 | 132 30.3 | 24.7 | Betelgeuse | 270 54.4 | N 7 24.6 |
| 23 | 104 18.8 | 180 56.5 | 18.9 | 197 56.0 | 44.6 | 127 35.3 | 46.3 | 147 32.5 | 24.6 | | | |
| **20** 00 | 119 21.2 | 195 59.9 | S16 18.8 | 212 56.5 | S23 44.7 | 142 37.2 | S10 46.1 | 162 34.6 | S17 24.5 | Canopus | 263 52.9 | S52 42.6 |
| 01 | 134 23.7 | 211 03.4 | 18.6 | 227 57.0 | 44.7 | 157 39.1 | 45.9 | 177 36.8 | 24.5 | Capella | 280 25.1 | N46 01.2 |
| 02 | 149 26.2 | 226 06.9 | 18.5 | 242 57.5 | 44.8 | 172 41.1 | 45.7 | 192 39.0 | 24.4 | Deneb | 49 27.9 | N45 21.5 |
| 03 | 164 28.6 | 241 10.3 .. | 18.4 | 257 58.0 .. | 44.9 | 187 43.0 .. | 45.5 | 207 41.2 .. | 24.3 | Denebola | 182 27.3 | N14 26.9 |
| 04 | 179 31.1 | 256 13.8 | 18.3 | 272 58.5 | 45.0 | 202 45.0 | 45.3 | 222 43.3 | 24.2 | Diphda | 348 49.8 | S17 52.2 |
| 05 | 194 33.6 | 271 17.2 | 18.2 | 287 59.0 | 45.0 | 217 46.9 | 45.1 | 237 45.5 | 24.1 | | | |
| 06 | 209 36.0 | 286 20.7 | S16 18.1 | 302 59.5 | S23 45.1 | 232 48.9 | S10 44.9 | 252 47.7 | S17 24.0 | Dubhe | 193 43.6 | N61 37.7 |
| T 07 | 224 38.5 | 301 24.1 | 17.9 | 318 00.0 | 45.2 | 247 50.8 | 44.7 | 267 49.8 | 24.0 | Elnath | 278 04.6 | N28 37.5 |
| H 08 | 239 41.0 | 316 27.5 | 17.8 | 333 00.5 | 45.2 | 262 52.7 | 44.5 | 282 52.0 | 23.9 | Eltanin | 90 43.8 | N51 29.0 |
| U 09 | 254 43.4 | 331 31.0 .. | 17.7 | 348 01.0 .. | 45.3 | 277 54.7 .. | 44.3 | 297 54.2 .. | 23.8 | Enif | 33 41.5 | N 9 58.5 |
| R 10 | 269 45.9 | 346 34.4 | 17.6 | 3 01.5 | 45.4 | 292 56.6 | 44.1 | 312 56.3 | 23.7 | Fomalhaut | 15 17.5 | S29 30.6 |
| S 11 | 284 48.3 | 1 37.8 | 17.5 | 18 01.9 | 45.5 | 307 58.6 | 43.9 | 327 58.5 | 23.6 | | | |
| D 12 | 299 50.8 | 16 41.2 | S16 17.4 | 33 02.4 | S23 45.5 | 323 00.5 | S10 43.7 | 343 00.7 | S17 23.5 | Gacrux | 171 54.1 | S57 13.9 |
| A 13 | 314 53.3 | 31 44.7 | 17.3 | 48 02.9 | 45.6 | 338 02.5 | 43.5 | 358 02.8 | 23.5 | Gienah | 175 45.9 | S17 39.7 |
| Y 14 | 329 55.7 | 46 48.1 | 17.2 | 63 03.4 | 45.7 | 353 04.4 | 43.3 | 13 05.0 | 23.4 | Hadar | 148 39.4 | S60 28.4 |
| 15 | 344 58.2 | 61 51.5 .. | 17.1 | 78 03.9 .. | 45.7 | 8 06.4 .. | 43.1 | 28 07.2 .. | 23.3 | Hamal | 327 53.9 | N23 34.0 |
| 16 | 0 00.7 | 76 54.9 | 17.0 | 93 04.4 | 45.8 | 23 08.3 | 42.9 | 43 09.3 | 23.2 | Kaus Aust. | 83 36.1 | S34 22.4 |
| 17 | 15 03.1 | 91 58.3 | 16.9 | 108 04.9 | 45.9 | 38 10.2 | 42.7 | 58 11.5 | 23.1 | | | |
| 18 | 30 05.6 | 107 01.7 | S16 16.7 | 123 05.4 | S23 45.9 | 53 12.2 | S10 42.4 | 73 13.7 | S17 23.0 | Kochab | 137 20.2 | N74 03.6 |
| 19 | 45 08.1 | 122 05.1 | 16.6 | 138 05.9 | 46.0 | 68 14.1 | 42.2 | 88 15.9 | 23.0 | Markab | 13 32.5 | N15 19.4 |
| 20 | 60 10.5 | 137 08.4 | 16.5 | 153 06.4 | 46.1 | 83 16.1 | 42.0 | 103 18.0 | 22.9 | Menkar | 314 08.6 | N 4 10.4 |
| 21 | 75 13.0 | 152 11.8 .. | 16.4 | 168 06.8 .. | 46.1 | 98 18.0 .. | 41.8 | 118 20.2 .. | 22.8 | Menkent | 148 00.5 | S36 28.5 |
| 22 | 90 15.5 | 167 15.2 | 16.3 | 183 07.3 | 46.2 | 113 19.9 | 41.6 | 133 22.4 | 22.7 | Miaplacidus | 221 37.8 | S69 48.3 |
| 23 | 105 17.9 | 182 18.6 | 16.2 | 198 07.8 | 46.3 | 128 21.9 | 41.4 | 148 24.5 | 22.6 | | | |
| **21** 00 | 120 20.4 | 197 21.9 | S16 16.1 | 213 08.3 | S23 46.3 | 143 23.8 | S10 41.2 | 163 26.7 | S17 22.5 | Mirfak | 308 31.5 | N49 56.5 |
| 01 | 135 22.8 | 212 25.3 | 16.0 | 228 08.8 | 46.4 | 158 25.8 | 41.0 | 178 28.9 | 22.5 | Nunki | 75 51.1 | S26 16.2 |
| 02 | 150 25.3 | 227 28.7 | 15.9 | 243 09.3 | 46.5 | 173 27.7 | 40.8 | 193 31.0 | 22.4 | Peacock | 53 10.2 | S56 39.9 |
| 03 | 165 27.8 | 242 32.0 .. | 15.8 | 258 09.8 .. | 46.5 | 188 29.7 .. | 40.6 | 208 33.2 .. | 22.3 | Pollux | 243 19.9 | N27 58.3 |
| 04 | 180 30.2 | 257 35.4 | 15.7 | 273 10.3 | 46.6 | 203 31.6 | 40.4 | 223 35.4 | 22.2 | Procyon | 244 53.0 | N 5 10.0 |
| 05 | 195 32.7 | 272 38.7 | 15.7 | 288 10.8 | 46.6 | 218 33.5 | 40.2 | 238 37.5 | 22.1 | | | |
| 06 | 210 35.2 | 287 42.1 | S16 15.6 | 303 11.3 | S23 46.7 | 233 35.5 | S10 40.0 | 253 39.7 | S17 22.0 | Rasalhague | 96 01.1 | N12 32.6 |
| 07 | 225 37.6 | 302 45.4 | 15.5 | 318 11.7 | 46.8 | 248 37.4 | 39.8 | 268 41.9 | 22.0 | Regulus | 207 36.7 | N11 51.5 |
| 08 | 240 40.1 | 317 48.7 | 15.4 | 333 12.2 | 46.8 | 263 39.4 | 39.6 | 283 44.0 | 21.9 | Rigel | 281 05.9 | S 8 10.7 |
| F 09 | 255 42.6 | 332 52.1 .. | 15.3 | 348 12.7 .. | 46.9 | 278 41.3 .. | 39.4 | 298 46.2 .. | 21.8 | Rigil Kent. | 139 43.7 | S60 55.2 |
| R 10 | 270 45.0 | 347 55.4 | 15.2 | 3 13.2 | 47.0 | 293 43.2 | 39.2 | 313 48.4 | 21.7 | Sabik | 102 05.8 | S15 45.1 |
| I 11 | 285 47.5 | 2 58.7 | 15.1 | 18 13.7 | 47.0 | 308 45.2 | 39.0 | 328 50.5 | 21.6 | | | |
| D 12 | 300 49.9 | 18 02.0 | S16 15.0 | 33 14.2 | S23 47.1 | 323 47.1 | S10 38.8 | 343 52.7 | S17 21.5 | Schedar | 349 33.9 | N56 39.6 |
| A 13 | 315 52.4 | 33 05.3 | 14.9 | 48 14.7 | 47.1 | 338 49.1 | 38.6 | 358 54.9 | 21.5 | Shaula | 96 14.0 | S37 07.1 |
| Y 14 | 330 54.9 | 48 08.6 | 14.8 | 63 15.2 | 47.2 | 353 51.0 | 38.4 | 13 57.0 | 21.4 | Sirius | 258 28.0 | S16 44.9 |
| 15 | 345 57.3 | 63 11.9 .. | 14.7 | 78 15.7 .. | 47.3 | 8 53.0 .. | 38.2 | 28 59.2 .. | 21.3 | Spica | 158 24.8 | S11 16.5 |
| 16 | 0 59.8 | 78 15.2 | 14.7 | 93 16.1 | 47.3 | 23 54.9 | 38.0 | 44 01.4 | 21.2 | Suhail | 222 47.6 | S43 31.2 |
| 17 | 16 02.3 | 93 18.5 | 14.6 | 108 16.6 | 47.4 | 38 56.8 | 37.8 | 59 03.6 | 21.1 | | | |
| 18 | 31 04.7 | 108 21.8 | S16 14.5 | 123 17.1 | S23 47.4 | 53 58.8 | S10 37.6 | 74 05.7 | S17 21.0 | Vega | 80 35.3 | N38 48.1 |
| 19 | 46 07.2 | 123 25.1 | 14.4 | 138 17.6 | 47.5 | 69 00.7 | 37.4 | 89 07.9 | 21.0 | Zuben'ubi | 136 58.8 | S16 07.9 |
| 20 | 61 09.7 | 138 28.4 | 14.3 | 153 18.1 | 47.5 | 84 02.7 | 37.1 | 104 10.1 | 20.9 | | SHA | Mer. Pass. |
| 21 | 76 12.1 | 153 31.7 .. | 14.2 | 168 18.6 .. | 47.6 | 99 04.6 .. | 36.9 | 119 12.2 .. | 20.8 | Venus | 76 38.7 | 10 53 |
| 22 | 91 14.6 | 168 35.0 | 14.2 | 183 19.1 | 47.6 | 114 06.5 | 36.7 | 134 14.4 | 20.7 | Mars | 93 35.3 | 9 48 |
| 23 | 106 17.1 | 183 38.2 | 14.1 | 198 19.6 | 47.7 | 129 08.5 | 36.5 | 149 16.6 | 20.6 | Jupiter | 23 16.0 | 14 28 |
| Mer. Pass. | 16 00.0 | v 3.4 | d 0.1 | v 0.5 | d 0.1 | v 1.9 | d 0.2 | v 2.2 | d 0.1 | Saturn | 43 13.4 | 13 08 |

## SUN / MOON

| UT | SUN GHA | SUN Dec | MOON GHA | v | MOON Dec | d | HP |
|---|---|---|---|---|---|---|---|
| d h | ° ′ | ° ′ | ° ′ | ′ | ° ′ | ′ | ′ |
| **19** 00 | 177 21.8 | S20 23.1 | 344 19.6 | 11.3 | N22 16.3 | 7.7 | 55.0 |
| 01 | 192 21.6 | 22.5 | 358 49.9 | 11.3 | 22 08.6 | 7.8 | 55.0 |
| 02 | 207 21.5 | 22.0 | 13 20.2 | 11.3 | 22 00.8 | 8.0 | 55.1 |
| 03 | 222 21.3 .. | 21.5 | 27 50.5 | 11.4 | 21 52.8 | 8.0 | 55.1 |
| 04 | 237 21.1 | 21.0 | 42 20.9 | 11.5 | 21 44.8 | 8.2 | 55.1 |
| 05 | 252 20.9 | 20.4 | 56 51.4 | 11.5 | 21 36.6 | 8.2 | 55.1 |
| 06 | 267 20.7 | S20 19.9 | 71 21.9 | 11.5 | N21 28.4 | 8.4 | 55.1 |
| W 07 | 282 20.5 | 19.4 | 85 52.4 | 11.5 | 21 20.0 | 8.4 | 55.1 |
| E 08 | 297 20.3 | 18.9 | 100 22.9 | 11.7 | 21 11.6 | 8.6 | 55.2 |
| D 09 | 312 20.1 .. | 18.3 | 114 53.6 | 11.6 | 21 03.0 | 8.7 | 55.2 |
| N 10 | 327 19.9 | 17.8 | 129 24.2 | 11.7 | 20 54.3 | 8.7 | 55.2 |
| E 11 | 342 19.7 | 17.3 | 143 54.9 | 11.8 | 20 45.6 | 8.9 | 55.2 |
| S 12 | 357 19.6 | S20 16.8 | 158 25.7 | 11.7 | N20 36.7 | 9.0 | 55.2 |
| D 13 | 12 19.4 | 16.2 | 172 56.4 | 11.9 | 20 27.7 | 9.1 | 55.2 |
| A 14 | 27 19.2 | 15.7 | 187 27.3 | 11.9 | 20 18.6 | 9.2 | 55.3 |
| Y 15 | 42 19.0 .. | 15.2 | 201 58.2 | 11.9 | 20 09.4 | 9.2 | 55.3 |
| 16 | 57 18.8 | 14.6 | 216 29.1 | 11.9 | 20 00.2 | 9.4 | 55.3 |
| 17 | 72 18.6 | 14.1 | 231 00.0 | 12.1 | 19 50.8 | 9.5 | 55.3 |
| 18 | 87 18.4 | S20 13.6 | 245 31.1 | 12.0 | N19 41.3 | 9.6 | 55.3 |
| 19 | 102 18.2 | 13.0 | 260 02.1 | 12.1 | 19 31.7 | 9.6 | 55.3 |
| 20 | 117 18.1 | 12.5 | 274 33.2 | 12.2 | 19 22.1 | 9.8 | 55.4 |
| 21 | 132 17.9 .. | 12.0 | 289 04.4 | 12.1 | 19 12.3 | 9.8 | 55.4 |
| 22 | 147 17.7 | 11.4 | 303 35.5 | 12.3 | 19 02.5 | 10.0 | 55.4 |
| 23 | 162 17.5 | 10.9 | 318 06.8 | 12.3 | 18 52.5 | 10.0 | 55.4 |
| **20** 00 | 177 17.3 | S20 10.4 | 332 38.1 | 12.3 | N18 42.5 | 10.2 | 55.4 |
| 01 | 192 17.1 | 09.8 | 347 09.4 | 12.3 | 18 32.3 | 10.2 | 55.5 |
| 02 | 207 16.9 | 09.3 | 1 40.7 | 12.4 | 18 22.1 | 10.3 | 55.5 |
| 03 | 222 16.8 .. | 08.7 | 16 12.1 | 12.5 | 18 11.8 | 10.4 | 55.5 |
| 04 | 237 16.6 | 08.2 | 30 43.6 | 12.5 | 18 01.4 | 10.5 | 55.5 |
| 05 | 252 16.4 | 07.7 | 45 15.1 | 12.5 | 17 50.9 | 10.6 | 55.5 |
| 06 | 267 16.2 | S20 07.1 | 59 46.6 | 12.6 | N17 40.3 | 10.7 | 55.5 |
| T 07 | 282 16.0 | 06.6 | 74 18.2 | 12.6 | 17 29.6 | 10.7 | 55.6 |
| H 08 | 297 15.8 | 06.0 | 88 49.8 | 12.7 | 17 18.9 | 10.9 | 55.6 |
| U 09 | 312 15.7 .. | 05.5 | 103 21.5 | 12.7 | 17 08.0 | 10.9 | 55.6 |
| R 10 | 327 15.5 | 05.0 | 117 53.2 | 12.8 | 16 57.1 | 11.0 | 55.6 |
| S 11 | 342 15.3 | 04.4 | 132 25.0 | 12.8 | 16 46.1 | 11.1 | 55.6 |
| D 12 | 357 15.1 | S20 03.9 | 146 56.8 | 12.8 | N16 35.0 | 11.2 | 55.7 |
| A 13 | 12 14.9 | 03.3 | 161 28.6 | 12.9 | 16 23.8 | 11.3 | 55.7 |
| Y 14 | 27 14.8 | 02.8 | 176 00.5 | 12.9 | 16 12.5 | 11.3 | 55.7 |
| 15 | 42 14.6 .. | 02.2 | 190 32.4 | 12.9 | 16 01.2 | 11.4 | 55.7 |
| 16 | 57 14.4 | 01.7 | 205 04.3 | 13.0 | 15 49.8 | 11.5 | 55.7 |
| 17 | 72 14.2 | 01.1 | 219 36.3 | 13.0 | 15 38.3 | 11.6 | 55.7 |
| 18 | 87 14.0 | S20 00.6 | 234 08.3 | 13.1 | N15 26.7 | 11.6 | 55.8 |
| 19 | 102 13.9 | 20 00.0 | 248 40.4 | 13.1 | 15 15.1 | 11.7 | 55.8 |
| 20 | 117 13.7 | 19 59.5 | 263 12.5 | 13.2 | 15 03.4 | 11.8 | 55.8 |
| 21 | 132 13.5 .. | 58.9 | 277 44.7 | 13.1 | 14 51.6 | 11.9 | 55.8 |
| 22 | 147 13.3 | 58.4 | 292 16.8 | 13.3 | 14 39.7 | 12.0 | 55.8 |
| 23 | 162 13.2 | 57.8 | 306 49.1 | 13.2 | 14 27.7 | 12.0 | 55.9 |
| **21** 00 | 177 13.0 | S19 57.3 | 321 21.3 | 13.3 | N14 15.7 | 12.1 | 55.9 |
| 01 | 192 12.8 | 56.7 | 335 53.6 | 13.3 | 14 03.6 | 12.1 | 55.9 |
| 02 | 207 12.6 | 56.2 | 350 25.9 | 13.4 | 13 51.5 | 12.2 | 55.9 |
| 03 | 222 12.4 .. | 55.6 | 4 58.3 | 13.4 | 13 39.3 | 12.3 | 55.9 |
| 04 | 237 12.3 | 55.1 | 19 30.7 | 13.4 | 13 27.0 | 12.4 | 56.0 |
| 05 | 252 12.1 | 54.5 | 34 03.1 | 13.4 | 13 14.6 | 12.4 | 56.0 |
| 06 | 267 11.9 | S19 54.0 | 48 35.5 | 13.5 | N13 02.2 | 12.5 | 56.0 |
| 07 | 282 11.7 | 53.4 | 63 08.0 | 13.5 | 12 49.7 | 12.6 | 56.0 |
| F 08 | 297 11.6 | 52.8 | 77 40.5 | 13.6 | 12 37.1 | 12.6 | 56.0 |
| R 09 | 312 11.4 .. | 52.3 | 92 13.1 | 13.5 | 12 24.5 | 12.7 | 56.1 |
| I 10 | 327 11.2 | 51.7 | 106 45.6 | 13.6 | 12 11.8 | 12.8 | 56.1 |
| D 11 | 342 11.0 | 51.2 | 121 18.2 | 13.7 | 11 59.0 | 12.8 | 56.1 |
| A 12 | 357 10.9 | S19 50.6 | 135 50.9 | 13.6 | N11 46.2 | 12.8 | 56.1 |
| Y 13 | 12 10.7 | 50.0 | 150 23.5 | 13.7 | 11 33.4 | 13.0 | 56.1 |
| 14 | 27 10.5 | 49.5 | 164 56.2 | 13.7 | 11 20.4 | 13.0 | 56.2 |
| 15 | 42 10.4 .. | 48.9 | 179 28.9 | 13.7 | 11 07.4 | 13.0 | 56.2 |
| 16 | 57 10.2 | 48.4 | 194 01.6 | 13.8 | 10 54.4 | 13.1 | 56.2 |
| 17 | 72 10.0 | 47.8 | 208 34.4 | 13.8 | 10 41.3 | 13.2 | 56.2 |
| 18 | 87 09.8 | S19 47.2 | 223 07.2 | 13.8 | N10 28.1 | 13.2 | 56.3 |
| 19 | 102 09.7 | 46.7 | 237 40.0 | 13.8 | 10 14.9 | 13.3 | 56.3 |
| 20 | 117 09.5 | 46.1 | 252 12.8 | 13.8 | 10 01.6 | 13.3 | 56.3 |
| 21 | 132 09.3 .. | 45.5 | 266 45.6 | 13.9 | 9 48.3 | 13.4 | 56.3 |
| 22 | 147 09.2 | 45.0 | 281 18.5 | 13.9 | 9 34.9 | 13.4 | 56.3 |
| 23 | 162 09.0 | 44.4 | 295 51.4 | 13.9 | N 9 21.5 | 13.5 | 56.4 |
| | SD 16.3 | d 0.5 | SD 15.0 | | 15.2 | | 15.3 |

## Twilight / Sunrise / Moonrise

| Lat. | Twilight Naut. | Twilight Civil | Sunrise | Moonrise 19 | 20 | 21 | 22 |
|---|---|---|---|---|---|---|---|
| ° | h m | h m | h m | h m | h m | h m | h m |
| N 72 | 07 48 | 09 31 | ■■■■ | ▭ | 16 22 | 18 56 | 21 05 |
| N 70 | 07 35 | 09 02 | 11 05 | ▭ | 17 03 | 19 13 | 21 11 |
| 68 | 07 24 | 08 41 | 10 10 | 15 15 | 17 30 | 19 26 | 21 16 |
| 66 | 07 15 | 08 24 | 09 37 | 15 56 | 17 51 | 19 37 | 21 20 |
| 64 | 07 08 | 08 10 | 09 13 | 16 24 | 18 07 | 19 46 | 21 24 |
| 62 | 07 01 | 07 58 | 08 55 | 16 45 | 18 21 | 19 54 | 21 27 |
| 60 | 06 55 | 07 48 | 08 39 | 17 02 | 18 32 | 20 01 | 21 29 |
| N 58 | 06 50 | 07 39 | 08 26 | 17 17 | 18 42 | 20 07 | 21 32 |
| 56 | 06 45 | 07 31 | 08 15 | 17 29 | 18 50 | 20 12 | 21 34 |
| 54 | 06 40 | 07 24 | 08 05 | 17 40 | 18 58 | 20 16 | 21 35 |
| 52 | 06 36 | 07 18 | 07 56 | 17 49 | 19 05 | 20 21 | 21 37 |
| 50 | 06 32 | 07 12 | 07 48 | 17 58 | 19 11 | 20 24 | 21 38 |
| 45 | 06 23 | 06 59 | 07 31 | 18 15 | 19 24 | 20 33 | 21 42 |
| N 40 | 06 15 | 06 48 | 07 18 | 18 30 | 19 34 | 20 39 | 21 44 |
| 35 | 06 08 | 06 39 | 07 06 | 18 42 | 19 44 | 20 45 | 21 47 |
| 30 | 06 01 | 06 30 | 06 56 | 18 53 | 19 52 | 20 50 | 21 49 |
| 20 | 05 47 | 06 14 | 06 38 | 19 11 | 20 05 | 20 59 | 21 52 |
| N 10 | 05 34 | 06 00 | 06 22 | 19 27 | 20 17 | 21 07 | 21 55 |
| 0 | 05 20 | 05 45 | 06 07 | 19 42 | 20 29 | 21 14 | 21 58 |
| S 10 | 05 04 | 05 30 | 05 52 | 19 56 | 20 40 | 21 21 | 22 01 |
| 20 | 04 44 | 05 13 | 05 36 | 20 12 | 20 51 | 21 29 | 22 04 |
| 30 | 04 19 | 04 51 | 05 18 | 20 30 | 21 05 | 21 37 | 22 08 |
| 35 | 04 04 | 04 38 | 05 07 | 20 40 | 21 13 | 21 42 | 22 10 |
| 40 | 03 44 | 04 23 | 04 54 | 20 52 | 21 22 | 21 48 | 22 12 |
| 45 | 03 20 | 04 04 | 04 39 | 21 06 | 21 32 | 21 54 | 22 15 |
| S 50 | 02 45 | 03 40 | 04 21 | 21 23 | 21 44 | 22 02 | 22 18 |
| 52 | 02 27 | 03 29 | 04 12 | 21 31 | 21 50 | 22 06 | 22 20 |
| 54 | 02 03 | 03 15 | 04 03 | 21 40 | 21 56 | 22 09 | 22 21 |
| 56 | 01 30 | 02 59 | 03 52 | 21 50 | 22 03 | 22 14 | 22 23 |
| 58 | //// | 02 39 | 03 39 | 22 01 | 22 11 | 22 18 | 22 25 |
| S 60 | //// | 02 14 | 03 24 | 22 14 | 22 20 | 22 24 | 22 27 |

## Sunset / Twilight / Moonset

| Lat | Sunset | Twilight Civil | Twilight Naut. | Moonset 19 | 20 | 21 | 22 |
|---|---|---|---|---|---|---|---|
| ° | h m | h m | h m | h m | h m | h m | h m |
| N 72 | ■■■■ | 14 52 | 16 35 | ▭ | 12 32 | 11 35 | 11 00 |
| N 70 | 13 18 | 15 21 | 16 48 | ▭ | 11 50 | 11 16 | 10 51 |
| 68 | 14 13 | 15 42 | 16 59 | 11 58 | 11 21 | 11 00 | 10 44 |
| 66 | 14 46 | 15 59 | 17 07 | 11 16 | 10 59 | 10 47 | 10 37 |
| 64 | 15 09 | 16 13 | 17 15 | 10 47 | 10 42 | 10 37 | 10 32 |
| 62 | 15 28 | 16 24 | 17 22 | 10 25 | 10 27 | 10 28 | 10 28 |
| 60 | 15 43 | 16 35 | 17 28 | 10 07 | 10 15 | 10 20 | 10 23 |
| N 58 | 15 56 | 16 43 | 17 33 | 09 52 | 10 04 | 10 13 | 10 20 |
| 56 | 16 08 | 16 51 | 17 38 | 09 39 | 09 55 | 10 07 | 10 17 |
| 54 | 16 18 | 16 58 | 17 42 | 09 28 | 09 47 | 10 01 | 10 14 |
| 52 | 16 26 | 17 05 | 17 47 | 09 18 | 09 39 | 09 56 | 10 11 |
| 50 | 16 34 | 17 11 | 17 50 | 09 09 | 09 32 | 09 52 | 10 09 |
| 45 | 16 51 | 17 23 | 17 59 | 08 50 | 09 18 | 09 42 | 10 03 |
| N 40 | 17 05 | 17 34 | 18 07 | 08 35 | 09 06 | 09 34 | 09 59 |
| 35 | 17 16 | 17 44 | 18 15 | 08 21 | 08 56 | 09 27 | 09 55 |
| 30 | 17 27 | 17 52 | 18 21 | 08 10 | 08 47 | 09 20 | 09 52 |
| 20 | 17 44 | 18 08 | 18 35 | 07 50 | 08 31 | 09 09 | 09 46 |
| N 10 | 18 00 | 18 22 | 18 48 | 07 33 | 08 17 | 09 00 | 09 40 |
| 0 | 18 15 | 18 37 | 19 02 | 07 17 | 08 04 | 08 50 | 09 35 |
| S 10 | 18 29 | 18 52 | 19 18 | 07 00 | 07 51 | 08 41 | 09 30 |
| 20 | 18 45 | 19 09 | 19 37 | 06 43 | 07 37 | 08 31 | 09 25 |
| 30 | 19 04 | 19 30 | 20 02 | 06 22 | 07 21 | 08 20 | 09 18 |
| 35 | 19 15 | 19 43 | 20 18 | 06 10 | 07 12 | 08 13 | 09 15 |
| 40 | 19 27 | 19 58 | 20 37 | 05 57 | 07 01 | 08 06 | 09 10 |
| 45 | 19 42 | 20 17 | 21 01 | 05 40 | 06 48 | 07 57 | 09 06 |
| S 50 | 20 00 | 20 40 | 21 35 | 05 20 | 06 32 | 07 46 | 09 00 |
| 52 | 20 09 | 20 52 | 21 53 | 05 10 | 06 25 | 07 41 | 08 57 |
| 54 | 20 18 | 21 06 | 22 16 | 05 00 | 06 17 | 07 35 | 08 54 |
| 56 | 20 29 | 21 21 | 22 48 | 04 47 | 06 08 | 07 29 | 08 51 |
| 58 | 20 42 | 21 40 | 23 58 | 04 33 | 05 57 | 07 22 | 08 47 |
| S 60 | 20 57 | 22 05 | //// | 04 16 | 05 45 | 07 14 | 08 43 |

## SUN / MOON

| Day | SUN Eqn. of Time 00h | SUN Eqn. of Time 12h | SUN Mer. Pass. | MOON Mer. Pass. Upper | MOON Mer. Pass. Lower | Age | Phase |
|---|---|---|---|---|---|---|---|
| d | m s | m s | h m | h m | h m | d | % |
| 19 | 10 32 | 10 41 | 12 11 | 01 05 | 13 29 | 17 | 98 |
| 20 | 10 50 | 10 59 | 12 11 | 01 53 | 14 16 | 18 | 94 |
| 21 | 11 08 | 11 16 | 12 11 | 02 39 | 15 02 | 19 | 88 |

## 2022 JANUARY 22, 23, 24 (SAT., SUN., MON.)

| UT | ARIES GHA | VENUS −4.6 GHA | Dec | MARS +1.4 GHA | Dec | JUPITER −2.1 GHA | Dec | SATURN +0.6 GHA | Dec | STARS Name | SHA | Dec |
|---|---|---|---|---|---|---|---|---|---|---|---|---|
| d h | ° ′ | ° ′ | ° ′ | ° ′ | ° ′ | ° ′ | ° ′ | ° ′ | ° ′ | | ° ′ | ° ′ |
| 22 00 | 121 19.5 | 198 41.5 | S16 14.0 | 213 20.0 | S23 47.8 | 144 10.4 | S10 36.3 | 164 18.7 | S17 20.5 | Acamar | 315 13.5 | S40 13.3 |
| 01 | 136 22.0 | 213 44.7 | 13.9 | 228 20.5 | 47.8 | 159 12.4 | 36.1 | 179 20.9 | 20.4 | Achernar | 335 22.1 | S57 07.9 |
| 02 | 151 24.4 | 228 48.0 | 13.8 | 243 21.0 | 47.9 | 174 14.3 | 35.9 | 194 23.1 | 20.4 | Acrux | 173 02.4 | S63 13.0 |
| 03 | 166 26.9 | 243 51.2 .. | 13.8 | 258 21.5 .. | 47.9 | 189 16.2 .. | 35.7 | 209 25.2 .. | 20.3 | Adhara | 255 07.4 | S29 00.2 |
| 04 | 181 29.4 | 258 54.5 | 13.7 | 273 22.0 | 48.0 | 204 18.2 | 35.5 | 224 27.4 | 20.2 | Aldebaran | 290 42.2 | N16 33.2 |
| 05 | 196 31.8 | 273 57.7 | 13.6 | 288 22.5 | 48.0 | 219 20.1 | 35.3 | 239 29.6 | 20.1 | | | |
| 06 | 211 34.3 | 289 01.0 | S16 13.5 | 303 23.0 | S23 48.1 | 234 22.1 | S10 35.1 | 254 31.7 | S17 20.0 | Alioth | 166 15.0 | N55 50.2 |
| S 07 | 226 36.8 | 304 04.2 | 13.5 | 318 23.5 | 48.1 | 249 24.0 | 34.9 | 269 33.9 | 19.9 | Alkaid | 152 53.9 | N49 12.0 |
| A 08 | 241 39.2 | 319 07.4 | 13.4 | 333 23.9 | 48.2 | 264 25.9 | 34.7 | 284 36.1 | 19.9 | Alnair | 27 36.4 | S46 51.5 |
| T 09 | 256 41.7 | 334 10.7 .. | 13.3 | 348 24.4 .. | 48.2 | 279 27.9 .. | 34.5 | 299 38.2 .. | 19.8 | Alnilam | 275 39.9 | S 1 11.4 |
| U 10 | 271 44.2 | 349 13.9 | 13.2 | 3 24.9 | 48.3 | 294 29.8 | 34.3 | 314 40.4 | 19.7 | Alphard | 217 49.8 | S 8 45.3 |
| R 11 | 286 46.6 | 4 17.1 | 13.2 | 18 25.4 | 48.3 | 309 31.8 | 34.1 | 329 42.6 | 19.6 | | | |
| D 12 | 301 49.1 | 19 20.3 | S16 13.1 | 33 25.9 | S23 48.4 | 324 33.7 | S10 33.9 | 344 44.7 | S17 19.5 | Alphecca | 126 06.0 | N26 38.3 |
| A 13 | 316 51.5 | 34 23.5 | 13.0 | 48 26.4 | 48.4 | 339 35.6 | 33.7 | 359 46.9 | 19.4 | Alpheratz | 357 37.4 | N29 12.7 |
| Y 14 | 331 54.0 | 49 26.7 | 13.0 | 63 26.9 | 48.5 | 354 37.6 | 33.5 | 14 49.1 | 19.4 | Altair | 62 02.6 | N 8 55.5 |
| 15 | 346 56.5 | 64 29.9 .. | 12.9 | 78 27.3 .. | 48.5 | 9 39.5 .. | 33.3 | 29 51.2 .. | 19.3 | Ankaa | 353 09.8 | S42 11.5 |
| 16 | 1 58.9 | 79 33.1 | 12.8 | 93 27.8 | 48.6 | 24 41.4 | 33.1 | 44 53.4 | 19.2 | Antares | 112 19.0 | S26 28.7 |
| 17 | 17 01.4 | 94 36.3 | 12.8 | 108 28.3 | 48.6 | 39 43.4 | 32.8 | 59 55.6 | 19.1 | | | |
| 18 | 32 03.9 | 109 39.5 | S16 12.7 | 123 28.8 | S23 48.7 | 54 45.3 | S10 32.6 | 74 57.7 | S17 19.0 | Arcturus | 145 50.2 | N19 03.9 |
| 19 | 47 06.3 | 124 42.7 | 12.6 | 138 29.3 | 48.7 | 69 47.3 | 32.4 | 89 59.9 | 18.9 | Atria | 107 15.8 | S69 03.7 |
| 20 | 62 08.8 | 139 45.8 | 12.6 | 153 29.8 | 48.8 | 84 49.2 | 32.2 | 105 02.1 | 18.9 | Avior | 234 15.0 | S59 34.8 |
| 21 | 77 11.3 | 154 49.0 .. | 12.5 | 168 30.3 .. | 48.8 | 99 51.1 .. | 32.0 | 120 04.2 .. | 18.8 | Bellatrix | 278 25.2 | N 6 22.1 |
| 22 | 92 13.7 | 169 52.2 | 12.4 | 183 30.7 | 48.9 | 114 53.1 | 31.8 | 135 06.4 | 18.7 | Betelgeuse | 270 54.4 | N 7 24.6 |
| 23 | 107 16.2 | 184 55.3 | 12.4 | 198 31.2 | 48.9 | 129 55.0 | 31.6 | 150 08.6 | 18.6 | | | |
| 23 00 | 122 18.7 | 199 58.5 | S16 12.3 | 213 31.7 | S23 49.0 | 144 57.0 | S10 31.4 | 165 10.7 | S17 18.5 | Canopus | 263 53.0 | S52 42.6 |
| 01 | 137 21.1 | 215 01.6 | 12.3 | 228 32.2 | 49.0 | 159 58.9 | 31.2 | 180 12.9 | 18.4 | Capella | 280 25.1 | N46 01.3 |
| 02 | 152 23.6 | 230 04.8 | 12.2 | 243 32.7 | 49.0 | 175 00.8 | 31.0 | 195 15.1 | 18.3 | Deneb | 49 27.9 | N45 21.5 |
| 03 | 167 26.0 | 245 07.9 .. | 12.1 | 258 33.2 .. | 49.1 | 190 02.8 .. | 30.8 | 210 17.2 .. | 18.3 | Denebola | 182 27.2 | N14 26.9 |
| 04 | 182 28.5 | 260 11.1 | 12.1 | 273 33.6 | 49.1 | 205 04.7 | 30.6 | 225 19.4 | 18.2 | Diphda | 348 49.9 | S17 52.2 |
| 05 | 197 31.0 | 275 14.2 | 12.0 | 288 34.1 | 49.2 | 220 06.6 | 30.4 | 240 21.6 | 18.1 | | | |
| 06 | 212 33.4 | 290 17.3 | S16 12.0 | 303 34.6 | S23 49.2 | 235 08.6 | S10 30.2 | 255 23.7 | S17 18.0 | Dubhe | 193 43.5 | N61 37.8 |
| 07 | 227 35.9 | 305 20.5 | 11.9 | 318 35.1 | 49.3 | 250 10.5 | 30.0 | 270 25.9 | 17.9 | Elnath | 278 04.6 | N28 37.5 |
| 08 | 242 38.4 | 320 23.6 | 11.9 | 333 35.6 | 49.3 | 265 12.5 | 29.8 | 285 28.1 | 17.8 | Eltanin | 90 43.8 | N51 29.0 |
| S 09 | 257 40.8 | 335 26.7 .. | 11.8 | 348 36.1 .. | 49.3 | 280 14.4 .. | 29.6 | 300 30.2 .. | 17.8 | Enif | 33 41.5 | N 9 58.5 |
| U 10 | 272 43.3 | 350 29.8 | 11.8 | 3 36.6 | 49.4 | 295 16.3 | 29.3 | 315 32.4 | 17.7 | Fomalhaut | 15 17.5 | S29 30.6 |
| N 11 | 287 45.8 | 5 32.9 | 11.7 | 18 37.0 | 49.4 | 310 18.3 | 29.1 | 330 34.6 | 17.6 | | | |
| D 12 | 302 48.2 | 20 36.0 | S16 11.7 | 33 37.5 | S23 49.5 | 325 20.2 | S10 28.9 | 345 36.7 | S17 17.5 | Gacrux | 171 54.1 | S57 13.9 |
| A 13 | 317 50.7 | 35 39.1 | 11.6 | 48 38.0 | 49.5 | 340 22.1 | 28.7 | 0 38.9 | 17.4 | Gienah | 175 45.9 | S17 39.8 |
| Y 14 | 332 53.2 | 50 42.2 | 11.6 | 63 38.5 | 49.5 | 355 24.1 | 28.5 | 15 41.1 | 17.3 | Hadar | 148 39.4 | S60 28.4 |
| 15 | 347 55.6 | 65 45.3 .. | 11.5 | 78 39.0 .. | 49.6 | 10 26.0 .. | 28.3 | 30 43.2 .. | 17.3 | Hamal | 327 53.9 | N23 34.0 |
| 16 | 2 58.1 | 80 48.4 | 11.5 | 93 39.5 | 49.6 | 25 27.9 | 28.1 | 45 45.4 | 17.2 | Kaus Aust. | 83 36.1 | S34 22.4 |
| 17 | 18 00.5 | 95 51.5 | 11.4 | 108 39.9 | 49.7 | 40 29.9 | 27.9 | 60 47.6 | 17.1 | | | |
| 18 | 33 03.0 | 110 54.5 | S16 11.4 | 123 40.4 | S23 49.7 | 55 31.8 | S10 27.7 | 75 49.7 | S17 17.0 | Kochab | 137 20.1 | N74 03.6 |
| 19 | 48 05.5 | 125 57.6 | 11.3 | 138 40.9 | 49.7 | 70 33.8 | 27.5 | 90 51.9 | 16.9 | Markab | 13 32.5 | N15 19.3 |
| 20 | 63 07.9 | 141 00.7 | 11.3 | 153 41.4 | 49.8 | 85 35.7 | 27.3 | 105 54.1 | 16.8 | Menkar | 314 08.6 | N 4 10.4 |
| 21 | 78 10.4 | 156 03.7 .. | 11.2 | 168 41.9 .. | 49.8 | 100 37.6 .. | 27.1 | 120 56.2 .. | 16.7 | Menkent | 148 00.5 | S36 28.5 |
| 22 | 93 12.9 | 171 06.8 | 11.2 | 183 42.4 | 49.8 | 115 39.6 | 26.9 | 135 58.4 | 16.7 | Miaplacidus | 221 37.8 | S69 48.3 |
| 23 | 108 15.3 | 186 09.9 | 11.1 | 198 42.8 | 49.9 | 130 41.5 | 26.7 | 151 00.6 | 16.6 | | | |
| 24 00 | 123 17.8 | 201 12.9 | S16 11.1 | 213 43.3 | S23 49.9 | 145 43.4 | S10 26.5 | 166 02.7 | S17 16.5 | Mirfak | 308 31.5 | N49 56.5 |
| 01 | 138 20.3 | 216 15.9 | 11.1 | 228 43.8 | 49.9 | 160 45.4 | 26.2 | 181 04.9 | 16.4 | Nunki | 75 51.1 | S26 16.2 |
| 02 | 153 22.7 | 231 19.0 | 11.0 | 243 44.3 | 50.0 | 175 47.3 | 26.0 | 196 07.1 | 16.3 | Peacock | 53 10.2 | S56 39.9 |
| 03 | 168 25.2 | 246 22.0 .. | 11.0 | 258 44.8 .. | 50.0 | 190 49.2 .. | 25.8 | 211 09.2 .. | 16.2 | Pollux | 243 19.9 | N27 58.3 |
| 04 | 183 27.6 | 261 25.0 | 10.9 | 273 45.2 | 50.0 | 205 51.2 | 25.6 | 226 11.4 | 16.2 | Procyon | 244 53.0 | N 5 10.0 |
| 05 | 198 30.1 | 276 28.1 | 10.9 | 288 45.7 | 50.1 | 220 53.1 | 25.4 | 241 13.6 | 16.1 | | | |
| 06 | 213 32.6 | 291 31.1 | S16 10.9 | 303 46.2 | S23 50.1 | 235 55.0 | S10 25.2 | 256 15.7 | S17 16.0 | Rasalhague | 96 01.1 | N12 32.5 |
| 07 | 228 35.0 | 306 34.1 | 10.8 | 318 46.7 | 50.1 | 250 57.0 | 25.0 | 271 17.9 | 15.9 | Regulus | 207 36.7 | N11 51.5 |
| 08 | 243 37.5 | 321 37.1 | 10.8 | 333 47.2 | 50.2 | 265 58.9 | 24.8 | 286 20.1 | 15.8 | Rigel | 281 05.9 | S 8 10.7 |
| M 09 | 258 40.0 | 336 40.1 .. | 10.8 | 348 47.7 .. | 50.2 | 281 00.9 .. | 24.6 | 301 22.2 .. | 15.7 | Rigil Kent. | 139 43.7 | S60 55.2 |
| O 10 | 273 42.4 | 351 43.1 | 10.7 | 3 48.1 | 50.2 | 296 02.8 | 24.4 | 316 24.4 | 15.7 | Sabik | 102 05.8 | S15 45.1 |
| N 11 | 288 44.9 | 6 46.1 | 10.7 | 18 48.6 | 50.3 | 311 04.7 | 24.2 | 331 26.6 | 15.6 | | | |
| D 12 | 303 47.4 | 21 49.1 | S16 10.7 | 33 49.1 | S23 50.3 | 326 06.7 | S10 24.0 | 346 28.7 | S17 15.5 | Schedar | 349 34.0 | N56 39.6 |
| A 13 | 318 49.8 | 36 52.1 | 10.6 | 48 49.6 | 50.3 | 341 08.6 | 23.8 | 1 30.9 | 15.4 | Shaula | 96 14.0 | S37 07.1 |
| Y 14 | 333 52.3 | 51 55.1 | 10.6 | 63 50.1 | 50.4 | 356 10.5 | 23.6 | 16 33.1 | 15.3 | Sirius | 258 28.0 | S16 44.9 |
| 15 | 348 54.8 | 66 58.1 .. | 10.6 | 78 50.5 .. | 50.4 | 11 12.5 .. | 23.3 | 31 35.2 .. | 15.2 | Spica | 158 24.8 | S11 16.5 |
| 16 | 3 57.2 | 82 01.1 | 10.5 | 93 51.0 | 50.4 | 26 14.4 | 23.1 | 46 37.4 | 15.1 | Suhail | 222 47.6 | S43 31.2 |
| 17 | 18 59.7 | 97 04.0 | 10.5 | 108 51.5 | 50.4 | 41 16.3 | 22.9 | 61 39.6 | 15.1 | | | |
| 18 | 34 02.1 | 112 07.0 | S16 10.5 | 123 52.0 | S23 50.5 | 56 18.3 | S10 22.7 | 76 41.7 | S17 15.0 | Vega | 80 35.3 | N38 48.1 |
| 19 | 49 04.6 | 127 10.0 | 10.4 | 138 52.5 | 50.5 | 71 20.2 | 22.5 | 91 43.9 | 14.9 | Zuben'ubi | 136 58.8 | S16 07.9 |
| 20 | 64 07.1 | 142 12.9 | 10.4 | 153 53.0 | 50.5 | 86 22.1 | 22.3 | 106 46.1 | 14.8 | | SHA | Mer. Pass. |
| 21 | 79 09.5 | 157 15.9 .. | 10.4 | 168 53.4 .. | 50.6 | 101 24.1 .. | 22.1 | 121 48.2 .. | 14.7 | | ° ′ | h m |
| 22 | 94 12.0 | 172 18.8 | 10.4 | 183 53.9 | 50.6 | 116 26.0 | 21.9 | 136 50.4 | 14.6 | Venus | 77 39.8 | 10 38 |
| 23 | 109 14.5 | 187 21.8 | 10.3 | 198 54.4 | 50.6 | 131 27.9 | 21.7 | 151 52.6 | 14.6 | Mars | 91 13.1 | 9 46 |
| | h m | | | | | | | | | Jupiter | 22 38.3 | 14 18 |
| Mer. Pass. 15 48.2 | | v 3.1 | d 0.1 | v 0.5 | d 0.0 | v 1.9 | d 0.2 | v 2.2 | d 0.1 | Saturn | 42 52.1 | 12 57 |

| UT | SUN GHA | SUN Dec | MOON GHA | v | MOON Dec | d | HP |
|---|---|---|---|---|---|---|---|
| d h | ° ′ | ° ′ | ° ′ | ′ | ° ′ | ′ | ′ |
| **22** 00 | 177 08.8 | S19 43.8 | 310 24.3 | 13.9 | N 9 08.0 | 13.5 | 56.4 |
| 01 | 192 08.6 | 43.3 | 324 57.2 | 13.9 | 8 54.5 | 13.6 | 56.4 |
| 02 | 207 08.5 | 42.7 | 339 30.1 | 14.0 | 8 40.9 | 13.6 | 56.4 |
| 03 | 222 08.3 | .. 42.1 | 354 03.1 | 14.0 | 8 27.3 | 13.7 | 56.5 |
| 04 | 237 08.1 | 41.6 | 8 36.1 | 13.9 | 8 13.6 | 13.7 | 56.5 |
| 05 | 252 08.0 | 41.0 | 23 09.0 | 14.0 | 7 59.9 | 13.7 | 56.5 |
| **S** 06 | 267 07.8 | S19 40.4 | 37 42.0 | 14.0 | N 7 46.2 | 13.8 | 56.5 |
| **A** 07 | 282 07.6 | 39.8 | 52 15.0 | 14.0 | 7 32.4 | 13.9 | 56.5 |
| **T** 08 | 297 07.5 | 39.3 | 66 48.0 | 14.0 | 7 18.5 | 13.9 | 56.6 |
| **U** 09 | 312 07.3 | .. 38.7 | 81 21.0 | 14.1 | 7 04.6 | 13.9 | 56.6 |
| **R** 10 | 327 07.1 | 38.1 | 95 54.1 | 14.0 | 6 50.7 | 14.0 | 56.6 |
| **D** 11 | 342 07.0 | 37.5 | 110 27.1 | 14.1 | 6 36.7 | 14.0 | 56.6 |
| **A** 12 | 357 06.8 | S19 37.0 | 125 00.2 | 14.0 | N 6 22.7 | 14.0 | 56.7 |
| **Y** 13 | 12 06.6 | 36.4 | 139 33.2 | 14.1 | 6 08.7 | 14.1 | 56.7 |
| 14 | 27 06.5 | 35.8 | 154 06.3 | 14.1 | 5 54.6 | 14.1 | 56.7 |
| 15 | 42 06.3 | .. 35.2 | 168 39.3 | 14.1 | 5 40.5 | 14.2 | 56.7 |
| 16 | 57 06.2 | 34.7 | 183 12.4 | 14.0 | 5 26.3 | 14.2 | 56.7 |
| 17 | 72 06.0 | 34.1 | 197 45.4 | 14.1 | 5 12.1 | 14.2 | 56.8 |
| 18 | 87 05.8 | S19 33.5 | 212 18.5 | 14.1 | N 4 57.9 | 14.3 | 56.8 |
| 19 | 102 05.7 | 32.9 | 226 51.6 | 14.0 | 4 43.6 | 14.3 | 56.8 |
| 20 | 117 05.5 | 32.3 | 241 24.6 | 14.1 | 4 29.3 | 14.3 | 56.8 |
| 21 | 132 05.3 | .. 31.8 | 255 57.7 | 14.0 | 4 15.0 | 14.3 | 56.9 |
| 22 | 147 05.2 | 31.2 | 270 30.7 | 14.1 | 4 00.7 | 14.4 | 56.9 |
| 23 | 162 05.0 | 30.6 | 285 03.8 | 14.0 | 3 46.3 | 14.4 | 56.9 |
| **23** 00 | 177 04.9 | S19 30.0 | 299 36.8 | 14.1 | N 3 31.9 | 14.4 | 56.9 |
| 01 | 192 04.7 | 29.4 | 314 09.9 | 14.0 | 3 17.5 | 14.5 | 57.0 |
| 02 | 207 04.5 | 28.8 | 328 42.9 | 14.0 | 3 03.0 | 14.5 | 57.0 |
| 03 | 222 04.4 | .. 28.3 | 343 15.9 | 14.0 | 2 48.5 | 14.5 | 57.0 |
| 04 | 237 04.2 | 27.7 | 357 48.9 | 14.0 | 2 34.0 | 14.5 | 57.0 |
| 05 | 252 04.0 | 27.1 | 12 21.9 | 14.0 | 2 19.5 | 14.5 | 57.1 |
| 06 | 267 03.9 | S19 26.5 | 26 54.9 | 14.0 | N 2 05.0 | 14.6 | 57.1 |
| 07 | 282 03.7 | 25.9 | 41 27.9 | 13.9 | 1 50.4 | 14.6 | 57.1 |
| **S** 08 | 297 03.6 | 25.3 | 56 00.8 | 13.9 | 1 35.8 | 14.6 | 57.1 |
| **U** 09 | 312 03.4 | .. 24.7 | 70 33.7 | 14.0 | 1 21.2 | 14.6 | 57.2 |
| **N** 10 | 327 03.3 | 24.1 | 85 06.7 | 13.9 | 1 06.6 | 14.7 | 57.2 |
| 11 | 342 03.1 | 23.6 | 99 39.6 | 13.9 | 0 51.9 | 14.6 | 57.2 |
| **D** 12 | 357 02.9 | S19 23.0 | 114 12.5 | 13.8 | N 0 37.3 | 14.7 | 57.2 |
| **A** 13 | 12 02.8 | 22.4 | 128 45.3 | 13.9 | 0 22.6 | 14.7 | 57.2 |
| **Y** 14 | 27 02.6 | 21.8 | 143 18.2 | 13.0 | N 0 07.9 | 14.7 | 57.3 |
| 15 | 42 02.5 | .. 21.2 | 157 51.0 | 13.8 | S 0 06.8 | 14.7 | 57.3 |
| 16 | 57 02.3 | 20.6 | 172 23.8 | 13.7 | 0 21.5 | 14.7 | 57.3 |
| 17 | 72 02.2 | 20.0 | 186 56.5 | 13.8 | 0 36.2 | 14.8 | 57.3 |
| 18 | 87 02.0 | S19 19.4 | 201 29.3 | 13.7 | S 0 51.0 | 14.7 | 57.4 |
| 19 | 102 01.8 | 18.8 | 216 02.0 | 13.7 | 1 05.7 | 14.8 | 57.4 |
| 20 | 117 01.7 | 18.2 | 230 34.7 | 13.6 | 1 20.5 | 14.7 | 57.4 |
| 21 | 132 01.5 | .. 17.6 | 245 07.3 | 13.6 | 1 35.2 | 14.8 | 57.4 |
| 22 | 147 01.4 | 17.0 | 259 39.9 | 13.6 | 1 50.0 | 14.7 | 57.5 |
| 23 | 162 01.2 | 16.4 | 274 12.5 | 13.5 | 2 04.7 | 14.8 | 57.5 |
| **24** 00 | 177 01.1 | S19 15.8 | 288 45.1 | 13.5 | S 2 19.5 | 14.8 | 57.5 |
| 01 | 192 00.9 | 15.2 | 303 17.6 | 13.5 | 2 34.3 | 14.7 | 57.5 |
| 02 | 207 00.8 | 14.6 | 317 50.1 | 13.4 | 2 49.0 | 14.8 | 57.6 |
| 03 | 222 00.6 | .. 14.0 | 332 22.5 | 13.4 | 3 03.8 | 14.8 | 57.6 |
| 04 | 237 00.5 | 13.4 | 346 54.9 | 13.4 | 3 18.6 | 14.7 | 57.6 |
| 05 | 252 00.3 | 12.8 | 1 27.3 | 13.3 | 3 33.3 | 14.8 | 57.7 |
| 06 | 267 00.2 | S19 12.2 | 15 59.6 | 13.3 | S 3 48.1 | 14.7 | 57.7 |
| 07 | 282 00.0 | 11.6 | 30 31.9 | 13.2 | 4 02.8 | 14.8 | 57.7 |
| **M** 08 | 296 59.9 | 11.0 | 45 04.1 | 13.2 | 4 17.6 | 14.7 | 57.7 |
| **O** 09 | 311 59.7 | .. 10.4 | 59 36.3 | 13.2 | 4 32.3 | 14.8 | 57.8 |
| **N** 10 | 326 59.6 | 09.8 | 74 08.5 | 13.0 | 4 47.1 | 14.7 | 57.8 |
| 11 | 341 59.4 | 09.2 | 88 40.5 | 13.1 | 5 01.8 | 14.7 | 57.8 |
| **D** 12 | 356 59.3 | S19 08.6 | 103 12.6 | 13.0 | S 5 16.5 | 14.7 | 57.9 |
| **A** 13 | 11 59.1 | 08.0 | 117 44.6 | 12.9 | 5 31.2 | 14.7 | 57.9 |
| **Y** 14 | 26 59.0 | 07.4 | 132 16.5 | 12.9 | 5 45.9 | 14.6 | 57.9 |
| 15 | 41 58.8 | .. 06.8 | 146 48.4 | 12.9 | 6 00.6 | 14.6 | 57.9 |
| 16 | 56 58.7 | 06.2 | 161 20.3 | 12.7 | 6 15.2 | 14.7 | 57.9 |
| 17 | 71 58.5 | 05.6 | 175 52.0 | 12.8 | 6 29.9 | 14.6 | 58.0 |
| 18 | 86 58.4 | S19 05.0 | 190 23.8 | 12.6 | S 6 44.5 | 14.6 | 58.0 |
| 19 | 101 58.2 | 04.4 | 204 55.4 | 12.6 | 6 59.1 | 14.6 | 58.0 |
| 20 | 116 58.1 | 03.7 | 219 27.0 | 12.6 | 7 13.7 | 14.5 | 58.0 |
| 21 | 131 57.9 | .. 03.1 | 233 58.6 | 12.5 | 7 28.2 | 14.6 | 58.1 |
| 22 | 146 57.8 | 02.5 | 248 30.1 | 12.4 | 7 42.8 | 14.5 | 58.1 |
| 23 | 161 57.6 | 01.9 | 263 01.5 | 12.3 | S 7 57.3 | 14.5 | 58.1 |
| | SD 16.3 | d 0.6 | SD 15.4 | | 15.6 | | 15.8 |

### Twilight / Sunrise / Moonrise

| Lat. | Naut. | Civil | Sunrise | Moonrise 22 | 23 | 24 | 25 |
|---|---|---|---|---|---|---|---|
| ° | h m | h m | h m | h m | h m | h m | h m |
| N 72 | 07 39 | 09 18 | ■■ | 21 05 | 23 11 | 25 25 | 01 25 |
| N 70 | 07 27 | 08 52 | 10 41 | 21 11 | 23 08 | 25 11 | 01 11 |
| 68 | 07 18 | 08 33 | 09 56 | 21 16 | 23 06 | 24 59 | 00 59 |
| 66 | 07 10 | 08 17 | 09 27 | 21 20 | 23 03 | 24 50 | 00 50 |
| 64 | 07 03 | 08 04 | 09 05 | 21 24 | 23 02 | 24 43 | 00 43 |
| 62 | 06 56 | 07 53 | 08 48 | 21 27 | 23 00 | 24 36 | 00 36 |
| 60 | 06 51 | 07 43 | 08 33 | 21 29 | 22 59 | 24 31 | 00 31 |
| N 58 | 06 46 | 07 35 | 08 21 | 21 32 | 22 57 | 24 26 | 00 26 |
| 56 | 06 41 | 07 28 | 08 10 | 21 34 | 22 56 | 24 21 | 00 21 |
| 54 | 06 37 | 07 21 | 08 01 | 21 35 | 22 55 | 24 17 | 00 17 |
| 52 | 06 33 | 07 15 | 07 53 | 21 37 | 22 54 | 24 14 | 00 14 |
| 50 | 06 30 | 07 09 | 07 45 | 21 38 | 22 54 | 24 11 | 00 11 |
| 45 | 06 21 | 06 57 | 07 29 | 21 42 | 22 52 | 24 04 | 00 04 |
| N 40 | 06 14 | 06 47 | 07 16 | 21 44 | 22 50 | 23 58 | 25 09 |
| 35 | 06 07 | 06 37 | 07 05 | 21 47 | 22 49 | 23 53 | 25 00 |
| 30 | 06 00 | 06 29 | 06 55 | 21 49 | 22 48 | 23 49 | 24 53 |
| 20 | 05 47 | 06 14 | 06 37 | 21 52 | 22 46 | 23 42 | 24 40 |
| N 10 | 05 35 | 06 00 | 06 22 | 21 55 | 22 45 | 23 35 | 24 29 |
| 0 | 05 21 | 05 46 | 06 08 | 21 58 | 22 43 | 23 29 | 24 18 |
| S 10 | 05 05 | 05 31 | 05 54 | 22 01 | 22 42 | 23 24 | 24 08 |
| 20 | 04 47 | 05 15 | 05 38 | 22 04 | 22 40 | 23 17 | 23 57 |
| 30 | 04 23 | 04 54 | 05 20 | 22 08 | 22 39 | 23 10 | 23 45 |
| 35 | 04 07 | 04 42 | 05 10 | 22 10 | 22 38 | 23 06 | 23 38 |
| 40 | 03 49 | 04 27 | 04 58 | 22 12 | 22 36 | 23 02 | 23 30 |
| 45 | 03 25 | 04 09 | 04 44 | 22 15 | 22 35 | 22 57 | 23 20 |
| S 50 | 02 52 | 03 46 | 04 26 | 22 18 | 22 34 | 22 50 | 23 09 |
| 52 | 02 35 | 03 35 | 04 18 | 22 20 | 22 33 | 22 47 | 23 04 |
| 54 | 02 14 | 03 22 | 04 08 | 22 21 | 22 32 | 22 44 | 22 58 |
| 56 | 01 45 | 03 07 | 03 58 | 22 23 | 22 32 | 22 41 | 22 52 |
| 58 | 00 54 | 02 48 | 03 46 | 22 25 | 22 31 | 22 37 | 22 45 |
| S 60 | //// | 02 26 | 03 32 | 22 27 | 22 30 | 22 33 | 22 37 |

### Sunset / Twilight / Moonset

| Lat. | Sunset | Civil | Naut. | Moonset 22 | 23 | 24 | 25 |
|---|---|---|---|---|---|---|---|
| ° | h m | h m | h m | h m | h m | h m | h m |
| N 72 | ■■ | 15 07 | 16 46 | 11 00 | 10 31 | 10 02 | 09 27 |
| N 70 | 13 44 | 15 32 | 16 57 | 10 51 | 10 30 | 10 08 | 09 44 |
| 68 | 14 28 | 15 52 | 17 07 | 10 44 | 10 29 | 10 14 | 09 57 |
| 66 | 14 57 | 16 08 | 17 15 | 10 37 | 10 28 | 10 19 | 10 08 |
| 64 | 15 19 | 16 21 | 17 22 | 10 32 | 10 27 | 10 23 | 10 18 |
| 62 | 15 36 | 16 31 | 17 28 | 10 28 | 10 27 | 10 26 | 10 26 |
| 60 | 15 51 | 16 41 | 17 33 | 10 23 | 10 26 | 10 29 | 10 32 |
| N 58 | 16 03 | 16 49 | 17 38 | 10 20 | 10 26 | 10 32 | 10 39 |
| 56 | 16 14 | 16 57 | 17 43 | 10 17 | 10 25 | 10 34 | 10 44 |
| 54 | 16 23 | 17 03 | 17 47 | 10 14 | 10 25 | 10 36 | 10 49 |
| 52 | 16 31 | 17 09 | 17 51 | 10 11 | 10 25 | 10 38 | 10 53 |
| 50 | 16 39 | 17 15 | 17 55 | 10 09 | 10 24 | 10 40 | 10 58 |
| 45 | 16 55 | 17 27 | 18 03 | 10 03 | 10 24 | 10 44 | 11 06 |
| N 40 | 17 08 | 17 37 | 18 10 | 09 59 | 10 23 | 10 47 | 11 14 |
| 35 | 17 19 | 17 47 | 18 17 | 09 55 | 10 22 | 10 50 | 11 20 |
| 30 | 17 29 | 17 55 | 18 24 | 09 52 | 10 22 | 10 53 | 11 26 |
| 20 | 17 46 | 18 10 | 18 36 | 09 46 | 10 21 | 10 57 | 11 36 |
| N 10 | 18 01 | 18 23 | 18 49 | 09 40 | 10 20 | 11 01 | 11 44 |
| 0 | 18 15 | 18 37 | 19 03 | 09 35 | 10 20 | 11 05 | 11 52 |
| S 10 | 18 30 | 18 52 | 19 18 | 09 30 | 10 19 | 11 09 | 12 00 |
| 20 | 18 45 | 19 09 | 19 37 | 09 25 | 10 18 | 11 13 | 12 09 |
| 30 | 19 03 | 19 29 | 20 01 | 09 18 | 10 17 | 11 19 | 12 19 |
| 35 | 19 13 | 19 41 | 20 16 | 09 15 | 10 17 | 11 20 | 12 25 |
| 40 | 19 25 | 19 56 | 20 34 | 09 10 | 10 16 | 11 23 | 12 32 |
| 45 | 19 39 | 20 14 | 20 58 | 09 06 | 10 15 | 11 26 | 12 39 |
| S 50 | 19 57 | 20 36 | 21 30 | 09 00 | 10 14 | 11 30 | 12 49 |
| 52 | 20 05 | 20 48 | 21 47 | 08 57 | 10 13 | 11 32 | 12 53 |
| 54 | 20 14 | 21 00 | 22 08 | 08 54 | 10 13 | 11 34 | 12 58 |
| 56 | 20 24 | 21 15 | 22 35 | 08 51 | 10 13 | 11 36 | 13 03 |
| 58 | 20 36 | 21 33 | 23 21 | 08 47 | 10 12 | 11 39 | 13 09 |
| S 60 | 20 50 | 21 55 | //// | 08 43 | 10 12 | 11 42 | 13 16 |

### SUN / MOON

| Day | Eqn. of Time 00h | Eqn. of Time 12h | Mer. Pass. | Mer. Pass. Upper | Mer. Pass. Lower | Age | Phase |
|---|---|---|---|---|---|---|---|
| d | m s | m s | h m | h m | h m | d | % |
| 22 | 11 24 | 11 32 | 12 12 | 03 25 | 15 47 | 20 | 81 |
| 23 | 11 40 | 11 48 | 12 12 | 04 09 | 16 31 | 21 | 72 |
| 24 | 11 55 | 12 03 | 12 12 | 04 54 | 17 17 | 22 | 62 |

| UT | ARIES | VENUS −4.7 | | MARS +1.4 | | JUPITER −2.1 | | SATURN +0.6 | | STARS | | |
|---|---|---|---|---|---|---|---|---|---|---|---|---|
| | GHA | GHA | Dec | GHA | Dec | GHA | Dec | GHA | Dec | Name | SHA | Dec |
| d h | ° ′ | ° ′ | ° ′ | ° ′ | ° ′ | ° ′ | ° ′ | ° ′ | ° ′ | | ° ′ | ° ′ |
| 25 00 | 124 16.9 | 202 24.7 | S16 10.3 | 213 54.9 | S23 50.6 | 146 29.9 | S10 21.5 | 166 54.7 | S17 14.5 | Acamar | 315 13.6 | S40 13.3 |
| 01 | 139 19.4 | 217 27.6 | 10.3 | 228 55.4 | 50.7 | 161 31.8 | 21.3 | 181 56.9 | 14.4 | Achernar | 335 22.1 | S57 07.9 |
| 02 | 154 21.9 | 232 30.6 | 10.3 | 243 55.8 | 50.7 | 176 33.7 | 21.1 | 196 59.1 | 14.3 | Acrux | 173 02.4 | S63 13.0 |
| 03 | 169 24.3 | 247 33.5 .. | 10.2 | 258 56.3 .. | 50.7 | 191 35.7 .. | 20.9 | 212 01.2 .. | 14.2 | Adhara | 255 07.4 | S29 00.2 |
| 04 | 184 26.8 | 262 36.4 | 10.2 | 273 56.8 | 50.7 | 206 37.6 | 20.6 | 227 03.4 | 14.1 | Aldebaran | 290 42.2 | N16 33.2 |
| 05 | 199 29.2 | 277 39.3 | 10.2 | 288 57.3 | 50.8 | 221 39.5 | 20.4 | 242 05.6 | 14.0 | | | |
| 06 | 214 31.7 | 292 42.2 | S16 10.2 | 303 57.8 | S23 50.8 | 236 41.5 | S10 20.2 | 257 07.7 | S17 14.0 | Alioth | 166 14.9 | N55 50.2 |
| 07 | 229 34.2 | 307 45.1 | 10.2 | 318 58.2 | 50.8 | 251 43.4 | 20.0 | 272 09.9 | 13.9 | Alkaid | 152 53.9 | N49 12.0 |
| T 08 | 244 36.6 | 322 48.0 | 10.1 | 333 58.7 | 50.8 | 266 45.3 | 19.8 | 287 12.1 | 13.8 | Alnair | 27 36.4 | S46 51.5 |
| U 09 | 259 39.1 | 337 50.9 .. | 10.1 | 348 59.2 .. | 50.8 | 281 47.3 .. | 19.6 | 302 14.2 .. | 13.7 | Alnilam | 275 39.9 | S 1 11.4 |
| E 10 | 274 41.6 | 352 53.8 | 10.1 | 3 59.7 | 50.9 | 296 49.2 | 19.4 | 317 16.4 | 13.6 | Alphard | 217 49.8 | S 8 45.3 |
| S 11 | 289 44.0 | 7 56.7 | 10.1 | 19 00.2 | 50.9 | 311 51.1 | 19.2 | 332 18.6 | 13.5 | | | |
| D 12 | 304 46.5 | 22 59.6 | S16 10.1 | 34 00.6 | S23 50.9 | 326 53.1 | S10 19.0 | 347 20.7 | S17 13.4 | Alphecca | 126 05.9 | N26 38.3 |
| A 13 | 319 49.0 | 38 02.5 | 10.1 | 49 01.1 | 50.9 | 341 55.0 | 18.8 | 2 22.9 | 13.4 | Alpheratz | 357 37.5 | N29 12.7 |
| Y 14 | 334 51.4 | 53 05.4 | 10.0 | 64 01.6 | 50.9 | 356 56.9 | 18.6 | 17 25.1 | 13.3 | Altair | 62 02.6 | N 8 55.5 |
| 15 | 349 53.9 | 68 08.2 .. | 10.0 | 79 02.1 .. | 51.0 | 11 58.9 .. | 18.4 | 32 27.2 .. | 13.2 | Ankaa | 353 09.8 | S42 11.5 |
| 16 | 4 56.4 | 83 11.1 | 10.0 | 94 02.6 | 51.0 | 27 00.8 | 18.1 | 47 29.4 | 13.1 | Antares | 112 19.0 | S26 28.7 |
| 17 | 19 58.8 | 98 13.9 | 10.0 | 109 03.0 | 51.0 | 42 02.7 | 17.9 | 62 31.6 | 13.0 | | | |
| 18 | 35 01.3 | 113 16.8 | S16 10.0 | 124 03.5 | S23 51.0 | 57 04.7 | S10 17.7 | 77 33.7 | S17 12.9 | Arcturus | 145 50.1 | N19 03.9 |
| 19 | 50 03.7 | 128 19.7 | 10.0 | 139 04.0 | 51.0 | 72 06.6 | 17.5 | 92 35.9 | 12.9 | Atria | 107 15.8 | S69 03.7 |
| 20 | 65 06.2 | 143 22.5 | 10.0 | 154 04.5 | 51.0 | 87 08.5 | 17.3 | 107 38.1 | 12.8 | Avior | 234 15.0 | S59 34.8 |
| 21 | 80 08.7 | 158 25.3 .. | 10.0 | 169 05.0 .. | 51.1 | 102 10.5 .. | 17.1 | 122 40.2 .. | 12.7 | Bellatrix | 278 25.2 | N 6 22.1 |
| 22 | 95 11.1 | 173 28.2 | 10.0 | 184 05.4 | 51.1 | 117 12.4 | 16.9 | 137 42.4 | 12.6 | Betelgeuse | 270 54.4 | N 7 24.6 |
| 23 | 110 13.6 | 188 31.0 | 10.0 | 199 05.9 | 51.1 | 132 14.3 | 16.7 | 152 44.6 | 12.5 | | | |
| 26 00 | 125 16.1 | 203 33.8 | S16 09.9 | 214 06.4 | S23 51.1 | 147 16.3 | S10 16.5 | 167 46.7 | S17 12.4 | Canopus | 263 53.0 | S52 42.6 |
| 01 | 140 18.5 | 218 36.7 | 09.9 | 229 06.9 | 51.1 | 162 18.2 | 16.3 | 182 48.9 | 12.3 | Capella | 280 25.1 | N46 01.3 |
| 02 | 155 21.0 | 233 39.5 | 09.9 | 244 07.3 | 51.1 | 177 20.1 | 16.1 | 197 51.1 | 12.3 | Deneb | 49 27.9 | N45 21.5 |
| 03 | 170 23.5 | 248 42.3 .. | 09.9 | 259 07.8 .. | 51.2 | 192 22.1 .. | 15.8 | 212 53.2 .. | 12.2 | Denebola | 182 27.2 | N14 26.9 |
| 04 | 185 25.9 | 263 45.1 | 09.9 | 274 08.3 | 51.2 | 207 24.0 | 15.6 | 227 55.4 | 12.1 | Diphda | 348 49.9 | S17 52.2 |
| 05 | 200 28.4 | 278 47.9 | 09.9 | 289 08.8 | 51.2 | 222 25.9 | 15.4 | 242 57.5 | 12.0 | | | |
| 06 | 215 30.9 | 293 50.7 | S16 09.9 | 304 09.3 | S23 51.2 | 237 27.9 | S10 15.2 | 257 59.7 | S17 11.9 | Dubhe | 193 43.5 | N61 37.8 |
| W 07 | 230 33.3 | 308 53.5 | 09.9 | 319 09.7 | 51.2 | 252 29.8 | 15.0 | 273 01.9 | 11.8 | Elnath | 278 04.6 | N28 37.5 |
| E 08 | 245 35.8 | 323 56.3 | 09.9 | 334 10.2 | 51.2 | 267 31.7 | 14.8 | 288 04.0 | 11.7 | Eltanin | 90 43.7 | N51 28.9 |
| D 09 | 260 38.2 | 338 59.1 .. | 09.9 | 349 10.7 .. | 51.2 | 282 33.6 .. | 14.6 | 303 06.2 .. | 11.7 | Enif | 33 41.5 | N 9 58.5 |
| N 10 | 275 40.7 | 354 01.9 | 09.9 | 4 11.2 | 51.2 | 297 35.6 | 14.4 | 318 08.4 | 11.6 | Fomalhaut | 15 17.5 | S29 30.6 |
| E 11 | 290 43.2 | 9 04.7 | 09.9 | 19 11.6 | 51.3 | 312 37.5 | 14.2 | 333 10.5 | 11.5 | | | |
| S 12 | 305 45.6 | 24 07.4 | S16 09.9 | 34 12.1 | S23 51.3 | 327 39.4 | S10 14.0 | 348 12.7 | S17 11.4 | Gacrux | 171 54.0 | S57 13.9 |
| D 13 | 320 48.1 | 39 10.2 | 09.9 | 49 12.6 | 51.3 | 342 41.4 | 13.7 | 3 14.9 | 11.3 | Gienah | 175 45.9 | S17 39.8 |
| A 14 | 335 50.6 | 54 13.0 | 09.9 | 64 13.1 | 51.3 | 357 43.3 | 13.5 | 18 17.0 | 11.2 | Hadar | 148 39.4 | S60 28.4 |
| Y 15 | 350 53.0 | 69 15.7 .. | 09.9 | 79 13.6 .. | 51.3 | 12 45.2 .. | 13.3 | 33 19.2 .. | 11.2 | Hamal | 327 53.9 | N23 34.0 |
| 16 | 5 55.5 | 84 18.5 | 09.9 | 94 14.0 | 51.3 | 27 47.2 | 13.1 | 48 21.4 | 11.1 | Kaus Aust. | 83 36.1 | S34 22.4 |
| 17 | 20 58.0 | 99 21.2 | 09.9 | 109 14.5 | 51.3 | 42 49.1 | 12.9 | 63 23.5 | 11.0 | | | |
| 18 | 36 00.4 | 114 24.0 | S16 09.9 | 124 15.0 | S23 51.3 | 57 51.0 | S10 12.7 | 78 25.7 | S17 10.9 | Kochab | 137 20.0 | N74 03.6 |
| 19 | 51 02.9 | 129 26.7 | 09.9 | 139 15.5 | 51.3 | 72 53.0 | 12.5 | 93 27.9 | 10.8 | Markab | 13 32.6 | N15 19.3 |
| 20 | 66 05.4 | 144 29.5 | 09.9 | 154 15.9 | 51.3 | 87 54.9 | 12.3 | 108 30.0 | 10.7 | Menkar | 314 08.6 | N 4 10.4 |
| 21 | 81 07.8 | 159 32.2 .. | 09.9 | 169 16.4 .. | 51.3 | 102 56.8 .. | 12.1 | 123 32.2 .. | 10.6 | Menkent | 148 00.4 | S36 28.5 |
| 22 | 96 10.3 | 174 34.9 | 09.9 | 184 16.9 | 51.3 | 117 58.7 | 11.9 | 138 34.4 | 10.6 | Miaplacidus | 221 37.8 | S69 48.3 |
| 23 | 111 12.7 | 189 37.6 | 10.0 | 199 17.4 | 51.4 | 133 00.7 | 11.6 | 153 36.5 | 10.5 | | | |
| 27 00 | 126 15.2 | 204 40.4 | S16 10.0 | 214 17.9 | S23 51.4 | 148 02.6 | S10 11.4 | 168 38.7 | S17 10.3 | Mirfak | 308 31.5 | N49 56.5 |
| 01 | 141 17.7 | 219 43.1 | 10.0 | 229 18.3 | 51.4 | 163 04.5 | 11.2 | 183 40.9 | 10.3 | Nunki | 75 51.1 | S26 16.2 |
| 02 | 156 20.1 | 234 45.8 | 10.0 | 244 18.8 | 51.4 | 178 06.5 | 11.0 | 198 43.0 | 10.2 | Peacock | 53 10.2 | S56 39.9 |
| 03 | 171 22.6 | 249 48.5 .. | 10.0 | 259 19.3 .. | 51.4 | 193 08.4 .. | 10.8 | 213 45.2 .. | 10.1 | Pollux | 243 19.9 | N27 58.3 |
| 04 | 186 25.1 | 264 51.2 | 10.0 | 274 19.8 | 51.4 | 208 10.3 | 10.6 | 228 47.4 | 10.0 | Procyon | 244 53.0 | N 5 10.0 |
| 05 | 201 27.5 | 279 53.9 | 10.0 | 289 20.2 | 51.4 | 223 12.3 | 10.4 | 243 49.5 | 10.0 | | | |
| 06 | 216 30.0 | 294 56.6 | S16 10.0 | 304 20.7 | S23 51.4 | 238 14.2 | S10 10.2 | 258 51.7 | S17 09.9 | Rasalhague | 96 01.1 | N12 32.5 |
| 07 | 231 32.5 | 309 59.3 | 10.0 | 319 21.2 | 51.4 | 253 16.1 | 10.0 | 273 53.8 | 09.8 | Regulus | 207 36.7 | N11 51.5 |
| T 08 | 246 34.9 | 325 01.9 | 10.0 | 334 21.7 | 51.4 | 268 18.0 | 09.8 | 288 56.0 | 09.7 | Rigel | 281 06.0 | S 8 10.7 |
| H 09 | 261 37.4 | 340 04.6 .. | 10.1 | 349 22.1 .. | 51.4 | 283 20.0 .. | 09.5 | 303 58.2 .. | 09.6 | Rigil Kent. | 139 43.6 | S60 55.2 |
| U 10 | 276 39.8 | 355 07.3 | 10.1 | 4 22.6 | 51.4 | 298 21.9 | 09.3 | 319 00.3 | 09.5 | Sabik | 102 05.8 | S15 45.1 |
| R 11 | 291 42.3 | 10 10.0 | 10.1 | 19 23.1 | 51.4 | 313 23.8 | 09.1 | 334 02.5 | 09.4 | | | |
| S 12 | 306 44.8 | 25 12.6 | S16 10.1 | 34 23.6 | S23 51.4 | 328 25.8 | S10 08.9 | 349 04.7 | S17 09.4 | Schedar | 349 34.0 | N56 39.6 |
| D 13 | 321 47.2 | 40 15.3 | 10.1 | 49 24.0 | 51.4 | 343 27.7 | 08.7 | 4 06.8 | 09.3 | Shaula | 96 14.0 | S37 07.1 |
| A 14 | 336 49.7 | 55 17.9 | 10.1 | 64 24.5 | 51.4 | 358 29.6 | 08.5 | 19 09.0 | 09.2 | Sirius | 258 28.0 | S16 44.9 |
| Y 15 | 351 52.2 | 70 20.6 .. | 10.2 | 79 25.0 .. | 51.4 | 13 31.5 .. | 08.3 | 34 11.2 .. | 09.1 | Spica | 158 24.8 | S11 16.5 |
| 16 | 6 54.6 | 85 23.2 | 10.2 | 94 25.5 | 51.4 | 28 33.5 | 08.1 | 49 13.3 | 09.0 | Suhail | 222 47.6 | S43 31.2 |
| 17 | 21 57.1 | 100 25.9 | 10.2 | 109 25.9 | 51.4 | 43 35.4 | 07.9 | 64 15.5 | 08.9 | | | |
| 18 | 36 59.6 | 115 28.5 | S16 10.2 | 124 26.4 | S23 51.4 | 58 37.3 | S10 07.7 | 79 17.7 | S17 08.8 | Vega | 80 35.2 | N38 48.1 |
| 19 | 52 02.0 | 130 31.2 | 10.2 | 139 26.9 | 51.4 | 73 39.3 | 07.4 | 94 19.8 | 08.8 | Zuben'ubi | 136 58.7 | S16 07.9 |
| 20 | 67 04.5 | 145 33.8 | 10.3 | 154 27.4 | 51.4 | 88 41.2 | 07.2 | 109 22.0 | 08.7 | | SHA | Mer. Pass. |
| 21 | 82 07.0 | 160 36.4 .. | 10.3 | 169 27.9 .. | 51.4 | 103 43.1 .. | 07.0 | 124 24.2 .. | 08.6 | | ° ′ | h m |
| 22 | 97 09.4 | 175 39.0 | 10.3 | 184 28.3 | 51.4 | 118 45.1 | 06.8 | 139 26.3 | 08.5 | Venus | 78 17.8 | 10 24 |
| 23 | 112 11.9 | 190 41.6 | 10.3 | 199 28.8 | 51.4 | 133 47.0 | 06.6 | 154 28.5 | 08.4 | Mars | 88 50.3 | 9 43 |
| | h m | | | | | | | | | Jupiter | 22 00.2 | 14 09 |
| Mer. Pass. 15 36.4 | v 2.8 d 0.0 | | | v 0.5 d 0.0 | | v 1.9 d 0.2 | | v 2.2 d 0.1 | | Saturn | 42 30.7 | 12 47 |

### SUN and MOON — GHA / Dec

| UT | SUN GHA | SUN Dec | MOON GHA | v | MOON Dec | d | HP |
|---|---|---|---|---|---|---|---|
| **25** d h | ° ′ | ° ′ | ° ′ | ′ | ° ′ | ′ | ′ |
| 00 | 176 57.5 | S19 01.3 | 277 32.8 | 12.3 | S 8 11.8 | 14.5 | 58.2 |
| 01 | 191 57.3 | 00.7 | 292 04.1 | 12.3 | 8 26.3 | 14.4 | 58.2 |
| 02 | 206 57.2 | 19 00.1 | 306 35.4 | 12.1 | 8 40.7 | 14.4 | 58.2 |
| 03 | 221 57.1 | 18 59.5 | 321 06.5 | 12.1 | 8 55.1 | 14.4 | 58.2 |
| 04 | 236 56.9 | 58.8 | 335 37.6 | 12.0 | 9 09.5 | 14.3 | 58.3 |
| 05 | 251 56.8 | 58.2 | 350 08.6 | 12.0 | 9 23.8 | 14.3 | 58.3 |
| 06 | 266 56.6 | S18 57.6 | 4 39.6 | 11.8 | S 9 38.1 | 14.3 | 58.3 |
| 07 | 281 56.5 | 57.0 | 19 10.4 | 11.8 | 9 52.4 | 14.2 | 58.3 |
| T 08 | 296 56.3 | 56.4 | 33 41.2 | 11.8 | 10 06.6 | 14.2 | 58.4 |
| U 09 | 311 56.2 | 55.8 | 48 12.0 | 11.6 | 10 20.8 | 14.2 | 58.4 |
| E 10 | 326 56.1 | 55.1 | 62 42.6 | 11.6 | 10 35.0 | 14.1 | 58.4 |
| S 11 | 341 55.9 | 54.5 | 77 13.2 | 11.5 | 10 49.1 | 14.1 | 58.4 |
| D 12 | 356 55.8 | S18 53.9 | 91 43.7 | 11.4 | S11 03.2 | 14.0 | 58.5 |
| A 13 | 11 55.6 | 53.3 | 106 14.1 | 11.3 | 11 17.2 | 14.0 | 58.5 |
| Y 14 | 26 55.5 | 52.7 | 120 44.4 | 11.2 | 11 31.2 | 14.0 | 58.5 |
| 15 | 41 55.3 | 52.0 | 135 14.6 | 11.2 | 11 45.2 | 13.9 | 58.6 |
| 16 | 56 55.2 | 51.4 | 149 44.8 | 11.1 | 11 59.1 | 13.8 | 58.6 |
| 17 | 71 55.1 | 50.8 | 164 14.9 | 11.0 | 12 12.9 | 13.8 | 58.6 |
| 18 | 86 54.9 | S18 50.2 | 178 44.9 | 10.9 | S12 26.7 | 13.8 | 58.6 |
| 19 | 101 54.8 | 49.5 | 193 14.8 | 10.8 | 12 40.5 | 13.7 | 58.7 |
| 20 | 116 54.6 | 48.9 | 207 44.6 | 10.7 | 12 54.2 | 13.6 | 58.7 |
| 21 | 131 54.5 | 48.3 | 222 14.3 | 10.6 | 13 07.8 | 13.6 | 58.7 |
| 22 | 146 54.4 | 47.7 | 236 43.9 | 10.6 | 13 21.4 | 13.5 | 58.7 |
| 23 | 161 54.2 | 47.0 | 251 13.5 | 10.4 | 13 34.9 | 13.5 | 58.8 |
| **26** 00 | 176 54.1 | S18 46.4 | 265 42.9 | 10.4 | S13 48.4 | 13.4 | 58.8 |
| 01 | 191 54.0 | 45.8 | 280 12.3 | 10.3 | 14 01.8 | 13.3 | 58.8 |
| 02 | 206 53.8 | 45.2 | 294 41.6 | 10.1 | 14 15.1 | 13.3 | 58.8 |
| 03 | 221 53.7 | 44.5 | 309 10.7 | 10.1 | 14 28.4 | 13.2 | 58.9 |
| 04 | 236 53.5 | 43.9 | 323 39.8 | 10.0 | 14 41.6 | 13.1 | 58.9 |
| 05 | 251 53.4 | 43.3 | 338 08.8 | 9.8 | 14 54.7 | 13.1 | 58.9 |
| 06 | 266 53.3 | S18 42.6 | 352 37.6 | 9.8 | S15 07.8 | 13.0 | 58.9 |
| W 07 | 281 53.1 | 42.0 | 7 06.4 | 9.7 | 15 20.8 | 12.9 | 59.0 |
| E 08 | 296 53.0 | 41.4 | 21 35.1 | 9.6 | 15 33.7 | 12.9 | 59.0 |
| D 09 | 311 52.9 | 40.7 | 36 03.7 | 9.4 | 15 46.6 | 12.7 | 59.0 |
| N 10 | 326 52.7 | 40.1 | 50 32.1 | 9.4 | 15 59.3 | 12.7 | 59.1 |
| E 11 | 341 52.6 | 39.5 | 65 00.5 | 9.3 | 16 12.0 | 12.6 | 59.1 |
| S 12 | 356 52.5 | S18 38.8 | 79 28.8 | 9.1 | S16 24.6 | 12.6 | 59.1 |
| D 13 | 11 52.3 | 38.2 | 93 56.9 | 9.1 | 16 37.2 | 12.4 | 59.1 |
| A 14 | 26 52.2 | 37.6 | 108 25.0 | 8.9 | 16 49.6 | 12.4 | 59.2 |
| Y 15 | 41 52.1 | 36.9 | 122 52.9 | 8.9 | 17 02.0 | 12.3 | 59.2 |
| 16 | 56 51.9 | 36.3 | 137 20.8 | 8.7 | 17 14.3 | 12.2 | 59.2 |
| 17 | 71 51.8 | 35.7 | 151 48.5 | 8.6 | 17 26.5 | 12.1 | 59.2 |
| 18 | 86 51.7 | S18 35.0 | 166 16.1 | 8.5 | S17 38.6 | 12.0 | 59.3 |
| 19 | 101 51.5 | 34.4 | 180 43.6 | 8.4 | 17 50.6 | 11.9 | 59.3 |
| 20 | 116 51.4 | 33.7 | 195 11.0 | 8.3 | 18 02.5 | 11.8 | 59.3 |
| 21 | 131 51.3 | 33.1 | 209 38.3 | 8.2 | 18 14.3 | 11.8 | 59.3 |
| 22 | 146 51.2 | 32.5 | 224 05.5 | 8.1 | 18 26.1 | 11.6 | 59.4 |
| 23 | 161 51.0 | 31.8 | 238 32.6 | 8.0 | 18 37.7 | 11.5 | 59.4 |
| **27** 00 | 176 50.9 | S18 31.2 | 252 59.6 | 7.8 | S18 49.2 | 11.4 | 59.4 |
| 01 | 191 50.8 | 30.5 | 267 26.4 | 7.8 | 19 00.6 | 11.4 | 59.4 |
| 02 | 206 50.6 | 29.9 | 281 53.2 | 7.6 | 19 12.0 | 11.2 | 59.5 |
| 03 | 221 50.5 | 29.3 | 296 19.8 | 7.5 | 19 23.2 | 11.1 | 59.5 |
| 04 | 236 50.4 | 28.6 | 310 46.3 | 7.4 | 19 34.3 | 11.0 | 59.5 |
| 05 | 251 50.3 | 28.0 | 325 12.7 | 7.3 | 19 45.3 | 10.8 | 59.5 |
| 06 | 266 50.1 | S18 27.3 | 339 39.0 | 7.2 | S19 56.1 | 10.8 | 59.5 |
| 07 | 281 50.0 | 26.7 | 354 05.2 | 7.0 | 20 06.9 | 10.7 | 59.6 |
| T 08 | 296 49.9 | 26.0 | 8 31.2 | 7.0 | 20 17.6 | 10.5 | 59.6 |
| H 09 | 311 49.7 | 25.4 | 22 57.2 | 6.8 | 20 28.1 | 10.5 | 59.6 |
| U 10 | 326 49.6 | 24.7 | 37 23.0 | 6.8 | 20 38.5 | 10.3 | 59.6 |
| R 11 | 341 49.5 | 24.1 | 51 48.8 | 6.6 | 20 48.8 | 10.2 | 59.7 |
| S 12 | 356 49.4 | S18 23.4 | 66 14.4 | 6.5 | S20 59.0 | 10.0 | 59.7 |
| D 13 | 11 49.2 | 22.8 | 80 39.9 | 6.3 | 21 09.0 | 10.0 | 59.7 |
| A 14 | 26 49.1 | 22.1 | 95 05.2 | 6.3 | 21 19.0 | 9.8 | 59.7 |
| Y 15 | 41 49.0 | 21.5 | 109 30.5 | 6.2 | 21 28.8 | 9.6 | 59.7 |
| 16 | 56 48.9 | 20.8 | 123 55.7 | 6.0 | 21 38.4 | 9.6 | 59.8 |
| 17 | 71 48.7 | 20.2 | 138 20.7 | 6.0 | 21 48.0 | 9.4 | 59.8 |
| 18 | 86 48.6 | S18 19.5 | 152 45.7 | 5.8 | S21 57.4 | 9.2 | 59.8 |
| 19 | 101 48.5 | 18.9 | 167 10.5 | 5.7 | 22 06.6 | 9.2 | 59.8 |
| 20 | 116 48.4 | 18.2 | 181 35.2 | 5.6 | 22 15.8 | 8.9 | 59.9 |
| 21 | 131 48.3 | 17.6 | 195 59.8 | 5.5 | 22 24.7 | 8.9 | 59.9 |
| 22 | 146 48.1 | 16.9 | 210 24.3 | 5.4 | 22 33.6 | 8.7 | 59.9 |
| 23 | 161 48.0 | 16.3 | 224 48.7 | 5.3 | S22 42.3 | 8.6 | 59.9 |
| | SD 16.3 | d 0.6 | SD 15.9 | | 16.1 | | 16.3 |

### Twilight, Sunrise, Moonrise

| Lat. | Naut. | Civil | Sunrise | Moonrise 25 | 26 | 27 | 28 |
|---|---|---|---|---|---|---|---|
| ° | h m | h m | h m | h m | h m | h m | h m |
| N 72 | 07 30 | 09 05 | 11 39 | 01 25 | 04 05 | ■■ | ■■ |
| N 70 | 07 19 | 08 42 | 10 21 | 01 11 | 03 29 | ■■ | ■■ |
| 68 | 07 11 | 08 24 | 09 43 | 00 59 | 03 05 | 05 38 | ■■ |
| 66 | 07 03 | 08 09 | 09 17 | 00 50 | 02 46 | 04 57 | ■■ |
| 64 | 06 57 | 07 57 | 08 57 | 00 43 | 02 31 | 04 29 | 06 41 |
| 62 | 06 51 | 07 47 | 08 41 | 00 36 | 02 18 | 04 07 | 06 02 |
| 60 | 06 46 | 07 38 | 08 27 | 00 31 | 02 07 | 03 50 | 05 35 |
| N 58 | 06 42 | 07 30 | 08 16 | 00 26 | 01 58 | 03 36 | 05 15 |
| 56 | 06 38 | 07 23 | 08 06 | 00 21 | 01 50 | 03 23 | 04 57 |
| 54 | 06 34 | 07 17 | 07 57 | 00 17 | 01 43 | 03 13 | 04 43 |
| 52 | 06 30 | 07 11 | 07 49 | 00 14 | 01 37 | 03 03 | 04 30 |
| 50 | 06 27 | 07 06 | 07 42 | 00 11 | 01 31 | 02 55 | 04 19 |
| 45 | 06 19 | 06 54 | 07 26 | 00 04 | 01 19 | 02 37 | 03 56 |
| N 40 | 06 12 | 06 45 | 07 14 | 25 09 | 01 09 | 02 22 | 03 38 |
| 35 | 06 05 | 06 36 | 07 03 | 25 00 | 01 00 | 02 10 | 03 22 |
| 30 | 05 59 | 06 28 | 06 53 | 24 53 | 00 53 | 02 00 | 03 09 |
| 20 | 05 47 | 06 14 | 06 37 | 24 40 | 00 40 | 01 42 | 02 47 |
| N 10 | 05 35 | 06 00 | 06 23 | 24 29 | 00 29 | 01 26 | 02 27 |
| 0 | 05 22 | 05 47 | 06 09 | 24 18 | 00 18 | 01 11 | 02 09 |
| S 10 | 05 07 | 05 33 | 05 55 | 24 08 | 00 08 | 00 57 | 01 51 |
| 20 | 04 49 | 05 17 | 05 40 | 23 57 | 24 42 | 00 42 | 01 32 |
| 30 | 04 26 | 04 57 | 05 23 | 23 45 | 24 24 | 00 24 | 01 10 |
| 35 | 04 11 | 04 45 | 05 13 | 23 38 | 24 14 | 00 14 | 00 57 |
| 40 | 03 53 | 04 31 | 05 02 | 23 30 | 24 03 | 00 03 | 00 43 |
| 45 | 03 30 | 04 14 | 04 48 | 23 20 | 23 49 | 24 25 | 00 25 |
| S 50 | 02 59 | 03 52 | 04 31 | 23 09 | 23 33 | 24 04 | 00 04 |
| 52 | 02 43 | 03 41 | 04 23 | 23 04 | 23 25 | 23 54 | 24 35 |
| 54 | 02 24 | 03 29 | 04 14 | 22 58 | 23 17 | 23 42 | 24 21 |
| 56 | 01 58 | 03 15 | 04 04 | 22 52 | 23 07 | 23 30 | 24 04 |
| 58 | 01 19 | 02 58 | 03 53 | 22 45 | 22 57 | 23 15 | 23 45 |
| S 60 | //// | 02 37 | 03 40 | 22 37 | 22 44 | 22 57 | 23 21 |

### Sunset, Twilight, Moonset

| Lat. | Sunset | Civil | Naut. | Moonset 25 | 26 | 27 | 28 |
|---|---|---|---|---|---|---|---|
| ° | h m | h m | h m | h m | h m | h m | h m |
| N 72 | 12 47 | 15 21 | 16 57 | 09 27 | 08 32 | ■■ | ■■ |
| N 70 | 14 05 | 15 44 | 17 07 | 09 44 | 09 09 | ■■ | ■■ |
| 68 | 14 43 | 16 02 | 17 15 | 09 57 | 09 35 | 08 54 | ■■ |
| 66 | 15 09 | 16 17 | 17 23 | 10 08 | 09 56 | 09 37 | ■■ |
| 64 | 15 29 | 16 29 | 17 29 | 10 18 | 10 12 | 10 06 | 09 56 |
| 62 | 15 45 | 16 39 | 17 34 | 10 26 | 10 26 | 10 28 | 10 35 |
| 60 | 15 58 | 16 48 | 17 39 | 10 32 | 10 38 | 10 46 | 11 02 |
| N 58 | 16 10 | 16 55 | 17 44 | 10 39 | 10 48 | 11 01 | 11 24 |
| 56 | 16 20 | 17 02 | 17 48 | 10 44 | 10 57 | 11 14 | 11 41 |
| 54 | 16 29 | 17 09 | 17 52 | 10 49 | 11 05 | 11 26 | 11 56 |
| 52 | 16 37 | 17 14 | 17 56 | 10 53 | 11 12 | 11 36 | 12 09 |
| 50 | 16 44 | 17 20 | 17 59 | 10 58 | 11 18 | 11 45 | 12 21 |
| 45 | 16 59 | 17 31 | 18 07 | 11 06 | 11 32 | 12 04 | 12 45 |
| N 40 | 17 12 | 17 41 | 18 14 | 11 14 | 11 44 | 12 20 | 13 04 |
| 35 | 17 22 | 17 49 | 18 20 | 11 20 | 11 54 | 12 33 | 13 20 |
| 30 | 17 32 | 17 57 | 18 26 | 11 26 | 12 02 | 12 44 | 13 34 |
| 20 | 17 48 | 18 11 | 18 38 | 11 36 | 12 17 | 13 04 | 13 58 |
| N 10 | 18 01 | 18 25 | 18 50 | 11 44 | 12 31 | 13 22 | 14 19 |
| 0 | 18 16 | 18 38 | 19 03 | 11 52 | 12 43 | 13 38 | 14 38 |
| S 10 | 18 30 | 18 52 | 19 18 | 12 00 | 12 55 | 13 55 | 14 57 |
| 20 | 18 44 | 19 08 | 19 36 | 12 09 | 13 09 | 14 12 | 15 18 |
| 30 | 19 01 | 19 28 | 19 59 | 12 19 | 13 24 | 14 32 | 15 42 |
| 35 | 19 11 | 19 39 | 20 13 | 12 25 | 13 33 | 14 44 | 15 56 |
| 40 | 19 23 | 19 53 | 20 31 | 12 32 | 13 43 | 14 58 | 16 13 |
| 45 | 19 36 | 20 10 | 20 53 | 12 39 | 13 56 | 15 14 | 16 33 |
| S 50 | 19 53 | 20 32 | 21 24 | 12 49 | 14 10 | 15 35 | 16 57 |
| 52 | 20 01 | 20 43 | 21 40 | 12 53 | 14 17 | 15 44 | 17 09 |
| 54 | 20 09 | 20 55 | 21 59 | 12 58 | 14 25 | 15 55 | 17 23 |
| 56 | 20 19 | 21 09 | 22 24 | 13 03 | 14 34 | 16 07 | 17 39 |
| 58 | 20 31 | 21 25 | 23 00 | 13 09 | 14 43 | 16 22 | 17 58 |
| S 60 | 20 44 | 21 46 | //// | 13 16 | 14 55 | 16 39 | 18 21 |

### SUN and MOON

| Day | Eqn. of Time 00ʰ | Eqn. of Time 12ʰ | Mer. Pass. | Mer. Pass. Upper | Lower | Age | Phase |
|---|---|---|---|---|---|---|---|
| d | m s | m s | h m | h m | h m | d | % |
| 25 | 12 10 | 12 17 | 12 12 | 05 41 | 18 05 | 23 | 51 |
| 26 | 12 23 | 12 30 | 12 12 | 06 31 | 18 57 | 24 | 40 |
| 27 | 12 36 | 12 42 | 12 13 | 07 25 | 19 53 | 25 | 29 |

| UT | ARIES | VENUS −4.8 | | MARS +1.4 | | JUPITER −2.1 | | SATURN +0.6 | | STARS | | |
|---|---|---|---|---|---|---|---|---|---|---|---|---|
| d h | GHA | GHA | Dec | GHA | Dec | GHA | Dec | GHA | Dec | Name | SHA | Dec |
| **28** 00 | 127 14.3 | 205 44.2 | S16 10.3 | 214 29.3 | S23 51.4 | 148 48.9 | S10 06.4 | 169 30.7 | S17 08.3 | Acamar | 315 13.6 | S40 13.3 |
| 01 | 142 16.8 | 220 46.9 | 10.4 | 229 29.8 | 51.4 | 163 50.8 | 06.2 | 184 32.8 | 08.2 | Achernar | 335 22.2 | S57 07.9 |
| 02 | 157 19.3 | 235 49.5 | 10.4 | 244 30.2 | 51.3 | 178 52.8 | 06.0 | 199 35.0 | 08.2 | Acrux | 173 02.3 | S63 13.0 |
| 03 | 172 21.7 | 250 52.1 .. | 10.4 | 259 30.7 .. | 51.3 | 193 54.7 .. | 05.7 | 214 37.2 .. | 08.1 | Adhara | 255 07.4 | S29 00.2 |
| 04 | 187 24.2 | 265 54.6 | 10.4 | 274 31.2 | 51.3 | 208 56.6 | 05.5 | 229 39.3 | 08.0 | Aldebaran | 290 42.2 | N16 33.2 |
| 05 | 202 26.7 | 280 57.2 | 10.5 | 289 31.7 | 51.3 | 223 58.5 | 05.3 | 244 41.5 | 07.9 | | | |
| 06 | 217 29.1 | 295 59.8 | S16 10.5 | 304 32.1 | S23 51.3 | 239 00.5 | S10 05.1 | 259 43.6 | S17 07.8 | Alioth | 166 14.9 | N55 50.2 |
| 07 | 232 31.6 | 311 02.4 | 10.5 | 319 32.6 | 51.3 | 254 02.4 | 04.9 | 274 45.8 | 07.7 | Alkaid | 152 53.9 | N49 12.0 |
| F 08 | 247 34.1 | 326 05.0 | 10.5 | 334 33.1 | 51.3 | 269 04.3 | 04.7 | 289 48.0 | 07.6 | Alnair | 27 36.4 | S46 51.5 |
| R 09 | 262 36.5 | 341 07.5 .. | 10.6 | 349 33.6 .. | 51.3 | 284 06.3 .. | 04.5 | 304 50.1 .. | 07.6 | Alnilam | 275 39.9 | S 1 11.4 |
| I 10 | 277 39.0 | 356 10.1 | 10.6 | 4 34.0 | 51.3 | 299 08.2 | 04.3 | 319 52.3 | 07.5 | Alphard | 217 49.8 | S 8 45.3 |
| D 11 | 292 41.5 | 11 12.7 | 10.6 | 19 34.5 | 51.3 | 314 10.1 | 04.1 | 334 54.5 | 07.4 | | | |
| A 12 | 307 43.9 | 26 15.2 | S16 10.7 | 34 35.0 | S23 51.3 | 329 12.0 | S10 03.8 | 349 56.6 | S17 07.3 | Alphecca | 126 05.9 | N26 38.3 |
| Y 13 | 322 46.4 | 41 17.8 | 10.7 | 49 35.4 | 51.3 | 344 14.0 | 03.6 | 4 58.8 | 07.2 | Alpheratz | 357 37.5 | N29 12.7 |
| 14 | 337 48.8 | 56 20.3 | 10.7 | 64 35.9 | 51.3 | 359 15.9 | 03.4 | 20 01.0 | 07.1 | Altair | 62 02.6 | N 8 55.5 |
| 15 | 352 51.3 | 71 22.9 .. | 10.8 | 79 36.4 .. | 51.2 | 14 17.8 .. | 03.2 | 35 03.1 .. | 07.0 | Ankaa | 353 09.8 | S42 11.5 |
| 16 | 7 53.8 | 86 25.4 | 10.8 | 94 36.9 | 51.2 | 29 19.8 | 03.0 | 50 05.3 | 07.0 | Antares | 112 19.0 | S26 28.7 |
| 17 | 22 56.2 | 101 27.9 | 10.8 | 109 37.3 | 51.2 | 44 21.7 | 02.8 | 65 07.5 | 06.9 | | | |
| 18 | 37 58.7 | 116 30.5 | S16 10.9 | 124 37.8 | S23 51.2 | 59 23.6 | S10 02.6 | 80 09.6 | S17 06.8 | Arcturus | 145 50.1 | N19 03.9 |
| 19 | 53 01.2 | 131 33.0 | 10.9 | 139 38.3 | 51.2 | 74 25.5 | 02.4 | 95 11.8 | 06.7 | Atria | 107 15.7 | S69 03.7 |
| 20 | 68 03.6 | 146 35.5 | 10.9 | 154 38.8 | 51.2 | 89 27.5 | 02.2 | 110 14.0 | 06.6 | Avior | 234 15.0 | S59 34.8 |
| 21 | 83 06.1 | 161 38.0 .. | 11.0 | 169 39.2 .. | 51.2 | 104 29.4 .. | 01.9 | 125 16.1 .. | 06.5 | Bellatrix | 278 25.2 | N 6 22.1 |
| 22 | 98 08.6 | 176 40.5 | 11.0 | 184 39.7 | 51.2 | 119 31.3 | 01.7 | 140 18.3 | 06.4 | Betelgeuse | 270 54.4 | N 7 24.6 |
| 23 | 113 11.0 | 191 43.0 | 11.0 | 199 40.2 | 51.1 | 134 33.2 | 01.5 | 155 20.4 | 06.4 | | | |
| **29** 00 | 128 13.5 | 206 45.5 | S16 11.1 | 214 40.7 | S23 51.1 | 149 35.2 | S10 01.3 | 170 22.6 | S17 06.3 | Canopus | 263 53.0 | S52 42.6 |
| 01 | 143 16.0 | 221 48.0 | 11.1 | 229 41.1 | 51.1 | 164 37.1 | 01.1 | 185 24.8 | 06.2 | Capella | 280 25.1 | N46 01.3 |
| 02 | 158 18.4 | 236 50.5 | 11.1 | 244 41.6 | 51.1 | 179 39.0 | 00.9 | 200 26.9 | 06.1 | Deneb | 49 27.9 | N45 21.4 |
| 03 | 173 20.9 | 251 53.0 .. | 11.2 | 259 42.1 .. | 51.1 | 194 40.9 .. | 00.7 | 215 29.1 .. | 06.0 | Denebola | 182 27.2 | N14 26.9 |
| 04 | 188 23.3 | 266 55.5 | 11.2 | 274 42.6 | 51.1 | 209 42.9 | 00.5 | 230 31.3 | 05.9 | Diphda | 348 49.9 | S17 52.2 |
| 05 | 203 25.8 | 281 58.0 | 11.3 | 289 43.0 | 51.0 | 224 44.8 | 00.2 | 245 33.4 | 05.8 | | | |
| 06 | 218 28.3 | 297 00.5 | S16 11.3 | 304 43.5 | S23 51.0 | 239 46.7 | S10 00.0 | 260 35.6 | S17 05.8 | Dubhe | 193 43.5 | N61 37.8 |
| 07 | 233 30.7 | 312 02.9 | 11.3 | 319 44.0 | 51.0 | 254 48.7 | 9 59.8 | 275 37.8 | 05.7 | Elnath | 278 04.6 | N28 37.5 |
| S 08 | 248 33.2 | 327 05.4 | 11.4 | 334 44.4 | 51.0 | 269 50.6 | 59.6 | 290 39.9 | 05.6 | Eltanin | 90 43.7 | N51 28.9 |
| A 09 | 263 35.7 | 342 07.9 .. | 11.4 | 349 44.9 .. | 51.0 | 284 52.5 .. | 59.4 | 305 42.1 .. | 05.5 | Enif | 33 41.5 | N 9 58.4 |
| T 10 | 278 38.1 | 357 10.3 | 11.5 | 4 45.4 | 51.0 | 299 54.4 | 59.2 | 320 44.3 | 05.4 | Fomalhaut | 15 17.5 | S29 30.6 |
| U 11 | 293 40.6 | 12 12.8 | 11.5 | 19 45.9 | 50.9 | 314 56.4 | 59.0 | 335 46.4 | 05.3 | | | |
| R 12 | 308 43.1 | 27 15.2 | S16 11.5 | 34 46.3 | S23 50.9 | 329 58.3 | S 9 58.8 | 350 48.6 | S17 05.2 | Gacrux | 171 54.0 | S57 13.9 |
| D 13 | 323 45.5 | 42 17.7 | 11.6 | 49 46.8 | 50.9 | 345 00.2 | 58.5 | 5 50.8 | 05.2 | Gienah | 175 45.9 | S17 39.8 |
| A 14 | 338 48.0 | 57 20.1 | 11.6 | 64 47.3 | 50.9 | 0 02.1 | 58.3 | 20 52.9 | 05.1 | Hadar | 148 39.3 | S60 28.4 |
| Y 15 | 353 50.5 | 72 22.5 .. | 11.7 | 79 47.8 .. | 50.9 | 15 04.1 .. | 58.1 | 35 55.1 .. | 05.0 | Hamal | 327 53.9 | N23 34.0 |
| 16 | 8 52.9 | 87 25.0 | 11.7 | 94 48.2 | 50.8 | 30 06.0 | 57.9 | 50 57.2 | 04.9 | Kaus Aust. | 83 36.1 | S34 22.4 |
| 17 | 23 55.4 | 102 27.4 | 11.8 | 109 48.7 | 50.8 | 45 07.9 | 57.7 | 65 59.4 | 04.8 | | | |
| 18 | 38 57.8 | 117 29.8 | S16 11.8 | 124 49.2 | S23 50.8 | 60 09.8 | S 9 57.5 | 81 01.6 | S17 04.7 | Kochab | 137 20.0 | N74 03.6 |
| 19 | 54 00.3 | 132 32.2 | 11.9 | 139 49.6 | 50.8 | 75 11.8 | 57.3 | 96 03.7 | 04.6 | Markab | 13 32.5 | N15 19.3 |
| 20 | 69 02.8 | 147 34.7 | 11.9 | 154 50.1 | 50.7 | 90 13.7 | 57.0 | 111 05.9 | 04.6 | Menkar | 314 08.6 | N 4 10.4 |
| 21 | 84 05.2 | 162 37.1 .. | 12.0 | 169 50.6 .. | 50.7 | 105 15.6 .. | 56.8 | 126 08.1 .. | 04.5 | Menkent | 148 00.4 | S36 28.5 |
| 22 | 99 07.7 | 177 39.5 | 12.0 | 184 51.1 | 50.7 | 120 17.5 | 56.6 | 141 10.2 | 04.4 | Miaplacidus | 221 37.7 | S69 48.4 |
| 23 | 114 10.2 | 192 41.9 | 12.1 | 199 51.5 | 50.7 | 135 19.5 | 56.4 | 156 12.4 | 04.3 | | | |
| **30** 00 | 129 12.6 | 207 44.3 | S16 12.1 | 214 52.0 | S23 50.6 | 150 21.4 | S 9 56.2 | 171 14.6 | S17 04.2 | Mirfak | 308 31.5 | N49 56.5 |
| 01 | 144 15.1 | 222 46.7 | 12.2 | 229 52.5 | 50.6 | 165 23.3 | 56.0 | 186 16.7 | 04.1 | Nunki | 75 51.1 | S26 16.2 |
| 02 | 159 17.6 | 237 49.0 | 12.2 | 244 53.0 | 50.6 | 180 25.2 | 55.8 | 201 18.9 | 04.0 | Peacock | 53 10.1 | S56 39.9 |
| 03 | 174 20.0 | 252 51.4 .. | 12.3 | 259 53.4 .. | 50.6 | 195 27.2 .. | 55.6 | 216 21.1 .. | 04.0 | Pollux | 243 19.9 | N27 58.3 |
| 04 | 189 22.5 | 267 53.8 | 12.3 | 274 53.9 | 50.5 | 210 29.1 | 55.3 | 231 23.2 | 03.9 | Procyon | 244 53.0 | N 5 10.0 |
| 05 | 204 25.0 | 282 56.2 | 12.4 | 289 54.4 | 50.5 | 225 31.0 | 55.1 | 246 25.4 | 03.8 | | | |
| 06 | 219 27.4 | 297 58.5 | S16 12.4 | 304 54.8 | S23 50.5 | 240 32.9 | S 9 54.9 | 261 27.5 | S17 03.7 | Rasalhague | 96 01.0 | N12 32.5 |
| 07 | 234 29.9 | 313 00.9 | 12.5 | 319 55.3 | 50.5 | 255 34.9 | 54.7 | 276 29.7 | 03.6 | Regulus | 207 36.7 | N11 51.5 |
| 08 | 249 32.3 | 328 03.3 | 12.5 | 334 55.8 | 50.4 | 270 36.8 | 54.5 | 291 31.9 | 03.5 | Rigel | 281 06.0 | S 8 10.7 |
| S 09 | 264 34.8 | 343 05.6 .. | 12.6 | 349 56.3 .. | 50.4 | 285 38.7 .. | 54.3 | 306 34.0 .. | 03.4 | Rigil Kent. | 139 43.6 | S60 55.2 |
| U 10 | 279 37.3 | 358 08.0 | 12.6 | 4 56.7 | 50.4 | 300 40.6 | 54.1 | 321 36.2 | 03.4 | Sabik | 102 05.8 | S15 45.1 |
| N 11 | 294 39.7 | 13 10.3 | 12.7 | 19 57.2 | 50.4 | 315 42.6 | 53.8 | 336 38.4 | 03.3 | | | |
| D 12 | 309 42.2 | 28 12.7 | S16 12.7 | 34 57.7 | S23 50.3 | 330 44.5 | S 9 53.6 | 351 40.5 | S17 03.2 | Schedar | 349 34.0 | N56 39.6 |
| A 13 | 324 44.7 | 43 15.0 | 12.8 | 49 58.1 | 50.3 | 345 46.4 | 53.4 | 6 42.7 | 03.1 | Shaula | 96 13.9 | S37 07.1 |
| Y 14 | 339 47.1 | 58 17.4 | 12.8 | 64 58.6 | 50.3 | 0 48.3 | 53.2 | 21 44.9 | 03.0 | Sirius | 258 28.0 | S16 44.9 |
| 15 | 354 49.6 | 73 19.7 .. | 12.9 | 79 59.1 .. | 50.2 | 15 50.3 .. | 53.0 | 36 47.0 .. | 02.9 | Spica | 158 24.7 | S11 16.5 |
| 16 | 9 52.1 | 88 22.0 | 13.0 | 94 59.6 | 50.2 | 30 52.2 | 52.8 | 51 49.2 | 02.8 | Suhail | 222 47.6 | S43 31.3 |
| 17 | 24 54.5 | 103 24.3 | 13.0 | 110 00.0 | 50.2 | 45 54.1 | 52.6 | 66 51.4 | 02.8 | | | |
| 18 | 39 57.0 | 118 26.6 | S16 13.1 | 125 00.5 | S23 50.1 | 60 56.0 | S 9 52.4 | 81 53.5 | S17 02.7 | Vega | 80 35.2 | N38 48.1 |
| 19 | 54 59.5 | 133 29.0 | 13.1 | 140 01.0 | 50.1 | 75 57.9 | 52.1 | 96 55.7 | 02.6 | Zuben'ubi | 136 58.7 | S16 07.9 |
| 20 | 70 01.9 | 148 31.3 | 13.2 | 155 01.4 | 50.1 | 90 59.9 | 51.9 | 111 57.8 | 02.5 | | SHA | Mer. Pass. |
| 21 | 85 04.4 | 163 33.6 .. | 13.2 | 170 01.9 .. | 50.0 | 106 01.8 .. | 51.7 | 127 00.0 .. | 02.4 | | ° ′ | h m |
| 22 | 100 06.8 | 178 35.9 | 13.3 | 185 02.4 | 50.0 | 121 03.7 | 51.5 | 142 02.2 | 02.3 | Venus | 78 32.0 | 10 11 |
| 23 | 115 09.3 | 193 38.2 | 13.4 | 200 02.9 | 50.0 | 136 05.6 | 51.3 | 157 04.3 | 02.2 | Mars | 86 27.2 | 9 41 |
| | h m | | | | | | | | | Jupiter | 21 21.7 | 14 00 |
| Mer.Pass. 15 24.6 | v 2.4   d 0.0 | | v 0.5   d 0.0 | | v 1.9   d 0.2 | | v 2.2   d 0.1 | | Saturn | 42 09.1 | 12 37 |

## SUN / MOON

| UT (d h) | SUN GHA | SUN Dec | MOON GHA | v | MOON Dec | d | HP |
|---|---|---|---|---|---|---|---|
| **28 00** | 176 47.9 | S18 15.6 | 239 13.0 | 5.1 | S22 50.9 | 8.4 | 59.9 |
| 01 | 191 47.8 | 15.0 | 253 37.1 | 5.1 | 22 59.3 | 8.2 | 60.0 |
| 02 | 206 47.7 | 14.3 | 268 01.2 | 5.0 | 23 07.5 | 8.1 | 60.0 |
| 03 | 221 47.5 | .. 13.6 | 282 25.2 | 4.8 | 23 15.6 | 8.0 | 60.0 |
| 04 | 236 47.4 | 13.0 | 296 49.0 | 4.8 | 23 23.6 | 7.8 | 60.0 |
| 05 | 251 47.3 | 12.3 | 311 12.8 | 4.6 | 23 31.4 | 7.7 | 60.0 |
| 06 | 266 47.2 | S18 11.7 | 325 36.4 | 4.6 | S23 39.1 | 7.5 | 60.0 |
| 07 | 281 47.1 | 11.0 | 340 00.0 | 4.4 | 23 46.6 | 7.3 | 60.1 |
| 08 | 296 46.9 | 10.4 | 354 23.4 | 4.4 | 23 53.9 | 7.2 | 60.1 |
| F 09 | 311 46.8 | .. 09.7 | 8 46.8 | 4.2 | 24 01.1 | 7.0 | 60.1 |
| R 10 | 326 46.7 | 09.0 | 23 10.0 | 4.2 | 24 08.1 | 6.9 | 60.1 |
| I 11 | 341 46.6 | 08.4 | 37 33.2 | 4.0 | 24 15.0 | 6.7 | 60.1 |
| D 12 | 356 46.5 | S18 07.7 | 51 56.2 | 4.0 | S24 21.7 | 6.5 | 60.2 |
| A 13 | 11 46.3 | 07.0 | 66 19.2 | 3.9 | 24 28.2 | 6.4 | 60.2 |
| Y 14 | 26 46.2 | 06.4 | 80 42.1 | 3.7 | 24 34.6 | 6.1 | 60.2 |
| 15 | 41 46.1 | .. 05.7 | 95 04.8 | 3.7 | 24 40.7 | 6.1 | 60.2 |
| 16 | 56 46.0 | 05.1 | 109 27.5 | 3.6 | 24 46.8 | 5.8 | 60.2 |
| 17 | 71 45.9 | 04.4 | 123 50.1 | 3.6 | 24 52.6 | 5.7 | 60.2 |
| 18 | 86 45.8 | S18 03.7 | 138 12.7 | 3.4 | S24 58.3 | 5.5 | 60.2 |
| 19 | 101 45.7 | 03.1 | 152 35.1 | 3.4 | 25 03.8 | 5.3 | 60.3 |
| 20 | 116 45.5 | 02.4 | 166 57.5 | 3.3 | 25 09.1 | 5.1 | 60.3 |
| 21 | 131 45.4 | .. 01.7 | 181 19.8 | 3.2 | 25 14.2 | 5.0 | 60.3 |
| 22 | 146 45.3 | 01.1 | 195 42.0 | 3.1 | 25 19.2 | 4.8 | 60.3 |
| 23 | 161 45.2 | 18 00.4 | 210 04.1 | 3.0 | 25 24.0 | 4.6 | 60.3 |
| **29 00** | 176 45.1 | S17 59.7 | 224 26.1 | 3.0 | S25 28.6 | 4.4 | 60.3 |
| 01 | 191 45.0 | 59.0 | 238 48.1 | 3.0 | 25 33.0 | 4.2 | 60.3 |
| 02 | 206 44.9 | 58.4 | 253 10.1 | 2.8 | 25 37.2 | 4.1 | 60.4 |
| 03 | 221 44.8 | .. 57.7 | 267 31.9 | 2.8 | 25 41.3 | 3.8 | 60.4 |
| 04 | 236 44.6 | 57.0 | 281 53.7 | 2.7 | 25 45.1 | 3.7 | 60.4 |
| 05 | 251 44.5 | 56.4 | 296 15.4 | 2.7 | 25 48.8 | 3.5 | 60.4 |
| 06 | 266 44.4 | S17 55.7 | 310 37.1 | 2.6 | S25 52.3 | 3.3 | 60.4 |
| 07 | 281 44.3 | 55.0 | 324 58.7 | 2.6 | 25 55.6 | 3.1 | 60.4 |
| S 08 | 296 44.2 | 54.3 | 339 20.3 | 2.5 | 25 58.7 | 2.9 | 60.4 |
| A 09 | 311 44.1 | .. 53.7 | 353 41.8 | 2.4 | 26 01.6 | 2.7 | 60.4 |
| T 10 | 326 44.0 | 53.0 | 8 03.2 | 2.4 | 26 04.3 | 2.6 | 60.4 |
| U 11 | 341 43.9 | 52.3 | 22 24.6 | 2.4 | 26 06.9 | 2.3 | 60.4 |
| R 12 | 356 43.8 | S17 51.6 | 36 46.0 | 2.4 | S26 09.2 | 2.2 | 60.5 |
| D 13 | 11 43.7 | 51.0 | 51 07.4 | 2.2 | 26 11.4 | 1.9 | 60.5 |
| A 14 | 26 43.5 | 50.3 | 65 28.6 | 2.3 | 26 13.3 | 1.8 | 60.5 |
| Y 15 | 41 43.4 | .. 49.6 | 79 49.9 | 2.2 | 26 15.1 | 1.5 | 60.5 |
| 16 | 56 43.3 | 48.9 | 94 11.1 | 2.2 | 26 16.6 | 1.4 | 60.5 |
| 17 | 71 43.2 | 48.3 | 108 32.3 | 2.2 | 26 18.0 | 1.1 | 60.5 |
| 18 | 86 43.1 | S17 47.6 | 122 53.5 | 2.2 | S26 19.1 | 1.0 | 60.5 |
| 19 | 101 43.0 | 46.9 | 137 14.7 | 2.1 | 26 20.1 | 0.8 | 60.5 |
| 20 | 116 42.9 | 46.2 | 151 35.8 | 2.1 | 26 20.9 | 0.6 | 60.5 |
| 21 | 131 42.8 | .. 45.5 | 165 56.9 | 2.1 | 26 21.5 | 0.3 | 60.5 |
| 22 | 146 42.7 | 44.9 | 180 18.0 | 2.1 | 26 21.8 | 0.2 | 60.5 |
| 23 | 161 42.6 | 44.2 | 194 39.1 | 2.0 | 26 22.0 | 0.0 | 60.5 |
| **30 00** | 176 42.5 | S17 43.5 | 209 00.1 | 2.1 | S26 22.0 | 0.2 | 60.5 |
| 01 | 191 42.4 | 42.8 | 223 21.2 | 2.1 | 26 21.8 | 0.5 | 60.5 |
| 02 | 206 42.3 | 42.1 | 237 42.3 | 2.1 | 26 21.3 | 0.6 | 60.5 |
| 03 | 221 42.2 | .. 41.4 | 252 03.4 | 2.0 | 26 20.7 | 0.8 | 60.5 |
| 04 | 236 42.1 | 40.8 | 266 24.4 | 2.1 | 26 19.9 | 1.0 | 60.5 |
| 05 | 251 42.0 | 40.1 | 280 45.5 | 2.1 | 26 18.9 | 1.2 | 60.5 |
| 06 | 266 41.9 | S17 39.4 | 295 06.6 | 2.1 | S26 17.7 | 1.5 | 60.5 |
| 07 | 281 41.8 | 38.7 | 309 27.7 | 2.1 | 26 16.2 | 1.6 | 60.5 |
| 08 | 296 41.7 | 38.0 | 323 48.8 | 2.2 | 26 14.6 | 1.8 | 60.5 |
| S 09 | 311 41.6 | .. 37.3 | 338 10.0 | 2.1 | 26 12.8 | 2.0 | 60.5 |
| U 10 | 326 41.5 | 36.6 | 352 31.1 | 2.2 | 26 10.8 | 2.2 | 60.5 |
| N 11 | 341 41.4 | 36.0 | 6 52.3 | 2.2 | 26 08.6 | 2.4 | 60.5 |
| D 12 | 356 41.3 | S17 35.3 | 21 13.5 | 2.2 | S26 06.2 | 2.6 | 60.5 |
| A 13 | 11 41.2 | 34.6 | 35 34.7 | 2.3 | 26 03.6 | 2.8 | 60.5 |
| Y 14 | 26 41.1 | 33.9 | 49 56.0 | 2.3 | 26 00.8 | 3.0 | 60.5 |
| 15 | 41 41.0 | .. 33.2 | 64 17.3 | 2.4 | 25 57.8 | 3.1 | 60.5 |
| 16 | 56 40.9 | 32.5 | 78 38.7 | 2.3 | 25 54.7 | 3.4 | 60.5 |
| 17 | 71 40.8 | 31.8 | 93 00.0 | 2.5 | 25 51.3 | 3.6 | 60.5 |
| 18 | 86 40.7 | S17 31.1 | 107 21.5 | 2.4 | S25 47.7 | 3.7 | 60.5 |
| 19 | 101 40.6 | 30.4 | 121 42.9 | 2.6 | 25 44.0 | 4.0 | 60.5 |
| 20 | 116 40.5 | 29.7 | 136 04.5 | 2.6 | 25 40.0 | 4.1 | 60.5 |
| 21 | 131 40.4 | .. 29.0 | 150 26.1 | 2.6 | 25 35.9 | 4.3 | 60.5 |
| 22 | 146 40.3 | 28.3 | 164 47.7 | 2.7 | 25 31.6 | 4.6 | 60.5 |
| 23 | 161 40.2 | 27.7 | 179 09.4 | 2.7 | S25 27.0 | 4.7 | 60.5 |
| | SD 16.3 | d 0.7 | SD 16.4 | | 16.5 | | 16.5 |

## Twilight / Moonrise

| Lat. | Naut. | Civil | Sunrise | Moonrise 28 | 29 | 30 | 31 |
|---|---|---|---|---|---|---|---|
| N 72 | 07 20 | 08 52 | 10 55 | ████ | ████ | ████ | ████ |
| N 70 | 07 11 | 08 31 | 10 02 | ████ | ████ | ████ | ████ |
| 68 | 07 03 | 08 15 | 09 30 | ████ | ████ | ████ | ████ |
| 66 | 06 57 | 08 01 | 09 07 | ████ | ████ | ████ | ████ |
| 64 | 06 51 | 07 50 | 08 48 | 06 41 | ████ | ████ | 10 10 |
| 62 | 06 46 | 07 41 | 08 33 | 06 02 | 07 52 | 09 03 | 09 28 |
| 60 | 06 41 | 07 33 | 08 21 | 05 35 | 07 13 | 08 23 | 09 00 |
| N 58 | 06 37 | 07 25 | 08 10 | 05 15 | 06 46 | 07 55 | 08 38 |
| 56 | 06 33 | 07 19 | 08 00 | 04 57 | 06 25 | 07 34 | 08 20 |
| 54 | 06 30 | 07 13 | 07 52 | 04 43 | 06 07 | 07 16 | 08 04 |
| 52 | 06 27 | 07 07 | 07 45 | 04 30 | 05 52 | 07 00 | 07 51 |
| 50 | 06 23 | 07 03 | 07 38 | 04 19 | 05 39 | 06 47 | 07 39 |
| 45 | 06 16 | 06 52 | 07 23 | 03 56 | 05 13 | 06 20 | 07 15 |
| N 40 | 06 10 | 06 42 | 07 11 | 03 38 | 04 51 | 05 59 | 06 56 |
| 35 | 06 04 | 06 34 | 07 01 | 03 22 | 04 34 | 05 41 | 06 39 |
| 30 | 05 58 | 06 27 | 06 52 | 03 09 | 04 19 | 05 25 | 06 25 |
| 20 | 05 47 | 06 13 | 06 36 | 02 47 | 03 53 | 04 59 | 06 01 |
| N 10 | 05 35 | 06 01 | 06 23 | 02 27 | 03 31 | 04 37 | 05 40 |
| 0 | 05 23 | 05 48 | 06 10 | 02 09 | 03 11 | 04 16 | 05 20 |
| S 10 | 05 08 | 05 34 | 05 56 | 01 51 | 02 51 | 03 55 | 05 01 |
| 20 | 04 51 | 05 19 | 05 42 | 01 32 | 02 29 | 03 32 | 04 40 |
| 30 | 04 29 | 05 00 | 05 26 | 01 10 | 02 04 | 03 07 | 04 15 |
| 35 | 04 15 | 04 48 | 05 16 | 00 57 | 01 49 | 02 51 | 04 01 |
| 40 | 03 58 | 04 35 | 05 05 | 00 43 | 01 32 | 02 33 | 03 44 |
| 45 | 03 36 | 04 18 | 04 52 | 00 25 | 01 12 | 02 12 | 03 24 |
| S 50 | 03 07 | 03 58 | 04 36 | 00 04 | 00 47 | 01 45 | 02 59 |
| 52 | 02 52 | 03 47 | 04 29 | 24 35 | 00 35 | 01 32 | 02 47 |
| 54 | 02 33 | 03 36 | 04 20 | 24 21 | 00 21 | 01 17 | 02 33 |
| 56 | 02 10 | 03 23 | 04 11 | 24 04 | 00 04 | 00 59 | 02 17 |
| 58 | 01 38 | 03 07 | 04 00 | 23 45 | 24 38 | 00 38 | 01 57 |
| S 60 | 00 19 | 02 47 | 03 48 | 23 21 | 24 11 | 00 11 | 01 33 |

## Sunset / Twilight / Moonset

| Lat. | Sunset | Civil | Naut. | Moonset 28 | 29 | 30 | 31 |
|---|---|---|---|---|---|---|---|
| N 72 | 13 32 | 15 36 | 17 08 | ████ | ████ | ████ | ████ |
| N 70 | 14 25 | 15 56 | 17 17 | ████ | ████ | ████ | ████ |
| 68 | 14 57 | 16 13 | 17 24 | ████ | ████ | ████ | ████ |
| 66 | 15 20 | 16 26 | 17 31 | ████ | ████ | ████ | ████ |
| 64 | 15 39 | 16 37 | 17 36 | 09 56 | ████ | ████ | 13 10 |
| 62 | 15 54 | 16 46 | 17 41 | 10 35 | 10 57 | 12 02 | 13 51 |
| 60 | 16 06 | 16 54 | 17 46 | 11 02 | 11 30 | 12 42 | 14 19 |
| N 58 | 16 17 | 17 02 | 17 50 | 11 24 | 12 04 | 13 10 | 14 40 |
| 56 | 16 26 | 17 08 | 17 54 | 11 41 | 12 25 | 13 31 | 14 58 |
| 54 | 16 35 | 17 14 | 17 57 | 11 56 | 12 43 | 13 49 | 15 13 |
| 52 | 16 42 | 17 19 | 18 00 | 12 09 | 12 58 | 14 04 | 15 26 |
| 50 | 16 49 | 17 24 | 18 03 | 12 21 | 13 11 | 14 17 | 15 37 |
| 45 | 17 03 | 17 35 | 18 10 | 12 45 | 13 38 | 14 44 | 16 01 |
| N 40 | 17 15 | 17 44 | 18 17 | 13 04 | 13 59 | 15 06 | 16 20 |
| 35 | 17 26 | 17 52 | 18 23 | 13 20 | 14 17 | 15 23 | 16 35 |
| 30 | 17 35 | 18 00 | 18 28 | 13 34 | 14 32 | 15 38 | 16 49 |
| 20 | 17 50 | 18 13 | 18 40 | 13 58 | 14 58 | 16 04 | 17 12 |
| N 10 | 18 04 | 18 26 | 18 51 | 14 19 | 15 21 | 16 26 | 17 31 |
| 0 | 18 17 | 18 38 | 19 04 | 14 38 | 15 42 | 16 47 | 17 50 |
| S 10 | 18 30 | 18 52 | 19 18 | 14 57 | 16 03 | 17 07 | 18 08 |
| 20 | 18 44 | 19 07 | 19 35 | 15 18 | 16 25 | 17 29 | 18 28 |
| 30 | 19 00 | 19 26 | 19 57 | 15 42 | 16 51 | 17 54 | 18 50 |
| 35 | 19 09 | 19 37 | 20 11 | 15 56 | 17 06 | 18 09 | 19 03 |
| 40 | 19 20 | 19 51 | 20 28 | 16 13 | 17 24 | 18 26 | 19 18 |
| 45 | 19 33 | 20 07 | 20 49 | 16 33 | 17 45 | 18 47 | 19 35 |
| S 50 | 19 49 | 20 27 | 21 18 | 16 57 | 18 12 | 19 12 | 19 57 |
| 52 | 19 56 | 20 37 | 21 34 | 17 09 | 18 25 | 19 25 | 20 08 |
| 54 | 20 05 | 20 49 | 21 50 | 17 23 | 18 40 | 19 39 | 20 19 |
| 56 | 20 14 | 21 02 | 22 13 | 17 39 | 18 58 | 19 55 | 20 33 |
| 58 | 20 24 | 21 17 | 22 43 | 17 58 | 19 19 | 20 15 | 20 48 |
| S 60 | 20 36 | 21 37 | 00 08 | 18 21 | 19 46 | 20 39 | 21 06 |

## SUN / MOON

| Day | Eqn. of Time 00h | 12h | Mer. Pass. | Mer. Pass. Upper | Lower | Age | Phase |
|---|---|---|---|---|---|---|---|
| d | m s | m s | h m | h m | h m | d | % |
| 28 | 12 48 | 12 54 | 12 13 | 08 23 | 20 54 | 26 | 19 |
| 29 | 12 59 | 13 05 | 12 13 | 09 26 | 21 59 | 27 | 11 |
| 30 | 13 10 | 13 15 | 12 13 | 10 31 | 23 04 | 28 | 4 |

| UT | ARIES GHA | VENUS −4·9 GHA | VENUS Dec | MARS +1·4 GHA | MARS Dec | JUPITER −2·1 GHA | JUPITER Dec | SATURN +0·6 GHA | SATURN Dec | STARS Name | SHA | Dec |
|---|---|---|---|---|---|---|---|---|---|---|---|---|
| **31 00** | 130 11.8 | 208 40.5 | S16 13.4 | 215 03.3 | S23 49.9 | 151 07.6 | S 9 51.1 | 172 06.5 | S17 02.2 | Acamar | 315 13.6 | S40 13.3 |
| 01 | 145 14.2 | 223 42.8 | 13.5 | 230 03.8 | 49.9 | 166 09.5 | 50.9 | 187 08.7 | 02.1 | Achernar | 335 22.2 | S57 07.9 |
| 02 | 160 16.7 | 238 45.0 | 13.5 | 245 04.3 | 49.9 | 181 11.4 | 50.6 | 202 10.8 | 02.0 | Acrux | 173 02.3 | S63 13.0 |
| 03 | 175 19.2 | 253 47.3 | .. 13.6 | 260 04.7 | .. 49.8 | 196 13.3 | .. 50.4 | 217 13.0 | .. 01.9 | Adhara | 255 07.4 | S29 00.3 |
| 04 | 190 21.6 | 268 49.6 | 13.7 | 275 05.2 | 49.8 | 211 15.3 | 50.2 | 232 15.2 | 01.8 | Aldebaran | 290 42.2 | N16 33.2 |
| 05 | 205 24.1 | 283 51.9 | 13.7 | 290 05.7 | 49.8 | 226 17.2 | 50.0 | 247 17.3 | 01.7 | | | |
| **M 06** | 220 26.6 | 298 54.1 | S16 13.8 | 305 06.2 | S23 49.7 | 241 19.1 | S 9 49.8 | 262 19.5 | S17 01.6 | Alioth | 166 14.9 | N55 50.2 |
| 07 | 235 29.0 | 313 56.4 | 13.9 | 320 06.6 | 49.7 | 256 21.0 | 49.6 | 277 21.7 | 01.5 | Alkaid | 152 53.8 | N49 11.9 |
| O 08 | 250 31.5 | 328 58.6 | 13.9 | 335 07.1 | 49.6 | 271 22.9 | 49.4 | 292 23.8 | 01.5 | Alnair | 27 36.4 | S46 51.5 |
| N 09 | 265 33.9 | 344 00.9 | .. 14.0 | 350 07.6 | .. 49.6 | 286 24.9 | .. 49.1 | 307 26.0 | .. 01.4 | Alnilam | 275 39.9 | S 1 11.4 |
| D 10 | 280 36.4 | 359 03.2 | 14.1 | 5 08.0 | 49.6 | 301 26.8 | 48.9 | 322 28.1 | 01.3 | Alphard | 217 49.8 | S 8 45.3 |
| A 11 | 295 38.9 | 14 05.4 | 14.1 | 20 08.5 | 49.5 | 316 28.7 | 48.7 | 337 30.3 | 01.2 | | | |
| Y 12 | 310 41.3 | 29 07.6 | S16 14.2 | 35 09.0 | S23 49.5 | 331 30.6 | S 9 48.5 | 352 32.5 | S17 01.1 | Alphecca | 126 05.9 | N26 38.2 |
| 13 | 325 43.8 | 44 09.9 | 14.2 | 50 09.4 | 49.4 | 346 32.6 | 48.3 | 7 34.6 | 01.0 | Alpheratz | 357 37.5 | N29 12.7 |
| 14 | 340 46.3 | 59 12.1 | 14.3 | 65 09.9 | 49.4 | 1 34.5 | 48.1 | 22 36.8 | 00.9 | Altair | 62 02.6 | N 8 55.5 |
| 15 | 355 48.7 | 74 14.3 | .. 14.4 | 80 10.4 | .. 49.4 | 16 36.4 | .. 47.9 | 37 39.0 | .. 00.9 | Ankaa | 353 09.8 | S42 11.5 |
| 16 | 10 51.2 | 89 16.6 | 14.4 | 95 10.9 | 49.3 | 31 38.3 | 47.6 | 52 41.1 | 00.8 | Antares | 112 18.9 | S26 28.7 |
| 17 | 25 53.7 | 104 18.8 | 14.5 | 110 11.3 | 49.3 | 46 40.3 | 47.4 | 67 43.3 | 00.7 | | | |
| 18 | 40 56.1 | 119 21.0 | S16 14.6 | 125 11.8 | S23 49.2 | 61 42.2 | S 9 47.2 | 82 45.5 | S17 00.6 | Arcturus | 145 50.1 | N19 03.9 |
| 19 | 55 58.6 | 134 23.2 | 14.7 | 140 12.3 | 49.2 | 76 44.1 | 47.0 | 97 47.6 | 00.5 | Atria | 107 15.6 | S69 03.7 |
| 20 | 71 01.1 | 149 25.4 | 14.7 | 155 12.7 | 49.2 | 91 46.0 | 46.8 | 112 49.8 | 00.4 | Avior | 234 15.0 | S59 34.8 |
| 21 | 86 03.5 | 164 27.6 | .. 14.8 | 170 13.2 | .. 49.1 | 106 47.9 | .. 46.6 | 127 51.9 | .. 00.3 | Bellatrix | 278 25.2 | N 6 22.1 |
| 22 | 101 06.0 | 179 29.8 | 14.9 | 185 13.7 | 49.1 | 121 49.9 | 46.3 | 142 54.1 | 00.3 | Betelgeuse | 270 54.4 | N 7 24.6 |
| 23 | 116 08.4 | 194 32.0 | 14.9 | 200 14.2 | 49.0 | 136 51.8 | 46.1 | 157 56.3 | 00.2 | | | |
| **1 00** | 131 10.9 | 209 34.2 | S16 15.0 | 215 14.6 | S23 49.0 | 151 53.7 | S 9 45.9 | 172 58.4 | S17 00.1 | Canopus | 263 53.0 | S52 42.6 |
| 01 | 146 13.4 | 224 36.4 | 15.1 | 230 15.1 | 48.9 | 166 55.6 | 45.7 | 188 00.6 | 17 00.0 | Capella | 280 25.1 | N46 01.3 |
| 02 | 161 15.8 | 239 38.6 | 15.1 | 245 15.6 | 48.9 | 181 57.5 | 45.5 | 203 02.8 | 16 59.9 | Deneb | 49 27.9 | N45 21.4 |
| 03 | 176 18.3 | 254 40.7 | .. 15.2 | 260 16.0 | .. 48.8 | 196 59.5 | .. 45.3 | 218 04.9 | .. 59.8 | Denebola | 182 27.2 | N14 26.8 |
| 04 | 191 20.8 | 269 42.9 | 15.3 | 275 16.5 | 48.8 | 212 01.4 | 45.1 | 233 07.1 | 59.7 | Diphda | 348 49.9 | S17 52.2 |
| 05 | 206 23.2 | 284 45.1 | 15.4 | 290 17.0 | 48.7 | 227 03.3 | 44.8 | 248 09.3 | 59.6 | | | |
| **T 06** | 221 25.7 | 299 47.3 | S16 15.4 | 305 17.4 | S23 48.7 | 242 05.2 | S 9 44.6 | 263 11.4 | S16 59.6 | Dubhe | 193 43.4 | N61 37.8 |
| U 07 | 236 28.2 | 314 49.4 | 15.5 | 320 17.9 | 48.7 | 257 07.2 | 44.4 | 278 13.6 | 59.5 | Elnath | 278 04.6 | N28 37.5 |
| E 08 | 251 30.6 | 329 51.6 | 15.6 | 335 18.4 | 48.6 | 272 09.1 | 44.2 | 293 15.8 | 59.4 | Eltanin | 90 43.7 | N51 28.9 |
| S 09 | 266 33.1 | 344 53.7 | .. 15.7 | 350 18.9 | .. 48.6 | 287 11.0 | .. 44.0 | 308 17.9 | .. 59.3 | Enif | 33 41.5 | N 9 58.4 |
| D 10 | 281 35.6 | 359 55.9 | 15.7 | 5 19.3 | 48.5 | 302 12.9 | 43.8 | 323 20.1 | 59.2 | Fomalhaut | 15 17.5 | S29 30.6 |
| A 11 | 296 38.0 | 14 58.0 | 15.8 | 20 19.8 | 48.5 | 317 14.8 | 43.5 | 338 22.2 | 59.1 | | | |
| Y 12 | 311 40.5 | 30 00.2 | S16 15.9 | 35 20.3 | S23 48.4 | 332 16.8 | S 9 43.3 | 353 24.4 | S16 59.0 | Gacrux | 171 53.9 | S57 13.9 |
| 13 | 326 42.9 | 45 02.3 | 16.0 | 50 20.7 | 48.4 | 347 18.7 | 43.1 | 8 26.6 | 59.0 | Gienah | 175 45.8 | S17 39.8 |
| 14 | 341 45.4 | 60 04.4 | 16.0 | 65 21.2 | 48.3 | 2 20.6 | 42.9 | 23 28.7 | 58.9 | Hadar | 148 39.3 | S60 28.4 |
| 15 | 356 47.9 | 75 06.5 | .. 16.1 | 80 21.7 | .. 48.3 | 17 22.5 | .. 42.7 | 38 30.9 | .. 58.8 | Hamal | 327 53.9 | N23 34.0 |
| 16 | 11 50.3 | 90 08.7 | 16.2 | 95 22.1 | 48.2 | 32 24.4 | 42.5 | 53 33.1 | 58.7 | Kaus Aust. | 83 36.0 | S34 22.4 |
| 17 | 26 52.8 | 105 10.8 | 16.3 | 110 22.6 | 48.2 | 47 26.4 | 42.3 | 68 35.2 | 58.6 | | | |
| 18 | 41 55.3 | 120 12.9 | S16 16.3 | 125 23.1 | S23 48.1 | 62 28.3 | S 9 42.0 | 83 37.4 | S16 58.5 | Kochab | 137 19.9 | N74 03.6 |
| 19 | 56 57.7 | 135 15.0 | 16.4 | 140 23.5 | 48.0 | 77 30.2 | 41.8 | 98 39.6 | 58.4 | Markab | 13 32.5 | N15 19.3 |
| 20 | 72 00.2 | 150 17.1 | 16.5 | 155 24.0 | 48.0 | 92 32.1 | 41.6 | 113 41.7 | 58.4 | Menkar | 314 08.6 | N 4 10.4 |
| 21 | 87 02.7 | 165 19.2 | .. 16.6 | 170 24.5 | .. 47.9 | 107 34.1 | .. 41.4 | 128 43.9 | .. 58.3 | Menkent | 148 00.4 | S36 28.5 |
| 22 | 102 05.1 | 180 21.3 | 16.6 | 185 25.0 | 47.9 | 122 36.0 | 41.2 | 143 46.1 | 58.2 | Miaplacidus | 221 37.7 | S69 48.4 |
| 23 | 117 07.6 | 195 23.4 | 16.7 | 200 25.4 | 47.8 | 137 37.9 | 41.0 | 158 48.2 | 58.1 | | | |
| **2 00** | 132 10.1 | 210 25.5 | S16 16.8 | 215 25.9 | S23 47.8 | 152 39.8 | S 9 40.7 | 173 50.4 | S16 58.0 | Mirfak | 308 31.6 | N49 56.5 |
| 01 | 147 12.5 | 225 27.6 | 16.9 | 230 26.4 | 47.7 | 167 41.7 | 40.5 | 188 52.5 | 57.9 | Nunki | 75 51.1 | S26 16.2 |
| 02 | 162 15.0 | 240 29.7 | 17.0 | 245 26.8 | 47.7 | 182 43.7 | 40.3 | 203 54.7 | 57.8 | Peacock | 53 10.1 | S56 39.9 |
| 03 | 177 17.4 | 255 31.8 | .. 17.0 | 260 27.3 | .. 47.6 | 197 45.6 | .. 40.1 | 218 56.9 | .. 57.7 | Pollux | 243 19.9 | N27 58.3 |
| 04 | 192 19.9 | 270 33.8 | 17.1 | 275 27.8 | 47.6 | 212 47.5 | 39.9 | 233 59.0 | 57.7 | Procyon | 244 53.0 | N 5 10.0 |
| 05 | 207 22.4 | 285 35.9 | 17.2 | 290 28.2 | 47.5 | 227 49.4 | 39.7 | 249 01.2 | 57.6 | | | |
| **W 06** | 222 24.8 | 300 38.0 | S16 17.3 | 305 28.7 | S23 47.4 | 242 51.3 | S 9 39.4 | 264 03.4 | S16 57.5 | Rasalhague | 96 01.0 | N12 32.5 |
| E 07 | 237 27.3 | 315 40.0 | 17.4 | 320 29.2 | 47.4 | 257 53.3 | 39.2 | 279 05.5 | 57.4 | Regulus | 207 36.7 | N11 51.5 |
| D 08 | 252 29.8 | 330 42.1 | 17.5 | 335 29.6 | 47.3 | 272 55.2 | 39.0 | 294 07.7 | 57.3 | Rigel | 281 06.0 | S 8 10.7 |
| N 09 | 267 32.2 | 345 44.1 | .. 17.5 | 350 30.1 | .. 47.3 | 287 57.1 | .. 38.8 | 309 09.9 | .. 57.2 | Rigil Kent. | 139 43.5 | S60 55.2 |
| E 10 | 282 34.7 | 0 46.2 | 17.6 | 5 30.6 | 47.2 | 302 59.0 | 38.6 | 324 12.0 | 57.1 | Sabik | 102 05.7 | S15 45.1 |
| S 11 | 297 37.2 | 15 48.2 | 17.7 | 20 31.0 | 47.1 | 318 00.9 | 38.4 | 339 14.2 | 57.1 | | | |
| D 12 | 312 39.6 | 30 50.3 | S16 17.8 | 35 31.5 | S23 47.1 | 333 02.9 | S 9 38.1 | 354 16.3 | S16 57.0 | Schedar | 349 34.0 | N56 39.6 |
| A 13 | 327 42.1 | 45 52.3 | 17.9 | 50 32.0 | 47.0 | 348 04.8 | 37.9 | 9 18.5 | 56.9 | Shaula | 96 13.9 | S37 07.1 |
| Y 14 | 342 44.5 | 60 54.4 | 18.0 | 65 32.5 | 47.0 | 3 06.7 | 37.7 | 24 20.7 | 56.8 | Sirius | 258 28.0 | S16 44.9 |
| 15 | 357 47.0 | 75 56.4 | .. 18.0 | 80 32.9 | .. 46.9 | 18 08.6 | .. 37.5 | 39 22.8 | .. 56.7 | Spica | 158 24.7 | S11 16.5 |
| 16 | 12 49.5 | 90 58.4 | 18.1 | 95 33.4 | 46.8 | 33 10.5 | 37.3 | 54 25.0 | 56.6 | Suhail | 222 47.6 | S43 31.3 |
| 17 | 27 51.9 | 106 00.4 | 18.2 | 110 33.9 | 46.8 | 48 12.4 | 37.1 | 69 27.2 | 56.5 | | | |
| 18 | 42 54.4 | 121 02.4 | S16 18.3 | 125 34.3 | S23 46.7 | 63 14.4 | S 9 36.9 | 84 29.3 | S16 56.4 | Vega | 80 35.2 | N38 48.0 |
| 19 | 57 56.9 | 136 04.5 | 18.4 | 140 34.8 | 46.7 | 78 16.3 | 36.6 | 99 31.5 | 56.4 | Zuben'ubi | 136 58.7 | S16 07.9 |
| 20 | 72 59.3 | 151 06.5 | 18.5 | 155 35.3 | 46.6 | 93 18.2 | 36.4 | 114 33.7 | 56.3 | | SHA | Mer. Pass. |
| 21 | 88 01.8 | 166 08.5 | .. 18.5 | 170 35.7 | .. 46.5 | 108 20.1 | .. 36.2 | 129 35.8 | .. 56.2 | | ° ' | h m |
| 22 | 103 04.3 | 181 10.5 | 18.6 | 185 36.2 | 46.5 | 123 22.0 | 36.0 | 144 38.0 | 56.1 | Venus | 78 23.3 | 10 00 |
| 23 | 118 06.7 | 196 12.5 | 18.7 | 200 36.7 | 46.4 | 138 24.0 | 35.8 | 159 40.2 | 56.0 | Mars | 84 03.7 | 9 39 |
| | h m | | | | | | | | | Jupiter | 20 42.8 | 13 51 |
| Mer. Pass. 15 12.8 | | v 2.1 | d 0.1 | v 0.5 | d 0.0 | v 1.9 | d 0.2 | v 2.2 | d 0.1 | Saturn | 41 47.5 | 12 26 |

| UT | SUN | | MOON | | | | Lat. | Twilight | | Sunrise | Moonrise | | | |
|---|---|---|---|---|---|---|---|---|---|---|---|---|---|---|
| | | | | | | | | Naut. | Civil | | 31 | 1 | 2 | 3 |
| | GHA | Dec | GHA | v | Dec | d | HP | | | | | | | |
| d h | ° ′ | ° ′ | ° ′ | ′ | ° ′ | ′ | ′ | ° | h m | h m | h m | h m | h m | h m | h m |
| 31 00 | 176 40.1 | S17 27.0 | 193 31.1 | 2.8 | S25 22.3 | 4.9 | 60.5 | N 72 | 07 10 | 08 38 | 10 27 | ▬ | ▬ | 11 40 | 10 40 |
| 01 | 191 40.0 | 26.3 | 207 52.9 | 2.9 | 25 17.4 | 5.0 | 60.5 | N 70 | 07 02 | 08 20 | 09 45 | ▬ | ▬ | 10 59 | 10 23 |
| 02 | 206 39.9 | 25.6 | 222 14.8 | 3.0 | 25 12.4 | 5.3 | 60.5 | 68 | 06 55 | 08 05 | 09 17 | ▬ | 11 18 | 10 32 | 10 09 |
| 03 | 221 39.8 .. | 24.9 | 236 36.8 | 3.0 | 25 07.1 | 5.4 | 60.4 | 66 | 06 49 | 07 53 | 08 56 | | 10 31 | 10 10 | 09 57 |
| 04 | 236 39.7 | 24.2 | 250 58.8 | 3.1 | 25 01.7 | 5.6 | 60.4 | 64 | 06 44 | 07 43 | 08 39 | 10 10 | 10 00 | 09 53 | 09 48 |
| 05 | 251 39.6 | 23.5 | 265 20.9 | 3.1 | 24 56.1 | 5.8 | 60.4 | 62 | 06 40 | 07 34 | 08 26 | 09 28 | 09 36 | 09 39 | 09 39 |
| 06 | 266 39.5 | S17 22.8 | 279 43.0 | 3.3 | S24 50.3 | 6.0 | 60.4 | 60 | 06 36 | 07 27 | 08 14 | 09 00 | 09 18 | 09 27 | 09 32 |
| 07 | 281 39.4 | 22.1 | 294 05.3 | 3.3 | 24 44.3 | 6.2 | 60.4 | N 58 | 06 32 | 07 20 | 08 04 | 08 38 | 09 02 | 09 16 | 09 26 |
| 08 | 296 39.3 | 21.4 | 308 27.6 | 3.4 | 24 38.1 | 6.3 | 60.4 | 56 | 06 29 | 07 14 | 07 55 | 08 20 | 08 49 | 09 07 | 09 20 |
| M 09 | 311 39.2 .. | 20.7 | 322 50.0 | 3.5 | 24 31.8 | 6.5 | 60.4 | 54 | 06 26 | 07 08 | 07 47 | 08 04 | 08 37 | 08 59 | 09 15 |
| O 10 | 326 39.1 | 20.0 | 337 12.5 | 3.5 | 24 25.3 | 6.7 | 60.4 | 52 | 06 23 | 07 03 | 07 40 | 07 51 | 08 27 | 08 52 | 09 10 |
| N 11 | 341 39.0 | 19.3 | 351 35.0 | 3.7 | 24 18.6 | 6.8 | 60.4 | 50 | 06 20 | 06 59 | 07 34 | 07 39 | 08 17 | 08 45 | 09 06 |
| D 12 | 356 38.9 | S17 18.6 | 5 57.7 | 3.7 | S24 11.8 | 7.0 | 60.3 | 45 | 06 13 | 06 49 | 07 20 | 07 15 | 07 58 | 08 31 | 08 57 |
| A 13 | 11 38.9 | 17.9 | 20 20.4 | 3.8 | 24 04.8 | 7.2 | 60.3 | N 40 | 06 08 | 06 40 | 07 09 | 06 56 | 07 42 | 08 19 | 08 49 |
| Y 14 | 26 38.8 | 17.2 | 34 43.2 | 4.0 | 23 57.6 | 7.4 | 60.3 | 35 | 06 02 | 06 32 | 06 59 | 06 39 | 07 28 | 08 09 | 08 43 |
| 15 | 41 38.7 .. | 16.5 | 49 06.2 | 4.0 | 23 50.2 | 7.5 | 60.3 | 30 | 05 57 | 06 25 | 06 50 | 06 25 | 07 16 | 08 00 | 08 37 |
| 16 | 56 38.6 | 15.8 | 63 29.2 | 4.1 | 23 42.7 | 7.7 | 60.3 | 20 | 05 46 | 06 12 | 06 35 | 06 01 | 06 56 | 07 44 | 08 27 |
| 17 | 71 38.5 | 15.1 | 77 52.3 | 4.2 | 23 35.0 | 7.8 | 60.3 | N 10 | 05 35 | 06 00 | 06 22 | 05 40 | 06 38 | 07 31 | 08 18 |
| 18 | 86 38.4 | S17 14.3 | 92 15.5 | 4.3 | S23 27.2 | 8.0 | 60.3 | 0 | 05 23 | 05 48 | 06 10 | 05 20 | 06 21 | 07 18 | 08 10 |
| 19 | 101 38.3 | 13.6 | 106 38.8 | 4.4 | 23 19.2 | 8.2 | 60.2 | S 10 | 05 10 | 05 35 | 05 58 | 05 01 | 06 05 | 07 05 | 08 01 |
| 20 | 116 38.2 | 12.9 | 121 02.2 | 4.5 | 23 11.0 | 8.3 | 60.2 | 20 | 04 53 | 05 21 | 05 44 | 04 40 | 05 47 | 06 51 | 07 52 |
| 21 | 131 38.1 .. | 12.2 | 135 25.7 | 4.6 | 23 02.7 | 8.5 | 60.2 | 30 | 04 32 | 05 03 | 05 28 | 04 15 | 05 26 | 06 36 | 07 42 |
| 22 | 146 38.0 | 11.5 | 149 49.3 | 4.7 | 22 54.2 | 8.6 | 60.2 | 35 | 04 18 | 04 52 | 05 19 | 04 01 | 05 14 | 06 26 | 07 36 |
| 23 | 161 38.0 | 10.8 | 164 13.0 | 4.8 | 22 45.6 | 8.8 | 60.2 | 40 | 04 02 | 04 39 | 05 09 | 03 44 | 05 00 | 06 16 | 07 29 |
| | | | | | | | | 45 | 03 41 | 04 23 | 04 57 | 03 24 | 04 43 | 06 03 | 07 21 |
| 1 00 | 176 37.9 | S17 10.1 | 178 36.8 | 4.9 | S22 36.8 | 8.9 | 60.2 | S 50 | 03 14 | 04 04 | 04 42 | 02 59 | 04 22 | 05 48 | 07 11 |
| 01 | 191 37.8 | 09.4 | 193 00.7 | 5.1 | 22 27.9 | 9.1 | 60.1 | 52 | 03 00 | 03 54 | 04 34 | 02 47 | 04 13 | 05 41 | 07 07 |
| 02 | 206 37.7 | 08.7 | 207 24.8 | 5.1 | 22 18.8 | 9.2 | 60.1 | 54 | 02 43 | 03 43 | 04 27 | 02 33 | 04 01 | 05 33 | 07 02 |
| 03 | 221 37.6 .. | 08.0 | 221 48.9 | 5.2 | 22 09.6 | 9.3 | 60.1 | 56 | 02 22 | 03 31 | 04 18 | 02 17 | 03 49 | 05 24 | 06 56 |
| 04 | 236 37.5 | 07.3 | 236 13.1 | 5.4 | 22 00.3 | 9.5 | 60.1 | 58 | 01 55 | 03 16 | 04 08 | 01 57 | 03 34 | 05 14 | 06 50 |
| 05 | 251 37.4 | 06.6 | 250 37.5 | 5.5 | 21 50.8 | 9.7 | 60.1 | S 60 | 01 10 | 02 58 | 03 56 | 01 33 | 03 16 | 05 02 | 06 43 |
| 06 | 266 37.4 | S17 05.8 | 265 02.0 | 5.5 | S21 41.1 | 9.8 | 60.0 | | | | | | | | |
| 07 | 281 37.3 | 05.1 | 279 26.5 | 5.7 | 21 31.3 | 9.9 | 60.0 | Lat. | Sunset | Twilight | | Moonset | | | |
| 08 | 296 37.2 | 04.4 | 293 51.2 | 5.8 | 21 21.4 | 10.0 | 60.0 | | | Civil | Naut. | 31 | 1 | 2 | 3 |
| T 09 | 311 37.1 .. | 03.7 | 308 16.0 | 5.9 | 21 11.4 | 10.2 | 60.0 | | | | | | | | |
| U 10 | 326 37.0 | 03.0 | 322 40.9 | 6.1 | 21 01.2 | 10.3 | 60.0 | ° | h m | h m | h m | h m | h m | h m | h m |
| E 11 | 341 36.9 | 02.3 | 337 06.0 | 6.1 | 20 50.9 | 10.4 | 59.9 | N 72 | 14 01 | 15 50 | 17 19 | ▬ | ▬ | 15 46 | 18 32 |
| S 12 | 356 36.8 | S17 01.6 | 351 31.1 | 6.3 | S20 40.5 | 10.6 | 59.9 | N 70 | 14 43 | 16 08 | 17 27 | ▬ | ▬ | 16 25 | 18 47 |
| D 13 | 11 36.8 | 00.9 | 5 56.4 | 6.3 | 20 29.9 | 10.7 | 59.9 | 68 | 15 11 | 16 23 | 17 33 | ▬ | 14 09 | 16 51 | 18 58 |
| A 14 | 26 36.7 | 17 00.1 | 20 21.7 | 6.5 | 20 19.2 | 10.8 | 59.9 | 66 | 15 32 | 16 35 | 17 39 | ▬ | 14 56 | 17 11 | 19 08 |
| Y 15 | 41 36.6 | 16 59.4 | 34 47.2 | 6.6 | 20 08.4 | 10.9 | 59.8 | 64 | 15 49 | 16 45 | 17 44 | 13 10 | 15 26 | 17 26 | 19 16 |
| 16 | 56 36.5 | 58.7 | 49 12.8 | 6.8 | 19 57.5 | 11.1 | 59.8 | 62 | 16 02 | 16 54 | 17 48 | 13 51 | 15 48 | 17 39 | 19 23 |
| 17 | 71 36.4 | 58.0 | 63 38.6 | 6.8 | 19 46.4 | 11.1 | 59.8 | 60 | 16 14 | 17 01 | 17 52 | 14 19 | 16 06 | 17 50 | 19 29 |
| 18 | 86 36.4 | S16 57.3 | 78 04.4 | 7.0 | S19 35.3 | 11.3 | 59.8 | N 58 | 16 24 | 17 08 | 17 56 | 14 40 | 16 21 | 18 00 | 19 34 |
| 19 | 101 36.3 | 56.6 | 92 30.4 | 7.0 | 19 24.0 | 11.4 | 59.7 | 56 | 16 33 | 17 14 | 17 59 | 14 58 | 16 33 | 18 08 | 19 38 |
| 20 | 116 36.2 | 55.8 | 106 56.4 | 7.2 | 19 12.6 | 11.5 | 59.7 | 54 | 16 41 | 17 19 | 18 02 | 15 13 | 16 45 | 18 16 | 19 42 |
| 21 | 131 36.1 .. | 55.1 | 121 22.6 | 7.3 | 19 01.1 | 11.6 | 59.7 | 52 | 16 48 | 17 24 | 18 05 | 15 26 | 16 54 | 18 22 | 19 46 |
| 22 | 146 36.0 | 54.4 | 135 48.9 | 7.4 | 18 49.5 | 11.7 | 59.7 | 50 | 16 54 | 17 29 | 18 08 | 15 37 | 17 03 | 18 28 | 19 49 |
| 23 | 161 36.0 | 53.7 | 150 15.3 | 7.6 | 18 37.8 | 11.8 | 59.6 | 45 | 17 08 | 17 39 | 18 14 | 16 01 | 17 21 | 18 41 | 19 57 |
| 2 00 | 176 35.9 | S16 53.0 | 164 41.9 | 7.6 | S18 26.0 | 11.9 | 59.6 | N 40 | 17 19 | 17 48 | 18 20 | 16 20 | 17 36 | 18 51 | 20 03 |
| 01 | 191 35.8 | 52.2 | 179 08.5 | 7.8 | 18 14.1 | 12.0 | 59.6 | 35 | 17 29 | 17 55 | 18 25 | 16 35 | 17 49 | 19 00 | 20 08 |
| 02 | 206 35.7 | 51.5 | 193 35.3 | 7.9 | 18 02.1 | 12.1 | 59.6 | 30 | 17 37 | 18 02 | 18 31 | 16 49 | 17 59 | 19 08 | 20 12 |
| 03 | 221 35.6 .. | 50.8 | 208 02.2 | 8.0 | 17 50.0 | 12.2 | 59.5 | 20 | 17 52 | 18 15 | 18 41 | 17 12 | 18 18 | 19 21 | 20 20 |
| 04 | 236 35.6 | 50.1 | 222 29.2 | 8.1 | 17 37.8 | 12.3 | 59.5 | N 10 | 18 05 | 18 27 | 18 52 | 17 31 | 18 34 | 19 32 | 20 26 |
| 05 | 251 35.5 | 49.3 | 236 56.3 | 8.2 | 17 25.5 | 12.4 | 59.5 | 0 | 18 17 | 18 39 | 19 04 | 17 50 | 18 49 | 19 43 | 20 33 |
| 06 | 266 35.4 | S16 48.6 | 251 23.5 | 8.4 | S17 13.1 | 12.5 | 59.4 | S 10 | 18 29 | 18 51 | 19 17 | 18 08 | 19 04 | 19 54 | 20 39 |
| W 07 | 281 35.3 | 47.9 | 265 50.9 | 8.4 | 17 00.6 | 12.6 | 59.4 | 20 | 18 43 | 19 06 | 19 34 | 18 28 | 19 19 | 20 05 | 20 45 |
| E 08 | 296 35.3 | 47.2 | 280 18.3 | 8.6 | 16 48.0 | 12.6 | 59.4 | 30 | 18 58 | 19 24 | 19 55 | 18 50 | 19 37 | 20 18 | 20 53 |
| D 09 | 311 35.2 .. | 46.4 | 294 45.9 | 8.7 | 16 35.4 | 12.8 | 59.4 | 35 | 19 07 | 19 35 | 20 08 | 19 03 | 19 48 | 20 25 | 20 57 |
| N 10 | 326 35.1 | 45.7 | 309 13.6 | 8.8 | 16 22.6 | 12.8 | 59.3 | 40 | 19 18 | 19 47 | 20 24 | 19 18 | 19 59 | 20 33 | 21 02 |
| E 11 | 341 35.0 | 45.0 | 323 41.4 | 8.9 | 16 09.8 | 12.9 | 59.3 | 45 | 19 30 | 20 03 | 20 44 | 19 35 | 20 13 | 20 43 | 21 07 |
| S 12 | 356 35.0 | S16 44.3 | 338 09.3 | 9.0 | S15 56.9 | 13.0 | 59.3 | S 50 | 19 45 | 20 22 | 21 11 | 19 57 | 20 30 | 20 54 | 21 14 |
| D 13 | 11 34.9 | 43.5 | 352 37.3 | 9.2 | 15 43.9 | 13.0 | 59.2 | 52 | 19 51 | 20 32 | 21 25 | 20 08 | 20 38 | 20 59 | 21 16 |
| A 14 | 26 34.8 | 42.8 | 7 05.5 | 9.2 | 15 30.9 | 13.2 | 59.2 | 54 | 19 59 | 20 42 | 21 42 | 20 19 | 20 46 | 21 05 | 21 20 |
| Y 15 | 41 34.7 .. | 42.1 | 21 33.7 | 9.4 | 15 17.7 | 13.2 | 59.2 | 56 | 20 08 | 20 55 | 22 02 | 20 33 | 20 56 | 21 12 | 21 23 |
| 16 | 56 34.7 | 41.4 | 36 02.1 | 9.4 | 15 04.5 | 13.2 | 59.1 | 58 | 20 18 | 21 09 | 22 28 | 20 48 | 21 07 | 21 19 | 21 27 |
| 17 | 71 34.6 | 40.6 | 50 30.5 | 9.6 | 14 51.3 | 13.4 | 59.1 | S 60 | 20 29 | 21 26 | 23 09 | 21 06 | 21 19 | 21 27 | 21 32 |
| 18 | 86 34.5 | S16 39.9 | 64 59.1 | 9.7 | S14 37.9 | 13.4 | 59.1 | | | SUN | | | MOON | | |
| 19 | 101 34.4 | 39.2 | 79 27.8 | 9.8 | 14 24.5 | 13.4 | 59.0 | Day | Eqn. of Time | | Mer. | Mer. Pass. | | Age | Phase |
| 20 | 116 34.4 | 38.4 | 93 56.6 | 9.9 | 14 11.1 | 13.6 | 59.0 | | 00ʰ | 12ʰ | Pass. | Upper | Lower | | |
| 21 | 131 34.3 .. | 37.7 | 108 25.5 | 10.0 | 13 57.5 | 13.6 | 59.0 | d | m s | m s | h m | h m | h m | d % | |
| 22 | 146 34.2 | 37.0 | 122 54.5 | 10.1 | 13 43.9 | 13.6 | 58.9 | 31 | 13 20 | 13 24 | 12 13 | 11 35 | 24 06 | 29 1 | ● |
| 23 | 161 34.2 | 36.2 | 137 23.6 | 10.2 | S13 30.3 | 13.7 | 58.9 | 1 | 13 28 | 13 32 | 12 14 | 12 35 | 00 06 | 00 0 | |
| | SD 16.3 | d 0.7 | SD 16.4 | | 16.3 | | 16.1 | 2 | 13 36 | 13 40 | 12 14 | 13 31 | 01 04 | 01 2 | |

| UT | ARIES GHA | VENUS −4.9 GHA | Dec | MARS +1.4 GHA | Dec | JUPITER −2.0 GHA | Dec | SATURN +0.5 GHA | Dec | STARS Name | SHA | Dec |
|---|---|---|---|---|---|---|---|---|---|---|---|---|
| **3** 00 | 133 09.2 | 211 14.5 | S16 18.8 | 215 37.1 | S23 46.3 | 153 25.9 | S 9 35.6 | 174 42.3 | S16 55.9 | Acamar | 315 13.6 | S40 13.3 |
| 01 | 148 11.7 | 226 16.5 | 18.9 | 230 37.6 | 46.3 | 168 27.8 | 35.3 | 189 44.5 | 55.8 | Achernar | 335 22.2 | S57 07.9 |
| 02 | 163 14.1 | 241 18.4 | 19.0 | 245 38.1 | 46.2 | 183 29.7 | 35.1 | 204 46.6 | 55.8 | Acrux | 173 02.2 | S63 13.0 |
| 03 | 178 16.6 | 256 20.4 .. | 19.1 | 260 38.5 .. | 46.1 | 198 31.6 .. | 34.9 | 219 48.8 .. | 55.7 | Adhara | 255 07.4 | S29 00.3 |
| 04 | 193 19.0 | 271 22.4 | 19.2 | 275 39.0 | 46.1 | 213 33.6 | 34.7 | 234 51.0 | 55.6 | Aldebaran | 290 42.2 | N16 33.2 |
| 05 | 208 21.5 | 286 24.4 | 19.2 | 290 39.5 | 46.0 | 228 35.5 | 34.5 | 249 53.1 | 55.5 | | | |
| T 06 | 223 24.0 | 301 26.3 | S16 19.3 | 305 40.0 | S23 45.9 | 243 37.4 | S 9 34.2 | 264 55.3 | S16 55.4 | Alioth | 166 14.8 | N55 50.2 |
| H 07 | 238 26.4 | 316 28.3 | 19.4 | 320 40.4 | 45.9 | 258 39.3 | 34.0 | 279 57.5 | 55.3 | Alkaid | 152 53.8 | N49 11.9 |
| U 08 | 253 28.9 | 331 30.3 | 19.5 | 335 40.9 | 45.8 | 273 41.2 | 33.8 | 294 59.6 | 55.2 | Alnair | 27 36.4 | S46 51.4 |
| R 09 | 268 31.4 | 346 32.2 .. | 19.6 | 350 41.4 .. | 45.7 | 288 43.2 .. | 33.6 | 310 01.8 .. | 55.2 | Alnilam | 275 39.9 | S 1 11.4 |
| S 10 | 283 33.8 | 1 34.2 | 19.7 | 5 41.8 | 45.7 | 303 45.1 | 33.4 | 325 04.0 | 55.1 | Alphard | 217 49.8 | S 8 45.3 |
| D 11 | 298 36.3 | 16 36.1 | 19.8 | 20 42.3 | 45.6 | 318 47.0 | 33.2 | 340 06.1 | 55.0 | | | |
| A 12 | 313 38.8 | 31 38.1 | S16 19.9 | 35 42.8 | S23 45.5 | 333 48.9 | S 9 32.9 | 355 08.3 | S16 54.9 | Alphecca | 126 05.8 | N26 38.2 |
| Y 13 | 328 41.2 | 46 40.0 | 20.0 | 50 43.2 | 45.5 | 348 50.8 | 32.7 | 10 10.4 | 54.8 | Alpheratz | 357 37.5 | N29 12.7 |
| 14 | 343 43.7 | 61 42.0 | 20.1 | 65 43.7 | 45.4 | 3 52.7 | 32.5 | 25 12.6 | 54.7 | Altair | 62 02.6 | N 8 55.5 |
| 15 | 358 46.2 | 76 43.9 .. | 20.1 | 80 44.2 .. | 45.3 | 18 54.7 .. | 32.3 | 40 14.8 .. | 54.6 | Ankaa | 353 09.8 | S42 11.5 |
| 16 | 13 48.6 | 91 45.8 | 20.2 | 95 44.6 | 45.2 | 33 56.6 | 32.1 | 55 16.9 | 54.5 | Antares | 112 18.9 | S26 28.7 |
| 17 | 28 51.1 | 106 47.8 | 20.3 | 110 45.1 | 45.2 | 48 58.5 | 31.9 | 70 19.1 | 54.5 | | | |
| 18 | 43 53.5 | 121 49.7 | S16 20.4 | 125 45.6 | S23 45.1 | 64 00.4 | S 9 31.6 | 85 21.3 | S16 54.4 | Arcturus | 145 50.1 | N19 03.9 |
| 19 | 58 56.0 | 136 51.6 | 20.5 | 140 46.0 | 45.0 | 79 02.3 | 31.4 | 100 23.4 | 54.3 | Atria | 107 15.6 | S69 03.7 |
| 20 | 73 58.5 | 151 53.5 | 20.6 | 155 46.5 | 45.0 | 94 04.2 | 31.2 | 115 25.6 | 54.2 | Avior | 234 15.0 | S59 34.8 |
| 21 | 89 00.9 | 166 55.4 .. | 20.7 | 170 47.0 .. | 44.9 | 109 06.2 .. | 31.0 | 130 27.8 .. | 54.1 | Bellatrix | 278 25.2 | N 6 22.1 |
| 22 | 104 03.4 | 181 57.3 | 20.8 | 185 47.4 | 44.8 | 124 08.1 | 30.8 | 145 29.9 | 54.0 | Betelgeuse | 270 54.4 | N 7 24.6 |
| 23 | 119 05.9 | 196 59.2 | 20.9 | 200 47.9 | 44.7 | 139 10.0 | 30.6 | 160 32.1 | 53.9 | | | |
| **4** 00 | 134 08.3 | 212 01.1 | S16 21.0 | 215 48.4 | S23 44.7 | 154 11.9 | S 9 30.3 | 175 34.3 | S16 53.9 | Canopus | 263 53.0 | S52 42.6 |
| 01 | 149 10.8 | 227 03.0 | 21.1 | 230 48.8 | 44.6 | 169 13.8 | 30.1 | 190 36.4 | 53.8 | Capella | 280 25.1 | N46 01.3 |
| 02 | 164 13.3 | 242 04.9 | 21.2 | 245 49.3 | 44.5 | 184 15.8 | 29.9 | 205 38.6 | 53.7 | Deneb | 49 27.9 | N45 21.4 |
| 03 | 179 15.7 | 257 06.8 .. | 21.3 | 260 49.8 .. | 44.4 | 199 17.7 .. | 29.7 | 220 40.7 .. | 53.6 | Denebola | 182 27.2 | N14 26.8 |
| 04 | 194 18.2 | 272 08.7 | 21.4 | 275 50.2 | 44.4 | 214 19.6 | 29.5 | 235 42.9 | 53.5 | Diphda | 348 49.9 | S17 52.2 |
| 05 | 209 20.6 | 287 10.6 | 21.4 | 290 50.7 | 44.3 | 229 21.5 | 29.2 | 250 45.1 | 53.4 | | | |
| 06 | 224 23.1 | 302 12.4 | S16 21.5 | 305 51.2 | S23 44.2 | 244 23.4 | S 9 29.0 | 265 47.2 | S16 53.3 | Dubhe | 193 43.4 | N61 37.8 |
| 07 | 239 25.6 | 317 14.3 | 21.6 | 320 51.6 | 44.1 | 259 25.3 | 28.8 | 280 49.4 | 53.2 | Elnath | 278 04.7 | N28 37.6 |
| 08 | 254 28.0 | 332 16.2 | 21.7 | 335 52.1 | 44.0 | 274 27.3 | 28.6 | 295 51.6 | 53.2 | Eltanin | 90 43.7 | N51 28.9 |
| F 09 | 269 30.5 | 347 18.0 .. | 21.8 | 350 52.6 .. | 44.0 | 289 29.2 .. | 28.4 | 310 53.7 .. | 53.1 | Enif | 33 41.5 | N 9 58.4 |
| R 10 | 284 33.0 | 2 19.9 | 21.9 | 5 53.1 | 43.9 | 304 31.1 | 28.2 | 325 55.9 | 53.0 | Fomalhaut | 15 17.5 | S29 30.6 |
| I 11 | 299 35.4 | 17 21.8 | 22.0 | 20 53.5 | 43.8 | 319 33.0 | 27.9 | 340 58.1 | 52.9 | | | |
| D 12 | 314 37.9 | 32 23.6 | S16 22.1 | 35 54.0 | S23 43.7 | 334 34.9 | S 9 27.7 | 356 00.2 | S16 52.8 | Gacrux | 171 53.9 | S57 13.9 |
| A 13 | 329 40.4 | 47 25.5 | 22.2 | 50 54.5 | 43.6 | 349 36.8 | 27.5 | 11 02.4 | 52.7 | Gienah | 175 45.8 | S17 39.8 |
| Y 14 | 344 42.8 | 62 27.3 | 22.3 | 65 54.9 | 43.6 | 4 38.8 | 27.3 | 26 04.5 | 52.6 | Hadar | 148 39.2 | S60 28.4 |
| 15 | 359 45.3 | 77 29.2 .. | 22.4 | 80 55.4 .. | 43.5 | 19 40.7 .. | 27.1 | 41 06.7 .. | 52.6 | Hamal | 327 54.0 | N23 34.0 |
| 16 | 14 47.8 | 92 31.0 | 22.5 | 95 55.9 | 43.4 | 34 42.6 | 26.8 | 56 08.9 | 52.5 | Kaus Aust. | 83 36.0 | S34 22.4 |
| 17 | 29 50.2 | 107 32.8 | 22.6 | 110 56.3 | 43.3 | 49 44.5 | 26.6 | 71 11.0 | 52.4 | | | |
| 18 | 44 52.7 | 122 34.7 | S16 22.7 | 125 56.8 | S23 43.2 | 64 46.4 | S 9 26.4 | 86 13.2 | S16 52.3 | Kochab | 137 19.8 | N74 03.6 |
| 19 | 59 55.1 | 137 36.5 | 22.8 | 140 57.3 | 43.2 | 79 48.3 | 26.2 | 101 15.4 | 52.2 | Markab | 13 32.6 | N15 19.3 |
| 20 | 74 57.6 | 152 38.3 | 22.9 | 155 57.7 | 43.1 | 94 50.3 | 26.0 | 116 17.5 | 52.1 | Menkar | 314 08.6 | N 4 10.4 |
| 21 | 90 00.1 | 167 40.1 .. | 23.0 | 170 58.2 .. | 43.0 | 109 52.2 .. | 25.8 | 131 19.7 .. | 52.0 | Menkent | 148 00.3 | S36 28.5 |
| 22 | 105 02.5 | 182 41.9 | 23.1 | 185 58.7 | 42.9 | 124 54.1 | 25.5 | 146 21.9 | 51.9 | Miaplacidus | 221 37.8 | S69 48.4 |
| 23 | 120 05.0 | 197 43.7 | 23.2 | 200 59.1 | 42.8 | 139 56.0 | 25.3 | 161 24.0 | 51.9 | | | |
| **5** 00 | 135 07.5 | 212 45.6 | S16 23.3 | 215 59.6 | S23 42.7 | 154 57.9 | S 9 25.1 | 176 26.2 | S16 51.8 | Mirfak | 308 31.6 | N49 56.5 |
| 01 | 150 09.9 | 227 47.4 | 23.4 | 231 00.1 | 42.6 | 169 59.8 | 24.9 | 191 28.4 | 51.7 | Nunki | 75 51.0 | S26 16.2 |
| 02 | 165 12.4 | 242 49.2 | 23.5 | 246 00.5 | 42.6 | 185 01.8 | 24.7 | 206 30.5 | 51.6 | Peacock | 53 10.1 | S56 39.9 |
| 03 | 180 14.9 | 257 50.9 .. | 23.6 | 261 01.0 .. | 42.5 | 200 03.7 .. | 24.4 | 221 32.7 .. | 51.5 | Pollux | 243 19.9 | N27 58.3 |
| 04 | 195 17.3 | 272 52.7 | 23.7 | 276 01.5 | 42.4 | 215 05.6 | 24.2 | 236 34.9 | 51.4 | Procyon | 244 53.0 | N 5 10.0 |
| 05 | 210 19.8 | 287 54.5 | 23.8 | 291 01.9 | 42.3 | 230 07.5 | 24.0 | 251 37.0 | 51.3 | | | |
| 06 | 225 22.2 | 302 56.3 | S16 23.9 | 306 02.4 | S23 42.2 | 245 09.4 | S 9 23.8 | 266 39.2 | S16 51.2 | Rasalhague | 96 01.0 | N12 32.5 |
| 07 | 240 24.7 | 317 58.1 | 24.0 | 321 02.9 | 42.1 | 260 11.3 | 23.6 | 281 41.3 | 51.2 | Regulus | 207 36.7 | N11 51.5 |
| 08 | 255 27.2 | 332 59.9 | 24.1 | 336 03.3 | 42.0 | 275 13.3 | 23.4 | 296 43.5 | 51.1 | Rigel | 281 06.0 | S 8 10.7 |
| S 09 | 270 29.6 | 348 01.6 .. | 24.2 | 351 03.8 .. | 42.0 | 290 15.2 .. | 23.1 | 311 45.7 .. | 51.0 | Rigil Kent. | 139 45.3 | S60 55.2 |
| A 10 | 285 32.1 | 3 03.4 | 24.3 | 6 04.3 | 41.9 | 305 17.1 | 22.9 | 326 47.8 | 50.9 | Sabik | 102 05.7 | S15 45.1 |
| T 11 | 300 34.6 | 18 05.2 | 24.4 | 21 04.7 | 41.8 | 320 19.0 | 22.7 | 341 50.0 | 50.8 | | | |
| U 12 | 315 37.0 | 33 06.9 | S16 24.5 | 36 05.2 | S23 41.7 | 335 20.9 | S 9 22.5 | 356 52.2 | S16 50.7 | Schedar | 349 34.0 | N56 39.6 |
| R 13 | 330 39.5 | 48 08.7 | 24.6 | 51 05.7 | 41.6 | 350 22.8 | 22.3 | 11 54.3 | 50.6 | Shaula | 96 13.9 | S37 07.1 |
| D 14 | 345 42.0 | 63 10.5 | 24.7 | 66 06.1 | 41.5 | 5 24.8 | 22.0 | 26 56.5 | 50.6 | Sirius | 258 28.1 | S16 44.9 |
| A 15 | 0 44.4 | 78 12.2 .. | 24.8 | 81 06.6 .. | 41.4 | 20 26.7 .. | 21.8 | 41 58.7 .. | 50.5 | Spica | 158 24.7 | S11 16.5 |
| Y 16 | 15 46.9 | 93 14.0 | 24.9 | 96 07.1 | 41.3 | 35 28.6 | 21.6 | 57 00.8 | 50.4 | Suhail | 222 47.6 | S43 31.3 |
| 17 | 30 49.4 | 108 15.7 | 25.0 | 111 07.5 | 41.2 | 50 30.5 | 21.4 | 72 03.0 | 50.3 | | | |
| 18 | 45 51.8 | 123 17.4 | S16 25.1 | 126 08.0 | S23 41.1 | 65 32.4 | S 9 21.2 | 87 05.2 | S16 50.2 | Vega | 80 35.2 | N38 48.0 |
| 19 | 60 54.3 | 138 19.2 | 25.2 | 141 08.5 | 41.0 | 80 34.3 | 20.9 | 102 07.3 | 50.1 | Zuben'ubi | 136 58.7 | S16 07.9 |
| 20 | 75 56.7 | 153 20.9 | 25.3 | 156 08.9 | 40.9 | 95 36.2 | 20.7 | 117 09.5 | 50.0 | | SHA | Mer. Pass. |
| 21 | 90 59.2 | 168 22.6 .. | 25.4 | 171 09.4 .. | 40.9 | 110 38.2 .. | 20.5 | 132 11.6 .. | 49.9 | Venus | 77 52.8 | 9 51 |
| 22 | 106 01.7 | 183 24.4 | 25.5 | 186 09.9 | 40.8 | 125 40.1 | 20.3 | 147 13.8 | 49.9 | Mars | 81 40.0 | 9 36 |
| 23 | 121 04.1 | 198 26.1 | 25.6 | 201 10.3 | 40.7 | 140 42.0 | 20.1 | 162 16.0 | 49.8 | Jupiter | 20 03.6 | 13 41 |
| Mer. Pass. 15 01.0 | | v 1.9 | d 0.1 | v 0.5 | d 0.1 | v 1.9 | d 0.2 | v 2.2 | d 0.1 | Saturn | 41 25.9 | 12 16 |

| UT | SUN | | MOON | | | | Lat. | Twilight | | Sunrise | Moonrise | | | |
|---|---|---|---|---|---|---|---|---|---|---|---|---|---|---|
| | | | | | | | | Naut. | Civil | | 3 | 4 | 5 | 6 |
| | GHA | Dec | GHA | v | Dec | d | HP | | | | | | | |
| d h | ° ′ | ° ′ | ° ′ | ′ | ° ′ | ′ | ′ | ° | h m | h m | h m | h m | h m | h m | h m |
| | | | | | | | | N 72 | 06 59 | 08 25 | 10 04 | 10 40 | 10 05 | 09 35 | 09 07 |
| 3 00 | 176 34.1 | S16 35.5 | 151 52.8 | 10.3 | S13 16.6 | 13.8 | 58.9 | N 70 | 06 52 | 08 09 | 09 29 | 10 23 | 09 57 | 09 36 | 09 15 |
| 01 | 191 34.0 | 34.8 | 166 22.1 | 10.4 | 13 02.8 | 13.8 | 58.8 | 68 | 06 46 | 07 55 | 09 05 | 10 09 | 09 52 | 09 37 | 09 22 |
| 02 | 206 33.9 | 34.0 | 180 51.5 | 10.5 | 12 49.0 | 13.9 | 58.8 | 66 | 06 42 | 07 44 | 08 46 | 09 57 | 09 47 | 09 37 | 09 28 |
| 03 | 221 33.9 . . | 33.3 | 195 21.0 | 10.6 | 12 35.1 | 13.9 | 58.8 | 64 | 06 37 | 07 35 | 08 30 | 09 48 | 09 42 | 09 37 | 09 33 |
| 04 | 236 33.8 | 32.6 | 209 50.6 | 10.7 | 12 21.2 | 14.0 | 58.7 | 62 | 06 34 | 07 27 | 08 18 | 09 39 | 09 39 | 09 38 | 09 37 |
| 05 | 251 33.7 | 31.8 | 224 20.3 | 10.8 | 12 07.2 | 14.0 | 58.7 | 60 | 06 30 | 07 20 | 08 07 | 09 32 | 09 36 | 09 38 | 09 41 |
| 06 | 266 33.7 | S16 31.1 | 238 50.1 | 10.9 | S11 53.2 | 14.1 | 58.7 | N 58 | 06 27 | 07 14 | 07 57 | 09 26 | 09 33 | 09 38 | 09 44 |
| 07 | 281 33.6 | 30.4 | 253 20.0 | 11.0 | 11 39.1 | 14.1 | 58.6 | 56 | 06 24 | 07 09 | 07 49 | 09 20 | 09 30 | 09 39 | 09 47 |
| T 08 | 296 33.5 | 29.6 | 267 50.0 | 11.1 | 11 25.0 | 14.1 | 58.6 | 54 | 06 21 | 07 03 | 07 42 | 09 15 | 09 28 | 09 39 | 09 50 |
| H 09 | 311 33.5 . . | 28.9 | 282 20.1 | 11.2 | 11 10.9 | 14.2 | 58.6 | 52 | 06 19 | 06 59 | 07 35 | 09 10 | 09 26 | 09 39 | 09 52 |
| U 10 | 326 33.4 | 28.2 | 296 50.3 | 11.3 | 10 56.7 | 14.2 | 58.5 | 50 | 06 16 | 06 55 | 07 29 | 09 06 | 09 24 | 09 39 | 09 54 |
| R 11 | 341 33.3 | 27.4 | 311 20.6 | 11.3 | 10 42.5 | 14.3 | 58.5 | 45 | 06 10 | 06 45 | 07 16 | 08 57 | 09 19 | 09 40 | 09 59 |
| S 12 | 356 33.3 | S16 26.7 | 325 50.9 | 11.5 | S10 28.2 | 14.3 | 58.5 | N 40 | 06 05 | 06 37 | 07 06 | 08 49 | 09 16 | 09 40 | 10 04 |
| D 13 | 11 33.2 | 25.9 | 340 21.4 | 11.5 | 10 13.9 | 14.3 | 58.4 | 35 | 06 00 | 06 30 | 06 57 | 08 43 | 09 13 | 09 40 | 10 07 |
| A 14 | 26 33.1 | 25.2 | 354 51.9 | 11.7 | 9 59.6 | 14.4 | 58.4 | 30 | 05 55 | 06 24 | 06 48 | 08 37 | 09 10 | 09 41 | 10 10 |
| Y 15 | 41 33.1 . . | 24.5 | 9 22.6 | 11.7 | 9 45.2 | 14.4 | 58.4 | 20 | 05 45 | 06 12 | 06 34 | 08 27 | 09 05 | 09 41 | 10 16 |
| 16 | 56 33.0 | 23.7 | 23 53.3 | 11.8 | 9 30.8 | 14.4 | 58.3 | N 10 | 05 35 | 06 00 | 06 22 | 08 18 | 09 01 | 09 42 | 10 21 |
| 17 | 71 32.9 | 23.0 | 38 24.1 | 11.9 | 9 16.4 | 14.5 | 58.3 | 0 | 05 24 | 05 49 | 06 10 | 08 10 | 08 57 | 09 42 | 10 26 |
| 18 | 86 32.9 | S16 22.2 | 52 55.0 | 12.0 | S 9 01.9 | 14.5 | 58.2 | S 10 | 05 11 | 05 37 | 05 59 | 08 01 | 08 53 | 09 43 | 10 30 |
| 19 | 101 32.8 | 21.5 | 67 26.0 | 12.0 | 8 47.4 | 14.5 | 58.2 | 20 | 04 55 | 05 23 | 05 46 | 07 52 | 08 49 | 09 43 | 10 35 |
| 20 | 116 32.7 | 20.7 | 81 57.0 | 12.2 | 8 32.9 | 14.5 | 58.2 | 30 | 04 35 | 05 06 | 05 31 | 07 42 | 08 44 | 09 44 | 10 41 |
| 21 | 131 32.7 . . | 20.0 | 96 28.2 | 12.2 | 8 18.4 | 14.6 | 58.1 | 35 | 04 22 | 04 55 | 05 22 | 07 36 | 08 42 | 09 44 | 10 45 |
| 22 | 146 32.6 | 19.3 | 110 59.4 | 12.3 | 8 03.8 | 14.5 | 58.1 | 40 | 04 07 | 04 43 | 05 13 | 07 29 | 08 38 | 09 45 | 10 49 |
| 23 | 161 32.6 | 18.5 | 125 30.7 | 12.4 | 7 49.3 | 14.6 | 58.1 | 45 | 03 47 | 04 28 | 05 01 | 07 21 | 08 35 | 09 45 | 10 53 |
| 4 00 | 176 32.5 | S16 17.8 | 140 02.1 | 12.4 | S 7 34.7 | 14.6 | 58.0 | S 50 | 03 21 | 04 09 | 04 47 | 07 11 | 08 30 | 09 46 | 10 59 |
| 01 | 191 32.4 | 17.0 | 154 33.5 | 12.6 | 7 20.1 | 14.7 | 58.0 | 52 | 03 08 | 04 00 | 04 40 | 07 07 | 08 28 | 09 46 | 11 01 |
| 02 | 206 32.4 | 16.3 | 169 05.1 | 12.6 | 7 05.4 | 14.6 | 58.0 | 54 | 02 52 | 03 50 | 04 33 | 07 02 | 08 26 | 09 46 | 11 04 |
| 03 | 221 32.3 . . | 15.5 | 183 36.7 | 12.7 | 6 50.8 | 14.6 | 57.9 | 56 | 02 34 | 03 39 | 04 25 | 06 56 | 08 24 | 09 47 | 11 07 |
| 04 | 236 32.2 | 14.8 | 198 08.4 | 12.7 | 6 36.2 | 14.7 | 57.9 | 58 | 02 09 | 03 25 | 04 15 | 06 50 | 08 21 | 09 47 | 11 10 |
| 05 | 251 32.2 | 14.0 | 212 40.1 | 12.8 | 6 21.5 | 14.7 | 57.8 | S 60 | 01 34 | 03 09 | 04 04 | 06 43 | 08 18 | 09 48 | 11 14 |

| UT | SUN | | MOON | | | | Lat. | Sunset | Twilight | | Moonset | | | |
|---|---|---|---|---|---|---|---|---|---|---|---|---|---|---|
| | GHA | Dec | GHA | v | Dec | d | HP | | Civil | Naut. | 3 | 4 | 5 | 6 |
| d h | ° ′ | ° ′ | ° ′ | ′ | ° ′ | ′ | ′ | ° | h m | h m | h m | h m | h m | h m | h m |
| 06 | 266 32.1 | S16 13.3 | 227 11.9 | 12.9 | S 6 06.8 | 14.7 | 57.8 | | | | | | | |
| 07 | 281 32.1 | 12.5 | 241 43.8 | 13.0 | 5 52.1 | 14.7 | 57.8 | N 72 | 14 25 | 16 04 | 17 31 | 18 32 | 20 46 | 22 50 | 24 56 |
| F 08 | 296 32.0 | 11.8 | 256 15.8 | 13.0 | 5 37.4 | 14.7 | 57.7 | N 70 | 15 00 | 16 21 | 17 37 | 18 47 | 20 50 | 22 45 | 24 40 |
| R 09 | 311 32.0 . . | 11.0 | 270 47.8 | 13.1 | 5 22.7 | 14.7 | 57.7 | 68 | 15 24 | 16 34 | 17 43 | 18 58 | 20 53 | 22 41 | 24 27 |
| I 10 | 326 31.9 | 10.3 | 285 19.9 | 13.1 | 5 08.0 | 14.7 | 57.7 | 66 | 15 43 | 16 44 | 17 47 | 19 08 | 20 55 | 22 37 | 24 17 |
| D 11 | 341 31.8 | 09.5 | 299 52.0 | 13.3 | 4 53.3 | 14.7 | 57.6 | 64 | 15 58 | 16 54 | 17 52 | 19 16 | 20 58 | 22 34 | 24 08 |
| A 12 | 356 31.8 | S16 08.8 | 314 24.3 | 13.2 | S 4 38.6 | 14.7 | 57.6 | 62 | 16 11 | 17 02 | 17 55 | 19 23 | 20 59 | 22 31 | 24 01 |
| Y 13 | 11 31.7 | 08.0 | 328 56.5 | 13.4 | 4 23.9 | 14.7 | 57.6 | 60 | 16 22 | 17 08 | 17 59 | 19 29 | 21 01 | 22 29 | 23 55 |
| 14 | 26 31.7 | 07.3 | 343 28.9 | 13.4 | 4 09.2 | 14.7 | 57.5 | N 58 | 16 31 | 17 15 | 18 02 | 19 34 | 21 02 | 22 27 | 23 49 |
| 15 | 41 31.6 . . | 06.5 | 358 01.3 | 13.5 | 3 54.5 | 14.7 | 57.5 | 56 | 16 39 | 17 20 | 18 05 | 19 38 | 21 04 | 22 25 | 23 45 |
| 16 | 56 31.5 | 05.8 | 12 33.8 | 13.5 | 3 39.8 | 14.7 | 57.4 | 54 | 16 47 | 17 25 | 18 07 | 19 42 | 21 05 | 22 24 | 23 40 |
| 17 | 71 31.5 | 05.0 | 27 06.3 | 13.5 | 3 25.1 | 14.8 | 57.4 | 52 | 16 53 | 17 30 | 18 10 | 19 46 | 21 06 | 22 22 | 23 36 |
| 18 | 86 31.4 | S16 04.3 | 41 38.0 | 13.7 | S 3 10.3 | 14.7 | 57.4 | 50 | 16 59 | 17 34 | 18 12 | 19 49 | 21 07 | 22 21 | 23 33 |
| 19 | 101 31.4 | 03.5 | 56 11.5 | 13.7 | 2 55.6 | 14.6 | 57.3 | 45 | 17 12 | 17 43 | 18 18 | 19 57 | 21 09 | 22 18 | 23 25 |
| 20 | 116 31.3 | 02.8 | 70 44.2 | 13.7 | 2 41.0 | 14.7 | 57.3 | N 40 | 17 23 | 17 51 | 18 23 | 20 03 | 21 10 | 22 16 | 23 19 |
| 21 | 131 31.3 . . | 02.0 | 85 16.9 | 13.8 | 2 26.3 | 14.7 | 57.3 | 35 | 17 32 | 17 58 | 18 28 | 20 08 | 21 12 | 22 13 | 23 13 |
| 22 | 146 31.2 | 01.3 | 99 49.7 | 13.8 | 2 11.6 | 14.7 | 57.2 | 30 | 17 40 | 18 05 | 18 33 | 20 12 | 21 13 | 22 12 | 23 09 |
| 23 | 161 31.2 | 16 00.5 | 114 22.5 | 13.9 | 1 56.9 | 14.6 | 57.2 | 20 | 17 54 | 18 16 | 18 43 | 20 20 | 21 15 | 22 08 | 23 00 |
| 5 00 | 176 31.1 | S15 59.8 | 128 55.4 | 13.9 | S 1 42.3 | 14.7 | 57.2 | N 10 | 18 07 | 18 28 | 18 53 | 20 26 | 21 17 | 22 06 | 22 53 |
| 01 | 191 31.1 | 59.0 | 143 28.3 | 14.0 | 1 27.6 | 14.6 | 57.1 | 0 | 18 17 | 18 39 | 19 04 | 20 33 | 21 19 | 22 03 | 22 46 |
| 02 | 206 31.0 | 58.2 | 158 01.3 | 14.0 | 1 13.0 | 14.6 | 57.1 | S 10 | 18 29 | 18 51 | 19 17 | 20 39 | 21 21 | 22 00 | 22 39 |
| 03 | 221 31.0 . . | 57.5 | 172 34.3 | 14.1 | 0 58.4 | 14.6 | 57.0 | 20 | 18 42 | 19 05 | 19 32 | 20 45 | 21 22 | 21 58 | 22 32 |
| 04 | 236 30.9 | 56.7 | 187 07.4 | 14.1 | 0 43.8 | 14.6 | 57.0 | 30 | 18 56 | 19 22 | 19 52 | 20 53 | 21 24 | 21 54 | 22 24 |
| 05 | 251 30.9 | 56.0 | 201 40.5 | 14.2 | 0 29.2 | 14.6 | 57.0 | 35 | 19 05 | 19 32 | 20 05 | 20 57 | 21 26 | 21 53 | 22 19 |
| 06 | 266 30.8 | S15 55.2 | 216 13.7 | 14.2 | S 0 14.6 | 14.5 | 56.9 | 40 | 19 14 | 19 44 | 20 20 | 21 02 | 21 27 | 21 51 | 22 14 |
| 07 | 281 30.7 | 54.4 | 230 46.9 | 14.2 | S 0 00.1 | 14.6 | 56.9 | 45 | 19 26 | 19 59 | 20 40 | 21 07 | 21 28 | 21 48 | 22 08 |
| S 08 | 296 30.7 | 53.7 | 245 20.1 | 14.3 | N 0 14.5 | 14.5 | 56.9 | S 50 | 19 40 | 20 17 | 21 05 | 21 14 | 21 30 | 21 45 | 22 01 |
| A 09 | 311 30.6 . . | 52.9 | 259 53.4 | 14.3 | 0 29.0 | 14.5 | 56.8 | 52 | 19 46 | 20 26 | 21 18 | 21 16 | 21 31 | 21 44 | 21 57 |
| T 10 | 326 30.6 | 52.2 | 274 26.7 | 14.3 | 0 43.5 | 14.4 | 56.8 | 54 | 19 54 | 20 36 | 21 33 | 21 20 | 21 32 | 21 43 | 21 54 |
| U 11 | 341 30.5 | 51.4 | 289 00.0 | 14.4 | 0 57.9 | 14.5 | 56.8 | 56 | 20 02 | 20 47 | 21 51 | 21 23 | 21 33 | 21 41 | 21 50 |
| R 12 | 356 30.5 | S15 50.6 | 303 33.4 | 14.4 | N 1 12.4 | 14.4 | 56.7 | 58 | 20 11 | 21 01 | 22 15 | 21 27 | 21 34 | 21 39 | 21 45 |
| D 13 | 11 30.5 | 49.9 | 318 06.8 | 14.4 | 1 26.8 | 14.6 | 56.7 | S 60 | 20 21 | 21 17 | 22 47 | 21 32 | 21 35 | 21 37 | 21 40 |
| A 14 | 26 30.4 | 49.1 | 332 40.2 | 14.5 | 1 41.2 | 14.4 | 56.7 | | | | | | | | |
| Y 15 | 41 30.4 . . | 48.3 | 347 13.7 | 14.5 | 1 55.6 | 14.3 | 56.6 | | SUN | | | MOON | | | |
| 16 | 56 30.3 | 47.6 | 1 47.2 | 14.6 | 2 09.9 | 14.3 | 56.6 | | | | | | | | |
| 17 | 71 30.3 | 46.8 | 16 20.7 | 14.6 | 2 24.2 | 14.3 | 56.6 | Day | Eqn. of Time | | Mer. | Mer. Pass. | | Age | Phase |
| 18 | 86 30.2 | S15 46.1 | 30 54.3 | 14.6 | N 2 38.5 | 14.3 | 56.5 | | 00ʰ | 12ʰ | Pass. | Upper | Lower | | |
| 19 | 101 30.2 | 45.3 | 45 27.9 | 14.6 | 2 52.8 | 14.2 | 56.5 | d | m s | m s | h m | h m | h m | d % | |
| 20 | 116 30.1 | 44.5 | 60 01.5 | 14.6 | 3 07.0 | 14.2 | 56.4 | 3 | 13 44 | 13 47 | 12 14 | 14 21 | 01 56 | 02 7 | |
| 21 | 131 30.1 . . | 43.8 | 74 35.1 | 14.7 | 3 21.2 | 14.2 | 56.4 | 4 | 13 50 | 13 53 | 12 14 | 15 08 | 02 45 | 03 13 | |
| 22 | 146 30.0 | 43.0 | 89 08.8 | 14.6 | 3 35.4 | 14.1 | 56.4 | 5 | 13 55 | 13 58 | 12 14 | 15 53 | 03 31 | 04 21 | |
| 23 | 161 30.0 | 42.2 | 103 42.4 | 14.7 | N 3 49.5 | 14.1 | 56.3 | | | | | | | | |
| | SD 16.3 | d 0.8 | SD 15.9 | | 15.7 | | 15.5 | | | | | | | | | |

| UT | ARIES | VENUS −4.9 | | MARS +1.4 | | JUPITER −2.0 | | SATURN +0.6 | | STARS | | |
|---|---|---|---|---|---|---|---|---|---|---|---|---|
| | GHA | GHA | Dec | GHA | Dec | GHA | Dec | GHA | Dec | Name | SHA | Dec |
| d h | ° ′ | ° ′ | ° ′ | ° ′ | ° ′ | ° ′ | ° ′ | ° ′ | ° ′ | | ° ′ | ° ′ |
| 6 00 | 136 06.6 | 213 27.8 | S16 25.7 | 216 10.8 | S23 40.7 | 155 43.9 | S 9 19.8 | 177 18.1 | S16 49.7 | Acamar | 315 13.6 | S40 13.3 |
| 01 | 151 09.1 | 228 29.5 | 25.8 | 231 11.3 | 40.5 | 170 45.8 | 19.6 | 192 20.3 | 49.6 | Achernar | 335 22.2 | S57 07.9 |
| 02 | 166 11.5 | 243 31.2 | 25.9 | 246 11.7 | 40.4 | 185 47.7 | 19.4 | 207 22.5 | 49.5 | Acrux | 173 02.2 | S63 13.0 |
| 03 | 181 14.0 | 258 32.9 .. | 26.0 | 261 12.2 .. | 40.3 | 200 49.6 .. | 19.2 | 222 24.6 .. | 49.4 | Adhara | 255 07.4 | S29 00.3 |
| 04 | 196 16.5 | 273 34.6 | 26.1 | 276 12.7 | 40.2 | 215 51.6 | 19.0 | 237 26.8 | 49.3 | Aldebaran | 290 42.2 | N16 33.2 |
| 05 | 211 18.9 | 288 36.3 | 26.2 | 291 13.1 | 40.1 | 230 53.5 | 18.7 | 252 29.0 | 49.2 | | | |
| 06 | 226 21.4 | 303 38.0 | S16 26.3 | 306 13.6 | S23 40.0 | 245 55.4 | S 9 18.5 | 267 31.1 | S16 49.2 | Alioth | 166 14.8 | N55 50.2 |
| 07 | 241 23.9 | 318 39.7 | 26.4 | 321 14.1 | 39.9 | 260 57.3 | 18.3 | 282 33.3 | 49.1 | Alkaid | 152 53.8 | N49 11.9 |
| 08 | 256 26.3 | 333 41.4 | 26.5 | 336 14.5 | 39.8 | 275 59.2 | 18.1 | 297 35.5 | 49.0 | Alnair | 27 36.4 | S46 51.4 |
| 09 | 271 28.8 | 348 43.1 .. | 26.6 | 351 15.0 .. | 39.7 | 291 01.1 .. | 17.9 | 312 37.6 .. | 48.9 | Alnilam | 275 39.9 | S 1 11.4 |
| 10 | 286 31.2 | 3 44.8 | 26.7 | 6 15.5 | 39.6 | 306 03.1 | 17.7 | 327 39.8 | 48.8 | Alphard | 217 49.8 | S 8 45.3 |
| 11 | 301 33.7 | 18 46.5 | 26.8 | 21 15.9 | 39.5 | 321 05.0 | 17.4 | 342 41.9 | 48.7 | | | |
| 12 | 316 36.2 | 33 48.1 | S16 26.9 | 36 16.4 | S23 39.4 | 336 06.9 | S 9 17.2 | 357 44.1 | S16 48.6 | Alphecca | 126 05.8 | N26 38.2 |
| 13 | 331 38.6 | 48 49.8 | 27.0 | 51 16.9 | 39.3 | 351 08.8 | 17.0 | 12 46.3 | 48.5 | Alpheratz | 357 37.5 | N29 12.7 |
| 14 | 346 41.1 | 63 51.5 | 27.2 | 66 17.3 | 39.2 | 6 10.7 | 16.8 | 27 48.4 | 48.5 | Altair | 62 02.6 | N 8 55.5 |
| 15 | 1 43.6 | 78 53.1 .. | 27.3 | 81 17.8 .. | 39.1 | 21 12.6 .. | 16.6 | 42 50.6 .. | 48.4 | Ankaa | 353 09.8 | S42 11.5 |
| 16 | 16 46.0 | 93 54.8 | 27.4 | 96 18.3 | 39.0 | 36 14.5 | 16.3 | 57 52.8 | 48.3 | Antares | 112 18.9 | S26 28.8 |
| 17 | 31 48.5 | 108 56.5 | 27.5 | 111 18.7 | 38.9 | 51 16.5 | 16.1 | 72 54.9 | 48.2 | | | |
| 18 | 46 51.0 | 123 58.1 | S16 27.6 | 126 19.2 | S23 38.8 | 66 18.4 | S 9 15.9 | 87 57.1 | S16 48.1 | Arcturus | 145 50.0 | N19 03.9 |
| 19 | 61 53.4 | 138 59.8 | 27.7 | 141 19.7 | 38.7 | 81 20.3 | 15.7 | 102 59.3 | 48.0 | Atria | 107 15.5 | S69 03.7 |
| 20 | 76 55.9 | 154 01.4 | 27.8 | 156 20.1 | 38.6 | 96 22.2 | 15.5 | 118 01.4 | 47.9 | Avior | 234 15.0 | S59 34.8 |
| 21 | 91 58.3 | 169 03.0 .. | 27.9 | 171 20.6 .. | 38.5 | 111 24.1 .. | 15.2 | 133 03.6 .. | 47.9 | Bellatrix | 278 25.2 | N 6 22.1 |
| 22 | 107 00.8 | 184 04.7 | 28.0 | 186 21.1 | 38.4 | 126 26.0 | 15.0 | 148 05.8 | 47.8 | Betelgeuse | 270 54.4 | N 7 24.6 |
| 23 | 122 03.3 | 199 06.3 | 28.1 | 201 21.5 | 38.3 | 141 27.9 | 14.8 | 163 07.9 | 47.7 | | | |
| 7 00 | 137 05.7 | 214 07.9 | S16 28.2 | 216 22.0 | S23 38.2 | 156 29.9 | S 9 14.6 | 178 10.1 | S16 47.6 | Canopus | 263 53.0 | S52 42.6 |
| 01 | 152 08.2 | 229 09.6 | 28.3 | 231 22.5 | 38.1 | 171 31.8 | 14.4 | 193 12.2 | 47.5 | Capella | 280 25.2 | N46 01.3 |
| 02 | 167 10.7 | 244 11.2 | 28.4 | 246 22.9 | 38.0 | 186 33.7 | 14.1 | 208 14.4 | 47.4 | Deneb | 49 27.9 | N45 21.4 |
| 03 | 182 13.1 | 259 12.8 .. | 28.5 | 261 23.4 .. | 37.8 | 201 35.6 .. | 13.9 | 223 16.6 .. | 47.3 | Denebola | 182 27.1 | N14 26.8 |
| 04 | 197 15.6 | 274 14.4 | 28.6 | 276 23.9 | 37.7 | 216 37.5 | 13.7 | 238 18.7 | 47.2 | Diphda | 348 49.9 | S17 52.2 |
| 05 | 212 18.1 | 289 16.0 | 28.7 | 291 24.3 | 37.6 | 231 39.4 | 13.5 | 253 20.9 | 47.2 | | | |
| 06 | 227 20.5 | 304 17.7 | S16 28.8 | 306 24.8 | S23 37.5 | 246 41.3 | S 9 13.3 | 268 23.1 | S16 47.1 | Dubhe | 193 43.4 | N61 37.8 |
| 07 | 242 23.0 | 319 19.3 | 28.9 | 321 25.3 | 37.4 | 261 43.2 | 13.0 | 283 25.2 | 47.0 | Elnath | 278 04.7 | N28 37.6 |
| 08 | 257 25.5 | 334 20.9 | 29.0 | 336 25.7 | 37.3 | 276 45.2 | 12.8 | 298 27.4 | 46.9 | Eltanin | 90 43.7 | N51 28.9 |
| 09 | 272 27.9 | 349 22.5 .. | 29.2 | 351 26.2 .. | 37.2 | 291 47.1 .. | 12.6 | 313 29.6 .. | 46.8 | Enif | 33 41.5 | N 9 58.4 |
| 10 | 287 30.4 | 4 24.1 | 29.3 | 6 26.7 | 37.1 | 306 49.0 | 12.4 | 328 31.7 | 46.7 | Fomalhaut | 15 17.5 | S29 30.6 |
| 11 | 302 32.8 | 19 25.7 | 29.4 | 21 27.1 | 37.0 | 321 50.9 | 12.1 | 343 33.9 | 46.6 | | | |
| 12 | 317 35.3 | 34 27.2 | S16 29.5 | 36 27.6 | S23 36.9 | 336 52.8 | S 9 11.9 | 358 36.1 | S16 46.5 | Gacrux | 171 53.9 | S57 14.0 |
| 13 | 332 37.8 | 49 28.8 | 29.6 | 51 28.1 | 36.8 | 351 54.7 | 11.7 | 13 38.2 | 46.5 | Gienah | 175 45.8 | S17 39.8 |
| 14 | 347 40.2 | 64 30.4 | 29.7 | 66 28.5 | 36.6 | 6 56.6 | 11.5 | 28 40.4 | 46.4 | Hadar | 148 39.2 | S60 28.5 |
| 15 | 2 42.7 | 79 32.0 .. | 29.8 | 81 29.0 .. | 36.5 | 21 58.6 .. | 11.3 | 43 42.6 .. | 46.3 | Hamal | 327 54.0 | N23 34.0 |
| 16 | 17 45.2 | 94 33.6 | 29.9 | 96 29.5 | 36.4 | 37 00.5 | 11.0 | 58 44.7 | 46.2 | Kaus Aust. | 83 36.5 | S34 22.4 |
| 17 | 32 47.6 | 109 35.1 | 30.0 | 111 29.9 | 36.3 | 52 02.4 | 10.8 | 73 46.9 | 46.1 | | | |
| 18 | 47 50.1 | 124 36.7 | S16 30.1 | 126 30.4 | S23 36.2 | 67 04.3 | S 9 10.6 | 88 49.0 | S16 46.0 | Kochab | 137 19.8 | N74 03.6 |
| 19 | 62 52.6 | 139 38.3 | 30.2 | 141 30.9 | 36.1 | 82 06.2 | 10.4 | 103 51.2 | 45.9 | Markab | 13 32.6 | N15 19.3 |
| 20 | 77 55.0 | 154 39.8 | 30.3 | 156 31.3 | 36.0 | 97 08.1 | 10.2 | 118 53.4 | 45.8 | Menkar | 314 08.6 | N 4 10.4 |
| 21 | 92 57.5 | 169 41.4 .. | 30.4 | 171 31.8 .. | 35.9 | 112 10.0 .. | 09.9 | 133 55.5 .. | 45.8 | Menkent | 148 00.3 | S36 28.5 |
| 22 | 107 59.9 | 184 42.9 | 30.5 | 186 32.3 | 35.7 | 127 11.9 | 09.7 | 148 57.7 | 45.7 | Miaplacidus | 221 37.8 | S69 48.4 |
| 23 | 123 02.4 | 199 44.5 | 30.6 | 201 32.7 | 35.6 | 142 13.9 | 09.5 | 163 59.9 | 45.6 | | | |
| 8 00 | 138 04.9 | 214 46.0 | S16 30.8 | 216 33.2 | S23 35.5 | 157 15.8 | S 9 09.3 | 179 02.0 | S16 45.5 | Mirfak | 308 31.6 | N49 56.5 |
| 01 | 153 07.3 | 229 47.6 | 30.9 | 231 33.7 | 35.4 | 172 17.7 | 09.1 | 194 04.2 | 45.4 | Nunki | 75 51.0 | S26 16.2 |
| 02 | 168 09.8 | 244 49.1 | 31.0 | 246 34.2 | 35.3 | 187 19.6 | 08.8 | 209 06.4 | 45.3 | Peacock | 53 10.1 | S56 39.9 |
| 03 | 183 12.3 | 259 50.7 .. | 31.1 | 261 34.6 .. | 35.2 | 202 21.5 .. | 08.6 | 224 08.5 .. | 45.2 | Pollux | 243 19.9 | N27 58.3 |
| 04 | 198 14.7 | 274 52.2 | 31.2 | 276 35.1 | 35.0 | 217 23.4 | 08.4 | 239 10.7 | 45.1 | Procyon | 244 53.0 | N 5 10.0 |
| 05 | 213 17.2 | 289 53.7 | 31.3 | 291 35.6 | 34.9 | 232 25.3 | 08.2 | 254 12.9 | 45.1 | | | |
| 06 | 228 19.7 | 304 55.3 | S16 31.4 | 306 36.0 | S23 34.8 | 247 27.3 | S 9 08.0 | 269 15.0 | S16 45.0 | Rasalhague | 96 01.0 | N12 32.5 |
| 07 | 243 22.1 | 319 56.8 | 31.5 | 321 36.5 | 34.7 | 262 29.2 | 07.7 | 284 17.2 | 44.9 | Regulus | 207 36.7 | N11 51.5 |
| 08 | 258 24.6 | 334 58.3 | 31.6 | 336 37.0 | 34.6 | 277 31.1 | 07.5 | 299 19.4 | 44.8 | Rigel | 281 06.0 | S 8 10.7 |
| 09 | 273 27.1 | 349 59.8 .. | 31.7 | 351 37.4 .. | 34.5 | 292 33.0 .. | 07.3 | 314 21.5 .. | 44.7 | Rigil Kent. | 139 43.5 | S60 55.2 |
| 10 | 288 29.5 | 5 01.3 | 31.8 | 6 37.9 | 34.3 | 307 34.9 | 07.1 | 329 23.7 | 44.6 | Sabik | 102 05.7 | S15 45.1 |
| 11 | 303 32.0 | 20 02.8 | 31.9 | 21 38.4 | 34.2 | 322 36.8 | 06.8 | 344 25.8 | 44.5 | | | |
| 12 | 318 34.4 | 35 04.3 | S16 32.0 | 36 38.8 | S23 34.1 | 337 38.7 | S 9 06.6 | 359 28.0 | S16 44.4 | Schedar | 349 34.1 | N56 39.6 |
| 13 | 333 36.9 | 50 05.9 | 32.2 | 51 39.3 | 34.0 | 352 40.6 | 06.4 | 14 30.2 | 44.4 | Shaula | 96 13.9 | S37 07.1 |
| 14 | 348 39.4 | 65 07.4 | 32.3 | 66 39.8 | 33.9 | 7 42.6 | 06.2 | 29 32.3 | 44.3 | Sirius | 258 28.1 | S16 44.9 |
| 15 | 3 41.8 | 80 08.8 .. | 32.4 | 81 40.2 .. | 33.7 | 22 44.5 .. | 06.0 | 44 34.5 .. | 44.2 | Spica | 158 24.7 | S11 16.6 |
| 16 | 18 44.3 | 95 10.3 | 32.5 | 96 40.7 | 33.6 | 37 46.4 | 05.7 | 59 36.7 | 44.1 | Suhail | 222 47.6 | S43 31.3 |
| 17 | 33 46.8 | 110 11.8 | 32.6 | 111 41.2 | 33.5 | 52 48.3 | 05.5 | 74 38.8 | 44.0 | | | |
| 18 | 48 49.2 | 125 13.3 | S16 32.7 | 126 41.6 | S23 33.4 | 67 50.2 | S 9 05.3 | 89 41.0 | S16 43.9 | Vega | 80 35.2 | N38 48.0 |
| 19 | 63 51.7 | 140 14.8 | 32.8 | 141 42.1 | 33.2 | 82 52.1 | 05.1 | 104 43.2 | 43.8 | Zuben'ubi | 136 58.6 | S16 07.9 |
| 20 | 78 54.2 | 155 16.3 | 32.9 | 156 42.6 | 33.1 | 97 54.0 | 04.9 | 119 45.3 | 43.8 | | SHA | Mer. Pass. |
| 21 | 93 56.6 | 170 17.8 .. | 33.0 | 171 43.0 .. | 33.0 | 112 55.9 .. | 04.6 | 134 47.5 .. | 43.7 | | ° ′ | h m |
| 22 | 108 59.1 | 185 19.3 | 33.1 | 186 43.5 | 32.9 | 127 57.8 | 04.4 | 149 49.7 | 43.6 | Venus | 77 02.2 | 9 42 |
| 23 | 124 01.6 | 200 20.7 | 33.2 | 201 44.0 | 32.8 | 142 59.8 | 04.2 | 164 51.8 | 43.5 | Mars | 79 16.3 | 9 34 |
| | h m | | | | | | | | | Jupiter | 19 24.1 | 13 32 |
| Mer. Pass. 14 49.2 | | v 1.6 | d 0.1 | v 0.5 | d 0.1 | v 1.9 | d 0.2 | v 2.2 | d 0.1 | Saturn | 41 04.3 | 12 06 |

| UT | SUN GHA | SUN Dec | MOON GHA | v | MOON Dec | d | HP |
|---|---|---|---|---|---|---|---|
| d h | ° ′ | ° ′ | ° ′ | ′ | ° ′ | ′ | ′ |
| 6 00 | 176 29.9 | S15 41.5 | 118 16.1 | 14.8 | N 4 03.6 | 14.1 | 56.3 |
| 01 | 191 29.9 | 40.7 | 132 49.9 | 14.7 | 4 17.7 | 14.0 | 56.3 |
| 02 | 206 29.8 | 39.9 | 147 23.6 | 14.7 | 4 31.7 | 14.0 | 56.2 |
| 03 | 221 29.8 .. | 39.1 | 161 57.3 | 14.8 | 4 45.7 | 14.0 | 56.2 |
| 04 | 236 29.8 | 38.4 | 176 31.1 | 14.8 | 4 59.7 | 13.9 | 56.2 |
| 05 | 251 29.7 | 37.6 | 191 04.9 | 14.8 | 5 13.6 | 13.9 | 56.1 |
| 06 | 266 29.7 | S15 36.8 | 205 38.7 | 14.8 | N 5 27.5 | 13.8 | 56.1 |
| 07 | 281 29.6 | 36.1 | 220 12.5 | 14.8 | 5 41.3 | 13.8 | 56.1 |
| 08 | 296 29.6 | 35.3 | 234 46.3 | 14.9 | 5 55.1 | 13.8 | 56.1 |
| S 09 | 311 29.5 .. | 34.5 | 249 20.2 | 14.8 | 6 08.9 | 13.7 | 56.0 |
| U 10 | 326 29.5 | 33.8 | 263 54.0 | 14.9 | 6 22.6 | 13.6 | 56.0 |
| N 11 | 341 29.5 | 33.0 | 278 27.9 | 14.8 | 6 36.2 | 13.7 | 56.0 |
| D 12 | 356 29.4 | S15 32.2 | 293 01.7 | 14.9 | N 6 49.9 | 13.6 | 55.9 |
| A 13 | 11 29.4 | 31.4 | 307 35.6 | 14.9 | 7 03.5 | 13.5 | 55.9 |
| Y 14 | 26 29.3 | 30.7 | 322 09.5 | 14.8 | 7 17.0 | 13.5 | 55.9 |
| 15 | 41 29.3 .. | 29.9 | 336 43.3 | 14.9 | 7 30.5 | 13.5 | 55.8 |
| 16 | 56 29.3 | 29.1 | 351 17.2 | 14.9 | 7 44.0 | 13.4 | 55.8 |
| 17 | 71 29.2 | 28.3 | 5 51.1 | 14.9 | 7 57.4 | 13.3 | 55.8 |
| 18 | 86 29.2 | S15 27.6 | 20 25.0 | 14.9 | N 8 10.7 | 13.3 | 55.7 |
| 19 | 101 29.2 | 26.8 | 34 58.9 | 14.8 | 8 24.0 | 13.3 | 55.7 |
| 20 | 116 29.1 | 26.0 | 49 32.7 | 14.9 | 8 37.3 | 13.2 | 55.7 |
| 21 | 131 29.1 .. | 25.2 | 64 06.6 | 14.9 | 8 50.5 | 13.2 | 55.7 |
| 22 | 146 29.0 | 24.4 | 78 40.5 | 14.9 | 9 03.7 | 13.1 | 55.6 |
| 23 | 161 29.0 | 23.7 | 93 14.4 | 14.8 | 9 16.8 | 13.1 | 55.6 |
| 7 00 | 176 29.0 | S15 22.9 | 107 48.2 | 14.9 | N 9 29.9 | 13.0 | 55.6 |
| 01 | 191 28.9 | 22.1 | 122 22.1 | 14.9 | 9 42.9 | 12.9 | 55.5 |
| 02 | 206 28.9 | 21.3 | 136 56.0 | 14.8 | 9 55.8 | 12.9 | 55.5 |
| 03 | 221 28.9 .. | 20.6 | 151 29.8 | 14.8 | 10 08.7 | 12.9 | 55.5 |
| 04 | 236 28.8 | 19.8 | 166 03.6 | 14.9 | 10 21.6 | 12.7 | 55.5 |
| 05 | 251 28.8 | 19.0 | 180 37.5 | 14.8 | 10 34.3 | 12.8 | 55.4 |
| 06 | 266 28.8 | S15 18.2 | 195 11.3 | 14.8 | N10 47.1 | 12.7 | 55.4 |
| 07 | 281 28.7 | 17.4 | 209 45.1 | 14.0 | 10 59.8 | 12.6 | 55.4 |
| 08 | 296 28.7 | 16.6 | 224 18.9 | 14.8 | 11 12.4 | 12.5 | 55.4 |
| M 09 | 311 28.7 .. | 15.9 | 238 52.7 | 14.8 | 11 24.9 | 12.5 | 55.3 |
| O 10 | 326 28.6 | 15.1 | 253 26.5 | 14.7 | 11 37.4 | 12.5 | 55.3 |
| N 11 | 341 28.6 | 14.3 | 268 00.2 | 14.8 | 11 49.9 | 12.4 | 55.3 |
| D 12 | 356 28.6 | S15 13.5 | 282 33.9 | 14.8 | N12 02.3 | 12.3 | 55.3 |
| A 13 | 11 28.5 | 12.7 | 297 07.7 | 14.7 | 12 14.6 | 12.3 | 55.2 |
| Y 14 | 26 28.5 | 11.9 | 311 41.4 | 14.7 | 12 26.9 | 12.2 | 55.2 |
| 15 | 41 28.5 .. | 11.2 | 326 15.1 | 14.6 | 12 39.1 | 12.1 | 55.2 |
| 16 | 56 28.4 | 10.4 | 340 48.7 | 14.7 | 12 51.2 | 12.1 | 55.2 |
| 17 | 71 28.4 | 09.6 | 355 22.4 | 14.6 | 13 03.3 | 12.0 | 55.1 |
| 18 | 86 28.4 | S15 08.8 | 9 56.0 | 14.6 | N13 15.3 | 11.9 | 55.1 |
| 19 | 101 28.3 | 08.0 | 24 29.6 | 14.6 | 13 27.2 | 11.9 | 55.1 |
| 20 | 116 28.3 | 07.2 | 39 03.2 | 14.5 | 13 39.1 | 11.8 | 55.1 |
| 21 | 131 28.3 .. | 06.4 | 53 36.7 | 14.6 | 13 50.9 | 11.8 | 55.0 |
| 22 | 146 28.3 | 05.6 | 68 10.3 | 14.5 | 14 02.7 | 11.6 | 55.0 |
| 23 | 161 28.2 | 04.9 | 82 43.8 | 14.5 | 14 14.3 | 11.7 | 55.0 |
| 8 00 | 176 28.2 | S15 04.1 | 97 17.3 | 14.4 | N14 26.0 | 11.5 | 55.0 |
| 01 | 191 28.2 | 03.3 | 111 50.7 | 14.4 | 14 37.5 | 11.5 | 54.9 |
| 02 | 206 28.1 | 02.5 | 126 24.1 | 14.4 | 14 49.0 | 11.4 | 54.9 |
| 03 | 221 28.1 .. | 01.7 | 140 57.5 | 14.4 | 15 00.4 | 11.3 | 54.9 |
| 04 | 236 28.1 | 00.9 | 155 30.9 | 14.4 | 15 11.7 | 11.3 | 54.9 |
| 05 | 251 28.1 | 15 00.1 | 170 04.3 | 14.3 | 15 23.0 | 11.2 | 54.9 |
| 06 | 266 28.0 | S14 59.3 | 184 37.6 | 14.2 | N15 34.2 | 11.1 | 54.8 |
| 07 | 281 28.0 | 58.5 | 199 10.8 | 14.3 | 15 45.3 | 11.0 | 54.8 |
| 08 | 296 28.0 | 57.7 | 213 44.1 | 14.2 | 15 56.3 | 11.0 | 54.8 |
| T 09 | 311 28.0 .. | 56.9 | 228 17.3 | 14.2 | 16 07.3 | 10.9 | 54.8 |
| U 10 | 326 27.9 | 56.2 | 242 50.5 | 14.1 | 16 18.2 | 10.8 | 54.8 |
| E 11 | 341 27.9 | 55.4 | 257 23.6 | 14.2 | 16 29.0 | 10.8 | 54.7 |
| S 12 | 356 27.9 | S14 54.6 | 271 56.8 | 14.0 | N16 39.8 | 10.7 | 54.7 |
| D 13 | 11 27.9 | 53.8 | 286 29.8 | 14.1 | 16 50.5 | 10.6 | 54.7 |
| A 14 | 26 27.8 | 53.0 | 301 02.9 | 14.0 | 17 01.1 | 10.5 | 54.7 |
| Y 15 | 41 27.8 .. | 52.2 | 315 35.9 | 14.0 | 17 11.6 | 10.4 | 54.7 |
| 16 | 56 27.8 | 51.4 | 330 08.9 | 13.9 | 17 22.0 | 10.4 | 54.7 |
| 17 | 71 27.8 | 50.6 | 344 41.8 | 13.9 | 17 32.4 | 10.3 | 54.6 |
| 18 | 86 27.8 | S14 49.8 | 359 14.7 | 13.9 | N17 42.7 | 10.2 | 54.6 |
| 19 | 101 27.7 | 49.0 | 13 47.6 | 13.8 | 17 52.9 | 10.1 | 54.6 |
| 20 | 116 27.7 | 48.2 | 28 20.4 | 13.8 | 18 03.0 | 10.0 | 54.6 |
| 21 | 131 27.7 .. | 47.4 | 42 53.2 | 13.7 | 18 13.0 | 10.0 | 54.6 |
| 22 | 146 27.7 | 46.6 | 57 25.9 | 13.7 | 18 23.0 | 9.9 | 54.6 |
| 23 | 161 27.7 | 45.8 | 71 58.6 | 13.7 | N18 32.9 | 9.8 | 54.5 |
| | SD 16.2 | d 0.8 | SD 15.2 | | 15.1 | | 14.9 |

| Lat. | Twilight Naut. | Twilight Civil | Sunrise | Moonrise 6 | Moonrise 7 | Moonrise 8 | Moonrise 9 |
|---|---|---|---|---|---|---|---|
| ° | h m | h m | h m | h m | h m | h m | h m |
| N 72 | 06 47 | 08 11 | 09 43 | 09 07 | 08 33 | 07 43 | ▭ |
| N 70 | 06 42 | 07 57 | 09 14 | 09 15 | 08 51 | 08 20 | 07 06 |
| 68 | 06 37 | 07 45 | 08 52 | 09 22 | 09 06 | 08 46 | 08 14 |
| 66 | 06 33 | 07 35 | 08 35 | 09 28 | 09 18 | 09 06 | 08 51 |
| 64 | 06 30 | 07 27 | 08 21 | 09 33 | 09 28 | 09 23 | 09 17 |
| 62 | 06 27 | 07 20 | 08 09 | 09 37 | 09 36 | 09 36 | 09 38 |
| 60 | 06 24 | 07 14 | 07 59 | 09 41 | 09 44 | 09 48 | 09 54 |
| N 58 | 06 21 | 07 08 | 07 51 | 09 44 | 09 50 | 09 58 | 10 08 |
| 56 | 06 19 | 07 03 | 07 43 | 09 47 | 09 56 | 10 07 | 10 21 |
| 54 | 06 16 | 06 58 | 07 36 | 09 50 | 10 01 | 10 15 | 10 31 |
| 52 | 06 14 | 06 54 | 07 30 | 09 52 | 10 06 | 10 22 | 10 41 |
| 50 | 06 12 | 06 50 | 07 24 | 09 54 | 10 10 | 10 28 | 10 49 |
| 45 | 06 07 | 06 42 | 07 12 | 09 59 | 10 20 | 10 42 | 11 08 |
| N 40 | 06 02 | 06 34 | 07 03 | 10 04 | 10 28 | 10 53 | 11 22 |
| 35 | 05 58 | 06 28 | 06 54 | 10 07 | 10 34 | 11 03 | 11 35 |
| 30 | 05 53 | 06 22 | 06 46 | 10 10 | 10 40 | 11 12 | 11 46 |
| 20 | 05 44 | 06 10 | 06 33 | 10 16 | 10 51 | 11 27 | 12 05 |
| N 10 | 05 35 | 06 00 | 06 22 | 10 21 | 11 00 | 11 40 | 12 22 |
| 0 | 05 24 | 05 49 | 06 11 | 10 26 | 11 09 | 11 52 | 12 38 |
| S 10 | 05 12 | 05 38 | 06 00 | 10 30 | 11 17 | 12 05 | 12 53 |
| 20 | 04 57 | 05 24 | 05 48 | 10 35 | 11 27 | 12 18 | 13 10 |
| 30 | 04 38 | 05 08 | 05 34 | 10 41 | 11 38 | 12 34 | 13 30 |
| 35 | 04 26 | 04 58 | 05 26 | 10 45 | 11 44 | 12 43 | 13 41 |
| 40 | 04 11 | 04 47 | 05 16 | 10 49 | 11 51 | 12 53 | 13 55 |
| 45 | 03 53 | 04 33 | 05 05 | 10 53 | 12 00 | 13 05 | 14 10 |
| S 50 | 03 28 | 04 15 | 04 52 | 10 59 | 12 10 | 13 20 | 14 30 |
| 52 | 03 16 | 04 07 | 04 46 | 11 01 | 12 15 | 13 27 | 14 39 |
| 54 | 03 02 | 03 57 | 04 39 | 11 04 | 12 20 | 13 35 | 14 49 |
| 56 | 02 44 | 03 47 | 04 31 | 11 07 | 12 26 | 13 44 | 15 01 |
| 58 | 02 23 | 03 34 | 04 23 | 11 10 | 12 32 | 13 54 | 15 15 |
| S 60 | 01 54 | 03 19 | 04 13 | 11 14 | 12 40 | 14 05 | 15 31 |

| Lat. | Sunset | Twilight Civil | Twilight Naut. | Moonset 6 | Moonset 7 | Moonset 8 | Moonset 9 |
|---|---|---|---|---|---|---|---|
| ° | h m | h m | h m | h m | h m | h m | h m |
| N 72 | 14 47 | 16 18 | 17 43 | 24 56 | 00 56 | 03 18 | ▭ |
| N 70 | 15 16 | 16 33 | 17 48 | 24 40 | 00 40 | 02 43 | 05 30 |
| 68 | 15 38 | 16 44 | 17 52 | 24 27 | 00 27 | 02 18 | 04 23 |
| 66 | 15 55 | 16 54 | 17 56 | 24 17 | 00 17 | 01 59 | 03 47 |
| 64 | 16 08 | 17 02 | 18 00 | 24 08 | 00 08 | 01 44 | 03 22 |
| 62 | 16 20 | 17 09 | 18 03 | 24 01 | 00 01 | 01 31 | 03 02 |
| 60 | 16 30 | 17 16 | 18 05 | 23 55 | 25 20 | 01 20 | 02 46 |
| N 58 | 16 38 | 17 21 | 18 08 | 23 49 | 25 11 | 01 11 | 02 32 |
| 56 | 16 46 | 17 26 | 18 10 | 23 45 | 25 03 | 01 03 | 02 21 |
| 54 | 16 53 | 17 31 | 18 13 | 23 40 | 24 56 | 00 56 | 02 11 |
| 52 | 16 59 | 17 35 | 18 15 | 23 36 | 24 49 | 00 49 | 02 02 |
| 50 | 17 04 | 17 39 | 18 17 | 23 33 | 24 44 | 00 44 | 01 54 |
| 45 | 17 16 | 17 47 | 18 22 | 23 25 | 24 31 | 00 31 | 01 37 |
| N 40 | 17 26 | 17 54 | 18 27 | 23 19 | 24 21 | 00 21 | 01 23 |
| 35 | 17 35 | 18 01 | 18 31 | 23 13 | 24 12 | 00 12 | 01 11 |
| 30 | 17 42 | 18 07 | 18 35 | 23 09 | 24 05 | 00 05 | 01 01 |
| 20 | 17 55 | 18 18 | 18 44 | 23 00 | 23 52 | 24 43 | 00 43 |
| N 10 | 18 07 | 18 28 | 18 53 | 22 53 | 23 40 | 24 28 | 00 28 |
| 0 | 18 18 | 18 39 | 19 04 | 22 46 | 23 30 | 24 14 | 00 14 |
| S 10 | 18 29 | 18 50 | 19 16 | 22 39 | 23 19 | 24 00 | 00 00 |
| 20 | 18 40 | 19 03 | 19 31 | 22 32 | 23 08 | 23 45 | 24 25 |
| 30 | 18 54 | 19 19 | 19 50 | 22 24 | 22 55 | 23 28 | 24 04 |
| 35 | 19 02 | 19 29 | 20 02 | 22 19 | 22 47 | 23 18 | 23 51 |
| 40 | 19 11 | 19 41 | 20 16 | 22 14 | 22 39 | 23 06 | 23 37 |
| 45 | 19 22 | 19 54 | 20 34 | 22 08 | 22 29 | 22 53 | 23 21 |
| S 50 | 19 35 | 20 12 | 20 58 | 22 01 | 22 17 | 22 37 | 23 00 |
| 52 | 19 41 | 20 20 | 21 10 | 21 57 | 22 12 | 22 29 | 22 51 |
| 54 | 19 48 | 20 29 | 21 24 | 21 54 | 22 06 | 22 21 | 22 40 |
| 56 | 19 55 | 20 40 | 21 41 | 21 51 | 21 59 | 22 11 | 22 28 |
| 58 | 20 04 | 20 52 | 22 02 | 21 45 | 21 52 | 22 01 | 22 13 |
| S 60 | 20 14 | 21 07 | 22 30 | 21 40 | 21 44 | 21 49 | 21 57 |

| | SUN | | | MOON | | | |
|---|---|---|---|---|---|---|---|
| Day | Eqn. of Time 00h | Eqn. of Time 12h | Mer. Pass. | Mer. Pass. Upper | Mer. Pass. Lower | Age | Phase |
| d | m s | m s | h m | h m | h m | d | % |
| 6 | 14 00 | 14 02 | 12 14 | 16 36 | 04 14 | 05 | 30 |
| 7 | 14 04 | 14 06 | 12 14 | 17 19 | 04 57 | 06 | 40 |
| 8 | 14 07 | 14 08 | 12 14 | 18 03 | 05 41 | 07 | 49 |

| UT | ARIES GHA | VENUS −4.9 GHA | VENUS Dec | MARS +1.4 GHA | MARS Dec | JUPITER −2.0 GHA | JUPITER Dec | SATURN +0.6 GHA | SATURN Dec | STARS Name | SHA | Dec |
|---|---|---|---|---|---|---|---|---|---|---|---|---|
| **9 00** | 139 04.0 | 215 22.2 | S16 33.3 | 216 44.4 | S23 32.6 | 158 01.7 | S 9 04.0 | 179 54.0 | S16 43.4 | Acamar | 315 13.6 | S40 13.3 |
| 01 | 154 06.5 | 230 23.6 | 33.4 | 231 44.9 | 32.5 | 173 03.6 | 03.7 | 194 56.2 | 43.3 | Achernar | 335 22.3 | S57 07.9 |
| 02 | 169 08.9 | 245 25.1 | 33.5 | 246 45.4 | 32.4 | 188 05.5 | 03.5 | 209 58.3 | 43.2 | Acrux | 173 02.2 | S63 13.0 |
| 03 | 184 11.4 | 260 26.5 .. | 33.7 | 261 45.8 .. | 32.2 | 203 07.4 .. | 03.3 | 225 00.5 .. | 43.1 | Adhara | 255 07.4 | S29 00.3 |
| 04 | 199 13.9 | 275 28.0 | 33.8 | 276 46.3 | 32.1 | 218 09.3 | 03.1 | 240 02.6 | 43.1 | Aldebaran | 290 42.2 | N16 33.2 |
| 05 | 214 16.3 | 290 29.4 | 33.9 | 291 46.8 | 32.0 | 233 11.2 | 02.9 | 255 04.8 | 43.0 | | | |
| W 06 | 229 18.8 | 305 30.9 | S16 34.0 | 306 47.2 | S23 31.9 | 248 13.1 | S 9 02.6 | 270 07.0 | S16 42.9 | Alioth | 166 14.8 | N55 50.2 |
| E 07 | 244 21.3 | 320 32.3 | 34.1 | 321 47.7 | 31.7 | 263 15.1 | 02.4 | 285 09.1 | 42.8 | Alkaid | 152 53.7 | N49 11.9 |
| D 08 | 259 23.7 | 335 33.8 | 34.2 | 336 48.2 | 31.6 | 278 17.0 | 02.2 | 300 11.3 | 42.7 | Alnair | 27 36.4 | S46 51.4 |
| N 09 | 274 26.2 | 350 35.2 .. | 34.3 | 351 48.6 .. | 31.5 | 293 18.9 .. | 02.0 | 315 13.5 .. | 42.6 | Alnilam | 275 40.0 | S 1 11.4 |
| E 10 | 289 28.7 | 5 36.6 | 34.4 | 6 49.1 | 31.4 | 308 20.8 | 01.7 | 330 15.6 | 42.5 | Alphard | 217 49.8 | S 8 45.3 |
| S 11 | 304 31.1 | 20 38.1 | 34.5 | 21 49.6 | 31.2 | 323 22.7 | 01.5 | 345 17.8 | 42.4 | | | |
| D 12 | 319 33.6 | 35 39.5 | S16 34.6 | 36 50.0 | S23 31.1 | 338 24.6 | S 9 01.3 | 0 20.0 | S16 42.3 | Alphecca | 126 05.8 | N26 38.2 |
| A 13 | 334 36.1 | 50 40.9 | 34.7 | 51 50.5 | 31.0 | 353 26.5 | 01.1 | 15 22.1 | 42.3 | Alpheratz | 357 37.5 | N29 12.7 |
| Y 14 | 349 38.5 | 65 42.3 | 34.8 | 66 51.0 | 30.8 | 8 28.4 | 00.9 | 30 24.3 | 42.2 | Altair | 62 02.6 | N 8 55.4 |
| 15 | 4 41.0 | 80 43.8 .. | 34.9 | 81 51.4 .. | 30.7 | 23 30.3 .. | 00.6 | 45 26.5 .. | 42.1 | Ankaa | 353 09.8 | S42 11.5 |
| 16 | 19 43.4 | 95 45.2 | 35.1 | 96 51.9 | 30.6 | 38 32.3 | 00.4 | 60 28.6 | 42.0 | Antares | 112 18.9 | S26 28.8 |
| 17 | 34 45.9 | 110 46.6 | 35.2 | 111 52.4 | 30.4 | 53 34.2 | 00.2 | 75 30.8 | 41.9 | | | |
| 18 | 49 48.4 | 125 48.0 | S16 35.3 | 126 52.8 | S23 30.3 | 68 36.1 | S 9 00.0 | 90 33.0 | S16 41.8 | Arcturus | 145 50.0 | N19 03.9 |
| 19 | 64 50.8 | 140 49.4 | 35.4 | 141 53.3 | 30.2 | 83 38.0 | 8 59.8 | 105 35.1 | 41.7 | Atria | 107 15.5 | S69 03.7 |
| 20 | 79 53.3 | 155 50.8 | 35.5 | 156 53.8 | 30.0 | 98 39.9 | 59.5 | 120 37.3 | 41.7 | Avior | 234 15.0 | S59 34.9 |
| 21 | 94 55.8 | 170 52.2 .. | 35.6 | 171 54.2 .. | 29.9 | 113 41.8 .. | 59.3 | 135 39.5 .. | 41.6 | Bellatrix | 278 25.3 | N 6 22.1 |
| 22 | 109 58.2 | 185 53.6 | 35.7 | 186 54.7 | 29.8 | 128 43.7 | 59.1 | 150 41.6 | 41.5 | Betelgeuse | 270 54.5 | N 7 24.6 |
| 23 | 125 00.7 | 200 55.0 | 35.8 | 201 55.2 | 29.6 | 143 45.6 | 58.9 | 165 43.8 | 41.4 | | | |
| **10 00** | 140 03.2 | 215 56.4 | S16 35.9 | 216 55.6 | S23 29.5 | 158 47.5 | S 8 58.6 | 180 46.0 | S16 41.3 | Canopus | 263 53.1 | S52 42.7 |
| 01 | 155 05.6 | 230 57.8 | 36.0 | 231 56.1 | 29.4 | 173 49.5 | 58.4 | 195 48.1 | 41.2 | Capella | 280 25.2 | N46 01.3 |
| 02 | 170 08.1 | 245 59.1 | 36.1 | 246 56.6 | 29.2 | 188 51.4 | 58.2 | 210 50.3 | 41.1 | Deneb | 49 27.9 | N45 21.4 |
| 03 | 185 10.5 | 261 00.5 .. | 36.2 | 261 57.0 .. | 29.1 | 203 53.3 .. | 58.0 | 225 52.4 .. | 41.0 | Denebola | 182 27.1 | N14 26.8 |
| 04 | 200 13.0 | 276 01.9 | 36.3 | 276 57.5 | 29.0 | 218 55.2 | 57.7 | 240 54.6 | 41.0 | Diphda | 348 49.9 | S17 52.2 |
| 05 | 215 15.5 | 291 03.3 | 36.4 | 291 58.0 | 28.8 | 233 57.1 | 57.5 | 255 56.8 | 40.9 | | | |
| T 06 | 230 17.9 | 306 04.6 | S16 36.5 | 306 58.4 | S23 28.7 | 248 59.0 | S 8 57.3 | 270 58.9 | S16 40.8 | Dubhe | 193 43.4 | N61 37.8 |
| H 07 | 245 20.4 | 321 06.0 | 36.7 | 321 58.9 | 28.5 | 264 00.9 | 57.1 | 286 01.1 | 40.7 | Elnath | 278 04.7 | N28 37.6 |
| U 08 | 260 22.9 | 336 07.4 | 36.8 | 336 59.4 | 28.4 | 279 02.8 | 56.9 | 301 03.3 | 40.6 | Eltanin | 90 43.6 | N51 28.9 |
| R 09 | 275 25.3 | 351 08.7 .. | 36.9 | 351 59.8 .. | 28.3 | 294 04.7 .. | 56.6 | 316 05.4 .. | 40.5 | Enif | 33 41.5 | N 9 58.4 |
| S 10 | 290 27.8 | 6 10.1 | 37.0 | 7 00.3 | 28.1 | 309 06.7 | 56.4 | 331 07.6 | 40.4 | Fomalhaut | 15 17.5 | S29 30.5 |
| D 11 | 305 30.3 | 21 11.4 | 37.1 | 22 00.8 | 28.0 | 324 08.6 | 56.2 | 346 09.8 | 40.3 | | | |
| A 12 | 320 32.7 | 36 12.8 | S16 37.2 | 37 01.2 | S23 27.8 | 339 10.5 | S 8 56.0 | 1 11.9 | S16 40.3 | Gacrux | 171 53.9 | S57 14.0 |
| Y 13 | 335 35.2 | 51 14.1 | 37.3 | 52 01.7 | 27.7 | 354 12.4 | 55.7 | 16 14.1 | 40.2 | Gienah | 175 45.8 | S17 39.8 |
| 14 | 350 37.7 | 66 15.5 | 37.4 | 67 02.2 | 27.6 | 9 14.3 | 55.5 | 31 16.3 | 40.1 | Hadar | 148 39.2 | S60 28.5 |
| 15 | 5 40.1 | 81 16.8 .. | 37.5 | 82 02.6 .. | 27.4 | 24 16.2 .. | 55.3 | 46 18.4 .. | 40.0 | Hamal | 327 54.0 | N23 34.0 |
| 16 | 20 42.6 | 96 18.1 | 37.6 | 97 03.1 | 27.3 | 39 18.1 | 55.1 | 61 20.6 | 39.9 | Kaus Aust. | 83 36.0 | S34 22.4 |
| 17 | 35 45.0 | 111 19.5 | 37.7 | 112 03.6 | 27.1 | 54 20.0 | 54.9 | 76 22.8 | 39.8 | | | |
| 18 | 50 47.5 | 126 20.8 | S16 37.8 | 127 04.0 | S23 27.0 | 69 21.9 | S 8 54.6 | 91 24.9 | S16 39.7 | Kochab | 137 19.7 | N74 03.6 |
| 19 | 65 50.0 | 141 22.1 | 37.9 | 142 04.5 | 26.8 | 84 23.8 | 54.4 | 106 27.1 | 39.6 | Markab | 13 32.6 | N15 19.3 |
| 20 | 80 52.4 | 156 23.5 | 38.0 | 157 05.0 | 26.7 | 99 25.8 | 54.2 | 121 29.3 | 39.6 | Menkar | 314 08.7 | N 4 10.4 |
| 21 | 95 54.9 | 171 24.8 .. | 38.1 | 172 05.4 .. | 26.6 | 114 27.7 .. | 54.0 | 136 31.4 .. | 39.5 | Menkent | 148 00.3 | S36 28.5 |
| 22 | 110 57.4 | 186 26.1 | 38.2 | 187 05.9 | 26.4 | 129 29.6 | 53.7 | 151 33.6 | 39.4 | Miaplacidus | 221 37.8 | S69 48.4 |
| 23 | 125 59.8 | 201 27.4 | 38.3 | 202 06.4 | 26.3 | 144 31.5 | 53.5 | 166 35.8 | 39.3 | | | |
| **11 00** | 141 02.3 | 216 28.7 | S16 38.5 | 217 06.8 | S23 26.1 | 159 33.4 | S 8 53.3 | 181 37.9 | S16 39.2 | Mirfak | 308 31.6 | N49 56.5 |
| 01 | 156 04.8 | 231 30.0 | 38.6 | 232 07.3 | 26.0 | 174 35.3 | 53.1 | 196 40.1 | 39.1 | Nunki | 75 51.0 | S26 16.2 |
| 02 | 171 07.2 | 246 31.3 | 38.7 | 247 07.8 | 25.8 | 189 37.2 | 52.8 | 211 42.3 | 39.0 | Peacock | 53 10.1 | S56 39.9 |
| 03 | 186 09.7 | 261 32.6 .. | 38.8 | 262 08.2 .. | 25.7 | 204 39.1 .. | 52.6 | 226 44.4 .. | 38.9 | Pollux | 243 19.9 | N27 58.3 |
| 04 | 201 12.2 | 276 33.9 | 38.9 | 277 08.7 | 25.5 | 219 41.0 | 52.4 | 241 46.6 | 38.9 | Procyon | 244 53.0 | N 5 10.0 |
| 05 | 216 14.6 | 291 35.2 | 39.0 | 292 09.2 | 25.4 | 234 42.9 | 52.2 | 256 48.8 | 38.8 | | | |
| F 06 | 231 17.1 | 306 36.5 | S16 39.1 | 307 09.6 | S23 25.2 | 249 44.9 | S 8 52.0 | 271 50.9 | S16 38.7 | Rasalhague | 96 00.9 | N12 32.5 |
| R 07 | 246 19.5 | 321 37.8 | 39.2 | 322 10.1 | 25.1 | 264 46.8 | 51.7 | 286 53.1 | 38.6 | Regulus | 207 36.7 | N11 51.5 |
| I 08 | 261 22.0 | 336 39.1 | 39.3 | 337 10.6 | 25.0 | 279 48.7 | 51.5 | 301 55.3 | 38.5 | Rigel | 281 06.0 | S 8 10.7 |
| D 09 | 276 24.5 | 351 40.4 .. | 39.4 | 352 11.0 .. | 24.8 | 294 50.6 .. | 51.3 | 316 57.4 .. | 38.4 | Rigil Kent. | 139 43.4 | S60 55.2 |
| A 10 | 291 26.9 | 6 41.7 | 39.5 | 7 11.5 | 24.7 | 309 52.5 | 51.1 | 331 59.6 | 38.3 | Sabik | 102 05.7 | S15 45.1 |
| Y 11 | 306 29.4 | 21 43.0 | 39.6 | 22 12.0 | 24.5 | 324 54.4 | 50.8 | 347 01.7 | 38.2 | | | |
| 12 | 321 31.9 | 36 44.2 | S16 39.7 | 37 12.4 | S23 24.4 | 339 56.3 | S 8 50.6 | 2 03.9 | S16 38.2 | Schedar | 349 34.1 | N56 39.6 |
| 13 | 336 34.3 | 51 45.5 | 39.8 | 52 12.9 | 24.2 | 354 58.2 | 50.4 | 17 06.1 | 38.1 | Shaula | 96 13.8 | S37 07.1 |
| 14 | 351 36.8 | 66 46.8 | 39.9 | 67 13.4 | 24.1 | 10 00.1 | 50.2 | 32 08.2 | 38.0 | Sirius | 258 28.1 | S16 44.9 |
| 15 | 6 39.3 | 81 48.0 .. | 40.0 | 82 13.8 .. | 23.9 | 25 02.0 .. | 49.9 | 47 10.4 .. | 37.9 | Spica | 158 24.7 | S11 16.6 |
| 16 | 21 41.7 | 96 49.3 | 40.1 | 97 14.3 | 23.7 | 40 03.9 | 49.7 | 62 12.6 | 37.8 | Suhail | 222 47.6 | S43 31.3 |
| 17 | 36 44.2 | 111 50.6 | 40.2 | 112 14.8 | 23.6 | 55 05.9 | 49.5 | 77 14.7 | 37.7 | | | |
| 18 | 51 46.7 | 126 51.8 | S16 40.3 | 127 15.2 | S23 23.4 | 70 07.8 | S 8 49.3 | 92 16.9 | S16 37.6 | Vega | 80 35.1 | N38 48.0 |
| 19 | 66 49.1 | 141 53.1 | 40.4 | 142 15.7 | 23.3 | 85 09.7 | 49.1 | 107 19.1 | 37.5 | Zuben'ubi | 136 58.6 | S16 08.0 |
| 20 | 81 51.6 | 156 54.3 | 40.5 | 157 16.2 | 23.1 | 100 11.6 | 48.8 | 122 21.2 | 37.5 | | | |
| 21 | 96 54.0 | 171 55.6 .. | 40.6 | 172 16.6 .. | 23.0 | 115 13.5 .. | 48.6 | 137 23.4 .. | 37.4 | | | |
| 22 | 111 56.5 | 186 56.8 | 40.7 | 187 17.1 | 22.8 | 130 15.4 | 48.4 | 152 25.6 | 37.3 | | | |
| 23 | 126 59.0 | 201 58.1 | 40.8 | 202 17.6 | 22.7 | 145 17.3 | 48.2 | 167 27.7 | 37.2 | | | |
| Mer. Pass. 14 37.4 | v 1.3 d 0.1 | v 0.5 d 0.1 | | v 1.9 d 0.2 | | v 2.2 d 0.1 | | | | | | |

| | SHA | Mer. Pass. |
|---|---|---|
| Venus | 75 53.2 | 9 35 |
| Mars | 76 52.5 | 9 32 |
| Jupiter | 18 44.4 | 13 23 |
| Saturn | 40 42.8 | 11 55 |

| UT | SUN GHA | SUN Dec | MOON GHA | v | MOON Dec | d | HP |
|---|---|---|---|---|---|---|---|
| d h | ° ′ | ° ′ | ° ′ | ′ | ° ′ | ′ | ′ |
| 9 00 | 176 27.6 | S14 45.0 | 86 31.3 | 13.6 | N18 42.7 | 9.7 | 54.5 |
| 01 | 191 27.6 | 44.2 | 101 03.9 | 13.6 | 18 52.4 | 9.6 | 54.5 |
| 02 | 206 27.6 | 43.4 | 115 36.5 | 13.5 | 19 02.0 | 9.5 | 54.5 |
| 03 | 221 27.6 | .. 42.6 | 130 09.0 | 13.5 | 19 11.5 | 9.5 | 54.5 |
| 04 | 236 27.6 | 41.8 | 144 41.5 | 13.4 | 19 21.0 | 9.4 | 54.5 |
| 05 | 251 27.5 | 41.0 | 159 13.9 | 13.4 | 19 30.4 | 9.2 | 54.5 |
| 06 | 266 27.5 | S14 40.2 | 173 46.3 | 13.4 | N19 39.6 | 9.2 | 54.4 |
| W 07 | 281 27.5 | 39.4 | 188 18.7 | 13.3 | 19 48.8 | 9.1 | 54.4 |
| E 08 | 296 27.5 | 38.6 | 202 51.0 | 13.3 | 19 57.9 | 9.1 | 54.4 |
| D 09 | 311 27.5 | .. 37.8 | 217 23.3 | 13.2 | 20 07.0 | 8.9 | 54.4 |
| N 10 | 326 27.5 | 37.0 | 231 55.5 | 13.2 | 20 15.9 | 8.8 | 54.4 |
| E 11 | 341 27.4 | 36.2 | 246 27.7 | 13.1 | 20 24.7 | 8.8 | 54.4 |
| S 12 | 356 27.4 | S14 35.4 | 260 59.8 | 13.1 | N20 33.5 | 8.6 | 54.4 |
| D 13 | 11 27.4 | 34.6 | 275 31.9 | 13.0 | 20 42.1 | 8.6 | 54.4 |
| A 14 | 26 27.4 | 33.7 | 290 03.9 | 13.0 | 20 50.7 | 8.5 | 54.3 |
| Y 15 | 41 27.4 | .. 32.9 | 304 35.9 | 13.0 | 20 59.2 | 8.3 | 54.3 |
| 16 | 56 27.4 | 32.1 | 319 07.9 | 12.9 | 21 07.5 | 8.3 | 54.3 |
| 17 | 71 27.4 | 31.3 | 333 39.8 | 12.8 | 21 15.8 | 8.2 | 54.3 |
| 18 | 86 27.3 | S14 30.5 | 348 11.6 | 12.8 | N21 24.0 | 8.1 | 54.3 |
| 19 | 101 27.3 | 29.7 | 2 43.4 | 12.8 | 21 32.1 | 8.0 | 54.3 |
| 20 | 116 27.3 | 28.9 | 17 15.2 | 12.7 | 21 40.1 | 7.9 | 54.3 |
| 21 | 131 27.3 | .. 28.1 | 31 46.9 | 12.7 | 21 48.0 | 7.8 | 54.3 |
| 22 | 146 27.3 | 27.3 | 46 18.6 | 12.6 | 21 55.8 | 7.7 | 54.3 |
| 23 | 161 27.3 | 26.5 | 60 50.2 | 12.5 | 22 03.5 | 7.6 | 54.3 |
| 10 00 | 176 27.3 | S14 25.7 | 75 21.7 | 12.6 | N22 11.1 | 7.5 | 54.3 |
| 01 | 191 27.3 | 24.9 | 89 53.3 | 12.4 | 22 18.6 | 7.4 | 54.2 |
| 02 | 206 27.3 | 24.0 | 104 24.7 | 12.5 | 22 26.0 | 7.3 | 54.2 |
| 03 | 221 27.2 | .. 23.2 | 118 56.2 | 12.3 | 22 33.3 | 7.2 | 54.2 |
| 04 | 236 27.2 | 22.4 | 133 27.5 | 12.4 | 22 40.5 | 7.1 | 54.2 |
| 05 | 251 27.2 | 21.6 | 147 58.9 | 12.2 | 22 47.6 | 7.0 | 54.2 |
| 06 | 266 27.2 | S14 20.8 | 162 30.1 | 12.3 | N22 54.6 | 6.9 | 54.2 |
| T 07 | 281 27.2 | 20.0 | 177 01.4 | 12.1 | 23 01.5 | 6.8 | 54.2 |
| H 08 | 296 27.2 | 19.2 | 191 32.5 | 12.2 | 23 08.3 | 6.7 | 54.2 |
| U 09 | 311 27.2 | .. 18.4 | 206 03.7 | 12.1 | 23 15.0 | 6.6 | 54.2 |
| R 10 | 326 27.2 | 17.5 | 220 34.8 | 12.0 | 23 21.6 | 6.5 | 54.2 |
| S 11 | 341 27.2 | 16.7 | 235 05.8 | 12.0 | 23 28.1 | 6.3 | 54.2 |
| D 12 | 356 27.2 | S14 15.9 | 249 36.8 | 11.9 | N23 34.4 | 6.3 | 54.2 |
| A 13 | 11 27.2 | 15.1 | 264 07.7 | 11.9 | 23 40.7 | 6.2 | 54.2 |
| Y 14 | 26 27.2 | 14.3 | 278 38.6 | 11.9 | 23 46.9 | 6.0 | 54.2 |
| 15 | 41 27.1 | 13.5 | 293 09.5 | 11.8 | 23 52.9 | 6.0 | 54.2 |
| 16 | 56 27.1 | 12.7 | 307 40.3 | 11.7 | 23 58.7 | 5.8 | 54.2 |
| 17 | 71 27.1 | 11.8 | 322 11.0 | 11.7 | 24 04.7 | 5.7 | 54.2 |
| 18 | 86 27.1 | S14 11.0 | 336 41.7 | 11.7 | N24 10.4 | 5.6 | 54.2 |
| 19 | 101 27.1 | 10.2 | 351 12.4 | 11.6 | 24 16.0 | 5.5 | 54.2 |
| 20 | 116 27.1 | 09.4 | 5 43.0 | 11.5 | 24 21.5 | 5.4 | 54.2 |
| 21 | 131 27.1 | .. 08.6 | 20 13.5 | 11.6 | 24 26.9 | 5.3 | 54.2 |
| 22 | 146 27.1 | 07.7 | 34 44.1 | 11.4 | 24 32.2 | 5.2 | 54.2 |
| 23 | 161 27.1 | 06.9 | 49 14.5 | 11.5 | 24 37.4 | 5.0 | 54.2 |
| 11 00 | 176 27.1 | S14 06.1 | 63 45.0 | 11.4 | N24 42.4 | 5.0 | 54.2 |
| 01 | 191 27.1 | 05.3 | 78 15.4 | 11.3 | 24 47.4 | 4.8 | 54.2 |
| 02 | 206 27.1 | 04.5 | 92 45.7 | 11.3 | 24 52.2 | 4.7 | 54.2 |
| 03 | 221 27.1 | .. 03.6 | 107 16.0 | 11.2 | 24 56.9 | 4.6 | 54.2 |
| 04 | 236 27.1 | 02.8 | 121 46.2 | 11.3 | 25 01.5 | 4.5 | 54.2 |
| 05 | 251 27.1 | 02.0 | 136 16.5 | 11.1 | 25 06.0 | 4.4 | 54.2 |
| 06 | 266 27.1 | S14 01.2 | 150 46.6 | 11.2 | N25 10.4 | 4.2 | 54.2 |
| F 07 | 281 27.1 | 14 00.4 | 165 16.8 | 11.0 | 25 14.6 | 4.2 | 54.2 |
| R 08 | 296 27.1 | 13 59.5 | 179 46.8 | 11.1 | 25 18.8 | 4.0 | 54.2 |
| I 09 | 311 27.1 | .. 58.7 | 194 16.9 | 11.0 | 25 22.8 | 3.9 | 54.2 |
| D 10 | 326 27.1 | 57.9 | 208 46.9 | 11.0 | 25 26.7 | 3.8 | 54.2 |
| A 11 | 341 27.1 | 57.1 | 223 16.9 | 10.9 | 25 30.5 | 3.6 | 54.2 |
| Y 12 | 356 27.1 | S13 56.2 | 237 46.8 | 10.9 | N25 34.1 | 3.6 | 54.2 |
| 13 | 11 27.1 | 55.4 | 252 16.7 | 10.8 | 25 37.7 | 3.4 | 54.2 |
| 14 | 26 27.1 | 54.6 | 266 46.5 | 10.8 | 25 41.1 | 3.3 | 54.2 |
| 15 | 41 27.1 | .. 53.8 | 281 16.3 | 10.8 | 25 44.4 | 3.2 | 54.2 |
| 16 | 56 27.1 | 52.9 | 295 46.1 | 10.8 | 25 47.6 | 3.0 | 54.2 |
| 17 | 71 27.1 | 52.1 | 310 15.9 | 10.7 | 25 50.6 | 3.0 | 54.2 |
| 18 | 86 27.1 | S13 51.3 | 324 45.6 | 10.6 | N25 53.6 | 2.8 | 54.2 |
| 19 | 101 27.1 | 50.5 | 339 15.2 | 10.7 | 25 56.4 | 2.7 | 54.2 |
| 20 | 116 27.1 | 49.6 | 353 44.9 | 10.6 | 25 59.1 | 2.5 | 54.2 |
| 21 | 131 27.1 | .. 48.8 | 8 14.5 | 10.6 | 26 01.6 | 2.5 | 54.2 |
| 22 | 146 27.1 | 48.0 | 22 44.1 | 10.5 | 26 04.1 | 2.3 | 54.2 |
| 23 | 161 27.1 | 47.1 | 37 13.6 | 10.5 | N26 06.4 | 2.2 | 54.2 |
| | SD 16.2 | d 0.8 | SD 14.8 | | 14.8 | | 14.8 |

### Twilight / Sunrise / Moonrise

| Lat. | Naut. | Civil | Sunrise | Moonrise 9 | 10 | 11 | 12 |
|---|---|---|---|---|---|---|---|
| ° | h m | h m | h m | h m | h m | h m | h m |
| N 72 | 06 35 | 07 58 | 09 24 | ▭ | ▭ | ▭ | ▭ |
| N 70 | 06 31 | 07 45 | 08 58 | 07 06 | ▭ | ▭ | ▭ |
| 68 | 06 28 | 07 35 | 08 39 | 08 14 | ▭ | ▭ | ▭ |
| 66 | 06 25 | 07 26 | 08 24 | 08 51 | 08 22 | ▭ | ▭ |
| 64 | 06 22 | 07 19 | 08 11 | 09 17 | 09 11 | 09 00 | ▭ |
| 62 | 06 20 | 07 12 | 08 01 | 09 38 | 09 42 | 09 53 | 10 21 |
| 60 | 06 17 | 07 07 | 07 52 | 09 54 | 10 05 | 10 25 | 11 00 |
| N 58 | 06 15 | 07 02 | 07 44 | 10 08 | 10 24 | 10 49 | 11 27 |
| 56 | 06 13 | 06 57 | 07 37 | 10 21 | 10 40 | 11 08 | 11 49 |
| 54 | 06 11 | 06 53 | 07 30 | 10 31 | 10 54 | 11 24 | 12 06 |
| 52 | 06 09 | 06 49 | 07 25 | 10 41 | 11 05 | 11 38 | 12 21 |
| 50 | 06 08 | 06 46 | 07 19 | 10 49 | 11 16 | 11 50 | 12 34 |
| 45 | 06 03 | 06 38 | 07 08 | 11 08 | 11 38 | 12 16 | 13 01 |
| N 40 | 05 59 | 06 31 | 06 59 | 11 22 | 11 56 | 12 36 | 13 22 |
| 35 | 05 55 | 06 25 | 06 51 | 11 35 | 12 11 | 12 53 | 13 40 |
| 30 | 05 51 | 06 19 | 06 44 | 11 46 | 12 24 | 13 07 | 13 55 |
| 20 | 05 43 | 06 09 | 06 32 | 12 05 | 12 47 | 13 32 | 14 21 |
| N 10 | 05 34 | 05 59 | 06 21 | 12 22 | 13 06 | 13 54 | 14 44 |
| 0 | 05 25 | 05 49 | 06 11 | 12 38 | 13 25 | 14 14 | 15 04 |
| S 10 | 05 13 | 05 39 | 06 00 | 12 53 | 13 43 | 14 34 | 15 25 |
| 20 | 04 59 | 05 26 | 05 49 | 13 10 | 14 03 | 14 56 | 15 48 |
| 30 | 04 41 | 05 11 | 05 36 | 13 30 | 14 26 | 15 21 | 16 14 |
| 35 | 04 29 | 05 02 | 05 29 | 13 41 | 14 39 | 15 36 | 16 29 |
| 40 | 04 15 | 04 51 | 05 20 | 13 55 | 14 55 | 15 53 | 16 47 |
| 45 | 03 58 | 04 38 | 05 10 | 14 10 | 15 14 | 16 14 | 17 08 |
| S 50 | 03 35 | 04 21 | 04 57 | 14 30 | 15 37 | 16 40 | 17 35 |
| 52 | 03 24 | 04 13 | 04 52 | 14 39 | 15 48 | 16 53 | 17 49 |
| 54 | 03 11 | 04 04 | 04 45 | 14 49 | 16 01 | 17 07 | 18 04 |
| 56 | 02 55 | 03 54 | 04 38 | 15 01 | 16 16 | 17 25 | 18 22 |
| 58 | 02 36 | 03 43 | 04 30 | 15 15 | 16 34 | 17 45 | 18 44 |
| S 60 | 02 10 | 03 29 | 04 21 | 15 31 | 16 55 | 18 12 | 19 12 |

### Sunset / Twilight / Moonset

| Lat. | Sunset | Civil | Naut. | Moonset 9 | 10 | 11 | 12 |
|---|---|---|---|---|---|---|---|
| ° | h m | h m | h m | h m | h m | h m | h m |
| N 72 | 15 06 | 16 32 | 17 55 | ▭ | ▭ | ▭ | ▭ |
| N 70 | 15 31 | 16 45 | 17 59 | 05 30 | ▭ | ▭ | ▭ |
| 68 | 15 50 | 16 55 | 18 02 | 04 23 | ▭ | ▭ | ▭ |
| 66 | 16 06 | 17 04 | 18 05 | 03 47 | 05 53 | ▭ | ▭ |
| 64 | 16 18 | 17 11 | 18 08 | 03 22 | 05 05 | 06 56 | ▭ |
| 62 | 16 29 | 17 17 | 18 10 | 03 02 | 04 34 | 06 04 | 07 20 |
| 60 | 16 38 | 17 23 | 18 12 | 02 46 | 04 11 | 05 32 | 06 41 |
| N 58 | 16 46 | 17 28 | 18 14 | 02 32 | 03 53 | 05 08 | 06 14 |
| 56 | 16 53 | 17 32 | 18 16 | 02 21 | 03 37 | 04 49 | 05 53 |
| 54 | 16 59 | 17 36 | 18 18 | 02 11 | 03 24 | 04 33 | 05 35 |
| 52 | 17 05 | 17 40 | 18 20 | 02 02 | 03 13 | 04 20 | 05 20 |
| 50 | 17 10 | 17 43 | 18 22 | 01 54 | 03 02 | 04 08 | 05 07 |
| 45 | 17 21 | 17 51 | 18 26 | 01 37 | 02 41 | 03 43 | 04 40 |
| N 40 | 17 30 | 17 58 | 18 30 | 01 23 | 02 24 | 03 23 | 04 19 |
| 35 | 17 38 | 18 04 | 18 34 | 01 11 | 02 09 | 03 07 | 04 02 |
| 30 | 17 45 | 18 09 | 18 38 | 01 01 | 01 57 | 02 53 | 03 47 |
| 20 | 17 57 | 18 19 | 18 46 | 00 43 | 01 36 | 02 28 | 03 21 |
| N 10 | 18 07 | 18 29 | 18 54 | 00 28 | 01 17 | 02 08 | 02 59 |
| 0 | 18 18 | 18 39 | 19 04 | 00 14 | 01 00 | 01 48 | 02 38 |
| S 10 | 18 28 | 18 50 | 19 15 | 00 00 | 00 43 | 01 29 | 02 17 |
| 20 | 18 39 | 19 02 | 19 29 | 24 25 | 00 25 | 01 08 | 01 55 |
| 30 | 18 52 | 19 17 | 19 47 | 24 04 | 00 04 | 00 44 | 01 30 |
| 35 | 18 59 | 19 26 | 19 58 | 23 51 | 24 30 | 00 30 | 01 15 |
| 40 | 19 08 | 19 37 | 20 12 | 23 37 | 24 14 | 00 14 | 00 57 |
| 45 | 19 18 | 19 50 | 20 29 | 23 21 | 23 55 | 24 36 | 00 36 |
| S 50 | 19 30 | 20 06 | 20 52 | 23 00 | 23 31 | 24 09 | 00 09 |
| 52 | 19 35 | 20 14 | 21 03 | 22 51 | 23 19 | 23 56 | 24 45 |
| 54 | 19 42 | 20 22 | 21 16 | 22 40 | 23 06 | 23 42 | 24 30 |
| 56 | 19 49 | 20 32 | 21 31 | 22 28 | 22 51 | 23 24 | 24 12 |
| 58 | 19 57 | 20 44 | 21 50 | 22 13 | 22 33 | 23 03 | 23 50 |
| S 60 | 20 06 | 20 57 | 22 14 | 21 57 | 22 11 | 22 37 | 23 22 |

### SUN / MOON

| Day | Eqn. of Time 00h | 12h | Mer. Pass. | Mer. Pass. Upper | Lower | Age | Phase |
|---|---|---|---|---|---|---|---|
| d | m s | m s | h m | h m | h m | d | % |
| 9 | 14 09 | 14 10 | 12 14 | 18 49 | 06 26 | 08 | 59 |
| 10 | 14 11 | 14 11 | 12 14 | 19 36 | 07 12 | 09 | 68 |
| 11 | 14 12 | 14 12 | 12 14 | 20 26 | 08 01 | 10 | 76 |

| UT | ARIES GHA | VENUS −4.9 GHA | Dec | MARS +1.3 GHA | Dec | JUPITER −2.0 GHA | Dec | SATURN +0.7 GHA | Dec | STARS Name | SHA | Dec |
|---|---|---|---|---|---|---|---|---|---|---|---|---|
| d h | ° ' | ° ' | ° ' | ° ' | ° ' | ° ' | ° ' | ° ' | ° ' | | ° ' | ° ' |
| 12 00 | 142 01.4 | 216 59.3 | S16 40.9 | 217 18.0 | S23 22.5 | 160 19.2 | S 8 47.9 | 182 29.9 | S16 37.1 | Acamar | 315 13.6 | S40 13.3 |
| 01 | 157 03.9 | 232 00.5 | 41.0 | 232 18.5 | 22.4 | 175 21.1 | 47.7 | 197 32.1 | 37.0 | Achernar | 335 22.3 | S57 07.8 |
| 02 | 172 06.4 | 247 01.8 | 41.1 | 247 19.0 | 22.2 | 190 23.0 | 47.5 | 212 34.2 | 36.9 | Acrux | 173 02.1 | S63 13.1 |
| 03 | 187 08.8 | 262 03.0 .. | 41.2 | 262 19.4 .. | 22.1 | 205 24.9 .. | 47.3 | 227 36.4 .. | 36.9 | Adhara | 255 07.4 | S29 00.3 |
| 04 | 202 11.3 | 277 04.2 | 41.3 | 277 19.9 | 21.9 | 220 26.9 | 47.0 | 242 38.6 | 36.8 | Aldebaran | 290 42.2 | N16 33.2 |
| 05 | 217 13.8 | 292 05.4 | 41.4 | 292 20.4 | 21.7 | 235 28.8 | 46.8 | 257 40.7 | 36.7 | | | |
| 06 | 232 16.2 | 307 06.7 | S16 41.6 | 307 20.9 | S23 21.6 | 250 30.7 | S 8 46.6 | 272 42.9 | S16 36.6 | Alioth | 166 14.7 | N55 50.2 |
| 07 | 247 18.7 | 322 07.9 | 41.7 | 322 21.3 | 21.4 | 265 32.6 | 46.4 | 287 45.1 | 36.5 | Alkaid | 152 53.7 | N49 11.9 |
| S 08 | 262 21.1 | 337 09.1 | 41.8 | 337 21.8 | 21.3 | 280 34.5 | 46.1 | 302 47.2 | 36.4 | Alnair | 27 36.4 | S46 51.4 |
| A 09 | 277 23.6 | 352 10.3 .. | 41.9 | 352 22.3 .. | 21.1 | 295 36.4 .. | 45.9 | 317 49.4 .. | 36.3 | Alnilam | 275 40.0 | S 1 11.4 |
| T 10 | 292 26.1 | 7 11.5 | 42.0 | 7 22.7 | 20.9 | 310 38.3 | 45.7 | 332 51.6 | 36.2 | Alphard | 217 49.8 | S 8 45.3 |
| U 11 | 307 28.5 | 22 12.7 | 42.1 | 22 23.2 | 20.8 | 325 40.2 | 45.5 | 347 53.7 | 36.2 | | | |
| R 12 | 322 31.0 | 37 13.9 | S16 42.2 | 37 23.7 | S23 20.6 | 340 42.1 | S 8 45.2 | 2 55.9 | S16 36.1 | Alphecca | 126 05.8 | N26 38.2 |
| D 13 | 337 33.5 | 52 15.1 | 42.3 | 52 24.1 | 20.5 | 355 44.0 | 45.0 | 17 58.1 | 36.0 | Alpheratz | 357 37.5 | N29 12.7 |
| A 14 | 352 35.9 | 67 16.3 | 42.4 | 67 24.6 | 20.3 | 10 45.9 | 44.8 | 33 00.2 | 35.9 | Altair | 62 02.6 | N 8 55.4 |
| Y 15 | 7 38.4 | 82 17.5 .. | 42.5 | 82 25.1 .. | 20.1 | 25 47.9 .. | 44.6 | 48 02.4 .. | 35.8 | Ankaa | 353 09.8 | S42 11.5 |
| 16 | 22 40.9 | 97 18.7 | 42.6 | 97 25.5 | 20.0 | 40 49.8 | 44.4 | 63 04.6 | 35.7 | Antares | 112 18.8 | S26 28.8 |
| 17 | 37 43.3 | 112 19.9 | 42.7 | 112 26.0 | 19.8 | 55 51.7 | 44.1 | 78 06.7 | 35.6 | | | |
| 18 | 52 45.8 | 127 21.1 | S16 42.8 | 127 26.5 | S23 19.7 | 70 53.6 | S 8 43.9 | 93 08.9 | S16 35.5 | Arcturus | 145 50.0 | N19 03.9 |
| 19 | 67 48.3 | 142 22.3 | 42.9 | 142 26.9 | 19.5 | 85 55.5 | 43.7 | 108 11.1 | 35.5 | Atria | 107 15.4 | S69 03.7 |
| 20 | 82 50.7 | 157 23.4 | 43.0 | 157 27.4 | 19.3 | 100 57.4 | 43.5 | 123 13.2 | 35.4 | Avior | 234 15.1 | S59 34.9 |
| 21 | 97 53.2 | 172 24.6 .. | 43.1 | 172 27.9 .. | 19.2 | 115 59.3 .. | 43.2 | 138 15.4 .. | 35.3 | Bellatrix | 278 25.3 | N 6 22.1 |
| 22 | 112 55.6 | 187 25.8 | 43.2 | 187 28.3 | 19.0 | 131 01.2 | 43.0 | 153 17.6 | 35.2 | Betelgeuse | 270 54.5 | N 7 24.6 |
| 23 | 127 58.1 | 202 27.0 | 43.2 | 202 28.8 | 18.8 | 146 03.1 | 42.8 | 168 19.7 | 35.1 | | | |
| 13 00 | 143 00.6 | 217 28.1 | S16 43.3 | 217 29.3 | S23 18.7 | 161 05.0 | S 8 42.6 | 183 21.9 | S16 35.0 | Canopus | 263 53.1 | S52 42.7 |
| 01 | 158 03.0 | 232 29.3 | 43.4 | 232 29.7 | 18.5 | 176 06.9 | 42.3 | 198 24.1 | 34.9 | Capella | 280 25.2 | N46 01.3 |
| 02 | 173 05.5 | 247 30.5 | 43.5 | 247 30.2 | 18.3 | 191 08.8 | 42.1 | 213 26.2 | 34.8 | Deneb | 49 27.8 | N45 21.4 |
| 03 | 188 08.0 | 262 31.6 .. | 43.6 | 262 30.7 .. | 18.2 | 206 10.8 .. | 41.9 | 228 28.4 .. | 34.8 | Denebola | 182 27.1 | N14 26.8 |
| 04 | 203 10.4 | 277 32.8 | 43.7 | 277 31.1 | 18.0 | 221 12.7 | 41.7 | 243 30.6 | 34.7 | Diphda | 348 49.9 | S17 52.2 |
| 05 | 218 12.9 | 292 33.9 | 43.8 | 292 31.6 | 17.8 | 236 14.6 | 41.4 | 258 32.7 | 34.6 | | | |
| 06 | 233 15.4 | 307 35.1 | S16 43.9 | 307 32.1 | S23 17.7 | 251 16.5 | S 8 41.2 | 273 34.9 | S16 34.5 | Dubhe | 193 43.3 | N61 37.8 |
| 07 | 248 17.8 | 322 36.2 | 44.0 | 322 32.5 | 17.5 | 266 18.4 | 41.0 | 288 37.1 | 34.4 | Elnath | 278 04.7 | N28 37.6 |
| 08 | 263 20.3 | 337 37.4 | 44.1 | 337 33.0 | 17.3 | 281 20.3 | 40.8 | 303 39.2 | 34.3 | Eltanin | 90 43.6 | N51 28.9 |
| S 09 | 278 22.8 | 352 38.5 .. | 44.2 | 352 33.5 .. | 17.2 | 296 22.2 .. | 40.5 | 318 41.4 .. | 34.2 | Enif | 33 41.4 | N 9 58.4 |
| U 10 | 293 25.2 | 7 39.7 | 44.3 | 7 34.0 | 17.0 | 311 24.1 | 40.3 | 333 43.6 | 34.1 | Fomalhaut | 15 17.5 | S29 30.5 |
| N 11 | 308 27.7 | 22 40.8 | 44.4 | 22 34.4 | 16.8 | 326 26.0 | 40.1 | 348 45.7 | 34.1 | | | |
| D 12 | 323 30.1 | 37 41.9 | S16 44.5 | 37 34.9 | S23 16.7 | 341 27.9 | S 8 39.9 | 3 47.9 | S16 34.0 | Gacrux | 171 53.8 | S57 14.0 |
| A 13 | 338 32.6 | 52 43.1 | 44.6 | 52 35.4 | 16.5 | 356 29.8 | 39.6 | 18 50.1 | 33.9 | Gienah | 175 45.8 | S17 39.8 |
| Y 14 | 353 35.1 | 67 44.2 | 44.7 | 67 35.8 | 16.3 | 11 31.7 | 39.4 | 33 52.2 | 33.8 | Hadar | 148 39.1 | S60 28.5 |
| 15 | 8 37.5 | 82 45.3 .. | 44.8 | 82 36.3 .. | 16.1 | 26 33.6 .. | 39.2 | 48 54.4 .. | 33.7 | Hamal | 327 54.0 | N23 34.0 |
| 16 | 23 40.0 | 97 46.4 | 44.9 | 97 36.8 | 16.0 | 41 35.6 | 39.0 | 63 56.6 | 33.6 | Kaus Aust. | 83 35.9 | S34 22.4 |
| 17 | 38 42.5 | 112 47.6 | 45.0 | 112 37.2 | 15.8 | 56 37.5 | 38.7 | 78 58.7 | 33.5 | | | |
| 18 | 53 44.9 | 127 48.7 | S16 45.1 | 127 37.7 | S23 15.6 | 71 39.4 | S 8 38.5 | 94 00.9 | S16 33.4 | Kochab | 137 19.6 | N74 03.6 |
| 19 | 68 47.4 | 142 49.8 | 45.2 | 142 38.2 | 15.5 | 86 41.3 | 38.3 | 109 03.1 | 33.4 | Markab | 13 32.6 | N15 19.3 |
| 20 | 83 49.9 | 157 50.9 | 45.3 | 157 38.6 | 15.3 | 101 43.2 | 38.1 | 124 05.2 | 33.3 | Menkar | 314 08.7 | N 4 10.4 |
| 21 | 98 52.3 | 172 52.0 .. | 45.4 | 172 39.1 .. | 15.1 | 116 45.1 .. | 37.8 | 139 07.4 .. | 33.2 | Menkent | 148 00.3 | S36 28.5 |
| 22 | 113 54.8 | 187 53.1 | 45.5 | 187 39.6 | 14.9 | 131 47.0 | 37.6 | 154 09.6 | 33.1 | Miaplacidus | 221 37.8 | S69 48.4 |
| 23 | 128 57.3 | 202 54.2 | 45.6 | 202 40.0 | 14.8 | 146 48.9 | 37.4 | 169 11.7 | 33.0 | | | |
| 14 00 | 143 59.7 | 217 55.3 | S16 45.6 | 217 40.5 | S23 14.6 | 161 50.8 | S 8 37.2 | 184 13.9 | S16 32.9 | Mirfak | 308 31.6 | N49 56.5 |
| 01 | 159 02.2 | 232 56.4 | 45.7 | 232 41.0 | 14.4 | 176 52.7 | 36.9 | 199 16.1 | 32.8 | Nunki | 75 51.0 | S26 16.2 |
| 02 | 174 04.6 | 247 57.5 | 45.8 | 247 41.4 | 14.2 | 191 54.6 | 36.7 | 214 18.2 | 32.7 | Peacock | 53 10.0 | S56 39.8 |
| 03 | 189 07.1 | 262 58.6 .. | 45.9 | 262 41.9 .. | 14.1 | 206 56.5 .. | 36.5 | 229 20.4 .. | 32.7 | Pollux | 243 19.9 | N27 58.3 |
| 04 | 204 09.6 | 277 59.7 | 46.0 | 277 42.4 | 13.9 | 221 58.4 | 36.3 | 244 22.6 | 32.6 | Procyon | 244 53.0 | N 5 10.0 |
| 05 | 219 12.0 | 293 00.8 | 46.1 | 292 42.9 | 13.7 | 237 00.4 | 36.0 | 259 24.7 | 32.5 | | | |
| 06 | 234 14.5 | 308 01.9 | S16 46.2 | 307 43.3 | S23 13.5 | 252 02.3 | S 8 35.8 | 274 26.9 | S16 32.4 | Rasalhague | 96 00.9 | N12 32.5 |
| 07 | 249 17.0 | 323 02.9 | 46.3 | 322 43.8 | 13.3 | 267 04.2 | 35.6 | 289 29.1 | 32.3 | Regulus | 207 36.6 | N11 51.5 |
| 08 | 264 19.4 | 338 04.0 | 46.4 | 337 44.3 | 13.2 | 282 06.1 | 35.4 | 304 31.2 | 32.2 | Rigel | 281 06.0 | S 8 10.7 |
| M 09 | 279 21.9 | 353 05.1 .. | 46.5 | 352 44.7 .. | 13.0 | 297 08.0 .. | 35.1 | 319 33.4 .. | 32.1 | Rigil Kent. | 139 43.4 | S60 55.3 |
| O 10 | 294 24.4 | 8 06.2 | 46.6 | 7 45.2 | 12.8 | 312 09.9 | 34.9 | 334 35.6 | 32.0 | Sabik | 102 05.6 | S15 45.1 |
| N 11 | 309 26.8 | 23 07.2 | 46.7 | 22 45.7 | 12.6 | 327 11.8 | 34.7 | 349 37.7 | 32.0 | | | |
| D 12 | 324 29.3 | 38 08.3 | S16 46.8 | 37 46.1 | S23 12.5 | 342 13.7 | S 8 34.5 | 4 39.9 | S16 31.9 | Schedar | 349 34.1 | N56 39.6 |
| A 13 | 339 31.7 | 53 09.4 | 46.8 | 52 46.6 | 12.3 | 357 15.6 | 34.2 | 19 42.1 | 31.8 | Shaula | 96 13.8 | S37 07.1 |
| Y 14 | 354 34.2 | 68 10.4 | 46.9 | 67 47.1 | 12.1 | 12 17.5 | 34.0 | 34 44.2 | 31.7 | Sirius | 258 28.1 | S16 44.9 |
| 15 | 9 36.7 | 83 11.5 .. | 47.0 | 82 47.5 .. | 11.9 | 27 19.4 .. | 33.8 | 49 46.4 .. | 31.6 | Spica | 158 24.6 | S11 16.6 |
| 16 | 24 39.1 | 98 12.5 | 47.1 | 97 48.0 | 11.7 | 42 21.3 | 33.6 | 64 48.6 | 31.5 | Suhail | 222 47.6 | S43 31.3 |
| 17 | 39 41.6 | 113 13.6 | 47.2 | 112 48.5 | 11.5 | 57 23.2 | 33.3 | 79 50.7 | 31.4 | | | |
| 18 | 54 44.1 | 128 14.6 | S16 47.3 | 127 48.9 | S23 11.4 | 72 25.1 | S 8 33.1 | 94 52.9 | S16 31.3 | Vega | 80 35.1 | N38 48.0 |
| 19 | 69 46.5 | 143 15.7 | 47.4 | 142 49.4 | 11.2 | 87 27.1 | 32.9 | 109 55.1 | 31.3 | Zuben'ubi | 136 58.6 | S16 08.0 |
| 20 | 84 49.0 | 158 16.7 | 47.5 | 157 49.9 | 11.0 | 102 29.0 | 32.7 | 124 57.2 | 31.2 | | SHA | Mer. Pass. |
| 21 | 99 51.5 | 173 17.8 .. | 47.6 | 172 50.4 .. | 10.8 | 117 30.9 .. | 32.4 | 139 59.4 .. | 31.1 | | ° ' | h m |
| 22 | 114 53.9 | 188 18.8 | 47.6 | 187 50.8 | 10.6 | 132 32.8 | 32.2 | 155 01.6 | 31.0 | Venus | 74 27.6 | 9 29 |
| 23 | 129 56.4 | 203 19.9 | 47.7 | 202 51.3 | 10.4 | 147 34.7 | 32.0 | 170 03.7 | 30.9 | Mars | 74 28.7 | 9 30 |
| | h m | | | | | | | | | Jupiter | 18 04.5 | 13 14 |
| Mer. Pass. 14 25.6 | | v 1.1 d 0.1 | | v 0.5 d 0.2 | | v 1.9 d 0.2 | | v 2.2 d 0.1 | | Saturn | 40 21.3 | 11 45 |

| UT | SUN | | MOON | | | | | Lat. | Twilight | | Sunrise | Moonrise | | | |
|---|---|---|---|---|---|---|---|---|---|---|---|---|---|---|---|
| | | | | | | | | | Naut. | Civil | | 12 | 13 | 14 | 15 |
| | GHA | Dec | GHA | v | Dec | d | HP | | | | | | | | |
| d h | ° ′ | ° ′ | ° ′ | ′ | ° ′ | ′ | ′ | ° | h m | h m | h m | h m | h m | h m | h m |
| 12 00 | 176 27.1 | S13 46.3 | 51 43.1 | 10.5 | N26 08.6 | 2.1 | 54.2 | N 72 | 06 23 | 07 44 | 09 05 | ⬜ | ⬜ | ⬜ | ⬜ |
| 01 | 191 27.1 | 45.5 | 66 12.6 | 10.4 | 26 10.7 | 1.9 | 54.2 | N 70 | 06 20 | 07 33 | 08 44 | ⬜ | ⬜ | ⬜ | 12 18 |
| 02 | 206 27.1 | 44.6 | 80 42.0 | 10.5 | 26 12.6 | 1.8 | 54.2 | 68 | 06 18 | 07 24 | 08 27 | ⬜ | ⬜ | ⬜ | 13 23 |
| 03 | 221 27.2 .. | 43.8 | 95 11.5 | 10.4 | 26 14.4 | 1.7 | 54.2 | 66 | 06 16 | 07 16 | 08 13 | ⬜ | ⬜ | 12 05 | 13 57 |
| 04 | 236 27.2 | 43.0 | 109 40.9 | 10.3 | 26 16.1 | 1.6 | 54.2 | 64 | 06 14 | 07 10 | 08 02 | ⬜ | ⬜ | 12 46 | 14 23 |
| 05 | 251 27.2 | 42.2 | 124 10.2 | 10.4 | 26 17.7 | 1.4 | 54.2 | 62 | 06 12 | 07 04 | 07 52 | 10 21 | 11 20 | 13 15 | 14 42 |
| 06 | 266 27.2 | S13 41.3 | 138 39.6 | 10.3 | N26 19.1 | 1.3 | 54.3 | 60 | 06 10 | 06 59 | 07 44 | 11 00 | 11 57 | 13 15 | 14 42 |
| S 07 | 281 27.2 | 40.5 | 153 08.9 | 10.3 | 26 20.4 | 1.2 | 54.3 | N 58 | 06 09 | 06 55 | 07 36 | 11 27 | 12 24 | 13 36 | 14 58 |
| A 08 | 296 27.2 | 39.7 | 167 38.2 | 10.3 | 26 21.6 | 1.1 | 54.3 | 56 | 06 07 | 06 51 | 07 30 | 11 49 | 12 44 | 13 54 | 15 12 |
| T 09 | 311 27.2 .. | 38.8 | 182 07.5 | 10.2 | 26 22.7 | 0.9 | 54.3 | 54 | 06 06 | 06 47 | 07 24 | 12 06 | 13 02 | 14 09 | 15 24 |
| U 10 | 326 27.2 | 38.0 | 196 36.7 | 10.3 | 26 23.6 | 0.8 | 54.3 | 52 | 06 04 | 06 44 | 07 19 | 12 21 | 13 16 | 14 22 | 15 34 |
| R 11 | 341 27.2 | 37.2 | 211 06.0 | 10.2 | 26 24.4 | 0.7 | 54.3 | 50 | 06 03 | 06 41 | 07 14 | 12 34 | 13 29 | 14 33 | 15 44 |
| D 12 | 356 27.2 | S13 36.3 | 225 35.2 | 10.2 | N26 25.1 | 0.6 | 54.3 | 45 | 05 59 | 06 34 | 07 04 | 13 01 | 13 55 | 14 57 | 16 03 |
| A 13 | 11 27.2 | 35.5 | 240 04.4 | 10.1 | 26 25.7 | 0.4 | 54.3 | N 40 | 05 56 | 06 28 | 06 56 | 13 22 | 14 16 | 15 16 | 16 19 |
| Y 14 | 26 27.2 | 34.7 | 254 33.5 | 10.1 | 26 26.1 | 0.3 | 54.3 | 35 | 05 52 | 06 22 | 06 48 | 13 40 | 14 33 | 15 31 | 16 32 |
| 15 | 41 27.3 .. | 33.8 | 269 02.7 | 10.1 | 26 26.4 | 0.1 | 54.3 | 30 | 05 49 | 06 17 | 06 42 | 13 55 | 14 48 | 15 45 | 16 44 |
| 16 | 56 27.3 | 33.0 | 283 31.8 | 10.2 | 26 26.5 | 0.1 | 54.3 | 20 | 05 42 | 06 08 | 06 30 | 14 21 | 15 14 | 16 00 | 17 03 |
| 17 | 71 27.3 | 32.2 | 298 01.0 | 10.1 | 26 26.6 | 0.1 | 54.3 | N 10 | 05 34 | 05 59 | 06 20 | 14 44 | 15 35 | 16 28 | 17 20 |
| 18 | 86 27.3 | S13 31.3 | 312 30.1 | 10.1 | N26 26.5 | 0.3 | 54.4 | 0 | 05 25 | 05 50 | 06 11 | 15 04 | 15 56 | 16 47 | 17 36 |
| 19 | 101 27.3 | 30.5 | 326 59.2 | 10.0 | 26 26.2 | 0.3 | 54.4 | S 10 | 05 14 | 05 39 | 06 01 | 15 25 | 16 16 | 17 05 | 17 52 |
| 20 | 116 27.3 | 29.6 | 341 28.2 | 10.1 | 26 25.9 | 0.5 | 54.4 | 20 | 05 01 | 05 28 | 05 51 | 15 48 | 16 38 | 17 25 | 18 09 |
| 21 | 131 27.3 .. | 28.8 | 355 57.3 | 10.1 | 26 25.4 | 0.6 | 54.4 | 30 | 04 44 | 05 14 | 05 39 | 16 14 | 17 03 | 17 48 | 18 29 |
| 22 | 146 27.3 | 28.0 | 10 26.4 | 10.0 | 26 24.8 | 0.8 | 54.4 | 35 | 04 33 | 05 05 | 05 32 | 16 29 | 17 18 | 18 01 | 18 40 |
| 23 | 161 27.3 | 27.1 | 24 55.4 | 10.1 | 26 24.0 | 0.8 | 54.4 | 40 | 04 20 | 04 55 | 05 24 | 16 47 | 17 35 | 18 17 | 18 53 |
| 13 00 | 176 27.4 | S13 26.3 | 39 24.5 | 10.0 | N26 23.2 | 1.0 | 54.4 | 45 | 04 03 | 04 42 | 05 14 | 17 08 | 17 55 | 18 35 | 19 08 |
| 01 | 191 27.4 | 25.4 | 53 53.5 | 10.0 | 26 22.2 | 1.2 | 54.4 | S 50 | 03 42 | 04 27 | 05 03 | 17 35 | 18 21 | 18 58 | 19 26 |
| 02 | 206 27.4 | 24.6 | 68 22.5 | 10.1 | 26 21.0 | 1.2 | 54.4 | 52 | 03 31 | 04 20 | 04 57 | 17 49 | 18 34 | 19 09 | 19 35 |
| 03 | 221 27.4 .. | 23.8 | 82 51.6 | 10.0 | 26 19.8 | 1.4 | 54.5 | 54 | 03 19 | 04 11 | 04 52 | 18 04 | 18 48 | 19 21 | 19 45 |
| 04 | 236 27.4 | 22.9 | 97 20.6 | 10.0 | 26 18.4 | 1.6 | 54.5 | 56 | 03 05 | 04 02 | 04 45 | 18 22 | 19 05 | 19 35 | 19 56 |
| 05 | 251 27.4 | 22.1 | 111 49.6 | 10.0 | 26 16.8 | 1.6 | 54.5 | 58 | 02 47 | 03 51 | 04 37 | 18 44 | 19 25 | 19 51 | 20 08 |
| 06 | 266 27.4 | S13 21.2 | 126 18.6 | 10.0 | N26 15.2 | 1.8 | 54.5 | S 60 | 02 26 | 03 39 | 04 29 | 19 12 | 19 50 | 20 11 | 20 23 |
| 07 | 281 27.5 | 20.4 | 140 47.6 | 10.0 | 26 13.4 | 1.9 | 54.5 | | | | | | | | |

| Lat. | Sunset | Twilight | | Moonset | | | |
|---|---|---|---|---|---|---|---|
| | | Civil | Naut. | 12 | 13 | 14 | 15 |
| S 08 | 296 27.5 | 19.6 | 155 16.6 | 10.1 | 26 11.5 | 2.1 | 54.5 |

| UT | SUN | | MOON | | | | | Lat. | Sunset | Twilight | | Moonset | | | |
|---|---|---|---|---|---|---|---|---|---|---|---|---|---|---|---|
| | | | | | | | | | | Civil | Naut. | 12 | 13 | 14 | 15 |
| | GHA | Dec | GHA | v | Dec | d | HP | ° | h m | h m | h m | h m | h m | h m | h m |
| S 09 | 311 27.5 .. | 18.7 | 169 45.7 | 10.0 | 26 09.4 | 2.1 | 54.5 | N 72 | 15 24 | 16 46 | 18 07 | ⬜ | ⬜ | ⬜ | ⬜ |
| U 10 | 326 27.5 | 17.9 | 184 14.7 | 10.0 | 26 07.3 | 2.3 | 54.5 | N 70 | 15 46 | 16 57 | 18 10 | ⬜ | ⬜ | ⬜ | 10 42 |
| N 11 | 341 27.5 | 17.0 | 198 43.7 | 10.0 | 26 05.0 | 2.5 | 54.5 | 68 | 16 03 | 17 06 | 18 12 | ⬜ | ⬜ | ⬜ | 09 37 |
| D 12 | 356 27.5 | S13 16.2 | 213 12.7 | 10.0 | N26 02.5 | 2.6 | 54.6 | 66 | 16 17 | 17 13 | 18 14 | ⬜ | ⬜ | 09 09 | 09 01 |
| A 13 | 11 27.6 | 15.4 | 227 41.7 | 10.1 | 25 59.9 | 2.7 | 54.6 | 64 | 16 28 | 17 20 | 18 16 | ⬜ | ⬜ | 09 09 | 09 01 |
| Y 14 | 26 27.6 | 14.5 | 242 10.8 | 10.0 | 25 57.2 | 2.8 | 54.6 | 62 | 16 37 | 17 25 | 18 17 | 07 20 | 08 07 | 08 28 | 08 36 |
| 15 | 41 27.6 .. | 13.7 | 256 39.8 | 10.1 | 25 54.4 | 2.9 | 54.6 | 60 | 16 46 | 17 30 | 18 19 | 06 41 | 07 30 | 07 59 | 08 15 |
| 16 | 56 27.6 | 12.8 | 271 08.9 | 10.0 | 25 51.5 | 3.1 | 54.6 | N 58 | 16 53 | 17 34 | 18 21 | 06 14 | 07 04 | 07 37 | 07 58 |
| 17 | 71 27.6 | 12.0 | 285 37.9 | 10.1 | 25 48.4 | 3.2 | 54.6 | 56 | 16 59 | 17 38 | 18 22 | 05 53 | 06 43 | 07 19 | 07 44 |
| 18 | 86 27.7 | S13 11.1 | 300 07.0 | 10.1 | N25 45.2 | 3.4 | 54.6 | 54 | 17 05 | 17 42 | 18 24 | 05 35 | 06 26 | 07 04 | 07 32 |
| 19 | 101 27.7 | 10.3 | 314 36.1 | 10.0 | 25 41.8 | 3.5 | 54.7 | 52 | 17 10 | 17 45 | 18 25 | 05 20 | 06 11 | 06 51 | 07 21 |
| 20 | 116 27.7 | 09.4 | 329 05.1 | 10.1 | 25 38.3 | 3.6 | 54.7 | 50 | 17 15 | 17 48 | 18 26 | 05 07 | 05 58 | 06 39 | 07 11 |
| 21 | 131 27.7 .. | 08.6 | 343 34.2 | 10.2 | 25 34.7 | 3.7 | 54.7 | 45 | 17 25 | 17 55 | 18 30 | 04 40 | 05 31 | 06 15 | 06 51 |
| 22 | 146 27.7 | 07.7 | 358 03.4 | 10.1 | 25 31.0 | 3.9 | 54.7 | N 40 | 17 33 | 18 01 | 18 33 | 04 19 | 05 10 | 05 55 | 06 34 |
| 23 | 161 27.8 | 06.9 | 12 32.5 | 10.1 | 25 27.1 | 4.0 | 54.7 | 35 | 17 41 | 18 07 | 18 36 | 04 02 | 04 53 | 05 39 | 06 20 |
| 14 00 | 176 27.8 | S13 06.0 | 27 01.6 | 10.2 | N25 23.1 | 4.1 | 54.7 | 30 | 17 47 | 18 12 | 18 40 | 03 47 | 04 38 | 05 25 | 06 08 |
| 01 | 191 27.8 | 05.2 | 41 30.8 | 10.2 | 25 19.0 | 4.2 | 54.7 | 20 | 17 58 | 18 21 | 18 47 | 03 21 | 04 12 | 05 01 | 05 47 |
| 02 | 206 27.8 | 04.4 | 56 00.0 | 10.1 | 25 14.8 | 4.4 | 54.8 | N 10 | 18 08 | 18 30 | 18 55 | 02 59 | 03 50 | 04 40 | 05 28 |
| 03 | 221 27.8 .. | 03.5 | 70 29.1 | 10.3 | 25 10.4 | 4.5 | 54.8 | 0 | 18 18 | 18 39 | 19 03 | 02 38 | 03 29 | 04 20 | 05 11 |
| 04 | 236 27.9 | 02.7 | 84 58.4 | 10.2 | 25 05.9 | 4.6 | 54.8 | S 10 | 18 27 | 18 49 | 19 14 | 02 17 | 03 08 | 04 01 | 04 53 |
| 05 | 251 27.9 | 01.8 | 99 27.6 | 10.2 | 25 01.3 | 4.8 | 54.8 | 20 | 18 37 | 19 00 | 19 27 | 01 55 | 02 46 | 03 40 | 04 35 |
| 06 | 266 27.9 | S13 01.0 | 113 56.8 | 10.3 | N24 56.5 | 4.9 | 54.8 | 30 | 18 49 | 19 14 | 19 44 | 01 30 | 02 20 | 03 15 | 04 13 |
| 07 | 281 27.9 | 13 00.1 | 128 26.1 | 10.3 | 24 51.6 | 5.0 | 54.8 | 35 | 18 56 | 19 23 | 19 55 | 01 15 | 02 05 | 03 01 | 04 00 |
| 08 | 296 28.0 | 12 59.3 | 142 55.4 | 10.3 | 24 46.6 | 5.1 | 54.9 | 40 | 19 04 | 19 33 | 20 08 | 00 57 | 01 47 | 02 44 | 03 46 |
| M 09 | 311 28.0 .. | 58.4 | 157 24.7 | 10.4 | 24 41.5 | 5.3 | 54.9 | 45 | 19 13 | 19 45 | 20 24 | 00 36 | 01 26 | 02 24 | 03 28 |
| O 10 | 326 28.0 | 57.6 | 171 54.1 | 10.3 | 24 36.2 | 5.3 | 54.9 | S 50 | 19 24 | 20 00 | 20 45 | 00 09 | 00 59 | 01 58 | 03 06 |
| N 11 | 341 28.0 | 56.7 | 186 23.4 | 10.4 | 24 30.9 | 5.5 | 54.9 | 52 | 19 30 | 20 07 | 20 55 | 24 45 | 00 45 | 01 46 | 02 56 |
| D 12 | 356 28.1 | S12 55.9 | 200 52.8 | 10.5 | N24 25.4 | 5.7 | 54.9 | 54 | 19 35 | 20 15 | 21 07 | 24 30 | 00 30 | 01 32 | 02 44 |
| A 13 | 11 28.1 | 55.0 | 215 22.3 | 10.4 | 24 19.7 | 5.7 | 54.9 | 56 | 19 42 | 20 24 | 21 21 | 24 12 | 00 12 | 01 15 | 02 30 |
| Y 14 | 26 28.1 | 54.1 | 229 51.7 | 10.5 | 24 14.0 | 5.9 | 55.0 | 58 | 19 49 | 20 35 | 21 38 | 23 50 | 24 56 | 00 56 | 02 14 |
| 15 | 41 28.1 .. | 53.3 | 244 21.2 | 10.5 | 24 08.1 | 6.0 | 55.0 | S 60 | 19 57 | 20 47 | 21 59 | 23 22 | 24 31 | 00 31 | 01 55 |
| 16 | 56 28.2 | 52.4 | 258 50.7 | 10.5 | 24 02.1 | 6.1 | 55.0 | | | | | | | | |
| 17 | 71 28.2 | 51.6 | 273 20.2 | 10.6 | 23 56.0 | 6.3 | 55.0 | | | | | | | | |
| 18 | 86 28.2 | S12 50.7 | 287 49.8 | 10.5 | N23 49.7 | 6.3 | 55.0 | | | SUN | | | MOON | | |
| 19 | 101 28.2 | 49.9 | 302 19.3 | 10.7 | 23 43.4 | 6.5 | 55.0 | Day | Eqn. of Time | | Mer. | Mer. Pass. | | Age | Phase |
| 20 | 116 28.3 | 49.0 | 316 49.0 | 10.6 | 23 36.9 | 6.6 | 55.1 | | 00ʰ | 12ʰ | Pass. | Upper | Lower | | |
| 21 | 131 28.3 .. | 48.2 | 331 18.6 | 10.7 | 23 30.3 | 6.7 | 55.1 | d | m s | m s | h m | h m | h m | d | % |
| 22 | 146 28.3 | 47.3 | 345 48.3 | 10.7 | 23 23.6 | 6.9 | 55.1 | 12 | 14 11 | 14 11 | 12 14 | 21 17 | 08 51 | 11 | 84 |
| 23 | 161 28.3 | 46.5 | 0 18.0 | 10.8 | N23 16.7 | 7.0 | 55.1 | 13 | 14 11 | 14 10 | 12 14 | 22 08 | 09 42 | 12 | 90 |
| | SD 16.2 | d 0.8 | SD 14.8 | | 14.9 | | 15.0 | 14 | 14 09 | 14 08 | 12 14 | 22 59 | 10 34 | 13 | 95 |

| UT | ARIES | VENUS −4.9 | | MARS +1.3 | | JUPITER −2.0 | | SATURN +0.7 | | STARS | | |
|---|---|---|---|---|---|---|---|---|---|---|---|---|
| | GHA | GHA | Dec | GHA | Dec | GHA | Dec | GHA | Dec | Name | SHA | Dec |
| d h | ° ′ | ° ′ | ° ′ | ° ′ | ° ′ | ° ′ | ° ′ | ° ′ | ° ′ | | ° ′ | ° ′ |
| 15 00 | 144 58.9 | 218 20.9 | S16 47.8 | 217 51.8 | S23 10.3 | 162 36.6 | S 8 31.8 | 185 05.9 | S16 30.8 | Acamar | 315 13.7 | S40 13.3 |
| 01 | 160 01.3 | 233 21.9 | 47.9 | 232 52.2 | 10.1 | 177 38.5 | 31.5 | 200 08.1 | 30.7 | Achernar | 335 22.3 | S57 07.8 |
| 02 | 175 03.8 | 248 23.0 | 48.0 | 247 52.7 | 09.9 | 192 40.4 | 31.3 | 215 10.3 | 30.7 | Acrux | 173 02.1 | S63 13.1 |
| 03 | 190 06.2 | 263 24.0 .. | 48.1 | 262 53.2 .. | 09.7 | 207 42.3 .. | 31.1 | 230 12.4 .. | 30.6 | Adhara | 255 07.4 | S29 00.3 |
| 04 | 205 08.7 | 278 25.0 | 48.2 | 277 53.6 | 09.5 | 222 44.2 | 30.9 | 245 14.6 | 30.5 | Aldebaran | 290 42.2 | N16 33.2 |
| 05 | 220 11.2 | 293 26.0 | 48.3 | 292 54.1 | 09.3 | 237 46.1 | 30.6 | 260 16.8 | 30.4 | | | |
| 06 | 235 13.6 | 308 27.0 | S16 48.3 | 307 54.6 | S23 09.1 | 252 48.0 | S 8 30.4 | 275 18.9 | S16 30.3 | Alioth | 166 14.7 | N55 50.2 |
| 07 | 250 16.1 | 323 28.1 | 48.4 | 322 55.0 | 09.0 | 267 49.9 | 30.2 | 290 21.1 | 30.2 | Alkaid | 152 53.7 | N49 11.9 |
| 08 | 265 18.6 | 338 29.1 | 48.5 | 337 55.5 | 08.8 | 282 51.8 | 30.0 | 305 23.3 | 30.1 | Alnair | 27 36.4 | S46 51.4 |
| T 09 | 280 21.0 | 353 30.1 .. | 48.6 | 352 56.0 .. | 08.6 | 297 53.7 .. | 29.7 | 320 25.4 .. | 30.0 | Alnilam | 275 40.0 | S 1 11.4 |
| U 10 | 295 23.5 | 8 31.1 | 48.7 | 7 56.5 | 08.4 | 312 55.7 | 29.5 | 335 27.6 | 30.0 | Alphard | 217 49.7 | S 8 45.3 |
| E 11 | 310 26.0 | 23 32.1 | 48.8 | 22 56.9 | 08.2 | 327 57.6 | 29.3 | 350 29.8 | 29.9 | | | |
| S 12 | 325 28.4 | 38 33.1 | S16 48.8 | 37 57.4 | S23 08.0 | 342 59.5 | S 8 29.1 | 5 31.9 | S16 29.8 | Alphecca | 126 05.7 | N26 38.2 |
| D 13 | 340 30.9 | 53 34.1 | 48.9 | 52 57.9 | 07.8 | 358 01.4 | 28.8 | 20 34.1 | 29.7 | Alpheratz | 357 37.5 | N29 12.7 |
| A 14 | 355 33.4 | 68 35.1 | 49.0 | 67 58.3 | 07.6 | 13 03.3 | 28.6 | 35 36.3 | 29.6 | Altair | 62 02.5 | N 8 55.4 |
| Y 15 | 10 35.8 | 83 36.1 .. | 49.1 | 82 58.8 .. | 07.4 | 28 05.2 .. | 28.4 | 50 38.4 .. | 29.5 | Ankaa | 353 09.8 | S42 11.5 |
| 16 | 25 38.3 | 98 37.1 | 49.2 | 97 59.3 | 07.2 | 43 07.1 | 28.1 | 65 40.6 | 29.4 | Antares | 112 18.8 | S26 28.8 |
| 17 | 40 40.7 | 113 38.1 | 49.3 | 112 59.7 | 07.1 | 58 09.0 | 27.9 | 80 42.8 | 29.3 | | | |
| 18 | 55 43.2 | 128 39.1 | S16 49.3 | 128 00.2 | S23 06.9 | 73 10.9 | S 8 27.7 | 95 44.9 | S16 29.3 | Arcturus | 145 50.0 | N19 03.9 |
| 19 | 70 45.7 | 143 40.0 | 49.4 | 143 00.7 | 06.7 | 88 12.8 | 27.5 | 110 47.1 | 29.2 | Atria | 107 15.3 | S69 03.7 |
| 20 | 85 48.1 | 158 41.0 | 49.5 | 158 01.2 | 06.5 | 103 14.7 | 27.2 | 125 49.3 | 29.1 | Avior | 234 15.1 | S59 34.9 |
| 21 | 100 50.6 | 173 42.0 .. | 49.6 | 173 01.6 .. | 06.3 | 118 16.6 .. | 27.0 | 140 51.4 .. | 29.0 | Bellatrix | 278 25.3 | N 6 22.1 |
| 22 | 115 53.1 | 188 43.0 | 49.7 | 188 02.1 | 06.1 | 133 18.5 | 26.8 | 155 53.6 | 28.9 | Betelgeuse | 270 54.5 | N 7 24.6 |
| 23 | 130 55.5 | 203 44.0 | 49.8 | 203 02.6 | 05.9 | 148 20.4 | 26.6 | 170 55.8 | 28.8 | | | |
| 16 00 | 145 58.0 | 218 44.9 | S16 49.8 | 218 03.0 | S23 05.7 | 163 22.3 | S 8 26.3 | 185 57.9 | S16 28.7 | Canopus | 263 53.1 | S52 42.7 |
| 01 | 161 00.5 | 233 45.9 | 49.9 | 233 03.5 | 05.5 | 178 24.2 | 26.1 | 201 00.1 | 28.6 | Capella | 280 25.2 | N46 01.3 |
| 02 | 176 02.9 | 248 46.9 | 50.0 | 248 04.0 | 05.3 | 193 26.1 | 25.9 | 216 02.3 | 28.6 | Deneb | 49 27.8 | N45 21.4 |
| 03 | 191 05.4 | 263 47.8 .. | 50.1 | 263 04.4 .. | 05.1 | 208 28.1 .. | 25.7 | 231 04.5 .. | 28.5 | Denebola | 182 27.1 | N14 26.8 |
| 04 | 206 07.9 | 278 48.8 | 50.2 | 278 04.9 | 04.9 | 223 30.0 | 25.4 | 246 06.6 | 28.4 | Diphda | 348 49.9 | S17 52.2 |
| 05 | 221 10.3 | 293 49.7 | 50.2 | 293 05.4 | 04.7 | 238 31.9 | 25.2 | 261 08.8 | 28.3 | | | |
| 06 | 236 12.8 | 308 50.7 | S16 50.3 | 308 05.9 | S23 04.5 | 253 33.8 | S 8 25.0 | 276 11.0 | S16 28.2 | Dubhe | 193 43.3 | N61 37.8 |
| W 07 | 251 15.2 | 323 51.7 | 50.4 | 323 06.3 | 04.3 | 268 35.7 | 24.8 | 291 13.1 | 28.1 | Elnath | 278 04.7 | N28 37.6 |
| E 08 | 266 17.7 | 338 52.6 | 50.5 | 338 06.8 | 04.1 | 283 37.6 | 24.5 | 306 15.3 | 28.0 | Eltanin | 90 43.6 | N51 28.9 |
| D 09 | 281 20.2 | 353 53.6 .. | 50.5 | 353 07.3 .. | 03.9 | 298 39.5 .. | 24.3 | 321 17.5 .. | 27.9 | Enif | 33 41.4 | N 9 58.4 |
| N 10 | 296 22.6 | 8 54.5 | 50.6 | 8 07.7 | 03.7 | 313 41.4 | 24.1 | 336 19.6 | 27.9 | Fomalhaut | 15 17.5 | S29 30.5 |
| E 11 | 311 25.1 | 23 55.4 | 50.7 | 23 08.2 | 03.5 | 328 43.3 | 23.9 | 351 21.8 | 27.8 | | | |
| S 12 | 326 27.6 | 38 56.4 | S16 50.8 | 38 08.7 | S23 03.3 | 343 45.2 | S 8 23.6 | 6 24.0 | S16 27.7 | Gacrux | 171 53.8 | S57 14.0 |
| D 13 | 341 30.0 | 53 57.3 | 50.9 | 53 09.1 | 03.1 | 358 47.1 | 23.4 | 21 26.1 | 27.6 | Gienah | 175 45.8 | S17 39.8 |
| A 14 | 356 32.5 | 68 58.3 | 50.9 | 68 09.6 | 02.9 | 13 49.0 | 23.2 | 36 28.3 | 27.5 | Hadar | 148 39.1 | S60 28.5 |
| Y 15 | 11 35.0 | 83 59.2 .. | 51.0 | 83 10.1 .. | 02.7 | 28 50.9 .. | 22.9 | 51 30.5 .. | 27.4 | Hamal | 327 54.0 | N23 34.0 |
| 16 | 26 37.4 | 99 00.1 | 51.1 | 98 10.6 | 02.5 | 43 52.8 | 22.7 | 66 32.6 | 27.3 | Kaus Aust. | 83 35.9 | S34 22.4 |
| 17 | 41 39.9 | 114 01.0 | 51.2 | 113 11.0 | 02.3 | 58 54.7 | 22.5 | 81 34.8 | 27.2 | | | |
| 18 | 56 42.3 | 129 02.0 | S16 51.2 | 128 11.5 | S23 02.1 | 73 56.6 | S 8 22.3 | 96 37.0 | S16 27.2 | Kochab | 137 19.6 | N74 03.6 |
| 19 | 71 44.8 | 144 02.9 | 51.3 | 143 12.0 | 01.9 | 88 58.5 | 22.0 | 111 39.1 | 27.1 | Markab | 13 32.6 | N15 19.3 |
| 20 | 86 47.3 | 159 03.8 | 51.4 | 158 12.4 | 01.7 | 104 00.5 | 21.8 | 126 41.3 | 27.0 | Menkar | 314 08.7 | N 4 10.4 |
| 21 | 101 49.7 | 174 04.7 .. | 51.5 | 173 12.9 .. | 01.5 | 119 02.4 .. | 21.6 | 141 43.5 .. | 26.9 | Menkent | 148 00.2 | S36 28.6 |
| 22 | 116 52.2 | 189 05.6 | 51.5 | 188 13.4 | 01.3 | 134 04.3 | 21.4 | 156 45.7 | 26.8 | Miaplacidus | 221 37.8 | S69 48.5 |
| 23 | 131 54.7 | 204 06.6 | 51.6 | 203 13.9 | 01.1 | 149 06.2 | 21.1 | 171 47.8 | 26.7 | | | |
| 17 00 | 146 57.1 | 219 07.5 | S16 51.7 | 218 14.3 | S23 00.9 | 164 08.1 | S 8 20.9 | 186 50.0 | S16 26.6 | Mirfak | 308 31.7 | N49 56.5 |
| 01 | 161 59.6 | 234 08.4 | 51.7 | 233 14.8 | 00.7 | 179 10.0 | 20.7 | 201 52.2 | 26.6 | Nunki | 75 51.0 | S26 16.2 |
| 02 | 177 02.1 | 249 09.3 | 51.8 | 248 15.3 | 00.5 | 194 11.9 | 20.5 | 216 54.3 | 26.5 | Peacock | 53 10.0 | S56 39.8 |
| 03 | 192 04.5 | 264 10.2 .. | 51.9 | 263 15.7 .. | 00.3 | 209 13.8 .. | 20.2 | 231 56.5 .. | 26.4 | Pollux | 243 19.9 | N27 58.3 |
| 04 | 207 07.0 | 279 11.1 | 52.0 | 278 16.2 | 23 00.1 | 224 15.7 | 20.0 | 246 58.7 | 26.3 | Procyon | 244 53.0 | N 5 10.0 |
| 05 | 222 09.5 | 294 12.0 | 52.0 | 293 16.7 | 22 59.9 | 239 17.6 | 19.8 | 262 00.8 | 26.2 | | | |
| 06 | 237 11.9 | 309 12.9 | S16 52.1 | 308 17.2 | S22 59.7 | 254 19.5 | S 8 19.5 | 277 03.0 | S16 26.1 | Rasalhague | 96 00.9 | N12 32.5 |
| 07 | 252 14.4 | 324 13.8 | 52.2 | 323 17.6 | 59.5 | 269 21.4 | 19.3 | 292 05.2 | 26.0 | Regulus | 207 36.6 | N11 51.5 |
| T 08 | 267 16.8 | 339 14.7 | 52.2 | 338 18.1 | 59.3 | 284 23.3 | 19.1 | 307 07.3 | 25.9 | Rigel | 281 06.0 | S 8 10.7 |
| H 09 | 282 19.3 | 354 15.6 .. | 52.3 | 353 18.6 .. | 59.0 | 299 25.2 .. | 18.9 | 322 09.5 .. | 25.9 | Rigil Kent. | 139 43.3 | S60 55.3 |
| U 10 | 297 21.8 | 9 16.4 | 52.4 | 8 19.0 | 58.8 | 314 27.1 | 18.6 | 337 11.7 | 25.8 | Sabik | 102 05.6 | S15 45.1 |
| R 11 | 312 24.2 | 24 17.3 | 52.4 | 23 19.5 | 58.6 | 329 29.0 | 18.4 | 352 13.8 | 25.7 | | | |
| S 12 | 327 26.7 | 39 18.2 | S16 52.5 | 38 20.0 | S22 58.4 | 344 30.9 | S 8 18.2 | 7 16.0 | S16 25.6 | Schedar | 349 34.1 | N56 39.6 |
| D 13 | 342 29.2 | 54 19.1 | 52.6 | 53 20.5 | 58.2 | 359 32.8 | 18.0 | 22 18.2 | 25.5 | Shaula | 96 13.8 | S37 07.1 |
| A 14 | 357 31.6 | 69 20.0 | 52.7 | 68 20.9 | 58.0 | 14 34.7 | 17.7 | 37 20.4 | 25.4 | Sirius | 258 28.1 | S16 45.0 |
| Y 15 | 12 34.1 | 84 20.8 .. | 52.7 | 83 21.4 .. | 57.8 | 29 36.7 .. | 17.5 | 52 22.5 .. | 25.3 | Spica | 158 24.6 | S11 16.6 |
| 16 | 27 36.6 | 99 21.7 | 52.8 | 98 21.9 | 57.6 | 44 38.6 | 17.3 | 67 24.7 | 25.2 | Suhail | 222 47.6 | S43 31.4 |
| 17 | 42 39.0 | 114 22.6 | 52.9 | 113 22.3 | 57.4 | 59 40.5 | 17.1 | 82 26.9 | 25.2 | | | |
| 18 | 57 41.5 | 129 23.4 | S16 52.9 | 128 22.8 | S22 57.1 | 74 42.4 | S 8 16.8 | 97 29.0 | S16 25.1 | Vega | 80 35.1 | N38 48.0 |
| 19 | 72 43.9 | 144 24.3 | 53.0 | 143 23.3 | 56.9 | 89 44.3 | 16.6 | 112 31.2 | 25.0 | Zuben'ubi | 136 58.6 | S16 08.0 |
| 20 | 87 46.4 | 159 25.2 | 53.0 | 158 23.8 | 56.7 | 104 46.2 | 16.4 | 127 33.4 | 24.9 | | SHA | Mer. Pass. |
| 21 | 102 48.9 | 174 26.0 .. | 53.1 | 173 24.2 .. | 56.5 | 119 48.1 .. | 16.1 | 142 35.5 .. | 24.8 | | ° ′ | h m |
| 22 | 117 51.3 | 189 26.9 | 53.2 | 188 24.7 | 56.3 | 134 50.0 | 15.9 | 157 37.7 | 24.7 | Venus | 72 46.9 | 9 24 |
| 23 | 132 53.8 | 204 27.7 | 53.2 | 203 25.2 | 56.1 | 149 51.9 | 15.7 | 172 39.9 | 24.6 | Mars | 72 05.0 | 9 28 |
| | h m | | | | | | | | | Jupiter | 17 24.3 | 13 05 |
| Mer. Pass. 14 13.8 | | v 0.9 | d 0.1 | v 0.5 | d 0.2 | v 1.9 | d 0.2 | v 2.2 | d 0.1 | Saturn | 40 00.0 | 11 34 |

| UT | SUN GHA | SUN Dec | MOON GHA | v | MOON Dec | d | HP |
|---|---|---|---|---|---|---|---|
| **15** 00 | 176 28.4 | S12 45.6 | 14 47.8 | 10.8 | N23 09.7 | 7.0 | 55.1 |
| 01 | 191 28.4 | 44.7 | 29 17.6 | 10.8 | 23 02.7 | 7.2 | 55.2 |
| 02 | 206 28.4 | 43.9 | 43 47.4 | 10.8 | 22 55.5 | 7.3 | 55.2 |
| 03 | 221 28.5 | .. 43.0 | 58 17.2 | 10.9 | 22 48.2 | 7.5 | 55.2 |
| 04 | 236 28.5 | 42.2 | 72 47.1 | 10.9 | 22 40.7 | 7.5 | 55.2 |
| 05 | 251 28.5 | 41.3 | 87 17.0 | 11.0 | 22 33.2 | 7.7 | 55.2 |
| 06 | 266 28.5 | S12 40.5 | 101 47.0 | 11.0 | N22 25.5 | 7.8 | 55.3 |
| T 07 | 281 28.6 | 39.6 | 116 17.0 | 11.0 | 22 17.7 | 7.9 | 55.3 |
| U 08 | 296 28.6 | 38.7 | 130 47.0 | 11.1 | 22 09.8 | 8.0 | 55.3 |
| E 09 | 311 28.6 | .. 37.9 | 145 17.1 | 11.1 | 22 01.8 | 8.1 | 55.3 |
| S 10 | 326 28.7 | 37.0 | 159 47.2 | 11.1 | 21 53.7 | 8.2 | 55.3 |
| D 11 | 341 28.7 | 36.2 | 174 17.3 | 11.2 | 21 45.5 | 8.3 | 55.3 |
| A 12 | 356 28.7 | S12 35.3 | 188 47.5 | 11.2 | N21 37.2 | 8.5 | 55.4 |
| Y 13 | 11 28.8 | 34.4 | 203 17.7 | 11.3 | 21 28.7 | 8.5 | 55.4 |
| 14 | 26 28.8 | 33.6 | 217 48.0 | 11.3 | 21 20.2 | 8.7 | 55.4 |
| 15 | 41 28.8 | .. 32.7 | 232 18.3 | 11.3 | 21 11.5 | 8.8 | 55.4 |
| 16 | 56 28.9 | 31.9 | 246 48.6 | 11.4 | 21 02.7 | 8.9 | 55.4 |
| 17 | 71 28.9 | 31.0 | 261 19.0 | 11.4 | 20 53.8 | 9.0 | 55.5 |
| 18 | 86 28.9 | S12 30.1 | 275 49.4 | 11.5 | N20 44.8 | 9.0 | 55.5 |
| 19 | 101 29.0 | 29.3 | 290 19.9 | 11.5 | 20 35.8 | 9.2 | 55.5 |
| 20 | 116 29.0 | 28.4 | 304 50.4 | 11.5 | 20 26.6 | 9.4 | 55.5 |
| 21 | 131 29.0 | .. 27.5 | 319 20.9 | 11.6 | 20 17.2 | 9.4 | 55.5 |
| 22 | 146 29.1 | 26.7 | 333 51.5 | 11.6 | 20 07.8 | 9.5 | 55.6 |
| 23 | 161 29.1 | 25.8 | 348 22.1 | 11.7 | 19 58.3 | 9.6 | 55.6 |
| **16** 00 | 176 29.2 | S12 24.9 | 2 52.8 | 11.7 | N19 48.7 | 9.7 | 55.6 |
| 01 | 191 29.2 | 24.1 | 17 23.5 | 11.7 | 19 39.0 | 9.8 | 55.6 |
| 02 | 206 29.2 | 23.2 | 31 54.2 | 11.8 | 19 29.2 | 9.9 | 55.6 |
| 03 | 221 29.3 | .. 22.3 | 46 25.0 | 11.8 | 19 19.3 | 10.0 | 55.7 |
| 04 | 236 29.3 | 21.5 | 60 55.8 | 11.9 | 19 09.3 | 10.2 | 55.7 |
| 05 | 251 29.3 | 20.6 | 75 26.7 | 11.9 | 18 59.1 | 10.2 | 55.7 |
| 06 | 266 29.4 | S12 19.7 | 89 57.6 | 12.0 | N18 48.9 | 10.3 | 55.7 |
| W 07 | 281 29.4 | 18.9 | 104 28.6 | 11.9 | 18 38.6 | 10.4 | 55.7 |
| E 08 | 296 29.5 | 18.0 | 118 59.5 | 12.1 | 18 28.2 | 10.5 | 55.8 |
| D 09 | 311 29.5 | .. 17.1 | 133 30.6 | 12.0 | 18 17.7 | 10.6 | 55.8 |
| N 10 | 326 29.5 | 16.3 | 148 01.6 | 12.1 | 18 07.1 | 10.7 | 55.8 |
| E 11 | 341 29.6 | 15.4 | 162 32.7 | 12.2 | 17 56.4 | 10.7 | 55.8 |
| S 12 | 356 29.6 | S12 14.5 | 177 03.9 | 12.2 | N17 45.7 | 10.9 | 55.9 |
| D 13 | 11 29.6 | 13.7 | 191 35.1 | 12.2 | 17 34.8 | 11.0 | 55.9 |
| A 14 | 26 29.7 | 12.8 | 206 06.3 | 12.3 | 17 23.8 | 11.0 | 55.9 |
| Y 15 | 41 29.7 | .. 11.9 | 220 37.6 | 12.3 | 17 12.8 | 11.1 | 55.9 |
| 16 | 56 29.8 | 11.1 | 235 08.9 | 12.3 | 17 01.7 | 11.3 | 55.9 |
| 17 | 71 29.8 | 10.2 | 249 40.2 | 12.4 | 16 50.4 | 11.3 | 56.0 |
| 18 | 86 29.9 | S12 09.3 | 264 11.6 | 12.4 | N16 39.1 | 11.4 | 56.0 |
| 19 | 101 29.9 | 08.5 | 278 43.0 | 12.5 | 16 27.7 | 11.5 | 56.0 |
| 20 | 116 29.9 | 07.6 | 293 14.5 | 12.5 | 16 16.2 | 11.5 | 56.0 |
| 21 | 131 30.0 | .. 06.7 | 307 46.0 | 12.5 | 16 04.7 | 11.7 | 56.0 |
| 22 | 146 30.0 | 05.8 | 322 17.5 | 12.6 | 15 53.0 | 11.7 | 56.1 |
| 23 | 161 30.1 | 05.0 | 336 49.1 | 12.6 | 15 41.3 | 11.8 | 56.1 |
| **17** 00 | 176 30.1 | S12 04.1 | 351 20.7 | 12.6 | N15 29.5 | 11.9 | 56.1 |
| 01 | 191 30.2 | 03.2 | 5 52.3 | 12.7 | 15 17.6 | 12.0 | 56.1 |
| 02 | 206 30.2 | 02.3 | 20 24.0 | 12.7 | 15 05.6 | 12.0 | 56.1 |
| 03 | 221 30.2 | .. 01.5 | 34 55.7 | 12.8 | 14 53.6 | 12.2 | 56.2 |
| 04 | 236 30.3 | 12 00.6 | 49 27.5 | 12.8 | 14 41.4 | 12.2 | 56.2 |
| 05 | 251 30.3 | 11 59.7 | 63 59.3 | 12.8 | 14 29.2 | 12.2 | 56.2 |
| 06 | 266 30.4 | S11 58.8 | 78 31.1 | 12.8 | N14 17.0 | 12.4 | 56.2 |
| T 07 | 281 30.4 | 58.0 | 93 02.9 | 12.9 | 14 04.6 | 12.4 | 56.2 |
| H 08 | 296 30.5 | 57.1 | 107 34.8 | 13.0 | 13 52.2 | 12.5 | 56.3 |
| U 09 | 311 30.5 | .. 56.2 | 122 06.8 | 12.9 | 13 39.7 | 12.6 | 56.3 |
| R 10 | 326 30.6 | 55.3 | 136 38.7 | 13.0 | 13 27.1 | 12.7 | 56.3 |
| S 11 | 341 30.6 | 54.5 | 151 10.7 | 13.0 | 13 14.4 | 12.7 | 56.3 |
| D 12 | 356 30.7 | S11 53.6 | 165 42.7 | 13.1 | N13 01.7 | 12.8 | 56.4 |
| A 13 | 11 30.7 | 52.7 | 180 14.8 | 13.0 | 12 48.9 | 12.8 | 56.4 |
| Y 14 | 26 30.8 | 51.8 | 194 46.8 | 13.1 | 12 36.1 | 12.9 | 56.4 |
| 15 | 41 30.8 | .. 51.0 | 209 18.9 | 13.2 | 12 23.2 | 13.0 | 56.4 |
| 16 | 56 30.8 | 50.1 | 223 51.1 | 13.1 | 12 10.2 | 13.0 | 56.4 |
| 17 | 71 30.9 | 49.2 | 238 23.2 | 13.2 | 11 57.2 | 13.2 | 56.5 |
| 18 | 86 30.9 | S11 48.3 | 252 55.4 | 13.2 | N11 44.0 | 13.1 | 56.5 |
| 19 | 101 31.0 | 47.4 | 267 27.6 | 13.3 | 11 30.9 | 13.3 | 56.5 |
| 20 | 116 31.0 | 46.6 | 281 59.9 | 13.2 | 11 17.6 | 13.3 | 56.5 |
| 21 | 131 31.1 | .. 45.7 | 296 32.1 | 13.3 | 11 04.3 | 13.3 | 56.5 |
| 22 | 146 31.1 | 44.8 | 311 04.4 | 13.4 | 10 51.0 | 13.4 | 56.6 |
| 23 | 161 31.2 | 43.9 | 325 36.8 | 13.3 | N10 37.6 | 13.5 | 56.6 |
| | SD 16.2 | d 0.9 | SD 15.1 | | 15.2 | | 15.4 |

| Lat. | Twilight Naut. | Twilight Civil | Sunrise | Moonrise 15 | 16 | 17 | 18 |
|---|---|---|---|---|---|---|---|
| N 72 | 06 10 | 07 30 | 08 48 | ▭ | 13 14 | 16 22 | 18 39 |
| N 70 | 06 09 | 07 21 | 08 29 | ▭ | 14 23 | 16 45 | 18 48 |
| 68 | 06 08 | 07 13 | 08 14 | 12 18 | 14 59 | 17 02 | 18 55 |
| 66 | 06 07 | 07 07 | 08 02 | 13 23 | 15 25 | 17 15 | 19 01 |
| 64 | 06 05 | 07 01 | 07 52 | 13 57 | 15 44 | 17 26 | 19 06 |
| 62 | 06 04 | 06 56 | 07 43 | 14 23 | 16 00 | 17 36 | 19 11 |
| 60 | 06 03 | 06 52 | 07 36 | 14 42 | 16 13 | 17 44 | 19 14 |
| N 58 | 06 02 | 06 48 | 07 29 | 14 58 | 16 24 | 17 51 | 19 18 |
| 56 | 06 01 | 06 44 | 07 23 | 15 12 | 16 34 | 17 57 | 19 21 |
| 54 | 06 00 | 06 41 | 07 18 | 15 24 | 16 43 | 18 03 | 19 23 |
| 52 | 05 59 | 06 38 | 07 13 | 15 34 | 16 50 | 18 08 | 19 26 |
| 50 | 05 58 | 06 36 | 07 09 | 15 44 | 16 57 | 18 12 | 19 28 |
| 45 | 05 55 | 06 29 | 07 00 | 16 03 | 17 12 | 18 22 | 19 32 |
| N 40 | 05 52 | 06 24 | 06 52 | 16 19 | 17 24 | 18 30 | 19 36 |
| 35 | 05 50 | 06 19 | 06 45 | 16 32 | 17 34 | 18 37 | 19 40 |
| 30 | 05 47 | 06 15 | 06 39 | 16 44 | 17 43 | 18 43 | 19 43 |
| 20 | 05 40 | 06 06 | 06 29 | 17 03 | 17 59 | 18 53 | 19 48 |
| N 10 | 05 33 | 05 58 | 06 19 | 17 20 | 18 12 | 19 03 | 19 52 |
| 0 | 05 25 | 05 49 | 06 11 | 17 36 | 18 24 | 19 11 | 19 56 |
| S 10 | 05 15 | 05 40 | 06 02 | 17 52 | 18 37 | 19 19 | 20 01 |
| 20 | 05 03 | 05 29 | 05 52 | 18 09 | 18 50 | 19 28 | 20 05 |
| 30 | 04 47 | 05 16 | 05 41 | 18 29 | 19 05 | 19 39 | 20 10 |
| 35 | 04 36 | 05 08 | 05 35 | 18 40 | 19 14 | 19 44 | 20 13 |
| 40 | 04 24 | 04 59 | 05 27 | 18 53 | 19 24 | 19 51 | 20 16 |
| 45 | 04 09 | 04 47 | 05 19 | 19 08 | 19 35 | 19 59 | 20 20 |
| S 50 | 03 49 | 04 33 | 05 08 | 19 26 | 19 49 | 20 08 | 20 25 |
| 52 | 03 39 | 04 26 | 05 03 | 19 35 | 19 56 | 20 12 | 20 27 |
| 54 | 03 28 | 04 18 | 04 58 | 19 45 | 20 03 | 20 17 | 20 29 |
| 56 | 03 14 | 04 10 | 04 52 | 19 56 | 20 11 | 20 22 | 20 31 |
| 58 | 02 59 | 04 00 | 04 45 | 20 08 | 20 20 | 20 28 | 20 34 |
| S 60 | 02 39 | 03 48 | 04 37 | 20 23 | 20 30 | 20 34 | 20 37 |

| Lat. | Sunset | Twilight Civil | Twilight Naut. | Moonset 15 | 16 | 17 | 18 |
|---|---|---|---|---|---|---|---|
| N 72 | 15 42 | 17 00 | 18 20 | ▭ | 11 30 | 10 01 | 09 21 |
| N 70 | 16 01 | 17 09 | 18 21 | ▭ | 10 20 | 09 36 | 09 09 |
| 68 | 16 15 | 17 17 | 18 22 | 10 42 | 09 43 | 09 18 | 09 00 |
| 66 | 16 28 | 17 23 | 18 23 | 09 37 | 09 16 | 09 02 | 08 52 |
| 64 | 16 38 | 17 28 | 18 24 | 09 01 | 08 55 | 08 50 | 08 45 |
| 62 | 16 46 | 17 33 | 18 25 | 08 36 | 08 38 | 08 39 | 08 39 |
| 60 | 16 54 | 17 37 | 18 26 | 08 15 | 08 24 | 08 30 | 08 34 |
| N 58 | 17 00 | 17 41 | 18 27 | 07 58 | 08 12 | 08 22 | 08 29 |
| 56 | 17 06 | 17 45 | 18 28 | 07 44 | 08 02 | 08 15 | 08 25 |
| 54 | 17 11 | 17 48 | 18 29 | 07 32 | 07 53 | 08 08 | 08 21 |
| 52 | 17 16 | 17 51 | 18 30 | 07 21 | 07 44 | 08 03 | 08 18 |
| 50 | 17 20 | 17 53 | 18 31 | 07 11 | 07 37 | 07 57 | 08 15 |
| 45 | 17 29 | 17 59 | 18 34 | 06 51 | 07 21 | 07 46 | 08 08 |
| N 40 | 17 37 | 18 05 | 18 36 | 06 34 | 07 07 | 07 36 | 08 03 |
| 35 | 17 44 | 18 09 | 18 39 | 06 20 | 06 56 | 07 28 | 07 58 |
| 30 | 17 49 | 18 14 | 18 42 | 06 08 | 06 46 | 07 21 | 07 53 |
| 20 | 18 00 | 18 22 | 18 48 | 05 47 | 06 29 | 07 08 | 07 46 |
| N 10 | 18 09 | 18 30 | 18 55 | 05 28 | 06 14 | 06 57 | 07 39 |
| 0 | 18 17 | 18 39 | 19 03 | 05 11 | 06 00 | 06 47 | 07 33 |
| S 10 | 18 26 | 18 48 | 19 13 | 04 53 | 05 45 | 06 36 | 07 26 |
| 20 | 18 36 | 18 58 | 19 25 | 04 35 | 05 30 | 06 25 | 07 20 |
| 30 | 18 47 | 19 11 | 19 41 | 04 13 | 05 12 | 06 12 | 07 12 |
| 35 | 18 53 | 19 19 | 19 51 | 04 00 | 05 02 | 06 04 | 07 07 |
| 40 | 19 00 | 19 29 | 20 03 | 03 46 | 04 50 | 05 56 | 07 02 |
| 45 | 19 09 | 19 40 | 20 18 | 03 28 | 04 36 | 05 46 | 06 56 |
| S 50 | 19 19 | 19 54 | 20 38 | 03 06 | 04 19 | 05 33 | 06 48 |
| 52 | 19 24 | 20 01 | 20 47 | 02 56 | 04 10 | 05 27 | 06 45 |
| 54 | 19 29 | 20 08 | 20 58 | 02 44 | 04 01 | 05 21 | 06 41 |
| 56 | 19 35 | 20 17 | 21 11 | 02 30 | 03 51 | 05 14 | 06 37 |
| 58 | 19 41 | 20 26 | 21 26 | 02 14 | 03 39 | 05 06 | 06 32 |
| S 60 | 19 49 | 20 37 | 21 45 | 01 55 | 03 25 | 04 56 | 06 27 |

| Day | SUN Eqn. of Time 00h | 12h | Mer. Pass. | MOON Mer. Pass. Upper | Lower | Age | Phase |
|---|---|---|---|---|---|---|---|
| 15 | 14 07 | 14 05 | 12 14 | 23 48 | 11 24 | 14 | 98 |
| 16 | 14 03 | 14 02 | 12 14 | 24 36 | 12 12 | 15 | 100 |
| 17 | 14 00 | 13 57 | 12 14 | 00 36 | 12 59 | 16 | 99 ○ |

| UT | ARIES GHA | VENUS −4.8 GHA | Dec | MARS +1.3 GHA | Dec | JUPITER −2.0 GHA | Dec | SATURN +0.7 GHA | Dec |
|---|---|---|---|---|---|---|---|---|---|
| **18 00** | 147 56.3 | 219 28.6 | S16 53.3 | 218 25.6 | S22 55.9 | 164 53.8 | S 8 15.5 | 187 42.1 | S16 24.5 |
| 01 | 162 58.7 | 234 29.4 | 53.4 | 233 26.1 | 55.7 | 179 55.7 | 15.2 | 202 44.2 | 24.5 |
| 02 | 178 01.2 | 249 30.3 | 53.4 | 248 26.6 | 55.4 | 194 57.6 | 15.0 | 217 46.4 | 24.4 |
| 03 | 193 03.7 | 264 31.1 . . | 53.5 | 263 27.1 . . | 55.2 | 209 59.5 . . | 14.8 | 232 48.6 . . | 24.3 |
| 04 | 208 06.1 | 279 32.0 | 53.6 | 278 27.5 | 55.0 | 225 01.4 | 14.6 | 247 50.7 | 24.2 |
| 05 | 223 08.6 | 294 32.8 | 53.6 | 293 28.0 | 54.8 | 240 03.3 | 14.3 | 262 52.9 | 24.1 |
| 06 | 238 11.1 | 309 33.6 | S16 53.7 | 308 28.5 | S22 54.6 | 255 05.2 | S 8 14.1 | 277 55.1 | S16 24.0 |
| 07 | 253 13.5 | 324 34.5 | 53.7 | 323 28.9 | 54.4 | 270 07.1 | 13.9 | 292 57.2 | 23.9 |
| 08 | 268 16.0 | 339 35.3 | 53.8 | 338 29.4 | 54.1 | 285 09.0 | 13.6 | 307 59.4 | 23.9 |
| 09 | 283 18.4 | 354 36.1 . . | 53.9 | 353 29.9 . . | 53.9 | 300 10.9 . . | 13.4 | 323 01.6 . . | 23.8 |
| 10 | 298 20.9 | 9 37.0 | 53.9 | 8 30.4 | 53.7 | 315 12.8 | 13.2 | 338 03.7 | 23.7 |
| 11 | 313 23.4 | 24 37.8 | 54.0 | 23 30.8 | 53.5 | 330 14.7 | 13.0 | 353 05.9 | 23.6 |
| 12 | 328 25.8 | 39 38.6 | S16 54.0 | 38 31.3 | S22 53.3 | 345 16.7 | S 8 12.7 | 8 08.1 | S16 23.5 |
| 13 | 343 28.3 | 54 39.4 | 54.1 | 53 31.8 | 53.0 | 0 18.6 | 12.5 | 23 10.3 | 23.4 |
| 14 | 358 30.8 | 69 40.3 | 54.2 | 68 32.3 | 52.8 | 15 20.5 | 12.3 | 38 12.4 | 23.3 |
| 15 | 13 33.2 | 84 41.1 . . | 54.2 | 83 32.7 . . | 52.6 | 30 22.4 . . | 12.1 | 53 14.6 . . | 23.2 |
| 16 | 28 35.7 | 99 41.9 | 54.3 | 98 33.2 | 52.4 | 45 24.3 | 11.8 | 68 16.8 | 23.2 |
| 17 | 43 38.2 | 114 42.7 | 54.3 | 113 33.7 | 52.2 | 60 26.2 | 11.6 | 83 18.9 | 23.1 |
| 18 | 58 40.6 | 129 43.5 | S16 54.4 | 128 34.1 | S22 51.9 | 75 28.1 | S 8 11.4 | 98 21.1 | S16 23.0 |
| 19 | 73 43.1 | 144 44.3 | 54.4 | 143 34.6 | 51.7 | 90 30.0 | 11.1 | 113 23.3 | 22.9 |
| 20 | 88 45.6 | 159 45.1 | 54.5 | 158 35.1 | 51.5 | 105 31.9 | 10.9 | 128 25.4 | 22.8 |
| 21 | 103 48.0 | 174 45.9 . . | 54.6 | 173 35.6 . . | 51.3 | 120 33.8 . . | 10.7 | 143 27.6 . . | 22.7 |
| 22 | 118 50.5 | 189 46.7 | 54.6 | 188 36.0 | 51.0 | 135 35.7 | 10.5 | 158 29.8 | 22.6 |
| 23 | 133 52.9 | 204 47.5 | 54.7 | 203 36.5 | 50.8 | 150 37.6 | 10.2 | 173 32.0 | 22.5 |
| **19 00** | 148 55.4 | 219 48.3 | S16 54.7 | 218 37.0 | S22 50.6 | 165 39.5 | S 8 10.0 | 188 34.1 | S16 22.5 |
| 01 | 163 57.9 | 234 49.1 | 54.8 | 233 37.5 | 50.4 | 180 41.4 | 09.8 | 203 36.3 | 22.4 |
| 02 | 179 00.3 | 249 49.9 | 54.8 | 248 37.9 | 50.2 | 195 43.3 | 09.5 | 218 38.5 | 22.3 |
| 03 | 194 02.8 | 264 50.7 . . | 54.9 | 263 38.4 . . | 49.9 | 210 45.2 . . | 09.3 | 233 40.6 . . | 22.2 |
| 04 | 209 05.3 | 279 51.5 | 54.9 | 278 38.9 | 49.7 | 225 47.1 | 09.1 | 248 42.8 | 22.1 |
| 05 | 224 07.7 | 294 52.3 | 55.0 | 293 39.3 | 49.5 | 240 49.0 | 08.9 | 263 45.0 | 22.0 |
| 06 | 239 10.2 | 309 53.1 | S16 55.0 | 308 39.8 | S22 49.2 | 255 50.9 | S 8 08.6 | 278 47.1 | S16 21.9 |
| 07 | 254 12.7 | 324 53.8 | 55.1 | 323 40.3 | 49.0 | 270 52.8 | 08.4 | 293 49.3 | 21.9 |
| 08 | 269 15.1 | 339 54.6 | 55.1 | 338 40.8 | 48.8 | 285 54.7 | 08.2 | 308 51.5 | 21.8 |
| 09 | 284 17.6 | 354 55.4 . . | 55.2 | 353 41.2 . . | 48.6 | 300 56.6 . . | 08.0 | 323 53.7 . . | 21.7 |
| 10 | 299 20.0 | 9 56.2 | 55.2 | 8 41.7 | 48.3 | 315 58.5 | 07.7 | 338 55.8 | 21.6 |
| 11 | 314 22.5 | 24 56.9 | 55.3 | 23 42.2 | 48.1 | 331 00.5 | 07.5 | 353 58.0 | 21.5 |
| 12 | 329 25.0 | 39 57.7 | S16 55.3 | 38 42.7 | S22 47.9 | 346 02.4 | S 8 07.3 | 9 00.2 | S16 21.4 |
| 13 | 344 27.4 | 54 58.5 | 55.4 | 53 43.1 | 47.6 | 1 04.3 | 07.0 | 24 02.3 | 21.3 |
| 14 | 359 29.9 | 69 59.2 | 55.4 | 68 43.6 | 47.4 | 16 06.2 | 06.8 | 39 04.5 | 21.2 |
| 15 | 14 32.4 | 85 00.0 . . | 55.5 | 83 44.1 . . | 47.2 | 31 08.1 . . | 06.6 | 54 06.7 . . | 21.2 |
| 16 | 29 34.8 | 100 00.8 | 55.5 | 98 44.6 | 47.0 | 46 10.0 | 06.4 | 69 08.9 | 21.1 |
| 17 | 44 37.3 | 115 01.5 | 55.6 | 113 45.0 | 46.7 | 61 11.9 | 06.1 | 84 11.0 | 21.0 |
| 18 | 59 39.8 | 130 02.3 | S16 55.6 | 128 45.5 | S22 46.5 | 76 13.8 | S 8 05.9 | 99 13.2 | S16 20.9 |
| 19 | 74 42.2 | 145 03.0 | 55.7 | 143 46.0 | 46.3 | 91 15.7 | 05.7 | 114 15.4 | 20.8 |
| 20 | 89 44.7 | 160 03.8 | 55.7 | 158 46.4 | 46.0 | 106 17.6 | 05.4 | 129 17.5 | 20.7 |
| 21 | 104 47.2 | 175 04.5 . . | 55.8 | 173 46.9 . . | 45.8 | 121 19.5 . . | 05.2 | 144 19.7 . . | 20.6 |
| 22 | 119 49.6 | 190 05.3 | 55.8 | 188 47.4 | 45.6 | 136 21.4 | 05.0 | 159 21.9 | 20.5 |
| 23 | 134 52.1 | 205 06.0 | 55.9 | 203 47.9 | 45.3 | 151 23.3 | 04.8 | 174 24.1 | 20.5 |
| **20 00** | 149 54.5 | 220 06.7 | S16 55.9 | 218 48.3 | S22 45.1 | 166 25.2 | S 8 04.5 | 189 26.2 | S16 20.4 |
| 01 | 164 57.0 | 235 07.5 | 55.9 | 233 48.8 | 44.9 | 181 27.1 | 04.3 | 204 28.4 | 20.3 |
| 02 | 179 59.5 | 250 08.2 | 56.0 | 248 49.3 | 44.6 | 196 29.0 | 04.1 | 219 30.6 | 20.2 |
| 03 | 195 01.9 | 265 09.0 . . | 56.0 | 263 49.8 . . | 44.4 | 211 30.9 . . | 03.9 | 234 32.7 . . | 20.1 |
| 04 | 210 04.4 | 280 09.7 | 56.1 | 278 50.2 | 44.2 | 226 32.8 | 03.6 | 249 34.9 | 20.0 |
| 05 | 225 06.9 | 295 10.4 | 56.1 | 293 50.7 | 43.9 | 241 34.7 | 03.4 | 264 37.1 | 19.9 |
| 06 | 240 09.3 | 310 11.2 | S16 56.2 | 308 51.2 | S22 43.7 | 256 36.6 | S 8 03.2 | 279 39.2 | S16 19.9 |
| 07 | 255 11.8 | 325 11.9 | 56.2 | 323 51.7 | 43.4 | 271 38.5 | 02.9 | 294 41.4 | 19.8 |
| 08 | 270 14.3 | 340 12.6 | 56.2 | 338 52.1 | 43.2 | 286 40.4 | 02.7 | 309 43.6 | 19.7 |
| 09 | 285 16.7 | 355 13.3 . . | 56.3 | 353 52.6 . . | 43.0 | 301 42.3 . . | 02.5 | 324 45.8 . . | 19.6 |
| 10 | 300 19.2 | 10 14.0 | 56.3 | 8 53.1 | 42.7 | 316 44.2 | 02.3 | 339 47.9 | 19.5 |
| 11 | 315 21.6 | 25 14.8 | 56.4 | 23 53.6 | 42.5 | 331 46.1 | 02.0 | 354 50.1 | 19.4 |
| 12 | 330 24.1 | 40 15.5 | S16 56.4 | 38 54.0 | S22 42.3 | 346 48.0 | S 8 01.8 | 9 52.3 | S16 19.3 |
| 13 | 345 26.6 | 55 16.2 | 56.4 | 53 54.5 | 42.0 | 1 49.9 | 01.6 | 24 54.4 | 19.2 |
| 14 | 0 29.0 | 70 16.9 | 56.5 | 68 55.0 | 41.8 | 16 51.9 | 01.3 | 39 56.6 | 19.2 |
| 15 | 15 31.5 | 85 17.6 . . | 56.5 | 83 55.5 . . | 41.5 | 31 53.8 . . | 01.1 | 54 58.8 . . | 19.1 |
| 16 | 30 34.0 | 100 18.3 | 56.5 | 98 55.9 | 41.3 | 46 55.7 | 00.9 | 70 01.0 | 19.0 |
| 17 | 45 36.4 | 115 19.0 | 56.6 | 113 56.4 | 41.1 | 61 57.6 | 00.7 | 85 03.1 | 18.9 |
| 18 | 60 38.9 | 130 19.7 | S16 56.6 | 128 56.9 | S22 40.8 | 76 59.5 | S 8 00.4 | 100 05.3 | S16 18.8 |
| 19 | 75 41.4 | 145 20.4 | 56.6 | 143 57.4 | 40.6 | 92 01.4 | 00.2 | 115 07.5 | 18.7 |
| 20 | 90 43.8 | 160 21.1 | 56.7 | 158 57.8 | 40.3 | 107 03.3 | 8 00.0 | 130 09.6 | 18.6 |
| 21 | 105 46.3 | 175 21.8 . . | 56.7 | 173 58.3 . . | 40.1 | 122 05.2 | 7 59.7 | 145 11.8 . . | 18.5 |
| 22 | 120 48.8 | 190 22.5 | 56.8 | 188 58.8 | 39.8 | 137 07.1 | 59.5 | 160 14.0 | 18.5 |
| 23 | 135 51.2 | 205 23.2 | 56.8 | 203 59.3 | 39.6 | 152 09.0 | 59.3 | 175 16.2 | 18.4 |
| Mer. Pass. | 14 02.0 | v 0.8 | d 0.0 | v 0.5 | d 0.2 | v 1.9 | d 0.2 | v 2.2 | d 0.1 |

**STARS**

| Name | SHA | Dec |
|---|---|---|
| Acamar | 315 13.7 | S40 13.3 |
| Achernar | 335 22.3 | S57 07.8 |
| Acrux | 173 02.1 | S63 13.1 |
| Adhara | 255 07.5 | S29 00.3 |
| Aldebaran | 290 42.3 | N16 33.2 |
| Alioth | 166 14.7 | N55 50.2 |
| Alkaid | 152 53.6 | N49 11.9 |
| Alnair | 27 36.4 | S46 51.4 |
| Alnilam | 275 40.0 | S 1 11.4 |
| Alphard | 217 49.8 | S 8 45.3 |
| Alphecca | 126 05.7 | N26 38.2 |
| Alpheratz | 357 37.5 | N29 12.7 |
| Altair | 62 02.5 | N 8 55.4 |
| Ankaa | 353 09.8 | S42 11.4 |
| Antares | 112 18.8 | S26 28.8 |
| Arcturus | 145 49.9 | N19 03.9 |
| Atria | 107 15.3 | S69 03.7 |
| Avior | 234 15.1 | S59 34.9 |
| Bellatrix | 278 25.3 | N 6 22.1 |
| Betelgeuse | 270 54.5 | N 7 24.6 |
| Canopus | 263 53.1 | S52 42.7 |
| Capella | 280 25.2 | N46 01.3 |
| Deneb | 49 27.8 | N45 21.3 |
| Denebola | 182 27.1 | N14 26.8 |
| Diphda | 348 49.9 | S17 52.2 |
| Dubhe | 193 43.3 | N61 37.8 |
| Elnath | 278 04.7 | N28 37.6 |
| Eltanin | 90 43.5 | N51 28.8 |
| Enif | 33 41.4 | N 9 58.4 |
| Fomalhaut | 15 17.5 | S29 30.5 |
| Gacrux | 171 53.8 | S57 14.0 |
| Gienah | 175 45.7 | S17 39.9 |
| Hadar | 148 39.0 | S60 28.5 |
| Hamal | 327 54.0 | N23 33.9 |
| Kaus Aust. | 83 35.9 | S34 22.4 |
| Kochab | 137 19.5 | N74 03.6 |
| Markab | 13 32.6 | N15 19.3 |
| Menkar | 314 08.7 | N 4 10.4 |
| Menkent | 148 00.2 | S36 28.6 |
| Miaplacidus | 221 37.8 | S69 48.5 |
| Mirfak | 308 31.7 | N49 56.5 |
| Nunki | 75 50.9 | S26 16.2 |
| Peacock | 53 10.0 | S56 39.8 |
| Pollux | 243 19.9 | N27 58.4 |
| Procyon | 244 53.0 | N 5 10.0 |
| Rasalhague | 96 00.9 | N12 32.5 |
| Regulus | 207 36.6 | N11 51.5 |
| Rigel | 281 06.0 | S 8 10.7 |
| Rigil Kent. | 139 43.3 | S60 55.3 |
| Sabik | 102 05.6 | S15 45.1 |
| Schedar | 349 34.1 | N56 39.6 |
| Shaula | 96 13.7 | S37 07.1 |
| Sirius | 258 28.1 | S16 45.0 |
| Spica | 158 24.6 | S11 16.6 |
| Suhail | 222 47.6 | S43 31.4 |
| Vega | 80 35.1 | N38 48.0 |
| Zuben'ubi | 136 58.5 | S16 08.0 |

| | SHA | Mer. Pass. |
|---|---|---|
| Venus | 70 52.9 | 9 20 |
| Mars | 69 41.6 | 9 25 |
| Jupiter | 16 44.1 | 12 56 |
| Saturn | 39 38.7 | 11 24 |

### SUN and MOON

| UT | SUN GHA | SUN Dec | MOON GHA | v | MOON Dec | d | HP |
|---|---|---|---|---|---|---|---|
| d h | ° ′ | ° ′ | ° ′ | ′ | ° ′ | ′ | ′ |
| **18** 00 | 176 31.2 | S11 43.0 | 340 09.1 | 13.4 | N10 24.1 | 13.5 | 56.6 |
| 01 | 191 31.3 | 42.2 | 354 41.5 | 13.3 | 10 10.6 | 13.6 | 56.6 |
| 02 | 206 31.3 | 41.3 | 9 13.8 | 13.5 | 9 57.0 | 13.7 | 56.6 |
| 03 | 221 31.4 .. | 40.4 | 23 46.3 | 13.4 | 9 43.3 | 13.7 | 56.7 |
| 04 | 236 31.5 | 39.5 | 38 18.7 | 13.4 | 9 29.6 | 13.7 | 56.7 |
| 05 | 251 31.5 | 38.6 | 52 51.1 | 13.5 | 9 15.9 | 13.8 | 56.7 |
| 06 | 266 31.6 | S11 37.8 | 67 23.6 | 13.5 | N 9 02.1 | 13.9 | 56.7 |
| 07 | 281 31.6 | 36.9 | 81 56.1 | 13.5 | 8 48.2 | 13.8 | 56.7 |
| 08 | 296 31.7 | 36.0 | 96 28.6 | 13.5 | 8 34.4 | 14.0 | 56.8 |
| F 09 | 311 31.7 .. | 35.1 | 111 01.1 | 13.5 | 8 20.4 | 14.0 | 56.8 |
| R 10 | 326 31.8 | 34.2 | 125 33.6 | 13.6 | 8 06.4 | 14.0 | 56.8 |
| I 11 | 341 31.8 | 33.3 | 140 06.2 | 13.5 | 7 52.4 | 14.1 | 56.8 |
| D 12 | 356 31.9 | S11 32.5 | 154 38.7 | 13.6 | N 7 38.3 | 14.1 | 56.9 |
| A 13 | 11 31.9 | 31.6 | 169 11.3 | 13.6 | 7 24.2 | 14.2 | 56.9 |
| Y 14 | 26 32.0 | 30.7 | 183 43.9 | 13.6 | 7 10.0 | 14.2 | 56.9 |
| 15 | 41 32.0 .. | 29.8 | 198 16.5 | 13.6 | 6 55.8 | 14.3 | 56.9 |
| 16 | 56 32.1 | 28.9 | 212 49.1 | 13.6 | 6 41.5 | 14.3 | 56.9 |
| 17 | 71 32.2 | 28.0 | 227 21.7 | 13.7 | 6 27.2 | 14.3 | 57.0 |
| 18 | 86 32.2 | S11 27.1 | 241 54.4 | 13.6 | N 6 12.9 | 14.4 | 57.0 |
| 19 | 101 32.3 | 26.3 | 256 27.0 | 13.6 | 5 58.5 | 14.4 | 57.0 |
| 20 | 116 32.3 | 25.4 | 270 59.6 | 13.7 | 5 44.1 | 14.4 | 57.0 |
| 21 | 131 32.4 .. | 24.5 | 285 32.3 | 13.6 | 5 29.7 | 14.5 | 57.0 |
| 22 | 146 32.4 | 23.6 | 300 04.9 | 13.7 | 5 15.2 | 14.5 | 57.1 |
| 23 | 161 32.5 | 22.7 | 314 37.6 | 13.7 | 5 00.7 | 14.5 | 57.1 |
| **19** 00 | 176 32.6 | S11 21.8 | 329 10.3 | 13.6 | N 4 46.2 | 14.6 | 57.1 |
| 01 | 191 32.6 | 20.9 | 343 42.9 | 13.7 | 4 31.6 | 14.6 | 57.1 |
| 02 | 206 32.7 | 20.0 | 358 15.6 | 13.7 | 4 17.0 | 14.6 | 57.1 |
| 03 | 221 32.7 .. | 19.1 | 12 48.3 | 13.6 | 4 02.4 | 14.7 | 57.2 |
| 04 | 236 32.8 | 18.3 | 27 20.9 | 13.7 | 3 47.7 | 14.7 | 57.2 |
| 05 | 251 32.8 | 17.4 | 41 53.6 | 13.7 | 3 33.0 | 14.7 | 57.2 |
| 06 | 266 32.9 | S11 16.5 | 56 26.3 | 13.6 | N 3 18.3 | 14.7 | 57.2 |
| 07 | 281 33.0 | 15.6 | 70 58.9 | 13.7 | 3 03.6 | 14.8 | 57.2 |
| S 08 | 296 33.0 | 14.7 | 85 31.6 | 13.6 | 2 48.8 | 14.8 | 57.3 |
| A 09 | 311 33.1 .. | 13.8 | 100 04.2 | 13.7 | 2 34.0 | 14.8 | 57.3 |
| T 10 | 326 33.1 | 12.9 | 114 36.9 | 13.6 | 2 19.2 | 14.8 | 57.3 |
| U 11 | 341 33.2 | 12.0 | 129 09.5 | 13.6 | 2 04.4 | 14.8 | 57.3 |
| R 12 | 356 33.3 | S11 11.1 | 143 42.1 | 13.6 | N 1 49.6 | 14.9 | 57.3 |
| D 13 | 11 33.3 | 10.2 | 158 14.7 | 13.6 | 1 34.7 | 14.9 | 57.4 |
| A 14 | 26 33.4 | 09.3 | 172 47.3 | 13.6 | 1 19.8 | 14.9 | 57.4 |
| Y 15 | 41 33.5 .. | 08.5 | 187 19.9 | 13.6 | 1 04.9 | 14.9 | 57.4 |
| 16 | 56 33.5 | 07.6 | 201 52.5 | 13.6 | 0 50.0 | 14.9 | 57.4 |
| 17 | 71 33.6 | 06.7 | 216 25.1 | 13.5 | 0 35.1 | 14.9 | 57.4 |
| 18 | 86 33.6 | S11 05.8 | 230 57.6 | 13.5 | N 0 20.2 | 14.9 | 57.5 |
| 19 | 101 33.7 | 04.9 | 245 30.1 | 13.6 | N 0 05.3 | 15.0 | 57.5 |
| 20 | 116 33.8 | 04.0 | 260 02.7 | 13.5 | S 0 09.7 | 15.0 | 57.5 |
| 21 | 131 33.8 .. | 03.1 | 274 35.2 | 13.4 | 0 24.7 | 14.9 | 57.5 |
| 22 | 146 33.9 | 02.2 | 289 07.6 | 13.5 | 0 39.6 | 15.0 | 57.5 |
| 23 | 161 34.0 | 01.3 | 303 40.1 | 13.4 | 0 54.6 | 15.0 | 57.5 |
| **20** 00 | 176 34.0 | S11 00.4 | 318 12.5 | 13.4 | S 1 09.6 | 14.9 | 57.6 |
| 01 | 191 34.1 | 10 59.5 | 332 44.9 | 13.4 | 1 24.5 | 15.0 | 57.6 |
| 02 | 206 34.2 | 58.6 | 347 17.3 | 13.4 | 1 39.5 | 15.0 | 57.6 |
| 03 | 221 34.2 .. | 57.7 | 1 49.7 | 13.3 | 1 54.5 | 15.0 | 57.6 |
| 04 | 236 34.3 | 56.8 | 16 22.0 | 13.4 | 2 09.5 | 15.0 | 57.7 |
| 05 | 251 34.3 | 55.9 | 30 54.4 | 13.2 | 2 24.5 | 15.0 | 57.7 |
| 06 | 266 34.4 | S10 55.0 | 45 26.6 | 13.3 | S 2 39.5 | 14.9 | 57.7 |
| 07 | 281 34.5 | 54.1 | 59 58.9 | 13.2 | 2 54.4 | 15.0 | 57.7 |
| 08 | 296 34.6 | 53.2 | 74 31.1 | 13.2 | 3 09.4 | 15.0 | 57.7 |
| S 09 | 311 34.6 .. | 52.3 | 89 03.3 | 13.2 | 3 24.4 | 14.9 | 57.8 |
| U 10 | 326 34.7 | 51.4 | 103 35.5 | 13.1 | 3 39.3 | 15.0 | 57.8 |
| N 11 | 341 34.8 | 50.5 | 118 07.6 | 13.1 | 3 54.3 | 14.9 | 57.8 |
| D 12 | 356 34.8 | S10 49.6 | 132 39.7 | 13.1 | S 4 09.2 | 15.0 | 57.8 |
| A 13 | 11 34.9 | 48.7 | 147 11.8 | 13.0 | 4 24.2 | 14.9 | 57.8 |
| Y 14 | 26 35.0 | 47.8 | 161 43.8 | 13.0 | 4 39.1 | 14.9 | 57.8 |
| 15 | 41 35.0 .. | 46.9 | 176 15.8 | 12.9 | 4 54.0 | 14.9 | 57.8 |
| 16 | 56 35.1 | 46.0 | 190 47.7 | 12.9 | 5 08.9 | 14.8 | 57.9 |
| 17 | 71 35.2 | 45.1 | 205 19.6 | 12.9 | 5 23.7 | 14.9 | 57.9 |
| 18 | 86 35.2 | S10 44.2 | 219 51.5 | 12.8 | S 5 38.6 | 14.8 | 57.9 |
| 19 | 101 35.3 | 43.3 | 234 23.3 | 12.8 | 5 53.4 | 14.9 | 57.9 |
| 20 | 116 35.4 | 42.4 | 248 55.1 | 12.7 | 6 08.3 | 14.8 | 57.9 |
| 21 | 131 35.4 .. | 41.5 | 263 26.8 | 12.7 | 6 23.1 | 14.7 | 58.0 |
| 22 | 146 35.5 | 40.6 | 277 58.5 | 12.6 | 6 37.8 | 14.8 | 58.0 |
| 23 | 161 35.6 | 39.7 | 292 30.1 | 12.6 | S 6 52.6 | 14.7 | 58.0 |
| | SD 16.2 | d 0.9 | SD 15.5 | | 15.6 | | 15.7 |

### Twilight, Sunrise, Moonrise

| Lat. | Twilight Naut. | Twilight Civil | Sunrise | Moonrise 18 | Moonrise 19 | Moonrise 20 | Moonrise 21 |
|---|---|---|---|---|---|---|---|
| ° | h m | h m | h m | h m | h m | h m | h m |
| N 72 | 05 57 | 07 16 | 08 31 | 18 39 | 20 47 | 22 59 | 25 28 |
| N 70 | 05 57 | 07 08 | 08 15 | 18 48 | 20 47 | 22 48 | 25 01 |
| 68 | 05 57 | 07 02 | 08 01 | 18 55 | 20 46 | 22 39 | 24 41 |
| 66 | 05 57 | 06 56 | 07 51 | 19 01 | 20 46 | 22 32 | 24 25 |
| 64 | 05 57 | 06 52 | 07 42 | 19 06 | 20 45 | 22 26 | 24 12 |
| 62 | 05 56 | 06 48 | 07 34 | 19 11 | 20 45 | 22 21 | 24 01 |
| 60 | 05 56 | 06 44 | 07 27 | 19 14 | 20 45 | 22 17 | 23 52 |
| N 58 | 05 55 | 06 41 | 07 21 | 19 18 | 20 44 | 22 13 | 23 44 |
| 56 | 05 55 | 06 38 | 07 16 | 19 21 | 20 44 | 22 09 | 23 37 |
| 54 | 05 54 | 06 35 | 07 11 | 19 23 | 20 44 | 22 06 | 23 31 |
| 52 | 05 53 | 06 33 | 07 07 | 19 26 | 20 44 | 22 03 | 23 25 |
| 50 | 05 53 | 06 30 | 07 03 | 19 28 | 20 44 | 22 01 | 23 20 |
| 45 | 05 51 | 06 25 | 06 55 | 19 32 | 20 43 | 21 55 | 23 10 |
| N 40 | 05 49 | 06 20 | 06 48 | 19 36 | 20 43 | 21 51 | 23 01 |
| 35 | 05 46 | 06 16 | 06 42 | 19 40 | 20 43 | 21 47 | 22 53 |
| 30 | 05 44 | 06 12 | 06 36 | 19 43 | 20 43 | 21 43 | 22 46 |
| 20 | 05 39 | 06 04 | 06 27 | 19 48 | 20 42 | 21 38 | 22 35 |
| N 10 | 05 32 | 05 57 | 06 18 | 19 52 | 20 42 | 21 32 | 22 25 |
| 0 | 05 25 | 05 49 | 06 10 | 19 56 | 20 42 | 21 28 | 22 16 |
| S 10 | 05 16 | 05 41 | 06 02 | 20 01 | 20 41 | 21 23 | 22 06 |
| 20 | 05 04 | 05 31 | 05 54 | 20 05 | 20 41 | 21 18 | 21 57 |
| 30 | 04 49 | 05 19 | 05 43 | 20 10 | 20 41 | 21 12 | 21 46 |
| 35 | 04 40 | 05 11 | 05 38 | 20 13 | 20 41 | 21 09 | 21 39 |
| 40 | 04 28 | 05 02 | 05 31 | 20 16 | 20 41 | 21 05 | 21 32 |
| 45 | 04 14 | 04 52 | 05 23 | 20 20 | 20 40 | 21 01 | 21 24 |
| S 50 | 03 55 | 04 39 | 05 13 | 20 25 | 20 40 | 20 56 | 21 14 |
| 52 | 03 46 | 04 32 | 05 09 | 20 27 | 20 40 | 20 54 | 21 10 |
| 54 | 03 36 | 04 25 | 05 04 | 20 29 | 20 40 | 20 52 | 21 05 |
| 56 | 03 24 | 04 17 | 04 59 | 20 31 | 20 40 | 20 49 | 20 59 |
| 58 | 03 09 | 04 08 | 04 52 | 20 34 | 20 40 | 20 46 | 20 53 |
| S 60 | 02 52 | 03 58 | 04 46 | 20 37 | 20 40 | 20 43 | 20 46 |

### Sunset, Twilight, Moonset

| Lat. | Sunset | Twilight Civil | Twilight Naut. | Moonset 18 | Moonset 19 | Moonset 20 | Moonset 21 |
|---|---|---|---|---|---|---|---|
| ° | h m | h m | h m | h m | h m | h m | h m |
| N 72 | 15 58 | 17 14 | 18 33 | 09 21 | 08 50 | 08 21 | 07 48 |
| N 70 | 16 15 | 17 21 | 18 32 | 09 09 | 08 47 | 08 25 | 08 01 |
| 68 | 16 28 | 17 27 | 18 32 | 09 00 | 08 44 | 08 29 | 08 12 |
| 66 | 16 38 | 17 33 | 18 32 | 08 52 | 08 42 | 08 32 | 08 21 |
| 64 | 16 47 | 17 37 | 18 32 | 08 45 | 08 40 | 08 35 | 08 29 |
| 62 | 16 55 | 17 41 | 18 33 | 08 39 | 08 38 | 08 37 | 08 36 |
| 60 | 17 01 | 17 45 | 18 33 | 08 34 | 08 36 | 08 39 | 08 42 |
| N 58 | 17 07 | 17 48 | 18 34 | 08 29 | 08 35 | 08 41 | 08 47 |
| 56 | 17 12 | 17 51 | 18 34 | 08 25 | 08 34 | 08 42 | 08 52 |
| 54 | 17 17 | 17 53 | 18 35 | 08 21 | 08 33 | 08 44 | 08 56 |
| 52 | 17 21 | 17 56 | 18 35 | 08 18 | 08 32 | 08 45 | 09 00 |
| 50 | 17 25 | 17 58 | 18 36 | 08 15 | 08 31 | 08 47 | 09 03 |
| 45 | 17 33 | 18 03 | 18 38 | 08 08 | 08 29 | 08 49 | 09 11 |
| N 40 | 17 40 | 18 08 | 18 40 | 08 03 | 08 27 | 08 51 | 09 17 |
| 35 | 17 46 | 18 12 | 18 42 | 07 58 | 08 26 | 08 53 | 09 22 |
| 30 | 17 52 | 18 16 | 18 44 | 07 53 | 08 24 | 08 55 | 09 27 |
| 20 | 18 01 | 18 23 | 18 49 | 07 46 | 08 22 | 08 58 | 09 36 |
| N 10 | 18 09 | 18 31 | 18 55 | 07 39 | 08 20 | 09 01 | 09 43 |
| 0 | 18 17 | 18 38 | 19 03 | 07 33 | 08 18 | 09 03 | 09 50 |
| S 10 | 18 25 | 18 47 | 19 12 | 07 26 | 08 16 | 09 06 | 09 57 |
| 20 | 18 34 | 18 56 | 19 23 | 07 20 | 08 14 | 09 08 | 10 05 |
| 30 | 18 44 | 19 08 | 19 38 | 07 12 | 08 11 | 09 12 | 10 13 |
| 35 | 18 49 | 19 16 | 19 47 | 07 07 | 08 10 | 09 13 | 10 18 |
| 40 | 18 56 | 19 24 | 19 58 | 07 02 | 08 08 | 09 15 | 10 24 |
| 45 | 19 04 | 19 35 | 20 12 | 06 56 | 08 06 | 09 18 | 10 30 |
| S 50 | 19 13 | 19 48 | 20 31 | 06 48 | 08 04 | 09 20 | 10 38 |
| 52 | 19 18 | 19 54 | 20 40 | 06 45 | 08 03 | 09 22 | 10 42 |
| 54 | 19 22 | 20 01 | 20 50 | 06 41 | 08 02 | 09 23 | 10 46 |
| 56 | 19 28 | 20 09 | 21 02 | 06 37 | 08 00 | 09 24 | 10 51 |
| 58 | 19 34 | 20 17 | 21 15 | 06 32 | 07 59 | 09 26 | 10 56 |
| S 60 | 19 40 | 20 28 | 21 32 | 06 27 | 07 57 | 09 28 | 11 01 |

### SUN and MOON

| Day | SUN Eqn. of Time 00h | SUN Eqn. of Time 12h | SUN Mer. Pass. | MOON Mer. Pass. Upper | MOON Mer. Pass. Lower | Age | Phase |
|---|---|---|---|---|---|---|---|
| d | m s | m s | h m | h m | h m | d | % |
| 18 | 13 55 | 13 53 | 12 14 | 01 22 | 13 45 | 17 | 96 |
| 19 | 13 50 | 13 47 | 12 14 | 02 07 | 14 30 | 18 | 92 |
| 20 | 13 44 | 13 41 | 12 14 | 02 52 | 15 15 | 19 | 85 |

| UT | ARIES GHA | VENUS −4.8 GHA | Dec | MARS +1.3 GHA | Dec | JUPITER −2.0 GHA | Dec | SATURN +0.7 GHA | Dec |
|---|---|---|---|---|---|---|---|---|---|
| **21** 00 | 150 53.7 | 220 23.9 | S16 56.8 | 218 59.7 | S22 39.4 | 167 10.9 | S 7 59.1 | 190 18.3 | S16 18.3 |
| 01 | 165 56.1 | 235 24.6 | 56.9 | 234 00.2 | 39.1 | 182 12.8 | 58.8 | 205 20.5 | 18.2 |
| 02 | 180 58.6 | 250 25.3 | 56.9 | 249 00.7 | 38.9 | 197 14.7 | 58.6 | 220 22.7 | 18.1 |
| 03 | 196 01.1 | 265 26.0 · · | 56.9 | 264 01.2 · · | 38.6 | 212 16.6 · · | 58.4 | 235 24.9 · · | 18.0 |
| 04 | 211 03.5 | 280 26.6 | 56.9 | 279 01.6 | 38.4 | 227 18.5 | 58.1 | 250 27.0 | 17.9 |
| 05 | 226 06.0 | 295 27.3 | 57.0 | 294 02.1 | 38.1 | 242 20.4 | 57.9 | 265 29.2 | 17.9 |
| 06 | 241 08.5 | 310 28.0 | S16 57.0 | 309 02.6 | S22 37.9 | 257 22.3 | S 7 57.7 | 280 31.4 | S16 17.8 |
| M 07 | 256 10.9 | 325 28.7 | 57.0 | 324 03.1 | 37.6 | 272 24.2 | 57.5 | 295 33.5 | 17.7 |
| O 08 | 271 13.4 | 340 29.4 | 57.1 | 339 03.5 | 37.4 | 287 26.1 | 57.2 | 310 35.7 | 17.6 |
| N 09 | 286 15.9 | 355 30.0 · · | 57.1 | 354 04.0 · · | 37.1 | 302 28.0 · · | 57.0 | 325 37.9 · · | 17.5 |
| D 10 | 301 18.3 | 10 30.7 | 57.1 | 9 04.5 | 36.9 | 317 29.9 | 56.8 | 340 40.1 | 17.4 |
| A 11 | 316 20.8 | 25 31.4 | 57.1 | 24 05.0 | 36.7 | 332 31.8 | 56.5 | 355 42.2 | 17.3 |
| Y 12 | 331 23.2 | 40 32.0 | S16 57.2 | 39 05.5 | S22 36.4 | 347 33.7 | S 7 56.3 | 10 44.4 | S16 17.2 |
| 13 | 346 25.7 | 55 32.7 | 57.2 | 54 05.9 | 36.2 | 2 35.6 | 56.1 | 25 46.6 | 17.2 |
| 14 | 1 28.2 | 70 33.3 | 57.2 | 69 06.4 | 35.9 | 17 37.5 | 55.9 | 40 48.7 | 17.1 |
| 15 | 16 30.6 | 85 34.0 · · | 57.3 | 84 06.9 · · | 35.7 | 32 39.4 · · | 55.6 | 55 50.9 · · | 17.0 |
| 16 | 31 33.1 | 100 34.7 | 57.3 | 99 07.4 | 35.4 | 47 41.3 | 55.4 | 70 53.1 | 16.9 |
| 17 | 46 35.6 | 115 35.3 | 57.3 | 114 07.8 | 35.2 | 62 43.2 | 55.2 | 85 55.3 | 16.8 |
| 18 | 61 38.0 | 130 36.0 | S16 57.3 | 129 08.3 | S22 34.9 | 77 45.1 | S 7 54.9 | 100 57.4 | S16 16.7 |
| 19 | 76 40.5 | 145 36.6 | 57.3 | 144 08.8 | 34.7 | 92 47.0 | 54.7 | 115 59.6 | 16.6 |
| 20 | 91 43.0 | 160 37.3 | 57.4 | 159 09.3 | 34.4 | 107 48.9 | 54.5 | 131 01.8 | 16.6 |
| 21 | 106 45.4 | 175 37.9 · · | 57.4 | 174 09.7 · · | 34.1 | 122 50.9 · · | 54.2 | 146 04.0 · · | 16.5 |
| 22 | 121 47.9 | 190 38.6 | 57.4 | 189 10.2 | 33.9 | 137 52.8 | 54.0 | 161 06.1 | 16.4 |
| 23 | 136 50.4 | 205 39.2 | 57.4 | 204 10.7 | 33.6 | 152 54.7 | 53.8 | 176 08.3 | 16.3 |
| **22** 00 | 151 52.8 | 220 39.8 | S16 57.5 | 219 11.2 | S22 33.4 | 167 56.6 | S 7 53.6 | 191 10.5 | S16 16.2 |
| 01 | 166 55.3 | 235 40.5 | 57.5 | 234 11.6 | 33.1 | 182 58.5 | 53.3 | 206 12.6 | 16.1 |
| 02 | 181 57.7 | 250 41.1 | 57.5 | 249 12.1 | 32.9 | 198 00.4 | 53.1 | 221 14.8 | 16.0 |
| 03 | 197 00.2 | 265 41.8 · · | 57.5 | 264 12.6 · · | 32.6 | 213 02.3 · · | 52.9 | 236 17.0 · · | 15.9 |
| 04 | 212 02.7 | 280 42.4 | 57.5 | 279 13.1 | 32.4 | 228 04.2 | 52.6 | 251 19.2 | 15.9 |
| 05 | 227 05.1 | 295 43.0 | 57.6 | 294 13.6 | 32.1 | 243 06.1 | 52.4 | 266 21.3 | 15.8 |
| 06 | 242 07.6 | 310 43.6 | S16 57.6 | 309 14.0 | S22 31.9 | 258 08.0 | S 7 52.2 | 281 23.5 | S16 15.7 |
| T 07 | 257 10.1 | 325 44.3 | 57.6 | 324 14.5 | 31.6 | 273 09.9 | 52.0 | 296 25.7 | 15.6 |
| U 08 | 272 12.5 | 340 44.9 | 57.6 | 339 15.0 | 31.3 | 288 11.8 | 51.7 | 311 27.9 | 15.5 |
| E 09 | 287 15.0 | 355 45.5 · · | 57.6 | 354 15.5 · · | 31.1 | 303 13.7 · · | 51.5 | 326 30.0 · · | 15.4 |
| S 10 | 302 17.5 | 10 46.1 | 57.6 | 9 15.9 | 30.8 | 318 15.6 | 51.3 | 341 32.2 | 15.3 |
| D 11 | 317 19.9 | 25 46.8 | 57.7 | 24 16.4 | 30.6 | 333 17.5 | 51.0 | 356 34.4 | 15.3 |
| A 12 | 332 22.4 | 40 47.4 | S16 57.7 | 39 16.9 | S22 30.3 | 348 19.4 | S 7 50.8 | 11 36.5 | S16 15.2 |
| Y 13 | 347 24.9 | 55 48.0 | 57.7 | 54 17.4 | 30.1 | 3 21.3 | 50.6 | 26 38.7 | 15.1 |
| 14 | 2 27.3 | 70 48.6 | 57.7 | 69 17.9 | 29.8 | 18 23.2 | 50.4 | 41 40.9 | 15.0 |
| 15 | 17 29.8 | 85 49.2 · · | 57.7 | 84 18.3 · · | 29.5 | 33 25.1 · · | 50.1 | 56 43.1 · · | 14.9 |
| 16 | 32 32.2 | 100 49.8 | 57.7 | 99 18.8 | 29.3 | 48 27.0 | 49.9 | 71 45.2 | 14.8 |
| 17 | 47 34.7 | 115 50.4 | 57.7 | 114 19.3 | 29.0 | 63 28.9 | 49.7 | 86 47.4 | 14.7 |
| 18 | 62 37.2 | 130 51.0 | S16 57.7 | 129 19.8 | S22 28.8 | 78 30.8 | S 7 49.4 | 101 49.6 | S16 14.6 |
| 19 | 77 39.6 | 145 51.6 | 57.8 | 144 20.2 | 28.5 | 93 32.7 | 49.2 | 116 51.8 | 14.6 |
| 20 | 92 42.1 | 160 52.2 | 57.8 | 159 20.7 | 28.2 | 108 34.6 | 49.0 | 131 53.9 | 14.5 |
| 21 | 107 44.6 | 175 52.8 · · | 57.8 | 174 21.2 · · | 28.0 | 123 36.5 · · | 48.7 | 146 56.1 · · | 14.4 |
| 22 | 122 47.0 | 190 53.4 | 57.8 | 189 21.7 | 27.7 | 138 38.4 | 48.5 | 161 58.3 | 14.3 |
| 23 | 137 49.5 | 205 54.0 | 57.8 | 204 22.2 | 27.5 | 153 40.3 | 48.3 | 177 00.4 | 14.2 |
| **23** 00 | 152 52.0 | 220 54.6 | S16 57.8 | 219 22.6 | S22 27.2 | 168 42.2 | S 7 48.1 | 192 02.6 | S16 14.1 |
| 01 | 167 54.4 | 235 55.2 | 57.8 | 234 23.1 | 26.9 | 183 44.1 | 47.8 | 207 04.8 | 14.0 |
| 02 | 182 56.9 | 250 55.8 | 57.8 | 249 23.6 | 26.7 | 198 46.0 | 47.6 | 222 07.0 | 14.0 |
| 03 | 197 59.3 | 265 56.4 · · | 57.8 | 264 24.1 · · | 26.4 | 213 47.9 · · | 47.4 | 237 09.1 · · | 13.9 |
| 04 | 213 01.8 | 280 57.0 | 57.8 | 279 24.5 | 26.1 | 228 49.8 | 47.1 | 252 11.3 | 13.8 |
| 05 | 228 04.3 | 295 57.6 | 57.8 | 294 25.0 | 25.9 | 243 51.7 | 46.9 | 267 13.5 | 13.7 |
| 06 | 243 06.7 | 310 58.1 | S16 57.8 | 309 25.5 | S22 25.6 | 258 53.6 | S 7 46.7 | 282 15.7 | S16 13.6 |
| W 07 | 258 09.2 | 325 58.7 | 57.8 | 324 26.0 | 25.3 | 273 55.5 | 46.5 | 297 17.8 | 13.5 |
| E 08 | 273 11.7 | 340 59.3 | 57.8 | 339 26.5 | 25.1 | 288 57.4 | 46.2 | 312 20.0 | 13.4 |
| D 09 | 288 14.1 | 355 59.9 · · | 57.8 | 354 26.9 · · | 24.8 | 303 59.3 · · | 46.0 | 327 22.2 · · | 13.3 |
| N 10 | 303 16.6 | 11 00.5 | 57.8 | 9 27.4 | 24.5 | 319 01.2 | 45.8 | 342 24.4 | 13.3 |
| E 11 | 318 19.1 | 26 01.0 | 57.8 | 24 27.9 | 24.3 | 334 03.1 | 45.5 | 357 26.5 | 13.2 |
| S 12 | 333 21.5 | 41 01.6 | S16 57.9 | 39 28.4 | S22 24.0 | 349 05.1 | S 7 45.3 | 12 28.7 | S16 13.1 |
| D 13 | 348 24.0 | 56 02.2 | 57.9 | 54 28.9 | 23.7 | 4 07.0 | 45.1 | 27 30.9 | 13.0 |
| A 14 | 3 26.5 | 71 02.7 | 57.9 | 69 29.3 | 23.5 | 19 08.9 | 44.8 | 42 33.1 | 12.9 |
| Y 15 | 18 28.9 | 86 03.3 · · | 57.9 | 84 29.8 · · | 23.2 | 34 10.8 · · | 44.6 | 57 35.2 · · | 12.8 |
| 16 | 33 31.4 | 101 03.9 | 57.9 | 99 30.3 | 22.9 | 49 12.7 | 44.4 | 72 37.4 | 12.7 |
| 17 | 48 33.8 | 116 04.4 | 57.9 | 114 30.8 | 22.7 | 64 14.6 | 44.2 | 87 39.6 | 12.7 |
| 18 | 63 36.3 | 131 05.0 | S16 57.9 | 129 31.3 | S22 22.4 | 79 16.5 | S 7 43.9 | 102 41.8 | S16 12.6 |
| 19 | 78 38.8 | 146 05.5 | 57.8 | 144 31.7 | 22.1 | 94 18.4 | 43.7 | 117 43.9 | 12.5 |
| 20 | 93 41.2 | 161 06.1 | 57.8 | 159 32.2 | 21.8 | 109 20.3 | 43.5 | 132 46.1 | 12.4 |
| 21 | 108 43.7 | 176 06.6 · · | 57.8 | 174 32.7 · · | 21.6 | 124 22.2 · · | 43.2 | 147 48.3 · · | 12.3 |
| 22 | 123 46.2 | 191 07.2 | 57.8 | 189 33.2 | 21.3 | 139 24.1 | 43.0 | 162 50.4 | 12.2 |
| 23 | 138 48.6 | 206 07.7 | 57.8 | 204 33.7 | 21.0 | 154 26.0 | 42.8 | 177 52.6 | 12.1 |
| Mer. Pass. 13 50.2 | | v 0.6 | d 0.0 | v 0.5 | d 0.3 | v 1.9 | d 0.2 | v 2.2 | d 0.1 |

**STARS**

| Name | SHA | Dec |
|---|---|---|
| Acamar | 315 13.7 | S40 13.3 |
| Achernar | 335 22.3 | S57 07.8 |
| Acrux | 173 02.1 | S63 13.1 |
| Adhara | 255 07.5 | S29 00.3 |
| Aldebaran | 290 42.3 | N16 33.1 |
| Alioth | 166 14.7 | N55 50.2 |
| Alkaid | 152 53.6 | N49 12.0 |
| Alnair | 27 36.4 | S46 51.4 |
| Alnilam | 275 40.0 | S 1 11.4 |
| Alphard | 217 49.8 | S 8 45.3 |
| Alphecca | 126 05.7 | N26 38.2 |
| Alpheratz | 357 37.5 | N29 12.6 |
| Altair | 62 02.5 | N 8 55.4 |
| Ankaa | 353 09.8 | S42 11.4 |
| Antares | 112 18.8 | S26 28.8 |
| Arcturus | 145 49.9 | N19 03.9 |
| Atria | 107 15.2 | S69 03.7 |
| Avior | 234 15.1 | S59 34.9 |
| Bellatrix | 278 25.3 | N 6 22.1 |
| Betelgeuse | 270 54.5 | N 7 24.6 |
| Canopus | 263 53.1 | S52 42.7 |
| Capella | 280 25.2 | N46 01.3 |
| Deneb | 49 27.8 | N45 21.3 |
| Denebola | 182 27.1 | N14 26.8 |
| Diphda | 348 49.9 | S17 52.2 |
| Dubhe | 193 43.3 | N61 37.8 |
| Elnath | 278 04.7 | N28 37.6 |
| Eltanin | 90 43.5 | N51 28.8 |
| Enif | 33 41.4 | N 9 58.4 |
| Fomalhaut | 15 17.5 | S29 30.5 |
| Gacrux | 171 53.8 | S57 14.0 |
| Gienah | 175 45.7 | S17 39.9 |
| Hadar | 148 39.0 | S60 28.5 |
| Hamal | 327 54.0 | N23 33.9 |
| Kaus Aust. | 83 35.9 | S34 22.4 |
| Kochab | 137 19.4 | N74 03.6 |
| Markab | 13 32.6 | N15 19.3 |
| Menkar | 314 08.7 | N 4 10.4 |
| Menkent | 148 00.2 | S36 28.6 |
| Miaplacidus | 221 37.8 | S69 48.5 |
| Mirfak | 308 31.7 | N49 56.5 |
| Nunki | 75 50.9 | S26 16.2 |
| Peacock | 53 10.0 | S56 39.8 |
| Pollux | 243 19.9 | N27 58.4 |
| Procyon | 244 53.1 | N 5 10.0 |
| Rasalhague | 96 00.9 | N12 32.5 |
| Regulus | 207 36.6 | N11 51.5 |
| Rigel | 281 06.0 | S 8 10.8 |
| Rigil Kent. | 139 43.3 | S60 55.3 |
| Sabik | 102 05.6 | S15 45.1 |
| Schedar | 349 34.1 | N56 39.5 |
| Shaula | 96 13.7 | S37 07.1 |
| Sirius | 258 28.1 | S16 45.0 |
| Spica | 158 24.6 | S11 16.6 |
| Suhail | 222 47.6 | S43 31.4 |
| Vega | 80 35.1 | N38 48.0 |
| Zuben'ubi | 136 58.5 | S16 08.0 |

| | SHA | Mer. Pass. |
|---|---|---|
| | ° ′ | h m |
| Venus | 68 47.0 | 9 17 |
| Mars | 67 18.4 | 9 23 |
| Jupiter | 16 03.7 | 12 47 |
| Saturn | 39 17.7 | 11 14 |

# INDEX TO SELECTED STARS, 2022

| Name | No | Mag | SHA | Dec | | No | Name | Mag | SHA | Dec |
|------|----|----|----|----|----|----|----|----|----|----|
| Acamar | 7 | 3·2 | 315 | S 40 | | 1 | Alpheratz | 2·1 | 358 | N 29 |
| Achernar | 5 | 0·5 | 335 | S 57 | | 2 | Ankaa | 2·4 | 353 | S 42 |
| Acrux | 30 | 1·3 | 173 | S 63 | | 3 | Schedar | 2·2 | 350 | N 57 |
| Adhara | 19 | 1·5 | 255 | S 29 | | 4 | Diphda | 2·0 | 349 | S 18 |
| Aldebaran | 10 | 0·9 | 291 | N 17 | | 5 | Achernar | 0·5 | 335 | S 57 |
| Alioth | 32 | 1·8 | 166 | N 56 | | 6 | Hamal | 2·0 | 328 | N 24 |
| Alkaid | 34 | 1·9 | 153 | N 49 | | 7 | Acamar | 3·2 | 315 | S 40 |
| Alnair | 55 | 1·7 | 28 | S 47 | | 8 | Menkar | 2·5 | 314 | N 4 |
| Alnilam | 15 | 1·7 | 276 | S 1 | | 9 | Mirfak | 1·8 | 309 | N 50 |
| Alphard | 25 | 2·0 | 218 | S 9 | | 10 | Aldebaran | 0·9 | 291 | N 17 |
| Alphecca | 41 | 2·2 | 126 | N 27 | | 11 | Rigel | 0·1 | 281 | S 8 |
| Alpheratz | 1 | 2·1 | 358 | N 29 | | 12 | Capella | 0·1 | 280 | N 46 |
| Altair | 51 | 0·8 | 62 | N 9 | | 13 | Bellatrix | 1·6 | 278 | N 6 |
| Ankaa | 2 | 2·4 | 353 | S 42 | | 14 | Elnath | 1·7 | 278 | N 29 |
| Antares | 42 | 1·0 | 112 | S 26 | | 15 | Alnilam | 1·7 | 276 | S 1 |
| Arcturus | 37 | 0·0 | 146 | N 19 | | 16 | Betelgeuse | Var.* | 271 | N 7 |
| Atria | 43 | 1·9 | 107 | S 69 | | 17 | Canopus | −0·7 | 264 | S 53 |
| Avior | 22 | 1·9 | 234 | S 60 | | 18 | Sirius | −1·5 | 258 | S 17 |
| Bellatrix | 13 | 1·6 | 278 | N 6 | | 19 | Adhara | 1·5 | 255 | S 29 |
| Betelgeuse | 16 | Var.* | 271 | N 7 | | 20 | Procyon | 0·4 | 245 | N 5 |
| Canopus | 17 | −0·7 | 264 | S 53 | | 21 | Pollux | 1·1 | 243 | N 28 |
| Capella | 12 | 0·1 | 280 | N 46 | | 22 | Avior | 1·9 | 234 | S 60 |
| Deneb | 53 | 1·3 | 49 | N 45 | | 23 | Suhail | 2·2 | 223 | S 44 |
| Denebola | 28 | 2·1 | 182 | N 14 | | 24 | Miaplacidus | 1·7 | 222 | S 70 |
| Diphda | 4 | 2·0 | 349 | S 18 | | 25 | Alphard | 2·0 | 218 | S 9 |
| Dubhe | 27 | 1·8 | 194 | N 62 | | 26 | Regulus | 1·4 | 208 | N 12 |
| Elnath | 14 | 1·7 | 278 | N 29 | | 27 | Dubhe | 1·8 | 194 | N 62 |
| Eltanin | 47 | 2·2 | 91 | N 51 | | 28 | Denebola | 2·1 | 182 | N 14 |
| Enif | 54 | 2·4 | 34 | N 10 | | 29 | Gienah | 2·6 | 176 | S 18 |
| Fomalhaut | 56 | 1·2 | 15 | S 30 | | 30 | Acrux | 1·3 | 173 | S 63 |
| Gacrux | 31 | 1·6 | 172 | S 57 | | 31 | Gacrux | 1·6 | 172 | S 57 |
| Gienah | 29 | 2·6 | 176 | S 18 | | 32 | Alioth | 1·8 | 166 | N 56 |
| Hadar | 35 | 0·6 | 149 | S 60 | | 33 | Spica | 1·0 | 158 | S 11 |
| Hamal | 6 | 2·0 | 328 | N 24 | | 34 | Alkaid | 1·9 | 153 | N 49 |
| Kaus Australis | 48 | 1·9 | 84 | S 34 | | 35 | Hadar | 0·6 | 149 | S 60 |
| Kochab | 40 | 2·1 | 137 | N 74 | | 36 | Menkent | 2·1 | 148 | S 36 |
| Markab | 57 | 2·5 | 14 | N 15 | | 37 | Arcturus | 0·0 | 146 | N 19 |
| Menkar | 8 | 2·5 | 314 | N 4 | | 38 | Rigil Kentaurus | −0·3 | 140 | S 61 |
| Menkent | 36 | 2·1 | 148 | S 36 | | 39 | Zubenelgenubi | 2·8 | 137 | S 16 |
| Miaplacidus | 24 | 1·7 | 222 | S 70 | | 40 | Kochab | 2·1 | 137 | N 74 |
| Mirfak | 9 | 1·8 | 309 | N 50 | | 41 | Alphecca | 2·2 | 126 | N 27 |
| Nunki | 50 | 2·0 | 76 | S 26 | | 42 | Antares | 1·0 | 112 | S 26 |
| Peacock | 52 | 1·9 | 53 | S 57 | | 43 | Atria | 1·9 | 107 | S 69 |
| Pollux | 21 | 1·1 | 243 | N 28 | | 44 | Sabik | 2·4 | 102 | S 16 |
| Procyon | 20 | 0·4 | 245 | N 5 | | 45 | Shaula | 1·6 | 96 | S 37 |
| Rasalhague | 46 | 2·1 | 96 | N 13 | | 46 | Rasalhague | 2·1 | 96 | N 13 |
| Regulus | 26 | 1·4 | 208 | N 12 | | 47 | Eltanin | 2·2 | 91 | N 51 |
| Rigel | 11 | 0·1 | 281 | S 8 | | 48 | Kaus Australis | 1·9 | 84 | S 34 |
| Rigil Kentaurus | 38 | −0·3 | 140 | S 61 | | 49 | Vega | 0·0 | 81 | N 39 |
| Sabik | 44 | 2·4 | 102 | S 16 | | 50 | Nunki | 2·0 | 76 | S 26 |
| Schedar | 3 | 2·2 | 350 | N 57 | | 51 | Altair | 0·8 | 62 | N 9 |
| Shaula | 45 | 1·6 | 96 | S 37 | | 52 | Peacock | 1·9 | 53 | S 57 |
| Sirius | 18 | −1·5 | 258 | S 17 | | 53 | Deneb | 1·3 | 49 | N 45 |
| Spica | 33 | 1·0 | 158 | S 11 | | 54 | Enif | 2·4 | 34 | N 10 |
| Suhail | 23 | 2·2 | 223 | S 44 | | 55 | Alnair | 1·7 | 28 | S 47 |
| Vega | 49 | 0·0 | 81 | N 39 | | 56 | Fomalhaut | 1·2 | 15 | S 30 |
| Zubenelgenubi | 39 | 2·8 | 137 | S 16 | | 57 | Markab | 2·5 | 14 | N 15 |

*0·1 — 1·2

# ALTITUDE CORRECTION TABLES 10°–90°—SUN, STARS, PLANETS

## OCT.—MAR. SUN APR.—SEPT.

| App. Alt. | Lower Limb | Upper Limb | App. Alt. | Lower Limb | Upper Limb |
|---|---|---|---|---|---|
| ° ′ | ′ | ′ | ° ′ | ′ | ′ |
| 9 33 | +10.8 | −21.5 | 9 39 | +10.6 | −21.2 |
| 9 45 | +10.9 | −21.4 | 9 50 | +10.7 | −21.1 |
| 9 56 | +11.0 | −21.3 | 10 02 | +10.8 | −21.0 |
| 10 08 | +11.1 | −21.2 | 10 14 | +10.9 | −20.9 |
| 10 20 | +11.2 | −21.1 | 10 27 | +11.0 | −20.8 |
| 10 33 | +11.3 | −21.0 | 10 40 | +11.1 | −20.7 |
| 10 46 | +11.4 | −20.9 | 10 53 | +11.2 | −20.6 |
| 11 00 | +11.5 | −20.8 | 11 07 | +11.3 | −20.5 |
| 11 15 | +11.6 | −20.7 | 11 22 | +11.4 | −20.4 |
| 11 30 | +11.7 | −20.6 | 11 37 | +11.5 | −20.3 |
| 11 45 | +11.8 | −20.5 | 11 53 | +11.6 | −20.2 |
| 12 01 | +11.9 | −20.4 | 12 10 | +11.7 | −20.1 |
| 12 18 | +12.0 | −20.3 | 12 27 | +11.8 | −20.0 |
| 12 36 | +12.1 | −20.2 | 12 45 | +11.9 | −19.9 |
| 12 54 | +12.2 | −20.1 | 13 04 | +12.0 | −19.8 |
| 13 14 | +12.3 | −20.0 | 13 24 | +12.1 | −19.7 |
| 13 34 | +12.4 | −19.9 | 13 44 | +12.2 | −19.6 |
| 13 55 | +12.5 | −19.8 | 14 06 | +12.3 | −19.5 |
| 14 17 | +12.6 | −19.7 | 14 29 | +12.4 | −19.4 |
| 14 41 | +12.7 | −19.6 | 14 53 | +12.5 | −19.3 |
| 15 05 | +12.8 | −19.5 | 15 18 | +12.6 | −19.2 |
| 15 31 | +12.9 | −19.4 | 15 45 | +12.7 | −19.1 |
| 15 59 | +13.0 | −19.3 | 16 13 | +12.8 | −19.0 |
| 16 27 | +13.1 | −19.2 | 16 43 | +12.9 | −18.9 |
| 16 58 | +13.2 | −19.1 | 17 14 | +13.0 | −18.8 |
| 17 30 | +13.3 | −19.0 | 17 47 | +13.1 | −18.7 |
| 18 05 | +13.4 | −18.9 | 18 23 | +13.2 | −18.6 |
| 18 41 | +13.5 | −18.8 | 19 00 | +13.3 | −18.5 |
| 19 20 | +13.6 | −18.7 | 19 41 | +13.4 | −18.4 |
| 20 02 | +13.7 | −18.6 | 20 24 | +13.5 | −18.3 |
| 20 46 | +13.8 | −18.5 | 21 10 | +13.6 | −18.2 |
| 21 34 | +13.9 | −18.4 | 21 59 | +13.7 | −18.1 |
| 22 25 | +14.0 | −18.3 | 22 52 | +13.8 | −18.0 |
| 23 20 | +14.1 | −18.2 | 23 49 | +13.9 | −17.9 |
| 24 20 | +14.2 | −18.1 | 24 51 | +14.0 | −17.8 |
| 25 24 | +14.3 | −18.0 | 25 58 | +14.1 | −17.7 |
| 26 34 | +14.4 | −17.9 | 27 11 | +14.2 | −17.6 |
| 27 50 | +14.5 | −17.8 | 28 31 | +14.3 | −17.5 |
| 29 13 | +14.6 | −17.7 | 29 58 | +14.4 | −17.4 |
| 30 44 | +14.7 | −17.6 | 31 33 | +14.5 | −17.3 |
| 32 24 | +14.8 | −17.5 | 33 18 | +14.6 | −17.2 |
| 34 15 | +14.9 | −17.4 | 35 15 | +14.7 | −17.1 |
| 36 17 | +15.0 | −17.3 | 37 24 | +14.8 | −17.0 |
| 38 34 | +15.1 | −17.2 | 39 48 | +14.9 | −16.9 |
| 41 06 | +15.2 | −17.1 | 42 28 | +15.0 | −16.8 |
| 43 56 | +15.3 | −17.0 | 45 29 | +15.1 | −16.7 |
| 47 07 | +15.4 | −16.9 | 48 52 | +15.2 | −16.6 |
| 50 43 | +15.5 | −16.8 | 52 41 | +15.3 | −16.5 |
| 54 46 | +15.6 | −16.7 | 56 59 | +15.4 | −16.4 |
| 59 21 | +15.7 | −16.6 | 61 50 | +15.5 | −16.3 |
| 64 28 | +15.8 | −16.5 | 67 15 | +15.6 | −16.2 |
| 70 10 | +15.9 | −16.4 | 73 14 | +15.7 | −16.1 |
| 76 24 | +16.0 | −16.3 | 79 42 | +15.8 | −16.0 |
| 83 05 | +16.1 | −16.2 | 86 31 | +15.9 | −15.9 |
| 90 00 | | | 90 00 | | |

## STARS AND PLANETS

| App Alt | Corrn |
|---|---|
| ° ′ | ′ |
| 9 55 | −5.3 |
| 10 07 | −5.2 |
| 10 20 | −5.1 |
| 10 32 | −5.0 |
| 10 46 | −4.9 |
| 10 59 | −4.8 |
| 11 14 | −4.7 |
| 11 29 | −4.6 |
| 11 44 | −4.5 |
| 12 00 | −4.4 |
| 12 17 | −4.3 |
| 12 35 | −4.2 |
| 12 53 | −4.1 |
| 13 12 | −4.0 |
| 13 32 | −3.9 |
| 13 53 | −3.8 |
| 14 16 | −3.7 |
| 14 39 | −3.6 |
| 15 03 | −3.5 |
| 15 29 | −3.4 |
| 15 56 | −3.3 |
| 16 25 | −3.2 |
| 16 55 | −3.1 |
| 17 27 | −3.0 |
| 18 01 | −2.9 |
| 18 37 | −2.8 |
| 19 16 | −2.7 |
| 19 56 | −2.6 |
| 20 40 | −2.5 |
| 21 27 | −2.4 |
| 22 17 | −2.3 |
| 23 11 | −2.2 |
| 24 09 | −2.1 |
| 25 12 | −2.0 |
| 26 20 | −1.9 |
| 27 34 | −1.8 |
| 28 54 | −1.7 |
| 30 22 | −1.6 |
| 31 58 | −1.5 |
| 33 43 | −1.4 |
| 35 38 | −1.3 |
| 37 45 | −1.2 |
| 40 06 | −1.1 |
| 42 42 | −1.0 |
| 45 34 | −0.9 |
| 48 45 | −0.8 |
| 52 16 | −0.7 |
| 56 00 | −0.6 |
| 60 26 | −0.5 |
| 65 06 | −0.4 |
| 70 09 | −0.3 |
| 75 32 | −0.2 |
| 81 12 | −0.1 |
| 87 03 | 0.0 |
| 90 00 | |

### App. Alt. Additional Corrn

**2022**

**VENUS**

Jan. 1–Jan. 6
Jan. 11–Jan. 29

| ° | ′ |
|---|---|
| 0 | +0.5 |
| 26 | +0.4 |
| 46 | +0.3 |
| 60 | +0.2 |
| 73 | +0.1 |
| 84 | |

Jan. 7–Jan. 10

| ° | ′ |
|---|---|
| 0 | +0.6 |
| 24 | +0.5 |
| 41 | +0.4 |
| 54 | +0.3 |
| 65 | +0.2 |
| 76 | +0.1 |
| 85 | |

Jan. 30–Feb. 13

| ° | ′ |
|---|---|
| 0 | +0.4 |
| 29 | +0.3 |
| 51 | +0.2 |
| 68 | +0.1 |
| 83 | |

Feb. 14–Mar. 8

| ° | ′ |
|---|---|
| 0 | +0.3 |
| 34 | +0.2 |
| 60 | +0.1 |
| 80 | |

Mar. 9–Apr. 28

| ° | ′ |
|---|---|
| 0 | +0.2 |
| 41 | +0.1 |
| 76 | |

Apr. 29–Dec. 31

| ° | ′ |
|---|---|
| 0 | +0.1 |
| 60 | |

**MARS**

Jan. 1–Aug. 28

| ° | ′ |
|---|---|
| 0 | +0.1 |
| 60 | |

Aug. 29–Nov. 9
Dec. 22–Dec. 31

| ° | ′ |
|---|---|
| 0 | +0.2 |
| 41 | +0.1 |
| 76 | |

Nov. 10–Dec. 21

| ° | ′ |
|---|---|
| 0 | +0.3 |
| 34 | +0.2 |
| 60 | +0.1 |
| 80 | |

## DIP

| Ht. of Eye | Corrn | Ht. of Eye | Ht. of Eye | Corrn |
|---|---|---|---|---|
| m | ′ | ft. | m | ′ |
| 2.4 | −2.8 | 8.0 | 1.0 | −1.8 |
| 2.6 | −2.9 | 8.6 | 1.5 | −2.2 |
| 2.8 | −3.0 | 9.2 | 2.0 | −2.5 |
| 3.0 | −3.1 | 9.8 | 2.5 | −2.8 |
| 3.2 | −3.2 | 10.5 | 3.0 | −3.0 |
| 3.4 | −3.3 | 11.2 | | |
| 3.6 | −3.4 | 11.9 | See table ← | |
| 3.8 | −3.5 | 12.6 | | |
| 4.0 | −3.6 | 13.3 | m | ′ |
| 4.3 | −3.7 | 14.1 | 20 | −7.9 |
| 4.5 | −3.8 | 14.9 | 22 | −8.3 |
| 4.7 | −3.9 | 15.7 | 24 | −8.6 |
| 5.0 | −4.0 | 16.5 | 26 | −9.0 |
| 5.2 | −4.1 | 17.4 | 28 | −9.3 |
| 5.5 | −4.2 | 18.3 | 30 | −9.6 |
| 5.8 | −4.3 | 19.1 | 32 | −10.0 |
| 6.1 | −4.4 | 20.1 | 34 | −10.3 |
| 6.3 | −4.5 | 21.0 | 36 | −10.6 |
| 6.6 | −4.6 | 22.0 | 38 | −10.8 |
| 6.9 | −4.7 | 22.9 | | |
| 7.2 | −4.8 | 23.9 | 40 | −11.1 |
| 7.5 | −4.9 | 24.9 | 42 | −11.4 |
| 7.9 | −5.0 | 26.0 | 44 | −11.7 |
| 8.2 | −5.1 | 27.1 | 46 | −11.9 |
| 8.5 | −5.2 | 28.1 | 48 | −12.2 |
| 8.8 | −5.3 | 29.2 | | |
| 9.2 | −5.4 | 30.4 | ft. | ′ |
| 9.5 | −5.5 | 31.5 | 2 | −1.4 |
| 9.9 | −5.6 | 32.7 | 4 | −1.9 |
| 10.3 | −5.7 | 33.9 | 6 | −2.4 |
| 10.6 | −5.8 | 35.1 | 8 | −2.7 |
| 11.0 | −5.9 | 36.3 | 10 | −3.1 |
| 11.4 | −6.0 | 37.6 | | |
| 11.8 | −6.1 | 38.9 | See table ← | |
| 12.2 | −6.2 | 40.1 | | |
| 12.6 | −6.3 | 41.5 | ft. | ′ |
| 13.0 | −6.4 | 42.8 | 70 | −8.1 |
| 13.4 | −6.5 | 44.2 | 75 | −8.4 |
| 13.8 | −6.6 | 45.5 | 80 | −8.7 |
| 14.2 | −6.7 | 46.9 | 85 | −8.9 |
| 14.7 | −6.8 | 48.4 | 90 | −9.2 |
| 15.1 | −6.9 | 49.8 | 95 | −9.5 |
| 15.5 | −7.0 | 51.3 | 100 | −9.7 |
| 16.0 | −7.1 | 52.8 | 105 | −9.9 |
| 16.5 | −7.2 | 54.3 | 110 | −10.2 |
| 16.9 | −7.3 | 55.8 | 115 | −10.4 |
| 17.4 | −7.4 | 57.4 | 120 | −10.6 |
| 17.9 | −7.5 | 58.9 | 125 | −10.8 |
| 18.4 | −7.6 | 60.5 | | |
| 18.8 | −7.7 | 62.1 | 130 | −11.1 |
| 19.3 | −7.8 | 63.8 | 135 | −11.3 |
| 19.8 | −7.9 | 65.4 | 140 | −11.5 |
| 20.4 | −8.0 | 67.1 | 145 | −11.7 |
| 20.9 | −8.1 | 68.8 | 150 | −11.9 |
| 21.4 | | 70.5 | 155 | −12.1 |

App. Alt. = Apparent altitude = Sextant altitude corrected for index error and dip.

| UT | SUN GHA | SUN Dec | MOON GHA | v | Dec | d | HP |
|---|---|---|---|---|---|---|---|
| d h | ° ′ | ° ′ | ° ′ | ′ | ° ′ | ′ | ′ |
| **21** 00 | 176 35.7 | S10 38.8 | 307 01.7 | 12.5 | S 7 07.3 | 14.7 | 58.0 |
| 01 | 191 35.7 | 37.9 | 321 33.2 | 12.5 | 7 22.0 | 14.7 | 58.0 |
| 02 | 206 35.8 | 37.0 | 336 04.7 | 12.5 | 7 36.7 | 14.6 | 58.0 |
| 03 | 221 35.9 | .. 36.1 | 350 36.2 | 12.3 | 7 51.3 | 14.7 | 58.1 |
| 04 | 236 35.9 | 35.2 | 5 07.5 | 12.4 | 8 06.0 | 14.5 | 58.1 |
| 05 | 251 36.0 | 34.3 | 19 38.9 | 12.2 | 8 20.5 | 14.6 | 58.1 |
| 06 | 266 36.1 | S10 33.4 | 34 10.1 | 12.3 | S 8 35.1 | 14.5 | 58.1 |
| 07 | 281 36.2 | 32.5 | 48 41.4 | 12.1 | 8 49.6 | 14.5 | 58.1 |
| 08 | 296 36.2 | 31.6 | 63 12.5 | 12.1 | 9 04.1 | 14.4 | 58.1 |
| M 09 | 311 36.3 | .. 30.7 | 77 43.6 | 12.1 | 9 18.5 | 14.5 | 58.2 |
| O 10 | 326 36.4 | 29.8 | 92 14.7 | 12.0 | 9 33.0 | 14.3 | 58.2 |
| N 11 | 341 36.5 | 28.9 | 106 45.7 | 11.9 | 9 47.3 | 14.3 | 58.2 |
| D 12 | 356 36.5 | S10 28.0 | 121 16.6 | 11.8 | S10 01.6 | 14.3 | 58.2 |
| A 13 | 11 36.6 | 27.1 | 135 47.4 | 11.8 | 10 15.9 | 14.3 | 58.2 |
| Y 14 | 26 36.7 | 26.2 | 150 18.2 | 11.8 | 10 30.2 | 14.2 | 58.2 |
| 15 | 41 36.8 | .. 25.2 | 164 49.0 | 11.6 | 10 44.4 | 14.1 | 58.3 |
| 16 | 56 36.8 | 24.3 | 179 19.6 | 11.6 | 10 58.5 | 14.1 | 58.3 |
| 17 | 71 36.9 | 23.4 | 193 50.2 | 11.6 | 11 12.6 | 14.1 | 58.3 |
| 18 | 86 37.0 | S10 22.5 | 208 20.8 | 11.4 | S11 26.7 | 14.0 | 58.3 |
| 19 | 101 37.1 | 21.6 | 222 51.2 | 11.4 | 11 40.7 | 13.9 | 58.3 |
| 20 | 116 37.1 | 20.7 | 237 21.6 | 11.3 | 11 54.6 | 13.9 | 58.4 |
| 21 | 131 37.2 | .. 19.8 | 251 51.9 | 11.3 | 12 08.5 | 13.9 | 58.4 |
| 22 | 146 37.3 | 18.9 | 266 22.2 | 11.1 | 12 22.4 | 13.8 | 58.4 |
| 23 | 161 37.4 | 18.0 | 280 52.3 | 11.1 | 12 36.2 | 13.7 | 58.4 |
| **22** 00 | 176 37.4 | S10 17.1 | 295 22.4 | 11.1 | S12 49.9 | 13.7 | 58.4 |
| 01 | 191 37.5 | 16.2 | 309 52.5 | 10.9 | 13 03.6 | 13.6 | 58.4 |
| 02 | 206 37.6 | 15.3 | 324 22.4 | 10.9 | 13 17.2 | 13.5 | 58.4 |
| 03 | 221 37.7 | .. 14.3 | 338 52.3 | 10.8 | 13 30.7 | 13.5 | 58.5 |
| 04 | 236 37.8 | 13.4 | 353 22.1 | 10.7 | 13 44.2 | 13.4 | 58.5 |
| 05 | 251 37.8 | 12.5 | 7 51.8 | 10.6 | 13 57.6 | 13.4 | 58.5 |
| 06 | 266 37.9 | S10 11.6 | 22 21.4 | 10.6 | S14 11.0 | 13.3 | 58.5 |
| 07 | 281 38.0 | 10.7 | 36 51.0 | 10.5 | 14 24.3 | 13.2 | 58.5 |
| T 08 | 296 38.1 | 09.8 | 51 20.5 | 10.4 | 14 37.5 | 13.1 | 58.5 |
| U 09 | 311 38.2 | .. 08.9 | 65 49.9 | 10.3 | 14 50.6 | 13.1 | 58.6 |
| E 10 | 326 38.2 | 08.0 | 80 19.2 | 10.2 | 15 03.7 | 13.0 | 58.6 |
| S 11 | 341 38.3 | 07.1 | 94 48.4 | 10.1 | 15 16.7 | 12.9 | 58.6 |
| D 12 | 356 38.4 | S10 06.1 | 109 17.5 | 10.1 | S15 29.6 | 12.9 | 58.6 |
| A 13 | 11 38.5 | 05.2 | 123 46.6 | 10.0 | 15 42.5 | 12.8 | 58.6 |
| Y 14 | 26 38.6 | 04.3 | 138 15.6 | 9.9 | 15 55.3 | 12.6 | 58.6 |
| 15 | 41 38.6 | .. 03.4 | 152 44.5 | 9.7 | 16 07.9 | 12.6 | 58.7 |
| 16 | 56 38.7 | 02.5 | 167 13.2 | 9.8 | 16 20.5 | 12.6 | 58.7 |
| 17 | 71 38.8 | 01.6 | 181 42.0 | 9.6 | 16 33.1 | 12.4 | 58.7 |
| 18 | 86 38.9 | S10 00.7 | 196 10.6 | 9.5 | S16 45.5 | 12.4 | 58.7 |
| 19 | 101 39.0 | 9 59.7 | 210 39.1 | 9.4 | 16 57.9 | 12.2 | 58.7 |
| 20 | 116 39.1 | 58.8 | 225 07.5 | 9.4 | 17 10.1 | 12.2 | 58.7 |
| 21 | 131 39.1 | .. 57.9 | 239 35.9 | 9.2 | 17 22.3 | 12.1 | 58.7 |
| 22 | 146 39.2 | 57.0 | 254 04.1 | 9.2 | 17 34.4 | 12.0 | 58.8 |
| 23 | 161 39.3 | 56.1 | 268 32.3 | 9.1 | 17 46.4 | 11.9 | 58.8 |
| **23** 00 | 176 39.4 | S 9 55.2 | 283 00.4 | 9.0 | S17 58.3 | 11.8 | 58.8 |
| 01 | 191 39.5 | 54.2 | 297 28.4 | 8.8 | 18 10.1 | 11.7 | 58.8 |
| 02 | 206 39.6 | 53.3 | 311 56.2 | 8.8 | 18 21.8 | 11.6 | 58.8 |
| 03 | 221 39.6 | .. 52.4 | 326 24.0 | 8.7 | 18 33.4 | 11.5 | 58.8 |
| 04 | 236 39.7 | 51.5 | 340 51.7 | 8.6 | 18 44.9 | 11.4 | 58.8 |
| 05 | 251 39.8 | 50.6 | 355 19.3 | 8.5 | 18 56.3 | 11.3 | 58.9 |
| 06 | 266 39.9 | S 9 49.7 | 9 46.8 | 8.4 | S19 07.6 | 11.2 | 58.9 |
| W 07 | 281 40.0 | 48.7 | 24 14.2 | 8.4 | 19 18.8 | 11.1 | 58.9 |
| E 08 | 296 40.1 | 47.8 | 38 41.6 | 8.2 | 19 29.9 | 10.8 | 58.9 |
| D 09 | 311 40.2 | .. 46.9 | 53 08.8 | 8.1 | 19 40.9 | 10.8 | 58.9 |
| N 10 | 326 40.2 | 46.0 | 67 35.9 | 8.0 | 19 51.7 | 10.8 | 58.9 |
| E 11 | 341 40.3 | 45.1 | 82 02.9 | 8.0 | 20 02.5 | 10.6 | 58.9 |
| S 12 | 356 40.4 | S 9 44.2 | 96 29.9 | 7.8 | S20 13.1 | 10.6 | 59.0 |
| D 13 | 11 40.5 | 43.2 | 110 56.7 | 7.7 | 20 23.7 | 10.4 | 59.0 |
| A 14 | 26 40.6 | 42.3 | 125 23.4 | 7.7 | 20 34.1 | 10.3 | 59.0 |
| Y 15 | 41 40.7 | .. 41.4 | 139 50.1 | 7.5 | 20 44.4 | 10.2 | 59.0 |
| 16 | 56 40.8 | 40.5 | 154 16.6 | 7.4 | 20 54.6 | 10.0 | 59.0 |
| 17 | 71 40.9 | 39.6 | 168 43.0 | 7.4 | 21 04.6 | 10.0 | 59.0 |
| 18 | 86 40.9 | S 9 38.6 | 183 09.4 | 7.2 | S21 14.6 | 9.8 | 59.0 |
| 19 | 101 41.0 | 37.7 | 197 35.6 | 7.2 | 21 24.4 | 9.7 | 59.1 |
| 20 | 116 41.1 | 36.8 | 212 01.8 | 7.1 | 21 34.1 | 9.5 | 59.1 |
| 21 | 131 41.2 | .. 35.9 | 226 27.9 | 6.9 | 21 43.6 | 9.4 | 59.1 |
| 22 | 146 41.3 | 34.9 | 240 53.8 | 6.9 | 21 53.0 | 9.3 | 59.1 |
| 23 | 161 41.4 | 34.0 | 255 19.7 | 6.8 | S22 02.3 | 9.2 | 59.1 |
| | SD 16.2 | d 0.9 | SD 15.9 | | 16.0 | | 16.1 |

| Lat. | Twilight Naut. | Twilight Civil | Sunrise | Moonrise 21 | 22 | 23 | 24 |
|---|---|---|---|---|---|---|---|
| ° | h m | h m | h m | h m | h m | h m | h m |
| N 72 | 05 44 | 07 02 | 08 14 | 25 28 | 01 28 | ■■ | ■■ |
| N 70 | 05 45 | 06 56 | 08 00 | 25 01 | 01 01 | 03 57 | ■■ |
| 68 | 05 46 | 06 51 | 07 49 | 24 41 | 00 41 | 03 02 | ■■ |
| 66 | 05 47 | 06 46 | 07 39 | 24 25 | 00 25 | 02 30 | 05 06 |
| 64 | 05 47 | 06 42 | 07 32 | 24 12 | 00 12 | 02 06 | 04 12 |
| 62 | 05 48 | 06 39 | 07 25 | 24 01 | 00 01 | 01 48 | 03 40 |
| 60 | 05 48 | 06 36 | 07 19 | 23 52 | 25 32 | 01 32 | 03 16 |
| N 58 | 05 48 | 06 33 | 07 14 | 23 44 | 25 19 | 01 19 | 02 57 |
| 56 | 05 48 | 06 31 | 07 09 | 23 37 | 25 08 | 01 08 | 02 41 |
| 54 | 05 48 | 06 29 | 07 05 | 23 31 | 24 59 | 00 59 | 02 27 |
| 52 | 05 48 | 06 27 | 07 01 | 23 25 | 24 50 | 00 50 | 02 16 |
| 50 | 05 47 | 06 25 | 06 58 | 23 20 | 24 42 | 00 42 | 02 05 |
| 45 | 05 46 | 06 20 | 06 50 | 23 10 | 24 26 | 00 26 | 01 44 |
| N 40 | 05 45 | 06 16 | 06 44 | 23 01 | 24 13 | 00 13 | 01 26 |
| 35 | 05 43 | 06 13 | 06 38 | 22 53 | 24 01 | 00 01 | 01 12 |
| 30 | 05 41 | 06 09 | 06 33 | 22 46 | 23 51 | 24 59 | 00 59 |
| 20 | 05 37 | 06 03 | 06 25 | 22 35 | 23 35 | 24 37 | 00 37 |
| N 10 | 05 31 | 05 56 | 06 17 | 22 25 | 23 20 | 24 19 | 00 19 |
| 0 | 05 25 | 05 49 | 06 10 | 22 16 | 23 07 | 24 02 | 00 02 |
| S 10 | 05 16 | 05 41 | 06 03 | 22 06 | 22 53 | 23 45 | 24 41 |
| 20 | 05 06 | 05 32 | 05 55 | 21 57 | 22 39 | 23 26 | 24 20 |
| 30 | 04 52 | 05 21 | 05 46 | 21 46 | 22 23 | 23 06 | 23 55 |
| 35 | 04 43 | 05 14 | 05 40 | 21 39 | 22 14 | 22 53 | 23 41 |
| 40 | 04 32 | 05 06 | 05 34 | 21 32 | 22 03 | 22 40 | 23 25 |
| 45 | 04 19 | 04 56 | 05 27 | 21 24 | 21 51 | 22 23 | 23 05 |
| S 50 | 04 02 | 04 44 | 05 19 | 21 14 | 21 36 | 22 03 | 22 40 |
| 52 | 03 53 | 04 38 | 05 15 | 21 10 | 21 29 | 21 54 | 22 29 |
| 54 | 03 44 | 04 32 | 05 10 | 21 05 | 21 21 | 21 43 | 22 15 |
| 56 | 03 33 | 04 25 | 05 05 | 20 59 | 21 12 | 21 31 | 22 00 |
| 58 | 03 20 | 04 16 | 05 00 | 20 53 | 21 03 | 21 17 | 21 42 |
| S 60 | 03 04 | 04 07 | 04 54 | 20 46 | 20 52 | 21 01 | 21 20 |

| Lat. | Sunset | Twilight Civil | Twilight Naut. | Moonset 21 | 22 | 23 | 24 |
|---|---|---|---|---|---|---|---|
| ° | h m | h m | h m | h m | h m | h m | h m |
| N 72 | 16 14 | 17 27 | 18 46 | 07 48 | 07 00 | ■■ | ■■ |
| N 70 | 16 28 | 17 33 | 18 44 | 08 01 | 07 30 | 06 23 | ■■ |
| 68 | 16 40 | 17 38 | 18 43 | 08 12 | 07 52 | 07 18 | ■■ |
| 66 | 16 49 | 17 42 | 18 42 | 08 21 | 08 09 | 07 52 | 07 13 |
| 64 | 16 57 | 17 46 | 18 41 | 08 29 | 08 24 | 08 17 | 08 07 |
| 62 | 17 03 | 17 49 | 18 41 | 08 36 | 08 36 | 08 36 | 08 40 |
| 60 | 17 09 | 17 52 | 18 40 | 08 42 | 08 46 | 08 53 | 09 05 |
| N 58 | 17 14 | 17 55 | 18 40 | 08 47 | 08 55 | 09 06 | 09 24 |
| 56 | 17 19 | 17 57 | 18 40 | 08 52 | 09 03 | 09 18 | 09 41 |
| 54 | 17 23 | 17 59 | 18 40 | 08 56 | 09 10 | 09 29 | 09 55 |
| 52 | 17 27 | 18 01 | 18 40 | 09 00 | 09 17 | 09 38 | 10 07 |
| 50 | 17 30 | 18 03 | 18 41 | 09 03 | 09 22 | 09 46 | 10 18 |
| 45 | 17 38 | 18 07 | 18 41 | 09 11 | 09 35 | 10 04 | 10 41 |
| N 40 | 17 44 | 18 11 | 18 43 | 09 17 | 09 45 | 10 19 | 10 59 |
| 35 | 17 49 | 18 15 | 18 44 | 09 22 | 09 54 | 10 31 | 11 14 |
| 30 | 17 54 | 18 18 | 18 46 | 09 27 | 10 02 | 10 42 | 11 28 |
| 20 | 18 02 | 18 25 | 18 50 | 09 36 | 10 16 | 11 01 | 11 51 |
| N 10 | 18 10 | 18 31 | 18 56 | 09 43 | 10 28 | 11 17 | 12 11 |
| 0 | 18 17 | 18 38 | 19 02 | 09 50 | 10 39 | 11 32 | 12 29 |
| S 10 | 18 24 | 18 45 | 19 10 | 09 57 | 10 51 | 11 48 | 12 48 |
| 20 | 18 32 | 18 54 | 19 21 | 10 05 | 11 03 | 12 04 | 13 08 |
| 30 | 18 41 | 19 05 | 19 34 | 10 13 | 11 17 | 12 23 | 13 31 |
| 35 | 18 46 | 19 12 | 19 43 | 10 18 | 11 25 | 12 35 | 13 49 |
| 40 | 18 52 | 19 20 | 19 54 | 10 24 | 11 35 | 12 47 | 14 01 |
| 45 | 18 59 | 19 30 | 20 07 | 10 30 | 11 46 | 13 03 | 14 20 |
| S 50 | 19 07 | 19 41 | 20 24 | 10 38 | 11 59 | 13 21 | 14 43 |
| 52 | 19 11 | 19 47 | 20 32 | 10 42 | 12 05 | 13 30 | 14 55 |
| 54 | 19 15 | 19 53 | 20 41 | 10 46 | 12 12 | 13 40 | 15 08 |
| 56 | 19 20 | 20 01 | 20 52 | 10 51 | 12 20 | 13 52 | 15 23 |
| 58 | 19 26 | 20 09 | 21 05 | 10 56 | 12 29 | 14 05 | 15 41 |
| S 60 | 19 32 | 20 18 | 21 20 | 11 01 | 12 39 | 14 20 | 16 02 |

| | SUN Eqn. of Time 00h | SUN Eqn. of Time 12h | SUN Mer. Pass. | MOON Mer. Pass. Upper | MOON Mer. Pass. Lower | Age | Phase |
|---|---|---|---|---|---|---|---|
| Day | m s | m s | h m | h m | h m | d | % |
| 21 | 13 38 | 13 34 | 12 14 | 03 39 | 16 03 | 20 | 76 |
| 22 | 13 30 | 13 27 | 12 13 | 04 27 | 16 53 | 21 | 66 |
| 23 | 13 23 | 13 19 | 12 13 | 05 19 | 17 47 | 22 | 55 |

| UT | ARIES GHA | VENUS −4.8 GHA | Dec | MARS +1.3 GHA | Dec | JUPITER −2.0 GHA | Dec | SATURN +0.7 GHA | Dec | STARS Name | SHA | Dec |
|---|---|---|---|---|---|---|---|---|---|---|---|---|
| **24 00** | 153 51.1 | 221 08.3 | S16 57.8 | 219 34.1 | S22 20.8 | 169 27.9 | S 7 42.5 | 192 54.8 | S16 12.1 | Acamar | 315 13.7 | S40 13.3 |
| 01 | 168 53.6 | 236 08.8 | 57.8 | 234 34.6 | 20.5 | 184 29.8 | 42.3 | 207 57.0 | 12.0 | Achernar | 335 22.4 | S57 07.8 |
| 02 | 183 56.0 | 251 09.4 | 57.8 | 249 35.1 | 20.2 | 199 31.7 | 42.1 | 222 59.1 | 11.9 | Acrux | 173 02.0 | S63 13.1 |
| 03 | 198 58.5 | 266 09.9 | .. 57.8 | 264 35.6 | .. 19.9 | 214 33.6 | .. 41.9 | 238 01.3 | .. 11.8 | Adhara | 255 07.5 | S29 00.3 |
| 04 | 214 01.0 | 281 10.5 | 57.8 | 279 36.1 | 19.7 | 229 35.5 | 41.6 | 253 03.5 | 11.7 | Aldebaran | 290 42.3 | N16 33.1 |
| 05 | 229 03.4 | 296 11.0 | 57.8 | 294 36.5 | 19.4 | 244 37.4 | 41.4 | 268 05.7 | 11.6 | | | |
| 06 | 244 05.9 | 311 11.5 | S16 57.8 | 309 37.0 | S22 19.1 | 259 39.3 | S 7 41.2 | 283 07.8 | S16 11.5 | Alioth | 166 14.6 | N55 50.2 |
| 07 | 259 08.3 | 326 12.1 | 57.8 | 324 37.5 | 18.8 | 274 41.2 | 40.9 | 298 10.0 | 11.4 | Alkaid | 152 53.6 | N49 12.0 |
| T 08 | 274 10.8 | 341 12.6 | 57.8 | 339 38.0 | 18.6 | 289 43.1 | 40.7 | 313 12.2 | 11.4 | Alnair | 27 36.4 | S46 51.4 |
| H 09 | 289 13.3 | 356 13.1 | .. 57.8 | 354 38.5 | .. 18.3 | 304 45.0 | .. 40.5 | 328 14.4 | .. 11.3 | Alnilam | 275 40.0 | S 1 11.4 |
| U 10 | 304 15.7 | 11 13.7 | 57.7 | 9 38.9 | 18.0 | 319 46.9 | 40.2 | 343 16.5 | 11.2 | Alphard | 217 49.7 | S 8 45.3 |
| R 11 | 319 18.2 | 26 14.2 | 57.7 | 24 39.4 | 17.7 | 334 48.8 | 40.0 | 358 18.7 | 11.1 | | | |
| S 12 | 334 20.7 | 41 14.7 | S16 57.7 | 39 39.9 | S22 17.5 | 349 50.7 | S 7 39.8 | 13 20.9 | S16 11.0 | Alphecca | 126 05.7 | N26 38.2 |
| D 13 | 349 23.1 | 56 15.3 | 57.7 | 54 40.4 | 17.2 | 4 52.6 | 39.6 | 28 23.1 | 10.9 | Alpheratz | 357 37.5 | N29 12.6 |
| A 14 | 4 25.6 | 71 15.8 | 57.7 | 69 40.9 | 16.9 | 19 54.5 | 39.3 | 43 25.2 | 10.8 | Altair | 62 02.5 | N 8 55.4 |
| Y 15 | 19 28.1 | 86 16.3 | .. 57.7 | 84 41.3 | .. 16.6 | 34 56.4 | .. 39.1 | 58 27.4 | .. 10.8 | Ankaa | 353 09.9 | S42 11.4 |
| 16 | 34 30.5 | 101 16.8 | 57.7 | 99 41.8 | 16.3 | 49 58.3 | 38.9 | 73 29.6 | 10.7 | Antares | 112 18.7 | S26 28.8 |
| 17 | 49 33.0 | 116 17.3 | 57.7 | 114 42.3 | 16.1 | 65 00.2 | 38.6 | 88 31.8 | 10.6 | | | |
| 18 | 64 35.5 | 131 17.8 | S16 57.6 | 129 42.8 | S22 15.8 | 80 02.1 | S 7 38.4 | 103 33.9 | S16 10.5 | Arcturus | 145 49.9 | N19 03.9 |
| 19 | 79 37.9 | 146 18.4 | 57.6 | 144 43.3 | 15.5 | 95 04.0 | 38.2 | 118 36.1 | 10.4 | Atria | 107 15.2 | S69 03.7 |
| 20 | 94 40.4 | 161 18.9 | 57.6 | 159 43.8 | 15.2 | 110 05.9 | 37.9 | 133 38.3 | 10.3 | Avior | 234 15.1 | S59 34.9 |
| 21 | 109 42.8 | 176 19.4 | .. 57.6 | 174 44.2 | .. 14.9 | 125 07.8 | .. 37.7 | 148 40.5 | .. 10.2 | Bellatrix | 278 25.3 | N 6 22.1 |
| 22 | 124 45.3 | 191 19.9 | 57.6 | 189 44.7 | 14.7 | 140 09.7 | 37.5 | 163 42.6 | 10.2 | Betelgeuse | 270 54.5 | N 7 24.6 |
| 23 | 139 47.8 | 206 20.4 | 57.5 | 204 45.2 | 14.4 | 155 11.6 | 37.3 | 178 44.8 | 10.1 | | | |
| **25 00** | 154 50.2 | 221 20.9 | S16 57.5 | 219 45.7 | S22 14.1 | 170 13.5 | S 7 37.0 | 193 47.0 | S16 10.0 | Canopus | 263 53.2 | S52 42.7 |
| 01 | 169 52.7 | 236 21.4 | 57.5 | 234 46.2 | 13.8 | 185 15.4 | 36.8 | 208 49.2 | 09.9 | Capella | 280 25.2 | N46 01.3 |
| 02 | 184 55.2 | 251 21.9 | 57.5 | 249 46.6 | 13.5 | 200 17.3 | 36.6 | 223 51.3 | 09.8 | Deneb | 49 27.8 | N45 21.3 |
| 03 | 199 57.6 | 266 22.4 | .. 57.5 | 264 47.1 | .. 13.2 | 215 19.2 | .. 36.3 | 238 53.5 | .. 09.7 | Denebola | 182 27.1 | N14 26.8 |
| 04 | 215 00.1 | 281 22.9 | 57.4 | 279 47.6 | 13.0 | 230 21.1 | 36.1 | 253 55.7 | 09.6 | Diphda | 348 49.9 | S17 52.2 |
| 05 | 230 02.6 | 296 23.4 | 57.4 | 294 48.1 | 12.7 | 245 23.0 | 35.9 | 268 57.9 | 09.6 | | | |
| 06 | 245 05.0 | 311 23.9 | S16 57.4 | 309 48.6 | S22 12.4 | 260 24.9 | S 7 35.6 | 284 00.0 | S16 09.5 | Dubhe | 193 43.3 | N61 37.9 |
| 07 | 260 07.5 | 326 24.4 | 57.4 | 324 49.1 | 12.1 | 275 26.8 | 35.4 | 299 02.2 | 09.4 | Elnath | 278 04.7 | N28 37.6 |
| 08 | 275 09.9 | 341 24.9 | 57.4 | 339 49.5 | 11.8 | 290 28.7 | 35.2 | 314 04.4 | 09.3 | Eltanin | 90 43.5 | N51 28.8 |
| F 09 | 290 12.4 | 356 25.4 | .. 57.3 | 354 50.0 | .. 11.5 | 305 30.6 | .. 34.9 | 329 06.6 | .. 09.2 | Enif | 33 41.4 | N 9 58.4 |
| R 10 | 305 14.9 | 11 25.9 | 57.3 | 9 50.5 | 11.3 | 320 32.5 | 34.7 | 344 08.8 | 09.1 | Fomalhaut | 15 17.5 | S29 30.5 |
| I 11 | 320 17.3 | 26 26.3 | 57.3 | 24 51.0 | 11.0 | 335 34.4 | 34.5 | 359 10.9 | 09.0 | | | |
| D 12 | 335 19.8 | 41 26.8 | S16 57.3 | 39 51.5 | S22 10.7 | 350 36.3 | S 7 34.3 | 14 13.1 | S16 08.9 | Gacrux | 171 53.7 | S57 14.1 |
| A 13 | 350 22.3 | 56 27.3 | 57.2 | 54 51.9 | 10.4 | 5 38.2 | 34.0 | 29 15.3 | 08.9 | Gienah | 175 45.7 | S17 39.9 |
| Y 14 | 5 24.7 | 71 27.8 | 57.2 | 69 52.4 | 10.1 | 20 40.1 | 33.8 | 44 17.5 | 08.8 | Hadar | 148 39.0 | S60 28.5 |
| 15 | 20 27.2 | 86 28.3 | .. 57.2 | 84 52.9 | .. 09.8 | 35 42.1 | .. 33.6 | 59 19.6 | .. 08.7 | Hamal | 327 54.0 | N23 33.9 |
| 16 | 35 29.7 | 101 28.7 | 57.1 | 99 53.4 | 09.5 | 50 44.0 | 33.3 | 74 21.8 | 08.6 | Kaus Aust. | 83 35.8 | S34 22.4 |
| 17 | 50 32.1 | 116 29.2 | 57.1 | 114 53.9 | 09.2 | 65 45.9 | 33.1 | 89 24.0 | 08.5 | | | |
| 18 | 65 34.6 | 131 29.7 | S16 57.1 | 129 54.4 | S22 09.0 | 80 47.8 | S 7 32.9 | 104 26.2 | S16 08.4 | Kochab | 137 19.4 | N74 03.6 |
| 19 | 80 37.1 | 146 30.2 | 57.1 | 144 54.8 | 08.7 | 95 49.7 | 32.6 | 119 28.3 | 08.3 | Markab | 13 32.6 | N15 19.3 |
| 20 | 95 39.5 | 161 30.6 | 57.0 | 159 55.3 | 08.4 | 110 51.6 | 32.4 | 134 30.5 | 08.3 | Menkar | 314 08.7 | N 4 10.4 |
| 21 | 110 42.0 | 176 31.1 | .. 57.0 | 174 55.8 | .. 08.1 | 125 53.5 | .. 32.2 | 149 32.7 | .. 08.2 | Menkent | 148 00.2 | S36 28.6 |
| 22 | 125 44.4 | 191 31.6 | 57.0 | 189 56.3 | 07.8 | 140 55.4 | 32.0 | 164 34.9 | 08.1 | Miaplacidus | 221 37.8 | S69 48.5 |
| 23 | 140 46.9 | 206 32.0 | 56.9 | 204 56.8 | 07.5 | 155 57.3 | 31.7 | 179 37.0 | 08.0 | | | |
| **26 00** | 155 49.4 | 221 32.5 | S16 56.9 | 219 57.3 | S22 07.2 | 170 59.2 | S 7 31.5 | 194 39.2 | S16 07.9 | Mirfak | 308 31.7 | N49 56.5 |
| 01 | 170 51.8 | 236 33.0 | 56.9 | 234 57.7 | 06.9 | 186 01.1 | 31.3 | 209 41.4 | 07.8 | Nunki | 75 50.9 | S26 16.1 |
| 02 | 185 54.3 | 251 33.4 | 56.8 | 249 58.2 | 06.6 | 201 03.0 | 31.0 | 224 43.6 | 07.7 | Peacock | 53 10.0 | S56 39.8 |
| 03 | 200 56.8 | 266 33.9 | .. 56.8 | 264 58.7 | .. 06.3 | 216 04.9 | .. 30.8 | 239 45.7 | .. 07.7 | Pollux | 243 19.9 | N27 58.4 |
| 04 | 215 59.2 | 281 34.3 | 56.8 | 279 59.2 | 06.0 | 231 06.8 | 30.6 | 254 47.9 | 07.6 | Procyon | 244 53.1 | N 5 10.0 |
| 05 | 231 01.7 | 296 34.8 | 56.7 | 294 59.7 | 05.7 | 246 08.7 | 30.3 | 269 50.1 | 07.5 | | | |
| 06 | 246 04.2 | 311 35.2 | S16 56.7 | 310 00.2 | S22 05.5 | 261 10.6 | S 7 30.1 | 284 52.3 | S16 07.4 | Rasalhague | 96 00.8 | N12 32.5 |
| 07 | 261 06.6 | 326 35.7 | 56.6 | 325 00.6 | 05.2 | 276 12.5 | 29.9 | 299 54.5 | 07.3 | Regulus | 207 36.6 | N11 51.5 |
| 08 | 276 09.1 | 341 36.1 | 56.6 | 340 01.1 | 04.9 | 291 14.4 | 29.6 | 314 56.6 | 07.2 | Rigel | 281 06.1 | S 8 10.8 |
| S 09 | 291 11.6 | 356 36.6 | .. 56.6 | 355 01.6 | .. 04.6 | 306 16.3 | .. 29.4 | 329 58.8 | .. 07.1 | Rigil Kent. | 139 43.2 | S60 55.3 |
| A 10 | 306 14.0 | 11 37.0 | 56.5 | 10 02.1 | 04.3 | 321 18.2 | 29.2 | 345 01.0 | 07.1 | Sabik | 102 05.6 | S15 45.1 |
| T 11 | 321 16.5 | 26 37.5 | 56.5 | 25 02.6 | 04.0 | 336 20.1 | 29.0 | 0 03.2 | 07.0 | | | |
| U 12 | 336 18.9 | 41 37.9 | S16 56.4 | 40 03.1 | S22 03.7 | 351 22.0 | S 7 28.7 | 15 05.3 | S16 06.9 | Schedar | 349 34.2 | N56 39.5 |
| R 13 | 351 21.4 | 56 38.4 | 56.4 | 55 03.6 | 03.4 | 6 23.9 | 28.5 | 30 07.5 | 06.8 | Shaula | 96 13.7 | S37 07.1 |
| D 14 | 6 23.9 | 71 38.8 | 56.4 | 70 04.0 | 03.1 | 21 25.8 | 28.3 | 45 09.7 | 06.7 | Sirius | 258 28.1 | S16 45.0 |
| A 15 | 21 26.3 | 86 39.2 | .. 56.3 | 85 04.5 | .. 02.8 | 36 27.7 | .. 28.0 | 60 11.9 | .. 06.6 | Spica | 158 24.6 | S11 16.6 |
| Y 16 | 36 28.8 | 101 39.7 | 56.3 | 100 05.0 | 02.5 | 51 29.6 | 27.8 | 75 14.0 | 06.5 | Suhail | 222 47.6 | S43 31.4 |
| 17 | 51 31.3 | 116 40.1 | 56.2 | 115 05.5 | 02.2 | 66 31.5 | 27.6 | 90 16.2 | 06.5 | | | |
| 18 | 66 33.7 | 131 40.6 | S16 56.2 | 130 06.0 | S22 01.9 | 81 33.4 | S 7 27.3 | 105 18.4 | S16 06.4 | Vega | 80 35.0 | N38 48.0 |
| 19 | 81 36.2 | 146 41.0 | 56.1 | 145 06.5 | 01.6 | 96 35.3 | 27.1 | 120 20.6 | 06.3 | Zuben'ubi | 136 58.5 | S16 08.0 |
| 20 | 96 38.7 | 161 41.4 | 56.1 | 160 07.0 | 01.3 | 111 37.2 | 26.9 | 135 22.8 | 06.2 | | SHA | Mer. Pass. |
| 21 | 111 41.1 | 176 41.8 | .. 56.0 | 175 07.4 | .. 01.0 | 126 39.1 | .. 26.6 | 150 24.9 | .. 06.1 | | ° ′ | h m |
| 22 | 126 43.6 | 191 42.3 | 56.0 | 190 07.9 | 00.7 | 141 41.0 | 26.4 | 165 27.1 | 06.0 | Venus | 66 30.7 | 9 14 |
| 23 | 141 46.1 | 206 42.7 | 55.9 | 205 08.4 | 00.4 | 156 42.9 | 26.2 | 180 29.3 | 05.9 | Mars | 64 55.4 | 9 21 |
| | h m | | | | | | | | | Jupiter | 15 23.3 | 12 37 |
| Mer. Pass. 13 38.4 | v 0.5 | d 0.0 | v 0.5 | d 0.3 | v 1.9 | d 0.2 | v 2.2 | d 0.1 | Saturn | 38 56.8 | 11 03 |

### SUN / MOON

| UT | SUN GHA | SUN Dec | MOON GHA | v | MOON Dec | d | HP |
|---|---|---|---|---|---|---|---|
| d h | ° ′ | ° ′ | ° ′ | ′ | ° ′ | ′ | ′ |
| 24 00 | 176 41.5 | S 9 33.1 | 269 45.5 | 6.6 | S22 11.5 | 9.0 | 59.1 |
| 01 | 191 41.6 | 32.2 | 284 11.1 | 6.6 | 22 20.5 | 8.9 | 59.1 |
| 02 | 206 41.7 | 31.3 | 298 36.7 | 6.5 | 22 29.4 | 8.8 | 59.1 |
| 03 | 221 41.8 | .. 30.3 | 313 02.2 | 6.4 | 22 38.2 | 8.6 | 59.2 |
| 04 | 236 41.8 | 29.4 | 327 27.6 | 6.3 | 22 46.8 | 8.5 | 59.2 |
| 05 | 251 41.9 | 28.5 | 341 52.9 | 6.2 | 22 55.3 | 8.3 | 59.2 |
| 06 | 266 42.0 | S 9 27.6 | 356 18.1 | 6.1 | S23 03.6 | 8.2 | 59.2 |
| 07 | 281 42.1 | 26.6 | 10 43.2 | 6.1 | 23 11.8 | 8.1 | 59.2 |
| T 08 | 296 42.2 | 25.7 | 25 08.3 | 5.9 | 23 19.9 | 7.9 | 59.2 |
| H 09 | 311 42.3 | .. 24.8 | 39 33.2 | 5.9 | 23 27.8 | 7.8 | 59.2 |
| U 10 | 326 42.4 | 23.9 | 53 58.1 | 5.7 | 23 35.6 | 7.6 | 59.2 |
| R 11 | 341 42.5 | 22.9 | 68 22.8 | 5.7 | 23 43.2 | 7.5 | 59.2 |
| S 12 | 356 42.6 | S 9 22.0 | 82 47.5 | 5.6 | S23 50.7 | 7.3 | 59.3 |
| D 13 | 11 42.7 | 21.1 | 97 12.1 | 5.5 | 23 58.0 | 7.1 | 59.3 |
| A 14 | 26 42.8 | 20.2 | 111 36.6 | 5.4 | 24 05.1 | 7.0 | 59.3 |
| Y 15 | 41 42.9 | .. 19.2 | 126 01.0 | 5.3 | 24 12.1 | 6.9 | 59.3 |
| 16 | 56 43.0 | 18.3 | 140 25.3 | 5.3 | 24 19.0 | 6.7 | 59.3 |
| 17 | 71 43.0 | 17.4 | 154 49.6 | 5.1 | 24 25.7 | 6.5 | 59.3 |
| 18 | 86 43.1 | S 9 16.5 | 169 13.7 | 5.1 | S24 32.2 | 6.4 | 59.3 |
| 19 | 101 43.2 | 15.5 | 183 37.8 | 5.0 | 24 38.6 | 6.2 | 59.3 |
| 20 | 116 43.3 | 14.6 | 198 01.8 | 4.9 | 24 44.8 | 6.1 | 59.3 |
| 21 | 131 43.4 | .. 13.7 | 212 25.7 | 4.9 | 24 50.9 | 5.9 | 59.4 |
| 22 | 146 43.5 | 12.8 | 226 49.6 | 4.8 | 24 56.8 | 5.7 | 59.4 |
| 23 | 161 43.6 | 11.8 | 241 13.4 | 4.7 | 25 02.5 | 5.6 | 59.4 |
| 25 00 | 176 43.7 | S 9 10.9 | 255 37.1 | 4.6 | S25 08.1 | 5.4 | 59.4 |
| 01 | 191 43.8 | 10.0 | 270 00.7 | 4.6 | 25 13.5 | 5.2 | 59.4 |
| 02 | 206 43.9 | 09.0 | 284 24.3 | 4.5 | 25 18.7 | 5.1 | 59.4 |
| 03 | 221 44.0 | .. 08.1 | 298 47.8 | 4.4 | 25 23.8 | 4.9 | 59.4 |
| 04 | 236 44.1 | 07.2 | 313 11.2 | 4.4 | 25 28.7 | 4.7 | 59.4 |
| 05 | 251 44.2 | 06.3 | 327 34.6 | 4.3 | 25 33.4 | 4.5 | 59.4 |
| 06 | 266 44.3 | S 9 05.3 | 341 57.9 | 4.2 | S25 37.9 | 4.4 | 59.4 |
| 07 | 281 44.4 | 04.4 | 356 21.1 | 4.2 | 25 42.3 | 4.2 | 59.4 |
| 08 | 296 44.5 | 03.5 | 10 44.3 | 4.1 | 25 46.5 | 4.0 | 59.5 |
| F 09 | 311 44.6 | .. 02.5 | 25 07.4 | 4.1 | 25 50.5 | 3.9 | 59.5 |
| R 10 | 326 44.7 | 01.6 | 39 30.5 | 4.0 | 25 54.4 | 3.7 | 59.5 |
| I 11 | 341 44.8 | 9 00.7 | 53 53.5 | 3.9 | 25 58.1 | 3.5 | 59.5 |
| D 12 | 356 44.9 | S 8 59.7 | 68 16.4 | 3.9 | S26 01.6 | 3.3 | 59.5 |
| A 13 | 11 45.0 | 58.8 | 82 39.3 | 3.9 | 26 04.9 | 3.1 | 59.5 |
| Y 14 | 26 45.1 | 57.9 | 97 02.2 | 3.8 | 26 08.0 | 3.0 | 59.5 |
| 15 | 41 45.2 | .. 56.9 | 111 25.0 | 3.8 | 26 11.0 | 2.8 | 59.5 |
| 16 | 56 45.3 | 56.0 | 125 47.8 | 3.7 | 26 13.8 | 2.6 | 59.5 |
| 17 | 71 45.4 | 55.1 | 140 10.5 | 3.7 | 26 16.4 | 2.4 | 59.5 |
| 18 | 86 45.5 | S 8 54.1 | 154 33.2 | 3.6 | S26 18.8 | 2.2 | 59.5 |
| 19 | 101 45.6 | 53.2 | 168 55.8 | 3.7 | 26 21.0 | 2.1 | 59.5 |
| 20 | 116 45.7 | 52.3 | 183 18.5 | 3.5 | 26 23.1 | 1.8 | 59.5 |
| 21 | 131 45.8 | .. 51.3 | 197 41.0 | 3.6 | 26 24.9 | 1.7 | 59.5 |
| 22 | 146 45.9 | 50.4 | 212 03.6 | 3.5 | 26 26.6 | 1.5 | 59.5 |
| 23 | 161 46.0 | 49.5 | 226 26.1 | 3.5 | 26 28.1 | 1.3 | 59.6 |
| 26 00 | 176 46.1 | S 8 48.5 | 240 48.6 | 3.5 | S26 29.4 | 1.1 | 59.6 |
| 01 | 191 46.2 | 47.6 | 255 11.1 | 3.4 | 26 30.5 | 1.0 | 59.6 |
| 02 | 206 46.3 | 46.7 | 269 33.5 | 3.5 | 26 31.5 | 0.7 | 59.6 |
| 03 | 221 46.4 | .. 45.7 | 283 56.0 | 3.4 | 26 32.2 | 0.6 | 59.6 |
| 04 | 236 46.5 | 44.8 | 298 18.4 | 3.4 | 26 32.8 | 0.4 | 59.6 |
| 05 | 251 46.6 | 43.9 | 312 40.8 | 3.4 | 26 33.2 | 0.2 | 59.6 |
| 06 | 266 46.7 | S 8 42.9 | 327 03.2 | 3.4 | S26 33.4 | 0.0 | 59.6 |
| 07 | 281 46.8 | 42.0 | 341 25.6 | 3.4 | 26 33.4 | 0.2 | 59.6 |
| 08 | 296 46.9 | 41.1 | 355 48.0 | 3.3 | 26 33.2 | 0.4 | 59.6 |
| S 09 | 311 47.0 | .. 40.1 | 10 10.3 | 3.4 | 26 32.8 | 0.5 | 59.6 |
| A 10 | 326 47.1 | 39.2 | 24 32.7 | 3.4 | 26 32.3 | 0.8 | 59.6 |
| T 11 | 341 47.2 | 38.3 | 38 55.1 | 3.4 | 26 31.5 | 0.9 | 59.6 |
| U 12 | 356 47.3 | S 8 37.3 | 53 17.5 | 3.3 | S26 30.6 | 1.1 | 59.6 |
| R 13 | 11 47.4 | 36.4 | 67 39.8 | 3.4 | 26 29.5 | 1.3 | 59.6 |
| D 14 | 26 47.5 | 35.5 | 82 02.2 | 3.4 | 26 28.2 | 1.5 | 59.6 |
| A 15 | 41 47.6 | .. 34.5 | 96 24.6 | 3.4 | 26 26.7 | 1.7 | 59.6 |
| Y 16 | 56 47.8 | 33.6 | 110 47.0 | 3.5 | 26 25.0 | 1.8 | 59.6 |
| 17 | 71 47.9 | 32.6 | 125 09.5 | 3.4 | 26 23.2 | 2.1 | 59.6 |
| 18 | 86 48.0 | S 8 31.7 | 139 31.9 | 3.5 | S26 21.1 | 2.2 | 59.6 |
| 19 | 101 48.1 | 30.8 | 153 54.4 | 3.5 | 26 18.9 | 2.4 | 59.6 |
| 20 | 116 48.2 | 29.8 | 168 16.9 | 3.5 | 26 16.5 | 2.6 | 59.6 |
| 21 | 131 48.3 | .. 28.9 | 182 39.4 | 3.5 | 26 13.9 | 2.8 | 59.6 |
| 22 | 146 48.4 | 27.9 | 197 01.9 | 3.6 | 26 11.1 | 3.0 | 59.6 |
| 23 | 161 48.5 | 27.0 | 211 24.5 | 3.6 | S26 08.1 | 3.2 | 59.6 |
| | SD 16.2 | d 0.9 | SD 16.1 | | 16.2 | | 16.2 |

### Twilight / Sunrise / Moonrise

| Lat. | Naut. | Civil | Sunrise | Moonrise 24 | 25 | 26 | 27 |
|---|---|---|---|---|---|---|---|
| ° | h m | h m | h m | h m | h m | h m | h m |
| N 72 | 05 30 | 06 47 | 07 58 | ▬▬ | ▬▬ | ▬▬ | ▬▬ |
| N 70 | 05 33 | 06 43 | 07 46 | ▬▬ | ▬▬ | ▬▬ | ▬▬ |
| 68 | 05 35 | 06 39 | 07 36 | ▬▬ | ▬▬ | ▬▬ | ▬▬ |
| 66 | 05 37 | 06 36 | 07 28 | 05 06 | ▬▬ | ▬▬ | ▬▬ |
| 64 | 05 38 | 06 33 | 07 21 | 04 12 | 06 47 | ▬▬ | 08 38 |
| 62 | 05 39 | 06 30 | 07 15 | 03 40 | 05 32 | 06 59 | 07 36 |
| 60 | 05 40 | 06 28 | 07 10 | 03 16 | 04 56 | 06 15 | 07 02 |
| N 58 | 05 41 | 06 26 | 07 06 | 02 57 | 04 30 | 05 46 | 06 36 |
| 56 | 05 41 | 06 24 | 07 02 | 02 41 | 04 09 | 05 23 | 06 16 |
| 54 | 05 41 | 06 22 | 06 58 | 02 27 | 03 52 | 05 05 | 05 59 |
| 52 | 05 42 | 06 21 | 06 55 | 02 16 | 03 38 | 04 49 | 05 45 |
| 50 | 05 42 | 06 19 | 06 52 | 02 05 | 03 25 | 04 36 | 05 32 |
| 45 | 05 41 | 06 15 | 06 45 | 01 44 | 02 59 | 04 08 | 05 06 |
| N 40 | 05 41 | 06 12 | 06 39 | 01 26 | 02 39 | 03 46 | 04 45 |
| 35 | 05 40 | 06 09 | 06 35 | 01 12 | 02 22 | 03 28 | 04 20 |
| 30 | 05 38 | 06 06 | 06 30 | 00 59 | 02 07 | 03 13 | 04 13 |
| 20 | 05 35 | 06 01 | 06 23 | 00 37 | 01 42 | 02 46 | 03 48 |
| N 10 | 05 30 | 05 55 | 06 16 | 00 19 | 01 21 | 02 24 | 03 26 |
| 0 | 05 24 | 05 49 | 06 10 | 00 02 | 01 01 | 02 03 | 03 05 |
| S 10 | 05 17 | 05 42 | 06 03 | 24 41 | 00 41 | 01 42 | 02 45 |
| 20 | 05 07 | 05 34 | 05 56 | 24 20 | 00 20 | 01 19 | 02 23 |
| 30 | 04 55 | 05 23 | 05 48 | 23 55 | 24 53 | 00 53 | 01 57 |
| 35 | 04 46 | 05 17 | 05 43 | 23 41 | 24 37 | 00 37 | 01 42 |
| 40 | 04 36 | 05 10 | 05 38 | 23 25 | 24 20 | 00 20 | 01 25 |
| 45 | 04 24 | 05 01 | 05 31 | 23 05 | 23 58 | 25 04 | 01 04 |
| S 50 | 04 08 | 04 50 | 05 24 | 22 40 | 23 31 | 24 37 | 00 37 |
| 52 | 04 00 | 04 44 | 05 20 | 22 29 | 23 18 | 24 24 | 00 24 |
| 54 | 03 51 | 04 39 | 05 16 | 22 15 | 23 03 | 24 10 | 00 10 |
| 56 | 03 41 | 04 32 | 05 12 | 22 00 | 22 45 | 23 52 | 25 17 |
| 58 | 03 30 | 04 24 | 05 07 | 21 42 | 22 24 | 23 31 | 25 00 |
| S 60 | 03 16 | 04 16 | 05 02 | 21 20 | 21 56 | 23 04 | 24 39 |

### Sunset / Twilight / Moonset

| Lat. | Sunset | Civil | Naut. | Moonset 24 | 25 | 26 | 27 |
|---|---|---|---|---|---|---|---|
| ° | h m | h m | h m | h m | h m | h m | h m |
| N 72 | 16 30 | 17 41 | 18 59 | ▬▬ | ▬▬ | ▬▬ | ▬▬ |
| N 70 | 16 42 | 17 45 | 18 56 | ▬▬ | ▬▬ | ▬▬ | ▬▬ |
| 68 | 16 51 | 17 49 | 18 53 | ▬▬ | ▬▬ | ▬▬ | ▬▬ |
| 66 | 16 59 | 17 52 | 18 51 | 07 13 | ▬▬ | ▬▬ | ▬▬ |
| 64 | 17 06 | 17 55 | 18 50 | 08 07 | 07 37 | ▬▬ | 10 09 |
| 62 | 17 12 | 17 57 | 18 48 | 08 40 | 08 53 | 09 37 | 11 10 |
| 60 | 17 17 | 17 59 | 18 47 | 09 05 | 09 30 | 10 20 | 11 45 |
| N 58 | 17 21 | 18 01 | 18 47 | 09 24 | 09 56 | 10 50 | 12 10 |
| 56 | 17 25 | 18 03 | 18 46 | 09 41 | 10 16 | 11 12 | 12 29 |
| 54 | 17 29 | 18 05 | 18 46 | 09 55 | 10 34 | 11 30 | 12 46 |
| 52 | 17 32 | 18 06 | 18 46 | 10 07 | 10 48 | 11 46 | 13 00 |
| 50 | 17 35 | 18 08 | 18 45 | 10 18 | 11 01 | 12 00 | 13 12 |
| 45 | 17 42 | 18 11 | 18 45 | 10 41 | 11 28 | 12 27 | 13 38 |
| N 40 | 17 47 | 18 15 | 18 46 | 10 59 | 11 49 | 12 49 | 13 58 |
| 35 | 17 52 | 18 17 | 18 47 | 11 14 | 12 06 | 13 07 | 14 15 |
| 30 | 17 56 | 18 20 | 18 48 | 11 28 | 12 21 | 13 23 | 14 29 |
| 20 | 18 03 | 18 26 | 18 51 | 11 51 | 12 47 | 13 49 | 14 54 |
| N 10 | 18 10 | 18 31 | 18 56 | 12 11 | 13 09 | 14 11 | 15 15 |
| 0 | 18 16 | 18 37 | 19 02 | 12 29 | 13 30 | 14 33 | 15 35 |
| S 10 | 18 23 | 18 44 | 19 09 | 12 48 | 13 51 | 14 53 | 15 54 |
| 20 | 18 30 | 18 52 | 19 18 | 13 08 | 14 13 | 15 16 | 16 15 |
| 30 | 18 38 | 19 02 | 19 31 | 13 31 | 14 39 | 15 42 | 16 39 |
| 35 | 18 42 | 19 08 | 19 39 | 13 45 | 14 54 | 15 57 | 16 53 |
| 40 | 18 48 | 19 15 | 19 49 | 14 01 | 15 11 | 16 15 | 17 09 |
| 45 | 18 54 | 19 24 | 20 01 | 14 20 | 15 32 | 16 36 | 17 28 |
| S 50 | 19 01 | 19 35 | 20 16 | 14 43 | 15 59 | 17 03 | 17 52 |
| 52 | 19 05 | 19 40 | 20 24 | 14 55 | 16 12 | 17 16 | 18 04 |
| 54 | 19 09 | 19 46 | 20 33 | 15 08 | 16 27 | 17 31 | 18 17 |
| 56 | 19 13 | 19 52 | 20 43 | 15 23 | 16 45 | 17 49 | 18 32 |
| 58 | 19 17 | 20 00 | 20 54 | 15 41 | 17 06 | 18 10 | 18 49 |
| S 60 | 19 23 | 20 08 | 21 08 | 16 02 | 17 33 | 18 37 | 19 10 |

### SUN / MOON

| Day | Eqn. of Time 00h | 12h | Mer. Pass. | Mer. Pass. Upper | Lower | Age | Phase |
|---|---|---|---|---|---|---|---|
| d | m s | m s | h m | h m | h m | d | % |
| 24 | 13 14 | 13 10 | 12 13 | 06 15 | 18 45 | 23 | 44 |
| 25 | 13 05 | 13 01 | 12 13 | 07 15 | 19 46 | 24 | 33 |
| 26 | 12 56 | 12 51 | 12 13 | 08 18 | 20 49 | 25 | 22 |

| UT | ARIES GHA | VENUS −4.7 GHA | Dec | MARS +1.3 GHA | Dec | JUPITER −2.0 GHA | Dec | SATURN +0.7 GHA | Dec | STARS Name | SHA | Dec |
|---|---|---|---|---|---|---|---|---|---|---|---|---|
| **27 00** | 156 48.5 | 221 43.1 | S16 55.9 | 220 08.9 | S22 00.1 | 171 44.8 | S 7 26.0 | 195 31.5 | S16 05.9 | Acamar | 315 13.7 | S40 13.3 |
| 01 | 171 51.0 | 236 43.5 | 55.8 | 235 09.4 | 21 59.8 | 186 46.7 | 25.7 | 210 33.6 | 05.8 | Achernar | 335 22.4 | S57 07.8 |
| 02 | 186 53.4 | 251 44.0 | 55.8 | 250 09.9 | 59.5 | 201 48.6 | 25.5 | 225 35.8 | 05.7 | Acrux | 173 02.0 | S63 13.2 |
| 03 | 201 55.9 | 266 44.4 .. | 55.7 | 265 10.4 .. | 59.2 | 216 50.5 .. | 25.3 | 240 38.0 .. | 05.6 | Adhara | 255 07.5 | S29 00.3 |
| 04 | 216 58.4 | 281 44.8 | 55.7 | 280 10.8 | 58.9 | 231 52.4 | 25.0 | 255 40.2 | 05.5 | Aldebaran | 290 42.3 | N16 33.1 |
| 05 | 232 00.8 | 296 45.2 | 55.6 | 295 11.3 | 58.6 | 246 54.3 | 24.8 | 270 42.4 | 05.4 | | | |
| 06 | 247 03.3 | 311 45.6 | S16 55.6 | 310 11.8 | S21 58.3 | 261 56.2 | S 7 24.6 | 285 44.5 | S16 05.3 | Alioth | 166 14.6 | N55 50.2 |
| 07 | 262 05.8 | 326 46.0 | 55.5 | 325 12.3 | 58.0 | 276 58.1 | 24.3 | 300 46.7 | 05.3 | Alkaid | 152 53.6 | N49 12.0 |
| 08 | 277 08.2 | 341 46.5 | 55.5 | 340 12.8 | 57.7 | 292 00.0 | 24.1 | 315 48.9 | 05.2 | Alnair | 27 36.3 | S46 51.3 |
| S 09 | 292 10.7 | 356 46.9 .. | 55.4 | 355 13.3 .. | 57.4 | 307 01.9 .. | 23.9 | 330 51.1 .. | 05.1 | Alnilam | 275 40.0 | S 1 11.4 |
| U 10 | 307 13.2 | 11 47.3 | 55.4 | 10 13.8 | 57.1 | 322 03.8 | 23.6 | 345 53.2 | 05.0 | Alphard | 217 49.7 | S 8 45.4 |
| N 11 | 322 15.6 | 26 47.7 | 55.3 | 25 14.2 | 56.8 | 337 05.7 | 23.4 | 0 55.4 | 04.9 | | | |
| D 12 | 337 18.1 | 41 48.1 | S16 55.3 | 40 14.7 | S21 56.5 | 352 07.6 | S 7 23.2 | 15 57.6 | S16 04.8 | Alphecca | 126 05.6 | N26 38.2 |
| A 13 | 352 20.6 | 56 48.5 | 55.2 | 55 15.2 | 56.1 | 7 09.5 | 22.9 | 30 59.8 | 04.7 | Alpheratz | 357 37.5 | N29 12.6 |
| Y 14 | 7 23.0 | 71 48.9 | 55.1 | 70 15.7 | 55.8 | 22 11.4 | 22.7 | 46 02.0 | 04.7 | Altair | 62 02.5 | N 8 55.4 |
| 15 | 22 25.5 | 86 49.3 .. | 55.1 | 85 16.2 .. | 55.5 | 37 13.3 .. | 22.5 | 61 04.1 .. | 04.6 | Ankaa | 353 09.9 | S42 11.4 |
| 16 | 37 27.9 | 101 49.7 | 55.0 | 100 16.7 | 55.2 | 52 15.2 | 22.3 | 76 06.3 | 04.5 | Antares | 112 18.7 | S26 28.8 |
| 17 | 52 30.4 | 116 50.1 | 55.0 | 115 17.2 | 54.9 | 67 17.1 | 22.0 | 91 08.5 | 04.4 | | | |
| 18 | 67 32.9 | 131 50.5 | S16 54.9 | 130 17.6 | S21 54.6 | 82 19.0 | S 7 21.8 | 106 10.7 | S16 04.3 | Arcturus | 145 49.9 | N19 03.9 |
| 19 | 82 35.3 | 146 50.9 | 54.9 | 145 18.1 | 54.3 | 97 20.9 | 21.6 | 121 12.8 | 04.2 | Atria | 107 15.1 | S69 03.7 |
| 20 | 97 37.8 | 161 51.3 | 54.8 | 160 18.6 | 54.0 | 112 22.8 | 21.3 | 136 15.0 | 04.1 | Avior | 234 15.1 | S59 35.0 |
| 21 | 112 40.3 | 176 51.7 .. | 54.7 | 175 19.1 .. | 53.7 | 127 24.7 .. | 21.1 | 151 17.2 .. | 04.1 | Bellatrix | 278 25.3 | N 6 22.1 |
| 22 | 127 42.7 | 191 52.1 | 54.7 | 190 19.6 | 53.4 | 142 26.6 | 20.9 | 166 19.4 | 04.0 | Betelgeuse | 270 54.5 | N 7 24.6 |
| 23 | 142 45.2 | 206 52.4 | 54.6 | 205 20.1 | 53.1 | 157 28.5 | 20.6 | 181 21.6 | 03.9 | | | |
| **28 00** | 157 47.7 | 221 52.8 | S16 54.5 | 220 20.6 | S21 52.8 | 172 30.4 | S 7 20.4 | 196 23.7 | S16 03.8 | Canopus | 263 53.2 | S52 42.7 |
| 01 | 172 50.1 | 236 53.2 | 54.5 | 235 21.1 | 52.4 | 187 32.3 | 20.2 | 211 25.9 | 03.7 | Capella | 280 25.3 | N46 01.3 |
| 02 | 187 52.6 | 251 53.6 | 54.4 | 250 21.6 | 52.1 | 202 34.2 | 19.9 | 226 28.1 | 03.6 | Deneb | 49 27.8 | N45 21.3 |
| 03 | 202 55.1 | 266 54.0 .. | 54.3 | 265 22.0 .. | 51.8 | 217 36.1 .. | 19.7 | 241 30.3 .. | 03.5 | Denebola | 182 27.0 | N14 26.8 |
| 04 | 217 57.5 | 281 54.4 | 54.3 | 280 22.5 | 51.5 | 232 38.0 | 19.5 | 256 32.5 | 03.5 | Diphda | 348 49.9 | S17 52.2 |
| 05 | 233 00.0 | 296 54.7 | 54.2 | 295 23.0 | 51.2 | 247 39.9 | 19.2 | 271 34.6 | 03.4 | | | |
| 06 | 248 02.4 | 311 55.1 | S16 54.1 | 310 23.5 | S21 50.9 | 262 41.8 | S 7 19.0 | 286 36.8 | S16 03.3 | Dubhe | 193 43.3 | N61 37.9 |
| 07 | 263 04.9 | 326 55.5 | 54.1 | 325 24.0 | 50.6 | 277 43.7 | 18.8 | 301 39.0 | 03.2 | Elnath | 278 04.7 | N28 37.6 |
| 08 | 278 07.4 | 341 55.9 | 54.0 | 340 24.5 | 50.3 | 292 45.6 | 18.6 | 316 41.2 | 03.1 | Eltanin | 90 43.5 | N51 28.8 |
| M 09 | 293 09.8 | 356 56.2 .. | 53.9 | 355 25.0 .. | 49.9 | 307 47.5 .. | 18.3 | 331 43.3 .. | 03.0 | Enif | 33 41.4 | N 9 58.4 |
| O 10 | 308 12.3 | 11 56.6 | 53.9 | 10 25.5 | 49.6 | 322 49.4 | 18.1 | 346 45.5 | 02.9 | Fomalhaut | 15 17.5 | S29 30.5 |
| N 11 | 323 14.8 | 26 57.0 | 53.8 | 25 25.9 | 49.3 | 337 51.3 | 17.9 | 1 47.7 | 02.9 | | | |
| D 12 | 338 17.2 | 41 57.4 | S16 53.7 | 40 26.4 | S21 49.0 | 352 53.2 | S 7 17.6 | 16 49.9 | S16 02.8 | Gacrux | 171 53.7 | S57 14.1 |
| A 13 | 353 19.7 | 56 57.7 | 53.6 | 55 26.9 | 48.7 | 7 55.2 | 17.4 | 31 52.1 | 02.7 | Gienah | 175 45.7 | S17 39.9 |
| Y 14 | 8 22.2 | 71 58.1 | 53.6 | 70 27.4 | 48.4 | 22 57.1 | 17.2 | 46 54.2 | 02.6 | Hadar | 148 38.9 | S60 28.5 |
| 15 | 23 24.6 | 86 58.4 .. | 53.5 | 85 27.9 .. | 48.1 | 37 59.0 .. | 16.9 | 61 56.4 .. | 02.5 | Hamal | 327 54.0 | N23 33.9 |
| 16 | 38 27.1 | 101 58.8 | 53.4 | 100 28.4 | 47.7 | 53 00.9 | 16.7 | 76 58.6 | 02.4 | Kaus Aust. | 83 35.8 | S34 22.4 |
| 17 | 53 29.5 | 116 59.2 | 53.3 | 115 28.9 | 47.4 | 68 02.8 | 16.5 | 92 00.8 | 02.3 | | | |
| 18 | 68 32.0 | 131 59.5 | S16 53.2 | 130 29.4 | S21 47.1 | 83 04.7 | S 7 16.2 | 107 03.0 | S16 02.3 | Kochab | 137 19.3 | N74 03.6 |
| 19 | 83 34.5 | 146 59.9 | 53.2 | 145 29.9 | 46.8 | 98 06.6 | 16.0 | 122 05.1 | 02.2 | Markab | 13 32.5 | N15 19.3 |
| 20 | 98 36.9 | 162 00.2 | 53.1 | 160 30.3 | 46.5 | 113 08.5 | 15.8 | 137 07.3 | 02.1 | Menkar | 314 08.7 | N 4 10.4 |
| 21 | 113 39.4 | 177 00.6 .. | 53.0 | 175 30.8 .. | 46.2 | 128 10.4 .. | 15.5 | 152 09.5 .. | 02.0 | Menkent | 148 00.1 | S36 28.6 |
| 22 | 128 41.9 | 192 01.0 | 53.0 | 190 31.3 | 45.8 | 143 12.3 | 15.3 | 167 11.7 | 01.9 | Miaplacidus | 221 37.8 | S69 48.5 |
| 23 | 143 44.3 | 207 01.3 | 52.9 | 205 31.8 | 45.5 | 158 14.2 | 15.1 | 182 13.9 | 01.8 | | | |
| **1 00** | 158 46.8 | 222 01.7 | S16 52.8 | 220 32.3 | S21 45.2 | 173 16.1 | S 7 14.8 | 197 16.0 | S16 01.8 | Mirfak | 308 31.7 | N49 56.5 |
| 01 | 173 49.3 | 237 02.0 | 52.7 | 235 32.8 | 44.9 | 188 18.0 | 14.6 | 212 18.2 | 01.7 | Nunki | 75 50.9 | S26 16.1 |
| 02 | 188 51.7 | 252 02.4 | 52.6 | 250 33.3 | 44.6 | 203 19.9 | 14.4 | 227 20.4 | 01.6 | Peacock | 53 09.9 | S56 39.8 |
| 03 | 203 54.2 | 267 02.7 .. | 52.6 | 265 33.8 .. | 44.2 | 218 21.8 .. | 14.2 | 242 22.6 .. | 01.5 | Pollux | 243 19.9 | N27 58.4 |
| 04 | 218 56.7 | 282 03.0 | 52.5 | 280 34.3 | 43.9 | 233 23.7 | 13.9 | 257 24.8 | 01.4 | Procyon | 244 53.1 | N 5 10.0 |
| 05 | 233 59.1 | 297 03.4 | 52.4 | 295 34.8 | 43.6 | 248 25.6 | 13.7 | 272 26.9 | 01.3 | | | |
| 06 | 249 01.6 | 312 03.7 | S16 52.3 | 310 35.3 | S21 43.3 | 263 27.5 | S 7 13.5 | 287 29.1 | S16 01.2 | Rasalhague | 96 00.8 | N12 32.5 |
| 07 | 264 04.0 | 327 04.1 | 52.2 | 325 35.7 | 42.9 | 278 29.4 | 13.2 | 302 31.3 | 01.2 | Regulus | 207 36.6 | N11 51.5 |
| 08 | 279 06.5 | 342 04.4 | 52.1 | 340 36.2 | 42.6 | 293 31.3 | 13.0 | 317 33.5 | 01.1 | Rigel | 281 06.1 | S 8 10.8 |
| T 09 | 294 09.0 | 357 04.8 .. | 52.0 | 355 36.7 .. | 42.3 | 308 33.2 .. | 12.8 | 332 35.7 .. | 01.0 | Rigil Kent. | 139 43.2 | S60 55.3 |
| U 10 | 309 11.4 | 12 05.1 | 52.0 | 10 37.2 | 42.0 | 323 35.1 | 12.5 | 347 37.8 | 00.9 | Sabik | 102 05.5 | S15 45.1 |
| E 11 | 324 13.9 | 27 05.4 | 51.9 | 25 37.7 | 41.7 | 338 37.0 | 12.3 | 2 40.0 | 00.8 | | | |
| S 12 | 339 16.4 | 42 05.8 | S16 51.8 | 40 38.2 | S21 41.3 | 353 38.9 | S 7 12.1 | 17 42.2 | S16 00.7 | Schedar | 349 34.2 | N56 39.5 |
| D 13 | 354 18.8 | 57 06.1 | 51.7 | 55 38.7 | 41.0 | 8 40.8 | 11.8 | 32 44.4 | 00.6 | Shaula | 96 13.7 | S37 07.1 |
| A 14 | 9 21.3 | 72 06.4 | 51.6 | 70 39.2 | 40.7 | 23 42.7 | 11.6 | 47 46.6 | 00.6 | Sirius | 258 28.1 | S16 45.0 |
| Y 15 | 24 23.8 | 87 06.8 .. | 51.5 | 85 39.7 .. | 40.4 | 38 44.6 .. | 11.4 | 62 48.7 .. | 00.5 | Spica | 158 24.5 | S11 16.6 |
| 16 | 39 26.2 | 102 07.1 | 51.4 | 100 40.2 | 40.0 | 53 46.5 | 11.1 | 77 50.9 | 00.4 | Suhail | 222 47.6 | S43 31.4 |
| 17 | 54 28.7 | 117 07.4 | 51.3 | 115 40.7 | 39.7 | 68 48.4 | 10.9 | 92 53.1 | 00.3 | | | |
| 18 | 69 31.2 | 132 07.7 | S16 51.2 | 130 41.1 | S21 39.4 | 83 50.3 | S 7 10.7 | 107 55.3 | S16 00.2 | Vega | 80 35.0 | N38 48.0 |
| 19 | 84 33.6 | 147 08.1 | 51.1 | 145 41.6 | 39.1 | 98 52.2 | 10.4 | 122 57.5 | 00.1 | Zuben'ubi | 136 58.5 | S16 08.0 |
| 20 | 99 36.1 | 162 08.4 | 51.1 | 160 42.1 | 38.7 | 113 54.1 | 10.2 | 137 59.6 | 00.0 | | SHA | Mer.Pass. |
| 21 | 114 38.5 | 177 08.7 .. | 51.0 | 175 42.6 .. | 38.4 | 128 56.0 .. | 10.0 | 153 01.8 | 16 00.0 | Venus | 64 05.2 | 9 12 |
| 22 | 129 41.0 | 192 09.0 | 50.9 | 190 43.1 | 38.1 | 143 57.9 | 09.8 | 168 04.0 | 15 59.9 | Mars | 62 32.9 | 9 18 |
| 23 | 144 43.5 | 207 09.3 | 50.8 | 205 43.6 | 37.7 | 158 59.8 | 09.5 | 183 06.2 | S15 59.8 | Jupiter | 14 42.8 | 12 28 |
| Mer.Pass. 13 26.6 | | v 0.4 | d 0.1 | v 0.5 | d 0.3 | v 1.9 | d 0.2 | v 2.2 | d 0.1 | Saturn | 38 36.1 | 10 53 |

| UT | SUN GHA | SUN Dec | MOON GHA | v | MOON Dec | d | HP |
|---|---|---|---|---|---|---|---|
| **27** 00 | 176 48.6 | S 8 26.1 | 225 47.1 | 3.6 | S26 04.9 | 3.3 | 59.6 |
| 01 | 191 48.7 | 25.1 | 240 09.7 | 3.7 | 26 01.6 | 3.5 | 59.6 |
| 02 | 206 48.8 | 24.2 | 254 32.4 | 3.7 | 25 58.1 | 3.7 | 59.6 |
| 03 | 221 48.9 | .. 23.2 | 268 55.1 | 3.8 | 25 54.4 | 3.9 | 59.6 |
| 04 | 236 49.0 | 22.3 | 283 17.9 | 3.8 | 25 50.5 | 4.1 | 59.6 |
| 05 | 251 49.1 | 21.4 | 297 40.7 | 3.8 | 25 46.4 | 4.2 | 59.6 |
| 06 | 266 49.3 | S 8 20.4 | 312 03.5 | 3.9 | S25 42.2 | 4.4 | 59.6 |
| 07 | 281 49.4 | 19.5 | 326 26.4 | 4.0 | 25 37.8 | 4.6 | 59.6 |
| 08 | 296 49.5 | 18.5 | 340 49.4 | 4.0 | 25 33.2 | 4.8 | 59.6 |
| S 09 | 311 49.6 | .. 17.6 | 355 12.4 | 4.0 | 25 28.4 | 5.0 | 59.6 |
| U 10 | 326 49.7 | 16.7 | 9 35.4 | 4.1 | 25 23.4 | 5.1 | 59.6 |
| N 11 | 341 49.8 | 15.7 | 23 58.5 | 4.2 | 25 18.3 | 5.3 | 59.6 |
| D 12 | 356 49.9 | S 8 14.8 | 38 21.7 | 4.2 | S25 13.0 | 5.5 | 59.6 |
| A 13 | 11 50.0 | 13.8 | 52 44.9 | 4.3 | 25 07.5 | 5.6 | 59.6 |
| Y 14 | 26 50.1 | 12.9 | 67 08.2 | 4.3 | 25 01.9 | 5.8 | 59.6 |
| 15 | 41 50.2 | .. 12.0 | 81 31.5 | 4.4 | 24 56.1 | 6.0 | 59.6 |
| 16 | 56 50.4 | 11.0 | 95 54.9 | 4.5 | 24 50.1 | 6.2 | 59.6 |
| 17 | 71 50.5 | 10.1 | 110 18.4 | 4.6 | 24 43.9 | 6.3 | 59.6 |
| 18 | 86 50.6 | S 8 09.1 | 124 42.0 | 4.6 | S24 37.6 | 6.5 | 59.6 |
| 19 | 101 50.7 | 08.2 | 139 05.6 | 4.7 | 24 31.1 | 6.6 | 59.6 |
| 20 | 116 50.8 | 07.2 | 153 29.3 | 4.7 | 24 24.5 | 6.9 | 59.6 |
| 21 | 131 50.9 | .. 06.3 | 167 53.0 | 4.9 | 24 17.6 | 6.9 | 59.6 |
| 22 | 146 51.0 | 05.3 | 182 16.9 | 4.9 | 24 10.7 | 7.2 | 59.5 |
| 23 | 161 51.1 | 04.4 | 196 40.8 | 5.0 | 24 03.5 | 7.3 | 59.5 |
| **28** 00 | 176 51.3 | S 8 03.5 | 211 04.8 | 5.1 | S23 56.2 | 7.4 | 59.5 |
| 01 | 191 51.4 | 02.5 | 225 28.9 | 5.1 | 23 48.8 | 7.7 | 59.5 |
| 02 | 206 51.5 | 01.6 | 239 53.0 | 5.2 | 23 41.1 | 7.7 | 59.5 |
| 03 | 221 51.6 | 8 00.6 | 254 17.2 | 5.4 | 23 33.4 | 8.0 | 59.5 |
| 04 | 236 51.7 | 7 59.7 | 268 41.6 | 5.4 | 23 25.4 | 8.0 | 59.5 |
| 05 | 251 51.8 | 58.7 | 283 06.0 | 5.5 | 23 17.4 | 8.3 | 59.5 |
| 06 | 266 51.9 | S 7 57.8 | 297 30.5 | 5.5 | S23 09.1 | 8.4 | 59.5 |
| 07 | 281 52.0 | 56.8 | 311 55.0 | 5.7 | 23 00.7 | 8.5 | 59.5 |
| 08 | 296 52.2 | 55.9 | 326 19.7 | 5.8 | 22 52.2 | 8.7 | 59.5 |
| M 09 | 311 52.3 | .. 55.0 | 340 44.5 | 5.8 | 22 43.5 | 8.8 | 59.5 |
| O 10 | 326 52.4 | 54.0 | 355 09.3 | 5.9 | 22 34.7 | 8.9 | 59.4 |
| N 11 | 341 52.5 | 53.1 | 9 34.2 | 6.1 | 22 25.8 | 9.2 | 59.4 |
| D 12 | 356 52.6 | S 7 52.1 | 23 59.3 | 6.1 | S22 16.6 | 9.2 | 59.4 |
| A 13 | 11 52.7 | 51.2 | 38 24.4 | 6.2 | 22 07.4 | 9.4 | 59.4 |
| Y 14 | 26 52.9 | 50.2 | 52 49.6 | 6.3 | 21 58.0 | 9.5 | 59.4 |
| 15 | 41 53.0 | .. 49.3 | 67 14.9 | 6.4 | 21 48.5 | 9.7 | 59.4 |
| 16 | 56 53.1 | 48.3 | 81 40.3 | 6.5 | 21 38.8 | 9.8 | 59.4 |
| 17 | 71 53.2 | 47.4 | 96 05.8 | 6.6 | 21 29.0 | 9.9 | 59.4 |
| 18 | 86 53.3 | S 7 46.4 | 110 31.4 | 6.7 | S21 19.1 | 10.0 | 59.4 |
| 19 | 101 53.4 | 45.5 | 124 57.1 | 6.8 | 21 09.1 | 10.2 | 59.3 |
| 20 | 116 53.6 | 44.5 | 139 22.9 | 6.9 | 20 58.9 | 10.3 | 59.3 |
| 21 | 131 53.7 | .. 43.6 | 153 48.8 | 7.0 | 20 48.6 | 10.5 | 59.3 |
| 22 | 146 53.8 | 42.6 | 168 14.8 | 7.0 | 20 38.1 | 10.5 | 59.3 |
| 23 | 161 53.9 | 41.7 | 182 40.8 | 7.2 | 20 27.6 | 10.7 | 59.3 |
| **1** 00 | 176 54.0 | S 7 40.7 | 197 07.0 | 7.3 | S20 16.9 | 10.8 | 59.3 |
| 01 | 191 54.1 | 39.8 | 211 33.3 | 7.4 | 20 06.1 | 10.9 | 59.3 |
| 02 | 206 54.3 | 38.8 | 225 59.7 | 7.4 | 19 55.2 | 11.1 | 59.3 |
| 03 | 221 54.4 | .. 37.9 | 240 26.1 | 7.6 | 19 44.1 | 11.1 | 59.2 |
| 04 | 236 54.5 | 36.9 | 254 52.7 | 7.7 | 19 33.0 | 11.3 | 59.2 |
| 05 | 251 54.6 | 36.0 | 269 19.4 | 7.8 | 19 21.7 | 11.4 | 59.2 |
| 06 | 266 54.7 | S 7 35.0 | 283 46.2 | 7.9 | S19 10.3 | 11.5 | 59.2 |
| 07 | 281 54.9 | 34.1 | 298 13.1 | 7.9 | 18 58.8 | 11.6 | 59.2 |
| T 08 | 296 55.0 | 33.1 | 312 40.0 | 8.1 | 18 47.2 | 11.7 | 59.2 |
| U 09 | 311 55.1 | .. 32.2 | 327 07.1 | 8.2 | 18 35.5 | 11.8 | 59.1 |
| E 10 | 326 55.2 | 31.2 | 341 34.3 | 8.3 | 18 23.7 | 11.9 | 59.1 |
| S 11 | 341 55.3 | 30.3 | 356 01.6 | 8.3 | 18 11.8 | 12.0 | 59.1 |
| D 12 | 356 55.5 | S 7 29.3 | 10 28.9 | 8.5 | S17 59.8 | 12.1 | 59.1 |
| A 13 | 11 55.6 | 28.4 | 24 56.4 | 8.6 | 17 47.7 | 12.2 | 59.1 |
| Y 14 | 26 55.7 | 27.4 | 39 24.0 | 8.6 | 17 35.5 | 12.3 | 59.1 |
| 15 | 41 55.8 | .. 26.5 | 53 51.6 | 8.8 | 17 23.2 | 12.4 | 59.0 |
| 16 | 56 55.9 | 25.5 | 68 19.4 | 8.9 | 17 10.8 | 12.5 | 59.0 |
| 17 | 71 56.1 | 24.6 | 82 47.3 | 8.9 | 16 58.3 | 12.5 | 59.0 |
| 18 | 86 56.2 | S 7 23.6 | 97 15.2 | 9.1 | S16 45.8 | 12.7 | 59.0 |
| 19 | 101 56.3 | 22.7 | 111 43.3 | 9.2 | 16 33.1 | 12.7 | 59.0 |
| 20 | 116 56.4 | 21.7 | 126 11.5 | 9.2 | 16 20.4 | 12.9 | 58.9 |
| 21 | 131 56.6 | .. 20.8 | 140 39.7 | 9.4 | 16 07.5 | 12.9 | 58.9 |
| 22 | 146 56.7 | 19.8 | 155 08.1 | 9.4 | 15 54.6 | 13.0 | 58.9 |
| 23 | 161 56.8 | 18.9 | 169 36.5 | 9.6 | S15 41.6 | 13.0 | 58.9 |
| | SD 16.2 | d 0.9 | SD 16.2 | | 16.2 | | 16.1 |

### Twilight / Sunrise / Moonrise

| Lat. | Naut. | Civil | Sunrise | 27 | 28 | 1 | 2 |
|---|---|---|---|---|---|---|---|
| N 72 | 05 15 | 06 33 | 07 42 | ■ | ■ | ■ | 09 14 |
| N 70 | 05 20 | 06 30 | 07 32 | ■ | ■ | 09 44 | 08 49 |
| 68 | 05 23 | 06 27 | 07 24 | ■ | ■ | 09 00 | 08 30 |
| 66 | 05 26 | 06 25 | 07 17 | ■ | 09 03 | 08 31 | 08 14 |
| 64 | 05 28 | 06 23 | 07 11 | 08 38 | 08 17 | 08 08 | 08 02 |
| 62 | 05 30 | 06 21 | 07 06 | 07 36 | 07 47 | 07 50 | 07 51 |
| 60 | 05 32 | 06 20 | 07 02 | 07 02 | 07 24 | 07 35 | 07 41 |
| N 58 | 05 33 | 06 18 | 06 58 | 06 36 | 07 05 | 07 22 | 07 33 |
| 56 | 05 34 | 06 17 | 06 54 | 06 16 | 06 50 | 07 11 | 07 26 |
| 54 | 05 35 | 06 15 | 06 51 | 05 59 | 06 36 | 07 01 | 07 19 |
| 52 | 05 35 | 06 14 | 06 48 | 05 45 | 06 25 | 06 53 | 07 13 |
| 50 | 05 36 | 06 13 | 06 46 | 05 32 | 06 14 | 06 45 | 07 08 |
| 45 | 05 36 | 06 10 | 06 40 | 05 06 | 05 52 | 06 28 | 06 56 |
| N 40 | 05 37 | 06 08 | 06 35 | 04 45 | 05 34 | 06 14 | 06 47 |
| 35 | 05 36 | 06 05 | 06 31 | 04 28 | 05 19 | 06 02 | 06 38 |
| 30 | 05 35 | 06 03 | 06 27 | 04 13 | 05 06 | 05 52 | 06 31 |
| 20 | 05 33 | 05 58 | 06 21 | 03 48 | 04 44 | 05 34 | 06 18 |
| N 10 | 05 29 | 05 54 | 06 15 | 03 26 | 04 24 | 05 18 | 06 07 |
| 0 | 05 24 | 05 48 | 06 09 | 03 05 | 04 06 | 05 03 | 05 57 |
| S 10 | 05 18 | 05 42 | 06 03 | 02 45 | 03 48 | 04 49 | 05 46 |
| 20 | 05 09 | 05 35 | 05 57 | 02 23 | 03 28 | 04 33 | 05 35 |
| 30 | 04 57 | 05 26 | 05 50 | 01 57 | 03 06 | 04 15 | 05 22 |
| 35 | 04 50 | 05 20 | 05 46 | 01 42 | 02 52 | 04 04 | 05 14 |
| 40 | 04 40 | 05 13 | 05 41 | 01 25 | 02 37 | 03 52 | 05 05 |
| 45 | 04 29 | 05 05 | 05 36 | 01 04 | 02 18 | 03 37 | 04 55 |
| S 50 | 04 14 | 04 55 | 05 29 | 00 37 | 01 55 | 03 19 | 04 43 |
| 52 | 04 07 | 04 50 | 05 26 | 00 24 | 01 44 | 03 11 | 04 37 |
| 54 | 03 59 | 04 45 | 05 22 | 00 10 | 01 32 | 03 01 | 04 31 |
| 56 | 03 50 | 04 39 | 05 18 | 25 17 | 01 17 | 02 51 | 04 24 |
| 58 | 03 39 | 04 32 | 05 14 | 25 00 | 01 00 | 02 38 | 04 16 |
| S 60 | 03 26 | 04 25 | 05 09 | 24 39 | 00 39 | 02 24 | 04 07 |

### Sunset / Twilight / Moonset

| Lat. | Sunset | Civil | Naut. | 27 | 28 | 1 | 2 |
|---|---|---|---|---|---|---|---|
| N 72 | 16 45 | 17 54 | 19 13 | ■ | ■ | ■ | 15 30 |
| N 70 | 16 55 | 17 57 | 19 08 | ■ | ■ | 13 10 | 15 53 |
| 68 | 17 03 | 18 00 | 19 04 | ■ | ■ | 13 52 | 16 10 |
| 66 | 17 10 | 18 02 | 19 01 | ■ | 11 51 | 14 20 | 16 24 |
| 64 | 17 15 | 18 03 | 18 58 | 10 09 | 12 36 | 14 41 | 16 36 |
| 62 | 17 20 | 18 05 | 18 56 | 11 10 | 13 05 | 14 58 | 16 45 |
| 60 | 17 25 | 18 07 | 18 55 | 11 45 | 13 27 | 15 13 | 16 53 |
| N 58 | 17 28 | 18 08 | 18 53 | 12 10 | 13 45 | 15 24 | 17 01 |
| 56 | 17 32 | 18 09 | 18 52 | 12 29 | 14 00 | 15 35 | 17 07 |
| 54 | 17 35 | 18 11 | 18 51 | 12 46 | 14 13 | 15 44 | 17 12 |
| 52 | 17 38 | 18 11 | 18 51 | 13 00 | 14 24 | 15 52 | 17 17 |
| 50 | 17 40 | 18 13 | 18 50 | 13 12 | 14 34 | 15 59 | 17 22 |
| 45 | 17 46 | 18 15 | 18 49 | 13 38 | 14 55 | 16 14 | 17 32 |
| N 40 | 17 51 | 18 18 | 18 49 | 13 58 | 15 12 | 16 27 | 17 40 |
| 35 | 17 55 | 18 20 | 18 49 | 14 15 | 15 26 | 16 38 | 17 47 |
| 30 | 17 58 | 18 22 | 18 50 | 14 29 | 15 39 | 16 47 | 17 53 |
| 20 | 18 05 | 18 27 | 18 52 | 14 54 | 15 59 | 17 03 | 18 03 |
| N 10 | 18 10 | 18 32 | 18 56 | 15 15 | 16 17 | 17 17 | 18 12 |
| 0 | 18 16 | 18 37 | 19 01 | 15 35 | 16 34 | 17 29 | 18 20 |
| S 10 | 18 21 | 18 43 | 19 07 | 15 54 | 16 51 | 17 42 | 18 29 |
| 20 | 18 27 | 18 50 | 19 16 | 16 15 | 17 08 | 17 55 | 18 38 |
| 30 | 18 34 | 18 59 | 19 27 | 16 39 | 17 28 | 18 11 | 18 47 |
| 35 | 18 38 | 19 04 | 19 35 | 16 53 | 17 40 | 18 19 | 18 53 |
| 40 | 18 43 | 19 11 | 19 44 | 17 09 | 17 53 | 18 29 | 19 00 |
| 45 | 18 49 | 19 19 | 19 55 | 17 28 | 18 09 | 18 41 | 19 07 |
| S 50 | 18 55 | 19 29 | 20 09 | 17 52 | 18 28 | 18 55 | 19 16 |
| 52 | 18 58 | 19 33 | 20 16 | 18 04 | 18 37 | 19 02 | 19 20 |
| 54 | 19 02 | 19 38 | 20 24 | 18 17 | 18 47 | 19 09 | 19 24 |
| 56 | 19 05 | 19 44 | 20 33 | 18 32 | 18 59 | 19 17 | 19 29 |
| 58 | 19 09 | 19 51 | 20 44 | 18 49 | 19 12 | 19 26 | 19 35 |
| S 60 | 19 14 | 19 57 | 20 56 | 19 10 | 19 27 | 19 36 | 19 41 |

### SUN / MOON

| Day | Eqn. of Time 00h | Eqn. of Time 12h | Mer. Pass. | Mer. Pass. Upper | Mer. Pass. Lower | Age | Phase |
|---|---|---|---|---|---|---|---|
| | m s | m s | h m | h m | h m | d | % |
| 27 | 12 46 | 12 41 | 12 13 | 09 20 | 21 50 | 26 | 13 |
| 28 | 12 35 | 12 30 | 12 12 | 10 20 | 22 49 | 27 | 7 |
| 1 | 12 24 | 12 18 | 12 12 | 11 16 | 23 43 | 28 | 2 |

| UT | ARIES GHA | VENUS −4.7 GHA | Dec | MARS +1.2 GHA | Dec | JUPITER −2.0 GHA | Dec | SATURN +0.7 GHA | Dec | STARS Name | SHA | Dec |
|---|---|---|---|---|---|---|---|---|---|---|---|---|
| **2 00** | 159 45.9 | 222 09.7 | S16 50.7 | 220 44.1 | S21 37.4 | 174 01.7 | S 7 09.3 | 198 08.4 | S15 59.7 | Acamar | 315 13.7 | S40 13.3 |
| 01 | 174 48.4 | 237 10.0 | 50.6 | 235 44.6 | 37.1 | 189 03.6 | 09.1 | 213 10.6 | 59.6 | Achernar | 335 22.4 | S57 07.8 |
| 02 | 189 50.9 | 252 10.3 | 50.5 | 250 45.1 | 36.8 | 204 05.5 | 08.8 | 228 12.7 | 59.5 | Acrux | 173 02.0 | S63 13.2 |
| 03 | 204 53.3 | 267 10.6 .. | 50.4 | 265 45.6 .. | 36.4 | 219 07.4 .. | 08.6 | 243 14.9 .. | 59.5 | Adhara | 255 07.5 | S29 00.3 |
| 04 | 219 55.8 | 282 10.9 | 50.3 | 280 46.1 | 36.1 | 234 09.3 | 08.4 | 258 17.1 | 59.4 | Aldebaran | 290 42.3 | N16 33.1 |
| 05 | 234 58.3 | 297 11.2 | 50.2 | 295 46.6 | 35.8 | 249 11.2 | 08.1 | 273 19.3 | 59.3 | | | |
| 06 | 250 00.7 | 312 11.5 | S16 50.1 | 310 47.1 | S21 35.4 | 264 13.1 | S 7 07.9 | 288 21.5 | S15 59.2 | Alioth | 166 14.6 | N55 50.2 |
| W 07 | 265 03.2 | 327 11.8 | 50.0 | 325 47.5 | 35.1 | 279 15.0 | 07.7 | 303 23.6 | 59.1 | Alkaid | 152 53.5 | N49 12.0 |
| E 08 | 280 05.6 | 342 12.1 | 49.9 | 340 48.0 | 34.8 | 294 16.9 | 07.4 | 318 25.8 | 59.0 | Alnair | 27 36.3 | S46 51.3 |
| D 09 | 295 08.1 | 357 12.5 .. | 49.8 | 355 48.5 .. | 34.4 | 309 18.8 .. | 07.2 | 333 28.0 .. | 58.9 | Alnilam | 275 40.0 | S 1 11.4 |
| N 10 | 310 10.6 | 12 12.8 | 49.7 | 10 49.0 | 34.1 | 324 20.7 | 07.0 | 348 30.2 | 58.9 | Alphard | 217 49.7 | S 8 45.4 |
| E 11 | 325 13.0 | 27 13.1 | 49.6 | 25 49.5 | 33.8 | 339 22.6 | 06.7 | 3 32.4 | 58.8 | | | |
| S 12 | 340 15.5 | 42 13.4 | S16 49.5 | 40 50.0 | S21 33.4 | 354 24.5 | S 7 06.5 | 18 34.5 | S15 58.7 | Alphecca | 126 05.6 | N26 38.2 |
| D 13 | 355 18.0 | 57 13.7 | 49.4 | 55 50.5 | 33.1 | 9 26.4 | 06.3 | 33 36.7 | 58.6 | Alpheratz | 357 37.5 | N29 12.6 |
| A 14 | 10 20.4 | 72 14.0 | 49.2 | 70 51.0 | 32.8 | 24 28.3 | 06.0 | 48 38.9 | 58.5 | Altair | 62 02.5 | N 8 55.4 |
| Y 15 | 25 22.9 | 87 14.3 .. | 49.1 | 85 51.5 .. | 32.4 | 39 30.2 .. | 05.8 | 63 41.1 .. | 58.4 | Ankaa | 353 09.9 | S42 11.4 |
| 16 | 40 25.4 | 102 14.6 | 49.0 | 100 52.0 | 32.1 | 54 32.1 | 05.6 | 78 43.3 | 58.4 | Antares | 112 18.7 | S26 28.8 |
| 17 | 55 27.8 | 117 14.8 | 48.9 | 115 52.5 | 31.8 | 69 34.0 | 05.3 | 93 45.5 | 58.3 | | | |
| 18 | 70 30.3 | 132 15.1 | S16 48.8 | 130 53.0 | S21 31.4 | 84 35.9 | S 7 05.1 | 108 47.6 | S15 58.2 | Arcturus | 145 49.9 | N19 03.9 |
| 19 | 85 32.8 | 147 15.4 | 48.7 | 145 53.5 | 31.1 | 99 37.8 | 04.9 | 123 49.8 | 58.1 | Atria | 107 15.1 | S69 03.7 |
| 20 | 100 35.2 | 162 15.7 | 48.6 | 160 54.0 | 30.8 | 114 39.7 | 04.7 | 138 52.0 | 58.0 | Avior | 234 15.2 | S59 35.0 |
| 21 | 115 37.7 | 177 16.0 .. | 48.5 | 175 54.5 .. | 30.4 | 129 41.6 .. | 04.4 | 153 54.2 .. | 57.9 | Bellatrix | 278 25.3 | N 6 22.1 |
| 22 | 130 40.1 | 192 16.3 | 48.4 | 190 55.0 | 30.1 | 144 43.5 | 04.2 | 168 56.4 | 57.8 | Betelgeuse | 270 54.5 | N 7 24.6 |
| 23 | 145 42.6 | 207 16.6 | 48.3 | 205 55.5 | 29.7 | 159 45.4 | 04.0 | 183 58.5 | 57.8 | | | |
| **3 00** | 160 45.1 | 222 16.9 | S16 48.1 | 220 55.9 | S21 29.4 | 174 47.3 | S 7 03.7 | 199 00.7 | S15 57.7 | Canopus | 263 53.2 | S52 42.7 |
| 01 | 175 47.5 | 237 17.2 | 48.0 | 235 56.4 | 29.1 | 189 49.2 | 03.5 | 214 02.9 | 57.6 | Capella | 280 25.3 | N46 01.3 |
| 02 | 190 50.0 | 252 17.4 | 47.9 | 250 56.9 | 28.7 | 204 51.1 | 03.3 | 229 05.1 | 57.5 | Deneb | 49 27.8 | N45 21.3 |
| 03 | 205 52.5 | 267 17.7 .. | 47.8 | 265 57.4 .. | 28.4 | 219 53.0 .. | 03.0 | 244 07.3 .. | 57.4 | Denebola | 182 27.0 | N14 26.8 |
| 04 | 220 54.9 | 282 18.0 | 47.7 | 280 57.9 | 28.1 | 234 54.9 | 02.8 | 259 09.5 | 57.3 | Diphda | 348 49.9 | S17 52.2 |
| 05 | 235 57.4 | 297 18.3 | 47.6 | 295 58.4 | 27.7 | 249 56.8 | 02.6 | 274 11.6 | 57.3 | | | |
| 06 | 250 59.9 | 312 18.6 | S16 47.4 | 310 58.9 | S21 27.4 | 264 58.7 | S 7 02.3 | 289 13.8 | S15 57.2 | Dubhe | 193 43.2 | N61 37.9 |
| T 07 | 266 02.3 | 327 18.8 | 47.3 | 325 59.4 | 27.0 | 280 00.6 | 02.1 | 304 16.0 | 57.1 | Elnath | 278 04.8 | N28 37.6 |
| H 08 | 281 04.8 | 342 19.1 | 47.2 | 340 59.9 | 26.7 | 295 02.5 | 01.9 | 319 18.2 | 57.0 | Eltanin | 90 43.4 | N51 28.8 |
| U 09 | 296 07.2 | 357 19.4 .. | 47.1 | 356 00.4 .. | 26.4 | 310 04.4 .. | 01.6 | 334 20.4 .. | 56.9 | Enif | 33 41.4 | N 9 58.4 |
| R 10 | 311 09.7 | 12 19.6 | 47.0 | 11 00.9 | 26.0 | 325 06.3 | 01.4 | 349 22.6 | 56.8 | Fomalhaut | 15 17.5 | S29 30.5 |
| S 11 | 326 12.2 | 27 19.9 | 46.8 | 26 01.4 | 25.7 | 340 08.2 | 01.2 | 4 24.7 | 56.7 | | | |
| D 12 | 341 14.6 | 42 20.2 | S16 46.7 | 41 01.9 | S21 25.3 | 355 10.1 | S 7 00.9 | 19 26.9 | S15 56.7 | Gacrux | 171 53.7 | S57 14.1 |
| A 13 | 356 17.1 | 57 20.5 | 46.6 | 56 02.4 | 25.0 | 10 12.0 | 00.7 | 34 29.1 | 56.6 | Gienah | 175 45.7 | S17 39.9 |
| Y 14 | 11 19.6 | 72 20.7 | 46.5 | 71 02.9 | 24.6 | 25 13.9 | 00.5 | 49 31.3 | 56.5 | Hadar | 148 38.9 | S60 28.6 |
| 15 | 26 22.0 | 87 21.0 .. | 46.4 | 86 03.4 .. | 24.3 | 40 15.8 .. | 00.2 | 64 33.5 .. | 56.4 | Hamal | 327 54.0 | N23 33.9 |
| 16 | 41 24.5 | 102 21.3 | 46.2 | 101 03.9 | 24.0 | 55 17.7 | 7 00.0 | 79 35.7 | 56.3 | Kaus Aust. | 83 35.8 | S34 22.4 |
| 17 | 56 27.0 | 117 21.5 | 46.1 | 116 04.4 | 23.6 | 70 19.6 | 6 59.8 | 94 37.8 | 56.2 | | | |
| 18 | 71 29.4 | 132 21.8 | S16 46.0 | 131 04.9 | S21 23.3 | 85 21.5 | S 6 59.5 | 109 40.0 | S15 56.2 | Kochab | 137 19.3 | N74 03.6 |
| 19 | 86 31.9 | 147 22.0 | 45.9 | 146 05.4 | 22.9 | 100 23.4 | 59.3 | 124 42.2 | 56.1 | Markab | 13 32.5 | N15 19.3 |
| 20 | 101 34.4 | 162 22.3 | 45.7 | 161 05.9 | 22.6 | 115 25.3 | 59.1 | 139 44.4 | 56.0 | Menkar | 314 08.7 | N 4 10.4 |
| 21 | 116 36.8 | 177 22.6 .. | 45.6 | 176 06.4 .. | 22.2 | 130 27.2 .. | 58.9 | 154 46.6 .. | 55.9 | Menkent | 148 00.1 | S36 28.6 |
| 22 | 131 39.3 | 192 22.8 | 45.5 | 191 06.9 | 21.9 | 145 29.1 | 58.6 | 169 48.8 | 55.8 | Miaplacidus | 221 37.9 | S69 48.6 |
| 23 | 146 41.7 | 207 23.1 | 45.3 | 206 07.4 | 21.5 | 160 31.0 | 58.4 | 184 50.9 | 55.7 | | | |
| **4 00** | 161 44.2 | 222 23.3 | S16 45.2 | 221 07.9 | S21 21.2 | 175 32.9 | S 6 58.2 | 199 53.1 | S15 55.6 | Mirfak | 308 31.8 | N49 56.5 |
| 01 | 176 46.7 | 237 23.6 | 45.1 | 236 08.4 | 20.8 | 190 34.9 | 57.9 | 214 55.3 | 55.6 | Nunki | 75 50.8 | S26 16.1 |
| 02 | 191 49.1 | 252 23.8 | 44.9 | 251 08.9 | 20.5 | 205 36.8 | 57.7 | 229 57.5 | 55.5 | Peacock | 53 09.9 | S56 39.8 |
| 03 | 206 51.6 | 267 24.1 .. | 44.8 | 266 09.3 .. | 20.1 | 220 38.7 .. | 57.5 | 244 59.7 .. | 55.4 | Pollux | 243 19.9 | N27 58.4 |
| 04 | 221 54.1 | 282 24.3 | 44.7 | 281 09.8 | 19.8 | 235 40.6 | 57.2 | 260 01.9 | 55.3 | Procyon | 244 53.1 | N 5 10.0 |
| 05 | 236 56.5 | 297 24.6 | 44.5 | 296 10.3 | 19.5 | 250 42.5 | 57.0 | 275 04.0 | 55.2 | | | |
| 06 | 251 59.0 | 312 24.8 | S16 44.4 | 311 10.8 | S21 19.1 | 265 44.4 | S 6 56.8 | 290 06.2 | S15 55.1 | Rasalhague | 96 00.8 | N12 32.4 |
| 07 | 267 01.5 | 327 25.1 | 44.3 | 326 11.3 | 18.8 | 280 46.3 | 56.5 | 305 08.4 | 55.1 | Regulus | 207 36.6 | N11 51.5 |
| 08 | 282 03.9 | 342 25.3 | 44.1 | 341 11.8 | 18.4 | 295 48.2 | 56.3 | 320 10.6 | 55.0 | Rigel | 281 06.1 | S 8 10.8 |
| F 09 | 297 06.4 | 357 25.6 .. | 44.0 | 356 12.3 .. | 18.1 | 310 50.1 .. | 56.1 | 335 12.8 .. | 54.9 | Rigil Kent. | 139 43.1 | S60 55.3 |
| R 10 | 312 08.8 | 12 25.8 | 43.9 | 11 12.8 | 17.7 | 325 52.0 | 55.8 | 350 15.0 | 54.8 | Sabik | 102 05.5 | S15 45.1 |
| I 11 | 327 11.3 | 27 26.0 | 43.7 | 26 13.3 | 17.3 | 340 53.9 | 55.6 | 5 17.1 | 54.7 | | | |
| D 12 | 342 13.8 | 42 26.3 | S16 43.6 | 41 13.8 | S21 17.0 | 355 55.8 | S 6 55.4 | 20 19.3 | S15 54.6 | Schedar | 349 34.2 | N56 39.5 |
| A 13 | 357 16.2 | 57 26.5 | 43.4 | 56 14.3 | 16.6 | 10 57.7 | 55.1 | 35 21.5 | 54.6 | Shaula | 96 13.6 | S37 07.1 |
| Y 14 | 12 18.7 | 72 26.8 | 43.3 | 71 14.8 | 16.3 | 25 59.6 | 54.9 | 50 23.7 | 54.5 | Sirius | 258 28.1 | S16 45.0 |
| 15 | 27 21.2 | 87 27.0 .. | 43.2 | 86 15.3 .. | 15.9 | 41 01.5 .. | 54.7 | 65 25.9 .. | 54.4 | Spica | 158 24.5 | S11 16.6 |
| 16 | 42 23.6 | 102 27.2 | 43.0 | 101 15.8 | 15.6 | 56 03.4 | 54.4 | 80 28.1 | 54.3 | Suhail | 222 47.6 | S43 31.4 |
| 17 | 57 26.1 | 117 27.5 | 42.9 | 116 16.3 | 15.2 | 71 05.3 | 54.2 | 95 30.3 | 54.2 | | | |
| 18 | 72 28.6 | 132 27.7 | S16 42.7 | 131 16.8 | S21 14.9 | 86 07.2 | S 6 54.0 | 110 32.4 | S15 54.1 | Vega | 80 35.0 | N38 47.9 |
| 19 | 87 31.0 | 147 27.9 | 42.6 | 146 17.3 | 14.5 | 101 09.1 | 53.7 | 125 34.6 | 54.0 | Zuben'ubi | 136 58.5 | S16 08.0 |
| 20 | 102 33.5 | 162 28.2 | 42.4 | 161 17.8 | 14.2 | 116 11.0 | 53.5 | 140 36.8 | 54.0 | | SHA | Mer. Pass. |
| 21 | 117 36.0 | 177 28.4 .. | 42.3 | 176 18.3 .. | 13.8 | 131 12.9 .. | 53.3 | 155 39.0 .. | 53.9 | Venus | 61 31.8 | 9 11 |
| 22 | 132 38.4 | 192 28.6 | 42.2 | 191 18.8 | 13.5 | 146 14.8 | 53.0 | 170 41.2 | 53.8 | Mars | 60 10.9 | 9 16 |
| 23 | 147 40.9 | 207 28.8 | 42.0 | 206 19.3 | 13.1 | 161 16.7 | 52.8 | 185 43.4 | 53.7 | Jupiter | 14 02.2 | 12 19 |
| Mer. Pass. 13 14.8 | | *v* 0.3 | *d* 0.1 | *v* 0.5 | *d* 0.3 | *v* 1.9 | *d* 0.2 | *v* 2.2 | *d* 0.1 | Saturn | 38 15.7 | 10 42 |

| UT | SUN GHA | SUN Dec | MOON GHA | v | MOON Dec | d | HP |
|---|---|---|---|---|---|---|---|
| d h | ° ′ | ° ′ | ° ′ | ′ | ° ′ | ′ | ′ |
| **2** 00 | 176 56.9 | S 7 17.9 | 184 05.1 | 9.6 | S15 28.6 | 13.2 | 58.9 |
| 01 | 191 57.1 | 16.9 | 198 33.7 | 9.7 | 15 15.4 | 13.2 | 58.8 |
| 02 | 206 57.2 | 16.0 | 213 02.4 | 9.8 | 15 02.2 | 13.3 | 58.8 |
| 03 | 221 57.3 | .. 15.0 | 227 31.2 | 10.0 | 14 48.9 | 13.4 | 58.8 |
| 04 | 236 57.4 | 14.1 | 242 00.2 | 10.0 | 14 35.5 | 13.4 | 58.8 |
| 05 | 251 57.5 | 13.1 | 256 29.2 | 10.1 | 14 22.1 | 13.6 | 58.8 |
| 06 | 266 57.7 | S 7 12.2 | 270 58.3 | 10.2 | S14 08.5 | 13.5 | 58.7 |
| W 07 | 281 57.8 | 11.2 | 285 27.5 | 10.2 | 13 55.0 | 13.7 | 58.7 |
| E 08 | 296 57.9 | 10.3 | 299 56.7 | 10.4 | 13 41.3 | 13.7 | 58.7 |
| D 09 | 311 58.0 | .. 09.3 | 314 26.1 | 10.5 | 13 27.6 | 13.8 | 58.7 |
| N 10 | 326 58.2 | 08.3 | 328 55.6 | 10.5 | 13 13.8 | 13.8 | 58.6 |
| E 11 | 341 58.3 | 07.4 | 343 25.1 | 10.6 | 13 00.0 | 13.9 | 58.6 |
| S 12 | 356 58.4 | S 7 06.4 | 357 54.7 | 10.8 | S12 46.1 | 13.9 | 58.6 |
| D 13 | 11 58.6 | 05.5 | 12 24.5 | 10.8 | 12 32.2 | 14.0 | 58.6 |
| A 14 | 26 58.7 | 04.5 | 26 54.3 | 10.9 | 12 18.2 | 14.1 | 58.6 |
| Y 15 | 41 58.8 | .. 03.6 | 41 24.2 | 10.9 | 12 04.1 | 14.1 | 58.5 |
| 16 | 56 58.9 | 02.6 | 55 54.1 | 11.1 | 11 50.0 | 14.2 | 58.5 |
| 17 | 71 59.1 | 01.7 | 70 24.2 | 11.1 | 11 35.8 | 14.2 | 58.5 |
| 18 | 86 59.2 | S 7 00.7 | 84 54.3 | 11.2 | S11 21.6 | 14.2 | 58.5 |
| 19 | 101 59.3 | 6 59.7 | 99 24.5 | 11.3 | 11 07.4 | 14.3 | 58.4 |
| 20 | 116 59.4 | 58.8 | 113 54.8 | 11.4 | 10 53.1 | 14.4 | 58.4 |
| 21 | 131 59.6 | .. 57.8 | 128 25.2 | 11.5 | 10 38.7 | 14.3 | 58.4 |
| 22 | 146 59.7 | 56.9 | 142 55.7 | 11.5 | 10 24.4 | 14.5 | 58.4 |
| 23 | 161 59.8 | 55.9 | 157 26.2 | 11.6 | 10 09.9 | 14.4 | 58.3 |
| **3** 00 | 177 00.0 | S 6 55.0 | 171 56.8 | 11.7 | S 9 55.5 | 14.5 | 58.3 |
| 01 | 192 00.1 | 54.0 | 186 27.5 | 11.8 | 9 41.0 | 14.6 | 58.3 |
| 02 | 207 00.2 | 53.0 | 200 58.3 | 11.8 | 9 26.4 | 14.5 | 58.3 |
| 03 | 222 00.3 | .. 52.1 | 215 29.1 | 11.9 | 9 11.9 | 14.6 | 58.2 |
| 04 | 237 00.5 | 51.1 | 230 00.0 | 12.0 | 8 57.3 | 14.7 | 58.2 |
| 05 | 252 00.6 | 50.2 | 244 31.0 | 12.1 | 8 42.6 | 14.6 | 58.2 |
| 06 | 267 00.7 | S 6 49.2 | 259 02.1 | 12.1 | S 8 28.0 | 14.7 | 58.1 |
| T 07 | 282 00.9 | 48.2 | 273 33.2 | 12.2 | 8 13.3 | 14.7 | 58.1 |
| H 08 | 297 01.0 | 47.3 | 288 04.4 | 12.2 | 7 58.6 | 14.8 | 58.1 |
| U 09 | 312 01.1 | .. 46.3 | 302 35.6 | 12.4 | 7 43.8 | 14.8 | 58.1 |
| R 10 | 327 01.2 | 45.4 | 317 07.0 | 12.3 | 7 29.0 | 14.7 | 58.0 |
| S 11 | 342 01.4 | 44.4 | 331 38.3 | 12.5 | 7 14.3 | 14.9 | 58.0 |
| D 12 | 357 01.5 | S 6 43.4 | 346 09.8 | 12.5 | S 6 59.4 | 14.8 | 58.0 |
| A 13 | 12 01.6 | 42.5 | 0 41.3 | 12.6 | 6 44.6 | 14.8 | 58.0 |
| Y 14 | 27 01.8 | 41.5 | 15 12.9 | 12.6 | 6 29.8 | 14.9 | 57.9 |
| 15 | 42 01.9 | .. 40.6 | 29 44.5 | 12.7 | 6 14.9 | 14.9 | 57.9 |
| 16 | 57 02.0 | 39.6 | 44 16.2 | 12.8 | 6 00.0 | 14.9 | 57.9 |
| 17 | 72 02.2 | 38.6 | 58 48.0 | 12.8 | 5 45.1 | 14.9 | 57.8 |
| 18 | 87 02.3 | S 6 37.7 | 73 19.8 | 12.9 | S 5 30.2 | 14.9 | 57.8 |
| 19 | 102 02.4 | 36.7 | 87 51.7 | 12.9 | 5 15.3 | 14.9 | 57.8 |
| 20 | 117 02.6 | 35.8 | 102 23.6 | 13.0 | 5 00.4 | 15.0 | 57.8 |
| 21 | 132 02.7 | .. 34.8 | 116 55.6 | 13.0 | 4 45.4 | 14.9 | 57.7 |
| 22 | 147 02.8 | 33.8 | 131 27.6 | 13.1 | 4 30.5 | 15.0 | 57.7 |
| 23 | 162 03.0 | 32.9 | 145 59.7 | 13.2 | 4 15.5 | 14.9 | 57.7 |
| **4** 00 | 177 03.1 | S 6 31.9 | 160 31.9 | 13.2 | S 4 00.6 | 15.0 | 57.6 |
| 01 | 192 03.2 | 31.0 | 175 04.1 | 13.2 | 3 45.6 | 14.9 | 57.6 |
| 02 | 207 03.4 | 30.0 | 189 36.3 | 13.3 | 3 30.7 | 15.0 | 57.6 |
| 03 | 222 03.5 | .. 29.0 | 204 08.6 | 13.4 | 3 15.7 | 15.0 | 57.6 |
| 04 | 237 03.6 | 28.1 | 218 41.0 | 13.4 | 3 00.7 | 14.9 | 57.5 |
| 05 | 252 03.8 | 27.1 | 233 13.4 | 13.4 | 2 45.8 | 15.0 | 57.5 |
| 06 | 267 03.9 | S 6 26.1 | 247 45.8 | 13.5 | S 2 30.8 | 14.9 | 57.5 |
| F 07 | 282 04.0 | 25.2 | 262 18.3 | 13.5 | 2 15.9 | 14.9 | 57.4 |
| R 08 | 297 04.2 | 24.2 | 276 50.8 | 13.6 | 2 00.9 | 14.9 | 57.4 |
| I 09 | 312 04.3 | .. 23.2 | 291 23.4 | 13.6 | 1 46.0 | 14.9 | 57.4 |
| D 10 | 327 04.4 | 22.3 | 305 56.0 | 13.6 | 1 31.1 | 15.0 | 57.3 |
| A 11 | 342 04.6 | 21.3 | 320 28.6 | 13.7 | 1 16.1 | 14.9 | 57.3 |
| Y 12 | 357 04.7 | S 6 20.4 | 335 01.3 | 13.7 | S 1 01.2 | 14.9 | 57.3 |
| 13 | 12 04.8 | 19.4 | 349 34.0 | 13.8 | 0 46.3 | 14.9 | 57.3 |
| 14 | 27 05.0 | 18.4 | 4 06.8 | 13.8 | 0 31.4 | 14.8 | 57.2 |
| 15 | 42 05.1 | .. 17.5 | 18 39.6 | 13.8 | 0 16.6 | 14.9 | 57.2 |
| 16 | 57 05.3 | 16.5 | 33 12.4 | 13.8 | S 0 01.7 | 14.8 | 57.2 |
| 17 | 72 05.4 | 15.5 | 47 45.2 | 13.9 | N 0 13.1 | 14.9 | 57.1 |
| 18 | 87 05.5 | S 6 14.6 | 62 18.1 | 14.0 | N 0 28.0 | 14.8 | 57.1 |
| 19 | 102 05.7 | 13.6 | 76 51.1 | 13.9 | 0 42.8 | 14.9 | 57.1 |
| 20 | 117 05.8 | 12.6 | 91 24.0 | 14.0 | 0 57.6 | 14.7 | 57.0 |
| 21 | 132 05.9 | .. 11.7 | 105 57.0 | 14.0 | 1 12.3 | 14.8 | 57.0 |
| 22 | 147 06.1 | 10.7 | 120 30.0 | 14.0 | 1 27.1 | 14.7 | 57.0 |
| 23 | 162 06.2 | 09.7 | 135 03.0 | 14.1 | N 1 41.8 | 14.7 | 57.0 |
| | SD 16.2 | d 1.0 | SD 16.0 | | 15.8 | | 15.6 |

### Twilight / Sunrise / Moonrise

| Lat. | Naut. | Civil | Sunrise | Moonrise 2 | 3 | 4 | 5 |
|---|---|---|---|---|---|---|---|
| ° | h m | h m | h m | h m | h m | h m | h m |
| N 72 | 05 00 | 06 18 | 07 26 | 09 14 | 08 31 | 07 59 | 07 30 |
| N 70 | 05 06 | 06 17 | 07 18 | 08 49 | 08 20 | 07 56 | 07 35 |
| 68 | 05 11 | 06 15 | 07 11 | 08 30 | 08 10 | 07 54 | 07 39 |
| 66 | 05 15 | 06 14 | 07 06 | 08 14 | 08 02 | 07 52 | 07 42 |
| 64 | 05 18 | 06 13 | 07 01 | 08 02 | 07 56 | 07 50 | 07 45 |
| 62 | 05 21 | 06 12 | 06 57 | 07 51 | 07 50 | 07 49 | 07 48 |
| 60 | 05 23 | 06 11 | 06 53 | 07 41 | 07 45 | 07 48 | 07 50 |
| N 58 | 05 25 | 06 10 | 06 50 | 07 33 | 07 41 | 07 46 | 07 52 |
| 56 | 05 27 | 06 09 | 06 47 | 07 26 | 07 37 | 07 45 | 07 54 |
| 54 | 05 28 | 06 09 | 06 44 | 07 19 | 07 33 | 07 44 | 07 55 |
| 52 | 05 29 | 06 08 | 06 42 | 07 13 | 07 30 | 07 44 | 07 57 |
| 50 | 05 30 | 06 07 | 06 39 | 07 08 | 07 27 | 07 43 | 07 58 |
| 45 | 05 31 | 06 05 | 06 35 | 06 56 | 07 20 | 07 41 | 08 01 |
| N 40 | 05 32 | 06 03 | 06 31 | 06 47 | 07 15 | 07 40 | 08 04 |
| 35 | 05 32 | 06 02 | 06 27 | 06 38 | 07 10 | 07 38 | 08 06 |
| 30 | 05 32 | 06 00 | 06 24 | 06 31 | 07 06 | 07 37 | 08 08 |
| 20 | 05 31 | 05 56 | 06 18 | 06 18 | 06 58 | 07 35 | 08 11 |
| N 10 | 05 28 | 05 52 | 06 13 | 06 07 | 06 52 | 07 34 | 08 14 |
| 0 | 05 24 | 05 48 | 06 09 | 05 57 | 06 46 | 07 32 | 08 17 |
| S 10 | 05 18 | 05 43 | 06 04 | 05 46 | 06 40 | 07 31 | 08 20 |
| 20 | 05 10 | 05 36 | 05 58 | 05 35 | 06 33 | 07 29 | 08 23 |
| 30 | 04 59 | 05 28 | 05 52 | 05 22 | 06 26 | 07 27 | 08 26 |
| 35 | 04 53 | 05 23 | 05 49 | 05 14 | 06 22 | 07 26 | 08 29 |
| 40 | 04 44 | 05 17 | 05 44 | 05 05 | 06 17 | 07 25 | 08 31 |
| 45 | 04 34 | 05 10 | 05 40 | 04 55 | 06 11 | 07 24 | 08 34 |
| S 50 | 04 20 | 05 01 | 05 34 | 04 43 | 06 04 | 07 22 | 08 37 |
| 52 | 04 14 | 04 56 | 05 31 | 04 37 | 06 01 | 07 21 | 08 39 |
| 54 | 04 06 | 04 51 | 05 28 | 04 31 | 05 57 | 07 20 | 08 40 |
| 56 | 03 58 | 04 46 | 05 25 | 04 24 | 05 54 | 07 19 | 08 42 |
| 58 | 03 48 | 04 40 | 05 21 | 04 16 | 05 49 | 07 18 | 08 44 |
| S 60 | 03 37 | 04 33 | 05 17 | 04 07 | 05 44 | 07 17 | 08 47 |

### Sunset / Twilight / Moonset

| Lat. | Sunset | Civil | Naut. | Moonset 2 | 3 | 4 | 5 |
|---|---|---|---|---|---|---|---|
| ° | h m | h m | h m | h m | h m | h m | h m |
| N 72 | 16 59 | 18 08 | 19 27 | 15 30 | 17 55 | 20 05 | 22 12 |
| N 70 | 17 08 | 18 09 | 19 20 | 15 53 | 18 04 | 20 04 | 22 01 |
| 68 | 17 14 | 18 10 | 19 15 | 16 10 | 18 11 | 20 03 | 21 52 |
| 66 | 17 20 | 18 11 | 19 11 | 16 24 | 18 16 | 20 02 | 21 44 |
| 64 | 17 24 | 18 12 | 19 07 | 16 36 | 18 21 | 20 01 | 21 38 |
| 62 | 17 29 | 18 13 | 19 05 | 16 45 | 18 25 | 20 01 | 21 33 |
| 60 | 17 32 | 18 14 | 19 02 | 16 53 | 18 29 | 20 00 | 21 29 |
| N 58 | 17 35 | 18 15 | 19 00 | 17 01 | 18 32 | 20 00 | 21 25 |
| 56 | 17 38 | 18 16 | 18 59 | 17 07 | 18 35 | 19 59 | 21 21 |
| 54 | 17 41 | 18 16 | 18 57 | 17 12 | 18 37 | 19 59 | 21 18 |
| 52 | 17 43 | 18 17 | 18 56 | 17 17 | 18 40 | 19 58 | 21 15 |
| 50 | 17 45 | 18 18 | 18 55 | 17 22 | 18 42 | 19 58 | 21 12 |
| 45 | 17 50 | 18 19 | 18 53 | 17 32 | 18 46 | 19 57 | 21 07 |
| N 40 | 17 54 | 18 21 | 18 52 | 17 40 | 18 50 | 19 56 | 21 02 |
| 35 | 17 57 | 18 23 | 18 52 | 17 47 | 18 53 | 19 56 | 20 58 |
| 30 | 18 00 | 18 24 | 18 52 | 17 53 | 18 56 | 19 56 | 20 54 |
| 20 | 18 06 | 18 28 | 18 53 | 18 03 | 19 00 | 19 55 | 20 48 |
| N 10 | 18 11 | 18 32 | 18 56 | 18 12 | 19 04 | 19 54 | 20 43 |
| 0 | 18 15 | 18 36 | 19 00 | 18 20 | 19 08 | 19 54 | 20 38 |
| S 10 | 18 20 | 18 41 | 19 06 | 18 29 | 19 12 | 19 53 | 20 33 |
| 20 | 18 25 | 18 47 | 19 13 | 18 38 | 19 16 | 19 52 | 20 28 |
| 30 | 18 31 | 18 55 | 19 24 | 18 47 | 19 21 | 19 51 | 20 22 |
| 35 | 18 35 | 19 00 | 19 31 | 18 53 | 19 23 | 19 51 | 20 18 |
| 40 | 18 39 | 19 06 | 19 39 | 19 00 | 19 26 | 19 50 | 20 14 |
| 45 | 18 43 | 19 13 | 19 49 | 19 07 | 19 29 | 19 50 | 20 10 |
| S 50 | 18 49 | 19 22 | 20 02 | 19 16 | 19 33 | 19 49 | 20 04 |
| 52 | 18 52 | 19 26 | 20 09 | 19 20 | 19 35 | 19 49 | 20 02 |
| 54 | 18 54 | 19 31 | 20 16 | 19 24 | 19 37 | 19 48 | 19 59 |
| 56 | 18 58 | 19 36 | 20 24 | 19 29 | 19 39 | 19 48 | 19 56 |
| 58 | 19 01 | 19 42 | 20 34 | 19 35 | 19 42 | 19 47 | 19 53 |
| S 60 | 19 05 | 19 49 | 20 45 | 19 41 | 19 44 | 19 47 | 19 49 |

| Day | SUN Eqn. of Time 00h | 12h | Mer. Pass. | MOON Mer. Pass. Upper | Lower | Age | Phase |
|---|---|---|---|---|---|---|---|
| d | m s | m s | h m | h m | h m | d | % |
| 2 | 12 13 | 12 07 | 12 12 | 12 09 | 24 33 | 29 | 0 |
| 3 | 12 00 | 11 54 | 12 12 | 12 57 | 00 33 | 01 | 1 |
| 4 | 11 48 | 11 41 | 12 12 | 13 43 | 01 20 | 02 | 4 |

# 2022 MARCH 5, 6, 7 (SAT., SUN., MON.)

| UT | ARIES | VENUS −4.7 | | MARS +1.2 | | JUPITER −2.0 | | SATURN +0.7 | | STARS | | |
|---|---|---|---|---|---|---|---|---|---|---|---|---|
| | GHA | GHA | Dec | GHA | Dec | GHA | Dec | GHA | Dec | Name | SHA | Dec |
| d h | ° ′ | ° ′ | ° ′ | ° ′ | ° ′ | ° ′ | ° ′ | ° ′ | ° ′ | | ° ′ | ° ′ |
| 5 00 | 162 43.3 | 222 29.1 | S16 41.9 | 221 19.8 | S21 12.8 | 176 18.6 | S 6 52.6 | 200 45.5 | S15 53.6 | Acamar | 315 13.8 | S40 13.3 |
| 01 | 177 45.8 | 237 29.3 | 41.7 | 236 20.3 | 12.4 | 191 20.5 | 52.4 | 215 47.7 | 53.5 | Achernar | 335 22.4 | S57 07.8 |
| 02 | 192 48.3 | 252 29.5 | 41.6 | 251 20.8 | 12.0 | 206 22.4 | 52.1 | 230 49.9 | 53.5 | Acrux | 173 02.0 | S63 13.2 |
| 03 | 207 50.7 | 267 29.7 . . | 41.4 | 266 21.3 . . | 11.7 | 221 24.3 . . | 51.9 | 245 52.1 . . | 53.4 | Adhara | 255 07.5 | S29 00.3 |
| 04 | 222 53.2 | 282 30.0 | 41.3 | 281 21.8 | 11.3 | 236 26.2 | 51.7 | 260 54.3 | 53.3 | Aldebaran | 290 42.3 | N16 33.1 |
| 05 | 237 55.7 | 297 30.2 | 41.1 | 296 22.3 | 11.0 | 251 28.1 | 51.4 | 275 56.5 | 53.2 | | | |
| 06 | 252 58.1 | 312 30.4 | S16 41.0 | 311 22.8 | S21 10.6 | 266 30.0 | S 6 51.2 | 290 58.7 | S15 53.1 | Alioth | 166 14.6 | N55 50.2 |
| 07 | 268 00.6 | 327 30.6 | 40.8 | 326 23.3 | 10.3 | 281 31.9 | 51.0 | 306 00.8 | 53.0 | Alkaid | 152 53.5 | N49 12.0 |
| S 08 | 283 03.1 | 342 30.8 | 40.6 | 341 23.8 | 09.9 | 296 33.8 | 50.7 | 321 03.0 | 53.0 | Al Na'ir | 27 36.3 | S46 51.3 |
| A 09 | 298 05.5 | 357 31.0 . . | 40.5 | 356 24.3 . . | 09.5 | 311 35.7 . . | 50.5 | 336 05.2 . . | 52.9 | Alnilam | 275 40.0 | S 1 11.4 |
| T 10 | 313 08.0 | 12 31.3 | 40.3 | 11 24.8 | 09.2 | 326 37.6 | 50.3 | 351 07.4 | 52.8 | Alphard | 217 49.8 | S 8 45.4 |
| U 11 | 328 10.5 | 27 31.5 | 40.2 | 26 25.3 | 08.8 | 341 39.5 | 50.0 | 6 09.6 | 52.7 | | | |
| R 12 | 343 12.9 | 42 31.7 | S16 40.0 | 41 25.8 | S21 08.5 | 356 41.4 | S 6 49.8 | 21 11.8 | S15 52.6 | Alphecca | 126 05.6 | N26 38.2 |
| D 13 | 358 15.4 | 57 31.9 | 39.9 | 56 26.3 | 08.1 | 11 43.3 | 49.6 | 36 14.0 | 52.5 | Alpheratz | 357 37.5 | N29 12.6 |
| A 14 | 13 17.8 | 72 32.1 | 39.7 | 71 26.8 | 07.7 | 26 45.2 | 49.3 | 51 16.1 | 52.4 | Altair | 62 02.4 | N 8 55.4 |
| Y 15 | 28 20.3 | 87 32.3 . . | 39.5 | 86 27.3 . . | 07.4 | 41 47.1 . . | 49.1 | 66 18.3 . . | 52.4 | Ankaa | 353 09.9 | S42 11.4 |
| 16 | 43 22.8 | 102 32.5 | 39.4 | 101 27.8 | 07.0 | 56 49.0 | 48.9 | 81 20.5 | 52.3 | Antares | 112 18.7 | S26 28.8 |
| 17 | 58 25.2 | 117 32.7 | 39.2 | 116 28.3 | 06.6 | 71 50.9 | 48.6 | 96 22.7 | 52.2 | | | |
| 18 | 73 27.7 | 132 32.9 | S16 39.1 | 131 28.9 | S21 06.3 | 86 52.8 | S 6 48.4 | 111 24.9 | S15 52.1 | Arcturus | 145 49.8 | N19 03.9 |
| 19 | 88 30.2 | 147 33.1 | 38.9 | 146 29.4 | 05.9 | 101 54.7 | 48.2 | 126 27.1 | 52.0 | Atria | 107 15.0 | S69 03.7 |
| 20 | 103 32.6 | 162 33.3 | 38.7 | 161 29.9 | 05.6 | 116 56.6 | 47.9 | 141 29.3 | 51.9 | Avior | 234 15.2 | S59 35.0 |
| 21 | 118 35.1 | 177 33.5 . . | 38.6 | 176 30.4 . . | 05.2 | 131 58.5 . . | 47.7 | 156 31.4 . . | 51.9 | Bellatrix | 278 25.3 | N 6 22.1 |
| 22 | 133 37.6 | 192 33.7 | 38.4 | 191 30.9 | 04.8 | 147 00.4 | 47.5 | 171 33.6 | 51.8 | Betelgeuse | 270 54.5 | N 7 24.6 |
| 23 | 148 40.0 | 207 33.9 | 38.2 | 206 31.4 | 04.5 | 162 02.3 | 47.2 | 186 35.8 | 51.7 | | | |
| 6 00 | 163 42.5 | 222 34.1 | S16 38.1 | 221 31.9 | S21 04.1 | 177 04.2 | S 6 47.0 | 201 38.0 | S15 51.6 | Canopus | 263 53.2 | S52 42.7 |
| 01 | 178 44.9 | 237 34.3 | 37.9 | 236 32.4 | 03.7 | 192 06.1 | 46.8 | 216 40.2 | 51.5 | Capella | 280 25.3 | N46 01.3 |
| 02 | 193 47.4 | 252 34.5 | 37.7 | 251 32.9 | 03.4 | 207 08.0 | 46.5 | 231 42.4 | 51.4 | Deneb | 49 27.8 | N45 21.3 |
| 03 | 208 49.9 | 267 34.7 . . | 37.6 | 266 33.4 . . | 03.0 | 222 09.9 . . | 46.3 | 246 44.6 . . | 51.4 | Denebola | 182 27.0 | N14 26.8 |
| 04 | 223 52.3 | 282 34.9 | 37.4 | 281 33.9 | 02.6 | 237 11.8 | 46.1 | 261 46.8 | 51.3 | Diphda | 348 49.9 | S17 52.2 |
| 05 | 238 54.8 | 297 35.1 | 37.2 | 296 34.4 | 02.3 | 252 13.7 | 45.8 | 276 48.9 | 51.2 | | | |
| 06 | 253 57.3 | 312 35.3 | S16 37.1 | 311 34.9 | S21 01.9 | 267 15.6 | S 6 45.6 | 291 51.1 | S15 51.1 | Dubhe | 193 43.2 | N61 37.9 |
| 07 | 268 59.7 | 327 35.5 | 36.9 | 326 35.4 | 01.5 | 282 17.5 | 45.4 | 306 53.3 | 51.0 | Elnath | 278 04.8 | N28 37.6 |
| 08 | 284 02.2 | 342 35.7 | 36.7 | 341 35.9 | 01.2 | 297 19.4 | 45.1 | 321 55.5 | 50.9 | Eltanin | 90 43.4 | N51 28.8 |
| S 09 | 299 04.7 | 357 35.9 . . | 36.6 | 356 36.4 . . | 00.8 | 312 21.3 . . | 44.9 | 336 57.7 . . | 50.9 | Enif | 33 41.4 | N 9 58.4 |
| U 10 | 314 07.1 | 12 36.1 | 36.4 | 11 36.9 | 00.4 | 327 23.2 | 44.7 | 351 59.9 | 50.8 | Fomalhaut | 15 17.5 | S29 30.5 |
| N 11 | 329 09.6 | 27 36.2 | 36.2 | 26 37.4 | 21 00.1 | 342 25.1 | 44.4 | 7 02.1 | 50.7 | | | |
| D 12 | 344 12.1 | 42 36.4 | S16 36.0 | 41 37.9 | S20 59.7 | 357 27.0 | S 6 44.2 | 22 04.2 | S15 50.6 | Gacrux | 171 53.7 | S57 14.1 |
| A 13 | 359 14.5 | 57 36.6 | 35.9 | 56 38.4 | 59.3 | 12 28.9 | 44.0 | 37 06.4 | 50.5 | Gienah | 175 45.7 | S17 39.9 |
| Y 14 | 14 17.0 | 72 36.8 | 35.7 | 71 38.9 | 59.0 | 27 30.9 | 43.8 | 52 08.6 | 50.4 | Hadar | 148 38.9 | S60 28.6 |
| 15 | 29 19.4 | 87 37.0 . . | 35.5 | 86 39.4 . . | 58.6 | 42 32.8 . . | 43.5 | 67 10.8 . . | 50.4 | Hamal | 327 54.1 | N23 33.9 |
| 16 | 44 21.9 | 102 37.2 | 35.3 | 101 39.9 | 58.2 | 57 34.7 | 43.3 | 82 13.0 | 50.3 | Kaus Aust. | 83 35.8 | S34 22.4 |
| 17 | 59 24.4 | 117 37.3 | 35.1 | 116 40.4 | 57.8 | 72 36.6 | 43.1 | 97 15.2 | 50.2 | | | |
| 18 | 74 26.8 | 132 37.5 | S16 35.0 | 131 40.9 | S20 57.5 | 87 38.5 | S 6 42.8 | 112 17.4 | S15 50.1 | Kochab | 137 19.2 | N74 03.6 |
| 19 | 89 29.3 | 147 37.7 | 34.8 | 146 41.4 | 57.1 | 102 40.4 | 42.6 | 127 19.6 | 50.0 | Markab | 13 32.5 | N15 19.3 |
| 20 | 104 31.8 | 162 37.9 | 34.6 | 161 41.9 | 56.7 | 117 42.3 | 42.4 | 142 21.7 | 49.9 | Menkar | 314 08.7 | N 4 10.4 |
| 21 | 119 34.2 | 177 38.0 . . | 34.4 | 176 42.5 . . | 56.4 | 132 44.2 . . | 42.1 | 157 23.9 . . | 49.9 | Menkent | 148 00.1 | S36 28.6 |
| 22 | 134 36.7 | 192 38.2 | 34.2 | 191 43.0 | 56.0 | 147 46.1 | 41.9 | 172 26.1 | 49.8 | Miaplacidus | 221 37.9 | S69 48.6 |
| 23 | 149 39.2 | 207 38.4 | 34.1 | 206 43.5 | 55.6 | 162 48.0 | 41.7 | 187 28.3 | 49.7 | | | |
| 7 00 | 164 41.6 | 222 38.6 | S16 33.9 | 221 44.0 | S20 55.2 | 177 49.9 | S 6 41.4 | 202 30.5 | S15 49.6 | Mirfak | 308 31.8 | N49 56.5 |
| 01 | 179 44.1 | 237 38.7 | 33.7 | 236 44.5 | 54.9 | 192 51.8 | 41.2 | 217 32.7 | 49.5 | Nunki | 75 50.8 | S26 16.1 |
| 02 | 194 46.5 | 252 38.9 | 33.5 | 251 45.0 | 54.5 | 207 53.7 | 41.0 | 232 34.9 | 49.4 | Peacock | 53 09.9 | S56 39.8 |
| 03 | 209 49.0 | 267 39.1 . . | 33.3 | 266 45.5 . . | 54.1 | 222 55.6 . . | 40.7 | 247 37.1 . . | 49.4 | Pollux | 243 19.9 | N27 58.4 |
| 04 | 224 51.5 | 282 39.2 | 33.1 | 281 46.0 | 53.7 | 237 57.5 | 40.5 | 262 39.3 | 49.3 | Procyon | 244 53.1 | N 5 10.0 |
| 05 | 239 53.9 | 297 39.4 | 32.9 | 296 46.5 | 53.4 | 252 59.4 | 40.3 | 277 41.4 | 49.2 | | | |
| 06 | 254 56.4 | 312 39.6 | S16 32.8 | 311 47.0 | S20 53.0 | 268 01.3 | S 6 40.0 | 292 43.6 | S15 49.1 | Rasalhague | 96 00.8 | N12 32.4 |
| 07 | 269 58.9 | 327 39.7 | 32.6 | 326 47.5 | 52.6 | 283 03.2 | 39.8 | 307 45.8 | 49.0 | Regulus | 207 36.6 | N11 51.5 |
| 08 | 285 01.3 | 342 39.9 | 32.4 | 341 48.0 | 52.2 | 298 05.1 | 39.6 | 322 48.0 | 48.9 | Rigel | 281 06.1 | S 8 10.8 |
| M 09 | 300 03.8 | 357 40.1 . . | 32.2 | 356 48.5 . . | 51.9 | 313 07.0 . . | 39.3 | 337 50.2 . . | 48.9 | Rigil Kent. | 139 43.1 | S60 55.3 |
| O 10 | 315 06.3 | 12 40.2 | 32.0 | 11 49.0 | 51.5 | 328 08.9 | 39.1 | 352 52.4 | 48.8 | Sabik | 102 05.5 | S15 45.1 |
| N 11 | 330 08.7 | 27 40.4 | 31.8 | 26 49.5 | 51.1 | 343 10.8 | 38.9 | 7 54.6 | 48.7 | | | |
| D 12 | 345 11.2 | 42 40.5 | S16 31.6 | 41 50.0 | S20 50.7 | 358 12.7 | S 6 38.6 | 22 56.8 | S15 48.6 | Schedar | 349 34.2 | N56 39.5 |
| A 13 | 0 13.7 | 57 40.7 | 31.4 | 56 50.6 | 50.3 | 13 14.6 | 38.4 | 37 58.9 | 48.5 | Shaula | 96 13.6 | S37 07.1 |
| Y 14 | 15 16.1 | 72 40.9 | 31.2 | 71 51.1 | 50.0 | 28 16.5 | 38.2 | 53 01.1 | 48.4 | Sirius | 258 28.2 | S16 45.0 |
| 15 | 30 18.6 | 87 41.0 . . | 31.0 | 86 51.6 . . | 49.6 | 43 18.4 . . | 37.9 | 68 03.3 . . | 48.4 | Spica | 158 24.5 | S11 16.6 |
| 16 | 45 21.0 | 102 41.2 | 30.8 | 101 52.1 | 49.2 | 58 20.3 | 37.7 | 83 05.5 | 48.3 | Suhail | 222 47.6 | S43 31.4 |
| 17 | 60 23.5 | 117 41.3 | 30.6 | 116 52.6 | 48.8 | 73 22.2 | 37.5 | 98 07.7 | 48.2 | | | |
| 18 | 75 26.0 | 132 41.5 | S16 30.4 | 131 53.1 | S20 48.4 | 88 24.1 | S 6 37.2 | 113 09.9 | S15 48.1 | Vega | 80 35.0 | N38 47.9 |
| 19 | 90 28.4 | 147 41.6 | 30.2 | 146 53.6 | 48.1 | 103 26.0 | 37.0 | 128 12.1 | 48.0 | Zuben'ubi | 136 58.4 | S16 08.0 |
| 20 | 105 30.9 | 162 41.8 | 30.0 | 161 54.1 | 47.7 | 118 27.9 | 36.8 | 143 14.3 | 47.9 | | SHA | Mer. Pass. |
| 21 | 120 33.4 | 177 41.9 . . | 29.8 | 176 54.6 . . | 47.3 | 133 29.8 . . | 36.5 | 158 16.5 . . | 47.9 | | ° ′ | h m |
| 22 | 135 35.8 | 192 42.1 | 29.6 | 191 55.1 | 46.9 | 148 31.7 | 36.3 | 173 18.6 | 47.8 | Venus | 58 51.7 | 9 10 |
| 23 | 150 38.3 | 207 42.2 | 29.4 | 206 55.6 | 46.5 | 163 33.6 | 36.1 | 188 20.8 | 47.7 | Mars | 57 49.4 | 9 14 |
| | h m | | | | | | | | | Jupiter | 13 21.7 | 12 10 |
| Mer. Pass. 13 03.0 | | v 0.2 | d 0.2 | v 0.5 | d 0.4 | v 1.9 | d 0.2 | v 2.2 | d 0.1 | Saturn | 37 55.5 | 10 32 |

### SUN and MOON

| UT | SUN GHA | SUN Dec | MOON GHA | v | MOON Dec | d | HP |
|---|---|---|---|---|---|---|---|
| d h | ° ′ | ° ′ | ° ′ | ′ | ° ′ | ′ | ′ |
| **5** 00 | 177 06.4 | S 6 08.8 | 149 36.1 | 14.1 | N 1 56.5 | 14.7 | 56.9 |
| 01 | 192 06.5 | 07.8 | 164 09.2 | 14.1 | 2 11.2 | 14.6 | 56.9 |
| 02 | 207 06.6 | 06.8 | 178 42.3 | 14.2 | 2 25.8 | 14.6 | 56.9 |
| 03 | 222 06.8 | .. 05.9 | 193 15.5 | 14.1 | 2 40.4 | 14.6 | 56.8 |
| 04 | 237 06.9 | 04.9 | 207 48.6 | 14.2 | 2 55.0 | 14.6 | 56.8 |
| 05 | 252 07.0 | 04.0 | 222 21.8 | 14.2 | 3 09.6 | 14.5 | 56.8 |
| 06 | 267 07.2 | S 6 03.0 | 236 55.0 | 14.2 | N 3 24.1 | 14.5 | 56.7 |
| S 07 | 282 07.3 | 02.0 | 251 28.2 | 14.2 | 3 38.6 | 14.5 | 56.7 |
| A 08 | 297 07.5 | 01.1 | 266 01.4 | 14.3 | 3 53.1 | 14.4 | 56.7 |
| T 09 | 312 07.6 | 6 00.1 | 280 34.7 | 14.3 | 4 07.5 | 14.4 | 56.6 |
| U 10 | 327 07.7 | 5 59.1 | 295 08.0 | 14.2 | 4 21.9 | 14.4 | 56.6 |
| R 11 | 342 07.9 | 58.2 | 309 41.2 | 14.3 | 4 36.3 | 14.3 | 56.6 |
| D 12 | 357 08.0 | S 5 57.2 | 324 14.5 | 14.4 | N 4 50.6 | 14.3 | 56.6 |
| A 13 | 12 08.2 | 56.2 | 338 47.9 | 14.3 | 5 04.9 | 14.3 | 56.5 |
| Y 14 | 27 08.3 | 55.2 | 353 21.2 | 14.3 | 5 19.2 | 14.2 | 56.5 |
| 15 | 42 08.4 | .. 54.3 | 7 54.5 | 14.3 | 5 33.4 | 14.2 | 56.5 |
| 16 | 57 08.6 | 53.3 | 22 27.8 | 14.4 | 5 47.6 | 14.1 | 56.4 |
| 17 | 72 08.7 | 52.3 | 37 01.2 | 14.4 | 6 01.7 | 14.1 | 56.4 |
| 18 | 87 08.9 | S 5 51.4 | 51 34.6 | 14.3 | N 6 15.8 | 14.1 | 56.4 |
| 19 | 102 09.0 | 50.4 | 66 07.9 | 14.4 | 6 29.9 | 14.0 | 56.4 |
| 20 | 117 09.2 | 49.4 | 80 41.3 | 14.4 | 6 43.9 | 14.0 | 56.3 |
| 21 | 132 09.3 | .. 48.5 | 95 14.7 | 14.3 | 6 57.9 | 13.9 | 56.3 |
| 22 | 147 09.4 | 47.5 | 109 48.0 | 14.4 | 7 11.8 | 13.9 | 56.3 |
| 23 | 162 09.6 | 46.5 | 124 21.4 | 14.4 | 7 25.7 | 13.8 | 56.2 |
| **6** 00 | 177 09.7 | S 5 45.6 | 138 54.8 | 14.4 | N 7 39.5 | 13.8 | 56.2 |
| 01 | 192 09.9 | 44.6 | 153 28.2 | 14.4 | 7 53.3 | 13.7 | 56.2 |
| 02 | 207 10.0 | 43.6 | 168 01.6 | 14.4 | 8 07.0 | 13.7 | 56.1 |
| 03 | 222 10.2 | .. 42.7 | 182 35.0 | 14.4 | 8 20.7 | 13.6 | 56.1 |
| 04 | 237 10.3 | 41.7 | 197 08.4 | 14.3 | 8 34.3 | 13.6 | 56.1 |
| 05 | 252 10.4 | 40.7 | 211 41.7 | 14.4 | 8 47.9 | 13.6 | 56.1 |
| 06 | 267 10.6 | S 5 39.7 | 226 15.1 | 14.4 | N 9 01.5 | 13.5 | 56.0 |
| 07 | 282 10.7 | 38.8 | 240 48.5 | 14.4 | 9 15.0 | 13.4 | 56.0 |
| S 08 | 297 10.9 | 37.8 | 255 21.9 | 14.3 | 9 28.4 | 13.4 | 56.0 |
| U 09 | 312 11.0 | .. 36.8 | 269 55.2 | 14.4 | 9 41.8 | 13.3 | 55.9 |
| N 10 | 327 11.2 | 35.9 | 284 28.6 | 14.3 | 9 55.1 | 13.2 | 55.9 |
| D 11 | 342 11.3 | 34.9 | 299 01.9 | 14.4 | 10 08.3 | 13.2 | 55.9 |
| A 12 | 357 11.5 | S 5 33.9 | 313 35.3 | 14.3 | N10 21.5 | 13.2 | 55.9 |
| Y 13 | 12 11.6 | 33.0 | 328 08.6 | 14.3 | 10 34.7 | 13.1 | 55.8 |
| 14 | 27 11.7 | 32.0 | 342 41.9 | 14.3 | 10 47.8 | 13.0 | 55.8 |
| 15 | 42 11.9 | .. 31.0 | 357 15.2 | 14.3 | 11 00.8 | 13.0 | 55.8 |
| 16 | 57 12.0 | 30.0 | 11 48.5 | 14.3 | 11 13.8 | 12.9 | 55.8 |
| 17 | 72 12.2 | 29.1 | 26 21.8 | 14.3 | 11 26.7 | 12.8 | 55.7 |
| 18 | 87 12.3 | S 5 28.1 | 40 55.1 | 14.2 | N11 39.5 | 12.8 | 55.7 |
| 19 | 102 12.5 | 27.1 | 55 28.3 | 14.3 | 11 52.3 | 12.8 | 55.7 |
| 20 | 117 12.6 | 26.2 | 70 01.6 | 14.2 | 12 05.1 | 12.6 | 55.6 |
| 21 | 132 12.8 | .. 25.2 | 84 34.8 | 14.2 | 12 17.7 | 12.6 | 55.6 |
| 22 | 147 12.9 | 24.2 | 99 08.0 | 14.2 | 12 30.3 | 12.5 | 55.6 |
| 23 | 162 13.1 | 23.2 | 113 41.2 | 14.1 | 12 42.8 | 12.5 | 55.6 |
| **7** 00 | 177 13.2 | S 5 22.3 | 128 14.3 | 14.2 | N12 55.3 | 12.4 | 55.5 |
| 01 | 192 13.4 | 21.3 | 142 47.5 | 14.1 | 13 07.7 | 12.3 | 55.5 |
| 02 | 207 13.5 | 20.3 | 157 20.6 | 14.1 | 13 20.0 | 12.3 | 55.5 |
| 03 | 222 13.6 | .. 19.4 | 171 53.7 | 14.1 | 13 32.3 | 12.2 | 55.5 |
| 04 | 237 13.8 | 18.4 | 186 26.8 | 14.1 | 13 44.5 | 12.1 | 55.4 |
| 05 | 252 13.9 | 17.4 | 200 59.9 | 14.0 | 13 56.6 | 12.1 | 55.4 |
| 06 | 267 14.1 | S 5 16.4 | 215 32.9 | 14.1 | N14 08.7 | 12.0 | 55.4 |
| 07 | 282 14.2 | 15.5 | 230 06.0 | 14.0 | 14 20.7 | 11.9 | 55.4 |
| 08 | 297 14.4 | 14.5 | 244 39.0 | 13.9 | 14 32.6 | 11.8 | 55.3 |
| M 09 | 312 14.5 | .. 13.5 | 259 11.9 | 14.0 | 14 44.4 | 11.8 | 55.3 |
| O 10 | 327 14.7 | 12.5 | 273 44.9 | 13.9 | 14 56.2 | 11.7 | 55.3 |
| N 11 | 342 14.8 | 11.6 | 288 17.8 | 13.9 | 15 07.9 | 11.6 | 55.3 |
| D 12 | 357 15.0 | S 5 10.6 | 302 50.7 | 13.9 | N15 19.5 | 11.5 | 55.3 |
| A 13 | 12 15.1 | 09.6 | 317 23.6 | 13.8 | 15 31.0 | 11.5 | 55.2 |
| Y 14 | 27 15.3 | 08.6 | 331 56.4 | 13.8 | 15 42.5 | 11.4 | 55.2 |
| 15 | 42 15.4 | .. 07.7 | 346 29.2 | 13.8 | 15 53.9 | 11.3 | 55.2 |
| 16 | 57 15.6 | 06.7 | 1 02.0 | 13.8 | 16 05.2 | 11.2 | 55.2 |
| 17 | 72 15.7 | 05.7 | 15 34.8 | 13.7 | 16 16.4 | 11.2 | 55.1 |
| 18 | 87 15.9 | S 5 04.8 | 30 07.5 | 13.7 | N16 27.6 | 11.0 | 55.1 |
| 19 | 102 16.0 | 03.8 | 44 40.2 | 13.6 | 16 38.6 | 11.0 | 55.1 |
| 20 | 117 16.2 | 02.8 | 59 12.8 | 13.7 | 16 49.6 | 11.0 | 55.1 |
| 21 | 132 16.3 | .. 01.8 | 73 45.5 | 13.6 | 17 00.6 | 10.8 | 55.1 |
| 22 | 147 16.5 | 5 00.9 | 88 18.1 | 13.5 | 17 11.4 | 10.7 | 55.0 |
| 23 | 162 16.6 | S 4 59.9 | 102 50.6 | 13.5 | N17 22.1 | 10.7 | 55.0 |
| | SD 16.1 | d 1.0 | SD 15.4 | | 15.2 | | 15.1 |

### Twilight — Sunrise — Moonrise

| Lat. | Naut. | Civil | Sunrise | Moonrise 5 | 6 | 7 | 8 |
|---|---|---|---|---|---|---|---|
| ° | h m | h m | h m | h m | h m | h m | h m |
| N 72 | 04 44 | 06 03 | 07 11 | 07 30 | 06 58 | 06 16 | ▭ |
| N 70 | 04 52 | 06 03 | 07 04 | 07 35 | 07 12 | 06 43 | 05 55 |
| 68 | 04 59 | 06 03 | 06 59 | 07 39 | 07 23 | 07 04 | 06 37 |
| 66 | 05 04 | 06 03 | 06 54 | 07 42 | 07 32 | 07 20 | 07 06 |
| 64 | 05 08 | 06 03 | 06 50 | 07 45 | 07 40 | 07 34 | 07 28 |
| 62 | 05 11 | 06 03 | 06 47 | 07 48 | 07 46 | 07 46 | 07 46 |
| 60 | 05 14 | 06 03 | 06 44 | 07 50 | 07 52 | 07 56 | 08 01 |
| N 58 | 05 17 | 06 02 | 06 41 | 07 52 | 07 57 | 08 04 | 08 13 |
| 56 | 05 19 | 06 02 | 06 39 | 07 54 | 08 02 | 08 12 | 08 24 |
| 54 | 05 21 | 06 02 | 06 37 | 07 55 | 08 06 | 08 19 | 08 34 |
| 52 | 05 22 | 06 01 | 06 35 | 07 57 | 08 10 | 08 25 | 08 42 |
| 50 | 05 24 | 06 01 | 06 33 | 07 58 | 08 14 | 08 30 | 08 50 |
| 45 | 05 26 | 06 00 | 06 29 | 08 01 | 08 21 | 08 43 | 09 07 |
| N 40 | 05 28 | 05 59 | 06 26 | 08 04 | 08 27 | 08 53 | 09 21 |
| 35 | 05 29 | 05 58 | 06 23 | 08 06 | 08 33 | 09 01 | 09 32 |
| 30 | 05 29 | 05 57 | 06 21 | 08 08 | 08 38 | 09 09 | 09 42 |
| 20 | 05 28 | 05 54 | 06 16 | 08 11 | 08 46 | 09 22 | 10 00 |
| N 10 | 05 26 | 05 51 | 06 12 | 08 14 | 08 54 | 09 34 | 10 16 |
| 0 | 05 23 | 05 47 | 06 08 | 08 17 | 09 01 | 09 45 | 10 30 |
| S 10 | 05 18 | 05 43 | 06 04 | 08 20 | 09 08 | 09 56 | 10 45 |
| 20 | 05 11 | 05 37 | 05 59 | 08 23 | 09 16 | 10 08 | 11 01 |
| 30 | 05 02 | 05 30 | 05 54 | 08 26 | 09 24 | 10 22 | 11 19 |
| 35 | 04 56 | 05 26 | 05 51 | 08 29 | 09 30 | 10 30 | 11 30 |
| 40 | 04 48 | 05 20 | 05 48 | 08 31 | 09 35 | 10 39 | 11 42 |
| 45 | 04 38 | 05 14 | 05 44 | 08 34 | 09 42 | 10 50 | 11 56 |
| S 50 | 04 26 | 05 06 | 05 39 | 08 37 | 09 50 | 11 03 | 12 14 |
| 52 | 04 20 | 05 02 | 05 37 | 08 39 | 09 54 | 11 09 | 12 23 |
| 54 | 04 13 | 04 58 | 05 34 | 08 40 | 09 59 | 11 16 | 12 32 |
| 56 | 04 06 | 04 53 | 05 31 | 08 42 | 10 03 | 11 23 | 12 43 |
| 58 | 03 57 | 04 48 | 05 28 | 08 44 | 10 08 | 11 32 | 12 55 |
| S 60 | 03 46 | 04 41 | 05 25 | 08 47 | 10 14 | 11 42 | 13 10 |

### Sunset — Twilight — Moonset

| Lat. | Sunset | Civil | Naut. | Moonset 5 | 6 | 7 | 8 |
|---|---|---|---|---|---|---|---|
| ° | h m | h m | h m | h m | h m | h m | h m |
| N 72 | 17 14 | 18 22 | 19 41 | 22 12 | 24 27 | 00 27 | ▭ |
| N 70 | 17 20 | 18 21 | 19 33 | 22 01 | 24 02 | 00 02 | 02 24 |
| 68 | 17 25 | 18 21 | 19 26 | 21 52 | 23 43 | 25 43 | 01 43 |
| 66 | 17 30 | 18 21 | 19 21 | 21 44 | 23 28 | 25 15 | 01 15 |
| 64 | 17 34 | 18 21 | 19 16 | 21 38 | 23 15 | 24 54 | 00 54 |
| 62 | 17 37 | 18 21 | 19 12 | 21 33 | 23 05 | 24 38 | 00 38 |
| 60 | 17 40 | 18 21 | 19 10 | 21 29 | 22 56 | 24 24 | 00 24 |
| N 58 | 17 42 | 18 22 | 19 07 | 21 25 | 22 48 | 24 12 | 00 12 |
| 56 | 17 45 | 18 22 | 19 05 | 21 21 | 22 42 | 24 02 | 00 02 |
| 54 | 17 47 | 18 22 | 19 03 | 21 18 | 22 36 | 23 52 | 25 08 |
| 52 | 17 48 | 18 22 | 19 01 | 21 15 | 22 30 | 23 44 | 24 57 |
| 50 | 17 50 | 18 23 | 19 00 | 21 12 | 22 25 | 23 37 | 24 48 |
| 45 | 17 54 | 18 23 | 18 57 | 21 07 | 22 15 | 23 22 | 24 28 |
| N 40 | 17 57 | 18 24 | 18 56 | 21 02 | 22 06 | 23 09 | 24 12 |
| 35 | 18 00 | 18 25 | 18 55 | 20 58 | 21 59 | 22 59 | 23 58 |
| 30 | 18 02 | 18 26 | 18 54 | 20 54 | 21 52 | 22 49 | 23 46 |
| 20 | 18 07 | 18 29 | 18 54 | 20 48 | 21 41 | 22 33 | 23 26 |
| N 10 | 18 11 | 18 32 | 18 56 | 20 43 | 21 31 | 22 20 | 23 09 |
| 0 | 18 15 | 18 35 | 18 59 | 20 38 | 21 22 | 22 07 | 22 53 |
| S 10 | 18 18 | 18 40 | 19 04 | 20 33 | 21 13 | 21 54 | 22 36 |
| 20 | 18 23 | 18 45 | 19 11 | 20 28 | 21 03 | 21 40 | 22 19 |
| 30 | 18 28 | 18 52 | 19 20 | 20 22 | 20 52 | 21 24 | 21 59 |
| 35 | 18 31 | 18 56 | 19 26 | 20 18 | 20 46 | 21 15 | 21 48 |
| 40 | 18 34 | 19 01 | 19 34 | 20 14 | 20 39 | 21 05 | 21 35 |
| 45 | 18 38 | 19 08 | 19 43 | 20 10 | 20 30 | 20 53 | 21 19 |
| S 50 | 18 43 | 19 15 | 19 55 | 20 04 | 20 20 | 20 38 | 21 00 |
| 52 | 18 45 | 19 19 | 20 01 | 20 02 | 20 16 | 20 32 | 20 51 |
| 54 | 18 47 | 19 23 | 20 08 | 19 59 | 20 11 | 20 24 | 20 41 |
| 56 | 18 50 | 19 28 | 20 15 | 19 56 | 20 05 | 20 16 | 20 30 |
| 58 | 18 53 | 19 33 | 20 24 | 19 53 | 19 59 | 20 06 | 20 17 |
| S 60 | 18 56 | 19 39 | 20 34 | 19 49 | 19 52 | 19 56 | 20 02 |

### SUN — MOON

| Day | Eqn. of Time 00h | 12h | Mer. Pass. | Mer. Pass. Upper | Lower | Age | Phase |
|---|---|---|---|---|---|---|---|
| d | m s | m s | h m | h m | h m | d | % |
| 5 | 11 35 | 11 28 | 12 11 | 14 27 | 02 05 | 03 | 9 |
| 6 | 11 21 | 11 14 | 12 11 | 15 11 | 02 49 | 04 | 15 |
| 7 | 11 07 | 11 00 | 12 11 | 15 56 | 03 33 | 05 | 23 |

| UT | ARIES | VENUS −4·6 | | MARS +1·2 | | JUPITER −2·0 | | SATURN +0·7 | | STARS | | |
|---|---|---|---|---|---|---|---|---|---|---|---|---|
| | GHA | GHA | Dec | GHA | Dec | GHA | Dec | GHA | Dec | Name | SHA | Dec |
| d h | ° ′ | ° ′ | ° ′ | ° ′ | ° ′ | ° ′ | ° ′ | ° ′ | ° ′ | | ° ′ | ° ′ |
| 8 00 | 165 40.8 | 222 42.4 | S16 29.2 | 221 56.1 | S20 46.2 | 178 35.5 | S 6 35.8 | 203 23.0 | S15 47.6 | Acamar | 315 13.8 | S40 13.3 |
| 01 | 180 43.2 | 237 42.5 | 29.0 | 236 56.7 | 45.8 | 193 37.4 | 35.6 | 218 25.2 | 47.5 | Achernar | 335 22.4 | S57 07.8 |
| 02 | 195 45.7 | 252 42.7 | 28.8 | 251 57.2 | 45.4 | 208 39.3 | 35.4 | 233 27.4 | 47.4 | Acrux | 173 02.0 | S63 13.2 |
| 03 | 210 48.2 | 267 42.8 · · | 28.6 | 266 57.7 · · | 45.0 | 223 41.2 · · | 35.1 | 248 29.6 · · | 47.4 | Adhara | 255 07.5 | S29 00.4 |
| 04 | 225 50.6 | 282 42.9 | 28.4 | 281 58.2 | 44.6 | 238 43.1 | 34.9 | 263 31.8 | 47.3 | Aldebaran | 290 42.3 | N16 33.1 |
| 05 | 240 53.1 | 297 43.1 | 28.2 | 296 58.7 | 44.2 | 253 45.0 | 34.7 | 278 34.0 | 47.2 | | | |
| 06 | 255 55.5 | 312 43.2 | S16 28.0 | 311 59.2 | S20 43.9 | 268 46.9 | S 6 34.4 | 293 36.2 | S15 47.1 | Alioth | 166 14.5 | N55 50.3 |
| 07 | 270 58.0 | 327 43.4 | 27.8 | 326 59.7 | 43.5 | 283 48.8 | 34.2 | 308 38.4 | 47.0 | Alkaid | 152 53.5 | N49 12.0 |
| 08 | 286 00.5 | 342 43.5 | 27.6 | 342 00.2 | 43.1 | 298 50.7 | 34.0 | 323 40.5 | 46.9 | Alnair | 27 36.3 | S46 51.3 |
| 09 | 301 02.9 | 357 43.6 · · | 27.4 | 357 00.7 · · | 42.7 | 313 52.6 · · | 33.7 | 338 42.7 · · | 46.9 | Alnilam | 275 40.1 | S 1 11.4 |
| 10 | 316 05.4 | 12 43.8 | 27.2 | 12 01.2 | 42.3 | 328 54.5 | 33.5 | 353 44.9 | 46.8 | Alphard | 217 49.8 | S 8 45.4 |
| 11 | 331 07.9 | 27 43.9 | 27.0 | 27 01.7 | 41.9 | 343 56.4 | 33.3 | 8 47.1 | 46.7 | | | |
| 12 | 346 10.3 | 42 44.1 | S16 26.8 | 42 02.3 | S20 41.5 | 358 58.3 | S 6 33.0 | 23 49.3 | S15 46.6 | Alphecca | 126 05.6 | N26 38.2 |
| 13 | 1 12.8 | 57 44.2 | 26.5 | 57 02.8 | 41.2 | 14 00.2 | 32.8 | 38 51.5 | 46.5 | Alpheratz | 357 37.5 | N29 12.6 |
| 14 | 16 15.3 | 72 44.3 | 26.3 | 72 03.3 | 40.8 | 29 02.2 | 32.6 | 53 53.7 | 46.4 | Altair | 62 02.4 | N 8 55.4 |
| 15 | 31 17.7 | 87 44.5 · · | 26.1 | 87 03.8 · · | 40.4 | 44 04.1 · · | 32.3 | 68 55.9 · · | 46.4 | Ankaa | 353 09.9 | S42 11.4 |
| 16 | 46 20.2 | 102 44.6 | 25.9 | 102 04.3 | 40.0 | 59 06.0 | 32.1 | 83 58.1 | 46.3 | Antares | 112 18.6 | S26 28.8 |
| 17 | 61 22.6 | 117 44.7 | 25.7 | 117 04.8 | 39.6 | 74 07.9 | 31.9 | 99 00.3 | 46.2 | | | |
| 18 | 76 25.1 | 132 44.8 | S16 25.5 | 132 05.3 | S20 39.2 | 89 09.8 | S 6 31.6 | 114 02.4 | S15 46.1 | Arcturus | 145 49.8 | N19 03.9 |
| 19 | 91 27.6 | 147 45.0 | 25.3 | 147 05.8 | 38.8 | 104 11.7 | 31.4 | 129 04.6 | 46.0 | Atria | 107 14.9 | S69 03.7 |
| 20 | 106 30.0 | 162 45.1 | 25.0 | 162 06.3 | 38.4 | 119 13.6 | 31.2 | 144 06.8 | 46.0 | Avior | 234 15.2 | S59 35.0 |
| 21 | 121 32.5 | 177 45.2 · · | 24.8 | 177 06.9 · · | 38.0 | 134 15.5 · · | 30.9 | 159 09.0 · · | 45.9 | Bellatrix | 278 25.4 | N 6 22.1 |
| 22 | 136 35.0 | 192 45.3 | 24.6 | 192 07.4 | 37.7 | 149 17.4 | 30.7 | 174 11.2 | 45.8 | Betelgeuse | 270 54.5 | N 7 24.6 |
| 23 | 151 37.4 | 207 45.5 | 24.4 | 207 07.9 | 37.3 | 164 19.3 | 30.5 | 189 13.4 | 45.7 | | | |
| 9 00 | 166 39.9 | 222 45.6 | S16 24.2 | 222 08.4 | S20 36.9 | 179 21.2 | S 6 30.3 | 204 15.6 | S15 45.6 | Canopus | 263 53.3 | S52 42.7 |
| 01 | 181 42.4 | 237 45.7 | 23.9 | 237 08.9 | 36.5 | 194 23.1 | 30.0 | 219 17.8 | 45.5 | Capella | 280 25.3 | N46 01.3 |
| 02 | 196 44.8 | 252 45.8 | 23.7 | 252 09.4 | 36.1 | 209 25.0 | 29.8 | 234 20.0 | 45.5 | Deneb | 49 27.7 | N45 21.3 |
| 03 | 211 47.3 | 267 46.0 · · | 23.5 | 267 09.9 · · | 35.7 | 224 26.9 · · | 29.6 | 249 22.2 · · | 45.4 | Denebola | 182 37.0 | N14 26.8 |
| 04 | 226 49.8 | 282 46.1 | 23.3 | 282 10.4 | 35.3 | 239 28.8 | 29.3 | 264 24.4 | 45.3 | Diphda | 348 49.9 | S17 52.1 |
| 05 | 241 52.2 | 297 46.2 | 23.0 | 297 10.9 | 34.9 | 254 30.7 | 29.1 | 279 26.5 | 45.2 | | | |
| 06 | 256 54.7 | 312 46.3 | S16 22.8 | 312 11.5 | S20 34.5 | 269 32.6 | S 6 28.9 | 294 28.7 | S15 45.1 | Dubhe | 193 43.2 | N61 37.9 |
| 07 | 271 57.1 | 327 46.4 | 22.6 | 327 12.0 | 34.1 | 284 34.5 | 28.6 | 309 30.9 | 45.0 | Elnath | 278 04.8 | N28 37.6 |
| 08 | 286 59.6 | 342 46.5 | 22.4 | 342 12.5 | 33.7 | 299 36.4 | 28.4 | 324 33.1 | 45.0 | Eltanin | 90 43.4 | N51 28.8 |
| 09 | 302 02.1 | 357 46.7 · · | 22.1 | 357 13.0 · · | 33.3 | 314 38.3 · · | 28.2 | 339 35.3 · · | 44.9 | Enif | 33 41.4 | N 9 58.4 |
| 10 | 317 04.5 | 12 46.8 | 21.9 | 12 13.5 | 32.9 | 329 40.2 | 27.9 | 354 37.5 | 44.8 | Fomalhaut | 15 17.5 | S29 30.5 |
| 11 | 332 07.0 | 27 46.9 | 21.7 | 27 14.0 | 32.5 | 344 42.1 | 27.7 | 9 39.7 | 44.7 | | | |
| 12 | 347 09.5 | 42 47.0 | S16 21.4 | 42 14.5 | S20 32.2 | 359 44.0 | S 6 27.5 | 24 41.9 | S15 44.6 | Gacrux | 171 53.7 | S57 14.1 |
| 13 | 2 11.9 | 57 47.1 | 21.2 | 57 15.1 | 31.8 | 14 45.9 | 27.2 | 39 44.1 | 44.5 | Gienah | 175 45.7 | S17 39.9 |
| 14 | 17 14.4 | 72 47.2 | 21.0 | 72 15.6 | 31.4 | 29 47.8 | 27.0 | 54 46.3 | 44.5 | Hadar | 148 38.8 | S60 28.6 |
| 15 | 32 16.9 | 87 47.3 · · | 20.8 | 87 16.1 · · | 31.0 | 44 49.7 · · | 26.8 | 69 48.5 · · | 44.4 | Hamal | 327 54.1 | N23 33.9 |
| 16 | 47 19.3 | 102 47.4 | 20.5 | 102 16.6 | 30.6 | 59 51.6 | 26.5 | 84 50.7 | 44.3 | Kaus Aust. | 83 35.7 | S34 22.4 |
| 17 | 62 21.8 | 117 47.5 | 20.3 | 117 17.1 | 30.2 | 74 53.5 | 26.3 | 99 52.8 | 44.2 | | | |
| 18 | 77 24.3 | 132 47.7 | S16 20.0 | 132 17.6 | S20 29.8 | 89 55.4 | S 6 26.1 | 114 55.0 | S15 44.1 | Kochab | 137 19.1 | N74 03.6 |
| 19 | 92 26.7 | 147 47.8 | 19.8 | 147 18.1 | 29.4 | 104 57.3 | 25.8 | 129 57.2 | 44.1 | Markab | 13 32.5 | N15 19.3 |
| 20 | 107 29.2 | 162 47.9 | 19.6 | 162 18.6 | 29.0 | 119 59.2 | 25.6 | 144 59.4 | 44.0 | Menkar | 314 08.8 | N 4 10.4 |
| 21 | 122 31.6 | 177 48.0 · · | 19.3 | 177 19.2 · · | 28.6 | 135 01.1 · · | 25.4 | 160 01.6 · · | 43.9 | Menkent | 148 00.1 | S36 28.6 |
| 22 | 137 34.1 | 192 48.1 | 19.1 | 192 19.7 | 28.2 | 150 03.0 | 25.1 | 175 03.8 | 43.8 | Miaplacidus | 221 37.9 | S69 48.6 |
| 23 | 152 36.6 | 207 48.2 | 18.9 | 207 20.2 | 27.8 | 165 04.9 | 24.9 | 190 06.0 | 43.7 | | | |
| 10 00 | 167 39.0 | 222 48.3 | S16 18.6 | 222 20.7 | S20 27.4 | 180 06.8 | S 6 24.7 | 205 08.2 | S15 43.6 | Mirfak | 308 31.8 | N49 56.4 |
| 01 | 182 41.5 | 237 48.4 | 18.4 | 237 21.2 | 27.0 | 195 08.7 | 24.4 | 220 10.4 | 43.6 | Nunki | 75 50.8 | S26 16.1 |
| 02 | 197 44.0 | 252 48.5 | 18.1 | 252 21.7 | 26.6 | 210 10.6 | 24.2 | 235 12.6 | 43.5 | Peacock | 53 09.8 | S56 39.7 |
| 03 | 212 46.4 | 267 48.6 · · | 17.9 | 267 22.2 · · | 26.2 | 225 12.6 · · | 24.0 | 250 14.8 · · | 43.4 | Pollux | 243 19.9 | N27 58.4 |
| 04 | 227 48.9 | 282 48.7 | 17.7 | 282 22.8 | 25.8 | 240 14.5 | 23.7 | 265 17.0 | 43.3 | Procyon | 244 53.1 | N 5 10.0 |
| 05 | 242 51.4 | 297 48.8 | 17.4 | 297 23.3 | 25.4 | 255 16.4 | 23.5 | 280 19.2 | 43.2 | | | |
| 06 | 257 53.8 | 312 48.9 | S16 17.2 | 312 23.8 | S20 25.0 | 270 18.3 | S 6 23.3 | 295 21.3 | S15 43.2 | Rasalhague | 96 00.8 | N12 32.4 |
| 07 | 272 56.3 | 327 49.0 | 16.9 | 327 24.3 | 24.6 | 285 20.2 | 23.0 | 310 23.5 | 43.1 | Regulus | 207 36.6 | N11 51.5 |
| 08 | 287 58.7 | 342 49.0 | 16.7 | 342 24.8 | 24.2 | 300 22.1 | 22.8 | 325 25.7 | 43.0 | Rigel | 281 06.1 | S 8 10.8 |
| 09 | 303 01.2 | 357 49.1 · · | 16.4 | 357 25.3 · · | 23.8 | 315 24.0 · · | 22.6 | 340 27.9 · · | 42.9 | Rigil Kent. | 139 43.1 | S60 55.3 |
| 10 | 318 03.7 | 12 49.2 | 16.2 | 12 25.9 | 23.4 | 330 25.9 | 22.3 | 355 30.1 | 42.8 | Sabik | 102 05.5 | S15 45.1 |
| 11 | 333 06.1 | 27 49.3 | 15.9 | 27 26.4 | 23.0 | 345 27.8 | 22.1 | 10 32.3 | 42.7 | | | |
| 12 | 348 08.6 | 42 49.4 | S16 15.7 | 42 26.9 | S20 22.6 | 0 29.7 | S 6 21.9 | 25 34.5 | S15 42.7 | Schedar | 349 34.2 | N56 39.5 |
| 13 | 3 11.1 | 57 49.5 | 15.4 | 57 27.4 | 22.2 | 15 31.6 | 21.6 | 40 36.7 | 42.6 | Shaula | 96 13.6 | S37 07.1 |
| 14 | 18 13.5 | 72 49.6 | 15.2 | 72 27.9 | 21.8 | 30 33.5 | 21.4 | 55 38.9 | 42.5 | Sirius | 258 28.2 | S16 45.0 |
| 15 | 33 16.0 | 87 49.7 · · | 14.9 | 87 28.4 · · | 21.3 | 45 35.4 · · | 21.2 | 70 41.1 · · | 42.5 | Spica | 158 24.5 | S11 16.6 |
| 16 | 48 18.5 | 102 49.8 | 14.7 | 102 29.0 | 20.9 | 60 37.3 | 20.9 | 85 43.3 | 42.4 | Suhail | 222 47.6 | S43 31.5 |
| 17 | 63 20.9 | 117 49.9 | 14.4 | 117 29.5 | 20.5 | 75 39.2 | 20.7 | 100 45.5 | 42.2 | | | |
| 18 | 78 23.4 | 132 49.9 | S16 14.2 | 132 30.0 | S20 20.1 | 90 41.1 | S 6 20.5 | 115 47.7 | S15 42.2 | Vega | 80 34.9 | N38 47.9 |
| 19 | 93 25.9 | 147 50.0 | 13.9 | 147 30.5 | 19.7 | 105 43.0 | 20.2 | 130 49.9 | 42.1 | Zuben'ubi | 136 58.4 | S16 08.0 |
| 20 | 108 28.3 | 162 50.1 | 13.7 | 162 31.0 | 19.3 | 120 44.9 | 20.0 | 145 52.1 | 42.0 | | SHA | Mer. Pass. |
| 21 | 123 30.8 | 177 50.2 · · | 13.4 | 177 31.5 · · | 18.9 | 135 46.8 · · | 19.8 | 160 54.3 · · | 41.9 | | ° ′ | h m |
| 22 | 138 33.2 | 192 50.3 | 13.2 | 192 32.1 | 18.5 | 150 48.7 | 19.5 | 175 56.4 | 41.8 | Venus | 56 05.7 | 9 09 |
| 23 | 153 35.7 | 207 50.4 | 12.9 | 207 32.6 | 18.1 | 165 50.6 | 19.3 | 190 58.6 | 41.8 | Mars | 55 28.5 | 9 11 |
| | h m | | | | | | | | | Jupiter | 12 41.3 | 12 01 |
| Mer. Pass. 12 51.2 | | v 0.1 | d 0.2 | v 0.5 | d 0.4 | v 1.9 | d 0.2 | v 2.2 | d 0.1 | Saturn | 37 35.7 | 10 21 |

| UT | SUN GHA | SUN Dec | MOON GHA | v | Dec | d | HP |
|---|---|---|---|---|---|---|---|
| d h | ° ′ | ° ′ | ° ′ | ′ | ° ′ | ′ | ′ |
| 8 00 | 177 16.8 | S 4 58.9 | 117 23.1 | 13.5 | N17 32.8 | 10.6 | 55.0 |
| 01 | 192 16.9 | 57.9 | 131 55.6 | 13.5 | 17 43.4 | 10.5 | 55.0 |
| 02 | 207 17.1 | 57.0 | 146 28.1 | 13.4 | 17 53.9 | 10.4 | 55.0 |
| 03 | 222 17.2 .. | 56.0 | 161 00.5 | 13.4 | 18 04.3 | 10.3 | 54.9 |
| 04 | 237 17.4 | 55.0 | 175 32.9 | 13.4 | 18 14.6 | 10.3 | 54.9 |
| 05 | 252 17.5 | 54.0 | 190 05.3 | 13.3 | 18 24.9 | 10.1 | 54.9 |
| 06 | 267 17.7 | S 4 53.1 | 204 37.6 | 13.3 | N18 35.0 | 10.1 | 54.9 |
| 07 | 282 17.8 | 52.1 | 219 09.9 | 13.2 | 18 45.1 | 10.0 | 54.9 |
| T 08 | 297 18.0 | 51.1 | 233 42.1 | 13.2 | 18 55.1 | 9.9 | 54.8 |
| U 09 | 312 18.2 .. | 50.1 | 248 14.3 | 13.2 | 19 05.0 | 9.8 | 54.8 |
| E 10 | 327 18.3 | 49.2 | 262 46.5 | 13.1 | 19 14.8 | 9.7 | 54.8 |
| S 11 | 342 18.5 | 48.2 | 277 18.6 | 13.1 | 19 24.5 | 9.6 | 54.8 |
| D 12 | 357 18.6 | S 4 47.2 | 291 50.7 | 13.0 | N19 34.1 | 9.6 | 54.8 |
| A 13 | 12 18.8 | 46.2 | 306 22.7 | 13.1 | 19 43.7 | 9.4 | 54.7 |
| Y 14 | 27 18.9 | 45.2 | 320 54.8 | 12.9 | 19 53.1 | 9.3 | 54.7 |
| 15 | 42 19.1 .. | 44.3 | 335 26.7 | 13.0 | 20 02.4 | 9.3 | 54.7 |
| 16 | 57 19.2 | 43.3 | 349 58.7 | 12.9 | 20 11.7 | 9.2 | 54.7 |
| 17 | 72 19.4 | 42.3 | 4 30.6 | 12.8 | 20 20.9 | 9.0 | 54.7 |
| 18 | 87 19.5 | S 4 41.3 | 19 02.4 | 12.8 | N20 29.9 | 9.0 | 54.7 |
| 19 | 102 19.7 | 40.4 | 33 34.2 | 12.8 | 20 38.9 | 8.9 | 54.6 |
| 20 | 117 19.8 | 39.4 | 48 06.0 | 12.7 | 20 47.8 | 8.7 | 54.6 |
| 21 | 132 20.0 .. | 38.4 | 62 37.7 | 12.7 | 20 56.5 | 8.7 | 54.6 |
| 22 | 147 20.2 | 37.4 | 77 09.4 | 12.6 | 21 05.2 | 8.6 | 54.6 |
| 23 | 162 20.3 | 36.5 | 91 41.0 | 12.7 | 21 13.8 | 8.5 | 54.6 |
| 9 00 | 177 20.5 | S 4 35.5 | 106 12.7 | 12.5 | N21 22.3 | 8.4 | 54.6 |
| 01 | 192 20.6 | 34.5 | 120 44.2 | 12.5 | 21 30.7 | 8.3 | 54.6 |
| 02 | 207 20.8 | 33.5 | 135 15.7 | 12.5 | 21 39.0 | 8.2 | 54.5 |
| 03 | 222 20.9 .. | 32.5 | 149 47.2 | 12.4 | 21 47.2 | 8.0 | 54.5 |
| 04 | 237 21.1 | 31.6 | 164 18.6 | 12.4 | 21 55.2 | 8.0 | 54.5 |
| 05 | 252 21.2 | 30.6 | 178 50.0 | 12.4 | 22 03.2 | 7.9 | 54.5 |
| 06 | 267 21.4 | S 4 29.6 | 193 21.4 | 12.3 | N22 11.1 | 7.8 | 54.5 |
| W 07 | 282 21.6 | 28.6 | 207 52.7 | 12.3 | 22 18.9 | 7.7 | 54.5 |
| E 08 | 297 21.7 | 27.7 | 222 24.0 | 12.2 | 22 26.6 | 7.5 | 54.5 |
| D 09 | 312 21.9 .. | 26.7 | 236 55.2 | 12.2 | 22 34.1 | 7.5 | 54.5 |
| N 10 | 327 22.0 | 25.7 | 251 26.4 | 12.1 | 22 41.6 | 7.4 | 54.4 |
| E 11 | 342 22.2 | 24.7 | 265 57.5 | 12.1 | 22 49.0 | 7.2 | 54.4 |
| S 12 | 357 22.3 | S 4 23.7 | 280 28.6 | 12.1 | N22 56.2 | 7.2 | 54.4 |
| D 13 | 12 22.5 | 22.8 | 294 59.7 | 12.0 | 23 03.4 | 7.0 | 54.4 |
| A 14 | 27 22.7 | 21.8 | 309 30.7 | 11.9 | 23 10.4 | 7.0 | 54.4 |
| Y 15 | 42 22.8 .. | 20.8 | 324 01.6 | 12.0 | 23 17.4 | 6.8 | 54.4 |
| 16 | 57 23.0 | 19.8 | 338 32.6 | 11.9 | 23 24.2 | 6.8 | 54.4 |
| 17 | 72 23.1 | 18.8 | 353 03.5 | 11.8 | 23 31.0 | 6.6 | 54.4 |
| 18 | 87 23.3 | S 4 17.9 | 7 34.3 | 11.8 | N23 37.6 | 6.5 | 54.4 |
| 19 | 102 23.4 | 16.9 | 22 05.1 | 11.8 | 23 44.1 | 6.4 | 54.4 |
| 20 | 117 23.6 | 15.9 | 36 35.9 | 11.7 | 23 50.5 | 6.3 | 54.4 |
| 21 | 132 23.8 .. | 14.9 | 51 06.6 | 11.7 | 23 56.8 | 6.1 | 54.4 |
| 22 | 147 23.9 | 13.9 | 65 37.3 | 11.6 | 24 02.9 | 6.1 | 54.3 |
| 23 | 162 24.1 | 13.0 | 80 07.9 | 11.6 | 24 09.0 | 6.0 | 54.3 |
| 10 00 | 177 24.2 | S 4 12.0 | 94 38.5 | 11.5 | N24 15.0 | 5.8 | 54.3 |
| 01 | 192 24.4 | 11.0 | 109 09.0 | 11.5 | 24 20.8 | 5.7 | 54.3 |
| 02 | 207 24.6 | 10.0 | 123 39.5 | 11.5 | 24 26.5 | 5.7 | 54.3 |
| 03 | 222 24.7 .. | 09.1 | 138 10.0 | 11.5 | 24 32.2 | 5.5 | 54.3 |
| 04 | 237 24.9 | 08.1 | 152 40.5 | 11.4 | 24 37.7 | 5.3 | 54.3 |
| 05 | 252 25.0 | 07.1 | 167 10.9 | 11.3 | 24 43.0 | 5.3 | 54.3 |
| 06 | 267 25.2 | S 4 06.1 | 181 41.2 | 11.3 | N24 48.3 | 5.2 | 54.3 |
| 07 | 282 25.4 | 05.1 | 196 11.5 | 11.3 | 24 53.5 | 5.0 | 54.3 |
| T 08 | 297 25.5 | 04.2 | 210 41.8 | 11.2 | 24 58.5 | 4.9 | 54.3 |
| H 09 | 312 25.7 .. | 03.2 | 225 12.0 | 11.3 | 25 03.4 | 4.8 | 54.3 |
| U 10 | 327 25.8 | 02.2 | 239 42.3 | 11.1 | 25 08.2 | 4.7 | 54.3 |
| R 11 | 342 26.0 | 01.2 | 254 12.4 | 11.1 | 25 12.9 | 4.6 | 54.3 |
| S 12 | 357 26.2 | S 4 00.2 | 268 42.5 | 11.1 | N25 17.5 | 4.5 | 54.3 |
| D 13 | 12 26.3 | 3 59.2 | 283 12.6 | 11.1 | 25 22.0 | 4.3 | 54.3 |
| A 14 | 27 26.5 | 58.3 | 297 42.7 | 11.0 | 25 26.3 | 4.2 | 54.3 |
| Y 15 | 42 26.6 .. | 57.3 | 312 12.7 | 11.0 | 25 30.5 | 4.1 | 54.2 |
| 16 | 57 26.8 | 56.3 | 326 42.7 | 11.0 | 25 34.6 | 4.0 | 54.2 |
| 17 | 72 27.0 | 55.3 | 341 12.7 | 10.9 | 25 38.6 | 3.9 | 54.2 |
| 18 | 87 27.1 | S 3 54.3 | 355 42.6 | 10.9 | N25 42.5 | 3.7 | 54.2 |
| 19 | 102 27.3 | 53.4 | 10 12.5 | 10.8 | 25 46.2 | 3.6 | 54.2 |
| 20 | 117 27.4 | 52.4 | 24 42.3 | 10.8 | 25 49.8 | 3.5 | 54.2 |
| 21 | 132 27.6 .. | 51.4 | 39 12.1 | 10.8 | 25 53.3 | 3.4 | 54.2 |
| 22 | 147 27.8 | 50.4 | 53 41.9 | 10.8 | 25 56.7 | 3.2 | 54.2 |
| 23 | 162 27.9 | 49.4 | 68 11.7 | 10.7 | N25 59.9 | 3.2 | 54.2 |
| SD | 16.1 | d 1.0 | SD 14.9 | | 14.8 | | 14.8 |

| Lat. | Naut. | Civil | Sunrise | Moonrise 8 | 9 | 10 | 11 |
|---|---|---|---|---|---|---|---|
| ° | h m | h m | h m | h m | h m | h m | h m |
| N 72 | 04 28 | 05 48 | 06 55 | □ | □ | □ | □ |
| N 70 | 04 38 | 05 50 | 06 50 | 05 55 | □ | □ | □ |
| 68 | 04 46 | 05 51 | 06 46 | 06 37 | 05 13 | □ | □ |
| 66 | 04 52 | 05 52 | 06 43 | 07 06 | 06 43 | □ | □ |
| 64 | 04 57 | 05 53 | 06 40 | 07 28 | 07 21 | 07 10 | □ |
| 62 | 05 02 | 05 53 | 06 37 | 07 46 | 07 48 | 07 54 | 08 12 |
| 60 | 05 05 | 05 54 | 06 35 | 08 01 | 08 09 | 08 24 | 08 51 |
| N 58 | 05 09 | 05 54 | 06 33 | 08 13 | 08 26 | 08 46 | 09 18 |
| 56 | 05 11 | 05 54 | 06 31 | 08 24 | 08 41 | 09 05 | 09 40 |
| 54 | 05 14 | 05 54 | 06 30 | 08 34 | 08 53 | 09 20 | 09 57 |
| 52 | 05 16 | 05 55 | 06 28 | 08 42 | 09 05 | 09 34 | 10 12 |
| 50 | 05 17 | 05 55 | 06 27 | 08 50 | 09 15 | 09 46 | 10 26 |
| 45 | 05 21 | 05 55 | 06 24 | 09 07 | 09 35 | 10 10 | 10 52 |
| N 40 | 05 23 | 05 54 | 06 21 | 09 21 | 09 52 | 10 30 | 11 14 |
| 35 | 05 25 | 05 54 | 06 19 | 09 32 | 10 07 | 10 46 | 11 31 |
| 30 | 05 26 | 05 53 | 06 17 | 09 42 | 10 19 | 11 01 | 11 47 |
| 20 | 05 26 | 05 52 | 06 14 | 10 00 | 10 41 | 11 25 | 12 13 |
| N 10 | 05 25 | 05 49 | 06 10 | 10 16 | 11 00 | 11 46 | 12 35 |
| 0 | 05 22 | 05 47 | 06 07 | 10 30 | 11 17 | 12 06 | 12 56 |
| S 10 | 05 18 | 05 43 | 06 04 | 10 45 | 11 35 | 12 26 | 13 17 |
| 20 | 05 13 | 05 38 | 06 00 | 11 01 | 11 54 | 12 47 | 13 39 |
| 30 | 05 04 | 05 32 | 05 56 | 11 19 | 12 16 | 13 12 | 14 05 |
| 35 | 04 58 | 05 28 | 05 54 | 11 30 | 12 29 | 13 26 | 14 21 |
| 40 | 04 51 | 05 24 | 05 51 | 11 42 | 12 44 | 13 43 | 14 39 |
| 45 | 04 43 | 05 18 | 05 48 | 11 56 | 13 01 | 14 04 | 15 01 |
| S 50 | 04 32 | 05 11 | 05 44 | 12 14 | 13 24 | 14 29 | 15 28 |
| 52 | 04 26 | 05 08 | 05 42 | 12 23 | 13 34 | 14 42 | 15 41 |
| 54 | 04 20 | 05 04 | 05 40 | 12 32 | 13 47 | 14 56 | 15 57 |
| 56 | 04 13 | 05 00 | 05 38 | 12 43 | 14 00 | 15 13 | 16 15 |
| 58 | 04 05 | 04 55 | 05 35 | 12 55 | 14 17 | 15 33 | 16 38 |
| S 60 | 03 56 | 04 50 | 05 32 | 13 10 | 14 37 | 15 59 | 17 07 |

| Lat. | Sunset | Civil | Naut. | Moonset 8 | 9 | 10 | 11 |
|---|---|---|---|---|---|---|---|
| ° | h m | h m | h m | h m | h m | h m | h m |
| N 72 | 17 28 | 18 35 | 19 56 | □ | □ | □ | □ |
| N 70 | 17 33 | 18 34 | 19 46 | 02 24 | □ | □ | □ |
| 68 | 17 37 | 18 32 | 19 38 | 01 43 | 04 44 | □ | □ |
| 66 | 17 40 | 18 31 | 19 31 | 01 15 | 03 15 | □ | □ |
| 64 | 17 43 | 18 30 | 19 26 | 00 54 | 02 30 | 04 29 | □ |
| 62 | 17 45 | 18 29 | 19 21 | 00 38 | 02 12 | 03 45 | 05 11 |
| 60 | 17 47 | 18 29 | 19 17 | 00 24 | 01 51 | 03 16 | 04 32 |
| N 58 | 17 49 | 18 28 | 19 14 | 00 11 | 01 34 | 02 54 | 04 05 |
| 56 | 17 51 | 18 28 | 19 11 | 00 02 | 01 20 | 02 36 | 03 43 |
| 54 | 17 52 | 18 28 | 19 09 | 25 08 | 01 08 | 02 20 | 03 26 |
| 52 | 17 54 | 18 27 | 19 07 | 24 57 | 00 57 | 02 07 | 03 11 |
| 50 | 17 55 | 18 27 | 19 05 | 24 48 | 00 48 | 01 56 | 02 58 |
| 45 | 17 58 | 18 27 | 19 01 | 24 28 | 00 28 | 01 32 | 02 31 |
| N 40 | 18 00 | 18 27 | 18 59 | 24 12 | 00 12 | 01 13 | 02 10 |
| 35 | 18 02 | 18 28 | 18 57 | 23 58 | 24 12 | 00 57 | 01 53 |
| 30 | 18 04 | 18 28 | 18 56 | 23 46 | 24 43 | 00 43 | 01 38 |
| 20 | 18 08 | 18 30 | 18 55 | 23 26 | 24 19 | 00 19 | 01 12 |
| N 10 | 18 11 | 18 32 | 18 56 | 23 09 | 23 59 | 24 50 | 00 50 |
| 0 | 18 14 | 18 35 | 18 59 | 22 53 | 23 40 | 24 30 | 00 30 |
| S 10 | 18 18 | 18 38 | 19 02 | 22 36 | 23 22 | 24 09 | 00 09 |
| 20 | 18 20 | 18 42 | 19 08 | 22 19 | 23 02 | 23 47 | 24 37 |
| 30 | 18 24 | 18 48 | 19 16 | 21 59 | 22 38 | 23 22 | 24 11 |
| 35 | 18 27 | 18 52 | 19 22 | 21 48 | 22 25 | 23 07 | 23 55 |
| 40 | 18 29 | 18 57 | 19 29 | 21 35 | 22 09 | 22 50 | 23 37 |
| 45 | 18 32 | 19 02 | 19 37 | 21 19 | 21 51 | 22 29 | 23 15 |
| S 50 | 18 36 | 19 09 | 19 48 | 21 00 | 21 28 | 22 03 | 22 48 |
| 52 | 18 38 | 19 12 | 19 53 | 20 51 | 21 17 | 21 50 | 22 34 |
| 54 | 18 40 | 19 16 | 19 59 | 20 41 | 21 04 | 21 35 | 22 19 |
| 56 | 18 42 | 19 20 | 20 06 | 20 30 | 20 50 | 21 19 | 22 00 |
| 58 | 18 44 | 19 24 | 20 14 | 20 17 | 20 33 | 20 58 | 21 38 |
| S 60 | 18 47 | 19 30 | 20 23 | 20 02 | 20 13 | 20 32 | 21 09 |

| | SUN | | | MOON | | | |
|---|---|---|---|---|---|---|---|
| Day | Eqn. of Time 00h | 12h | Mer. Pass. | Mer. Pass. Upper | Lower | Age | Phase |
| d | m s | m s | h m | h m | h m | d | % |
| 8 | 10 53 | 10 46 | 12 11 | 16 41 | 04 18 | 06 | 32 |
| 9 | 10 38 | 10 31 | 12 11 | 17 29 | 05 05 | 07 | 41 |
| 10 | 10 23 | 10 16 | 12 10 | 18 18 | 05 53 | 08 | 51 |

| UT | ARIES GHA | VENUS −4.6 GHA | Dec | MARS +1.2 GHA | Dec | JUPITER −2.0 GHA | Dec | SATURN +0.7 GHA | Dec |
|---|---|---|---|---|---|---|---|---|---|
| **11 00** | 168 38.2 | 222 50.4 | S16 12.6 | 222 33.1 | S20 17.7 | 180 52.5 | S 6 19.1 | 206 00.8 | S15 41.7 |
| 01 | 183 40.6 | 237 50.5 | 12.4 | 237 33.6 | 17.3 | 195 54.4 | 18.8 | 221 03.0 | 41.6 |
| 02 | 198 43.1 | 252 50.6 | 12.1 | 252 34.1 | 16.9 | 210 56.3 | 18.6 | 236 05.2 | 41.5 |
| 03 | 213 45.6 | 267 50.7 .. | 11.9 | 267 34.6 .. | 16.5 | 225 58.2 .. | 18.4 | 251 07.4 .. | 41.4 |
| 04 | 228 48.0 | 282 50.7 | 11.6 | 282 35.2 | 16.1 | 241 00.1 | 18.1 | 266 09.6 | 41.3 |
| 05 | 243 50.5 | 297 50.8 | 11.3 | 297 35.7 | 15.6 | 256 02.0 | 17.9 | 281 11.8 | 41.3 |
| **F 06** | 258 53.0 | 312 50.9 | S16 11.1 | 312 36.2 | S20 15.2 | 271 03.9 | S 6 17.7 | 296 14.0 | S15 41.2 |
| R 07 | 273 55.4 | 327 51.0 | 10.8 | 327 36.7 | 14.8 | 286 05.8 | 17.4 | 311 16.2 | 41.1 |
| I 08 | 288 57.9 | 342 51.0 | 10.5 | 342 37.2 | 14.4 | 301 07.7 | 17.2 | 326 18.4 | 41.0 |
| D 09 | 304 00.4 | 357 51.1 .. | 10.3 | 357 37.8 .. | 14.0 | 316 09.6 .. | 17.0 | 341 20.6 .. | 40.9 |
| A 10 | 319 02.8 | 12 51.2 | 10.0 | 12 38.3 | 13.6 | 331 11.6 | 16.7 | 356 22.8 | 40.9 |
| Y 11 | 334 05.3 | 27 51.3 | 09.7 | 27 38.8 | 13.2 | 346 13.5 | 16.5 | 11 25.0 | 40.8 |
| 12 | 349 07.7 | 42 51.3 | S16 09.5 | 42 39.3 | S20 12.8 | 1 15.4 | S 6 16.3 | 26 27.2 | S15 40.7 |
| 13 | 4 10.2 | 57 51.4 | 09.2 | 57 39.8 | 12.4 | 16 17.3 | 16.0 | 41 29.4 | 40.6 |
| 14 | 19 12.7 | 72 51.5 | 08.9 | 72 40.4 | 11.9 | 31 19.2 | 15.8 | 56 31.6 | 40.5 |
| 15 | 34 15.1 | 87 51.5 .. | 08.7 | 87 40.9 .. | 11.5 | 46 21.1 .. | 15.6 | 71 33.8 .. | 40.5 |
| 16 | 49 17.6 | 102 51.6 | 08.4 | 102 41.4 | 11.1 | 61 23.0 | 15.3 | 86 35.9 | 40.4 |
| 17 | 64 20.1 | 117 51.7 | 08.1 | 117 41.9 | 10.7 | 76 24.9 | 15.1 | 101 38.1 | 40.3 |
| 18 | 79 22.5 | 132 51.7 | S16 07.9 | 132 42.4 | S20 10.3 | 91 26.8 | S 6 14.9 | 116 40.3 | S15 40.2 |
| 19 | 94 25.0 | 147 51.8 | 07.6 | 147 43.0 | 09.9 | 106 28.7 | 14.7 | 131 42.5 | 40.1 |
| 20 | 109 27.5 | 162 51.9 | 07.3 | 162 43.5 | 09.5 | 121 30.6 | 14.4 | 146 44.7 | 40.0 |
| 21 | 124 29.9 | 177 51.9 .. | 07.0 | 177 44.0 .. | 09.0 | 136 32.5 .. | 14.2 | 161 46.9 .. | 40.0 |
| 22 | 139 32.4 | 192 52.0 | 06.8 | 192 44.5 | 08.6 | 151 34.4 | 14.0 | 176 49.1 | 39.9 |
| 23 | 154 34.9 | 207 52.0 | 06.5 | 207 45.0 | 08.2 | 166 36.3 | 13.7 | 191 51.3 | 39.8 |
| **12 00** | 169 37.3 | 222 52.1 | S16 06.2 | 222 45.6 | S20 07.8 | 181 38.2 | S 6 13.5 | 206 53.5 | S15 39.7 |
| 01 | 184 39.8 | 237 52.2 | 05.9 | 237 46.1 | 07.4 | 196 40.1 | 13.3 | 221 55.7 | 39.6 |
| 02 | 199 42.2 | 252 52.2 | 05.6 | 252 46.6 | 07.0 | 211 42.0 | 13.0 | 236 57.9 | 39.6 |
| 03 | 214 44.7 | 267 52.3 .. | 05.4 | 267 47.1 .. | 06.5 | 226 43.9 .. | 12.8 | 252 00.1 .. | 39.5 |
| 04 | 229 47.2 | 282 52.3 | 05.1 | 282 47.6 | 06.1 | 241 45.8 | 12.6 | 267 02.3 | 39.4 |
| 05 | 244 49.6 | 297 52.4 | 04.8 | 297 48.2 | 05.7 | 256 47.7 | 12.3 | 282 04.5 | 39.3 |
| **S 06** | 259 52.1 | 312 52.4 | S16 04.5 | 312 48.7 | S20 05.3 | 271 49.6 | S 6 12.1 | 297 06.7 | S15 39.2 |
| A 07 | 274 54.6 | 327 52.5 | 04.2 | 327 49.2 | 04.9 | 286 51.5 | 11.9 | 312 08.9 | 39.1 |
| T 08 | 289 57.0 | 342 52.5 | 04.0 | 342 49.7 | 04.4 | 301 53.4 | 11.6 | 327 11.1 | 39.1 |
| U 09 | 304 59.5 | 357 52.6 .. | 03.7 | 357 50.3 .. | 04.0 | 316 55.3 .. | 11.4 | 342 13.3 .. | 39.0 |
| R 10 | 320 02.0 | 12 52.6 | 03.4 | 12 50.8 | 03.6 | 331 57.2 | 11.2 | 357 15.5 | 38.9 |
| D 11 | 335 04.4 | 27 52.7 | 03.1 | 27 51.3 | 03.2 | 346 59.1 | 10.9 | 12 17.7 | 38.8 |
| A 12 | 350 06.9 | 42 52.7 | S16 02.8 | 42 51.8 | S20 02.8 | 2 01.1 | S 6 10.7 | 27 19.9 | S15 38.7 |
| Y 13 | 5 09.3 | 57 52.8 | 02.5 | 57 52.3 | 02.3 | 17 03.0 | 10.5 | 42 22.1 | 38.7 |
| 14 | 20 11.8 | 72 52.8 | 02.2 | 72 52.9 | 01.9 | 32 04.9 | 10.2 | 57 24.3 | 38.6 |
| 15 | 35 14.3 | 87 52.9 .. | 02.0 | 87 53.4 .. | 01.5 | 47 06.8 .. | 10.0 | 72 26.5 .. | 38.5 |
| 16 | 50 16.7 | 102 52.9 | 01.7 | 102 53.9 | 01.1 | 62 08.7 | 09.8 | 87 28.7 | 38.4 |
| 17 | 65 19.2 | 117 53.0 | 01.4 | 117 54.4 | 00.7 | 77 10.6 | 09.5 | 102 30.9 | 38.3 |
| 18 | 80 21.7 | 132 53.0 | S16 01.1 | 132 55.0 | S20 00.2 | 92 12.5 | S 6 09.3 | 117 33.0 | S15 38.3 |
| 19 | 95 24.1 | 147 53.1 | 00.8 | 147 55.5 | 19 59.8 | 107 14.4 | 09.1 | 132 35.2 | 38.2 |
| 20 | 110 26.6 | 162 53.1 | 00.5 | 162 56.0 | 59.4 | 122 16.3 | 08.8 | 147 37.4 | 38.1 |
| 21 | 125 29.1 | 177 53.2 | 16 00.2 | 177 56.5 .. | 59.0 | 137 18.2 .. | 08.6 | 162 39.6 .. | 38.0 |
| 22 | 140 31.5 | 192 53.2 | 15 59.9 | 192 57.0 | 58.5 | 152 20.1 | 08.4 | 177 41.8 | 37.9 |
| 23 | 155 34.0 | 207 53.2 | 59.6 | 207 57.6 | 58.1 | 167 22.0 | 08.1 | 192 44.0 | 37.9 |
| **13 00** | 170 36.5 | 222 53.3 | S15 59.3 | 222 58.1 | S19 57.7 | 182 23.9 | S 6 07.9 | 207 46.2 | S15 37.8 |
| 01 | 185 38.9 | 237 53.3 | 59.0 | 237 58.6 | 57.3 | 197 25.8 | 07.7 | 222 48.4 | 37.7 |
| 02 | 200 41.4 | 252 53.4 | 58.7 | 252 59.1 | 56.8 | 212 27.7 | 07.4 | 237 50.6 | 37.6 |
| 03 | 215 43.8 | 267 53.4 .. | 58.4 | 267 59.7 .. | 56.4 | 227 29.6 .. | 07.2 | 252 52.8 .. | 37.5 |
| 04 | 230 46.3 | 282 53.5 | 58.1 | 283 00.2 | 56.0 | 242 31.5 | 07.0 | 267 55.0 | 37.4 |
| 05 | 245 48.8 | 297 53.5 | 57.8 | 298 00.7 | 55.6 | 257 33.4 | 06.7 | 282 57.2 | 37.4 |
| **S 06** | 260 51.2 | 312 53.5 | S15 57.5 | 313 01.2 | S19 55.1 | 272 35.3 | S 6 06.5 | 297 59.4 | S15 37.3 |
| U 07 | 275 53.7 | 327 53.6 | 57.2 | 328 01.8 | 54.7 | 287 37.2 | 06.3 | 313 01.6 | 37.2 |
| N 08 | 290 56.2 | 342 53.6 | 56.9 | 343 02.3 | 54.3 | 302 39.1 | 06.0 | 328 03.8 | 37.1 |
| D 09 | 305 58.6 | 357 53.6 .. | 56.6 | 358 02.8 .. | 53.9 | 317 41.0 .. | 05.8 | 343 06.0 .. | 37.0 |
| A 10 | 321 01.1 | 12 53.7 | 56.3 | 13 03.3 | 53.4 | 332 42.9 | 05.6 | 358 08.2 | 37.0 |
| Y 11 | 336 03.6 | 27 53.7 | 56.0 | 28 03.9 | 53.0 | 347 44.9 | 05.3 | 13 10.4 | 36.9 |
| 12 | 351 06.0 | 42 53.7 | S15 55.7 | 43 04.4 | S19 52.6 | 2 46.8 | S 6 05.1 | 28 12.6 | S15 36.8 |
| 13 | 6 08.5 | 57 53.8 | 55.4 | 58 04.9 | 52.1 | 17 48.7 | 04.9 | 43 14.8 | 36.7 |
| 14 | 21 11.0 | 72 53.8 | 55.1 | 73 05.4 | 51.7 | 32 50.6 | 04.6 | 58 17.0 | 36.6 |
| 15 | 36 13.4 | 87 53.8 .. | 54.8 | 88 06.0 .. | 51.3 | 47 52.5 .. | 04.4 | 73 19.2 .. | 36.6 |
| 16 | 51 15.9 | 102 53.8 | 54.5 | 103 06.5 | 50.8 | 62 54.4 | 04.2 | 88 21.4 | 36.5 |
| 17 | 66 18.3 | 117 53.9 | 54.1 | 118 07.0 | 50.4 | 77 56.3 | 03.9 | 103 23.6 | 36.4 |
| 18 | 81 20.8 | 132 53.9 | S15 53.8 | 133 07.6 | S19 50.0 | 92 58.2 | S 6 03.7 | 118 25.8 | S15 36.3 |
| 19 | 96 23.3 | 147 53.9 | 53.5 | 148 08.1 | 49.6 | 108 00.1 | 03.5 | 133 28.0 | 36.2 |
| 20 | 111 25.7 | 162 53.9 | 53.2 | 163 08.6 | 49.1 | 123 02.0 | 03.2 | 148 30.2 | 36.2 |
| 21 | 126 28.2 | 177 54.0 .. | 52.9 | 178 09.1 .. | 48.7 | 138 03.9 .. | 03.0 | 163 32.4 .. | 36.1 |
| 22 | 141 30.7 | 192 54.0 | 52.6 | 193 09.7 | 48.3 | 153 05.8 | 02.8 | 178 34.6 | 36.0 |
| 23 | 156 33.1 | 207 54.0 | 52.3 | 208 10.2 | 47.8 | 168 07.7 | 02.5 | 193 36.8 | 35.9 |
| Mer. Pass. 12 39.4 | | v 0.0 | d 0.3 | v 0.5 | d 0.4 | v 1.9 | d 0.2 | v 2.2 | d 0.1 |

**STARS**

| Name | SHA | Dec |
|---|---|---|
| Acamar | 315 13.8 | S40 13.3 |
| Achernar | 335 22.4 | S57 07.7 |
| Acrux | 173 01.9 | S63 13.2 |
| Adhara | 255 07.5 | S29 00.4 |
| Aldebaran | 290 42.4 | N16 33.1 |
| Alioth | 166 14.5 | N55 50.3 |
| Alkaid | 152 53.5 | N49 12.0 |
| Alnair | 27 36.3 | S46 51.3 |
| Alnilam | 275 40.1 | S 1 11.4 |
| Alphard | 217 49.8 | S 8 45.4 |
| Alphecca | 126 05.6 | N26 38.2 |
| Alpheratz | 357 37.5 | N29 12.6 |
| Altair | 62 02.4 | N 8 55.4 |
| Ankaa | 353 09.9 | S42 11.4 |
| Antares | 112 18.6 | S26 28.8 |
| Arcturus | 145 49.8 | N19 03.9 |
| Atria | 107 14.9 | S69 03.7 |
| Avior | 234 15.2 | S59 35.0 |
| Bellatrix | 278 25.4 | N 6 22.1 |
| Betelgeuse | 270 54.6 | N 7 24.6 |
| Canopus | 263 53.3 | S52 42.7 |
| Capella | 280 25.3 | N46 01.3 |
| Deneb | 49 27.7 | N45 21.3 |
| Denebola | 182 27.0 | N14 26.8 |
| Diphda | 348 49.9 | S17 52.1 |
| Dubhe | 193 43.2 | N61 37.9 |
| Elnath | 278 04.8 | N28 37.6 |
| Eltanin | 90 47.3 | N51 28.8 |
| Enif | 33 41.4 | N 9 58.4 |
| Fomalhaut | 15 17.4 | S29 30.5 |
| Gacrux | 171 53.7 | S57 14.1 |
| Gienah | 175 45.7 | S17 39.9 |
| Hadar | 148 38.8 | S60 28.6 |
| Hamal | 327 54.1 | N23 33.9 |
| Kaus Aust. | 83 35.7 | S34 22.4 |
| Kochab | 137 19.1 | N74 03.6 |
| Markab | 13 32.5 | N15 19.3 |
| Menkar | 314 08.8 | N 4 10.4 |
| Menkent | 148 00.1 | S36 28.5 |
| Miaplacidus | 221 37.9 | S69 48.6 |
| Mirfak | 308 31.8 | N49 56.4 |
| Nunki | 75 50.8 | S26 16.1 |
| Peacock | 53 09.8 | S56 39.7 |
| Pollux | 243 20.0 | N27 58.4 |
| Procyon | 244 53.1 | N 5 10.0 |
| Rasalhague | 96 00.7 | N12 32.4 |
| Regulus | 207 36.6 | N11 51.5 |
| Rigel | 281 06.1 | S 8 10.8 |
| Rigil Kent. | 139 43.0 | S60 55.4 |
| Sabik | 102 05.4 | S15 45.1 |
| Schedar | 349 34.2 | N56 39.5 |
| Shaula | 96 13.5 | S37 07.1 |
| Sirius | 258 28.2 | S16 45.0 |
| Spica | 158 24.5 | S11 16.6 |
| Suhail | 222 47.6 | S43 31.5 |
| Vega | 80 34.9 | N38 47.9 |
| Zuben'ubi | 136 58.4 | S16 08.0 |

| | SHA | Mer. Pass. |
|---|---|---|
| | ° ′ | h m |
| Venus | 53 14.8 | 9 08 |
| Mars | 53 08.2 | 9 09 |
| Jupiter | 12 00.9 | 11 52 |
| Saturn | 37 16.2 | 10 11 |

| UT | SUN | | MOON | | | | | Lat. | Twilight | | Sunrise | Moonrise | | | |
|---|---|---|---|---|---|---|---|---|---|---|---|---|---|---|---|
| | GHA | Dec | GHA | v | Dec | d | HP | | Naut. | Civil | | 11 | 12 | 13 | 14 |
| d h | ° ′ | ° ′ | ° ′ | ′ | ° ′ | ′ | ′ | ° | h m | h m | h m | h m | h m | h m | h m |
| 11 00 | 177 28.1 | S 3 48.5 | 82 41.4 | 10.7 | N26 03.1 | 3.0 | 54.2 | N 72 | 04 11 | 05 33 | 06 40 | ▭ | ▭ | ▭ | ▭ |
| 01 | 192 28.3 | 47.5 | 97 11.1 | 10.7 | 26 06.1 | 2.8 | 54.2 | N 70 | 04 23 | 05 36 | 06 36 | ▭ | ▭ | ▭ | ▭ |
| 02 | 207 28.4 | 46.5 | 111 40.8 | 10.6 | 26 08.9 | 2.8 | 54.2 | 68 | 04 33 | 05 39 | 06 34 | ▭ | ▭ | ▭ | 10 30 |
| 03 | 222 28.6 | 45.5 | 126 10.4 | 10.7 | 26 11.7 | 2.6 | 54.2 | 66 | 04 40 | 05 41 | 06 31 | ▭ | ▭ | 09 20 | 11 21 |
| 04 | 237 28.8 | 44.5 | 140 40.1 | 10.6 | 26 14.3 | 2.5 | 54.2 | 64 | 04 47 | 05 42 | 06 29 | ▭ | 08 58 | 10 17 | 11 52 |
| 05 | 252 28.9 | 43.5 | 155 09.7 | 10.5 | 26 16.8 | 2.4 | 54.2 | 62 | 04 52 | 05 44 | 06 28 | 08 12 | 09 39 | 10 50 | 12 15 |
| 06 | 267 29.1 | S 3 42.6 | 169 39.2 | 10.6 | N26 19.2 | 2.3 | 54.2 | 60 | 04 56 | 05 45 | 06 26 | 08 51 | 09 39 | | |
| 07 | 282 29.2 | 41.6 | 184 08.8 | 10.5 | 26 21.5 | 2.1 | 54.2 | N 58 | 05 00 | 05 46 | 06 25 | 09 18 | 10 08 | 11 15 | 12 34 |
| 08 | 297 29.4 | 40.6 | 198 38.3 | 10.5 | 26 23.6 | 2.0 | 54.3 | 56 | 05 03 | 05 47 | 06 23 | 09 40 | 10 30 | 11 34 | 12 50 |
| F 09 | 312 29.6 | 39.6 | 213 07.8 | 10.4 | 26 25.6 | 1.9 | 54.3 | 54 | 05 06 | 05 47 | 06 22 | 09 57 | 10 47 | 11 50 | 13 03 |
| R 10 | 327 29.7 | 38.6 | 227 37.2 | 10.5 | 26 27.5 | 1.8 | 54.3 | 52 | 05 09 | 05 48 | 06 20 | 10 12 | 11 03 | 12 04 | 13 14 |
| I 11 | 342 29.9 | 37.7 | 242 06.7 | 10.4 | 26 29.3 | 1.6 | 54.3 | 50 | 05 11 | 05 48 | 06 20 | 10 26 | 11 16 | 12 16 | 13 25 |
| D 12 | 357 30.1 | S 3 36.7 | 256 36.1 | 10.4 | N26 30.9 | 1.5 | 54.3 | 45 | 05 15 | 05 49 | 06 18 | 10 52 | 11 43 | 12 42 | 13 46 |
| A 13 | 12 30.2 | 35.7 | 271 05.5 | 10.4 | 26 32.4 | 1.4 | 54.3 | N 40 | 05 18 | 05 50 | 06 17 | 11 14 | 12 05 | 13 02 | 14 04 |
| Y 14 | 27 30.4 | 34.7 | 285 34.9 | 10.3 | 26 33.8 | 1.2 | 54.3 | 35 | 05 20 | 05 50 | 06 15 | 11 31 | 12 22 | 13 18 | 14 18 |
| 15 | 42 30.6 | 33.7 | 300 04.2 | 10.4 | 26 35.0 | 1.1 | 54.3 | 30 | 05 22 | 05 50 | 06 14 | 11 47 | 12 38 | 13 33 | 14 31 |
| 16 | 57 30.7 | 32.7 | 314 33.6 | 10.3 | 26 36.1 | 1.0 | 54.3 | 20 | 05 24 | 05 49 | 06 11 | 12 13 | 13 04 | 13 57 | 14 52 |
| 17 | 72 30.9 | 31.8 | 329 02.9 | 10.3 | 26 37.1 | 0.9 | 54.3 | N 10 | 05 23 | 05 48 | 06 09 | 12 35 | 13 26 | 14 18 | 15 11 |
| | | | | | | | | 0 | 05 22 | 05 46 | 06 06 | 12 56 | 13 47 | 14 38 | 15 28 |
| 18 | 87 31.1 | S 3 30.8 | 343 32.2 | 10.3 | N26 38.0 | 0.7 | 54.3 | S 10 | 05 19 | 05 43 | 06 04 | 13 17 | 14 08 | 14 57 | 15 45 |
| 19 | 102 31.2 | 29.8 | 358 01.5 | 10.3 | 26 38.7 | 0.6 | 54.3 | 20 | 05 14 | 05 39 | 06 01 | 13 39 | 14 30 | 15 18 | 16 04 |
| 20 | 117 31.4 | 28.8 | 12 30.8 | 10.2 | 26 39.3 | 0.5 | 54.3 | 30 | 05 06 | 05 34 | 05 58 | 14 05 | 14 56 | 15 43 | 16 25 |
| 21 | 132 31.5 | 27.8 | 27 00.0 | 10.2 | 26 39.8 | 0.4 | 54.3 | 35 | 05 01 | 05 31 | 05 56 | 14 21 | 15 11 | 15 57 | 16 37 |
| 22 | 147 31.7 | 26.8 | 41 29.3 | 10.2 | 26 40.2 | 0.2 | 54.3 | 40 | 04 55 | 05 27 | 05 54 | 14 39 | 15 29 | 16 13 | 16 51 |
| 23 | 162 31.9 | 25.9 | 55 58.5 | 10.2 | 26 40.4 | 0.1 | 54.3 | 45 | 04 47 | 05 22 | 05 52 | 15 01 | 15 51 | 16 33 | 17 08 |
| 12 00 | 177 32.0 | S 3 24.9 | 70 27.7 | 10.3 | N26 40.5 | 0.0 | 54.3 | S 50 | 04 37 | 05 16 | 05 49 | 15 28 | 16 18 | 16 57 | 17 28 |
| 01 | 192 32.2 | 23.9 | 84 57.0 | 10.2 | 26 40.5 | 0.2 | 54.3 | 52 | 04 32 | 05 13 | 05 47 | 15 41 | 16 31 | 17 09 | 17 38 |
| 02 | 207 32.4 | 22.9 | 99 26.2 | 10.1 | 26 40.3 | 0.3 | 54.4 | 54 | 04 27 | 05 10 | 05 46 | 15 57 | 16 46 | 17 22 | 17 49 |
| 03 | 222 32.5 | 21.9 | 113 55.3 | 10.2 | 26 40.0 | 0.4 | 54.4 | 56 | 04 21 | 05 06 | 05 44 | 16 15 | 17 04 | 17 38 | 18 01 |
| 04 | 237 32.7 | 20.9 | 128 24.5 | 10.2 | 26 39.6 | 0.6 | 54.4 | 58 | 04 13 | 05 02 | 05 42 | 16 38 | 17 25 | 17 56 | 18 16 |
| 05 | 252 32.9 | 20.0 | 142 53.7 | 10.2 | 26 39.0 | 0.7 | 54.4 | S 60 | 04 05 | 04 58 | 05 40 | 17 07 | 17 53 | 18 19 | 18 32 |

| UT | SUN | | MOON | | | | | Lat. | Sunset | Twilight | | Moonset | | | |
|---|---|---|---|---|---|---|---|---|---|---|---|---|---|---|---|
| | | | | | | | | | | Civil | Naut. | 11 | 12 | 13 | 14 |
| 06 | 267 33.0 | S 3 19.0 | 157 22.9 | 10.1 | N26 38.3 | 0.8 | 54.4 | ° | h m | h m | h m | h m | h m | h m | h m |
| 07 | 282 33.2 | 18.0 | 171 52.0 | 10.2 | 26 37.5 | 0.9 | 54.4 | N 72 | 17 42 | 18 49 | 20 12 | ▭ | ▭ | ▭ | ▭ |
| 08 | 297 33.4 | 17.0 | 186 21.2 | 10.2 | 26 36.6 | 1.1 | 54.4 | N 70 | 17 45 | 18 46 | 19 59 | ▭ | ▭ | ▭ | ▭ |
| S 09 | 312 33.5 | 16.0 | 200 50.4 | 10.1 | 26 35.5 | 1.2 | 54.4 | 68 | 17 48 | 18 43 | 19 50 | ▭ | ▭ | ▭ | 08 11 |
| A 10 | 327 33.7 | 15.0 | 215 19.5 | 10.2 | 26 34.3 | 1.3 | 54.4 | 66 | 17 50 | 18 41 | 19 42 | ▭ | ▭ | 07 36 | 07 20 |
| T 11 | 342 33.9 | 14.1 | 229 48.7 | 10.1 | 26 33.0 | 1.5 | 54.4 | 64 | 17 52 | 18 39 | 19 35 | ▭ | ▭ | 07 36 | 07 20 |
| U 12 | 357 34.0 | S 3 13.1 | 244 17.8 | 10.2 | N26 31.5 | 1.6 | 54.4 | 62 | 17 53 | 18 37 | 19 30 | 05 11 | 06 11 | 06 58 | 06 48 |
| R 13 | 12 34.2 | 12.1 | 258 47.0 | 10.1 | 26 29.9 | 1.7 | 54.5 | 60 | 17 55 | 18 36 | 19 25 | 04 32 | 05 29 | 06 04 | 06 24 |
| D 14 | 27 34.4 | 11.1 | 273 16.1 | 10.2 | 26 28.2 | 1.8 | 54.5 | N 58 | 17 56 | 18 35 | 19 21 | 04 05 | 05 01 | 05 40 | 06 05 |
| A 15 | 42 34.6 | 10.1 | 287 45.3 | 10.1 | 26 26.4 | 2.0 | 54.5 | 56 | 17 57 | 18 34 | 19 18 | 03 43 | 04 39 | 05 20 | 05 49 |
| Y 16 | 57 34.7 | 09.1 | 302 14.4 | 10.2 | 26 24.4 | 2.1 | 54.5 | 54 | 17 58 | 18 33 | 19 15 | 03 26 | 04 21 | 05 04 | 05 35 |
| 17 | 72 34.9 | 08.1 | 316 43.6 | 10.1 | 26 22.3 | 2.3 | 54.5 | 52 | 17 59 | 18 33 | 19 12 | 03 11 | 04 06 | 04 49 | 05 23 |
| 18 | 87 35.1 | S 3 07.2 | 331 12.7 | 10.2 | N26 20.0 | 2.3 | 54.5 | 50 | 18 00 | 18 32 | 19 10 | 02 58 | 03 52 | 04 37 | 05 12 |
| 19 | 102 35.2 | 06.2 | 345 41.9 | 10.1 | 26 17.7 | 2.5 | 54.5 | 45 | 18 02 | 18 31 | 19 05 | 02 31 | 03 25 | 04 11 | 04 50 |
| 20 | 117 35.4 | 05.2 | 0 11.0 | 10.2 | 26 15.2 | 2.7 | 54.5 | N 40 | 18 04 | 18 31 | 19 02 | 02 10 | 03 04 | 03 51 | 04 32 |
| 21 | 132 35.6 | 04.2 | 14 40.2 | 10.2 | 26 12.5 | 2.7 | 54.6 | 35 | 18 05 | 18 30 | 19 00 | 01 53 | 02 46 | 03 34 | 04 16 |
| 22 | 147 35.7 | 03.2 | 29 09.4 | 10.2 | 26 09.8 | 2.9 | 54.6 | 30 | 18 06 | 18 30 | 18 58 | 01 38 | 02 30 | 03 19 | 04 03 |
| 23 | 162 35.9 | 02.2 | 43 38.6 | 10.2 | 26 06.9 | 3.0 | 54.6 | 20 | 18 09 | 18 31 | 18 56 | 01 12 | 02 04 | 02 54 | 03 40 |
| 13 00 | 177 36.1 | S 3 01.3 | 58 07.8 | 10.2 | N26 03.9 | 3.2 | 54.6 | N 10 | 18 11 | 18 32 | 18 56 | 00 50 | 01 42 | 02 32 | 03 21 |
| 01 | 192 36.2 | 3 00.3 | 72 37.0 | 10.2 | 26 00.7 | 3.2 | 54.6 | 0 | 18 13 | 18 34 | 18 58 | 00 30 | 01 20 | 02 12 | 03 02 |
| 02 | 207 36.4 | 2 59.3 | 87 06.2 | 10.2 | 25 57.5 | 3.4 | 54.6 | S 10 | 18 15 | 18 36 | 19 01 | 00 09 | 00 59 | 01 51 | 02 44 |
| 03 | 222 36.6 | 58.3 | 101 35.4 | 10.3 | 25 54.1 | 3.6 | 54.6 | 20 | 18 18 | 18 40 | 19 06 | 24 37 | 00 37 | 01 29 | 02 24 |
| 04 | 237 36.7 | 57.3 | 116 04.7 | 10.2 | 25 50.5 | 3.6 | 54.7 | 30 | 18 21 | 18 45 | 19 13 | 24 11 | 00 11 | 01 04 | 02 00 |
| 05 | 252 36.9 | 56.3 | 130 33.9 | 10.3 | 25 46.9 | 3.8 | 54.7 | 35 | 18 22 | 18 48 | 19 18 | 23 55 | 24 49 | 00 49 | 01 47 |
| 06 | 267 37.1 | S 2 55.3 | 145 03.2 | 10.3 | N25 43.1 | 3.9 | 54.7 | 40 | 18 24 | 18 52 | 19 24 | 23 37 | 24 31 | 00 31 | 01 31 |
| 07 | 282 37.3 | 54.4 | 159 32.5 | 10.3 | 25 39.2 | 4.1 | 54.7 | 45 | 18 27 | 18 56 | 19 31 | 23 15 | 24 10 | 00 10 | 01 12 |
| 08 | 297 37.4 | 53.4 | 174 01.8 | 10.3 | 25 35.1 | 4.2 | 54.7 | S 50 | 18 30 | 19 02 | 19 41 | 22 48 | 23 43 | 24 48 | 00 48 |
| S 09 | 312 37.6 | 52.4 | 188 31.1 | 10.3 | 25 30.9 | 4.3 | 54.7 | 52 | 18 31 | 19 05 | 19 46 | 22 34 | 23 30 | 24 37 | 00 37 |
| U 10 | 327 37.8 | 51.4 | 203 00.4 | 10.4 | 25 26.6 | 4.4 | 54.7 | 54 | 18 33 | 19 08 | 19 51 | 22 19 | 23 15 | 24 24 | 00 24 |
| N 11 | 342 37.9 | 50.4 | 217 29.8 | 10.4 | 25 22.2 | 4.5 | 54.8 | 56 | 18 34 | 19 12 | 19 57 | 22 02 | 22 58 | 24 08 | 00 08 |
| D 12 | 357 38.1 | S 2 49.4 | 231 59.2 | 10.3 | N25 17.7 | 4.7 | 54.8 | 58 | 18 36 | 19 16 | 20 04 | 21 38 | 22 36 | 23 51 | 25 14 |
| A 13 | 12 38.3 | 48.4 | 246 28.5 | 10.4 | 25 13.0 | 4.8 | 54.8 | S 60 | 18 38 | 19 20 | 20 12 | 21 09 | 22 09 | 23 29 | 24 58 |
| Y 14 | 27 38.4 | 47.5 | 260 57.9 | 10.5 | 25 08.2 | 5.0 | 54.8 | | | | | | | | |
| 15 | 42 38.6 | 46.5 | 275 27.4 | 10.4 | 25 03.2 | 5.0 | 54.8 | | | | | | | | |
| 16 | 57 38.8 | 45.5 | 289 56.8 | 10.5 | 24 58.2 | 5.2 | 54.8 | | | | | | | | |
| 17 | 72 39.0 | 44.5 | 304 26.3 | 10.5 | 24 53.0 | 5.3 | 54.9 | | | | | | | | |
| 18 | 87 39.1 | S 2 43.5 | 318 55.8 | 10.5 | N24 47.7 | 5.4 | 54.9 | | | | | | | | |
| 19 | 102 39.3 | 42.5 | 333 25.3 | 10.5 | 24 42.3 | 5.6 | 54.9 | | | | | | | | |
| 20 | 117 39.5 | 41.5 | 347 54.8 | 10.6 | 24 36.7 | 5.7 | 54.9 | | | | | | | | |
| 21 | 132 39.6 | 40.6 | 2 24.4 | 10.6 | 24 31.0 | 5.8 | 54.9 | | | | | | | | |
| 22 | 147 39.8 | 39.6 | 16 54.0 | 10.6 | 24 25.2 | 5.9 | 55.0 | | | | | | | | |
| 23 | 162 40.0 | 38.6 | 31 23.6 | 10.6 | N24 19.3 | 6.0 | 55.0 | | | | | | | | |
| | SD 16.1 | d 1.0 | SD 14.8 | | 14.8 | | 14.9 | | | | | | | | | |

| | SUN | | | MOON | | | |
|---|---|---|---|---|---|---|---|
| Day | Eqn. of Time | | Mer. | Mer. Pass. | | Age | Phase |
| | 00ʰ | 12ʰ | Pass. | Upper | Lower | | |
| d | m s | m s | h m | h m | h m | d | % |
| 11 | 10 08 | 10 00 | 12 10 | 19 08 | 06 43 | 09 | 60 |
| 12 | 09 52 | 09 44 | 12 10 | 19 59 | 07 34 | 10 | 69 |
| 13 | 09 36 | 09 28 | 12 09 | 20 50 | 08 25 | 11 | 77 |

| UT | ARIES | VENUS −4·5 | | MARS +1·2 | | JUPITER −2·0 | | SATURN +0·7 | | STARS | | |
|---|---|---|---|---|---|---|---|---|---|---|---|---|
| | GHA | GHA | Dec | GHA | Dec | GHA | Dec | GHA | Dec | Name | SHA | Dec |
| d h | ° ′ | ° ′ | ° ′ | ° ′ | ° ′ | ° ′ | ° ′ | ° ′ | ° ′ | | ° ′ | ° ′ |
| **14** 00 | 171 35.6 | 222 54.0 | S15 52.0 | 223 10.7 | S19 47.4 | 183 09.6 | S 6 02.3 | 208 39.0 | S15 35.8 | Acamar | 315 13.8 | S40 13.3 |
| 01 | 186 38.1 | 237 54.1 | 51.6 | 238 11.2 | 47.0 | 198 11.5 | 02.1 | 223 41.2 | 35.8 | Achernar | 335 22.4 | S57 07.7 |
| 02 | 201 40.5 | 252 54.1 | 51.3 | 253 11.8 | 46.5 | 213 13.4 | 01.8 | 238 43.4 | 35.7 | Acrux | 173 01.9 | S63 13.2 |
| 03 | 216 43.0 | 267 54.1 .. | 51.0 | 268 12.3 .. | 46.1 | 228 15.3 .. | 01.6 | 253 45.6 .. | 35.6 | Adhara | 255 07.6 | S29 00.4 |
| 04 | 231 45.5 | 282 54.1 | 50.7 | 283 12.8 | 45.7 | 243 17.2 | 01.4 | 268 47.8 | 35.5 | Aldebaran | 290 42.4 | N16 33.1 |
| 05 | 246 47.9 | 297 54.1 | 50.4 | 298 13.3 | 45.2 | 258 19.1 | 01.2 | 283 50.0 | 35.4 | | | |
| 06 | 261 50.4 | 312 54.2 | S15 50.0 | 313 13.9 | S19 44.8 | 273 21.0 | S 6 00.9 | 298 52.2 | S15 35.4 | Alioth | 166 14.5 | N55 50.3 |
| 07 | 276 52.8 | 327 54.2 | 49.7 | 328 14.4 | 44.4 | 288 23.0 | 00.7 | 313 54.4 | 35.3 | Alkaid | 152 53.5 | N49 12.0 |
| 08 | 291 55.3 | 342 54.2 | 49.4 | 343 14.9 | 43.9 | 303 24.9 | 00.5 | 328 56.6 | 35.2 | Alnair | 27 36.3 | S46 51.3 |
| M 09 | 306 57.8 | 357 54.2 .. | 49.1 | 358 15.5 .. | 43.5 | 318 26.8 .. | 00.2 | 343 58.8 .. | 35.1 | Alnilam | 275 40.1 | S 1 11.4 |
| O 10 | 322 00.2 | 12 54.2 | 48.8 | 13 16.0 | 43.0 | 333 28.7 | 6 00.0 | 359 01.0 | 35.0 | Alphard | 217 49.8 | S 8 45.4 |
| N 11 | 337 02.7 | 27 54.3 | 48.4 | 28 16.5 | 42.6 | 348 30.6 | 5 59.8 | 14 03.2 | 35.0 | | | |
| D 12 | 352 05.2 | 42 54.3 | S15 48.1 | 43 17.0 | S19 42.2 | 3 32.5 | S 5 59.5 | 29 05.4 | S15 34.9 | Alphecca | 126 05.5 | N26 38.2 |
| A 13 | 7 07.6 | 57 54.3 | 47.8 | 58 17.6 | 41.7 | 18 34.4 | 59.3 | 44 07.6 | 34.8 | Alpheratz | 357 37.5 | N29 12.6 |
| Y 14 | 22 10.1 | 72 54.3 | 47.5 | 73 18.1 | 41.3 | 33 36.3 | 59.1 | 59 09.8 | 34.7 | Altair | 62 02.4 | N 8 55.4 |
| 15 | 37 12.6 | 87 54.3 .. | 47.1 | 88 18.6 .. | 40.9 | 48 38.2 .. | 58.8 | 74 12.0 .. | 34.6 | Ankaa | 353 09.9 | S42 11.4 |
| 16 | 52 15.0 | 102 54.3 | 46.8 | 103 19.2 | 40.4 | 63 40.1 | 58.6 | 89 14.2 | 34.6 | Antares | 112 18.6 | S26 28.8 |
| 17 | 67 17.5 | 117 54.3 | 46.5 | 118 19.7 | 40.0 | 78 42.0 | 58.4 | 104 16.4 | 34.5 | | | |
| 18 | 82 19.9 | 132 54.3 | S15 46.1 | 133 20.2 | S19 39.5 | 93 43.9 | S 5 58.1 | 119 18.6 | S15 34.4 | Arcturus | 145 49.8 | N19 03.9 |
| 19 | 97 22.4 | 147 54.3 | 45.8 | 148 20.8 | 39.1 | 108 45.8 | 57.9 | 134 20.8 | 34.3 | Atria | 107 14.8 | S69 03.7 |
| 20 | 112 24.9 | 162 54.4 | 45.5 | 163 21.3 | 38.7 | 123 47.7 | 57.7 | 149 23.0 | 34.2 | Avior | 234 15.2 | S59 35.0 |
| 21 | 127 27.3 | 177 54.4 .. | 45.1 | 178 21.8 .. | 38.2 | 138 49.6 .. | 57.4 | 164 25.2 .. | 34.2 | Bellatrix | 278 25.4 | N 6 22.1 |
| 22 | 142 29.8 | 192 54.4 | 44.8 | 193 22.3 | 37.8 | 153 51.5 | 57.2 | 179 27.4 | 34.1 | Betelgeuse | 270 54.6 | N 7 24.6 |
| 23 | 157 32.3 | 207 54.4 | 44.5 | 208 22.9 | 37.3 | 168 53.4 | 57.0 | 194 29.6 | 34.0 | | | |
| **15** 00 | 172 34.7 | 222 54.4 | S15 44.1 | 223 23.4 | S19 36.9 | 183 55.3 | S 5 56.7 | 209 31.8 | S15 33.9 | Canopus | 263 53.3 | S52 42.7 |
| 01 | 187 37.2 | 237 54.4 | 43.8 | 238 23.9 | 36.5 | 198 57.2 | 56.5 | 224 34.0 | 33.8 | Capella | 280 25.4 | N46 01.3 |
| 02 | 202 39.7 | 252 54.4 | 43.5 | 253 24.5 | 36.0 | 213 59.2 | 56.3 | 239 36.2 | 33.8 | Deneb | 49 27.7 | N45 21.3 |
| 03 | 217 42.1 | 267 54.4 .. | 43.1 | 268 25.0 .. | 35.6 | 229 01.1 .. | 56.0 | 254 38.4 .. | 33.7 | Denebola | 182 27.0 | N14 26.8 |
| 04 | 232 44.6 | 282 54.4 | 42.8 | 283 25.5 | 35.1 | 244 03.0 | 55.8 | 269 40.6 | 33.6 | Diphda | 348 49.9 | S17 52.1 |
| 05 | 247 47.1 | 297 54.4 | 42.4 | 298 26.1 | 34.7 | 259 04.9 | 55.6 | 284 42.8 | 33.5 | | | |
| 06 | 262 49.5 | 312 54.4 | S15 42.1 | 313 26.6 | S19 34.2 | 274 06.8 | S 5 55.3 | 299 45.0 | S15 33.4 | Dubhe | 193 43.2 | N61 37.9 |
| 07 | 277 52.0 | 327 54.4 | 41.8 | 328 27.1 | 33.8 | 289 08.7 | 55.1 | 314 47.2 | 33.4 | Elnath | 278 04.8 | N28 37.6 |
| T 08 | 292 54.4 | 342 54.4 | 41.4 | 343 27.7 | 33.4 | 304 10.6 | 54.9 | 329 49.4 | 33.3 | Eltanin | 90 43.3 | N51 28.8 |
| U 09 | 307 56.9 | 357 54.4 .. | 41.1 | 358 28.2 .. | 32.9 | 319 12.5 .. | 54.6 | 344 51.6 .. | 33.2 | Enif | 33 41.4 | N 9 58.4 |
| E 10 | 322 59.4 | 12 54.4 | 40.7 | 13 28.7 | 32.5 | 334 14.4 | 54.4 | 359 53.8 | 33.1 | Fomalhaut | 15 17.4 | S29 30.5 |
| S 11 | 338 01.8 | 27 54.4 | 40.4 | 28 29.2 | 32.0 | 349 16.3 | 54.2 | 14 56.0 | 33.0 | | | |
| D 12 | 353 04.3 | 42 54.4 | S15 40.1 | 43 29.8 | S19 31.6 | 4 18.2 | S 5 53.9 | 29 58.2 | S15 33.0 | Gacrux | 171 53.6 | S57 14.2 |
| A 13 | 8 06.8 | 57 54.4 | 39.7 | 58 30.3 | 31.1 | 19 20.1 | 53.7 | 45 00.4 | 32.9 | Gienah | 175 45.6 | S17 39.9 |
| Y 14 | 23 09.2 | 72 54.4 | 39.4 | 73 30.8 | 30.7 | 34 22.0 | 53.5 | 60 02.6 | 32.8 | Hadar | 148 38.8 | S60 28.6 |
| 15 | 38 11.7 | 87 54.4 .. | 39.0 | 88 31.4 .. | 30.2 | 49 23.9 .. | 53.2 | 75 04.8 .. | 32.7 | Hamal | 327 54.1 | N23 33.9 |
| 16 | 53 14.2 | 102 54.4 | 38.7 | 103 31.9 | 29.8 | 64 25.8 | 53.0 | 90 07.0 | 32.6 | Kaus Aust. | 83 35.7 | S34 22.4 |
| 17 | 68 16.6 | 117 54.4 | 38.3 | 118 32.4 | 29.3 | 79 27.7 | 52.8 | 105 09.2 | 32.6 | | | |
| 18 | 83 19.1 | 132 54.4 | S15 38.0 | 133 33.0 | S19 28.9 | 94 29.6 | S 5 52.5 | 120 11.4 | S15 32.5 | Kochab | 137 19.0 | N74 03.6 |
| 19 | 98 21.6 | 147 54.4 | 37.6 | 148 33.5 | 28.5 | 109 31.6 | 52.3 | 135 13.6 | 32.4 | Markab | 13 32.5 | N15 19.3 |
| 20 | 113 24.0 | 162 54.4 | 37.3 | 163 34.0 | 28.0 | 124 33.5 | 52.1 | 150 15.8 | 32.3 | Menkar | 314 08.8 | N 4 10.4 |
| 21 | 128 26.5 | 177 54.4 .. | 36.9 | 178 34.6 .. | 27.6 | 139 35.4 .. | 51.8 | 165 18.0 .. | 32.2 | Menkent | 148 00.0 | S36 28.7 |
| 22 | 143 28.9 | 192 54.3 | 36.6 | 193 35.1 | 27.1 | 154 37.3 | 51.6 | 180 20.2 | 32.2 | Miaplacidus | 221 38.0 | S69 48.6 |
| 23 | 158 31.4 | 207 54.3 | 36.2 | 208 35.6 | 26.7 | 169 39.2 | 51.4 | 195 22.4 | 32.1 | | | |
| **16** 00 | 173 33.9 | 222 54.3 | S15 35.9 | 223 36.2 | S19 26.2 | 184 41.1 | S 5 51.1 | 210 24.6 | S15 32.0 | Mirfak | 308 31.8 | N49 56.4 |
| 01 | 188 36.3 | 237 54.3 | 35.5 | 238 36.7 | 25.8 | 199 43.0 | 50.9 | 225 26.9 | 31.9 | Nunki | 75 50.8 | S26 16.1 |
| 02 | 203 38.8 | 252 54.3 | 35.1 | 253 37.2 | 25.3 | 214 44.9 | 50.7 | 240 29.1 | 31.8 | Peacock | 53 09.8 | S56 39.7 |
| 03 | 218 41.3 | 267 54.3 .. | 34.8 | 268 37.8 .. | 24.9 | 229 46.8 .. | 50.5 | 255 31.3 .. | 31.8 | Pollux | 243 20.0 | N27 58.4 |
| 04 | 233 43.7 | 282 54.3 | 34.4 | 283 38.3 | 24.4 | 244 48.7 | 50.2 | 270 33.5 | 31.7 | Procyon | 244 53.1 | N 5 10.0 |
| 05 | 248 46.2 | 297 54.3 | 34.1 | 298 38.8 | 24.0 | 259 50.6 | 50.0 | 285 35.7 | 31.6 | | | |
| 06 | 263 48.7 | 312 54.3 | S15 33.7 | 313 39.4 | S19 23.5 | 274 52.5 | S 5 49.8 | 300 37.9 | S15 31.5 | Rasalhague | 96 00.7 | N12 32.4 |
| W 07 | 278 51.1 | 327 54.2 | 33.3 | 328 39.9 | 23.1 | 289 54.4 | 49.5 | 315 40.1 | 31.4 | Regulus | 207 36.6 | N11 51.5 |
| E 08 | 293 53.6 | 342 54.2 | 33.0 | 343 40.4 | 22.6 | 304 56.3 | 49.3 | 330 42.3 | 31.4 | Rigel | 281 06.1 | S 8 10.8 |
| D 09 | 308 56.0 | 357 54.2 .. | 32.6 | 358 41.0 .. | 22.2 | 319 58.2 .. | 49.1 | 345 44.5 .. | 31.3 | Rigil Kent. | 139 43.0 | S60 55.4 |
| N 10 | 323 58.5 | 12 54.2 | 32.3 | 13 41.5 | 21.7 | 335 00.1 | 48.8 | 0 46.7 | 31.2 | Sabik | 102 05.4 | S15 45.2 |
| E 11 | 339 01.0 | 27 54.2 | 31.9 | 28 42.1 | 21.2 | 350 02.1 | 48.6 | 15 48.9 | 31.1 | | | |
| S 12 | 354 03.4 | 42 54.2 | S15 31.5 | 43 42.6 | S19 20.8 | 5 04.0 | S 5 48.4 | 30 51.1 | S15 31.1 | Schedar | 349 34.2 | N56 39.5 |
| D 13 | 9 05.9 | 57 54.1 | 31.2 | 58 43.1 | 20.3 | 20 05.9 | 48.1 | 45 53.3 | 31.0 | Shaula | 96 13.5 | S37 07.1 |
| A 14 | 24 08.4 | 72 54.1 | 30.8 | 73 43.7 | 19.9 | 35 07.8 | 47.9 | 60 55.5 | 30.9 | Sirius | 258 28.2 | S16 45.0 |
| Y 15 | 39 10.8 | 87 54.1 .. | 30.4 | 88 44.2 .. | 19.4 | 50 09.7 .. | 47.7 | 75 57.7 .. | 30.8 | Spica | 158 24.5 | S11 16.6 |
| 16 | 54 13.3 | 102 54.1 | 30.1 | 103 44.7 | 19.0 | 65 11.6 | 47.4 | 90 59.9 | 30.7 | Suhail | 222 47.7 | S43 31.5 |
| 17 | 69 15.8 | 117 54.1 | 29.7 | 118 45.3 | 18.5 | 80 13.5 | 47.2 | 106 02.1 | 30.7 | | | |
| 18 | 84 18.2 | 132 54.0 | S15 29.3 | 133 45.8 | S19 18.1 | 95 15.4 | S 5 47.0 | 121 04.3 | S15 30.6 | Vega | 80 34.9 | N38 47.9 |
| 19 | 99 20.7 | 147 54.0 | 29.0 | 148 46.3 | 17.6 | 110 17.3 | 46.7 | 136 06.5 | 30.5 | Zuben'ubi | 136 58.4 | S16 08.0 |
| 20 | 114 23.2 | 162 54.0 | 28.6 | 163 46.9 | 17.2 | 125 19.2 | 46.5 | 151 08.7 | 30.4 | | SHA | Mer.Pass. |
| 21 | 129 25.6 | 177 54.0 .. | 28.2 | 178 47.4 .. | 16.7 | 140 21.1 .. | 46.3 | 166 10.9 .. | 30.3 | | ° ′ | h m |
| 22 | 144 28.1 | 192 54.0 | 27.8 | 193 48.0 | 16.2 | 155 23.0 | 46.0 | 181 13.1 | 30.3 | Venus | 50 19.7 | 9 08 |
| 23 | 159 30.5 | 207 53.9 | 27.5 | 208 48.5 | 15.8 | 170 24.9 | 45.8 | 196 15.3 | 30.2 | Mars | 50 48.7 | 9 06 |
| | h m | | | | | | | | | Jupiter | 11 20.6 | 11 43 |
| Mer. Pass. 12 27.6 | | v 0.0 | d 0.3 | v 0.5 | d 0.4 | v 1.9 | d 0.2 | v 2.2 | d 0.1 | Saturn | 36 57.1 | 10 00 |

| UT | SUN GHA | SUN Dec | MOON GHA | v | MOON Dec | d | HP |
|---|---|---|---|---|---|---|---|
| d h | ° ′ | ° ′ | ° ′ | ′ | ° ′ | ′ | ′ |
| **14** 00 | 177 40.2 | S 2 37.6 | 45 53.2 | 10.7 | N24 13.3 | 6.2 | 55.0 |
| 01 | 192 40.3 | 36.6 | 60 22.9 | 10.7 | 24 07.1 | 6.3 | 55.0 |
| 02 | 207 40.5 | 35.6 | 74 52.6 | 10.7 | 24 00.8 | 6.4 | 55.0 |
| 03 | 222 40.7 .. | 34.6 | 89 22.3 | 10.7 | 23 54.4 | 6.6 | 55.1 |
| 04 | 237 40.9 | 33.7 | 103 52.0 | 10.8 | 23 47.8 | 6.6 | 55.1 |
| 05 | 252 41.0 | 32.7 | 118 21.8 | 10.8 | 23 41.2 | 6.8 | 55.1 |
| 06 | 267 41.2 | S 2 31.7 | 132 51.6 | 10.8 | N23 34.4 | 6.9 | 55.1 |
| 07 | 282 41.4 | 30.7 | 147 21.4 | 10.9 | 23 27.5 | 7.0 | 55.1 |
| **M** 08 | 297 41.5 | 29.7 | 161 51.3 | 10.9 | 23 20.5 | 7.1 | 55.2 |
| **O** 09 | 312 41.7 .. | 28.7 | 176 21.2 | 10.9 | 23 13.4 | 7.3 | 55.2 |
| **N** 10 | 327 41.9 | 27.7 | 190 51.1 | 11.0 | 23 06.1 | 7.4 | 55.2 |
| **D** 11 | 342 42.1 | 26.8 | 205 21.1 | 11.0 | 22 58.7 | 7.4 | 55.2 |
| **A** 12 | 357 42.2 | S 2 25.8 | 219 51.1 | 11.0 | N22 51.3 | 7.6 | 55.2 |
| **Y** 13 | 12 42.4 | 24.8 | 234 21.1 | 11.0 | 22 43.7 | 7.8 | 55.3 |
| 14 | 27 42.6 | 23.8 | 248 51.1 | 11.1 | 22 35.9 | 7.8 | 55.3 |
| 15 | 42 42.8 .. | 22.8 | 263 21.2 | 11.1 | 22 28.1 | 7.9 | 55.3 |
| 16 | 57 42.9 | 21.8 | 277 51.3 | 11.2 | 22 20.2 | 8.1 | 55.3 |
| 17 | 72 43.1 | 20.8 | 292 21.5 | 11.1 | 22 12.1 | 8.2 | 55.4 |
| 18 | 87 43.3 | S 2 19.8 | 306 51.6 | 11.2 | N22 03.9 | 8.3 | 55.4 |
| 19 | 102 43.5 | 18.9 | 321 21.8 | 11.3 | 21 55.6 | 8.4 | 55.4 |
| 20 | 117 43.6 | 17.9 | 335 52.1 | 11.3 | 21 47.2 | 8.5 | 55.4 |
| 21 | 132 43.8 .. | 16.9 | 350 22.4 | 11.3 | 21 38.7 | 8.6 | 55.4 |
| 22 | 147 44.0 | 15.9 | 4 52.7 | 11.3 | 21 30.1 | 8.8 | 55.5 |
| 23 | 162 44.2 | 14.9 | 19 23.0 | 11.4 | 21 21.3 | 8.8 | 55.5 |
| **15** 00 | 177 44.3 | S 2 13.9 | 33 53.4 | 11.4 | N21 12.5 | 9.0 | 55.5 |
| 01 | 192 44.5 | 12.9 | 48 23.8 | 11.5 | 21 03.5 | 9.0 | 55.5 |
| 02 | 207 44.7 | 12.0 | 62 54.3 | 11.5 | 20 54.5 | 9.2 | 55.6 |
| 03 | 222 44.9 .. | 11.0 | 77 24.8 | 11.5 | 20 45.3 | 9.3 | 55.6 |
| 04 | 237 45.0 | 10.0 | 91 55.3 | 11.5 | 20 36.0 | 9.4 | 55.6 |
| 05 | 252 45.2 | 09.0 | 106 25.0 | 11.6 | 20 26.6 | 9.5 | 55.6 |
| 06 | 267 45.4 | S 2 08.0 | 120 56.4 | 11.7 | N20 17.1 | 9.6 | 55.7 |
| 07 | 282 45.6 | 07.0 | 135 27.1 | 11.6 | 20 07.5 | 9.7 | 55.7 |
| **T** 08 | 297 45.7 | 06.0 | 149 57.7 | 11.7 | 19 57.8 | 9.8 | 55.7 |
| **U** 09 | 312 45.9 .. | 05.0 | 164 28.4 | 11.7 | 19 48.0 | 9.9 | 55.7 |
| **E** 10 | 327 46.1 | 04.1 | 178 59.1 | 11.8 | 19 38.1 | 10.0 | 55.8 |
| **S** 11 | 342 46.3 | 03.1 | 193 29.9 | 11.8 | 19 28.1 | 10.1 | 55.8 |
| **D** 12 | 357 46.4 | S 2 02.1 | 208 00.7 | 11.8 | N19 18.0 | 10.3 | 55.8 |
| **A** 13 | 12 46.6 | 01.1 | 222 31.5 | 11.9 | 19 07.7 | 10.3 | 55.8 |
| **Y** 14 | 27 46.8 | 2 00.1 | 237 02.4 | 11.9 | 18 57.4 | 10.4 | 55.9 |
| 15 | 42 47.0 | 1 59.1 | 251 33.3 | 11.9 | 18 47.0 | 10.5 | 55.9 |
| 16 | 57 47.1 | 58.1 | 266 04.2 | 12.0 | 18 36.5 | 10.6 | 55.9 |
| 17 | 72 47.3 | 57.1 | 280 35.2 | 12.0 | 18 25.9 | 10.8 | 55.9 |
| 18 | 87 47.5 | S 1 56.2 | 295 06.2 | 12.1 | N18 15.1 | 10.8 | 56.0 |
| 19 | 102 47.7 | 55.2 | 309 37.3 | 12.0 | 18 04.3 | 10.9 | 56.0 |
| 20 | 117 47.8 | 54.2 | 324 08.3 | 12.1 | 17 53.4 | 11.0 | 56.0 |
| 21 | 132 48.0 .. | 53.2 | 338 39.4 | 12.2 | 17 42.4 | 11.1 | 56.0 |
| 22 | 147 48.2 | 52.2 | 353 10.6 | 12.1 | 17 31.3 | 11.2 | 56.1 |
| 23 | 162 48.4 | 51.2 | 7 41.7 | 12.3 | 17 20.1 | 11.2 | 56.1 |
| **16** 00 | 177 48.6 | S 1 50.2 | 22 13.0 | 12.2 | N17 08.9 | 11.4 | 56.1 |
| 01 | 192 48.7 | 49.2 | 36 44.2 | 12.3 | 16 57.5 | 11.5 | 56.1 |
| 02 | 207 48.9 | 48.3 | 51 15.5 | 12.3 | 16 46.0 | 11.5 | 56.2 |
| 03 | 222 49.1 .. | 47.3 | 65 46.8 | 12.3 | 16 34.5 | 11.7 | 56.2 |
| 04 | 237 49.3 | 46.3 | 80 18.1 | 12.3 | 16 22.8 | 11.7 | 56.2 |
| 05 | 252 49.4 | 45.3 | 94 49.4 | 12.4 | 16 11.1 | 11.8 | 56.3 |
| 06 | 267 49.6 | S 1 44.3 | 109 20.8 | 12.5 | N15 59.3 | 11.9 | 56.3 |
| 07 | 282 49.8 | 43.3 | 123 52.3 | 12.4 | 15 47.4 | 12.0 | 56.3 |
| **W** 08 | 297 50.0 | 42.3 | 138 23.7 | 12.5 | 15 35.4 | 12.1 | 56.3 |
| **E** 09 | 312 50.2 .. | 41.3 | 152 55.2 | 12.5 | 15 23.3 | 12.2 | 56.4 |
| **D** 10 | 327 50.3 | 40.4 | 167 26.7 | 12.6 | 15 11.1 | 12.2 | 56.4 |
| **N** 11 | 342 50.5 | 39.4 | 181 58.3 | 12.5 | 14 58.9 | 12.3 | 56.4 |
| **E** 12 | 357 50.7 | S 1 38.4 | 196 29.8 | 12.6 | N14 46.6 | 12.4 | 56.4 |
| **S** 13 | 12 50.9 | 37.4 | 211 01.4 | 12.6 | 14 34.2 | 12.5 | 56.5 |
| **D** 14 | 27 51.0 | 36.4 | 225 33.0 | 12.7 | 14 21.7 | 12.6 | 56.5 |
| **A** 15 | 42 51.2 .. | 35.4 | 240 04.7 | 12.7 | 14 09.1 | 12.6 | 56.5 |
| **Y** 16 | 57 51.4 | 34.4 | 254 36.4 | 12.7 | 13 56.5 | 12.7 | 56.5 |
| 17 | 72 51.6 | 33.4 | 269 08.1 | 12.7 | 13 43.8 | 12.8 | 56.6 |
| 18 | 87 51.8 | S 1 32.4 | 283 39.8 | 12.7 | N13 31.0 | 12.9 | 56.6 |
| 19 | 102 51.9 | 31.5 | 298 11.5 | 12.8 | 13 18.1 | 13.0 | 56.6 |
| 20 | 117 52.1 | 30.5 | 312 43.3 | 12.8 | 13 05.1 | 13.0 | 56.7 |
| 21 | 132 52.3 .. | 29.5 | 327 15.1 | 12.8 | 12 52.1 | 13.1 | 56.7 |
| 22 | 147 52.5 | 28.5 | 341 46.9 | 12.9 | 12 39.0 | 13.1 | 56.7 |
| 23 | 162 52.7 | 27.5 | 356 18.8 | 12.9 | N12 25.9 | 13.3 | 56.7 |
| | SD 16.1 | d 1.0 | SD 15.1 | | 15.2 | | 15.4 |

## Twilight / Sunrise / Moonrise

| Lat. | Twilight Naut. | Twilight Civil | Sunrise | Moonrise 14 | 15 | 16 | 17 |
|---|---|---|---|---|---|---|---|
| ° | h m | h m | h m | h m | h m | h m | h m |
| N 72 | 03 54 | 05 17 | 06 24 | ☐ | ☐ | 13 29 | 15 58 |
| N 70 | 04 08 | 05 22 | 06 23 | ☐ | 11 08 | 14 01 | 16 12 |
| 68 | 04 19 | 05 26 | 06 21 | ☐ | 12 11 | 14 24 | 16 22 |
| 66 | 04 28 | 05 29 | 06 20 | 10 30 | 12 46 | 14 42 | 16 31 |
| 64 | 04 35 | 05 32 | 06 19 | 11 21 | 13 11 | 14 56 | 16 39 |
| 62 | 04 42 | 05 34 | 06 18 | 11 52 | 13 30 | 15 08 | 16 45 |
| 60 | 04 47 | 05 36 | 06 17 | 12 15 | 13 46 | 15 18 | 16 50 |
| N 58 | 04 51 | 05 37 | 06 16 | 12 34 | 13 59 | 15 27 | 16 55 |
| 56 | 04 55 | 05 39 | 06 16 | 12 50 | 14 11 | 15 35 | 16 59 |
| 54 | 04 59 | 05 40 | 06 15 | 13 03 | 14 21 | 15 42 | 17 03 |
| 52 | 05 02 | 05 41 | 06 14 | 13 14 | 14 30 | 15 48 | 17 06 |
| 50 | 05 04 | 05 42 | 06 14 | 13 25 | 14 38 | 15 53 | 17 10 |
| 45 | 05 09 | 05 44 | 06 13 | 13 46 | 14 55 | 16 05 | 17 16 |
| N 40 | 05 13 | 05 45 | 06 12 | 14 04 | 15 08 | 16 15 | 17 22 |
| 35 | 05 16 | 05 46 | 06 11 | 14 18 | 15 20 | 16 23 | 17 27 |
| 30 | 05 18 | 05 46 | 06 10 | 14 31 | 15 30 | 16 30 | 17 31 |
| 20 | 05 21 | 05 47 | 06 09 | 14 52 | 15 48 | 16 43 | 17 38 |
| N 10 | 05 22 | 05 46 | 06 07 | 15 11 | 16 03 | 16 54 | 17 44 |
| 0 | 05 21 | 05 45 | 06 06 | 15 28 | 16 17 | 17 04 | 17 50 |
| S 10 | 05 19 | 05 43 | 06 04 | 15 45 | 16 31 | 17 14 | 17 56 |
| 20 | 05 15 | 05 40 | 06 02 | 16 04 | 16 46 | 17 25 | 18 03 |
| 30 | 05 08 | 05 36 | 06 00 | 16 25 | 17 03 | 17 37 | 18 10 |
| 35 | 05 04 | 05 34 | 05 59 | 16 37 | 17 13 | 17 44 | 18 14 |
| 40 | 04 58 | 05 30 | 05 57 | 16 51 | 17 24 | 17 52 | 18 18 |
| 45 | 04 51 | 05 26 | 05 56 | 17 08 | 17 37 | 18 02 | 18 24 |
| S 50 | 04 42 | 05 21 | 05 54 | 17 28 | 17 53 | 18 13 | 18 30 |
| 52 | 04 38 | 05 19 | 05 53 | 17 38 | 18 00 | 18 18 | 18 33 |
| 54 | 04 33 | 05 16 | 05 52 | 17 49 | 18 09 | 18 24 | 18 36 |
| 56 | 04 28 | 05 13 | 05 50 | 18 01 | 18 18 | 18 30 | 18 40 |
| 58 | 04 21 | 05 09 | 05 49 | 18 16 | 18 28 | 18 37 | 18 44 |
| S 60 | 04 14 | 05 05 | 05 47 | 18 32 | 18 40 | 18 45 | 18 49 |

## Sunset / Twilight / Moonset

| Lat. | Sunset | Twilight Civil | Twilight Naut. | Moonset 14 | 15 | 16 | 17 |
|---|---|---|---|---|---|---|---|
| ° | h m | h m | h m | h m | h m | h m | h m |
| N 72 | 17 56 | 19 03 | 20 28 | ☐ | ☐ | 08 38 | 07 48 |
| N 70 | 17 57 | 18 58 | 20 13 | ☐ | 09 17 | 08 04 | 07 32 |
| 68 | 17 59 | 18 54 | 20 02 | ☐ | 08 13 | 07 40 | 07 19 |
| 66 | 18 00 | 18 51 | 19 52 | 08 11 | 07 37 | 07 20 | 07 08 |
| 64 | 18 01 | 18 48 | 19 45 | 07 20 | 07 11 | 07 05 | 06 59 |
| 62 | 18 01 | 18 46 | 19 39 | 06 40 | 06 51 | 06 52 | 06 51 |
| 60 | 18 02 | 18 44 | 19 33 | 06 24 | 06 34 | 06 41 | 06 45 |
| N 58 | 18 03 | 18 42 | 19 28 | 06 05 | 06 20 | 06 31 | 06 39 |
| 56 | 18 03 | 18 40 | 19 24 | 05 49 | 06 08 | 06 22 | 06 33 |
| 54 | 18 04 | 18 39 | 19 21 | 05 35 | 05 58 | 06 15 | 06 28 |
| 52 | 18 04 | 18 38 | 19 17 | 05 23 | 05 48 | 06 08 | 06 24 |
| 50 | 18 05 | 18 37 | 19 15 | 05 12 | 05 40 | 06 02 | 06 20 |
| 45 | 18 06 | 18 35 | 19 09 | 04 50 | 05 22 | 05 48 | 06 12 |
| N 40 | 18 07 | 18 34 | 19 05 | 04 32 | 05 07 | 05 37 | 06 04 |
| 35 | 18 07 | 18 33 | 19 02 | 04 16 | 04 54 | 05 28 | 05 58 |
| 30 | 18 08 | 18 32 | 19 00 | 04 03 | 04 43 | 05 19 | 05 53 |
| 20 | 18 10 | 18 32 | 18 57 | 03 40 | 04 24 | 05 05 | 05 43 |
| N 10 | 18 11 | 18 32 | 18 56 | 03 21 | 04 07 | 04 52 | 05 34 |
| 0 | 18 12 | 18 33 | 18 57 | 03 02 | 03 52 | 04 40 | 05 26 |
| S 10 | 18 14 | 18 35 | 18 59 | 02 44 | 03 36 | 04 27 | 05 18 |
| 20 | 18 15 | 18 37 | 19 03 | 02 24 | 03 19 | 04 14 | 05 09 |
| 30 | 18 17 | 18 41 | 19 09 | 02 00 | 02 59 | 03 59 | 04 59 |
| 35 | 18 18 | 18 44 | 19 13 | 01 47 | 02 48 | 03 50 | 04 54 |
| 40 | 18 20 | 18 47 | 19 19 | 01 31 | 02 34 | 03 40 | 04 47 |
| 45 | 18 21 | 18 51 | 19 25 | 01 12 | 02 19 | 03 28 | 04 39 |
| S 50 | 18 23 | 18 56 | 19 34 | 00 48 | 01 59 | 03 14 | 04 30 |
| 52 | 18 24 | 18 58 | 19 38 | 00 37 | 01 50 | 03 07 | 04 25 |
| 54 | 18 25 | 19 01 | 19 43 | 00 24 | 01 40 | 02 59 | 04 20 |
| 56 | 18 26 | 19 04 | 19 48 | 00 08 | 01 28 | 02 51 | 04 15 |
| 58 | 18 27 | 19 07 | 19 55 | 25 14 | 01 14 | 02 41 | 04 09 |
| S 60 | 18 29 | 19 11 | 20 02 | 24 58 | 00 58 | 02 30 | 04 02 |

## SUN and MOON

| Day | SUN Eqn. of Time 00h | 12h | Mer. Pass. | MOON Mer. Pass. Upper | Lower | Age | Phase |
|---|---|---|---|---|---|---|---|
| d | m s | m s | h m | h m | h m | d | % |
| 14 | 09 20 | 09 11 | 12 09 | 21 40 | 09 15 | 12 | 85 |
| 15 | 09 03 | 08 55 | 12 09 | 22 28 | 10 04 | 13 | 91 |
| 16 | 08 46 | 08 38 | 12 09 | 23 15 | 10 52 | 14 | 96 |

| UT | ARIES | VENUS −4.5 | | MARS +1.2 | | JUPITER −2.0 | | SATURN +0.7 | | STARS | | |
|---|---|---|---|---|---|---|---|---|---|---|---|---|
| | GHA | GHA | Dec | GHA | Dec | GHA | Dec | GHA | Dec | Name | SHA | Dec |
| d h | ° ′ | ° ′ | ° ′ | ° ′ | ° ′ | ° ′ | ° ′ | ° ′ | ° ′ | | ° ′ | ° ′ |
| 17 00 | 174 33.0 | 222 53.9 | S15 27.1 | 223 49.0 | S19 15.3 | 185 26.8 | S 5 45.6 | 211 17.5 | S15 30.1 | Acamar | 315 13.8 | S40 13.2 |
| 01 | 189 35.5 | 237 53.9 | 26.7 | 238 49.6 | 14.9 | 200 28.7 | 45.3 | 226 19.7 | 30.0 | Achernar | 335 22.5 | S57 07.7 |
| 02 | 204 37.9 | 252 53.9 | 26.4 | 253 50.1 | 14.4 | 215 30.7 | 45.1 | 241 21.9 | 29.9 | Acrux | 173 01.9 | S63 13.3 |
| 03 | 219 40.4 | 267 53.8 . . | 26.0 | 268 50.6 . . | 14.0 | 230 32.6 . . | 44.9 | 256 24.2 . . | 29.9 | Adhara | 255 07.6 | S29 00.4 |
| 04 | 234 42.9 | 282 53.8 | 25.6 | 283 51.2 | 13.5 | 245 34.5 | 44.6 | 271 26.4 | 29.8 | Aldebaran | 290 42.4 | N16 33.1 |
| 05 | 249 45.3 | 297 53.8 | 25.2 | 298 51.7 | 13.0 | 260 36.4 | 44.4 | 286 28.6 | 29.7 | | | |
| 06 | 264 47.8 | 312 53.7 | S15 24.8 | 313 52.2 | S19 12.6 | 275 38.3 | S 5 44.2 | 301 30.8 | S15 29.6 | Alioth | 166 14.5 | N55 50.3 |
| 07 | 279 50.3 | 327 53.7 | 24.5 | 328 52.8 | 12.1 | 290 40.2 | 43.9 | 316 33.0 | 29.6 | Alkaid | 152 53.4 | N49 12.0 |
| T 08 | 294 52.7 | 342 53.7 | 24.1 | 343 53.3 | 11.7 | 305 42.1 | 43.7 | 331 35.2 | 29.5 | Alnair | 27 36.2 | S46 51.3 |
| H 09 | 309 55.2 | 357 53.7 . . | 23.7 | 358 53.9 . . | 11.2 | 320 44.0 . . | 43.5 | 346 37.4 . . | 29.4 | Alnilam | 275 40.1 | S 1 11.4 |
| U 10 | 324 57.6 | 12 53.6 | 23.3 | 13 54.4 | 10.7 | 335 45.9 | 43.2 | 1 39.6 | 29.3 | Alphard | 217 49.8 | S 8 45.4 |
| R 11 | 340 00.1 | 27 53.6 | 22.9 | 28 54.9 | 10.3 | 350 47.8 | 43.0 | 16 41.8 | 29.2 | | | |
| S 12 | 355 02.6 | 42 53.6 | S15 22.6 | 43 55.5 | S19 09.8 | 5 49.7 | S 5 42.8 | 31 44.0 | S15 29.2 | Alphecca | 126 05.5 | N26 38.2 |
| D 13 | 10 05.0 | 57 53.5 | 22.2 | 58 56.0 | 09.4 | 20 51.6 | 42.6 | 46 46.2 | 29.1 | Alpheratz | 357 37.5 | N29 12.6 |
| A 14 | 25 07.5 | 72 53.5 | 21.8 | 73 56.6 | 08.9 | 35 53.5 | 42.3 | 61 48.4 | 29.0 | Altair | 62 02.4 | N 8 55.4 |
| Y 15 | 40 10.0 | 87 53.5 . . | 21.4 | 88 57.1 . . | 08.4 | 50 55.4 . . | 42.1 | 76 50.6 . . | 28.9 | Ankaa | 353 09.9 | S42 11.3 |
| 16 | 55 12.4 | 102 53.4 | 21.0 | 103 57.6 | 08.0 | 65 57.4 | 41.9 | 91 52.8 | 28.8 | Antares | 112 18.6 | S26 28.8 |
| 17 | 70 14.9 | 117 53.4 | 20.6 | 118 58.2 | 07.5 | 80 59.3 | 41.6 | 106 55.0 | 28.8 | | | |
| 18 | 85 17.4 | 132 53.4 | S15 20.2 | 133 58.7 | S19 07.0 | 96 01.2 | S 5 41.4 | 121 57.2 | S15 28.7 | Arcturus | 145 49.8 | N19 03.9 |
| 19 | 100 19.8 | 147 53.3 | 19.8 | 148 59.3 | 06.6 | 111 03.1 | 41.2 | 136 59.4 | 28.6 | Atria | 107 14.8 | S69 03.7 |
| 20 | 115 22.3 | 162 53.3 | 19.5 | 163 59.8 | 06.1 | 126 05.0 | 40.9 | 152 01.7 | 28.5 | Avior | 234 15.3 | S59 35.0 |
| 21 | 130 24.8 | 177 53.2 . . | 19.1 | 179 00.3 . . | 05.7 | 141 06.9 . . | 40.7 | 167 03.9 . . | 28.5 | Bellatrix | 278 25.4 | N 6 22.1 |
| 22 | 145 27.2 | 192 53.2 | 18.7 | 194 00.9 | 05.2 | 156 08.8 | 40.5 | 182 06.1 | 28.4 | Betelgeuse | 270 54.6 | N 7 24.6 |
| 23 | 160 29.7 | 207 53.2 | 18.3 | 209 01.4 | 04.7 | 171 10.7 | 40.2 | 197 08.3 | 28.3 | | | |
| 18 00 | 175 32.1 | 222 53.1 | S15 17.9 | 224 02.0 | S19 04.3 | 186 12.6 | S 5 40.0 | 212 10.5 | S15 28.2 | Canopus | 263 53.3 | S52 42.7 |
| 01 | 190 34.6 | 237 53.1 | 17.5 | 239 02.5 | 03.8 | 201 14.5 | 39.8 | 227 12.7 | 28.1 | Capella | 280 25.4 | N46 01.3 |
| 02 | 205 37.1 | 252 53.1 | 17.1 | 254 03.0 | 03.3 | 216 16.4 | 39.5 | 242 14.9 | 28.1 | Deneb | 49 27.7 | N45 21.2 |
| 03 | 220 39.5 | 267 53.0 . . | 16.7 | 269 03.6 . . | 02.9 | 231 18.3 . . | 39.3 | 257 17.1 . . | 28.0 | Denebola | 182 27.0 | N14 26.8 |
| 04 | 235 42.0 | 282 53.0 | 16.3 | 284 04.1 | 02.4 | 246 20.2 | 39.1 | 272 19.3 | 27.9 | Diphda | 348 49.9 | S17 52.1 |
| 05 | 250 44.5 | 297 52.9 | 15.9 | 299 04.7 | 01.9 | 261 22.2 | 38.8 | 287 21.5 | 27.8 | | | |
| 06 | 265 46.9 | 312 52.9 | S15 15.5 | 314 05.2 | S19 01.5 | 276 24.1 | S 5 38.6 | 302 23.7 | S15 27.8 | Dubhe | 193 43.2 | N61 37.9 |
| 07 | 280 49.4 | 327 52.8 | 15.1 | 329 05.7 | 01.0 | 291 26.0 | 38.4 | 317 25.9 | 27.7 | Elnath | 278 04.8 | N28 37.6 |
| 08 | 295 51.9 | 342 52.8 | 14.7 | 344 06.3 | 00.5 | 306 27.9 | 38.1 | 332 28.1 | 27.6 | Eltanin | 90 43.3 | N51 28.8 |
| F 09 | 310 54.3 | 357 52.8 . . | 14.3 | 359 06.8 | 19 00.1 | 321 29.8 . . | 37.9 | 347 30.3 . . | 27.5 | Enif | 33 41.3 | N 9 58.4 |
| R 10 | 325 56.8 | 12 52.7 | 13.9 | 14 07.4 | 18 59.6 | 336 31.7 | 37.7 | 2 32.5 | 27.4 | Fomalhaut | 15 17.4 | S29 30.4 |
| I 11 | 340 59.2 | 27 52.7 | 13.5 | 29 07.9 | 59.1 | 351 33.6 | 37.4 | 17 34.8 | 27.4 | | | |
| D 12 | 356 01.7 | 42 52.6 | S15 13.1 | 44 08.4 | S18 58.7 | 6 35.5 | S 5 37.2 | 32 37.0 | S15 27.3 | Gacrux | 171 53.6 | S57 14.2 |
| A 13 | 11 04.2 | 57 52.6 | 12.7 | 59 09.0 | 58.2 | 21 37.4 | 37.0 | 47 39.2 | 27.2 | Gienah | 175 45.6 | S17 39.9 |
| Y 14 | 26 06.6 | 72 52.5 | 12.3 | 74 09.5 | 57.7 | 36 39.3 | 36.7 | 62 41.4 | 27.1 | Hadar | 148 38.8 | S60 28.6 |
| 15 | 41 09.1 | 87 52.5 . . | 11.9 | 89 10.1 . . | 57.2 | 51 41.2 . . | 36.5 | 77 43.6 . . | 27.0 | Hamal | 327 54.1 | N23 33.9 |
| 16 | 56 11.6 | 102 52.4 | 11.5 | 104 10.6 | 56.8 | 66 43.1 | 36.3 | 92 45.8 | 27.0 | Kaus Aust. | 83 35.6 | S34 22.4 |
| 17 | 71 14.0 | 117 52.4 | 11.1 | 119 11.2 | 56.3 | 81 45.0 | 36.0 | 107 48.0 | 26.9 | | | |
| 18 | 86 16.5 | 132 52.3 | S15 10.7 | 134 11.7 | S18 55.8 | 96 47.0 | S 5 35.8 | 122 50.2 | S15 26.8 | Kochab | 137 19.0 | N74 03.6 |
| 19 | 101 19.0 | 147 52.3 | 10.3 | 149 12.2 | 55.4 | 111 48.9 | 35.6 | 137 52.4 | 26.7 | Markab | 13 32.5 | N15 19.3 |
| 20 | 116 21.4 | 162 52.2 | 09.8 | 164 12.8 | 54.9 | 126 50.8 | 35.4 | 152 54.6 | 26.7 | Menkar | 314 08.8 | N 4 10.4 |
| 21 | 131 23.9 | 177 52.2 . . | 09.4 | 179 13.3 . . | 54.4 | 141 52.7 . . | 35.1 | 167 56.8 . . | 26.6 | Menkent | 148 00.0 | S36 28.7 |
| 22 | 146 26.4 | 192 52.1 | 09.0 | 194 13.9 | 53.9 | 156 54.6 | 34.9 | 182 59.0 | 26.5 | Miaplacidus | 221 38.0 | S69 48.6 |
| 23 | 161 28.8 | 207 52.1 | 08.6 | 209 14.4 | 53.5 | 171 56.5 | 34.7 | 198 01.3 | 26.4 | | | |
| 19 00 | 176 31.3 | 222 52.0 | S15 08.2 | 224 15.0 | S18 53.0 | 186 58.4 | S 5 34.4 | 213 03.5 | S15 26.3 | Mirfak | 308 31.8 | N49 56.4 |
| 01 | 191 33.7 | 237 52.0 | 07.8 | 239 15.5 | 52.5 | 202 00.3 | 34.2 | 228 05.7 | 26.3 | Nunki | 75 50.7 | S26 16.1 |
| 02 | 206 36.2 | 252 51.9 | 07.4 | 254 16.0 | 52.1 | 217 02.2 | 34.0 | 243 07.9 | 26.2 | Peacock | 53 09.7 | S56 39.7 |
| 03 | 221 38.7 | 267 51.9 . . | 07.0 | 269 16.6 . . | 51.6 | 232 04.1 . . | 33.7 | 258 10.1 . . | 26.1 | Pollux | 243 20.0 | N27 58.4 |
| 04 | 236 41.1 | 282 51.8 | 06.5 | 284 17.1 | 51.1 | 247 06.0 | 33.5 | 273 12.3 | 26.0 | Procyon | 244 53.1 | N 5 10.0 |
| 05 | 251 43.6 | 297 51.8 | 06.1 | 299 17.7 | 50.6 | 262 07.9 | 33.3 | 288 14.5 | 26.0 | | | |
| 06 | 266 46.1 | 312 51.7 | S15 05.7 | 314 18.2 | S18 50.2 | 277 09.9 | S 5 33.0 | 303 16.7 | S15 25.9 | Rasalhague | 96 00.7 | N12 32.4 |
| 07 | 281 48.5 | 327 51.7 | 05.3 | 329 18.8 | 49.7 | 292 11.8 | 32.8 | 318 18.9 | 25.8 | Regulus | 207 36.6 | N11 51.5 |
| S 08 | 296 51.0 | 342 51.6 | 04.9 | 344 19.3 | 49.2 | 307 13.7 | 32.6 | 333 21.1 | 25.7 | Rigel | 281 06.1 | S 8 10.8 |
| A 09 | 311 53.5 | 357 51.5 . . | 04.4 | 359 19.9 . . | 48.7 | 322 15.6 . . | 32.3 | 348 23.3 . . | 25.6 | Rigil Kent. | 139 43.0 | S60 55.4 |
| T 10 | 326 55.9 | 12 51.5 | 04.0 | 14 20.4 | 48.3 | 337 17.5 | 32.1 | 3 25.6 | 25.6 | Sabik | 102 05.4 | S15 45.2 |
| U 11 | 341 58.4 | 27 51.4 | 03.6 | 29 20.9 | 47.8 | 352 19.4 | 31.9 | 18 27.8 | 25.5 | | | |
| R 12 | 357 00.9 | 42 51.4 | S15 03.2 | 44 21.5 | S18 47.3 | 7 21.3 | S 5 31.6 | 33 30.0 | S15 25.4 | Schedar | 349 34.2 | N56 39.4 |
| D 13 | 12 03.3 | 57 51.3 | 02.8 | 59 22.0 | 46.8 | 22 23.2 | 31.4 | 48 32.2 | 25.3 | Shaula | 96 13.5 | S37 07.1 |
| A 14 | 27 05.8 | 72 51.2 | 02.3 | 74 22.6 | 46.3 | 37 25.1 | 31.2 | 63 34.4 | 25.3 | Sirius | 258 28.2 | S16 45.0 |
| Y 15 | 42 08.2 | 87 51.2 . . | 01.9 | 89 23.1 . . | 45.9 | 52 27.0 . . | 30.9 | 78 36.6 . . | 25.2 | Spica | 158 24.5 | S11 16.7 |
| 16 | 57 10.7 | 102 51.1 | 01.5 | 104 23.7 | 45.4 | 67 28.9 | 30.7 | 93 38.8 | 25.1 | Suhail | 222 47.7 | S43 31.5 |
| 17 | 72 13.2 | 117 51.1 | 01.1 | 119 24.2 | 44.9 | 82 30.9 | 30.5 | 108 41.0 | 25.0 | | | |
| 18 | 87 15.6 | 132 51.0 | S15 00.6 | 134 24.8 | S18 44.4 | 97 32.8 | S 5 30.3 | 123 43.2 | S15 25.0 | Vega | 80 34.9 | N38 47.9 |
| 19 | 102 18.1 | 147 50.9 | 15 00.2 | 149 25.3 | 44.0 | 112 34.7 | 30.0 | 138 45.4 | 24.9 | Zuben'ubi | 136 58.4 | S16 08.0 |
| 20 | 117 20.6 | 162 50.9 | 14 59.8 | 164 25.9 | 43.5 | 127 36.6 | 29.8 | 153 47.6 | 24.8 | | SHA | Mer. Pass. |
| 21 | 132 23.0 | 177 50.8 . . | 59.3 | 179 26.4 . . | 43.0 | 142 38.5 . . | 29.6 | 168 49.9 . . | 24.7 | | ° ′ | h m |
| 22 | 147 25.5 | 192 50.8 | 58.9 | 194 27.0 | 42.5 | 157 40.4 | 29.3 | 183 52.1 | 24.6 | Venus | 47 21.0 | 9 08 |
| 23 | 162 28.0 | 207 50.7 | 58.5 | 209 27.5 | 42.0 | 172 42.3 | 29.1 | 198 54.3 | 24.6 | Mars | 48 29.8 | 9 04 |
| | h m | | | | | | | | | Jupiter | 10 40.5 | 11 34 |
| Mer. Pass. 12 15.8 | | v 0.0 | d 0.4 | v 0.5 | d 0.5 | v 1.9 | d 0.2 | v 2.2 | d 0.1 | Saturn | 36 38.3 | 9 50 |

### SUN and MOON

| UT (d h) | SUN GHA | SUN Dec | MOON GHA | v | Dec | d | HP |
|---|---|---|---|---|---|---|---|
|  | ° ′ | ° ′ | ° ′ | ′ | ° ′ | ′ | ′ |
| **17 00** | 177 52.8 | S 1 26.5 | 10 50.7 | 12.8 | N12 12.6 | 13.3 | 56.8 |
| 01 | 192 53.0 | 25.5 | 25 22.5 | 12.9 | 11 59.3 | 13.4 | 56.8 |
| 02 | 207 53.2 | 24.5 | 39 54.4 | 13.0 | 11 45.9 | 13.4 | 56.8 |
| 03 | 222 53.4 | .. 23.6 | 54 26.4 | 12.9 | 11 32.5 | 13.5 | 56.8 |
| 04 | 237 53.6 | 22.6 | 68 58.3 | 13.0 | 11 19.0 | 13.6 | 56.9 |
| 05 | 252 53.7 | 21.6 | 83 30.3 | 13.0 | 11 05.4 | 13.6 | 56.9 |
| 06 | 267 53.9 | S 1 20.6 | 98 02.3 | 13.0 | N10 51.8 | 13.7 | 56.9 |
| 07 | 282 54.1 | 19.6 | 112 34.3 | 13.0 | 10 38.1 | 13.8 | 57.0 |
| **T** 08 | 297 54.3 | 18.6 | 127 06.3 | 13.0 | 10 24.3 | 13.8 | 57.0 |
| **H** 09 | 312 54.5 | .. 17.6 | 141 38.3 | 13.1 | 10 10.5 | 13.9 | 57.0 |
| **U** 10 | 327 54.6 | 16.6 | 156 10.4 | 13.0 | 9 56.6 | 14.0 | 57.0 |
| **R** 11 | 342 54.8 | 15.7 | 170 42.4 | 13.1 | 9 42.6 | 14.0 | 57.1 |
| **S** 12 | 357 55.0 | S 1 14.7 | 185 14.5 | 13.1 | N 9 28.6 | 14.0 | 57.1 |
| **D** 13 | 12 55.2 | 13.7 | 199 46.6 | 13.1 | 9 14.6 | 14.2 | 57.1 |
| **A** 14 | 27 55.4 | 12.7 | 214 18.7 | 13.1 | 9 00.4 | 14.1 | 57.1 |
| **Y** 15 | 42 55.5 | .. 11.7 | 228 50.8 | 13.1 | 8 46.3 | 14.3 | 57.2 |
| 16 | 57 55.7 | 10.7 | 243 22.9 | 13.1 | 8 32.0 | 14.3 | 57.2 |
| 17 | 72 55.9 | 09.7 | 257 55.0 | 13.2 | 8 17.7 | 14.3 | 57.2 |
| 18 | 87 56.1 | S 1 08.7 | 272 27.2 | 13.1 | N 8 03.4 | 14.4 | 57.2 |
| 19 | 102 56.3 | 07.7 | 286 59.3 | 13.2 | 7 49.0 | 14.4 | 57.3 |
| 20 | 117 56.4 | 06.8 | 301 31.5 | 13.1 | 7 34.6 | 14.5 | 57.3 |
| 21 | 132 56.6 | .. 05.8 | 316 03.6 | 13.2 | 7 20.1 | 14.5 | 57.3 |
| 22 | 147 56.8 | 04.8 | 330 35.8 | 13.2 | 7 05.6 | 14.6 | 57.3 |
| 23 | 162 57.0 | 03.8 | 345 08.0 | 13.1 | 6 51.0 | 14.6 | 57.4 |
| **18 00** | 177 57.2 | S 1 02.8 | 359 40.1 | 13.2 | N 6 36.4 | 14.7 | 57.4 |
| 01 | 192 57.3 | 01.8 | 14 12.3 | 13.2 | 6 21.7 | 14.7 | 57.4 |
| 02 | 207 57.5 | 1 00.8 | 28 44.5 | 13.2 | 6 07.0 | 14.7 | 57.4 |
| 03 | 222 57.7 | 0 59.8 | 43 16.7 | 13.1 | 5 52.3 | 14.8 | 57.5 |
| 04 | 237 57.9 | 58.8 | 57 48.8 | 13.2 | 5 37.5 | 14.9 | 57.5 |
| 05 | 252 58.1 | 57.9 | 72 21.0 | 13.2 | 5 22.6 | 14.8 | 57.5 |
| 06 | 267 58.3 | S 0 56.9 | 86 53.2 | 13.2 | N 5 07.8 | 14.9 | 57.5 |
| 07 | 282 58.4 | 55.9 | 101 25.4 | 13.1 | 4 52.9 | 15.0 | 57.6 |
| **F** 08 | 297 58.6 | 54.9 | 115 57.5 | 13.2 | 4 37.9 | 15.0 | 57.6 |
| **R** 09 | 312 58.8 | .. 53.9 | 130 29.7 | 13.2 | 4 22.9 | 15.0 | 57.6 |
| **I** 10 | 327 59.0 | 52.9 | 145 01.9 | 13.1 | 4 07.9 | 15.0 | 57.6 |
| **D** 11 | 342 59.2 | 51.9 | 159 34.0 | 13.2 | 3 52.9 | 15.1 | 57.7 |
| **A** 12 | 357 59.4 | S 0 50.9 | 174 06.2 | 13.1 | N 3 37.8 | 15.1 | 57.7 |
| **Y** 13 | 12 59.5 | 50.0 | 188 38.3 | 13.1 | 3 22.7 | 15.1 | 57.7 |
| 14 | 27 59.7 | 49.0 | 203 10.4 | 13.2 | 3 07.6 | 15.2 | 57.7 |
| 15 | 42 59.9 | .. 48.0 | 217 42.6 | 13.1 | 2 52.4 | 15.2 | 57.8 |
| 16 | 58 00.1 | 47.0 | 232 14.7 | 13.1 | 2 37.2 | 15.2 | 57.8 |
| 17 | 73 00.3 | 46.0 | 246 46.8 | 13.0 | 2 22.0 | 15.2 | 57.8 |
| 18 | 88 00.5 | S 0 45.0 | 261 18.8 | 13.1 | N 2 06.8 | 15.3 | 57.8 |
| 19 | 103 00.6 | 44.0 | 275 50.9 | 13.1 | 1 51.5 | 15.2 | 57.9 |
| 20 | 118 00.8 | 43.0 | 290 23.0 | 13.0 | 1 36.3 | 15.3 | 57.9 |
| 21 | 133 01.0 | .. 42.0 | 304 55.0 | 13.0 | 1 21.0 | 15.4 | 57.9 |
| 22 | 148 01.2 | 41.1 | 319 27.0 | 13.0 | 1 05.6 | 15.3 | 57.9 |
| 23 | 163 01.4 | 40.1 | 333 59.0 | 13.0 | 0 50.3 | 15.3 | 58.0 |
| **19 00** | 178 01.5 | S 0 39.1 | 348 31.0 | 13.0 | N 0 35.0 | 15.4 | 58.0 |
| 01 | 193 01.7 | 38.1 | 3 03.0 | 12.9 | 0 19.6 | 15.4 | 58.0 |
| 02 | 208 01.9 | 37.1 | 17 34.9 | 12.9 | N 0 04.2 | 15.4 | 58.0 |
| 03 | 223 02.1 | .. 36.1 | 32 06.8 | 12.9 | S 0 11.2 | 15.4 | 58.0 |
| 04 | 238 02.3 | 35.1 | 46 38.7 | 12.9 | 0 26.6 | 15.4 | 58.1 |
| 05 | 253 02.5 | 34.1 | 61 10.6 | 12.9 | 0 42.0 | 15.4 | 58.1 |
| 06 | 268 02.6 | S 0 33.2 | 75 42.5 | 12.8 | S 0 57.4 | 15.4 | 58.1 |
| 07 | 283 02.8 | 32.2 | 90 14.3 | 12.8 | 1 12.8 | 15.4 | 58.1 |
| **S** 08 | 298 03.0 | 31.2 | 104 46.1 | 12.7 | 1 28.2 | 15.5 | 58.1 |
| **A** 09 | 313 03.2 | .. 30.2 | 119 17.8 | 12.8 | 1 43.7 | 15.4 | 58.2 |
| **T** 10 | 328 03.4 | 29.2 | 133 49.6 | 12.7 | 1 59.1 | 15.4 | 58.2 |
| **U** 11 | 343 03.6 | 28.2 | 148 21.3 | 12.7 | 2 14.5 | 15.5 | 58.2 |
| **R** 12 | 358 03.8 | S 0 27.2 | 162 53.0 | 12.6 | S 2 30.0 | 15.4 | 58.2 |
| **D** 13 | 13 03.9 | 26.2 | 177 24.6 | 12.6 | 2 45.4 | 15.5 | 58.3 |
| **A** 14 | 28 04.1 | 25.2 | 191 56.2 | 12.6 | 3 00.9 | 15.4 | 58.3 |
| **Y** 15 | 43 04.3 | .. 24.3 | 206 27.8 | 12.5 | 3 16.3 | 15.4 | 58.3 |
| 16 | 58 04.5 | 23.3 | 220 59.3 | 12.5 | 3 31.7 | 15.4 | 58.3 |
| 17 | 73 04.7 | 22.3 | 235 30.8 | 12.5 | 3 47.1 | 15.4 | 58.3 |
| 18 | 88 04.9 | S 0 21.3 | 250 02.3 | 12.4 | S 4 02.5 | 15.4 | 58.4 |
| 19 | 103 05.0 | 20.3 | 264 33.7 | 12.4 | 4 17.9 | 15.4 | 58.4 |
| 20 | 118 05.2 | 19.3 | 279 05.1 | 12.4 | 4 33.3 | 15.4 | 58.4 |
| 21 | 133 05.4 | .. 18.3 | 293 36.5 | 12.3 | 4 48.7 | 15.3 | 58.4 |
| 22 | 148 05.6 | 17.3 | 308 07.8 | 12.2 | 5 04.0 | 15.4 | 58.4 |
| 23 | 163 05.8 | 16.4 | 322 39.0 | 12.3 | S 5 19.4 | 15.3 | 58.4 |
| **SD** | 16.1 | d 1.0 | SD 15.6 | | 15.7 | | 15.9 |

### Twilight — Sunrise — Moonrise

| Lat. | Naut. | Civil | Sunrise | 17 | 18 | 19 | 20 |
|---|---|---|---|---|---|---|---|
| ° | h m | h m | h m | h m | h m | h m | h m |
| N 72 | 03 35 | 05 02 | 06 09 | 15 58 | 18 11 | 20 24 | 22 50 |
| N 70 | 03 52 | 05 08 | 06 09 | 16 12 | 18 14 | 20 17 | 22 29 |
| 68 | 04 05 | 05 13 | 06 09 | 16 22 | 18 16 | 20 12 | 22 13 |
| 66 | 04 15 | 05 17 | 06 08 | 16 31 | 18 18 | 20 07 | 22 00 |
| 64 | 04 24 | 05 21 | 06 08 | 16 39 | 18 20 | 20 03 | 21 50 |
| 62 | 04 31 | 05 24 | 06 08 | 16 45 | 18 21 | 19 59 | 21 41 |
| 60 | 04 37 | 05 27 | 06 08 | 16 50 | 18 23 | 19 56 | 21 33 |
| N 58 | 04 42 | 05 29 | 06 08 | 16 55 | 18 24 | 19 54 | 21 27 |
| 56 | 04 47 | 05 31 | 06 08 | 16 59 | 18 25 | 19 51 | 21 21 |
| 54 | 04 51 | 05 32 | 06 08 | 17 03 | 18 25 | 19 49 | 21 15 |
| 52 | 04 54 | 05 34 | 06 08 | 17 06 | 18 26 | 19 47 | 21 11 |
| 50 | 04 57 | 05 35 | 06 07 | 17 10 | 18 27 | 19 46 | 21 06 |
| 45 | 05 04 | 05 38 | 06 07 | 17 16 | 18 28 | 19 42 | 20 57 |
| N 40 | 05 08 | 05 40 | 06 07 | 17 22 | 18 30 | 19 39 | 20 50 |
| 35 | 05 12 | 05 41 | 06 07 | 17 27 | 18 31 | 19 36 | 20 43 |
| 30 | 05 15 | 05 43 | 06 06 | 17 31 | 18 32 | 19 34 | 20 38 |
| 20 | 05 18 | 05 44 | 06 06 | 17 38 | 18 33 | 19 30 | 20 28 |
| N 10 | 05 20 | 05 44 | 06 05 | 17 44 | 18 35 | 19 26 | 20 19 |
| 0 | 05 20 | 05 44 | 06 05 | 17 50 | 18 36 | 19 23 | 20 11 |
| S 10 | 05 19 | 05 43 | 06 04 | 17 56 | 18 38 | 19 20 | 20 04 |
| 20 | 05 16 | 05 41 | 06 03 | 18 03 | 18 39 | 19 17 | 19 55 |
| 30 | 05 10 | 05 38 | 06 02 | 18 10 | 18 41 | 19 13 | 19 46 |
| 35 | 05 07 | 05 36 | 06 01 | 18 14 | 18 42 | 19 11 | 19 41 |
| 40 | 05 02 | 05 34 | 06 01 | 18 18 | 18 43 | 19 08 | 19 35 |
| 45 | 04 56 | 05 30 | 06 00 | 18 24 | 18 45 | 19 05 | 19 28 |
| S 50 | 04 48 | 05 26 | 05 58 | 18 30 | 18 46 | 19 02 | 19 19 |
| 52 | 04 44 | 05 24 | 05 58 | 18 33 | 18 47 | 19 01 | 19 16 |
| 54 | 04 40 | 05 22 | 05 57 | 18 36 | 18 48 | 18 59 | 19 11 |
| 56 | 04 35 | 05 19 | 05 57 | 18 40 | 18 49 | 18 57 | 19 07 |
| 58 | 04 29 | 05 16 | 05 56 | 18 44 | 18 50 | 18 55 | 19 02 |
| S 60 | 04 22 | 05 13 | 05 55 | 18 48 | 18 51 | 18 53 | 18 56 |

### Sunset — Twilight — Moonset

| Lat. | Sunset | Civil | Naut. | 17 | 18 | 19 | 20 |
|---|---|---|---|---|---|---|---|
| ° | h m | h m | h m | h m | h m | h m | h m |
| N 72 | 18 10 | 19 18 | 20 46 | 07 48 | 07 13 | 06 43 | 06 10 |
| N 70 | 18 10 | 19 11 | 20 28 | 07 32 | 07 07 | 06 44 | 06 21 |
| 68 | 18 09 | 19 05 | 20 14 | 07 19 | 07 02 | 06 46 | 06 29 |
| 66 | 18 09 | 19 01 | 20 04 | 07 08 | 06 57 | 06 47 | 06 36 |
| 64 | 18 09 | 18 57 | 19 55 | 06 59 | 06 53 | 06 48 | 06 42 |
| 62 | 18 09 | 18 54 | 19 47 | 06 51 | 06 50 | 06 49 | 06 47 |
| 60 | 18 09 | 18 51 | 19 41 | 06 45 | 06 47 | 06 49 | 06 52 |
| N 58 | 18 09 | 18 49 | 19 35 | 06 39 | 06 45 | 06 50 | 06 56 |
| 56 | 18 10 | 18 47 | 19 31 | 06 33 | 06 42 | 06 51 | 07 00 |
| 54 | 18 10 | 18 45 | 19 27 | 06 28 | 06 40 | 06 51 | 07 03 |
| 52 | 18 10 | 18 43 | 19 23 | 06 24 | 06 38 | 06 52 | 07 06 |
| 50 | 18 10 | 18 42 | 19 20 | 06 20 | 06 37 | 06 52 | 07 09 |
| 45 | 18 10 | 18 39 | 19 13 | 06 12 | 06 33 | 06 53 | 07 15 |
| N 40 | 18 10 | 18 37 | 19 08 | 06 04 | 06 30 | 06 54 | 07 20 |
| 35 | 18 10 | 18 35 | 19 05 | 05 58 | 06 27 | 06 55 | 07 24 |
| 30 | 18 10 | 18 34 | 19 02 | 05 53 | 06 24 | 06 55 | 07 28 |
| 20 | 18 10 | 18 32 | 18 58 | 05 43 | 06 20 | 06 57 | 07 34 |
| N 10 | 18 11 | 18 32 | 18 56 | 05 34 | 06 16 | 06 58 | 07 40 |
| 0 | 18 11 | 18 32 | 18 56 | 05 26 | 06 12 | 06 58 | 07 46 |
| S 10 | 18 12 | 18 33 | 18 57 | 05 18 | 06 09 | 06 59 | 07 51 |
| 20 | 18 13 | 18 35 | 19 00 | 05 09 | 06 05 | 07 00 | 07 57 |
| 30 | 18 14 | 18 37 | 19 05 | 04 59 | 06 00 | 07 01 | 08 04 |
| 35 | 18 14 | 18 39 | 19 09 | 04 54 | 05 57 | 07 02 | 08 08 |
| 40 | 18 15 | 18 42 | 19 14 | 04 47 | 05 54 | 07 03 | 08 12 |
| 45 | 18 16 | 18 46 | 19 19 | 04 39 | 05 51 | 07 03 | 08 18 |
| S 50 | 18 17 | 18 49 | 19 27 | 04 30 | 05 46 | 07 04 | 08 24 |
| 52 | 18 17 | 18 51 | 19 31 | 04 25 | 05 44 | 07 05 | 08 27 |
| 54 | 18 18 | 18 53 | 19 35 | 04 20 | 05 42 | 07 05 | 08 30 |
| 56 | 18 19 | 18 56 | 19 40 | 04 15 | 05 40 | 07 06 | 08 33 |
| 58 | 18 19 | 18 58 | 19 45 | 04 09 | 05 37 | 07 06 | 08 37 |
| S 60 | 18 20 | 19 01 | 19 52 | 04 02 | 05 34 | 07 07 | 08 42 |

### SUN and MOON

| Day | Eqn. of Time 00h | Eqn. of Time 12h | Mer. Pass. | Mer. Pass. Upper | Mer. Pass. Lower | Age | Phase |
|---|---|---|---|---|---|---|---|
| d | m s | m s | h m | h m | h m | d | % |
| 17 | 08 29 | 08 20 | 12 08 | 24 01 | 11 38 | 15 | 99 |
| 18 | 08 12 | 08 03 | 12 08 | 00 01 | 12 24 | 16 | 100 |
| 19 | 07 54 | 07 45 | 12 08 | 00 47 | 13 11 | 17 | 98 |

| UT | ARIES | VENUS −4.5 | | MARS +1.1 | | JUPITER −2.0 | | SATURN +0.7 | | STARS | | |
|---|---|---|---|---|---|---|---|---|---|---|---|---|
| | GHA | GHA | Dec | GHA | Dec | GHA | Dec | GHA | Dec | Name | SHA | Dec |
| d h | ° ′ | ° ′ | ° ′ | ° ′ | ° ′ | ° ′ | ° ′ | ° ′ | ° ′ | | ° ′ | ° ′ |
| 20 00 | 177 30.4 | 222 50.6 | S14 58.0 | 224 28.0 | S18 41.6 | 187 44.2 | S 5 28.9 | 213 56.5 | S15 24.5 | Acamar | 315 13.8 | S40 13.2 |
| 01 | 192 32.9 | 237 50.6 | 57.6 | 239 28.6 | 41.1 | 202 46.1 | 28.6 | 228 58.7 | 24.4 | Achernar | 335 22.5 | S57 07.7 |
| 02 | 207 35.3 | 252 50.5 | 57.2 | 254 29.1 | 40.6 | 217 48.0 | 28.4 | 244 00.9 | 24.3 | Acrux | 173 01.9 | S63 13.3 |
| 03 | 222 37.8 | 267 50.4 | 56.7 | 269 29.7 | 40.1 | 232 49.9 | 28.2 | 259 03.1 | 24.3 | Adhara | 255 07.6 | S29 00.4 |
| 04 | 237 40.3 | 282 50.4 | 56.3 | 284 30.2 | 39.6 | 247 51.9 | 27.9 | 274 05.3 | 24.2 | Aldebaran | 290 42.4 | N16 33.1 |
| 05 | 252 42.7 | 297 50.3 | 55.9 | 299 30.8 | 39.1 | 262 53.8 | 27.7 | 289 07.5 | 24.1 | | | |
| 06 | 267 45.2 | 312 50.2 | S14 55.4 | 314 31.3 | S18 38.7 | 277 55.7 | S 5 27.5 | 304 09.8 | S15 24.0 | Alioth | 166 14.5 | N55 50.3 |
| 07 | 282 47.7 | 327 50.2 | 55.0 | 329 31.9 | 38.2 | 292 57.6 | 27.2 | 319 12.0 | 23.9 | Alkaid | 152 53.4 | N49 12.0 |
| 08 | 297 50.1 | 342 50.1 | 54.6 | 344 32.4 | 37.7 | 307 59.5 | 27.0 | 334 14.2 | 23.9 | Alnair | 27 36.2 | S46 51.3 |
| S 09 | 312 52.6 | 357 50.0 | 54.1 | 359 33.0 | 37.2 | 323 01.4 | 26.8 | 349 16.4 | 23.8 | Alnilam | 275 40.1 | S 1 11.4 |
| U 10 | 327 55.1 | 12 50.0 | 53.7 | 14 33.5 | 36.7 | 338 03.3 | 26.5 | 4 18.6 | 23.7 | Alphard | 217 49.8 | S 8 45.4 |
| N 11 | 342 57.5 | 27 49.9 | 53.2 | 29 34.1 | 36.2 | 353 05.2 | 26.3 | 19 20.8 | 23.6 | | | |
| D 12 | 358 00.0 | 42 49.8 | S14 52.8 | 44 34.6 | S18 35.8 | 8 07.1 | S 5 26.1 | 34 23.0 | S15 23.6 | Alphecca | 126 05.5 | N26 38.2 |
| A 13 | 13 02.5 | 57 49.7 | 52.3 | 59 35.2 | 35.3 | 23 09.0 | 25.8 | 49 25.2 | 23.5 | Alpheratz | 357 37.5 | N29 12.6 |
| Y 14 | 28 04.9 | 72 49.7 | 51.9 | 74 35.7 | 34.8 | 38 11.0 | 25.6 | 64 27.4 | 23.4 | Altair | 62 02.4 | N 8 55.4 |
| 15 | 43 07.4 | 87 49.6 | 51.5 | 89 36.3 | 34.3 | 53 12.9 | 25.4 | 79 29.7 | 23.3 | Ankaa | 353 09.9 | S42 11.3 |
| 16 | 58 09.8 | 102 49.5 | 51.0 | 104 36.8 | 33.8 | 68 14.8 | 25.2 | 94 31.9 | 23.3 | Antares | 112 18.5 | S26 28.8 |
| 17 | 73 12.3 | 117 49.5 | 50.6 | 119 37.4 | 33.3 | 83 16.7 | 24.9 | 109 34.1 | 23.2 | | | |
| 18 | 88 14.8 | 132 49.4 | S14 50.1 | 134 37.9 | S18 32.9 | 98 18.6 | S 5 24.7 | 124 36.3 | S15 23.1 | Arcturus | 145 49.8 | N19 03.9 |
| 19 | 103 17.2 | 147 49.3 | 49.7 | 149 38.5 | 32.4 | 113 20.5 | 24.5 | 139 38.5 | 23.0 | Atria | 107 14.7 | S69 03.7 |
| 20 | 118 19.7 | 162 49.2 | 49.2 | 164 39.0 | 31.9 | 128 22.4 | 24.2 | 154 40.7 | 22.9 | Avior | 234 15.3 | S59 35.0 |
| 21 | 133 22.2 | 177 49.2 | 48.8 | 179 39.6 | 31.4 | 143 24.3 | 24.0 | 169 42.9 | 22.9 | Bellatrix | 278 25.4 | N 6 22.1 |
| 22 | 148 24.6 | 192 49.1 | 48.3 | 194 40.1 | 30.9 | 158 26.2 | 23.8 | 184 45.1 | 22.8 | Betelgeuse | 270 54.6 | N 7 24.6 |
| 23 | 163 27.1 | 207 49.0 | 47.9 | 209 40.7 | 30.4 | 173 28.1 | 23.5 | 199 47.4 | 22.7 | | | |
| 21 00 | 178 29.6 | 222 48.9 | S14 47.4 | 224 41.2 | S18 29.9 | 188 30.0 | S 5 23.3 | 214 49.6 | S15 22.6 | Canopus | 263 53.4 | S52 42.7 |
| 01 | 193 32.0 | 237 48.9 | 47.0 | 239 41.8 | 29.4 | 203 32.0 | 23.1 | 229 51.8 | 22.6 | Capella | 280 25.4 | N46 01.3 |
| 02 | 208 34.5 | 252 48.8 | 46.5 | 254 42.3 | 29.0 | 218 33.9 | 22.8 | 244 54.0 | 22.5 | Deneb | 49 27.7 | N45 21.2 |
| 03 | 223 36.9 | 267 48.7 | 46.1 | 269 42.9 | 28.5 | 233 35.8 | 22.6 | 259 56.2 | 22.4 | Denebola | 182 27.0 | N14 26.8 |
| 04 | 238 39.4 | 282 48.6 | 45.6 | 284 43.4 | 28.0 | 248 37.7 | 22.4 | 274 58.4 | 22.3 | Diphda | 348 49.9 | S17 52.1 |
| 05 | 253 41.9 | 297 48.5 | 45.2 | 299 44.0 | 27.5 | 263 39.6 | 22.1 | 290 00.6 | 22.3 | | | |
| 06 | 268 44.3 | 312 48.5 | S14 44.7 | 314 44.5 | S18 27.0 | 278 41.5 | S 5 21.9 | 305 02.8 | S15 22.2 | Dubhe | 193 43.2 | N61 38.0 |
| 07 | 283 46.8 | 327 48.4 | 44.2 | 329 45.1 | 26.5 | 293 43.4 | 21.7 | 320 05.1 | 22.1 | Elnath | 278 04.8 | N28 37.6 |
| 08 | 298 49.3 | 342 48.3 | 43.8 | 344 45.6 | 26.0 | 308 45.3 | 21.4 | 335 07.3 | 22.0 | Eltanin | 90 43.2 | N51 28.8 |
| M 09 | 313 51.7 | 357 48.2 | 43.3 | 359 46.2 | 25.5 | 323 47.2 | 21.2 | 350 09.5 | 22.0 | Enif | 33 41.3 | N 9 58.4 |
| O 10 | 328 54.2 | 12 48.1 | 42.9 | 14 46.7 | 25.0 | 338 49.2 | 21.0 | 5 11.7 | 21.9 | Fomalhaut | 15 17.4 | S29 30.4 |
| N 11 | 343 56.7 | 27 48.1 | 42.4 | 29 47.3 | 24.5 | 353 51.1 | 20.8 | 20 13.9 | 21.8 | | | |
| D 12 | 358 59.1 | 42 48.0 | S14 41.9 | 44 47.8 | S18 24.0 | 8 53.0 | S 5 20.5 | 35 16.1 | S15 21.7 | Gacrux | 171 53.6 | S57 14.2 |
| A 13 | 14 01.6 | 57 47.9 | 41.5 | 59 48.4 | 23.6 | 23 54.9 | 20.3 | 50 18.3 | 21.6 | Gienah | 175 45.6 | S17 39.9 |
| Y 14 | 29 04.1 | 72 47.8 | 41.0 | 74 48.9 | 23.1 | 38 56.8 | 20.1 | 65 20.6 | 21.6 | Hadar | 148 38.7 | S60 28.6 |
| 15 | 44 06.5 | 87 47.7 | 40.5 | 89 49.5 | 22.6 | 53 58.7 | 19.8 | 80 22.8 | 21.5 | Hamal | 327 54.1 | N23 33.9 |
| 16 | 59 09.0 | 102 47.7 | 40.1 | 104 50.0 | 22.1 | 69 00.6 | 19.6 | 95 25.0 | 21.4 | Kaus Aust. | 83 35.6 | S34 22.4 |
| 17 | 74 11.4 | 117 47.6 | 39.6 | 119 50.6 | 21.6 | 84 02.5 | 19.4 | 110 27.2 | 21.3 | | | |
| 18 | 89 13.9 | 132 47.5 | S14 39.2 | 134 51.1 | S18 21.1 | 99 04.4 | S 5 19.1 | 125 29.4 | S15 21.3 | Kochab | 137 19.0 | N74 03.6 |
| 19 | 104 16.4 | 147 47.4 | 38.7 | 149 51.7 | 20.6 | 114 06.3 | 18.9 | 140 31.6 | 21.2 | Markab | 13 32.5 | N15 19.2 |
| 20 | 119 18.8 | 162 47.3 | 38.2 | 164 52.3 | 20.1 | 129 08.3 | 18.7 | 155 33.8 | 21.1 | Menkar | 314 08.8 | N 4 10.4 |
| 21 | 134 21.3 | 177 47.2 | 37.7 | 179 52.8 | 19.6 | 144 10.2 | 18.4 | 170 36.1 | 21.0 | Menkent | 148 00.0 | S36 28.7 |
| 22 | 149 23.8 | 192 47.1 | 37.3 | 194 53.4 | 19.1 | 159 12.1 | 18.2 | 185 38.3 | 21.0 | Miaplacidus | 221 38.0 | S69 48.6 |
| 23 | 164 26.2 | 207 47.1 | 36.8 | 209 53.9 | 18.6 | 174 14.0 | 18.0 | 200 40.5 | 20.9 | | | |
| 22 00 | 179 28.7 | 222 47.0 | S14 36.3 | 224 54.5 | S18 18.1 | 189 15.9 | S 5 17.7 | 215 42.7 | S15 20.8 | Mirfak | 308 31.9 | N49 56.4 |
| 01 | 194 31.2 | 237 46.9 | 35.9 | 239 55.0 | 17.6 | 204 17.8 | 17.5 | 230 44.9 | 20.7 | Nunki | 75 50.7 | S26 16.1 |
| 02 | 209 33.6 | 252 46.8 | 35.4 | 254 55.6 | 17.1 | 219 19.7 | 17.3 | 245 47.1 | 20.7 | Peacock | 53 09.7 | S56 39.7 |
| 03 | 224 36.1 | 267 46.7 | 34.9 | 269 56.1 | 16.6 | 234 21.6 | 17.0 | 260 49.3 | 20.6 | Pollux | 243 20.0 | N27 58.4 |
| 04 | 239 38.5 | 282 46.6 | 34.4 | 284 56.7 | 16.1 | 249 23.5 | 16.8 | 275 51.6 | 20.5 | Procyon | 244 53.1 | N 5 10.0 |
| 05 | 254 41.0 | 297 46.5 | 34.0 | 299 57.2 | 15.6 | 264 25.5 | 16.6 | 290 53.8 | 20.4 | | | |
| 06 | 269 43.5 | 312 46.4 | S14 33.5 | 314 57.8 | S18 15.1 | 279 27.4 | S 5 16.4 | 305 56.0 | S15 20.4 | Rasalhague | 96 00.7 | N12 32.4 |
| 07 | 284 45.9 | 327 46.4 | 33.0 | 329 58.3 | 14.6 | 294 29.3 | 16.1 | 320 58.2 | 20.3 | Regulus | 207 36.6 | N11 51.5 |
| 08 | 299 48.4 | 342 46.3 | 32.5 | 344 58.9 | 14.1 | 309 31.2 | 15.9 | 336 00.4 | 20.2 | Rigel | 281 06.2 | S 8 10.8 |
| T 09 | 314 50.9 | 357 46.2 | 32.1 | 359 59.5 | 13.6 | 324 33.1 | 15.7 | 351 02.6 | 20.1 | Rigil Kent. | 139 43.0 | S60 55.4 |
| U 10 | 329 53.3 | 12 46.1 | 31.6 | 15 00.0 | 13.1 | 339 35.0 | 15.4 | 6 04.8 | 20.0 | Sabik | 102 05.4 | S15 45.2 |
| E 11 | 344 55.8 | 27 46.0 | 31.1 | 30 00.6 | 12.6 | 354 36.9 | 15.2 | 21 07.1 | 20.0 | | | |
| S 12 | 359 58.3 | 42 45.9 | S14 30.6 | 45 01.1 | S18 12.1 | 9 38.8 | S 5 15.0 | 36 09.3 | S15 19.9 | Schedar | 349 34.2 | N56 39.4 |
| D 13 | 15 00.7 | 57 45.8 | 30.1 | 60 01.7 | 11.6 | 24 40.7 | 14.7 | 51 11.5 | 19.8 | Shaula | 96 13.5 | S37 07.1 |
| A 14 | 30 03.2 | 72 45.7 | 29.7 | 75 02.2 | 11.1 | 39 42.7 | 14.5 | 66 13.7 | 19.7 | Sirius | 258 28.2 | S16 45.0 |
| Y 15 | 45 05.7 | 87 45.6 | 29.2 | 90 02.8 | 10.6 | 54 44.6 | 14.3 | 81 15.9 | 19.7 | Spica | 158 24.4 | S11 16.7 |
| 16 | 60 08.1 | 102 45.5 | 28.7 | 105 03.3 | 10.1 | 69 46.5 | 14.0 | 96 18.1 | 19.6 | Suhail | 222 47.7 | S43 31.5 |
| 17 | 75 10.6 | 117 45.4 | 28.2 | 120 03.9 | 09.6 | 84 48.4 | 13.8 | 111 20.4 | 19.5 | | | |
| 18 | 90 13.0 | 132 45.3 | S14 27.7 | 135 04.5 | S18 09.1 | 99 50.3 | S 5 13.6 | 126 22.6 | S15 19.4 | Vega | 80 34.8 | N38 47.9 |
| 19 | 105 15.5 | 147 45.2 | 27.2 | 150 05.0 | 08.6 | 114 52.2 | 13.3 | 141 24.8 | 19.4 | Zuben'ubi | 136 58.3 | S16 08.0 |
| 20 | 120 18.0 | 162 45.1 | 26.7 | 165 05.6 | 08.1 | 129 54.1 | 13.1 | 156 27.0 | 19.3 | | SHA | Mer. Pass. |
| 21 | 135 20.4 | 177 45.1 | 26.3 | 180 06.1 | 07.6 | 144 56.0 | 12.9 | 171 29.2 | 19.2 | | ° ′ | h m |
| 22 | 150 22.9 | 192 45.0 | 25.8 | 195 06.7 | 07.1 | 159 57.9 | 12.7 | 186 31.4 | 19.1 | Venus | 44 19.4 | 9 09 |
| 23 | 165 25.4 | 207 44.9 | 25.3 | 210 07.2 | 06.6 | 174 59.9 | 12.4 | 201 33.7 | 19.1 | Mars | 46 11.7 | 9 01 |
| | h m | | | | | | | | | Jupiter | 10 00.5 | 11 25 |
| Mer. Pass. 12 04.0 | | v −0.1 | d 0.5 | v 0.6 | d 0.5 | v 1.9 | d 0.2 | v 2.2 | d 0.1 | Saturn | 36 20.0 | 9 39 |

| UT | SUN GHA | SUN Dec | MOON GHA | v | MOON Dec | d | HP |
|---|---|---|---|---|---|---|---|
| d h | ° ′ | ° ′ | ° ′ | ′ | ° ′ | ′ | ′ |
| **20** 00 | 178 06.0 | S 0 15.4 | 337 10.3 | 12.1 | S 5 34.7 | 15.3 | 58.5 |
| 01 | 193 06.1 | 14.4 | 351 41.4 | 12.2 | 5 50.0 | 15.3 | 58.5 |
| 02 | 208 06.3 | 13.4 | 6 12.6 | 12.0 | 6 05.3 | 15.3 | 58.5 |
| 03 | 223 06.5 | .. 12.4 | 20 43.6 | 12.1 | 6 20.6 | 15.2 | 58.5 |
| 04 | 238 06.7 | 11.4 | 35 14.7 | 11.9 | 6 35.8 | 15.3 | 58.5 |
| 05 | 253 06.9 | 10.4 | 49 45.6 | 12.0 | 6 51.1 | 15.1 | 58.6 |
| 06 | 268 07.1 | S 0 09.4 | 64 16.6 | 11.9 | S 7 06.2 | 15.2 | 58.6 |
| 07 | 283 07.3 | 08.5 | 78 47.5 | 11.8 | 7 21.4 | 15.2 | 58.6 |
| S 08 | 298 07.4 | 07.5 | 93 18.3 | 11.8 | 7 36.6 | 15.1 | 58.6 |
| U 09 | 313 07.6 | .. 06.5 | 107 49.1 | 11.7 | 7 51.7 | 15.0 | 58.6 |
| N 10 | 328 07.8 | 05.5 | 122 19.8 | 11.6 | 8 06.7 | 15.1 | 58.6 |
| D 11 | 343 08.0 | 04.5 | 136 50.4 | 11.7 | 8 21.8 | 15.0 | 58.7 |
| A 12 | 358 08.2 | S 0 03.5 | 151 21.1 | 11.5 | S 8 36.8 | 15.0 | 58.7 |
| Y 13 | 13 08.4 | 02.5 | 165 51.6 | 11.5 | 8 51.8 | 14.9 | 58.7 |
| 14 | 28 08.6 | 01.5 | 180 22.1 | 11.4 | 9 06.7 | 14.9 | 58.7 |
| 15 | 43 08.7 | S 00.5 | 194 52.5 | 11.4 | 9 21.6 | 14.9 | 58.7 |
| 16 | 58 08.9 | N 00.4 | 209 22.9 | 11.3 | 9 36.5 | 14.8 | 58.7 |
| 17 | 73 09.1 | 01.4 | 223 53.2 | 11.3 | 9 51.3 | 14.7 | 58.7 |
| 18 | 88 09.3 | N 0 02.4 | 238 23.5 | 11.2 | S10 06.0 | 14.8 | 58.8 |
| 19 | 103 09.5 | 03.4 | 252 53.7 | 11.1 | 10 20.8 | 14.6 | 58.8 |
| 20 | 118 09.7 | 04.4 | 267 23.8 | 11.1 | 10 35.4 | 14.7 | 58.8 |
| 21 | 133 09.9 | .. 05.4 | 281 53.9 | 10.9 | 10 50.1 | 14.5 | 58.8 |
| 22 | 148 10.0 | 06.4 | 296 23.8 | 11.0 | 11 04.6 | 14.6 | 58.8 |
| 23 | 163 10.2 | 07.4 | 310 53.8 | 10.8 | 11 19.2 | 14.4 | 58.8 |
| **21** 00 | 178 10.4 | N 0 08.3 | 325 23.6 | 10.8 | S11 33.6 | 14.5 | 58.8 |
| 01 | 193 10.6 | 09.3 | 339 53.4 | 10.7 | 11 48.1 | 14.3 | 58.9 |
| 02 | 208 10.8 | 10.3 | 354 23.1 | 10.7 | 12 02.4 | 14.3 | 58.9 |
| 03 | 223 11.0 | .. 11.3 | 8 52.8 | 10.6 | 12 16.7 | 14.3 | 58.9 |
| 04 | 238 11.2 | 12.3 | 23 22.4 | 10.5 | 12 31.0 | 14.1 | 58.9 |
| 05 | 253 11.3 | 13.3 | 37 51.9 | 10.4 | 12 45.1 | 14.2 | 58.9 |
| 06 | 268 11.5 | N 0 14.3 | 52 21.3 | 10.4 | S12 59.3 | 14.0 | 58.9 |
| 07 | 283 11.7 | 15.3 | 66 50.7 | 10.3 | 13 13.3 | 14.0 | 58.9 |
| M 08 | 298 11.9 | 16.2 | 81 20.0 | 10.2 | 13 27.3 | 13.9 | 58.9 |
| O 09 | 313 12.1 | .. 17.2 | 95 49.2 | 10.1 | 13 41.2 | 13.9 | 59.0 |
| N 10 | 328 12.3 | 18.2 | 110 18.3 | 10.1 | 13 55.1 | 13.7 | 59.0 |
| D 11 | 343 12.5 | 19.2 | 124 47.4 | 10.0 | 14 08.8 | 13.7 | 59.0 |
| A 12 | 358 12.6 | N 0 20.2 | 139 16.4 | 9.9 | S14 22.5 | 13.7 | 59.0 |
| Y 13 | 13 12.8 | 21.2 | 153 45.3 | 9.8 | 14 36.2 | 13.5 | 59.0 |
| 14 | 28 13.0 | 22.2 | 168 14.1 | 9.7 | 14 49.7 | 13.5 | 59.0 |
| 15 | 43 13.2 | .. 23.1 | 182 42.8 | 9.7 | 15 03.2 | 13.4 | 59.0 |
| 16 | 58 13.4 | 24.1 | 197 11.5 | 9.6 | 15 16.6 | 13.3 | 59.0 |
| 17 | 73 13.6 | 25.1 | 211 40.1 | 9.5 | 15 29.9 | 13.3 | 59.0 |
| 18 | 88 13.8 | N 0 26.1 | 226 08.6 | 9.4 | S15 43.2 | 13.1 | 59.1 |
| 19 | 103 14.0 | 27.1 | 240 37.0 | 9.3 | 15 56.3 | 13.1 | 59.1 |
| 20 | 118 14.1 | 28.1 | 255 05.3 | 9.3 | 16 09.4 | 13.0 | 59.1 |
| 21 | 133 14.3 | .. 29.1 | 269 33.6 | 9.2 | 16 22.4 | 12.9 | 59.1 |
| 22 | 148 14.5 | 30.1 | 284 01.8 | 9.1 | 16 35.3 | 12.8 | 59.1 |
| 23 | 163 14.7 | 31.0 | 298 29.9 | 9.0 | 16 48.1 | 12.7 | 59.1 |
| **22** 00 | 178 14.9 | N 0 32.0 | 312 57.9 | 8.9 | S17 00.8 | 12.6 | 59.1 |
| 01 | 193 15.1 | 33.0 | 327 25.8 | 8.8 | 17 13.4 | 12.5 | 59.1 |
| 02 | 208 15.3 | 34.0 | 341 53.6 | 8.8 | 17 25.9 | 12.4 | 59.1 |
| 03 | 223 15.4 | .. 35.0 | 356 21.4 | 8.6 | 17 38.3 | 12.3 | 59.1 |
| 04 | 238 15.6 | 36.0 | 10 49.0 | 8.6 | 17 50.6 | 12.2 | 59.1 |
| 05 | 253 15.8 | 37.0 | 25 16.6 | 8.5 | 18 02.8 | 12.2 | 59.1 |
| 06 | 268 16.0 | N 0 38.0 | 39 44.1 | 8.4 | S18 15.0 | 12.0 | 59.2 |
| 07 | 283 16.2 | 38.9 | 54 11.5 | 8.3 | 18 27.0 | 11.9 | 59.2 |
| T 08 | 298 16.4 | 39.9 | 68 38.8 | 8.2 | 18 38.9 | 11.8 | 59.2 |
| U 09 | 313 16.6 | .. 40.9 | 83 06.0 | 8.2 | 18 50.7 | 11.7 | 59.2 |
| E 10 | 328 16.8 | 41.9 | 97 33.2 | 8.0 | 19 02.4 | 11.6 | 59.2 |
| S 11 | 343 16.9 | 42.9 | 112 00.2 | 8.0 | 19 14.0 | 11.4 | 59.2 |
| D 12 | 358 17.1 | N 0 43.9 | 126 27.2 | 7.8 | S19 25.4 | 11.4 | 59.2 |
| A 13 | 13 17.3 | 44.9 | 140 54.0 | 7.8 | 19 36.8 | 11.2 | 59.2 |
| Y 14 | 28 17.5 | 45.8 | 155 20.8 | 7.7 | 19 48.0 | 11.2 | 59.2 |
| 15 | 43 17.7 | .. 46.8 | 169 47.5 | 7.6 | 19 59.2 | 11.0 | 59.2 |
| 16 | 58 17.9 | 47.8 | 184 14.1 | 7.6 | 20 10.2 | 10.9 | 59.2 |
| 17 | 73 18.1 | 48.8 | 198 40.7 | 7.4 | 20 21.1 | 10.7 | 59.2 |
| 18 | 88 18.3 | N 0 49.8 | 213 07.1 | 7.3 | S20 31.8 | 10.7 | 59.2 |
| 19 | 103 18.4 | 50.8 | 227 33.4 | 7.3 | 20 42.5 | 10.5 | 59.2 |
| 20 | 118 18.6 | 51.8 | 241 59.7 | 7.2 | 20 53.0 | 10.4 | 59.2 |
| 21 | 133 18.8 | .. 52.7 | 256 25.9 | 7.1 | 21 03.4 | 10.2 | 59.2 |
| 22 | 148 19.0 | 53.7 | 270 52.0 | 7.0 | 21 13.6 | 10.2 | 59.2 |
| 23 | 163 19.2 | 54.7 | 285 18.0 | 6.9 | S21 23.8 | 10.0 | 59.3 |
| | SD 16.1 | d 1.0 | SD 16.0 | | 16.1 | | 16.1 |

## Moonrise

| Lat. | Twilight Naut. | Twilight Civil | Sunrise | Moonrise 20 | 21 | 22 | 23 |
|---|---|---|---|---|---|---|---|
| ° | h m | h m | h m | h m | h m | h m | h m |
| N 72 | 03 15 | 04 45 | 05 54 | 22 50 | 26 29 | 02 29 | ▬ |
| N 70 | 03 35 | 04 54 | 05 55 | 22 29 | 25 08 | 01 08 | ▬ |
| 68 | 03 50 | 05 00 | 05 56 | 22 13 | 24 31 | 00 31 | ▬ |
| 66 | 04 02 | 05 06 | 05 57 | 22 00 | 24 04 | 00 04 | 02 31 |
| 64 | 04 12 | 05 10 | 05 58 | 21 50 | 23 44 | 25 49 | 01 49 |
| 62 | 04 20 | 05 14 | 05 58 | 21 41 | 23 28 | 25 21 | 01 21 |
| 60 | 04 27 | 05 17 | 05 59 | 21 33 | 23 15 | 25 00 | 01 00 |
| N 58 | 04 33 | 05 20 | 05 59 | 21 27 | 23 03 | 24 42 | 00 42 |
| 56 | 04 39 | 05 23 | 06 00 | 21 21 | 22 53 | 24 28 | 00 28 |
| 54 | 04 43 | 05 25 | 06 00 | 21 15 | 22 44 | 24 15 | 00 15 |
| 52 | 04 47 | 05 27 | 06 01 | 21 11 | 22 37 | 24 04 | 00 04 |
| 50 | 04 51 | 05 29 | 06 01 | 21 06 | 22 30 | 23 54 | 25 16 |
| 45 | 04 58 | 05 32 | 06 02 | 20 57 | 22 15 | 23 34 | 24 51 |
| N 40 | 05 03 | 05 35 | 06 02 | 20 50 | 22 03 | 23 17 | 24 31 |
| 35 | 05 08 | 05 37 | 06 02 | 20 43 | 21 52 | 23 03 | 24 14 |
| 30 | 05 11 | 05 39 | 06 03 | 20 38 | 21 43 | 22 51 | 24 00 |
| 20 | 05 16 | 05 41 | 06 03 | 20 28 | 21 28 | 22 31 | 23 36 |
| N 10 | 05 18 | 05 43 | 06 04 | 20 19 | 21 15 | 22 13 | 23 15 |
| 0 | 05 19 | 05 43 | 06 04 | 20 11 | 21 02 | 21 57 | 22 55 |
| S 10 | 05 19 | 05 43 | 06 04 | 20 04 | 20 50 | 21 41 | 22 36 |
| 20 | 05 16 | 05 42 | 06 04 | 19 55 | 20 37 | 21 24 | 22 15 |
| 30 | 05 12 | 05 40 | 06 04 | 19 46 | 20 22 | 21 04 | 21 52 |
| 35 | 05 09 | 05 39 | 06 04 | 19 41 | 20 14 | 20 52 | 21 38 |
| 40 | 05 05 | 05 37 | 06 04 | 19 35 | 20 04 | 20 39 | 21 22 |
| 45 | 05 00 | 05 34 | 06 03 | 19 28 | 19 53 | 20 24 | 21 03 |
| S 50 | 04 53 | 05 31 | 06 03 | 19 19 | 19 40 | 20 05 | 20 39 |
| 52 | 04 49 | 05 29 | 06 03 | 19 16 | 19 33 | 19 56 | 20 28 |
| 54 | 04 46 | 05 28 | 06 03 | 19 11 | 19 26 | 19 46 | 20 15 |
| 56 | 04 41 | 05 26 | 06 03 | 19 07 | 19 19 | 19 35 | 20 00 |
| 58 | 04 36 | 05 23 | 06 02 | 19 02 | 19 10 | 19 23 | 19 43 |
| S 60 | 04 31 | 05 21 | 06 02 | 18 56 | 19 00 | 19 08 | 19 22 |

## Moonset

| Lat. | Sunset | Twilight Civil | Twilight Naut. | Moonset 20 | 21 | 22 | 23 |
|---|---|---|---|---|---|---|---|
| ° | h m | h m | h m | h m | h m | h m | h m |
| N 72 | 18 23 | 19 32 | 21 04 | 06 10 | 05 28 | 03 38 | ▬ |
| N 70 | 18 22 | 19 24 | 20 44 | 06 21 | 05 51 | 05 00 | ▬ |
| 68 | 18 20 | 19 17 | 20 28 | 06 29 | 06 09 | 05 40 | ▬ |
| 66 | 18 19 | 19 11 | 20 15 | 06 36 | 06 24 | 06 07 | 05 37 |
| 64 | 18 18 | 19 06 | 20 05 | 06 42 | 06 36 | 06 29 | 06 19 |
| 62 | 18 17 | 19 02 | 19 56 | 06 47 | 06 46 | 06 48 | 06 48 |
| 60 | 18 17 | 18 59 | 19 49 | 06 52 | 06 55 | 07 00 | 07 10 |
| N 58 | 18 16 | 18 56 | 19 43 | 06 56 | 07 03 | 07 13 | 07 28 |
| 56 | 18 16 | 18 53 | 19 37 | 07 00 | 07 10 | 07 24 | 07 43 |
| 54 | 18 15 | 18 51 | 19 33 | 07 03 | 07 16 | 07 33 | 07 56 |
| 52 | 18 15 | 18 49 | 19 29 | 07 06 | 07 22 | 07 42 | 08 08 |
| 50 | 18 14 | 18 47 | 19 25 | 07 09 | 07 27 | 07 49 | 08 18 |
| 45 | 18 14 | 18 43 | 19 17 | 07 15 | 07 38 | 08 06 | 08 40 |
| N 40 | 18 13 | 18 40 | 19 12 | 07 20 | 07 47 | 08 19 | 08 57 |
| 35 | 18 12 | 18 38 | 19 07 | 07 24 | 07 55 | 08 31 | 09 12 |
| 30 | 18 12 | 18 36 | 19 04 | 07 28 | 08 02 | 08 41 | 09 25 |
| 20 | 18 11 | 18 33 | 18 59 | 07 34 | 08 14 | 08 58 | 09 47 |
| N 10 | 18 11 | 18 32 | 18 56 | 07 40 | 08 25 | 09 14 | 10 06 |
| 0 | 18 10 | 18 31 | 18 55 | 07 46 | 08 35 | 09 28 | 10 24 |
| S 10 | 18 10 | 18 31 | 18 56 | 07 51 | 08 45 | 09 42 | 10 42 |
| 20 | 18 10 | 18 32 | 18 58 | 07 57 | 08 56 | 09 58 | 11 02 |
| 30 | 18 10 | 18 34 | 19 02 | 08 04 | 09 09 | 10 16 | 11 24 |
| 35 | 18 10 | 18 35 | 19 05 | 08 08 | 09 16 | 10 26 | 11 37 |
| 40 | 18 10 | 18 37 | 19 08 | 08 13 | 09 24 | 10 38 | 11 53 |
| 45 | 18 10 | 18 39 | 19 14 | 08 18 | 09 34 | 10 52 | 12 11 |
| S 50 | 18 10 | 18 42 | 19 20 | 08 24 | 09 46 | 11 10 | 12 33 |
| 52 | 18 10 | 18 44 | 19 24 | 08 27 | 09 51 | 11 18 | 12 44 |
| 54 | 18 10 | 18 46 | 19 27 | 08 30 | 09 57 | 11 27 | 12 57 |
| 56 | 18 11 | 18 47 | 19 31 | 08 33 | 10 04 | 11 38 | 13 11 |
| 58 | 18 11 | 18 50 | 19 36 | 08 37 | 10 12 | 11 49 | 13 28 |
| S 60 | 18 11 | 18 52 | 19 42 | 08 42 | 10 20 | 12 03 | 13 48 |

| Day | SUN Eqn. of Time 00h | SUN Eqn. of Time 12h | SUN Mer. Pass. | MOON Mer. Pass. Upper | MOON Mer. Pass. Lower | Age | Phase |
|---|---|---|---|---|---|---|---|
| d | m s | m s | h m | h m | h m | d | % |
| 20 | 07 37 | 07 28 | 12 07 | 01 34 | 13 58 | 18 | 94 |
| 21 | 07 19 | 07 10 | 12 07 | 02 23 | 14 49 | 19 | 88 |
| 22 | 07 01 | 06 52 | 12 07 | 03 15 | 15 42 | 20 | 79 |

| UT (d h) | ARIES GHA | VENUS −4.4 GHA | Dec | MARS +1.1 GHA | Dec | JUPITER −2.0 GHA | Dec | SATURN +0.7 GHA | Dec | Star Name | SHA | Dec |
|---|---|---|---|---|---|---|---|---|---|---|---|---|
| 23 00 | 180 27.8 | 222 44.8 | S14 24.8 | 225 07.8 | S18 06.1 | 190 01.8 | S 5 12.2 | 216 35.9 | S15 19.0 | Acamar | 315 13.9 | S40 13.2 |
| 01 | 195 30.3 | 237 44.7 | 24.3 | 240 08.4 | 05.6 | 205 03.7 | 12.0 | 231 38.1 | 18.9 | Achernar | 335 22.5 | S57 07.7 |
| 02 | 210 32.8 | 252 44.6 | 23.8 | 255 08.9 | 05.1 | 220 05.6 | 11.7 | 246 40.3 | 18.8 | Acrux | 173 01.9 | S63 13.3 |
| 03 | 225 35.2 | 267 44.5 .. | 23.3 | 270 09.5 .. | 04.6 | 235 07.5 .. | 11.5 | 261 42.5 .. | 18.8 | Adhara | 255 07.6 | S29 00.4 |
| 04 | 240 37.7 | 282 44.4 | 22.8 | 285 10.0 | 04.1 | 250 09.4 | 11.3 | 276 44.7 | 18.7 | Aldebaran | 290 42.4 | N16 33.1 |
| 05 | 255 40.2 | 297 44.3 | 22.3 | 300 10.6 | 03.6 | 265 11.3 | 11.0 | 291 47.0 | 18.6 | | | |
| 06 | 270 42.6 | 312 44.2 | S14 21.8 | 315 11.1 | S18 03.1 | 280 13.2 | S 5 10.8 | 306 49.2 | S15 18.5 | Alioth | 166 14.5 | N55 50.3 |
| W 07 | 285 45.1 | 327 44.1 | 21.3 | 330 11.7 | 02.6 | 295 15.2 | 10.6 | 321 51.4 | 18.5 | Alkaid | 152 53.4 | N49 12.0 |
| E 08 | 300 47.5 | 342 44.0 | 20.8 | 345 12.3 | 02.1 | 310 17.1 | 10.3 | 336 53.6 | 18.4 | Alnair | 27 36.2 | S46 51.2 |
| D 09 | 315 50.0 | 357 43.9 .. | 20.3 | 0 12.8 .. | 01.6 | 325 19.0 .. | 10.1 | 351 55.8 .. | 18.3 | Alnilam | 275 40.1 | S 1 11.4 |
| N 10 | 330 52.5 | 12 43.8 | 19.8 | 15 13.4 | 01.1 | 340 20.9 | 09.9 | 6 58.0 | 18.2 | Alphard | 217 49.8 | S 8 45.4 |
| E 11 | 345 54.9 | 27 43.7 | 19.3 | 30 13.9 | 00.6 | 355 22.8 | 09.6 | 22 00.3 | 18.2 | | | |
| S 12 | 0 57.4 | 42 43.6 | S14 18.8 | 45 14.5 | S18 00.1 | 10 24.7 | S 5 09.4 | 37 02.5 | S15 18.1 | Alphecca | 126 05.5 | N26 38.2 |
| D 13 | 15 59.9 | 57 43.5 | 18.3 | 60 15.1 | 17 59.6 | 25 26.6 | 09.2 | 52 04.7 | 18.0 | Alpheratz | 357 37.5 | N29 12.6 |
| A 14 | 31 02.3 | 72 43.4 | 17.8 | 75 15.6 | 59.1 | 40 28.5 | 09.0 | 67 06.9 | 17.9 | Altair | 62 02.3 | N 8 55.4 |
| Y 15 | 46 04.8 | 87 43.3 .. | 17.3 | 90 16.2 .. | 58.5 | 55 30.5 .. | 08.7 | 82 09.1 .. | 17.9 | Ankaa | 353 09.9 | S42 11.3 |
| 16 | 61 07.3 | 102 43.2 | 16.8 | 105 16.7 | 58.0 | 70 32.4 | 08.5 | 97 11.4 | 17.8 | Antares | 112 18.5 | S26 28.8 |
| 17 | 76 09.7 | 117 43.1 | 16.3 | 120 17.3 | 57.5 | 85 34.3 | 08.3 | 112 13.6 | 17.7 | | | |
| 18 | 91 12.2 | 132 43.0 | S14 15.8 | 135 17.9 | S17 57.0 | 100 36.2 | S 5 08.0 | 127 15.8 | S15 17.6 | Arcturus | 145 49.7 | N19 03.9 |
| 19 | 106 14.7 | 147 42.9 | 15.3 | 150 18.4 | 56.5 | 115 38.1 | 07.8 | 142 18.0 | 17.6 | Atria | 107 14.7 | S69 03.7 |
| 20 | 121 17.1 | 162 42.7 | 14.8 | 165 19.0 | 56.0 | 130 40.0 | 07.6 | 157 20.2 | 17.5 | Avior | 234 15.3 | S59 35.1 |
| 21 | 136 19.6 | 177 42.6 .. | 14.3 | 180 19.5 .. | 55.5 | 145 41.9 .. | 07.3 | 172 22.4 .. | 17.4 | Bellatrix | 278 25.4 | N 6 22.1 |
| 22 | 151 22.0 | 192 42.5 | 13.8 | 195 20.1 | 55.0 | 160 43.8 | 07.1 | 187 24.7 | 17.3 | Betelgeuse | 270 54.6 | N 7 24.6 |
| 23 | 166 24.5 | 207 42.4 | 13.3 | 210 20.7 | 54.5 | 175 45.8 | 06.9 | 202 26.9 | 17.3 | | | |
| 24 00 | 181 27.0 | 222 42.3 | S14 12.8 | 225 21.2 | S17 54.0 | 190 47.7 | S 5 06.6 | 217 29.1 | S15 17.2 | Canopus | 263 53.4 | S52 42.7 |
| 01 | 196 29.4 | 237 42.2 | 12.3 | 240 21.8 | 53.5 | 205 49.6 | 06.4 | 232 31.3 | 17.1 | Capella | 280 25.4 | N46 01.3 |
| 02 | 211 31.9 | 252 42.1 | 11.8 | 255 22.3 | 52.9 | 220 51.5 | 06.2 | 247 33.5 | 17.0 | Deneb | 49 27.6 | N45 21.2 |
| 03 | 226 34.4 | 267 42.0 .. | 11.2 | 270 22.9 .. | 52.4 | 235 53.4 .. | 06.0 | 262 35.8 .. | 17.0 | Denebola | 182 27.0 | N14 26.8 |
| 04 | 241 36.8 | 282 41.9 | 10.7 | 285 23.5 | 51.9 | 250 55.3 | 05.7 | 277 38.0 | 16.9 | Diphda | 348 49.9 | S17 52.1 |
| 05 | 256 39.3 | 297 41.8 | 10.2 | 300 24.0 | 51.4 | 265 57.2 | 05.5 | 292 40.2 | 16.8 | | | |
| 06 | 271 41.8 | 312 41.7 | S14 09.7 | 315 24.6 | S17 50.9 | 280 59.1 | S 5 05.3 | 307 42.4 | S15 16.7 | Dubhe | 193 43.2 | N61 38.0 |
| T 07 | 286 44.2 | 327 41.6 | 09.2 | 330 25.1 | 50.4 | 296 01.1 | 05.0 | 322 44.6 | 16.7 | Elnath | 278 04.9 | N28 37.6 |
| H 08 | 301 46.7 | 342 41.5 | 08.7 | 345 25.7 | 49.9 | 311 03.0 | 04.8 | 337 46.9 | 16.6 | Eltanin | 90 43.2 | N51 28.8 |
| U 09 | 316 49.1 | 357 41.4 .. | 08.2 | 0 26.3 .. | 49.4 | 326 04.9 .. | 04.6 | 352 49.1 .. | 16.5 | Enif | 33 41.3 | N 9 58.4 |
| R 10 | 331 51.6 | 12 41.2 | 07.6 | 15 26.8 | 48.8 | 341 06.8 | 04.3 | 7 51.3 | 16.4 | Fomalhaut | 15 17.4 | S29 30.4 |
| S 11 | 346 54.1 | 27 41.1 | 07.1 | 30 27.4 | 48.3 | 356 08.7 | 04.1 | 22 53.5 | 16.4 | | | |
| D 12 | 1 56.5 | 42 41.0 | S14 06.6 | 45 28.0 | S17 47.8 | 11 10.6 | S 5 03.9 | 37 55.7 | S15 16.3 | Gacrux | 171 53.6 | S57 14.2 |
| A 13 | 16 59.0 | 57 40.9 | 06.1 | 60 28.5 | 47.3 | 26 12.5 | 03.6 | 52 58.0 | 16.2 | Gienah | 175 45.6 | S17 40.0 |
| Y 14 | 32 01.5 | 72 40.8 | 05.6 | 75 29.1 | 46.8 | 41 14.4 | 03.4 | 68 00.2 | 16.1 | Hadar | 148 38.7 | S60 28.7 |
| 15 | 47 03.9 | 87 40.7 .. | 05.0 | 90 29.6 .. | 46.3 | 56 16.4 .. | 03.2 | 83 02.4 .. | 16.1 | Hamal | 327 54.1 | N23 33.9 |
| 16 | 62 06.4 | 102 40.6 | 04.5 | 105 30.2 | 45.8 | 71 18.3 | 03.0 | 98 04.6 | 16.0 | Kaus Aust. | 83 35.6 | S34 22.4 |
| 17 | 77 08.9 | 117 40.5 | 04.0 | 120 30.8 | 45.2 | 86 20.2 | 02.7 | 113 06.8 | 15.9 | | | |
| 18 | 92 11.3 | 132 40.4 | S14 03.5 | 135 31.3 | S17 44.7 | 101 22.1 | S 5 02.5 | 128 09.1 | S15 15.8 | Kochab | 137 18.9 | N74 03.7 |
| 19 | 107 13.8 | 147 40.2 | 02.9 | 150 31.9 | 44.2 | 116 24.0 | 02.3 | 143 11.3 | 15.8 | Markab | 13 32.5 | N15 19.2 |
| 20 | 122 16.3 | 162 40.1 | 02.4 | 165 32.5 | 43.7 | 131 25.9 | 02.0 | 158 13.5 | 15.7 | Menkar | 314 08.8 | N 4 10.4 |
| 21 | 137 18.7 | 177 40.0 .. | 01.9 | 180 33.0 .. | 43.2 | 146 27.8 .. | 01.8 | 173 15.7 .. | 15.6 | Menkent | 148 00.0 | S36 28.7 |
| 22 | 152 21.2 | 192 39.9 | 01.4 | 195 33.6 | 42.7 | 161 29.8 | 01.6 | 188 17.9 | 15.5 | Miaplacidus | 221 38.1 | S69 48.7 |
| 23 | 167 23.6 | 207 39.8 | 00.8 | 210 34.1 | 42.1 | 176 31.7 | 01.3 | 203 20.2 | 15.5 | | | |
| 25 00 | 182 26.1 | 222 39.7 | S14 00.3 | 225 34.7 | S17 41.6 | 191 33.6 | S 5 01.1 | 218 22.4 | S15 15.4 | Mirfak | 308 31.9 | N49 56.4 |
| 01 | 197 28.6 | 237 39.6 | 13 59.8 | 240 35.3 | 41.1 | 206 35.5 | 00.9 | 233 24.6 | 15.3 | Nunki | 75 50.7 | S26 16.1 |
| 02 | 212 31.0 | 252 39.4 | 59.3 | 255 35.8 | 40.6 | 221 37.4 | 00.6 | 248 26.8 | 15.3 | Peacock | 53 09.7 | S56 39.7 |
| 03 | 227 33.5 | 267 39.3 .. | 58.7 | 270 36.4 .. | 40.1 | 236 39.3 .. | 00.4 | 263 29.0 .. | 15.2 | Pollux | 243 20.0 | N27 58.4 |
| 04 | 242 36.0 | 282 39.2 | 58.2 | 285 37.0 | 39.5 | 251 41.2 | 00.2 | 278 31.3 | 15.1 | Procyon | 244 53.1 | N 5 10.0 |
| 05 | 257 38.4 | 297 39.1 | 57.7 | 300 37.5 | 39.0 | 266 43.2 | 5 00.0 | 293 33.5 | 15.0 | | | |
| 06 | 272 40.9 | 312 39.0 | S13 57.1 | 315 38.1 | S17 38.5 | 281 45.1 | S 4 59.7 | 308 35.7 | S15 15.0 | Rasalhague | 96 00.6 | N12 32.4 |
| 07 | 287 43.4 | 327 38.9 | 56.6 | 330 38.7 | 38.0 | 296 47.0 | 59.5 | 323 37.9 | 14.9 | Regulus | 207 36.6 | N11 51.5 |
| 08 | 302 45.8 | 342 38.7 | 56.1 | 345 39.2 | 37.5 | 311 48.9 | 59.3 | 338 40.1 | 14.8 | Rigel | 281 06.2 | S 8 10.8 |
| F 09 | 317 48.3 | 357 38.6 .. | 55.5 | 0 39.8 .. | 37.0 | 326 50.8 .. | 59.0 | 353 42.4 .. | 14.7 | Rigil Kent. | 139 42.9 | S60 55.4 |
| R 10 | 332 50.8 | 12 38.5 | 55.0 | 15 40.4 | 36.4 | 341 52.7 | 58.8 | 8 44.6 | 14.7 | Sabik | 102 05.3 | S15 45.2 |
| I 11 | 347 53.2 | 27 38.4 | 54.4 | 30 40.9 | 35.9 | 356 54.6 | 58.6 | 23 46.8 | 14.6 | | | |
| D 12 | 2 55.7 | 42 38.3 | S13 53.9 | 45 41.5 | S17 35.4 | 11 56.6 | S 4 58.3 | 38 49.0 | S15 14.5 | Schedar | 349 34.2 | N56 39.4 |
| A 13 | 17 58.1 | 57 38.2 | 53.4 | 60 42.1 | 34.9 | 26 58.5 | 58.1 | 53 51.3 | 14.4 | Shaula | 96 13.4 | S37 07.1 |
| Y 14 | 33 00.6 | 72 38.0 | 52.8 | 75 42.6 | 34.3 | 42 00.4 | 57.9 | 68 53.5 | 14.4 | Sirius | 258 28.2 | S16 45.0 |
| 15 | 48 03.1 | 87 37.9 .. | 52.3 | 90 43.2 .. | 33.8 | 57 02.3 .. | 57.6 | 83 55.7 .. | 14.3 | Spica | 158 24.4 | S11 16.7 |
| 16 | 63 05.5 | 102 37.8 | 51.7 | 105 43.8 | 33.3 | 72 04.2 | 57.4 | 98 57.9 | 14.2 | Suhail | 222 47.7 | S43 31.5 |
| 17 | 78 08.0 | 117 37.7 | 51.2 | 120 44.3 | 32.8 | 87 06.1 | 57.2 | 114 00.1 | 14.1 | | | |
| 18 | 93 10.5 | 132 37.6 | S13 50.7 | 135 44.9 | S17 32.3 | 102 08.0 | S 4 57.0 | 129 02.4 | S15 14.1 | Vega | 80 34.8 | N38 47.9 |
| 19 | 108 12.9 | 147 37.4 | 50.1 | 150 45.5 | 31.7 | 117 10.0 | 56.7 | 144 04.6 | 14.0 | Zuben'ubi | 136 58.3 | S16 08.0 |
| 20 | 123 15.4 | 162 37.3 | 49.6 | 165 46.0 | 31.2 | 132 11.9 | 56.5 | 159 06.8 | 13.9 | | | |
| 21 | 138 17.9 | 177 37.2 .. | 49.0 | 180 46.6 .. | 30.7 | 147 13.8 .. | 56.3 | 174 09.0 .. | 13.8 | | SHA | Mer. Pass. |
| 22 | 153 20.3 | 192 37.1 | 48.5 | 195 47.2 | 30.2 | 162 15.7 | 56.0 | 189 11.3 | 13.8 | Venus | 41 15.4 | 9 09 |
| 23 | 168 22.8 | 207 37.0 | 47.9 | 210 47.7 | 29.6 | 177 17.6 | 55.8 | 204 13.5 | 13.7 | Mars | 43 54.2 | 8 58 |
| Mer. Pass. | h m 11 52.3 | v −0.1 | d 0.5 | v 0.6 | d 0.5 | v 1.9 | d 0.2 | v 2.2 | d 0.1 | Jupiter / Saturn | 9 20.7 / 36 02.1 | 11 15 / 9 29 |

| UT | SUN GHA | SUN Dec | MOON GHA | v | MOON Dec | d | HP |
|---|---|---|---|---|---|---|---|
| d h | ° ′ | ° ′ | ° ′ | ′ | ° ′ | ′ | ′ |
| **23** 00 | 178 19.4 | N 0 55.7 | 299 43.9 | 6.8 | S21 33.8 | 9.9 | 59.3 |
| 01 | 193 19.6 | 56.7 | 314 09.7 | 6.7 | 21 43.7 | 9.7 | 59.3 |
| 02 | 208 19.8 | 57.7 | 328 35.4 | 6.7 | 21 53.4 | 9.6 | 59.3 |
| 03 | 223 19.9 | .. 58.7 | 343 01.1 | 6.6 | 22 03.0 | 9.5 | 59.3 |
| 04 | 238 20.1 | 0 59.6 | 357 26.7 | 6.5 | 22 12.5 | 9.3 | 59.3 |
| 05 | 253 20.3 | 1 00.6 | 11 52.2 | 6.4 | 22 21.8 | 9.2 | 59.3 |
| W 06 | 268 20.5 | N 1 01.6 | 26 17.6 | 6.3 | S22 31.0 | 9.0 | 59.3 |
| E 07 | 283 20.7 | 02.6 | 40 42.9 | 6.2 | 22 40.0 | 8.9 | 59.3 |
| D 08 | 298 20.9 | 03.6 | 55 08.1 | 6.2 | 22 48.9 | 8.8 | 59.3 |
| N 09 | 313 21.1 | .. 04.6 | 69 33.3 | 6.0 | 22 57.7 | 8.6 | 59.3 |
| E 10 | 328 21.3 | 05.6 | 83 58.3 | 6.0 | 23 06.3 | 8.5 | 59.3 |
| S 11 | 343 21.4 | 06.5 | 98 23.3 | 6.0 | 23 14.8 | 8.3 | 59.3 |
| D 12 | 358 21.6 | N 1 07.5 | 112 48.3 | 5.8 | S23 23.1 | 8.2 | 59.3 |
| A 13 | 13 21.8 | 08.5 | 127 13.1 | 5.8 | 23 31.3 | 8.0 | 59.3 |
| Y 14 | 28 22.0 | 09.5 | 141 37.9 | 5.6 | 23 39.3 | 7.8 | 59.3 |
| 15 | 43 22.2 | .. 10.5 | 156 02.5 | 5.6 | 23 47.1 | 7.8 | 59.3 |
| 16 | 58 22.4 | 11.5 | 170 27.1 | 5.6 | 23 54.9 | 7.5 | 59.3 |
| 17 | 73 22.6 | 12.5 | 184 51.7 | 5.4 | 24 02.4 | 7.4 | 59.3 |
| 18 | 88 22.8 | N 1 13.4 | 199 16.1 | 5.4 | S24 09.8 | 7.3 | 59.3 |
| 19 | 103 22.9 | 14.4 | 213 40.5 | 5.4 | 24 17.1 | 7.1 | 59.3 |
| 20 | 118 23.1 | 15.4 | 228 04.9 | 5.2 | 24 24.2 | 6.9 | 59.3 |
| 21 | 133 23.3 | .. 16.4 | 242 29.1 | 5.2 | 24 31.1 | 6.8 | 59.3 |
| 22 | 148 23.5 | 17.4 | 256 53.3 | 5.1 | 24 37.9 | 6.6 | 59.3 |
| 23 | 163 23.7 | 18.4 | 271 17.4 | 5.0 | 24 44.5 | 6.4 | 59.3 |
| **24** 00 | 178 23.9 | N 1 19.4 | 285 41.4 | 5.0 | S24 50.9 | 6.3 | 59.3 |
| 01 | 193 24.1 | 20.3 | 300 05.4 | 4.9 | 24 57.2 | 6.1 | 59.3 |
| 02 | 208 24.3 | 21.3 | 314 29.3 | 4.9 | 25 03.3 | 5.9 | 59.3 |
| 03 | 223 24.4 | .. 22.3 | 328 53.2 | 4.8 | 25 09.2 | 5.8 | 59.3 |
| 04 | 238 24.6 | 23.3 | 343 17.0 | 4.7 | 25 15.0 | 5.6 | 59.3 |
| 05 | 253 24.8 | 24.3 | 357 40.7 | 4.7 | 25 20.6 | 5.5 | 59.3 |
| T 06 | 268 25.0 | N 1 25.3 | 12 04.4 | 4.7 | S25 26.1 | 5.2 | 59.3 |
| H 07 | 283 25.2 | 26.2 | 26 28.1 | 4.5 | 25 31.3 | 5.1 | 59.3 |
| U 08 | 298 25.4 | 27.2 | 40 51.6 | 4.6 | 25 36.4 | 5.0 | 59.3 |
| R 09 | 313 25.6 | .. 28.2 | 55 15.2 | 4.6 | 25 41.4 | 4.7 | 59.3 |
| S 10 | 328 25.8 | 29.2 | 69 38.6 | 4.5 | 25 46.1 | 4.6 | 59.3 |
| D 11 | 343 26.0 | 30.2 | 84 02.1 | 4.3 | 25 50.7 | 4.4 | 59.3 |
| A 12 | 358 26.1 | N 1 31.2 | 98 25.4 | 4.4 | S25 55.1 | 4.3 | 59.3 |
| Y 13 | 13 26.3 | 32.2 | 112 48.8 | 4.3 | 25 59.4 | 4.0 | 59.3 |
| 14 | 28 26.5 | 33.1 | 127 12.1 | 4.2 | 26 03.4 | 3.9 | 59.3 |
| 15 | 43 26.7 | .. 34.1 | 141 35.3 | 4.3 | 26 07.3 | 3.7 | 59.3 |
| 16 | 58 26.9 | 35.1 | 155 58.6 | 4.1 | 26 11.0 | 3.5 | 59.3 |
| 17 | 73 27.1 | 36.1 | 170 21.7 | 4.2 | 26 14.5 | 3.4 | 59.3 |
| 18 | 88 27.3 | N 1 37.1 | 184 44.9 | 4.1 | S26 17.9 | 3.1 | 59.3 |
| 19 | 103 27.5 | 38.1 | 199 08.0 | 4.1 | 26 21.0 | 3.0 | 59.3 |
| 20 | 118 27.6 | 39.0 | 213 31.1 | 4.0 | 26 24.0 | 2.8 | 59.3 |
| 21 | 133 27.8 | .. 40.0 | 227 54.1 | 4.0 | 26 26.8 | 2.7 | 59.3 |
| 22 | 148 28.0 | 41.0 | 242 17.1 | 4.0 | 26 29.5 | 2.4 | 59.3 |
| 23 | 163 28.2 | 42.0 | 256 40.1 | 4.0 | 26 31.9 | 2.3 | 59.3 |
| **25** 00 | 178 28.4 | N 1 43.0 | 271 03.1 | 4.0 | S26 34.2 | 2.1 | 59.2 |
| 01 | 193 28.6 | 44.0 | 285 26.1 | 3.9 | 26 36.3 | 1.9 | 59.2 |
| 02 | 208 28.8 | 44.9 | 299 49.0 | 4.0 | 26 38.2 | 1.7 | 59.2 |
| 03 | 223 29.0 | .. 45.9 | 314 11.9 | 4.0 | 26 39.9 | 1.5 | 59.2 |
| 04 | 238 29.2 | 46.9 | 328 34.9 | 3.9 | 26 41.4 | 1.4 | 59.2 |
| 05 | 253 29.3 | 47.9 | 342 57.8 | 3.9 | 26 42.8 | 1.1 | 59.2 |
| F 06 | 268 29.5 | N 1 48.9 | 357 20.7 | 3.8 | S26 43.9 | 1.0 | 59.2 |
| R 07 | 283 29.7 | 49.9 | 11 43.5 | 3.9 | 26 44.9 | 0.8 | 59.2 |
| I 08 | 298 29.9 | 50.8 | 26 06.4 | 3.9 | 26 45.7 | 0.6 | 59.2 |
| D 09 | 313 30.1 | .. 51.8 | 40 29.3 | 3.9 | 26 46.3 | 0.5 | 59.2 |
| A 10 | 328 30.3 | 52.8 | 54 52.2 | 3.9 | 26 46.8 | 0.2 | 59.2 |
| Y 11 | 343 30.5 | 53.8 | 69 15.1 | 3.8 | 26 47.0 | 0.1 | 59.2 |
| 12 | 358 30.7 | N 1 54.8 | 83 37.9 | 3.9 | S26 47.1 | 0.1 | 59.2 |
| 13 | 13 30.9 | 55.7 | 98 00.8 | 3.9 | 26 47.0 | 0.3 | 59.2 |
| 14 | 28 31.0 | 56.7 | 112 23.7 | 3.9 | 26 46.7 | 0.5 | 59.2 |
| 15 | 43 31.2 | .. 57.7 | 126 46.6 | 4.0 | 26 46.2 | 0.6 | 59.2 |
| 16 | 58 31.4 | 58.7 | 141 09.6 | 3.9 | 26 45.6 | 0.9 | 59.2 |
| 17 | 73 31.6 | 1 59.7 | 155 32.5 | 4.0 | 26 44.7 | 1.0 | 59.2 |
| 18 | 88 31.8 | N 2 00.7 | 169 55.5 | 3.9 | S26 43.7 | 1.2 | 59.2 |
| 19 | 103 32.0 | 01.6 | 184 18.4 | 4.0 | 26 42.5 | 1.4 | 59.2 |
| 20 | 118 32.2 | 02.6 | 198 41.4 | 4.1 | 26 41.1 | 1.6 | 59.2 |
| 21 | 133 32.4 | .. 03.6 | 213 04.5 | 4.0 | 26 39.5 | 1.7 | 59.2 |
| 22 | 148 32.5 | 04.6 | 227 27.5 | 4.1 | 26 37.8 | 2.0 | 59.2 |
| 23 | 163 32.7 | 05.6 | 241 50.6 | 4.1 | S26 35.8 | 2.1 | 59.1 |
| | SD 16.1 | d 1.0 | SD 16.2 | | 16.2 | | 16.1 |

### Twilight / Sunrise / Moonrise

| Lat. | Naut. | Civil | Sunrise | Moonrise 23 | 24 | 25 | 26 |
|---|---|---|---|---|---|---|---|
| ° | h m | h m | h m | h m | h m | h m | h m |
| N 72 | 02 53 | 04 29 | 05 38 | ▬▬ | ▬▬ | ▬▬ | ▬▬ |
| N 70 | 03 17 | 04 39 | 05 41 | ▬▬ | ▬▬ | ▬▬ | ▬▬ |
| 68 | 03 35 | 04 47 | 05 43 | ▬▬ | ▬▬ | ▬▬ | ▬▬ |
| 66 | 03 49 | 04 54 | 05 45 | 02 31 | ▬▬ | ▬▬ | ▬▬ |
| 64 | 04 00 | 04 59 | 05 47 | 01 49 | 04 16 | ▬▬ | ▬▬ |
| 62 | 04 09 | 05 04 | 05 49 | 01 21 | 03 17 | 04 57 | 05 47 |
| 60 | 04 17 | 05 08 | 05 50 | 01 00 | 02 43 | 04 11 | 05 06 |
| N 58 | 04 24 | 05 12 | 05 51 | 00 42 | 02 19 | 03 41 | 04 38 |
| 56 | 04 30 | 05 15 | 05 52 | 00 28 | 01 59 | 03 18 | 04 17 |
| 54 | 04 35 | 05 17 | 05 53 | 00 15 | 01 43 | 03 00 | 03 59 |
| 52 | 04 40 | 05 20 | 05 54 | 00 04 | 01 29 | 02 44 | 03 43 |
| 50 | 04 44 | 05 22 | 05 54 | 25 16 | 01 16 | 02 30 | 03 30 |
| 45 | 04 52 | 05 27 | 05 56 | 24 51 | 00 51 | 02 02 | 03 03 |
| N 40 | 04 58 | 05 30 | 05 57 | 24 31 | 00 31 | 01 40 | 02 41 |
| 35 | 05 03 | 05 33 | 05 58 | 24 14 | 00 14 | 01 22 | 02 23 |
| 30 | 05 07 | 05 35 | 05 59 | 24 00 | 00 00 | 01 07 | 02 08 |
| 20 | 05 13 | 05 39 | 06 01 | 23 36 | 24 40 | 00 40 | 01 42 |
| N 10 | 05 17 | 05 41 | 06 02 | 23 15 | 24 17 | 00 17 | 01 19 |
| 0 | 05 18 | 05 42 | 06 03 | 22 55 | 23 56 | 24 58 | 00 58 |
| S 10 | 05 19 | 05 43 | 06 04 | 22 36 | 23 35 | 24 37 | 00 37 |
| 20 | 05 17 | 05 43 | 06 05 | 22 15 | 23 13 | 24 14 | 00 14 |
| 30 | 05 14 | 05 42 | 06 06 | 21 52 | 22 47 | 23 48 | 24 54 |
| 35 | 05 12 | 05 41 | 06 06 | 21 38 | 22 31 | 23 33 | 24 40 |
| 40 | 05 08 | 05 40 | 06 07 | 21 22 | 22 13 | 23 15 | 24 24 |
| 45 | 05 04 | 05 38 | 06 07 | 21 03 | 21 52 | 22 53 | 24 04 |
| S 50 | 04 58 | 05 36 | 06 08 | 20 39 | 21 25 | 22 26 | 23 39 |
| 52 | 04 55 | 05 35 | 06 08 | 20 28 | 21 12 | 22 12 | 23 27 |
| 54 | 04 52 | 05 33 | 06 09 | 20 15 | 20 57 | 21 57 | 23 14 |
| 56 | 04 48 | 05 32 | 06 09 | 20 00 | 20 39 | 21 39 | 22 58 |
| 58 | 04 44 | 05 30 | 06 09 | 19 43 | 20 18 | 21 17 | 22 39 |
| S 60 | 04 39 | 05 28 | 06 10 | 19 22 | 19 51 | 20 48 | 22 15 |

### Sunset / Twilight / Moonset

| Lat. | Sunset | Civil | Naut. | Moonset 23 | 24 | 25 | 26 |
|---|---|---|---|---|---|---|---|
| ° | h m | h m | h m | h m | h m | h m | h m |
| N 72 | 18 37 | 19 47 | 21 25 | ▬▬ | ▬▬ | ▬▬ | ▬▬ |
| N 70 | 18 34 | 19 37 | 21 00 | ▬▬ | ▬▬ | ▬▬ | ▬▬ |
| 68 | 18 31 | 19 28 | 20 41 | ▬▬ | ▬▬ | ▬▬ | ▬▬ |
| 66 | 18 29 | 19 21 | 20 27 | 05 37 | ▬▬ | ▬▬ | ▬▬ |
| 64 | 18 27 | 19 15 | 20 15 | 06 19 | 05 56 | ▬▬ | ▬▬ |
| 62 | 18 26 | 19 10 | 20 05 | 06 48 | 06 55 | 07 24 | 08 44 |
| 60 | 18 24 | 19 06 | 19 57 | 07 10 | 07 29 | 08 10 | 09 24 |
| N 58 | 18 23 | 19 02 | 19 50 | 07 28 | 07 54 | 08 40 | 09 51 |
| 56 | 18 22 | 18 59 | 19 44 | 07 43 | 08 14 | 09 03 | 10 13 |
| 54 | 18 21 | 18 56 | 19 39 | 07 56 | 08 31 | 09 21 | 10 30 |
| 52 | 18 20 | 18 54 | 19 34 | 08 08 | 08 45 | 09 37 | 10 46 |
| 50 | 18 19 | 18 52 | 19 30 | 08 18 | 08 58 | 09 51 | 10 59 |
| 45 | 18 17 | 18 47 | 19 21 | 08 40 | 09 24 | 10 19 | 11 25 |
| N 40 | 18 16 | 18 43 | 19 15 | 08 57 | 09 44 | 10 41 | 11 47 |
| 35 | 18 15 | 18 40 | 19 10 | 09 12 | 10 02 | 10 59 | 12 04 |
| 30 | 18 14 | 18 38 | 19 06 | 09 25 | 10 16 | 11 15 | 12 19 |
| 20 | 18 12 | 18 34 | 19 00 | 09 47 | 10 42 | 11 42 | 12 45 |
| N 10 | 18 11 | 18 32 | 18 56 | 10 06 | 11 04 | 12 05 | 13 07 |
| 0 | 18 10 | 18 30 | 18 54 | 10 24 | 11 24 | 12 26 | 13 27 |
| S 10 | 18 08 | 18 29 | 18 54 | 10 42 | 11 45 | 12 47 | 13 48 |
| 20 | 18 07 | 18 29 | 18 55 | 11 02 | 12 07 | 13 10 | 14 09 |
| 30 | 18 06 | 18 30 | 18 58 | 11 24 | 12 32 | 13 36 | 14 30 |
| 35 | 18 06 | 18 31 | 19 00 | 11 37 | 12 47 | 13 52 | 14 49 |
| 40 | 18 05 | 18 32 | 19 04 | 11 53 | 13 05 | 14 10 | 15 06 |
| 45 | 18 04 | 18 34 | 19 08 | 12 11 | 13 26 | 14 32 | 15 26 |
| S 50 | 18 04 | 18 36 | 19 13 | 12 33 | 13 52 | 14 59 | 15 52 |
| 52 | 18 03 | 18 37 | 19 16 | 12 44 | 14 05 | 15 13 | 16 04 |
| 54 | 18 03 | 18 38 | 19 19 | 12 57 | 14 20 | 15 28 | 16 18 |
| 56 | 18 03 | 18 39 | 19 23 | 13 11 | 14 37 | 15 47 | 16 34 |
| 58 | 18 02 | 18 41 | 19 27 | 13 28 | 14 58 | 16 09 | 16 54 |
| S 60 | 18 02 | 18 43 | 19 32 | 13 48 | 15 25 | 16 37 | 17 17 |

### SUN and MOON

| Day | SUN Eqn. of Time 00h | 12h | Mer. Pass. | MOON Mer. Pass. Upper | Lower | Age | Phase |
|---|---|---|---|---|---|---|---|
| d | m s | m s | h m | h m | h m | d | % |
| 23 | 06 43 | 06 34 | 12 07 | 04 11 | 16 40 | 21 | 69 |
| 24 | 06 25 | 06 16 | 12 06 | 05 10 | 17 40 | 22 | 58 |
| 25 | 06 07 | 05 58 | 12 06 | 06 11 | 18 42 | 23 | 47 |

| UT | ARIES | VENUS −4.4 | | MARS +1.1 | | JUPITER −2.0 | | SATURN +0.7 | | STARS | | |
|---|---|---|---|---|---|---|---|---|---|---|---|---|
| | GHA | GHA | Dec | GHA | Dec | GHA | Dec | GHA | Dec | Name | SHA | Dec |
| d h | ° ′ | ° ′ | ° ′ | ° ′ | ° ′ | ° ′ | ° ′ | ° ′ | ° ′ | | ° ′ | ° ′ |
| 26 00 | 183 25.3 | 222 36.8 | S13 47.4 | 225 48.3 | S17 29.1 | 192 19.5 | S 4 55.6 | 219 15.7 | S15 13.6 | Acamar | 315 13.9 | S40 13.2 |
| 01 | 198 27.7 | 237 36.7 | 46.8 | 240 48.9 | 28.6 | 207 21.4 | 55.3 | 234 17.9 | 13.6 | Achernar | 335 22.5 | S57 07.7 |
| 02 | 213 30.2 | 252 36.6 | 46.3 | 255 49.4 | 28.1 | 222 23.4 | 55.1 | 249 20.2 | 13.5 | Acrux | 173 01.9 | S63 13.3 |
| 03 | 228 32.6 | 267 36.5 .. | 45.7 | 270 50.0 .. | 27.5 | 237 25.3 .. | 54.9 | 264 22.4 .. | 13.4 | Adhara | 255 07.6 | S29 00.4 |
| 04 | 243 35.1 | 282 36.3 | 45.2 | 285 50.6 | 27.0 | 252 27.2 | 54.7 | 279 24.6 | 13.3 | Aldebaran | 290 42.4 | N16 33.1 |
| 05 | 258 37.6 | 297 36.2 | 44.6 | 300 51.1 | 26.5 | 267 29.1 | 54.4 | 294 26.8 | 13.3 | | | |
| 06 | 273 40.0 | 312 36.1 | S13 44.1 | 315 51.7 | S17 26.0 | 282 31.0 | S 4 54.2 | 309 29.0 | S15 13.2 | Alioth | 166 14.5 | N55 50.3 |
| 07 | 288 42.5 | 327 36.0 | 43.5 | 330 52.3 | 25.4 | 297 32.9 | 54.0 | 324 31.3 | 13.1 | Alkaid | 152 53.4 | N49 12.0 |
| S 08 | 303 45.0 | 342 35.8 | 43.0 | 345 52.8 | 24.9 | 312 34.8 | 53.7 | 339 33.5 | 13.0 | Alnair | 27 36.2 | S46 51.2 |
| A 09 | 318 47.4 | 357 35.7 .. | 42.4 | 0 53.4 .. | 24.4 | 327 36.8 .. | 53.5 | 354 35.7 .. | 13.0 | Alnilam | 275 40.1 | S 1 11.4 |
| T 10 | 333 49.9 | 12 35.6 | 41.9 | 15 54.0 | 23.8 | 342 38.7 | 53.3 | 9 37.9 | 12.9 | Alphard | 217 49.8 | S 8 45.4 |
| U 11 | 348 52.4 | 27 35.5 | 41.3 | 30 54.6 | 23.3 | 357 40.6 | 53.0 | 24 40.2 | 12.8 | | | |
| R 12 | 3 54.8 | 42 35.3 | S13 40.8 | 45 55.1 | S17 22.8 | 12 42.5 | S 4 52.8 | 39 42.4 | S15 12.7 | Alphecca | 126 05.5 | N26 38.2 |
| D 13 | 18 57.3 | 57 35.2 | 40.2 | 60 55.7 | 22.3 | 27 44.4 | 52.6 | 54 44.6 | 12.7 | Alpheratz | 357 37.5 | N29 12.6 |
| A 14 | 33 59.8 | 72 35.1 | 39.6 | 75 56.3 | 21.7 | 42 46.3 | 52.4 | 69 46.8 | 12.6 | Altair | 62 03.4 | N 8 55.4 |
| Y 15 | 49 02.2 | 87 35.0 .. | 39.1 | 90 56.8 .. | 21.2 | 57 48.3 .. | 52.1 | 84 49.1 .. | 12.5 | Ankaa | 353 09.9 | S42 11.3 |
| 16 | 64 04.7 | 102 34.8 | 38.5 | 105 57.4 | 20.7 | 72 50.2 | 51.9 | 99 51.3 | 12.5 | Antares | 112 18.5 | S26 28.8 |
| 17 | 79 07.1 | 117 34.7 | 38.0 | 120 58.0 | 20.1 | 87 52.1 | 51.7 | 114 53.5 | 12.4 | | | |
| 18 | 94 09.6 | 132 34.6 | S13 37.4 | 135 58.5 | S17 19.6 | 102 54.0 | S 4 51.4 | 129 55.7 | S15 12.3 | Arcturus | 145 49.7 | N19 03.9 |
| 19 | 109 12.1 | 147 34.5 | 36.8 | 150 59.1 | 19.1 | 117 55.9 | 51.2 | 144 58.0 | 12.2 | Atria | 107 14.6 | S69 03.8 |
| 20 | 124 14.5 | 162 34.3 | 36.3 | 165 59.7 | 18.6 | 132 57.8 | 51.0 | 160 00.2 | 12.2 | Avior | 234 15.4 | S59 35.1 |
| 21 | 139 17.0 | 177 34.2 .. | 35.7 | 181 00.3 .. | 18.0 | 147 59.7 .. | 50.7 | 175 02.4 .. | 12.1 | Bellatrix | 278 25.4 | N 6 22.1 |
| 22 | 154 19.5 | 192 34.1 | 35.2 | 196 00.8 | 17.5 | 163 01.7 | 50.5 | 190 04.6 | 12.0 | Betelgeuse | 270 54.6 | N 7 24.6 |
| 23 | 169 21.9 | 207 33.9 | 34.6 | 211 01.4 | 17.0 | 178 03.6 | 50.3 | 205 06.9 | 11.9 | | | |
| 27 00 | 184 24.4 | 222 33.8 | S13 34.0 | 226 02.0 | S17 16.4 | 193 05.5 | S 4 50.1 | 220 09.1 | S15 11.9 | Canopus | 263 53.4 | S52 42.7 |
| 01 | 199 26.9 | 237 33.7 | 33.5 | 241 02.5 | 15.9 | 208 07.4 | 49.8 | 235 11.3 | 11.8 | Capella | 280 25.4 | N46 01.3 |
| 02 | 214 29.3 | 252 33.6 | 32.9 | 256 03.1 | 15.4 | 223 09.3 | 49.6 | 250 13.5 | 11.7 | Deneb | 49 27.6 | N45 21.2 |
| 03 | 229 31.8 | 267 33.4 .. | 32.3 | 271 03.7 .. | 14.8 | 238 11.2 .. | 49.4 | 265 15.8 .. | 11.7 | Denebola | 182 27.0 | N14 26.8 |
| 04 | 244 34.2 | 282 33.3 | 31.7 | 286 04.3 | 14.3 | 253 13.2 | 49.1 | 280 18.0 | 11.6 | Diphda | 348 49.9 | S17 52.1 |
| 05 | 259 36.7 | 297 33.2 | 31.2 | 301 04.8 | 13.8 | 268 15.1 | 48.9 | 295 20.2 | 11.5 | | | |
| 06 | 274 39.2 | 312 33.0 | S13 30.6 | 316 05.4 | S17 13.2 | 283 17.0 | S 4 48.7 | 310 22.4 | S15 11.4 | Dubhe | 193 43.2 | N61 38.0 |
| 07 | 289 41.6 | 327 32.9 | 30.0 | 331 06.0 | 12.7 | 298 18.9 | 48.4 | 325 24.7 | 11.4 | Elnath | 278 04.9 | N28 37.6 |
| 08 | 304 44.1 | 342 32.8 | 29.5 | 346 06.5 | 12.2 | 313 20.8 | 48.2 | 340 26.9 | 11.3 | Eltanin | 90 43.2 | N51 28.8 |
| S 09 | 319 46.6 | 357 32.6 .. | 28.9 | 1 07.1 .. | 11.6 | 328 22.7 .. | 48.0 | 355 29.1 .. | 11.2 | Enif | 33 41.3 | N 9 58.4 |
| U 10 | 334 49.0 | 12 32.5 | 28.3 | 16 07.7 | 11.1 | 343 24.7 | 47.8 | 10 31.4 | 11.1 | Fomalhaut | 15 17.4 | S29 30.4 |
| N 11 | 349 51.5 | 27 32.4 | 27.7 | 31 08.3 | 10.6 | 358 26.6 | 47.5 | 25 33.6 | 11.1 | | | |
| D 12 | 4 54.0 | 42 32.2 | S13 27.2 | 46 08.8 | S17 10.0 | 13 28.5 | S 4 47.3 | 40 35.8 | S15 11.0 | Gacrux | 171 53.6 | S57 14.2 |
| A 13 | 19 56.4 | 57 32.1 | 26.6 | 61 09.4 | 09.5 | 28 30.4 | 47.1 | 55 38.0 | 10.9 | Gienah | 175 45.6 | S17 40.0 |
| Y 14 | 34 58.9 | 72 32.0 | 26.0 | 76 10.0 | 09.0 | 43 32.3 | 46.8 | 70 40.3 | 10.9 | Hadar | 148 38.7 | S60 28.7 |
| 15 | 50 01.4 | 87 31.8 .. | 25.4 | 91 10.6 .. | 08.4 | 58 34.2 .. | 46.6 | 85 42.5 .. | 10.8 | Hamal | 327 54.1 | N23 33.9 |
| 16 | 65 03.8 | 102 31.7 | 24.9 | 106 11.2 | 07.9 | 73 36.2 | 46.4 | 100 44.7 | 10.7 | Kaus Aust. | 83 35.6 | S34 22.4 |
| 17 | 80 06.3 | 117 31.6 | 24.3 | 121 11.7 | 07.3 | 88 38.1 | 46.1 | 115 46.9 | 10.6 | | | |
| 18 | 95 08.7 | 132 31.4 | S13 23.7 | 136 12.3 | S17 06.8 | 103 40.0 | S 4 45.9 | 130 49.2 | S15 10.6 | Kochab | 137 18.9 | N74 03.7 |
| 19 | 110 11.2 | 147 31.3 | 23.1 | 151 12.8 | 06.3 | 118 41.9 | 45.7 | 145 51.4 | 10.5 | Markab | 13 32.5 | N15 19.2 |
| 20 | 125 13.7 | 162 31.2 | 22.5 | 166 13.4 | 05.7 | 133 43.8 | 45.5 | 160 53.6 | 10.4 | Menkar | 314 08.8 | N 4 10.4 |
| 21 | 140 16.1 | 177 31.0 .. | 22.0 | 181 14.0 .. | 05.2 | 148 45.7 .. | 45.2 | 175 55.9 .. | 10.3 | Menkent | 148 00.0 | S36 28.7 |
| 22 | 155 18.6 | 192 30.9 | 21.4 | 196 14.6 | 04.7 | 163 47.7 | 45.0 | 190 58.1 | 10.3 | Miaplacidus | 221 38.1 | S69 48.7 |
| 23 | 170 21.1 | 207 30.8 | 20.8 | 211 15.1 | 04.1 | 178 49.6 | 44.8 | 206 00.3 | 10.2 | | | |
| 28 00 | 185 23.5 | 222 30.6 | S13 20.2 | 226 15.7 | S17 03.6 | 193 51.5 | S 4 44.5 | 221 02.5 | S15 10.1 | Mirfak | 308 31.9 | N49 56.4 |
| 01 | 200 26.0 | 237 30.5 | 19.6 | 241 16.3 | 03.0 | 208 53.4 | 44.3 | 236 04.8 | 10.1 | Nunki | 75 50.7 | S26 16.1 |
| 02 | 215 28.5 | 252 30.4 | 19.0 | 256 16.9 | 02.5 | 223 55.3 | 44.1 | 251 07.0 | 10.0 | Peacock | 53 09.6 | S56 39.7 |
| 03 | 230 30.9 | 267 30.2 .. | 18.4 | 271 17.4 .. | 02.0 | 238 57.2 .. | 43.9 | 266 09.2 .. | 09.9 | Pollux | 243 20.0 | N27 58.4 |
| 04 | 245 33.4 | 282 30.1 | 17.9 | 286 18.0 | 01.4 | 253 59.2 | 43.6 | 281 11.4 | 09.8 | Procyon | 244 53.2 | N 5 10.0 |
| 05 | 260 35.9 | 297 29.9 | 17.3 | 301 18.6 | 00.9 | 269 01.1 | 43.4 | 296 13.7 | 09.8 | | | |
| 06 | 275 38.3 | 312 29.8 | S13 16.7 | 316 19.2 | S17 00.3 | 284 03.0 | S 4 43.2 | 311 15.9 | S15 09.7 | Rasalhague | 96 00.6 | N12 32.4 |
| 07 | 290 40.8 | 327 29.7 | 16.1 | 331 19.7 | 16 59.8 | 299 04.9 | 42.9 | 326 18.1 | 09.6 | Regulus | 207 36.6 | N11 51.5 |
| 08 | 305 43.2 | 342 29.5 | 15.5 | 346 20.3 | 59.3 | 314 06.8 | 42.7 | 341 20.4 | 09.6 | Rigel | 281 06.2 | S 8 10.8 |
| M 09 | 320 45.7 | 357 29.4 .. | 14.9 | 1 20.9 .. | 58.7 | 329 08.7 .. | 42.5 | 356 22.6 .. | 09.5 | Rigil Kent. | 139 42.9 | S60 55.4 |
| O 10 | 335 48.2 | 12 29.3 | 14.3 | 16 21.5 | 58.2 | 344 10.7 | 42.2 | 11 24.8 | 09.4 | Sabik | 102 05.3 | S15 45.2 |
| N 11 | 350 50.6 | 27 29.1 | 13.7 | 31 22.1 | 57.6 | 359 12.6 | 42.0 | 26 27.0 | 09.3 | | | |
| D 12 | 5 53.1 | 42 29.0 | S13 13.1 | 46 22.6 | S16 57.1 | 14 14.5 | S 4 41.8 | 41 29.3 | S15 09.3 | Schedar | 349 34.2 | N56 39.4 |
| A 13 | 20 55.6 | 57 28.8 | 12.5 | 61 23.2 | 56.6 | 29 16.4 | 41.6 | 56 31.5 | 09.2 | Shaula | 96 13.4 | S37 07.1 |
| Y 14 | 35 58.0 | 72 28.7 | 11.9 | 76 23.8 | 56.0 | 44 18.3 | 41.3 | 71 33.7 | 09.1 | Sirius | 258 28.2 | S16 45.0 |
| 15 | 51 00.5 | 87 28.6 .. | 11.3 | 91 24.4 .. | 55.5 | 59 20.3 .. | 41.1 | 86 36.0 .. | 09.1 | Spica | 158 24.4 | S11 16.7 |
| 16 | 66 03.0 | 102 28.4 | 10.8 | 106 24.9 | 54.9 | 74 22.2 | 40.9 | 101 38.2 | 09.0 | Suhail | 222 47.7 | S43 31.5 |
| 17 | 81 05.4 | 117 28.3 | 10.2 | 121 25.5 | 54.4 | 89 24.1 | 40.6 | 116 40.4 | 08.9 | | | |
| 18 | 96 07.9 | 132 28.1 | S13 09.6 | 136 26.1 | S16 53.8 | 104 26.0 | S 4 40.4 | 131 42.6 | S15 08.8 | Vega | 80 34.8 | N38 47.9 |
| 19 | 111 10.3 | 147 28.0 | 09.0 | 151 26.7 | 53.3 | 119 27.9 | 40.2 | 146 44.9 | 08.8 | Zuben'ubi | 136 58.3 | S16 08.1 |
| 20 | 126 12.8 | 162 27.9 | 08.4 | 166 27.3 | 52.8 | 134 29.8 | 40.0 | 161 47.1 | 08.7 | | SHA | Mer. Pass. |
| 21 | 141 15.3 | 177 27.7 .. | 07.8 | 181 27.8 .. | 52.2 | 149 31.8 .. | 39.7 | 176 49.3 .. | 08.6 | Venus | 38 09.4 | 9 10 |
| 22 | 156 17.7 | 192 27.6 | 07.2 | 196 28.4 | 51.7 | 164 33.7 | 39.5 | 191 51.6 | 08.6 | Mars | 41 37.6 | 8 56 |
| 23 | 171 20.2 | 207 27.4 | 06.6 | 211 29.0 | 51.1 | 179 35.6 | 39.3 | 206 53.8 | 08.5 | Jupiter | 8 41.1 | 11 06 |
| Mer. Pass. 11 40.5 | | v −0.1 | d 0.6 | v 0.6 | d 0.5 | v 1.9 | d 0.2 | v 2.2 | d 0.1 | Saturn | 35 44.7 | 9 18 |

### SUN / MOON

| UT | SUN GHA | SUN Dec | MOON GHA | v | MOON Dec | d | HP |
|----|---------|---------|----------|---|----------|---|----|
| d h | ° ′ | ° ′ | ° ′ | ′ | ° ′ | ′ | ′ |
| 26 00 | 178 32.9 | N 2 06.6 | 256 13.7 | 4.2 | S26 33.7 | 2.3 | 59.1 |
| 01 | 193 33.1 | 07.5 | 270 36.9 | 4.1 | 26 31.4 | 2.5 | 59.1 |
| 02 | 208 33.3 | 08.5 | 285 00.0 | 4.2 | 26 28.9 | 2.6 | 59.1 |
| 03 | 223 33.5 .. | 09.5 | 299 23.2 | 4.3 | 26 26.3 | 2.8 | 59.1 |
| 04 | 238 33.7 | 10.5 | 313 46.5 | 4.3 | 26 23.5 | 3.1 | 59.1 |
| 05 | 253 33.9 | 11.5 | 328 09.8 | 4.3 | 26 20.4 | 3.1 | 59.1 |
| 06 | 268 34.1 | N 2 12.4 | 342 33.1 | 4.4 | S26 17.3 | 3.4 | 59.1 |
| 07 | 283 34.2 | 13.4 | 356 56.5 | 4.5 | 26 13.9 | 3.5 | 59.1 |
| S 08 | 298 34.4 | 14.4 | 11 20.0 | 4.4 | 26 10.4 | 3.7 | 59.1 |
| A 09 | 313 34.6 .. | 15.4 | 25 43.4 | 4.6 | 26 06.7 | 3.9 | 59.1 |
| T 10 | 328 34.8 | 16.4 | 40 07.0 | 4.5 | 26 02.8 | 4.1 | 59.1 |
| U 11 | 343 35.0 | 17.3 | 54 30.5 | 4.7 | 25 58.7 | 4.2 | 59.1 |
| R 12 | 358 35.2 | N 2 18.3 | 68 54.2 | 4.7 | S25 54.5 | 4.4 | 59.1 |
| D 13 | 13 35.4 | 19.3 | 83 17.9 | 4.7 | 25 50.1 | 4.6 | 59.0 |
| A 14 | 28 35.6 | 20.3 | 97 41.6 | 4.8 | 25 45.5 | 4.7 | 59.0 |
| Y 15 | 43 35.7 .. | 21.3 | 112 05.4 | 4.9 | 25 40.8 | 4.9 | 59.0 |
| 16 | 58 35.9 | 22.2 | 126 29.3 | 4.9 | 25 35.9 | 5.1 | 59.0 |
| 17 | 73 36.1 | 23.2 | 140 53.2 | 5.1 | 25 30.8 | 5.3 | 59.0 |
| 18 | 88 36.3 | N 2 24.2 | 155 17.3 | 5.0 | S25 25.5 | 5.4 | 59.0 |
| 19 | 103 36.5 | 25.2 | 169 41.3 | 5.2 | 25 20.1 | 5.5 | 59.0 |
| 20 | 118 36.7 | 26.2 | 184 05.5 | 5.2 | 25 14.6 | 5.8 | 59.0 |
| 21 | 133 36.9 .. | 27.2 | 198 29.7 | 5.2 | 25 08.8 | 5.9 | 59.0 |
| 22 | 148 37.1 | 28.1 | 212 53.9 | 5.4 | 25 02.9 | 6.0 | 59.0 |
| 23 | 163 37.3 | 29.1 | 227 18.3 | 5.4 | 24 56.9 | 6.2 | 59.0 |
| 27 00 | 178 37.4 | N 2 30.1 | 241 42.7 | 5.5 | S24 50.7 | 6.4 | 58.9 |
| 01 | 193 37.6 | 31.1 | 256 07.2 | 5.6 | 24 44.3 | 6.5 | 58.9 |
| 02 | 208 37.8 | 32.0 | 270 31.8 | 5.6 | 24 37.8 | 6.7 | 58.9 |
| 03 | 223 38.0 .. | 33.0 | 284 56.4 | 5.7 | 24 31.1 | 6.9 | 58.9 |
| 04 | 238 38.2 | 34.0 | 299 21.1 | 5.8 | 24 24.2 | 7.0 | 58.9 |
| 05 | 253 38.4 | 35.0 | 313 45.9 | 5.9 | 24 17.2 | 7.1 | 58.9 |
| 06 | 268 38.6 | N 2 36.0 | 328 10.8 | 6.0 | S24 10.1 | 7.3 | 58.9 |
| 07 | 283 38.8 | 36.9 | 342 35.8 | 6.0 | 24 02.8 | 7.5 | 58.9 |
| S 08 | 298 38.9 | 37.9 | 357 00.8 | 6.2 | 23 55.3 | 7.6 | 58.9 |
| U 09 | 313 39.1 .. | 38.9 | 11 26.0 | 6.2 | 23 47.7 | 7.7 | 58.9 |
| N 10 | 328 39.3 | 39.9 | 25 51.2 | 6.3 | 23 40.0 | 7.9 | 58.8 |
| D 11 | 343 39.5 | 40.9 | 40 16.5 | 6.4 | 23 32.1 | 8.1 | 58.8 |
| A 12 | 358 39.7 | N 2 41.8 | 54 41.9 | 6.5 | S23 24.0 | 8.1 | 58.8 |
| Y 13 | 13 39.9 | 42.8 | 69 07.4 | 6.5 | 23 15.9 | 8.4 | 58.8 |
| 14 | 28 40.1 | 43.8 | 83 32.9 | 6.7 | 23 07.5 | 8.4 | 58.8 |
| 15 | 43 40.3 | 44.8 | 97 58.6 | 6.7 | 22 59.1 | 8.6 | 58.8 |
| 16 | 58 40.5 | 45.8 | 112 24.3 | 6.9 | 22 50.5 | 8.8 | 58.8 |
| 17 | 73 40.6 | 46.7 | 126 50.2 | 6.9 | 22 41.7 | 8.9 | 58.8 |
| 18 | 88 40.8 | N 2 47.7 | 141 16.1 | 7.0 | S22 32.8 | 9.0 | 58.8 |
| 19 | 103 41.0 | 48.7 | 155 42.1 | 7.1 | 22 23.8 | 9.1 | 50.7 |
| 20 | 118 41.2 | 49.7 | 170 08.2 | 7.2 | 22 14.7 | 9.3 | 58.7 |
| 21 | 133 41.4 .. | 50.6 | 184 34.4 | 7.3 | 22 05.4 | 9.4 | 58.7 |
| 22 | 148 41.6 | 51.6 | 199 00.7 | 7.4 | 21 56.0 | 9.5 | 58.7 |
| 23 | 163 41.8 | 52.6 | 213 27.1 | 7.4 | 21 46.5 | 9.7 | 58.7 |
| 28 00 | 178 42.0 | N 2 53.6 | 227 53.5 | 7.6 | S21 36.8 | 9.8 | 58.7 |
| 01 | 193 42.1 | 54.6 | 242 20.1 | 7.7 | 21 27.0 | 9.9 | 58.7 |
| 02 | 208 42.3 | 55.5 | 256 46.8 | 7.7 | 21 17.1 | 10.0 | 58.7 |
| 03 | 223 42.5 .. | 56.5 | 271 13.5 | 7.9 | 21 07.1 | 10.2 | 58.6 |
| 04 | 238 42.7 | 57.5 | 285 40.4 | 7.9 | 20 56.9 | 10.2 | 58.6 |
| 05 | 253 42.9 | 58.5 | 300 07.3 | 8.0 | 20 46.7 | 10.4 | 58.6 |
| 06 | 268 43.1 | N 2 59.4 | 314 34.3 | 8.2 | S20 36.3 | 10.5 | 58.6 |
| 07 | 283 43.3 | 3 00.4 | 329 01.5 | 8.2 | 20 25.8 | 10.6 | 58.6 |
| 08 | 298 43.5 | 01.4 | 343 28.7 | 8.3 | 20 15.2 | 10.8 | 58.6 |
| M 09 | 313 43.6 .. | 02.4 | 357 56.0 | 8.4 | 20 04.4 | 10.8 | 58.6 |
| O 10 | 328 43.8 | 03.3 | 12 23.4 | 8.5 | 19 53.6 | 11.0 | 58.6 |
| N 11 | 343 44.0 | 04.3 | 26 50.9 | 8.6 | 19 42.6 | 11.0 | 58.5 |
| D 12 | 358 44.2 | N 3 05.3 | 41 18.5 | 8.7 | S19 31.6 | 11.2 | 58.5 |
| A 13 | 13 44.4 | 06.3 | 55 46.2 | 8.8 | 19 20.4 | 11.3 | 58.5 |
| Y 14 | 28 44.6 | 07.3 | 70 14.0 | 8.9 | 19 09.1 | 11.4 | 58.5 |
| 15 | 43 44.8 .. | 08.2 | 84 41.9 | 9.0 | 18 57.7 | 11.4 | 58.5 |
| 16 | 58 45.0 | 09.2 | 99 09.9 | 9.1 | 18 46.3 | 11.6 | 58.5 |
| 17 | 73 45.1 | 10.2 | 113 38.0 | 9.1 | 18 34.7 | 11.7 | 58.5 |
| 18 | 88 45.3 | N 3 11.2 | 128 06.1 | 9.3 | S18 23.0 | 11.8 | 58.4 |
| 19 | 103 45.5 | 12.1 | 142 34.4 | 9.3 | 18 11.2 | 11.9 | 58.4 |
| 20 | 118 45.7 | 13.1 | 157 02.7 | 9.5 | 17 59.3 | 11.9 | 58.4 |
| 21 | 133 45.9 .. | 14.1 | 171 31.2 | 9.5 | 17 47.4 | 12.1 | 58.4 |
| 22 | 148 46.1 | 15.1 | 185 59.7 | 9.6 | 17 35.3 | 12.1 | 58.4 |
| 23 | 163 46.3 | 16.0 | 200 28.3 | 9.7 | S17 23.2 | 12.3 | 58.4 |
| | SD 16.1 | d 1.0 | SD 16.1 | | 16.0 | | 15.9 |

### Twilight / Sunrise / Moonrise

| Lat. | Twilight Naut. | Twilight Civil | Sunrise | Moonrise 26 | Moonrise 27 | Moonrise 28 | Moonrise 29 |
|------|------|------|------|------|------|------|------|
| ° | h m | h m | h m | h m | h m | h m | h m |
| N 72 | 02 29 | 04 12 | 05 22 | ■■■ | ■■■ | ■■■ | 07 55 |
| N 70 | 02 58 | 04 24 | 05 27 | ■■■ | ■■■ | ■■■ | 07 19 |
| 68 | 03 18 | 04 33 | 05 31 | ■■■ | ■■■ | 07 35 | 06 53 |
| 66 | 03 35 | 04 41 | 05 34 | ■■■ | ■■■ | 06 54 | 06 34 |
| 64 | 03 47 | 04 48 | 05 36 | ■■■ | 06 38 | 06 25 | 06 17 |
| 62 | 03 58 | 04 54 | 05 39 | 05 47 | 06 00 | 06 04 | 06 04 |
| 60 | 04 07 | 04 59 | 05 41 | 05 06 | 05 33 | 05 46 | 05 52 |
| N 58 | 04 15 | 05 03 | 05 42 | 04 38 | 05 12 | 05 31 | 05 42 |
| 56 | 04 21 | 05 07 | 05 44 | 04 17 | 04 54 | 05 18 | 05 34 |
| 54 | 04 27 | 05 10 | 05 45 | 03 59 | 04 39 | 05 07 | 05 26 |
| 52 | 04 32 | 05 13 | 05 47 | 03 43 | 04 27 | 04 57 | 05 19 |
| 50 | 04 37 | 05 15 | 05 48 | 03 30 | 04 15 | 04 48 | 05 12 |
| 45 | 04 46 | 05 21 | 05 50 | 03 03 | 03 51 | 04 29 | 04 59 |
| N 40 | 04 53 | 05 25 | 05 52 | 02 41 | 03 32 | 04 13 | 04 47 |
| 35 | 04 59 | 05 29 | 05 54 | 02 23 | 03 16 | 04 00 | 04 37 |
| 30 | 05 04 | 05 32 | 05 56 | 02 08 | 03 02 | 03 49 | 04 29 |
| 20 | 05 10 | 05 36 | 05 58 | 01 42 | 02 38 | 03 29 | 04 14 |
| N 10 | 05 15 | 05 39 | 06 00 | 01 19 | 02 18 | 03 12 | 04 01 |
| 0 | 05 17 | 05 41 | 06 02 | 00 58 | 01 58 | 02 56 | 03 49 |
| S 10 | 05 19 | 05 43 | 06 04 | 00 37 | 01 39 | 02 39 | 03 36 |
| 20 | 05 18 | 05 44 | 06 06 | 00 14 | 01 18 | 02 22 | 03 23 |
| 30 | 05 16 | 05 44 | 06 08 | 24 54 | 00 54 | 02 02 | 03 08 |
| 35 | 05 14 | 05 43 | 06 09 | 24 40 | 00 40 | 01 50 | 02 59 |
| 40 | 05 11 | 05 43 | 06 10 | 24 24 | 00 24 | 01 36 | 02 49 |
| 45 | 05 08 | 05 42 | 06 11 | 24 04 | 00 04 | 01 20 | 02 37 |
| S 50 | 05 03 | 05 40 | 06 13 | 23 39 | 25 00 | 01 00 | 02 22 |
| 52 | 05 00 | 05 40 | 06 13 | 23 27 | 24 51 | 00 51 | 02 16 |
| 54 | 04 58 | 05 39 | 06 14 | 23 14 | 24 40 | 00 40 | 02 08 |
| 56 | 04 54 | 05 38 | 06 15 | 22 58 | 24 28 | 00 28 | 01 59 |
| 58 | 04 51 | 05 37 | 06 16 | 22 39 | 24 13 | 00 13 | 01 50 |
| S 60 | 04 46 | 05 35 | 06 17 | 22 15 | 23 57 | 25 38 | 01 38 |

### Sunset / Twilight / Moonset

| Lat. | Sunset | Twilight Civil | Twilight Naut. | Moonset 26 | Moonset 27 | Moonset 28 | Moonset 29 |
|------|------|------|------|------|------|------|------|
| ° | h m | h m | h m | h m | h m | h m | h m |
| N 72 | 18 51 | 20 03 | 21 49 | ■■■ | ■■■ | ■■■ | 12 32 |
| N 70 | 18 46 | 19 50 | 21 18 | ■■■ | ■■■ | ■■■ | 13 05 |
| 68 | 18 42 | 19 40 | 20 56 | ■■■ | ■■■ | 10 59 | 13 29 |
| 66 | 18 39 | 19 32 | 20 39 | ■■■ | ■■■ | 11 39 | 13 48 |
| 64 | 18 36 | 19 25 | 20 26 | ■■■ | 09 57 | 12 07 | 14 03 |
| 62 | 18 34 | 19 19 | 20 15 | 08 44 | 10 35 | 12 28 | 14 15 |
| 60 | 18 31 | 19 14 | 20 06 | 09 24 | 11 01 | 12 45 | 14 25 |
| N 58 | 10 30 | 19 09 | 19 50 | 09 51 | 11 22 | 12 59 | 14 34 |
| 56 | 10 20 | 19 06 | 19 51 | 10 13 | 11 39 | 13 11 | 14 42 |
| 54 | 18 26 | 19 02 | 19 45 | 10 30 | 11 53 | 13 21 | 14 49 |
| 52 | 18 25 | 18 59 | 19 40 | 10 46 | 12 06 | 13 31 | 14 55 |
| 50 | 18 24 | 18 56 | 19 35 | 10 59 | 12 17 | 13 39 | 15 01 |
| 45 | 18 21 | 18 51 | 19 26 | 11 25 | 12 40 | 13 57 | 15 13 |
| N 40 | 18 19 | 18 46 | 19 18 | 11 47 | 12 58 | 14 11 | 15 23 |
| 35 | 18 17 | 18 43 | 19 12 | 12 04 | 13 13 | 14 23 | 15 31 |
| 30 | 18 16 | 18 40 | 19 08 | 12 19 | 13 26 | 14 34 | 15 39 |
| 20 | 18 13 | 18 35 | 19 01 | 12 45 | 13 49 | 14 51 | 15 51 |
| N 10 | 18 11 | 18 32 | 18 56 | 13 07 | 14 08 | 15 07 | 16 02 |
| 0 | 18 09 | 18 29 | 18 53 | 13 27 | 14 26 | 15 21 | 16 13 |
| S 10 | 18 07 | 18 28 | 18 52 | 13 48 | 14 44 | 15 36 | 16 23 |
| 20 | 18 05 | 18 27 | 18 52 | 14 09 | 15 03 | 15 51 | 16 34 |
| 30 | 18 03 | 18 27 | 18 54 | 14 34 | 15 25 | 16 08 | 16 46 |
| 35 | 18 02 | 18 27 | 18 56 | 14 49 | 15 38 | 16 18 | 16 53 |
| 40 | 18 00 | 18 27 | 18 59 | 15 06 | 15 52 | 16 29 | 17 01 |
| 45 | 17 59 | 18 28 | 19 02 | 15 26 | 16 09 | 16 43 | 17 10 |
| S 50 | 17 57 | 18 29 | 19 07 | 15 52 | 16 30 | 16 59 | 17 21 |
| 52 | 17 56 | 18 30 | 19 09 | 16 04 | 16 41 | 17 06 | 17 26 |
| 54 | 17 56 | 18 31 | 19 12 | 16 18 | 16 52 | 17 15 | 17 31 |
| 56 | 17 55 | 18 32 | 19 15 | 16 34 | 17 05 | 17 24 | 17 37 |
| 58 | 17 54 | 18 33 | 19 18 | 16 54 | 17 19 | 17 35 | 17 44 |
| S 60 | 17 53 | 18 34 | 19 23 | 17 17 | 17 37 | 17 47 | 17 52 |

### SUN / MOON

| Day | SUN Eqn. of Time 00h | SUN Eqn. of Time 12h | SUN Mer. Pass. | MOON Mer. Pass. Upper | MOON Mer. Pass. Lower | Age | Phase |
|-----|------|------|------|------|------|------|------|
| d | m s | m s | h m | h m | h m | d % | |
| 26 | 05 49 | 05 40 | 12 06 | 07 13 | 19 43 | 24 36 | |
| 27 | 05 31 | 05 22 | 12 05 | 08 12 | 20 41 | 25 25 | |
| 28 | 05 13 | 05 04 | 12 05 | 09 09 | 21 35 | 26 16 | |

| UT | ARIES | VENUS −4.4 | | MARS +1.1 | | JUPITER −2.0 | | SATURN +0.7 | | STARS | | |
|---|---|---|---|---|---|---|---|---|---|---|---|---|
| | GHA | GHA | Dec | GHA | Dec | GHA | Dec | GHA | Dec | Name | SHA | Dec |
| d h | ° ′ | ° ′ | ° ′ | ° ′ | ° ′ | ° ′ | ° ′ | ° ′ | ° ′ | | ° ′ | ° ′ |
| 29 00 | 186 22.7 | 222 27.3 | S13 06.0 | 226 29.6 | S16 50.6 | 194 37.5 | S 4 39.0 | 221 56.0 | S15 08.4 | Acamar | 315 13.9 | S40 13.2 |
| 01 | 201 25.1 | 237 27.2 | 05.3 | 241 30.1 | 50.0 | 209 39.4 | 38.8 | 236 58.3 | 08.3 | Achernar | 335 22.5 | S57 07.6 |
| 02 | 216 27.6 | 252 27.0 | 04.7 | 256 30.7 | 49.5 | 224 41.3 | 38.6 | 252 00.5 | 08.3 | Acrux | 173 01.9 | S63 13.3 |
| 03 | 231 30.1 | 267 26.9 · · | 04.1 | 271 31.3 · · | 48.9 | 239 43.3 · · | 38.4 | 267 02.7 · · | 08.2 | Adhara | 255 07.6 | S29 00.4 |
| 04 | 246 32.5 | 282 26.7 | 03.5 | 286 31.9 | 48.4 | 254 45.2 | 38.1 | 282 05.0 | 08.1 | Aldebaran | 290 42.4 | N16 33.1 |
| 05 | 261 35.0 | 297 26.6 | 02.9 | 301 32.5 | 47.8 | 269 47.1 | 37.9 | 297 07.2 | 08.1 | | | |
| 06 | 276 37.5 | 312 26.4 | S13 02.3 | 316 33.0 | S16 47.3 | 284 49.0 | S 4 37.7 | 312 09.4 | S15 08.0 | Alioth | 166 14.5 | N55 50.3 |
| 07 | 291 39.9 | 327 26.3 | 01.7 | 331 33.6 | 46.8 | 299 50.9 | 37.4 | 327 11.6 | 07.9 | Alkaid | 152 53.4 | N49 12.0 |
| T 08 | 306 42.4 | 342 26.2 | 01.1 | 346 34.2 | 46.2 | 314 52.9 | 37.2 | 342 13.9 | 07.8 | Alnair | 27 36.2 | S46 51.2 |
| U 09 | 321 44.8 | 357 26.0 | 13 00.5 | 1 34.8 · · | 45.7 | 329 54.8 · · | 37.0 | 357 16.1 · · | 07.8 | Alnilam | 275 40.1 | S 1 11.4 |
| E 10 | 336 47.3 | 12 25.9 | 12 59.9 | 16 35.4 | 45.1 | 344 56.7 | 36.7 | 12 18.3 | 07.7 | Alphard | 217 49.8 | S 8 45.4 |
| S 11 | 351 49.8 | 27 25.7 | 59.3 | 31 35.9 | 44.6 | 359 58.6 | 36.5 | 27 20.6 | 07.6 | | | |
| D 12 | 6 52.2 | 42 25.6 | S12 58.7 | 46 36.5 | S16 44.0 | 15 00.5 | S 4 36.3 | 42 22.8 | S15 07.6 | Alphecca | 126 05.4 | N26 38.2 |
| A 13 | 21 54.7 | 57 25.4 | 58.1 | 61 37.1 | 43.5 | 30 02.5 | 36.1 | 57 25.0 | 07.5 | Alpheratz | 357 37.5 | N29 12.6 |
| Y 14 | 36 57.2 | 72 25.3 | 57.4 | 76 37.7 | 42.9 | 45 04.4 | 35.8 | 72 27.3 | 07.4 | Altair | 62 02.3 | N 8 55.4 |
| 15 | 51 59.6 | 87 25.2 · · | 56.8 | 91 38.3 · · | 42.4 | 60 06.3 · · | 35.6 | 87 29.5 · · | 07.3 | Ankaa | 353 09.8 | S42 11.3 |
| 16 | 67 02.1 | 102 25.0 | 56.2 | 106 38.8 | 41.8 | 75 08.2 | 35.4 | 102 31.7 | 07.3 | Antares | 112 18.5 | S26 28.8 |
| 17 | 82 04.6 | 117 24.9 | 55.6 | 121 39.4 | 41.3 | 90 10.1 | 35.1 | 117 34.0 | 07.2 | | | |
| 18 | 97 07.0 | 132 24.7 | S12 55.0 | 136 40.0 | S16 40.7 | 105 12.0 | S 4 34.9 | 132 36.2 | S15 07.1 | Arcturus | 145 49.7 | N19 03.9 |
| 19 | 112 09.5 | 147 24.6 | 54.4 | 151 40.6 | 40.2 | 120 14.0 | 34.7 | 147 38.4 | 07.1 | Atria | 107 14.5 | S69 03.8 |
| 20 | 127 12.0 | 162 24.4 | 53.7 | 166 41.2 | 39.6 | 135 15.9 | 34.5 | 162 40.7 | 07.0 | Avior | 234 15.4 | S59 35.1 |
| 21 | 142 14.4 | 177 24.3 · · | 53.1 | 181 41.8 · · | 39.1 | 150 17.8 · · | 34.2 | 177 42.9 · · | 06.9 | Bellatrix | 278 25.4 | N 6 22.1 |
| 22 | 157 16.9 | 192 24.1 | 52.5 | 196 42.3 | 38.5 | 165 19.7 | 34.0 | 192 45.1 | 06.8 | Betelgeuse | 270 54.6 | N 7 24.6 |
| 23 | 172 19.3 | 207 24.0 | 51.9 | 211 42.9 | 38.0 | 180 21.6 | 33.8 | 207 47.3 | 06.8 | | | |
| 30 00 | 187 21.8 | 222 23.8 | S12 51.3 | 226 43.5 | S16 37.4 | 195 23.6 | S 4 33.5 | 222 49.6 | S15 06.7 | Canopus | 263 53.4 | S52 42.7 |
| 01 | 202 24.3 | 237 23.7 | 50.6 | 241 44.1 | 36.9 | 210 25.5 | 33.3 | 237 51.8 | 06.6 | Capella | 280 25.4 | N46 01.3 |
| 02 | 217 26.7 | 252 23.5 | 50.0 | 256 44.7 | 36.3 | 225 27.4 | 33.1 | 252 54.0 | 06.6 | Deneb | 49 27.6 | N45 21.2 |
| 03 | 232 29.2 | 267 23.4 · · | 49.4 | 271 45.2 · · | 35.8 | 240 29.3 · · | 32.9 | 267 56.3 · · | 06.5 | Denebola | 182 20.9 | N14 26.8 |
| 04 | 247 31.7 | 282 23.3 | 48.8 | 286 45.8 | 35.2 | 255 31.2 | 32.6 | 282 58.5 | 06.4 | Diphda | 348 49.9 | S17 52.1 |
| 05 | 262 34.1 | 297 23.1 | 48.2 | 301 46.4 | 34.6 | 270 33.2 | 32.4 | 298 00.7 | 06.4 | | | |
| 06 | 277 36.6 | 312 23.0 | S12 47.5 | 316 47.0 | S16 34.1 | 285 35.1 | S 4 32.2 | 313 03.0 | S15 06.3 | Dubhe | 193 43.2 | N61 38.0 |
| W 07 | 292 39.1 | 327 22.8 | 46.9 | 331 47.6 | 33.5 | 300 37.0 | 31.9 | 328 05.2 | 06.2 | Elnath | 278 04.9 | N28 37.6 |
| E 08 | 307 41.5 | 342 22.7 | 46.3 | 346 48.2 | 33.0 | 315 38.9 | 31.7 | 343 07.4 | 06.1 | Eltanin | 90 43.2 | N51 28.8 |
| D 09 | 322 44.0 | 357 22.5 · · | 45.6 | 1 48.7 · · | 32.4 | 330 40.8 · · | 31.5 | 358 09.7 · · | 06.1 | Enif | 33 41.3 | N 9 58.4 |
| N 10 | 337 46.4 | 12 22.4 | 45.0 | 16 49.3 | 31.9 | 345 42.8 | 31.3 | 13 11.9 | 06.0 | Fomalhaut | 15 17.4 | S29 30.4 |
| E 11 | 352 48.9 | 27 22.2 | 44.4 | 31 49.9 | 31.3 | 0 44.7 | 31.0 | 28 14.1 | 05.9 | | | |
| S 12 | 7 51.4 | 42 22.1 | S12 43.8 | 46 50.5 | S16 30.8 | 15 46.6 | S 4 30.8 | 43 16.4 | S15 05.9 | Gacrux | 171 53.6 | S57 14.3 |
| D 13 | 22 53.8 | 57 21.9 | 43.1 | 61 51.1 | 30.2 | 30 48.5 | 30.6 | 58 18.6 | 05.8 | Gienah | 175 45.6 | S17 40.0 |
| A 14 | 37 56.3 | 72 21.8 | 42.5 | 76 51.7 | 29.7 | 45 50.4 | 30.3 | 73 20.8 | 05.7 | Hadar | 148 38.7 | S60 28.7 |
| Y 15 | 52 58.8 | 87 21.6 · · | 41.9 | 91 52.3 · · | 29.1 | 60 52.4 · · | 30.1 | 88 23.1 · · | 05.7 | Hamal | 327 54.1 | N23 33.9 |
| 16 | 68 01.2 | 102 21.5 | 41.2 | 106 52.8 | 28.5 | 75 54.3 | 29.9 | 103 25.3 | 05.6 | Kaus Aust. | 83 35.5 | S34 22.4 |
| 17 | 83 03.7 | 117 21.3 | 40.6 | 121 53.4 | 28.0 | 90 56.2 | 29.7 | 118 27.5 | 05.5 | | | |
| 18 | 98 06.2 | 132 21.2 | S12 40.0 | 136 54.0 | S16 27.4 | 105 58.1 | S 4 29.4 | 133 29.8 | S15 05.4 | Kochab | 137 18.8 | N74 03.7 |
| 19 | 113 08.6 | 147 21.0 | 39.3 | 151 54.6 | 26.9 | 121 00.0 | 29.2 | 148 32.0 | 05.4 | Markab | 13 32.5 | N15 19.2 |
| 20 | 128 11.1 | 162 20.9 | 38.7 | 166 55.2 | 26.3 | 136 02.0 | 29.0 | 163 34.3 | 05.3 | Menkar | 314 08.8 | N 4 10.4 |
| 21 | 143 13.6 | 177 20.7 · · | 38.1 | 181 55.8 · · | 25.8 | 151 03.9 · · | 28.7 | 178 36.5 · · | 05.2 | Menkent | 148 00.0 | S36 28.7 |
| 22 | 158 16.0 | 192 20.6 | 37.4 | 196 56.3 | 25.2 | 166 05.8 | 28.5 | 193 38.7 | 05.2 | Miaplacidus | 221 38.2 | S69 48.7 |
| 23 | 173 18.5 | 207 20.4 | 36.8 | 211 56.9 | 24.6 | 181 07.7 | 28.3 | 208 41.0 | 05.1 | | | |
| 31 00 | 188 20.9 | 222 20.3 | S12 36.2 | 226 57.5 | S16 24.1 | 196 09.6 | S 4 28.1 | 223 43.2 | S15 05.0 | Mirfak | 308 31.9 | N49 56.4 |
| 01 | 203 23.4 | 237 20.1 | 35.5 | 241 58.1 | 23.5 | 211 11.6 | 27.8 | 238 45.4 | 05.0 | Nunki | 75 50.6 | S26 16.1 |
| 02 | 218 25.9 | 252 20.0 | 34.9 | 256 58.7 | 23.0 | 226 13.5 | 27.6 | 253 47.7 | 04.9 | Peacock | 53 09.6 | S56 39.7 |
| 03 | 233 28.3 | 267 19.8 · · | 34.2 | 271 59.3 · · | 22.4 | 241 15.4 · · | 27.4 | 268 49.9 · · | 04.8 | Pollux | 243 20.0 | N27 58.4 |
| 04 | 248 30.8 | 282 19.7 | 33.6 | 286 59.9 | 21.8 | 256 17.3 | 27.2 | 283 52.1 | 04.7 | Procyon | 244 53.2 | N 5 10.0 |
| 05 | 263 33.3 | 297 19.5 | 33.0 | 302 00.5 | 21.3 | 271 19.3 | 26.9 | 298 54.4 | 04.7 | | | |
| 06 | 278 35.7 | 312 19.4 | S12 32.3 | 317 01.0 | S16 20.7 | 286 21.2 | S 4 26.7 | 313 56.6 | S15 04.6 | Rasalhague | 96 00.6 | N12 32.4 |
| 07 | 293 38.2 | 327 19.2 | 31.7 | 332 01.6 | 20.2 | 301 23.1 | 26.5 | 328 58.8 | 04.5 | Regulus | 207 36.6 | N11 51.5 |
| T 08 | 308 40.7 | 342 19.0 | 31.0 | 347 02.2 | 19.6 | 316 25.0 | 26.2 | 344 01.1 | 04.5 | Rigel | 281 06.2 | S 8 10.7 |
| H 09 | 323 43.1 | 357 18.9 · · | 30.4 | 2 02.8 · · | 19.0 | 331 26.9 · · | 26.0 | 359 03.3 · · | 04.4 | Rigil Kent. | 139 42.9 | S60 55.4 |
| U 10 | 338 45.6 | 12 18.7 | 29.7 | 17 03.4 | 18.5 | 346 28.9 | 25.8 | 14 05.5 | 04.3 | Sabik | 102 05.3 | S15 45.2 |
| R 11 | 353 48.0 | 27 18.6 | 29.1 | 32 04.0 | 17.9 | 1 30.8 | 25.6 | 29 07.8 | 04.3 | | | |
| S 12 | 8 50.5 | 42 18.4 | S12 28.4 | 47 04.6 | S16 17.4 | 16 32.7 | S 4 25.3 | 44 10.0 | S15 04.2 | Schedar | 349 34.2 | N56 39.4 |
| D 13 | 23 53.0 | 57 18.3 | 27.8 | 62 05.2 | 16.8 | 31 34.6 | 25.1 | 59 12.3 | 04.1 | Shaula | 96 13.4 | S37 07.1 |
| A 14 | 38 55.4 | 72 18.1 | 27.1 | 77 05.7 | 16.2 | 46 36.5 | 24.9 | 74 14.5 | 04.0 | Sirius | 258 28.3 | S16 45.0 |
| Y 15 | 53 57.9 | 87 18.0 · · | 26.5 | 92 06.3 · · | 15.7 | 61 38.5 · · | 24.6 | 89 16.7 · · | 04.0 | Spica | 158 24.4 | S11 16.7 |
| 16 | 69 00.4 | 102 17.8 | 25.8 | 107 06.9 | 15.1 | 76 40.4 | 24.4 | 104 19.0 | 03.9 | Suhail | 222 47.7 | S43 31.5 |
| 17 | 84 02.8 | 117 17.7 | 25.2 | 122 07.5 | 14.6 | 91 42.3 | 24.2 | 119 21.2 | 03.8 | | | |
| 18 | 99 05.3 | 132 17.5 | S12 24.5 | 137 08.1 | S16 14.0 | 106 44.2 | S 4 24.0 | 134 23.4 | S15 03.8 | Vega | 80 34.8 | N38 47.9 |
| 19 | 114 07.8 | 147 17.4 | 23.9 | 152 08.7 | 13.4 | 121 46.2 | 23.7 | 149 25.7 | 03.7 | Zuben'ubi | 136 58.3 | S16 08.1 |
| 20 | 129 10.2 | 162 17.2 | 23.2 | 167 09.3 | 12.9 | 136 48.1 | 23.5 | 164 27.9 | 03.6 | | SHA | Mer. Pass. |
| 21 | 144 12.7 | 177 17.1 · · | 22.6 | 182 09.9 · · | 12.3 | 151 50.0 · · | 23.3 | 179 30.2 · · | 03.6 | | ° ′ | h m |
| 22 | 159 15.2 | 192 16.9 | 21.9 | 197 10.5 | 11.7 | 166 51.9 | 23.0 | 194 32.4 | 03.5 | Venus | 35 02.0 | 9 10 |
| 23 | 174 17.6 | 207 16.7 | 21.3 | 212 11.0 | 11.2 | 181 53.8 | 22.8 | 209 34.6 | 03.4 | Mars | 39 21.7 | 8 53 |
| | h m | | | | | | | | | Jupiter | 8 01.8 | 10 57 |
| Mer. Pass. 11 28.7 | | v −0.1 | d 0.6 | v 0.6 | d 0.6 | v 1.9 | d 0.2 | v 2.2 | d 0.1 | Saturn | 35 27.8 | 9 07 |

| UT | SUN | | MOON | | | | Lat. | Twilight | | Sunrise | Moonrise | | | |
|---|---|---|---|---|---|---|---|---|---|---|---|---|---|---|
| | | | | | | | | Naut. | Civil | | 29 | 30 | 31 | 1 |
| | GHA | Dec | GHA | v | Dec | d | HP | | | | | | | |
| d h | ° ′ | ° ′ | ° ′ | ′ | ° ′ | ′ | ′ | ° | h m | h m | h m | h m | h m | h m | h m |
| 29 00 | 178 46.5 | N 3 17.0 | 214 57.0 | 9.8 | S17 10.9 | 12.3 | 58.3 | N 72 | 02 01 | 03 54 | 05 07 | 07 55 | 07 00 | 06 24 | 05 54 |
| 01 | 193 46.6 | 18.0 | 229 25.8 | 9.9 | 16 58.6 | 12.4 | 58.3 | N 70 | 02 37 | 04 08 | 05 13 | 07 19 | 06 44 | 06 18 | 05 56 |
| 02 | 208 46.8 | 19.0 | 243 54.7 | 10.0 | 16 46.2 | 12.5 | 58.3 | 68 | 03 01 | 04 20 | 05 18 | 06 53 | 06 31 | 06 13 | 05 57 |
| 03 | 223 47.0 | .. 19.9 | 258 23.7 | 10.1 | 16 33.7 | 12.6 | 58.3 | 66 | 03 20 | 04 29 | 05 22 | 06 34 | 06 20 | 06 09 | 05 58 |
| 04 | 238 47.2 | 20.9 | 272 52.8 | 10.1 | 16 21.1 | 12.7 | 58.3 | 64 | 03 34 | 04 37 | 05 26 | 06 17 | 06 11 | 06 05 | 05 59 |
| 05 | 253 47.4 | 21.9 | 287 21.9 | 10.3 | 16 08.4 | 12.7 | 58.3 | 62 | 03 47 | 04 43 | 05 29 | 06 04 | 06 03 | 06 01 | 06 00 |
| 06 | 268 47.6 | N 3 22.9 | 301 51.2 | 10.3 | S15 55.7 | 12.8 | 58.2 | 60 | 03 57 | 04 49 | 05 32 | 05 52 | 05 56 | 05 59 | 06 01 |
| 07 | 283 47.8 | 23.8 | 316 20.5 | 10.4 | 15 42.9 | 12.9 | 58.2 | N 58 | 04 05 | 04 54 | 05 34 | 05 42 | 05 50 | 05 56 | 06 01 |
| 08 | 298 48.0 | 24.8 | 330 49.9 | 10.5 | 15 30.0 | 13.0 | 58.2 | 56 | 04 13 | 04 58 | 05 36 | 05 34 | 05 45 | 05 54 | 06 02 |
| T 09 | 313 48.1 | .. 25.8 | 345 19.4 | 10.6 | 15 17.0 | 13.1 | 58.2 | 54 | 04 19 | 05 02 | 05 38 | 05 26 | 05 40 | 05 52 | 06 02 |
| U 10 | 328 48.3 | 26.8 | 359 49.0 | 10.7 | 15 03.9 | 13.1 | 58.2 | 52 | 04 25 | 05 06 | 05 40 | 05 19 | 05 36 | 05 50 | 06 03 |
| E 11 | 343 48.5 | 27.7 | 14 18.7 | 10.8 | 14 50.8 | 13.2 | 58.2 | 50 | 04 30 | 05 09 | 05 41 | 05 12 | 05 32 | 05 48 | 06 03 |
| S 12 | 358 48.7 | N 3 28.7 | 28 48.5 | 10.8 | S14 37.6 | 13.2 | 58.1 | 45 | 04 40 | 05 15 | 05 45 | 04 59 | 05 23 | 05 44 | 06 04 |
| D 13 | 13 48.9 | 29.7 | 43 18.3 | 10.9 | 14 24.4 | 13.4 | 58.1 | N 40 | 04 48 | 05 20 | 05 48 | 04 47 | 05 16 | 05 41 | 06 05 |
| A 14 | 28 49.1 | 30.7 | 57 48.2 | 11.0 | 14 11.0 | 13.4 | 58.1 | 35 | 04 55 | 05 24 | 05 50 | 04 37 | 05 10 | 05 38 | 06 06 |
| Y 15 | 43 49.3 | .. 31.6 | 72 18.2 | 11.1 | 13 57.6 | 13.4 | 58.1 | 30 | 05 00 | 05 28 | 05 52 | 04 29 | 05 04 | 05 36 | 06 06 |
| 16 | 58 49.5 | 32.6 | 86 48.3 | 11.2 | 13 44.2 | 13.5 | 58.1 | 20 | 05 08 | 05 33 | 05 55 | 04 14 | 04 55 | 05 32 | 06 07 |
| 17 | 73 49.6 | 33.6 | 101 18.5 | 11.2 | 13 30.7 | 13.6 | 58.1 | N 10 | 05 13 | 05 37 | 05 58 | 04 01 | 04 46 | 05 28 | 06 08 |
| 18 | 88 49.8 | N 3 34.5 | 115 48.7 | 11.3 | S13 17.1 | 13.7 | 58.0 | 0 | 05 16 | 05 40 | 06 01 | 03 49 | 04 38 | 05 25 | 06 09 |
| 19 | 103 50.0 | 35.5 | 130 19.0 | 11.4 | 13 03.4 | 13.7 | 58.0 | S 10 | 05 18 | 05 43 | 06 04 | 03 36 | 04 30 | 05 21 | 06 10 |
| 20 | 118 50.2 | 36.5 | 144 49.4 | 11.5 | 12 49.7 | 13.7 | 58.0 | 20 | 05 19 | 05 44 | 06 06 | 03 23 | 04 22 | 05 17 | 06 11 |
| 21 | 133 50.4 | .. 37.5 | 159 19.9 | 11.5 | 12 36.0 | 13.9 | 58.0 | 30 | 05 18 | 05 46 | 06 09 | 03 08 | 04 12 | 05 13 | 06 13 |
| 22 | 148 50.6 | 38.4 | 173 50.4 | 11.6 | 12 22.1 | 13.8 | 58.0 | 35 | 05 16 | 05 46 | 06 11 | 02 59 | 04 06 | 05 11 | 06 13 |
| 23 | 163 50.8 | 39.4 | 188 21.0 | 11.7 | 12 08.3 | 14.0 | 58.0 | 40 | 05 14 | 05 46 | 06 13 | 02 49 | 04 00 | 05 08 | 06 14 |
| 30 00 | 178 50.9 | N 3 40.4 | 202 51.7 | 11.8 | S11 54.3 | 13.9 | 57.9 | 45 | 05 12 | 05 46 | 06 15 | 02 37 | 03 52 | 05 05 | 06 15 |
| 01 | 193 51.1 | 41.4 | 217 22.5 | 11.8 | 11 40.4 | 14.1 | 57.9 | S 50 | 05 08 | 05 45 | 06 17 | 02 22 | 03 43 | 05 01 | 06 16 |
| 02 | 208 51.3 | 42.3 | 231 53.3 | 11.9 | 11 26.3 | 14.0 | 57.9 | 52 | 05 06 | 05 45 | 06 18 | 02 16 | 03 39 | 04 59 | 06 17 |
| 03 | 223 51.5 | .. 43.3 | 246 24.2 | 12.0 | 11 12.3 | 14.2 | 57.9 | 54 | 05 03 | 05 44 | 06 20 | 02 08 | 03 34 | 04 57 | 06 17 |
| 04 | 238 51.7 | 44.3 | 260 55.2 | 12.1 | 10 58.1 | 14.1 | 57.9 | 56 | 05 01 | 05 44 | 06 21 | 01 59 | 03 29 | 04 55 | 06 18 |
| 05 | 253 51.9 | 45.2 | 275 26.3 | 12.1 | 10 44.0 | 14.2 | 57.8 | 58 | 04 58 | 05 43 | 06 22 | 01 50 | 03 23 | 04 52 | 06 19 |
| 06 | 268 52.1 | N 3 46.2 | 289 57.4 | 12.2 | S10 29.8 | 14.3 | 57.8 | S 60 | 04 54 | 05 43 | 06 24 | 01 38 | 03 16 | 04 50 | 06 20 |

| UT | SUN | | MOON | | | | Lat. | Sunset | Twilight | | Moonset | | | |
|---|---|---|---|---|---|---|---|---|---|---|---|---|---|---|
| | | | | | | | | | Civil | Naut. | 29 | 30 | 31 | 1 |
| d h | ° ′ | ° ′ | ° ′ | ′ | ° ′ | ′ | ′ | ° | h m | h m | h m | h m | h m | h m | h m |
| 07 | 283 52.3 | 47.2 | 304 28.6 | 12.2 | 10 15.5 | 14.3 | 57.8 | | h m | h m | h m | h m | h m | h m | h m |
| W 08 | 298 52.4 | 48.2 | 318 59.8 | 12.3 | 10 01.2 | 14.3 | 57.8 | N 72 | 19 05 | 20 19 | 22 17 | 12 32 | 15 09 | 17 22 | 19 28 |
| E 09 | 313 52.6 | .. 49.1 | 333 31.1 | 12.4 | 9 46.9 | 14.4 | 57.8 | N 70 | 18 58 | 20 04 | 21 38 | 13 05 | 15 22 | 17 24 | 19 21 |
| D 10 | 328 52.8 | 50.1 | 348 02.5 | 12.5 | 9 32.5 | 14.4 | 57.7 | 68 | 18 53 | 19 52 | 21 12 | 13 29 | 15 33 | 17 27 | 19 16 |
| N 11 | 343 53.0 | 51.1 | 2 34.0 | 12.5 | 9 18.1 | 14.4 | 57.7 | 66 | 18 49 | 19 42 | 20 53 | 13 48 | 15 42 | 17 29 | 19 12 |
| E 12 | 358 53.2 | N 3 52.0 | 17 05.5 | 12.5 | S 9 03.7 | 14.5 | 57.7 | 64 | 18 45 | 19 34 | 20 37 | 14 03 | 15 49 | 17 30 | 19 08 |
| S 13 | 13 53.4 | 53.0 | 31 37.0 | 12.7 | 8 49.2 | 14.5 | 57.7 | 62 | 18 42 | 19 27 | 20 25 | 14 15 | 15 56 | 17 32 | 19 05 |
| D 14 | 28 53.6 | 54.0 | 46 08.7 | 12.7 | 8 34.7 | 14.6 | 57.7 | 60 | 18 39 | 19 22 | 20 15 | 14 25 | 16 01 | 17 33 | 19 02 |
| A 15 | 43 53.7 | .. 55.0 | 60 40.4 | 12.7 | 8 20.1 | 14.6 | 57.6 | N 58 | 18 36 | 19 16 | 20 06 | 14 34 | 16 06 | 17 34 | 19 00 |
| Y 16 | 58 53.9 | 55.9 | 75 12.1 | 12.8 | 8 05.5 | 14.6 | 57.6 | 56 | 18 34 | 19 12 | 19 58 | 14 42 | 16 10 | 17 35 | 18 57 |
| 17 | 73 54.1 | 56.9 | 89 43.9 | 12.9 | 7 50.9 | 14.6 | 57.6 | 54 | 18 32 | 19 08 | 19 52 | 14 49 | 16 14 | 17 36 | 18 55 |
| 18 | 88 54.3 | N 3 57.9 | 104 15.8 | 12.9 | S 7 36.3 | 14.6 | 57.6 | 52 | 18 30 | 19 04 | 19 46 | 14 55 | 16 17 | 17 36 | 18 54 |
| 19 | 103 54.5 | 58.8 | 118 47.7 | 12.9 | 7 21.7 | 14.7 | 57.6 | 50 | 18 29 | 19 01 | 19 41 | 15 01 | 16 20 | 17 37 | 18 52 |
| 20 | 118 54.7 | 3 59.8 | 133 19.6 | 13.1 | 7 07.0 | 14.7 | 57.5 | 45 | 18 25 | 18 55 | 19 30 | 15 13 | 16 27 | 17 39 | 18 48 |
| 21 | 133 54.9 | 4 00.8 | 147 51.7 | 13.0 | 6 52.3 | 14.8 | 57.5 | N 40 | 18 22 | 18 49 | 19 22 | 15 23 | 16 33 | 17 40 | 18 45 |
| 22 | 148 55.0 | 01.7 | 162 23.7 | 13.2 | 6 37.5 | 14.7 | 57.5 | 35 | 18 20 | 18 45 | 19 15 | 15 31 | 16 37 | 17 41 | 18 43 |
| 23 | 163 55.2 | 02.7 | 176 55.9 | 13.1 | 6 22.8 | 14.8 | 57.5 | 30 | 18 17 | 18 41 | 19 10 | 15 39 | 16 41 | 17 42 | 18 41 |
| 31 00 | 178 55.4 | N 4 03.7 | 191 28.0 | 13.3 | S 6 08.0 | 14.8 | 57.5 | 20 | 18 14 | 18 36 | 19 02 | 15 51 | 16 49 | 17 43 | 18 37 |
| 01 | 193 55.6 | 04.7 | 206 00.3 | 13.2 | 5 53.2 | 14.8 | 57.4 | N 10 | 18 11 | 18 32 | 18 56 | 16 02 | 16 55 | 17 45 | 18 34 |
| 02 | 208 55.8 | 05.6 | 220 32.5 | 13.4 | 5 38.4 | 14.8 | 57.4 | 0 | 18 08 | 18 28 | 18 52 | 16 13 | 17 01 | 17 46 | 18 30 |
| 03 | 223 56.0 | .. 06.6 | 235 04.9 | 13.3 | 5 23.6 | 14.8 | 57.4 | S 10 | 18 05 | 18 26 | 18 50 | 16 23 | 17 06 | 17 47 | 18 27 |
| 04 | 238 56.2 | 07.6 | 249 37.2 | 13.4 | 5 08.8 | 14.9 | 57.4 | 20 | 18 02 | 18 24 | 18 50 | 16 34 | 17 12 | 17 49 | 18 24 |
| 05 | 253 56.3 | 08.5 | 264 09.6 | 13.5 | 4 53.9 | 14.8 | 57.3 | 30 | 17 59 | 18 23 | 18 51 | 16 46 | 17 19 | 17 50 | 18 20 |
| 06 | 268 56.5 | N 4 09.5 | 278 42.1 | 13.5 | S 4 39.1 | 14.9 | 57.3 | 35 | 17 57 | 18 23 | 18 52 | 16 53 | 17 23 | 17 51 | 18 18 |
| 07 | 283 56.7 | 10.5 | 293 14.6 | 13.5 | 4 24.2 | 14.9 | 57.3 | 40 | 17 55 | 18 22 | 18 54 | 17 01 | 17 27 | 17 52 | 18 15 |
| 08 | 298 56.9 | 11.4 | 307 47.1 | 13.6 | 4 09.3 | 14.9 | 57.3 | 45 | 17 53 | 18 22 | 18 56 | 17 10 | 17 33 | 17 53 | 18 12 |
| T 09 | 313 57.1 | .. 12.4 | 322 19.7 | 13.6 | 3 54.4 | 14.9 | 57.3 | S 50 | 17 51 | 18 23 | 19 00 | 17 21 | 17 39 | 17 54 | 18 09 |
| H 10 | 328 57.3 | 13.4 | 336 52.3 | 13.7 | 3 39.5 | 14.9 | 57.2 | 52 | 17 49 | 18 23 | 19 02 | 17 26 | 17 41 | 17 55 | 18 08 |
| U 11 | 343 57.5 | 14.3 | 351 25.0 | 13.7 | 3 24.6 | 14.9 | 57.2 | 54 | 17 48 | 18 23 | 19 04 | 17 31 | 17 44 | 17 55 | 18 06 |
| R 12 | 358 57.6 | N 4 15.3 | 5 57.7 | 13.7 | S 3 09.7 | 14.9 | 57.2 | 56 | 17 47 | 18 24 | 19 07 | 17 37 | 17 48 | 17 56 | 18 04 |
| S 13 | 13 57.8 | 16.3 | 20 30.4 | 13.8 | 2 54.8 | 14.9 | 57.2 | 58 | 17 45 | 18 24 | 19 10 | 17 44 | 17 51 | 17 57 | 18 02 |
| D 14 | 28 58.0 | 17.2 | 35 03.2 | 13.8 | 2 39.9 | 14.9 | 57.1 | S 60 | 17 44 | 18 25 | 19 13 | 17 52 | 17 55 | 17 58 | 18 00 |
| A 15 | 43 58.2 | .. 18.2 | 49 36.0 | 13.8 | 2 25.0 | 14.9 | 57.1 | | | | | | | | |
| Y 16 | 58 58.4 | 19.2 | 64 08.8 | 13.9 | 2 10.1 | 14.9 | 57.1 | | | | | | | | |
| 17 | 73 58.6 | 20.1 | 78 41.7 | 13.9 | 1 55.2 | 14.9 | 57.1 | | | | | | | | |

| UT | SUN | | MOON | | | | Day | SUN | | | MOON | | | |
|---|---|---|---|---|---|---|---|---|---|---|---|---|---|---|
| | | | | | | | | Eqn. of Time | | Mer. | Mer. Pass. | | Age | Phase |
| | | | | | | | | 00ʰ | 12ʰ | Pass. | Upper | Lower | | |
| 18 | 88 58.8 | N 4 21.1 | 93 14.6 | 13.9 | S 1 40.3 | 14.9 | 57.1 | d | m s | m s | h m | h m | h m | d % | |
| 19 | 103 58.9 | 22.1 | 107 47.5 | 14.0 | 1 25.4 | 14.9 | 57.0 | 29 | 04 55 | 04 46 | 12 05 | 10 01 | 22 25 | 27 9 | ● |
| 20 | 118 59.1 | 23.0 | 122 20.5 | 14.0 | 1 10.5 | 14.9 | 57.0 | 30 | 04 37 | 04 28 | 12 04 | 10 49 | 23 13 | 28 4 | |
| 21 | 133 59.3 | .. 24.0 | 136 53.5 | 14.0 | 0 55.6 | 14.9 | 57.0 | 31 | 04 19 | 04 10 | 12 04 | 11 35 | 23 58 | 29 1 | |
| 22 | 148 59.5 | 25.0 | 151 26.5 | 14.1 | 0 40.7 | 14.9 | 57.0 | | | | | | | | |
| 23 | 163 59.7 | 25.9 | 165 59.6 | 14.0 | S 0 25.8 | 14.9 | 56.9 | | | | | | | | |
| | SD 16.0 | d 1.0 | SD 15.8 | | 15.7 | | 15.6 | | | | | | | | |

| UT | ARIES GHA | VENUS −4.3 GHA | Dec | MARS +1.1 GHA | Dec | JUPITER −2.0 GHA | Dec | SATURN +0.7 GHA | Dec |
|---|---|---|---|---|---|---|---|---|---|
| **1 00** | 189 20.1 | 222 16.6 | S12 20.6 | 227 11.6 | S16 10.6 | 196 55.8 | S 4 22.6 | 224 36.9 | S15 03.4 |
| 01 | 204 22.5 | 237 16.4 | 20.0 | 242 12.2 | 10.0 | 211 57.7 | 22.4 | 239 39.1 | 03.3 |
| 02 | 219 25.0 | 252 16.3 | 19.3 | 257 12.8 | 09.5 | 226 59.6 | 22.1 | 254 41.3 | 03.2 |
| 03 | 234 27.5 | 267 16.1 .. | 18.6 | 272 13.4 .. | 08.9 | 242 01.5 .. | 21.9 | 269 43.6 .. | 03.1 |
| 04 | 249 29.9 | 282 16.0 | 18.0 | 287 14.0 | 08.3 | 257 03.4 | 21.7 | 284 45.8 | 03.1 |
| 05 | 264 32.4 | 297 15.8 | 17.3 | 302 14.6 | 07.8 | 272 05.4 | 21.5 | 299 48.1 | 03.0 |
| 06 | 279 34.9 | 312 15.6 | S12 16.7 | 317 15.2 | S16 07.2 | 287 07.3 | S 4 21.2 | 314 50.3 | S15 02.9 |
| 07 | 294 37.3 | 327 15.5 | 16.0 | 332 15.8 | 06.6 | 302 09.2 | 21.0 | 329 52.5 | 02.9 |
| 08 | 309 39.8 | 342 15.3 | 15.3 | 347 16.4 | 06.1 | 317 11.1 | 20.8 | 344 54.8 | 02.8 |
| F 09 | 324 42.3 | 357 15.2 .. | 14.7 | 2 16.9 .. | 05.5 | 332 13.1 .. | 20.5 | 359 57.0 .. | 02.7 |
| R 10 | 339 44.7 | 12 15.0 | 14.0 | 17 17.5 | 04.9 | 347 15.0 | 20.3 | 14 59.2 | 02.7 |
| I 11 | 354 47.2 | 27 14.9 | 13.4 | 32 18.1 | 04.4 | 2 16.9 | 20.1 | 30 01.5 | 02.6 |
| D 12 | 9 49.6 | 42 14.7 | S12 12.7 | 47 18.7 | S16 03.8 | 17 18.8 | S 4 19.9 | 45 03.7 | S15 02.5 |
| A 13 | 24 52.1 | 57 14.6 | 12.0 | 62 19.3 | 03.2 | 32 20.8 | 19.6 | 60 06.0 | 02.5 |
| Y 14 | 39 54.6 | 72 14.4 | 11.4 | 77 19.9 | 02.7 | 47 22.7 | 19.4 | 75 08.2 | 02.4 |
| 15 | 54 57.0 | 87 14.2 .. | 10.7 | 92 20.5 .. | 02.1 | 62 24.6 .. | 19.2 | 90 10.4 .. | 02.3 |
| 16 | 69 59.5 | 102 14.1 | 10.0 | 107 21.1 | 01.5 | 77 26.5 | 19.0 | 105 12.7 | 02.3 |
| 17 | 85 02.0 | 117 13.9 | 09.4 | 122 21.7 | 01.0 | 92 28.4 | 18.7 | 120 14.9 | 02.2 |
| 18 | 100 04.4 | 132 13.8 | S12 08.7 | 137 22.3 | S16 00.4 | 107 30.4 | S 4 18.5 | 135 17.2 | S15 02.1 |
| 19 | 115 06.9 | 147 13.6 | 08.0 | 152 22.9 | 15 59.8 | 122 32.3 | 18.3 | 150 19.4 | 02.0 |
| 20 | 130 09.4 | 162 13.4 | 07.4 | 167 23.5 | 59.3 | 137 34.2 | 18.0 | 165 21.6 | 02.0 |
| 21 | 145 11.8 | 177 13.3 .. | 06.7 | 182 24.1 .. | 58.7 | 152 36.1 .. | 17.8 | 180 23.9 .. | 01.9 |
| 22 | 160 14.3 | 192 13.1 | 06.0 | 197 24.6 | 58.1 | 167 38.1 | 17.6 | 195 26.1 | 01.8 |
| 23 | 175 16.8 | 207 13.0 | 05.3 | 212 25.2 | 57.5 | 182 40.0 | 17.4 | 210 28.4 | 01.8 |
| **2 00** | 190 19.2 | 222 12.8 | S12 04.7 | 227 25.8 | S15 57.0 | 197 41.9 | S 4 17.1 | 225 30.6 | S15 01.7 |
| 01 | 205 21.7 | 237 12.7 | 04.0 | 242 26.4 | 56.4 | 212 43.8 | 16.9 | 240 32.8 | 01.6 |
| 02 | 220 24.1 | 252 12.5 | 03.3 | 257 27.0 | 55.8 | 227 45.8 | 16.7 | 255 35.1 | 01.6 |
| 03 | 235 26.6 | 267 12.3 .. | 02.6 | 272 27.6 .. | 55.3 | 242 47.7 .. | 16.5 | 270 37.3 .. | 01.5 |
| 04 | 250 29.1 | 282 12.2 | 02.0 | 287 28.2 | 54.7 | 257 49.6 | 16.2 | 285 39.6 | 01.4 |
| 05 | 265 31.5 | 297 12.0 | 01.3 | 302 28.8 | 54.1 | 272 51.5 | 16.0 | 300 41.8 | 01.4 |
| 06 | 280 34.0 | 312 11.9 | S12 00.6 | 317 29.4 | S15 53.5 | 287 53.5 | S 4 15.8 | 315 44.0 | S15 01.3 |
| S 07 | 295 36.5 | 327 11.7 | 11 59.9 | 332 30.0 | 53.0 | 302 55.4 | 15.5 | 330 46.3 | 01.2 |
| A 08 | 310 38.9 | 342 11.5 | 59.3 | 347 30.6 | 52.4 | 317 57.3 | 15.3 | 345 48.5 | 01.2 |
| T 09 | 325 41.4 | 357 11.4 .. | 58.6 | 2 31.2 .. | 51.8 | 332 59.2 .. | 15.1 | 0 50.8 .. | 01.1 |
| U 10 | 340 43.9 | 12 11.2 | 57.9 | 17 31.8 | 51.3 | 348 01.1 | 14.9 | 15 53.0 | 01.0 |
| R 11 | 355 46.3 | 27 11.1 | 57.2 | 32 32.4 | 50.7 | 3 03.1 | 14.6 | 30 55.2 | 01.0 |
| D 12 | 10 48.8 | 42 10.9 | S11 56.5 | 47 33.0 | S15 50.1 | 18 05.0 | S 4 14.4 | 45 57.5 | S15 00.9 |
| A 13 | 25 51.3 | 57 10.7 | 55.9 | 62 33.6 | 49.5 | 33 06.9 | 14.2 | 60 59.7 | 00.8 |
| Y 14 | 40 53.7 | 72 10.6 | 55.2 | 77 34.2 | 49.0 | 48 08.8 | 14.0 | 76 02.0 | 00.7 |
| 15 | 55 56.2 | 87 10.4 .. | 54.5 | 92 34.8 .. | 48.4 | 63 10.8 .. | 13.7 | 91 04.2 .. | 00.7 |
| 16 | 70 58.6 | 102 10.3 | 53.8 | 107 35.4 | 47.8 | 78 12.7 | 13.5 | 106 06.4 | 00.6 |
| 17 | 86 01.1 | 117 10.1 | 53.1 | 122 35.9 | 47.2 | 93 14.6 | 13.3 | 121 08.7 | 00.5 |
| 18 | 101 03.6 | 132 09.9 | S11 52.4 | 137 36.5 | S15 46.7 | 108 16.5 | S 4 13.1 | 136 10.9 | S15 00.5 |
| 19 | 116 06.0 | 147 09.8 | 51.8 | 152 37.1 | 46.1 | 123 18.5 | 12.8 | 151 13.2 | 00.4 |
| 20 | 131 08.5 | 162 09.6 | 51.1 | 167 37.7 | 45.5 | 138 20.4 | 12.6 | 166 15.4 | 00.3 |
| 21 | 146 11.0 | 177 09.4 .. | 50.4 | 182 38.3 .. | 44.9 | 153 22.3 .. | 12.4 | 181 17.7 .. | 00.3 |
| 22 | 161 13.4 | 192 09.3 | 49.7 | 197 38.9 | 44.3 | 168 24.2 | 12.1 | 196 19.9 | 00.2 |
| 23 | 176 15.9 | 207 09.1 | 49.0 | 212 39.5 | 43.8 | 183 26.2 | 11.9 | 211 22.1 | 00.1 |
| **3 00** | 191 18.4 | 222 09.0 | S11 48.3 | 227 40.1 | S15 43.2 | 198 28.1 | S 4 11.7 | 226 24.4 | S15 00.1 |
| 01 | 206 20.8 | 237 08.8 | 47.6 | 242 40.7 | 42.6 | 213 30.0 | 11.5 | 241 26.6 | 15 00.0 |
| 02 | 221 23.3 | 252 08.6 | 46.9 | 257 41.3 | 42.0 | 228 31.9 | 11.2 | 256 28.9 | 14 59.9 |
| 03 | 236 25.7 | 267 08.5 .. | 46.2 | 272 41.9 .. | 41.5 | 243 33.9 .. | 11.0 | 271 31.1 .. | 59.9 |
| 04 | 251 28.2 | 282 08.3 | 45.5 | 287 42.5 | 40.9 | 258 35.8 | 10.8 | 286 33.4 | 59.8 |
| 05 | 266 30.7 | 297 08.1 | 44.9 | 302 43.1 | 40.3 | 273 37.7 | 10.6 | 301 35.6 | 59.7 |
| 06 | 281 33.1 | 312 08.0 | S11 44.2 | 317 43.7 | S15 39.7 | 288 39.6 | S 4 10.3 | 316 37.8 | S14 59.7 |
| 07 | 296 35.6 | 327 07.8 | 43.5 | 332 44.3 | 39.1 | 303 41.6 | 10.1 | 331 40.1 | 59.6 |
| 08 | 311 38.1 | 342 07.7 | 42.8 | 347 44.9 | 38.6 | 318 43.5 | 09.9 | 346 42.3 | 59.5 |
| S 09 | 326 40.5 | 357 07.5 .. | 42.1 | 2 45.5 .. | 38.0 | 333 45.4 .. | 09.7 | 1 44.6 .. | 59.5 |
| U 10 | 341 43.0 | 12 07.3 | 41.4 | 17 46.1 | 37.4 | 348 47.3 | 09.4 | 16 46.8 | 59.4 |
| N 11 | 356 45.5 | 27 07.2 | 40.7 | 32 46.7 | 36.8 | 3 49.3 | 09.2 | 31 49.1 | 59.3 |
| D 12 | 11 47.9 | 42 07.0 | S11 40.0 | 47 47.3 | S15 36.2 | 18 51.2 | S 4 09.0 | 46 51.3 | S14 59.3 |
| A 13 | 26 50.4 | 57 06.8 | 39.3 | 62 47.9 | 35.7 | 33 53.1 | 08.7 | 61 53.5 | 59.2 |
| Y 14 | 41 52.9 | 72 06.7 | 38.6 | 77 48.5 | 35.1 | 48 55.0 | 08.5 | 76 55.8 | 59.1 |
| 15 | 56 55.3 | 87 06.5 .. | 37.9 | 92 49.1 .. | 34.5 | 63 57.0 .. | 08.3 | 91 58.0 .. | 59.1 |
| 16 | 71 57.8 | 102 06.3 | 37.2 | 107 49.7 | 33.9 | 78 58.9 | 08.1 | 107 00.3 | 59.0 |
| 17 | 87 00.2 | 117 06.2 | 36.5 | 122 50.3 | 33.3 | 94 00.8 | 07.8 | 122 02.5 | 58.9 |
| 18 | 102 02.7 | 132 06.0 | S11 35.8 | 137 50.9 | S15 32.8 | 109 02.7 | S 4 07.6 | 137 04.8 | S14 58.9 |
| 19 | 117 05.2 | 147 05.9 | 35.1 | 152 51.5 | 32.2 | 124 04.7 | 07.4 | 152 07.0 | 58.8 |
| 20 | 132 07.6 | 162 05.7 | 34.4 | 167 52.1 | 31.6 | 139 06.6 | 07.2 | 167 09.3 | 58.7 |
| 21 | 147 10.1 | 177 05.5 .. | 33.7 | 182 52.7 .. | 31.0 | 154 08.5 .. | 06.9 | 182 11.5 .. | 58.7 |
| 22 | 162 12.6 | 192 05.4 | 33.0 | 197 53.3 | 30.4 | 169 10.5 | 06.7 | 197 13.7 | 58.6 |
| 23 | 177 15.0 | 207 05.2 | 32.3 | 212 53.9 | 29.9 | 184 12.4 | 06.5 | 212 16.0 | 58.5 |
| Mer. Pass. 11 16.9 | | v −0.2 | d 0.7 | v 0.6 | d 0.6 | v 1.9 | d 0.2 | v 2.2 | d 0.1 |

**STARS**

| Name | SHA | Dec |
|---|---|---|
| Acamar | 315 13.9 | S40 13.2 |
| Achernar | 335 22.5 | S57 07.6 |
| Acrux | 173 01.9 | S63 13.3 |
| Adhara | 255 07.7 | S29 00.4 |
| Aldebaran | 290 42.4 | N16 33.1 |
| Alioth | 166 14.5 | N55 50.4 |
| Alkaid | 152 53.4 | N49 12.1 |
| Al Na'ir | 27 36.2 | S46 51.2 |
| Alnilam | 275 40.2 | S 1 11.4 |
| Alphard | 217 49.8 | S 8 45.4 |
| Alphecca | 126 05.4 | N26 38.2 |
| Alpheratz | 357 37.5 | N29 12.6 |
| Altair | 62 02.3 | N 8 55.4 |
| Ankaa | 353 09.8 | S42 11.3 |
| Antares | 112 18.4 | S26 28.8 |
| Arcturus | 145 49.7 | N19 03.9 |
| Atria | 107 14.5 | S69 03.8 |
| Avior | 234 15.4 | S59 35.1 |
| Bellatrix | 278 25.5 | N 6 22.1 |
| Betelgeuse | 270 54.6 | N 7 24.6 |
| Canopus | 263 53.5 | S52 42.7 |
| Capella | 280 25.5 | N46 01.3 |
| Deneb | 49 27.6 | N45 21.2 |
| Denebola | 182 27.0 | N14 26.8 |
| Diphda | 348 49.9 | S17 52.1 |
| Dubhe | 193 43.3 | N61 38.0 |
| Elnath | 278 04.9 | N28 37.6 |
| Eltanin | 90 43.1 | N51 28.8 |
| Enif | 33 41.3 | N 9 58.4 |
| Fomalhaut | 15 17.4 | S29 30.4 |
| Gacrux | 171 53.6 | S57 14.3 |
| Gienah | 175 45.6 | S17 40.0 |
| Hadar | 148 38.6 | S60 28.7 |
| Hamal | 327 54.1 | N23 33.9 |
| Kaus Aust. | 83 35.5 | S34 22.4 |
| Kochab | 137 18.8 | N74 03.7 |
| Markab | 13 32.5 | N15 19.2 |
| Menkar | 314 08.8 | N 4 10.4 |
| Menkent | 148 00.0 | S36 28.7 |
| Miaplacidus | 221 38.2 | S69 48.7 |
| Mirfak | 308 31.9 | N49 56.4 |
| Nunki | 75 50.6 | S26 16.1 |
| Peacock | 53 09.6 | S56 39.7 |
| Pollux | 243 20.0 | N27 58.4 |
| Procyon | 244 53.2 | N 5 10.0 |
| Rasalhague | 96 00.6 | N12 32.4 |
| Regulus | 207 36.6 | N11 51.5 |
| Rigel | 281 06.2 | S 8 10.7 |
| Rigil Kent. | 139 42.9 | S60 55.5 |
| Sabik | 102 05.3 | S15 45.2 |
| Schedar | 349 34.2 | N56 39.4 |
| Shaula | 96 13.4 | S37 07.1 |
| Sirius | 258 28.3 | S16 45.0 |
| Spica | 158 24.4 | S11 16.7 |
| Suhail | 222 47.7 | S43 31.5 |
| Vega | 80 34.7 | N38 47.9 |
| Zuben'ubi | 136 58.3 | S16 08.1 |

| | SHA | Mer. Pass. |
|---|---|---|
| Venus | 31 53.6 | 9 11 |
| Mars | 37 06.6 | 8 50 |
| Jupiter | 7 22.7 | 10 48 |
| Saturn | 35 11.4 | 8 57 |

| UT | SUN GHA | SUN Dec | MOON GHA | v | MOON Dec | d | HP |
|---|---|---|---|---|---|---|---|
| d h | ° ′ | ° ′ | ° ′ | ′ | ° ′ | ′ | ′ |
| **1** 00 | 178 59.9 | N 4 26.9 | 180 32.6 | 14.1 | S 0 11.0 | 14.9 | 56.9 |
| 01 | 194 00.1 | 27.9 | 195 05.7 | 14.2 | N 0 03.9 | 14.8 | 56.9 |
| 02 | 209 00.2 | 28.8 | 209 38.9 | 14.1 | 0 18.7 | 14.8 | 56.9 |
| 03 | 224 00.4 .. | 29.8 | 224 12.0 | 14.2 | 0 33.5 | 14.9 | 56.9 |
| 04 | 239 00.6 | 30.8 | 238 45.2 | 14.1 | 0 48.4 | 14.8 | 56.8 |
| 05 | 254 00.8 | 31.7 | 253 18.3 | 14.2 | 1 03.2 | 14.7 | 56.8 |
| 06 | 269 01.0 | N 4 32.7 | 267 51.5 | 14.3 | N 1 17.9 | 14.8 | 56.8 |
| 07 | 284 01.2 | 33.7 | 282 24.8 | 14.2 | 1 32.7 | 14.8 | 56.8 |
| 08 | 299 01.3 | 34.6 | 296 58.0 | 14.3 | 1 47.5 | 14.7 | 56.7 |
| F 09 | 314 01.5 .. | 35.6 | 311 31.3 | 14.2 | 2 02.2 | 14.7 | 56.7 |
| R 10 | 329 01.7 | 36.6 | 326 04.5 | 14.3 | 2 16.9 | 14.7 | 56.7 |
| I 11 | 344 01.9 | 37.5 | 340 37.8 | 14.3 | 2 31.6 | 14.6 | 56.7 |
| D 12 | 359 02.1 | N 4 38.5 | 355 11.1 | 14.3 | N 2 46.2 | 14.7 | 56.6 |
| A 13 | 14 02.3 | 39.5 | 9 44.4 | 14.3 | 3 00.9 | 14.6 | 56.6 |
| Y 14 | 29 02.5 | 40.4 | 24 17.7 | 14.4 | 3 15.5 | 14.6 | 56.6 |
| 15 | 44 02.6 .. | 41.4 | 38 51.1 | 14.3 | 3 30.1 | 14.5 | 56.6 |
| 16 | 59 02.8 | 42.4 | 53 24.4 | 14.4 | 3 44.6 | 14.5 | 56.5 |
| 17 | 74 03.0 | 43.3 | 67 57.8 | 14.3 | 3 59.2 | 14.5 | 56.5 |
| 18 | 89 03.2 | N 4 44.3 | 82 31.1 | 14.4 | N 4 13.7 | 14.4 | 56.5 |
| 19 | 104 03.4 | 45.2 | 97 04.5 | 14.4 | 4 28.1 | 14.5 | 56.5 |
| 20 | 119 03.6 | 46.2 | 111 37.9 | 14.4 | 4 42.6 | 14.4 | 56.5 |
| 21 | 134 03.7 .. | 47.2 | 126 11.3 | 14.3 | 4 57.0 | 14.4 | 56.4 |
| 22 | 149 03.9 | 48.1 | 140 44.6 | 14.4 | 5 11.4 | 14.3 | 56.4 |
| 23 | 164 04.1 | 49.1 | 155 18.0 | 14.4 | 5 25.7 | 14.3 | 56.4 |
| **2** 00 | 179 04.3 | N 4 50.0 | 169 51.4 | 14.4 | N 5 40.0 | 14.3 | 56.4 |
| 01 | 194 04.5 | 51.0 | 184 24.8 | 14.4 | 5 54.3 | 14.2 | 56.3 |
| 02 | 209 04.7 | 52.0 | 198 58.2 | 14.4 | 6 08.5 | 14.2 | 56.3 |
| 03 | 224 04.8 .. | 53.0 | 213 31.6 | 14.4 | 6 22.7 | 14.2 | 56.3 |
| 04 | 239 05.0 | 53.9 | 228 05.0 | 14.3 | 6 36.9 | 14.1 | 56.3 |
| 05 | 254 05.2 | 54.9 | 242 38.3 | 14.4 | 6 51.0 | 14.1 | 56.2 |
| 06 | 269 05.4 | N 4 55.8 | 257 11.7 | 14.4 | N 7 05.1 | 14.0 | 56.2 |
| S 07 | 284 05.6 | 56.8 | 271 45.1 | 14.4 | 7 19.1 | 14.0 | 56.2 |
| A 08 | 299 05.8 | 57.8 | 286 18.5 | 14.3 | 7 33.1 | 13.9 | 56.2 |
| T 09 | 314 05.9 .. | 58.7 | 300 51.8 | 14.4 | 7 47.0 | 13.9 | 56.1 |
| U 10 | 329 06.1 | 4 59.7 | 315 25.2 | 14.4 | 8 00.9 | 13.9 | 56.1 |
| R 11 | 344 06.3 | 5 00.6 | 329 58.6 | 14.3 | 8 14.8 | 13.8 | 56.1 |
| D 12 | 359 06.5 | N 5 01.6 | 344 31.9 | 14.3 | N 8 28.6 | 13.7 | 56.1 |
| A 13 | 14 06.7 | 02.6 | 359 05.2 | 14.4 | 8 42.3 | 13.8 | 56.1 |
| Y 14 | 29 06.9 | 03.5 | 13 38.6 | 14.3 | 8 56.1 | 13.6 | 56.0 |
| 15 | 44 07.0 .. | 04.5 | 28 11.9 | 14.3 | 9 09.7 | 13.6 | 56.0 |
| 16 | 59 07.2 | 05.4 | 42 45.2 | 14.3 | 9 23.3 | 13.6 | 56.0 |
| 17 | 74 07.4 | 06.4 | 57 18.5 | 14.3 | 9 36.9 | 13.5 | 56.0 |
| 18 | 89 07.6 | N 5 07.4 | 71 51.8 | 14.2 | N 9 50.4 | 13.4 | 55.9 |
| 19 | 104 07.8 | 08.3 | 86 25.0 | 14.3 | 10 03.8 | 13.4 | 55.9 |
| 20 | 119 08.0 | 09.3 | 100 58.3 | 14.2 | 10 17.2 | 13.4 | 55.9 |
| 21 | 134 08.1 .. | 10.2 | 115 31.5 | 14.2 | 10 30.6 | 13.3 | 55.9 |
| 22 | 149 08.3 | 11.2 | 130 04.7 | 14.2 | 10 43.9 | 13.2 | 55.8 |
| 23 | 164 08.5 | 12.2 | 144 37.9 | 14.2 | 10 57.1 | 13.2 | 55.8 |
| **3** 00 | 179 08.7 | N 5 13.1 | 159 11.1 | 14.2 | N11 10.3 | 13.1 | 55.8 |
| 01 | 194 08.9 | 14.1 | 173 44.3 | 14.1 | 11 23.4 | 13.0 | 55.8 |
| 02 | 209 09.0 | 15.0 | 188 17.4 | 14.1 | 11 36.4 | 13.0 | 55.7 |
| 03 | 224 09.2 .. | 16.0 | 202 50.5 | 14.1 | 11 49.4 | 13.0 | 55.7 |
| 04 | 239 09.4 | 17.0 | 217 23.6 | 14.1 | 12 02.4 | 12.8 | 55.7 |
| 05 | 254 09.6 | 17.9 | 231 56.7 | 14.1 | 12 15.2 | 12.8 | 55.7 |
| 06 | 269 09.8 | N 5 18.9 | 246 29.8 | 14.0 | N12 28.0 | 12.8 | 55.7 |
| 07 | 284 10.0 | 19.8 | 261 02.8 | 14.0 | 12 40.8 | 12.7 | 55.6 |
| 08 | 299 10.1 | 20.8 | 275 35.8 | 14.0 | 12 53.5 | 12.6 | 55.6 |
| S 09 | 314 10.3 .. | 21.8 | 290 08.8 | 14.0 | 13 06.1 | 12.5 | 55.6 |
| U 10 | 329 10.5 | 22.7 | 304 41.8 | 13.9 | 13 18.6 | 12.5 | 55.6 |
| N 11 | 344 10.7 | 23.7 | 319 14.7 | 14.0 | 13 31.1 | 12.4 | 55.5 |
| D 12 | 359 10.9 | N 5 24.6 | 333 47.7 | 13.8 | N13 43.5 | 12.4 | 55.5 |
| A 13 | 14 11.0 | 25.6 | 348 20.5 | 13.9 | 13 55.9 | 12.2 | 55.5 |
| Y 14 | 29 11.2 | 26.5 | 2 53.4 | 13.8 | 14 08.1 | 12.2 | 55.5 |
| 15 | 44 11.4 .. | 27.5 | 17 26.2 | 13.9 | 14 20.3 | 12.2 | 55.4 |
| 16 | 59 11.6 | 28.4 | 31 59.1 | 13.7 | 14 32.5 | 12.0 | 55.4 |
| 17 | 74 11.8 | 29.4 | 46 31.8 | 13.7 | 14 44.5 | 12.0 | 55.4 |
| 18 | 89 12.0 | N 5 30.4 | 61 04.6 | 13.7 | N14 56.5 | 11.9 | 55.4 |
| 19 | 104 12.1 | 31.3 | 75 37.3 | 13.7 | 15 08.4 | 11.9 | 55.4 |
| 20 | 119 12.3 | 32.3 | 90 10.0 | 13.6 | 15 20.3 | 11.7 | 55.4 |
| 21 | 134 12.5 .. | 33.2 | 104 42.6 | 13.7 | 15 32.0 | 11.7 | 55.3 |
| 22 | 149 12.7 | 34.2 | 119 15.3 | 13.6 | 15 43.7 | 11.6 | 55.3 |
| 23 | 164 12.9 | 35.1 | 133 47.9 | 13.5 | N15 55.3 | 11.5 | 55.3 |
| | SD 16.0 | d 1.0 | SD 15.4 | 15.3 | | | 15.1 |

| Lat. | Twilight Naut. | Twilight Civil | Sunrise | Moonrise 1 | 2 | 3 | 4 |
|---|---|---|---|---|---|---|---|
| ° | h m | h m | h m | h m | h m | h m | h m |
| N 72 | 01 26 | 03 35 | 04 51 | 05 54 | 05 24 | 04 47 | 03 43 |
| N 70 | 02 13 | 03 52 | 04 59 | 05 56 | 05 33 | 05 07 | 04 29 |
| 68 | 02 43 | 04 06 | 05 05 | 05 57 | 05 41 | 05 23 | 05 00 |
| 66 | 03 04 | 04 17 | 05 11 | 05 58 | 05 48 | 05 36 | 05 23 |
| 64 | 03 21 | 04 26 | 05 15 | 05 59 | 05 53 | 05 47 | 05 41 |
| 62 | 03 35 | 04 33 | 05 19 | 06 00 | 05 58 | 05 57 | 05 56 |
| 60 | 03 46 | 04 40 | 05 23 | 06 01 | 06 02 | 06 05 | 06 09 |
| N 58 | 03 55 | 04 45 | 05 26 | 06 01 | 06 06 | 06 12 | 06 20 |
| 56 | 04 04 | 04 50 | 05 28 | 06 02 | 06 10 | 06 18 | 06 29 |
| 54 | 04 11 | 04 55 | 05 31 | 06 02 | 06 13 | 06 24 | 06 38 |
| 52 | 04 17 | 04 59 | 05 33 | 06 03 | 06 15 | 06 29 | 06 45 |
| 50 | 04 23 | 05 02 | 05 35 | 06 03 | 06 18 | 06 34 | 06 52 |
| 45 | 04 34 | 05 09 | 05 39 | 06 04 | 06 24 | 06 44 | 07 07 |
| N 40 | 04 43 | 05 15 | 05 43 | 06 05 | 06 28 | 06 53 | 07 19 |
| 35 | 04 50 | 05 20 | 05 46 | 06 06 | 06 32 | 07 00 | 07 30 |
| 30 | 04 56 | 05 24 | 05 48 | 06 06 | 06 36 | 07 07 | 07 39 |
| 20 | 05 05 | 05 31 | 05 53 | 06 07 | 06 42 | 07 18 | 07 55 |
| N 10 | 05 11 | 05 36 | 05 57 | 06 08 | 06 48 | 07 28 | 08 09 |
| 0 | 05 15 | 05 40 | 06 00 | 06 09 | 06 53 | 07 37 | 08 22 |
| S 10 | 05 18 | 05 43 | 06 04 | 06 10 | 06 59 | 07 47 | 08 36 |
| 20 | 05 20 | 05 45 | 06 07 | 06 11 | 07 04 | 07 57 | 08 50 |
| 30 | 05 20 | 05 47 | 06 11 | 06 13 | 07 11 | 08 09 | 09 07 |
| 35 | 05 19 | 05 48 | 06 13 | 06 13 | 07 15 | 08 16 | 09 16 |
| 40 | 05 17 | 05 49 | 06 16 | 06 14 | 07 19 | 08 23 | 09 27 |
| 45 | 05 15 | 05 49 | 06 19 | 06 15 | 07 24 | 08 33 | 09 40 |
| S 50 | 05 12 | 05 50 | 06 22 | 06 16 | 07 30 | 08 44 | 09 57 |
| 52 | 05 11 | 05 50 | 06 24 | 06 17 | 07 33 | 08 49 | 10 04 |
| 54 | 05 09 | 05 50 | 06 25 | 06 17 | 07 36 | 08 55 | 10 13 |
| 56 | 05 07 | 05 50 | 06 27 | 06 18 | 07 40 | 09 01 | 10 22 |
| 58 | 05 04 | 05 50 | 06 29 | 06 19 | 07 44 | 09 00 | 10 33 |
| S 60 | 05 01 | 05 50 | 06 31 | 06 20 | 07 48 | 09 16 | 10 45 |

| Lat. | Sunset | Twilight Civil | Naut. | Moonset 1 | 2 | 3 | 4 |
|---|---|---|---|---|---|---|---|
| ° | h m | h m | h m | h m | h m | h m | h m |
| N 72 | 19 19 | 20 36 | 22 55 | 19 28 | 21 39 | 24 17 | 00 17 |
| N 70 | 19 11 | 20 18 | 22 01 | 19 21 | 21 21 | 23 32 | ▭ |
| 68 | 19 04 | 20 04 | 21 29 | 19 16 | 21 06 | 23 03 | 25 22 |
| 66 | 18 59 | 19 53 | 21 07 | 19 12 | 20 55 | 22 41 | 24 37 |
| 64 | 18 54 | 19 44 | 20 49 | 19 08 | 20 45 | 22 24 | 24 00 |
| 62 | 18 50 | 19 36 | 20 35 | 19 05 | 20 37 | 22 10 | 23 46 |
| 60 | 18 46 | 19 29 | 20 24 | 19 02 | 20 30 | 21 59 | 23 28 |
| N 58 | 18 43 | 19 24 | 20 14 | 19 00 | 20 24 | 21 49 | 23 13 |
| 56 | 18 40 | 19 18 | 20 05 | 18 57 | 20 19 | 21 40 | 23 00 |
| 54 | 18 38 | 19 14 | 19 58 | 18 55 | 20 14 | 21 32 | 22 49 |
| 52 | 18 35 | 19 10 | 19 52 | 18 54 | 20 10 | 21 25 | 22 39 |
| 50 | 18 33 | 19 06 | 19 46 | 18 52 | 20 06 | 21 19 | 22 31 |
| 45 | 18 29 | 18 59 | 19 34 | 18 48 | 19 57 | 21 05 | 22 13 |
| N 40 | 18 25 | 18 53 | 19 25 | 18 45 | 19 50 | 20 54 | 21 58 |
| 35 | 18 22 | 18 48 | 19 18 | 18 43 | 19 44 | 20 45 | 21 45 |
| 30 | 18 19 | 18 43 | 19 12 | 18 41 | 19 39 | 20 37 | 21 35 |
| 20 | 18 15 | 18 37 | 19 03 | 18 37 | 19 30 | 20 23 | 21 16 |
| N 10 | 18 11 | 18 32 | 18 56 | 18 34 | 19 22 | 20 10 | 21 00 |
| 0 | 18 07 | 18 28 | 18 52 | 18 30 | 19 14 | 19 59 | 20 45 |
| S 10 | 18 03 | 18 24 | 18 49 | 18 27 | 19 07 | 19 47 | 20 30 |
| 20 | 18 00 | 18 22 | 18 47 | 18 24 | 18 59 | 19 35 | 20 14 |
| 30 | 17 56 | 18 19 | 18 47 | 18 20 | 18 50 | 19 22 | 19 55 |
| 35 | 17 53 | 18 18 | 18 48 | 18 18 | 18 45 | 19 14 | 19 45 |
| 40 | 17 51 | 18 17 | 18 49 | 18 15 | 18 39 | 19 05 | 19 33 |
| 45 | 17 48 | 18 17 | 18 51 | 18 12 | 18 32 | 18 54 | 19 19 |
| S 50 | 17 44 | 18 16 | 18 54 | 18 09 | 18 24 | 18 41 | 19 01 |
| 52 | 17 43 | 18 16 | 18 55 | 18 08 | 18 21 | 18 35 | 18 53 |
| 54 | 17 41 | 18 16 | 18 57 | 18 06 | 18 17 | 18 29 | 18 44 |
| 56 | 17 39 | 18 16 | 18 59 | 18 04 | 18 12 | 18 22 | 18 34 |
| 58 | 17 37 | 18 16 | 19 01 | 18 02 | 18 07 | 18 14 | 18 23 |
| S 60 | 17 35 | 18 16 | 19 04 | 18 00 | 18 02 | 18 05 | 18 09 |

| Day | SUN Eqn. of Time 00h | SUN Eqn. of Time 12h | Mer. Pass. | MOON Mer. Pass. Upper | Lower | Age | Phase |
|---|---|---|---|---|---|---|---|
| d | m s | m s | h m | h m | h m | d | % |
| 1 | 04 01 | 03 52 | 12 04 | 12 20 | 24 42 | 00 | 0 |
| 2 | 03 43 | 03 34 | 12 04 | 13 04 | 00 42 | 01 | 2 |
| 3 | 03 26 | 03 17 | 12 03 | 13 48 | 01 26 | 02 | 5 |

| UT | ARIES GHA | VENUS GHA | VENUS Dec | MARS GHA | MARS Dec | JUPITER GHA | JUPITER Dec | SATURN GHA | SATURN Dec | STARS Name | SHA | Dec |
|---|---|---|---|---|---|---|---|---|---|---|---|---|
| **4 00** | 192 17.5 | 222 05.0 | S11 31.6 | 227 54.5 | S15 29.3 | 199 14.3 | S 4 06.3 | 227 18.2 | S14 58.5 | Acamar | 315 13.9 | S40 13.2 |
| 01 | 207 20.0 | 237 04.9 | 30.8 | 242 55.1 | 28.7 | 214 16.2 | 06.0 | 242 20.5 | 58.4 | Achernar | 335 22.5 | S57 07.6 |
| 02 | 222 22.4 | 252 04.7 | 30.1 | 257 55.7 | 28.1 | 229 18.2 | 05.8 | 257 22.7 | 58.3 | Acrux | 173 01.9 | S63 13.4 |
| 03 | 237 24.9 | 267 04.5 | .. 29.4 | 272 56.3 | .. 27.5 | 244 20.1 | .. 05.6 | 272 25.0 | .. 58.3 | Adhara | 255 07.7 | S29 00.4 |
| 04 | 252 27.3 | 282 04.4 | 28.7 | 287 56.9 | 26.9 | 259 22.0 | 05.4 | 287 27.2 | 58.2 | Aldebaran | 290 42.4 | N16 33.1 |
| 05 | 267 29.8 | 297 04.2 | 28.0 | 302 57.5 | 26.3 | 274 23.9 | 05.1 | 302 29.5 | 58.1 | | | |
| 06 | 282 32.3 | 312 04.0 | S11 27.3 | 317 58.1 | S15 25.8 | 289 25.9 | S 4 04.9 | 317 31.7 | S14 58.1 | Alioth | 166 14.5 | N55 50.4 |
| 07 | 297 34.7 | 327 03.9 | 26.6 | 332 58.7 | 25.2 | 304 27.8 | 04.7 | 332 34.0 | 58.0 | Alkaid | 152 53.4 | N49 12.1 |
| 08 | 312 37.2 | 342 03.7 | 25.9 | 347 59.3 | 24.6 | 319 29.7 | 04.5 | 347 36.2 | 57.9 | Alnair | 27 36.1 | S46 51.2 |
| M 09 | 327 39.7 | 357 03.5 | .. 25.2 | 2 59.9 | .. 24.0 | 334 31.6 | .. 04.2 | 2 38.4 | .. 57.9 | Alnilam | 275 40.2 | S 1 11.4 |
| O 10 | 342 42.1 | 12 03.4 | 24.5 | 18 00.5 | 23.4 | 349 33.6 | 04.0 | 17 40.7 | 57.8 | Alphard | 217 49.8 | S 8 45.4 |
| N 11 | 357 44.6 | 27 03.2 | 23.7 | 33 01.1 | 22.8 | 4 35.5 | 03.8 | 32 42.9 | 57.7 | | | |
| D 12 | 12 47.1 | 42 03.0 | S11 23.0 | 48 01.7 | S15 22.3 | 19 37.4 | S 4 03.5 | 47 45.2 | S14 57.7 | Alphecca | 126 05.4 | N26 38.2 |
| A 13 | 27 49.5 | 57 02.9 | 22.3 | 63 02.3 | 21.7 | 34 39.4 | 03.3 | 62 47.4 | 57.6 | Alpheratz | 357 37.5 | N29 12.6 |
| Y 14 | 42 52.0 | 72 02.7 | 21.6 | 78 02.9 | 21.1 | 49 41.3 | 03.1 | 77 49.7 | 57.5 | Altair | 62 02.2 | N 8 55.4 |
| 15 | 57 54.5 | 87 02.5 | .. 20.9 | 93 03.5 | .. 20.5 | 64 43.2 | .. 02.9 | 92 51.9 | .. 57.5 | Ankaa | 353 09.8 | S42 11.3 |
| 16 | 72 56.9 | 102 02.4 | 20.2 | 108 04.2 | 19.9 | 79 45.1 | 02.6 | 107 54.2 | 57.4 | Antares | 112 18.4 | S26 28.8 |
| 17 | 87 59.4 | 117 02.2 | 19.4 | 123 04.8 | 19.3 | 94 47.1 | 02.4 | 122 56.4 | 57.3 | | | |
| 18 | 103 01.8 | 132 02.0 | S11 18.7 | 138 05.4 | S15 18.7 | 109 49.0 | S 4 02.2 | 137 58.7 | S14 57.2 | Arcturus | 145 49.7 | N19 03.9 |
| 19 | 118 04.3 | 147 01.9 | 18.0 | 153 06.0 | 18.1 | 124 50.9 | 02.0 | 153 00.9 | 57.2 | Atria | 107 14.4 | S69 03.8 |
| 20 | 133 06.8 | 162 01.7 | 17.3 | 168 06.6 | 17.6 | 139 52.8 | 01.7 | 168 03.2 | 57.1 | Avior | 234 15.4 | S59 35.1 |
| 21 | 148 09.2 | 177 01.5 | .. 16.6 | 183 07.2 | .. 17.0 | 154 54.8 | .. 01.5 | 183 05.4 | .. 57.1 | Bellatrix | 278 25.5 | N 6 22.1 |
| 22 | 163 11.7 | 192 01.4 | 15.8 | 198 07.8 | 16.4 | 169 56.7 | 01.3 | 198 07.7 | 57.0 | Betelgeuse | 270 54.7 | N 7 24.6 |
| 23 | 178 14.2 | 207 01.2 | 15.1 | 213 08.4 | 15.8 | 184 58.6 | 01.1 | 213 09.9 | 56.9 | | | |
| **5 00** | 193 16.6 | 222 01.0 | S11 14.4 | 228 09.0 | S15 15.2 | 200 00.6 | S 4 00.8 | 228 12.2 | S14 56.9 | Canopus | 263 53.5 | S52 42.7 |
| 01 | 208 19.1 | 237 00.9 | 13.7 | 243 09.6 | 14.6 | 215 02.5 | 00.6 | 243 14.4 | 56.8 | Capella | 280 25.5 | N46 01.3 |
| 02 | 223 21.6 | 252 00.7 | 13.0 | 258 10.2 | 14.0 | 230 04.4 | 00.4 | 258 16.6 | 56.7 | Deneb | 49 27.5 | N45 21.2 |
| 03 | 238 24.0 | 267 00.5 | .. 12.2 | 273 10.8 | .. 13.4 | 245 06.3 | 4 00.2 | 273 18.9 | .. 56.7 | Denebola | 182 27.0 | N14 26.9 |
| 04 | 253 26.5 | 282 00.4 | 11.5 | 288 11.4 | 12.8 | 260 08.3 | 3 59.9 | 288 21.1 | 56.6 | Diphda | 348 49.9 | S17 52.1 |
| 05 | 268 29.0 | 297 00.2 | 10.8 | 303 12.0 | 12.2 | 275 10.2 | 59.7 | 303 23.4 | 56.5 | | | |
| 06 | 283 31.4 | 312 00.0 | S11 10.1 | 318 12.6 | S15 11.7 | 290 12.1 | S 3 59.5 | 318 25.6 | S14 56.5 | Dubhe | 193 43.3 | N61 38.0 |
| 07 | 298 33.9 | 326 59.9 | 09.3 | 333 13.2 | 11.1 | 305 14.1 | 59.3 | 333 27.9 | 56.4 | Elnath | 278 04.9 | N28 37.6 |
| 08 | 313 36.3 | 341 59.7 | 08.6 | 348 13.8 | 10.5 | 320 16.0 | 59.0 | 348 30.1 | 56.3 | Eltanin | 90 43.1 | N51 28.8 |
| T 09 | 328 38.8 | 356 59.5 | .. 07.9 | 3 14.4 | .. 09.9 | 335 17.9 | .. 58.8 | 3 32.4 | .. 56.3 | Enif | 33 41.2 | N 9 58.4 |
| U 10 | 343 41.3 | 11 59.4 | 07.1 | 18 15.0 | 09.3 | 350 19.8 | 58.6 | 18 34.6 | 56.2 | Fomalhaut | 15 17.4 | S29 30.4 |
| E 11 | 358 43.7 | 26 59.2 | 06.4 | 33 15.7 | 08.7 | 5 21.8 | 58.4 | 33 36.9 | 56.1 | | | |
| S 12 | 13 46.2 | 41 59.0 | S11 05.7 | 48 16.3 | S15 08.1 | 20 23.7 | S 3 58.1 | 48 39.1 | S14 56.1 | Gacrux | 171 53.6 | S57 14.3 |
| D 13 | 28 48.7 | 56 58.9 | 04.9 | 63 16.9 | 07.5 | 35 25.6 | 57.9 | 63 41.4 | 56.0 | Gienah | 175 45.6 | S17 40.0 |
| A 14 | 43 51.1 | 71 58.7 | 04.2 | 78 17.5 | 06.9 | 50 27.6 | 57.7 | 78 43.6 | 55.9 | Hadar | 148 38.6 | S60 28.7 |
| Y 15 | 58 53.6 | 86 58.5 | .. 03.5 | 93 18.1 | .. 06.3 | 65 29.5 | .. 57.5 | 93 45.9 | .. 55.9 | Hamal | 327 54.1 | N23 33.9 |
| 16 | 73 56.1 | 101 58.3 | 02.8 | 108 18.7 | 05.7 | 80 31.4 | 57.2 | 108 48.1 | 55.8 | Kaus Aust. | 83 35.5 | S34 22.4 |
| 17 | 88 58.5 | 116 58.2 | 02.0 | 123 19.3 | 05.1 | 95 33.3 | 57.0 | 123 50.4 | 55.8 | | | |
| 18 | 104 01.0 | 131 58.0 | S11 01.3 | 138 19.9 | S15 04.6 | 110 35.3 | S 3 56.8 | 138 52.6 | S14 55.7 | Kochab | 137 18.8 | N74 03.7 |
| 19 | 119 03.4 | 146 57.8 | 11 00.5 | 153 20.5 | 04.0 | 125 37.2 | 56.6 | 153 54.9 | 55.6 | Markab | 13 32.5 | N15 19.2 |
| 20 | 134 05.9 | 161 57.7 | 10 59.8 | 168 21.1 | 03.4 | 140 39.1 | 56.3 | 168 57.1 | 55.6 | Menkar | 314 08.8 | N 4 10.4 |
| 21 | 149 08.4 | 176 57.5 | .. 59.1 | 183 21.7 | .. 02.8 | 155 41.1 | .. 56.1 | 183 59.4 | .. 55.5 | Menkent | 147 59.9 | S36 28.7 |
| 22 | 164 10.8 | 191 57.3 | 58.3 | 198 22.3 | 02.2 | 170 43.0 | 55.9 | 199 01.6 | 55.4 | Miaplacidus | 221 38.2 | S69 48.7 |
| 23 | 179 13.3 | 206 57.2 | 57.6 | 213 22.9 | 01.6 | 185 44.9 | 55.7 | 214 03.9 | 55.4 | | | |
| **6 00** | 194 15.8 | 221 57.0 | S10 56.9 | 228 23.6 | S15 01.0 | 200 46.9 | S 3 55.4 | 229 06.1 | S14 55.3 | Mirfak | 308 31.9 | N49 56.4 |
| 01 | 209 18.2 | 236 56.8 | 56.1 | 243 24.2 | 15 00.4 | 215 48.8 | 55.2 | 244 08.4 | 55.2 | Nunki | 75 50.6 | S26 16.1 |
| 02 | 224 20.7 | 251 56.7 | 55.4 | 258 24.8 | 14 59.8 | 230 50.7 | 55.0 | 259 10.6 | 55.2 | Peacock | 53 09.5 | S56 39.7 |
| 03 | 239 23.2 | 266 56.5 | .. 54.6 | 273 25.4 | .. 59.2 | 245 52.6 | .. 54.8 | 274 12.9 | .. 55.1 | Pollux | 243 20.1 | N27 58.4 |
| 04 | 254 25.6 | 281 56.3 | 53.9 | 288 26.0 | 58.6 | 260 54.6 | 54.5 | 289 15.1 | 55.0 | Procyon | 244 53.2 | N 5 10.0 |
| 05 | 269 28.1 | 296 56.1 | 53.2 | 303 26.6 | 58.0 | 275 56.5 | 54.3 | 304 17.4 | 55.0 | | | |
| 06 | 284 30.6 | 311 56.0 | S10 52.4 | 318 27.2 | S14 57.4 | 290 58.4 | S 3 54.1 | 319 19.6 | S14 54.9 | Rasalhague | 96 00.6 | N12 32.4 |
| W 07 | 299 33.0 | 326 55.8 | 51.7 | 333 27.8 | 56.8 | 306 00.4 | 53.9 | 334 21.9 | 54.8 | Regulus | 207 36.7 | N11 51.5 |
| E 08 | 314 35.5 | 341 55.6 | 50.9 | 348 28.4 | 56.2 | 321 02.3 | 53.6 | 349 24.1 | 54.8 | Rigel | 281 06.2 | S 8 10.7 |
| D 09 | 329 37.9 | 356 55.5 | .. 50.2 | 3 29.0 | .. 55.6 | 336 04.2 | .. 53.4 | 4 26.4 | .. 54.7 | Rigil Kent. | 139 42.8 | S60 55.5 |
| N 10 | 344 40.4 | 11 55.3 | 49.4 | 18 29.7 | 55.0 | 351 06.2 | 53.2 | 19 28.6 | 54.6 | Sabik | 102 05.3 | S15 45.2 |
| E 11 | 359 42.9 | 26 55.1 | 48.7 | 33 30.3 | 54.4 | 6 08.1 | 53.0 | 34 30.9 | 54.6 | | | |
| S 12 | 14 45.3 | 41 54.9 | S10 48.0 | 48 30.9 | S14 53.8 | 21 10.0 | S 3 52.7 | 49 33.1 | S14 54.5 | Schedar | 349 34.2 | N56 39.4 |
| D 13 | 29 47.8 | 56 54.8 | 47.2 | 63 31.5 | 53.2 | 36 11.9 | 52.5 | 64 35.4 | 54.5 | Shaula | 96 13.3 | S37 07.1 |
| A 14 | 44 50.3 | 71 54.6 | 46.5 | 78 32.1 | 52.6 | 51 13.9 | 52.3 | 79 37.6 | 54.4 | Sirius | 258 28.3 | S16 45.0 |
| Y 15 | 59 52.7 | 86 54.4 | .. 45.7 | 93 32.7 | .. 52.0 | 66 15.8 | .. 52.1 | 94 39.9 | .. 54.3 | Spica | 158 24.4 | S11 16.7 |
| 16 | 74 55.2 | 101 54.3 | 45.0 | 108 33.3 | 51.4 | 81 17.7 | 51.8 | 109 42.2 | 54.3 | Suhail | 222 47.8 | S43 31.5 |
| 17 | 89 57.7 | 116 54.1 | 44.2 | 123 33.9 | 50.8 | 96 19.7 | 51.6 | 124 44.4 | 54.2 | | | |
| 18 | 105 00.1 | 131 53.9 | S10 43.5 | 138 34.5 | S14 50.2 | 111 21.6 | S 3 51.4 | 139 46.7 | S14 54.1 | Vega | 80 34.7 | N38 47.9 |
| 19 | 120 02.6 | 146 53.8 | 42.7 | 153 35.2 | 49.6 | 126 23.5 | 51.2 | 154 48.9 | 54.1 | Zuben'ubi | 136 58.3 | S16 08.1 |
| 20 | 135 05.1 | 161 53.6 | 42.0 | 168 35.8 | 49.0 | 141 25.5 | 50.9 | 169 51.2 | 54.0 | | SHA | Mer. Pass. |
| 21 | 150 07.5 | 176 53.4 | .. 41.2 | 183 36.4 | .. 48.4 | 156 27.4 | .. 50.7 | 184 53.4 | .. 53.9 | | | |
| 22 | 165 10.0 | 191 53.2 | 40.5 | 198 37.0 | 47.8 | 171 29.3 | 50.5 | 199 55.7 | 53.9 | Venus | 28 44.4 | 9 12 |
| 23 | 180 12.4 | 206 53.1 | 39.7 | 213 37.6 | 47.2 | 186 31.3 | 50.3 | 214 57.9 | 53.8 | Mars | 34 52.4 | 8 47 |
| | | | | | | | | | | Jupiter | 6 43.9 | 10 39 |
| Mer. Pass. 11 05.1 | | v −0.2   d 0.7 | | v 0.6   d 0.6 | | v 1.9   d 0.2 | | v 2.2   d 0.1 | | Saturn | 34 55.5 | 8 46 |

## SUN / MOON

| UT | SUN GHA | SUN Dec | MOON GHA | v | Dec | d | HP |
|---|---|---|---|---|---|---|---|
| d h | ° ′ | ° ′ | ° ′ | ′ | ° ′ | ′ | ′ |
| **4** 00 | 179 13.0 | N 5 36.1 | 148 20.4 | 13.5 | N16 06.8 | 11.5 | 55.3 |
| 01 | 194 13.2 | 37.1 | 162 52.9 | 13.5 | 16 18.3 | 11.4 | 55.2 |
| 02 | 209 13.4 | 38.0 | 177 25.4 | 13.5 | 16 29.7 | 11.3 | 55.2 |
| 03 | 224 13.6 | .. 39.0 | 191 57.9 | 13.4 | 16 41.0 | 11.2 | 55.2 |
| 04 | 239 13.8 | 39.9 | 206 30.3 | 13.4 | 16 52.2 | 11.1 | 55.2 |
| 05 | 254 13.9 | 40.9 | 221 02.7 | 13.4 | 17 03.3 | 11.0 | 55.2 |
| 06 | 269 14.1 | N 5 41.8 | 235 35.1 | 13.3 | N17 14.3 | 11.0 | 55.1 |
| 07 | 284 14.3 | 42.8 | 250 07.4 | 13.3 | 17 25.3 | 10.9 | 55.1 |
| **M** 08 | 299 14.5 | 43.7 | 264 39.7 | 13.2 | 17 36.2 | 10.8 | 55.1 |
| **O** 09 | 314 14.7 | .. 44.7 | 279 11.9 | 13.2 | 17 47.0 | 10.7 | 55.1 |
| **N** 10 | 329 14.8 | 45.6 | 293 44.1 | 13.2 | 17 57.7 | 10.6 | 55.1 |
| **D** 11 | 344 15.0 | 46.6 | 308 16.3 | 13.1 | 18 08.3 | 10.5 | 55.1 |
| **A** 12 | 359 15.2 | N 5 47.5 | 322 48.4 | 13.1 | N18 18.8 | 10.5 | 55.0 |
| **Y** 13 | 14 15.4 | 48.5 | 337 20.5 | 13.1 | 18 29.3 | 10.4 | 55.0 |
| 14 | 29 15.6 | 49.5 | 351 52.6 | 13.0 | 18 39.7 | 10.2 | 55.0 |
| 15 | 44 15.7 | .. 50.4 | 6 24.6 | 13.0 | 18 49.9 | 10.2 | 55.0 |
| 16 | 59 15.9 | 51.4 | 20 56.6 | 12.9 | 19 00.1 | 10.1 | 55.0 |
| 17 | 74 16.1 | 52.3 | 35 28.5 | 12.9 | 19 10.2 | 10.0 | 54.9 |
| 18 | 89 16.3 | N 5 53.3 | 50 00.4 | 12.9 | N19 20.2 | 9.9 | 54.9 |
| 19 | 104 16.5 | 54.2 | 64 32.3 | 12.8 | 19 30.1 | 9.8 | 54.9 |
| 20 | 119 16.6 | 55.2 | 79 04.1 | 12.8 | 19 39.9 | 9.7 | 54.9 |
| 21 | 134 16.8 | .. 56.1 | 93 35.9 | 12.7 | 19 49.6 | 9.7 | 54.9 |
| 22 | 149 17.0 | 57.1 | 108 07.6 | 12.7 | 19 59.3 | 9.5 | 54.9 |
| 23 | 164 17.2 | 58.0 | 122 39.3 | 12.7 | 20 08.8 | 9.4 | 54.8 |
| **5** 00 | 179 17.4 | N 5 59.0 | 137 11.0 | 12.6 | N20 18.2 | 9.4 | 54.8 |
| 01 | 194 17.5 | 5 59.9 | 151 42.6 | 12.6 | 20 27.6 | 9.2 | 54.8 |
| 02 | 209 17.7 | 6 00.9 | 166 14.2 | 12.5 | 20 36.8 | 9.1 | 54.8 |
| 03 | 224 17.9 | .. 01.8 | 180 45.7 | 12.5 | 20 45.9 | 9.1 | 54.8 |
| 04 | 239 18.1 | 02.8 | 195 17.2 | 12.5 | 20 55.0 | 8.9 | 54.8 |
| 05 | 254 18.3 | 03.7 | 209 48.7 | 12.4 | 21 03.9 | 8.9 | 54.7 |
| 06 | 269 18.4 | N 6 04.7 | 224 20.1 | 12.4 | N21 12.8 | 8.7 | 54.7 |
| **T** 07 | 284 18.6 | 05.6 | 238 51.5 | 12.3 | 21 21.5 | 8.7 | 54.7 |
| **U** 08 | 299 18.8 | 06.6 | 253 22.8 | 12.3 | 21 30.2 | 8.5 | 54.7 |
| **E** 09 | 314 19.0 | .. 07.5 | 267 54.1 | 12.2 | 21 38.7 | 8.5 | 54.7 |
| **S** 10 | 329 19.1 | 08.5 | 282 25.3 | 12.3 | 21 47.2 | 8.3 | 54.7 |
| **D** 11 | 344 19.3 | 09.4 | 296 56.6 | 12.1 | 21 55.5 | 8.2 | 54.6 |
| **A** 12 | 359 19.5 | N 6 10.4 | 311 27.7 | 12.2 | N22 03.7 | 8.2 | 54.6 |
| **Y** 13 | 14 19.7 | 11.3 | 325 58.9 | 12.0 | 22 11.9 | 8.0 | 54.6 |
| 14 | 29 19.9 | 12.3 | 340 29.9 | 12.1 | 22 19.9 | 7.9 | 54.6 |
| 15 | 44 20.0 | 13.2 | 355 01.0 | 12.0 | 22 27.8 | 7.8 | 54.6 |
| 16 | 59 20.2 | 14.2 | 9 32.0 | 11.9 | 22 35.6 | 7.7 | 54.6 |
| 17 | 74 20.4 | 15.1 | 24 02.9 | 12.0 | 22 43.3 | 7.6 | 54.6 |
| 18 | 89 20.6 | N 6 16.1 | 38 33.9 | 11.9 | N22 50.9 | 7.5 | 54.6 |
| 19 | 104 20.8 | 17.0 | 53 04.8 | 11.8 | 22 58.4 | 7.4 | 54.5 |
| 20 | 119 20.9 | 17.9 | 67 35.6 | 11.8 | 23 05.8 | 7.3 | 54.5 |
| 21 | 134 21.1 | .. 18.9 | 82 06.4 | 11.8 | 23 13.1 | 7.2 | 54.5 |
| 22 | 149 21.3 | 19.8 | 96 37.2 | 11.7 | 23 20.3 | 7.0 | 54.5 |
| 23 | 164 21.5 | 20.8 | 111 07.9 | 11.7 | 23 27.3 | 7.0 | 54.5 |
| **6** 00 | 179 21.6 | N 6 21.7 | 125 38.6 | 11.6 | N23 34.3 | 6.8 | 54.5 |
| 01 | 194 21.8 | 22.7 | 140 09.2 | 11.6 | 23 41.1 | 6.7 | 54.5 |
| 02 | 209 22.0 | 23.6 | 154 39.8 | 11.6 | 23 47.8 | 6.6 | 54.5 |
| 03 | 224 22.2 | .. 24.6 | 169 10.4 | 11.5 | 23 54.4 | 6.5 | 54.4 |
| 04 | 239 22.3 | 25.5 | 183 40.9 | 11.5 | 24 00.9 | 6.4 | 54.4 |
| 05 | 254 22.5 | 26.5 | 198 11.4 | 11.4 | 24 07.3 | 6.3 | 54.4 |
| 06 | 269 22.7 | N 6 27.4 | 212 41.8 | 11.4 | N24 13.6 | 6.2 | 54.4 |
| **W** 07 | 284 22.9 | 28.4 | 227 12.2 | 11.4 | 24 19.8 | 6.0 | 54.4 |
| **E** 08 | 299 23.1 | 29.3 | 241 42.6 | 11.3 | 24 25.8 | 5.9 | 54.4 |
| **D** 09 | 314 23.2 | .. 30.2 | 256 12.9 | 11.4 | 24 31.7 | 5.8 | 54.4 |
| **N** 10 | 329 23.4 | 31.2 | 270 43.3 | 11.2 | 24 37.5 | 5.7 | 54.4 |
| **E** 11 | 344 23.6 | 32.1 | 285 13.5 | 11.2 | 24 43.2 | 5.6 | 54.4 |
| **S** 12 | 359 23.8 | N 6 33.1 | 299 43.7 | 11.2 | N24 48.8 | 5.5 | 54.3 |
| **D** 13 | 14 23.9 | 34.0 | 314 13.9 | 11.2 | 24 54.3 | 5.3 | 54.3 |
| **A** 14 | 29 24.1 | 35.0 | 328 44.1 | 11.1 | 24 59.6 | 5.2 | 54.3 |
| **Y** 15 | 44 24.3 | .. 35.9 | 343 14.2 | 11.1 | 25 04.8 | 5.1 | 54.3 |
| 16 | 59 24.5 | 36.9 | 357 44.3 | 11.1 | 25 09.9 | 5.0 | 54.3 |
| 17 | 74 24.6 | 37.8 | 12 14.4 | 11.0 | 25 14.9 | 4.9 | 54.3 |
| 18 | 89 24.8 | N 6 38.7 | 26 44.4 | 11.0 | N25 19.8 | 4.7 | 54.3 |
| 19 | 104 25.0 | 39.7 | 41 14.4 | 11.0 | 25 24.5 | 4.7 | 54.3 |
| 20 | 119 25.2 | 40.6 | 55 44.4 | 10.9 | 25 29.2 | 4.5 | 54.3 |
| 21 | 134 25.3 | .. 41.6 | 70 14.3 | 10.9 | 25 33.7 | 4.4 | 54.3 |
| 22 | 149 25.5 | 42.5 | 84 44.2 | 10.9 | 25 38.1 | 4.2 | 54.3 |
| 23 | 164 25.7 | 43.4 | 99 14.1 | 10.8 | N25 42.3 | 4.2 | 54.3 |
| | SD 16.0 | d 0.9 | SD 15.0 | | 14.9 | | 14.8 |

## Twilight / Moonrise

| Lat. | Naut. | Civil | Sunrise | Moonrise 4 | 5 | 6 | 7 |
|---|---|---|---|---|---|---|---|
| ° | h m | h m | h m | h m | h m | h m | h m |
| N 72 | 00 12 | 03 16 | 04 35 | 03 43 | □ | □ | □ |
| N 70 | 01 46 | 03 36 | 04 45 | 04 29 | □ | □ | □ |
| 68 | 02 23 | 03 51 | 04 53 | 05 00 | 04 17 | □ | □ |
| 66 | 02 48 | 04 04 | 04 59 | 05 23 | 05 03 | 04 04 | □ |
| 64 | 03 07 | 04 14 | 05 05 | 05 41 | 05 33 | 05 23 | 04 44 |
| 62 | 03 22 | 04 23 | 05 09 | 05 56 | 05 56 | 06 00 | 06 10 |
| 60 | 03 35 | 04 30 | 05 14 | 06 09 | 06 15 | 06 26 | 06 47 |
| N 58 | 03 45 | 04 36 | 05 17 | 06 20 | 06 30 | 06 47 | 07 13 |
| 56 | 03 55 | 04 42 | 05 20 | 06 29 | 06 44 | 07 04 | 07 34 |
| 54 | 04 02 | 04 47 | 05 23 | 06 38 | 06 55 | 07 18 | 07 51 |
| 52 | 04 09 | 04 51 | 05 26 | 06 45 | 07 05 | 07 31 | 08 06 |
| 50 | 04 15 | 04 55 | 05 28 | 06 52 | 07 14 | 07 42 | 08 19 |
| 45 | 04 28 | 05 04 | 05 34 | 07 07 | 07 34 | 08 06 | 08 45 |
| N 40 | 04 38 | 05 10 | 05 38 | 07 19 | 07 50 | 08 25 | 09 06 |
| 35 | 04 46 | 05 16 | 05 42 | 07 30 | 08 03 | 08 41 | 09 24 |
| 30 | 04 52 | 05 21 | 05 45 | 07 39 | 08 15 | 08 54 | 09 39 |
| 20 | 05 02 | 05 28 | 05 50 | 07 55 | 08 35 | 09 18 | 10 04 |
| N 10 | 05 09 | 05 34 | 05 55 | 08 09 | 08 53 | 09 38 | 10 27 |
| 0 | 05 15 | 05 39 | 05 59 | 08 22 | 09 09 | 09 57 | 10 47 |
| S 10 | 05 18 | 05 43 | 06 04 | 08 36 | 09 26 | 10 17 | 11 08 |
| 20 | 05 20 | 05 46 | 06 08 | 08 50 | 09 44 | 10 37 | 11 30 |
| 30 | 05 21 | 05 49 | 06 13 | 09 07 | 10 04 | 11 01 | 11 56 |
| 35 | 05 21 | 05 50 | 06 16 | 09 16 | 10 17 | 11 15 | 12 12 |
| 40 | 05 20 | 05 52 | 06 19 | 09 27 | 10 31 | 11 32 | 12 30 |
| 45 | 05 19 | 05 53 | 06 22 | 09 40 | 10 47 | 11 52 | 12 51 |
| S 50 | 05 17 | 05 54 | 06 27 | 09 57 | 11 08 | 12 16 | 13 19 |
| 52 | 05 16 | 05 55 | 06 29 | 10 04 | 11 18 | 12 28 | 13 32 |
| 54 | 05 14 | 05 55 | 06 31 | 10 13 | 11 29 | 12 42 | 13 47 |
| 56 | 05 13 | 05 56 | 06 33 | 10 22 | 11 42 | 12 58 | 14 06 |
| 58 | 05 11 | 05 56 | 06 36 | 10 33 | 11 57 | 13 17 | 14 28 |
| S 60 | 05 09 | 05 57 | 06 39 | 10 45 | 12 15 | 13 41 | 14 57 |

## Sunset / Twilight / Moonset

| Lat. | Sunset | Civil | Naut. | Moonset 4 | 5 | 6 | 7 |
|---|---|---|---|---|---|---|---|
| ° | h m | h m | h m | h m | h m | h m | h m |
| N 72 | 19 34 | 20 54 | //// | 00 17 | □ | □ | □ |
| N 70 | 19 23 | 20 33 | 22 28 | □ | □ | □ | □ |
| 68 | 19 15 | 20 17 | 21 48 | 25 22 | 01 22 | □ | □ |
| 66 | 19 08 | 20 04 | 21 22 | 24 37 | 00 37 | 03 16 | □ |
| 64 | 19 03 | 19 54 | 21 02 | 24 08 | 00 08 | 01 58 | 04 20 |
| 62 | 18 59 | 19 45 | 20 46 | 23 46 | 23 22 | 01 22 | 02 54 |
| 60 | 18 53 | 19 37 | 20 33 | 23 28 | 24 56 | 00 56 | 02 18 |
| N 58 | 18 50 | 19 31 | 20 22 | 23 13 | 24 35 | 00 35 | 01 52 |
| 56 | 18 46 | 19 25 | 20 13 | 23 00 | 24 19 | 00 19 | 01 31 |
| 54 | 18 43 | 19 20 | 20 05 | 22 49 | 24 04 | 00 04 | 01 14 |
| 52 | 18 41 | 19 15 | 19 58 | 22 40 | 23 52 | 24 59 | 00 59 |
| 50 | 18 38 | 19 11 | 19 52 | 22 31 | 23 41 | 24 47 | 00 47 |
| 45 | 18 33 | 19 03 | 19 38 | 22 13 | 23 18 | 24 21 | 00 21 |
| N 40 | 18 28 | 18 56 | 19 28 | 21 58 | 23 00 | 24 00 | 00 00 |
| 35 | 18 24 | 18 50 | 19 20 | 21 45 | 22 45 | 23 43 | 24 37 |
| 30 | 18 21 | 18 45 | 19 14 | 21 35 | 22 32 | 23 28 | 24 22 |
| 20 | 18 15 | 18 38 | 19 04 | 21 16 | 22 10 | 23 03 | 23 56 |
| N 10 | 18 10 | 18 32 | 18 56 | 21 00 | 21 50 | 22 41 | 23 33 |
| 0 | 18 06 | 18 27 | 18 51 | 20 45 | 21 32 | 22 21 | 23 12 |
| S 10 | 18 02 | 18 23 | 18 47 | 20 30 | 21 14 | 22 01 | 22 51 |
| 20 | 17 57 | 18 19 | 18 45 | 20 14 | 20 55 | 21 40 | 22 28 |
| 30 | 17 52 | 18 16 | 18 44 | 19 55 | 20 33 | 21 15 | 22 02 |
| 35 | 17 49 | 18 14 | 18 44 | 19 45 | 20 20 | 21 00 | 21 46 |
| 40 | 17 46 | 18 13 | 18 44 | 19 33 | 20 05 | 20 43 | 21 28 |
| 45 | 17 42 | 18 12 | 18 45 | 19 19 | 19 48 | 20 23 | 21 08 |
| S 50 | 17 38 | 18 10 | 18 47 | 19 01 | 19 26 | 19 58 | 20 39 |
| 52 | 17 36 | 18 10 | 18 49 | 18 53 | 19 16 | 19 45 | 20 25 |
| 54 | 17 34 | 18 09 | 18 50 | 18 44 | 19 04 | 19 31 | 20 10 |
| 56 | 17 31 | 18 08 | 18 51 | 18 34 | 18 51 | 19 15 | 19 53 |
| 58 | 17 29 | 18 08 | 18 53 | 18 23 | 18 35 | 18 56 | 19 29 |
| S 60 | 17 26 | 18 07 | 18 55 | 18 09 | 18 17 | 18 32 | 19 00 |

## SUN / MOON

| Day | SUN Eqn. of Time 00h | SUN Eqn. of Time 12h | SUN Mer. Pass. | MOON Mer. Pass. Upper | MOON Mer. Pass. Lower | Age | Phase |
|---|---|---|---|---|---|---|---|
| d | m s | m s | h m | h m | h m | d | % |
| 4 | 03 08 | 03 00 | 12 03 | 14 34 | 02 11 | 03 | 10 |
| 5 | 02 51 | 02 42 | 12 03 | 15 21 | 02 57 | 04 | 17 |
| 6 | 02 34 | 02 25 | 12 02 | 16 09 | 03 45 | 05 | 25 |

| UT | ARIES GHA | VENUS −4.3 GHA | Dec | MARS +1.0 GHA | Dec | JUPITER −2.1 GHA | Dec | SATURN +0.7 GHA | Dec | STARS Name | SHA | Dec |
|---|---|---|---|---|---|---|---|---|---|---|---|---|
| d h | ° ′ | ° ′ | ° ′ | ° ′ | ° ′ | ° ′ | ° ′ | ° ′ | ° ′ | | ° ′ | ° ′ |
| **7 00** | 195 14.9 | 221 52.9 | S10 38.9 | 228 38.2 | S14 46.6 | 201 33.2 | S 3 50.1 | 230 00.2 | S14 53.7 | Acamar | 315 13.9 | S40 13.2 |
| 01 | 210 17.4 | 236 52.7 | 38.2 | 243 38.8 | 46.0 | 216 35.1 | 49.8 | 245 02.4 | 53.7 | Achernar | 335 22.5 | S57 07.6 |
| 02 | 225 19.8 | 251 52.6 | 37.4 | 258 39.4 | 45.4 | 231 37.0 | 49.6 | 260 04.7 | 53.6 | Acrux | 173 01.9 | S63 13.4 |
| 03 | 240 22.3 | 266 52.4 .. | 36.7 | 273 40.1 .. | 44.8 | 246 39.0 .. | 49.4 | 275 06.9 .. | 53.6 | Adhara | 255 07.7 | S29 00.4 |
| 04 | 255 24.8 | 281 52.2 | 35.9 | 288 40.7 | 44.2 | 261 40.9 | 49.2 | 290 09.2 | 53.5 | Aldebaran | 290 42.5 | N16 33.1 |
| 05 | 270 27.2 | 296 52.0 | 35.2 | 303 41.3 | 43.6 | 276 42.8 | 48.9 | 305 11.4 | 53.4 | | | |
| 06 | 285 29.7 | 311 51.9 | S10 34.4 | 318 41.9 | S14 43.0 | 291 44.8 | S 3 48.7 | 320 13.7 | S14 53.4 | Alioth | 166 14.4 | N55 50.4 |
| 07 | 300 32.2 | 326 51.7 | 33.7 | 333 42.5 | 42.4 | 306 46.7 | 48.5 | 335 16.0 | 53.3 | Alkaid | 152 53.4 | N49 12.1 |
| 08 | 315 34.6 | 341 51.5 | 32.9 | 348 43.1 | 41.8 | 321 48.6 | 48.3 | 350 18.2 | 53.2 | Alnair | 27 36.1 | S46 51.2 |
| 09 | 330 37.1 | 356 51.3 .. | 32.1 | 3 43.7 .. | 41.2 | 336 50.6 .. | 48.0 | 5 20.5 .. | 53.2 | Alnilam | 275 40.2 | S 1 11.4 |
| 10 | 345 39.6 | 11 51.2 | 31.4 | 18 44.3 | 40.6 | 351 52.5 | 47.8 | 20 22.7 | 53.1 | Alphard | 217 49.8 | S 8 45.4 |
| 11 | 0 42.0 | 26 51.0 | 30.6 | 33 45.0 | 40.0 | 6 54.4 | 47.6 | 35 25.0 | 53.0 | | | |
| 12 | 15 44.5 | 41 50.8 | S10 29.8 | 48 45.6 | S14 39.4 | 21 56.4 | S 3 47.4 | 50 27.2 | S14 53.0 | Alphecca | 126 05.4 | N26 38.2 |
| 13 | 30 46.9 | 56 50.7 | 29.1 | 63 46.2 | 38.8 | 36 58.3 | 47.1 | 65 29.5 | 52.9 | Alpheratz | 357 37.5 | N29 12.5 |
| 14 | 45 49.4 | 71 50.5 | 28.3 | 78 46.8 | 38.2 | 52 00.2 | 46.9 | 80 31.7 | 52.9 | Altair | 62 02.2 | N 8 55.4 |
| 15 | 60 51.9 | 86 50.3 .. | 27.6 | 93 47.4 .. | 37.6 | 67 02.2 .. | 46.7 | 95 34.0 .. | 52.8 | Ankaa | 353 09.8 | S42 11.2 |
| 16 | 75 54.3 | 101 50.1 | 26.8 | 108 48.0 | 37.0 | 82 04.1 | 46.5 | 110 36.2 | 52.7 | Antares | 112 18.4 | S26 28.8 |
| 17 | 90 56.8 | 116 50.0 | 26.0 | 123 48.6 | 36.4 | 97 06.0 | 46.2 | 125 38.5 | 52.7 | | | |
| 18 | 105 59.3 | 131 49.8 | S10 25.3 | 138 49.3 | S14 35.8 | 112 08.0 | S 3 46.0 | 140 40.8 | S14 52.6 | Arcturus | 145 49.7 | N19 03.9 |
| 19 | 121 01.7 | 146 49.6 | 24.5 | 153 49.9 | 35.2 | 127 09.9 | 45.8 | 155 43.0 | 52.5 | Atria | 107 14.4 | S69 03.8 |
| 20 | 136 04.2 | 161 49.4 | 23.7 | 168 50.5 | 34.6 | 142 11.8 | 45.6 | 170 45.3 | 52.5 | Avior | 234 15.5 | S59 35.1 |
| 21 | 151 06.7 | 176 49.3 .. | 23.0 | 183 51.1 .. | 34.0 | 157 13.8 .. | 45.4 | 185 47.5 .. | 52.4 | Bellatrix | 278 25.5 | N 6 22.1 |
| 22 | 166 09.1 | 191 49.1 | 22.2 | 198 51.7 | 33.4 | 172 15.7 | 45.1 | 200 49.8 | 52.3 | Betelgeuse | 270 54.7 | N 7 24.6 |
| 23 | 181 11.6 | 206 48.9 | 21.4 | 213 52.3 | 32.8 | 187 17.6 | 44.9 | 215 52.0 | 52.3 | | | |
| **8 00** | 196 14.0 | 221 48.8 | S10 20.7 | 228 53.0 | S14 32.2 | 202 19.6 | S 3 44.7 | 230 54.3 | S14 52.2 | Canopus | 263 53.5 | S52 42.7 |
| 01 | 211 16.5 | 236 48.6 | 19.9 | 243 53.6 | 31.6 | 217 21.5 | 44.5 | 245 56.5 | 52.2 | Capella | 280 25.5 | N46 01.3 |
| 02 | 226 19.0 | 251 48.4 | 19.1 | 258 54.2 | 30.9 | 232 23.4 | 44.2 | 260 58.8 | 52.1 | Deneb | 49 27.5 | N45 21.2 |
| 03 | 241 21.4 | 266 48.2 .. | 18.3 | 273 54.8 .. | 30.3 | 247 25.4 .. | 44.0 | 276 01.1 .. | 52.0 | Denebola | 182 27.0 | N14 26.9 |
| 04 | 256 23.9 | 281 48.1 | 17.6 | 288 55.4 | 29.7 | 262 27.3 | 43.8 | 291 03.3 | 52.0 | Diphda | 348 49.9 | S17 52.1 |
| 05 | 271 26.4 | 296 47.9 | 16.8 | 303 56.0 | 29.1 | 277 29.2 | 43.6 | 306 05.6 | 51.9 | | | |
| 06 | 286 28.8 | 311 47.7 | S10 16.0 | 318 56.7 | S14 28.5 | 292 31.2 | S 3 43.3 | 321 07.8 | S14 51.8 | Dubhe | 193 43.3 | N61 38.0 |
| 07 | 301 31.3 | 326 47.5 | 15.3 | 333 57.3 | 27.9 | 307 33.1 | 43.1 | 336 10.1 | 51.8 | Elnath | 278 04.9 | N28 37.6 |
| 08 | 316 33.8 | 341 47.4 | 14.5 | 348 57.9 | 27.3 | 322 35.0 | 42.9 | 351 12.3 | 51.7 | Eltanin | 90 43.1 | N51 28.8 |
| 09 | 331 36.2 | 356 47.2 .. | 13.7 | 3 58.5 .. | 26.7 | 337 37.0 .. | 42.7 | 6 14.6 .. | 51.6 | Enif | 33 41.2 | N 9 58.4 |
| 10 | 346 38.7 | 11 47.0 | 12.9 | 18 59.1 | 26.1 | 352 38.9 | 42.4 | 21 16.9 | 51.6 | Fomalhaut | 15 17.3 | S29 30.4 |
| 11 | 1 41.2 | 26 46.8 | 12.2 | 33 59.7 | 25.5 | 7 40.8 | 42.2 | 36 19.1 | 51.5 | | | |
| 12 | 16 43.6 | 41 46.7 | S10 11.4 | 49 00.4 | S14 24.9 | 22 42.8 | S 3 42.0 | 51 21.4 | S14 51.5 | Gacrux | 171 53.6 | S57 14.3 |
| 13 | 31 46.1 | 56 46.5 | 10.6 | 64 01.0 | 24.3 | 37 44.7 | 41.8 | 66 23.6 | 51.4 | Gienah | 175 45.6 | S17 40.0 |
| 14 | 46 48.5 | 71 46.3 | 09.8 | 79 01.6 | 23.7 | 52 46.6 | 41.6 | 81 25.9 | 51.3 | Hadar | 148 38.6 | S60 28.7 |
| 15 | 61 51.0 | 86 46.2 .. | 09.0 | 94 02.2 .. | 23.0 | 67 48.6 .. | 41.3 | 96 28.1 .. | 51.3 | Hamal | 327 54.1 | N23 33.9 |
| 16 | 76 53.5 | 101 46.0 | 08.3 | 109 02.8 | 22.4 | 82 50.5 | 41.1 | 111 30.4 | 51.2 | Kaus Aust. | 83 35.5 | S34 22.4 |
| 17 | 91 55.9 | 116 45.8 | 07.5 | 124 03.5 | 21.8 | 97 52.4 | 40.9 | 126 32.7 | 51.1 | | | |
| 18 | 106 58.4 | 131 45.6 | S10 06.7 | 139 04.1 | S14 21.2 | 112 54.4 | S 3 40.7 | 141 34.9 | S14 51.1 | Kochab | 137 18.7 | N74 03.7 |
| 19 | 122 00.9 | 146 45.5 | 05.9 | 154 04.7 | 20.6 | 127 56.3 | 40.4 | 156 37.2 | 51.0 | Markab | 13 32.4 | N15 19.2 |
| 20 | 137 03.3 | 161 45.3 | 05.1 | 169 05.3 | 20.0 | 142 58.2 | 40.2 | 171 39.4 | 51.0 | Menkar | 314 08.8 | N 4 10.4 |
| 21 | 152 05.8 | 176 45.1 .. | 04.4 | 184 05.9 .. | 19.4 | 158 00.2 .. | 40.0 | 186 41.7 .. | 50.9 | Menkent | 147 59.9 | S36 28.7 |
| 22 | 167 08.3 | 191 44.9 | 03.6 | 199 06.6 | 18.8 | 173 02.1 | 39.8 | 201 43.9 | 50.8 | Miaplacidus | 221 38.3 | S69 48.7 |
| 23 | 182 10.7 | 206 44.8 | 02.8 | 214 07.2 | 18.2 | 188 04.0 | 39.5 | 216 46.2 | 50.8 | | | |
| **9 00** | 197 13.2 | 221 44.6 | S10 02.0 | 229 07.8 | S14 17.5 | 203 06.0 | S 3 39.3 | 231 48.5 | S14 50.7 | Mirfak | 308 31.9 | N49 56.4 |
| 01 | 212 15.7 | 236 44.4 | 01.2 | 244 08.4 | 16.9 | 218 07.9 | 39.1 | 246 50.7 | 50.6 | Nunki | 75 50.6 | S26 16.1 |
| 02 | 227 18.1 | 251 44.2 | 10 00.4 | 259 09.0 | 16.3 | 233 09.8 | 38.9 | 261 53.0 | 50.6 | Peacock | 53 09.5 | S56 39.7 |
| 03 | 242 20.6 | 266 44.1 | 9 59.7 | 274 09.7 .. | 15.7 | 248 11.8 .. | 38.7 | 276 55.2 .. | 50.5 | Pollux | 243 20.1 | N27 58.4 |
| 04 | 257 23.0 | 281 43.9 | 58.9 | 289 10.3 | 15.1 | 263 13.7 | 38.4 | 291 57.5 | 50.5 | Procyon | 244 53.2 | N 5 10.0 |
| 05 | 272 25.5 | 296 43.7 | 58.1 | 304 10.9 | 14.5 | 278 15.6 | 38.2 | 306 59.8 | 50.4 | | | |
| 06 | 287 28.0 | 311 43.5 | S 9 57.3 | 319 11.5 | S14 13.9 | 293 17.6 | S 3 38.0 | 322 02.0 | S14 50.3 | Rasalhague | 96 00.5 | N12 32.5 |
| 07 | 302 30.4 | 326 43.4 | 56.5 | 334 12.1 | 13.3 | 308 19.5 | 37.8 | 337 04.3 | 50.3 | Regulus | 207 36.7 | N11 51.5 |
| 08 | 317 32.9 | 341 43.2 | 55.7 | 349 12.8 | 12.6 | 323 21.4 | 37.5 | 352 06.5 | 50.2 | Rigel | 281 06.2 | S 8 10.7 |
| 09 | 332 35.4 | 356 43.0 .. | 54.9 | 4 13.4 .. | 12.0 | 338 23.4 .. | 37.3 | 7 08.8 .. | 50.1 | Rigil Kent. | 139 42.8 | S60 55.5 |
| 10 | 347 37.8 | 11 42.8 | 54.1 | 19 14.0 | 11.4 | 353 25.3 | 37.1 | 22 11.1 | 50.1 | Sabik | 102 05.2 | S15 45.2 |
| 11 | 2 40.3 | 26 42.7 | 53.3 | 34 14.6 | 10.8 | 8 27.3 | 36.9 | 37 13.3 | 50.0 | | | |
| 12 | 17 42.8 | 41 42.5 | S 9 52.6 | 49 15.2 | S14 10.2 | 23 29.2 | S 3 36.7 | 52 15.6 | S14 50.0 | Schedar | 349 34.2 | N56 39.4 |
| 13 | 32 45.2 | 56 42.3 | 51.8 | 64 15.9 | 09.6 | 38 31.1 | 36.4 | 67 17.8 | 49.9 | Shaula | 96 13.3 | S37 07.1 |
| 14 | 47 47.7 | 71 42.1 | 51.0 | 79 16.5 | 09.0 | 53 33.1 | 36.2 | 82 20.1 | 49.8 | Sirius | 258 28.3 | S16 45.0 |
| 15 | 62 50.2 | 86 42.0 .. | 50.2 | 94 17.1 .. | 08.4 | 68 35.0 .. | 36.0 | 97 22.4 .. | 49.8 | Spica | 158 24.4 | S11 16.7 |
| 16 | 77 52.6 | 101 41.8 | 49.4 | 109 17.7 | 07.7 | 83 36.9 | 35.8 | 112 24.6 | 49.7 | Suhail | 222 47.8 | S43 31.5 |
| 17 | 92 55.1 | 116 41.6 | 48.6 | 124 18.4 | 07.1 | 98 38.9 | 35.5 | 127 26.9 | 49.7 | | | |
| 18 | 107 57.5 | 131 41.4 | S 9 47.8 | 139 19.0 | S14 06.5 | 113 40.8 | S 3 35.3 | 142 29.1 | S14 49.6 | Vega | 80 34.7 | N38 47.9 |
| 19 | 123 00.0 | 146 41.3 | 47.0 | 154 19.6 | 05.9 | 128 42.7 | 35.1 | 157 31.4 | 49.5 | Zuben'ubi | 136 58.2 | S16 08.1 |
| 20 | 138 02.5 | 161 41.1 | 46.2 | 169 20.2 | 05.3 | 143 44.7 | 34.9 | 172 33.7 | 49.5 | | SHA | Mer. Pass. |
| 21 | 153 04.9 | 176 40.9 .. | 45.4 | 184 20.9 .. | 04.7 | 158 46.6 .. | 34.7 | 187 35.9 .. | 49.4 | | ° ′ | h m |
| 22 | 168 07.4 | 191 40.7 | 44.6 | 199 21.5 | 04.0 | 173 48.5 | 34.4 | 202 38.2 | 49.3 | Venus | 25 34.7 | 9 13 |
| 23 | 183 09.9 | 206 40.6 | 43.8 | 214 22.1 | 03.4 | 188 50.5 | 34.2 | 217 40.4 | 49.3 | Mars | 32 38.9 | 8 44 |
| | h m | | | | | | | | | Jupiter | 6 05.5 | 10 29 |
| Mer. Pass. | 10 53.3 | v −0.2 | d 0.8 | v 0.6 | d 0.6 | v 1.9 | d 0.2 | v 2.3 | d 0.1 | Saturn | 34 40.2 | 8 35 |

| UT | SUN GHA | SUN Dec | MOON GHA | v | Dec | d | HP |
|---|---|---|---|---|---|---|---|
| d h | ° ′ | ° ′ | ° ′ | ′ | ° ′ | ′ | ′ |
| **7** 00 | 179 25.9 | N 6 44.4 | 113 43.9 | 10.8 | N25 46.5 | 4.0 | 54.3 |
| 01 | 194 26.0 | 45.3 | 128 13.7 | 10.8 | 25 50.5 | 3.9 | 54.3 |
| 02 | 209 26.2 | 46.3 | 142 43.5 | 10.8 | 25 54.4 | 3.8 | 54.3 |
| 03 | 224 26.4 | .. 47.2 | 157 13.3 | 10.7 | 25 58.2 | 3.6 | 54.3 |
| 04 | 239 26.6 | 48.2 | 171 43.0 | 10.7 | 26 01.8 | 3.5 | 54.3 |
| 05 | 254 26.7 | 49.1 | 186 12.7 | 10.7 | 26 05.3 | 3.4 | 54.2 |
| 06 | 269 26.9 | N 6 50.0 | 200 42.4 | 10.6 | N26 08.7 | 3.3 | 54.2 |
| 07 | 284 27.1 | 51.0 | 215 12.0 | 10.7 | 26 12.0 | 3.2 | 54.2 |
| T 08 | 299 27.3 | 51.9 | 229 41.7 | 10.6 | 26 15.2 | 3.0 | 54.2 |
| H 09 | 314 27.4 | .. 52.9 | 244 11.3 | 10.6 | 26 18.2 | 2.9 | 54.2 |
| U 10 | 329 27.6 | 53.8 | 258 40.9 | 10.5 | 26 21.1 | 2.8 | 54.2 |
| R 11 | 344 27.8 | 54.7 | 273 10.4 | 10.6 | 26 23.9 | 2.6 | 54.2 |
| S 12 | 359 28.0 | N 6 55.7 | 287 40.0 | 10.5 | N26 26.5 | 2.6 | 54.2 |
| D 13 | 14 28.1 | 56.6 | 302 09.5 | 10.5 | 26 29.1 | 2.4 | 54.2 |
| A 14 | 29 28.3 | 57.6 | 316 39.0 | 10.5 | 26 31.5 | 2.2 | 54.2 |
| Y 15 | 44 28.5 | .. 58.5 | 331 08.5 | 10.5 | 26 33.7 | 2.2 | 54.2 |
| 16 | 59 28.7 | 6 59.4 | 345 38.0 | 10.4 | 26 35.9 | 2.0 | 54.2 |
| 17 | 74 28.8 | 7 00.4 | 0 07.4 | 10.4 | 26 37.9 | 1.9 | 54.2 |
| 18 | 89 29.0 | N 7 01.3 | 14 36.8 | 10.5 | N26 39.8 | 1.7 | 54.2 |
| 19 | 104 29.2 | 02.2 | 29 06.3 | 10.4 | 26 41.5 | 1.7 | 54.2 |
| 20 | 119 29.4 | 03.2 | 43 35.7 | 10.3 | 26 43.2 | 1.5 | 54.2 |
| 21 | 134 29.5 | .. 04.1 | 58 05.0 | 10.4 | 26 44.7 | 1.4 | 54.2 |
| 22 | 149 29.7 | 05.1 | 72 34.4 | 10.4 | 26 46.1 | 1.2 | 54.2 |
| 23 | 164 29.9 | 06.0 | 87 03.8 | 10.3 | 26 47.3 | 1.2 | 54.2 |
| **8** 00 | 179 30.1 | N 7 06.9 | 101 33.1 | 10.4 | N26 48.5 | 1.0 | 54.2 |
| 01 | 194 30.2 | 07.9 | 116 02.5 | 10.3 | 26 49.5 | 0.8 | 54.2 |
| 02 | 209 30.4 | 08.8 | 130 31.8 | 10.3 | 26 50.3 | 0.8 | 54.2 |
| 03 | 224 30.6 | .. 09.7 | 145 01.1 | 10.3 | 26 51.1 | 0.6 | 54.2 |
| 04 | 239 30.7 | 10.7 | 159 30.4 | 10.3 | 26 51.7 | 0.5 | 54.2 |
| 05 | 254 30.9 | 11.6 | 173 59.7 | 10.3 | 26 52.2 | 0.3 | 54.2 |
| 06 | 269 31.1 | N 7 12.5 | 188 29.0 | 10.3 | N26 52.5 | 0.2 | 54.2 |
| 07 | 284 31.3 | 13.5 | 202 58.3 | 10.3 | 26 52.7 | 0.1 | 54.2 |
| F 08 | 299 31.4 | 14.4 | 217 27.6 | 10.3 | 26 52.8 | 0.0 | 54.2 |
| R 09 | 314 31.6 | .. 15.3 | 231 56.9 | 10.3 | 26 52.8 | 0.2 | 54.2 |
| I 10 | 329 31.8 | 16.3 | 246 26.2 | 10.3 | 26 52.6 | 0.3 | 54.2 |
| D 11 | 344 32.0 | 17.2 | 260 55.5 | 10.3 | 26 52.3 | 0.4 | 54.3 |
| A 12 | 359 32.1 | N 7 18.2 | 275 24.8 | 10.2 | N26 51.9 | 0.5 | 54.3 |
| Y 13 | 14 32.3 | 19.1 | 289 54.0 | 10.3 | 26 51.4 | 0.7 | 54.3 |
| 14 | 29 32.5 | 20.0 | 304 23.3 | 10.3 | 26 50.7 | 0.8 | 54.3 |
| 15 | 44 32.6 | .. 21.0 | 318 52.6 | 10.3 | 26 49.9 | 1.0 | 54.3 |
| 16 | 59 32.8 | 21.9 | 333 21.9 | 10.3 | 26 48.9 | 1.0 | 54.3 |
| 17 | 74 33.0 | 22.8 | 347 51.2 | 10.3 | 26 47.9 | 1.2 | 54.3 |
| 18 | 89 33.2 | N 7 23.8 | 2 20.5 | 10.2 | N26 46.7 | 1.3 | 54.3 |
| 19 | 104 33.3 | 24.7 | 16 49.7 | 10.3 | 26 45.4 | 1.5 | 54.3 |
| 20 | 119 33.5 | 25.6 | 31 19.0 | 10.3 | 26 43.9 | 1.6 | 54.3 |
| 21 | 134 33.7 | .. 26.5 | 45 48.3 | 10.4 | 26 42.3 | 1.7 | 54.3 |
| 22 | 149 33.8 | 27.5 | 60 17.7 | 10.3 | 26 40.6 | 1.8 | 54.3 |
| 23 | 164 34.0 | 28.4 | 74 47.0 | 10.3 | 26 38.8 | 2.0 | 54.3 |
| **9** 00 | 179 34.2 | N 7 29.3 | 89 16.3 | 10.3 | N26 36.8 | 2.1 | 54.3 |
| 01 | 194 34.4 | 30.3 | 103 45.6 | 10.4 | 26 34.7 | 2.2 | 54.3 |
| 02 | 209 34.5 | 31.2 | 118 15.0 | 10.3 | 26 32.5 | 2.4 | 54.4 |
| 03 | 224 34.7 | .. 32.1 | 132 44.3 | 10.4 | 26 30.1 | 2.5 | 54.4 |
| 04 | 239 34.9 | 33.1 | 147 13.7 | 10.4 | 26 27.6 | 2.6 | 54.4 |
| 05 | 254 35.0 | 34.0 | 161 43.1 | 10.4 | 26 25.0 | 2.7 | 54.4 |
| 06 | 269 35.2 | N 7 34.9 | 176 12.5 | 10.4 | N26 22.3 | 2.9 | 54.4 |
| 07 | 284 35.4 | 35.9 | 190 41.9 | 10.4 | 26 19.4 | 3.0 | 54.4 |
| S 08 | 299 35.5 | 36.8 | 205 11.3 | 10.5 | 26 16.4 | 3.1 | 54.4 |
| A 09 | 314 35.7 | .. 37.7 | 219 40.8 | 10.4 | 26 13.3 | 3.2 | 54.4 |
| T 10 | 329 35.9 | 38.6 | 234 10.2 | 10.5 | 26 10.1 | 3.4 | 54.4 |
| U 11 | 344 36.1 | 39.6 | 248 39.7 | 10.5 | 26 06.7 | 3.5 | 54.5 |
| R 12 | 359 36.2 | N 7 40.5 | 263 09.2 | 10.5 | N26 03.2 | 3.6 | 54.5 |
| D 13 | 14 36.4 | 41.4 | 277 38.7 | 10.5 | 25 59.6 | 3.8 | 54.5 |
| A 14 | 29 36.6 | 42.4 | 292 08.2 | 10.6 | 25 55.8 | 3.9 | 54.5 |
| Y 15 | 44 36.7 | .. 43.3 | 306 37.8 | 10.6 | 25 51.9 | 4.0 | 54.5 |
| 16 | 59 36.9 | 44.2 | 321 07.4 | 10.5 | 25 47.9 | 4.1 | 54.5 |
| 17 | 74 37.1 | 45.1 | 335 36.9 | 10.7 | 25 43.8 | 4.3 | 54.5 |
| 18 | 89 37.2 | N 7 46.1 | 350 06.6 | 10.6 | N25 39.5 | 4.3 | 54.5 |
| 19 | 104 37.4 | 47.0 | 4 36.2 | 10.6 | 25 35.2 | 4.5 | 54.6 |
| 20 | 119 37.6 | 47.9 | 19 05.8 | 10.7 | 25 30.7 | 4.7 | 54.6 |
| 21 | 134 37.7 | .. 48.9 | 33 35.5 | 10.7 | 25 26.0 | 4.7 | 54.6 |
| 22 | 149 37.9 | 49.8 | 48 05.2 | 10.8 | 25 21.3 | 4.9 | 54.6 |
| 23 | 164 38.1 | 50.7 | 62 35.0 | 10.7 | N25 16.4 | 5.0 | 54.6 |
| | SD 16.0 | d 0.9 | SD 14.8 | | 14.8 | | 14.8 |

### Twilight / Sunrise / Moonrise

| Lat. | Naut. | Civil | Sunrise | Moonrise 7 | 8 | 9 | 10 |
|---|---|---|---|---|---|---|---|
| ° | h m | h m | h m | h m | h m | h m | h m |
| N 72 | //// | 02 55 | 04 19 | □ | □ | □ | □ |
| N 70 | 01 10 | 03 19 | 04 30 | □ | □ | □ | □ |
| 68 | 02 00 | 03 37 | 04 40 | □ | □ | □ | □ |
| 66 | 02 31 | 03 51 | 04 47 | □ | □ | □ | □ |
| 64 | 02 53 | 04 02 | 04 54 | 04 44 | □ | □ | 08 38 |
| 62 | 03 10 | 04 12 | 05 00 | 06 10 | 06 41 | 07 48 | 09 19 |
| 60 | 03 24 | 04 20 | 05 05 | 06 47 | 07 25 | 08 27 | 09 47 |
| N 58 | 03 35 | 04 27 | 05 09 | 07 13 | 07 54 | 08 54 | 10 09 |
| 56 | 03 45 | 04 34 | 05 13 | 07 34 | 08 17 | 09 15 | 10 27 |
| 54 | 03 54 | 04 39 | 05 16 | 07 51 | 08 35 | 09 33 | 10 41 |
| 52 | 04 02 | 04 44 | 05 19 | 08 06 | 08 51 | 09 48 | 10 54 |
| 50 | 04 08 | 04 49 | 05 22 | 08 19 | 09 05 | 10 01 | 11 06 |
| 45 | 04 22 | 04 58 | 05 28 | 08 45 | 09 32 | 10 27 | 11 29 |
| N 40 | 04 33 | 05 06 | 05 33 | 09 06 | 09 54 | 10 48 | 11 48 |
| 35 | 04 41 | 05 12 | 05 38 | 09 24 | 10 12 | 11 06 | 12 04 |
| 30 | 04 49 | 05 17 | 05 41 | 09 39 | 10 28 | 11 21 | 12 17 |
| 20 | 05 00 | 05 26 | 05 48 | 10 04 | 10 54 | 11 46 | 12 40 |
| N 10 | 05 08 | 05 32 | 05 53 | 10 27 | 11 17 | 12 08 | 13 00 |
| 0 | 05 14 | 05 38 | 05 59 | 10 47 | 11 38 | 12 29 | 13 19 |
| S 10 | 05 18 | 05 43 | 06 04 | 11 08 | 11 59 | 12 49 | 13 37 |
| 20 | 05 21 | 05 47 | 06 09 | 11 30 | 12 22 | 13 11 | 13 57 |
| 30 | 05 23 | 05 51 | 06 15 | 11 56 | 12 49 | 13 36 | 14 20 |
| 35 | 05 23 | 05 53 | 06 18 | 12 12 | 13 04 | 13 51 | 14 33 |
| 40 | 05 23 | 05 55 | 06 22 | 12 30 | 13 22 | 14 09 | 14 48 |
| 45 | 05 23 | 05 57 | 06 26 | 12 51 | 13 44 | 14 29 | 15 07 |
| S 50 | 05 22 | 05 59 | 06 31 | 13 19 | 14 12 | 14 55 | 15 29 |
| 52 | 05 21 | 06 00 | 06 34 | 13 32 | 14 26 | 15 08 | 15 40 |
| 54 | 05 20 | 06 01 | 06 36 | 13 47 | 14 41 | 15 22 | 15 52 |
| 56 | 05 19 | 06 02 | 06 39 | 14 06 | 15 00 | 15 39 | 16 06 |
| 58 | 05 17 | 06 03 | 06 42 | 14 28 | 15 23 | 15 59 | 16 22 |
| S 60 | 05 16 | 06 04 | 06 46 | 14 57 | 15 52 | 16 25 | 16 42 |

### Sunset / Twilight / Moonset

| Lat. | Sunset | Civil | Naut. | Moonset 7 | 8 | 9 | 10 |
|---|---|---|---|---|---|---|---|
| ° | h m | h m | h m | h m | h m | h m | h m |
| N 72 | 19 48 | 21 14 | //// | □ | □ | □ | □ |
| N 70 | 19 36 | 20 49 | 23 09 | □ | □ | □ | □ |
| 68 | 19 27 | 20 31 | 22 10 | □ | □ | □ | □ |
| 66 | 19 18 | 20 16 | 21 38 | □ | □ | □ | □ |
| 64 | 19 12 | 20 04 | 21 15 | 04 20 | □ | □ | 05 42 |
| 62 | 19 06 | 19 54 | 20 57 | 02 54 | 04 09 | 04 47 | 05 00 |
| 60 | 19 01 | 19 45 | 20 43 | 02 18 | 03 24 | 04 08 | 04 32 |
| N 58 | 18 56 | 19 38 | 20 31 | 01 52 | 02 55 | 03 41 | 04 10 |
| 56 | 18 52 | 19 32 | 20 20 | 01 31 | 02 32 | 03 19 | 03 52 |
| 54 | 18 49 | 19 26 | 20 11 | 01 14 | 02 14 | 03 01 | 03 37 |
| 52 | 18 46 | 19 21 | 20 04 | 01 00 | 01 58 | 02 46 | 03 23 |
| 50 | 18 43 | 19 16 | 19 57 | 00 47 | 01 45 | 02 33 | 03 12 |
| 45 | 18 36 | 19 07 | 19 43 | 00 21 | 01 17 | 02 06 | 02 48 |
| N 40 | 18 31 | 18 59 | 19 32 | 00 00 | 00 56 | 01 45 | 02 28 |
| 35 | 18 27 | 18 53 | 19 23 | 24 37 | 00 37 | 01 27 | 02 12 |
| 30 | 18 23 | 18 47 | 19 16 | 24 22 | 00 22 | 01 12 | 01 58 |
| 20 | 18 16 | 18 38 | 19 05 | 23 56 | 24 46 | 00 46 | 01 34 |
| N 10 | 18 10 | 18 32 | 18 56 | 23 33 | 24 24 | 00 24 | 01 13 |
| 0 | 18 05 | 18 26 | 18 50 | 23 12 | 24 03 | 00 03 | 00 53 |
| S 10 | 18 00 | 18 21 | 18 46 | 22 51 | 23 42 | 24 33 | 00 33 |
| 20 | 17 55 | 18 17 | 18 42 | 22 28 | 23 19 | 24 12 | 00 12 |
| 30 | 17 49 | 18 13 | 18 40 | 22 02 | 22 53 | 23 48 | 24 45 |
| 35 | 17 45 | 18 10 | 18 40 | 21 46 | 22 37 | 23 33 | 24 32 |
| 40 | 17 41 | 18 08 | 18 40 | 21 28 | 22 19 | 23 16 | 24 18 |
| 45 | 17 37 | 18 06 | 18 40 | 21 06 | 21 57 | 22 56 | 24 00 |
| S 50 | 17 32 | 18 04 | 18 41 | 20 39 | 21 30 | 22 31 | 23 39 |
| 52 | 17 29 | 18 03 | 18 42 | 20 25 | 21 16 | 22 18 | 23 28 |
| 54 | 17 26 | 18 02 | 18 43 | 20 10 | 21 01 | 22 04 | 23 17 |
| 56 | 17 24 | 18 01 | 18 44 | 19 51 | 20 42 | 21 47 | 23 03 |
| 58 | 17 20 | 18 00 | 18 45 | 19 29 | 20 19 | 21 28 | 22 47 |
| S 60 | 17 17 | 17 59 | 18 47 | 19 00 | 19 50 | 21 02 | 22 28 |

| | SUN | | | MOON | | | |
|---|---|---|---|---|---|---|---|
| Day | Eqn. of Time 00h | 12h | Mer. Pass. | Mer. Pass. Upper | Lower | Age | Phase |
| d | m s | m s | h m | h m | h m | d | % |
| 7 | 02 17 | 02 08 | 12 02 | 16 59 | 04 34 | 06 | 34 |
| 8 | 02 00 | 01 52 | 12 02 | 17 50 | 05 25 | 07 | 43 |
| 9 | 01 44 | 01 35 | 12 02 | 18 41 | 06 16 | 08 | 52 |

| UT | ARIES | VENUS −4.3 | | MARS +1.0 | | JUPITER −2.1 | | SATURN +0.7 | | STARS | | |
|---|---|---|---|---|---|---|---|---|---|---|---|---|
| | GHA | GHA | Dec | GHA | Dec | GHA | Dec | GHA | Dec | Name | SHA | Dec |
| d h | ° ′ | ° ′ | ° ′ | ° ′ | ° ′ | ° ′ | ° ′ | ° ′ | ° ′ | | ° ′ | ° ′ |
| 10 00 | 198 12.3 | 221 40.4 | S 9 43.0 | 229 22.7 | S14 02.8 | 203 52.4 | S 3 34.0 | 232 42.7 | S14 49.2 | Acamar | 315 13.9 | S40 13.2 |
| 01 | 213 14.8 | 236 40.2 | 42.2 | 244 23.3 | 02.2 | 218 54.4 | 33.8 | 247 45.0 | 49.2 | Achernar | 335 22.5 | S57 07.6 |
| 02 | 228 17.3 | 251 40.0 | 41.4 | 259 24.0 | 01.6 | 233 56.3 | 33.5 | 262 47.2 | 49.1 | Acrux | 173 10.9 | S63 13.4 |
| 03 | 243 19.7 | 266 39.8 .. | 40.6 | 274 24.6 .. | 01.0 | 248 58.2 .. | 33.3 | 277 49.5 .. | 49.0 | Adhara | 255 07.7 | S29 00.4 |
| 04 | 258 22.2 | 281 39.7 | 39.8 | 289 25.2 | 14 00.3 | 264 00.2 | 33.1 | 292 51.8 | 49.0 | Aldebaran | 290 42.5 | N16 33.1 |
| 05 | 273 24.6 | 296 39.5 | 39.0 | 304 25.8 | 13 59.7 | 279 02.1 | 32.9 | 307 54.0 | 48.9 | | | |
| 06 | 288 27.1 | 311 39.3 | S 9 38.2 | 319 26.5 | S13 59.1 | 294 04.0 | S 3 32.7 | 322 56.3 | S14 48.9 | Alioth | 166 14.4 | N55 50.4 |
| 07 | 303 29.6 | 326 39.1 | 37.4 | 334 27.1 | 58.5 | 309 06.0 | 32.4 | 337 58.5 | 48.8 | Alkaid | 152 53.3 | N49 12.1 |
| 08 | 318 32.0 | 341 39.0 | 36.6 | 349 27.7 | 57.9 | 324 07.9 | 32.2 | 353 00.8 | 48.7 | Alnair | 27 36.1 | S46 51.2 |
| S 09 | 333 34.5 | 356 38.8 .. | 35.8 | 4 28.3 .. | 57.2 | 339 09.9 .. | 32.0 | 8 03.1 .. | 48.7 | Alnilam | 275 40.2 | S 1 11.4 |
| U 10 | 348 36.9 | 11 38.6 | 35.0 | 19 29.0 | 56.6 | 354 11.8 | 31.8 | 23 05.3 | 48.6 | Alphard | 217 49.8 | S 8 45.4 |
| N 11 | 3 39.4 | 26 38.4 | 34.2 | 34 29.6 | 56.0 | 9 13.7 | 31.5 | 38 07.6 | 48.5 | | | |
| D 12 | 18 41.9 | 41 38.3 | S 9 33.4 | 49 30.2 | S13 55.4 | 24 15.7 | S 3 31.3 | 53 09.9 | S14 48.5 | Alphecca | 126 05.4 | N26 38.2 |
| A 13 | 33 44.4 | 56 38.1 | 32.6 | 64 30.8 | 54.8 | 39 17.6 | 31.1 | 68 12.1 | 48.4 | Alpheratz | 357 37.5 | N29 12.5 |
| Y 14 | 48 46.8 | 71 37.9 | 31.8 | 79 31.5 | 54.2 | 54 19.5 | 30.9 | 83 14.4 | 48.4 | Altair | 62 02.2 | N 8 55.4 |
| 15 | 63 49.3 | 86 37.7 .. | 30.9 | 94 32.1 .. | 53.5 | 69 21.5 .. | 30.7 | 98 16.6 .. | 48.3 | Ankaa | 353 09.8 | S42 11.2 |
| 16 | 78 51.8 | 101 37.6 | 30.1 | 109 32.7 | 52.9 | 84 23.4 | 30.4 | 113 18.9 | 48.2 | Antares | 112 18.4 | S26 28.8 |
| 17 | 93 54.2 | 116 37.4 | 29.3 | 124 33.3 | 52.3 | 99 25.4 | 30.2 | 128 21.2 | 48.2 | | | |
| 18 | 108 56.7 | 131 37.2 | S 9 28.5 | 139 34.0 | S13 51.7 | 114 27.3 | S 3 30.0 | 143 23.4 | S14 48.1 | Arcturus | 145 49.7 | N19 03.9 |
| 19 | 123 59.1 | 146 37.0 | 27.7 | 154 34.6 | 51.1 | 129 29.2 | 29.8 | 158 25.7 | 48.1 | Atria | 107 14.3 | S69 03.8 |
| 20 | 139 01.6 | 161 36.8 | 26.9 | 169 35.2 | 50.4 | 144 31.2 | 29.6 | 173 28.0 | 48.0 | Avior | 234 15.5 | S59 35.1 |
| 21 | 154 04.1 | 176 36.7 .. | 26.1 | 184 35.9 .. | 49.8 | 159 33.1 .. | 29.3 | 188 30.2 .. | 47.9 | Bellatrix | 278 25.5 | N 6 22.1 |
| 22 | 169 06.5 | 191 36.5 | 25.3 | 199 36.5 | 49.2 | 174 35.0 | 29.1 | 203 32.5 | 47.9 | Betelgeuse | 270 54.7 | N 7 24.6 |
| 23 | 184 09.0 | 206 36.3 | 24.5 | 214 37.1 | 48.6 | 189 37.0 | 28.9 | 218 34.8 | 47.8 | | | |
| 11 00 | 199 11.5 | 221 36.1 | S 9 23.7 | 229 37.7 | S13 47.9 | 204 38.9 | S 3 28.7 | 233 37.0 | S14 47.8 | Canopus | 263 53.6 | S52 42.7 |
| 01 | 214 13.9 | 236 36.0 | 22.8 | 244 38.4 | 47.3 | 219 40.9 | 28.4 | 248 39.3 | 47.7 | Capella | 280 25.5 | N46 01.3 |
| 02 | 229 16.4 | 251 35.8 | 22.0 | 259 39.0 | 46.7 | 234 42.8 | 28.2 | 263 41.5 | 47.6 | Deneb | 49 27.5 | N45 21.2 |
| 03 | 244 18.9 | 266 35.6 .. | 21.2 | 274 39.6 .. | 46.1 | 249 44.7 .. | 28.0 | 278 43.8 .. | 47.6 | Denebola | 182 27.0 | N14 26.9 |
| 04 | 259 21.3 | 281 35.4 | 20.4 | 289 40.2 | 45.5 | 264 46.7 | 27.8 | 293 46.1 | 47.5 | Diphda | 348 49.9 | S17 52.1 |
| 05 | 274 23.8 | 296 35.3 | 19.6 | 304 40.9 | 44.8 | 279 48.6 | 27.6 | 308 48.3 | 47.5 | | | |
| 06 | 289 26.3 | 311 35.1 | S 9 18.8 | 319 41.5 | S13 44.2 | 294 50.5 | S 3 27.3 | 323 50.6 | S14 47.4 | Dubhe | 193 43.3 | N61 38.0 |
| 07 | 304 28.7 | 326 34.9 | 17.9 | 334 42.1 | 43.6 | 309 52.5 | 27.1 | 338 52.9 | 47.3 | Elnath | 278 04.9 | N28 37.6 |
| 08 | 319 31.2 | 341 34.7 | 17.1 | 349 42.8 | 43.0 | 324 54.4 | 26.9 | 353 55.1 | 47.3 | Eltanin | 90 43.0 | N51 28.8 |
| M 09 | 334 33.6 | 356 34.5 .. | 16.3 | 4 43.4 .. | 42.3 | 339 56.4 .. | 26.7 | 8 57.4 .. | 47.2 | Enif | 33 41.2 | N 9 58.4 |
| O 10 | 349 36.1 | 11 34.4 | 15.5 | 19 44.0 | 41.7 | 354 58.3 | 26.5 | 23 59.7 | 47.2 | Fomalhaut | 15 17.3 | S29 30.4 |
| N 11 | 4 38.6 | 26 34.2 | 14.7 | 34 44.6 | 41.1 | 10 00.2 | 26.2 | 39 01.9 | 47.1 | | | |
| D 12 | 19 41.0 | 41 34.0 | S 9 13.8 | 49 45.3 | S13 40.5 | 25 02.2 | S 3 26.0 | 54 04.2 | S14 47.0 | Gacrux | 171 53.6 | S57 14.3 |
| A 13 | 34 43.5 | 56 33.8 | 13.0 | 64 45.9 | 39.8 | 40 04.1 | 25.8 | 69 06.5 | 47.0 | Gienah | 175 45.6 | S17 40.0 |
| Y 14 | 49 46.0 | 71 33.7 | 12.2 | 79 46.5 | 39.2 | 55 06.1 | 25.6 | 84 08.7 | 46.9 | Hadar | 148 38.6 | S60 28.7 |
| 15 | 64 48.4 | 86 33.5 .. | 11.4 | 94 47.2 .. | 38.6 | 70 08.0 .. | 25.4 | 99 11.0 .. | 46.9 | Hamal | 327 54.1 | N23 33.9 |
| 16 | 79 50.9 | 101 33.3 | 10.6 | 109 47.8 | 38.0 | 85 09.9 | 25.1 | 114 13.3 | 46.8 | Kaus Aust. | 83 35.4 | S34 22.4 |
| 17 | 94 53.4 | 116 33.1 | 09.7 | 124 48.4 | 37.3 | 100 11.9 | 24.9 | 129 15.5 | 46.7 | | | |
| 18 | 109 55.8 | 131 32.9 | S 9 08.9 | 139 49.1 | S13 36.7 | 115 13.8 | S 3 24.7 | 144 17.8 | S14 46.7 | Kochab | 137 18.7 | N74 03.7 |
| 19 | 124 58.3 | 146 32.8 | 08.1 | 154 49.7 | 36.1 | 130 15.8 | 24.5 | 159 20.1 | 46.6 | Markab | 13 32.4 | N15 19.2 |
| 20 | 140 00.7 | 161 32.6 | 07.3 | 169 50.3 | 35.5 | 145 17.7 | 24.3 | 174 22.3 | 46.6 | Menkar | 314 08.8 | N 4 10.4 |
| 21 | 155 03.2 | 176 32.4 .. | 06.4 | 184 50.9 .. | 34.8 | 160 19.6 .. | 24.0 | 189 24.6 .. | 46.5 | Menkent | 147 59.9 | S36 28.8 |
| 22 | 170 05.7 | 191 32.2 | 05.6 | 199 51.6 | 34.2 | 175 21.6 | 23.8 | 204 26.9 | 46.4 | Miaplacidus | 221 38.3 | S69 48.7 |
| 23 | 185 08.1 | 206 32.1 | 04.8 | 214 52.2 | 33.6 | 190 23.5 | 23.6 | 219 29.1 | 46.4 | | | |
| 12 00 | 200 10.6 | 221 31.9 | S 9 04.0 | 229 52.8 | S13 33.0 | 205 25.5 | S 3 23.4 | 234 31.4 | S14 46.3 | Mirfak | 308 31.9 | N49 56.4 |
| 01 | 215 13.1 | 236 31.7 | 03.1 | 244 53.5 | 32.3 | 220 27.4 | 23.1 | 249 33.7 | 46.3 | Nunki | 75 50.5 | S26 16.1 |
| 02 | 230 15.5 | 251 31.5 | 02.3 | 259 54.1 | 31.7 | 235 29.3 | 22.9 | 264 35.9 | 46.2 | Peacock | 53 09.5 | S56 39.6 |
| 03 | 245 18.0 | 266 31.3 .. | 01.5 | 274 54.7 .. | 31.1 | 250 31.3 .. | 22.7 | 279 38.2 .. | 46.1 | Pollux | 243 20.1 | N27 58.4 |
| 04 | 260 20.5 | 281 31.2 | 9 00.6 | 289 55.4 | 30.4 | 265 33.2 | 22.5 | 294 40.5 | 46.1 | Procyon | 244 53.2 | N 5 10.0 |
| 05 | 275 22.9 | 296 31.0 | 8 59.8 | 304 56.0 | 29.8 | 280 35.2 | 22.3 | 309 42.7 | 46.0 | | | |
| 06 | 290 25.4 | 311 30.8 | S 8 59.0 | 319 56.6 | S13 29.2 | 295 37.1 | S 3 22.0 | 324 45.0 | S14 46.0 | Rasalhague | 96 00.5 | N12 32.5 |
| 07 | 305 27.9 | 326 30.6 | 58.2 | 334 57.3 | 28.6 | 310 39.0 | 21.8 | 339 47.3 | 45.9 | Regulus | 207 36.7 | N11 51.5 |
| 08 | 320 30.3 | 341 30.5 | 57.3 | 349 57.9 | 27.9 | 325 41.0 | 21.6 | 354 49.5 | 45.8 | Rigel | 281 06.2 | S 8 10.7 |
| T 09 | 335 32.8 | 356 30.3 .. | 56.5 | 4 58.5 .. | 27.3 | 340 42.9 .. | 21.4 | 9 51.8 .. | 45.8 | Rigil Kent. | 139 42.8 | S60 55.5 |
| U 10 | 350 35.2 | 11 30.1 | 55.7 | 19 59.2 | 26.7 | 355 44.9 | 21.2 | 24 54.1 | 45.7 | Sabik | 102 05.2 | S15 45.2 |
| E 11 | 5 37.7 | 26 29.9 | 54.8 | 34 59.8 | 26.0 | 10 46.8 | 20.9 | 39 56.3 | 45.7 | | | |
| S 12 | 20 40.2 | 41 29.7 | S 8 54.0 | 50 00.4 | S13 25.4 | 25 48.7 | S 3 20.7 | 54 58.6 | S14 45.6 | Schedar | 349 34.2 | N56 39.3 |
| D 13 | 35 42.6 | 56 29.6 | 53.2 | 65 01.1 | 24.8 | 40 50.7 | 20.5 | 70 00.9 | 45.5 | Shaula | 96 13.3 | S37 07.1 |
| A 14 | 50 45.1 | 71 29.4 | 52.3 | 80 01.7 | 24.2 | 55 52.6 | 20.3 | 85 03.1 | 45.5 | Sirius | 258 28.3 | S16 45.0 |
| Y 15 | 65 47.6 | 86 29.2 .. | 51.5 | 95 02.3 .. | 23.5 | 70 54.6 .. | 20.1 | 100 05.4 .. | 45.4 | Spica | 158 24.4 | S11 16.7 |
| 16 | 80 50.0 | 101 29.0 | 50.7 | 110 03.0 | 22.9 | 85 56.5 | 19.8 | 115 07.7 | 45.4 | Suhail | 222 47.8 | S43 31.6 |
| 17 | 95 52.5 | 116 28.9 | 49.8 | 125 03.6 | 22.3 | 100 58.5 | 19.6 | 130 10.0 | 45.3 | | | |
| 18 | 110 55.0 | 131 28.7 | S 8 49.0 | 140 04.2 | S13 21.6 | 116 00.4 | S 3 19.4 | 145 12.2 | S14 45.3 | Vega | 80 34.7 | N38 47.9 |
| 19 | 125 57.4 | 146 28.5 | 48.1 | 155 04.9 | 21.0 | 131 02.3 | 19.2 | 160 14.5 | 45.2 | Zuben'ubi | 136 58.2 | S16 08.1 |
| 20 | 140 59.9 | 161 28.3 | 47.3 | 170 05.5 | 20.4 | 146 04.3 | 19.0 | 175 16.8 | 45.1 | | SHA | Mer. Pass. |
| 21 | 156 02.4 | 176 28.1 .. | 46.5 | 185 06.1 .. | 19.7 | 161 06.2 .. | 18.7 | 190 19.0 .. | 45.1 | | ° ′ | h m |
| 22 | 171 04.8 | 191 28.0 | 45.6 | 200 06.8 | 19.1 | 176 08.2 | 18.5 | 205 21.3 .. | 45.0 | Venus | 22 24.7 | 9 14 |
| 23 | 186 07.3 | 206 27.8 | 44.8 | 215 07.4 | 18.5 | 191 10.1 | 18.3 | 220 23.6 | 45.0 | Mars | 30 26.3 | 8 41 |
| | h m | | | | | | | | | Jupiter | 5 27.4 | 10 20 |
| Mer. Pass. 10 41.5 | | v −0.2 | d 0.8 | v 0.6 | d 0.6 | v 1.9 | d 0.2 | v 2.3 | d 0.1 | Saturn | 34 25.5 | 8 24 |

| UT | SUN GHA | SUN Dec | MOON GHA | v | MOON Dec | d | HP |
|---|---|---|---|---|---|---|---|
| d h | ° ′ | ° ′ | ° ′ | ′ | ° ′ | ′ | ′ |
| 10 00 | 179 38.3 | N 7 51.6 | 77 04.7 | 10.8 | N25 11.4 | 5.1 | 54.6 |
| 01 | 194 38.4 | 52.6 | 91 34.5 | 10.8 | 25 06.3 | 5.3 | 54.6 |
| 02 | 209 38.6 | 53.5 | 106 04.3 | 10.8 | 25 01.0 | 5.3 | 54.7 |
| 03 | 224 38.8 | .. 54.4 | 120 34.1 | 10.9 | 24 55.7 | 5.5 | 54.7 |
| 04 | 239 38.9 | 55.3 | 135 04.0 | 10.9 | 24 50.2 | 5.6 | 54.7 |
| 05 | 254 39.1 | 56.3 | 149 33.9 | 10.9 | 24 44.6 | 5.7 | 54.7 |
| 06 | 269 39.3 | N 7 57.2 | 164 03.8 | 10.9 | N24 38.9 | 5.9 | 54.7 |
| 07 | 284 39.4 | 58.1 | 178 33.7 | 11.0 | 24 33.0 | 6.0 | 54.8 |
| 08 | 299 39.6 | 7 59.0 | 193 03.7 | 11.0 | 24 27.0 | 6.1 | 54.8 |
| S 09 | 314 39.8 | 8 00.0 | 207 33.7 | 11.0 | 24 20.9 | 6.2 | 54.8 |
| U 10 | 329 39.9 | 00.9 | 222 03.7 | 11.1 | 24 14.7 | 6.3 | 54.8 |
| N 11 | 344 40.1 | 01.8 | 236 33.8 | 11.1 | 24 08.4 | 6.4 | 54.8 |
| D 12 | 359 40.3 | N 8 02.7 | 251 03.9 | 11.1 | N24 02.0 | 6.6 | 54.8 |
| A 13 | 14 40.4 | 03.6 | 265 34.0 | 11.2 | 23 55.4 | 6.7 | 54.9 |
| Y 14 | 29 40.6 | 04.6 | 280 04.2 | 11.1 | 23 48.7 | 6.8 | 54.9 |
| 15 | 44 40.8 | .. 05.5 | 294 34.3 | 11.3 | 23 41.9 | 6.9 | 54.9 |
| 16 | 59 40.9 | 06.4 | 309 04.6 | 11.2 | 23 35.0 | 7.1 | 54.9 |
| 17 | 74 41.1 | 07.3 | 323 34.8 | 11.3 | 23 27.9 | 7.1 | 54.9 |
| 18 | 89 41.3 | N 8 08.3 | 338 05.1 | 11.3 | N23 20.8 | 7.3 | 55.0 |
| 19 | 104 41.4 | 09.2 | 352 35.4 | 11.4 | 23 13.5 | 7.3 | 55.0 |
| 20 | 119 41.6 | 10.1 | 7 05.8 | 11.3 | 23 06.2 | 7.5 | 55.0 |
| 21 | 134 41.8 | .. 11.0 | 21 36.1 | 11.4 | 22 58.7 | 7.7 | 55.0 |
| 22 | 149 41.9 | 11.9 | 36 06.5 | 11.5 | 22 51.0 | 7.7 | 55.0 |
| 23 | 164 42.1 | 12.9 | 50 37.0 | 11.5 | 22 43.3 | 7.8 | 55.1 |
| 11 00 | 179 42.3 | N 8 13.8 | 65 07.5 | 11.5 | N22 35.5 | 8.0 | 55.1 |
| 01 | 194 42.4 | 14.7 | 79 38.0 | 11.5 | 22 27.5 | 8.0 | 55.1 |
| 02 | 209 42.6 | 15.6 | 94 08.5 | 11.6 | 22 19.5 | 8.2 | 55.1 |
| 03 | 224 42.8 | .. 16.5 | 108 39.1 | 11.6 | 22 11.3 | 8.3 | 55.2 |
| 04 | 239 42.9 | 17.5 | 123 09.7 | 11.7 | 22 03.0 | 8.4 | 55.2 |
| 05 | 254 43.1 | 18.4 | 137 40.4 | 11.6 | 21 54.6 | 8.5 | 55.2 |
| 06 | 269 43.2 | N 8 19.3 | 152 11.0 | 11.8 | N21 46.1 | 8.6 | 55.2 |
| 07 | 284 43.4 | 20.2 | 166 41.8 | 11.7 | 21 37.5 | 8.7 | 55.3 |
| 08 | 299 43.6 | 21.1 | 181 12.5 | 11.8 | 21 28.8 | 8.8 | 55.3 |
| M 09 | 314 43.7 | .. 22.1 | 195 43.3 | 11.8 | 21 20.0 | 8.9 | 55.3 |
| O 10 | 329 43.9 | 23.0 | 210 14.1 | 11.8 | 21 11.1 | 9.1 | 55.3 |
| N 11 | 344 44.1 | 23.9 | 224 44.9 | 11.9 | 21 02.0 | 9.1 | 55.4 |
| D 12 | 359 44.2 | N 8 24.8 | 239 15.8 | 11.9 | N20 52.9 | 9.3 | 55.4 |
| A 13 | 14 44.4 | 25.7 | 253 46.7 | 12.0 | 20 43.6 | 9.3 | 55.4 |
| Y 14 | 29 44.6 | 26.6 | 268 17.7 | 12.0 | 20 34.3 | 9.5 | 55.4 |
| 15 | 44 44.7 | .. 27.6 | 282 48.7 | 12.0 | 20 24.8 | 9.6 | 55.5 |
| 16 | 59 44.9 | 28.5 | 297 19.7 | 12.1 | 20 15.2 | 9.6 | 55.5 |
| 17 | 74 45.1 | 29.4 | 311 50.8 | 12.0 | 20 05.6 | 9.8 | 55.5 |
| 18 | 89 45.2 | N 8 30.3 | 326 21.8 | 12.1 | N19 55.8 | 9.9 | 55.5 |
| 19 | 104 45.4 | 31.2 | 340 52.9 | 12.2 | 19 45.9 | 10.0 | 55.6 |
| 20 | 119 45.5 | 32.1 | 355 24.1 | 12.2 | 19 35.9 | 10.0 | 55.6 |
| 21 | 134 45.7 | .. 33.1 | 9 55.3 | 12.2 | 19 25.9 | 10.2 | 55.6 |
| 22 | 149 45.9 | 34.0 | 24 26.5 | 12.2 | 19 15.7 | 10.3 | 55.6 |
| 23 | 164 46.0 | 34.9 | 38 57.7 | 12.3 | 19 05.4 | 10.4 | 55.7 |
| 12 00 | 179 46.2 | N 8 35.8 | 53 29.0 | 12.3 | N18 55.0 | 10.4 | 55.7 |
| 01 | 194 46.4 | 36.7 | 68 00.3 | 12.4 | 18 44.6 | 10.6 | 55.7 |
| 02 | 209 46.5 | 37.6 | 82 31.7 | 12.3 | 18 34.0 | 10.7 | 55.8 |
| 03 | 224 46.7 | .. 38.5 | 97 03.0 | 12.4 | 18 23.3 | 10.7 | 55.8 |
| 04 | 239 46.8 | 39.5 | 111 34.4 | 12.5 | 18 12.6 | 10.9 | 55.8 |
| 05 | 254 47.0 | 40.4 | 126 05.9 | 12.4 | 18 01.7 | 10.9 | 55.8 |
| 06 | 269 47.2 | N 8 41.3 | 140 37.3 | 12.5 | N17 50.8 | 11.1 | 55.9 |
| 07 | 284 47.3 | 42.2 | 155 08.8 | 12.5 | 17 39.7 | 11.1 | 55.9 |
| T 08 | 299 47.5 | 43.1 | 169 40.3 | 12.6 | 17 28.6 | 11.2 | 55.9 |
| U 09 | 314 47.7 | .. 44.0 | 184 11.9 | 12.6 | 17 17.4 | 11.4 | 56.0 |
| E 10 | 329 47.8 | 44.9 | 198 43.5 | 12.6 | 17 06.0 | 11.4 | 56.0 |
| S 11 | 344 48.0 | 45.8 | 213 15.1 | 12.6 | 16 54.6 | 11.5 | 56.0 |
| D 12 | 359 48.1 | N 8 46.8 | 227 46.7 | 12.6 | N16 43.1 | 11.6 | 56.0 |
| A 13 | 14 48.3 | 47.7 | 242 18.3 | 12.7 | 16 31.5 | 11.7 | 56.1 |
| Y 14 | 29 48.5 | 48.6 | 256 50.0 | 12.7 | 16 19.8 | 11.7 | 56.1 |
| 15 | 44 48.6 | .. 49.5 | 271 21.7 | 12.8 | 16 08.1 | 11.9 | 56.1 |
| 16 | 59 48.8 | 50.4 | 285 53.5 | 12.7 | 15 56.2 | 11.9 | 56.2 |
| 17 | 74 48.9 | 51.3 | 300 25.2 | 12.8 | 15 44.3 | 12.0 | 56.2 |
| 18 | 89 49.1 | N 8 52.2 | 314 57.0 | 12.8 | N15 32.3 | 12.2 | 56.2 |
| 19 | 104 49.3 | 53.1 | 329 28.8 | 12.9 | 15 20.1 | 12.2 | 56.3 |
| 20 | 119 49.4 | 54.0 | 344 00.7 | 12.8 | 15 07.9 | 12.2 | 56.3 |
| 21 | 134 49.6 | .. 54.9 | 358 32.5 | 12.9 | 14 55.7 | 12.4 | 56.3 |
| 22 | 149 49.7 | 55.8 | 13 04.4 | 12.9 | 14 43.3 | 12.5 | 56.4 |
| 23 | 164 49.9 | 56.8 | 27 36.3 | 12.9 | N14 30.8 | 12.5 | 56.4 |
| | SD 16.0 | d 0.9 | SD 14.9 | | 15.1 | | 15.3 |

| Lat. | Naut. | Civil | Sunrise | Moonrise 10 | 11 | 12 | 13 |
|---|---|---|---|---|---|---|---|
| ° | h m | h m | h m | h m | h m | h m | h m |
| N 72 | //// | 02 33 | 04 02 | ▢ | ▢ | 10 06 | 13 03 |
| N 70 | //// | 03 01 | 04 16 | ▢ | ▢ | 11 03 | 13 24 |
| 68 | 01 34 | 03 21 | 04 27 | ▢ | 09 01 | 11 37 | 13 40 |
| 66 | 02 11 | 03 37 | 04 36 | ▢ | 09 59 | 12 01 | 13 52 |
| 64 | 02 37 | 03 51 | 04 43 | 08 38 | 10 33 | 12 20 | 14 03 |
| 62 | 02 57 | 04 01 | 04 50 | 09 19 | 10 57 | 12 35 | 14 12 |
| 60 | 03 12 | 04 11 | 04 56 | 09 47 | 11 16 | 12 47 | 14 19 |
| N 58 | 03 25 | 04 19 | 05 01 | 10 09 | 11 32 | 12 58 | 14 26 |
| 56 | 03 36 | 04 26 | 05 05 | 10 27 | 11 45 | 13 08 | 14 32 |
| 54 | 03 45 | 04 32 | 05 09 | 10 41 | 11 57 | 13 16 | 14 37 |
| 52 | 03 54 | 04 37 | 05 12 | 10 54 | 12 07 | 13 24 | 14 42 |
| 50 | 04 01 | 04 42 | 05 16 | 11 06 | 12 16 | 13 30 | 14 46 |
| 45 | 04 16 | 04 52 | 05 23 | 11 29 | 12 36 | 13 44 | 14 55 |
| N 40 | 04 28 | 05 01 | 05 29 | 11 48 | 12 51 | 13 56 | 15 03 |
| 35 | 04 37 | 05 08 | 05 33 | 12 04 | 13 04 | 14 06 | 15 09 |
| 30 | 04 45 | 05 14 | 05 37 | 12 17 | 13 16 | 14 15 | 15 15 |
| 20 | 04 57 | 05 23 | 05 45 | 12 40 | 13 35 | 14 30 | 15 25 |
| N 10 | 05 06 | 05 31 | 05 52 | 13 00 | 13 52 | 14 43 | 15 33 |
| 0 | 05 13 | 05 37 | 05 58 | 13 19 | 14 08 | 14 55 | 15 41 |
| S 10 | 05 18 | 05 42 | 06 04 | 13 37 | 14 23 | 15 07 | 15 49 |
| 20 | 05 22 | 05 48 | 06 10 | 13 57 | 14 40 | 15 20 | 15 58 |
| 30 | 05 25 | 05 53 | 06 17 | 14 20 | 14 59 | 15 34 | 16 07 |
| 35 | 05 26 | 05 55 | 06 21 | 14 33 | 15 10 | 15 43 | 16 13 |
| 40 | 05 26 | 05 58 | 06 25 | 14 48 | 15 23 | 15 52 | 16 19 |
| 45 | 05 26 | 06 00 | 06 30 | 15 07 | 15 38 | 16 04 | 16 26 |
| S 50 | 05 26 | 06 03 | 06 36 | 15 29 | 15 56 | 16 17 | 16 35 |
| 52 | 05 26 | 06 05 | 06 39 | 15 40 | 16 04 | 16 23 | 16 39 |
| 54 | 05 25 | 06 06 | 06 42 | 15 52 | 16 14 | 16 30 | 16 43 |
| 56 | 05 25 | 06 08 | 06 45 | 16 06 | 16 25 | 16 38 | 16 48 |
| 58 | 05 24 | 06 09 | 06 49 | 16 22 | 16 37 | 16 46 | 16 54 |
| S 60 | 05 23 | 06 11 | 06 53 | 16 42 | 16 51 | 16 56 | 17 00 |

| Lat. | Sunset | Civil | Naut. | Moonset 10 | 11 | 12 | 13 |
|---|---|---|---|---|---|---|---|
| ° | h m | h m | h m | h m | h m | h m | h m |
| N 72 | 20 04 | 21 36 | //// | ▢ | ▢ | 07 41 | 06 21 |
| N 70 | 19 49 | 21 06 | //// | ▢ | ▢ | 06 42 | 05 59 |
| 68 | 19 38 | 20 44 | 22 38 | ▢ | 07 03 | 06 07 | 05 41 |
| 66 | 19 29 | 20 28 | 21 56 | ▢ | 06 04 | 05 41 | 05 27 |
| 64 | 19 21 | 20 14 | 21 29 | 05 42 | 05 30 | 05 22 | 05 15 |
| 62 | 19 14 | 20 03 | 21 09 | 05 00 | 05 04 | 05 05 | 05 05 |
| 60 | 19 08 | 19 53 | 20 53 | 04 32 | 04 45 | 04 52 | 04 56 |
| N 58 | 19 03 | 19 45 | 20 39 | 04 10 | 04 28 | 04 40 | 04 48 |
| 56 | 18 59 | 19 38 | 20 28 | 03 52 | 04 14 | 04 30 | 04 41 |
| 54 | 18 54 | 19 32 | 20 18 | 03 37 | 04 02 | 04 21 | 04 35 |
| 52 | 18 51 | 19 26 | 20 10 | 03 23 | 03 51 | 04 13 | 04 30 |
| 50 | 18 47 | 19 21 | 20 03 | 03 12 | 03 42 | 04 05 | 04 25 |
| 45 | 18 40 | 19 11 | 19 47 | 02 48 | 03 21 | 03 50 | 04 14 |
| N 40 | 18 34 | 19 02 | 19 35 | 02 28 | 03 05 | 03 37 | 04 05 |
| 35 | 18 29 | 18 55 | 19 26 | 02 12 | 02 51 | 03 26 | 03 57 |
| 30 | 18 25 | 18 49 | 19 18 | 01 58 | 02 39 | 03 16 | 03 50 |
| 20 | 18 17 | 18 39 | 19 06 | 01 34 | 02 18 | 02 59 | 03 38 |
| N 10 | 18 10 | 18 32 | 18 57 | 01 13 | 02 00 | 02 44 | 03 27 |
| 0 | 18 04 | 18 25 | 18 50 | 00 53 | 01 42 | 02 30 | 03 17 |
| S 10 | 17 58 | 18 20 | 18 44 | 00 33 | 01 25 | 02 16 | 03 07 |
| 20 | 17 52 | 18 14 | 18 40 | 00 12 | 01 07 | 02 01 | 02 56 |
| 30 | 17 45 | 18 09 | 18 37 | 24 45 | 00 45 | 01 44 | 02 44 |
| 35 | 17 41 | 18 07 | 18 36 | 24 32 | 00 32 | 01 34 | 02 37 |
| 40 | 17 37 | 18 04 | 18 35 | 24 18 | 00 18 | 01 22 | 02 28 |
| 45 | 17 31 | 18 01 | 18 35 | 24 00 | 00 00 | 01 08 | 02 18 |
| S 50 | 17 25 | 17 58 | 18 35 | 23 39 | 24 51 | 00 51 | 02 06 |
| 52 | 17 22 | 17 56 | 18 35 | 23 28 | 24 43 | 00 43 | 02 01 |
| 54 | 17 19 | 17 55 | 18 36 | 23 17 | 24 34 | 00 34 | 01 54 |
| 56 | 17 16 | 17 54 | 18 36 | 23 03 | 24 24 | 00 24 | 01 48 |
| 58 | 17 12 | 17 52 | 18 37 | 22 47 | 24 13 | 00 13 | 01 40 |
| S 60 | 17 08 | 17 50 | 18 38 | 22 28 | 23 59 | 25 31 | 01 31 |

| | SUN | | | MOON | | | |
|---|---|---|---|---|---|---|---|
| Day | Eqn. of Time 00h | 12h | Mer. Pass. | Mer. Pass. Upper | Lower | Age | Phase |
| d | m s | m s | h m | h m | h m | d | % |
| 10 | 01 27 | 01 19 | 12 01 | 19 31 | 07 06 | 09 | 62 |
| 11 | 01 11 | 01 03 | 12 01 | 20 19 | 07 55 | 10 | 71 |
| 12 | 00 56 | 00 48 | 12 01 | 21 06 | 08 43 | 11 | 80 |

| UT | ARIES GHA | VENUS −4.2 GHA | Dec | MARS +1.0 GHA | Dec | JUPITER −2.1 GHA | Dec | SATURN +0.7 GHA | Dec | STARS Name | SHA | Dec |
|---|---|---|---|---|---|---|---|---|---|---|---|---|
| **13 00** | 201 09.7 | 221 27.6 | S 8 43.9 | 230 08.0 | S13 17.8 | 206 12.0 | S 3 18.1 | 235 25.8 | S14 44.9 | Acamar | 315 13.9 | S40 13.1 |
| 01 | 216 12.2 | 236 27.4 | 43.1 | 245 08.7 | 17.2 | 221 14.0 | 17.9 | 250 28.1 | 44.8 | Achernar | 335 22.5 | S57 07.6 |
| 02 | 231 14.7 | 251 27.2 | 42.3 | 260 09.3 | 16.6 | 236 15.9 | 17.6 | 265 30.4 | 44.8 | Acrux | 173 01.9 | S63 13.4 |
| 03 | 246 17.1 | 266 27.1 .. | 41.4 | 275 09.9 .. | 15.9 | 251 17.9 .. | 17.4 | 280 32.7 .. | 44.7 | Adhara | 255 07.7 | S29 00.4 |
| 04 | 261 19.6 | 281 26.9 | 40.6 | 290 10.6 | 15.3 | 266 19.8 | 17.2 | 295 34.9 | 44.7 | Aldebaran | 290 42.5 | N16 33.1 |
| 05 | 276 22.1 | 296 26.7 | 39.7 | 305 11.2 | 14.7 | 281 21.8 | 17.0 | 310 37.2 | 44.6 | | | |
| 06 | 291 24.5 | 311 26.5 | S 8 38.9 | 320 11.8 | S13 14.1 | 296 23.7 | S 3 16.8 | 325 39.5 | S14 44.5 | Alioth | 166 14.4 | N55 50.4 |
| W 07 | 306 27.0 | 326 26.4 | 38.0 | 335 12.5 | 13.4 | 311 25.6 | 16.6 | 340 41.7 | 44.5 | Alkaid | 152 53.3 | N49 12.1 |
| E 08 | 321 29.5 | 341 26.2 | 37.2 | 350 13.1 | 12.8 | 326 27.6 | 16.3 | 355 44.0 | 44.4 | Alnair | 27 36.1 | S46 51.2 |
| D 09 | 336 31.9 | 356 26.0 .. | 36.3 | 5 13.7 .. | 12.2 | 341 29.5 .. | 16.1 | 10 46.3 .. | 44.4 | Alnilam | 275 40.2 | S 1 11.4 |
| N 10 | 351 34.4 | 11 25.8 | 35.5 | 20 14.4 | 11.5 | 356 31.5 | 15.9 | 25 48.6 | 44.3 | Alphard | 217 49.8 | S 8 45.4 |
| E 11 | 6 36.8 | 26 25.6 | 34.7 | 35 15.0 | 10.9 | 11 33.4 | 15.7 | 40 50.8 | 44.3 | | | |
| S 12 | 21 39.3 | 41 25.5 | S 8 33.8 | 50 15.6 | S13 10.2 | 26 35.4 | S 3 15.5 | 55 53.1 | S14 44.2 | Alphecca | 126 05.4 | N26 38.3 |
| D 13 | 36 41.8 | 56 25.3 | 33.0 | 65 16.3 | 09.6 | 41 37.3 | 15.2 | 70 55.4 | 44.1 | Alpheratz | 357 37.4 | N29 12.5 |
| A 14 | 51 44.2 | 71 25.1 | 32.1 | 80 16.9 | 09.0 | 56 39.2 | 15.0 | 85 57.6 | 44.1 | Altair | 62 02.2 | N 8 55.4 |
| Y 15 | 66 46.7 | 86 24.9 .. | 31.3 | 95 17.6 .. | 08.3 | 71 41.2 .. | 14.8 | 100 59.9 .. | 44.0 | Ankaa | 353 09.8 | S42 11.2 |
| 16 | 81 49.2 | 101 24.7 | 30.4 | 110 18.2 | 07.7 | 86 43.1 | 14.6 | 116 02.2 | 44.0 | Antares | 112 18.4 | S26 28.8 |
| 17 | 96 51.6 | 116 24.6 | 29.6 | 125 18.8 | 07.1 | 101 45.1 | 14.4 | 131 04.5 | 43.9 | | | |
| 18 | 111 54.1 | 131 24.4 | S 8 28.7 | 140 19.5 | S13 06.4 | 116 47.0 | S 3 14.1 | 146 06.7 | S14 43.8 | Arcturus | 145 49.7 | N19 03.9 |
| 19 | 126 56.6 | 146 24.2 | 27.9 | 155 20.1 | 05.8 | 131 49.0 | 13.9 | 161 09.0 | 43.8 | Atria | 107 14.3 | S69 03.8 |
| 20 | 141 59.0 | 161 24.0 | 27.0 | 170 20.7 | 05.2 | 146 50.9 | 13.7 | 176 11.3 | 43.7 | Avior | 234 15.5 | S59 35.1 |
| 21 | 157 01.5 | 176 23.8 .. | 26.2 | 185 21.4 .. | 04.5 | 161 52.8 .. | 13.5 | 191 13.5 .. | 43.7 | Bellatrix | 278 25.5 | N 6 22.1 |
| 22 | 172 04.0 | 191 23.7 | 25.3 | 200 22.0 | 03.9 | 176 54.8 | 13.3 | 206 15.8 | 43.6 | Betelgeuse | 270 54.7 | N 7 24.6 |
| 23 | 187 06.4 | 206 23.5 | 24.5 | 215 22.7 | 03.3 | 191 56.7 | 13.0 | 221 18.1 | 43.6 | | | |
| **14 00** | 202 08.9 | 221 23.3 | S 8 23.6 | 230 23.3 | S13 02.6 | 206 58.7 | S 3 12.8 | 236 20.4 | S14 43.5 | Canopus | 263 53.6 | S52 42.7 |
| 01 | 217 11.3 | 236 23.1 | 22.7 | 245 23.9 | 02.0 | 222 00.6 | 12.6 | 251 22.6 | 43.4 | Capella | 280 25.5 | N46 01.3 |
| 02 | 232 13.8 | 251 22.9 | 21.9 | 260 24.6 | 01.3 | 237 02.6 | 12.4 | 266 24.9 | 43.4 | Deneb | 49 27.4 | N45 21.2 |
| 03 | 247 16.3 | 266 22.8 .. | 21.0 | 275 25.2 .. | 00.7 | 252 04.5 .. | 12.2 | 281 27.2 .. | 43.3 | Denebola | 182 27.0 | N14 26.9 |
| 04 | 262 18.7 | 281 22.6 | 20.2 | 290 25.8 | 13 00.1 | 267 06.5 | 12.0 | 296 29.5 | 43.3 | Diphda | 348 49.9 | S17 52.0 |
| 05 | 277 21.2 | 296 22.4 | 19.3 | 305 26.5 | 12 59.4 | 282 08.4 | 11.7 | 311 31.7 | 43.2 | | | |
| 06 | 292 23.7 | 311 22.2 | S 8 18.5 | 320 27.1 | S12 58.8 | 297 10.3 | S 3 11.5 | 326 34.0 | S14 43.2 | Dubhe | 193 43.3 | N61 38.1 |
| T 07 | 307 26.1 | 326 22.0 | 17.6 | 335 27.8 | 58.2 | 312 12.3 | 11.3 | 341 36.3 | 43.1 | Elnath | 278 04.9 | N28 37.6 |
| H 08 | 322 28.6 | 341 21.9 | 16.7 | 350 28.4 | 57.5 | 327 14.2 | 11.1 | 356 38.6 | 43.0 | Eltanin | 90 43.0 | N51 28.8 |
| U 09 | 337 31.1 | 356 21.7 .. | 15.9 | 5 29.0 .. | 56.9 | 342 16.2 .. | 10.9 | 11 40.8 .. | 43.0 | Enif | 33 41.2 | N 9 58.4 |
| R 10 | 352 33.5 | 11 21.5 | 15.0 | 20 29.7 | 56.2 | 357 18.1 | 10.6 | 26 43.1 | 42.9 | Fomalhaut | 15 17.3 | S29 30.3 |
| S 11 | 7 36.0 | 26 21.3 | 14.2 | 35 30.3 | 55.6 | 12 20.1 | 10.4 | 41 45.4 | 42.9 | | | |
| D 12 | 22 38.4 | 41 21.2 | S 8 13.3 | 50 31.0 | S12 55.0 | 27 22.0 | S 3 10.2 | 56 47.6 | S14 42.8 | Gacrux | 171 53.6 | S57 14.3 |
| A 13 | 37 40.9 | 56 21.0 | 12.4 | 65 31.6 | 54.3 | 42 24.0 | 10.0 | 71 49.9 | 42.8 | Gienah | 175 45.6 | S17 40.0 |
| Y 14 | 52 43.4 | 71 20.8 | 11.6 | 80 32.2 | 53.7 | 57 25.9 | 09.8 | 86 52.2 | 42.7 | Hadar | 148 38.6 | S60 28.8 |
| 15 | 67 45.8 | 86 20.6 .. | 10.7 | 95 32.9 .. | 53.0 | 72 27.8 .. | 09.5 | 101 54.5 .. | 42.6 | Hamal | 327 54.1 | N23 33.9 |
| 16 | 82 48.3 | 101 20.4 | 09.9 | 110 33.5 | 52.4 | 87 29.8 | 09.3 | 116 56.7 | 42.6 | Kaus Aust. | 83 35.4 | S34 22.4 |
| 17 | 97 50.8 | 116 20.3 | 09.0 | 125 34.2 | 51.8 | 102 31.7 | 09.1 | 131 59.0 | 42.5 | | | |
| 18 | 112 53.2 | 131 20.1 | S 8 08.1 | 140 34.8 | S12 51.1 | 117 33.7 | S 3 08.9 | 147 01.3 | S14 42.5 | Kochab | 137 18.7 | N74 03.7 |
| 19 | 127 55.7 | 146 19.9 | 07.3 | 155 35.4 | 50.5 | 132 35.6 | 08.7 | 162 03.6 | 42.4 | Markab | 13 32.4 | N15 19.2 |
| 20 | 142 58.2 | 161 19.7 | 06.4 | 170 36.1 | 49.8 | 147 37.6 | 08.5 | 177 05.8 | 42.4 | Menkar | 314 08.8 | N 4 10.4 |
| 21 | 158 00.6 | 176 19.5 .. | 05.5 | 185 36.7 .. | 49.2 | 162 39.5 .. | 08.2 | 192 08.1 .. | 42.3 | Menkent | 147 59.9 | S36 28.8 |
| 22 | 173 03.1 | 191 19.4 | 04.7 | 200 37.4 | 48.6 | 177 41.5 | 08.0 | 207 10.4 | 42.2 | Miaplacidus | 221 38.4 | S69 48.7 |
| 23 | 188 05.6 | 206 19.2 | 03.8 | 215 38.0 | 47.9 | 192 43.4 | 07.8 | 222 12.7 | 42.2 | | | |
| **15 00** | 203 08.0 | 221 19.0 | S 8 02.9 | 230 38.7 | S12 47.3 | 207 45.4 | S 3 07.6 | 237 15.0 | S14 42.1 | Mirfak | 308 31.9 | N49 56.4 |
| 01 | 218 10.5 | 236 18.8 | 02.1 | 245 39.3 | 46.6 | 222 47.3 | 07.4 | 252 17.2 | 42.1 | Nunki | 75 50.5 | S26 16.1 |
| 02 | 233 12.9 | 251 18.6 | 01.2 | 260 39.9 | 46.0 | 237 49.2 | 07.2 | 267 19.5 | 42.0 | Peacock | 53 09.4 | S56 39.6 |
| 03 | 248 15.4 | 266 18.5 | 8 00.3 | 275 40.6 .. | 45.4 | 252 51.2 .. | 06.9 | 282 21.8 .. | 42.0 | Pollux | 243 20.1 | N27 58.4 |
| 04 | 263 17.9 | 281 18.3 | 7 59.5 | 290 41.2 | 44.7 | 267 53.1 | 06.7 | 297 24.1 | 41.9 | Procyon | 244 53.2 | N 5 10.0 |
| 05 | 278 20.3 | 296 18.1 | 58.6 | 305 41.9 | 44.1 | 282 55.1 | 06.5 | 312 26.3 | 41.8 | | | |
| 06 | 293 22.8 | 311 17.9 | S 7 57.7 | 320 42.5 | S12 43.4 | 297 57.0 | S 3 06.3 | 327 28.6 | S14 41.8 | Rasalhague | 96 00.5 | N12 32.5 |
| 07 | 308 25.3 | 326 17.7 | 56.9 | 335 43.1 | 42.8 | 312 59.0 | 06.1 | 342 30.9 | 41.7 | Regulus | 207 36.7 | N11 51.5 |
| F 08 | 323 27.7 | 341 17.6 | 56.0 | 350 43.8 | 42.1 | 328 00.9 | 05.8 | 357 33.2 | 41.7 | Rigel | 281 06.2 | S 8 10.7 |
| R 09 | 338 30.2 | 356 17.4 .. | 55.1 | 5 44.4 .. | 41.5 | 343 02.9 .. | 05.6 | 12 35.4 .. | 41.6 | Rigil Kent. | 139 42.8 | S60 55.5 |
| I 10 | 353 32.7 | 11 17.2 | 54.2 | 20 45.1 | 40.9 | 358 04.8 | 05.4 | 27 37.7 | 41.6 | Sabik | 102 05.2 | S15 45.2 |
| 11 | 8 35.1 | 26 17.0 | 53.4 | 35 45.7 | 40.2 | 13 06.8 | 05.2 | 42 40.0 | 41.5 | | | |
| D 12 | 23 37.6 | 41 16.8 | S 7 52.5 | 50 46.4 | S12 39.6 | 28 08.7 | S 3 05.0 | 57 42.3 | S14 41.5 | Schedar | 349 34.2 | N56 39.3 |
| A 13 | 38 40.1 | 56 16.6 | 51.6 | 65 47.0 | 38.9 | 43 10.7 | 04.8 | 72 44.6 | 41.4 | Shaula | 96 13.2 | S37 07.1 |
| Y 14 | 53 42.5 | 71 16.5 | 50.8 | 80 47.6 | 38.3 | 58 12.6 | 04.5 | 87 46.8 | 41.3 | Sirius | 258 28.3 | S16 45.0 |
| 15 | 68 45.0 | 86 16.3 .. | 49.9 | 95 48.3 .. | 37.6 | 73 14.6 .. | 04.3 | 102 49.1 .. | 41.3 | Spica | 158 24.4 | S11 16.7 |
| 16 | 83 47.4 | 101 16.1 | 49.0 | 110 48.9 | 37.0 | 88 16.5 | 04.1 | 117 51.4 | 41.2 | Suhail | 222 47.8 | S43 31.6 |
| 17 | 98 49.9 | 116 15.9 | 48.1 | 125 49.6 | 36.3 | 103 18.4 | 03.9 | 132 53.7 | 41.2 | | | |
| 18 | 113 52.4 | 131 15.7 | S 7 47.2 | 140 50.2 | S12 35.7 | 118 20.4 | S 3 03.7 | 147 55.9 | S14 41.1 | Vega | 80 34.6 | N38 47.9 |
| 19 | 128 54.8 | 146 15.6 | 46.4 | 155 50.9 | 35.1 | 133 22.3 | 03.5 | 162 58.2 | 41.1 | Zuben'ubi | 136 58.2 | S16 08.1 |
| 20 | 143 57.3 | 161 15.4 | 45.5 | 170 51.5 | 34.4 | 148 24.3 | 03.2 | 178 00.5 | 41.0 | | SHA | Mer.Pass. |
| 21 | 158 59.8 | 176 15.2 .. | 44.6 | 185 52.2 .. | 33.8 | 163 26.2 .. | 03.0 | 193 02.8 .. | 41.0 | | ° ′ | h m |
| 22 | 174 02.2 | 191 15.0 | 43.7 | 200 52.8 | 33.1 | 178 28.2 | 02.8 | 208 05.1 | 40.9 | Venus | 19 14.4 | 9 15 |
| 23 | 189 04.7 | 206 14.8 | 42.9 | 215 53.4 | 32.5 | 193 30.1 | 02.6 | 223 07.3 | 40.8 | Mars | 28 14.4 | 8 38 |
| Mer.Pass. 10 29.7 | | v −0.2 | d 0.9 | v 0.6 | d 0.6 | v 1.9 | d 0.2 | v 2.3 | d 0.1 | Jupiter | 4 49.8 | 10 11 |
| | | | | | | | | | | Saturn | 34 11.5 | 8 13 |

| UT | SUN | | MOON | | | | | Lat. | Twilight | | Sunrise | Moonrise | | | |
|---|---|---|---|---|---|---|---|---|---|---|---|---|---|---|---|
| | GHA | Dec | GHA | v | Dec | d | HP | | Naut. | Civil | | 13 | 14 | 15 | 16 |
| d h | ° ′ | ° ′ | ° ′ | ′ | ° ′ | ′ | ′ | ° | h m | h m | h m | h m | h m | h m | h m |
| 13 00 | 179 50.1 | N 8 57.7 | 42 08.2 | 12.9 | N14 18.3 | 12.6 | 56.4 | N 72 | //// | 02 08 | 03 45 | 13 03 | 15 22 | 17 35 | 19 56 |
| 01 | 194 50.2 | 58.6 | 56 40.1 | 13.0 | 14 05.7 | 12.7 | 56.4 | N 70 | //// | 02 42 | 04 01 | 13 24 | 15 29 | 17 33 | 19 42 |
| 02 | 209 50.4 | 8 59.5 | 71 12.1 | 13.0 | 13 53.0 | 12.7 | 56.5 | 68 | 00 57 | 03 05 | 04 14 | 13 40 | 15 35 | 17 31 | 19 31 |
| 03 | 224 50.5 | 9 00.4 | 85 44.1 | 13.0 | 13 40.3 | 12.9 | 56.5 | 66 | 01 50 | 03 24 | 04 24 | 13 52 | 15 40 | 17 29 | 19 22 |
| 04 | 239 50.7 | 01.3 | 100 16.1 | 13.0 | 13 27.4 | 12.9 | 56.5 | 64 | 02 21 | 03 38 | 04 33 | 14 03 | 15 45 | 17 27 | 19 15 |
| 05 | 254 50.9 | 02.2 | 114 48.1 | 13.0 | 13 14.5 | 13.0 | 56.6 | 62 | 02 43 | 03 51 | 04 40 | 14 12 | 15 48 | 17 26 | 19 08 |
| 06 | 269 51.0 | N 9 03.1 | 129 20.1 | 13.1 | N13 01.5 | 13.1 | 56.6 | 60 | 03 00 | 04 01 | 04 47 | 14 19 | 15 51 | 17 25 | 19 03 |
| W 07 | 284 51.2 | 04.0 | 143 52.2 | 13.0 | 12 48.4 | 13.1 | 56.6 | N 58 | 03 15 | 04 10 | 04 52 | 14 26 | 15 54 | 17 24 | 18 58 |
| E 08 | 299 51.3 | 04.9 | 158 24.2 | 13.1 | 12 35.3 | 13.2 | 56.7 | 56 | 03 27 | 04 17 | 04 57 | 14 32 | 15 57 | 17 23 | 18 53 |
| D 09 | 314 51.5 | .. 05.8 | 172 56.3 | 13.1 | 12 22.1 | 13.3 | 56.7 | 54 | 03 37 | 04 24 | 05 02 | 14 37 | 15 59 | 17 23 | 18 49 |
| N 10 | 329 51.7 | 06.7 | 187 28.4 | 13.1 | 12 08.8 | 13.4 | 56.7 | 52 | 03 46 | 04 30 | 05 06 | 14 42 | 16 01 | 17 22 | 18 46 |
| E 11 | 344 51.8 | 07.6 | 202 00.5 | 13.1 | 11 55.4 | 13.4 | 56.8 | 50 | 03 54 | 04 35 | 05 09 | 14 46 | 16 03 | 17 21 | 18 43 |
| S 12 | 359 52.0 | N 9 08.5 | 216 32.6 | 13.1 | N11 42.0 | 13.5 | 56.8 | 45 | 04 10 | 04 47 | 05 17 | 14 55 | 16 07 | 17 20 | 18 36 |
| D 13 | 14 52.1 | 09.4 | 231 04.7 | 13.2 | 11 28.5 | 13.6 | 56.8 | N 40 | 04 23 | 04 56 | 05 24 | 15 03 | 16 10 | 17 19 | 18 30 |
| A 14 | 29 52.3 | 10.4 | 245 36.9 | 13.1 | 11 14.9 | 13.6 | 56.9 | 35 | 04 33 | 05 04 | 05 30 | 15 09 | 16 13 | 17 18 | 18 26 |
| Y 15 | 44 52.4 | .. 11.3 | 260 09.0 | 13.2 | 11 01.3 | 13.7 | 56.9 | 30 | 04 41 | 05 10 | 05 34 | 15 15 | 16 15 | 17 17 | 18 21 |
| 16 | 59 52.6 | 12.2 | 274 41.2 | 13.2 | 10 47.6 | 13.8 | 56.9 | 20 | 04 54 | 05 21 | 05 43 | 15 25 | 16 20 | 17 16 | 18 14 |
| 17 | 74 52.8 | 13.1 | 289 13.4 | 13.1 | 10 33.8 | 13.9 | 57.0 | N 10 | 05 04 | 05 29 | 05 50 | 15 33 | 16 24 | 17 15 | 18 08 |
| 18 | 89 52.9 | N 9 14.0 | 303 45.5 | 13.2 | N10 19.9 | 13.9 | 57.0 | 0 | 05 12 | 05 36 | 05 57 | 15 41 | 16 27 | 17 14 | 18 02 |
| 19 | 104 53.1 | 14.9 | 318 17.7 | 13.2 | 10 06.0 | 13.9 | 57.0 | S 10 | 05 18 | 05 42 | 06 04 | 15 49 | 16 31 | 17 13 | 17 56 |
| 20 | 119 53.2 | 15.8 | 332 49.9 | 13.2 | 9 52.1 | 14.1 | 57.1 | 20 | 05 23 | 05 48 | 06 11 | 15 58 | 16 35 | 17 12 | 17 50 |
| 21 | 134 53.4 | .. 16.7 | 347 22.1 | 13.2 | 9 38.0 | 14.1 | 57.1 | 30 | 05 26 | 05 54 | 06 18 | 16 07 | 16 39 | 17 10 | 17 43 |
| 22 | 149 53.5 | 17.6 | 1 54.3 | 13.2 | 9 23.9 | 14.1 | 57.1 | 35 | 05 28 | 05 57 | 06 23 | 16 13 | 16 41 | 17 10 | 17 39 |
| 23 | 164 53.7 | 18.5 | 16 26.5 | 13.2 | 9 09.8 | 14.2 | 57.2 | 40 | 05 29 | 06 01 | 06 28 | 16 19 | 16 44 | 17 09 | 17 35 |
| 14 00 | 179 53.9 | N 9 19.4 | 30 58.7 | 13.2 | N 8 55.6 | 14.3 | 57.2 | 45 | 05 30 | 06 04 | 06 34 | 16 26 | 16 47 | 17 08 | 17 30 |
| 01 | 194 54.0 | 20.3 | 45 30.9 | 13.2 | 8 41.3 | 14.3 | 57.2 | S 50 | 05 30 | 06 08 | 06 41 | 16 35 | 16 51 | 17 07 | 17 23 |
| 02 | 209 54.2 | 21.2 | 60 03.1 | 13.2 | 8 27.0 | 14.4 | 57.3 | 52 | 05 30 | 06 10 | 06 44 | 16 39 | 16 53 | 17 06 | 17 21 |
| 03 | 224 54.3 | .. 22.1 | 74 35.3 | 13.3 | 8 12.6 | 14.4 | 57.3 | 54 | 05 30 | 06 11 | 06 47 | 16 43 | 16 55 | 17 06 | 17 18 |
| 04 | 239 54.5 | 23.0 | 89 07.6 | 13.2 | 7 58.2 | 14.5 | 57.3 | 56 | 05 30 | 06 13 | 06 51 | 16 48 | 16 57 | 17 05 | 17 14 |
| 05 | 254 54.6 | 23.9 | 103 39.8 | 13.2 | 7 43.7 | 14.6 | 57.4 | 58 | 05 30 | 06 15 | 06 55 | 16 54 | 16 59 | 17 05 | 17 11 |
| 06 | 269 54.8 | N 9 24.8 | 118 12.0 | 13.2 | N 7 29.1 | 14.6 | 57.4 | S 60 | 05 29 | 06 18 | 07 00 | 17 00 | 17 02 | 17 04 | 17 06 |

| UT | SUN | | MOON | | | | | Lat. | Sunset | Twilight | | Moonset | | | |
|---|---|---|---|---|---|---|---|---|---|---|---|---|---|---|---|
| | | | | | | | | | | Civil | Naut. | 13 | 14 | 15 | 16 |
| d h | ° ′ | ° ′ | ° ′ | ′ | ° ′ | ′ | ′ | ° | h m | h m | h m | h m | h m | h m | h m |
| 07 | 284 54.9 | 25.7 | 132 44.2 | 13.2 | 7 14.5 | 14.6 | 57.4 | N 72 | 20 19 | 22 00 | //// | 06 21 | 05 41 | 05 09 | 04 37 |
| T 08 | 299 55.1 | 26.6 | 147 16.4 | 13.2 | 6 59.9 | 14.7 | 57.5 | N 70 | 20 03 | 21 24 | //// | 05 59 | 05 31 | 05 07 | 04 44 |
| H 09 | 314 55.3 | .. 27.5 | 161 48.6 | 13.1 | 6 45.2 | 14.8 | 57.5 | 68 | 19 49 | 20 59 | 23 20 | 05 41 | 05 22 | 05 05 | 04 49 |
| U 10 | 329 55.4 | 28.4 | 176 20.7 | 13.2 | 6 30.4 | 14.8 | 57.5 | 66 | 19 39 | 20 40 | 22 17 | 05 27 | 05 15 | 05 04 | 04 53 |
| R 11 | 344 55.6 | 29.3 | 190 52.9 | 13.2 | 6 15.6 | 14.8 | 57.6 | 64 | 19 30 | 20 25 | 21 44 | 05 15 | 05 09 | 05 03 | 04 57 |
| S 12 | 359 55.7 | N 9 30.2 | 205 25.1 | 13.1 | N 6 00.8 | 14.9 | 57.6 | 62 | 19 22 | 20 12 | 21 21 | 05 05 | 05 03 | 05 02 | 05 00 |
| D 13 | 14 55.9 | 31.1 | 219 57.2 | 13.2 | 5 45.9 | 15.0 | 57.6 | 60 | 19 16 | 20 02 | 21 03 | 04 56 | 04 59 | 05 01 | 05 03 |
| A 14 | 29 56.0 | 32.0 | 234 29.4 | 13.1 | 5 30.9 | 15.0 | 57.7 | N 58 | 19 10 | 19 53 | 20 48 | 04 48 | 04 54 | 05 00 | 05 05 |
| Y 15 | 44 56.2 | 32.9 | 249 01.5 | 13.2 | 5 15.9 | 15.0 | 57.7 | 56 | 19 05 | 19 45 | 20 36 | 04 41 | 04 51 | 04 59 | 05 07 |
| 16 | 59 56.3 | 33.8 | 263 33.7 | 13.1 | 5 00.9 | 15.1 | 57.7 | 54 | 19 00 | 19 38 | 20 25 | 04 35 | 04 47 | 04 58 | 05 10 |
| 17 | 74 56.5 | 34.7 | 278 05.8 | 13.1 | 4 45.8 | 15.1 | 57.8 | 52 | 18 56 | 19 32 | 20 16 | 04 30 | 04 44 | 04 58 | 05 11 |
| 18 | 89 56.6 | N 9 35.6 | 292 37.9 | 13.1 | N 4 30.7 | 15.1 | 57.8 | 50 | 18 52 | 19 26 | 20 08 | 04 25 | 04 42 | 04 57 | 05 13 |
| 19 | 104 56.8 | 36.5 | 307 10.0 | 13.0 | 4 15.6 | 15.2 | 57.8 | 45 | 18 44 | 19 15 | 19 52 | 04 14 | 04 35 | 04 56 | 05 17 |
| 20 | 119 56.9 | 37.4 | 321 42.0 | 13.1 | 4 00.4 | 15.2 | 57.9 | N 40 | 18 37 | 19 05 | 19 39 | 04 05 | 04 30 | 04 55 | 05 20 |
| 21 | 134 57.1 | .. 38.3 | 336 14.1 | 13.0 | 3 45.2 | 15.3 | 57.9 | 35 | 18 32 | 18 58 | 19 29 | 03 57 | 04 26 | 04 54 | 05 23 |
| 22 | 149 57.3 | 39.2 | 350 46.1 | 13.0 | 3 29.9 | 15.3 | 57.9 | 30 | 18 27 | 18 51 | 19 20 | 03 50 | 04 22 | 04 53 | 05 25 |
| 23 | 164 57.4 | 40.0 | 5 18.1 | 13.0 | 3 14.6 | 15.3 | 58.0 | 20 | 18 18 | 18 40 | 19 07 | 03 38 | 04 15 | 04 52 | 05 29 |
| 15 00 | 179 57.6 | N 9 40.9 | 19 50.1 | 13.0 | N 2 59.3 | 15.4 | 58.0 | N 10 | 18 10 | 18 32 | 18 57 | 03 27 | 04 09 | 04 50 | 05 33 |
| 01 | 194 57.7 | 41.8 | 34 22.1 | 13.0 | 2 43.9 | 15.3 | 58.0 | 0 | 18 04 | 18 25 | 18 49 | 03 17 | 04 03 | 04 49 | 05 36 |
| 02 | 209 57.9 | 42.7 | 48 54.1 | 12.9 | 2 28.6 | 15.5 | 58.1 | S 10 | 17 57 | 18 18 | 18 43 | 03 07 | 03 57 | 04 48 | 05 40 |
| 03 | 224 58.0 | .. 43.6 | 63 26.0 | 12.9 | 2 13.1 | 15.4 | 58.1 | 20 | 17 50 | 18 12 | 18 38 | 02 56 | 03 51 | 04 46 | 05 43 |
| 04 | 239 58.2 | 44.5 | 77 57.9 | 12.9 | 1 57.7 | 15.5 | 58.1 | 30 | 17 42 | 18 06 | 18 34 | 02 44 | 03 44 | 04 45 | 05 48 |
| 05 | 254 58.3 | 45.4 | 92 29.8 | 12.8 | 1 42.2 | 15.5 | 58.2 | 35 | 17 37 | 18 03 | 18 32 | 02 36 | 03 39 | 04 44 | 05 50 |
| 06 | 269 58.5 | N 9 46.3 | 107 01.6 | 12.8 | N 1 26.7 | 15.5 | 58.2 | 40 | 17 32 | 17 59 | 18 31 | 02 28 | 03 35 | 04 43 | 05 53 |
| 07 | 284 58.6 | 47.2 | 121 33.4 | 12.8 | 1 11.2 | 15.6 | 58.2 | 45 | 17 26 | 17 56 | 18 30 | 02 18 | 03 29 | 04 42 | 05 56 |
| 08 | 299 58.8 | 48.1 | 136 05.2 | 12.8 | 0 55.6 | 15.6 | 58.3 | S 50 | 17 19 | 17 52 | 18 29 | 02 06 | 03 22 | 04 40 | 06 00 |
| F 09 | 314 58.9 | .. 49.0 | 150 37.0 | 12.7 | 0 40.1 | 15.6 | 58.3 | 52 | 17 16 | 17 50 | 18 29 | 02 01 | 03 19 | 04 39 | 06 02 |
| R 10 | 329 59.1 | 49.9 | 165 08.7 | 12.7 | 0 24.5 | 15.6 | 58.3 | 54 | 17 12 | 17 48 | 18 29 | 01 54 | 03 16 | 04 39 | 06 04 |
| I 11 | 344 59.2 | 50.8 | 179 40.4 | 12.7 | N 0 08.9 | 15.7 | 58.3 | 56 | 17 08 | 17 46 | 18 29 | 01 48 | 03 12 | 04 38 | 06 06 |
| D 12 | 359 59.4 | N 9 51.7 | 194 12.1 | 12.6 | S 0 06.8 | 15.6 | 58.4 | 58 | 17 04 | 17 44 | 18 29 | 01 40 | 03 08 | 04 37 | 06 08 |
| A 13 | 14 59.5 | 52.6 | 208 43.7 | 12.6 | 0 22.4 | 15.7 | 58.4 | S 60 | 16 59 | 17 42 | 18 30 | 01 31 | 03 03 | 04 36 | 06 11 |
| Y 14 | 29 59.7 | 53.4 | 223 15.3 | 12.6 | 0 38.1 | 15.6 | 58.4 | | | | | | | | |
| 15 | 44 59.8 | .. 54.3 | 237 46.9 | 12.5 | 0 53.7 | 15.7 | 58.5 | | | | | | | | |
| 16 | 60 00.0 | 55.2 | 252 18.4 | 12.5 | 1 09.4 | 15.7 | 58.5 | | | | | | | | |
| 17 | 75 00.1 | 56.1 | 266 49.9 | 12.5 | 1 25.1 | 15.7 | 58.5 | | | | | | | | |
| 18 | 90 00.3 | N 9 57.0 | 281 21.4 | 12.4 | S 1 40.8 | 15.7 | 58.6 | | | | | | | | |
| 19 | 105 00.4 | 57.9 | 295 52.8 | 12.3 | 1 56.5 | 15.8 | 58.6 | | | | | | | | |
| 20 | 120 00.6 | 58.8 | 310 24.1 | 12.3 | 2 12.3 | 15.7 | 58.6 | | | | | | | | |
| 21 | 135 00.7 | 9 59.7 | 324 55.4 | 12.3 | 2 28.0 | 15.7 | 58.6 | | | | | | | | |
| 22 | 150 00.9 | 10 00.6 | 339 26.7 | 12.3 | 2 43.7 | 15.8 | 58.7 | | | | | | | | |
| 23 | 165 01.0 | N10 01.4 | 353 58.0 | 12.1 | S 2 59.5 | 15.7 | 58.7 | | | | | | | | |
| | SD 16.0 | d 0.9 | SD 15.5 | | 15.7 | | 15.9 | | | | | | | | | |

| | SUN | | | MOON | | | |
|---|---|---|---|---|---|---|---|
| Day | Eqn. of Time | | Mer. | Mer. Pass. | | Age | Phase |
| | 00ʰ | 12ʰ | Pass. | Upper | Lower | | |
| d | m s | m s | h m | h m | h m | d | % |
| 13 | 00 40 | 00 32 | 12 01 | 21 52 | 09 29 | 12 | 87 |
| 14 | 00 25 | 00 17 | 12 00 | 22 38 | 10 15 | 13 | 93 |
| 15 | 00 10 | 00 03 | 12 00 | 23 25 | 11 01 | 14 | 98 |

| UT | ARIES GHA | VENUS −4.2 GHA | Dec | MARS +1.0 GHA | Dec | JUPITER −2.1 GHA | Dec | SATURN +0.7 GHA | Dec | STARS Name | SHA | Dec |
|---|---|---|---|---|---|---|---|---|---|---|---|---|
| 16 00 | 204 07.2 | 221 14.7 | S 7 42.0 | 230 54.1 | S12 31.8 | 208 32.1 | S 3 02.4 | 238 09.6 | S14 40.8 | Acamar | 315 13.9 | S40 13.1 |
| 01 | 219 09.6 | 236 14.5 | 41.1 | 245 54.7 | 31.2 | 223 34.0 | 02.1 | 253 11.9 | 40.7 | Achernar | 335 22.5 | S57 07.5 |
| 02 | 234 12.1 | 251 14.3 | 40.2 | 260 55.4 | 30.5 | 238 36.0 | 01.9 | 268 14.2 | 40.7 | Acrux | 173 01.9 | S63 13.4 |
| 03 | 249 14.5 | 266 14.1 .. | 39.3 | 275 56.0 .. | 29.9 | 253 37.9 .. | 01.7 | 283 16.5 .. | 40.6 | Adhara | 255 07.7 | S29 00.4 |
| 04 | 264 17.0 | 281 13.9 | 38.5 | 290 56.7 | 29.2 | 268 39.9 | 01.5 | 298 18.7 | 40.6 | Aldebaran | 290 42.5 | N16 33.1 |
| 05 | 279 19.5 | 296 13.8 | 37.6 | 305 57.3 | 28.6 | 283 41.8 | 01.3 | 313 21.0 | 40.5 | | | |
| 06 | 294 21.9 | 311 13.6 | S 7 36.7 | 320 58.0 | S12 27.9 | 298 43.8 | S 3 01.1 | 328 23.3 | S14 40.5 | Alioth | 166 14.5 | N55 50.4 |
| 07 | 309 24.4 | 326 13.4 | 35.8 | 335 58.6 | 27.3 | 313 45.7 | 00.8 | 343 25.6 | 40.4 | Alkaid | 152 53.3 | N49 12.1 |
| S 08 | 324 26.9 | 341 13.2 | 34.9 | 350 59.3 | 26.7 | 328 47.7 | 00.6 | 358 27.8 | 40.3 | Alnair | 27 36.0 | S46 51.1 |
| A 09 | 339 29.3 | 356 13.0 .. | 34.0 | 5 59.9 .. | 26.0 | 343 49.6 .. | 00.4 | 13 30.1 .. | 40.3 | Alnilam | 275 40.2 | S 1 11.4 |
| T 10 | 354 31.8 | 11 12.9 | 33.2 | 21 00.5 | 25.4 | 358 51.6 | 00.2 | 28 32.4 | 40.2 | Alphard | 217 49.9 | S 8 45.4 |
| U 11 | 9 34.3 | 26 12.7 | 32.3 | 36 01.2 | 24.7 | 13 53.5 | 3 00.0 | 43 34.7 | 40.2 | | | |
| R 12 | 24 36.7 | 41 12.5 | S 7 31.4 | 51 01.8 | S12 24.1 | 28 55.5 | S 2 59.8 | 58 37.0 | S14 40.1 | Alphecca | 126 05.4 | N26 38.3 |
| D 13 | 39 39.2 | 56 12.3 | 30.5 | 66 02.5 | 23.4 | 43 57.4 | 59.5 | 73 39.3 | 40.1 | Alpheratz | 357 37.4 | N29 12.5 |
| A 14 | 54 41.7 | 71 12.1 | 29.6 | 81 03.1 | 22.8 | 58 59.4 | 59.3 | 88 41.5 | 40.0 | Altair | 62 02.2 | N 8 55.4 |
| Y 15 | 69 44.1 | 86 11.9 .. | 28.7 | 96 03.8 .. | 22.1 | 74 01.3 .. | 59.1 | 103 43.8 .. | 40.0 | Ankaa | 353 09.8 | S42 11.2 |
| 16 | 84 46.6 | 101 11.8 | 27.8 | 111 04.4 | 21.5 | 89 03.3 | 58.9 | 118 46.1 | 39.9 | Antares | 112 18.3 | S26 28.8 |
| 17 | 99 49.0 | 116 11.6 | 27.0 | 126 05.1 | 20.8 | 104 05.2 | 58.7 | 133 48.4 | 39.8 | | | |
| 18 | 114 51.5 | 131 11.4 | S 7 26.1 | 141 05.7 | S12 20.2 | 119 07.2 | S 2 58.5 | 148 50.7 | S14 39.8 | Arcturus | 145 49.7 | N19 03.9 |
| 19 | 129 54.0 | 146 11.2 | 25.2 | 156 06.4 | 19.5 | 134 09.1 | 58.2 | 163 52.9 | 39.7 | Atria | 107 14.2 | S69 03.8 |
| 20 | 144 56.4 | 161 11.0 | 24.3 | 171 07.0 | 18.9 | 149 11.1 | 58.0 | 178 55.2 | 39.7 | Avior | 234 15.6 | S59 35.1 |
| 21 | 159 58.9 | 176 10.9 .. | 23.4 | 186 07.7 .. | 18.2 | 164 13.0 .. | 57.8 | 193 57.5 .. | 39.6 | Bellatrix | 278 25.5 | N 6 22.1 |
| 22 | 175 01.4 | 191 10.7 | 22.5 | 201 08.3 | 17.6 | 179 15.0 | 57.6 | 208 59.8 | 39.6 | Betelgeuse | 270 54.7 | N 7 24.6 |
| 23 | 190 03.8 | 206 10.5 | 21.6 | 216 09.0 | 16.9 | 194 16.9 | 57.4 | 224 02.1 | 39.5 | | | |
| 17 00 | 205 06.3 | 221 10.3 | S 7 20.7 | 231 09.6 | S12 16.3 | 209 18.9 | S 2 57.2 | 239 04.3 | S14 39.5 | Canopus | 263 53.6 | S52 42.7 |
| 01 | 220 08.8 | 236 10.1 | 19.8 | 246 10.3 | 15.6 | 224 20.8 | 57.0 | 254 06.6 | 39.4 | Capella | 280 25.5 | N46 01.3 |
| 02 | 235 11.2 | 251 10.0 | 18.9 | 261 10.9 | 15.0 | 239 22.8 | 56.7 | 269 08.9 | 39.3 | Deneb | 49 27.4 | N45 21.2 |
| 03 | 250 13.7 | 266 09.8 .. | 18.0 | 276 11.6 .. | 14.3 | 254 24.7 .. | 56.5 | 284 11.2 .. | 39.3 | Denebola | 182 27.0 | N14 26.9 |
| 04 | 265 16.1 | 281 09.6 | 17.2 | 291 12.2 | 13.7 | 269 26.7 | 56.3 | 299 13.5 | 39.2 | Diphda | 348 49.9 | S17 52.0 |
| 05 | 280 18.6 | 296 09.4 | 16.3 | 306 12.9 | 13.0 | 284 28.6 | 56.1 | 314 15.8 | 39.2 | | | |
| 06 | 295 21.1 | 311 09.2 | S 7 15.4 | 321 13.5 | S12 12.4 | 299 30.6 | S 2 55.9 | 329 18.0 | S14 39.1 | Dubhe | 193 43.3 | N61 38.1 |
| 07 | 310 23.5 | 326 09.0 | 14.5 | 336 14.1 | 11.7 | 314 32.5 | 55.7 | 344 20.3 | 39.1 | Elnath | 278 05.0 | N28 37.5 |
| 08 | 325 26.0 | 341 08.9 | 13.6 | 351 14.8 | 11.1 | 329 34.5 | 55.4 | 359 22.6 | 39.0 | Eltanin | 90 43.0 | N51 28.8 |
| S 09 | 340 28.5 | 356 08.7 .. | 12.7 | 6 15.4 .. | 10.4 | 344 36.4 .. | 55.2 | 14 24.9 .. | 39.0 | Enif | 33 41.2 | N 9 58.4 |
| U 10 | 355 30.9 | 11 08.5 | 11.8 | 21 16.1 | 09.7 | 359 38.4 | 55.0 | 29 27.2 | 38.9 | Fomalhaut | 15 17.3 | S29 30.3 |
| N 11 | 10 33.4 | 26 08.3 | 10.9 | 36 16.7 | 09.1 | 14 40.3 | 54.8 | 44 29.5 | 38.9 | | | |
| D 12 | 25 35.9 | 41 08.1 | S 7 10.0 | 51 17.4 | S12 08.4 | 29 42.3 | S 2 54.6 | 59 31.7 | S14 38.8 | Gacrux | 171 53.6 | S57 14.3 |
| A 13 | 40 38.3 | 56 08.0 | 09.1 | 66 18.0 | 07.8 | 44 44.2 | 54.4 | 74 34.0 | 38.8 | Gienah | 175 45.6 | S17 40.0 |
| Y 14 | 55 40.8 | 71 07.8 | 08.2 | 81 18.7 | 07.1 | 59 46.2 | 54.1 | 89 36.3 | 38.7 | Hadar | 148 38.6 | S60 28.8 |
| 15 | 70 43.3 | 86 07.6 .. | 07.3 | 96 19.3 .. | 06.5 | 74 48.1 .. | 53.9 | 104 38.6 .. | 38.6 | Hamal | 327 54.1 | N23 33.9 |
| 16 | 85 45.7 | 101 07.4 | 06.4 | 111 20.0 | 05.8 | 89 50.1 | 53.7 | 119 40.9 | 38.6 | Kaus Aust. | 83 35.4 | S34 22.4 |
| 17 | 100 48.2 | 116 07.2 | 05.5 | 126 20.6 | 05.2 | 104 52.0 | 53.5 | 134 43.2 | 38.5 | | | |
| 18 | 115 50.6 | 131 07.1 | S 7 04.6 | 141 21.3 | S12 04.5 | 119 54.0 | S 2 53.3 | 149 45.4 | S14 38.5 | Kochab | 137 18.7 | N74 03.8 |
| 19 | 130 53.1 | 146 06.9 | 03.7 | 156 22.0 | 03.9 | 134 55.9 | 53.1 | 164 47.7 | 38.4 | Markab | 13 32.4 | N15 19.2 |
| 20 | 145 55.6 | 161 06.7 | 02.8 | 171 22.6 | 03.2 | 149 57.9 | 52.9 | 179 50.0 | 38.4 | Menkar | 314 08.8 | N 4 10.4 |
| 21 | 160 58.0 | 176 06.5 .. | 01.9 | 186 23.3 .. | 02.6 | 164 59.8 .. | 52.6 | 194 52.3 .. | 38.3 | Menkent | 147 59.9 | S36 28.8 |
| 22 | 176 00.5 | 191 06.3 | 01.0 | 201 23.9 | 01.9 | 180 01.8 | 52.4 | 209 54.6 | 38.3 | Miaplacidus | 221 38.4 | S69 48.7 |
| 23 | 191 03.0 | 206 06.1 | 7 00.1 | 216 24.6 | 01.3 | 195 03.7 | 52.2 | 224 56.9 | 38.2 | | | |
| 18 00 | 206 05.4 | 221 06.0 | S 6 59.2 | 231 25.2 | S12 00.6 | 210 05.7 | S 2 52.0 | 239 59.2 | S14 38.2 | Mirfak | 308 32.0 | N49 56.3 |
| 01 | 221 07.9 | 236 05.8 | 58.3 | 246 25.9 | 11 59.9 | 225 07.6 | 51.8 | 255 01.4 | 38.1 | Nunki | 75 50.5 | S26 16.1 |
| 02 | 236 10.4 | 251 05.6 | 57.4 | 261 26.5 | 59.3 | 240 09.6 | 51.6 | 270 03.7 | 38.1 | Peacock | 53 09.4 | S56 39.6 |
| 03 | 251 12.8 | 266 05.4 .. | 56.5 | 276 27.2 .. | 58.6 | 255 11.5 .. | 51.3 | 285 06.0 .. | 38.0 | Pollux | 243 20.1 | N27 58.4 |
| 04 | 266 15.3 | 281 05.2 | 55.6 | 291 27.8 | 58.0 | 270 13.5 | 51.1 | 300 08.3 | 37.9 | Procyon | 244 53.2 | N 5 10.0 |
| 05 | 281 17.8 | 296 05.1 | 54.7 | 306 28.5 | 57.3 | 285 15.4 | 50.9 | 315 10.6 | 37.9 | | | |
| 06 | 296 20.2 | 311 04.9 | S 6 53.7 | 321 29.1 | S11 56.7 | 300 17.4 | S 2 50.7 | 330 12.9 | S14 37.8 | Rasalhague | 96 00.5 | N12 32.5 |
| 07 | 311 22.7 | 326 04.7 | 52.8 | 336 29.8 | 56.0 | 315 19.4 | 50.5 | 345 15.2 | 37.8 | Regulus | 207 36.7 | N11 51.5 |
| 08 | 326 25.1 | 341 04.5 | 51.9 | 351 30.4 | 55.3 | 330 21.3 | 50.3 | 0 17.4 | 37.7 | Rigel | 281 06.3 | S 8 10.7 |
| M 09 | 341 27.6 | 356 04.3 .. | 51.0 | 6 31.1 .. | 54.7 | 345 23.3 .. | 50.1 | 15 19.7 .. | 37.7 | Rigil Kent. | 139 42.8 | S60 55.5 |
| O 10 | 356 30.1 | 11 04.1 | 50.1 | 21 31.7 | 54.0 | 0 25.2 | 49.8 | 30 22.0 | 37.6 | Sabik | 102 05.2 | S15 45.2 |
| N 11 | 11 32.5 | 26 04.0 | 49.2 | 36 32.4 | 53.4 | 15 27.2 | 49.6 | 45 24.3 | 37.6 | | | |
| D 12 | 26 35.0 | 41 03.8 | S 6 48.3 | 51 33.0 | S11 52.7 | 30 29.1 | S 2 49.4 | 60 26.6 | S14 37.5 | Schedar | 349 34.2 | N56 39.3 |
| A 13 | 41 37.5 | 56 03.6 | 47.4 | 66 33.7 | 52.1 | 45 31.1 | 49.2 | 75 28.9 | 37.5 | Shaula | 96 13.2 | S37 07.1 |
| Y 14 | 56 39.9 | 71 03.4 | 46.5 | 81 34.3 | 51.4 | 60 33.0 | 49.0 | 90 31.2 | 37.4 | Sirius | 258 28.3 | S16 45.0 |
| 15 | 71 42.4 | 86 03.2 .. | 45.6 | 96 35.0 .. | 50.7 | 75 35.0 .. | 48.8 | 105 33.4 .. | 37.4 | Spica | 158 24.4 | S11 16.7 |
| 16 | 86 44.9 | 101 03.0 | 44.7 | 111 35.7 | 50.1 | 90 36.9 | 48.6 | 120 35.7 | 37.3 | Suhail | 222 47.8 | S43 31.6 |
| 17 | 101 47.3 | 116 02.9 | 43.7 | 126 36.3 | 49.4 | 105 38.9 | 48.3 | 135 38.0 | 37.3 | | | |
| 18 | 116 49.8 | 131 02.7 | S 6 42.8 | 141 37.0 | S11 48.8 | 120 40.8 | S 2 48.1 | 150 40.3 | S14 37.2 | Vega | 80 34.6 | N38 47.9 |
| 19 | 131 52.2 | 146 02.5 | 41.9 | 156 37.6 | 48.1 | 135 42.8 | 47.9 | 165 42.6 | 37.1 | Zuben'ubi | 136 58.2 | S16 08.1 |
| 20 | 146 54.7 | 161 02.3 | 41.0 | 171 38.3 | 47.5 | 150 44.7 | 47.7 | 180 44.9 | 37.1 | | | |
| 21 | 161 57.2 | 176 02.1 .. | 40.1 | 186 38.9 .. | 46.8 | 165 46.7 .. | 47.5 | 195 47.2 .. | 37.0 | | | |
| 22 | 176 59.6 | 191 02.0 | 39.2 | 201 39.6 | 46.1 | 180 48.7 | 47.3 | 210 49.5 | 37.0 | | | |
| 23 | 192 02.1 | 206 01.8 | 38.3 | 216 40.2 | 45.5 | 195 50.6 | 47.0 | 225 51.7 | 36.9 | | | |

| | | SHA | Mer. Pass. |
|---|---|---|---|
| | | ° ′ | h m |
| Venus | | 16 04.0 | 9 15 |
| Mars | | 26 03.3 | 8 35 |
| Jupiter | | 4 12.6 | 10 01 |
| Saturn | | 33 58.1 | 8 02 |

| | h m | | | | | | |
|---|---|---|---|---|---|---|---|
| Mer. Pass. | 10 17.9 | v −0.2 | d 0.9 | v 0.6   d 0.7 | v 2.0   d 0.2 | v 2.3   d 0.1 | |

| UT | SUN GHA | SUN Dec | MOON GHA | v | MOON Dec | d | HP |
|---|---|---|---|---|---|---|---|
| d h | ° ′ | ° ′ | ° ′ | ′ | ° ′ | ′ | ′ |
| **16 00** | 180 01.2 | N10 02.3 | 8 29.1 | 12.2 | S 3 15.2 | 15.7 | 58.7 |
| 01 | 195 01.3 | 03.2 | 23 00.3 | 12.1 | 3 30.9 | 15.8 | 58.8 |
| 02 | 210 01.5 | 04.1 | 37 31.4 | 12.0 | 3 46.7 | 15.7 | 58.8 |
| 03 | 225 01.6 .. | 05.0 | 52 02.4 | 12.0 | 4 02.4 | 15.7 | 58.8 |
| 04 | 240 01.8 | 05.9 | 66 33.4 | 11.9 | 4 18.1 | 15.8 | 58.8 |
| 05 | 255 01.9 | 06.8 | 81 04.3 | 11.9 | 4 33.9 | 15.7 | 58.9 |
| 06 | 270 02.1 | N10 07.7 | 95 35.2 | 11.9 | S 4 49.6 | 15.7 | 58.9 |
| **S** 07 | 285 02.2 | 08.5 | 110 06.1 | 11.7 | 5 05.3 | 15.7 | 58.9 |
| **A** 08 | 300 02.4 | 09.4 | 124 36.8 | 11.8 | 5 21.0 | 15.6 | 58.9 |
| **T** 09 | 315 02.5 .. | 10.3 | 139 07.6 | 11.6 | 5 36.6 | 15.7 | 59.0 |
| **U** 10 | 330 02.7 | 11.2 | 153 38.2 | 11.6 | 5 52.3 | 15.7 | 59.0 |
| **R** 11 | 345 02.8 | 12.1 | 168 08.8 | 11.6 | 6 08.0 | 15.6 | 59.0 |
| **D** 12 | 0 03.0 | N10 13.0 | 182 39.4 | 11.4 | S 6 23.6 | 15.6 | 59.1 |
| **A** 13 | 15 03.1 | 13.9 | 197 09.8 | 11.5 | 6 39.2 | 15.6 | 59.1 |
| **Y** 14 | 30 03.3 | 14.7 | 211 40.3 | 11.3 | 6 54.8 | 15.6 | 59.1 |
| 15 | 45 03.4 .. | 15.6 | 226 10.6 | 11.3 | 7 10.4 | 15.5 | 59.1 |
| 16 | 60 03.6 | 16.5 | 240 40.9 | 11.3 | 7 25.9 | 15.5 | 59.2 |
| 17 | 75 03.7 | 17.4 | 255 11.2 | 11.1 | 7 41.4 | 15.5 | 59.2 |
| 18 | 90 03.8 | N10 18.3 | 269 41.3 | 11.1 | S 7 56.9 | 15.5 | 59.2 |
| 19 | 105 04.0 | 19.2 | 284 11.4 | 11.1 | 8 12.4 | 15.4 | 59.2 |
| 20 | 120 04.1 | 20.0 | 298 41.5 | 10.9 | 8 27.8 | 15.4 | 59.2 |
| 21 | 135 04.3 .. | 20.9 | 313 11.4 | 10.9 | 8 43.2 | 15.4 | 59.3 |
| 22 | 150 04.4 | 21.8 | 327 41.3 | 10.8 | 8 58.6 | 15.3 | 59.3 |
| 23 | 165 04.6 | 22.7 | 342 11.1 | 10.8 | 9 13.9 | 15.3 | 59.3 |
| **17 00** | 180 04.7 | N10 23.6 | 356 40.9 | 10.7 | S 9 29.2 | 15.3 | 59.3 |
| 01 | 195 04.9 | 24.4 | 11 10.6 | 10.6 | 9 44.5 | 15.2 | 59.4 |
| 02 | 210 05.0 | 25.3 | 25 40.2 | 10.5 | 9 59.7 | 15.2 | 59.4 |
| 03 | 225 05.2 .. | 26.2 | 40 09.7 | 10.5 | 10 14.9 | 15.1 | 59.4 |
| 04 | 240 05.3 | 27.1 | 54 39.2 | 10.3 | 10 30.0 | 15.1 | 59.4 |
| 05 | 255 05.4 | 28.0 | 69 08.5 | 10.3 | 10 45.1 | 15.0 | 59.4 |
| 06 | 270 05.6 | N10 28.8 | 83 37.8 | 10.2 | S11 00.1 | 15.0 | 59.5 |
| 07 | 285 05.7 | 29.7 | 98 07.0 | 10.2 | 11 15.1 | 14.9 | 59.5 |
| **S** 08 | 300 05.9 | 30.6 | 112 36.2 | 10.1 | 11 30.0 | 14.9 | 59.5 |
| **U** 09 | 315 06.0 .. | 31.5 | 127 05.3 | 9.9 | 11 44.9 | 14.8 | 59.5 |
| **N** 10 | 330 06.2 | 32.4 | 141 34.2 | 9.9 | 11 59.7 | 14.8 | 59.5 |
| **D** 11 | 345 06.3 | 33.2 | 156 03.1 | 9.8 | 12 14.5 | 14.7 | 59.6 |
| **A** 12 | 0 06.5 | N10 34.1 | 170 31.9 | 9.8 | S12 29.2 | 14.7 | 59.6 |
| **Y** 13 | 15 06.6 | 35.0 | 185 00.7 | 9.6 | 12 43.9 | 14.5 | 59.6 |
| 14 | 30 06.7 | 35.9 | 199 29.3 | 9.6 | 12 58.4 | 14.6 | 59.6 |
| 15 | 45 06.9 .. | 36.8 | 213 57.9 | 9.5 | 13 13.0 | 14.4 | 59.6 |
| 16 | 60 07.0 | 37.6 | 228 26.4 | 9.4 | 13 27.4 | 14.4 | 59.7 |
| 17 | 75 07.2 | 38.5 | 242 54.8 | 9.3 | 13 41.8 | 14.3 | 59.7 |
| 18 | 90 07.3 | N10 39.4 | 257 23.1 | 9.2 | S13 56.1 | 14.3 | 59.7 |
| 19 | 105 07.5 | 40.3 | 271 51.3 | 9.1 | 14 10.4 | 14.1 | 59.7 |
| 20 | 120 07.6 | 41.1 | 286 19.4 | 9.0 | 14 24.5 | 14.1 | 59.7 |
| 21 | 135 07.7 .. | 42.0 | 300 47.4 | 9.0 | 14 38.6 | 14.0 | 59.7 |
| 22 | 150 07.9 | 42.9 | 315 15.4 | 8.8 | 14 52.6 | 14.0 | 59.7 |
| 23 | 165 08.0 | 43.8 | 329 43.2 | 8.8 | 15 06.6 | 13.8 | 59.8 |
| **18 00** | 180 08.2 | N10 44.6 | 344 11.0 | 8.7 | S15 20.4 | 13.8 | 59.8 |
| 01 | 195 08.3 | 45.5 | 358 38.7 | 8.6 | 15 34.2 | 13.7 | 59.8 |
| 02 | 210 08.4 | 46.4 | 13 06.3 | 8.4 | 15 47.9 | 13.6 | 59.8 |
| 03 | 225 08.6 .. | 47.2 | 27 33.7 | 8.4 | 16 01.5 | 13.5 | 59.8 |
| 04 | 240 08.7 | 48.1 | 42 01.1 | 8.3 | 16 15.0 | 13.4 | 59.8 |
| 05 | 255 08.9 | 49.0 | 56 28.4 | 8.2 | 16 28.4 | 13.3 | 59.8 |
| 06 | 270 09.0 | N10 49.9 | 70 55.6 | 8.2 | S16 41.7 | 13.3 | 59.9 |
| 07 | 285 09.1 | 50.7 | 85 22.8 | 8.0 | 16 55.0 | 13.1 | 59.9 |
| 08 | 300 09.3 | 51.6 | 99 49.8 | 7.9 | 17 08.1 | 13.0 | 59.9 |
| **M** 09 | 315 09.4 .. | 52.5 | 114 16.7 | 7.8 | 17 21.1 | 13.0 | 59.9 |
| **O** 10 | 330 09.6 | 53.4 | 128 43.5 | 7.8 | 17 34.1 | 12.8 | 59.9 |
| **N** 11 | 345 09.7 | 54.2 | 143 10.3 | 7.6 | 17 46.9 | 12.7 | 59.9 |
| **D** 12 | 0 09.8 | N10 55.1 | 157 36.9 | 7.5 | S17 59.6 | 12.6 | 59.9 |
| **A** 13 | 15 10.0 | 56.0 | 172 03.4 | 7.5 | 18 12.2 | 12.5 | 59.9 |
| **Y** 14 | 30 10.1 | 56.8 | 186 29.9 | 7.3 | 18 24.7 | 12.5 | 59.9 |
| 15 | 45 10.3 .. | 57.7 | 200 56.2 | 7.3 | 18 37.2 | 12.2 | 59.9 |
| 16 | 60 10.4 | 58.6 | 215 22.5 | 7.2 | 18 49.4 | 12.2 | 60.0 |
| 17 | 75 10.5 | 10 59.4 | 229 48.7 | 7.0 | 19 01.6 | 12.1 | 60.0 |
| 18 | 90 10.7 | N11 00.3 | 244 14.7 | 7.0 | S19 13.7 | 11.9 | 60.0 |
| 19 | 105 10.8 | 01.2 | 258 40.7 | 6.9 | 19 25.6 | 11.8 | 60.0 |
| 20 | 120 10.9 | 02.0 | 273 06.6 | 6.7 | 19 37.4 | 11.7 | 60.0 |
| 21 | 135 11.1 .. | 02.9 | 287 32.3 | 6.7 | 19 49.1 | 11.6 | 60.0 |
| 22 | 150 11.2 | 03.8 | 301 58.0 | 6.6 | 20 00.7 | 11.5 | 60.0 |
| 23 | 165 11.4 | 04.6 | 316 23.6 | 6.5 | S20 12.2 | 11.3 | 60.0 |
| | SD 16.0 | d 0.9 | SD 16.1 | | 16.2 | | 16.3 |

| Lat. | Twilight Naut. | Twilight Civil | Sunrise | Moonrise 16 | 17 | 18 | 19 |
|---|---|---|---|---|---|---|---|
| ° | h m | h m | h m | h m | h m | h m | h m |
| N 72 | //// | 01 38 | 03 28 | 19 56 | 22 48 | ■ | ■ |
| N 70 | //// | 02 21 | 03 46 | 19 42 | 22 10 | ■ | ■ |
| 68 | //// | 02 49 | 04 01 | 19 31 | 21 44 | 24 34 | 00 34 |
| 66 | 01 24 | 03 10 | 04 12 | 19 22 | 21 25 | 23 45 | ■ |
| 64 | 02 03 | 03 26 | 04 22 | 19 15 | 21 09 | 23 14 | 25 36 |
| 62 | 02 28 | 03 40 | 04 31 | 19 08 | 20 56 | 22 51 | 24 52 |
| 60 | 02 48 | 03 51 | 04 38 | 19 03 | 20 45 | 22 33 | 24 22 |
| N 58 | 03 04 | 04 01 | 04 44 | 18 58 | 20 35 | 22 17 | 24 00 |
| 56 | 03 17 | 04 09 | 04 50 | 18 53 | 20 27 | 22 05 | 23 42 |
| 54 | 03 28 | 04 17 | 04 55 | 18 49 | 20 20 | 21 53 | 23 26 |
| 52 | 03 38 | 04 23 | 04 59 | 18 46 | 20 13 | 21 44 | 23 13 |
| 50 | 03 47 | 04 29 | 05 03 | 18 43 | 20 07 | 21 35 | 23 01 |
| 45 | 04 04 | 04 41 | 05 12 | 18 36 | 19 55 | 21 16 | 22 37 |
| N 40 | 04 18 | 04 51 | 05 19 | 18 30 | 19 45 | 21 01 | 22 18 |
| 35 | 04 28 | 05 00 | 05 26 | 18 26 | 19 36 | 20 49 | 22 02 |
| 30 | 04 38 | 05 07 | 05 31 | 18 21 | 19 28 | 20 38 | 21 49 |
| 20 | 04 52 | 05 18 | 05 41 | 18 14 | 19 15 | 20 19 | 21 25 |
| N 10 | 05 02 | 05 27 | 05 49 | 18 08 | 19 04 | 20 03 | 21 05 |
| 0 | 05 11 | 05 35 | 05 56 | 18 02 | 18 53 | 19 48 | 20 47 |
| S 10 | 05 18 | 05 42 | 06 04 | 17 56 | 18 42 | 19 33 | 20 28 |
| 20 | 05 23 | 05 49 | 06 11 | 17 50 | 18 31 | 19 17 | 20 08 |
| 30 | 05 28 | 05 56 | 06 20 | 17 43 | 18 19 | 18 59 | 19 46 |
| 35 | 05 30 | 06 00 | 06 25 | 17 39 | 18 12 | 18 49 | 19 33 |
| 40 | 05 32 | 06 03 | 06 31 | 17 35 | 18 03 | 18 37 | 19 17 |
| 45 | 05 33 | 06 08 | 06 37 | 17 30 | 17 54 | 18 23 | 18 59 |
| S 50 | 05 35 | 06 12 | 06 45 | 17 23 | 17 42 | 18 06 | 18 37 |
| 52 | 05 35 | 06 14 | 06 49 | 17 21 | 17 37 | 17 58 | 18 27 |
| 54 | 05 35 | 06 17 | 06 53 | 17 18 | 17 31 | 17 49 | 18 15 |
| 56 | 05 36 | 06 19 | 06 57 | 17 14 | 17 25 | 17 40 | 18 01 |
| 58 | 05 36 | 06 22 | 07 02 | 17 11 | 17 18 | 17 29 | 17 46 |
| S 60 | 05 36 | 06 24 | 07 07 | 17 06 | 17 10 | 17 16 | 17 27 |

| Lat. | Sunset | Twilight Civil | Naut. | Moonset 16 | 17 | 18 | 19 |
|---|---|---|---|---|---|---|---|
| ° | h m | h m | h m | h m | h m | h m | h m |
| N 72 | 20 35 | 22 31 | //// | 04 37 | 04 00 | 02 57 | ■ |
| N 70 | 20 16 | 21 44 | //// | 04 44 | 04 16 | 03 37 | ■ |
| 68 | 20 01 | 21 14 | //// | 04 49 | 04 30 | 04 05 | 03 11 |
| 66 | 19 49 | 20 53 | 22 44 | 04 53 | 04 41 | 04 26 | 04 02 |
| 64 | 19 39 | 20 36 | 22 02 | 04 57 | 04 50 | 04 43 | 04 34 |
| 62 | 19 30 | 20 22 | 21 34 | 05 00 | 04 58 | 04 57 | 04 57 |
| 60 | 19 23 | 20 10 | 21 14 | 05 03 | 05 05 | 05 09 | 05 17 |
| N 58 | 19 16 | 20 00 | 20 58 | 05 05 | 05 11 | 05 20 | 05 33 |
| 56 | 19 11 | 19 52 | 20 44 | 05 07 | 05 17 | 05 29 | 05 46 |
| 54 | 19 06 | 19 44 | 20 33 | 05 10 | 05 22 | 05 37 | 05 58 |
| 52 | 19 01 | 19 37 | 20 23 | 05 11 | 05 26 | 05 45 | 06 09 |
| 50 | 18 57 | 19 31 | 20 14 | 05 13 | 05 30 | 05 51 | 06 18 |
| 45 | 18 48 | 19 19 | 19 56 | 05 17 | 05 39 | 06 06 | 06 38 |
| N 40 | 18 40 | 19 09 | 19 43 | 05 20 | 05 47 | 06 17 | 06 54 |
| 35 | 18 34 | 19 00 | 19 31 | 05 23 | 05 53 | 06 28 | 07 08 |
| 30 | 18 28 | 18 53 | 19 22 | 05 25 | 05 59 | 06 37 | 07 20 |
| 20 | 18 19 | 18 41 | 19 08 | 05 29 | 06 09 | 06 52 | 07 40 |
| N 10 | 18 11 | 18 32 | 18 57 | 05 33 | 06 18 | 07 06 | 07 58 |
| 0 | 18 03 | 18 24 | 18 48 | 05 36 | 06 26 | 07 18 | 08 15 |
| S 10 | 17 55 | 18 17 | 18 41 | 05 40 | 06 34 | 07 31 | 08 32 |
| 20 | 17 47 | 18 10 | 18 36 | 05 43 | 06 43 | 07 45 | 08 50 |
| 30 | 17 39 | 18 03 | 18 31 | 05 48 | 06 53 | 08 01 | 09 11 |
| 35 | 17 33 | 17 59 | 18 29 | 05 50 | 06 59 | 08 10 | 09 24 |
| 40 | 17 28 | 17 55 | 18 27 | 05 53 | 07 05 | 08 21 | 09 38 |
| 45 | 17 21 | 17 51 | 18 25 | 05 56 | 07 13 | 08 33 | 09 55 |
| S 50 | 17 13 | 17 46 | 18 24 | 06 00 | 07 23 | 08 49 | 10 16 |
| 52 | 17 10 | 17 44 | 18 23 | 06 02 | 07 27 | 08 56 | 10 26 |
| 54 | 17 06 | 17 42 | 18 23 | 06 04 | 07 32 | 09 04 | 10 37 |
| 56 | 17 01 | 17 39 | 18 22 | 06 06 | 07 37 | 09 13 | 10 50 |
| 58 | 16 56 | 17 37 | 18 22 | 06 08 | 07 43 | 09 23 | 11 05 |
| S 60 | 16 51 | 17 34 | 18 22 | 06 11 | 07 50 | 09 35 | 11 23 |

| Day | SUN Eqn. of Time 00ʰ | SUN Eqn. of Time 12ʰ | SUN Mer. Pass. | MOON Mer. Pass. Upper | MOON Mer. Pass. Lower | Age | Phase |
|---|---|---|---|---|---|---|---|
| d | m s | m s | h m | h m | h m | d % | |
| 16 | 00 04 | 00 12 | 12 00 | 24 14 | 11 49 | 15 100 | ◯ |
| 17 | 00 19 | 00 26 | 12 00 | 00 14 | 12 39 | 16 99 | |
| 18 | 00 32 | 00 39 | 11 59 | 01 06 | 13 33 | 17 96 | |

| UT | ARIES GHA | VENUS −4·2 GHA | Dec | MARS +0·9 GHA | Dec | JUPITER −2·1 GHA | Dec | SATURN +0·7 GHA | Dec | STARS Name | SHA | Dec |
|---|---|---|---|---|---|---|---|---|---|---|---|---|
| **19 00** | 207 04.6 | 221 01.6 | S 6 37.4 | 231 40.9 | S11 44.8 | 210 52.6 | S 2 46.8 | 240 54.0 | S14 36.9 | Acamar | 315 13.9 | S40 13.1 |
| 01 | 222 07.0 | 236 01.4 | 36.4 | 246 41.5 | 44.2 | 225 54.5 | 46.6 | 255 56.3 | 36.8 | Achernar | 335 22.5 | S57 07.5 |
| 02 | 237 09.5 | 251 01.2 | 35.5 | 261 42.2 | 43.5 | 240 56.5 | 46.4 | 270 58.6 | 36.8 | Acrux | 173 01.9 | S63 13.4 |
| 03 | 252 12.0 | 266 01.0 | .. 34.6 | 276 42.9 | .. 42.8 | 255 58.4 | .. 46.2 | 286 00.9 | .. 36.7 | Adhara | 255 07.8 | S29 00.4 |
| 04 | 267 14.4 | 281 00.9 | 33.7 | 291 43.5 | 42.2 | 271 00.4 | 46.0 | 301 03.2 | 36.7 | Aldebaran | 290 42.5 | N16 33.1 |
| 05 | 282 16.9 | 296 00.7 | 32.8 | 306 44.2 | 41.5 | 286 02.3 | 45.8 | 316 05.5 | 36.6 | | | |
| 06 | 297 19.4 | 311 00.5 | S 6 31.9 | 321 44.8 | S11 40.9 | 301 04.3 | S 2 45.5 | 331 07.8 | S14 36.6 | Alioth | 166 14.5 | N55 50.4 |
| 07 | 312 21.8 | 326 00.3 | 30.9 | 336 45.5 | 40.2 | 316 06.2 | 45.3 | 346 10.1 | 36.5 | Alkaid | 152 53.3 | N49 12.1 |
| T 08 | 327 24.3 | 341 00.1 | 30.0 | 351 46.1 | 39.5 | 331 08.2 | 45.1 | 1 12.3 | 36.5 | Alnair | 27 36.6 | S46 51.1 |
| U 09 | 342 26.7 | 355 59.9 | .. 29.1 | 6 46.8 | .. 38.9 | 346 10.2 | .. 44.9 | 16 14.6 | .. 36.4 | Alnilam | 275 40.2 | S 1 11.4 |
| E 10 | 357 29.2 | 10 59.8 | 28.2 | 21 47.4 | 38.2 | 1 12.1 | 44.7 | 31 16.9 | 36.4 | Alphard | 217 49.9 | S 8 45.4 |
| S 11 | 12 31.7 | 25 59.6 | 27.3 | 36 48.1 | 37.6 | 16 14.1 | 44.5 | 46 19.2 | 36.3 | | | |
| D 12 | 27 34.1 | 40 59.4 | S 6 26.3 | 51 48.8 | S11 36.9 | 31 16.0 | S 2 44.3 | 61 21.5 | S14 36.3 | Alphecca | 126 05.3 | N26 38.3 |
| A 13 | 42 36.6 | 55 59.2 | 25.4 | 66 49.4 | 36.2 | 46 18.0 | 44.1 | 76 23.8 | 36.2 | Alpheratz | 357 37.4 | N29 12.5 |
| Y 14 | 57 39.1 | 70 59.0 | 24.5 | 81 50.1 | 35.6 | 61 19.9 | 43.8 | 91 26.1 | 36.1 | Altair | 62 02.1 | N 8 55.4 |
| 15 | 72 41.5 | 85 58.8 | .. 23.6 | 96 50.7 | .. 34.9 | 76 21.9 | .. 43.6 | 106 28.4 | .. 36.1 | Ankaa | 353 09.8 | S42 11.2 |
| 16 | 87 44.0 | 100 58.7 | 22.7 | 111 51.4 | 34.2 | 91 23.8 | 43.4 | 121 30.7 | 36.0 | Antares | 112 18.3 | S26 28.8 |
| 17 | 102 46.5 | 115 58.5 | 21.7 | 126 52.0 | 33.6 | 106 25.8 | 43.2 | 136 33.0 | 36.0 | | | |
| 18 | 117 48.9 | 130 58.3 | S 6 20.8 | 141 52.7 | S11 32.9 | 121 27.8 | S 2 43.0 | 151 35.2 | S14 35.9 | Arcturus | 145 49.7 | N19 03.9 |
| 19 | 132 51.4 | 145 58.1 | 19.9 | 156 53.4 | 32.3 | 136 29.7 | 42.8 | 166 37.5 | 35.9 | Atria | 107 14.2 | S69 03.8 |
| 20 | 147 53.9 | 160 57.9 | 19.0 | 171 54.0 | 31.6 | 151 31.7 | 42.6 | 181 39.8 | 35.8 | Avior | 234 15.6 | S59 35.1 |
| 21 | 162 56.3 | 175 57.8 | .. 18.0 | 186 54.7 | .. 30.9 | 166 33.6 | .. 42.3 | 196 42.1 | .. 35.8 | Bellatrix | 278 25.5 | N 6 22.1 |
| 22 | 177 58.8 | 190 57.6 | 17.1 | 201 55.3 | 30.3 | 181 35.6 | 42.1 | 211 44.4 | 35.7 | Betelgeuse | 270 54.7 | N 7 24.6 |
| 23 | 193 01.2 | 205 57.4 | 16.2 | 216 56.0 | 29.6 | 196 37.5 | 41.9 | 226 46.7 | 35.7 | | | |
| **20 00** | 208 03.7 | 220 57.2 | S 6 15.3 | 231 56.6 | S11 28.9 | 211 39.5 | S 2 41.7 | 241 49.0 | S14 35.6 | Canopus | 263 53.6 | S52 42.7 |
| 01 | 223 06.2 | 235 57.0 | 14.3 | 246 57.3 | 28.3 | 226 41.4 | 41.5 | 256 51.3 | 35.6 | Capella | 280 25.5 | N46 01.3 |
| 02 | 238 08.6 | 250 56.8 | 13.4 | 261 58.0 | 27.6 | 241 43.4 | 41.3 | 271 53.6 | 35.5 | Deneb | 49 27.4 | N45 21.2 |
| 03 | 253 11.1 | 265 56.7 | .. 12.5 | 276 58.6 | .. 27.0 | 256 45.4 | .. 41.1 | 286 55.9 | .. 35.5 | Denebola | 182 27.0 | N14 26.9 |
| 04 | 268 13.6 | 280 56.5 | 11.5 | 291 59.3 | 26.3 | 271 47.3 | 40.8 | 301 58.2 | 35.4 | Diphda | 348 49.9 | S17 52.0 |
| 05 | 283 16.0 | 295 56.3 | 10.6 | 306 59.9 | 25.6 | 286 49.3 | 40.6 | 317 00.4 | 35.4 | | | |
| 06 | 298 18.5 | 310 56.1 | S 6 09.7 | 322 00.6 | S11 25.0 | 301 51.2 | S 2 40.4 | 332 02.7 | S14 35.3 | Dubhe | 193 43.4 | N61 38.1 |
| W 07 | 313 21.0 | 325 55.9 | 08.8 | 337 01.3 | 24.3 | 316 53.2 | 40.2 | 347 05.0 | 35.3 | Elnath | 278 05.0 | N28 37.5 |
| E 08 | 328 23.4 | 340 55.7 | 07.8 | 352 01.9 | 23.6 | 331 55.1 | 40.0 | 2 07.3 | 35.2 | Eltanin | 90 43.0 | N51 28.8 |
| D 09 | 343 25.9 | 355 55.6 | .. 06.9 | 7 02.6 | .. 23.0 | 346 57.1 | .. 39.8 | 17 09.6 | .. 35.2 | Enif | 33 41.1 | N 9 58.4 |
| N 10 | 358 28.4 | 10 55.4 | 06.0 | 22 03.2 | 22.3 | 1 59.1 | 39.6 | 32 11.9 | 35.1 | Fomalhaut | 15 17.3 | S29 30.3 |
| E 11 | 13 30.8 | 25 55.2 | 05.0 | 37 03.9 | 21.6 | 17 01.0 | 39.4 | 47 14.2 | 35.1 | | | |
| S 12 | 28 33.3 | 40 55.0 | S 6 04.1 | 52 04.6 | S11 21.0 | 32 03.0 | S 2 39.1 | 62 16.5 | S14 35.0 | Gacrux | 171 53.6 | S57 14.4 |
| D 13 | 43 35.7 | 55 54.8 | 03.2 | 67 05.2 | 20.3 | 47 04.9 | 38.9 | 77 18.8 | 35.0 | Gienah | 175 45.6 | S17 40.0 |
| A 14 | 58 38.2 | 70 54.6 | 02.2 | 82 05.9 | 19.6 | 62 06.9 | 38.7 | 92 21.1 | 34.9 | Hadar | 148 38.6 | S60 28.8 |
| Y 15 | 73 40.7 | 85 54.5 | .. 01.3 | 97 06.5 | .. 19.0 | 77 08.8 | .. 38.5 | 107 23.4 | .. 34.9 | Hamal | 327 54.1 | N23 33.9 |
| 16 | 88 43.1 | 100 54.3 | 6 00.4 | 112 07.2 | 18.3 | 92 10.8 | 38.3 | 122 25.7 | 34.8 | Kaus Aust. | 83 35.4 | S34 22.4 |
| 17 | 103 45.6 | 115 54.1 | 5 59.4 | 127 07.9 | 17.6 | 107 12.8 | 38.1 | 137 28.0 | 34.8 | | | |
| 18 | 118 48.1 | 130 53.9 | S 5 58.5 | 142 08.5 | S11 17.0 | 122 14.7 | S 2 37.9 | 152 30.3 | S14 34.7 | Kochab | 137 18.7 | N74 03.8 |
| 19 | 133 50.5 | 145 53.7 | 57.6 | 157 09.2 | 16.3 | 137 16.7 | 37.7 | 167 32.5 | 34.7 | Markab | 13 32.4 | N15 19.2 |
| 20 | 148 53.0 | 160 53.5 | 56.6 | 172 09.8 | 15.6 | 152 18.6 | 37.4 | 182 34.8 | 34.6 | Menkar | 314 08.8 | N 4 10.4 |
| 21 | 163 55.5 | 175 53.4 | .. 55.7 | 187 10.5 | .. 15.0 | 167 20.6 | .. 37.2 | 197 37.1 | .. 34.6 | Menkent | 147 59.9 | S36 28.8 |
| 22 | 178 57.9 | 190 53.2 | 54.8 | 202 11.2 | 14.3 | 182 22.6 | 37.0 | 212 39.4 | 34.5 | Miaplacidus | 221 38.4 | S69 48.7 |
| 23 | 194 00.4 | 205 53.0 | 53.8 | 217 11.8 | 13.6 | 197 24.5 | 36.8 | 227 41.7 | 34.5 | | | |
| **21 00** | 209 02.8 | 220 52.8 | S 5 52.9 | 232 12.5 | S11 13.0 | 212 26.5 | S 2 36.6 | 242 44.0 | S14 34.4 | Mirfak | 308 32.0 | N49 56.3 |
| 01 | 224 05.3 | 235 52.6 | 52.0 | 247 13.1 | 12.3 | 227 28.4 | 36.4 | 257 46.3 | 34.4 | Nunki | 75 50.5 | S26 16.1 |
| 02 | 239 07.8 | 250 52.4 | 51.0 | 262 13.8 | 11.6 | 242 30.4 | 36.2 | 272 48.6 | 34.3 | Peacock | 53 09.4 | S56 39.6 |
| 03 | 254 10.2 | 265 52.3 | .. 50.1 | 277 14.5 | .. 11.0 | 257 32.3 | .. 36.0 | 287 50.9 | .. 34.3 | Pollux | 243 20.1 | N27 58.4 |
| 04 | 269 12.7 | 280 52.1 | 49.2 | 292 15.1 | 10.3 | 272 34.3 | 35.7 | 302 53.2 | 34.2 | Procyon | 244 53.3 | N 5 10.0 |
| 05 | 284 15.2 | 295 51.9 | 48.2 | 307 15.8 | 09.6 | 287 36.3 | 35.5 | 317 55.5 | 34.2 | | | |
| 06 | 299 17.6 | 310 51.7 | S 5 47.3 | 322 16.4 | S11 09.0 | 302 38.2 | S 2 35.3 | 332 57.8 | S14 34.1 | Rasalhague | 96 00.4 | N12 32.5 |
| T 07 | 314 20.1 | 325 51.5 | 46.3 | 337 17.1 | 08.3 | 317 40.2 | 35.1 | 348 00.1 | 34.0 | Regulus | 207 36.7 | N11 51.5 |
| H 08 | 329 22.6 | 340 51.3 | 45.4 | 352 17.8 | 07.6 | 332 42.1 | 34.9 | 3 02.4 | 34.0 | Rigel | 281 06.3 | S 8 10.7 |
| U 09 | 344 25.0 | 355 51.2 | .. 44.5 | 7 18.4 | .. 07.0 | 347 44.1 | .. 34.7 | 18 04.7 | .. 33.9 | Rigil Kent. | 139 42.7 | S60 55.5 |
| R 10 | 359 27.5 | 10 51.0 | 43.5 | 22 19.1 | 06.3 | 2 46.1 | 34.5 | 33 07.0 | 33.9 | Sabik | 102 05.1 | S15 45.2 |
| S 11 | 14 30.0 | 25 50.8 | 42.6 | 37 19.8 | 05.6 | 17 48.0 | 34.3 | 48 09.3 | 33.8 | | | |
| D 12 | 29 32.4 | 40 50.6 | S 5 41.6 | 52 20.4 | S11 05.0 | 32 50.0 | S 2 34.0 | 63 11.6 | S14 33.8 | Schedar | 349 34.1 | N56 39.3 |
| A 13 | 44 34.9 | 55 50.4 | 40.7 | 67 21.1 | 04.3 | 47 51.9 | 33.8 | 78 13.9 | 33.7 | Shaula | 96 13.2 | S37 07.1 |
| Y 14 | 59 37.3 | 70 50.2 | 39.7 | 82 21.7 | 03.6 | 62 53.9 | 33.6 | 93 16.2 | 33.7 | Sirius | 258 28.4 | S16 45.0 |
| 15 | 74 39.8 | 85 50.0 | .. 38.8 | 97 22.4 | .. 02.9 | 77 55.9 | .. 33.4 | 108 18.5 | .. 33.6 | Spica | 158 24.4 | S11 16.7 |
| 16 | 89 42.3 | 100 49.9 | 37.9 | 112 23.1 | 02.3 | 92 57.8 | 33.2 | 123 20.7 | 33.6 | Suhail | 222 47.8 | S43 31.6 |
| 17 | 104 44.7 | 115 49.7 | 36.9 | 127 23.7 | 01.6 | 107 59.8 | 33.0 | 138 23.0 | 33.5 | | | |
| 18 | 119 47.2 | 130 49.5 | S 5 36.0 | 142 24.4 | S11 00.9 | 123 01.7 | S 2 32.8 | 153 25.3 | S14 33.5 | Vega | 80 34.6 | N38 48.0 |
| 19 | 134 49.7 | 145 49.3 | 35.0 | 157 25.1 | 11 00.3 | 138 03.7 | 32.6 | 168 27.6 | 33.5 | Zuben'ubi | 136 58.2 | S16 08.1 |
| 20 | 149 52.1 | 160 49.1 | 34.1 | 172 25.7 | 10 59.6 | 153 05.7 | 32.3 | 183 29.9 | 33.4 | | | |
| 21 | 164 54.6 | 175 48.9 | .. 33.1 | 187 26.4 | .. 58.9 | 168 07.6 | .. 32.1 | 198 32.2 | .. 33.4 | | | |
| 22 | 179 57.1 | 190 48.8 | 32.2 | 202 27.1 | 58.2 | 183 09.6 | 31.9 | 213 34.5 | 33.3 | | | |
| 23 | 194 59.5 | 205 48.6 | 31.2 | 217 27.7 | 57.6 | 198 11.5 | 31.7 | 228 36.8 | 33.3 | | | |

| | SHA | Mer. Pass. |
|---|---|---|
| | ° ′ | h m |
| Venus | 12 53.5 | 9 16 |
| Mars | 23 52.9 | 8 32 |
| Jupiter | 3 35.8 | 9 52 |
| Saturn | 33 45.3 | 7 52 |

| | h m | | | | |
|---|---|---|---|---|---|
| Mer. Pass. | 10 06.1 | v −0.2 d 0.9 | v 0.7 d 0.7 | v 2.0 d 0.2 | v 2.3 d 0.1 |

### SUN / MOON

| UT | SUN GHA | SUN Dec | MOON GHA | v | MOON Dec | d | HP |
|---|---|---|---|---|---|---|---|
| **19** 00 | 180 11.5 | N11 05.5 | 330 49.1 | 6.4 | S20 23.5 | 11.2 | 60.0 |
| 01 | 195 11.6 | 06.4 | 345 14.5 | 6.3 | 20 34.7 | 11.1 | 60.0 |
| 02 | 210 11.8 | 07.2 | 359 39.8 | 6.2 | 20 45.8 | 10.9 | 60.0 |
| 03 | 225 11.9 | .. 08.1 | 14 05.0 | 6.1 | 20 56.7 | 10.8 | 60.0 |
| 04 | 240 12.0 | 09.0 | 28 30.1 | 6.0 | 21 07.5 | 10.7 | 60.0 |
| 05 | 255 12.2 | 09.8 | 42 55.1 | 6.0 | 21 18.2 | 10.5 | 60.0 |
| 06 | 270 12.3 | N11 10.7 | 57 20.1 | 5.8 | S21 28.7 | 10.4 | 60.0 |
| 07 | 285 12.5 | 11.6 | 71 44.9 | 5.7 | 21 39.1 | 10.2 | 60.0 |
| **T** 08 | 300 12.6 | 12.4 | 86 09.6 | 5.7 | 21 49.3 | 10.1 | 60.0 |
| **U** 09 | 315 12.7 | .. 13.3 | 100 34.3 | 5.6 | 21 59.4 | 10.0 | 60.0 |
| **E** 10 | 330 12.9 | 14.2 | 114 58.9 | 5.5 | 22 09.4 | 9.8 | 60.0 |
| **S** 11 | 345 13.0 | 15.0 | 129 23.4 | 5.3 | 22 19.2 | 9.7 | 60.0 |
| **D** 12 | 0 13.1 | N11 15.9 | 143 47.7 | 5.4 | S22 28.9 | 9.5 | 60.1 |
| **A** 13 | 15 13.3 | 16.7 | 158 12.1 | 5.2 | 22 38.4 | 9.4 | 60.1 |
| **Y** 14 | 30 13.4 | 17.6 | 172 36.3 | 5.1 | 22 47.8 | 9.2 | 60.1 |
| 15 | 45 13.5 | .. 18.5 | 187 00.4 | 5.1 | 22 57.0 | 9.0 | 60.1 |
| 16 | 60 13.7 | 19.3 | 201 24.5 | 4.9 | 23 06.0 | 8.9 | 60.1 |
| 17 | 75 13.8 | 20.2 | 215 48.4 | 4.9 | 23 14.9 | 8.8 | 60.1 |
| 18 | 90 13.9 | N11 21.1 | 230 12.3 | 4.8 | S23 23.7 | 8.6 | 60.1 |
| 19 | 105 14.1 | 21.9 | 244 36.1 | 4.7 | 23 32.3 | 8.4 | 60.0 |
| 20 | 120 14.2 | 22.8 | 258 59.8 | 4.7 | 23 40.7 | 8.3 | 60.0 |
| 21 | 135 14.3 | .. 23.6 | 273 23.5 | 4.6 | 23 49.0 | 8.1 | 60.0 |
| 22 | 150 14.5 | 24.5 | 287 47.1 | 4.5 | 23 57.1 | 7.9 | 60.0 |
| 23 | 165 14.6 | 25.4 | 302 10.6 | 4.4 | 24 05.0 | 7.8 | 60.0 |
| **20** 00 | 180 14.7 | N11 26.2 | 316 34.0 | 4.3 | S24 12.8 | 7.6 | 60.0 |
| 01 | 195 14.9 | 27.1 | 330 57.3 | 4.3 | 24 20.4 | 7.4 | 60.0 |
| 02 | 210 15.0 | 27.9 | 345 20.6 | 4.2 | 24 27.8 | 7.3 | 60.0 |
| 03 | 225 15.1 | .. 28.8 | 359 43.8 | 4.2 | 24 35.1 | 7.1 | 60.0 |
| 04 | 240 15.3 | 29.6 | 14 07.0 | 4.1 | 24 42.2 | 6.9 | 60.0 |
| 05 | 255 15.4 | 30.5 | 28 30.1 | 4.0 | 24 49.1 | 6.7 | 60.0 |
| 06 | 270 15.5 | N11 31.4 | 42 53.1 | 3.9 | S24 55.8 | 6.6 | 60.0 |
| **W** 07 | 285 15.7 | 32.2 | 57 16.0 | 3.9 | 25 02.4 | 6.4 | 60.0 |
| **E** 08 | 300 15.8 | 33.1 | 71 38.9 | 3.9 | 25 08.8 | 6.2 | 60.0 |
| **D** 09 | 315 15.9 | .. 33.9 | 86 01.8 | 3.8 | 25 15.0 | 6.1 | 60.0 |
| **N** 10 | 330 16.0 | 34.8 | 100 24.6 | 3.7 | 25 21.1 | 5.8 | 60.0 |
| **E** 11 | 345 16.2 | 35.6 | 114 47.3 | 3.7 | 25 26.9 | 5.7 | 60.0 |
| **S** 12 | 0 16.3 | N11 36.5 | 129 10.0 | 3.6 | S25 32.6 | 5.5 | 60.0 |
| **D** 13 | 15 16.4 | 37.3 | 143 32.6 | 3.6 | 25 38.1 | 5.3 | 60.0 |
| **A** 14 | 30 16.6 | 38.2 | 157 55.2 | 3.5 | 25 43.4 | 5.2 | 60.0 |
| **Y** 15 | 45 16.7 | .. 39.1 | 172 17.7 | 3.5 | 25 48.6 | 4.9 | 60.0 |
| 16 | 60 16.8 | 39.9 | 186 40.2 | 3.4 | 25 53.5 | 4.8 | 60.0 |
| 17 | 75 17.0 | 40.8 | 201 02.6 | 3.4 | 25 58.3 | 4.6 | 59.9 |
| 18 | 90 17.1 | N11 41.6 | 215 25.0 | 3.4 | S26 02.9 | 4.4 | 59.9 |
| 19 | 105 17.2 | 42.5 | 229 47.4 | 3.3 | 26 07.3 | 4.2 | 59.9 |
| 20 | 120 17.3 | 43.3 | 244 09.7 | 3.3 | 26 11.5 | 4.0 | 59.9 |
| 21 | 135 17.5 | .. 44.2 | 258 32.0 | 3.3 | 26 15.5 | 3.8 | 59.9 |
| 22 | 150 17.6 | 45.0 | 272 54.3 | 3.2 | 26 19.3 | 3.7 | 59.9 |
| 23 | 165 17.7 | 45.9 | 287 16.5 | 3.2 | 26 23.0 | 3.5 | 59.9 |
| **21** 00 | 180 17.9 | N11 46.7 | 301 38.7 | 3.2 | S26 26.5 | 3.2 | 59.9 |
| 01 | 195 18.0 | 47.6 | 316 00.9 | 3.2 | 26 29.7 | 3.1 | 59.9 |
| 02 | 210 18.1 | 48.4 | 330 23.1 | 3.2 | 26 32.8 | 2.9 | 59.9 |
| 03 | 225 18.2 | .. 49.3 | 344 45.3 | 3.1 | 26 35.7 | 2.7 | 59.8 |
| 04 | 240 18.4 | 50.1 | 359 07.4 | 3.1 | 26 38.4 | 2.5 | 59.8 |
| 05 | 255 18.5 | 51.0 | 13 29.5 | 3.1 | 26 40.9 | 2.3 | 59.8 |
| 06 | 270 18.6 | N11 51.8 | 27 51.6 | 3.2 | S26 43.2 | 2.2 | 59.8 |
| 07 | 285 18.7 | 52.7 | 42 13.8 | 3.1 | 26 45.4 | 1.9 | 59.8 |
| **T** 08 | 300 18.9 | 53.5 | 56 35.9 | 3.1 | 26 47.3 | 1.7 | 59.8 |
| **H** 09 | 315 19.0 | .. 54.4 | 70 58.0 | 3.0 | 26 49.0 | 1.6 | 59.7 |
| **U** 10 | 330 19.1 | 55.2 | 85 20.0 | 3.1 | 26 50.6 | 1.4 | 59.7 |
| **R** 11 | 345 19.3 | 56.1 | 99 42.1 | 3.2 | 26 52.0 | 1.1 | 59.7 |
| **S** 12 | 0 19.4 | N11 56.9 | 114 04.3 | 3.1 | S26 53.1 | 1.0 | 59.7 |
| **D** 13 | 15 19.5 | 57.8 | 128 26.4 | 3.1 | 26 54.1 | 0.8 | 59.7 |
| **A** 14 | 30 19.6 | 58.6 | 142 48.5 | 3.1 | 26 54.9 | 0.6 | 59.7 |
| **Y** 15 | 45 19.8 | 11 59.5 | 157 10.6 | 3.2 | 26 55.5 | 0.4 | 59.7 |
| 16 | 60 19.9 | 12 00.3 | 171 32.8 | 3.1 | 26 55.9 | 0.2 | 59.7 |
| 17 | 75 20.0 | 01.1 | 185 54.9 | 3.2 | 26 56.1 | 0.0 | 59.7 |
| 18 | 90 20.1 | N12 02.0 | 200 17.1 | 3.2 | S26 56.1 | 0.1 | 59.7 |
| 19 | 105 20.3 | 02.8 | 214 39.3 | 3.2 | 26 56.0 | 0.4 | 59.6 |
| 20 | 120 20.4 | 03.7 | 229 01.5 | 3.3 | 26 55.6 | 0.5 | 59.6 |
| 21 | 135 20.5 | .. 04.5 | 243 23.8 | 3.3 | 26 55.1 | 0.8 | 59.6 |
| 22 | 150 20.6 | 05.4 | 257 46.1 | 3.3 | 26 54.3 | 0.9 | 59.6 |
| 23 | 165 20.7 | 06.2 | 272 08.4 | 3.3 | S26 53.4 | 1.1 | 59.6 |
| | SD 15.9 | d 0.9 | SD 16.4 | | 16.3 | | 16.3 |

### Twilight / Sunrise / Moonrise

| Lat. | Naut. | Civil | Sunrise | Moonrise 19 | 20 | 21 | 22 |
|---|---|---|---|---|---|---|---|
| N 72 | //// | 00 57 | 03 10 | ■ | ■ | ■ | ■ |
| N 70 | //// | 01 58 | 03 31 | ■ | ■ | ■ | ■ |
| 68 | //// | 02 31 | 03 47 | 00 34 | ■ | ■ | ■ |
| 66 | 00 49 | 02 55 | 04 01 | ■ | ■ | ■ | ■ |
| 64 | 01 43 | 03 14 | 04 12 | 25 36 | 01 36 | ■ | ■ |
| 62 | 02 13 | 03 29 | 04 21 | 24 52 | 00 52 | 02 46 | 03 55 |
| 60 | 02 35 | 03 41 | 04 29 | 24 22 | 00 22 | 02 01 | 03 09 |
| N 58 | 02 53 | 03 52 | 04 36 | 24 00 | 00 00 | 01 32 | 02 39 |
| 56 | 03 07 | 04 01 | 04 42 | 23 42 | 25 09 | 01 09 | 02 16 |
| 54 | 03 20 | 04 09 | 04 48 | 23 26 | 24 50 | 00 50 | 01 57 |
| 52 | 03 30 | 04 16 | 04 53 | 23 13 | 24 35 | 00 35 | 01 41 |
| 50 | 03 39 | 04 23 | 04 57 | 23 01 | 24 21 | 00 21 | 01 27 |
| 45 | 03 58 | 04 36 | 05 07 | 22 37 | 23 54 | 24 59 | 00 59 |
| N 40 | 04 13 | 04 47 | 05 15 | 22 18 | 23 32 | 24 37 | 00 37 |
| 35 | 04 24 | 04 56 | 05 22 | 22 02 | 23 14 | 24 19 | 00 19 |
| 30 | 04 34 | 05 03 | 05 28 | 21 49 | 22 58 | 24 03 | 00 03 |
| 20 | 04 49 | 05 16 | 05 38 | 21 25 | 22 32 | 23 36 | 24 35 |
| N 10 | 05 01 | 05 26 | 05 47 | 21 05 | 22 10 | 23 13 | 24 14 |
| 0 | 05 10 | 05 34 | 05 56 | 20 47 | 21 49 | 22 52 | 23 54 |
| S 10 | 05 18 | 05 42 | 06 04 | 20 28 | 21 28 | 22 30 | 23 33 |
| 20 | 05 24 | 05 50 | 06 12 | 20 08 | 21 05 | 22 07 | 23 12 |
| 30 | 05 30 | 05 58 | 06 22 | 19 46 | 20 40 | 21 41 | 22 47 |
| 35 | 05 32 | 06 02 | 06 28 | 19 33 | 20 25 | 21 25 | 22 32 |
| 40 | 05 35 | 06 06 | 06 34 | 19 17 | 20 07 | 21 07 | 22 15 |
| 45 | 05 37 | 06 11 | 06 41 | 18 59 | 19 46 | 20 45 | 21 54 |
| S 50 | 05 39 | 06 17 | 06 50 | 18 37 | 19 20 | 20 17 | 21 28 |
| 52 | 05 40 | 06 19 | 06 54 | 18 27 | 19 07 | 20 03 | 21 15 |
| 54 | 05 41 | 06 22 | 06 58 | 18 15 | 18 52 | 19 48 | 21 01 |
| 56 | 05 41 | 06 25 | 07 03 | 18 01 | 18 35 | 19 29 | 20 44 |
| 58 | 05 42 | 06 28 | 07 08 | 17 46 | 18 15 | 19 06 | 20 23 |
| S 60 | 05 43 | 06 31 | 07 15 | 17 27 | 17 49 | 18 37 | 19 57 |

### Sunset / Twilight / Moonset

| Lat. | Sunset | Civil | Naut. | Moonset 19 | 20 | 21 | 22 |
|---|---|---|---|---|---|---|---|
| N 72 | 20 53 | 23 22 | //// | ■ | ■ | ■ | ■ |
| N 70 | 20 30 | 22 07 | //// | ■ | ■ | ■ | ■ |
| 68 | 20 13 | 21 31 | //// | 03 11 | ■ | ■ | ■ |
| 66 | 20 00 | 21 06 | 23 27 | 04 02 | ■ | ■ | ■ |
| 64 | 19 48 | 20 47 | 22 21 | 04 34 | 04 16 | ■ | ■ |
| 62 | 19 39 | 20 31 | 21 49 | 04 57 | 05 01 | 05 18 | 06 22 |
| 60 | 19 30 | 20 19 | 21 26 | 05 17 | 05 31 | 06 03 | 07 07 |
| N 58 | 19 23 | 20 08 | 21 07 | 05 33 | 05 54 | 06 33 | 07 37 |
| 56 | 19 17 | 19 58 | 20 53 | 05 46 | 06 13 | 06 56 | 08 00 |
| 54 | 19 11 | 19 50 | 20 40 | 05 58 | 06 28 | 07 14 | 08 19 |
| 52 | 19 06 | 19 43 | 20 29 | 06 09 | 06 42 | 07 30 | 08 35 |
| 50 | 19 02 | 19 36 | 20 20 | 06 18 | 06 54 | 07 44 | 08 48 |
| 45 | 18 53 | 19 23 | 20 01 | 06 38 | 07 19 | 08 12 | 09 16 |
| N 40 | 18 43 | 19 12 | 19 46 | 06 54 | 07 39 | 08 34 | 09 38 |
| 35 | 18 36 | 19 03 | 19 34 | 07 08 | 07 56 | 08 52 | 09 56 |
| 30 | 18 30 | 18 55 | 19 24 | 07 20 | 08 10 | 09 08 | 10 12 |
| 20 | 18 20 | 18 42 | 19 09 | 07 40 | 08 35 | 09 34 | 10 38 |
| N 10 | 18 11 | 18 32 | 18 57 | 07 58 | 08 56 | 09 57 | 11 01 |
| 0 | 18 02 | 18 23 | 18 48 | 08 15 | 09 16 | 10 19 | 11 22 |
| S 10 | 17 54 | 18 15 | 18 40 | 08 32 | 09 36 | 10 40 | 11 43 |
| 20 | 17 45 | 18 08 | 18 33 | 08 50 | 09 57 | 11 03 | 12 05 |
| 30 | 17 35 | 18 00 | 18 28 | 09 11 | 10 22 | 11 30 | 12 31 |
| 35 | 17 30 | 17 56 | 18 25 | 09 24 | 10 37 | 11 45 | 12 46 |
| 40 | 17 23 | 17 51 | 18 23 | 09 38 | 10 54 | 12 04 | 13 04 |
| 45 | 17 16 | 17 46 | 18 20 | 09 55 | 11 14 | 12 26 | 13 25 |
| S 50 | 17 07 | 17 40 | 18 18 | 10 16 | 11 40 | 12 53 | 13 51 |
| 52 | 17 03 | 17 38 | 18 17 | 10 26 | 11 52 | 13 07 | 14 04 |
| 54 | 16 59 | 17 35 | 18 16 | 10 37 | 12 07 | 13 23 | 14 19 |
| 56 | 16 54 | 17 32 | 18 16 | 10 50 | 12 23 | 13 41 | 14 36 |
| 58 | 16 48 | 17 29 | 18 15 | 11 05 | 12 43 | 14 04 | 14 57 |
| S 60 | 16 42 | 17 26 | 18 14 | 11 23 | 13 09 | 14 34 | 15 23 |

### SUN / MOON

| Day | Eqn. of Time 00h | 12h | Mer. Pass. | Mer. Pass. Upper | Lower | Age | Phase |
|---|---|---|---|---|---|---|---|
| | m s | m s | h m | h m | h m | d | % |
| 19 | 00 46 | 00 52 | 11 59 | 02 01 | 14 31 | 18 | 90 |
| 20 | 00 59 | 01 05 | 11 59 | 03 01 | 15 32 | 19 | 82 |
| 21 | 01 11 | 01 17 | 11 59 | 04 04 | 16 35 | 20 | 72 |

| UT | ARIES GHA | VENUS −4.2 GHA | Dec | MARS +0.9 GHA | Dec | JUPITER −2.1 GHA | Dec | SATURN +0.7 GHA | Dec | STARS Name | SHA | Dec |
|---|---|---|---|---|---|---|---|---|---|---|---|---|
| **22** 00 | 210 02.0 | 220 48.4 | S 5 30.3 | 232 28.4 | S10 56.9 | 213 13.5 | S 2 31.5 | 243 39.1 | S14 33.2 | Acamar | 315 13.9 | S40 13.1 |
| 01 | 225 04.5 | 235 48.2 | 29.4 | 247 29.1 | 56.2 | 228 15.5 | 31.3 | 258 41.4 | 33.2 | Achernar | 335 22.5 | S57 07.5 |
| 02 | 240 06.9 | 250 48.0 | 28.4 | 262 29.7 | 55.6 | 243 17.4 | 31.1 | 273 43.7 | 33.1 | Acrux | 173 01.9 | S63 13.5 |
| 03 | 255 09.4 | 265 47.8 .. | 27.5 | 277 30.4 .. | 54.9 | 258 19.4 .. | 30.9 | 288 46.0 .. | 33.1 | Adhara | 255 07.8 | S29 00.4 |
| 04 | 270 11.8 | 280 47.7 | 26.5 | 292 31.0 | 54.2 | 273 21.4 | 30.7 | 303 48.3 | 33.0 | Aldebaran | 290 42.5 | N16 33.1 |
| 05 | 285 14.3 | 295 47.5 | 25.6 | 307 31.7 | 53.5 | 288 23.3 | 30.4 | 318 50.6 | 33.0 | | | |
| 06 | 300 16.8 | 310 47.3 | S 5 24.6 | 322 32.4 | S10 52.9 | 303 25.3 | S 2 30.2 | 333 52.9 | S14 32.9 | Alioth | 166 14.5 | N55 50.4 |
| 07 | 315 19.2 | 325 47.1 | 23.7 | 337 33.0 | 52.2 | 318 27.2 | 30.0 | 348 55.2 | 32.9 | Alkaid | 152 53.3 | N49 12.2 |
| F 08 | 330 21.7 | 340 46.9 | 22.7 | 352 33.7 | 51.5 | 333 29.2 | 29.8 | 3 57.5 | 32.8 | Alnair | 27 36.0 | S46 51.1 |
| R 09 | 345 24.2 | 355 46.7 .. | 21.8 | 7 34.4 .. | 50.9 | 348 31.2 .. | 29.6 | 18 59.8 .. | 32.8 | Alnilam | 275 40.2 | S 1 11.4 |
| I 10 | 0 26.6 | 10 46.5 | 20.8 | 22 35.0 | 50.2 | 3 33.1 | 29.4 | 34 02.1 | 32.7 | Alphard | 217 49.9 | S 8 45.4 |
| D 11 | 15 29.1 | 25 46.4 | 19.9 | 37 35.7 | 49.5 | 18 35.1 | 29.2 | 49 04.4 | 32.7 | | | |
| A 12 | 30 31.6 | 40 46.2 | S 5 18.9 | 52 36.4 | S10 48.8 | 33 37.0 | S 2 29.0 | 64 06.7 | S14 32.6 | Alphecca | 126 05.3 | N26 38.3 |
| Y 13 | 45 34.0 | 55 46.0 | 18.0 | 67 37.0 | 48.2 | 48 39.0 | 28.8 | 79 09.0 | 32.6 | Alpheratz | 357 37.4 | N29 12.5 |
| 14 | 60 36.5 | 70 45.8 | 17.0 | 82 37.7 | 47.5 | 63 41.0 | 28.5 | 94 11.3 | 32.5 | Altair | 62 02.1 | N 8 55.4 |
| 15 | 75 39.0 | 85 45.6 .. | 16.0 | 97 38.4 .. | 46.8 | 78 42.9 .. | 28.3 | 109 13.6 .. | 32.5 | Ankaa | 353 09.8 | S42 11.2 |
| 16 | 90 41.4 | 100 45.4 | 15.1 | 112 39.0 | 46.1 | 93 44.9 | 28.1 | 124 15.9 | 32.4 | Antares | 112 18.3 | S26 28.9 |
| 17 | 105 43.9 | 115 45.3 | 14.1 | 127 39.7 | 45.5 | 108 46.9 | 27.9 | 139 18.2 | 32.4 | | | |
| 18 | 120 46.3 | 130 45.1 | S 5 13.2 | 142 40.4 | S10 44.8 | 123 48.8 | S 2 27.7 | 154 20.5 | S14 32.3 | Arcturus | 145 49.6 | N19 03.9 |
| 19 | 135 48.8 | 145 44.9 | 12.2 | 157 41.0 | 44.1 | 138 50.8 | 27.5 | 169 22.8 | 32.3 | Atria | 107 14.1 | S69 03.8 |
| 20 | 150 51.3 | 160 44.7 | 11.3 | 172 41.7 | 43.4 | 153 52.7 | 27.3 | 184 25.1 | 32.2 | Avior | 234 15.6 | S59 35.1 |
| 21 | 165 53.7 | 175 44.5 .. | 10.3 | 187 42.4 .. | 42.8 | 168 54.7 .. | 27.1 | 199 27.4 .. | 32.2 | Bellatrix | 278 25.5 | N 6 22.1 |
| 22 | 180 56.2 | 190 44.3 | 09.4 | 202 43.0 | 42.1 | 183 56.7 | 26.9 | 214 29.7 | 32.1 | Betelgeuse | 270 54.7 | N 7 24.6 |
| 23 | 195 58.7 | 205 44.1 | 08.4 | 217 43.7 | 41.4 | 198 58.6 | 26.7 | 229 32.0 | 32.1 | | | |
| **23** 00 | 211 01.1 | 220 44.0 | S 5 07.5 | 232 44.4 | S10 40.7 | 214 00.6 | S 2 26.4 | 244 34.3 | S14 32.0 | Canopus | 263 53.6 | S52 42.7 |
| 01 | 226 03.6 | 235 43.8 | 06.5 | 247 45.0 | 40.1 | 229 02.6 | 26.2 | 259 36.6 | 32.0 | Capella | 280 25.5 | N46 01.3 |
| 02 | 241 06.1 | 250 43.6 | 05.5 | 262 45.7 | 39.4 | 244 04.5 | 26.0 | 274 38.9 | 31.9 | Deneb | 49 27.4 | N45 21.2 |
| 03 | 256 08.5 | 265 43.4 .. | 04.6 | 277 46.4 .. | 38.7 | 259 06.5 .. | 25.8 | 289 41.2 .. | 31.9 | Denebola | 182 27.0 | N14 26.9 |
| 04 | 271 11.0 | 280 43.2 | 03.6 | 292 47.0 | 38.0 | 274 08.5 | 25.6 | 304 43.5 | 31.8 | Diphda | 348 49.9 | S17 52.0 |
| 05 | 286 13.5 | 295 43.0 | 02.7 | 307 47.7 | 37.4 | 289 10.4 | 25.4 | 319 45.8 | 31.8 | | | |
| 06 | 301 15.9 | 310 42.9 | S 5 01.7 | 322 48.4 | S10 36.7 | 304 12.4 | S 2 25.2 | 334 48.1 | S14 31.7 | Dubhe | 193 43.4 | N61 38.1 |
| 07 | 316 18.4 | 325 42.7 | 5 00.7 | 337 49.1 | 36.0 | 319 14.3 | 25.0 | 349 50.4 | 31.7 | Elnath | 278 05.0 | N28 37.5 |
| S 08 | 331 20.8 | 340 42.5 | 4 59.8 | 352 49.7 | 35.3 | 334 16.3 | 24.8 | 4 52.7 | 31.6 | Eltanin | 90 42.9 | N51 28.9 |
| A 09 | 346 23.3 | 355 42.3 .. | 58.8 | 7 50.4 .. | 34.7 | 349 18.3 .. | 24.5 | 19 55.0 .. | 31.6 | Enif | 33 41.1 | N 9 58.4 |
| T 10 | 1 25.8 | 10 42.1 | 57.9 | 22 51.1 | 34.0 | 4 20.2 | 24.3 | 34 57.3 | 31.5 | Fomalhaut | 15 17.2 | S29 30.3 |
| U 11 | 16 28.2 | 25 41.9 | 56.9 | 37 51.7 | 33.3 | 19 22.2 | 24.1 | 49 59.6 | 31.5 | | | |
| R 12 | 31 30.7 | 40 41.7 | S 4 55.9 | 52 52.4 | S10 32.6 | 34 24.2 | S 2 23.9 | 65 01.9 | S14 31.5 | Gacrux | 171 53.6 | S57 14.4 |
| D 13 | 46 33.2 | 55 41.6 | 55.0 | 67 53.1 | 32.0 | 49 26.1 | 23.7 | 80 04.2 | 31.4 | Gienah | 175 45.6 | S17 40.0 |
| A 14 | 61 35.6 | 70 41.4 | 54.0 | 82 53.7 | 31.3 | 64 28.1 | 23.5 | 95 06.5 | 31.4 | Hadar | 148 38.5 | S60 28.8 |
| Y 15 | 76 38.1 | 85 41.2 .. | 53.1 | 97 54.4 .. | 30.6 | 79 30.1 .. | 23.3 | 110 08.8 .. | 31.3 | Hamal | 327 54.1 | N23 33.9 |
| 16 | 91 40.6 | 100 41.0 | 52.1 | 112 55.1 | 29.9 | 94 32.0 | 23.1 | 125 11.1 | 31.3 | Kaus Aust. | 83 35.3 | S34 22.4 |
| 17 | 106 43.0 | 115 40.8 | 51.1 | 127 55.7 | 29.2 | 109 34.0 | 22.9 | 140 13.4 | 31.2 | | | |
| 18 | 121 45.5 | 130 40.6 | S 4 50.2 | 142 56.4 | S10 28.6 | 124 36.0 | S 2 22.7 | 155 15.7 | S14 31.2 | Kochab | 137 18.7 | N74 03.8 |
| 19 | 136 48.0 | 145 40.4 | 49.2 | 157 57.1 | 27.9 | 139 37.9 | 22.5 | 170 18.1 | 31.1 | Markab | 13 32.4 | N15 19.3 |
| 20 | 151 50.4 | 160 40.3 | 48.2 | 172 57.8 | 27.2 | 154 39.9 | 22.2 | 185 20.4 | 31.1 | Menkar | 314 08.8 | N 4 10.4 |
| 21 | 166 52.9 | 175 40.1 .. | 47.3 | 187 58.4 .. | 26.5 | 169 41.8 .. | 22.0 | 200 22.7 .. | 31.0 | Menkent | 147 59.5 | S36 28.8 |
| 22 | 181 55.3 | 190 39.9 | 46.3 | 202 59.1 | 25.9 | 184 43.8 | 21.8 | 215 25.0 | 31.0 | Miaplacidus | 221 38.5 | S69 48.8 |
| 23 | 196 57.8 | 205 39.7 | 45.3 | 217 59.8 | 25.2 | 199 45.8 | 21.6 | 230 27.3 | 30.9 | | | |
| **24** 00 | 212 00.3 | 220 39.5 | S 4 44.4 | 233 00.4 | S10 24.5 | 214 47.7 | S 2 21.4 | 245 29.6 | S14 30.9 | Mirfak | 308 31.9 | N49 56.3 |
| 01 | 227 02.7 | 235 39.3 | 43.4 | 248 01.1 | 23.8 | 229 49.7 | 21.2 | 260 31.9 | 30.8 | Nunki | 75 50.4 | S26 16.1 |
| 02 | 242 05.2 | 250 39.1 | 42.4 | 263 01.8 | 23.1 | 244 51.7 | 21.0 | 275 34.2 | 30.8 | Peacock | 53 09.3 | S56 39.6 |
| 03 | 257 07.7 | 265 39.0 .. | 41.5 | 278 02.4 .. | 22.5 | 259 53.6 .. | 20.8 | 290 36.5 .. | 30.7 | Pollux | 243 20.1 | N27 58.4 |
| 04 | 272 10.1 | 280 38.8 | 40.5 | 293 03.1 | 21.8 | 274 55.6 | 20.6 | 305 38.8 | 30.7 | Procyon | 244 53.3 | N 5 10.0 |
| 05 | 287 12.6 | 295 38.6 | 39.5 | 308 03.8 | 21.1 | 289 57.6 | 20.4 | 320 41.1 | 30.6 | | | |
| 06 | 302 15.1 | 310 38.4 | S 4 38.6 | 323 04.5 | S10 20.4 | 304 59.5 | S 2 20.1 | 335 43.4 | S14 30.6 | Rasalhague | 96 00.4 | N12 32.5 |
| 07 | 317 17.5 | 325 38.2 | 37.6 | 338 05.1 | 19.7 | 320 01.5 | 19.9 | 350 45.7 | 30.6 | Regulus | 207 36.7 | N11 51.5 |
| S 08 | 332 20.0 | 340 38.0 | 36.6 | 353 05.8 | 19.1 | 335 03.5 | 19.7 | 5 48.0 | 30.5 | Rigel | 281 06.3 | S 8 10.7 |
| U 09 | 347 22.4 | 355 37.8 .. | 35.7 | 8 06.5 .. | 18.4 | 350 05.4 .. | 19.5 | 20 50.3 .. | 30.5 | Rigil Kent. | 139 42.7 | S60 55.6 |
| N 10 | 2 24.9 | 10 37.7 | 34.7 | 23 07.2 | 17.7 | 5 07.4 | 19.3 | 35 52.6 | 30.4 | Sabik | 102 05.1 | S15 45.2 |
| D 11 | 17 27.4 | 25 37.5 | 33.7 | 38 07.8 | 17.0 | 20 09.4 | 19.1 | 50 54.9 | 30.4 | | | |
| A 12 | 32 29.8 | 40 37.3 | S 4 32.8 | 53 08.5 | S10 16.3 | 35 11.3 | S 2 18.9 | 65 57.2 | S14 30.3 | Schedar | 349 34.1 | N56 39.3 |
| Y 13 | 47 32.3 | 55 37.1 | 31.8 | 68 09.2 | 15.7 | 50 13.3 | 18.7 | 80 59.5 | 30.3 | Shaula | 96 13.2 | S37 07.1 |
| 14 | 62 34.8 | 70 36.9 | 30.8 | 83 09.8 | 15.0 | 65 15.3 | 18.5 | 96 01.8 | 30.2 | Sirius | 258 28.4 | S16 45.0 |
| 15 | 77 37.2 | 85 36.7 .. | 29.8 | 98 10.5 .. | 14.3 | 80 17.2 .. | 18.3 | 111 04.1 .. | 30.2 | Spica | 158 24.4 | S11 16.7 |
| 16 | 92 39.7 | 100 36.5 | 28.9 | 113 11.2 | 13.6 | 95 19.2 | 18.1 | 126 06.5 | 30.1 | Suhail | 222 47.9 | S43 31.6 |
| 17 | 107 42.2 | 115 36.4 | 27.9 | 128 11.9 | 12.9 | 110 21.2 | 17.9 | 141 08.8 | 30.1 | | | |
| 18 | 122 44.6 | 130 36.2 | S 4 26.9 | 143 12.5 | S10 12.3 | 125 23.1 | S 2 17.6 | 156 11.1 | S14 30.0 | Vega | 80 34.6 | N38 48.0 |
| 19 | 137 47.1 | 145 36.0 | 26.0 | 158 13.2 | 11.6 | 140 25.1 | 17.4 | 171 13.4 | 30.0 | Zuben'ubi | 136 58.2 | S16 08.1 |
| 20 | 152 49.6 | 160 35.8 | 25.0 | 173 13.9 | 10.9 | 155 27.1 | 17.2 | 186 15.7 | 29.9 | | SHA | Mer.Pass. |
| 21 | 167 52.0 | 175 35.6 .. | 24.0 | 188 14.6 .. | 10.2 | 170 29.0 .. | 17.0 | 201 18.0 .. | 29.9 | Venus | 9 42.8 | 9 17 |
| 22 | 182 54.5 | 190 35.4 | 23.0 | 203 15.2 | 09.5 | 185 31.0 | 16.8 | 216 20.3 | 29.9 | Mars | 21 43.2 | 8 29 |
| 23 | 197 56.9 | 205 35.2 | 22.1 | 218 15.9 | 08.8 | 200 33.0 | 16.6 | 231 22.6 | 29.8 | Jupiter | 2 59.5 | 9 43 |
| Mer.Pass. 9 54.3 | | v −0.2 | d 1.0 | v 0.7 | d 0.7 | v 2.0 | d 0.2 | v 2.3 | d 0.0 | Saturn | 33 33.2 | 7 41 |

## SUN / MOON

| UT | SUN GHA | SUN Dec | MOON GHA | v | MOON Dec | d | HP |
|---|---|---|---|---|---|---|---|
| d h | ° ′ | ° ′ | ° ′ | ′ | ° ′ | ′ | ′ |
| 22 00 | 180 20.9 | N12 07.1 | 286 30.7 | 3.4 | S26 52.3 | 1.3 | 59.6 |
| 01 | 195 21.0 | 07.9 | 300 53.1 | 3.5 | 26 51.0 | 1.5 | 59.6 |
| 02 | 210 21.1 | 08.7 | 315 15.6 | 3.4 | 26 49.5 | 1.7 | 59.5 |
| 03 | 225 21.2 | .. 09.6 | 329 38.0 | 3.5 | 26 47.8 | 1.8 | 59.5 |
| 04 | 240 21.4 | 10.4 | 344 00.5 | 3.6 | 26 46.0 | 2.1 | 59.5 |
| 05 | 255 21.5 | 11.3 | 358 23.1 | 3.6 | 26 43.9 | 2.2 | 59.5 |
| 06 | 270 21.6 | N12 12.1 | 12 45.7 | 3.7 | S26 41.7 | 2.4 | 59.5 |
| 07 | 285 21.7 | 12.9 | 27 08.4 | 3.7 | 26 39.3 | 2.6 | 59.5 |
| 08 | 300 21.9 | 13.8 | 41 31.1 | 3.7 | 26 36.7 | 2.8 | 59.4 |
| F 09 | 315 22.0 | .. 14.6 | 55 53.8 | 3.8 | 26 33.9 | 3.0 | 59.4 |
| R 10 | 330 22.1 | 15.5 | 70 16.6 | 3.9 | 26 30.9 | 3.1 | 59.4 |
| I 11 | 345 22.2 | 16.3 | 84 39.5 | 4.0 | 26 27.8 | 3.3 | 59.4 |
| D 12 | 0 22.3 | N12 17.1 | 99 02.5 | 4.0 | S26 24.5 | 3.5 | 59.4 |
| A 13 | 15 22.5 | 18.0 | 113 25.5 | 4.0 | 26 21.0 | 3.7 | 59.4 |
| Y 14 | 30 22.6 | 18.8 | 127 48.5 | 4.2 | 26 17.3 | 3.8 | 59.3 |
| 15 | 45 22.7 | .. 19.7 | 142 11.7 | 4.2 | 26 13.5 | 4.1 | 59.3 |
| 16 | 60 22.8 | 20.5 | 156 34.9 | 4.3 | 26 09.4 | 4.2 | 59.3 |
| 17 | 75 22.9 | 21.3 | 170 58.2 | 4.3 | 26 05.2 | 4.4 | 59.3 |
| 18 | 90 23.1 | N12 22.2 | 185 21.5 | 4.4 | S26 00.8 | 4.5 | 59.3 |
| 19 | 105 23.2 | 23.0 | 199 44.9 | 4.5 | 25 56.3 | 4.7 | 59.3 |
| 20 | 120 23.3 | 23.8 | 214 08.4 | 4.6 | 25 51.6 | 4.9 | 59.2 |
| 21 | 135 23.4 | .. 24.7 | 228 32.0 | 4.6 | 25 46.7 | 5.1 | 59.2 |
| 22 | 150 23.5 | 25.5 | 242 55.6 | 4.8 | 25 41.6 | 5.2 | 59.2 |
| 23 | 165 23.7 | 26.3 | 257 19.4 | 4.8 | 25 36.4 | 5.4 | 59.2 |
| 23 00 | 180 23.8 | N12 27.2 | 271 43.2 | 4.9 | S25 31.0 | 5.5 | 59.2 |
| 01 | 195 23.9 | 28.0 | 286 07.1 | 5.0 | 25 25.5 | 5.8 | 59.1 |
| 02 | 210 24.0 | 28.8 | 300 31.1 | 5.1 | 25 19.7 | 5.9 | 59.1 |
| 03 | 225 24.1 | .. 29.7 | 314 55.2 | 5.1 | 25 13.8 | 6.0 | 59.1 |
| 04 | 240 24.2 | 30.5 | 329 19.3 | 5.3 | 25 07.8 | 6.2 | 59.1 |
| 05 | 255 24.4 | 31.3 | 343 43.6 | 5.3 | 25 01.6 | 6.4 | 59.1 |
| 06 | 270 24.5 | N12 32.2 | 358 07.9 | 5.4 | S24 55.2 | 6.5 | 59.0 |
| S 07 | 285 24.6 | 33.0 | 12 32.3 | 5.6 | 24 48.7 | 6.7 | 59.0 |
| A 08 | 300 24.7 | 33.8 | 26 56.9 | 5.6 | 24 42.0 | 6.8 | 59.0 |
| T 09 | 315 24.8 | .. 34.7 | 41 21.5 | 5.7 | 24 35.2 | 7.0 | 59.0 |
| U 10 | 330 24.9 | 35.5 | 55 46.2 | 5.8 | 24 28.2 | 7.1 | 59.0 |
| R 11 | 345 25.1 | 36.3 | 70 11.0 | 5.9 | 24 21.1 | 7.3 | 59.0 |
| D 12 | 0 25.2 | N12 37.2 | 84 35.9 | 6.0 | S24 13.8 | 7.4 | 58.9 |
| A 13 | 15 25.3 | 38.0 | 99 00.9 | 6.1 | 24 06.4 | 7.6 | 58.9 |
| Y 14 | 30 25.4 | 38.8 | 113 26.0 | 6.2 | 23 58.8 | 7.7 | 58.9 |
| 15 | 45 25.5 | .. 39.7 | 127 51.2 | 6.3 | 23 51.1 | 7.9 | 58.9 |
| 16 | 60 25.6 | 40.5 | 142 16.5 | 6.4 | 23 43.2 | 8.0 | 58.9 |
| 17 | 75 25.8 | 41.3 | 156 41.9 | 6.5 | 23 35.2 | 8.1 | 58.8 |
| 18 | 90 25.9 | N12 42.1 | 171 07.4 | 6.6 | S23 27.1 | 8.3 | 58.8 |
| 19 | 105 26.0 | 43.0 | 185 33.0 | 6.7 | 23 18.8 | 8.5 | 58.8 |
| 20 | 120 26.1 | 43.8 | 199 58.7 | 6.8 | 23 10.3 | 8.5 | 58.8 |
| 21 | 135 26.2 | .. 44.6 | 214 24.5 | 6.9 | 23 01.8 | 8.7 | 58.8 |
| 22 | 150 26.3 | 45.4 | 228 50.4 | 7.0 | 22 53.1 | 8.8 | 58.7 |
| 23 | 165 26.4 | 46.3 | 243 16.4 | 7.2 | 22 44.3 | 9.0 | 58.7 |
| 24 00 | 180 26.5 | N12 47.1 | 257 42.6 | 7.2 | S22 35.3 | 9.1 | 58.7 |
| 01 | 195 26.7 | 47.9 | 272 08.8 | 7.3 | 22 26.2 | 9.2 | 58.7 |
| 02 | 210 26.8 | 48.8 | 286 35.1 | 7.4 | 22 17.0 | 9.4 | 58.6 |
| 03 | 225 26.9 | .. 49.6 | 301 01.5 | 7.6 | 22 07.6 | 9.4 | 58.6 |
| 04 | 240 27.0 | 50.4 | 315 28.1 | 7.6 | 21 58.2 | 9.6 | 58.6 |
| 05 | 255 27.1 | 51.2 | 329 54.7 | 7.8 | 21 48.6 | 9.7 | 58.6 |
| 06 | 270 27.2 | N12 52.0 | 344 21.5 | 7.8 | S21 38.9 | 9.9 | 58.6 |
| 07 | 285 27.3 | 52.9 | 358 48.3 | 8.0 | 21 29.0 | 9.9 | 58.5 |
| 08 | 300 27.4 | 53.7 | 13 15.3 | 8.0 | 21 19.1 | 10.1 | 58.5 |
| S 09 | 315 27.6 | .. 54.5 | 27 42.3 | 8.2 | 21 09.0 | 10.2 | 58.5 |
| U 10 | 330 27.7 | 55.3 | 42 09.5 | 8.3 | 20 58.8 | 10.3 | 58.5 |
| N 11 | 345 27.8 | 56.2 | 56 36.8 | 8.3 | 20 48.5 | 10.4 | 58.5 |
| D 12 | 0 27.9 | N12 57.0 | 71 04.1 | 8.5 | S20 38.1 | 10.5 | 58.4 |
| A 13 | 15 28.0 | 57.8 | 85 31.6 | 8.6 | 20 27.6 | 10.7 | 58.4 |
| Y 14 | 30 28.1 | 58.6 | 99 59.2 | 8.7 | 20 16.9 | 10.7 | 58.4 |
| 15 | 45 28.2 | 12 59.4 | 114 26.9 | 8.8 | 20 06.2 | 10.8 | 58.4 |
| 16 | 60 28.3 | 13 00.3 | 128 54.7 | 8.9 | 19 55.4 | 11.0 | 58.4 |
| 17 | 75 28.4 | 01.1 | 143 22.6 | 9.0 | 19 44.4 | 11.0 | 58.3 |
| 18 | 90 28.6 | N13 01.9 | 157 50.6 | 9.1 | S19 33.4 | 11.2 | 58.3 |
| 19 | 105 28.7 | 02.7 | 172 18.7 | 9.2 | 19 22.2 | 11.2 | 58.3 |
| 20 | 120 28.8 | 03.5 | 186 46.9 | 9.3 | 19 11.0 | 11.4 | 58.3 |
| 21 | 135 28.9 | .. 04.4 | 201 15.2 | 9.4 | 18 59.6 | 11.4 | 58.2 |
| 22 | 150 29.0 | 05.2 | 215 43.6 | 9.5 | 18 48.2 | 11.6 | 58.2 |
| 23 | 165 29.1 | 06.0 | 230 12.1 | 9.6 | S18 36.6 | 11.6 | 58.2 |
| | SD 15.9 | d 0.8 | SD 16.2 | | 16.1 | | 15.9 |

## Twilight / Sunrise / Moonrise

| Lat. | Twilight Naut. | Twilight Civil | Sunrise | Moonrise 22 | Moonrise 23 | Moonrise 24 | Moonrise 25 |
|---|---|---|---|---|---|---|---|
| ° | h m | h m | h m | h m | h m | h m | h m |
| N 72 | //// | //// | 02 51 | ■■■ | ■■■ | ■■■ | 06 45 |
| N 70 | //// | 01 30 | 03 15 | ■■■ | ■■■ | ■■■ | 05 51 |
| 68 | //// | 02 12 | 03 34 | ■■■ | ■■■ | 06 25 | 05 18 |
| 66 | //// | 02 40 | 03 49 | ■■■ | ■■■ | 05 19 | 04 53 |
| 64 | 01 19 | 03 01 | 04 01 | ■■■ | 05 03 | 04 43 | 04 34 |
| 62 | 01 57 | 03 18 | 04 12 | 03 55 | 04 13 | 04 18 | 04 18 |
| 60 | 02 22 | 03 31 | 04 21 | 03 09 | 03 42 | 03 57 | 04 05 |
| N 58 | 02 42 | 03 43 | 04 28 | 02 39 | 03 18 | 03 40 | 03 53 |
| 56 | 02 58 | 03 53 | 04 35 | 02 16 | 02 59 | 03 26 | 03 43 |
| 54 | 03 11 | 04 02 | 04 41 | 01 57 | 02 43 | 03 14 | 03 34 |
| 52 | 03 22 | 04 09 | 04 47 | 01 41 | 02 29 | 03 03 | 03 26 |
| 50 | 03 32 | 04 16 | 04 51 | 01 27 | 02 17 | 02 53 | 03 19 |
| 45 | 03 52 | 04 31 | 05 02 | 00 59 | 01 52 | 02 32 | 03 03 |
| N 40 | 04 08 | 04 42 | 05 11 | 00 37 | 01 32 | 02 15 | 02 51 |
| 35 | 04 20 | 04 52 | 05 18 | 00 19 | 01 15 | 02 01 | 02 40 |
| 30 | 04 31 | 05 00 | 05 25 | 00 03 | 01 00 | 01 49 | 02 30 |
| 20 | 04 47 | 05 13 | 05 36 | 24 35 | 00 35 | 01 28 | 02 14 |
| N 10 | 04 59 | 05 24 | 05 46 | 24 14 | 00 14 | 01 09 | 01 59 |
| 0 | 05 09 | 05 34 | 05 55 | 23 54 | 24 52 | 00 52 | 01 46 |
| S 10 | 05 18 | 05 42 | 06 04 | 23 33 | 24 34 | 00 34 | 01 32 |
| 20 | 05 25 | 05 51 | 06 13 | 23 12 | 24 16 | 00 16 | 01 17 |
| 30 | 05 31 | 05 59 | 06 24 | 22 47 | 23 54 | 25 00 | 01 00 |
| 35 | 05 34 | 06 04 | 06 30 | 22 32 | 23 41 | 24 50 | 00 50 |
| 40 | 05 37 | 06 09 | 06 37 | 22 15 | 23 27 | 24 39 | 00 39 |
| 45 | 05 40 | 06 15 | 06 45 | 21 54 | 23 09 | 24 26 | 00 26 |
| S 50 | 05 43 | 06 21 | 06 54 | 21 28 | 22 48 | 24 09 | 00 09 |
| 52 | 05 44 | 06 24 | 06 59 | 21 15 | 22 37 | 24 02 | 00 02 |
| 54 | 05 45 | 06 27 | 07 04 | 21 01 | 22 25 | 23 53 | 25 19 |
| 56 | 05 47 | 06 30 | 07 09 | 20 44 | 22 12 | 23 43 | 25 12 |
| 58 | 05 48 | 06 34 | 07 15 | 20 23 | 21 56 | 23 32 | 25 05 |
| S 60 | 05 49 | 06 38 | 07 22 | 19 57 | 21 37 | 23 19 | 24 57 |

## Sunset / Twilight / Moonset

| Lat. | Sunset | Twilight Civil | Twilight Naut. | Moonset 22 | Moonset 23 | Moonset 24 | Moonset 25 |
|---|---|---|---|---|---|---|---|
| ° | h m | h m | h m | h m | h m | h m | h m |
| N 72 | 21 11 | //// | //// | ■■■ | ■■■ | ■■■ | 09 34 |
| N 70 | 20 45 | 22 36 | //// | ■■■ | ■■■ | ■■■ | 10 26 |
| 68 | 20 26 | 21 50 | //// | ■■■ | ■■■ | 08 01 | 10 58 |
| 66 | 20 10 | 21 20 | //// | ■■■ | ■■■ | 09 05 | 11 21 |
| 64 | 19 58 | 20 59 | 22 46 | ■■■ | 07 22 | 09 40 | 11 39 |
| 62 | 19 47 | 20 41 | 22 05 | 06 22 | 08 11 | 10 05 | 11 54 |
| 60 | 19 38 | 20 27 | 21 38 | 07 07 | 08 42 | 10 25 | 12 06 |
| N 58 | 19 30 | 20 16 | 21 18 | 07 37 | 09 05 | 10 41 | 12 17 |
| 56 | 19 23 | 20 05 | 21 01 | 08 00 | 09 23 | 10 55 | 12 26 |
| 54 | 19 17 | 19 56 | 20 48 | 08 19 | 09 39 | 11 07 | 12 34 |
| 52 | 19 11 | 19 49 | 20 36 | 08 35 | 09 53 | 11 17 | 12 41 |
| 50 | 19 06 | 19 42 | 20 26 | 08 48 | 10 05 | 11 26 | 12 48 |
| 45 | 18 55 | 19 27 | 20 06 | 09 16 | 10 29 | 11 46 | 13 02 |
| N 40 | 18 46 | 19 15 | 19 50 | 09 38 | 10 49 | 12 01 | 13 13 |
| 35 | 18 39 | 19 05 | 19 37 | 09 56 | 11 05 | 12 14 | 13 23 |
| 30 | 18 32 | 18 57 | 19 27 | 10 12 | 11 19 | 12 26 | 13 31 |
| 20 | 18 21 | 18 44 | 19 10 | 10 38 | 11 42 | 12 45 | 13 45 |
| N 10 | 18 11 | 18 32 | 18 58 | 11 01 | 12 03 | 13 02 | 13 58 |
| 0 | 18 02 | 18 23 | 18 47 | 11 22 | 12 22 | 13 18 | 14 10 |
| S 10 | 17 53 | 18 14 | 18 39 | 11 43 | 12 41 | 13 33 | 14 21 |
| 20 | 17 43 | 18 06 | 18 32 | 12 05 | 13 01 | 13 50 | 14 33 |
| 30 | 17 32 | 17 57 | 18 25 | 12 31 | 13 24 | 14 09 | 14 47 |
| 35 | 17 26 | 17 52 | 18 22 | 12 46 | 13 37 | 14 20 | 14 55 |
| 40 | 17 19 | 17 47 | 18 19 | 13 04 | 13 53 | 14 32 | 15 04 |
| 45 | 17 11 | 17 41 | 18 16 | 13 25 | 14 11 | 14 47 | 15 15 |
| S 50 | 17 02 | 17 35 | 18 13 | 13 51 | 14 34 | 15 05 | 15 28 |
| 52 | 16 57 | 17 32 | 18 11 | 14 04 | 14 45 | 15 13 | 15 34 |
| 54 | 16 52 | 17 29 | 18 10 | 14 19 | 14 57 | 15 22 | 15 40 |
| 56 | 16 47 | 17 26 | 18 09 | 14 36 | 15 11 | 15 33 | 15 47 |
| 58 | 16 41 | 17 22 | 18 08 | 14 57 | 15 27 | 15 45 | 15 55 |
| S 60 | 16 34 | 17 18 | 18 06 | 15 23 | 15 47 | 15 58 | 16 04 |

## SUN / MOON

| Day | SUN Eqn. of Time 00ʰ | SUN Eqn. of Time 12ʰ | SUN Mer. Pass. | MOON Mer. Pass. Upper | MOON Mer. Pass. Lower | Age | Phase |
|---|---|---|---|---|---|---|---|
| d | m s | m s | h m | h m | h m | d % | |
| 22 | 01 23 | 01 29 | 11 59 | 05 07 | 17 38 | 21 61 | |
| 23 | 01 35 | 01 40 | 11 58 | 06 08 | 18 37 | 22 50 | |
| 24 | 01 46 | 01 51 | 11 58 | 07 05 | 19 32 | 23 39 | |

| UT | ARIES | VENUS −4.1 | | MARS +0.9 | | JUPITER −2.1 | | SATURN +0.7 | | STARS | | |
|---|---|---|---|---|---|---|---|---|---|---|---|---|
| d h | GHA | GHA | Dec | GHA | Dec | GHA | Dec | GHA | Dec | Name | SHA | Dec |
| | ° ′ | ° ′ | ° ′ | ° ′ | ° ′ | ° ′ | ° ′ | ° ′ | ° ′ | | ° ′ | ° ′ |
| 25 00 | 212 59.4 | 220 35.1 | S 4 21.1 | 233 16.6 | S10 08.2 | 215 34.9 | S 2 16.4 | 246 24.9 | S14 29.8 | Acamar | 315 13.9 | S40 13.1 |
| 01 | 228 01.9 | 235 34.9 | 20.1 | 248 17.2 | 07.5 | 230 36.9 | 16.2 | 261 27.2 | 29.7 | Achernar | 335 22.5 | S57 07.5 |
| 02 | 243 04.3 | 250 34.7 | 19.1 | 263 17.9 | 06.8 | 245 38.9 | 16.0 | 276 29.5 | 29.7 | Acrux | 173 01.9 | S63 13.5 |
| 03 | 258 06.8 | 265 34.5 .. | 18.2 | 278 18.6 .. | 06.1 | 260 40.9 .. | 15.8 | 291 31.8 .. | 29.6 | Adhara | 255 07.8 | S29 00.3 |
| 04 | 273 09.3 | 280 34.3 | 17.2 | 293 19.3 | 05.4 | 275 42.8 | 15.6 | 306 34.1 | 29.6 | Aldebaran | 290 42.5 | N16 33.1 |
| 05 | 288 11.7 | 295 34.1 | 16.2 | 308 19.9 | 04.7 | 290 44.8 | 15.4 | 321 36.4 | 29.5 | | | |
| 06 | 303 14.2 | 310 33.9 | S 4 15.2 | 323 20.6 | S10 04.1 | 305 46.8 | S 2 15.1 | 336 38.8 | S14 29.5 | Alioth | 166 14.5 | N55 50.5 |
| 07 | 318 16.7 | 325 33.8 | 14.3 | 338 21.3 | 03.4 | 320 48.7 | 14.9 | 351 41.1 | 29.4 | Alkaid | 152 53.3 | N49 12.2 |
| 08 | 333 19.1 | 340 33.6 | 13.3 | 353 22.0 | 02.7 | 335 50.7 | 14.7 | 6 43.4 | 29.4 | Alnair | 27 35.9 | S46 51.1 |
| M 09 | 348 21.6 | 355 33.4 .. | 12.3 | 8 22.6 .. | 02.0 | 350 52.7 .. | 14.5 | 21 45.7 .. | 29.3 | Alnilam | 275 40.2 | S 1 11.4 |
| O 10 | 3 24.1 | 10 33.2 | 11.3 | 23 23.3 | 01.3 | 5 54.6 | 14.3 | 36 48.0 | 29.3 | Alphard | 217 49.9 | S 8 45.4 |
| N 11 | 18 26.5 | 25 33.0 | 10.3 | 38 24.0 | 00.6 | 20 56.6 | 14.1 | 51 50.3 | 29.3 | | | |
| D 12 | 33 29.0 | 40 32.8 | S 4 09.4 | 53 24.7 | S10 00.0 | 35 58.6 | S 2 13.9 | 66 52.6 | S14 29.2 | Alphecca | 126 05.3 | N26 38.3 |
| A 13 | 48 31.4 | 55 32.6 | 08.4 | 68 25.3 | 9 59.3 | 51 00.5 | 13.7 | 81 54.9 | 29.2 | Alpheratz | 357 37.4 | N29 12.5 |
| Y 14 | 63 33.9 | 70 32.5 | 07.4 | 83 26.0 | 58.6 | 66 02.5 | 13.5 | 96 57.2 | 29.1 | Altair | 62 02.1 | N 8 55.4 |
| 15 | 78 36.4 | 85 32.3 .. | 06.4 | 98 26.7 .. | 57.9 | 81 04.5 .. | 13.3 | 111 59.5 .. | 29.1 | Ankaa | 353 09.8 | S42 11.1 |
| 16 | 93 38.8 | 100 32.1 | 05.4 | 113 27.4 | 57.2 | 96 06.4 | 13.1 | 127 01.8 | 29.0 | Antares | 112 18.3 | S26 28.9 |
| 17 | 108 41.3 | 115 31.9 | 04.5 | 128 28.1 | 56.5 | 111 08.4 | 12.9 | 142 04.2 | 29.0 | | | |
| 18 | 123 43.8 | 130 31.7 | S 4 03.5 | 143 28.7 | S 9 55.9 | 126 10.4 | S 2 12.7 | 157 06.5 | S14 28.9 | Arcturus | 145 49.6 | N19 04.0 |
| 19 | 138 46.2 | 145 31.5 | 02.5 | 158 29.4 | 55.2 | 141 12.4 | 12.4 | 172 08.8 | 28.9 | Atria | 107 14.1 | S69 03.9 |
| 20 | 153 48.7 | 160 31.3 | 01.5 | 173 30.1 | 54.5 | 156 14.3 | 12.2 | 187 11.1 | 28.8 | Avior | 234 15.7 | S59 35.1 |
| 21 | 168 51.2 | 175 31.1 | 4 00.5 | 188 30.8 .. | 53.8 | 171 16.3 .. | 12.0 | 202 13.4 .. | 28.8 | Bellatrix | 278 25.5 | N 6 22.1 |
| 22 | 183 53.6 | 190 31.0 | 3 59.6 | 203 31.4 | 53.1 | 186 18.3 | 11.8 | 217 15.7 | 28.8 | Betelgeuse | 270 54.7 | N 7 24.6 |
| 23 | 198 56.1 | 205 30.8 | 58.6 | 218 32.1 | 52.4 | 201 20.2 | 11.6 | 232 18.0 | 28.7 | | | |
| 26 00 | 213 58.5 | 220 30.6 | S 3 57.6 | 233 32.8 | S 9 51.7 | 216 22.2 | S 2 11.4 | 247 20.3 | S14 28.7 | Canopus | 263 53.7 | S52 42.7 |
| 01 | 229 01.0 | 235 30.4 | 56.6 | 248 33.5 | 51.1 | 231 24.2 | 11.2 | 262 22.6 | 28.6 | Capella | 280 25.6 | N46 01.2 |
| 02 | 244 03.5 | 250 30.2 | 55.6 | 263 34.1 | 50.4 | 246 26.2 | 11.0 | 277 25.0 | 28.6 | Deneb | 49 27.3 | N45 21.2 |
| 03 | 259 05.9 | 265 30.0 .. | 54.6 | 278 34.8 .. | 49.7 | 261 28.1 .. | 10.8 | 292 27.3 .. | 28.5 | Denebola | 182 27.0 | N14 26.9 |
| 04 | 274 08.4 | 280 29.8 | 53.6 | 293 35.5 | 49.0 | 276 30.1 | 10.6 | 307 29.6 | 28.5 | Diphda | 348 49.9 | S17 52.0 |
| 05 | 289 10.9 | 295 29.7 | 52.7 | 308 36.2 | 48.3 | 291 32.1 | 10.4 | 322 31.9 | 28.4 | | | |
| 06 | 304 13.3 | 310 29.5 | S 3 51.7 | 323 36.9 | S 9 47.6 | 306 34.0 | S 2 10.2 | 337 34.2 | S14 28.4 | Dubhe | 193 43.4 | N61 38.1 |
| 07 | 319 15.8 | 325 29.3 | 50.7 | 338 37.5 | 46.9 | 321 36.0 | 10.0 | 352 36.5 | 28.4 | Elnath | 278 05.0 | N28 37.5 |
| 08 | 334 18.3 | 340 29.1 | 49.7 | 353 38.2 | 46.3 | 336 38.0 | 09.8 | 7 38.8 | 28.3 | Eltanin | 90 42.9 | N51 28.9 |
| T 09 | 349 20.7 | 355 28.9 .. | 48.7 | 8 38.9 .. | 45.6 | 351 39.9 .. | 09.5 | 22 41.1 .. | 28.3 | Enif | 33 41.1 | N 9 58.4 |
| U 10 | 4 23.2 | 10 28.7 | 47.7 | 23 39.6 | 44.9 | 6 41.9 | 09.3 | 37 43.4 | 28.2 | Fomalhaut | 15 17.2 | S29 30.3 |
| E 11 | 19 25.7 | 25 28.5 | 46.7 | 38 40.2 | 44.2 | 21 43.9 | 09.1 | 52 45.8 | 28.2 | | | |
| S 12 | 34 28.1 | 40 28.3 | S 3 45.8 | 53 40.9 | S 9 43.5 | 36 45.9 | S 2 08.9 | 67 48.1 | S14 28.1 | Gacrux | 171 53.6 | S57 14.4 |
| D 13 | 49 30.6 | 55 28.2 | 44.8 | 68 41.6 | 42.8 | 51 47.8 | 08.7 | 82 50.4 | 28.1 | Gienah | 175 45.6 | S17 40.0 |
| A 14 | 64 33.0 | 70 28.0 | 43.8 | 83 42.3 | 42.1 | 66 49.8 | 08.5 | 97 52.7 | 28.0 | Hadar | 148 38.5 | S60 28.8 |
| Y 15 | 79 35.5 | 85 27.8 .. | 42.8 | 98 43.0 .. | 41.4 | 81 51.8 .. | 08.3 | 112 55.0 .. | 28.0 | Hamal | 327 54.1 | N23 33.9 |
| 16 | 94 38.0 | 100 27.6 | 41.8 | 113 43.6 | 40.8 | 96 53.8 | 08.1 | 127 57.3 | 28.0 | Kaus Aust. | 83 35.3 | S34 22.4 |
| 17 | 109 40.4 | 115 27.4 | 40.8 | 128 44.3 | 40.1 | 111 55.7 | 07.9 | 142 59.6 | 27.9 | | | |
| 18 | 124 42.9 | 130 27.2 | S 3 39.8 | 143 45.0 | S 9 39.4 | 126 57.7 | S 2 07.7 | 158 01.9 | S14 27.9 | Kochab | 137 18.6 | N74 03.8 |
| 19 | 139 45.4 | 145 27.0 | 38.8 | 158 45.7 | 38.7 | 141 59.7 | 07.5 | 173 04.3 | 27.8 | Markab | 13 32.3 | N15 19.3 |
| 20 | 154 47.8 | 160 26.8 | 37.8 | 173 46.4 | 38.0 | 157 01.6 | 07.3 | 188 06.6 | 27.8 | Menkar | 314 08.8 | N 4 10.5 |
| 21 | 169 50.3 | 175 26.7 .. | 36.9 | 188 47.0 .. | 37.3 | 172 03.6 .. | 07.1 | 203 08.9 .. | 27.7 | Menkent | 147 59.9 | S36 28.8 |
| 22 | 184 52.8 | 190 26.5 | 35.9 | 203 47.7 | 36.6 | 187 05.6 | 06.9 | 218 11.2 | 27.7 | Miaplacidus | 221 38.5 | S69 48.8 |
| 23 | 199 55.2 | 205 26.3 | 34.9 | 218 48.4 | 35.9 | 202 07.6 | 06.7 | 233 13.5 | 27.6 | | | |
| 27 00 | 214 57.7 | 220 26.1 | S 3 33.9 | 233 49.1 | S 9 35.3 | 217 09.5 | S 2 06.5 | 248 15.8 | S14 27.6 | Mirfak | 308 31.9 | N49 56.3 |
| 01 | 230 00.1 | 235 25.9 | 32.9 | 248 49.8 | 34.6 | 232 11.5 | 06.2 | 263 18.1 | 27.6 | Nunki | 75 50.4 | S26 16.1 |
| 02 | 245 02.6 | 250 25.7 | 31.9 | 263 50.4 | 33.9 | 247 13.5 | 06.0 | 278 20.5 | 27.5 | Peacock | 53 09.3 | S56 39.6 |
| 03 | 260 05.1 | 265 25.5 .. | 30.9 | 278 51.1 .. | 33.2 | 262 15.5 .. | 05.8 | 293 22.8 .. | 27.5 | Pollux | 243 20.1 | N27 58.4 |
| 04 | 275 07.5 | 280 25.3 | 29.9 | 293 51.8 | 32.5 | 277 17.4 | 05.6 | 308 25.1 | 27.4 | Procyon | 244 53.3 | N 5 10.0 |
| 05 | 290 10.0 | 295 25.2 | 28.9 | 308 52.5 | 31.8 | 292 19.4 | 05.4 | 323 27.4 | 27.4 | | | |
| 06 | 305 12.5 | 310 25.0 | S 3 27.9 | 323 53.2 | S 9 31.1 | 307 21.4 | S 2 05.2 | 338 29.7 | S14 27.3 | Rasalhague | 96 00.4 | N12 32.5 |
| W 07 | 320 14.9 | 325 24.8 | 26.9 | 338 53.8 | 30.4 | 322 23.3 | 05.0 | 353 32.0 | 27.3 | Regulus | 207 36.7 | N11 51.5 |
| E 08 | 335 17.4 | 340 24.6 | 25.9 | 353 54.5 | 29.7 | 337 25.3 | 04.8 | 8 34.3 | 27.3 | Rigel | 281 06.3 | S 8 10.7 |
| D 09 | 350 19.9 | 355 24.4 .. | 24.9 | 8 55.2 .. | 29.0 | 352 27.3 .. | 04.6 | 23 36.7 .. | 27.2 | Rigil Kent. | 139 42.7 | S60 55.6 |
| N 10 | 5 22.3 | 10 24.2 | 24.0 | 23 55.9 | 28.4 | 7 29.3 | 04.4 | 38 39.0 | 27.2 | Sabik | 102 05.1 | S15 45.2 |
| E 11 | 20 24.8 | 25 24.0 | 23.0 | 38 56.6 | 27.7 | 22 31.2 | 04.2 | 53 41.3 | 27.1 | | | |
| S 12 | 35 27.3 | 40 23.8 | S 3 22.0 | 53 57.2 | S 9 27.0 | 37 33.2 | S 2 04.0 | 68 43.6 | S14 27.1 | Schedar | 349 34.1 | N56 39.3 |
| D 13 | 50 29.7 | 55 23.6 | 21.0 | 68 57.9 | 26.3 | 52 35.2 | 03.8 | 83 45.9 | 27.0 | Shaula | 96 13.1 | S37 07.1 |
| A 14 | 65 32.2 | 70 23.5 | 20.0 | 83 58.6 | 25.6 | 67 37.2 | 03.6 | 98 48.2 | 27.0 | Sirius | 258 28.4 | S16 45.0 |
| Y 15 | 80 34.6 | 85 23.3 .. | 19.0 | 98 59.3 .. | 24.9 | 82 39.1 .. | 03.4 | 113 50.6 .. | 26.9 | Spica | 158 24.4 | S11 16.7 |
| 16 | 95 37.1 | 100 23.1 | 18.0 | 114 00.0 | 24.2 | 97 41.1 | 03.2 | 128 52.9 | 26.9 | Suhail | 222 47.9 | S43 31.6 |
| 17 | 110 39.6 | 115 22.9 | 17.0 | 129 00.7 | 23.5 | 112 43.1 | 03.0 | 143 55.2 | 26.9 | | | |
| 18 | 125 42.0 | 130 22.7 | S 3 16.0 | 144 01.3 | S 9 22.8 | 127 45.1 | S 2 02.8 | 158 57.5 | S14 26.8 | Vega | 80 34.5 | N38 48.0 |
| 19 | 140 44.5 | 145 22.5 | 15.0 | 159 02.0 | 22.1 | 142 47.0 | 02.5 | 173 59.8 | 26.8 | Zuben'ubi | 136 58.2 | S16 08.1 |
| 20 | 155 47.0 | 160 22.3 | 14.0 | 174 02.7 | 21.4 | 157 49.0 | 02.3 | 189 02.1 | 26.7 | | SHA | Mer. Pass. |
| 21 | 170 49.4 | 175 22.1 .. | 13.0 | 189 03.4 .. | 20.8 | 172 51.0 .. | 02.1 | 204 04.5 .. | 26.7 | | ° ′ | h m |
| 22 | 185 51.9 | 190 22.0 | 12.0 | 204 04.1 | 20.1 | 187 53.0 | 01.9 | 219 06.8 | 26.6 | Venus | 6 32.0 | 9 18 |
| 23 | 200 54.4 | 205 21.8 | 11.0 | 219 04.8 | 19.4 | 202 54.9 | 01.7 | 234 09.1 | 26.6 | Mars | 19 34.2 | 8 25 |
| | h m | | | | | | | | | Jupiter | 2 23.7 | 9 33 |
| Mer. Pass. | 9 42.5 | v −0.2 | d 1.0 | v 0.7 | d 0.7 | v 2.0 | d 0.2 | v 2.3 | d 0.0 | Saturn | 33 21.8 | 7 29 |

| UT | SUN GHA | Dec | MOON GHA | v | Dec | d | HP | Lat. | Twilight Naut. | Civil | Sunrise | Moonrise 25 | 26 | 27 | 28 |
|---|---|---|---|---|---|---|---|---|---|---|---|---|---|---|---|
| d h | ° ′ | ° ′ | ° ′ | ′ | ° ′ | ′ | ′ | ° | h m | h m | h m | h m | h m | h m | h m |
| **25** 00 | 180 29.2 | N13 06.8 | 244 40.7 | 9.7 | S18 25.0 | 11.7 | 58.2 | N 72 | //// | //// | 02 31 | 06 45 | 05 28 | 04 49 | 04 18 |
| 01 | 195 29.3 | 07.6 | 259 09.4 | 9.8 | 18 13.3 | 11.9 | 58.2 | N 70 | //// | 00 53 | 02 59 | 05 51 | 05 07 | 04 40 | 04 17 |
| 02 | 210 29.4 | 08.4 | 273 38.2 | 9.9 | 18 01.4 | 11.9 | 58.1 | 68 | //// | 01 52 | 03 21 | 05 18 | 04 51 | 04 32 | 04 16 |
| 03 | 225 29.5 .. | 09.3 | 288 07.1 | 10.0 | 17 49.5 | 12.0 | 58.1 | 66 | //// | 02 24 | 03 37 | 04 53 | 04 38 | 04 25 | 04 15 |
| 04 | 240 29.6 | 10.1 | 302 36.1 | 10.1 | 17 37.5 | 12.0 | 58.1 | 64 | 00 46 | 02 48 | 03 51 | 04 34 | 04 26 | 04 20 | 04 14 |
| 05 | 255 29.7 | 10.9 | 317 05.2 | 10.2 | 17 25.5 | 12.2 | 58.1 | 62 | 01 38 | 03 07 | 04 02 | 04 18 | 04 17 | 04 15 | 04 13 |
| 06 | 270 29.9 | N13 11.7 | 331 34.4 | 10.3 | S17 13.3 | 12.2 | 58.1 | 60 | 02 08 | 03 22 | 04 12 | 04 05 | 04 09 | 04 11 | 04 13 |
| 07 | 285 30.0 | 12.5 | 346 03.7 | 10.4 | 17 01.1 | 12.4 | 58.0 | N 58 | 02 30 | 03 34 | 04 20 | 03 53 | 04 01 | 04 07 | 04 12 |
| M 08 | 300 30.1 | 13.3 | 0 33.1 | 10.5 | 16 48.7 | 12.4 | 58.0 | 56 | 02 48 | 03 45 | 04 28 | 03 43 | 03 55 | 04 04 | 04 12 |
| O 09 | 315 30.2 .. | 14.2 | 15 02.6 | 10.6 | 16 36.3 | 12.5 | 58.0 | 54 | 03 02 | 03 54 | 04 34 | 03 34 | 03 49 | 04 01 | 04 11 |
| N 10 | 330 30.3 | 15.0 | 29 32.2 | 10.7 | 16 23.8 | 12.5 | 58.0 | 52 | 03 14 | 04 03 | 04 40 | 03 26 | 03 44 | 03 58 | 04 11 |
| D 11 | 345 30.4 | 15.8 | 44 01.9 | 10.7 | 16 11.3 | 12.6 | 57.9 | 50 | 03 25 | 04 10 | 04 46 | 03 19 | 03 39 | 03 56 | 04 10 |
| A 12 | 0 30.5 | N13 16.6 | 58 31.6 | 10.9 | S15 58.7 | 12.8 | 57.9 | 45 | 03 47 | 04 26 | 04 57 | 03 03 | 03 29 | 03 50 | 04 10 |
| Y 13 | 15 30.6 | 17.4 | 73 01.5 | 10.9 | 15 45.9 | 12.7 | 57.9 | N 40 | 04 03 | 04 38 | 05 07 | 02 51 | 03 20 | 03 46 | 04 09 |
| 14 | 30 30.7 | 18.2 | 87 31.4 | 11.0 | 15 33.2 | 12.9 | 57.9 | 35 | 04 16 | 04 48 | 05 15 | 02 40 | 03 13 | 03 42 | 04 09 |
| 15 | 45 30.8 .. | 19.0 | 102 01.4 | 11.2 | 15 20.3 | 12.9 | 57.9 | 30 | 04 27 | 04 57 | 05 22 | 02 30 | 03 06 | 03 38 | 04 08 |
| 16 | 60 30.9 | 19.8 | 116 31.6 | 11.2 | 15 07.4 | 13.0 | 57.8 | 20 | 04 44 | 05 11 | 05 34 | 02 14 | 02 55 | 03 32 | 04 07 |
| 17 | 75 31.0 | 20.7 | 131 01.8 | 11.3 | 14 54.4 | 13.0 | 57.8 | N 10 | 04 58 | 05 23 | 05 45 | 01 59 | 02 45 | 03 27 | 04 06 |
| 18 | 90 31.1 | N13 21.5 | 145 32.1 | 11.4 | S14 41.4 | 13.2 | 57.8 | 0 | 05 08 | 05 33 | 05 54 | 01 46 | 02 35 | 03 22 | 04 06 |
| 19 | 105 31.2 | 22.3 | 160 02.5 | 11.4 | 14 28.2 | 13.1 | 57.8 | S 10 | 05 18 | 05 43 | 06 04 | 01 32 | 02 26 | 03 16 | 04 05 |
| 20 | 120 31.3 | 23.1 | 174 32.9 | 11.6 | 14 15.1 | 13.3 | 57.8 | 20 | 05 26 | 05 52 | 06 14 | 01 17 | 02 16 | 03 11 | 04 04 |
| 21 | 135 31.4 .. | 23.9 | 189 03.5 | 11.6 | 14 01.8 | 13.3 | 57.7 | 30 | 05 33 | 06 01 | 06 26 | 01 00 | 02 04 | 03 05 | 04 04 |
| 22 | 150 31.5 | 24.7 | 203 34.1 | 11.7 | 13 48.5 | 13.3 | 57.7 | 35 | 05 37 | 06 06 | 06 32 | 00 50 | 01 57 | 03 01 | 04 03 |
| 23 | 165 31.6 | 25.5 | 218 04.8 | 11.8 | 13 35.2 | 13.5 | 57.7 | 40 | 05 40 | 06 12 | 06 40 | 00 39 | 01 49 | 02 57 | 04 03 |
| **26** 00 | 180 31.7 | N13 26.3 | 232 35.6 | 11.9 | S13 21.7 | 13.4 | 57.7 | 45 | 05 44 | 06 18 | 06 49 | 00 26 | 01 40 | 02 52 | 04 02 |
| 01 | 195 31.8 | 27.1 | 247 06.5 | 12.0 | 13 08.3 | 13.6 | 57.6 | S 50 | 05 47 | 06 25 | 06 59 | 00 09 | 01 29 | 02 47 | 04 02 |
| 02 | 210 31.9 | 27.9 | 261 37.5 | 12.0 | 12 54.7 | 13.6 | 57.6 | 52 | 05 49 | 06 28 | 07 04 | 00 02 | 01 24 | 02 44 | 04 01 |
| 03 | 225 32.0 .. | 28.7 | 276 08.5 | 12.1 | 12 41.1 | 13.6 | 57.6 | 54 | 05 50 | 06 32 | 07 09 | 25 19 | 01 19 | 02 41 | 04 01 |
| 04 | 240 32.1 | 29.5 | 290 39.6 | 12.2 | 12 27.5 | 13.7 | 57.6 | 56 | 05 52 | 06 36 | 07 15 | 25 12 | 01 12 | 02 38 | 04 00 |
| 05 | 255 32.2 | 30.4 | 305 10.8 | 12.3 | 12 13.8 | 13.7 | 57.6 | 58 | 05 54 | 06 40 | 07 22 | 25 05 | 01 05 | 02 34 | 04 00 |
| 06 | 270 32.4 | N13 31.2 | 319 42.1 | 12.3 | S12 00.1 | 13.8 | 57.5 | S 60 | 05 55 | 06 44 | 07 29 | 24 57 | 00 57 | 02 30 | 04 00 |

| UT | SUN GHA | Dec | MOON GHA | v | Dec | d | HP | Lat. | Sunset | Twilight Civil | Naut. | Moonset 25 | 26 | 27 | 28 |
|---|---|---|---|---|---|---|---|---|---|---|---|---|---|---|---|
| d h | ° ′ | ° ′ | ° ′ | ′ | ° ′ | ′ | ′ | ° | h m | h m | h m | h m | h m | h m | h m |
| 07 | 285 32.5 | 32.0 | 334 13.4 | 12.4 | 11 46.3 | 13.8 | 57.5 | N 72 | 21 30 | //// | //// | 09 34 | 12 33 | 14 48 | 16 54 |
| T 08 | 300 32.6 | 32.8 | 348 44.8 | 12.5 | 11 32.5 | 13.9 | 57.5 | N 70 | 21 00 | 23 21 | //// | 10 26 | 12 51 | 14 55 | 16 51 |
| U 09 | 315 32.7 .. | 33.6 | 3 16.3 | 12.5 | 11 18.6 | 13.9 | 57.5 | 68 | 20 38 | 22 10 | //// | 10 58 | 13 06 | 15 00 | 16 48 |
| E 10 | 330 32.8 | 34.4 | 17 47.8 | 12.7 | 11 04.7 | 14.0 | 57.5 | 66 | 20 21 | 21 35 | //// | 11 21 | 13 17 | 15 04 | 16 46 |
| S 11 | 345 32.9 | 35.2 | 32 19.5 | 12.7 | 10 50.7 | 14.0 | 57.4 | 64 | 20 07 | 21 11 | 23 25 | 11 39 | 13 27 | 15 07 | 16 44 |
| D 12 | 0 33.0 | N13 36.0 | 46 51.2 | 12.7 | S10 36.7 | 14.1 | 57.4 | 62 | 19 55 | 20 52 | 22 23 | 11 54 | 13 35 | 15 11 | 16 43 |
| A 13 | 15 33.1 | 36.8 | 61 22.9 | 12.9 | 10 22.6 | 14.1 | 57.4 | 60 | 19 45 | 20 36 | 21 51 | 12 06 | 13 42 | 15 13 | 16 41 |
| Y 14 | 30 33.2 | 37.6 | 75 54.8 | 12.8 | 10 08.5 | 14.1 | 57.4 | N 58 | 19 37 | 20 23 | 21 28 | 12 17 | 13 48 | 15 16 | 16 40 |
| 15 | 45 33.3 .. | 38.4 | 90 26.6 | 13.0 | 9 54.4 | 14.1 | 57.3 | 56 | 19 29 | 20 12 | 21 10 | 12 26 | 13 53 | 15 18 | 16 39 |
| 16 | 60 33.4 | 39.2 | 104 58.6 | 13.0 | 9 40.3 | 14.2 | 57.3 | 54 | 19 22 | 20 03 | 20 55 | 12 34 | 13 58 | 15 19 | 16 38 |
| 17 | 75 33.5 | 40.0 | 119 30.6 | 13.1 | 9 26.1 | 14.3 | 57.3 | 52 | 19 16 | 19 54 | 20 43 | 12 41 | 14 03 | 15 21 | 16 37 |
| 18 | 90 33.6 | N13 40.8 | 134 02.7 | 13.1 | S 9 11.8 | 14.2 | 57.3 | 50 | 19 11 | 19 47 | 20 32 | 12 48 | 14 07 | 15 23 | 16 37 |
| 19 | 105 33.7 | 41.6 | 148 34.8 | 13.2 | 8 57.6 | 14.3 | 57.3 | 45 | 18 59 | 19 31 | 20 10 | 13 02 | 14 15 | 15 26 | 16 35 |
| 20 | 120 33.8 | 42.4 | 163 07.0 | 13.3 | 8 43.3 | 14.4 | 57.2 | N 40 | 18 50 | 19 18 | 19 54 | 13 13 | 14 22 | 15 29 | 16 34 |
| 21 | 135 33.8 .. | 43.2 | 177 39.3 | 13.3 | 8 28.9 | 14.3 | 57.2 | 35 | 18 41 | 19 08 | 19 40 | 13 23 | 14 28 | 15 31 | 16 33 |
| 22 | 150 33.9 | 44.0 | 192 11.6 | 13.4 | 8 14.6 | 14.4 | 57.2 | 30 | 18 34 | 18 59 | 19 29 | 13 31 | 14 33 | 15 33 | 16 32 |
| 23 | 165 34.0 | 44.8 | 206 44.0 | 13.4 | 8 00.2 | 14.4 | 57.2 | 20 | 18 22 | 18 45 | 19 12 | 13 45 | 14 42 | 15 37 | 16 30 |
| **27** 00 | 180 34.1 | N13 45.6 | 221 16.4 | 13.5 | S 7 45.8 | 14.4 | 57.2 | N 10 | 18 11 | 18 33 | 18 58 | 13 58 | 14 50 | 15 40 | 16 28 |
| 01 | 195 34.2 | 46.4 | 235 48.9 | 13.6 | 7 31.4 | 14.5 | 57.1 | 0 | 18 01 | 18 22 | 18 47 | 14 10 | 14 58 | 15 43 | 16 27 |
| 02 | 210 34.3 | 47.2 | 250 21.5 | 13.6 | 7 16.9 | 14.5 | 57.1 | S 10 | 17 51 | 18 13 | 18 38 | 14 21 | 15 05 | 15 46 | 16 25 |
| 03 | 225 34.4 .. | 48.0 | 264 54.1 | 13.6 | 7 02.4 | 14.5 | 57.1 | 20 | 17 41 | 18 04 | 18 30 | 14 33 | 15 13 | 15 49 | 16 23 |
| 04 | 240 34.5 | 48.8 | 279 26.7 | 13.7 | 6 47.9 | 14.5 | 57.1 | 30 | 17 29 | 17 54 | 18 22 | 14 47 | 15 21 | 15 52 | 16 22 |
| 05 | 255 34.6 | 49.6 | 293 59.4 | 13.7 | 6 33.4 | 14.6 | 57.0 | 35 | 17 23 | 17 49 | 18 19 | 14 55 | 15 26 | 15 54 | 16 20 |
| 06 | 270 34.7 | N13 50.4 | 308 32.1 | 13.8 | S 6 18.8 | 14.5 | 57.0 | 40 | 17 15 | 17 43 | 18 15 | 15 04 | 15 32 | 15 56 | 16 18 |
| W 07 | 285 34.8 | 51.2 | 323 04.9 | 13.9 | 6 04.3 | 14.6 | 57.0 | 45 | 17 06 | 17 37 | 18 11 | 15 15 | 15 38 | 15 59 | 16 18 |
| E 08 | 300 34.9 | 52.0 | 337 37.8 | 13.8 | 5 49.7 | 14.6 | 57.0 | S 50 | 16 56 | 17 30 | 18 08 | 15 28 | 15 46 | 16 02 | 16 16 |
| D 09 | 315 35.0 .. | 52.8 | 352 10.6 | 14.0 | 5 35.1 | 14.6 | 57.0 | 52 | 16 51 | 17 26 | 18 06 | 15 34 | 15 50 | 16 03 | 16 15 |
| N 10 | 330 35.1 | 53.6 | 6 43.6 | 13.9 | 5 20.5 | 14.6 | 56.9 | 54 | 16 46 | 17 23 | 18 04 | 15 40 | 15 53 | 16 04 | 16 15 |
| E 11 | 345 35.2 | 54.4 | 21 16.5 | 14.0 | 5 05.9 | 14.7 | 56.9 | 56 | 16 40 | 17 19 | 18 03 | 15 47 | 15 58 | 16 06 | 16 14 |
| S 12 | 0 35.3 | N13 55.2 | 35 49.5 | 14.1 | S 4 51.2 | 14.6 | 56.9 | 58 | 16 33 | 17 15 | 18 01 | 15 55 | 16 02 | 16 08 | 16 13 |
| D 13 | 15 35.4 | 55.9 | 50 22.6 | 14.1 | 4 36.6 | 14.7 | 56.9 | S 60 | 16 26 | 17 10 | 17 59 | 16 04 | 16 08 | 16 10 | 16 12 |
| A 14 | 30 35.5 | 56.7 | 64 55.7 | 14.1 | 4 21.9 | 14.7 | 56.9 | | | | | | | | |
| Y 15 | 45 35.6 .. | 57.5 | 79 28.8 | 14.2 | 4 07.2 | 14.6 | 56.8 | | | | | | | | |
| 16 | 60 35.7 | 58.3 | 94 02.0 | 14.2 | 3 52.6 | 14.7 | 56.8 | | | | | | | | |
| 17 | 75 35.8 | 59.1 | 108 35.2 | 14.2 | 3 37.9 | 14.7 | 56.8 | | | | | | | | |

| Day | Eqn. of Time 00h | 12h | Mer. Pass. | Mer. Pass. Upper | Lower | Age | Phase |
|---|---|---|---|---|---|---|---|
| | m s | m s | h m | h m | h m | d | % |
| 25 | 01 57 | 02 02 | 11 58 | 07 58 | 20 23 | 24 | 28 |
| 26 | 02 07 | 02 12 | 11 58 | 08 46 | 21 10 | 25 | 19 |
| 27 | 02 16 | 02 21 | 11 58 | 09 32 | 21 54 | 26 | 12 |

| 18 | 90 35.9 | N13 59.9 | 123 08.4 | 14.3 | S 3 23.2 | 14.7 | 56.8 |
| 19 | 105 36.0 | 14 00.7 | 137 41.7 | 14.3 | 3 08.5 | 14.7 | 56.8 |
| 20 | 120 36.0 | 01.5 | 152 15.0 | 14.3 | 2 53.8 | 14.9 | 56.7 |
| 21 | 135 36.1 .. | 02.3 | 166 48.3 | 14.4 | 2 39.1 | 14.7 | 56.7 |
| 22 | 150 36.2 | 03.1 | 181 21.7 | 14.4 | 2 24.4 | 14.7 | 56.7 |
| 23 | 165 36.3 | 03.9 | 195 55.1 | 14.4 | S 2 09.7 | 14.7 | 56.7 |

| | SD 15.9 | d 0.8 | SD 15.8 | | 15.6 | | 15.5 |

| UT | ARIES GHA | VENUS −4·1 GHA | Dec | MARS +0·9 GHA | Dec | JUPITER −2·1 GHA | Dec | SATURN +0·7 GHA | Dec | STARS Name | SHA | Dec |
|---|---|---|---|---|---|---|---|---|---|---|---|---|
| 28 00 | 215 56.8 | 220 21.6 | S 3 10.0 | 234 05.4 | S 9 18.7 | 217 56.9 | S 2 01.5 | 249 11.4 | S14 26.6 | Acamar | 315 13.9 | S40 13.1 |
| 01 | 230 59.3 | 235 21.4 | 09.0 | 249 06.1 | 18.0 | 232 58.9 | 01.3 | 264 13.7 | 26.5 | Achernar | 335 22.5 | S57 07.5 |
| 02 | 246 01.8 | 250 21.2 | 08.0 | 264 06.8 | 17.3 | 248 00.9 | 01.1 | 279 16.0 | 26.5 | Acrux | 173 01.9 | S63 13.5 |
| 03 | 261 04.2 | 265 21.0 | .. 07.0 | 279 07.5 | .. 16.6 | 263 02.8 | .. 00.9 | 294 18.4 | .. 26.4 | Adhara | 255 07.8 | S29 00.3 |
| 04 | 276 06.7 | 280 20.8 | 06.0 | 294 08.2 | 15.9 | 278 04.8 | 00.7 | 309 20.7 | 26.4 | Aldebaran | 290 42.5 | N16 33.1 |
| 05 | 291 09.1 | 295 20.6 | 05.0 | 309 08.9 | 15.2 | 293 06.8 | 00.5 | 324 23.0 | 26.3 | | | |
| 06 | 306 11.6 | 310 20.4 | S 3 04.0 | 324 09.5 | S 9 14.5 | 308 08.8 | S 2 00.3 | 339 25.3 | S14 26.3 | Alioth | 166 14.5 | N55 50.5 |
| T 07 | 321 14.1 | 325 20.3 | 03.0 | 339 10.2 | 13.8 | 323 10.8 | 2 00.1 | 354 27.6 | 26.3 | Alkaid | 152 53.3 | N49 12.2 |
| H 08 | 336 16.5 | 340 20.1 | 02.0 | 354 10.9 | 13.1 | 338 12.7 | 1 59.9 | 9 30.0 | 26.2 | Alnair | 27 35.9 | S46 51.1 |
| U 09 | 351 19.0 | 355 19.9 | .. 01.0 | 9 11.6 | .. 12.4 | 353 14.7 | .. 59.7 | 24 32.3 | .. 26.2 | Alnilam | 275 40.2 | S 1 11.4 |
| R 10 | 6 21.5 | 10 19.7 | 3 00.0 | 24 12.3 | 11.8 | 8 16.7 | 59.5 | 39 34.6 | 26.1 | Alphard | 217 49.9 | S 8 45.4 |
| S 11 | 21 23.9 | 25 19.5 | 2 59.0 | 39 13.0 | 11.1 | 23 18.7 | 59.3 | 54 36.9 | 26.1 | | | |
| D 12 | 36 26.4 | 40 19.3 | S 2 58.0 | 54 13.6 | S 9 10.4 | 38 20.6 | S 1 59.1 | 69 39.2 | S14 26.1 | Alphecca | 126 05.3 | N26 38.3 |
| A 13 | 51 28.9 | 55 19.1 | 57.0 | 69 14.3 | 09.7 | 53 22.6 | 58.9 | 84 41.6 | 26.0 | Alpheratz | 357 37.4 | N29 12.5 |
| Y 14 | 66 31.3 | 70 18.9 | 56.0 | 84 15.0 | 09.0 | 68 24.6 | 58.7 | 99 43.9 | 26.0 | Altair | 62 02.1 | N 8 55.4 |
| 15 | 81 33.8 | 85 18.7 | .. 55.0 | 99 15.7 | .. 08.3 | 83 26.6 | .. 58.5 | 114 46.2 | .. 25.9 | Ankaa | 353 09.7 | S42 11.1 |
| 16 | 96 36.2 | 100 18.6 | 54.0 | 114 16.4 | 07.6 | 98 28.5 | 58.3 | 129 48.5 | 25.9 | Antares | 112 18.3 | S26 28.9 |
| 17 | 111 38.7 | 115 18.4 | 53.0 | 129 17.1 | 06.9 | 113 30.5 | 58.1 | 144 50.8 | 25.8 | | | |
| 18 | 126 41.2 | 130 18.2 | S 2 52.0 | 144 17.8 | S 9 06.2 | 128 32.5 | S 1 57.8 | 159 53.2 | S14 25.8 | Arcturus | 145 49.6 | N19 04.0 |
| 19 | 141 43.6 | 145 18.0 | 51.0 | 159 18.4 | 05.5 | 143 34.5 | 57.6 | 174 55.5 | 25.8 | Atria | 107 14.1 | S69 03.9 |
| 20 | 156 46.1 | 160 17.8 | 50.0 | 174 19.1 | 04.8 | 158 36.5 | 57.4 | 189 57.8 | 25.7 | Avior | 234 15.7 | S59 35.1 |
| 21 | 171 48.6 | 175 17.6 | .. 49.0 | 189 19.8 | .. 04.1 | 173 38.4 | .. 57.2 | 205 00.1 | .. 25.7 | Bellatrix | 278 25.5 | N 6 22.1 |
| 22 | 186 51.0 | 190 17.4 | 47.9 | 204 20.5 | 03.4 | 188 40.4 | 57.0 | 220 02.4 | 25.6 | Betelgeuse | 270 54.7 | N 7 24.6 |
| 23 | 201 53.5 | 205 17.2 | 46.9 | 219 21.2 | 02.7 | 203 42.4 | 56.8 | 235 04.8 | 25.6 | | | |
| 29 00 | 216 56.0 | 220 17.0 | S 2 45.9 | 234 21.9 | S 9 02.0 | 218 44.4 | S 1 56.6 | 250 07.1 | S14 25.6 | Canopus | 263 53.7 | S52 42.7 |
| 01 | 231 58.4 | 235 16.9 | 44.9 | 249 22.6 | 01.3 | 233 46.3 | 56.4 | 265 09.4 | 25.5 | Capella | 280 25.6 | N46 01.2 |
| 02 | 247 00.9 | 250 16.7 | 43.9 | 264 23.2 | 00.6 | 248 48.3 | 56.2 | 280 11.7 | 25.5 | Deneb | 49 27.3 | N45 21.2 |
| 03 | 262 03.4 | 265 16.5 | .. 42.9 | 279 23.9 | 9 00.0 | 263 50.3 | .. 56.0 | 295 14.0 | .. 25.4 | Denebola | 182 27.0 | N14 26.9 |
| 04 | 277 05.8 | 280 16.3 | 41.9 | 294 24.6 | 8 59.3 | 278 52.3 | 55.8 | 310 16.4 | 25.4 | Diphda | 348 49.9 | S17 52.0 |
| 05 | 292 08.3 | 295 16.1 | 40.9 | 309 25.3 | 58.6 | 293 54.3 | 55.6 | 325 18.7 | 25.3 | | | |
| 06 | 307 10.7 | 310 15.9 | S 2 39.9 | 324 26.0 | S 8 57.9 | 308 56.2 | S 1 55.4 | 340 21.0 | S14 25.3 | Dubhe | 193 43.4 | N61 38.1 |
| 07 | 322 13.2 | 325 15.7 | 38.9 | 339 26.7 | 57.2 | 323 58.2 | 55.2 | 355 23.3 | 25.3 | Elnath | 278 05.0 | N28 37.5 |
| F 08 | 337 15.7 | 340 15.5 | 37.9 | 354 27.4 | 56.5 | 339 00.2 | 55.0 | 10 25.6 | 25.2 | Eltanin | 90 42.9 | N51 28.9 |
| R 09 | 352 18.1 | 355 15.3 | .. 36.9 | 9 28.1 | .. 55.8 | 354 02.2 | .. 54.8 | 25 28.0 | .. 25.2 | Enif | 33 41.1 | N 9 58.4 |
| I 10 | 7 20.6 | 10 15.1 | 35.9 | 24 28.7 | 55.1 | 9 04.2 | 54.6 | 40 30.3 | 25.1 | Fomalhaut | 15 17.2 | S29 30.3 |
| D 11 | 22 23.1 | 25 15.0 | 34.8 | 39 29.4 | 54.4 | 24 06.1 | 54.4 | 55 32.6 | 25.1 | | | |
| A 12 | 37 25.5 | 40 14.8 | S 2 33.8 | 54 30.1 | S 8 53.7 | 39 08.1 | S 1 54.2 | 70 34.9 | S14 25.1 | Gacrux | 171 53.6 | S57 14.4 |
| Y 13 | 52 28.0 | 55 14.6 | 32.8 | 69 30.8 | 53.0 | 54 10.1 | 54.0 | 85 37.3 | 25.0 | Gienah | 175 45.6 | S17 40.0 |
| 14 | 67 30.5 | 70 14.4 | 31.8 | 84 31.5 | 52.3 | 69 12.1 | 53.8 | 100 39.6 | 25.0 | Hadar | 148 38.5 | S60 28.8 |
| 15 | 82 32.9 | 85 14.2 | .. 30.8 | 99 32.2 | .. 51.6 | 84 14.1 | .. 53.6 | 115 41.9 | .. 24.9 | Hamal | 327 54.1 | N23 33.9 |
| 16 | 97 35.4 | 100 14.0 | 29.8 | 114 32.9 | 50.9 | 99 16.0 | 53.4 | 130 44.2 | 24.9 | Kaus Aust. | 83 35.3 | S34 22.4 |
| 17 | 112 37.8 | 115 13.8 | 28.8 | 129 33.6 | 50.2 | 114 18.0 | 53.2 | 145 46.6 | 24.9 | | | |
| 18 | 127 40.3 | 130 13.6 | S 2 27.8 | 144 34.2 | S 8 49.5 | 129 20.0 | S 1 53.0 | 160 48.9 | S14 24.8 | Kochab | 137 18.6 | N74 03.8 |
| 19 | 142 42.8 | 145 13.4 | 26.8 | 159 34.9 | 48.8 | 144 22.0 | 52.8 | 175 51.2 | 24.8 | Markab | 13 32.3 | N15 19.3 |
| 20 | 157 45.2 | 160 13.2 | 25.8 | 174 35.6 | 48.1 | 159 24.0 | 52.6 | 190 53.5 | 24.7 | Menkar | 314 08.8 | N 4 10.5 |
| 21 | 172 47.7 | 175 13.1 | .. 24.7 | 189 36.3 | .. 47.4 | 174 25.9 | .. 52.4 | 205 55.8 | .. 24.7 | Menkent | 147 59.9 | S36 28.8 |
| 22 | 187 50.2 | 190 12.9 | 23.7 | 204 37.0 | 46.7 | 189 27.9 | 52.2 | 220 58.2 | 24.6 | Miaplacidus | 221 38.6 | S69 48.8 |
| 23 | 202 52.6 | 205 12.7 | 22.7 | 219 37.7 | 46.0 | 204 29.9 | 52.0 | 236 00.5 | 24.6 | | | |
| 30 00 | 217 55.1 | 220 12.5 | S 2 21.7 | 234 38.4 | S 8 45.3 | 219 31.9 | S 1 51.8 | 251 02.8 | S14 24.6 | Mirfak | 308 32.0 | N49 56.3 |
| 01 | 232 57.6 | 235 12.3 | 20.7 | 249 39.1 | 44.6 | 234 33.9 | 51.6 | 266 05.1 | 24.5 | Nunki | 75 50.4 | S26 16.1 |
| 02 | 248 00.0 | 250 12.1 | 19.7 | 264 39.8 | 43.9 | 249 35.8 | 51.3 | 281 07.5 | 24.5 | Peacock | 53 09.2 | S56 39.6 |
| 03 | 263 02.5 | 265 11.9 | .. 18.7 | 279 40.5 | .. 43.2 | 264 37.8 | .. 51.1 | 296 09.8 | .. 24.4 | Pollux | 243 20.2 | N27 58.4 |
| 04 | 278 05.0 | 280 11.7 | 17.7 | 294 41.1 | 42.5 | 279 39.8 | 50.9 | 311 12.1 | 24.4 | Procyon | 244 53.3 | N 5 10.0 |
| 05 | 293 07.4 | 295 11.5 | 16.6 | 309 41.8 | 41.8 | 294 41.8 | 50.7 | 326 14.4 | 24.4 | | | |
| 06 | 308 09.9 | 310 11.3 | S 2 15.6 | 324 42.5 | S 8 41.1 | 309 43.8 | S 1 50.5 | 341 16.8 | S14 24.3 | Rasalhague | 96 00.4 | N12 32.5 |
| 07 | 323 12.3 | 325 11.2 | 14.6 | 339 43.2 | 40.4 | 324 45.7 | 50.3 | 356 19.1 | 24.3 | Regulus | 207 36.7 | N11 51.5 |
| S 08 | 338 14.8 | 340 11.0 | 13.6 | 354 43.9 | 39.7 | 339 47.7 | 50.1 | 11 21.4 | 24.2 | Rigel | 281 06.3 | S 8 10.7 |
| A 09 | 353 17.3 | 355 10.8 | .. 12.6 | 9 44.6 | .. 39.0 | 354 49.7 | .. 49.9 | 26 23.7 | .. 24.2 | Rigil Kent. | 139 42.7 | S60 55.6 |
| T 10 | 8 19.7 | 10 10.6 | 11.6 | 24 45.3 | 38.3 | 9 51.7 | 49.7 | 41 26.1 | 24.2 | Sabik | 102 05.1 | S15 45.2 |
| U 11 | 23 22.2 | 25 10.4 | 10.5 | 39 46.0 | 37.6 | 24 53.7 | 49.5 | 56 28.4 | 24.1 | | | |
| R 12 | 38 24.7 | 40 10.2 | S 2 09.5 | 54 46.7 | S 8 36.9 | 39 55.7 | S 1 49.3 | 71 30.7 | S14 24.1 | Schedar | 349 34.1 | N56 39.3 |
| D 13 | 53 27.1 | 55 10.0 | 08.5 | 69 47.4 | 36.2 | 54 57.6 | 49.1 | 86 33.1 | 24.0 | Shaula | 96 13.1 | S37 07.1 |
| A 14 | 68 29.6 | 70 09.8 | 07.5 | 84 48.0 | 35.5 | 69 59.6 | 48.9 | 101 35.4 | 24.0 | Sirius | 258 28.4 | S16 45.0 |
| Y 15 | 83 32.1 | 85 09.6 | .. 06.5 | 99 48.7 | .. 34.8 | 85 01.6 | .. 48.7 | 116 37.7 | .. 24.0 | Spica | 158 24.4 | S11 16.7 |
| 16 | 98 34.5 | 100 09.4 | 05.5 | 114 49.4 | 34.1 | 100 03.6 | 48.5 | 131 40.0 | 23.9 | Suhail | 222 47.9 | S43 31.6 |
| 17 | 113 37.0 | 115 09.2 | 04.4 | 129 50.1 | 33.4 | 115 05.6 | 48.3 | 146 42.4 | 23.9 | | | |
| 18 | 128 39.5 | 130 09.0 | S 2 03.4 | 144 50.8 | S 8 32.7 | 130 07.6 | S 1 48.1 | 161 44.7 | S14 23.8 | Vega | 80 34.5 | N38 48.0 |
| 19 | 143 41.9 | 145 08.9 | 02.4 | 159 51.5 | 32.0 | 145 09.5 | 47.9 | 176 47.0 | 23.8 | Zuben'ubi | 136 58.2 | S16 08.1 |
| 20 | 158 44.4 | 160 08.7 | 01.4 | 174 52.2 | 31.3 | 160 11.5 | 47.7 | 191 49.3 | 23.8 | | | |
| 21 | 173 46.8 | 175 08.5 | 2 00.4 | 189 52.9 | .. 30.6 | 175 13.5 | .. 47.5 | 206 51.7 | .. 23.7 | | SHA | Mer. Pass. |
| 22 | 188 49.3 | 190 08.3 | 1 59.4 | 204 53.6 | 29.9 | 190 15.5 | 47.3 | 221 54.0 | 23.7 | Venus | 3 21.1 | 9 19 |
| 23 | 203 51.8 | 205 08.1 | S 1 58.3 | 219 54.3 | 29.2 | 205 17.5 | 47.1 | 236 56.3 | 23.7 | Mars | 17 25.9 | 8 22 |
| Mer. Pass. 9 30.7 | | v −0.2 | d 1.0 | v 0.7 | d 0.7 | v 2.0 | d 0.2 | v 2.3 | d 0.0 | Jupiter | 1 48.4 | 9 24 |
| | | | | | | | | | | Saturn | 33 11.1 | 7 18 |

| UT | SUN GHA | SUN Dec | MOON GHA | v | MOON Dec | d | HP |
|---|---|---|---|---|---|---|---|
| d h | ° ′ | ° ′ | ° ′ | ′ | ° ′ | ′ | ′ |
| **28** 00 | 180 36.4 | N14 04.7 | 210 28.5 | 14.5 | S 1 55.0 | 14.7 | 56.6 |
| 01 | 195 36.5 | 05.4 | 225 02.0 | 14.5 | 1 40.3 | 14.7 | 56.6 |
| 02 | 210 36.6 | 06.2 | 239 35.5 | 14.5 | 1 25.6 | 14.7 | 56.6 |
| 03 | 225 36.7 | .. 07.0 | 254 09.0 | 14.5 | 1 10.9 | 14.7 | 56.6 |
| 04 | 240 36.8 | 07.8 | 268 42.5 | 14.6 | 0 56.2 | 14.7 | 56.6 |
| 05 | 255 36.9 | 08.6 | 283 16.1 | 14.5 | 0 41.5 | 14.7 | 56.5 |
| 06 | 270 37.0 | N14 09.4 | 297 49.6 | 14.6 | S 0 26.8 | 14.7 | 56.5 |
| 07 | 285 37.1 | 10.2 | 312 23.2 | 14.6 | S 0 12.1 | 14.6 | 56.5 |
| 08 | 300 37.1 | 11.0 | 326 56.8 | 14.7 | N 0 02.5 | 14.7 | 56.5 |
| 09 | 315 37.2 | .. 11.7 | 341 30.5 | 14.6 | 0 17.2 | 14.6 | 56.5 |
| 10 | 330 37.3 | 12.5 | 356 04.1 | 14.7 | 0 31.8 | 14.7 | 56.4 |
| 11 | 345 37.4 | 13.3 | 10 37.8 | 14.7 | 0 46.5 | 14.6 | 56.4 |
| 12 | 0 37.5 | N14 14.1 | 25 11.5 | 14.7 | N 1 01.1 | 14.6 | 56.4 |
| 13 | 15 37.6 | 14.9 | 39 45.2 | 14.7 | 1 15.7 | 14.6 | 56.4 |
| 14 | 30 37.7 | 15.7 | 54 18.9 | 14.7 | 1 30.3 | 14.6 | 56.4 |
| 15 | 45 37.8 | .. 16.4 | 68 52.6 | 14.8 | 1 44.9 | 14.5 | 56.3 |
| 16 | 60 37.9 | 17.2 | 83 26.4 | 14.7 | 1 59.4 | 14.6 | 56.3 |
| 17 | 75 38.0 | 18.0 | 98 00.1 | 14.8 | 2 14.0 | 14.6 | 56.3 |
| 18 | 90 38.0 | N14 18.8 | 112 33.9 | 14.8 | N 2 28.5 | 14.5 | 56.3 |
| 19 | 105 38.1 | 19.6 | 127 07.7 | 14.7 | 2 43.0 | 14.5 | 56.3 |
| 20 | 120 38.2 | 20.4 | 141 41.4 | 14.8 | 2 57.5 | 14.4 | 56.2 |
| 21 | 135 38.3 | .. 21.1 | 156 15.2 | 14.8 | 3 11.9 | 14.5 | 56.2 |
| 22 | 150 38.4 | 21.9 | 170 49.0 | 14.8 | 3 26.4 | 14.4 | 56.2 |
| 23 | 165 38.5 | 22.7 | 185 22.8 | 14.8 | 3 40.8 | 14.3 | 56.2 |
| **29** 00 | 180 38.6 | N14 23.5 | 199 56.6 | 14.8 | N 3 55.1 | 14.4 | 56.2 |
| 01 | 195 38.7 | 24.3 | 214 30.4 | 14.8 | 4 09.5 | 14.3 | 56.1 |
| 02 | 210 38.7 | 25.0 | 229 04.2 | 14.8 | 4 23.8 | 14.4 | 56.1 |
| 03 | 225 38.8 | .. 25.8 | 243 38.0 | 14.8 | 4 38.2 | 14.2 | 56.1 |
| 04 | 240 38.9 | 26.6 | 258 11.8 | 14.8 | 4 52.4 | 14.3 | 56.1 |
| 05 | 255 39.0 | 27.4 | 272 45.6 | 14.8 | 5 06.7 | 14.2 | 56.1 |
| 06 | 270 39.1 | N14 28.1 | 287 19.4 | 14.8 | N 5 20.9 | 14.2 | 56.0 |
| 07 | 285 39.2 | 28.9 | 301 53.2 | 14.8 | 5 35.1 | 14.1 | 56.0 |
| 08 | 300 39.3 | 29.7 | 316 27.0 | 14.8 | 5 49.2 | 14.2 | 56.0 |
| 09 | 315 39.3 | .. 30.5 | 331 00.8 | 14.7 | 6 03.4 | 14.0 | 56.0 |
| 10 | 330 39.4 | 31.2 | 345 34.5 | 14.8 | 6 17.4 | 14.1 | 56.0 |
| 11 | 345 39.5 | 32.0 | 0 08.3 | 14.8 | 6 31.5 | 14.0 | 55.9 |
| 12 | 0 39.6 | N14 32.8 | 14 42.1 | 14.7 | N 6 45.5 | 14.0 | 55.9 |
| 13 | 15 39.7 | 33.6 | 29 15.8 | 14.8 | 6 59.5 | 13.9 | 55.9 |
| 14 | 30 39.8 | 34.3 | 43 49.6 | 14.7 | 7 13.4 | 13.9 | 55.9 |
| 15 | 45 39.8 | .. 35.1 | 58 23.3 | 14.7 | 7 27.3 | 13.9 | 55.9 |
| 16 | 60 39.9 | 35.9 | 72 57.0 | 14.8 | 7 41.2 | 13.8 | 55.0 |
| 17 | 75 40.0 | 36.7 | 87 30.8 | 14.7 | 7 55.0 | 13.8 | 55.8 |
| 18 | 90 40.1 | N14 37.4 | 102 04.5 | 14.6 | N 8 08.8 | 13.7 | 55.8 |
| 19 | 105 40.2 | 38.2 | 116 30.1 | 14.7 | 8 22.5 | 13.7 | 55.8 |
| 20 | 120 40.3 | 39.0 | 131 11.8 | 14.7 | 8 36.2 | 13.7 | 55.8 |
| 21 | 135 40.3 | .. 39.8 | 145 45.5 | 14.6 | 8 49.9 | 13.6 | 55.7 |
| 22 | 150 40.4 | 40.5 | 160 19.1 | 14.6 | 9 03.5 | 13.5 | 55.7 |
| 23 | 165 40.5 | 41.3 | 174 52.7 | 14.6 | 9 17.0 | 13.5 | 55.7 |
| **30** 00 | 180 40.6 | N14 42.1 | 189 26.3 | 14.6 | N 9 30.5 | 13.5 | 55.7 |
| 01 | 195 40.7 | 42.8 | 203 59.9 | 14.6 | 9 44.0 | 13.4 | 55.7 |
| 02 | 210 40.7 | 43.6 | 218 33.5 | 14.5 | 9 57.4 | 13.3 | 55.6 |
| 03 | 225 40.8 | .. 44.4 | 233 07.0 | 14.6 | 10 10.7 | 13.4 | 55.6 |
| 04 | 240 40.9 | 45.1 | 247 40.6 | 14.5 | 10 24.1 | 13.2 | 55.6 |
| 05 | 255 41.0 | 45.9 | 262 14.1 | 14.4 | 10 37.3 | 13.2 | 55.6 |
| 06 | 270 41.1 | N14 46.7 | 276 47.5 | 14.5 | N10 50.5 | 13.2 | 55.6 |
| 07 | 285 41.1 | 47.4 | 291 21.0 | 14.4 | 11 03.7 | 13.1 | 55.5 |
| 08 | 300 41.2 | 48.2 | 305 54.4 | 14.4 | 11 16.8 | 13.0 | 55.5 |
| 09 | 315 41.3 | .. 49.0 | 320 27.8 | 14.4 | 11 29.8 | 13.0 | 55.5 |
| 10 | 330 41.4 | 49.7 | 335 01.2 | 14.4 | 11 42.8 | 12.9 | 55.5 |
| 11 | 345 41.4 | 50.5 | 349 34.6 | 14.3 | 11 55.7 | 12.9 | 55.5 |
| 12 | 0 41.5 | N14 51.3 | 4 07.9 | 14.3 | N12 08.6 | 12.8 | 55.5 |
| 13 | 15 41.6 | 52.0 | 18 41.2 | 14.3 | 12 21.4 | 12.7 | 55.4 |
| 14 | 30 41.7 | 52.8 | 33 14.5 | 14.2 | 12 34.1 | 12.7 | 55.4 |
| 15 | 45 41.8 | .. 53.6 | 47 47.7 | 14.2 | 12 46.8 | 12.6 | 55.4 |
| 16 | 60 41.8 | 54.3 | 62 20.9 | 14.2 | 12 59.4 | 12.6 | 55.4 |
| 17 | 75 41.9 | 55.1 | 76 54.1 | 14.2 | N13 12.0 | 12.5 | 55.4 |
| 18 | 90 42.0 | N14 55.8 | | | | | |
| 19 | 105 42.1 | 56.6 | | | | | |
| 20 | 120 42.2 | 57.4 | | | | | |
| 21 | 135 42.2 | .. 58.1 | | | | | |
| 22 | 150 42.3 | 58.9 | | | | | |
| 23 | 165 42.4 | 59.6 | | | | | |
| | SD 15.9 | d 0.8 | SD 15.4 | | 15.2 | | 15.1 |

THURSDAY (28), FRIDAY (29), SATURDAY (30)

### Twilight / Sunrise / Moonrise

| Lat. | Naut. | Civil | Sunrise | Moonrise 28 | 29 | 30 | 1 |
|---|---|---|---|---|---|---|---|
| ° | h m | h m | h m | h m | h m | h m | h m |
| N 72 | //// | //// | 02 09 | 04 18 | 03 48 | 03 15 | 02 27 |
| N 70 | //// | //// | 02 43 | 04 17 | 03 54 | 03 30 | 02 59 |
| 68 | //// | 01 27 | 03 07 | 04 16 | 04 00 | 03 43 | 03 22 |
| 66 | //// | 02 08 | 03 26 | 04 15 | 04 04 | 03 53 | 03 40 |
| 64 | //// | 02 35 | 03 41 | 04 14 | 04 08 | 04 02 | 03 56 |
| 62 | 01 17 | 02 55 | 03 53 | 04 13 | 04 11 | 04 09 | 04 08 |
| 60 | 01 53 | 03 12 | 04 04 | 04 13 | 04 14 | 04 16 | 04 19 |
| N 58 | 02 18 | 03 25 | 04 13 | 04 12 | 04 17 | 04 22 | 04 28 |
| 56 | 02 38 | 03 37 | 04 21 | 04 12 | 04 19 | 04 27 | 04 37 |
| 54 | 02 53 | 03 47 | 04 28 | 04 11 | 04 21 | 04 32 | 04 44 |
| 52 | 03 07 | 03 56 | 04 34 | 04 11 | 04 23 | 04 36 | 04 51 |
| 50 | 03 18 | 04 04 | 04 40 | 04 10 | 04 25 | 04 40 | 04 57 |
| 45 | 03 41 | 04 21 | 04 53 | 04 10 | 04 29 | 04 48 | 05 10 |
| N 40 | 03 58 | 04 34 | 05 03 | 04 09 | 04 32 | 04 55 | 05 21 |
| 35 | 04 12 | 04 45 | 05 12 | 04 09 | 04 35 | 05 01 | 05 30 |
| 30 | 04 24 | 04 54 | 05 19 | 04 08 | 04 37 | 05 07 | 05 38 |
| 20 | 04 42 | 05 09 | 05 32 | 04 07 | 04 42 | 05 16 | 05 52 |
| N 10 | 04 56 | 05 22 | 05 43 | 04 06 | 04 45 | 05 25 | 06 05 |
| 0 | 05 08 | 05 33 | 05 54 | 04 06 | 04 49 | 05 32 | 06 17 |
| S 10 | 05 18 | 05 43 | 06 04 | 04 05 | 04 53 | 05 40 | 06 29 |
| 20 | 05 26 | 05 53 | 06 15 | 04 04 | 04 57 | 05 49 | 06 41 |
| 30 | 05 35 | 06 03 | 06 28 | 04 04 | 05 01 | 05 59 | 06 56 |
| 35 | 05 39 | 06 09 | 06 35 | 04 03 | 05 04 | 06 04 | 07 05 |
| 40 | 05 43 | 06 15 | 06 43 | 04 03 | 05 07 | 06 11 | 07 15 |
| 45 | 05 47 | 06 22 | 06 52 | 04 02 | 05 11 | 06 18 | 07 26 |
| S 50 | 05 51 | 06 30 | 07 03 | 04 02 | 05 15 | 06 28 | 07 40 |
| 52 | 05 53 | 06 33 | 07 09 | 04 01 | 05 17 | 06 32 | 07 47 |
| 54 | 05 55 | 06 37 | 07 14 | 04 01 | 05 19 | 06 37 | 07 54 |
| 56 | 05 57 | 06 41 | 07 21 | 04 00 | 05 21 | 06 42 | 08 03 |
| 58 | 05 59 | 06 46 | 07 28 | 04 00 | 05 24 | 06 48 | 08 12 |
| S 60 | 06 01 | 06 51 | 07 36 | 04 00 | 05 27 | 06 54 | 08 23 |

### Sunset / Twilight / Moonset

| Lat. | Sunset | Civil | Naut. | Moonset 28 | 29 | 30 | 1 |
|---|---|---|---|---|---|---|---|
| ° | h m | h m | h m | h m | h m | h m | h m |
| N 72 | 21 52 | //// | //// | 16 54 | 19 00 | 21 20 | □ |
| N 70 | 21 16 | //// | //// | 16 51 | 18 46 | 20 50 | 23 29 |
| 68 | 20 51 | 22 36 | //// | 16 48 | 18 36 | 20 29 | 22 35 |
| 66 | 20 32 | 21 52 | //// | 16 46 | 18 27 | 20 11 | 22 03 |
| 64 | 20 16 | 21 24 | //// | 16 44 | 18 20 | 19 58 | 21 39 |
| 62 | 20 04 | 21 02 | 22 45 | 16 43 | 18 14 | 19 46 | 21 20 |
| 60 | 19 53 | 20 45 | 22 06 | 16 41 | 18 09 | 19 36 | 21 05 |
| N 58 | 19 43 | 20 31 | 21 39 | 16 40 | 18 04 | 19 28 | 20 52 |
| 56 | 19 35 | 20 19 | 21 20 | 16 39 | 18 00 | 19 20 | 20 41 |
| 54 | 19 28 | 20 09 | 21 03 | 16 38 | 17 56 | 19 14 | 20 31 |
| 52 | 19 21 | 20 00 | 20 50 | 16 38 | 17 53 | 19 08 | 20 23 |
| 50 | 19 16 | 19 52 | 20 38 | 16 37 | 17 50 | 19 03 | 20 15 |
| 45 | 19 03 | 19 35 | 20 15 | 16 35 | 17 43 | 18 51 | 19 59 |
| N 40 | 18 53 | 19 22 | 19 57 | 16 34 | 17 38 | 18 42 | 19 45 |
| 35 | 18 44 | 19 11 | 19 43 | 16 33 | 17 33 | 18 33 | 19 34 |
| 30 | 18 36 | 19 01 | 19 31 | 16 32 | 17 29 | 18 26 | 19 24 |
| 20 | 18 23 | 18 46 | 19 13 | 16 30 | 17 22 | 18 14 | 19 07 |
| N 10 | 18 11 | 18 33 | 18 59 | 16 28 | 17 16 | 18 03 | 18 52 |
| 0 | 18 01 | 18 22 | 18 47 | 16 27 | 17 10 | 17 54 | 18 39 |
| S 10 | 17 50 | 18 12 | 18 37 | 16 25 | 17 04 | 17 44 | 18 25 |
| 20 | 17 39 | 18 02 | 18 28 | 16 23 | 16 58 | 17 33 | 18 10 |
| 30 | 17 27 | 17 51 | 18 20 | 16 22 | 16 51 | 17 21 | 17 54 |
| 35 | 17 20 | 17 46 | 18 16 | 16 20 | 16 47 | 17 14 | 17 44 |
| 40 | 17 11 | 17 39 | 18 11 | 16 19 | 16 42 | 17 07 | 17 33 |
| 45 | 17 02 | 17 33 | 18 07 | 16 17 | 16 37 | 16 57 | 17 20 |
| S 50 | 16 51 | 17 25 | 18 03 | 16 16 | 16 31 | 16 47 | 17 05 |
| 52 | 16 45 | 17 21 | 18 01 | 16 15 | 16 28 | 16 42 | 16 58 |
| 54 | 16 40 | 17 17 | 17 59 | 16 15 | 16 25 | 16 36 | 16 50 |
| 56 | 16 33 | 17 13 | 17 57 | 16 14 | 16 21 | 16 30 | 16 41 |
| 58 | 16 26 | 17 08 | 17 55 | 16 13 | 16 18 | 16 23 | 16 31 |
| S 60 | 16 18 | 17 03 | 17 52 | 16 12 | 16 13 | 16 15 | 16 19 |

A partial eclipse of the Sun occurs on this date. See page 5.

### SUN / MOON

| Day | Eqn. of Time 00h | 12h | Mer. Pass. | Mer. Pass. Upper | Lower | Age | Phase |
|---|---|---|---|---|---|---|---|
| d | m s | m s | h m | h m | h m | d | % |
| 28 | 02 25 | 02 30 | 11 58 | 10 16 | 22 38 | 27 | 6 |
| 29 | 02 34 | 02 38 | 11 57 | 10 59 | 23 21 | 28 | 2 |
| 30 | 02 42 | 02 46 | 11 57 | 11 43 | 24 05 | 29 | 0 |

| UT | ARIES GHA | VENUS −4.1 GHA | Dec | MARS +0.9 GHA | Dec | JUPITER −2.1 GHA | Dec | SATURN +0.7 GHA | Dec | STARS Name | SHA | Dec |
|---|---|---|---|---|---|---|---|---|---|---|---|---|
| **d h** | ° ′ | ° ′ | ° ′ | ° ′ | ° ′ | ° ′ | ° ′ | ° ′ | ° ′ | | ° ′ | ° ′ |
| **1 00** | 218 54.2 | 220 07.9 | S 1 57.3 | 234 55.0 | S 8 28.5 | 220 19.5 | S 1 46.9 | 251 58.7 | S14 23.6 | Acamar | 315 13.9 | S40 13.1 |
| 01 | 233 56.7 | 235 07.7 | 56.3 | 249 55.7 | 27.8 | 235 21.4 | 46.7 | 267 01.0 | 23.6 | Achernar | 335 22.5 | S57 07.5 |
| 02 | 248 59.2 | 250 07.5 | 55.3 | 264 56.4 | 27.1 | 250 23.4 | 46.5 | 282 03.3 | 23.5 | Acrux | 173 01.9 | S63 13.5 |
| 03 | 264 01.6 | 265 07.3 | .. 54.3 | 279 57.0 | .. 26.4 | 265 25.4 | .. 46.3 | 297 05.6 | .. 23.5 | Adhara | 255 07.8 | S29 00.3 |
| 04 | 279 04.1 | 280 07.1 | 53.2 | 294 57.7 | 25.7 | 280 27.4 | 46.1 | 312 08.0 | 23.5 | Aldebaran | 290 42.5 | N16 33.1 |
| 05 | 294 06.6 | 295 06.9 | 52.2 | 309 58.4 | 25.0 | 295 29.4 | 45.9 | 327 10.3 | 23.4 | | | |
| 06 | 309 09.0 | 310 06.7 | S 1 51.2 | 324 59.1 | S 8 24.3 | 310 31.4 | S 1 45.7 | 342 12.6 | S14 23.4 | Alioth | 166 14.5 | N55 50.5 |
| 07 | 324 11.5 | 325 06.6 | 50.2 | 339 59.8 | 23.6 | 325 33.3 | 45.5 | 357 15.0 | 23.3 | Alkaid | 152 53.3 | N49 12.2 |
| 08 | 339 13.9 | 340 06.4 | 49.2 | 355 00.5 | 22.9 | 340 35.3 | 45.3 | 12 17.3 | 23.3 | Alnair | 27 35.9 | S46 51.1 |
| 09 | 354 16.4 | 355 06.2 | .. 48.1 | 10 01.2 | .. 22.2 | 355 37.3 | .. 45.1 | 27 19.6 | .. 23.3 | Alnilam | 275 40.3 | S 1 11.4 |
| 10 | 9 18.9 | 10 06.0 | 47.1 | 25 01.9 | 21.5 | 10 39.3 | 44.9 | 42 21.9 | 23.2 | Alphard | 217 49.9 | S 8 45.4 |
| 11 | 24 21.3 | 25 05.8 | 46.1 | 40 02.6 | 20.8 | 25 41.3 | 44.7 | 57 24.3 | 23.2 | | | |
| 12 | 39 23.8 | 40 05.6 | S 1 45.1 | 55 03.3 | S 8 20.1 | 40 43.3 | S 1 44.5 | 72 26.6 | S14 23.1 | Alphecca | 126 05.3 | N26 38.3 |
| 13 | 54 26.3 | 55 05.4 | 44.0 | 70 04.0 | 19.4 | 55 45.3 | 44.3 | 87 28.9 | 23.1 | Alpheratz | 357 37.4 | N29 12.5 |
| 14 | 69 28.7 | 70 05.2 | 43.0 | 85 04.7 | 18.7 | 70 47.2 | 44.1 | 102 31.3 | 23.1 | Altair | 62 02.0 | N 8 55.4 |
| 15 | 84 31.2 | 85 05.0 | .. 42.0 | 100 05.4 | .. 18.0 | 85 49.2 | .. 43.9 | 117 33.6 | .. 23.0 | Ankaa | 353 09.7 | S42 11.1 |
| 16 | 99 33.7 | 100 04.8 | 41.0 | 115 06.1 | 17.3 | 100 51.2 | 43.7 | 132 35.9 | 23.0 | Antares | 112 18.3 | S26 28.9 |
| 17 | 114 36.1 | 115 04.6 | 40.0 | 130 06.8 | 16.6 | 115 53.2 | 43.5 | 147 38.2 | 23.0 | | | |
| 18 | 129 38.6 | 130 04.4 | S 1 38.9 | 145 07.4 | S 8 15.9 | 130 55.2 | S 1 43.3 | 162 40.6 | S14 22.9 | Arcturus | 145 49.6 | N19 04.0 |
| 19 | 144 41.1 | 145 04.2 | 37.9 | 160 08.1 | 15.2 | 145 57.2 | 43.1 | 177 42.9 | 22.9 | Atria | 107 14.0 | S69 03.9 |
| 20 | 159 43.5 | 160 04.1 | 36.9 | 175 08.8 | 14.5 | 160 59.2 | 42.9 | 192 45.2 | 22.8 | Avior | 234 15.7 | S59 35.1 |
| 21 | 174 46.0 | 175 03.9 | .. 35.9 | 190 09.5 | .. 13.8 | 176 01.1 | .. 42.7 | 207 47.6 | .. 22.8 | Bellatrix | 278 25.5 | N 6 22.1 |
| 22 | 189 48.4 | 190 03.7 | 34.8 | 205 10.2 | 13.1 | 191 03.1 | 42.5 | 222 49.9 | 22.8 | Betelgeuse | 270 54.7 | N 7 24.6 |
| 23 | 204 50.9 | 205 03.5 | 33.8 | 220 10.9 | 12.4 | 206 05.1 | 42.3 | 237 52.2 | 22.7 | | | |
| **2 00** | 219 53.4 | 220 03.3 | S 1 32.8 | 235 11.6 | S 8 11.7 | 221 07.1 | S 1 42.1 | 252 54.6 | S14 22.7 | Canopus | 263 53.7 | S52 42.7 |
| 01 | 234 55.8 | 235 03.1 | 31.8 | 250 12.3 | 11.0 | 236 09.1 | 41.9 | 267 56.9 | 22.7 | Capella | 280 25.6 | N46 01.2 |
| 02 | 249 58.3 | 250 02.9 | 30.7 | 265 13.0 | 10.3 | 251 11.1 | 41.7 | 282 59.2 | 22.6 | Deneb | 49 27.3 | N45 21.2 |
| 03 | 265 00.8 | 265 02.7 | .. 29.7 | 280 13.7 | .. 09.6 | 266 13.1 | .. 41.5 | 298 01.6 | .. 22.6 | Denebola | 182 27.0 | N14 26.9 |
| 04 | 280 03.2 | 280 02.5 | 28.7 | 295 14.4 | 08.9 | 281 15.1 | 41.3 | 313 03.9 | 22.5 | Diphda | 348 49.8 | S17 52.0 |
| 05 | 295 05.7 | 295 02.3 | 27.7 | 310 15.1 | 08.2 | 296 17.0 | 41.1 | 328 06.2 | 22.5 | | | |
| 06 | 310 08.2 | 310 02.1 | S 1 26.6 | 325 15.8 | S 8 07.5 | 311 19.0 | S 1 40.9 | 343 08.6 | S14 22.4 | Dubhe | 193 43.4 | N61 38.1 |
| 07 | 325 10.6 | 325 01.9 | 25.6 | 340 16.5 | 06.8 | 326 21.0 | 40.7 | 358 10.9 | 22.4 | Elnath | 278 05.0 | N28 37.5 |
| 08 | 340 13.1 | 340 01.7 | 24.6 | 355 17.2 | 06.1 | 341 23.0 | 40.5 | 13 13.2 | 22.4 | Eltanin | 90 42.9 | N51 28.9 |
| 09 | 355 15.6 | 355 01.5 | .. 23.6 | 10 17.9 | .. 05.4 | 356 25.0 | .. 40.3 | 28 15.6 | .. 22.3 | Enif | 33 41.1 | N 9 58.4 |
| 10 | 10 18.0 | 10 01.4 | 22.5 | 25 18.6 | 04.7 | 11 27.0 | 40.1 | 43 17.9 | 22.3 | Fomalhaut | 15 17.2 | S29 30.3 |
| 11 | 25 20.5 | 25 01.2 | 21.5 | 40 19.3 | 04.0 | 26 29.0 | 39.9 | 58 20.2 | 22.3 | | | |
| 12 | 40 22.9 | 40 01.0 | S 1 20.5 | 55 20.0 | S 8 03.3 | 41 31.0 | S 1 39.7 | 73 22.6 | S14 22.2 | Gacrux | 171 53.6 | S57 14.4 |
| 13 | 55 25.4 | 55 00.8 | 19.4 | 70 20.7 | 02.6 | 56 32.9 | 39.5 | 88 24.9 | 22.2 | Gienah | 175 45.6 | S17 40.0 |
| 14 | 70 27.9 | 70 00.6 | 18.4 | 85 21.4 | 01.9 | 71 34.9 | 39.3 | 103 27.2 | 22.2 | Hadar | 148 38.5 | S60 28.8 |
| 15 | 85 30.3 | 85 00.4 | .. 17.4 | 100 22.1 | .. 01.1 | 86 36.9 | .. 39.1 | 118 29.6 | .. 22.1 | Hamal | 327 54.1 | N23 33.9 |
| 16 | 100 32.8 | 100 00.2 | 16.4 | 115 22.8 | 8 00.4 | 101 38.9 | 38.9 | 133 31.9 | 22.1 | Kaus Aust. | 83 35.2 | S34 22.4 |
| 17 | 115 35.3 | 115 00.0 | 15.3 | 130 23.5 | 7 59.7 | 116 40.9 | 38.7 | 148 34.2 | 22.1 | | | |
| 18 | 130 37.7 | 129 59.8 | S 1 14.3 | 145 24.2 | S 7 59.0 | 131 42.9 | S 1 38.5 | 163 36.6 | S14 22.0 | Kochab | 137 18.6 | N74 03.8 |
| 19 | 145 40.2 | 144 59.6 | 13.3 | 160 24.9 | 58.3 | 146 44.9 | 38.3 | 178 38.9 | 22.0 | Markab | 13 32.3 | N15 19.3 |
| 20 | 160 42.7 | 159 59.4 | 12.2 | 175 25.6 | 57.6 | 161 46.9 | 38.1 | 193 41.2 | 21.9 | Menkar | 314 08.8 | N 4 10.5 |
| 21 | 175 45.1 | 174 59.2 | .. 11.2 | 190 26.2 | .. 56.9 | 176 48.8 | .. 37.9 | 208 43.6 | .. 21.9 | Menkent | 147 59.9 | S36 28.8 |
| 22 | 190 47.6 | 189 59.0 | 10.2 | 205 26.9 | 56.2 | 191 50.8 | 37.7 | 223 45.9 | 21.9 | Miaplacidus | 221 38.6 | S69 48.8 |
| 23 | 205 50.0 | 204 58.8 | 09.2 | 220 27.6 | 55.5 | 206 52.8 | 37.5 | 238 48.2 | 21.8 | | | |
| **3 00** | 220 52.5 | 219 58.6 | S 1 08.1 | 235 28.3 | S 7 54.8 | 221 54.8 | S 1 37.3 | 253 50.6 | S14 21.8 | Mirfak | 308 32.0 | N49 56.3 |
| 01 | 235 55.0 | 234 58.4 | 07.1 | 250 29.0 | 54.1 | 236 56.8 | 37.1 | 268 52.9 | 21.8 | Nunki | 75 50.4 | S26 16.1 |
| 02 | 250 57.4 | 249 58.2 | 06.1 | 265 29.7 | 53.4 | 251 58.8 | 36.9 | 283 55.2 | 21.7 | Peacock | 53 09.2 | S56 39.6 |
| 03 | 265 59.9 | 264 58.0 | .. 05.0 | 280 30.4 | .. 52.7 | 267 00.8 | .. 36.7 | 298 57.6 | .. 21.7 | Pollux | 243 20.2 | N27 58.4 |
| 04 | 281 02.4 | 279 57.9 | 04.0 | 295 31.1 | 52.0 | 282 02.8 | 36.5 | 313 59.9 | 21.6 | Procyon | 244 53.3 | N 5 10.0 |
| 05 | 296 04.8 | 294 57.7 | 03.0 | 310 31.8 | 51.3 | 297 04.8 | 36.3 | 329 02.2 | 21.6 | | | |
| 06 | 311 07.3 | 309 57.5 | S 1 01.9 | 325 32.5 | S 7 50.6 | 312 06.8 | S 1 36.1 | 344 04.6 | S14 21.6 | Rasalhague | 96 00.4 | N12 32.5 |
| 07 | 326 09.8 | 324 57.3 | 00.9 | 340 33.2 | 49.9 | 327 08.7 | 35.9 | 359 06.9 | 21.5 | Regulus | 207 36.7 | N11 51.5 |
| 08 | 341 12.2 | 339 57.1 | 0 59.9 | 355 33.9 | 49.2 | 342 10.7 | 35.7 | 14 09.2 | 21.5 | Rigel | 281 06.3 | S 8 10.7 |
| 09 | 356 14.7 | 354 56.9 | .. 58.8 | 10 34.6 | .. 48.5 | 357 12.7 | .. 35.5 | 29 11.6 | .. 21.5 | Rigil Kent. | 139 42.7 | S60 55.6 |
| 10 | 11 17.2 | 9 56.7 | 57.8 | 25 35.3 | 47.7 | 12 14.7 | 35.3 | 44 13.9 | 21.4 | Sabik | 102 05.1 | S15 45.2 |
| 11 | 26 19.6 | 24 56.5 | 56.8 | 40 36.0 | 47.0 | 27 16.7 | 35.1 | 59 16.3 | 21.4 | | | |
| 12 | 41 22.1 | 39 56.3 | S 0 55.7 | 55 36.7 | S 7 46.3 | 42 18.7 | S 1 34.9 | 74 18.6 | S14 21.4 | Schedar | 349 34.1 | N56 39.3 |
| 13 | 56 24.5 | 54 56.1 | 54.7 | 70 37.4 | 45.6 | 57 20.7 | 34.7 | 89 20.9 | 21.3 | Shaula | 96 13.1 | S37 07.1 |
| 14 | 71 27.0 | 69 55.9 | 53.7 | 85 38.1 | 44.9 | 72 22.7 | 34.6 | 104 23.3 | 21.3 | Sirius | 258 28.4 | S16 45.0 |
| 15 | 86 29.5 | 84 55.7 | .. 52.6 | 100 38.8 | .. 44.2 | 87 24.7 | .. 34.4 | 119 25.6 | .. 21.2 | Spica | 158 24.4 | S11 16.7 |
| 16 | 101 31.9 | 99 55.5 | 51.6 | 115 39.5 | 43.5 | 102 26.7 | 34.2 | 134 27.9 | 21.2 | Suhail | 222 47.9 | S43 31.6 |
| 17 | 116 34.4 | 114 55.3 | 50.6 | 130 40.2 | 42.8 | 117 28.7 | 34.0 | 149 30.3 | 21.2 | | | |
| 18 | 131 36.9 | 129 55.1 | S 0 49.5 | 145 40.9 | S 7 42.1 | 132 30.6 | S 1 33.8 | 164 32.6 | S14 21.1 | Vega | 80 34.5 | N38 48.0 |
| 19 | 146 39.3 | 144 54.9 | 48.5 | 160 41.6 | 41.4 | 147 32.6 | 33.6 | 179 35.0 | 21.1 | Zuben'ubi | 136 58.2 | S16 08.1 |
| 20 | 161 41.8 | 159 54.7 | 47.5 | 175 42.3 | 40.7 | 162 34.6 | 33.4 | 194 37.3 | 21.1 | | | |
| 21 | 176 44.3 | 174 54.5 | .. 46.4 | 190 43.0 | .. 40.0 | 177 36.6 | .. 33.2 | 209 39.6 | .. 21.0 | | SHA | Mer. Pass. |
| 22 | 191 46.7 | 189 54.3 | 45.4 | 205 43.7 | 39.3 | 192 38.6 | 33.0 | 224 42.0 | 21.0 | Venus | 0 09.9 | 9 20 |
| 23 | 206 49.2 | 204 54.1 | 44.4 | 220 44.4 | 38.6 | 207 40.6 | 32.8 | 239 44.3 | 21.0 | Mars | 15 18.2 | 8 19 |
| Mer. Pass. | h m   9 18.9 | v −0.2 | d 1.0 | v 0.7 | d 0.7 | v 2.0 | d 0.2 | v 2.3 | d 0.0 | Jupiter   Saturn | 1 13.7   33 01.2 | 9 14   7 07 |

## SUN / MOON

| UT | SUN GHA | SUN Dec | MOON GHA | v | MOON Dec | d | HP |
|---|---|---|---|---|---|---|---|
| d h | ° ′ | ° ′ | ° ′ | ′ | ° ′ | ′ | ′ |
| **1** 00 | 180 42.5 | N15 00.4 | 178 45.5 | 13.9 | N14 38.1 | 12.0 | 55.2 |
| 01 | 195 42.5 | 01.2 | 193 18.4 | 13.9 | 14 50.1 | 12.0 | 55.2 |
| 02 | 210 42.6 | 01.9 | 207 51.3 | 13.9 | 15 02.1 | 11.9 | 55.2 |
| 03 | 225 42.7 .. | 02.7 | 222 24.2 | 13.8 | 15 14.0 | 11.8 | 55.2 |
| 04 | 240 42.8 | 03.4 | 236 57.0 | 13.7 | 15 25.8 | 11.7 | 55.2 |
| 05 | 255 42.8 | 04.2 | 251 29.7 | 13.8 | 15 37.5 | 11.7 | 55.1 |
| 06 | 270 42.9 | N15 05.0 | 266 02.5 | 13.7 | N15 49.2 | 11.6 | 55.1 |
| 07 | 285 43.0 | 05.7 | 280 35.2 | 13.6 | 16 00.8 | 11.5 | 55.1 |
| 08 | 300 43.1 | 06.5 | 295 07.8 | 13.7 | 16 12.3 | 11.5 | 55.1 |
| S 09 | 315 43.1 .. | 07.2 | 309 40.5 | 13.5 | 16 23.8 | 11.3 | 55.1 |
| U 10 | 330 43.2 | 08.0 | 324 13.0 | 13.6 | 16 35.1 | 11.3 | 55.1 |
| N 11 | 345 43.3 | 08.7 | 338 45.6 | 13.5 | 16 46.4 | 11.2 | 55.0 |
| D 12 | 0 43.4 | N15 09.5 | 353 18.1 | 13.4 | N16 57.6 | 11.2 | 55.0 |
| A 13 | 15 43.4 | 10.2 | 7 50.5 | 13.5 | 17 08.8 | 11.0 | 55.0 |
| Y 14 | 30 43.5 | 11.0 | 22 23.0 | 13.3 | 17 19.8 | 11.0 | 55.0 |
| 15 | 45 43.6 .. | 11.7 | 36 55.3 | 13.4 | 17 30.8 | 10.8 | 55.0 |
| 16 | 60 43.6 | 12.5 | 51 27.7 | 13.3 | 17 41.6 | 10.8 | 55.0 |
| 17 | 75 43.7 | 13.3 | 66 00.0 | 13.2 | 17 52.4 | 10.8 | 54.9 |
| 18 | 90 43.8 | N15 14.0 | 80 32.2 | 13.2 | N18 03.2 | 10.6 | 54.9 |
| 19 | 105 43.9 | 14.8 | 95 04.4 | 13.2 | 18 13.8 | 10.5 | 54.9 |
| 20 | 120 43.9 | 15.5 | 109 36.6 | 13.1 | 18 24.3 | 10.5 | 54.9 |
| 21 | 135 44.0 .. | 16.3 | 124 08.7 | 13.1 | 18 34.8 | 10.4 | 54.9 |
| 22 | 150 44.1 | 17.0 | 138 40.8 | 13.0 | 18 45.2 | 10.2 | 54.9 |
| 23 | 165 44.1 | 17.8 | 153 12.8 | 13.0 | 18 55.4 | 10.2 | 54.9 |
| **2** 00 | 180 44.2 | N15 18.5 | 167 44.8 | 13.0 | N19 05.6 | 10.1 | 54.8 |
| 01 | 195 44.3 | 19.3 | 182 16.8 | 12.9 | 19 15.7 | 10.1 | 54.8 |
| 02 | 210 44.4 | 20.0 | 196 48.7 | 12.8 | 19 25.8 | 9.9 | 54.8 |
| 03 | 225 44.4 .. | 20.7 | 211 20.5 | 12.9 | 19 35.7 | 9.8 | 54.8 |
| 04 | 240 44.5 | 21.5 | 225 52.4 | 12.7 | 19 45.5 | 9.8 | 54.8 |
| 05 | 255 44.6 | 22.2 | 240 24.1 | 12.8 | 19 55.3 | 9.6 | 54.8 |
| 06 | 270 44.6 | N15 23.0 | 254 55.9 | 12.6 | N20 04.9 | 9.5 | 54.7 |
| 07 | 285 44.7 | 23.7 | 269 27.5 | 12.7 | 20 14.4 | 9.5 | 54.7 |
| 08 | 300 44.8 | 24.5 | 283 59.2 | 12.6 | 20 23.9 | 9.4 | 54.7 |
| M 09 | 315 44.8 .. | 25.2 | 298 30.8 | 12.5 | 20 33.3 | 9.2 | 54.7 |
| O 10 | 330 44.9 | 26.0 | 313 02.3 | 12.5 | 20 42.5 | 9.2 | 54.7 |
| N 11 | 345 45.0 | 26.7 | 327 33.8 | 12.5 | 20 51.7 | 9.1 | 54.7 |
| D 12 | 0 45.0 | N15 27.5 | 342 05.3 | 12.4 | N21 00.8 | 8.9 | 54.7 |
| A 13 | 15 45.1 | 28.2 | 356 36.7 | 12.3 | 21 09.7 | 8.9 | 54.6 |
| Y 14 | 30 45.2 | 28.9 | 11 08.0 | 12.4 | 21 18.6 | 8.8 | 54.6 |
| 15 | 45 45.2 .. | 29.7 | 25 39.4 | 12.2 | 21 27.4 | 8.6 | 54.6 |
| 16 | 60 45.3 | 30.4 | 40 10.6 | 12.3 | 21 36.0 | 8.6 | 54.6 |
| 17 | 75 45.4 | 31.2 | 54 41.9 | 12.2 | 21 44.6 | 8.5 | 54.6 |
| 18 | 90 45.4 | N15 31.9 | 69 13.1 | 12.1 | N21 53.1 | 8.3 | 54.6 |
| 19 | 105 45.5 | 32.6 | 83 44.2 | 12.1 | 22 01.4 | 8.3 | 54.6 |
| 20 | 120 45.6 | 33.4 | 98 15.3 | 12.0 | 22 09.7 | 8.1 | 54.6 |
| 21 | 135 45.6 .. | 34.1 | 112 46.3 | 12.1 | 22 17.8 | 8.1 | 54.5 |
| 22 | 150 45.7 | 34.9 | 127 17.4 | 11.9 | 22 25.9 | 7.9 | 54.5 |
| 23 | 165 45.8 | 35.6 | 141 48.3 | 11.9 | 22 33.8 | 7.9 | 54.5 |
| **3** 00 | 180 45.8 | N15 36.3 | 156 19.2 | 11.9 | N22 41.7 | 7.7 | 54.5 |
| 01 | 195 45.9 | 37.1 | 170 50.1 | 11.9 | 22 49.4 | 7.6 | 54.5 |
| 02 | 210 46.0 | 37.8 | 185 21.0 | 11.7 | 22 57.0 | 7.5 | 54.5 |
| 03 | 225 46.0 .. | 38.6 | 199 51.7 | 11.8 | 23 04.5 | 7.4 | 54.5 |
| 04 | 240 46.1 | 39.3 | 214 22.5 | 11.7 | 23 11.9 | 7.3 | 54.5 |
| 05 | 255 46.1 | 40.0 | 228 53.2 | 11.7 | 23 19.2 | 7.2 | 54.4 |
| 06 | 270 46.2 | N15 40.8 | 243 23.9 | 11.6 | N23 26.4 | 7.1 | 54.4 |
| 07 | 285 46.3 | 41.5 | 257 54.5 | 11.6 | 23 33.5 | 7.0 | 54.4 |
| 08 | 300 46.3 | 42.2 | 272 25.1 | 11.5 | 23 40.5 | 6.8 | 54.4 |
| T 09 | 315 46.4 .. | 43.0 | 286 55.6 | 11.5 | 23 47.3 | 6.7 | 54.4 |
| U 10 | 330 46.5 | 43.7 | 301 26.1 | 11.5 | 23 54.0 | 6.7 | 54.4 |
| E 11 | 345 46.5 | 44.4 | 315 56.6 | 11.4 | 24 00.7 | 6.5 | 54.4 |
| S 12 | 0 46.6 | N15 45.2 | 330 27.0 | 11.4 | N24 07.2 | 6.4 | 54.4 |
| D 13 | 15 46.6 | 45.9 | 344 57.4 | 11.3 | 24 13.6 | 6.2 | 54.4 |
| A 14 | 30 46.7 | 46.6 | 359 27.7 | 11.3 | 24 19.8 | 6.2 | 54.3 |
| Y 15 | 45 46.8 .. | 47.4 | 13 58.0 | 11.3 | 24 26.0 | 6.1 | 54.3 |
| 16 | 60 46.8 | 48.1 | 28 28.3 | 11.2 | 24 32.1 | 5.9 | 54.3 |
| 17 | 75 46.9 | 48.8 | 42 58.5 | 11.2 | 24 38.0 | 5.8 | 54.3 |
| 18 | 90 46.9 | N15 49.6 | 57 28.7 | 11.1 | N24 43.8 | 5.7 | 54.3 |
| 19 | 105 47.0 | 50.3 | 71 58.8 | 11.1 | 24 49.5 | 5.6 | 54.3 |
| 20 | 120 47.1 | 51.0 | 86 28.9 | 11.1 | 24 55.1 | 5.4 | 54.3 |
| 21 | 135 47.1 .. | 51.7 | 100 59.0 | 11.1 | 25 00.5 | 5.4 | 54.3 |
| 22 | 150 47.2 | 52.5 | 115 29.1 | 11.0 | 25 05.9 | 5.2 | 54.3 |
| 23 | 165 47.2 | 53.2 | 129 59.1 | 11.0 | N25 11.1 | 5.1 | 54.3 |
| | SD 15.9 | d 0.7 | SD 15.0 | | 14.9 | | 14.8 |

## Twilight / Sunrise / Moonrise

| Lat. | Twilight Naut. | Twilight Civil | Sunrise | Moonrise 1 | 2 | 3 | 4 |
|---|---|---|---|---|---|---|---|
| ° | h m | h m | h m | h m | h m | h m | h m |
| N 72 | //// | //// | 01 44 | 02 27 | ☐ | ☐ | ☐ |
| N 70 | //// | //// | 02 25 | 02 59 | 01 55 | ☐ | ☐ |
| 68 | //// | 00 56 | 02 53 | 03 22 | 02 50 | ☐ | ☐ |
| 66 | //// | 01 49 | 03 14 | 03 40 | 03 24 | 02 52 | ☐ |
| 64 | //// | 02 21 | 03 30 | 03 56 | 03 48 | 03 39 | 03 19 |
| 62 | 00 49 | 02 44 | 03 44 | 04 08 | 04 08 | 04 09 | 04 15 |
| 60 | 01 37 | 03 02 | 03 55 | 04 19 | 04 24 | 04 32 | 04 48 |
| N 58 | 02 06 | 03 17 | 04 05 | 04 28 | 04 37 | 04 51 | 05 12 |
| 56 | 02 27 | 03 29 | 04 14 | 04 37 | 04 49 | 05 07 | 05 32 |
| 54 | 02 45 | 03 40 | 04 22 | 04 44 | 05 00 | 05 20 | 05 48 |
| 52 | 02 59 | 03 50 | 04 29 | 04 51 | 05 09 | 05 32 | 06 03 |
| 50 | 03 11 | 03 58 | 04 35 | 04 57 | 05 17 | 05 42 | 06 15 |
| 45 | 03 35 | 04 16 | 04 48 | 05 10 | 05 35 | 06 04 | 06 41 |
| N 40 | 03 54 | 04 30 | 04 59 | 05 21 | 05 49 | 06 22 | 07 01 |
| 35 | 04 09 | 04 41 | 05 08 | 05 30 | 06 02 | 06 37 | 07 10 |
| 30 | 04 21 | 04 51 | 05 16 | 05 38 | 06 12 | 06 50 | 07 33 |
| 20 | 04 40 | 05 07 | 05 30 | 05 52 | 06 31 | 07 13 | 07 58 |
| N 10 | 04 55 | 05 21 | 05 42 | 06 05 | 06 47 | 07 32 | 08 20 |
| 0 | 05 07 | 05 32 | 05 53 | 06 17 | 07 03 | 07 50 | 08 40 |
| S 10 | 05 18 | 05 43 | 06 05 | 06 29 | 07 18 | 08 09 | 09 00 |
| 20 | 05 27 | 05 54 | 06 16 | 06 41 | 07 35 | 08 29 | 09 22 |
| 30 | 05 36 | 06 05 | 06 30 | 06 56 | 07 54 | 08 51 | 09 48 |
| 35 | 05 41 | 06 11 | 06 37 | 07 05 | 08 05 | 09 05 | 10 03 |
| 40 | 05 45 | 06 18 | 06 46 | 07 15 | 08 18 | 09 21 | 10 20 |
| 45 | 05 50 | 06 25 | 06 56 | 07 26 | 08 33 | 09 39 | 10 41 |
| S 50 | 05 55 | 06 34 | 07 08 | 07 40 | 08 52 | 10 03 | 11 08 |
| 52 | 05 57 | 06 38 | 07 14 | 07 47 | 09 02 | 10 14 | 11 21 |
| 54 | 06 00 | 06 42 | 07 20 | 07 54 | 09 12 | 10 27 | 11 36 |
| 56 | 06 02 | 06 47 | 07 27 | 08 03 | 09 23 | 10 42 | 11 54 |
| 58 | 06 05 | 06 52 | 07 34 | 08 12 | 09 36 | 10 59 | 12 15 |
| S 60 | 06 07 | 06 57 | 07 43 | 08 23 | 09 52 | 11 21 | 12 43 |

## Sunset / Twilight / Moonset

| Lat. | Sunset | Twilight Civil | Twilight Naut. | Moonset 1 | 2 | 3 | 4 |
|---|---|---|---|---|---|---|---|
| ° | h m | h m | h m | h m | h m | h m | h m |
| N 72 | 22 17 | //// | //// | ☐ | ☐ | ☐ | ☐ |
| N 70 | 21 33 | //// | //// | 23 29 | ☐ | ☐ | ☐ |
| 68 | 21 04 | 23 12 | //// | 22 35 | ☐ | ☐ | ☐ |
| 66 | 20 43 | 22 10 | //// | 22 03 | 24 13 | 00 13 | ☐ |
| 64 | 20 26 | 21 37 | //// | 21 39 | 23 27 | 25 28 | 01 28 |
| 62 | 20 12 | 21 13 | 23 17 | 21 20 | 22 57 | 24 33 | 00 33 |
| 60 | 20 00 | 20 55 | 22 22 | 21 05 | 22 34 | 24 00 | 00 00 |
| N 58 | 19 50 | 20 39 | 21 51 | 20 52 | 22 16 | 23 36 | 24 46 |
| 56 | 19 41 | 20 26 | 21 29 | 20 41 | 22 01 | 23 17 | 24 23 |
| 54 | 19 33 | 20 15 | 21 12 | 20 31 | 21 48 | 23 01 | 24 05 |
| 52 | 19 26 | 20 06 | 20 57 | 20 23 | 21 37 | 22 47 | 23 50 |
| 50 | 19 20 | 19 57 | 20 45 | 20 15 | 21 26 | 22 35 | 23 36 |
| 45 | 19 07 | 19 39 | 20 20 | 19 59 | 21 05 | 22 10 | 23 09 |
| N 40 | 18 56 | 19 25 | 20 01 | 19 45 | 20 48 | 21 50 | 22 47 |
| 35 | 18 46 | 19 13 | 19 46 | 19 34 | 20 34 | 21 33 | 22 29 |
| 30 | 18 38 | 19 03 | 19 34 | 19 24 | 20 22 | 21 19 | 22 14 |
| 20 | 18 24 | 18 47 | 19 14 | 19 07 | 20 01 | 20 55 | 21 48 |
| N 10 | 18 12 | 18 34 | 18 59 | 18 52 | 19 42 | 20 34 | 21 25 |
| 0 | 18 00 | 18 22 | 18 47 | 18 39 | 19 25 | 20 14 | 21 04 |
| S 10 | 17 49 | 18 11 | 18 36 | 18 25 | 19 09 | 19 55 | 20 43 |
| 20 | 17 37 | 18 00 | 18 26 | 18 10 | 18 50 | 19 34 | 20 21 |
| 30 | 17 24 | 17 49 | 18 17 | 17 54 | 18 30 | 19 10 | 19 55 |
| 35 | 17 16 | 17 43 | 18 13 | 17 44 | 18 18 | 18 56 | 19 39 |
| 40 | 17 08 | 17 36 | 18 08 | 17 33 | 18 04 | 18 40 | 19 22 |
| 45 | 16 58 | 17 28 | 18 03 | 17 20 | 17 48 | 18 20 | 19 00 |
| S 50 | 16 45 | 17 20 | 17 58 | 17 05 | 17 27 | 17 56 | 18 33 |
| 52 | 16 40 | 17 16 | 17 56 | 16 58 | 17 18 | 17 44 | 18 20 |
| 54 | 16 33 | 17 11 | 17 53 | 16 50 | 17 07 | 17 31 | 18 05 |
| 56 | 16 27 | 17 07 | 17 51 | 16 41 | 16 55 | 17 16 | 17 47 |
| 58 | 16 19 | 17 02 | 17 48 | 16 31 | 16 41 | 16 58 | 17 25 |
| S 60 | 16 10 | 16 56 | 17 46 | 16 19 | 16 25 | 16 36 | 16 58 |

## SUN / MOON

| Day | SUN Eqn. of Time 00h | SUN Eqn. of Time 12h | Mer. Pass. | MOON Mer. Pass. Upper | MOON Mer. Pass. Lower | Age | Phase |
|---|---|---|---|---|---|---|---|
| d | m s | m s | h m | h m | h m | d | % |
| 1 | 02 50 | 02 53 | 11 57 | 12 28 | 00 05 | 01 | 0 | |
| 2 | 02 57 | 03 00 | 11 57 | 13 14 | 00 51 | 02 | 3 | |
| 3 | 03 03 | 03 06 | 11 57 | 14 02 | 01 38 | 03 | 7 | ● |

| UT | ARIES | VENUS −4·1 | | MARS +0·8 | | JUPITER −2·1 | | SATURN +0·7 | | STARS | | |
|---|---|---|---|---|---|---|---|---|---|---|---|---|
| | GHA | GHA | Dec | GHA | Dec | GHA | Dec | GHA | Dec | Name | SHA | Dec |
| d h | ° ′ | ° ′ | ° ′ | ° ′ | ° ′ | ° ′ | ° ′ | ° ′ | ° ′ | | ° ′ | ° ′ |
| 4 00 | 221 51.7 | 219 53.9 | S 0 43.3 | 235 45.1 | S 7 37.8 | 222 42.6 | S 1 32.6 | 254 46.6 | S14 20.9 | Acamar | 315 13.9 | S40 13.0 |
| 01 | 236 54.1 | 234 53.7 | 42.3 | 250 45.8 | 37.1 | 237 44.6 | 32.4 | 269 49.0 | 20.9 | Achernar | 335 22.4 | S57 07.4 |
| 02 | 251 56.6 | 249 53.6 | 41.3 | 265 46.5 | 36.4 | 252 46.6 | 32.2 | 284 51.3 | 20.9 | Acrux | 173 02.0 | S63 13.5 |
| 03 | 266 59.0 | 264 53.4 . . | 40.2 | 280 47.2 . . | 35.7 | 267 48.6 . . | 32.0 | 299 53.7 . . | 20.8 | Adhara | 255 07.8 | S29 00.3 |
| 04 | 282 01.5 | 279 53.2 | 39.2 | 295 47.9 | 35.0 | 282 50.6 | 31.8 | 314 56.0 | 20.8 | Aldebaran | 290 42.5 | N16 33.1 |
| 05 | 297 04.0 | 294 53.0 | 38.2 | 310 48.6 | 34.3 | 297 52.6 | 31.6 | 329 58.3 | 20.7 | | | |
| 06 | 312 06.4 | 309 52.8 | S 0 37.1 | 325 49.3 | S 7 33.6 | 312 54.6 | S 1 31.4 | 345 00.7 | S14 20.7 | Alioth | 166 14.5 | N55 50.5 |
| W 07 | 327 08.9 | 324 52.6 | 36.1 | 340 50.1 | 32.9 | 327 56.6 | 31.2 | 0 03.0 | 20.7 | Alkaid | 152 53.3 | N49 12.2 |
| E 08 | 342 11.4 | 339 52.4 | 35.1 | 355 50.8 | 32.2 | 342 58.5 | 31.0 | 15 05.4 | 20.6 | Alnair | 27 35.9 | S46 51.1 |
| D 09 | 357 13.8 | 354 52.2 . . | 34.0 | 10 51.5 . . | 31.5 | 358 00.5 . . | 30.8 | 30 07.7 . . | 20.6 | Alnilam | 275 40.3 | S 1 11.4 |
| N 10 | 12 16.3 | 9 52.0 | 33.0 | 25 52.2 | 30.8 | 13 02.5 | 30.6 | 45 10.0 | 20.6 | Alphard | 217 49.9 | S 8 45.4 |
| E 11 | 27 18.8 | 24 51.8 | 31.9 | 40 52.9 | 30.1 | 28 04.5 | 30.4 | 60 12.4 | 20.5 | | | |
| S 12 | 42 21.2 | 39 51.6 | S 0 30.9 | 55 53.6 | S 7 29.3 | 43 06.5 | S 1 30.2 | 75 14.7 | S14 20.5 | Alphecca | 126 05.3 | N26 38.3 |
| D 13 | 57 23.7 | 54 51.4 | 29.9 | 70 54.3 | 28.6 | 58 08.5 | 30.0 | 90 17.1 | 20.5 | Alpheratz | 357 37.3 | N29 12.5 |
| A 14 | 72 26.2 | 69 51.2 | 28.8 | 85 55.0 | 27.9 | 73 10.5 | 29.8 | 105 19.4 | 20.4 | Altair | 62 02.0 | N 8 55.5 |
| Y 15 | 87 28.6 | 84 51.0 . . | 27.8 | 100 55.7 . . | 27.2 | 88 12.5 . . | 29.6 | 120 21.7 . . | 20.4 | Ankaa | 353 09.7 | S42 11.1 |
| 16 | 102 31.1 | 99 50.8 | 26.7 | 115 56.4 | 26.5 | 103 14.5 | 29.4 | 135 24.1 | 20.4 | Antares | 112 18.2 | S26 28.9 |
| 17 | 117 33.5 | 114 50.6 | 25.7 | 130 57.1 | 25.8 | 118 16.5 | 29.2 | 150 26.4 | 20.3 | | | |
| 18 | 132 36.0 | 129 50.4 | S 0 24.7 | 145 57.8 | S 7 25.1 | 133 18.5 | S 1 29.0 | 165 28.8 | S14 20.3 | Arcturus | 145 49.6 | N19 04.0 |
| 19 | 147 38.5 | 144 50.2 | 23.6 | 160 58.5 | 24.4 | 148 20.5 | 28.8 | 180 31.1 | 20.3 | Atria | 107 14.0 | S69 03.9 |
| 20 | 162 40.9 | 159 50.0 | 22.6 | 175 59.2 | 23.7 | 163 22.5 | 28.6 | 195 33.5 | 20.2 | Avior | 234 15.7 | S59 35.1 |
| 21 | 177 43.4 | 174 49.8 . . | 21.6 | 190 59.9 . . | 23.0 | 178 24.5 . . | 28.4 | 210 35.8 . . | 20.2 | Bellatrix | 278 25.5 | N 6 22.1 |
| 22 | 192 45.9 | 189 49.6 | 20.5 | 206 00.6 | 22.3 | 193 26.5 | 28.3 | 225 38.1 | 20.2 | Betelgeuse | 270 54.7 | N 7 24.6 |
| 23 | 207 48.3 | 204 49.4 | 19.5 | 221 01.3 | 21.5 | 208 28.5 | 28.1 | 240 40.5 | 20.1 | | | |
| 5 00 | 222 50.8 | 219 49.2 | S 0 18.4 | 236 02.0 | S 7 20.8 | 223 30.5 | S 1 27.9 | 255 42.8 | S14 20.1 | Canopus | 263 53.7 | S52 42.7 |
| 01 | 237 53.3 | 234 49.0 | 17.4 | 251 02.7 | 20.1 | 238 32.5 | 27.7 | 270 45.2 | 20.1 | Capella | 280 25.6 | N46 01.2 |
| 02 | 252 55.7 | 249 48.8 | 16.4 | 266 03.4 | 19.4 | 253 34.4 | 27.5 | 285 47.5 | 20.0 | Deneb | 49 27.2 | N45 21.2 |
| 03 | 267 58.2 | 264 48.6 . . | 15.3 | 281 04.1 . . | 18.7 | 268 36.4 . . | 27.3 | 300 49.8 . . | 20.0 | Denebola | 182 27.0 | N14 26.9 |
| 04 | 283 00.6 | 279 48.4 | 14.3 | 296 04.8 | 18.0 | 283 38.4 | 27.1 | 315 52.2 | 20.0 | Diphda | 348 49.8 | S17 52.0 |
| 05 | 298 03.1 | 294 48.2 | 13.2 | 311 05.5 | 17.3 | 298 40.4 | 26.9 | 330 54.5 | 19.9 | | | |
| 06 | 313 05.6 | 309 48.0 | S 0 12.2 | 326 06.2 | S 7 16.6 | 313 42.4 | S 1 26.7 | 345 56.9 | S14 19.9 | Dubhe | 193 43.5 | N61 38.1 |
| T 07 | 328 08.0 | 324 47.8 | 11.2 | 341 06.9 | 15.9 | 328 44.4 | 26.5 | 0 59.2 | 19.8 | Elnath | 278 05.0 | N28 37.5 |
| H 08 | 343 10.5 | 339 47.6 | 10.1 | 356 07.6 | 15.2 | 343 46.4 | 26.3 | 16 01.6 | 19.8 | Eltanin | 90 42.8 | N51 28.9 |
| U 09 | 358 13.0 | 354 47.4 . . | 09.1 | 11 08.3 . . | 14.4 | 358 48.4 . . | 26.1 | 31 03.9 . . | 19.8 | Enif | 33 41.0 | N 9 58.4 |
| R 10 | 13 15.4 | 9 47.2 | 08.0 | 26 09.0 | 13.7 | 13 50.4 | 25.9 | 46 06.2 | 19.7 | Fomalhaut | 15 17.2 | S29 30.3 |
| S 11 | 28 17.9 | 24 47.0 | 07.0 | 41 09.8 | 13.0 | 28 52.4 | 25.7 | 61 08.6 | 19.7 | | | |
| D 12 | 43 20.4 | 39 46.8 | S 0 05.9 | 56 10.5 | S 7 12.3 | 43 54.4 | S 1 25.5 | 76 10.9 | S14 19.7 | Gacrux | 171 53.6 | S57 14.4 |
| A 13 | 58 22.8 | 54 46.6 | 04.9 | 71 11.2 | 11.6 | 58 56.4 | 25.3 | 91 13.3 | 19.6 | Gienah | 175 45.6 | S17 40.0 |
| Y 14 | 73 25.3 | 69 46.4 | 03.9 | 86 11.9 | 10.9 | 73 58.4 | 25.1 | 106 15.6 | 19.6 | Hadar | 148 38.5 | S60 28.9 |
| 15 | 88 27.8 | 84 46.2 . . | 02.8 | 101 12.6 . . | 10.2 | 89 00.4 . . | 24.9 | 121 18.0 . . | 19.6 | Hamal | 327 54.1 | N23 33.9 |
| 16 | 103 30.2 | 99 46.0 | 01.8 | 116 13.3 | 09.5 | 104 02.4 | 24.7 | 136 20.3 | 19.5 | Kaus Aust. | 83 35.2 | S34 22.4 |
| 17 | 118 32.7 | 114 45.8 | S 00.7 | 131 14.0 | 08.8 | 119 04.4 | 24.5 | 151 22.7 | 19.5 | | | |
| 18 | 133 35.1 | 129 45.6 | N 0 00.3 | 146 14.7 | S 7 08.0 | 134 06.4 | S 1 24.3 | 166 25.0 | S14 19.5 | Kochab | 137 18.6 | N74 03.9 |
| 19 | 148 37.6 | 144 45.4 | 01.3 | 161 15.4 | 07.3 | 149 08.4 | 24.2 | 181 27.3 | 19.4 | Markab | 13 32.3 | N15 19.3 |
| 20 | 163 40.1 | 159 45.2 | 02.4 | 176 16.1 | 06.6 | 164 10.4 | 24.0 | 196 29.7 | 19.4 | Menkar | 314 08.8 | N 4 10.5 |
| 21 | 178 42.5 | 174 45.0 . . | 03.4 | 191 16.8 . . | 05.9 | 179 12.4 . . | 23.8 | 211 32.0 . . | 19.4 | Menkent | 147 59.9 | S36 28.8 |
| 22 | 193 45.0 | 189 44.8 | 04.5 | 206 17.5 | 05.2 | 194 14.4 | 23.6 | 226 34.4 | 19.3 | Miaplacidus | 221 38.7 | S69 48.8 |
| 23 | 208 47.5 | 204 44.6 | 05.5 | 221 18.2 | 04.5 | 209 16.4 | 23.4 | 241 36.7 | 19.3 | | | |
| 6 00 | 223 49.9 | 219 44.4 | N 0 06.6 | 236 18.9 | S 7 03.8 | 224 18.4 | S 1 23.2 | 256 39.1 | S14 19.3 | Mirfak | 308 31.9 | N49 56.3 |
| 01 | 238 52.4 | 234 44.2 | 07.6 | 251 19.6 | 03.1 | 239 20.4 | 23.0 | 271 41.4 | 19.2 | Nunki | 75 50.3 | S26 16.1 |
| 02 | 253 54.9 | 249 44.0 | 08.7 | 266 20.3 | 02.4 | 254 22.4 | 22.8 | 286 43.8 | 19.2 | Peacock | 53 09.1 | S56 39.6 |
| 03 | 268 57.3 | 264 43.8 . . | 09.7 | 281 21.1 . . | 01.6 | 269 24.4 . . | 22.6 | 301 46.1 . . | 19.2 | Pollux | 243 20.2 | N27 58.4 |
| 04 | 283 59.8 | 279 43.6 | 10.7 | 296 21.8 | 00.9 | 284 26.4 | 22.4 | 316 48.5 | 19.1 | Procyon | 244 53.3 | N 5 10.0 |
| 05 | 299 02.3 | 294 43.4 | 11.8 | 311 22.5 | 7 00.2 | 299 28.4 | 22.2 | 331 50.8 | 19.1 | | | |
| 06 | 314 04.7 | 309 43.2 | N 0 12.8 | 326 23.2 | S 6 59.5 | 314 30.4 | S 1 22.0 | 346 53.2 | S14 19.1 | Rasalhague | 96 00.4 | N12 32.5 |
| 07 | 329 07.2 | 324 43.0 | 13.9 | 341 23.9 | 58.8 | 329 32.4 | 21.8 | 1 55.5 | 19.1 | Regulus | 207 36.7 | N11 51.5 |
| 08 | 344 09.6 | 339 42.8 | 14.9 | 356 24.6 | 58.1 | 344 34.4 | 21.6 | 16 57.8 | 19.0 | Rigel | 281 06.3 | S 8 10.7 |
| F 09 | 359 12.1 | 354 42.6 . . | 16.0 | 11 25.3 . . | 57.4 | 359 36.4 . . | 21.4 | 32 00.2 . . | 19.0 | Rigil Kent. | 139 42.7 | S60 55.6 |
| R 10 | 14 14.6 | 9 42.4 | 17.0 | 26 26.0 | 56.7 | 14 38.4 | 21.2 | 47 02.5 | 19.0 | Sabik | 102 05.1 | S15 45.2 |
| I 11 | 29 17.0 | 24 42.2 | 18.1 | 41 26.7 | 55.9 | 29 40.4 | 21.0 | 62 04.9 | 18.9 | | | |
| D 12 | 44 19.5 | 39 42.0 | N 0 19.1 | 56 27.4 | S 6 55.2 | 44 42.4 | S 1 20.9 | 77 07.2 | S14 18.9 | Schedar | 349 34.0 | N56 39.3 |
| A 13 | 59 22.0 | 54 41.8 | 20.1 | 71 28.1 | 54.5 | 59 44.4 | 20.7 | 92 09.6 | 18.9 | Shaula | 96 13.1 | S37 07.1 |
| Y 14 | 74 24.4 | 69 41.6 | 21.2 | 86 28.8 | 53.8 | 74 46.4 | 20.5 | 107 11.9 | 18.8 | Sirius | 258 28.4 | S16 45.0 |
| 15 | 89 26.9 | 84 41.4 . . | 22.2 | 101 29.5 . . | 53.1 | 89 48.4 . . | 20.3 | 122 14.3 . . | 18.8 | Spica | 158 24.4 | S11 16.7 |
| 16 | 104 29.4 | 99 41.2 | 23.3 | 116 30.3 | 52.4 | 104 50.4 | 20.1 | 137 16.6 | 18.8 | Suhail | 222 47.9 | S43 31.6 |
| 17 | 119 31.8 | 114 41.0 | 24.3 | 131 31.0 | 51.7 | 119 52.4 | 19.9 | 152 19.0 | 18.7 | | | |
| 18 | 134 34.3 | 129 40.8 | N 0 25.4 | 146 31.7 | S 6 50.9 | 134 54.4 | S 1 19.7 | 167 21.3 | S14 18.7 | Vega | 80 34.5 | N38 48.0 |
| 19 | 149 36.8 | 144 40.6 | 26.4 | 161 32.4 | 50.2 | 149 56.4 | 19.5 | 182 23.7 | 18.7 | Zuben'ubi | 136 58.1 | S16 08.1 |
| 20 | 164 39.2 | 159 40.4 | 27.5 | 176 33.1 | 49.5 | 164 58.4 | 19.3 | 197 26.0 | 18.6 | | SHA | Mer. Pass. |
| 21 | 179 41.7 | 174 40.2 . . | 28.5 | 191 33.8 . . | 48.8 | 180 00.4 . . | 19.1 | 212 28.4 . . | 18.6 | | ° ′ | h m |
| 22 | 194 44.1 | 189 40.0 | 29.6 | 206 34.5 | 48.1 | 195 02.4 | 18.9 | 227 30.7 | 18.6 | Venus | 356 58.4 | 9 21 |
| 23 | 209 46.6 | 204 39.8 | 30.6 | 221 35.2 | 47.4 | 210 04.4 | 18.7 | 242 33.1 | 18.5 | Mars | 13 11.2 | 8 15 |
| | h m | | | | | | | | | Jupiter | 0 39.7 | 9 05 |
| Mer. Pass. 9 07.1 | | v −0.2 | d 1.0 | v 0.7 | d 0.7 | v 2.0 | d 0.2 | v 2.3 | d 0.0 | Saturn | 32 52.0 | 6 56 |

| UT | SUN GHA | SUN Dec | MOON GHA | v | MOON Dec | d | HP |
|---|---|---|---|---|---|---|---|
| d h | ° ′ | ° ′ | ° ′ | ′ | ° ′ | ′ | ′ |
| 4 00 | 180 47.3 | N15 53.9 | 144 29.1 | 10.9 | N25 16.2 | 5.0 | 54.3 |
| 01 | 195 47.4 | 54.7 | 158 59.0 | 10.9 | 25 21.2 | 4.9 | 54.3 |
| 02 | 210 47.4 | 55.4 | 173 28.9 | 10.9 | 25 26.1 | 4.7 | 54.2 |
| 03 | 225 47.5 | .. 56.1 | 187 58.8 | 10.9 | 25 30.8 | 4.6 | 54.2 |
| 04 | 240 47.5 | 56.8 | 202 28.7 | 10.8 | 25 35.4 | 4.5 | 54.2 |
| 05 | 255 47.6 | 57.6 | 216 58.5 | 10.8 | 25 39.9 | 4.4 | 54.2 |
| 06 | 270 47.7 | N15 58.3 | 231 28.3 | 10.8 | N25 44.3 | 4.2 | 54.2 |
| W 07 | 285 47.7 | 59.0 | 245 58.1 | 10.7 | 25 48.5 | 4.2 | 54.2 |
| E 08 | 300 47.8 | 15 59.7 | 260 27.8 | 10.7 | 25 52.7 | 4.0 | 54.2 |
| D 09 | 315 47.8 | 16 00.5 | 274 57.5 | 10.7 | 25 56.7 | 3.8 | 54.2 |
| N 10 | 330 47.9 | 01.2 | 289 27.2 | 10.7 | 26 00.5 | 3.8 | 54.2 |
| E 11 | 345 47.9 | 01.9 | 303 56.9 | 10.6 | 26 04.3 | 3.6 | 54.2 |
| S 12 | 0 48.0 | N16 02.6 | 318 26.5 | 10.6 | N26 07.9 | 3.5 | 54.2 |
| D 13 | 15 48.0 | 03.3 | 332 56.1 | 10.6 | 26 11.4 | 3.4 | 54.2 |
| A 14 | 30 48.1 | 04.1 | 347 25.7 | 10.6 | 26 14.8 | 3.3 | 54.2 |
| Y 15 | 45 48.2 | .. 04.8 | 1 55.3 | 10.5 | 26 18.1 | 3.1 | 54.2 |
| 16 | 60 48.2 | 05.5 | 16 24.8 | 10.5 | 26 21.2 | 3.0 | 54.2 |
| 17 | 75 48.3 | 06.2 | 30 54.3 | 10.5 | 26 24.2 | 2.9 | 54.1 |
| 18 | 90 48.3 | N16 06.9 | 45 23.8 | 10.5 | N26 27.1 | 2.7 | 54.1 |
| 19 | 105 48.4 | 07.7 | 59 53.3 | 10.5 | 26 29.8 | 2.6 | 54.1 |
| 20 | 120 48.4 | 08.4 | 74 22.8 | 10.5 | 26 32.4 | 2.5 | 54.1 |
| 21 | 135 48.5 | .. 09.1 | 88 52.3 | 10.4 | 26 34.9 | 2.4 | 54.1 |
| 22 | 150 48.5 | 09.8 | 103 21.7 | 10.4 | 26 37.3 | 2.2 | 54.1 |
| 23 | 165 48.6 | 10.5 | 117 51.1 | 10.4 | 26 39.5 | 2.2 | 54.1 |
| 5 00 | 180 48.6 | N16 11.2 | 132 20.5 | 10.4 | N26 41.7 | 1.9 | 54.1 |
| 01 | 195 48.7 | 12.0 | 146 49.9 | 10.4 | 26 43.6 | 1.9 | 54.1 |
| 02 | 210 48.8 | 12.7 | 161 19.3 | 10.4 | 26 45.5 | 1.7 | 54.1 |
| 03 | 225 48.8 | .. 13.4 | 175 48.7 | 10.3 | 26 47.2 | 1.6 | 54.1 |
| 04 | 240 48.9 | 14.1 | 190 18.0 | 10.4 | 26 48.8 | 1.5 | 54.1 |
| 05 | 255 48.9 | 14.8 | 204 47.4 | 10.3 | 26 50.3 | 1.3 | 54.1 |
| 06 | 270 49.0 | N16 15.5 | 219 16.7 | 10.3 | N26 51.6 | 1.2 | 54.1 |
| T 07 | 285 49.0 | 16.2 | 233 46.1 | 10.3 | 26 52.8 | 1.1 | 54.1 |
| H 08 | 300 49.1 | 17.0 | 248 15.4 | 10.3 | 26 53.9 | 1.0 | 54.1 |
| U 09 | 315 49.1 | .. 17.7 | 262 44.7 | 10.3 | 26 54.9 | 0.8 | 54.1 |
| R 10 | 330 49.2 | 18.4 | 277 14.0 | 10.3 | 26 55.7 | 0.7 | 54.1 |
| S 11 | 345 49.2 | 19.1 | 291 43.4 | 10.3 | 26 56.4 | 0.6 | 54.1 |
| D 12 | 0 49.3 | N16 19.8 | 306 12.7 | 10.3 | N26 57.0 | 0.4 | 54.1 |
| A 13 | 15 49.3 | 20.5 | 320 42.0 | 10.3 | 26 57.4 | 0.3 | 54.1 |
| Y 14 | 30 49.4 | 21.2 | 335 11.3 | 10.3 | 26 57.7 | 0.2 | 54.1 |
| 15 | 45 49.4 | .. 21.9 | 349 40.6 | 10.3 | 26 57.9 | 0.1 | 54.1 |
| 16 | 60 49.5 | 22.6 | 4 09.9 | 10.3 | 26 58.0 | 0.1 | 54.1 |
| 17 | 75 49.5 | 23.4 | 18 39.2 | 10.3 | 26 57.9 | 0.2 | 54.1 |
| 18 | 90 49.6 | N16 24.1 | 33 08.5 | 10.4 | N26 57.7 | 0.4 | 54.1 |
| 19 | 105 49.6 | 24.8 | 47 37.9 | 10.3 | 26 57.3 | 0.4 | 54.1 |
| 20 | 120 49.7 | 25.5 | 62 07.2 | 10.3 | 26 56.9 | 0.6 | 54.1 |
| 21 | 135 49.7 | .. 26.2 | 76 36.5 | 10.4 | 26 56.3 | 0.8 | 54.1 |
| 22 | 150 49.8 | 26.9 | 91 05.9 | 10.3 | 26 55.5 | 0.8 | 54.1 |
| 23 | 165 49.8 | 27.6 | 105 35.2 | 10.4 | 26 54.7 | 1.0 | 54.1 |
| 6 00 | 180 49.9 | N16 28.3 | 120 04.6 | 10.3 | N26 53.7 | 1.1 | 54.1 |
| 01 | 195 49.9 | 29.0 | 134 33.9 | 10.4 | 26 52.6 | 1.2 | 54.1 |
| 02 | 210 49.9 | 29.7 | 149 03.3 | 10.4 | 26 51.4 | 1.4 | 54.1 |
| 03 | 225 50.0 | .. 30.4 | 163 32.7 | 10.4 | 26 50.0 | 1.5 | 54.1 |
| 04 | 240 50.0 | 31.1 | 178 02.1 | 10.4 | 26 48.5 | 1.6 | 54.1 |
| 05 | 255 50.1 | 31.8 | 192 31.5 | 10.4 | 26 46.9 | 1.8 | 54.1 |
| 06 | 270 50.1 | N16 32.5 | 207 00.9 | 10.4 | N26 45.1 | 1.9 | 54.1 |
| 07 | 285 50.2 | 33.2 | 221 30.3 | 10.5 | 26 43.2 | 2.0 | 54.1 |
| F 08 | 300 50.2 | 33.9 | 235 59.8 | 10.5 | 26 41.2 | 2.1 | 54.2 |
| R 09 | 315 50.3 | .. 34.6 | 250 29.3 | 10.4 | 26 39.1 | 2.3 | 54.2 |
| I 10 | 330 50.3 | 35.3 | 264 58.7 | 10.5 | 26 36.8 | 2.3 | 54.2 |
| D 11 | 345 50.4 | 36.0 | 279 28.2 | 10.6 | 26 34.5 | 2.6 | 54.2 |
| A 12 | 0 50.4 | N16 36.7 | 293 57.8 | 10.5 | N26 31.9 | 2.6 | 54.2 |
| Y 13 | 15 50.4 | 37.4 | 308 27.3 | 10.6 | 26 29.3 | 2.8 | 54.2 |
| 14 | 30 50.5 | 38.1 | 322 56.9 | 10.6 | 26 26.5 | 2.9 | 54.2 |
| 15 | 45 50.5 | .. 38.8 | 337 26.5 | 10.6 | 26 23.6 | 3.0 | 54.2 |
| 16 | 60 50.6 | 39.5 | 351 56.1 | 10.6 | 26 20.6 | 3.1 | 54.2 |
| 17 | 75 50.6 | 40.2 | 6 25.7 | 10.6 | 26 17.5 | 3.3 | 54.2 |
| 18 | 90 50.7 | N16 40.9 | 20 55.3 | 10.7 | N26 14.2 | 3.4 | 54.2 |
| 19 | 105 50.7 | 41.6 | 35 25.0 | 10.7 | 26 10.8 | 3.5 | 54.2 |
| 20 | 120 50.8 | 42.3 | 49 54.7 | 10.7 | 26 07.3 | 3.6 | 54.2 |
| 21 | 135 50.8 | .. 43.0 | 64 24.4 | 10.8 | 26 03.7 | 3.8 | 54.2 |
| 22 | 150 50.8 | 43.7 | 78 54.2 | 10.8 | 25 59.9 | 3.9 | 54.2 |
| 23 | 165 50.9 | 44.4 | 93 24.0 | 10.8 | N25 56.0 | 4.0 | 54.3 |
| | SD 15.9 | d 0.7 | SD 14.8 | | 14.7 | | 14.8 |

| Lat. | Twilight Naut. | Twilight Civil | Sunrise | Moonrise 4 | 5 | 6 | 7 |
|---|---|---|---|---|---|---|---|
| ° | h m | h m | h m | h m | h m | h m | h m |
| N 72 | //// | //// | 01 14 | ☐ | ☐ | ☐ | ☐ |
| N 70 | //// | //// | 02 07 | ☐ | ☐ | ☐ | ☐ |
| 68 | //// | //// | 02 39 | ☐ | ☐ | ☐ | ☐ |
| 66 | //// | 01 29 | 03 02 | ☐ | ☐ | ☐ | ☐ |
| 64 | //// | 02 06 | 03 20 | 03 19 | ☐ | ☐ | 05 56 |
| 62 | //// | 02 32 | 03 35 | 04 15 | 04 35 | 05 27 | 06 52 |
| 60 | 01 19 | 02 52 | 03 47 | 04 48 | 05 18 | 06 11 | 07 25 |
| N 58 | 01 53 | 03 08 | 03 58 | 05 12 | 05 47 | 06 40 | 07 49 |
| 56 | 02 17 | 03 22 | 04 07 | 05 32 | 06 10 | 07 02 | 08 08 |
| 54 | 02 36 | 03 33 | 04 16 | 05 48 | 06 28 | 07 20 | 08 25 |
| 52 | 02 51 | 03 43 | 04 23 | 06 03 | 06 43 | 07 36 | 08 38 |
| 50 | 03 04 | 03 52 | 04 30 | 06 15 | 06 57 | 07 49 | 08 51 |
| 45 | 03 30 | 04 11 | 04 44 | 06 41 | 07 25 | 08 17 | 09 16 |
| N 40 | 03 50 | 04 26 | 04 55 | 07 01 | 07 46 | 08 38 | 09 36 |
| 35 | 04 05 | 04 38 | 05 05 | 07 18 | 08 04 | 08 56 | 09 52 |
| 30 | 04 18 | 04 48 | 05 14 | 07 33 | 08 20 | 09 12 | 10 06 |
| 20 | 04 38 | 05 05 | 05 29 | 07 58 | 08 46 | 09 38 | 10 31 |
| N 10 | 04 54 | 05 19 | 05 41 | 08 20 | 09 09 | 10 00 | 10 52 |
| 0 | 05 07 | 05 32 | 05 53 | 08 40 | 09 30 | 10 21 | 11 11 |
| S 10 | 05 18 | 05 43 | 06 05 | 09 00 | 09 52 | 10 42 | 11 31 |
| 20 | 05 28 | 05 55 | 06 17 | 09 22 | 10 15 | 11 05 | 11 52 |
| 30 | 05 38 | 06 07 | 06 31 | 09 48 | 10 41 | 11 31 | 12 16 |
| 35 | 05 43 | 06 13 | 06 40 | 10 03 | 10 57 | 11 46 | 12 30 |
| 40 | 05 48 | 06 20 | 06 49 | 10 20 | 11 15 | 12 04 | 12 46 |
| 45 | 05 53 | 06 28 | 06 59 | 10 41 | 11 37 | 12 25 | 13 05 |
| S 50 | 05 59 | 06 38 | 07 12 | 11 08 | 12 05 | 12 52 | 13 30 |
| 52 | 06 02 | 06 42 | 07 18 | 11 21 | 12 19 | 13 06 | 13 41 |
| 54 | 06 04 | 06 47 | 07 25 | 11 36 | 12 35 | 13 21 | 13 54 |
| 56 | 06 07 | 06 52 | 07 32 | 11 54 | 12 54 | 13 39 | 14 10 |
| 58 | 06 10 | 06 57 | 07 41 | 12 15 | 13 17 | 14 00 | 14 28 |
| S 60 | 06 13 | 07 04 | 07 50 | 12 43 | 13 48 | 14 28 | 14 50 |

| Lat. | Sunset | Twilight Civil | Twilight Naut. | Moonset 4 | 5 | 6 | 7 |
|---|---|---|---|---|---|---|---|
| ° | h m | h m | h m | h m | h m | h m | h m |
| N 72 | 22 50 | //// | //// | ☐ | ☐ | ☐ | ☐ |
| N 70 | 21 52 | //// | //// | ☐ | ☐ | ☐ | ☐ |
| 68 | 21 18 | //// | //// | ☐ | ☐ | ☐ | ☐ |
| 66 | 20 54 | 22 31 | //// | ☐ | ☐ | ☐ | ☐ |
| 64 | 20 36 | 21 51 | //// | 01 28 | ☐ | ☐ | 04 07 |
| 62 | 20 20 | 21 24 | //// | 00 33 | 01 58 | 02 51 | 03 11 |
| 60 | 20 00 | 21 04 | 22 40 | 00 00 | 01 15 | 02 07 | 02 38 |
| N 58 | 19 57 | 20 47 | 22 04 | 24 46 | 00 46 | 01 38 | 02 13 |
| 56 | 19 47 | 20 34 | 21 39 | 24 23 | 00 23 | 01 16 | 01 54 |
| 54 | 19 39 | 20 22 | 21 20 | 24 05 | 00 05 | 00 58 | 01 37 |
| 52 | 19 31 | 20 11 | 21 04 | 23 50 | 24 42 | 00 42 | 01 23 |
| 50 | 19 25 | 20 02 | 20 51 | 23 36 | 24 29 | 00 29 | 01 11 |
| 45 | 19 10 | 19 43 | 20 25 | 23 09 | 24 01 | 00 01 | 00 45 |
| N 40 | 18 59 | 19 28 | 20 05 | 22 47 | 23 39 | 24 25 | 00 25 |
| 35 | 18 49 | 19 16 | 19 49 | 22 29 | 23 21 | 24 07 | 00 07 |
| 30 | 18 40 | 19 06 | 19 36 | 22 14 | 23 06 | 23 53 | 24 35 |
| 20 | 18 25 | 18 48 | 19 16 | 21 48 | 22 39 | 23 28 | 24 13 |
| N 10 | 18 12 | 18 34 | 19 00 | 21 25 | 22 16 | 23 06 | 23 53 |
| 0 | 18 00 | 18 22 | 18 47 | 21 04 | 21 55 | 22 46 | 23 35 |
| S 10 | 17 48 | 18 10 | 18 35 | 20 43 | 21 34 | 22 25 | 23 16 |
| 20 | 17 36 | 17 59 | 18 25 | 20 21 | 21 11 | 22 03 | 22 57 |
| 30 | 17 22 | 17 47 | 18 15 | 19 55 | 20 44 | 21 38 | 22 34 |
| 35 | 17 13 | 17 40 | 18 10 | 19 39 | 20 29 | 21 23 | 22 20 |
| 40 | 17 04 | 17 33 | 18 05 | 19 22 | 20 10 | 21 05 | 22 04 |
| 45 | 16 53 | 17 24 | 17 59 | 19 00 | 19 48 | 20 44 | 21 46 |
| S 50 | 16 40 | 17 15 | 17 54 | 18 33 | 19 20 | 20 17 | 21 22 |
| 52 | 16 34 | 17 11 | 17 51 | 18 20 | 19 06 | 20 04 | 21 11 |
| 54 | 16 28 | 17 06 | 17 48 | 18 05 | 18 50 | 19 49 | 20 58 |
| 56 | 16 20 | 17 01 | 17 44 | 17 47 | 18 32 | 19 31 | 20 43 |
| 58 | 16 12 | 16 55 | 17 42 | 17 25 | 18 08 | 19 10 | 20 25 |
| S 60 | 16 02 | 16 49 | 17 39 | 16 58 | 17 38 | 18 42 | 20 04 |

| Day | SUN Eqn. of Time 00h | SUN Eqn. of Time 12h | SUN Mer. Pass. | MOON Mer. Pass. Upper | MOON Mer. Pass. Lower | Age | Phase |
|---|---|---|---|---|---|---|---|
| d | m s | m s | h m | h m | h m | d % | |
| 4 | 03 09 | 03 12 | 11 57 | 14 52 | 02 27 | 04 12 | |
| 5 | 03 14 | 03 17 | 11 57 | 15 43 | 03 17 | 05 19 | |
| 6 | 03 19 | 03 22 | 11 57 | 16 33 | 04 08 | 06 27 | ◑ |

| UT | ARIES GHA | VENUS −4.1 GHA | Dec | MARS +0.8 GHA | Dec | JUPITER −2.1 GHA | Dec | SATURN +0.7 GHA | Dec |
|---|---|---|---|---|---|---|---|---|---|
| **SATURDAY** | | | | | | | | | |
| 7 00 | 224 49.1 | 219 39.6 | N 0 31.7 | 236 35.9 | S 6 46.7 | 225 06.4 | S 1 18.5 | 257 35.4 | S14 18.5 |
| 01 | 239 51.5 | 234 39.4 | 32.7 | 251 36.6 | 46.0 | 240 08.4 | 18.3 | 272 37.8 | 18.5 |
| 02 | 254 54.0 | 249 39.2 | 33.8 | 266 37.4 | 45.2 | 255 10.4 | 18.1 | 287 40.1 | 18.4 |
| 03 | 269 56.5 | 264 39.0 | .. 34.8 | 281 38.1 | .. 44.5 | 270 12.4 | .. 18.0 | 302 42.5 | .. 18.4 |
| 04 | 284 58.9 | 279 38.8 | 35.8 | 296 38.8 | 43.8 | 285 14.4 | 17.8 | 317 44.8 | 18.4 |
| 05 | 300 01.4 | 294 38.6 | 36.9 | 311 39.5 | 43.1 | 300 16.4 | 17.6 | 332 47.2 | 18.3 |
| 06 | 315 03.9 | 309 38.4 | N 0 37.9 | 326 40.2 | S 6 42.4 | 315 18.4 | S 1 17.4 | 347 49.5 | S14 18.3 |
| 07 | 330 06.3 | 324 38.2 | 39.0 | 341 40.9 | 41.7 | 330 20.4 | 17.2 | 2 51.9 | 18.3 |
| 08 | 345 08.8 | 339 38.0 | 40.0 | 356 41.6 | 41.0 | 345 22.4 | 17.0 | 17 54.2 | 18.3 |
| 09 | 0 11.3 | 354 37.8 | .. 41.1 | 11 42.3 | .. 40.2 | 0 24.4 | .. 16.8 | 32 56.6 | .. 18.2 |
| 10 | 15 13.7 | 9 37.6 | 42.1 | 26 43.0 | 39.5 | 15 26.4 | 16.6 | 47 58.9 | 18.2 |
| 11 | 30 16.2 | 24 37.4 | 43.2 | 41 43.7 | 38.8 | 30 28.4 | 16.4 | 63 01.3 | 18.2 |
| 12 | 45 18.6 | 39 37.2 | N 0 44.2 | 56 44.5 | S 6 38.1 | 45 30.4 | S 1 16.2 | 78 03.6 | S14 18.1 |
| 13 | 60 21.1 | 54 37.0 | 45.3 | 71 45.2 | 37.4 | 60 32.4 | 16.0 | 93 06.0 | 18.1 |
| 14 | 75 23.6 | 69 36.8 | 46.3 | 86 45.9 | 36.7 | 75 34.4 | 15.8 | 108 08.3 | 18.1 |
| 15 | 90 26.0 | 84 36.5 | .. 47.4 | 101 46.6 | .. 36.0 | 90 36.4 | .. 15.6 | 123 10.7 | .. 18.0 |
| 16 | 105 28.5 | 99 36.3 | 48.4 | 116 47.3 | 35.2 | 105 38.4 | 15.5 | 138 13.0 | 18.0 |
| 17 | 120 31.0 | 114 36.1 | 49.5 | 131 48.0 | 34.5 | 120 40.4 | 15.3 | 153 15.4 | 18.0 |
| 18 | 135 33.4 | 129 35.9 | N 0 50.5 | 146 48.7 | S 6 33.8 | 135 42.4 | S 1 15.1 | 168 17.7 | S14 17.9 |
| 19 | 150 35.9 | 144 35.7 | 51.6 | 161 49.4 | 33.1 | 150 44.4 | 14.9 | 183 20.1 | 17.9 |
| 20 | 165 38.4 | 159 35.5 | 52.6 | 176 50.1 | 32.4 | 165 46.4 | 14.7 | 198 22.4 | 17.9 |
| 21 | 180 40.8 | 174 35.3 | .. 53.7 | 191 50.9 | .. 31.7 | 180 48.4 | .. 14.5 | 213 24.8 | .. 17.8 |
| 22 | 195 43.3 | 189 35.1 | 54.7 | 206 51.6 | 30.9 | 195 50.5 | 14.3 | 228 27.1 | 17.8 |
| 23 | 210 45.7 | 204 34.9 | 55.8 | 221 52.3 | 30.2 | 210 52.5 | 14.1 | 243 29.5 | 17.8 |
| **SUNDAY** | | | | | | | | | |
| 8 00 | 225 48.2 | 219 34.7 | N 0 56.8 | 236 53.0 | S 6 29.5 | 225 54.5 | S 1 13.9 | 258 31.9 | S14 17.8 |
| 01 | 240 50.7 | 234 34.5 | 57.9 | 251 53.7 | 28.8 | 240 56.5 | 13.7 | 273 34.2 | 17.7 |
| 02 | 255 53.1 | 249 34.3 | 0 58.9 | 266 54.4 | 28.1 | 255 58.5 | 13.5 | 288 36.6 | 17.7 |
| 03 | 270 55.6 | 264 34.1 | 1 00.0 | 281 55.1 | .. 27.4 | 271 00.5 | .. 13.3 | 303 38.9 | .. 17.7 |
| 04 | 285 58.1 | 279 33.9 | 01.0 | 296 55.8 | 26.7 | 286 02.5 | 13.2 | 318 41.3 | 17.6 |
| 05 | 301 00.5 | 294 33.7 | 02.1 | 311 56.6 | 25.9 | 301 04.5 | 13.0 | 333 43.6 | 17.6 |
| 06 | 316 03.0 | 309 33.5 | N 1 03.1 | 326 57.3 | S 6 25.2 | 316 06.5 | S 1 12.8 | 348 46.0 | S14 17.6 |
| 07 | 331 05.5 | 324 33.3 | 04.2 | 341 58.0 | 24.5 | 331 08.5 | 12.6 | 3 48.3 | 17.5 |
| 08 | 346 07.9 | 339 33.1 | 05.2 | 356 58.7 | 23.8 | 346 10.5 | 12.4 | 18 50.7 | 17.5 |
| 09 | 1 10.4 | 354 32.9 | .. 06.3 | 11 59.4 | .. 23.1 | 1 12.5 | .. 12.2 | 33 53.0 | .. 17.5 |
| 10 | 16 12.9 | 9 32.6 | 07.3 | 27 00.1 | 22.4 | 16 14.5 | 12.0 | 48 55.4 | 17.5 |
| 11 | 31 15.3 | 24 32.4 | 08.4 | 42 00.8 | 21.6 | 31 16.5 | 11.8 | 63 57.7 | 17.4 |
| 12 | 46 17.8 | 39 32.2 | N 1 09.4 | 57 01.5 | S 6 20.9 | 46 18.5 | S 1 11.6 | 79 00.1 | S14 17.4 |
| 13 | 61 20.2 | 54 32.0 | 10.5 | 72 02.3 | 20.2 | 61 20.5 | 11.4 | 94 02.5 | 17.4 |
| 14 | 76 22.7 | 69 31.8 | 11.5 | 87 03.0 | 19.5 | 76 22.5 | 11.2 | 109 04.8 | 17.3 |
| 15 | 91 25.2 | 84 31.6 | .. 12.6 | 102 03.7 | .. 18.8 | 91 24.5 | .. 11.1 | 124 07.2 | .. 17.3 |
| 16 | 106 27.6 | 99 31.4 | 13.7 | 117 04.4 | 18.1 | 106 26.6 | 10.9 | 139 09.5 | 17.3 |
| 17 | 121 30.1 | 114 31.2 | 14.7 | 132 05.1 | 17.3 | 121 28.6 | 10.7 | 154 11.9 | 17.2 |
| 18 | 136 32.6 | 129 31.0 | N 1 15.8 | 147 05.8 | S 6 16.6 | 136 30.6 | S 1 10.5 | 169 14.2 | S14 17.2 |
| 19 | 151 35.0 | 144 30.8 | 16.8 | 162 06.5 | 15.9 | 151 32.6 | 10.3 | 184 16.6 | 17.2 |
| 20 | 166 37.5 | 159 30.6 | 17.9 | 177 07.3 | 15.2 | 166 34.6 | 10.1 | 199 18.9 | 17.2 |
| 21 | 181 40.0 | 174 30.4 | .. 18.9 | 192 08.0 | .. 14.5 | 181 36.6 | .. 09.9 | 214 21.3 | .. 17.1 |
| 22 | 196 42.4 | 189 30.2 | 20.0 | 207 08.7 | 13.8 | 196 38.6 | 09.7 | 229 23.7 | 17.1 |
| 23 | 211 44.9 | 204 30.0 | 21.0 | 222 09.4 | 13.0 | 211 40.6 | 09.5 | 244 26.0 | 17.1 |
| **MONDAY** | | | | | | | | | |
| 9 00 | 226 47.4 | 219 29.7 | N 1 22.1 | 237 10.1 | S 6 12.3 | 226 42.6 | S 1 09.3 | 259 28.4 | S14 17.0 |
| 01 | 241 49.8 | 234 29.5 | 23.1 | 252 10.8 | 11.6 | 241 44.6 | 09.2 | 274 30.7 | 17.0 |
| 02 | 256 52.3 | 249 29.3 | 24.2 | 267 11.5 | 10.9 | 256 46.6 | 09.0 | 289 33.1 | 17.0 |
| 03 | 271 54.7 | 264 29.1 | .. 25.2 | 282 12.3 | .. 10.2 | 271 48.6 | .. 08.8 | 304 35.4 | .. 17.0 |
| 04 | 286 57.2 | 279 28.9 | 26.3 | 297 13.0 | 09.5 | 286 50.6 | 08.7 | 319 37.8 | 16.9 |
| 05 | 301 59.7 | 294 28.7 | 27.3 | 312 13.7 | 08.7 | 301 52.7 | 08.4 | 334 40.2 | 16.9 |
| 06 | 317 02.1 | 309 28.5 | N 1 28.4 | 327 14.4 | S 6 08.0 | 316 54.7 | S 1 08.2 | 349 42.5 | S14 16.9 |
| 07 | 332 04.6 | 324 28.3 | 29.4 | 342 15.1 | 07.3 | 331 56.7 | 08.0 | 4 44.9 | 16.8 |
| 08 | 347 07.1 | 339 28.1 | 30.5 | 357 15.8 | 06.6 | 346 58.7 | 07.8 | 19 47.2 | 16.8 |
| 09 | 2 09.5 | 354 27.9 | .. 31.6 | 12 16.6 | .. 05.9 | 2 00.7 | .. 07.6 | 34 49.6 | .. 16.8 |
| 10 | 17 12.0 | 9 27.7 | 32.6 | 27 17.3 | 05.1 | 17 02.7 | 07.4 | 49 51.9 | 16.8 |
| 11 | 32 14.5 | 24 27.5 | 33.7 | 42 18.0 | 04.4 | 32 04.7 | 07.3 | 64 54.3 | 16.7 |
| 12 | 47 16.9 | 39 27.2 | N 1 34.7 | 57 18.7 | S 6 03.7 | 47 06.7 | S 1 07.1 | 79 56.7 | S14 16.7 |
| 13 | 62 19.4 | 54 27.0 | 35.8 | 72 19.4 | 03.0 | 62 08.7 | 06.9 | 94 59.0 | 16.7 |
| 14 | 77 21.8 | 69 26.8 | 36.8 | 87 20.1 | 02.3 | 77 10.7 | 06.7 | 110 01.4 | 16.6 |
| 15 | 92 24.3 | 84 26.6 | .. 37.9 | 102 20.9 | .. 01.6 | 92 12.7 | .. 06.5 | 125 03.7 | .. 16.6 |
| 16 | 107 26.8 | 99 26.4 | 38.9 | 117 21.6 | 00.8 | 107 14.8 | 06.3 | 140 06.1 | 16.6 |
| 17 | 122 29.2 | 114 26.2 | 40.0 | 132 22.3 | 6 00.1 | 122 16.8 | 06.1 | 155 08.5 | 16.6 |
| 18 | 137 31.7 | 129 26.0 | N 1 41.0 | 147 23.0 | S 5 59.4 | 137 18.8 | S 1 05.9 | 170 10.8 | S14 16.5 |
| 19 | 152 34.2 | 144 25.8 | 42.1 | 162 23.7 | 58.7 | 152 20.8 | 05.7 | 185 13.2 | 16.5 |
| 20 | 167 36.6 | 159 25.6 | 43.2 | 177 24.4 | 58.0 | 167 22.8 | 05.6 | 200 15.5 | 16.5 |
| 21 | 182 39.1 | 174 25.4 | .. 44.2 | 192 25.2 | .. 57.2 | 182 24.8 | .. 05.4 | 215 17.9 | .. 16.4 |
| 22 | 197 41.6 | 189 25.1 | 45.3 | 207 25.9 | 56.5 | 197 26.8 | 05.2 | 230 20.3 | 16.4 |
| 23 | 212 44.0 | 204 24.9 | 46.3 | 222 26.6 | 55.8 | 212 28.8 | 05.0 | 245 22.6 | 16.4 |
| Mer. Pass. 8 55.3 | | v −0.2 d 1.1 | | v 0.7 d 0.7 | | v 2.0 d 0.2 | | v 2.4 d 0.0 | |

### STARS

| Name | SHA | Dec |
|---|---|---|
| Acamar | 315 13.9 | S40 13.0 |
| Achernar | 335 22.4 | S57 07.4 |
| Acrux | 173 02.0 | S63 13.5 |
| Adhara | 255 07.8 | S29 00.3 |
| Aldebaran | 290 42.5 | N16 33.1 |
| Alioth | 166 14.5 | N55 50.5 |
| Alkaid | 152 53.3 | N49 12.2 |
| Alnair | 27 35.8 | S46 51.1 |
| Alnilam | 275 40.3 | S 1 11.4 |
| Alphard | 217 49.9 | S 8 45.4 |
| Alphecca | 126 05.3 | N26 38.3 |
| Alpheratz | 357 37.3 | N29 12.5 |
| Altair | 62 02.0 | N 8 55.5 |
| Ankaa | 353 09.7 | S42 11.1 |
| Antares | 112 18.2 | S26 28.9 |
| Arcturus | 145 49.6 | N19 04.0 |
| Atria | 107 13.9 | S69 03.9 |
| Avior | 234 15.8 | S59 35.1 |
| Bellatrix | 278 25.5 | N 6 22.1 |
| Betelgeuse | 270 54.7 | N 7 24.6 |
| Canopus | 263 53.8 | S52 42.7 |
| Capella | 280 25.6 | N46 01.2 |
| Deneb | 49 27.2 | N45 21.2 |
| Denebola | 182 27.0 | N14 26.9 |
| Diphda | 348 49.8 | S17 52.0 |
| Dubhe | 193 43.5 | N61 38.1 |
| Elnath | 278 05.0 | N28 37.5 |
| Eltanin | 90 42.8 | N51 28.9 |
| Enif | 33 41.0 | N 9 58.4 |
| Fomalhaut | 15 17.1 | S29 30.3 |
| Gacrux | 171 53.6 | S57 14.4 |
| Gienah | 175 45.6 | S17 40.0 |
| Hadar | 148 38.5 | S60 28.9 |
| Hamal | 327 54.0 | N23 33.9 |
| Kaus Aust. | 83 35.2 | S34 22.4 |
| Kochab | 137 18.6 | N74 03.9 |
| Markab | 13 32.3 | N15 19.3 |
| Menkar | 314 08.8 | N 4 10.5 |
| Menkent | 147 59.8 | S36 28.8 |
| Miaplacidus | 221 38.7 | S69 48.8 |
| Mirfak | 308 31.9 | N49 56.3 |
| Nunki | 75 50.3 | S26 16.1 |
| Peacock | 53 09.1 | S56 39.6 |
| Pollux | 243 20.2 | N27 58.4 |
| Procyon | 244 53.3 | N 5 10.0 |
| Rasalhague | 96 00.3 | N12 32.5 |
| Regulus | 207 36.7 | N11 51.5 |
| Rigel | 281 06.3 | S 8 10.7 |
| Rigil Kent. | 139 42.7 | S60 55.6 |
| Sabik | 102 05.0 | S15 45.2 |
| Schedar | 349 34.0 | N56 39.3 |
| Shaula | 96 13.0 | S37 07.1 |
| Sirius | 258 28.4 | S16 44.9 |
| Spica | 158 24.4 | S11 16.7 |
| Suhail | 222 48.0 | S43 31.6 |
| Vega | 80 34.4 | N38 48.0 |
| Zuben'ubi | 136 58.1 | S16 08.1 |

| | SHA | Mer. Pass. |
|---|---|---|
| Venus | 353 46.5 | 9 22 |
| Mars | 11 04.8 | 8 12 |
| Jupiter | 0 06.2 | 8 55 |
| Saturn | 32 43.6 | 6 45 |

| UT | SUN GHA | SUN Dec | MOON GHA | v | MOON Dec | d | HP |
|---|---|---|---|---|---|---|---|
| d h | ° ′ | ° ′ | ° ′ | ′ | ° ′ | ′ | ′ |
| 7 00 | 180 50.9 | N16 45.1 | 107 53.8 | 10.8 | N25 52.0 | 4.1 | 54.3 |
| 01 | 195 51.0 | 45.8 | 122 23.6 | 10.9 | 25 47.9 | 4.3 | 54.3 |
| 02 | 210 51.0 | 46.5 | 136 53.5 | 10.9 | 25 43.6 | 4.4 | 54.3 |
| 03 | 225 51.0 .. | 47.1 | 151 23.4 | 10.9 | 25 39.2 | 4.5 | 54.3 |
| 04 | 240 51.1 | 47.8 | 165 53.3 | 11.0 | 25 34.7 | 4.6 | 54.3 |
| 05 | 255 51.1 | 48.5 | 180 23.3 | 10.9 | 25 30.1 | 4.8 | 54.3 |
| 06 | 270 51.2 | N16 49.2 | 194 53.2 | 11.1 | N25 25.3 | 4.8 | 54.3 |
| 07 | 285 51.2 | 49.9 | 209 23.3 | 11.0 | 25 20.5 | 5.0 | 54.3 |
| 08 | 300 51.2 | 50.6 | 223 53.3 | 11.1 | 25 15.5 | 5.1 | 54.3 |
| 09 | 315 51.3 .. | 51.3 | 238 23.4 | 11.1 | 25 10.4 | 5.2 | 54.4 |
| 10 | 330 51.3 | 52.0 | 252 53.5 | 11.2 | 25 05.2 | 5.4 | 54.4 |
| 11 | 345 51.4 | 52.7 | 267 23.7 | 11.1 | 24 59.8 | 5.4 | 54.4 |
| 12 | 0 51.4 | N16 53.4 | 281 53.8 | 11.3 | N24 54.4 | 5.6 | 54.4 |
| 13 | 15 51.4 | 54.0 | 296 24.1 | 11.2 | 24 48.8 | 5.7 | 54.4 |
| 14 | 30 51.5 | 54.7 | 310 54.3 | 11.3 | 24 43.1 | 5.8 | 54.4 |
| 15 | 45 51.5 .. | 55.4 | 325 24.6 | 11.3 | 24 37.3 | 6.0 | 54.4 |
| 16 | 60 51.6 | 56.1 | 339 54.9 | 11.4 | 24 31.3 | 6.0 | 54.5 |
| 17 | 75 51.6 | 56.8 | 354 25.3 | 11.4 | 24 25.3 | 6.2 | 54.5 |
| 18 | 90 51.6 | N16 57.5 | 8 55.7 | 11.4 | N24 19.1 | 6.2 | 54.5 |
| 19 | 105 51.7 | 58.2 | 23 26.1 | 11.5 | 24 12.9 | 6.4 | 54.5 |
| 20 | 120 51.7 | 58.8 | 37 56.6 | 11.5 | 24 06.5 | 6.5 | 54.5 |
| 21 | 135 51.7 | 16 59.5 | 52 27.1 | 11.5 | 24 00.0 | 6.7 | 54.5 |
| 22 | 150 51.8 | 17 00.2 | 66 57.6 | 11.6 | 23 53.3 | 6.7 | 54.5 |
| 23 | 165 51.8 | 00.9 | 81 28.2 | 11.6 | 23 46.6 | 6.8 | 54.6 |
| 8 00 | 180 51.9 | N17 01.6 | 95 58.8 | 11.7 | N23 39.8 | 7.0 | 54.6 |
| 01 | 195 51.9 | 02.2 | 110 29.5 | 11.7 | 23 32.8 | 7.1 | 54.6 |
| 02 | 210 51.9 | 02.9 | 125 00.2 | 11.7 | 23 25.7 | 7.2 | 54.6 |
| 03 | 225 52.0 .. | 03.6 | 139 30.9 | 11.8 | 23 18.5 | 7.2 | 54.6 |
| 04 | 240 52.0 | 04.3 | 154 01.7 | 11.8 | 23 11.3 | 7.4 | 54.6 |
| 05 | 255 52.0 | 05.0 | 168 32.5 | 11.8 | 23 03.9 | 7.6 | 54.7 |
| 06 | 270 52.1 | N17 05.6 | 183 03.3 | 11.9 | N22 56.3 | 7.6 | 54.7 |
| 07 | 285 52.1 | 06.3 | 197 34.2 | 11.9 | 22 48.7 | 7.7 | 54.7 |
| 08 | 300 52.1 | 07.0 | 212 05.1 | 12.0 | 22 41.0 | 7.8 | 54.7 |
| 09 | 315 52.2 .. | 07.7 | 226 36.1 | 12.0 | 22 33.2 | 8.0 | 54.7 |
| 10 | 330 52.2 | 08.4 | 241 07.1 | 12.1 | 22 25.2 | 8.0 | 54.8 |
| 11 | 345 52.2 | 09.0 | 255 38.2 | 12.0 | 22 17.2 | 8.2 | 54.8 |
| 12 | 0 52.3 | N17 09.7 | 270 09.2 | 12.2 | N22 09.0 | 8.3 | 54.8 |
| 13 | 15 52.3 | 10.4 | 284 40.4 | 12.1 | 22 00.7 | 8.3 | 54.8 |
| 14 | 30 52.3 | 11.1 | 299 11.5 | 12.2 | 21 52.4 | 8.5 | 54.8 |
| 15 | 45 52.4 .. | 11.7 | 313 42.7 | 12.2 | 21 43.9 | 8.6 | 54.9 |
| 16 | 60 52.4 | 12.4 | 328 13.9 | 12.3 | 21 35.3 | 8.7 | 54.9 |
| 17 | 75 52.4 | 13.1 | 342 45.2 | 12.3 | 21 26.6 | 8.7 | 54.9 |
| 18 | 90 52.5 | N17 13.7 | 357 16.5 | 12.4 | N21 17.9 | 8.9 | 54.9 |
| 19 | 105 52.5 | 14.4 | 11 47.9 | 12.4 | 21 09.0 | 9.0 | 54.9 |
| 20 | 120 52.5 | 15.1 | 26 19.3 | 12.4 | 21 00.0 | 9.1 | 55.0 |
| 21 | 135 52.6 .. | 15.8 | 40 50.7 | 12.5 | 20 50.9 | 9.2 | 55.0 |
| 22 | 150 52.6 | 16.4 | 55 22.2 | 12.5 | 20 41.7 | 9.3 | 55.0 |
| 23 | 165 52.6 | 17.1 | 69 53.7 | 12.5 | 20 32.4 | 9.4 | 55.0 |
| 9 00 | 180 52.6 | N17 17.8 | 84 25.2 | 12.6 | N20 23.0 | 9.5 | 55.0 |
| 01 | 195 52.7 | 18.4 | 98 56.8 | 12.6 | 20 13.5 | 9.5 | 55.1 |
| 02 | 210 52.7 | 19.1 | 113 28.4 | 12.7 | 20 04.0 | 9.7 | 55.1 |
| 03 | 225 52.7 .. | 19.8 | 128 00.1 | 12.7 | 19 54.3 | 9.8 | 55.1 |
| 04 | 240 52.8 | 20.4 | 142 31.8 | 12.7 | 19 44.5 | 9.9 | 55.1 |
| 05 | 255 52.8 | 21.1 | 157 03.5 | 12.7 | 19 34.6 | 9.9 | 55.2 |
| 06 | 270 52.8 | N17 21.8 | 171 35.2 | 12.8 | N19 24.7 | 10.1 | 55.2 |
| 07 | 285 52.9 | 22.4 | 186 07.0 | 12.9 | 19 14.6 | 10.2 | 55.2 |
| 08 | 300 52.9 | 23.1 | 200 38.9 | 12.8 | 19 04.4 | 10.2 | 55.2 |
| 09 | 315 52.9 .. | 23.8 | 215 10.7 | 12.9 | 18 54.2 | 10.4 | 55.3 |
| 10 | 330 52.9 | 24.4 | 229 42.6 | 13.0 | 18 43.8 | 10.4 | 55.3 |
| 11 | 345 53.0 | 25.1 | 244 14.6 | 12.9 | 18 33.4 | 10.5 | 55.3 |
| 12 | 0 53.0 | N17 25.8 | 258 46.5 | 13.0 | N18 22.9 | 10.7 | 55.3 |
| 13 | 15 53.0 | 26.4 | 273 18.5 | 13.0 | 18 12.2 | 10.7 | 55.4 |
| 14 | 30 53.0 | 27.1 | 287 50.5 | 13.1 | 18 01.5 | 10.8 | 55.4 |
| 15 | 45 53.1 .. | 27.8 | 302 22.6 | 13.1 | 17 50.7 | 10.9 | 55.4 |
| 16 | 60 53.1 | 28.4 | 316 54.7 | 13.1 | 17 39.8 | 10.9 | 55.5 |
| 17 | 75 53.1 | 29.1 | 331 26.8 | 13.2 | 17 28.9 | 11.1 | 55.5 |
| 18 | 90 53.2 | N17 29.7 | 345 59.0 | 13.2 | N17 17.8 | 11.2 | 55.5 |
| 19 | 105 53.2 | 30.4 | 0 31.2 | 13.2 | 17 06.6 | 11.2 | 55.5 |
| 20 | 120 53.2 | 31.1 | 15 03.4 | 13.2 | 16 55.4 | 11.3 | 55.6 |
| 21 | 135 53.2 .. | 31.7 | 29 35.6 | 13.3 | 16 44.1 | 11.4 | 55.6 |
| 22 | 150 53.3 | 32.4 | 44 07.9 | 13.3 | 16 32.7 | 11.5 | 55.6 |
| 23 | 165 53.3 | 33.0 | 58 40.2 | 13.3 | N16 21.2 | 11.6 | 55.7 |
| | SD 15.9 | d 0.7 | SD 14.8 | | 14.9 | | 15.1 |

Days labelled in left margin: SATURDAY (7), SUNDAY (8), MONDAY (9)

| Lat. | Twilight Naut. | Twilight Civil | Sunrise | Moonrise 7 | Moonrise 8 | Moonrise 9 | Moonrise 10 |
|---|---|---|---|---|---|---|---|
| ° | h m | h m | h m | h m | h m | h m | h m |
| N 72 | //// | //// | 00 26 | □ | □ | □ | 10 05 |
| N 70 | //// | //// | 01 47 | □ | □ | 07 53 | 10 35 |
| 68 | //// | //// | 02 24 | □ | □ | 08 49 | 10 57 |
| 66 | //// | 01 04 | 02 50 | □ | 07 10 | 09 22 | 11 14 |
| 64 | //// | 01 51 | 03 10 | 05 56 | 07 57 | 09 45 | 11 28 |
| 62 | //// | 02 20 | 03 26 | 06 52 | 08 28 | 10 04 | 11 40 |
| 60 | 00 57 | 02 42 | 03 40 | 07 25 | 08 50 | 10 20 | 11 49 |
| N 58 | 01 39 | 03 00 | 03 51 | 07 49 | 09 09 | 10 33 | 11 58 |
| 56 | 02 06 | 03 14 | 04 01 | 08 08 | 09 24 | 10 44 | 12 05 |
| 54 | 02 27 | 03 27 | 04 10 | 08 25 | 09 37 | 10 53 | 12 12 |
| 52 | 02 44 | 03 37 | 04 18 | 08 38 | 09 48 | 11 02 | 12 18 |
| 50 | 02 58 | 03 47 | 04 25 | 08 51 | 09 58 | 11 10 | 12 23 |
| 45 | 03 25 | 04 07 | 04 40 | 09 16 | 10 20 | 11 26 | 12 35 |
| N 40 | 03 45 | 04 22 | 04 52 | 09 36 | 10 37 | 11 40 | 12 44 |
| 35 | 04 02 | 04 35 | 05 02 | 09 52 | 10 51 | 11 51 | 12 52 |
| 30 | 04 15 | 04 46 | 05 12 | 10 06 | 11 03 | 12 01 | 13 00 |
| 20 | 04 36 | 05 04 | 05 27 | 10 31 | 11 24 | 12 18 | 13 12 |
| N 10 | 04 53 | 05 18 | 05 41 | 10 52 | 11 43 | 12 33 | 13 23 |
| 0 | 05 06 | 05 31 | 05 53 | 11 11 | 12 00 | 12 47 | 13 32 |
| S 10 | 05 18 | 05 44 | 06 05 | 11 31 | 12 17 | 13 01 | 13 42 |
| 20 | 05 29 | 05 56 | 06 19 | 11 52 | 12 35 | 13 15 | 13 53 |
| 30 | 05 40 | 06 08 | 06 33 | 12 16 | 12 56 | 13 32 | 14 05 |
| 35 | 05 45 | 06 15 | 06 42 | 12 30 | 13 08 | 13 41 | 14 12 |
| 40 | 05 51 | 06 23 | 06 52 | 12 46 | 13 22 | 13 52 | 14 20 |
| 45 | 05 57 | 06 32 | 07 03 | 13 05 | 13 38 | 14 05 | 14 29 |
| S 50 | 06 03 | 06 42 | 07 17 | 13 30 | 13 58 | 14 21 | 14 40 |
| 52 | 06 06 | 06 46 | 07 23 | 13 41 | 14 08 | 14 28 | 14 45 |
| 54 | 06 09 | 06 51 | 07 30 | 13 54 | 14 19 | 14 36 | 14 50 |
| 56 | 06 12 | 06 57 | 07 38 | 14 10 | 14 31 | 14 45 | 14 56 |
| 58 | 06 15 | 07 03 | 07 47 | 14 28 | 14 45 | 14 55 | 15 03 |
| S 60 | 06 19 | 07 10 | 07 57 | 14 50 | 15 01 | 15 07 | 15 11 |

| Lat. | Sunset | Twilight Civil | Twilight Naut. | Moonset 7 | Moonset 8 | Moonset 9 | Moonset 10 |
|---|---|---|---|---|---|---|---|
| ° | h m | h m | h m | h m | h m | h m | h m |
| N 72 | □ | □ | □ | □ | □ | □ | 05 00 |
| N 70 | 22 13 | //// | //// | □ | □ | 05 33 | 04 28 |
| 68 | 21 33 | //// | //// | □ | □ | 04 37 | 04 04 |
| 66 | 21 06 | 22 58 | //// | □ | 04 35 | 04 03 | 03 46 |
| 64 | 20 45 | 22 07 | //// | 04 07 | 03 48 | 03 38 | 03 31 |
| 62 | 20 29 | 21 36 | //// | 03 11 | 03 17 | 03 18 | 03 18 |
| 60 | 20 15 | 21 13 | 23 05 | 02 30 | 02 54 | 03 02 | 03 07 |
| N 58 | 20 03 | 20 55 | 22 18 | 02 13 | 02 35 | 02 49 | 02 58 |
| 56 | 19 53 | 20 41 | 21 49 | 01 54 | 02 19 | 02 37 | 02 49 |
| 54 | 19 44 | 20 28 | 21 28 | 01 37 | 02 06 | 02 26 | 02 42 |
| 52 | 19 36 | 20 17 | 21 11 | 01 23 | 01 54 | 02 17 | 02 35 |
| 50 | 19 29 | 20 07 | 20 57 | 01 11 | 01 43 | 02 09 | 02 29 |
| 45 | 19 14 | 19 47 | 20 29 | 00 45 | 01 21 | 01 51 | 02 16 |
| N 40 | 19 02 | 19 32 | 20 09 | 00 25 | 01 03 | 01 36 | 02 05 |
| 35 | 18 51 | 19 19 | 19 52 | 00 07 | 00 48 | 01 24 | 01 56 |
| 30 | 18 42 | 19 08 | 19 39 | 24 35 | 00 35 | 01 13 | 01 48 |
| 20 | 18 26 | 18 50 | 19 17 | 24 13 | 00 13 | 00 54 | 01 33 |
| N 10 | 18 13 | 18 35 | 19 01 | 23 53 | 24 38 | 00 38 | 01 21 |
| 0 | 18 00 | 18 22 | 18 47 | 23 35 | 24 23 | 00 23 | 01 09 |
| S 10 | 17 48 | 18 09 | 18 35 | 23 16 | 24 07 | 00 07 | 00 57 |
| 20 | 17 34 | 17 57 | 18 24 | 22 57 | 23 50 | 24 44 | 00 44 |
| 30 | 17 19 | 17 44 | 18 13 | 22 34 | 23 31 | 24 29 | 00 29 |
| 35 | 17 11 | 17 37 | 18 08 | 22 20 | 23 20 | 24 21 | 00 21 |
| 40 | 17 01 | 17 30 | 18 02 | 22 04 | 23 07 | 24 11 | 00 11 |
| 45 | 16 49 | 17 21 | 17 56 | 21 46 | 22 51 | 23 59 | 25 08 |
| S 50 | 16 36 | 17 11 | 17 49 | 21 22 | 22 32 | 23 45 | 24 59 |
| 52 | 16 29 | 17 06 | 17 47 | 21 11 | 22 23 | 23 38 | 24 55 |
| 54 | 16 22 | 17 01 | 17 44 | 20 58 | 22 13 | 23 31 | 24 50 |
| 56 | 16 14 | 16 55 | 17 40 | 20 43 | 22 01 | 23 22 | 24 45 |
| 58 | 16 05 | 16 49 | 17 37 | 20 25 | 21 48 | 23 13 | 24 39 |
| S 60 | 15 55 | 16 42 | 17 33 | 20 04 | 21 32 | 23 02 | 24 32 |

| Day | SUN Eqn. of Time 00h | SUN Eqn. of Time 12h | SUN Mer. Pass. | MOON Mer. Pass. Upper | MOON Mer. Pass. Lower | Age | Phase |
|---|---|---|---|---|---|---|---|
| d | m s | m s | h m | h m | h m | d | % |
| 7 | 03 24 | 03 26 | 11 57 | 17 23 | 04 58 | 07 | 36 |
| 8 | 03 27 | 03 29 | 11 57 | 18 11 | 05 47 | 08 | 45 |
| 9 | 03 31 | 03 32 | 11 56 | 18 58 | 06 35 | 09 | 55 |

| UT | ARIES | VENUS −4.0 | | MARS +0.8 | | JUPITER −2.1 | | SATURN +0.7 | | STARS | | |
|---|---|---|---|---|---|---|---|---|---|---|---|---|
| | GHA | GHA | Dec | GHA | Dec | GHA | Dec | GHA | Dec | Name | SHA | Dec |
| d h | ° ′ | ° ′ | ° ′ | ° ′ | ° ′ | ° ′ | ° ′ | ° ′ | ° ′ | | ° ′ | ° ′ |
| 10 00 | 227 46.5 | 219 24.7 | N 1 47.4 | 237 27.3 | S 5 55.1 | 227 30.8 | S 1 04.8 | 260 25.0 | S14 16.4 | Acamar | 315 13.9 | S40 13.0 |
| 01 | 242 49.0 | 234 24.5 | 48.4 | 252 28.0 | 54.4 | 242 32.9 | 04.6 | 275 27.3 | 16.3 | Achernar | 335 22.4 | S57 07.4 |
| 02 | 257 51.4 | 249 24.3 | 49.5 | 267 28.7 | 53.7 | 257 34.9 | 04.4 | 290 29.7 | 16.3 | Acrux | 173 02.0 | S63 13.5 |
| 03 | 272 53.9 | 264 24.1 .. | 50.5 | 282 29.5 .. | 52.9 | 272 36.9 .. | 04.2 | 305 32.1 .. | 16.3 | Adhara | 255 07.8 | S29 00.3 |
| 04 | 287 56.3 | 279 23.9 | 51.6 | 297 30.2 | 52.2 | 287 38.9 | 04.0 | 320 34.4 | 16.2 | Aldebaran | 290 42.5 | N16 33.1 |
| 05 | 302 58.8 | 294 23.7 | 52.7 | 312 30.9 | 51.5 | 302 40.9 | 03.9 | 335 36.8 | 16.2 | | | |
| 06 | 318 01.3 | 309 23.5 | N 1 53.7 | 327 31.6 | S 5 50.8 | 317 42.9 | S 1 03.7 | 350 39.1 | S14 16.2 | Alioth | 166 14.5 | N55 50.5 |
| 07 | 333 03.7 | 324 23.2 | 54.8 | 342 32.3 | 50.1 | 332 44.9 | 03.5 | 5 41.5 | 16.2 | Alkaid | 152 53.3 | N49 12.2 |
| 08 | 348 06.2 | 339 23.0 | 55.8 | 357 33.0 | 49.3 | 347 46.9 | 03.3 | 20 43.9 | 16.1 | Alnair | 27 35.8 | S46 51.1 |
| 09 | 3 08.7 | 354 22.8 .. | 56.9 | 12 33.8 .. | 48.6 | 2 48.9 .. | 03.1 | 35 46.2 .. | 16.1 | Alnilam | 275 40.3 | S 1 11.4 |
| 10 | 18 11.1 | 9 22.6 | 57.9 | 27 34.5 | 47.9 | 17 51.0 | 02.9 | 50 48.6 | 16.1 | Alphard | 217 49.9 | S 8 45.4 |
| 11 | 33 13.6 | 24 22.4 | 1 59.0 | 42 35.2 | 47.2 | 32 53.0 | 02.7 | 65 51.0 | 16.1 | | | |
| 12 | 48 16.1 | 39 22.2 | N 2 00.0 | 57 35.9 | S 5 46.5 | 47 55.0 | S 1 02.5 | 80 53.3 | S14 16.0 | Alphecca | 126 05.3 | N26 38.3 |
| 13 | 63 18.5 | 54 22.0 | 01.1 | 72 36.6 | 45.7 | 62 57.0 | 02.4 | 95 55.7 | 16.0 | Alpheratz | 357 37.3 | N29 12.5 |
| 14 | 78 21.0 | 69 21.8 | 02.2 | 87 37.4 | 45.0 | 77 59.0 | 02.2 | 110 58.0 | 16.0 | Altair | 62 02.0 | N 8 55.5 |
| 15 | 93 23.5 | 84 21.5 .. | 03.2 | 102 38.1 .. | 44.3 | 93 01.0 .. | 02.0 | 126 00.4 .. | 15.9 | Ankaa | 353 09.7 | S42 11.1 |
| 16 | 108 25.9 | 99 21.3 | 04.3 | 117 38.8 | 43.6 | 108 03.0 | 01.8 | 141 02.8 | 15.9 | Antares | 112 18.2 | S26 28.9 |
| 17 | 123 28.4 | 114 21.1 | 05.3 | 132 39.5 | 42.9 | 123 05.1 | 01.6 | 156 05.1 | 15.9 | | | |
| 18 | 138 30.8 | 129 20.9 | N 2 06.4 | 147 40.2 | S 5 42.1 | 138 07.1 | S 1 01.4 | 171 07.5 | S14 15.9 | Arcturus | 145 49.6 | N19 04.0 |
| 19 | 153 33.3 | 144 20.7 | 07.4 | 162 41.0 | 41.4 | 153 09.1 | 01.2 | 186 09.9 | 15.8 | Atria | 107 13.9 | S69 03.9 |
| 20 | 168 35.8 | 159 20.5 | 08.5 | 177 41.7 | 40.7 | 168 11.1 | 01.0 | 201 12.2 | 15.8 | Avior | 234 15.8 | S59 35.1 |
| 21 | 183 38.2 | 174 20.3 .. | 09.6 | 192 42.4 .. | 40.0 | 183 13.1 .. | 00.9 | 216 14.6 .. | 15.8 | Bellatrix | 278 25.6 | N 6 22.1 |
| 22 | 198 40.7 | 189 20.0 | 10.6 | 207 43.1 | 39.3 | 198 15.1 | 00.7 | 231 16.9 | 15.8 | Betelgeuse | 270 54.8 | N 7 24.6 |
| 23 | 213 43.2 | 204 19.8 | 11.7 | 222 43.8 | 38.5 | 213 17.1 | 00.5 | 246 19.3 | 15.7 | | | |
| 11 00 | 228 45.6 | 219 19.6 | N 2 12.7 | 237 44.6 | S 5 37.8 | 228 19.2 | S 1 00.3 | 261 21.7 | S14 15.7 | Canopus | 263 53.8 | S52 42.6 |
| 01 | 243 48.1 | 234 19.4 | 13.8 | 252 45.3 | 37.1 | 243 21.2 | 1 00.1 | 276 24.0 | 15.7 | Capella | 280 25.6 | N46 01.2 |
| 02 | 258 50.6 | 249 19.2 | 14.8 | 267 46.0 | 36.4 | 258 23.2 | 0 59.9 | 291 26.4 | 15.7 | Deneb | 49 27.2 | N45 21.2 |
| 03 | 273 53.0 | 264 19.0 .. | 15.9 | 282 46.7 .. | 35.7 | 273 25.2 .. | 59.7 | 306 28.8 .. | 15.6 | Denebola | 182 27.0 | N14 26.9 |
| 04 | 288 55.5 | 279 18.8 | 17.0 | 297 47.4 | 34.9 | 288 27.2 | 59.6 | 321 31.1 | 15.6 | Diphda | 348 49.8 | S17 51.9 |
| 05 | 303 57.9 | 294 18.5 | 18.0 | 312 48.2 | 34.2 | 303 29.2 | 59.4 | 336 33.5 | 15.6 | | | |
| 06 | 319 00.4 | 309 18.3 | N 2 19.1 | 327 48.9 | S 5 33.5 | 318 31.2 | S 0 59.2 | 351 35.9 | S14 15.5 | Dubhe | 193 43.5 | N61 38.1 |
| 07 | 334 02.9 | 324 18.1 | 20.1 | 342 49.6 | 32.8 | 333 33.3 | 59.0 | 6 38.2 | 15.5 | Elnath | 278 05.0 | N28 37.5 |
| 08 | 349 05.3 | 339 17.9 | 21.2 | 357 50.3 | 32.1 | 348 35.3 | 58.8 | 21 40.6 | 15.5 | Eltanin | 90 42.8 | N51 28.9 |
| 09 | 4 07.8 | 354 17.7 .. | 22.2 | 12 51.0 .. | 31.3 | 3 37.3 .. | 58.6 | 36 43.0 .. | 15.5 | Enif | 33 41.0 | N 9 58.4 |
| 10 | 19 10.3 | 9 17.5 | 23.3 | 27 51.8 | 30.6 | 18 39.3 | 58.4 | 51 45.3 | 15.4 | Fomalhaut | 15 17.1 | S29 30.2 |
| 11 | 34 12.7 | 24 17.3 | 24.4 | 42 52.5 | 29.9 | 33 41.3 | 58.2 | 66 47.7 | 15.4 | | | |
| 12 | 49 15.2 | 39 17.0 | N 2 25.4 | 57 53.2 | S 5 29.2 | 48 43.3 | S 0 58.1 | 81 50.1 | S14 15.4 | Gacrux | 171 53.7 | S57 14.4 |
| 13 | 64 17.7 | 54 16.8 | 26.5 | 72 53.9 | 28.5 | 63 45.3 | 57.9 | 96 52.4 | 15.4 | Gienah | 175 45.6 | S17 40.0 |
| 14 | 79 20.1 | 69 16.6 | 27.5 | 87 54.6 | 27.7 | 78 47.4 | 57.7 | 111 54.8 | 15.3 | Hadar | 148 38.5 | S60 28.9 |
| 15 | 94 22.6 | 84 16.4 .. | 28.6 | 102 55.4 .. | 27.0 | 93 49.4 .. | 57.5 | 126 57.2 .. | 15.3 | Hamal | 327 54.0 | N23 33.9 |
| 16 | 109 25.1 | 99 16.2 | 29.6 | 117 56.1 | 26.3 | 108 51.4 | 57.3 | 141 59.5 | 15.3 | Kaus Aust. | 83 35.2 | S34 22.4 |
| 17 | 124 27.5 | 114 16.0 | 30.7 | 132 56.8 | 25.6 | 123 53.4 | 57.1 | 157 01.9 | 15.3 | | | |
| 18 | 139 30.0 | 129 15.7 | N 2 31.8 | 147 57.5 | S 5 24.9 | 138 55.4 | S 0 56.9 | 172 04.3 | S14 15.2 | Kochab | 137 18.6 | N74 03.9 |
| 19 | 154 32.4 | 144 15.5 | 32.8 | 162 58.3 | 24.1 | 153 57.4 | 56.8 | 187 06.6 | 15.2 | Markab | 13 32.2 | N15 19.3 |
| 20 | 169 34.9 | 159 15.3 | 33.9 | 177 59.0 | 23.4 | 168 59.5 | 56.6 | 202 09.0 | 15.2 | Menkar | 314 08.8 | N 4 10.5 |
| 21 | 184 37.4 | 174 15.1 .. | 34.9 | 192 59.7 .. | 22.7 | 184 01.5 .. | 56.4 | 217 11.4 .. | 15.2 | Menkent | 147 59.8 | S36 28.8 |
| 22 | 199 39.8 | 189 14.9 | 36.0 | 208 00.4 | 22.0 | 199 03.5 | 56.2 | 232 13.7 | 15.1 | Miaplacidus | 221 38.8 | S69 48.8 |
| 23 | 214 42.3 | 204 14.7 | 37.1 | 223 01.1 | 21.2 | 214 05.5 | 56.0 | 247 16.1 | 15.1 | | | |
| 12 00 | 229 44.8 | 219 14.4 | N 2 38.1 | 238 01.9 | S 5 20.5 | 229 07.5 | S 0 55.8 | 262 18.5 | S14 15.1 | Mirfak | 308 31.9 | N49 56.3 |
| 01 | 244 47.2 | 234 14.2 | 39.2 | 253 02.6 | 19.8 | 244 09.6 | 55.6 | 277 20.8 | 15.1 | Nunki | 75 50.3 | S26 16.1 |
| 02 | 259 49.7 | 249 14.0 | 40.2 | 268 03.3 | 19.1 | 259 11.6 | 55.5 | 292 23.2 | 15.0 | Peacock | 53 09.1 | S56 39.6 |
| 03 | 274 52.2 | 264 13.8 .. | 41.3 | 283 04.0 .. | 18.4 | 274 13.6 .. | 55.3 | 307 25.6 .. | 15.0 | Pollux | 243 20.2 | N27 58.4 |
| 04 | 289 54.6 | 279 13.6 | 42.4 | 298 04.8 | 17.6 | 289 15.6 | 55.1 | 322 27.9 | 15.0 | Procyon | 244 53.3 | N 5 10.0 |
| 05 | 304 57.1 | 294 13.3 | 43.4 | 313 05.5 | 16.9 | 304 17.6 | 54.9 | 337 30.3 | 15.0 | | | |
| 06 | 319 59.6 | 309 13.1 | N 2 44.5 | 328 06.2 | S 5 16.2 | 319 19.6 | S 0 54.7 | 352 32.7 | S14 14.9 | Rasalhague | 96 00.3 | N12 32.5 |
| 07 | 335 02.0 | 324 12.9 | 45.5 | 343 06.9 | 15.5 | 334 21.7 | 54.5 | 7 35.0 | 14.9 | Regulus | 207 36.8 | N11 51.5 |
| 08 | 350 04.5 | 339 12.7 | 46.6 | 358 07.6 | 14.8 | 349 23.7 | 54.3 | 22 37.4 | 14.9 | Rigel | 281 06.3 | S 8 10.7 |
| 09 | 5 06.9 | 354 12.5 .. | 47.6 | 13 08.4 .. | 14.0 | 4 25.7 .. | 54.2 | 37 39.8 .. | 14.9 | Rigil Kent. | 139 42.7 | S60 55.6 |
| 10 | 20 09.4 | 9 12.3 | 48.7 | 28 09.1 | 13.3 | 19 27.7 | 54.0 | 52 42.2 | 14.8 | Sabik | 102 05.0 | S15 45.2 |
| 11 | 35 11.9 | 24 12.0 | 49.8 | 43 09.8 | 12.6 | 34 29.7 | 53.8 | 67 44.5 | 14.8 | | | |
| 12 | 50 14.3 | 39 11.8 | N 2 50.8 | 58 10.5 | S 5 11.9 | 49 31.8 | S 0 53.6 | 82 46.9 | S14 14.8 | Schedar | 349 34.0 | N56 39.3 |
| 13 | 65 16.8 | 54 11.6 | 51.9 | 73 11.3 | 11.1 | 64 33.8 | 53.4 | 97 49.3 | 14.8 | Shaula | 96 13.0 | S37 07.1 |
| 14 | 80 19.3 | 69 11.4 | 52.9 | 88 12.0 | 10.4 | 79 35.8 | 53.2 | 112 51.6 | 14.7 | Sirius | 258 28.4 | S16 44.9 |
| 15 | 95 21.7 | 84 11.2 .. | 54.0 | 103 12.7 .. | 09.7 | 94 37.8 .. | 53.1 | 127 54.0 .. | 14.7 | Spica | 158 24.4 | S11 16.7 |
| 16 | 110 24.2 | 99 11.0 | 55.1 | 118 13.4 | 09.0 | 109 39.8 | 52.9 | 142 56.4 | 14.7 | Suhail | 222 48.0 | S43 31.6 |
| 17 | 125 26.7 | 114 10.7 | 56.1 | 133 14.2 | 08.3 | 124 41.9 | 52.7 | 157 58.7 | 14.7 | | | |
| 18 | 140 29.1 | 129 10.5 | N 2 57.2 | 148 14.9 | S 5 07.5 | 139 43.9 | S 0 52.5 | 173 01.1 | S14 14.6 | Vega | 80 34.4 | N38 48.0 |
| 19 | 155 31.6 | 144 10.3 | 58.2 | 163 15.6 | 06.8 | 154 45.9 | 52.3 | 188 03.5 | 14.6 | Zuben'ubi | 136 58.1 | S16 08.1 |
| 20 | 170 34.0 | 159 10.0 | 2 59.3 | 178 16.3 | 06.1 | 169 47.9 | 52.1 | 203 05.9 | 14.6 | | SHA | Mer. Pass. |
| 21 | 185 36.5 | 174 09.8 | 3 00.4 | 193 17.0 .. | 05.4 | 184 49.9 .. | 52.0 | 218 08.2 .. | 14.6 | | ° ′ | h m |
| 22 | 200 39.0 | 189 09.6 | 01.4 | 208 17.8 | 04.6 | 199 52.0 | 51.8 | 233 10.6 | 14.5 | Venus | 350 34.0 | 9 23 |
| 23 | 215 41.4 | 204 09.4 | 02.5 | 223 18.5 | 03.9 | 214 54.0 | 51.6 | 248 13.0 | 14.5 | Mars | 8 58.9 | 8 09 |
| | h m | | | | | | | | | Jupiter | 359 33.5 | 8 46 |
| Mer. Pass. 8 43.5 | | v −0.2 | d 1.1 | v 0.7 | d 0.7 | v 2.0 | d 0.2 | v 2.4 | d 0.0 | Saturn | 32 36.0 | 6 34 |

| UT | SUN GHA | SUN Dec | MOON GHA | v | Dec | d | HP |
|---|---|---|---|---|---|---|---|
| **d h** | ° ′ | ° ′ | ° ′ | ′ | ° ′ | ′ | ′ |
| **10 00** | 180 53.3 | N17 33.7 | 73 12.5 | 13.4 | N16 09.6 | 11.7 | 55.7 |
| 01 | 195 53.3 | 34.3 | 87 44.9 | 13.3 | 15 57.9 | 11.7 | 55.7 |
| 02 | 210 53.4 | 35.0 | 102 17.2 | 13.4 | 15 46.2 | 11.9 | 55.7 |
| 03 | 225 53.4 | .. 35.7 | 116 49.6 | 13.5 | 15 34.3 | 11.9 | 55.8 |
| 04 | 240 53.4 | 36.3 | 131 22.1 | 13.4 | 15 22.4 | 12.0 | 55.8 |
| 05 | 255 53.4 | 37.0 | 145 54.5 | 13.5 | 15 10.4 | 12.0 | 55.8 |
| 06 | 270 53.4 | N17 37.6 | 160 27.0 | 13.5 | N14 58.4 | 12.2 | 55.9 |
| 07 | 285 53.5 | 38.3 | 174 59.5 | 13.5 | 14 46.2 | 12.2 | 55.9 |
| 08 | 300 53.5 | 38.9 | 189 32.0 | 13.5 | 14 34.0 | 12.3 | 55.9 |
| 09 | 315 53.5 | .. 39.6 | 204 04.5 | 13.6 | 14 21.7 | 12.4 | 56.0 |
| 10 | 330 53.5 | 40.2 | 218 37.1 | 13.6 | 14 09.3 | 12.5 | 56.0 |
| 11 | 345 53.6 | 40.9 | 233 09.7 | 13.5 | 13 56.8 | 12.5 | 56.0 |
| 12 | 0 53.6 | N17 41.5 | 247 42.2 | 13.7 | N13 44.3 | 12.6 | 56.1 |
| 13 | 15 53.6 | 42.2 | 262 14.9 | 13.6 | 13 31.7 | 12.7 | 56.1 |
| 14 | 30 53.6 | 42.8 | 276 47.5 | 13.6 | 13 19.0 | 12.7 | 56.1 |
| 15 | 45 53.6 | .. 43.5 | 291 20.1 | 13.7 | 13 06.3 | 12.9 | 56.1 |
| 16 | 60 53.7 | 44.1 | 305 52.8 | 13.7 | 12 53.4 | 12.9 | 56.2 |
| 17 | 75 53.7 | 44.8 | 320 25.5 | 13.7 | 12 40.5 | 12.9 | 56.2 |
| 18 | 90 53.7 | N17 45.4 | 334 58.2 | 13.7 | N12 27.6 | 13.1 | 56.2 |
| 19 | 105 53.7 | 46.1 | 349 30.9 | 13.7 | 12 14.5 | 13.1 | 56.3 |
| 20 | 120 53.7 | 46.7 | 4 03.6 | 13.7 | 12 01.4 | 13.2 | 56.3 |
| 21 | 135 53.8 | .. 47.4 | 18 36.3 | 13.7 | 11 48.2 | 13.2 | 56.3 |
| 22 | 150 53.8 | 48.0 | 33 09.0 | 13.8 | 11 35.0 | 13.3 | 56.4 |
| 23 | 165 53.8 | 48.7 | 47 41.8 | 13.7 | 11 21.7 | 13.4 | 56.4 |
| **11 00** | 180 53.8 | N17 49.3 | 62 14.5 | 13.8 | N11 08.3 | 13.5 | 56.5 |
| 01 | 195 53.8 | 49.9 | 76 47.3 | 13.8 | 10 54.8 | 13.5 | 56.5 |
| 02 | 210 53.9 | 50.6 | 91 20.1 | 13.7 | 10 41.3 | 13.6 | 56.5 |
| 03 | 225 53.9 | .. 51.2 | 105 52.8 | 13.8 | 10 27.7 | 13.6 | 56.6 |
| 04 | 240 53.9 | 51.9 | 120 25.6 | 13.8 | 10 14.1 | 13.7 | 56.6 |
| 05 | 255 53.9 | 52.5 | 134 58.4 | 13.8 | 10 00.4 | 13.8 | 56.6 |
| 06 | 270 53.9 | N17 53.2 | 149 31.2 | 13.8 | N 9 46.6 | 13.8 | 56.7 |
| 07 | 285 53.9 | 53.8 | 164 04.0 | 13.7 | 9 32.8 | 13.9 | 56.7 |
| 08 | 300 54.0 | 54.4 | 178 36.7 | 13.8 | 9 18.9 | 14.0 | 56.7 |
| 09 | 315 54.0 | .. 55.1 | 193 09.5 | 13.8 | 9 04.9 | 14.0 | 56.8 |
| 10 | 330 54.0 | 55.7 | 207 42.3 | 13.8 | 8 50.9 | 14.0 | 56.8 |
| 11 | 345 54.0 | 56.4 | 222 15.1 | 13.8 | 8 36.9 | 14.1 | 56.8 |
| 12 | 0 54.0 | N17 57.0 | 236 47.9 | 13.8 | N 8 22.8 | 14.2 | 56.9 |
| 13 | 15 54.0 | 57.6 | 251 20.7 | 13.7 | 8 08.6 | 14.3 | 56.9 |
| 14 | 30 54.1 | 58.3 | 265 53.4 | 13.8 | 7 54.3 | 14.2 | 56.9 |
| 15 | 45 54.1 | .. 58.9 | 280 26.2 | 13.8 | 7 40.1 | 14.4 | 57.0 |
| 16 | 60 54.1 | 17 59.6 | 294 59.0 | 13.7 | 7 25.7 | 14.4 | 57.0 |
| 17 | 75 54.1 | 18 00.2 | 309 31.7 | 13.8 | 7 11.3 | 14.4 | 57.1 |
| 18 | 90 54.1 | N18 00.8 | 324 04.5 | 13.7 | N 6 56.9 | 14.5 | 57.1 |
| 19 | 105 54.1 | 01.5 | 338 37.2 | 13.7 | 6 42.4 | 14.6 | 57.1 |
| 20 | 120 54.1 | 02.1 | 353 09.9 | 13.7 | 6 27.8 | 14.5 | 57.2 |
| 21 | 135 54.2 | .. 02.7 | 7 42.6 | 13.7 | 6 13.3 | 14.7 | 57.2 |
| 22 | 150 54.2 | 03.4 | 22 15.3 | 13.7 | 5 58.6 | 14.7 | 57.2 |
| 23 | 165 54.2 | 04.0 | 36 48.0 | 13.7 | 5 43.9 | 14.7 | 57.3 |
| **12 00** | 180 54.2 | N18 04.6 | 51 20.7 | 13.6 | N 5 29.2 | 14.8 | 57.3 |
| 01 | 195 54.2 | 05.3 | 65 53.3 | 13.6 | 5 14.4 | 14.8 | 57.4 |
| 02 | 210 54.2 | 05.9 | 80 25.9 | 13.6 | 4 59.6 | 14.9 | 57.4 |
| 03 | 225 54.2 | .. 06.5 | 94 58.5 | 13.6 | 4 44.7 | 14.9 | 57.4 |
| 04 | 240 54.2 | 07.1 | 109 31.1 | 13.6 | 4 29.8 | 14.9 | 57.5 |
| 05 | 255 54.3 | 07.8 | 124 03.7 | 13.6 | 4 14.9 | 15.0 | 57.5 |
| 06 | 270 54.3 | N18 08.4 | 138 36.3 | 13.5 | N 3 59.9 | 15.1 | 57.5 |
| 07 | 285 54.3 | 09.0 | 153 08.8 | 13.5 | 3 44.8 | 15.0 | 57.6 |
| 08 | 300 54.3 | 09.7 | 167 41.3 | 13.5 | 3 29.8 | 15.1 | 57.6 |
| 09 | 315 54.3 | .. 10.3 | 182 13.8 | 13.4 | 3 14.7 | 15.2 | 57.7 |
| 10 | 330 54.3 | 10.9 | 196 46.2 | 13.4 | 2 59.5 | 15.1 | 57.7 |
| 11 | 345 54.3 | 11.5 | 211 18.6 | 13.4 | 2 44.4 | 15.2 | 57.7 |
| 12 | 0 54.3 | N18 12.2 | 225 51.0 | 13.4 | N 2 29.2 | 15.3 | 57.8 |
| 13 | 15 54.3 | 12.8 | 240 23.4 | 13.3 | 2 13.9 | 15.3 | 57.8 |
| 14 | 30 54.4 | 13.4 | 254 55.7 | 13.3 | 1 58.6 | 15.3 | 57.9 |
| 15 | 45 54.4 | .. 14.0 | 269 28.0 | 13.2 | 1 43.3 | 15.3 | 57.9 |
| 16 | 60 54.4 | 14.7 | 284 00.2 | 13.3 | 1 28.0 | 15.4 | 57.9 |
| 17 | 75 54.4 | 15.3 | 298 32.5 | 13.2 | 1 12.6 | 15.3 | 58.0 |
| 18 | 90 54.4 | N18 15.9 | 313 04.7 | 13.1 | N 0 57.3 | 15.5 | 58.0 |
| 19 | 105 54.4 | 16.5 | 327 36.8 | 13.1 | 0 41.8 | 15.4 | 58.0 |
| 20 | 120 54.4 | 17.2 | 342 08.9 | 13.1 | 0 26.4 | 15.5 | 58.1 |
| 21 | 135 54.4 | .. 17.8 | 356 41.0 | 13.0 | N 0 10.9 | 15.4 | 58.1 |
| 22 | 150 54.4 | 18.4 | 11 13.0 | 13.0 | S 0 04.5 | 15.5 | 58.2 |
| 23 | 165 54.4 | 19.0 | 25 45.0 | 13.0 | S 0 20.0 | 15.6 | 58.2 |
| | SD 15.9 | d 0.6 | SD 15.3 | | 15.5 | | 15.7 |

Days (left margin): 10 TUESDAY, 11 WEDNESDAY, 12 THURSDAY

| Lat. | Twilight Naut. | Twilight Civil | Sunrise | Moonrise 10 | 11 | 12 | 13 |
|---|---|---|---|---|---|---|---|
| ° | h m | h m | h m | h m | h m | h m | h m |
| N 72 | □ | □ | □ | 10 05 | 12 29 | 14 41 | 16 56 |
| N 70 | //// | //// | 01 23 | 10 35 | 12 42 | 14 43 | 16 48 |
| 68 | //// | //// | 02 09 | 10 57 | 12 53 | 14 45 | 16 42 |
| 66 | //// | 00 25 | 02 38 | 11 14 | 13 01 | 14 47 | 16 36 |
| 64 | //// | 01 34 | 03 00 | 11 28 | 13 08 | 14 48 | 16 32 |
| 62 | //// | 02 08 | 03 18 | 11 40 | 13 14 | 14 50 | 16 28 |
| 60 | 00 22 | 02 32 | 03 32 | 11 49 | 13 19 | 14 51 | 16 25 |
| N 58 | 01 24 | 02 51 | 03 44 | 11 58 | 13 24 | 14 52 | 16 22 |
| 56 | 01 56 | 03 07 | 03 55 | 12 05 | 13 28 | 14 52 | 16 20 |
| 54 | 02 18 | 03 20 | 04 04 | 12 12 | 13 32 | 14 53 | 16 18 |
| 52 | 02 36 | 03 32 | 04 13 | 12 18 | 13 35 | 14 54 | 16 16 |
| 50 | 02 51 | 03 42 | 04 20 | 12 23 | 13 38 | 14 54 | 16 14 |
| 45 | 03 20 | 04 02 | 04 36 | 12 35 | 13 45 | 14 56 | 16 10 |
| N 40 | 03 41 | 04 19 | 04 49 | 12 44 | 13 50 | 14 57 | 16 06 |
| 35 | 03 58 | 04 32 | 05 00 | 12 52 | 13 55 | 14 58 | 16 04 |
| 30 | 04 12 | 04 43 | 05 09 | 13 00 | 13 59 | 14 59 | 16 01 |
| 20 | 04 35 | 05 02 | 05 26 | 13 12 | 14 06 | 15 00 | 15 57 |
| N 10 | 04 52 | 05 18 | 05 40 | 13 23 | 14 12 | 15 02 | 15 53 |
| 0 | 05 06 | 05 31 | 05 53 | 13 32 | 14 17 | 15 03 | 15 50 |
| S 10 | 05 18 | 05 44 | 06 06 | 13 42 | 14 23 | 15 04 | 15 46 |
| 20 | 05 30 | 05 57 | 06 20 | 13 53 | 14 29 | 15 05 | 15 42 |
| 30 | 05 41 | 06 10 | 06 35 | 14 05 | 14 36 | 15 07 | 15 38 |
| 35 | 05 47 | 06 18 | 06 44 | 14 12 | 14 40 | 15 08 | 15 36 |
| 40 | 05 53 | 06 26 | 06 55 | 14 20 | 14 45 | 15 09 | 15 34 |
| 45 | 06 00 | 06 35 | 07 07 | 14 29 | 14 50 | 15 10 | 15 31 |
| S 50 | 06 07 | 06 46 | 07 21 | 14 40 | 14 56 | 15 11 | 15 27 |
| 52 | 06 10 | 06 51 | 07 28 | 14 45 | 14 59 | 15 12 | 15 25 |
| 54 | 06 13 | 06 56 | 07 35 | 14 50 | 15 02 | 15 13 | 15 24 |
| 56 | 06 17 | 07 02 | 07 44 | 14 56 | 15 05 | 15 13 | 15 22 |
| 58 | 06 20 | 07 09 | 07 53 | 15 03 | 15 09 | 15 14 | 15 20 |
| S 60 | 06 24 | 07 16 | 08 04 | 15 11 | 15 13 | 15 15 | 15 17 |

| Lat. | Sunset | Twilight Civil | Twilight Naut. | Moonset 10 | 11 | 12 | 13 |
|---|---|---|---|---|---|---|---|
| ° | h m | h m | h m | h m | h m | h m | h m |
| N 72 | □ | □ | □ | 05 00 | 04 11 | 03 37 | 03 06 |
| N 70 | 22 37 | //// | //// | 04 28 | 03 56 | 03 31 | 03 08 |
| 68 | 21 48 | //// | //// | 04 04 | 03 43 | 03 26 | 03 09 |
| 66 | 21 18 | //// | //// | 03 46 | 03 33 | 03 22 | 03 11 |
| 64 | 20 55 | 22 24 | //// | 03 31 | 03 24 | 03 18 | 03 12 |
| 62 | 20 37 | 21 48 | //// | 03 18 | 03 17 | 03 15 | 03 13 |
| 60 | 20 22 | 21 23 | //// | 03 07 | 03 10 | 03 12 | 03 14 |
| N 58 | 20 10 | 21 04 | 22 33 | 02 58 | 03 04 | 03 10 | 03 15 |
| 56 | 19 59 | 20 48 | 22 00 | 02 49 | 02 59 | 03 07 | 03 15 |
| 54 | 19 50 | 20 34 | 21 37 | 02 42 | 02 54 | 03 05 | 03 16 |
| 52 | 19 41 | 20 23 | 21 19 | 02 35 | 02 50 | 03 04 | 03 17 |
| 50 | 19 34 | 20 12 | 21 03 | 02 29 | 02 46 | 03 02 | 03 17 |
| 45 | 19 18 | 19 51 | 20 34 | 02 16 | 02 38 | 02 58 | 03 18 |
| N 40 | 19 05 | 19 35 | 20 12 | 02 05 | 02 31 | 02 55 | 03 19 |
| 35 | 18 53 | 19 21 | 19 55 | 01 56 | 02 25 | 02 53 | 03 20 |
| 30 | 18 44 | 19 10 | 19 41 | 01 48 | 02 20 | 02 50 | 03 21 |
| 20 | 18 27 | 18 51 | 19 19 | 01 33 | 02 10 | 02 46 | 03 22 |
| N 10 | 18 13 | 18 35 | 19 01 | 01 21 | 02 02 | 02 42 | 03 24 |
| 0 | 18 00 | 18 22 | 18 47 | 01 09 | 01 54 | 02 39 | 03 25 |
| S 10 | 17 47 | 18 09 | 18 34 | 00 57 | 01 46 | 02 35 | 03 26 |
| 20 | 17 33 | 17 56 | 18 23 | 00 44 | 01 38 | 02 32 | 03 27 |
| 30 | 17 17 | 17 42 | 18 11 | 00 29 | 01 28 | 02 27 | 03 28 |
| 35 | 17 08 | 17 35 | 18 05 | 00 21 | 01 22 | 02 25 | 03 29 |
| 40 | 16 58 | 17 27 | 17 59 | 00 11 | 01 16 | 02 22 | 03 30 |
| 45 | 16 46 | 17 17 | 17 53 | 25 08 | 01 08 | 02 18 | 03 31 |
| S 50 | 16 31 | 17 06 | 17 46 | 24 59 | 00 59 | 02 14 | 03 32 |
| 52 | 16 24 | 17 01 | 17 42 | 24 55 | 00 55 | 02 12 | 03 32 |
| 54 | 16 17 | 16 56 | 17 39 | 24 50 | 00 50 | 02 10 | 03 33 |
| 56 | 16 08 | 16 50 | 17 36 | 24 45 | 00 45 | 02 08 | 03 34 |
| 58 | 15 59 | 16 44 | 17 32 | 24 39 | 00 39 | 02 05 | 03 34 |
| S 60 | 15 48 | 16 36 | 17 27 | 24 32 | 00 32 | 02 03 | 03 35 |

| Day | SUN Eqn. of Time 00h | SUN Eqn. of Time 12h | SUN Mer. Pass. | MOON Mer. Pass. Upper | MOON Mer. Pass. Lower | Age | Phase |
|---|---|---|---|---|---|---|---|
| d | m s | m s | h m | h m | h m | d | % |
| 10 | 03 33 | 03 34 | 11 56 | 19 43 | 07 21 | 10 | 65 |
| 11 | 03 35 | 03 36 | 11 56 | 20 28 | 08 06 | 11 | 74 |
| 12 | 03 37 | 03 37 | 11 56 | 21 14 | 08 51 | 12 | 83 |

| UT | ARIES | VENUS −4.0 | | MARS +0.8 | | JUPITER −2.2 | | SATURN +0.7 | | STARS | | |
|---|---|---|---|---|---|---|---|---|---|---|---|---|
| | GHA | GHA | Dec | GHA | Dec | GHA | Dec | GHA | Dec | Name | SHA | Dec |
| d h | ° ′ | ° ′ | ° ′ | ° ′ | ° ′ | ° ′ | ° ′ | ° ′ | ° ′ | | ° ′ | ° ′ |
| **13** 00 | 230 43.9 | 219 09.2 | N 3 03.5 | 238 19.2 | S 5 03.2 | 229 56.0 | S 0 51.4 | 263 15.3 | S14 14.5 | Acamar | 315 13.9 | S40 13.0 |
| 01 | 245 46.4 | 234 08.9 | 04.6 | 253 19.9 | 02.5 | 244 58.0 | 51.2 | 278 17.7 | 14.5 | Achernar | 335 22.4 | S57 07.4 |
| 02 | 260 48.8 | 249 08.7 | 05.7 | 268 20.7 | 01.8 | 260 00.0 | 51.0 | 293 20.1 | 14.4 | Acrux | 173 02.0 | S63 13.5 |
| 03 | 275 51.3 | 264 08.5 .. | 06.7 | 283 21.4 .. | 01.0 | 275 02.1 .. | 50.8 | 308 22.5 .. | 14.4 | Adhara | 255 07.9 | S29 00.3 |
| 04 | 290 53.8 | 279 08.3 | 07.8 | 298 22.1 | 5 00.3 | 290 04.1 | 50.7 | 323 24.8 | 14.4 | Aldebaran | 290 42.5 | N16 33.1 |
| 05 | 305 56.2 | 294 08.1 | 08.8 | 313 22.8 | 4 59.6 | 305 06.1 | 50.5 | 338 27.2 | 14.4 | | | |
| 06 | 320 58.7 | 309 07.8 | N 3 09.9 | 328 23.6 | S 4 58.9 | 320 08.1 | S 0 50.3 | 353 29.6 | S14 14.4 | Alioth | 166 14.5 | N55 50.5 |
| 07 | 336 01.2 | 324 07.6 | 11.0 | 343 24.3 | 58.1 | 335 10.2 | 50.1 | 8 31.9 | 14.3 | Alkaid | 152 53.3 | N49 12.2 |
| 08 | 351 03.6 | 339 07.4 | 12.0 | 358 25.0 | 57.4 | 350 12.2 | 49.9 | 23 34.3 | 14.3 | Alnair | 27 35.8 | S46 51.1 |
| F 09 | 6 06.1 | 354 07.2 .. | 13.1 | 13 25.7 .. | 56.7 | 5 14.2 .. | 49.7 | 38 36.7 .. | 14.3 | Alnilam | 275 40.3 | S 1 11.4 |
| R 10 | 21 08.5 | 9 06.9 | 14.1 | 28 26.5 | 56.0 | 20 16.2 | 49.6 | 53 39.1 | 14.3 | Alphard | 217 50.0 | S 8 45.4 |
| I 11 | 36 11.0 | 24 06.7 | 15.2 | 43 27.2 | 55.2 | 35 18.2 | 49.4 | 68 41.4 | 14.2 | | | |
| D 12 | 51 13.5 | 39 06.5 | N 3 16.3 | 58 27.9 | S 4 54.5 | 50 20.3 | S 0 49.2 | 83 43.8 | S14 14.2 | Alphecca | 126 05.3 | N26 38.4 |
| A 13 | 66 15.9 | 54 06.3 | 17.3 | 73 28.7 | 53.8 | 65 22.3 | 49.0 | 98 46.2 | 14.2 | Alpheratz | 357 37.3 | N29 12.5 |
| Y 14 | 81 18.4 | 69 06.0 | 18.4 | 88 29.4 | 53.1 | 80 24.3 | 48.8 | 113 48.6 | 14.2 | Altair | 62 02.0 | N 8 55.5 |
| 15 | 96 20.9 | 84 05.8 .. | 19.4 | 103 30.1 .. | 52.4 | 95 26.3 .. | 48.7 | 128 50.9 .. | 14.1 | Ankaa | 353 09.6 | S42 11.1 |
| 16 | 111 23.3 | 99 05.6 | 20.5 | 118 30.8 | 51.6 | 110 28.4 | 48.5 | 143 53.3 | 14.1 | Antares | 112 18.2 | S26 28.9 |
| 17 | 126 25.8 | 114 05.4 | 21.5 | 133 31.6 | 50.9 | 125 30.4 | 48.3 | 158 55.7 | 14.1 | | | |
| 18 | 141 28.3 | 129 05.1 | N 3 22.6 | 148 32.3 | S 4 50.2 | 140 32.4 | S 0 48.1 | 173 58.1 | S14 14.1 | Arcturus | 145 49.6 | N19 04.0 |
| 19 | 156 30.7 | 144 04.9 | 23.7 | 163 33.0 | 49.5 | 155 34.4 | 47.9 | 189 00.4 | 14.0 | Atria | 107 13.9 | S69 03.9 |
| 20 | 171 33.2 | 159 04.7 | 24.7 | 178 33.7 | 48.7 | 170 36.5 | 47.7 | 204 02.8 | 14.0 | Avior | 234 15.8 | S59 35.1 |
| 21 | 186 35.6 | 174 04.5 .. | 25.8 | 193 34.5 .. | 48.0 | 185 38.5 .. | 47.6 | 219 05.2 .. | 14.0 | Bellatrix | 278 25.6 | N 6 22.1 |
| 22 | 201 38.1 | 189 04.2 | 26.8 | 208 35.2 | 47.3 | 200 40.5 | 47.4 | 234 07.6 | 14.0 | Betelgeuse | 270 54.8 | N 7 24.6 |
| 23 | 216 40.6 | 204 04.0 | 27.9 | 223 35.9 | 46.6 | 215 42.5 | 47.2 | 249 09.9 | 14.0 | | | |
| **14** 00 | 231 43.0 | 219 03.8 | N 3 29.0 | 238 36.6 | S 4 45.8 | 230 44.6 | S 0 47.0 | 264 12.3 | S14 13.9 | Canopus | 263 53.8 | S52 42.6 |
| 01 | 246 45.5 | 234 03.6 | 30.0 | 253 37.4 | 45.1 | 245 46.6 | 46.8 | 279 14.7 | 13.9 | Capella | 280 25.6 | N46 01.2 |
| 02 | 261 48.0 | 249 03.3 | 31.1 | 268 38.1 | 44.4 | 260 48.6 | 46.6 | 294 17.1 | 13.9 | Deneb | 49 27.2 | N45 21.3 |
| 03 | 276 50.4 | 264 03.1 .. | 32.1 | 283 38.8 .. | 43.7 | 275 50.6 .. | 46.5 | 309 19.4 .. | 13.9 | Denebola | 182 27.0 | N14 26.9 |
| 04 | 291 52.9 | 279 02.9 | 33.2 | 298 39.5 | 42.9 | 290 52.7 | 46.3 | 324 21.8 | 13.8 | Diphda | 348 49.8 | S17 51.9 |
| 05 | 306 55.4 | 294 02.7 | 34.3 | 313 40.3 | 42.2 | 305 54.7 | 46.1 | 339 24.2 | 13.8 | | | |
| 06 | 321 57.8 | 309 02.4 | N 3 35.3 | 328 41.0 | S 4 41.5 | 320 56.7 | S 0 45.9 | 354 26.6 | S14 13.8 | Dubhe | 193 43.5 | N61 38.1 |
| 07 | 337 00.3 | 324 02.2 | 36.4 | 343 41.7 | 40.8 | 335 58.7 | 45.7 | 9 28.9 | 13.8 | Elnath | 278 05.0 | N28 37.5 |
| S 08 | 352 02.8 | 339 02.0 | 37.4 | 358 42.5 | 40.1 | 351 00.8 | 45.6 | 24 31.3 | 13.8 | Eltanin | 90 42.8 | N51 28.9 |
| A 09 | 7 05.2 | 354 01.8 .. | 38.5 | 13 43.2 .. | 39.3 | 6 02.8 .. | 45.4 | 39 33.7 .. | 13.7 | Enif | 33 41.0 | N 9 58.4 |
| T 10 | 22 07.7 | 9 01.5 | 39.6 | 28 43.9 | 38.6 | 21 04.8 | 45.2 | 54 36.1 | 13.7 | Fomalhaut | 15 17.1 | S29 30.2 |
| U 11 | 37 10.1 | 24 01.3 | 40.6 | 43 44.6 | 37.9 | 36 06.8 | 45.0 | 69 38.4 | 13.7 | | | |
| R 12 | 52 12.6 | 39 01.1 | N 3 41.7 | 58 45.4 | S 4 37.2 | 51 08.9 | S 0 44.8 | 84 40.8 | S14 13.6 | Gacrux | 171 53.7 | S57 14.5 |
| D 13 | 67 15.1 | 54 00.8 | 42.8 | 73 46.1 | 36.4 | 66 10.9 | 44.6 | 99 43.2 | 13.6 | Gienah | 175 45.6 | S17 40.0 |
| A 14 | 82 17.5 | 69 00.6 | 43.8 | 88 46.8 | 35.7 | 81 12.9 | 44.5 | 114 45.6 | 13.6 | Hadar | 148 38.5 | S60 28.9 |
| Y 15 | 97 20.0 | 84 00.4 .. | 44.9 | 103 47.6 .. | 35.0 | 96 14.9 .. | 44.3 | 129 48.0 .. | 13.6 | Hamal | 327 54.0 | N23 33.9 |
| 16 | 112 22.5 | 99 00.2 | 45.9 | 118 48.3 | 34.3 | 111 17.0 | 44.1 | 144 50.3 | 13.6 | Kaus Aust. | 83 35.2 | S34 22.4 |
| 17 | 127 24.9 | 113 59.9 | 47.0 | 133 49.0 | 33.5 | 126 19.0 | 43.9 | 159 52.7 | 13.6 | | | |
| 18 | 142 27.4 | 128 59.7 | N 3 48.1 | 148 49.7 | S 4 32.8 | 141 21.0 | S 0 43.7 | 174 55.1 | S14 13.5 | Kochab | 137 18.6 | N74 03.9 |
| 19 | 157 29.9 | 143 59.5 | 49.1 | 163 50.5 | 32.1 | 156 23.0 | 43.6 | 189 57.5 | 13.5 | Markab | 13 32.2 | N15 19.3 |
| 20 | 172 32.3 | 158 59.2 | 50.2 | 178 51.2 | 31.4 | 171 25.1 | 43.4 | 204 59.8 | 13.5 | Menkar | 314 08.8 | N 4 10.5 |
| 21 | 187 34.8 | 173 59.0 .. | 51.2 | 193 51.9 .. | 30.6 | 186 27.1 .. | 43.2 | 220 02.2 .. | 13.5 | Menkent | 147 59.9 | S36 28.8 |
| 22 | 202 37.3 | 188 58.8 | 52.3 | 208 52.7 | 29.9 | 201 29.1 | 43.0 | 235 04.6 | 13.4 | Miaplacidus | 221 38.8 | S69 48.8 |
| 23 | 217 39.7 | 203 58.5 | 53.4 | 223 53.4 | 29.2 | 216 31.2 | 42.8 | 250 07.0 | 13.4 | | | |
| **15** 00 | 232 42.2 | 218 58.3 | N 3 54.4 | 238 54.1 | S 4 28.5 | 231 33.2 | S 0 42.7 | 265 09.4 | S14 13.4 | Mirfak | 308 31.9 | N49 56.3 |
| 01 | 247 44.6 | 233 58.1 | 55.5 | 253 54.8 | 27.7 | 246 35.2 | 42.5 | 280 11.7 | 13.4 | Nunki | 75 50.3 | S26 16.1 |
| 02 | 262 47.1 | 248 57.9 | 56.5 | 268 55.6 | 27.0 | 261 37.2 | 42.3 | 295 14.1 | 13.4 | Peacock | 53 09.0 | S56 39.6 |
| 03 | 277 49.6 | 263 57.6 .. | 57.6 | 283 56.3 .. | 26.3 | 276 39.3 .. | 42.1 | 310 16.5 .. | 13.3 | Pollux | 243 20.2 | N27 58.4 |
| 04 | 292 52.0 | 278 57.4 | 58.7 | 298 57.0 | 25.6 | 291 41.3 | 41.9 | 325 18.9 | 13.3 | Procyon | 244 53.3 | N 5 10.0 |
| 05 | 307 54.5 | 293 57.2 | 3 59.7 | 313 57.8 | 24.8 | 306 43.3 | 41.8 | 340 21.3 | 13.3 | | | |
| 06 | 322 57.0 | 308 56.9 | N 4 00.8 | 328 58.5 | S 4 24.1 | 321 45.4 | S 0 41.6 | 355 23.6 | S14 13.3 | Rasalhague | 96 00.3 | N12 32.5 |
| 07 | 337 59.4 | 323 56.7 | 01.8 | 343 59.2 | 23.4 | 336 47.4 | 41.4 | 10 26.0 | 13.3 | Regulus | 207 36.8 | N11 51.5 |
| 08 | 353 01.9 | 338 56.5 | 02.9 | 358 59.9 | 22.7 | 351 49.4 | 41.2 | 25 28.4 | 13.2 | Rigel | 281 06.3 | S 8 10.7 |
| S 09 | 8 04.4 | 353 56.2 .. | 04.0 | 14 00.7 .. | 21.9 | 6 51.4 .. | 41.0 | 40 30.8 .. | 13.2 | Rigil Kent. | 139 42.7 | S60 55.7 |
| U 10 | 23 06.8 | 8 56.0 | 05.0 | 29 01.4 | 21.2 | 21 53.5 | 40.9 | 55 33.2 | 13.2 | Sabik | 102 05.0 | S15 45.2 |
| N 11 | 38 09.3 | 23 55.8 | 06.1 | 44 02.1 | 20.5 | 36 55.5 | 40.7 | 70 35.5 | 13.2 | | | |
| D 12 | 53 11.7 | 38 55.5 | N 4 07.1 | 59 02.9 | S 4 19.8 | 51 57.5 | S 0 40.5 | 85 37.9 | S14 13.2 | Schedar | 349 34.0 | N56 39.3 |
| A 13 | 68 14.2 | 53 55.3 | 08.2 | 74 03.6 | 19.0 | 66 59.6 | 40.3 | 100 40.3 | 13.1 | Shaula | 96 13.0 | S37 07.1 |
| Y 14 | 83 16.7 | 68 55.1 | 09.3 | 89 04.3 | 18.3 | 82 01.6 | 40.1 | 115 42.7 | 13.1 | Sirius | 258 28.4 | S16 44.9 |
| 15 | 98 19.1 | 83 54.8 .. | 10.3 | 104 05.1 .. | 17.6 | 97 03.6 .. | 40.0 | 130 45.1 .. | 13.1 | Spica | 158 24.4 | S11 16.7 |
| 16 | 113 21.6 | 98 54.6 | 11.4 | 119 05.8 | 16.9 | 112 05.7 | 39.8 | 145 47.5 | 13.1 | Suhail | 222 48.0 | S43 31.6 |
| 17 | 128 24.1 | 113 54.4 | 12.4 | 134 06.5 | 16.1 | 127 07.7 | 39.6 | 160 49.8 | 13.1 | | | |
| 18 | 143 26.5 | 128 54.1 | N 4 13.5 | 149 07.2 | S 4 15.4 | 142 09.7 | S 0 39.4 | 175 52.2 | S14 13.0 | Vega | 80 34.4 | N38 48.0 |
| 19 | 158 29.0 | 143 53.9 | 14.6 | 164 08.0 | 14.7 | 157 11.7 | 39.2 | 190 54.6 | 13.0 | Zuben'ubi | 136 58.1 | S16 08.1 |
| 20 | 173 31.5 | 158 53.7 | 15.6 | 179 08.7 | 14.0 | 172 13.8 | 39.1 | 205 57.0 | 13.0 | | SHA | Mer. Pass. |
| 21 | 188 33.9 | 173 53.4 .. | 16.7 | 194 09.4 .. | 13.2 | 187 15.8 .. | 38.9 | 220 59.4 .. | 13.0 | | ° ′ | h m |
| 22 | 203 36.4 | 188 53.2 | 17.7 | 209 10.2 | 12.5 | 202 17.8 | 38.7 | 236 01.7 | 12.9 | Venus | 347 20.8 | 9 24 |
| 23 | 218 38.9 | 203 53.0 | 18.8 | 224 10.9 | 11.8 | 217 19.9 | 38.5 | 251 04.1 | 12.9 | Mars | 6 53.6 | 8 05 |
| | h m | | | | | | | | | Jupiter | 359 01.5 | 8 36 |
| Mer. Pass. 8 31.7 | v −0.2 d 1.1 | v 0.7 | d 0.7 | v 2.0 | d 0.2 | v 2.4 | d 0.0 | | | Saturn | 32 29.3 | 6 22 |

| UT | SUN | | MOON | | | | | Lat. | Twilight | | Sunrise | Moonrise | | | |
|---|---|---|---|---|---|---|---|---|---|---|---|---|---|---|---|
| | | | | | | | | | Naut. | Civil | | 13 | 14 | 15 | 16 |
| | GHA | Dec | GHA | v | Dec | d | HP | | | | | | | | |
| d h | ° ' | ° ' | ° ' | ' | ° ' | ' | ' | ° | h m | h m | h m | h m | h m | h m | h m |
| 13 00 | 180 54.4 | N18 19.6 | 40 17.0 | 12.9 | S 0 35.6 | 15.5 | 58.2 | N 72 | ☐ | ☐ | ☐ | 16 56 | 19 27 | ■■ | ■■ |
| 01 | 195 54.4 | 20.3 | 54 48.9 | 12.8 | 0 51.1 | 15.6 | 58.3 | N 70 | //// | //// | 00 54 | 16 48 | 19 05 | 22 00 | ■■ |
| 02 | 210 54.5 | 20.9 | 69 20.7 | 12.8 | 1 06.7 | 15.5 | 58.3 | 68 | //// | //// | 01 53 | 16 42 | 18 47 | 21 15 | ■■ |
| 03 | 225 54.5 .. | 21.5 | 83 52.5 | 12.8 | 1 22.2 | 15.6 | 58.4 | 66 | //// | //// | 02 26 | 16 36 | 18 34 | 20 46 | 23 33 |
| 04 | 240 54.5 | 22.1 | 98 24.3 | 12.7 | 1 37.8 | 15.6 | 58.4 | 64 | //// | 01 16 | 02 50 | 16 32 | 18 23 | 20 24 | 22 40 |
| 05 | 255 54.5 | 22.7 | 112 56.0 | 12.6 | 1 53.4 | 15.7 | 58.4 | 62 | //// | 01 56 | 03 09 | 16 28 | 18 13 | 20 06 | 22 08 |
| 06 | 270 54.5 | N18 23.3 | 127 27.6 | 12.6 | S 2 09.1 | 15.6 | 58.5 | 60 | //// | 02 23 | 03 25 | 16 25 | 18 05 | 19 52 | 21 44 |
| 07 | 285 54.5 | 24.0 | 141 59.2 | 12.6 | 2 24.7 | 15.6 | 58.5 | N 58 | 01 08 | 02 43 | 03 38 | 16 22 | 17 58 | 19 39 | 21 25 |
| 08 | 300 54.5 | 24.6 | 156 30.8 | 12.5 | 2 40.3 | 15.7 | 58.5 | 56 | 01 44 | 03 00 | 03 49 | 16 20 | 17 52 | 19 29 | 21 09 |
| F 09 | 315 54.5 .. | 25.2 | 171 02.3 | 12.4 | 2 56.0 | 15.6 | 58.6 | 54 | 02 09 | 03 14 | 03 59 | 16 18 | 17 46 | 19 20 | 20 56 |
| R 10 | 330 54.5 | 25.8 | 185 33.7 | 12.4 | 3 11.6 | 15.7 | 58.6 | 52 | 02 29 | 03 26 | 04 08 | 16 16 | 17 41 | 19 11 | 20 44 |
| I 11 | 345 54.5 | 26.4 | 200 05.1 | 12.3 | 3 27.3 | 15.7 | 58.7 | 50 | 02 45 | 03 37 | 04 16 | 16 14 | 17 37 | 19 04 | 20 34 |
| D 12 | 0 54.5 | N18 27.0 | 214 36.4 | 12.3 | S 3 43.0 | 15.6 | 58.7 | 45 | 03 15 | 03 58 | 04 32 | 16 10 | 17 27 | 18 48 | 20 12 |
| A 13 | 15 54.5 | 27.6 | 229 07.7 | 12.2 | 3 58.6 | 15.7 | 58.7 | N 40 | 03 38 | 04 15 | 04 46 | 16 06 | 17 19 | 18 36 | 19 55 |
| Y 14 | 30 54.5 | 28.3 | 243 38.9 | 12.1 | 4 14.3 | 15.7 | 58.8 | 35 | 03 55 | 04 29 | 04 57 | 16 04 | 17 12 | 18 25 | 19 40 |
| 15 | 45 54.5 .. | 28.9 | 258 10.0 | 12.1 | 4 30.0 | 15.6 | 58.8 | 30 | 04 10 | 04 41 | 05 07 | 16 01 | 17 06 | 18 15 | 19 28 |
| 16 | 60 54.5 | 29.5 | 272 41.1 | 12.0 | 4 45.6 | 15.7 | 58.8 | 20 | 04 33 | 05 01 | 05 24 | 15 57 | 16 56 | 17 59 | 19 06 |
| 17 | 75 54.5 | 30.1 | 287 12.1 | 11.9 | 5 01.3 | 15.6 | 58.9 | N 10 | 04 51 | 05 17 | 05 39 | 15 53 | 16 47 | 17 45 | 18 48 |
| 18 | 90 54.5 | N18 30.7 | 301 43.0 | 11.9 | S 5 16.9 | 15.7 | 58.9 | 0 | 05 06 | 05 31 | 05 53 | 15 50 | 16 39 | 17 32 | 18 31 |
| 19 | 105 54.5 | 31.3 | 316 13.9 | 11.8 | 5 32.6 | 15.6 | 58.9 | S 10 | 05 19 | 05 44 | 06 06 | 15 46 | 16 31 | 17 20 | 18 14 |
| 20 | 120 54.5 | 31.9 | 330 44.7 | 11.7 | 5 48.2 | 15.7 | 59.0 | 20 | 05 31 | 05 58 | 06 21 | 15 42 | 16 22 | 17 06 | 17 56 |
| 21 | 135 54.5 .. | 32.5 | 345 15.4 | 11.7 | 6 03.9 | 15.6 | 59.0 | 30 | 05 43 | 06 12 | 06 37 | 15 38 | 16 12 | 16 51 | 17 35 |
| 22 | 150 54.5 | 33.1 | 359 46.1 | 11.6 | 6 19.5 | 15.6 | 59.0 | 35 | 05 49 | 06 20 | 06 47 | 15 36 | 16 07 | 16 42 | 17 23 |
| 23 | 165 54.5 | 33.7 | 14 16.7 | 11.5 | 6 35.1 | 15.6 | 59.1 | 40 | 05 56 | 06 28 | 06 57 | 15 34 | 16 01 | 16 32 | 17 09 |
| | | | | | | | | 45 | 06 03 | 06 38 | 07 10 | 15 31 | 15 53 | 16 20 | 16 53 |
| 14 00 | 180 54.5 | N18 34.3 | 28 47.2 | 11.5 | S 6 50.7 | 15.6 | 59.1 | S 50 | 06 10 | 06 50 | 07 25 | 15 27 | 15 45 | 16 06 | 16 33 |
| 01 | 195 54.5 | 34.9 | 43 17.7 | 11.3 | 7 06.3 | 15.5 | 59.2 | 52 | 06 14 | 06 55 | 07 32 | 15 25 | 15 41 | 15 59 | 16 24 |
| 02 | 210 54.5 | 35.6 | 57 48.0 | 11.3 | 7 21.8 | 15.6 | 59.2 | 54 | 06 17 | 07 01 | 07 40 | 15 24 | 15 36 | 15 52 | 16 14 |
| 03 | 225 54.5 .. | 36.2 | 72 18.3 | 11.2 | 7 37.4 | 15.5 | 59.2 | 56 | 06 21 | 07 07 | 07 49 | 15 22 | 15 31 | 15 44 | 16 02 |
| 04 | 240 54.5 | 36.8 | 86 48.5 | 11.2 | 7 52.9 | 15.5 | 59.3 | 58 | 06 25 | 07 14 | 07 59 | 15 20 | 15 26 | 15 35 | 15 48 |
| 05 | 255 54.5 | 37.4 | 101 18.7 | 11.0 | 8 08.4 | 15.5 | 59.3 | S 60 | 06 30 | 07 22 | 08 11 | 15 17 | 15 20 | 15 25 | 15 33 |
| 06 | 270 54.5 | N18 38.0 | 115 48.7 | 11.0 | S 8 23.9 | 15.4 | 59.3 | Lat. | Sunset | Twilight | | Moonset | | | |
| 07 | 285 54.5 | 38.6 | 130 18.7 | 10.9 | 8 39.3 | 15.4 | 59.4 | | | Civil | Naut. | 13 | 14 | 15 | 16 |
| S 08 | 300 54.5 | 39.2 | 144 48.6 | 10.8 | 8 54.7 | 15.4 | 59.4 | | | | | | | | |
| A 09 | 315 54.5 .. | 39.8 | 159 18.4 | 10.7 | 9 10.1 | 15.4 | 59.4 | ° | h m | h m | h m | h m | h m | h m | h m |
| T 10 | 330 54.5 | 40.4 | 173 48.1 | 10.6 | 9 25.5 | 15.3 | 59.5 | N 72 | ☐ | ☐ | ☐ | 03 06 | 02 32 | 01 46 | ■■ |
| U 11 | 345 54.5 | 41.0 | 188 17.7 | 10.6 | 9 40.8 | 15.3 | 59.5 | N 70 | 23 11 | //// | //// | 03 08 | 02 43 | 02 11 | 01 09 |
| R 12 | 0 54.5 | N18 41.6 | 202 47.3 | 10.4 | S 9 56.1 | 15.3 | 59.5 | 68 | 22 05 | //// | //// | 03 09 | 02 52 | 02 30 | 01 56 |
| D 13 | 15 54.5 | 42.2 | 217 16.7 | 10.4 | 10 11.4 | 15.2 | 59.6 | 66 | 21 30 | //// | //// | 03 11 | 02 59 | 02 46 | 02 27 |
| A 14 | 30 54.5 | 42.8 | 231 46.1 | 10.3 | 10 26.6 | 15.2 | 59.6 | 64 | 21 05 | 22 43 | //// | 03 12 | 03 06 | 02 59 | 02 50 |
| Y 15 | 45 54.5 .. | 43.4 | 246 15.4 | 10.2 | 10 41.8 | 15.1 | 59.6 | 62 | 20 45 | 22 01 | //// | 03 13 | 03 11 | 03 10 | 03 09 |
| 16 | 60 54.5 | 44.0 | 260 44.6 | 10.2 | 10 56.9 | 15.1 | 59.7 | 60 | 20 30 | 21 33 | //// | 03 14 | 03 16 | 03 19 | 03 24 |
| 17 | 75 54.5 | 44.6 | 275 13.6 | 10.0 | 11 12.0 | 15.1 | 59.7 | N 58 | 20 16 | 21 12 | 22 51 | 03 15 | 03 20 | 03 27 | 03 37 |
| 18 | 90 54.5 | N18 45.2 | 289 42.6 | 9.9 | S11 27.1 | 15.0 | 59.7 | 56 | 20 05 | 20 55 | 22 12 | 03 15 | 03 24 | 03 35 | 03 49 |
| 19 | 105 54.5 | 45.8 | 304 11.5 | 9.8 | 11 42.1 | 14.9 | 59.7 | 54 | 19 55 | 20 40 | 21 46 | 03 16 | 03 27 | 03 41 | 03 59 |
| 20 | 120 54.5 | 46.4 | 318 40.3 | 9.7 | 11 57.0 | 14.9 | 59.8 | 52 | 19 46 | 20 28 | 21 26 | 03 17 | 03 31 | 03 47 | 04 08 |
| 21 | 135 54.5 .. | 46.9 | 333 09.0 | 9.7 | 12 11.9 | 14.9 | 59.8 | 50 | 19 38 | 20 17 | 21 10 | 03 17 | 03 33 | 03 52 | 04 16 |
| 22 | 150 54.5 | 47.5 | 347 37.7 | 9.5 | 12 26.8 | 14.8 | 59.8 | 45 | 19 21 | 19 55 | 20 39 | 03 18 | 03 40 | 04 04 | 04 33 |
| 23 | 165 54.5 | 48.1 | 2 06.2 | 9.4 | 12 41.6 | 14.7 | 59.9 | N 40 | 19 07 | 19 38 | 20 16 | 03 19 | 03 45 | 04 14 | 04 47 |
| 15 00 | 180 54.5 | N18 48.7 | 16 34.6 | 9.3 | S12 56.3 | 14.7 | 59.9 | 35 | 18 56 | 19 24 | 19 58 | 03 20 | 03 50 | 04 22 | 05 00 |
| 01 | 195 54.5 | 49.3 | 31 02.9 | 9.2 | 13 11.0 | 14.6 | 59.9 | 30 | 18 46 | 19 12 | 19 43 | 03 21 | 03 54 | 04 29 | 05 10 |
| 02 | 210 54.5 | 49.9 | 45 31.1 | 9.1 | 13 25.6 | 14.5 | 60.0 | 20 | 18 29 | 18 52 | 19 20 | 03 22 | 04 01 | 04 42 | 05 28 |
| 03 | 225 54.5 .. | 50.5 | 59 59.2 | 9.0 | 13 40.1 | 14.5 | 60.0 | N 10 | 18 14 | 18 36 | 19 02 | 03 24 | 04 07 | 04 53 | 05 44 |
| 04 | 240 54.5 | 51.1 | 74 27.2 | 8.9 | 13 54.6 | 14.5 | 60.0 | 0 | 18 00 | 18 22 | 18 47 | 03 25 | 04 13 | 05 04 | 05 59 |
| 05 | 255 54.5 | 51.7 | 88 55.1 | 8.8 | 14 09.1 | 14.3 | 60.0 | S 10 | 17 46 | 18 08 | 18 34 | 03 26 | 04 18 | 05 14 | 06 15 |
| 06 | 270 54.5 | N18 52.3 | 103 22.9 | 8.6 | S14 23.4 | 14.3 | 60.1 | 20 | 17 32 | 17 55 | 18 22 | 03 27 | 04 25 | 05 26 | 06 31 |
| 07 | 285 54.5 | 52.9 | 117 50.5 | 8.6 | 14 37.7 | 14.2 | 60.1 | 30 | 17 15 | 17 41 | 18 10 | 03 28 | 04 32 | 05 39 | 06 49 |
| 08 | 300 54.5 | 53.5 | 132 18.1 | 8.5 | 14 51.9 | 14.1 | 60.1 | 35 | 17 06 | 17 33 | 18 03 | 03 29 | 04 36 | 05 46 | 07 00 |
| S 09 | 315 54.4 .. | 54.0 | 146 45.6 | 8.3 | 15 06.0 | 14.1 | 60.1 | 40 | 16 55 | 17 24 | 17 57 | 03 30 | 04 41 | 05 55 | 07 13 |
| U 10 | 330 54.4 | 54.6 | 161 12.9 | 8.3 | 15 20.1 | 13.9 | 60.2 | 45 | 16 42 | 17 14 | 17 50 | 03 31 | 04 46 | 06 05 | 07 28 |
| N 11 | 345 54.4 | 55.2 | 175 40.2 | 8.1 | 15 34.0 | 13.9 | 60.2 | S 50 | 16 27 | 17 03 | 17 42 | 03 32 | 04 53 | 06 18 | 07 46 |
| D 12 | 0 54.4 | N18 55.8 | 190 07.3 | 8.1 | S15 47.9 | 13.8 | 60.2 | 52 | 16 20 | 16 57 | 17 39 | 03 32 | 04 56 | 06 23 | 07 55 |
| A 13 | 15 54.4 | 56.4 | 204 34.4 | 7.9 | 16 01.7 | 13.8 | 60.2 | 54 | 16 12 | 16 52 | 17 35 | 03 33 | 04 59 | 06 30 | 08 05 |
| Y 14 | 30 54.4 | 57.0 | 219 01.3 | 7.8 | 16 15.5 | 13.6 | 60.3 | 56 | 16 03 | 16 45 | 17 31 | 03 34 | 05 03 | 06 37 | 08 16 |
| 15 | 45 54.4 .. | 57.6 | 233 28.1 | 7.7 | 16 29.1 | 13.5 | 60.3 | 58 | 15 53 | 16 38 | 17 27 | 03 34 | 05 07 | 06 45 | 08 28 |
| 16 | 60 54.4 | 58.1 | 247 54.8 | 7.6 | 16 42.6 | 13.5 | 60.3 | S 60 | 15 41 | 16 30 | 17 22 | 03 35 | 05 12 | 06 54 | 08 43 |
| 17 | 75 54.4 | 58.7 | 262 21.4 | 7.5 | 16 56.1 | 13.3 | 60.3 | | | SUN | | | MOON | | |
| 18 | 90 54.4 | N18 59.3 | 276 47.9 | 7.3 | S17 09.4 | 13.3 | 60.4 | Day | Eqn. of Time | | Mer. | Mer. Pass. | | Age | Phase |
| 19 | 105 54.4 | 18 59.9 | 291 14.2 | 7.3 | 17 22.7 | 13.2 | 60.4 | | 00ʰ | 12ʰ | Pass. | Upper | Lower | | |
| 20 | 120 54.4 | 19 00.5 | 305 40.5 | 7.1 | 17 35.9 | 13.0 | 60.4 | d | m s | m s | h m | h m | h m | d % | |
| 21 | 135 54.3 .. | 01.1 | 320 06.6 | 7.0 | 17 48.9 | 13.0 | 60.4 | 13 | 03 38 | 03 38 | 11 56 | 22 01 | 09 37 | 13 90 | |
| 22 | 150 54.3 | 01.6 | 334 32.6 | 6.9 | 18 01.9 | 12.8 | 60.4 | 14 | 03 38 | 03 38 | 11 56 | 22 51 | 10 26 | 14 96 | |
| 23 | 165 54.3 | 02.2 | 348 58.5 | 6.8 | S18 14.7 | 12.8 | 60.5 | 15 | 03 38 | 03 38 | 11 56 | 23 46 | 11 18 | 15 99 | ◯ |
| | SD 15.9 | d 0.6 | SD 16.0 | | 16.2 | | 16.4 | | | | | | | | | |

| UT | ARIES | VENUS −4.0 | | MARS +0.7 | | JUPITER −2.2 | | SATURN +0.7 | | STARS | | |
|---|---|---|---|---|---|---|---|---|---|---|---|---|
| d h | GHA | GHA | Dec | GHA | Dec | GHA | Dec | GHA | Dec | Name | SHA | Dec |
| **16 00** | 233 41.3 | 218 52.7 N 4 19.9 | | 239 11.6 S 4 11.1 | | 232 21.9 S 0 38.3 | | 266 06.5 S14 12.9 | | Acamar | 315 13.9 | S40 13.0 |
| 01 | 248 43.8 | 233 52.5 | 20.9 | 254 12.4 | 10.3 | 247 23.9 | 38.2 | 281 08.9 | 12.9 | Achernar | 335 22.4 | S57 07.4 |
| 02 | 263 46.2 | 248 52.3 | 22.0 | 269 13.1 | 09.6 | 262 26.0 | 38.0 | 296 11.3 | 12.9 | Acrux | 173 02.0 | S63 13.6 |
| 03 | 278 48.7 | 263 52.0 . . | 23.0 | 284 13.8 . . | 08.9 | 277 28.0 . . | 37.8 | 311 13.7 . . | 12.8 | Adhara | 255 07.9 | S29 00.3 |
| 04 | 293 51.2 | 278 51.8 | 24.1 | 299 14.6 | 08.2 | 292 30.0 | 37.6 | 326 16.0 | 12.8 | Aldebaran | 290 42.5 | N16 33.1 |
| 05 | 308 53.6 | 293 51.6 | 25.2 | 314 15.3 | 07.4 | 307 32.1 | 37.4 | 341 18.4 | 12.8 | | | |
| 06 | 323 56.1 | 308 51.3 N 4 26.2 | | 329 16.0 S 4 06.7 | | 322 34.1 S 0 37.3 | | 356 20.8 S14 12.8 | | Alioth | 166 14.5 | N55 50.5 |
| M 07 | 338 58.6 | 323 51.1 | 27.3 | 344 16.8 | 06.0 | 337 36.1 | 37.1 | 11 23.2 | 12.8 | Alkaid | 152 53.3 | N49 12.3 |
| O 08 | 354 01.0 | 338 50.8 | 28.3 | 359 17.5 | 05.3 | 352 38.2 | 36.9 | 26 25.6 | 12.7 | Alnair | 27 35.7 | S46 51.0 |
| N 09 | 9 03.5 | 353 50.6 . . | 29.4 | 14 18.2 . . | 04.5 | 7 40.2 . . | 36.7 | 41 28.0 . . | 12.7 | Alnilam | 275 40.3 | S 1 11.4 |
| D 10 | 24 06.0 | 8 50.4 | 30.4 | 29 18.9 | 03.8 | 22 42.2 | 36.6 | 56 30.3 | 12.7 | Alphard | 217 50.0 | S 8 45.4 |
| A 11 | 39 08.4 | 23 50.1 | 31.5 | 44 19.7 | 03.1 | 37 44.3 | 36.4 | 71 32.7 | 12.7 | | | |
| Y 12 | 54 10.9 | 38 49.9 N 4 32.6 | | 59 20.4 S 4 02.3 | | 52 46.3 S 0 36.2 | | 86 35.1 S14 12.7 | | Alphecca | 126 05.3 | N26 38.4 |
| 13 | 69 13.4 | 53 49.7 | 33.6 | 74 21.1 | 01.6 | 67 48.3 | 36.0 | 101 37.5 | 12.7 | Alpheratz | 357 37.3 | N29 12.5 |
| 14 | 84 15.8 | 68 49.4 | 34.7 | 89 21.9 | 00.9 | 82 50.4 | 35.8 | 116 39.9 | 12.6 | Altair | 62 01.9 | N 8 55.5 |
| 15 | 99 18.3 | 83 49.2 . . | 35.7 | 104 22.6 | 4 00.2 | 97 52.4 . . | 35.7 | 131 42.3 . . | 12.6 | Ankaa | 353 09.6 | S42 11.0 |
| 16 | 114 20.7 | 98 48.9 | 36.8 | 119 23.3 | 3 59.4 | 112 54.4 | 35.5 | 146 44.7 | 12.6 | Antares | 112 18.2 | S26 28.9 |
| 17 | 129 23.2 | 113 48.7 | 37.9 | 134 24.1 | 58.7 | 127 56.5 | 35.3 | 161 47.0 | 12.6 | | | |
| 18 | 144 25.7 | 128 48.5 N 4 38.9 | | 149 24.8 S 3 58.0 | | 142 58.5 S 0 35.1 | | 176 49.4 S14 12.6 | | Arcturus | 145 49.6 | N19 04.0 |
| 19 | 159 28.1 | 143 48.2 | 40.0 | 164 25.5 | 57.3 | 158 00.5 | 35.0 | 191 51.8 | 12.5 | Atria | 107 13.8 | S69 03.9 |
| 20 | 174 30.6 | 158 48.0 | 41.0 | 179 26.3 | 56.5 | 173 02.6 | 34.8 | 206 54.2 | 12.5 | Avior | 234 15.9 | S59 35.1 |
| 21 | 189 33.1 | 173 47.8 . . | 42.1 | 194 27.0 . . | 55.8 | 188 04.6 . . | 34.6 | 221 56.6 . . | 12.5 | Bellatrix | 278 25.6 | N 6 22.1 |
| 22 | 204 35.5 | 188 47.5 | 43.2 | 209 27.7 | 55.1 | 203 06.6 | 34.4 | 236 59.0 | 12.5 | Betelgeuse | 270 54.8 | N 7 24.6 |
| 23 | 219 38.0 | 203 47.3 | 44.2 | 224 28.5 | 54.4 | 218 08.7 | 34.2 | 252 01.4 | 12.5 | | | |
| **17 00** | 234 40.5 | 218 47.0 N 4 45.3 | | 239 29.2 S 3 53.6 | | 233 10.7 S 0 34.1 | | 267 03.7 S14 12.4 | | Canopus | 263 53.8 | S52 42.6 |
| 01 | 249 42.9 | 233 46.8 | 46.3 | 254 29.9 | 52.9 | 248 12.7 | 33.9 | 282 06.1 | 12.4 | Capella | 280 25.6 | N46 01.2 |
| 02 | 264 45.4 | 248 46.6 | 47.4 | 269 30.7 | 52.2 | 263 14.8 | 33.7 | 297 08.5 | 12.4 | Deneb | 49 27.1 | N45 21.3 |
| 03 | 279 47.9 | 263 46.3 . . | 48.5 | 284 31.4 . . | 51.5 | 278 16.8 . . | 33.5 | 312 10.9 . . | 12.4 | Denebola | 182 27.0 | N14 26.9 |
| 04 | 294 50.3 | 278 46.1 | 49.5 | 299 32.1 | 50.7 | 293 18.8 | 33.4 | 327 13.3 | 12.4 | Diphda | 348 49.8 | S17 51.9 |
| 05 | 309 52.8 | 293 45.8 | 50.6 | 314 32.9 | 50.0 | 308 20.9 | 33.2 | 342 15.7 | 12.3 | | | |
| 06 | 324 55.2 | 308 45.6 N 4 51.6 | | 329 33.6 S 3 49.3 | | 323 22.9 S 0 33.0 | | 357 18.1 S14 12.3 | | Dubhe | 193 43.6 | N61 38.1 |
| T 07 | 339 57.7 | 323 45.3 | 52.7 | 344 34.3 | 48.6 | 338 25.0 | 32.8 | 12 20.5 | 12.3 | Elnath | 278 05.0 | N28 37.5 |
| U 08 | 355 00.2 | 338 45.1 | 53.7 | 359 35.1 | 47.8 | 353 27.0 | 32.6 | 27 22.8 | 12.3 | Eltanin | 90 42.8 | N51 29.0 |
| E 09 | 10 02.6 | 353 44.9 . . | 54.8 | 14 35.8 . . | 47.1 | 8 29.0 . . | 32.5 | 42 25.2 . . | 12.3 | Enif | 33 40.9 | N 9 58.4 |
| S 10 | 25 05.1 | 8 44.6 | 55.9 | 29 36.5 | 46.4 | 23 31.1 | 32.3 | 57 27.6 | 12.3 | Fomalhaut | 15 17.1 | S29 30.2 |
| D 11 | 40 07.6 | 23 44.4 | 56.9 | 44 37.3 | 45.6 | 38 33.1 | 32.1 | 72 30.0 | 12.2 | | | |
| A 12 | 55 10.0 | 38 44.1 N 4 58.0 | | 59 38.0 S 3 44.9 | | 53 35.1 S 0 31.9 | | 87 32.4 S14 12.2 | | Gacrux | 171 53.7 | S57 14.5 |
| Y 13 | 70 12.5 | 53 43.9 | 4 59.0 | 74 38.7 | 44.2 | 68 37.2 | 31.8 | 102 34.8 | 12.2 | Gienah | 175 45.7 | S17 40.0 |
| 14 | 85 15.0 | 68 43.6 | 5 00.1 | 89 39.5 | 43.5 | 83 39.2 | 31.6 | 117 37.2 | 12.2 | Hadar | 148 38.5 | S60 28.9 |
| 15 | 100 17.4 | 83 43.4 . . | 01.2 | 104 40.2 . . | 42.7 | 98 41.2 . . | 31.4 | 132 39.6 . . | 12.2 | Hamal | 327 54.0 | N23 33.9 |
| 16 | 115 19.9 | 98 43.2 | 02.2 | 119 40.9 | 42.0 | 113 43.3 | 31.2 | 147 42.0 | 12.1 | Kaus Aust. | 83 35.1 | S34 22.4 |
| 17 | 130 22.4 | 113 42.9 | 03.3 | 134 41.7 | 41.3 | 128 45.3 | 31.1 | 162 44.3 | 12.1 | | | |
| 18 | 145 24.8 | 128 42.7 N 5 04.3 | | 149 42.4 S 3 40.6 | | 143 47.4 S 0 30.9 | | 177 46.7 S14 12.1 | | Kochab | 137 18.7 | N74 03.9 |
| 19 | 160 27.3 | 143 42.4 | 05.4 | 164 43.1 | 39.8 | 158 49.4 | 30.7 | 192 49.1 | 12.1 | Markab | 13 32.2 | N15 19.3 |
| 20 | 175 29.7 | 158 42.2 | 06.5 | 179 43.9 | 39.1 | 173 51.4 | 30.5 | 207 51.5 | 12.1 | Menkar | 314 08.8 | N 4 10.5 |
| 21 | 190 32.2 | 173 41.9 . . | 07.5 | 194 44.6 . . | 38.4 | 188 53.5 . . | 30.4 | 222 53.9 . . | 12.1 | Menkent | 147 59.8 | S36 28.9 |
| 22 | 205 34.7 | 188 41.7 | 08.6 | 209 45.4 | 37.6 | 203 55.5 | 30.2 | 237 56.3 | 12.0 | Miaplacidus | 221 38.8 | S69 48.8 |
| 23 | 220 37.1 | 203 41.4 | 09.6 | 224 46.1 | 36.9 | 218 57.6 | 30.0 | 252 58.7 | 12.0 | | | |
| **18 00** | 235 39.6 | 218 41.2 N 5 10.7 | | 239 46.8 S 3 36.2 | | 233 59.6 S 0 29.8 | | 268 01.1 S14 12.0 | | Mirfak | 308 31.9 | N49 56.3 |
| 01 | 250 42.1 | 233 41.0 | 11.7 | 254 47.6 | 35.5 | 249 01.6 | 29.7 | 283 03.5 | 12.0 | Nunki | 75 50.2 | S26 16.1 |
| 02 | 265 44.5 | 248 40.7 | 12.8 | 269 48.3 | 34.7 | 264 03.7 | 29.5 | 298 05.9 | 12.0 | Peacock | 53 09.0 | S56 39.6 |
| 03 | 280 47.0 | 263 40.5 . . | 13.9 | 284 49.0 . . | 34.0 | 279 05.7 . . | 29.3 | 313 08.3 . . | 12.0 | Pollux | 243 20.2 | N27 58.4 |
| 04 | 295 49.5 | 278 40.2 | 14.9 | 299 49.8 | 33.3 | 294 07.7 | 29.1 | 328 10.6 | 11.9 | Procyon | 244 53.3 | N 5 10.0 |
| 05 | 310 51.9 | 293 40.0 | 16.0 | 314 50.5 | 32.6 | 309 09.8 | 29.0 | 343 13.0 | 11.9 | | | |
| 06 | 325 54.4 | 308 39.7 N 5 17.0 | | 329 51.2 S 3 31.8 | | 324 11.8 S 0 28.8 | | 358 15.4 S14 11.9 | | Rasalhague | 96 00.3 | N12 32.5 |
| W 07 | 340 56.9 | 323 39.5 | 18.1 | 344 52.0 | 31.1 | 339 13.9 | 28.6 | 13 17.8 | 11.9 | Regulus | 207 36.8 | N11 51.5 |
| E 08 | 355 59.3 | 338 39.2 | 19.1 | 359 52.7 | 30.4 | 354 15.9 | 28.4 | 28 20.2 | 11.9 | Rigel | 281 06.3 | S 8 10.7 |
| D 09 | 11 01.8 | 353 39.0 . . | 20.2 | 14 53.4 . . | 29.7 | 9 17.9 . . | 28.2 | 43 22.6 . . | 11.9 | Rigil Kent. | 139 42.7 | S60 55.7 |
| N 10 | 26 04.2 | 8 38.7 | 21.3 | 29 54.2 | 28.9 | 24 20.0 | 28.1 | 58 25.0 | 11.8 | Sabik | 102 05.0 | S15 45.2 |
| E 11 | 41 06.7 | 23 38.5 | 22.3 | 44 54.9 | 28.2 | 39 22.0 | 27.9 | 73 27.4 | 11.8 | | | |
| S 12 | 56 09.2 | 38 38.2 N 5 23.4 | | 59 55.6 S 3 27.5 | | 54 24.1 S 0 27.7 | | 88 29.8 S14 11.8 | | Schedar | 349 33.9 | N56 39.3 |
| D 13 | 71 11.6 | 53 38.0 | 24.4 | 74 56.4 | 26.7 | 69 26.1 | 27.6 | 103 32.2 | 11.8 | Shaula | 96 13.0 | S37 07.1 |
| A 14 | 86 14.1 | 68 37.7 | 25.5 | 89 57.1 | 26.0 | 84 28.1 | 27.4 | 118 34.6 | 11.8 | Sirius | 258 28.4 | S16 44.9 |
| Y 15 | 101 16.6 | 83 37.5 . . | 26.5 | 104 57.9 . . | 25.3 | 99 30.2 . . | 27.2 | 133 37.0 . . | 11.8 | Spica | 158 24.4 | S11 16.7 |
| 16 | 116 19.0 | 98 37.2 | 27.6 | 119 58.6 | 24.6 | 114 32.2 | 27.0 | 148 39.4 | 11.7 | Suhail | 222 48.0 | S43 31.6 |
| 17 | 131 21.5 | 113 37.0 | 28.7 | 134 59.3 | 23.8 | 129 34.3 | 26.9 | 163 41.7 | 11.7 | | | |
| 18 | 146 24.0 | 128 36.7 N 5 29.7 | | 150 00.1 S 3 23.1 | | 144 36.3 S 0 26.7 | | 178 44.1 S14 11.7 | | Vega | 80 34.4 | N38 48.0 |
| 19 | 161 26.4 | 143 36.5 | 30.8 | 165 00.8 | 22.4 | 159 38.4 | 26.5 | 193 46.5 | 11.7 | Zuben'ubi | 136 58.1 | S16 08.1 |
| 20 | 176 28.9 | 158 36.2 | 31.8 | 180 01.5 | 21.7 | 174 40.4 | 26.3 | 208 48.9 | 11.7 | | SHA | Mer. Pass. |
| 21 | 191 31.3 | 173 36.0 . . | 32.9 | 195 02.3 . . | 20.9 | 189 42.4 . . | 26.2 | 223 51.3 . . | 11.7 | | ° ' | h m |
| 22 | 206 33.8 | 188 35.7 | 33.9 | 210 03.0 | 20.2 | 204 44.5 | 26.0 | 238 53.7 | 11.6 | Venus | 344 06.6 | 9 25 |
| 23 | 221 36.3 | 203 35.5 | 35.0 | 225 03.8 | 19.5 | 219 46.5 | 25.8 | 253 56.1 | 11.6 | Mars | 4 48.7 | 8 02 |
| | h m | | | | | | | | | Jupiter | 358 30.2 | 8 26 |
| Mer. Pass. | 8 19.9 | v −0.2 | d 1.1 | v 0.7 | d 0.7 | v 2.0 | d 0.2 | v 2.4 | d 0.0 | Saturn | 32 23.3 | 6 11 |

### SUN and MOON

| UT | SUN GHA | SUN Dec | MOON GHA | v | MOON Dec | d | HP |
|---|---|---|---|---|---|---|---|
| d h | ° ′ | ° ′ | ° ′ | ′ | ° ′ | ′ | ′ |
| **16 00** | 180 54.3 | N19 02.8 | 3 24.3 | 6.7 | S18 27.5 | 12.6 | 60.5 |
| 01 | 195 54.3 | 03.4 | 17 50.0 | 6.6 | 18 40.1 | 12.5 | 60.5 |
| 02 | 210 54.3 | 04.0 | 32 15.6 | 6.4 | 18 52.6 | 12.4 | 60.5 |
| 03 | 225 54.3 .. | 04.5 | 46 41.0 | 6.4 | 19 05.0 | 12.3 | 60.5 |
| 04 | 240 54.3 | 05.1 | 61 06.4 | 6.2 | 19 17.3 | 12.2 | 60.5 |
| 05 | 255 54.3 | 05.7 | 75 31.6 | 6.1 | 19 29.5 | 12.0 | 60.6 |
| 06 | 270 54.2 | N19 06.3 | 89 56.7 | 6.0 | S19 41.5 | 12.0 | 60.6 |
| 07 | 285 54.2 | 06.8 | 104 21.7 | 5.9 | 19 53.5 | 11.8 | 60.6 |
| 08 | 300 54.2 | 07.4 | 118 46.6 | 5.8 | 20 05.3 | 11.7 | 60.6 |
| M 09 | 315 54.2 .. | 08.0 | 133 11.4 | 5.6 | 20 17.0 | 11.5 | 60.6 |
| O 10 | 330 54.2 | 08.6 | 147 36.0 | 5.6 | 20 28.5 | 11.4 | 60.6 |
| N 11 | 345 54.2 | 09.1 | 162 00.6 | 5.4 | 20 39.9 | 11.3 | 60.7 |
| D 12 | 0 54.2 | N19 09.7 | 176 25.0 | 5.3 | S20 51.2 | 11.2 | 60.7 |
| A 13 | 15 54.2 | 10.3 | 190 49.3 | 5.2 | 21 02.4 | 11.0 | 60.7 |
| Y 14 | 30 54.1 | 10.9 | 205 13.5 | 5.1 | 21 13.4 | 10.8 | 60.7 |
| 15 | 45 54.1 .. | 11.4 | 219 37.6 | 5.0 | 21 24.2 | 10.8 | 60.7 |
| 16 | 60 54.1 | 12.0 | 234 01.6 | 4.9 | 21 35.0 | 10.6 | 60.7 |
| 17 | 75 54.1 | 12.6 | 248 25.5 | 4.8 | 21 45.6 | 10.4 | 60.7 |
| 18 | 90 54.1 | N19 13.1 | 262 49.3 | 4.7 | S21 56.0 | 10.3 | 60.7 |
| 19 | 105 54.1 | 13.7 | 277 13.0 | 4.5 | 22 06.3 | 10.1 | 60.8 |
| 20 | 120 54.1 | 14.3 | 291 36.5 | 4.5 | 22 16.4 | 10.0 | 60.8 |
| 21 | 135 54.0 .. | 14.8 | 306 00.0 | 4.3 | 22 26.4 | 9.9 | 60.8 |
| 22 | 150 54.0 | 15.4 | 320 23.3 | 4.3 | 22 36.3 | 9.6 | 60.8 |
| 23 | 165 54.0 | 16.0 | 334 46.6 | 4.1 | 22 45.9 | 9.6 | 60.8 |
| **17 00** | 180 54.0 | N19 16.5 | 349 09.7 | 4.1 | S22 55.5 | 9.3 | 60.8 |
| 01 | 195 54.0 | 17.1 | 3 32.8 | 3.9 | 23 04.8 | 9.2 | 60.8 |
| 02 | 210 54.0 | 17.7 | 17 55.7 | 3.9 | 23 14.0 | 9.1 | 60.8 |
| 03 | 225 53.9 .. | 18.2 | 32 18.6 | 3.7 | 23 23.1 | 8.8 | 60.8 |
| 04 | 240 53.9 | 18.8 | 46 41.3 | 3.7 | 23 31.9 | 8.7 | 60.8 |
| 05 | 255 53.9 | 19.4 | 61 04.0 | 3.6 | 23 40.6 | 8.6 | 60.8 |
| 06 | 270 53.9 | N19 19.9 | 75 26.6 | 3.4 | S23 49.2 | 8.3 | 60.8 |
| 07 | 285 53.9 | 20.5 | 89 49.0 | 3.4 | 23 57.5 | 8.2 | 60.8 |
| T 08 | 300 53.9 | 21.1 | 104 11.4 | 3.3 | 24 05.7 | 8.1 | 60.8 |
| U 09 | 315 53.8 .. | 21.6 | 118 33.7 | 3.2 | 24 13.8 | 7.8 | 60.8 |
| E 10 | 330 53.8 | 22.2 | 132 55.9 | 3.2 | 24 21.6 | 7.7 | 60.9 |
| S 11 | 345 53.8 | 22.7 | 147 18.1 | 3.0 | 24 29.3 | 7.5 | 60.9 |
| D 12 | 0 53.8 | N19 23.3 | 161 40.1 | 3.0 | S24 36.8 | 7.3 | 60.9 |
| A 13 | 15 53.8 | 23.9 | 176 02.1 | 2.9 | 24 44.1 | 7.1 | 60.9 |
| Y 14 | 30 53.7 | 24.4 | 190 24.0 | 2.8 | 24 51.2 | 6.9 | 60.9 |
| 15 | 45 53.7 .. | 25.0 | 204 45.8 | 2.7 | 24 58.1 | 6.8 | 60.9 |
| 16 | 60 53.7 | 25.5 | 219 07.5 | 2.7 | 25 04.9 | 6.6 | 60.9 |
| 17 | 75 53.7 | 26.1 | 233 29.2 | 2.6 | 25 11.5 | 6.4 | 60.9 |
| 18 | 90 53.7 | N19 26.6 | 247 50.8 | 2.5 | S25 17.9 | 6.2 | 60.9 |
| 19 | 105 53.6 | 27.2 | 262 12.3 | 2.4 | 25 24.1 | 6.0 | 60.9 |
| 20 | 120 53.6 | 27.8 | 276 33.7 | 2.5 | 25 30.1 | 5.8 | 60.9 |
| 21 | 135 53.6 .. | 28.3 | 290 55.2 | 2.3 | 25 35.9 | 5.6 | 60.9 |
| 22 | 150 53.6 | 28.9 | 305 16.5 | 2.3 | 25 41.5 | 5.4 | 60.8 |
| 23 | 165 53.6 | 29.4 | 319 37.8 | 2.2 | 25 46.9 | 5.3 | 60.8 |
| **18 00** | 180 53.5 | N19 30.0 | 333 59.0 | 2.2 | S25 52.2 | 5.0 | 60.8 |
| 01 | 195 53.5 | 30.5 | 348 20.2 | 2.1 | 25 57.2 | 4.9 | 60.8 |
| 02 | 210 53.5 | 31.1 | 2 41.3 | 2.1 | 26 02.1 | 4.6 | 60.8 |
| 03 | 225 53.5 .. | 31.6 | 17 02.4 | 2.0 | 26 06.7 | 4.5 | 60.8 |
| 04 | 240 53.4 | 32.2 | 31 23.4 | 2.0 | 26 11.2 | 4.2 | 60.8 |
| 05 | 255 53.4 | 32.7 | 45 44.4 | 2.0 | 26 15.4 | 4.1 | 60.8 |
| 06 | 270 53.4 | N19 33.3 | 60 05.4 | 1.9 | S26 19.5 | 3.8 | 60.8 |
| W 07 | 285 53.4 | 33.8 | 74 26.3 | 1.9 | 26 23.3 | 3.7 | 60.8 |
| E 08 | 300 53.4 | 34.4 | 88 47.2 | 1.9 | 26 27.0 | 3.4 | 60.8 |
| D 09 | 315 53.3 .. | 34.9 | 103 08.1 | 1.8 | 26 30.4 | 3.2 | 60.8 |
| N 10 | 330 53.3 | 35.5 | 117 28.9 | 1.8 | 26 33.6 | 3.1 | 60.8 |
| E 11 | 345 53.3 | 36.0 | 131 49.7 | 1.8 | 26 36.7 | 2.8 | 60.8 |
| S 12 | 0 53.3 | N19 36.6 | 146 10.5 | 1.8 | S26 39.5 | 2.7 | 60.8 |
| D 13 | 15 53.2 | 37.1 | 160 31.3 | 1.7 | 26 42.2 | 2.4 | 60.7 |
| A 14 | 30 53.2 | 37.6 | 174 52.0 | 1.8 | 26 44.6 | 2.2 | 60.7 |
| Y 15 | 45 53.2 .. | 38.2 | 189 12.8 | 1.7 | 26 46.8 | 2.0 | 60.7 |
| 16 | 60 53.1 | 38.7 | 203 33.5 | 1.7 | 26 48.8 | 1.9 | 60.7 |
| 17 | 75 53.1 | 39.3 | 217 54.2 | 1.8 | 26 50.7 | 1.6 | 60.7 |
| 18 | 90 53.1 | N19 39.8 | 232 15.0 | 1.7 | S26 52.3 | 1.4 | 60.7 |
| 19 | 105 53.1 | 40.4 | 246 35.7 | 1.7 | 26 53.7 | 1.2 | 60.7 |
| 20 | 120 53.0 | 40.9 | 260 56.4 | 1.8 | 26 54.9 | 1.0 | 60.7 |
| 21 | 135 53.0 .. | 41.4 | 275 17.2 | 1.8 | 26 55.9 | 0.8 | 60.7 |
| 22 | 150 53.0 | 42.0 | 289 38.0 | 1.7 | 26 56.7 | 0.6 | 60.6 |
| 23 | 165 53.0 | 42.5 | 303 58.7 | 1.8 | S26 57.3 | 0.3 | 60.6 |
| | SD 15.8 | d 0.6 | SD 16.5 | | 16.6 | | 16.6 |

### Twilight, Sunrise and Moonrise

| Lat. | Naut. | Civil | Sunrise | Moonrise 16 | 17 | 18 | 19 |
|---|---|---|---|---|---|---|---|
| ° | h m | h m | h m | h m | h m | h m | h m |
| N 72 | □ | □ | □ | ■ | ■ | ■ | ■ |
| N 70 | □ | □ | □ | ■ | ■ | ■ | ■ |
| 68 | //// | //// | 01 36 | ■ | ■ | ■ | ■ |
| 66 | //// | //// | 02 14 | 23 33 | ■ | ■ | ■ |
| 64 | //// | 00 53 | 02 41 | 22 40 | ■ | ■ | ■ |
| 62 | //// | 01 43 | 03 01 | 22 08 | 24 12 | 00 12 | 01 50 |
| 60 | //// | 02 13 | 03 18 | 21 44 | 23 34 | 25 00 | 01 00 |
| N 58 | 00 47 | 02 35 | 03 32 | 21 25 | 23 07 | 24 28 | 00 28 |
| 56 | 01 33 | 02 53 | 03 44 | 21 09 | 22 46 | 24 05 | 00 05 |
| 54 | 02 01 | 03 08 | 03 54 | 20 56 | 22 28 | 23 46 | 24 41 |
| 52 | 02 22 | 03 21 | 04 03 | 20 44 | 22 13 | 23 29 | 24 26 |
| 50 | 02 39 | 03 32 | 04 12 | 20 34 | 22 00 | 23 15 | 24 13 |
| 45 | 03 11 | 03 55 | 04 29 | 20 12 | 21 34 | 22 47 | 23 47 |
| N 40 | 03 34 | 04 12 | 04 43 | 19 55 | 21 13 | 22 25 | 23 26 |
| 35 | 03 53 | 04 27 | 04 55 | 19 40 | 20 55 | 22 06 | 23 08 |
| 30 | 04 08 | 04 39 | 05 06 | 19 28 | 20 41 | 21 50 | 22 53 |
| 20 | 04 32 | 05 00 | 05 23 | 19 06 | 20 15 | 21 23 | 22 27 |
| N 10 | 04 50 | 05 16 | 05 39 | 18 48 | 19 54 | 21 00 | 22 04 |
| 0 | 05 05 | 05 31 | 05 53 | 18 31 | 19 33 | 20 39 | 21 44 |
| S 10 | 05 19 | 05 45 | 06 07 | 18 14 | 19 13 | 20 17 | 21 23 |
| 20 | 05 32 | 05 59 | 06 22 | 17 56 | 18 52 | 19 54 | 21 00 |
| 30 | 05 45 | 06 14 | 06 39 | 17 35 | 18 27 | 19 28 | 20 34 |
| 35 | 05 51 | 06 22 | 06 49 | 17 23 | 18 13 | 19 12 | 20 19 |
| 40 | 05 58 | 06 31 | 07 00 | 17 09 | 17 56 | 18 54 | 20 01 |
| 45 | 06 05 | 06 41 | 07 13 | 16 53 | 17 36 | 18 32 | 19 40 |
| S 50 | 06 14 | 06 53 | 07 29 | 16 33 | 17 11 | 18 04 | 19 12 |
| 52 | 06 17 | 06 59 | 07 37 | 16 24 | 17 00 | 17 50 | 18 59 |
| 54 | 06 21 | 07 05 | 07 45 | 16 14 | 16 46 | 17 35 | 18 44 |
| 56 | 06 25 | 07 12 | 07 55 | 16 02 | 16 30 | 17 17 | 18 26 |
| 58 | 06 30 | 07 19 | 08 05 | 15 48 | 16 12 | 16 54 | 18 04 |
| S 60 | 06 35 | 07 27 | 08 18 | 15 33 | 15 49 | 16 25 | 17 36 |

### Sunset, Twilight and Moonset

| Lat. | Sunset | Civil | Naut. | Moonset 16 | 17 | 18 | 19 |
|---|---|---|---|---|---|---|---|
| ° | h m | h m | h m | h m | h m | h m | h m |
| N 72 | □ | □ | □ | ■ | ■ | ■ | ■ |
| N 70 | □ | □ | □ | 01 09 | ■ | ■ | ■ |
| 68 | 22 22 | //// | //// | 01 56 | ■ | ■ | ■ |
| 66 | 21 42 | //// | //// | 02 27 | 01 44 | ■ | ■ |
| 64 | 21 14 | 23 09 | //// | 02 50 | 02 37 | ■ | ■ |
| 62 | 20 53 | 22 14 | //// | 03 09 | 03 10 | 03 19 | 03 59 |
| 60 | 20 37 | 21 43 | //// | 03 24 | 03 35 | 03 58 | 04 49 |
| N 58 | 20 22 | 21 20 | 23 14 | 03 37 | 03 54 | 04 25 | 05 21 |
| 56 | 20 10 | 21 01 | 22 24 | 03 49 | 04 11 | 04 47 | 05 44 |
| 54 | 20 00 | 20 46 | 21 55 | 03 59 | 04 25 | 05 04 | 06 03 |
| 52 | 19 50 | 20 33 | 21 33 | 04 08 | 04 37 | 05 20 | 06 19 |
| 50 | 19 42 | 20 22 | 21 16 | 04 16 | 04 48 | 05 33 | 06 33 |
| 45 | 19 25 | 19 59 | 20 43 | 04 33 | 05 11 | 06 00 | 07 02 |
| N 40 | 19 10 | 19 41 | 20 19 | 04 47 | 05 29 | 06 21 | 07 24 |
| 35 | 18 58 | 19 26 | 20 01 | 05 00 | 05 45 | 06 39 | 07 43 |
| 30 | 18 48 | 19 14 | 19 46 | 05 10 | 05 58 | 06 55 | 07 59 |
| 20 | 18 30 | 18 54 | 19 22 | 05 28 | 06 21 | 07 21 | 08 25 |
| N 10 | 18 14 | 18 37 | 19 03 | 05 44 | 06 41 | 07 43 | 08 48 |
| 0 | 18 00 | 18 22 | 18 47 | 05 59 | 07 00 | 08 04 | 09 10 |
| S 10 | 17 46 | 18 08 | 18 34 | 06 15 | 07 19 | 08 25 | 09 31 |
| 20 | 17 31 | 17 54 | 18 21 | 06 31 | 07 39 | 08 48 | 09 54 |
| 30 | 17 14 | 17 39 | 18 08 | 06 49 | 08 02 | 09 14 | 10 21 |
| 35 | 17 04 | 17 31 | 18 01 | 07 00 | 08 16 | 09 30 | 10 36 |
| 40 | 16 52 | 17 22 | 17 55 | 07 13 | 08 32 | 09 48 | 10 54 |
| 45 | 16 39 | 17 11 | 17 47 | 07 28 | 08 51 | 10 09 | 11 16 |
| S 50 | 16 23 | 16 59 | 17 39 | 07 45 | 09 15 | 10 37 | 11 44 |
| 52 | 16 15 | 16 53 | 17 35 | 07 55 | 09 27 | 10 50 | 11 57 |
| 54 | 16 07 | 16 47 | 17 31 | 08 05 | 09 40 | 11 06 | 12 13 |
| 56 | 15 58 | 16 41 | 17 27 | 08 16 | 09 55 | 11 24 | 12 31 |
| 58 | 15 47 | 16 33 | 17 22 | 08 28 | 10 13 | 11 46 | 12 53 |
| S 60 | 15 35 | 16 25 | 17 17 | 08 43 | 10 35 | 12 15 | 13 21 |

### SUN and MOON notes

| Day | SUN Eqn. of Time 00h | 12h | Mer. Pass. | MOON Mer. Pass. Upper | Lower | Age | Phase |
|---|---|---|---|---|---|---|---|
| d | m s | m s | h m | h m | h m | d | % |
| 16 | 03 37 | 03 37 | 11 56 | 24 45 | 12 15 | 16 | 100 |
| 17 | 03 36 | 03 35 | 11 56 | 00 45 | 13 17 | 17 | 97 |
| 18 | 03 34 | 03 33 | 11 56 | 01 49 | 14 21 | 18 | 92 |

| UT | ARIES | VENUS −4.0 | | MARS +0.7 | | JUPITER −2.2 | | SATURN +0.6 | | STARS | | |
|---|---|---|---|---|---|---|---|---|---|---|---|---|
| | GHA | GHA | Dec | GHA | Dec | GHA | Dec | GHA | Dec | Name | SHA | Dec |
| d h | ° ′ | ° ′ | ° ′ | ° ′ | ° ′ | ° ′ | ° ′ | ° ′ | ° ′ | | ° ′ | ° ′ |
| 19 00 | 236 38.7 | 218 35.2 | N 5 36.1 | 240 04.5 | S 3 18.7 | 234 48.6 | S 0 25.6 | 268 58.5 | S14 11.6 | Acamar | 315 13.9 | S40 13.0 |
| 01 | 251 41.2 | 233 35.0 | 37.1 | 255 05.2 | 18.0 | 249 50.6 | ·· 25.5 | 284 00.9 | 11.6 | Achernar | 335 22.4 | S57 07.3 |
| 02 | 266 43.7 | 248 34.7 | 38.2 | 270 06.0 | 17.3 | 264 52.7 | 25.3 | 299 03.3 | 11.6 | Acrux | 173 02.0 | S63 13.6 |
| 03 | 281 46.1 | 263 34.5 | ·· 39.2 | 285 06.7 | ·· 16.6 | 279 54.7 | ·· 25.1 | 314 05.7 | ·· 11.6 | Adhara | 255 07.9 | S29 00.3 |
| 04 | 296 48.6 | 278 34.2 | 40.3 | 300 07.4 | 15.8 | 294 56.7 | 24.9 | 329 08.1 | 11.5 | Aldebaran | 290 42.5 | N16 33.1 |
| 05 | 311 51.1 | 293 34.0 | 41.3 | 315 08.2 | 15.1 | 309 58.8 | 24.8 | 344 10.5 | 11.5 | | | |
| 06 | 326 53.5 | 308 33.7 | N 5 42.4 | 330 08.9 | S 3 14.4 | 325 00.8 | S 0 24.6 | 359 12.9 | S14 11.5 | Alioth | 166 14.5 | N55 50.6 |
| 07 | 341 56.0 | 323 33.5 | 43.4 | 345 09.6 | 13.6 | 340 02.9 | 24.4 | 14 15.3 | 11.5 | Alkaid | 152 53.3 | N49 12.3 |
| T 08 | 356 58.5 | 338 33.2 | 44.5 | 0 10.4 | 12.9 | 355 04.9 | 24.2 | 29 17.7 | 11.5 | Alnair | 27 35.7 | S46 51.0 |
| H 09 | 12 00.9 | 353 33.0 | ·· 45.6 | 15 11.1 | ·· 12.2 | 10 07.0 | ·· 24.1 | 44 20.1 | ·· 11.5 | Alnilam | 275 40.3 | S 1 11.4 |
| U 10 | 27 03.4 | 8 32.7 | 46.6 | 30 11.9 | 11.5 | 25 09.0 | 23.9 | 59 22.5 | 11.4 | Alphard | 217 50.0 | S 8 45.4 |
| R 11 | 42 05.8 | 23 32.5 | 47.7 | 45 12.6 | 10.7 | 40 11.0 | 23.7 | 74 24.9 | 11.4 | | | |
| S 12 | 57 08.3 | 38 32.2 | N 5 48.7 | 60 13.3 | S 3 10.0 | 55 13.1 | S 0 23.5 | 89 27.2 | S14 11.4 | Alphecca | 126 05.2 | N26 38.4 |
| D 13 | 72 10.8 | 53 32.0 | 49.8 | 75 14.1 | 09.3 | 70 15.1 | 23.4 | 104 29.6 | 11.4 | Alpheratz | 357 37.2 | N29 12.5 |
| A 14 | 87 13.2 | 68 31.7 | 50.8 | 90 14.8 | 08.6 | 85 17.2 | 23.2 | 119 32.0 | 11.4 | Altair | 62 01.9 | N 8 55.5 |
| Y 15 | 102 15.7 | 83 31.5 | ·· 51.9 | 105 15.6 | ·· 07.8 | 100 19.2 | ·· 23.0 | 134 34.4 | ·· 11.4 | Ankaa | 353 09.6 | S42 11.0 |
| 16 | 117 18.2 | 98 31.2 | 52.9 | 120 16.3 | 07.1 | 115 21.3 | 22.9 | 149 36.8 | 11.4 | Antares | 112 18.2 | S26 28.9 |
| 17 | 132 20.6 | 113 30.9 | 54.0 | 135 17.0 | 06.4 | 130 23.3 | 22.7 | 164 39.2 | 11.3 | | | |
| 18 | 147 23.1 | 128 30.7 | N 5 55.0 | 150 17.8 | S 3 05.6 | 145 25.4 | S 0 22.5 | 179 41.6 | S14 11.3 | Arcturus | 145 49.6 | N19 04.0 |
| 19 | 162 25.6 | 143 30.4 | 56.1 | 165 18.5 | 04.9 | 160 27.4 | 22.3 | 194 44.0 | 11.3 | Atria | 107 13.8 | S69 03.9 |
| 20 | 177 28.0 | 158 30.2 | 57.2 | 180 19.2 | 04.2 | 175 29.4 | 22.2 | 209 46.4 | 11.3 | Avior | 234 15.9 | S59 35.1 |
| 21 | 192 30.5 | 173 29.9 | ·· 58.2 | 195 20.0 | ·· 03.5 | 190 31.5 | ·· 22.0 | 224 48.8 | ·· 11.3 | Bellatrix | 278 25.5 | N 6 22.1 |
| 22 | 207 33.0 | 188 29.7 | 5 59.3 | 210 20.7 | 02.7 | 205 33.5 | 21.8 | 239 51.2 | 11.3 | Betelgeuse | 270 54.8 | N 7 24.6 |
| 23 | 222 35.4 | 203 29.4 | 6 00.3 | 225 21.5 | 02.0 | 220 35.6 | 21.6 | 254 53.6 | 11.3 | | | |
| 20 00 | 237 37.9 | 218 29.1 | N 6 01.4 | 240 22.2 | S 3 01.3 | 235 37.6 | S 0 21.5 | 269 56.0 | S14 11.2 | Canopus | 263 53.8 | S52 42.6 |
| 01 | 252 40.3 | 233 28.9 | 02.4 | 255 22.9 | 3 00.5 | 250 39.7 | 21.3 | 284 58.4 | 11.2 | Capella | 280 25.6 | N46 01.2 |
| 02 | 267 42.8 | 248 28.6 | 03.5 | 270 23.7 | 2 59.8 | 265 41.7 | 21.1 | 300 00.8 | 11.2 | Deneb | 49 27.1 | N45 21.3 |
| 03 | 282 45.3 | 263 28.4 | ·· 04.5 | 285 24.4 | ·· 59.1 | 280 43.8 | ·· 21.0 | 315 03.2 | ·· 11.2 | Denebola | 182 27.0 | N14 26.9 |
| 04 | 297 47.7 | 278 28.1 | 05.6 | 300 25.2 | 58.4 | 295 45.8 | 20.8 | 330 05.6 | 11.2 | Diphda | 348 49.7 | S17 51.9 |
| 05 | 312 50.2 | 293 27.9 | 06.6 | 315 25.9 | 57.6 | 310 47.9 | 20.6 | 345 08.0 | 11.2 | | | |
| 06 | 327 52.7 | 308 27.6 | N 6 07.7 | 330 26.6 | S 2 56.9 | 325 49.9 | S 0 20.4 | 0 10.4 | S14 11.2 | Dubhe | 193 43.6 | N61 38.2 |
| 07 | 342 55.1 | 323 27.3 | 08.7 | 345 27.4 | 56.2 | 340 52.0 | 20.3 | 15 12.8 | 11.1 | Elnath | 278 05.0 | N28 37.5 |
| 08 | 357 57.6 | 338 27.1 | 09.8 | 0 28.1 | 55.5 | 355 54.0 | 20.1 | 30 15.2 | 11.1 | Eltanin | 90 42.7 | N51 29.0 |
| F 09 | 13 00.1 | 353 26.8 | ·· 10.9 | 15 28.9 | ·· 54.7 | 10 56.1 | ·· 19.9 | 45 17.6 | ·· 11.1 | Enif | 33 40.9 | N 9 58.5 |
| R 10 | 28 02.5 | 8 26.6 | 11.9 | 30 29.6 | 54.0 | 25 58.1 | 19.8 | 60 20.0 | 11.1 | Fomalhaut | 15 17.0 | S29 30.2 |
| I 11 | 43 05.0 | 23 26.3 | 13.0 | 45 30.3 | 53.3 | 41 00.1 | 19.6 | 75 22.4 | 11.1 | | | |
| D 12 | 58 07.5 | 38 26.0 | N 6 14.0 | 60 31.1 | S 2 52.5 | 56 02.2 | S 0 19.4 | 90 24.8 | S14 11.1 | Gacrux | 171 53.7 | S57 14.5 |
| A 13 | 73 09.9 | 53 25.8 | 15.1 | 75 31.8 | 51.8 | 71 04.2 | 19.2 | 105 27.2 | 11.1 | Gienah | 175 45.7 | S17 40.0 |
| Y 14 | 88 12.4 | 68 25.5 | 16.1 | 90 32.6 | 51.1 | 86 06.3 | 19.1 | 120 29.6 | 11.0 | Hadar | 148 38.5 | S60 28.9 |
| 15 | 103 14.8 | 83 25.3 | ·· 17.2 | 105 33.3 | ·· 50.4 | 101 08.3 | ·· 18.9 | 135 32.0 | ·· 11.0 | Hamal | 327 54.0 | N23 33.9 |
| 16 | 118 17.3 | 98 25.0 | 18.2 | 120 34.0 | 49.6 | 116 10.4 | 18.7 | 150 34.4 | 11.0 | Kaus Aust. | 83 35.1 | S34 22.4 |
| 17 | 133 19.8 | 113 24.7 | 19.3 | 135 34.8 | 48.9 | 131 12.4 | 18.6 | 165 36.8 | 11.0 | | | |
| 18 | 148 22.2 | 128 24.5 | N 6 20.3 | 150 35.5 | S 2 48.2 | 146 14.5 | S 0 18.4 | 180 39.2 | S14 11.0 | Kochab | 137 18.7 | N74 03.9 |
| 19 | 163 24.7 | 143 24.2 | 21.4 | 165 36.3 | 47.4 | 161 16.5 | 18.2 | 195 41.6 | 11.0 | Markab | 13 32.2 | N15 19.3 |
| 20 | 178 27.2 | 158 24.0 | 22.4 | 180 37.0 | 46.7 | 176 18.6 | 18.0 | 210 44.0 | 11.0 | Menkar | 314 08.8 | N 4 10.5 |
| 21 | 193 29.6 | 173 23.7 | ·· 23.5 | 195 37.7 | ·· 46.0 | 191 20.6 | ·· 17.9 | 225 46.4 | ·· 10.9 | Menkent | 147 59.8 | S36 28.9 |
| 22 | 208 32.1 | 188 23.4 | 24.5 | 210 38.5 | 45.3 | 206 22.7 | 17.7 | 240 48.8 | 10.9 | Miaplacidus | 221 38.9 | S69 48.8 |
| 23 | 223 34.6 | 203 23.2 | 25.6 | 225 39.2 | 44.5 | 221 24.7 | 17.5 | 255 51.2 | 10.9 | | | |
| 21 00 | 238 37.0 | 218 22.9 | N 6 26.6 | 240 40.0 | S 2 43.8 | 236 26.8 | S 0 17.4 | 270 53.6 | S14 10.9 | Mirfak | 308 31.9 | N49 56.3 |
| 01 | 253 39.5 | 233 22.6 | 27.7 | 255 40.7 | 43.1 | 251 28.8 | 17.2 | 285 56.0 | 10.9 | Nunki | 75 50.2 | S26 16.1 |
| 02 | 268 42.0 | 248 22.4 | 28.7 | 270 41.4 | 42.3 | 266 30.9 | 17.0 | 300 58.4 | 10.9 | Peacock | 53 08.9 | S56 39.6 |
| 03 | 283 44.4 | 263 22.1 | ·· 29.8 | 285 42.2 | ·· 41.6 | 281 32.9 | ·· 16.9 | 316 00.8 | ·· 10.9 | Pollux | 243 20.2 | N27 58.4 |
| 04 | 298 46.9 | 278 21.8 | 30.8 | 300 42.9 | 40.9 | 296 35.0 | 16.7 | 331 03.2 | 10.8 | Procyon | 244 53.3 | N 5 10.0 |
| 05 | 313 49.3 | 293 21.6 | 31.9 | 315 43.7 | 40.2 | 311 37.0 | 16.5 | 346 05.6 | 10.8 | | | |
| 06 | 328 51.8 | 308 21.3 | N 6 32.9 | 330 44.4 | S 2 39.4 | 326 39.1 | S 0 16.3 | 1 08.0 | S14 10.8 | Rasalhague | 96 00.3 | N12 32.5 |
| 07 | 343 54.3 | 323 21.1 | 34.0 | 345 45.1 | 38.7 | 341 41.1 | 16.2 | 16 10.4 | 10.8 | Regulus | 207 36.8 | N11 51.5 |
| S 08 | 358 56.7 | 338 20.8 | 35.0 | 0 45.9 | 38.0 | 356 43.2 | 16.0 | 31 12.8 | 10.8 | Rigel | 281 06.3 | S 8 10.7 |
| A 09 | 13 59.2 | 353 20.5 | ·· 36.1 | 15 46.6 | ·· 37.3 | 11 45.2 | ·· 15.8 | 46 15.3 | ·· 10.8 | Rigil Kent. | 139 42.7 | S60 55.7 |
| T 10 | 29 01.7 | 8 20.3 | 37.1 | 30 47.4 | 36.5 | 26 47.3 | 15.7 | 61 17.7 | 10.8 | Sabik | 102 05.0 | S15 45.2 |
| U 11 | 44 04.1 | 23 20.0 | 38.2 | 45 48.1 | 35.8 | 41 49.3 | 15.5 | 76 20.1 | 10.8 | | | |
| R 12 | 59 06.6 | 38 19.7 | N 6 39.2 | 60 48.8 | S 2 35.1 | 56 51.4 | S 0 15.3 | 91 22.5 | S14 10.7 | Schedar | 349 33.9 | N56 39.3 |
| D 13 | 74 09.1 | 53 19.5 | 40.3 | 75 49.6 | 34.3 | 71 53.4 | 15.2 | 106 24.9 | 10.7 | Shaula | 96 13.0 | S37 07.1 |
| A 14 | 89 11.5 | 68 19.2 | 41.3 | 90 50.3 | 33.6 | 86 55.5 | 15.0 | 121 27.3 | 10.7 | Sirius | 258 28.4 | S16 44.9 |
| Y 15 | 104 14.0 | 83 18.9 | ·· 42.4 | 105 51.1 | ·· 32.9 | 101 57.6 | ·· 14.8 | 136 29.7 | ·· 10.7 | Spica | 158 24.4 | S11 16.7 |
| 16 | 119 16.5 | 98 18.7 | 43.4 | 120 51.8 | 32.2 | 116 59.6 | 14.6 | 151 32.1 | 10.7 | Suhail | 222 48.0 | S43 31.6 |
| 17 | 134 18.9 | 113 18.4 | 44.5 | 135 52.6 | 31.4 | 132 01.7 | 14.5 | 166 34.5 | 10.7 | | | |
| 18 | 149 21.4 | 128 18.1 | N 6 45.5 | 150 53.3 | S 2 30.7 | 147 03.7 | S 0 14.3 | 181 36.9 | S14 10.7 | Vega | 80 34.4 | N38 48.1 |
| 19 | 164 23.8 | 143 17.9 | 46.6 | 165 54.0 | 30.0 | 162 05.8 | 14.1 | 196 39.3 | 10.7 | Zuben'ubi | 136 58.1 | S16 08.1 |
| 20 | 179 26.3 | 158 17.6 | 47.6 | 180 54.8 | 29.2 | 177 07.8 | 14.0 | 211 41.7 | 10.6 | | SHA | Mer. Pass. |
| 21 | 194 28.8 | 173 17.3 | ·· 48.7 | 195 55.5 | ·· 28.5 | 192 09.9 | ·· 13.8 | 226 44.1 | ·· 10.6 | | ° ′ | h m |
| 22 | 209 31.2 | 188 17.0 | 49.7 | 210 56.3 | 27.8 | 207 11.9 | 13.6 | 241 46.5 | 10.6 | Venus | 340 51.3 | 9 26 |
| 23 | 224 33.7 | 203 16.8 | 50.8 | 225 57.0 | 27.1 | 222 14.0 | 13.5 | 256 48.9 | 10.6 | Mars | 2 44.3 | 7 58 |
| | h m | | | | | | | | | Jupiter | 357 59.7 | 8 16 |
| Mer. Pass. 8 08.1 | | v −0.3 | d 1.1 | v 0.7 | d 0.7 | v 2.0 | d 0.2 | v 2.4 | d 0.0 | Saturn | 32 18.1 | 5 59 |

| UT | SUN GHA | SUN Dec | MOON GHA | v | MOON Dec | d | HP |
|---|---|---|---|---|---|---|---|
| d h | ° ' | ° ' | ° ' | ' | ° ' | ' | ' |
| **19** 00 | 180 52.9 | N19 43.1 | 318 19.5 | 1.8 | S26 57.6 | 0.2 | 60.6 |
| 01 | 195 52.9 | 43.6 | 332 40.3 | 1.8 | 26 57.8 | 0.0 | 60.6 |
| 02 | 210 52.9 | 44.1 | 347 01.1 | 1.9 | 26 57.8 | 0.2 | 60.6 |
| 03 | 225 52.8 | .. 44.7 | 1 22.0 | 1.9 | 26 57.6 | 0.5 | 60.6 |
| 04 | 240 52.8 | 45.2 | 15 42.9 | 1.9 | 26 57.1 | 0.6 | 60.5 |
| 05 | 255 52.8 | 45.7 | 30 03.8 | 1.9 | 26 56.5 | 0.8 | 60.5 |
| 06 | 270 52.8 | N19 46.3 | 44 24.7 | 2.0 | S26 55.7 | 1.1 | 60.5 |
| 07 | 285 52.7 | 46.8 | 58 45.7 | 2.1 | 26 54.6 | 1.2 | 60.5 |
| T 08 | 300 52.7 | 47.4 | 73 06.8 | 2.0 | 26 53.4 | 1.5 | 60.5 |
| H 09 | 315 52.7 | .. 47.9 | 87 27.8 | 2.1 | 26 51.9 | 1.6 | 60.5 |
| U 10 | 330 52.6 | 48.4 | 101 48.9 | 2.2 | 26 50.3 | 1.8 | 60.4 |
| R 11 | 345 52.6 | 49.0 | 116 10.1 | 2.2 | 26 48.5 | 2.1 | 60.4 |
| S 12 | 0 52.6 | N19 49.5 | 130 31.3 | 2.3 | S26 46.4 | 2.2 | 60.4 |
| D 13 | 15 52.5 | 50.0 | 144 52.6 | 2.3 | 26 44.2 | 2.4 | 60.4 |
| A 14 | 30 52.5 | 50.5 | 159 13.9 | 2.4 | 26 41.8 | 2.7 | 60.4 |
| Y 15 | 45 52.5 | .. 51.1 | 173 35.3 | 2.5 | 26 39.1 | 2.8 | 60.3 |
| 16 | 60 52.5 | 51.6 | 187 56.8 | 2.5 | 26 36.3 | 3.0 | 60.3 |
| 17 | 75 52.4 | 52.1 | 202 18.3 | 2.6 | 26 33.3 | 3.2 | 60.3 |
| 18 | 90 52.4 | N19 52.7 | 216 39.9 | 2.6 | S26 30.1 | 3.4 | 60.3 |
| 19 | 105 52.4 | 53.2 | 231 01.5 | 2.8 | 26 26.7 | 3.6 | 60.3 |
| 20 | 120 52.3 | 53.7 | 245 23.3 | 2.8 | 26 23.1 | 3.8 | 60.2 |
| 21 | 135 52.3 | .. 54.2 | 259 45.1 | 2.9 | 26 19.3 | 3.9 | 60.2 |
| 22 | 150 52.3 | 54.8 | 274 07.0 | 2.9 | 26 15.4 | 4.2 | 60.2 |
| 23 | 165 52.2 | 55.3 | 288 28.9 | 3.1 | 26 11.2 | 4.3 | 60.2 |
| **20** 00 | 180 52.2 | N19 55.8 | 302 51.0 | 3.1 | S26 06.9 | 4.5 | 60.2 |
| 01 | 195 52.2 | 56.3 | 317 13.1 | 3.2 | 26 02.4 | 4.7 | 60.1 |
| 02 | 210 52.1 | 56.9 | 331 35.3 | 3.3 | 25 57.7 | 4.9 | 60.1 |
| 03 | 225 52.1 | .. 57.4 | 345 57.6 | 3.4 | 25 52.8 | 5.1 | 60.1 |
| 04 | 240 52.1 | 57.9 | 0 20.0 | 3.5 | 25 47.7 | 5.2 | 60.1 |
| 05 | 255 52.0 | 58.4 | 14 42.5 | 3.6 | 25 42.5 | 5.4 | 60.0 |
| 06 | 270 52.0 | N19 59.0 | 29 05.1 | 3.7 | S25 37.1 | 5.6 | 60.0 |
| 07 | 285 51.9 | 19 59.5 | 43 27.8 | 3.8 | 25 31.5 | 5.8 | 60.0 |
| F 08 | 300 51.9 | 20 00.0 | 57 50.6 | 3.9 | 25 25.7 | 5.9 | 60.0 |
| R 09 | 315 51.9 | .. 00.5 | 72 13.5 | 3.9 | 25 19.8 | 6.1 | 59.9 |
| I 10 | 330 51.8 | 01.0 | 86 36.4 | 4.1 | 25 13.7 | 6.3 | 59.9 |
| D 11 | 345 51.8 | 01.6 | 100 59.5 | 4.2 | 25 07.4 | 6.5 | 59.9 |
| A 12 | 0 51.8 | N20 02.1 | 115 22.7 | 4.3 | S25 00.9 | 6.6 | 59.9 |
| Y 13 | 15 51.7 | 02.6 | 129 46.0 | 4.4 | 24 54.3 | 6.7 | 59.8 |
| 14 | 30 51.7 | 03.1 | 144 09.4 | 4.5 | 24 47.6 | 7.0 | 59.8 |
| 15 | 45 51.7 | .. 03.6 | 158 32.9 | 4.6 | 24 40.6 | 7.1 | 59.8 |
| 16 | 60 51.6 | 04.1 | 172 56.5 | 4.8 | 24 33.5 | 7.2 | 59.8 |
| 17 | 75 51.6 | 04.7 | 187 20.3 | 4.8 | 24 26.3 | 7.4 | 59.7 |
| 18 | 90 51.5 | N20 05.2 | 201 44.1 | 5.0 | S24 18.9 | 7.6 | 59.7 |
| 19 | 105 51.5 | 05.7 | 216 08.1 | 5.0 | 24 11.3 | 7.7 | 59.7 |
| 20 | 120 51.5 | 06.2 | 230 32.1 | 5.2 | 24 03.6 | 7.9 | 59.6 |
| 21 | 135 51.4 | .. 06.7 | 244 56.3 | 5.3 | 23 55.7 | 8.0 | 59.6 |
| 22 | 150 51.4 | 07.2 | 259 20.6 | 5.4 | 23 47.7 | 8.2 | 59.6 |
| 23 | 165 51.3 | 07.7 | 273 45.0 | 5.6 | 23 39.5 | 8.3 | 59.6 |
| **21** 00 | 180 51.3 | N20 08.2 | 288 09.6 | 5.6 | S23 31.2 | 8.5 | 59.5 |
| 01 | 195 51.3 | 08.7 | 302 34.2 | 5.8 | 23 22.7 | 8.6 | 59.5 |
| 02 | 210 51.2 | 09.3 | 316 59.0 | 5.9 | 23 14.1 | 8.7 | 59.5 |
| 03 | 225 51.2 | .. 09.8 | 331 23.9 | 6.0 | 23 05.4 | 8.9 | 59.4 |
| 04 | 240 51.1 | 10.3 | 345 48.9 | 6.1 | 22 56.5 | 9.0 | 59.4 |
| 05 | 255 51.1 | 10.8 | 0 14.0 | 6.3 | 22 47.5 | 9.2 | 59.4 |
| 06 | 270 51.1 | N20 11.3 | 14 39.3 | 6.4 | S22 38.3 | 9.2 | 59.4 |
| 07 | 285 51.0 | 11.8 | 29 04.7 | 6.5 | 22 29.1 | 9.5 | 59.3 |
| S 08 | 300 51.0 | 12.3 | 43 30.2 | 6.6 | 22 19.6 | 9.5 | 59.3 |
| A 09 | 315 50.9 | .. 12.8 | 57 55.8 | 6.7 | 22 10.1 | 9.7 | 59.3 |
| T 10 | 330 50.9 | 13.3 | 72 21.5 | 6.9 | 22 00.4 | 9.8 | 59.2 |
| U 11 | 345 50.9 | 13.8 | 86 47.4 | 7.0 | 21 50.6 | 9.9 | 59.2 |
| R 12 | 0 50.8 | N20 14.3 | 101 13.4 | 7.1 | S21 40.7 | 10.1 | 59.2 |
| D 13 | 15 50.8 | 14.8 | 115 39.5 | 7.2 | 21 30.6 | 10.2 | 59.2 |
| A 14 | 30 50.7 | 15.3 | 130 05.7 | 7.4 | 21 20.5 | 10.3 | 59.1 |
| Y 15 | 45 50.7 | .. 15.8 | 144 32.1 | 7.4 | 21 10.2 | 10.4 | 59.1 |
| 16 | 60 50.6 | 16.3 | 158 58.5 | 7.6 | 20 59.8 | 10.5 | 59.1 |
| 17 | 75 50.6 | 16.8 | 173 25.1 | 7.7 | 20 49.3 | 10.7 | 59.0 |
| 18 | 90 50.6 | N20 17.3 | 187 51.8 | 7.9 | S20 38.6 | 10.7 | 59.0 |
| 19 | 105 50.5 | 17.8 | 202 18.7 | 7.9 | 20 27.9 | 10.8 | 59.0 |
| 20 | 120 50.5 | 18.3 | 216 45.6 | 8.1 | 20 17.1 | 11.0 | 58.9 |
| 21 | 135 50.4 | .. 18.8 | 231 12.7 | 8.2 | 20 06.1 | 11.1 | 58.9 |
| 22 | 150 50.4 | 19.3 | 245 39.9 | 8.3 | 19 55.0 | 11.1 | 58.9 |
| 23 | 165 50.3 | 19.8 | 260 07.2 | 8.5 | S19 43.9 | 11.3 | 58.9 |
| | SD 15.8 | d 0.5 | SD 16.5 | | 16.3 | | 16.1 |

| Lat. | Naut. | Civil | Sunrise | Moonrise 19 | 20 | 21 | 22 |
|---|---|---|---|---|---|---|---|
| ° | h m | h m | h m | h m | h m | h m | h m |
| N 72 | □ | □ | □ | ■ | ■ | ■ | ■ |
| N 70 | □ | □ | □ | ■ | ■ | ■ | 04 29 |
| 68 | //// | //// | 01 17 | ■ | ■ | ■ | 03 43 |
| 66 | //// | //// | 02 02 | ■ | ■ | 03 50 | 03 12 |
| 64 | //// | 00 14 | 02 32 | ■ | 03 47 | 03 01 | 02 49 |
| 62 | //// | 01 29 | 02 54 | 01 50 | 02 23 | 02 30 | 02 31 |
| 60 | //// | 02 03 | 03 11 | 01 00 | 01 46 | 02 06 | 02 16 |
| N 58 | 00 12 | 02 27 | 03 26 | 00 28 | 01 20 | 01 47 | 02 03 |
| 56 | 01 21 | 02 47 | 03 39 | 00 05 | 00 59 | 01 31 | 01 51 |
| 54 | 01 52 | 03 02 | 03 50 | 24 41 | 00 41 | 01 18 | 01 41 |
| 52 | 02 15 | 03 16 | 03 59 | 24 26 | 00 26 | 01 06 | 01 32 |
| 50 | 02 33 | 03 27 | 04 08 | 24 13 | 00 13 | 00 55 | 01 24 |
| 45 | 03 06 | 03 51 | 04 26 | 23 47 | 24 32 | 00 32 | 01 07 |
| N 40 | 03 31 | 04 10 | 04 41 | 23 26 | 24 14 | 00 14 | 00 53 |
| 35 | 03 50 | 04 25 | 04 53 | 23 08 | 23 59 | 24 41 | 00 41 |
| 30 | 04 06 | 04 37 | 05 04 | 22 53 | 23 46 | 24 31 | 00 31 |
| 20 | 04 30 | 04 58 | 05 22 | 22 27 | 23 23 | 24 12 | 00 12 |
| N 10 | 04 49 | 05 16 | 05 38 | 22 04 | 23 04 | 23 57 | 24 44 |
| 0 | 05 05 | 05 31 | 05 53 | 21 44 | 22 45 | 23 42 | 24 33 |
| S 10 | 05 20 | 05 45 | 06 08 | 21 23 | 22 27 | 23 27 | 24 22 |
| 20 | 05 33 | 06 00 | 06 23 | 21 00 | 22 07 | 23 11 | 24 11 |
| 30 | 05 46 | 06 15 | 06 41 | 20 34 | 21 44 | 22 52 | 23 57 |
| 35 | 05 53 | 06 24 | 06 51 | 20 19 | 21 30 | 22 41 | 23 50 |
| 40 | 06 00 | 06 33 | 07 03 | 20 01 | 21 14 | 22 29 | 23 43 |
| 45 | 06 08 | 06 44 | 07 17 | 19 40 | 20 56 | 22 14 | 23 30 |
| S 50 | 06 17 | 06 57 | 07 33 | 19 12 | 20 32 | 21 56 | 23 18 |
| 52 | 06 21 | 07 03 | 07 41 | 18 59 | 20 21 | 21 47 | 23 12 |
| 54 | 06 25 | 07 09 | 07 50 | 18 44 | 20 08 | 21 38 | 23 05 |
| 56 | 06 30 | 07 16 | 08 00 | 18 26 | 19 53 | 21 27 | 22 58 |
| 58 | 06 34 | 07 24 | 08 11 | 18 04 | 19 36 | 21 14 | 22 50 |
| S 60 | 06 40 | 07 33 | 08 24 | 17 36 | 19 14 | 20 59 | 22 40 |

| Lat. | Sunset | Civil | Naut. | Moonset 19 | 20 | 21 | 22 |
|---|---|---|---|---|---|---|---|
| ° | h m | h m | h m | h m | h m | h m | h m |
| N 72 | □ | □ | □ | ■ | ■ | ■ | ■ |
| N 70 | □ | □ | □ | ■ | ■ | ■ | 07 40 |
| 68 | 22 43 | //// | //// | ■ | ■ | ■ | 08 25 |
| 66 | 21 54 | //// | //// | ■ | ■ | 06 21 | 08 54 |
| 64 | 21 24 | //// | //// | ■ | 04 18 | 07 09 | 09 16 |
| 62 | 21 01 | 22 28 | //// | 03 59 | 05 41 | 07 40 | 09 33 |
| 60 | 20 43 | 21 53 | //// | 04 49 | 06 18 | 08 03 | 09 48 |
| N 58 | 20 28 | 21 28 | //// | 05 21 | 06 44 | 08 21 | 10 00 |
| 56 | 20 16 | 21 08 | 22 36 | 05 44 | 07 04 | 08 37 | 10 10 |
| 54 | 20 05 | 20 52 | 22 04 | 06 03 | 07 21 | 08 50 | 10 20 |
| 52 | 19 55 | 20 39 | 21 40 | 06 19 | 07 36 | 09 01 | 10 28 |
| 50 | 19 46 | 20 27 | 21 22 | 06 33 | 07 49 | 09 12 | 10 35 |
| 45 | 19 28 | 20 03 | 20 48 | 07 02 | 08 15 | 09 33 | 10 51 |
| N 40 | 19 13 | 19 44 | 20 23 | 07 24 | 08 35 | 09 50 | 11 04 |
| 35 | 19 00 | 19 29 | 20 04 | 07 43 | 08 52 | 10 04 | 11 14 |
| 30 | 18 50 | 19 16 | 19 48 | 07 59 | 09 07 | 10 17 | 11 24 |
| 20 | 18 31 | 18 55 | 19 23 | 08 25 | 09 32 | 10 38 | 11 40 |
| N 10 | 18 15 | 18 37 | 19 04 | 08 48 | 09 54 | 10 56 | 11 54 |
| 0 | 18 00 | 18 22 | 18 48 | 09 10 | 10 13 | 11 13 | 12 07 |
| S 10 | 17 45 | 18 08 | 18 33 | 09 31 | 10 33 | 11 29 | 12 20 |
| 20 | 17 30 | 17 53 | 18 20 | 09 54 | 10 54 | 11 47 | 12 33 |
| 30 | 17 12 | 17 38 | 18 07 | 10 21 | 11 19 | 12 08 | 12 49 |
| 35 | 17 02 | 17 29 | 18 00 | 10 36 | 11 33 | 12 19 | 12 58 |
| 40 | 16 50 | 17 19 | 17 52 | 10 54 | 11 49 | 12 33 | 13 08 |
| 45 | 16 36 | 17 09 | 17 45 | 11 16 | 12 09 | 12 49 | 13 20 |
| S 50 | 16 19 | 16 56 | 17 36 | 11 44 | 12 33 | 13 08 | 13 34 |
| 52 | 16 12 | 16 50 | 17 32 | 11 57 | 12 45 | 13 18 | 13 41 |
| 54 | 16 03 | 16 43 | 17 27 | 12 13 | 12 58 | 13 28 | 13 48 |
| 56 | 15 53 | 16 36 | 17 23 | 12 31 | 13 14 | 13 40 | 13 56 |
| 58 | 15 42 | 16 29 | 17 18 | 12 53 | 13 32 | 13 53 | 14 05 |
| S 60 | 15 29 | 16 20 | 17 13 | 13 21 | 13 54 | 14 08 | 14 16 |

| | SUN Eqn. of Time 00h | SUN Eqn. of Time 12h | SUN Mer. Pass. | MOON Mer. Pass. Upper | MOON Mer. Pass. Lower | Age | Phase |
|---|---|---|---|---|---|---|---|
| d | m s | m s | h m | h m | h m | d | % |
| 19 | 03 32 | 03 30 | 11 56 | 02 54 | 15 27 | 19 | 84 |
| 20 | 03 29 | 03 27 | 11 57 | 03 59 | 16 29 | 20 | 75 |
| 21 | 03 25 | 03 23 | 11 57 | 04 59 | 17 27 | 21 | 64 |

| UT | ARIES GHA | VENUS −4.0 GHA | Dec | MARS +0.7 GHA | Dec | JUPITER −2.2 GHA | Dec | SATURN +0.6 GHA | Dec | STARS Name | SHA | Dec |
|---|---|---|---|---|---|---|---|---|---|---|---|---|
| **d h** | ° ′ | ° ′ | ° ′ | ° ′ | ° ′ | ° ′ | ° ′ | ° ′ | ° ′ | | ° ′ | ° ′ |
| **22 00** | 239 36.2 | 218 16.5 | N 6 51.8 | 240 57.8 | S 2 26.3 | 237 16.0 | S 0 13.3 | 271 51.3 | S14 10.6 | Acamar | 315 13.9 | S40 12.9 |
| 01 | 254 38.6 | 233 16.2 | 52.9 | 255 58.5 | 25.6 | 252 18.1 | 13.1 | 286 53.7 | 10.6 | Achernar | 335 22.3 | S57 07.3 |
| 02 | 269 41.1 | 248 16.0 | 53.9 | 270 59.2 | 24.9 | 267 20.1 | 13.0 | 301 56.1 | 10.6 | Acrux | 173 02.1 | S63 13.6 |
| 03 | 284 43.6 | 263 15.7 .. | 55.0 | 286 00.0 .. | 24.1 | 282 22.2 .. | 12.8 | 316 58.5 .. | 10.6 | Adhara | 255 07.9 | S29 00.3 |
| 04 | 299 46.0 | 278 15.4 | 56.0 | 301 00.7 | 23.4 | 297 24.2 | 12.6 | 332 01.0 | 10.6 | Aldebaran | 290 42.5 | N16 33.1 |
| 05 | 314 48.5 | 293 15.2 | 57.1 | 316 01.5 | 22.7 | 312 26.3 | 12.5 | 347 03.4 | 10.5 | | | |
| **S** 06 | 329 50.9 | 308 14.9 | N 6 58.1 | 331 02.2 | S 2 22.0 | 327 28.4 | S 0 12.3 | 2 05.8 | S14 10.5 | Alioth | 166 14.6 | N55 50.6 |
| **U** 07 | 344 53.4 | 323 14.6 | 6 59.2 | 346 03.0 | 21.2 | 342 30.4 | 12.1 | 17 08.2 | 10.5 | Alkaid | 152 53.4 | N49 12.3 |
| **N** 08 | 359 55.9 | 338 14.3 | 7 00.2 | 1 03.7 | 20.5 | 357 32.5 | 11.9 | 32 10.6 | 10.5 | Alnair | 27 35.7 | S46 51.0 |
| **D** 09 | 14 58.3 | 353 14.1 .. | 01.3 | 16 04.4 .. | 19.8 | 12 34.5 .. | 11.8 | 47 13.0 .. | 10.5 | Alnilam | 275 45.3 | S 1 11.3 |
| **A** 10 | 30 00.8 | 8 13.8 | 02.3 | 31 05.2 | 19.0 | 27 36.6 | 11.6 | 62 15.4 | 10.5 | Alphard | 217 50.0 | S 8 45.4 |
| **Y** 11 | 45 03.3 | 23 13.5 | 03.4 | 46 05.9 | 18.3 | 42 38.6 | 11.4 | 77 17.8 | 10.5 | | | |
| 12 | 60 05.7 | 38 13.3 | N 7 04.4 | 61 06.7 | S 2 17.6 | 57 40.7 | S 0 11.3 | 92 20.2 | S14 10.5 | Alphecca | 126 05.2 | N26 38.4 |
| 13 | 75 08.2 | 53 13.0 | 05.5 | 76 07.4 | 16.9 | 72 42.7 | 11.1 | 107 22.6 | 10.4 | Alpheratz | 357 37.2 | N29 12.6 |
| 14 | 90 10.7 | 68 12.7 | 06.5 | 91 08.2 | 16.1 | 87 44.8 | 10.9 | 122 25.0 | 10.4 | Altair | 62 01.9 | N 8 55.5 |
| 15 | 105 13.1 | 83 12.4 .. | 07.5 | 106 08.9 .. | 15.4 | 102 46.9 .. | 10.8 | 137 27.4 .. | 10.4 | Ankaa | 353 09.6 | S42 11.0 |
| 16 | 120 15.6 | 98 12.2 | 08.6 | 121 09.6 | 14.7 | 117 48.9 | 10.6 | 152 29.8 | 10.4 | Antares | 112 18.1 | S26 28.9 |
| 17 | 135 18.1 | 113 11.9 | 09.6 | 136 10.4 | 13.9 | 132 51.0 | 10.4 | 167 32.3 | 10.4 | | | |
| 18 | 150 20.5 | 128 11.6 | N 7 10.7 | 151 11.1 | S 2 13.2 | 147 53.0 | S 0 10.3 | 182 34.7 | S14 10.4 | Arcturus | 145 49.6 | N19 04.0 |
| 19 | 165 23.0 | 143 11.3 | 11.7 | 166 11.9 | 12.5 | 162 55.1 | 10.1 | 197 37.1 | 10.4 | Atria | 107 13.8 | S69 04.0 |
| 20 | 180 25.4 | 158 11.1 | 12.8 | 181 12.6 | 11.8 | 177 57.1 | 09.9 | 212 39.5 | 10.4 | Avior | 234 15.9 | S59 35.1 |
| 21 | 195 27.9 | 173 10.8 .. | 13.8 | 196 13.4 .. | 11.0 | 192 59.2 .. | 09.8 | 227 41.9 .. | 10.4 | Bellatrix | 278 25.5 | N 6 22.1 |
| 22 | 210 30.4 | 188 10.5 | 14.9 | 211 14.1 | 10.3 | 208 01.3 | 09.6 | 242 44.3 | 10.4 | Betelgeuse | 270 54.8 | N 7 24.6 |
| 23 | 225 32.8 | 203 10.2 | 15.9 | 226 14.9 | 09.6 | 223 03.3 | 09.4 | 257 46.7 | 10.3 | | | |
| **23 00** | 240 35.3 | 218 10.0 | N 7 17.0 | 241 15.6 | S 2 08.9 | 238 05.4 | S 0 09.3 | 272 49.1 | S14 10.3 | Canopus | 263 53.8 | S52 42.6 |
| 01 | 255 37.8 | 233 09.7 | 18.0 | 256 16.3 | 08.1 | 253 07.4 | 09.1 | 287 51.5 | 10.3 | Capella | 280 25.6 | N46 01.2 |
| 02 | 270 40.2 | 248 09.4 | 19.0 | 271 17.1 | 07.4 | 268 09.5 | 08.9 | 302 53.9 | 10.3 | Deneb | 49 27.1 | N45 21.3 |
| 03 | 285 42.7 | 263 09.1 .. | 20.1 | 286 17.8 .. | 06.7 | 283 11.5 .. | 08.8 | 317 56.4 .. | 10.3 | Denebola | 182 27.1 | N14 26.9 |
| 04 | 300 45.2 | 278 08.9 | 21.1 | 301 18.6 | 05.9 | 298 13.6 | 08.6 | 332 58.8 | 10.3 | Diphda | 348 49.7 | S17 51.9 |
| 05 | 315 47.6 | 293 08.6 | 22.2 | 316 19.3 | 05.2 | 313 15.7 | 08.4 | 348 01.2 | 10.3 | | | |
| **M** 06 | 330 50.1 | 308 08.3 | N 7 23.2 | 331 20.1 | S 2 04.5 | 328 17.7 | S 0 08.3 | 3 03.6 | S14 10.3 | Dubhe | 193 43.6 | N61 38.2 |
| **O** 07 | 345 52.6 | 323 08.0 | 24.3 | 346 20.8 | 03.8 | 343 19.8 | 08.1 | 18 06.0 | 10.3 | Elnath | 278 05.0 | N28 37.5 |
| **N** 08 | 0 55.0 | 338 07.7 | 25.3 | 1 21.6 | 03.0 | 358 21.8 | 07.9 | 33 08.4 | 10.2 | Eltanin | 90 42.7 | N51 29.0 |
| **D** 09 | 15 57.5 | 353 07.5 .. | 26.3 | 16 22.3 .. | 02.3 | 13 23.9 .. | 07.8 | 48 10.8 .. | 10.2 | Enif | 33 40.9 | N 9 58.5 |
| **A** 10 | 30 59.9 | 8 07.2 | 27.4 | 31 23.0 | 01.6 | 28 26.0 | 07.6 | 63 13.2 | 10.2 | Fomalhaut | 15 17.0 | S29 30.2 |
| **Y** 11 | 46 02.4 | 23 06.9 | 28.4 | 46 23.8 | 00.8 | 43 28.0 | 07.4 | 78 15.6 | 10.2 | | | |
| 12 | 61 04.9 | 38 06.6 | N 7 29.5 | 61 24.5 | S 2 00.1 | 58 30.1 | S 0 07.3 | 93 18.1 | S14 10.2 | Gacrux | 171 53.7 | S57 14.5 |
| 13 | 76 07.3 | 53 06.3 | 30.5 | 76 25.3 | 1 59.4 | 73 32.1 | 07.1 | 108 20.5 | 10.2 | Gienah | 175 45.7 | S17 40.0 |
| 14 | 91 09.8 | 68 06.1 | 31.6 | 91 26.0 | 58.7 | 88 34.2 | 06.9 | 123 22.9 | 10.2 | Hadar | 148 38.5 | S60 28.9 |
| 15 | 106 12.3 | 83 05.8 .. | 32.6 | 106 26.8 .. | 57.9 | 103 36.3 .. | 06.8 | 138 25.3 .. | 10.2 | Hamal | 327 54.0 | N23 33.9 |
| 16 | 121 14.7 | 98 05.5 | 33.6 | 121 27.5 | 57.2 | 118 38.3 | 06.6 | 153 27.7 | 10.2 | Kaus Aust. | 83 35.1 | S34 22.4 |
| 17 | 136 17.2 | 113 05.2 | 34.7 | 136 28.3 | 56.5 | 133 40.4 | 06.4 | 168 30.1 | 10.2 | | | |
| 18 | 151 19.7 | 128 04.9 | N 7 35.7 | 151 29.0 | S 1 55.7 | 148 42.4 | S 0 06.3 | 183 32.5 | S14 10.1 | Kochab | 137 18.7 | N74 03.9 |
| 19 | 166 22.1 | 143 04.7 | 36.8 | 166 29.8 | 55.0 | 163 44.5 | 06.1 | 198 34.9 | 10.1 | Markab | 13 32.1 | N15 19.3 |
| 20 | 181 24.6 | 158 04.4 | 37.8 | 181 30.5 | 54.3 | 178 46.6 | 06.0 | 213 37.4 | 10.1 | Menkar | 314 08.8 | N 4 10.5 |
| 21 | 196 27.0 | 173 04.1 .. | 38.9 | 196 31.2 .. | 53.6 | 193 48.6 .. | 05.8 | 228 39.8 .. | 10.1 | Menkent | 147 59.8 | S36 28.9 |
| 22 | 211 29.5 | 188 03.8 | 39.9 | 211 32.0 | 52.8 | 208 50.7 | 05.6 | 243 42.2 | 10.1 | Miaplacidus | 221 38.9 | S69 48.8 |
| 23 | 226 32.0 | 203 03.5 | 40.9 | 226 32.7 | 52.1 | 223 52.7 | 05.5 | 258 44.6 | 10.1 | | | |
| **24 00** | 241 34.4 | 218 03.2 | N 7 42.0 | 241 33.5 | S 1 51.4 | 238 54.8 | S 0 05.3 | 273 47.0 | S14 10.1 | Mirfak | 308 31.9 | N49 56.3 |
| 01 | 256 36.9 | 233 03.0 | 43.0 | 256 34.2 | 50.6 | 253 56.9 | 05.1 | 288 49.4 | 10.1 | Nunki | 75 50.2 | S26 16.1 |
| 02 | 271 39.4 | 248 02.7 | 44.1 | 271 35.0 | 49.9 | 268 58.9 | 05.0 | 303 51.8 | 10.1 | Peacock | 53 08.9 | S56 39.6 |
| 03 | 286 41.8 | 263 02.4 .. | 45.1 | 286 35.7 .. | 49.2 | 284 01.0 .. | 04.8 | 318 54.3 .. | 10.1 | Pollux | 243 20.2 | N27 58.4 |
| 04 | 301 44.3 | 278 02.1 | 46.1 | 301 36.5 | 48.5 | 299 03.1 | 04.6 | 333 56.7 | 10.1 | Procyon | 244 53.3 | N 5 10.0 |
| 05 | 316 46.8 | 293 01.8 | 47.2 | 316 37.2 | 47.7 | 314 05.1 | 04.5 | 348 59.1 | 10.0 | | | |
| **T** 06 | 331 49.2 | 308 01.5 | N 7 48.2 | 331 38.0 | S 1 47.0 | 329 07.2 | S 0 04.3 | 4 01.5 | S14 10.0 | Rasalhague | 96 00.3 | N12 32.6 |
| **U** 07 | 346 51.7 | 323 01.3 | 49.3 | 346 38.7 | 46.3 | 344 09.2 | 04.1 | 19 03.9 | 10.0 | Regulus | 207 36.8 | N11 51.5 |
| **E** 08 | 1 54.2 | 338 01.0 | 50.3 | 1 39.5 | 45.6 | 359 11.3 | 04.0 | 34 06.3 | 10.0 | Rigel | 281 06.3 | S 8 10.6 |
| **S** 09 | 16 56.6 | 353 00.7 .. | 51.3 | 16 40.2 .. | 44.8 | 14 13.4 .. | 03.8 | 49 08.7 .. | 10.0 | Rigil Kent. | 139 42.7 | S60 55.7 |
| **D** 10 | 31 59.1 | 8 00.4 | 52.4 | 31 41.0 | 44.1 | 29 15.4 | 03.6 | 64 11.2 | 10.0 | Sabik | 102 05.0 | S15 45.2 |
| **A** 11 | 47 01.5 | 23 00.1 | 53.4 | 46 41.7 | 43.4 | 44 17.5 | 03.5 | 79 13.6 | 10.0 | | | |
| **Y** 12 | 62 04.0 | 37 59.8 | N 7 54.5 | 61 42.4 | S 1 42.6 | 59 19.6 | S 0 03.3 | 94 16.0 | S14 10.0 | Schedar | 349 33.9 | N56 39.3 |
| 13 | 77 06.5 | 52 59.5 | 55.5 | 76 43.2 | 41.9 | 74 21.6 | 03.2 | 109 18.4 | 10.0 | Shaula | 96 12.9 | S37 07.1 |
| 14 | 92 08.9 | 67 59.2 | 56.5 | 91 43.9 | 41.2 | 89 23.7 | 03.0 | 124 20.8 | 10.0 | Sirius | 258 28.4 | S16 44.9 |
| 15 | 107 11.4 | 82 59.0 .. | 57.6 | 106 44.7 .. | 40.5 | 104 25.8 .. | 02.8 | 139 23.2 .. | 10.0 | Spica | 158 24.4 | S11 16.7 |
| 16 | 122 13.9 | 97 58.7 | 58.6 | 121 45.4 | 39.7 | 119 27.8 | 02.7 | 154 25.7 | 10.0 | Suhail | 222 48.0 | S43 31.6 |
| 17 | 137 16.3 | 112 58.4 | 7 59.6 | 136 46.2 | 39.0 | 134 29.9 | 02.5 | 169 28.1 | 09.9 | | | |
| 18 | 152 18.8 | 127 58.1 | N 8 00.7 | 151 46.9 | S 1 38.3 | 149 31.9 | S 0 02.3 | 184 30.5 | S14 09.9 | Vega | 80 34.3 | N38 48.1 |
| 19 | 167 21.3 | 142 57.8 | 01.7 | 166 47.7 | 37.5 | 164 34.0 | 02.2 | 199 32.9 | 09.9 | Zuben'ubi | 136 58.1 | S16 08.1 |
| 20 | 182 23.7 | 157 57.5 | 02.8 | 181 48.4 | 36.8 | 179 36.1 | 02.0 | 214 35.3 | 09.9 | | SHA | Mer. Pass. |
| 21 | 197 26.2 | 172 57.2 .. | 03.8 | 196 49.2 .. | 36.1 | 194 38.1 .. | 01.8 | 229 37.7 .. | 09.9 | | ° ′ | h m |
| 22 | 212 28.7 | 187 56.9 | 04.8 | 211 49.9 | 35.4 | 209 40.2 | 01.7 | 244 40.2 | 09.9 | Venus | 337 34.7 | 9 28 |
| 23 | 227 31.1 | 202 56.6 | 05.9 | 226 50.7 | 34.6 | 224 42.3 | 01.5 | 259 42.6 | 09.9 | Mars | 0 40.3 | 7 55 |
| | h m | | | | | | | | | Jupiter | 357 30.1 | 8 07 |
| Mer. Pass. 7 56.3 | | v −0.3 | d 1.0 | v 0.7 | d 0.7 | v 2.1 | d 0.2 | v 2.4 | d 0.0 | Saturn | 32 13.8 | 5 48 |

| UT | SUN | | MOON | | | | | Lat. | Twilight | | Sunrise | Moonrise | | | |
|---|---|---|---|---|---|---|---|---|---|---|---|---|---|---|---|
| | GHA | Dec | GHA | v | Dec | d | HP | | Naut. | Civil | | 22 | 23 | 24 | 25 |
| d h | ° ′ | ° ′ | ° ′ | ′ | ° ′ | ′ | ′ | ° | h m | h m | h m | h m | h m | h m | h m |
| 22 00 | 180 50.3 | N20 20.3 | 274 34.7 | 8.5 | S19 32.6 | 11.4 | 58.8 | N 72 | ▢ | ▢ | ▢ | ▆ | 03 57 | 03 12 | 02 40 |
| 01 | 195 50.2 | 20.8 | 289 02.2 | 8.7 | 19 21.2 | 11.4 | 58.8 | N 70 | ▢ | ▢ | ▢ | 04 29 | 03 31 | 03 00 | 02 36 |
| 02 | 210 50.2 | 21.3 | 303 29.9 | 8.8 | 19 09.8 | 11.6 | 58.8 | 68 | //// | //// | 00 54 | 03 43 | 03 11 | 02 50 | 02 33 |
| 03 | 225 50.1 | .. 21.8 | 317 57.7 | 8.9 | 18 58.2 | 11.7 | 58.7 | 66 | //// | //// | 01 50 | 03 12 | 02 55 | 02 42 | 02 31 |
| 04 | 240 50.1 | 22.3 | 332 25.6 | 9.0 | 18 46.5 | 11.7 | 58.7 | 64 | //// | //// | 02 23 | 02 49 | 02 41 | 02 35 | 02 28 |
| 05 | 255 50.1 | 22.8 | 346 53.6 | 9.2 | 18 34.8 | 11.8 | 58.7 | 62 | //// | 01 15 | 02 46 | 02 31 | 02 30 | 02 28 | 02 27 |
| 06 | 270 50.0 | N20 23.3 | 1 21.8 | 9.2 | S18 23.0 | 12.0 | 58.6 | 60 | //// | 01 54 | 03 05 | 02 16 | 02 20 | 02 23 | 02 27 |
| 07 | 285 50.0 | 23.8 | 15 50.0 | 9.4 | 18 11.0 | 12.0 | 58.6 | N 58 | //// | 02 20 | 03 21 | 02 03 | 02 12 | 02 18 | 02 23 |
| 08 | 300 49.9 | 24.3 | 30 18.4 | 9.5 | 17 59.0 | 12.1 | 58.6 | 56 | 01 08 | 02 40 | 03 34 | 01 51 | 02 04 | 02 14 | 02 22 |
| S 09 | 315 49.9 | .. 24.8 | 44 46.9 | 9.6 | 17 46.9 | 12.2 | 58.5 | 54 | 01 43 | 02 57 | 03 45 | 01 41 | 01 58 | 02 10 | 02 21 |
| U 10 | 330 49.8 | 25.2 | 59 15.5 | 9.7 | 17 34.7 | 12.3 | 58.5 | 52 | 02 08 | 03 11 | 03 55 | 01 32 | 01 52 | 02 07 | 02 20 |
| N 11 | 345 49.8 | 25.7 | 73 44.2 | 9.8 | 17 22.4 | 12.3 | 58.5 | 50 | 02 27 | 03 23 | 04 04 | 01 24 | 01 46 | 02 04 | 02 19 |
| D 12 | 0 49.7 | N20 26.2 | 88 13.0 | 9.9 | S17 10.1 | 12.4 | 58.5 | 45 | 03 03 | 03 48 | 04 23 | 01 07 | 01 34 | 01 57 | 02 17 |
| A 13 | 15 49.7 | 26.7 | 102 41.9 | 10.1 | 16 57.7 | 12.6 | 58.4 | N 40 | 03 28 | 04 07 | 04 38 | 00 53 | 01 24 | 01 51 | 02 15 |
| Y 14 | 30 49.6 | 27.2 | 117 11.0 | 10.1 | 16 45.1 | 12.5 | 58.4 | 35 | 03 48 | 04 23 | 04 51 | 00 41 | 01 16 | 01 46 | 02 13 |
| 15 | 45 49.6 | .. 27.7 | 131 40.1 | 10.3 | 16 32.6 | 12.7 | 58.4 | 30 | 04 04 | 04 36 | 05 02 | 00 31 | 01 08 | 01 42 | 02 12 |
| 16 | 60 49.5 | 28.2 | 146 09.4 | 10.4 | 16 19.9 | 12.7 | 58.3 | 20 | 04 29 | 04 58 | 05 21 | 00 12 | 00 55 | 01 34 | 02 09 |
| 17 | 75 49.5 | 28.7 | 160 38.8 | 10.4 | 16 07.2 | 12.8 | 58.3 | N 10 | 04 49 | 05 15 | 05 38 | 24 44 | 00 44 | 01 27 | 02 07 |
| 18 | 90 49.4 | N20 29.1 | 175 08.2 | 10.6 | S15 54.4 | 12.9 | 58.3 | 0 | 05 05 | 05 31 | 05 53 | 24 33 | 00 33 | 01 21 | 02 05 |
| 19 | 105 49.4 | 29.6 | 189 37.8 | 10.7 | 15 41.5 | 13.0 | 58.2 | S 10 | 05 20 | 05 46 | 06 08 | 24 22 | 00 22 | 01 14 | 02 03 |
| 20 | 120 49.3 | 30.1 | 204 07.5 | 10.8 | 15 28.5 | 13.0 | 58.2 | 20 | 05 34 | 06 01 | 06 24 | 24 11 | 00 11 | 01 07 | 02 01 |
| 21 | 135 49.3 | .. 30.6 | 218 37.3 | 10.9 | 15 15.5 | 13.0 | 58.2 | 30 | 05 48 | 06 17 | 06 43 | 23 57 | 24 59 | 00 59 | 01 59 |
| 22 | 150 49.2 | 31.1 | 233 07.2 | 10.9 | 15 02.5 | 13.2 | 58.1 | 35 | 05 55 | 06 26 | 06 53 | 23 50 | 24 55 | 00 55 | 01 57 |
| 23 | 165 49.2 | 31.6 | 247 37.1 | 11.1 | 14 49.3 | 13.2 | 58.1 | 40 | 06 03 | 06 36 | 07 05 | 23 41 | 24 50 | 00 50 | 01 56 |
| | | | | | | | | 45 | 06 11 | 06 47 | 07 20 | 23 30 | 24 44 | 00 44 | 01 54 |
| 23 00 | 180 49.1 | N20 32.0 | 262 07.2 | 11.2 | S14 36.1 | 13.2 | 58.1 | S 50 | 06 20 | 07 00 | 07 37 | 23 18 | 24 36 | 00 36 | 01 52 |
| 01 | 195 49.1 | 32.5 | 276 37.4 | 11.3 | 14 22.9 | 13.4 | 58.1 | 52 | 06 24 | 07 06 | 07 45 | 23 12 | 24 33 | 00 33 | 01 51 |
| 02 | 210 49.0 | 33.0 | 291 07.7 | 11.4 | 14 09.5 | 13.3 | 58.0 | 54 | 06 29 | 07 13 | 07 55 | 23 05 | 24 29 | 00 29 | 01 49 |
| 03 | 225 49.0 | .. 33.5 | 305 38.1 | 11.4 | 13 56.2 | 13.5 | 58.0 | 56 | 06 34 | 07 21 | 08 05 | 22 58 | 24 25 | 00 25 | 01 48 |
| 04 | 240 48.9 | 34.0 | 320 08.5 | 11.6 | 13 42.7 | 13.5 | 58.0 | 58 | 06 39 | 07 29 | 08 16 | 22 50 | 24 21 | 00 21 | 01 47 |
| 05 | 255 48.9 | 34.4 | 334 39.1 | 11.7 | 13 29.2 | 13.5 | 57.9 | S 60 | 06 44 | 07 38 | 08 30 | 22 40 | 24 15 | 00 15 | 01 45 |
| 06 | 270 48.8 | N20 34.9 | 349 09.8 | 11.7 | S13 15.7 | 13.6 | 57.9 | | | | | | | | |
| 07 | 285 48.8 | 35.4 | 3 40.5 | 11.9 | 13 02.1 | 13.6 | 57.9 | Lat. | Sunset | Twilight | | Moonset | | | |
| 08 | 300 48.7 | 35.9 | 18 11.4 | 11.9 | 12 48.5 | 13.7 | 57.8 | | | Civil | Naut. | 22 | 23 | 24 | 25 |
| M 09 | 315 48.7 | .. 36.4 | 32 42.3 | 12.0 | 12 34.8 | 13.7 | 57.8 | ° | h m | h m | h m | h m | h m | h m | h m |
| O 10 | 330 48.6 | 36.8 | 47 13.3 | 12.1 | 12 21.1 | 13.8 | 57.8 | N 72 | ▢ | ▢ | ▢ | ▆ | 09 59 | 12 22 | 14 28 |
| N 11 | 345 48.6 | 37.3 | 61 44.4 | 12.2 | 12 07.3 | 13.9 | 57.8 | N 70 | ▢ | ▢ | ▢ | 07 40 | 10 23 | 12 31 | 14 28 |
| D 12 | 0 48.5 | N20 37.8 | 76 15.6 | 12.3 | S11 53.4 | 13.8 | 57.7 | 68 | 23 08 | //// | //// | 08 25 | 10 41 | 12 39 | 14 27 |
| A 13 | 15 48.4 | 38.3 | 90 46.9 | 12.4 | 11 39.6 | 13.9 | 57.7 | 66 | 22 07 | //// | //// | 08 54 | 10 56 | 12 45 | 14 27 |
| Y 14 | 30 48.4 | 38.7 | 105 18.3 | 12.4 | 11 25.7 | 14.0 | 57.7 | 64 | 21 33 | //// | //// | 09 16 | 11 08 | 12 50 | 14 27 |
| 15 | 45 48.3 | .. 39.2 | 119 49.7 | 12.5 | 11 11.7 | 14.0 | 57.6 | 62 | 21 09 | 22 43 | //// | 09 33 | 11 18 | 12 55 | 14 27 |
| 16 | 60 48.3 | 39.7 | 134 21.2 | 12.6 | 10 57.7 | 14.0 | 57.6 | 60 | 20 50 | 22 03 | //// | 09 48 | 11 26 | 12 59 | 14 27 |
| 17 | 75 48.2 | 40.1 | 148 52.8 | 12.7 | 10 43.7 | 14.1 | 57.6 | N 58 | 20 34 | 21 35 | //// | 10 00 | 11 34 | 13 02 | 14 27 |
| 18 | 90 48.2 | N20 40.6 | 163 24.5 | 12.8 | S10 29.6 | 14.1 | 57.5 | 56 | 20 21 | 21 15 | 22 50 | 10 10 | 11 40 | 13 05 | 14 27 |
| 19 | 105 48.1 | 41.1 | 177 56.3 | 12.8 | 10 15.5 | 14.1 | 57.5 | 54 | 20 09 | 20 58 | 22 13 | 10 20 | 11 46 | 13 08 | 14 27 |
| 20 | 120 48.1 | 41.6 | 192 28.1 | 12.9 | 10 01.4 | 14.2 | 57.5 | 52 | 19 59 | 20 44 | 21 47 | 10 28 | 11 51 | 13 10 | 14 27 |
| 21 | 135 48.0 | .. 42.0 | 207 00.0 | 13.0 | 9 47.2 | 14.2 | 57.5 | 50 | 19 50 | 20 31 | 21 28 | 10 35 | 11 56 | 13 13 | 14 27 |
| 22 | 150 48.0 | 42.5 | 221 32.0 | 13.1 | 9 33.0 | 14.2 | 57.4 | 45 | 19 31 | 20 06 | 20 52 | 10 51 | 12 06 | 13 18 | 14 27 |
| 23 | 165 47.9 | 43.0 | 236 04.1 | 13.1 | 9 18.8 | 14.3 | 57.4 | N 40 | 19 16 | 19 47 | 20 26 | 11 04 | 12 14 | 13 22 | 14 26 |
| 24 00 | 180 47.8 | N20 43.4 | 250 36.2 | 13.2 | S 9 04.5 | 14.2 | 57.4 | 35 | 19 03 | 19 31 | 20 06 | 11 14 | 12 21 | 13 25 | 14 26 |
| 01 | 195 47.8 | 43.9 | 265 08.4 | 13.3 | 8 50.3 | 14.4 | 57.3 | 30 | 18 51 | 19 18 | 19 50 | 11 24 | 12 28 | 13 28 | 14 26 |
| 02 | 210 47.7 | 44.4 | 279 40.7 | 13.3 | 8 35.9 | 14.3 | 57.3 | 20 | 18 32 | 18 56 | 19 25 | 11 40 | 12 38 | 13 33 | 14 26 |
| 03 | 225 47.7 | .. 44.8 | 294 13.0 | 13.4 | 8 21.6 | 14.4 | 57.3 | N 10 | 18 16 | 18 38 | 19 05 | 11 54 | 12 48 | 13 38 | 14 26 |
| 04 | 240 47.6 | 45.3 | 308 45.4 | 13.5 | 8 07.2 | 14.3 | 57.3 | 0 | 18 00 | 18 22 | 18 48 | 12 07 | 12 56 | 13 42 | 14 26 |
| 05 | 255 47.6 | 45.8 | 323 17.9 | 13.5 | 7 52.9 | 14.4 | 57.2 | S 10 | 17 45 | 18 08 | 18 33 | 12 20 | 13 05 | 13 46 | 14 26 |
| 06 | 270 47.5 | N20 46.2 | 337 50.4 | 13.6 | S 7 38.5 | 14.5 | 57.2 | 20 | 17 29 | 17 53 | 18 20 | 12 33 | 13 14 | 13 51 | 14 25 |
| 07 | 285 47.4 | 46.7 | 352 23.0 | 13.6 | 7 24.0 | 14.4 | 57.2 | 30 | 17 11 | 17 36 | 18 06 | 12 49 | 13 24 | 13 56 | 14 25 |
| 08 | 300 47.4 | 47.1 | 6 55.6 | 13.7 | 7 09.6 | 14.5 | 57.1 | 35 | 17 00 | 17 27 | 17 58 | 12 58 | 13 30 | 13 59 | 14 25 |
| T 09 | 315 47.3 | .. 47.6 | 21 28.3 | 13.8 | 6 55.1 | 14.5 | 57.1 | 40 | 16 48 | 17 17 | 17 51 | 13 08 | 13 37 | 14 02 | 14 25 |
| U 10 | 330 47.3 | 48.1 | 36 01.1 | 13.8 | 6 40.6 | 14.5 | 57.1 | 45 | 16 34 | 17 06 | 17 42 | 13 20 | 13 44 | 14 05 | 14 25 |
| E 11 | 345 47.2 | 48.5 | 50 33.9 | 13.9 | 6 26.1 | 14.5 | 57.1 | S 50 | 16 16 | 16 53 | 17 33 | 13 34 | 13 54 | 14 10 | 14 24 |
| S 12 | 0 47.1 | N20 49.0 | 65 06.8 | 13.9 | S 6 11.6 | 14.5 | 57.0 | 52 | 16 08 | 16 47 | 17 29 | 13 41 | 13 58 | 14 12 | 14 24 |
| D 13 | 15 47.1 | 49.4 | 79 39.7 | 14.0 | 5 57.1 | 14.5 | 57.0 | 54 | 15 59 | 16 40 | 17 24 | 13 48 | 14 02 | 14 14 | 14 24 |
| A 14 | 30 47.0 | 49.9 | 94 12.7 | 14.1 | 5 42.6 | 14.6 | 57.0 | 56 | 15 48 | 16 33 | 17 19 | 13 56 | 14 08 | 14 16 | 14 24 |
| Y 15 | 45 47.0 | .. 50.4 | 108 45.8 | 14.1 | 5 28.0 | 14.6 | 56.9 | 58 | 15 37 | 16 24 | 17 14 | 14 05 | 14 13 | 14 19 | 14 24 |
| 16 | 60 46.9 | 50.8 | 123 18.9 | 14.1 | 5 13.4 | 14.5 | 56.9 | S 60 | 15 23 | 16 15 | 17 09 | 14 16 | 14 20 | 14 22 | 14 24 |
| 17 | 75 46.8 | 51.3 | 137 52.0 | 14.2 | 4 58.9 | 14.6 | 56.9 | | | | | | | | |
| 18 | 90 46.8 | N20 51.7 | 152 25.2 | 14.2 | S 4 44.3 | 14.6 | 56.9 | | | SUN | | | MOON | | |
| 19 | 105 46.7 | 52.2 | 166 58.4 | 14.3 | 4 29.7 | 14.6 | 56.8 | Day | Eqn. of Time | | Mer. | Mer. Pass. | | Age | Phase |
| 20 | 120 46.7 | 52.6 | 181 31.7 | 14.3 | 4 15.1 | 14.6 | 56.8 | | 00ʰ | 12ʰ | Pass. | Upper | Lower | | |
| 21 | 135 46.6 | .. 53.1 | 196 05.0 | 14.4 | 4 00.5 | 14.6 | 56.8 | d | m s | m s | h m | h m | h m | d | % |
| 22 | 150 46.5 | 53.5 | 210 38.4 | 14.4 | 3 45.9 | 14.6 | 56.8 | 22 | 03 21 | 03 19 | 11 57 | 05 54 | 18 20 | 22 | 53 |
| 23 | 165 46.5 | 54.0 | 225 11.8 | 14.5 | S 3 31.3 | 14.6 | 56.7 | 23 | 03 17 | 03 14 | 11 57 | 06 45 | 19 09 | 23 | 42 |
| | SD 15.8 | d 0.5 | SD 15.9 | | 15.7 | | 15.5 | 24 | 03 11 | 03 09 | 11 57 | 07 31 | 19 54 | 24 | 32 |

| UT | ARIES | VENUS −4.0 | | MARS +0.7 | | JUPITER −2.2 | | SATURN +0.6 | | STARS | | |
|---|---|---|---|---|---|---|---|---|---|---|---|---|
| | GHA | GHA | Dec | GHA | Dec | GHA | Dec | GHA | Dec | Name | SHA | Dec |
| d h | ° ′ | ° ′ | ° ′ | ° ′ | ° ′ | ° ′ | ° ′ | ° ′ | ° ′ | | ° ′ | ° ′ |
| 25 00 | 242 33.6 | 217 56.4 N 8 06.9 | | 241 51.4 S 1 33.9 | | 239 44.3 S 0 01.4 | | 274 45.0 S14 09.9 | | Acamar | 315 13.9 | S40 12.9 |
| 01 | 257 36.0 | 232 56.1 | 07.9 | 256 52.2 | 33.2 | 254 46.4 | 01.2 | 289 47.4 | 09.9 | Achernar | 335 22.3 | S57 07.3 |
| 02 | 272 38.5 | 247 55.8 | 09.0 | 271 52.9 | 32.5 | 269 48.5 | 01.0 | 304 49.8 | 09.9 | Acrux | 173 02.1 | S63 13.6 |
| 03 | 287 41.0 | 262 55.5 . . | 10.0 | 286 53.7 . . | 31.7 | 284 50.5 . . | 00.9 | 319 52.2 . . | 09.9 | Adhara | 255 07.9 | S29 00.3 |
| 04 | 302 43.4 | 277 55.2 | 11.0 | 301 54.4 | 31.0 | 299 52.6 | 00.7 | 334 54.7 | 09.9 | Aldebaran | 290 42.5 | N16 33.2 |
| 05 | 317 45.9 | 292 54.9 | 12.1 | 316 55.2 | 30.3 | 314 54.7 | 00.5 | 349 57.1 | 09.9 | | | |
| 06 | 332 48.4 | 307 54.6 N 8 13.1 | | 331 55.9 S 1 29.5 | | 329 56.7 S 0 00.4 | | 4 59.5 S14 09.8 | | Alioth | 166 14.6 | N55 50.6 |
| W 07 | 347 50.8 | 322 54.3 | 14.1 | 346 56.7 | 28.8 | 344 58.8 | 00.2 | 20 01.9 | 09.8 | Alkaid | 152 53.4 | N49 12.3 |
| E 08 | 2 53.3 | 337 54.0 | 15.2 | 1 57.4 | 28.1 | 0 00.9 S | 00.1 | 35 04.3 | 09.8 | Alnair | 27 35.6 | S46 51.0 |
| D 09 | 17 55.8 | 352 53.7 . . | 16.2 | 16 58.1 . . | 27.4 | 15 02.9 N | 00.1 | 50 06.8 . . | 09.8 | Alnilam | 275 40.3 | S 1 11.3 |
| N 10 | 32 58.2 | 7 53.4 | 17.2 | 31 58.9 | 26.6 | 30 05.0 | 00.3 | 65 09.2 | 09.8 | Alphard | 217 50.0 | S 8 45.4 |
| E 11 | 48 00.7 | 22 53.1 | 18.3 | 46 59.6 | 25.9 | 45 07.1 | 00.4 | 80 11.6 | 09.8 | | | |
| S 12 | 63 03.1 | 37 52.9 N 8 19.3 | | 62 00.4 S 1 25.2 | | 60 09.1 N 0 00.6 | | 95 14.0 S14 09.8 | | Alphecca | 126 05.2 | N26 38.4 |
| D 13 | 78 05.6 | 52 52.6 | 20.4 | 77 01.1 | 24.4 | 75 11.2 | 00.8 | 110 16.4 | 09.8 | Alpheratz | 357 37.2 | N29 12.6 |
| A 14 | 93 08.1 | 67 52.3 | 21.4 | 92 01.9 | 23.7 | 90 13.3 | 00.9 | 125 18.9 | 09.8 | Altair | 62 01.9 | N 8 55.5 |
| Y 15 | 108 10.5 | 82 52.0 . . | 22.4 | 107 02.6 . . | 23.0 | 105 15.3 . . | 01.1 | 140 21.3 . . | 09.8 | Ankaa | 353 09.5 | S42 11.0 |
| 16 | 123 13.0 | 97 51.7 | 23.4 | 122 03.4 | 22.3 | 120 17.4 | 01.2 | 155 23.7 | 09.8 | Antares | 112 18.1 | S26 28.9 |
| 17 | 138 15.5 | 112 51.4 | 24.5 | 137 04.1 | 21.5 | 135 19.5 | 01.4 | 170 26.1 | 09.8 | | | |
| 18 | 153 17.9 | 127 51.1 N 8 25.5 | | 152 04.9 S 1 20.8 | | 150 21.6 N 0 01.6 | | 185 28.5 S14 09.8 | | Arcturus | 145 49.6 | N19 04.0 |
| 19 | 168 20.4 | 142 50.8 | 26.5 | 167 05.6 | 20.1 | 165 23.6 | 01.7 | 200 31.0 | 09.8 | Atria | 107 13.8 | S69 04.0 |
| 20 | 183 22.9 | 157 50.5 | 27.6 | 182 06.4 | 19.4 | 180 25.7 | 01.9 | 215 33.4 | 09.7 | Avior | 234 15.9 | S59 35.1 |
| 21 | 198 25.3 | 172 50.2 . . | 28.6 | 197 07.1 . . | 18.6 | 195 27.8 . . | 02.1 | 230 35.8 . . | 09.7 | Bellatrix | 278 25.5 | N 6 22.1 |
| 22 | 213 27.8 | 187 49.9 | 29.6 | 212 07.9 | 17.9 | 210 29.8 | 02.2 | 245 38.2 | 09.7 | Betelgeuse | 270 54.8 | N 7 24.6 |
| 23 | 228 30.3 | 202 49.6 | 30.7 | 227 08.6 | 17.2 | 225 31.9 | 02.4 | 260 40.7 | 09.7 | | | |
| 26 00 | 243 32.7 | 217 49.3 N 8 31.7 | | 242 09.4 S 1 16.4 | | 240 34.0 N 0 02.5 | | 275 43.1 S14 09.7 | | Canopus | 263 53.8 | S52 42.6 |
| 01 | 258 35.2 | 232 49.0 | 32.7 | 257 10.1 | 15.7 | 255 36.0 | 02.7 | 290 45.5 | 09.7 | Capella | 280 25.6 | N46 01.2 |
| 02 | 273 37.6 | 247 48.7 | 33.8 | 272 10.9 | 15.0 | 270 38.1 | 02.9 | 305 47.9 | 09.7 | Deneb | 49 27.1 | N45 21.3 |
| 03 | 288 40.1 | 262 48.4 . . | 34.8 | 287 11.6 . . | 14.3 | 285 40.2 . . | 03.0 | 320 50.3 . . | 09.7 | Denebola | 182 27.1 | N14 26.9 |
| 04 | 303 42.6 | 277 48.1 | 35.8 | 302 12.4 | 13.5 | 300 42.2 | 03.2 | 335 52.8 | 09.7 | Diphda | 348 49.7 | S17 51.9 |
| 05 | 318 45.0 | 292 47.8 | 36.9 | 317 13.1 | 12.8 | 315 44.3 | 03.3 | 350 55.2 | 09.7 | | | |
| 06 | 333 47.5 | 307 47.5 N 8 37.9 | | 332 13.9 S 1 12.1 | | 330 46.4 N 0 03.5 | | 5 57.6 S14 09.7 | | Dubhe | 193 43.6 | N61 38.2 |
| T 07 | 348 50.0 | 322 47.2 | 38.9 | 347 14.6 | 11.4 | 345 48.5 | 03.7 | 21 00.0 | 09.7 | Elnath | 278 05.0 | N28 37.5 |
| H 08 | 3 52.4 | 337 46.9 | 39.9 | 2 15.4 | 10.6 | 0 50.5 | 03.8 | 36 02.5 | 09.7 | Eltanin | 90 42.7 | N51 29.0 |
| U 09 | 18 54.9 | 352 46.6 . . | 41.0 | 17 16.1 . . | 09.9 | 15 52.6 . . | 04.0 | 51 04.9 . . | 09.7 | Enif | 33 40.9 | N 9 58.5 |
| R 10 | 33 57.4 | 7 46.3 | 42.0 | 32 16.9 | 09.2 | 30 54.7 | 04.1 | 66 07.3 | 09.7 | Fomalhaut | 15 17.0 | S29 30.2 |
| S 11 | 48 59.8 | 22 46.0 | 43.0 | 47 17.6 | 08.4 | 45 56.7 | 04.3 | 81 09.7 | 09.7 | | | |
| D 12 | 64 02.3 | 37 45.7 N 8 44.1 | | 62 18.4 S 1 07.7 | | 60 58.8 N 0 04.5 | | 96 12.1 S14 09.6 | | Gacrux | 171 53.7 | S57 14.5 |
| A 13 | 79 04.7 | 52 45.4 | 45.1 | 77 19.1 | 07.0 | 76 00.9 | 04.6 | 111 14.6 | 09.6 | Gienah | 175 45.7 | S17 40.0 |
| Y 14 | 94 07.2 | 67 45.1 | 46.1 | 92 19.9 | 06.3 | 91 03.0 | 04.8 | 126 17.0 | 09.6 | Hadar | 148 38.5 | S60 29.0 |
| 15 | 109 09.7 | 82 44.8 . . | 47.1 | 107 20.6 . . | 05.5 | 106 05.0 . . | 04.9 | 141 19.4 . . | 09.6 | Hamal | 327 54.0 | N23 33.9 |
| 16 | 124 12.1 | 97 44.5 | 48.2 | 122 21.4 | 04.8 | 121 07.1 | 05.1 | 156 21.8 | 09.6 | Kaus Aust. | 83 35.1 | S34 22.4 |
| 17 | 139 14.6 | 112 44.2 | 49.2 | 137 22.1 | 04.1 | 136 09.2 | 05.3 | 171 24.3 | 09.6 | | | |
| 18 | 154 17.1 | 127 43.9 N 8 50.2 | | 152 22.9 S 1 03.4 | | 151 11.3 N 0 05.4 | | 186 26.7 S14 09.6 | | Kochab | 137 18.7 | N74 04.0 |
| 19 | 169 19.5 | 142 43.6 | 51.3 | 167 23.6 | 02.6 | 166 13.3 | 05.6 | 201 29.1 | 09.6 | Markab | 13 32.1 | N15 19.3 |
| 20 | 184 22.0 | 157 43.3 | 52.3 | 182 24.4 | 01.9 | 181 15.4 | 05.7 | 216 31.5 | 09.6 | Menkar | 314 08.7 | N 4 10.5 |
| 21 | 199 24.5 | 172 43.0 . . | 53.3 | 197 25.1 . . | 01.2 | 196 17.5 . . | 05.9 | 231 34.0 . . | 09.6 | Menkent | 147 59.8 | S36 28.9 |
| 22 | 214 26.9 | 187 42.7 | 54.3 | 212 25.9 | 1 00.4 | 211 19.5 | 06.1 | 246 36.4 | 09.6 | Miaplacidus | 221 39.0 | S69 48.8 |
| 23 | 229 29.4 | 202 42.4 | 55.4 | 227 26.6 | 0 59.7 | 226 21.6 | 06.2 | 261 38.8 | 09.6 | | | |
| 27 00 | 244 31.9 | 217 42.1 N 8 56.4 | | 242 27.4 S 0 59.0 | | 241 23.7 N 0 06.4 | | 276 41.2 S14 09.6 | | Mirfak | 308 31.9 | N49 56.2 |
| 01 | 259 34.3 | 232 41.8 | 57.4 | 257 28.2 | 58.3 | 256 25.8 | 06.5 | 291 43.7 | 09.6 | Nunki | 75 50.2 | S26 16.1 |
| 02 | 274 36.8 | 247 41.4 | 58.5 | 272 28.9 | 57.5 | 271 27.8 | 06.7 | 306 46.1 | 09.6 | Peacock | 53 08.9 | S56 39.6 |
| 03 | 289 39.2 | 262 41.1 | 8 59.5 | 287 29.7 . . | 56.8 | 286 29.9 . . | 06.9 | 321 48.5 . . | 09.6 | Pollux | 243 20.2 | N27 58.4 |
| 04 | 304 41.7 | 277 40.8 | 9 00.5 | 302 30.4 | 56.1 | 301 32.0 | 07.0 | 336 51.0 | 09.6 | Procyon | 244 53.4 | N 5 10.0 |
| 05 | 319 44.2 | 292 40.5 | 01.5 | 317 31.2 | 55.4 | 316 34.1 | 07.2 | 351 53.4 | 09.6 | | | |
| 06 | 334 46.6 | 307 40.2 N 9 02.5 | | 332 31.9 S 0 54.6 | | 331 36.1 N 0 07.3 | | 6 55.8 S14 09.6 | | Rasalhague | 96 00.2 | N12 32.6 |
| 07 | 349 49.1 | 322 39.9 | 03.6 | 347 32.7 | 53.9 | 346 38.2 | 07.5 | 21 58.2 | 09.5 | Regulus | 207 36.8 | N11 51.6 |
| 08 | 4 51.6 | 337 39.6 | 04.6 | 2 33.4 | 53.2 | 1 40.3 | 07.7 | 37 00.7 | 09.5 | Rigel | 281 06.3 | S 8 10.6 |
| F 09 | 19 54.0 | 352 39.3 . . | 05.6 | 17 34.2 . . | 52.5 | 16 42.4 . . | 07.8 | 52 03.1 . . | 09.5 | Rigil Kent. | 139 42.7 | S60 55.7 |
| R 10 | 34 56.5 | 7 39.0 | 06.6 | 32 34.9 | 51.7 | 31 44.4 | 08.0 | 67 05.5 | 09.5 | Sabik | 102 04.9 | S15 45.2 |
| I 11 | 49 59.0 | 22 38.7 | 07.7 | 47 35.7 | 51.0 | 46 46.5 | 08.1 | 82 07.9 | 09.5 | | | |
| D 12 | 65 01.4 | 37 38.4 N 9 08.7 | | 62 36.4 S 0 50.3 | | 61 48.6 N 0 08.3 | | 97 10.4 S14 09.5 | | Schedar | 349 33.8 | N56 39.3 |
| A 13 | 80 03.9 | 52 38.1 | 09.7 | 77 37.2 | 49.5 | 76 50.7 | 08.4 | 112 12.8 | 09.5 | Shaula | 96 12.9 | S37 07.1 |
| Y 14 | 95 06.4 | 67 37.7 | 10.7 | 92 37.9 | 48.8 | 91 52.8 | 08.6 | 127 15.2 | 09.5 | Sirius | 258 28.5 | S16 44.9 |
| 15 | 110 08.8 | 82 37.4 . . | 11.7 | 107 38.7 . . | 48.1 | 106 54.8 . . | 08.8 | 142 17.7 . . | 09.5 | Spica | 158 24.4 | S11 16.7 |
| 16 | 125 11.3 | 97 37.1 | 12.8 | 122 39.4 | 47.4 | 121 56.9 | 08.9 | 157 20.1 | 09.5 | Suhail | 222 48.1 | S43 31.6 |
| 17 | 140 13.7 | 112 36.8 | 13.8 | 137 40.2 | 46.6 | 136 59.0 | 09.1 | 172 22.5 | 09.5 | | | |
| 18 | 155 16.2 | 127 36.5 N 9 14.8 | | 152 40.9 S 0 45.9 | | 152 01.1 N 0 09.2 | | 187 24.9 S14 09.5 | | Vega | 80 34.3 | N38 48.1 |
| 19 | 170 18.7 | 142 36.2 | 15.8 | 167 41.7 | 45.2 | 167 03.1 | 09.4 | 202 27.4 | 09.5 | Zuben'ubi | 136 58.1 | S16 08.1 |
| 20 | 185 21.1 | 157 35.9 | 16.8 | 182 42.4 | 44.5 | 182 05.2 | 09.5 | 217 29.8 | 09.5 | | SHA | Mer. Pass. |
| 21 | 200 23.6 | 172 35.6 . . | 17.9 | 197 43.2 . . | 43.7 | 197 07.3 . . | 09.7 | 232 32.2 . . | 09.5 | | ° ′ | h m |
| 22 | 215 26.1 | 187 35.3 | 18.9 | 212 43.9 | 43.0 | 212 09.4 | 09.9 | 247 34.7 | 09.5 | Venus | 334 16.6 | 9 29 |
| 23 | 230 28.5 | 202 34.9 | 19.9 | 227 44.7 | 42.3 | 227 11.5 | 10.0 | 262 37.1 | 09.5 | Mars | 358 36.7 | 7 51 |
| | h m | | | | | | | | | Jupiter | 357 01.3 | 7 57 |
| Mer. Pass. | 7 44.5 | v −0.3 | d 1.0 | v 0.8 | d 0.7 | v 2.1 | d 0.2 | v 2.4 | d 0.0 | Saturn | 32 10.4 | 5 36 |

| UT | SUN GHA | SUN Dec | MOON GHA | v | MOON Dec | d | HP |
|---|---|---|---|---|---|---|---|
| d h | ° ′ | ° ′ | ° ′ | ′ | ° ′ | ′ | ′ |
| 25 00 | 180 46.4 | N20 54.4 | 239 45.3 | 14.4 | S 3 16.7 | 14.6 | 56.7 |
| 01 | 195 46.4 | 54.9 | 254 18.7 | 14.6 | 3 02.1 | 14.6 | 56.7 |
| 02 | 210 46.3 | 55.4 | 268 52.3 | 14.5 | 2 47.5 | 14.6 | 56.6 |
| 03 | 225 46.2 | .. 55.8 | 283 25.8 | 14.6 | 2 32.9 | 14.6 | 56.6 |
| 04 | 240 46.2 | 56.3 | 297 59.4 | 14.7 | 2 18.3 | 14.6 | 56.6 |
| 05 | 255 46.1 | 56.7 | 312 33.1 | 14.6 | 2 03.7 | 14.6 | 56.6 |
| 06 | 270 46.0 | N20 57.1 | 327 06.7 | 14.7 | S 1 49.1 | 14.6 | 56.5 |
| W 07 | 285 46.0 | 57.6 | 341 40.4 | 14.8 | 1 34.5 | 14.6 | 56.5 |
| E 08 | 300 45.9 | 58.0 | 356 14.2 | 14.7 | 1 19.9 | 14.6 | 56.5 |
| D 09 | 315 45.9 | .. 58.5 | 10 47.9 | 14.8 | 1 05.3 | 14.6 | 56.5 |
| N 10 | 330 45.8 | 58.9 | 25 21.7 | 14.8 | 0 50.7 | 14.5 | 56.4 |
| E 11 | 345 45.7 | 59.4 | 39 55.5 | 14.9 | 0 36.2 | 14.6 | 56.4 |
| S 12 | 0 45.7 | N20 59.8 | 54 29.4 | 14.8 | S 0 21.6 | 14.5 | 56.4 |
| D 13 | 15 45.6 | 21 00.3 | 69 03.2 | 14.9 | S 0 07.1 | 14.6 | 56.4 |
| A 14 | 30 45.5 | 00.7 | 83 37.1 | 14.9 | N 0 07.5 | 14.5 | 56.3 |
| Y 15 | 45 45.5 | .. 01.2 | 98 11.0 | 15.0 | 0 22.0 | 14.5 | 56.3 |
| 16 | 60 45.4 | 01.6 | 112 45.0 | 14.9 | 0 36.5 | 14.5 | 56.3 |
| 17 | 75 45.3 | 02.0 | 127 18.9 | 15.0 | 0 51.0 | 14.5 | 56.3 |
| 18 | 90 45.3 | N21 02.5 | 141 52.9 | 15.0 | N 1 05.5 | 14.5 | 56.2 |
| 19 | 105 45.2 | 02.9 | 156 26.9 | 15.0 | 1 20.0 | 14.4 | 56.2 |
| 20 | 120 45.1 | 03.4 | 171 00.9 | 15.0 | 1 34.4 | 14.4 | 56.2 |
| 21 | 135 45.1 | .. 03.8 | 185 34.9 | 15.0 | 1 48.8 | 14.4 | 56.2 |
| 22 | 150 45.0 | 04.2 | 200 08.9 | 15.1 | 2 03.2 | 14.4 | 56.1 |
| 23 | 165 44.9 | 04.7 | 214 43.0 | 15.1 | 2 17.6 | 14.4 | 56.1 |
| 26 00 | 180 44.9 | N21 05.1 | 229 17.1 | 15.0 | N 2 32.0 | 14.4 | 56.1 |
| 01 | 195 44.8 | 05.5 | 243 51.1 | 15.1 | 2 46.4 | 14.3 | 56.1 |
| 02 | 210 44.7 | 06.0 | 258 25.2 | 15.1 | 3 00.7 | 14.3 | 56.0 |
| 03 | 225 44.7 | .. 06.4 | 272 59.3 | 15.1 | 3 15.0 | 14.3 | 56.0 |
| 04 | 240 44.6 | 06.9 | 287 33.4 | 15.1 | 3 29.3 | 14.2 | 56.0 |
| 05 | 255 44.5 | 07.3 | 302 07.5 | 15.1 | 3 43.5 | 14.3 | 56.0 |
| 06 | 270 44.5 | N21 07.7 | 316 41.6 | 15.1 | N 3 57.8 | 14.2 | 56.0 |
| T 07 | 285 44.4 | 08.2 | 331 15.7 | 15.2 | 4 12.0 | 14.1 | 55.9 |
| H 08 | 300 44.3 | 08.6 | 345 49.9 | 15.1 | 4 26.1 | 14.2 | 55.9 |
| U 09 | 315 44.3 | .. 09.0 | 0 24.0 | 15.1 | 4 40.3 | 14.1 | 55.9 |
| R 10 | 330 44.2 | 09.4 | 14 58.1 | 15.1 | 4 54.4 | 14.1 | 55.9 |
| S 11 | 345 44.1 | 09.9 | 29 32.2 | 15.1 | 5 08.5 | 14.1 | 55.8 |
| D 12 | 0 44.0 | N21 10.3 | 44 06.3 | 15.2 | N 5 22.6 | 14.0 | 55.8 |
| A 13 | 15 44.0 | 10.7 | 58 40.5 | 15.1 | 5 36.6 | 14.0 | 55.8 |
| Y 14 | 30 43.9 | 11.2 | 73 14.6 | 15.1 | 5 50.6 | 13.9 | 55.8 |
| 15 | 45 43.8 | .. 11.6 | 87 48.7 | 15.1 | 6 04.5 | 14.0 | 55.8 |
| 16 | 60 43.8 | 12.0 | 102 22.8 | 15.1 | 6 18.5 | 13.9 | 55.7 |
| 17 | 75 43.7 | 12.4 | 116 56.9 | 15.1 | 6 32.4 | 13.8 | 55.7 |
| 18 | 90 43.6 | N21 12.9 | 131 31.0 | 15.1 | N 6 46.2 | 13.8 | 55.7 |
| 19 | 105 43.5 | 13.3 | 146 05.1 | 15.1 | 7 00.0 | 13.8 | 55.7 |
| 20 | 120 43.5 | 13.7 | 160 39.2 | 15.1 | 7 13.8 | 13.8 | 55.7 |
| 21 | 135 43.4 | .. 14.1 | 175 13.3 | 15.0 | 7 27.6 | 13.7 | 55.6 |
| 22 | 150 43.3 | 14.6 | 189 47.3 | 15.1 | 7 41.3 | 13.6 | 55.6 |
| 23 | 165 43.3 | 15.0 | 204 21.4 | 15.0 | 7 54.9 | 13.6 | 55.6 |
| 27 00 | 180 43.2 | N21 15.4 | 218 55.4 | 15.0 | N 8 08.5 | 13.6 | 55.6 |
| 01 | 195 43.1 | 15.8 | 233 29.4 | 15.0 | 8 22.1 | 13.5 | 55.6 |
| 02 | 210 43.0 | 16.3 | 248 03.4 | 15.0 | 8 35.6 | 13.5 | 55.5 |
| 03 | 225 43.0 | .. 16.7 | 262 37.4 | 15.0 | 8 49.1 | 13.5 | 55.5 |
| 04 | 240 42.9 | 17.1 | 277 11.4 | 15.0 | 9 02.6 | 13.4 | 55.5 |
| 05 | 255 42.8 | 17.5 | 291 45.4 | 14.9 | 9 16.0 | 13.3 | 55.5 |
| 06 | 270 42.8 | N21 17.9 | 306 19.3 | 14.9 | N 9 29.3 | 13.4 | 55.5 |
| 07 | 285 42.7 | 18.3 | 320 53.2 | 14.9 | 9 42.7 | 13.2 | 55.4 |
| 08 | 300 42.6 | 18.8 | 335 27.1 | 14.9 | 9 55.9 | 13.2 | 55.4 |
| F 09 | 315 42.5 | .. 19.2 | 350 01.0 | 14.9 | 10 09.1 | 13.2 | 55.4 |
| R 10 | 330 42.5 | 19.6 | 4 34.9 | 14.8 | 10 22.3 | 13.1 | 55.4 |
| I 11 | 345 42.4 | 20.0 | 19 08.7 | 14.8 | 10 35.4 | 13.1 | 55.4 |
| D 12 | 0 42.3 | N21 20.4 | 33 42.5 | 14.8 | N10 48.5 | 13.0 | 55.3 |
| A 13 | 15 42.2 | 20.8 | 48 16.3 | 14.8 | 11 01.5 | 12.9 | 55.3 |
| Y 14 | 30 42.2 | 21.3 | 62 50.1 | 14.7 | 11 14.4 | 12.9 | 55.3 |
| 15 | 45 42.1 | .. 21.7 | 77 23.8 | 14.7 | 11 27.3 | 12.9 | 55.3 |
| 16 | 60 42.0 | 22.1 | 91 57.5 | 14.7 | 11 40.2 | 12.8 | 55.3 |
| 17 | 75 41.9 | 22.5 | 106 31.2 | 14.7 | 11 53.0 | 12.7 | 55.2 |
| 18 | 90 41.9 | N21 22.9 | 121 04.9 | 14.6 | N12 05.7 | 12.7 | 55.2 |
| 19 | 105 41.8 | 23.3 | 135 38.5 | 14.6 | 12 18.4 | 12.6 | 55.2 |
| 20 | 120 41.7 | 23.7 | 150 12.1 | 14.5 | 12 31.0 | 12.6 | 55.2 |
| 21 | 135 41.6 | .. 24.1 | 164 45.6 | 14.6 | 12 43.6 | 12.5 | 55.2 |
| 22 | 150 41.5 | 24.5 | 179 19.2 | 14.5 | 12 56.1 | 12.4 | 55.2 |
| 23 | 165 41.5 | 24.9 | 193 52.7 | 14.5 | N13 08.5 | 12.4 | 55.1 |
| | SD 15.8 | d 0.4 | SD 15.4 | | 15.2 | | 15.1 |

### Twilight / Sunrise / Moonrise

| Lat. | Twilight Naut. | Twilight Civil | Sunrise | Moonrise 25 | Moonrise 26 | Moonrise 27 | Moonrise 28 |
|---|---|---|---|---|---|---|---|
| ° | h m | h m | h m | h m | h m | h m | h m |
| N 72 | ▭ | ▭ | ▭ | 02 40 | 02 10 | 01 39 | {00 58 / 23 27} |
| N 70 | ▭ | ▭ | ▭ | 02 36 | 02 14 | 01 51 | 01 23 |
| 68 | //// | //// | 00 17 | 02 33 | 02 17 | 02 01 | 01 42 |
| 66 | //// | //// | 01 38 | 02 31 | 02 20 | 02 09 | 01 58 |
| 64 | //// | //// | 02 14 | 02 28 | 02 22 | 02 17 | 02 10 |
| 62 | //// | 00 59 | 02 39 | 02 27 | 02 25 | 02 23 | 02 21 |
| 60 | //// | 01 44 | 02 59 | 02 25 | 02 26 | 02 28 | 02 30 |
| N 58 | //// | 02 13 | 03 16 | 02 23 | 02 28 | 02 33 | 02 39 |
| 56 | 00 53 | 02 35 | 03 29 | 02 22 | 02 29 | 02 37 | 02 46 |
| 54 | 01 35 | 02 52 | 03 41 | 02 21 | 02 31 | 02 41 | 02 52 |
| 52 | 02 02 | 03 07 | 03 52 | 02 20 | 02 32 | 02 44 | 02 58 |
| 50 | 02 22 | 03 20 | 04 01 | 02 19 | 02 33 | 02 47 | 03 03 |
| 45 | 02 59 | 03 45 | 04 21 | 02 17 | 02 35 | 02 54 | 03 15 |
| N 40 | 03 25 | 04 05 | 04 36 | 02 15 | 02 37 | 03 00 | 03 24 |
| 35 | 03 46 | 04 21 | 04 50 | 02 13 | 02 39 | 03 05 | 03 33 |
| 30 | 04 02 | 04 34 | 05 01 | 02 12 | 02 41 | 03 10 | 03 40 |
| 20 | 04 28 | 04 57 | 05 21 | 02 09 | 02 43 | 03 17 | 03 53 |
| N 10 | 04 49 | 05 15 | 05 38 | 02 07 | 02 46 | 03 24 | 04 04 |
| 0 | 05 06 | 05 31 | 05 53 | 02 05 | 02 48 | 03 31 | 04 14 |
| S 10 | 05 21 | 05 47 | 06 09 | 02 03 | 02 50 | 03 37 | 04 25 |
| 20 | 05 35 | 06 02 | 06 26 | 02 01 | 02 53 | 03 44 | 04 36 |
| 30 | 05 49 | 06 19 | 06 44 | 01 59 | 02 56 | 03 53 | 04 49 |
| 35 | 05 57 | 06 28 | 06 55 | 01 57 | 02 58 | 03 57 | 04 57 |
| 40 | 06 05 | 06 38 | 07 08 | 01 56 | 03 00 | 04 03 | 05 06 |
| 45 | 06 13 | 06 50 | 07 23 | 01 54 | 03 02 | 04 09 | 05 16 |
| S 50 | 06 23 | 07 04 | 07 41 | 01 52 | 03 04 | 04 16 | 05 28 |
| 52 | 06 28 | 07 10 | 07 49 | 01 51 | 03 06 | 04 20 | 05 34 |
| 54 | 06 32 | 07 17 | 07 59 | 01 49 | 03 07 | 04 24 | 05 41 |
| 56 | 06 37 | 07 25 | 08 09 | 01 48 | 03 09 | 04 28 | 05 48 |
| 58 | 06 43 | 07 33 | 08 22 | 01 47 | 03 10 | 04 33 | 05 56 |
| S 60 | 06 49 | 07 43 | 08 36 | 01 45 | 03 12 | 04 38 | 06 05 |

### Sunset / Twilight / Moonset

| Lat. | Sunset | Twilight Civil | Twilight Naut. | Moonset 25 | Moonset 26 | Moonset 27 | Moonset 28 |
|---|---|---|---|---|---|---|---|
| ° | h m | h m | h m | h m | h m | h m | h m |
| N 72 | ▭ | ▭ | ▭ | 14 28 | 16 31 | 18 43 | 21 48 |
| N 70 | ▭ | ▭ | ▭ | 14 28 | 16 21 | 18 20 | 20 38 |
| 68 | ▭ | ▭ | ▭ | 14 27 | 16 14 | 18 03 | 20 01 |
| 66 | 22 20 | //// | //// | 14 27 | 16 07 | 17 49 | 19 36 |
| 64 | 21 43 | //// | //// | 14 27 | 16 02 | 17 37 | 19 16 |
| 62 | 21 16 | 23 01 | //// | 14 27 | 15 57 | 17 28 | 19 00 |
| 60 | 20 56 | 22 13 | //// | 14 27 | 15 53 | 17 20 | 18 47 |
| N 58 | 20 40 | 21 43 | //// | 14 27 | 15 50 | 17 12 | 18 36 |
| 56 | 20 26 | 21 21 | 23 06 | 14 27 | 15 47 | 17 06 | 18 26 |
| 54 | 20 14 | 21 03 | 22 22 | 14 27 | 15 44 | 17 01 | 18 17 |
| 52 | 20 03 | 20 48 | 21 54 | 14 27 | 15 41 | 16 55 | 18 10 |
| 50 | 19 54 | 20 36 | 21 34 | 14 27 | 15 39 | 16 51 | 18 03 |
| 45 | 19 34 | 20 10 | 20 56 | 14 27 | 15 34 | 16 41 | 17 48 |
| N 40 | 19 18 | 19 50 | 20 30 | 14 26 | 15 30 | 16 33 | 17 36 |
| 35 | 19 05 | 19 34 | 20 09 | 14 26 | 15 26 | 16 26 | 17 26 |
| 30 | 18 53 | 19 20 | 19 52 | 14 26 | 15 23 | 16 20 | 17 17 |
| 20 | 18 33 | 18 58 | 19 26 | 14 26 | 15 18 | 16 09 | 17 01 |
| N 10 | 18 16 | 18 39 | 19 06 | 14 26 | 15 13 | 16 00 | 16 48 |
| 0 | 18 01 | 18 23 | 18 49 | 14 26 | 15 09 | 15 51 | 16 36 |
| S 10 | 17 45 | 18 08 | 18 33 | 14 26 | 15 04 | 15 43 | 16 23 |
| 20 | 17 28 | 17 52 | 18 19 | 14 25 | 14 59 | 15 34 | 16 10 |
| 30 | 17 10 | 17 35 | 18 05 | 14 25 | 14 54 | 15 24 | 15 55 |
| 35 | 16 59 | 17 26 | 17 57 | 14 25 | 14 51 | 15 18 | 15 46 |
| 40 | 16 46 | 17 16 | 17 49 | 14 25 | 14 47 | 15 11 | 15 36 |
| 45 | 16 31 | 17 04 | 17 40 | 14 25 | 14 43 | 15 03 | 15 25 |
| S 50 | 16 13 | 16 50 | 17 31 | 14 24 | 14 39 | 14 54 | 15 11 |
| 52 | 16 05 | 16 44 | 17 26 | 14 24 | 14 37 | 14 49 | 15 04 |
| 54 | 15 55 | 16 37 | 17 21 | 14 24 | 14 34 | 14 45 | 14 57 |
| 56 | 15 44 | 16 29 | 17 16 | 14 24 | 14 31 | 14 40 | 14 49 |
| 58 | 15 32 | 16 20 | 17 11 | 14 24 | 14 29 | 14 34 | 14 40 |
| S 60 | 15 18 | 16 11 | 17 05 | 14 24 | 14 25 | 14 27 | 14 30 |

### SUN / MOON

| Day | SUN Eqn. of Time 00h | SUN Eqn. of Time 12h | SUN Mer. Pass. | MOON Mer. Pass. Upper | MOON Mer. Pass. Lower | Age | Phase |
|---|---|---|---|---|---|---|---|
| d | m s | m s | h m | h m | h m | d | % |
| 25 | 03 06 | 03 03 | 11 57 | 08 16 | 20 37 | 25 | 23 |
| 26 | 03 00 | 02 56 | 11 57 | 08 58 | 21 20 | 26 | 15 |
| 27 | 02 53 | 02 49 | 11 57 | 09 41 | 22 03 | 27 | 8 |

| UT | ARIES GHA | VENUS −4.0 GHA | Dec | MARS +0.7 GHA | Dec | JUPITER −2.2 GHA | Dec | SATURN +0.6 GHA | Dec | STARS Name | SHA | Dec |
|---|---|---|---|---|---|---|---|---|---|---|---|---|
| d h | ° ′ | ° ′ | ° ′ | ° ′ | ° ′ | ° ′ | ° ′ | ° ′ | ° ′ | | ° ′ | ° ′ |
| 28 00 | 245 31.0 | 217 34.6 | N 9 20.9 | 242 45.5 | S 0 41.6 | 242 13.5 | N 0 10.2 | 277 39.5 | S14 09.5 | Acamar | 315 13.8 | S40 12.9 |
| 01 | 260 33.5 | 232 34.3 | 21.9 | 257 46.2 | 40.8 | 257 15.6 | 10.3 | 292 41.9 | 09.5 | Achernar | 335 22.3 | S57 07.3 |
| 02 | 275 35.9 | 247 34.0 | 23.0 | 272 47.0 | 40.1 | 272 17.7 | 10.5 | 307 44.4 | 09.5 | Acrux | 173 02.1 | S63 13.6 |
| 03 | 290 38.4 | 262 33.7 . . | 24.0 | 287 47.7 . . | 39.4 | 287 19.8 . . | 10.6 | 322 46.8 . . | 09.5 | Adhara | 255 07.9 | S29 00.3 |
| 04 | 305 40.8 | 277 33.4 | 25.0 | 302 48.5 | 38.7 | 302 21.8 | 10.8 | 337 49.2 | 09.5 | Aldebaran | 290 42.5 | N16 33.2 |
| 05 | 320 43.3 | 292 33.1 | 26.0 | 317 49.2 | 37.9 | 317 23.9 | 11.0 | 352 51.7 | 09.5 | | | |
| 06 | 335 45.8 | 307 32.7 | N 9 27.0 | 332 50.0 | S 0 37.2 | 332 26.0 | N 0 11.1 | 7 54.1 | S14 09.5 | Alioth | 166 14.6 | N55 50.6 |
| 07 | 350 48.2 | 322 32.4 | 28.1 | 347 50.7 | 36.5 | 347 28.1 | 11.3 | 22 56.5 | 09.5 | Alkaid | 152 53.4 | N49 12.3 |
| S 08 | 5 50.7 | 337 32.1 | 29.1 | 2 51.5 | 35.8 | 2 30.2 | 11.4 | 37 59.0 | 09.4 | Alnair | 27 35.6 | S46 51.0 |
| A 09 | 20 53.2 | 352 31.8 . . | 30.1 | 17 52.2 . . | 35.0 | 17 32.2 . . | 11.6 | 53 01.4 . . | 09.4 | Alnilam | 275 40.3 | S 1 11.3 |
| T 10 | 35 55.6 | 7 31.5 | 31.1 | 32 53.0 | 34.3 | 32 34.3 | 11.7 | 68 03.8 | 09.4 | Alphard | 217 50.0 | S 8 45.4 |
| U 11 | 50 58.1 | 22 31.2 | 32.1 | 47 53.7 | 33.6 | 47 36.4 | 11.9 | 83 06.3 | 09.4 | | | |
| R 12 | 66 00.6 | 37 30.8 | N 9 33.1 | 62 54.5 | S 0 32.8 | 62 38.5 | N 0 12.1 | 98 08.7 | S14 09.4 | Alphecca | 126 05.2 | N26 38.4 |
| D 13 | 81 03.0 | 52 30.5 | 34.2 | 77 55.3 | 32.1 | 77 40.6 | 12.2 | 113 11.1 | 09.4 | Alpheratz | 357 37.2 | N29 12.6 |
| A 14 | 96 05.5 | 67 30.2 | 35.2 | 92 56.0 | 31.4 | 92 42.6 | 12.4 | 128 13.6 | 09.4 | Altair | 62 01.8 | N 8 55.5 |
| Y 15 | 111 08.0 | 82 29.9 . . | 36.2 | 107 56.8 . . | 30.7 | 107 44.7 . . | 12.5 | 143 16.0 . . | 09.4 | Ankaa | 353 09.5 | S42 11.0 |
| 16 | 126 10.4 | 97 29.6 | 37.2 | 122 57.5 | 29.9 | 122 46.8 | 12.7 | 158 18.4 | 09.4 | Antares | 112 18.1 | S26 28.9 |
| 17 | 141 12.9 | 112 29.3 | 38.2 | 137 58.3 | 29.2 | 137 48.9 | 12.8 | 173 20.8 | 09.4 | | | |
| 18 | 156 15.3 | 127 28.9 | N 9 39.2 | 152 59.0 | S 0 28.5 | 152 51.0 | N 0 13.0 | 188 23.3 | S14 09.4 | Arcturus | 145 49.6 | N19 04.0 |
| 19 | 171 17.8 | 142 28.6 | 40.3 | 167 59.8 | 27.8 | 167 53.1 | 13.2 | 203 25.7 | 09.4 | Atria | 107 13.7 | S69 04.0 |
| 20 | 186 20.3 | 157 28.3 | 41.3 | 183 00.5 | 27.0 | 182 55.1 | 13.3 | 218 28.1 | 09.4 | Avior | 234 16.0 | S59 35.1 |
| 21 | 201 22.7 | 172 28.0 . . | 42.3 | 198 01.3 . . | 26.3 | 197 57.2 . . | 13.5 | 233 30.6 . . | 09.4 | Bellatrix | 278 25.5 | N 6 22.1 |
| 22 | 216 25.2 | 187 27.7 | 43.3 | 213 02.0 | 25.6 | 212 59.3 | 13.6 | 248 33.0 | 09.4 | Betelgeuse | 270 54.8 | N 7 24.6 |
| 23 | 231 27.7 | 202 27.3 | 44.3 | 228 02.8 | 24.9 | 228 01.4 | 13.8 | 263 35.4 | 09.4 | | | |
| 29 00 | 246 30.1 | 217 27.0 | N 9 45.3 | 243 03.6 | S 0 24.1 | 243 03.5 | N 0 13.9 | 278 37.9 | S14 09.4 | Canopus | 263 53.9 | S52 42.6 |
| 01 | 261 32.6 | 232 26.7 | 46.3 | 258 04.3 | 23.4 | 258 05.5 | 14.1 | 293 40.3 | 09.4 | Capella | 280 25.6 | N46 01.2 |
| 02 | 276 35.1 | 247 26.4 | 47.3 | 273 05.1 | 22.7 | 273 07.6 | 14.2 | 308 42.7 | 09.4 | Deneb | 49 27.0 | N45 21.3 |
| 03 | 291 37.5 | 262 26.0 . . | 48.4 | 288 05.8 . . | 22.0 | 288 09.7 . . | 14.4 | 323 45.2 . . | 09.4 | Denebola | 182 27.1 | N14 26.9 |
| 04 | 306 40.0 | 277 25.7 | 49.4 | 303 06.6 | 21.2 | 303 11.8 | 14.5 | 338 47.6 | 09.4 | Diphda | 348 49.7 | S17 51.9 |
| 05 | 321 42.5 | 292 25.4 | 50.4 | 318 07.3 | 20.5 | 318 13.9 | 14.7 | 353 50.1 | 09.4 | | | |
| 06 | 336 44.9 | 307 25.1 | N 9 51.4 | 333 08.1 | S 0 19.8 | 333 16.0 | N 0 14.9 | 8 52.5 | S14 09.4 | Dubhe | 193 43.6 | N61 38.2 |
| 07 | 351 47.4 | 322 24.8 | 52.4 | 348 08.8 | 19.1 | 348 18.0 | 15.0 | 23 54.9 | 09.4 | Elnath | 278 05.0 | N28 37.5 |
| 08 | 6 49.8 | 337 24.4 | 53.4 | 3 09.6 | 18.3 | 3 20.1 | 15.2 | 38 57.4 | 09.4 | Eltanin | 90 42.7 | N51 29.0 |
| S 09 | 21 52.3 | 352 24.1 . . | 54.4 | 18 10.3 . . | 17.6 | 18 22.2 . . | 15.3 | 53 59.8 . . | 09.4 | Enif | 33 40.8 | N 9 58.5 |
| U 10 | 36 54.8 | 7 23.8 | 55.4 | 33 11.1 | 16.9 | 33 24.3 | 15.5 | 69 02.2 | 09.4 | Fomalhaut | 15 17.0 | S29 30.2 |
| N 11 | 51 57.2 | 22 23.5 | 56.5 | 48 11.9 | 16.2 | 48 26.4 | 15.6 | 84 04.7 | 09.4 | | | |
| D 12 | 66 59.7 | 37 23.1 | N 9 57.5 | 63 12.6 | S 0 15.4 | 63 28.5 | N 0 15.8 | 99 07.1 | S14 09.4 | Gacrux | 171 53.7 | S57 14.5 |
| A 13 | 82 02.2 | 52 22.8 | 58.5 | 78 13.4 | 14.7 | 78 30.6 | 15.9 | 114 09.5 | 09.4 | Gienah | 175 45.7 | S17 40.0 |
| Y 14 | 97 04.6 | 67 22.5 | 9 59.5 | 93 14.1 | 14.0 | 93 32.6 | 16.1 | 129 12.0 | 09.4 | Hadar | 148 38.5 | S60 29.0 |
| 15 | 112 07.1 | 82 22.1 | 10 00.5 | 108 14.9 . . | 13.3 | 108 34.7 . . | 16.2 | 144 14.4 . . | 09.4 | Hamal | 327 53.9 | N23 33.9 |
| 16 | 127 09.6 | 97 21.8 | 01.5 | 123 15.6 | 12.5 | 123 36.8 | 16.4 | 159 16.8 | 09.4 | Kaus Aust. | 83 35.0 | S34 22.4 |
| 17 | 142 12.0 | 112 21.5 | 02.5 | 138 16.4 | 11.8 | 138 38.9 | 16.6 | 174 19.3 | 09.4 | | | |
| 18 | 157 14.5 | 127 21.2 | N10 03.5 | 153 17.1 | S 0 11.1 | 153 41.0 | N 0 16.7 | 189 21.7 | S14 09.4 | Kochab | 137 18.7 | N74 04.0 |
| 19 | 172 17.0 | 142 20.8 | 04.5 | 168 17.9 | 10.4 | 168 43.1 | 16.9 | 204 24.2 | 09.4 | Markab | 13 32.1 | N15 19.3 |
| 20 | 187 19.4 | 157 20.5 | 05.5 | 183 18.7 | 09.6 | 183 45.2 | 17.0 | 219 26.6 | 09.4 | Menkar | 314 08.7 | N 4 10.5 |
| 21 | 202 21.9 | 172 20.2 . . | 06.5 | 198 19.4 . . | 08.9 | 198 47.2 . . | 17.2 | 234 29.0 . . | 09.4 | Menkent | 147 59.8 | S36 28.9 |
| 22 | 217 24.3 | 187 19.9 | 07.5 | 213 20.2 | 08.2 | 213 49.3 | 17.3 | 249 31.5 | 09.4 | Miaplacidus | 221 39.0 | S69 48.8 |
| 23 | 232 26.8 | 202 19.5 | 08.5 | 228 20.9 | 07.5 | 228 51.4 | 17.5 | 264 33.9 | 09.4 | | | |
| 30 00 | 247 29.3 | 217 19.2 | N10 09.6 | 243 21.7 | S 0 06.7 | 243 53.5 | N 0 17.6 | 279 36.3 | S14 09.4 | Mirfak | 308 31.8 | N49 56.2 |
| 01 | 262 31.7 | 232 18.9 | 10.6 | 258 22.4 | 06.0 | 258 55.6 | 17.8 | 294 38.8 | 09.4 | Nunki | 75 50.1 | S26 16.1 |
| 02 | 277 34.2 | 247 18.5 | 11.6 | 273 23.2 | 05.3 | 273 57.7 | 17.9 | 309 41.2 | 09.4 | Peacock | 53 08.8 | S56 39.6 |
| 03 | 292 36.7 | 262 18.2 . . | 12.6 | 288 24.0 . . | 04.6 | 288 59.8 . . | 18.1 | 324 43.7 . . | 09.4 | Pollux | 243 20.2 | N27 58.4 |
| 04 | 307 39.1 | 277 17.9 | 13.6 | 303 24.7 | 03.8 | 304 01.9 | 18.2 | 339 46.1 | 09.4 | Procyon | 244 53.4 | N 5 10.0 |
| 05 | 322 41.6 | 292 17.5 | 14.6 | 318 25.5 | 03.1 | 319 03.9 | 18.4 | 354 48.5 | 09.4 | | | |
| 06 | 337 44.1 | 307 17.2 | N10 15.6 | 333 26.2 | S 0 02.4 | 334 06.0 | N 0 18.5 | 9 51.0 | S14 09.4 | Rasalhague | 96 00.2 | N12 32.6 |
| 07 | 352 46.5 | 322 16.9 | 16.6 | 348 27.0 | 01.7 | 349 08.1 | 18.7 | 24 53.4 | 09.4 | Regulus | 207 36.8 | N11 51.6 |
| 08 | 7 49.0 | 337 16.5 | 17.6 | 3 27.7 | 01.0 | 4 10.2 | 18.9 | 39 55.9 | 09.4 | Rigel | 281 06.3 | S 8 10.6 |
| M 09 | 22 51.4 | 352 16.2 . . | 18.6 | 18 28.5 | S 00.2 | 19 12.3 . . | 19.0 | 54 58.3 . . | 09.4 | Rigil Kent. | 139 42.7 | S60 55.7 |
| O 10 | 37 53.9 | 7 15.9 | 19.6 | 33 29.3 | N 00.5 | 34 14.4 | 19.2 | 70 00.7 | 09.4 | Sabik | 102 04.9 | S15 45.1 |
| N 11 | 52 56.4 | 22 15.5 | 20.6 | 48 30.0 | 01.2 | 49 16.5 | 19.3 | 85 03.2 | 09.4 | | | |
| D 12 | 67 58.8 | 37 15.2 | N10 21.6 | 63 30.8 | N 0 01.9 | 64 18.6 | N 0 19.5 | 100 05.6 | S14 09.4 | Schedar | 349 33.8 | N56 39.2 |
| A 13 | 83 01.3 | 52 14.9 | 22.6 | 78 31.5 | 02.7 | 79 20.7 | 19.6 | 115 08.0 | 09.4 | Shaula | 96 12.9 | S37 07.1 |
| Y 14 | 98 03.8 | 67 14.5 | 23.6 | 93 32.3 | 03.4 | 94 22.7 | 19.8 | 130 10.5 | 09.4 | Sirius | 258 28.5 | S16 44.9 |
| 15 | 113 06.2 | 82 14.2 . . | 24.6 | 108 33.0 . . | 04.1 | 109 24.8 . . | 19.9 | 145 12.9 . . | 09.4 | Spica | 158 24.4 | S11 16.7 |
| 16 | 128 08.7 | 97 13.9 | 25.6 | 123 33.8 | 04.8 | 124 26.9 | 20.1 | 160 15.4 | 09.4 | Suhail | 222 48.1 | S43 31.6 |
| 17 | 143 11.2 | 112 13.5 | 26.6 | 138 34.6 | 05.6 | 139 29.0 | 20.2 | 175 17.8 | 09.4 | | | |
| 18 | 158 13.6 | 127 13.2 | N10 27.6 | 153 35.3 | N 0 06.3 | 154 31.1 | N 0 20.4 | 190 20.3 | S14 09.4 | Vega | 80 34.3 | N38 48.1 |
| 19 | 173 16.1 | 142 12.9 | 28.6 | 168 36.1 | 07.0 | 169 33.2 | 20.5 | 205 22.7 | 09.4 | Zuben'ubi | 136 58.1 | S16 08.1 |
| 20 | 188 18.6 | 157 12.5 | 29.6 | 183 36.8 | 07.7 | 184 35.3 | 20.7 | 220 25.1 | 09.4 | | SHA | Mer. Pass. |
| 21 | 203 21.0 | 172 12.2 . . | 30.6 | 198 37.6 . . | 08.5 | 199 37.4 . . | 20.8 | 235 27.6 . . | 09.4 | | ° ′ | h m |
| 22 | 218 23.5 | 187 11.8 | 31.6 | 213 38.3 | 09.2 | 214 39.5 | 21.0 | 250 30.0 | 09.4 | Venus | 330 56.9 | 9 30 |
| 23 | 233 25.9 | 202 11.5 | 32.6 | 228 39.1 | 09.9 | 229 41.6 | 21.1 | 265 32.5 | 09.4 | Mars | 356 33.4 | 7 47 |
| | h m | | | | | | | | | Jupiter | 356 33.3 | 7 47 |
| Mer. Pass. 7 32.8 | v −0.3 | d 1.0 | v 0.8 | d 0.7 | v 2.1 | d 0.2 | v 2.4 | d 0.0 | Saturn | 32 07.7 | 5 25 |

| UT | SUN GHA | SUN Dec | MOON GHA | v | MOON Dec | d | HP |
|---|---|---|---|---|---|---|---|
| d h | ° ′ | ° ′ | ° ′ | ′ | ° ′ | ′ | ′ |
| **28** 00 | 180 41.4 | N21 25.3 | 208 26.2 | 14.4 | N13 20.9 | 12.3 | 55.1 |
| 01 | 195 41.3 | 25.8 | 222 59.6 | 14.4 | 13 33.2 | 12.3 | 55.1 |
| 02 | 210 41.2 | 26.2 | 237 33.0 | 14.4 | 13 45.5 | 12.2 | 55.1 |
| 03 | 225 41.2 .. | 26.6 | 252 06.4 | 14.3 | 13 57.7 | 12.1 | 55.1 |
| 04 | 240 41.1 | 27.0 | 266 39.7 | 14.3 | 14 09.8 | 12.1 | 55.0 |
| 05 | 255 41.0 | 27.4 | 281 13.0 | 14.3 | 14 21.9 | 12.0 | 55.0 |
| 06 | 270 40.9 | N21 27.8 | 295 46.3 | 14.2 | N14 33.9 | 11.9 | 55.0 |
| 07 | 285 40.8 | 28.2 | 310 19.5 | 14.2 | 14 45.8 | 11.9 | 55.0 |
| 08 | 300 40.8 | 28.6 | 324 52.7 | 14.1 | 14 57.7 | 11.8 | 55.0 |
| 09 | 315 40.7 .. | 29.0 | 339 25.8 | 14.2 | 15 09.5 | 11.7 | 55.0 |
| 10 | 330 40.6 | 29.4 | 353 59.0 | 14.0 | 15 21.2 | 11.6 | 54.9 |
| 11 | 345 40.5 | 29.8 | 8 32.0 | 14.1 | 15 32.8 | 11.6 | 54.9 |
| 12 | 0 40.5 | N21 30.2 | 23 05.1 | 14.0 | N15 44.4 | 11.5 | 54.9 |
| 13 | 15 40.4 | 30.6 | 37 38.1 | 13.9 | 15 55.9 | 11.5 | 54.9 |
| 14 | 30 40.3 | 31.0 | 52 11.0 | 13.9 | 16 07.4 | 11.3 | 54.9 |
| 15 | 45 40.2 .. | 31.4 | 66 43.9 | 13.9 | 16 18.7 | 11.3 | 54.9 |
| 16 | 60 40.1 | 31.8 | 81 16.8 | 13.8 | 16 30.0 | 11.2 | 54.9 |
| 17 | 75 40.0 | 32.2 | 95 49.6 | 13.8 | 16 41.2 | 11.2 | 54.8 |
| 18 | 90 40.0 | N21 32.6 | 110 22.4 | 13.7 | N16 52.4 | 11.0 | 54.8 |
| 19 | 105 39.9 | 32.9 | 124 55.1 | 13.7 | 17 03.4 | 11.0 | 54.8 |
| 20 | 120 39.8 | 33.3 | 139 27.8 | 13.7 | 17 14.4 | 10.9 | 54.8 |
| 21 | 135 39.7 .. | 33.7 | 154 00.5 | 13.6 | 17 25.3 | 10.8 | 54.8 |
| 22 | 150 39.6 | 34.1 | 168 33.1 | 13.6 | 17 36.1 | 10.8 | 54.8 |
| 23 | 165 39.6 | 34.5 | 183 05.7 | 13.5 | 17 46.9 | 10.7 | 54.7 |
| **29** 00 | 180 39.5 | N21 34.9 | 197 38.2 | 13.4 | N17 57.6 | 10.5 | 54.7 |
| 01 | 195 39.4 | 35.3 | 212 10.6 | 13.5 | 18 08.1 | 10.5 | 54.7 |
| 02 | 210 39.3 | 35.7 | 226 43.1 | 13.3 | 18 18.6 | 10.5 | 54.7 |
| 03 | 225 39.2 .. | 36.1 | 241 15.4 | 13.4 | 18 29.1 | 10.3 | 54.7 |
| 04 | 240 39.1 | 36.5 | 255 47.8 | 13.3 | 18 39.4 | 10.2 | 54.7 |
| 05 | 255 39.1 | 36.9 | 270 20.1 | 13.2 | 18 49.6 | 10.2 | 54.7 |
| 06 | 270 39.0 | N21 37.2 | 284 52.3 | 13.2 | N18 59.8 | 10.1 | 54.7 |
| 07 | 285 38.9 | 37.6 | 299 24.5 | 13.1 | 19 09.9 | 10.0 | 54.6 |
| 08 | 300 38.8 | 38.0 | 313 56.6 | 13.1 | 19 19.9 | 9.9 | 54.6 |
| 09 | 315 38.7 .. | 38.4 | 328 28.7 | 13.1 | 19 29.8 | 9.8 | 54.6 |
| 10 | 330 38.6 | 38.8 | 343 00.8 | 13.0 | 19 39.6 | 9.7 | 54.6 |
| 11 | 345 38.6 | 39.2 | 357 32.8 | 12.9 | 19 49.3 | 9.6 | 54.6 |
| 12 | 0 38.5 | N21 39.5 | 12 04.7 | 12.9 | N19 58.9 | 9.5 | 54.6 |
| 13 | 15 38.4 | 39.9 | 26 36.6 | 12.9 | 20 08.4 | 9.5 | 54.6 |
| 14 | 30 38.3 | 40.3 | 41 08.5 | 12.8 | 20 17.9 | 9.3 | 54.5 |
| 15 | 45 38.2 .. | 40.7 | 55 40.3 | 12.7 | 20 27.2 | 9.3 | 54.5 |
| 16 | 60 38.1 | 41.1 | 70 12.0 | 12.6 | 20 36.5 | 9.2 | 54.5 |
| 17 | 75 38.1 | 41.5 | 84 43.8 | 12.6 | 20 45.7 | 9.0 | 54.5 |
| 18 | 90 38.0 | N21 41.8 | 99 15.4 | 12.6 | N20 54.7 | 9.0 | 54.5 |
| 19 | 105 37.9 | 42.2 | 113 47.0 | 12.6 | 21 03.7 | 8.9 | 54.5 |
| 20 | 120 37.8 | 42.6 | 128 18.6 | 12.5 | 21 12.6 | 8.8 | 54.5 |
| 21 | 135 37.7 .. | 43.0 | 142 50.1 | 12.5 | 21 21.4 | 8.6 | 54.5 |
| 22 | 150 37.6 | 43.3 | 157 21.6 | 12.4 | 21 30.0 | 8.6 | 54.4 |
| 23 | 165 37.5 | 43.7 | 171 53.0 | 12.3 | 21 38.6 | 8.5 | 54.4 |
| **30** 00 | 180 37.5 | N21 44.1 | 186 24.3 | 12.4 | N21 47.1 | 8.4 | 54.4 |
| 01 | 195 37.4 | 44.5 | 200 55.7 | 12.2 | 21 55.5 | 8.3 | 54.4 |
| 02 | 210 37.3 | 44.8 | 215 26.9 | 12.3 | 22 03.8 | 8.1 | 54.4 |
| 03 | 225 37.2 .. | 45.2 | 229 58.2 | 12.1 | 22 11.9 | 8.1 | 54.4 |
| 04 | 240 37.1 | 45.6 | 244 29.3 | 12.2 | 22 20.0 | 8.0 | 54.4 |
| 05 | 255 37.0 | 46.0 | 259 00.5 | 12.0 | 22 28.0 | 7.8 | 54.4 |
| 06 | 270 36.9 | N21 46.3 | 273 31.5 | 12.1 | N22 35.8 | 7.8 | 54.4 |
| 07 | 285 36.8 | 46.7 | 288 02.6 | 11.9 | 22 43.6 | 7.7 | 54.3 |
| 08 | 300 36.8 | 47.1 | 302 33.5 | 12.0 | 22 51.3 | 7.5 | 54.3 |
| 09 | 315 36.7 .. | 47.4 | 317 04.5 | 11.9 | 22 58.8 | 7.4 | 54.3 |
| 10 | 330 36.6 | 47.8 | 331 35.4 | 11.8 | 23 06.2 | 7.4 | 54.3 |
| 11 | 345 36.5 | 48.2 | 346 06.2 | 11.8 | 23 13.6 | 7.2 | 54.3 |
| 12 | 0 36.4 | N21 48.5 | 0 37.0 | 11.8 | N23 20.8 | 7.1 | 54.3 |
| 13 | 15 36.3 | 48.9 | 15 07.8 | 11.7 | 23 27.9 | 7.0 | 54.3 |
| 14 | 30 36.2 | 49.3 | 29 38.5 | 11.6 | 23 34.9 | 6.9 | 54.3 |
| 15 | 45 36.1 .. | 49.6 | 44 09.1 | 11.6 | 23 41.8 | 6.8 | 54.3 |
| 16 | 60 36.0 | 50.0 | 58 39.7 | 11.6 | 23 48.6 | 6.7 | 54.3 |
| 17 | 75 35.9 | 50.4 | 73 10.3 | 11.5 | 23 55.3 | 6.6 | 54.3 |
| 18 | 90 35.9 | N21 50.7 | 87 40.8 | 11.5 | N24 01.9 | 6.4 | 54.2 |
| 19 | 105 35.8 | 51.1 | 102 11.3 | 11.5 | 24 08.3 | 6.3 | 54.2 |
| 20 | 120 35.7 | 51.5 | 116 41.8 | 11.4 | 24 14.6 | 6.3 | 54.2 |
| 21 | 135 35.6 .. | 51.8 | 131 12.2 | 11.3 | 24 20.9 | 6.1 | 54.2 |
| 22 | 150 35.5 | 52.2 | 145 42.5 | 11.4 | 24 27.0 | 6.0 | 54.2 |
| 23 | 165 35.4 | 52.5 | 160 12.9 | 11.2 | N24 33.0 | 5.8 | 54.2 |
| | SD 15.8 | d 0.4 | SD 15.0 | | 14.9 | | 14.8 |

Days at left margin: **SATURDAY** (28), **SUNDAY** (29), **MONDAY** (30).

### Twilight / Sunrise / Moonrise

| Lat. | Naut. | Civil | Sunrise | Moonrise 28 | 29 | 30 | 31 |
|---|---|---|---|---|---|---|---|
| ° | h m | h m | h m | h m | h m | h m | h m |
| N 72 | □ | □ | □ | (00 58 / 23 27) | □ | □ | □ |
| N 70 | □ | □ | □ | 01 23 | 00 38 | □ | □ |
| 68 | □ | □ | □ | 01 42 | 01 16 | 00 13 | □ |
| 66 | //// | //// | 01 25 | 01 58 | 01 43 | 01 19 | □ |
| 64 | //// | //// | 02 06 | 02 10 | 02 03 | 01 55 | 01 42 |
| 62 | //// | 00 39 | 02 33 | 02 21 | 02 20 | 02 21 | 02 25 |
| 60 | //// | 01 35 | 02 54 | 02 30 | 02 34 | 02 41 | 02 54 |
| N 58 | //// | 02 06 | 03 11 | 02 39 | 02 46 | 02 58 | 03 16 |
| 56 | 00 35 | 02 29 | 03 26 | 02 46 | 02 57 | 03 12 | 03 34 |
| 54 | 01 27 | 02 48 | 03 38 | 02 52 | 03 06 | 03 25 | 03 50 |
| 52 | 01 56 | 03 03 | 03 49 | 02 58 | 03 15 | 03 36 | 04 03 |
| 50 | 02 17 | 03 16 | 03 58 | 03 03 | 03 22 | 03 45 | 04 15 |
| 45 | 02 56 | 03 43 | 04 18 | 03 15 | 03 38 | 04 06 | 04 39 |
| N 40 | 03 23 | 04 03 | 04 35 | 03 24 | 03 51 | 04 22 | 04 59 |
| 35 | 03 44 | 04 19 | 04 48 | 03 33 | 04 03 | 04 37 | 05 15 |
| 30 | 04 01 | 04 33 | 05 00 | 03 40 | 04 13 | 04 49 | 05 30 |
| 20 | 04 28 | 04 56 | 05 20 | 03 53 | 04 30 | 05 10 | 05 54 |
| N 10 | 04 48 | 05 15 | 05 38 | 04 04 | 04 45 | 05 29 | 06 15 |
| 0 | 05 06 | 05 32 | 05 54 | 04 14 | 04 59 | 05 46 | 06 35 |
| S 10 | 05 21 | 05 47 | 06 10 | 04 25 | 05 13 | 06 03 | 06 54 |
| 20 | 05 36 | 06 03 | 06 27 | 04 36 | 05 29 | 06 22 | 07 16 |
| 30 | 05 51 | 06 20 | 06 46 | 04 49 | 05 46 | 06 44 | 07 40 |
| 35 | 05 58 | 06 30 | 06 57 | 04 57 | 05 57 | 06 56 | 07 55 |
| 40 | 06 07 | 06 40 | 07 10 | 05 06 | 06 09 | 07 11 | 08 12 |
| 45 | 06 16 | 06 52 | 07 25 | 05 16 | 06 23 | 07 29 | 08 32 |
| S 50 | 06 26 | 07 07 | 07 44 | 05 28 | 06 40 | 07 51 | 08 58 |
| 52 | 06 31 | 07 13 | 07 53 | 05 34 | 06 48 | 08 01 | 09 10 |
| 54 | 06 35 | 07 20 | 08 03 | 05 41 | 06 57 | 08 13 | 09 25 |
| 56 | 06 41 | 07 28 | 08 14 | 05 48 | 07 08 | 08 27 | 09 41 |
| 58 | 06 46 | 07 37 | 08 26 | 05 56 | 07 20 | 08 43 | 10 02 |
| S 60 | 06 53 | 07 47 | 08 41 | 06 05 | 07 33 | 09 02 | 10 27 |

### Sunset / Twilight / Moonset

| Lat. | Sunset | Civil | Naut. | Moonset 28 | 29 | 30 | 31 |
|---|---|---|---|---|---|---|---|
| ° | h m | h m | h m | h m | h m | h m | h m |
| N 72 | □ | □ | □ | 21 48 | □ | □ | □ |
| N 70 | □ | □ | □ | 20 38 | □ | □ | □ |
| 68 | □ | □ | □ | 20 01 | 22 41 | □ | □ |
| 66 | 22 33 | //// | //// | 19 36 | 21 35 | □ | □ |
| 64 | 21 51 | //// | //// | 19 16 | 21 00 | 22 54 | □ |
| 62 | 21 23 | 23 24 | //// | 19 00 | 20 35 | 22 11 | 23 42 |
| 60 | 21 02 | 22 22 | //// | 18 47 | 20 15 | 21 43 | 23 02 |
| N 58 | 20 45 | 21 50 | //// | 18 36 | 19 59 | 21 21 | 22 35 |
| 56 | 20 30 | 21 27 | 23 27 | 18 26 | 19 46 | 21 03 | 22 13 |
| 54 | 20 18 | 21 08 | 22 31 | 18 17 | 19 34 | 20 48 | 21 56 |
| 52 | 20 07 | 20 53 | 22 01 | 18 10 | 19 23 | 20 35 | 21 41 |
| 50 | 19 57 | 20 40 | 21 39 | 18 03 | 19 14 | 20 23 | 21 28 |
| 45 | 19 37 | 20 13 | 21 00 | 17 48 | 18 55 | 20 00 | 21 01 |
| N 40 | 19 21 | 19 52 | 20 33 | 17 36 | 18 39 | 19 41 | 20 40 |
| 35 | 19 07 | 19 36 | 20 11 | 17 26 | 18 26 | 19 25 | 20 22 |
| 30 | 18 55 | 19 22 | 19 54 | 17 17 | 18 14 | 19 11 | 20 07 |
| 20 | 18 35 | 18 59 | 19 28 | 17 01 | 17 54 | 18 48 | 19 41 |
| N 10 | 18 17 | 18 40 | 19 07 | 16 48 | 17 37 | 18 28 | 19 19 |
| 0 | 18 01 | 18 23 | 18 49 | 16 36 | 17 21 | 18 09 | 18 59 |
| S 10 | 17 45 | 18 08 | 18 34 | 16 23 | 17 06 | 17 51 | 18 38 |
| 20 | 17 28 | 17 52 | 18 19 | 16 10 | 16 49 | 17 31 | 18 16 |
| 30 | 17 09 | 17 35 | 18 04 | 15 55 | 16 29 | 17 08 | 17 51 |
| 35 | 16 57 | 17 25 | 17 56 | 15 46 | 16 18 | 16 54 | 17 36 |
| 40 | 16 44 | 17 14 | 17 48 | 15 36 | 16 05 | 16 39 | 17 18 |
| 45 | 16 29 | 17 02 | 17 39 | 15 25 | 15 50 | 16 20 | 16 58 |
| S 50 | 16 11 | 16 48 | 17 29 | 15 11 | 15 32 | 15 58 | 16 31 |
| 52 | 16 02 | 16 41 | 17 24 | 15 04 | 15 23 | 15 47 | 16 19 |
| 54 | 15 52 | 16 34 | 17 19 | 14 57 | 15 13 | 15 34 | 16 04 |
| 56 | 15 41 | 16 26 | 17 14 | 14 49 | 15 02 | 15 20 | 15 47 |
| 58 | 15 28 | 16 17 | 17 08 | 14 40 | 14 50 | 15 04 | 15 27 |
| S 60 | 15 13 | 16 07 | 17 02 | 14 30 | 14 35 | 14 44 | 15 01 |

### SUN / MOON

| Day | Eqn. of Time 00ʰ | Eqn. of Time 12ʰ | Mer. Pass. | Mer. Pass. Upper | Mer. Pass. Lower | Age | Phase |
|---|---|---|---|---|---|---|---|
| d | m s | m s | h m | h m | h m | d | % |
| 28 | 02 46 | 02 42 | 11 57 | 10 25 | 22 47 | 28 | 4 |
| 29 | 02 38 | 02 34 | 11 57 | 11 10 | 23 34 | 29 | 1 |
| 30 | 02 30 | 02 26 | 11 58 | 11 57 | 24 22 | 00 | 0 |

| UT | ARIES GHA | VENUS −3.9 GHA | Dec | MARS +0.6 GHA | Dec | JUPITER −2.2 GHA | Dec | SATURN +0.6 GHA | Dec | STARS Name | SHA | Dec |
|---|---|---|---|---|---|---|---|---|---|---|---|---|
| 31 00 | 248 28.4 | 217 11.2 N10 33.6 | | 243 39.9 N 0 10.6 | | 244 43.6 N 0 21.3 | | 280 34.9 S14 09.4 | | Acamar | 315 13.8 | S40 12.9 |
| 01 | 263 30.9 | 232 10.8 | 34.6 | 258 40.6 | 11.3 | 259 45.7 | 21.4 | 295 37.3 | 09.4 | Achernar | 335 22.3 | S57 07.3 |
| 02 | 278 33.3 | 247 10.5 | 35.6 | 273 41.4 | 12.1 | 274 47.8 | 21.6 | 310 39.8 | 09.4 | Acrux | 173 02.1 | S63 13.6 |
| 03 | 293 35.8 | 262 10.2 .. | 36.6 | 288 42.1 .. | 12.8 | 289 49.9 .. | 21.7 | 325 42.2 .. | 09.4 | Adhara | 255 07.9 | S29 00.3 |
| 04 | 308 38.3 | 277 09.8 | 37.6 | 303 42.9 | 13.5 | 304 52.0 | 21.9 | 340 44.7 | 09.4 | Aldebaran | 290 42.5 | N16 33.2 |
| 05 | 323 40.7 | 292 09.5 | 38.6 | 318 43.7 | 14.2 | 319 54.1 | 22.0 | 355 47.1 | 09.4 | | | |
| 06 | 338 43.2 | 307 09.1 N10 39.6 | | 333 44.4 N 0 15.0 | | 334 56.2 N 0 22.2 | | 10 49.6 S14 09.4 | | Alioth | 166 14.6 | N55 50.6 |
| 07 | 353 45.7 | 322 08.8 | 40.6 | 348 45.2 | 15.7 | 349 58.3 | 22.3 | 25 52.0 | 09.4 | Alkaid | 152 53.6 | N49 12.3 |
| T 08 | 8 48.1 | 337 08.5 | 41.6 | 3 45.9 | 16.4 | 5 00.4 | 22.5 | 40 54.4 | 09.4 | Alnair | 27 35.6 | S46 51.0 |
| U 09 | 23 50.6 | 352 08.1 .. | 42.6 | 18 46.7 .. | 17.1 | 20 02.5 .. | 22.6 | 55 56.9 .. | 09.4 | Alnilam | 275 40.3 | S 1 11.3 |
| E 10 | 38 53.1 | 7 07.8 | 43.6 | 33 47.4 | 17.9 | 35 04.6 | 22.8 | 70 59.3 | 09.4 | Alphard | 217 50.0 | S 8 45.4 |
| S 11 | 53 55.5 | 22 07.4 | 44.6 | 48 48.2 | 18.6 | 50 06.7 | 22.9 | 86 01.8 | 09.4 | | | |
| D 12 | 68 58.0 | 37 07.1 N10 45.6 | | 63 49.0 N 0 19.3 | | 65 08.8 N 0 23.1 | | 101 04.2 S14 09.4 | | Alphecca | 126 05.2 | N26 38.4 |
| A 13 | 84 00.4 | 52 06.7 | 46.6 | 78 49.7 | 20.0 | 80 10.9 | 23.2 | 116 06.7 | 09.4 | Alpheratz | 357 37.1 | N29 12.6 |
| Y 14 | 99 02.9 | 67 06.4 | 47.6 | 93 50.5 | 20.7 | 95 13.0 | 23.4 | 131 09.1 | 09.4 | Altair | 62 01.8 | N 8 55.5 |
| 15 | 114 05.4 | 82 06.1 .. | 48.6 | 108 51.2 .. | 21.5 | 110 15.0 .. | 23.5 | 146 11.5 .. | 09.4 | Ankaa | 353 09.5 | S42 11.0 |
| 16 | 129 07.8 | 97 05.7 | 49.6 | 123 52.0 | 22.2 | 125 17.1 | 23.7 | 161 14.0 | 09.4 | Antares | 112 18.1 | S26 28.9 |
| 17 | 144 10.3 | 112 05.4 | 50.5 | 138 52.8 | 22.9 | 140 19.2 | 23.8 | 176 16.4 | 09.4 | | | |
| 18 | 159 12.8 | 127 05.0 N10 51.5 | | 153 53.5 N 0 23.6 | | 155 21.3 N 0 24.0 | | 191 18.9 S14 09.4 | | Arcturus | 145 49.6 | N19 04.0 |
| 19 | 174 15.2 | 142 04.7 | 52.5 | 168 54.3 | 24.4 | 170 23.4 | 24.1 | 206 21.3 | 09.4 | Atria | 107 13.7 | S69 04.0 |
| 20 | 189 17.7 | 157 04.3 | 53.5 | 183 55.0 | 25.1 | 185 25.5 | 24.3 | 221 23.8 | 09.4 | Avior | 234 16.0 | S59 35.1 |
| 21 | 204 20.2 | 172 04.0 .. | 54.5 | 198 55.8 .. | 25.8 | 200 27.6 .. | 24.4 | 236 26.2 .. | 09.4 | Bellatrix | 278 25.5 | N 6 22.1 |
| 22 | 219 22.6 | 187 03.6 | 55.5 | 213 56.6 | 26.5 | 215 29.7 | 24.6 | 251 28.7 | 09.4 | Betelgeuse | 270 54.8 | N 7 24.6 |
| 23 | 234 25.1 | 202 03.3 | 56.5 | 228 57.3 | 27.2 | 230 31.8 | 24.7 | 266 31.1 | 09.4 | | | |
| 1 00 | 249 27.6 | 217 02.9 N10 57.5 | | 243 58.1 N 0 28.0 | | 245 33.9 N 0 24.9 | | 281 33.6 S14 09.4 | | Canopus | 263 53.9 | S52 42.6 |
| 01 | 264 30.0 | 232 02.6 | 58.5 | 258 58.8 | 28.7 | 260 36.0 | 25.0 | 296 36.0 | 09.4 | Capella | 280 25.6 | N46 01.2 |
| 02 | 279 32.5 | 247 02.2 | 10 59.5 | 273 59.6 | 29.4 | 275 38.1 | 25.2 | 311 38.4 | 09.4 | Deneb | 49 27.0 | N45 21.3 |
| 03 | 294 34.9 | 262 01.9 | 11 00.5 | 289 00.4 .. | 30.1 | 290 40.2 .. | 25.3 | 326 40.9 .. | 09.4 | Denebola | 182 27.1 | N14 26.9 |
| 04 | 309 37.4 | 277 01.6 | 01.5 | 304 01.1 | 30.9 | 305 42.3 | 25.5 | 341 43.3 | 09.4 | Diphda | 348 49.6 | S17 51.9 |
| 05 | 324 39.9 | 292 01.2 | 02.4 | 319 01.9 | 31.6 | 320 44.4 | 25.6 | 356 45.8 | 09.4 | | | |
| 06 | 339 42.3 | 307 00.9 N11 03.4 | | 334 02.6 N 0 32.3 | | 335 46.5 N 0 25.8 | | 11 48.2 S14 09.4 | | Dubhe | 193 43.7 | N61 38.2 |
| W 07 | 354 44.8 | 322 00.5 | 04.4 | 349 03.4 | 33.0 | 350 48.6 | 25.9 | 26 50.7 | 09.4 | Elnath | 278 05.0 | N28 37.5 |
| E 08 | 9 47.3 | 337 00.2 | 05.4 | 4 04.2 | 33.7 | 5 50.7 | 26.1 | 41 53.1 | 09.4 | Eltanin | 90 42.7 | N51 29.0 |
| D 09 | 24 49.7 | 351 59.8 .. | 06.4 | 19 04.9 .. | 34.5 | 20 52.8 .. | 26.2 | 56 55.6 .. | 09.4 | Enif | 33 40.8 | N 9 58.5 |
| N 10 | 39 52.2 | 6 59.5 | 07.4 | 34 05.7 | 35.2 | 35 54.9 | 26.4 | 71 58.0 | 09.4 | Fomalhaut | 15 16.9 | S29 30.2 |
| E 11 | 54 54.7 | 21 59.1 | 08.4 | 49 06.4 | 35.9 | 50 57.0 | 26.5 | 87 00.5 | 09.4 | | | |
| S 12 | 69 57.1 | 36 58.7 N11 09.4 | | 64 07.2 N 0 36.6 | | 65 59.1 N 0 26.7 | | 102 02.9 S14 09.4 | | Gacrux | 171 53.8 | S57 14.5 |
| D 13 | 84 59.6 | 51 58.4 | 10.3 | 79 08.0 | 37.4 | 81 01.2 | 26.8 | 117 05.4 | 09.4 | Gienah | 175 45.7 | S17 40.0 |
| A 14 | 100 02.1 | 66 58.0 | 11.3 | 94 08.7 | 38.1 | 96 03.3 | 27.0 | 132 07.8 | 09.4 | Hadar | 148 38.5 | S60 29.0 |
| Y 15 | 115 04.5 | 81 57.7 .. | 12.3 | 109 09.5 .. | 38.8 | 111 05.4 .. | 27.1 | 147 10.3 .. | 09.4 | Hamal | 327 53.9 | N23 33.9 |
| 16 | 130 07.0 | 96 57.3 | 13.3 | 124 10.2 | 39.5 | 126 07.5 | 27.3 | 162 12.7 | 09.4 | Kaus Aust. | 83 35.0 | S34 22.4 |
| 17 | 145 09.4 | 111 57.0 | 14.3 | 139 11.0 | 40.2 | 141 09.6 | 27.4 | 177 15.2 | 09.4 | | | |
| 18 | 160 11.9 | 126 56.6 N11 15.3 | | 154 11.8 N 0 41.0 | | 156 11.7 N 0 27.6 | | 192 17.6 S14 09.4 | | Kochab | 137 18.8 | N74 04.0 |
| 19 | 175 14.4 | 141 56.3 | 16.3 | 169 12.5 | 41.7 | 171 13.8 | 27.7 | 207 20.1 | 09.4 | Markab | 13 32.1 | N15 19.3 |
| 20 | 190 16.8 | 156 55.9 | 17.2 | 184 13.3 | 42.4 | 186 15.9 | 27.8 | 222 22.5 | 09.4 | Menkar | 314 08.7 | N 4 10.5 |
| 21 | 205 19.3 | 171 55.6 .. | 18.2 | 199 14.0 .. | 43.1 | 201 18.0 .. | 28.0 | 237 25.0 .. | 09.4 | Menkent | 147 59.8 | S36 28.9 |
| 22 | 220 21.8 | 186 55.2 | 19.2 | 214 14.8 | 43.8 | 216 20.1 | 28.1 | 252 27.4 | 09.4 | Miaplacidus | 221 39.1 | S69 48.8 |
| 23 | 235 24.2 | 201 54.9 | 20.2 | 229 15.6 | 44.6 | 231 22.2 | 28.3 | 267 29.9 | 09.4 | | | |
| 2 00 | 250 26.7 | 216 54.5 N11 21.2 | | 244 16.3 N 0 45.3 | | 246 24.3 N 0 28.4 | | 282 32.3 S14 09.4 | | Mirfak | 308 31.8 | N49 56.2 |
| 01 | 265 29.2 | 231 54.1 | 22.2 | 259 17.1 | 46.0 | 261 26.4 | 28.6 | 297 34.8 | 09.5 | Nunki | 75 50.1 | S26 16.1 |
| 02 | 280 31.6 | 246 53.8 | 23.1 | 274 17.9 | 46.7 | 276 28.5 | 28.7 | 312 37.2 | 09.5 | Peacock | 53 08.8 | S56 39.6 |
| 03 | 295 34.1 | 261 53.4 .. | 24.1 | 289 18.6 .. | 47.4 | 291 30.6 .. | 28.9 | 327 39.7 .. | 09.5 | Pollux | 243 20.2 | N27 58.4 |
| 04 | 310 36.6 | 276 53.1 | 25.1 | 304 19.4 | 48.2 | 306 32.7 | 29.0 | 342 42.1 | 09.5 | Procyon | 244 53.4 | N 5 10.0 |
| 05 | 325 39.0 | 291 52.7 | 26.1 | 319 20.1 | 48.9 | 321 34.8 | 29.2 | 357 44.6 | 09.5 | | | |
| 06 | 340 41.5 | 306 52.4 N11 27.1 | | 334 20.9 N 0 49.6 | | 336 36.9 N 0 29.3 | | 12 47.0 S14 09.5 | | Rasalhague | 96 00.2 | N12 32.6 |
| 07 | 355 43.9 | 321 52.0 | 28.0 | 349 21.7 | 50.3 | 351 39.0 | 29.5 | 27 49.5 | 09.5 | Regulus | 207 36.8 | N11 51.6 |
| T 08 | 10 46.4 | 336 51.6 | 29.0 | 4 22.4 | 51.1 | 6 41.1 | 29.6 | 42 51.9 | 09.5 | Rigel | 281 06.3 | S 8 10.6 |
| H 09 | 25 48.9 | 351 51.3 .. | 30.0 | 19 23.2 .. | 51.8 | 21 43.2 .. | 29.8 | 57 54.4 .. | 09.5 | Rigil Kent. | 139 42.7 | S60 55.7 |
| U 10 | 40 51.3 | 6 50.9 | 31.0 | 34 23.9 | 52.5 | 36 45.3 | 29.9 | 72 56.8 | 09.5 | Sabik | 102 04.9 | S15 45.1 |
| R 11 | 55 53.8 | 21 50.6 | 32.0 | 49 24.7 | 53.2 | 51 47.4 | 30.0 | 87 59.3 | 09.5 | | | |
| S 12 | 70 56.3 | 36 50.2 N11 32.9 | | 64 25.5 N 0 53.9 | | 66 49.5 N 0 30.2 | | 103 01.7 S14 09.5 | | Schedar | 349 33.8 | N56 39.2 |
| D 13 | 85 58.7 | 51 49.8 | 33.9 | 79 26.2 | 54.7 | 81 51.6 | 30.3 | 118 04.2 | 09.5 | Shaula | 96 12.9 | S37 07.1 |
| A 14 | 101 01.2 | 66 49.5 | 34.9 | 94 27.0 | 55.4 | 96 53.7 | 30.5 | 133 06.6 | 09.5 | Sirius | 258 28.5 | S16 44.9 |
| Y 15 | 116 03.7 | 81 49.1 .. | 35.9 | 109 27.8 .. | 56.1 | 111 55.8 .. | 30.6 | 148 09.1 .. | 09.5 | Spica | 158 24.4 | S11 16.7 |
| 16 | 131 06.1 | 96 48.7 | 36.8 | 124 28.5 | 56.8 | 126 57.9 | 30.8 | 163 11.5 | 09.5 | Suhail | 222 48.1 | S43 31.5 |
| 17 | 146 08.6 | 111 48.4 | 37.8 | 139 29.3 | 57.5 | 142 00.0 | 30.9 | 178 14.0 | 09.5 | | | |
| 18 | 161 11.0 | 126 48.0 N11 38.8 | | 154 30.0 N 0 58.3 | | 157 02.1 N 0 31.1 | | 193 16.4 S14 09.5 | | Vega | 80 34.3 | N38 48.1 |
| 19 | 176 13.5 | 141 47.7 | 39.8 | 169 30.8 | 59.0 | 172 04.2 | 31.2 | 208 18.9 | 09.5 | Zuben'ubi | 136 58.1 | S16 08.1 |
| 20 | 191 16.0 | 156 47.3 | 40.7 | 184 31.6 | 0 59.7 | 187 06.3 | 31.4 | 223 21.3 | 09.5 | | SHA | Mer. Pass. |
| 21 | 206 18.4 | 171 46.9 .. | 41.7 | 199 32.3 | 1 00.4 | 202 08.4 .. | 31.5 | 238 23.8 .. | 09.5 | | | h m |
| 22 | 221 20.9 | 186 46.6 | 42.7 | 214 33.1 | 01.1 | 217 10.5 | 31.6 | 253 26.2 | 09.5 | Venus | 327 35.4 | 9 32 |
| 23 | 236 23.4 | 201 46.2 | 43.7 | 229 33.9 | 01.8 | 232 12.6 | 31.8 | 268 28.7 | 09.5 | Mars | 354 30.5 | 7 44 |
| Mer. Pass. h m 7 21.0 | | v −0.4 | d 1.0 | v 0.8 | d 0.7 | v 2.1 | d 0.1 | v 2.4 | d 0.0 | Jupiter | 356 06.4 | 7 37 |
| | | | | | | | | | | Saturn | 32 06.0 | 5 13 |

| UT | SUN GHA | SUN Dec | MOON GHA | v | MOON Dec | d | HP |
|---|---|---|---|---|---|---|---|
| d h | ° ′ | ° ′ | ° ′ | ′ | ° ′ | ′ | ′ |
| **31** 00 | 180 35.3 | N21 52.9 | 174 43.1 | 11.3 | N24 38.8 | 5.8 | 54.2 |
| 01 | 195 35.2 | 53.3 | 189 13.4 | 11.2 | 24 44.6 | 5.6 | 54.2 |
| 02 | 210 35.1 | 53.6 | 203 43.6 | 11.1 | 24 50.2 | 5.6 | 54.2 |
| 03 | 225 35.0 .. | 54.0 | 218 13.7 | 11.2 | 24 55.8 | 5.4 | 54.2 |
| 04 | 240 34.9 | 54.3 | 232 43.9 | 11.0 | 25 01.2 | 5.3 | 54.2 |
| 05 | 255 34.9 | 54.7 | 247 13.9 | 11.1 | 25 06.5 | 5.1 | 54.2 |
| 06 | 270 34.8 | N21 55.0 | 261 44.0 | 11.0 | N25 11.6 | 5.1 | 54.1 |
| 07 | 285 34.7 | 55.4 | 276 14.0 | 11.0 | 25 16.7 | 4.9 | 54.1 |
| 08 | 300 34.6 | 55.8 | 290 44.0 | 10.9 | 25 21.6 | 4.8 | 54.1 |
| 09 | 315 34.5 .. | 56.1 | 305 13.9 | 10.9 | 25 26.4 | 4.7 | 54.1 |
| 10 | 330 34.4 | 56.5 | 319 43.8 | 10.9 | 25 31.1 | 4.6 | 54.1 |
| 11 | 345 34.3 | 56.8 | 334 13.7 | 10.9 | 25 35.7 | 4.4 | 54.1 |
| 12 | 0 34.2 | N21 57.2 | 348 43.6 | 10.8 | N25 40.1 | 4.3 | 54.1 |
| 13 | 15 34.1 | 57.5 | 3 13.4 | 10.8 | 25 44.4 | 4.2 | 54.1 |
| 14 | 30 34.0 | 57.9 | 17 43.2 | 10.7 | 25 48.6 | 4.1 | 54.1 |
| 15 | 45 33.9 .. | 58.2 | 32 12.9 | 10.7 | 25 52.7 | 4.0 | 54.1 |
| 16 | 60 33.8 | 58.6 | 46 42.6 | 10.7 | 25 56.7 | 3.8 | 54.1 |
| 17 | 75 33.7 | 58.9 | 61 12.3 | 10.7 | 26 00.5 | 3.7 | 54.1 |
| 18 | 90 33.6 | N21 59.3 | 75 42.0 | 10.6 | N26 04.2 | 3.6 | 54.1 |
| 19 | 105 33.6 | 21 59.6 | 90 11.6 | 10.7 | 26 07.8 | 3.5 | 54.1 |
| 20 | 120 33.5 | 22 00.0 | 104 41.3 | 10.5 | 26 11.3 | 3.3 | 54.1 |
| 21 | 135 33.4 .. | 00.3 | 119 10.8 | 10.6 | 26 14.6 | 3.2 | 54.1 |
| 22 | 150 33.3 | 00.6 | 133 40.4 | 10.6 | 26 17.8 | 3.1 | 54.0 |
| 23 | 165 33.2 | 01.0 | 148 10.0 | 10.5 | 26 20.9 | 2.9 | 54.0 |
| **1** 00 | 180 33.1 | N22 01.3 | 162 39.5 | 10.5 | N26 23.8 | 2.9 | 54.0 |
| 01 | 195 33.0 | 01.7 | 177 09.0 | 10.5 | 26 26.7 | 2.7 | 54.0 |
| 02 | 210 32.9 | 02.0 | 191 38.5 | 10.4 | 26 29.4 | 2.5 | 54.0 |
| 03 | 225 32.8 .. | 02.4 | 206 07.9 | 10.5 | 26 31.9 | 2.5 | 54.0 |
| 04 | 240 32.7 | 02.7 | 220 37.4 | 10.4 | 26 34.4 | 2.3 | 54.0 |
| 05 | 255 32.6 | 03.0 | 235 06.8 | 10.4 | 26 36.7 | 2.2 | 54.0 |
| 06 | 270 32.5 | N22 03.4 | 249 36.2 | 10.5 | 26 38.9 | 2.0 | 54.0 |
| 07 | 285 32.4 | 03.7 | 264 05.7 | 10.3 | 26 40.9 | 2.0 | 54.0 |
| 08 | 300 32.3 | 04.1 | 278 35.0 | 10.4 | 26 42.9 | 1.8 | 54.0 |
| 09 | 315 32.2 .. | 04.4 | 293 04.4 | 10.4 | 26 44.7 | 1.7 | 54.0 |
| 10 | 330 32.1 | 04.7 | 307 33.8 | 10.3 | 26 46.4 | 1.5 | 54.0 |
| 11 | 345 32.0 | 05.1 | 322 03.1 | 10.4 | 26 47.9 | 1.4 | 54.0 |
| 12 | 0 31.9 | N22 05.4 | 336 32.5 | 10.3 | N26 49.3 | 1.3 | 54.0 |
| 13 | 15 31.8 | 05.7 | 351 01.8 | 10.4 | 26 50.6 | 1.2 | 54.0 |
| 14 | 30 31.7 | 06.1 | 5 31.2 | 10.3 | 26 51.8 | 1.0 | 54.0 |
| 15 | 45 31.6 .. | 06.4 | 20 00.5 | 10.3 | 26 52.8 | 0.9 | 54.0 |
| 16 | 60 31.5 | 06.7 | 34 29.8 | 10.3 | 26 53.7 | 0.8 | 54.0 |
| 17 | 75 31.4 | 07.1 | 48 59.1 | 10.3 | 26 54.5 | 0.7 | 54.0 |
| 18 | 90 31.3 | N22 07.4 | 63 28.4 | 10.3 | N26 55.2 | 0.5 | 54.0 |
| 19 | 105 31.2 | 07.7 | 77 57.7 | 10.3 | 26 55.7 | 0.4 | 54.0 |
| 20 | 120 31.1 | 00.1 | 92 27.0 | 10.4 | 26 56.1 | 0.2 | 54.0 |
| 21 | 135 31.0 .. | 08.4 | 106 56.4 | 10.3 | 26 56.3 | 0.1 | 54.0 |
| 22 | 150 30.9 | 08.7 | 121 25.7 | 10.3 | 26 56.4 | 0.0 | 54.0 |
| 23 | 165 30.8 | 09.1 | 135 55.0 | 10.3 | 26 56.4 | 0.1 | 54.0 |
| **2** 00 | 180 30.7 | N22 09.4 | 150 24.3 | 10.3 | N26 56.3 | 0.2 | 54.0 |
| 01 | 195 30.6 | 09.7 | 164 53.6 | 10.3 | 26 56.1 | 0.4 | 54.0 |
| 02 | 210 30.5 | 10.0 | 179 22.9 | 10.4 | 26 55.7 | 0.5 | 54.0 |
| 03 | 225 30.4 .. | 10.4 | 193 52.3 | 10.3 | 26 55.2 | 0.7 | 54.0 |
| 04 | 240 30.3 | 10.7 | 208 21.6 | 10.4 | 26 54.5 | 0.8 | 54.0 |
| 05 | 255 30.2 | 11.0 | 222 51.0 | 10.3 | 26 53.7 | 0.9 | 54.0 |
| 06 | 270 30.1 | N22 11.3 | 237 20.3 | 10.4 | N26 52.8 | 1.0 | 54.0 |
| 07 | 285 30.0 | 11.7 | 251 49.7 | 10.4 | 26 51.8 | 1.2 | 54.0 |
| 08 | 300 29.9 | 12.0 | 266 19.1 | 10.4 | 26 50.6 | 1.2 | 54.0 |
| 09 | 315 29.8 .. | 12.3 | 280 48.5 | 10.4 | 26 49.4 | 1.5 | 54.0 |
| 10 | 330 29.7 | 12.6 | 295 17.9 | 10.4 | 26 47.9 | 1.5 | 54.0 |
| 11 | 345 29.6 | 12.9 | 309 47.3 | 10.5 | 26 46.4 | 1.7 | 54.0 |
| 12 | 0 29.5 | N22 13.3 | 324 16.8 | 10.4 | N26 44.7 | 1.8 | 54.0 |
| 13 | 15 29.4 | 13.6 | 338 46.2 | 10.5 | 26 42.9 | 1.9 | 54.0 |
| 14 | 30 29.3 | 13.9 | 353 15.7 | 10.5 | 26 41.0 | 2.1 | 54.0 |
| 15 | 45 29.2 .. | 14.2 | 7 45.2 | 10.5 | 26 38.9 | 2.1 | 54.0 |
| 16 | 60 29.1 | 14.5 | 22 14.7 | 10.5 | 26 36.8 | 2.4 | 54.0 |
| 17 | 75 29.0 | 14.8 | 36 44.2 | 10.6 | 26 34.4 | 2.4 | 54.0 |
| 18 | 90 28.9 | N22 15.2 | 51 13.8 | 10.6 | N26 32.0 | 2.5 | 54.0 |
| 19 | 105 28.8 | 15.5 | 65 43.4 | 10.6 | 26 29.5 | 2.7 | 54.0 |
| 20 | 120 28.7 | 15.8 | 80 13.0 | 10.6 | 26 26.8 | 2.8 | 54.0 |
| 21 | 135 28.6 .. | 16.1 | 94 42.6 | 10.6 | 26 24.0 | 3.0 | 54.0 |
| 22 | 150 28.5 | 16.4 | 109 12.2 | 10.7 | 26 21.0 | 3.0 | 54.0 |
| 23 | 165 28.4 | 16.7 | 123 41.9 | 10.7 | N26 18.0 | 3.2 | 54.0 |
| | SD 15.8 | d 0.3 | SD 14.7 | | 14.7 | | 14.7 |

Day labels: 31 TUESDAY, 1 WEDNESDAY, 2 THURSDAY.

| Lat. | Twilight Naut. | Twilight Civil | Sunrise | Moonrise 31 | 1 | 2 | 3 |
|---|---|---|---|---|---|---|---|
| ° | h m | h m | h m | h m | h m | h m | h m |
| N 72 | □ | □ | □ | □ | □ | □ | □ |
| N 70 | □ | □ | □ | □ | □ | □ | □ |
| 68 | □ | □ | □ | □ | □ | □ | □ |
| 66 | //// | //// | 01 12 | □ | □ | □ | □ |
| 64 | //// | //// | 01 58 | 01 42 | □ | □ | 03 02 |
| 62 | //// | //// | 02 27 | 02 25 | 02 38 | 03 17 | 04 33 |
| 60 | //// | 01 26 | 02 49 | 02 54 | 03 18 | 04 02 | 05 09 |
| N 58 | //// | 02 00 | 03 07 | 03 16 | 03 46 | 04 32 | 05 36 |
| 56 | //// | 02 25 | 03 22 | 03 34 | 04 07 | 04 54 | 05 56 |
| 54 | 01 19 | 02 44 | 03 35 | 03 50 | 04 25 | 05 13 | 06 13 |
| 52 | 01 50 | 03 00 | 03 46 | 04 03 | 04 40 | 05 29 | 06 28 |
| 50 | 02 13 | 03 13 | 03 56 | 04 15 | 04 53 | 05 42 | 06 40 |
| 45 | 02 53 | 03 40 | 04 17 | 04 39 | 05 21 | 06 10 | 07 06 |
| N 40 | 03 21 | 04 01 | 04 33 | 04 59 | 05 42 | 06 32 | 07 27 |
| 35 | 03 42 | 04 18 | 04 47 | 05 15 | 06 00 | 06 50 | 07 44 |
| 30 | 04 00 | 04 32 | 04 59 | 05 30 | 06 15 | 07 05 | 07 59 |
| 20 | 04 27 | 04 56 | 05 20 | 05 54 | 06 41 | 07 32 | 08 24 |
| N 10 | 04 48 | 05 15 | 05 38 | 06 15 | 07 04 | 07 54 | 08 46 |
| 0 | 05 06 | 05 32 | 05 54 | 06 35 | 07 25 | 08 16 | 09 06 |
| S 10 | 05 22 | 05 48 | 06 11 | 06 54 | 07 46 | 08 37 | 09 26 |
| 20 | 05 37 | 06 04 | 06 28 | 07 16 | 08 09 | 09 00 | 09 48 |
| 30 | 05 52 | 06 22 | 06 48 | 07 40 | 08 35 | 09 26 | 10 12 |
| 35 | 06 00 | 06 31 | 06 59 | 07 55 | 08 51 | 09 42 | 10 27 |
| 40 | 06 09 | 06 42 | 07 12 | 08 12 | 09 09 | 10 00 | 10 44 |
| 45 | 06 18 | 06 55 | 07 28 | 08 32 | 09 31 | 10 21 | 11 04 |
| S 50 | 06 29 | 07 09 | 07 47 | 08 58 | 09 58 | 10 49 | 11 30 |
| 52 | 06 33 | 07 16 | 07 56 | 09 10 | 10 12 | 11 03 | 11 42 |
| 54 | 06 38 | 07 24 | 08 06 | 09 25 | 10 28 | 11 18 | 11 56 |
| 56 | 06 44 | 07 32 | 08 18 | 09 41 | 10 46 | 11 37 | 12 12 |
| 58 | 06 50 | 07 41 | 08 31 | 10 02 | 11 09 | 11 59 | 12 31 |
| S 60 | 06 57 | 07 52 | 08 46 | 10 27 | 11 39 | 12 28 | 12 56 |

| Lat. | Sunset | Twilight Civil | Twilight Naut. | Moonset 31 | 1 | 2 | 3 |
|---|---|---|---|---|---|---|---|
| ° | h m | h m | h m | h m | h m | h m | h m |
| N 72 | □ | □ | □ | □ | □ | □ | □ |
| N 70 | □ | □ | □ | □ | □ | □ | □ |
| 68 | □ | □ | □ | □ | □ | □ | □ |
| 66 | 22 47 | //// | //// | □ | □ | □ | □ |
| 64 | 22 00 | //// | //// | □ | □ | □ | 02 49 |
| 62 | 21 30 | //// | //// | 23 42 | 24 49 | 00 49 | 01 18 |
| 60 | 21 08 | 22 32 | //// | 23 02 | 24 04 | 00 04 | 00 41 |
| N 58 | 20 50 | 21 57 | //// | 22 35 | 23 34 | 24 15 | 00 15 |
| 56 | 20 34 | 21 32 | //// | 22 13 | 23 11 | 23 54 | 24 23 |
| 54 | 20 22 | 21 13 | 22 40 | 21 56 | 22 53 | 23 37 | 24 09 |
| 52 | 20 10 | 20 57 | 22 07 | 21 41 | 22 37 | 23 22 | 23 56 |
| 50 | 20 00 | 20 43 | 21 44 | 21 28 | 22 23 | 23 09 | 23 45 |
| 45 | 19 40 | 20 16 | 21 04 | 21 01 | 21 56 | 22 43 | 23 21 |
| N 40 | 19 23 | 19 55 | 20 35 | 20 40 | 21 34 | 22 21 | 23 02 |
| 35 | 19 09 | 19 38 | 20 14 | 20 22 | 21 16 | 22 04 | 22 47 |
| 30 | 18 57 | 19 24 | 19 56 | 20 07 | 21 00 | 21 49 | 22 33 |
| 20 | 18 36 | 19 00 | 19 29 | 19 41 | 20 34 | 21 23 | 22 09 |
| N 10 | 18 18 | 18 41 | 19 08 | 19 19 | 20 11 | 21 01 | 21 49 |
| 0 | 18 02 | 18 24 | 18 50 | 18 59 | 19 49 | 20 40 | 21 30 |
| S 10 | 17 45 | 18 08 | 18 34 | 18 38 | 19 28 | 20 19 | 21 11 |
| 20 | 17 28 | 17 52 | 18 18 | 18 16 | 19 05 | 19 57 | 20 50 |
| 30 | 17 08 | 17 34 | 18 04 | 17 51 | 18 39 | 19 31 | 20 26 |
| 35 | 16 56 | 17 24 | 17 55 | 17 36 | 18 23 | 19 15 | 20 12 |
| 40 | 16 43 | 17 13 | 17 47 | 17 18 | 18 05 | 18 58 | 19 55 |
| 45 | 16 28 | 17 01 | 17 37 | 16 58 | 17 43 | 18 36 | 19 36 |
| S 50 | 16 08 | 16 46 | 17 27 | 16 31 | 17 15 | 18 09 | 19 11 |
| 52 | 15 59 | 16 39 | 17 22 | 16 19 | 17 01 | 17 55 | 18 59 |
| 54 | 15 49 | 16 32 | 17 17 | 16 04 | 16 45 | 17 40 | 18 45 |
| 56 | 15 38 | 16 23 | 17 11 | 15 47 | 16 27 | 17 21 | 18 29 |
| 58 | 15 24 | 16 14 | 17 05 | 15 27 | 16 04 | 16 59 | 18 10 |
| S 60 | 15 09 | 16 04 | 16 59 | 15 01 | 15 34 | 16 30 | 17 46 |

| Day | SUN Eqn. of Time 00h | SUN Eqn. of Time 12h | Mer. Pass. | MOON Mer. Pass. Upper | MOON Mer. Pass. Lower | Age | Phase |
|---|---|---|---|---|---|---|---|
| d | m s | m s | h m | h m | h m | d | % |
| 31 | 02 21 | 02 17 | 11 58 | 12 47 | 00 22 | 01 | 1 |
| 1 | 02 12 | 02 08 | 11 58 | 13 37 | 01 12 | 02 | 4 |
| 2 | 02 03 | 01 58 | 11 58 | 14 28 | 02 03 | 03 | 8 |

| UT | ARIES GHA | VENUS −3.9 GHA | Dec | MARS +0.6 GHA | Dec | JUPITER −2.3 GHA | Dec | SATURN +0.6 GHA | Dec | STARS Name | SHA | Dec |
|---|---|---|---|---|---|---|---|---|---|---|---|---|
| **3 00** | 251 25.8 | 216 45.8 | N11 44.6 | 244 34.6 | N 1 02.6 | 247 14.7 | N 0 31.9 | 283 31.1 | S14 09.5 | Acamar | 315 13.8 | S40 12.9 |
| 01 | 266 28.3 | 231 45.5 | 45.6 | 259 35.4 | 03.3 | 262 16.8 | 32.1 | 298 33.6 | 09.5 | Achernar | 335 22.2 | S57 07.3 |
| 02 | 281 30.8 | 246 45.1 | 46.6 | 274 36.1 | 04.0 | 277 19.0 | 32.2 | 313 36.1 | 09.6 | Acrux | 173 02.1 | S63 13.6 |
| 03 | 296 33.2 | 261 44.7 .. | 47.6 | 289 36.9 .. | 04.7 | 292 21.1 .. | 32.4 | 328 38.5 .. | 09.6 | Adhara | 255 07.9 | S29 00.2 |
| 04 | 311 35.7 | 276 44.4 | 48.5 | 304 37.7 | 05.4 | 307 23.2 | 32.5 | 343 41.0 | 09.6 | Aldebaran | 290 42.4 | N16 33.2 |
| 05 | 326 38.2 | 291 44.0 | 49.5 | 319 38.4 | 06.2 | 322 25.3 | 32.7 | 358 43.4 | 09.6 | | | |
| 06 | 341 40.6 | 306 43.6 | N11 50.5 | 334 39.2 | N 1 06.9 | 337 27.4 | N 0 32.8 | 13 45.9 | S14 09.6 | Alioth | 166 14.6 | N55 50.6 |
| 07 | 356 43.1 | 321 43.3 | 51.4 | 349 40.0 | 07.6 | 352 29.5 | 33.0 | 28 48.3 | 09.6 | Alkaid | 152 53.4 | N49 12.3 |
| F 08 | 11 45.5 | 336 42.9 | 52.4 | 4 40.7 | 08.3 | 7 31.6 | 33.1 | 43 50.8 | 09.6 | Alnair | 27 35.5 | S46 51.0 |
| R 09 | 26 48.0 | 351 42.5 .. | 53.4 | 19 41.5 .. | 09.0 | 22 33.7 .. | 33.2 | 58 53.2 .. | 09.6 | Alnilam | 275 40.3 | S 1 11.3 |
| I 10 | 41 50.5 | 6 42.2 | 54.4 | 34 42.3 | 09.8 | 37 35.8 | 33.4 | 73 55.7 | 09.6 | Alphard | 217 50.0 | S 8 45.4 |
| D 11 | 56 52.9 | 21 41.8 | 55.3 | 49 43.0 | 10.5 | 52 37.9 | 33.5 | 88 58.1 | 09.6 | | | |
| A 12 | 71 55.4 | 36 41.4 | N11 56.3 | 64 43.8 | N 1 11.2 | 67 40.0 | N 0 33.7 | 104 00.6 | S14 09.6 | Alphecca | 126 05.2 | N26 38.4 |
| Y 13 | 86 57.9 | 51 41.1 | 57.3 | 79 44.5 | 11.9 | 82 42.1 | 33.8 | 119 03.1 | 09.6 | Alpheratz | 357 37.1 | N29 12.6 |
| 14 | 102 00.3 | 66 40.7 | 58.2 | 94 45.3 | 12.6 | 97 44.2 | 34.0 | 134 05.5 | 09.6 | Altair | 62 01.8 | N 8 55.5 |
| 15 | 117 02.8 | 81 40.3 | 11 59.2 | 109 46.1 .. | 13.4 | 112 46.3 .. | 34.1 | 149 08.0 .. | 09.6 | Ankaa | 353 09.5 | S42 11.0 |
| 16 | 132 05.3 | 96 39.9 | 12 00.2 | 124 46.8 | 14.1 | 127 48.5 | 34.2 | 164 10.4 | 09.6 | Antares | 112 18.1 | S26 28.9 |
| 17 | 147 07.7 | 111 39.6 | 01.1 | 139 47.6 | 14.8 | 142 50.6 | 34.4 | 179 12.9 | 09.6 | | | |
| 18 | 162 10.2 | 126 39.2 | N12 02.1 | 154 48.4 | N 1 15.5 | 157 52.7 | N 0 34.5 | 194 15.3 | S14 09.6 | Arcturus | 145 49.6 | N19 04.1 |
| 19 | 177 12.7 | 141 38.8 | 03.1 | 169 49.1 | 16.2 | 172 54.8 | 34.7 | 209 17.8 | 09.6 | Atria | 107 13.7 | S69 04.0 |
| 20 | 192 15.1 | 156 38.4 | 04.0 | 184 49.9 | 16.9 | 187 56.9 | 34.8 | 224 20.3 | 09.6 | Avior | 234 16.0 | S59 35.0 |
| 21 | 207 17.6 | 171 38.1 .. | 05.0 | 199 50.7 .. | 17.7 | 202 59.0 .. | 35.0 | 239 22.7 .. | 09.7 | Bellatrix | 278 25.5 | N 6 22.1 |
| 22 | 222 20.0 | 186 37.7 | 06.0 | 214 51.4 | 18.4 | 218 01.1 | 35.1 | 254 25.2 | 09.7 | Betelgeuse | 270 54.7 | N 7 24.6 |
| 23 | 237 22.5 | 201 37.3 | 06.9 | 229 52.2 | 19.1 | 233 03.2 | 35.2 | 269 27.6 | 09.7 | | | |
| **4 00** | 252 25.0 | 216 36.9 | N12 07.9 | 244 52.9 | N 1 19.8 | 248 05.3 | N 0 35.4 | 284 30.1 | S14 09.7 | Canopus | 263 53.9 | S52 42.5 |
| 01 | 267 27.4 | 231 36.6 | 08.9 | 259 53.7 | 20.5 | 263 07.4 | 35.5 | 299 32.5 | 09.7 | Capella | 280 25.6 | N46 01.2 |
| 02 | 282 29.9 | 246 36.2 | 09.8 | 274 54.5 | 21.2 | 278 09.5 | 35.7 | 314 35.0 | 09.7 | Deneb | 49 27.0 | N45 21.3 |
| 03 | 297 32.4 | 261 35.8 .. | 10.8 | 289 55.2 .. | 22.0 | 293 11.7 .. | 35.8 | 329 37.5 .. | 09.7 | Denebola | 182 27.1 | N14 26.9 |
| 04 | 312 34.8 | 276 35.4 | 11.8 | 304 56.0 | 22.7 | 308 13.8 | 36.0 | 344 39.9 | 09.7 | Diphda | 348 49.6 | S17 51.8 |
| 05 | 327 37.3 | 291 35.1 | 12.7 | 319 56.8 | 23.4 | 323 15.9 | 36.1 | 359 42.4 | 09.7 | | | |
| 06 | 342 39.8 | 306 34.7 | N12 13.7 | 334 57.5 | N 1 24.1 | 338 18.0 | N 0 36.2 | 14 44.8 | S14 09.7 | Dubhe | 193 43.7 | N61 38.2 |
| 07 | 357 42.2 | 321 34.3 | 14.6 | 349 58.3 | 24.8 | 353 20.1 | 36.4 | 29 47.3 | 09.7 | Elnath | 278 05.0 | N28 37.5 |
| S 08 | 12 44.7 | 336 33.9 | 15.6 | 4 59.1 | 25.6 | 8 22.2 | 36.5 | 44 49.8 | 09.7 | Eltanin | 90 42.7 | N51 29.0 |
| A 09 | 27 47.2 | 351 33.6 .. | 16.6 | 19 59.8 .. | 26.3 | 23 24.3 .. | 36.7 | 59 52.2 .. | 09.7 | Enif | 33 40.8 | N 9 58.5 |
| T 10 | 42 49.6 | 6 33.2 | 17.5 | 35 00.6 | 27.0 | 38 26.4 | 36.8 | 74 54.7 | 09.7 | Fomalhaut | 15 16.9 | S29 30.2 |
| U 11 | 57 52.1 | 21 32.8 | 18.5 | 50 01.4 | 27.7 | 53 28.6 | 37.0 | 89 57.1 | 09.7 | | | |
| R 12 | 72 54.5 | 36 32.4 | N12 19.4 | 65 02.1 | N 1 28.4 | 68 30.7 | N 0 37.1 | 104 59.6 | S14 09.8 | Gacrux | 171 53.8 | S57 14.5 |
| D 13 | 87 57.0 | 51 32.0 | 20.4 | 80 02.9 | 29.1 | 83 32.8 | 37.2 | 120 02.1 | 09.8 | Gienah | 175 45.7 | S17 40.0 |
| A 14 | 102 59.5 | 66 31.7 | 21.4 | 95 03.7 | 29.9 | 98 34.9 | 37.4 | 135 04.5 | 09.8 | Hadar | 148 38.5 | S60 29.0 |
| Y 15 | 118 01.9 | 81 31.3 .. | 22.3 | 110 04.4 .. | 30.6 | 113 37.0 .. | 37.5 | 150 07.0 .. | 09.8 | Hamal | 327 53.9 | N23 33.9 |
| 16 | 133 04.4 | 96 30.9 | 23.3 | 125 05.2 | 31.3 | 128 39.1 | 37.7 | 165 09.4 | 09.8 | Kaus Aust. | 83 35.0 | S34 22.4 |
| 17 | 148 06.9 | 111 30.5 | 24.2 | 140 06.0 | 32.0 | 143 41.2 | 37.8 | 180 11.9 | 09.8 | | | |
| 18 | 163 09.3 | 126 30.1 | N12 25.2 | 155 06.7 | N 1 32.7 | 158 43.3 | N 0 37.9 | 195 14.4 | S14 09.8 | Kochab | 137 18.8 | N74 04.0 |
| 19 | 178 11.8 | 141 29.7 | 26.1 | 170 07.5 | 33.4 | 173 45.5 | 38.1 | 210 16.8 | 09.8 | Markab | 13 32.0 | N15 19.3 |
| 20 | 193 14.3 | 156 29.4 | 27.1 | 185 08.2 | 34.2 | 188 47.6 | 38.2 | 225 19.3 | 09.8 | Menkar | 314 08.7 | N 4 10.5 |
| 21 | 208 16.7 | 171 29.0 .. | 28.1 | 200 09.0 .. | 34.9 | 203 49.7 .. | 38.4 | 240 21.7 .. | 09.8 | Menkent | 147 59.8 | S36 28.9 |
| 22 | 223 19.2 | 186 28.6 | 29.0 | 215 09.8 | 35.6 | 218 51.8 | 38.5 | 255 24.2 | 09.8 | Miaplacidus | 221 39.1 | S69 48.8 |
| 23 | 238 21.6 | 201 28.2 | 30.0 | 230 10.5 | 36.3 | 233 53.9 | 38.6 | 270 26.7 | 09.8 | | | |
| **5 00** | 253 24.1 | 216 27.8 | N12 30.9 | 245 11.3 | N 1 37.0 | 248 56.0 | N 0 38.8 | 285 29.1 | S14 09.8 | Mirfak | 308 31.8 | N49 56.2 |
| 01 | 268 26.6 | 231 27.4 | 31.9 | 260 12.1 | 37.7 | 263 58.1 | 38.9 | 300 31.6 | 09.9 | Nunki | 75 50.1 | S26 16.1 |
| 02 | 283 29.0 | 246 27.1 | 32.8 | 275 12.8 | 38.5 | 279 00.3 | 39.1 | 315 34.0 | 09.9 | Peacock | 53 08.8 | S56 39.6 |
| 03 | 298 31.5 | 261 26.7 .. | 33.8 | 290 13.6 .. | 39.2 | 294 02.4 .. | 39.2 | 330 36.5 .. | 09.9 | Pollux | 243 20.2 | N27 58.4 |
| 04 | 313 34.0 | 276 26.3 | 34.7 | 305 14.4 | 39.9 | 309 04.5 | 39.3 | 345 39.0 | 09.9 | Procyon | 244 53.4 | N 5 10.1 |
| 05 | 328 36.4 | 291 25.9 | 35.7 | 320 15.1 | 40.6 | 324 06.6 | 39.5 | 0 41.4 | 09.9 | | | |
| 06 | 343 38.9 | 306 25.5 | N12 36.6 | 335 15.9 | N 1 41.3 | 339 08.7 | N 0 39.6 | 15 43.9 | S14 09.9 | Rasalhague | 96 00.2 | N12 32.6 |
| 07 | 358 41.4 | 321 25.1 | 37.6 | 350 16.7 | 42.0 | 354 10.8 | 39.8 | 30 46.4 | 09.9 | Regulus | 207 36.8 | N11 51.6 |
| S 08 | 13 43.8 | 336 24.7 | 38.5 | 5 17.4 | 42.7 | 9 13.0 | 39.9 | 45 48.8 | 09.9 | Rigel | 281 06.3 | S 8 10.6 |
| U 09 | 28 46.3 | 351 24.4 .. | 39.5 | 20 18.2 .. | 43.5 | 24 15.1 .. | 40.0 | 60 51.3 .. | 09.9 | Rigil Kent. | 139 42.7 | S60 55.7 |
| N 10 | 43 48.8 | 6 24.0 | 40.4 | 35 19.0 | 44.2 | 39 17.2 | 40.2 | 75 53.7 | 09.9 | Sabik | 102 04.9 | S15 45.1 |
| D 11 | 58 51.2 | 21 23.6 | 41.4 | 50 19.7 | 44.9 | 54 19.3 | 40.3 | 90 56.2 | 09.9 | | | |
| A 12 | 73 53.7 | 36 23.2 | N12 42.3 | 65 20.5 | N 1 45.6 | 69 21.4 | N 0 40.5 | 105 58.7 | S14 09.9 | Schedar | 349 33.7 | N56 39.3 |
| Y 13 | 88 56.1 | 51 22.8 | 43.3 | 80 21.3 | 46.3 | 84 23.5 | 40.6 | 121 01.1 | 09.9 | Shaula | 96 12.9 | S37 07.2 |
| 14 | 103 58.6 | 66 22.4 | 44.2 | 95 22.0 | 47.0 | 99 25.7 | 40.7 | 136 03.6 | 09.9 | Sirius | 258 28.5 | S16 44.9 |
| 15 | 119 01.1 | 81 22.0 .. | 45.2 | 110 22.8 .. | 47.8 | 114 27.8 .. | 40.9 | 151 06.1 .. | 10.0 | Spica | 158 24.4 | S11 16.7 |
| 16 | 134 03.5 | 96 21.6 | 46.1 | 125 23.6 | 48.5 | 129 29.9 | 41.0 | 166 08.5 | 10.0 | Suhail | 222 48.1 | S43 31.5 |
| 17 | 149 06.0 | 111 21.2 | 47.1 | 140 24.3 | 49.2 | 144 32.0 | 41.2 | 181 11.0 | 10.0 | | | |
| 18 | 164 08.5 | 126 20.8 | N12 48.0 | 155 25.1 | N 1 49.9 | 159 34.1 | N 0 41.3 | 196 13.5 | S14 10.0 | Vega | 80 34.3 | N38 48.1 |
| 19 | 179 10.9 | 141 20.4 | 49.0 | 170 25.9 | 50.6 | 174 36.2 | 41.4 | 211 15.9 | 10.0 | Zuben'ubi | 136 58.1 | S16 08.1 |
| 20 | 194 13.4 | 156 20.1 | 49.9 | 185 26.6 | 51.3 | 189 38.4 | 41.6 | 226 18.4 | 10.0 | | SHA | Mer. Pass. |
| 21 | 209 15.9 | 171 19.7 .. | 50.9 | 200 27.4 .. | 52.0 | 204 40.5 .. | 41.7 | 241 20.9 .. | 10.0 | | ° ' | h m |
| 22 | 224 18.3 | 186 19.3 | 51.8 | 215 28.2 | 52.8 | 219 42.6 | 41.9 | 256 23.3 | 10.0 | Venus | 324 12.0 | 9 34 |
| 23 | 239 20.8 | 201 18.9 | 52.8 | 230 28.9 | 53.5 | 234 44.7 | 42.0 | 271 25.8 | 10.0 | Mars | 352 28.0 | 7 40 |
| | h m | | | | | | | | | Jupiter | 355 40.4 | 7 27 |
| Mer. Pass. | 7 09.2 | v −0.4 | d 1.0 | v 0.8 | d 0.7 | v 2.1 | d 0.1 | v 2.5 | d 0.0 | Saturn | 32 05.1 | 5 01 |

| UT | SUN GHA | SUN Dec | MOON GHA | v | Dec | d | HP |
|---|---|---|---|---|---|---|---|
| d h | ° ′ | ° ′ | ° ′ | ′ | ° ′ | ′ | ′ |
| 3 00 | 180 28.3 | N22 17.0 | 138 11.6 | 10.8 | N26 14.8 | 3.3 | 54.0 |
| 01 | 195 28.2 | 17.3 | 152 41.4 | 10.7 | 26 11.5 | 3.5 | 54.0 |
| 02 | 210 28.1 | 17.7 | 167 11.1 | 10.8 | 26 08.0 | 3.5 | 54.0 |
| 03 | 225 28.0 .. | 18.0 | 181 40.9 | 10.8 | 26 04.5 | 3.7 | 54.0 |
| 04 | 240 27.9 | 18.3 | 196 10.7 | 10.9 | 26 00.8 | 3.8 | 54.1 |
| 05 | 255 27.8 | 18.6 | 210 40.6 | 10.9 | 25 57.0 | 3.9 | 54.1 |
| 06 | 270 27.7 | N22 18.9 | 225 10.5 | 10.9 | N25 53.1 | 4.1 | 54.1 |
| 07 | 285 27.6 | 19.2 | 239 40.4 | 10.9 | 25 49.0 | 4.2 | 54.1 |
| 08 | 300 27.5 | 19.5 | 254 10.3 | 11.0 | 25 44.8 | 4.2 | 54.1 |
| F 09 | 315 27.4 .. | 19.8 | 268 40.3 | 11.0 | 25 40.6 | 4.4 | 54.1 |
| R 10 | 330 27.3 | 20.1 | 283 10.3 | 11.1 | 25 36.2 | 4.6 | 54.1 |
| I 11 | 345 27.2 | 20.4 | 297 40.4 | 11.1 | 25 31.6 | 4.6 | 54.1 |
| D 12 | 0 27.1 | N22 20.7 | 312 10.5 | 11.1 | N25 27.0 | 4.8 | 54.1 |
| A 13 | 15 27.0 | 21.0 | 326 40.6 | 11.1 | 25 22.2 | 4.9 | 54.1 |
| Y 14 | 30 26.8 | 21.3 | 341 10.7 | 11.2 | 25 17.3 | 5.0 | 54.1 |
| 15 | 45 26.7 .. | 21.6 | 355 40.9 | 11.3 | 25 12.3 | 5.1 | 54.1 |
| 16 | 60 26.6 | 21.9 | 10 11.2 | 11.2 | 25 07.2 | 5.3 | 54.1 |
| 17 | 75 26.5 | 22.2 | 24 41.4 | 11.4 | 25 01.9 | 5.3 | 54.1 |
| 18 | 90 26.4 | N22 22.5 | 39 11.8 | 11.3 | N24 56.6 | 5.5 | 54.2 |
| 19 | 105 26.3 | 22.8 | 53 42.1 | 11.4 | 24 51.1 | 5.6 | 54.2 |
| 20 | 120 26.2 | 23.1 | 68 12.5 | 11.4 | 24 45.5 | 5.7 | 54.2 |
| 21 | 135 26.1 .. | 23.4 | 82 42.9 | 11.5 | 24 39.8 | 5.8 | 54.2 |
| 22 | 150 26.0 | 23.7 | 97 13.4 | 11.5 | 24 34.0 | 5.9 | 54.2 |
| 23 | 165 25.9 | 24.0 | 111 43.9 | 11.6 | 24 28.1 | 6.1 | 54.2 |
| 4 00 | 180 25.8 | N22 24.3 | 126 14.5 | 11.6 | N24 22.0 | 6.1 | 54.2 |
| 01 | 195 25.7 | 24.6 | 140 45.1 | 11.6 | 24 15.9 | 6.3 | 54.2 |
| 02 | 210 25.6 | 24.9 | 155 15.7 | 11.7 | 24 09.6 | 6.4 | 54.2 |
| 03 | 225 25.5 .. | 25.2 | 169 46.4 | 11.7 | 24 03.2 | 6.5 | 54.2 |
| 04 | 240 25.4 | 25.5 | 184 17.1 | 11.8 | 23 56.7 | 6.6 | 54.3 |
| 05 | 255 25.3 | 25.8 | 198 47.9 | 11.8 | 23 50.1 | 6.7 | 54.3 |
| 06 | 270 25.1 | N22 26.1 | 213 18.7 | 11.9 | N23 43.4 | 6.8 | 54.3 |
| S 07 | 285 25.0 | 26.4 | 227 49.6 | 11.9 | 23 36.6 | 7.0 | 54.3 |
| A 08 | 300 24.9 | 26.6 | 242 20.5 | 11.9 | 23 29.6 | 7.0 | 54.3 |
| T 09 | 315 24.8 | 26.9 | 256 51.4 | 12.0 | 23 22.6 | 7.2 | 54.3 |
| U 10 | 330 24.7 | 27.2 | 271 22.4 | 12.1 | 23 15.4 | 7.2 | 54.3 |
| R 11 | 345 24.6 | 27.5 | 285 53.5 | 12.0 | 23 08.2 | 7.4 | 54.3 |
| D 12 | 0 24.5 | N22 27.8 | 300 24.5 | 12.2 | N23 00.8 | 7.5 | 54.3 |
| A 13 | 15 24.4 | 28.1 | 314 55.7 | 12.1 | 22 53.3 | 7.5 | 54.4 |
| Y 14 | 30 24.3 | 28.4 | 329 26.8 | 12.3 | 22 45.8 | 7.7 | 54.4 |
| 15 | 45 24.2 .. | 28.6 | 343 58.1 | 12.2 | 22 38.1 | 7.8 | 54.4 |
| 16 | 60 24.1 | 28.9 | 358 29.3 | 12.3 | 22 30.3 | 7.9 | 54.4 |
| 17 | 75 24.0 | 29.2 | 13 00.6 | 12.4 | 22 22.4 | 8.0 | 54.4 |
| 18 | 90 23.8 | N22 29.5 | 27 32.0 | 12.4 | N22 14.4 | 8.1 | 54.4 |
| 19 | 105 23.7 | 29.8 | 42 03.4 | 12.4 | 22 06.3 | 8.2 | 54.4 |
| 20 | 120 23.6 | 30.1 | 56 34.8 | 12.5 | 21 58.1 | 8.3 | 54.5 |
| 21 | 135 23.5 .. | 30.3 | 71 06.3 | 12.5 | 21 49.8 | 8.4 | 54.5 |
| 22 | 150 23.4 | 30.6 | 85 37.8 | 12.6 | 21 41.4 | 8.5 | 54.5 |
| 23 | 165 23.3 | 30.9 | 100 09.4 | 12.7 | 21 32.9 | 8.5 | 54.5 |
| 5 00 | 180 23.2 | N22 31.2 | 114 41.1 | 12.6 | N21 24.4 | 8.7 | 54.5 |
| 01 | 195 23.1 | 31.5 | 129 12.7 | 12.7 | 21 15.7 | 8.8 | 54.5 |
| 02 | 210 23.0 | 31.7 | 143 44.4 | 12.8 | 21 06.9 | 8.9 | 54.6 |
| 03 | 225 22.9 .. | 32.0 | 158 16.2 | 12.8 | 20 58.0 | 9.0 | 54.6 |
| 04 | 240 22.7 | 32.3 | 172 48.0 | 12.8 | 20 49.0 | 9.1 | 54.6 |
| 05 | 255 22.6 | 32.6 | 187 19.8 | 12.9 | 20 39.9 | 9.2 | 54.6 |
| 06 | 270 22.5 | N22 32.8 | 201 51.7 | 13.0 | N20 30.7 | 9.2 | 54.6 |
| 07 | 285 22.4 | 33.1 | 216 23.7 | 12.9 | 20 21.5 | 9.4 | 54.6 |
| 08 | 300 22.3 | 33.4 | 230 55.6 | 13.1 | 20 12.1 | 9.5 | 54.7 |
| S 09 | 315 22.2 .. | 33.7 | 245 27.7 | 13.0 | 20 02.6 | 9.5 | 54.7 |
| U 10 | 330 22.1 | 33.9 | 259 59.7 | 13.1 | 19 53.1 | 9.6 | 54.7 |
| N 11 | 345 22.0 | 34.2 | 274 31.8 | 13.2 | 19 43.5 | 9.8 | 54.7 |
| D 12 | 0 21.9 | N22 34.5 | 289 04.0 | 13.2 | N19 33.7 | 9.8 | 54.7 |
| A 13 | 15 21.7 | 34.7 | 303 36.2 | 13.2 | 19 23.9 | 9.9 | 54.8 |
| Y 14 | 30 21.6 | 35.0 | 318 08.4 | 13.3 | 19 14.0 | 10.0 | 54.8 |
| 15 | 45 21.5 .. | 35.3 | 332 40.7 | 13.3 | 19 04.0 | 10.1 | 54.8 |
| 16 | 60 21.4 | 35.5 | 347 13.0 | 13.4 | 18 53.9 | 10.2 | 54.8 |
| 17 | 75 21.3 | 35.8 | 1 45.4 | 13.4 | 18 43.7 | 10.3 | 54.8 |
| 18 | 90 21.2 | N22 36.1 | 16 17.8 | 13.4 | N18 33.4 | 10.3 | 54.9 |
| 19 | 105 21.1 | 36.3 | 30 50.2 | 13.5 | 18 23.1 | 10.4 | 54.9 |
| 20 | 120 21.0 | 36.6 | 45 22.7 | 13.5 | 18 12.7 | 10.6 | 54.9 |
| 21 | 135 20.8 .. | 36.9 | 59 55.2 | 13.5 | 18 02.1 | 10.6 | 54.9 |
| 22 | 150 20.7 | 37.1 | 74 27.7 | 13.6 | 17 51.5 | 10.7 | 54.9 |
| 23 | 165 20.6 | 37.4 | 89 00.3 | 13.6 | N17 40.8 | 10.7 | 55.0 |
| SD | 15.8 | d 0.3 | SD 14.7 | | 14.8 | | 14.9 |

| Lat. | Naut. | Civil | Sunrise | Moonrise 3 | 4 | 5 | 6 |
|---|---|---|---|---|---|---|---|
| ° | h m | h m | h m | h m | h m | h m | h m |
| N 72 | ☐ | ☐ | ☐ | ☐ | ☐ | ☐ | 07 09 |
| N 70 | ☐ | ☐ | ☐ | ☐ | ☐ | ☐ | 07 54 |
| 68 | ☐ | ☐ | ☐ | ☐ | ☐ | 06 05 | 08 23 |
| 66 | //// | //// | 00 59 | ☐ | 04 12 | 06 50 | 08 44 |
| 64 | //// | //// | 01 51 | 03 02 | 05 29 | 07 19 | 09 01 |
| 62 | //// | //// | 02 22 | 04 33 | 06 06 | 07 41 | 09 15 |
| 60 | //// | 01 18 | 02 45 | 05 09 | 06 32 | 07 59 | 09 27 |
| N 58 | //// | 01 55 | 03 04 | 05 36 | 06 52 | 08 14 | 09 37 |
| 56 | //// | 02 20 | 03 19 | 05 56 | 07 09 | 08 26 | 09 46 |
| 54 | 01 11 | 02 40 | 03 32 | 06 13 | 07 23 | 08 37 | 09 54 |
| 52 | 01 45 | 02 57 | 03 44 | 06 28 | 07 35 | 08 47 | 10 01 |
| 50 | 02 09 | 03 11 | 03 54 | 06 40 | 07 46 | 08 56 | 10 07 |
| 45 | 02 51 | 03 39 | 04 15 | 07 06 | 08 09 | 09 14 | 10 20 |
| N 40 | 03 19 | 04 00 | 04 32 | 07 27 | 08 27 | 09 29 | 10 32 |
| 35 | 03 41 | 04 17 | 04 47 | 07 44 | 08 42 | 09 41 | 10 41 |
| 30 | 03 59 | 04 32 | 04 59 | 07 59 | 08 55 | 09 52 | 10 49 |
| 20 | 04 27 | 04 56 | 05 20 | 08 24 | 09 17 | 10 11 | 11 03 |
| N 10 | 04 48 | 05 15 | 05 38 | 08 46 | 09 37 | 10 27 | 11 16 |
| 0 | 05 06 | 05 32 | 05 55 | 09 06 | 09 55 | 10 42 | 11 27 |
| S 10 | 05 23 | 05 49 | 06 11 | 09 26 | 10 13 | 10 57 | 11 38 |
| 20 | 05 38 | 06 05 | 06 29 | 09 48 | 10 32 | 11 13 | 11 51 |
| 30 | 05 53 | 06 23 | 06 49 | 10 12 | 10 54 | 11 31 | 12 04 |
| 35 | 06 02 | 06 33 | 07 01 | 10 27 | 11 07 | 11 41 | 12 12 |
| 40 | 06 10 | 06 44 | 07 14 | 10 44 | 11 22 | 11 54 | 12 21 |
| 45 | 06 20 | 06 57 | 07 30 | 11 04 | 11 39 | 12 08 | 12 32 |
| S 50 | 06 31 | 07 12 | 07 50 | 11 30 | 12 01 | 12 25 | 12 45 |
| 52 | 06 36 | 07 19 | 07 59 | 11 42 | 12 11 | 12 33 | 12 50 |
| 54 | 06 41 | 07 27 | 08 10 | 11 56 | 12 23 | 12 42 | 12 57 |
| 56 | 06 47 | 07 35 | 08 21 | 12 12 | 12 36 | 12 52 | 13 04 |
| 58 | 06 53 | 07 45 | 08 35 | 12 31 | 12 51 | 13 04 | 13 12 |
| S 60 | 07 00 | 07 56 | 08 51 | 12 56 | 13 10 | 13 17 | 13 21 |

| Lat. | Sunset | Civil | Naut. | Moonset 3 | 4 | 5 | 6 |
|---|---|---|---|---|---|---|---|
| ° | h m | h m | h m | h m | h m | h m | h m |
| N 72 | ☐ | ☐ | ☐ | ☐ | ☐ | ☐ | 03 43 |
| N 70 | ☐ | ☐ | ☐ | ☐ | ☐ | ☐ | 02 57 |
| 68 | ☐ | ☐ | ☐ | ☐ | ☐ | 03 09 | 02 26 |
| 66 | 23 02 | //// | //// | ☐ | 03 22 | 02 23 | 02 03 |
| 64 | 22 08 | //// | //// | 02 49 | 02 04 | 01 53 | 01 45 |
| 62 | 21 36 | //// | //// | 01 18 | 01 27 | 01 30 | 01 30 |
| 60 | 21 13 | 22 42 | //// | 00 41 | 01 01 | 01 12 | 01 17 |
| N 58 | 20 51 | 22 03 | //// | 00 15 | 00 40 | 00 56 | 01 06 |
| 56 | 20 38 | 21 37 | //// | 24 23 | 00 23 | 00 43 | 00 57 |
| 54 | 20 25 | 21 17 | 22 48 | 24 09 | 00 09 | 00 31 | 00 48 |
| 52 | 20 13 | 21 01 | 22 13 | 23 56 | 24 21 | 00 21 | 00 41 |
| 50 | 20 03 | 20 47 | 21 49 | 23 45 | 24 12 | 00 12 | 00 34 |
| 45 | 19 42 | 20 19 | 21 07 | 23 21 | 23 53 | 24 19 | 00 19 |
| N 40 | 19 25 | 19 57 | 20 38 | 23 02 | 23 37 | 24 07 | 00 07 |
| 35 | 19 10 | 19 40 | 20 16 | 22 47 | 23 24 | 23 56 | 24 26 |
| 30 | 18 58 | 19 25 | 19 58 | 22 33 | 23 12 | 23 47 | 24 19 |
| 20 | 18 37 | 19 01 | 19 30 | 22 09 | 22 52 | 23 31 | 24 08 |
| N 10 | 18 19 | 18 42 | 19 09 | 21 49 | 22 34 | 23 17 | 23 58 |
| 0 | 18 02 | 18 24 | 18 50 | 21 30 | 22 18 | 23 04 | 23 48 |
| S 10 | 17 45 | 18 08 | 18 34 | 21 11 | 22 01 | 22 50 | 23 39 |
| 20 | 17 28 | 17 51 | 18 19 | 20 50 | 21 43 | 22 36 | 23 28 |
| 30 | 17 07 | 17 34 | 18 03 | 20 26 | 21 22 | 22 20 | 23 17 |
| 35 | 16 56 | 17 23 | 17 55 | 20 12 | 21 10 | 22 10 | 23 10 |
| 40 | 16 42 | 17 12 | 17 46 | 19 55 | 20 56 | 21 59 | 23 02 |
| 45 | 16 26 | 17 00 | 17 36 | 19 36 | 20 40 | 21 46 | 22 53 |
| S 50 | 16 07 | 16 44 | 17 25 | 19 11 | 20 19 | 21 30 | 22 42 |
| 52 | 15 57 | 16 37 | 17 21 | 18 59 | 20 09 | 21 22 | 22 36 |
| 54 | 15 47 | 16 30 | 17 15 | 18 45 | 19 58 | 21 14 | 22 31 |
| 56 | 15 35 | 16 21 | 17 10 | 18 29 | 19 45 | 21 04 | 22 24 |
| 58 | 15 21 | 16 12 | 17 03 | 18 10 | 19 30 | 20 53 | 22 17 |
| S 60 | 15 05 | 16 01 | 16 56 | 17 46 | 19 13 | 20 41 | 22 09 |

| Day | SUN Eqn. of Time 00h | 12h | Mer. Pass. | MOON Mer. Pass. Upper | Lower | Age | Phase |
|---|---|---|---|---|---|---|---|
| d | m s | m s | h m | h m | h m | d % | |
| 3 | 01 53 | 01 48 | 11 58 | 15 18 | 02 53 | 04 14 | |
| 4 | 01 43 | 01 38 | 11 58 | 16 06 | 03 42 | 05 21 | |
| 5 | 01 33 | 01 28 | 11 59 | 16 53 | 04 30 | 06 30 | |

| UT | ARIES GHA | VENUS −3·9 GHA | Dec | MARS +0·6 GHA | Dec | JUPITER −2·3 GHA | Dec | SATURN +0·6 GHA | Dec | STARS Name | SHA | Dec |
|---|---|---|---|---|---|---|---|---|---|---|---|---|
| d h | ° ′ | ° ′ | ° ′ | ° ′ | ° ′ | ° ′ | ° ′ | ° ′ | ° ′ | | ° ′ | ° ′ |
| **6 00** | 254 23.3 | 216 18.5 | N12 53.7 | 245 29.7 | N 1 54.2 | 249 46.8 | N 0 42.1 | 286 28.3 | S14 10.0 | Acamar | 315 13.8 | S40 12.9 |
| 01 | 269 25.7 | 231 18.1 | 54.6 | 260 30.5 | 54.9 | 264 49.0 | 42.3 | 301 30.7 | 10.0 | Achernar | 335 22.2 | S57 07.2 |
| 02 | 284 28.2 | 246 17.7 | 55.6 | 275 31.2 | 55.6 | 279 51.1 | 42.4 | 316 33.2 | 10.0 | Acrux | 173 02.2 | S63 13.6 |
| 03 | 299 30.6 | 261 17.3 .. | 56.5 | 290 32.0 .. | 56.3 | 294 53.2 .. | 42.5 | 331 35.7 .. | 10.1 | Adhara | 255 07.9 | S29 00.2 |
| 04 | 314 33.1 | 276 16.9 | 57.5 | 305 32.8 | 57.0 | 309 55.3 | 42.7 | 346 38.1 | 10.1 | Aldebaran | 290 42.4 | N16 33.2 |
| 05 | 329 35.6 | 291 16.5 | 58.4 | 320 33.5 | 57.8 | 324 57.4 | 42.8 | 1 40.6 | 10.1 | | | |
| 06 | 344 38.0 | 306 16.1 | N12 59.4 | 335 34.3 | N 1 58.5 | 339 59.6 | N 0 43.0 | 16 43.0 | S14 10.1 | Alioth | 166 14.6 | N55 50.6 |
| 07 | 359 40.5 | 321 15.7 | 13 00.3 | 350 35.1 | 59.2 | 355 01.7 | 43.1 | 31 45.5 | 10.1 | Alkaid | 152 53.4 | N49 12.3 |
| 08 | 14 43.0 | 336 15.3 | 01.2 | 5 35.8 | 1 59.9 | 10 03.8 | 43.2 | 46 48.0 | 10.1 | Alnair | 27 35.5 | S46 51.0 |
| M 09 | 29 45.4 | 351 14.9 .. | 02.2 | 20 36.6 | 2 00.6 | 25 05.9 .. | 43.4 | 61 50.5 .. | 10.1 | Alnilam | 275 40.2 | S 1 11.3 |
| O 10 | 44 47.9 | 6 14.5 | 03.1 | 35 37.4 | 01.3 | 40 08.1 | 43.5 | 76 52.9 | 10.1 | Alphard | 217 50.0 | S 8 45.4 |
| N 11 | 59 50.4 | 21 14.1 | 04.1 | 50 38.1 | 02.0 | 55 10.2 | 43.6 | 91 55.4 | 10.1 | | | |
| D 12 | 74 52.8 | 36 13.7 | N13 05.0 | 65 38.9 | N 2 02.8 | 70 12.3 | N 0 43.8 | 106 57.9 | S14 10.1 | Alphecca | 126 05.2 | N26 38.4 |
| A 13 | 89 55.3 | 51 13.3 | 05.9 | 80 39.7 | 03.5 | 85 14.4 | 43.9 | 122 00.3 | 10.2 | Alpheratz | 357 37.1 | N29 12.6 |
| Y 14 | 104 57.8 | 66 12.9 | 06.9 | 95 40.5 | 04.2 | 100 16.5 | 44.1 | 137 02.8 | 10.2 | Altair | 62 01.8 | N 8 55.6 |
| 15 | 120 00.2 | 81 12.5 .. | 07.8 | 110 41.2 .. | 04.9 | 115 18.7 .. | 44.2 | 152 05.3 .. | 10.2 | Ankaa | 353 09.4 | S42 10.9 |
| 16 | 135 02.7 | 96 12.1 | 08.7 | 125 42.0 | 05.6 | 130 20.8 | 44.3 | 167 07.7 | 10.2 | Antares | 112 18.1 | S26 28.9 |
| 17 | 150 05.1 | 111 11.7 | 09.7 | 140 42.8 | 06.3 | 145 22.9 | 44.5 | 182 10.2 | 10.2 | | | |
| 18 | 165 07.6 | 126 11.3 | N13 10.6 | 155 43.5 | N 2 07.0 | 160 25.0 | N 0 44.6 | 197 12.7 | S14 10.2 | Arcturus | 145 49.6 | N19 04.1 |
| 19 | 180 10.1 | 141 10.9 | 11.6 | 170 44.3 | 07.7 | 175 27.2 | 44.7 | 212 15.1 | 10.2 | Atria | 107 13.7 | S69 04.0 |
| 20 | 195 12.5 | 156 10.5 | 12.5 | 185 45.1 | 08.5 | 190 29.3 | 44.9 | 227 17.6 | 10.2 | Avior | 234 16.0 | S59 35.0 |
| 21 | 210 15.0 | 171 10.1 .. | 13.4 | 200 45.8 .. | 09.2 | 205 31.4 .. | 45.0 | 242 20.1 .. | 10.2 | Bellatrix | 278 25.5 | N 6 22.1 |
| 22 | 225 17.5 | 186 09.7 | 14.4 | 215 46.6 | 09.9 | 220 33.5 | 45.1 | 257 22.5 | 10.2 | Betelgeuse | 270 54.7 | N 7 24.6 |
| 23 | 240 19.9 | 201 09.3 | 15.3 | 230 47.4 | 10.6 | 235 35.7 | 45.3 | 272 25.0 | 10.3 | | | |
| **7 00** | 255 22.4 | 216 08.9 | N13 16.2 | 245 48.1 | N 2 11.3 | 250 37.8 | N 0 45.4 | 287 27.5 | S14 10.3 | Canopus | 263 53.9 | S52 42.5 |
| 01 | 270 24.9 | 231 08.5 | 17.2 | 260 48.9 | 12.0 | 265 39.9 | 45.6 | 302 29.9 | 10.3 | Capella | 280 25.5 | N46 01.2 |
| 02 | 285 27.3 | 246 08.1 | 18.1 | 275 49.7 | 12.7 | 280 42.0 | 45.7 | 317 32.4 | 10.3 | Deneb | 49 27.0 | N45 21.3 |
| 03 | 300 29.8 | 261 07.7 .. | 19.0 | 290 50.4 .. | 13.4 | 295 44.2 .. | 45.8 | 332 34.9 .. | 10.3 | Denebola | 182 27.1 | N14 26.9 |
| 04 | 315 32.2 | 276 07.3 | 20.0 | 305 51.2 | 14.2 | 310 46.3 | 46.0 | 347 37.4 | 10.3 | Diphda | 348 49.6 | S17 51.8 |
| 05 | 330 34.7 | 291 06.9 | 20.9 | 320 52.0 | 14.9 | 325 48.4 | 46.1 | 2 39.8 | 10.3 | | | |
| 06 | 345 37.2 | 306 06.4 | N13 21.8 | 335 52.7 | N 2 15.6 | 340 50.5 | N 0 46.2 | 17 42.3 | S14 10.3 | Dubhe | 193 43.7 | N61 38.2 |
| 07 | 0 39.6 | 321 06.0 | 22.7 | 350 53.5 | 16.3 | 355 52.7 | 46.4 | 32 44.8 | 10.3 | Elnath | 278 05.0 | N28 37.5 |
| T 08 | 15 42.1 | 336 05.6 | 23.7 | 5 54.3 | 17.0 | 10 54.8 | 46.5 | 47 47.2 | 10.3 | Eltanin | 90 42.6 | N51 29.1 |
| U 09 | 30 44.6 | 351 05.2 .. | 24.6 | 20 55.1 .. | 17.7 | 25 56.9 .. | 46.6 | 62 49.7 .. | 10.4 | Enif | 33 40.8 | N 9 58.5 |
| E 10 | 45 47.0 | 6 04.8 | 25.5 | 35 55.8 | 18.4 | 40 59.0 | 46.8 | 77 52.2 | 10.4 | Fomalhaut | 15 16.9 | S29 30.1 |
| S 11 | 60 49.5 | 21 04.4 | 26.5 | 50 56.6 | 19.1 | 56 01.2 | 46.9 | 92 54.7 | 10.4 | | | |
| D 12 | 75 52.0 | 36 04.0 | N13 27.4 | 65 57.4 | N 2 19.9 | 71 03.3 | N 0 47.0 | 107 57.1 | S14 10.4 | Gacrux | 171 53.8 | S57 14.5 |
| A 13 | 90 54.4 | 51 03.6 | 28.3 | 80 58.1 | 20.6 | 86 05.4 | 47.2 | 122 59.6 | 10.4 | Gienah | 175 45.7 | S17 40.0 |
| Y 14 | 105 56.9 | 66 03.2 | 29.2 | 95 58.9 | 21.3 | 101 07.5 | 47.3 | 138 02.1 | 10.4 | Hadar | 148 38.6 | S60 29.0 |
| 15 | 120 59.4 | 81 02.8 .. | 30.2 | 110 59.7 .. | 22.0 | 116 09.7 .. | 47.4 | 153 04.5 .. | 10.4 | Hamal | 327 53.9 | N23 33.9 |
| 16 | 136 01.8 | 96 02.3 | 31.1 | 126 00.4 | 22.7 | 131 11.8 | 47.6 | 168 07.0 | 10.4 | Kaus Aust. | 83 35.0 | S34 22.4 |
| 17 | 151 04.3 | 111 01.9 | 32.0 | 141 01.2 | 23.4 | 146 13.9 | 47.7 | 183 09.5 | 10.4 | | | |
| 18 | 166 06.7 | 126 01.5 | N13 32.9 | 156 02.0 | N 2 24.1 | 161 16.1 | N 0 47.8 | 198 12.0 | S14 10.5 | Kochab | 137 18.8 | N74 04.0 |
| 19 | 181 09.2 | 141 01.1 | 33.9 | 171 02.8 | 24.8 | 176 18.2 | 48.0 | 213 14.4 | 10.5 | Markab | 13 32.0 | N15 19.4 |
| 20 | 196 11.7 | 156 00.7 | 34.8 | 186 03.5 | 25.5 | 191 20.3 | 48.1 | 228 16.9 | 10.5 | Menkar | 314 08.7 | N 4 10.5 |
| 21 | 211 14.1 | 171 00.3 .. | 35.7 | 201 04.3 .. | 26.3 | 206 22.4 .. | 48.3 | 243 19.4 .. | 10.5 | Menkent | 147 59.9 | S36 28.9 |
| 22 | 226 16.6 | 185 59.9 | 36.6 | 216 05.1 | 27.0 | 221 24.6 | 48.4 | 258 21.9 | 10.5 | Miaplacidus | 221 39.1 | S69 48.7 |
| 23 | 241 19.1 | 200 59.5 | 37.6 | 231 05.8 | 27.7 | 236 26.7 | 48.5 | 273 24.3 | 10.5 | | | |
| **8 00** | 256 21.5 | 215 59.0 | N13 38.5 | 246 06.6 | N 2 28.4 | 251 28.8 | N 0 48.7 | 288 26.8 | S14 10.5 | Mirfak | 308 31.8 | N49 56.2 |
| 01 | 271 24.0 | 230 58.6 | 39.4 | 261 07.4 | 29.1 | 266 31.0 | 48.8 | 303 29.3 | 10.5 | Nunki | 75 50.1 | S26 16.1 |
| 02 | 286 26.5 | 245 58.2 | 40.3 | 276 08.1 | 29.8 | 281 33.1 | 48.9 | 318 31.7 | 10.5 | Peacock | 53 08.7 | S56 39.6 |
| 03 | 301 28.9 | 260 57.8 .. | 41.2 | 291 08.9 .. | 30.5 | 296 35.2 .. | 49.1 | 333 34.2 .. | 10.6 | Pollux | 243 20.2 | N27 58.4 |
| 04 | 316 31.4 | 275 57.4 | 42.2 | 306 09.7 | 31.2 | 311 37.3 | 49.2 | 348 36.7 | 10.6 | Procyon | 244 53.4 | N 5 10.1 |
| 05 | 331 33.9 | 290 57.0 | 43.1 | 321 10.5 | 31.9 | 326 39.5 | 49.3 | 3 39.2 | 10.6 | | | |
| 06 | 346 36.3 | 305 56.5 | N13 44.0 | 336 11.2 | N 2 32.6 | 341 41.6 | N 0 49.5 | 18 41.6 | S14 10.6 | Rasalhague | 96 00.2 | N12 32.6 |
| W 07 | 1 38.8 | 320 56.1 | 44.9 | 351 12.0 | 33.4 | 356 43.7 | 49.6 | 33 44.1 | 10.6 | Regulus | 207 36.8 | N11 51.6 |
| E 08 | 16 41.2 | 335 55.7 | 45.8 | 6 12.8 | 34.1 | 11 45.9 | 49.7 | 48 46.6 | 10.6 | Rigel | 281 06.3 | S 8 10.6 |
| D 09 | 31 43.7 | 350 55.3 .. | 46.8 | 21 13.5 .. | 34.8 | 26 48.0 .. | 49.9 | 63 49.1 .. | 10.6 | Rigil Kent. | 139 42.7 | S60 55.8 |
| N 10 | 46 46.2 | 5 54.9 | 47.7 | 36 14.3 | 35.5 | 41 50.1 | 50.0 | 78 51.5 | 10.6 | Sabik | 102 04.9 | S15 45.1 |
| E 11 | 61 48.6 | 20 54.4 | 48.6 | 51 15.1 | 36.2 | 56 52.3 | 50.1 | 93 54.0 | 10.7 | | | |
| S 12 | 76 51.1 | 35 54.0 | N13 49.5 | 66 15.8 | N 2 36.9 | 71 54.4 | N 0 50.2 | 108 56.5 | S14 10.7 | Schedar | 349 33.7 | N56 39.3 |
| D 13 | 91 53.6 | 50 53.6 | 50.4 | 81 16.6 | 37.6 | 86 56.5 | 50.4 | 123 59.0 | 10.7 | Shaula | 96 12.9 | S37 07.2 |
| A 14 | 106 56.0 | 65 53.2 | 51.3 | 96 17.4 | 38.3 | 101 58.7 | 50.5 | 139 01.4 | 10.7 | Sirius | 258 28.5 | S16 44.9 |
| Y 15 | 121 58.5 | 80 52.8 .. | 52.3 | 111 18.2 .. | 39.0 | 117 00.8 .. | 50.6 | 154 03.9 .. | 10.7 | Spica | 158 24.4 | S11 16.7 |
| 16 | 137 01.0 | 95 52.3 | 53.2 | 126 18.9 | 39.7 | 132 02.9 | 50.8 | 169 06.4 | 10.7 | Suhail | 222 48.1 | S43 31.5 |
| 17 | 152 03.4 | 110 51.9 | 54.1 | 141 19.7 | 40.4 | 147 05.1 | 50.9 | 184 08.9 | 10.7 | | | |
| 18 | 167 05.9 | 125 51.5 | N13 55.0 | 156 20.5 | N 2 41.2 | 162 07.2 | N 0 51.0 | 199 11.4 | S14 10.7 | Vega | 80 34.3 | N38 48.1 |
| 19 | 182 08.3 | 140 51.1 | 55.9 | 171 21.2 | 41.9 | 177 09.3 | 51.2 | 214 13.8 | 10.8 | Zuben'ubi | 136 58.1 | S16 08.1 |
| 20 | 197 10.8 | 155 50.7 | 56.8 | 186 22.0 | 42.6 | 192 11.5 | 51.3 | 229 16.3 | 10.8 | | SHA | Mer. Pass. |
| 21 | 212 13.3 | 170 50.2 .. | 57.7 | 201 22.8 .. | 43.3 | 207 13.6 .. | 51.4 | 244 18.8 .. | 10.8 | Venus | 320 46.5 | 9 36 |
| 22 | 227 15.7 | 185 49.8 | 58.6 | 216 23.6 | 44.0 | 222 15.7 | 51.6 | 259 21.3 | 10.8 | Mars | 350 25.7 | 7 36 |
| 23 | 242 18.2 | 200 49.4 | 59.6 | 231 24.3 | 44.7 | 237 17.9 | 51.7 | 274 23.7 | 10.8 | Jupiter | 355 15.4 | 7 16 |
| Mer. Pass. 6 57.4 | | v −0.4 | d 0.9 | v 0.8 | d 0.7 | v 2.1 | d 0.1 | v 2.5 | d 0.0 | Saturn | 32 05.1 | 4 49 |

| UT | SUN | | MOON | | | | | Lat. | Twilight | | Sunrise | Moonrise | | | |
|---|---|---|---|---|---|---|---|---|---|---|---|---|---|---|---|
| | GHA | Dec | GHA | v | Dec | d | HP | | Naut. | Civil | | 6 | 7 | 8 | 9 |
| d h | ° ′ | ° ′ | ° ′ | ′ | ° ′ | ′ | ′ | ° | h m | h m | h m | h m | h m | h m | h m |
| **6** 00 | 180 20.5 | N22 37.7 | 103 32.9 | 13.7 | N17 30.1 | 10.9 | 55.0 | N 72 | ▢ | ▢ | ▢ | 07 09 | 09 46 | 11 56 | 14 04 |
| 01 | 195 20.4 | 37.9 | 118 05.6 | 13.7 | 17 19.2 | 10.9 | 55.0 | N 70 | ▢ | ▢ | ▢ | 07 54 | 10 04 | 12 03 | 14 01 |
| 02 | 210 20.3 | 38.2 | 132 38.3 | 13.7 | 17 08.3 | 11.1 | 55.0 | 68 | ▢ | ▢ | ▢ | 08 23 | 10 18 | 12 08 | 13 59 |
| 03 | 225 20.2 .. | 38.4 | 147 11.0 | 13.8 | 16 57.2 | 11.1 | 55.0 | 66 | //// | //// | 00 45 | 08 44 | 10 30 | 12 13 | 13 57 |
| 04 | 240 20.0 | 38.7 | 161 43.8 | 13.8 | 16 46.1 | 11.1 | 55.1 | 64 | //// | //// | 01 45 | 09 01 | 10 40 | 12 17 | 13 55 |
| 05 | 255 19.9 | 39.0 | 176 16.6 | 13.8 | 16 35.0 | 11.3 | 55.1 | 62 | //// | //// | 02 18 | 09 15 | 10 48 | 12 20 | 13 54 |
| 06 | 270 19.8 | N22 39.2 | 190 49.4 | 13.9 | N16 23.7 | 11.3 | 55.1 | 60 | //// | 01 10 | 02 42 | 09 27 | 10 55 | 12 23 | 13 53 |
| 07 | 285 19.7 | 39.5 | 205 22.3 | 13.9 | 16 12.4 | 11.5 | 55.1 | N 58 | //// | 01 50 | 03 01 | 09 37 | 11 01 | 12 25 | 13 52 |
| 08 | 300 19.6 | 39.7 | 219 55.2 | 13.9 | 16 00.9 | 11.5 | 55.2 | 56 | //// | 02 17 | 03 17 | 09 46 | 11 06 | 12 27 | 13 51 |
| M 09 | 315 19.5 .. | 40.0 | 234 28.1 | 14.0 | 15 49.4 | 11.5 | 55.2 | 54 | 01 04 | 02 38 | 03 30 | 09 54 | 11 11 | 12 29 | 13 50 |
| O 10 | 330 19.4 | 40.2 | 249 01.1 | 14.0 | 15 37.9 | 11.7 | 55.2 | 52 | 01 41 | 02 54 | 03 42 | 10 01 | 11 15 | 12 31 | 13 49 |
| N 11 | 345 19.2 | 40.5 | 263 34.1 | 14.0 | 15 26.2 | 11.7 | 55.2 | 50 | 02 06 | 03 09 | 03 52 | 10 07 | 11 19 | 12 33 | 13 48 |
| D 12 | 0 19.1 | N22 40.8 | 278 07.1 | 14.1 | N15 14.5 | 11.8 | 55.3 | 45 | 02 49 | 03 37 | 04 14 | 10 20 | 11 28 | 12 36 | 13 47 |
| A 13 | 15 19.0 | 41.0 | 292 40.2 | 14.1 | 15 02.7 | 11.8 | 55.3 | N 40 | 03 18 | 03 59 | 04 31 | 10 32 | 11 35 | 12 39 | 13 46 |
| Y 14 | 30 18.9 | 41.3 | 307 13.3 | 14.1 | 14 50.9 | 12.0 | 55.3 | 35 | 03 40 | 04 16 | 04 46 | 10 41 | 11 41 | 12 42 | 13 45 |
| 15 | 45 18.8 .. | 41.5 | 321 46.4 | 14.1 | 14 38.9 | 12.0 | 55.3 | 30 | 03 58 | 04 31 | 04 58 | 10 49 | 11 46 | 12 44 | 13 44 |
| 16 | 60 18.7 | 41.8 | 336 19.5 | 14.2 | 14 26.9 | 12.1 | 55.4 | 20 | 04 26 | 04 55 | 05 20 | 11 03 | 11 56 | 12 48 | 13 42 |
| 17 | 75 18.6 | 42.0 | 350 52.7 | 14.1 | 14 14.8 | 12.1 | 55.4 | N 10 | 04 48 | 05 15 | 05 38 | 11 16 | 12 04 | 12 52 | 13 41 |
| | | | | | | | | 0 | 05 07 | 05 33 | 05 55 | 11 27 | 12 11 | 12 55 | 13 39 |
| 18 | 90 18.4 | N22 42.3 | 5 25.8 | 14.3 | N14 02.7 | 12.3 | 55.4 | S 10 | 05 23 | 05 49 | 06 12 | 11 38 | 12 18 | 12 58 | 13 38 |
| 19 | 105 18.3 | 42.5 | 19 59.1 | 14.2 | 13 50.4 | 12.3 | 55.5 | 20 | 05 39 | 06 06 | 06 30 | 11 51 | 12 26 | 13 01 | 13 37 |
| 20 | 120 18.2 | 42.8 | 34 32.3 | 14.3 | 13 38.1 | 12.3 | 55.5 | 30 | 05 55 | 06 24 | 06 51 | 12 04 | 12 35 | 13 05 | 13 35 |
| 21 | 135 18.1 .. | 43.0 | 49 05.5 | 14.3 | 13 25.8 | 12.5 | 55.5 | 35 | 06 03 | 06 35 | 07 03 | 12 12 | 12 41 | 13 07 | 13 34 |
| 22 | 150 18.0 | 43.3 | 63 38.8 | 14.3 | 13 13.3 | 12.5 | 55.5 | 40 | 06 12 | 06 46 | 07 16 | 12 21 | 12 46 | 13 10 | 13 34 |
| 23 | 165 17.9 | 43.5 | 78 12.1 | 14.3 | 13 00.8 | 12.5 | 55.6 | 45 | 06 22 | 06 59 | 07 32 | 12 32 | 12 53 | 13 13 | 13 32 |
| **7** 00 | 180 17.7 | N22 43.7 | 92 45.4 | 14.4 | N12 48.3 | 12.7 | 55.6 | S 50 | 06 33 | 07 14 | 07 52 | 12 45 | 13 01 | 13 16 | 13 31 |
| 01 | 195 17.6 | 44.0 | 107 18.8 | 14.3 | 12 35.6 | 12.7 | 55.6 | 52 | 06 38 | 07 22 | 08 02 | 12 50 | 13 05 | 13 18 | 13 31 |
| 02 | 210 17.5 | 44.2 | 121 52.1 | 14.4 | 12 22.9 | 12.7 | 55.6 | 54 | 06 44 | 07 29 | 08 13 | 12 57 | 13 09 | 13 20 | 13 30 |
| 03 | 225 17.4 .. | 44.4 | 136 25.5 | 14.4 | 12 10.2 | 12.8 | 55.7 | 56 | 06 49 | 07 38 | 08 25 | 13 04 | 13 13 | 13 22 | 13 29 |
| 04 | 240 17.3 | 44.7 | 150 58.9 | 14.4 | 11 57.4 | 12.9 | 55.7 | 58 | 06 56 | 07 48 | 08 39 | 13 12 | 13 18 | 13 24 | 13 29 |
| 05 | 255 17.2 | 45.0 | 165 32.3 | 14.4 | 11 44.5 | 13.0 | 55.7 | S 60 | 07 03 | 07 59 | 08 55 | 13 21 | 13 24 | 13 26 | 13 28 |
| 06 | 270 17.0 | N22 45.2 | 180 05.7 | 14.5 | N11 31.5 | 13.0 | 55.8 | Lat. | Sunset | Twilight | | Moonset | | | |
| 07 | 285 16.9 | 45.4 | 194 39.2 | 14.4 | 11 18.5 | 13.1 | 55.8 | | | Civil | Naut. | 6 | 7 | 8 | 9 |
| 08 | 300 16.8 | 45.7 | 209 12.6 | 14.5 | 11 05.4 | 13.1 | 55.8 | ° | h m | h m | h m | h m | h m | h m | h m |
| T 09 | 315 16.7 .. | 45.9 | 223 46.1 | 14.4 | 10 52.3 | 13.2 | 55.9 | N 72 | ▢ | ▢ | ▢ | 03 43 | 02 39 | 02 02 | 01 31 |
| U 10 | 330 16.6 | 46.2 | 238 19.5 | 14.5 | 10 39.1 | 13.3 | 55.9 | N 70 | ▢ | ▢ | ▢ | 02 57 | 02 19 | 01 53 | 01 30 |
| E 11 | 345 16.5 | 46.4 | 252 53.0 | 14.5 | 10 25.8 | 13.3 | 55.9 | 68 | ▢ | ▢ | ▢ | 02 26 | 02 03 | 01 45 | 01 28 |
| S 12 | 0 16.3 | N22 46.6 | 267 26.5 | 14.5 | N10 12.5 | 13.3 | 55.9 | 66 | 23 18 | //// | //// | 02 03 | 01 50 | 01 38 | 01 27 |
| D 13 | 15 16.2 | 46.9 | 282 00.0 | 14.5 | 9 59.2 | 13.5 | 56.0 | 64 | 22 15 | //// | //// | 01 45 | 01 38 | 01 32 | 01 26 |
| A 14 | 30 16.1 | 47.1 | 296 33.5 | 14.5 | 9 45.7 | 13.5 | 56.0 | 62 | 21 41 | //// | //// | 01 30 | 01 29 | 01 27 | 01 26 |
| Y 15 | 45 16.0 .. | 47.3 | 311 07.0 | 14.5 | 9 32.2 | 13.5 | 56.0 | 60 | 21 17 | 22 50 | //// | 01 17 | 01 21 | 01 23 | 01 25 |
| 16 | 60 15.9 | 47.6 | 325 40.5 | 14.6 | 9 18.7 | 13.6 | 56.1 | N 58 | 20 58 | 22 09 | //// | 01 06 | 01 14 | 01 19 | 01 24 |
| 17 | 75 15.8 | 47.8 | 340 14.1 | 14.5 | 9 05.1 | 13.6 | 56.1 | 56 | 20 42 | 21 42 | //// | 00 57 | 01 07 | 01 16 | 01 24 |
| 18 | 90 15.6 | N22 48.0 | 354 47.6 | 14.5 | N 8 51.5 | 13.7 | 56.1 | 54 | 20 28 | 21 21 | //// | 00 48 | 01 02 | 01 13 | 01 23 |
| 19 | 105 15.5 | 48.3 | 9 21.1 | 14.5 | 8 37.8 | 13.8 | 56.2 | 52 | 20 16 | 21 04 | 22 18 | 00 41 | 00 56 | 01 10 | 01 23 |
| 20 | 120 15.4 | 48.5 | 23 54.6 | 14.6 | 8 24.0 | 13.8 | 56.2 | 50 | 20 06 | 20 50 | 21 53 | 00 34 | 00 52 | 01 07 | 01 22 |
| 21 | 135 15.3 .. | 48.7 | 38 28.2 | 14.5 | 8 10.2 | 13.8 | 56.2 | 45 | 19 44 | 20 21 | 21 10 | 00 19 | 00 41 | 01 02 | 01 21 |
| 22 | 150 15.2 | 49.0 | 53 01.7 | 14.5 | 7 56.4 | 13.9 | 56.3 | N 40 | 19 27 | 19 59 | 20 40 | 00 07 | 00 33 | 00 57 | 01 20 |
| 23 | 165 15.0 | 49.2 | 67 35.2 | 14.5 | 7 42.5 | 14.0 | 56.3 | 35 | 19 12 | 19 42 | 20 18 | 24 26 | 00 26 | 00 53 | 01 20 |
| **8** 00 | 180 14.9 | N22 49.4 | 82 08.7 | 14.5 | N 7 28.5 | 14.0 | 56.3 | 30 | 18 59 | 19 27 | 20 00 | 24 19 | 00 19 | 00 49 | 01 19 |
| 01 | 195 14.8 | 49.7 | 96 42.2 | 14.5 | 7 14.5 | 14.1 | 56.4 | 20 | 18 38 | 19 03 | 19 32 | 24 08 | 00 08 | 00 43 | 01 18 |
| 02 | 210 14.7 | 49.9 | 111 15.7 | 14.5 | 7 00.4 | 14.0 | 56.4 | N 10 | 18 20 | 18 43 | 19 10 | 23 58 | 24 37 | 00 37 | 01 17 |
| 03 | 225 14.6 .. | 50.1 | 125 49.2 | 14.5 | 6 46.4 | 14.2 | 56.4 | 0 | 18 03 | 18 25 | 18 51 | 23 48 | 24 32 | 00 32 | 01 16 |
| 04 | 240 14.4 | 50.3 | 140 22.7 | 14.5 | 6 32.2 | 14.2 | 56.5 | S 10 | 17 46 | 18 08 | 18 35 | 23 39 | 24 26 | 00 26 | 01 15 |
| 05 | 255 14.3 | 50.6 | 154 56.2 | 14.5 | 6 18.0 | 14.2 | 56.5 | 20 | 17 28 | 17 52 | 18 19 | 23 28 | 24 21 | 00 21 | 01 14 |
| 06 | 270 14.2 | N22 50.8 | 169 29.7 | 14.5 | N 6 03.8 | 14.3 | 56.6 | 30 | 17 07 | 17 33 | 18 03 | 23 17 | 24 14 | 00 14 | 01 12 |
| W 07 | 285 14.1 | 51.0 | 184 03.2 | 14.4 | 5 49.5 | 14.3 | 56.6 | 35 | 16 55 | 17 23 | 17 55 | 23 10 | 24 10 | 00 10 | 01 12 |
| E 08 | 300 14.0 | 51.2 | 198 36.6 | 14.5 | 5 35.2 | 14.4 | 56.6 | 40 | 16 41 | 17 12 | 17 46 | 23 02 | 24 06 | 00 06 | 01 11 |
| D 09 | 315 13.9 .. | 51.4 | 213 10.1 | 14.4 | 5 20.8 | 14.4 | 56.7 | 45 | 16 25 | 16 59 | 17 36 | 22 53 | 24 01 | 00 01 | 01 10 |
| N 10 | 330 13.7 | 51.7 | 227 43.5 | 14.4 | 5 06.4 | 14.4 | 56.7 | S 50 | 16 05 | 16 43 | 17 24 | 22 42 | 23 54 | 25 09 | 01 09 |
| E 11 | 345 13.6 | 51.9 | 242 16.9 | 14.4 | 4 52.0 | 14.5 | 56.7 | 52 | 15 56 | 16 36 | 17 19 | 22 36 | 23 52 | 25 08 | 01 08 |
| S 12 | 0 13.5 | N22 52.1 | 256 50.3 | 14.4 | N 4 37.5 | 14.5 | 56.8 | 54 | 15 45 | 16 28 | 17 14 | 22 31 | 23 48 | 25 07 | 01 07 |
| D 13 | 15 13.4 | 52.3 | 271 23.7 | 14.3 | 4 23.0 | 14.6 | 56.8 | 56 | 15 33 | 16 20 | 17 08 | 22 24 | 23 45 | 25 07 | 01 07 |
| A 14 | 30 13.2 | 52.6 | 285 57.0 | 14.3 | 4 08.4 | 14.6 | 56.8 | 58 | 15 19 | 16 10 | 17 02 | 22 17 | 23 41 | 25 06 | 01 06 |
| Y 15 | 45 13.1 .. | 52.8 | 300 30.3 | 14.4 | 3 53.8 | 14.6 | 56.9 | S 60 | 15 02 | 15 59 | 16 55 | 22 09 | 23 37 | 25 05 | 01 05 |
| 16 | 60 13.0 | 53.0 | 315 03.7 | 14.2 | 3 39.2 | 14.7 | 56.9 | | | SUN | | | MOON | | |
| 17 | 75 12.9 | 53.2 | 329 36.9 | 14.3 | 3 24.5 | 14.7 | 56.9 | Day | Eqn. of Time | | Mer. | Mer. Pass. | | Age | Phase |
| 18 | 90 12.8 | N22 53.4 | 344 10.2 | 14.3 | N 3 09.8 | 14.7 | 57.0 | | 00h | 12h | Pass. | Upper | Lower | | |
| 19 | 105 12.6 | 53.6 | 358 43.5 | 14.2 | 2 55.1 | 14.8 | 57.0 | d | m s | m s | h m | h m | h m | d % | |
| 20 | 120 12.5 | 53.9 | 13 16.7 | 14.1 | 2 40.3 | 14.8 | 57.1 | 6 | 01 22 | 01 17 | 11 59 | 17 38 | 05 15 | 07 39 | |
| 21 | 135 12.4 .. | 54.1 | 27 49.8 | 14.2 | 2 25.5 | 14.8 | 57.1 | 7 | 01 11 | 01 06 | 11 59 | 18 21 | 06 00 | 08 49 | |
| 22 | 150 12.3 | 54.3 | 42 23.0 | 14.1 | 2 10.7 | 14.9 | 57.1 | 8 | 01 00 | 00 54 | 11 59 | 19 05 | 06 43 | 09 59 | |
| 23 | 165 12.2 | 54.5 | 56 56.1 | 14.1 | N 1 55.8 | 14.8 | 57.2 | | | | | | | | |
| | SD 15.8 | d 0.2 | SD 15.1 | | 15.2 | | 15.5 | | | | | | | | | |

| UT | ARIES GHA | VENUS −3.9 GHA | VENUS Dec | MARS +0.6 GHA | MARS Dec | JUPITER −2.3 GHA | JUPITER Dec | SATURN +0.6 GHA | SATURN Dec | STARS Name | STARS SHA | STARS Dec |
|---|---|---|---|---|---|---|---|---|---|---|---|---|
| **9 00** | 257 20.7 | 215 49.0 | N14 00.5 | 246 25.1 | N 2 45.4 | 252 20.0 | N 0 51.8 | 289 26.2 | S14 10.8 | Acamar | 315 13.8 | S40 12.8 |
| 01 | 272 23.1 | 230 48.5 | 01.4 | 261 25.9 | 46.1 | 267 22.1 | 52.0 | 304 28.7 | 10.8 | Achernar | 335 22.2 | S57 07.2 |
| 02 | 287 25.6 | 245 48.1 | 02.3 | 276 26.6 | 46.8 | 282 24.3 | 52.1 | 319 31.2 | 10.8 | Acrux | 173 02.2 | S63 13.6 |
| 03 | 302 28.1 | 260 47.7 .. | 03.2 | 291 27.4 .. | 47.5 | 297 26.4 .. | 52.2 | 334 33.6 .. | 10.9 | Adhara | 255 07.9 | S29 00.2 |
| 04 | 317 30.5 | 275 47.2 | 04.1 | 306 28.2 | 48.2 | 312 28.5 | 52.4 | 349 36.1 | 10.9 | Aldebaran | 290 42.4 | N16 33.2 |
| 05 | 332 33.0 | 290 46.8 | 05.0 | 321 29.0 | 48.9 | 327 30.7 | 52.5 | 4 38.6 | 10.9 | | | |
| T 06 | 347 35.5 | 305 46.4 | N14 05.9 | 336 29.7 | N 2 49.7 | 342 32.8 | N 0 52.6 | 19 41.1 | S14 10.9 | Alioth | 166 14.7 | N55 50.6 |
| H 07 | 2 37.9 | 320 46.0 | 06.8 | 351 30.5 | 50.4 | 357 34.9 | 52.8 | 34 43.6 | 10.9 | Alkaid | 152 53.4 | N49 12.3 |
| U 08 | 17 40.4 | 335 45.5 | 07.7 | 6 31.3 | 51.1 | 12 37.1 | 52.9 | 49 46.0 | 10.9 | Alnair | 27 35.5 | S46 51.0 |
| R 09 | 32 42.8 | 350 45.1 .. | 08.6 | 21 32.0 .. | 51.8 | 27 39.2 .. | 53.0 | 64 48.5 .. | 10.9 | Alnilam | 275 40.2 | S 1 11.3 |
| S 10 | 47 45.3 | 5 44.7 | 09.5 | 36 32.8 | 52.5 | 42 41.4 | 53.1 | 79 51.0 | 10.9 | Alphard | 217 50.0 | S 8 45.4 |
| D 11 | 62 47.8 | 20 44.2 | 10.4 | 51 33.6 | 53.2 | 57 43.5 | 53.3 | 94 53.5 | 11.0 | | | |
| A 12 | 77 50.2 | 35 43.8 | N14 11.4 | 66 34.4 | N 2 53.9 | 72 45.6 | N 0 53.4 | 109 56.0 | S14 11.0 | Alphecca | 126 05.2 | N26 38.4 |
| Y 13 | 92 52.7 | 50 43.4 | 12.3 | 81 35.1 | 54.6 | 87 47.8 | 53.5 | 124 58.4 | 11.0 | Alpheratz | 357 37.1 | N29 12.6 |
| 14 | 107 55.2 | 65 43.0 | 13.2 | 96 35.9 | 55.3 | 102 49.9 | 53.7 | 140 00.9 | 11.0 | Altair | 62 01.8 | N 8 55.6 |
| 15 | 122 57.6 | 80 42.5 .. | 14.1 | 111 36.7 .. | 56.0 | 117 52.0 .. | 53.8 | 155 03.4 .. | 11.0 | Ankaa | 353 09.4 | S42 10.9 |
| 16 | 138 00.1 | 95 42.1 | 15.0 | 126 37.4 | 56.7 | 132 54.2 | 53.9 | 170 05.9 | 11.0 | Antares | 112 18.1 | S26 28.9 |
| 17 | 153 02.6 | 110 41.7 | 15.9 | 141 38.2 | 57.4 | 147 56.3 | 54.1 | 185 08.4 | 11.0 | | | |
| 18 | 168 05.0 | 125 41.2 | N14 16.8 | 156 39.0 | N 2 58.1 | 162 58.5 | N 0 54.2 | 200 10.8 | S14 11.1 | Arcturus | 145 49.6 | N19 04.1 |
| 19 | 183 07.5 | 140 40.8 | 17.7 | 171 39.8 | 58.9 | 178 00.6 | 54.3 | 215 13.3 | 11.1 | Atria | 107 13.7 | S69 04.0 |
| 20 | 198 09.9 | 155 40.4 | 18.6 | 186 40.5 | 2 59.6 | 193 02.7 | 54.4 | 230 15.8 | 11.1 | Avior | 234 16.0 | S59 35.0 |
| 21 | 213 12.4 | 170 39.9 .. | 19.5 | 201 41.3 | 3 00.3 | 208 04.9 .. | 54.6 | 245 18.3 .. | 11.1 | Bellatrix | 278 25.5 | N 6 22.1 |
| 22 | 228 14.9 | 185 39.5 | 20.4 | 216 42.1 | 01.0 | 223 07.0 | 54.7 | 260 20.8 | 11.1 | Betelgeuse | 270 54.7 | N 7 24.6 |
| 23 | 243 17.3 | 200 39.0 | 21.3 | 231 42.8 | 01.7 | 238 09.2 | 54.8 | 275 23.2 | 11.1 | | | |
| **10 00** | 258 19.8 | 215 38.6 | N14 22.2 | 246 43.6 | N 3 02.4 | 253 11.3 | N 0 55.0 | 290 25.7 | S14 11.1 | Canopus | 263 53.9 | S52 42.5 |
| 01 | 273 22.3 | 230 38.2 | 23.1 | 261 44.4 | 03.1 | 268 13.4 | 55.1 | 305 28.2 | 11.2 | Capella | 280 25.5 | N46 01.2 |
| 02 | 288 24.7 | 245 37.7 | 24.0 | 276 45.2 | 03.8 | 283 15.6 | 55.2 | 320 30.7 | 11.2 | Deneb | 49 26.9 | N45 21.4 |
| 03 | 303 27.2 | 260 37.3 .. | 24.9 | 291 45.9 .. | 04.5 | 298 17.7 .. | 55.3 | 335 33.2 .. | 11.2 | Denebola | 182 27.1 | N14 26.9 |
| 04 | 318 29.7 | 275 36.9 | 25.7 | 306 46.7 | 05.2 | 313 19.9 | 55.5 | 350 35.7 | 11.2 | Diphda | 348 49.6 | S17 51.8 |
| 05 | 333 32.1 | 290 36.4 | 26.6 | 321 47.5 | 05.9 | 328 22.0 | 55.6 | 5 38.1 | 11.2 | | | |
| F 06 | 348 34.6 | 305 36.0 | N14 27.5 | 336 48.3 | N 3 06.6 | 343 24.1 | N 0 55.7 | 20 40.6 | S14 11.2 | Dubhe | 193 43.7 | N61 38.2 |
| R 07 | 3 37.1 | 320 35.5 | 28.4 | 351 49.0 | 07.3 | 358 26.3 | 55.9 | 35 43.1 | 11.2 | Elnath | 278 05.0 | N28 37.5 |
| I 08 | 18 39.5 | 335 35.1 | 29.3 | 6 49.8 | 08.0 | 13 28.4 | 56.0 | 50 45.6 | 11.3 | Eltanin | 90 42.6 | N51 29.1 |
| D 09 | 33 42.0 | 350 34.7 .. | 30.2 | 21 50.6 .. | 08.7 | 28 30.6 .. | 56.1 | 65 48.1 .. | 11.3 | Enif | 33 40.8 | N 9 58.5 |
| A 10 | 48 44.4 | 5 34.2 | 31.1 | 36 51.3 | 09.4 | 43 32.7 | 56.2 | 80 50.6 | 11.3 | Fomalhaut | 15 16.9 | S29 30.1 |
| Y 11 | 63 46.9 | 20 33.8 | 32.0 | 51 52.1 | 10.1 | 58 34.8 | 56.4 | 95 53.0 | 11.3 | | | |
| 12 | 78 49.4 | 35 33.3 | N14 32.9 | 66 52.9 | N 3 10.8 | 73 37.0 | N 0 56.5 | 110 55.5 | S14 11.3 | Gacrux | 171 53.8 | S57 14.5 |
| 13 | 93 51.8 | 50 32.9 | 33.8 | 81 53.7 | 11.6 | 88 39.1 | 56.6 | 125 58.0 | 11.3 | Gienah | 175 45.7 | S17 40.0 |
| 14 | 108 54.3 | 65 32.5 | 34.7 | 96 54.4 | 12.3 | 103 41.3 | 56.8 | 141 00.5 | 11.3 | Hadar | 148 38.6 | S60 29.0 |
| 15 | 123 56.8 | 80 32.0 .. | 35.6 | 111 55.2 .. | 13.0 | 118 43.4 .. | 56.9 | 156 03.0 .. | 11.4 | Hamal | 327 53.9 | N23 33.9 |
| 16 | 138 59.2 | 95 31.6 | 36.5 | 126 56.0 | 13.7 | 133 45.6 | 57.0 | 171 05.5 | 11.4 | Kaus Aust. | 83 35.0 | S34 22.4 |
| 17 | 154 01.7 | 110 31.1 | 37.3 | 141 56.8 | 14.4 | 148 47.7 | 57.1 | 186 07.9 | 11.4 | | | |
| 18 | 169 04.2 | 125 30.7 | N14 38.2 | 156 57.5 | N 3 15.1 | 163 49.8 | N 0 57.3 | 201 10.4 | S14 11.4 | Kochab | 137 18.9 | N74 04.0 |
| 19 | 184 06.6 | 140 30.2 | 39.1 | 171 58.3 | 15.8 | 178 52.0 | 57.4 | 216 12.9 | 11.4 | Markab | 13 32.0 | N15 19.4 |
| 20 | 199 09.1 | 155 29.8 | 40.0 | 186 59.1 | 16.5 | 193 54.1 | 57.5 | 231 15.4 | 11.4 | Menkar | 314 08.7 | N 4 10.5 |
| 21 | 214 11.6 | 170 29.3 .. | 40.9 | 201 59.9 .. | 17.2 | 208 56.3 .. | 57.6 | 246 17.9 .. | 11.5 | Menkent | 147 59.9 | S36 28.9 |
| 22 | 229 14.0 | 185 28.9 | 41.8 | 217 00.6 | 17.9 | 223 58.4 | 57.8 | 261 20.4 | 11.5 | Miaplacidus | 221 39.2 | S69 48.7 |
| 23 | 244 16.5 | 200 28.5 | 42.7 | 232 01.4 | 18.6 | 239 00.6 | 57.9 | 276 22.8 | 11.5 | | | |
| **11 00** | 259 18.9 | 215 28.0 | N14 43.6 | 247 02.2 | N 3 19.3 | 254 02.7 | N 0 58.0 | 291 25.3 | S14 11.5 | Mirfak | 308 31.8 | N49 56.2 |
| 01 | 274 21.4 | 230 27.6 | 44.4 | 262 02.9 | 20.0 | 269 04.8 | 58.2 | 306 27.8 | 11.5 | Nunki | 75 50.1 | S26 16.1 |
| 02 | 289 23.9 | 245 27.1 | 45.3 | 277 03.7 | 20.7 | 284 07.0 | 58.3 | 321 30.3 | 11.5 | Peacock | 53 08.7 | S56 39.6 |
| 03 | 304 26.3 | 260 26.7 .. | 46.2 | 292 04.5 .. | 21.4 | 299 09.1 .. | 58.4 | 336 32.8 .. | 11.5 | Pollux | 243 20.3 | N27 58.4 |
| 04 | 319 28.8 | 275 26.2 | 47.1 | 307 05.3 | 22.1 | 314 11.3 | 58.5 | 351 35.3 | 11.6 | Procyon | 244 53.4 | N 5 10.1 |
| 05 | 334 31.3 | 290 25.8 | 48.0 | 322 06.0 | 22.8 | 329 13.4 | 58.7 | 6 37.8 | 11.6 | | | |
| S 06 | 349 33.7 | 305 25.3 | N14 48.9 | 337 06.8 | N 3 23.5 | 344 15.6 | N 0 58.8 | 21 40.2 | S14 11.6 | Rasalhague | 96 00.2 | N12 32.6 |
| A 07 | 4 36.2 | 320 24.9 | 49.7 | 352 07.6 | 24.2 | 359 17.7 | 58.9 | 36 42.7 | 11.6 | Regulus | 207 36.8 | N11 51.6 |
| T 08 | 19 38.7 | 335 24.4 | 50.6 | 7 08.4 | 24.9 | 14 19.9 | 59.0 | 51 45.2 | 11.6 | Rigel | 281 06.3 | S 8 10.6 |
| U 09 | 34 41.1 | 350 24.0 .. | 51.5 | 22 09.1 .. | 25.6 | 29 22.0 .. | 59.2 | 66 47.7 .. | 11.6 | Rigil Kent. | 139 42.7 | S60 55.8 |
| R 10 | 49 43.6 | 5 23.5 | 52.4 | 37 09.9 | 26.3 | 44 24.2 | 59.3 | 81 50.2 | 11.7 | Sabik | 102 04.9 | S15 45.1 |
| D 11 | 64 46.0 | 20 23.1 | 53.3 | 52 10.7 | 27.0 | 59 26.3 | 59.4 | 96 52.7 | 11.7 | | | |
| A 12 | 79 48.5 | 35 22.6 | N14 54.1 | 67 11.5 | N 3 27.7 | 74 28.5 | N 0 59.5 | 111 55.2 | S14 11.7 | Schedar | 349 33.7 | N56 39.3 |
| Y 13 | 94 51.0 | 50 22.2 | 55.0 | 82 12.2 | 28.4 | 89 30.6 | 59.7 | 126 57.7 | 11.7 | Shaula | 96 12.9 | S37 07.2 |
| 14 | 109 53.4 | 65 21.7 | 55.9 | 97 13.0 | 29.1 | 104 32.8 | 59.8 | 142 00.1 | 11.7 | Sirius | 258 28.5 | S16 44.9 |
| 15 | 124 55.9 | 80 21.2 .. | 56.8 | 112 13.8 .. | 29.8 | 119 34.9 | 0 59.9 | 157 02.6 .. | 11.7 | Spica | 158 24.4 | S11 16.7 |
| 16 | 139 58.4 | 95 20.8 | 57.6 | 127 14.6 | 30.6 | 134 37.0 | 1 00.0 | 172 05.1 | 11.8 | Suhail | 222 48.1 | S43 31.5 |
| 17 | 155 00.8 | 110 20.3 | 58.5 | 142 15.3 | 31.3 | 149 39.2 | 00.2 | 187 07.6 | 11.8 | | | |
| 18 | 170 03.3 | 125 19.9 | N14 59.4 | 157 16.1 | N 3 32.0 | 164 41.3 | N 1 00.3 | 202 10.1 | S14 11.8 | Vega | 80 34.3 | N38 48.2 |
| 19 | 185 05.8 | 140 19.4 | 15 00.3 | 172 16.9 | 32.7 | 179 43.5 | 00.4 | 217 12.6 | 11.8 | Zuben'ubi | 136 58.1 | S16 08.1 |
| 20 | 200 08.2 | 155 19.0 | 01.2 | 187 17.7 | 33.4 | 194 45.6 | 00.5 | 232 15.1 | 11.8 | | | |
| 21 | 215 10.7 | 170 18.5 .. | 02.1 | 202 18.4 .. | 34.1 | 209 47.8 .. | 00.7 | 247 17.6 .. | 11.8 | | | |
| 22 | 230 13.2 | 185 18.1 | 02.9 | 217 19.2 | 34.8 | 224 49.9 | 00.8 | 262 20.1 | 11.9 | | | |
| 23 | 245 15.6 | 200 17.6 | 03.8 | 232 20.0 | 35.5 | 239 52.1 | 00.9 | 277 22.5 | 11.9 | | | |
| **Mer. Pass.** | 6 45.6 | v −0.4 | d 0.9 | v 0.8 | d 0.7 | v 2.1 | d 0.1 | v 2.5 | d 0.0 | | | |

| | SHA | Mer. Pass. |
|---|---|---|
| Venus | 317 18.8 | 9 38 |
| Mars | 348 23.8 | 7 33 |
| Jupiter | 354 51.5 | 7 06 |
| Saturn | 32 05.9 | 4 38 |

### SUN and MOON

| UT | SUN GHA | SUN Dec | MOON GHA | v | MOON Dec | d | HP |
|---|---|---|---|---|---|---|---|
| d h | ° ' | ° ' | ° ' | ' | ° ' | ' | ' |
| 9 00 | 180 12.0 | N22 54.7 | 71 29.2 | 14.1 | N 1 41.0 | 15.0 | 57.2 |
| 01 | 195 11.9 | 54.9 | 86 02.3 | 14.0 | 1 26.0 | 14.9 | 57.3 |
| 02 | 210 11.8 | 55.1 | 100 35.3 | 14.0 | 1 11.1 | 15.0 | 57.3 |
| 03 | 225 11.7 .. | 55.3 | 115 08.3 | 13.9 | 0 56.1 | 15.0 | 57.3 |
| 04 | 240 11.6 | 55.5 | 129 41.2 | 14.0 | 0 41.1 | 15.0 | 57.4 |
| 05 | 255 11.4 | 55.8 | 144 14.2 | 13.8 | 0 26.1 | 15.0 | 57.4 |
| 06 | 270 11.3 | N22 56.0 | 158 47.0 | 13.9 | N 0 11.1 | 15.1 | 57.4 |
| 07 | 285 11.2 | 56.2 | 173 19.9 | 13.8 | S 0 04.0 | 15.1 | 57.5 |
| T 08 | 300 11.1 | 56.4 | 187 52.7 | 13.7 | 0 19.1 | 15.1 | 57.5 |
| H 09 | 315 10.9 .. | 56.6 | 202 25.4 | 13.7 | 0 34.2 | 15.1 | 57.6 |
| U 10 | 330 10.8 | 56.8 | 216 58.1 | 13.7 | 0 49.3 | 15.1 | 57.6 |
| R 11 | 345 10.7 | 57.0 | 231 30.8 | 13.6 | 1 04.4 | 15.2 | 57.6 |
| S 12 | 0 10.6 | N22 57.2 | 246 03.4 | 13.6 | S 1 19.6 | 15.2 | 57.7 |
| D 13 | 15 10.5 | 57.4 | 260 36.0 | 13.5 | 1 34.8 | 15.2 | 57.7 |
| A 14 | 30 10.3 | 57.6 | 275 08.5 | 13.4 | 1 50.0 | 15.2 | 57.8 |
| Y 15 | 45 10.2 .. | 57.8 | 289 40.9 | 13.4 | 2 05.2 | 15.2 | 57.8 |
| 16 | 60 10.1 | 58.0 | 304 13.3 | 13.4 | 2 20.4 | 15.2 | 57.8 |
| 17 | 75 10.0 | 58.2 | 318 45.7 | 13.3 | 2 35.6 | 15.2 | 57.9 |
| 18 | 90 09.8 | N22 58.4 | 333 18.0 | 13.2 | S 2 50.8 | 15.3 | 57.9 |
| 19 | 105 09.7 | 58.6 | 347 50.2 | 13.2 | 3 06.1 | 15.2 | 58.0 |
| 20 | 120 09.6 | 58.8 | 2 22.4 | 13.1 | 3 21.3 | 15.3 | 58.0 |
| 21 | 135 09.5 .. | 59.0 | 16 54.5 | 13.1 | 3 36.6 | 15.2 | 58.0 |
| 22 | 150 09.3 | 59.2 | 31 26.6 | 13.0 | 3 51.8 | 15.3 | 58.1 |
| 23 | 165 09.2 | 59.4 | 45 58.6 | 12.9 | 4 07.1 | 15.3 | 58.1 |
| 10 00 | 180 09.1 | N22 59.6 | 60 30.5 | 12.9 | S 4 22.4 | 15.2 | 58.2 |
| 01 | 195 09.0 | 22 59.8 | 75 02.4 | 12.8 | 4 37.6 | 15.3 | 58.2 |
| 02 | 210 08.9 | 23 00.0 | 89 34.2 | 12.8 | 4 52.9 | 15.3 | 58.2 |
| 03 | 225 08.7 .. | 00.2 | 104 06.0 | 12.6 | 5 08.2 | 15.3 | 58.3 |
| 04 | 240 08.6 | 00.3 | 118 37.6 | 12.6 | 5 23.4 | 15.3 | 58.3 |
| 05 | 255 08.5 | 00.5 | 133 09.2 | 12.6 | 5 38.7 | 15.2 | 58.4 |
| 06 | 270 08.4 | N23 00.7 | 147 40.8 | 12.4 | S 5 53.9 | 15.3 | 58.4 |
| 07 | 285 08.2 | 00.9 | 162 12.2 | 12.4 | 6 09.2 | 15.2 | 58.4 |
| 08 | 300 08.1 | 01.1 | 176 43.6 | 12.3 | 6 24.4 | 15.3 | 58.5 |
| F 09 | 315 08.0 | 01.3 | 191 14.9 | 12.2 | 6 39.7 | 15.2 | 58.5 |
| R 10 | 330 07.9 | 01.5 | 205 46.1 | 12.2 | 6 54.9 | 15.2 | 58.6 |
| I 11 | 345 07.7 | 01.7 | 220 17.3 | 12.0 | 7 10.1 | 15.2 | 58.6 |
| D 12 | 0 07.6 | N23 01.9 | 234 48.3 | 12.0 | S 7 25.3 | 15.2 | 58.6 |
| A 13 | 15 07.5 | 02.0 | 249 19.3 | 11.9 | 7 40.5 | 15.1 | 58.7 |
| Y 14 | 30 07.4 | 02.2 | 263 50.2 | 11.9 | 7 55.6 | 15.2 | 58.7 |
| 15 | 45 07.2 .. | 02.4 | 278 21.1 | 11.7 | 8 10.8 | 15.1 | 58.8 |
| 16 | 60 07.1 | 02.6 | 292 51.8 | 11.6 | 8 25.9 | 15.1 | 58.8 |
| 17 | 75 07.0 | 02.8 | 307 22.4 | 11.6 | 8 41.0 | 15.1 | 58.8 |
| 18 | 90 06.9 | N23 03.0 | 321 53.0 | 11.5 | S 8 56.1 | 15.0 | 58.9 |
| 19 | 105 06.7 | 03.1 | 336 23.5 | 11.4 | 9 11.1 | 15.1 | 58.9 |
| 20 | 120 06.6 | 03.3 | 350 53.9 | 11.2 | 9 26.2 | 15.0 | 59.0 |
| 21 | 135 06.5 .. | 03.5 | 5 24.1 | 11.2 | 9 41.2 | 14.9 | 59.0 |
| 22 | 150 06.4 | 03.7 | 19 54.3 | 11.1 | 9 56.1 | 15.0 | 59.0 |
| 23 | 165 06.2 | 03.9 | 34 24.4 | 11.0 | 10 11.1 | 14.9 | 59.1 |
| 11 00 | 180 06.1 | N23 04.0 | 48 54.4 | 11.0 | S10 26.0 | 14.9 | 59.1 |
| 01 | 195 06.0 | 04.2 | 63 24.4 | 10.8 | 10 40.9 | 14.8 | 59.2 |
| 02 | 210 05.9 | 04.4 | 77 54.2 | 10.7 | 10 55.7 | 14.8 | 59.2 |
| 03 | 225 05.7 .. | 04.6 | 92 23.9 | 10.6 | 11 10.5 | 14.8 | 59.2 |
| 04 | 240 05.6 | 04.8 | 106 53.5 | 10.5 | 11 25.3 | 14.7 | 59.3 |
| 05 | 255 05.5 | 04.9 | 121 23.0 | 10.4 | 11 40.0 | 14.7 | 59.3 |
| 06 | 270 05.3 | N23 05.1 | 135 52.4 | 10.3 | S11 54.7 | 14.6 | 59.3 |
| 07 | 285 05.2 | 05.3 | 150 21.7 | 10.2 | 12 09.3 | 14.6 | 59.4 |
| 08 | 300 05.1 | 05.4 | 164 50.9 | 10.1 | 12 23.9 | 14.5 | 59.4 |
| S 09 | 315 05.0 .. | 05.6 | 179 20.0 | 9.9 | 12 38.4 | 14.5 | 59.5 |
| A 10 | 330 04.8 | 05.8 | 193 48.9 | 9.9 | 12 52.9 | 14.4 | 59.5 |
| T 11 | 345 04.7 | 06.0 | 208 17.8 | 9.8 | 13 07.3 | 14.4 | 59.5 |
| U 12 | 0 04.6 | N23 06.1 | 222 46.6 | 9.6 | S13 21.7 | 14.4 | 59.6 |
| R 13 | 15 04.5 | 06.3 | 237 15.2 | 9.6 | 13 36.1 | 14.2 | 59.6 |
| D 14 | 30 04.3 | 06.5 | 251 43.8 | 9.4 | 13 50.3 | 14.2 | 59.6 |
| A 15 | 45 04.2 .. | 06.6 | 266 12.2 | 9.3 | 14 04.5 | 14.2 | 59.7 |
| Y 16 | 60 04.1 | 06.8 | 280 40.5 | 9.2 | 14 18.7 | 14.1 | 59.7 |
| 17 | 75 04.0 | 07.0 | 295 08.7 | 9.1 | 14 32.8 | 14.0 | 59.8 |
| 18 | 90 03.8 | N23 07.1 | 309 36.8 | 8.9 | S14 46.8 | 13.9 | 59.8 |
| 19 | 105 03.7 | 07.3 | 324 04.7 | 8.8 | 15 00.7 | 13.9 | 59.8 |
| 20 | 120 03.6 | 07.5 | 338 32.5 | 8.8 | 15 14.6 | 13.8 | 59.9 |
| 21 | 135 03.4 .. | 07.6 | 353 00.3 | 8.6 | 15 28.4 | 13.8 | 59.9 |
| 22 | 150 03.3 | 07.8 | 7 27.9 | 8.4 | 15 42.2 | 13.6 | 59.9 |
| 23 | 165 03.2 | 07.9 | 21 55.3 | 8.4 | S15 55.8 | 13.6 | 60.0 |
| | SD 15.8 | d 0.2 | SD 15.7 | | 16.0 | | 16.2 |

### Twilight, Sunrise and Moonrise

| Lat. | Naut. | Civil | Sunrise | Moonrise 9 | 10 | 11 | 12 |
|---|---|---|---|---|---|---|---|
| ° | h m | h m | h m | h m | h m | h m | h m |
| N 72 | ☐ | ☐ | ☐ | 14 04 | 16 21 | 19 11 | ▬ |
| N 70 | ☐ | ☐ | ☐ | 14 01 | 16 07 | 18 34 | ▬ |
| 68 | ☐ | ☐ | 00 28 | 13 59 | 15 56 | 18 08 | 21 00 |
| 66 | //// | //// | 01 39 | 13 57 | 15 47 | 17 48 | 20 10 |
| 64 | //// | //// | 02 14 | 13 55 | 15 39 | 17 32 | 19 39 |
| 62 | //// | //// | 02 39 | 13 54 | 15 33 | 17 19 | 19 15 |
| 60 | //// | 01 03 | 02 59 | 13 53 | 15 27 | 17 08 | 18 57 |
| N 58 | //// | 01 46 | 03 15 | 13 52 | 15 22 | 16 59 | 18 42 |
| 56 | //// | 02 14 | 03 29 | 13 51 | 15 18 | 16 51 | 18 29 |
| 54 | 00 57 | 02 35 | 03 41 | 13 50 | 15 14 | 16 43 | 18 18 |
| 52 | 01 37 | 02 53 | 03 51 | 13 49 | 15 11 | 16 37 | 18 08 |
| 50 | 02 03 | 03 07 | 04 13 | 13 48 | 15 07 | 16 31 | 17 59 |
| 45 | 02 47 | 03 36 | 04 13 | 13 47 | 15 01 | 16 18 | 17 40 |
| N 40 | 03 17 | 03 58 | 04 31 | 13 46 | 14 55 | 16 08 | 17 25 |
| 35 | 03 40 | 04 16 | 04 46 | 13 45 | 14 50 | 15 59 | 17 13 |
| 30 | 03 58 | 04 31 | 04 58 | 13 44 | 14 46 | 15 52 | 17 02 |
| 20 | 04 26 | 04 55 | 05 20 | 13 42 | 14 38 | 15 38 | 16 43 |
| N 10 | 04 49 | 05 16 | 05 39 | 13 41 | 14 32 | 15 27 | 16 27 |
| 0 | 05 07 | 05 33 | 05 56 | 13 39 | 14 26 | 15 16 | 16 12 |
| S 10 | 05 24 | 05 50 | 06 13 | 13 38 | 14 20 | 15 06 | 15 57 |
| 20 | 05 40 | 06 07 | 06 31 | 13 37 | 14 14 | 14 55 | 15 41 |
| 30 | 05 56 | 06 26 | 06 52 | 13 35 | 14 07 | 14 42 | 15 23 |
| 35 | 06 04 | 06 36 | 07 04 | 13 34 | 14 03 | 14 35 | 15 12 |
| 40 | 06 11 | 06 48 | 07 10 | 13 34 | 13 59 | 14 27 | 15 00 |
| 45 | 06 24 | 07 01 | 07 34 | 13 32 | 13 53 | 14 17 | 14 47 |
| S 50 | 06 35 | 07 16 | 07 55 | 13 31 | 13 47 | 14 06 | 14 30 |
| 52 | 06 40 | 07 24 | 08 04 | 13 31 | 13 44 | 14 01 | 14 22 |
| 54 | 06 46 | 07 32 | 08 15 | 13 30 | 13 41 | 13 55 | 14 13 |
| 56 | 06 52 | 07 40 | 08 27 | 13 29 | 13 38 | 13 49 | 14 03 |
| 58 | 06 58 | 07 50 | 08 42 | 13 29 | 13 34 | 13 41 | 13 52 |
| S 60 | 07 05 | 08 02 | 08 59 | 13 28 | 13 30 | 13 33 | 13 39 |

### Sunset, Twilight and Moonset

| Lat. | Sunset | Civil | Naut. | Moonset 9 | 10 | 11 | 12 |
|---|---|---|---|---|---|---|---|
| ° | h m | h m | h m | h m | h m | h m | h m |
| N 72 | ☐ | ☐ | ☐ | 01 31 | 01 00 | 00 23 / 23 20 | ▬ |
| N 70 | ☐ | ☐ | ☐ | 01 30 | 01 07 | 00 40 | 00 00 |
| 68 | ☐ | ☐ | ☐ | 01 28 | 01 12 | 00 53 | 00 23 / 23 33 |
| 66 | 23 37 | //// | //// | 01 27 | 01 16 | 01 04 | 00 49 |
| 64 | 22 21 | //// | //// | 01 26 | 01 20 | 01 14 | 01 06 |
| 62 | 21 46 | //// | //// | 01 26 | 01 24 | 01 22 | 01 21 |
| 60 | 21 21 | 22 59 | //// | 01 25 | 01 26 | 01 29 | 01 33 |
| N 58 | 21 01 | 22 14 | //// | 01 24 | 01 29 | 01 35 | 01 43 |
| 56 | 20 45 | 21 46 | //// | 01 24 | 01 31 | 01 41 | 01 52 |
| 54 | 20 31 | 21 23 | 23 04 | 01 23 | 01 34 | 01 46 | 02 01 |
| 52 | 20 19 | 21 07 | 22 23 | 01 23 | 01 35 | 01 50 | 02 08 |
| 50 | 20 08 | 20 52 | 21 56 | 01 22 | 01 37 | 01 54 | 02 15 |
| 45 | 19 46 | 20 23 | 21 12 | 01 21 | 01 41 | 02 03 | 02 29 |
| N 40 | 19 28 | 20 01 | 20 42 | 01 20 | 01 44 | 02 10 | 02 41 |
| 35 | 19 14 | 19 43 | 20 20 | 01 20 | 01 47 | 02 17 | 02 51 |
| 30 | 19 01 | 19 28 | 20 01 | 01 19 | 01 50 | 02 23 | 03 00 |
| 20 | 18 39 | 19 04 | 19 33 | 01 18 | 01 54 | 02 32 | 03 16 |
| N 10 | 18 20 | 18 43 | 19 10 | 01 17 | 01 58 | 02 41 | 03 29 |
| 0 | 18 03 | 18 26 | 18 52 | 01 16 | 02 01 | 02 49 | 03 42 |
| S 10 | 17 46 | 18 09 | 18 35 | 01 15 | 02 05 | 02 58 | 03 55 |
| 20 | 17 28 | 17 52 | 18 19 | 01 14 | 02 09 | 03 06 | 04 09 |
| 30 | 17 07 | 17 33 | 18 03 | 01 12 | 02 13 | 03 17 | 04 24 |
| 35 | 16 55 | 17 23 | 17 54 | 01 12 | 02 15 | 03 22 | 04 34 |
| 40 | 16 41 | 17 11 | 17 45 | 01 11 | 02 18 | 03 29 | 04 44 |
| 45 | 16 24 | 16 58 | 17 35 | 01 10 | 02 22 | 03 37 | 04 57 |
| S 50 | 16 04 | 16 42 | 17 24 | 01 09 | 02 26 | 03 46 | 05 12 |
| 52 | 15 55 | 16 35 | 17 19 | 01 08 | 02 27 | 03 51 | 05 19 |
| 54 | 15 44 | 16 27 | 17 13 | 01 07 | 02 29 | 03 56 | 05 27 |
| 56 | 15 31 | 16 18 | 17 07 | 01 07 | 02 32 | 04 01 | 05 36 |
| 58 | 15 17 | 16 08 | 17 01 | 01 06 | 02 34 | 04 07 | 05 46 |
| S 60 | 15 00 | 15 57 | 16 53 | 01 05 | 02 37 | 04 14 | 05 58 |

### SUN and MOON — passages

| Day | Eqn. of Time 00h | 12h | Mer. Pass. | Mer. Pass. Upper | Lower | Age | Phase |
|---|---|---|---|---|---|---|---|
| d | m s | m s | h m | h m | h m | d | % |
| 9 | 00 48 | 00 43 | 11 59 | 19 50 | 07 27 | 10 | 69 |
| 10 | 00 37 | 00 31 | 11 59 | 20 38 | 08 14 | 11 | 79 |
| 11 | 00 25 | 00 19 | 12 00 | 21 29 | 09 03 | 12 | 87 |

| UT (d h) | ARIES GHA | VENUS −3.9 GHA | VENUS Dec | MARS +0.6 GHA | MARS Dec | JUPITER −2.3 GHA | JUPITER Dec | SATURN +0.5 GHA | SATURN Dec | STARS Name | SHA | Dec |
|---|---|---|---|---|---|---|---|---|---|---|---|---|
| 12 00 | 260 18.1 | 215 17.1 | N15 04.6 | 247 20.8 | N 3 36.2 | 254 54.2 | N 1 01.0 | 292 25.0 | S14 11.9 | Acamar | 315 13.8 | S40 12.8 |
| 01 | 275 20.5 | 230 16.7 | 05.5 | 262 21.5 | 36.9 | 269 56.4 | 01.2 | 307 27.5 | 11.9 | Achernar | 335 22.2 | S57 07.2 |
| 02 | 290 23.0 | 245 16.2 | 06.4 | 277 22.3 | 37.6 | 284 58.5 | 01.3 | 322 30.0 | 11.9 | Acrux | 173 02.2 | S63 13.6 |
| 03 | 305 25.5 | 260 15.8 .. | 07.3 | 292 23.1 .. | 38.3 | 300 00.7 .. | 01.4 | 337 32.5 .. | 11.9 | Adhara | 255 07.9 | S29 00.2 |
| 04 | 320 27.9 | 275 15.3 | 08.1 | 307 23.9 | 39.0 | 315 02.8 | 01.5 | 352 35.0 | 12.0 | Aldebaran | 290 42.4 | N16 33.2 |
| 05 | 335 30.4 | 290 14.8 | 09.0 | 322 24.6 | 39.7 | 330 05.0 | 01.7 | 7 37.5 | 12.0 | | | |
| 06 | 350 32.9 | 305 14.4 | N15 09.9 | 337 25.4 | N 3 40.4 | 345 07.1 | N 1 01.8 | 22 40.0 | S14 12.0 | Alioth | 166 14.7 | N55 50.6 |
| 07 | 5 35.3 | 320 13.9 | 10.7 | 352 26.2 | 41.1 | 0 09.3 | 01.9 | 37 42.5 | 12.0 | Alkaid | 152 53.4 | N49 12.3 |
| 08 | 20 37.8 | 335 13.5 | 11.6 | 7 27.0 | 41.8 | 15 11.4 | 02.0 | 52 45.0 | 12.0 | Alnair | 27 35.4 | S46 51.0 |
| S 09 | 35 40.3 | 350 13.0 .. | 12.5 | 22 27.7 .. | 42.5 | 30 13.6 .. | 02.2 | 67 47.4 .. | 12.0 | Alnilam | 275 40.2 | S 1 11.3 |
| U 10 | 50 42.7 | 5 12.5 | 13.3 | 37 28.5 | 43.2 | 45 15.8 | 02.3 | 82 49.9 | 12.1 | Alphard | 217 50.0 | S 8 45.4 |
| N 11 | 65 45.2 | 20 12.1 | 14.2 | 52 29.3 | 43.9 | 60 17.9 | 02.4 | 97 52.4 | 12.1 | | | |
| D 12 | 80 47.7 | 35 11.6 | N15 15.1 | 67 30.1 | N 3 44.6 | 75 20.1 | N 1 02.5 | 112 54.9 | S14 12.1 | Alphecca | 126 05.2 | N26 38.5 |
| A 13 | 95 50.1 | 50 11.1 | 15.9 | 82 30.8 | 45.3 | 90 22.2 | 02.6 | 127 57.4 | 12.1 | Alpheratz | 357 37.0 | N29 12.6 |
| Y 14 | 110 52.6 | 65 10.7 | 16.8 | 97 31.6 | 46.0 | 105 24.4 | 02.8 | 142 59.9 | 12.1 | Altair | 62 01.8 | N 8 55.6 |
| 15 | 125 55.0 | 80 10.2 .. | 17.7 | 112 32.4 .. | 46.7 | 120 26.5 .. | 02.9 | 158 02.4 .. | 12.2 | Ankaa | 353 09.4 | S42 10.9 |
| 16 | 140 57.5 | 95 09.7 | 18.5 | 127 33.2 | 47.4 | 135 28.7 | 03.0 | 173 04.9 | 12.2 | Antares | 112 18.1 | S26 28.9 |
| 17 | 156 00.0 | 110 09.3 | 19.4 | 142 33.9 | 48.1 | 150 30.8 | 03.1 | 188 07.4 | 12.2 | | | |
| 18 | 171 02.4 | 125 08.8 | N15 20.2 | 157 34.7 | N 3 48.8 | 165 33.0 | N 1 03.3 | 203 09.9 | S14 12.2 | Arcturus | 145 49.6 | N19 04.1 |
| 19 | 186 04.9 | 140 08.3 | 21.1 | 172 35.5 | 49.5 | 180 35.1 | 03.4 | 218 12.4 | 12.2 | Atria | 107 13.7 | S69 04.1 |
| 20 | 201 07.4 | 155 07.9 | 22.0 | 187 36.3 | 50.2 | 195 37.3 | 03.5 | 233 14.9 | 12.2 | Avior | 234 16.1 | S59 35.0 |
| 21 | 216 09.8 | 170 07.4 .. | 22.8 | 202 37.0 .. | 50.9 | 210 39.4 .. | 03.6 | 248 17.3 .. | 12.3 | Bellatrix | 278 25.5 | N 6 22.1 |
| 22 | 231 12.3 | 185 06.9 | 23.7 | 217 37.8 | 51.6 | 225 41.6 | 03.8 | 263 19.8 | 12.3 | Betelgeuse | 270 54.7 | N 7 24.6 |
| 23 | 246 14.8 | 200 06.5 | 24.5 | 232 38.6 | 52.3 | 240 43.7 | 03.9 | 278 22.3 | 12.3 | | | |
| 13 00 | 261 17.2 | 215 06.0 | N15 25.4 | 247 39.4 | N 3 53.0 | 255 45.9 | N 1 04.0 | 293 24.8 | S14 12.3 | Canopus | 263 53.9 | S52 42.5 |
| 01 | 276 19.7 | 230 05.5 | 26.3 | 262 40.1 | 53.7 | 270 48.1 | 04.1 | 308 27.3 | 12.3 | Capella | 280 25.5 | N46 01.1 |
| 02 | 291 22.2 | 245 05.1 | 27.1 | 277 40.9 | 54.4 | 285 50.2 | 04.2 | 323 29.8 | 12.4 | Deneb | 49 26.9 | N45 21.4 |
| 03 | 306 24.6 | 260 04.6 .. | 28.0 | 292 41.7 .. | 55.1 | 300 52.4 .. | 04.4 | 338 32.3 .. | 12.4 | Denebola | 182 27.1 | N14 27.0 |
| 04 | 321 27.1 | 275 04.1 | 28.8 | 307 42.5 | 55.8 | 315 54.5 | 04.5 | 353 34.8 | 12.4 | Diphda | 348 49.6 | S17 51.8 |
| 05 | 336 29.5 | 290 03.7 | 29.7 | 322 43.2 | 56.5 | 330 56.7 | 04.6 | 8 37.3 | 12.4 | | | |
| 06 | 351 32.0 | 305 03.2 | N15 30.5 | 337 44.0 | N 3 57.2 | 345 58.8 | N 1 04.7 | 23 39.8 | S14 12.4 | Dubhe | 193 43.8 | N61 38.2 |
| 07 | 6 34.5 | 320 02.7 | 31.4 | 352 44.7 | 57.9 | 1 01.0 | 04.8 | 38 42.3 | 12.4 | Elnath | 278 05.0 | N28 37.5 |
| 08 | 21 36.9 | 335 02.2 | 32.3 | 7 45.6 | 58.6 | 16 03.1 | 05.0 | 53 44.8 | 12.5 | Eltanin | 90 42.6 | N51 29.1 |
| M 09 | 36 39.4 | 350 01.8 .. | 33.1 | 22 46.3 | 3 59.3 | 31 05.3 .. | 05.1 | 68 47.3 .. | 12.5 | Enif | 33 40.7 | N 9 58.5 |
| O 10 | 51 41.9 | 5 01.3 | 34.0 | 37 47.1 | 4 00.0 | 46 07.5 | 05.2 | 83 49.8 | 12.5 | Fomalhaut | 15 16.8 | S29 30.1 |
| N 11 | 66 44.3 | 20 00.8 | 34.8 | 52 47.9 | 00.7 | 61 09.6 | 05.3 | 98 52.3 | 12.5 | | | |
| D 12 | 81 46.8 | 35 00.3 | N15 35.7 | 67 48.7 | N 4 01.4 | 76 11.8 | N 1 05.5 | 113 54.8 | S14 12.5 | Gacrux | 171 53.8 | S57 14.5 |
| A 13 | 96 49.3 | 49 59.9 | 36.5 | 82 49.4 | 02.1 | 91 13.9 | 05.6 | 128 57.2 | 12.6 | Gienah | 175 45.7 | S17 40.0 |
| Y 14 | 111 51.7 | 64 59.4 | 37.4 | 97 50.2 | 02.8 | 106 16.1 | 05.7 | 143 59.7 | 12.6 | Hadar | 148 38.6 | S60 29.0 |
| 15 | 126 54.2 | 79 58.9 .. | 38.2 | 112 51.0 .. | 03.4 | 121 18.3 .. | 05.8 | 159 02.2 .. | 12.6 | Hamal | 327 53.8 | N23 33.9 |
| 16 | 141 56.7 | 94 58.4 | 39.1 | 127 51.8 | 04.1 | 136 20.4 | 05.9 | 174 04.7 | 12.6 | Kaus Aust. | 83 35.0 | S34 22.4 |
| 17 | 156 59.1 | 109 58.0 | 39.9 | 142 52.6 | 04.8 | 151 22.6 | 06.1 | 189 07.2 | 12.6 | | | |
| 18 | 172 01.6 | 124 57.5 | N15 40.8 | 157 53.3 | N 4 05.5 | 166 24.7 | N 1 06.2 | 204 09.7 | S14 12.7 | Kochab | 137 18.9 | N74 04.0 |
| 19 | 187 04.0 | 139 57.0 | 41.6 | 172 54.1 | 06.2 | 181 26.9 | 06.3 | 219 12.2 | 12.7 | Markab | 13 32.0 | N15 19.4 |
| 20 | 202 06.5 | 154 56.5 | 42.5 | 187 54.9 | 06.9 | 196 29.0 | 06.4 | 234 14.7 | 12.7 | Menkar | 314 08.7 | N 4 10.6 |
| 21 | 217 09.0 | 169 56.0 .. | 43.3 | 202 55.7 .. | 07.6 | 211 31.2 .. | 06.5 | 249 17.2 .. | 12.7 | Menkent | 147 59.9 | S36 28.9 |
| 22 | 232 11.4 | 184 55.6 | 44.1 | 217 56.4 | 08.3 | 226 33.4 | 06.7 | 264 19.7 | 12.7 | Miaplacidus | 221 39.2 | S69 48.7 |
| 23 | 247 13.9 | 199 55.1 | 45.0 | 232 57.2 | 09.0 | 241 35.5 | 06.8 | 279 22.2 | 12.7 | | | |
| 14 00 | 262 16.4 | 214 54.6 | N15 45.8 | 247 58.0 | N 4 09.7 | 256 37.7 | N 1 06.9 | 294 24.7 | S14 12.8 | Mirfak | 308 31.7 | N49 56.2 |
| 01 | 277 18.8 | 229 54.1 | 46.7 | 262 58.8 | 10.4 | 271 39.8 | 07.0 | 309 27.2 | 12.8 | Nunki | 75 50.1 | S26 16.1 |
| 02 | 292 21.3 | 244 53.6 | 47.5 | 277 59.5 | 11.1 | 286 42.0 | 07.1 | 324 29.7 | 12.8 | Peacock | 53 08.7 | S56 39.6 |
| 03 | 307 23.8 | 259 53.2 .. | 48.4 | 293 00.3 .. | 11.8 | 301 44.2 .. | 07.3 | 339 32.2 .. | 12.8 | Pollux | 243 20.3 | N27 58.4 |
| 04 | 322 26.2 | 274 52.7 | 49.2 | 308 01.1 | 12.5 | 316 46.3 | 07.4 | 354 34.7 | 12.8 | Procyon | 244 53.4 | N 5 10.1 |
| 05 | 337 28.7 | 289 52.2 | 50.1 | 323 01.9 | 13.2 | 331 48.5 | 07.5 | 9 37.2 | 12.9 | | | |
| 06 | 352 31.2 | 304 51.7 | N15 50.9 | 338 02.7 | N 4 13.9 | 346 50.7 | N 1 07.6 | 24 39.7 | S14 12.9 | Rasalhague | 96 00.2 | N12 32.6 |
| 07 | 7 33.6 | 319 51.2 | 51.7 | 353 03.4 | 14.6 | 1 52.8 | 07.7 | 39 42.2 | 12.9 | Regulus | 207 36.8 | N11 51.6 |
| 08 | 22 36.1 | 334 50.7 | 52.6 | 8 04.2 | 15.3 | 16 55.0 | 07.9 | 54 44.7 | 12.9 | Rigel | 281 06.3 | S 8 10.6 |
| T 09 | 37 38.5 | 349 50.3 .. | 53.4 | 23 05.0 .. | 16.0 | 31 57.1 .. | 08.0 | 69 47.2 .. | 12.9 | Rigil Kent. | 139 42.7 | S60 55.8 |
| U 10 | 52 41.0 | 4 49.8 | 54.3 | 38 05.8 | 16.7 | 46 59.3 | 08.1 | 84 49.7 | 13.0 | Sabik | 102 04.9 | S15 45.1 |
| E 11 | 67 43.5 | 19 49.3 | 55.1 | 53 06.5 | 17.4 | 62 01.5 | 08.2 | 99 52.2 | 13.0 | | | |
| S 12 | 82 45.9 | 34 48.8 | N15 55.9 | 68 07.3 | N 4 18.1 | 77 03.6 | N 1 08.3 | 114 54.7 | S14 13.0 | Schedar | 349 33.6 | N56 39.3 |
| D 13 | 97 48.4 | 49 48.3 | 56.8 | 83 08.1 | 18.8 | 92 05.8 | 08.4 | 129 57.2 | 13.0 | Shaula | 96 12.8 | S37 07.2 |
| A 14 | 112 50.9 | 64 47.8 | 57.6 | 98 08.9 | 19.5 | 107 08.0 | 08.6 | 144 59.7 | 13.0 | Sirius | 258 28.5 | S16 44.8 |
| Y 15 | 127 53.3 | 79 47.3 .. | 58.4 | 113 09.6 .. | 20.2 | 122 10.1 .. | 08.7 | 160 02.2 .. | 13.1 | Spica | 158 24.4 | S11 16.7 |
| 16 | 142 55.8 | 94 46.8 | 15 59.3 | 128 10.4 | 20.9 | 137 12.3 | 08.8 | 175 04.7 | 13.1 | Suhail | 222 48.1 | S43 31.5 |
| 17 | 157 58.3 | 109 46.4 | 16 00.1 | 143 11.2 | 21.5 | 152 14.4 | 08.9 | 190 07.2 | 13.1 | | | |
| 18 | 173 00.7 | 124 45.9 | N16 00.9 | 158 12.0 | N 4 22.2 | 167 16.6 | N 1 09.0 | 205 09.7 | S14 13.1 | Vega | 80 34.2 | N38 48.2 |
| 19 | 188 03.2 | 139 45.4 | 01.8 | 173 12.8 | 22.9 | 182 18.8 | 09.2 | 220 12.2 | 13.2 | Zuben'ubi | 136 58.1 | S16 08.1 |
| 20 | 203 05.6 | 154 44.9 | 02.6 | 188 13.5 | 23.6 | 197 20.9 | 09.3 | 235 14.7 | 13.2 | | SHA | Mer. Pass. |
| 21 | 218 08.1 | 169 44.4 .. | 03.4 | 203 14.3 .. | 24.3 | 212 23.1 .. | 09.4 | 250 17.2 .. | 13.2 | Venus | 313 48.8 | 9 40 |
| 22 | 233 10.6 | 184 43.9 | 04.3 | 218 15.1 | 25.0 | 227 25.3 | 09.5 | 265 19.7 | 13.2 | Mars | 346 22.1 | 7 29 |
| 23 | 248 13.0 | 199 43.4 | 05.1 | 233 15.9 | 25.7 | 242 27.4 | 09.6 | 280 22.2 | 13.2 | Jupiter | 354 28.7 | 6 56 |
| Mer. Pass. 6 33.8 | | v −0.5 d 0.9 | | v 0.8 d 0.7 | | v 2.2 d 0.1 | | v 2.5 d 0.0 | | Saturn | 32 07.6 | 4 26 |

### SUN / MOON

| UT | SUN GHA | SUN Dec | MOON GHA | v | Dec | d | HP |
|---|---|---|---|---|---|---|---|
| d h | ° ′ | ° ′ | ° ′ | ′ | ° ′ | ′ | ′ |
| **12 00** | 180 03.1 | N23 08.1 | 36 22.7 | 8.2 | S16 09.4 | 13.5 | 60.0 |
| 01 | 195 02.9 | 08.3 | 50 49.9 | 8.1 | 16 22.9 | 13.4 | 60.0 |
| 02 | 210 02.8 | 08.4 | 65 17.0 | 8.0 | 16 36.3 | 13.4 | 60.1 |
| 03 | 225 02.7 · · | 08.6 | 79 44.0 | 7.9 | 16 49.7 | 13.2 | 60.1 |
| 04 | 240 02.5 | 08.7 | 94 10.9 | 7.7 | 17 02.9 | 13.2 | 60.1 |
| 05 | 255 02.4 | 08.9 | 108 37.6 | 7.6 | 17 16.1 | 13.1 | 60.2 |
| 06 | 270 02.3 | N23 09.1 | 123 04.2 | 7.5 | S17 29.2 | 12.9 | 60.2 |
| 07 | 285 02.2 | 09.2 | 137 30.7 | 7.4 | 17 42.1 | 12.9 | 60.2 |
| 08 | 300 02.0 | 09.4 | 151 57.1 | 7.2 | 17 55.0 | 12.8 | 60.3 |
| S 09 | 315 01.9 · · | 09.5 | 166 23.3 | 7.1 | 18 07.8 | 12.7 | 60.3 |
| U 10 | 330 01.8 | 09.7 | 180 49.4 | 7.0 | 18 20.5 | 12.6 | 60.3 |
| N 11 | 345 01.7 | 09.8 | 195 15.4 | 6.8 | 18 33.1 | 12.6 | 60.4 |
| D 12 | 0 01.5 | N23 10.0 | 209 41.2 | 6.7 | S18 45.5 | 12.4 | 60.4 |
| A 13 | 15 01.4 | 10.1 | 224 06.9 | 6.6 | 18 57.9 | 12.3 | 60.4 |
| Y 14 | 30 01.3 | 10.3 | 238 32.5 | 6.5 | 19 10.2 | 12.1 | 60.4 |
| 15 | 45 01.1 · · | 10.4 | 252 58.0 | 6.3 | 19 22.3 | 12.1 | 60.5 |
| 16 | 60 01.0 | 10.6 | 267 23.3 | 6.2 | 19 34.4 | 11.9 | 60.5 |
| 17 | 75 00.9 | 10.7 | 281 48.5 | 6.1 | 19 46.3 | 11.8 | 60.5 |
| 18 | 90 00.8 | N23 10.9 | 296 13.6 | 5.9 | S19 58.1 | 11.7 | 60.6 |
| 19 | 105 00.6 | 11.0 | 310 38.5 | 5.8 | 20 09.8 | 11.6 | 60.6 |
| 20 | 120 00.5 | 11.2 | 325 03.3 | 5.7 | 20 21.4 | 11.4 | 60.6 |
| 21 | 135 00.4 · · | 11.3 | 339 28.0 | 5.6 | 20 32.8 | 11.3 | 60.6 |
| 22 | 150 00.2 | 11.5 | 353 52.6 | 5.4 | 20 44.1 | 11.2 | 60.7 |
| 23 | 165 00.1 | 11.6 | 8 17.0 | 5.3 | 20 55.3 | 11.1 | 60.7 |
| **13 00** | 180 00.0 | N23 11.8 | 22 41.3 | 5.2 | S21 06.4 | 10.9 | 60.7 |
| 01 | 194 59.8 | 11.9 | 37 05.5 | 5.0 | 21 17.3 | 10.8 | 60.7 |
| 02 | 209 59.7 | 12.0 | 51 29.5 | 4.9 | 21 28.1 | 10.6 | 60.8 |
| 03 | 224 59.6 · · | 12.2 | 65 53.4 | 4.8 | 21 38.7 | 10.5 | 60.8 |
| 04 | 239 59.5 | 12.3 | 80 17.2 | 4.7 | 21 49.2 | 10.4 | 60.8 |
| 05 | 254 59.3 | 12.5 | 94 40.9 | 4.5 | 21 59.6 | 10.2 | 60.8 |
| 06 | 269 59.2 | N23 12.6 | 109 04.4 | 4.4 | S22 09.8 | 10.1 | 60.9 |
| 07 | 284 59.1 | 12.8 | 123 27.8 | 4.3 | 22 19.9 | 9.9 | 60.9 |
| 08 | 299 58.9 | 12.9 | 137 51.1 | 4.2 | 22 29.8 | 9.8 | 60.9 |
| M 09 | 314 58.8 · · | 13.0 | 152 14.3 | 4.0 | 22 39.6 | 9.6 | 60.9 |
| N 10 | 329 58.7 | 13.2 | 166 37.3 | 3.9 | 22 49.2 | 9.5 | 61.0 |
| O 11 | 344 58.5 | 13.3 | 181 00.2 | 3.8 | 22 58.7 | 9.3 | 61.0 |
| D 12 | 359 58.4 | N23 13.4 | 195 23.0 | 3.7 | S23 08.0 | 9.1 | 61.0 |
| A 13 | 14 58.3 | 13.6 | 209 45.7 | 3.6 | 23 17.1 | 9.0 | 61.0 |
| Y 14 | 29 58.2 | 13.7 | 224 08.3 | 3.4 | 23 26.1 | 8.8 | 61.0 |
| 15 | 44 58.0 | 13.8 | 238 30.7 | 3.4 | 23 34.9 | 8.7 | 61.0 |
| 16 | 59 57.9 | 14.0 | 252 53.1 | 3.2 | 23 43.6 | 8.5 | 61.1 |
| 17 | 74 57.8 | 14.1 | 267 15.3 | 3.1 | 23 52.1 | 8.3 | 61.1 |
| 18 | 89 57.6 | N23 14.2 | 281 37.4 | 3.0 | S24 00.4 | 8.1 | 61.1 |
| 19 | 104 57.5 | 14.4 | 295 59.4 | 2.9 | 24 08.5 | 8.0 | 61.1 |
| 20 | 119 57.4 | 14.5 | 310 21.3 | 2.8 | 24 16.5 | 7.8 | 61.1 |
| 21 | 134 57.2 · · | 14.6 | 324 43.1 | 2.7 | 24 24.3 | 7.6 | 61.1 |
| 22 | 149 57.1 | 14.8 | 339 04.8 | 2.6 | 24 31.9 | 7.5 | 61.2 |
| 23 | 164 57.0 | 14.9 | 353 26.4 | 2.5 | 24 39.4 | 7.2 | 61.2 |
| **14 00** | 179 56.9 | N23 15.0 | 7 47.9 | 2.4 | S24 46.6 | 7.1 | 61.2 |
| 01 | 194 56.7 | 15.1 | 22 09.3 | 2.3 | 24 53.7 | 6.9 | 61.2 |
| 02 | 209 56.6 | 15.3 | 36 30.6 | 2.2 | 25 00.6 | 6.7 | 61.2 |
| 03 | 224 56.5 · · | 15.4 | 50 51.8 | 2.1 | 25 07.3 | 6.5 | 61.2 |
| 04 | 239 56.3 | 15.5 | 65 12.9 | 2.0 | 25 13.8 | 6.3 | 61.2 |
| 05 | 254 56.2 | 15.6 | 79 33.9 | 2.0 | 25 20.1 | 6.2 | 61.2 |
| 06 | 269 56.1 | N23 15.8 | 93 54.9 | 1.8 | S25 26.3 | 5.9 | 61.3 |
| 07 | 284 55.9 | 15.9 | 108 15.7 | 1.8 | 25 32.2 | 5.7 | 61.3 |
| T 08 | 299 55.8 | 16.0 | 122 36.5 | 1.7 | 25 37.9 | 5.6 | 61.3 |
| U 09 | 314 55.7 · · | 16.1 | 136 57.2 | 1.6 | 25 43.5 | 5.3 | 61.3 |
| E 10 | 329 55.5 | 16.2 | 151 17.8 | 1.6 | 25 48.8 | 5.2 | 61.3 |
| S 11 | 344 55.4 | 16.4 | 165 38.4 | 1.5 | 25 54.0 | 4.9 | 61.3 |
| D 12 | 359 55.3 | N23 16.5 | 179 58.9 | 1.4 | S25 58.9 | 4.8 | 61.3 |
| A 13 | 14 55.1 | 16.6 | 194 19.3 | 1.3 | 26 03.7 | 4.5 | 61.3 |
| Y 14 | 29 55.0 | 16.7 | 208 39.6 | 1.3 | 26 08.2 | 4.4 | 61.3 |
| 15 | 44 54.9 · · | 16.8 | 222 59.9 | 1.2 | 26 12.6 | 4.1 | 61.3 |
| 16 | 59 54.7 | 16.9 | 237 20.1 | 1.2 | 26 16.7 | 4.0 | 61.3 |
| 17 | 74 54.6 | 17.1 | 251 40.3 | 1.1 | 26 20.7 | 3.7 | 61.3 |
| 18 | 89 54.5 | N23 17.2 | 266 00.4 | 1.1 | S26 24.4 | 3.5 | 61.3 |
| 19 | 104 54.4 | 17.3 | 280 20.5 | 1.1 | 26 27.9 | 3.3 | 61.3 |
| 20 | 119 54.2 | 17.4 | 294 40.6 | 0.9 | 26 31.2 | 3.1 | 61.3 |
| 21 | 134 54.1 · · | 17.5 | 309 00.5 | 1.0 | 26 34.3 | 2.9 | 61.3 |
| 22 | 149 54.0 | 17.6 | 323 20.5 | 0.9 | 26 37.2 | 2.7 | 61.3 |
| 23 | 164 53.8 | 17.7 | 337 40.4 | 0.9 | S26 39.9 | 2.4 | 61.3 |
| | SD 15.8 | d 0.1 | SD | 16.5 | 16.6 | | 16.7 |

### Twilight / Sunrise / Moonrise

| Lat. | Naut. | Civil | Sunrise | 12 | 13 | 14 | 15 |
|---|---|---|---|---|---|---|---|
| ° | h m | h m | h m | h m | h m | h m | h m |
| N 72 | ☐ | ☐ | ☐ | ■ | ■ | ■ | ■ |
| N 70 | ☐ | ☐ | ☐ | ■ | ■ | ■ | ■ |
| 68 | ☐ | ☐ | ☐ | 21 00 | ■ | ■ | ■ |
| 66 | ☐ | ☐ | ☐ | 20 10 | ■ | ■ | ■ |
| 64 | //// | //// | 01 35 | 19 39 | 22 07 | ■ | ■ |
| 62 | //// | //// | 02 12 | 19 15 | 21 20 | 23 19 | 24 24 |
| 60 | //// | 00 57 | 02 37 | 18 57 | 20 50 | 22 33 | 23 40 |
| N 58 | //// | 01 43 | 02 57 | 18 42 | 20 27 | 22 03 | 23 10 |
| 56 | //// | 02 12 | 03 14 | 18 29 | 20 09 | 21 40 | 22 48 |
| 54 | 00 52 | 02 34 | 03 28 | 18 18 | 19 53 | 21 21 | 22 29 |
| 52 | 01 35 | 02 51 | 03 40 | 18 08 | 19 40 | 21 05 | 22 13 |
| 50 | 02 02 | 03 06 | 03 51 | 17 59 | 19 28 | 20 51 | 22 00 |
| 45 | 02 46 | 03 36 | 04 13 | 17 40 | 19 04 | 20 23 | 21 32 |
| N 40 | 03 16 | 03 58 | 04 31 | 17 25 | 18 45 | 20 01 | 21 10 |
| 35 | 03 39 | 04 16 | 04 45 | 17 13 | 18 29 | 19 43 | 20 52 |
| 30 | 03 58 | 04 31 | 04 58 | 17 02 | 18 15 | 19 28 | 20 36 |
| 20 | 04 27 | 04 56 | 05 20 | 16 43 | 17 51 | 19 01 | 20 09 |
| N 10 | 04 49 | 05 16 | 05 39 | 16 27 | 17 31 | 18 39 | 19 46 |
| 0 | 05 08 | 05 34 | 05 56 | 16 12 | 17 12 | 18 18 | 19 25 |
| S 10 | 05 25 | 05 51 | 06 14 | 15 57 | 16 54 | 17 57 | 19 03 |
| 20 | 05 41 | 06 08 | 06 32 | 15 41 | 16 34 | 17 34 | 18 40 |
| 30 | 05 57 | 06 27 | 06 53 | 15 23 | 16 11 | 17 08 | 18 14 |
| 35 | 06 06 | 06 37 | 07 05 | 15 12 | 15 58 | 16 53 | 17 58 |
| 40 | 06 15 | 06 49 | 07 19 | 15 00 | 15 42 | 16 35 | 17 40 |
| 45 | 06 25 | 07 02 | 07 36 | 14 47 | 15 24 | 16 14 | 17 18 |
| S 50 | 06 37 | 07 18 | 07 57 | 14 30 | 15 02 | 15 48 | 16 50 |
| 52 | 06 42 | 07 25 | 08 06 | 14 22 | 14 51 | 15 35 | 16 36 |
| 54 | 06 47 | 07 34 | 08 17 | 14 13 | 14 39 | 15 20 | 16 21 |
| 56 | 06 54 | 07 43 | 08 30 | 14 03 | 14 26 | 15 03 | 16 02 |
| 58 | 07 00 | 07 53 | 08 44 | 13 52 | 14 10 | 14 42 | 15 40 |
| S 60 | 07 08 | 08 04 | 09 01 | 13 39 | 13 51 | 14 16 | 15 10 |

### Sunset / Twilight / Moonset

| Lat. | Sunset | Civil | Naut. | 12 | 13 | 14 | 15 |
|---|---|---|---|---|---|---|---|
| ° | h m | h m | h m | h m | h m | h m | h m |
| N 72 | ☐ | ☐ | ☐ | ■ | ■ | ■ | ■ |
| N 70 | ☐ | ☐ | ☐ | 00 00 | ■ | ■ | ■ |
| 68 | ☐ | ☐ | ☐ | (00 28 / 23 33) | ■ | ■ | ■ |
| 66 | ☐ | ☐ | ☐ | 00 49 | 00 25 | ■ | ■ |
| 64 | 22 26 | //// | //// | 01 06 | 00 57 | 00 38 | ■ |
| 62 | 21 49 | //// | //// | 01 21 | 01 21 | 01 25 | 01 45 |
| 60 | 21 24 | 23 05 | //// | 01 33 | 01 40 | 01 56 | 02 31 |
| N 58 | 21 03 | 22 18 | //// | 01 43 | 01 56 | 02 19 | 03 02 |
| 56 | 20 47 | 21 49 | //// | 01 52 | 02 10 | 02 38 | 03 25 |
| 54 | 20 33 | 21 27 | 23 10 | 02 01 | 02 22 | 02 54 | 03 44 |
| 52 | 20 21 | 21 09 | 22 26 | 02 08 | 02 32 | 03 08 | 04 00 |
| 50 | 20 10 | 20 54 | 21 59 | 02 15 | 02 42 | 03 20 | 04 13 |
| 45 | 19 48 | 20 25 | 21 14 | 02 29 | 03 02 | 03 45 | 04 42 |
| N 40 | 19 30 | 20 03 | 20 44 | 02 41 | 03 18 | 04 05 | 05 04 |
| 35 | 19 15 | 19 44 | 20 21 | 02 51 | 03 32 | 04 22 | 05 22 |
| 30 | 19 02 | 19 29 | 20 03 | 03 00 | 03 44 | 04 36 | 05 38 |
| 20 | 18 40 | 19 05 | 19 34 | 03 16 | 04 05 | 05 01 | 06 05 |
| N 10 | 18 21 | 18 44 | 19 11 | 03 29 | 04 23 | 05 23 | 06 28 |
| 0 | 18 04 | 18 26 | 18 52 | 03 42 | 04 40 | 05 43 | 06 50 |
| S 10 | 17 46 | 18 09 | 18 36 | 03 55 | 04 57 | 06 03 | 07 11 |
| 20 | 17 28 | 17 52 | 18 20 | 04 09 | 05 15 | 06 25 | 07 34 |
| 30 | 17 07 | 17 33 | 18 03 | 04 24 | 05 36 | 06 50 | 08 01 |
| 35 | 16 55 | 17 23 | 17 55 | 04 34 | 05 49 | 07 04 | 08 16 |
| 40 | 16 41 | 17 11 | 17 45 | 04 44 | 06 03 | 07 21 | 08 35 |
| 45 | 16 24 | 16 58 | 17 35 | 04 57 | 06 20 | 07 42 | 08 57 |
| S 50 | 16 04 | 16 42 | 17 23 | 05 12 | 06 41 | 08 08 | 09 25 |
| 52 | 15 54 | 16 35 | 17 18 | 05 19 | 06 51 | 08 21 | 09 38 |
| 54 | 15 43 | 16 26 | 17 13 | 05 27 | 07 03 | 08 35 | 09 54 |
| 56 | 15 30 | 16 17 | 17 07 | 05 36 | 07 16 | 08 52 | 10 13 |
| 58 | 15 16 | 16 07 | 17 00 | 05 46 | 07 31 | 09 12 | 10 35 |
| S 60 | 14 59 | 15 56 | 16 52 | 05 58 | 07 49 | 09 38 | 11 05 |

### SUN / MOON

| Day | Eqn. of Time 00ʰ | Eqn. of Time 12ʰ | Mer. Pass. | Mer. Pass. Upper | Mer. Pass. Lower | Age | Phase |
|---|---|---|---|---|---|---|---|
| d | m s | m s | h m | h m | h m | d | % |
| 12 | 00 12 | 00 06 | 12 00 | 22 26 | 09 57 | 13 | 94 |
| 13 | 00 00 | 00 06 | 12 00 | 23 27 | 10 56 | 14 | 98 |
| 14 | 00 12 | 00 19 | 12 00 | 24 33 | 12 00 | 15 | 100 |

| UT | ARIES | VENUS −3·9 | | MARS +0·5 | | JUPITER −2·3 | | SATURN +0·5 | | STARS | | |
|---|---|---|---|---|---|---|---|---|---|---|---|---|
| | GHA | GHA | Dec | GHA | Dec | GHA | Dec | GHA | Dec | Name | SHA | Dec |
| d h | ° ′ | ° ′ | ° ′ | ° ′ | ° ′ | ° ′ | ° ′ | ° ′ | ° ′ | | ° ′ | ° ′ |
| 15 00 | 263 15.5 | 214 42.9 | N16 05.9 | 248 16.6 | N 4 26.4 | 257 29.6 | N 1 09.7 | 295 24.7 | S14 13.3 | Acamar | 315 13.7 | S40 12.8 |
| 01 | 278 18.0 | 229 42.4 | 06.8 | 263 17.4 | 27.1 | 272 31.8 | 09.9 | 310 27.2 | 13.3 | Achernar | 335 22.1 | S57 07.2 |
| 02 | 293 20.4 | 244 41.9 | 07.6 | 278 18.2 | 27.8 | 287 33.9 | 10.0 | 325 29.7 | 13.3 | Acrux | 173 02.2 | S63 13.6 |
| 03 | 308 22.9 | 259 41.4 .. | 08.4 | 293 19.0 .. | 28.5 | 302 36.1 .. | 10.1 | 340 32.2 .. | 13.3 | Adhara | 255 07.9 | S29 00.2 |
| 04 | 323 25.4 | 274 40.9 | 09.2 | 308 19.8 | 29.2 | 317 38.3 | 10.2 | 355 34.7 | 13.3 | Aldebaran | 290 42.4 | N16 33.2 |
| 05 | 338 27.8 | 289 40.5 | 10.1 | 323 20.5 | 29.9 | 332 40.4 | 10.3 | 10 37.2 | 13.4 | | | |
| 06 | 353 30.3 | 304 40.0 | N16 10.9 | 338 21.3 | N 4 30.6 | 347 42.6 | N 1 10.4 | 25 39.7 | S14 13.4 | Alioth | 166 14.7 | N55 50.6 |
| W 07 | 8 32.8 | 319 39.5 | 11.7 | 353 22.1 | 31.3 | 2 44.8 | 10.6 | 40 42.2 | 13.4 | Alkaid | 152 53.4 | N49 12.4 |
| E 08 | 23 35.2 | 334 39.0 | 12.5 | 8 22.9 | 32.0 | 17 46.9 | 10.7 | 55 44.7 | 13.4 | Alnair | 27 35.4 | S46 51.0 |
| D 09 | 38 37.7 | 349 38.5 .. | 13.4 | 23 23.6 .. | 32.6 | 32 49.1 .. | 10.8 | 70 47.2 .. | 13.4 | Alnilam | 275 40.2 | S 1 11.3 |
| N 10 | 53 40.1 | 4 38.0 | 14.2 | 38 24.4 | 33.3 | 47 51.3 | 10.9 | 85 49.7 | 13.5 | Alphard | 217 50.0 | S 8 45.3 |
| E 11 | 68 42.6 | 19 37.5 | 15.0 | 53 25.2 | 34.0 | 62 53.4 | 11.0 | 100 52.2 | 13.5 | | | |
| S 12 | 83 45.1 | 34 37.0 | N16 15.8 | 68 26.0 | N 4 34.7 | 77 55.6 | N 1 11.1 | 115 54.7 | S14 13.5 | Alphecca | 126 05.2 | N26 38.5 |
| D 13 | 98 47.5 | 49 36.5 | 16.7 | 83 26.8 | 35.4 | 92 57.8 | 11.3 | 130 57.2 | 13.5 | Alpheratz | 357 37.0 | N29 12.6 |
| A 14 | 113 50.0 | 64 36.0 | 17.5 | 98 27.5 | 36.1 | 107 59.9 | 11.4 | 145 59.7 | 13.6 | Altair | 62 01.7 | N 8 55.6 |
| Y 15 | 128 52.5 | 79 35.5 .. | 18.3 | 113 28.3 .. | 36.8 | 123 02.1 .. | 11.5 | 161 02.2 .. | 13.6 | Ankaa | 353 09.4 | S42 10.9 |
| 16 | 143 54.9 | 94 35.0 | 19.1 | 128 29.1 | 37.5 | 138 04.3 | 11.6 | 176 04.7 | 13.6 | Antares | 112 18.1 | S26 28.9 |
| 17 | 158 57.4 | 109 34.5 | 19.9 | 143 29.9 | 38.2 | 153 06.5 | 11.7 | 191 07.2 | 13.6 | | | |
| 18 | 173 59.9 | 124 34.0 | N16 20.8 | 158 30.6 | N 4 38.9 | 168 08.6 | N 1 11.8 | 206 09.7 | S14 13.6 | Arcturus | 145 49.6 | N19 04.1 |
| 19 | 189 02.3 | 139 33.5 | 21.6 | 173 31.4 | 39.6 | 183 10.8 | 11.9 | 221 12.2 | 13.7 | Atria | 107 13.6 | S69 04.1 |
| 20 | 204 04.8 | 154 33.0 | 22.4 | 188 32.2 | 40.3 | 198 13.0 | 12.1 | 236 14.7 | 13.7 | Avior | 234 16.1 | S59 35.0 |
| 21 | 219 07.3 | 169 32.5 .. | 23.2 | 203 33.0 .. | 41.0 | 213 15.1 .. | 12.2 | 251 17.2 .. | 13.7 | Bellatrix | 278 25.5 | N 6 22.2 |
| 22 | 234 09.7 | 184 32.0 | 24.0 | 218 33.8 | 41.6 | 228 17.3 | 12.3 | 266 19.7 | 13.7 | Betelgeuse | 270 54.7 | N 7 24.6 |
| 23 | 249 12.2 | 199 31.5 | 24.8 | 233 34.5 | 42.3 | 243 19.5 | 12.4 | 281 22.2 | 13.7 | | | |
| 16 00 | 264 14.6 | 214 31.0 | N16 25.7 | 248 35.3 | N 4 43.0 | 258 21.6 | N 1 12.5 | 296 24.8 | S14 13.8 | Canopus | 263 53.9 | S52 42.5 |
| 01 | 279 17.1 | 229 30.5 | 26.5 | 263 36.1 | 43.7 | 273 23.8 | 12.6 | 311 27.3 | 13.8 | Capella | 280 25.5 | N46 01.1 |
| 02 | 294 19.6 | 244 30.0 | 27.3 | 278 36.9 | 44.4 | 288 26.0 | 12.8 | 326 29.8 | 13.8 | Deneb | 49 26.9 | N45 21.4 |
| 03 | 309 22.0 | 259 29.4 .. | 28.1 | 293 37.7 .. | 45.1 | 303 28.2 .. | 12.9 | 341 32.3 .. | 13.8 | Denebola | 182 27.1 | N14 27.0 |
| 04 | 324 24.5 | 274 28.9 | 28.9 | 308 38.4 | 45.8 | 318 30.3 | 13.0 | 356 34.8 | 13.9 | Diphda | 348 49.5 | S17 51.8 |
| 05 | 339 27.0 | 289 28.4 | 29.7 | 323 39.2 | 46.5 | 333 32.5 | 13.1 | 11 37.3 | 13.9 | | | |
| 06 | 354 29.4 | 304 27.9 | N16 30.5 | 338 40.0 | N 4 47.2 | 348 34.7 | N 1 13.2 | 26 39.8 | S14 13.9 | Dubhe | 193 43.8 | N61 38.2 |
| 07 | 9 31.9 | 319 27.4 | 31.3 | 353 40.8 | 47.9 | 3 36.9 | 13.3 | 41 42.3 | 13.9 | Elnath | 278 04.9 | N28 37.5 |
| T 08 | 24 34.4 | 334 26.9 | 32.2 | 8 41.6 | 48.5 | 18 39.0 | 13.4 | 56 44.8 | 14.0 | Eltanin | 90 42.6 | N51 29.1 |
| H 09 | 39 36.8 | 349 26.4 .. | 33.0 | 23 42.3 .. | 49.2 | 33 41.2 .. | 13.6 | 71 47.3 .. | 14.0 | Enif | 33 40.7 | N 9 58.6 |
| U 10 | 54 39.3 | 4 25.9 | 33.8 | 38 43.1 | 49.9 | 48 43.4 | 13.7 | 86 49.8 | 14.0 | Fomalhaut | 15 16.8 | S29 30.1 |
| R 11 | 69 41.8 | 19 25.4 | 34.6 | 53 43.9 | 50.6 | 63 45.5 | 13.8 | 101 52.3 | 14.0 | | | |
| S 12 | 84 44.2 | 34 24.9 | N16 35.4 | 68 44.7 | N 4 51.3 | 78 47.7 | N 1 13.9 | 116 54.8 | S14 14.0 | Gacrux | 171 53.8 | S57 14.5 |
| D 13 | 99 46.7 | 49 24.4 | 36.2 | 83 45.4 | 52.0 | 93 49.9 | 14.0 | 131 57.3 | 14.1 | Gienah | 175 45.7 | S17 40.0 |
| A 14 | 114 49.1 | 64 23.9 | 37.0 | 98 46.2 | 52.7 | 108 52.1 | 14.1 | 146 59.8 | 14.1 | Hadar | 148 38.6 | S60 29.0 |
| Y 15 | 129 51.6 | 79 23.3 .. | 37.8 | 113 47.0 .. | 53.4 | 123 54.2 .. | 14.2 | 162 02.3 .. | 14.1 | Hamal | 327 53.8 | N23 33.9 |
| 16 | 144 54.1 | 94 22.8 | 38.6 | 128 47.8 | 54.1 | 138 56.4 | 14.3 | 177 04.9 | 14.1 | Kaus Aust. | 83 34.9 | S34 22.4 |
| 17 | 159 56.5 | 109 22.3 | 39.4 | 143 48.6 | 54.8 | 153 58.6 | 14.5 | 192 07.4 | 14.2 | | | |
| 18 | 174 59.0 | 124 21.8 | N16 40.2 | 158 49.3 | N 4 55.4 | 169 00.8 | N 1 14.6 | 207 09.9 | S14 14.2 | Kochab | 137 18.9 | N74 04.0 |
| 19 | 190 01.5 | 139 21.3 | 41.0 | 173 50.1 | 56.1 | 184 02.9 | 14.7 | 222 12.4 | 14.2 | Markab | 13 31.9 | N15 19.4 |
| 20 | 205 03.9 | 154 20.8 | 41.8 | 188 50.9 | 56.8 | 199 05.1 | 14.8 | 237 14.9 | 14.2 | Menkar | 314 08.6 | N 4 10.6 |
| 21 | 220 06.4 | 169 20.3 .. | 42.6 | 203 51.7 .. | 57.5 | 214 07.3 .. | 14.9 | 252 17.4 .. | 14.3 | Menkent | 147 59.9 | S36 28.9 |
| 22 | 235 08.9 | 184 19.8 | 43.4 | 218 52.5 | 58.2 | 229 09.5 | 15.0 | 267 19.9 | 14.3 | Miaplacidus | 221 39.2 | S69 48.7 |
| 23 | 250 11.3 | 199 19.2 | 44.2 | 233 53.2 | 58.9 | 244 11.6 | 15.1 | 282 22.4 | 14.3 | | | |
| 17 00 | 265 13.8 | 214 18.7 | N16 45.0 | 248 54.0 | N 4 59.6 | 259 13.8 | N 1 15.2 | 297 24.9 | S14 14.3 | Mirfak | 308 31.7 | N49 56.2 |
| 01 | 280 16.3 | 229 18.2 | 45.8 | 263 54.8 | 5 00.3 | 274 16.0 | 15.4 | 312 27.4 | 14.3 | Nunki | 75 50.0 | S26 16.1 |
| 02 | 295 18.7 | 244 17.7 | 46.6 | 278 55.6 | 01.0 | 289 18.2 | 15.5 | 327 29.9 | 14.4 | Peacock | 53 08.6 | S56 39.6 |
| 03 | 310 21.2 | 259 17.2 .. | 47.4 | 293 56.4 .. | 01.6 | 304 20.4 .. | 15.6 | 342 32.4 .. | 14.4 | Pollux | 243 20.2 | N27 58.4 |
| 04 | 325 23.6 | 274 16.7 | 48.2 | 308 57.1 | 02.3 | 319 22.5 | 15.7 | 357 35.0 | 14.4 | Procyon | 244 53.4 | N 5 10.1 |
| 05 | 340 26.1 | 289 16.1 | 49.0 | 323 57.9 | 03.0 | 334 24.7 | 15.8 | 12 37.5 | 14.4 | | | |
| 06 | 355 28.6 | 304 15.6 | N16 49.8 | 338 58.7 | N 5 03.7 | 349 26.9 | N 1 15.9 | 27 40.0 | S14 14.5 | Rasalhague | 96 00.2 | N12 32.6 |
| 07 | 10 31.0 | 319 15.1 | 50.6 | 353 59.5 | 04.4 | 4 29.1 | 16.0 | 42 42.5 | 14.5 | Regulus | 207 36.8 | N11 51.6 |
| 08 | 25 33.5 | 334 14.6 | 51.4 | 9 00.3 | 05.1 | 19 31.2 | 16.1 | 57 45.0 | 14.5 | Rigel | 281 06.2 | S 8 10.6 |
| F 09 | 40 36.0 | 349 14.1 .. | 52.2 | 24 01.0 .. | 05.8 | 34 33.4 .. | 16.3 | 72 47.5 .. | 14.5 | Rigil Kent. | 139 42.7 | S60 55.8 |
| R 10 | 55 38.4 | 4 13.5 | 53.0 | 39 01.8 | 06.5 | 49 35.6 | 16.4 | 87 50.0 | 14.6 | Sabik | 102 04.9 | S15 45.1 |
| I 11 | 70 40.9 | 19 13.0 | 53.8 | 54 02.6 | 07.1 | 64 37.8 | 16.5 | 102 52.5 | 14.6 | | | |
| D 12 | 85 43.4 | 34 12.5 | N16 54.6 | 69 03.4 | N 5 07.8 | 79 40.0 | N 1 16.6 | 117 55.0 | S14 14.6 | Schedar | 349 33.6 | N56 39.3 |
| A 13 | 100 45.8 | 49 12.0 | 55.4 | 84 04.2 | 08.5 | 94 42.1 | 16.7 | 132 57.5 | 14.6 | Shaula | 96 12.8 | S37 07.2 |
| Y 14 | 115 48.3 | 64 11.5 | 56.1 | 99 04.9 | 09.2 | 109 44.3 | 16.8 | 148 00.1 | 14.7 | Sirius | 258 28.4 | S16 44.8 |
| 15 | 130 50.8 | 79 10.9 .. | 56.9 | 114 05.7 .. | 09.9 | 124 46.5 .. | 16.9 | 163 02.6 .. | 14.7 | Spica | 158 24.4 | S11 16.7 |
| 16 | 145 53.2 | 94 10.4 | 57.7 | 129 06.5 | 10.6 | 139 48.7 | 17.0 | 178 05.1 | 14.7 | Suhail | 222 48.1 | S43 31.5 |
| 17 | 160 55.7 | 109 09.9 | 58.5 | 144 07.3 | 11.3 | 154 50.9 | 17.1 | 193 07.6 | 14.7 | | | |
| 18 | 175 58.1 | 124 09.4 | N16 59.3 | 159 08.1 | N 5 11.9 | 169 53.0 | N 1 17.3 | 208 10.1 | S14 14.8 | Vega | 80 34.2 | N38 48.2 |
| 19 | 191 00.6 | 139 08.8 | 17 00.1 | 174 08.8 | 12.6 | 184 55.2 | 17.4 | 223 12.6 | 14.8 | Zuben'ubi | 136 58.1 | S16 08.1 |
| 20 | 206 03.1 | 154 08.3 | 00.9 | 189 09.6 | 13.3 | 199 57.4 | 17.5 | 238 15.1 | 14.8 | | SHA | Mer. Pass. |
| 21 | 221 05.5 | 169 07.8 .. | 01.7 | 204 10.4 .. | 14.0 | 214 59.6 .. | 17.6 | 253 17.6 .. | 14.8 | | ° ′ | h m |
| 22 | 236 08.0 | 184 07.3 | 02.4 | 219 11.2 | 14.7 | 230 01.8 | 17.7 | 268 20.1 | 14.9 | Venus | 310 16.3 | 9 42 |
| 23 | 251 10.5 | 199 06.7 | 03.2 | 234 12.0 | 15.4 | 245 03.9 | 17.8 | 283 22.7 | 14.9 | Mars | 344 20.7 | 7 25 |
| | h m | | | | | | | | | Jupiter | 354 07.0 | 6 46 |
| Mer. Pass. 6 22.0 | | v −0.5 | d 0.8 | v 0.8 | d 0.7 | v 2.2 | d 0.1 | v 2.5 | d 0.0 | Saturn | 32 10.1 | 4 14 |

## SUN / MOON

| UT (d h) | SUN GHA | SUN Dec | MOON GHA | v | MOON Dec | d | HP |
|---|---|---|---|---|---|---|---|
| 15 00 | 179 53.7 | N23 17.8 | 352 00.3 | 0.9 | S26 42.3 | 2.3 | 61.3 |
| 01 | 194 53.6 | 18.0 | 6 20.2 | 0.8 | 26 44.6 | 2.0 | 61.3 |
| 02 | 209 53.4 | 18.1 | 20 40.0 | 0.8 | 26 46.6 | 1.9 | 61.3 |
| 03 | 224 53.3 | .. 18.2 | 34 59.8 | 0.8 | 26 48.5 | 1.6 | 61.3 |
| 04 | 239 53.2 | 18.3 | 49 19.6 | 0.8 | 26 50.1 | 1.4 | 61.3 |
| 05 | 254 53.0 | 18.4 | 63 39.4 | 0.7 | 26 51.5 | 1.2 | 61.3 |
| 06 | 269 52.9 | N23 18.5 | 77 59.1 | 0.8 | S26 52.7 | 0.9 | 61.3 |
| W 07 | 284 52.8 | 18.6 | 92 18.9 | 0.7 | 26 53.6 | 0.8 | 61.3 |
| E 08 | 299 52.6 | 18.7 | 106 38.6 | 0.8 | 26 54.4 | 0.5 | 61.3 |
| D 09 | 314 52.5 | .. 18.8 | 120 58.4 | 0.8 | 26 54.9 | 0.4 | 61.3 |
| N 10 | 329 52.4 | 18.9 | 135 18.2 | 0.7 | 26 55.3 | 0.1 | 61.3 |
| E 11 | 344 52.2 | 19.0 | 149 37.9 | 0.8 | 26 55.4 | 0.1 | 61.3 |
| S 12 | 359 52.1 | N23 19.1 | 163 57.7 | 0.8 | S26 55.3 | 0.3 | 61.3 |
| D 13 | 14 52.0 | 19.2 | 178 17.5 | 0.8 | 26 55.0 | 0.5 | 61.3 |
| A 14 | 29 51.8 | 19.3 | 192 37.3 | 0.8 | 26 54.5 | 0.8 | 61.3 |
| Y 15 | 44 51.7 | .. 19.4 | 206 57.1 | 0.9 | 26 53.7 | 0.9 | 61.3 |
| 16 | 59 51.6 | 19.5 | 221 17.0 | 0.9 | 26 52.8 | 1.2 | 61.3 |
| 17 | 74 51.4 | 19.6 | 235 36.9 | 0.9 | 26 51.6 | 1.4 | 61.3 |
| 18 | 89 51.3 | N23 19.7 | 249 56.8 | 0.9 | S26 50.2 | 1.6 | 61.2 |
| 19 | 104 51.2 | 19.8 | 264 16.7 | 1.0 | 26 48.6 | 1.8 | 61.2 |
| 20 | 119 51.0 | 19.9 | 278 36.7 | 1.0 | 26 46.8 | 2.0 | 61.2 |
| 21 | 134 50.9 | .. 20.0 | 292 56.7 | 1.1 | 26 44.8 | 2.2 | 61.2 |
| 22 | 149 50.8 | 20.1 | 307 16.8 | 1.1 | 26 42.6 | 2.4 | 61.2 |
| 23 | 164 50.6 | 20.2 | 321 36.9 | 1.2 | 26 40.2 | 2.7 | 61.2 |
| 16 00 | 179 50.5 | N23 20.3 | 335 57.1 | 1.2 | S26 37.5 | 2.8 | 61.2 |
| 01 | 194 50.4 | 20.4 | 350 17.3 | 1.3 | 26 34.7 | 3.1 | 61.2 |
| 02 | 209 50.2 | 20.5 | 4 37.6 | 1.4 | 26 31.6 | 3.2 | 61.1 |
| 03 | 224 50.1 | .. 20.5 | 18 58.0 | 1.4 | 26 28.4 | 3.5 | 61.1 |
| 04 | 239 50.0 | 20.6 | 33 18.4 | 1.5 | 26 24.9 | 3.7 | 61.1 |
| 05 | 254 49.8 | 20.7 | 47 38.9 | 1.5 | 26 21.2 | 3.8 | 61.1 |
| 06 | 269 49.7 | N23 20.8 | 61 59.4 | 1.6 | S26 17.4 | 4.1 | 61.1 |
| T 07 | 284 49.6 | 20.9 | 76 20.0 | 1.7 | 26 13.3 | 4.2 | 61.1 |
| H 08 | 299 49.4 | 21.0 | 90 40.7 | 1.8 | 26 09.1 | 4.5 | 61.0 |
| U 09 | 314 49.3 | .. 21.1 | 105 01.5 | 1.9 | 26 04.6 | 4.7 | 61.0 |
| R 10 | 329 49.2 | 21.2 | 119 22.4 | 1.9 | 25 59.9 | 4.8 | 61.0 |
| S 11 | 344 49.0 | 21.2 | 133 43.3 | 2.0 | 25 55.1 | 5.1 | 61.0 |
| D 12 | 359 48.9 | N23 21.3 | 148 04.3 | 2.1 | S25 50.0 | 5.2 | 61.0 |
| A 13 | 14 48.8 | 21.4 | 162 25.4 | 2.2 | 25 44.8 | 5.4 | 61.0 |
| Y 14 | 29 48.6 | 21.5 | 176 46.6 | 2.3 | 25 39.4 | 5.7 | 60.9 |
| 15 | 44 48.5 | .. 21.6 | 191 07.9 | 2.4 | 25 33.7 | 5.8 | 60.9 |
| 16 | 59 48.4 | 21.7 | 205 29.3 | 2.5 | 25 27.9 | 6.0 | 60.9 |
| 17 | 74 48.2 | 21.7 | 219 50.8 | 2.6 | 25 21.9 | 6.1 | 60.9 |
| 18 | 89 48.1 | N23 21.8 | 234 12.4 | 2.7 | S25 15.8 | 6.4 | 60.8 |
| 19 | 104 48.0 | 21.9 | 248 34.1 | 2.8 | 25 09.4 | 6.5 | 60.8 |
| 20 | 119 47.8 | 22.0 | 262 55.9 | 2.9 | 25 02.9 | 6.7 | 60.8 |
| 21 | 134 47.7 | .. 22.1 | 277 17.8 | 3.1 | 24 56.2 | 6.9 | 60.8 |
| 22 | 149 47.6 | 22.1 | 291 39.9 | 3.1 | 24 49.3 | 7.1 | 60.8 |
| 23 | 164 47.4 | 22.2 | 306 02.0 | 3.2 | 24 42.2 | 7.2 | 60.7 |
| 17 00 | 179 47.3 | N23 22.3 | 320 24.2 | 3.4 | S24 35.0 | 7.5 | 60.7 |
| 01 | 194 47.2 | 22.4 | 334 46.6 | 3.5 | 24 27.5 | 7.5 | 60.7 |
| 02 | 209 47.0 | 22.4 | 349 09.1 | 3.5 | 24 20.0 | 7.8 | 60.7 |
| 03 | 224 46.9 | .. 22.5 | 3 31.6 | 3.8 | 24 12.2 | 7.9 | 60.6 |
| 04 | 239 46.8 | 22.6 | 17 54.4 | 3.8 | 24 04.3 | 8.1 | 60.6 |
| 05 | 254 46.6 | 22.7 | 32 17.2 | 3.9 | 23 56.2 | 8.2 | 60.6 |
| 06 | 269 46.5 | N23 22.7 | 46 40.1 | 4.1 | S23 48.0 | 8.4 | 60.6 |
| 07 | 284 46.4 | 22.8 | 61 03.2 | 4.2 | 23 39.6 | 8.6 | 60.5 |
| 08 | 299 46.2 | 22.9 | 75 26.4 | 4.3 | 23 31.0 | 8.7 | 60.5 |
| F 09 | 314 46.1 | .. 22.9 | 89 49.7 | 4.5 | 23 22.3 | 8.9 | 60.5 |
| R 10 | 329 45.9 | 23.0 | 104 13.2 | 4.5 | 23 13.4 | 9.0 | 60.4 |
| I 11 | 344 45.8 | 23.1 | 118 36.7 | 4.7 | 23 04.4 | 9.1 | 60.4 |
| D 12 | 359 45.7 | N23 23.1 | 133 00.4 | 4.8 | S22 55.3 | 9.4 | 60.4 |
| A 13 | 14 45.5 | 23.2 | 147 24.2 | 5.0 | 22 45.9 | 9.4 | 60.3 |
| Y 14 | 29 45.4 | 23.3 | 161 48.2 | 5.1 | 22 36.5 | 9.6 | 60.3 |
| 15 | 44 45.3 | .. 23.3 | 176 12.3 | 5.2 | 22 26.9 | 9.8 | 60.3 |
| 16 | 59 45.1 | 23.4 | 190 36.5 | 5.3 | 22 17.1 | 9.8 | 60.3 |
| 17 | 74 45.0 | 23.5 | 205 00.8 | 5.5 | 22 07.3 | 10.0 | 60.2 |
| 18 | 89 44.9 | N23 23.5 | 219 25.3 | 5.6 | S21 57.3 | 10.2 | 60.2 |
| 19 | 104 44.7 | 23.6 | 233 49.9 | 5.8 | 21 47.1 | 10.3 | 60.2 |
| 20 | 119 44.6 | 23.7 | 248 14.7 | 5.8 | 21 36.8 | 10.4 | 60.1 |
| 21 | 134 44.5 | .. 23.7 | 262 39.5 | 6.0 | 21 26.4 | 10.5 | 60.1 |
| 22 | 149 44.3 | 23.8 | 277 04.5 | 6.2 | 21 15.9 | 10.7 | 60.1 |
| 23 | 164 44.2 | 23.8 | 291 29.7 | 6.2 | S21 05.2 | 10.8 | 60.0 |
| | SD 15.8 | d 0.1 | SD 16.7 | | 16.6 | | 16.5 |

## Twilight / Sunrise / Moonrise

| Lat. | Naut. | Civil | Sunrise | Moonrise 15 | 16 | 17 | 18 |
|---|---|---|---|---|---|---|---|
| N 72 | ☐ | ☐ | ☐ | ■ | ■ | ■ | ■ |
| N 70 | ☐ | ☐ | ☐ | ■ | ■ | ■ | 02 17 |
| 68 | ☐ | ☐ | ☐ | ■ | ■ | ■ | 01 34 |
| 66 | ☐ | ☐ | ☐ | ■ | ■ | ■ | 01 21 |
| 64 | //// | //// | 01 32 | ■ | ■ | ■ | 01 05 |
| 62 | //// | //// | 02 10 | 24 24 | 24 11 | 00 39 | 00 42 |
| 60 | //// | 00 52 | 02 36 | 23 40 | 24 11 | 00 11 | 00 24 |
| N 58 | //// | 01 41 | 02 56 | 23 10 | 23 49 | 24 09 | 00 09 |
| 56 | //// | 02 11 | 03 13 | 22 48 | 23 30 | 23 56 | 24 12 |
| 54 | 00 48 | 02 33 | 03 27 | 22 29 | 23 15 | 23 44 | 24 04 |
| 52 | 01 33 | 02 51 | 03 39 | 22 13 | 23 02 | 23 34 | 23 57 |
| 50 | 02 00 | 03 06 | 03 50 | 22 00 | 22 50 | 23 25 | 23 50 |
| 45 | 02 46 | 03 35 | 04 13 | 21 32 | 22 26 | 23 06 | 23 37 |
| N 40 | 03 16 | 03 58 | 04 31 | 21 10 | 22 06 | 22 50 | 23 25 |
| 35 | 03 39 | 04 16 | 04 46 | 20 52 | 21 50 | 22 37 | 23 16 |
| 30 | 03 58 | 04 31 | 04 59 | 20 36 | 21 35 | 22 25 | 23 07 |
| 20 | 04 27 | 04 56 | 05 21 | 20 09 | 21 11 | 22 05 | 22 52 |
| N 10 | 04 49 | 05 16 | 05 40 | 19 46 | 20 50 | 21 48 | 22 39 |
| 0 | 05 08 | 05 35 | 05 57 | 19 25 | 20 30 | 21 31 | 22 27 |
| S 10 | 05 25 | 05 52 | 06 14 | 19 03 | 20 11 | 21 15 | 22 14 |
| 20 | 05 41 | 06 09 | 06 33 | 18 40 | 19 49 | 20 57 | 22 01 |
| 30 | 05 58 | 06 28 | 06 54 | 18 14 | 19 25 | 20 37 | 21 46 |
| 35 | 06 07 | 06 38 | 07 06 | 17 58 | 19 10 | 20 25 | 21 37 |
| 40 | 06 16 | 06 50 | 07 21 | 17 40 | 18 54 | 20 11 | 21 27 |
| 45 | 06 26 | 07 04 | 07 37 | 17 18 | 18 33 | 19 54 | 21 15 |
| S 50 | 06 38 | 07 20 | 07 58 | 16 50 | 18 08 | 19 34 | 21 00 |
| 52 | 06 43 | 07 27 | 08 08 | 16 36 | 17 56 | 19 24 | 20 53 |
| 54 | 06 49 | 07 35 | 08 19 | 16 21 | 17 42 | 19 13 | 20 46 |
| 56 | 06 55 | 07 44 | 08 32 | 16 02 | 17 25 | 19 01 | 20 37 |
| 58 | 07 02 | 07 54 | 08 46 | 15 40 | 17 06 | 18 46 | 20 27 |
| S 60 | 07 09 | 08 06 | 09 04 | 15 10 | 16 41 | 18 29 | 20 16 |

## Sunset / Twilight / Moonset

| Lat. | Sunset | Civil | Naut. | Moonset 15 | 16 | 17 | 18 |
|---|---|---|---|---|---|---|---|
| N 72 | ☐ | ☐ | ☐ | ■ | ■ | ■ | ■ |
| N 70 | ☐ | ☐ | ☐ | ■ | ■ | ■ | ■ |
| 68 | ☐ | ☐ | ☐ | ■ | ■ | ■ | 05 31 |
| 66 | ☐ | ☐ | ☐ | ■ | ■ | ■ | 06 13 |
| 64 | 22 30 | //// | //// | ■ | ■ | 04 21 | 06 41 |
| 62 | 21 52 | //// | //// | 01 45 | 03 02 | 05 02 | 07 02 |
| 60 | 21 26 | 23 11 | //// | 02 31 | 03 45 | 05 30 | 07 20 |
| N 58 | 21 05 | 22 21 | //// | 03 02 | 04 15 | 05 51 | 07 34 |
| 56 | 20 49 | 21 51 | //// | 03 25 | 04 37 | 06 09 | 07 46 |
| 54 | 20 35 | 21 29 | 23 15 | 03 44 | 04 55 | 06 24 | 07 57 |
| 52 | 20 22 | 21 11 | 22 29 | 04 00 | 05 11 | 06 37 | 08 07 |
| 50 | 20 11 | 20 56 | 22 00 | 04 13 | 05 24 | 06 48 | 08 15 |
| 45 | 19 49 | 20 26 | 21 16 | 04 42 | 05 52 | 07 11 | 08 33 |
| N 40 | 19 31 | 20 04 | 20 45 | 05 04 | 06 14 | 07 30 | 08 47 |
| 35 | 19 16 | 19 46 | 20 22 | 05 22 | 06 32 | 07 46 | 08 59 |
| 30 | 19 03 | 19 30 | 20 04 | 05 38 | 06 47 | 07 59 | 09 10 |
| 20 | 18 41 | 19 05 | 19 35 | 06 05 | 07 13 | 08 22 | 09 28 |
| N 10 | 18 22 | 18 45 | 19 12 | 06 28 | 07 36 | 08 42 | 09 44 |
| 0 | 18 04 | 18 27 | 18 53 | 06 50 | 07 56 | 09 00 | 09 58 |
| S 10 | 17 47 | 18 10 | 18 36 | 07 11 | 08 17 | 09 18 | 10 13 |
| 20 | 17 29 | 17 53 | 18 22 | 07 34 | 08 39 | 09 37 | 10 28 |
| 30 | 17 07 | 17 34 | 18 04 | 08 01 | 09 05 | 10 00 | 10 45 |
| 35 | 16 55 | 17 23 | 17 55 | 08 16 | 09 20 | 10 13 | 10 55 |
| 40 | 16 41 | 17 11 | 17 45 | 08 35 | 09 37 | 10 27 | 11 07 |
| 45 | 16 24 | 16 58 | 17 35 | 08 57 | 09 58 | 10 45 | 11 21 |
| S 50 | 16 03 | 16 42 | 17 23 | 09 25 | 10 24 | 11 06 | 11 37 |
| 52 | 15 54 | 16 34 | 17 18 | 09 38 | 10 37 | 11 17 | 11 44 |
| 54 | 15 42 | 16 26 | 17 12 | 09 54 | 10 51 | 11 28 | 11 52 |
| 56 | 15 30 | 16 17 | 17 06 | 10 13 | 11 08 | 11 41 | 12 02 |
| 58 | 15 15 | 16 07 | 17 00 | 10 35 | 11 28 | 11 56 | 12 12 |
| S 60 | 14 58 | 15 55 | 16 52 | 11 05 | 11 53 | 12 14 | 12 25 |

## SUN / MOON

| Day | SUN Eqn. of Time 00h | 12h | Mer. Pass. | MOON Mer. Pass. Upper | Lower | Age | Phase |
|---|---|---|---|---|---|---|---|
| | m s | m s | h m | h m | h m | d | % |
| 15 | 00 25 | 00 31 | 12 01 | 00 33 | 13 07 | 16 | 98 |
| 16 | 00 38 | 00 44 | 12 01 | 01 41 | 14 13 | 17 | 94 |
| 17 | 00 51 | 00 57 | 12 01 | 02 45 | 15 16 | 18 | 87 | ◯

| UT | ARIES GHA | VENUS −3.9 GHA | Dec | MARS +0.5 GHA | Dec | JUPITER −2.3 GHA | Dec | SATURN +0.5 GHA | Dec | STARS Name | SHA | Dec |
|---|---|---|---|---|---|---|---|---|---|---|---|---|
| d h | ° ′ | ° ′ | ° ′ | ° ′ | ° ′ | ° ′ | ° ′ | ° ′ | ° ′ | | ° ′ | ° ′ |
| 18 00 | 266 12.9 | 214 06.2 | N17 04.0 | 249 12.7 | N 5 16.1 | 260 06.1 | N 1 17.9 | 298 25.2 | S14 14.9 | Acamar | 315 13.7 | S40 12.8 |
| 01 | 281 15.4 | 229 05.7 | 04.8 | 264 13.5 | 16.7 | 275 08.3 | 18.0 | 313 27.7 | 14.9 | Achernar | 335 22.1 | S57 07.2 |
| 02 | 296 17.9 | 244 05.1 | 05.6 | 279 14.3 | 17.4 | 290 10.5 | 18.1 | 328 30.2 | 15.0 | Acrux | 173 02.3 | S63 13.6 |
| 03 | 311 20.3 | 259 04.6 .. | 06.4 | 294 15.1 .. | 18.1 | 305 12.7 .. | 18.2 | 343 32.7 .. | 15.0 | Adhara | 255 07.9 | S29 00.2 |
| 04 | 326 22.8 | 274 04.1 | 07.1 | 309 15.9 | 18.8 | 320 14.9 | 18.4 | 358 35.2 | 15.0 | Aldebaran | 290 42.4 | N16 33.2 |
| 05 | 341 25.3 | 289 03.6 | 07.9 | 324 16.6 | 19.5 | 335 17.0 | 18.5 | 13 37.7 | 15.0 | | | |
| 06 | 356 27.7 | 304 03.0 | N17 08.7 | 339 17.4 | N 5 20.2 | 350 19.2 | N 1 18.6 | 28 40.2 | S14 15.1 | Alioth | 166 14.7 | N55 50.6 |
| S 07 | 11 30.2 | 319 02.5 | 09.5 | 354 18.2 | 20.8 | 5 21.4 | 18.7 | 43 42.8 | 15.1 | Alkaid | 152 53.5 | N49 12.4 |
| A 08 | 26 32.6 | 334 02.0 | 10.3 | 9 19.0 | 21.5 | 20 23.6 | 18.8 | 58 45.3 | 15.1 | Alnair | 27 35.4 | S46 51.0 |
| T 09 | 41 35.1 | 349 01.4 .. | 11.0 | 24 19.8 .. | 22.2 | 35 25.8 .. | 18.9 | 73 47.8 .. | 15.1 | Alnilam | 275 40.2 | S 1 11.3 |
| U 10 | 56 37.6 | 4 00.9 | 11.8 | 39 20.6 | 22.9 | 50 28.0 | 19.0 | 88 50.3 | 15.2 | Alphard | 217 50.0 | S 8 45.3 |
| R 11 | 71 40.0 | 19 00.4 | 12.6 | 54 21.3 | 23.6 | 65 30.1 | 19.1 | 103 52.8 | 15.2 | | | |
| D 12 | 86 42.5 | 33 59.8 | N17 13.4 | 69 22.1 | N 5 24.3 | 80 32.3 | N 1 19.2 | 118 55.3 | S14 15.2 | Alphecca | 126 05.2 | N26 38.5 |
| A 13 | 101 45.0 | 48 59.3 | 14.1 | 84 22.9 | 25.0 | 95 34.5 | 19.3 | 133 57.8 | 15.2 | Alpheratz | 357 37.0 | N29 12.6 |
| Y 14 | 116 47.4 | 63 58.8 | 14.9 | 99 23.7 | 25.6 | 110 36.7 | 19.4 | 149 00.4 | 15.3 | Altair | 62 01.7 | N 8 55.6 |
| 15 | 131 49.9 | 78 58.2 .. | 15.7 | 114 24.5 .. | 26.3 | 125 38.9 .. | 19.5 | 164 02.9 .. | 15.3 | Ankaa | 353 09.3 | S42 10.9 |
| 16 | 146 52.4 | 93 57.7 | 16.5 | 129 25.2 | 27.0 | 140 41.1 | 19.7 | 179 05.4 | 15.3 | Antares | 112 18.1 | S26 28.9 |
| 17 | 161 54.8 | 108 57.2 | 17.2 | 144 26.0 | 27.7 | 155 43.3 | 19.8 | 194 07.9 | 15.3 | | | |
| 18 | 176 57.3 | 123 56.6 | N17 18.0 | 159 26.8 | N 5 28.4 | 170 45.4 | N 1 19.9 | 209 10.4 | S14 15.4 | Arcturus | 145 49.6 | N19 04.1 |
| 19 | 191 59.7 | 138 56.1 | 18.8 | 174 27.6 | 29.1 | 185 47.6 | 20.0 | 224 12.9 | 15.4 | Atria | 107 13.6 | S69 04.1 |
| 20 | 207 02.2 | 153 55.6 | 19.5 | 189 28.4 | 29.7 | 200 49.8 | 20.1 | 239 15.5 | 15.4 | Avior | 234 16.1 | S59 35.0 |
| 21 | 222 04.7 | 168 55.0 .. | 20.3 | 204 29.1 .. | 30.4 | 215 52.0 .. | 20.2 | 254 18.0 .. | 15.4 | Bellatrix | 278 25.5 | N 6 22.2 |
| 22 | 237 07.1 | 183 54.5 | 21.1 | 219 29.9 | 31.1 | 230 54.2 | 20.3 | 269 20.5 | 15.5 | Betelgeuse | 270 54.7 | N 7 24.6 |
| 23 | 252 09.6 | 198 53.9 | 21.8 | 234 30.7 | 31.8 | 245 56.4 | 20.4 | 284 23.0 | 15.5 | | | |
| 19 00 | 267 12.1 | 213 53.4 | N17 22.6 | 249 31.5 | N 5 32.5 | 260 58.6 | N 1 20.5 | 299 25.5 | S14 15.5 | Canopus | 263 53.9 | S52 42.5 |
| 01 | 282 14.5 | 228 52.9 | 23.4 | 264 32.3 | 33.1 | 276 00.8 | 20.6 | 314 28.0 | 15.5 | Capella | 280 25.5 | N46 01.1 |
| 02 | 297 17.0 | 243 52.3 | 24.1 | 279 33.1 | 33.8 | 291 02.9 | 20.7 | 329 30.5 | 15.6 | Deneb | 49 26.9 | N45 21.4 |
| 03 | 312 19.5 | 258 51.8 .. | 24.9 | 294 33.8 .. | 34.5 | 306 05.1 .. | 20.8 | 344 33.1 .. | 15.6 | Denebola | 182 27.1 | N14 27.0 |
| 04 | 327 21.9 | 273 51.2 | 25.7 | 309 34.6 | 35.2 | 321 07.3 | 20.9 | 359 35.6 | 15.6 | Diphda | 348 49.5 | S17 51.8 |
| 05 | 342 24.4 | 288 50.7 | 26.4 | 324 35.4 | 35.9 | 336 09.5 | 21.1 | 14 38.1 | 15.6 | | | |
| 06 | 357 26.9 | 303 50.2 | N17 27.2 | 339 36.2 | N 5 36.6 | 351 11.7 | N 1 21.2 | 29 40.6 | S14 15.7 | Dubhe | 193 43.8 | N61 38.2 |
| 07 | 12 29.3 | 318 49.6 | 28.0 | 354 37.0 | 37.2 | 6 13.9 | 21.3 | 44 43.1 | 15.7 | Elnath | 278 04.9 | N28 37.5 |
| S 08 | 27 31.8 | 333 49.1 | 28.7 | 9 37.7 | 37.9 | 21 16.1 | 21.4 | 59 45.6 | 15.7 | Eltanin | 90 42.6 | N51 29.1 |
| U 09 | 42 34.2 | 348 48.5 .. | 29.5 | 24 38.5 .. | 38.6 | 36 18.3 .. | 21.5 | 74 48.2 .. | 15.8 | Enif | 33 40.7 | N 9 58.6 |
| N 10 | 57 36.7 | 3 48.0 | 30.2 | 39 39.3 | 39.3 | 51 20.5 | 21.6 | 89 50.7 | 15.8 | Fomalhaut | 15 16.8 | S29 30.1 |
| 11 | 72 39.2 | 18 47.4 | 31.0 | 54 40.1 | 40.0 | 66 22.6 | 21.7 | 104 53.2 | 15.8 | | | |
| D 12 | 87 41.6 | 33 46.9 | N17 31.8 | 69 40.9 | N 5 40.6 | 81 24.8 | N 1 21.8 | 119 55.7 | S14 15.8 | Gacrux | 171 53.9 | S57 14.5 |
| A 13 | 102 44.1 | 48 46.3 | 32.5 | 84 41.7 | 41.3 | 96 27.0 | 21.9 | 134 58.2 | 15.9 | Gienah | 175 45.7 | S17 40.0 |
| Y 14 | 117 46.6 | 63 45.8 | 33.3 | 99 42.4 | 42.0 | 111 29.2 | 22.0 | 150 00.8 | 15.9 | Hadar | 148 38.6 | S60 29.0 |
| 15 | 132 49.0 | 78 45.3 .. | 34.0 | 114 43.2 .. | 42.7 | 126 31.4 .. | 22.1 | 165 03.3 .. | 15.9 | Hamal | 327 53.8 | N23 33.9 |
| 16 | 147 51.5 | 93 44.7 | 34.8 | 129 44.0 | 43.4 | 141 33.6 | 22.2 | 180 05.8 | 15.9 | Kaus Aust. | 83 34.9 | S34 22.4 |
| 17 | 162 54.0 | 108 44.2 | 35.5 | 144 44.8 | 44.0 | 156 35.8 | 22.3 | 195 08.3 | 16.0 | | | |
| 18 | 177 56.4 | 123 43.6 | N17 36.3 | 159 45.6 | N 5 44.7 | 171 38.0 | N 1 22.4 | 210 10.8 | S14 16.0 | Kochab | 137 19.0 | N74 04.0 |
| 19 | 192 58.9 | 138 43.1 | 37.1 | 174 46.3 | 45.4 | 186 40.2 | 22.5 | 225 13.4 | 16.0 | Markab | 13 31.9 | N15 19.4 |
| 20 | 208 01.4 | 153 42.5 | 37.8 | 189 47.1 | 46.1 | 201 42.4 | 22.6 | 240 15.9 | 16.0 | Menkar | 314 08.6 | N 4 10.6 |
| 21 | 223 03.8 | 168 42.0 .. | 38.6 | 204 47.9 .. | 46.8 | 216 44.6 .. | 22.7 | 255 18.4 .. | 16.1 | Menkent | 147 59.9 | S36 28.9 |
| 22 | 238 06.3 | 183 41.4 | 39.3 | 219 48.7 | 47.4 | 231 46.8 | 22.8 | 270 20.9 | 16.1 | Miaplacidus | 221 39.3 | S69 48.7 |
| 23 | 253 08.7 | 198 40.9 | 40.1 | 234 49.5 | 48.1 | 246 49.0 | 23.0 | 285 23.4 | 16.1 | | | |
| 20 00 | 268 11.2 | 213 40.3 | N17 40.8 | 249 50.3 | N 5 48.8 | 261 51.1 | N 1 23.1 | 300 26.0 | S14 16.2 | Mirfak | 308 31.7 | N49 56.2 |
| 01 | 283 13.7 | 228 39.8 | 41.6 | 264 51.0 | 49.5 | 276 53.3 | 23.2 | 315 28.5 | 16.2 | Nunki | 75 50.0 | S26 16.1 |
| 02 | 298 16.1 | 243 39.2 | 42.3 | 279 51.8 | 50.2 | 291 55.5 | 23.3 | 330 31.0 | 16.2 | Peacock | 53 08.6 | S56 39.6 |
| 03 | 313 18.6 | 258 38.7 .. | 43.1 | 294 52.6 .. | 50.8 | 306 57.7 .. | 23.4 | 345 33.5 .. | 16.2 | Pollux | 243 20.2 | N27 58.4 |
| 04 | 328 21.1 | 273 38.1 | 43.8 | 309 53.4 | 51.5 | 321 59.9 | 23.5 | 0 36.0 | 16.3 | Procyon | 244 53.4 | N 5 10.1 |
| 05 | 343 23.5 | 288 37.6 | 44.5 | 324 54.2 | 52.2 | 337 02.1 | 23.6 | 15 38.6 | 16.3 | | | |
| 06 | 358 26.0 | 303 37.0 | N17 45.3 | 339 55.0 | N 5 52.9 | 352 04.3 | N 1 23.7 | 30 41.1 | S14 16.3 | Rasalhague | 96 00.2 | N12 32.6 |
| 07 | 13 28.5 | 318 36.4 | 46.0 | 354 55.7 | 53.5 | 7 06.5 | 23.8 | 45 43.6 | 16.3 | Regulus | 207 36.8 | N11 51.6 |
| 08 | 28 30.9 | 333 35.9 | 46.8 | 9 56.5 | 54.2 | 22 08.7 | 23.9 | 60 46.1 | 16.4 | Rigel | 281 06.2 | S 8 10.6 |
| M 09 | 43 33.4 | 348 35.3 .. | 47.5 | 24 57.3 .. | 54.9 | 37 10.9 .. | 24.0 | 75 48.6 .. | 16.4 | Rigil Kent. | 139 42.7 | S60 55.8 |
| O 10 | 58 35.8 | 3 34.8 | 48.3 | 39 58.1 | 55.6 | 52 13.1 | 24.1 | 90 51.2 | 16.4 | Sabik | 102 04.9 | S15 45.1 |
| N 11 | 73 38.3 | 18 34.2 | 49.0 | 54 58.9 | 56.3 | 67 15.3 | 24.2 | 105 53.7 | 16.5 | | | |
| D 12 | 88 40.8 | 33 33.7 | N17 49.8 | 69 59.7 | N 5 56.9 | 82 17.5 | N 1 24.3 | 120 56.2 | S14 16.5 | Schedar | 349 33.5 | N56 39.3 |
| A 13 | 103 43.2 | 48 33.1 | 50.5 | 85 00.4 | 57.6 | 97 19.7 | 24.4 | 135 58.7 | 16.5 | Shaula | 96 12.8 | S37 07.2 |
| Y 14 | 118 45.7 | 63 32.5 | 51.2 | 100 01.2 | 58.3 | 112 21.9 | 24.5 | 151 01.2 | 16.5 | Sirius | 258 28.4 | S16 44.8 |
| 15 | 133 48.2 | 78 32.0 .. | 51.9 | 115 02.0 .. | 59.0 | 127 24.1 .. | 24.6 | 166 03.8 .. | 16.6 | Spica | 158 24.4 | S11 16.7 |
| 16 | 148 50.6 | 93 31.4 | 52.7 | 130 02.8 | 5 59.6 | 142 26.3 | 24.7 | 181 06.3 | 16.6 | Suhail | 222 48.2 | S43 31.5 |
| 17 | 163 53.1 | 108 30.9 | 53.5 | 145 03.6 | 6 00.3 | 157 28.5 | 24.8 | 196 08.8 | 16.6 | | | |
| 18 | 178 55.6 | 123 30.3 | N17 54.2 | 160 04.4 | N 6 01.0 | 172 30.7 | N 1 24.9 | 211 11.3 | S14 16.7 | Vega | 80 34.2 | N38 48.2 |
| 19 | 193 58.0 | 138 29.8 | 54.9 | 175 05.1 | 01.7 | 187 32.9 | 25.0 | 226 13.9 | 16.7 | Zuben'ubi | 136 58.1 | S16 08.1 |
| 20 | 209 00.5 | 153 29.2 | 55.7 | 190 05.9 | 02.3 | 202 35.1 | 25.1 | 241 16.4 | 16.7 | | SHA | Mer. Pass. |
| 21 | 224 03.0 | 168 28.6 .. | 56.4 | 205 06.7 .. | 03.0 | 217 37.3 .. | 25.2 | 256 18.9 .. | 16.7 | | ° ′ | h m |
| 22 | 239 05.4 | 183 28.1 | 57.1 | 220 07.5 | 03.7 | 232 39.5 | 25.3 | 271 21.4 | 16.8 | Venus | 306 41.3 | 9 45 |
| 23 | 254 07.9 | 198 27.5 | 57.9 | 235 08.3 | 04.4 | 247 41.7 | 25.4 | 286 24.0 | 16.8 | Mars | 342 19.4 | 7 22 |
| | h m | | | | | | | | | Jupiter | 353 46.5 | 6 35 |
| Mer. Pass. 6 10.2 | | v −0.5 d 0.8 | | v 0.8 d 0.7 | | v 2.2 d 0.1 | | v 2.5 d 0.0 | | Saturn | 32 13.4 | 4 02 |

| UT | SUN GHA | SUN Dec | MOON GHA | v | MOON Dec | d | HP |
|---|---|---|---|---|---|---|---|
| **d h** | ° ′ | ° ′ | ° ′ | ′ | ° ′ | ′ | ′ |
| **18 00** | 179 44.1 | N23 23.9 | 305 54.9 | 6.4 | S20 54.4 | 10.9 | 60.0 |
| 01 | 194 43.9 | 24.0 | 320 20.3 | 6.6 | 20 43.5 | 11.0 | 60.0 |
| 02 | 209 43.8 | 24.0 | 334 45.9 | 6.6 | 20 32.5 | 11.2 | 59.9 |
| 03 | 224 43.7 .. | 24.1 | 349 11.5 | 6.8 | 20 21.3 | 11.2 | 59.9 |
| 04 | 239 43.5 | 24.1 | 3 37.3 | 7.0 | 20 10.1 | 11.4 | 59.9 |
| 05 | 254 43.4 | 24.2 | 18 03.3 | 7.0 | 19 58.7 | 11.5 | 59.8 |
| **S** 06 | 269 43.2 N23 24.2 | | 32 29.3 | 7.2 | S19 47.2 | 11.6 | 59.8 |
| **A** 07 | 284 43.1 | 24.3 | 46 55.5 | 7.4 | 19 35.6 | 11.7 | 59.8 |
| **T** 08 | 299 43.0 | 24.3 | 61 21.9 | 7.4 | 19 23.9 | 11.8 | 59.7 |
| **U** 09 | 314 42.8 .. | 24.4 | 75 48.3 | 7.6 | 19 12.1 | 11.9 | 59.7 |
| **R** 10 | 329 42.7 | 24.4 | 90 14.9 | 7.7 | 19 00.2 | 12.0 | 59.7 |
| **D** 11 | 344 42.6 | 24.5 | 104 41.6 | 7.9 | 18 48.2 | 12.1 | 59.6 |
| **A** 12 | 359 42.4 N23 24.5 | | 119 08.5 | 7.9 | S18 36.1 | 12.2 | 59.6 |
| **Y** 13 | 14 42.3 | 24.6 | 133 35.4 | 8.1 | 18 23.9 | 12.3 | 59.6 |
| 14 | 29 42.2 | 24.6 | 148 02.5 | 8.3 | 18 11.6 | 12.4 | 59.5 |
| 15 | 44 42.0 .. | 24.7 | 162 29.8 | 8.3 | 17 59.2 | 12.4 | 59.5 |
| 16 | 59 41.9 | 24.7 | 176 57.1 | 8.5 | 17 46.8 | 12.6 | 59.5 |
| 17 | 74 41.8 | 24.8 | 191 24.6 | 8.6 | 17 34.2 | 12.7 | 59.4 |
| 18 | 89 41.6 N23 24.8 | | 205 52.2 | 8.8 | S17 21.5 | 12.7 | 59.4 |
| 19 | 104 41.5 | 24.9 | 220 20.0 | 8.8 | 17 08.8 | 12.8 | 59.3 |
| 20 | 119 41.4 | 24.9 | 234 47.8 | 9.0 | 16 56.0 | 12.9 | 59.3 |
| 21 | 134 41.2 .. | 25.0 | 249 15.8 | 9.1 | 16 43.1 | 13.0 | 59.3 |
| 22 | 149 41.1 | 25.0 | 263 43.9 | 9.2 | 16 30.1 | 13.0 | 59.2 |
| 23 | 164 40.9 | 25.0 | 278 12.1 | 9.4 | 16 17.1 | 13.2 | 59.2 |
| **19 00** | 179 40.8 N23 25.1 | | 292 40.5 | 9.4 | S16 03.9 | 13.2 | 59.2 |
| 01 | 194 40.7 | 25.1 | 307 08.9 | 9.6 | 15 50.7 | 13.2 | 59.1 |
| 02 | 209 40.5 | 25.2 | 321 37.5 | 9.7 | 15 37.5 | 13.4 | 59.1 |
| 03 | 224 40.4 .. | 25.2 | 336 06.2 | 9.8 | 15 24.1 | 13.4 | 59.1 |
| 04 | 239 40.3 | 25.2 | 350 35.0 | 10.0 | 15 10.7 | 13.5 | 59.0 |
| 05 | 254 40.1 | 25.3 | 5 04.0 | 10.0 | 14 57.2 | 13.5 | 59.0 |
| **S** 06 | 269 40.0 N23 25.3 | | 19 33.0 | 10.2 | S14 43.7 | 13.6 | 58.9 |
| **U** 07 | 284 39.9 | 25.4 | 34 02.2 | 10.2 | 14 30.1 | 13.6 | 58.9 |
| **N** 08 | 299 39.7 | 25.4 | 48 31.4 | 10.4 | 14 16.5 | 13.8 | 58.9 |
| **D** 09 | 314 39.6 .. | 25.4 | 63 00.8 | 10.5 | 14 02.7 | 13.7 | 58.8 |
| **A** 10 | 329 39.4 | 25.5 | 77 30.3 | 10.6 | 13 49.0 | 13.9 | 58.8 |
| **Y** 11 | 344 39.3 | 25.5 | 91 59.9 | 10.7 | 13 35.1 | 13.8 | 58.8 |
| 12 | 359 39.2 N23 25.5 | | 106 29.6 | 10.8 | S13 21.3 | 14.0 | 58.7 |
| 13 | 14 39.0 | 25.6 | 120 59.4 | 11.0 | 13 07.3 | 14.0 | 58.7 |
| 14 | 29 38.9 | 25.6 | 135 29.4 | 11.0 | 12 53.3 | 14.0 | 58.6 |
| 15 | 44 38.8 .. | 25.6 | 149 59.4 | 11.1 | 12 39.3 | 14.1 | 58.6 |
| 16 | 59 38.6 | 25.7 | 164 29.5 | 11.2 | 12 25.2 | 14.1 | 58.6 |
| 17 | 74 38.5 | 25.7 | 178 59.7 | 11.4 | 12 11.1 | 14.2 | 58.5 |
| 18 | 89 38.4 N23 25.7 | | 193 30.1 | 11.4 | S11 56.9 | 14.2 | 58.5 |
| 19 | 104 38.2 | 25.7 | 208 00.5 | 11.5 | 11 42.7 | 14.2 | 58.5 |
| 20 | 119 38.1 | 25.8 | 222 31.0 | 11.6 | 11 28.5 | 14.3 | 58.4 |
| 21 | 134 38.0 .. | 25.8 | 237 01.6 | 11.8 | 11 14.2 | 14.3 | 58.4 |
| 22 | 149 37.8 | 25.8 | 251 32.4 | 11.8 | 10 59.9 | 14.4 | 58.3 |
| 23 | 164 37.7 | 25.8 | 266 03.2 | 11.9 | 10 45.5 | 14.4 | 58.3 |
| **20 00** | 179 37.5 N23 25.9 | | 280 34.1 | 11.9 | S10 31.1 | 14.4 | 58.3 |
| 01 | 194 37.4 | 25.9 | 295 05.0 | 12.1 | 10 16.7 | 14.5 | 58.2 |
| 02 | 209 37.3 | 25.9 | 309 36.1 | 12.2 | 10 02.2 | 14.5 | 58.2 |
| 03 | 224 37.1 .. | 25.9 | 324 07.3 | 12.2 | 9 47.7 | 14.5 | 58.2 |
| 04 | 239 37.0 | 26.0 | 338 38.5 | 12.4 | 9 33.2 | 14.5 | 58.1 |
| 05 | 254 36.9 | 26.0 | 353 09.9 | 12.4 | 9 18.7 | 14.6 | 58.1 |
| **M** 06 | 269 36.7 N23 26.0 | | 7 41.3 | 12.5 | S 9 04.1 | 14.6 | 58.0 |
| **O** 07 | 284 36.6 | 26.0 | 22 12.8 | 12.6 | 8 49.5 | 14.6 | 58.0 |
| **N** 08 | 299 36.5 | 26.0 | 36 44.4 | 12.7 | 8 34.9 | 14.6 | 58.0 |
| **D** 09 | 314 36.3 .. | 26.1 | 51 16.1 | 12.7 | 8 20.3 | 14.7 | 57.9 |
| **A** 10 | 329 36.2 | 26.1 | 65 47.8 | 12.8 | 8 05.6 | 14.7 | 57.9 |
| **Y** 11 | 344 36.0 | 26.1 | 80 19.6 | 12.9 | 7 50.9 | 14.7 | 57.9 |
| 12 | 359 35.9 N23 26.1 | | 94 51.5 | 13.0 | S 7 36.2 | 14.7 | 57.8 |
| 13 | 14 35.8 | 26.1 | 109 23.5 | 13.1 | 7 21.5 | 14.7 | 57.8 |
| 14 | 29 35.6 | 26.1 | 123 55.6 | 13.1 | 7 06.8 | 14.8 | 57.8 |
| 15 | 44 35.5 .. | 26.1 | 138 27.7 | 13.2 | 6 52.0 | 14.8 | 57.7 |
| 16 | 59 35.4 | 26.2 | 152 59.9 | 13.2 | 6 37.3 | 14.8 | 57.7 |
| 17 | 74 35.2 | 26.2 | 167 32.1 | 13.3 | 6 22.5 | 14.8 | 57.6 |
| 18 | 89 35.1 N23 26.2 | | 182 04.4 | 13.4 | S 6 07.7 | 14.8 | 57.6 |
| 19 | 104 35.0 | 26.2 | 196 36.8 | 13.5 | 5 52.9 | 14.8 | 57.5 |
| 20 | 119 34.8 | 26.2 | 211 09.3 | 13.5 | 5 38.1 | 14.8 | 57.5 |
| 21 | 134 34.7 .. | 26.2 | 225 41.8 | 13.6 | 5 23.3 | 14.8 | 57.5 |
| 22 | 149 34.6 | 26.2 | 240 14.4 | 13.6 | 5 08.5 | 14.8 | 57.5 |
| 23 | 164 34.4 | 26.2 | 254 47.0 | 13.7 | S 4 53.7 | 14.8 | 57.4 |
| | SD 15.8  d 0.0 | | SD 16.2 | | 16.0 | | 15.8 |

| Lat. | Twilight Naut. | Twilight Civil | Sunrise | Moonrise 18 | 19 | 20 | 21 |
|---|---|---|---|---|---|---|---|
| ° | h m | h m | h m | h m | h m | h m | h m |
| N 72 | □ | □ | □ | ■■■ | 02 33 | 01 36 | 01 01 |
| N 70 | □ | □ | □ | ■■■ | 01 57 | 01 21 | 00 55 |
| 68 | □ | □ | □ | 02 17 | 01 32 | 01 08 | 00 50 |
| 66 | □ | □ | □ | 01 34 | 01 12 | 00 57 | 00 46 |
| 64 | //// | //// | 01 31 | 01 05 | 00 56 | 00 48 | 00 42 |
| 62 | //// | //// | 02 09 | 00 42 | 00 42 | 00 41 | 00 39 |
| 60 | //// | 00 49 | 02 36 | 00 24 | 00 31 | 00 34 | 00 36 |
| N 58 | //// | 01 40 | 02 56 | 00 09 | 00 21 | 00 28 | 00 34 |
| 56 | //// | 02 10 | 03 13 | 24 12 | 00 12 | 00 23 | 00 31 |
| 54 | 00 45 | 02 33 | 03 27 | 24 04 | 00 04 | 00 18 | 00 29 |
| 52 | 01 32 | 02 51 | 03 39 | 23 57 | 24 14 | 00 14 | 00 28 |
| 50 | 02 00 | 03 06 | 03 50 | 23 50 | 24 10 | 00 10 | 00 26 |
| 45 | 02 46 | 03 35 | 04 13 | 23 37 | 24 01 | 00 01 | 00 22 |
| N 40 | 03 16 | 03 58 | 04 31 | 23 25 | 23 54 | 24 19 | 00 19 |
| 35 | 03 40 | 04 16 | 04 46 | 23 16 | 23 48 | 24 17 | 00 17 |
| 30 | 03 58 | 04 32 | 04 59 | 23 07 | 23 43 | 24 14 | 00 14 |
| 20 | 04 27 | 04 57 | 05 21 | 22 52 | 23 33 | 24 10 | 00 10 |
| N 10 | 04 50 | 05 17 | 05 40 | 22 39 | 23 25 | 24 07 | 00 07 |
| 0 | 05 09 | 05 35 | 05 58 | 22 27 | 23 17 | 24 03 | 00 03 |
| S 10 | 05 26 | 05 52 | 06 15 | 22 14 | 23 09 | 24 00 | 00 00 |
| 20 | 05 42 | 06 10 | 06 34 | 22 01 | 23 01 | 23 56 | 24 49 |
| 30 | 05 59 | 06 29 | 06 55 | 21 46 | 22 51 | 23 52 | 24 51 |
| 35 | 06 07 | 06 39 | 07 07 | 21 37 | 22 45 | 23 50 | 24 52 |
| 40 | 06 17 | 06 51 | 07 22 | 21 27 | 22 39 | 23 47 | 24 52 |
| 45 | 06 27 | 07 04 | 07 38 | 21 15 | 22 31 | 23 44 | 24 54 |
| S 50 | 06 39 | 07 21 | 07 59 | 21 00 | 22 22 | 23 40 | 24 55 |
| 52 | 06 44 | 07 28 | 08 09 | 20 53 | 22 18 | 23 39 | 24 55 |
| 54 | 06 50 | 07 36 | 08 20 | 20 46 | 22 14 | 23 37 | 24 56 |
| 56 | 06 56 | 07 45 | 08 33 | 20 37 | 22 08 | 23 35 | 24 57 |
| 58 | 07 03 | 07 56 | 08 48 | 20 27 | 22 03 | 23 32 | 24 57 |
| S 60 | 07 10 | 08 07 | 09 05 | 20 16 | 21 56 | 23 30 | 24 58 |

| Lat. | Sunset | Twilight Civil | Twilight Naut. | Moonset 18 | 19 | 20 | 21 |
|---|---|---|---|---|---|---|---|
| ° | h m | h m | h m | h m | h m | h m | h m |
| N 72 | □ | □ | □ | ■■■ | 07 11 | 09 50 | 12 02 |
| N 70 | □ | □ | □ | ■■■ | 07 45 | 10 03 | 12 05 |
| 68 | □ | □ | □ | 05 31 | 08 08 | 10 14 | 12 07 |
| 66 | □ | □ | □ | 06 13 | 08 27 | 10 22 | 12 08 |
| 64 | 22 32 | //// | //// | 06 41 | 08 42 | 10 30 | 12 10 |
| 62 | 21 54 | //// | //// | 07 02 | 08 54 | 10 36 | 12 11 |
| 60 | 21 27 | 23 14 | //// | 07 20 | 09 04 | 10 41 | 12 12 |
| N 58 | 21 07 | 22 23 | //// | 07 34 | 09 13 | 10 46 | 12 13 |
| 56 | 20 50 | 21 53 | //// | 07 46 | 09 21 | 10 50 | 12 14 |
| 54 | 20 36 | 21 30 | 23 18 | 07 57 | 09 28 | 10 54 | 12 15 |
| 52 | 20 23 | 21 12 | 22 31 | 08 07 | 09 34 | 10 57 | 12 16 |
| 50 | 20 12 | 20 57 | 22 03 | 08 15 | 09 40 | 11 00 | 12 16 |
| 45 | 19 50 | 20 27 | 21 17 | 08 33 | 09 52 | 11 07 | 12 18 |
| N 40 | 19 32 | 20 05 | 20 46 | 08 47 | 10 02 | 11 12 | 12 19 |
| 35 | 19 17 | 19 47 | 20 23 | 08 59 | 10 10 | 11 17 | 12 20 |
| 30 | 19 04 | 19 31 | 20 05 | 09 10 | 10 17 | 11 21 | 12 21 |
| 20 | 18 42 | 19 06 | 19 35 | 09 28 | 10 30 | 11 28 | 12 22 |
| N 10 | 18 23 | 18 46 | 19 13 | 09 44 | 10 41 | 11 34 | 12 23 |
| 0 | 18 05 | 18 28 | 18 54 | 09 58 | 10 51 | 11 39 | 12 24 |
| S 10 | 17 48 | 18 10 | 18 37 | 10 13 | 11 01 | 11 45 | 12 26 |
| 20 | 17 29 | 17 53 | 18 21 | 10 28 | 11 12 | 11 51 | 12 27 |
| 30 | 17 08 | 17 34 | 18 04 | 10 45 | 11 24 | 11 58 | 12 28 |
| 35 | 16 55 | 17 24 | 17 55 | 10 55 | 11 31 | 12 01 | 12 29 |
| 40 | 16 41 | 17 12 | 17 46 | 11 07 | 11 39 | 12 06 | 12 30 |
| 45 | 16 24 | 16 58 | 17 36 | 11 20 | 11 48 | 12 11 | 12 31 |
| S 50 | 16 04 | 16 42 | 17 24 | 11 37 | 11 59 | 12 17 | 12 32 |
| 52 | 15 54 | 16 35 | 17 18 | 11 44 | 12 04 | 12 19 | 12 32 |
| 54 | 15 43 | 16 26 | 17 13 | 11 52 | 12 09 | 12 22 | 12 33 |
| 56 | 15 30 | 16 17 | 17 07 | 12 02 | 12 15 | 12 25 | 12 34 |
| 58 | 15 15 | 16 07 | 17 00 | 12 12 | 12 22 | 12 29 | 12 34 |
| S 60 | 14 58 | 15 55 | 16 52 | 12 25 | 12 30 | 12 33 | 12 35 |

| Day | SUN Eqn. of Time 00h | 12h | Mer. Pass. | MOON Mer. Pass. Upper | Lower | Age | Phase |
|---|---|---|---|---|---|---|---|
| d | m s | m s | h m | h m | h m | d | % |
| 18 | 01 03 | 01 10 | 12 01 | 03 45 | 16 13 | 19 | 78 |
| 19 | 01 16 | 01 23 | 12 01 | 04 39 | 17 04 | 20 | 68 |
| 20 | 01 30 | 01 36 | 12 02 | 05 28 | 17 51 | 21 | 57 |

| UT | ARIES GHA | VENUS −3.9 GHA | Dec | MARS +0.5 GHA | Dec | JUPITER −2.4 GHA | Dec | SATURN +0.5 GHA | Dec | STARS Name | SHA | Dec |
|---|---|---|---|---|---|---|---|---|---|---|---|---|
| **21 00** | 269 10.3 | 213 26.9 | N17 58.6 | 250 09.1 | N 6 05.0 | 262 43.9 | N 1 25.5 | 301 26.5 | S14 16.8 | Acamar | 315 13.7 | S40 12.8 |
| 01 | 284 12.8 | 228 26.4 | 17 59.3 | 265 09.8 | 05.7 | 277 46.1 | 25.6 | 316 29.0 | 16.9 | Achernar | 335 22.1 | S57 07.2 |
| 02 | 299 15.3 | 243 25.8 | 18 00.1 | 280 10.6 | 06.4 | 292 48.3 | 25.7 | 331 31.5 | 16.9 | Acrux | 173 02.3 | S63 13.6 |
| 03 | 314 17.7 | 258 25.3 .. | 00.8 | 295 11.4 .. | 07.1 | 307 50.5 .. | 25.8 | 346 34.0 .. | 16.9 | Adhara | 255 07.9 | S29 00.2 |
| 04 | 329 20.2 | 273 24.7 | 01.5 | 310 12.2 | 07.7 | 322 52.7 | 25.9 | 1 36.6 | 16.9 | Aldebaran | 290 42.4 | N16 33.2 |
| 05 | 344 22.7 | 288 24.1 | 02.2 | 325 13.0 | 08.4 | 337 54.9 | 26.0 | 16 39.1 | 17.0 | | | |
| T 06 | 359 25.1 | 303 23.6 | N18 03.0 | 340 13.8 | N 6 09.1 | 352 57.1 | N 1 26.1 | 31 41.6 | S14 17.0 | Alioth | 166 14.7 | N55 50.6 |
| U 07 | 14 27.6 | 318 23.0 | 03.7 | 355 14.5 | 09.8 | 7 59.3 | 26.3 | 46 44.1 | 17.0 | Alkaid | 152 53.5 | N49 12.4 |
| E 08 | 29 30.1 | 333 22.4 | 04.4 | 10 15.3 | 10.4 | 23 01.5 | 26.4 | 61 46.7 | 17.1 | Alnair | 27 35.3 | S46 51.0 |
| S 09 | 44 32.5 | 348 21.9 .. | 05.2 | 25 16.1 .. | 11.1 | 38 03.7 .. | 26.5 | 76 49.2 .. | 17.1 | Alnilam | 275 40.2 | S 1 11.3 |
| D 10 | 59 35.0 | 3 21.3 | 05.9 | 40 16.9 | 11.8 | 53 05.9 | 26.6 | 91 51.7 | 17.1 | Alphard | 217 50.0 | S 8 45.3 |
| A 11 | 74 37.5 | 18 20.7 | 06.6 | 55 17.7 | 12.5 | 68 08.1 | 26.7 | 106 54.2 | 17.1 | | | |
| Y 12 | 89 39.9 | 33 20.1 | N18 07.3 | 70 18.5 | N 6 13.1 | 83 10.3 | N 1 26.8 | 121 56.8 | S14 17.2 | Alphecca | 126 05.2 | N26 38.5 |
| 13 | 104 42.4 | 48 19.6 | 08.1 | 85 19.2 | 13.8 | 98 12.5 | 26.9 | 136 59.3 | 17.2 | Alpheratz | 357 36.9 | N29 12.6 |
| 14 | 119 44.8 | 63 19.0 | 08.8 | 100 20.0 | 14.5 | 113 14.7 | 27.0 | 152 01.8 | 17.2 | Altair | 62 01.7 | N 8 55.6 |
| 15 | 134 47.3 | 78 18.4 .. | 09.5 | 115 20.8 .. | 15.2 | 128 16.9 .. | 27.1 | 167 04.4 .. | 17.3 | Ankaa | 353 09.3 | S42 10.9 |
| 16 | 149 49.8 | 93 17.9 | 10.2 | 130 21.6 | 15.8 | 143 19.1 | 27.2 | 182 06.9 | 17.3 | Antares | 112 18.1 | S26 28.9 |
| 17 | 164 52.2 | 108 17.3 | 10.9 | 145 22.4 | 16.5 | 158 21.3 | 27.3 | 197 09.4 | 17.3 | | | |
| 18 | 179 54.7 | 123 16.7 | N18 11.7 | 160 23.2 | N 6 17.2 | 173 23.5 | N 1 27.4 | 212 11.9 | S14 17.4 | Arcturus | 145 49.7 | N19 04.1 |
| 19 | 194 57.2 | 138 16.2 | 12.4 | 175 23.9 | 17.9 | 188 25.7 | 27.5 | 227 14.5 | 17.4 | Atria | 107 13.6 | S69 04.1 |
| 20 | 209 59.6 | 153 15.6 | 13.1 | 190 24.7 | 18.5 | 203 27.9 | 27.6 | 242 17.0 | 17.4 | Avior | 234 16.1 | S59 35.0 |
| 21 | 225 02.1 | 168 15.0 .. | 13.8 | 205 25.5 .. | 19.2 | 218 30.1 .. | 27.7 | 257 19.5 .. | 17.4 | Bellatrix | 278 25.5 | N 6 22.2 |
| 22 | 240 04.6 | 183 14.4 | 14.5 | 220 26.3 | 19.9 | 233 32.3 | 27.8 | 272 22.0 | 17.5 | Betelgeuse | 270 54.7 | N 7 24.7 |
| 23 | 255 07.0 | 198 13.9 | 15.2 | 235 27.1 | 20.5 | 248 34.5 | 27.9 | 287 24.6 | 17.5 | | | |
| **22 00** | 270 09.5 | 213 13.3 | N18 16.0 | 250 27.9 | N 6 21.2 | 263 36.7 | N 1 28.0 | 302 27.1 | S14 17.5 | Canopus | 263 53.9 | S52 42.4 |
| 01 | 285 11.9 | 228 12.7 | 16.7 | 265 28.7 | 21.9 | 278 38.9 | 28.1 | 317 29.6 | 17.6 | Capella | 280 25.5 | N46 01.1 |
| 02 | 300 14.4 | 243 12.1 | 17.4 | 280 29.4 | 22.6 | 293 41.1 | 28.2 | 332 32.2 | 17.6 | Deneb | 49 26.8 | N45 21.4 |
| 03 | 315 16.9 | 258 11.6 .. | 18.1 | 295 30.2 .. | 23.2 | 308 43.3 .. | 28.3 | 347 34.7 .. | 17.6 | Denebola | 182 27.1 | N14 27.0 |
| 04 | 330 19.3 | 273 11.0 | 18.8 | 310 31.0 | 23.9 | 323 45.5 | 28.4 | 2 37.2 | 17.7 | Diphda | 348 49.5 | S17 51.8 |
| 05 | 345 21.8 | 288 10.4 | 19.5 | 325 31.8 | 24.6 | 338 47.7 | 28.5 | 17 39.7 | 17.7 | | | |
| W 06 | 0 24.3 | 303 09.8 | N18 20.2 | 340 32.6 | N 6 25.2 | 353 49.9 | N 1 28.6 | 32 42.3 | S14 17.7 | Dubhe | 193 43.8 | N61 38.2 |
| E 07 | 15 26.7 | 318 09.2 | 20.9 | 355 33.4 | 25.9 | 8 52.2 | 28.6 | 47 44.8 | 17.7 | Elnath | 278 04.9 | N28 37.5 |
| D 08 | 30 29.2 | 333 08.7 | 21.6 | 10 34.1 | 26.6 | 23 54.4 | 28.7 | 62 47.3 | 17.8 | Eltanin | 90 42.6 | N51 29.1 |
| N 09 | 45 31.7 | 348 08.1 .. | 22.4 | 25 34.9 .. | 27.3 | 38 56.6 .. | 28.8 | 77 49.8 .. | 17.8 | Enif | 33 40.7 | N 9 58.6 |
| E 10 | 60 34.1 | 3 07.5 | 23.1 | 40 35.7 | 27.9 | 53 58.8 | 28.9 | 92 52.4 | 17.8 | Fomalhaut | 15 16.7 | S29 30.1 |
| S 11 | 75 36.6 | 18 06.9 | 23.8 | 55 36.5 | 28.6 | 69 01.0 | 29.0 | 107 54.9 | 17.9 | | | |
| D 12 | 90 39.1 | 33 06.4 | N18 24.5 | 70 37.3 | N 6 29.3 | 84 03.2 | N 1 29.1 | 122 57.4 | S14 17.9 | Gacrux | 171 53.9 | S57 14.5 |
| A 13 | 105 41.5 | 48 05.8 | 25.2 | 85 38.1 | 29.9 | 99 05.4 | 29.2 | 138 00.0 | 17.9 | Gienah | 175 45.7 | S17 40.0 |
| Y 14 | 120 44.0 | 63 05.2 | 25.9 | 100 38.9 | 30.6 | 114 07.6 | 29.3 | 153 02.5 | 18.0 | Hadar | 148 38.6 | S60 29.0 |
| 15 | 135 46.4 | 78 04.6 .. | 26.6 | 115 39.6 .. | 31.3 | 129 09.8 .. | 29.4 | 168 05.0 .. | 18.0 | Hamal | 327 53.8 | N23 33.9 |
| 16 | 150 48.9 | 93 04.0 | 27.3 | 130 40.4 | 31.9 | 144 12.0 | 29.5 | 183 07.6 | 18.0 | Kaus Aust. | 83 34.9 | S34 22.4 |
| 17 | 165 51.4 | 108 03.4 | 28.0 | 145 41.2 | 32.6 | 159 14.2 | 29.6 | 198 10.1 | 18.0 | | | |
| 18 | 180 53.8 | 123 02.9 | N18 28.7 | 160 42.0 | N 6 33.3 | 174 16.4 | N 1 29.7 | 213 12.6 | S14 18.1 | Kochab | 137 19.0 | N74 04.1 |
| 19 | 195 56.3 | 138 02.3 | 29.4 | 175 42.8 | 34.0 | 189 18.7 | 29.8 | 228 15.1 | 18.1 | Markab | 13 31.9 | N15 19.4 |
| 20 | 210 58.8 | 153 01.7 | 30.1 | 190 43.6 | 34.6 | 204 20.9 | 29.9 | 243 17.7 | 18.1 | Menkar | 314 08.6 | N 4 10.6 |
| 21 | 226 01.2 | 168 01.1 .. | 30.8 | 205 44.4 .. | 35.3 | 219 23.1 .. | 30.0 | 258 20.2 .. | 18.2 | Menkent | 147 59.9 | S36 28.9 |
| 22 | 241 03.7 | 183 00.5 | 31.5 | 220 45.1 | 36.0 | 234 25.3 | 30.1 | 273 22.7 | 18.2 | Miaplacidus | 221 39.3 | S69 48.7 |
| 23 | 256 06.2 | 197 59.9 | 32.2 | 235 45.9 | 36.6 | 249 27.5 | 30.2 | 288 25.3 | 18.2 | | | |
| **23 00** | 271 08.6 | 212 59.3 | N18 32.9 | 250 46.7 | N 6 37.3 | 264 29.7 | N 1 30.3 | 303 27.8 | S14 18.3 | Mirfak | 308 31.7 | N49 56.2 |
| 01 | 286 11.1 | 227 58.8 | 33.6 | 265 47.5 | 38.0 | 279 31.9 | 30.4 | 318 30.3 | 18.3 | Nunki | 75 50.0 | S26 16.1 |
| 02 | 301 13.6 | 242 58.2 | 34.3 | 280 48.3 | 38.6 | 294 34.1 | 30.5 | 333 32.9 | 18.3 | Peacock | 53 08.6 | S56 39.6 |
| 03 | 316 16.0 | 257 57.6 .. | 35.0 | 295 49.1 .. | 39.3 | 309 36.3 .. | 30.6 | 348 35.4 .. | 18.4 | Pollux | 243 20.2 | N27 58.4 |
| 04 | 331 18.5 | 272 57.0 | 35.7 | 310 49.9 | 40.0 | 324 38.6 | 30.7 | 3 37.9 | 18.4 | Procyon | 244 53.4 | N 5 10.1 |
| 05 | 346 20.9 | 287 56.4 | 36.4 | 325 50.6 | 40.6 | 339 40.8 | 30.8 | 18 40.5 | 18.4 | | | |
| T 06 | 1 23.4 | 302 55.8 | N18 37.0 | 340 51.4 | N 6 41.3 | 354 43.0 | N 1 30.9 | 33 43.0 | S14 18.5 | Rasalhague | 96 00.2 | N12 32.6 |
| H 07 | 16 25.9 | 317 55.2 | 37.7 | 355 52.2 | 42.0 | 9 45.2 | 31.0 | 48 45.5 | 18.5 | Regulus | 207 36.9 | N11 51.6 |
| U 08 | 31 28.3 | 332 54.6 | 38.4 | 10 53.0 | 42.6 | 24 47.4 | 31.1 | 63 48.1 | 18.5 | Rigel | 281 06.2 | S 8 10.6 |
| R 09 | 46 30.8 | 347 54.0 .. | 39.1 | 25 53.8 .. | 43.3 | 39 49.6 .. | 31.2 | 78 50.6 .. | 18.5 | Rigil Kent. | 139 42.8 | S60 55.8 |
| S 10 | 61 33.3 | 2 53.5 | 39.8 | 40 54.6 | 44.0 | 54 51.8 | 31.3 | 93 53.1 | 18.6 | Sabik | 102 04.9 | S15 45.1 |
| D 11 | 76 35.7 | 17 52.9 | 40.5 | 55 55.4 | 44.6 | 69 54.0 | 31.4 | 108 55.7 | 18.6 | | | |
| A 12 | 91 38.2 | 32 52.3 | N18 41.2 | 70 56.1 | N 6 45.3 | 84 56.3 | N 1 31.5 | 123 58.2 | S14 18.6 | Schedar | 349 33.5 | N56 39.3 |
| Y 13 | 106 40.7 | 47 51.7 | 41.9 | 85 56.9 | 46.0 | 99 58.5 | 31.6 | 139 00.7 | 18.7 | Shaula | 96 12.8 | S37 07.2 |
| 14 | 121 43.1 | 62 51.1 | 42.6 | 100 57.7 | 46.6 | 115 00.7 | 31.7 | 154 03.3 | 18.7 | Sirius | 258 28.4 | S16 44.8 |
| 15 | 136 45.6 | 77 50.5 .. | 43.2 | 115 58.5 .. | 47.3 | 130 02.9 .. | 31.7 | 169 05.8 .. | 18.7 | Spica | 158 24.4 | S11 16.7 |
| 16 | 151 48.0 | 92 49.9 | 43.9 | 130 59.3 | 48.0 | 145 05.1 | 31.8 | 184 08.3 | 18.8 | Suhail | 222 48.2 | S43 31.5 |
| 17 | 166 50.5 | 107 49.3 | 44.6 | 146 00.1 | 48.6 | 160 07.3 | 31.9 | 199 10.9 | 18.8 | | | |
| 18 | 181 53.0 | 122 48.7 | N18 45.3 | 161 00.9 | N 6 49.3 | 175 09.5 | N 1 32.0 | 214 13.4 | S14 18.8 | Vega | 80 34.2 | N38 48.2 |
| 19 | 196 55.4 | 137 48.1 | 46.0 | 176 01.6 | 50.0 | 190 11.8 | 32.1 | 229 15.9 | 18.9 | Zuben'ubi | 136 58.1 | S16 08.1 |
| 20 | 211 57.9 | 152 47.5 | 46.6 | 191 02.4 | 50.6 | 205 14.0 | 32.2 | 244 18.5 | 18.9 | | SHA | Mer. Pass. |
| 21 | 227 00.4 | 167 46.9 .. | 47.3 | 206 03.2 .. | 51.3 | 220 16.2 .. | 32.3 | 259 21.0 .. | 18.9 | | ° ′ | h m |
| 22 | 242 02.8 | 182 46.3 | 48.0 | 221 04.0 | 52.0 | 235 18.4 | 32.4 | 274 23.5 | 19.0 | Venus | 303 03.8 | 9 47 |
| 23 | 257 05.3 | 197 45.7 | 48.7 | 236 04.8 | 52.6 | 250 20.6 | 32.5 | 289 26.1 | 19.0 | Mars | 340 18.4 | 7 18 |
| Mer. Pass. | h m 5 58.4 | v −0.6 | d 0.7 | v 0.8 | d 0.7 | v 2.2 | d 0.1 | v 2.5 | d 0.0 | Jupiter | 353 27.2 | 6 25 |
| | | | | | | | | | | Saturn | 32 17.6 | 3 50 |

| UT | SUN | | MOON | | | | Lat. | Twilight | | Sunrise | Moonrise | | | |
|---|---|---|---|---|---|---|---|---|---|---|---|---|---|---|
| | | | | | | | | Naut. | Civil | | 21 | 22 | 23 | 24 |
| | GHA | Dec | GHA | v | Dec | d | HP | | | | | | | |
| d h | ° ′ | ° ′ | ° ′ | ′ | ° ′ | ′ | ′ | N 72 | h m ☐ | h m ☐ | h m ☐ | h m 01 01 | h m 00 31 | h m (00 01 / 23 24) | h m 22 23 |
| 21 00 | 179 34.3 | N23 26.2 | 269 19.7 | 13.8 | S 4 38.9 | 14.8 | 57.4 | N 70 | ☐ | ☐ | ☐ | 00 55 | 00 33 | (00 10 / 23 40) | 23 07 |
| 01 | 194 34.1 | 26.2 | 283 52.5 | 13.8 | 4 24.1 | 14.8 | 57.4 | 68 | ☐ | ☐ | ☐ | 00 50 | 00 34 | 00 18 | (00 00 / 23 37) |
| 02 | 209 34.0 | 26.2 | 298 25.3 | 13.9 | 4 09.3 | 14.9 | 57.3 | 66 | ☐ | ☐ | ☐ | 00 46 | 00 35 | 00 25 | 00 13 |
| 03 | 224 33.9 | 26.3 | 312 58.2 | 13.9 | 3 54.4 | 14.8 | 57.3 | 64 | //// | //// | 01 31 | 00 42 | 00 36 | 00 30 | 00 24 |
| 04 | 239 33.7 | 26.3 | 327 31.1 | 14.0 | 3 39.6 | 14.8 | 57.2 | 62 | //// | //// | 02 10 | 00 39 | 00 37 | 00 35 | 00 33 |
| 05 | 254 33.6 | 26.3 | 342 04.1 | 14.0 | 3 24.8 | 14.8 | 57.2 | 60 | //// | 00 49 | 02 36 | 00 36 | 00 38 | 00 39 | 00 42 |
| 06 | 269 33.5 | N23 26.3 | 356 37.1 | 14.1 | S 3 10.0 | 14.8 | 57.2 | N 58 | //// | 01 41 | 02 57 | 00 34 | 00 38 | 00 43 | 00 49 |
| T 07 | 284 33.3 | 26.3 | 11 10.2 | 14.1 | 2 55.2 | 14.8 | 57.1 | 56 | //// | 02 11 | 03 13 | 00 31 | 00 39 | 00 47 | 00 55 |
| U 08 | 299 33.2 | 26.3 | 25 43.3 | 14.2 | 2 40.4 | 14.8 | 57.1 | 54 | 00 45 | 02 33 | 03 28 | 00 29 | 00 40 | 00 50 | 01 01 |
| E 09 | 314 33.1 | 26.3 | 40 16.5 | 14.2 | 2 25.6 | 14.8 | 57.1 | 52 | 01 33 | 02 51 | 03 40 | 00 28 | 00 40 | 00 52 | 01 06 |
| S 10 | 329 32.9 | 26.3 | 54 49.7 | 14.2 | 2 10.8 | 14.8 | 57.0 | 50 | 02 01 | 03 06 | 03 51 | 00 26 | 00 41 | 00 55 | 01 10 |
| D 11 | 344 32.8 | 26.3 | 69 22.9 | 14.3 | 1 56.0 | 14.8 | 57.0 | 45 | 02 46 | 03 36 | 04 13 | 00 22 | 00 42 | 01 01 | 01 20 |
| A 12 | 359 32.6 | N23 26.3 | 83 56.2 | 14.4 | S 1 41.2 | 14.7 | 57.0 | N 40 | 03 17 | 03 59 | 04 32 | 00 19 | 00 43 | 01 05 | 01 29 |
| Y 13 | 14 32.5 | 26.3 | 98 29.6 | 14.4 | 1 26.5 | 14.8 | 56.9 | 35 | 03 40 | 04 17 | 04 47 | 00 17 | 00 43 | 01 09 | 01 36 |
| 14 | 29 32.4 | 26.3 | 113 03.0 | 14.4 | 1 11.7 | 14.7 | 56.9 | 30 | 03 59 | 04 32 | 05 00 | 00 14 | 00 44 | 01 13 | 01 43 |
| 15 | 44 32.2 | 26.3 | 127 36.4 | 14.5 | 0 57.0 | 14.8 | 56.9 | 20 | 04 28 | 04 57 | 05 22 | 00 10 | 00 45 | 01 19 | 01 54 |
| 16 | 59 32.1 | 26.3 | 142 09.9 | 14.5 | 0 42.2 | 14.7 | 56.8 | N 10 | 04 51 | 05 18 | 05 41 | 00 07 | 00 46 | 01 25 | 02 04 |
| 17 | 74 32.0 | 26.2 | 156 43.4 | 14.5 | 0 27.5 | 14.7 | 56.8 | 0 | 05 10 | 05 36 | 05 58 | 00 03 | 00 47 | 01 30 | 02 13 |
| 18 | 89 31.8 | N23 26.2 | 171 16.9 | 14.6 | S 0 12.8 | 14.7 | 56.8 | S 10 | 05 27 | 05 53 | 06 16 | 00 00 | 00 48 | 01 36 | 02 23 |
| 19 | 104 31.7 | 26.2 | 185 50.5 | 14.6 | N 0 01.9 | 14.6 | 56.7 | 20 | 05 43 | 06 10 | 06 34 | 24 49 | 00 49 | 01 41 | 02 33 |
| 20 | 119 31.6 | 26.2 | 200 24.1 | 14.6 | 0 16.5 | 14.7 | 56.7 | 30 | 05 59 | 06 29 | 06 56 | 24 51 | 00 51 | 01 48 | 02 44 |
| 21 | 134 31.4 | 26.2 | 214 57.7 | 14.7 | 0 31.2 | 14.6 | 56.7 | 35 | 06 08 | 06 40 | 07 08 | 24 52 | 00 52 | 01 52 | 02 51 |
| 22 | 149 31.3 | 26.2 | 229 31.4 | 14.6 | 0 45.8 | 14.6 | 56.6 | 40 | 06 18 | 06 52 | 07 22 | 24 52 | 00 52 | 01 56 | 02 59 |
| 23 | 164 31.2 | 26.2 | 244 05.0 | 14.8 | 1 00.4 | 14.6 | 56.6 | 45 | 06 28 | 07 05 | 07 39 | 24 54 | 00 54 | 02 01 | 03 08 |
| 22 00 | 179 31.0 | N23 26.2 | 258 38.8 | 14.7 | N 1 15.0 | 14.6 | 56.6 | S 50 | 06 40 | 07 21 | 08 00 | 24 55 | 00 55 | 02 07 | 03 19 |
| 01 | 194 30.9 | 26.2 | 273 12.5 | 14.8 | 1 29.6 | 14.5 | 56.5 | 52 | 06 45 | 07 29 | 08 10 | 24 55 | 00 55 | 02 10 | 03 24 |
| 02 | 209 30.7 | 26.2 | 287 46.3 | 14.8 | 1 44.1 | 14.5 | 56.5 | 54 | 06 51 | 07 37 | 08 21 | 24 56 | 00 56 | 02 13 | 03 30 |
| 03 | 224 30.6 | 26.2 | 302 20.1 | 14.8 | 1 58.6 | 14.5 | 56.5 | 56 | 06 57 | 07 46 | 08 34 | 24 57 | 00 57 | 02 17 | 03 36 |
| 04 | 239 30.5 | 26.1 | 316 53.9 | 14.8 | 2 13.1 | 14.5 | 56.5 | 58 | 07 04 | 07 56 | 08 48 | 24 57 | 00 57 | 02 21 | 03 43 |
| 05 | 254 30.3 | 26.1 | 331 27.7 | 14.9 | 2 27.6 | 14.5 | 56.4 | S 60 | 07 11 | 08 08 | 09 06 | 24 58 | 00 58 | 02 25 | 03 51 |
| 06 | 269 30.2 | N23 26.1 | 346 01.6 | 14.9 | N 2 42.1 | 14.4 | 56.4 | | | | | | | | |
| W 07 | 284 30.1 | 26.1 | 0 35.5 | 14.9 | 2 56.5 | 14.4 | 56.4 | Lat. | Sunset | Twilight | | Moonset | | | |
| E 08 | 299 29.9 | 26.1 | 15 09.4 | 14.9 | 3 10.9 | 14.3 | 56.3 | | | Civil | Naut. | 21 | 22 | 23 | 24 |
| D 09 | 314 29.8 | 26.1 | 29 43.3 | 14.9 | 3 25.2 | 14.4 | 56.3 | | | | | | | | |
| N 10 | 329 29.7 | 26.0 | 44 17.2 | 14.9 | 3 39.6 | 14.3 | 56.3 | ° | h m | h m | h m | h m | h m | h m | h m |
| E 11 | 344 29.5 | 26.0 | 58 51.1 | 15.0 | 3 53.9 | 14.3 | 56.2 | N 72 | ☐ | ☐ | ☐ | 12 02 | 14 06 | 16 14 | 18 47 |
| S 12 | 359 29.4 | N23 26.0 | 73 25.1 | 15.0 | N 4 08.2 | 14.2 | 56.2 | N 70 | ☐ | ☐ | ☐ | 12 05 | 14 00 | 15 56 | 18 05 |
| D 13 | 14 29.2 | 26.0 | 87 59.1 | 14.9 | 4 22.4 | 14.2 | 56.2 | 68 | ☐ | ☐ | ☐ | 12 07 | 13 54 | 15 42 | 17 36 |
| A 14 | 29 29.1 | 26.0 | 102 33.0 | 15.0 | 4 36.6 | 14.2 | 56.1 | 66 | ☐ | ☐ | ☐ | 12 08 | 13 50 | 15 31 | 17 15 |
| Y 15 | 44 29.0 | 26.0 | 117 07.0 | 15.0 | 4 50.8 | 14.1 | 56.1 | 64 | 22 33 | //// | //// | 12 10 | 13 46 | 15 21 | 16 58 |
| 16 | 59 28.8 | 25.9 | 131 41.0 | 15.0 | 5 04.9 | 14.2 | 56.1 | 62 | 21 54 | //// | //// | 12 11 | 13 43 | 15 13 | 16 44 |
| 17 | 74 28.7 | 25.9 | 146 15.0 | 15.0 | 5 19.1 | 14.0 | 56.1 | 60 | 21 28 | 23 14 | //// | 12 12 | 13 40 | 15 06 | 16 33 |
| 18 | 89 28.6 | N23 25.9 | 160 49.0 | 15.0 | N 5 33.1 | 14.1 | 56.0 | N 58 | 21 07 | 22 23 | //// | 12 13 | 13 37 | 15 00 | 16 23 |
| 19 | 104 28.4 | 25.9 | 175 23.0 | 15.0 | 5 47.2 | 14.0 | 56.0 | 56 | 20 51 | 21 53 | //// | 12 14 | 13 35 | 14 55 | 16 14 |
| 20 | 119 28.3 | 25.8 | 189 57.0 | 15.1 | 6 01.2 | 13.9 | 56.0 | 54 | 20 36 | 21 31 | 23 19 | 12 15 | 13 33 | 14 50 | 16 06 |
| 21 | 134 28.2 | 25.8 | 204 31.1 | 15.0 | 6 15.1 | 14.0 | 55.9 | 52 | 20 24 | 21 13 | 22 31 | 12 16 | 13 31 | 14 46 | 15 59 |
| 22 | 149 28.0 | 25.8 | 219 05.1 | 15.0 | 6 29.1 | 13.9 | 55.9 | 50 | 20 13 | 20 58 | 22 03 | 12 16 | 13 30 | 14 42 | 15 53 |
| 23 | 164 27.9 | 25.8 | 233 39.1 | 15.0 | 6 43.0 | 13.8 | 55.9 | 45 | 19 51 | 20 28 | 21 18 | 12 18 | 13 26 | 14 33 | 15 40 |
| 23 00 | 179 27.8 | N23 25.7 | 248 13.1 | 15.0 | N 6 56.8 | 13.8 | 55.9 | N 40 | 19 33 | 20 05 | 20 47 | 12 19 | 13 23 | 14 26 | 15 29 |
| 01 | 194 27.6 | 25.7 | 262 47.1 | 15.1 | 7 10.6 | 13.8 | 55.8 | 35 | 19 17 | 19 47 | 20 24 | 12 20 | 13 21 | 14 20 | 15 20 |
| 02 | 209 27.5 | 25.7 | 277 21.2 | 15.0 | 7 24.4 | 13.7 | 55.8 | 30 | 19 04 | 19 32 | 20 05 | 12 21 | 13 18 | 14 15 | 15 12 |
| 03 | 224 27.3 | 25.6 | 291 55.2 | 15.0 | 7 38.1 | 13.7 | 55.8 | 20 | 18 42 | 19 07 | 19 36 | 12 22 | 13 14 | 14 06 | 14 58 |
| 04 | 239 27.2 | 25.6 | 306 29.2 | 15.0 | 7 51.8 | 13.6 | 55.8 | N 10 | 18 23 | 18 46 | 19 13 | 12 23 | 13 11 | 13 58 | 14 46 |
| 05 | 254 27.1 | 25.6 | 321 03.2 | 15.0 | 8 05.4 | 13.6 | 55.7 | 0 | 18 06 | 18 28 | 18 54 | 12 24 | 13 08 | 13 51 | 14 34 |
| 06 | 269 26.9 | N23 25.6 | 335 37.2 | 15.0 | N 8 19.0 | 13.5 | 55.7 | S 10 | 17 48 | 18 11 | 18 37 | 12 26 | 13 05 | 13 43 | 14 23 |
| T 07 | 284 26.8 | 25.5 | 350 11.2 | 14.9 | 8 32.5 | 13.5 | 55.7 | 20 | 17 30 | 17 54 | 18 21 | 12 27 | 13 01 | 13 36 | 14 11 |
| H 08 | 299 26.7 | 25.5 | 4 45.1 | 15.0 | 8 46.0 | 13.5 | 55.7 | 30 | 17 08 | 17 35 | 18 05 | 12 28 | 12 57 | 13 27 | 13 57 |
| U 09 | 314 26.5 | 25.5 | 19 19.1 | 15.0 | 8 59.5 | 13.4 | 55.6 | 35 | 16 56 | 17 24 | 17 56 | 12 29 | 12 55 | 13 22 | 13 49 |
| R 10 | 329 26.4 | 25.4 | 33 53.1 | 14.9 | 9 12.9 | 13.3 | 55.6 | 40 | 16 42 | 17 12 | 17 47 | 12 30 | 12 53 | 13 16 | 13 40 |
| S 11 | 344 26.3 | 25.4 | 48 27.0 | 14.9 | 9 26.2 | 13.3 | 55.6 | 45 | 16 25 | 16 59 | 17 36 | 12 31 | 12 50 | 13 09 | 13 30 |
| D 12 | 359 26.1 | N23 25.3 | 63 00.9 | 15.0 | N 9 39.5 | 13.3 | 55.6 | S 50 | 16 04 | 16 43 | 17 24 | 12 32 | 12 46 | 13 01 | 13 17 |
| A 13 | 14 26.0 | 25.3 | 77 34.9 | 14.9 | 9 52.8 | 13.2 | 55.5 | 52 | 15 54 | 16 35 | 17 19 | 12 32 | 12 45 | 12 57 | 13 12 |
| Y 14 | 29 25.9 | 25.3 | 92 08.8 | 14.8 | 10 06.0 | 13.1 | 55.5 | 54 | 15 43 | 16 27 | 17 13 | 12 33 | 12 43 | 12 53 | 13 05 |
| 15 | 44 25.7 | 25.2 | 106 42.6 | 14.9 | 10 19.1 | 13.1 | 55.5 | 56 | 15 30 | 16 18 | 17 07 | 12 34 | 12 41 | 12 49 | 12 58 |
| 16 | 59 25.6 | 25.2 | 121 16.5 | 14.9 | 10 32.2 | 13.0 | 55.5 | 58 | 15 16 | 16 08 | 17 00 | 12 34 | 12 39 | 12 44 | 12 50 |
| 17 | 74 25.5 | 25.2 | 135 50.4 | 14.8 | 10 45.2 | 13.0 | 55.4 | S 60 | 14 58 | 15 56 | 16 53 | 12 35 | 12 37 | 12 39 | 12 41 |
| 18 | 89 25.3 | N23 25.1 | 150 24.2 | 14.8 | N10 58.2 | 13.0 | 55.4 | | | SUN | | | MOON | | |
| 19 | 104 25.2 | 25.1 | 164 58.0 | 14.8 | 11 11.2 | 12.8 | 55.4 | Day | Eqn. of Time | | Mer. | Mer. Pass. | | Age | Phase |
| 20 | 119 25.0 | 25.0 | 179 31.8 | 14.8 | 11 24.0 | 12.9 | 55.4 | | 00ʰ | 12ʰ | Pass. | Upper | Lower | | |
| 21 | 134 24.9 | 25.0 | 194 05.6 | 14.7 | 11 36.9 | 12.7 | 55.3 | d | m s | m s | h m | h m | h m | d % | |
| 22 | 149 24.8 | 24.9 | 208 39.3 | 14.8 | 11 49.6 | 12.7 | 55.3 | 21 | 01 43 | 01 49 | 12 02 | 06 14 | 18 36 | 22 46 | |
| 23 | 164 24.6 | 24.9 | 223 13.1 | 14.7 | N12 02.3 | 12.7 | 55.3 | 22 | 01 56 | 02 02 | 12 02 | 06 58 | 19 19 | 23 36 | |
| | SD 15.8 | d 0.0 | SD 15.5 | | 15.3 | | 15.1 | 23 | 02 09 | 02 15 | 12 02 | 07 40 | 20 02 | 24 27 | |

| UT | ARIES | VENUS −3.9 | | MARS +0.5 | | JUPITER −2.4 | | SATURN +0.5 | | STARS | | |
|---|---|---|---|---|---|---|---|---|---|---|---|---|
| | GHA | GHA | Dec | GHA | Dec | GHA | Dec | GHA | Dec | Name | SHA | Dec |
| d h | ° ′ | ° ′ | ° ′ | ° ′ | ° ′ | ° ′ | ° ′ | ° ′ | ° ′ | | ° ′ | ° ′ |
| 24 00 | 272 07.8 | 212 45.1 | N18 49.4 | 251 05.6 | N 6 53.3 | 265 22.8 | N 1 32.6 | 304 28.6 | S14 19.0 | Acamar | 315 13.7 | S40 12.8 |
| 01 | 287 10.2 | 227 44.5 | 50.0 | 266 06.4 | 54.0 | 280 25.1 | 32.7 | 319 31.1 | 19.1 | Achernar | 335 22.0 | S57 07.2 |
| 02 | 302 12.7 | 242 43.9 | 50.7 | 281 07.1 | 54.6 | 295 27.3 | 32.8 | 334 33.7 | 19.1 | Acrux | 173 02.3 | S63 13.6 |
| 03 | 317 15.2 | 257 43.3 . . | 51.4 | 296 07.9 . . | 55.3 | 310 29.5 . . | 32.9 | 349 36.2 . . | 19.1 | Adhara | 255 07.9 | S29 00.2 |
| 04 | 332 17.6 | 272 42.7 | 52.1 | 311 08.7 | 56.0 | 325 31.7 | 33.0 | 4 38.7 | 19.2 | Aldebaran | 290 42.4 | N16 33.2 |
| 05 | 347 20.1 | 287 42.1 | 52.7 | 326 09.5 | 56.6 | 340 33.9 | 33.1 | 19 41.3 | 19.2 | | | |
| 06 | 2 22.5 | 302 41.5 | N18 53.4 | 341 10.3 | N 6 57.3 | 355 36.1 | N 1 33.2 | 34 43.8 | S14 19.2 | Alioth | 166 14.8 | N55 50.6 |
| 07 | 17 25.0 | 317 40.9 | 54.1 | 356 11.1 | 57.9 | 10 38.4 | 33.3 | 49 46.3 | 19.3 | Alkaid | 152 53.5 | N49 12.4 |
| 08 | 32 27.5 | 332 40.3 | 54.8 | 11 11.9 | 58.6 | 25 40.6 | 33.4 | 64 48.9 | 19.3 | Alnair | 27 35.3 | S46 51.0 |
| F 09 | 47 29.9 | 347 39.7 . . | 55.4 | 26 12.7 . . | 59.3 | 40 42.8 . . | 33.4 | 79 51.4 . . | 19.3 | Alnilam | 275 40.2 | S 1 11.3 |
| R 10 | 62 32.4 | 2 39.1 | 56.1 | 41 13.4 | 6 59.9 | 55 45.0 | 33.5 | 94 54.0 | 19.4 | Alphard | 217 50.0 | S 8 45.3 |
| I 11 | 77 34.9 | 17 38.5 | 56.8 | 56 14.2 | 7 00.6 | 70 47.2 | 33.6 | 109 56.5 | 19.4 | | | |
| D 12 | 92 37.3 | 32 37.9 | N18 57.4 | 71 15.0 | N 7 01.3 | 85 49.5 | N 1 33.7 | 124 59.0 | S14 19.4 | Alphecca | 126 05.2 | N26 38.5 |
| A 13 | 107 39.8 | 47 37.3 | 58.1 | 86 15.8 | 01.9 | 100 51.7 | 33.8 | 140 01.6 | 19.5 | Alpheratz | 357 36.9 | N29 12.6 |
| Y 14 | 122 42.3 | 62 36.7 | 58.8 | 101 16.6 | 02.6 | 115 53.9 | 33.9 | 155 04.1 | 19.5 | Altair | 62 01.7 | N 8 55.6 |
| 15 | 137 44.7 | 77 36.1 | 18 59.4 | 116 17.4 . . | 03.3 | 130 56.1 . . | 34.0 | 170 06.6 . . | 19.5 | Ankaa | 353 09.3 | S42 10.9 |
| 16 | 152 47.2 | 92 35.5 | 19 00.1 | 131 18.2 | 03.9 | 145 58.3 | 34.1 | 185 09.2 | 19.6 | Antares | 112 18.1 | S26 28.9 |
| 17 | 167 49.7 | 107 34.9 | 00.8 | 146 19.0 | 04.6 | 161 00.6 | 34.2 | 200 11.7 | 19.6 | | | |
| 18 | 182 52.1 | 122 34.3 | N19 01.4 | 161 19.7 | N 7 05.2 | 176 02.8 | N 1 34.3 | 215 14.3 | S14 19.6 | Arcturus | 145 49.7 | N19 04.1 |
| 19 | 197 54.6 | 137 33.7 | 02.1 | 176 20.5 | 05.9 | 191 05.0 | 34.4 | 230 16.8 | 19.7 | Atria | 107 13.6 | S69 04.1 |
| 20 | 212 57.0 | 152 33.1 | 02.7 | 191 21.3 | 06.6 | 206 07.2 | 34.5 | 245 19.3 | 19.7 | Avior | 234 16.1 | S59 35.0 |
| 21 | 227 59.5 | 167 32.5 . . | 03.4 | 206 22.1 . . | 07.2 | 221 09.5 . . | 34.6 | 260 21.9 . . | 19.7 | Bellatrix | 278 25.5 | N 6 22.2 |
| 22 | 243 02.0 | 182 31.8 | 04.1 | 221 22.9 | 07.9 | 236 11.7 | 34.6 | 275 24.4 | 19.8 | Betelgeuse | 270 54.7 | N 7 24.7 |
| 23 | 258 04.4 | 197 31.2 | 04.7 | 236 23.7 | 08.5 | 251 13.9 | 34.7 | 290 26.9 | 19.8 | | | |
| 25 00 | 273 06.9 | 212 30.6 | N19 05.4 | 251 24.5 | N 7 09.2 | 266 16.1 | N 1 34.8 | 305 29.5 | S14 19.8 | Canopus | 263 53.9 | S52 42.4 |
| 01 | 288 09.4 | 227 30.0 | 06.0 | 266 25.3 | 09.9 | 281 18.3 | 34.9 | 320 32.0 | 19.9 | Capella | 280 25.5 | N46 01.1 |
| 02 | 303 11.8 | 242 29.4 | 06.7 | 281 26.0 | 10.5 | 296 20.6 | 35.0 | 335 34.6 | 19.9 | Deneb | 49 26.8 | N45 21.4 |
| 03 | 318 14.3 | 257 28.8 . . | 07.4 | 296 26.8 . . | 11.2 | 311 22.8 . . | 35.1 | 350 37.1 . . | 19.9 | Denebola | 182 27.1 | N14 27.0 |
| 04 | 333 16.8 | 272 28.2 | 08.0 | 311 27.6 | 11.9 | 326 25.0 | 35.2 | 5 39.6 | 20.0 | Diphda | 348 49.5 | S17 51.8 |
| 05 | 348 19.2 | 287 27.6 | 08.7 | 326 28.4 | 12.5 | 341 27.2 | 35.3 | 20 42.2 | 20.0 | | | |
| 06 | 3 21.7 | 302 27.0 | N19 09.3 | 341 29.2 | N 7 13.2 | 356 29.5 | N 1 35.4 | 35 44.7 | S14 20.0 | Dubhe | 193 43.8 | N61 38.2 |
| 07 | 18 24.1 | 317 26.3 | 10.0 | 356 30.0 | 13.8 | 11 31.7 | 35.5 | 50 47.3 | 20.1 | Elnath | 278 04.9 | N28 37.5 |
| S 08 | 33 26.6 | 332 25.7 | 10.6 | 11 30.8 | 14.5 | 26 33.9 | 35.6 | 65 49.8 | 20.1 | Eltanin | 90 42.6 | N51 29.2 |
| A 09 | 48 29.1 | 347 25.1 . . | 11.3 | 26 31.6 . . | 15.2 | 41 36.1 . . | 35.6 | 80 52.3 . . | 20.1 | Enif | 33 40.6 | N 9 58.6 |
| T 10 | 63 31.5 | 2 24.5 | 11.9 | 41 32.3 | 15.8 | 56 38.4 | 35.7 | 95 54.9 | 20.2 | Fomalhaut | 15 16.7 | S29 30.1 |
| U 11 | 78 34.0 | 17 23.9 | 12.6 | 56 33.1 | 16.5 | 71 40.6 | 35.8 | 110 57.4 | 20.2 | | | |
| R 12 | 93 36.5 | 32 23.3 | N19 13.2 | 71 33.9 | N 7 17.1 | 86 42.8 | N 1 35.9 | 126 00.0 | S14 20.2 | Gacrux | 171 53.9 | S57 14.5 |
| D 13 | 108 38.9 | 47 22.7 | 13.9 | 86 34.7 | 17.8 | 101 45.0 | 36.0 | 141 02.5 | 20.3 | Gienah | 175 45.7 | S17 40.0 |
| A 14 | 123 41.4 | 62 22.0 | 14.5 | 101 35.5 | 18.4 | 116 47.3 | 36.1 | 156 05.0 | 20.3 | Hadar | 148 38.6 | S60 29.0 |
| Y 15 | 138 43.9 | 77 21.4 . . | 15.2 | 116 36.3 . . | 19.1 | 131 49.5 . . | 36.2 | 171 07.6 . . | 20.3 | Hamal | 327 53.7 | N23 33.9 |
| 16 | 153 46.3 | 92 20.8 | 15.8 | 131 37.1 | 19.8 | 146 51.7 | 36.3 | 186 10.1 | 20.4 | Kaus Aust. | 83 34.9 | S34 22.4 |
| 17 | 168 48.8 | 107 20.2 | 16.5 | 146 37.9 | 20.4 | 161 54.0 | 36.4 | 201 12.7 | 20.4 | | | |
| 18 | 183 51.3 | 122 19.6 | N19 17.1 | 161 38.7 | N 7 21.1 | 176 56.2 | N 1 36.5 | 216 15.2 | S14 20.4 | Kochab | 137 19.1 | N74 04.1 |
| 19 | 198 53.7 | 137 19.0 | 17.7 | 176 39.4 | 21.7 | 191 58.4 | 36.5 | 231 17.7 | 20.5 | Markab | 13 31.9 | N15 19.4 |
| 20 | 213 56.2 | 152 18.3 | 18.4 | 191 40.2 | 22.4 | 207 00.6 | 36.6 | 246 20.3 | 20.5 | Menkar | 314 08.6 | N 4 10.6 |
| 21 | 228 58.6 | 167 17.7 . . | 19.0 | 206 41.0 . . | 23.1 | 222 02.9 . . | 36.7 | 261 22.8 . . | 20.5 | Menkent | 147 59.9 | S36 28.9 |
| 22 | 244 01.1 | 182 17.1 | 19.7 | 221 41.8 | 23.7 | 237 05.1 | 36.8 | 276 25.4 | 20.6 | Miaplacidus | 221 39.3 | S69 48.7 |
| 23 | 259 03.6 | 197 16.5 | 20.3 | 236 42.6 | 24.4 | 252 07.3 | 36.9 | 291 27.9 | 20.6 | | | |
| 26 00 | 274 06.0 | 212 15.9 | N19 20.9 | 251 43.4 | N 7 25.0 | 267 09.6 | N 1 37.0 | 306 30.5 | S14 20.6 | Mirfak | 308 31.6 | N49 56.2 |
| 01 | 289 08.5 | 227 15.2 | 21.6 | 266 44.2 | 25.7 | 282 11.8 | 37.1 | 321 33.0 | 20.7 | Nunki | 75 50.0 | S26 16.1 |
| 02 | 304 11.0 | 242 14.6 | 22.2 | 281 45.0 | 26.3 | 297 14.0 | 37.2 | 336 35.5 | 20.7 | Peacock | 53 08.5 | S56 39.6 |
| 03 | 319 13.4 | 257 14.0 . . | 22.9 | 296 45.8 . . | 27.0 | 312 16.2 . . | 37.3 | 351 38.1 . . | 20.7 | Pollux | 243 20.2 | N27 58.4 |
| 04 | 334 15.9 | 272 13.4 | 23.5 | 311 46.5 | 27.7 | 327 18.5 | 37.3 | 6 40.6 | 20.8 | Procyon | 244 53.4 | N 5 10.1 |
| 05 | 349 18.4 | 287 12.7 | 24.1 | 326 47.3 | 28.3 | 342 20.7 | 37.4 | 21 43.2 | 20.8 | | | |
| 06 | 4 20.8 | 302 12.1 | N19 24.8 | 341 48.1 | N 7 29.0 | 357 22.9 | N 1 37.5 | 36 45.7 | S14 20.8 | Rasalhague | 96 00.2 | N12 32.7 |
| 07 | 19 23.3 | 317 11.5 | 25.4 | 356 48.9 | 29.6 | 12 25.2 | 37.6 | 51 48.3 | 20.9 | Regulus | 207 36.9 | N11 51.6 |
| 08 | 34 25.8 | 332 10.9 | 26.0 | 11 49.7 | 30.3 | 27 27.4 | 37.7 | 66 50.8 | 20.9 | Rigel | 281 06.2 | S 8 10.5 |
| S 09 | 49 28.2 | 347 10.2 . . | 26.7 | 26 50.5 . . | 30.9 | 42 29.6 . . | 37.8 | 81 53.3 . . | 21.0 | Rigil Kent. | 139 42.8 | S60 55.8 |
| U 10 | 64 30.7 | 2 09.6 | 27.3 | 41 51.3 | 31.6 | 57 31.9 | 37.9 | 96 55.9 | 21.0 | Sabik | 102 04.9 | S15 45.1 |
| N 11 | 79 33.1 | 17 09.0 | 27.9 | 56 52.1 | 32.2 | 72 34.1 | 38.0 | 111 58.4 | 21.0 | | | |
| D 12 | 94 35.6 | 32 08.4 | N19 28.5 | 71 52.9 | N 7 32.9 | 87 36.3 | N 1 38.0 | 127 01.0 | S14 21.1 | Schedar | 349 33.5 | N56 39.3 |
| A 13 | 109 38.1 | 47 07.7 | 29.2 | 86 53.6 | 33.6 | 102 38.6 | 38.1 | 142 03.5 | 21.1 | Shaula | 96 12.8 | S37 07.2 |
| Y 14 | 124 40.5 | 62 07.1 | 29.8 | 101 54.4 | 34.2 | 117 40.8 | 38.2 | 157 06.1 | 21.1 | Sirius | 258 28.4 | S16 44.8 |
| 15 | 139 43.0 | 77 06.5 . . | 30.4 | 116 55.2 . . | 34.9 | 132 43.0 . . | 38.3 | 172 08.6 . . | 21.2 | Spica | 158 24.4 | S11 16.7 |
| 16 | 154 45.5 | 92 05.9 | 31.0 | 131 56.0 | 35.5 | 147 45.3 | 38.4 | 187 11.1 | 21.2 | Suhail | 222 48.2 | S43 31.5 |
| 17 | 169 47.9 | 107 05.2 | 31.7 | 146 56.8 | 36.2 | 162 47.5 | 38.5 | 202 13.7 | 21.2 | | | |
| 18 | 184 50.4 | 122 04.6 | N19 32.3 | 161 57.6 | N 7 36.8 | 177 49.7 | N 1 38.6 | 217 16.2 | S14 21.3 | Vega | 80 34.2 | N38 48.2 |
| 19 | 199 52.9 | 137 04.0 | 32.9 | 176 58.4 | 37.5 | 192 52.0 | 38.7 | 232 18.8 | 21.3 | Zuben'ubi | 136 58.1 | S16 08.1 |
| 20 | 214 55.3 | 152 03.3 | 33.5 | 191 59.2 | 38.1 | 207 54.2 | 38.7 | 247 21.3 | 21.3 | | SHA | Mer. Pass. |
| 21 | 229 57.8 | 167 02.7 . . | 34.2 | 207 00.0 . . | 38.8 | 222 56.4 . . | 38.8 | 262 23.9 . . | 21.4 | | ° ′ | h m |
| 22 | 245 00.3 | 182 02.1 | 34.8 | 222 00.8 | 39.4 | 237 58.7 | 38.9 | 277 26.4 | 21.4 | Venus | 299 23.7 | 9 50 |
| 23 | 260 02.7 | 197 01.4 | 35.4 | 237 01.5 | 40.1 | 253 00.9 | 39.0 | 292 29.0 | 21.5 | Mars | 338 17.6 | 7 14 |
| | h m | | | | | | | | | Jupiter | 353 09.2 | 6 14 |
| Mer. Pass. 5 46.6 | | v −0.6 | d 0.6 | v 0.8 | d 0.7 | v 2.2 | d 0.1 | v 2.5 | d 0.0 | Saturn | 32 22.6 | 3 37 |

| UT | SUN | | MOON | | | | | Lat. | Twilight | | Sunrise | Moonrise | | | |
|---|---|---|---|---|---|---|---|---|---|---|---|---|---|---|---|
| | | | | | | | | | Naut. | Civil | | 24 | 25 | 26 | 27 |
| | GHA | Dec | GHA | v | Dec | d | HP | ° | h m | h m | h m | h m | h m | h m | h m |
| d h | ° ′ | ° ′ | ° ′ | ′ | ° ′ | ′ | ′ | N 72 | ▭ | ▭ | ▭ | 22 23 | ▭ | ▭ | ▭ |
| 24 00 | 179 24.5 | N23 24.9 | 237 46.8 | 14.6 | N12 15.0 | 12.6 | 55.3 | N 70 | ▭ | ▭ | ▭ | 23 07 | ▭ | ▭ | ▭ |
| 01 | 194 24.4 | 24.8 | 252 20.4 | 14.7 | 12 27.6 | 12.5 | 55.2 | 68 | ▭ | ▭ | ▭ | (00 00 / 23 37) | 22 56 | ▭ | ▭ |
| 02 | 209 24.2 | 24.8 | 266 54.1 | 14.6 | 12 40.1 | 12.5 | 55.2 | 66 | ▭ | ▭ | ▭ | 00 13 | (00 00 / 23 40) | 22 49 | ▭ |
| 03 | 224 24.1 .. | 24.7 | 281 27.7 | 14.6 | 12 52.6 | 12.4 | 55.2 | 64 | //// | //// | 01 33 | 00 24 | 00 18 | (00 10 / 23 59) | 23 26 |
| 04 | 239 24.0 | 24.7 | 296 01.3 | 14.6 | 13 05.0 | 12.3 | 55.2 | 62 | //// | //// | 02 11 | 00 33 | 00 32 | 00 33 | 00 35 |
| 05 | 254 23.8 | 24.6 | 310 34.9 | 14.5 | 13 17.3 | 12.3 | 55.2 | 60 | //// | 00 52 | 02 37 | 00 42 | 00 45 | 00 51 | 01 01 |
| 06 | 269 23.7 | N23 24.6 | 325 08.4 | 14.6 | N13 29.6 | 12.2 | 55.1 | N 58 | //// | 01 42 | 02 58 | 00 49 | 00 56 | 01 06 | 01 22 |
| 07 | 284 23.6 | 24.5 | 339 42.0 | 14.4 | 13 41.8 | 12.2 | 55.1 | 56 | //// | 02 12 | 03 14 | 00 55 | 01 05 | 01 19 | 01 39 |
| 08 | 299 23.4 | 24.5 | 354 15.4 | 14.5 | 13 54.0 | 12.0 | 55.1 | 54 | 00 48 | 02 34 | 03 29 | 01 01 | 01 14 | 01 30 | 01 53 |
| F 09 | 314 23.3 .. | 24.4 | 8 48.9 | 14.4 | 14 06.0 | 12.1 | 55.1 | 52 | 01 34 | 02 52 | 03 41 | 01 06 | 01 21 | 01 41 | 02 06 |
| R 10 | 329 23.2 | 24.4 | 23 22.3 | 14.4 | 14 18.1 | 11.9 | 55.1 | 50 | 02 02 | 03 07 | 03 52 | 01 10 | 01 28 | 01 50 | 02 17 |
| I 11 | 344 23.0 | 24.3 | 37 55.7 | 14.3 | 14 30.0 | 11.9 | 55.0 | 45 | 02 47 | 03 37 | 04 14 | 01 20 | 01 43 | 02 09 | 02 40 |
| D 12 | 359 22.9 | N23 24.3 | 52 29.0 | 14.4 | N14 41.9 | 11.8 | 55.0 | N 40 | 03 18 | 04 00 | 04 32 | 01 29 | 01 55 | 02 24 | 02 59 |
| A 13 | 14 22.8 | 24.2 | 67 02.4 | 14.3 | 14 53.7 | 11.8 | 55.0 | 35 | 03 41 | 04 18 | 04 47 | 01 36 | 02 05 | 02 38 | 03 15 |
| Y 14 | 29 22.6 | 24.2 | 81 35.7 | 14.2 | 15 05.5 | 11.6 | 55.0 | 30 | 04 00 | 04 33 | 05 00 | 01 43 | 02 14 | 02 49 | 03 28 |
| 15 | 44 22.5 .. | 24.1 | 96 08.9 | 14.2 | 15 17.1 | 11.6 | 55.0 | 20 | 04 29 | 04 58 | 05 22 | 01 54 | 02 30 | 03 09 | 03 52 |
| 16 | 59 22.4 | 24.0 | 110 42.1 | 14.2 | 15 28.7 | 11.6 | 54.9 | N 10 | 04 51 | 05 18 | 05 41 | 02 04 | 02 44 | 03 27 | 04 12 |
| 17 | 74 22.2 | 24.0 | 125 15.3 | 14.1 | 15 40.3 | 11.4 | 54.9 | 0 | 05 10 | 05 36 | 05 59 | 02 13 | 02 57 | 03 43 | 04 31 |
| 18 | 89 22.1 | N23 23.9 | 139 48.4 | 14.1 | N15 51.7 | 11.4 | 54.9 | S 10 | 05 27 | 05 54 | 06 16 | 02 23 | 03 11 | 04 00 | 04 50 |
| 19 | 104 22.0 | 23.9 | 154 21.5 | 14.1 | 16 03.1 | 11.4 | 54.9 | 20 | 05 43 | 06 11 | 06 35 | 02 33 | 03 25 | 04 17 | 05 11 |
| 20 | 119 21.8 | 23.8 | 168 54.6 | 14.0 | 16 14.5 | 11.3 | 54.9 | 30 | 06 00 | 06 30 | 06 56 | 02 44 | 03 41 | 04 38 | 05 35 |
| 21 | 134 21.7 .. | 23.8 | 183 27.6 | 14.0 | 16 25.7 | 11.2 | 54.8 | 35 | 06 09 | 06 40 | 07 09 | 02 51 | 03 51 | 04 50 | 05 49 |
| 22 | 149 21.6 | 23.7 | 198 00.6 | 14.0 | 16 36.9 | 11.1 | 54.8 | 40 | 06 18 | 06 52 | 07 23 | 02 59 | 04 02 | 05 04 | 06 05 |
| 23 | 164 21.4 | 23.6 | 212 33.6 | 13.9 | 16 48.0 | 11.0 | 54.8 | 45 | 06 28 | 07 06 | 07 39 | 03 08 | 04 15 | 05 21 | 06 25 |
| 25 00 | 179 21.3 | N23 23.6 | 227 06.5 | 13.8 | N16 59.0 | 10.9 | 54.8 | S 50 | 06 40 | 07 22 | 08 00 | 03 19 | 04 30 | 05 41 | 06 49 |
| 01 | 194 21.2 | 23.5 | 241 39.3 | 13.8 | 17 09.9 | 10.9 | 54.8 | 52 | 06 45 | 07 29 | 08 10 | 03 24 | 04 38 | 05 51 | 07 01 |
| 02 | 209 21.0 | 23.4 | 256 12.1 | 13.8 | 17 20.8 | 10.7 | 54.8 | 54 | 06 51 | 07 37 | 08 21 | 03 30 | 04 46 | 06 02 | 07 15 |
| 03 | 224 20.9 .. | 23.4 | 270 44.9 | 13.8 | 17 31.5 | 10.7 | 54.7 | 56 | 06 57 | 07 46 | 08 34 | 03 36 | 04 56 | 06 15 | 07 31 |
| 04 | 239 20.7 | 23.3 | 285 17.7 | 13.7 | 17 42.2 | 10.7 | 54.7 | 58 | 07 04 | 07 57 | 08 48 | 03 43 | 05 06 | 06 29 | 07 49 |
| 05 | 254 20.6 | 23.3 | 299 50.4 | 13.6 | 17 52.9 | 10.5 | 54.7 | S 60 | 07 11 | 08 08 | 09 06 | 03 51 | 05 19 | 06 47 | 08 13 |

| Lat. | Sunset | Twilight | | Moonset | | | |
|---|---|---|---|---|---|---|---|
| | | Civil | Naut. | 24 | 25 | 26 | 27 |
| 25 06 | 269 20.5 N23 23.2 | 314 23.0 13.6 N18 03.4 10.5 54.7 | | | | | |

| | | Twilight | | Moonset | | | |
|---|---|---|---|---|---|---|---|
| Lat. | Sunset | Civil | Naut. | 24 | 25 | 26 | 27 |
| ° | h m | h m | h m | h m | h m | h m | h m |
| N 72 | ▭ | ▭ | ▭ | 18 47 | ▭ | ▭ | ▭ |
| N 70 | ▭ | ▭ | ▭ | 18 05 | ▭ | ▭ | ▭ |
| 68 | ▭ | ▭ | ▭ | 17 36 | 19 52 | ▭ | ▭ |
| 66 | ▭ | ▭ | ▭ | 17 15 | 19 08 | 21 39 | ▭ |
| 64 | 22 32 | //// | //// | 16 58 | 18 40 | 20 29 | 22 45 |
| 62 | 21 54 | //// | //// | 16 44 | 18 18 | 19 53 | 21 26 |
| 60 | 21 28 | 23 12 | //// | 16 33 | 18 00 | 19 28 | 20 50 |
| N 58 | 21 07 | 22 23 | //// | 16 23 | 17 46 | 19 08 | 20 24 |
| 56 | 20 51 | 21 53 | //// | 16 14 | 17 33 | 18 51 | 20 04 |
| 54 | 20 37 | 21 31 | 23 17 | 16 06 | 17 23 | 18 37 | 19 47 |
| 52 | 20 24 | 21 13 | 22 31 | 15 59 | 17 13 | 18 25 | 19 33 |
| 50 | 20 13 | 20 58 | 22 03 | 15 53 | 17 04 | 18 14 | 19 20 |
| 45 | 19 51 | 20 28 | 21 18 | 15 40 | 16 46 | 17 52 | 18 54 |
| N 40 | 19 33 | 20 06 | 20 47 | 15 29 | 16 32 | 17 34 | 18 33 |
| 35 | 19 18 | 19 48 | 20 24 | 15 20 | 16 19 | 17 19 | 18 16 |
| 30 | 19 05 | 19 32 | 20 06 | 15 12 | 16 09 | 17 05 | 18 02 |
| 20 | 18 43 | 19 07 | 19 37 | 14 58 | 15 50 | 16 43 | 17 37 |
| N 10 | 18 24 | 18 47 | 19 14 | 14 46 | 15 34 | 16 24 | 17 15 |
| 0 | 18 06 | 18 29 | 18 55 | 14 34 | 15 19 | 16 06 | 16 55 |
| S 10 | 17 49 | 18 12 | 18 38 | 14 23 | 15 04 | 15 48 | 16 35 |
| 20 | 17 30 | 17 54 | 18 22 | 14 11 | 14 49 | 15 29 | 16 14 |
| 30 | 17 09 | 17 36 | 18 05 | 13 57 | 14 30 | 15 07 | 15 49 |
| 35 | 16 57 | 17 25 | 17 57 | 13 49 | 14 20 | 14 55 | 15 34 |
| 40 | 16 43 | 17 13 | 17 47 | 13 40 | 14 08 | 14 40 | 15 17 |
| 45 | 16 26 | 17 00 | 17 37 | 13 30 | 13 54 | 14 22 | 14 57 |
| S 50 | 16 05 | 16 44 | 17 25 | 13 17 | 13 37 | 14 01 | 14 32 |
| 52 | 15 55 | 16 36 | 17 20 | 13 12 | 13 29 | 13 51 | 14 20 |
| 54 | 15 44 | 16 28 | 17 14 | 13 05 | 13 20 | 13 39 | 14 06 |
| 56 | 15 32 | 16 19 | 17 08 | 12 58 | 13 10 | 13 26 | 13 50 |
| 58 | 15 17 | 16 09 | 17 01 | 12 50 | 12 58 | 13 11 | 13 31 |
| S 60 | 14 59 | 15 57 | 16 54 | 12 41 | 12 45 | 12 53 | 13 07 |

The SUN / MOON section (UT 25 06 through 26 23):

| UT | SUN GHA | SUN Dec | MOON GHA | v | MOON Dec | d | HP |
|---|---|---|---|---|---|---|---|
| 25 06 | 269 20.5 | N23 23.2 | 314 23.0 | 13.6 | N18 03.4 | 10.5 | 54.7 |
| 07 | 284 20.3 | 23.1 | 328 55.6 | 13.6 | 18 13.9 | 10.3 | 54.7 |
| 08 | 299 20.2 | 23.1 | 343 28.2 | 13.5 | 18 24.2 | 10.3 | 54.7 |
| 09 | 314 20.1 .. | 23.0 | 358 00.7 | 13.5 | 18 34.5 | 10.2 | 54.6 |
| 10 | 329 19.9 | 22.9 | 12 33.2 | 13.4 | 18 44.7 | 10.2 | 54.6 |
| 11 | 344 19.8 | 22.8 | 27 05.6 | 13.4 | 18 54.9 | 10.0 | 54.6 |
| 12 | 359 19.7 | N23 22.8 | 41 38.0 | 13.3 | N19 04.9 | 9.9 | 54.6 |
| 13 | 14 19.5 | 22.7 | 56 10.3 | 13.3 | 19 14.8 | 9.9 | 54.6 |
| 14 | 29 19.4 | 22.6 | 70 42.6 | 13.2 | 19 24.7 | 9.8 | 54.6 |
| 15 | 44 19.3 .. | 22.6 | 85 14.8 | 13.2 | 19 34.5 | 9.7 | 54.5 |
| 16 | 59 19.1 | 22.5 | 99 47.0 | 13.2 | 19 44.2 | 9.6 | 54.5 |
| 17 | 74 19.0 | 22.4 | 114 19.2 | 13.1 | 19 53.8 | 9.5 | 54.5 |
| 18 | 89 18.9 | N23 22.3 | 128 51.3 | 13.0 | N20 03.3 | 9.4 | 54.5 |
| 19 | 104 18.7 | 22.3 | 143 23.3 | 13.0 | 20 12.7 | 9.3 | 54.5 |
| 20 | 119 18.6 | 22.2 | 157 55.3 | 13.0 | 20 22.0 | 9.2 | 54.5 |
| 21 | 134 18.5 .. | 22.1 | 172 27.3 | 12.9 | 20 31.2 | 9.2 | 54.5 |
| 22 | 149 18.4 | 22.0 | 186 59.2 | 12.8 | 20 40.4 | 9.0 | 54.4 |
| 23 | 164 18.2 | 22.0 | 201 31.0 | 12.8 | 20 49.4 | 9.0 | 54.4 |
| 26 00 | 179 18.1 | N23 21.9 | 216 02.8 | 12.8 | N20 58.4 | 8.8 | 54.4 |
| 01 | 194 18.0 | 21.8 | 230 34.6 | 12.7 | 21 07.2 | 8.8 | 54.4 |
| 02 | 209 17.8 | 21.7 | 245 06.3 | 12.7 | 21 16.0 | 8.6 | 54.4 |
| 03 | 224 17.7 .. | 21.6 | 259 38.0 | 12.6 | 21 24.6 | 8.6 | 54.4 |
| 04 | 239 17.6 | 21.6 | 274 09.6 | 12.5 | 21 33.2 | 8.5 | 54.4 |
| 05 | 254 17.4 | 21.5 | 288 41.1 | 12.5 | 21 41.7 | 8.3 | 54.4 |
| 06 | 269 17.3 | N23 21.4 | 303 12.6 | 12.5 | N21 50.0 | 8.3 | 54.3 |
| 07 | 284 17.2 | 21.3 | 317 44.1 | 12.4 | 21 58.3 | 8.2 | 54.3 |
| 08 | 299 17.0 | 21.2 | 332 15.5 | 12.3 | 22 06.5 | 8.0 | 54.3 |
| 09 | 314 16.9 .. | 21.1 | 346 46.9 | 12.3 | 22 14.5 | 8.0 | 54.3 |
| 10 | 329 16.8 | 21.0 | 1 18.2 | 12.3 | 22 22.5 | 7.9 | 54.3 |
| 11 | 344 16.6 | 21.0 | 15 49.5 | 12.2 | 22 30.4 | 7.7 | 54.3 |
| 12 | 359 16.5 | N23 20.9 | 30 20.7 | 12.2 | N22 38.1 | 7.7 | 54.3 |
| 13 | 14 16.4 | 20.8 | 44 51.9 | 12.1 | 22 45.8 | 7.5 | 54.3 |
| 14 | 29 16.2 | 20.7 | 59 23.0 | 12.1 | 22 53.3 | 7.5 | 54.3 |
| 15 | 44 16.1 .. | 20.6 | 73 54.1 | 12.0 | 23 00.8 | 7.3 | 54.2 |
| 16 | 59 16.0 | 20.5 | 88 25.1 | 12.0 | 23 08.1 | 7.3 | 54.2 |
| 17 | 74 15.8 | 20.4 | 102 56.1 | 11.9 | 23 15.4 | 7.1 | 54.2 |
| 18 | 89 15.7 | N23 20.3 | 117 27.0 | 11.9 | N23 22.5 | 7.0 | 54.2 |
| 19 | 104 15.6 | 20.2 | 131 57.9 | 11.8 | 23 29.5 | 6.9 | 54.2 |
| 20 | 119 15.4 | 20.1 | 146 28.7 | 11.8 | 23 36.4 | 6.8 | 54.2 |
| 21 | 134 15.3 .. | 20.1 | 160 59.5 | 11.8 | 23 43.2 | 6.7 | 54.2 |
| 22 | 149 15.2 | 20.0 | 175 30.3 | 11.7 | 23 49.9 | 6.6 | 54.2 |
| 23 | 164 15.0 | 19.9 | 190 01.0 | 11.6 | N23 56.5 | 6.5 | 54.2 |
| | SD 15.8 | d 0.1 | SD 15.0 | | 14.9 | | 14.8 |

| | SUN | | | MOON | | | |
|---|---|---|---|---|---|---|---|
| Day | Eqn. of Time | | Mer. | Mer. Pass. | | Age | Phase |
| | 00h | 12h | Pass. | Upper | Lower | | |
| d | m s | m s | h m | h m | h m | d | % |
| 24 | 02 22 | 02 28 | 12 02 | 08 24 | 20 46 | 25 | 18 |
| 25 | 02 35 | 02 41 | 12 03 | 09 08 | 21 31 | 26 | 11 |
| 26 | 02 47 | 02 54 | 12 03 | 09 55 | 22 19 | 27 | 6 |

| UT | ARIES GHA | VENUS −3.9 GHA | Dec | MARS +0.4 GHA | Dec | JUPITER −2.4 GHA | Dec | SATURN +0.5 GHA | Dec | STARS Name | SHA | Dec |
|---|---|---|---|---|---|---|---|---|---|---|---|---|
| d h | ° ′ | ° ′ | ° ′ | ° ′ | ° ′ | ° ′ | ° ′ | ° ′ | ° ′ | | ° ′ | ° ′ |
| 27 00 | 275 05.2 | 212 00.8 | N19 36.0 | 252 02.3 | N 7 40.7 | 268 03.1 | N 1 39.1 | 307 31.5 | S14 21.5 | Acamar | 315 13.7 | S40 12.7 |
| 01 | 290 07.6 | 227 00.2 | 36.6 | 267 03.1 | 41.4 | 283 05.4 | 39.2 | 322 34.1 | 21.5 | Achernar | 335 22.0 | S57 07.2 |
| 02 | 305 10.1 | 241 59.5 | 37.3 | 282 03.9 | 42.1 | 298 07.6 | 39.3 | 337 36.6 | 21.6 | Acrux | 173 02.3 | S63 13.6 |
| 03 | 320 12.6 | 256 58.9 . . | 37.9 | 297 04.7 . . | 42.7 | 313 09.8 . . | 39.3 | 352 39.1 . . | 21.6 | Adhara | 255 07.9 | S29 00.1 |
| 04 | 335 15.0 | 271 58.3 | 38.5 | 312 05.5 | 43.4 | 328 12.1 | 39.4 | 7 41.7 | 21.6 | Aldebaran | 290 42.3 | N16 33.2 |
| 05 | 350 17.5 | 286 57.6 | 39.1 | 327 06.3 | 44.0 | 343 14.3 | 39.5 | 22 44.2 | 21.7 | | | |
| 06 | 5 20.0 | 301 57.0 | N19 39.7 | 342 07.1 | N 7 44.7 | 358 16.5 | N 1 39.6 | 37 46.8 | S14 21.7 | Alioth | 166 14.8 | N55 50.6 |
| 07 | 20 22.4 | 316 56.4 | 40.3 | 357 07.9 | 45.3 | 13 18.8 | 39.7 | 52 49.3 | 21.7 | Alkaid | 152 53.5 | N49 12.4 |
| 08 | 35 24.9 | 331 55.7 | 40.9 | 12 08.7 | 46.0 | 28 21.0 | 39.8 | 67 51.9 | 21.8 | Alnair | 27 35.3 | S46 51.0 |
| M 09 | 50 27.4 | 346 55.1 . . | 41.6 | 27 09.4 . . | 46.6 | 43 23.3 . . | 39.9 | 82 54.4 . . | 21.8 | Alnilam | 275 40.2 | S 1 11.3 |
| O 10 | 65 29.8 | 1 54.5 | 42.2 | 42 10.2 | 47.3 | 58 25.5 | 39.9 | 97 57.0 | 21.8 | Alphard | 217 50.0 | S 8 45.3 |
| N 11 | 80 32.3 | 16 53.8 | 42.8 | 57 11.0 | 47.9 | 73 27.7 | 40.0 | 112 59.5 | 21.9 | | | |
| D 12 | 95 34.8 | 31 53.2 | N19 43.4 | 72 11.8 | N 7 48.6 | 88 30.0 | N 1 40.1 | 128 02.1 | S14 21.9 | Alphecca | 126 05.2 | N26 38.5 |
| A 13 | 110 37.2 | 46 52.5 | 44.0 | 87 12.6 | 49.2 | 103 32.2 | 40.2 | 143 04.6 | 22.0 | Alpheratz | 357 36.9 | N29 12.6 |
| Y 14 | 125 39.7 | 61 51.9 | 44.6 | 102 13.4 | 49.9 | 118 34.4 | 40.3 | 158 07.2 | 22.0 | Altair | 62 01.7 | N 8 55.6 |
| 15 | 140 42.1 | 76 51.3 . . | 45.2 | 117 14.2 . . | 50.5 | 133 36.7 . . | 40.4 | 173 09.7 . . | 22.0 | Ankaa | 353 09.2 | S42 10.9 |
| 16 | 155 44.6 | 91 50.6 | 45.8 | 132 15.0 | 51.2 | 148 38.9 | 40.4 | 188 12.3 | 22.1 | Antares | 112 18.1 | S26 28.9 |
| 17 | 170 47.1 | 106 50.0 | 46.4 | 147 15.8 | 51.8 | 163 41.2 | 40.5 | 203 14.8 | 22.1 | | | |
| 18 | 185 49.5 | 121 49.3 | N19 47.0 | 162 16.6 | N 7 52.5 | 178 43.4 | N 1 40.6 | 218 17.4 | S14 22.1 | Arcturus | 145 49.7 | N19 04.1 |
| 19 | 200 52.0 | 136 48.7 | 47.6 | 177 17.4 | 53.1 | 193 45.6 | 40.7 | 233 19.9 | 22.2 | Atria | 107 13.6 | S69 04.1 |
| 20 | 215 54.5 | 151 48.1 | 48.2 | 192 18.1 | 53.8 | 208 47.9 | 40.8 | 248 22.5 | 22.2 | Avior | 234 16.1 | S59 35.0 |
| 21 | 230 56.9 | 166 47.4 . . | 48.8 | 207 18.9 . . | 54.4 | 223 50.1 . . | 40.9 | 263 25.0 . . | 22.3 | Bellatrix | 278 25.5 | N 6 22.2 |
| 22 | 245 59.4 | 181 46.8 | 49.4 | 222 19.7 | 55.1 | 238 52.4 | 40.9 | 278 27.6 | 22.3 | Betelgeuse | 270 54.7 | N 7 24.7 |
| 23 | 261 01.9 | 196 46.1 | 50.0 | 237 20.5 | 55.7 | 253 54.6 | 41.0 | 293 30.1 | 22.3 | | | |
| 28 00 | 276 04.3 | 211 45.5 | N19 50.6 | 252 21.3 | N 7 56.4 | 268 56.9 | N 1 41.1 | 308 32.7 | S14 22.4 | Canopus | 263 53.9 | S52 42.4 |
| 01 | 291 06.8 | 226 44.8 | 51.2 | 267 22.1 | 57.0 | 283 59.1 | 41.2 | 323 35.2 | 22.4 | Capella | 280 25.4 | N46 01.1 |
| 02 | 306 09.2 | 241 44.2 | 51.8 | 282 22.9 | 57.7 | 299 01.3 | 41.3 | 338 37.8 | 22.4 | Deneb | 49 26.8 | N45 21.4 |
| 03 | 321 11.7 | 256 43.6 . . | 52.4 | 297 23.7 . . | 58.3 | 314 03.6 . . | 41.4 | 353 40.3 . . | 22.5 | Denebola | 182 27.1 | N14 27.0 |
| 04 | 336 14.2 | 271 42.9 | 53.0 | 312 24.5 | 59.0 | 329 05.8 | 41.4 | 8 42.9 | 22.5 | Diphda | 348 49.4 | S17 51.8 |
| 05 | 351 16.6 | 286 42.3 | 53.6 | 327 25.3 | 7 59.6 | 344 08.1 | 41.5 | 23 45.4 | 22.6 | | | |
| 06 | 6 19.1 | 301 41.6 | N19 54.2 | 342 26.1 | N 8 00.3 | 359 10.3 | N 1 41.6 | 38 48.0 | S14 22.6 | Dubhe | 193 43.9 | N61 38.1 |
| 07 | 21 21.6 | 316 41.0 | 54.8 | 357 26.9 | 00.9 | 14 12.5 | 41.7 | 53 50.5 | 22.6 | Elnath | 278 04.9 | N28 37.5 |
| 08 | 36 24.0 | 331 40.3 | 55.4 | 12 27.6 | 01.6 | 29 14.8 | 41.8 | 68 53.1 | 22.7 | Eltanin | 90 42.6 | N51 29.2 |
| T 09 | 51 26.5 | 346 39.7 . . | 56.0 | 27 28.4 . . | 02.2 | 44 17.0 . . | 41.9 | 83 55.6 . . | 22.7 | Enif | 33 40.6 | N 9 58.6 |
| U 10 | 66 29.0 | 1 39.0 | 56.5 | 42 29.2 | 02.9 | 59 19.3 | 41.9 | 98 58.2 | 22.7 | Fomalhaut | 15 16.7 | S29 30.1 |
| E 11 | 81 31.4 | 16 38.4 | 57.1 | 57 30.0 | 03.5 | 74 21.5 | 42.0 | 114 00.7 | 22.8 | | | |
| S 12 | 96 33.9 | 31 37.7 | N19 57.7 | 72 30.8 | N 8 04.1 | 89 23.8 | N 1 42.1 | 129 03.3 | S14 22.8 | Gacrux | 171 53.9 | S57 14.5 |
| D 13 | 111 36.4 | 46 37.1 | 58.3 | 87 31.6 | 04.8 | 104 26.0 | 42.2 | 144 05.8 | 22.9 | Gienah | 175 45.7 | S17 40.0 |
| A 14 | 126 38.8 | 61 36.4 | 58.9 | 102 32.4 | 05.4 | 119 28.3 | 42.3 | 159 08.4 | 22.9 | Hadar | 148 38.7 | S60 29.1 |
| Y 15 | 141 41.3 | 76 35.8 | 19 59.5 | 117 33.2 . . | 06.1 | 134 30.5 . . | 42.3 | 174 10.9 . . | 22.9 | Hamal | 327 53.7 | N23 33.9 |
| 16 | 156 43.7 | 91 35.1 | 20 00.1 | 132 34.0 | 06.7 | 149 32.8 | 42.4 | 189 13.5 | 23.0 | Kaus Aust. | 83 34.9 | S34 22.4 |
| 17 | 171 46.2 | 106 34.5 | 00.6 | 147 34.8 | 07.4 | 164 35.0 | 42.5 | 204 16.0 | 23.0 | | | |
| 18 | 186 48.7 | 121 33.8 | N20 01.2 | 162 35.6 | N 8 08.0 | 179 37.2 | N 1 42.6 | 219 18.6 | S14 23.0 | Kochab | 137 19.1 | N74 04.1 |
| 19 | 201 51.1 | 136 33.2 | 01.8 | 177 36.4 | 08.7 | 194 39.5 | 42.7 | 234 21.1 | 23.1 | Markab | 13 31.9 | N15 19.4 |
| 20 | 216 53.6 | 151 32.5 | 02.4 | 192 37.1 | 09.3 | 209 41.7 | 42.8 | 249 23.7 | 23.1 | Menkar | 314 08.6 | N 4 10.6 |
| 21 | 231 56.1 | 166 31.9 . . | 03.0 | 207 37.9 . . | 10.0 | 224 44.0 . . | 42.8 | 264 26.2 . . | 23.2 | Menkent | 147 59.9 | S36 28.9 |
| 22 | 246 58.5 | 181 31.2 | 03.5 | 222 38.7 | 10.6 | 239 46.2 | 42.9 | 279 28.8 | 23.2 | Miaplacidus | 221 39.4 | S69 48.7 |
| 23 | 262 01.0 | 196 30.6 | 04.1 | 237 39.5 | 11.2 | 254 48.5 | 43.0 | 294 31.3 | 23.2 | | | |
| 29 00 | 277 03.5 | 211 29.9 | N20 04.7 | 252 40.3 | N 8 11.9 | 269 50.7 | N 1 43.1 | 309 33.9 | S14 23.3 | Mirfak | 308 31.6 | N49 56.2 |
| 01 | 292 05.9 | 226 29.3 | 05.3 | 267 41.1 | 12.5 | 284 53.0 | 43.2 | 324 36.4 | 23.3 | Nunki | 75 50.0 | S26 16.1 |
| 02 | 307 08.4 | 241 28.6 | 05.9 | 282 41.9 | 13.2 | 299 55.2 | 43.2 | 339 39.0 | 23.3 | Peacock | 53 08.5 | S56 39.6 |
| 03 | 322 10.9 | 256 27.9 . . | 06.4 | 297 42.7 . . | 13.8 | 314 57.5 . . | 43.3 | 354 41.5 . . | 23.4 | Pollux | 243 20.2 | N27 58.4 |
| 04 | 337 13.3 | 271 27.3 | 07.0 | 312 43.5 | 14.5 | 329 59.7 | 43.4 | 9 44.1 | 23.4 | Procyon | 244 53.4 | N 5 10.1 |
| 05 | 352 15.8 | 286 26.6 | 07.6 | 327 44.3 | 15.1 | 345 02.0 | 43.5 | 24 46.7 | 23.5 | | | |
| 06 | 7 18.2 | 301 26.0 | N20 08.1 | 342 45.1 | N 8 15.8 | 0 04.2 | N 1 43.6 | 39 49.2 | S14 23.5 | Rasalhague | 96 00.2 | N12 32.7 |
| 07 | 22 20.7 | 316 25.3 | 08.7 | 357 45.9 | 16.4 | 15 06.5 | 43.6 | 54 51.8 | 23.5 | Regulus | 207 36.9 | N11 51.6 |
| W 08 | 37 23.2 | 331 24.7 | 09.3 | 12 46.7 | 17.0 | 30 08.7 | 43.7 | 69 54.3 | 23.6 | Rigel | 281 06.2 | S 8 10.5 |
| E 09 | 52 25.6 | 346 24.0 . . | 09.9 | 27 47.5 . . | 17.7 | 45 11.0 . . | 43.8 | 84 56.9 . . | 23.6 | Rigil Kent. | 139 42.8 | S60 55.8 |
| D 10 | 67 28.1 | 1 23.3 | 10.4 | 42 48.2 | 18.3 | 60 13.2 | 43.9 | 99 59.4 | 23.7 | Sabik | 102 04.8 | S15 45.1 |
| N 11 | 82 30.6 | 16 22.7 | 11.0 | 57 49.0 | 19.0 | 75 15.5 | 44.0 | 115 02.0 | 23.7 | | | |
| E 12 | 97 33.0 | 31 22.0 | N20 11.6 | 72 49.8 | N 8 19.6 | 90 17.7 | N 1 44.0 | 130 04.5 | S14 23.7 | Schedar | 349 33.4 | N56 39.3 |
| S 13 | 112 35.5 | 46 21.4 | 12.1 | 87 50.6 | 20.3 | 105 20.0 | 44.1 | 145 07.1 | 23.8 | Shaula | 96 12.8 | S37 07.2 |
| D 14 | 127 38.0 | 61 20.7 | 12.7 | 102 51.4 | 20.9 | 120 22.2 | 44.2 | 160 09.6 | 23.8 | Sirius | 258 28.4 | S16 44.8 |
| A 15 | 142 40.4 | 76 20.0 . . | 13.2 | 117 52.2 . . | 21.5 | 135 24.5 . . | 44.3 | 175 12.2 . . | 23.8 | Spica | 158 24.4 | S11 16.7 |
| Y 16 | 157 42.9 | 91 19.4 | 13.8 | 132 53.0 | 22.2 | 150 26.7 | 44.3 | 190 14.7 | 23.9 | Suhail | 222 48.2 | S43 31.5 |
| 17 | 172 45.4 | 106 18.7 | 14.4 | 147 53.8 | 22.8 | 165 29.0 | 44.4 | 205 17.3 | 23.9 | | | |
| 18 | 187 47.8 | 121 18.1 | N20 14.9 | 162 54.6 | N 8 23.5 | 180 31.2 | N 1 44.5 | 220 19.9 | S14 24.0 | Vega | 80 34.2 | N38 48.2 |
| 19 | 202 50.3 | 136 17.4 | 15.5 | 177 55.4 | 24.1 | 195 33.5 | 44.6 | 235 22.4 | 24.0 | Zuben'ubi | 136 58.1 | S16 08.1 |
| 20 | 217 52.7 | 151 16.7 | 16.1 | 192 56.2 | 24.8 | 210 35.7 | 44.7 | 250 25.0 | 24.0 | | SHA | Mer. Pass. |
| 21 | 232 55.2 | 166 16.1 . . | 16.6 | 207 57.0 . . | 25.4 | 225 38.0 . . | 44.7 | 265 27.5 . . | 24.1 | | ° ′ | h m |
| 22 | 247 57.7 | 181 15.4 | 17.2 | 222 57.8 | 26.0 | 240 40.2 | 44.8 | 280 30.1 | 24.1 | Venus | 295 41.2 | 9 53 |
| 23 | 263 00.1 | 196 14.7 | 17.7 | 237 58.6 | 26.7 | 255 42.5 | 44.9 | 295 32.6 | 24.2 | Mars | 336 17.0 | 7 10 |
| | h m | | | | | | | | | Jupiter | 352 52.5 | 6 03 |
| Mer. Pass. 5 34.8 | v −0.6 | d 0.6 | | v 0.8 | d 0.6 | v 2.2 | d 0.1 | v 2.6 | d 0.0 | Saturn | 32 28.3 | 3 25 |

| UT | SUN GHA | SUN Dec | MOON GHA | v | Dec | d | HP |
|---|---|---|---|---|---|---|---|
| d h | ° ′ | ° ′ | ° ′ | ′ | ° ′ | ′ | ′ |
| 27 00 | 179 14.9 | N23 19.8 | 204 31.6 | 11.7 | N24 03.0 | 6.3 | 54.2 |
| 01 | 194 14.8 | 19.7 | 219 02.3 | 11.5 | 24 09.3 | 6.3 | 54.2 |
| 02 | 209 14.7 | 19.6 | 233 32.8 | 11.6 | 24 15.6 | 6.1 | 54.1 |
| 03 | 224 14.5 | .. 19.5 | 248 03.4 | 11.4 | 24 21.7 | 6.0 | 54.1 |
| 04 | 239 14.4 | 19.4 | 262 33.8 | 11.5 | 24 27.7 | 5.9 | 54.1 |
| 05 | 254 14.3 | 19.3 | 277 04.3 | 11.4 | 24 33.6 | 5.8 | 54.1 |
| 06 | 269 14.1 | N23 19.2 | 291 34.7 | 11.3 | N24 39.4 | 5.7 | 54.1 |
| M 07 | 284 14.0 | 19.1 | 306 05.0 | 11.3 | 24 45.1 | 5.5 | 54.1 |
| O 08 | 299 13.9 | 19.0 | 320 35.3 | 11.3 | 24 50.6 | 5.5 | 54.1 |
| N 09 | 314 13.7 | .. 18.9 | 335 05.6 | 11.2 | 24 56.1 | 5.3 | 54.1 |
| D 10 | 329 13.6 | 18.8 | 349 35.8 | 11.2 | 25 01.4 | 5.2 | 54.1 |
| A 11 | 344 13.5 | 18.7 | 4 06.0 | 11.2 | 25 06.6 | 5.1 | 54.1 |
| Y 12 | 359 13.3 | N23 18.6 | 18 36.2 | 11.1 | N25 11.7 | 5.0 | 54.1 |
| 13 | 14 13.2 | 18.5 | 33 06.3 | 11.1 | 25 16.7 | 4.8 | 54.1 |
| 14 | 29 13.1 | 18.3 | 47 36.4 | 11.0 | 25 21.5 | 4.8 | 54.1 |
| 15 | 44 13.0 | .. 18.2 | 62 06.4 | 11.0 | 25 26.3 | 4.6 | 54.1 |
| 16 | 59 12.8 | 18.1 | 76 36.4 | 11.0 | 25 30.9 | 4.5 | 54.0 |
| 17 | 74 12.7 | 18.0 | 91 06.4 | 10.9 | 25 35.4 | 4.4 | 54.0 |
| 18 | 89 12.6 | N23 17.9 | 105 36.3 | 10.9 | N25 39.8 | 4.2 | 54.0 |
| 19 | 104 12.4 | 17.8 | 120 06.2 | 10.9 | 25 44.0 | 4.1 | 54.0 |
| 20 | 119 12.3 | 17.7 | 134 36.1 | 10.8 | 25 48.1 | 3.9 | 54.0 |
| 21 | 134 12.2 | .. 17.6 | 149 05.9 | 10.8 | 25 52.1 | 3.9 | 54.0 |
| 22 | 149 12.0 | 17.5 | 163 35.7 | 10.8 | 25 56.0 | 3.8 | 54.0 |
| 23 | 164 11.9 | 17.4 | 178 05.5 | 10.8 | 25 59.8 | 3.6 | 54.0 |
| 28 00 | 179 11.8 | N23 17.2 | 192 35.3 | 10.7 | N26 03.4 | 3.5 | 54.0 |
| 01 | 194 11.7 | 17.1 | 207 05.0 | 10.7 | 26 06.9 | 3.4 | 54.0 |
| 02 | 209 11.5 | 17.0 | 221 34.7 | 10.6 | 26 10.3 | 3.3 | 54.0 |
| 03 | 224 11.4 | .. 16.9 | 236 04.3 | 10.7 | 26 13.6 | 3.1 | 54.0 |
| 04 | 239 11.3 | 16.8 | 250 34.0 | 10.6 | 26 16.7 | 3.1 | 54.0 |
| 05 | 254 11.1 | 16.7 | 265 03.6 | 10.6 | 26 19.8 | 2.9 | 54.0 |
| 06 | 269 11.0 | N23 16.6 | 279 33.2 | 10.5 | N26 22.7 | 2.7 | 54.0 |
| T 07 | 284 10.9 | 16.4 | 294 02.7 | 10.6 | 26 25.4 | 2.7 | 54.0 |
| U 08 | 299 10.8 | 16.3 | 308 32.3 | 10.5 | 26 28.1 | 2.5 | 54.0 |
| E 09 | 314 10.6 | .. 16.2 | 323 01.8 | 10.5 | 26 30.6 | 2.4 | 54.0 |
| S 10 | 329 10.5 | 16.1 | 337 31.3 | 10.5 | 26 33.0 | 2.2 | 54.0 |
| D 11 | 344 10.4 | 16.0 | 352 00.8 | 10.4 | 26 35.2 | 2.2 | 54.0 |
| A 12 | 359 10.2 | N23 15.8 | 6 30.2 | 10.5 | N26 37.4 | 2.0 | 54.0 |
| Y 13 | 14 10.1 | 15.7 | 20 59.7 | 10.4 | 26 39.4 | 1.8 | 54.0 |
| 14 | 29 10.0 | 15.6 | 35 29.1 | 10.4 | 26 41.2 | 1.8 | 54.0 |
| 15 | 44 09.9 | .. 15.5 | 49 58.5 | 10.4 | 26 43.0 | 1.6 | 53.9 |
| 16 | 59 09.7 | 15.3 | 64 27.9 | 10.4 | 26 44.6 | 1.5 | 53.9 |
| 17 | 74 09.6 | 15.2 | 78 57.3 | 10.4 | 26 46.1 | 1.4 | 53.9 |
| 18 | 89 09.5 | N23 15.1 | 93 26.7 | 10.4 | N26 47.5 | 1.2 | 53.9 |
| 19 | 104 09.3 | 15.0 | 107 56.1 | 10.3 | 26 48.7 | 1.1 | 53.9 |
| 20 | 119 09.2 | 14.8 | 122 25.4 | 10.4 | 26 49.8 | 1.0 | 53.9 |
| 21 | 134 09.1 | .. 14.7 | 136 54.8 | 10.3 | 26 50.8 | 0.8 | 53.9 |
| 22 | 149 09.0 | 14.6 | 151 24.1 | 10.3 | 26 51.6 | 0.7 | 53.9 |
| 23 | 164 08.8 | 14.5 | 165 53.4 | 10.4 | 26 52.3 | 0.6 | 53.9 |
| 29 00 | 179 08.7 | N23 14.3 | 180 22.8 | 10.3 | N26 52.9 | 0.5 | 53.9 |
| 01 | 194 08.6 | 14.2 | 194 52.1 | 10.3 | 26 53.4 | 0.3 | 53.9 |
| 02 | 209 08.5 | 14.1 | 209 21.4 | 10.3 | 26 53.7 | 0.2 | 53.9 |
| 03 | 224 08.3 | .. 13.9 | 223 50.7 | 10.3 | 26 53.9 | 0.1 | 53.9 |
| 04 | 239 08.2 | 13.8 | 238 20.0 | 10.4 | 26 54.0 | 0.1 | 53.9 |
| 05 | 254 08.1 | 13.7 | 252 49.4 | 10.3 | 26 53.9 | 0.1 | 53.9 |
| 06 | 269 07.9 | N23 13.5 | 267 18.7 | 10.3 | N26 53.8 | 0.3 | 53.9 |
| W 07 | 284 07.8 | 13.4 | 281 48.0 | 10.3 | 26 53.5 | 0.5 | 53.9 |
| E 08 | 299 07.7 | 13.3 | 296 17.3 | 10.4 | 26 53.0 | 0.6 | 53.9 |
| D 09 | 314 07.6 | .. 13.1 | 310 46.7 | 10.3 | 26 52.4 | 0.7 | 53.9 |
| N 10 | 329 07.4 | 13.0 | 325 16.0 | 10.3 | 26 51.7 | 0.8 | 53.9 |
| E 11 | 344 07.3 | 12.8 | 339 45.3 | 10.4 | 26 50.9 | 1.0 | 53.9 |
| S 12 | 359 07.2 | N23 12.7 | 354 14.7 | 10.4 | N26 49.9 | 1.0 | 53.9 |
| D 13 | 14 07.1 | 12.6 | 8 44.1 | 10.3 | 26 48.9 | 1.3 | 53.9 |
| A 14 | 29 06.9 | 12.4 | 23 13.4 | 10.4 | 26 47.6 | 1.3 | 53.9 |
| Y 15 | 44 06.8 | .. 12.3 | 37 42.8 | 10.4 | 26 46.3 | 1.5 | 53.9 |
| 16 | 59 06.7 | 12.1 | 52 12.2 | 10.4 | 26 44.8 | 1.6 | 53.9 |
| 17 | 74 06.6 | 12.0 | 66 41.6 | 10.5 | 26 43.2 | 1.7 | 53.9 |
| 18 | 89 06.4 | N23 11.9 | 81 11.1 | 10.4 | N26 41.5 | 1.9 | 53.9 |
| 19 | 104 06.3 | 11.7 | 95 40.5 | 10.5 | 26 39.6 | 2.0 | 53.9 |
| 20 | 119 06.2 | 11.6 | 110 10.0 | 10.4 | 26 37.6 | 2.1 | 53.9 |
| 21 | 134 06.1 | .. 11.4 | 124 39.4 | 10.5 | 26 35.5 | 2.2 | 53.9 |
| 22 | 149 05.9 | 11.3 | 139 08.9 | 10.5 | 26 33.3 | 2.4 | 54.0 |
| 23 | 164 05.8 | 11.1 | 153 38.4 | 10.6 | N26 30.9 | 2.5 | 54.0 |
| | SD 15.8  d 0.1 | | SD 14.7 | 14.7 | | | 14.7 |

| Lat. | Twilight Naut. | Twilight Civil | Sunrise | Moonrise 27 | 28 | 29 | 30 |
|---|---|---|---|---|---|---|---|
| ° | h m | h m | h m | h m | h m | h m | h m |
| N 72 | ☐ | ☐ | ☐ | ☐ | ☐ | ☐ | ☐ |
| N 70 | ☐ | ☐ | ☐ | ☐ | ☐ | ☐ | ☐ |
| 68 | ☐ | ☐ | ☐ | ☐ | ☐ | ☐ | ☐ |
| 66 | ☐ | ☐ | ☐ | ☐ | ☐ | ☐ | ☐ |
| 64 | //// | //// | 01 36 | 23 26 | ☐ | ☐ | ☐ |
| 62 | //// | //// | 02 13 | 00 35 | 00 45 | 01 14 | 02 19 |
| 60 | //// | 00 57 | 02 39 | 01 01 | 01 21 | 01 58 | 02 59 |
| N 58 | //// | 01 45 | 03 00 | 01 22 | 01 47 | 02 28 | 03 26 |
| 56 | //// | 02 14 | 03 16 | 01 39 | 02 08 | 02 50 | 03 48 |
| 54 | 00 52 | 02 36 | 03 30 | 01 53 | 02 25 | 03 09 | 04 05 |
| 52 | 01 36 | 02 54 | 03 42 | 02 06 | 02 40 | 03 24 | 04 20 |
| 50 | 02 04 | 03 09 | 03 53 | 02 17 | 02 52 | 03 38 | 04 33 |
| 45 | 02 49 | 03 38 | 04 16 | 02 40 | 03 19 | 04 06 | 05 00 |
| N 40 | 03 19 | 04 01 | 04 33 | 02 59 | 03 40 | 04 27 | 05 21 |
| 35 | 03 42 | 04 19 | 04 48 | 03 15 | 03 57 | 04 46 | 05 39 |
| 30 | 04 01 | 04 34 | 05 01 | 03 28 | 04 12 | 05 01 | 05 54 |
| 20 | 04 30 | 04 59 | 05 23 | 03 52 | 04 38 | 05 28 | 06 20 |
| N 10 | 04 52 | 05 19 | 05 42 | 04 12 | 05 00 | 05 50 | 06 42 |
| 0 | 05 11 | 05 37 | 06 00 | 04 31 | 05 21 | 06 12 | 07 02 |
| S 10 | 05 28 | 05 54 | 06 17 | 04 50 | 05 42 | 06 33 | 07 23 |
| 20 | 05 44 | 06 11 | 06 35 | 05 11 | 06 04 | 06 56 | 07 45 |
| 30 | 06 00 | 06 30 | 06 56 | 05 35 | 06 30 | 07 22 | 08 10 |
| 35 | 06 09 | 06 41 | 07 09 | 05 49 | 06 45 | 07 38 | 08 25 |
| 40 | 06 18 | 06 52 | 07 23 | 06 05 | 07 03 | 07 56 | 08 42 |
| 45 | 06 29 | 07 06 | 07 40 | 06 25 | 07 25 | 08 18 | 09 03 |
| S 50 | 06 40 | 07 22 | 08 00 | 06 49 | 07 52 | 08 46 | 09 29 |
| 52 | 06 45 | 07 29 | 08 10 | 07 01 | 08 05 | 08 59 | 09 42 |
| 54 | 06 51 | 07 37 | 08 21 | 07 15 | 08 21 | 09 15 | 09 57 |
| 56 | 06 57 | 07 46 | 08 33 | 07 31 | 08 39 | 09 34 | 10 14 |
| 58 | 07 04 | 07 56 | 08 48 | 07 49 | 09 01 | 09 57 | 10 34 |
| S 60 | 07 11 | 08 08 | 09 05 | 08 13 | 09 30 | 10 27 | 11 00 |

| Lat. | Sunset | Twilight Civil | Twilight Naut. | Moonset 27 | 28 | 29 | 30 |
|---|---|---|---|---|---|---|---|
| ° | h m | h m | h m | h m | h m | h m | h m |
| N 72 | ☐ | ☐ | ☐ | ☐ | ☐ | ☐ | ☐ |
| N 70 | ☐ | ☐ | ☐ | ☐ | ☐ | ☐ | ☐ |
| 68 | ☐ | ☐ | ☐ | ☐ | ☐ | ☐ | ☐ |
| 66 | ☐ | ☐ | ☐ | ☐ | ☐ | ☐ | ☐ |
| 64 | 22 29 | //// | //// | 22 45 | ☐ | ☐ | ☐ |
| 62 | 21 53 | //// | //// | 21 26 | 22 42 | 23 23 | 23 36 |
| 60 | 21 27 | 23 08 | //// | 20 50 | 21 58 | 22 43 | 23 07 |
| N 58 | 21 07 | 22 21 | //// | 20 24 | 21 29 | 22 15 | 22 45 |
| 56 | 20 50 | 21 52 | //// | 20 04 | 21 06 | 21 53 | 22 27 |
| 54 | 20 36 | 21 30 | 23 13 | 19 47 | 20 48 | 21 36 | 22 11 |
| 52 | 20 24 | 21 12 | 22 29 | 19 33 | 20 32 | 21 21 | 21 58 |
| 50 | 20 13 | 20 58 | 22 02 | 19 20 | 20 18 | 21 07 | 21 46 |
| 45 | 19 51 | 20 28 | 21 18 | 18 54 | 19 51 | 20 40 | 21 21 |
| N 40 | 19 33 | 20 06 | 20 47 | 18 33 | 19 29 | 20 19 | 21 02 |
| 35 | 19 18 | 19 48 | 20 24 | 18 16 | 19 11 | 20 01 | 20 45 |
| 30 | 19 05 | 19 33 | 20 06 | 18 02 | 18 55 | 19 46 | 20 31 |
| 20 | 18 43 | 19 08 | 19 37 | 17 37 | 18 29 | 19 20 | 20 07 |
| N 10 | 18 24 | 18 47 | 19 15 | 17 15 | 18 06 | 18 57 | 19 46 |
| 0 | 18 07 | 18 29 | 18 56 | 16 55 | 17 45 | 18 36 | 19 26 |
| S 10 | 17 50 | 18 12 | 18 39 | 16 35 | 17 24 | 18 15 | 19 06 |
| 20 | 17 31 | 17 55 | 18 23 | 16 14 | 17 01 | 17 52 | 18 45 |
| 30 | 17 10 | 17 37 | 18 06 | 15 49 | 16 35 | 17 26 | 18 20 |
| 35 | 16 58 | 17 26 | 17 58 | 15 34 | 16 20 | 17 11 | 18 06 |
| 40 | 16 44 | 17 14 | 17 48 | 15 17 | 16 02 | 16 52 | 17 49 |
| 45 | 16 27 | 17 01 | 17 38 | 14 57 | 15 40 | 16 31 | 17 29 |
| S 50 | 16 07 | 16 45 | 17 27 | 14 32 | 15 12 | 16 03 | 17 03 |
| 52 | 15 57 | 16 38 | 17 21 | 14 20 | 14 59 | 15 49 | 16 50 |
| 54 | 15 46 | 16 30 | 17 16 | 14 06 | 14 43 | 15 34 | 16 36 |
| 56 | 15 33 | 16 21 | 17 10 | 13 50 | 14 25 | 15 15 | 16 19 |
| 58 | 15 19 | 16 10 | 17 03 | 13 31 | 14 03 | 14 52 | 15 59 |
| S 60 | 15 01 | 15 59 | 16 56 | 13 07 | 13 34 | 14 22 | 15 34 |

| | SUN | | | MOON | | | |
|---|---|---|---|---|---|---|---|
| Day | Eqn. of Time 00h | 12h | Mer. Pass. | Mer. Pass. Upper | Lower | Age | Phase |
| d | m s | m s | h m | h m | h m | d | % |
| 27 | 03 00 | 03 06 | 12 03 | 10 43 | 23 08 | 28 | 2 |
| 28 | 03 13 | 03 19 | 12 03 | 11 33 | 23 58 | 29 | 0 |
| 29 | 03 25 | 03 31 | 12 04 | 12 24 | 24 49 | 00 | 0 |

| UT | ARIES GHA | VENUS −3.9 GHA | VENUS Dec | MARS +0.4 GHA | MARS Dec | JUPITER −2.4 GHA | JUPITER Dec | SATURN +0.5 GHA | SATURN Dec | STARS Name | SHA | Dec |
|---|---|---|---|---|---|---|---|---|---|---|---|---|
| **30** 00 | 278 02.6 | 211 14.1 | N20 18.3 | 252 59.4 | N 8 27.3 | 270 44.8 | N 1 45.0 | 310 35.2 | S14 24.2 | Acamar | 315 13.6 | S40 12.7 |
| 01 | 293 05.1 | 226 13.4 | 18.8 | 268 00.1 | 28.0 | 285 47.0 | 45.0 | 325 37.8 | 24.2 | Achernar | 335 21.9 | S57 07.1 |
| 02 | 308 07.5 | 241 12.7 | 19.4 | 283 00.9 | 28.6 | 300 49.3 | 45.1 | 340 40.3 | 24.3 | Acrux | 173 02.4 | S63 13.6 |
| 03 | 323 10.0 | 256 12.1 .. | 19.9 | 298 01.7 .. | 29.2 | 315 51.5 .. | 45.2 | 355 42.9 .. | 24.3 | Adhara | 255 07.9 | S29 00.1 |
| 04 | 338 12.5 | 271 11.4 | 20.5 | 313 02.5 | 29.9 | 330 53.8 | 45.3 | 10 45.4 | 24.4 | Aldebaran | 290 42.3 | N16 33.2 |
| 05 | 353 14.9 | 286 10.7 | 21.0 | 328 03.3 | 30.5 | 345 56.0 | 45.4 | 25 48.0 | 24.4 | | | |
| T 06 | 8 17.4 | 301 10.1 | N20 21.6 | 343 04.1 | N 8 31.2 | 0 58.3 | N 1 45.4 | 40 50.5 | S14 24.4 | Alioth | 166 14.8 | N55 50.6 |
| H 07 | 23 19.9 | 316 09.4 | 22.1 | 358 04.9 | 31.8 | 16 00.5 | 45.5 | 55 53.1 | 24.5 | Alkaid | 152 53.5 | N49 12.4 |
| U 08 | 38 22.3 | 331 08.7 | 22.7 | 13 05.7 | 32.4 | 31 02.8 | 45.6 | 70 55.7 | 24.5 | Alnair | 27 35.3 | S46 51.0 |
| R 09 | 53 24.8 | 346 08.1 .. | 23.2 | 28 06.5 .. | 33.1 | 46 05.1 .. | 45.7 | 85 58.2 .. | 24.6 | Alnilam | 275 40.2 | S 1 11.3 |
| S 10 | 68 27.2 | 1 07.4 | 23.8 | 43 07.3 | 33.7 | 61 07.3 | 45.7 | 101 00.8 | 24.6 | Alphard | 217 50.0 | S 8 45.3 |
| D 11 | 83 29.7 | 16 06.7 | 24.3 | 58 08.1 | 34.3 | 76 09.6 | 45.8 | 116 03.3 | 24.6 | | | |
| A 12 | 98 32.2 | 31 06.1 | N20 24.9 | 73 08.9 | N 8 35.0 | 91 11.8 | N 1 45.9 | 131 05.9 | S14 24.7 | Alphecca | 126 05.2 | N26 38.5 |
| Y 13 | 113 34.6 | 46 05.4 | 25.4 | 88 09.7 | 35.6 | 106 14.1 | 46.0 | 146 08.4 | 24.7 | Alpheratz | 357 36.9 | N29 12.7 |
| 14 | 128 37.1 | 61 04.7 | 26.0 | 103 10.5 | 36.3 | 121 16.3 | 46.0 | 161 11.0 | 24.8 | Altair | 62 01.7 | N 8 55.6 |
| 15 | 143 39.6 | 76 04.0 .. | 26.5 | 118 11.3 .. | 36.9 | 136 18.6 .. | 46.1 | 176 13.6 .. | 24.8 | Ankaa | 353 09.2 | S42 10.9 |
| 16 | 158 42.0 | 91 03.4 | 27.0 | 133 12.1 | 37.5 | 151 20.9 | 46.2 | 191 16.1 | 24.8 | Antares | 112 18.1 | S26 28.9 |
| 17 | 173 44.5 | 106 02.7 | 27.6 | 148 12.9 | 38.2 | 166 23.1 | 46.3 | 206 18.7 | 24.9 | | | |
| 18 | 188 47.0 | 121 02.0 | N20 28.1 | 163 13.7 | N 8 38.8 | 181 25.4 | N 1 46.3 | 221 21.2 | S14 24.9 | Arcturus | 145 49.7 | N19 04.1 |
| 19 | 203 49.4 | 136 01.3 | 28.7 | 178 14.4 | 39.5 | 196 27.6 | 46.4 | 236 23.8 | 25.0 | Atria | 107 13.6 | S69 04.1 |
| 20 | 218 51.9 | 151 00.7 | 29.2 | 193 15.2 | 40.1 | 211 29.9 | 46.5 | 251 26.4 | 25.0 | Avior | 234 16.1 | S59 34.9 |
| 21 | 233 54.4 | 166 00.0 .. | 29.7 | 208 16.0 .. | 40.7 | 226 32.2 .. | 46.6 | 266 28.9 .. | 25.0 | Bellatrix | 278 25.4 | N 6 22.2 |
| 22 | 248 56.8 | 180 59.3 | 30.3 | 223 16.8 | 41.4 | 241 34.4 | 46.6 | 281 31.5 | 25.1 | Betelgeuse | 270 54.7 | N 7 24.7 |
| 23 | 263 59.3 | 195 58.6 | 30.8 | 238 17.6 | 42.0 | 256 36.7 | 46.7 | 296 34.0 | 25.1 | | | |
| **1** 00 | 279 01.7 | 210 58.0 | N20 31.3 | 253 18.4 | N 8 42.6 | 271 38.9 | N 1 46.8 | 311 36.6 | S14 25.2 | Canopus | 263 53.9 | S52 42.4 |
| 01 | 294 04.2 | 225 57.3 | 31.9 | 268 19.2 | 43.3 | 286 41.2 | 46.9 | 326 39.2 | 25.2 | Capella | 280 25.4 | N46 01.1 |
| 02 | 309 06.7 | 240 56.6 | 32.4 | 283 20.0 | 43.9 | 301 43.5 | 46.9 | 341 41.7 | 25.2 | Deneb | 49 26.8 | N45 21.5 |
| 03 | 324 09.1 | 255 55.9 .. | 32.9 | 298 20.8 .. | 44.5 | 316 45.7 .. | 47.0 | 356 44.3 .. | 25.3 | Denebola | 182 27.2 | N14 27.0 |
| 04 | 339 11.6 | 270 55.3 | 33.5 | 313 21.6 | 45.2 | 331 48.0 | 47.1 | 11 46.8 | 25.3 | Diphda | 348 49.4 | S17 51.7 |
| 05 | 354 14.1 | 285 54.6 | 34.0 | 328 22.4 | 45.8 | 346 50.2 | 47.2 | 26 49.4 | 25.4 | | | |
| F 06 | 9 16.5 | 300 53.9 | N20 34.5 | 343 23.2 | N 8 46.4 | 1 52.5 | N 1 47.2 | 41 52.0 | S14 25.4 | Dubhe | 193 43.9 | N61 38.1 |
| R 07 | 24 19.0 | 315 53.2 | 35.1 | 358 24.0 | 47.1 | 16 54.8 | 47.3 | 56 54.5 | 25.4 | Elnath | 278 04.9 | N28 37.5 |
| I 08 | 39 21.5 | 330 52.6 | 35.6 | 13 24.8 | 47.7 | 31 57.0 | 47.4 | 71 57.1 | 25.5 | Eltanin | 90 42.6 | N51 29.2 |
| D 09 | 54 23.9 | 345 51.9 .. | 36.1 | 28 25.6 .. | 48.3 | 46 59.3 .. | 47.5 | 86 59.6 .. | 25.5 | Enif | 33 40.6 | N 9 58.6 |
| A 10 | 69 26.4 | 0 51.2 | 36.6 | 43 26.4 | 49.0 | 62 01.6 | 47.5 | 102 02.2 | 25.6 | Fomalhaut | 15 16.7 | S29 30.1 |
| Y 11 | 84 28.8 | 15 50.5 | 37.2 | 58 27.2 | 49.6 | 77 03.8 | 47.6 | 117 04.8 | 25.6 | | | |
| 12 | 99 31.3 | 30 49.8 | N20 37.7 | 73 28.0 | N 8 50.3 | 92 06.1 | N 1 47.7 | 132 07.3 | S14 25.7 | Gacrux | 171 53.9 | S57 14.5 |
| 13 | 114 33.8 | 45 49.1 | 38.2 | 88 28.8 | 50.9 | 107 08.4 | 47.8 | 147 09.9 | 25.7 | Gienah | 175 45.8 | S17 40.0 |
| 14 | 129 36.2 | 60 48.5 | 38.7 | 103 29.6 | 51.5 | 122 10.6 | 47.8 | 162 12.4 | 25.7 | Hadar | 148 38.7 | S60 29.1 |
| 15 | 144 38.7 | 75 47.8 .. | 39.2 | 118 30.4 .. | 52.2 | 137 12.9 .. | 47.9 | 177 15.0 .. | 25.8 | Hamal | 327 53.7 | N23 33.9 |
| 16 | 159 41.2 | 90 47.1 | 39.8 | 133 31.1 | 52.8 | 152 15.1 | 48.0 | 192 17.6 | 25.8 | Kaus Aust. | 83 34.9 | S34 22.4 |
| 17 | 174 43.6 | 105 46.4 | 40.3 | 148 31.9 | 53.4 | 167 17.4 | 48.0 | 207 20.1 | 25.9 | | | |
| 18 | 189 46.1 | 120 45.7 | N20 40.8 | 163 32.7 | N 8 54.1 | 182 19.7 | N 1 48.1 | 222 22.7 | S14 25.9 | Kochab | 137 19.1 | N74 04.1 |
| 19 | 204 48.6 | 135 45.1 | 41.3 | 178 33.5 | 54.7 | 197 21.9 | 48.2 | 237 25.3 | 25.9 | Markab | 13 31.8 | N15 19.4 |
| 20 | 219 51.0 | 150 44.4 | 41.8 | 193 34.3 | 55.3 | 212 24.2 | 48.3 | 252 27.8 | 26.0 | Menkar | 314 08.5 | N 4 10.6 |
| 21 | 234 53.5 | 165 43.7 .. | 42.3 | 208 35.1 .. | 55.9 | 227 26.5 .. | 48.3 | 267 30.4 .. | 26.0 | Menkent | 147 59.9 | S36 28.9 |
| 22 | 249 56.0 | 180 43.0 | 42.9 | 223 35.9 | 56.6 | 242 28.7 | 48.4 | 282 32.9 | 26.1 | Miaplacidus | 221 39.4 | S69 48.7 |
| 23 | 264 58.4 | 195 42.3 | 43.4 | 238 36.7 | 57.2 | 257 31.0 | 48.5 | 297 35.5 | 26.1 | | | |
| **2** 00 | 280 00.9 | 210 41.6 | N20 43.9 | 253 37.5 | N 8 57.8 | 272 33.3 | N 1 48.6 | 312 38.1 | S14 26.1 | Mirfak | 308 31.6 | N49 56.2 |
| 01 | 295 03.3 | 225 40.9 | 44.4 | 268 38.3 | 58.5 | 287 35.5 | 48.6 | 327 40.6 | 26.2 | Nunki | 75 50.0 | S26 16.1 |
| 02 | 310 05.8 | 240 40.3 | 44.9 | 283 39.1 | 59.1 | 302 37.8 | 48.7 | 342 43.2 | 26.2 | Peacock | 53 08.5 | S56 39.6 |
| 03 | 325 08.3 | 255 39.6 .. | 45.4 | 298 39.9 | 8 59.7 | 317 40.1 .. | 48.8 | 357 45.8 .. | 26.3 | Pollux | 243 20.2 | N27 58.4 |
| 04 | 340 10.7 | 270 38.9 | 45.9 | 313 40.7 | 9 00.4 | 332 42.3 | 48.8 | 12 48.3 | 26.3 | Procyon | 244 53.3 | N 5 10.1 |
| 05 | 355 13.2 | 285 38.2 | 46.4 | 328 41.5 | 01.0 | 347 44.6 | 48.9 | 27 50.9 | 26.4 | | | |
| S 06 | 10 15.7 | 300 37.5 | N20 46.9 | 343 42.3 | N 9 01.6 | 2 46.9 | N 1 49.0 | 42 53.5 | S14 26.4 | Rasalhague | 96 00.1 | N12 32.7 |
| A 07 | 25 18.1 | 315 36.8 | 47.4 | 358 43.1 | 02.3 | 17 49.2 | 49.1 | 57 56.0 | 26.4 | Regulus | 207 36.9 | N11 51.6 |
| T 08 | 40 20.6 | 330 36.1 | 47.9 | 13 43.9 | 02.9 | 32 51.4 | 49.1 | 72 58.6 | 26.5 | Rigel | 281 06.2 | S 8 10.5 |
| U 09 | 55 23.1 | 345 35.4 .. | 48.4 | 28 44.7 .. | 03.5 | 47 53.7 .. | 49.2 | 88 01.1 .. | 26.5 | Rigil Kent. | 139 42.8 | S60 55.8 |
| R 10 | 70 25.5 | 0 34.7 | 48.9 | 43 45.5 | 04.1 | 62 56.0 | 49.3 | 103 03.7 | 26.6 | Sabik | 102 04.8 | S15 45.1 |
| D 11 | 85 28.0 | 15 34.1 | 49.4 | 58 46.3 | 04.8 | 77 58.2 | 49.3 | 118 06.3 | 26.6 | | | |
| A 12 | 100 30.5 | 30 33.4 | N20 49.9 | 73 47.1 | N 9 05.4 | 93 00.5 | N 1 49.4 | 133 08.8 | S14 26.7 | Schedar | 349 33.4 | N56 39.3 |
| Y 13 | 115 32.9 | 45 32.7 | 50.4 | 88 47.9 | 06.0 | 108 02.8 | 49.5 | 148 11.4 | 26.7 | Shaula | 96 12.8 | S37 07.2 |
| 14 | 130 35.4 | 60 32.0 | 50.9 | 103 48.7 | 06.7 | 123 05.0 | 49.5 | 163 14.0 | 26.7 | Sirius | 258 28.4 | S16 44.8 |
| 15 | 145 37.8 | 75 31.3 .. | 51.4 | 118 49.5 .. | 07.3 | 138 07.3 .. | 49.6 | 178 16.5 .. | 26.8 | Spica | 158 24.4 | S11 16.7 |
| 16 | 160 40.3 | 90 30.6 | 51.9 | 133 50.3 | 07.9 | 153 09.6 | 49.7 | 193 19.1 | 26.8 | Suhail | 222 48.2 | S43 31.5 |
| 17 | 175 42.8 | 105 29.9 | 52.4 | 148 51.1 | 08.5 | 168 11.9 | 49.8 | 208 21.7 | 26.9 | | | |
| 18 | 190 45.2 | 120 29.2 | N20 52.9 | 163 51.9 | N 9 09.2 | 183 14.1 | N 1 49.8 | 223 24.2 | S14 26.9 | Vega | 80 34.2 | N38 48.3 |
| 19 | 205 47.7 | 135 28.5 | 53.4 | 178 52.7 | 09.8 | 198 16.4 | 49.9 | 238 26.8 | 26.9 | Zuben'ubi | 136 58.1 | S16 08.1 |
| 20 | 220 50.2 | 150 27.8 | 53.9 | 193 53.5 | 10.4 | 213 18.7 | 50.0 | 253 29.4 | 27.0 | | SHA | Mer. Pass. |
| 21 | 235 52.6 | 165 27.1 .. | 54.4 | 208 54.3 .. | 11.1 | 228 20.9 .. | 50.0 | 268 31.9 .. | 27.0 | | | |
| 22 | 250 55.1 | 180 26.4 | 54.9 | 223 55.1 | 11.7 | 243 23.2 | 50.1 | 283 34.5 | 27.1 | Venus | 291 56.2 | 9 57 |
| 23 | 265 57.6 | 195 25.7 | 55.4 | 238 55.9 | 12.3 | 258 25.5 | 50.2 | 298 37.1 | 27.1 | Mars | 334 16.7 | 7 06 |
| Mer. Pass. | 5 23.0 | v −0.7 | d 0.5 | v 0.8 | d 0.6 | v 2.3 | d 0.1 | v 2.6 | d 0.0 | Jupiter | 352 37.2 | 5 53 |
| | | | | | | | | | | Saturn | 32 34.8 | 3 13 |

### SUN and MOON

| UT | SUN GHA | SUN Dec | MOON GHA | v | MOON Dec | d | HP |
|---|---|---|---|---|---|---|---|
| **30** d h | ° ′ | ° ′ | ° ′ | ′ | ° ′ | ′ | ′ |
| 00 | 179 05.7 | N23 11.0 | 168 08.0 | 10.5 | N26 28.4 | 2.6 | 54.0 |
| 01 | 194 05.6 | 10.8 | 182 37.5 | 10.6 | 26 25.8 | 2.7 | 54.0 |
| 02 | 209 05.4 | 10.7 | 197 07.1 | 10.6 | 26 23.1 | 2.9 | 54.0 |
| 03 | 224 05.3 | .. 10.5 | 211 36.7 | 10.6 | 26 20.2 | 3.0 | 54.0 |
| 04 | 239 05.2 | 10.4 | 226 06.3 | 10.7 | 26 17.2 | 3.1 | 54.0 |
| 05 | 254 05.1 | 10.2 | 240 36.0 | 10.7 | 26 14.1 | 3.3 | 54.0 |
| **T** 06 | 269 04.9 | N23 10.1 | 255 05.7 | 10.7 | N26 10.8 | 3.3 | 54.0 |
| **H** 07 | 284 04.8 | 09.9 | 269 35.4 | 10.7 | 26 07.5 | 3.5 | 54.0 |
| **U** 08 | 299 04.7 | 09.8 | 284 05.1 | 10.8 | 26 04.0 | 3.6 | 54.0 |
| **R** 09 | 314 04.6 | .. 09.6 | 298 34.9 | 10.8 | 26 00.4 | 3.8 | 54.0 |
| **S** 10 | 329 04.4 | 09.5 | 313 04.7 | 10.8 | 25 56.6 | 3.9 | 54.0 |
| **D** 11 | 344 04.3 | 09.3 | 327 34.5 | 10.9 | 25 52.7 | 3.9 | 54.0 |
| **A** 12 | 359 04.2 | N23 09.2 | 342 04.4 | 10.9 | N25 48.8 | 4.1 | 54.0 |
| **Y** 13 | 14 04.1 | 09.0 | 356 34.3 | 10.9 | 25 44.7 | 4.3 | 54.0 |
| 14 | 29 03.9 | 08.9 | 11 04.2 | 11.0 | 25 40.4 | 4.3 | 54.0 |
| 15 | 44 03.8 | .. 08.7 | 25 34.2 | 11.0 | 25 36.1 | 4.5 | 54.0 |
| 16 | 59 03.7 | 08.5 | 40 04.2 | 11.0 | 25 31.6 | 4.6 | 54.0 |
| 17 | 74 03.6 | 08.4 | 54 34.2 | 11.1 | 25 27.0 | 4.7 | 54.0 |
| 18 | 89 03.4 | N23 08.2 | 69 04.3 | 11.1 | N25 22.3 | 4.8 | 54.0 |
| 19 | 104 03.3 | 08.1 | 83 34.4 | 11.1 | 25 17.5 | 5.0 | 54.0 |
| 20 | 119 03.2 | 07.9 | 98 04.5 | 11.2 | 25 12.5 | 5.0 | 54.0 |
| 21 | 134 03.1 | .. 07.7 | 112 34.7 | 11.2 | 25 07.5 | 5.2 | 54.1 |
| 22 | 149 03.0 | 07.6 | 127 04.9 | 11.3 | 25 02.3 | 5.3 | 54.1 |
| 23 | 164 02.8 | 07.4 | 141 35.2 | 11.3 | 24 57.0 | 5.4 | 54.1 |
| **1** 00 | 179 02.7 | N23 07.2 | 156 05.5 | 11.3 | N24 51.6 | 5.6 | 54.1 |
| 01 | 194 02.6 | 07.1 | 170 35.0 | 11.4 | 24 46.0 | 5.6 | 54.1 |
| 02 | 209 02.5 | 06.9 | 185 06.2 | 11.4 | 24 40.4 | 5.8 | 54.1 |
| 03 | 224 02.3 | .. 06.7 | 199 36.6 | 11.5 | 24 34.6 | 5.9 | 54.1 |
| 04 | 239 02.2 | 06.6 | 214 07.1 | 11.5 | 24 28.7 | 6.0 | 54.1 |
| 05 | 254 02.1 | 06.4 | 228 37.6 | 11.6 | 24 22.7 | 6.1 | 54.1 |
| **F** 06 | 269 02.0 | N23 06.2 | 243 08.2 | 11.6 | N24 16.6 | 6.2 | 54.1 |
| **R** 07 | 284 01.9 | 06.1 | 257 38.8 | 11.6 | 24 10.4 | 6.3 | 54.1 |
| **I** 08 | 299 01.7 | 05.9 | 272 09.4 | 11.7 | 24 04.1 | 6.5 | 54.1 |
| **D** 09 | 314 01.6 | .. 05.7 | 286 40.1 | 11.8 | 23 57.6 | 6.5 | 54.1 |
| **A** 10 | 329 01.5 | 05.6 | 301 10.9 | 11.7 | 23 51.1 | 6.7 | 54.1 |
| **Y** 11 | 344 01.4 | 05.4 | 315 41.6 | 11.9 | 23 44.4 | 6.8 | 54.2 |
| 12 | 359 01.2 | N23 05.2 | 330 12.5 | 11.9 | N23 37.6 | 6.8 | 54.2 |
| 13 | 14 01.1 | 05.0 | 344 43.4 | 11.9 | 23 30.8 | 7.0 | 54.2 |
| 14 | 29 01.0 | 04.9 | 359 14.3 | 12.0 | 23 23.8 | 7.1 | 54.2 |
| 15 | 44 00.9 | .. 04.7 | 13 45.3 | 12.0 | 23 16.7 | 7.2 | 54.2 |
| 16 | 59 00.8 | 04.5 | 28 16.3 | 12.0 | 23 09.5 | 7.3 | 54.2 |
| 17 | 74 00.6 | 04.3 | 42 47.3 | 12.2 | 23 02.2 | 7.4 | 54.2 |
| 18 | 89 00.5 | N23 04.2 | 57 18.5 | 12.1 | N22 54.8 | 7.6 | 54.2 |
| 19 | 104 00.4 | 04.0 | 71 49.6 | 12.2 | 22 47.2 | 7.6 | 54.2 |
| 20 | 119 00.3 | 03.8 | 86 20.8 | 12.3 | 22 39.6 | 7.7 | 54.2 |
| 21 | 134 00.2 | .. 03.6 | 100 52.1 | 12.3 | 22 31.9 | 7.8 | 54.3 |
| 22 | 149 00.0 | 03.5 | 115 23.4 | 12.4 | 22 24.1 | 8.0 | 54.3 |
| 23 | 163 59.9 | 03.3 | 129 54.8 | 12.4 | 22 16.1 | 8.0 | 54.3 |
| **2** 00 | 178 59.8 | N23 03.1 | 144 26.2 | 12.4 | N22 08.1 | 8.1 | 54.3 |
| 01 | 193 59.7 | 02.9 | 158 57.6 | 12.5 | 22 00.0 | 8.3 | 54.3 |
| 02 | 208 59.6 | 02.7 | 173 29.1 | 12.6 | 21 51.7 | 8.3 | 54.3 |
| 03 | 223 59.4 | .. 02.5 | 188 00.7 | 12.6 | 21 43.4 | 8.4 | 54.3 |
| 04 | 238 59.3 | 02.4 | 202 32.3 | 12.7 | 21 35.0 | 8.6 | 54.3 |
| 05 | 253 59.2 | 02.2 | 217 04.0 | 12.7 | 21 26.4 | 8.6 | 54.3 |
| **S** 06 | 268 59.1 | N23 02.0 | 231 35.7 | 12.7 | N21 17.8 | 8.7 | 54.4 |
| **A** 07 | 283 59.0 | 01.8 | 246 07.4 | 12.8 | 21 09.1 | 8.8 | 54.4 |
| **T** 08 | 298 58.9 | 01.6 | 260 39.2 | 12.9 | 21 00.3 | 9.0 | 54.4 |
| **U** 09 | 313 58.7 | .. 01.4 | 275 11.1 | 12.9 | 20 51.3 | 9.0 | 54.4 |
| **R** 10 | 328 58.6 | 01.2 | 289 43.0 | 12.9 | 20 42.3 | 9.1 | 54.4 |
| **D** 11 | 343 58.5 | 01.1 | 304 14.9 | 13.0 | 20 33.2 | 9.2 | 54.4 |
| **A** 12 | 358 58.4 | N23 00.9 | 318 46.9 | 13.1 | N20 24.0 | 9.2 | 54.4 |
| **Y** 13 | 13 58.3 | 00.7 | 333 19.0 | 13.1 | 20 14.8 | 9.4 | 54.4 |
| 14 | 28 58.1 | 00.5 | 347 51.1 | 13.1 | 20 05.4 | 9.5 | 54.5 |
| 15 | 43 58.0 | .. 00.3 | 2 23.2 | 13.2 | 19 55.9 | 9.6 | 54.5 |
| 16 | 58 57.9 | 23 00.1 | 16 55.4 | 13.2 | 19 46.3 | 9.6 | 54.5 |
| 17 | 73 57.8 | 22 59.9 | 31 27.6 | 13.3 | 19 36.7 | 9.7 | 54.5 |
| 18 | 88 57.7 | N22 59.7 | 45 59.9 | 13.4 | N19 27.0 | 9.9 | 54.5 |
| 19 | 103 57.6 | 59.5 | 60 32.3 | 13.3 | 19 17.1 | 9.9 | 54.5 |
| 20 | 118 57.4 | 59.3 | 75 04.6 | 13.5 | 19 07.2 | 10.0 | 54.5 |
| 21 | 133 57.3 | .. 59.1 | 89 37.1 | 13.4 | 18 57.2 | 10.1 | 54.6 |
| 22 | 148 57.2 | 58.9 | 104 09.5 | 13.6 | 18 47.1 | 10.1 | 54.6 |
| 23 | 163 57.1 | 58.7 | 118 42.1 | 13.5 | N18 37.0 | 10.3 | 54.6 |
| | SD 15.8 | d 0.2 | SD 14.7 | | 14.8 | | 14.8 |

### Twilight — Sunrise — Moonrise

| Lat. | Naut. | Civil | Sunrise | 30 | 1 | 2 | 3 |
|---|---|---|---|---|---|---|---|
| ° | h m | h m | h m | h m | h m | h m | h m |
| N 72 | □ | □ | □ | □ | □ | □ | 04 01 |
| N 70 | □ | □ | □ | □ | □ | □ | 05 19 |
| 68 | □ | □ | □ | □ | □ | 03 15 | 05 56 |
| 66 | //// | //// | 00 19 | □ | □ | 04 23 | 06 22 |
| 64 | //// | //// | 01 41 | □ | 03 06 | 04 59 | 06 42 |
| 62 | //// | //// | 02 17 | 02 19 | 03 49 | 05 24 | 06 58 |
| 60 | //// | 01 03 | 02 42 | 02 59 | 04 18 | 05 44 | 07 13 |
| N 58 | //// | 01 48 | 03 02 | 03 26 | 04 40 | 06 00 | 07 23 |
| 56 | //// | 02 17 | 03 18 | 03 48 | 04 57 | 06 14 | 07 33 |
| 54 | 00 58 | 02 38 | 03 32 | 04 05 | 05 13 | 06 26 | 07 42 |
| 52 | 01 40 | 02 56 | 03 44 | 04 20 | 05 26 | 06 36 | 07 49 |
| 50 | 02 06 | 03 11 | 03 55 | 04 33 | 05 37 | 06 46 | 07 56 |
| 45 | 02 51 | 03 40 | 04 17 | 05 00 | 06 01 | 07 05 | 08 11 |
| N 40 | 03 21 | 04 02 | 04 35 | 05 21 | 06 20 | 07 21 | 08 24 |
| 35 | 03 44 | 04 20 | 04 50 | 05 39 | 06 36 | 07 35 | 08 34 |
| 30 | 04 02 | 04 35 | 05 02 | 05 54 | 06 49 | 07 46 | 08 43 |
| 20 | 04 31 | 05 00 | 05 24 | 06 20 | 07 13 | 08 06 | 08 58 |
| N 10 | 04 53 | 05 20 | 05 43 | 06 42 | 07 33 | 08 23 | 09 12 |
| 0 | 05 12 | 05 38 | 06 00 | 07 02 | 07 51 | 08 39 | 09 24 |
| S 10 | 05 28 | 05 55 | 06 17 | 07 23 | 08 10 | 08 55 | 09 37 |
| 20 | 05 44 | 06 12 | 06 36 | 07 45 | 08 30 | 09 12 | 09 50 |
| 30 | 06 00 | 06 30 | 06 57 | 08 10 | 08 53 | 09 31 | 10 06 |
| 35 | 06 09 | 06 41 | 07 09 | 08 25 | 09 07 | 09 43 | 10 14 |
| 40 | 06 18 | 06 52 | 07 23 | 08 42 | 09 22 | 09 56 | 10 24 |
| 45 | 06 28 | 07 06 | 07 39 | 09 03 | 09 40 | 10 11 | 10 36 |
| S 50 | 06 40 | 07 21 | 08 00 | 09 29 | 10 03 | 10 29 | 10 50 |
| 52 | 06 45 | 07 29 | 08 09 | 09 42 | 10 14 | 10 38 | 10 57 |
| 54 | 06 51 | 07 37 | 08 20 | 09 57 | 10 27 | 10 48 | 11 04 |
| 56 | 06 57 | 07 46 | 08 33 | 10 14 | 10 41 | 10 59 | 11 12 |
| 58 | 07 03 | 07 56 | 08 47 | 10 34 | 10 57 | 11 12 | 11 21 |
| S 60 | 07 11 | 08 07 | 09 04 | 11 00 | 11 17 | 11 26 | 11 31 |

### Sunset — Twilight — Moonset

| Lat. | Sunset | Civil | Naut. | 30 | 1 | 2 | 3 |
|---|---|---|---|---|---|---|---|
| ° | h m | h m | h m | h m | h m | h m | h m |
| N 72 | □ | □ | □ | □ | □ | □ | 02 44 |
| N 70 | □ | □ | □ | □ | □ | □ | 01 25 |
| 68 | □ | □ | □ | □ | □ | 01 52 | 00 47 |
| 66 | 23 40 | //// | //// | □ | 00 43 | 00 20 | 00 19 |
| 64 | 22 25 | //// | //// | □ | (00 07) | (23 56) | 23 52 |
| 62 | 21 50 | //// | //// | 23 36 | 23 41 | 23 41 | 23 41 |
| 60 | 21 25 | 23 03 | //// | 23 07 | 23 20 | 23 27 | 23 31 |
| N 58 | 21 05 | 22 18 | //// | 22 45 | 23 03 | 23 15 | 23 23 |
| 56 | 20 49 | 21 50 | //// | 22 27 | 22 49 | 23 04 | 23 15 |
| 54 | 20 35 | 21 29 | 23 08 | 22 11 | 22 36 | 22 55 | 23 09 |
| 52 | 20 23 | 21 11 | 22 27 | 21 58 | 22 25 | 22 46 | 23 03 |
| 50 | 20 13 | 20 57 | 22 01 | 21 46 | 22 16 | 22 39 | 22 58 |
| 45 | 19 50 | 20 28 | 21 17 | 21 21 | 21 55 | 22 23 | 22 46 |
| N 40 | 19 33 | 20 05 | 20 47 | 21 02 | 21 38 | 22 09 | 22 36 |
| 35 | 19 18 | 19 48 | 20 24 | 20 45 | 21 24 | 21 58 | 22 28 |
| 30 | 19 05 | 19 33 | 20 06 | 20 31 | 21 12 | 21 48 | 22 21 |
| 20 | 18 44 | 19 08 | 19 37 | 20 07 | 20 51 | 21 31 | 22 08 |
| N 10 | 18 25 | 18 48 | 19 15 | 19 46 | 20 32 | 21 15 | 21 56 |
| 0 | 18 08 | 18 30 | 18 56 | 19 26 | 20 15 | 21 01 | 21 46 |
| S 10 | 17 50 | 18 13 | 18 39 | 19 06 | 19 57 | 20 47 | 21 35 |
| 20 | 17 32 | 17 56 | 18 24 | 18 45 | 19 38 | 20 31 | 21 23 |
| 30 | 17 11 | 17 38 | 18 07 | 18 20 | 19 17 | 20 14 | 21 10 |
| 35 | 16 59 | 17 27 | 17 59 | 18 06 | 19 04 | 20 03 | 21 02 |
| 40 | 16 45 | 17 16 | 17 50 | 17 49 | 18 49 | 19 51 | 20 54 |
| 45 | 16 29 | 17 02 | 17 40 | 17 29 | 18 31 | 19 37 | 20 43 |
| S 50 | 16 08 | 16 47 | 17 28 | 17 03 | 18 09 | 19 19 | 20 31 |
| 52 | 15 59 | 16 39 | 17 23 | 16 50 | 17 59 | 19 11 | 20 23 |
| 54 | 15 48 | 16 31 | 17 17 | 16 36 | 17 47 | 19 02 | 20 18 |
| 56 | 15 35 | 16 22 | 17 11 | 16 19 | 17 33 | 18 52 | 20 11 |
| 58 | 15 21 | 16 12 | 17 05 | 15 59 | 17 17 | 18 40 | 20 03 |
| S 60 | 15 04 | 16 01 | 16 58 | 15 34 | 16 58 | 18 26 | 19 53 |

### SUN and MOON — Eqn. of Time / Mer. Pass. / Age / Phase

| Day | Eqn. of Time 00h | Eqn. of Time 12h | Mer. Pass. | Mer. Pass. Upper | Mer. Pass. Lower | Age | Phase |
|---|---|---|---|---|---|---|---|
| d | m s | m s | h m | h m | h m | d | % |
| 30 | 03 37 | 03 43 | 12 04 | 13 14 | 00 49 | 01 | 2 |
| 1 | 03 49 | 03 55 | 12 04 | 14 03 | 01 39 | 02 | 5 |
| 2 | 04 01 | 04 06 | 12 04 | 14 50 | 02 27 | 03 | 10 |

| UT | ARIES | VENUS −3.9 | | MARS +0.4 | | JUPITER −2.4 | | SATURN +0.4 | | STARS | | |
|---|---|---|---|---|---|---|---|---|---|---|---|---|
| | GHA | GHA | Dec | GHA | Dec | GHA | Dec | GHA | Dec | Name | SHA | Dec |
| d h | ° ′ | ° ′ | ° ′ | ° ′ | ° ′ | ° ′ | ° ′ | ° ′ | ° ′ | | ° ′ | ° ′ |
| 3 00 | 281 00.0 | 210 25.0 | N20 55.9 | 253 56.6 | N 9 12.9 | 273 27.8 | N 1 50.2 | 313 39.6 | S14 27.2 | Acamar | 315 13.6 | S40 12.7 |
| 01 | 296 02.5 | 225 24.3 | 56.4 | 268 57.4 | 13.6 | 288 30.0 | 50.3 | 328 42.2 | 27.2 | Achernar | 335 21.9 | S57 07.1 |
| 02 | 311 05.0 | 240 23.6 | 56.9 | 283 58.2 | 14.2 | 303 32.3 | 50.4 | 343 44.8 | 27.2 | Acrux | 173 02.4 | S63 13.6 |
| 03 | 326 07.4 | 255 22.9 .. | 57.3 | 298 59.0 .. | 14.8 | 318 34.6 .. | 50.4 | 358 47.3 .. | 27.3 | Adhara | 255 07.9 | S29 00.1 |
| 04 | 341 09.9 | 270 22.2 | 57.8 | 313 59.8 | 15.4 | 333 36.9 | 50.5 | 13 49.9 | 27.3 | Aldebaran | 290 42.3 | N16 33.2 |
| 05 | 356 12.3 | 285 21.6 | 58.3 | 329 00.6 | 16.1 | 348 39.1 | 50.6 | 28 52.5 | 27.4 | | | |
| 06 | 11 14.8 | 300 20.9 | N20 58.8 | 344 01.4 | N 9 16.7 | 3 41.4 | N 1 50.6 | 43 55.0 | S14 27.4 | Alioth | 166 14.8 | N55 50.6 |
| 07 | 26 17.3 | 315 20.2 | 59.3 | 359 02.2 | 17.3 | 18 43.7 | 50.7 | 58 57.6 | 27.5 | Alkaid | 152 53.5 | N49 12.4 |
| 08 | 41 19.7 | 330 19.5 | 20 59.8 | 14 03.0 | 18.0 | 33 46.0 | 50.8 | 74 00.2 | 27.5 | Alnair | 27 35.2 | S46 51.0 |
| S 09 | 56 22.2 | 345 18.8 | 21 00.3 | 29 03.8 .. | 18.6 | 48 48.2 .. | 50.9 | 89 02.7 .. | 27.5 | Alnilam | 275 40.2 | S 1 11.2 |
| U 10 | 71 24.7 | 0 18.1 | 00.7 | 44 04.6 | 19.2 | 63 50.5 | 50.9 | 104 05.3 | 27.6 | Alphard | 217 50.1 | S 8 45.3 |
| N 11 | 86 27.1 | 15 17.4 | 01.2 | 59 05.4 | 19.8 | 78 52.8 | 51.0 | 119 07.9 | 27.6 | | | |
| D 12 | 101 29.6 | 30 16.7 | N21 01.7 | 74 06.2 | N 9 20.5 | 93 55.1 | N 1 51.1 | 134 10.4 | S14 27.7 | Alphecca | 126 05.3 | N26 38.5 |
| A 13 | 116 32.1 | 45 16.0 | 02.1 | 89 07.0 | 21.1 | 108 57.4 | 51.1 | 149 13.0 | 27.7 | Alpheratz | 357 36.8 | N29 12.7 |
| Y 14 | 131 34.5 | 60 15.2 | 02.6 | 104 07.8 | 21.7 | 123 59.6 | 51.2 | 164 15.6 | 27.8 | Altair | 62 01.6 | N 8 55.6 |
| 15 | 146 37.0 | 75 14.5 .. | 03.1 | 119 08.6 .. | 22.3 | 139 01.9 .. | 51.3 | 179 18.1 .. | 27.8 | Ankaa | 353 09.2 | S42 10.9 |
| 16 | 161 39.4 | 90 13.8 | 03.6 | 134 09.4 | 22.9 | 154 04.2 | 51.3 | 194 20.7 | 27.9 | Antares | 112 18.1 | S26 28.9 |
| 17 | 176 41.9 | 105 13.1 | 04.0 | 149 10.2 | 23.6 | 169 06.5 | 51.4 | 209 23.3 | 27.9 | | | |
| 18 | 191 44.4 | 120 12.4 | N21 04.5 | 164 11.0 | N 9 24.2 | 184 08.7 | N 1 51.5 | 224 25.8 | S14 27.9 | Arcturus | 145 49.7 | N19 04.1 |
| 19 | 206 46.8 | 135 11.7 | 05.0 | 179 11.8 | 24.8 | 199 11.0 | 51.5 | 239 28.4 | 28.0 | Atria | 107 13.6 | S69 04.1 |
| 20 | 221 49.3 | 150 11.0 | 05.5 | 194 12.6 | 25.4 | 214 13.3 | 51.6 | 254 31.0 | 28.0 | Avior | 234 16.2 | S59 34.9 |
| 21 | 236 51.8 | 165 10.3 .. | 05.9 | 209 13.4 .. | 26.1 | 229 15.6 .. | 51.7 | 269 33.6 .. | 28.1 | Bellatrix | 278 25.4 | N 6 22.2 |
| 22 | 251 54.2 | 180 09.6 | 06.4 | 224 14.2 | 26.7 | 244 17.9 | 51.7 | 284 36.1 | 28.1 | Betelgeuse | 270 54.7 | N 7 24.7 |
| 23 | 266 56.7 | 195 08.9 | 06.9 | 239 15.0 | 27.3 | 259 20.1 | 51.8 | 299 38.7 | 28.2 | | | |
| 4 00 | 281 59.2 | 210 08.2 | N21 07.3 | 254 15.8 | N 9 27.9 | 274 22.4 | N 1 51.9 | 314 41.3 | S14 28.2 | Canopus | 263 53.9 | S52 42.4 |
| 01 | 297 01.6 | 225 07.5 | 07.8 | 269 16.6 | 28.6 | 289 24.7 | 51.9 | 329 43.8 | 28.2 | Capella | 280 25.4 | N46 01.1 |
| 02 | 312 04.1 | 240 06.8 | 08.3 | 284 17.4 | 29.2 | 304 27.0 | 52.0 | 344 46.4 | 28.3 | Deneb | 49 26.8 | N45 21.5 |
| 03 | 327 06.6 | 255 06.1 .. | 08.7 | 299 18.2 .. | 29.8 | 319 29.3 .. | 52.1 | 359 49.0 .. | 28.3 | Denebola | 182 27.2 | N14 27.0 |
| 04 | 342 09.0 | 270 05.4 | 09.2 | 314 19.0 | 30.4 | 334 31.5 | 52.1 | 14 51.5 | 28.4 | Diphda | 348 49.4 | S17 51.7 |
| 05 | 357 11.5 | 285 04.7 | 09.6 | 329 19.8 | 31.0 | 349 33.8 | 52.2 | 29 54.1 | 28.4 | | | |
| 06 | 12 13.9 | 300 04.0 | N21 10.1 | 344 20.6 | N 9 31.7 | 4 36.1 | N 1 52.2 | 44 56.7 | S14 28.5 | Dubhe | 193 43.9 | N61 38.1 |
| 07 | 27 16.4 | 315 03.3 | 10.6 | 359 21.4 | 32.3 | 19 38.4 | 52.3 | 59 59.3 | 28.5 | Elnath | 278 04.9 | N28 37.5 |
| 08 | 42 18.9 | 330 02.5 | 11.0 | 14 22.2 | 32.9 | 34 40.7 | 52.4 | 75 01.8 | 28.6 | Eltanin | 90 42.6 | N51 29.2 |
| M 09 | 57 21.3 | 345 01.8 .. | 11.5 | 29 23.0 .. | 33.5 | 49 43.0 .. | 52.4 | 90 04.4 .. | 28.6 | Enif | 33 40.6 | N 9 58.6 |
| O 10 | 72 23.8 | 0 01.1 | 11.9 | 44 23.8 | 34.1 | 64 45.2 | 52.5 | 105 07.0 | 28.6 | Fomalhaut | 15 16.6 | S29 30.1 |
| N 11 | 87 26.3 | 15 00.4 | 12.4 | 59 24.6 | 34.8 | 79 47.5 | 52.6 | 120 09.5 | 28.7 | | | |
| D 12 | 102 28.7 | 29 59.7 | N21 12.8 | 74 25.4 | N 9 35.4 | 94 49.8 | N 1 52.6 | 135 12.1 | S14 28.7 | Gacrux | 171 54.0 | S57 14.5 |
| A 13 | 117 31.2 | 44 59.0 | 13.3 | 89 26.2 | 36.0 | 109 52.1 | 52.7 | 150 14.7 | 28.8 | Gienah | 175 45.8 | S17 40.0 |
| Y 14 | 132 33.7 | 59 58.3 | 13.7 | 104 27.0 | 36.6 | 124 54.4 | 52.8 | 165 17.3 | 28.8 | Hadar | 148 38.7 | S60 29.1 |
| 15 | 147 36.1 | 74 57.6 .. | 14.2 | 119 27.8 .. | 37.2 | 139 56.7 .. | 52.8 | 180 19.8 .. | 28.9 | Hamal | 327 53.7 | N23 33.9 |
| 16 | 162 38.6 | 89 56.9 | 14.6 | 134 28.6 | 37.9 | 154 58.9 | 52.9 | 195 22.4 | 28.9 | Kaus Aust. | 83 34.9 | S34 22.4 |
| 17 | 177 41.1 | 104 56.1 | 15.1 | 149 29.4 | 38.5 | 170 01.2 | 53.0 | 210 25.0 | 29.0 | | | |
| 18 | 192 43.5 | 119 55.4 | N21 15.5 | 164 30.2 | N 9 39.1 | 185 03.5 | N 1 53.0 | 225 27.5 | S14 29.0 | Kochab | 137 19.2 | N74 04.1 |
| 19 | 207 46.0 | 134 54.7 | 16.0 | 179 31.0 | 39.7 | 200 05.8 | 53.1 | 240 30.1 | 29.0 | Markab | 13 31.8 | N15 19.5 |
| 20 | 222 48.4 | 149 54.0 | 16.4 | 194 31.8 | 40.3 | 215 08.1 | 53.1 | 255 32.7 | 29.1 | Menkar | 314 08.5 | N 4 10.6 |
| 21 | 237 50.9 | 164 53.3 .. | 16.9 | 209 32.6 .. | 41.0 | 230 10.4 .. | 53.2 | 270 35.3 .. | 29.1 | Menkent | 147 59.9 | S36 28.9 |
| 22 | 252 53.4 | 179 52.6 | 17.3 | 224 33.4 | 41.6 | 245 12.7 | 53.3 | 285 37.8 | 29.2 | Miaplacidus | 221 39.4 | S69 48.7 |
| 23 | 267 55.8 | 194 51.9 | 17.8 | 239 34.2 | 42.2 | 260 14.9 | 53.3 | 300 40.4 | 29.2 | | | |
| 5 00 | 282 58.3 | 209 51.2 | N21 18.2 | 254 35.0 | N 9 42.8 | 275 17.2 | N 1 53.4 | 315 43.0 | S14 29.3 | Mirfak | 308 31.5 | N49 56.2 |
| 01 | 298 00.8 | 224 50.4 | 18.7 | 269 35.8 | 43.4 | 290 19.5 | 53.5 | 330 45.6 | 29.3 | Nunki | 75 50.0 | S26 16.1 |
| 02 | 313 03.2 | 239 49.7 | 19.1 | 284 36.6 | 44.0 | 305 21.8 | 53.5 | 345 48.1 | 29.4 | Peacock | 53 08.5 | S56 39.6 |
| 03 | 328 05.7 | 254 49.0 .. | 19.5 | 299 37.4 .. | 44.7 | 320 24.1 .. | 53.6 | 0 50.7 .. | 29.4 | Pollux | 243 20.2 | N27 58.4 |
| 04 | 343 08.2 | 269 48.3 | 20.0 | 314 38.2 | 45.3 | 335 26.4 | 53.7 | 15 53.3 | 29.4 | Procyon | 244 53.3 | N 5 10.1 |
| 05 | 358 10.6 | 284 47.6 | 20.4 | 329 39.0 | 45.9 | 350 28.7 | 53.7 | 30 55.8 | 29.5 | | | |
| 06 | 13 13.1 | 299 46.9 | N21 20.9 | 344 39.8 | N 9 46.5 | 5 31.0 | N 1 53.8 | 45 58.4 | S14 29.5 | Rasalhague | 96 00.1 | N12 32.7 |
| 07 | 28 15.5 | 314 46.1 | 21.3 | 359 40.6 | 47.1 | 20 33.2 | 53.8 | 61 01.0 | 29.6 | Regulus | 207 36.9 | N11 51.6 |
| 08 | 43 18.0 | 329 45.4 | 21.7 | 14 41.4 | 47.7 | 35 35.5 | 53.9 | 76 03.6 | 29.6 | Rigel | 281 06.2 | S 8 10.5 |
| T 09 | 58 20.5 | 344 44.7 .. | 22.2 | 29 42.2 .. | 48.4 | 50 37.8 .. | 54.0 | 91 06.1 .. | 29.7 | Rigil Kent. | 139 42.8 | S60 55.8 |
| U 10 | 73 22.9 | 359 44.0 | 22.6 | 44 43.0 | 49.0 | 65 40.1 | 54.0 | 106 08.7 | 29.7 | Sabik | 102 04.8 | S15 45.1 |
| E 11 | 88 25.4 | 14 43.3 | 23.0 | 59 43.8 | 49.6 | 80 42.4 | 54.1 | 121 11.3 | 29.8 | | | |
| S 12 | 103 27.9 | 29 42.5 | N21 23.5 | 74 44.6 | N 9 50.2 | 95 44.7 | N 1 54.1 | 136 13.9 | S14 29.8 | Schedar | 349 33.4 | N56 39.3 |
| D 13 | 118 30.3 | 44 41.8 | 23.9 | 89 45.4 | 50.8 | 110 47.0 | 54.2 | 151 16.4 | 29.9 | Shaula | 96 12.8 | S37 07.2 |
| A 14 | 133 32.8 | 59 41.1 | 24.3 | 104 46.2 | 51.4 | 125 49.3 | 54.3 | 166 19.0 | 29.9 | Sirius | 258 28.4 | S16 44.8 |
| Y 15 | 148 35.3 | 74 40.4 .. | 24.7 | 119 47.0 .. | 52.0 | 140 51.6 .. | 54.3 | 181 21.6 .. | 29.9 | Spica | 158 24.4 | S11 16.7 |
| 16 | 163 37.7 | 89 39.7 | 25.2 | 134 47.8 | 52.7 | 155 53.9 | 54.4 | 196 24.2 | 30.0 | Suhail | 222 48.2 | S43 31.4 |
| 17 | 178 40.2 | 104 38.9 | 25.6 | 149 48.6 | 53.3 | 170 56.2 | 54.5 | 211 26.7 | 30.0 | | | |
| 18 | 193 42.7 | 119 38.2 | N21 26.0 | 164 49.4 | N 9 53.9 | 185 58.4 | N 1 54.5 | 226 29.3 | S14 30.1 | Vega | 80 34.2 | N38 48.3 |
| 19 | 208 45.1 | 134 37.5 | 26.4 | 179 50.2 | 54.5 | 201 00.7 | 54.6 | 241 31.9 | 30.1 | Zuben'ubi | 136 58.1 | S16 08.1 |
| 20 | 223 47.6 | 149 36.8 | 26.9 | 194 51.0 | 55.1 | 216 03.0 | 54.6 | 256 34.5 | 30.2 | | SHA | Mer. Pass. |
| 21 | 238 50.0 | 164 36.0 .. | 27.3 | 209 51.8 .. | 55.7 | 231 05.3 .. | 54.7 | 271 37.0 .. | 30.2 | | ° ′ | h m |
| 22 | 253 52.5 | 179 35.3 | 27.7 | 224 52.6 | 56.3 | 246 07.6 | 54.8 | 286 39.6 | 30.3 | Venus | 288 09.0 | 10 00 |
| 23 | 268 55.0 | 194 34.6 | 28.1 | 239 53.4 | 57.0 | 261 09.9 | 54.8 | 301 42.2 | 30.3 | Mars | 332 16.7 | 7 03 |
| | h m | | | | | | | | | Jupiter | 352 23.3 | 5 42 |
| Mer. Pass. 5 11.2 | | v −0.7 | d 0.5 | v 0.8 | d 0.6 | v 2.3 | d 0.1 | v 2.6 | d 0.0 | Saturn | 32 42.1 | 3 01 |

| UT | SUN GHA | SUN Dec | MOON GHA | MOON v | MOON Dec | MOON d | MOON HP |
|---|---|---|---|---|---|---|---|
| d h | ° ′ | ° ′ | ° ′ | ′ | ° ′ | ′ | ′ |
| 3 00 | 178 57.0 | N22 58.5 | 133 14.6 | 13.6 | N18 26.7 | 10.3 | 54.6 |
| 01 | 193 56.9 | 58.3 | 147 47.2 | 13.7 | 18 16.4 | 10.4 | 54.6 |
| 02 | 208 56.7 | 58.1 | 162 19.9 | 13.7 | 18 06.0 | 10.5 | 54.6 |
| 03 | 223 56.6 .. | 57.9 | 176 52.6 | 13.7 | 17 55.5 | 10.6 | 54.7 |
| 04 | 238 56.5 | 57.7 | 191 25.3 | 13.8 | 17 44.9 | 10.7 | 54.7 |
| 05 | 253 56.4 | 57.5 | 205 58.1 | 13.8 | 17 34.2 | 10.7 | 54.7 |
| 06 | 268 56.3 | N22 57.3 | 220 30.9 | 13.9 | N17 23.5 | 10.8 | 54.7 |
| 07 | 283 56.2 | 57.1 | 235 03.8 | 13.9 | 17 12.7 | 10.9 | 54.7 |
| S 08 | 298 56.0 | 56.9 | 249 36.7 | 14.0 | 17 01.8 | 11.0 | 54.7 |
| U 09 | 313 55.9 .. | 56.7 | 264 09.7 | 14.0 | 16 50.8 | 11.0 | 54.8 |
| N 10 | 328 55.8 | 56.5 | 278 42.7 | 14.0 | 16 39.8 | 11.2 | 54.8 |
| D 11 | 343 55.7 | 56.3 | 293 15.7 | 14.1 | 16 28.6 | 11.2 | 54.8 |
| A 12 | 358 55.6 | N22 56.1 | 307 48.8 | 14.1 | N16 17.4 | 11.2 | 54.8 |
| Y 13 | 13 55.5 | 55.9 | 322 21.9 | 14.1 | 16 06.2 | 11.4 | 54.8 |
| 14 | 28 55.4 | 55.7 | 336 55.0 | 14.2 | 15 54.8 | 11.4 | 54.8 |
| 15 | 43 55.2 .. | 55.5 | 351 28.2 | 14.3 | 15 43.4 | 11.5 | 54.9 |
| 16 | 58 55.1 | 55.3 | 6 01.5 | 14.2 | 15 31.9 | 11.6 | 54.9 |
| 17 | 73 55.0 | 55.1 | 20 34.7 | 14.3 | 15 20.3 | 11.6 | 54.9 |
| 18 | 88 54.9 | N22 54.9 | 35 08.0 | 14.4 | N15 08.7 | 11.7 | 54.9 |
| 19 | 103 54.8 | 54.7 | 49 41.4 | 14.3 | 14 57.0 | 11.8 | 54.9 |
| 20 | 118 54.7 | 54.4 | 64 14.7 | 14.4 | 14 45.2 | 11.8 | 55.0 |
| 21 | 133 54.6 .. | 54.2 | 78 48.1 | 14.5 | 14 33.4 | 11.9 | 55.0 |
| 22 | 148 54.4 | 54.0 | 93 21.6 | 14.4 | 14 21.5 | 12.0 | 55.0 |
| 23 | 163 54.3 | 53.8 | 107 55.0 | 14.5 | 14 09.5 | 12.1 | 55.0 |
| 4 00 | 178 54.2 | N22 53.6 | 122 28.5 | 14.6 | N13 57.4 | 12.1 | 55.0 |
| 01 | 193 54.1 | 53.4 | 137 02.1 | 14.5 | 13 45.3 | 12.1 | 55.1 |
| 02 | 208 54.0 | 53.2 | 151 35.6 | 14.6 | 13 33.2 | 12.3 | 55.1 |
| 03 | 223 53.9 .. | 52.9 | 166 09.2 | 14.6 | 13 20.9 | 12.3 | 55.1 |
| 04 | 238 53.8 | 52.7 | 180 42.9 | 14.6 | 13 08.6 | 12.3 | 55.1 |
| 05 | 253 53.7 | 52.5 | 195 16.5 | 14.7 | 12 56.3 | 12.5 | 55.1 |
| 06 | 268 53.5 | N22 52.3 | 209 50.2 | 14.7 | N12 43.8 | 12.5 | 55.2 |
| 07 | 283 53.4 | 52.1 | 224 23.9 | 14.7 | 12 31.3 | 12.5 | 55.2 |
| M 08 | 298 53.3 | 51.9 | 238 57.6 | 14.8 | 12 18.8 | 12.6 | 55.2 |
| O 09 | 313 53.2 .. | 51.6 | 253 31.4 | 14.8 | 12 06.2 | 12.7 | 55.2 |
| N 10 | 328 53.1 | 51.4 | 268 05.2 | 14.8 | 11 53.5 | 12.7 | 55.3 |
| D 11 | 343 53.0 | 51.2 | 282 39.0 | 14.8 | 11 40.8 | 12.8 | 55.3 |
| A 12 | 358 52.9 | N22 51.0 | 297 12.8 | 14.8 | N11 28.0 | 12.8 | 55.3 |
| Y 13 | 13 52.8 | 50.7 | 311 46.6 | 14.9 | 11 15.2 | 12.9 | 55.3 |
| 14 | 28 52.6 | 50.5 | 326 20.5 | 14.9 | 11 02.3 | 12.9 | 55.4 |
| 15 | 43 52.5 .. | 50.3 | 340 54.4 | 14.9 | 10 49.4 | 13.0 | 55.4 |
| 16 | 58 52.4 | 50.1 | 355 28.3 | 14.9 | 10 36.4 | 13.1 | 55.4 |
| 17 | 73 52.3 | 49.8 | 10 02.2 | 15.0 | 10 23.3 | 13.1 | 55.4 |
| 18 | 88 52.2 | N22 49.6 | 24 36.2 | 14.9 | N10 10.2 | 13.2 | 55.4 |
| 19 | 103 52.1 | 49.4 | 39 10.1 | 15.0 | 9 57.0 | 13.2 | 55.5 |
| 20 | 118 52.0 | 49.2 | 53 44.1 | 15.0 | 9 43.8 | 13.2 | 55.5 |
| 21 | 133 51.9 .. | 48.9 | 68 18.1 | 15.0 | 9 30.6 | 13.3 | 55.5 |
| 22 | 148 51.8 | 48.7 | 82 52.1 | 15.0 | 9 17.3 | 13.4 | 55.5 |
| 23 | 163 51.7 | 48.5 | 97 26.1 | 15.0 | 9 03.9 | 13.4 | 55.6 |
| 5 00 | 178 51.5 | N22 48.2 | 112 00.1 | 15.0 | N 8 50.5 | 13.5 | 55.6 |
| 01 | 193 51.4 | 48.0 | 126 34.1 | 15.1 | 8 37.0 | 13.5 | 55.6 |
| 02 | 208 51.3 | 47.8 | 141 08.2 | 15.0 | 8 23.5 | 13.5 | 55.6 |
| 03 | 223 51.2 .. | 47.5 | 155 42.2 | 15.1 | 8 10.0 | 13.6 | 55.7 |
| 04 | 238 51.1 | 47.3 | 170 16.3 | 15.0 | 7 56.4 | 13.6 | 55.7 |
| 05 | 253 51.0 | 47.1 | 184 50.3 | 15.1 | 7 42.8 | 13.7 | 55.7 |
| 06 | 268 50.9 | N22 46.8 | 199 24.4 | 15.0 | N 7 29.1 | 13.8 | 55.8 |
| 07 | 283 50.8 | 46.6 | 213 58.4 | 15.1 | 7 15.3 | 13.7 | 55.8 |
| T 08 | 298 50.7 | 46.4 | 228 32.5 | 15.1 | 7 01.6 | 13.8 | 55.8 |
| U 09 | 313 50.6 .. | 46.1 | 243 06.6 | 15.1 | 6 47.8 | 13.9 | 55.8 |
| E 10 | 328 50.5 | 45.9 | 257 40.7 | 15.0 | 6 33.9 | 13.9 | 55.9 |
| S 11 | 343 50.3 | 45.7 | 272 14.7 | 15.1 | 6 20.0 | 13.9 | 55.9 |
| D 12 | 358 50.2 | N22 45.4 | 286 48.8 | 15.1 | N 6 06.1 | 14.0 | 55.9 |
| A 13 | 13 50.1 | 45.2 | 301 22.9 | 15.0 | 5 52.1 | 14.0 | 56.0 |
| Y 14 | 28 50.0 | 44.9 | 315 56.9 | 15.1 | 5 38.1 | 14.0 | 56.0 |
| 15 | 43 49.9 .. | 44.7 | 330 31.0 | 15.0 | 5 24.1 | 14.1 | 56.0 |
| 16 | 58 49.8 | 44.5 | 345 05.0 | 15.1 | 5 10.0 | 14.1 | 56.0 |
| 17 | 73 49.7 | 44.2 | 359 39.1 | 15.0 | 4 55.9 | 14.1 | 56.1 |
| 18 | 88 49.6 | N22 44.0 | 14 13.1 | 15.1 | N 4 41.8 | 14.2 | 56.1 |
| 19 | 103 49.5 | 43.7 | 28 47.2 | 15.0 | 4 27.6 | 14.2 | 56.1 |
| 20 | 118 49.4 | 43.5 | 43 21.2 | 15.0 | 4 13.4 | 14.3 | 56.2 |
| 21 | 133 49.3 .. | 43.2 | 57 55.2 | 15.0 | 3 59.1 | 14.2 | 56.2 |
| 22 | 148 49.2 | 43.0 | 72 29.2 | 15.0 | 3 44.9 | 14.3 | 56.2 |
| 23 | 163 49.1 | 42.7 | 87 03.2 | 14.9 | N 3 30.6 | 14.4 | 56.2 |
| | SD 15.8 | d 0.2 | SD 14.9 | | 15.1 | | 15.2 |

| Lat. | Twilight Naut. | Twilight Civil | Sunrise | Moonrise 3 | Moonrise 4 | Moonrise 5 | Moonrise 6 |
|---|---|---|---|---|---|---|---|
| ° | h m | h m | h m | h m | h m | h m | h m |
| N 72 | ☐ | ☐ | ☐ | 04 01 | 07 13 | 09 25 | 11 29 |
| N 70 | ☐ | ☐ | ☐ | 05 19 | 07 36 | 09 35 | 11 30 |
| 68 | ☐ | ☐ | ☐ | 05 56 | 07 54 | 09 43 | 11 30 |
| 66 | //// | //// | 00 41 | 06 22 | 08 08 | 09 50 | 11 30 |
| 64 | //// | //// | 01 47 | 06 42 | 08 20 | 09 55 | 11 31 |
| 62 | //// | //// | 02 21 | 06 58 | 08 30 | 10 00 | 11 31 |
| 60 | //// | 01 11 | 02 46 | 07 12 | 08 38 | 10 04 | 11 31 |
| N 58 | //// | 01 53 | 03 05 | 07 23 | 08 46 | 10 08 | 11 31 |
| 56 | //// | 02 21 | 03 21 | 07 33 | 08 52 | 10 11 | 11 32 |
| 54 | 01 05 | 02 42 | 03 35 | 07 42 | 08 58 | 10 14 | 11 32 |
| 52 | 01 44 | 02 59 | 03 47 | 07 49 | 09 03 | 10 17 | 11 32 |
| 50 | 02 10 | 03 13 | 03 57 | 07 56 | 09 08 | 10 19 | 11 32 |
| 45 | 02 53 | 03 42 | 04 19 | 08 11 | 09 18 | 10 25 | 11 32 |
| N 40 | 03 23 | 04 04 | 04 36 | 08 24 | 09 26 | 10 29 | 11 33 |
| 35 | 03 45 | 04 22 | 04 51 | 08 34 | 09 33 | 10 33 | 11 33 |
| 30 | 04 03 | 04 36 | 05 04 | 08 43 | 09 39 | 10 36 | 11 33 |
| 20 | 04 32 | 05 01 | 05 25 | 08 58 | 09 50 | 10 42 | 11 34 |
| N 10 | 04 54 | 05 21 | 05 44 | 09 12 | 10 00 | 10 47 | 11 34 |
| 0 | 05 12 | 05 38 | 06 01 | 09 24 | 10 08 | 10 51 | 11 34 |
| S 10 | 05 29 | 05 55 | 06 18 | 09 37 | 10 17 | 10 56 | 11 35 |
| 20 | 05 45 | 06 12 | 06 36 | 09 50 | 10 26 | 11 01 | 11 35 |
| 30 | 06 01 | 06 30 | 06 57 | 10 06 | 10 37 | 11 06 | 11 35 |
| 35 | 06 09 | 06 41 | 07 09 | 10 14 | 10 43 | 11 10 | 11 36 |
| 40 | 06 18 | 06 52 | 07 22 | 10 24 | 10 50 | 11 13 | 11 36 |
| 45 | 06 28 | 07 05 | 07 39 | 10 36 | 10 58 | 11 17 | 11 36 |
| S 50 | 06 39 | 07 21 | 07 59 | 10 50 | 11 07 | 11 22 | 11 37 |
| 52 | 06 44 | 07 28 | 08 08 | 10 57 | 11 12 | 11 25 | 11 37 |
| 54 | 06 50 | 07 36 | 08 19 | 11 04 | 11 16 | 11 27 | 11 37 |
| 56 | 06 56 | 07 44 | 08 31 | 11 12 | 11 22 | 11 30 | 11 37 |
| 58 | 07 02 | 07 54 | 08 45 | 11 21 | 11 28 | 11 33 | 11 38 |
| S 60 | 07 09 | 08 05 | 09 02 | 11 31 | 11 34 | 11 36 | 11 38 |

| Lat. | Sunset | Twilight Civil | Twilight Naut. | Moonset 3 | Moonset 4 | Moonset 5 | Moonset 6 |
|---|---|---|---|---|---|---|---|
| ° | h m | h m | h m | h m | h m | h m | h m |
| N 72 | ☐ | ☐ | ☐ | 02 44 | 01 05 | 00 24 / 23 53 | 23 23 |
| N 70 | ☐ | ☐ | ☐ | 01 25 | 00 40 | 00 12 / 23 48 | 23 26 |
| 68 | ☐ | ☐ | ☐ | 00 47 | 00 20 | 00 01 / 23 45 | 23 29 |
| 66 | 23 23 | //// | //// | 00 19 | 23 53 | 23 42 | 23 32 |
| 64 | 22 20 | //// | //// | 23 52 | 23 15 | 23 39 | 23 34 |
| 62 | 21 47 | //// | //// | 23 41 | 23 39 | 23 37 | 23 35 |
| 60 | 21 22 | 22 56 | //// | 23 31 | 23 34 | 23 35 | 23 37 |
| N 58 | 21 03 | 22 15 | //// | 23 23 | 23 29 | 23 34 | 23 38 |
| 56 | 20 47 | 21 47 | //// | 23 15 | 23 24 | 23 32 | 23 39 |
| 54 | 20 34 | 21 27 | 23 02 | 23 09 | 23 20 | 23 31 | 23 41 |
| 52 | 20 22 | 21 10 | 22 24 | 23 03 | 23 17 | 23 29 | 23 42 |
| 50 | 20 11 | 20 55 | 21 58 | 22 58 | 23 14 | 23 28 | 23 42 |
| 45 | 19 50 | 20 27 | 21 15 | 22 46 | 23 06 | 23 26 | 23 44 |
| N 40 | 19 32 | 20 05 | 20 46 | 22 36 | 23 00 | 23 23 | 23 46 |
| 35 | 19 18 | 19 47 | 20 23 | 22 28 | 22 55 | 23 21 | 23 47 |
| 30 | 19 05 | 19 32 | 20 05 | 22 21 | 22 51 | 23 20 | 23 49 |
| 20 | 18 44 | 19 08 | 19 37 | 22 08 | 22 43 | 23 17 | 23 51 |
| N 10 | 18 25 | 18 48 | 19 15 | 21 56 | 22 36 | 23 14 | 23 53 |
| 0 | 18 08 | 18 31 | 18 57 | 21 46 | 22 29 | 23 12 | 23 55 |
| S 10 | 17 51 | 18 14 | 18 40 | 21 35 | 22 22 | 23 09 | 23 57 |
| 20 | 17 33 | 17 57 | 18 24 | 21 23 | 22 15 | 23 06 | 23 59 |
| 30 | 17 13 | 17 39 | 18 09 | 21 10 | 22 07 | 23 03 | 24 01 |
| 35 | 17 01 | 17 29 | 18 00 | 21 02 | 22 02 | 23 01 | 24 02 |
| 40 | 16 47 | 17 17 | 17 51 | 20 54 | 21 56 | 22 59 | 24 04 |
| 45 | 16 31 | 17 04 | 17 41 | 20 43 | 21 50 | 22 57 | 24 06 |
| S 50 | 16 10 | 16 49 | 17 30 | 20 31 | 21 42 | 22 54 | 24 08 |
| 52 | 16 01 | 16 41 | 17 25 | 20 25 | 21 38 | 22 53 | 24 09 |
| 54 | 15 50 | 16 34 | 17 19 | 20 18 | 21 34 | 22 51 | 24 10 |
| 56 | 15 38 | 16 25 | 17 14 | 20 11 | 21 30 | 22 50 | 24 11 |
| 58 | 15 24 | 16 15 | 17 07 | 20 03 | 21 25 | 22 48 | 24 12 |
| S 60 | 15 07 | 16 04 | 17 00 | 19 53 | 21 20 | 22 46 | 24 13 |

| | SUN | | | MOON | | | |
|---|---|---|---|---|---|---|---|
| Day | Eqn. of Time 00h | Eqn. of Time 12h | Mer. Pass. | Mer. Pass. Upper | Mer. Pass. Lower | Age | Phase |
| d | m s | m s | h m | h m | h m | d | % |
| 3 | 04 12 | 04 17 | 12 04 | 15 35 | 03 13 | 04 | 17 |
| 4 | 04 23 | 04 28 | 12 04 | 16 19 | 03 57 | 05 | 25 |
| 5 | 04 34 | 04 39 | 12 05 | 17 01 | 04 40 | 06 | 34 |

| UT | ARIES GHA | VENUS −3.9 GHA | Dec | MARS +0.4 GHA | Dec | JUPITER −2.5 GHA | Dec | SATURN +0.4 GHA | Dec | STARS Name | SHA | Dec |
|---|---|---|---|---|---|---|---|---|---|---|---|---|
| d h 6 00 | 283 57.4 | 209 33.9 | N21 28.5 | 254 54.2 | N 9 57.6 | 276 12.2 | N 1 54.9 | 316 44.8 | S14 30.4 | Acamar | 315 13.6 | S40 12.7 |
| 01 | 298 59.9 | 224 33.1 | 29.0 | 269 55.0 | 58.2 | 291 14.5 | 54.9 | 331 47.4 | 30.4 | Achernar | 335 21.9 | S57 07.1 |
| 02 | 314 02.4 | 239 32.4 | 29.4 | 284 55.8 | 58.8 | 306 16.8 | 55.0 | 346 49.9 | 30.4 | Acrux | 173 02.4 | S63 13.6 |
| 03 | 329 04.8 | 254 31.7 .. | 29.8 | 299 56.6 | 9 59.4 | 321 19.1 .. | 55.1 | 1 52.5 .. | 30.5 | Adhara | 255 07.9 | S29 00.1 |
| 04 | 344 07.3 | 269 31.0 | 30.2 | 314 57.4 | 10 00.0 | 336 21.4 | 55.1 | 16 55.1 | 30.5 | Aldebaran | 290 42.3 | N16 33.2 |
| 05 | 359 09.8 | 284 30.2 | 30.6 | 329 58.2 | 00.6 | 351 23.7 | 55.2 | 31 57.7 | 30.6 | | | |
| W 06 | 14 12.2 | 299 29.5 | N21 31.0 | 344 59.0 | N10 01.2 | 6 26.0 | N 1 55.2 | 47 00.2 | S14 30.6 | Alioth | 166 14.8 | N55 50.6 |
| E 07 | 29 14.7 | 314 28.8 | 31.5 | 359 59.9 | 01.8 | 21 28.3 | 55.3 | 62 02.8 | 30.7 | Alkaid | 152 53.6 | N49 12.4 |
| D 08 | 44 17.1 | 329 28.1 | 31.9 | 15 00.7 | 02.5 | 36 30.6 | 55.4 | 77 05.4 | 30.7 | Alnair | 27 35.2 | S46 51.0 |
| N 09 | 59 19.6 | 344 27.3 .. | 32.3 | 30 01.5 .. | 03.1 | 51 32.9 .. | 55.4 | 92 08.0 .. | 30.8 | Alnilam | 275 40.1 | S 1 11.2 |
| E 10 | 74 22.1 | 359 26.6 | 32.7 | 45 02.3 | 03.7 | 66 35.2 | 55.5 | 107 10.5 | 30.8 | Alphard | 217 50.1 | S 8 45.3 |
| S 11 | 89 24.5 | 14 25.9 | 33.1 | 60 03.1 | 04.3 | 81 37.5 | 55.5 | 122 13.1 | 30.9 | | | |
| D 12 | 104 27.0 | 29 25.1 | N21 33.5 | 75 03.9 | N10 04.9 | 96 39.8 | N 1 55.6 | 137 15.7 | S14 30.9 | Alphecca | 126 05.3 | N26 38.5 |
| A 13 | 119 29.5 | 44 24.4 | 33.9 | 90 04.7 | 05.5 | 111 42.0 | 55.6 | 152 18.3 | 31.0 | Alpheratz | 357 36.8 | N29 12.7 |
| Y 14 | 134 31.9 | 59 23.7 | 34.3 | 105 05.5 | 06.1 | 126 44.3 | 55.7 | 167 20.9 | 31.0 | Altair | 62 01.6 | N 8 55.7 |
| 15 | 149 34.4 | 74 23.0 .. | 34.7 | 120 06.3 .. | 06.7 | 141 46.6 .. | 55.8 | 182 23.4 .. | 31.0 | Ankaa | 353 09.1 | S42 10.8 |
| 16 | 164 36.9 | 89 22.2 | 35.1 | 135 07.1 | 07.3 | 156 48.9 | 55.8 | 197 26.0 | 31.1 | Antares | 112 18.1 | S26 28.9 |
| 17 | 179 39.3 | 104 21.5 | 35.5 | 150 07.9 | 08.0 | 171 51.2 | 55.9 | 212 28.6 | 31.1 | | | |
| 18 | 194 41.8 | 119 20.8 | N21 35.9 | 165 08.7 | N10 08.6 | 186 53.5 | N 1 55.9 | 227 31.2 | S14 31.2 | Arcturus | 145 49.7 | N19 04.1 |
| 19 | 209 44.3 | 134 20.0 | 36.3 | 180 09.5 | 09.2 | 201 55.8 | 56.0 | 242 33.7 | 31.2 | Atria | 107 13.6 | S69 04.2 |
| 20 | 224 46.7 | 149 19.3 | 36.7 | 195 10.3 | 09.8 | 216 58.1 | 56.1 | 257 36.3 | 31.3 | Avior | 234 16.2 | S59 34.9 |
| 21 | 239 49.2 | 164 18.6 .. | 37.1 | 210 11.1 .. | 10.4 | 232 00.4 .. | 56.1 | 272 38.9 .. | 31.3 | Bellatrix | 278 25.4 | N 6 22.2 |
| 22 | 254 51.6 | 179 17.8 | 37.5 | 225 11.9 | 11.0 | 247 02.7 | 56.2 | 287 41.5 | 31.4 | Betelgeuse | 270 54.7 | N 7 24.7 |
| 23 | 269 54.1 | 194 17.1 | 37.9 | 240 12.7 | 11.6 | 262 05.0 | 56.2 | 302 44.1 | 31.4 | | | |
| 7 00 | 284 56.6 | 209 16.4 | N21 38.3 | 255 13.5 | N10 12.2 | 277 07.3 | N 1 56.3 | 317 46.6 | S14 31.5 | Canopus | 263 53.9 | S52 42.4 |
| 01 | 299 59.0 | 224 15.6 | 38.7 | 270 14.3 | 12.8 | 292 09.6 | 56.3 | 332 49.2 | 31.5 | Capella | 280 25.4 | N46 01.1 |
| 02 | 315 01.5 | 239 14.9 | 39.1 | 285 15.1 | 13.4 | 307 11.9 | 56.4 | 347 51.8 | 31.6 | Deneb | 49 26.8 | N45 21.5 |
| 03 | 330 04.0 | 254 14.2 .. | 39.5 | 300 15.9 .. | 14.0 | 322 14.2 .. | 56.5 | 2 54.4 .. | 31.6 | Denebola | 182 27.2 | N14 27.0 |
| 04 | 345 06.4 | 269 13.4 | 39.9 | 315 16.7 | 14.6 | 337 16.5 | 56.5 | 17 57.0 | 31.7 | Diphda | 348 49.4 | S17 51.7 |
| 05 | 0 08.9 | 284 12.7 | 40.3 | 330 17.5 | 15.2 | 352 18.8 | 56.6 | 32 59.5 | 31.7 | | | |
| T 06 | 15 11.4 | 299 12.0 | N21 40.7 | 345 18.3 | N10 15.9 | 7 21.1 | N 1 56.6 | 48 02.1 | S14 31.7 | Dubhe | 193 43.9 | N61 38.1 |
| H 07 | 30 13.8 | 314 11.2 | 41.0 | 0 19.1 | 16.5 | 22 23.4 | 56.7 | 63 04.7 | 31.8 | Elnath | 278 04.8 | N28 37.5 |
| U 08 | 45 16.3 | 329 10.5 | 41.4 | 15 19.9 | 17.1 | 37 25.8 | 56.7 | 78 07.3 | 31.8 | Eltanin | 90 42.6 | N51 29.2 |
| R 09 | 60 18.8 | 344 09.8 .. | 41.8 | 30 20.7 .. | 17.7 | 52 28.1 .. | 56.8 | 93 09.9 .. | 31.9 | Enif | 33 40.6 | N 9 58.6 |
| S 10 | 75 21.2 | 359 09.0 | 42.2 | 45 21.5 | 18.3 | 67 30.4 | 56.8 | 108 12.4 | 31.9 | Fomalhaut | 15 16.6 | S29 30.1 |
| D 11 | 90 23.7 | 14 08.3 | 42.6 | 60 22.3 | 18.9 | 82 32.7 | 56.9 | 123 15.0 | 32.0 | | | |
| A 12 | 105 26.1 | 29 07.5 | N21 43.0 | 75 23.1 | N10 19.5 | 97 35.0 | N 1 57.0 | 138 17.6 | S14 32.0 | Gacrux | 171 54.0 | S57 14.5 |
| Y 13 | 120 28.6 | 44 06.8 | 43.3 | 90 23.9 | 20.1 | 112 37.3 | 57.0 | 153 20.2 | 32.1 | Gienah | 175 45.8 | S17 40.0 |
| 14 | 135 31.1 | 59 06.1 | 43.7 | 105 24.8 | 20.7 | 127 39.6 | 57.1 | 168 22.8 | 32.1 | Hadar | 148 38.7 | S60 29.1 |
| 15 | 150 33.5 | 74 05.3 .. | 44.1 | 120 25.6 .. | 21.3 | 142 41.9 .. | 57.1 | 183 25.3 .. | 32.2 | Hamal | 327 53.6 | N23 34.0 |
| 16 | 165 36.0 | 89 04.6 | 44.5 | 135 26.4 | 21.9 | 157 44.2 | 57.2 | 198 27.9 | 32.2 | Kaus Aust. | 83 34.9 | S34 22.4 |
| 17 | 180 38.5 | 104 03.9 | 44.9 | 150 27.2 | 22.5 | 172 46.5 | 57.2 | 213 30.5 | 32.3 | | | |
| 18 | 195 40.9 | 119 03.1 | N21 45.2 | 165 28.0 | N10 23.1 | 187 48.8 | N 1 57.3 | 228 33.1 | S14 32.3 | Kochab | 137 19.2 | N74 04.1 |
| 19 | 210 43.4 | 134 02.4 | 45.6 | 180 28.8 | 23.7 | 202 51.1 | 57.3 | 243 35.7 | 32.4 | Markab | 13 31.8 | N15 19.5 |
| 20 | 225 45.9 | 149 01.6 | 46.0 | 195 29.6 | 24.3 | 217 53.4 | 57.4 | 258 38.3 | 32.4 | Menkar | 314 08.5 | N 4 10.6 |
| 21 | 240 48.3 | 164 00.9 .. | 46.4 | 210 30.4 .. | 24.9 | 232 55.7 .. | 57.5 | 273 40.8 .. | 32.5 | Menkent | 147 59.9 | S36 28.9 |
| 22 | 255 50.8 | 179 00.1 | 46.7 | 225 31.2 | 25.5 | 247 58.0 | 57.5 | 288 43.4 | 32.5 | Miaplacidus | 221 39.5 | S69 48.6 |
| 23 | 270 53.2 | 193 59.4 | 47.1 | 240 32.0 | 26.1 | 263 00.3 | 57.6 | 303 46.0 | 32.6 | | | |
| 8 00 | 285 55.7 | 208 58.7 | N21 47.5 | 255 32.8 | N10 26.7 | 278 02.6 | N 1 57.6 | 318 48.6 | S14 32.6 | Mirfak | 308 31.5 | N49 56.2 |
| 01 | 300 58.2 | 223 57.9 | 47.8 | 270 33.6 | 27.3 | 293 04.9 | 57.7 | 333 51.2 | 32.6 | Nunki | 75 49.9 | S26 16.1 |
| 02 | 316 00.6 | 238 57.2 | 48.2 | 285 34.4 | 27.9 | 308 07.3 | 57.7 | 348 53.8 | 32.7 | Peacock | 53 08.4 | S56 39.6 |
| 03 | 331 03.1 | 253 56.4 .. | 48.6 | 300 35.2 .. | 28.5 | 323 09.6 .. | 57.8 | 3 56.3 .. | 32.7 | Pollux | 243 20.2 | N27 58.4 |
| 04 | 346 05.6 | 268 55.7 | 49.0 | 315 36.0 | 29.1 | 338 11.9 | 57.8 | 18 58.9 | 32.8 | Procyon | 244 53.3 | N 5 10.1 |
| 05 | 1 08.0 | 283 55.0 | 49.3 | 330 36.8 | 29.7 | 353 14.2 | 57.9 | 34 01.5 | 32.8 | | | |
| F 06 | 16 10.5 | 298 54.2 | N21 49.7 | 345 37.6 | N10 30.3 | 8 16.5 | N 1 57.9 | 49 04.1 | S14 32.9 | Rasalhague | 96 00.1 | N12 32.7 |
| R 07 | 31 13.0 | 313 53.5 | 50.0 | 0 38.4 | 30.9 | 23 18.8 | 58.0 | 64 06.7 | 32.9 | Regulus | 207 36.9 | N11 51.6 |
| I 08 | 46 15.4 | 328 52.7 | 50.4 | 15 39.2 | 31.5 | 38 21.1 | 58.0 | 79 09.3 | 33.0 | Rigel | 281 06.2 | S 8 10.5 |
| D 09 | 61 17.9 | 343 52.0 .. | 50.8 | 30 40.0 .. | 32.1 | 53 23.4 .. | 58.1 | 94 11.8 .. | 33.0 | Rigil Kent. | 139 42.8 | S60 55.8 |
| A 10 | 76 20.4 | 358 51.2 | 51.1 | 45 40.8 | 32.8 | 68 25.7 | 58.1 | 109 14.4 | 33.1 | Sabik | 102 04.8 | S15 45.1 |
| Y 11 | 91 22.8 | 13 50.5 | 51.5 | 60 41.7 | 33.4 | 83 28.0 | 58.2 | 124 17.0 | 33.1 | | | |
| 12 | 106 25.3 | 28 49.7 | N21 51.8 | 75 42.5 | N10 34.0 | 98 30.3 | N 1 58.3 | 139 19.6 | S14 33.2 | Schedar | 349 33.3 | N56 39.3 |
| 13 | 121 27.7 | 43 49.0 | 52.2 | 90 43.3 | 34.6 | 113 32.7 | 58.3 | 154 22.2 | 33.2 | Shaula | 96 12.8 | S37 07.2 |
| 14 | 136 30.2 | 58 48.2 | 52.6 | 105 44.1 | 35.2 | 128 35.0 | 58.4 | 169 24.8 | 33.3 | Sirius | 258 28.4 | S16 44.8 |
| 15 | 151 32.7 | 73 47.5 .. | 52.9 | 120 44.9 .. | 35.8 | 143 37.3 .. | 58.4 | 184 27.3 .. | 33.3 | Spica | 158 24.4 | S11 16.7 |
| 16 | 166 35.1 | 88 46.8 | 53.3 | 135 45.7 | 36.4 | 158 39.6 | 58.5 | 199 29.9 | 33.4 | Suhail | 222 48.2 | S43 31.4 |
| 17 | 181 37.6 | 103 46.0 | 53.6 | 150 46.5 | 36.9 | 173 41.9 | 58.5 | 214 32.5 | 33.4 | | | |
| 18 | 196 40.1 | 118 45.3 | N21 54.0 | 165 47.3 | N10 37.5 | 188 44.2 | N 1 58.6 | 229 35.1 | S14 33.5 | Vega | 80 34.2 | N38 48.3 |
| 19 | 211 42.5 | 133 44.5 | 54.3 | 180 48.1 | 38.1 | 203 46.5 | 58.6 | 244 37.7 | 33.5 | Zuben'ubi | 136 58.1 | S16 08.1 |
| 20 | 226 45.0 | 148 43.8 | 54.7 | 195 48.9 | 38.7 | 218 48.8 | 58.7 | 259 40.3 | 33.6 | | SHA | Mer. Pass. |
| 21 | 241 47.5 | 163 43.0 .. | 55.0 | 210 49.7 .. | 39.3 | 233 51.2 .. | 58.7 | 274 42.8 .. | 33.6 | Venus | 284 19.8 | 10 03 |
| 22 | 256 49.9 | 178 42.3 | 55.4 | 225 50.5 | 39.9 | 248 53.5 | 58.8 | 289 45.4 | 33.7 | Mars | 330 16.9 | 6 59 |
| 23 | 271 52.4 | 193 41.5 | 55.7 | 240 51.3 | 40.5 | 263 55.8 | 58.8 | 304 48.0 | 33.7 | Jupiter | 352 10.8 | 5 31 |
| Mer. Pass. 4 59.4 | | v −0.7 d 0.4 | | v 0.8 d 0.6 | | v 2.3 d 0.1 | | v 2.6 d 0.0 | | Saturn | 32 50.1 | 2 48 |

## SUN / MOON

| UT (d h) | SUN GHA | SUN Dec | MOON GHA | v | MOON Dec | d | HP |
|---|---|---|---|---|---|---|---|
| **6 00** | 178 49.0 | N22 42.5 | 101 37.1 | 15.0 | N 3 16.2 | 14.3 | 56.3 |
| 01 | 193 48.9 | 42.3 | 116 11.1 | 14.9 | 3 01.9 | 14.4 | 56.3 |
| 02 | 208 48.7 | 42.0 | 130 45.0 | 14.9 | 2 47.5 | 14.5 | 56.3 |
| 03 | 223 48.6 | .. 41.8 | 145 18.9 | 14.9 | 2 33.0 | 14.4 | 56.4 |
| 04 | 238 48.5 | 41.5 | 159 52.8 | 14.9 | 2 18.6 | 14.5 | 56.4 |
| 05 | 253 48.4 | 41.3 | 174 26.7 | 14.8 | 2 04.1 | 14.5 | 56.4 |
| **W** 06 | 268 48.3 | N22 41.0 | 189 00.5 | 14.8 | N 1 49.6 | 14.5 | 56.5 |
| **E** 07 | 283 48.2 | 40.7 | 203 34.3 | 14.8 | 1 35.1 | 14.5 | 56.5 |
| **D** 08 | 298 48.1 | 40.5 | 218 08.1 | 14.8 | 1 20.6 | 14.6 | 56.5 |
| **N** 09 | 313 48.0 | .. 40.2 | 232 41.9 | 14.7 | 1 06.0 | 14.6 | 56.6 |
| **E** 10 | 328 47.9 | 40.0 | 247 15.6 | 14.8 | 0 51.4 | 14.6 | 56.6 |
| **S** 11 | 343 47.8 | 39.7 | 261 49.4 | 14.6 | 0 36.8 | 14.6 | 56.6 |
| **D** 12 | 358 47.7 | N22 39.5 | 276 23.0 | 14.7 | N 0 22.2 | 14.6 | 56.7 |
| **A** 13 | 13 47.6 | 39.2 | 290 56.7 | 14.6 | N 0 07.6 | 14.7 | 56.7 |
| **Y** 14 | 28 47.5 | 39.0 | 305 30.3 | 14.6 | S 0 07.1 | 14.7 | 56.7 |
| 15 | 43 47.4 | .. 38.7 | 320 03.9 | 14.6 | 0 21.8 | 14.7 | 56.8 |
| 16 | 58 47.3 | 38.4 | 334 37.5 | 14.5 | 0 36.5 | 14.7 | 56.8 |
| 17 | 73 47.2 | 38.2 | 349 11.0 | 14.4 | 0 51.2 | 14.7 | 56.8 |
| 18 | 88 47.1 | N22 37.9 | 3 44.4 | 14.5 | S 1 05.9 | 14.7 | 56.9 |
| 19 | 103 47.0 | 37.7 | 18 17.9 | 14.4 | 1 20.6 | 14.8 | 56.9 |
| 20 | 118 46.9 | 37.4 | 32 51.3 | 14.3 | 1 35.4 | 14.7 | 56.9 |
| 21 | 133 46.8 | .. 37.1 | 47 24.6 | 14.4 | 1 50.1 | 14.8 | 57.0 |
| 22 | 148 46.7 | 36.9 | 61 58.0 | 14.2 | 2 04.9 | 14.8 | 57.0 |
| 23 | 163 46.6 | 36.6 | 76 31.2 | 14.2 | 2 19.7 | 14.7 | 57.0 |
| **7 00** | 178 46.5 | N22 36.4 | 91 04.4 | 14.2 | S 2 34.4 | 14.8 | 57.1 |
| 01 | 193 46.4 | 36.1 | 105 37.6 | 14.2 | 2 49.2 | 14.8 | 57.1 |
| 02 | 208 46.3 | 35.8 | 120 10.8 | 14.0 | 3 04.0 | 14.8 | 57.1 |
| 03 | 223 46.2 | .. 35.6 | 134 43.8 | 14.1 | 3 18.8 | 14.8 | 57.2 |
| 04 | 238 46.1 | 35.3 | 149 16.9 | 13.9 | 3 33.6 | 14.8 | 57.2 |
| 05 | 253 46.0 | 35.0 | 163 49.8 | 14.0 | 3 48.4 | 14.8 | 57.2 |
| **T** 06 | 268 45.9 | N22 34.8 | 178 22.8 | 13.8 | S 4 03.2 | 14.8 | 57.3 |
| **H** 07 | 283 45.8 | 34.5 | 192 55.6 | 13.8 | 4 18.0 | 14.8 | 57.3 |
| **U** 08 | 298 45.7 | 34.2 | 207 28.4 | 13.8 | 4 32.8 | 14.9 | 57.3 |
| **R** 09 | 313 45.6 | .. 34.0 | 222 01.2 | 13.7 | 4 47.7 | 14.8 | 57.4 |
| **S** 10 | 328 45.5 | 33.7 | 236 33.9 | 13.6 | 5 02.5 | 14.8 | 57.4 |
| **D** 11 | 343 45.4 | 33.4 | 251 06.5 | 13.6 | 5 17.3 | 14.7 | 57.5 |
| **A** 12 | 358 45.3 | N22 33.1 | 265 39.1 | 13.5 | S 5 32.0 | 14.8 | 57.5 |
| **Y** 13 | 13 45.2 | 32.9 | 280 11.6 | 13.4 | 5 46.8 | 14.8 | 57.5 |
| 14 | 28 45.1 | 32.6 | 294 44.0 | 13.4 | 6 01.6 | 14.8 | 57.6 |
| 15 | 43 45.0 | .. 32.3 | 309 16.4 | 13.3 | 6 16.4 | 14.8 | 57.6 |
| 16 | 58 44.9 | 32.0 | 323 48.7 | 13.3 | 6 31.2 | 14.7 | 57.6 |
| 17 | 73 44.8 | 31.8 | 338 21.0 | 13.1 | 6 45.9 | 14.7 | 57.7 |
| 18 | 88 44.7 | N22 31.5 | 352 53.1 | 13.1 | S 7 00.6 | 14.8 | 57.7 |
| 19 | 103 44.6 | 31.2 | 7 25.2 | 13.0 | 7 15.4 | 14.7 | 57.8 |
| 20 | 118 44.5 | 30.9 | 21 57.2 | 13.0 | 7 30.1 | 14.7 | 57.8 |
| 21 | 133 44.4 | .. 30.7 | 36 29.2 | 12.9 | 7 44.8 | 14.7 | 57.8 |
| 22 | 148 44.3 | 30.4 | 51 01.1 | 12.8 | 7 59.5 | 14.6 | 57.9 |
| 23 | 163 44.2 | 30.1 | 65 32.9 | 12.7 | 8 14.1 | 14.7 | 57.9 |
| **8 00** | 178 44.1 | N22 29.8 | 80 04.6 | 12.6 | S 8 28.8 | 14.6 | 57.9 |
| 01 | 193 44.0 | 29.5 | 94 36.2 | 12.6 | 8 43.4 | 14.6 | 58.0 |
| 02 | 208 43.9 | 29.3 | 109 07.8 | 12.5 | 8 58.0 | 14.6 | 58.0 |
| 03 | 223 43.8 | .. 29.0 | 123 39.3 | 12.4 | 9 12.6 | 14.5 | 58.1 |
| 04 | 238 43.7 | 28.7 | 138 10.7 | 12.3 | 9 27.1 | 14.5 | 58.1 |
| 05 | 253 43.6 | 28.4 | 152 42.0 | 12.2 | 9 41.6 | 14.5 | 58.1 |
| **F** 06 | 268 43.5 | N22 28.1 | 167 13.2 | 12.1 | S 9 56.1 | 14.5 | 58.2 |
| **R** 07 | 283 43.4 | 27.8 | 181 44.3 | 12.1 | 10 10.6 | 14.4 | 58.2 |
| **I** 08 | 298 43.3 | 27.6 | 196 15.4 | 11.9 | 10 25.0 | 14.4 | 58.2 |
| 09 | 313 43.2 | .. 27.3 | 210 46.3 | 11.9 | 10 39.4 | 14.4 | 58.3 |
| **D** 10 | 328 43.1 | 27.0 | 225 17.2 | 11.7 | 10 53.8 | 14.3 | 58.3 |
| **A** 11 | 343 43.0 | 26.7 | 239 47.9 | 11.7 | 11 08.1 | 14.3 | 58.4 |
| **Y** 12 | 358 42.9 | N22 26.4 | 254 18.6 | 11.6 | S11 22.4 | 14.3 | 58.4 |
| 13 | 13 42.8 | 26.1 | 268 49.2 | 11.4 | 11 36.7 | 14.2 | 58.4 |
| 14 | 28 42.7 | 25.8 | 283 19.6 | 11.4 | 11 50.9 | 14.2 | 58.5 |
| 15 | 43 42.6 | .. 25.5 | 297 50.0 | 11.3 | 12 05.1 | 14.1 | 58.5 |
| 16 | 58 42.5 | 25.3 | 312 20.3 | 11.2 | 12 19.2 | 14.1 | 58.5 |
| 17 | 73 42.4 | 25.0 | 326 50.5 | 11.1 | 12 33.3 | 14.1 | 58.6 |
| 18 | 88 42.4 | N22 24.7 | 341 20.6 | 10.9 | S12 47.4 | 14.0 | 58.6 |
| 19 | 103 42.3 | 24.4 | 355 50.5 | 10.9 | 13 01.4 | 13.9 | 58.7 |
| 20 | 118 42.2 | 24.1 | 10 20.4 | 10.8 | 13 15.3 | 14.0 | 58.7 |
| 21 | 133 42.1 | .. 23.8 | 24 50.2 | 10.6 | 13 29.3 | 13.8 | 58.7 |
| 22 | 148 42.0 | 23.5 | 39 19.8 | 10.5 | 13 43.1 | 13.8 | 58.8 |
| 23 | 163 41.9 | 23.2 | 53 49.3 | 10.5 | S13 56.9 | 13.7 | 58.8 |
| **SD** | 15.8 | d 0.3 | SD 15.4 | | 15.7 | | 15.9 |

## Twilight / Moonrise

| Lat. | Naut. | Civil | Sunrise | Moonrise 6 | 7 | 8 | 9 |
|---|---|---|---|---|---|---|---|
| N 72 | ☐ | ☐ | ☐ | 11 29 | 13 37 | 16 02 | ■ |
| N 70 | ☐ | ☐ | ☐ | 11 30 | 13 28 | 15 38 | 18 29 |
| 68 | ☐ | ☐ | ☐ | 11 30 | 13 20 | 15 20 | 17 42 |
| 66 | //// | //// | 00 58 | 11 30 | 13 14 | 15 06 | 17 12 |
| 64 | //// | //// | 01 54 | 11 31 | 13 09 | 14 54 | 16 50 |
| 62 | //// | //// | 02 26 | 11 31 | 13 05 | 14 44 | 16 32 |
| 60 | //// | 01 20 | 02 50 | 11 31 | 13 01 | 14 35 | 16 17 |
| N 58 | //// | 01 58 | 03 09 | 11 31 | 12 57 | 14 28 | 16 05 |
| 56 | //// | 02 25 | 03 24 | 11 32 | 12 54 | 14 22 | 15 54 |
| 54 | 01 13 | 02 45 | 03 38 | 11 32 | 12 52 | 14 16 | 15 45 |
| 52 | 01 49 | 03 02 | 03 49 | 11 32 | 12 49 | 14 11 | 15 37 |
| 50 | 02 14 | 03 16 | 04 00 | 11 32 | 12 47 | 14 06 | 15 29 |
| 45 | 02 56 | 03 44 | 04 21 | 11 32 | 12 42 | 13 56 | 15 13 |
| N 40 | 03 25 | 04 06 | 04 38 | 11 33 | 12 38 | 13 47 | 15 00 |
| 35 | 03 47 | 04 23 | 04 53 | 11 33 | 12 35 | 13 40 | 14 50 |
| 30 | 04 05 | 04 38 | 05 05 | 11 33 | 12 32 | 13 34 | 14 40 |
| 20 | 04 33 | 05 02 | 05 26 | 11 34 | 12 27 | 13 23 | 14 24 |
| N 10 | 04 55 | 05 22 | 05 44 | 11 34 | 12 23 | 13 14 | 14 10 |
| 0 | 05 13 | 05 39 | 06 01 | 11 34 | 12 18 | 13 05 | 13 57 |
| S 10 | 05 29 | 05 55 | 06 18 | 11 35 | 12 14 | 12 57 | 13 44 |
| 20 | 05 45 | 06 12 | 06 36 | 11 35 | 12 10 | 12 48 | 13 30 |
| 30 | 06 00 | 06 30 | 06 56 | 11 35 | 12 05 | 12 38 | 13 14 |
| 35 | 06 09 | 06 40 | 07 08 | 11 36 | 12 03 | 12 32 | 13 05 |
| 40 | 06 18 | 06 51 | 07 22 | 11 36 | 11 59 | 12 25 | 12 55 |
| 45 | 06 27 | 07 04 | 07 38 | 11 36 | 11 56 | 12 17 | 12 43 |
| S 50 | 06 38 | 07 19 | 07 57 | 11 37 | 11 52 | 12 08 | 12 29 |
| 52 | 06 43 | 07 26 | 08 07 | 11 37 | 11 50 | 12 04 | 12 22 |
| 54 | 06 49 | 07 34 | 08 17 | 11 37 | 11 48 | 11 59 | 12 15 |
| 56 | 06 54 | 07 43 | 08 29 | 11 37 | 11 45 | 11 54 | 12 06 |
| 58 | 07 01 | 07 52 | 08 43 | 11 38 | 11 43 | 11 49 | 11 57 |
| S 60 | 07 08 | 08 03 | 08 59 | 11 38 | 11 40 | 11 42 | 11 47 |

## Sunset / Twilight / Moonset

| Lat. | Sunset | Civil | Naut. | Moonset 6 | 7 | 8 | 9 |
|---|---|---|---|---|---|---|---|
| N 72 | ☐ | ☐ | ☐ | 23 23 | 22 50 | 22 05 | ■ |
| N 70 | ☐ | ☐ | ☐ | 23 26 | 23 02 | 22 31 | 21 29 |
| 68 | ☐ | ☐ | ☐ | 23 29 | 23 12 | 22 51 | 22 17 |
| 66 | 23 08 | //// | //// | 23 32 | 23 20 | 23 07 | 22 49 |
| 64 | 22 14 | //// | //// | 23 34 | 23 27 | 23 21 | 23 12 |
| 62 | 21 43 | //// | //// | 23 35 | 23 33 | 23 32 | 23 31 |
| 60 | 21 19 | 22 48 | //// | 23 37 | 23 39 | 23 42 | 23 47 |
| N 58 | 21 00 | 22 10 | //// | 23 38 | 23 43 | 23 50 | 24 00 |
| 56 | 20 45 | 21 44 | //// | 23 39 | 23 48 | 23 58 | 24 12 |
| 54 | 20 32 | 21 24 | 22 55 | 23 41 | 23 51 | 24 04 | 00 04 |
| 52 | 20 21 | 21 07 | 22 20 | 23 42 | 23 55 | 24 10 | 00 10 |
| 50 | 20 10 | 20 53 | 21 55 | 23 42 | 23 58 | 24 16 | 00 16 |
| 45 | 19 49 | 20 25 | 21 13 | 23 44 | 24 05 | 00 05 | 00 28 |
| N 40 | 19 32 | 20 04 | 20 45 | 23 46 | 24 10 | 00 10 | 00 38 |
| 35 | 19 17 | 19 46 | 20 23 | 23 48 | 24 15 | 00 15 | 00 46 |
| 30 | 19 05 | 19 32 | 20 05 | 23 49 | 24 20 | 00 20 | 00 54 |
| 20 | 18 44 | 19 08 | 19 37 | 23 51 | 24 27 | 00 27 | 01 07 |
| N 10 | 18 25 | 18 48 | 19 15 | 23 53 | 24 34 | 00 34 | 01 18 |
| 0 | 18 09 | 18 31 | 18 57 | 23 55 | 24 40 | 00 40 | 01 29 |
| S 10 | 17 52 | 18 15 | 18 41 | 23 57 | 24 47 | 00 47 | 01 40 |
| 20 | 17 34 | 17 58 | 18 25 | 23 59 | 24 54 | 00 54 | 01 52 |
| 30 | 17 14 | 17 40 | 18 10 | 24 01 | 00 01 | 01 01 | 02 05 |
| 35 | 17 02 | 17 30 | 18 01 | 24 02 | 00 02 | 01 06 | 02 13 |
| 40 | 16 49 | 17 19 | 17 53 | 24 04 | 00 04 | 01 11 | 02 22 |
| 45 | 16 33 | 17 06 | 17 43 | 24 06 | 00 06 | 01 17 | 02 32 |
| S 50 | 16 13 | 16 51 | 17 32 | 24 08 | 00 08 | 01 24 | 02 45 |
| 52 | 16 04 | 16 44 | 17 27 | 24 09 | 00 09 | 01 27 | 02 51 |
| 54 | 15 53 | 16 36 | 17 22 | 24 10 | 00 10 | 01 31 | 02 57 |
| 56 | 15 41 | 16 28 | 17 16 | 24 11 | 00 11 | 01 35 | 03 05 |
| 58 | 15 28 | 16 18 | 17 10 | 24 12 | 00 12 | 01 40 | 03 13 |
| S 60 | 15 11 | 16 07 | 17 03 | 24 13 | 00 13 | 01 45 | 03 22 |

## SUN / MOON

| Day | Eqn. of Time 00h | Eqn. of Time 12h | Mer. Pass. | Mer. Pass. Upper | Mer. Pass. Lower | Age | Phase |
|---|---|---|---|---|---|---|---|
| d | m s | m s | h m | h m | h m | d | % |
| 6 | 04 44 | 04 49 | 12 05 | 17 45 | 05 23 | 07 | 44 |
| 7 | 04 54 | 04 59 | 12 05 | 18 29 | 06 07 | 08 | 54 |
| 8 | 05 04 | 05 08 | 12 05 | 19 17 | 06 53 | 09 | 65 |

| UT | ARIES GHA | VENUS −3.9 GHA | Dec | MARS +0.3 GHA | Dec | JUPITER −2.5 GHA | Dec | SATURN +0.4 GHA | Dec |
|---|---|---|---|---|---|---|---|---|---|
| **9 00** | 286 54.9 | 208 40.8 | N21 56.1 | 255 52.1 | N10 41.1 | 278 58.1 | N 1 58.9 | 319 50.6 | S14 33.8 |
| 01 | 301 57.3 | 223 40.0 | 56.4 | 270 52.9 | 41.7 | 294 00.4 | 58.9 | 334 53.2 | 33.8 |
| 02 | 316 59.8 | 238 39.3 | 56.8 | 285 53.7 | 42.3 | 309 02.7 | 59.0 | 349 55.8 | 33.9 |
| 03 | 332 02.2 | 253 38.5 .. | 57.1 | 300 54.5 .. | 42.9 | 324 05.0 .. | 59.0 | 4 58.4 .. | 33.9 |
| 04 | 347 04.7 | 268 37.8 | 57.4 | 315 55.4 | 43.5 | 339 07.4 | 59.1 | 20 00.9 | 34.0 |
| 05 | 2 07.2 | 283 37.0 | 57.8 | 330 56.2 | 44.1 | 354 09.7 | 59.1 | 35 03.5 | 34.0 |
| S 06 | 17 09.6 | 298 36.3 | N21 58.1 | 345 57.0 | N10 44.7 | 9 12.0 | N 1 59.2 | 50 06.1 | S14 34.1 |
| A 07 | 32 12.1 | 313 35.5 | 58.5 | 0 57.8 | 45.3 | 24 14.3 | 59.2 | 65 08.7 | 34.1 |
| T 08 | 47 14.6 | 328 34.7 | 58.8 | 15 58.6 | 45.9 | 39 16.6 | 59.3 | 80 11.3 | 34.2 |
| U 09 | 62 17.0 | 343 34.0 .. | 59.1 | 30 59.4 .. | 46.5 | 54 18.9 .. | 59.3 | 95 13.9 .. | 34.2 |
| R 10 | 77 19.5 | 358 33.2 | 59.5 | 46 00.2 | 47.1 | 69 21.3 | 59.4 | 110 16.5 | 34.2 |
| D 11 | 92 22.0 | 13 32.5 | 21 59.8 | 61 01.0 | 47.7 | 84 23.6 | 59.4 | 125 19.1 | 34.3 |
| A 12 | 107 24.4 | 28 31.7 | N22 00.1 | 76 01.8 | N10 48.3 | 99 25.9 | N 1 59.5 | 140 21.6 | S14 34.3 |
| Y 13 | 122 26.9 | 43 31.0 | 00.5 | 91 02.6 | 48.9 | 114 28.2 | 59.5 | 155 24.2 | 34.4 |
| 14 | 137 29.3 | 58 30.2 | 00.8 | 106 03.4 | 49.5 | 129 30.5 | 59.6 | 170 26.8 | 34.4 |
| 15 | 152 31.8 | 73 29.5 .. | 01.1 | 121 04.2 .. | 50.1 | 144 32.8 .. | 59.6 | 185 29.4 .. | 34.5 |
| 16 | 167 34.3 | 88 28.7 | 01.5 | 136 05.0 | 50.7 | 159 35.2 | 59.7 | 200 32.0 | 34.5 |
| 17 | 182 36.7 | 103 28.0 | 01.8 | 151 05.8 | 51.3 | 174 37.5 | 59.7 | 215 34.6 | 34.6 |
| 18 | 197 39.2 | 118 27.2 | N22 02.1 | 166 06.7 | N10 51.9 | 189 39.8 | N 1 59.8 | 230 37.2 | S14 34.6 |
| 19 | 212 41.7 | 133 26.5 | 02.4 | 181 07.5 | 52.5 | 204 42.1 | 59.8 | 245 39.7 | 34.7 |
| 20 | 227 44.1 | 148 25.7 | 02.8 | 196 08.3 | 53.0 | 219 44.4 | 59.9 | 260 42.3 | 34.7 |
| 21 | 242 46.6 | 163 24.9 .. | 03.1 | 211 09.1 .. | 53.6 | 234 46.8 | 1 59.9 | 275 44.9 .. | 34.8 |
| 22 | 257 49.1 | 178 24.2 | 03.4 | 226 09.9 | 54.2 | 249 49.1 | 2 00.0 | 290 47.5 | 34.8 |
| 23 | 272 51.5 | 193 23.4 | 03.7 | 241 10.7 | 54.8 | 264 51.4 | 00.0 | 305 50.1 | 34.9 |
| **10 00** | 287 54.0 | 208 22.7 | N22 04.1 | 256 11.5 | N10 55.4 | 279 53.7 | N 2 00.1 | 320 52.7 | S14 34.9 |
| 01 | 302 56.5 | 223 21.9 | 04.4 | 271 12.3 | 56.0 | 294 56.0 | 00.1 | 335 55.3 | 35.0 |
| 02 | 317 58.9 | 238 21.1 | 04.7 | 286 13.1 | 56.6 | 309 58.4 | 00.2 | 350 57.9 | 35.0 |
| 03 | 333 01.4 | 253 20.4 .. | 05.0 | 301 13.9 .. | 57.2 | 325 00.7 .. | 00.2 | 6 00.5 .. | 35.1 |
| 04 | 348 03.8 | 268 19.6 | 05.3 | 316 14.7 | 57.8 | 340 03.0 | 00.3 | 21 03.0 | 35.1 |
| 05 | 3 06.3 | 283 18.9 | 05.6 | 331 15.5 | 58.4 | 355 05.3 | 00.3 | 36 05.6 | 35.2 |
| S 06 | 18 08.8 | 298 18.1 | N22 06.0 | 346 16.3 | N10 59.0 | 10 07.7 | N 2 00.4 | 51 08.2 | S14 35.2 |
| U 07 | 33 11.2 | 313 17.4 | 06.3 | 1 17.2 | 10 59.6 | 25 10.0 | 00.4 | 66 10.8 | 35.3 |
| N 08 | 48 13.7 | 328 16.6 | 06.6 | 16 18.0 | 11 00.2 | 40 12.3 | 00.4 | 81 13.4 | 35.3 |
| D 09 | 63 16.2 | 343 15.8 .. | 06.9 | 31 18.8 .. | 00.7 | 55 14.6 .. | 00.5 | 96 16.0 .. | 35.4 |
| A 10 | 78 18.6 | 358 15.1 | 07.2 | 46 19.6 | 01.3 | 70 16.9 | 00.5 | 111 18.6 | 35.4 |
| Y 11 | 93 21.1 | 13 14.3 | 07.5 | 61 20.4 | 01.9 | 85 19.3 | 00.6 | 126 21.2 | 35.5 |
| 12 | 108 23.6 | 28 13.5 | N22 07.8 | 76 21.2 | N11 02.5 | 100 21.6 | N 2 00.6 | 141 23.8 | S14 35.5 |
| 13 | 123 26.0 | 43 12.8 | 08.1 | 91 22.0 | 03.1 | 115 23.9 | 00.7 | 156 26.4 | 35.6 |
| 14 | 138 28.5 | 58 12.0 | 08.4 | 106 22.8 | 03.7 | 130 26.2 | 00.7 | 171 28.9 | 35.6 |
| 15 | 153 31.0 | 73 11.3 .. | 08.7 | 121 23.6 .. | 04.3 | 145 28.6 .. | 00.8 | 186 31.5 .. | 35.7 |
| 16 | 168 33.4 | 88 10.5 | 09.1 | 136 24.4 | 04.9 | 160 30.9 | 00.8 | 201 34.1 | 35.7 |
| 17 | 183 35.9 | 103 09.7 | 09.4 | 151 25.2 | 05.5 | 175 33.2 | 00.9 | 216 36.7 | 35.8 |
| 18 | 198 38.3 | 118 09.0 | N22 09.7 | 166 26.0 | N11 06.1 | 190 35.5 | N 2 00.9 | 231 39.3 | S14 35.8 |
| 19 | 213 40.8 | 133 08.2 | 10.0 | 181 26.9 | 06.6 | 205 37.9 | 01.0 | 246 41.9 | 35.9 |
| 20 | 228 43.3 | 148 07.4 | 10.3 | 196 27.7 | 07.2 | 220 40.2 | 01.0 | 261 44.5 | 35.9 |
| 21 | 243 45.7 | 163 06.7 .. | 10.6 | 211 28.5 .. | 07.8 | 235 42.5 .. | 01.0 | 276 47.1 .. | 36.0 |
| 22 | 258 48.2 | 178 05.9 | 10.9 | 226 29.3 | 08.4 | 250 44.9 | 01.1 | 291 49.7 | 36.0 |
| 23 | 273 50.7 | 193 05.2 | 11.2 | 241 30.1 | 09.0 | 265 47.2 | 01.1 | 306 52.3 | 36.1 |
| **11 00** | 288 53.1 | 208 04.4 | N22 11.5 | 256 30.9 | N11 09.6 | 280 49.5 | N 2 01.2 | 321 54.8 | S14 36.1 |
| 01 | 303 55.6 | 223 03.6 | 11.7 | 271 31.7 | 10.2 | 295 51.8 | 01.2 | 336 57.4 | 36.2 |
| 02 | 318 58.1 | 238 02.9 | 12.0 | 286 32.5 | 10.8 | 310 54.2 | 01.3 | 352 00.0 | 36.2 |
| 03 | 334 00.5 | 253 02.1 .. | 12.3 | 301 33.3 .. | 11.3 | 325 56.5 .. | 01.3 | 7 02.6 .. | 36.3 |
| 04 | 349 03.0 | 268 01.3 | 12.6 | 316 34.1 | 11.9 | 340 58.8 | 01.4 | 22 05.2 | 36.3 |
| 05 | 4 05.5 | 283 00.6 | 12.9 | 331 34.9 | 12.5 | 356 01.2 | 01.4 | 37 07.8 | 36.4 |
| M 06 | 19 07.9 | 297 59.8 | N22 13.2 | 346 35.8 | N11 13.1 | 11 03.5 | N 2 01.5 | 52 10.4 | S14 36.4 |
| O 07 | 34 10.4 | 312 59.0 | 13.5 | 1 36.6 | 13.7 | 26 05.8 | 01.5 | 67 13.0 | 36.5 |
| N 08 | 49 12.8 | 327 58.3 | 13.8 | 16 37.4 | 14.3 | 41 08.1 | 01.5 | 82 15.6 | 36.5 |
| D 09 | 64 15.3 | 342 57.5 .. | 14.1 | 31 38.2 .. | 14.9 | 56 10.5 .. | 01.6 | 97 18.2 .. | 36.6 |
| A 10 | 79 17.8 | 357 56.7 | 14.4 | 46 39.0 | 15.4 | 71 12.8 | 01.6 | 112 20.8 | 36.6 |
| Y 11 | 94 20.2 | 12 55.9 | 14.6 | 61 39.8 | 16.0 | 86 15.1 | 01.7 | 127 23.4 | 36.7 |
| 12 | 109 22.7 | 27 55.2 | N22 14.9 | 76 40.6 | N11 16.6 | 101 17.5 | N 2 01.7 | 142 26.0 | S14 36.7 |
| 13 | 124 25.2 | 42 54.4 | 15.2 | 91 41.4 | 17.2 | 116 19.8 | 01.8 | 157 28.5 | 36.8 |
| 14 | 139 27.6 | 57 53.6 | 15.5 | 106 42.2 | 17.8 | 131 22.1 | 01.8 | 172 31.1 | 36.8 |
| 15 | 154 30.1 | 72 52.9 .. | 15.8 | 121 43.0 .. | 18.4 | 146 24.5 .. | 01.8 | 187 33.7 .. | 36.9 |
| 16 | 169 32.6 | 87 52.1 | 16.0 | 136 43.9 | 19.0 | 161 26.8 | 01.9 | 202 36.3 | 37.0 |
| 17 | 184 35.0 | 102 51.3 | 16.3 | 151 44.7 | 19.5 | 176 29.1 | 01.9 | 217 38.9 | 37.0 |
| 18 | 199 37.5 | 117 50.6 | N22 16.6 | 166 45.5 | N11 20.1 | 191 31.5 | N 2 02.0 | 232 41.5 | S14 37.1 |
| 19 | 214 40.0 | 132 49.8 | 16.9 | 181 46.3 | 20.7 | 206 33.8 | 02.0 | 247 44.1 | 37.1 |
| 20 | 229 42.4 | 147 49.0 | 17.1 | 196 47.1 | 21.3 | 221 36.1 | 02.1 | 262 46.7 | 37.2 |
| 21 | 244 44.9 | 162 48.2 .. | 17.4 | 211 47.9 .. | 21.9 | 236 38.5 .. | 02.1 | 277 49.3 .. | 37.2 |
| 22 | 259 47.3 | 177 47.5 | 17.7 | 226 48.7 | 22.5 | 251 40.8 | 02.1 | 292 51.9 | 37.3 |
| 23 | 274 49.8 | 192 46.7 | 18.0 | 241 49.5 | 23.0 | 266 43.1 | 02.2 | 307 54.5 | 37.3 |
| Mer. Pass. | h m 4 47.6 | v −0.8 | d 0.3 | v 0.8 | d 0.6 | v 2.3 | d 0.0 | v 2.6 | d 0.1 |

**STARS**

| Name | SHA | Dec |
|---|---|---|
| Acamar | 315 13.6 | S40 12.7 |
| Achernar | 335 21.8 | S57 07.1 |
| Acrux | 173 02.4 | S63 13.6 |
| Adhara | 255 07.9 | S29 00.1 |
| Aldebaran | 290 42.3 | N16 33.2 |
| Alioth | 166 14.9 | N55 50.6 |
| Alkaid | 152 53.6 | N49 12.4 |
| Al Na'ir | 27 35.2 | S46 51.0 |
| Alnilam | 275 40.1 | S 1 11.2 |
| Alphard | 217 50.1 | S 8 45.3 |
| Alphecca | 126 05.3 | N26 38.5 |
| Alpheratz | 357 36.8 | N29 12.7 |
| Altair | 62 01.6 | N 8 55.7 |
| Ankaa | 353 09.1 | S42 10.8 |
| Antares | 112 18.1 | S26 28.9 |
| Arcturus | 145 49.7 | N19 04.1 |
| Atria | 107 13.7 | S69 04.2 |
| Avior | 234 16.2 | S59 34.9 |
| Bellatrix | 278 25.4 | N 6 22.2 |
| Betelgeuse | 270 54.6 | N 7 24.7 |
| Canopus | 263 53.9 | S52 42.3 |
| Capella | 280 25.4 | N46 01.1 |
| Deneb | 49 26.7 | N45 21.5 |
| Denebola | 182 27.2 | N14 27.0 |
| Diphda | 348 49.3 | S17 51.7 |
| Dubhe | 193 43.9 | N61 38.1 |
| Elnath | 278 04.8 | N28 37.5 |
| Eltanin | 90 42.6 | N51 29.2 |
| Enif | 33 40.6 | N 9 58.6 |
| Fomalhaut | 15 16.6 | S29 30.1 |
| Gacrux | 171 54.0 | S57 14.5 |
| Gienah | 175 45.8 | S17 40.0 |
| Hadar | 148 38.7 | S60 29.1 |
| Hamal | 327 53.6 | N23 34.0 |
| Kaus Aust. | 83 34.9 | S34 22.4 |
| Kochab | 137 19.3 | N74 04.1 |
| Markab | 13 31.8 | N15 19.5 |
| Menkar | 314 08.5 | N 4 10.6 |
| Menkent | 147 59.9 | S36 28.9 |
| Miaplacidus | 221 39.5 | S69 48.6 |
| Mirfak | 308 31.5 | N49 56.2 |
| Nunki | 75 49.9 | S26 16.1 |
| Peacock | 53 08.4 | S56 39.7 |
| Pollux | 243 20.2 | N27 58.4 |
| Procyon | 244 53.3 | N 5 10.1 |
| Rasalhague | 96 00.1 | N12 32.7 |
| Regulus | 207 36.9 | N11 51.6 |
| Rigel | 281 06.2 | S 8 10.5 |
| Rigil Kent. | 139 42.9 | S60 55.8 |
| Sabik | 102 04.8 | S15 45.1 |
| Schedar | 349 33.3 | N56 39.3 |
| Shaula | 96 12.8 | S37 07.2 |
| Sirius | 258 28.4 | S16 44.8 |
| Spica | 158 24.4 | S11 16.7 |
| Suhail | 222 48.2 | S43 31.4 |
| Vega | 80 34.2 | N38 48.3 |
| Zuben'ubi | 136 58.1 | S16 08.1 |

| | SHA | Mer. Pass. |
|---|---|---|
| Venus | 280 28.7 | h m 10 07 |
| Mars | 328 17.5 | 6 55 |
| Jupiter | 351 59.7 | 5 20 |
| Saturn | 32 58.7 | 2 36 |

| UT | SUN GHA | SUN Dec | MOON GHA | v | MOON Dec | d | HP |
|---|---|---|---|---|---|---|---|
| d h | ° ′ | ° ′ | ° ′ | ′ | ° ′ | ′ | ′ |
| **9** 00 | 178 41.8 | N22 22.9 | 68 18.8 | 10.3 | S14 10.6 | 13.7 | 58.9 |
| 01 | 193 41.7 | 22.6 | 82 48.1 | 10.2 | 14 24.3 | 13.6 | 58.9 |
| 02 | 208 41.6 | 22.3 | 97 17.3 | 10.1 | 14 37.9 | 13.6 | 58.9 |
| 03 | 223 41.5 | .. 22.0 | 111 46.4 | 10.0 | 14 51.5 | 13.5 | 59.0 |
| 04 | 238 41.4 | 21.7 | 126 15.4 | 9.9 | 15 05.0 | 13.4 | 59.0 |
| 05 | 253 41.3 | 21.4 | 140 44.3 | 9.7 | 15 18.4 | 13.4 | 59.0 |
| 06 | 268 41.2 | N22 21.1 | 155 13.0 | 9.6 | S15 31.8 | 13.3 | 59.1 |
| 07 | 283 41.1 | 20.8 | 169 41.6 | 9.5 | 15 45.1 | 13.3 | 59.1 |
| 08 | 298 41.0 | 20.5 | 184 10.1 | 9.4 | 15 58.4 | 13.1 | 59.2 |
| 09 | 313 41.0 | .. 20.2 | 198 38.5 | 9.3 | 16 11.5 | 13.1 | 59.2 |
| 10 | 328 40.9 | 19.9 | 213 06.8 | 9.2 | 16 24.6 | 13.0 | 59.2 |
| 11 | 343 40.8 | 19.6 | 227 35.0 | 9.0 | 16 37.6 | 12.9 | 59.3 |
| 12 | 358 40.7 | N22 19.3 | 242 03.0 | 8.9 | S16 50.5 | 12.9 | 59.3 |
| 13 | 13 40.6 | 19.0 | 256 30.9 | 8.8 | 17 03.4 | 12.8 | 59.3 |
| 14 | 28 40.5 | 18.7 | 270 58.7 | 8.6 | 17 16.2 | 12.7 | 59.4 |
| 15 | 43 40.4 | .. 18.4 | 285 26.3 | 8.6 | 17 28.9 | 12.6 | 59.4 |
| 16 | 58 40.3 | 18.1 | 299 53.9 | 8.4 | 17 41.5 | 12.5 | 59.4 |
| 17 | 73 40.2 | 17.8 | 314 21.3 | 8.2 | 17 54.0 | 12.4 | 59.5 |
| 18 | 88 40.1 | N22 17.5 | 328 48.5 | 8.2 | S18 06.4 | 12.3 | 59.5 |
| 19 | 103 40.1 | 17.2 | 343 15.7 | 8.0 | 18 18.7 | 12.3 | 59.6 |
| 20 | 118 40.0 | 16.8 | 357 42.7 | 7.9 | 18 31.0 | 12.1 | 59.6 |
| 21 | 133 39.9 | .. 16.5 | 12 09.6 | 7.7 | 18 43.1 | 12.1 | 59.6 |
| 22 | 148 39.8 | 16.2 | 26 36.3 | 7.7 | 18 55.2 | 11.9 | 59.7 |
| 23 | 163 39.7 | 15.9 | 41 03.0 | 7.5 | 19 07.1 | 11.9 | 59.7 |
| **10** 00 | 178 39.6 | N22 15.6 | 55 29.5 | 7.3 | S19 19.0 | 11.7 | 59.7 |
| 01 | 193 39.5 | 15.3 | 69 55.8 | 7.3 | 19 30.7 | 11.7 | 59.8 |
| 02 | 208 39.4 | 15.0 | 84 22.1 | 7.1 | 19 42.4 | 11.5 | 59.8 |
| 03 | 223 39.3 | .. 14.7 | 98 48.2 | 6.9 | 19 53.9 | 11.4 | 59.8 |
| 04 | 238 39.3 | 14.3 | 113 14.1 | 6.9 | 20 05.3 | 11.4 | 59.9 |
| 05 | 253 39.2 | 14.0 | 127 40.0 | 6.7 | 20 16.7 | 11.2 | 59.9 |
| 06 | 268 39.1 | N22 13.7 | 142 05.7 | 6.6 | S20 27.9 | 11.0 | 59.9 |
| 07 | 283 39.0 | 13.4 | 156 31.3 | 6.4 | 20 38.9 | 11.0 | 60.0 |
| 08 | 298 38.9 | 13.1 | 170 56.7 | 6.3 | 20 49.9 | 10.8 | 60.0 |
| 09 | 313 38.8 | .. 12.8 | 185 22.0 | 6.2 | 21 00.7 | 10.8 | 60.0 |
| 10 | 328 38.7 | 12.4 | 199 47.2 | 6.0 | 21 11.5 | 10.6 | 60.1 |
| 11 | 343 38.6 | 12.1 | 214 12.2 | 5.9 | 21 22.1 | 10.4 | 60.1 |
| 12 | 358 38.6 | N22 11.8 | 228 37.1 | 5.8 | S21 32.5 | 10.2 | 60.1 |
| 13 | 13 38.5 | 11.5 | 243 01.9 | 5.6 | 21 42.9 | 10.2 | 60.2 |
| 14 | 28 38.4 | 11.2 | 257 26.5 | 5.5 | 21 53.1 | 10.1 | 60.2 |
| 15 | 43 38.3 | .. 10.8 | 271 51.0 | 5.4 | 22 03.2 | 9.9 | 60.2 |
| 16 | 58 38.2 | 10.5 | 286 15.4 | 5.2 | 22 13.1 | 9.8 | 60.3 |
| 17 | 73 38.1 | 10.2 | 300 39.6 | 5.2 | 22 22.9 | 9.7 | 60.3 |
| 18 | 88 38.0 | N22 09.9 | 315 03.8 | 4.9 | S22 32.6 | 9.5 | 60.3 |
| 19 | 103 38.0 | 09.5 | 329 27.7 | 4.9 | 22 42.1 | 9.4 | 60.4 |
| 20 | 118 37.9 | 09.2 | 343 51.6 | 4.7 | 22 51.5 | 9.2 | 60.4 |
| 21 | 133 37.8 | .. 08.9 | 358 15.3 | 4.6 | 23 00.7 | 9.1 | 60.4 |
| 22 | 148 37.7 | 08.5 | 12 38.9 | 4.5 | 23 09.8 | 8.9 | 60.4 |
| 23 | 163 37.6 | 08.2 | 27 02.4 | 4.3 | 23 18.7 | 8.8 | 60.5 |
| **11** 00 | 178 37.5 | N22 07.9 | 41 25.7 | 4.2 | S23 27.5 | 8.6 | 60.5 |
| 01 | 193 37.5 | 07.6 | 55 48.9 | 4.1 | 23 36.1 | 8.5 | 60.5 |
| 02 | 208 37.4 | 07.2 | 70 12.0 | 4.0 | 23 44.6 | 8.3 | 60.6 |
| 03 | 223 37.3 | .. 06.9 | 84 35.0 | 3.8 | 23 52.9 | 8.1 | 60.6 |
| 04 | 238 37.2 | 06.6 | 98 57.8 | 3.8 | 24 01.0 | 8.0 | 60.6 |
| 05 | 253 37.1 | 06.3 | 113 20.6 | 3.6 | 24 09.0 | 7.8 | 60.6 |
| 06 | 268 37.0 | N22 05.9 | 127 43.2 | 3.5 | S24 16.8 | 7.7 | 60.7 |
| 07 | 283 37.0 | 05.6 | 142 05.7 | 3.3 | 24 24.5 | 7.5 | 60.7 |
| 08 | 298 36.9 | 05.3 | 156 28.0 | 3.3 | 24 32.0 | 7.3 | 60.7 |
| 09 | 313 36.8 | .. 04.9 | 170 50.3 | 3.1 | 24 39.3 | 7.1 | 60.7 |
| 10 | 328 36.7 | 04.6 | 185 12.4 | 3.0 | 24 46.4 | 7.0 | 60.8 |
| 11 | 343 36.6 | 04.3 | 199 34.4 | 3.0 | 24 53.4 | 6.8 | 60.8 |
| 12 | 358 36.5 | N22 03.9 | 213 56.4 | 2.8 | S25 00.2 | 6.6 | 60.8 |
| 13 | 13 36.5 | 03.6 | 228 18.2 | 2.7 | 25 06.8 | 6.4 | 60.8 |
| 14 | 28 36.4 | 03.2 | 242 39.9 | 2.6 | 25 13.2 | 6.3 | 60.9 |
| 15 | 43 36.3 | .. 02.9 | 257 01.5 | 2.5 | 25 19.5 | 6.0 | 60.9 |
| 16 | 58 36.2 | 02.6 | 271 23.0 | 2.4 | 25 25.5 | 5.9 | 60.9 |
| 17 | 73 36.1 | 02.2 | 285 44.4 | 2.3 | 25 31.4 | 5.7 | 60.9 |
| 18 | 88 36.1 | N22 01.9 | 300 05.7 | 2.2 | S25 37.1 | 5.5 | 60.9 |
| 19 | 103 36.0 | 01.6 | 314 26.9 | 2.1 | 25 42.6 | 5.3 | 61.0 |
| 20 | 118 35.9 | 01.2 | 328 48.0 | 2.0 | 25 47.9 | 5.2 | 61.0 |
| 21 | 133 35.8 | .. 00.9 | 343 09.0 | 2.0 | 25 53.1 | 4.9 | 61.0 |
| 22 | 148 35.7 | 00.5 | 357 30.0 | 1.8 | 25 58.0 | 4.7 | 61.0 |
| 23 | 163 35.7 | 00.2 | 11 50.8 | 1.8 | S26 02.7 | 4.6 | 61.0 |
| | SD 15.8 | d 0.3 | SD 16.2 | | 16.4 | | 16.6 |

Day labels: SATURDAY (9), SUNDAY (10), MONDAY (11)

### Moonrise

| Lat. | Twilight Naut. | Twilight Civil | Sunrise | Moonrise 9 | 10 | 11 | 12 |
|---|---|---|---|---|---|---|---|
| ° | h m | h m | h m | h m | h m | h m | h m |
| N 72 | □ | □ | □ | ■■ | ■■ | ■■ | ■■ |
| N 70 | □ | □ | □ | 18 29 | ■■ | ■■ | ■■ |
| 68 | □ | □ | □ | 17 42 | ■■ | ■■ | ■■ |
| 66 | //// | //// | 01 12 | 17 12 | 19 54 | ■■ | ■■ |
| 64 | //// | //// | 02 01 | 16 50 | 19 02 | ■■ | ■■ |
| 62 | //// | //// | 02 32 | 16 32 | 18 30 | 20 33 | 22 11 |
| 60 | //// | 01 29 | 02 55 | 16 17 | 18 06 | 19 55 | 21 22 |
| N 58 | //// | 02 05 | 03 13 | 16 05 | 17 47 | 19 28 | 20 51 |
| 56 | //// | 02 30 | 03 28 | 15 54 | 17 31 | 19 07 | 20 27 |
| 54 | 01 21 | 02 49 | 03 41 | 15 45 | 17 18 | 18 49 | 20 08 |
| 52 | 01 55 | 03 05 | 03 52 | 15 37 | 17 06 | 18 35 | 19 52 |
| 50 | 02 18 | 03 19 | 04 02 | 15 29 | 16 56 | 18 22 | 19 38 |
| 45 | 02 59 | 03 47 | 04 23 | 15 13 | 16 34 | 17 55 | 19 09 |
| N 40 | 03 27 | 04 08 | 04 40 | 15 00 | 16 17 | 17 34 | 18 47 |
| 35 | 03 49 | 04 25 | 04 54 | 14 50 | 16 02 | 17 17 | 18 29 |
| 30 | 04 07 | 04 39 | 05 06 | 14 40 | 15 50 | 17 02 | 18 13 |
| 20 | 04 34 | 05 03 | 05 27 | 14 24 | 15 29 | 16 37 | 17 46 |
| N 10 | 04 56 | 05 22 | 05 45 | 14 10 | 15 10 | 16 15 | 17 23 |
| 0 | 05 13 | 05 39 | 06 02 | 13 57 | 14 53 | 15 55 | 17 01 |
| S 10 | 05 29 | 05 56 | 06 18 | 13 44 | 14 36 | 15 35 | 16 40 |
| 20 | 05 45 | 06 12 | 06 36 | 13 30 | 14 18 | 15 14 | 16 17 |
| 30 | 06 00 | 06 30 | 06 56 | 13 14 | 13 57 | 14 49 | 15 50 |
| 35 | 06 08 | 06 39 | 07 07 | 13 05 | 13 45 | 14 35 | 15 34 |
| 40 | 06 17 | 06 50 | 07 21 | 12 55 | 13 32 | 14 18 | 15 16 |
| 45 | 06 26 | 07 03 | 07 36 | 12 43 | 13 15 | 13 58 | 14 54 |
| S 50 | 06 37 | 07 18 | 07 56 | 12 29 | 12 56 | 13 33 | 14 27 |
| 52 | 06 42 | 07 25 | 08 05 | 12 22 | 12 46 | 13 21 | 14 13 |
| 54 | 06 47 | 07 32 | 08 15 | 12 15 | 12 36 | 13 08 | 13 58 |
| 56 | 06 53 | 07 41 | 08 26 | 12 06 | 12 24 | 12 52 | 13 39 |
| 58 | 06 59 | 07 50 | 08 40 | 11 57 | 12 11 | 12 34 | 13 17 |
| S 60 | 07 05 | 08 01 | 08 55 | 11 47 | 11 55 | 12 11 | 12 48 |

### Moonset

| Lat. | Sunset | Twilight Civil | Twilight Naut. | Moonset 9 | 10 | 11 | 12 |
|---|---|---|---|---|---|---|---|
| ° | h m | h m | h m | h m | h m | h m | h m |
| N 72 | □ | □ | □ | ■■ | ■■ | ■■ | ■■ |
| N 70 | □ | □ | □ | 21 29 | ■■ | ■■ | ■■ |
| 68 | □ | □ | □ | 22 17 | ■■ | ■■ | ■■ |
| 66 | 22 54 | //// | //// | 22 49 | 22 07 | ■■ | ■■ |
| 64 | 22 07 | //// | //// | 23 12 | 23 00 | ■■ | ■■ |
| 62 | 21 38 | //// | //// | 23 31 | 23 33 | 23 42 | 24 24 |
| 60 | 21 15 | 22 39 | //// | 23 47 | 23 57 | 24 20 | 00 20 |
| N 58 | 20 57 | 22 05 | //// | 24 00 | 00 00 | 00 17 | 00 47 |
| 56 | 20 42 | 21 40 | //// | 24 12 | 00 12 | 00 33 | 01 09 |
| 54 | 20 29 | 21 21 | 22 47 | 00 04 | 00 22 | 00 47 | 01 26 |
| 52 | 20 18 | 21 05 | 22 15 | 00 10 | 00 31 | 00 59 | 01 42 |
| 50 | 20 08 | 20 51 | 21 52 | 00 16 | 00 39 | 01 10 | 01 55 |
| 45 | 19 47 | 20 24 | 21 11 | 00 28 | 00 56 | 01 33 | 02 22 |
| N 40 | 19 30 | 20 03 | 20 43 | 00 38 | 01 10 | 01 51 | 02 43 |
| 35 | 19 16 | 19 46 | 20 21 | 00 46 | 01 23 | 02 07 | 03 01 |
| 30 | 19 04 | 19 31 | 20 04 | 00 54 | 01 33 | 02 20 | 03 16 |
| 20 | 18 43 | 19 08 | 19 37 | 01 07 | 01 52 | 02 43 | 03 43 |
| N 10 | 18 26 | 18 48 | 19 15 | 01 18 | 02 08 | 03 03 | 04 05 |
| 0 | 18 09 | 18 31 | 18 57 | 01 29 | 02 23 | 03 22 | 04 26 |
| S 10 | 17 53 | 18 15 | 18 41 | 01 40 | 02 38 | 03 41 | 04 47 |
| 20 | 17 35 | 17 59 | 18 26 | 01 52 | 02 54 | 04 01 | 05 10 |
| 30 | 17 15 | 17 41 | 18 11 | 02 05 | 03 13 | 04 24 | 05 36 |
| 35 | 17 04 | 17 32 | 18 03 | 02 13 | 03 24 | 04 38 | 05 51 |
| 40 | 16 50 | 17 21 | 17 54 | 02 22 | 03 36 | 04 54 | 06 09 |
| 45 | 16 35 | 17 08 | 17 45 | 02 32 | 03 51 | 05 13 | 06 31 |
| S 50 | 16 16 | 16 53 | 17 34 | 02 45 | 04 10 | 05 37 | 06 58 |
| 52 | 16 06 | 16 46 | 17 29 | 02 51 | 04 19 | 05 48 | 07 12 |
| 54 | 15 56 | 16 39 | 17 24 | 02 57 | 04 28 | 06 01 | 07 27 |
| 56 | 15 45 | 16 31 | 17 19 | 03 05 | 04 39 | 06 16 | 07 45 |
| 58 | 15 31 | 16 21 | 17 13 | 03 13 | 04 52 | 06 34 | 08 07 |
| S 60 | 15 16 | 16 11 | 17 06 | 03 22 | 05 07 | 06 56 | 08 36 |

### SUN / MOON

| Day | SUN Eqn. of Time 00h | 12h | Mer. Pass. | MOON Mer. Pass. Upper | Lower | Age | Phase |
|---|---|---|---|---|---|---|---|
| d | m s | m s | h m | h m | h m | d | % |
| 9 | 05 13 | 05 17 | 12 05 | 20 10 | 07 43 | 10 | 75 |
| 10 | 05 21 | 05 26 | 12 05 | 21 07 | 08 38 | 11 | 85 |
| 11 | 05 30 | 05 34 | 12 06 | 22 10 | 09 38 | 12 | 92 |

| UT | ARIES | VENUS −3.9 | | MARS +0.3 | | JUPITER −2.5 | | SATURN +0.4 | | STARS | | |
|---|---|---|---|---|---|---|---|---|---|---|---|---|
| | GHA | GHA | Dec | GHA | Dec | GHA | Dec | GHA | Dec | Name | SHA | Dec |
| d h | ° ′ | ° ′ | ° ′ | ° ′ | ° ′ | ° ′ | ° ′ | ° ′ | ° ′ | | ° ′ | ° ′ |
| 12 00 | 289 52.3 | 207 45.9 | N22 18.2 | 256 50.3 | N11 23.6 | 281 45.5 | N 2 02.2 | 322 57.1 | S14 37.4 | Acamar | 315 13.5 | S40 12.7 |
| 01 | 304 54.7 | 222 45.2 | 18.5 | 271 51.1 | 24.2 | 296 47.8 | 02.3 | 337 59.7 | 37.4 | Achernar | 335 21.8 | S57 07.1 |
| 02 | 319 57.2 | 237 44.4 | 18.8 | 286 52.0 | 24.8 | 311 50.1 | 02.3 | 353 02.3 | 37.5 | Acrux | 173 02.5 | S63 13.6 |
| 03 | 334 59.7 | 252 43.6 .. | 19.0 | 301 52.8 .. | 25.4 | 326 52.5 .. | 02.4 | 8 04.9 .. | 37.5 | Adhara | 255 07.9 | S29 00.1 |
| 04 | 350 02.1 | 267 42.8 | 19.3 | 316 53.6 | 25.9 | 341 54.8 | 02.4 | 23 07.5 | 37.6 | Aldebaran | 290 42.2 | N16 33.2 |
| 05 | 5 04.6 | 282 42.1 | 19.6 | 331 54.4 | 26.5 | 356 57.1 | 02.4 | 38 10.0 | 37.6 | | | |
| 06 | 20 07.1 | 297 41.3 | N22 19.8 | 346 55.2 | N11 27.1 | 11 59.5 | N 2 02.5 | 53 12.6 | S14 37.7 | Alioth | 166 14.9 | N55 50.6 |
| 07 | 35 09.5 | 312 40.5 | 20.1 | 1 56.0 | 27.7 | 27 01.8 | 02.5 | 68 15.2 | 37.7 | Alkaid | 152 53.6 | N49 12.4 |
| 08 | 50 12.0 | 327 39.7 | 20.4 | 16 56.8 | 28.3 | 42 04.2 | 02.6 | 83 17.8 | 37.8 | Alnair | 27 35.1 | S46 51.0 |
| 09 | 65 14.5 | 342 39.0 .. | 20.6 | 31 57.6 .. | 28.8 | 57 06.5 .. | 02.6 | 98 20.4 .. | 37.8 | Alnilam | 275 40.1 | S 1 11.2 |
| 10 | 80 16.9 | 357 38.2 | 20.9 | 46 58.4 | 29.4 | 72 08.8 | 02.6 | 113 23.0 | 37.9 | Alphard | 217 50.1 | S 8 45.3 |
| 11 | 95 19.4 | 12 37.4 | 21.1 | 61 59.3 | 30.0 | 87 11.2 | 02.7 | 128 25.6 | 37.9 | | | |
| 12 | 110 21.8 | 27 36.6 | N22 21.4 | 77 00.1 | N11 30.6 | 102 13.5 | N 2 02.7 | 143 28.2 | S14 38.0 | Alphecca | 126 05.3 | N26 38.5 |
| 13 | 125 24.3 | 42 35.9 | 21.7 | 92 00.9 | 31.2 | 117 15.8 | 02.8 | 158 30.8 | 38.0 | Alpheratz | 357 36.8 | N29 12.7 |
| 14 | 140 26.8 | 57 35.1 | 21.9 | 107 01.7 | 31.7 | 132 18.2 | 02.8 | 173 33.4 | 38.1 | Altair | 62 01.6 | N 8 55.7 |
| 15 | 155 29.2 | 72 34.3 .. | 22.2 | 122 02.5 .. | 32.3 | 147 20.5 .. | 02.8 | 188 36.0 .. | 38.1 | Ankaa | 353 09.1 | S42 10.8 |
| 16 | 170 31.7 | 87 33.5 | 22.4 | 137 03.3 | 32.9 | 162 22.9 | 02.9 | 203 38.6 | 38.2 | Antares | 112 18.1 | S26 28.9 |
| 17 | 185 34.2 | 102 32.8 | 22.7 | 152 04.1 | 33.5 | 177 25.2 | 02.9 | 218 41.2 | 38.2 | | | |
| 18 | 200 36.6 | 117 32.0 | N22 22.9 | 167 04.9 | N11 34.1 | 192 27.5 | N 2 03.0 | 233 43.8 | S14 38.3 | Arcturus | 145 49.7 | N19 04.1 |
| 19 | 215 39.1 | 132 31.2 | 23.2 | 182 05.8 | 34.6 | 207 29.9 | 03.0 | 248 46.4 | 38.3 | Atria | 107 13.7 | S69 04.2 |
| 20 | 230 41.6 | 147 30.4 | 23.4 | 197 06.6 | 35.2 | 222 32.2 | 03.0 | 263 49.0 | 38.4 | Avior | 234 16.2 | S59 34.9 |
| 21 | 245 44.0 | 162 29.7 .. | 23.7 | 212 07.4 .. | 35.8 | 237 34.6 .. | 03.1 | 278 51.6 .. | 38.4 | Bellatrix | 278 25.4 | N 6 22.2 |
| 22 | 260 46.5 | 177 28.9 | 23.9 | 227 08.2 | 36.4 | 252 36.9 | 03.1 | 293 54.2 | 38.5 | Betelgeuse | 270 54.6 | N 7 24.7 |
| 23 | 275 49.0 | 192 28.1 | 24.2 | 242 09.0 | 37.0 | 267 39.3 | 03.2 | 308 56.8 | 38.6 | | | |
| 13 00 | 290 51.4 | 207 27.3 | N22 24.4 | 257 09.8 | N11 37.5 | 282 41.6 | N 2 03.2 | 323 59.4 | S14 38.6 | Canopus | 263 53.8 | S52 42.3 |
| 01 | 305 53.9 | 222 26.5 | 24.6 | 272 10.6 | 38.1 | 297 43.9 | 03.2 | 339 02.0 | 38.7 | Capella | 280 25.3 | N46 01.1 |
| 02 | 320 56.3 | 237 25.8 | 24.9 | 287 11.4 | 38.7 | 312 46.3 | 03.3 | 354 04.6 | 38.7 | Deneb | 49 26.7 | N45 21.5 |
| 03 | 335 58.8 | 252 25.0 .. | 25.1 | 302 12.2 .. | 39.3 | 327 48.6 .. | 03.3 | 9 07.2 .. | 38.8 | Denebola | 182 27.2 | N14 27.0 |
| 04 | 351 01.3 | 267 24.2 | 25.4 | 317 13.1 | 39.8 | 342 51.0 | 03.4 | 24 09.8 | 38.8 | Diphda | 348 49.3 | S17 51.7 |
| 05 | 6 03.7 | 282 23.4 | 25.6 | 332 13.9 | 40.4 | 357 53.3 | 03.4 | 39 12.4 | 38.9 | | | |
| 06 | 21 06.2 | 297 22.6 | N22 25.9 | 347 14.7 | N11 41.0 | 12 55.7 | N 2 03.4 | 54 15.0 | S14 38.9 | Dubhe | 193 44.0 | N61 38.1 |
| 07 | 36 08.7 | 312 21.9 | 26.1 | 2 15.5 | 41.6 | 27 58.0 | 03.5 | 69 17.6 | 39.0 | Elnath | 278 04.8 | N28 37.5 |
| 08 | 51 11.1 | 327 21.1 | 26.3 | 17 16.3 | 42.1 | 43 00.3 | 03.5 | 84 20.1 | 39.0 | Eltanin | 90 42.6 | N51 29.3 |
| 09 | 66 13.6 | 342 20.3 .. | 26.6 | 32 17.1 .. | 42.7 | 58 02.7 .. | 03.6 | 99 22.7 .. | 39.1 | Enif | 33 40.5 | N 9 58.7 |
| 10 | 81 16.1 | 357 19.5 | 26.8 | 47 17.9 | 43.3 | 73 05.0 | 03.6 | 114 25.3 | 39.1 | Fomalhaut | 15 16.6 | S29 30.1 |
| 11 | 96 18.5 | 12 18.7 | 27.0 | 62 18.7 | 43.9 | 88 07.4 | 03.6 | 129 27.9 | 39.2 | | | |
| 12 | 111 21.0 | 27 18.0 | N22 27.3 | 77 19.6 | N11 44.4 | 103 09.7 | N 2 03.7 | 144 30.5 | S14 39.2 | Gacrux | 171 54.0 | S57 14.5 |
| 13 | 126 23.5 | 42 17.2 | 27.5 | 92 20.4 | 45.0 | 118 12.1 | 03.7 | 159 33.1 | 39.3 | Gienah | 175 45.8 | S17 40.0 |
| 14 | 141 25.9 | 57 16.4 | 27.7 | 107 21.2 | 45.6 | 133 14.4 | 03.7 | 174 35.7 | 39.3 | Hadar | 148 38.7 | S60 29.1 |
| 15 | 156 28.4 | 72 15.6 .. | 27.9 | 122 22.0 .. | 46.2 | 148 16.8 .. | 03.8 | 189 38.3 .. | 39.4 | Hamal | 327 53.6 | N23 34.0 |
| 16 | 171 30.8 | 87 14.8 | 28.2 | 137 22.8 | 46.7 | 163 19.1 | 03.8 | 204 40.9 | 39.4 | Kaus Aust. | 83 34.8 | S34 22.4 |
| 17 | 186 33.3 | 102 14.0 | 28.4 | 152 23.6 | 47.3 | 178 21.5 | 03.8 | 219 43.5 | 39.5 | | | |
| 18 | 201 35.8 | 117 13.3 | N22 28.7 | 167 24.4 | N11 47.9 | 193 23.8 | N 2 03.9 | 234 46.1 | S14 39.5 | Kochab | 137 19.3 | N74 04.1 |
| 19 | 216 38.2 | 132 12.5 | 28.9 | 182 25.3 | 48.5 | 208 26.1 | 03.9 | 249 48.7 | 39.6 | Markab | 13 31.7 | N15 19.5 |
| 20 | 231 40.7 | 147 11.7 | 29.1 | 197 26.1 | 49.0 | 223 28.5 | 04.0 | 264 51.3 | 39.7 | Menkar | 314 08.4 | N 4 10.6 |
| 21 | 246 43.2 | 162 10.9 .. | 29.3 | 212 26.9 .. | 49.6 | 238 30.8 .. | 04.0 | 279 53.9 .. | 39.7 | Menkent | 147 59.9 | S36 28.9 |
| 22 | 261 45.6 | 177 10.1 | 29.5 | 227 27.7 | 50.2 | 253 33.2 | 04.0 | 294 56.5 | 39.8 | Miaplacidus | 221 39.5 | S69 48.6 |
| 23 | 276 48.1 | 192 09.3 | 29.7 | 242 28.5 | 50.7 | 268 35.5 | 04.1 | 309 59.1 | 39.8 | | | |
| 14 00 | 291 50.6 | 207 08.5 | N22 30.0 | 257 29.3 | N11 51.3 | 283 37.9 | N 2 04.1 | 325 01.7 | S14 39.9 | Mirfak | 308 31.4 | N49 56.2 |
| 01 | 306 53.0 | 222 07.8 | 30.2 | 272 30.1 | 51.9 | 298 40.2 | 04.1 | 340 04.3 | 39.9 | Nunki | 75 49.9 | S26 16.1 |
| 02 | 321 55.5 | 237 07.0 | 30.4 | 287 30.9 | 52.5 | 313 42.6 | 04.2 | 355 06.9 | 40.0 | Peacock | 53 08.4 | S56 39.7 |
| 03 | 336 58.0 | 252 06.2 .. | 30.6 | 302 31.8 .. | 53.0 | 328 44.9 .. | 04.2 | 10 09.5 .. | 40.0 | Pollux | 243 20.2 | N27 58.4 |
| 04 | 352 00.4 | 267 05.4 | 30.8 | 317 32.6 | 53.6 | 343 47.3 | 04.2 | 25 12.1 | 40.1 | Procyon | 244 53.3 | N 5 10.1 |
| 05 | 7 02.9 | 282 04.6 | 31.0 | 332 33.4 | 54.2 | 358 49.6 | 04.3 | 40 14.7 | 40.1 | | | |
| 06 | 22 05.3 | 297 03.8 | N22 31.2 | 347 34.2 | N11 54.7 | 13 52.0 | N 2 04.3 | 55 17.3 | S14 40.2 | Rasalhague | 96 00.1 | N12 32.7 |
| 07 | 37 07.8 | 312 03.0 | 31.5 | 2 35.0 | 55.3 | 28 54.3 | 04.4 | 70 19.9 | 40.2 | Regulus | 207 36.9 | N11 51.6 |
| 08 | 52 10.3 | 327 02.3 | 31.7 | 17 35.8 | 55.9 | 43 56.7 | 04.4 | 85 22.5 | 40.3 | Rigel | 281 06.1 | S 8 10.5 |
| 09 | 67 12.7 | 342 01.5 .. | 31.9 | 32 36.6 .. | 56.4 | 58 59.0 .. | 04.4 | 100 25.1 .. | 40.3 | Rigil Kent. | 139 42.9 | S60 55.8 |
| 10 | 82 15.2 | 357 00.7 | 32.1 | 47 37.5 | 57.0 | 74 01.4 | 04.5 | 115 27.7 | 40.4 | Sabik | 102 04.8 | S15 45.1 |
| 11 | 97 17.7 | 11 59.9 | 32.3 | 62 38.3 | 57.6 | 89 03.7 | 04.5 | 130 30.3 | 40.5 | | | |
| 12 | 112 20.1 | 26 59.1 | N22 32.5 | 77 39.1 | N11 58.2 | 104 06.1 | N 2 04.5 | 145 32.9 | S14 40.5 | Schedar | 349 33.2 | N56 39.3 |
| 13 | 127 22.6 | 41 58.3 | 32.7 | 92 39.9 | 58.7 | 119 08.5 | 04.6 | 160 35.5 | 40.6 | Shaula | 96 12.8 | S37 07.2 |
| 14 | 142 25.1 | 56 57.5 | 32.9 | 107 40.7 | 59.3 | 134 10.8 | 04.6 | 175 38.1 | 40.6 | Sirius | 258 28.4 | S16 44.7 |
| 15 | 157 27.5 | 71 56.7 .. | 33.1 | 122 41.5 | 11 59.9 | 149 13.2 .. | 04.6 | 190 40.7 .. | 40.7 | Spica | 158 24.4 | S11 16.7 |
| 16 | 172 30.0 | 86 56.0 | 33.3 | 137 42.4 | 12 00.4 | 164 15.5 | 04.7 | 205 43.3 | 40.7 | Suhail | 222 48.2 | S43 31.4 |
| 17 | 187 32.4 | 101 55.2 | 33.5 | 152 43.2 | 01.0 | 179 17.9 | 04.7 | 220 45.9 | 40.8 | | | |
| 18 | 202 34.9 | 116 54.4 | N22 33.7 | 167 44.0 | N12 01.6 | 194 20.2 | N 2 04.7 | 235 48.5 | S14 40.8 | Vega | 80 34.2 | N38 48.3 |
| 19 | 217 37.4 | 131 53.6 | 33.9 | 182 44.8 | 02.1 | 209 22.6 | 04.8 | 250 51.1 | 40.9 | Zuben'ubi | 136 58.1 | S16 08.1 |
| 20 | 232 39.8 | 146 52.8 | 34.1 | 197 45.6 | 02.7 | 224 24.9 | 04.8 | 265 53.7 | 40.9 | | SHA | Mer. Pass. |
| 21 | 247 42.3 | 161 52.0 .. | 34.3 | 212 46.4 .. | 03.3 | 239 27.3 .. | 04.8 | 280 56.3 .. | 41.0 | | ° ′ | h m |
| 22 | 262 44.8 | 176 51.2 | 34.5 | 227 47.2 | 03.8 | 254 29.6 | 04.9 | 295 58.9 | 41.0 | Venus | 276 35.9 | 10 11 |
| 23 | 277 47.2 | 191 50.4 | 34.7 | 242 48.1 | 04.4 | 269 32.0 | 04.9 | 311 01.6 | 41.1 | Mars | 326 18.4 | 6 51 |
| | h m | | | | | | | | | Jupiter | 351 50.2 | 5 08 |
| Mer. Pass. 4 35.8 | | v −0.8 | d 0.2 | v 0.8 | d 0.6 | v 2.3 | d 0.0 | v 2.6 | d 0.1 | Saturn | 33 08.0 | 2 24 |

| UT | SUN | | MOON | | | | | Lat. | Twilight | | Sunrise | Moonrise | | | |
|---|---|---|---|---|---|---|---|---|---|---|---|---|---|---|---|
| | GHA | Dec | GHA | v | Dec | d | HP | | Naut. | Civil | | 12 | 13 | 14 | 15 |
| d h | ° ′ | ° ′ | ° ′ | ′ | ° ′ | ′ | ′ | ° | h m | h m | h m | h m | h m | h m | h m |
| 12 00 | 178 35.6 | N21 59.8 | 26 11.6 | 1.7 | S26 07.3 | 4.3 | 61.1 | N 72 | ☐ | ☐ | ☐ | ▬▬ | ▬▬ | ▬▬ | ▬▬ |
| 01 | 193 35.5 | 59.5 | 40 32.3 | 1.6 | 26 11.6 | 4.1 | 61.1 | N 70 | ☐ | ☐ | ☐ | ▬▬ | ▬▬ | ▬▬ | 23 57 |
| 02 | 208 35.4 | 59.1 | 54 52.9 | 1.5 | 26 15.7 | 4.0 | 61.1 | 66 | //// | //// | 01 26 | ▬▬ | ▬▬ | ▬▬ | (00 04 / 23 31) |
| 03 | 223 35.3 .. | 58.8 | 69 13.4 | 1.5 | 26 19.7 | 3.7 | 61.1 | 64 | //// | //// | 02 10 | ▬▬ | 23 56 | 23 21 | 23 10 |
| 04 | 238 35.3 | 58.5 | 83 33.9 | 1.4 | 26 23.4 | 3.5 | 61.1 | 62 | //// | 00 31 | 02 38 | 22 11 | 22 45 | 22 52 | 22 53 |
| 05 | 253 35.2 | 58.1 | 97 54.3 | 1.3 | 26 26.9 | 3.4 | 61.2 | 60 | //// | 01 38 | 03 00 | 21 22 | 22 09 | 22 29 | 22 39 |
| 06 | 268 35.1 | N21 57.8 | 112 14.6 | 1.3 | S26 30.3 | 3.1 | 61.2 | N 58 | //// | 02 11 | 03 17 | 20 51 | 21 43 | 22 11 | 22 26 |
| 07 | 283 35.0 | 57.4 | 126 34.9 | 1.2 | 26 33.4 | 2.9 | 61.2 | 56 | 00 28 | 02 35 | 03 32 | 20 27 | 21 22 | 21 56 | 22 16 |
| 08 | 298 35.0 | 57.1 | 140 55.1 | 1.2 | 26 36.3 | 2.7 | 61.2 | 54 | 01 30 | 02 54 | 03 44 | 20 08 | 21 05 | 21 42 | 22 06 |
| 09 | 313 34.9 .. | 56.7 | 155 15.3 | 1.1 | 26 39.0 | 2.5 | 61.2 | 52 | 02 01 | 03 09 | 03 56 | 19 52 | 20 50 | 21 31 | 21 58 |
| 10 | 328 34.8 | 56.4 | 169 35.4 | 1.0 | 26 41.5 | 2.3 | 61.2 | 50 | 02 23 | 03 23 | 04 05 | 19 38 | 20 37 | 21 20 | 21 51 |
| 11 | 343 34.7 | 56.0 | 183 55.4 | 1.0 | 26 43.8 | 2.1 | 61.2 | 45 | 03 02 | 03 50 | 04 26 | 19 09 | 20 11 | 20 58 | 21 34 |
| 12 | 358 34.7 | N21 55.7 | 198 15.4 | 1.0 | S26 45.9 | 1.9 | 61.2 | N 40 | 03 30 | 04 10 | 04 42 | 18 47 | 19 50 | 20 41 | 21 21 |
| 13 | 13 34.6 | 55.3 | 212 35.4 | 0.9 | 26 47.8 | 1.7 | 61.3 | 35 | 03 51 | 04 27 | 04 56 | 18 29 | 19 32 | 20 26 | 21 10 |
| 14 | 28 34.5 | 55.0 | 226 55.3 | 0.9 | 26 49.5 | 1.4 | 61.3 | 30 | 04 08 | 04 41 | 05 08 | 18 13 | 19 17 | 20 13 | 20 59 |
| 15 | 43 34.4 .. | 54.6 | 241 15.2 | 0.9 | 26 50.9 | 1.3 | 61.3 | 20 | 04 35 | 05 04 | 05 28 | 17 46 | 18 51 | 19 51 | 20 42 |
| 16 | 58 34.3 | 54.3 | 255 35.1 | 0.8 | 26 52.2 | 1.0 | 61.3 | N 10 | 04 56 | 05 23 | 05 46 | 17 23 | 18 29 | 19 31 | 20 27 |
| 17 | 73 34.3 | 53.9 | 269 54.9 | 0.8 | 26 53.2 | 0.8 | 61.3 | 0 | 05 14 | 05 40 | 06 02 | 17 01 | 18 08 | 19 13 | 20 13 |
| 18 | 88 34.2 | N21 53.5 | 284 14.7 | 0.8 | S26 54.0 | 0.6 | 61.3 | S 10 | 05 30 | 05 56 | 06 18 | 16 40 | 17 48 | 18 55 | 19 58 |
| 19 | 103 34.1 | 53.2 | 298 34.5 | 0.7 | 26 54.6 | 0.4 | 61.3 | 20 | 05 45 | 06 12 | 06 35 | 16 17 | 17 25 | 18 35 | 19 43 |
| 20 | 118 34.0 | 52.8 | 312 54.2 | 0.8 | 26 55.0 | 0.2 | 61.3 | 30 | 05 59 | 06 29 | 06 55 | 15 50 | 16 59 | 18 13 | 19 25 |
| 21 | 133 34.0 .. | 52.5 | 327 14.0 | 0.7 | 26 55.2 | 0.1 | 61.3 | 35 | 06 07 | 06 39 | 07 06 | 15 34 | 16 44 | 17 59 | 19 15 |
| 22 | 148 33.9 | 52.1 | 341 33.7 | 0.7 | 26 55.1 | 0.2 | 61.3 | 40 | 06 16 | 06 49 | 07 19 | 15 16 | 16 26 | 17 44 | 19 03 |
| 23 | 163 33.8 | 51.8 | 355 53.4 | 0.7 | 26 54.9 | 0.5 | 61.3 | 45 | 06 25 | 07 02 | 07 35 | 14 54 | 16 05 | 17 26 | 18 49 |
| 13 00 | 178 33.7 | N21 51.4 | 10 13.1 | 0.8 | S26 54.4 | 0.7 | 61.4 | S 50 | 06 35 | 07 16 | 07 53 | 14 27 | 15 38 | 17 03 | 18 32 |
| 01 | 193 33.7 | 51.0 | 24 32.9 | 0.7 | 26 53.7 | 0.9 | 61.4 | 52 | 06 40 | 07 23 | 08 02 | 14 13 | 15 25 | 16 52 | 18 24 |
| 02 | 208 33.6 | 50.7 | 38 52.6 | 0.7 | 26 52.8 | 1.1 | 61.4 | 54 | 06 45 | 07 30 | 08 12 | 13 58 | 15 10 | 16 39 | 18 15 |
| 03 | 223 33.5 .. | 50.3 | 53 12.3 | 0.7 | 26 51.7 | 1.4 | 61.4 | 56 | 06 50 | 07 38 | 08 23 | 13 39 | 14 52 | 16 25 | 18 04 |
| 04 | 238 33.5 | 49.9 | 67 32.0 | 0.8 | 26 50.3 | 1.5 | 61.4 | 58 | 06 56 | 07 47 | 08 36 | 13 17 | 14 30 | 16 08 | 17 52 |
| 05 | 253 33.4 | 49.6 | 81 51.8 | 0.8 | 26 48.8 | 1.8 | 61.4 | S 60 | 07 03 | 07 57 | 08 51 | 12 48 | 14 02 | 15 47 | 17 39 |
| 06 | 268 33.3 | N21 49.2 | 96 11.6 | 0.7 | S26 47.0 | 1.9 | 61.4 | Lat. | Sunset | Twilight | | Moonset | | | |
| 07 | 283 33.2 | 48.9 | 110 31.3 | 0.9 | 26 45.1 | 2.2 | 61.4 | | | Civil | Naut. | 12 | 13 | 14 | 15 |
| 08 | 298 33.2 | 48.5 | 124 51.2 | 0.8 | 26 42.9 | 2.4 | 61.4 | ° | h m | h m | h m | h m | h m | h m | h m |
| 09 | 313 33.1 .. | 48.1 | 139 11.0 | 0.9 | 26 40.5 | 2.6 | 61.4 | N 72 | ☐ | ☐ | ☐ | ▬▬ | ▬▬ | ▬▬ | ▬▬ |
| 10 | 328 33.0 | 47.8 | 153 30.9 | 0.9 | 26 37.9 | 2.9 | 61.4 | N 70 | ☐ | ☐ | ☐ | ▬▬ | ▬▬ | ▬▬ | ▬▬ |
| 11 | 343 32.9 | 47.4 | 167 50.8 | 0.9 | 26 35.0 | 3.0 | 61.4 | 68 | ☐ | ☐ | ☐ | ▬▬ | ▬▬ | ▬▬ | 03 06 |
| 12 | 358 32.9 | N21 47.0 | 182 10.7 | 1.0 | S26 32.0 | 3.3 | 61.4 | 66 | 22 42 | //// | //// | ▬▬ | ▬▬ | 01 01 | 03 49 |
| 13 | 13 32.8 | 46.7 | 196 30.7 | 1.0 | 26 28.7 | 3.4 | 61.4 | 64 | 22 00 | //// | //// | ▬▬ | ▬▬ | 01 01 | 03 49 |
| 14 | 28 32.7 | 46.3 | 210 50.7 | 1.1 | 26 25.3 | 3.7 | 61.4 | 62 | 21 32 | 23 31 | //// | 24 24 | 00 24 | 02 11 | 04 17 |
| 15 | 43 32.7 .. | 45.9 | 225 10.8 | 1.1 | 26 21.6 | 3.9 | 61.4 | 60 | 21 11 | 22 31 | //// | 00 20 | 01 13 | 02 46 | 04 39 |
| 16 | 58 32.6 | 45.6 | 239 30.9 | 1.2 | 26 17.7 | 4.0 | 61.4 | N 58 | 20 53 | 21 59 | //// | 00 47 | 01 44 | 03 12 | 04 56 |
| 17 | 73 32.5 | 45.2 | 253 51.1 | 1.2 | 26 13.7 | 4.3 | 61.4 | 56 | 20 39 | 21 35 | 23 34 | 01 09 | 02 08 | 03 32 | 05 11 |
| 18 | 88 32.4 | N21 44.8 | 268 11.3 | 1.3 | S26 09.4 | 4.5 | 61.4 | 54 | 20 26 | 21 17 | 22 39 | 01 26 | 02 27 | 03 49 | 05 24 |
| 19 | 103 32.4 | 44.4 | 282 31.6 | 1.4 | 26 04.9 | 4.7 | 61.3 | 52 | 20 15 | 21 01 | 22 09 | 01 42 | 02 43 | 04 04 | 05 35 |
| 20 | 118 32.3 | 44.1 | 296 52.0 | 1.4 | 26 00.2 | 4.9 | 61.3 | 50 | 20 06 | 20 48 | 21 47 | 01 55 | 02 57 | 04 16 | 05 44 |
| 21 | 133 32.2 .. | 43.7 | 311 12.4 | 1.5 | 25 55.3 | 5.1 | 61.3 | 45 | 19 45 | 20 21 | 21 08 | 02 22 | 03 25 | 04 42 | 06 05 |
| 22 | 148 32.2 | 43.3 | 325 32.9 | 1.5 | 25 50.2 | 5.3 | 61.3 | N 40 | 19 29 | 20 01 | 20 41 | 02 43 | 03 48 | 05 02 | 06 22 |
| 23 | 163 32.1 | 43.0 | 339 53.4 | 1.7 | 25 44.9 | 5.5 | 61.3 | 35 | 19 15 | 19 44 | 20 20 | 03 01 | 04 06 | 05 19 | 06 36 |
| 14 00 | 178 32.0 | N21 42.6 | 354 14.1 | 1.7 | S25 39.4 | 5.7 | 61.3 | 30 | 19 03 | 19 30 | 20 03 | 03 16 | 04 22 | 05 34 | 06 48 |
| 01 | 193 32.0 | 42.2 | 8 34.8 | 1.8 | 25 33.7 | 5.9 | 61.3 | 20 | 18 43 | 19 07 | 19 36 | 03 43 | 04 49 | 05 59 | 07 08 |
| 02 | 208 31.9 | 41.8 | 22 55.6 | 1.9 | 25 27.8 | 6.0 | 61.3 | N 10 | 18 26 | 18 48 | 19 15 | 04 05 | 05 12 | 06 20 | 07 26 |
| 03 | 223 31.8 .. | 41.4 | 37 16.5 | 1.9 | 25 21.8 | 6.3 | 61.3 | 0 | 18 09 | 18 32 | 18 58 | 04 26 | 05 33 | 06 40 | 07 42 |
| 04 | 238 31.8 | 41.1 | 51 37.4 | 2.1 | 25 15.5 | 6.5 | 61.3 | S 10 | 17 53 | 18 16 | 18 42 | 04 47 | 05 55 | 06 59 | 07 58 |
| 05 | 253 31.7 | 40.7 | 65 58.5 | 2.1 | 25 09.0 | 6.6 | 61.3 | 20 | 17 36 | 18 00 | 18 27 | 05 10 | 06 18 | 07 20 | 08 16 |
| 06 | 268 31.6 | N21 40.3 | 80 19.6 | 2.3 | S25 02.4 | 6.9 | 61.2 | 30 | 17 17 | 17 43 | 18 12 | 05 36 | 06 44 | 07 44 | 08 35 |
| 07 | 283 31.6 | 39.9 | 94 40.9 | 2.3 | 24 55.5 | 7.0 | 61.2 | 35 | 17 05 | 17 33 | 18 04 | 05 51 | 07 00 | 07 58 | 08 47 |
| 08 | 298 31.5 | 39.6 | 109 02.2 | 2.4 | 24 48.5 | 7.2 | 61.2 | 40 | 16 53 | 17 23 | 17 56 | 06 09 | 07 18 | 08 15 | 09 00 |
| 09 | 313 31.4 .. | 39.2 | 123 23.6 | 2.5 | 24 41.3 | 7.4 | 61.2 | 45 | 16 37 | 17 10 | 17 47 | 06 31 | 07 39 | 08 34 | 09 15 |
| 10 | 328 31.3 | 38.8 | 137 45.1 | 2.7 | 24 33.9 | 7.6 | 61.2 | S 50 | 16 19 | 16 56 | 17 37 | 06 58 | 08 07 | 08 58 | 09 34 |
| 11 | 343 31.3 | 38.4 | 152 06.8 | 2.7 | 24 26.3 | 7.7 | 61.2 | 52 | 16 10 | 16 49 | 17 32 | 07 12 | 08 20 | 09 09 | 09 43 |
| 12 | 358 31.2 | N21 38.0 | 166 28.5 | 2.8 | S24 18.6 | 8.0 | 61.2 | 54 | 16 00 | 16 42 | 17 27 | 07 27 | 08 35 | 09 22 | 09 53 |
| 13 | 13 31.2 | 37.6 | 180 50.3 | 3.0 | 24 10.6 | 8.1 | 61.2 | 56 | 15 49 | 16 34 | 17 22 | 07 45 | 08 53 | 09 37 | 10 04 |
| 14 | 28 31.1 | 37.3 | 195 12.3 | 3.0 | 24 02.5 | 8.3 | 61.1 | 58 | 15 36 | 16 25 | 17 16 | 08 07 | 09 15 | 09 55 | 10 16 |
| 15 | 43 31.0 .. | 36.9 | 209 34.3 | 3.2 | 23 54.2 | 8.4 | 61.1 | S 60 | 15 21 | 16 15 | 17 09 | 08 36 | 09 43 | 10 16 | 10 31 |
| 16 | 58 31.0 | 36.5 | 223 56.5 | 3.3 | 23 45.8 | 8.6 | 61.1 | | | | | | | | |
| 17 | 73 30.9 | 36.1 | 238 18.8 | 3.3 | 23 37.2 | 8.8 | 61.1 | | | | | | | | |

| | SUN | | | MOON | | | |
|---|---|---|---|---|---|---|---|
| Day | Eqn. of Time | | Mer. | Mer. Pass. | | Age | Phase |
| | 00ʰ | 12ʰ | Pass. | Upper | Lower | | |
| d | m s | m s | h m | h m | h m | d | % |
| 12 | 05 38 | 05 41 | 12 06 | 23 17 | 10 44 | 13 | 97 |
| 13 | 05 45 | 05 48 | 12 06 | 24 24 | 11 51 | 14 | 100 |
| 14 | 05 52 | 05 55 | 12 06 | 00 24 | 12 56 | 15 | 99 |

Additional SUN rows (18–23):

| UT | GHA | Dec |
|---|---|---|
| 18 | 88 30.8 | N21 35.7 |
| 19 | 103 30.8 | 35.3 |
| 20 | 118 30.7 | 34.9 |
| 21 | 133 30.6 .. | 34.6 |
| 22 | 148 30.6 | 34.2 |
| 23 | 163 30.5 | 33.8 |

Additional MOON rows (18–23):

| UT | GHA | v | Dec | d | HP |
|---|---|---|---|---|---|
| 18 | 252 41.1 | 3.6 | S23 28.4 | 9.0 | 61.1 |
| 19 | 267 03.7 | 3.6 | 23 19.4 | 9.1 | 61.0 |
| 20 | 281 26.3 | 3.7 | 23 10.3 | 9.2 | 61.0 |
| 21 | 295 49.0 | 3.9 | 23 01.1 | 9.5 | 61.0 |
| 22 | 310 11.9 | 3.9 | 22 51.6 | 9.6 | 61.0 |
| 23 | 324 34.8 | 4.1 | S22 42.0 | 9.7 | 61.0 |

| | SD | | | | | |
|---|---|---|---|---|---|---|
| SUN | SD 15.8 | d 0.4 | MOON | SD 16.7 | 16.7 | 16.7 |

## Planetary Ephemeris

| UT (d h) | ARIES GHA | VENUS −3.9 GHA | Dec | MARS +0.3 GHA | Dec | JUPITER −2.5 GHA | Dec | SATURN +0.4 GHA | Dec |
|---|---|---|---|---|---|---|---|---|---|
| 15 00 | 292 49.7 | 206 49.6 | N22 34.9 | 257 48.9 | N12 05.0 | 284 34.4 | N 2 04.9 | 326 04.2 | S14 41.1 |
| 01 | 307 52.2 | 221 48.8 | 35.1 | 272 49.7 | 05.5 | 299 36.7 | 05.0 | 341 06.8 | 41.2 |
| 02 | 322 54.6 | 236 48.0 | 35.3 | 287 50.5 | 06.1 | 314 39.1 | 05.0 | 356 09.4 | 41.3 |
| 03 | 337 57.1 | 251 47.3 .. | 35.5 | 302 51.3 .. | 06.7 | 329 41.4 .. | 05.0 | 11 12.0 .. | 41.3 |
| 04 | 352 59.6 | 266 46.5 | 35.6 | 317 52.1 | 07.2 | 344 43.8 | 05.1 | 26 14.6 | 41.4 |
| 05 | 8 02.0 | 281 45.7 | 35.8 | 332 52.9 | 07.8 | 359 46.1 | 05.1 | 41 17.2 | 41.4 |
| 06 | 23 04.5 | 296 44.9 | N22 36.0 | 347 53.8 | N12 08.4 | 14 48.5 | N 2 05.1 | 56 19.8 | S14 41.5 |
| 07 | 38 06.9 | 311 44.1 | 36.2 | 2 54.6 | 08.9 | 29 50.9 | 05.2 | 71 22.4 | 41.5 |
| 08 | 53 09.4 | 326 43.3 | 36.4 | 17 55.4 | 09.5 | 44 53.2 | 05.2 | 86 25.0 | 41.6 |
| F 09 | 68 11.9 | 341 42.5 .. | 36.6 | 32 56.2 .. | 10.1 | 59 55.6 .. | 05.2 | 101 27.6 .. | 41.6 |
| R 10 | 83 14.3 | 356 41.7 | 36.8 | 47 57.0 | 10.6 | 74 57.9 | 05.3 | 116 30.2 | 41.7 |
| I 11 | 98 16.8 | 11 40.9 | 36.9 | 62 57.8 | 11.2 | 90 00.3 | 05.3 | 131 32.8 | 41.7 |
| D 12 | 113 19.3 | 26 40.1 | N22 37.1 | 77 58.7 | N12 11.7 | 105 02.7 | N 2 05.3 | 146 35.4 | S14 41.8 |
| A 13 | 128 21.7 | 41 39.3 | 37.3 | 92 59.5 | 12.3 | 120 05.0 | 05.3 | 161 38.0 | 41.9 |
| Y 14 | 143 24.2 | 56 38.5 | 37.5 | 108 00.3 | 12.9 | 135 07.4 | 05.4 | 176 40.6 | 41.9 |
| 15 | 158 26.7 | 71 37.7 .. | 37.6 | 123 01.1 .. | 13.4 | 150 09.7 .. | 05.4 | 191 43.2 .. | 42.0 |
| 16 | 173 29.1 | 86 36.9 | 37.8 | 138 01.9 | 14.0 | 165 12.1 | 05.4 | 206 45.8 | 42.0 |
| 17 | 188 31.6 | 101 36.2 | 38.0 | 153 02.7 | 14.6 | 180 14.5 | 05.5 | 221 48.4 | 42.1 |
| 18 | 203 34.1 | 116 35.4 | N22 38.2 | 168 03.6 | N12 15.1 | 195 16.8 | N 2 05.5 | 236 51.0 | S14 42.1 |
| 19 | 218 36.5 | 131 34.6 | 38.3 | 183 04.4 | 15.7 | 210 19.2 | 05.5 | 251 53.6 | 42.2 |
| 20 | 233 39.0 | 146 33.8 | 38.5 | 198 05.2 | 16.2 | 225 21.5 | 05.6 | 266 56.2 | 42.2 |
| 21 | 248 41.4 | 161 33.0 .. | 38.7 | 213 06.0 .. | 16.8 | 240 23.9 .. | 05.6 | 281 58.8 .. | 42.3 |
| 22 | 263 43.9 | 176 32.2 | 38.8 | 228 06.8 | 17.4 | 255 26.3 | 05.6 | 297 01.4 | 42.3 |
| 23 | 278 46.4 | 191 31.4 | 39.0 | 243 07.6 | 17.9 | 270 28.6 | 05.7 | 312 04.0 | 42.4 |
| 16 00 | 293 48.8 | 206 30.6 | N22 39.2 | 258 08.5 | N12 18.5 | 285 31.0 | N 2 05.7 | 327 06.6 | S14 42.5 |
| 01 | 308 51.3 | 221 29.8 | 39.3 | 273 09.3 | 19.1 | 300 33.4 | 05.7 | 342 09.2 | 42.5 |
| 02 | 323 53.8 | 236 29.0 | 39.5 | 288 10.1 | 19.6 | 315 35.7 | 05.7 | 357 11.9 | 42.6 |
| 03 | 338 56.2 | 251 28.2 .. | 39.7 | 303 10.9 .. | 20.2 | 330 38.1 .. | 05.8 | 12 14.5 .. | 42.6 |
| 04 | 353 58.7 | 266 27.4 | 39.8 | 318 11.7 | 20.7 | 345 40.4 | 05.8 | 27 17.1 | 42.7 |
| 05 | 9 01.2 | 281 26.6 | 40.0 | 333 12.5 | 21.3 | 0 42.8 | 05.8 | 42 19.7 | 42.7 |
| 06 | 24 03.6 | 296 25.8 | N22 40.2 | 348 13.4 | N12 21.9 | 15 45.2 | N 2 05.9 | 57 22.3 | S14 42.8 |
| 07 | 39 06.1 | 311 25.0 | 40.3 | 3 14.2 | 22.4 | 30 47.5 | 05.9 | 72 24.9 | 42.8 |
| S 08 | 54 08.6 | 326 24.2 | 40.5 | 18 15.0 | 23.0 | 45 49.9 | 05.9 | 87 27.5 | 42.9 |
| A 09 | 69 11.0 | 341 23.4 .. | 40.6 | 33 15.8 .. | 23.5 | 60 52.3 .. | 05.9 | 102 30.1 .. | 42.9 |
| T 10 | 84 13.5 | 356 22.6 | 40.8 | 48 16.6 | 24.1 | 75 54.6 | 06.0 | 117 32.7 | 43.0 |
| U 11 | 99 15.9 | 11 21.8 | 40.9 | 63 17.5 | 24.6 | 90 57.0 | 06.0 | 132 35.3 | 43.1 |
| R 12 | 114 18.4 | 26 21.0 | N22 41.1 | 78 18.3 | N12 25.2 | 105 59.4 | N 2 06.0 | 147 37.9 | S14 43.1 |
| D 13 | 129 20.9 | 41 20.2 | 41.2 | 93 19.1 | 25.8 | 121 01.7 | 06.1 | 162 40.5 | 43.2 |
| A 14 | 144 23.3 | 56 19.4 | 41.4 | 108 19.9 | 26.3 | 136 04.1 | 06.1 | 177 43.1 | 43.2 |
| Y 15 | 159 25.8 | 71 18.6 .. | 41.5 | 123 20.7 .. | 26.9 | 151 06.5 .. | 06.1 | 192 45.7 .. | 43.3 |
| 16 | 174 28.3 | 86 17.8 | 41.7 | 138 21.5 | 27.4 | 166 08.8 | 06.1 | 207 48.3 | 43.3 |
| 17 | 189 30.7 | 101 17.0 | 41.8 | 153 22.4 | 28.0 | 181 11.2 | 06.2 | 222 50.9 | 43.4 |
| 18 | 204 33.2 | 116 16.2 | N22 42.0 | 168 23.2 | N12 28.5 | 196 13.6 | N 2 06.2 | 237 53.5 | S14 43.4 |
| 19 | 219 35.7 | 131 15.4 | 42.1 | 183 24.0 | 29.1 | 211 15.9 | 06.2 | 252 56.2 | 43.5 |
| 20 | 234 38.1 | 146 14.6 | 42.3 | 198 24.8 | 29.7 | 226 18.3 | 06.3 | 267 58.8 | 43.5 |
| 21 | 249 40.6 | 161 13.8 .. | 42.4 | 213 25.6 .. | 30.2 | 241 20.7 .. | 06.3 | 283 01.4 .. | 43.6 |
| 22 | 264 43.0 | 176 13.0 | 42.6 | 228 26.5 | 30.8 | 256 23.1 | 06.3 | 298 04.0 | 43.7 |
| 23 | 279 45.5 | 191 12.2 | 42.7 | 243 27.3 | 31.3 | 271 25.4 | 06.3 | 313 06.6 | 43.7 |
| 17 00 | 294 48.0 | 206 11.4 | N22 42.8 | 258 28.1 | N12 31.9 | 286 27.8 | N 2 06.4 | 328 09.2 | S14 43.8 |
| 01 | 309 50.4 | 221 10.6 | 43.0 | 273 28.9 | 32.4 | 301 30.2 | 06.4 | 343 11.8 | 43.8 |
| 02 | 324 52.9 | 236 09.8 | 43.1 | 288 29.7 | 33.0 | 316 32.5 | 06.4 | 358 14.4 | 43.9 |
| 03 | 339 55.4 | 251 09.0 .. | 43.3 | 303 30.5 .. | 33.6 | 331 34.9 .. | 06.4 | 13 17.0 .. | 43.9 |
| 04 | 354 57.8 | 266 08.2 | 43.4 | 318 31.4 | 34.1 | 346 37.3 | 06.5 | 28 19.6 | 44.0 |
| 05 | 10 00.3 | 281 07.4 | 43.5 | 333 32.2 | 34.7 | 1 39.7 | 06.5 | 43 22.2 | 44.0 |
| 06 | 25 02.8 | 296 06.6 | N22 43.7 | 348 33.0 | N12 35.2 | 16 42.0 | N 2 06.5 | 58 24.8 | S14 44.1 |
| 07 | 40 05.2 | 311 05.8 | 43.8 | 3 33.8 | 35.8 | 31 44.4 | 06.5 | 73 27.4 | 44.2 |
| 08 | 55 07.7 | 326 05.0 | 43.9 | 18 34.6 | 36.3 | 46 46.8 | 06.6 | 88 30.1 | 44.2 |
| S 09 | 70 10.2 | 341 04.2 .. | 44.1 | 33 35.5 .. | 36.9 | 61 49.1 .. | 06.6 | 103 32.7 .. | 44.3 |
| U 10 | 85 12.6 | 356 03.4 | 44.2 | 48 36.3 | 37.4 | 76 51.5 | 06.6 | 118 35.3 | 44.3 |
| N 11 | 100 15.1 | 11 02.6 | 44.3 | 63 37.1 | 38.0 | 91 53.9 | 06.6 | 133 37.9 | 44.4 |
| D 12 | 115 17.5 | 26 01.8 | N22 44.4 | 78 37.9 | N12 38.5 | 106 56.3 | N 2 06.7 | 148 40.5 | S14 44.4 |
| A 13 | 130 20.0 | 41 01.0 | 44.6 | 93 38.7 | 39.1 | 121 58.6 | 06.7 | 163 43.1 | 44.5 |
| Y 14 | 145 22.5 | 56 00.2 | 44.7 | 108 39.6 | 39.6 | 137 01.0 | 06.7 | 178 45.7 | 44.5 |
| 15 | 160 24.9 | 70 59.4 .. | 44.8 | 123 40.4 .. | 40.2 | 152 03.4 .. | 06.7 | 193 48.3 .. | 44.6 |
| 16 | 175 27.4 | 85 58.6 | 44.9 | 138 41.2 | 40.7 | 167 05.8 | 06.8 | 208 50.9 | 44.7 |
| 17 | 190 29.9 | 100 57.8 | 45.0 | 153 42.0 | 41.3 | 182 08.1 | 06.8 | 223 53.5 | 44.7 |
| 18 | 205 32.3 | 115 57.0 | N22 45.2 | 168 42.8 | N12 41.8 | 197 10.5 | N 2 06.8 | 238 56.1 | S14 44.8 |
| 19 | 220 34.8 | 130 56.2 | 45.3 | 183 43.7 | 42.4 | 212 12.9 | 06.8 | 253 58.8 | 44.8 |
| 20 | 235 37.3 | 145 55.4 | 45.4 | 198 44.5 | 42.9 | 227 15.3 | 06.9 | 269 01.4 | 44.9 |
| 21 | 250 39.7 | 160 54.5 .. | 45.5 | 213 45.3 .. | 43.5 | 242 17.6 .. | 06.9 | 284 04.0 .. | 44.9 |
| 22 | 265 42.2 | 175 53.7 | 45.6 | 228 46.1 | 44.0 | 257 20.0 | 06.9 | 299 06.6 | 45.0 |
| 23 | 280 44.7 | 190 52.9 | 45.8 | 243 46.9 | 44.6 | 272 22.4 | 06.9 | 314 09.2 | 45.1 |
| Mer. Pass. | h m 4 24.0 | v −0.8 | d 0.2 | v 0.8 | d 0.6 | v 2.4 | d 0.0 | v 2.6 | d 0.1 |

## Stars

| Name | SHA | Dec |
|---|---|---|
| Acamar | 315 13.5 | S40 12.7 |
| Achernar | 335 21.8 | S57 07.1 |
| Acrux | 173 02.5 | S63 13.6 |
| Adhara | 255 07.8 | S29 00.1 |
| Aldebaran | 290 42.2 | N16 33.2 |
| Alioth | 166 14.9 | N55 50.6 |
| Alkaid | 152 53.6 | N49 12.4 |
| Alnair | 27 35.1 | S46 51.0 |
| Alnilam | 275 40.1 | S 1 11.2 |
| Alphard | 217 50.0 | S 8 45.3 |
| Alphecca | 126 05.3 | N26 38.5 |
| Alpheratz | 357 36.7 | N29 12.7 |
| Altair | 62 01.6 | N 8 55.7 |
| Ankaa | 353 09.1 | S42 10.8 |
| Antares | 112 18.1 | S26 28.9 |
| Arcturus | 145 49.7 | N19 04.1 |
| Atria | 107 13.7 | S69 04.2 |
| Avior | 234 16.2 | S59 34.9 |
| Bellatrix | 278 25.4 | N 6 22.2 |
| Betelgeuse | 270 54.6 | N 7 24.7 |
| Canopus | 263 53.8 | S52 42.3 |
| Capella | 280 25.3 | N46 01.1 |
| Deneb | 49 26.7 | N45 21.5 |
| Denebola | 182 27.2 | N14 27.0 |
| Diphda | 348 49.3 | S17 51.7 |
| Dubhe | 193 44.0 | N61 38.1 |
| Elnath | 278 04.8 | N28 37.5 |
| Eltanin | 90 42.6 | N51 29.3 |
| Enif | 33 40.5 | N 9 58.7 |
| Fomalhaut | 15 16.5 | S29 30.1 |
| Gacrux | 171 54.0 | S57 14.5 |
| Gienah | 175 45.8 | S17 40.0 |
| Hadar | 148 38.8 | S60 29.1 |
| Hamal | 327 53.6 | N23 34.0 |
| Kaus Aust. | 83 34.8 | S34 22.4 |
| Kochab | 137 19.4 | N74 04.1 |
| Markab | 13 31.7 | N15 19.5 |
| Menkar | 314 08.4 | N 4 10.7 |
| Menkent | 147 59.9 | S36 28.9 |
| Miaplacidus | 221 39.5 | S69 48.6 |
| Mirfak | 308 31.4 | N49 56.2 |
| Nunki | 75 49.9 | S26 16.1 |
| Peacock | 53 08.4 | S56 39.7 |
| Pollux | 243 20.2 | N27 58.4 |
| Procyon | 244 53.3 | N 5 10.1 |
| Rasalhague | 96 00.1 | N12 32.7 |
| Regulus | 207 36.9 | N11 51.6 |
| Rigel | 281 06.1 | S 8 10.5 |
| Rigil Kent. | 139 42.9 | S60 55.8 |
| Sabik | 102 04.8 | S15 45.1 |
| Schedar | 349 33.2 | N56 39.3 |
| Shaula | 96 12.8 | S37 07.2 |
| Sirius | 258 28.4 | S16 44.7 |
| Spica | 158 24.5 | S11 16.7 |
| Suhail | 222 48.2 | S43 31.4 |
| Vega | 80 34.2 | N38 48.3 |
| Zuben'ubi | 136 58.2 | S16 08.1 |

| | SHA | Mer. Pass. |
|---|---|---|
| | ° ′ | h m |
| Venus | 272 41.7 | 10 15 |
| Mars | 324 19.6 | 6 47 |
| Jupiter | 351 42.2 | 4 57 |
| Saturn | 33 17.8 | 2 11 |

| UT | SUN GHA | SUN Dec | MOON GHA | v | MOON Dec | d | HP |
|---|---|---|---|---|---|---|---|
| **15 FRIDAY** | ° ′ | ° ′ | ° ′ | ′ | ° ′ | ′ | ′ |
| 00 | 178 30.4 | N21 33.4 | 338 57.9 | 4.3 | S22 32.3 | 9.9 | 60.9 |
| 01 | 193 30.4 | 33.0 | 353 21.2 | 4.3 | 22 22.4 | 10.1 | 60.9 |
| 02 | 208 30.3 | 32.6 | 7 44.5 | 4.5 | 22 12.3 | 10.1 | 60.9 |
| 03 | 223 30.2 .. | 32.2 | 22 08.0 | 4.6 | 22 02.2 | 10.4 | 60.9 |
| 04 | 238 30.2 | 31.8 | 36 31.6 | 4.7 | 21 51.8 | 10.5 | 60.9 |
| 05 | 253 30.1 | 31.4 | 50 55.3 | 4.8 | 21 41.3 | 10.6 | 60.8 |
| 06 | 268 30.1 | N21 31.0 | 65 19.1 | 5.0 | S21 30.7 | 10.8 | 60.8 |
| 07 | 283 30.0 | 30.6 | 79 43.1 | 5.1 | 21 19.9 | 10.9 | 60.8 |
| 08 | 298 29.9 | 30.2 | 94 07.2 | 5.2 | 21 09.0 | 11.0 | 60.8 |
| 09 | 313 29.9 .. | 29.9 | 108 31.4 | 5.4 | 20 58.0 | 11.2 | 60.7 |
| 10 | 328 29.8 | 29.5 | 122 55.8 | 5.5 | 20 46.8 | 11.2 | 60.7 |
| 11 | 343 29.7 | 29.1 | 137 20.3 | 5.6 | 20 35.6 | 11.5 | 60.7 |
| 12 | 358 29.7 | N21 28.7 | 151 44.9 | 5.8 | S20 24.1 | 11.5 | 60.7 |
| 13 | 13 29.6 | 28.3 | 166 09.7 | 5.8 | 20 12.6 | 11.7 | 60.6 |
| 14 | 28 29.6 | 27.9 | 180 34.5 | 6.0 | 20 00.9 | 11.8 | 60.6 |
| 15 | 43 29.5 .. | 27.5 | 194 59.5 | 6.2 | 19 49.1 | 11.9 | 60.6 |
| 16 | 58 29.4 | 27.1 | 209 24.7 | 6.2 | 19 37.2 | 12.0 | 60.5 |
| 17 | 73 29.4 | 26.7 | 223 49.9 | 6.4 | 19 25.2 | 12.2 | 60.5 |
| 18 | 88 29.3 | N21 26.3 | 238 15.3 | 6.5 | S19 13.0 | 12.2 | 60.5 |
| 19 | 103 29.3 | 25.9 | 252 40.8 | 6.7 | 19 00.8 | 12.4 | 60.5 |
| 20 | 118 29.2 | 25.5 | 267 06.5 | 6.8 | 18 48.4 | 12.4 | 60.4 |
| 21 | 133 29.1 .. | 25.1 | 281 32.3 | 6.9 | 18 36.0 | 12.6 | 60.4 |
| 22 | 148 29.1 | 24.6 | 295 58.2 | 7.0 | 18 23.4 | 12.7 | 60.4 |
| 23 | 163 29.0 | 24.2 | 310 24.2 | 7.2 | 18 10.7 | 12.8 | 60.3 |
| **16 SATURDAY** | | | | | | | |
| 00 | 178 29.0 | N21 23.8 | 324 50.4 | 7.3 | S17 57.9 | 12.8 | 60.3 |
| 01 | 193 28.9 | 23.4 | 339 17.7 | 7.4 | 17 45.1 | 13.0 | 60.3 |
| 02 | 208 28.8 | 23.0 | 353 43.1 | 7.6 | 17 32.1 | 13.1 | 60.2 |
| 03 | 223 28.8 .. | 22.6 | 8 09.7 | 7.7 | 17 19.0 | 13.1 | 60.2 |
| 04 | 238 28.7 | 22.2 | 22 36.4 | 7.8 | 17 05.9 | 13.3 | 60.2 |
| 05 | 253 28.7 | 21.8 | 37 03.2 | 7.9 | 16 52.6 | 13.3 | 60.1 |
| 06 | 268 28.6 | N21 21.4 | 51 30.1 | 8.0 | S16 39.3 | 13.4 | 60.1 |
| 07 | 283 28.6 | 21.0 | 65 57.1 | 8.2 | 16 25.9 | 13.5 | 60.1 |
| 08 | 298 28.5 | 20.6 | 80 24.3 | 8.3 | 16 12.4 | 13.6 | 60.0 |
| 09 | 313 28.4 .. | 20.2 | 94 51.6 | 8.4 | 15 58.8 | 13.7 | 60.0 |
| 10 | 328 28.4 | 19.7 | 109 19.0 | 8.6 | 15 45.1 | 13.7 | 60.0 |
| 11 | 343 28.3 | 19.3 | 123 46.6 | 8.6 | 15 31.4 | 13.8 | 59.9 |
| 12 | 358 28.3 | N21 18.9 | 138 14.2 | 8.8 | S15 17.6 | 13.9 | 59.9 |
| 13 | 13 28.2 | 18.5 | 152 42.0 | 8.9 | 15 03.7 | 13.9 | 59.9 |
| 14 | 28 28.2 | 18.1 | 167 09.9 | 9.0 | 14 49.8 | 14.1 | 59.8 |
| 15 | 43 28.1 .. | 17.7 | 181 37.9 | 9.2 | 14 35.7 | 14.1 | 59.8 |
| 16 | 58 28.0 | 17.3 | 196 06.1 | 9.2 | 14 21.6 | 14.1 | 59.8 |
| 17 | 73 28.0 | 16.9 | 210 34.3 | 9.4 | 14 07.5 | 14.2 | 59.7 |
| 18 | 88 27.9 | N21 16.4 | 225 02.7 | 9.5 | S13 53.3 | 14.3 | 59.7 |
| 19 | 103 27.9 | 16.0 | 239 31.2 | 9.6 | 13 39.0 | 14.3 | 59.7 |
| 20 | 118 27.8 | 15.6 | 253 59.8 | 9.7 | 13 24.7 | 14.4 | 59.6 |
| 21 | 133 27.8 .. | 15.2 | 268 28.5 | 9.8 | 13 10.3 | 14.5 | 59.6 |
| 22 | 148 27.7 | 14.8 | 282 57.3 | 9.9 | 12 55.8 | 14.5 | 59.5 |
| 23 | 163 27.7 | 14.3 | 297 26.2 | 10.0 | 12 41.3 | 14.5 | 59.5 |
| **17 SUNDAY** | | | | | | | |
| 00 | 178 27.6 | N21 13.9 | 311 55.2 | 10.2 | S12 26.8 | 14.6 | 59.5 |
| 01 | 193 27.6 | 13.5 | 326 24.4 | 10.2 | 12 12.2 | 14.7 | 59.4 |
| 02 | 208 27.5 | 13.1 | 340 53.6 | 10.4 | 11 57.5 | 14.6 | 59.4 |
| 03 | 223 27.5 .. | 12.7 | 355 23.0 | 10.4 | 11 42.9 | 14.8 | 59.4 |
| 04 | 238 27.4 | 12.2 | 9 52.4 | 10.6 | 11 28.1 | 14.8 | 59.3 |
| 05 | 253 27.3 | 11.8 | 24 22.0 | 10.7 | 11 13.3 | 14.8 | 59.3 |
| 06 | 268 27.3 | N21 11.4 | 38 51.7 | 10.7 | S10 58.5 | 14.8 | 59.2 |
| 07 | 283 27.2 | 11.0 | 53 21.4 | 10.9 | 10 43.7 | 14.9 | 59.2 |
| 08 | 298 27.2 | 10.5 | 67 51.3 | 10.9 | 10 28.8 | 14.9 | 59.2 |
| 09 | 313 27.1 .. | 10.1 | 82 21.2 | 11.1 | 10 13.9 | 15.0 | 59.1 |
| 10 | 328 27.1 | 09.7 | 96 51.3 | 11.1 | 9 58.9 | 15.0 | 59.1 |
| 11 | 343 27.0 | 09.3 | 111 21.4 | 11.3 | 9 43.9 | 15.0 | 59.0 |
| 12 | 358 27.0 | N21 08.8 | 125 51.7 | 11.3 | S 9 28.9 | 15.0 | 59.0 |
| 13 | 13 26.9 | 08.4 | 140 22.0 | 11.4 | 9 13.9 | 15.1 | 59.0 |
| 14 | 28 26.9 | 08.0 | 154 52.4 | 11.5 | 8 58.8 | 15.1 | 58.9 |
| 15 | 43 26.8 .. | 07.5 | 169 22.9 | 11.6 | 8 43.7 | 15.1 | 58.9 |
| 16 | 58 26.8 | 07.1 | 183 53.5 | 11.7 | 8 28.6 | 15.2 | 58.8 |
| 17 | 73 26.7 | 06.7 | 198 24.2 | 11.8 | 8 13.4 | 15.1 | 58.8 |
| 18 | 88 26.7 | N21 06.2 | 212 55.0 | 11.9 | S 7 58.3 | 15.2 | 58.8 |
| 19 | 103 26.6 | 05.8 | 227 25.9 | 11.9 | 7 43.1 | 15.2 | 58.7 |
| 20 | 118 26.6 | 05.4 | 241 56.8 | 12.0 | 7 27.9 | 15.2 | 58.7 |
| 21 | 133 26.5 .. | 04.9 | 256 27.8 | 12.1 | 7 12.7 | 15.3 | 58.6 |
| 22 | 148 26.5 | 04.5 | 270 58.9 | 12.2 | 6 57.4 | 15.2 | 58.6 |
| 23 | 163 26.4 | 04.1 | 285 30.1 | 12.3 | S 6 42.2 | 15.3 | 58.6 |
| SD | 15.8 | d 0.4 | SD 16.5 | | 16.3 | | 16.1 |

### Twilight / Sunrise / Moonrise

| Lat. | Naut. | Civil | Sunrise | Moonrise 15 | 16 | 17 | 18 |
|---|---|---|---|---|---|---|---|
| ° | h m | h m | h m | h m | h m | h m | h m |
| N 72 | — | — | — | ■■■ | 01 45 | (00 06 / 23 24) | 22 52 |
| N 70 | — | — | — | ■■■ | (00 35 / 23 44) | 23 15 | 22 51 |
| 68 | — | — | — | 23 57 | 23 27 | 23 07 | 22 50 |
| 66 | //// | //// | 01 40 | (00 04 / 23 31) | 23 13 | 23 01 | 22 50 |
| 64 | //// | //// | 02 18 | 23 10 | 23 02 | 22 55 | 22 49 |
| 62 | //// | 00 57 | 02 45 | 22 53 | 22 52 | 22 50 | 22 49 |
| 60 | //// | 01 48 | 03 05 | 22 39 | 22 43 | 22 46 | 22 48 |
| N 58 | //// | 02 18 | 03 22 | 22 26 | 22 36 | 22 42 | 22 48 |
| 56 | 00 52 | 02 41 | 03 36 | 22 16 | 22 29 | 22 39 | 22 47 |
| 54 | 01 39 | 02 59 | 03 48 | 22 06 | 22 23 | 22 36 | 22 47 |
| 52 | 02 07 | 03 14 | 03 59 | 21 58 | 22 18 | 22 33 | 22 47 |
| 50 | 02 28 | 03 27 | 04 09 | 21 51 | 22 13 | 22 31 | 22 46 |
| 45 | 03 06 | 03 53 | 04 28 | 21 34 | 22 02 | 22 25 | 22 46 |
| N 40 | 03 33 | 04 13 | 04 44 | 21 21 | 21 53 | 22 21 | 22 45 |
| 35 | 03 54 | 04 29 | 04 58 | 21 10 | 21 46 | 22 17 | 22 45 |
| 30 | 04 10 | 04 43 | 05 10 | 20 59 | 21 39 | 22 13 | 22 44 |
| 20 | 04 37 | 05 05 | 05 30 | 20 42 | 21 27 | 22 07 | 22 44 |
| N 10 | 04 57 | 05 24 | 05 47 | 20 27 | 21 17 | 22 02 | 22 43 |
| 0 | 05 14 | 05 40 | 06 03 | 20 13 | 21 07 | 21 57 | 22 43 |
| S 10 | 05 30 | 05 56 | 06 18 | 19 58 | 20 57 | 21 51 | 22 42 |
| 20 | 05 44 | 06 11 | 06 35 | 19 43 | 20 47 | 21 46 | 22 42 |
| 30 | 05 59 | 06 28 | 06 54 | 19 25 | 20 35 | 21 40 | 22 41 |
| 35 | 06 06 | 06 38 | 07 05 | 19 15 | 20 28 | 21 36 | 22 41 |
| 40 | 06 14 | 06 48 | 07 18 | 19 03 | 20 20 | 21 32 | 22 41 |
| 45 | 06 23 | 07 00 | 07 33 | 18 49 | 20 10 | 21 27 | 22 40 |
| S 50 | 06 33 | 07 14 | 07 51 | 18 32 | 19 59 | 21 22 | 22 40 |
| 52 | 06 38 | 07 20 | 07 59 | 18 24 | 19 54 | 21 19 | 22 39 |
| 54 | 06 43 | 07 27 | 08 09 | 18 15 | 19 48 | 21 16 | 22 39 |
| 56 | 06 48 | 07 35 | 08 20 | 18 04 | 19 41 | 21 13 | 22 39 |
| 58 | 06 53 | 07 44 | 08 32 | 17 52 | 19 34 | 21 09 | 22 39 |
| S 60 | 06 59 | 07 54 | 08 47 | 17 39 | 19 26 | 21 05 | 22 38 |

### Sunset / Twilight / Moonset

| Lat. | Sunset | Civil | Naut. | Moonset 15 | 16 | 17 | 18 |
|---|---|---|---|---|---|---|---|
| ° | h m | h m | h m | h m | h m | h m | h m |
| N 72 | — | — | — | ■■■ | 03 32 | 07 02 | 09 26 |
| N 70 | — | — | — | ■■■ | 04 40 | 07 21 | 09 32 |
| 68 | — | — | — | ■■■ | 05 16 | 07 36 | 09 37 |
| 66 | 22 29 | //// | //// | 03 06 | 05 41 | 07 48 | 09 41 |
| 64 | 21 52 | //// | //// | 03 49 | 06 01 | 07 58 | 09 44 |
| 62 | 21 26 | 23 10 | //// | 04 17 | 06 17 | 08 06 | 09 47 |
| 60 | 21 05 | 22 22 | //// | 04 39 | 06 30 | 08 13 | 09 50 |
| N 58 | 20 49 | 21 52 | //// | 04 56 | 06 41 | 08 20 | 09 52 |
| 56 | 20 35 | 21 30 | 23 15 | 05 11 | 06 51 | 08 25 | 09 54 |
| 54 | 20 23 | 21 12 | 22 31 | 05 24 | 06 59 | 08 30 | 09 56 |
| 52 | 20 12 | 20 58 | 22 03 | 05 35 | 07 07 | 08 35 | 09 58 |
| 50 | 20 03 | 20 45 | 21 43 | 05 44 | 07 14 | 08 39 | 09 59 |
| 45 | 19 43 | 20 19 | 21 05 | 06 05 | 07 28 | 08 47 | 10 02 |
| N 40 | 19 27 | 19 59 | 20 39 | 06 22 | 07 40 | 08 55 | 10 05 |
| 35 | 19 14 | 19 43 | 20 18 | 06 36 | 07 50 | 09 01 | 10 08 |
| 30 | 19 02 | 19 29 | 20 01 | 06 48 | 07 59 | 09 06 | 10 10 |
| 20 | 18 43 | 19 07 | 19 35 | 07 08 | 08 14 | 09 15 | 10 13 |
| N 10 | 18 26 | 18 48 | 19 15 | 07 26 | 08 27 | 09 24 | 10 16 |
| 0 | 18 10 | 18 32 | 18 58 | 07 42 | 08 39 | 09 31 | 10 19 |
| S 10 | 17 54 | 18 17 | 18 42 | 07 58 | 08 51 | 09 38 | 10 22 |
| 20 | 17 37 | 18 01 | 18 28 | 08 16 | 09 04 | 09 46 | 10 25 |
| 30 | 17 18 | 17 44 | 18 14 | 08 35 | 09 18 | 09 55 | 10 28 |
| 35 | 17 07 | 17 35 | 18 06 | 08 47 | 09 27 | 10 00 | 10 30 |
| 40 | 16 55 | 17 25 | 17 58 | 09 00 | 09 36 | 10 06 | 10 32 |
| 45 | 16 40 | 17 13 | 17 49 | 09 15 | 09 47 | 10 12 | 10 34 |
| S 50 | 16 22 | 16 59 | 17 39 | 09 34 | 10 00 | 10 20 | 10 37 |
| 52 | 16 13 | 16 52 | 17 35 | 09 43 | 10 06 | 10 24 | 10 38 |
| 54 | 16 04 | 16 45 | 17 30 | 09 53 | 10 13 | 10 28 | 10 40 |
| 56 | 15 53 | 16 38 | 17 25 | 10 04 | 10 20 | 10 32 | 10 41 |
| 58 | 15 40 | 16 29 | 17 19 | 10 16 | 10 29 | 10 37 | 10 43 |
| S 60 | 15 26 | 16 19 | 17 13 | 10 31 | 10 38 | 10 42 | 10 45 |

### SUN / MOON

| Day | SUN Eqn. of Time 00h | 12h | Mer. Pass. | MOON Mer. Pass. Upper | Lower | Age | Phase |
|---|---|---|---|---|---|---|---|
| d | m s | m s | h m | h m | h m | d | % |
| 15 | 05 58 | 06 01 | 12 06 | 01 28 | 13 58 | 16 | 95 |
| 16 | 06 04 | 06 07 | 12 06 | 02 26 | 14 53 | 17 | 89 |
| 17 | 06 09 | 06 12 | 12 06 | 03 19 | 15 44 | 18 | 81 |

| UT | ARIES GHA | VENUS −3.9 GHA | Dec | MARS +0.3 GHA | Dec | JUPITER −2.6 GHA | Dec | SATURN +0.4 GHA | Dec | STARS Name | SHA | Dec |
|---|---|---|---|---|---|---|---|---|---|---|---|---|
| **18** 00 | 295 47.1 | 205 52.1 | N22 45.9 | 258 47.8 | N12 45.1 | 287 24.8 | N 2 07.0 | 329 11.8 | S14 45.1 | Acamar | 315 13.5 | S40 12.7 |
| 01 | 310 49.6 | 220 51.3 | 46.0 | 273 48.6 | 45.7 | 302 27.2 | 07.0 | 344 14.4 | 45.2 | Achernar | 335 21.7 | S57 07.1 |
| 02 | 325 52.0 | 235 50.5 | 46.1 | 288 49.4 | 46.2 | 317 29.5 | 07.0 | 359 17.0 | 45.2 | Acrux | 173 02.5 | S63 13.6 |
| 03 | 340 54.5 | 250 49.7 .. | 46.2 | 303 50.2 .. | 46.8 | 332 31.9 .. | 07.0 | 14 19.6 .. | 45.3 | Adhara | 255 07.8 | S29 00.0 |
| 04 | 355 57.0 | 265 48.9 | 46.3 | 318 51.0 | 47.3 | 347 34.3 | 07.1 | 29 22.2 | 45.3 | Aldebaran | 290 42.2 | N16 33.2 |
| 05 | 10 59.4 | 280 48.1 | 46.4 | 333 51.9 | 47.9 | 2 36.7 | 07.1 | 44 24.9 | 45.4 | | | |
| 06 | 26 01.9 | 295 47.3 | N22 46.5 | 348 52.7 | N12 48.4 | 17 39.1 | N 2 07.1 | 59 27.5 | S14 45.4 | Alioth | 166 14.9 | N55 50.6 |
| 07 | 41 04.4 | 310 46.5 | 46.6 | 3 53.5 | 49.0 | 32 41.4 | 07.1 | 74 30.1 | 45.5 | Alkaid | 152 53.6 | N49 12.4 |
| M 08 | 56 06.8 | 325 45.7 | 46.7 | 18 54.3 | 49.5 | 47 43.8 | 07.1 | 89 32.7 | 45.6 | Alnair | 27 35.1 | S46 51.0 |
| O 09 | 71 09.3 | 340 44.9 .. | 46.8 | 33 55.2 .. | 50.1 | 62 46.2 .. | 07.2 | 104 35.3 .. | 45.6 | Alnilam | 275 40.1 | S 1 11.2 |
| N 10 | 86 11.8 | 355 44.1 | 46.9 | 48 56.0 | 50.6 | 77 48.6 | 07.2 | 119 37.9 | 45.7 | Alphard | 217 50.1 | S 8 45.3 |
| D 11 | 101 14.2 | 10 43.3 | 47.0 | 63 56.8 | 51.2 | 92 51.0 | 07.2 | 134 40.5 | 45.7 | | | |
| A 12 | 116 16.7 | 25 42.5 | N22 47.1 | 78 57.6 | N12 51.7 | 107 53.3 | N 2 07.2 | 149 43.1 | S14 45.8 | Alphecca | 126 05.3 | N26 38.6 |
| Y 13 | 131 19.1 | 40 41.6 | 47.2 | 93 58.4 | 52.3 | 122 55.7 | 07.3 | 164 45.7 | 45.8 | Alpheratz | 357 36.7 | N29 12.7 |
| 14 | 146 21.6 | 55 40.8 | 47.3 | 108 59.3 | 52.8 | 137 58.1 | 07.3 | 179 48.4 | 45.9 | Altair | 62 01.6 | N 8 55.7 |
| 15 | 161 24.1 | 70 40.0 .. | 47.4 | 124 00.1 .. | 53.4 | 153 00.5 .. | 07.3 | 194 51.0 .. | 46.0 | Ankaa | 353 09.0 | S42 10.8 |
| 16 | 176 26.5 | 85 39.2 | 47.5 | 139 00.9 | 53.9 | 168 02.9 | 07.3 | 209 53.6 | 46.0 | Antares | 112 18.1 | S26 28.9 |
| 17 | 191 29.0 | 100 38.4 | 47.6 | 154 01.7 | 54.5 | 183 05.3 | 07.3 | 224 56.2 | 46.1 | | | |
| 18 | 206 31.5 | 115 37.6 | N22 47.7 | 169 02.5 | N12 55.0 | 198 07.6 | N 2 07.4 | 239 58.8 | S14 46.1 | Arcturus | 145 49.7 | N19 04.1 |
| 19 | 221 33.9 | 130 36.8 | 47.8 | 184 03.4 | 55.5 | 213 10.0 | 07.4 | 255 01.4 | 46.2 | Atria | 107 13.7 | S69 04.2 |
| 20 | 236 36.4 | 145 36.0 | 47.9 | 199 04.2 | 56.1 | 228 12.4 | 07.4 | 270 04.0 | 46.2 | Avior | 234 16.2 | S59 34.9 |
| 21 | 251 38.9 | 160 35.2 .. | 48.0 | 214 05.0 .. | 56.6 | 243 14.8 .. | 07.4 | 285 06.6 .. | 46.3 | Bellatrix | 278 25.3 | N 6 22.2 |
| 22 | 266 41.3 | 175 34.4 | 48.1 | 229 05.8 | 57.2 | 258 17.2 | 07.4 | 300 09.2 | 46.3 | Betelgeuse | 270 54.6 | N 7 24.7 |
| 23 | 281 43.8 | 190 33.6 | 48.2 | 244 06.7 | 57.7 | 273 19.6 | 07.5 | 315 11.9 | 46.4 | | | |
| **19** 00 | 296 46.3 | 205 32.8 | N22 48.2 | 259 07.5 | N12 58.3 | 288 21.9 | N 2 07.5 | 330 14.5 | S14 46.5 | Canopus | 263 53.8 | S52 42.3 |
| 01 | 311 48.7 | 220 31.9 | 48.3 | 274 08.3 | 58.8 | 303 24.3 | 07.5 | 345 17.1 | 46.5 | Capella | 280 25.3 | N46 01.1 |
| 02 | 326 51.2 | 235 31.1 | 48.4 | 289 09.1 | 59.4 | 318 26.7 | 07.5 | 0 19.7 | 46.6 | Deneb | 49 26.7 | N45 21.6 |
| 03 | 341 53.6 | 250 30.3 .. | 48.5 | 304 10.0 | 12 59.9 | 333 29.1 .. | 07.5 | 15 22.3 .. | 46.6 | Denebola | 182 27.2 | N14 27.0 |
| 04 | 356 56.1 | 265 29.5 | 48.6 | 319 10.8 | 13 00.4 | 348 31.5 | 07.6 | 30 24.9 | 46.7 | Diphda | 348 49.3 | S17 51.7 |
| 05 | 11 58.6 | 280 28.7 | 48.7 | 334 11.6 | 01.0 | 3 33.9 | 07.6 | 45 27.5 | 46.7 | | | |
| 06 | 27 01.0 | 295 27.9 | N22 48.7 | 349 12.4 | N13 01.5 | 18 36.3 | N 2 07.6 | 60 30.2 | S14 46.8 | Dubhe | 193 44.0 | N61 38.1 |
| 07 | 42 03.5 | 310 27.1 | 48.8 | 4 13.2 | 02.1 | 33 38.6 | 07.6 | 75 32.8 | 46.9 | Elnath | 278 04.8 | N28 37.5 |
| T 08 | 57 06.0 | 325 26.3 | 48.9 | 19 14.1 | 02.6 | 48 41.0 | 07.6 | 90 35.4 | 46.9 | Eltanin | 90 42.6 | N51 29.3 |
| U 09 | 72 08.4 | 340 25.5 .. | 49.0 | 34 14.9 .. | 03.1 | 63 43.4 .. | 07.7 | 105 38.0 .. | 47.0 | Enif | 33 40.5 | N 9 58.7 |
| E 10 | 87 10.9 | 355 24.6 | 49.0 | 49 15.7 | 03.7 | 78 45.8 | 07.7 | 120 40.6 | 47.0 | Fomalhaut | 15 16.5 | S29 30.1 |
| S 11 | 102 13.4 | 10 23.8 | 49.1 | 64 16.5 | 04.2 | 93 48.2 | 07.7 | 135 43.2 | 47.1 | | | |
| D 12 | 117 15.8 | 25 23.0 | N22 49.2 | 79 17.4 | N13 04.8 | 108 50.6 | N 2 07.7 | 150 45.8 | S14 47.1 | Gacrux | 171 54.1 | S57 14.5 |
| A 13 | 132 18.3 | 40 22.2 | 49.3 | 94 18.2 | 05.3 | 123 53.0 | 07.7 | 165 48.4 | 47.2 | Gienah | 175 45.8 | S17 40.0 |
| Y 14 | 147 20.7 | 55 21.4 | 49.3 | 109 19.0 | 05.9 | 138 55.4 | 07.8 | 180 51.1 | 47.3 | Hadar | 148 38.8 | S60 29.1 |
| 15 | 162 23.2 | 70 20.6 .. | 49.4 | 124 19.8 .. | 06.4 | 153 57.8 .. | 07.8 | 195 53.7 .. | 47.3 | Hamal | 327 53.5 | N23 34.0 |
| 16 | 177 25.7 | 85 19.8 | 49.5 | 139 20.7 | 06.9 | 169 00.1 | 07.8 | 210 56.3 | 47.4 | Kaus Aust. | 83 34.8 | S34 22.4 |
| 17 | 192 28.1 | 100 19.0 | 49.5 | 154 21.5 | 07.5 | 184 02.5 | 07.8 | 225 58.9 | 47.4 | | | |
| 18 | 207 30.6 | 115 18.2 | N22 49.6 | 169 22.3 | N13 08.0 | 199 04.9 | N 2 07.8 | 241 01.5 | S14 47.5 | Kochab | 137 19.4 | N74 04.1 |
| 19 | 222 33.1 | 130 17.3 | 49.7 | 184 23.1 | 08.6 | 214 07.3 | 07.8 | 256 04.1 | 47.5 | Markab | 13 31.7 | N15 19.5 |
| 20 | 237 35.5 | 145 16.5 | 49.7 | 199 24.0 | 09.1 | 229 09.7 | 07.9 | 271 06.7 | 47.6 | Menkar | 314 08.4 | N 4 10.7 |
| 21 | 252 38.0 | 160 15.7 .. | 49.8 | 214 24.8 .. | 09.6 | 244 12.1 .. | 07.9 | 286 09.4 .. | 47.7 | Menkent | 148 00.0 | S36 28.9 |
| 22 | 267 40.5 | 175 14.9 | 49.9 | 229 25.6 | 10.2 | 259 14.5 | 07.9 | 301 12.0 | 47.7 | Miaplacidus | 221 39.5 | S69 48.6 |
| 23 | 282 42.9 | 190 14.1 | 49.9 | 244 26.4 | 10.7 | 274 16.9 | 07.9 | 316 14.6 | 47.8 | | | |
| **20** 00 | 297 45.4 | 205 13.3 | N22 50.0 | 259 27.3 | N13 11.2 | 289 19.3 | N 2 07.9 | 331 17.2 | S14 47.8 | Mirfak | 308 31.4 | N49 56.2 |
| 01 | 312 47.9 | 220 12.5 | 50.0 | 274 28.1 | 11.8 | 304 21.7 | 08.0 | 346 19.8 | 47.9 | Nunki | 75 49.9 | S26 16.1 |
| 02 | 327 50.3 | 235 11.7 | 50.1 | 289 28.9 | 12.3 | 319 24.1 | 08.0 | 1 22.4 | 47.9 | Peacock | 53 08.3 | S56 39.7 |
| 03 | 342 52.8 | 250 10.8 .. | 50.1 | 304 29.7 .. | 12.9 | 334 26.5 .. | 08.0 | 16 25.0 .. | 48.0 | Pollux | 243 20.2 | N27 58.4 |
| 04 | 357 55.2 | 265 10.0 | 50.2 | 319 30.6 | 13.4 | 349 28.8 | 08.0 | 31 27.7 | 48.1 | Procyon | 244 53.3 | N 5 10.1 |
| 05 | 12 57.7 | 280 09.2 | 50.2 | 334 31.4 | 13.9 | 4 31.2 | 08.0 | 46 30.3 | 48.1 | | | |
| 06 | 28 00.2 | 295 08.4 | N22 50.3 | 349 32.2 | N13 14.5 | 19 33.6 | N 2 08.0 | 61 32.9 | S14 48.2 | Rasalhague | 96 00.1 | N12 32.7 |
| W 07 | 43 02.6 | 310 07.6 | 50.4 | 4 33.0 | 15.0 | 34 36.0 | 08.1 | 76 35.5 | 48.2 | Regulus | 207 36.9 | N11 51.6 |
| E 08 | 58 05.1 | 325 06.8 | 50.4 | 19 33.9 | 15.5 | 49 38.4 | 08.1 | 91 38.1 | 48.3 | Rigel | 281 06.1 | S 8 10.5 |
| D 09 | 73 07.6 | 340 06.0 .. | 50.5 | 34 34.7 .. | 16.1 | 64 40.8 .. | 08.1 | 106 40.7 .. | 48.4 | Rigil Kent. | 139 42.9 | S60 55.8 |
| N 10 | 88 10.0 | 355 05.2 | 50.5 | 49 35.5 | 16.6 | 79 43.2 | 08.1 | 121 43.4 | 48.4 | Sabik | 102 04.8 | S15 45.1 |
| E 11 | 103 12.5 | 10 04.3 | 50.5 | 64 36.3 | 17.2 | 94 45.6 | 08.1 | 136 46.0 | 48.5 | | | |
| S 12 | 118 15.0 | 25 03.5 | N22 50.6 | 79 37.2 | N13 17.7 | 109 48.0 | N 2 08.1 | 151 48.6 | S14 48.5 | Schedar | 349 33.2 | N56 39.3 |
| D 13 | 133 17.4 | 40 02.7 | 50.6 | 94 38.0 | 18.2 | 124 50.4 | 08.1 | 166 51.2 | 48.6 | Shaula | 96 12.8 | S37 07.2 |
| A 14 | 148 19.9 | 55 01.9 | 50.7 | 109 38.8 | 18.8 | 139 52.8 | 08.2 | 181 53.8 | 48.6 | Sirius | 258 28.4 | S16 44.7 |
| Y 15 | 163 22.4 | 70 01.1 .. | 50.7 | 124 39.6 .. | 19.3 | 154 55.2 .. | 08.2 | 196 56.4 .. | 48.7 | Spica | 158 24.5 | S11 16.7 |
| 16 | 178 24.8 | 85 00.3 | 50.8 | 139 40.5 | 19.8 | 169 57.6 | 08.2 | 211 59.1 | 48.8 | Suhail | 222 48.2 | S43 31.4 |
| 17 | 193 27.3 | 99 59.5 | 50.8 | 154 41.3 | 20.4 | 185 00.0 | 08.2 | 227 01.7 | 48.8 | | | |
| 18 | 208 29.7 | 114 58.6 | N22 50.8 | 169 42.1 | N13 20.9 | 200 02.4 | N 2 08.2 | 242 04.3 | S14 48.9 | Vega | 80 34.2 | N38 48.3 |
| 19 | 223 32.2 | 129 57.8 | 50.9 | 184 42.9 | 21.4 | 215 04.8 | 08.2 | 257 06.9 | 48.9 | Zuben'ubi | 136 58.2 | S16 08.1 |
| 20 | 238 34.7 | 144 57.0 | 50.9 | 199 43.8 | 22.0 | 230 07.2 | 08.3 | 272 09.5 | 49.0 | | | |
| 21 | 253 37.1 | 159 56.2 .. | 51.0 | 214 44.6 .. | 22.5 | 245 09.6 .. | 08.3 | 287 12.1 .. | 49.0 | | SHA | Mer. Pass. |
| 22 | 268 39.6 | 174 55.4 | 51.0 | 229 45.4 | 23.0 | 260 12.0 | 08.3 | 302 14.8 | 49.1 | Venus | 268 46.5 | 10 18 |
| 23 | 283 42.1 | 189 54.6 | 51.0 | 244 46.2 | 23.6 | 275 14.4 | 08.3 | 317 17.4 | 49.2 | Mars | 322 21.2 | 6 43 |
| Mer. Pass. 4 12.2 | | v −0.8 | d 0.1 | v 0.8 | d 0.5 | v 2.4 | d 0.0 | v 2.6 | d 0.1 | Jupiter | 351 35.7 | 4 46 |
| | | | | | | | | | | Saturn | 33 28.2 | 1 59 |

| UT | SUN | | MOON | | | | | Lat. | Twilight | | Sunrise | Moonrise | | | |
|---|---|---|---|---|---|---|---|---|---|---|---|---|---|---|---|
| | | | | | | | | | Naut. | Civil | | 18 | 19 | 20 | 21 |
| | GHA | Dec | GHA | v | Dec | d | HP | | | | | | | | |
| d h | ° ′ | ° ′ | ° ′ | ′ | ° ′ | ′ | ′ | N 72 | h m ▭ | h m ▭ | h m ▭ | h m 22 52 | h m 22 22 | h m 21 47 | h m 20 57 |
| 18 00 | 178 26.4 | N21 03.6 | 300 01.4 | 12.3 | S 6 26.9 | 15.2 | 58.5 | N 70 | ▭ | ▭ | ▭ | 22 51 | 22 28 | 22 04 | 21 31 |
| 01 | 193 26.3 | 03.2 | 314 32.7 | 12.4 | 6 11.7 | 15.3 | 58.5 | 68 | //// | //// | 00 45 | 22 50 | 22 34 | 22 17 | 21 56 |
| 02 | 208 26.3 | 02.8 | 329 04.1 | 12.5 | 5 56.4 | 15.3 | 58.4 | 66 | //// | //// | 01 53 | 22 50 | 22 39 | 22 28 | 22 15 |
| 03 | 223 26.3 .. | 02.3 | 343 35.6 | 12.6 | 5 41.1 | 15.3 | 58.4 | 64 | //// | //// | 02 27 | 22 49 | 22 43 | 22 37 | 22 30 |
| 04 | 238 26.2 | 01.9 | 358 07.2 | 12.6 | 5 25.8 | 15.2 | 58.4 | 62 | //// | 01 15 | 02 52 | 22 48 | 22 46 | 22 45 | 22 43 |
| 05 | 253 26.2 | 01.5 | 12 38.8 | 12.7 | 5 10.6 | 15.3 | 58.3 | 60 | //// | 01 58 | 03 11 | 22 48 | 22 50 | 22 52 | 22 54 |
| 06 | 268 26.1 | N21 01.0 | 27 10.5 | 12.7 | S 4 55.3 | 15.3 | 58.3 | N 58 | //// | 02 26 | 03 27 | 22 48 | 22 52 | 22 58 | 23 04 |
| 07 | 283 26.1 | 00.6 | 41 42.2 | 12.9 | 4 40.0 | 15.3 | 58.2 | 56 | 01 09 | 02 47 | 03 41 | 22 47 | 22 55 | 23 03 | 23 13 |
| 08 | 298 26.0 | 21 00.1 | 56 14.1 | 12.9 | 4 24.7 | 15.3 | 58.2 | 54 | 01 48 | 03 04 | 03 53 | 22 47 | 22 57 | 23 08 | 23 20 |
| M 09 | 313 26.0 | 20 59.7 | 70 46.0 | 12.9 | 4 09.4 | 15.3 | 58.2 | 52 | 02 14 | 03 18 | 04 03 | 22 47 | 22 59 | 23 12 | 23 27 |
| O 10 | 328 25.9 | 59.3 | 85 17.9 | 13.1 | 3 54.1 | 15.3 | 58.1 | 50 | 02 34 | 03 31 | 04 12 | 22 46 | 23 01 | 23 16 | 23 33 |
| N 11 | 343 25.9 | 58.8 | 99 50.0 | 13.0 | 3 38.8 | 15.3 | 58.1 | 45 | 03 10 | 03 56 | 04 31 | 22 46 | 23 05 | 23 25 | 23 47 |
| D 12 | 358 25.8 | N20 58.4 | 114 22.0 | 13.2 | S 3 23.5 | 15.2 | 58.0 | N 40 | 03 36 | 04 15 | 04 47 | 22 45 | 23 09 | 23 32 | 23 58 |
| A 13 | 13 25.8 | 57.9 | 128 54.2 | 13.2 | 3 08.3 | 15.3 | 58.0 | 35 | 03 56 | 04 31 | 05 00 | 22 45 | 23 12 | 23 39 | 24 07 |
| Y 14 | 28 25.7 | 57.5 | 143 26.4 | 13.2 | 2 53.0 | 15.3 | 58.0 | 30 | 04 12 | 04 45 | 05 11 | 22 44 | 23 14 | 23 44 | 24 16 |
| 15 | 43 25.7 .. | 57.0 | 157 58.6 | 13.3 | 2 37.7 | 15.2 | 57.9 | 20 | 04 38 | 05 07 | 05 31 | 22 44 | 23 19 | 23 54 | 24 30 |
| 16 | 58 25.7 | 56.6 | 172 30.9 | 13.4 | 2 22.5 | 15.3 | 57.9 | N 10 | 04 58 | 05 25 | 05 47 | 22 43 | 23 23 | 24 03 | 00 03 |
| 17 | 73 25.6 | 56.1 | 187 03.3 | 13.4 | 2 07.2 | 15.2 | 57.8 | 0 | 05 15 | 05 41 | 06 03 | 22 43 | 23 27 | 24 11 | 00 11 |
| 18 | 88 25.6 | N20 55.7 | 201 35.7 | 13.5 | S 1 52.0 | 15.2 | 57.8 | S 10 | 05 30 | 05 56 | 06 18 | 22 42 | 23 31 | 24 19 | 00 19 |
| 19 | 103 25.5 | 55.3 | 216 08.2 | 13.5 | 1 36.8 | 15.2 | 57.8 | 20 | 05 44 | 06 11 | 06 34 | 22 42 | 23 35 | 24 28 | 00 28 |
| 20 | 118 25.5 | 54.8 | 230 40.7 | 13.6 | 1 21.6 | 15.2 | 57.7 | 30 | 05 58 | 06 27 | 06 53 | 22 41 | 23 40 | 24 38 | 00 38 |
| 21 | 133 25.4 .. | 54.4 | 245 13.3 | 13.6 | 1 06.4 | 15.1 | 57.7 | 35 | 06 05 | 06 36 | 07 04 | 22 41 | 23 43 | 24 44 | 00 44 |
| 22 | 148 25.4 | 53.9 | 259 45.9 | 13.7 | 0 51.3 | 15.2 | 57.6 | 40 | 06 13 | 06 46 | 07 16 | 22 41 | 23 46 | 24 51 | 00 51 |
| 23 | 163 25.3 | 53.5 | 274 18.6 | 13.7 | 0 36.1 | 15.1 | 57.6 | 45 | 06 21 | 06 58 | 07 30 | 22 40 | 23 50 | 24 59 | 00 59 |
| 19 00 | 178 25.3 | N20 53.0 | 288 51.3 | 13.7 | S 0 21.0 | 15.1 | 57.6 | S 50 | 06 31 | 07 11 | 07 40 | 22 40 | 23 55 | 25 08 | 01 08 |
| 01 | 193 25.3 | 52.6 | 303 24.0 | 13.8 | S 0 05.9 | 15.1 | 57.5 | 52 | 06 35 | 07 17 | 07 56 | 22 39 | 23 57 | 25 12 | 01 12 |
| 02 | 208 25.2 | 52.1 | 317 56.8 | 13.9 | N 0 09.2 | 15.1 | 57.5 | 54 | 06 40 | 07 24 | 08 06 | 22 39 | 23 59 | 25 17 | 01 17 |
| 03 | 223 25.2 .. | 51.7 | 332 29.7 | 13.8 | 0 24.3 | 15.1 | 57.5 | 56 | 06 45 | 07 32 | 08 16 | 22 39 | 24 02 | 00 02 | 01 23 |
| 04 | 238 25.1 | 51.2 | 347 02.5 | 13.9 | 0 39.4 | 15.0 | 57.4 | 58 | 06 50 | 07 40 | 08 28 | 22 39 | 24 05 | 00 05 | 01 29 |
| 05 | 253 25.1 | 50.8 | 1 35.4 | 14.0 | 0 54.4 | 15.0 | 57.4 | S 60 | 06 56 | 07 50 | 08 42 | 22 38 | 24 08 | 00 08 | 01 36 |
| 06 | 268 25.1 | N20 50.3 | 16 08.4 | 14.0 | N 1 09.4 | 15.0 | 57.3 | | | | | | | | |
| 07 | 283 25.0 | 49.8 | 30 41.4 | 14.0 | 1 24.4 | 14.9 | 57.3 | Lat. | Sunset | Twilight | | Moonset | | | |
| T 08 | 298 25.0 | 49.4 | 45 14.4 | 14.1 | 1 39.3 | 14.9 | 57.3 | | | Civil | Naut. | 18 | 19 | 20 | 21 |
| U 09 | 313 24.9 .. | 48.9 | 59 47.5 | 14.0 | 1 54.2 | 14.9 | 57.2 | | | | | | | | |
| E 10 | 328 24.9 | 48.5 | 74 20.5 | 14.2 | 2 09.1 | 14.9 | 57.2 | ° | h m | h m | h m | h m | h m | h m | h m |
| S 11 | 343 24.8 | 48.0 | 88 53.7 | 14.1 | 2 24.0 | 14.8 | 57.1 | N 72 | ▭ | ▭ | ▭ | 09 26 | 11 35 | 13 44 | 16 07 |
| D 12 | 358 24.8 | N20 47.6 | 103 26.8 | 14.2 | N 2 38.8 | 14.8 | 57.1 | N 70 | ▭ | ▭ | ▭ | 09 32 | 11 32 | 13 30 | 15 35 |
| A 13 | 13 24.8 | 47.1 | 118 00.0 | 14.2 | 2 53.6 | 14.8 | 57.1 | 68 | 23 17 | //// | //// | 09 37 | 11 29 | 13 19 | 15 12 |
| Y 14 | 28 24.7 | 46.6 | 132 33.2 | 14.2 | 3 08.4 | 14.7 | 57.0 | 66 | 22 17 | //// | //// | 09 41 | 11 27 | 13 10 | 14 54 |
| 15 | 43 24.7 .. | 46.2 | 147 06.4 | 14.2 | 3 23.1 | 14.7 | 57.0 | 64 | 21 43 | //// | //// | 09 44 | 11 25 | 13 02 | 14 40 |
| 16 | 58 24.7 | 45.7 | 161 39.6 | 14.3 | 3 37.8 | 14.7 | 57.0 | 62 | 21 19 | 22 53 | //// | 09 47 | 11 23 | 12 56 | 14 28 |
| 17 | 73 24.6 | 45.3 | 176 12.9 | 14.3 | 3 52.5 | 14.6 | 56.9 | 60 | 21 00 | 22 12 | //// | 09 50 | 11 21 | 12 50 | 14 18 |
| 18 | 88 24.6 | N20 44.8 | 190 46.2 | 14.3 | N 4 07.1 | 14.6 | 56.9 | N 58 | 20 44 | 21 45 | //// | 09 52 | 11 20 | 12 45 | 14 09 |
| 19 | 103 24.5 | 44.3 | 205 19.5 | 14.4 | 4 21.7 | 14.5 | 56.8 | 56 | 20 31 | 21 24 | 23 00 | 09 54 | 11 19 | 12 41 | 14 01 |
| 20 | 118 24.5 | 43.9 | 219 52.9 | 14.3 | 4 36.2 | 14.6 | 56.8 | 54 | 20 19 | 21 08 | 22 22 | 09 56 | 11 18 | 12 37 | 13 54 |
| 21 | 133 24.5 .. | 43.4 | 234 26.2 | 14.4 | 4 50.8 | 14.4 | 56.8 | 52 | 20 09 | 20 53 | 21 57 | 09 58 | 11 17 | 12 33 | 13 48 |
| 22 | 148 24.4 | 43.0 | 248 59.6 | 14.4 | 5 05.2 | 14.5 | 56.7 | 50 | 20 00 | 20 41 | 21 38 | 09 59 | 11 16 | 12 30 | 13 43 |
| 23 | 163 24.4 | 42.5 | 263 33.0 | 14.4 | 5 19.7 | 14.4 | 56.7 | 45 | 19 41 | 20 16 | 21 02 | 10 02 | 11 14 | 12 23 | 13 31 |
| 20 00 | 178 24.3 | N20 42.0 | 278 06.4 | 14.4 | N 5 34.1 | 14.3 | 56.7 | N 40 | 19 25 | 19 57 | 20 36 | 10 05 | 11 12 | 12 17 | 13 21 |
| 01 | 193 24.3 | 41.6 | 292 39.8 | 14.4 | 5 48.4 | 14.3 | 56.6 | 35 | 19 12 | 19 41 | 20 16 | 10 08 | 11 11 | 12 12 | 13 13 |
| 02 | 208 24.3 | 41.1 | 307 13.2 | 14.4 | 6 02.7 | 14.3 | 56.6 | 30 | 19 01 | 19 28 | 20 00 | 10 10 | 11 10 | 12 08 | 13 06 |
| 03 | 223 24.2 .. | 40.6 | 321 46.6 | 14.5 | 6 17.0 | 14.2 | 56.5 | 20 | 18 42 | 19 06 | 19 34 | 10 13 | 11 08 | 12 01 | 12 53 |
| 04 | 238 24.2 | 40.2 | 336 20.1 | 14.4 | 6 31.2 | 14.2 | 56.5 | N 10 | 18 25 | 18 48 | 19 14 | 10 16 | 11 06 | 11 54 | 12 42 |
| 05 | 253 24.2 | 39.7 | 350 53.5 | 14.5 | 6 45.4 | 14.1 | 56.5 | 0 | 18 10 | 18 32 | 18 58 | 10 19 | 11 04 | 11 48 | 12 32 |
| 06 | 268 24.1 | N20 39.2 | 5 27.0 | 14.5 | N 6 59.5 | 14.1 | 56.5 | S 10 | 17 55 | 18 17 | 18 43 | 10 22 | 11 02 | 11 42 | 12 22 |
| W 07 | 283 24.1 | 38.8 | 20 00.5 | 14.4 | 7 13.6 | 14.0 | 56.4 | 20 | 17 38 | 18 02 | 18 29 | 10 25 | 11 00 | 11 35 | 12 11 |
| E 08 | 298 24.1 | 38.3 | 34 33.9 | 14.5 | 7 27.6 | 14.0 | 56.4 | 30 | 17 20 | 17 46 | 18 15 | 10 28 | 10 58 | 11 28 | 11 59 |
| D 09 | 313 24.0 .. | 37.8 | 49 07.4 | 14.5 | 7 41.6 | 14.0 | 56.4 | 35 | 17 09 | 17 37 | 18 08 | 10 30 | 10 57 | 11 24 | 11 52 |
| N 10 | 328 24.0 | 37.3 | 63 40.9 | 14.5 | 7 55.6 | 13.9 | 56.3 | 40 | 16 57 | 17 27 | 18 00 | 10 32 | 10 56 | 11 19 | 11 44 |
| E 11 | 343 24.0 | 36.9 | 78 14.4 | 14.5 | 8 09.5 | 13.8 | 56.3 | 45 | 16 43 | 17 15 | 17 52 | 10 34 | 10 54 | 11 14 | 11 34 |
| S 12 | 358 23.9 | N20 36.4 | 92 47.9 | 14.4 | N 8 23.3 | 13.8 | 56.3 | S 50 | 16 25 | 17 02 | 17 42 | 10 37 | 10 52 | 11 07 | 11 23 |
| D 13 | 13 23.9 | 35.9 | 107 21.3 | 14.5 | 8 37.1 | 13.7 | 56.2 | 52 | 16 17 | 16 56 | 17 38 | 10 38 | 10 51 | 11 04 | 11 18 |
| A 14 | 28 23.8 | 35.5 | 121 54.8 | 14.5 | 8 50.8 | 13.7 | 56.2 | 54 | 16 08 | 16 49 | 17 33 | 10 40 | 10 50 | 11 01 | 11 12 |
| Y 15 | 43 23.8 .. | 35.0 | 136 28.3 | 14.5 | 9 04.5 | 13.6 | 56.2 | 56 | 15 57 | 16 41 | 17 29 | 10 41 | 10 49 | 10 57 | 11 06 |
| 16 | 58 23.8 | 34.5 | 151 01.8 | 14.5 | 9 18.1 | 13.6 | 56.1 | 58 | 15 45 | 16 33 | 17 23 | 10 43 | 10 48 | 10 53 | 10 59 |
| 17 | 73 23.7 | 34.0 | 165 35.3 | 14.4 | 9 31.7 | 13.5 | 56.1 | S 60 | 15 31 | 16 24 | 17 17 | 10 45 | 10 47 | 10 49 | 10 51 |
| 18 | 88 23.7 | N20 33.6 | 180 08.7 | 14.5 | N 9 45.2 | 13.5 | 56.1 | | SUN | | | MOON | | | |
| 19 | 103 23.7 | 33.1 | 194 42.2 | 14.5 | 9 58.7 | 13.4 | 56.0 | Day | Eqn. of Time | | Mer. | Mer. Pass. | | Age | Phase |
| 20 | 118 23.6 | 32.6 | 209 15.7 | 14.4 | 10 12.1 | 13.3 | 56.0 | | 00 h | 12 h | Pass. | Upper | Lower | | |
| 21 | 133 23.6 .. | 32.1 | 223 49.1 | 14.4 | 10 25.4 | 13.3 | 56.0 | d | m s | m s | h m | h m | h m | d % | |
| 22 | 148 23.6 | 31.6 | 238 22.5 | 14.5 | 10 38.7 | 13.2 | 55.9 | 18 | 06 14 | 06 17 | 12 06 | 04 08 | 16 31 | 19 72 | |
| 23 | 163 23.6 | 31.2 | 252 56.0 | 14.4 | N10 51.9 | 13.2 | 55.9 | 19 | 06 19 | 06 21 | 12 06 | 04 53 | 17 16 | 20 61 | ◑ |
| | SD 15.8 | d 0.5 | SD 15.8 | | 15.6 | | 15.3 | 20 | 06 23 | 06 24 | 12 06 | 05 38 | 17 59 | 21 51 | |

| UT | ARIES | VENUS −3.9 | | MARS +0.2 | | JUPITER −2.6 | | SATURN +0.4 | | STARS | | |
|---|---|---|---|---|---|---|---|---|---|---|---|---|
| | GHA | GHA | Dec | GHA | Dec | GHA | Dec | GHA | Dec | Name | SHA | Dec |
| d h | ° ′ | ° ′ | ° ′ | ° ′ | ° ′ | ° ′ | ° ′ | ° ′ | ° ′ | | ° ′ | ° ′ |
| 21 00 | 298 44.5 | 204 53.7 | N22 51.1 | 259 47.1 | N13 24.1 | 290 16.8 | N 2 08.3 | 332 20.0 | S14 49.2 | Acamar | 315 13.5 | S40 12.6 |
| 01 | 313 47.0 | 219 52.9 | 51.1 | 274 47.9 | 24.6 | 305 19.2 | 08.3 | 347 22.6 | 49.3 | Achernar | 335 21.7 | S57 07.1 |
| 02 | 328 49.5 | 234 52.1 | 51.1 | 289 48.7 | 25.2 | 320 21.6 | 08.3 | 2 25.2 | 49.3 | Acrux | 173 02.6 | S63 13.6 |
| 03 | 343 51.9 | 249 51.3 .. | 51.1 | 304 49.6 .. | 25.7 | 335 24.0 .. | 08.4 | 17 27.8 .. | 49.4 | Adhara | 255 07.8 | S29 00.0 |
| 04 | 358 54.4 | 264 50.5 | 51.2 | 319 50.4 | 26.2 | 350 26.4 | 08.4 | 32 30.5 | 49.5 | Aldebaran | 290 42.2 | N16 33.2 |
| 05 | 13 56.8 | 279 49.7 | 51.2 | 334 51.2 | 26.7 | 5 28.8 | 08.4 | 47 33.1 | 49.5 | | | |
| 06 | 28 59.3 | 294 48.8 | N22 51.2 | 349 52.0 | N13 27.3 | 20 31.2 | N 2 08.4 | 62 35.7 | S14 49.6 | Alioth | 166 14.9 | N55 50.6 |
| 07 | 44 01.8 | 309 48.0 | 51.2 | 4 52.9 | 27.8 | 35 33.6 | 08.4 | 77 38.3 | 49.6 | Alkaid | 152 53.6 | N49 12.4 |
| T 08 | 59 04.2 | 324 47.2 | 51.3 | 19 53.7 | 28.3 | 50 36.0 | 08.4 | 92 40.9 | 49.7 | Alnair | 27 35.1 | S46 51.0 |
| H 09 | 74 06.7 | 339 46.4 .. | 51.3 | 34 54.5 .. | 28.9 | 65 38.4 .. | 08.4 | 107 43.5 .. | 49.7 | Alnilam | 275 40.1 | S 1 11.2 |
| U 10 | 89 09.2 | 354 45.6 | 51.3 | 49 55.4 | 29.4 | 80 40.8 | 08.4 | 122 46.2 | 49.8 | Alphard | 217 50.1 | S 8 45.3 |
| R 11 | 104 11.6 | 9 44.8 | 51.3 | 64 56.2 | 29.9 | 95 43.2 | 08.5 | 137 48.8 | 49.9 | | | |
| S 12 | 119 14.1 | 24 44.0 | N22 51.3 | 79 57.0 | N13 30.5 | 110 45.6 | N 2 08.5 | 152 51.4 | S14 49.9 | Alphecca | 126 05.3 | N26 38.6 |
| D 13 | 134 16.6 | 39 43.1 | 51.4 | 94 57.8 | 31.0 | 125 48.0 | 08.5 | 167 54.0 | 50.0 | Alpheratz | 357 36.7 | N29 12.7 |
| A 14 | 149 19.0 | 54 42.3 | 51.4 | 109 58.7 | 31.5 | 140 50.4 | 08.5 | 182 56.6 | 50.0 | Altair | 62 01.6 | N 8 55.7 |
| Y 15 | 164 21.5 | 69 41.5 .. | 51.4 | 124 59.5 .. | 32.0 | 155 52.8 .. | 08.5 | 197 59.3 .. | 50.1 | Ankaa | 353 09.0 | S42 10.8 |
| 16 | 179 24.0 | 84 40.7 | 51.4 | 140 00.3 | 32.6 | 170 55.2 | 08.5 | 213 01.9 | 50.2 | Antares | 112 18.1 | S26 28.9 |
| 17 | 194 26.4 | 99 39.9 | 51.4 | 155 01.1 | 33.1 | 185 57.6 | 08.5 | 228 04.5 | 50.2 | | | |
| 18 | 209 28.9 | 114 39.0 | N22 51.4 | 170 02.0 | N13 33.6 | 201 00.0 | N 2 08.5 | 243 07.1 | S14 50.3 | Arcturus | 145 49.7 | N19 04.1 |
| 19 | 224 31.3 | 129 38.2 | 51.4 | 185 02.8 | 34.2 | 216 02.4 | 08.6 | 258 09.7 | 50.3 | Atria | 107 13.7 | S69 04.2 |
| 20 | 239 33.8 | 144 37.4 | 51.5 | 200 03.6 | 34.7 | 231 04.8 | 08.6 | 273 12.3 | 50.4 | Avior | 234 16.2 | S59 34.8 |
| 21 | 254 36.3 | 159 36.6 .. | 51.5 | 215 04.5 .. | 35.2 | 246 07.3 .. | 08.6 | 288 15.0 .. | 50.4 | Bellatrix | 278 25.3 | N 6 22.2 |
| 22 | 269 38.7 | 174 35.8 | 51.5 | 230 05.3 | 35.7 | 261 09.7 | 08.6 | 303 17.6 | 50.5 | Betelgeuse | 270 54.6 | N 7 24.7 |
| 23 | 284 41.2 | 189 35.0 | 51.5 | 245 06.1 | 36.3 | 276 12.1 | 08.6 | 318 20.2 | 50.6 | | | |
| 22 00 | 299 43.7 | 204 34.1 | N22 51.5 | 260 07.0 | N13 36.8 | 291 14.5 | N 2 08.6 | 333 22.8 | S14 50.6 | Canopus | 263 53.8 | S52 42.3 |
| 01 | 314 46.1 | 219 33.3 | 51.5 | 275 07.8 | 37.3 | 306 16.9 | 08.6 | 348 25.4 | 50.7 | Capella | 280 25.3 | N46 01.1 |
| 02 | 329 48.6 | 234 32.5 | 51.5 | 290 08.6 | 37.8 | 321 19.3 | 08.6 | 3 28.1 | 50.7 | Deneb | 49 26.7 | N45 21.6 |
| 03 | 344 51.1 | 249 31.7 .. | 51.5 | 305 09.4 .. | 38.4 | 336 21.7 .. | 08.6 | 18 30.7 .. | 50.8 | Denebola | 182 27.2 | N14 27.0 |
| 04 | 359 53.5 | 264 30.9 | 51.5 | 320 10.3 | 38.9 | 351 24.1 | 08.6 | 33 33.3 | 50.9 | Diphda | 348 49.2 | S17 51.7 |
| 05 | 14 56.0 | 279 30.1 | 51.5 | 335 11.1 | 39.4 | 6 26.5 | 08.7 | 48 35.9 | 50.9 | | | |
| 06 | 29 58.5 | 294 29.2 | N22 51.5 | 350 11.9 | N13 39.9 | 21 28.9 | N 2 08.7 | 63 38.5 | S14 51.0 | Dubhe | 193 44.0 | N61 38.1 |
| 07 | 45 00.9 | 309 28.4 | 51.5 | 5 12.8 | 40.5 | 36 31.3 | 08.7 | 78 41.2 | 51.0 | Elnath | 278 04.7 | N28 37.5 |
| 08 | 60 03.4 | 324 27.6 | 51.5 | 20 13.6 | 41.0 | 51 33.7 | 08.7 | 93 43.8 | 51.1 | Eltanin | 90 42.7 | N51 29.3 |
| F 09 | 75 05.8 | 339 26.8 .. | 51.5 | 35 14.4 .. | 41.5 | 66 36.2 .. | 08.7 | 108 46.4 .. | 51.2 | Enif | 33 40.5 | N 9 58.7 |
| R 10 | 90 08.3 | 354 26.0 | 51.5 | 50 15.3 | 42.0 | 81 38.6 | 08.7 | 123 49.0 | 51.2 | Fomalhaut | 15 16.5 | S29 30.1 |
| I 11 | 105 10.8 | 9 25.1 | 51.5 | 65 16.1 | 42.6 | 96 41.0 | 08.7 | 138 51.6 | 51.3 | | | |
| D 12 | 120 13.2 | 24 24.3 | N22 51.4 | 80 16.9 | N13 43.1 | 111 43.4 | N 2 08.7 | 153 54.3 | S14 51.3 | Gacrux | 171 54.1 | S57 14.5 |
| A 13 | 135 15.7 | 39 23.5 | 51.4 | 95 17.7 | 43.6 | 126 45.8 | 08.7 | 168 56.9 | 51.4 | Gienah | 175 45.8 | S17 40.0 |
| Y 14 | 150 18.2 | 54 22.7 | 51.4 | 110 18.6 | 44.1 | 141 48.2 | 08.7 | 183 59.5 | 51.4 | Hadar | 148 38.8 | S60 29.1 |
| 15 | 165 20.6 | 69 21.9 .. | 51.4 | 125 19.4 .. | 44.7 | 156 50.6 .. | 08.8 | 199 02.1 .. | 51.5 | Hamal | 327 53.5 | N23 34.0 |
| 16 | 180 23.1 | 84 21.0 | 51.4 | 140 20.2 | 45.2 | 171 53.0 | 08.8 | 214 04.7 | 51.6 | Kaus Aust. | 83 34.8 | S34 22.4 |
| 17 | 195 25.6 | 99 20.2 | 51.4 | 155 21.1 | 45.7 | 186 55.4 | 08.8 | 229 07.4 | 51.6 | | | |
| 18 | 210 28.0 | 114 19.4 | N22 51.4 | 170 21.9 | N13 46.2 | 201 57.9 | N 2 08.8 | 244 10.0 | S14 51.7 | Kochab | 137 19.5 | N74 04.1 |
| 19 | 225 30.5 | 129 18.6 | 51.4 | 185 22.7 | 46.7 | 217 00.3 | 08.8 | 259 12.6 | 51.7 | Markab | 13 31.7 | N15 19.5 |
| 20 | 240 32.9 | 144 17.8 | 51.3 | 200 23.6 | 47.3 | 232 02.7 | 08.8 | 274 15.2 | 51.8 | Menkar | 314 08.4 | N 4 10.7 |
| 21 | 255 35.4 | 159 17.0 .. | 51.3 | 215 24.4 .. | 47.8 | 247 05.1 .. | 08.8 | 289 17.8 .. | 51.9 | Menkent | 148 00.0 | S36 28.9 |
| 22 | 270 37.9 | 174 16.1 | 51.3 | 230 25.2 | 48.3 | 262 07.5 | 08.8 | 304 20.5 | 51.9 | Miaplacidus | 221 39.6 | S69 48.6 |
| 23 | 285 40.3 | 189 15.3 | 51.3 | 245 26.1 | 48.8 | 277 09.9 | 08.8 | 319 23.1 | 52.0 | | | |
| 23 00 | 300 42.8 | 204 14.5 | N22 51.3 | 260 26.9 | N13 49.4 | 292 12.3 | N 2 08.8 | 334 25.7 | S14 52.0 | Mirfak | 308 31.4 | N49 56.2 |
| 01 | 315 45.3 | 219 13.7 | 51.2 | 275 27.7 | 49.9 | 307 14.8 | 08.8 | 349 28.3 | 52.1 | Nunki | 75 49.9 | S26 16.1 |
| 02 | 330 47.7 | 234 12.9 | 51.2 | 290 28.5 | 50.4 | 322 17.2 | 08.8 | 4 31.0 | 52.2 | Peacock | 53 08.3 | S56 39.7 |
| 03 | 345 50.2 | 249 12.0 .. | 51.2 | 305 29.4 .. | 50.9 | 337 19.6 .. | 08.9 | 19 33.6 .. | 52.2 | Pollux | 243 20.2 | N27 58.4 |
| 04 | 0 52.7 | 264 11.2 | 51.1 | 320 30.2 | 51.4 | 352 22.0 | 08.9 | 34 36.2 | 52.3 | Procyon | 244 53.3 | N 5 10.1 |
| 05 | 15 55.1 | 279 10.4 | 51.1 | 335 31.0 | 52.0 | 7 24.4 | 08.9 | 49 38.8 | 52.3 | | | |
| 06 | 30 57.6 | 294 09.6 | N22 51.1 | 350 31.9 | N13 52.5 | 22 26.8 | N 2 08.9 | 64 41.4 | S14 52.4 | Rasalhague | 96 00.2 | N12 32.7 |
| 07 | 46 00.1 | 309 08.8 | 51.1 | 5 32.7 | 53.0 | 37 29.3 | 08.9 | 79 44.1 | 52.5 | Regulus | 207 36.9 | N11 51.6 |
| S 08 | 61 02.5 | 324 07.9 | 51.0 | 20 33.5 | 53.5 | 52 31.7 | 08.9 | 94 46.7 | 52.5 | Rigel | 281 06.1 | S 8 10.5 |
| A 09 | 76 05.0 | 339 07.1 .. | 51.0 | 35 34.4 .. | 54.0 | 67 34.1 .. | 08.9 | 109 49.3 .. | 52.6 | Rigil Kent. | 139 43.0 | S60 55.8 |
| T 10 | 91 07.4 | 354 06.3 | 51.0 | 50 35.2 | 54.5 | 82 36.5 | 08.9 | 124 51.9 | 52.6 | Sabik | 102 04.8 | S15 45.1 |
| U 11 | 106 09.9 | 9 05.5 | 50.9 | 65 36.0 | 55.1 | 97 38.9 | 08.9 | 139 54.6 | 52.7 | | | |
| R 12 | 121 12.4 | 24 04.7 | N22 50.9 | 80 36.9 | N13 55.6 | 112 41.3 | N 2 08.9 | 154 57.2 | S14 52.7 | Schedar | 349 33.1 | N56 39.4 |
| D 13 | 136 14.8 | 39 03.8 | 50.9 | 95 37.7 | 56.1 | 127 43.8 | 08.9 | 169 59.8 | 52.8 | Shaula | 96 12.8 | S37 07.2 |
| A 14 | 151 17.3 | 54 03.0 | 50.8 | 110 38.5 | 56.6 | 142 46.2 | 08.9 | 185 02.4 | 52.9 | Sirius | 258 28.4 | S16 44.7 |
| Y 15 | 166 19.8 | 69 02.2 .. | 50.8 | 125 39.4 .. | 57.1 | 157 48.6 .. | 08.9 | 200 05.0 .. | 52.9 | Spica | 158 24.5 | S11 16.7 |
| 16 | 181 22.2 | 84 01.4 | 50.7 | 140 40.2 | 57.6 | 172 51.0 | 08.9 | 215 07.7 | 53.0 | Suhail | 222 48.2 | S43 31.4 |
| 17 | 196 24.7 | 99 00.6 | 50.7 | 155 41.0 | 58.2 | 187 53.4 | 08.9 | 230 10.3 | 53.0 | | | |
| 18 | 211 27.2 | 113 59.7 | N22 50.6 | 170 41.9 | N13 58.7 | 202 55.9 | N 2 08.9 | 245 12.9 | S14 53.1 | Vega | 80 34.2 | N38 48.4 |
| 19 | 226 29.6 | 128 58.9 | 50.6 | 185 42.7 | 59.2 | 217 58.3 | 08.9 | 260 15.5 | 53.2 | Zuben'ubi | 136 58.2 | S16 08.1 |
| 20 | 241 32.1 | 143 58.1 | 50.6 | 200 43.5 | 13 59.7 | 233 00.7 | 09.0 | 275 18.2 | 53.2 | | SHA | Mer.Pass. |
| 21 | 256 34.6 | 158 57.3 .. | 50.5 | 215 44.4 | 14 00.2 | 248 03.1 .. | 09.0 | 290 20.8 .. | 53.3 | | ° ′ | h m |
| 22 | 271 37.0 | 173 56.5 | 50.5 | 230 45.2 | 00.7 | 263 05.5 | 09.0 | 305 23.4 | 53.3 | Venus | 264 50.5 | 10 22 |
| 23 | 286 39.5 | 188 55.6 | 50.4 | 245 46.0 | 01.3 | 278 08.0 | 09.0 | 320 26.0 | 53.4 | Mars | 320 23.3 | 6 39 |
| | h m | | | | | | | | | Jupiter | 351 30.8 | 4 34 |
| Mer.Pass. 4 00.4 | | v −0.8 | d 0.0 | v 0.8 | d 0.5 | v 2.4 | d 0.0 | v 2.6 | d 0.1 | Saturn | 33 39.2 | 1 46 |

| UT | SUN | | MOON | | | | | Lat. | Twilight | | Sunrise | Moonrise | | | |
|---|---|---|---|---|---|---|---|---|---|---|---|---|---|---|---|
| | | | | | | | | | Naut. | Civil | | 21 | 22 | 23 | 24 |
| | GHA | Dec | GHA | v | Dec | d | HP | ° | h m | h m | h m | h m | h m | h m | h m |
| d h | ° ′ | ° ′ | ° ′ | ′ | ° ′ | ′ | ′ | N 72 | ▭ | ▭ | ▭ | 20 57 | ▭ | ▭ | ▭ |
| 21 00 | 178 23.5 | N20 30.7 | 267 29.4 | 14.4 | N11 05.1 | 13.1 | 55.9 | N 70 | ▭ | ▭ | ▭ | 21 31 | 20 22 | ▭ | ▭ |
| 01 | 193 23.5 | 30.2 | 282 02.8 | 14.4 | 11 18.2 | 13.0 | 55.8 | 68 | //// | //// | 01 14 | 21 56 | 21 23 | ▭ | ▭ |
| 02 | 208 23.5 | 29.7 | 296 36.2 | 14.4 | 11 31.2 | 13.0 | 55.8 | 66 | //// | //// | 02 05 | 22 15 | 21 58 | 21 24 | ▭ |
| 03 | 223 23.4 .. | 29.3 | 311 09.6 | 14.3 | 11 44.2 | 12.9 | 55.8 | 64 | //// | //// | 02 36 | 22 30 | 22 23 | 22 13 | 21 53 |
| 04 | 238 23.4 | 28.8 | 325 42.9 | 14.4 | 11 57.1 | 12.9 | 55.7 | 62 | //// | 01 31 | 02 59 | 22 43 | 22 43 | 22 44 | 22 51 |
| 05 | 253 23.4 | 28.3 | 340 16.3 | 14.3 | 12 10.0 | 12.8 | 55.7 | 60 | //// | 02 08 | 03 18 | 22 54 | 22 59 | 23 08 | 23 24 |
| 06 | 268 23.3 | N20 27.8 | 354 49.6 | 14.3 | N12 22.8 | 12.7 | 55.7 | N 58 | //// | 02 33 | 03 33 | 23 04 | 23 13 | 23 27 | 23 49 |
| T 07 | 283 23.3 | 27.3 | 9 22.9 | 14.3 | 12 35.5 | 12.7 | 55.7 | 56 | 01 23 | 02 53 | 03 46 | 23 13 | 23 25 | 23 43 | 24 09 |
| H 08 | 298 23.3 | 26.8 | 23 56.2 | 14.3 | 12 48.2 | 12.6 | 55.6 | 54 | 01 57 | 03 09 | 03 57 | 23 20 | 23 36 | 23 56 | 24 25 |
| U 09 | 313 23.2 .. | 26.4 | 38 29.5 | 14.2 | 13 00.8 | 12.5 | 55.6 | 52 | 02 21 | 03 23 | 04 07 | 23 27 | 23 45 | 24 08 | 00 08 |
| R 10 | 328 23.2 | 25.9 | 53 02.7 | 14.3 | 13 13.3 | 12.5 | 55.6 | 50 | 02 39 | 03 35 | 04 16 | 23 33 | 23 54 | 24 19 | 00 19 |
| S 11 | 343 23.2 | 25.4 | 67 36.0 | 14.2 | 13 25.8 | 12.4 | 55.5 | 45 | 03 14 | 03 59 | 04 34 | 23 47 | 24 11 | 00 11 | 00 41 |
| D 12 | 358 23.2 | N20 24.9 | 82 09.2 | 14.2 | N13 38.2 | 12.3 | 55.5 | N 40 | 03 39 | 04 18 | 04 49 | 23 58 | 24 26 | 00 26 | 00 59 |
| A 13 | 13 23.1 | 24.4 | 96 42.4 | 14.1 | 13 50.5 | 12.2 | 55.5 | 35 | 03 59 | 04 33 | 05 02 | 24 07 | 00 07 | 00 39 | 01 14 |
| Y 14 | 28 23.1 | 23.9 | 111 15.5 | 14.2 | 14 02.7 | 12.2 | 55.4 | 30 | 04 15 | 04 46 | 05 13 | 24 16 | 00 16 | 00 50 | 01 27 |
| 15 | 43 23.1 .. | 23.4 | 125 48.7 | 14.1 | 14 14.9 | 12.1 | 55.4 | 20 | 04 40 | 05 08 | 05 32 | 24 30 | 00 30 | 01 09 | 01 50 |
| 16 | 58 23.0 | 22.9 | 140 21.8 | 14.1 | 14 27.0 | 12.1 | 55.4 | N 10 | 04 59 | 05 25 | 05 48 | 00 03 | 00 43 | 01 25 | 02 10 |
| 17 | 73 23.0 | 22.5 | 154 54.9 | 14.0 | 14 39.1 | 11.9 | 55.4 | 0 | 05 15 | 05 41 | 06 03 | 00 11 | 00 55 | 01 41 | 02 28 |
| 18 | 88 23.0 | N20 22.0 | 169 27.9 | 14.1 | N14 51.0 | 11.9 | 55.4 | S 10 | 05 30 | 05 55 | 06 18 | 00 19 | 01 07 | 01 56 | 02 46 |
| 19 | 103 23.0 | 21.5 | 184 01.0 | 14.0 | 15 02.9 | 11.9 | 55.3 | 20 | 05 43 | 06 10 | 06 34 | 00 28 | 01 20 | 02 13 | 03 06 |
| 20 | 118 22.9 | 21.0 | 198 34.0 | 14.0 | 15 14.8 | 11.7 | 55.3 | 30 | 05 57 | 06 26 | 06 52 | 00 38 | 01 35 | 02 32 | 03 29 |
| 21 | 133 22.9 .. | 20.5 | 213 07.0 | 13.9 | 15 26.5 | 11.7 | 55.3 | 35 | 06 04 | 06 35 | 07 02 | 00 44 | 01 44 | 02 44 | 03 43 |
| 22 | 148 22.9 | 20.0 | 227 39.9 | 13.9 | 15 38.2 | 11.6 | 55.3 | 40 | 06 11 | 06 44 | 07 14 | 00 51 | 01 54 | 02 57 | 03 59 |
| 23 | 163 22.9 | 19.5 | 242 12.8 | 13.9 | 15 49.8 | 11.5 | 55.2 | 45 | 06 19 | 06 55 | 07 28 | 00 59 | 02 06 | 03 13 | 04 17 |
| 22 00 | 178 22.8 | N20 19.0 | 256 45.7 | 13.9 | N16 01.3 | 11.4 | 55.2 | S 50 | 06 28 | 07 08 | 07 45 | 01 08 | 02 20 | 03 32 | 04 41 |
| 01 | 193 22.8 | 18.5 | 271 18.6 | 13.8 | 16 12.7 | 11.4 | 55.2 | 52 | 06 32 | 07 14 | 07 53 | 01 12 | 02 27 | 03 41 | 04 52 |
| 02 | 208 22.8 | 18.0 | 285 51.4 | 13.8 | 16 24.1 | 11.3 | 55.2 | 54 | 06 37 | 07 21 | 08 02 | 01 17 | 02 35 | 03 51 | 05 05 |
| 03 | 223 22.8 .. | 17.5 | 300 24.2 | 13.7 | 16 35.4 | 11.2 | 55.1 | 56 | 06 41 | 07 28 | 08 12 | 01 23 | 02 43 | 04 03 | 05 20 |
| 04 | 238 22.7 | 17.0 | 314 56.9 | 13.8 | 16 46.6 | 11.1 | 55.1 | 58 | 06 46 | 07 36 | 08 23 | 01 29 | 02 53 | 04 16 | 05 38 |
| 05 | 253 22.7 | 16.5 | 329 29.7 | 13.7 | 16 57.7 | 11.1 | 55.1 | S 60 | 06 52 | 07 45 | 08 36 | 01 36 | 03 04 | 04 32 | 06 00 |

| UT | SUN | | MOON | | | | | Lat. | Sunset | Twilight | | Moonset | | | |
|---|---|---|---|---|---|---|---|---|---|---|---|---|---|---|---|
| | | | | | | | | | | Civil | Naut. | 21 | 22 | 23 | 24 |
| 06 | 268 22.7 | N20 16.0 | 344 02.4 | 13.6 | N17 08.8 | 10.9 | 55.1 | ° | h m | h m | h m | h m | h m | h m | h m |
| 07 | 283 22.7 | 15.5 | 358 35.0 | 13.6 | 17 19.7 | 10.9 | 55.0 | N 72 | ▭ | ▭ | ▭ | 16 07 | ▭ | ▭ | ▭ |
| 08 | 298 22.6 | 15.0 | 13 07.6 | 13.6 | 17 30.6 | 10.8 | 55.0 | N 70 | ▭ | ▭ | ▭ | 15 35 | 18 19 | ▭ | ▭ |
| F 09 | 313 22.6 .. | 14.5 | 27 40.2 | 13.6 | 17 41.4 | 10.7 | 55.0 | 68 | 22 53 | //// | //// | 15 12 | 17 19 | ▭ | ▭ |
| R 10 | 328 22.6 | 14.0 | 42 12.8 | 13.5 | 17 52.1 | 10.6 | 55.0 | 66 | 22 04 | //// | //// | 14 54 | 16 45 | 18 56 | ▭ |
| I 11 | 343 22.6 | 13.5 | 56 45.3 | 13.4 | 18 02.7 | 10.6 | 55.0 | 64 | 21 34 | //// | //// | 14 40 | 16 21 | 18 08 | 20 09 |
| D 12 | 358 22.5 | N20 13.0 | 71 17.7 | 13.5 | N18 13.3 | 10.4 | 54.9 | 62 | 21 12 | 22 38 | //// | 14 28 | 16 02 | 17 37 | 19 12 |
| A 13 | 13 22.5 | 12.5 | 85 50.2 | 13.3 | 18 23.7 | 10.4 | 54.9 | 60 | 20 54 | 22 03 | //// | 14 18 | 15 46 | 17 14 | 18 39 |
| Y 14 | 28 22.5 | 12.0 | 100 22.5 | 13.4 | 18 34.1 | 10.3 | 54.9 | N 58 | 20 39 | 21 38 | //// | 14 09 | 15 33 | 16 56 | 18 14 |
| 15 | 43 22.5 .. | 11.5 | 114 54.9 | 13.3 | 18 44.4 | 10.2 | 54.9 | 56 | 20 26 | 21 18 | 22 46 | 14 01 | 15 21 | 16 40 | 17 55 |
| 16 | 58 22.5 | 11.0 | 129 27.2 | 13.3 | 18 54.6 | 10.1 | 54.8 | 54 | 20 15 | 21 02 | 22 14 | 13 54 | 15 11 | 16 27 | 17 39 |
| 17 | 73 22.4 | 10.5 | 143 59.5 | 13.2 | 19 04.7 | 10.0 | 54.8 | 52 | 20 05 | 20 49 | 21 50 | 13 48 | 15 03 | 16 16 | 17 25 |
| 18 | 88 22.4 | N20 10.0 | 158 31.7 | 13.2 | N19 14.7 | 9.9 | 54.8 | 50 | 19 56 | 20 37 | 21 32 | 13 43 | 14 55 | 16 05 | 17 13 |
| 19 | 103 22.4 | 09.5 | 173 03.9 | 13.1 | 19 24.6 | 9.9 | 54.8 | 45 | 19 38 | 20 13 | 20 58 | 13 31 | 14 38 | 15 44 | 16 47 |
| 20 | 118 22.4 | 09.0 | 187 36.0 | 13.1 | 19 34.5 | 9.7 | 54.8 | N 40 | 19 23 | 19 54 | 20 33 | 13 21 | 14 24 | 15 27 | 16 27 |
| 21 | 133 22.3 .. | 08.5 | 202 08.1 | 13.1 | 19 44.2 | 9.7 | 54.7 | 35 | 19 11 | 19 39 | 20 14 | 13 13 | 14 13 | 15 12 | 16 11 |
| 22 | 148 22.3 | 08.0 | 216 40.2 | 13.0 | 19 53.9 | 9.6 | 54.7 | 30 | 19 00 | 19 26 | 19 58 | 13 06 | 14 03 | 15 00 | 15 56 |
| 23 | 163 22.3 | 07.5 | 231 12.2 | 13.0 | 20 03.5 | 9.4 | 54.7 | 20 | 18 41 | 19 05 | 19 33 | 12 53 | 13 46 | 14 39 | 15 32 |
| 23 00 | 178 22.3 | N20 07.0 | 245 44.2 | 12.9 | N20 12.9 | 9.4 | 54.7 | N 10 | 18 25 | 18 47 | 19 14 | 12 42 | 13 31 | 14 20 | 15 11 |
| 01 | 193 22.3 | 06.5 | 260 16.1 | 12.9 | 20 22.3 | 9.3 | 54.7 | 0 | 18 10 | 18 32 | 18 58 | 12 32 | 13 17 | 14 03 | 14 52 |
| 02 | 208 22.2 | 06.0 | 274 48.0 | 12.9 | 20 31.6 | 9.2 | 54.7 | S 10 | 17 55 | 18 18 | 18 43 | 12 22 | 13 03 | 13 46 | 14 32 |
| 03 | 223 22.2 .. | 05.5 | 289 19.9 | 12.8 | 20 40.8 | 9.1 | 54.6 | 20 | 17 40 | 18 03 | 18 30 | 12 11 | 12 48 | 13 28 | 14 11 |
| 04 | 238 22.2 | 05.0 | 303 51.7 | 12.7 | 20 49.9 | 9.0 | 54.6 | 30 | 17 22 | 17 47 | 18 17 | 11 59 | 12 31 | 13 07 | 13 47 |
| 05 | 253 22.2 | 04.4 | 318 23.4 | 12.7 | 20 58.9 | 8.9 | 54.6 | 35 | 17 11 | 17 39 | 18 10 | 11 52 | 12 21 | 12 55 | 13 33 |
| 06 | 268 22.2 | N20 03.9 | 332 55.1 | 12.7 | N21 07.8 | 8.8 | 54.6 | 40 | 17 00 | 17 29 | 18 02 | 11 44 | 12 10 | 12 41 | 13 17 |
| S 07 | 283 22.2 | 03.4 | 347 26.8 | 12.6 | 21 16.6 | 8.7 | 54.6 | 45 | 16 46 | 17 18 | 17 54 | 11 34 | 11 57 | 12 24 | 12 57 |
| A 08 | 298 22.1 | 02.9 | 1 58.4 | 12.6 | 21 25.3 | 8.6 | 54.5 | S 50 | 16 29 | 17 05 | 17 45 | 11 23 | 11 41 | 12 04 | 12 33 |
| T 09 | 313 22.1 .. | 02.4 | 16 30.0 | 12.6 | 21 33.9 | 8.5 | 54.5 | 52 | 16 21 | 16 59 | 17 41 | 11 18 | 11 34 | 11 54 | 12 21 |
| U 10 | 328 22.1 | 01.9 | 31 01.6 | 12.4 | 21 42.4 | 8.4 | 54.5 | 54 | 16 12 | 16 53 | 17 37 | 11 12 | 11 26 | 11 44 | 12 08 |
| R 11 | 343 22.1 | 01.4 | 45 33.0 | 12.5 | 21 50.8 | 8.3 | 54.5 | 56 | 16 02 | 16 46 | 17 32 | 11 06 | 11 17 | 11 31 | 11 52 |
| D 12 | 358 22.1 | N20 00.9 | 60 04.5 | 12.4 | N21 59.1 | 8.2 | 54.5 | 58 | 15 51 | 16 38 | 17 27 | 10 59 | 11 06 | 11 17 | 11 34 |
| A 13 | 13 22.0 | 20 00.3 | 74 35.9 | 12.3 | 22 07.3 | 8.1 | 54.5 | S 60 | 15 37 | 16 29 | 17 22 | 10 51 | 10 55 | 11 01 | 11 12 |
| Y 14 | 28 22.0 | 19 59.8 | 89 07.2 | 12.4 | 22 15.4 | 8.0 | 54.5 | | | | | | | | |
| 15 | 43 22.0 .. | 59.3 | 103 38.6 | 12.2 | 22 23.4 | 7.9 | 54.4 | | | SUN | | | MOON | | |
| 16 | 58 22.0 | 58.8 | 118 09.8 | 12.2 | 22 31.3 | 7.8 | 54.4 | | | | | | | | |
| 17 | 73 22.0 | 58.3 | 132 41.0 | 12.2 | 22 39.1 | 7.7 | 54.4 | Day | Eqn. of Time | | Mer. | Mer. Pass. | | Age | Phase |
| 18 | 88 22.0 | N19 57.8 | 147 12.2 | 12.1 | N22 46.8 | 7.5 | 54.4 | | 00ʰ | 12ʰ | Pass. | Upper | Lower | | |
| 19 | 103 22.0 | 57.2 | 161 43.3 | 12.1 | 22 54.3 | 7.5 | 54.4 | d | m s | m s | h m | h m | h m | d | % |
| 20 | 118 21.9 | 56.7 | 176 14.4 | 12.1 | 23 01.8 | 7.4 | 54.4 | 21 | 06 26 | 06 27 | 12 06 | 06 21 | 18 43 | 22 | 41 |
| 21 | 133 21.9 .. | 56.2 | 190 45.5 | 12.0 | 23 09.2 | 7.2 | 54.4 | 22 | 06 29 | 06 30 | 12 06 | 07 06 | 19 29 | 23 | 32 |
| 22 | 148 21.9 | 55.7 | 205 16.5 | 11.9 | 23 16.4 | 7.2 | 54.3 | 23 | 06 31 | 06 32 | 12 07 | 07 52 | 20 16 | 24 | 23 |
| 23 | 163 21.9 | 55.2 | 219 47.4 | 11.9 | N23 23.6 | 7.0 | 54.3 | | | | | | | | |
| | SD 15.8 | d 0.5 | SD 15.1 | | 15.0 | | 14.8 | | | | | | | | | |

| UT | ARIES | VENUS −3.9 | | MARS +0.2 | | JUPITER −2.6 | | SATURN +0.3 | | STARS | | |
|---|---|---|---|---|---|---|---|---|---|---|---|---|
| d h | GHA | GHA | Dec | GHA | Dec | GHA | Dec | GHA | Dec | Name | SHA | Dec |
| **24** 00 | 301 41.9 | 203 54.8 | N22 50.4 | 260 46.9 | N14 01.8 | 293 10.4 | N 2 09.0 | 335 28.7 | S14 53.5 | Acamar | 315 13.4 | S40 12.6 |
| 01 | 316 44.4 | 218 54.0 | 50.3 | 275 47.7 | 02.3 | 308 12.8 | 09.0 | 350 31.3 | 53.5 | Achernar | 335 21.7 | S57 07.1 |
| 02 | 331 46.9 | 233 53.2 | 50.3 | 290 48.6 | 02.8 | 323 15.2 | 09.0 | 5 33.9 | 53.6 | Acrux | 173 02.6 | S63 13.6 |
| 03 | 346 49.3 | 248 52.4 | .. 50.2 | 305 49.4 | .. 03.3 | 338 17.7 | .. 09.0 | 20 36.5 | .. 53.6 | Adhara | 255 07.8 | S29 00.0 |
| 04 | 1 51.8 | 263 51.5 | 50.2 | 320 50.2 | 03.8 | 353 20.1 | 09.0 | 35 39.1 | 53.7 | Aldebaran | 290 42.2 | N16 33.2 |
| 05 | 16 54.3 | 278 50.7 | 50.1 | 335 51.1 | 04.3 | 8 22.5 | 09.0 | 50 41.8 | 53.8 | | | |
| 06 | 31 56.7 | 293 49.9 | N22 50.0 | 350 51.9 | N14 04.9 | 23 24.9 | N 2 09.0 | 65 44.4 | S14 53.8 | Alioth | 166 14.9 | N55 50.6 |
| 07 | 46 59.2 | 308 49.1 | 50.0 | 5 52.7 | 05.4 | 38 27.4 | 09.0 | 80 47.0 | 53.9 | Alkaid | 152 53.7 | N49 12.4 |
| 08 | 62 01.7 | 323 48.2 | 49.9 | 20 53.6 | 05.9 | 53 29.8 | 09.0 | 95 49.6 | 53.9 | Alnair | 27 35.1 | S46 51.0 |
| S 09 | 77 04.1 | 338 47.4 | .. 49.9 | 35 54.4 | .. 06.4 | 68 32.2 | .. 09.0 | 110 52.3 | .. 54.0 | Alnilam | 275 40.0 | S 1 11.2 |
| U 10 | 92 06.6 | 353 46.6 | 49.8 | 50 55.2 | 06.9 | 83 34.6 | 09.0 | 125 54.9 | 54.1 | Alphard | 217 50.1 | S 8 45.3 |
| N 11 | 107 09.1 | 8 45.8 | 49.7 | 65 56.1 | 07.4 | 98 37.1 | 09.0 | 140 57.5 | 54.1 | | | |
| D 12 | 122 11.5 | 23 45.0 | N22 49.7 | 80 56.9 | N14 07.9 | 113 39.5 | N 2 09.0 | 156 00.1 | S14 54.2 | Alphecca | 126 05.3 | N26 38.6 |
| A 13 | 137 14.0 | 38 44.1 | 49.6 | 95 57.7 | 08.4 | 128 41.9 | 09.0 | 171 02.8 | 54.2 | Alpheratz | 357 36.7 | N29 12.7 |
| Y 14 | 152 16.4 | 53 43.3 | 49.5 | 110 58.6 | 08.9 | 143 44.3 | 09.0 | 186 05.4 | 54.3 | Altair | 62 01.6 | N 8 55.7 |
| 15 | 167 18.9 | 68 42.5 | .. 49.5 | 125 59.4 | .. 09.5 | 158 46.8 | .. 09.0 | 201 08.0 | .. 54.4 | Ankaa | 353 09.0 | S42 10.8 |
| 16 | 182 21.4 | 83 41.7 | 49.4 | 141 00.2 | 10.0 | 173 49.2 | 09.0 | 216 10.6 | 54.4 | Antares | 112 18.1 | S26 28.9 |
| 17 | 197 23.8 | 98 40.9 | 49.3 | 156 01.1 | 10.5 | 188 51.6 | 09.0 | 231 13.3 | 54.5 | | | |
| 18 | 212 26.3 | 113 40.0 | N22 49.3 | 171 01.9 | N14 11.0 | 203 54.0 | N 2 09.0 | 246 15.9 | S14 54.5 | Arcturus | 145 49.7 | N19 04.1 |
| 19 | 227 28.8 | 128 39.2 | 49.2 | 186 02.8 | 11.5 | 218 56.5 | 09.0 | 261 18.5 | 54.6 | Atria | 107 13.7 | S69 04.2 |
| 20 | 242 31.2 | 143 38.4 | 49.1 | 201 03.6 | 12.0 | 233 58.9 | 09.0 | 276 21.1 | 54.7 | Avior | 234 16.2 | S59 34.8 |
| 21 | 257 33.7 | 158 37.6 | .. 49.1 | 216 04.4 | .. 12.5 | 249 01.3 | .. 09.0 | 291 23.8 | .. 54.7 | Bellatrix | 278 25.3 | N 6 22.2 |
| 22 | 272 36.2 | 173 36.8 | 49.0 | 231 05.3 | 13.0 | 264 03.8 | 09.0 | 306 26.4 | 54.8 | Betelgeuse | 270 54.6 | N 7 24.7 |
| 23 | 287 38.6 | 188 35.9 | 48.9 | 246 06.1 | 13.5 | 279 06.2 | 09.0 | 321 29.0 | 54.8 | | | |
| **25** 00 | 302 41.1 | 203 35.1 | N22 48.8 | 261 06.9 | N14 14.0 | 294 08.6 | N 2 09.0 | 336 31.6 | S14 54.9 | Canopus | 263 53.8 | S52 42.3 |
| 01 | 317 43.6 | 218 34.3 | 48.7 | 276 07.8 | 14.5 | 309 11.1 | 09.0 | 351 34.3 | 55.0 | Capella | 280 25.2 | N46 01.1 |
| 02 | 332 46.0 | 233 33.5 | 48.7 | 291 08.6 | 15.1 | 324 13.5 | 09.0 | 6 36.9 | 55.0 | Deneb | 49 26.7 | N45 21.6 |
| 03 | 347 48.5 | 248 32.6 | .. 48.6 | 306 09.5 | .. 15.6 | 339 15.9 | .. 09.0 | 21 39.5 | .. 55.1 | Denebola | 182 27.2 | N14 27.0 |
| 04 | 2 50.9 | 263 31.8 | 48.5 | 321 10.3 | 16.1 | 354 18.3 | 09.0 | 36 42.1 | 55.1 | Diphda | 348 49.2 | S17 51.7 |
| 05 | 17 53.4 | 278 31.0 | 48.4 | 336 11.1 | 16.6 | 9 20.8 | 09.0 | 51 44.8 | 55.2 | | | |
| 06 | 32 55.9 | 293 30.2 | N22 48.3 | 351 12.0 | N14 17.1 | 24 23.2 | N 2 09.0 | 66 47.4 | S14 55.3 | Dubhe | 193 44.0 | N61 38.1 |
| 07 | 47 58.3 | 308 29.4 | 48.3 | 6 12.8 | 17.6 | 39 25.6 | 09.0 | 81 50.0 | 55.3 | Elnath | 278 04.7 | N28 37.5 |
| 08 | 63 00.8 | 323 28.5 | 48.2 | 21 13.6 | 18.1 | 54 28.1 | 09.0 | 96 52.7 | 55.4 | Eltanin | 90 42.7 | N51 29.3 |
| M 09 | 78 03.3 | 338 27.7 | .. 48.1 | 36 14.5 | .. 18.6 | 69 30.5 | .. 09.0 | 111 55.3 | .. 55.5 | Enif | 33 40.5 | N 9 58.7 |
| O 10 | 93 05.7 | 353 26.9 | 48.0 | 51 15.3 | 19.1 | 84 32.9 | 09.0 | 126 57.9 | 55.5 | Fomalhaut | 15 16.5 | S29 30.1 |
| N 11 | 108 08.2 | 8 26.1 | 47.9 | 66 16.2 | 19.6 | 99 35.4 | 09.0 | 142 00.5 | 55.6 | | | |
| D 12 | 123 10.7 | 23 25.3 | N22 47.8 | 81 17.0 | N14 20.1 | 114 37.8 | N 2 09.0 | 157 03.2 | S14 55.6 | Gacrux | 171 54.1 | S57 14.5 |
| A 13 | 138 13.1 | 38 24.4 | 47.7 | 96 17.8 | 20.6 | 129 40.2 | 09.0 | 172 05.8 | 55.7 | Gienah | 175 45.8 | S17 40.0 |
| Y 14 | 153 15.6 | 53 23.6 | 47.6 | 111 18.7 | 21.1 | 144 42.7 | 09.0 | 187 08.4 | 55.8 | Hadar | 148 38.8 | S60 29.1 |
| 15 | 168 18.0 | 68 22.8 | .. 47.5 | 126 19.5 | .. 21.6 | 159 45.1 | .. 09.0 | 202 11.0 | .. 55.8 | Hamal | 327 53.5 | N23 34.0 |
| 16 | 183 20.5 | 83 22.0 | 47.4 | 141 20.4 | 22.1 | 174 47.5 | 09.0 | 217 13.7 | 55.9 | Kaus Aust. | 83 34.8 | S34 22.4 |
| 17 | 198 23.0 | 98 21.1 | 47.3 | 156 21.2 | 22.6 | 189 50.0 | 09.0 | 232 16.3 | 55.9 | | | |
| 18 | 213 25.4 | 113 20.3 | N22 47.2 | 171 22.0 | N14 23.1 | 204 52.4 | N 2 09.0 | 247 18.9 | S14 56.0 | Kochab | 137 19.6 | N74 04.1 |
| 19 | 228 27.9 | 128 19.5 | 47.1 | 186 22.9 | 23.7 | 219 54.8 | 09.0 | 262 21.5 | 56.1 | Markab | 13 31.7 | N15 19.5 |
| 20 | 243 30.4 | 143 18.7 | 47.0 | 201 23.7 | 24.2 | 234 57.3 | 09.0 | 277 24.2 | 56.1 | Menkar | 314 08.3 | N 4 10.7 |
| 21 | 258 32.8 | 158 17.9 | .. 46.9 | 216 24.5 | .. 24.7 | 249 59.7 | .. 09.0 | 292 26.8 | .. 56.2 | Menkent | 148 00.0 | S36 28.9 |
| 22 | 273 35.3 | 173 17.0 | 46.8 | 231 25.4 | 25.2 | 265 02.2 | 09.0 | 307 29.4 | 56.2 | Miaplacidus | 221 39.6 | S69 48.6 |
| 23 | 288 37.8 | 188 16.2 | 46.7 | 246 26.2 | 25.7 | 280 04.6 | 09.0 | 322 32.1 | 56.3 | | | |
| **26** 00 | 303 40.2 | 203 15.4 | N22 46.6 | 261 27.1 | N14 26.2 | 295 07.0 | N 2 09.0 | 337 34.7 | S14 56.4 | Mirfak | 308 31.3 | N49 56.2 |
| 01 | 318 42.7 | 218 14.6 | 46.5 | 276 27.9 | 26.7 | 310 09.5 | 09.0 | 352 37.3 | 56.4 | Nunki | 75 49.9 | S26 16.1 |
| 02 | 333 45.2 | 233 13.8 | 46.4 | 291 28.7 | 27.2 | 325 11.9 | 09.0 | 7 39.9 | 56.5 | Peacock | 53 08.3 | S56 39.7 |
| 03 | 348 47.6 | 248 12.9 | .. 46.3 | 306 29.6 | .. 27.7 | 340 14.3 | .. 09.0 | 22 42.6 | .. 56.5 | Pollux | 243 20.2 | N27 58.4 |
| 04 | 3 50.1 | 263 12.1 | 46.2 | 321 30.4 | 28.2 | 355 16.8 | 09.0 | 37 45.2 | 56.6 | Procyon | 244 53.3 | N 5 10.1 |
| 05 | 18 52.5 | 278 11.3 | 46.1 | 336 31.3 | 28.7 | 10 19.2 | 09.0 | 52 47.8 | 56.7 | | | |
| 06 | 33 55.0 | 293 10.5 | N22 46.0 | 351 32.1 | N14 29.2 | 25 21.7 | N 2 09.0 | 67 50.4 | S14 56.7 | Rasalhague | 96 00.2 | N12 32.7 |
| 07 | 48 57.5 | 308 09.7 | 45.9 | 6 33.0 | 29.7 | 40 24.1 | 09.0 | 82 53.1 | 56.8 | Regulus | 207 36.9 | N11 51.6 |
| 08 | 63 59.9 | 323 08.8 | 45.7 | 21 33.8 | 30.2 | 55 26.5 | 09.0 | 97 55.7 | 56.8 | Rigel | 281 06.1 | S 8 10.4 |
| T 09 | 79 02.4 | 338 08.0 | .. 45.6 | 36 34.6 | .. 30.7 | 70 29.0 | .. 09.0 | 112 58.3 | .. 56.9 | Rigil Kent. | 139 43.0 | S60 55.8 |
| U 10 | 94 04.9 | 353 07.2 | 45.5 | 51 35.5 | 31.2 | 85 31.4 | 09.0 | 128 01.0 | 57.0 | Sabik | 102 04.8 | S15 45.1 |
| E 11 | 109 07.3 | 8 06.4 | 45.4 | 66 36.3 | 31.7 | 100 33.9 | 09.0 | 143 03.6 | 57.0 | | | |
| S 12 | 124 09.8 | 23 05.5 | N22 45.3 | 81 37.2 | N14 32.2 | 115 36.3 | N 2 09.0 | 158 06.2 | S14 57.1 | Schedar | 349 33.1 | N56 39.4 |
| D 13 | 139 12.3 | 38 04.7 | 45.2 | 96 38.0 | 32.7 | 130 38.7 | 09.0 | 173 08.8 | 57.2 | Shaula | 96 12.8 | S37 07.2 |
| A 14 | 154 14.7 | 53 03.9 | 45.0 | 111 38.8 | 33.2 | 145 41.2 | 09.0 | 188 11.5 | 57.2 | Sirius | 258 28.3 | S16 44.7 |
| Y 15 | 169 17.2 | 68 03.1 | .. 44.9 | 126 39.7 | .. 33.7 | 160 43.6 | .. 09.0 | 203 14.1 | .. 57.3 | Spica | 158 24.5 | S11 16.7 |
| 16 | 184 19.7 | 83 02.3 | 44.8 | 141 40.5 | 34.2 | 175 46.1 | 09.0 | 218 16.7 | 57.3 | Suhail | 222 48.2 | S43 31.4 |
| 17 | 199 22.1 | 98 01.4 | 44.7 | 156 41.4 | 34.7 | 190 48.5 | 09.0 | 233 19.4 | 57.4 | | | |
| 18 | 214 24.6 | 113 00.6 | N22 44.5 | 171 42.2 | N14 35.2 | 205 51.0 | N 2 09.0 | 248 22.0 | S14 57.5 | Vega | 80 34.2 | N38 48.4 |
| 19 | 229 27.0 | 127 59.8 | 44.4 | 186 43.1 | 35.7 | 220 53.4 | 09.0 | 263 24.6 | 57.5 | Zuben'ubi | 136 58.2 | S16 08.1 |
| 20 | 244 29.5 | 142 59.0 | 44.3 | 201 43.9 | 36.2 | 235 55.8 | 09.0 | 278 27.2 | 57.6 | | SHA | Mer. Pass. |
| 21 | 259 32.0 | 157 58.2 | .. 44.2 | 216 44.7 | .. 36.7 | 250 58.3 | .. 09.0 | 293 29.9 | .. 57.6 | | ° ′ | h m |
| 22 | 274 34.4 | 172 57.3 | 44.0 | 231 45.6 | 37.1 | 266 00.7 | 09.0 | 308 32.5 | 57.7 | Venus | 260 54.0 | 10 26 |
| 23 | 289 36.9 | 187 56.5 | 43.9 | 246 46.4 | 37.6 | 281 03.2 | 08.9 | 323 35.1 | 57.8 | Mars | 318 25.9 | 6 35 |
| | h m | | | | | | | | | Jupiter | 351 27.5 | 4 23 |
| Mer. Pass. | 3 48.6 | v −0.8 | d 0.1 | v 0.8 | d 0.5 | v 2.4 | d 0.0 | v 2.6 | d 0.1 | Saturn | 33 50.6 | 1 34 |

| UT | SUN GHA | SUN Dec | MOON GHA | v | MOON Dec | d | HP |
|---|---|---|---|---|---|---|---|
| d h | ° ′ | ° ′ | ° ′ | ′ | ° ′ | ′ | ′ |
| 24 00 | 178 21.9 | N19 54.6 | 234 18.3 | 11.9 | N23 30.6 | 7.0 | 54.3 |
| 01 | 193 21.9 | 54.1 | 248 49.2 | 11.8 | 23 37.6 | 6.8 | 54.3 |
| 02 | 208 21.9 | 53.6 | 263 20.0 | 11.8 | 23 44.4 | 6.7 | 54.3 |
| 03 | 223 21.8 · · | 53.1 | 277 50.8 | 11.7 | 23 51.1 | 6.6 | 54.3 |
| 04 | 238 21.8 | 52.5 | 292 21.5 | 11.7 | 23 57.7 | 6.5 | 54.3 |
| 05 | 253 21.8 | 52.0 | 306 52.2 | 11.7 | 24 04.2 | 6.4 | 54.3 |
| 06 | 268 21.8 | N19 51.5 | 321 22.9 | 11.6 | N24 10.6 | 6.3 | 54.2 |
| 07 | 283 21.8 | 51.0 | 335 53.5 | 11.5 | 24 16.9 | 6.1 | 54.2 |
| 08 | 298 21.8 | 50.4 | 350 24.0 | 11.5 | 24 23.0 | 6.1 | 54.2 |
| S 09 | 313 21.8 · · | 49.9 | 4 54.5 | 11.5 | 24 29.1 | 5.9 | 54.2 |
| U 10 | 328 21.8 | 49.4 | 19 25.0 | 11.5 | 24 35.0 | 5.8 | 54.2 |
| N 11 | 343 21.7 | 48.9 | 33 55.5 | 11.4 | 24 40.8 | 5.7 | 54.2 |
| D 12 | 358 21.7 | N19 48.3 | 48 25.9 | 11.3 | N24 46.5 | 5.6 | 54.2 |
| A 13 | 13 21.7 | 47.8 | 62 56.2 | 11.3 | 24 52.1 | 5.4 | 54.2 |
| Y 14 | 28 21.7 | 47.3 | 77 26.5 | 11.3 | 24 57.5 | 5.4 | 54.2 |
| 15 | 43 21.7 · · | 46.7 | 91 56.8 | 11.3 | 25 02.9 | 5.2 | 54.2 |
| 16 | 58 21.7 | 46.2 | 106 27.1 | 11.2 | 25 08.1 | 5.1 | 54.1 |
| 17 | 73 21.7 | 45.7 | 120 57.3 | 11.1 | 25 13.2 | 5.0 | 54.1 |
| 18 | 88 21.7 | N19 45.1 | 135 27.4 | 11.2 | N25 18.2 | 4.9 | 54.1 |
| 19 | 103 21.7 | 44.6 | 149 57.6 | 11.1 | 25 23.1 | 4.8 | 54.1 |
| 20 | 118 21.6 | 44.1 | 164 27.7 | 11.0 | 25 27.9 | 4.6 | 54.1 |
| 21 | 133 21.6 · · | 43.5 | 178 57.7 | 11.0 | 25 32.5 | 4.5 | 54.1 |
| 22 | 148 21.6 | 43.0 | 193 27.7 | 11.0 | 25 37.0 | 4.4 | 54.1 |
| 23 | 163 21.6 | 42.5 | 207 57.7 | 11.0 | 25 41.4 | 4.3 | 54.1 |
| 25 00 | 178 21.6 | N19 41.9 | 222 27.7 | 10.9 | N25 45.7 | 4.2 | 54.1 |
| 01 | 193 21.6 | 41.4 | 236 57.6 | 10.9 | 25 49.9 | 4.0 | 54.1 |
| 02 | 208 21.6 | 40.9 | 251 27.5 | 10.9 | 25 53.9 | 3.9 | 54.1 |
| 03 | 223 21.6 · · | 40.3 | 265 57.4 | 10.8 | 25 57.8 | 3.8 | 54.1 |
| 04 | 238 21.6 | 39.8 | 280 27.2 | 10.8 | 26 01.6 | 3.7 | 54.1 |
| 05 | 253 21.6 | 39.3 | 294 57.0 | 10.7 | 26 05.3 | 3.5 | 54.1 |
| 06 | 268 21.6 | N19 38.7 | 309 26.7 | 10.8 | N26 08.8 | 3.4 | 54.0 |
| 07 | 283 21.6 | 38.2 | 323 56.5 | 10.7 | 26 12.2 | 3.3 | 54.0 |
| 08 | 298 21.6 | 37.6 | 338 26.2 | 10.7 | 26 15.5 | 3.2 | 54.0 |
| M 09 | 313 21.6 · · | 37.1 | 352 55.9 | 10.6 | 26 18.7 | 3.0 | 54.0 |
| O 10 | 328 21.5 | 36.6 | 7 25.5 | 10.7 | 26 21.7 | 2.9 | 54.0 |
| N 11 | 343 21.5 | 36.0 | 21 55.2 | 10.6 | 26 24.6 | 2.8 | 54.0 |
| D 12 | 358 21.5 | N19 35.5 | 36 24.8 | 10.6 | N26 27.4 | 2.7 | 54.0 |
| A 13 | 13 21.5 | 34.9 | 50 54.4 | 10.5 | 26 30.1 | 2.5 | 54.0 |
| Y 14 | 28 21.5 | 34.4 | 65 23.9 | 10.6 | 26 32.6 | 2.4 | 54.0 |
| 15 | 43 21.5 · · | 33.8 | 79 53.5 | 10.5 | 26 35.0 | 2.3 | 54.0 |
| 16 | 58 21.5 | 33.3 | 94 23.0 | 10.5 | 26 37.3 | 2.2 | 54.0 |
| 17 | 73 21.5 | 32.8 | 108 52.5 | 10.5 | 26 39.5 | 2.0 | 54.0 |
| 18 | 88 21.5 | N19 32.2 | 123 22.0 | 10.5 | N26 41.5 | 1.9 | 54.0 |
| 19 | 103 21.5 | 31.7 | 137 51.5 | 10.4 | 26 43.4 | 1.8 | 54.0 |
| 20 | 118 21.5 | 31.1 | 152 20.9 | 10.4 | 26 45.2 | 1.7 | 54.0 |
| 21 | 133 21.5 · · | 30.6 | 166 50.3 | 10.5 | 26 46.9 | 1.5 | 54.0 |
| 22 | 148 21.5 | 30.0 | 181 19.8 | 10.4 | 26 48.4 | 1.4 | 54.0 |
| 23 | 163 21.5 | 29.5 | 195 49.2 | 10.4 | 26 49.8 | 1.2 | 54.0 |
| 26 00 | 178 21.5 | N19 28.9 | 210 18.6 | 10.3 | N26 51.0 | 1.2 | 54.0 |
| 01 | 193 21.5 | 28.4 | 224 47.9 | 10.4 | 26 52.2 | 1.0 | 54.0 |
| 02 | 208 21.5 | 27.8 | 239 17.3 | 10.3 | 26 53.2 | 0.9 | 54.0 |
| 03 | 223 21.5 · · | 27.3 | 253 46.7 | 10.3 | 26 54.1 | 0.7 | 54.0 |
| 04 | 238 21.5 | 26.7 | 268 16.0 | 10.4 | 26 54.8 | 0.6 | 54.0 |
| 05 | 253 21.5 | 26.2 | 282 45.4 | 10.3 | 26 55.4 | 0.5 | 54.0 |
| 06 | 268 21.5 | N19 25.6 | 297 14.7 | 10.3 | N26 55.9 | 0.4 | 54.0 |
| 07 | 283 21.5 | 25.1 | 311 44.0 | 10.4 | 26 56.3 | 0.2 | 54.0 |
| 08 | 298 21.5 | 24.5 | 326 13.4 | 10.3 | 26 56.5 | 0.1 | 54.0 |
| T 09 | 313 21.5 · · | 24.0 | 340 42.7 | 10.3 | 26 56.6 | 0.0 | 54.0 |
| U 10 | 328 21.5 | 23.4 | 355 12.0 | 10.3 | 26 56.6 | 0.2 | 54.0 |
| E 11 | 343 21.5 | 22.8 | 9 41.3 | 10.3 | 26 56.4 | 0.2 | 54.0 |
| S 12 | 358 21.5 | N19 22.3 | 24 10.6 | 10.4 | N26 56.2 | 0.5 | 54.0 |
| D 13 | 13 21.5 | 21.7 | 38 40.0 | 10.3 | 26 55.7 | 0.5 | 54.0 |
| A 14 | 28 21.5 | 21.2 | 53 09.3 | 10.3 | 26 55.2 | 0.7 | 54.0 |
| Y 15 | 43 21.5 · · | 20.6 | 67 38.6 | 10.3 | 26 54.5 | 0.8 | 54.0 |
| 16 | 58 21.5 | 20.1 | 82 07.9 | 10.4 | 26 53.7 | 0.9 | 54.0 |
| 17 | 73 21.5 | 19.5 | 96 37.3 | 10.3 | 26 52.8 | 1.1 | 54.0 |
| 18 | 88 21.5 | N19 18.9 | 111 06.6 | 10.4 | N26 51.7 | 1.2 | 54.0 |
| 19 | 103 21.5 | 18.4 | 125 36.0 | 10.3 | 26 50.5 | 1.3 | 54.0 |
| 20 | 118 21.5 | 17.8 | 140 05.3 | 10.4 | 26 49.2 | 1.4 | 54.0 |
| 21 | 133 21.5 · · | 17.3 | 154 34.7 | 10.4 | 26 47.8 | 1.6 | 54.0 |
| 22 | 148 21.5 | 16.7 | 169 04.1 | 10.4 | 26 46.2 | 1.7 | 54.0 |
| 23 | 163 21.5 | 16.1 | 183 33.5 | 10.4 | N26 44.5 | 1.9 | 54.0 |
| | SD 15.8 | d 0.5 | SD 14.8 | | 14.7 | | 14.7 |

| Lat. | Twilight Naut. | Twilight Civil | Sunrise | Moonrise 24 | Moonrise 25 | Moonrise 26 | Moonrise 27 |
|---|---|---|---|---|---|---|---|
| ° | h m | h m | h m | h m | h m | h m | h m |
| N 72 | ▭ | ▭ | ▭ | ▭ | ▭ | ▭ | ▭ |
| N 70 | ▭ | ▭ | ▭ | ▭ | ▭ | ▭ | ▭ |
| 68 | //// | //// | 01 35 | ▭ | ▭ | ▭ | ▭ |
| 66 | //// | //// | 02 17 | ▭ | ▭ | ▭ | ▭ |
| 64 | //// | 00 43 | 02 46 | 21 53 | ▭ | ▭ | ▭ |
| 62 | //// | 01 45 | 03 07 | 22 51 | 23 12 | 24 06 | 00 06 |
| 60 | //// | 02 17 | 03 24 | 23 24 | 23 55 | 24 49 | 00 49 |
| N 58 | 00 40 | 02 41 | 03 39 | 23 49 | 24 24 | 00 24 | 01 18 |
| 56 | 01 36 | 03 00 | 03 51 | 24 09 | 00 09 | 00 47 | 01 40 |
| 54 | 02 06 | 03 15 | 04 02 | 24 25 | 00 25 | 01 05 | 01 58 |
| 52 | 02 28 | 03 28 | 04 11 | 00 08 | 00 39 | 01 21 | 02 13 |
| 50 | 02 45 | 03 39 | 04 20 | 00 19 | 00 52 | 01 34 | 02 27 |
| 45 | 03 18 | 04 03 | 04 37 | 00 41 | 01 17 | 02 02 | 02 54 |
| N 40 | 03 42 | 04 21 | 04 52 | 00 59 | 01 38 | 02 23 | 03 16 |
| 35 | 04 01 | 04 36 | 05 04 | 01 14 | 01 55 | 02 42 | 03 34 |
| 30 | 04 17 | 04 48 | 05 15 | 01 27 | 02 10 | 02 57 | 03 49 |
| 20 | 04 41 | 05 09 | 05 33 | 01 50 | 02 35 | 03 24 | 04 15 |
| N 10 | 05 00 | 05 26 | 05 49 | 02 10 | 02 57 | 03 46 | 04 37 |
| 0 | 05 16 | 05 41 | 06 03 | 02 28 | 03 17 | 04 08 | 04 58 |
| S 10 | 05 29 | 05 55 | 06 17 | 02 46 | 03 38 | 04 29 | 05 19 |
| 20 | 05 42 | 06 09 | 06 33 | 03 06 | 04 00 | 04 52 | 05 42 |
| 30 | 05 55 | 06 24 | 06 50 | 03 29 | 04 25 | 05 18 | 06 08 |
| 35 | 06 02 | 06 33 | 07 00 | 03 43 | 04 40 | 05 34 | 06 23 |
| 40 | 06 09 | 06 42 | 07 11 | 03 59 | 04 58 | 05 52 | 06 41 |
| 45 | 06 17 | 06 53 | 07 25 | 04 17 | 05 19 | 06 14 | 07 02 |
| S 50 | 06 25 | 07 05 | 07 41 | 04 41 | 05 46 | 06 42 | 07 29 |
| 52 | 06 29 | 07 11 | 07 49 | 04 52 | 05 59 | 06 56 | 07 42 |
| 54 | 06 33 | 07 17 | 07 57 | 05 05 | 06 14 | 07 12 | 07 57 |
| 56 | 06 37 | 07 24 | 08 07 | 05 20 | 06 31 | 07 31 | 08 15 |
| 58 | 06 42 | 07 31 | 08 18 | 05 38 | 06 53 | 07 54 | 08 36 |
| S 60 | 06 47 | 07 40 | 08 30 | 06 00 | 07 21 | 08 24 | 09 04 |

| Lat. | Sunset | Twilight Civil | Twilight Naut. | Moonset 24 | Moonset 25 | Moonset 26 | Moonset 27 |
|---|---|---|---|---|---|---|---|
| ° | h m | h m | h m | h m | h m | h m | h m |
| N 72 | ▭ | ▭ | ▭ | ▭ | ▭ | ▭ | ▭ |
| N 70 | ▭ | ▭ | ▭ | ▭ | ▭ | ▭ | ▭ |
| 68 | 22 33 | //// | //// | ▭ | ▭ | ▭ | ▭ |
| 66 | 21 52 | //// | //// | ▭ | ▭ | ▭ | ▭ |
| 64 | 21 25 | 23 19 | //// | 20 09 | ▭ | ▭ | 22 39 |
| 62 | 21 04 | 22 24 | //// | 19 12 | 20 36 | 21 27 | 21 46 |
| 60 | 20 47 | 21 53 | //// | 18 39 | 19 52 | 20 44 | 21 13 |
| N 58 | 20 33 | 21 30 | 23 24 | 18 14 | 19 23 | 20 15 | 20 49 |
| 56 | 20 21 | 21 12 | 22 34 | 17 55 | 19 01 | 19 53 | 20 30 |
| 54 | 20 10 | 20 57 | 22 05 | 17 39 | 18 42 | 19 34 | 20 13 |
| 52 | 20 01 | 20 44 | 21 44 | 17 25 | 18 27 | 19 19 | 19 59 |
| 50 | 19 53 | 20 33 | 21 26 | 17 13 | 18 14 | 19 05 | 19 47 |
| 45 | 19 35 | 20 10 | 20 54 | 16 47 | 17 46 | 18 38 | 19 21 |
| N 40 | 19 21 | 19 52 | 20 30 | 16 27 | 17 24 | 18 16 | 19 01 |
| 35 | 19 09 | 19 37 | 20 11 | 16 11 | 17 07 | 17 58 | 18 44 |
| 30 | 18 58 | 19 24 | 19 56 | 15 56 | 16 51 | 17 43 | 18 30 |
| 20 | 18 40 | 19 04 | 19 32 | 15 32 | 16 25 | 17 16 | 18 05 |
| N 10 | 18 25 | 18 47 | 19 13 | 15 11 | 16 02 | 16 53 | 17 43 |
| 0 | 18 10 | 18 32 | 18 58 | 14 52 | 15 41 | 16 32 | 17 23 |
| S 10 | 17 56 | 18 18 | 18 44 | 14 32 | 15 20 | 16 11 | 17 02 |
| 20 | 17 41 | 18 04 | 18 31 | 14 11 | 14 58 | 15 48 | 16 41 |
| 30 | 17 23 | 17 49 | 18 18 | 13 47 | 14 32 | 15 22 | 16 15 |
| 35 | 17 13 | 17 41 | 18 11 | 13 33 | 14 17 | 15 06 | 16 00 |
| 40 | 17 02 | 17 31 | 18 04 | 13 17 | 13 59 | 14 48 | 15 43 |
| 45 | 16 49 | 17 21 | 17 57 | 12 57 | 13 37 | 14 26 | 15 22 |
| S 50 | 16 32 | 17 09 | 17 48 | 12 33 | 13 10 | 13 58 | 14 55 |
| 52 | 16 25 | 17 03 | 17 45 | 12 21 | 12 57 | 13 44 | 14 42 |
| 54 | 16 16 | 16 57 | 17 41 | 12 08 | 12 42 | 13 28 | 14 27 |
| 56 | 16 07 | 16 50 | 17 36 | 11 52 | 12 24 | 13 09 | 14 10 |
| 58 | 15 56 | 16 42 | 17 32 | 11 34 | 12 02 | 12 46 | 13 48 |
| S 60 | 15 44 | 16 34 | 17 27 | 11 12 | 11 34 | 12 16 | 13 21 |

| | SUN Eqn. of Time 00ʰ | SUN Eqn. of Time 12ʰ | SUN Mer. Pass. | MOON Mer. Pass. Upper | MOON Mer. Pass. Lower | MOON Age | MOON Phase |
|---|---|---|---|---|---|---|---|
| Day | m s | m s | h m | h m | h m | d | % |
| d | | | | | | | |
| 24 | 06 32 | 06 33 | 12 07 | 08 40 | 21 04 | 25 | 16 |
| 25 | 06 34 | 06 34 | 12 07 | 09 29 | 21 54 | 26 | 9 |
| 26 | 06 34 | 06 34 | 12 07 | 10 20 | 22 45 | 27 | 5 |

| UT | ARIES GHA | VENUS −3.9 GHA | Dec | MARS +0.2 GHA | Dec | JUPITER −2.6 GHA | Dec | SATURN +0.3 GHA | Dec |
|---|---|---|---|---|---|---|---|---|---|
| **27 00** | 304 39.4 | 202 55.7 | N22 43.8 | 261 47.3 | N14 38.1 | 296 05.6 | N 2 08.9 | 338 37.8 | S14 57.8 |
| 01 | 319 41.8 | 217 54.9 | 43.6 | 276 48.1 | 38.6 | 311 08.1 | 08.9 | 353 40.4 | 57.9 |
| 02 | 334 44.3 | 232 54.1 | 43.5 | 291 49.0 | 39.1 | 326 10.5 | 08.9 | 8 43.0 | 57.9 |
| 03 | 349 46.8 | 247 53.2 .. | 43.4 | 306 49.8 .. | 39.6 | 341 13.0 .. | 08.9 | 23 45.6 .. | 58.0 |
| 04 | 4 49.2 | 262 52.4 | 43.2 | 321 50.6 | 40.1 | 356 15.4 | 08.9 | 38 48.3 | 58.1 |
| 05 | 19 51.7 | 277 51.6 | 43.1 | 336 51.5 | 40.6 | 11 17.9 | 08.9 | 53 50.9 | 58.1 |
| 06 | 34 54.2 | 292 50.8 | N22 43.0 | 351 52.3 | N14 41.1 | 26 20.3 | N 2 08.9 | 68 53.5 | S14 58.2 |
| W 07 | 49 56.6 | 307 50.0 | 42.8 | 6 53.2 | 41.6 | 41 22.8 | 08.9 | 83 56.2 | 58.3 |
| E 08 | 64 59.1 | 322 49.1 | 42.7 | 21 54.0 | 42.1 | 56 25.2 | 08.9 | 98 58.8 | 58.3 |
| D 09 | 80 01.5 | 337 48.3 .. | 42.5 | 36 54.9 .. | 42.6 | 71 27.6 .. | 08.9 | 114 01.4 .. | 58.4 |
| N 10 | 95 04.0 | 352 47.5 | 42.4 | 51 55.7 | 43.1 | 86 30.1 | 08.9 | 129 04.1 | 58.4 |
| E 11 | 110 06.5 | 7 46.7 | 42.2 | 66 56.5 | 43.6 | 101 32.5 | 08.9 | 144 06.7 | 58.5 |
| S 12 | 125 08.9 | 22 45.8 | N22 42.1 | 81 57.4 | N14 44.1 | 116 35.0 | N 2 08.9 | 159 09.3 | S14 58.6 |
| D 13 | 140 11.4 | 37 45.0 | 41.9 | 96 58.2 | 44.6 | 131 37.4 | 08.9 | 174 11.9 | 58.6 |
| A 14 | 155 13.9 | 52 44.2 | 41.8 | 111 59.1 | 45.1 | 146 39.9 | 08.9 | 189 14.6 | 58.7 |
| Y 15 | 170 16.3 | 67 43.4 .. | 41.6 | 126 59.9 .. | 45.5 | 161 42.3 .. | 08.8 | 204 17.2 .. | 58.7 |
| 16 | 185 18.8 | 82 42.6 | 41.5 | 142 00.8 | 46.0 | 176 44.8 | 08.8 | 219 19.8 | 58.8 |
| 17 | 200 21.3 | 97 41.7 | 41.3 | 157 01.6 | 46.5 | 191 47.2 | 08.8 | 234 22.5 | 58.9 |
| 18 | 215 23.7 | 112 40.9 | N22 41.2 | 172 02.5 | N14 47.0 | 206 49.7 | N 2 08.8 | 249 25.1 | S14 59.0 |
| 19 | 230 26.2 | 127 40.1 | 41.0 | 187 03.3 | 47.5 | 221 52.1 | 08.8 | 264 27.7 | 59.0 |
| 20 | 245 28.7 | 142 39.3 | 40.9 | 202 04.2 | 48.0 | 236 54.6 | 08.8 | 279 30.4 | 59.1 |
| 21 | 260 31.1 | 157 38.5 .. | 40.7 | 217 05.0 .. | 48.5 | 251 57.0 .. | 08.8 | 294 33.0 .. | 59.1 |
| 22 | 275 33.6 | 172 37.7 | 40.6 | 232 05.8 | 49.0 | 266 59.5 | 08.8 | 309 35.6 | 59.2 |
| 23 | 290 36.0 | 187 36.8 | 40.4 | 247 06.7 | 49.5 | 282 01.9 | 08.8 | 324 38.3 | 59.2 |
| **28 00** | 305 38.5 | 202 36.0 | N22 40.3 | 262 07.5 | N14 50.0 | 297 04.4 | N 2 08.8 | 339 40.9 | S14 59.3 |
| 01 | 320 41.0 | 217 35.2 | 40.1 | 277 08.4 | 50.5 | 312 06.9 | 08.8 | 354 43.5 | 59.4 |
| 02 | 335 43.4 | 232 34.4 | 39.9 | 292 09.2 | 50.9 | 327 09.3 | 08.8 | 9 46.1 | 59.4 |
| 03 | 350 45.9 | 247 33.6 .. | 39.8 | 307 10.1 .. | 51.4 | 342 11.8 .. | 08.8 | 24 48.8 .. | 59.5 |
| 04 | 5 48.4 | 262 32.7 | 39.6 | 322 10.9 | 51.9 | 357 14.2 | 08.7 | 39 51.4 | 59.5 |
| 05 | 20 50.8 | 277 31.9 | 39.4 | 337 11.8 | 52.4 | 12 16.7 | 08.7 | 54 54.0 | 59.6 |
| 06 | 35 53.3 | 292 31.1 | N22 39.3 | 352 12.6 | N14 52.9 | 27 19.1 | N 2 08.7 | 69 56.7 | S14 59.7 |
| T 07 | 50 55.8 | 307 30.3 | 39.1 | 7 13.5 | 53.4 | 42 21.6 | 08.7 | 84 59.3 | 59.7 |
| H 08 | 65 58.2 | 322 29.5 | 38.9 | 22 14.3 | 53.9 | 57 24.0 | 08.7 | 100 01.9 | 59.8 |
| U 09 | 81 00.7 | 337 28.6 .. | 38.8 | 37 15.2 .. | 54.4 | 72 26.5 .. | 08.7 | 115 04.6 .. | 59.9 |
| R 10 | 96 03.1 | 352 27.8 | 38.6 | 52 16.0 | 54.8 | 87 28.9 | 08.7 | 130 07.2 | 14 59.9 |
| S 11 | 111 05.6 | 7 27.0 | 38.4 | 67 16.9 | 55.3 | 102 31.4 | 08.7 | 145 09.8 | 15 00.0 |
| D 12 | 126 08.1 | 22 26.2 | N22 38.3 | 82 17.7 | N14 55.8 | 117 33.9 | N 2 08.7 | 160 12.5 | S15 00.0 |
| A 13 | 141 10.5 | 37 25.4 | 38.1 | 97 18.6 | 56.3 | 132 36.3 | 08.7 | 175 15.1 | 00.1 |
| Y 14 | 156 13.0 | 52 24.5 | 37.9 | 112 19.4 | 56.8 | 147 38.8 | 08.6 | 190 17.7 | 00.2 |
| 15 | 171 15.5 | 67 23.7 .. | 37.7 | 127 20.2 .. | 57.3 | 162 41.2 .. | 08.6 | 205 20.4 .. | 00.2 |
| 16 | 186 17.9 | 82 22.9 | 37.5 | 142 21.1 | 57.8 | 177 43.7 | 08.6 | 220 23.0 | 00.3 |
| 17 | 201 20.4 | 97 22.1 | 37.4 | 157 21.9 | 58.3 | 192 46.1 | 08.6 | 235 25.6 | 00.4 |
| 18 | 216 22.9 | 112 21.3 | N22 37.2 | 172 22.8 | N14 58.7 | 207 48.6 | N 2 08.6 | 250 28.3 | S15 00.4 |
| 19 | 231 25.3 | 127 20.5 | 37.0 | 187 23.6 | 59.2 | 222 51.1 | 08.6 | 265 30.9 | 00.5 |
| 20 | 246 27.8 | 142 19.6 | 36.8 | 202 24.5 | 14 59.7 | 237 53.5 | 08.6 | 280 33.5 | 00.5 |
| 21 | 261 30.3 | 157 18.8 .. | 36.6 | 217 25.3 | 15 00.2 | 252 56.0 .. | 08.6 | 295 36.1 .. | 00.6 |
| 22 | 276 32.7 | 172 18.0 | 36.5 | 232 26.2 | 00.7 | 267 58.4 | 08.6 | 310 38.8 | 00.7 |
| 23 | 291 35.2 | 187 17.2 | 36.3 | 247 27.0 | 01.2 | 283 00.9 | 08.5 | 325 41.4 | 00.7 |
| **29 00** | 306 37.6 | 202 16.4 | N22 36.1 | 262 27.9 | N15 01.6 | 298 03.4 | N 2 08.5 | 340 44.0 | S15 00.8 |
| 01 | 321 40.1 | 217 15.5 | 35.9 | 277 28.7 | 02.1 | 313 05.8 | 08.5 | 355 46.7 | 00.9 |
| 02 | 336 42.6 | 232 14.7 | 35.7 | 292 29.6 | 02.6 | 328 08.3 | 08.5 | 10 49.3 | 00.9 |
| 03 | 351 45.0 | 247 13.9 .. | 35.5 | 307 30.4 .. | 03.1 | 343 10.7 .. | 08.5 | 25 51.9 .. | 01.0 |
| 04 | 6 47.5 | 262 13.0 | 35.3 | 322 31.3 | 03.6 | 358 13.2 | 08.5 | 40 54.6 | 01.0 |
| 05 | 21 50.0 | 277 12.3 | 35.1 | 337 32.1 | 04.1 | 13 15.7 | 08.5 | 55 57.2 | 01.1 |
| 06 | 36 52.4 | 292 11.5 | N22 34.9 | 352 33.0 | N15 04.5 | 28 18.1 | N 2 08.5 | 70 59.8 | S15 01.2 |
| F 07 | 51 54.9 | 307 10.6 | 34.7 | 7 33.8 | 05.0 | 43 20.6 | 08.4 | 86 02.5 | 01.2 |
| R 08 | 66 57.4 | 322 09.8 | 34.5 | 22 34.7 | 05.5 | 58 23.1 | 08.4 | 101 05.1 | 01.3 |
| I 09 | 81 59.8 | 337 09.0 .. | 34.3 | 37 35.5 .. | 06.0 | 73 25.5 .. | 08.4 | 116 07.7 .. | 01.4 |
| D 10 | 97 02.3 | 352 08.2 | 34.2 | 52 36.4 | 06.5 | 88 28.0 | 08.4 | 131 10.4 | 01.4 |
| A 11 | 112 04.8 | 7 07.4 | 34.0 | 67 37.2 | 06.9 | 103 30.4 | 08.4 | 146 13.0 | 01.5 |
| Y 12 | 127 07.2 | 22 06.6 | N22 33.8 | 82 38.1 | N15 07.4 | 118 32.9 | N 2 08.4 | 161 15.6 | S15 01.5 |
| 13 | 142 09.7 | 37 05.7 | 33.5 | 97 38.9 | 07.9 | 133 35.4 | 08.4 | 176 18.3 | 01.6 |
| 14 | 157 12.1 | 52 04.9 | 33.3 | 112 39.8 | 08.4 | 148 37.8 | 08.4 | 191 20.9 | 01.7 |
| 15 | 172 14.6 | 67 04.1 .. | 33.1 | 127 40.6 .. | 08.9 | 163 40.3 .. | 08.3 | 206 23.5 .. | 01.7 |
| 16 | 187 17.1 | 82 03.3 | 32.9 | 142 41.5 | 09.3 | 178 42.8 | 08.3 | 221 26.2 | 01.8 |
| 17 | 202 19.5 | 97 02.5 | 32.7 | 157 42.4 | 09.8 | 193 45.2 | 08.3 | 236 28.8 | 01.8 |
| 18 | 217 22.0 | 112 01.7 | N22 32.5 | 172 43.2 | N15 10.3 | 208 47.7 | N 2 08.3 | 251 31.4 | S15 01.9 |
| 19 | 232 24.5 | 127 00.8 | 32.3 | 187 44.1 | 10.8 | 223 50.2 | 08.3 | 266 34.1 | 02.0 |
| 20 | 247 26.9 | 142 00.0 | 32.1 | 202 44.9 | 11.3 | 238 52.6 | 08.3 | 281 36.7 | 02.0 |
| 21 | 262 29.4 | 156 59.2 .. | 31.9 | 217 45.8 .. | 11.7 | 253 55.1 .. | 08.3 | 296 39.3 .. | 02.1 |
| 22 | 277 31.9 | 171 58.4 | 31.7 | 232 46.6 | 12.2 | 268 57.6 | 08.2 | 311 42.0 | 02.2 |
| 23 | 292 34.3 | 186 57.6 | 31.5 | 247 47.5 | 12.7 | 284 00.0 | 08.2 | 326 44.6 | 02.2 |
| Mer. Pass. | h m 3 36.8 | v −0.8  d 0.2 | | v 0.8  d 0.5 | | v 2.5  d 0.0 | | v 2.6  d 0.1 | |

### STARS

| Name | SHA | Dec |
|---|---|---|
| Acamar | 315 13.4 | S40 12.6 |
| Achernar | 335 21.6 | S57 07.1 |
| Acrux | 173 02.6 | S63 13.6 |
| Adhara | 255 07.8 | S29 00.0 |
| Aldebaran | 290 42.1 | N16 33.2 |
| Alioth | 166 15.0 | N55 50.6 |
| Alkaid | 152 53.7 | N49 12.4 |
| Alnair | 27 35.0 | S46 51.0 |
| Alnilam | 275 40.0 | S 1 11.2 |
| Alphard | 217 50.0 | S 8 45.3 |
| Alphecca | 126 05.3 | N26 38.6 |
| Alpheratz | 357 36.6 | N29 12.8 |
| Altair | 62 01.6 | N 8 55.7 |
| Ankaa | 353 08.9 | S42 10.8 |
| Antares | 112 18.1 | S26 28.9 |
| Arcturus | 145 49.8 | N19 04.1 |
| Atria | 107 13.7 | S69 04.2 |
| Avior | 234 16.2 | S59 34.8 |
| Bellatrix | 278 25.3 | N 6 22.2 |
| Betelgeuse | 270 54.5 | N 7 24.7 |
| Canopus | 263 53.8 | S52 42.3 |
| Capella | 280 25.2 | N46 01.1 |
| Deneb | 49 26.7 | N45 21.6 |
| Denebola | 182 27.2 | N14 27.0 |
| Diphda | 348 49.2 | S17 51.7 |
| Dubhe | 193 44.0 | N61 38.1 |
| Elnath | 278 04.7 | N28 37.5 |
| Eltanin | 90 42.7 | N51 29.3 |
| Enif | 33 40.5 | N 9 58.7 |
| Fomalhaut | 15 16.5 | S29 30.1 |
| Gacrux | 171 54.1 | S57 14.5 |
| Gienah | 175 45.8 | S17 40.0 |
| Hadar | 148 38.9 | S60 29.1 |
| Hamal | 327 53.5 | N23 34.0 |
| Kaus Aust. | 83 34.8 | S34 22.4 |
| Kochab | 137 19.6 | N74 04.1 |
| Markab | 13 31.6 | N15 19.5 |
| Menkar | 314 08.3 | N 4 10.7 |
| Menkent | 148 00.5 | S36 28.9 |
| Miaplacidus | 221 39.6 | S69 48.6 |
| Mirfak | 308 31.3 | N49 56.2 |
| Nunki | 75 49.9 | S26 16.1 |
| Peacock | 53 08.3 | S56 39.7 |
| Pollux | 243 20.1 | N27 58.4 |
| Procyon | 244 53.3 | N 5 10.1 |
| Rasalhague | 96 00.2 | N12 32.7 |
| Regulus | 207 36.9 | N11 51.6 |
| Rigel | 281 06.0 | S 8 10.4 |
| Rigil Kent. | 139 43.0 | S60 55.8 |
| Sabik | 102 04.8 | S15 45.1 |
| Schedar | 349 33.1 | N56 39.4 |
| Shaula | 96 12.8 | S37 07.2 |
| Sirius | 258 28.3 | S16 44.7 |
| Spica | 158 24.5 | S11 16.7 |
| Suhail | 222 48.2 | S43 31.3 |
| Vega | 80 34.2 | N38 48.4 |
| Zuben'ubi | 136 58.2 | S16 08.1 |

| | SHA | Mer. Pass. |
|---|---|---|
| | ° ' | h m |
| Venus | 256 57.5 | 10 30 |
| Mars | 316 29.0 | 6 31 |
| Jupiter | 351 25.9 | 4 11 |
| Saturn | 34 02.4 | 1 21 |

| UT | SUN | | MOON | | | | | Lat. | Twilight | | Sunrise | Moonrise | | | |
|---|---|---|---|---|---|---|---|---|---|---|---|---|---|---|---|
| | | | | | | | | | Naut. | Civil | | 27 | 28 | 29 | 30 |
| | GHA | Dec | GHA | v | Dec | d | HP | | | | | | | | |
| d h | ° ′ | ° ′ | ° ′ | ′ | ° ′ | ′ | ′ | ° | h m | h m | h m | h m | h m | h m | h m |
| | | | | | | | | N 72 | ▭ | ▭ | ▭ | ▭ | ▭ | ▭ | ▭ |
| 27 00 | 178 21.5 | N19 15.6 | 198 02.9 | 10.4 | N26 42.6 | 1.9 | 54.0 | N 70 | //// | //// | 00 35 | ▭ | ▭ | ▭ | 02 38 |
| 01 | 193 21.5 | 15.0 | 212 32.3 | 10.4 | 26 40.7 | 2.1 | 54.0 | 68 | //// | //// | 01 53 | ▭ | ▭ | ▭ | 03 29 |
| 02 | 208 21.5 | 14.5 | 227 01.7 | 10.5 | 26 38.6 | 2.2 | 54.0 | 66 | //// | //// | 02 30 | ▭ | ▭ | 01 53 | 04 01 |
| 03 | 223 21.5 . . | 13.9 | 241 31.2 | 10.4 | 26 36.4 | 2.4 | 54.0 | 64 | //// | 01 12 | 02 55 | ▭ | 00 39 | 02 38 | 04 24 |
| 04 | 238 21.5 | 13.3 | 256 00.6 | 10.5 | 26 34.0 | 2.4 | 54.0 | 62 | //// | 01 58 | 03 15 | 00 06 | 01 32 | 03 07 | 04 43 |
| 05 | 253 21.5 | 12.8 | 270 30.1 | 10.5 | 26 31.6 | 2.6 | 54.0 | 60 | //// | 02 27 | 03 31 | 00 49 | 02 04 | 03 29 | 04 58 |
| 06 | 268 21.6 | N19 12.2 | 284 59.6 | 10.5 | N26 29.0 | 2.8 | 54.0 | N 58 | 01 06 | 02 49 | 03 45 | 01 18 | 02 28 | 03 47 | 05 10 |
| W 07 | 283 21.6 | 11.6 | 299 29.1 | 10.6 | 26 26.2 | 2.8 | 54.0 | 56 | 01 48 | 03 06 | 03 56 | 01 40 | 02 47 | 04 02 | 05 21 |
| E 08 | 298 21.6 | 11.1 | 313 58.7 | 10.5 | 26 23.4 | 3.0 | 54.0 | 54 | 02 14 | 03 21 | 04 07 | 01 58 | 03 03 | 04 15 | 05 31 |
| D 09 | 313 21.6 . . | 10.5 | 328 28.2 | 10.6 | 26 20.4 | 3.1 | 54.0 | 52 | 02 35 | 03 33 | 04 16 | 02 13 | 03 17 | 04 27 | 05 40 |
| N 10 | 328 21.6 | 09.9 | 342 57.8 | 10.6 | 26 17.3 | 3.2 | 54.0 | 50 | 02 51 | 03 44 | 04 24 | 02 27 | 03 29 | 04 37 | 05 47 |
| E 11 | 343 21.6 | 09.4 | 357 27.4 | 10.7 | 26 14.1 | 3.4 | 54.0 | 45 | 03 23 | 04 06 | 04 41 | 02 54 | 03 53 | 04 57 | 06 04 |
| S 12 | 358 21.6 | N19 08.8 | 11 57.1 | 10.6 | N26 10.7 | 3.5 | 54.0 | N 40 | 03 46 | 04 24 | 04 55 | 03 16 | 04 13 | 05 14 | 06 17 |
| D 13 | 13 21.6 | 08.2 | 26 26.7 | 10.7 | 26 07.2 | 3.6 | 54.0 | 35 | 04 04 | 04 38 | 05 06 | 03 34 | 04 30 | 05 28 | 06 28 |
| A 14 | 28 21.6 | 07.7 | 40 56.4 | 10.7 | 26 03.6 | 3.7 | 54.0 | 30 | 04 19 | 04 50 | 05 17 | 03 49 | 04 44 | 05 41 | 06 38 |
| Y 15 | 43 21.6 . . | 07.1 | 55 26.1 | 10.8 | 25 59.9 | 3.9 | 54.0 | 20 | 04 42 | 05 10 | 05 34 | 04 15 | 05 08 | 06 02 | 06 55 |
| 16 | 58 21.6 | 06.5 | 69 55.9 | 10.7 | 25 56.0 | 4.0 | 54.0 | N 10 | 05 01 | 05 27 | 05 49 | 04 37 | 05 29 | 06 20 | 07 09 |
| 17 | 73 21.6 | 05.9 | 84 25.6 | 10.8 | 25 52.0 | 4.1 | 54.1 | 0 | 05 16 | 05 41 | 06 03 | 04 58 | 05 48 | 06 37 | 07 23 |
| 18 | 88 21.6 | N19 05.4 | 98 55.4 | 10.9 | N25 47.9 | 4.2 | 54.1 | S 10 | 05 29 | 05 55 | 06 17 | 05 19 | 06 08 | 06 53 | 07 36 |
| 19 | 103 21.6 | 04.8 | 113 25.3 | 10.8 | 25 43.7 | 4.3 | 54.1 | 20 | 05 42 | 06 08 | 06 32 | 05 42 | 06 28 | 07 11 | 07 51 |
| 20 | 118 21.7 | 04.2 | 127 55.1 | 10.9 | 25 39.4 | 4.5 | 54.1 | 30 | 05 54 | 06 23 | 06 48 | 06 08 | 06 52 | 07 32 | 08 07 |
| 21 | 133 21.7 . . | 03.6 | 142 25.0 | 10.9 | 25 34.9 | 4.6 | 54.1 | 35 | 06 00 | 06 31 | 06 58 | 06 23 | 07 06 | 07 44 | 08 17 |
| 22 | 148 21.7 | 03.1 | 156 54.9 | 11.0 | 25 30.3 | 4.7 | 54.1 | 40 | 06 07 | 06 40 | 07 09 | 06 41 | 07 22 | 07 58 | 08 28 |
| 23 | 163 21.7 | 02.5 | 171 24.9 | 11.0 | 25 25.6 | 4.9 | 54.1 | 45 | 06 14 | 06 50 | 07 22 | 07 02 | 07 42 | 08 14 | 08 40 |
| 28 00 | 178 21.7 | N19 01.9 | 185 54.9 | 11.0 | N25 20.7 | 4.9 | 54.1 | S 50 | 06 22 | 07 02 | 07 37 | 07 29 | 08 06 | 08 34 | 08 56 |
| 01 | 193 21.7 | 01.3 | 200 24.9 | 11.1 | 25 15.8 | 5.1 | 54.1 | 52 | 06 26 | 07 07 | 07 45 | 07 42 | 08 17 | 08 43 | 09 03 |
| 02 | 208 21.7 | 00.8 | 214 55.0 | 11.1 | 25 10.7 | 5.2 | 54.1 | 54 | 06 29 | 07 13 | 07 53 | 07 57 | 08 30 | 08 54 | 09 11 |
| 03 | 223 21.7 | 19 00.2 | 229 25.1 | 11.2 | 25 05.5 | 5.3 | 54.1 | 56 | 06 33 | 07 19 | 08 02 | 08 15 | 08 45 | 09 06 | 09 20 |
| 04 | 238 21.7 | 18 59.6 | 243 55.3 | 11.1 | 25 00.2 | 5.4 | 54.1 | 58 | 06 38 | 07 26 | 08 12 | 08 36 | 09 03 | 09 19 | 09 30 |
| 05 | 253 21.8 | 59.0 | 258 25.4 | 11.3 | 24 54.8 | 5.6 | 54.1 | S 60 | 06 42 | 07 34 | 08 24 | 09 04 | 09 25 | 09 35 | 09 41 |

| UT | SUN | | MOON | | | | | Lat. | Sunset | Twilight | | Moonset | | | |
|---|---|---|---|---|---|---|---|---|---|---|---|---|---|---|---|
| | | | | | | | | | | Civil | Naut. | 27 | 28 | 29 | 30 |
| | | | | | | | | ° | h m | h m | h m | h m | h m | h m | h m |
| 06 | 268 21.8 | N18 58.5 | 272 55.7 | 11.2 | N24 49.2 | 5.6 | 54.1 | N 72 | ▭ | ▭ | ▭ | ▭ | ▭ | ▭ | 23 32 |
| 07 | 283 21.8 | 57.9 | 287 25.9 | 11.3 | 24 43.6 | 5.8 | 54.1 | N 70 | 23 21 | //// | //// | ▭ | ▭ | ▭ | 22 58 |
| 08 | 298 21.8 | 57.3 | 301 56.2 | 11.4 | 24 37.8 | 5.9 | 54.1 | 68 | 22 15 | //// | //// | ▭ | ▭ | 23 09 | 22 38 |
| T 09 | 313 21.8 . . | 56.7 | 316 26.6 | 11.3 | 24 31.9 | 6.0 | 54.2 | 66 | 21 40 | //// | //// | ▭ | 23 07 | 22 36 | 22 19 |
| H 10 | 328 21.8 | 56.1 | 330 56.9 | 11.5 | 24 25.9 | 6.2 | 54.2 | 64 | 21 15 | 22 54 | //// | 22 39 | 22 21 | 22 12 | 22 05 |
| U 11 | 343 21.8 | 55.6 | 345 27.4 | 11.4 | 24 19.7 | 6.2 | 54.2 | 62 | 20 56 | 22 11 | //// | 21 46 | 21 51 | 21 53 | 21 52 |
| R 12 | 358 21.8 | N18 55.0 | 359 57.8 | 11.5 | N24 13.5 | 6.4 | 54.2 | 60 | 20 40 | 21 43 | //// | 21 13 | 21 29 | 21 37 | 21 41 |
| S 13 | 13 21.9 | 54.4 | 14 28.3 | 11.6 | 24 07.1 | 6.4 | 54.2 | N 58 | 20 27 | 21 22 | 23 01 | 20 49 | 21 10 | 21 23 | 21 32 |
| D 14 | 28 21.9 | 53.8 | 28 58.9 | 11.6 | 24 00.7 | 6.6 | 54.2 | 56 | 20 15 | 21 05 | 22 22 | 20 30 | 20 55 | 21 12 | 21 24 |
| A 15 | 43 21.9 . . | 53.2 | 43 29.5 | 11.6 | 23 54.1 | 6.7 | 54.2 | 54 | 20 05 | 20 51 | 21 56 | 20 13 | 20 41 | 21 01 | 21 16 |
| Y 16 | 58 21.9 | 52.6 | 58 00.1 | 11.7 | 23 47.4 | 6.8 | 54.2 | 52 | 19 57 | 20 39 | 21 36 | 19 59 | 20 30 | 20 52 | 21 10 |
| 17 | 73 21.9 | 52.1 | 72 30.8 | 11.8 | 23 40.6 | 6.9 | 54.2 | 50 | 19 49 | 20 28 | 21 20 | 19 47 | 20 19 | 20 44 | 21 04 |
| 18 | 88 21.9 | N18 51.5 | 87 01.6 | 11.7 | N23 33.7 | 7.0 | 54.2 | 45 | 19 32 | 20 06 | 20 49 | 19 21 | 19 57 | 20 27 | 20 51 |
| 19 | 103 21.9 | 50.9 | 101 32.3 | 11.9 | 23 26.7 | 7.2 | 54.2 | N 40 | 19 18 | 19 49 | 20 26 | 19 01 | 19 40 | 20 12 | 20 40 |
| 20 | 118 22.0 | 50.3 | 116 03.2 | 11.8 | 23 19.5 | 7.2 | 54.2 | 35 | 19 06 | 19 34 | 20 08 | 18 44 | 19 25 | 20 00 | 20 31 |
| 21 | 133 22.0 . . | 49.7 | 130 34.0 | 12.0 | 23 12.3 | 7.4 | 54.3 | 30 | 18 56 | 19 22 | 19 54 | 18 30 | 19 12 | 19 49 | 20 23 |
| 22 | 148 22.0 | 49.1 | 145 05.0 | 11.9 | 23 04.9 | 7.4 | 54.3 | 20 | 18 39 | 19 03 | 19 30 | 18 05 | 18 49 | 19 31 | 20 09 |
| 23 | 163 22.0 | 48.5 | 159 35.9 | 12.0 | 22 57.5 | 7.6 | 54.3 | N 10 | 18 24 | 18 46 | 19 11 | 17 43 | 18 30 | 19 14 | 19 56 |
| 29 00 | 178 22.0 | N18 47.9 | 174 06.9 | 12.1 | N22 49.9 | 7.6 | 54.3 | 0 | 18 10 | 18 32 | 18 57 | 17 23 | 18 12 | 18 59 | 19 45 |
| 01 | 193 22.0 | 47.4 | 188 38.0 | 12.1 | 22 42.3 | 7.8 | 54.3 | S 10 | 17 56 | 18 18 | 18 44 | 17 02 | 17 54 | 18 44 | 19 33 |
| 02 | 208 22.1 | 46.8 | 203 09.1 | 12.2 | 22 34.5 | 7.9 | 54.3 | 20 | 17 42 | 18 05 | 18 32 | 16 41 | 17 34 | 18 27 | 19 20 |
| 03 | 223 22.1 . . | 46.2 | 217 40.3 | 12.2 | 22 26.6 | 8.0 | 54.3 | 30 | 17 25 | 17 51 | 18 20 | 16 15 | 17 11 | 18 08 | 19 05 |
| 04 | 238 22.1 | 45.6 | 232 11.5 | 12.2 | 22 18.6 | 8.1 | 54.3 | 35 | 17 16 | 17 43 | 18 13 | 16 00 | 16 58 | 17 57 | 18 57 |
| 05 | 253 22.1 | 45.0 | 246 42.7 | 12.3 | 22 10.5 | 8.2 | 54.3 | 40 | 17 05 | 17 34 | 18 07 | 15 43 | 16 42 | 17 44 | 18 47 |
| 06 | 268 22.1 | N18 44.4 | 261 14.0 | 12.4 | N22 02.3 | 8.2 | 54.3 | 45 | 16 52 | 17 24 | 17 59 | 15 22 | 16 24 | 17 29 | 18 36 |
| 07 | 283 22.1 | 43.8 | 275 45.4 | 12.4 | 21 54.1 | 8.4 | 54.4 | S 50 | 16 36 | 17 12 | 17 52 | 14 55 | 16 01 | 17 10 | 18 22 |
| 08 | 298 22.2 | 43.2 | 290 16.8 | 12.4 | 21 45.7 | 8.5 | 54.4 | 52 | 16 29 | 17 07 | 17 49 | 14 42 | 15 49 | 17 01 | 18 15 |
| F 09 | 313 22.2 . . | 42.6 | 304 48.2 | 12.5 | 21 37.2 | 8.6 | 54.4 | 54 | 16 21 | 17 01 | 17 44 | 14 27 | 15 37 | 16 51 | 18 08 |
| R 10 | 328 22.2 | 42.0 | 319 19.7 | 12.6 | 21 28.6 | 8.7 | 54.4 | 56 | 16 12 | 16 55 | 17 40 | 14 10 | 15 22 | 16 40 | 18 00 |
| I 11 | 343 22.2 | 41.4 | 333 51.3 | 12.6 | 21 19.9 | 8.8 | 54.4 | 58 | 16 02 | 16 47 | 17 36 | 13 48 | 15 05 | 16 27 | 17 50 |
| D 12 | 358 22.2 | N18 40.8 | 348 22.9 | 12.6 | N21 11.1 | 8.9 | 54.4 | S 60 | 15 50 | 16 39 | 17 31 | 13 21 | 14 43 | 16 11 | 17 40 |
| A 13 | 13 22.3 | 40.2 | 2 54.5 | 12.7 | 21 02.2 | 9.0 | 54.4 | | | | | | | | |
| Y 14 | 28 22.3 | 39.7 | 17 26.2 | 12.8 | 20 53.2 | 9.0 | 54.4 | | | | | | | | |
| 15 | 43 22.3 . . | 39.1 | 31 58.0 | 12.8 | 20 44.2 | 9.2 | 54.4 | | | | | | | | |
| 16 | 58 22.3 | 38.5 | 46 29.8 | 12.8 | 20 35.0 | 9.3 | 54.5 | | | | | | | | |
| 17 | 73 22.3 | 37.9 | 61 01.6 | 12.9 | 20 25.7 | 9.3 | 54.5 | | | | | | | | |
| 18 | 88 22.4 | N18 37.3 | 75 33.5 | 13.0 | N20 16.4 | 9.5 | 54.5 | | | | | | | | |
| 19 | 103 22.4 | 36.7 | 90 05.5 | 13.0 | 20 06.9 | 9.5 | 54.5 | | | | | | | | |
| 20 | 118 22.4 | 36.1 | 104 37.5 | 13.0 | 19 57.4 | 9.6 | 54.5 | | | | | | | | |
| 21 | 133 22.4 . . | 35.5 | 119 09.5 | 13.1 | 19 47.8 | 9.8 | 54.5 | | | | | | | | |
| 22 | 148 22.5 | 34.9 | 133 41.6 | 13.1 | 19 38.0 | 9.8 | 54.5 | | | | | | | | |
| 23 | 163 22.5 | 34.3 | 148 13.7 | 13.2 | N19 28.2 | 9.9 | 54.5 | | | | | | | | |

| Day | SUN | | | | MOON | | | |
|---|---|---|---|---|---|---|---|---|
| | Eqn. of Time | | Mer. | | Mer. Pass. | | Age | Phase |
| | 00ʰ | 12ʰ | Pass. | | Upper | Lower | | |
| d | m s | m s | h m | | h m | h m | d | % |
| 27 | 06 34 | 06 34 | 12 07 | | 11 11 | 23 36 | 28 | 2 |
| 28 | 06 33 | 06 33 | 12 07 | | 12 00 | 24 24 | 29 | 0 |
| 29 | 06 32 | 06 31 | 12 07 | | 12 48 | 00 24 | 01 | 1 |

SD 15.8   d 0.6    SD 14.7   14.8   14.8

## 2022 JULY 30, 31, AUG. 1 (SAT., SUN., MON.)

| UT | ARIES | VENUS −3.9 | | MARS +0.2 | | JUPITER −2.6 | | SATURN +0.3 | | STARS | | |
|---|---|---|---|---|---|---|---|---|---|---|---|---|
| | GHA | GHA | Dec | GHA | Dec | GHA | Dec | GHA | Dec | Name | SHA | Dec |
| d h | ° ′ | ° ′ | ° ′ | ° ′ | ° ′ | ° ′ | ° ′ | ° ′ | ° ′ | | ° ′ | ° ′ |
| 30 00 | 307 36.8 | 201 56.8 | N22 31.3 | 262 48.3 | N15 13.2 | 299 02.5 | N 2 08.2 | 341 47.2 | S15 02.3 | Acamar | 315 13.4 | S40 12.6 |
| 01 | 322 39.3 | 216 55.9 | 31.0 | 277 49.2 | 13.6 | 314 05.0 | 08.2 | 356 49.9 | 02.3 | Achernar | 335 21.6 | S57 07.1 |
| 02 | 337 41.7 | 231 55.1 | 30.8 | 292 50.0 | 14.1 | 329 07.4 | 08.2 | 11 52.5 | 02.4 | Acrux | 173 02.6 | S63 13.6 |
| 03 | 352 44.2 | 246 54.3 .. | 30.6 | 307 50.9 .. | 14.6 | 344 09.9 .. | 08.2 | 26 55.2 .. | 02.5 | Adhara | 255 07.8 | S29 00.0 |
| 04 | 7 46.6 | 261 53.5 | 30.4 | 322 51.7 | 15.1 | 359 12.4 | 08.2 | 41 57.8 | 02.5 | Aldebaran | 290 42.1 | N16 33.2 |
| 05 | 22 49.1 | 276 52.7 | 30.2 | 337 52.6 | 15.5 | 14 14.8 | 08.1 | 57 00.4 | 02.6 | | | |
| 06 | 37 51.6 | 291 51.9 | N22 29.9 | 352 53.4 | N15 16.0 | 29 17.3 | N 2 08.1 | 72 03.1 | S15 02.7 | Alioth | 166 15.0 | N55 50.6 |
| 07 | 52 54.0 | 306 51.0 | 29.7 | 7 54.3 | 16.5 | 44 19.8 | 08.1 | 87 05.7 | 02.7 | Alkaid | 152 53.7 | N49 12.4 |
| S 08 | 67 56.5 | 321 50.2 | 29.5 | 22 55.1 | 17.0 | 59 22.3 | 08.1 | 102 08.3 | 02.8 | Alnair | 27 35.0 | S46 51.0 |
| A 09 | 82 59.0 | 336 49.4 .. | 29.3 | 37 56.0 .. | 17.4 | 74 24.7 .. | 08.1 | 117 11.0 .. | 02.8 | Alnilam | 275 40.0 | S 1 11.2 |
| T 10 | 98 01.4 | 351 48.6 | 29.1 | 52 56.9 | 17.9 | 89 27.2 | 08.1 | 132 13.6 | 02.9 | Alphard | 217 50.0 | S 8 45.3 |
| U 11 | 113 03.9 | 6 47.8 | 28.8 | 67 57.7 | 18.4 | 104 29.7 | 08.0 | 147 16.2 | 03.0 | | | |
| R 12 | 128 06.4 | 21 47.0 | N22 28.6 | 82 58.6 | N15 18.9 | 119 32.1 | N 2 08.0 | 162 18.9 | S15 03.0 | Alphecca | 126 05.3 | N26 38.6 |
| D 13 | 143 08.8 | 36 46.2 | 28.4 | 97 59.4 | 19.3 | 134 34.6 | 08.0 | 177 21.5 | 03.1 | Alpheratz | 357 36.6 | N29 12.8 |
| A 14 | 158 11.3 | 51 45.3 | 28.1 | 113 00.3 | 19.8 | 149 37.1 | 08.0 | 192 24.1 | 03.2 | Altair | 62 01.6 | N 8 55.7 |
| Y 15 | 173 13.7 | 66 44.5 .. | 27.9 | 128 01.1 .. | 20.3 | 164 39.6 .. | 08.0 | 207 26.8 .. | 03.2 | Ankaa | 353 08.9 | S42 10.8 |
| 16 | 188 16.2 | 81 43.7 | 27.7 | 143 02.0 | 20.8 | 179 42.0 | 08.0 | 222 29.4 | 03.3 | Antares | 112 18.1 | S26 28.9 |
| 17 | 203 18.7 | 96 42.9 | 27.4 | 158 02.8 | 21.2 | 194 44.5 | 07.9 | 237 32.0 | 03.4 | | | |
| 18 | 218 21.1 | 111 42.1 | N22 27.2 | 173 03.7 | N15 21.7 | 209 47.0 | N 2 07.9 | 252 34.7 | S15 03.4 | Arcturus | 145 49.8 | N19 04.1 |
| 19 | 233 23.6 | 126 41.3 | 27.0 | 188 04.6 | 22.2 | 224 49.5 | 07.9 | 267 37.3 | 03.5 | Atria | 107 13.8 | S69 04.2 |
| 20 | 248 26.1 | 141 40.5 | 26.7 | 203 05.4 | 22.6 | 239 51.9 | 07.9 | 282 39.9 | 03.5 | Avior | 234 16.2 | S59 34.8 |
| 21 | 263 28.5 | 156 39.6 .. | 26.5 | 218 06.3 .. | 23.1 | 254 54.4 .. | 07.9 | 297 42.6 .. | 03.6 | Bellatrix | 278 25.3 | N 6 22.2 |
| 22 | 278 31.0 | 171 38.8 | 26.3 | 233 07.1 | 23.6 | 269 56.9 | 07.9 | 312 45.2 | 03.7 | Betelgeuse | 270 54.5 | N 7 24.7 |
| 23 | 293 33.5 | 186 38.0 | 26.0 | 248 08.0 | 24.1 | 284 59.3 | 07.8 | 327 47.9 | 03.7 | | | |
| 31 00 | 308 35.9 | 201 37.2 | N22 25.8 | 263 08.8 | N15 24.5 | 300 01.8 | N 2 07.8 | 342 50.5 | S15 03.8 | Canopus | 263 53.8 | S52 42.2 |
| 01 | 323 38.4 | 216 36.4 | 25.5 | 278 09.7 | 25.0 | 315 04.3 | 07.8 | 357 53.1 | 03.9 | Capella | 280 25.2 | N46 01.1 |
| 02 | 338 40.9 | 231 35.6 | 25.3 | 293 10.5 | 25.5 | 330 06.8 | 07.8 | 12 55.8 | 03.9 | Deneb | 49 26.7 | N45 21.6 |
| 03 | 353 43.3 | 246 34.8 .. | 25.0 | 308 11.4 .. | 25.9 | 345 09.3 .. | 07.8 | 27 58.4 .. | 04.0 | Denebola | 182 27.2 | N14 27.0 |
| 04 | 8 45.8 | 261 34.0 | 24.8 | 323 12.3 | 26.4 | 0 11.7 | 07.7 | 43 01.0 | 04.0 | Diphda | 348 49.2 | S17 51.7 |
| 05 | 23 48.2 | 276 33.1 | 24.5 | 338 13.1 | 26.9 | 15 14.2 | 07.7 | 58 03.7 | 04.1 | | | |
| 06 | 38 50.7 | 291 32.3 | N22 24.3 | 353 14.0 | N15 27.4 | 30 16.7 | N 2 07.7 | 73 06.3 | S15 04.2 | Dubhe | 193 44.0 | N61 38.0 |
| 07 | 53 53.2 | 306 31.5 | 24.1 | 8 14.8 | 27.8 | 45 19.2 | 07.7 | 88 08.9 | 04.2 | Elnath | 278 04.7 | N28 37.5 |
| S 08 | 68 55.6 | 321 30.7 | 23.8 | 23 15.7 | 28.3 | 60 21.6 | 07.7 | 103 11.6 | 04.3 | Eltanin | 90 42.7 | N51 29.3 |
| U 09 | 83 58.1 | 336 29.9 .. | 23.5 | 38 16.5 .. | 28.8 | 75 24.1 .. | 07.6 | 118 14.2 .. | 04.4 | Enif | 33 40.4 | N 9 58.7 |
| N 10 | 99 00.6 | 351 29.1 | 23.3 | 53 17.4 | 29.2 | 90 26.6 | 07.6 | 133 16.8 | 04.4 | Fomalhaut | 15 16.4 | S29 30.1 |
| 11 | 114 03.0 | 6 28.3 | 23.0 | 68 18.3 | 29.7 | 105 29.1 | 07.6 | 148 19.5 | 04.5 | | | |
| D 12 | 129 05.5 | 21 27.5 | N22 22.8 | 83 19.1 | N15 30.2 | 120 31.6 | N 2 07.6 | 163 22.1 | S15 04.5 | Gacrux | 171 54.1 | S57 14.5 |
| A 13 | 144 08.0 | 36 26.7 | 22.5 | 98 20.0 | 30.6 | 135 34.0 | 07.6 | 178 24.8 | 04.6 | Gienah | 175 45.8 | S17 40.0 |
| Y 14 | 159 10.4 | 51 25.8 | 22.3 | 113 20.8 | 31.1 | 150 36.5 | 07.5 | 193 27.4 | 04.7 | Hadar | 148 38.9 | S60 29.1 |
| 15 | 174 12.9 | 66 25.0 .. | 22.0 | 128 21.7 .. | 31.6 | 165 39.0 .. | 07.5 | 208 30.0 .. | 04.7 | Hamal | 327 53.4 | N23 34.0 |
| 16 | 189 15.4 | 81 24.2 | 21.8 | 143 22.6 | 32.0 | 180 41.5 | 07.5 | 223 32.7 | 04.8 | Kaus Aust. | 83 34.8 | S34 22.4 |
| 17 | 204 17.8 | 96 23.4 | 21.5 | 158 23.4 | 32.5 | 195 44.0 | 07.5 | 238 35.3 | 04.9 | | | |
| 18 | 219 20.3 | 111 22.6 | N22 21.2 | 173 24.3 | N15 33.0 | 210 46.4 | N 2 07.5 | 253 37.9 | S15 04.9 | Kochab | 137 19.7 | N74 04.1 |
| 19 | 234 22.7 | 126 21.8 | 21.0 | 188 25.1 | 33.4 | 225 48.9 | 07.4 | 268 40.6 | 05.0 | Markab | 13 31.6 | N15 19.6 |
| 20 | 249 25.2 | 141 21.0 | 20.7 | 203 26.0 | 33.9 | 240 51.4 | 07.4 | 283 43.2 | 05.1 | Menkar | 314 08.3 | N 4 10.7 |
| 21 | 264 27.7 | 156 20.2 .. | 20.4 | 218 26.9 .. | 34.4 | 255 53.9 .. | 07.4 | 298 45.9 .. | 05.1 | Menkent | 148 00.0 | S36 28.9 |
| 22 | 279 30.1 | 171 19.4 | 20.2 | 233 27.7 | 34.8 | 270 56.4 | 07.4 | 313 48.5 | 05.2 | Miaplacidus | 221 39.6 | S69 48.5 |
| 23 | 294 32.6 | 186 18.5 | 19.9 | 248 28.6 | 35.3 | 285 58.8 | 07.4 | 328 51.1 | 05.2 | | | |
| 1 00 | 309 35.1 | 201 17.7 | N22 19.6 | 263 29.4 | N15 35.7 | 301 01.3 | N 2 07.3 | 343 53.8 | S15 05.3 | Mirfak | 308 31.2 | N49 56.2 |
| 01 | 324 37.5 | 216 16.9 | 19.4 | 278 30.3 | 36.2 | 316 03.8 | 07.3 | 358 56.4 | 05.4 | Nunki | 75 49.9 | S26 16.1 |
| 02 | 339 40.0 | 231 16.1 | 19.1 | 293 31.2 | 36.7 | 331 06.3 | 07.3 | 13 59.0 | 05.4 | Peacock | 53 08.3 | S56 39.7 |
| 03 | 354 42.5 | 246 15.3 .. | 18.8 | 308 32.0 .. | 37.1 | 346 08.8 .. | 07.3 | 29 01.7 .. | 05.5 | Pollux | 243 20.1 | N27 58.4 |
| 04 | 9 44.9 | 261 14.5 | 18.6 | 323 32.9 | 37.6 | 1 11.3 | 07.3 | 44 04.3 | 05.6 | Procyon | 244 53.3 | N 5 10.1 |
| 05 | 24 47.4 | 276 13.7 | 18.3 | 338 33.7 | 38.1 | 16 13.8 | 07.2 | 59 06.9 | 05.6 | | | |
| 06 | 39 49.8 | 291 12.9 | N22 18.0 | 353 34.6 | N15 38.5 | 31 16.2 | N 2 07.2 | 74 09.6 | S15 05.7 | Rasalhague | 96 00.2 | N12 32.7 |
| 07 | 54 52.3 | 306 12.1 | 17.7 | 8 35.5 | 39.0 | 46 18.7 | 07.2 | 89 12.2 | 05.7 | Regulus | 207 36.9 | N11 51.6 |
| 08 | 69 54.8 | 321 11.3 | 17.5 | 23 36.3 | 39.5 | 61 21.2 | 07.2 | 104 14.9 | 05.8 | Rigel | 281 06.0 | S 8 10.4 |
| M 09 | 84 57.2 | 336 10.5 .. | 17.2 | 38 37.2 .. | 39.9 | 76 23.7 .. | 07.1 | 119 17.5 .. | 05.9 | Rigil Kent. | 139 43.0 | S60 55.9 |
| O 10 | 99 59.7 | 351 09.6 | 16.9 | 53 38.0 | 40.4 | 91 26.2 | 07.1 | 134 20.1 | 05.9 | Sabik | 102 04.9 | S15 45.1 |
| N 11 | 115 02.2 | 6 08.8 | 16.6 | 68 38.9 | 40.8 | 106 28.7 | 07.1 | 149 22.8 | 06.0 | | | |
| D 12 | 130 04.6 | 21 08.0 | N22 16.3 | 83 39.8 | N15 41.3 | 121 31.2 | N 2 07.1 | 164 25.4 | S15 06.1 | Schedar | 349 33.0 | N56 39.4 |
| A 13 | 145 07.1 | 36 07.2 | 16.0 | 98 40.6 | 41.8 | 136 33.6 | 07.1 | 179 28.0 | 06.1 | Shaula | 96 12.8 | S37 07.2 |
| Y 14 | 160 09.6 | 51 06.4 | 15.8 | 113 41.5 | 42.2 | 151 36.1 | 07.0 | 194 30.7 | 06.2 | Sirius | 258 28.3 | S16 44.7 |
| 15 | 175 12.0 | 66 05.6 .. | 15.5 | 128 42.4 .. | 42.7 | 166 38.6 .. | 07.0 | 209 33.3 .. | 06.3 | Spica | 158 24.5 | S11 16.7 |
| 16 | 190 14.5 | 81 04.8 | 15.2 | 143 43.2 | 43.1 | 181 41.1 | 07.0 | 224 36.0 | 06.3 | Suhail | 222 48.2 | S43 31.3 |
| 17 | 205 17.0 | 96 04.0 | 14.9 | 158 44.1 | 43.6 | 196 43.6 | 07.0 | 239 38.6 | 06.4 | | | |
| 18 | 220 19.4 | 111 03.2 | N22 14.6 | 173 44.9 | N15 44.1 | 211 46.1 | N 2 06.9 | 254 41.2 | S15 06.4 | Vega | 80 34.2 | N38 48.4 |
| 19 | 235 21.9 | 126 02.4 | 14.3 | 188 45.8 | 44.5 | 226 48.6 | 06.9 | 269 43.9 | 06.5 | Zuben'ubi | 136 58.2 | S16 08.1 |
| 20 | 250 24.3 | 141 01.6 | 14.0 | 203 46.7 | 45.0 | 241 51.1 | 06.9 | 284 46.5 | 06.6 | | SHA | Mer. Pass. |
| 21 | 265 26.8 | 156 00.8 .. | 13.7 | 218 47.5 .. | 45.4 | 256 53.5 .. | 06.9 | 299 49.2 .. | 06.6 | | ° ′ | h m |
| 22 | 280 29.3 | 171 00.0 | 13.4 | 233 48.4 | 45.9 | 271 56.0 | 06.8 | 314 51.8 | 06.7 | Venus | 253 01.3 | 10 34 |
| 23 | 295 31.7 | 185 59.2 | 13.2 | 248 49.3 | 46.4 | 286 58.5 | 06.8 | 329 54.4 | 06.8 | Mars | 314 32.9 | 6 27 |
| | h m | | | | | | | | | Jupiter | 351 25.9 | 3 59 |
| Mer. Pass. 3 25.0 | | v −0.8 | d 0.3 | v 0.9 | d 0.5 | v 2.5 | d 0.0 | v 2.6 | d 0.1 | Saturn | 34 14.6 | 1 08 |

| UT | SUN GHA | SUN Dec | MOON GHA | v | MOON Dec | d | HP |
|---|---|---|---|---|---|---|---|
| d h | ° ′ | ° ′ | ° ′ | ′ | ° ′ | ′ | ′ |
| **30** 00 | 178 22.5 | N18 33.7 | 162 45.9 | 13.3 | N19 18.3 | 10.0 | 54.6 |
| 01 | 193 22.5 | 33.1 | 177 18.2 | 13.2 | 19 08.3 | 10.0 | 54.6 |
| 02 | 208 22.6 | 32.5 | 191 50.4 | 13.4 | 18 58.3 | 10.2 | 54.6 |
| 03 | 223 22.6 .. | 31.9 | 206 22.8 | 13.3 | 18 48.1 | 10.2 | 54.6 |
| 04 | 238 22.6 | 31.3 | 220 55.1 | 13.5 | 18 37.9 | 10.4 | 54.6 |
| 05 | 253 22.6 | 30.6 | 235 27.6 | 13.4 | 18 27.5 | 10.4 | 54.6 |
| **S** 06 | 268 22.6 | N18 30.0 | 250 00.0 | 13.6 | N18 17.1 | 10.5 | 54.6 |
| **A** 07 | 283 22.7 | 29.4 | 264 32.6 | 13.5 | 18 06.6 | 10.5 | 54.7 |
| **T** 08 | 298 22.7 | 28.8 | 279 05.1 | 13.6 | 17 56.0 | 10.6 | 54.7 |
| **U** 09 | 313 22.7 .. | 28.2 | 293 37.7 | 13.7 | 17 45.4 | 10.6 | 54.7 |
| **R** 10 | 328 22.7 | 27.6 | 308 10.4 | 13.7 | 17 34.6 | 10.8 | 54.7 |
| **D** 11 | 343 22.8 | 27.0 | 322 43.1 | 13.8 | 17 23.8 | 10.9 | 54.7 |
| **A** 12 | 358 22.8 | N18 26.4 | 337 15.9 | 13.8 | N17 12.9 | 11.0 | 54.7 |
| **Y** 13 | 13 22.8 | 25.8 | 351 48.7 | 13.0 | 17 01.9 | 11.0 | 54.7 |
| 14 | 28 22.9 | 25.2 | 6 21.5 | 13.9 | 16 50.9 | 11.2 | 54.8 |
| 15 | 43 22.9 .. | 24.6 | 20 54.4 | 13.9 | 16 39.7 | 11.2 | 54.8 |
| 16 | 58 22.9 | 24.0 | 35 27.3 | 14.0 | 16 28.5 | 11.3 | 54.8 |
| 17 | 73 22.9 | 23.4 | 50 00.3 | 14.0 | 16 17.2 | 11.3 | 54.8 |
| 18 | 88 23.0 | N18 22.8 | 64 33.3 | 14.0 | N16 05.9 | 11.5 | 54.8 |
| 19 | 103 23.0 | 22.1 | 79 06.3 | 14.1 | 15 54.4 | 11.5 | 54.8 |
| 20 | 118 23.0 | 21.5 | 93 39.4 | 14.1 | 15 42.9 | 11.5 | 54.8 |
| 21 | 133 23.0 .. | 20.9 | 108 12.5 | 14.2 | 15 31.4 | 11.7 | 54.9 |
| 22 | 148 23.1 | 20.3 | 122 45.7 | 14.2 | 15 19.7 | 11.7 | 54.9 |
| 23 | 163 23.1 | 19.7 | 137 18.9 | 14.3 | 15 08.0 | 11.8 | 54.9 |
| **31** 00 | 178 23.1 | N18 19.1 | 151 52.2 | 14.3 | N14 56.2 | 11.8 | 54.9 |
| 01 | 193 23.2 | 18.5 | 166 25.5 | 14.3 | 14 44.4 | 12.0 | 54.9 |
| 02 | 208 23.2 | 17.8 | 180 58.8 | 14.4 | 14 32.4 | 11.9 | 54.9 |
| 03 | 223 23.2 .. | 17.2 | 195 32.2 | 14.4 | 14 20.5 | 12.1 | 55.0 |
| 04 | 238 23.3 | 16.6 | 210 05.6 | 14.4 | 14 08.4 | 12.1 | 55.0 |
| 05 | 253 23.3 | 16.0 | 224 39.0 | 14.5 | 13 56.3 | 12.2 | 55.0 |
| 06 | 268 23.3 | N18 15.4 | 239 12.5 | 14.5 | N13 44.1 | 12.2 | 55.0 |
| **S** 07 | 283 23.4 | 14.8 | 253 46.0 | 14.5 | 13 31.9 | 12.3 | 55.0 |
| **U** 08 | 298 23.4 | 14.1 | 268 19.5 | 14.6 | 13 19.6 | 12.4 | 55.0 |
| **N** 09 | 313 23.4 .. | 13.5 | 282 53.1 | 14.6 | 13 07.2 | 12.4 | 55.1 |
| **D** 10 | 328 23.4 | 12.9 | 297 26.7 | 14.6 | 12 54.8 | 12.5 | 55.1 |
| **A** 11 | 343 23.5 | 12.3 | 312 00.3 | 14.7 | 12 42.3 | 12.6 | 55.1 |
| **Y** 12 | 358 23.5 | N18 11.7 | 326 34.0 | 14.7 | N12 29.7 | 12.6 | 55.1 |
| 13 | 13 23.5 | 11.0 | 341 07.7 | 14.7 | 12 17.1 | 12.7 | 55.1 |
| 14 | 28 23.6 | 10.4 | 355 41.4 | 14.8 | 12 04.4 | 12.7 | 55.1 |
| 15 | 43 23.6 .. | 09.8 | 10 15.2 | 14.8 | 11 51.7 | 12.8 | 55.2 |
| 16 | 58 23.6 | 09.2 | 24 49.0 | 14.8 | 11 38.9 | 12.8 | 55.2 |
| 17 | 73 23.7 | 08.6 | 39 22.8 | 14.8 | 11 26.1 | 12.9 | 55.2 |
| 18 | 88 23.7 | N18 07.9 | 53 56.6 | 14.9 | N11 13.2 | 12.9 | 55.2 |
| 19 | 103 23.7 | 07.3 | 68 30.5 | 14.9 | 11 00.3 | 13.0 | 55.2 |
| 20 | 118 23.8 | 06.7 | 83 04.4 | 14.9 | 10 47.3 | 13.1 | 55.3 |
| 21 | 133 23.8 .. | 06.1 | 97 38.3 | 14.9 | 10 34.2 | 13.1 | 55.3 |
| 22 | 148 23.9 | 05.4 | 112 12.2 | 15.0 | 10 21.1 | 13.1 | 55.3 |
| 23 | 163 23.9 | 04.8 | 126 46.2 | 15.0 | 10 08.0 | 13.2 | 55.3 |
| **1** 00 | 178 23.9 | N18 04.2 | 141 20.2 | 15.0 | N 9 54.8 | 13.3 | 55.3 |
| 01 | 193 24.0 | 03.6 | 155 54.2 | 15.0 | 9 41.5 | 13.3 | 55.4 |
| 02 | 208 24.0 | 02.9 | 170 28.2 | 15.1 | 9 28.2 | 13.3 | 55.4 |
| 03 | 223 24.0 .. | 02.3 | 185 02.3 | 15.0 | 9 14.9 | 13.4 | 55.4 |
| 04 | 238 24.1 | 01.7 | 199 36.3 | 15.1 | 9 01.5 | 13.4 | 55.4 |
| 05 | 253 24.1 | 01.0 | 214 10.4 | 15.1 | 8 48.1 | 13.5 | 55.4 |
| 06 | 268 24.1 | N18 00.4 | 228 44.5 | 15.1 | N 8 34.6 | 13.5 | 55.5 |
| 07 | 283 24.2 | 17 59.8 | 243 18.6 | 15.1 | 8 21.1 | 13.6 | 55.5 |
| **M** 08 | 298 24.2 | 59.2 | 257 52.7 | 15.1 | 8 07.5 | 13.6 | 55.5 |
| **O** 09 | 313 24.3 .. | 58.5 | 272 26.8 | 15.2 | 7 53.9 | 13.6 | 55.5 |
| **N** 10 | 328 24.3 | 57.9 | 287 01.0 | 15.2 | 7 40.3 | 13.7 | 55.5 |
| **D** 11 | 343 24.3 | 57.3 | 301 35.2 | 15.1 | 7 26.6 | 13.7 | 55.6 |
| **A** 12 | 358 24.4 | N17 56.6 | 316 09.3 | 15.2 | N 7 12.9 | 13.8 | 55.6 |
| **Y** 13 | 13 24.4 | 56.0 | 330 43.5 | 15.2 | 6 59.1 | 13.8 | 55.6 |
| 14 | 28 24.5 | 55.4 | 345 17.7 | 15.2 | 6 45.3 | 13.8 | 55.6 |
| 15 | 43 24.5 .. | 54.7 | 359 51.9 | 15.2 | 6 31.5 | 13.9 | 55.6 |
| 16 | 58 24.5 | 54.1 | 14 26.1 | 15.2 | 6 17.6 | 13.9 | 55.7 |
| 17 | 73 24.6 | 53.5 | 29 00.3 | 15.2 | 6 03.7 | 14.0 | 55.7 |
| 18 | 88 24.6 | N17 52.8 | 43 34.5 | 15.2 | N 5 49.7 | 13.9 | 55.7 |
| 19 | 103 24.7 | 52.2 | 58 08.7 | 15.2 | 5 35.8 | 14.1 | 55.7 |
| 20 | 118 24.7 | 51.6 | 72 42.9 | 15.3 | 5 21.7 | 14.0 | 55.8 |
| 21 | 133 24.7 .. | 50.9 | 87 17.2 | 15.2 | 5 07.7 | 14.1 | 55.8 |
| 22 | 148 24.8 | 50.3 | 101 51.4 | 15.2 | 4 53.6 | 14.1 | 55.8 |
| 23 | 163 24.8 | 49.6 | 116 25.6 | 15.2 | N 4 39.5 | 14.1 | 55.8 |
| | SD 15.8 | d 0.6 | SD 14.9 | | 15.0 | | 15.1 |

| Lat. | Twilight Naut. | Civil | Sunrise | Moonrise 30 | 31 | 1 | 2 |
|---|---|---|---|---|---|---|---|
| ° | h m | h m | h m | h m | h m | h m | h m |
| N 72 | ☐ | ☐ | ☐ | ☐ | 04 43 | 07 01 | 09 05 |
| N 70 | //// | //// | 01 16 | 02 38 | 05 12 | 07 14 | 09 08 |
| 68 | //// | //// | 02 10 | 03 29 | 05 34 | 07 24 | 09 11 |
| 66 | //// | //// | 02 41 | 04 01 | 05 51 | 07 33 | 09 13 |
| 64 | //// | 01 33 | 03 05 | 04 24 | 06 04 | 07 40 | 09 15 |
| 62 | //// | 02 11 | 03 23 | 04 43 | 06 16 | 07 46 | 09 16 |
| 60 | //// | 02 37 | 03 38 | 04 58 | 06 25 | 07 52 | 09 18 |
| N 58 | 01 24 | 02 57 | 03 51 | 05 10 | 06 34 | 07 56 | 09 19 |
| 56 | 01 59 | 03 13 | 04 02 | 05 21 | 06 41 | 08 00 | 09 20 |
| 54 | 02 23 | 03 27 | 04 12 | 05 31 | 06 48 | 08 04 | 09 21 |
| 52 | 02 42 | 03 39 | 04 20 | 05 40 | 06 54 | 08 07 | 09 22 |
| 50 | 02 57 | 03 49 | 04 28 | 05 47 | 06 59 | 08 10 | 09 22 |
| 45 | 03 27 | 04 10 | 04 44 | 06 04 | 07 10 | 08 17 | 09 24 |
| N 40 | 03 49 | 04 27 | 04 57 | 06 17 | 07 20 | 08 22 | 09 25 |
| 35 | 04 07 | 04 41 | 05 09 | 06 28 | 07 28 | 08 27 | 09 27 |
| 30 | 04 21 | 04 52 | 05 18 | 06 38 | 07 35 | 08 31 | 09 28 |
| 20 | 04 44 | 05 12 | 05 35 | 06 55 | 07 47 | 08 38 | 09 30 |
| N 10 | 05 01 | 05 27 | 05 50 | 07 09 | 07 57 | 08 45 | 09 31 |
| 0 | 05 16 | 05 41 | 06 03 | 07 23 | 08 07 | 08 50 | 09 33 |
| S 10 | 05 29 | 05 54 | 06 16 | 07 36 | 08 17 | 08 56 | 09 34 |
| 20 | 05 41 | 06 07 | 06 30 | 07 51 | 08 28 | 09 02 | 09 36 |
| 30 | 05 52 | 06 21 | 06 46 | 08 07 | 08 39 | 09 09 | 09 38 |
| 35 | 05 58 | 06 29 | 06 55 | 08 17 | 08 46 | 09 13 | 09 39 |
| 40 | 06 04 | 06 37 | 07 06 | 08 28 | 08 54 | 09 18 | 09 40 |
| 45 | 06 11 | 06 47 | 07 18 | 08 40 | 09 03 | 09 23 | 09 42 |
| S 50 | 06 19 | 06 58 | 07 33 | 08 56 | 09 14 | 09 29 | 09 44 |
| 52 | 06 22 | 07 03 | 07 40 | 09 03 | 09 19 | 09 32 | 09 44 |
| 54 | 06 25 | 07 08 | 07 48 | 09 11 | 09 24 | 09 35 | 09 45 |
| 56 | 06 29 | 07 14 | 07 56 | 09 20 | 09 30 | 09 39 | 09 46 |
| 58 | 06 33 | 07 21 | 08 06 | 09 30 | 09 37 | 09 42 | 09 47 |
| S 60 | 06 37 | 07 29 | 08 17 | 09 41 | 09 45 | 09 47 | 09 48 |

| Lat. | Sunset | Twilight Civil | Naut. | Moonset 30 | 31 | 1 | 2 |
|---|---|---|---|---|---|---|---|
| ° | h m | h m | h m | h m | h m | h m | h m |
| N 72 | ☐ | ☐ | ☐ | 23 32 | 22 45 | 22 12 | 21 42 |
| N 70 | 22 48 | //// | //// | {00 02 / 23 01} | 22 30 | 22 06 | 21 44 |
| 68 | 21 59 | //// | //// | 22 38 | 22 17 | 22 00 | 21 44 |
| 66 | 21 28 | //// | //// | 22 19 | 22 07 | 21 56 | 21 45 |
| 64 | 21 06 | 22 34 | //// | 22 05 | 21 58 | 21 52 | 21 46 |
| 62 | 20 48 | 21 59 | //// | 21 52 | 21 51 | 21 49 | 21 47 |
| 60 | 20 33 | 21 34 | //// | 21 41 | 21 44 | 21 46 | 21 47 |
| N 58 | 20 20 | 21 14 | 22 44 | 21 32 | 21 38 | 21 43 | 21 48 |
| 56 | 20 10 | 20 58 | 22 11 | 21 24 | 21 33 | 21 41 | 21 48 |
| 54 | 20 00 | 20 45 | 21 47 | 21 16 | 21 28 | 21 39 | 21 48 |
| 52 | 19 52 | 20 33 | 21 29 | 21 10 | 21 24 | 21 37 | 21 49 |
| 50 | 19 44 | 20 23 | 21 14 | 21 04 | 21 20 | 21 35 | 21 49 |
| 45 | 19 28 | 20 02 | 20 44 | 20 51 | 21 12 | 21 31 | 21 50 |
| N 40 | 19 15 | 19 45 | 20 23 | 20 40 | 21 05 | 21 28 | 21 50 |
| 35 | 19 04 | 19 32 | 20 05 | 20 31 | 20 59 | 21 25 | 21 51 |
| 30 | 18 54 | 19 20 | 19 51 | 20 23 | 20 54 | 21 23 | 21 51 |
| 20 | 18 38 | 19 01 | 19 29 | 20 09 | 20 44 | 21 18 | 21 52 |
| N 10 | 18 23 | 18 45 | 19 09 | 19 56 | 20 36 | 21 14 | 21 53 |
| 0 | 18 10 | 18 32 | 18 57 | 19 45 | 20 28 | 21 11 | 21 53 |
| S 10 | 17 57 | 18 19 | 18 44 | 19 33 | 20 20 | 21 07 | 21 54 |
| 20 | 17 43 | 18 06 | 18 33 | 19 20 | 20 12 | 21 03 | 21 55 |
| 30 | 17 27 | 17 52 | 18 21 | 19 05 | 20 02 | 20 58 | 21 55 |
| 35 | 17 18 | 17 45 | 18 15 | 18 57 | 19 56 | 20 56 | 21 56 |
| 40 | 17 07 | 17 36 | 18 09 | 18 47 | 19 50 | 20 53 | 21 56 |
| 45 | 16 55 | 17 27 | 18 02 | 18 36 | 19 42 | 20 49 | 21 57 |
| S 50 | 16 40 | 17 16 | 17 55 | 18 22 | 19 33 | 20 45 | 21 57 |
| 52 | 16 33 | 17 11 | 17 48 | 18 15 | 19 29 | 20 43 | 21 57 |
| 54 | 16 26 | 17 05 | 17 48 | 18 08 | 19 24 | 20 41 | 21 58 |
| 56 | 16 17 | 16 59 | 17 45 | 18 00 | 19 19 | 20 38 | 21 58 |
| 58 | 16 08 | 16 53 | 17 41 | 17 50 | 19 13 | 20 36 | 21 58 |
| S 60 | 15 56 | 16 45 | 17 37 | 17 40 | 19 07 | 20 33 | 21 59 |

| | SUN | | | MOON | | | |
|---|---|---|---|---|---|---|---|
| Day | Eqn. of Time 00h | 12h | Mer. Pass. | Mer. Pass. Upper | Lower | Age | Phase |
| d | m s | m s | h m | h m | h m | d | % |
| 30 | 06 30 | 06 29 | 12 06 | 13 34 | 01 11 | 02 | 3 |
| 31 | 06 28 | 06 26 | 12 06 | 14 18 | 01 56 | 03 | 7 |
| 1 | 06 24 | 06 23 | 12 06 | 15 01 | 02 39 | 04 | 13 |

| UT | ARIES GHA | VENUS −3.9 GHA | Dec | MARS +0.1 GHA | Dec | JUPITER −2.7 GHA | Dec | SATURN +0.3 GHA | Dec | STARS Name | SHA | Dec |
|---|---|---|---|---|---|---|---|---|---|---|---|---|
| d h | ° ′ | ° ′ | ° ′ | ° ′ | ° ′ | ° ′ | ° ′ | ° ′ | ° ′ | | ° ′ | ° ′ |
| 2 00 | 310 34.2 | 200 58.3 | N22 12.9 | 263 50.1 | N15 46.8 | 302 01.0 | N 2 06.8 | 344 57.1 | S15 06.8 | Acamar | 315 13.3 | S40 12.6 |
| 01 | 325 36.7 | 215 57.5 | 12.6 | 278 51.0 | 47.3 | 317 03.5 | 06.8 | 359 59.7 | 06.9 | Achernar | 335 21.6 | S57 07.1 |
| 02 | 340 39.1 | 230 56.7 | 12.3 | 293 51.9 | 47.7 | 332 06.0 | 06.7 | 15 02.3 | 07.0 | Acrux | 173 02.7 | S63 13.6 |
| 03 | 355 41.6 | 245 55.9 . . | 12.0 | 308 52.7 . . | 48.2 | 347 08.5 . . | 06.7 | 30 05.0 . . | 07.0 | Adhara | 255 07.8 | S29 00.0 |
| 04 | 10 44.1 | 260 55.1 | 11.7 | 323 53.6 | 48.6 | 2 11.0 | 06.7 | 45 07.6 | 07.1 | Aldebaran | 290 42.1 | N16 33.2 |
| 05 | 25 46.5 | 275 54.3 | 11.4 | 338 54.4 | 49.1 | 17 13.5 | 06.7 | 60 10.3 | 07.1 | | | |
| 06 | 40 49.0 | 290 53.5 | N22 11.1 | 353 55.3 | N15 49.6 | 32 16.0 | N 2 06.6 | 75 12.9 | S15 07.2 | Alioth | 166 15.0 | N55 50.6 |
| 07 | 55 51.4 | 305 52.7 | 10.8 | 8 56.2 | 50.0 | 47 18.5 | 06.6 | 90 15.5 | 07.3 | Alkaid | 152 53.7 | N49 12.4 |
| 08 | 70 53.9 | 320 51.9 | 10.5 | 23 57.0 | 50.5 | 62 21.0 | 06.6 | 105 18.2 | 07.3 | Alnair | 27 35.0 | S46 51.0 |
| 09 | 85 56.4 | 335 51.1 . . | 10.1 | 38 57.9 . . | 50.9 | 77 23.5 . . | 06.6 | 120 20.8 . . | 07.4 | Alnilam | 275 40.0 | S 1 11.2 |
| 10 | 100 58.8 | 350 50.3 | 09.8 | 53 58.8 | 51.4 | 92 25.9 | 06.5 | 135 23.5 | 07.5 | Alphard | 217 50.0 | S 8 45.3 |
| 11 | 116 01.3 | 5 49.5 | 09.5 | 68 59.6 | 51.8 | 107 28.4 | 06.5 | 150 26.1 | 07.5 | | | |
| 12 | 131 03.8 | 20 48.7 | N22 09.2 | 84 00.5 | N15 52.3 | 122 30.9 | N 2 06.5 | 165 28.7 | S15 07.6 | Alphecca | 126 05.4 | N26 38.6 |
| 13 | 146 06.2 | 35 47.9 | 08.9 | 99 01.4 | 52.7 | 137 33.4 | 06.5 | 180 31.4 | 07.6 | Alpheratz | 357 36.6 | N29 12.8 |
| 14 | 161 08.7 | 50 47.1 | 08.6 | 114 02.2 | 53.2 | 152 35.9 | 06.4 | 195 34.0 | 07.7 | Altair | 62 01.6 | N 8 55.7 |
| 15 | 176 11.2 | 65 46.3 . . | 08.3 | 129 03.1 . . | 53.6 | 167 38.4 . . | 06.4 | 210 36.6 . . | 07.8 | Ankaa | 353 08.9 | S42 10.8 |
| 16 | 191 13.6 | 80 45.5 | 08.0 | 144 04.0 | 54.1 | 182 40.9 | 06.4 | 225 39.3 | 07.8 | Antares | 112 18.1 | S26 28.9 |
| 17 | 206 16.1 | 95 44.7 | 07.7 | 159 04.8 | 54.6 | 197 43.4 | 06.3 | 240 41.9 | 07.9 | | | |
| 18 | 221 18.6 | 110 43.9 | N22 07.3 | 174 05.7 | N15 55.0 | 212 45.9 | N 2 06.3 | 255 44.6 | S15 08.0 | Arcturus | 145 49.8 | N19 04.1 |
| 19 | 236 21.0 | 125 43.1 | 07.0 | 189 06.6 | 55.5 | 227 48.4 | 06.3 | 270 47.2 | 08.0 | Atria | 107 13.8 | S69 04.2 |
| 20 | 251 23.5 | 140 42.3 | 06.7 | 204 07.4 | 55.9 | 242 50.9 | 06.3 | 285 49.8 | 08.1 | Avior | 234 16.2 | S59 34.8 |
| 21 | 266 25.9 | 155 41.5 . . | 06.4 | 219 08.3 . . | 56.4 | 257 53.4 . . | 06.2 | 300 52.5 . . | 08.2 | Bellatrix | 278 25.3 | N 6 22.3 |
| 22 | 281 28.4 | 170 40.7 | 06.1 | 234 09.2 | 56.8 | 272 55.9 | 06.2 | 315 55.1 | 08.2 | Betelgeuse | 270 54.5 | N 7 24.7 |
| 23 | 296 30.9 | 185 39.9 | 05.8 | 249 10.0 | 57.3 | 287 58.4 | 06.2 | 330 57.8 | 08.3 | | | |
| 3 00 | 311 33.3 | 200 39.0 | N22 05.4 | 264 10.9 | N15 57.7 | 303 00.9 | N 2 06.2 | 346 00.4 | S15 08.3 | Canopus | 263 53.7 | S52 42.2 |
| 01 | 326 35.8 | 215 38.2 | 05.1 | 279 11.8 | 58.2 | 318 03.4 | 06.1 | 1 03.0 | 08.4 | Capella | 280 25.2 | N46 01.1 |
| 02 | 341 38.3 | 230 37.4 | 04.8 | 294 12.6 | 58.6 | 333 05.9 | 06.1 | 16 05.7 | 08.5 | Deneb | 49 26.7 | N45 21.6 |
| 03 | 356 40.7 | 245 36.6 . . | 04.5 | 309 13.5 . . | 59.1 | 348 08.4 . . | 06.1 | 31 08.3 . . | 08.5 | Denebola | 182 27.2 | N14 27.0 |
| 04 | 11 43.2 | 260 35.8 | 04.1 | 324 14.4 | 15 59.5 | 3 10.9 | 06.0 | 46 11.0 | 08.6 | Diphda | 348 49.1 | S17 51.7 |
| 05 | 26 45.7 | 275 35.0 | 03.8 | 339 15.3 | 16 00.0 | 18 13.4 | 06.0 | 61 13.6 | 08.7 | | | |
| 06 | 41 48.1 | 290 34.2 | N22 03.5 | 354 16.1 | N16 00.4 | 33 15.9 | N 2 06.0 | 76 16.2 | S15 08.7 | Dubhe | 193 44.0 | N61 38.0 |
| 07 | 56 50.6 | 305 33.4 | 03.1 | 9 17.0 | 00.9 | 48 18.4 | 06.0 | 91 18.9 | 08.8 | Elnath | 278 04.7 | N28 37.5 |
| 08 | 71 53.0 | 320 32.6 | 02.8 | 24 17.9 | 01.3 | 63 20.9 | 05.9 | 106 21.5 | 08.8 | Eltanin | 90 42.7 | N51 29.3 |
| 09 | 86 55.5 | 335 31.8 . . | 02.5 | 39 18.7 . . | 01.8 | 78 23.4 . . | 05.9 | 121 24.2 . . | 08.9 | Enif | 33 40.4 | N 9 58.7 |
| 10 | 101 58.0 | 350 31.0 | 02.1 | 54 19.6 | 02.2 | 93 25.9 | 05.9 | 136 26.8 | 09.0 | Fomalhaut | 15 16.4 | S29 30.1 |
| 11 | 117 00.4 | 5 30.2 | 01.8 | 69 20.5 | 02.7 | 108 28.4 | 05.8 | 151 29.4 | 09.0 | | | |
| 12 | 132 02.9 | 20 29.4 | N22 01.5 | 84 21.3 | N16 03.1 | 123 30.9 | N 2 05.8 | 166 32.1 | S15 09.1 | Gacrux | 171 54.2 | S57 14.5 |
| 13 | 147 05.4 | 35 28.6 | 01.1 | 99 22.2 | 03.6 | 138 33.4 | 05.8 | 181 34.7 | 09.2 | Gienah | 175 45.8 | S17 40.0 |
| 14 | 162 07.8 | 50 27.8 | 00.8 | 114 23.1 | 04.0 | 153 35.9 | 05.8 | 196 37.4 | 09.2 | Hadar | 148 38.9 | S60 29.1 |
| 15 | 177 10.3 | 65 27.0 . . | 00.5 | 129 23.9 . . | 04.5 | 168 38.4 . . | 05.7 | 211 40.0 . . | 09.3 | Hamal | 327 53.4 | N23 34.0 |
| 16 | 192 12.8 | 80 26.2 | 22 00.1 | 144 24.8 | 04.9 | 183 40.9 | 05.7 | 226 42.6 | 09.4 | Kaus Aust. | 83 34.8 | S34 22.4 |
| 17 | 207 15.2 | 95 25.4 | 21 59.8 | 159 25.7 | 05.3 | 198 43.4 | 05.7 | 241 45.3 | 09.4 | | | |
| 18 | 222 17.7 | 110 24.6 | N21 59.4 | 174 26.6 | N16 05.8 | 213 45.9 | N 2 05.6 | 256 47.9 | S15 09.5 | Kochab | 137 19.7 | N74 04.1 |
| 19 | 237 20.2 | 125 23.9 | 59.1 | 189 27.4 | 06.2 | 228 48.4 | 05.6 | 271 50.6 | 09.6 | Markab | 13 31.6 | N15 19.6 |
| 20 | 252 22.6 | 140 23.1 | 58.7 | 204 28.3 | 06.7 | 243 50.9 | 05.6 | 286 53.2 | 09.6 | Menkar | 314 08.3 | N 4 10.7 |
| 21 | 267 25.1 | 155 22.3 . . | 58.4 | 219 29.2 . . | 07.1 | 258 53.4 . . | 05.5 | 301 55.8 . . | 09.7 | Menkent | 148 00.0 | S36 28.9 |
| 22 | 282 27.5 | 170 21.5 | 58.1 | 234 30.0 | 07.6 | 273 55.9 | 05.5 | 316 58.5 | 09.8 | Miaplacidus | 221 39.6 | S69 48.5 |
| 23 | 297 30.0 | 185 20.7 | 57.7 | 249 30.9 | 08.0 | 288 58.4 | 05.5 | 332 01.1 | 09.8 | | | |
| 4 00 | 312 32.5 | 200 19.9 | N21 57.4 | 264 31.8 | N16 08.5 | 304 00.9 | N 2 05.5 | 347 03.8 | S15 09.9 | Mirfak | 308 31.2 | N49 56.2 |
| 01 | 327 34.9 | 215 19.1 | 57.0 | 279 32.7 | 08.9 | 319 03.5 | 05.4 | 2 06.4 | 09.9 | Nunki | 75 49.9 | S26 16.1 |
| 02 | 342 37.4 | 230 18.3 | 56.7 | 294 33.5 | 09.4 | 334 06.0 | 05.4 | 17 09.0 | 10.0 | Peacock | 53 08.3 | S56 39.7 |
| 03 | 357 39.9 | 245 17.5 . . | 56.3 | 309 34.4 . . | 09.8 | 349 08.5 . . | 05.4 | 32 11.7 . . | 10.1 | Pollux | 243 20.1 | N27 58.4 |
| 04 | 12 42.3 | 260 16.7 | 56.0 | 324 35.3 | 10.2 | 4 11.0 | 05.3 | 47 14.3 | 10.1 | Procyon | 244 53.3 | N 5 10.1 |
| 05 | 27 44.8 | 275 15.9 | 55.6 | 339 36.2 | 10.7 | 19 13.5 | 05.3 | 62 17.0 | 10.2 | | | |
| 06 | 42 47.3 | 290 15.1 | N21 55.2 | 354 37.0 | N16 11.1 | 34 16.0 | N 2 05.3 | 77 19.6 | S15 10.3 | Rasalhague | 96 00.2 | N12 32.8 |
| 07 | 57 49.7 | 305 14.3 | 54.9 | 9 37.9 | 11.6 | 49 18.5 | 05.2 | 92 22.3 | 10.3 | Regulus | 207 36.9 | N11 51.6 |
| 08 | 72 52.2 | 320 13.5 | 54.5 | 24 38.8 | 12.0 | 64 21.0 | 05.2 | 107 24.9 | 10.4 | Rigel | 281 06.0 | S 8 10.4 |
| 09 | 87 54.7 | 335 12.7 . . | 54.2 | 39 39.6 . . | 12.5 | 79 23.5 . . | 05.2 | 122 27.5 . . | 10.5 | Rigil Kent. | 139 43.1 | S60 55.8 |
| 10 | 102 57.1 | 350 11.9 | 53.8 | 54 40.5 | 12.9 | 94 26.0 | 05.1 | 137 30.2 | 10.5 | Sabik | 102 04.9 | S15 45.1 |
| 11 | 117 59.6 | 5 11.1 | 53.4 | 69 41.4 | 13.3 | 109 28.5 | 05.1 | 152 32.8 | 10.6 | | | |
| 12 | 133 02.0 | 20 10.3 | N21 53.1 | 84 42.3 | N16 13.8 | 124 31.0 | N 2 05.1 | 167 35.5 | S15 10.6 | Schedar | 349 33.0 | N56 39.4 |
| 13 | 148 04.5 | 35 09.5 | 52.7 | 99 43.1 | 14.2 | 139 33.5 | 05.0 | 182 38.1 | 10.7 | Shaula | 96 12.8 | S37 07.2 |
| 14 | 163 07.0 | 50 08.7 | 52.4 | 114 44.0 | 14.7 | 154 36.1 | 05.0 | 197 40.7 | 10.8 | Sirius | 258 28.3 | S16 44.7 |
| 15 | 178 09.4 | 65 07.9 . . | 52.0 | 129 44.9 . . | 15.1 | 169 38.6 . . | 05.0 | 212 43.4 . . | 10.8 | Spica | 158 24.5 | S11 16.7 |
| 16 | 193 11.9 | 80 07.1 | 51.6 | 144 45.8 | 15.6 | 184 41.1 | 04.9 | 227 46.0 | 10.9 | Suhail | 222 48.2 | S43 31.3 |
| 17 | 208 14.4 | 95 06.3 | 51.3 | 159 46.6 | 16.0 | 199 43.6 | 04.9 | 242 48.7 | 11.0 | | | |
| 18 | 223 16.8 | 110 05.5 | N21 50.9 | 174 47.5 | N16 16.4 | 214 46.1 | N 2 04.9 | 257 51.3 | S15 11.0 | Vega | 80 34.2 | N38 48.4 |
| 19 | 238 19.3 | 125 04.8 | 50.5 | 189 48.4 | 16.9 | 229 48.6 | 04.8 | 272 53.9 | 11.1 | Zuben'ubi | 136 58.2 | S16 08.1 |
| 20 | 253 21.8 | 140 04.0 | 50.1 | 204 49.3 | 17.3 | 244 51.1 | 04.8 | 287 56.6 | 11.2 | | SHA | Mer. Pass. |
| 21 | 268 24.2 | 155 03.2 . . | 49.8 | 219 50.1 . . | 17.8 | 259 53.6 . . | 04.8 | 302 59.2 . . | 11.2 | | ° ′ | h m |
| 22 | 283 26.7 | 170 02.4 | 49.4 | 234 51.0 | 18.2 | 274 56.2 | 04.7 | 318 01.9 | 11.3 | Venus | 249 05.7 | 10 38 |
| 23 | 298 29.1 | 185 01.6 | 49.0 | 249 51.9 | 18.6 | 289 58.7 | 04.7 | 333 04.5 | 11.3 | Mars | 312 37.6 | 6 23 |
| Mer. Pass. | h m 3 13.2 | v −0.8 | d 0.3 | v 0.9 | d 0.4 | v 2.5 | d 0.0 | v 2.6 | d 0.1 | Jupiter | 351 27.6 | 3 47 |
| | | | | | | | | | | Saturn | 34 27.1 | 0 56 |

### SUN and MOON

| UT | SUN GHA | SUN Dec | MOON GHA | v | MOON Dec | d | HP |
|---|---|---|---|---|---|---|---|
| d h | ° ′ | ° ′ | ° ′ | ′ | ° ′ | ′ | ′ |
| **2 00** | 178 24.9 | N17 49.0 | 130 59.8 | 15.2 | N 4 25.4 | 14.2 | 55.8 |
| 01 | 193 24.9 | 48.4 | 145 34.0 | 15.3 | 4 11.2 | 14.2 | 55.9 |
| 02 | 208 25.0 | 47.7 | 160 08.3 | 15.2 | 3 57.0 | 14.2 | 55.9 |
| 03 | 223 25.0 .. | 47.1 | 174 42.5 | 15.2 | 3 42.8 | 14.2 | 55.9 |
| 04 | 238 25.0 | 46.4 | 189 16.7 | 15.2 | 3 28.6 | 14.3 | 55.9 |
| 05 | 253 25.1 | 45.8 | 203 50.9 | 15.2 | 3 14.3 | 14.3 | 56.0 |
| 06 | 268 25.1 | N17 45.2 | 218 25.1 | 15.1 | N 3 00.0 | 14.3 | 56.0 |
| 07 | 283 25.2 | 44.5 | 232 59.2 | 15.2 | 2 45.7 | 14.3 | 56.0 |
| T 08 | 298 25.2 | 43.9 | 247 33.4 | 15.2 | 2 31.4 | 14.4 | 56.0 |
| U 09 | 313 25.3 .. | 43.2 | 262 07.6 | 15.1 | 2 17.0 | 14.4 | 56.1 |
| E 10 | 328 25.3 | 42.6 | 276 41.7 | 15.1 | 2 02.6 | 14.4 | 56.1 |
| S 11 | 343 25.3 | 41.9 | 291 15.8 | 15.1 | 1 48.2 | 14.4 | 56.1 |
| D 12 | 358 25.4 | N17 41.3 | 305 49.9 | 15.1 | N 1 33.8 | 14.4 | 56.1 |
| A 13 | 13 25.4 | 40.7 | 320 24.0 | 15.1 | 1 19.4 | 14.5 | 56.1 |
| Y 14 | 28 25.5 | 40.0 | 334 58.1 | 15.1 | 1 04.9 | 14.4 | 56.2 |
| 15 | 43 25.5 .. | 39.4 | 349 32.2 | 15.0 | 0 50.5 | 14.5 | 56.2 |
| 16 | 58 25.6 | 38.7 | 4 06.2 | 15.1 | 0 36.0 | 14.5 | 56.2 |
| 17 | 73 25.6 | 38.1 | 18 40.3 | 15.0 | 0 21.5 | 14.5 | 56.2 |
| 18 | 88 25.7 | N17 37.4 | 33 14.3 | 14.9 | N 0 07.0 | 14.6 | 56.3 |
| 19 | 103 25.7 | 36.8 | 47 48.2 | 15.0 | S 0 07.6 | 14.5 | 56.3 |
| 20 | 118 25.8 | 36.1 | 62 22.2 | 14.9 | 0 22.1 | 14.6 | 56.3 |
| 21 | 133 25.8 .. | 35.5 | 76 56.1 | 14.9 | 0 36.7 | 14.5 | 56.3 |
| 22 | 148 25.9 | 34.8 | 91 30.0 | 14.9 | 0 51.2 | 14.6 | 56.4 |
| 23 | 163 25.9 | 34.2 | 106 03.9 | 14.9 | 1 05.8 | 14.6 | 56.4 |
| **3 00** | 178 26.0 | N17 33.5 | 120 37.8 | 14.8 | S 1 20.4 | 14.5 | 56.4 |
| 01 | 193 26.0 | 32.9 | 135 11.6 | 14.8 | 1 34.9 | 14.6 | 56.5 |
| 02 | 208 26.1 | 32.2 | 149 45.4 | 14.7 | 1 49.5 | 14.6 | 56.5 |
| 03 | 223 26.1 .. | 31.6 | 164 19.1 | 14.7 | 2 04.1 | 14.6 | 56.5 |
| 04 | 238 26.2 | 30.9 | 178 52.8 | 14.7 | 2 18.7 | 14.6 | 56.5 |
| 05 | 253 26.2 | 30.3 | 193 26.5 | 14.7 | 2 33.3 | 14.6 | 56.6 |
| 06 | 268 26.3 | N17 29.6 | 208 00.2 | 14.6 | S 2 47.9 | 14.6 | 56.6 |
| W 07 | 283 26.3 | 29.0 | 222 33.8 | 14.6 | 3 02.5 | 14.6 | 56.6 |
| E 08 | 298 26.4 | 28.3 | 237 07.4 | 14.5 | 3 17.1 | 14.6 | 56.6 |
| D 09 | 313 26.4 .. | 27.7 | 251 40.9 | 14.5 | 3 31.7 | 14.6 | 56.7 |
| N 10 | 328 26.5 | 27.0 | 266 14.4 | 14.4 | 3 46.3 | 14.6 | 56.7 |
| E 11 | 343 26.5 | 26.3 | 280 47.8 | 14.4 | 4 00.9 | 14.6 | 56.7 |
| S 12 | 358 26.6 | N17 25.7 | 295 21.2 | 14.4 | S 4 15.5 | 14.6 | 56.7 |
| D 13 | 13 26.6 | 25.0 | 309 54.6 | 14.3 | 4 30.1 | 14.6 | 56.8 |
| A 14 | 28 26.7 | 24.4 | 324 27.9 | 14.3 | 4 44.7 | 14.6 | 56.8 |
| Y 15 | 43 26.7 .. | 23.7 | 339 01.2 | 14.2 | 4 59.3 | 14.6 | 56.8 |
| 16 | 58 26.8 | 23.1 | 353 34.4 | 14.2 | 5 13.9 | 14.5 | 56.9 |
| 17 | 73 26.8 | 22.4 | 8 07.6 | 14.1 | 5 28.4 | 14.6 | 56.9 |
| 18 | 88 26.9 | N17 21.7 | 22 40.7 | 14.1 | S 5 43.0 | 14.5 | 56.9 |
| 19 | 103 26.9 | 21.1 | 37 13.8 | 14.0 | 5 57.5 | 14.5 | 56.9 |
| 20 | 118 27.0 | 20.4 | 51 46.8 | 13.9 | 6 12.0 | 14.5 | 57.0 |
| 21 | 133 27.1 .. | 19.8 | 66 19.7 | 13.9 | 6 26.6 | 14.5 | 57.0 |
| 22 | 148 27.1 | 19.1 | 80 52.6 | 13.9 | 6 41.1 | 14.4 | 57.0 |
| 23 | 163 27.2 | 18.4 | 95 25.5 | 13.8 | 6 55.5 | 14.5 | 57.1 |
| **4 00** | 178 27.2 | N17 17.8 | 109 58.3 | 13.7 | S 7 10.0 | 14.5 | 57.1 |
| 01 | 193 27.3 | 17.1 | 124 31.0 | 13.7 | 7 24.5 | 14.4 | 57.1 |
| 02 | 208 27.3 | 16.4 | 139 03.7 | 13.6 | 7 38.9 | 14.4 | 57.1 |
| 03 | 223 27.4 .. | 15.8 | 153 36.3 | 13.5 | 7 53.3 | 14.4 | 57.2 |
| 04 | 238 27.4 | 15.1 | 168 08.8 | 13.5 | 8 07.7 | 14.4 | 57.2 |
| 05 | 253 27.5 | 14.5 | 182 41.3 | 13.4 | 8 22.1 | 14.3 | 57.2 |
| 06 | 268 27.6 | N17 13.8 | 197 13.7 | 13.3 | S 8 36.4 | 14.3 | 57.3 |
| 07 | 283 27.6 | 13.1 | 211 46.0 | 13.3 | 8 50.7 | 14.3 | 57.3 |
| T 08 | 298 27.7 | 12.5 | 226 18.3 | 13.2 | 9 05.0 | 14.3 | 57.3 |
| H 09 | 313 27.7 .. | 11.8 | 240 50.5 | 13.1 | 9 19.3 | 14.3 | 57.4 |
| U 10 | 328 27.8 | 11.1 | 255 22.6 | 13.0 | 9 33.6 | 14.2 | 57.4 |
| R 11 | 343 27.8 | 10.5 | 269 54.6 | 13.0 | 9 47.8 | 14.1 | 57.4 |
| S 12 | 358 27.9 | N17 09.8 | 284 26.6 | 12.9 | S10 01.9 | 14.2 | 57.4 |
| D 13 | 13 28.0 | 09.1 | 298 58.5 | 12.8 | 10 16.1 | 14.1 | 57.5 |
| A 14 | 28 28.0 | 08.5 | 313 30.3 | 12.8 | 10 30.2 | 14.1 | 57.5 |
| Y 15 | 43 28.1 .. | 07.8 | 328 02.1 | 12.7 | 10 44.3 | 14.0 | 57.5 |
| 16 | 58 28.1 | 07.1 | 342 33.8 | 12.5 | 10 58.3 | 14.0 | 57.6 |
| 17 | 73 28.2 | 06.4 | 357 05.3 | 12.5 | 11 12.3 | 14.0 | 57.6 |
| 18 | 88 28.3 | N17 05.8 | 11 36.8 | 12.5 | S11 26.3 | 13.9 | 57.6 |
| 19 | 103 28.3 | 05.1 | 26 08.3 | 12.3 | 11 40.2 | 13.9 | 57.7 |
| 20 | 118 28.4 | 04.4 | 40 39.6 | 12.3 | 11 54.1 | 13.9 | 57.7 |
| 21 | 133 28.4 .. | 03.8 | 55 10.9 | 12.1 | 12 08.0 | 13.8 | 57.7 |
| 22 | 148 28.5 | 03.1 | 69 42.0 | 12.1 | 12 21.8 | 13.7 | 57.7 |
| 23 | 163 28.6 | 02.4 | 84 13.1 | 12.0 | S12 35.5 | 13.7 | 57.8 |
| | SD 15.8 | d 0.7 | SD 15.3 | | 15.5 | | 15.7 |

### Twilight, Sunrise and Moonrise

| Lat. | Twilight Naut. | Twilight Civil | Sunrise | Moonrise 2 | 3 | 4 | 5 |
|---|---|---|---|---|---|---|---|
| ° | h m | h m | h m | h m | h m | h m | h m |
| N 72 | ☐ | ☐ | ☐ | 09 05 | 11 09 | 13 24 | 16 23 |
| N 70 | //// | //// | 01 43 | 09 08 | 11 03 | 13 06 | 15 32 |
| 68 | //// | //// | 02 25 | 09 11 | 10 58 | 12 52 | 15 00 |
| 66 | //// | 00 52 | 02 53 | 09 13 | 10 54 | 12 40 | 14 37 |
| 64 | //// | 01 51 | 03 14 | 09 15 | 10 50 | 12 31 | 14 19 |
| 62 | //// | 02 23 | 03 31 | 09 16 | 10 47 | 12 23 | 14 04 |
| 60 | 00 47 | 02 46 | 03 45 | 09 18 | 10 45 | 12 16 | 13 52 |
| N 58 | 01 40 | 03 05 | 03 57 | 09 19 | 10 43 | 12 10 | 13 42 |
| 56 | 02 10 | 03 20 | 04 08 | 09 20 | 10 41 | 12 04 | 13 32 |
| 54 | 02 32 | 03 33 | 04 17 | 09 21 | 10 39 | 11 59 | 13 24 |
| 52 | 02 49 | 03 44 | 04 25 | 09 22 | 10 37 | 11 55 | 13 17 |
| 50 | 03 04 | 03 54 | 04 32 | 09 22 | 10 36 | 11 51 | 13 11 |
| 45 | 03 32 | 04 14 | 04 47 | 09 24 | 10 32 | 11 43 | 12 57 |
| N 40 | 03 53 | 04 30 | 05 00 | 09 25 | 10 30 | 11 36 | 12 45 |
| 35 | 04 10 | 04 43 | 05 11 | 09 27 | 10 27 | 11 30 | 12 36 |
| 30 | 04 23 | 04 54 | 05 20 | 09 28 | 10 25 | 11 25 | 12 27 |
| 20 | 04 45 | 05 13 | 05 36 | 09 30 | 10 22 | 11 16 | 12 13 |
| N 10 | 05 02 | 05 28 | 05 50 | 09 31 | 10 19 | 11 08 | 12 01 |
| 0 | 05 16 | 05 41 | 06 03 | 09 33 | 10 16 | 11 01 | 11 49 |
| S 10 | 05 28 | 05 53 | 06 15 | 09 34 | 10 13 | 10 54 | 11 37 |
| 20 | 05 39 | 06 06 | 06 29 | 09 36 | 10 10 | 10 46 | 11 25 |
| 30 | 05 50 | 06 19 | 06 44 | 09 38 | 10 07 | 10 38 | 11 11 |
| 35 | 05 56 | 06 26 | 06 53 | 09 39 | 10 05 | 10 33 | 11 03 |
| 40 | 06 02 | 06 34 | 07 03 | 09 40 | 10 03 | 10 27 | 10 54 |
| 45 | 06 08 | 06 43 | 07 14 | 09 42 | 10 01 | 10 21 | 10 44 |
| S 50 | 06 15 | 06 54 | 07 29 | 09 44 | 09 58 | 10 13 | 10 31 |
| 52 | 06 18 | 06 58 | 07 35 | 09 44 | 09 56 | 10 10 | 10 25 |
| 54 | 06 21 | 07 03 | 07 42 | 09 45 | 09 55 | 10 06 | 10 19 |
| 56 | 06 24 | 07 09 | 07 51 | 09 46 | 09 53 | 10 02 | 10 12 |
| 58 | 06 28 | 07 15 | 08 00 | 09 47 | 09 52 | 09 57 | 10 04 |
| S 60 | 06 31 | 07 22 | 08 10 | 09 48 | 09 50 | 09 52 | 09 55 |

### Sunset, Twilight and Moonset

| Lat. | Sunset | Twilight Civil | Twilight Naut. | Moonset 2 | 3 | 4 | 5 |
|---|---|---|---|---|---|---|---|
| ° | h m | h m | h m | h m | h m | h m | h m |
| N 72 | ☐ | ☐ | ☐ | 21 42 | 21 11 | 20 32 | 19 15 |
| N 70 | 22 23 | //// | //// | 21 44 | 21 21 | 20 53 | 20 09 |
| 68 | 21 44 | //// | //// | 21 44 | 21 28 | 21 09 | 20 42 |
| 66 | 21 16 | 23 09 | //// | 21 45 | 21 34 | 21 22 | 21 06 |
| 64 | 20 56 | 22 17 | //// | 21 46 | 21 40 | 21 33 | 21 25 |
| 62 | 20 39 | 21 46 | //// | 21 47 | 21 44 | 21 43 | 21 41 |
| 60 | 20 26 | 21 24 | 23 15 | 21 47 | 21 49 | 21 51 | 21 55 |
| N 58 | 20 14 | 21 06 | 22 28 | 21 48 | 21 52 | 21 58 | 22 06 |
| 56 | 20 04 | 20 51 | 22 00 | 21 48 | 21 56 | 22 04 | 22 14 |
| 54 | 19 55 | 20 38 | 21 39 | 21 48 | 21 58 | 22 10 | 22 25 |
| 52 | 19 47 | 20 27 | 21 22 | 21 49 | 22 01 | 22 15 | 22 33 |
| 50 | 19 39 | 20 18 | 21 07 | 21 49 | 22 04 | 22 20 | 22 40 |
| 45 | 19 24 | 19 58 | 20 39 | 21 50 | 22 09 | 22 30 | 22 55 |
| N 40 | 19 12 | 19 42 | 20 19 | 21 50 | 22 13 | 22 39 | 23 08 |
| 35 | 19 01 | 19 29 | 20 02 | 21 51 | 22 17 | 22 46 | 23 19 |
| 30 | 18 52 | 19 18 | 19 49 | 21 51 | 22 21 | 22 53 | 23 29 |
| 20 | 18 36 | 18 59 | 19 27 | 21 52 | 22 27 | 23 04 | 23 45 |
| N 10 | 18 22 | 18 44 | 19 10 | 21 53 | 22 32 | 23 14 | 24 00 |
| 0 | 18 10 | 18 31 | 18 57 | 21 53 | 22 37 | 23 23 | 24 13 |
| S 10 | 17 57 | 18 19 | 18 44 | 21 54 | 22 42 | 23 33 | 24 27 |
| 20 | 17 44 | 18 07 | 18 33 | 21 55 | 22 47 | 23 43 | 24 44 |
| 30 | 17 29 | 17 54 | 18 23 | 21 55 | 22 54 | 23 54 | 24 59 |
| 35 | 17 20 | 17 47 | 18 17 | 21 56 | 22 57 | 24 01 | 00 01 |
| 40 | 17 10 | 17 39 | 18 11 | 21 56 | 23 01 | 24 09 | 00 09 |
| 45 | 16 58 | 17 30 | 18 05 | 21 57 | 23 06 | 24 18 | 00 18 |
| S 50 | 16 44 | 17 20 | 17 58 | 21 57 | 23 11 | 24 29 | 00 29 |
| 52 | 16 38 | 17 15 | 17 56 | 21 57 | 23 14 | 24 34 | 00 34 |
| 54 | 16 31 | 17 10 | 17 53 | 21 58 | 23 17 | 24 39 | 00 39 |
| 56 | 16 23 | 17 04 | 17 49 | 21 58 | 23 20 | 24 46 | 00 46 |
| 58 | 16 14 | 16 58 | 17 46 | 21 58 | 23 24 | 24 53 | 00 53 |
| S 60 | 16 03 | 16 51 | 17 42 | 21 59 | 23 27 | 25 00 | 01 00 |

### SUN and MOON

| | SUN | | | MOON | | | |
|---|---|---|---|---|---|---|---|
| Day | Eqn. of Time 00h | 12h | Mer. Pass. | Mer. Pass. Upper | Lower | Age | Phase |
| d | m s | m s | h m | h m | h m | d | % |
| 2 | 06 21 | 06 19 | 12 06 | 15 43 | 03 22 | 05 | 21 |
| 3 | 06 16 | 06 14 | 12 06 | 16 27 | 04 05 | 06 | 30 |
| 4 | 06 11 | 06 09 | 12 06 | 17 12 | 04 49 | 07 | 40 |

| UT | ARIES GHA | VENUS −3.9 GHA | Dec | MARS +0.1 GHA | Dec | JUPITER −2.7 GHA | Dec | SATURN +0.3 GHA | Dec | STARS Name | SHA | Dec |
|---|---|---|---|---|---|---|---|---|---|---|---|---|
| **5 00** | 313 31.6 | 200 00.8 | N21 48.6 | 264 52.8 | N16 19.1 | 305 01.2 | N 2 04.7 | 348 07.2 | S15 11.4 | Acamar | 315 13.3 | S40 12.6 |
| 01 | 328 34.1 | 215 00.0 | 48.3 | 279 53.6 | 19.5 | 320 03.7 | 04.6 | 3 09.8 | 11.5 | Achernar | 335 21.5 | S57 07.1 |
| 02 | 343 36.5 | 229 59.2 | 47.9 | 294 54.5 | 19.9 | 335 06.2 | 04.6 | 18 12.4 | 11.5 | Acrux | 173 02.7 | S63 13.6 |
| 03 | 358 39.0 | 244 58.4 .. | 47.5 | 309 55.4 .. | 20.4 | 350 08.7 .. | 04.6 | 33 15.1 .. | 11.6 | Adhara | 255 07.8 | S29 00.0 |
| 04 | 13 41.5 | 259 57.6 | 47.1 | 324 56.3 | 20.8 | 5 11.2 | 04.5 | 48 17.7 | 11.7 | Aldebaran | 290 42.1 | N16 33.2 |
| 05 | 28 43.9 | 274 56.8 | 46.8 | 339 57.2 | 21.3 | 20 13.8 | 04.5 | 63 20.4 | 11.7 | | | |
| 06 | 43 46.4 | 289 56.0 | N21 46.4 | 354 58.0 | N16 21.7 | 35 16.3 | N 2 04.5 | 78 23.0 | S15 11.8 | Alioth | 166 15.0 | N55 50.6 |
| 07 | 58 48.9 | 304 55.3 | 46.0 | 9 58.9 | 22.1 | 50 18.8 | 04.4 | 93 25.6 | 11.9 | Alkaid | 152 53.7 | N49 12.4 |
| F 08 | 73 51.3 | 319 54.5 | 45.6 | 24 59.8 | 22.6 | 65 21.3 | 04.4 | 108 28.3 | 11.9 | Alnair | 27 35.0 | S46 51.0 |
| R 09 | 88 53.8 | 334 53.7 .. | 45.2 | 40 00.7 .. | 23.0 | 80 23.8 .. | 04.4 | 123 30.9 .. | 12.0 | Alnilam | 275 40.0 | S 1 11.2 |
| I 10 | 103 56.3 | 349 52.9 | 44.8 | 55 01.5 | 23.4 | 95 26.3 | 04.3 | 138 33.6 | 12.1 | Alphard | 217 50.0 | S 8 45.2 |
| D 11 | 118 58.7 | 4 52.1 | 44.4 | 70 02.4 | 23.9 | 110 28.8 | 04.3 | 153 36.2 | 12.1 | | | |
| A 12 | 134 01.2 | 19 51.3 | N21 44.1 | 85 03.3 | N16 24.3 | 125 31.4 | N 2 04.3 | 168 38.9 | S15 12.2 | Alphecca | 126 05.4 | N26 38.6 |
| Y 13 | 149 03.6 | 34 50.5 | 43.7 | 100 04.2 | 24.7 | 140 33.9 | 04.2 | 183 41.5 | 12.2 | Alpheratz | 357 36.6 | N29 12.8 |
| 14 | 164 06.1 | 49 49.7 | 43.3 | 115 05.1 | 25.2 | 155 36.4 | 04.2 | 198 44.1 | 12.3 | Altair | 62 01.6 | N 8 55.7 |
| 15 | 179 08.6 | 64 48.9 .. | 42.9 | 130 05.9 .. | 25.6 | 170 38.9 .. | 04.1 | 213 46.8 .. | 12.4 | Ankaa | 353 08.9 | S42 10.8 |
| 16 | 194 11.0 | 79 48.2 | 42.5 | 145 06.8 | 26.0 | 185 41.4 | 04.1 | 228 49.4 | 12.4 | Antares | 112 18.1 | S26 28.9 |
| 17 | 209 13.5 | 94 47.4 | 42.1 | 160 07.7 | 26.5 | 200 44.0 | 04.1 | 243 52.1 | 12.5 | | | |
| 18 | 224 16.0 | 109 46.6 | N21 41.7 | 175 08.6 | N16 26.9 | 215 46.5 | N 2 04.0 | 258 54.7 | S15 12.6 | Arcturus | 145 49.8 | N19 04.1 |
| 19 | 239 18.4 | 124 45.8 | 41.3 | 190 09.5 | 27.3 | 230 49.0 | 04.0 | 273 57.4 | 12.6 | Atria | 107 13.8 | S69 04.2 |
| 20 | 254 20.9 | 139 45.0 | 40.9 | 205 10.3 | 27.8 | 245 51.5 | 04.0 | 289 00.0 | 12.7 | Avior | 234 16.2 | S59 34.8 |
| 21 | 269 23.4 | 154 44.2 .. | 40.5 | 220 11.2 .. | 28.2 | 260 54.0 .. | 03.9 | 304 02.6 .. | 12.8 | Bellatrix | 278 25.2 | N 6 22.3 |
| 22 | 284 25.8 | 169 43.4 | 40.1 | 235 12.1 | 28.6 | 275 56.6 | 03.9 | 319 05.3 | 12.8 | Betelgeuse | 270 54.5 | N 7 24.7 |
| 23 | 299 28.3 | 184 42.6 | 39.7 | 250 13.0 | 29.1 | 290 59.1 | 03.8 | 334 07.9 | 12.9 | | | |
| **6 00** | 314 30.8 | 199 41.9 | N21 39.3 | 265 13.9 | N16 29.5 | 306 01.6 | N 2 03.8 | 349 10.6 | S15 13.0 | Canopus | 263 53.7 | S52 42.2 |
| 01 | 329 33.2 | 214 41.1 | 38.9 | 280 14.7 | 29.9 | 321 04.1 | 03.8 | 4 13.2 | 13.0 | Capella | 280 25.1 | N46 01.1 |
| 02 | 344 35.7 | 229 40.3 | 38.5 | 295 15.6 | 30.4 | 336 06.6 | 03.7 | 19 15.9 | 13.1 | Deneb | 49 26.7 | N45 21.7 |
| 03 | 359 38.1 | 244 39.5 .. | 38.1 | 310 16.5 .. | 30.8 | 351 09.2 .. | 03.7 | 34 18.5 .. | 13.1 | Denebola | 182 27.2 | N14 27.0 |
| 04 | 14 40.6 | 259 38.7 | 37.7 | 325 17.4 | 31.2 | 6 11.7 | 03.7 | 49 21.1 | 13.2 | Diphda | 348 49.1 | S17 51.7 |
| 05 | 29 43.1 | 274 37.9 | 37.3 | 340 18.3 | 31.7 | 21 14.2 | 03.6 | 64 23.8 | 13.2 | | | |
| 06 | 44 45.5 | 289 37.1 | N21 36.9 | 355 19.1 | N16 32.1 | 36 16.7 | N 2 03.6 | 79 26.4 | S15 13.3 | Dubhe | 193 44.0 | N61 38.0 |
| S 07 | 59 48.0 | 304 36.4 | 36.5 | 10 20.0 | 32.5 | 51 19.2 | 03.5 | 94 29.1 | 13.4 | Elnath | 278 04.6 | N28 37.5 |
| A 08 | 74 50.5 | 319 35.6 | 36.1 | 25 20.9 | 33.0 | 66 21.8 | 03.5 | 109 31.7 | 13.5 | Eltanin | 90 42.7 | N51 29.4 |
| T 09 | 89 52.9 | 334 34.8 .. | 35.6 | 40 21.8 .. | 33.4 | 81 24.3 .. | 03.5 | 124 34.4 .. | 13.5 | Enif | 33 40.4 | N 9 58.7 |
| U 10 | 104 55.4 | 349 34.0 | 35.2 | 55 22.7 | 33.8 | 96 26.8 | 03.4 | 139 37.0 | 13.6 | Fomalhaut | 15 16.4 | S29 30.1 |
| R 11 | 119 57.9 | 4 33.2 | 34.8 | 70 23.5 | 34.2 | 111 29.3 | 03.4 | 154 39.6 | 13.7 | | | |
| D 12 | 135 00.3 | 19 32.4 | N21 34.4 | 85 24.4 | N16 34.7 | 126 31.9 | N 2 03.4 | 169 42.3 | S15 13.7 | Gacrux | 171 54.2 | S57 14.5 |
| A 13 | 150 02.8 | 34 31.7 | 34.0 | 100 25.3 | 35.1 | 141 34.4 | 03.3 | 184 44.9 | 13.8 | Gienah | 175 45.9 | S17 40.0 |
| Y 14 | 165 05.2 | 49 30.9 | 33.6 | 115 26.2 | 35.5 | 156 36.9 | 03.3 | 199 47.6 | 13.8 | Hadar | 148 38.9 | S60 29.1 |
| 15 | 180 07.7 | 64 30.1 .. | 33.1 | 130 27.1 .. | 36.0 | 171 39.4 .. | 03.2 | 214 50.2 .. | 13.9 | Hamal | 327 53.4 | N23 34.0 |
| 16 | 195 10.2 | 79 29.3 | 32.7 | 145 28.0 | 36.4 | 186 42.0 | 03.2 | 229 52.9 | 14.0 | Kaus Aust. | 83 34.8 | S34 22.4 |
| 17 | 210 12.6 | 94 28.5 | 32.3 | 160 28.8 | 36.8 | 201 44.5 | 03.2 | 244 55.5 | 14.0 | | | |
| 18 | 225 15.1 | 109 27.7 | N21 31.9 | 175 29.7 | N16 37.2 | 216 47.0 | N 2 03.1 | 259 58.1 | S15 14.1 | Kochab | 137 19.8 | N74 04.1 |
| 19 | 240 17.6 | 124 27.0 | 31.5 | 190 30.6 | 37.7 | 231 49.6 | 03.1 | 275 00.8 | 14.2 | Markab | 13 31.6 | N15 19.6 |
| 20 | 255 20.0 | 139 26.2 | 31.0 | 205 31.5 | 38.1 | 246 52.1 | 03.0 | 290 03.4 | 14.2 | Menkar | 314 08.3 | N 4 10.7 |
| 21 | 270 22.5 | 154 25.4 .. | 30.6 | 220 32.4 .. | 38.5 | 261 54.6 .. | 03.0 | 305 06.1 .. | 14.3 | Menkent | 148 00.0 | S36 28.9 |
| 22 | 285 25.0 | 169 24.6 | 30.2 | 235 33.3 | 38.9 | 276 57.1 | 03.0 | 320 08.7 | 14.4 | Miaplacidus | 221 39.6 | S69 48.5 |
| 23 | 300 27.4 | 184 23.8 | 29.8 | 250 34.2 | 39.4 | 291 59.7 | 02.9 | 335 11.4 | 14.4 | | | |
| **7 00** | 315 29.9 | 199 23.1 | N21 29.3 | 265 35.0 | N16 39.8 | 307 02.2 | N 2 02.9 | 350 14.0 | S15 14.5 | Mirfak | 308 31.2 | N49 56.2 |
| 01 | 330 32.4 | 214 22.3 | 28.9 | 280 35.9 | 40.2 | 322 04.7 | 02.8 | 5 16.6 | 14.6 | Nunki | 75 49.9 | S26 16.1 |
| 02 | 345 34.8 | 229 21.5 | 28.5 | 295 36.8 | 40.6 | 337 07.2 | 02.8 | 20 19.3 | 14.6 | Peacock | 53 08.3 | S56 39.7 |
| 03 | 0 37.3 | 244 20.7 .. | 28.0 | 310 37.7 .. | 41.1 | 352 09.8 .. | 02.8 | 35 21.9 .. | 14.7 | Pollux | 243 20.1 | N27 58.4 |
| 04 | 15 39.7 | 259 19.9 | 27.6 | 325 38.6 | 41.5 | 7 12.3 | 02.7 | 50 24.6 | 14.7 | Procyon | 244 53.2 | N 5 10.1 |
| 05 | 30 42.2 | 274 19.2 | 27.2 | 340 39.5 | 41.9 | 22 14.8 | 02.7 | 65 27.2 | 14.8 | | | |
| 06 | 45 44.7 | 289 18.4 | N21 26.7 | 355 40.4 | N16 42.3 | 37 17.4 | N 2 02.6 | 80 29.9 | S15 14.9 | Rasalhague | 96 00.2 | N12 32.8 |
| 07 | 60 47.1 | 304 17.6 | 26.3 | 10 41.2 | 42.8 | 52 19.9 | 02.6 | 95 32.5 | 14.9 | Regulus | 207 36.9 | N11 51.6 |
| S 08 | 75 49.6 | 319 16.8 | 25.9 | 25 42.1 | 43.2 | 67 22.4 | 02.6 | 110 35.1 | 15.0 | Rigel | 281 06.0 | S 8 10.4 |
| U 09 | 90 52.1 | 334 16.0 .. | 25.4 | 40 43.0 .. | 43.6 | 82 25.0 .. | 02.5 | 125 37.8 .. | 15.1 | Rigil Kent. | 139 43.1 | S60 55.8 |
| N 10 | 105 54.5 | 349 15.3 | 25.0 | 55 43.9 | 44.0 | 97 27.5 | 02.5 | 140 40.4 | 15.1 | Sabik | 102 04.9 | S15 45.1 |
| D 11 | 120 57.0 | 4 14.5 | 24.6 | 70 44.8 | 44.5 | 112 30.0 | 02.4 | 155 43.1 | 15.2 | | | |
| A 12 | 135 59.5 | 19 13.7 | N21 24.1 | 85 45.7 | N16 44.9 | 127 32.6 | N 2 02.4 | 170 45.7 | S15 15.3 | Schedar | 349 33.0 | N56 39.4 |
| Y 13 | 151 01.9 | 34 12.9 | 23.7 | 100 46.6 | 45.3 | 142 35.1 | 02.3 | 185 48.4 | 15.3 | Shaula | 96 12.8 | S37 07.2 |
| 14 | 166 04.4 | 49 12.2 | 23.2 | 115 47.4 | 45.7 | 157 37.6 | 02.3 | 200 51.0 | 15.4 | Sirius | 258 28.3 | S16 44.7 |
| 15 | 181 06.9 | 64 11.4 .. | 22.8 | 130 48.3 .. | 46.1 | 172 40.2 .. | 02.3 | 215 53.7 .. | 15.5 | Spica | 158 24.5 | S11 16.6 |
| 16 | 196 09.3 | 79 10.6 | 22.3 | 145 49.2 | 46.6 | 187 42.7 | 02.2 | 230 56.3 | 15.5 | Suhail | 222 48.2 | S43 31.3 |
| 17 | 211 11.8 | 94 09.8 | 21.9 | 160 50.1 | 47.0 | 202 45.2 | 02.2 | 245 58.9 | 15.6 | | | |
| 18 | 226 14.2 | 109 09.1 | N21 21.4 | 175 51.0 | N16 47.4 | 217 47.8 | N 2 02.1 | 261 01.6 | S15 15.6 | Vega | 80 34.2 | N38 48.4 |
| 19 | 241 16.7 | 124 08.3 | 21.0 | 190 51.9 | 47.8 | 232 50.3 | 02.1 | 276 04.2 | 15.7 | Zuben'ubi | 136 58.2 | S16 08.1 |
| 20 | 256 19.2 | 139 07.5 | 20.5 | 205 52.8 | 48.2 | 247 52.8 | 02.0 | 291 06.9 | 15.8 | | SHA | Mer.Pass. |
| 21 | 271 21.6 | 154 06.7 .. | 20.1 | 220 53.7 .. | 48.7 | 262 55.4 .. | 02.0 | 306 09.5 .. | 15.8 | | | |
| 22 | 286 24.1 | 169 06.0 | 19.6 | 235 54.6 | 49.1 | 277 57.9 | 02.0 | 321 12.2 | 15.9 | Venus | 245 11.1 | 10 42 |
| 23 | 301 26.6 | 184 05.2 | 19.2 | 250 55.4 | 49.5 | 293 00.4 | 01.9 | 336 14.8 | 16.0 | Mars | 310 43.1 | 6 19 |
| Mer.Pass. | 3 01.5 | v −0.8 | d 0.4 | v 0.9 | d 0.4 | v 2.5 | d 0.0 | v 2.6 | d 0.1 | Jupiter | 351 30.8 | 3 35 |
| | | | | | | | | | | Saturn | 34 39.8 | 0 43 |

### SUN and MOON

| UT | SUN GHA | SUN Dec | MOON GHA | v | MOON Dec | d | HP |
|---|---|---|---|---|---|---|---|
| d h | ° ′ | ° ′ | ° ′ | ′ | ° ′ | ′ | ′ |
| **5** 00 | 178 28.6 | N17 01.7 | 98 44.1 | 11.9 | S12 49.2 | 13.7 | 57.8 |
| 01 | 193 28.7 | 01.1 | 113 15.0 | 11.8 | 13 02.9 | 13.6 | 57.8 |
| 02 | 208 28.8 | 17 00.4 | 127 45.8 | 11.7 | 13 16.5 | 13.6 | 57.9 |
| 03 | 223 28.8 | 16 59.7 | 142 16.5 | 11.6 | 13 30.1 | 13.5 | 57.9 |
| 04 | 238 28.9 | 59.0 | 156 47.1 | 11.5 | 13 43.6 | 13.5 | 57.9 |
| 05 | 253 28.9 | 58.4 | 171 17.6 | 11.5 | 13 57.1 | 13.4 | 58.0 |
| 06 | 268 29.0 | N16 57.7 | 185 48.1 | 11.3 | S14 10.5 | 13.3 | 58.0 |
| 07 | 283 29.1 | 57.0 | 200 18.4 | 11.2 | 14 23.8 | 13.3 | 58.0 |
| 08 | 298 29.1 | 56.3 | 214 48.6 | 11.2 | 14 37.1 | 13.2 | 58.1 |
| F 09 | 313 29.2 | 55.7 | 229 18.8 | 11.0 | 14 50.3 | 13.2 | 58.1 |
| R 10 | 328 29.3 | 55.0 | 243 48.8 | 10.9 | 15 03.5 | 13.1 | 58.1 |
| I 11 | 343 29.3 | 54.3 | 258 18.7 | 10.8 | 15 16.6 | 13.0 | 58.2 |
| D 12 | 358 29.4 | N16 53.6 | 272 48.5 | 10.8 | S15 29.6 | 13.0 | 58.2 |
| A 13 | 13 29.5 | 52.9 | 287 18.3 | 10.6 | 15 42.6 | 12.9 | 58.2 |
| Y 14 | 28 29.5 | 52.3 | 301 47.9 | 10.5 | 15 55.5 | 12.8 | 58.2 |
| 15 | 43 29.6 | 51.6 | 316 17.4 | 10.4 | 16 08.3 | 12.8 | 58.3 |
| 16 | 58 29.7 | 50.9 | 330 46.8 | 10.3 | 16 21.1 | 12.7 | 58.3 |
| 17 | 73 29.7 | 50.2 | 345 16.1 | 10.2 | 16 33.8 | 12.6 | 58.3 |
| 18 | 88 29.8 | N16 49.5 | 359 45.3 | 10.0 | S16 46.4 | 12.6 | 58.4 |
| 19 | 103 29.9 | 48.8 | 14 14.3 | 10.0 | 16 59.0 | 12.4 | 58.4 |
| 20 | 118 29.9 | 48.2 | 28 43.3 | 9.8 | 17 11.4 | 12.4 | 58.4 |
| 21 | 133 30.0 | 47.5 | 43 12.1 | 9.8 | 17 23.8 | 12.3 | 58.5 |
| 22 | 148 30.1 | 46.8 | 57 40.9 | 9.6 | 17 36.1 | 12.2 | 58.5 |
| 23 | 163 30.1 | 46.1 | 72 09.5 | 9.5 | 17 48.3 | 12.2 | 58.5 |
| **6** 00 | 178 30.2 | N16 45.4 | 86 38.0 | 9.4 | S18 00.5 | 12.0 | 58.6 |
| 01 | 193 30.3 | 44.7 | 101 06.4 | 9.3 | 18 12.5 | 12.0 | 58.6 |
| 02 | 208 30.3 | 44.1 | 115 34.7 | 9.2 | 18 24.5 | 11.9 | 58.6 |
| 03 | 223 30.4 | 43.4 | 130 02.9 | 9.0 | 18 36.4 | 11.8 | 58.7 |
| 04 | 238 30.5 | 42.7 | 144 30.9 | 8.9 | 18 48.2 | 11.7 | 58.7 |
| 05 | 253 30.5 | 42.0 | 158 58.8 | 8.8 | 18 59.9 | 11.6 | 58.7 |
| 06 | 268 30.6 | N16 41.3 | 173 26.6 | 8.7 | S19 11.5 | 11.5 | 58.8 |
| S 07 | 283 30.7 | 40.6 | 187 54.3 | 8.6 | 19 23.0 | 11.4 | 58.8 |
| A 08 | 298 30.7 | 39.9 | 202 21.9 | 8.4 | 19 34.4 | 11.3 | 58.8 |
| T 09 | 313 30.8 | 39.2 | 216 49.3 | 8.4 | 19 45.7 | 11.2 | 58.9 |
| U 10 | 328 30.9 | 38.5 | 231 16.7 | 8.2 | 19 56.9 | 11.1 | 58.9 |
| R 11 | 343 31.0 | 37.9 | 245 43.9 | 8.0 | 20 08.0 | 11.0 | 58.9 |
| D 12 | 358 31.0 | N16 37.2 | 260 10.9 | 8.0 | S20 19.0 | 10.9 | 58.9 |
| A 13 | 13 31.1 | 36.5 | 274 37.9 | 7.8 | 20 29.9 | 10.8 | 59.0 |
| Y 14 | 28 31.2 | 35.8 | 289 04.7 | 7.7 | 20 40.7 | 10.6 | 59.0 |
| 15 | 43 31.2 | 35.1 | 303 31.4 | 7.6 | 20 51.3 | 10.6 | 59.0 |
| 16 | 58 31.3 | 34.4 | 317 58.0 | 7.5 | 21 01.9 | 10.4 | 59.1 |
| 17 | 73 31.4 | 33.7 | 332 24.5 | 7.3 | 21 12.3 | 10.4 | 59.1 |
| 18 | 88 31.5 | N16 33.0 | 346 50.8 | 7.3 | S21 22.7 | 10.2 | 59.1 |
| 19 | 103 31.5 | 32.3 | 1 17.1 | 7.1 | 21 32.9 | 10.1 | 59.2 |
| 20 | 118 31.6 | 31.6 | 15 43.2 | 6.9 | 21 43.0 | 9.9 | 59.2 |
| 21 | 133 31.7 | 30.9 | 30 09.1 | 6.9 | 21 52.9 | 9.9 | 59.2 |
| 22 | 148 31.8 | 30.2 | 44 35.0 | 6.7 | 22 02.8 | 9.7 | 59.3 |
| 23 | 163 31.8 | 29.5 | 59 00.7 | 6.6 | 22 12.5 | 9.6 | 59.3 |
| **7** 00 | 178 31.9 | N16 28.8 | 73 26.3 | 6.5 | S22 22.1 | 9.4 | 59.3 |
| 01 | 193 32.0 | 28.1 | 87 51.8 | 6.3 | 22 31.5 | 9.4 | 59.3 |
| 02 | 208 32.1 | 27.5 | 102 17.1 | 6.3 | 22 40.9 | 9.1 | 59.4 |
| 03 | 223 32.1 | 26.8 | 116 42.4 | 6.1 | 22 50.0 | 9.1 | 59.4 |
| 04 | 238 32.2 | 26.1 | 131 07.5 | 5.9 | 22 59.1 | 8.9 | 59.4 |
| 05 | 253 32.3 | 25.4 | 145 32.4 | 5.9 | 23 08.0 | 8.8 | 59.5 |
| 06 | 268 32.4 | N16 24.7 | 159 57.3 | 5.8 | S23 16.8 | 8.7 | 59.5 |
| 07 | 283 32.4 | 24.0 | 174 22.1 | 5.6 | 23 25.5 | 8.5 | 59.5 |
| 08 | 298 32.5 | 23.3 | 188 46.7 | 5.5 | 23 34.0 | 8.3 | 59.6 |
| S 09 | 313 32.6 | 22.6 | 203 11.2 | 5.4 | 23 42.3 | 8.2 | 59.6 |
| U 10 | 328 32.7 | 21.9 | 217 35.6 | 5.2 | 23 50.5 | 8.1 | 59.6 |
| N 11 | 343 32.7 | 21.2 | 231 59.8 | 5.2 | 23 58.6 | 7.9 | 59.6 |
| D 12 | 358 32.8 | N16 20.5 | 246 24.0 | 5.0 | S24 06.5 | 7.7 | 59.7 |
| A 13 | 13 32.9 | 19.8 | 260 48.0 | 4.9 | 24 14.2 | 7.6 | 59.7 |
| Y 14 | 28 33.0 | 19.1 | 275 11.9 | 4.8 | 24 21.8 | 7.5 | 59.7 |
| 15 | 43 33.1 | 18.3 | 289 35.7 | 4.7 | 24 29.3 | 7.3 | 59.8 |
| 16 | 58 33.1 | 17.6 | 303 59.4 | 4.5 | 24 36.6 | 7.1 | 59.8 |
| 17 | 73 33.2 | 16.9 | 318 22.9 | 4.5 | 24 43.7 | 7.0 | 59.8 |
| 18 | 88 33.3 | N16 16.2 | 332 46.4 | 4.3 | S24 50.7 | 6.8 | 59.8 |
| 19 | 103 33.4 | 15.5 | 347 09.7 | 4.3 | 24 57.5 | 6.6 | 59.9 |
| 20 | 118 33.5 | 14.8 | 1 33.0 | 4.1 | 25 04.1 | 6.5 | 59.9 |
| 21 | 133 33.5 | 14.1 | 15 56.1 | 4.0 | 25 10.6 | 6.3 | 59.9 |
| 22 | 148 33.6 | 13.4 | 30 19.1 | 3.9 | 25 16.9 | 6.2 | 59.9 |
| 23 | 163 33.7 | 12.7 | 44 42.0 | 3.9 | S25 23.1 | 5.9 | 60.0 |
| SD | 15.8 | d 0.7 | 15.9 | | 16.1 | | 16.3 |

### Twilight, Sunrise, Moonrise

| Lat. | Naut. | Civil | Sunrise | 5 | 6 | 7 | 8 |
|---|---|---|---|---|---|---|---|
| ° | h m | h m | h m | h m | h m | h m | h m |
| N 72 | //// | //// | 00 57 | 16 23 | ████ | ████ | ████ |
| N 70 | //// | //// | 02 04 | 15 32 | ████ | ████ | ████ |
| 68 | //// | //// | 02 39 | 15 00 | 18 03 | ████ | ████ |
| 66 | //// | 01 23 | 03 04 | 14 37 | 16 56 | ████ | ████ |
| 64 | //// | 02 06 | 03 24 | 14 19 | 16 20 | 18 46 | ████ |
| 62 | //// | 02 34 | 03 39 | 14 04 | 15 55 | 17 54 | 19 47 |
| 60 | 01 15 | 02 55 | 03 52 | 13 52 | 15 35 | 17 22 | 18 59 |
| N 58 | 01 54 | 03 12 | 04 04 | 13 42 | 15 19 | 16 58 | 18 28 |
| 56 | 02 20 | 03 27 | 04 13 | 13 32 | 15 05 | 16 39 | 18 05 |
| 54 | 02 40 | 03 39 | 04 22 | 13 24 | 14 53 | 16 23 | 17 46 |
| 52 | 02 56 | 03 49 | 04 29 | 13 17 | 14 43 | 16 10 | 17 30 |
| 50 | 03 10 | 03 59 | 04 36 | 13 11 | 14 34 | 15 58 | 17 16 |
| 45 | 03 36 | 04 18 | 04 51 | 12 57 | 14 14 | 15 33 | 16 48 |
| N 40 | 03 57 | 04 33 | 05 03 | 12 45 | 13 58 | 15 13 | 16 26 |
| 35 | 04 12 | 04 46 | 05 13 | 12 36 | 13 45 | 14 57 | 16 08 |
| 30 | 04 26 | 04 56 | 05 22 | 12 27 | 13 34 | 14 43 | 15 52 |
| 20 | 04 46 | 05 14 | 05 37 | 12 13 | 13 14 | 14 19 | 15 26 |
| N 10 | 05 03 | 05 28 | 05 51 | 12 01 | 12 57 | 13 58 | 15 03 |
| 0 | 05 16 | 05 41 | 06 02 | 11 49 | 12 41 | 13 39 | 14 42 |
| S 10 | 05 27 | 05 53 | 06 15 | 11 37 | 12 26 | 13 20 | 14 21 |
| 20 | 05 38 | 06 04 | 06 27 | 11 25 | 12 09 | 13 00 | 13 58 |
| 30 | 05 48 | 06 17 | 06 42 | 11 11 | 11 50 | 12 37 | 13 32 |
| 35 | 05 53 | 06 24 | 06 50 | 11 03 | 11 39 | 12 23 | 13 16 |
| 40 | 05 59 | 06 31 | 07 00 | 10 54 | 11 27 | 12 07 | 12 59 |
| 45 | 06 04 | 06 39 | 07 11 | 10 44 | 11 12 | 11 49 | 12 37 |
| S 50 | 06 10 | 06 49 | 07 24 | 10 31 | 10 54 | 11 26 | 12 10 |
| 52 | 06 13 | 06 54 | 07 30 | 10 25 | 10 46 | 11 15 | 11 57 |
| 54 | 06 16 | 06 58 | 07 37 | 10 19 | 10 37 | 11 03 | 11 42 |
| 56 | 06 19 | 07 04 | 07 44 | 10 12 | 10 26 | 10 48 | 11 25 |
| 58 | 06 22 | 07 09 | 07 53 | 10 04 | 10 14 | 10 32 | 11 04 |
| S 60 | 06 25 | 07 16 | 08 03 | 09 55 | 10 01 | 10 12 | 10 37 |

### Sunset, Twilight, Moonset

| Lat. | Sunset | Civil | Naut. | 5 | 6 | 7 | 8 |
|---|---|---|---|---|---|---|---|
| ° | h m | h m | h m | h m | h m | h m | h m |
| N 72 | 23 01 | //// | //// | 19 15 | ████ | ████ | ████ |
| N 70 | 22 02 | //// | //// | 20 09 | ████ | ████ | ████ |
| 68 | 21 29 | //// | //// | 20 42 | 19 30 | ████ | ████ |
| 66 | 21 05 | 22 42 | //// | 21 06 | 20 39 | ████ | ████ |
| 64 | 20 46 | 22 01 | //// | 21 25 | 21 15 | 20 52 | ████ |
| 62 | 20 31 | 21 34 | //// | 21 41 | 21 41 | 21 45 | 22 04 |
| 60 | 20 18 | 21 14 | 22 51 | 21 55 | 22 02 | 22 17 | 22 52 |
| N 58 | 20 07 | 20 57 | 22 14 | 22 06 | 22 19 | 22 41 | 23 23 |
| 56 | 19 57 | 20 43 | 21 49 | 22 16 | 22 33 | 23 01 | 23 47 |
| 54 | 19 49 | 20 32 | 21 30 | 22 25 | 22 46 | 23 17 | 24 06 |
| 52 | 19 41 | 20 21 | 21 14 | 22 33 | 22 57 | 23 31 | 24 22 |
| 50 | 19 35 | 20 12 | 21 01 | 22 40 | 23 06 | 23 43 | 24 36 |
| 45 | 19 20 | 19 53 | 20 34 | 22 55 | 23 27 | 24 09 | 00 09 |
| N 40 | 19 08 | 19 38 | 20 14 | 23 08 | 23 44 | 24 29 | 00 29 |
| 35 | 18 58 | 19 26 | 19 59 | 23 19 | 23 58 | 24 46 | 00 46 |
| 30 | 18 49 | 19 15 | 19 46 | 23 29 | 24 11 | 00 11 | 01 01 |
| 20 | 18 34 | 18 58 | 19 25 | 23 45 | 24 32 | 00 32 | 01 26 |
| N 10 | 18 21 | 18 43 | 19 09 | 24 00 | 00 00 | 00 51 | 01 48 |
| 0 | 18 09 | 18 31 | 18 56 | 24 13 | 00 13 | 01 08 | 02 08 |
| S 10 | 17 57 | 18 19 | 18 45 | 24 27 | 00 27 | 01 26 | 02 29 |
| 20 | 17 45 | 18 08 | 18 34 | 24 42 | 00 42 | 01 44 | 02 50 |
| 30 | 17 30 | 17 55 | 18 24 | 24 59 | 00 59 | 02 06 | 03 11 |
| 35 | 17 22 | 17 49 | 18 19 | 00 01 | 01 08 | 02 19 | 03 31 |
| 40 | 17 13 | 17 41 | 18 14 | 00 09 | 01 20 | 02 34 | 03 48 |
| 45 | 17 02 | 17 33 | 18 08 | 00 18 | 01 33 | 02 51 | 04 09 |
| S 50 | 16 49 | 17 23 | 18 02 | 00 29 | 01 50 | 03 13 | 04 35 |
| 52 | 16 42 | 17 19 | 17 59 | 00 34 | 01 57 | 03 24 | 04 48 |
| 54 | 16 36 | 17 14 | 17 57 | 00 39 | 02 06 | 03 36 | 05 03 |
| 56 | 16 28 | 17 09 | 17 54 | 00 46 | 02 16 | 03 49 | 05 21 |
| 58 | 16 20 | 17 03 | 17 51 | 00 53 | 02 27 | 04 05 | 05 41 |
| S 60 | 16 10 | 16 57 | 17 47 | 01 00 | 02 40 | 04 24 | 06 07 |

### SUN / MOON

| | SUN | | | MOON | | | |
|---|---|---|---|---|---|---|---|
| Day | Eqn. of Time 00h | 12h | Mer. Pass. | Mer. Pass. Upper | Lower | Age | Phase |
| d | m s | m s | h m | h m | h m | d | % |
| 5 | 06 06 | 06 03 | 12 06 | 18 01 | 05 36 | 08 | 51 |
| 6 | 05 59 | 05 56 | 12 06 | 18 55 | 06 27 | 09 | 62 |
| 7 | 05 53 | 05 49 | 12 06 | 19 54 | 07 23 | 10 | 72 |

| UT | ARIES | VENUS −3.9 | | MARS +0.1 | | JUPITER −2.7 | | SATURN +0.3 | | STARS | | |
|---|---|---|---|---|---|---|---|---|---|---|---|---|
| | GHA | GHA | Dec | GHA | Dec | GHA | Dec | GHA | Dec | Name | SHA | Dec |
| d h | ° ′ | ° ′ | ° ′ | ° ′ | ° ′ | ° ′ | ° ′ | ° ′ | ° ′ | | ° ′ | ° ′ |
| 8 00 | 316 29.0 | 199 04.4 | N21 18.7 | 265 56.3 | N16 49.9 | 308 03.0 | N 2 01.9 | 351 17.4 | S15 16.0 | Acamar | 315 13.3 | S40 12.6 |
| 01 | 331 31.5 | 214 03.6 | 18.3 | 280 57.2 | 50.3 | 323 05.5 | 01.8 | 6 20.1 | 16.1 | Achernar | 335 21.5 | S57 07.1 |
| 02 | 346 34.0 | 229 02.9 | 17.8 | 295 58.1 | 50.8 | 338 08.0 | 01.8 | 21 22.7 | 16.2 | Acrux | 173 02.7 | S63 13.6 |
| 03 | 1 36.4 | 244 02.1 .. | 17.4 | 310 59.0 .. | 51.2 | 353 10.6 .. | 01.7 | 36 25.4 .. | 16.2 | Adhara | 255 07.7 | S29 00.0 |
| 04 | 16 38.9 | 259 01.3 | 16.9 | 325 59.9 | 51.6 | 8 13.1 | 01.7 | 51 28.0 | 16.3 | Aldebaran | 290 42.0 | N16 33.3 |
| 05 | 31 41.4 | 274 00.5 | 16.5 | 341 00.8 | 52.0 | 23 15.6 | 01.7 | 66 30.7 | 16.4 | | | |
| 06 | 46 43.8 | 288 59.8 | N21 16.0 | 356 01.7 | N16 52.4 | 38 18.2 | N 2 01.6 | 81 33.3 | S15 16.4 | Alioth | 166 15.0 | N55 50.6 |
| 07 | 61 46.3 | 303 59.0 | 15.5 | 11 02.6 | 52.9 | 53 20.7 | 01.6 | 96 36.0 | 16.5 | Alkaid | 152 53.7 | N49 12.4 |
| 08 | 76 48.7 | 318 58.2 | 15.1 | 26 03.5 | 53.3 | 68 23.3 | 01.5 | 111 38.6 | 16.5 | Alnair | 27 35.0 | S46 51.0 |
| M 09 | 91 51.2 | 333 57.4 .. | 14.6 | 41 04.3 .. | 53.7 | 83 25.8 .. | 01.5 | 126 41.2 .. | 16.6 | Alnilam | 275 40.0 | S 1 11.2 |
| O 10 | 106 53.7 | 348 56.7 | 14.1 | 56 05.2 | 54.1 | 98 28.3 | 01.4 | 141 43.9 | 16.7 | Alphard | 217 50.0 | S 8 45.2 |
| N 11 | 121 56.1 | 3 55.9 | 13.7 | 71 06.1 | 54.5 | 113 30.9 | 01.4 | 156 46.5 | 16.7 | | | |
| D 12 | 136 58.6 | 18 55.1 | N21 13.2 | 86 07.0 | N16 54.9 | 128 33.4 | N 2 01.3 | 171 49.2 | S15 16.8 | Alphecca | 126 05.4 | N26 38.6 |
| A 13 | 152 01.1 | 33 54.4 | 12.7 | 101 07.9 | 55.4 | 143 36.0 | 01.3 | 186 51.8 | 16.9 | Alpheratz | 357 36.6 | N29 12.8 |
| Y 14 | 167 03.5 | 48 53.6 | 12.3 | 116 08.8 | 55.8 | 158 38.5 | 01.3 | 201 54.5 | 16.9 | Altair | 62 01.6 | N 8 55.8 |
| 15 | 182 06.0 | 63 52.8 .. | 11.8 | 131 09.7 .. | 56.2 | 173 41.0 .. | 01.2 | 216 57.1 .. | 17.0 | Ankaa | 353 08.8 | S42 10.8 |
| 16 | 197 08.5 | 78 52.1 | 11.3 | 146 10.6 | 56.6 | 188 43.6 | 01.2 | 231 59.8 | 17.1 | Antares | 112 18.1 | S26 28.9 |
| 17 | 212 10.9 | 93 51.3 | 10.9 | 161 11.5 | 57.0 | 203 46.1 | 01.1 | 247 02.4 | 17.1 | | | |
| 18 | 227 13.4 | 108 50.5 | N21 10.4 | 176 12.4 | N16 57.4 | 218 48.7 | N 2 01.1 | 262 05.0 | S15 17.2 | Arcturus | 145 49.8 | N19 04.1 |
| 19 | 242 15.9 | 123 49.7 | 09.9 | 191 13.3 | 57.8 | 233 51.2 | 01.0 | 277 07.7 | 17.3 | Atria | 107 13.8 | S69 04.3 |
| 20 | 257 18.3 | 138 49.0 | 09.4 | 206 14.2 | 58.3 | 248 53.7 | 01.0 | 292 10.3 | 17.3 | Avior | 234 16.2 | S59 34.7 |
| 21 | 272 20.8 | 153 48.2 .. | 09.0 | 221 15.1 .. | 58.7 | 263 56.3 .. | 00.9 | 307 13.0 .. | 17.4 | Bellatrix | 278 25.2 | N 6 22.3 |
| 22 | 287 23.2 | 168 47.4 | 08.5 | 236 16.0 | 59.1 | 278 58.8 | 00.9 | 322 15.6 | 17.4 | Betelgeuse | 270 54.5 | N 7 24.7 |
| 23 | 302 25.7 | 183 46.7 | 08.0 | 251 16.8 | 59.5 | 294 01.4 | 00.8 | 337 18.3 | 17.5 | | | |
| 9 00 | 317 28.2 | 198 45.9 | N21 07.5 | 266 17.7 | N16 59.9 | 309 03.9 | N 2 00.8 | 352 20.9 | S15 17.6 | Canopus | 263 53.7 | S52 42.2 |
| 01 | 332 30.6 | 213 45.1 | 07.0 | 281 18.6 | 17 00.3 | 324 06.5 | 00.7 | 7 23.6 | 17.6 | Capella | 280 25.1 | N46 01.1 |
| 02 | 347 33.1 | 228 44.4 | 06.6 | 296 19.5 | 00.7 | 339 09.0 | 00.7 | 22 26.2 | 17.7 | Deneb | 49 26.7 | N45 21.7 |
| 03 | 2 35.6 | 243 43.6 .. | 06.1 | 311 20.4 .. | 01.1 | 354 11.5 .. | 00.7 | 37 28.9 .. | 17.8 | Denebola | 182 27.2 | N14 27.0 |
| 04 | 17 38.0 | 258 42.8 | 05.6 | 326 21.3 | 01.6 | 9 14.1 | 00.6 | 52 31.5 | 17.8 | Diphda | 348 49.1 | S17 51.7 |
| 05 | 32 40.5 | 273 42.1 | 05.1 | 341 22.2 | 02.0 | 24 16.6 | 00.6 | 67 34.1 | 17.9 | | | |
| 06 | 47 43.0 | 288 41.3 | N21 04.6 | 356 23.1 | N17 02.4 | 39 19.2 | N 2 00.5 | 82 36.8 | S15 18.0 | Dubhe | 193 44.1 | N61 38.0 |
| 07 | 62 45.4 | 303 40.5 | 04.1 | 11 24.0 | 02.8 | 54 21.7 | 00.5 | 97 39.4 | 18.0 | Elnath | 278 04.6 | N28 37.5 |
| 08 | 77 47.9 | 318 39.8 | 03.7 | 26 24.9 | 03.2 | 69 24.3 | 00.4 | 112 42.1 | 18.1 | Eltanin | 90 42.7 | N51 29.4 |
| T 09 | 92 50.4 | 333 39.0 .. | 03.2 | 41 25.8 .. | 03.6 | 84 26.8 .. | 00.4 | 127 44.7 .. | 18.2 | Enif | 33 40.4 | N 9 58.7 |
| U 10 | 107 52.8 | 348 38.3 | 02.7 | 56 26.7 | 04.0 | 99 29.4 | 00.3 | 142 47.4 | 18.2 | Fomalhaut | 15 16.4 | S29 30.1 |
| E 11 | 122 55.3 | 3 37.5 | 02.2 | 71 27.6 | 04.4 | 114 31.9 | 00.3 | 157 50.0 | 18.3 | | | |
| S 12 | 137 57.7 | 18 36.7 | N21 01.7 | 86 28.5 | N17 04.8 | 129 34.5 | N 2 00.2 | 172 52.7 | S15 18.3 | Gacrux | 171 54.2 | S57 14.5 |
| D 13 | 153 00.2 | 33 36.0 | 01.2 | 101 29.4 | 05.2 | 144 37.0 | 00.2 | 187 55.3 | 18.4 | Gienah | 175 45.8 | S17 40.0 |
| A 14 | 168 02.7 | 48 35.2 | 00.7 | 116 30.3 | 05.7 | 159 39.6 | 00.1 | 202 57.9 | 18.5 | Hadar | 148 39.0 | S60 29.1 |
| Y 15 | 183 05.1 | 63 34.4 | 21 00.2 | 131 31.2 .. | 06.1 | 174 42.1 .. | 00.1 | 218 00.6 .. | 18.5 | Hamal | 327 53.4 | N23 34.1 |
| 16 | 198 07.6 | 78 33.7 | 20 59.7 | 146 32.1 | 06.5 | 189 44.7 | 00.0 | 233 03.2 | 18.6 | Kaus Aust. | 83 34.8 | S34 22.4 |
| 17 | 213 10.1 | 93 32.9 | 59.2 | 161 33.0 | 06.9 | 204 47.2 | 2 00.0 | 248 05.9 | 18.7 | | | |
| 18 | 228 12.5 | 108 32.1 | N20 58.7 | 176 33.9 | N17 07.3 | 219 49.7 | N 1 59.9 | 263 08.5 | S15 18.7 | Kochab | 137 19.8 | N74 04.1 |
| 19 | 243 15.0 | 123 31.4 | 58.2 | 191 34.8 | 07.7 | 234 52.3 | 59.9 | 278 11.2 | 18.8 | Markab | 13 31.6 | N15 19.6 |
| 20 | 258 17.5 | 138 30.6 | 57.7 | 206 35.7 | 08.1 | 249 54.8 | 59.8 | 293 13.8 | 18.9 | Menkar | 314 08.2 | N 4 10.7 |
| 21 | 273 19.9 | 153 29.9 .. | 57.2 | 221 36.6 .. | 08.5 | 264 57.4 .. | 59.8 | 308 16.5 .. | 18.9 | Menkent | 148 00.0 | S36 28.9 |
| 22 | 288 22.4 | 168 29.1 | 56.7 | 236 37.5 | 08.9 | 279 59.9 | 59.7 | 323 19.1 | 19.0 | Miaplacidus | 221 39.6 | S69 48.5 |
| 23 | 303 24.9 | 183 28.3 | 56.2 | 251 38.4 | 09.3 | 295 02.5 | 59.7 | 338 21.8 | 19.1 | | | |
| 10 00 | 318 27.3 | 198 27.6 | N20 55.7 | 266 39.3 | N17 09.7 | 310 05.0 | N 1 59.6 | 353 24.4 | S15 19.1 | Mirfak | 308 31.1 | N49 56.2 |
| 01 | 333 29.8 | 213 26.8 | 55.2 | 281 40.2 | 10.1 | 325 07.6 | 59.6 | 8 27.0 | 19.2 | Nunki | 75 49.9 | S26 16.1 |
| 02 | 348 32.2 | 228 26.1 | 54.7 | 296 41.1 | 10.5 | 340 10.2 | 59.5 | 23 29.7 | 19.2 | Peacock | 53 08.3 | S56 39.7 |
| 03 | 3 34.7 | 243 25.3 .. | 54.2 | 311 42.0 .. | 10.9 | 355 12.7 .. | 59.5 | 38 32.3 .. | 19.3 | Pollux | 243 20.1 | N27 58.3 |
| 04 | 18 37.2 | 258 24.5 | 53.7 | 326 42.9 | 11.3 | 10 15.3 | 59.4 | 53 35.0 | 19.4 | Procyon | 244 53.2 | N 5 10.1 |
| 05 | 33 39.6 | 273 23.8 | 53.2 | 341 43.8 | 11.8 | 25 17.8 | 59.4 | 68 37.6 | 19.4 | | | |
| 06 | 48 42.1 | 288 23.0 | N20 52.6 | 356 44.7 | N17 12.2 | 40 20.4 | N 1 59.3 | 83 40.3 | S15 19.5 | Rasalhague | 96 00.2 | N12 32.8 |
| W 07 | 63 44.6 | 303 22.3 | 52.1 | 11 45.6 | 12.6 | 55 22.9 | 59.3 | 98 42.9 | 19.6 | Regulus | 207 36.9 | N11 51.6 |
| E 08 | 78 47.0 | 318 21.5 | 51.6 | 26 46.5 | 13.0 | 70 25.5 | 59.2 | 113 45.6 | 19.6 | Rigel | 281 06.0 | S 8 10.4 |
| D 09 | 93 49.5 | 333 20.8 .. | 51.1 | 41 47.4 .. | 13.4 | 85 28.0 .. | 59.2 | 128 48.2 .. | 19.7 | Rigil Kent. | 139 43.1 | S60 55.8 |
| N 10 | 108 52.0 | 348 20.0 | 50.6 | 56 48.3 | 13.8 | 100 30.6 | 59.1 | 143 50.9 | 19.8 | Sabik | 102 04.9 | S15 45.1 |
| E 11 | 123 54.4 | 3 19.2 | 50.1 | 71 49.2 | 14.2 | 115 33.1 | 59.1 | 158 53.5 | 19.8 | | | |
| S 12 | 138 56.9 | 18 18.5 | N20 49.6 | 86 50.1 | N17 14.6 | 130 35.7 | N 1 59.0 | 173 56.1 | S15 19.9 | Schedar | 349 32.9 | N56 39.4 |
| D 13 | 153 59.3 | 33 17.7 | 49.0 | 101 51.0 | 15.0 | 145 38.2 | 59.0 | 188 58.8 | 20.0 | Shaula | 96 12.8 | S37 07.2 |
| A 14 | 169 01.8 | 48 17.0 | 48.5 | 116 51.9 | 15.4 | 160 40.8 | 58.9 | 204 01.4 | 20.0 | Sirius | 258 28.3 | S16 44.7 |
| Y 15 | 184 04.3 | 63 16.2 .. | 48.0 | 131 52.8 .. | 15.8 | 175 43.3 .. | 58.9 | 219 04.1 .. | 20.1 | Spica | 158 24.5 | S11 16.6 |
| 16 | 199 06.7 | 78 15.5 | 47.5 | 146 53.7 | 16.2 | 190 45.9 | 58.8 | 234 06.7 | 20.1 | Suhail | 222 48.2 | S43 31.3 |
| 17 | 214 09.2 | 93 14.7 | 47.0 | 161 54.6 | 16.6 | 205 48.5 | 58.8 | 249 09.4 | 20.2 | | | |
| 18 | 229 11.7 | 108 13.9 | N20 46.4 | 176 55.5 | N17 17.0 | 220 51.0 | N 1 58.7 | 264 12.0 | S15 20.3 | Vega | 80 34.2 | N38 48.4 |
| 19 | 244 14.1 | 123 13.2 | 45.9 | 191 56.4 | 17.4 | 235 53.6 | 58.7 | 279 14.7 | 20.3 | Zuben'ubi | 136 58.2 | S16 08.1 |
| 20 | 259 16.6 | 138 12.4 | 45.4 | 206 57.3 | 17.8 | 250 56.1 | 58.6 | 294 17.3 | 20.4 | | SHA | Mer. Pass. |
| 21 | 274 19.1 | 153 11.7 .. | 44.9 | 221 58.2 .. | 18.2 | 265 58.7 .. | 58.6 | 309 20.0 .. | 20.5 | | ° ′ | h m |
| 22 | 289 21.5 | 168 10.9 | 44.3 | 236 59.1 | 18.6 | 281 01.2 | 58.5 | 324 22.6 | 20.5 | Venus | 241 17.7 | 10 45 |
| 23 | 304 24.0 | 183 10.2 | 43.8 | 252 00.0 | 19.0 | 296 03.8 | 58.5 | 339 25.2 | 20.6 | Mars | 308 49.6 | 6 14 |
| | h m | | | | | | | | | Jupiter | 351 35.7 | 3 23 |
| Mer. Pass. 2 49.7 | | v −0.8 | d 0.5 | v 0.9 | d 0.4 | v 2.5 | d 0.0 | v 2.6 | d 0.1 | Saturn | 34 52.7 | 0 31 |

| UT | SUN GHA | SUN Dec | MOON GHA | v | Dec | d | HP |
|---|---|---|---|---|---|---|---|
| d h | ° ′ | ° ′ | ° ′ | ′ | ° ′ | ′ | ′ |
| **8** 00 | 178 33.8 | N16 12.0 | 59 04.9 | 3.7 | S25 29.0 | 5.8 | 60.0 |
| 01 | 193 33.9 | 11.3 | 73 27.6 | 3.6 | 25 34.8 | 5.6 | 60.0 |
| 02 | 208 33.9 | 10.6 | 87 50.2 | 3.5 | 25 40.4 | 5.5 | 60.0 |
| 03 | 223 34.0 | .. 09.9 | 102 12.7 | 3.4 | 25 45.9 | 5.3 | 60.1 |
| 04 | 238 34.1 | 09.2 | 116 35.1 | 3.3 | 25 51.2 | 5.0 | 60.1 |
| 05 | 253 34.2 | 08.5 | 130 57.4 | 3.3 | 25 56.2 | 5.0 | 60.1 |
| 06 | 268 34.3 | N16 07.7 | 145 19.7 | 3.1 | S26 01.2 | 4.7 | 60.1 |
| 07 | 283 34.4 | 07.0 | 159 41.8 | 3.1 | 26 05.9 | 4.5 | 60.2 |
| 08 | 298 34.4 | 06.3 | 174 03.9 | 2.9 | 26 10.4 | 4.4 | 60.2 |
| M 09 | 313 34.5 | .. 05.6 | 188 25.8 | 2.9 | 26 14.8 | 4.1 | 60.2 |
| O 10 | 328 34.6 | 04.9 | 202 47.7 | 2.8 | 26 18.9 | 4.0 | 60.2 |
| N 11 | 343 34.7 | 04.2 | 217 09.5 | 2.7 | 26 22.9 | 3.8 | 60.3 |
| D 12 | 358 34.8 | N16 03.5 | 231 31.2 | 2.7 | S26 26.7 | 3.6 | 60.3 |
| A 13 | 13 34.9 | 02.8 | 245 52.9 | 2.5 | 26 30.3 | 3.4 | 60.3 |
| Y 14 | 28 34.9 | 02.1 | 260 14.4 | 2.5 | 26 33.7 | 3.3 | 60.3 |
| 15 | 43 35.0 | .. 01.3 | 274 35.9 | 2.5 | 26 37.0 | 3.0 | 60.4 |
| 16 | 58 35.1 | 16 00.6 | 288 57.4 | 2.3 | 26 40.0 | 2.8 | 60.4 |
| 17 | 73 35.2 | 15 59.9 | 303 18.7 | 2.3 | 26 42.8 | 2.7 | 60.4 |
| 18 | 88 35.3 | N15 59.2 | 317 40.0 | 2.3 | S26 45.5 | 2.4 | 60.4 |
| 19 | 103 35.4 | 58.5 | 332 01.3 | 2.1 | 26 47.9 | 2.2 | 60.4 |
| 20 | 118 35.5 | 57.8 | 346 22.4 | 2.2 | 26 50.1 | 2.1 | 60.5 |
| 21 | 133 35.5 | .. 57.0 | 0 43.6 | 2.0 | 26 52.2 | 1.8 | 60.5 |
| 22 | 148 35.6 | 56.3 | 15 04.6 | 2.0 | 26 54.0 | 1.7 | 60.5 |
| 23 | 163 35.7 | 55.6 | 29 25.6 | 2.0 | 26 55.7 | 1.4 | 60.5 |
| **9** 00 | 178 35.8 | N15 54.9 | 43 46.6 | 1.9 | S26 57.1 | 1.2 | 60.5 |
| 01 | 193 35.9 | 54.2 | 58 07.5 | 1.9 | 26 58.3 | 1.1 | 60.6 |
| 02 | 208 36.0 | 53.5 | 72 28.4 | 1.8 | 26 59.4 | 0.8 | 60.6 |
| 03 | 223 36.1 | .. 52.7 | 86 49.2 | 1.9 | 27 00.2 | 0.6 | 60.6 |
| 04 | 238 36.2 | 52.0 | 101 10.1 | 1.7 | 27 00.8 | 0.5 | 60.6 |
| 05 | 253 36.2 | 51.3 | 115 30.8 | 1.8 | 27 01.3 | 0.2 | 60.6 |
| 06 | 268 36.3 | N15 50.6 | 129 51.6 | 1.7 | S27 01.5 | 0.0 | 60.6 |
| 07 | 283 36.4 | 49.9 | 144 12.3 | 1.7 | 27 01.5 | 0.2 | 60.7 |
| T 08 | 298 36.5 | 49.1 | 158 33.0 | 1.7 | 27 01.3 | 0.4 | 60.7 |
| U 09 | 313 36.6 | .. 48.4 | 172 53.7 | 1.6 | 27 00.9 | 0.6 | 60.7 |
| E 10 | 328 36.7 | 47.7 | 187 14.3 | 1.7 | 27 00.3 | 0.8 | 60.7 |
| S 11 | 343 36.8 | 47.0 | 201 35.0 | 1.6 | 26 59.5 | 1.0 | 60.7 |
| D 12 | 358 36.9 | N15 46.3 | 215 55.6 | 1.6 | S26 58.5 | 1.2 | 60.7 |
| A 13 | 13 37.0 | 45.5 | 230 16.2 | 1.6 | 26 57.3 | 1.5 | 60.7 |
| Y 14 | 28 37.1 | 44.8 | 244 36.8 | 1.6 | 26 55.8 | 1.6 | 60.8 |
| 15 | 43 37.1 | .. 44.1 | 258 57.4 | 1.7 | 26 54.2 | 1.9 | 60.8 |
| 16 | 58 37.2 | 43.4 | 273 18.1 | 1.6 | 26 52.3 | 2.0 | 60.8 |
| 17 | 73 37.3 | 42.6 | 287 38.7 | 1.6 | 26 50.3 | 2.3 | 60.8 |
| 18 | 88 37.4 | N15 41.9 | 301 59.3 | 1.7 | S26 48.0 | 2.4 | 60.8 |
| 19 | 103 37.5 | 41.2 | 316 20.0 | 1.6 | 26 45.6 | 2.7 | 60.8 |
| 20 | 118 37.6 | 40.5 | 330 40.6 | 1.7 | 26 42.9 | 2.9 | 60.8 |
| 21 | 133 37.7 | .. 39.7 | 345 01.3 | 1.7 | 26 40.0 | 3.1 | 60.8 |
| 22 | 148 37.8 | 39.0 | 359 22.0 | 1.7 | 26 36.9 | 3.2 | 60.8 |
| 23 | 163 37.9 | 38.3 | 13 42.7 | 1.8 | 26 33.7 | 3.5 | 60.8 |
| **10** 00 | 178 38.0 | N15 37.5 | 28 03.5 | 1.7 | S26 30.2 | 3.7 | 60.9 |
| 01 | 193 38.1 | 36.8 | 42 24.2 | 1.8 | 26 26.5 | 3.9 | 60.9 |
| 02 | 208 38.2 | 36.1 | 56 45.0 | 1.9 | 26 22.6 | 4.1 | 60.9 |
| 03 | 223 38.3 | .. 35.4 | 71 05.9 | 1.9 | 26 18.5 | 4.3 | 60.9 |
| 04 | 238 38.4 | 34.6 | 85 26.8 | 1.9 | 26 14.2 | 4.5 | 60.9 |
| 05 | 253 38.4 | 33.9 | 99 47.7 | 2.0 | 26 09.7 | 4.7 | 60.9 |
| 06 | 268 38.5 | N15 33.2 | 114 08.7 | 2.0 | S26 05.0 | 4.9 | 60.9 |
| W 07 | 283 38.6 | 32.4 | 128 29.7 | 2.0 | 26 00.1 | 5.1 | 60.9 |
| E 08 | 298 38.7 | 31.7 | 142 50.7 | 2.1 | 25 55.0 | 5.3 | 60.9 |
| D 09 | 313 38.8 | .. 31.0 | 157 11.8 | 2.2 | 25 49.7 | 5.5 | 60.9 |
| N 10 | 328 38.9 | 30.2 | 171 33.0 | 2.2 | 25 44.2 | 5.7 | 60.9 |
| E 11 | 343 39.0 | 29.5 | 185 54.2 | 2.3 | 25 38.5 | 5.9 | 60.9 |
| S 12 | 358 39.1 | N15 28.8 | 200 15.5 | 2.4 | S25 32.6 | 6.0 | 60.9 |
| D 13 | 13 39.2 | 28.0 | 214 36.9 | 2.4 | 25 26.6 | 6.3 | 60.9 |
| A 14 | 28 39.3 | 27.3 | 228 58.3 | 2.5 | 25 20.3 | 6.5 | 60.9 |
| Y 15 | 43 39.4 | .. 26.6 | 243 19.8 | 2.6 | 25 13.8 | 6.6 | 60.9 |
| 16 | 58 39.5 | 25.8 | 257 41.4 | 2.6 | 25 07.2 | 6.8 | 60.9 |
| 17 | 73 39.6 | 25.1 | 272 03.0 | 2.7 | 25 00.4 | 7.0 | 60.9 |
| 18 | 88 39.7 | N15 24.4 | 286 24.7 | 2.8 | S24 53.4 | 7.2 | 60.9 |
| 19 | 103 39.8 | 23.6 | 300 46.5 | 2.8 | 24 46.2 | 7.4 | 60.9 |
| 20 | 118 39.9 | 22.9 | 315 08.3 | 3.0 | 24 38.8 | 7.6 | 60.9 |
| 21 | 133 40.0 | .. 22.2 | 329 30.3 | 3.0 | 24 31.2 | 7.7 | 60.9 |
| 22 | 148 40.1 | 21.4 | 343 52.3 | 3.1 | 24 23.5 | 8.0 | 60.9 |
| 23 | 163 40.2 | 20.7 | 358 14.4 | 3.2 | S24 15.5 | 8.1 | 60.9 |
| | SD 15.8 | d 0.7 | SD 16.4 | | 16.5 | | 16.6 |

| Lat. | Naut. | Civil | Sunrise | Moonrise 8 | 9 | 10 | 11 |
|---|---|---|---|---|---|---|---|
| ° | h m | h m | h m | h m | h m | h m | h m |
| N 72 | //// | //// | 01 35 | ■■■■ | ■■■■ | ■■■■ | ■■■■ |
| N 70 | //// | //// | 02 23 | ■■■■ | ■■■■ | ■■■■ | ■■■■ |
| 68 | //// | 00 27 | 02 53 | ■■■■ | ■■■■ | ■■■■ | 22 36 |
| 66 | //// | 01 45 | 03 15 | ■■■■ | ■■■■ | ■■■■ | 21 55 |
| 64 | //// | 02 21 | 03 33 | ■■■■ | ■■■■ | 21 43 | 21 26 |
| 62 | 00 25 | 02 45 | 03 47 | 19 47 | 20 48 | 21 02 | 21 04 |
| 60 | 01 35 | 03 05 | 04 00 | 18 59 | 20 03 | 20 33 | 20 46 |
| N 58 | 02 07 | 03 20 | 04 10 | 18 28 | 19 33 | 20 11 | 20 31 |
| 56 | 02 30 | 03 34 | 04 19 | 18 05 | 19 11 | 19 53 | 20 18 |
| 54 | 02 48 | 03 45 | 04 27 | 17 46 | 18 52 | 19 37 | 20 07 |
| 52 | 03 03 | 03 55 | 04 34 | 17 30 | 18 36 | 19 24 | 19 57 |
| 50 | 03 16 | 04 04 | 04 41 | 17 16 | 18 22 | 19 12 | 19 48 |
| 45 | 03 41 | 04 22 | 04 54 | 16 48 | 17 54 | 18 48 | 19 28 |
| N 40 | 04 00 | 04 36 | 05 06 | 16 26 | 17 32 | 18 28 | 19 13 |
| 35 | 04 15 | 04 48 | 05 15 | 16 08 | 17 14 | 18 12 | 19 00 |
| 30 | 04 28 | 04 58 | 05 24 | 15 52 | 16 58 | 17 57 | 18 48 |
| 20 | 04 48 | 05 15 | 05 38 | 15 26 | 16 31 | 17 33 | 18 28 |
| N 10 | 05 03 | 05 29 | 05 51 | 15 03 | 16 08 | 17 12 | 18 11 |
| 0 | 05 16 | 05 41 | 06 02 | 14 42 | 15 47 | 16 52 | 17 54 |
| S 10 | 05 27 | 05 52 | 06 14 | 14 20 | 15 26 | 16 32 | 17 38 |
| 20 | 05 36 | 06 03 | 06 26 | 13 58 | 15 03 | 16 11 | 17 20 |
| 30 | 05 46 | 06 14 | 06 39 | 13 32 | 14 36 | 15 47 | 17 00 |
| 35 | 05 51 | 06 21 | 06 47 | 13 16 | 14 20 | 15 32 | 16 48 |
| 40 | 05 55 | 06 28 | 06 56 | 12 59 | 14 02 | 15 15 | 16 34 |
| 45 | 06 01 | 06 35 | 07 06 | 12 37 | 13 40 | 14 55 | 16 18 |
| S 50 | 06 06 | 06 44 | 07 19 | 12 10 | 13 12 | 14 30 | 15 58 |
| 52 | 06 08 | 06 49 | 07 25 | 11 57 | 12 58 | 14 17 | 15 48 |
| 54 | 06 11 | 06 53 | 07 31 | 11 42 | 12 42 | 14 03 | 15 37 |
| 56 | 06 13 | 06 58 | 07 38 | 11 25 | 12 24 | 13 47 | 15 25 |
| 58 | 06 16 | 07 03 | 07 46 | 11 04 | 12 01 | 13 27 | 15 10 |
| S 60 | 06 19 | 07 09 | 07 55 | 10 37 | 11 31 | 13 02 | 14 53 |

| Lat. | Sunset | Civil | Naut. | Moonset 8 | 9 | 10 | 11 |
|---|---|---|---|---|---|---|---|
| ° | h m | h m | h m | h m | h m | h m | h m |
| N 72 | 22 28 | //// | //// | ■■■■ | ■■■■ | ■■■■ | ■■■■ |
| N 70 | 21 43 | //// | //// | ■■■■ | ■■■■ | ■■■■ | ■■■■ |
| 68 | 21 14 | 23 22 | //// | ■■■■ | ■■■■ | ■■■■ | ■■■■ |
| 66 | 20 53 | 22 20 | //// | ■■■■ | ■■■■ | ■■■■ | ■■■■ |
| 64 | 20 36 | 21 47 | //// | ■■■■ | ■■■■ | ■■■■ | 00 43 |
| 62 | 20 22 | 21 23 | 23 27 | 22 04 | 23 21 | 25 24 | 01 24 |
| 60 | 20 10 | 21 04 | 22 31 | 22 52 | 24 06 | 00 06 | 01 52 |
| N 58 | 20 00 | 20 49 | 22 01 | 23 23 | 24 36 | 00 36 | 02 13 |
| 56 | 19 51 | 20 36 | 21 39 | 23 47 | 24 58 | 00 58 | 02 31 |
| 54 | 19 43 | 20 25 | 21 21 | 24 06 | 00 06 | 01 17 | 02 46 |
| 52 | 19 36 | 20 15 | 21 06 | 24 22 | 00 22 | 01 32 | 02 59 |
| 50 | 19 29 | 20 06 | 20 54 | 24 36 | 00 36 | 01 46 | 03 10 |
| 45 | 19 16 | 19 48 | 20 29 | 00 09 | 01 04 | 02 14 | 03 34 |
| N 40 | 19 05 | 19 34 | 20 10 | 00 29 | 01 24 | 02 35 | 03 52 |
| 35 | 18 55 | 19 22 | 19 55 | 00 46 | 01 45 | 02 53 | 04 08 |
| 30 | 18 47 | 19 12 | 19 43 | 01 01 | 02 01 | 03 09 | 04 21 |
| 20 | 18 33 | 18 56 | 19 23 | 01 26 | 02 28 | 03 35 | 04 44 |
| N 10 | 18 20 | 18 42 | 19 08 | 01 48 | 02 51 | 03 57 | 05 04 |
| 0 | 18 09 | 18 30 | 18 55 | 02 08 | 03 13 | 04 18 | 05 22 |
| S 10 | 17 58 | 18 19 | 18 45 | 02 29 | 03 34 | 04 39 | 05 40 |
| 20 | 17 46 | 18 09 | 18 35 | 02 50 | 03 57 | 05 01 | 06 00 |
| 30 | 17 32 | 17 57 | 18 26 | 03 16 | 04 24 | 05 27 | 06 22 |
| 35 | 17 24 | 17 51 | 18 21 | 03 31 | 04 40 | 05 42 | 06 35 |
| 40 | 17 16 | 17 44 | 18 16 | 03 48 | 04 58 | 05 59 | 06 50 |
| 45 | 17 05 | 17 36 | 18 11 | 04 09 | 05 20 | 06 20 | 07 07 |
| S 50 | 16 53 | 17 27 | 18 06 | 04 35 | 05 48 | 06 46 | 07 29 |
| 52 | 16 47 | 17 23 | 18 03 | 04 48 | 06 02 | 06 59 | 07 39 |
| 54 | 16 41 | 17 19 | 18 01 | 05 03 | 06 18 | 07 13 | 07 50 |
| 56 | 16 34 | 17 14 | 17 59 | 05 20 | 06 37 | 07 30 | 08 03 |
| 58 | 16 27 | 17 09 | 17 56 | 05 41 | 07 00 | 07 50 | 08 18 |
| S 60 | 16 17 | 17 03 | 17 53 | 06 07 | 07 30 | 08 15 | 08 36 |

| | SUN Eqn. of Time 00h | 12h | Mer. Pass. | MOON Mer. Pass. Upper | Lower | Age | Phase |
|---|---|---|---|---|---|---|---|
| Day | m s | m s | h m | h m | h m | d | % |
| 8 | 05 45 | 05 41 | 12 06 | 20 57 | 08 25 | 11 | 82 |
| 9 | 05 37 | 05 33 | 12 06 | 22 03 | 09 30 | 12 | 90 |
| 10 | 05 28 | 05 24 | 12 05 | 23 07 | 10 35 | 13 | 96 |

| UT | ARIES | VENUS −3·9 | | MARS +0·0 | | JUPITER −2·7 | | SATURN +0·2 | | STARS | | |
|---|---|---|---|---|---|---|---|---|---|---|---|---|
| | GHA | GHA | Dec | GHA | Dec | GHA | Dec | GHA | Dec | Name | SHA | Dec |
| d h | ° ′ | ° ′ | ° ′ | ° ′ | ° ′ | ° ′ | ° ′ | ° ′ | ° ′ | | ° ′ | ° ′ |
| 11 00 | 319 26.5 | 198 09.4 | N20 43.3 | 267 00.9 | N17 19.4 | 311 06.4 | N 1 58.4 | 354 27.9 | S15 20.7 | Acamar | 315 13.3 | S40 12.6 |
| 01 | 334 28.9 | 213 08.7 | 42.7 | 282 01.8 | 19.8 | 326 08.9 | 58.4 | 9 30.5 | 20.7 | Achernar | 335 21.4 | S57 07.1 |
| 02 | 349 31.4 | 228 07.9 | 42.2 | 297 02.7 | 20.2 | 341 11.5 | 58.3 | 24 33.2 | 20.8 | Acrux | 173 02.7 | S63 13.6 |
| 03 | 4 33.8 | 243 07.2 .. | 41.7 | 312 03.6 .. | 20.6 | 356 14.0 .. | 58.3 | 39 35.8 .. | 20.9 | Adhara | 255 07.7 | S29 00.0 |
| 04 | 19 36.3 | 258 06.4 | 41.1 | 327 04.5 | 21.0 | 11 16.6 | 58.2 | 54 38.5 | 20.9 | Aldebaran | 290 42.0 | N16 33.3 |
| 05 | 34 38.8 | 273 05.7 | 40.6 | 342 05.4 | 21.4 | 26 19.2 | 58.1 | 69 41.1 | 21.0 | | | |
| 06 | 49 41.2 | 288 04.9 | N20 40.1 | 357 06.3 | N17 21.8 | 41 21.7 | N 1 58.1 | 84 43.8 | S15 21.0 | Alioth | 166 15.0 | N55 50.6 |
| 07 | 64 43.7 | 303 04.2 | 39.5 | 12 07.2 | 22.2 | 56 24.3 | 58.0 | 99 46.4 | 21.1 | Alkaid | 152 53.8 | N49 12.4 |
| T 08 | 79 46.2 | 318 03.4 | 39.0 | 27 08.1 | 22.6 | 71 26.8 | 58.0 | 114 49.1 | 21.2 | Alnair | 27 34.9 | S46 51.0 |
| H 09 | 94 48.6 | 333 02.7 .. | 38.5 | 42 09.0 .. | 23.0 | 86 29.4 .. | 57.9 | 129 51.7 .. | 21.2 | Alnilam | 275 39.9 | S 1 11.1 |
| U 10 | 109 51.1 | 348 01.9 | 37.9 | 57 09.9 | 23.4 | 101 32.0 | 57.9 | 144 54.4 | 21.3 | Alphard | 217 50.0 | S 8 45.2 |
| R 11 | 124 53.6 | 3 01.2 | 37.4 | 72 10.9 | 23.8 | 116 34.5 | 57.8 | 159 57.0 | 21.4 | | | |
| S 12 | 139 56.0 | 18 00.4 | N20 36.8 | 87 11.8 | N17 24.2 | 131 37.1 | N 1 57.8 | 174 59.6 | S15 21.4 | Alphecca | 126 05.4 | N26 38.6 |
| D 13 | 154 58.5 | 32 59.7 | 36.3 | 102 12.7 | 24.6 | 146 39.6 | 57.7 | 190 02.3 | 21.5 | Alpheratz | 357 36.5 | N29 12.8 |
| A 14 | 170 01.0 | 47 58.9 | 35.7 | 117 13.6 | 25.0 | 161 42.2 | 57.7 | 205 04.9 | 21.6 | Altair | 62 01.6 | N 8 55.8 |
| Y 15 | 185 03.4 | 62 58.2 .. | 35.2 | 132 14.5 .. | 25.4 | 176 44.8 .. | 57.6 | 220 07.6 .. | 21.6 | Ankaa | 353 08.8 | S42 10.8 |
| 16 | 200 05.9 | 77 57.4 | 34.7 | 147 15.4 | 25.8 | 191 47.3 | 57.6 | 235 10.2 | 21.7 | Antares | 112 18.1 | S26 28.9 |
| 17 | 215 08.3 | 92 56.7 | 34.1 | 162 16.3 | 26.1 | 206 49.9 | 57.5 | 250 12.9 | 21.8 | | | |
| 18 | 230 10.8 | 107 55.9 | N20 33.6 | 177 17.2 | N17 26.5 | 221 52.5 | N 1 57.4 | 265 15.5 | S15 21.8 | Arcturus | 145 49.8 | N19 04.1 |
| 19 | 245 13.3 | 122 55.2 | 33.0 | 192 18.1 | 26.9 | 236 55.0 | 57.4 | 280 18.2 | 21.9 | Atria | 107 13.9 | S69 04.3 |
| 20 | 260 15.7 | 137 54.4 | 32.5 | 207 19.0 | 27.3 | 251 57.6 | 57.3 | 295 20.8 | 21.9 | Avior | 234 16.2 | S59 34.7 |
| 21 | 275 18.2 | 152 53.7 .. | 31.9 | 222 19.9 .. | 27.7 | 267 00.1 .. | 57.3 | 310 23.5 .. | 22.0 | Bellatrix | 278 25.2 | N 6 22.3 |
| 22 | 290 20.7 | 167 52.9 | 31.4 | 237 20.8 | 28.1 | 282 02.7 | 57.2 | 325 26.1 | 22.1 | Betelgeuse | 270 54.4 | N 7 24.7 |
| 23 | 305 23.1 | 182 52.2 | 30.8 | 252 21.7 | 28.5 | 297 05.3 | 57.2 | 340 28.8 | 22.1 | | | |
| 12 00 | 320 25.6 | 197 51.5 | N20 30.2 | 267 22.7 | N17 28.9 | 312 07.8 | N 1 57.1 | 355 31.4 | S15 22.2 | Canopus | 263 53.7 | S52 42.2 |
| 01 | 335 28.1 | 212 50.7 | 29.7 | 282 23.6 | 29.3 | 327 10.4 | 57.1 | 10 34.0 | 22.3 | Capella | 280 25.1 | N46 01.1 |
| 02 | 350 30.5 | 227 50.0 | 29.1 | 297 24.5 | 29.7 | 342 13.0 | 57.0 | 25 36.7 | 22.3 | Deneb | 49 26.7 | N45 21.7 |
| 03 | 5 33.0 | 242 49.2 .. | 28.6 | 312 25.4 .. | 30.1 | 357 15.5 .. | 56.9 | 40 39.3 .. | 22.4 | Denebola | 182 27.2 | N14 27.0 |
| 04 | 20 35.5 | 257 48.5 | 28.0 | 327 26.3 | 30.5 | 12 18.1 | 56.9 | 55 42.0 | 22.5 | Diphda | 348 49.1 | S17 51.6 |
| 05 | 35 37.9 | 272 47.7 | 27.5 | 342 27.2 | 30.9 | 27 20.7 | 56.8 | 70 44.6 | 22.5 | | | |
| 06 | 50 40.4 | 287 47.0 | N20 26.9 | 357 28.1 | N17 31.3 | 42 23.2 | N 1 56.8 | 85 47.3 | S15 22.6 | Dubhe | 193 44.0 | N61 38.0 |
| 07 | 65 42.8 | 302 46.2 | 26.3 | 12 29.0 | 31.7 | 57 25.8 | 56.7 | 100 49.9 | 22.7 | Elnath | 278 04.6 | N28 37.5 |
| 08 | 80 45.3 | 317 45.5 | 25.8 | 27 29.9 | 32.0 | 72 28.4 | 56.7 | 115 52.6 | 22.7 | Eltanin | 90 42.8 | N51 29.4 |
| F 09 | 95 47.8 | 332 44.8 .. | 25.2 | 42 30.8 .. | 32.4 | 87 30.9 .. | 56.6 | 130 55.2 .. | 22.8 | Enif | 33 40.4 | N 9 58.8 |
| R 10 | 110 50.2 | 347 44.0 | 24.6 | 57 31.8 | 32.8 | 102 33.5 | 56.5 | 145 57.9 | 22.8 | Fomalhaut | 15 16.4 | S29 30.1 |
| I 11 | 125 52.7 | 2 43.3 | 24.1 | 72 32.7 | 33.2 | 117 36.1 | 56.5 | 161 00.5 | 22.9 | | | |
| D 12 | 140 55.2 | 17 42.5 | N20 23.5 | 87 33.6 | N17 33.6 | 132 38.6 | N 1 56.4 | 176 03.2 | S15 23.0 | Gacrux | 171 54.2 | S57 14.5 |
| A 13 | 155 57.6 | 32 41.8 | 22.9 | 102 34.5 | 34.0 | 147 41.2 | 56.4 | 191 05.8 | 23.0 | Gienah | 175 45.9 | S17 39.9 |
| Y 14 | 171 00.1 | 47 41.1 | 22.4 | 117 35.4 | 34.4 | 162 43.8 | 56.3 | 206 08.4 | 23.1 | Hadar | 148 39.0 | S60 29.1 |
| 15 | 186 02.6 | 62 40.3 .. | 21.8 | 132 36.3 .. | 34.8 | 177 46.4 .. | 56.3 | 221 11.1 .. | 23.2 | Hamal | 327 53.3 | N23 34.1 |
| 16 | 201 05.0 | 77 39.6 | 21.2 | 147 37.2 | 35.2 | 192 48.9 | 56.2 | 236 13.7 | 23.2 | Kaus Aust. | 83 34.8 | S34 22.5 |
| 17 | 216 07.5 | 92 38.8 | 20.7 | 162 38.1 | 35.6 | 207 51.5 | 56.1 | 251 16.4 | 23.3 | | | |
| 18 | 231 09.9 | 107 38.1 | N20 20.1 | 177 39.1 | N17 35.9 | 222 54.1 | N 1 56.1 | 266 19.0 | S15 23.4 | Kochab | 137 19.9 | N74 04.1 |
| 19 | 246 12.4 | 122 37.4 | 19.5 | 192 40.0 | 36.3 | 237 56.6 | 56.0 | 281 21.7 | 23.4 | Markab | 13 31.6 | N15 19.6 |
| 20 | 261 14.9 | 137 36.6 | 18.9 | 207 40.9 | 36.7 | 252 59.2 | 56.0 | 296 24.3 | 23.5 | Menkar | 314 08.2 | N 4 10.7 |
| 21 | 276 17.3 | 152 35.9 .. | 18.4 | 222 41.8 .. | 37.1 | 268 01.8 .. | 55.9 | 311 27.0 .. | 23.6 | Menkent | 148 00.1 | S36 28.9 |
| 22 | 291 19.8 | 167 35.1 | 17.8 | 237 42.7 | 37.5 | 283 04.4 | 55.9 | 326 29.6 | 23.6 | Miaplacidus | 221 39.6 | S69 48.5 |
| 23 | 306 22.3 | 182 34.4 | 17.2 | 252 43.6 | 37.9 | 298 06.9 | 55.8 | 341 32.3 | 23.7 | | | |
| 13 00 | 321 24.7 | 197 33.7 | N20 16.6 | 267 44.5 | N17 38.3 | 313 09.5 | N 1 55.7 | 356 34.9 | S15 23.7 | Mirfak | 308 31.1 | N49 56.9 |
| 01 | 336 27.2 | 212 32.9 | 16.0 | 282 45.4 | 38.7 | 328 12.1 | 55.7 | 11 37.6 | 23.8 | Nunki | 75 49.9 | S26 16.1 |
| 02 | 351 29.7 | 227 32.2 | 15.5 | 297 46.4 | 39.0 | 343 14.6 | 55.6 | 26 40.2 | 23.9 | Peacock | 53 08.3 | S56 39.8 |
| 03 | 6 32.1 | 242 31.5 .. | 14.9 | 312 47.3 .. | 39.4 | 358 17.2 .. | 55.6 | 41 42.9 .. | 23.9 | Pollux | 243 20.1 | N27 58.3 |
| 04 | 21 34.6 | 257 30.7 | 14.3 | 327 48.2 | 39.8 | 13 19.8 | 55.5 | 56 45.5 | 24.0 | Procyon | 244 53.2 | N 5 10.1 |
| 05 | 36 37.1 | 272 30.0 | 13.7 | 342 49.1 | 40.2 | 28 22.4 | 55.4 | 71 48.1 | 24.1 | | | |
| 06 | 51 39.5 | 287 29.2 | N20 13.1 | 357 50.0 | N17 40.6 | 43 24.9 | N 1 55.4 | 86 50.8 | S15 24.1 | Rasalhague | 96 00.2 | N12 32.8 |
| 07 | 66 42.0 | 302 28.5 | 12.5 | 12 50.9 | 41.0 | 58 27.5 | 55.3 | 101 53.4 | 24.2 | Regulus | 207 36.9 | N11 51.6 |
| S 08 | 81 44.4 | 317 27.8 | 12.0 | 27 51.9 | 41.4 | 73 30.1 | 55.3 | 116 56.1 | 24.3 | Rigel | 281 05.9 | S 8 10.4 |
| A 09 | 96 46.9 | 332 27.0 .. | 11.4 | 42 52.8 .. | 41.7 | 88 32.7 .. | 55.2 | 131 58.7 .. | 24.3 | Rigil Kent. | 139 43.1 | S60 55.8 |
| T 10 | 111 49.4 | 347 26.3 | 10.8 | 57 53.7 | 42.1 | 103 35.2 | 55.1 | 147 01.4 | 24.4 | Sabik | 102 04.9 | S15 45.1 |
| U 11 | 126 51.8 | 2 25.6 | 10.2 | 72 54.6 | 42.5 | 118 37.8 | 55.1 | 162 04.0 | 24.5 | | | |
| R 12 | 141 54.3 | 17 24.8 | N20 09.6 | 87 55.5 | N17 42.9 | 133 40.4 | N 1 55.0 | 177 06.7 | S15 24.5 | Schedar | 349 32.9 | N56 39.5 |
| D 13 | 156 56.8 | 32 24.1 | 09.0 | 102 56.4 | 43.3 | 148 43.0 | 55.0 | 192 09.3 | 24.6 | Shaula | 96 12.8 | S37 07.3 |
| A 14 | 171 59.2 | 47 23.4 | 08.4 | 117 57.4 | 43.7 | 163 45.5 | 54.9 | 207 12.0 | 24.6 | Sirius | 258 28.2 | S16 44.6 |
| Y 15 | 187 01.7 | 62 22.6 .. | 07.8 | 132 58.3 .. | 44.0 | 178 48.1 .. | 54.8 | 222 14.6 .. | 24.7 | Spica | 158 24.5 | S11 16.6 |
| 16 | 202 04.2 | 77 21.9 | 07.2 | 147 59.2 | 44.4 | 193 50.7 | 54.8 | 237 17.3 | 24.8 | Suhail | 222 48.2 | S43 31.3 |
| 17 | 217 06.6 | 92 21.2 | 06.6 | 163 00.1 | 44.8 | 208 53.3 | 54.7 | 252 19.9 | 24.8 | | | |
| 18 | 232 09.1 | 107 20.5 | N20 06.0 | 178 01.0 | N17 45.2 | 223 55.9 | N 1 54.7 | 267 22.6 | S15 24.9 | Vega | 80 34.2 | N38 48.4 |
| 19 | 247 11.6 | 122 19.7 | 05.4 | 193 02.0 | 45.6 | 238 58.4 | 54.6 | 282 25.2 | 25.0 | Zuben'ubi | 136 58.2 | S16 08.1 |
| 20 | 262 14.0 | 137 19.0 | 04.8 | 208 02.9 | 45.9 | 254 01.0 | 54.5 | 297 27.8 | 25.0 | | SHA | Mer. Pass. |
| 21 | 277 16.5 | 152 18.3 .. | 04.2 | 223 03.8 .. | 46.3 | 269 03.6 .. | 54.5 | 312 30.5 .. | 25.1 | | ° ′ | h m |
| 22 | 292 18.9 | 167 17.5 | 03.6 | 238 04.7 | 46.7 | 284 06.2 | 54.4 | 327 33.1 | 25.2 | Venus | 237 25.9 | 10 49 |
| 23 | 307 21.4 | 182 16.8 | 03.0 | 253 05.6 | 47.1 | 299 08.8 | 54.4 | 342 35.8 | 25.2 | Mars | 306 57.1 | 6 10 |
| | h m | | | | | | | | | Jupiter | 351 42.2 | 3 11 |
| Mer. Pass. 2 37.9 | | v −0.7 | d 0.6 | v 0.9 | d 0.4 | v 2.6 | d 0.1 | v 2.6 | d 0.1 | Saturn | 35 05.8 | 0 18 |

| UT | SUN GHA | SUN Dec | MOON GHA | v | MOON Dec | d | HP |
|---|---|---|---|---|---|---|---|
| d h | ° ' | ° ' | ° ' | ' | ° ' | ' | ' |
| 11 00 | 178 40.3 | N15 19.9 | 12 36.6 | 3.3 | S24 07.4 | 8.3 | 60.9 |
| 01 | 193 40.4 | 19.2 | 26 58.9 | 3.4 | 23 59.1 | 8.4 | 60.9 |
| 02 | 208 40.5 | 18.5 | 41 21.3 | 3.4 | 23 50.7 | 8.6 | 60.9 |
| 03 | 223 40.6 | .. 17.7 | 55 43.7 | 3.6 | 23 42.1 | 8.8 | 60.9 |
| 04 | 238 40.7 | 17.0 | 70 06.3 | 3.7 | 23 33.3 | 9.0 | 60.9 |
| 05 | 253 40.8 | 16.2 | 84 29.0 | 3.7 | 23 24.3 | 9.1 | 60.9 |
| 06 | 268 40.9 | N15 15.5 | 98 51.7 | 3.9 | S23 15.2 | 9.3 | 60.9 |
| 07 | 283 41.0 | 14.8 | 113 14.6 | 4.0 | 23 05.9 | 9.5 | 60.9 |
| T 08 | 298 41.1 | 14.0 | 127 37.6 | 4.0 | 22 56.4 | 9.6 | 60.9 |
| H 09 | 313 41.2 | .. 13.3 | 142 00.6 | 4.2 | 22 46.8 | 9.7 | 60.9 |
| U 10 | 328 41.3 | 12.5 | 156 23.8 | 4.2 | 22 37.1 | 10.0 | 60.9 |
| R 11 | 343 41.4 | 11.8 | 170 47.0 | 4.4 | 22 27.1 | 10.1 | 60.9 |
| S 12 | 358 41.5 | N15 11.0 | 185 10.4 | 4.5 | S22 17.0 | 10.2 | 60.8 |
| D 13 | 13 41.6 | 10.3 | 199 33.9 | 4.6 | 22 06.8 | 10.4 | 60.8 |
| A 14 | 28 41.7 | 09.6 | 213 57.5 | 4.7 | 21 56.4 | 10.5 | 60.8 |
| Y 15 | 43 41.8 | .. 08.8 | 228 21.2 | 4.8 | 21 45.9 | 10.7 | 60.8 |
| 16 | 58 41.9 | 08.1 | 242 45.0 | 4.9 | 21 35.2 | 10.9 | 60.8 |
| 17 | 73 42.0 | 07.3 | 257 08.9 | 5.0 | 21 24.3 | 10.9 | 60.8 |
| 18 | 88 42.1 | N15 06.6 | 271 32.9 | 5.2 | S21 13.4 | 11.1 | 60.8 |
| 19 | 103 42.2 | 05.8 | 285 57.1 | 5.2 | 21 02.3 | 11.3 | 60.8 |
| 20 | 118 42.3 | 05.1 | 300 21.3 | 5.4 | 20 51.0 | 11.4 | 60.7 |
| 21 | 133 42.4 | .. 04.3 | 314 45.7 | 5.4 | 20 39.6 | 11.5 | 60.7 |
| 22 | 148 42.5 | 03.6 | 329 10.1 | 5.6 | 20 28.1 | 11.7 | 60.7 |
| 23 | 163 42.6 | 02.8 | 343 34.7 | 5.7 | 20 16.4 | 11.7 | 60.7 |
| 12 00 | 178 42.8 | N15 02.1 | 357 59.4 | 5.8 | S20 04.7 | 12.0 | 60.7 |
| 01 | 193 42.9 | 01.3 | 12 24.2 | 6.0 | 19 52.7 | 12.0 | 60.7 |
| 02 | 208 43.0 | 15 00.6 | 26 49.2 | 6.0 | 19 40.7 | 12.2 | 60.7 |
| 03 | 223 43.1 | 14 59.8 | 41 14.2 | 6.2 | 19 28.5 | 12.2 | 60.6 |
| 04 | 238 43.2 | 59.1 | 55 39.4 | 6.2 | 19 16.3 | 12.4 | 60.6 |
| 05 | 253 43.3 | 58.3 | 70 04.6 | 6.4 | 19 03.9 | 12.6 | 60.6 |
| 06 | 268 43.4 | N14 57.6 | 84 30.0 | 6.5 | S18 51.3 | 12.6 | 60.6 |
| 07 | 283 43.5 | 56.8 | 98 55.5 | 6.7 | 18 38.7 | 12.7 | 60.6 |
| 08 | 298 43.6 | 56.1 | 113 21.2 | 6.7 | 18 26.0 | 12.9 | 60.6 |
| F 09 | 313 43.7 | .. 55.3 | 127 46.9 | 6.9 | 18 13.1 | 13.0 | 60.5 |
| R 10 | 328 43.8 | 54.6 | 142 12.8 | 6.9 | 18 00.1 | 13.0 | 60.5 |
| I 11 | 343 43.9 | 53.8 | 156 38.7 | 7.1 | 17 47.1 | 13.2 | 60.5 |
| D 12 | 358 44.0 | N14 53.1 | 171 04.8 | 7.2 | S17 33.9 | 13.3 | 60.5 |
| A 13 | 13 44.1 | 52.3 | 185 31.0 | 7.3 | 17 20.6 | 13.4 | 60.5 |
| Y 14 | 28 44.3 | 51.6 | 199 57.3 | 7.4 | 17 07.2 | 13.4 | 60.4 |
| 15 | 43 44.4 | .. 50.8 | 214 23.7 | 7.6 | 16 53.8 | 13.6 | 60.4 |
| 16 | 58 44.5 | 50.1 | 228 50.3 | 7.6 | 16 40.2 | 13.7 | 60.4 |
| 17 | 73 44.6 | 49.3 | 243 16.9 | 7.8 | 16 26.5 | 13.7 | 60.4 |
| 18 | 88 44.7 | N14 48.5 | 257 43.7 | 7.9 | S16 12.8 | 13.8 | 60.3 |
| 19 | 103 44.8 | 47.8 | 272 10.6 | 7.9 | 15 59.0 | 14.0 | 60.3 |
| 20 | 118 44.9 | 47.0 | 286 37.5 | 8.1 | 15 45.0 | 14.0 | 60.3 |
| 21 | 133 45.0 | .. 46.3 | 301 04.6 | 8.3 | 15 31.0 | 14.1 | 60.3 |
| 22 | 148 45.1 | 45.5 | 315 31.9 | 8.3 | 15 16.9 | 14.1 | 60.2 |
| 23 | 163 45.2 | 44.8 | 329 59.2 | 8.4 | 15 02.8 | 14.3 | 60.2 |
| 13 00 | 178 45.4 | N14 44.0 | 344 26.6 | 8.5 | S14 48.5 | 14.3 | 60.2 |
| 01 | 193 45.5 | 43.2 | 358 54.1 | 8.7 | 14 34.2 | 14.4 | 60.2 |
| 02 | 208 45.6 | 42.5 | 13 21.8 | 8.7 | 14 19.8 | 14.5 | 60.1 |
| 03 | 223 45.7 | .. 41.7 | 27 49.5 | 8.9 | 14 05.3 | 14.5 | 60.1 |
| 04 | 238 45.8 | 41.0 | 42 17.4 | 8.9 | 13 50.8 | 14.6 | 60.1 |
| 05 | 253 45.9 | 40.2 | 56 45.3 | 9.1 | 13 36.2 | 14.7 | 60.1 |
| 06 | 268 46.0 | N14 39.4 | 71 13.4 | 9.2 | S13 21.5 | 14.7 | 60.0 |
| S 07 | 283 46.1 | 38.7 | 85 41.6 | 9.2 | 13 06.8 | 14.8 | 60.0 |
| A 08 | 298 46.3 | 37.9 | 100 09.8 | 9.4 | 12 52.0 | 14.9 | 60.0 |
| T 09 | 313 46.4 | .. 37.2 | 114 38.2 | 9.5 | 12 37.1 | 14.9 | 59.9 |
| U 10 | 328 46.5 | 36.4 | 129 06.7 | 9.6 | 12 22.2 | 14.9 | 59.9 |
| R 11 | 343 46.6 | 35.6 | 143 35.3 | 9.6 | 12 07.3 | 15.1 | 59.9 |
| D 12 | 358 46.7 | N14 34.9 | 158 03.9 | 9.8 | S11 52.2 | 15.0 | 59.9 |
| A 13 | 13 46.8 | 34.1 | 172 32.7 | 9.9 | 11 37.2 | 15.1 | 59.8 |
| Y 14 | 28 46.9 | 33.3 | 187 01.6 | 9.9 | 11 22.1 | 15.2 | 59.8 |
| 15 | 43 47.0 | .. 32.6 | 201 30.5 | 10.1 | 11 06.9 | 15.2 | 59.8 |
| 16 | 58 47.2 | 31.8 | 215 59.6 | 10.2 | 10 51.7 | 15.3 | 59.7 |
| 17 | 73 47.3 | 31.1 | 230 28.8 | 10.2 | 10 36.4 | 15.3 | 59.7 |
| 18 | 88 47.4 | N14 30.3 | 244 58.0 | 10.3 | S10 21.1 | 15.3 | 59.7 |
| 19 | 103 47.5 | 29.5 | 259 27.3 | 10.5 | 10 05.8 | 15.4 | 59.6 |
| 20 | 118 47.6 | 28.8 | 273 56.8 | 10.5 | 9 50.4 | 15.4 | 59.6 |
| 21 | 133 47.7 | .. 28.0 | 288 26.3 | 10.6 | 9 35.0 | 15.4 | 59.6 |
| 22 | 148 47.9 | 27.2 | 302 55.9 | 10.7 | 9 19.6 | 15.5 | 59.5 |
| 23 | 163 48.0 | 26.5 | 317 25.6 | 10.8 | S 9 04.1 | 15.5 | 59.5 |
| | SD 15.8 | d 0.8 | SD 16.6 | | 16.5 | | 16.3 |

| Lat. | Twilight Naut. | Twilight Civil | Sunrise | Moonrise 11 | Moonrise 12 | Moonrise 13 | Moonrise 14 |
|---|---|---|---|---|---|---|---|
| ° | h m | h m | h m | h m | h m | h m | h m |
| N 72 | //// | //// | 02 01 | ■■ | 22 48 | 21 52 | 21 16 |
| N 70 | //// | //// | 02 40 | ■■ | 22 15 | 21 38 | 21 12 |
| 68 | //// | 01 16 | 03 06 | 22 36 | 21 51 | 21 27 | 21 08 |
| 66 | //// | 02 04 | 03 26 | 21 55 | 21 32 | 21 17 | 21 05 |
| 64 | //// | 02 34 | 03 42 | 21 26 | 21 16 | 21 09 | 21 02 |
| 62 | 01 08 | 02 56 | 03 56 | 21 04 | 21 03 | 21 02 | 21 00 |
| 60 | 01 51 | 03 14 | 04 07 | 20 46 | 20 52 | 20 56 | 20 58 |
| N 58 | 02 19 | 03 28 | 04 16 | 20 31 | 20 43 | 20 50 | 20 56 |
| 56 | 02 39 | 03 40 | 04 25 | 20 18 | 20 34 | 20 45 | 20 54 |
| 54 | 02 56 | 03 51 | 04 32 | 20 07 | 20 26 | 20 41 | 20 53 |
| 52 | 03 10 | 04 00 | 04 39 | 19 57 | 20 20 | 20 37 | 20 51 |
| 50 | 03 22 | 04 08 | 04 45 | 19 48 | 20 13 | 20 33 | 20 50 |
| 45 | 03 46 | 04 26 | 04 58 | 19 28 | 20 00 | 20 26 | 20 47 |
| N 40 | 04 04 | 04 39 | 05 09 | 19 13 | 19 49 | 20 19 | 20 45 |
| 35 | 04 18 | 04 51 | 05 18 | 19 00 | 19 39 | 20 13 | 20 43 |
| 30 | 04 30 | 05 00 | 05 26 | 18 48 | 19 31 | 20 08 | 20 41 |
| 20 | 04 49 | 05 16 | 05 39 | 18 28 | 19 16 | 19 59 | 20 38 |
| N 10 | 05 03 | 05 29 | 05 51 | 18 11 | 19 04 | 19 52 | 20 36 |
| 0 | 05 15 | 05 40 | 06 02 | 17 54 | 18 52 | 19 44 | 20 33 |
| S 10 | 05 26 | 05 51 | 06 12 | 17 38 | 18 40 | 19 37 | 20 31 |
| 20 | 05 35 | 06 01 | 06 24 | 17 20 | 18 27 | 19 29 | 20 28 |
| 30 | 05 43 | 06 12 | 06 37 | 17 00 | 18 12 | 19 20 | 20 25 |
| 35 | 05 48 | 06 18 | 06 44 | 16 48 | 18 03 | 19 15 | 20 23 |
| 40 | 05 52 | 06 24 | 06 52 | 16 34 | 17 53 | 19 09 | 20 21 |
| 45 | 05 57 | 06 31 | 07 02 | 16 18 | 17 41 | 19 02 | 20 19 |
| S 50 | 06 01 | 06 40 | 07 14 | 15 58 | 17 27 | 18 54 | 20 16 |
| 52 | 06 03 | 06 43 | 07 19 | 15 48 | 17 21 | 18 50 | 20 15 |
| 54 | 06 05 | 06 47 | 07 25 | 15 37 | 17 13 | 18 46 | 20 14 |
| 56 | 06 08 | 06 52 | 07 32 | 15 25 | 17 05 | 18 41 | 20 12 |
| 58 | 06 10 | 06 57 | 07 39 | 15 10 | 16 55 | 18 36 | 20 10 |
| S 60 | 06 13 | 07 02 | 07 47 | 14 53 | 16 44 | 18 30 | 20 08 |

| Lat. | Sunset | Twilight Civil | Twilight Naut. | Moonset 11 | Moonset 12 | Moonset 13 | Moonset 14 |
|---|---|---|---|---|---|---|---|
| ° | h m | h m | h m | h m | h m | h m | h m |
| N 72 | 22 02 | //// | //// | ■■ | ■■ | 03 49 | 06 33 |
| N 70 | 21 26 | //// | //// | ■■ | ■■ | 04 20 | 06 44 |
| 68 | 21 00 | 22 45 | //// | ■■ | 01 59 | 04 42 | 06 53 |
| 66 | 20 41 | 22 01 | //// | ■■ | 02 40 | 04 59 | 07 01 |
| 64 | 20 25 | 21 33 | //// | 00 43 | 03 07 | 05 13 | 07 07 |
| 62 | 20 13 | 21 11 | 22 54 | 01 24 | 03 32 | 05 25 | 07 12 |
| 60 | 20 02 | 20 54 | 22 15 | 01 52 | 03 45 | 05 35 | 07 17 |
| N 58 | 19 52 | 20 40 | 21 48 | 02 13 | 04 00 | 05 43 | 07 21 |
| 56 | 19 44 | 20 28 | 21 20 | 02 31 | 04 12 | 05 51 | 07 25 |
| 54 | 19 37 | 20 10 | 21 12 | 02 46 | 04 22 | 05 57 | 07 28 |
| 52 | 19 30 | 20 09 | 20 58 | 02 59 | 04 32 | 06 03 | 07 31 |
| 50 | 19 24 | 20 00 | 20 47 | 03 10 | 04 40 | 06 09 | 07 34 |
| 45 | 19 11 | 19 44 | 20 23 | 03 34 | 04 58 | 06 20 | 07 39 |
| N 40 | 19 01 | 19 30 | 20 06 | 03 52 | 05 12 | 06 30 | 07 44 |
| 35 | 18 52 | 19 19 | 19 51 | 04 08 | 05 24 | 06 38 | 07 48 |
| 30 | 18 44 | 19 09 | 19 40 | 04 21 | 05 34 | 06 45 | 07 52 |
| 20 | 18 31 | 18 54 | 19 21 | 04 44 | 05 52 | 06 57 | 07 58 |
| N 10 | 18 19 | 18 41 | 19 06 | 05 04 | 06 08 | 07 07 | 08 03 |
| 0 | 18 08 | 18 30 | 18 55 | 05 22 | 06 22 | 07 17 | 08 08 |
| S 10 | 17 58 | 18 20 | 18 45 | 05 40 | 06 36 | 07 27 | 08 13 |
| 20 | 17 47 | 18 09 | 18 36 | 06 00 | 06 51 | 07 37 | 08 18 |
| 30 | 17 34 | 17 59 | 18 27 | 06 22 | 07 09 | 07 49 | 08 24 |
| 35 | 17 27 | 17 53 | 18 23 | 06 35 | 07 19 | 07 55 | 08 27 |
| 40 | 17 18 | 17 47 | 18 19 | 06 50 | 07 30 | 08 03 | 08 31 |
| 45 | 17 09 | 17 39 | 18 14 | 07 07 | 07 43 | 08 11 | 08 35 |
| S 50 | 16 57 | 17 31 | 18 09 | 07 29 | 07 59 | 08 22 | 08 40 |
| 52 | 16 52 | 17 28 | 18 08 | 07 39 | 08 06 | 08 27 | 08 42 |
| 54 | 16 46 | 17 24 | 18 05 | 07 50 | 08 15 | 08 32 | 08 45 |
| 56 | 16 39 | 17 19 | 18 03 | 08 03 | 08 24 | 08 38 | 08 48 |
| 58 | 16 32 | 17 14 | 18 01 | 08 18 | 08 34 | 08 44 | 08 51 |
| S 60 | 16 24 | 17 09 | 17 59 | 08 36 | 08 46 | 08 51 | 08 54 |

| | SUN Eqn. of Time 00h | SUN Eqn. of Time 12h | SUN Mer. Pass. | MOON Mer. Pass. Upper | MOON Mer. Pass. Lower | Age | Phase |
|---|---|---|---|---|---|---|---|
| Day | | | | | | | |
| d | m s | m s | h m | h m | h m | d % | |
| 11 | 05 19 | 05 14 | 12 05 | 24 08 | 11 38 | 14 99 | |
| 12 | 05 09 | 05 04 | 12 05 | 00 08 | 12 37 | 15 100 | |
| 13 | 04 59 | 04 53 | 12 05 | 01 05 | 13 31 | 16 97 | |

| UT | ARIES GHA | VENUS −3.9 GHA | Dec | MARS +0.0 GHA | Dec | JUPITER −2.8 GHA | Dec | SATURN +0.2 GHA | Dec | STARS Name | SHA | Dec |
|---|---|---|---|---|---|---|---|---|---|---|---|---|
| d h | ° ′ | ° ′ | ° ′ | ° ′ | ° ′ | ° ′ | ° ′ | ° ′ | ° ′ | | ° ′ | ° ′ |
| 14 00 | 322 23.9 | 197 16.1 | N20 02.4 | 268 06.5 | N17 47.5 | 314 11.3 | N 1 54.3 | 357 38.4 | S15 25.3 | Acamar | 315 13.2 | S40 12.6 |
| 01 | 337 26.3 | 212 15.3 | 01.8 | 283 07.5 | 47.8 | 329 13.9 | 54.2 | 12 41.1 | 25.4 | Achernar | 335 21.4 | S57 07.1 |
| 02 | 352 28.8 | 227 14.6 | 01.2 | 298 08.4 | 48.2 | 344 16.5 | 54.2 | 27 43.7 | 25.4 | Acrux | 173 02.7 | S63 13.6 |
| 03 | 7 31.3 | 242 13.9 .. | 00.6 | 313 09.3 .. | 48.6 | 359 19.1 .. | 54.1 | 42 46.4 .. | 25.5 | Adhara | 255 07.7 | S28 59.9 |
| 04 | 22 33.7 | 257 13.2 | 20 00.0 | 328 10.2 | 49.0 | 14 21.7 | 54.0 | 57 49.0 | 25.5 | Aldebaran | 290 42.0 | N16 33.3 |
| 05 | 37 36.2 | 272 12.4 | 19 59.4 | 343 11.1 | 49.4 | 29 24.2 | 54.0 | 72 51.7 | 25.6 | | | |
| 06 | 52 38.7 | 287 11.7 | N19 58.8 | 358 12.1 | N17 49.7 | 44 26.8 | N 1 53.9 | 87 54.3 | S15 25.7 | Alioth | 166 15.1 | N55 50.6 |
| 07 | 67 41.1 | 302 11.0 | 58.2 | 13 13.0 | 50.1 | 59 29.4 | 53.9 | 102 57.0 | 25.7 | Alkaid | 152 53.8 | N49 12.4 |
| 08 | 82 43.6 | 317 10.3 | 57.6 | 28 13.9 | 50.5 | 74 32.0 | 53.8 | 117 59.6 | 25.8 | Alnair | 27 34.9 | S46 51.0 |
| S 09 | 97 46.0 | 332 09.5 .. | 56.9 | 43 14.8 .. | 50.9 | 89 34.6 .. | 53.7 | 133 02.3 .. | 25.9 | Alnilam | 275 39.9 | S 1 11.1 |
| U 10 | 112 48.5 | 347 08.8 | 56.3 | 58 15.8 | 51.3 | 104 37.1 | 53.7 | 148 04.9 | 25.9 | Alphard | 217 50.0 | S 8 45.2 |
| N 11 | 127 51.0 | 2 08.1 | 55.7 | 73 16.7 | 51.6 | 119 39.7 | 53.6 | 163 07.5 | 26.0 | | | |
| D 12 | 142 53.4 | 17 07.4 | N19 55.1 | 88 17.6 | N17 52.0 | 134 42.3 | N 1 53.5 | 178 10.2 | S15 26.1 | Alphecca | 126 05.4 | N26 38.6 |
| A 13 | 157 55.9 | 32 06.6 | 54.5 | 103 18.5 | 52.4 | 149 44.9 | 53.5 | 193 12.8 | 26.1 | Alpheratz | 357 36.5 | N29 12.8 |
| Y 14 | 172 58.4 | 47 05.9 | 53.9 | 118 19.4 | 52.8 | 164 47.5 | 53.4 | 208 15.5 | 26.2 | Altair | 62 01.6 | N 8 55.8 |
| 15 | 188 00.8 | 62 05.2 .. | 53.2 | 133 20.4 .. | 53.1 | 179 50.1 .. | 53.4 | 223 18.1 .. | 26.2 | Ankaa | 353 08.8 | S42 10.8 |
| 16 | 203 03.3 | 77 04.5 | 52.6 | 148 21.3 | 53.5 | 194 52.6 | 53.3 | 238 20.8 | 26.3 | Antares | 112 18.1 | S26 28.9 |
| 17 | 218 05.8 | 92 03.7 | 52.0 | 163 22.2 | 53.9 | 209 55.2 | 53.2 | 253 23.4 | 26.4 | | | |
| 18 | 233 08.2 | 107 03.0 | N19 51.4 | 178 23.1 | N17 54.3 | 224 57.8 | N 1 53.2 | 268 26.1 | S15 26.4 | Arcturus | 145 49.8 | N19 04.1 |
| 19 | 248 10.7 | 122 02.3 | 50.8 | 193 24.1 | 54.6 | 240 00.4 | 53.1 | 283 28.7 | 26.5 | Atria | 107 13.9 | S69 04.3 |
| 20 | 263 13.2 | 137 01.6 | 50.1 | 208 25.0 | 55.0 | 255 03.0 | 53.0 | 298 31.4 | 26.6 | Avior | 234 16.1 | S59 34.7 |
| 21 | 278 15.6 | 152 00.8 .. | 49.5 | 223 25.9 .. | 55.4 | 270 05.6 .. | 53.0 | 313 34.0 .. | 26.6 | Bellatrix | 278 25.2 | N 6 22.3 |
| 22 | 293 18.1 | 167 00.1 | 48.9 | 238 26.8 | 55.8 | 285 08.2 | 52.9 | 328 36.7 | 26.7 | Betelgeuse | 270 54.4 | N 7 24.7 |
| 23 | 308 20.5 | 181 59.4 | 48.3 | 253 27.8 | 56.1 | 300 10.7 | 52.8 | 343 39.3 | 26.8 | | | |
| 15 00 | 323 23.0 | 196 58.7 | N19 47.6 | 268 28.7 | N17 56.5 | 315 13.3 | N 1 52.8 | 358 42.0 | S15 26.8 | Canopus | 263 53.6 | S52 42.2 |
| 01 | 338 25.5 | 211 58.0 | 47.0 | 283 29.6 | 56.9 | 330 15.9 | 52.7 | 13 44.6 | 26.9 | Capella | 280 25.0 | N46 01.1 |
| 02 | 353 27.9 | 226 57.2 | 46.4 | 298 30.5 | 57.3 | 345 18.5 | 52.6 | 28 47.2 | 27.0 | Deneb | 49 26.7 | N45 21.7 |
| 03 | 8 30.4 | 241 56.5 .. | 45.7 | 313 31.5 .. | 57.6 | 0 21.1 .. | 52.6 | 43 49.9 .. | 27.0 | Denebola | 182 27.2 | N14 27.0 |
| 04 | 23 32.9 | 256 55.8 | 45.1 | 328 32.4 | 58.0 | 15 23.7 | 52.5 | 58 52.5 | 27.1 | Diphda | 348 49.1 | S17 51.6 |
| 05 | 38 35.3 | 271 55.1 | 44.5 | 343 33.3 | 58.4 | 30 26.3 | 52.5 | 73 55.2 | 27.1 | | | |
| 06 | 53 37.8 | 286 54.4 | N19 43.9 | 358 34.3 | N17 58.8 | 45 28.9 | N 1 52.4 | 88 57.8 | S15 27.2 | Dubhe | 193 44.1 | N61 38.0 |
| 07 | 68 40.3 | 301 53.6 | 43.2 | 13 35.2 | 59.1 | 60 31.5 | 52.3 | 104 00.5 | 27.3 | Elnath | 278 04.6 | N28 37.5 |
| 08 | 83 42.7 | 316 52.9 | 42.6 | 28 36.1 | 59.5 | 75 34.0 | 52.3 | 119 03.1 | 27.3 | Eltanin | 90 42.8 | N51 29.4 |
| M 09 | 98 45.2 | 331 52.2 .. | 41.9 | 43 37.0 | 17 59.9 | 90 36.6 .. | 52.2 | 134 05.8 .. | 27.4 | Enif | 33 40.4 | N 9 58.8 |
| O 10 | 113 47.6 | 346 51.5 | 41.3 | 58 38.0 | 18 00.2 | 105 39.2 | 52.1 | 149 08.4 | 27.5 | Fomalhaut | 15 16.4 | S29 30.1 |
| N 11 | 128 50.1 | 1 50.8 | 40.7 | 73 38.9 | 00.6 | 120 41.8 | 52.1 | 164 11.1 | 27.5 | | | |
| D 12 | 143 52.6 | 16 50.1 | N19 40.0 | 88 39.8 | N18 01.0 | 135 44.4 | N 1 52.0 | 179 13.7 | S15 27.6 | Gacrux | 171 54.2 | S57 14.5 |
| A 13 | 158 55.0 | 31 49.3 | 39.4 | 103 40.7 | 01.4 | 150 47.0 | 51.9 | 194 16.4 | 27.7 | Gienah | 175 45.9 | S17 39.9 |
| Y 14 | 173 57.5 | 46 48.6 | 38.7 | 118 41.7 | 01.7 | 165 49.6 | 51.9 | 209 19.0 | 27.7 | Hadar | 148 39.0 | S60 29.1 |
| 15 | 189 00.0 | 61 47.9 .. | 38.1 | 133 42.6 .. | 02.1 | 180 52.2 .. | 51.8 | 224 21.7 .. | 27.8 | Hamal | 327 53.3 | N23 34.1 |
| 16 | 204 02.4 | 76 47.2 | 37.5 | 148 43.5 | 02.5 | 195 54.8 | 51.7 | 239 24.3 | 27.8 | Kaus Aust. | 83 34.9 | S34 22.5 |
| 17 | 219 04.9 | 91 46.5 | 36.8 | 163 44.5 | 02.8 | 210 57.4 | 51.7 | 254 27.0 | 27.9 | | | |
| 18 | 234 07.4 | 106 45.8 | N19 36.2 | 178 45.4 | N18 03.2 | 226 00.0 | N 1 51.6 | 269 29.6 | S15 28.0 | Kochab | 137 19.9 | N74 04.1 |
| 19 | 249 09.8 | 121 45.1 | 35.5 | 193 46.3 | 03.6 | 241 02.5 | 51.5 | 284 32.2 | 28.0 | Markab | 13 31.6 | N15 19.6 |
| 20 | 264 12.3 | 136 44.3 | 34.9 | 208 47.3 | 03.9 | 256 05.1 | 51.5 | 299 34.9 | 28.1 | Menkar | 314 08.2 | N 4 10.7 |
| 21 | 279 14.8 | 151 43.6 .. | 34.2 | 223 48.2 .. | 04.3 | 271 07.7 .. | 51.4 | 314 37.5 .. | 28.2 | Menkent | 148 00.1 | S36 28.9 |
| 22 | 294 17.2 | 166 42.9 | 33.6 | 238 49.1 | 04.7 | 286 10.3 | 51.3 | 329 40.2 | 28.2 | Miaplacidus | 221 39.6 | S69 48.5 |
| 23 | 309 19.7 | 181 42.2 | 32.9 | 253 50.0 | 05.0 | 301 12.9 | 51.3 | 344 42.8 | 28.3 | | | |
| 16 00 | 324 22.1 | 196 41.5 | N19 32.3 | 268 51.0 | N18 05.4 | 316 15.5 | N 1 51.2 | 359 45.5 | S15 28.4 | Mirfak | 308 31.1 | N49 56.2 |
| 01 | 339 24.6 | 211 40.8 | 31.6 | 283 51.9 | 05.8 | 331 18.1 | 51.1 | 14 48.1 | 28.4 | Nunki | 75 49.9 | S26 16.1 |
| 02 | 354 27.1 | 226 40.1 | 31.0 | 298 52.8 | 06.1 | 346 20.7 | 51.1 | 29 50.8 | 28.5 | Peacock | 53 08.3 | S56 39.8 |
| 03 | 9 29.5 | 241 39.4 .. | 30.3 | 313 53.8 .. | 06.5 | 1 23.3 .. | 51.0 | 44 53.4 .. | 28.5 | Pollux | 243 20.1 | N27 58.3 |
| 04 | 24 32.0 | 256 38.7 | 29.7 | 328 54.7 | 06.9 | 16 25.9 | 50.9 | 59 56.1 | 28.6 | Procyon | 244 53.2 | N 5 10.1 |
| 05 | 39 34.5 | 271 37.9 | 29.0 | 343 55.6 | 07.2 | 31 28.5 | 50.8 | 74 58.7 | 28.7 | | | |
| 06 | 54 36.9 | 286 37.2 | N19 28.4 | 358 56.6 | N18 07.6 | 46 31.1 | N 1 50.8 | 90 01.4 | S15 28.7 | Rasalhague | 96 00.2 | N12 32.8 |
| 07 | 69 39.4 | 301 36.5 | 27.7 | 13 57.5 | 08.0 | 61 33.7 | 50.7 | 105 04.0 | 28.8 | Regulus | 207 36.9 | N11 51.6 |
| 08 | 84 41.9 | 316 35.8 | 27.0 | 28 58.4 | 08.3 | 76 36.3 | 50.6 | 120 06.7 | 28.9 | Rigel | 281 05.9 | S 8 10.4 |
| T 09 | 99 44.3 | 331 35.1 .. | 26.4 | 43 59.4 .. | 08.7 | 91 38.9 .. | 50.6 | 135 09.3 .. | 28.9 | Rigil Kent. | 139 43.2 | S60 55.8 |
| U 10 | 114 46.8 | 346 34.4 | 25.7 | 59 00.3 | 09.1 | 106 41.5 | 50.5 | 150 11.9 | 29.0 | Sabik | 102 04.9 | S15 45.1 |
| E 11 | 129 49.3 | 1 33.7 | 25.1 | 74 01.2 | 09.4 | 121 44.1 | 50.4 | 165 14.6 | 29.1 | | | |
| S 12 | 144 51.7 | 16 33.0 | N19 24.4 | 89 02.2 | N18 09.8 | 136 46.7 | N 1 50.4 | 180 17.2 | S15 29.1 | Schedar | 349 32.9 | N56 39.5 |
| D 13 | 159 54.2 | 31 32.3 | 23.7 | 104 03.1 | 10.2 | 151 49.3 | 50.3 | 195 19.9 | 29.2 | Shaula | 96 12.8 | S37 07.3 |
| A 14 | 174 56.6 | 46 31.6 | 23.1 | 119 04.0 | 10.5 | 166 51.9 | 50.2 | 210 22.5 | 29.2 | Sirius | 258 28.2 | S16 44.6 |
| Y 15 | 189 59.1 | 61 30.9 .. | 22.4 | 134 05.0 .. | 10.9 | 181 54.5 .. | 50.2 | 225 25.2 .. | 29.3 | Spica | 158 24.5 | S11 16.6 |
| 16 | 205 01.6 | 76 30.2 | 21.7 | 149 05.9 | 11.3 | 196 57.1 | 50.1 | 240 27.8 | 29.4 | Suhail | 222 48.2 | S43 31.3 |
| 17 | 220 04.0 | 91 29.4 | 21.1 | 164 06.9 | 11.6 | 211 59.7 | 50.0 | 255 30.5 | 29.4 | | | |
| 18 | 235 06.5 | 106 28.7 | N19 20.4 | 179 07.8 | N18 12.0 | 227 02.3 | N 1 50.0 | 270 33.1 | S15 29.5 | Vega | 80 34.2 | N38 48.5 |
| 19 | 250 09.0 | 121 28.0 | 19.7 | 194 08.7 | 12.3 | 242 04.9 | 49.9 | 285 35.8 | 29.6 | Zuben'ubi | 136 58.2 | S16 08.1 |
| 20 | 265 11.4 | 136 27.3 | 19.1 | 209 09.7 | 12.7 | 257 07.5 | 49.8 | 300 38.4 | 29.6 | | SHA | Mer. Pass. |
| 21 | 280 13.9 | 151 26.6 .. | 18.4 | 224 10.6 .. | 13.1 | 272 10.1 .. | 49.7 | 315 41.1 .. | 29.7 | | ° ′ | h m |
| 22 | 295 16.4 | 166 25.9 | 17.7 | 239 11.5 | 13.4 | 287 12.7 | 49.7 | 330 43.7 | 29.8 | Venus | 233 35.7 | 10 53 |
| 23 | 310 18.8 | 181 25.2 | 17.0 | 254 12.5 | 13.8 | 302 15.3 | 49.6 | 345 46.4 | 29.8 | Mars | 305 05.7 | 6 06 |
| | h m | | | | | | | | | Jupiter | 351 50.3 | 2 59 |
| Mer. Pass. 2 26.1 | | v −0.7 | d 0.6 | v 0.9 | d 0.4 | v 2.6 | d 0.1 | v 2.6 | d 0.1 | Saturn | 35 18.9 | 0 05 |

| UT | SUN GHA | SUN Dec | MOON GHA | v | MOON Dec | d | HP |
|---|---|---|---|---|---|---|---|
| d h | ° ′ | ° ′ | ° ′ | ′ | ° ′ | ′ | ′ |
| 14 00 | 178 48.1 | N14 25.7 | 331 55.4 | 10.8 | S 8 48.6 | 15.6 | 59.5 |
| 01 | 193 48.2 | 24.9 | 346 25.2 | 11.0 | 8 33.0 | 15.5 | 59.4 |
| 02 | 208 48.3 | 24.1 | 0 55.2 | 11.0 | 8 17.5 | 15.6 | 59.4 |
| 03 | 223 48.4 .. | 23.4 | 15 25.2 | 11.1 | 8 01.9 | 15.6 | 59.4 |
| 04 | 238 48.6 | 22.6 | 29 55.3 | 11.2 | 7 46.3 | 15.7 | 59.3 |
| 05 | 253 48.7 | 21.8 | 44 25.5 | 11.3 | 7 30.6 | 15.6 | 59.3 |
| 06 | 268 48.8 | N14 21.1 | 58 55.8 | 11.3 | S 7 15.0 | 15.7 | 59.3 |
| 07 | 283 48.9 | 20.3 | 73 26.1 | 11.4 | 6 59.3 | 15.7 | 59.2 |
| 08 | 298 49.0 | 19.5 | 87 56.5 | 11.5 | 6 43.6 | 15.7 | 59.2 |
| S 09 | 313 49.2 .. | 18.8 | 102 27.0 | 11.6 | 6 27.9 | 15.7 | 59.2 |
| U 10 | 328 49.3 | 18.0 | 116 57.6 | 11.6 | 6 12.2 | 15.8 | 59.1 |
| N 11 | 343 49.4 | 17.2 | 131 28.2 | 11.7 | 5 56.5 | 15.8 | 59.1 |
| D 12 | 358 49.5 | N14 16.4 | 145 58.9 | 11.8 | S 5 40.7 | 15.7 | 59.0 |
| A 13 | 13 49.6 | 15.7 | 160 29.7 | 11.9 | 5 25.0 | 15.8 | 59.0 |
| Y 14 | 28 49.7 | 14.9 | 175 00.6 | 11.9 | 5 09.2 | 15.7 | 59.0 |
| 15 | 43 49.9 .. | 14.1 | 189 31.5 | 12.0 | 4 53.5 | 15.8 | 58.9 |
| 16 | 58 50.0 | 13.3 | 204 02.5 | 12.0 | 4 37.7 | 15.8 | 58.9 |
| 17 | 73 50.1 | 12.6 | 218 33.5 | 12.1 | 4 21.9 | 15.7 | 58.9 |
| 18 | 88 50.2 | N14 11.8 | 233 04.6 | 12.2 | S 4 06.2 | 15.8 | 58.8 |
| 19 | 103 50.4 | 11.0 | 247 35.8 | 12.3 | 3 50.4 | 15.8 | 58.8 |
| 20 | 118 50.5 | 10.2 | 262 07.1 | 12.3 | 3 34.6 | 15.8 | 58.8 |
| 21 | 133 50.6 .. | 09.5 | 276 38.4 | 12.3 | 3 18.9 | 15.8 | 58.7 |
| 22 | 148 50.7 | 08.7 | 291 09.7 | 12.4 | 3 03.1 | 15.8 | 58.7 |
| 23 | 163 50.8 | 07.9 | 305 41.1 | 12.5 | 2 47.3 | 15.7 | 58.6 |
| 15 00 | 178 51.0 | N14 07.1 | 320 12.6 | 12.5 | S 2 31.6 | 15.7 | 58.6 |
| 01 | 193 51.1 | 06.4 | 334 44.1 | 12.6 | 2 15.9 | 15.8 | 58.6 |
| 02 | 208 51.2 | 05.6 | 349 15.7 | 12.6 | 2 00.1 | 15.7 | 58.5 |
| 03 | 223 51.3 .. | 04.8 | 3 47.3 | 12.7 | 1 44.4 | 15.7 | 58.5 |
| 04 | 238 51.5 | 04.0 | 18 19.0 | 12.8 | 1 28.7 | 15.7 | 58.5 |
| 05 | 253 51.6 | 03.2 | 32 50.8 | 12.7 | 1 13.0 | 15.6 | 58.4 |
| 06 | 268 51.7 | N14 02.5 | 47 22.5 | 12.9 | S 0 57.4 | 15.7 | 58.4 |
| 07 | 283 51.8 | 01.7 | 61 54.4 | 12.8 | 0 41.7 | 15.6 | 58.3 |
| 08 | 298 51.9 | 00.9 | 76 26.2 | 13.0 | 0 26.1 | 15.7 | 58.3 |
| M 09 | 313 52.1 | 14 00.1 | 90 58.2 | 12.9 | S 0 10.4 | 15.7 | 58.3 |
| O 10 | 328 52.2 | 13 59.3 | 105 30.1 | 13.0 | N 0 05.2 | 15.5 | 58.2 |
| N 11 | 343 52.3 | 58.6 | 120 02.1 | 13.1 | 0 20.7 | 15.6 | 58.2 |
| D 12 | 358 52.4 | N13 57.8 | 134 34.2 | 13.1 | N 0 36.3 | 15.5 | 58.1 |
| A 13 | 13 52.6 | 57.0 | 149 06.3 | 13.1 | 0 51.8 | 15.5 | 58.1 |
| Y 14 | 28 52.7 | 56.2 | 163 38.4 | 13.2 | 1 07.3 | 15.5 | 58.1 |
| 15 | 43 52.8 .. | 55.4 | 178 10.6 | 13.2 | 1 22.0 | 15.4 | 58.0 |
| 16 | 58 52.9 | 54.6 | 192 42.8 | 13.2 | 1 38.2 | 15.5 | 58.0 |
| 17 | 73 53.1 | 53.9 | 207 15.0 | 13.3 | 1 53.7 | 15.4 | 58.0 |
| 18 | 88 53.2 | N13 53.1 | 221 47.3 | 13.3 | N 2 09.1 | 15.3 | 57.9 |
| 19 | 103 53.3 | 52.3 | 236 19.6 | 13.3 | 2 24.4 | 15.3 | 57.9 |
| 20 | 118 53.5 | 51.5 | 250 51.9 | 13.3 | 2 39.7 | 15.3 | 57.8 |
| 21 | 133 53.6 .. | 50.7 | 265 24.2 | 13.4 | 2 55.0 | 15.3 | 57.8 |
| 22 | 148 53.7 | 49.9 | 279 56.6 | 13.4 | 3 10.3 | 15.2 | 57.8 |
| 23 | 163 53.8 | 49.2 | 294 29.0 | 13.5 | 3 25.5 | 15.2 | 57.7 |
| 16 00 | 178 54.0 | N13 48.4 | 309 01.5 | 13.5 | N 3 40.7 | 15.1 | 57.7 |
| 01 | 193 54.1 | 47.6 | 323 34.0 | 13.5 | 3 55.8 | 15.1 | 57.6 |
| 02 | 208 54.2 | 46.8 | 338 06.5 | 13.5 | 4 10.9 | 15.1 | 57.6 |
| 03 | 223 54.3 .. | 46.0 | 352 39.0 | 13.5 | 4 26.0 | 15.0 | 57.6 |
| 04 | 238 54.5 | 45.2 | 7 11.5 | 13.6 | 4 41.0 | 15.0 | 57.5 |
| 05 | 253 54.6 | 44.4 | 21 44.1 | 13.5 | 4 56.0 | 15.0 | 57.5 |
| 06 | 268 54.7 | N13 43.6 | 36 16.6 | 13.6 | N 5 11.0 | 14.9 | 57.5 |
| 07 | 283 54.9 | 42.8 | 50 49.2 | 13.7 | 5 25.9 | 14.8 | 57.4 |
| 08 | 298 55.0 | 42.1 | 65 21.9 | 13.6 | 5 40.7 | 14.8 | 57.4 |
| T 09 | 313 55.1 .. | 41.3 | 79 54.5 | 13.6 | 5 55.5 | 14.8 | 57.3 |
| U 10 | 328 55.3 | 40.5 | 94 27.1 | 13.7 | 6 10.3 | 14.7 | 57.3 |
| E 11 | 343 55.4 | 39.7 | 108 59.8 | 13.7 | 6 25.0 | 14.7 | 57.3 |
| S 12 | 358 55.5 | N13 38.9 | 123 32.5 | 13.6 | N 6 39.7 | 14.6 | 57.2 |
| D 13 | 13 55.6 | 38.1 | 138 05.1 | 13.7 | 6 54.3 | 14.5 | 57.2 |
| A 14 | 28 55.8 | 37.3 | 152 37.8 | 13.7 | 7 08.8 | 14.5 | 57.1 |
| Y 15 | 43 55.9 .. | 36.5 | 167 10.5 | 13.8 | 7 23.3 | 14.5 | 57.1 |
| 16 | 58 56.0 | 35.7 | 181 43.3 | 13.7 | 7 37.8 | 14.4 | 57.1 |
| 17 | 73 56.2 | 34.9 | 196 16.0 | 13.7 | 7 52.2 | 14.4 | 57.0 |
| 18 | 88 56.3 | N13 34.1 | 210 48.7 | 13.7 | N 8 06.6 | 14.3 | 57.0 |
| 19 | 103 56.4 | 33.3 | 225 21.4 | 13.8 | 8 20.9 | 14.2 | 57.0 |
| 20 | 118 56.6 | 32.5 | 239 54.2 | 13.7 | 8 35.1 | 14.2 | 56.9 |
| 21 | 133 56.7 .. | 31.8 | 254 26.9 | 13.8 | 8 49.3 | 14.1 | 56.9 |
| 22 | 148 56.8 | 31.0 | 268 59.7 | 13.7 | 9 03.4 | 14.1 | 56.9 |
| 23 | 163 57.0 | 30.2 | 283 32.4 | 13.7 | N 9 17.5 | 14.0 | 56.8 |
| SD | 15.8 | d 0.8 | SD 16.1 | | 15.8 | | 15.6 |

**Moonrise**

| Lat. | Naut. | Civil | Sunrise | 14 | 15 | 16 | 17 |
|---|---|---|---|---|---|---|---|
| ° | h m | h m | h m | h m | h m | h m | h m |
| N 72 | //// | //// | 02 24 | 21 16 | 20 44 | 20 11 | 19 28 |
| N 70 | //// | //// | 02 56 | 21 12 | 20 48 | 20 24 | 19 54 |
| 68 | //// | 01 43 | 03 19 | 21 08 | 20 51 | 20 34 | 20 14 |
| 66 | //// | 02 21 | 03 37 | 21 05 | 20 54 | 20 42 | 20 29 |
| 64 | //// | 02 47 | 03 52 | 21 02 | 20 56 | 20 49 | 20 43 |
| 62 | 01 31 | 03 06 | 04 04 | 21 00 | 20 58 | 20 55 | 20 54 |
| 60 | 02 06 | 03 22 | 04 14 | 20 58 | 20 59 | 21 01 | 21 03 |
| N 58 | 02 30 | 03 36 | 04 23 | 20 56 | 21 01 | 21 06 | 21 12 |
| 56 | 02 48 | 03 47 | 04 31 | 20 54 | 21 02 | 21 10 | 21 19 |
| 54 | 03 04 | 03 57 | 04 38 | 20 53 | 21 03 | 21 14 | 21 26 |
| 52 | 03 17 | 04 06 | 04 44 | 20 51 | 21 04 | 21 17 | 21 32 |
| 50 | 03 28 | 04 13 | 04 50 | 20 50 | 21 05 | 21 21 | 21 37 |
| 45 | 03 50 | 04 30 | 05 02 | 20 47 | 21 08 | 21 28 | 21 49 |
| N 40 | 04 07 | 04 42 | 05 11 | 20 45 | 21 09 | 21 34 | 21 59 |
| 35 | 04 21 | 04 53 | 05 20 | 20 43 | 21 11 | 21 39 | 22 07 |
| 30 | 04 32 | 05 02 | 05 27 | 20 41 | 21 13 | 21 43 | 22 15 |
| 20 | 04 50 | 05 17 | 05 40 | 20 38 | 21 15 | 21 51 | 22 28 |
| N 10 | 05 04 | 05 29 | 05 51 | 20 36 | 21 17 | 21 58 | 22 39 |
| 0 | 05 15 | 05 40 | 06 01 | 20 33 | 21 20 | 22 05 | 22 50 |
| S 10 | 05 25 | 05 50 | 06 11 | 20 31 | 21 22 | 22 11 | 23 01 |
| 20 | 05 33 | 05 59 | 06 22 | 20 28 | 21 24 | 22 19 | 23 12 |
| 30 | 05 41 | 06 09 | 06 34 | 20 25 | 21 27 | 22 27 | 23 26 |
| 35 | 05 45 | 06 15 | 06 41 | 20 23 | 21 28 | 22 32 | 23 34 |
| 40 | 05 49 | 06 20 | 06 48 | 20 21 | 21 30 | 22 37 | 23 43 |
| 45 | 05 52 | 06 27 | 06 57 | 20 19 | 21 32 | 22 43 | 23 53 |
| S 50 | 05 56 | 06 34 | 07 08 | 20 16 | 21 35 | 22 51 | 24 06 |
| 52 | 05 58 | 06 38 | 07 13 | 20 15 | 21 36 | 22 55 | 24 12 |
| 54 | 06 00 | 06 42 | 07 19 | 20 14 | 21 37 | 22 59 | 24 19 |
| 56 | 06 02 | 06 46 | 07 25 | 20 12 | 21 39 | 23 03 | 24 26 |
| 58 | 06 04 | 06 50 | 07 32 | 20 10 | 21 40 | 23 08 | 24 34 |
| S 60 | 06 06 | 06 55 | 07 39 | 20 08 | 21 42 | 23 14 | 24 44 |

**Moonset**

| Lat. | Sunset | Civil | Naut. | 14 | 15 | 16 | 17 |
|---|---|---|---|---|---|---|---|
| ° | h m | h m | h m | h m | h m | h m | h m |
| N 72 | 21 39 | //// | //// | 06 33 | 08 51 | 11 04 | 13 23 |
| N 70 | 21 09 | 23 32 | //// | 06 44 | 08 52 | 10 54 | 12 59 |
| 68 | 20 47 | 22 19 | //// | 06 53 | 08 52 | 10 46 | 12 41 |
| 66 | 20 29 | 21 44 | //// | 07 01 | 08 53 | 10 40 | 12 27 |
| 64 | 20 15 | 21 19 | 23 36 | 07 07 | 08 53 | 10 34 | 12 15 |
| 62 | 20 03 | 21 00 | 22 31 | 07 12 | 08 53 | 10 30 | 12 05 |
| 60 | 19 53 | 20 44 | 21 59 | 07 17 | 08 53 | 10 26 | 11 57 |
| N 58 | 19 45 | 20 31 | 21 36 | 07 21 | 08 54 | 10 22 | 11 49 |
| 56 | 19 37 | 20 20 | 21 18 | 07 25 | 08 54 | 10 19 | 11 43 |
| 54 | 19 30 | 20 10 | 21 03 | 07 28 | 08 54 | 10 16 | 11 37 |
| 52 | 19 24 | 20 02 | 20 51 | 07 31 | 08 54 | 10 14 | 11 32 |
| 50 | 19 18 | 19 54 | 20 40 | 07 34 | 08 54 | 10 12 | 11 27 |
| 45 | 19 07 | 19 39 | 20 18 | 07 39 | 08 54 | 10 07 | 11 17 |
| N 40 | 18 57 | 19 26 | 20 01 | 07 44 | 08 55 | 10 02 | 11 09 |
| 35 | 18 49 | 19 15 | 19 47 | 07 48 | 08 55 | 09 59 | 11 01 |
| 30 | 18 41 | 19 06 | 19 36 | 07 52 | 08 55 | 09 56 | 10 55 |
| 20 | 18 29 | 18 52 | 19 19 | 07 58 | 08 55 | 09 50 | 10 44 |
| N 10 | 18 18 | 18 40 | 19 05 | 08 03 | 08 55 | 09 46 | 10 35 |
| 0 | 18 08 | 18 29 | 18 54 | 08 08 | 08 55 | 09 41 | 10 26 |
| S 10 | 17 58 | 18 20 | 18 45 | 08 13 | 08 56 | 09 37 | 10 17 |
| 20 | 17 47 | 18 10 | 18 36 | 08 18 | 08 56 | 09 32 | 10 08 |
| 30 | 17 36 | 18 00 | 18 28 | 08 24 | 08 56 | 09 27 | 09 58 |
| 35 | 17 29 | 17 55 | 18 25 | 08 27 | 08 56 | 09 23 | 09 51 |
| 40 | 17 21 | 17 49 | 18 21 | 08 31 | 08 56 | 09 20 | 09 45 |
| 45 | 17 12 | 17 43 | 18 17 | 08 35 | 08 56 | 09 16 | 09 37 |
| S 50 | 17 01 | 17 35 | 18 13 | 08 40 | 08 56 | 09 11 | 09 27 |
| 52 | 16 56 | 17 32 | 18 12 | 08 42 | 08 56 | 09 09 | 09 23 |
| 54 | 16 51 | 17 28 | 18 10 | 08 45 | 08 56 | 09 07 | 09 18 |
| 56 | 16 45 | 17 24 | 18 08 | 08 48 | 08 56 | 09 04 | 09 12 |
| 58 | 16 38 | 17 20 | 18 06 | 08 51 | 08 56 | 09 01 | 09 07 |
| S 60 | 16 30 | 17 15 | 18 05 | 08 54 | 08 56 | 08 58 | 09 00 |

| Day | SUN Eqn. of Time 00h | SUN Eqn. of Time 12h | SUN Mer. Pass. | MOON Mer. Pass. Upper | MOON Mer. Pass. Lower | Age | Phase |
|---|---|---|---|---|---|---|---|
| d | m s | m s | h m | h m | h m | d | % |
| 14 | 04 48 | 04 42 | 12 05 | 01 56 | 14 21 | 17 | 92 |
| 15 | 04 36 | 04 30 | 12 05 | 02 44 | 15 08 | 18 | 85 |
| 16 | 04 24 | 04 18 | 12 04 | 03 30 | 15 53 | 19 | 76 |

| UT | ARIES | VENUS −3·9 | | MARS +0·0 | | JUPITER −2·8 | | SATURN +0·2 | | STARS | | |
|---|---|---|---|---|---|---|---|---|---|---|---|---|
| | GHA | GHA | Dec | GHA | Dec | GHA | Dec | GHA | Dec | Name | SHA | Dec |
| d h | ° ′ | ° ′ | ° ′ | ° ′ | ° ′ | ° ′ | ° ′ | ° ′ | ° ′ | | ° ′ | ° ′ |
| 17 00 | 325 21.3 | 196 24.5 | N19 16.4 | 269 13.4 | N18 14.1 | 317 17.9 | N 1 49.5 | 0 49.0 | S15 29.9 | Acamar | 315 13.2 | S40 12.6 |
| 01 | 340 23.7 | 211 23.8 | 15.7 | 284 14.4 | 14.5 | 332 20.5 | 49.5 | 15 51.7 | 29.9 | Achernar | 335 21.4 | S57 07.1 |
| 02 | 355 26.2 | 226 23.1 | 15.0 | 299 15.3 | 14.9 | 347 23.1 | 49.4 | 30 54.3 | 30.0 | Acrux | 173 02.8 | S63 13.5 |
| 03 | 10 28.7 | 241 22.4 .. | 14.3 | 314 16.2 .. | 15.2 | 2 25.7 .. | 49.3 | 45 56.9 .. | 30.1 | Adhara | 255 07.7 | S28 59.9 |
| 04 | 25 31.1 | 256 21.7 | 13.7 | 329 17.2 | 15.6 | 17 28.3 | 49.2 | 60 59.6 | 30.1 | Aldebaran | 290 42.0 | N16 33.3 |
| 05 | 40 33.6 | 271 21.0 | 13.0 | 344 18.1 | 15.9 | 32 30.9 | 49.2 | 76 02.2 | 30.2 | | | |
| 06 | 55 36.1 | 286 20.3 | N19 12.3 | 359 19.0 | N18 16.3 | 47 33.5 | N 1 49.1 | 91 04.9 | S15 30.3 | Alioth | 166 15.1 | N55 50.6 |
| W 07 | 70 38.5 | 301 19.6 | 11.6 | 14 20.0 | 16.7 | 62 36.1 | 49.0 | 106 07.5 | 30.3 | Alkaid | 152 53.8 | N49 12.4 |
| E 08 | 85 41.0 | 316 18.9 | 10.9 | 29 20.9 | 17.0 | 77 38.7 | 49.0 | 121 10.2 | 30.4 | Al Na'ir | 27 34.9 | S46 51.0 |
| D 09 | 100 43.5 | 331 18.2 .. | 10.3 | 44 21.9 .. | 17.4 | 92 41.3 .. | 48.9 | 136 12.8 .. | 30.5 | Alnilam | 275 39.9 | S 1 11.1 |
| N 10 | 115 45.9 | 346 17.5 | 09.6 | 59 22.8 | 17.7 | 107 43.9 | 48.8 | 151 15.5 | 30.5 | Alphard | 217 50.0 | S 8 45.2 |
| E 11 | 130 48.4 | 1 16.8 | 08.9 | 74 23.7 | 18.1 | 122 46.5 | 48.7 | 166 18.1 | 30.6 | | | |
| S 12 | 145 50.9 | 16 16.1 | N19 08.2 | 89 24.7 | N18 18.5 | 137 49.1 | N 1 48.7 | 181 20.8 | S15 30.6 | Alphecca | 126 05.4 | N26 38.6 |
| D 13 | 160 53.3 | 31 15.4 | 07.5 | 104 25.6 | 18.8 | 152 51.7 | 48.6 | 196 23.4 | 30.7 | Alpheratz | 357 36.5 | N29 12.8 |
| A 14 | 175 55.8 | 46 14.7 | 06.8 | 119 26.6 | 19.2 | 167 54.3 | 48.5 | 211 26.1 | 30.8 | Altair | 62 01.6 | N 8 55.8 |
| Y 15 | 190 58.2 | 61 14.0 .. | 06.1 | 134 27.5 .. | 19.5 | 182 56.9 .. | 48.5 | 226 28.7 .. | 30.8 | Ankaa | 353 08.8 | S42 10.8 |
| 16 | 206 00.7 | 76 13.3 | 05.5 | 149 28.5 | 19.9 | 197 59.5 | 48.4 | 241 31.4 | 30.9 | Antares | 112 18.2 | S26 28.9 |
| 17 | 221 03.2 | 91 12.6 | 04.8 | 164 29.4 | 20.2 | 213 02.1 | 48.3 | 256 34.0 | 31.0 | | | |
| 18 | 236 05.6 | 106 11.9 | N19 04.1 | 179 30.3 | N18 20.6 | 228 04.7 | N 1 48.2 | 271 36.6 | S15 31.0 | Arcturus | 145 49.8 | N19 04.1 |
| 19 | 251 08.1 | 121 11.2 | 03.4 | 194 31.3 | 21.0 | 243 07.3 | 48.2 | 286 39.3 | 31.1 | Atria | 107 14.0 | S69 04.3 |
| 20 | 266 10.6 | 136 10.5 | 02.7 | 209 32.2 | 21.3 | 258 09.9 | 48.1 | 301 41.9 | 31.1 | Avior | 234 16.1 | S59 34.7 |
| 21 | 281 13.0 | 151 09.8 .. | 02.0 | 224 33.2 .. | 21.7 | 273 12.6 .. | 48.0 | 316 44.6 .. | 31.2 | Bellatrix | 278 25.1 | N 6 22.3 |
| 22 | 296 15.5 | 166 09.1 | 01.3 | 239 34.1 | 22.0 | 288 15.2 | 48.0 | 331 47.2 | 31.3 | Betelgeuse | 270 54.4 | N 7 24.8 |
| 23 | 311 18.0 | 181 08.5 | 19 00.6 | 254 35.1 | 22.4 | 303 17.8 | 47.9 | 346 49.9 | 31.3 | | | |
| 18 00 | 326 20.4 | 196 07.8 | N18 59.9 | 269 36.0 | N18 22.7 | 318 20.4 | N 1 47.8 | 1 52.5 | S15 31.4 | Canopus | 263 53.6 | S52 42.2 |
| 01 | 341 22.9 | 211 07.1 | 59.2 | 284 36.9 | 23.1 | 333 23.0 | 47.7 | 16 55.2 | 31.5 | Capella | 280 25.0 | N46 01.1 |
| 02 | 356 25.3 | 226 06.4 | 58.5 | 299 37.9 | 23.4 | 348 25.6 | 47.7 | 31 57.8 | 31.5 | Deneb | 49 26.7 | N45 21.7 |
| 03 | 11 27.8 | 241 05.7 .. | 57.8 | 314 38.8 .. | 23.8 | 3 28.2 .. | 47.6 | 47 00.5 .. | 31.6 | Denebola | 182 27.2 | N14 27.0 |
| 04 | 26 30.3 | 256 05.0 | 57.1 | 329 39.8 | 24.1 | 18 30.8 | 47.5 | 62 03.1 | 31.7 | Diphda | 348 49.0 | S17 51.6 |
| 05 | 41 32.7 | 271 04.3 | 56.4 | 344 40.7 | 24.5 | 33 33.4 | 47.4 | 77 05.8 | 31.7 | | | |
| 06 | 56 35.2 | 286 03.6 | N18 55.7 | 359 41.7 | N18 24.8 | 48 36.0 | N 1 47.4 | 92 08.4 | S15 31.8 | Dubhe | 193 44.1 | N61 38.0 |
| T 07 | 71 37.7 | 301 02.9 | 55.0 | 14 42.6 | 25.2 | 63 38.6 | 47.3 | 107 11.1 | 31.8 | Elnath | 278 04.5 | N28 37.5 |
| H 08 | 86 40.1 | 316 02.2 | 54.3 | 29 43.6 | 25.6 | 78 41.3 | 47.2 | 122 13.7 | 31.9 | Eltanin | 90 42.8 | N51 29.4 |
| U 09 | 101 42.6 | 331 01.5 .. | 53.6 | 44 44.5 .. | 25.9 | 93 43.9 .. | 47.1 | 137 16.3 .. | 32.0 | Enif | 33 40.4 | N 9 58.8 |
| R 10 | 116 45.1 | 346 00.8 | 52.9 | 59 45.5 | 26.3 | 108 46.5 | 47.1 | 152 19.0 | 32.0 | Fomalhaut | 15 16.3 | S29 30.1 |
| S 11 | 131 47.5 | 1 00.2 | 52.2 | 74 46.4 | 26.6 | 123 49.1 | 47.0 | 167 21.6 | 32.1 | | | |
| D 12 | 146 50.0 | 15 59.5 | N18 51.5 | 89 47.3 | N18 27.0 | 138 51.7 | N 1 46.9 | 182 24.3 | S15 32.2 | Gacrux | 171 54.3 | S57 14.4 |
| A 13 | 161 52.5 | 30 58.8 | 50.8 | 104 48.3 | 27.3 | 153 54.3 | 46.8 | 197 26.9 | 32.2 | Gienah | 175 45.9 | S17 39.9 |
| Y 14 | 176 54.9 | 45 58.1 | 50.0 | 119 49.2 | 27.7 | 168 56.9 | 46.8 | 212 29.6 | 32.3 | Hadar | 148 39.0 | S60 29.1 |
| 15 | 191 57.4 | 60 57.4 .. | 49.3 | 134 50.2 .. | 28.0 | 183 59.5 .. | 46.7 | 227 32.2 .. | 32.4 | Hamal | 327 53.3 | N23 34.1 |
| 16 | 206 59.8 | 75 56.7 | 48.6 | 149 51.1 | 28.4 | 199 02.2 | 46.6 | 242 34.9 | 32.4 | Kaus Aust. | 83 34.9 | S34 22.5 |
| 17 | 222 02.3 | 90 56.0 | 47.9 | 164 52.1 | 28.7 | 214 04.8 | 46.5 | 257 37.5 | 32.5 | | | |
| 18 | 237 04.8 | 105 55.3 | N18 47.2 | 179 53.0 | N18 29.1 | 229 07.4 | N 1 46.5 | 272 40.2 | S15 32.5 | Kochab | 137 20.0 | N74 04.1 |
| 19 | 252 07.2 | 120 54.6 | 46.5 | 194 54.0 | 29.4 | 244 10.0 | 46.4 | 287 42.8 | 32.6 | Markab | 13 31.5 | N15 19.6 |
| 20 | 267 09.7 | 135 54.0 | 45.8 | 209 54.9 | 29.8 | 259 12.6 | 46.3 | 302 45.5 | 32.7 | Menkar | 314 08.2 | N 4 10.7 |
| 21 | 282 12.2 | 150 53.3 .. | 45.0 | 224 55.9 .. | 30.1 | 274 15.2 .. | 46.2 | 317 48.1 .. | 32.7 | Menkent | 148 00.1 | S36 28.9 |
| 22 | 297 14.6 | 165 52.6 | 44.3 | 239 56.8 | 30.5 | 289 17.8 | 46.2 | 332 50.8 | 32.8 | Miaplacidus | 221 39.6 | S69 48.4 |
| 23 | 312 17.1 | 180 51.9 | 43.6 | 254 57.8 | 30.8 | 304 20.4 | 46.1 | 347 53.4 | 32.9 | | | |
| 19 00 | 327 19.6 | 195 51.2 | N18 42.9 | 269 58.7 | N18 31.2 | 319 23.1 | N 1 46.0 | 2 56.0 | S15 32.9 | Mirfak | 308 31.1 | N49 56.3 |
| 01 | 342 22.0 | 210 50.5 | 42.2 | 284 59.7 | 31.5 | 334 25.7 | 45.9 | 17 58.7 | 33.0 | Nunki | 75 49.9 | S26 16.1 |
| 02 | 357 24.5 | 225 49.9 | 41.4 | 300 00.6 | 31.9 | 349 28.3 | 45.9 | 33 01.3 | 33.0 | Peacock | 53 08.3 | S56 39.8 |
| 03 | 12 27.0 | 240 49.2 .. | 40.7 | 315 01.6 .. | 32.2 | 4 30.9 .. | 45.8 | 48 04.0 .. | 33.1 | Pollux | 243 20.0 | N27 58.3 |
| 04 | 27 29.4 | 255 48.5 | 40.0 | 330 02.5 | 32.5 | 19 33.5 | 45.7 | 63 06.6 | 33.2 | Procyon | 244 53.2 | N 5 10.1 |
| 05 | 42 31.9 | 270 47.8 | 39.3 | 345 03.5 | 32.9 | 34 36.1 | 45.6 | 78 09.3 | 33.2 | | | |
| 06 | 57 34.3 | 285 47.1 | N18 38.6 | 0 04.4 | N18 33.2 | 49 38.8 | N 1 45.6 | 93 11.9 | S15 33.3 | Rasalhague | 96 00.2 | N12 32.8 |
| 07 | 72 36.8 | 300 46.4 | 37.8 | 15 05.4 | 33.6 | 64 41.4 | 45.5 | 108 14.6 | 33.4 | Regulus | 207 36.9 | N11 51.6 |
| F 08 | 87 39.3 | 315 45.8 | 37.1 | 30 06.4 | 33.9 | 79 44.0 | 45.4 | 123 17.2 | 33.4 | Rigel | 281 05.9 | S 8 10.4 |
| R 09 | 102 41.7 | 330 45.1 .. | 36.4 | 45 07.3 .. | 34.3 | 94 46.6 .. | 45.3 | 138 19.9 .. | 33.5 | Rigil Kent. | 139 43.2 | S60 55.8 |
| I 10 | 117 44.2 | 345 44.4 | 35.6 | 60 08.3 | 34.6 | 109 49.2 | 45.2 | 153 22.5 | 33.5 | Sabik | 102 04.9 | S15 45.1 |
| D 11 | 132 46.7 | 0 43.7 | 34.9 | 75 09.2 | 35.0 | 124 51.9 | 45.2 | 168 25.2 | 33.6 | | | |
| A 12 | 147 49.1 | 15 43.0 | N18 34.2 | 90 10.2 | N18 35.3 | 139 54.5 | N 1 45.1 | 183 27.8 | S15 33.7 | Schedar | 349 32.9 | N56 39.5 |
| Y 13 | 162 51.6 | 30 42.4 | 33.4 | 105 11.1 | 35.7 | 154 57.1 | 45.0 | 198 30.4 | 33.7 | Shaula | 96 12.8 | S37 07.3 |
| 14 | 177 54.1 | 45 41.7 | 32.7 | 120 12.1 | 36.0 | 169 59.7 | 44.9 | 213 33.1 | 33.8 | Sirius | 258 28.2 | S16 44.6 |
| 15 | 192 56.5 | 60 41.0 .. | 32.0 | 135 13.0 .. | 36.3 | 185 02.3 .. | 44.9 | 228 35.7 .. | 33.9 | Spica | 158 24.6 | S11 16.6 |
| 16 | 207 59.0 | 75 40.3 | 31.2 | 150 14.0 | 36.7 | 200 04.9 | 44.8 | 243 38.4 | 33.9 | Suhail | 222 48.2 | S43 31.3 |
| 17 | 223 01.4 | 90 39.6 | 30.5 | 165 14.9 | 37.0 | 215 07.6 | 44.7 | 258 41.0 | 34.0 | | | |
| 18 | 238 03.9 | 105 39.0 | N18 29.8 | 180 15.9 | N18 37.4 | 230 10.2 | N 1 44.6 | 273 43.7 | S15 34.0 | Vega | 80 34.3 | N38 48.5 |
| 19 | 253 06.4 | 120 38.3 | 29.0 | 195 16.9 | 37.7 | 245 12.8 | 44.5 | 288 46.3 | 34.1 | Zuben'ubi | 136 58.3 | S16 08.1 |
| 20 | 268 08.8 | 135 37.6 | 28.3 | 210 17.8 | 38.1 | 260 15.4 | 44.5 | 303 49.0 | 34.2 | | SHA | Mer.Pass. |
| 21 | 283 11.3 | 150 36.9 .. | 27.6 | 225 18.8 .. | 38.4 | 275 18.1 .. | 44.4 | 318 51.6 .. | 34.2 | | ° ′ | h m |
| 22 | 298 13.8 | 165 36.3 | 26.8 | 240 19.7 | 38.7 | 290 20.7 | 44.3 | 333 54.3 | 34.3 | Venus | 229 47.3 | 10 56 |
| 23 | 313 16.2 | 180 35.6 | 26.1 | 255 20.7 | 39.1 | 305 23.3 | 44.2 | 348 56.9 | 34.4 | Mars | 303 15.6 | 6 01 |
| | h m | | | | | | | | | Jupiter | 352 00.0 | 2 46 |
| Mer.Pass. 2 14.3 | | v −0.7 d 0.7 | | v 0.9 d 0.4 | | v 2.6 d 0.1 | | v 2.6 d 0.1 | | Saturn | 35 32.1 | 23 48 |

| UT | SUN | | MOON | | | | | Lat. | Twilight | | Sunrise | Moonrise | | | |
|---|---|---|---|---|---|---|---|---|---|---|---|---|---|---|---|
| | | | | | | | | | Naut. | Civil | | 17 | 18 | 19 | 20 |
| | GHA | Dec | GHA | v | Dec | d | HP | | | | | | | | |
| d h | ° ′ | ° ′ | ° ′ | ′ | ° ′ | ′ | ′ | N 72 | h m /// | h m /// | h m 02 44 | h m 19 28 | h m ▢ | h m ▢ | h m ▢ |
| 17 00 | 178 57.1 | N13 29.4 | 298 05.1 | 13.8 | N 9 31.5 | 13.9 | 56.8 | N 70 | //// | 01 12 | 03 11 | 19 54 | 19 04 | ▢ | ▢ |
| 01 | 193 57.2 | 28.6 | 312 37.9 | 13.7 | 9 45.4 | 13.9 | 56.7 | 68 | //// | 02 05 | 03 32 | 20 14 | 19 45 | ▢ | ▢ |
| 02 | 208 57.4 | 27.8 | 327 10.6 | 13.8 | 9 59.3 | 13.8 | 56.7 | 66 | //// | 02 36 | 03 48 | 20 29 | 20 13 | 19 47 | ▢ |
| 03 | 223 57.5 .. | 27.0 | 341 43.4 | 13.7 | 10 13.1 | 13.8 | 56.7 | 64 | 01 04 | 02 59 | 04 01 | 20 43 | 20 35 | 20 25 | 20 09 |
| 04 | 238 57.6 | 26.2 | 356 16.1 | 13.7 | 10 26.9 | 13.7 | 56.6 | 62 | 01 50 | 03 17 | 04 12 | 20 54 | 20 52 | 20 53 | 20 56 |
| 05 | 253 57.8 | 25.4 | 10 48.8 | 13.7 | 10 40.6 | 13.6 | 56.6 | 60 | 02 19 | 03 31 | 04 21 | 21 03 | 21 07 | 21 14 | 21 27 |
| 06 | 268 57.9 | N13 24.6 | 25 21.5 | 13.8 | N10 54.2 | 13.6 | 56.6 | N 58 | 02 40 | 03 43 | 04 29 | 21 12 | 21 20 | 21 31 | 21 50 |
| W 07 | 283 58.0 | 23.8 | 39 54.3 | 13.7 | 11 07.8 | 13.5 | 56.5 | 56 | 02 57 | 03 54 | 04 37 | 21 19 | 21 30 | 21 46 | 22 09 |
| E 08 | 298 58.2 | 23.0 | 54 27.0 | 13.7 | 11 21.3 | 13.4 | 56.5 | 54 | 03 11 | 04 03 | 04 43 | 21 26 | 21 40 | 21 59 | 22 24 |
| D 09 | 313 58.3 .. | 22.2 | 68 59.7 | 13.7 | 11 34.7 | 13.4 | 56.5 | 52 | 03 23 | 04 11 | 04 49 | 21 32 | 21 49 | 22 10 | 22 38 |
| N 10 | 328 58.4 | 21.4 | 83 32.4 | 13.6 | 11 48.1 | 13.3 | 56.4 | 50 | 03 34 | 04 18 | 04 54 | 21 37 | 21 56 | 22 20 | 22 51 |
| E 11 | 343 58.6 | 20.6 | 98 05.0 | 13.7 | 12 01.4 | 13.2 | 56.4 | 45 | 03 55 | 04 33 | 05 05 | 21 49 | 22 13 | 22 41 | 23 15 |
| S 12 | 358 58.7 | N13 19.8 | 112 37.7 | 13.7 | N12 14.6 | 13.2 | 56.4 | N 40 | 04 11 | 04 46 | 05 14 | 21 59 | 22 26 | 22 50 | 23 35 |
| D 13 | 13 58.8 | 19.0 | 127 10.4 | 13.6 | 12 27.8 | 13.0 | 56.3 | 35 | 04 24 | 04 56 | 05 22 | 22 07 | 22 38 | 23 12 | 23 52 |
| A 14 | 28 59.0 | 18.2 | 141 43.0 | 13.7 | 12 40.8 | 13.1 | 56.3 | 30 | 04 34 | 05 04 | 05 29 | 22 15 | 22 48 | 23 25 | 24 06 |
| Y 15 | 43 59.1 .. | 17.4 | 156 15.7 | 13.6 | 12 53.9 | 12.9 | 56.3 | 20 | 04 51 | 05 18 | 05 41 | 22 28 | 23 06 | 23 47 | 24 31 |
| 16 | 58 59.2 | 16.6 | 170 48.3 | 13.6 | 13 06.8 | 12.9 | 56.2 | N 10 | 05 04 | 05 29 | 05 51 | 22 39 | 23 21 | 24 05 | 00 05 |
| 17 | 73 59.4 | 15.8 | 185 20.9 | 13.6 | 13 19.7 | 12.8 | 56.2 | 0 | 05 15 | 05 39 | 06 01 | 22 50 | 23 36 | 24 23 | 00 23 |
| 18 | 88 59.5 | N13 15.0 | 199 53.5 | 13.5 | N13 32.5 | 12.7 | 56.2 | S 10 | 05 23 | 05 48 | 06 10 | 23 01 | 23 50 | 24 41 | 00 41 |
| 19 | 103 59.7 | 14.2 | 214 26.0 | 13.6 | 13 45.2 | 12.6 | 56.1 | 20 | 05 31 | 05 57 | 06 20 | 23 12 | 24 06 | 00 06 | 01 00 |
| 20 | 118 59.8 | 13.4 | 228 58.6 | 13.5 | 13 57.8 | 12.6 | 56.1 | 30 | 05 38 | 06 06 | 06 31 | 23 26 | 24 24 | 00 24 | 01 22 |
| 21 | 133 59.9 .. | 12.6 | 243 31.1 | 13.5 | 14 10.4 | 12.5 | 56.1 | 35 | 05 41 | 06 11 | 06 37 | 23 34 | 24 35 | 00 35 | 01 35 |
| 22 | 149 00.1 | 11.8 | 258 03.6 | 13.5 | 14 22.9 | 12.4 | 56.0 | 40 | 05 45 | 06 17 | 06 44 | 23 43 | 24 47 | 00 47 | 01 50 |
| 23 | 164 00.2 | 11.0 | 272 36.1 | 13.5 | 14 35.3 | 12.3 | 56.0 | 45 | 05 49 | 06 22 | 06 53 | 23 53 | 25 01 | 01 01 | 02 08 |
| 18 00 | 179 00.3 | N13 10.2 | 287 08.6 | 13.4 | N14 47.6 | 12.3 | 56.0 | S 50 | 05 51 | 06 29 | 07 03 | 24 06 | 00 06 | 01 19 | 02 31 |
| 01 | 194 00.5 | 09.4 | 301 41.0 | 13.5 | 14 59.9 | 12.2 | 55.9 | 52 | 05 53 | 06 32 | 07 07 | 24 12 | 00 12 | 01 28 | 02 41 |
| 02 | 209 00.6 | 08.5 | 316 13.5 | 13.4 | 15 12.1 | 12.1 | 55.9 | 54 | 05 54 | 06 35 | 07 12 | 24 19 | 00 19 | 01 37 | 02 54 |
| 03 | 224 00.8 .. | 07.7 | 330 45.9 | 13.4 | 15 24.2 | 12.0 | 55.9 | 56 | 05 55 | 06 39 | 07 18 | 24 26 | 00 26 | 01 48 | 03 08 |
| 04 | 239 00.9 | 06.9 | 345 18.3 | 13.3 | 15 36.2 | 11.9 | 55.8 | 58 | 05 57 | 06 43 | 07 24 | 24 34 | 00 34 | 02 00 | 03 24 |
| 05 | 254 01.0 | 06.1 | 359 50.6 | 13.3 | 15 48.1 | 11.9 | 55.8 | S 60 | 05 58 | 06 47 | 07 31 | 24 44 | 00 44 | 02 15 | 03 44 |
| 06 | 269 01.2 | N13 05.3 | 14 22.9 | 13.4 | N16 00.0 | 11.8 | 55.8 | Lat. | Sunset | Twilight | | Moonset | | | |
| T 07 | 284 01.3 | 04.5 | 28 55.3 | 13.2 | 16 11.8 | 11.6 | 55.7 | | | Civil | Naut. | 17 | 18 | 19 | 20 |
| H 08 | 299 01.5 | 03.7 | 43 27.5 | 13.3 | 16 23.4 | 11.6 | 55.7 | | | | | | | | |
| U 09 | 314 01.6 .. | 02.9 | 57 59.8 | 13.2 | 16 35.0 | 11.6 | 55.7 | ° | h m | h m | h m | h m | h m | h m | h m |
| R 10 | 329 01.7 | 02.1 | 72 32.0 | 13.2 | 16 46.6 | 11.4 | 55.7 | N 72 | 21 19 | //// | //// | 13 23 | ▢ | ▢ | ▢ |
| S 11 | 344 01.9 | 01.3 | 87 04.2 | 13.2 | 16 58.0 | 11.3 | 55.6 | N 70 | 20 53 | 22 45 | //// | 12 59 | 15 24 | ▢ | ▢ |
| D 12 | 359 02.0 | N13 00.5 | 101 36.4 | 13.1 | N17 09.3 | 11.3 | 55.6 | 68 | 20 33 | 21 57 | //// | 12 41 | 14 45 | ▢ | ▢ |
| A 13 | 14 02.2 | 12 59.7 | 116 08.5 | 13.1 | 17 20.6 | 11.3 | 55.6 | 66 | 20 18 | 21 28 | //// | 12 27 | 14 18 | 16 22 | ▢ |
| Y 14 | 29 02.3 | 58.9 | 130 40.6 | 13.1 | 17 31.8 | 11.0 | 55.5 | 64 | 20 05 | 21 06 | 22 54 | 12 15 | 13 57 | 15 44 | 17 42 |
| 15 | 44 02.4 .. | 58.0 | 145 12.7 | 13.1 | 17 42.8 | 11.0 | 55.5 | 62 | 19 54 | 20 49 | 22 12 | 12 05 | 13 41 | 15 18 | 16 55 |
| 16 | 59 02.6 | 57.2 | 159 44.8 | 13.0 | 17 53.8 | 10.9 | 55.5 | 60 | 19 45 | 20 34 | 21 45 | 11 57 | 13 27 | 14 57 | 16 25 |
| 17 | 74 02.7 | 56.4 | 174 16.8 | 13.0 | 18 04.7 | 10.8 | 55.5 | N 58 | 19 37 | 20 22 | 21 25 | 11 49 | 13 15 | 14 40 | 16 02 |
| 18 | 89 02.9 | N12 55.6 | 188 48.8 | 12.9 | N18 15.5 | 10.8 | 55.4 | 56 | 19 30 | 20 12 | 21 08 | 11 43 | 13 05 | 14 26 | 15 44 |
| 19 | 104 03.0 | 54.8 | 203 20.7 | 12.9 | 18 26.3 | 10.6 | 55.4 | 54 | 19 24 | 20 03 | 20 54 | 11 37 | 12 56 | 14 14 | 15 28 |
| 20 | 119 03.1 | 54.0 | 217 52.6 | 12.9 | 18 36.9 | 10.5 | 55.4 | 52 | 19 18 | 19 55 | 20 43 | 11 32 | 12 48 | 14 03 | 15 15 |
| 21 | 134 03.3 .. | 53.2 | 232 24.5 | 12.9 | 18 47.4 | 10.5 | 55.3 | 50 | 19 13 | 19 48 | 20 33 | 11 27 | 12 41 | 13 54 | 15 03 |
| 22 | 149 03.4 | 52.4 | 246 56.4 | 12.8 | 18 57.9 | 10.3 | 55.3 | 45 | 19 02 | 19 33 | 20 12 | 11 17 | 12 26 | 13 34 | 14 39 |
| 23 | 164 03.6 | 51.6 | 261 28.2 | 12.8 | 19 08.2 | 10.3 | 55.3 | N 40 | 18 53 | 19 21 | 19 56 | 11 09 | 12 14 | 13 18 | 14 20 |
| 19 00 | 179 03.7 | N12 50.7 | 276 00.0 | 12.7 | N19 18.5 | 10.1 | 55.3 | 35 | 18 45 | 19 12 | 19 43 | 11 01 | 12 03 | 13 04 | 14 04 |
| 01 | 194 03.9 | 49.9 | 290 31.7 | 12.7 | 19 28.6 | 10.1 | 55.2 | 30 | 18 38 | 19 03 | 19 33 | 10 55 | 11 54 | 12 52 | 13 50 |
| 02 | 209 04.0 | 49.1 | 305 03.4 | 12.7 | 19 38.7 | 10.0 | 55.2 | 20 | 18 27 | 18 49 | 19 16 | 10 44 | 11 38 | 12 32 | 13 26 |
| 03 | 224 04.1 .. | 48.3 | 319 35.1 | 12.6 | 19 48.7 | 9.8 | 55.2 | N 10 | 18 17 | 18 38 | 19 03 | 10 35 | 11 24 | 12 15 | 13 06 |
| 04 | 239 04.3 | 47.5 | 334 06.7 | 12.6 | 19 58.5 | 9.8 | 55.2 | 0 | 18 07 | 18 28 | 18 53 | 10 26 | 11 12 | 11 58 | 12 47 |
| 05 | 254 04.4 | 46.7 | 348 38.3 | 12.6 | 20 08.3 | 9.7 | 55.1 | S 10 | 17 58 | 18 20 | 18 44 | 10 17 | 10 59 | 11 42 | 12 28 |
| 06 | 269 04.6 | N12 45.9 | 3 09.9 | 12.5 | N20 18.0 | 9.5 | 55.1 | 20 | 17 48 | 18 11 | 18 37 | 10 08 | 10 45 | 11 25 | 12 07 |
| 07 | 284 04.7 | 45.0 | 17 41.4 | 12.5 | 20 27.5 | 9.5 | 55.1 | 30 | 17 37 | 18 02 | 18 30 | 09 58 | 10 30 | 11 05 | 11 44 |
| 08 | 299 04.9 | 44.2 | 32 12.9 | 12.5 | 20 37.0 | 9.4 | 55.1 | 35 | 17 31 | 17 57 | 18 27 | 09 51 | 10 21 | 10 54 | 11 32 |
| F 09 | 314 05.0 .. | 43.4 | 46 44.4 | 12.4 | 20 46.4 | 9.3 | 55.1 | 40 | 17 24 | 17 52 | 18 24 | 09 45 | 10 11 | 10 40 | 11 15 |
| R 10 | 329 05.2 | 42.6 | 61 15.8 | 12.4 | 20 55.7 | 9.1 | 55.0 | 45 | 17 16 | 17 46 | 18 20 | 09 37 | 09 59 | 10 25 | 10 56 |
| I 11 | 344 05.3 | 41.8 | 75 47.2 | 12.3 | 21 04.8 | 9.1 | 55.0 | S 50 | 17 06 | 17 39 | 18 17 | 09 27 | 09 45 | 10 06 | 10 32 |
| D 12 | 359 05.4 | N12 41.0 | 90 18.5 | 12.3 | N21 13.9 | 9.0 | 55.0 | 52 | 17 01 | 17 36 | 18 16 | 09 23 | 09 38 | 09 57 | 10 21 |
| A 13 | 14 05.6 | 40.1 | 104 49.8 | 12.3 | 21 22.9 | 8.9 | 55.0 | 54 | 16 56 | 17 33 | 18 15 | 09 18 | 09 31 | 09 47 | 10 09 |
| Y 14 | 29 05.7 | 39.3 | 119 21.1 | 12.2 | 21 31.8 | 8.7 | 54.9 | 56 | 16 51 | 17 30 | 18 13 | 09 12 | 09 22 | 09 36 | 09 54 |
| 15 | 44 05.9 .. | 38.5 | 133 52.3 | 12.2 | 21 40.5 | 8.7 | 54.9 | 58 | 16 44 | 17 26 | 18 12 | 09 07 | 09 13 | 09 23 | 09 37 |
| 16 | 59 06.0 | 37.7 | 148 23.5 | 12.1 | 21 49.2 | 8.5 | 54.9 | S 60 | 16 37 | 17 22 | 18 10 | 09 00 | 09 03 | 09 08 | 09 17 |
| 17 | 74 06.2 | 36.9 | 162 54.6 | 12.1 | 21 57.7 | 8.5 | 54.9 | | | | | | | | |

| | | | | | | | | SUN | | | | MOON | | | |
|---|---|---|---|---|---|---|---|---|---|---|---|---|---|---|---|
| 18 | 89 06.3 | N12 36.0 | 177 25.8 | 12.0 | N22 06.2 | 8.3 | 54.9 | Day | Eqn. of Time | | Mer. | Mer. Pass. | | Age | Phase |
| 19 | 104 06.5 | 35.2 | 191 56.8 | 12.1 | 22 14.5 | 8.2 | 54.8 | | 00ʰ | 12ʰ | Pass. | Upper | Lower | | |
| 20 | 119 06.6 | 34.4 | 206 27.9 | 11.9 | 22 22.7 | 8.2 | 54.8 | d | m s | m s | h m | h m | h m | d % | |
| 21 | 134 06.8 .. | 33.6 | 220 58.8 | 12.0 | 22 30.9 | 8.0 | 54.8 | 17 | 04 12 | 04 05 | 12 04 | 04 15 | 16 38 | 20 67 | |
| 22 | 149 06.9 | 32.8 | 235 29.8 | 11.9 | 22 38.9 | 7.9 | 54.8 | 18 | 03 59 | 03 52 | 12 04 | 05 01 | 17 24 | 21 57 | |
| 23 | 164 07.1 | 31.9 | 250 00.7 | 11.9 | N22 46.8 | 7.8 | 54.8 | 19 | 03 45 | 03 38 | 12 04 | 05 47 | 18 11 | 22 47 | |
| | SD 15.8 | d 0.8 | SD 15.4 | | 15.1 | | 15.0 | | | | | | | | | |

| UT | ARIES GHA | VENUS −3.9 GHA | Dec | MARS −0.1 GHA | Dec | JUPITER −2.8 GHA | Dec | SATURN +0.3 GHA | Dec | STARS Name | SHA | Dec |
|---|---|---|---|---|---|---|---|---|---|---|---|---|
| d h | ° ′ | ° ′ | ° ′ | ° ′ | ° ′ | ° ′ | ° ′ | ° ′ | ° ′ | | ° ′ | ° ′ |
| 20 00 | 328 18.7 | 195 34.9 | N18 25.3 | 270 21.6 | N18 39.4 | 320 25.9 | N 1 44.1 | 3 59.6 | S15 34.4 | Acamar | 315 13.2 | S40 12.6 |
| 01 | 343 21.2 | 210 34.2 | 24.6 | 285 22.6 | 39.8 | 335 28.5 | 44.1 | 19 02.2 | 34.5 | Achernar | 335 21.4 | S57 07.1 |
| 02 | 358 23.6 | 225 33.6 | 23.9 | 300 23.6 | 40.1 | 350 31.2 | 44.0 | 34 04.8 | 34.6 | Acrux | 173 02.8 | S63 13.5 |
| 03 | 13 26.1 | 240 32.9 . . | 23.1 | 315 24.5 . . | 40.5 | 5 33.8 . . | 43.9 | 49 07.5 . . | 34.6 | Adhara | 255 07.7 | S28 59.9 |
| 04 | 28 28.6 | 255 32.2 | 22.4 | 330 25.5 | 40.8 | 20 36.4 | 43.8 | 64 10.1 | 34.7 | Aldebaran | 290 41.9 | N16 33.3 |
| 05 | 43 31.0 | 270 31.5 | 21.6 | 345 26.4 | 41.1 | 35 39.0 | 43.8 | 79 12.8 | 34.7 | | | |
| 06 | 58 33.5 | 285 30.9 | N18 20.9 | 0 27.4 | N18 41.5 | 50 41.7 | N 1 43.7 | 94 15.4 | S15 34.8 | Alioth | 166 15.1 | N55 50.5 |
| 07 | 73 35.9 | 300 30.2 | 20.1 | 15 28.4 | 41.8 | 65 44.3 | 43.6 | 109 18.1 | 34.9 | Alkaid | 152 53.8 | N49 12.4 |
| S 08 | 88 38.4 | 315 29.5 | 19.4 | 30 29.3 | 42.2 | 80 46.9 | 43.5 | 124 20.7 | 34.9 | Alnair | 27 34.9 | S46 51.0 |
| A 09 | 103 40.9 | 330 28.8 . . | 18.6 | 45 30.3 . . | 42.5 | 95 49.5 . . | 43.4 | 139 23.4 . . | 35.0 | Alnilam | 275 39.9 | S 1 11.1 |
| T 10 | 118 43.3 | 345 28.2 | 17.9 | 60 31.2 | 42.8 | 110 52.2 | 43.4 | 154 26.0 | 35.1 | Alphard | 217 50.0 | S 8 45.2 |
| U 11 | 133 45.8 | 0 27.5 | 17.1 | 75 32.2 | 43.2 | 125 54.8 | 43.3 | 169 28.7 | 35.1 | | | |
| R 12 | 148 48.3 | 15 26.8 | N18 16.4 | 90 33.2 | N18 43.5 | 140 57.4 | N 1 43.2 | 184 31.3 | S15 35.2 | Alphecca | 126 05.4 | N26 38.6 |
| D 13 | 163 50.7 | 30 26.2 | 15.6 | 105 34.1 | 43.8 | 156 00.0 | 43.1 | 199 34.0 | 35.2 | Alpheratz | 357 36.5 | N29 12.9 |
| A 14 | 178 53.2 | 45 25.5 | 14.9 | 120 35.1 | 44.2 | 171 02.7 | 43.0 | 214 36.6 | 35.3 | Altair | 62 01.6 | N 8 55.8 |
| Y 15 | 193 55.7 | 60 24.8 . . | 14.1 | 135 36.0 . . | 44.5 | 186 05.3 . . | 43.0 | 229 39.2 . . | 35.4 | Ankaa | 353 08.8 | S42 10.8 |
| 16 | 208 58.1 | 75 24.2 | 13.3 | 150 37.0 | 44.9 | 201 07.9 | 42.9 | 244 41.9 | 35.4 | Antares | 112 18.2 | S26 28.9 |
| 17 | 224 00.6 | 90 23.5 | 12.6 | 165 38.0 | 45.2 | 216 10.5 | 42.8 | 259 44.5 | 35.5 | | | |
| 18 | 239 03.1 | 105 22.8 | N18 11.8 | 180 38.9 | N18 45.5 | 231 13.2 | N 1 42.7 | 274 47.2 | S15 35.6 | Arcturus | 145 49.8 | N19 04.1 |
| 19 | 254 05.5 | 120 22.2 | 11.1 | 195 39.9 | 45.9 | 246 15.8 | 42.6 | 289 49.8 | 35.6 | Atria | 107 14.0 | S69 04.3 |
| 20 | 269 08.0 | 135 21.5 | 10.3 | 210 40.9 | 46.2 | 261 18.4 | 42.5 | 304 52.5 | 35.7 | Avior | 234 16.1 | S59 34.7 |
| 21 | 284 10.4 | 150 20.8 . . | 09.6 | 225 41.8 . . | 46.5 | 276 21.0 . . | 42.5 | 319 55.1 . . | 35.7 | Bellatrix | 278 25.1 | N 6 22.3 |
| 22 | 299 12.9 | 165 20.2 | 08.8 | 240 42.8 | 46.9 | 291 23.7 | 42.4 | 334 57.8 | 35.8 | Betelgeuse | 270 54.4 | N 7 24.8 |
| 23 | 314 15.4 | 180 19.5 | 08.0 | 255 43.8 | 47.2 | 306 26.3 | 42.3 | 350 00.4 | 35.9 | | | |
| 21 00 | 329 17.8 | 195 18.8 | N18 07.3 | 270 44.7 | N18 47.5 | 321 28.9 | N 1 42.2 | 5 03.1 | S15 35.9 | Canopus | 263 53.6 | S52 42.1 |
| 01 | 344 20.3 | 210 18.2 | 06.5 | 285 45.7 | 47.9 | 336 31.6 | 42.1 | 20 05.7 | 36.0 | Capella | 280 25.0 | N46 01.1 |
| 02 | 359 22.8 | 225 17.5 | 05.7 | 300 46.7 | 48.2 | 351 34.2 | 42.1 | 35 08.3 | 36.1 | Deneb | 49 26.7 | N45 21.7 |
| 03 | 14 25.2 | 240 16.8 . . | 05.0 | 315 47.6 . . | 48.6 | 6 36.8 . . | 42.0 | 50 11.0 . . | 36.1 | Denebola | 182 27.2 | N14 27.0 |
| 04 | 29 27.7 | 255 16.2 | 04.2 | 330 48.6 | 48.9 | 21 39.5 | 41.9 | 65 13.6 | 36.2 | Diphda | 348 49.0 | S17 51.6 |
| 05 | 44 30.2 | 270 15.5 | 03.4 | 345 49.6 | 49.2 | 36 42.1 | 41.8 | 80 16.3 | 36.2 | | | |
| 06 | 59 32.6 | 285 14.8 | N18 02.7 | 0 50.5 | N18 49.6 | 51 44.7 | N 1 41.7 | 95 18.9 | S15 36.3 | Dubhe | 193 44.1 | N61 38.0 |
| 07 | 74 35.1 | 300 14.2 | 01.9 | 15 51.5 | 49.9 | 66 47.3 | 41.6 | 110 21.6 | 36.4 | Elnath | 278 04.5 | N28 37.5 |
| 08 | 89 37.6 | 315 13.5 | 01.1 | 30 52.5 | 50.2 | 81 50.0 | 41.6 | 125 24.2 | 36.4 | Eltanin | 90 42.8 | N51 29.4 |
| S 09 | 104 40.0 | 330 12.8 | 18 00.4 | 45 53.4 . . | 50.6 | 96 52.6 . . | 41.5 | 140 26.9 . . | 36.5 | Enif | 33 40.4 | N 9 58.8 |
| U 10 | 119 42.5 | 345 12.2 | 17 59.6 | 60 54.4 | 50.9 | 111 55.2 | 41.4 | 155 29.5 | 36.5 | Fomalhaut | 15 16.3 | S29 30.1 |
| N 11 | 134 44.9 | 0 11.5 | 58.8 | 75 55.4 | 51.2 | 126 57.9 | 41.3 | 170 32.2 | 36.6 | | | |
| D 12 | 149 47.4 | 15 10.9 | N17 58.0 | 90 56.3 | N18 51.5 | 142 00.5 | N 1 41.2 | 185 34.8 | S15 36.7 | Gacrux | 171 54.3 | S57 14.4 |
| A 13 | 164 49.9 | 30 10.2 | 57.3 | 105 57.3 | 51.9 | 157 03.1 | 41.1 | 200 37.4 | 36.7 | Gienah | 175 45.9 | S17 39.9 |
| Y 14 | 179 52.3 | 45 09.5 | 56.5 | 120 58.3 | 52.2 | 172 05.8 | 41.1 | 215 40.1 | 36.8 | Hadar | 148 39.1 | S60 29.0 |
| 15 | 194 54.8 | 60 08.9 . . | 55.7 | 135 59.2 . . | 52.5 | 187 08.4 . . | 41.0 | 230 42.7 . . | 36.9 | Hamal | 327 53.3 | N23 34.1 |
| 16 | 209 57.3 | 75 08.2 | 54.9 | 151 00.2 | 52.9 | 202 11.0 | 40.9 | 245 45.4 | 36.9 | Kaus Aust. | 83 34.9 | S34 22.5 |
| 17 | 224 59.7 | 90 07.6 | 54.2 | 166 01.2 | 53.2 | 217 13.7 | 40.8 | 260 48.0 | 37.0 | | | |
| 18 | 240 02.2 | 105 06.9 | N17 53.4 | 181 02.1 | N18 53.5 | 232 16.3 | N 1 40.7 | 275 50.7 | S15 37.0 | Kochab | 137 20.1 | N74 04.1 |
| 19 | 255 04.7 | 120 06.2 | 52.6 | 196 03.1 | 53.9 | 247 18.9 | 40.6 | 290 53.3 | 37.1 | Markab | 13 31.5 | N15 19.6 |
| 20 | 270 07.1 | 135 05.6 | 51.8 | 211 04.1 | 54.2 | 262 21.6 | 40.6 | 305 56.0 | 37.2 | Menkar | 314 08.1 | N 4 10.7 |
| 21 | 285 09.6 | 150 04.9 . . | 51.0 | 226 05.1 . . | 54.5 | 277 24.2 . . | 40.5 | 320 58.6 . . | 37.2 | Menkent | 148 00.1 | S36 28.9 |
| 22 | 300 12.1 | 165 04.3 | 50.2 | 241 06.0 | 54.9 | 292 26.8 | 40.4 | 336 01.3 | 37.3 | Miaplacidus | 221 39.6 | S69 48.4 |
| 23 | 315 14.5 | 180 03.6 | 49.5 | 256 07.0 | 55.2 | 307 29.5 | 40.3 | 351 03.9 | 37.4 | | | |
| 22 00 | 330 17.0 | 195 03.0 | N17 48.7 | 271 08.0 | N18 55.5 | 322 32.1 | N 1 40.2 | 6 06.5 | S15 37.4 | Mirfak | 308 31.0 | N49 56.3 |
| 01 | 345 19.4 | 210 02.3 | 47.9 | 286 08.9 | 55.8 | 337 34.7 | 40.1 | 21 09.2 | 37.5 | Nunki | 75 49.9 | S26 16.1 |
| 02 | 0 21.9 | 225 01.7 | 47.1 | 301 09.9 | 56.2 | 352 37.4 | 40.1 | 36 11.8 | 37.5 | Peacock | 53 08.3 | S56 39.8 |
| 03 | 15 24.4 | 240 01.0 . . | 46.3 | 316 10.9 . . | 56.5 | 7 40.0 . . | 40.0 | 51 14.5 . . | 37.6 | Pollux | 243 20.0 | N27 58.3 |
| 04 | 30 26.8 | 255 00.3 | 45.5 | 331 11.9 | 56.8 | 22 42.7 | 39.9 | 66 17.1 | 37.7 | Procyon | 244 53.2 | N 5 10.1 |
| 05 | 45 29.3 | 269 59.7 | 44.7 | 346 12.8 | 57.2 | 37 45.3 | 39.8 | 81 19.8 | 37.7 | | | |
| 06 | 60 31.8 | 284 59.0 | N17 44.0 | 1 13.8 | N18 57.5 | 52 47.9 | N 1 39.7 | 96 22.4 | S15 37.8 | Rasalhague | 96 00.2 | N12 32.8 |
| 07 | 75 34.2 | 299 58.4 | 43.2 | 16 14.8 | 57.8 | 67 50.6 | 39.6 | 111 25.1 | 37.9 | Regulus | 207 36.9 | N11 51.6 |
| 08 | 90 36.7 | 314 57.7 | 42.4 | 31 15.8 | 58.1 | 82 53.2 | 39.5 | 126 27.7 | 37.9 | Rigel | 281 05.9 | S 8 10.4 |
| M 09 | 105 39.2 | 329 57.1 . . | 41.6 | 46 16.7 . . | 58.5 | 97 55.8 . . | 39.5 | 141 30.3 . . | 38.0 | Rigil Kent. | 139 43.2 | S60 55.8 |
| O 10 | 120 41.6 | 344 56.4 | 40.8 | 61 17.7 | 58.8 | 112 58.5 | 39.4 | 156 33.0 | 38.0 | Sabik | 102 04.9 | S15 45.1 |
| N 11 | 135 44.1 | 359 55.8 | 40.0 | 76 18.7 | 59.1 | 128 01.1 | 39.3 | 171 35.6 | 38.1 | | | |
| D 12 | 150 46.5 | 14 55.1 | N17 39.2 | 91 19.7 | N18 59.4 | 143 03.8 | N 1 39.2 | 186 38.3 | S15 38.2 | Schedar | 349 32.8 | N56 39.5 |
| A 13 | 165 49.0 | 29 54.5 | 38.4 | 106 20.6 | 18 59.8 | 158 06.4 | 39.1 | 201 40.9 | 38.2 | Shaula | 96 12.8 | S37 07.3 |
| Y 14 | 180 51.5 | 44 53.8 | 37.6 | 121 21.6 | 19 00.1 | 173 09.0 | 39.0 | 216 43.6 | 38.3 | Sirius | 258 28.2 | S16 44.6 |
| 15 | 195 53.9 | 59 53.2 . . | 36.8 | 136 22.6 . . | 00.4 | 188 11.7 . . | 38.9 | 231 46.2 . . | 38.3 | Spica | 158 24.6 | S11 16.6 |
| 16 | 210 56.4 | 74 52.5 | 36.0 | 151 23.6 | 00.7 | 203 14.3 | 38.9 | 246 48.9 | 38.4 | Suhail | 222 48.2 | S43 31.2 |
| 17 | 225 58.9 | 89 51.9 | 35.2 | 166 24.6 | 01.1 | 218 17.0 | 38.8 | 261 51.5 | 38.5 | | | |
| 18 | 241 01.3 | 104 51.2 | N17 34.4 | 181 25.5 | N19 01.4 | 233 19.6 | N 1 38.7 | 276 54.2 | S15 38.5 | Vega | 80 34.3 | N38 48.5 |
| 19 | 256 03.8 | 119 50.6 | 33.6 | 196 26.5 | 01.7 | 248 22.2 | 38.6 | 291 56.8 | 38.6 | Zuben'ubi | 136 58.3 | S16 08.1 |
| 20 | 271 06.3 | 134 49.9 | 32.8 | 211 27.5 | 02.0 | 263 24.9 | 38.5 | 306 59.4 | 38.7 | | SHA | Mer. Pass. |
| 21 | 286 08.7 | 149 49.3 . . | 32.0 | 226 28.5 . . | 02.4 | 278 27.5 . . | 38.4 | 322 02.1 . . | 38.7 | | ° ′ | h m |
| 22 | 301 11.2 | 164 48.6 | 31.2 | 241 29.5 | 02.7 | 293 30.2 | 38.3 | 337 04.7 | 38.8 | Venus | 226 01.0 | 10 59 |
| 23 | 316 13.7 | 179 48.0 | 30.4 | 256 30.4 | 03.0 | 308 32.8 | 38.3 | 352 07.4 | 38.8 | Mars | 301 26.9 | 5 57 |
| | h m | | | | | | | | | Jupiter | 352 11.1 | 2 34 |
| Mer. Pass. 2 02.5 | | v −0.7 | d 0.8 | v 1.0 | d 0.3 | v 2.6 | d 0.1 | v 2.6 | d 0.1 | Saturn | 35 45.2 | 23 36 |

### SUN and MOON

| UT | SUN GHA | SUN Dec | MOON GHA | v | Dec | d | HP |
|---|---|---|---|---|---|---|---|
| d h | ° ′ | ° ′ | ° ′ | ′ | ° ′ | ′ | ′ |
| 20 00 | 179 07.2 | N12 31.1 | 264 31.6 | 11.8 | N22 54.6 | 7.7 | 54.7 |
| 01 | 194 07.4 | 30.3 | 279 02.4 | 11.8 | 23 02.3 | 7.6 | 54.7 |
| 02 | 209 07.5 | 29.5 | 293 33.2 | 11.8 | 23 09.9 | 7.4 | 54.7 |
| 03 | 224 07.7 .. | 28.6 | 308 04.0 | 11.7 | 23 17.3 | 7.4 | 54.7 |
| 04 | 239 07.8 | 27.8 | 322 34.7 | 11.7 | 23 24.7 | 7.3 | 54.7 |
| 05 | 254 08.0 | 27.0 | 337 05.4 | 11.6 | 23 32.0 | 7.1 | 54.6 |
| 06 | 269 08.1 | N12 26.2 | 351 36.0 | 11.6 | N23 39.1 | 7.0 | 54.6 |
| S 07 | 284 08.2 | 25.4 | 6 06.6 | 11.6 | 23 46.1 | 6.9 | 54.6 |
| A 08 | 299 08.4 | 24.5 | 20 37.2 | 11.5 | 23 53.0 | 6.8 | 54.6 |
| T 09 | 314 08.5 .. | 23.7 | 35 07.7 | 11.5 | 23 59.8 | 6.7 | 54.6 |
| U 10 | 329 08.7 | 22.9 | 49 38.2 | 11.4 | 24 06.5 | 6.6 | 54.6 |
| R 11 | 344 08.8 | 22.1 | 64 08.6 | 11.5 | 24 13.1 | 6.4 | 54.5 |
| D 12 | 359 09.0 | N12 21.2 | 78 39.1 | 11.3 | N24 19.5 | 6.4 | 54.5 |
| A 13 | 14 09.1 | 20.4 | 93 09.4 | 11.4 | 24 25.9 | 6.2 | 54.5 |
| Y 14 | 29 09.3 | 19.6 | 107 39.8 | 11.3 | 24 32.1 | 6.1 | 54.5 |
| 15 | 44 09.4 .. | 18.7 | 122 10.1 | 11.2 | 24 38.2 | 6.0 | 54.5 |
| 16 | 59 09.6 | 17.9 | 136 40.3 | 11.3 | 24 44.2 | 5.8 | 54.5 |
| 17 | 74 09.8 | 17.1 | 151 10.6 | 11.2 | 24 50.0 | 5.8 | 54.5 |
| 18 | 89 09.9 | N12 16.3 | 165 40.8 | 11.1 | N24 55.8 | 5.6 | 54.4 |
| 19 | 104 10.1 | 15.4 | 180 10.9 | 11.2 | 25 01.4 | 5.5 | 54.4 |
| 20 | 119 10.2 | 14.6 | 194 41.1 | 11.1 | 25 06.9 | 5.4 | 54.4 |
| 21 | 134 10.4 .. | 13.8 | 209 11.2 | 11.0 | 25 12.3 | 5.3 | 54.4 |
| 22 | 149 10.5 | 13.0 | 223 41.2 | 11.1 | 25 17.6 | 5.2 | 54.4 |
| 23 | 164 10.7 | 12.1 | 238 11.3 | 11.0 | 25 22.8 | 5.0 | 54.4 |
| 21 00 | 179 10.8 | N12 11.3 | 252 41.3 | 10.9 | N25 27.8 | 4.9 | 54.4 |
| 01 | 194 11.0 | 10.5 | 267 11.2 | 10.9 | 25 32.7 | 4.8 | 54.3 |
| 02 | 209 11.1 | 09.6 | 281 41.1 | 10.9 | 25 37.5 | 4.7 | 54.3 |
| 03 | 224 11.3 .. | 08.8 | 296 11.0 | 10.9 | 25 42.2 | 4.5 | 54.3 |
| 04 | 239 11.4 | 08.0 | 310 40.9 | 10.9 | 25 46.7 | 4.4 | 54.3 |
| 05 | 254 11.6 | 07.1 | 325 10.8 | 10.8 | 25 51.1 | 4.3 | 54.3 |
| 06 | 269 11.7 | N12 06.3 | 339 40.6 | 10.8 | N25 55.4 | 4.2 | 54.3 |
| 07 | 284 11.9 | 05.5 | 354 10.4 | 10.7 | 25 59.6 | 4.1 | 54.3 |
| S 08 | 299 12.0 | 04.6 | 8 40.1 | 10.7 | 26 03.7 | 3.9 | 54.3 |
| U 09 | 314 12.2 .. | 03.8 | 23 09.8 | 10.7 | 26 07.6 | 3.8 | 54.3 |
| N 10 | 329 12.4 | 03.0 | 37 39.5 | 10.7 | 26 11.4 | 3.7 | 54.2 |
| D 11 | 344 12.5 | 02.1 | 52 09.2 | 10.7 | 26 15.1 | 3.5 | 54.2 |
| A 12 | 359 12.7 | N12 01.3 | 66 38.9 | 10.6 | N26 18.6 | 3.4 | 54.2 |
| Y 13 | 14 12.8 | 12 00.5 | 81 08.5 | 10.6 | 26 22.0 | 3.3 | 54.2 |
| 14 | 29 13.0 | 11 59.6 | 95 38.1 | 10.6 | 26 25.3 | 3.2 | 54.2 |
| 15 | 44 13.1 .. | 58.8 | 110 07.7 | 10.5 | 26 28.5 | 3.1 | 54.2 |
| 16 | 59 13.3 | 58.0 | 124 37.2 | 10.6 | 26 31.6 | 2.9 | 54.2 |
| 17 | 74 13.4 | 57.1 | 139 06.8 | 10.5 | 26 34.5 | 2.8 | 54.2 |
| 18 | 89 13.6 | N11 56.3 | 153 36.3 | 10.5 | N26 37.3 | 2.6 | 54.2 |
| 19 | 104 13.8 | 55.5 | 168 05.8 | 10.5 | 26 39.9 | 2.6 | 54.2 |
| 20 | 119 13.9 | 54.6 | 182 35.3 | 10.4 | 26 42.5 | 2.4 | 54.2 |
| 21 | 134 14.1 .. | 53.8 | 197 04.7 | 10.5 | 26 44.9 | 2.3 | 54.2 |
| 22 | 149 14.2 | 52.9 | 211 34.2 | 10.4 | 26 47.2 | 2.1 | 54.2 |
| 23 | 164 14.4 | 52.1 | 226 03.6 | 10.4 | 26 49.3 | 2.1 | 54.2 |
| 22 00 | 179 14.5 | N11 51.3 | 240 33.0 | 10.4 | N26 51.4 | 1.9 | 54.1 |
| 01 | 194 14.7 | 50.4 | 255 02.4 | 10.4 | 26 53.3 | 1.7 | 54.1 |
| 02 | 209 14.9 | 49.6 | 269 31.8 | 10.3 | 26 55.0 | 1.7 | 54.1 |
| 03 | 224 15.0 .. | 48.8 | 284 01.1 | 10.4 | 26 56.7 | 1.5 | 54.1 |
| 04 | 239 15.2 | 47.9 | 298 30.5 | 10.3 | 26 58.2 | 1.4 | 54.1 |
| 05 | 254 15.3 | 47.1 | 312 59.8 | 10.4 | 26 59.6 | 1.2 | 54.1 |
| 06 | 269 15.5 | N11 46.2 | 327 29.2 | 10.3 | N27 00.8 | 1.1 | 54.1 |
| 07 | 284 15.6 | 45.4 | 341 58.5 | 10.3 | 27 01.9 | 1.0 | 54.1 |
| 08 | 299 15.8 | 44.6 | 356 27.8 | 10.3 | 27 02.9 | 0.9 | 54.1 |
| M 09 | 314 16.0 .. | 43.7 | 10 57.1 | 10.3 | 27 03.8 | 0.7 | 54.1 |
| O 10 | 329 16.1 | 42.9 | 25 26.4 | 10.3 | 27 04.5 | 0.6 | 54.1 |
| N 11 | 344 16.3 | 42.0 | 39 55.7 | 10.3 | 27 05.1 | 0.5 | 54.1 |
| D 12 | 359 16.4 | N11 41.2 | 54 25.0 | 10.3 | N27 05.6 | 0.3 | 54.1 |
| A 13 | 14 16.6 | 40.3 | 68 54.3 | 10.3 | 27 05.9 | 0.3 | 54.1 |
| Y 14 | 29 16.8 | 39.5 | 83 23.6 | 10.2 | 27 06.2 | 0.0 | 54.1 |
| 15 | 44 16.9 .. | 38.7 | 97 52.8 | 10.3 | 27 06.2 | 0.0 | 54.1 |
| 16 | 59 17.1 | 37.8 | 112 22.1 | 10.3 | 27 06.2 | 0.2 | 54.1 |
| 17 | 74 17.2 | 37.0 | 126 51.4 | 10.3 | 27 06.0 | 0.3 | 54.1 |
| 18 | 89 17.4 | N11 36.1 | 141 20.7 | 10.3 | N27 05.7 | 0.4 | 54.1 |
| 19 | 104 17.6 | 35.3 | 155 50.0 | 10.3 | 27 05.3 | 0.6 | 54.1 |
| 20 | 119 17.7 | 34.4 | 170 19.3 | 10.2 | 27 04.7 | 0.7 | 54.1 |
| 21 | 134 17.9 .. | 33.6 | 184 48.5 | 10.2 | 27 04.0 | 0.8 | 54.1 |
| 22 | 149 18.0 | 32.8 | 199 17.8 | 10.3 | 27 03.2 | 1.0 | 54.1 |
| 23 | 164 18.2 | 31.9 | 213 47.1 | 10.4 | N27 02.2 | 1.1 | 54.1 |
| | SD 15.8 | d 0.8 | SD 14.9 | | 14.8 | | 14.7 |

### Twilight / Moonrise

| Lat. | Twilight Naut. | Twilight Civil | Sunrise | Moonrise 20 | 21 | 22 | 23 |
|---|---|---|---|---|---|---|---|
| ° | h m | h m | h m | h m | h m | h m | h m |
| N 72 | //// | //// | 03 02 | ▯ | ▯ | ▯ | ▯ |
| N 70 | //// | 01 44 | 03 26 | ▯ | ▯ | ▯ | ▯ |
| 68 | //// | 02 24 | 03 44 | ▯ | ▯ | ▯ | ▯ |
| 66 | //// | 02 50 | 03 58 | ▯ | ▯ | ▯ | ▯ |
| 64 | 01 31 | 03 10 | 04 10 | 20 09 | ▯ | ▯ | ▯ |
| 62 | 02 07 | 03 26 | 04 20 | 20 56 | 21 09 | 21 50 | 23 10 |
| 60 | 02 31 | 03 40 | 04 28 | 21 27 | 21 51 | 22 37 | 23 47 |
| N 58 | 02 50 | 03 51 | 04 36 | 21 50 | 22 20 | 23 07 | 24 13 |
| 56 | 03 06 | 04 01 | 04 42 | 22 09 | 22 42 | 23 30 | 24 34 |
| 54 | 03 19 | 04 09 | 04 48 | 22 24 | 23 00 | 23 49 | 24 51 |
| 52 | 03 30 | 04 17 | 04 54 | 22 38 | 23 16 | 24 05 | 00 05 |
| 50 | 03 39 | 04 23 | 04 58 | 22 50 | 23 29 | 24 19 | 00 19 |
| 45 | 03 59 | 04 37 | 05 09 | 23 15 | 23 57 | 24 47 | 00 47 |
| N 40 | 04 14 | 04 49 | 05 17 | 23 35 | 24 18 | 00 18 | 01 09 |
| 35 | 04 26 | 04 58 | 05 24 | 23 52 | 24 36 | 00 36 | 01 27 |
| 30 | 04 36 | 05 06 | 05 31 | 24 06 | 00 06 | 00 52 | 01 43 |
| 20 | 04 52 | 05 19 | 05 42 | 24 31 | 00 31 | 01 18 | 02 09 |
| N 10 | 05 04 | 05 30 | 05 51 | 00 05 | 00 52 | 01 41 | 02 32 |
| 0 | 05 14 | 05 39 | 06 00 | 00 23 | 01 12 | 02 02 | 02 53 |
| S 10 | 05 22 | 05 47 | 06 08 | 00 41 | 01 32 | 02 24 | 03 15 |
| 20 | 05 29 | 05 55 | 06 17 | 01 00 | 01 54 | 02 47 | 03 37 |
| 30 | 05 35 | 06 03 | 06 28 | 01 22 | 02 19 | 03 13 | 04 04 |
| 35 | 05 38 | 06 08 | 06 34 | 01 35 | 02 34 | 03 29 | 04 20 |
| 40 | 05 41 | 06 12 | 06 40 | 01 50 | 02 51 | 03 47 | 04 38 |
| 45 | 05 43 | 06 18 | 06 48 | 02 08 | 03 11 | 04 09 | 05 00 |
| S 50 | 05 46 | 06 24 | 06 57 | 02 31 | 03 38 | 04 37 | 05 28 |
| 52 | 05 47 | 06 26 | 07 01 | 02 41 | 03 50 | 04 51 | 05 41 |
| 54 | 05 48 | 06 29 | 07 06 | 02 54 | 04 05 | 05 07 | 05 57 |
| 56 | 05 49 | 06 32 | 07 11 | 03 08 | 04 22 | 05 26 | 06 15 |
| 58 | 05 50 | 06 36 | 07 17 | 03 24 | 04 43 | 05 50 | 06 38 |
| S 60 | 05 51 | 06 39 | 07 23 | 03 44 | 05 10 | 06 21 | 07 08 |

### Twilight / Moonset

| Lat. | Sunset | Twilight Civil | Twilight Naut. | Moonset 20 | 21 | 22 | 23 |
|---|---|---|---|---|---|---|---|
| ° | h m | h m | h m | h m | h m | h m | h m |
| N 72 | 21 00 | 23 34 | //// | ▯ | ▯ | ▯ | ▯ |
| N 70 | 20 37 | 22 15 | //// | ▯ | ▯ | ▯ | ▯ |
| 68 | 20 20 | 21 38 | //// | ▯ | ▯ | ▯ | ▯ |
| 66 | 20 06 | 21 13 | 23 38 | ▯ | ▯ | ▯ | ▯ |
| 64 | 19 54 | 20 53 | 22 28 | 17 42 | ▯ | ▯ | ▯ |
| 62 | 19 45 | 20 37 | 21 55 | 16 55 | 18 26 | 19 31 | 19 56 |
| 60 | 19 36 | 20 25 | 21 32 | 16 25 | 17 44 | 18 44 | 19 19 |
| N 58 | 19 29 | 20 14 | 21 13 | 16 02 | 17 16 | 18 14 | 18 53 |
| 56 | 19 22 | 20 04 | 20 50 | 15 44 | 16 54 | 17 51 | 18 33 |
| 54 | 19 17 | 19 56 | 20 46 | 15 28 | 16 36 | 17 32 | 18 15 |
| 52 | 19 12 | 19 48 | 20 35 | 15 15 | 16 20 | 17 16 | 18 00 |
| 50 | 19 07 | 19 42 | 20 25 | 15 03 | 16 07 | 17 02 | 17 47 |
| 45 | 18 57 | 19 28 | 20 06 | 14 39 | 15 40 | 16 34 | 17 20 |
| N 40 | 18 48 | 19 17 | 19 51 | 14 20 | 15 18 | 16 12 | 16 59 |
| 35 | 18 41 | 19 08 | 19 39 | 14 04 | 15 01 | 15 54 | 16 42 |
| 30 | 18 35 | 19 00 | 19 29 | 13 50 | 14 45 | 15 38 | 16 27 |
| 20 | 18 24 | 18 47 | 19 14 | 13 26 | 14 19 | 15 11 | 16 01 |
| N 10 | 18 15 | 18 37 | 19 02 | 13 06 | 13 57 | 14 48 | 15 39 |
| 0 | 18 07 | 18 28 | 18 52 | 12 47 | 13 36 | 14 27 | 15 18 |
| S 10 | 17 58 | 18 19 | 18 44 | 12 28 | 13 15 | 14 05 | 14 57 |
| 20 | 17 49 | 18 12 | 18 37 | 12 07 | 12 53 | 13 42 | 14 34 |
| 30 | 17 39 | 18 03 | 18 31 | 11 44 | 12 27 | 13 16 | 14 08 |
| 35 | 17 33 | 17 59 | 18 29 | 11 30 | 12 12 | 13 00 | 13 53 |
| 40 | 17 27 | 17 54 | 18 26 | 11 15 | 11 55 | 12 41 | 13 35 |
| 45 | 17 19 | 17 49 | 18 24 | 10 56 | 11 33 | 12 19 | 13 13 |
| S 50 | 17 10 | 17 43 | 18 21 | 10 32 | 11 07 | 11 51 | 12 46 |
| 52 | 17 06 | 17 41 | 18 20 | 10 21 | 10 54 | 11 37 | 12 32 |
| 54 | 17 01 | 17 38 | 18 19 | 10 09 | 10 39 | 11 21 | 12 17 |
| 56 | 16 56 | 17 35 | 18 18 | 09 54 | 10 22 | 11 02 | 11 58 |
| 58 | 16 51 | 17 32 | 18 17 | 09 37 | 10 00 | 10 39 | 11 35 |
| S 60 | 16 44 | 17 28 | 18 17 | 09 17 | 09 34 | 10 08 | 11 06 |

### SUN / MOON

| Day | SUN Eqn. of Time 00h | SUN Eqn. of Time 12h | SUN Mer. Pass. | MOON Mer. Pass. Upper | MOON Mer. Pass. Lower | Age | Phase |
|---|---|---|---|---|---|---|---|
| d | m s | m s | h m | h m | h m | d | % |
| 20 | 03 31 | 03 24 | 12 03 | 06 35 | 18 59 | 23 | 38 |
| 21 | 03 17 | 03 10 | 12 03 | 07 24 | 19 49 | 24 | 29 |
| 22 | 03 02 | 02 55 | 12 03 | 08 15 | 20 40 | 25 | 21 |

| UT d h | ARIES GHA | VENUS −3.9 GHA | Dec | MARS −0.1 GHA | Dec | JUPITER −2.8 GHA | Dec | SATURN +0.3 GHA | Dec |
|---|---|---|---|---|---|---|---|---|---|
| **23** 00 | 331 16.1 | 194 47.3 | N17 29.6 | 271 31.4 | N19 03.3 | 323 35.4 | N 1 38.2 | 7 10.0 | S15 38.9 |
| 01 | 346 18.6 | 209 46.7 | 28.8 | 286 32.4 | 03.6 | 338 38.1 | 38.1 | 22 12.7 | 39.0 |
| 02 | 1 21.0 | 224 46.0 | 28.0 | 301 33.4 | 04.0 | 353 40.7 | 38.0 | 37 15.3 | 39.0 |
| 03 | 16 23.5 | 239 45.4 .. | 27.2 | 316 34.4 .. | 04.3 | 8 43.4 .. | 37.9 | 52 18.0 .. | 39.1 |
| 04 | 31 26.0 | 254 44.8 | 26.3 | 331 35.3 | 04.6 | 23 46.0 | 37.8 | 67 20.6 | 39.1 |
| 05 | 46 28.4 | 269 44.1 | 25.5 | 346 36.3 | 04.9 | 38 48.7 | 37.7 | 82 23.2 | 39.2 |
| 06 | 61 30.9 | 284 43.5 | N17 24.7 | 1 37.3 | N19 05.3 | 53 51.3 | N 1 37.6 | 97 25.9 | S15 39.3 |
| 07 | 76 33.4 | 299 42.8 | 23.9 | 16 38.3 | 05.6 | 68 54.0 | 37.6 | 112 28.5 | 39.3 |
| 08 | 91 35.8 | 314 42.2 | 23.1 | 31 39.3 | 05.9 | 83 56.6 | 37.5 | 127 31.2 | 39.4 |
| 09 | 106 38.3 | 329 41.5 .. | 22.3 | 46 40.3 .. | 06.2 | 98 59.2 .. | 37.4 | 142 33.8 .. | 39.5 |
| 10 | 121 40.8 | 344 40.9 | 21.5 | 61 41.2 | 06.5 | 114 01.9 | 37.3 | 157 36.5 | 39.5 |
| 11 | 136 43.2 | 359 40.3 | 20.7 | 76 42.2 | 06.9 | 129 04.5 | 37.2 | 172 39.1 | 39.6 |
| 12 | 151 45.7 | 14 39.6 | N17 19.8 | 91 43.2 | N19 07.2 | 144 07.2 | N 1 37.1 | 187 41.8 | S15 39.6 |
| 13 | 166 48.2 | 29 39.0 | 19.0 | 106 44.2 | 07.5 | 159 09.8 | 37.0 | 202 44.4 | 39.7 |
| 14 | 181 50.6 | 44 38.3 | 18.2 | 121 45.2 | 07.8 | 174 12.5 | 36.9 | 217 47.0 | 39.8 |
| 15 | 196 53.1 | 59 37.7 .. | 17.4 | 136 46.2 .. | 08.1 | 189 15.1 .. | 36.8 | 232 49.7 .. | 39.8 |
| 16 | 211 55.5 | 74 37.1 | 16.6 | 151 47.1 | 08.4 | 204 17.8 | 36.8 | 247 52.3 | 39.9 |
| 17 | 226 58.0 | 89 36.4 | 15.8 | 166 48.1 | 08.8 | 219 20.4 | 36.7 | 262 55.0 | 39.9 |
| 18 | 242 00.5 | 104 35.8 | N17 14.9 | 181 49.1 | N19 09.1 | 234 23.1 | N 1 36.6 | 277 57.6 | S15 40.0 |
| 19 | 257 02.9 | 119 35.1 | 14.1 | 196 50.1 | 09.4 | 249 25.7 | 36.5 | 293 00.3 | 40.1 |
| 20 | 272 05.4 | 134 34.5 | 13.3 | 211 51.1 | 09.7 | 264 28.3 | 36.4 | 308 02.9 | 40.1 |
| 21 | 287 07.9 | 149 33.9 .. | 12.5 | 226 52.1 .. | 10.0 | 279 31.0 .. | 36.3 | 323 05.5 .. | 40.2 |
| 22 | 302 10.3 | 164 33.2 | 11.6 | 241 53.1 | 10.3 | 294 33.6 | 36.2 | 338 08.2 | 40.3 |
| 23 | 317 12.8 | 179 32.6 | 10.8 | 256 54.1 | 10.7 | 309 36.3 | 36.1 | 353 10.8 | 40.3 |
| **24** 00 | 332 15.3 | 194 32.0 | N17 10.0 | 271 55.0 | N19 11.0 | 324 38.9 | N 1 36.0 | 8 13.5 | S15 40.4 |
| 01 | 347 17.7 | 209 31.3 | 09.2 | 286 56.0 | 11.3 | 339 41.6 | 36.0 | 23 16.1 | 40.4 |
| 02 | 2 20.2 | 224 30.7 | 08.3 | 301 57.0 | 11.6 | 354 44.2 | 35.9 | 38 18.8 | 40.5 |
| 03 | 17 22.7 | 239 30.0 .. | 07.5 | 316 58.0 .. | 11.9 | 9 46.9 .. | 35.8 | 53 21.4 .. | 40.6 |
| 04 | 32 25.1 | 254 29.4 | 06.7 | 331 59.0 | 12.2 | 24 49.5 | 35.7 | 68 24.1 | 40.6 |
| 05 | 47 27.6 | 269 28.8 | 05.8 | 347 00.0 | 12.6 | 39 52.2 | 35.6 | 83 26.7 | 40.7 |
| 06 | 62 30.0 | 284 28.1 | N17 05.0 | 2 01.0 | N19 12.9 | 54 54.8 | N 1 35.5 | 98 29.3 | S15 40.7 |
| 07 | 77 32.5 | 299 27.5 | 04.2 | 17 02.0 | 13.2 | 69 57.5 | 35.4 | 113 32.0 | 40.8 |
| 08 | 92 35.0 | 314 26.9 | 03.3 | 32 03.0 | 13.5 | 85 00.1 | 35.3 | 128 34.6 | 40.9 |
| 09 | 107 37.4 | 329 26.2 .. | 02.5 | 47 04.0 .. | 13.8 | 100 02.8 .. | 35.2 | 143 37.3 .. | 40.9 |
| 10 | 122 39.9 | 344 25.6 | 01.7 | 62 04.9 | 14.1 | 115 05.4 | 35.1 | 158 39.9 | 41.0 |
| 11 | 137 42.4 | 359 25.0 | 00.8 | 77 05.9 | 14.4 | 130 08.1 | 35.1 | 173 42.6 | 41.0 |
| 12 | 152 44.8 | 14 24.3 | N17 00.0 | 92 06.9 | N19 14.8 | 145 10.7 | N 1 35.0 | 188 45.2 | S15 41.1 |
| 13 | 167 47.3 | 29 23.7 | 16 59.2 | 107 07.9 | 15.1 | 160 13.4 | 34.9 | 203 47.8 | 41.2 |
| 14 | 182 49.8 | 44 23.1 | 58.3 | 122 08.9 | 15.4 | 175 16.1 | 34.8 | 218 50.5 | 41.2 |
| 15 | 197 52.2 | 59 22.5 .. | 57.5 | 137 09.9 .. | 15.7 | 190 18.7 .. | 34.7 | 233 53.1 .. | 41.3 |
| 16 | 212 54.7 | 74 21.8 | 56.7 | 152 10.9 | 16.0 | 205 21.4 | 34.6 | 248 55.8 | 41.4 |
| 17 | 227 57.1 | 89 21.2 | 55.8 | 167 11.9 | 16.3 | 220 24.0 | 34.5 | 263 58.4 | 41.4 |
| 18 | 242 59.6 | 104 20.6 | N16 55.0 | 182 12.9 | N19 16.6 | 235 26.7 | N 1 34.4 | 279 01.1 | S15 41.5 |
| 19 | 258 02.1 | 119 19.9 | 54.1 | 197 13.9 | 16.9 | 250 29.3 | 34.3 | 294 03.7 | 41.5 |
| 20 | 273 04.5 | 134 19.3 | 53.3 | 212 14.9 | 17.2 | 265 32.0 | 34.2 | 309 06.3 | 41.6 |
| 21 | 288 07.0 | 149 18.7 .. | 52.4 | 227 15.9 .. | 17.6 | 280 34.6 .. | 34.1 | 324 09.0 .. | 41.7 |
| 22 | 303 09.5 | 164 18.1 | 51.6 | 242 16.9 | 17.9 | 295 37.3 | 34.0 | 339 11.6 | 41.7 |
| 23 | 318 11.9 | 179 17.4 | 50.8 | 257 17.9 | 18.2 | 310 39.9 | 34.0 | 354 14.3 | 41.8 |
| **25** 00 | 333 14.4 | 194 16.8 | N16 49.9 | 272 18.9 | N19 18.5 | 325 42.6 | N 1 33.9 | 9 16.9 | S15 41.8 |
| 01 | 348 16.9 | 209 16.2 | 49.1 | 287 19.9 | 18.8 | 340 45.2 | 33.8 | 24 19.6 | 41.9 |
| 02 | 3 19.3 | 224 15.6 | 48.2 | 302 20.9 | 19.1 | 355 47.9 | 33.7 | 39 22.2 | 42.0 |
| 03 | 18 21.8 | 239 14.9 .. | 47.4 | 317 21.9 .. | 19.4 | 10 50.6 .. | 33.6 | 54 24.8 .. | 42.0 |
| 04 | 33 24.3 | 254 14.3 | 46.5 | 332 22.9 | 19.7 | 25 53.2 | 33.5 | 69 27.5 | 42.1 |
| 05 | 48 26.7 | 269 13.7 | 45.7 | 347 23.9 | 20.0 | 40 55.9 | 33.4 | 84 30.1 | 42.1 |
| 06 | 63 29.2 | 284 13.1 | N16 44.8 | 2 24.9 | N19 20.3 | 55 58.5 | N 1 33.3 | 99 32.8 | S15 42.2 |
| 07 | 78 31.6 | 299 12.4 | 44.0 | 17 25.9 | 20.6 | 71 01.2 | 33.2 | 114 35.4 | 42.3 |
| 08 | 93 34.1 | 314 11.8 | 43.1 | 32 26.9 | 21.0 | 86 03.8 | 33.1 | 129 38.1 | 42.3 |
| 09 | 108 36.6 | 329 11.2 .. | 42.3 | 47 27.9 .. | 21.3 | 101 06.5 .. | 33.0 | 144 40.7 .. | 42.4 |
| 10 | 123 39.0 | 344 10.6 | 41.4 | 62 28.9 | 21.6 | 116 09.2 | 32.9 | 159 43.3 | 42.4 |
| 11 | 138 41.5 | 359 09.9 | 40.5 | 77 29.9 | 21.9 | 131 11.8 | 32.8 | 174 46.0 | 42.5 |
| 12 | 153 44.0 | 14 09.3 | N16 39.7 | 92 30.9 | N19 22.2 | 146 14.5 | N 1 32.7 | 189 48.6 | S15 42.6 |
| 13 | 168 46.4 | 29 08.7 | 38.8 | 107 31.9 | 22.5 | 161 17.1 | 32.7 | 204 51.3 | 42.6 |
| 14 | 183 48.9 | 44 08.1 | 38.0 | 122 32.9 | 22.8 | 176 19.8 | 32.6 | 219 53.9 | 42.7 |
| 15 | 198 51.4 | 59 07.5 .. | 37.1 | 137 33.9 .. | 23.1 | 191 22.5 .. | 32.5 | 234 56.6 .. | 42.7 |
| 16 | 213 53.8 | 74 06.8 | 36.3 | 152 34.9 | 23.4 | 206 25.1 | 32.4 | 249 59.2 | 42.8 |
| 17 | 228 56.3 | 89 06.2 | 35.4 | 167 35.9 | 23.7 | 221 27.8 | 32.3 | 265 01.8 | 42.9 |
| 18 | 243 58.8 | 104 05.6 | N16 34.5 | 182 36.9 | N19 24.0 | 236 30.4 | N 1 32.2 | 280 04.5 | S15 42.9 |
| 19 | 259 01.2 | 119 05.0 | 33.7 | 197 37.9 | 24.3 | 251 33.1 | 32.1 | 295 07.1 | 43.0 |
| 20 | 274 03.7 | 134 04.4 | 32.8 | 212 38.9 | 24.6 | 266 35.7 | 32.0 | 310 09.8 | 43.0 |
| 21 | 289 06.1 | 149 03.7 .. | 31.9 | 227 39.9 .. | 24.9 | 281 38.4 .. | 31.9 | 325 12.4 .. | 43.1 |
| 22 | 304 08.6 | 164 03.1 | 31.1 | 242 40.9 | 25.2 | 296 41.1 | 31.8 | 340 15.1 | 43.2 |
| 23 | 319 11.1 | 179 02.5 | 30.2 | 257 41.9 | 25.5 | 311 43.7 | 31.7 | 355 17.7 | 43.2 |
| Mer. Pass. | h m 1 50.7 | v −0.6 | d 0.8 | v 1.0 | d 0.3 | v 2.7 | d 0.1 | v 2.6 | d 0.1 |

Side column: T U E S D A Y (Aug 23), W E D N E S D A Y (Aug 24), T H U R S D A Y (Aug 25)

### STARS

| Name | SHA | Dec |
|---|---|---|
| Acamar | 315 13.2 | S40 12.6 |
| Achernar | 335 21.3 | S57 07.1 |
| Acrux | 173 02.8 | S63 13.5 |
| Adhara | 255 07.7 | S28 59.9 |
| Aldebaran | 290 41.9 | N16 33.3 |
| Alioth | 166 15.1 | N55 50.5 |
| Alkaid | 152 53.8 | N49 12.3 |
| Alnair | 27 34.9 | S46 51.0 |
| Alnilam | 275 39.8 | S 1 11.1 |
| Alphard | 217 50.0 | S 8 45.2 |
| Alphecca | 126 05.4 | N26 38.6 |
| Alpheratz | 357 36.5 | N29 12.9 |
| Altair | 62 01.6 | N 8 55.8 |
| Ankaa | 353 08.7 | S42 10.8 |
| Antares | 112 18.2 | S26 28.9 |
| Arcturus | 145 49.9 | N19 04.1 |
| Atria | 107 14.0 | S69 04.3 |
| Avior | 234 16.1 | S59 34.7 |
| Bellatrix | 278 25.1 | N 6 22.3 |
| Betelgeuse | 270 54.4 | N 7 24.8 |
| Canopus | 263 53.6 | S52 42.1 |
| Capella | 280 24.9 | N46 01.1 |
| Deneb | 49 26.7 | N45 21.8 |
| Denebola | 182 27.2 | N14 27.0 |
| Diphda | 348 49.0 | S17 51.6 |
| Dubhe | 193 44.1 | N61 37.9 |
| Elnath | 278 04.5 | N28 37.5 |
| Eltanin | 90 42.8 | N51 29.4 |
| Enif | 33 40.4 | N 9 58.8 |
| Fomalhaut | 15 16.3 | S29 30.1 |
| Gacrux | 171 54.3 | S57 14.4 |
| Gienah | 175 45.9 | S17 39.9 |
| Hadar | 148 39.1 | S60 29.0 |
| Hamal | 327 53.2 | N23 34.1 |
| Kaus Aust. | 83 34.9 | S34 22.5 |
| Kochab | 137 20.1 | N74 04.1 |
| Markab | 13 31.5 | N15 19.6 |
| Menkar | 314 08.1 | N 4 10.8 |
| Menkent | 148 00.1 | S36 28.9 |
| Miaplacidus | 221 39.6 | S69 48.4 |
| Mirfak | 308 31.0 | N49 56.3 |
| Nunki | 75 49.9 | S26 16.1 |
| Peacock | 53 08.3 | S56 39.8 |
| Pollux | 243 20.0 | N27 58.3 |
| Procyon | 244 53.1 | N 5 10.1 |
| Rasalhague | 96 00.2 | N12 32.8 |
| Regulus | 207 36.9 | N11 51.6 |
| Rigel | 281 05.9 | S 8 10.4 |
| Rigil Kent. | 139 43.2 | S60 55.8 |
| Sabik | 102 04.9 | S15 45.1 |
| Schedar | 349 32.8 | N56 39.5 |
| Shaula | 96 12.9 | S37 07.3 |
| Sirius | 258 28.2 | S16 44.6 |
| Spica | 158 24.6 | S11 16.6 |
| Suhail | 222 48.2 | S43 31.2 |
| Vega | 80 34.3 | N38 48.5 |
| Zuben'ubi | 136 58.3 | S16 08.1 |

| | SHA | Mer. Pass. |
|---|---|---|
| Venus | 222 16.7 | h m 11 02 |
| Mars | 299 39.8 | 5 52 |
| Jupiter | 352 23.7 | 2 21 |
| Saturn | 35 58.2 | 23 23 |

| UT | SUN GHA | SUN Dec | MOON GHA | v | MOON Dec | d | HP |
|---|---|---|---|---|---|---|---|
| d h | ° ′ | ° ′ | ° ′ | ′ | ° ′ | ′ | ′ |
| 23 00 | 179 18.4 | N11 31.1 | 228 16.5 | 10.3 | N27 01.1 | 1.2 | 54.1 |
| 01 | 194 18.5 | 30.2 | 242 45.8 | 10.3 | 26 59.9 | 1.3 | 54.1 |
| 02 | 209 18.7 | 29.4 | 257 15.1 | 10.3 | 26 58.6 | 1.5 | 54.1 |
| 03 | 224 18.9 | 28.5 | 271 44.4 | 10.4 | 26 57.1 | 1.6 | 54.1 |
| 04 | 239 19.0 | 27.7 | 286 13.8 | 10.3 | 26 55.5 | 1.8 | 54.1 |
| 05 | 254 19.2 | 26.8 | 300 43.1 | 10.4 | 26 53.7 | 1.8 | 54.1 |
| 06 | 269 19.3 | N11 26.0 | 315 12.5 | 10.4 | N26 51.9 | 2.0 | 54.1 |
| 07 | 284 19.5 | 25.1 | 329 41.9 | 10.4 | 26 49.9 | 2.1 | 54.1 |
| T 08 | 299 19.7 | 24.3 | 344 11.3 | 10.4 | 26 47.8 | 2.3 | 54.1 |
| U 09 | 314 19.8 | 23.4 | 358 40.7 | 10.4 | 26 45.5 | 2.4 | 54.1 |
| E 10 | 329 20.0 | 22.6 | 13 10.1 | 10.5 | 26 43.1 | 2.5 | 54.1 |
| S 11 | 344 20.2 | 21.7 | 27 39.6 | 10.5 | 26 40.6 | 2.6 | 54.1 |
| D 12 | 359 20.3 | N11 20.9 | 42 09.1 | 10.4 | N26 38.0 | 2.8 | 54.1 |
| A 13 | 14 20.5 | 20.0 | 56 38.5 | 10.5 | 26 35.2 | 2.9 | 54.1 |
| Y 14 | 29 20.7 | 19.2 | 71 08.0 | 10.6 | 26 32.3 | 3.0 | 54.1 |
| 15 | 44 20.8 | 18.3 | 85 37.6 | 10.5 | 26 29.3 | 3.1 | 54.1 |
| 16 | 59 21.0 | 17.5 | 100 07.1 | 10.6 | 26 26.2 | 3.3 | 54.1 |
| 17 | 74 21.1 | 16.6 | 114 36.7 | 10.6 | 26 22.9 | 3.4 | 54.1 |
| 18 | 89 21.3 | N11 15.8 | 129 06.3 | 10.6 | N26 19.5 | 3.5 | 54.1 |
| 19 | 104 21.5 | 14.9 | 143 35.9 | 10.6 | 26 16.0 | 3.7 | 54.1 |
| 20 | 119 21.6 | 14.1 | 158 05.5 | 10.7 | 26 12.3 | 3.8 | 54.1 |
| 21 | 134 21.8 | 13.2 | 172 35.2 | 10.7 | 26 08.5 | 3.9 | 54.1 |
| 22 | 149 22.0 | 12.4 | 187 04.9 | 10.7 | 26 04.6 | 4.0 | 54.2 |
| 23 | 164 22.1 | 11.5 | 201 34.6 | 10.8 | 26 00.6 | 4.1 | 54.2 |
| 24 00 | 179 22.3 | N11 10.7 | 216 04.4 | 10.8 | N25 56.5 | 4.3 | 54.2 |
| 01 | 194 22.5 | 09.8 | 230 34.2 | 10.8 | 25 52.2 | 4.4 | 54.2 |
| 02 | 209 22.6 | 09.0 | 245 04.0 | 10.8 | 25 47.8 | 4.5 | 54.2 |
| 03 | 224 22.8 | 08.1 | 259 33.8 | 10.9 | 25 43.3 | 4.7 | 54.2 |
| 04 | 239 23.0 | 07.3 | 274 03.7 | 10.9 | 25 38.6 | 4.7 | 54.2 |
| 05 | 254 23.1 | 06.4 | 288 33.6 | 11.0 | 25 33.9 | 4.9 | 54.2 |
| 06 | 269 23.3 | N11 05.5 | 303 03.6 | 10.9 | N25 29.0 | 5.0 | 54.2 |
| W 07 | 284 23.5 | 04.7 | 317 33.5 | 11.0 | 25 24.0 | 5.1 | 54.2 |
| E 08 | 299 23.6 | 03.8 | 332 03.5 | 11.1 | 25 18.9 | 5.3 | 54.2 |
| D 09 | 314 23.8 | 03.0 | 346 33.6 | 11.1 | 25 13.6 | 5.4 | 54.2 |
| N 10 | 329 24.0 | 02.1 | 1 03.7 | 11.1 | 25 08.2 | 5.5 | 54.2 |
| E 11 | 344 24.1 | 01.3 | 15 33.8 | 11.1 | 25 02.7 | 5.6 | 54.2 |
| S 12 | 359 24.3 | N11 00.4 | 30 03.9 | 11.2 | N24 57.1 | 5.7 | 54.2 |
| D 13 | 14 24.5 | 10 59.6 | 44 34.1 | 11.3 | 24 51.4 | 5.8 | 54.3 |
| A 14 | 29 24.6 | 58.7 | 59 04.4 | 11.2 | 24 45.6 | 6.0 | 54.3 |
| Y 15 | 44 24.8 | 57.8 | 73 34.6 | 11.3 | 24 39.6 | 6.1 | 54.3 |
| 16 | 59 25.0 | 57.0 | 88 04.9 | 11.4 | 24 33.5 | 6.2 | 54.3 |
| 17 | 74 25.2 | 56.1 | 102 35.3 | 11.4 | 24 27.3 | 6.3 | 54.3 |
| 18 | 89 25.3 | N10 55.3 | 117 05.7 | 11.4 | N24 21.0 | 6.4 | 54.3 |
| 19 | 104 25.5 | 54.4 | 131 36.1 | 11.4 | 24 14.6 | 6.6 | 54.3 |
| 20 | 119 25.7 | 53.5 | 146 06.5 | 11.6 | 24 08.0 | 6.6 | 54.3 |
| 21 | 134 25.8 | 52.7 | 160 37.1 | 11.5 | 24 01.4 | 6.8 | 54.3 |
| 22 | 149 26.0 | 51.8 | 175 07.6 | 11.6 | 23 54.6 | 6.9 | 54.3 |
| 23 | 164 26.2 | 51.0 | 189 38.2 | 11.6 | 23 47.7 | 7.0 | 54.3 |
| 25 00 | 179 26.3 | N10 50.1 | 204 08.8 | 11.7 | N23 40.7 | 7.1 | 54.4 |
| 01 | 194 26.5 | 49.2 | 218 39.5 | 11.7 | 23 33.6 | 7.2 | 54.4 |
| 02 | 209 26.7 | 48.4 | 233 10.2 | 11.8 | 23 26.4 | 7.3 | 54.4 |
| 03 | 224 26.9 | 47.5 | 247 41.0 | 11.8 | 23 19.1 | 7.4 | 54.4 |
| 04 | 239 27.0 | 46.7 | 262 11.8 | 11.9 | 23 11.7 | 7.6 | 54.4 |
| 05 | 254 27.2 | 45.8 | 276 42.7 | 11.9 | 23 04.1 | 7.6 | 54.4 |
| 06 | 269 27.4 | N10 44.9 | 291 13.6 | 11.9 | N22 56.5 | 7.8 | 54.4 |
| 07 | 284 27.5 | 44.1 | 305 44.5 | 12.0 | 22 48.7 | 7.9 | 54.4 |
| T 08 | 299 27.7 | 43.2 | 320 15.5 | 12.0 | 22 40.8 | 8.0 | 54.4 |
| H 09 | 314 27.9 | 42.3 | 334 46.5 | 12.1 | 22 32.8 | 8.0 | 54.5 |
| U 10 | 329 28.1 | 41.5 | 349 17.6 | 12.1 | 22 24.8 | 8.2 | 54.5 |
| R 11 | 344 28.2 | 40.6 | 3 48.7 | 12.2 | 22 16.6 | 8.3 | 54.5 |
| S 12 | 359 28.4 | N10 39.8 | 18 19.9 | 12.2 | N22 08.3 | 8.4 | 54.5 |
| D 13 | 14 28.6 | 38.9 | 32 51.1 | 12.3 | 21 59.9 | 8.5 | 54.5 |
| A 14 | 29 28.8 | 38.0 | 47 22.4 | 12.3 | 21 51.4 | 8.6 | 54.5 |
| Y 15 | 44 28.9 | 37.2 | 61 53.7 | 12.4 | 21 42.8 | 8.7 | 54.5 |
| 16 | 59 29.1 | 36.3 | 76 25.1 | 12.4 | 21 34.1 | 8.8 | 54.5 |
| 17 | 74 29.3 | 35.4 | 90 56.5 | 12.4 | 21 25.3 | 8.9 | 54.6 |
| 18 | 89 29.4 | N10 34.6 | 105 27.9 | 12.5 | N21 16.4 | 9.0 | 54.6 |
| 19 | 104 29.6 | 33.7 | 119 59.4 | 12.6 | 21 07.4 | 9.1 | 54.6 |
| 20 | 119 29.8 | 32.8 | 134 31.0 | 12.6 | 20 58.3 | 9.2 | 54.6 |
| 21 | 134 30.0 | 32.0 | 149 02.6 | 12.6 | 20 49.1 | 9.3 | 54.6 |
| 22 | 149 30.1 | 31.1 | 163 34.2 | 12.7 | 20 39.8 | 9.4 | 54.6 |
| 23 | 164 30.3 | 30.2 | 178 05.9 | 12.7 | N20 30.4 | 9.5 | 54.6 |
| | SD 15.8 | d 0.9 | SD 14.7 | | 14.8 | | 14.8 |

| Lat. | Twilight Naut. | Twilight Civil | Sunrise | Moonrise 23 | Moonrise 24 | Moonrise 25 | Moonrise 26 |
|---|---|---|---|---|---|---|---|
| ° | h m | h m | h m | h m | h m | h m | h m |
| N 72 | //// | 01 14 | 03 19 | ☐ | ☐ | ☐ | ☐ |
| N 70 | //// | 02 08 | 03 40 | ☐ | ☐ | ☐ | ☐ |
| 68 | //// | 02 40 | 03 55 | ☐ | ☐ | ☐ | 00 51 |
| 66 | 01 04 | 03 03 | 04 08 | ☐ | 23 00 | 25 33 | 01 33 |
| 64 | 01 52 | 03 21 | 04 19 | ☐ | ☐ | 00 10 | 02 01 |
| 62 | 02 21 | 03 36 | 04 28 | 23 10 | 24 46 | 00 46 | 02 23 |
| 60 | 02 43 | 03 48 | 04 36 | 23 47 | 25 11 | 01 11 | 02 40 |
| N 58 | 03 00 | 03 58 | 04 42 | 24 13 | 00 13 | 01 31 | 02 54 |
| 56 | 03 14 | 04 07 | 04 48 | 24 34 | 00 34 | 01 48 | 03 07 |
| 54 | 03 26 | 04 15 | 04 54 | 24 51 | 00 51 | 02 02 | 03 18 |
| 52 | 03 36 | 04 22 | 04 59 | 00 05 | 01 05 | 02 14 | 03 27 |
| 50 | 03 45 | 04 28 | 05 03 | 00 19 | 01 18 | 02 25 | 03 36 |
| 45 | 04 03 | 04 41 | 05 12 | 00 47 | 01 44 | 02 47 | 03 53 |
| N 40 | 04 18 | 04 52 | 05 20 | 01 09 | 02 05 | 03 05 | 04 08 |
| 35 | 04 29 | 05 00 | 05 27 | 01 27 | 02 22 | 03 20 | 04 20 |
| 30 | 04 39 | 05 08 | 05 32 | 01 43 | 02 37 | 03 33 | 04 31 |
| 20 | 04 53 | 05 20 | 05 42 | 02 09 | 03 02 | 03 56 | 04 49 |
| N 10 | 05 05 | 05 30 | 05 51 | 02 32 | 03 23 | 04 15 | 05 05 |
| 0 | 05 14 | 05 38 | 05 59 | 02 53 | 03 44 | 04 33 | 05 20 |
| S 10 | 05 21 | 05 46 | 06 07 | 03 15 | 04 04 | 04 51 | 05 35 |
| 20 | 05 27 | 05 53 | 06 15 | 03 37 | 04 25 | 05 10 | 05 50 |
| 30 | 05 32 | 06 00 | 06 24 | 04 04 | 04 50 | 05 31 | 06 08 |
| 35 | 05 35 | 06 04 | 06 30 | 04 20 | 05 05 | 05 44 | 06 19 |
| 40 | 05 37 | 06 08 | 06 36 | 04 38 | 05 22 | 05 59 | 06 31 |
| 45 | 05 39 | 06 13 | 06 43 | 05 00 | 05 42 | 06 16 | 06 44 |
| S 50 | 05 40 | 06 18 | 06 51 | 05 28 | 06 07 | 06 38 | 07 01 |
| 52 | 05 41 | 06 20 | 06 55 | 05 41 | 06 19 | 06 48 | 07 09 |
| 54 | 05 42 | 06 23 | 06 59 | 05 57 | 06 33 | 06 59 | 07 18 |
| 56 | 05 42 | 06 25 | 07 04 | 06 15 | 06 50 | 07 12 | 07 28 |
| 58 | 05 43 | 06 28 | 07 09 | 06 38 | 07 09 | 07 28 | 07 39 |
| S 60 | 05 43 | 06 31 | 07 15 | 07 08 | 07 33 | 07 46 | 07 52 |

| Lat | Sunset | Twilight Civil | Twilight Naut. | Moonset 23 | Moonset 24 | Moonset 25 | Moonset 26 |
|---|---|---|---|---|---|---|---|
| ° | h m | h m | h m | h m | h m | h m | h m |
| N 72 | 20 41 | 22 39 | //// | ☐ | ☐ | ☐ | 22 09 |
| N 70 | 20 22 | 21 50 | //// | ☐ | ☐ | ☐ | 21 27 |
| 68 | 20 06 | 21 20 | //// | ☐ | ☐ | 21 40 | 20 58 |
| 66 | 19 54 | 20 58 | 22 50 | ☐ | 21 51 | 20 57 | 20 36 |
| 64 | 19 44 | 20 41 | 22 07 | ☐ | 20 40 | 20 27 | 20 19 |
| 62 | 19 35 | 20 26 | 21 39 | 19 56 | 20 04 | 20 05 | 20 05 |
| 60 | 19 27 | 20 15 | 21 19 | 19 19 | 19 38 | 19 47 | 19 52 |
| N 58 | 19 21 | 20 05 | 21 02 | 18 53 | 19 17 | 19 32 | 19 42 |
| 56 | 19 15 | 19 56 | 20 49 | 18 32 | 19 00 | 19 19 | 19 32 |
| 54 | 19 10 | 19 48 | 20 37 | 18 15 | 18 46 | 19 08 | 19 24 |
| 52 | 19 05 | 19 41 | 20 27 | 18 00 | 18 33 | 18 58 | 19 17 |
| 50 | 19 01 | 19 35 | 20 18 | 17 47 | 18 22 | 18 49 | 19 10 |
| 45 | 18 52 | 19 23 | 20 00 | 17 20 | 17 59 | 18 30 | 18 56 |
| N 40 | 18 44 | 19 12 | 19 46 | 16 59 | 17 40 | 18 14 | 18 44 |
| 35 | 18 38 | 19 04 | 19 35 | 16 42 | 17 24 | 18 01 | 18 33 |
| 30 | 18 32 | 18 56 | 19 26 | 16 27 | 17 10 | 17 49 | 18 24 |
| 20 | 18 22 | 18 45 | 19 11 | 16 01 | 16 47 | 17 29 | 18 09 |
| N 10 | 18 14 | 18 35 | 19 00 | 15 39 | 16 27 | 17 12 | 17 55 |
| 0 | 18 06 | 18 27 | 18 51 | 15 18 | 16 08 | 16 56 | 17 42 |
| S 10 | 17 58 | 18 19 | 18 44 | 14 57 | 15 48 | 16 39 | 17 29 |
| 20 | 17 50 | 18 12 | 18 38 | 14 34 | 15 28 | 16 22 | 17 15 |
| 30 | 17 41 | 18 05 | 18 33 | 14 08 | 15 04 | 16 01 | 16 59 |
| 35 | 17 35 | 18 01 | 18 31 | 13 53 | 14 50 | 15 49 | 16 49 |
| 40 | 17 30 | 17 57 | 18 29 | 13 35 | 14 33 | 15 35 | 16 39 |
| 45 | 17 23 | 17 53 | 18 27 | 13 13 | 14 14 | 15 19 | 16 26 |
| S 50 | 17 15 | 17 48 | 18 25 | 12 46 | 13 49 | 14 58 | 16 10 |
| 52 | 17 11 | 17 45 | 18 25 | 12 32 | 13 37 | 14 49 | 16 03 |
| 54 | 17 07 | 17 43 | 18 24 | 12 17 | 13 23 | 14 38 | 15 55 |
| 56 | 17 02 | 17 40 | 18 24 | 11 58 | 13 08 | 14 25 | 15 45 |
| 58 | 16 57 | 17 38 | 18 23 | 11 36 | 12 49 | 14 10 | 15 35 |
| S 60 | 16 51 | 17 34 | 18 23 | 11 06 | 12 25 | 13 53 | 15 23 |

| | SUN | | | MOON | | | |
|---|---|---|---|---|---|---|---|
| Day | Eqn. of Time 00h | Eqn. of Time 12h | Mer. Pass. | Mer. Pass. Upper | Mer. Pass. Lower | Age | Phase |
| d | m s | m s | h m | h m | h m | d | % |
| 23 | 02 47 | 02 39 | 12 03 | 09 05 | 21 31 | 26 | 14 |
| 24 | 02 31 | 02 23 | 12 02 | 09 56 | 22 20 | 27 | 8 |
| 25 | 02 15 | 02 07 | 12 02 | 10 44 | 23 08 | 28 | 3 |

| UT | ARIES GHA | VENUS −3.9 GHA | VENUS Dec | MARS −0.1 GHA | MARS Dec | JUPITER −2.8 GHA | JUPITER Dec | SATURN +0.3 GHA | SATURN Dec | STARS Name | SHA | Dec |
|---|---|---|---|---|---|---|---|---|---|---|---|---|
| d h | ° ′ | ° ′ | ° ′ | ° ′ | ° ′ | ° ′ | ° ′ | ° ′ | ° ′ | | ° ′ | ° ′ |
| 26 00 | 334 13.5 | 194 01.9 | N16 29.4 | 272 42.9 | N19 25.8 | 326 46.4 | N 1 31.6 | 10 20.3 | S15 43.3 | Acamar | 315 13.1 | S40 12.6 |
| 01 | 349 16.0 | 209 01.3 | 28.5 | 287 43.9 | 26.1 | 341 49.1 | 31.5 | 25 23.0 | 43.4 | Achernar | 335 21.3 | S57 07.1 |
| 02 | 4 18.5 | 224 00.7 | 27.6 | 302 44.9 | 26.4 | 356 51.7 | 31.4 | 40 25.6 | 43.4 | Acrux | 173 02.8 | S63 13.5 |
| 03 | 19 20.9 | 239 00.0 . . | 26.8 | 317 45.9 . . | 26.8 | 11 54.4 . . | 31.3 | 55 28.3 . . | 43.5 | Adhara | 255 07.6 | S28 59.9 |
| 04 | 34 23.4 | 253 59.4 | 25.9 | 332 46.9 | 27.1 | 26 57.0 | 31.2 | 70 30.9 | 43.5 | Aldebaran | 290 41.9 | N16 33.3 |
| 05 | 49 25.9 | 268 58.8 | 25.0 | 347 47.9 | 27.4 | 41 59.7 | 31.1 | 85 33.5 | 43.6 | | | |
| 06 | 64 28.3 | 283 58.2 | N16 24.1 | 2 48.9 | N19 27.7 | 57 02.4 | N 1 31.0 | 100 36.2 | S15 43.7 | Alioth | 166 15.1 | N55 50.5 |
| 07 | 79 30.8 | 298 57.6 | 23.3 | 17 50.0 | 28.0 | 72 05.0 | 31.0 | 115 38.8 | 43.7 | Alkaid | 152 53.8 | N49 12.3 |
| 08 | 94 33.2 | 313 57.0 | 22.4 | 32 51.0 | 28.3 | 87 07.7 | 30.9 | 130 41.5 | 43.8 | Alnair | 27 34.9 | S46 51.1 |
| F 09 | 109 35.7 | 328 56.4 . . | 21.5 | 47 52.0 . . | 28.6 | 102 10.4 . . | 30.8 | 145 44.1 . . | 43.8 | Alnilam | 275 39.8 | S 1 11.1 |
| R 10 | 124 38.2 | 343 55.8 | 20.7 | 62 53.0 | 28.9 | 117 13.0 | 30.7 | 160 46.8 | 43.9 | Alphard | 217 50.0 | S 8 45.2 |
| I 11 | 139 40.6 | 358 55.1 | 19.8 | 77 54.0 | 29.2 | 132 15.7 | 30.6 | 175 49.4 | 44.0 | | | |
| D 12 | 154 43.1 | 13 54.5 | N16 18.9 | 92 55.0 | N19 29.5 | 147 18.4 | N 1 30.5 | 190 52.0 | S15 44.0 | Alphecca | 126 05.5 | N26 38.6 |
| A 13 | 169 45.6 | 28 53.9 | 18.0 | 107 56.0 | 29.8 | 162 21.0 | 30.4 | 205 54.7 | 44.1 | Alpheratz | 357 36.5 | N29 12.9 |
| Y 14 | 184 48.0 | 43 53.3 | 17.1 | 122 57.0 | 30.1 | 177 23.7 | 30.3 | 220 57.3 | 44.1 | Altair | 62 01.6 | N 8 55.8 |
| 15 | 199 50.5 | 58 52.7 . . | 16.3 | 137 58.0 . . | 30.4 | 192 26.3 . . | 30.2 | 236 00.0 . . | 44.2 | Ankaa | 353 08.7 | S42 10.8 |
| 16 | 214 53.0 | 73 52.1 | 15.4 | 152 59.0 | 30.7 | 207 29.0 | 30.1 | 251 02.6 | 44.3 | Antares | 112 18.2 | S26 28.9 |
| 17 | 229 55.4 | 88 51.5 | 14.5 | 168 00.1 | 31.0 | 222 31.7 | 30.0 | 266 05.2 | 44.3 | | | |
| 18 | 244 57.9 | 103 50.9 | N16 13.6 | 183 01.1 | N19 31.3 | 237 34.3 | N 1 29.9 | 281 07.9 | S15 44.4 | Arcturus | 145 49.9 | N19 04.1 |
| 19 | 260 00.4 | 118 50.3 | 12.8 | 198 02.1 | 31.6 | 252 37.0 | 29.8 | 296 10.5 | 44.4 | Atria | 107 14.0 | S69 04.3 |
| 20 | 275 02.8 | 133 49.7 | 11.9 | 213 03.1 | 31.9 | 267 39.7 | 29.7 | 311 13.2 | 44.5 | Avior | 234 16.1 | S59 34.7 |
| 21 | 290 05.3 | 148 49.0 . . | 11.0 | 228 04.1 . . | 32.2 | 282 42.3 . . | 29.6 | 326 15.8 . . | 44.6 | Bellatrix | 278 25.1 | N 6 22.3 |
| 22 | 305 07.7 | 163 48.4 | 10.1 | 243 05.1 | 32.5 | 297 45.0 | 29.5 | 341 18.4 | 44.6 | Betelgeuse | 270 54.3 | N 7 24.8 |
| 23 | 320 10.2 | 178 47.8 | 09.2 | 258 06.1 | 32.8 | 312 47.7 | 29.4 | 356 21.1 | 44.7 | | | |
| 27 00 | 335 12.7 | 193 47.2 | N16 08.3 | 273 07.1 | N19 33.0 | 327 50.3 | N 1 29.3 | 11 23.7 | S15 44.7 | Canopus | 263 53.5 | S52 42.1 |
| 01 | 350 15.1 | 208 46.6 | 07.4 | 288 08.2 | 33.3 | 342 53.0 | 29.2 | 26 26.4 | 44.8 | Capella | 280 24.9 | N46 01.1 |
| 02 | 5 17.6 | 223 46.0 | 06.6 | 303 09.2 | 33.6 | 357 55.7 | 29.1 | 41 29.0 | 44.9 | Deneb | 49 26.7 | N45 21.8 |
| 03 | 20 20.1 | 238 45.4 . . | 05.7 | 318 10.2 . . | 33.9 | 12 58.3 . . | 29.0 | 56 31.7 . . | 44.9 | Denebola | 182 27.2 | N14 27.0 |
| 04 | 35 22.5 | 253 44.8 | 04.8 | 333 11.2 | 34.2 | 28 01.0 | 28.9 | 71 34.3 | 45.0 | Diphda | 348 49.0 | S17 51.6 |
| 05 | 50 25.0 | 268 44.2 | 03.9 | 348 12.2 | 34.5 | 43 03.7 | 28.8 | 86 36.9 | 45.0 | | | |
| 06 | 65 27.5 | 283 43.6 | N16 03.0 | 3 13.2 | N19 34.8 | 58 06.4 | N 1 28.7 | 101 39.6 | S15 45.1 | Dubhe | 193 44.1 | N61 37.9 |
| 07 | 80 29.9 | 298 43.0 | 02.1 | 18 14.3 | 35.1 | 73 09.0 | 28.6 | 116 42.2 | 45.1 | Elnath | 278 04.5 | N28 37.5 |
| S 08 | 95 32.4 | 313 42.4 | 01.2 | 33 15.3 | 35.4 | 88 11.7 | 28.5 | 131 44.9 | 45.2 | Eltanin | 90 42.9 | N51 29.4 |
| A 09 | 110 34.9 | 328 41.8 | 16 00.3 | 48 16.3 . . | 35.7 | 103 14.4 . . | 28.4 | 146 47.5 . . | 45.3 | Enif | 33 40.4 | N 9 58.8 |
| T 10 | 125 37.3 | 343 41.2 | 15 59.4 | 63 17.3 | 36.0 | 118 17.0 | 28.3 | 161 50.1 | 45.3 | Fomalhaut | 15 16.3 | S29 30.1 |
| U 11 | 140 39.8 | 358 40.6 | 58.5 | 78 18.3 | 36.3 | 133 19.7 | 28.2 | 176 52.8 | 45.4 | | | |
| R 12 | 155 42.2 | 13 40.0 | N15 57.7 | 93 19.4 | N19 36.6 | 148 22.4 | N 1 28.1 | 191 55.4 | S15 45.4 | Gacrux | 171 54.3 | S57 14.4 |
| D 13 | 170 44.7 | 28 39.4 | 56.8 | 108 20.4 | 36.9 | 163 25.0 | 28.0 | 206 58.1 | 45.5 | Gienah | 175 45.9 | S17 39.9 |
| A 14 | 185 47.2 | 43 38.8 | 55.9 | 123 21.4 | 37.2 | 178 27.7 | 27.9 | 222 00.7 | 45.6 | Hadar | 148 39.1 | S60 29.0 |
| Y 15 | 200 49.6 | 58 38.2 . . | 55.0 | 138 22.4 . . | 37.5 | 193 30.4 . . | 27.8 | 237 03.3 . . | 45.6 | Hamal | 327 53.2 | N23 34.1 |
| 16 | 215 52.1 | 73 37.6 | 54.1 | 153 23.4 | 37.8 | 208 33.1 | 27.7 | 252 06.0 | 45.7 | Kaus Aust. | 83 34.9 | S34 22.5 |
| 17 | 230 54.6 | 88 37.0 | 53.2 | 168 24.5 | 38.1 | 223 35.7 | 27.6 | 267 08.6 | 45.7 | | | |
| 18 | 245 57.0 | 103 36.4 | N15 52.3 | 183 25.5 | N19 38.4 | 238 38.4 | N 1 27.5 | 282 11.3 | S15 45.8 | Kochab | 137 20.2 | N74 04.1 |
| 19 | 260 59.5 | 118 35.8 | 51.4 | 198 26.5 | 38.6 | 253 41.1 | 27.4 | 297 13.9 | 45.9 | Markab | 13 31.5 | N15 19.7 |
| 20 | 276 02.0 | 133 35.2 | 50.5 | 213 27.5 | 38.9 | 268 43.7 | 27.3 | 312 16.5 | 45.9 | Menkar | 314 08.1 | N 4 10.8 |
| 21 | 291 04.4 | 148 34.6 . . | 49.6 | 228 28.5 . . | 39.2 | 283 46.4 . . | 27.2 | 327 19.2 . . | 46.0 | Menkent | 148 00.1 | S36 28.9 |
| 22 | 306 06.9 | 163 34.0 | 48.7 | 243 29.6 | 39.5 | 298 49.1 | 27.1 | 342 21.8 | 46.0 | Miaplacidus | 221 39.6 | S69 48.4 |
| 23 | 321 09.3 | 178 33.4 | 47.8 | 258 30.6 | 39.8 | 313 51.8 | 27.0 | 357 24.5 | 46.1 | | | |
| 28 00 | 336 11.8 | 193 32.8 | N15 46.9 | 273 31.6 | N19 40.1 | 328 54.4 | N 1 26.9 | 12 27.1 | S15 46.2 | Mirfak | 308 30.9 | N49 56.3 |
| 01 | 351 14.3 | 208 32.2 | 46.0 | 288 32.6 | 40.4 | 343 57.1 | 26.8 | 27 29.7 | 46.2 | Nunki | 75 49.9 | S26 16.1 |
| 02 | 6 16.7 | 223 31.6 | 45.0 | 303 33.7 | 40.7 | 358 59.8 | 26.7 | 42 32.4 | 46.3 | Peacock | 53 08.3 | S56 39.8 |
| 03 | 21 19.2 | 238 31.0 . . | 44.1 | 318 34.7 . . | 41.0 | 14 02.5 . . | 26.6 | 57 35.0 . . | 46.3 | Pollux | 243 20.0 | N27 58.3 |
| 04 | 36 21.7 | 253 30.4 | 43.2 | 333 35.7 | 41.3 | 29 05.1 | 26.5 | 72 37.7 | 46.4 | Procyon | 244 53.1 | N 5 10.2 |
| 05 | 51 24.1 | 268 29.8 | 42.3 | 348 36.7 | 41.6 | 44 07.8 | 26.4 | 87 40.3 | 46.5 | | | |
| 06 | 66 26.6 | 283 29.2 | N15 41.4 | 3 37.8 | N19 41.8 | 59 10.5 | N 1 26.3 | 102 42.9 | S15 46.5 | Rasalhague | 96 00.2 | N12 32.8 |
| 07 | 81 29.1 | 298 28.6 | 40.5 | 18 38.8 | 42.1 | 74 13.2 | 26.2 | 117 45.6 | 46.6 | Regulus | 207 36.8 | N11 51.6 |
| 08 | 96 31.5 | 313 28.0 | 39.6 | 33 39.8 | 42.4 | 89 15.8 | 26.1 | 132 48.2 | 46.6 | Rigel | 281 05.8 | S 8 10.4 |
| S 09 | 111 34.0 | 328 27.4 . . | 38.7 | 48 40.8 . . | 42.7 | 104 18.5 . . | 26.0 | 147 50.9 . . | 46.7 | Rigil Kent. | 139 43.3 | S60 55.8 |
| U 10 | 126 36.5 | 343 26.8 | 37.8 | 63 41.9 | 43.0 | 119 21.2 | 25.9 | 162 53.5 | 46.8 | Sabik | 102 04.9 | S15 45.1 |
| N 11 | 141 38.9 | 358 26.3 | 36.9 | 78 42.9 | 43.3 | 134 23.9 | 25.8 | 177 56.1 | 46.8 | | | |
| D 12 | 156 41.4 | 13 25.7 | N15 36.0 | 93 43.9 | N19 43.6 | 149 26.5 | N 1 25.7 | 192 58.8 | S15 46.9 | Schedar | 349 32.8 | N56 39.5 |
| A 13 | 171 43.8 | 28 25.1 | 35.0 | 108 45.0 | 43.9 | 164 29.2 | 25.6 | 208 01.4 | 46.9 | Shaula | 96 12.9 | S37 07.3 |
| Y 14 | 186 46.3 | 43 24.5 | 34.1 | 123 46.0 | 44.2 | 179 31.9 | 25.5 | 223 04.1 | 47.0 | Sirius | 258 28.2 | S16 44.6 |
| 15 | 201 48.8 | 58 23.9 . . | 33.2 | 138 47.0 . . | 44.4 | 194 34.6 . . | 25.4 | 238 06.7 . . | 47.0 | Spica | 158 24.6 | S11 16.6 |
| 16 | 216 51.2 | 73 23.3 | 32.3 | 153 48.0 | 44.7 | 209 37.3 | 25.3 | 253 09.3 | 47.1 | Suhail | 222 48.2 | S43 31.2 |
| 17 | 231 53.7 | 88 22.7 | 31.4 | 168 49.1 | 45.0 | 224 39.9 | 25.2 | 268 12.0 | 47.2 | | | |
| 18 | 246 56.2 | 103 22.1 | N15 30.5 | 183 50.1 | N19 45.3 | 239 42.6 | N 1 25.1 | 283 14.6 | S15 47.2 | Vega | 80 34.3 | N38 48.5 |
| 19 | 261 58.6 | 118 21.5 | 29.5 | 198 51.1 | 45.6 | 254 45.3 | 25.0 | 298 17.2 | 47.3 | Zuben'ubi | 136 58.3 | S16 08.1 |
| 20 | 277 01.1 | 133 20.9 | 28.6 | 213 52.2 | 45.9 | 269 48.0 | 24.9 | 313 19.9 | 47.3 | | | |
| 21 | 292 03.6 | 148 20.4 . . | 27.7 | 228 53.2 . . | 46.2 | 284 50.6 . . | 24.8 | 328 22.5 . . | 47.4 | | SHA | Mer. Pass. |
| 22 | 307 06.0 | 163 19.8 | 26.8 | 243 54.2 | 46.4 | 299 53.3 | 24.7 | 343 25.2 | 47.5 | Venus | ° ′ 218 34.5 | h m 11 05 |
| 23 | 322 08.5 | 178 19.2 | 25.9 | 258 55.3 | 46.7 | 314 56.0 | 24.6 | 358 27.8 | 47.5 | Mars | 297 54.5 | 5 47 |
| Mer. Pass. | h m 1 38.9 | v −0.6 | d 0.9 | v 1.0 | d 0.3 | v 2.7 | d 0.1 | v 2.6 | d 0.1 | Jupiter | 352 37.7 | 2 08 |
| | | | | | | | | | | Saturn | 36 11.1 | 23 10 |

| UT | SUN GHA | SUN Dec | MOON GHA | v | MOON Dec | d | HP |
|---|---|---|---|---|---|---|---|
| d h | ° ′ | ° ′ | ° ′ | ′ | ° ′ | ′ | ′ |
| **26** 00 | 179 30.5 | N10 29.4 | 192 37.6 | 12.8 | N20 20.9 | 9.6 | 54.6 |
| 01 | 194 30.7 | 28.5 | 207 09.4 | 12.8 | 20 11.3 | 9.7 | 54.7 |
| 02 | 209 30.8 | 27.6 | 221 41.2 | 12.9 | 20 01.6 | 9.8 | 54.7 |
| 03 | 224 31.0 | .. 26.8 | 236 13.1 | 12.9 | 19 51.8 | 9.8 | 54.7 |
| 04 | 239 31.2 | 25.9 | 250 45.0 | 13.0 | 19 42.0 | 10.0 | 54.7 |
| 05 | 254 31.4 | 25.0 | 265 17.0 | 13.0 | 19 32.0 | 10.0 | 54.7 |
| 06 | 269 31.5 | N10 24.2 | 279 49.0 | 13.0 | N19 22.0 | 10.2 | 54.7 |
| 07 | 284 31.7 | 23.3 | 294 21.0 | 13.1 | 19 11.8 | 10.2 | 54.7 |
| 08 | 299 31.9 | 22.4 | 308 53.1 | 13.2 | 19 01.6 | 10.3 | 54.8 |
| F 09 | 314 32.1 | .. 21.5 | 323 25.3 | 13.2 | 18 51.3 | 10.4 | 54.8 |
| R 10 | 329 32.2 | 20.7 | 337 57.5 | 13.2 | 18 40.9 | 10.5 | 54.8 |
| I 11 | 344 32.4 | 19.8 | 352 29.7 | 13.3 | 18 30.4 | 10.6 | 54.8 |
| D 12 | 359 32.6 | N10 18.9 | 7 02.0 | 13.3 | N18 19.8 | 10.7 | 54.8 |
| A 13 | 14 32.8 | 18.1 | 21 34.3 | 13.4 | 18 09.1 | 10.7 | 54.8 |
| Y 14 | 29 33.0 | 17.2 | 36 06.7 | 13.4 | 17 58.4 | 10.9 | 54.9 |
| 15 | 44 33.1 | .. 16.3 | 50 39.1 | 13.5 | 17 47.5 | 10.9 | 54.9 |
| 16 | 59 33.3 | 15.4 | 65 11.6 | 13.5 | 17 36.6 | 11.0 | 54.9 |
| 17 | 74 33.5 | 14.6 | 79 44.1 | 13.5 | 17 25.6 | 11.1 | 54.9 |
| 18 | 89 33.7 | N10 13.7 | 94 16.6 | 13.6 | N17 14.5 | 11.1 | 54.9 |
| 19 | 104 33.8 | 12.8 | 108 49.2 | 13.6 | 17 03.4 | 11.3 | 54.9 |
| 20 | 119 34.0 | 12.0 | 123 21.8 | 13.7 | 16 52.1 | 11.3 | 54.9 |
| 21 | 134 34.2 | .. 11.1 | 137 54.5 | 13.7 | 16 40.8 | 11.4 | 55.0 |
| 22 | 149 34.4 | 10.2 | 152 27.2 | 13.7 | 16 29.4 | 11.5 | 55.0 |
| 23 | 164 34.6 | 09.3 | 166 59.9 | 13.8 | 16 17.9 | 11.5 | 55.0 |
| **27** 00 | 179 34.7 | N10 08.5 | 181 32.7 | 13.8 | N16 06.4 | 11.7 | 55.0 |
| 01 | 194 34.9 | 07.6 | 196 05.5 | 13.9 | 15 54.7 | 11.7 | 55.0 |
| 02 | 209 35.1 | 06.7 | 210 38.4 | 13.9 | 15 43.0 | 11.7 | 55.0 |
| 03 | 224 35.3 | .. 05.8 | 225 11.3 | 14.0 | 15 31.3 | 11.9 | 55.1 |
| 04 | 239 35.4 | 05.0 | 239 44.3 | 14.0 | 15 19.4 | 11.9 | 55.1 |
| 05 | 254 35.6 | 04.1 | 254 17.3 | 14.0 | 15 07.5 | 12.0 | 55.1 |
| 06 | 269 35.8 | N10 03.2 | 268 50.3 | 14.0 | N14 55.5 | 12.1 | 55.1 |
| 07 | 284 36.0 | 02.3 | 283 23.3 | 14.1 | 14 43.4 | 12.1 | 55.1 |
| S 08 | 299 36.2 | 01.4 | 297 56.4 | 14.2 | 14 31.3 | 12.2 | 55.1 |
| A 09 | 314 36.3 | 10 00.6 | 312 29.6 | 14.1 | 14 19.1 | 12.3 | 55.2 |
| T 10 | 329 36.5 | 9 59.7 | 327 02.7 | 14.2 | 14 06.8 | 12.3 | 55.2 |
| U 11 | 344 36.7 | 58.8 | 341 35.9 | 14.3 | 13 54.5 | 12.4 | 55.2 |
| R 12 | 359 36.9 | N 9 57.9 | 356 09.2 | 14.2 | N13 42.1 | 12.5 | 55.2 |
| D 13 | 14 37.1 | 57.1 | 10 42.4 | 14.3 | 13 29.6 | 12.5 | 55.2 |
| A 14 | 29 37.2 | 56.2 | 25 15.7 | 14.4 | 13 17.1 | 12.6 | 55.3 |
| Y 15 | 44 37.4 | .. 55.3 | 39 49.1 | 14.3 | 13 04.5 | 12.7 | 55.3 |
| 16 | 59 37.6 | 54.4 | 54 22.4 | 14.4 | 12 51.8 | 12.7 | 55.3 |
| 17 | 74 37.8 | 53.5 | 68 55.8 | 14.4 | 12 39.1 | 12.8 | 55.3 |
| 18 | 89 38.0 | N 9 52.7 | 83 29.2 | 14.5 | N12 26.3 | 12.8 | 55.3 |
| 19 | 104 38.2 | 51.8 | 98 02.7 | 14.5 | 12 13.5 | 12.9 | 55.3 |
| 20 | 119 38.3 | 50.9 | 112 36.2 | 14.5 | 12 00.6 | 13.0 | 55.4 |
| 21 | 134 38.5 | .. 50.0 | 127 09.7 | 14.5 | 11 47.6 | 13.0 | 55.4 |
| 22 | 149 38.7 | 49.1 | 141 43.2 | 14.6 | 11 34.6 | 13.1 | 55.4 |
| 23 | 164 38.9 | 48.3 | 156 16.8 | 14.6 | 11 21.5 | 13.1 | 55.4 |
| **28** 00 | 179 39.1 | N 9 47.4 | 170 50.4 | 14.6 | N11 08.4 | 13.2 | 55.4 |
| 01 | 194 39.3 | 46.5 | 185 24.0 | 14.6 | 10 55.2 | 13.3 | 55.5 |
| 02 | 209 39.4 | 45.6 | 199 57.6 | 14.7 | 10 41.9 | 13.2 | 55.5 |
| 03 | 224 39.6 | .. 44.7 | 214 31.3 | 14.7 | 10 28.7 | 13.4 | 55.5 |
| 04 | 239 39.8 | 43.9 | 229 05.0 | 14.7 | 10 15.3 | 13.4 | 55.5 |
| 05 | 254 40.0 | 43.0 | 243 38.7 | 14.7 | 10 01.9 | 13.4 | 55.5 |
| 06 | 269 40.2 | N 9 42.1 | 258 12.4 | 14.8 | N 9 48.5 | 13.5 | 55.5 |
| 07 | 284 40.4 | 41.2 | 272 46.2 | 14.7 | 9 35.0 | 13.6 | 55.6 |
| 08 | 299 40.5 | 40.3 | 287 19.9 | 14.8 | 9 21.4 | 13.6 | 55.6 |
| S 09 | 314 40.7 | .. 39.4 | 301 53.7 | 14.8 | 9 07.8 | 13.6 | 55.6 |
| U 10 | 329 40.9 | 38.6 | 316 27.5 | 14.9 | 8 54.2 | 13.7 | 55.6 |
| N 11 | 344 41.1 | 37.7 | 331 01.4 | 14.8 | 8 40.5 | 13.7 | 55.6 |
| D 12 | 359 41.3 | N 9 36.8 | 345 35.2 | 14.9 | N 8 26.8 | 13.8 | 55.7 |
| A 13 | 14 41.5 | 35.9 | 0 09.1 | 14.8 | 8 13.0 | 13.8 | 55.7 |
| Y 14 | 29 41.6 | 35.0 | 14 42.9 | 14.9 | 7 59.2 | 13.9 | 55.7 |
| 15 | 44 41.8 | .. 34.1 | 29 16.8 | 14.9 | 7 45.3 | 13.9 | 55.7 |
| 16 | 59 42.0 | 33.3 | 43 50.7 | 14.9 | 7 31.4 | 13.9 | 55.7 |
| 17 | 74 42.2 | 32.4 | 58 24.6 | 14.9 | 7 17.5 | 14.0 | 55.8 |
| 18 | 89 42.4 | N 9 31.5 | 72 58.5 | 15.0 | N 7 03.5 | 14.0 | 55.8 |
| 19 | 104 42.6 | 30.6 | 87 32.5 | 14.9 | 6 49.5 | 14.1 | 55.8 |
| 20 | 119 42.8 | 29.7 | 102 06.4 | 15.0 | 6 35.4 | 14.0 | 55.8 |
| 21 | 134 42.9 | .. 28.8 | 116 40.4 | 14.9 | 6 21.4 | 14.2 | 55.8 |
| 22 | 149 43.1 | 27.9 | 131 14.3 | 15.0 | 6 07.2 | 14.1 | 55.9 |
| 23 | 164 43.3 | 27.0 | 145 48.3 | 14.9 | N 5 53.1 | 14.2 | 55.9 |
| | SD 15.9 | d 0.9 | SD 14.9 | | 15.0 | | 15.2 |

### Twilight / Sunrise / Moonrise

| Lat. | Naut. | Civil | Sunrise | 26 | 27 | 28 | 29 |
|---|---|---|---|---|---|---|---|
| ° | h m | h m | h m | h m | h m | h m | h m |
| N 72 | //// | 01 49 | 03 35 | ▭ | 02 00 | 04 33 | 06 41 |
| N 70 | //// | 02 29 | 03 53 | ▭ | 02 40 | 04 50 | 06 47 |
| 68 | //// | 02 56 | 04 07 | 00 51 | 03 08 | 05 03 | 06 52 |
| 66 | 01 34 | 03 16 | 04 18 | 01 33 | 03 28 | 05 14 | 06 56 |
| 64 | 02 10 | 03 32 | 04 28 | 02 01 | 03 44 | 05 23 | 06 59 |
| 62 | 02 35 | 03 45 | 04 36 | 02 23 | 03 58 | 05 31 | 07 02 |
| 60 | 02 54 | 03 56 | 04 43 | 02 40 | 04 09 | 05 37 | 07 04 |
| N 58 | 03 09 | 04 06 | 04 49 | 02 54 | 04 19 | 05 43 | 07 06 |
| 56 | 03 22 | 04 14 | 04 54 | 03 07 | 04 27 | 05 48 | 07 08 |
| 54 | 03 33 | 04 21 | 04 59 | 03 18 | 04 35 | 05 52 | 07 10 |
| 52 | 03 42 | 04 27 | 05 03 | 03 27 | 04 42 | 05 57 | 07 12 |
| 50 | 03 51 | 04 33 | 05 07 | 03 36 | 04 48 | 06 00 | 07 13 |
| 45 | 04 08 | 04 45 | 05 16 | 03 53 | 05 01 | 06 08 | 07 16 |
| N 40 | 04 21 | 04 55 | 05 23 | 04 08 | 05 11 | 06 15 | 07 19 |
| 35 | 04 32 | 05 03 | 05 29 | 04 20 | 05 21 | 06 21 | 07 21 |
| 30 | 04 41 | 05 10 | 05 34 | 04 31 | 05 29 | 06 26 | 07 23 |
| 20 | 04 54 | 05 21 | 05 43 | 04 49 | 05 42 | 06 34 | 07 26 |
| N 10 | 05 05 | 05 30 | 05 51 | 05 05 | 05 54 | 06 42 | 07 29 |
| 0 | 05 13 | 05 37 | 05 58 | 05 20 | 06 05 | 06 49 | 07 32 |
| S 10 | 05 19 | 05 44 | 06 05 | 05 35 | 06 16 | 06 56 | 07 35 |
| 20 | 05 25 | 05 51 | 06 13 | 05 50 | 06 28 | 07 04 | 07 38 |
| 30 | 05 29 | 05 57 | 06 21 | 06 08 | 06 41 | 07 12 | 07 41 |
| 35 | 05 31 | 06 00 | 06 26 | 06 19 | 06 49 | 07 17 | 07 43 |
| 40 | 05 32 | 06 04 | 06 31 | 06 31 | 06 58 | 07 22 | 07 45 |
| 45 | 05 34 | 06 08 | 06 38 | 06 44 | 07 00 | 07 29 | 07 48 |
| S 50 | 05 35 | 06 12 | 06 45 | 07 01 | 07 20 | 07 36 | 07 51 |
| 52 | 05 35 | 06 14 | 06 48 | 07 09 | 07 26 | 07 40 | 07 52 |
| 54 | 05 35 | 06 16 | 06 52 | 07 18 | 07 32 | 07 44 | 07 54 |
| 56 | 05 35 | 06 18 | 06 56 | 07 28 | 07 39 | 07 48 | 07 55 |
| 58 | 05 35 | 06 21 | 07 01 | 07 39 | 07 47 | 07 53 | 07 57 |
| S 60 | 05 35 | 06 23 | 07 06 | 07 52 | 07 56 | 07 58 | 07 59 |

### Sunset / Twilight / Moonset

| Lat. | Sunset | Civil | Naut. | 26 | 27 | 28 | 29 |
|---|---|---|---|---|---|---|---|
| ° | h m | h m | h m | h m | h m | h m | h m |
| N 72 | 20 24 | 22 06 | //// | 22 09 | 21 09 | 20 33 | 20 02 |
| N 70 | 20 07 | 21 29 | //// | 21 27 | 20 50 | 20 24 | 20 01 |
| 68 | 19 53 | 21 03 | 23 30 | 20 58 | 20 35 | 20 17 | 20 00 |
| 66 | 19 42 | 20 44 | 22 22 | 20 36 | 20 22 | 20 11 | 20 00 |
| 64 | 19 33 | 20 28 | 21 48 | 20 19 | 20 12 | 20 05 | 19 59 |
| 62 | 19 25 | 20 16 | 21 25 | 20 05 | 20 03 | 20 01 | 19 58 |
| 60 | 19 19 | 20 05 | 21 06 | 19 52 | 19 55 | 19 57 | 19 58 |
| N 58 | 19 13 | 19 56 | 20 51 | 19 42 | 19 48 | 19 53 | 19 58 |
| 56 | 19 07 | 19 48 | 20 39 | 19 32 | 19 42 | 19 50 | 19 57 |
| 54 | 19 03 | 19 41 | 20 28 | 19 24 | 19 37 | 19 47 | 19 57 |
| 52 | 18 59 | 19 34 | 20 19 | 19 17 | 19 32 | 19 45 | 19 57 |
| 50 | 18 55 | 19 29 | 20 11 | 19 10 | 19 27 | 19 42 | 19 56 |
| 45 | 18 46 | 19 17 | 19 54 | 18 56 | 19 18 | 19 37 | 19 56 |
| N 40 | 18 40 | 19 08 | 19 41 | 18 44 | 19 09 | 19 33 | 19 55 |
| 35 | 18 34 | 19 00 | 19 31 | 18 33 | 19 02 | 19 29 | 19 55 |
| 30 | 18 28 | 18 53 | 19 22 | 18 24 | 18 56 | 19 26 | 19 55 |
| 20 | 18 20 | 18 42 | 19 08 | 18 09 | 18 45 | 19 21 | 19 54 |
| N 10 | 18 12 | 18 33 | 18 58 | 17 55 | 18 35 | 19 15 | 19 53 |
| 0 | 18 05 | 18 26 | 18 50 | 17 42 | 18 26 | 19 10 | 19 53 |
| S 10 | 17 58 | 18 19 | 18 44 | 17 29 | 18 17 | 19 05 | 19 52 |
| 20 | 17 51 | 18 14 | 18 39 | 17 15 | 18 07 | 18 59 | 19 51 |
| 30 | 17 42 | 18 07 | 18 34 | 16 59 | 17 56 | 18 53 | 19 50 |
| 35 | 17 38 | 18 03 | 18 33 | 16 49 | 17 50 | 18 50 | 19 50 |
| 40 | 17 32 | 18 00 | 18 31 | 16 39 | 17 42 | 18 46 | 19 49 |
| 45 | 17 26 | 17 56 | 18 30 | 16 26 | 17 33 | 18 41 | 19 49 |
| S 50 | 17 19 | 17 52 | 18 29 | 16 10 | 17 23 | 18 35 | 19 48 |
| 52 | 17 16 | 17 50 | 18 29 | 16 03 | 17 18 | 18 32 | 19 48 |
| 54 | 17 12 | 17 48 | 18 29 | 15 55 | 17 12 | 18 30 | 19 47 |
| 56 | 17 08 | 17 46 | 18 29 | 15 45 | 17 06 | 18 26 | 19 47 |
| 58 | 17 03 | 17 43 | 18 29 | 15 35 | 16 59 | 18 23 | 19 46 |
| S 60 | 16 58 | 17 41 | 18 29 | 15 23 | 16 51 | 18 19 | 19 46 |

### SUN / MOON

| Day | Eqn. of Time 00ʰ | Eqn. of Time 12ʰ | Mer. Pass. | Mer. Pass. Upper | Mer. Pass. Lower | Age | Phase |
|---|---|---|---|---|---|---|---|
| d | m s | m s | h m | h m | h m | d | % |
| 26 | 01 58 | 01 50 | 12 02 | 11 31 | 23 54 | 29 | 1 |
| 27 | 01 41 | 01 33 | 12 02 | 12 16 | 24 38 | 00 | 0 |
| 28 | 01 24 | 01 15 | 12 01 | 12 59 | 00 38 | 01 | 1 |

| UT | ARIES GHA | VENUS −3.9 GHA | VENUS Dec | MARS −0.2 GHA | MARS Dec | JUPITER −2.9 GHA | JUPITER Dec | SATURN +0.3 GHA | SATURN Dec | STARS Name | SHA | Dec |
|---|---|---|---|---|---|---|---|---|---|---|---|---|
| **29 00** | 337 10.9 | 193 18.6 | N15 24.9 | 273 56.3 | N19 47.0 | 329 58.7 | N 1 24.5 | 13 30.4 | S15 47.6 | Acamar | 315 13.1 | S40 12.6 |
| 01 | 352 13.4 | 208 18.0 | 24.0 | 288 57.3 | 47.3 | 345 01.4 | 24.4 | 28 33.1 | 47.6 | Achernar | 335 21.3 | S57 07.1 |
| 02 | 7 15.9 | 223 17.4 | 23.1 | 303 58.4 | 47.6 | 0 04.0 | 24.3 | 43 35.7 | 47.7 | Acrux | 173 02.8 | S63 13.5 |
| 03 | 22 18.3 | 238 16.8 .. | 22.2 | 318 59.4 .. | 47.9 | 15 06.7 .. | 24.2 | 58 38.4 .. | 47.7 | Adhara | 255 07.6 | S28 59.9 |
| 04 | 37 20.8 | 253 16.3 | 21.2 | 334 00.4 | 48.1 | 30 09.4 | 24.1 | 73 41.0 | 47.8 | Aldebaran | 290 41.9 | N16 33.3 |
| 05 | 52 23.3 | 268 15.7 | 20.3 | 349 01.5 | 48.4 | 45 12.1 | 24.0 | 88 43.6 | 47.9 | | | |
| 06 | 67 25.7 | 283 15.1 | N15 19.4 | 4 02.5 | N19 48.7 | 60 14.8 | N 1 23.9 | 103 46.3 | S15 47.9 | Alioth | 166 15.1 | N55 50.5 |
| 07 | 82 28.2 | 298 14.5 | 18.5 | 19 03.5 | 49.0 | 75 17.4 | 23.8 | 118 48.9 | 48.0 | Alkaid | 152 53.9 | N49 12.3 |
| 08 | 97 30.7 | 313 13.9 | 17.5 | 34 04.6 | 49.3 | 90 20.1 | 23.7 | 133 51.5 | 48.0 | Alnair | 27 34.9 | S46 51.1 |
| M 09 | 112 33.1 | 328 13.3 .. | 16.6 | 49 05.6 .. | 49.6 | 105 22.8 .. | 23.6 | 148 54.2 .. | 48.1 | Alnilam | 275 39.8 | S 1 11.1 |
| O 10 | 127 35.6 | 343 12.8 | 15.7 | 64 06.7 | 49.8 | 120 25.5 | 23.5 | 163 56.8 | 48.2 | Alphard | 217 50.0 | S 8 45.2 |
| N 11 | 142 38.1 | 358 12.2 | 14.8 | 79 07.7 | 50.1 | 135 28.2 | 23.4 | 178 59.5 | 48.2 | | | |
| D 12 | 157 40.5 | 13 11.6 | N15 13.8 | 94 08.7 | N19 50.4 | 150 30.9 | N 1 23.3 | 194 02.1 | S15 48.3 | Alphecca | 126 05.5 | N26 38.6 |
| A 13 | 172 43.0 | 28 11.0 | 12.9 | 109 09.8 | 50.7 | 165 33.5 | 23.2 | 209 04.7 | 48.3 | Alpheratz | 357 36.5 | N29 12.9 |
| Y 14 | 187 45.4 | 43 10.4 | 12.0 | 124 10.8 | 51.0 | 180 36.2 | 23.1 | 224 07.4 | 48.4 | Altair | 62 01.6 | N 8 55.8 |
| 15 | 202 47.9 | 58 09.8 .. | 11.0 | 139 11.8 .. | 51.3 | 195 38.9 .. | 23.0 | 239 10.0 .. | 48.5 | Ankaa | 353 08.7 | S42 10.8 |
| 16 | 217 50.4 | 73 09.3 | 10.1 | 154 12.9 | 51.5 | 210 41.6 | 22.9 | 254 12.7 | 48.5 | Antares | 112 18.2 | S26 28.9 |
| 17 | 232 52.8 | 88 08.7 | 09.2 | 169 13.9 | 51.8 | 225 44.3 | 22.8 | 269 15.3 | 48.6 | | | |
| 18 | 247 55.3 | 103 08.1 | N15 08.2 | 184 15.0 | N19 52.1 | 240 47.0 | N 1 22.7 | 284 17.9 | S15 48.6 | Arcturus | 145 49.9 | N19 04.1 |
| 19 | 262 57.8 | 118 07.5 | 07.3 | 199 16.0 | 52.4 | 255 49.6 | 22.6 | 299 20.6 | 48.7 | Atria | 107 14.1 | S69 04.3 |
| 20 | 278 00.2 | 133 06.9 | 06.3 | 214 17.0 | 52.7 | 270 52.3 | 22.5 | 314 23.2 | 48.7 | Avior | 234 16.1 | S59 34.6 |
| 21 | 293 02.7 | 148 06.4 .. | 05.4 | 229 18.1 .. | 52.9 | 285 55.0 .. | 22.4 | 329 25.8 .. | 48.8 | Bellatrix | 278 25.1 | N 6 22.3 |
| 22 | 308 05.2 | 163 05.8 | 04.5 | 244 19.1 | 53.2 | 300 57.7 | 22.3 | 344 28.5 | 48.9 | Betelgeuse | 270 54.3 | N 7 24.8 |
| 23 | 323 07.6 | 178 05.2 | 03.5 | 259 20.2 | 53.5 | 316 00.4 | 22.2 | 359 31.1 | 48.9 | | | |
| **30 00** | 338 10.1 | 193 04.6 | N15 02.6 | 274 21.2 | N19 53.8 | 331 03.1 | N 1 22.1 | 14 33.8 | S15 49.0 | Canopus | 263 53.5 | S52 42.1 |
| 01 | 353 12.5 | 208 04.1 | 01.7 | 289 22.3 | 54.1 | 346 05.7 | 21.9 | 29 36.4 | 49.0 | Capella | 280 24.9 | N46 01.1 |
| 02 | 8 15.0 | 223 03.5 | 15 00.7 | 304 23.3 | 54.3 | 1 08.4 | 21.8 | 44 39.0 | 49.1 | Deneb | 49 26.7 | N45 21.8 |
| 03 | 23 17.5 | 238 02.9 | 14 59.8 | 319 24.3 .. | 54.6 | 16 11.1 .. | 21.7 | 59 41.7 .. | 49.1 | Denebola | 182 27.2 | N14 27.0 |
| 04 | 38 19.9 | 253 02.3 | 58.8 | 334 25.4 | 54.9 | 31 13.8 | 21.6 | 74 44.3 | 49.2 | Diphda | 348 49.0 | S17 51.6 |
| 05 | 53 22.4 | 268 01.8 | 57.9 | 349 26.4 | 55.2 | 46 16.5 | 21.5 | 89 46.9 | 49.3 | | | |
| 06 | 68 24.9 | 283 01.2 | N14 56.9 | 4 27.5 | N19 55.4 | 61 19.2 | N 1 21.4 | 104 49.6 | S15 49.3 | Dubhe | 193 44.1 | N61 37.9 |
| 07 | 83 27.3 | 298 00.6 | 56.0 | 19 28.5 | 55.7 | 76 21.9 | 21.3 | 119 52.2 | 49.4 | Elnath | 278 04.4 | N28 37.5 |
| T 08 | 98 29.8 | 313 00.0 | 55.0 | 34 29.6 | 56.0 | 91 24.6 | 21.2 | 134 54.8 | 49.4 | Eltanin | 90 42.9 | N51 29.4 |
| U 09 | 113 32.3 | 327 59.5 .. | 54.1 | 49 30.6 .. | 56.3 | 106 27.2 .. | 21.1 | 149 57.5 .. | 49.5 | Enif | 33 40.4 | N 9 58.8 |
| E 10 | 128 34.7 | 342 58.9 | 53.2 | 64 31.7 | 56.5 | 121 29.9 | 21.0 | 165 00.1 | 49.6 | Fomalhaut | 15 16.3 | S29 30.1 |
| S 11 | 143 37.2 | 357 58.3 | 52.2 | 79 32.7 | 56.8 | 136 32.6 | 20.9 | 180 02.8 | 49.6 | | | |
| D 12 | 158 39.7 | 12 57.7 | N14 51.3 | 94 33.8 | N19 57.1 | 151 35.3 | N 1 20.8 | 195 05.4 | S15 49.7 | Gacrux | 171 54.3 | S57 14.4 |
| A 13 | 173 42.1 | 27 57.2 | 50.3 | 109 34.8 | 57.4 | 166 38.0 | 20.7 | 210 08.0 | 49.7 | Gienah | 175 45.9 | S17 39.9 |
| Y 14 | 188 44.6 | 42 56.6 | 49.4 | 124 35.9 | 57.7 | 181 40.7 | 20.6 | 225 10.7 | 49.8 | Hadar | 148 39.1 | S60 29.0 |
| 15 | 203 47.0 | 57 56.0 .. | 48.4 | 139 36.9 .. | 57.9 | 196 43.4 .. | 20.5 | 240 13.3 .. | 49.8 | Hamal | 327 53.2 | N23 34.1 |
| 16 | 218 49.5 | 72 55.5 | 47.5 | 154 38.0 | 58.2 | 211 46.1 | 20.4 | 255 15.9 | 49.9 | Kaus Aust. | 83 34.9 | S34 22.5 |
| 17 | 233 52.0 | 87 54.9 | 46.5 | 169 39.0 | 58.5 | 226 48.7 | 20.3 | 270 18.6 | 50.0 | | | |
| 18 | 248 54.4 | 102 54.3 | N14 45.6 | 184 40.1 | N19 58.8 | 241 51.4 | N 1 20.2 | 285 21.2 | S15 50.0 | Kochab | 137 20.2 | N74 04.1 |
| 19 | 263 56.9 | 117 53.8 | 44.6 | 199 41.1 | 59.0 | 256 54.1 | 20.1 | 300 23.8 | 50.1 | Markab | 13 31.5 | N15 19.7 |
| 20 | 278 59.4 | 132 53.2 | 43.6 | 214 42.2 | 59.3 | 271 56.8 | 19.9 | 315 26.5 | 50.1 | Menkar | 314 08.1 | N 4 10.8 |
| 21 | 294 01.8 | 147 52.6 .. | 42.7 | 229 43.2 .. | 59.6 | 286 59.5 .. | 19.8 | 330 29.1 .. | 50.2 | Menkent | 148 00.1 | S36 28.9 |
| 22 | 309 04.3 | 162 52.1 | 41.7 | 244 44.3 | 19 59.8 | 302 02.2 | 19.7 | 345 31.8 | 50.2 | Miaplacidus | 221 39.5 | S69 48.4 |
| 23 | 324 06.8 | 177 51.5 | 40.8 | 259 45.3 | 20 00.1 | 317 04.9 | 19.6 | 0 34.4 | 50.3 | | | |
| **31 00** | 339 09.2 | 192 50.9 | N14 39.8 | 274 46.4 | N20 00.4 | 332 07.6 | N 1 19.5 | 15 37.0 | S15 50.4 | Mirfak | 308 30.9 | N49 56.3 |
| 01 | 354 11.7 | 207 50.4 | 38.9 | 289 47.4 | 00.7 | 347 10.3 | 19.4 | 30 39.7 | 50.4 | Nunki | 75 50.0 | S26 16.1 |
| 02 | 9 14.2 | 222 49.8 | 37.9 | 304 48.5 | 00.9 | 2 13.0 | 19.3 | 45 42.3 | 50.5 | Peacock | 53 08.3 | S56 39.8 |
| 03 | 24 16.6 | 237 49.2 .. | 36.9 | 319 49.5 .. | 01.2 | 17 15.6 .. | 19.2 | 60 44.9 .. | 50.5 | Pollux | 243 20.0 | N27 58.3 |
| 04 | 39 19.1 | 252 48.7 | 36.0 | 334 50.6 | 01.5 | 32 18.3 | 19.1 | 75 47.6 | 50.6 | Procyon | 244 53.1 | N 5 10.2 |
| 05 | 54 21.5 | 267 48.1 | 35.0 | 349 51.6 | 01.8 | 47 21.0 | 19.0 | 90 50.2 | 50.6 | | | |
| 06 | 69 24.0 | 282 47.5 | N14 34.1 | 4 52.7 | N20 02.0 | 62 23.7 | N 1 18.9 | 105 52.8 | S15 50.7 | Rasalhague | 96 00.3 | N12 32.8 |
| W 07 | 84 26.5 | 297 47.0 | 33.1 | 19 53.8 | 02.3 | 77 26.4 | 18.8 | 120 55.5 | 50.8 | Regulus | 207 36.8 | N11 51.6 |
| E 08 | 99 28.9 | 312 46.4 | 32.1 | 34 54.8 | 02.6 | 92 29.1 | 18.7 | 135 58.1 | 50.8 | Rigel | 281 05.8 | S 8 10.4 |
| D 09 | 114 31.4 | 327 45.8 .. | 31.2 | 49 55.9 .. | 02.8 | 107 31.8 .. | 18.6 | 151 00.7 .. | 50.9 | Rigil Kent. | 139 43.3 | S60 55.8 |
| N 10 | 129 33.9 | 342 45.3 | 30.2 | 64 56.9 | 03.1 | 122 34.5 | 18.5 | 166 03.4 | 50.9 | Sabik | 102 04.9 | S15 45.1 |
| E 11 | 144 36.3 | 357 44.7 | 29.2 | 79 58.0 | 03.4 | 137 37.2 | 18.3 | 181 06.0 | 51.0 | | | |
| S 12 | 159 38.8 | 12 44.1 | N14 28.3 | 94 59.0 | N20 03.6 | 152 39.9 | N 1 18.2 | 196 08.7 | S15 51.0 | Schedar | 349 32.8 | N56 39.5 |
| D 13 | 174 41.3 | 27 43.6 | 27.3 | 110 00.1 | 03.9 | 167 42.6 | 18.1 | 211 11.3 | 51.1 | Shaula | 96 12.9 | S37 07.3 |
| A 14 | 189 43.7 | 42 43.0 | 26.3 | 125 01.2 | 04.2 | 182 45.3 | 18.0 | 226 13.9 | 51.2 | Sirius | 258 28.1 | S16 44.6 |
| Y 15 | 204 46.2 | 57 42.5 .. | 25.4 | 140 02.2 .. | 04.5 | 197 48.0 .. | 17.9 | 241 16.6 .. | 51.2 | Spica | 158 24.6 | S11 16.6 |
| 16 | 219 48.6 | 72 41.9 | 24.4 | 155 03.3 | 04.7 | 212 50.7 | 17.8 | 256 19.2 | 51.3 | Suhail | 222 48.2 | S43 31.2 |
| 17 | 234 51.1 | 87 41.3 | 23.4 | 170 04.3 | 05.0 | 227 53.4 | 17.7 | 271 21.8 | 51.3 | | | |
| 18 | 249 53.6 | 102 40.8 | N14 22.5 | 185 05.4 | N20 05.3 | 242 56.0 | N 1 17.6 | 286 24.5 | S15 51.4 | Vega | 80 34.3 | N38 48.5 |
| 19 | 264 56.0 | 117 40.2 | 21.5 | 200 06.5 | 05.5 | 257 58.7 | 17.5 | 301 27.1 | 51.4 | Zuben'ubi | 136 58.3 | S16 08.1 |
| 20 | 278 58.5 | 132 39.7 | 20.5 | 215 07.5 | 05.8 | 273 01.4 | 17.4 | 316 29.7 | 51.5 | | SHA | Mer. Pass. |
| 21 | 295 01.0 | 147 39.1 .. | 19.6 | 230 08.6 .. | 06.1 | 288 04.1 .. | 17.3 | 331 32.4 .. | 51.6 | Venus | 214 54.6 | 11 08 |
| 22 | 310 03.4 | 162 38.5 | 18.6 | 245 09.7 | 06.3 | 303 06.8 | 17.2 | 346 35.0 | 51.6 | Mars | 296 11.1 | 5 42 |
| 23 | 325 05.9 | 177 38.0 | 17.6 | 260 10.7 | 06.6 | 318 09.5 | 17.1 | 1 37.6 | 51.7 | Jupiter | 352 53.0 | 1 55 |
| Mer. Pass. h m 1 27.1 | | v −0.6 | d 0.9 | v 1.0 | d 0.3 | v 2.7 | d 0.1 | v 2.6 | d 0.1 | Saturn | 36 23.7 | 22 58 |

| UT | SUN GHA | SUN Dec | MOON GHA | v | MOON Dec | d | HP |
|---|---|---|---|---|---|---|---|
| d h | ° ′ | ° ′ | ° ′ | ′ | ° ′ | ′ | ′ |
| 29 00 | 179 43.5 | N 9 26.2 | 160 22.2 | 15.0 | N 5 38.9 | 14.3 | 55.9 |
| 01 | 194 43.7 | 25.3 | 174 56.2 | 15.0 | 5 24.6 | 14.2 | 55.9 |
| 02 | 209 43.9 | 24.4 | 189 30.2 | 15.0 | 5 10.4 | 14.3 | 55.9 |
| 03 | 224 44.1 | .. 23.5 | 204 04.2 | 15.0 | 4 56.1 | 14.3 | 56.0 |
| 04 | 239 44.2 | 22.6 | 218 38.2 | 14.9 | 4 41.8 | 14.4 | 56.0 |
| 05 | 254 44.4 | 21.7 | 233 12.1 | 15.0 | 4 27.4 | 14.4 | 56.0 |
| 06 | 269 44.6 | N 9 20.8 | 247 46.1 | 15.0 | N 4 13.0 | 14.4 | 56.0 |
| 07 | 284 44.8 | 19.9 | 262 20.1 | 15.0 | 3 58.6 | 14.4 | 56.0 |
| 08 | 299 45.0 | 19.1 | 276 54.1 | 15.0 | 3 44.2 | 14.5 | 56.1 |
| M 09 | 314 45.2 | .. 18.2 | 291 28.1 | 14.9 | 3 29.7 | 14.4 | 56.1 |
| O 10 | 329 45.4 | 17.3 | 306 02.0 | 15.0 | 3 15.3 | 14.5 | 56.1 |
| N 11 | 344 45.6 | 16.4 | 320 36.0 | 14.9 | 3 00.8 | 14.6 | 56.1 |
| D 12 | 359 45.7 | N 9 15.5 | 335 09.9 | 15.0 | N 2 46.2 | 14.5 | 56.1 |
| A 13 | 14 45.9 | 14.6 | 349 43.9 | 14.9 | 2 31.7 | 14.6 | 56.2 |
| Y 14 | 29 46.1 | 13.7 | 4 17.8 | 15.0 | 2 17.1 | 14.6 | 56.2 |
| 15 | 44 46.3 | .. 12.8 | 18 51.8 | 14.9 | 2 02.5 | 14.6 | 56.2 |
| 16 | 59 46.5 | 11.9 | 33 25.7 | 14.9 | 1 47.9 | 14.6 | 56.2 |
| 17 | 74 46.7 | 11.0 | 47 59.6 | 14.9 | 1 33.3 | 14.6 | 56.2 |
| 18 | 89 46.9 | N 9 10.1 | 62 33.5 | 14.9 | N 1 18.7 | 14.7 | 56.3 |
| 19 | 104 47.1 | 09.3 | 77 07.4 | 14.9 | 1 04.0 | 14.7 | 56.3 |
| 20 | 119 47.3 | 08.4 | 91 41.3 | 14.8 | 0 49.3 | 14.7 | 56.3 |
| 21 | 134 47.4 | .. 07.5 | 106 15.1 | 14.9 | 0 34.6 | 14.7 | 56.3 |
| 22 | 149 47.6 | 06.6 | 120 49.0 | 14.8 | 0 19.9 | 14.7 | 56.3 |
| 23 | 164 47.8 | 05.7 | 135 22.8 | 14.8 | N 0 05.2 | 14.7 | 56.4 |
| 30 00 | 179 48.0 | N 9 04.8 | 149 56.6 | 14.8 | S 0 09.5 | 14.7 | 56.4 |
| 01 | 194 48.2 | 03.9 | 164 30.4 | 14.8 | 0 24.2 | 14.8 | 56.4 |
| 02 | 209 48.4 | 03.0 | 179 04.2 | 14.7 | 0 39.0 | 14.7 | 56.4 |
| 03 | 224 48.6 | .. 02.1 | 193 37.9 | 14.7 | 0 53.7 | 14.8 | 56.5 |
| 04 | 239 48.8 | 01.2 | 208 11.6 | 14.7 | 1 08.5 | 14.7 | 56.5 |
| 05 | 254 49.0 | 9 00.3 | 222 45.3 | 14.7 | 1 23.2 | 14.8 | 56.5 |
| 06 | 269 49.2 | N 8 59.4 | 237 19.0 | 14.7 | S 1 38.0 | 14.7 | 56.5 |
| 07 | 284 49.4 | 58.5 | 251 52.7 | 14.6 | 1 52.7 | 14.8 | 56.5 |
| T 08 | 299 49.5 | 57.6 | 266 26.3 | 14.6 | 2 07.5 | 14.8 | 56.5 |
| U 09 | 314 49.7 | .. 56.7 | 280 59.9 | 14.5 | 2 22.3 | 14.7 | 56.6 |
| E 10 | 329 49.9 | 55.8 | 295 33.4 | 14.5 | 2 37.0 | 14.8 | 56.6 |
| S 11 | 344 50.1 | 54.9 | 310 06.9 | 14.5 | 2 51.8 | 14.8 | 56.6 |
| D 12 | 359 50.3 | N 8 54.0 | 324 40.4 | 14.5 | S 3 06.6 | 14.7 | 56.6 |
| A 13 | 14 50.5 | 53.1 | 339 13.9 | 14.4 | 3 21.3 | 14.8 | 56.7 |
| Y 14 | 29 50.7 | 52.3 | 353 47.3 | 14.4 | 3 36.1 | 14.7 | 56.7 |
| 15 | 44 50.9 | .. 51.4 | 8 20.7 | 14.4 | 3 50.8 | 14.8 | 56.7 |
| 16 | 59 51.1 | 50.5 | 22 54.1 | 14.3 | 4 05.6 | 14.7 | 56.7 |
| 17 | 74 51.3 | 49.6 | 37 27.4 | 14.3 | 4 20.3 | 14.8 | 56.7 |
| 18 | 89 51.5 | N 8 48.7 | 52 00.7 | 14.3 | S 4 35.1 | 14.7 | 56.8 |
| 19 | 104 51.7 | 47.8 | 66 33.9 | 14.2 | 4 49.8 | 14.7 | 56.8 |
| 20 | 119 51.8 | 46.9 | 81 07.1 | 14.2 | 5 04.5 | 14.7 | 56.8 |
| 21 | 134 52.0 | .. 46.0 | 95 40.3 | 14.1 | 5 19.2 | 14.7 | 56.8 |
| 22 | 149 52.2 | 45.1 | 110 13.4 | 14.1 | 5 33.9 | 14.7 | 56.8 |
| 23 | 164 52.4 | 44.2 | 124 46.5 | 14.0 | 5 48.6 | 14.6 | 56.9 |
| 31 00 | 179 52.6 | N 8 43.3 | 139 19.5 | 14.0 | S 6 03.2 | 14.7 | 56.9 |
| 01 | 194 52.8 | 42.4 | 153 52.5 | 13.9 | 6 17.9 | 14.6 | 56.9 |
| 02 | 209 53.0 | 41.5 | 168 25.4 | 13.9 | 6 32.5 | 14.6 | 56.9 |
| 03 | 224 53.2 | .. 40.6 | 182 58.3 | 13.8 | 6 47.1 | 14.6 | 57.0 |
| 04 | 239 53.4 | 39.7 | 197 31.1 | 13.8 | 7 01.7 | 14.6 | 57.0 |
| 05 | 254 53.6 | 38.8 | 212 03.9 | 13.8 | 7 16.3 | 14.5 | 57.0 |
| 06 | 269 53.8 | N 8 37.9 | 226 36.7 | 13.6 | S 7 30.8 | 14.5 | 57.0 |
| W 07 | 284 54.0 | 37.0 | 241 09.3 | 13.7 | 7 45.3 | 14.5 | 57.0 |
| E 08 | 299 54.2 | 36.1 | 255 42.0 | 13.5 | 7 59.8 | 14.5 | 57.1 |
| D 09 | 314 54.4 | .. 35.2 | 270 14.5 | 13.5 | 8 14.3 | 14.4 | 57.1 |
| N 10 | 329 54.6 | 34.3 | 284 47.0 | 13.5 | 8 28.7 | 14.5 | 57.1 |
| E 11 | 344 54.8 | 33.4 | 299 19.5 | 13.4 | 8 43.2 | 14.3 | 57.1 |
| S 12 | 359 55.0 | N 8 32.5 | 313 51.9 | 13.3 | S 8 57.5 | 14.4 | 57.2 |
| D 13 | 14 55.2 | 31.6 | 328 24.2 | 13.3 | 9 11.9 | 14.3 | 57.2 |
| A 14 | 29 55.3 | 30.6 | 342 56.5 | 13.2 | 9 26.2 | 14.3 | 57.2 |
| Y 15 | 44 55.5 | .. 29.7 | 357 28.7 | 13.1 | 9 40.5 | 14.3 | 57.2 |
| 16 | 59 55.7 | 28.8 | 12 00.8 | 13.1 | 9 54.8 | 14.2 | 57.2 |
| 17 | 74 55.9 | 27.9 | 26 32.9 | 13.0 | 10 09.0 | 14.2 | 57.3 |
| 18 | 89 56.1 | N 8 27.0 | 41 04.9 | 12.9 | S10 23.2 | 14.1 | 57.3 |
| 19 | 104 56.3 | 26.1 | 55 36.8 | 12.9 | 10 37.3 | 14.1 | 57.3 |
| 20 | 119 56.5 | 25.2 | 70 08.7 | 12.8 | 10 51.4 | 14.1 | 57.3 |
| 21 | 134 56.7 | .. 24.3 | 84 40.5 | 12.8 | 11 05.5 | 14.0 | 57.4 |
| 22 | 149 56.9 | 23.4 | 99 12.3 | 12.6 | 11 19.5 | 14.0 | 57.4 |
| 23 | 164 57.1 | 22.5 | 113 43.9 | 12.6 | S11 33.5 | 14.0 | 57.4 |
| | SD 15.9 | d 0.9 | SD 15.3 | | 15.4 | | 15.6 |

| Lat. | Twilight Naut. | Twilight Civil | Sunrise | Moonrise 29 | 30 | 31 | 1 |
|---|---|---|---|---|---|---|---|
| ° | h m | h m | h m | h m | h m | h m | h m |
| N 72 | //// | 02 15 | 03 51 | 06 41 | 08 46 | 10 57 | 13 35 |
| N 70 | //// | 02 48 | 04 06 | 06 47 | 08 42 | 10 43 | 12 59 |
| 68 | 01 08 | 03 11 | 04 18 | 06 52 | 08 39 | 10 31 | 12 34 |
| 66 | 01 56 | 03 28 | 04 28 | 06 56 | 08 37 | 10 22 | 12 15 |
| 64 | 02 26 | 03 43 | 04 37 | 06 59 | 08 35 | 10 14 | 12 00 |
| 62 | 02 47 | 03 54 | 04 44 | 07 02 | 08 33 | 10 08 | 11 47 |
| 60 | 03 04 | 04 04 | 04 50 | 07 04 | 08 32 | 10 02 | 11 36 |
| N 58 | 03 18 | 04 13 | 04 55 | 07 06 | 08 30 | 09 57 | 11 27 |
| 56 | 03 30 | 04 20 | 05 00 | 07 08 | 08 29 | 09 52 | 11 19 |
| 54 | 03 40 | 04 27 | 05 04 | 07 10 | 08 28 | 09 48 | 11 12 |
| 52 | 03 49 | 04 33 | 05 08 | 07 12 | 08 27 | 09 45 | 11 06 |
| 50 | 03 56 | 04 38 | 05 12 | 07 13 | 08 26 | 09 42 | 11 00 |
| 45 | 04 12 | 04 49 | 05 19 | 07 16 | 08 25 | 09 35 | 10 47 |
| N 40 | 04 24 | 04 58 | 05 26 | 07 19 | 08 23 | 09 29 | 10 37 |
| 35 | 04 34 | 05 05 | 05 31 | 07 21 | 08 22 | 09 24 | 10 29 |
| 30 | 04 43 | 05 11 | 05 36 | 07 23 | 08 21 | 09 20 | 10 21 |
| 20 | 04 55 | 05 22 | 05 44 | 07 26 | 08 19 | 09 12 | 10 08 |
| N 10 | 05 05 | 05 30 | 05 51 | 07 29 | 08 17 | 09 06 | 09 57 |
| 0 | 05 12 | 05 36 | 05 57 | 07 32 | 08 15 | 09 00 | 09 46 |
| S 10 | 05 18 | 05 42 | 06 04 | 07 35 | 08 14 | 08 54 | 09 36 |
| 20 | 05 22 | 05 48 | 06 10 | 07 38 | 08 12 | 08 47 | 09 25 |
| 30 | 05 26 | 05 54 | 06 18 | 07 41 | 08 10 | 08 40 | 09 12 |
| 35 | 05 27 | 05 57 | 06 22 | 07 43 | 08 09 | 08 36 | 09 05 |
| 40 | 05 28 | 05 59 | 06 27 | 07 45 | 08 08 | 08 31 | 08 57 |
| 45 | 05 29 | 06 03 | 06 32 | 07 48 | 08 06 | 08 26 | 00 48 |
| S 50 | 05 29 | 06 06 | 06 39 | 07 51 | 08 05 | 08 20 | 08 36 |
| 52 | 05 29 | 06 08 | 06 42 | 07 52 | 08 04 | 08 17 | 08 31 |
| 54 | 05 29 | 06 09 | 06 45 | 07 54 | 08 03 | 08 14 | 08 26 |
| 56 | 05 28 | 06 11 | 06 49 | 07 55 | 08 02 | 08 10 | 08 19 |
| 58 | 05 28 | 06 13 | 06 53 | 07 57 | 08 02 | 08 06 | 08 12 |
| S 60 | 05 27 | 06 15 | 06 57 | 07 59 | 08 00 | 08 02 | 08 04 |

| Lat. | Sunset | Twilight Civil | Twilight Naut. | Moonset 29 | 30 | 31 | 1 |
|---|---|---|---|---|---|---|---|
| ° | h m | h m | h m | h m | h m | h m | h m |
| N 72 | 20 07 | 21 39 | //// | 20 02 | 19 31 | 18 55 | 17 56 |
| N 70 | 19 52 | 21 09 | //// | 20 01 | 19 38 | 19 11 | 18 34 |
| 68 | 19 40 | 20 47 | 22 42 | 20 00 | 19 44 | 19 25 | 19 00 |
| 66 | 19 31 | 20 30 | 21 59 | 20 00 | 19 48 | 19 36 | 19 21 |
| 64 | 19 23 | 20 16 | 21 31 | 19 59 | 19 52 | 19 46 | 19 38 |
| 62 | 19 16 | 20 05 | 21 11 | 19 58 | 19 56 | 19 54 | 19 52 |
| 60 | 19 10 | 19 55 | 20 54 | 19 58 | 19 59 | 20 01 | 20 03 |
| N 58 | 19 04 | 19 47 | 20 41 | 19 58 | 20 02 | 20 07 | 20 14 |
| 56 | 19 00 | 19 39 | 20 29 | 19 57 | 20 04 | 20 12 | 20 23 |
| 54 | 18 56 | 19 33 | 20 20 | 19 57 | 20 07 | 20 17 | 20 31 |
| 52 | 18 52 | 19 27 | 20 11 | 19 57 | 20 09 | 20 22 | 20 38 |
| 50 | 18 48 | 19 22 | 20 04 | 19 56 | 20 11 | 20 26 | 20 44 |
| 45 | 18 41 | 19 11 | 19 48 | 19 56 | 20 15 | 20 35 | 20 58 |
| N 40 | 18 35 | 19 03 | 19 36 | 19 55 | 20 18 | 20 42 | 21 10 |
| 35 | 18 30 | 18 56 | 19 26 | 19 55 | 20 21 | 20 49 | 21 20 |
| 30 | 18 25 | 18 49 | 19 18 | 19 55 | 20 24 | 20 55 | 21 29 |
| 20 | 18 17 | 18 39 | 19 06 | 19 54 | 20 28 | 21 04 | 21 44 |
| N 10 | 18 10 | 18 32 | 18 56 | 19 53 | 20 32 | 21 13 | 21 57 |
| 0 | 18 04 | 18 25 | 18 49 | 19 53 | 20 36 | 21 21 | 22 10 |
| S 10 | 17 58 | 18 19 | 18 44 | 19 52 | 20 40 | 21 30 | 22 22 |
| 20 | 17 51 | 18 13 | 18 39 | 19 51 | 20 44 | 21 39 | 22 36 |
| 30 | 17 44 | 18 08 | 18 36 | 19 50 | 20 49 | 21 49 | 22 51 |
| 35 | 17 40 | 18 05 | 18 35 | 19 50 | 20 51 | 21 55 | 23 00 |
| 40 | 17 35 | 18 02 | 18 34 | 19 49 | 20 54 | 22 01 | 23 11 |
| 45 | 17 30 | 17 59 | 18 33 | 19 49 | 20 58 | 22 09 | 23 23 |
| S 50 | 17 23 | 17 56 | 18 33 | 19 48 | 21 02 | 22 19 | 23 38 |
| 52 | 17 20 | 17 54 | 18 34 | 19 48 | 21 04 | 22 23 | 23 45 |
| 54 | 17 17 | 17 53 | 18 34 | 19 47 | 21 06 | 22 28 | 23 53 |
| 56 | 17 14 | 17 51 | 18 34 | 19 47 | 21 09 | 22 33 | 24 01 |
| 58 | 17 10 | 17 49 | 18 35 | 19 46 | 21 11 | 22 39 | 24 11 |
| S 60 | 17 05 | 17 48 | 18 36 | 19 46 | 21 14 | 22 46 | 24 23 |

| | SUN | | | MOON | | | |
|---|---|---|---|---|---|---|---|
| Day | Eqn. of Time 00ʰ | 12ʰ | Mer. Pass. | Mer. Pass. Upper | Lower | Age | Phase |
| d | m s | m s | h m | h m | h m | d | % |
| 29 | 01 06 | 00 57 | 12 01 | 13 42 | 01 21 | 02 | 5 |
| 30 | 00 48 | 00 39 | 12 01 | 14 26 | 02 04 | 03 | 10 |
| 31 | 00 30 | 00 21 | 12 00 | 15 10 | 02 48 | 04 | 17 |

| UT | ARIES GHA | VENUS −3.9 GHA | Dec | MARS −0.2 GHA | Dec | JUPITER −2.9 GHA | Dec | SATURN +0.3 GHA | Dec |
|---|---|---|---|---|---|---|---|---|---|
| **1** 00 | 340 08.4 | 192 37.4 | N14 16.6 | 275 11.8 | N20 06.9 | 333 12.2 | N 1 16.9 | 16 40.3 | S15 51.7 |
| 01 | 355 10.8 | 207 36.9 | 15.7 | 290 12.8 | 07.1 | 348 14.9 | 16.8 | 31 42.9 | 51.8 |
| 02 | 10 13.3 | 222 36.3 | 14.7 | 305 13.9 | 07.4 | 3 17.6 | 16.7 | 46 45.5 | 51.8 |
| 03 | 25 15.8 | 237 35.8 .. | 13.7 | 320 15.0 .. | 07.7 | 18 20.3 .. | 16.6 | 61 48.2 .. | 51.9 |
| 04 | 40 18.2 | 252 35.2 | 12.7 | 335 16.0 | 07.9 | 33 23.0 | 16.5 | 76 50.8 | 52.0 |
| 05 | 55 20.7 | 267 34.7 | 11.8 | 350 17.1 | 08.2 | 48 25.7 | 16.4 | 91 53.4 | 52.0 |
| T 06 | 70 23.1 | 282 34.1 | N14 10.8 | 5 18.2 | N20 08.5 | 63 28.4 | N 1 16.3 | 106 56.1 | S15 52.1 |
| H 07 | 85 25.6 | 297 33.5 | 09.8 | 20 19.2 | 08.7 | 78 31.1 | 16.2 | 121 58.7 | 52.1 |
| U 08 | 100 28.1 | 312 33.0 | 08.8 | 35 20.3 | 09.0 | 93 33.8 | 16.1 | 137 01.3 | 52.2 |
| R 09 | 115 30.5 | 327 32.4 .. | 07.8 | 50 21.4 .. | 09.3 | 108 36.5 .. | 16.0 | 152 04.0 .. | 52.2 |
| S 10 | 130 33.0 | 342 31.9 | 06.9 | 65 22.4 | 09.5 | 123 39.2 | 15.9 | 167 06.6 | 52.3 |
| D 11 | 145 35.5 | 357 31.3 | 05.9 | 80 23.5 | 09.8 | 138 41.9 | 15.7 | 182 09.2 | 52.3 |
| A 12 | 160 37.9 | 12 30.8 | N14 04.9 | 95 24.6 | N20 10.0 | 153 44.6 | N 1 15.6 | 197 11.9 | S15 52.4 |
| Y 13 | 175 40.4 | 27 30.2 | 03.9 | 110 25.6 | 10.3 | 168 47.3 | 15.5 | 212 14.5 | 52.5 |
| 14 | 190 42.9 | 42 29.7 | 02.9 | 125 26.7 | 10.6 | 183 50.0 | 15.4 | 227 17.1 | 52.5 |
| 15 | 205 45.3 | 57 29.1 .. | 01.9 | 140 27.8 .. | 10.8 | 198 52.7 .. | 15.3 | 242 19.8 .. | 52.6 |
| 16 | 220 47.8 | 72 28.6 | 01.0 | 155 28.9 | 11.1 | 213 55.4 | 15.2 | 257 22.4 | 52.6 |
| 17 | 235 50.2 | 87 28.0 | 14 00.0 | 170 29.9 | 11.4 | 228 58.1 | 15.1 | 272 25.0 | 52.7 |
| 18 | 250 52.7 | 102 27.5 | N13 59.0 | 185 31.0 | N20 11.6 | 244 00.8 | N 1 15.0 | 287 27.7 | S15 52.7 |
| 19 | 265 55.2 | 117 26.9 | 58.0 | 200 32.1 | 11.9 | 259 03.5 | 14.9 | 302 30.3 | 52.8 |
| 20 | 280 57.6 | 132 26.4 | 57.0 | 215 33.1 | 12.2 | 274 06.2 | 14.8 | 317 32.9 | 52.9 |
| 21 | 296 00.1 | 147 25.8 .. | 56.0 | 230 34.2 .. | 12.4 | 289 08.9 .. | 14.6 | 332 35.6 .. | 52.9 |
| 22 | 311 02.6 | 162 25.3 | 55.0 | 245 35.3 | 12.7 | 304 11.6 | 14.5 | 347 38.2 | 53.0 |
| 23 | 326 05.0 | 177 24.7 | 54.0 | 260 36.4 | 12.9 | 319 14.3 | 14.4 | 2 40.8 | 53.0 |
| **2** 00 | 341 07.5 | 192 24.2 | N13 53.1 | 275 37.4 | N20 13.2 | 334 17.0 | N 1 14.3 | 17 43.5 | S15 53.1 |
| 01 | 356 10.0 | 207 23.6 | 52.1 | 290 38.5 | 13.5 | 349 19.7 | 14.2 | 32 46.1 | 53.1 |
| 02 | 11 12.4 | 222 23.1 | 51.1 | 305 39.6 | 13.7 | 4 22.4 | 14.1 | 47 48.7 | 53.2 |
| 03 | 26 14.9 | 237 22.5 .. | 50.1 | 320 40.7 .. | 14.0 | 19 25.1 .. | 14.0 | 62 51.4 .. | 53.2 |
| 04 | 41 17.4 | 252 22.0 | 49.1 | 335 41.7 | 14.2 | 34 27.8 | 13.9 | 77 54.0 | 53.3 |
| 05 | 56 19.8 | 267 21.4 | 48.1 | 350 42.8 | 14.5 | 49 30.5 | 13.8 | 92 56.6 | 53.4 |
| F 06 | 71 22.3 | 282 20.9 | N13 47.1 | 5 43.9 | N20 14.8 | 64 33.2 | N 1 13.7 | 107 59.3 | S15 53.4 |
| R 07 | 86 24.7 | 297 20.4 | 46.1 | 20 45.0 | 15.0 | 79 35.9 | 13.5 | 123 01.9 | 53.5 |
| I 08 | 101 27.2 | 312 19.8 | 45.1 | 35 46.0 | 15.3 | 94 38.6 | 13.4 | 138 04.5 | 53.5 |
| D 09 | 116 29.7 | 327 19.3 .. | 44.1 | 50 47.1 .. | 15.5 | 109 41.3 .. | 13.3 | 153 07.2 .. | 53.6 |
| A 10 | 131 32.1 | 342 18.7 | 43.1 | 65 48.2 | 15.8 | 124 44.0 | 13.2 | 168 09.8 | 53.6 |
| Y 11 | 146 34.6 | 357 18.2 | 42.1 | 80 49.3 | 16.1 | 139 46.7 | 13.1 | 183 12.4 | 53.7 |
| 12 | 161 37.1 | 12 17.6 | N13 41.1 | 95 50.4 | N20 16.3 | 154 49.4 | N 1 13.0 | 198 15.1 | S15 53.7 |
| 13 | 176 39.5 | 27 17.1 | 40.1 | 110 51.4 | 16.6 | 169 52.1 | 12.9 | 213 17.7 | 53.8 |
| 14 | 191 42.0 | 42 16.6 | 39.1 | 125 52.5 | 16.8 | 184 54.8 | 12.8 | 228 20.3 | 53.9 |
| 15 | 206 44.5 | 57 16.0 .. | 38.1 | 140 53.6 .. | 17.1 | 199 57.5 .. | 12.6 | 243 23.0 .. | 53.9 |
| 16 | 221 46.9 | 72 15.5 | 37.1 | 155 54.7 | 17.3 | 215 00.2 | 12.5 | 258 25.6 | 54.0 |
| 17 | 236 49.4 | 87 14.9 | 36.1 | 170 55.8 | 17.6 | 230 03.0 | 12.4 | 273 28.2 | 54.0 |
| 18 | 251 51.9 | 102 14.4 | N13 35.1 | 185 56.8 | N20 17.9 | 245 05.7 | N 1 12.3 | 288 30.9 | S15 54.1 |
| 19 | 266 54.3 | 117 13.8 | 34.1 | 200 57.9 | 18.1 | 260 08.4 | 12.2 | 303 33.5 | 54.1 |
| 20 | 281 56.8 | 132 13.3 | 33.1 | 215 59.0 | 18.4 | 275 11.1 | 12.1 | 318 36.1 | 54.2 |
| 21 | 296 59.2 | 147 12.8 .. | 32.1 | 231 00.1 .. | 18.6 | 290 13.8 .. | 12.0 | 333 38.7 .. | 54.2 |
| 22 | 312 01.7 | 162 12.2 | 31.1 | 246 01.2 | 18.9 | 305 16.5 | 11.9 | 348 41.4 | 54.3 |
| 23 | 327 04.2 | 177 11.7 | 30.1 | 261 02.3 | 19.1 | 320 19.2 | 11.8 | 3 44.0 | 54.4 |
| **3** 00 | 342 06.6 | 192 11.2 | N13 29.1 | 276 03.3 | N20 19.4 | 335 21.9 | N 1 11.6 | 18 46.6 | S15 54.4 |
| 01 | 357 09.1 | 207 10.6 | 28.1 | 291 04.4 | 19.6 | 350 24.6 | 11.5 | 33 49.3 | 54.5 |
| 02 | 12 11.6 | 222 10.1 | 27.1 | 306 05.5 | 19.9 | 5 27.3 | 11.4 | 48 51.9 | 54.5 |
| 03 | 27 14.0 | 237 09.5 .. | 26.1 | 321 06.6 .. | 20.2 | 20 30.0 .. | 11.3 | 63 54.5 .. | 54.6 |
| 04 | 42 16.5 | 252 09.0 | 25.1 | 336 07.7 | 20.4 | 35 32.7 | 11.2 | 78 57.2 | 54.6 |
| 05 | 57 19.0 | 267 08.5 | 24.0 | 351 08.8 | 20.7 | 50 35.4 | 11.1 | 93 59.8 | 54.7 |
| S 06 | 72 21.4 | 282 07.9 | N13 23.0 | 6 09.9 | N20 20.9 | 65 38.1 | N 1 11.0 | 109 02.4 | S15 54.7 |
| A 07 | 87 23.9 | 297 07.4 | 22.0 | 21 10.9 | 21.2 | 80 40.8 | 10.8 | 124 05.1 | 54.8 |
| T 08 | 102 26.3 | 312 06.9 | 21.0 | 36 12.0 | 21.4 | 95 43.6 | 10.7 | 139 07.7 | 54.9 |
| U 09 | 117 28.8 | 327 06.3 .. | 20.0 | 51 13.1 .. | 21.7 | 110 46.3 .. | 10.6 | 154 10.3 .. | 54.9 |
| R 10 | 132 31.3 | 342 05.8 | 19.0 | 66 14.2 | 21.9 | 125 49.0 | 10.5 | 169 12.9 | 55.0 |
| D 11 | 147 33.7 | 357 05.3 | 18.0 | 81 15.3 | 22.2 | 140 51.7 | 10.4 | 184 15.6 | 55.0 |
| A 12 | 162 36.2 | 12 04.7 | N13 17.0 | 96 16.4 | N20 22.4 | 155 54.4 | N 1 10.3 | 199 18.2 | S15 55.1 |
| Y 13 | 177 38.7 | 27 04.2 | 15.9 | 111 17.5 | 22.7 | 170 57.1 | 10.2 | 214 20.8 | 55.1 |
| 14 | 192 41.1 | 42 03.7 | 14.9 | 126 18.6 | 22.9 | 185 59.8 | 10.1 | 229 23.5 | 55.2 |
| 15 | 207 43.6 | 57 03.1 .. | 13.9 | 141 19.7 .. | 23.2 | 201 02.5 .. | 09.9 | 244 26.1 .. | 55.2 |
| 16 | 222 46.1 | 72 02.6 | 12.9 | 156 20.8 | 23.4 | 216 05.2 | 09.8 | 259 28.7 | 55.3 |
| 17 | 237 48.5 | 87 02.1 | 11.9 | 171 21.9 | 23.7 | 231 07.9 | 09.7 | 274 31.4 | 55.3 |
| 18 | 252 51.0 | 102 01.5 | N13 10.9 | 186 22.9 | N20 23.9 | 246 10.6 | N 1 09.6 | 289 34.0 | S15 55.4 |
| 19 | 267 53.5 | 117 01.0 | 09.8 | 201 24.0 | 24.2 | 261 13.4 | 09.5 | 304 36.6 | 55.5 |
| 20 | 282 55.9 | 132 00.5 | 08.8 | 216 25.1 | 24.4 | 276 16.1 | 09.4 | 319 39.2 | 55.5 |
| 21 | 297 58.4 | 146 59.9 .. | 07.8 | 231 26.2 .. | 24.7 | 291 18.8 .. | 09.3 | 334 41.9 .. | 55.6 |
| 22 | 313 00.8 | 161 59.4 | 06.8 | 246 27.3 | 24.9 | 306 21.5 | 09.1 | 349 44.5 | 55.6 |
| 23 | 328 03.3 | 176 58.9 | 05.8 | 261 28.4 | 25.2 | 321 24.2 | 09.0 | 4 47.1 | 55.7 |
| Mer. Pass. 1 15.3 | | v −0.5 d 1.0 | | v 1.1 d 0.3 | | v 2.7 d 0.1 | | v 2.6 d 0.1 | |

**STARS**

| Name | SHA | Dec |
|---|---|---|
| Acamar | 315 13.1 | S40 12.6 |
| Achernar | 335 21.2 | S57 07.1 |
| Acrux | 173 02.8 | S63 13.5 |
| Adhara | 255 07.6 | S28 59.9 |
| Aldebaran | 290 41.9 | N16 33.3 |
| Alioth | 166 15.2 | N55 50.5 |
| Alkaid | 152 53.9 | N49 12.3 |
| Alnair | 27 34.9 | S46 51.1 |
| Alnilam | 275 39.8 | S 1 11.1 |
| Alphard | 217 50.0 | S 8 45.2 |
| Alphecca | 126 05.5 | N26 38.6 |
| Alpheratz | 357 36.5 | N29 12.9 |
| Altair | 62 01.6 | N 8 55.8 |
| Ankaa | 353 08.7 | S42 10.8 |
| Antares | 112 18.2 | S26 28.9 |
| Arcturus | 145 49.9 | N19 04.1 |
| Atria | 107 14.1 | S69 04.3 |
| Avior | 234 16.0 | S59 34.6 |
| Bellatrix | 278 25.0 | N 6 22.3 |
| Betelgeuse | 270 54.3 | N 7 24.8 |
| Canopus | 263 53.5 | S52 42.1 |
| Capella | 280 24.8 | N46 01.1 |
| Deneb | 49 26.7 | N45 21.8 |
| Denebola | 182 27.2 | N14 26.9 |
| Diphda | 348 49.0 | S17 51.6 |
| Dubhe | 193 44.1 | N61 37.9 |
| Elnath | 278 04.4 | N28 37.5 |
| Eltanin | 90 42.9 | N51 29.4 |
| Enif | 33 40.4 | N 9 58.8 |
| Fomalhaut | 15 16.3 | S29 30.1 |
| Gacrux | 171 54.3 | S57 14.4 |
| Gienah | 175 45.9 | S17 39.9 |
| Hadar | 148 39.2 | S60 29.0 |
| Hamal | 327 53.2 | N23 34.1 |
| Kaus Aust. | 83 34.9 | S34 22.5 |
| Kochab | 137 20.3 | N74 04.1 |
| Markab | 13 31.5 | N15 19.7 |
| Menkar | 314 08.1 | N 4 10.8 |
| Menkent | 148 00.2 | S36 28.9 |
| Miaplacidus | 221 39.5 | S69 48.4 |
| Mirfak | 308 30.9 | N49 56.3 |
| Nunki | 75 50.0 | S26 16.1 |
| Peacock | 53 08.3 | S56 39.8 |
| Pollux | 243 20.0 | N27 58.3 |
| Procyon | 244 53.1 | N 5 10.2 |
| Rasalhague | 96 00.3 | N12 32.8 |
| Regulus | 207 36.8 | N11 51.6 |
| Rigel | 281 05.8 | S 8 10.4 |
| Rigil Kent. | 139 43.3 | S60 55.8 |
| Sabik | 102 05.0 | S15 45.1 |
| Schedar | 349 32.8 | N56 39.6 |
| Shaula | 96 12.9 | S37 07.3 |
| Sirius | 258 28.1 | S16 44.6 |
| Spica | 158 24.6 | S11 16.6 |
| Suhail | 222 48.1 | S43 31.2 |
| Vega | 80 34.3 | N38 48.5 |
| Zuben'ubi | 136 58.3 | S16 08.1 |

| | SHA | Mer. Pass. |
|---|---|---|
| Venus | 211 16.7 | 11 11 |
| Mars | 294 29.9 | 5 37 |
| Jupiter | 353 09.5 | 1 43 |
| Saturn | 36 36.0 | 22 45 |

| UT | SUN GHA | SUN Dec | MOON GHA | v | Dec | d | HP |
|---|---|---|---|---|---|---|---|
| d h | ° ′ | ° ′ | ° ′ | ′ | ° ′ | ′ | ′ |
| 1 00 | 179 57.3 | N 8 21.6 | 128 15.5 | 12.5 | S11 47.5 | 13.9 | 57.4 |
| 01 | 194 57.5 | 20.7 | 142 47.0 | 12.5 | 12 01.4 | 13.8 | 57.4 |
| 02 | 209 57.7 | 19.8 | 157 18.5 | 12.3 | 12 15.2 | 13.8 | 57.5 |
| 03 | 224 57.9 | .. 18.9 | 171 49.8 | 12.3 | 12 29.0 | 13.8 | 57.5 |
| 04 | 239 58.1 | 18.0 | 186 21.1 | 12.2 | 12 42.8 | 13.7 | 57.5 |
| 05 | 254 58.3 | 17.1 | 200 52.3 | 12.2 | 12 56.5 | 13.6 | 57.5 |
| 06 | 269 58.5 | N 8 16.2 | 215 23.5 | 12.0 | S13 10.1 | 13.6 | 57.6 |
| 07 | 284 58.7 | 15.3 | 229 54.5 | 12.0 | 13 23.7 | 13.5 | 57.6 |
| 08 | 299 58.9 | 14.4 | 244 25.5 | 11.9 | 13 37.2 | 13.5 | 57.6 |
| 09 | 314 59.1 | .. 13.5 | 258 56.4 | 11.8 | 13 50.7 | 13.5 | 57.6 |
| 10 | 329 59.3 | 12.5 | 273 27.2 | 11.7 | 14 04.2 | 13.3 | 57.6 |
| 11 | 344 59.5 | 11.6 | 287 57.9 | 11.6 | 14 17.5 | 13.3 | 57.7 |
| 12 | 359 59.7 | N 8 10.7 | 302 28.5 | 11.6 | S14 30.8 | 13.3 | 57.7 |
| 13 | 14 59.9 | 09.8 | 316 59.1 | 11.4 | 14 44.1 | 13.2 | 57.7 |
| 14 | 30 00.1 | 08.9 | 331 29.5 | 11.4 | 14 57.3 | 13.1 | 57.7 |
| 15 | 45 00.3 | .. 08.0 | 345 59.9 | 11.3 | 15 10.4 | 13.0 | 57.8 |
| 16 | 60 00.5 | 07.1 | 0 30.2 | 11.2 | 15 23.4 | 13.0 | 57.8 |
| 17 | 75 00.7 | 06.2 | 15 00.4 | 11.1 | 15 36.4 | 12.9 | 57.8 |
| 18 | 90 00.9 | N 8 05.3 | 29 30.5 | 11.0 | S15 49.3 | 12.9 | 57.8 |
| 19 | 105 01.1 | 04.4 | 44 00.5 | 10.9 | 16 02.2 | 12.7 | 57.8 |
| 20 | 120 01.3 | 03.5 | 58 30.4 | 10.8 | 16 14.9 | 12.7 | 57.9 |
| 21 | 135 01.5 | .. 02.5 | 73 00.2 | 10.7 | 16 27.6 | 12.6 | 57.9 |
| 22 | 150 01.7 | 01.6 | 87 29.9 | 10.7 | 16 40.2 | 12.6 | 57.9 |
| 23 | 165 01.9 | 8 00.7 | 101 59.6 | 10.5 | 16 52.8 | 12.4 | 57.9 |
| 2 00 | 180 02.1 | N 7 59.8 | 116 29.1 | 10.4 | S17 05.2 | 12.4 | 58.0 |
| 01 | 195 02.3 | 58.9 | 130 58.5 | 10.4 | 17 17.6 | 12.3 | 58.0 |
| 02 | 210 02.5 | 58.0 | 145 27.9 | 10.2 | 17 29.9 | 12.3 | 58.0 |
| 03 | 225 02.7 | .. 57.1 | 159 57.1 | 10.1 | 17 42.2 | 12.1 | 58.0 |
| 04 | 240 02.9 | 56.2 | 174 26.2 | 10.1 | 17 54.3 | 12.0 | 58.1 |
| 05 | 255 03.1 | 55.3 | 188 55.3 | 9.9 | 18 06.3 | 12.0 | 58.1 |
| 06 | 270 03.3 | N 7 54.3 | 203 24.2 | 9.9 | S18 18.3 | 11.9 | 58.1 |
| 07 | 285 03.5 | 53.4 | 217 53.1 | 9.7 | 18 30.2 | 11.8 | 58.1 |
| 08 | 300 03.7 | 52.5 | 232 21.0 | 9.6 | 18 42.0 | 11.7 | 58.1 |
| 09 | 315 03.9 | .. 51.6 | 246 50.4 | 9.6 | 18 53.7 | 11.6 | 58.2 |
| 10 | 330 04.1 | 50.7 | 261 19.0 | 9.4 | 19 05.3 | 11.5 | 58.2 |
| 11 | 345 04.3 | 49.8 | 275 47.4 | 9.3 | 19 16.8 | 11.4 | 58.2 |
| 12 | 0 04.5 | N 7 48.9 | 290 15.7 | 9.2 | S19 28.2 | 11.3 | 58.2 |
| 13 | 15 04.7 | 48.0 | 304 43.9 | 9.1 | 19 39.5 | 11.2 | 58.3 |
| 14 | 30 04.9 | 47.0 | 319 12.0 | 9.0 | 19 50.7 | 11.1 | 58.3 |
| 15 | 45 05.1 | .. 46.1 | 333 40.0 | 8.9 | 20 01.8 | 11.0 | 58.3 |
| 16 | 60 05.3 | 45.2 | 348 07.9 | 8.8 | 20 12.8 | 10.9 | 58.3 |
| 17 | 75 05.5 | 44.3 | 2 35.7 | 8.7 | 20 23.7 | 10.8 | 58.3 |
| 18 | 90 05.7 | N 7 43.4 | 17 03.4 | 8.6 | S20 34.5 | 10.7 | 58.4 |
| 19 | 105 05.9 | 42.5 | 31 31.0 | 8.5 | 20 45.2 | 10.5 | 58.4 |
| 20 | 120 06.1 | 41.6 | 45 58.5 | 8.3 | 20 55.7 | 10.5 | 58.4 |
| 21 | 135 06.3 | .. 40.6 | 60 25.8 | 8.3 | 21 06.2 | 10.4 | 58.4 |
| 22 | 150 06.5 | 39.7 | 74 53.1 | 8.1 | 21 16.6 | 10.2 | 58.5 |
| 23 | 165 06.7 | 38.8 | 89 20.2 | 8.1 | 21 26.8 | 10.1 | 58.5 |
| 3 00 | 180 06.9 | N 7 37.9 | 103 47.3 | 7.9 | S21 36.9 | 10.0 | 58.5 |
| 01 | 195 07.1 | 37.0 | 118 14.2 | 7.8 | 21 46.9 | 9.9 | 58.5 |
| 02 | 210 07.3 | 36.1 | 132 41.0 | 7.7 | 21 56.8 | 9.8 | 58.5 |
| 03 | 225 07.5 | .. 35.2 | 147 07.7 | 7.6 | 22 06.6 | 9.6 | 58.6 |
| 04 | 240 07.7 | 34.2 | 161 34.3 | 7.5 | 22 16.2 | 9.5 | 58.6 |
| 05 | 255 07.9 | 33.3 | 176 00.8 | 7.4 | 22 25.7 | 9.4 | 58.6 |
| 06 | 270 08.1 | N 7 32.4 | 190 27.2 | 7.3 | S22 35.1 | 9.3 | 58.6 |
| 07 | 285 08.3 | 31.5 | 204 53.5 | 7.2 | 22 44.4 | 9.1 | 58.7 |
| 08 | 300 08.6 | 30.6 | 219 19.7 | 7.0 | 22 53.5 | 9.0 | 58.7 |
| 09 | 315 08.8 | .. 29.6 | 233 45.7 | 7.0 | 23 02.5 | 8.8 | 58.7 |
| 10 | 330 09.0 | 28.7 | 248 11.7 | 6.8 | 23 11.3 | 8.8 | 58.7 |
| 11 | 345 09.2 | 27.8 | 262 37.5 | 6.8 | 23 20.1 | 8.6 | 58.7 |
| 12 | 0 09.4 | N 7 26.9 | 277 03.3 | 6.6 | S23 28.7 | 8.4 | 58.8 |
| 13 | 15 09.6 | 26.0 | 291 28.9 | 6.5 | 23 37.1 | 8.4 | 58.8 |
| 14 | 30 09.8 | 25.1 | 305 54.4 | 6.5 | 23 45.5 | 8.1 | 58.8 |
| 15 | 45 10.0 | .. 24.1 | 320 19.9 | 6.3 | 23 53.6 | 8.1 | 58.8 |
| 16 | 60 10.2 | 23.2 | 334 45.2 | 6.2 | 24 01.7 | 7.9 | 58.9 |
| 17 | 75 10.4 | 22.3 | 349 10.4 | 6.1 | 24 09.6 | 7.7 | 58.9 |
| 18 | 90 10.6 | N 7 21.4 | 3 35.5 | 6.0 | S24 17.3 | 7.6 | 58.9 |
| 19 | 105 10.8 | 20.5 | 18 00.5 | 5.9 | 24 24.9 | 7.5 | 58.9 |
| 20 | 120 11.0 | 19.5 | 32 25.4 | 5.9 | 24 32.4 | 7.3 | 58.9 |
| 21 | 135 11.2 | .. 18.6 | 46 50.3 | 5.7 | 24 39.7 | 7.1 | 59.0 |
| 22 | 150 11.4 | 17.7 | 61 15.0 | 5.6 | 24 46.8 | 7.0 | 59.0 |
| 23 | 165 11.6 | 16.8 | 75 39.6 | 5.5 | S24 53.8 | 6.8 | 59.0 |
| | SD 15.9 | d 0.9 | SD 15.7 | | 15.9 | | 16.0 |

| Lat. | Twilight Naut. | Twilight Civil | Sunrise | Moonrise 1 | Moonrise 2 | Moonrise 3 | Moonrise 4 |
|---|---|---|---|---|---|---|---|
| ° | h m | h m | h m | h m | h m | h m | h m |
| N 72 | //// | 02 38 | 04 06 | 13 35 | ■■■ | ■■■ | ■■■ |
| N 70 | 00 05 | 03 05 | 04 19 | 12 59 | ■■■ | ■■■ | ■■■ |
| 68 | 01 39 | 03 24 | 04 30 | 12 34 | 15 08 | ■■■ | ■■■ |
| 66 | 02 15 | 03 40 | 04 38 | 12 15 | 14 25 | ■■■ | ■■■ |
| 64 | 02 40 | 03 53 | 04 45 | 12 00 | 13 56 | 16 10 | ■■■ |
| 62 | 02 59 | 04 03 | 04 52 | 11 47 | 13 34 | 15 29 | 17 27 |
| 60 | 03 14 | 04 12 | 04 57 | 11 36 | 13 17 | 15 01 | 16 42 |
| N 58 | 03 27 | 04 20 | 05 02 | 11 27 | 13 02 | 14 40 | 16 12 |
| 56 | 03 37 | 04 27 | 05 06 | 11 19 | 12 50 | 14 22 | 15 50 |
| 54 | 03 47 | 04 33 | 05 10 | 11 12 | 12 39 | 14 07 | 15 32 |
| 52 | 03 55 | 04 38 | 05 13 | 11 06 | 12 29 | 13 54 | 15 16 |
| 50 | 04 02 | 04 43 | 05 16 | 11 00 | 12 21 | 13 43 | 15 02 |
| 45 | 04 16 | 04 53 | 05 23 | 10 47 | 12 03 | 13 20 | 14 35 |
| N 40 | 04 28 | 05 01 | 05 29 | 10 37 | 11 48 | 13 01 | 14 13 |
| 35 | 04 37 | 05 07 | 05 33 | 10 29 | 11 36 | 12 46 | 13 55 |
| 30 | 04 44 | 05 13 | 05 37 | 10 21 | 11 25 | 12 32 | 13 40 |
| 20 | 04 56 | 05 22 | 05 45 | 10 08 | 11 07 | 12 09 | 13 14 |
| N 10 | 05 05 | 05 30 | 05 51 | 09 57 | 10 51 | 11 50 | 12 51 |
| 0 | 05 11 | 05 36 | 05 56 | 09 46 | 10 37 | 11 31 | 12 31 |
| S 10 | 05 16 | 05 41 | 06 02 | 09 36 | 10 22 | 11 13 | 12 10 |
| 20 | 05 20 | 05 46 | 06 08 | 09 25 | 10 07 | 10 54 | 11 48 |
| 30 | 05 23 | 05 50 | 06 14 | 09 12 | 09 49 | 10 32 | 11 22 |
| 35 | 05 23 | 05 53 | 06 18 | 09 05 | 09 39 | 10 19 | 11 07 |
| 40 | 05 24 | 05 55 | 06 22 | 08 57 | 09 27 | 10 04 | 10 50 |
| 45 | 05 23 | 05 57 | 06 27 | 08 48 | 09 14 | 09 46 | 10 29 |
| S 50 | 05 23 | 06 00 | 06 33 | 08 36 | 08 57 | 09 25 | 10 03 |
| 52 | 05 22 | 06 01 | 06 35 | 08 31 | 08 50 | 09 15 | 09 50 |
| 54 | 05 22 | 06 02 | 06 38 | 08 26 | 08 41 | 09 03 | 09 36 |
| 56 | 05 21 | 06 04 | 06 41 | 08 19 | 08 32 | 08 50 | 09 19 |
| 58 | 05 20 | 06 05 | 06 45 | 08 12 | 08 21 | 08 35 | 08 59 |
| S 60 | 05 19 | 06 07 | 06 48 | 08 04 | 08 08 | 00 17 | 08 34 |

| Lat. | Sunset | Twilight Civil | Twilight Naut. | Moonset 1 | Moonset 2 | Moonset 3 | Moonset 4 |
|---|---|---|---|---|---|---|---|
| ° | h m | h m | h m | h m | h m | h m | h m |
| N 72 | 19 50 | 21 16 | //// | 17 56 | ■■■ | ■■■ | ■■■ |
| N 70 | 19 38 | 20 51 | 23 16 | 18 34 | ■■■ | ■■■ | ■■■ |
| 68 | 19 27 | 20 32 | 22 13 | 19 00 | 18 13 | ■■■ | ■■■ |
| 66 | 19 19 | 20 17 | 21 39 | 19 21 | 18 58 | ■■■ | ■■■ |
| 64 | 19 12 | 20 04 | 21 16 | 19 38 | 19 28 | 19 10 | ■■■ |
| 62 | 19 06 | 19 54 | 20 57 | 19 52 | 19 50 | 19 51 | 19 59 |
| 60 | 19 01 | 19 45 | 20 43 | 20 03 | 20 09 | 20 19 | 20 44 |
| N 58 | 18 56 | 19 38 | 20 30 | 20 14 | 20 24 | 20 41 | 21 14 |
| 56 | 18 52 | 19 31 | 20 20 | 20 23 | 20 37 | 20 59 | 21 36 |
| 54 | 18 48 | 19 25 | 20 11 | 20 31 | 20 49 | 21 15 | 21 55 |
| 52 | 18 45 | 19 20 | 20 03 | 20 38 | 20 59 | 21 28 | 22 11 |
| 50 | 18 42 | 19 16 | 19 56 | 20 44 | 21 08 | 21 40 | 22 25 |
| 45 | 18 36 | 19 06 | 19 42 | 20 58 | 21 27 | 22 04 | 22 53 |
| N 40 | 18 30 | 18 58 | 19 31 | 21 10 | 21 43 | 22 24 | 23 15 |
| 35 | 18 26 | 18 51 | 19 22 | 21 20 | 21 56 | 22 40 | 23 33 |
| 30 | 18 21 | 18 46 | 19 14 | 21 29 | 22 08 | 22 54 | 23 49 |
| 20 | 18 15 | 18 37 | 19 03 | 21 44 | 22 28 | 23 18 | 24 16 |
| N 10 | 18 09 | 18 30 | 18 54 | 21 57 | 22 46 | 23 39 | 24 39 |
| 0 | 18 03 | 18 24 | 18 48 | 22 10 | 23 02 | 23 59 | 25 00 |
| S 10 | 17 58 | 18 19 | 18 43 | 22 22 | 23 19 | 24 19 | 00 19 |
| 20 | 17 52 | 18 14 | 18 40 | 22 36 | 23 36 | 24 40 | 00 40 |
| 30 | 17 46 | 18 10 | 18 37 | 22 51 | 23 57 | 25 04 | 01 04 |
| 35 | 17 42 | 18 07 | 18 37 | 23 00 | 24 09 | 00 09 | 01 19 |
| 40 | 17 38 | 18 05 | 18 36 | 23 11 | 24 23 | 00 23 | 01 36 |
| 45 | 17 33 | 18 03 | 18 37 | 23 23 | 24 39 | 00 39 | 01 56 |
| S 50 | 17 28 | 18 00 | 18 38 | 23 38 | 25 00 | 01 00 | 02 21 |
| 52 | 17 25 | 17 59 | 18 38 | 23 45 | 25 09 | 01 09 | 02 33 |
| 54 | 17 22 | 17 58 | 18 39 | 23 53 | 25 20 | 01 20 | 02 47 |
| 56 | 17 19 | 17 57 | 18 40 | 24 01 | 00 01 | 01 33 | 03 04 |
| 58 | 17 16 | 17 56 | 18 41 | 24 11 | 00 11 | 01 48 | 03 23 |
| S 60 | 17 12 | 17 54 | 18 42 | 24 23 | 00 23 | 02 05 | 03 48 |

| | SUN | | | MOON | | | |
|---|---|---|---|---|---|---|---|
| Day | Eqn. of Time 00h | Eqn. of Time 12h | Mer. Pass. | Mer. Pass. Upper | Mer. Pass. Lower | Age | Phase |
| d | m s | m s | h m | h m | h m | d % | |
| 1 | 00 11 | 00 02 | 12 00 | 15 58 | 03 34 | 05 26 | |
| 2 | 00 08 | 00 18 | 12 00 | 16 49 | 04 23 | 06 36 | |
| 3 | 00 27 | 00 37 | 11 59 | 17 45 | 05 17 | 07 47 | |

| UT | ARIES | VENUS −3.9 | | MARS −0.2 | | JUPITER −2.9 | | SATURN +0.3 | | STARS | | |
|---|---|---|---|---|---|---|---|---|---|---|---|---|
| | GHA | GHA | Dec | GHA | Dec | GHA | Dec | GHA | Dec | Name | SHA | Dec |
| d h | ° ′ | ° ′ | ° ′ | ° ′ | ° ′ | ° ′ | ° ′ | ° ′ | ° ′ | | ° ′ | ° ′ |
| 4 00 | 343 05.8 | 191 58.3 | N13 04.7 | 276 29.5 | N20 25.4 | 336 26.9 | N 1 08.9 | 19 49.8 | S15 55.7 | Acamar | 315 13.1 | S40 12.6 |
| 01 | 358 08.2 | 206 57.8 | 03.7 | 291 30.6 | 25.7 | 351 29.6 | 08.8 | 34 52.4 | 55.8 | Achernar | 335 21.2 | S57 07.1 |
| 02 | 13 10.7 | 221 57.3 | 02.7 | 306 31.7 | 25.9 | 6 32.3 | 08.7 | 49 55.0 | 55.8 | Acrux | 173 02.8 | S63 13.5 |
| 03 | 28 13.2 | 236 56.8 .. | 01.7 | 321 32.8 .. | 26.2 | 21 35.1 .. | 08.6 | 64 57.7 .. | 55.9 | Adhara | 255 07.6 | S28 59.9 |
| 04 | 43 15.6 | 251 56.2 | 13 00.7 | 336 33.9 | 26.4 | 36 37.8 | 08.5 | 80 00.3 | 55.9 | Aldebaran | 290 41.8 | N16 33.3 |
| 05 | 58 18.1 | 266 55.7 | 12 59.6 | 351 35.0 | 26.7 | 51 40.5 | 08.3 | 95 02.9 | 56.0 | | | |
| 06 | 73 20.6 | 281 55.2 | N12 58.6 | 6 36.1 | N20 26.9 | 66 43.2 | N 1 08.2 | 110 05.5 | S15 56.1 | Alioth | 166 15.2 | N55 50.5 |
| 07 | 88 23.0 | 296 54.7 | 57.6 | 21 37.2 | 27.2 | 81 45.9 | 08.1 | 125 08.2 | 56.1 | Alkaid | 152 53.9 | N49 12.3 |
| 08 | 103 25.5 | 311 54.1 | 56.5 | 36 38.3 | 27.4 | 96 48.6 | 08.0 | 140 10.8 | 56.2 | Alnair | 27 34.9 | S46 51.1 |
| S 09 | 118 28.0 | 326 53.6 .. | 55.5 | 51 39.4 .. | 27.7 | 111 51.3 .. | 07.9 | 155 13.4 .. | 56.2 | Alnilam | 275 39.8 | S 1 11.1 |
| U 10 | 133 30.4 | 341 53.1 | 54.5 | 66 40.5 | 27.9 | 126 54.0 | 07.8 | 170 16.1 | 56.3 | Alphard | 217 50.0 | S 8 45.2 |
| N 11 | 148 32.9 | 356 52.6 | 53.5 | 81 41.6 | 28.2 | 141 56.8 | 07.7 | 185 18.7 | 56.3 | | | |
| D 12 | 163 35.3 | 11 52.0 | N12 52.4 | 96 42.7 | N20 28.4 | 156 59.5 | N 1 07.5 | 200 21.3 | S15 56.4 | Alphecca | 126 05.5 | N26 38.6 |
| A 13 | 178 37.8 | 26 51.5 | 51.4 | 111 43.8 | 28.7 | 172 02.2 | 07.4 | 215 23.9 | 56.4 | Alpheratz | 357 36.4 | N29 12.9 |
| Y 14 | 193 40.3 | 41 51.0 | 50.4 | 126 44.9 | 28.9 | 187 04.9 | 07.3 | 230 26.6 | 56.5 | Altair | 62 01.6 | N 8 55.8 |
| 15 | 208 42.7 | 56 50.5 .. | 49.3 | 141 46.0 .. | 29.2 | 202 07.6 .. | 07.2 | 245 29.2 .. | 56.5 | Ankaa | 353 08.7 | S42 10.9 |
| 16 | 223 45.2 | 71 49.9 | 48.3 | 156 47.1 | 29.4 | 217 10.3 | 07.1 | 260 31.8 | 56.6 | Antares | 112 18.2 | S26 28.9 |
| 17 | 238 47.7 | 86 49.4 | 47.3 | 171 48.2 | 29.7 | 232 13.0 | 07.0 | 275 34.4 | 56.7 | | | |
| 18 | 253 50.1 | 101 48.9 | N12 46.2 | 186 49.3 | N20 29.9 | 247 15.8 | N 1 06.8 | 290 37.1 | S15 56.7 | Arcturus | 145 49.9 | N19 04.1 |
| 19 | 268 52.6 | 116 48.4 | 45.2 | 201 50.4 | 30.1 | 262 18.5 | 06.7 | 305 39.7 | 56.8 | Atria | 107 14.2 | S69 04.3 |
| 20 | 283 55.1 | 131 47.8 | 44.2 | 216 51.5 | 30.4 | 277 21.2 | 06.6 | 320 42.3 | 56.8 | Avior | 234 16.0 | S59 34.6 |
| 21 | 298 57.5 | 146 47.3 .. | 43.1 | 231 52.6 .. | 30.6 | 292 23.9 .. | 06.5 | 335 45.0 .. | 56.9 | Bellatrix | 278 25.0 | N 6 22.3 |
| 22 | 314 00.0 | 161 46.8 | 42.1 | 246 53.7 | 30.9 | 307 26.6 | 06.4 | 350 47.6 | 56.9 | Betelgeuse | 270 54.3 | N 7 24.8 |
| 23 | 329 02.5 | 176 46.3 | 41.1 | 261 54.9 | 31.1 | 322 29.3 | 06.3 | 5 50.2 | 57.0 | | | |
| 5 00 | 344 04.9 | 191 45.8 | N12 40.0 | 276 56.0 | N20 31.4 | 337 32.0 | N 1 06.2 | 20 52.8 | S15 57.0 | Canopus | 263 53.5 | S52 42.1 |
| 01 | 359 07.4 | 206 45.2 | 39.0 | 291 57.1 | 31.6 | 352 34.8 | 06.0 | 35 55.5 | 57.1 | Capella | 280 24.8 | N46 01.1 |
| 02 | 14 09.8 | 221 44.7 | 38.0 | 306 58.2 | 31.9 | 7 37.5 | 05.9 | 50 58.1 | 57.1 | Deneb | 49 26.7 | N45 21.8 |
| 03 | 29 12.3 | 236 44.2 .. | 36.9 | 321 59.3 .. | 32.1 | 22 40.2 .. | 05.8 | 66 00.7 .. | 57.2 | Denebola | 182 27.2 | N14 26.9 |
| 04 | 44 14.8 | 251 43.7 | 35.9 | 337 00.4 | 32.3 | 37 42.9 | 05.7 | 81 03.4 | 57.2 | Diphda | 348 49.0 | S17 51.6 |
| 05 | 59 17.2 | 266 43.2 | 34.8 | 352 01.5 | 32.6 | 52 45.6 | 05.6 | 96 06.0 | 57.3 | | | |
| 06 | 74 19.7 | 281 42.7 | N12 33.8 | 7 02.6 | N20 32.8 | 67 48.4 | N 1 05.5 | 111 08.6 | S15 57.4 | Dubhe | 193 44.1 | N61 37.9 |
| 07 | 89 22.2 | 296 42.1 | 32.8 | 22 03.7 | 33.1 | 82 51.1 | 05.3 | 126 11.2 | 57.4 | Elnath | 278 04.4 | N28 37.5 |
| 08 | 104 24.6 | 311 41.6 | 31.7 | 37 04.8 | 33.3 | 97 53.8 | 05.2 | 141 13.9 | 57.5 | Eltanin | 90 42.9 | N51 29.4 |
| M 09 | 119 27.1 | 326 41.1 .. | 30.7 | 52 05.9 .. | 33.6 | 112 56.5 .. | 05.1 | 156 16.5 .. | 57.5 | Enif | 33 40.4 | N 9 58.8 |
| O 10 | 134 29.6 | 341 40.6 | 29.6 | 67 07.1 | 33.8 | 127 59.2 | 05.0 | 171 19.1 | 57.6 | Fomalhaut | 15 16.3 | S29 30.1 |
| N 11 | 149 32.0 | 356 40.1 | 28.6 | 82 08.2 | 34.0 | 143 01.9 | 04.9 | 186 21.7 | 57.6 | | | |
| D 12 | 164 34.5 | 11 39.6 | N12 27.6 | 97 09.3 | N20 34.3 | 158 04.7 | N 1 04.8 | 201 24.4 | S15 57.7 | Gacrux | 171 54.3 | S57 14.4 |
| A 13 | 179 37.0 | 26 39.0 | 26.5 | 112 10.4 | 34.5 | 173 07.4 | 04.6 | 216 27.0 | 57.7 | Gienah | 175 45.9 | S17 39.9 |
| Y 14 | 194 39.4 | 41 38.5 | 25.5 | 127 11.5 | 34.8 | 188 10.1 | 04.5 | 231 29.6 | 57.8 | Hadar | 148 39.2 | S60 29.0 |
| 15 | 209 41.9 | 56 38.0 .. | 24.4 | 142 12.6 .. | 35.0 | 203 12.8 .. | 04.4 | 246 32.2 .. | 57.8 | Hamal | 327 53.2 | N23 34.1 |
| 16 | 224 44.3 | 71 37.5 | 23.4 | 157 13.7 | 35.2 | 218 15.5 | 04.3 | 261 34.9 | 57.9 | Kaus Aust. | 83 34.9 | S34 22.5 |
| 17 | 239 46.8 | 86 37.0 | 22.3 | 172 14.9 | 35.5 | 233 18.3 | 04.2 | 276 37.5 | 57.9 | | | |
| 18 | 254 49.3 | 101 36.5 | N12 21.3 | 187 16.0 | N20 35.7 | 248 21.0 | N 1 04.0 | 291 40.1 | S15 58.0 | Kochab | 137 20.3 | N74 04.0 |
| 19 | 269 51.7 | 116 36.0 | 20.2 | 202 17.1 | 36.0 | 263 23.7 | 03.9 | 306 42.7 | 58.0 | Markab | 13 31.5 | N15 19.7 |
| 20 | 284 54.2 | 131 35.4 | 19.2 | 217 18.2 | 36.2 | 278 26.4 | 03.8 | 321 45.4 | 58.1 | Menkar | 314 08.0 | N 4 10.8 |
| 21 | 299 56.7 | 146 34.9 .. | 18.1 | 232 19.3 .. | 36.4 | 293 29.1 .. | 03.7 | 336 48.0 .. | 58.1 | Menkent | 148 00.2 | S36 28.9 |
| 22 | 314 59.1 | 161 34.4 | 17.1 | 247 20.4 | 36.7 | 308 31.9 | 03.6 | 351 50.6 | 58.2 | Miaplacidus | 221 39.5 | S69 48.4 |
| 23 | 330 01.6 | 176 33.9 | 16.0 | 262 21.6 | 36.9 | 323 34.6 | 03.5 | 6 53.3 | 58.3 | | | |
| 6 00 | 345 04.1 | 191 33.4 | N12 15.0 | 277 22.7 | N20 37.2 | 338 37.3 | N 1 03.3 | 21 55.9 | S15 58.3 | Mirfak | 308 30.9 | N49 56.3 |
| 01 | 0 06.5 | 206 32.9 | 13.9 | 292 23.8 | 37.4 | 353 40.0 | 03.2 | 36 58.5 | 58.4 | Nunki | 75 50.0 | S26 16.1 |
| 02 | 15 09.0 | 221 32.4 | 12.9 | 307 24.9 | 37.6 | 8 42.7 | 03.1 | 52 01.1 | 58.4 | Peacock | 53 08.3 | S56 39.8 |
| 03 | 30 11.5 | 236 31.9 .. | 11.8 | 322 26.0 .. | 37.9 | 23 45.5 .. | 03.0 | 67 03.8 .. | 58.5 | Pollux | 243 19.9 | N27 58.3 |
| 04 | 45 13.9 | 251 31.4 | 10.8 | 337 27.2 | 38.1 | 38 48.2 | 02.9 | 82 06.4 | 58.5 | Procyon | 244 53.1 | N 5 10.2 |
| 05 | 60 16.4 | 266 30.9 | 09.7 | 352 28.3 | 38.3 | 53 50.9 | 02.8 | 97 09.0 | 58.6 | | | |
| 06 | 75 18.8 | 281 30.3 | N12 08.7 | 7 29.4 | N20 38.6 | 68 53.6 | N 1 02.6 | 112 11.6 | S15 58.6 | Rasalhague | 96 00.3 | N12 32.8 |
| 07 | 90 21.3 | 296 29.8 | 07.6 | 22 30.5 | 38.8 | 83 56.3 | 02.5 | 127 14.3 | 58.7 | Regulus | 207 36.8 | N11 51.6 |
| 08 | 105 23.8 | 311 29.3 | 06.5 | 37 31.6 | 39.1 | 98 59.1 | 02.4 | 142 16.9 | 58.7 | Rigel | 281 05.8 | S 8 10.4 |
| T 09 | 120 26.2 | 326 28.8 .. | 05.5 | 52 32.8 .. | 39.3 | 114 01.8 .. | 02.3 | 157 19.5 .. | 58.8 | Rigil Kent. | 139 43.3 | S60 55.8 |
| U 10 | 135 28.7 | 341 28.3 | 04.4 | 67 33.9 | 39.5 | 129 04.5 | 02.2 | 172 22.1 | 58.8 | Sabik | 102 05.0 | S15 45.1 |
| E 11 | 150 31.2 | 356 27.8 | 03.4 | 82 35.0 | 39.8 | 144 07.2 | 02.0 | 187 24.8 | 58.9 | | | |
| S 12 | 165 33.6 | 11 27.3 | N12 02.3 | 97 36.1 | N20 40.0 | 159 10.0 | N 1 01.9 | 202 27.4 | S15 58.9 | Schedar | 349 32.7 | N56 39.6 |
| D 13 | 180 36.1 | 26 26.8 | 01.3 | 112 37.3 | 40.2 | 174 12.7 | 01.8 | 217 30.0 | 59.0 | Shaula | 96 12.9 | S37 07.3 |
| A 14 | 195 38.6 | 41 26.3 | 12 00.2 | 127 38.4 | 40.5 | 189 15.4 | 01.7 | 232 32.6 | 59.0 | Sirius | 258 28.1 | S16 44.6 |
| Y 15 | 210 41.0 | 56 25.8 .. | 11 59.1 | 142 39.5 .. | 40.7 | 204 18.1 .. | 01.6 | 247 35.2 .. | 59.1 | Spica | 158 24.6 | S11 16.6 |
| 16 | 225 43.5 | 71 25.3 | 58.1 | 157 40.7 | 40.9 | 219 20.9 | 01.4 | 262 37.9 | 59.2 | Suhail | 222 48.1 | S43 31.2 |
| 17 | 240 45.9 | 86 24.8 | 57.0 | 172 41.8 | 41.2 | 234 23.6 | 01.3 | 277 40.5 | 59.2 | | | |
| 18 | 255 48.4 | 101 24.3 | N11 56.0 | 187 42.9 | N20 41.4 | 249 26.3 | N 1 01.2 | 292 43.1 | S15 59.3 | Vega | 80 34.3 | N38 48.5 |
| 19 | 270 50.9 | 116 23.8 | 54.9 | 202 44.0 | 41.6 | 264 29.0 | 01.1 | 307 45.7 | 59.3 | Zuben'ubi | 136 58.3 | S16 08.1 |
| 20 | 285 53.3 | 131 23.3 | 53.8 | 217 45.2 | 41.9 | 279 31.8 | 01.0 | 322 48.4 | 59.4 | | SHA | Mer. Pass. |
| 21 | 300 55.8 | 146 22.8 .. | 52.8 | 232 46.3 .. | 42.1 | 294 34.5 .. | 00.9 | 337 51.0 .. | 59.4 | | ° ′ | h m |
| 22 | 315 58.3 | 161 22.3 | 51.7 | 247 47.4 | 42.3 | 309 37.2 | 00.7 | 352 53.6 | 59.5 | Venus | 207 40.9 | 11 13 |
| 23 | 331 00.7 | 176 21.7 | 50.6 | 262 48.6 | 42.6 | 324 39.9 | 00.6 | 7 56.2 | 59.5 | Mars | 292 51.0 | 5 32 |
| | h m | | | | | | | | | Jupiter | 353 27.1 | 1 30 |
| Mer. Pass. 1 03.5 | v −0.5 d 1.0 | | | v 1.1 d 0.2 | | v 2.7 d 0.1 | | v 2.6 d 0.1 | | Saturn | 36 47.9 | 22 33 |

| UT | SUN GHA | SUN Dec | MOON GHA | v | MOON Dec | d | HP |
|---|---|---|---|---|---|---|---|
| d h | ° ′ | ° ′ | ° ′ | ′ | ° ′ | ′ | ′ |
| 4 00 | 180 11.8 | N 7 15.9 | 90 04.1 | 5.4 | S25 00.6 | 6.7 | 59.0 |
| 01 | 195 12.0 | 14.9 | 104 28.5 | 5.3 | 25 07.3 | 6.6 | 59.0 |
| 02 | 210 12.3 | 14.0 | 118 52.8 | 5.3 | 25 13.9 | 6.3 | 59.1 |
| 03 | 225 12.5 | . . 13.1 | 133 17.1 | 5.1 | 25 20.2 | 6.2 | 59.1 |
| 04 | 240 12.7 | 12.2 | 147 41.2 | 5.0 | 25 26.4 | 6.1 | 59.1 |
| 05 | 255 12.9 | 11.3 | 162 05.2 | 5.0 | 25 32.5 | 5.9 | 59.1 |
| 06 | 270 13.1 | N 7 10.3 | 176 29.2 | 4.8 | S25 38.4 | 5.7 | 59.1 |
| 07 | 285 13.3 | 09.4 | 190 53.0 | 4.8 | 25 44.1 | 5.5 | 59.2 |
| 08 | 300 13.5 | 08.5 | 205 16.8 | 4.7 | 25 49.6 | 5.4 | 59.2 |
| S 09 | 315 13.7 | . . 07.6 | 219 40.5 | 4.6 | 25 55.0 | 5.2 | 59.2 |
| U 10 | 330 13.9 | 06.6 | 234 04.1 | 4.5 | 26 00.2 | 5.1 | 59.2 |
| N 11 | 345 14.1 | 05.7 | 248 27.6 | 4.4 | 26 05.3 | 4.9 | 59.2 |
| D 12 | 0 14.3 | N 7 04.8 | 262 51.0 | 4.4 | S26 10.2 | 4.7 | 59.3 |
| A 13 | 15 14.5 | 03.9 | 277 14.4 | 4.3 | 26 14.9 | 4.5 | 59.3 |
| Y 14 | 30 14.7 | 02.9 | 291 37.7 | 4.2 | 26 19.4 | 4.3 | 59.3 |
| 15 | 45 14.9 | . . 02.0 | 306 00.9 | 4.1 | 26 23.7 | 4.2 | 59.3 |
| 16 | 60 15.2 | 01.1 | 320 24.0 | 4.0 | 26 27.9 | 4.0 | 59.3 |
| 17 | 75 15.4 | 7 00.2 | 334 47.0 | 4.0 | 26 31.9 | 3.8 | 59.4 |
| 18 | 90 15.6 | N 6 59.3 | 349 10.0 | 3.9 | S26 35.7 | 3.7 | 59.4 |
| 19 | 105 15.8 | 58.3 | 3 32.9 | 3.9 | 26 39.4 | 3.5 | 59.4 |
| 20 | 120 16.0 | 57.4 | 17 55.8 | 3.8 | 26 42.9 | 3.2 | 59.4 |
| 21 | 135 16.2 | . . 56.5 | 32 18.6 | 3.7 | 26 46.1 | 3.1 | 59.4 |
| 22 | 150 16.4 | 55.6 | 46 41.3 | 3.6 | 26 49.2 | 2.9 | 59.5 |
| 23 | 165 16.6 | 54.6 | 61 03.9 | 3.6 | 26 52.1 | 2.8 | 59.5 |
| 5 00 | 180 16.8 | N 6 53.7 | 75 26.5 | 3.6 | S26 54.9 | 2.5 | 59.5 |
| 01 | 195 17.0 | 52.8 | 89 49.1 | 3.4 | 26 57.4 | 2.4 | 59.5 |
| 02 | 210 17.2 | 51.9 | 104 11.5 | 3.5 | 26 59.8 | 2.1 | 59.5 |
| 03 | 225 17.4 | . . 50.9 | 118 34.0 | 3.4 | 27 01.9 | 2.0 | 59.5 |
| 04 | 240 17.7 | 50.0 | 132 56.4 | 3.3 | 27 03.9 | 1.8 | 59.6 |
| 05 | 255 17.9 | 49.1 | 147 18.7 | 3.3 | 27 05.7 | 1.6 | 59.6 |
| 06 | 270 18.1 | N 6 48.1 | 161 41.0 | 3.2 | S27 07.3 | 1.5 | 59.6 |
| 07 | 285 18.3 | 47.2 | 176 03.2 | 3.2 | 27 08.8 | 1.2 | 59.6 |
| 08 | 300 18.5 | 46.3 | 190 25.4 | 3.2 | 27 10.0 | 1.0 | 59.6 |
| M 09 | 315 18.7 | . . 45.4 | 204 47.6 | 3.1 | 27 11.0 | 0.9 | 59.6 |
| O 10 | 330 18.9 | 44.4 | 219 09.7 | 3.1 | 27 11.9 | 0.6 | 59.7 |
| N 11 | 345 19.1 | 43.5 | 233 31.8 | 3.1 | 27 12.5 | 0.5 | 59.7 |
| D 12 | 0 19.3 | N 6 42.6 | 247 53.9 | 3.0 | S27 13.0 | 0.2 | 59.7 |
| A 13 | 15 19.5 | 41.7 | 262 15.9 | 3.1 | 27 13.2 | 0.1 | 59.7 |
| Y 14 | 30 19.8 | 40.7 | 276 38.0 | 3.0 | 27 13.3 | 0.1 | 59.7 |
| 15 | 45 20.0 | . . 39.8 | 291 00.0 | 2.9 | 27 13.2 | 0.3 | 59.7 |
| 16 | 60 20.2 | 38.9 | 305 21.9 | 3.0 | 27 12.9 | 0.6 | 59.8 |
| 17 | 75 20.4 | 37.9 | 319 43.9 | 2.9 | 27 12.3 | 0.7 | 59.8 |
| 18 | 90 20.6 | N 6 37.0 | 334 05.8 | 3.0 | S27 11.6 | 0.9 | 59.8 |
| 19 | 105 20.8 | 36.1 | 348 27.8 | 2.9 | 27 10.7 | 1.1 | 59.8 |
| 20 | 120 21.0 | 35.2 | 2 49.7 | 2.9 | 27 09.6 | 1.2 | 59.8 |
| 21 | 135 21.2 | . . 34.2 | 17 11.6 | 2.9 | 27 08.4 | 1.5 | 59.8 |
| 22 | 150 21.4 | 33.3 | 31 33.5 | 2.9 | 27 06.9 | 1.7 | 59.8 |
| 23 | 165 21.7 | 32.4 | 45 55.4 | 2.9 | 27 05.2 | 1.9 | 59.9 |
| 6 00 | 180 21.9 | N 6 31.4 | 60 17.3 | 2.9 | S27 03.3 | 2.1 | 59.9 |
| 01 | 195 22.1 | 30.5 | 74 39.2 | 3.0 | 27 01.2 | 2.2 | 59.9 |
| 02 | 210 22.3 | 29.6 | 89 01.2 | 2.9 | 26 59.0 | 2.5 | 59.9 |
| 03 | 225 22.5 | . . 28.6 | 103 23.1 | 2.9 | 26 56.5 | 2.6 | 59.9 |
| 04 | 240 22.7 | 27.7 | 117 45.0 | 3.0 | 26 53.9 | 2.9 | 59.9 |
| 05 | 255 22.9 | 26.8 | 132 07.0 | 2.9 | 26 51.0 | 3.0 | 59.9 |
| 06 | 270 23.1 | N 6 25.9 | 146 28.9 | 3.0 | S26 48.0 | 3.3 | 59.9 |
| 07 | 285 23.3 | 24.9 | 160 50.9 | 3.0 | 26 44.7 | 3.4 | 60.0 |
| 08 | 300 23.6 | 24.0 | 175 12.9 | 3.1 | 26 41.3 | 3.6 | 60.0 |
| T 09 | 315 23.8 | . . 23.1 | 189 35.0 | 3.0 | 26 37.7 | 3.8 | 60.0 |
| U 10 | 330 24.0 | 22.1 | 203 57.0 | 3.1 | 26 33.9 | 4.0 | 60.0 |
| E 11 | 345 24.2 | 21.2 | 218 19.1 | 3.2 | 26 29.9 | 4.2 | 60.0 |
| S 12 | 0 24.4 | N 6 20.3 | 232 41.3 | 3.1 | S26 25.7 | 4.4 | 60.0 |
| D 13 | 15 24.6 | 19.3 | 247 03.4 | 3.2 | 26 21.3 | 4.6 | 60.0 |
| A 14 | 30 24.8 | 18.4 | 261 25.6 | 3.2 | 26 16.7 | 4.8 | 60.0 |
| Y 15 | 45 25.0 | . . 17.5 | 275 47.8 | 3.3 | 26 11.9 | 4.9 | 60.0 |
| 16 | 60 25.3 | 16.5 | 290 10.1 | 3.3 | 26 07.0 | 5.2 | 60.0 |
| 17 | 75 25.5 | 15.6 | 304 32.4 | 3.4 | 26 01.8 | 5.3 | 60.0 |
| 18 | 90 25.7 | N 6 14.7 | 318 54.8 | 3.4 | S25 56.5 | 5.5 | 60.1 |
| 19 | 105 25.9 | 13.7 | 333 17.2 | 3.5 | 25 51.0 | 5.7 | 60.1 |
| 20 | 120 26.1 | 12.8 | 347 39.7 | 3.5 | 25 45.3 | 5.9 | 60.1 |
| 21 | 135 26.3 | . . 11.9 | 2 02.2 | 3.5 | 25 39.4 | 6.1 | 60.1 |
| 22 | 150 26.5 | 10.9 | 16 24.7 | 3.7 | 25 33.3 | 6.2 | 60.1 |
| 23 | 165 26.8 | 10.0 | 30 47.4 | 3.6 | S25 27.1 | 6.4 | 60.1 |
| | SD 15.9 | d 0.9 | SD 16.1 | | 16.3 | | 16.3 |

### Twilight / Moonrise

| Lat. | Naut. | Civil | Sunrise | Moonrise 4 | 5 | 6 | 7 |
|---|---|---|---|---|---|---|---|
| ° | h m | h m | h m | h m | h m | h m | h m |
| N 72 | //// | 02 58 | 04 21 | ■■■■ | ■■■■ | ■■■■ | ■■■■ |
| N 70 | 01 16 | 03 20 | 04 32 | ■■■■ | ■■■■ | ■■■■ | ■■■■ |
| 68 | 02 03 | 03 38 | 04 40 | ■■■■ | ■■■■ | ■■■■ | ■■■■ |
| 66 | 02 32 | 03 51 | 04 48 | ■■■■ | ■■■■ | ■■■■ | 20 29 |
| 64 | 02 53 | 04 03 | 04 54 | ■■■■ | ■■■■ | 20 26 | 19 46 |
| 62 | 03 10 | 04 12 | 04 59 | 17 27 | 18 52 | 19 13 | 19 17 |
| 60 | 03 24 | 04 20 | 05 04 | 16 42 | 17 58 | 18 37 | 18 54 |
| N 58 | 03 35 | 04 27 | 05 08 | 16 12 | 17 26 | 18 11 | 18 36 |
| 56 | 03 45 | 04 33 | 05 12 | 15 50 | 17 02 | 17 51 | 18 21 |
| 54 | 03 53 | 04 38 | 05 15 | 15 32 | 16 42 | 17 33 | 18 07 |
| 52 | 04 01 | 04 43 | 05 18 | 15 16 | 16 26 | 17 19 | 17 56 |
| 50 | 04 07 | 04 47 | 05 21 | 15 02 | 16 12 | 17 06 | 17 45 |
| 45 | 04 21 | 04 57 | 05 27 | 14 35 | 15 43 | 16 39 | 17 24 |
| N 40 | 04 31 | 05 04 | 05 31 | 14 13 | 15 20 | 16 18 | 17 06 |
| 35 | 04 39 | 05 10 | 05 36 | 13 55 | 15 01 | 16 01 | 16 51 |
| 30 | 04 46 | 05 15 | 05 39 | 13 40 | 14 45 | 15 45 | 16 38 |
| 20 | 04 57 | 05 23 | 05 45 | 13 14 | 14 18 | 15 20 | 16 16 |
| N 10 | 05 05 | 05 29 | 05 51 | 12 51 | 13 55 | 14 57 | 15 56 |
| 0 | 05 10 | 05 35 | 05 55 | 12 31 | 13 33 | 14 37 | 15 38 |
| S 10 | 05 15 | 05 39 | 06 00 | 12 10 | 13 11 | 14 16 | 15 20 |
| 20 | 05 17 | 05 43 | 06 05 | 11 48 | 12 48 | 13 53 | 15 01 |
| 30 | 05 19 | 05 47 | 06 11 | 11 22 | 12 21 | 13 27 | 14 38 |
| 35 | 05 19 | 05 48 | 06 14 | 11 07 | 12 05 | 13 12 | 14 25 |
| 40 | 05 19 | 05 50 | 06 17 | 10 50 | 11 47 | 12 54 | 14 09 |
| 45 | 05 19 | 05 52 | 06 21 | 10 29 | 11 24 | 12 33 | 13 51 |
| S 50 | 05 17 | 05 54 | 06 26 | 10 03 | 10 56 | 12 06 | 13 28 |
| 52 | 05 16 | 05 55 | 06 28 | 09 50 | 10 42 | 11 52 | 13 17 |
| 54 | 05 15 | 05 55 | 06 31 | 09 36 | 10 26 | 11 37 | 13 04 |
| 56 | 05 13 | 05 56 | 06 33 | 09 19 | 10 07 | 11 19 | 12 50 |
| 58 | 05 12 | 05 57 | 06 36 | 08 59 | 09 44 | 10 57 | 12 33 |
| S 60 | 05 10 | 05 58 | 06 40 | 08 34 | 09 13 | 10 29 | 12 12 |

### Sunset / Twilight / Moonset

| Lat. | Sunset | Civil | Naut. | Moonset 4 | 5 | 6 | 7 |
|---|---|---|---|---|---|---|---|
| ° | h m | h m | h m | h m | h m | h m | h m |
| N 72 | 19 34 | 20 55 | //// | ■■■■ | ■■■■ | ■■■■ | ■■■■ |
| N 70 | 19 23 | 20 33 | 22 31 | ■■■■ | ■■■■ | ■■■■ | ■■■■ |
| 68 | 19 15 | 20 17 | 21 49 | ■■■■ | ■■■■ | ■■■■ | ■■■■ |
| 66 | 19 07 | 20 03 | 21 21 | ■■■■ | ■■■■ | ■■■■ | 23 31 |
| 64 | 19 01 | 19 53 | 21 01 | ■■■■ | ■■■■ | 21 25 | 24 14 |
| 62 | 18 56 | 19 43 | 20 45 | 19 59 | 20 46 | 22 37 | 24 42 |
| 60 | 18 52 | 19 36 | 20 31 | 20 44 | 21 40 | 23 13 | 25 03 |
| N 58 | 18 48 | 19 29 | 20 20 | 21 14 | 22 12 | 23 39 | 25 21 |
| 56 | 18 44 | 19 23 | 20 11 | 21 36 | 22 36 | 23 59 | 25 36 |
| 54 | 18 41 | 19 18 | 20 03 | 21 55 | 22 55 | 24 16 | 00 16 |
| 52 | 18 38 | 19 13 | 19 55 | 22 11 | 23 12 | 24 30 | 00 30 |
| 50 | 18 36 | 19 09 | 19 49 | 22 25 | 23 26 | 24 43 | 00 43 |
| 45 | 18 30 | 19 00 | 19 36 | 22 53 | 23 55 | 25 09 | 01 09 |
| N 40 | 18 25 | 18 53 | 19 26 | 23 15 | 24 17 | 00 17 | 01 29 |
| 35 | 18 21 | 18 47 | 19 17 | 23 33 | 24 36 | 00 36 | 01 46 |
| 30 | 18 18 | 18 42 | 19 10 | 23 49 | 24 52 | 00 52 | 02 01 |
| 20 | 18 12 | 18 34 | 19 00 | 24 16 | 00 16 | 01 19 | 02 25 |
| N 10 | 18 07 | 18 28 | 18 53 | 24 39 | 00 39 | 01 42 | 02 47 |
| 0 | 18 02 | 18 23 | 18 47 | 25 00 | 01 00 | 02 03 | 03 06 |
| S 10 | 17 57 | 18 18 | 18 43 | 00 19 | 01 22 | 02 25 | 03 26 |
| 20 | 17 53 | 18 15 | 18 40 | 00 40 | 01 45 | 02 48 | 03 47 |
| 30 | 17 47 | 18 11 | 18 39 | 01 04 | 02 11 | 03 14 | 04 11 |
| 35 | 17 44 | 18 09 | 18 39 | 01 19 | 02 27 | 03 30 | 04 25 |
| 40 | 17 41 | 18 08 | 18 39 | 01 36 | 02 46 | 03 48 | 04 41 |
| 45 | 17 37 | 18 06 | 18 40 | 01 56 | 03 08 | 04 10 | 05 00 |
| S 50 | 17 32 | 18 04 | 18 42 | 02 21 | 03 36 | 04 38 | 05 24 |
| 52 | 17 30 | 18 04 | 18 43 | 02 33 | 03 50 | 04 51 | 05 36 |
| 54 | 17 28 | 18 03 | 18 44 | 02 47 | 04 06 | 05 07 | 05 49 |
| 56 | 17 25 | 18 02 | 18 45 | 03 04 | 04 25 | 05 25 | 06 04 |
| 58 | 17 22 | 18 02 | 18 47 | 03 23 | 04 48 | 05 47 | 06 21 |
| S 60 | 17 19 | 18 01 | 18 49 | 03 48 | 05 18 | 06 16 | 06 43 |

### SUN / MOON

| Day | Eqn. of Time 00ʰ | Eqn. of Time 12ʰ | Mer. Pass. | Mer. Pass. Upper | Mer. Pass. Lower | Age | Phase |
|---|---|---|---|---|---|---|---|
| d | m s | m s | h m | h m | h m | d | % |
| 4 | 00 47 | 00 57 | 11 59 | 18 45 | 06 15 | 08 | 59 |
| 5 | 01 07 | 01 17 | 11 59 | 19 48 | 07 16 | 09 | 70 |
| 6 | 01 27 | 01 37 | 11 58 | 20 51 | 08 20 | 10 | 80 |

## 2022 SEPTEMBER 7, 8, 9 (WED., THURS., FRI.)

| UT | ARIES GHA | VENUS −3.9 GHA | Dec | MARS −0.3 GHA | Dec | JUPITER −2.9 GHA | Dec | SATURN +0.3 GHA | Dec | STARS Name | SHA | Dec |
|---|---|---|---|---|---|---|---|---|---|---|---|---|
| d h | ° ′ | ° ′ | ° ′ | ° ′ | ° ′ | ° ′ | ° ′ | ° ′ | ° ′ | | ° ′ | ° ′ |
| 7 00 | 346 03.2 | 191 21.2 | N11 49.6 | 277 49.7 | N20 42.8 | 339 42.7 | N 1 00.5 | 22 58.9 | S15 59.6 | Acamar | 315 13.0 | S40 12.6 |
| 01 | 1 05.7 | 206 20.7 | 48.5 | 292 50.8 | 43.0 | 354 45.4 | 00.4 | 38 01.5 | 59.6 | Achernar | 335 21.2 | S57 07.1 |
| 02 | 16 08.1 | 221 20.2 | 47.4 | 307 51.9 | 43.3 | 9 48.1 | 00.3 | 53 04.1 | 59.7 | Acrux | 173 02.9 | S63 13.5 |
| 03 | 31 10.6 | 236 19.7 | .. 46.4 | 322 53.1 | .. 43.5 | 24 50.8 | .. 00.1 | 68 06.7 | .. 59.7 | Adhara | 255 07.6 | S28 59.9 |
| 04 | 46 13.1 | 251 19.2 | 45.3 | 337 54.2 | 43.7 | 39 53.6 | 1 00.0 | 83 09.4 | 59.8 | Aldebaran | 290 41.8 | N16 33.3 |
| 05 | 61 15.5 | 266 18.7 | 44.2 | 352 55.3 | 44.0 | 54 56.3 | 0 59.9 | 98 12.0 | 59.8 | | | |
| 06 | 76 18.0 | 281 18.2 | N11 43.2 | 7 56.5 | N20 44.2 | 69 59.0 | N 0 59.8 | 113 14.6 | S15 59.9 | Alioth | 166 15.2 | N55 50.5 |
| W 07 | 91 20.4 | 296 17.7 | 42.1 | 22 57.6 | 44.4 | 85 01.7 | 59.7 | 128 17.2 | 15 59.9 | Alkaid | 152 53.9 | N49 12.3 |
| E 08 | 106 22.9 | 311 17.2 | 41.0 | 37 58.7 | 44.7 | 100 04.5 | 59.5 | 143 19.8 | 16 00.0 | Alnair | 27 34.9 | S46 51.1 |
| D 09 | 121 25.4 | 326 16.7 | .. 40.0 | 52 59.9 | .. 44.9 | 115 07.2 | .. 59.4 | 158 22.5 | .. 00.0 | Alnilam | 275 39.7 | S 1 11.1 |
| N 10 | 136 27.8 | 341 16.2 | 38.9 | 68 01.0 | 45.1 | 130 09.9 | 59.3 | 173 25.1 | 00.1 | Alphard | 217 49.9 | S 8 45.2 |
| E 11 | 151 30.3 | 356 15.7 | 37.8 | 83 02.2 | 45.4 | 145 12.6 | 59.2 | 188 27.7 | 00.1 | | | |
| S 12 | 166 32.8 | 11 15.2 | N11 36.8 | 98 03.3 | N20 45.6 | 160 15.4 | N 0 59.1 | 203 30.3 | S16 00.2 | Alphecca | 126 05.5 | N26 38.6 |
| D 13 | 181 35.2 | 26 14.7 | 35.7 | 113 04.4 | 45.8 | 175 18.1 | 58.9 | 218 33.0 | 00.2 | Alpheratz | 357 36.4 | N29 12.9 |
| A 14 | 196 37.7 | 41 14.3 | 34.6 | 128 05.6 | 46.1 | 190 20.8 | 58.8 | 233 35.6 | 00.3 | Altair | 62 01.6 | N 8 55.8 |
| Y 15 | 211 40.2 | 56 13.8 | .. 33.5 | 143 06.7 | .. 46.3 | 205 23.5 | .. 58.7 | 248 38.2 | .. 00.3 | Ankaa | 353 08.7 | S42 10.9 |
| 16 | 226 42.6 | 71 13.3 | 32.5 | 158 07.8 | 46.5 | 220 26.3 | 58.6 | 263 40.8 | 00.4 | Antares | 112 18.2 | S26 28.9 |
| 17 | 241 45.1 | 86 12.8 | 31.4 | 173 09.0 | 46.7 | 235 29.0 | 58.5 | 278 43.4 | 00.5 | | | |
| 18 | 256 47.6 | 101 12.3 | N11 30.3 | 188 10.1 | N20 47.0 | 250 31.7 | N 0 58.3 | 293 46.1 | S16 00.5 | Arcturus | 145 49.9 | N19 04.1 |
| 19 | 271 50.0 | 116 11.8 | 29.2 | 203 11.3 | 47.2 | 265 34.5 | 58.2 | 308 48.7 | 00.6 | Atria | 107 14.2 | S69 04.3 |
| 20 | 286 52.5 | 131 11.3 | 28.2 | 218 12.4 | 47.4 | 280 37.2 | 58.1 | 323 51.3 | 00.6 | Avior | 234 16.0 | S59 34.6 |
| 21 | 301 54.9 | 146 10.8 | .. 27.1 | 233 13.6 | .. 47.7 | 295 39.9 | .. 58.0 | 338 53.9 | .. 00.7 | Bellatrix | 278 25.0 | N 6 22.3 |
| 22 | 316 57.4 | 161 10.3 | 26.0 | 248 14.7 | 47.9 | 310 42.6 | 57.9 | 353 56.6 | 00.7 | Betelgeuse | 270 54.2 | N 7 24.8 |
| 23 | 331 59.9 | 176 09.8 | 24.9 | 263 15.8 | 48.1 | 325 45.4 | 57.7 | 8 59.2 | 00.8 | | | |
| 8 00 | 347 02.3 | 191 09.3 | N11 23.8 | 278 17.0 | N20 48.3 | 340 48.1 | N 0 57.6 | 24 01.8 | S16 00.8 | Canopus | 263 53.4 | S52 42.1 |
| 01 | 2 04.8 | 206 08.8 | 22.8 | 293 18.1 | 48.6 | 355 50.8 | 57.5 | 39 04.4 | 00.9 | Capella | 280 24.8 | N46 01.1 |
| 02 | 17 07.3 | 221 08.3 | 21.7 | 308 19.3 | 48.8 | 10 53.6 | 57.4 | 54 07.0 | 00.9 | Deneb | 49 26.7 | N45 21.8 |
| 03 | 32 09.7 | 236 07.8 | .. 20.6 | 323 20.4 | .. 49.0 | 25 56.3 | .. 57.2 | 69 09.7 | .. 01.0 | Denebola | 182 27.2 | N14 26.9 |
| 04 | 47 12.2 | 251 07.3 | 19.5 | 338 21.6 | 49.3 | 40 59.0 | 57.1 | 84 12.3 | 01.0 | Diphda | 348 48.9 | S17 51.6 |
| 05 | 62 14.7 | 266 06.8 | 18.4 | 353 22.7 | 49.5 | 56 01.8 | 57.0 | 99 14.9 | 01.1 | | | |
| 06 | 77 17.1 | 281 06.3 | N11 17.4 | 8 23.8 | N20 49.7 | 71 04.5 | N 0 56.9 | 114 17.5 | S16 01.1 | Dubhe | 193 44.0 | N61 37.9 |
| 07 | 92 19.6 | 296 05.8 | 16.3 | 23 25.0 | 49.9 | 86 07.2 | 56.8 | 129 20.1 | 01.2 | Elnath | 278 04.3 | N28 37.5 |
| T 08 | 107 22.1 | 311 05.4 | 15.2 | 38 26.1 | 50.2 | 101 09.9 | 56.6 | 144 22.8 | 01.2 | Eltanin | 90 43.0 | N51 29.4 |
| H 09 | 122 24.5 | 326 04.9 | .. 14.1 | 53 27.3 | .. 50.4 | 116 12.7 | .. 56.5 | 159 25.4 | .. 01.3 | Enif | 33 40.4 | N 9 58.8 |
| U 10 | 137 27.0 | 341 04.4 | 13.0 | 68 28.4 | 50.6 | 131 15.4 | 56.4 | 174 28.0 | 01.3 | Fomalhaut | 15 16.3 | S29 30.1 |
| R 11 | 152 29.4 | 356 03.9 | 12.0 | 83 29.6 | 50.8 | 146 18.1 | 56.3 | 189 30.6 | 01.4 | | | |
| S 12 | 167 31.9 | 11 03.4 | N11 10.9 | 98 30.7 | N20 51.1 | 161 20.9 | N 0 56.2 | 204 33.2 | S16 01.4 | Gacrux | 171 54.3 | S57 14.4 |
| D 13 | 182 34.4 | 26 02.9 | 09.8 | 113 31.9 | 51.3 | 176 23.6 | 56.0 | 219 35.9 | 01.5 | Gienah | 175 45.9 | S17 39.4 |
| A 14 | 197 36.8 | 41 02.4 | 08.7 | 128 33.0 | 51.5 | 191 26.3 | 55.9 | 234 38.5 | 01.5 | Hadar | 148 39.2 | S60 29.0 |
| Y 15 | 212 39.3 | 56 01.9 | .. 07.6 | 143 34.2 | .. 51.7 | 206 29.1 | .. 55.8 | 249 41.1 | .. 01.6 | Hamal | 327 53.1 | N23 34.1 |
| 16 | 227 41.8 | 71 01.4 | 06.5 | 158 35.3 | 52.0 | 221 31.8 | 55.7 | 264 43.7 | 01.6 | Kaus Aust. | 83 34.9 | S34 22.5 |
| 17 | 242 44.2 | 86 01.0 | 05.4 | 173 36.5 | 52.2 | 236 34.5 | 55.5 | 279 46.3 | 01.7 | | | |
| 18 | 257 46.7 | 101 00.5 | N11 04.3 | 188 37.6 | N20 52.4 | 251 37.3 | N 0 55.4 | 294 49.0 | S16 01.7 | Kochab | 137 20.4 | N74 04.0 |
| 19 | 272 49.2 | 116 00.0 | 03.3 | 203 38.8 | 52.6 | 266 40.0 | 55.3 | 309 51.6 | 01.8 | Markab | 13 31.5 | N15 19.7 |
| 20 | 287 51.6 | 130 59.5 | 02.2 | 218 40.0 | 52.9 | 281 42.7 | 55.2 | 324 54.2 | 01.8 | Menkar | 314 08.0 | N 4 10.8 |
| 21 | 302 54.1 | 145 59.0 | .. 01.1 | 233 41.1 | .. 53.1 | 296 45.5 | .. 55.1 | 339 56.8 | .. 01.9 | Menkent | 148 00.2 | S36 28.9 |
| 22 | 317 56.5 | 160 58.5 | 11 00.0 | 248 42.3 | 53.3 | 311 48.2 | 54.9 | 354 59.4 | 01.9 | Miaplacidus | 221 39.5 | S69 48.3 |
| 23 | 332 59.0 | 175 58.0 | 10 58.9 | 263 43.4 | 53.5 | 326 50.9 | 54.8 | 10 02.1 | 02.0 | | | |
| 9 00 | 348 01.5 | 190 57.5 | N10 57.8 | 278 44.6 | N20 53.7 | 341 53.7 | N 0 54.7 | 25 04.7 | S16 02.0 | Mirfak | 308 30.8 | N49 56.3 |
| 01 | 3 03.9 | 205 57.1 | 56.7 | 293 45.7 | 54.0 | 356 56.4 | 54.6 | 40 07.3 | 02.1 | Nunki | 75 50.0 | S26 16.1 |
| 02 | 18 06.4 | 220 56.6 | 55.6 | 308 46.9 | 54.2 | 11 59.1 | 54.4 | 55 09.9 | 02.1 | Peacock | 53 08.3 | S56 39.8 |
| 03 | 33 08.9 | 235 56.1 | .. 54.5 | 323 48.0 | .. 54.4 | 27 01.9 | .. 54.3 | 70 12.5 | .. 02.2 | Pollux | 243 19.9 | N27 58.3 |
| 04 | 48 11.3 | 250 55.6 | 53.4 | 338 49.2 | 54.6 | 42 04.6 | 54.2 | 85 15.2 | 02.2 | Procyon | 244 53.1 | N 5 10.2 |
| 05 | 63 13.8 | 265 55.1 | 52.3 | 353 50.4 | 54.9 | 57 07.3 | 54.1 | 100 17.8 | 02.3 | | | |
| 06 | 78 16.3 | 280 54.6 | N10 51.2 | 8 51.5 | N20 55.1 | 72 10.1 | N 0 53.9 | 115 20.4 | S16 02.3 | Rasalhague | 96 00.3 | N12 32.8 |
| 07 | 93 18.7 | 295 54.2 | 50.1 | 23 52.7 | 55.3 | 87 12.8 | 53.8 | 130 23.0 | 02.4 | Regulus | 207 36.8 | N11 51.6 |
| 08 | 108 21.2 | 310 53.7 | 49.1 | 38 53.8 | 55.5 | 102 15.5 | 53.7 | 145 25.6 | 02.4 | Rigel | 281 05.7 | S 8 10.4 |
| F 09 | 123 23.7 | 325 53.2 | .. 48.0 | 53 55.0 | .. 55.7 | 117 18.3 | .. 53.6 | 160 28.3 | .. 02.5 | Rigil Kent. | 139 43.3 | S60 55.8 |
| R 10 | 138 26.1 | 340 52.7 | 46.9 | 68 56.2 | 56.0 | 132 21.0 | 53.5 | 175 30.9 | 02.5 | Sabik | 102 05.0 | S15 45.1 |
| I 11 | 153 28.6 | 355 52.2 | 45.8 | 83 57.3 | 56.2 | 147 23.7 | 53.3 | 190 33.5 | 02.6 | | | |
| D 12 | 168 31.0 | 10 51.7 | N10 44.7 | 98 58.5 | N20 56.4 | 162 26.5 | N 0 53.2 | 205 36.1 | S16 02.6 | Schedar | 349 32.7 | N56 39.6 |
| A 13 | 183 33.5 | 25 51.3 | 43.6 | 113 59.6 | 56.6 | 177 29.2 | 53.1 | 220 38.7 | 02.7 | Shaula | 96 12.9 | S37 07.3 |
| Y 14 | 198 36.0 | 40 50.8 | 42.5 | 129 00.8 | 56.8 | 192 32.0 | 53.0 | 235 41.3 | 02.7 | Sirius | 258 28.1 | S16 44.6 |
| 15 | 213 38.4 | 55 50.3 | .. 41.4 | 144 02.0 | .. 57.1 | 207 34.7 | .. 52.8 | 250 44.0 | .. 02.8 | Spica | 158 24.6 | S11 16.6 |
| 16 | 228 40.9 | 70 49.8 | 40.3 | 159 03.1 | 57.3 | 222 37.4 | 52.7 | 265 46.6 | 02.8 | Suhail | 222 48.1 | S43 31.2 |
| 17 | 243 43.4 | 85 49.3 | 39.2 | 174 04.3 | 57.5 | 237 40.2 | 52.6 | 280 49.2 | 02.9 | | | |
| 18 | 258 45.8 | 100 48.9 | N10 38.1 | 189 05.5 | N20 57.7 | 252 42.9 | N 0 52.5 | 295 51.8 | S16 02.9 | Vega | 80 34.4 | N38 48.5 |
| 19 | 273 48.3 | 115 48.4 | 37.0 | 204 06.6 | 57.9 | 267 45.6 | 52.3 | 310 54.4 | 03.0 | Zuben'ubi | 136 58.3 | S16 08.1 |
| 20 | 288 50.8 | 130 47.9 | 35.9 | 219 07.8 | 58.2 | 282 48.4 | 52.2 | 325 57.0 | 03.0 | | SHA | Mer. Pass. |
| 21 | 303 53.2 | 145 47.4 | .. 34.8 | 234 09.0 | .. 58.4 | 297 51.1 | .. 52.1 | 340 59.7 | .. 03.1 | | ° ′ | h m |
| 22 | 318 55.7 | 160 46.9 | 33.7 | 249 10.1 | 58.6 | 312 53.8 | 52.0 | 356 02.3 | 03.1 | Venus | 204 07.0 | 11 16 |
| 23 | 333 58.1 | 175 46.5 | 32.6 | 264 11.3 | 58.8 | 327 56.6 | 51.9 | 11 04.9 | 03.2 | Mars | 291 14.6 | 5 26 |
| | h m | | | | | | | | | Jupiter | 353 45.8 | 1 17 |
| Mer. Pass. 0 51.7 | | v −0.5 | d 1.1 | v 1.1 | d 0.2 | v 2.7 | d 0.1 | v 2.6 | d 0.1 | Saturn | 36 59.5 | 22 20 |

| UT | SUN GHA | SUN Dec | MOON GHA | v | MOON Dec | d | HP |
|---|---|---|---|---|---|---|---|
| d h | ° ′ | ° ′ | ° ′ | ′ | ° ′ | ′ | ′ |
| **7** 00 | 180 27.0 | N 6 09.1 | 45 10.0 | 3.8 | S25 20.7 | 6.7 | 60.1 |
| 01 | 195 27.2 | 08.1 | 59 32.8 | 3.8 | 25 14.0 | 6.7 | 60.1 |
| 02 | 210 27.4 | 07.2 | 73 55.6 | 3.9 | 25 07.3 | 7.0 | 60.1 |
| 03 | 225 27.6 | .. 06.3 | 88 18.5 | 3.9 | 25 00.3 | 7.2 | 60.1 |
| 04 | 240 27.8 | 05.3 | 102 41.4 | 4.0 | 24 53.1 | 7.3 | 60.1 |
| 05 | 255 28.0 | 04.4 | 117 04.4 | 4.1 | 24 45.8 | 7.5 | 60.1 |
| 06 | 270 28.3 | N 6 03.5 | 131 27.5 | 4.1 | S24 38.3 | 7.6 | 60.1 |
| W 07 | 285 28.5 | 02.5 | 145 50.6 | 4.2 | 24 30.7 | 7.9 | 60.1 |
| E 08 | 300 28.7 | 01.6 | 160 13.8 | 4.3 | 24 22.8 | 8.0 | 60.1 |
| D 09 | 315 28.9 | 6 00.7 | 174 37.1 | 4.4 | 24 14.8 | 8.1 | 60.1 |
| N 10 | 330 29.1 | 5 59.7 | 189 00.5 | 4.4 | 24 06.7 | 8.4 | 60.1 |
| E 11 | 345 29.3 | 58.8 | 203 23.9 | 4.5 | 23 58.3 | 8.5 | 60.1 |
| S 12 | 0 29.5 | N 5 57.8 | 217 47.4 | 4.6 | S23 49.8 | 8.7 | 60.2 |
| D 13 | 15 29.8 | 56.9 | 232 11.0 | 4.7 | 23 41.1 | 8.8 | 60.2 |
| A 14 | 30 30.0 | 56.0 | 246 34.7 | 4.8 | 23 32.3 | 9.0 | 60.2 |
| Y 15 | 45 30.2 | .. 55.0 | 260 58.5 | 4.9 | 23 23.3 | 9.2 | 60.2 |
| 16 | 60 30.4 | 54.1 | 275 22.4 | 4.9 | 23 14.1 | 9.3 | 60.2 |
| 17 | 75 30.6 | 53.2 | 289 46.3 | 5.0 | 23 04.8 | 9.4 | 60.2 |
| 18 | 90 30.8 | N 5 52.2 | 304 10.3 | 5.1 | S22 55.4 | 9.7 | 60.2 |
| 19 | 105 31.0 | 51.3 | 318 34.4 | 5.2 | 22 45.7 | 9.7 | 60.2 |
| 20 | 120 31.3 | 50.4 | 332 58.6 | 5.3 | 22 36.0 | 10.0 | 60.2 |
| 21 | 135 31.5 | .. 49.4 | 347 22.9 | 5.4 | 22 26.0 | 10.0 | 60.2 |
| 22 | 150 31.7 | 48.5 | 1 47.3 | 5.5 | 22 16.0 | 10.3 | 60.2 |
| 23 | 165 31.9 | 47.5 | 16 11.8 | 5.5 | 22 05.7 | 10.3 | 60.2 |
| **8** 00 | 180 32.1 | N 5 46.6 | 30 36.3 | 5.7 | S21 55.4 | 10.6 | 60.2 |
| 01 | 195 32.3 | 45.7 | 45 01.0 | 5.7 | 21 44.8 | 10.6 | 60.2 |
| 02 | 210 32.6 | 44.7 | 59 25.7 | 5.9 | 21 34.2 | 10.8 | 60.1 |
| 03 | 225 32.8 | .. 43.8 | 73 50.6 | 5.9 | 21 23.4 | 11.0 | 60.1 |
| 04 | 240 33.0 | 42.8 | 88 15.5 | 6.1 | 21 12.4 | 11.1 | 60.1 |
| 05 | 255 33.2 | 41.9 | 102 40.6 | 6.1 | 21 01.3 | 11.2 | 60.1 |
| 06 | 270 33.4 | N 5 41.0 | 117 05.7 | 6.2 | S20 50.1 | 11.3 | 60.1 |
| T 07 | 285 33.6 | 40.0 | 131 30.9 | 6.3 | 20 38.8 | 11.5 | 60.1 |
| H 08 | 300 33.9 | 39.1 | 145 56.2 | 6.5 | 20 27.3 | 11.6 | 60.1 |
| U 09 | 315 34.1 | .. 38.1 | 160 21.7 | 6.5 | 20 15.7 | 11.7 | 60.1 |
| R 10 | 330 34.3 | 37.2 | 174 47.2 | 6.6 | 20 04.0 | 11.9 | 60.1 |
| S 11 | 345 34.5 | 36.3 | 189 12.8 | 6.7 | 19 52.1 | 12.0 | 60.1 |
| D 12 | 0 34.7 | N 5 35.3 | 203 38.5 | 6.8 | S19 40.1 | 12.1 | 60.1 |
| A 13 | 15 34.9 | 34.4 | 218 04.3 | 6.9 | 19 28.0 | 12.2 | 60.1 |
| Y 14 | 30 35.2 | 33.4 | 232 30.2 | 7.0 | 19 15.8 | 12.4 | 60.1 |
| 15 | 45 35.4 | .. 32.5 | 246 56.2 | 7.1 | 19 03.4 | 12.5 | 60.1 |
| 16 | 60 35.6 | 31.5 | 261 22.3 | 7.2 | 18 50.9 | 12.6 | 60.1 |
| 17 | 75 35.8 | 30.6 | 275 48.5 | 7.3 | 18 38.4 | 12.7 | 60.1 |
| 18 | 90 36.0 | N 5 29.7 | 290 14.8 | 7.5 | S18 25.7 | 12.8 | 60.1 |
| 19 | 105 36.2 | 28.7 | 304 41.3 | 7.5 | 18 12.9 | 13.0 | 60.0 |
| 20 | 120 36.5 | 27.8 | 319 07.8 | 7.7 | 17 59.9 | 13.0 | 60.0 |
| 21 | 135 36.7 | .. 26.9 | 333 34.3 | 7.7 | 17 46.9 | 13.1 | 60.0 |
| 22 | 150 36.9 | 25.9 | 348 01.0 | 7.8 | 17 33.8 | 13.2 | 60.0 |
| 23 | 165 37.1 | 25.0 | 2 27.8 | 7.9 | 17 20.6 | 13.4 | 60.0 |
| **9** 00 | 180 37.3 | N 5 24.0 | 16 54.7 | 8.0 | S17 07.2 | 13.4 | 60.0 |
| 01 | 195 37.5 | 23.1 | 31 21.7 | 8.1 | 16 53.8 | 13.5 | 60.0 |
| 02 | 210 37.8 | 22.2 | 45 48.8 | 8.2 | 16 40.3 | 13.7 | 60.0 |
| 03 | 225 38.0 | .. 21.2 | 60 16.0 | 8.3 | 16 26.6 | 13.7 | 60.0 |
| 04 | 240 38.2 | 20.3 | 74 43.3 | 8.3 | 16 12.9 | 13.8 | 59.9 |
| 05 | 255 38.4 | 19.3 | 89 10.6 | 8.5 | 15 59.1 | 13.9 | 59.9 |
| 06 | 270 38.6 | N 5 18.4 | 103 38.1 | 8.6 | S15 45.2 | 14.0 | 59.9 |
| F 07 | 285 38.8 | 17.4 | 118 05.7 | 8.6 | 15 31.2 | 14.0 | 59.9 |
| R 08 | 300 39.1 | 16.5 | 132 33.3 | 8.8 | 15 17.2 | 14.2 | 59.9 |
| I 09 | 315 39.3 | .. 15.6 | 147 01.1 | 8.8 | 15 03.0 | 14.2 | 59.9 |
| D 10 | 330 39.5 | 14.6 | 161 28.9 | 8.9 | 14 48.8 | 14.3 | 59.9 |
| A 11 | 345 39.7 | 13.7 | 175 56.8 | 9.1 | 14 34.5 | 14.4 | 59.8 |
| Y 12 | 0 39.9 | N 5 12.7 | 190 24.9 | 9.1 | S14 20.1 | 14.5 | 59.8 |
| 13 | 15 40.2 | 11.8 | 204 53.0 | 9.2 | 14 05.6 | 14.6 | 59.8 |
| 14 | 30 40.4 | 10.8 | 219 21.2 | 9.3 | 13 51.0 | 14.6 | 59.8 |
| 15 | 45 40.6 | .. 09.9 | 233 49.5 | 9.4 | 13 36.4 | 14.7 | 59.8 |
| 16 | 60 40.8 | 08.9 | 248 17.9 | 9.5 | 13 21.7 | 14.7 | 59.8 |
| 17 | 75 41.0 | 08.0 | 262 46.4 | 9.5 | 13 07.0 | 14.8 | 59.7 |
| 18 | 90 41.3 | N 5 07.1 | 277 14.9 | 9.7 | S12 52.2 | 14.9 | 59.7 |
| 19 | 105 41.5 | 06.1 | 291 43.6 | 9.7 | 12 37.3 | 15.0 | 59.7 |
| 20 | 120 41.7 | 05.2 | 306 12.3 | 9.8 | 12 22.3 | 15.0 | 59.7 |
| 21 | 135 41.9 | .. 04.2 | 320 41.1 | 9.9 | 12 07.3 | 15.0 | 59.7 |
| 22 | 150 42.1 | 03.3 | 335 10.0 | 10.0 | 11 52.3 | 15.1 | 59.7 |
| 23 | 165 42.3 | 02.3 | 349 39.0 | 10.1 | S11 37.2 | 15.2 | 59.6 |
| | SD 15.9 | d 0.9 | SD 16.4 | | 16.4 | | 16.3 |

### Twilight / Sunrise / Moonrise

| Lat. | Naut. | Civil | Sunrise | 7 | 8 | 9 | 10 |
|---|---|---|---|---|---|---|---|
| ° | h m | h m | h m | h m | h m | h m | h m |
| N 72 | 00 35 | 03 16 | 04 35 | ▬▬ | 22 05 | 20 27 | 19 44 |
| N 70 | 01 48 | 03 35 | 04 44 | ▬▬ | 20 57 | 20 06 | 19 35 |
| 68 | 02 23 | 03 50 | 04 51 | ▬▬ | 20 20 | 19 49 | 19 28 |
| 66 | 02 47 | 04 02 | 04 57 | 20 29 | 19 54 | 19 35 | 19 22 |
| 64 | 03 06 | 04 12 | 05 03 | 19 46 | 19 33 | 19 24 | 19 16 |
| 62 | 03 21 | 04 21 | 05 07 | 19 17 | 19 16 | 19 14 | 19 12 |
| 60 | 03 33 | 04 28 | 05 11 | 18 54 | 19 02 | 19 06 | 19 08 |
| N 58 | 03 43 | 04 34 | 05 15 | 18 36 | 18 50 | 18 58 | 19 04 |
| 56 | 03 52 | 04 39 | 05 18 | 18 21 | 18 39 | 18 52 | 19 01 |
| 54 | 04 00 | 04 44 | 05 20 | 18 07 | 18 30 | 18 46 | 18 58 |
| 52 | 04 06 | 04 48 | 05 23 | 17 56 | 18 22 | 18 41 | 18 56 |
| 50 | 04 12 | 04 52 | 05 25 | 17 45 | 18 14 | 18 36 | 18 53 |
| 45 | 04 25 | 05 00 | 05 30 | 17 24 | 17 58 | 18 25 | 18 48 |
| N 40 | 04 34 | 05 07 | 05 34 | 17 06 | 17 45 | 18 16 | 18 44 |
| 35 | 04 42 | 05 12 | 05 38 | 16 51 | 17 33 | 18 09 | 18 40 |
| 30 | 04 48 | 05 17 | 05 41 | 16 38 | 17 23 | 18 02 | 18 37 |
| 20 | 04 58 | 05 24 | 05 46 | 16 16 | 17 06 | 17 51 | 18 31 |
| N 10 | 05 05 | 05 29 | 05 50 | 15 56 | 16 51 | 17 40 | 18 26 |
| 0 | 05 10 | 05 34 | 05 54 | 15 38 | 16 37 | 17 31 | 18 21 |
| S 10 | 05 13 | 05 37 | 05 58 | 15 20 | 16 22 | 17 21 | 18 16 |
| 20 | 05 15 | 05 40 | 06 03 | 15 01 | 16 07 | 17 11 | 18 11 |
| 30 | 05 15 | 05 43 | 06 07 | 14 38 | 15 49 | 16 59 | 18 05 |
| 35 | 05 15 | 05 44 | 06 10 | 14 25 | 15 39 | 16 52 | 18 02 |
| 40 | 05 14 | 05 45 | 06 13 | 14 09 | 15 27 | 16 44 | 17 58 |
| 45 | 05 13 | 05 47 | 06 16 | 13 51 | 15 13 | 16 35 | 17 53 |
| S 50 | 05 10 | 05 48 | 06 20 | 13 28 | 14 56 | 16 23 | 17 48 |
| 52 | 05 09 | 05 48 | 06 22 | 13 17 | 14 48 | 16 18 | 17 45 |
| 54 | 05 07 | 05 48 | 06 23 | 13 04 | 14 39 | 16 12 | 17 43 |
| 56 | 05 06 | 05 49 | 06 26 | 12 50 | 14 28 | 16 06 | 17 40 |
| 58 | 05 04 | 05 49 | 06 28 | 12 33 | 14 17 | 15 59 | 17 36 |
| S 60 | 05 01 | 05 49 | 06 31 | 12 12 | 14 03 | 15 50 | 17 32 |

### Sunset / Twilight / Moonset

| Lat. | Sunset | Civil | Naut. | 7 | 8 | 9 | 10 |
|---|---|---|---|---|---|---|---|
| ° | h m | h m | h m | h m | h m | h m | h m |
| N 72 | 19 18 | 20 35 | 22 59 | ▬▬ | 23 59 | 27 29 | 03 29 |
| N 70 | 19 09 | 20 16 | 22 00 | ▬▬ | ▬▬ | 01 05 | 03 48 |
| 68 | 19 02 | 20 02 | 21 28 | ▬▬ | ▬▬ | 01 41 | 04 03 |
| 66 | 18 56 | 19 51 | 21 04 | 23 31 | 26 06 | 02 06 | 04 14 |
| 64 | 18 51 | 19 41 | 20 46 | 24 14 | 00 14 | 02 25 | 04 24 |
| 62 | 18 46 | 19 33 | 20 32 | 24 42 | 00 42 | 02 41 | 04 32 |
| 60 | 18 43 | 19 26 | 20 20 | 25 03 | 01 03 | 02 54 | 04 39 |
| N 58 | 18 39 | 19 20 | 20 10 | 25 21 | 01 21 | 03 05 | 04 45 |
| 56 | 18 36 | 19 15 | 20 02 | 25 36 | 01 36 | 03 15 | 04 51 |
| 54 | 18 34 | 19 10 | 19 54 | 00 16 | 01 48 | 03 23 | 04 56 |
| 52 | 18 31 | 19 06 | 19 48 | 00 30 | 01 59 | 03 31 | 05 00 |
| 50 | 18 29 | 19 02 | 19 42 | 00 43 | 02 09 | 03 38 | 05 04 |
| 45 | 18 24 | 18 54 | 19 30 | 01 09 | 02 30 | 03 52 | 05 12 |
| N 40 | 18 20 | 18 48 | 19 20 | 01 29 | 02 46 | 04 04 | 05 19 |
| 35 | 18 17 | 18 43 | 19 13 | 01 46 | 03 00 | 04 14 | 05 25 |
| 30 | 18 14 | 18 38 | 19 07 | 02 01 | 03 12 | 04 23 | 05 31 |
| 20 | 18 09 | 18 31 | 18 57 | 02 25 | 03 33 | 04 38 | 05 40 |
| N 10 | 18 05 | 18 26 | 18 51 | 02 47 | 03 50 | 04 51 | 05 48 |
| 0 | 18 01 | 18 22 | 18 46 | 03 06 | 04 07 | 05 03 | 05 55 |
| S 10 | 17 57 | 18 18 | 18 43 | 03 26 | 04 23 | 05 15 | 06 02 |
| 20 | 17 53 | 18 15 | 18 41 | 03 47 | 04 40 | 05 27 | 06 10 |
| 30 | 17 49 | 18 13 | 18 40 | 04 11 | 05 00 | 05 42 | 06 18 |
| 35 | 17 46 | 18 12 | 18 41 | 04 25 | 05 11 | 05 50 | 06 23 |
| 40 | 17 43 | 18 11 | 18 42 | 04 41 | 05 24 | 05 59 | 06 29 |
| 45 | 17 40 | 18 10 | 18 44 | 05 00 | 05 40 | 06 10 | 06 35 |
| S 50 | 17 36 | 18 09 | 18 46 | 05 24 | 05 58 | 06 23 | 06 43 |
| 52 | 17 35 | 18 08 | 18 48 | 05 36 | 06 07 | 06 29 | 06 46 |
| 54 | 17 33 | 18 08 | 18 49 | 05 49 | 06 17 | 06 36 | 06 50 |
| 56 | 17 31 | 18 08 | 18 51 | 06 04 | 06 28 | 06 43 | 06 54 |
| 58 | 17 29 | 18 08 | 18 53 | 06 21 | 06 40 | 06 52 | 06 59 |
| S 60 | 17 26 | 18 08 | 18 56 | 06 43 | 06 55 | 07 01 | 07 04 |

### SUN / MOON

| Day | Eqn. of Time 00h | Eqn. of Time 12h | Mer. Pass. | Mer. Pass. Upper | Mer. Pass. Lower | Age | Phase |
|---|---|---|---|---|---|---|---|
| d | m s | m s | h m | h m | h m | d | % |
| 7 | 01 47 | 01 58 | 11 58 | 21 53 | 09 22 | 11 | 88 |
| 8 | 02 08 | 02 18 | 11 58 | 22 50 | 10 22 | 12 | 95 |
| 9 | 02 29 | 02 39 | 11 57 | 23 43 | 11 17 | 13 | 99 |

| UT | ARIES GHA | VENUS −3.9 GHA | Dec | MARS −0.3 GHA | Dec | JUPITER −2.9 GHA | Dec | SATURN +0.4 GHA | Dec | STARS Name | SHA | Dec |
|---|---|---|---|---|---|---|---|---|---|---|---|---|
| **10 00** | 349 00.6 | 190 46.0 | N10 31.5 | 279 12.5 | N20 59.0 | 342 59.3 | N 0 51.7 | 26 07.5 | S16 03.2 | Acamar | 315 13.0 | S40 12.6 |
| 01 | 4 03.1 | 205 45.5 | 30.3 | 294 13.6 | 59.2 | 358 02.1 | 51.6 | 41 10.1 | 03.3 | Achernar | 335 21.2 | S57 07.1 |
| 02 | 19 05.5 | 220 45.0 | 29.2 | 309 14.8 | 59.5 | 13 04.8 | 51.5 | 56 12.8 | 03.3 | Acrux | 173 02.9 | S63 13.4 |
| 03 | 34 08.0 | 235 44.6 .. | 28.1 | 324 16.0 .. | 59.7 | 28 07.5 .. | 51.4 | 71 15.4 .. | 03.4 | Adhara | 255 07.5 | S28 59.9 |
| 04 | 49 10.5 | 250 44.1 | 27.0 | 339 17.1 | 20 59.9 | 43 10.3 | 51.2 | 86 18.0 | 03.4 | Aldebaran | 290 41.8 | N16 33.3 |
| 05 | 64 12.9 | 265 43.6 | 25.9 | 354 18.3 | 21 00.1 | 58 13.0 | 51.1 | 101 20.6 | 03.5 | | | |
| 06 | 79 15.4 | 280 43.1 | N10 24.8 | 9 19.5 | N21 00.3 | 73 15.7 | N 0 51.0 | 116 23.2 | S16 03.5 | Alioth | 166 15.2 | N55 50.5 |
| 07 | 94 17.9 | 295 42.6 | 23.7 | 24 20.7 | 00.5 | 88 18.5 | 50.9 | 131 25.8 | 03.6 | Alkaid | 152 53.9 | N49 12.3 |
| S 08 | 109 20.3 | 310 42.2 | 22.6 | 39 21.8 | 00.8 | 103 21.2 | 50.7 | 146 28.4 | 03.6 | Alnair | 27 34.9 | S46 51.1 |
| A 09 | 124 22.8 | 325 41.7 .. | 21.5 | 54 23.0 .. | 01.0 | 118 24.0 .. | 50.6 | 161 31.1 .. | 03.7 | Alnilam | 275 39.7 | S 1 11.1 |
| T 10 | 139 25.3 | 340 41.2 | 20.4 | 69 24.2 | 01.2 | 133 26.7 | 50.5 | 176 33.7 | 03.7 | Alphard | 217 49.9 | S 8 45.2 |
| U 11 | 154 27.7 | 355 40.7 | 19.3 | 84 25.4 | 01.4 | 148 29.4 | 50.4 | 191 36.3 | 03.8 | | | |
| R 12 | 169 30.2 | 10 40.3 | N10 18.2 | 99 26.5 | N21 01.6 | 163 32.2 | N 0 50.2 | 206 38.9 | S16 03.8 | Alphecca | 126 05.5 | N26 38.6 |
| D 13 | 184 32.6 | 25 39.8 | 17.1 | 114 27.7 | 01.8 | 178 34.9 | 50.1 | 221 41.5 | 03.9 | Alpheratz | 357 36.4 | N29 12.9 |
| A 14 | 199 35.1 | 40 39.3 | 15.9 | 129 28.9 | 02.1 | 193 37.7 | 50.0 | 236 44.1 | 03.9 | Altair | 62 01.6 | N 8 55.8 |
| Y 15 | 214 37.6 | 55 38.9 .. | 14.8 | 144 30.1 .. | 02.3 | 208 40.4 .. | 49.9 | 251 46.8 .. | 04.0 | Ankaa | 353 08.6 | S42 10.9 |
| 16 | 229 40.0 | 70 38.4 | 13.7 | 159 31.2 | 02.5 | 223 43.1 | 49.7 | 266 49.4 | 04.0 | Antares | 112 18.3 | S26 28.9 |
| 17 | 244 42.5 | 85 37.9 | 12.6 | 174 32.4 | 02.7 | 238 45.9 | 49.6 | 281 52.0 | 04.1 | | | |
| 18 | 259 45.0 | 100 37.4 | N10 11.5 | 189 33.6 | N21 02.9 | 253 48.6 | N 0 49.5 | 296 54.6 | S16 04.1 | Arcturus | 145 49.9 | N19 04.1 |
| 19 | 274 47.4 | 115 37.0 | 10.4 | 204 34.8 | 03.1 | 268 51.4 | 49.4 | 311 57.2 | 04.2 | Atria | 107 14.2 | S69 04.3 |
| 20 | 289 49.9 | 130 36.5 | 09.3 | 219 36.0 | 03.3 | 283 54.1 | 49.2 | 326 59.8 | 04.2 | Avior | 234 16.0 | S59 34.6 |
| 21 | 304 52.4 | 145 36.0 .. | 08.2 | 234 37.1 .. | 03.5 | 298 56.8 .. | 49.1 | 342 02.4 .. | 04.3 | Bellatrix | 278 25.0 | N 6 22.3 |
| 22 | 319 54.8 | 160 35.6 | 07.0 | 249 38.3 | 03.8 | 313 59.6 | 49.0 | 357 05.1 | 04.3 | Betelgeuse | 270 54.2 | N 7 24.8 |
| 23 | 334 57.3 | 175 35.1 | 05.9 | 264 39.5 | 04.0 | 329 02.3 | 48.9 | 12 07.7 | 04.4 | | | |
| **11 00** | 349 59.8 | 190 34.6 | N10 04.8 | 279 40.7 | N21 04.2 | 344 05.1 | N 0 48.7 | 27 10.3 | S16 04.4 | Canopus | 263 53.4 | S52 42.1 |
| 01 | 5 02.2 | 205 34.1 | 03.7 | 294 41.9 | 04.4 | 359 07.8 | 48.6 | 42 12.9 | 04.5 | Capella | 280 24.7 | N46 01.1 |
| 02 | 20 04.7 | 220 33.7 | 02.6 | 309 43.0 | 04.6 | 14 10.5 | 48.5 | 57 15.5 | 04.5 | Deneb | 49 26.8 | N45 21.8 |
| 03 | 35 07.1 | 235 33.2 .. | 01.5 | 324 44.2 .. | 04.8 | 29 13.3 .. | 48.4 | 72 18.1 .. | 04.6 | Denebola | 182 27.2 | N14 26.9 |
| 04 | 50 09.6 | 250 32.7 | 10 00.3 | 339 45.4 | 05.0 | 44 16.0 | 48.2 | 87 20.8 | 04.6 | Diphda | 348 48.9 | S17 51.6 |
| 05 | 65 12.1 | 265 32.3 | 9 59.2 | 354 46.6 | 05.2 | 59 18.8 | 48.1 | 102 23.4 | 04.7 | | | |
| 06 | 80 14.5 | 280 31.8 | N 9 58.1 | 9 47.8 | N21 05.5 | 74 21.5 | N 0 48.0 | 117 26.0 | S16 04.7 | Dubhe | 193 44.0 | N61 37.8 |
| 07 | 95 17.0 | 295 31.3 | 57.0 | 24 49.0 | 05.7 | 89 24.2 | 47.9 | 132 28.6 | 04.8 | Elnath | 278 04.3 | N28 37.5 |
| S 08 | 110 19.5 | 310 30.9 | 55.9 | 39 50.2 | 05.9 | 104 27.0 | 47.7 | 147 31.2 | 04.8 | Eltanin | 90 43.0 | N51 29.4 |
| U 09 | 125 21.9 | 325 30.4 .. | 54.7 | 54 51.3 .. | 06.1 | 119 29.7 .. | 47.6 | 162 33.8 .. | 04.8 | Enif | 33 40.4 | N 9 58.8 |
| N 10 | 140 24.4 | 340 29.9 | 53.6 | 69 52.5 | 06.3 | 134 32.5 | 47.5 | 177 36.4 | 04.9 | Fomalhaut | 15 16.3 | S29 30.1 |
| D 11 | 155 26.9 | 355 29.5 | 52.5 | 84 53.7 | 06.5 | 149 35.2 | 47.4 | 192 39.0 | 04.9 | | | |
| A 12 | 170 29.3 | 10 29.0 | N 9 51.4 | 99 54.9 | N21 06.7 | 164 38.0 | N 0 47.2 | 207 41.7 | S16 05.0 | Gacrux | 171 54.3 | S57 14.4 |
| Y 13 | 185 31.8 | 25 28.5 | 50.3 | 114 56.1 | 06.9 | 179 40.7 | 47.1 | 222 44.3 | 05.0 | Gienah | 175 45.9 | S17 39.9 |
| 14 | 200 34.2 | 40 28.1 | 49.1 | 129 57.3 | 07.1 | 194 43.4 | 47.0 | 237 46.9 | 05.1 | Hadar | 148 39.2 | S60 29.0 |
| 15 | 215 36.7 | 55 27.6 .. | 48.0 | 144 58.5 .. | 07.3 | 209 46.2 .. | 46.9 | 252 49.5 .. | 05.1 | Hamal | 327 53.1 | N23 34.2 |
| 16 | 230 39.2 | 70 27.1 | 46.9 | 159 59.7 | 07.6 | 224 48.9 | 46.7 | 267 52.1 | 05.2 | Kaus Aust. | 83 34.9 | S34 22.5 |
| 17 | 245 41.6 | 85 26.7 | 45.8 | 175 00.9 | 07.8 | 239 51.7 | 46.6 | 282 54.7 | 05.2 | | | |
| 18 | 260 44.1 | 100 26.2 | N 9 44.6 | 190 02.0 | N21 08.0 | 254 54.4 | N 0 46.5 | 297 57.3 | S16 05.3 | Kochab | 137 20.4 | N74 04.0 |
| 19 | 275 46.6 | 115 25.7 | 43.5 | 205 03.2 | 08.2 | 269 57.2 | 46.3 | 313 00.0 | 05.3 | Markab | 13 31.5 | N15 19.7 |
| 20 | 290 49.0 | 130 25.3 | 42.4 | 220 04.4 | 08.4 | 284 59.9 | 46.2 | 328 02.6 | 05.4 | Menkar | 314 08.0 | N 4 10.8 |
| 21 | 305 51.5 | 145 24.8 .. | 41.3 | 235 05.6 .. | 08.6 | 300 02.7 .. | 46.1 | 343 05.2 .. | 05.4 | Menkent | 148 00.2 | S36 28.8 |
| 22 | 320 54.0 | 160 24.3 | 40.1 | 250 06.8 | 08.8 | 315 05.4 | 46.0 | 358 07.8 | 05.5 | Miaplacidus | 221 39.5 | S69 48.3 |
| 23 | 335 56.4 | 175 23.9 | 39.0 | 265 08.0 | 09.0 | 330 08.1 | 45.8 | 13 10.4 | 05.5 | | | |
| **12 00** | 350 58.9 | 190 23.4 | N 9 37.9 | 280 09.2 | N21 09.2 | 345 10.9 | N 0 45.7 | 28 13.0 | S16 05.6 | Mirfak | 308 30.8 | N49 56.3 |
| 01 | 6 01.4 | 205 22.9 | 36.7 | 295 10.4 | 09.4 | 0 13.6 | 45.6 | 43 15.6 | 05.6 | Nunki | 75 50.0 | S26 16.1 |
| 02 | 21 03.8 | 220 22.5 | 35.6 | 310 11.6 | 09.6 | 15 16.4 | 45.5 | 58 18.2 | 05.7 | Peacock | 53 08.3 | S56 39.9 |
| 03 | 36 06.3 | 235 22.0 .. | 34.5 | 325 12.8 .. | 09.8 | 30 19.1 .. | 45.3 | 73 20.9 .. | 05.7 | Pollux | 243 19.9 | N27 58.3 |
| 04 | 51 08.7 | 250 21.6 | 33.4 | 340 14.0 | 10.1 | 45 21.9 | 45.2 | 88 23.5 | 05.8 | Procyon | 244 53.0 | N 5 10.2 |
| 05 | 66 11.2 | 265 21.1 | 32.2 | 355 15.2 | 10.3 | 60 24.6 | 45.1 | 103 26.1 | 05.8 | | | |
| 06 | 81 13.7 | 280 20.6 | N 9 31.1 | 10 16.4 | N21 10.5 | 75 27.4 | N 0 45.0 | 118 28.7 | S16 05.9 | Rasalhague | 96 00.3 | N12 32.8 |
| 07 | 96 16.1 | 295 20.2 | 30.0 | 25 17.6 | 10.7 | 90 30.1 | 44.8 | 133 31.3 | 05.9 | Regulus | 207 36.8 | N11 51.6 |
| M 08 | 111 18.6 | 310 19.7 | 28.8 | 40 18.8 | 10.9 | 105 32.8 | 44.7 | 148 33.9 | 06.0 | Rigel | 281 05.7 | S 8 10.3 |
| O 09 | 126 21.1 | 325 19.3 .. | 27.7 | 55 20.0 .. | 11.1 | 120 35.6 .. | 44.6 | 163 36.5 .. | 06.0 | Rigil Kent. | 139 43.4 | S60 55.8 |
| N 10 | 141 23.5 | 340 18.8 | 26.6 | 70 21.2 | 11.3 | 135 38.3 | 44.4 | 178 39.1 | 06.0 | Sabik | 102 05.0 | S15 45.1 |
| D 11 | 156 26.0 | 355 18.3 | 25.4 | 85 22.4 | 11.5 | 150 41.1 | 44.3 | 193 41.7 | 06.1 | | | |
| A 12 | 171 28.5 | 10 17.9 | N 9 24.3 | 100 23.6 | N21 11.7 | 165 43.8 | N 0 44.2 | 208 44.4 | S16 06.1 | Schedar | 349 32.7 | N56 39.6 |
| Y 13 | 186 30.9 | 25 17.4 | 23.2 | 115 24.8 | 11.9 | 180 46.6 | 44.1 | 223 47.0 | 06.2 | Shaula | 96 12.9 | S37 07.3 |
| 14 | 201 33.4 | 40 17.0 | 22.0 | 130 26.0 | 12.1 | 195 49.3 | 43.9 | 238 49.6 | 06.2 | Sirius | 258 28.1 | S16 44.6 |
| 15 | 216 35.8 | 55 16.5 .. | 20.9 | 145 27.2 .. | 12.3 | 210 52.1 .. | 43.8 | 253 52.2 .. | 06.3 | Spica | 158 24.6 | S11 16.6 |
| 16 | 231 38.3 | 70 16.0 | 19.8 | 160 28.4 | 12.5 | 225 54.8 | 43.7 | 268 54.8 | 06.3 | Suhail | 222 48.1 | S43 31.2 |
| 17 | 246 40.8 | 85 15.6 | 18.6 | 175 29.6 | 12.7 | 240 57.6 | 43.6 | 283 57.4 | 06.4 | | | |
| 18 | 261 43.2 | 100 15.1 | N 9 17.5 | 190 30.8 | N21 12.9 | 256 00.3 | N 0 43.4 | 299 00.0 | S16 06.4 | Vega | 80 34.4 | N38 48.5 |
| 19 | 276 45.7 | 115 14.7 | 16.4 | 205 32.0 | 13.1 | 271 03.1 | 43.3 | 314 02.6 | 06.5 | Zuben'ubi | 136 58.3 | S16 08.1 |
| 20 | 291 48.2 | 130 14.2 | 15.2 | 220 33.2 | 13.3 | 286 05.8 | 43.2 | 329 05.2 | 06.5 | | | |
| 21 | 306 50.6 | 145 13.8 .. | 14.1 | 235 34.4 .. | 13.5 | 301 08.6 .. | 43.1 | 344 07.8 .. | 06.6 | | SHA | Mer. Pass. |
| 22 | 321 53.1 | 160 13.3 | 13.0 | 250 35.7 | 13.7 | 316 11.3 | 42.9 | 359 10.5 | 06.6 | Venus | 200 34.9 | 11 18 |
| 23 | 336 55.6 | 175 12.8 | 11.8 | 265 36.9 | 13.9 | 331 14.0 | 42.8 | 14 13.1 | 06.7 | Mars | 289 40.9 | 5 21 |
| | h m | | | | | | | | | Jupiter | 354 05.3 | 1 03 |
| Mer. Pass. | 0 39.9 | v −0.5 | d 1.1 | v 1.2 | d 0.2 | v 2.7 | d 0.1 | v 2.6 | d 0.0 | Saturn | 37 10.5 | 22 07 |

| UT | SUN GHA | SUN Dec | MOON GHA | v | MOON Dec | d | HP |
|---|---|---|---|---|---|---|---|
| d h | ° ′ | ° ′ | ° ′ | ′ | ° ′ | ′ | ′ |
| **10 00** | 180 42.6 | N 5 01.4 | 4 08.1 | 10.1 | S11 22.0 | 15.2 | 59.6 |
| 01 | 195 42.8 | 5 00.4 | 18 37.2 | 10.2 | 11 06.8 | 15.3 | 59.6 |
| 02 | 210 43.0 | 4 59.5 | 33 06.4 | 10.4 | 10 51.5 | 15.4 | 59.6 |
| 03 | 225 43.2 | .. 58.5 | 47 35.8 | 10.3 | 10 36.1 | 15.3 | 59.6 |
| 04 | 240 43.4 | 57.6 | 62 05.1 | 10.5 | 10 20.8 | 15.5 | 59.5 |
| 05 | 255 43.7 | 56.7 | 76 34.6 | 10.6 | 10 05.3 | 15.4 | 59.5 |
| 06 | 270 43.9 | N 4 55.7 | 91 04.2 | 10.6 | S 9 49.9 | 15.5 | 59.5 |
| 07 | 285 44.1 | 54.8 | 105 33.8 | 10.7 | 9 34.4 | 15.6 | 59.5 |
| S 08 | 300 44.3 | 53.8 | 120 03.5 | 10.7 | 9 18.8 | 15.6 | 59.4 |
| A 09 | 315 44.5 | .. 52.9 | 134 33.2 | 10.9 | 9 03.2 | 15.6 | 59.4 |
| T 10 | 330 44.8 | 51.9 | 149 03.1 | 10.9 | 8 47.6 | 15.6 | 59.4 |
| U 11 | 345 45.0 | 51.0 | 163 33.0 | 10.9 | 8 32.0 | 15.7 | 59.4 |
| R 12 | 0 45.2 | N 4 50.0 | 178 02.9 | 11.1 | S 8 16.3 | 15.8 | 59.4 |
| D 13 | 15 45.4 | 49.1 | 192 33.0 | 11.1 | 8 00.5 | 15.7 | 59.3 |
| A 14 | 30 45.6 | 48.1 | 207 03.1 | 11.2 | 7 44.8 | 15.8 | 59.3 |
| Y 15 | 45 45.9 | .. 47.2 | 221 33.3 | 11.2 | 7 29.0 | 15.8 | 59.3 |
| 16 | 60 46.1 | 46.2 | 236 03.5 | 11.4 | 7 13.2 | 15.8 | 59.3 |
| 17 | 75 46.3 | 45.3 | 250 33.9 | 11.3 | 6 57.4 | 15.9 | 59.2 |
| 18 | 90 46.5 | N 4 44.3 | 265 04.2 | 11.5 | S 6 41.5 | 15.8 | 59.2 |
| 19 | 105 46.7 | 43.4 | 279 34.7 | 11.5 | 6 25.7 | 15.9 | 59.2 |
| 20 | 120 47.0 | 42.4 | 294 05.2 | 11.6 | 6 09.8 | 16.0 | 59.2 |
| 21 | 135 47.2 | .. 41.5 | 308 35.8 | 11.6 | 5 53.8 | 15.9 | 59.1 |
| 22 | 150 47.4 | 40.5 | 323 06.4 | 11.7 | 5 37.9 | 15.9 | 59.1 |
| 23 | 165 47.6 | 39.6 | 337 37.1 | 11.7 | 5 22.0 | 16.0 | 59.1 |
| **11 00** | 180 47.8 | N 4 38.6 | 352 07.8 | 11.8 | S 5 06.0 | 15.9 | 59.0 |
| 01 | 195 48.1 | 37.7 | 6 38.6 | 11.8 | 4 50.1 | 16.0 | 59.0 |
| 02 | 210 48.3 | 36.7 | 21 09.4 | 12.0 | 4 34.1 | 16.0 | 59.0 |
| 03 | 225 48.5 | .. 35.8 | 35 40.4 | 11.9 | 4 18.1 | 16.0 | 59.0 |
| 04 | 240 48.7 | 34.8 | 50 11.3 | 12.0 | 4 02.1 | 16.0 | 58.9 |
| 05 | 255 48.9 | 33.9 | 64 42.3 | 12.1 | 3 46.1 | 16.0 | 58.9 |
| 06 | 270 49.2 | N 4 32.9 | 79 13.4 | 12.1 | S 3 30.1 | 16.0 | 58.9 |
| 07 | 285 49.4 | 32.0 | 93 44.5 | 12.1 | 3 14.1 | 16.0 | 58.9 |
| S 08 | 300 49.6 | 31.0 | 108 15.6 | 12.3 | 2 58.1 | 16.0 | 58.8 |
| U 09 | 315 49.8 | .. 30.1 | 122 46.9 | 12.2 | 2 42.1 | 16.0 | 58.8 |
| N 10 | 330 50.1 | 29.1 | 137 18.1 | 12.3 | 2 26.1 | 16.0 | 58.8 |
| D 11 | 345 50.3 | 28.2 | 151 49.4 | 12.3 | 2 10.1 | 16.0 | 58.7 |
| A 12 | 0 50.5 | N 4 27.2 | 166 20.7 | 12.4 | S 1 54.1 | 15.9 | 58.7 |
| Y 13 | 15 50.7 | 26.3 | 180 52.1 | 12.4 | 1 38.2 | 16.0 | 58.7 |
| 14 | 30 50.9 | 25.3 | 195 23.5 | 12.5 | 1 22.2 | 16.0 | 58.6 |
| 15 | 45 51.2 | .. 24.4 | 209 55.0 | 12.5 | 1 06.2 | 15.9 | 58.6 |
| 16 | 60 51.4 | 23.4 | 224 26.5 | 12.5 | 0 50.3 | 16.0 | 58.6 |
| 17 | 75 51.6 | 22.5 | 238 58.0 | 12.6 | 0 34.3 | 15.9 | 58.6 |
| 18 | 90 51.8 | N 4 21.5 | 253 29.6 | 12.6 | S 0 18.4 | 15.9 | 58.5 |
| 19 | 105 52.0 | 20.6 | 268 01.2 | 12.7 | S 0 02.5 | 15.9 | 58.5 |
| 20 | 120 52.3 | 19.6 | 282 32.9 | 12.7 | N 0 13.4 | 15.9 | 58.5 |
| 21 | 135 52.5 | .. 18.7 | 297 04.6 | 12.7 | 0 29.2 | 15.9 | 58.4 |
| 22 | 150 52.7 | 17.7 | 311 36.3 | 12.7 | 0 45.1 | 15.8 | 58.4 |
| 23 | 165 52.9 | 16.8 | 326 08.0 | 12.8 | 1 00.9 | 15.8 | 58.4 |
| **12 00** | 180 53.2 | N 4 15.8 | 340 39.8 | 12.8 | N 1 16.7 | 15.8 | 58.3 |
| 01 | 195 53.4 | 14.9 | 355 11.6 | 12.8 | 1 32.5 | 15.8 | 58.3 |
| 02 | 210 53.6 | 13.9 | 9 43.4 | 12.9 | 1 48.3 | 15.7 | 58.3 |
| 03 | 225 53.8 | .. 13.0 | 24 15.3 | 12.9 | 2 04.0 | 15.7 | 58.2 |
| 04 | 240 54.0 | 12.0 | 38 47.2 | 12.9 | 2 19.7 | 15.7 | 58.2 |
| 05 | 255 54.3 | 11.1 | 53 19.1 | 12.9 | 2 35.4 | 15.6 | 58.2 |
| 06 | 270 54.5 | N 4 10.1 | 67 51.0 | 13.0 | N 2 51.0 | 15.6 | 58.1 |
| 07 | 285 54.7 | 09.2 | 82 23.0 | 12.9 | 3 06.6 | 15.6 | 58.1 |
| M 08 | 300 54.9 | 08.2 | 96 54.9 | 13.0 | 3 22.2 | 15.6 | 58.1 |
| O 09 | 315 55.1 | .. 07.3 | 111 26.9 | 13.0 | 3 37.8 | 15.5 | 58.0 |
| N 10 | 330 55.4 | 06.3 | 125 58.9 | 13.1 | 3 53.3 | 15.5 | 58.0 |
| D 11 | 345 55.6 | 05.3 | 140 31.0 | 13.0 | 4 08.8 | 15.4 | 58.0 |
| A 12 | 0 55.8 | N 4 04.4 | 155 03.0 | 13.1 | N 4 24.2 | 15.4 | 57.9 |
| Y 13 | 15 56.0 | 03.4 | 169 35.1 | 13.1 | 4 39.6 | 15.3 | 57.9 |
| 14 | 30 56.3 | 02.5 | 184 07.2 | 13.1 | 4 54.9 | 15.4 | 57.9 |
| 15 | 45 56.5 | .. 01.5 | 198 39.3 | 13.1 | 5 10.3 | 15.2 | 57.8 |
| 16 | 60 56.7 | 4 00.6 | 213 11.4 | 13.1 | 5 25.5 | 15.3 | 57.8 |
| 17 | 75 56.9 | 3 59.6 | 227 43.5 | 13.1 | 5 40.8 | 15.1 | 57.8 |
| 18 | 90 57.1 | N 3 58.7 | 242 15.6 | 13.2 | N 5 55.9 | 15.2 | 57.7 |
| 19 | 105 57.4 | 57.7 | 256 47.8 | 13.1 | 6 11.1 | 15.1 | 57.7 |
| 20 | 120 57.6 | 56.8 | 271 19.9 | 13.2 | 6 26.2 | 15.0 | 57.7 |
| 21 | 135 57.8 | .. 55.8 | 285 52.1 | 13.1 | 6 41.2 | 15.0 | 57.6 |
| 22 | 150 58.0 | 54.8 | 300 24.2 | 13.2 | 6 56.2 | 15.0 | 57.6 |
| 23 | 165 58.3 | 53.9 | 314 56.4 | 13.2 | N 7 11.2 | 14.9 | 57.6 |
| | SD 15.9 | d 1.0 | SD 16.2 | | 16.0 | | 15.8 |

| Lat. | Twilight Naut. | Twilight Civil | Sunrise | Moonrise 10 | 11 | 12 | 13 |
|---|---|---|---|---|---|---|---|
| ° | h m | h m | h m | h m | h m | h m | h m |
| N 72 | 01 27 | 03 33 | 04 49 | 19 44 | 19 10 | 18 37 | 17 59 |
| N 70 | 02 12 | 03 50 | 04 56 | 19 35 | 19 10 | 18 45 | 18 18 |
| 68 | 02 40 | 04 02 | 05 02 | 19 28 | 19 10 | 18 52 | 18 33 |
| 66 | 03 01 | 04 13 | 05 07 | 19 22 | 19 10 | 18 58 | 18 45 |
| 64 | 03 17 | 04 22 | 05 11 | 19 16 | 19 10 | 19 03 | 18 56 |
| 62 | 03 31 | 04 29 | 05 15 | 19 12 | 19 09 | 19 07 | 19 05 |
| 60 | 03 42 | 04 35 | 05 18 | 19 08 | 19 09 | 19 11 | 19 12 |
| N 58 | 03 51 | 04 41 | 05 21 | 19 04 | 19 09 | 19 14 | 19 19 |
| 56 | 03 59 | 04 45 | 05 24 | 19 01 | 19 09 | 19 17 | 19 25 |
| 54 | 04 06 | 04 50 | 05 26 | 18 58 | 19 09 | 19 20 | 19 31 |
| 52 | 04 12 | 04 53 | 05 28 | 18 56 | 19 09 | 19 22 | 19 36 |
| 50 | 04 17 | 04 57 | 05 30 | 18 53 | 19 09 | 19 24 | 19 40 |
| 45 | 04 29 | 05 04 | 05 34 | 18 48 | 19 09 | 19 29 | 19 50 |
| N 40 | 04 37 | 05 10 | 05 37 | 18 44 | 19 09 | 19 33 | 19 58 |
| 35 | 04 44 | 05 14 | 05 40 | 18 40 | 19 09 | 19 37 | 20 05 |
| 30 | 04 50 | 05 18 | 05 42 | 18 37 | 19 09 | 19 40 | 20 11 |
| 20 | 04 59 | 05 24 | 05 47 | 18 31 | 19 09 | 19 45 | 20 22 |
| N 10 | 05 05 | 05 29 | 05 50 | 18 26 | 19 09 | 19 50 | 20 32 |
| 0 | 05 09 | 05 33 | 05 53 | 18 21 | 19 09 | 19 55 | 20 41 |
| S 10 | 05 11 | 05 36 | 05 57 | 18 16 | 19 09 | 20 00 | 20 50 |
| 20 | 05 12 | 05 38 | 06 00 | 18 11 | 19 09 | 20 05 | 21 00 |
| 30 | 05 12 | 05 40 | 06 03 | 18 05 | 19 09 | 20 11 | 21 11 |
| 35 | 05 11 | 05 40 | 06 05 | 18 02 | 19 09 | 20 14 | 21 18 |
| 40 | 05 09 | 05 41 | 06 08 | 17 58 | 19 09 | 20 18 | 21 25 |
| 45 | 05 07 | 05 41 | 06 10 | 17 53 | 19 09 | 20 22 | 21 34 |
| S 50 | 05 04 | 05 41 | 06 13 | 17 48 | 19 09 | 20 28 | 21 45 |
| 52 | 05 02 | 05 41 | 06 15 | 17 45 | 19 09 | 20 30 | 21 50 |
| 54 | 05 00 | 05 41 | 06 16 | 17 43 | 19 09 | 20 33 | 21 56 |
| 56 | 04 58 | 05 41 | 06 18 | 17 40 | 19 09 | 20 36 | 22 02 |
| 58 | 04 55 | 05 41 | 06 20 | 17 36 | 19 09 | 20 40 | 22 09 |
| S 60 | 04 52 | 05 40 | 06 22 | 17 32 | 19 09 | 20 43 | 22 16 |

| Lat. | Sunset | Twilight Civil | Twilight Naut. | Moonset 10 | 11 | 12 | 13 |
|---|---|---|---|---|---|---|---|
| ° | h m | h m | h m | h m | h m | h m | h m |
| N 72 | 19 02 | 20 16 | 22 16 | 03 29 | 05 58 | 08 13 | 10 31 |
| N 70 | 18 55 | 20 00 | 21 35 | 03 48 | 06 03 | 08 09 | 10 14 |
| 68 | 18 49 | 19 48 | 21 08 | 04 03 | 06 07 | 08 05 | 10 01 |
| 66 | 18 44 | 19 38 | 20 49 | 04 14 | 06 11 | 08 01 | 09 51 |
| 64 | 18 40 | 19 29 | 20 33 | 04 24 | 06 14 | 07 59 | 09 42 |
| 62 | 18 37 | 19 22 | 20 20 | 04 32 | 06 17 | 07 56 | 09 34 |
| 60 | 18 34 | 19 16 | 20 09 | 04 39 | 06 19 | 07 54 | 09 28 |
| N 58 | 18 31 | 19 11 | 20 00 | 04 45 | 06 21 | 07 52 | 09 22 |
| 56 | 18 28 | 19 06 | 19 53 | 04 51 | 06 23 | 07 51 | 09 17 |
| 54 | 18 26 | 19 02 | 19 46 | 04 56 | 06 24 | 07 49 | 09 13 |
| 52 | 18 24 | 18 59 | 19 40 | 05 00 | 06 26 | 07 48 | 09 09 |
| 50 | 18 23 | 18 55 | 19 35 | 05 04 | 06 27 | 07 47 | 09 05 |
| 45 | 18 19 | 18 48 | 19 24 | 05 12 | 06 30 | 07 44 | 08 57 |
| N 40 | 18 16 | 18 43 | 19 15 | 05 19 | 06 32 | 07 42 | 08 50 |
| 35 | 18 13 | 18 38 | 19 08 | 05 25 | 06 34 | 07 40 | 08 45 |
| 30 | 18 10 | 18 35 | 19 03 | 05 31 | 06 36 | 07 39 | 08 40 |
| 20 | 18 06 | 18 29 | 18 54 | 05 40 | 06 39 | 07 36 | 08 31 |
| N 10 | 18 03 | 18 24 | 18 49 | 05 48 | 06 41 | 07 33 | 08 24 |
| 0 | 18 00 | 18 21 | 18 45 | 05 55 | 06 44 | 07 31 | 08 17 |
| S 10 | 17 57 | 18 18 | 18 42 | 06 02 | 06 46 | 07 29 | 08 10 |
| 20 | 17 54 | 18 16 | 18 41 | 06 10 | 06 49 | 07 26 | 08 03 |
| 30 | 17 50 | 18 14 | 18 42 | 06 18 | 06 52 | 07 23 | 07 54 |
| 35 | 17 48 | 18 13 | 18 43 | 06 23 | 06 53 | 07 21 | 07 49 |
| 40 | 17 46 | 18 13 | 18 45 | 06 29 | 06 55 | 07 20 | 07 44 |
| 45 | 17 44 | 18 13 | 18 47 | 06 35 | 06 57 | 07 17 | 07 38 |
| S 50 | 17 41 | 18 13 | 18 51 | 06 43 | 07 00 | 07 15 | 07 30 |
| 52 | 17 40 | 18 13 | 18 52 | 06 46 | 07 01 | 07 14 | 07 27 |
| 54 | 17 38 | 18 13 | 18 54 | 06 50 | 07 02 | 07 12 | 07 23 |
| 56 | 17 37 | 18 14 | 18 56 | 06 54 | 07 03 | 07 11 | 07 19 |
| 58 | 17 35 | 18 14 | 19 00 | 06 59 | 07 05 | 07 09 | 07 14 |
| S 60 | 17 33 | 18 14 | 19 03 | 07 04 | 07 06 | 07 08 | 07 09 |

| | SUN Eqn. of Time 00h | SUN Eqn. of Time 12h | SUN Mer. Pass. | MOON Mer. Pass. Upper | MOON Mer. Pass. Lower | Age | Phase |
|---|---|---|---|---|---|---|---|
| Day | m s | m s | h m | h m | h m | d | % |
| 10 | 02 50 | 03 00 | 11 57 | 24 33 | 12 08 | 14 | 100 |
| 11 | 03 11 | 03 22 | 11 57 | 00 33 | 12 56 | 15 | 98 |
| 12 | 03 32 | 03 43 | 11 56 | 01 20 | 13 43 | 16 | 94 |

| UT | ARIES | VENUS −3·9 | | MARS −0·4 | | JUPITER −2·9 | | SATURN +0·4 | | STARS | | |
|---|---|---|---|---|---|---|---|---|---|---|---|---|
| | GHA | GHA | Dec | GHA | Dec | GHA | Dec | GHA | Dec | Name | SHA | Dec |
| d h | ° ′ | ° ′ | ° ′ | ° ′ | ° ′ | ° ′ | ° ′ | ° ′ | ° ′ | | ° ′ | ° ′ |
| 13 00 | 351 58.0 | 190 12.4 N 9 10.7 | | 280 38.1 N21 14.1 | | 346 16.8 N 0 42.7 | | 29 15.7 S16 06.7 | | Acamar | 315 13.0 | S40 12.6 |
| 01 | 7 00.5 | 205 11.9 | 09.5 | 295 39.3 | 14.3 | 1 19.5 | 42.5 | 44 18.3 | 06.8 | Achernar | 335 21.1 | S57 07.1 |
| 02 | 22 03.0 | 220 11.5 | 08.4 | 310 40.5 | 14.5 | 16 22.3 | 42.4 | 59 20.9 | 06.8 | Acrux | 173 02.9 | S63 13.4 |
| 03 | 37 05.4 | 235 11.0 . . | 07.3 | 325 41.7 . . | 14.7 | 31 25.0 . . | 42.3 | 74 23.5 . . | 06.8 | Adhara | 255 07.5 | S28 59.9 |
| 04 | 52 07.9 | 250 10.6 | 06.1 | 340 42.9 | 15.0 | 46 27.8 | 42.2 | 89 26.1 | 06.9 | Aldebaran | 290 41.8 | N16 33.3 |
| 05 | 67 10.3 | 265 10.1 | 05.0 | 355 44.1 | 15.2 | 61 30.5 | 42.0 | 104 28.7 | 06.9 | | | |
| 06 | 82 12.8 | 280 09.7 N 9 03.8 | | 10 45.3 N21 15.4 | | 76 33.3 N 0 41.9 | | 119 31.3 S16 07.0 | | Alioth | 166 15.2 | N55 50.4 |
| 07 | 97 15.3 | 295 09.2 | 02.7 | 25 46.6 | 15.6 | 91 36.0 | 41.8 | 134 33.9 | 07.0 | Alkaid | 152 53.9 | N49 12.3 |
| T 08 | 112 17.7 | 310 08.7 | 01.6 | 40 47.8 | 15.8 | 106 38.8 | 41.6 | 149 36.6 | 07.1 | Alnair | 27 34.9 | S46 51.1 |
| U 09 | 127 20.2 | 325 08.3 9 00.4 | | 55 49.0 . . | 16.0 | 121 41.5 . . | 41.5 | 164 39.2 . . | 07.1 | Alnilam | 275 39.7 | S 1 11.1 |
| E 10 | 142 22.7 | 340 07.8 8 59.3 | | 70 50.2 | 16.2 | 136 44.3 | 41.4 | 179 41.8 | 07.2 | Alphard | 217 49.9 | S 8 45.2 |
| S 11 | 157 25.1 | 355 07.4 | 58.1 | 85 51.4 | 16.4 | 151 47.0 | 41.3 | 194 44.4 | 07.2 | | | |
| D 12 | 172 27.6 | 10 06.9 N 8 57.0 | | 100 52.6 N21 16.6 | | 166 49.8 N 0 41.1 | | 209 47.0 S16 07.3 | | Alphecca | 126 05.5 | N26 38.6 |
| A 13 | 187 30.1 | 25 06.5 | 55.8 | 115 53.8 | 16.8 | 181 52.5 | 41.0 | 224 49.6 | 07.3 | Alpheratz | 357 36.4 | N29 13.0 |
| Y 14 | 202 32.5 | 40 06.0 | 54.7 | 130 55.1 | 17.0 | 196 55.3 | 40.9 | 239 52.2 | 07.4 | Altair | 62 01.6 | N 8 55.8 |
| 15 | 217 35.0 | 55 05.6 . . | 53.5 | 145 56.3 . . | 17.2 | 211 58.0 . . | 40.7 | 254 54.8 . . | 07.4 | Ankaa | 353 08.6 | S42 10.9 |
| 16 | 232 37.4 | 70 05.1 | 52.4 | 160 57.5 | 17.4 | 227 00.8 | 40.6 | 269 57.4 | 07.4 | Antares | 112 18.3 | S26 28.9 |
| 17 | 247 39.9 | 85 04.7 | 51.3 | 175 58.7 | 17.6 | 242 03.5 | 40.5 | 285 00.0 | 07.5 | | | |
| 18 | 262 42.4 | 100 04.2 N 8 50.1 | | 190 59.9 N21 17.8 | | 257 06.3 N 0 40.4 | | 300 02.6 S16 07.6 | | Arcturus | 145 49.9 | N19 04.1 |
| 19 | 277 44.8 | 115 03.8 | 49.0 | 206 01.2 | 18.0 | 272 09.0 | 40.2 | 315 05.2 | 07.6 | Atria | 107 14.3 | S69 04.3 |
| 20 | 292 47.3 | 130 03.3 | 47.8 | 221 02.4 | 18.2 | 287 11.8 | 40.1 | 330 07.9 | 07.6 | Avior | 234 15.9 | S59 34.6 |
| 21 | 307 49.8 | 145 02.9 . . | 46.7 | 236 03.6 . . | 18.4 | 302 14.5 . . | 40.0 | 345 10.5 . . | 07.7 | Bellatrix | 278 24.9 | N 6 22.3 |
| 22 | 322 52.2 | 160 02.4 | 45.5 | 251 04.8 | 18.5 | 317 17.3 | 39.8 | 0 13.1 | 07.7 | Betelgeuse | 270 54.2 | N 7 24.8 |
| 23 | 337 54.7 | 175 02.0 | 44.4 | 266 06.1 | 18.7 | 332 20.0 | 39.7 | 15 15.7 | 07.8 | | | |
| 14 00 | 352 57.2 | 190 01.5 N 8 43.2 | | 281 07.3 N21 18.9 | | 347 22.8 N 0 39.6 | | 30 18.3 S16 07.8 | | Canopus | 263 53.4 | S52 42.1 |
| 01 | 7 59.6 | 205 01.1 | 42.1 | 296 08.5 | 19.1 | 2 25.5 | 39.5 | 45 20.9 | 07.9 | Capella | 280 24.7 | N46 01.1 |
| 02 | 23 02.1 | 220 00.6 | 40.9 | 311 09.7 | 19.3 | 17 28.3 | 39.3 | 60 23.5 | 07.9 | Deneb | 49 26.8 | N45 21.8 |
| 03 | 38 04.6 | 235 00.2 . . | 39.8 | 326 11.0 . . | 19.5 | 32 31.0 . . | 39.2 | 75 26.1 . . | 08.0 | Denebola | 182 27.2 | N14 26.9 |
| 04 | 53 07.0 | 249 59.7 | 38.6 | 341 12.2 | 19.7 | 47 33.8 | 39.1 | 90 28.7 | 08.0 | Diphda | 348 48.9 | S17 51.6 |
| 05 | 68 09.5 | 264 59.3 | 37.5 | 356 13.4 | 19.9 | 62 36.5 | 38.9 | 105 31.3 | 08.0 | | | |
| 06 | 83 11.9 | 279 58.8 N 8 36.3 | | 11 14.6 N21 20.1 | | 77 39.3 N 0 38.8 | | 120 33.9 S16 08.1 | | Dubhe | 193 44.0 | N61 37.8 |
| W 07 | 98 14.4 | 294 58.4 | 35.2 | 26 15.9 | 20.3 | 92 42.0 | 38.7 | 135 36.5 | 08.1 | Elnath | 278 04.3 | N28 37.5 |
| E 08 | 113 16.9 | 309 57.9 | 34.0 | 41 17.1 | 20.5 | 107 44.8 | 38.6 | 150 39.1 | 08.2 | Eltanin | 90 43.0 | N51 29.4 |
| D 09 | 128 19.3 | 324 57.5 . . | 32.9 | 56 18.3 . . | 20.7 | 122 47.5 . . | 38.4 | 165 41.7 . . | 08.2 | Enif | 33 40.4 | N 9 58.8 |
| N 10 | 143 21.8 | 339 57.0 | 31.7 | 71 19.5 | 20.9 | 137 50.3 | 38.3 | 180 44.3 | 08.3 | Fomalhaut | 15 16.3 | S29 30.1 |
| E 11 | 158 24.3 | 354 56.6 | 30.5 | 86 20.8 | 21.1 | 152 53.1 | 38.2 | 195 47.0 | 08.3 | | | |
| S 12 | 173 26.7 | 9 56.1 N 8 29.4 | | 101 22.0 N21 21.3 | | 167 55.8 N 0 38.0 | | 210 49.6 S16 08.4 | | Gacrux | 171 54.3 | S57 14.3 |
| D 13 | 188 29.2 | 24 55.7 | 28.2 | 116 23.2 | 21.5 | 182 58.6 | 37.9 | 225 52.2 | 08.4 | Gienah | 175 45.9 | S17 39.9 |
| A 14 | 203 31.7 | 39 55.3 | 27.1 | 131 24.5 | 21.7 | 198 01.3 | 37.8 | 240 54.8 | 08.5 | Hadar | 148 39.2 | S60 29.0 |
| Y 15 | 218 34.1 | 54 54.8 . . | 25.9 | 146 25.7 . . | 21.9 | 213 04.1 . . | 37.7 | 255 57.4 . . | 08.5 | Hamal | 327 53.1 | N23 34.2 |
| 16 | 233 36.6 | 69 54.4 | 24.8 | 161 26.9 | 22.1 | 228 06.8 | 37.5 | 271 00.0 | 08.5 | Kaus Aust. | 83 35.0 | S34 22.5 |
| 17 | 248 39.1 | 84 53.9 | 23.6 | 176 28.2 | 22.3 | 243 09.6 | 37.4 | 286 02.6 | 08.6 | | | |
| 18 | 263 41.5 | 99 53.5 N 8 22.5 | | 191 29.4 N21 22.5 | | 258 12.3 N 0 37.3 | | 301 05.2 S16 08.6 | | Kochab | 137 20.5 | N74 04.0 |
| 19 | 278 44.0 | 114 53.0 | 21.3 | 206 30.6 | 22.7 | 273 15.1 | 37.1 | 316 07.8 | 08.7 | Markab | 13 31.5 | N15 19.7 |
| 20 | 293 46.4 | 129 52.6 | 20.1 | 221 31.9 | 22.9 | 288 17.8 | 37.0 | 331 10.4 | 08.7 | Menkar | 314 08.0 | N 4 10.8 |
| 21 | 308 48.9 | 144 52.1 . . | 19.0 | 236 33.1 . . | 23.1 | 303 20.6 . . | 36.9 | 346 13.0 . . | 08.8 | Menkent | 148 00.2 | S36 28.8 |
| 22 | 323 51.4 | 159 51.7 | 17.8 | 251 34.4 | 23.2 | 318 23.3 | 36.8 | 1 15.6 | 08.8 | Miaplacidus | 221 39.4 | S69 48.3 |
| 23 | 338 53.8 | 174 51.3 | 16.7 | 266 35.6 | 23.4 | 333 26.1 | 36.6 | 16 18.2 | 08.9 | | | |
| 15 00 | 353 56.3 | 189 50.8 N 8 15.5 | | 281 36.8 N21 23.6 | | 348 28.8 N 0 36.5 | | 31 20.8 S16 08.9 | | Mirfak | 308 30.8 | N49 56.3 |
| 01 | 8 58.8 | 204 50.4 | 14.3 | 296 38.1 | 23.8 | 3 31.6 | 36.4 | 46 23.4 | 08.9 | Nunki | 75 50.0 | S26 16.1 |
| 02 | 24 01.2 | 219 49.9 | 13.2 | 311 39.3 | 24.0 | 18 34.4 | 36.2 | 61 26.0 | 09.0 | Peacock | 53 08.3 | S56 39.9 |
| 03 | 39 03.7 | 234 49.5 . . | 12.0 | 326 40.6 . . | 24.2 | 33 37.1 . . | 36.1 | 76 28.6 . . | 09.0 | Pollux | 243 19.9 | N27 58.3 |
| 04 | 54 06.2 | 249 49.0 | 10.9 | 341 41.8 | 24.4 | 48 39.9 | 36.0 | 91 31.2 | 09.1 | Procyon | 244 53.0 | N 5 10.2 |
| 05 | 69 08.6 | 264 48.6 | 09.7 | 356 43.0 | 24.6 | 63 42.6 | 35.8 | 106 33.8 | 09.1 | | | |
| 06 | 84 11.1 | 279 48.2 N 8 08.5 | | 11 44.3 N21 24.8 | | 78 45.4 N 0 35.7 | | 121 36.4 S16 09.2 | | Rasalhague | 96 00.3 | N12 32.8 |
| 07 | 99 13.5 | 294 47.7 | 07.4 | 26 45.5 | 25.0 | 93 48.1 | 35.6 | 136 39.0 | 09.2 | Regulus | 207 36.8 | N11 51.6 |
| T 08 | 114 16.0 | 309 47.3 | 06.2 | 41 46.8 | 25.2 | 108 50.9 | 35.5 | 151 41.7 | 09.3 | Rigel | 281 05.7 | S 8 10.3 |
| H 09 | 129 18.5 | 324 46.8 . . | 05.1 | 56 48.0 . . | 25.4 | 123 53.6 . . | 35.3 | 166 44.3 . . | 09.3 | Rigil Kent. | 139 43.4 | S60 55.8 |
| U 10 | 144 20.9 | 339 46.4 | 03.9 | 71 49.3 | 25.6 | 138 56.4 | 35.2 | 181 46.9 | 09.3 | Sabik | 102 05.0 | S15 45.1 |
| R 11 | 159 23.4 | 354 46.0 | 02.7 | 86 50.5 | 25.7 | 153 59.1 | 35.1 | 196 49.5 | 09.4 | | | |
| S 12 | 174 25.9 | 9 45.5 N 8 01.6 | | 101 51.7 N21 25.9 | | 169 01.9 N 0 34.9 | | 211 52.1 S16 09.4 | | Schedar | 349 32.7 | N56 39.6 |
| D 13 | 189 28.3 | 24 45.1 8 00.4 | | 116 53.0 | 26.1 | 184 04.7 | 34.8 | 226 54.7 | 09.5 | Shaula | 96 13.0 | S37 07.3 |
| A 14 | 204 30.8 | 39 44.6 7 59.2 | | 131 54.2 | 26.3 | 199 07.4 | 34.7 | 241 57.3 | 09.5 | Sirius | 258 28.0 | S16 44.6 |
| Y 15 | 219 33.3 | 54 44.2 . . | 58.1 | 146 55.5 . . | 26.5 | 214 10.2 . . | 34.5 | 256 59.9 . . | 09.6 | Spica | 158 24.6 | S11 16.6 |
| 16 | 234 35.7 | 69 43.8 | 56.9 | 161 56.7 | 26.7 | 229 12.9 | 34.4 | 272 02.5 | 09.6 | Suhail | 222 48.1 | S43 31.1 |
| 17 | 249 38.2 | 84 43.3 | 55.7 | 176 58.0 | 26.9 | 244 15.7 | 34.3 | 287 05.1 | 09.7 | | | |
| 18 | 264 40.7 | 99 42.9 N 7 54.6 | | 191 59.2 N21 27.1 | | 259 18.4 N 0 34.2 | | 302 07.7 S16 09.7 | | Vega | 80 34.4 | N38 48.5 |
| 19 | 279 43.1 | 114 42.4 | 53.4 | 207 00.5 | 27.3 | 274 21.2 | 34.0 | 317 10.3 | 09.7 | Zuben'ubi | 136 58.4 | S16 08.0 |
| 20 | 294 45.6 | 129 42.0 | 52.2 | 222 01.7 | 27.5 | 289 23.9 | 33.9 | 332 12.9 | 09.8 | | SHA | Mer. Pass. |
| 21 | 309 48.0 | 144 41.6 . . | 51.1 | 237 03.0 . . | 27.6 | 304 26.7 . . | 33.8 | 347 15.5 . . | 09.8 | | ° ′ | h m |
| 22 | 324 50.5 | 159 41.1 | 49.9 | 252 04.2 | 27.8 | 319 29.5 | 33.6 | 2 18.1 | 09.9 | Venus | 197 04.4 | 11 20 |
| 23 | 339 53.0 | 174 40.7 | 48.7 | 267 05.5 | 28.0 | 334 32.2 | 33.5 | 17 20.7 | 09.9 | Mars | 288 10.1 | 5 15 |
| | h m | | | | | | | | | Jupiter | 354 25.6 | 0 50 |
| Mer. Pass. 0 28.1 | | v −0.4 | d 1.2 | v 1.2 | d 0.2 | v 2.8 | d 0.1 | v 2.6 | d 0.0 | Saturn | 37 21.1 | 21 55 |

| UT | SUN GHA | SUN Dec | MOON GHA | $v$ | MOON Dec | $d$ | HP |
|---|---|---|---|---|---|---|---|
| d h | ° ′ | ° ′ | ° ′ | ′ | ° ′ | ′ | ′ |
| **13** 00 | 180 58.5 | N 3 52.9 | 329 28.6 | 13.1 | N 7 26.1 | 14.8 | 57.5 |
| 01 | 195 58.7 | 52.0 | 344 00.7 | 13.2 | 7 40.9 | 14.8 | 57.5 |
| 02 | 210 58.9 | 51.0 | 358 32.9 | 13.2 | 7 55.7 | 14.7 | 57.5 |
| 03 | 225 59.2 | .. 50.1 | 13 05.1 | 13.2 | 8 10.4 | 14.7 | 57.4 |
| 04 | 240 59.4 | 49.1 | 27 37.3 | 13.2 | 8 25.1 | 14.6 | 57.4 |
| 05 | 255 59.6 | 48.2 | 42 09.5 | 13.2 | 8 39.7 | 14.6 | 57.4 |
| 06 | 270 59.8 | N 3 47.2 | 56 41.7 | 13.1 | N 8 54.3 | 14.5 | 57.3 |
| 07 | 286 00.0 | 46.2 | 71 13.8 | 13.2 | 9 08.8 | 14.4 | 57.3 |
| T 08 | 301 00.3 | 45.3 | 85 46.0 | 13.2 | 9 23.2 | 14.4 | 57.3 |
| U 09 | 316 00.5 | .. 44.3 | 100 18.2 | 13.1 | 9 37.6 | 14.3 | 57.2 |
| F 10 | 331 00.7 | 43.4 | 114 50.3 | 13.2 | 9 51.9 | 14.3 | 57.2 |
| S 11 | 346 00.9 | 42.4 | 129 22.5 | 13.2 | 10 06.2 | 14.2 | 57.2 |
| D 12 | 1 01.2 | N 3 41.5 | 143 54.7 | 13.1 | N10 20.4 | 14.1 | 57.1 |
| A 13 | 16 01.4 | 40.5 | 158 26.8 | 13.2 | 10 34.5 | 14.1 | 57.1 |
| Y 14 | 31 01.6 | 39.6 | 172 59.0 | 13.1 | 10 48.6 | 14.0 | 57.1 |
| 15 | 46 01.8 | .. 38.6 | 187 31.1 | 13.1 | 11 02.6 | 13.9 | 57.0 |
| 16 | 61 02.0 | 37.6 | 202 03.2 | 13.1 | 11 16.5 | 13.8 | 57.0 |
| 17 | 76 02.3 | 36.7 | 216 35.3 | 13.1 | 11 30.3 | 13.8 | 57.0 |
| 18 | 91 02.5 | N 3 35.7 | 231 07.4 | 13.1 | N11 44.1 | 13.8 | 56.9 |
| 19 | 106 02.7 | 34.8 | 245 39.5 | 13.1 | 11 57.9 | 13.6 | 56.9 |
| 20 | 121 02.9 | 33.8 | 260 11.6 | 13.1 | 12 11.5 | 13.6 | 56.9 |
| 21 | 136 03.2 | .. 32.8 | 274 43.7 | 13.0 | 12 25.1 | 13.5 | 56.8 |
| 22 | 151 03.4 | 31.9 | 289 15.7 | 13.0 | 12 38.6 | 13.4 | 56.8 |
| 23 | 166 03.6 | 30.9 | 303 47.7 | 13.1 | 12 52.0 | 13.4 | 56.8 |
| **14** 00 | 181 03.8 | N 3 30.0 | 318 19.8 | 13.0 | N13 05.4 | 13.3 | 56.7 |
| 01 | 196 04.1 | 29.0 | 332 51.8 | 12.9 | 13 18.7 | 13.2 | 56.7 |
| 02 | 211 04.3 | 28.1 | 347 23.7 | 13.0 | 13 31.9 | 13.1 | 56.7 |
| 03 | 226 04.5 | .. 27.1 | 1 55.7 | 12.9 | 13 45.0 | 13.0 | 56.6 |
| 04 | 241 04.7 | 26.1 | 16 27.6 | 13.0 | 13 58.0 | 13.0 | 56.6 |
| 05 | 256 04.9 | 25.2 | 30 59.6 | 12.9 | 14 11.0 | 12.9 | 56.6 |
| 06 | 271 05.2 | N 3 24.2 | 45 31.5 | 12.9 | N14 23.9 | 12.8 | 56.5 |
| W 07 | 286 05.4 | 23.3 | 60 03.4 | 12.8 | 14 36.7 | 12.7 | 56.5 |
| E 08 | 301 05.6 | 22.3 | 74 35.2 | 12.9 | 14 49.4 | 12.6 | 56.5 |
| D 09 | 316 05.8 | .. 21.3 | 89 07.1 | 12.8 | 15 02.0 | 12.6 | 56.4 |
| N 10 | 331 06.1 | 20.4 | 103 38.9 | 12.8 | 15 14.6 | 12.5 | 56.4 |
| E 11 | 346 06.3 | 19.4 | 118 10.7 | 12.7 | 15 27.1 | 12.4 | 56.4 |
| S 12 | 1 06.5 | N 3 18.5 | 132 42.4 | 12.8 | N15 39.5 | 12.3 | 56.3 |
| D 13 | 16 06.7 | 17.5 | 147 14.2 | 12.7 | 15 51.8 | 12.2 | 56.3 |
| A 14 | 31 07.0 | 16.6 | 161 45.9 | 12.7 | 16 04.0 | 12.1 | 56.3 |
| Y 15 | 46 07.2 | .. 15.6 | 176 17.6 | 12.7 | 16 16.1 | 12.0 | 56.2 |
| 16 | 61 07.4 | 14.6 | 190 49.3 | 12.6 | 16 28.1 | 12.0 | 56.2 |
| 17 | 76 07.6 | 13.7 | 205 20.9 | 12.6 | 16 40.1 | 11.8 | 56.2 |
| 18 | 91 07.9 | N 3 12.7 | 219 52.5 | 12.6 | N16 51.9 | 11.8 | 56.2 |
| 19 | 106 08.1 | 11.8 | 234 24.1 | 12.6 | 17 03.7 | 11.7 | 56.1 |
| 20 | 121 08.3 | 10.8 | 248 55.7 | 12.5 | 17 15.4 | 11.6 | 56.1 |
| 21 | 136 08.5 | .. 09.8 | 263 27.2 | 12.5 | 17 27.0 | 11.5 | 56.1 |
| 22 | 151 08.7 | 08.9 | 277 58.7 | 12.5 | 17 38.5 | 11.4 | 56.0 |
| 23 | 166 09.0 | 07.9 | 292 30.2 | 12.4 | 17 49.9 | 11.3 | 56.0 |
| **15** 00 | 181 09.2 | N 3 06.9 | 307 01.6 | 12.4 | N18 01.2 | 11.2 | 56.0 |
| 01 | 196 09.4 | 06.0 | 321 33.0 | 12.4 | 18 12.4 | 11.1 | 55.9 |
| 02 | 211 09.6 | 05.0 | 336 04.4 | 12.3 | 18 23.5 | 11.0 | 55.9 |
| 03 | 226 09.9 | .. 04.1 | 350 35.7 | 12.3 | 18 34.5 | 10.9 | 55.9 |
| 04 | 241 10.1 | 03.1 | 5 07.0 | 12.3 | 18 45.4 | 10.9 | 55.9 |
| 05 | 256 10.3 | 02.1 | 19 38.3 | 12.3 | 18 56.3 | 10.7 | 55.8 |
| 06 | 271 10.5 | N 3 01.2 | 34 09.6 | 12.2 | N19 07.0 | 10.6 | 55.8 |
| 07 | 286 10.8 | 3 00.2 | 48 40.8 | 12.2 | 19 17.6 | 10.5 | 55.8 |
| T 08 | 301 11.0 | 2 59.3 | 63 12.0 | 12.1 | 19 28.1 | 10.4 | 55.7 |
| H 09 | 316 11.2 | .. 58.3 | 77 43.1 | 12.1 | 19 38.5 | 10.4 | 55.7 |
| U 10 | 331 11.4 | 57.3 | 92 14.2 | 12.1 | 19 48.9 | 10.2 | 55.7 |
| R 11 | 346 11.7 | 56.4 | 106 45.3 | 12.1 | 19 59.1 | 10.1 | 55.7 |
| S 12 | 1 11.9 | N 2 55.4 | 121 16.4 | 12.0 | N20 09.2 | 10.0 | 55.6 |
| D 13 | 16 12.1 | 54.5 | 135 47.4 | 12.0 | 20 19.2 | 9.9 | 55.6 |
| A 14 | 31 12.3 | 53.5 | 150 18.4 | 11.9 | 20 29.1 | 9.8 | 55.6 |
| Y 15 | 46 12.5 | .. 52.5 | 164 49.3 | 11.9 | 20 38.9 | 9.7 | 55.5 |
| 16 | 61 12.8 | 51.6 | 179 20.2 | 11.9 | 20 48.6 | 9.6 | 55.5 |
| 17 | 76 13.0 | 50.6 | 193 51.1 | 11.9 | 20 58.2 | 9.5 | 55.5 |
| 18 | 91 13.2 | N 2 49.6 | 208 22.0 | 11.8 | N21 07.7 | 9.4 | 55.5 |
| 19 | 106 13.4 | 48.7 | 222 52.8 | 11.7 | 21 17.1 | 9.3 | 55.4 |
| 20 | 121 13.7 | 47.7 | 237 23.5 | 11.8 | 21 26.4 | 9.1 | 55.4 |
| 21 | 136 13.9 | .. 46.8 | 251 54.3 | 11.7 | 21 35.5 | 9.1 | 55.4 |
| 22 | 151 14.1 | 45.8 | 266 25.0 | 11.6 | 21 44.6 | 8.9 | 55.4 |
| 23 | 166 14.3 | 44.8 | 280 55.6 | 11.7 | N21 53.5 | 8.8 | 55.3 |
| | SD 15.9 | $d$ 1.0 | SD 15.6 | | 15.4 | | 15.2 |

| Lat. | Twilight Naut. | Twilight Civil | Sunrise | Moonrise 13 | Moonrise 14 | Moonrise 15 | Moonrise 16 |
|---|---|---|---|---|---|---|---|
| ° | h m | h m | h m | h m | h m | h m | h m |
| N 72 | 01 58 | 03 49 | 05 02 | 17 59 | 16 54 | ▭ | ▭ |
| N 70 | 02 32 | 04 03 | 05 08 | 18 18 | 17 38 | ▭ | ▭ |
| 68 | 02 56 | 04 14 | 05 13 | 18 33 | 18 08 | 17 21 | ▭ |
| 66 | 03 14 | 04 23 | 05 17 | 18 45 | 18 30 | 18 08 | ▭ |
| 64 | 03 29 | 04 31 | 05 20 | 18 56 | 18 48 | 18 38 | 18 23 |
| 62 | 03 40 | 04 37 | 05 23 | 19 05 | 19 03 | 19 01 | 19 02 |
| 60 | 03 50 | 04 43 | 05 25 | 19 12 | 19 15 | 19 20 | 19 22 |
| N 58 | 03 59 | 04 47 | 05 27 | 19 19 | 19 26 | 19 36 | 19 51 |
| 56 | 04 06 | 04 52 | 05 29 | 19 25 | 19 35 | 19 49 | 20 08 |
| 54 | 04 12 | 04 55 | 05 31 | 19 31 | 19 44 | 20 00 | 20 23 |
| 52 | 04 18 | 04 59 | 05 33 | 19 36 | 19 51 | 20 11 | 20 36 |
| 50 | 04 23 | 05 02 | 05 34 | 19 40 | 19 58 | 20 20 | 20 48 |
| 45 | 04 33 | 05 08 | 05 37 | 19 50 | 20 13 | 20 39 | 21 11 |
| N 40 | 04 41 | 05 13 | 05 40 | 19 58 | 20 25 | 20 55 | 21 31 |
| 35 | 04 47 | 05 17 | 05 42 | 20 05 | 20 35 | 21 09 | 21 47 |
| 30 | 04 52 | 05 20 | 05 44 | 20 11 | 20 45 | 21 21 | 22 01 |
| 20 | 04 59 | 05 25 | 05 47 | 20 22 | 21 00 | 21 41 | 22 24 |
| N 10 | 05 04 | 05 29 | 05 50 | 20 32 | 21 14 | 21 59 | 22 45 |
| 0 | 05 08 | 05 32 | 05 52 | 20 41 | 21 28 | 22 15 | 23 04 |
| S 10 | 05 09 | 05 34 | 05 55 | 20 50 | 21 41 | 22 32 | 23 24 |
| 20 | 05 10 | 05 35 | 05 57 | 21 00 | 21 55 | 22 50 | 23 45 |
| 30 | 05 08 | 05 36 | 06 00 | 21 11 | 22 11 | 23 11 | 24 09 |
| 35 | 05 07 | 05 36 | 06 01 | 21 18 | 22 21 | 23 23 | 24 24 |
| 40 | 05 04 | 05 36 | 06 03 | 21 25 | 22 32 | 23 37 | 24 40 |
| 45 | 05 01 | 05 35 | 06 05 | 21 34 | 22 45 | 23 54 | 25 00 |
| S 50 | 04 57 | 05 35 | 06 07 | 21 45 | 23 01 | 24 15 | 00 15 |
| 52 | 04 55 | 05 34 | 06 08 | 21 50 | 23 09 | 24 25 | 00 25 |
| 54 | 04 53 | 05 34 | 06 10 | 21 56 | 23 17 | 24 36 | 00 36 |
| 56 | 04 50 | 05 33 | 06 10 | 22 02 | 23 26 | 24 49 | 00 49 |
| 58 | 04 46 | 05 32 | 06 11 | 22 09 | 23 37 | 25 05 | 01 05 |
| S 60 | 04 43 | 05 31 | 06 13 | 22 16 | 23 50 | 25 23 | 01 23 |

| Lat. | Sunset | Twilight Civil | Twilight Naut. | Moonset 13 | Moonset 14 | Moonset 15 | Moonset 16 |
|---|---|---|---|---|---|---|---|
| ° | h m | h m | h m | h m | h m | h m | h m |
| N 72 | 18 46 | 19 58 | 21 45 | 10 31 | 13 13 | ▭ | ▭ |
| N 70 | 18 41 | 19 45 | 21 13 | 10 14 | 12 31 | ▭ | ▭ |
| 68 | 18 36 | 19 34 | 20 51 | 10 01 | 12 03 | 14 29 | ▭ |
| 66 | 18 33 | 19 25 | 20 34 | 09 51 | 11 42 | 13 44 | ▭ |
| 64 | 18 30 | 19 18 | 20 20 | 09 42 | 11 26 | 13 11 | 15 10 |
| 62 | 18 27 | 19 12 | 20 08 | 09 34 | 11 12 | 12 51 | 14 32 |
| 60 | 18 24 | 19 07 | 19 59 | 09 28 | 11 01 | 12 34 | 14 05 |
| N 58 | 18 22 | 19 02 | 19 51 | 09 22 | 10 51 | 12 19 | 13 45 |
| 56 | 18 21 | 18 58 | 19 44 | 09 17 | 10 42 | 12 06 | 13 27 |
| 54 | 18 19 | 18 55 | 19 38 | 09 13 | 10 34 | 11 55 | 13 13 |
| 52 | 18 17 | 18 51 | 19 32 | 09 09 | 10 28 | 11 45 | 13 00 |
| 50 | 18 16 | 18 49 | 19 27 | 09 05 | 10 21 | 11 37 | 12 49 |
| 45 | 18 13 | 18 43 | 19 17 | 08 57 | 10 08 | 11 18 | 12 26 |
| N 40 | 18 11 | 18 38 | 19 10 | 08 50 | 09 58 | 11 04 | 12 08 |
| 35 | 18 09 | 18 34 | 19 04 | 08 45 | 09 48 | 10 51 | 11 53 |
| 30 | 18 07 | 18 31 | 18 59 | 08 40 | 09 40 | 10 40 | 11 39 |
| 20 | 18 04 | 18 26 | 18 51 | 08 31 | 09 26 | 10 21 | 11 17 |
| N 10 | 18 01 | 18 22 | 18 47 | 08 24 | 09 14 | 10 05 | 10 57 |
| 0 | 17 59 | 18 20 | 18 44 | 08 17 | 09 03 | 09 50 | 10 39 |
| S 10 | 17 57 | 18 18 | 18 42 | 08 10 | 08 52 | 09 35 | 10 21 |
| 20 | 17 54 | 18 16 | 18 42 | 08 03 | 08 40 | 09 19 | 10 01 |
| 30 | 17 52 | 18 16 | 18 44 | 07 54 | 08 27 | 09 01 | 09 39 |
| 35 | 17 51 | 18 16 | 18 45 | 07 49 | 08 19 | 08 50 | 09 26 |
| 40 | 17 49 | 18 16 | 18 47 | 07 44 | 08 10 | 08 38 | 09 11 |
| 45 | 17 47 | 18 17 | 18 51 | 07 38 | 08 00 | 08 24 | 08 53 |
| S 50 | 17 45 | 18 18 | 18 55 | 07 30 | 07 47 | 08 07 | 08 31 |
| 52 | 17 44 | 18 19 | 18 57 | 07 27 | 07 41 | 07 59 | 08 21 |
| 54 | 17 43 | 18 19 | 19 00 | 07 23 | 07 35 | 07 50 | 08 09 |
| 56 | 17 42 | 18 19 | 19 03 | 07 19 | 07 28 | 07 40 | 07 56 |
| 58 | 17 41 | 18 20 | 19 07 | 07 14 | 07 20 | 07 28 | 07 40 |
| S 60 | 17 40 | 18 21 | 19 10 | 07 09 | 07 11 | 07 15 | 07 21 |

| | SUN | | | MOON | | | |
|---|---|---|---|---|---|---|---|
| Day | Eqn. of Time 00h | 12h | Mer. Pass. | Mer. Pass. Upper | Lower | Age | Phase |
| d | m s | m s | h m | h m | h m | d | % |
| 13 | 03 53 | 04 04 | 11 56 | 02 06 | 14 29 | 17 | 89 |
| 14 | 04 15 | 04 26 | 11 56 | 02 52 | 15 15 | 18 | 81 |
| 15 | 04 36 | 04 47 | 11 55 | 03 39 | 16 03 | 19 | 73 |

| UT | ARIES | VENUS −3.9 | | MARS −0.4 | | JUPITER −2.9 | | SATURN +0.4 | | STARS | | |
|---|---|---|---|---|---|---|---|---|---|---|---|---|
| | GHA | GHA | Dec | GHA | Dec | GHA | Dec | GHA | Dec | Name | SHA | Dec |
| d h | ° ′ | ° ′ | ° ′ | ° ′ | ° ′ | ° ′ | ° ′ | ° ′ | ° ′ | | ° ′ | ° ′ |
| 16 00 | 354 55.4 | 189 40.3 | N 7 47.6 | 282 06.8 | N21 28.2 | 349 35.0 | N 0 33.4 | 32 23.3 | S16 10.0 | Acamar | 315 13.0 | S40 12.6 |
| 01 | 9 57.9 | 204 39.8 | 46.4 | 297 08.0 | 28.4 | 4 37.7 | 33.2 | 47 25.9 | 10.0 | Achernar | 335 21.1 | S57 07.1 |
| 02 | 25 00.4 | 219 39.4 | 45.2 | 312 09.3 | 28.6 | 19 40.5 | 33.1 | 62 28.5 | 10.1 | Acrux | 173 02.9 | S63 13.4 |
| 03 | 40 02.8 | 234 38.9 | .. 44.1 | 327 10.5 | .. 28.8 | 34 43.2 | .. 33.0 | 77 31.1 | .. 10.1 | Adhara | 255 07.5 | S28 59.9 |
| 04 | 55 05.3 | 249 38.5 | 42.9 | 342 11.8 | 29.0 | 49 46.0 | 32.9 | 92 33.7 | 10.1 | Aldebaran | 290 41.7 | N16 33.3 |
| 05 | 70 07.8 | 264 38.1 | 41.7 | 357 13.0 | 29.2 | 64 48.8 | 32.7 | 107 36.3 | 10.2 | | | |
| 06 | 85 10.2 | 279 37.6 | N 7 40.5 | 12 14.3 | N21 29.3 | 79 51.5 | N 0 32.6 | 122 38.9 | S16 10.2 | Alioth | 166 15.2 | N55 50.4 |
| 07 | 100 12.7 | 294 37.2 | 39.4 | 27 15.6 | 29.5 | 94 54.3 | 32.5 | 137 41.5 | 10.3 | Alkaid | 152 53.9 | N49 12.3 |
| 08 | 115 15.2 | 309 36.8 | 38.2 | 42 16.8 | 29.7 | 109 57.0 | 32.3 | 152 44.1 | 10.3 | Alnair | 27 34.9 | S46 51.1 |
| 09 | 130 17.6 | 324 36.3 | .. 37.0 | 57 18.1 | .. 29.9 | 124 59.8 | .. 32.2 | 167 46.7 | .. 10.4 | Alnilam | 275 39.7 | S 1 11.1 |
| 10 | 145 20.1 | 339 35.9 | 35.8 | 72 19.3 | 30.1 | 140 02.5 | 32.1 | 182 49.3 | 10.4 | Alphard | 217 49.9 | S 8 45.2 |
| 11 | 160 22.5 | 354 35.5 | 34.7 | 87 20.6 | 30.3 | 155 05.3 | 31.9 | 197 51.9 | 10.4 | | | |
| 12 | 175 25.0 | 9 35.0 | N 7 33.5 | 102 21.9 | N21 30.5 | 170 08.1 | N 0 31.8 | 212 54.5 | S16 10.5 | Alphecca | 126 05.5 | N26 38.6 |
| 13 | 190 27.5 | 24 34.6 | 32.3 | 117 23.1 | 30.7 | 185 10.8 | 31.7 | 227 57.1 | 10.5 | Alpheratz | 357 36.4 | N29 13.0 |
| 14 | 205 29.9 | 39 34.2 | 31.2 | 132 24.4 | 30.8 | 200 13.6 | 31.5 | 242 59.7 | 10.6 | Altair | 62 01.6 | N 8 55.8 |
| 15 | 220 32.4 | 54 33.7 | .. 30.0 | 147 25.6 | .. 31.0 | 215 16.3 | .. 31.4 | 258 02.3 | .. 10.6 | Ankaa | 353 08.6 | S42 10.9 |
| 16 | 235 34.9 | 69 33.3 | 28.8 | 162 26.9 | 31.2 | 230 19.1 | 31.3 | 273 04.9 | 10.7 | Antares | 112 18.3 | S26 28.9 |
| 17 | 250 37.3 | 84 32.9 | 27.6 | 177 28.2 | 31.4 | 245 21.8 | 31.1 | 288 07.5 | 10.7 | | | |
| 18 | 265 39.8 | 99 32.4 | N 7 26.5 | 192 29.4 | N21 31.6 | 260 24.6 | N 0 31.0 | 303 10.1 | S16 10.7 | Arcturus | 145 49.9 | N19 04.1 |
| 19 | 280 42.3 | 114 32.0 | 25.3 | 207 30.7 | 31.8 | 275 27.4 | 30.9 | 318 12.7 | 10.8 | Atria | 107 14.3 | S69 04.3 |
| 20 | 295 44.7 | 129 31.6 | 24.1 | 222 32.0 | 31.9 | 290 30.1 | 30.8 | 333 15.3 | 10.8 | Avior | 234 15.9 | S59 34.6 |
| 21 | 310 47.2 | 144 31.1 | .. 22.9 | 237 33.2 | .. 32.1 | 305 32.9 | .. 30.6 | 348 17.9 | .. 10.9 | Bellatrix | 278 24.9 | N 6 22.3 |
| 22 | 325 49.6 | 159 30.7 | 21.7 | 252 34.5 | 32.3 | 320 35.6 | 30.5 | 3 20.5 | 10.9 | Betelgeuse | 270 54.2 | N 7 24.8 |
| 23 | 340 52.1 | 174 30.3 | 20.6 | 267 35.8 | 32.5 | 335 38.4 | 30.4 | 18 23.1 | 11.0 | | | |
| 17 00 | 355 54.6 | 189 29.8 | N 7 19.4 | 282 37.0 | N21 32.7 | 350 41.2 | N 0 30.2 | 33 25.7 | S16 11.0 | Canopus | 263 53.3 | S52 42.1 |
| 01 | 10 57.0 | 204 29.4 | 18.2 | 297 38.3 | 32.9 | 5 43.9 | 30.1 | 48 28.3 | 11.0 | Capella | 280 24.7 | N46 01.1 |
| 02 | 25 59.5 | 219 29.0 | 17.0 | 312 39.6 | 33.1 | 20 46.7 | 30.0 | 63 30.9 | 11.1 | Deneb | 49 26.8 | N45 21.9 |
| 03 | 41 02.0 | 234 28.5 | .. 15.9 | 327 40.9 | .. 33.2 | 35 49.4 | .. 29.8 | 78 33.5 | .. 11.1 | Denebola | 182 27.2 | N14 26.9 |
| 04 | 56 04.4 | 249 28.1 | 14.7 | 342 42.1 | 33.4 | 50 52.2 | 29.7 | 93 36.1 | 11.2 | Diphda | 348 48.9 | S17 51.6 |
| 05 | 71 06.9 | 264 27.7 | 13.5 | 357 43.4 | 33.6 | 65 55.0 | 29.6 | 108 38.7 | 11.2 | | | |
| 06 | 86 09.4 | 279 27.2 | N 7 12.3 | 12 44.7 | N21 33.8 | 80 57.7 | N 0 29.4 | 123 41.3 | S16 11.3 | Dubhe | 193 44.0 | N61 37.8 |
| 07 | 101 11.8 | 294 26.8 | 11.1 | 27 46.0 | 34.0 | 96 00.5 | 29.3 | 138 43.9 | 11.3 | Elnath | 278 04.3 | N28 37.5 |
| 08 | 116 14.3 | 309 26.4 | 10.0 | 42 47.2 | 34.2 | 111 03.2 | 29.2 | 153 46.5 | 11.3 | Eltanin | 90 43.0 | N51 29.4 |
| 09 | 131 16.8 | 324 26.0 | .. 08.8 | 57 48.5 | .. 34.3 | 126 06.0 | .. 29.0 | 168 49.1 | .. 11.4 | Enif | 33 40.4 | N 9 58.8 |
| 10 | 146 19.2 | 339 25.5 | 07.6 | 72 49.8 | 34.5 | 141 08.8 | 28.9 | 183 51.7 | 11.4 | Fomalhaut | 15 16.3 | S29 30.1 |
| 11 | 161 21.7 | 354 25.1 | 06.4 | 87 51.1 | 34.7 | 156 11.5 | 28.8 | 198 54.3 | 11.5 | | | |
| 12 | 176 24.1 | 9 24.7 | N 7 05.2 | 102 52.3 | N21 34.9 | 171 14.3 | N 0 28.7 | 213 56.9 | S16 11.5 | Gacrux | 171 54.3 | S57 14.3 |
| 13 | 191 26.6 | 24 24.2 | 04.0 | 117 53.6 | 35.1 | 186 17.0 | 28.5 | 228 59.5 | 11.6 | Gienah | 175 45.9 | S17 39.9 |
| 14 | 206 29.1 | 39 23.8 | 02.9 | 132 54.9 | 35.2 | 201 19.8 | 28.4 | 244 02.1 | 11.6 | Hadar | 148 39.2 | S60 29.0 |
| 15 | 221 31.5 | 54 23.4 | .. 01.7 | 147 56.2 | .. 35.4 | 216 22.6 | .. 28.3 | 259 04.7 | .. 11.6 | Hamal | 327 53.1 | N23 34.2 |
| 16 | 236 34.0 | 69 23.0 | 7 00.5 | 162 57.5 | 35.6 | 231 25.3 | 28.1 | 274 07.3 | 11.7 | Kaus Aust. | 83 35.0 | S34 22.5 |
| 17 | 251 36.5 | 84 22.5 | 6 59.3 | 177 58.7 | 35.8 | 246 28.1 | 28.0 | 289 09.9 | 11.7 | | | |
| 18 | 266 38.9 | 99 22.1 | N 6 58.1 | 193 00.0 | N21 36.0 | 261 30.8 | N 0 27.9 | 304 12.5 | S16 11.8 | Kochab | 137 20.5 | N74 04.0 |
| 19 | 281 41.4 | 114 21.7 | 56.9 | 208 01.3 | 36.2 | 276 33.6 | 27.7 | 319 15.1 | 11.8 | Markab | 13 31.5 | N15 19.7 |
| 20 | 296 43.9 | 129 21.2 | 55.8 | 223 02.6 | 36.3 | 291 36.4 | 27.6 | 334 17.7 | 11.9 | Menkar | 314 08.0 | N 4 10.8 |
| 21 | 311 46.3 | 144 20.8 | .. 54.6 | 238 03.9 | .. 36.5 | 306 39.1 | .. 27.5 | 349 20.3 | .. 11.9 | Menkent | 148 00.2 | S36 28.8 |
| 22 | 326 48.8 | 159 20.4 | 53.4 | 253 05.2 | 36.7 | 321 41.9 | 27.3 | 4 22.9 | 11.9 | Miaplacidus | 221 39.4 | S69 48.3 |
| 23 | 341 51.3 | 174 20.0 | 52.2 | 268 06.4 | 36.9 | 336 44.6 | 27.2 | 19 25.5 | 12.0 | | | |
| 18 00 | 356 53.7 | 189 19.5 | N 6 51.0 | 283 07.7 | N21 37.1 | 351 47.4 | N 0 27.1 | 34 28.1 | S16 12.0 | Mirfak | 308 30.7 | N49 56.3 |
| 01 | 11 56.2 | 204 19.1 | 49.8 | 298 09.0 | 37.2 | 6 50.2 | 26.9 | 49 30.6 | 12.1 | Nunki | 75 50.0 | S26 16.1 |
| 02 | 26 58.6 | 219 18.7 | 48.6 | 313 10.3 | 37.4 | 21 52.9 | 26.8 | 64 33.2 | 12.1 | Peacock | 53 08.4 | S56 39.9 |
| 03 | 42 01.1 | 234 18.3 | .. 47.4 | 328 11.6 | .. 37.6 | 36 55.7 | .. 26.7 | 79 35.8 | .. 12.1 | Pollux | 243 19.8 | N27 58.3 |
| 04 | 57 03.6 | 249 17.8 | 46.3 | 343 12.9 | 37.8 | 51 58.5 | 26.5 | 94 38.4 | 12.2 | Procyon | 244 53.0 | N 5 10.2 |
| 05 | 72 06.0 | 264 17.4 | 45.1 | 358 14.2 | 38.0 | 67 01.2 | 26.4 | 109 41.0 | 12.2 | | | |
| 06 | 87 08.5 | 279 17.0 | N 6 43.9 | 13 15.5 | N21 38.1 | 82 04.0 | N 0 26.3 | 124 43.6 | S16 12.3 | Rasalhague | 96 00.3 | N12 32.8 |
| 07 | 102 11.0 | 294 16.6 | 42.7 | 28 16.8 | 38.3 | 97 06.7 | 26.1 | 139 46.2 | 12.3 | Regulus | 207 36.8 | N11 51.6 |
| 08 | 117 13.4 | 309 16.1 | 41.5 | 43 18.0 | 38.5 | 112 09.5 | 26.0 | 154 48.8 | 12.4 | Rigel | 281 05.7 | S 8 10.3 |
| 09 | 132 15.9 | 324 15.7 | .. 40.3 | 58 19.3 | .. 38.7 | 127 12.3 | .. 25.9 | 169 51.4 | .. 12.4 | Rigil Kent. | 139 43.4 | S60 55.8 |
| 10 | 147 18.4 | 339 15.3 | 39.1 | 73 20.6 | 38.8 | 142 15.0 | 25.8 | 184 54.0 | 12.4 | Sabik | 102 05.0 | S15 45.1 |
| 11 | 162 20.8 | 354 14.9 | 37.9 | 88 21.9 | 39.0 | 157 17.8 | 25.6 | 199 56.6 | 12.5 | | | |
| 12 | 177 23.3 | 9 14.4 | N 6 36.7 | 103 23.2 | N21 39.2 | 172 20.5 | N 0 25.5 | 214 59.2 | S16 12.5 | Schedar | 349 32.7 | N56 39.6 |
| 13 | 192 25.8 | 24 14.0 | 35.5 | 118 24.5 | 39.4 | 187 23.3 | 25.4 | 230 01.8 | 12.6 | Shaula | 96 13.0 | S37 07.3 |
| 14 | 207 28.2 | 39 13.6 | 34.4 | 133 25.8 | 39.6 | 202 26.1 | 25.2 | 245 04.4 | 12.6 | Sirius | 258 28.0 | S16 44.6 |
| 15 | 222 30.7 | 54 13.2 | .. 33.2 | 148 27.1 | .. 39.7 | 217 28.8 | .. 25.1 | 260 07.0 | .. 12.6 | Spica | 158 24.6 | S11 16.6 |
| 16 | 237 33.1 | 69 12.7 | 32.0 | 163 28.4 | 39.9 | 232 31.6 | 25.0 | 275 09.6 | 12.7 | Suhail | 222 48.1 | S43 31.1 |
| 17 | 252 35.6 | 84 12.3 | 30.8 | 178 29.7 | 40.1 | 247 34.4 | 24.8 | 290 12.2 | 12.7 | | | |
| 18 | 267 38.1 | 99 11.9 | N 6 29.6 | 193 31.0 | N21 40.3 | 262 37.1 | N 0 24.7 | 305 14.8 | S16 12.8 | Vega | 80 34.4 | N38 48.5 |
| 19 | 282 40.5 | 114 11.5 | 28.4 | 208 32.3 | 40.4 | 277 39.9 | 24.6 | 320 17.4 | 12.8 | Zuben'ubi | 136 58.4 | S16 08.0 |
| 20 | 297 43.0 | 129 11.1 | 27.2 | 223 33.6 | 40.6 | 292 42.7 | 24.4 | 335 20.0 | 12.8 | | SHA | Mer.Pass. |
| 21 | 312 45.5 | 144 10.6 | .. 26.0 | 238 34.9 | .. 40.8 | 307 45.4 | .. 24.3 | 350 22.5 | .. 12.9 | | ° ′ | h m |
| 22 | 327 47.9 | 159 10.2 | 24.8 | 253 36.2 | 41.0 | 322 48.2 | 24.2 | 5 25.1 | 12.9 | Venus | 193 35.3 | 11 22 |
| 23 | 342 50.4 | 174 09.8 | 23.6 | 268 37.5 | 41.1 | 337 50.9 | 24.0 | 20 27.7 | 13.0 | Mars | 286 42.5 | 5 09 |
| | h m | | | | | | | | | Jupiter | 354 46.6 | 0 37 |
| Mer.Pass. | 0 16.3 | v −0.4 | d 1.2 | v 1.3 | d 0.2 | v 2.8 | d 0.1 | v 2.6 | d 0.0 | Saturn | 37 31.1 | 21 43 |

| UT | SUN GHA | Dec | MOON GHA | v | Dec | d | HP |
|---|---|---|---|---|---|---|---|
| | ° ′ | ° ′ | ° ′ | ′ | ° ′ | ′ | ′ |
| **16** 00 | 181 14.6 | N 2 43.9 | 295 26.3 | 11.6 | N22 02.3 | 8.8 | 55.3 |
| 01 | 196 14.8 | 42.9 | 309 56.9 | 11.5 | 22 11.1 | 8.6 | 55.3 |
| 02 | 211 15.0 | 41.9 | 324 27.4 | 11.6 | 22 19.7 | 8.5 | 55.3 |
| 03 | 226 15.2 | .. 41.0 | 338 58.0 | 11.4 | 22 28.2 | 8.4 | 55.2 |
| 04 | 241 15.5 | 40.0 | 353 28.4 | 11.5 | 22 36.6 | 8.2 | 55.2 |
| 05 | 256 15.7 | 39.0 | 7 58.9 | 11.4 | 22 44.8 | 8.2 | 55.2 |
| 06 | 271 15.9 | N 2 38.1 | 22 29.3 | 11.4 | N22 53.0 | 8.0 | 55.2 |
| 07 | 286 16.1 | 37.1 | 36 59.7 | 11.4 | 23 01.0 | 8.0 | 55.1 |
| **F** 08 | 301 16.3 | 36.2 | 51 30.1 | 11.3 | 23 09.0 | 7.8 | 55.1 |
| **R** 09 | 316 16.6 | .. 35.2 | 66 00.4 | 11.2 | 23 16.8 | 7.7 | 55.1 |
| **I** 10 | 331 16.8 | 34.2 | 80 30.6 | 11.3 | 23 24.5 | 7.6 | 55.1 |
| **D** 11 | 346 17.0 | 33.3 | 95 00.9 | 11.2 | 23 32.1 | 7.4 | 55.0 |
| **A** 12 | 1 17.2 | N 2 32.3 | 109 31.1 | 11.2 | N23 39.5 | 7.4 | 55.0 |
| **Y** 13 | 16 17.5 | 31.3 | 124 01.3 | 11.1 | 23 46.9 | 7.2 | 55.0 |
| 14 | 31 17.7 | 30.4 | 138 31.4 | 11.1 | 23 54.1 | 7.1 | 55.0 |
| 15 | 46 17.9 | .. 29.4 | 153 01.5 | 11.1 | 24 01.2 | 7.0 | 55.0 |
| 16 | 61 18.1 | 28.4 | 167 31.6 | 11.1 | 24 08.2 | 6.9 | 54.9 |
| 17 | 76 18.4 | 27.5 | 182 01.7 | 11.0 | 24 15.1 | 6.7 | 54.9 |
| 18 | 91 18.6 | N 2 26.5 | 196 31.7 | 11.0 | N24 21.8 | 6.7 | 54.9 |
| 19 | 106 18.8 | 25.5 | 211 01.7 | 10.9 | 24 28.5 | 6.5 | 54.9 |
| 20 | 121 19.0 | 24.6 | 225 31.6 | 10.9 | 24 35.0 | 6.4 | 54.9 |
| 21 | 136 19.3 | .. 23.6 | 240 01.5 | 10.9 | 24 41.4 | 6.2 | 54.8 |
| 22 | 151 19.5 | 22.7 | 254 31.4 | 10.9 | 24 47.6 | 6.2 | 54.8 |
| 23 | 166 19.7 | 21.7 | 269 01.3 | 10.8 | 24 53.8 | 6.0 | 54.8 |
| **17** 00 | 181 19.9 | N 2 20.7 | 283 31.1 | 10.8 | N24 59.8 | 5.9 | 54.8 |
| 01 | 196 20.2 | 19.8 | 298 00.9 | 10.8 | 25 05.7 | 5.8 | 54.8 |
| 02 | 211 20.4 | 18.8 | 312 30.7 | 10.7 | 25 11.5 | 5.6 | 54.7 |
| 03 | 226 20.6 | .. 17.8 | 327 00.4 | 10.7 | 25 17.1 | 5.6 | 54.7 |
| 04 | 241 20.8 | 16.9 | 341 30.1 | 10.7 | 25 22.7 | 5.4 | 54.7 |
| 05 | 256 21.0 | 15.9 | 355 59.8 | 10.6 | 25 28.1 | 5.3 | 54.7 |
| 06 | 271 21.3 | N 2 14.9 | 10 29.4 | 10.7 | N25 33.4 | 5.1 | 54.7 |
| **S** 07 | 286 21.5 | 14.0 | 24 59.1 | 10.6 | 25 38.5 | 5.1 | 54.7 |
| **A** 08 | 301 21.7 | 13.0 | 39 28.7 | 10.5 | 25 43.6 | 4.9 | 54.6 |
| **T** 09 | 316 21.9 | .. 12.0 | 53 58.2 | 10.6 | 25 48.5 | 4.7 | 54.6 |
| **U** 10 | 331 22.2 | 11.1 | 68 27.8 | 10.5 | 25 53.2 | 4.7 | 54.6 |
| **R** 11 | 346 22.4 | 10.1 | 82 57.3 | 10.5 | 25 57.9 | 4.5 | 54.6 |
| **D** 12 | 1 22.6 | N 2 09.1 | 97 26.8 | 10.5 | N26 02.4 | 4.4 | 54.6 |
| **A** 13 | 16 22.8 | 08.2 | 111 56.3 | 10.5 | 26 06.8 | 4.3 | 54.6 |
| **Y** 14 | 31 23.1 | 07.2 | 126 25.8 | 10.4 | 26 11.1 | 4.1 | 54.6 |
| 15 | 46 23.3 | .. 06.2 | 140 55.2 | 10.4 | 26 15.2 | 4.0 | 54.5 |
| 16 | 61 23.5 | 05.3 | 155 24.6 | 10.4 | 26 19.2 | 3.9 | 54.5 |
| 17 | 76 23.7 | 04.3 | 169 54.0 | 10.4 | 26 23.1 | 3.8 | 54.5 |
| 18 | 91 24.0 | N 2 03.3 | 184 23.4 | 10.3 | N26 26.9 | 3.6 | 54.5 |
| 19 | 106 24.2 | 02.4 | 198 52.7 | 10.4 | 26 30.5 | 3.5 | 54.5 |
| 20 | 121 24.4 | 01.4 | 213 22.1 | 10.3 | 26 34.0 | 3.4 | 54.5 |
| 21 | 136 24.6 | 2 00.4 | 227 51.4 | 10.3 | 26 37.4 | 3.2 | 54.5 |
| 22 | 151 24.8 | 1 59.5 | 242 20.7 | 10.3 | 26 40.6 | 3.1 | 54.4 |
| 23 | 166 25.1 | 58.5 | 256 50.0 | 10.3 | 26 43.7 | 3.0 | 54.4 |
| **18** 00 | 181 25.3 | N 1 57.5 | 271 19.3 | 10.2 | N26 46.7 | 2.8 | 54.4 |
| 01 | 196 25.5 | 56.6 | 285 48.5 | 10.3 | 26 49.5 | 2.8 | 54.4 |
| 02 | 211 25.7 | 55.6 | 300 17.8 | 10.2 | 26 52.3 | 2.6 | 54.4 |
| 03 | 226 26.0 | .. 54.6 | 314 47.0 | 10.2 | 26 54.9 | 2.4 | 54.4 |
| 04 | 241 26.2 | 53.7 | 329 16.2 | 10.2 | 26 57.3 | 2.3 | 54.4 |
| 05 | 256 26.4 | 52.7 | 343 45.4 | 10.2 | 26 59.6 | 2.2 | 54.4 |
| 06 | 271 26.6 | N 1 51.7 | 358 14.6 | 10.2 | N27 01.8 | 2.1 | 54.4 |
| 07 | 286 26.9 | 50.8 | 12 43.8 | 10.2 | 27 03.9 | 1.9 | 54.3 |
| **S** 08 | 301 27.1 | 49.8 | 27 13.0 | 10.2 | 27 05.8 | 1.8 | 54.3 |
| **U** 09 | 316 27.3 | .. 48.8 | 41 42.2 | 10.1 | 27 07.6 | 1.7 | 54.3 |
| **N** 10 | 331 27.5 | 47.9 | 56 11.3 | 10.2 | 27 09.3 | 1.5 | 54.3 |
| **D** 11 | 346 27.7 | 46.9 | 70 40.5 | 10.1 | 27 10.8 | 1.5 | 54.3 |
| **A** 12 | 1 28.0 | N 1 45.9 | 85 09.6 | 10.2 | N27 12.3 | 1.2 | 54.3 |
| **Y** 13 | 16 28.2 | 45.0 | 99 38.8 | 10.1 | 27 13.5 | 1.2 | 54.3 |
| 14 | 31 28.4 | 44.0 | 114 07.9 | 10.2 | 27 14.7 | 1.0 | 54.3 |
| 15 | 46 28.6 | .. 43.0 | 128 37.1 | 10.1 | 27 15.7 | 0.9 | 54.3 |
| 16 | 61 28.9 | 42.0 | 143 06.2 | 10.1 | 27 16.6 | 0.7 | 54.3 |
| 17 | 76 29.1 | 41.1 | 157 35.4 | 10.1 | 27 17.3 | 0.6 | 54.3 |
| 18 | 91 29.3 | N 1 40.1 | 172 04.5 | 10.1 | N27 17.9 | 0.5 | 54.3 |
| 19 | 106 29.5 | 39.1 | 186 33.6 | 10.2 | 27 18.4 | 0.4 | 54.3 |
| 20 | 121 29.8 | 38.2 | 201 02.8 | 10.1 | 27 18.8 | 0.2 | 54.3 |
| 21 | 136 30.0 | .. 37.2 | 215 31.9 | 10.2 | 27 19.0 | 0.1 | 54.2 |
| 22 | 151 30.2 | 36.2 | 230 01.1 | 10.1 | 27 19.1 | 0.1 | 54.2 |
| 23 | 166 30.4 | 35.3 | 244 30.2 | 10.2 | N27 19.0 | 0.1 | 54.2 |
| | SD 15.9 | d 1.0 | SD 15.0 | | 14.9 | | 14.8 |

| Lat. | Twilight Naut. | Civil | Sunrise | Moonrise 16 | 17 | 18 | 19 |
|---|---|---|---|---|---|---|---|
| ° | h m | h m | h m | h m | h m | h m | h m |
| N 72 | 02 23 | 04 05 | 05 16 | □ | □ | □ | □ |
| N 70 | 02 51 | 04 17 | 05 20 | □ | □ | □ | □ |
| 68 | 03 11 | 04 26 | 05 23 | □ | □ | □ | □ |
| 66 | 03 27 | 04 34 | 05 26 | □ | □ | □ | □ |
| 64 | 03 39 | 04 40 | 05 28 | 18 23 | □ | □ | □ |
| 62 | 03 50 | 04 45 | 05 30 | 19 02 | 19 08 | 19 34 | 20 43 |
| 60 | 03 59 | 04 50 | 05 32 | 19 29 | 19 48 | 20 25 | 21 27 |
| N 58 | 04 06 | 04 54 | 05 34 | 19 51 | 20 16 | 20 56 | 21 56 |
| 56 | 04 12 | 04 58 | 05 35 | 20 08 | 20 37 | 21 20 | 22 18 |
| 54 | 04 18 | 05 01 | 05 36 | 20 23 | 20 55 | 21 39 | 22 36 |
| 52 | 04 23 | 05 04 | 05 38 | 20 36 | 21 10 | 21 55 | 22 52 |
| 50 | 04 27 | 05 06 | 05 39 | 20 48 | 21 23 | 22 09 | 23 05 |
| 45 | 04 37 | 05 11 | 05 41 | 21 11 | 21 50 | 22 37 | 23 33 |
| N 40 | 04 44 | 05 16 | 05 43 | 21 31 | 22 12 | 23 00 | 23 54 |
| 35 | 04 49 | 05 19 | 05 44 | 21 47 | 22 30 | 23 18 | 24 12 |
| 30 | 04 54 | 05 22 | 05 46 | 22 01 | 22 45 | 23 34 | 24 27 |
| 20 | 05 00 | 05 26 | 05 48 | 22 24 | 23 11 | 24 01 | 00 01 |
| N 10 | 05 04 | 05 29 | 05 50 | 22 45 | 23 34 | 24 24 | 00 24 |
| 0 | 05 07 | 05 31 | 05 51 | 23 04 | 23 55 | 24 46 | 00 46 |
| S 10 | 05 07 | 05 32 | 05 53 | 23 24 | 24 16 | 00 16 | 01 08 |
| 20 | 05 07 | 05 32 | 05 54 | 23 45 | 24 39 | 00 39 | 01 31 |
| 30 | 05 04 | 05 32 | 05 56 | 24 09 | 00 09 | 01 05 | 01 58 |
| 35 | 05 02 | 05 32 | 05 57 | 24 24 | 00 24 | 01 21 | 02 14 |
| 40 | 04 59 | 05 31 | 05 58 | 24 40 | 00 40 | 01 39 | 02 33 |
| 45 | 04 56 | 05 30 | 05 59 | 25 00 | 01 00 | 02 01 | 02 55 |
| S 50 | 04 50 | 05 28 | 06 00 | 00 15 | 01 26 | 02 29 | 03 24 |
| 52 | 04 48 | 05 27 | 06 01 | 00 25 | 01 38 | 02 43 | 03 38 |
| 54 | 04 45 | 05 26 | 06 01 | 00 36 | 01 52 | 02 59 | 03 54 |
| 56 | 04 42 | 05 25 | 06 02 | 00 49 | 02 08 | 03 18 | 04 13 |
| 58 | 04 38 | 05 24 | 06 03 | 01 05 | 02 28 | 03 41 | 04 37 |
| S 60 | 04 33 | 05 22 | 06 04 | 01 23 | 02 53 | 04 12 | 05 09 |

| Lat. | Sunset | Twilight Civil | Naut. | Moonset 16 | 17 | 18 | 19 |
|---|---|---|---|---|---|---|---|
| ° | h m | h m | h m | h m | h m | h m | h m |
| N 72 | 18 31 | 19 41 | 21 20 | □ | □ | □ | □ |
| N 70 | 18 27 | 19 30 | 20 54 | □ | □ | □ | □ |
| 68 | 18 24 | 19 21 | 20 34 | □ | □ | □ | □ |
| 66 | 18 21 | 19 13 | 20 19 | □ | □ | □ | □ |
| 64 | 18 19 | 19 07 | 20 07 | 15 10 | □ | □ | □ |
| 62 | 18 17 | 19 02 | 19 57 | 14 32 | 16 11 | 17 31 | 18 08 |
| 60 | 18 15 | 18 57 | 19 48 | 14 05 | 15 31 | 16 40 | 17 24 |
| N 58 | 18 14 | 18 53 | 19 41 | 13 45 | 15 04 | 16 09 | 16 55 |
| 56 | 18 13 | 18 50 | 19 35 | 13 27 | 14 42 | 15 45 | 16 33 |
| 54 | 18 11 | 18 47 | 19 29 | 13 13 | 14 25 | 15 26 | 16 14 |
| 52 | 18 10 | 18 44 | 19 25 | 13 00 | 14 10 | 15 10 | 15 58 |
| 50 | 18 09 | 18 42 | 19 20 | 12 49 | 13 57 | 14 56 | 15 45 |
| 45 | 18 07 | 18 37 | 19 11 | 12 26 | 13 30 | 14 28 | 15 17 |
| N 40 | 18 06 | 18 33 | 19 05 | 12 08 | 13 09 | 14 05 | 14 55 |
| 35 | 18 04 | 18 30 | 18 59 | 11 53 | 12 52 | 13 47 | 14 37 |
| 30 | 18 03 | 18 27 | 18 55 | 11 39 | 12 37 | 13 31 | 14 22 |
| 20 | 18 01 | 18 23 | 18 49 | 11 17 | 12 11 | 13 04 | 13 55 |
| N 10 | 17 59 | 18 20 | 18 45 | 10 57 | 11 49 | 12 41 | 13 32 |
| 0 | 17 58 | 18 18 | 18 42 | 10 39 | 11 29 | 12 20 | 13 11 |
| S 10 | 17 56 | 18 17 | 18 42 | 10 21 | 11 08 | 11 58 | 12 49 |
| 20 | 17 55 | 18 17 | 18 43 | 10 01 | 10 46 | 11 35 | 12 26 |
| 30 | 17 54 | 18 17 | 18 45 | 09 39 | 10 21 | 11 08 | 11 59 |
| 35 | 17 53 | 18 18 | 18 47 | 09 26 | 10 06 | 10 52 | 11 44 |
| 40 | 17 52 | 18 19 | 18 50 | 09 11 | 09 49 | 10 34 | 11 25 |
| 45 | 17 51 | 18 20 | 18 54 | 08 53 | 09 28 | 10 11 | 11 03 |
| S 50 | 17 50 | 18 22 | 19 00 | 08 31 | 09 03 | 09 43 | 10 34 |
| 52 | 17 49 | 18 23 | 19 02 | 08 21 | 08 50 | 09 29 | 10 20 |
| 54 | 17 49 | 18 24 | 19 05 | 08 09 | 08 36 | 09 13 | 10 04 |
| 56 | 17 48 | 18 25 | 19 09 | 07 56 | 08 19 | 08 54 | 09 45 |
| 58 | 17 48 | 18 27 | 19 13 | 07 40 | 07 59 | 08 31 | 09 21 |
| S 60 | 17 47 | 18 28 | 19 17 | 07 21 | 07 34 | 08 00 | 08 49 |

| Day | SUN Eqn. of Time 00h | 12h | Mer. Pass. | MOON Mer. Pass. Upper | Lower | Age | Phase |
|---|---|---|---|---|---|---|---|
| d | m s | m s | h m | h m | h m | d % | |
| 16 | 04 58 | 05 09 | 11 55 | 04 27 | 16 52 | 20 64 | ◗ |
| 17 | 05 19 | 05 30 | 11 55 | 05 17 | 17 42 | 21 54 | |
| 18 | 05 41 | 05 51 | 11 54 | 06 07 | 18 33 | 22 45 | |

| UT | ARIES GHA | VENUS −3·9 GHA | Dec | MARS −0·4 GHA | Dec | JUPITER −2·9 GHA | Dec | SATURN +0·4 GHA | Dec | STARS Name | SHA | Dec |
|---|---|---|---|---|---|---|---|---|---|---|---|---|
| **19 00** | 357 52.9 | 189 09.4 N 6 22.4 | | 283 38.8 N21 41.3 | | 352 53.7 N 0 23.9 | | 35 30.3 S16 13.0 | | Acamar | 315 12.9 | S40 12.6 |
| 01 | 12 55.3 | 204 08.9 | 21.2 | 298 40.1 | 41.5 | 7 56.5 | 23.8 | 50 32.9 | 13.1 | Achernar | 335 21.1 | S57 07.2 |
| 02 | 27 57.8 | 219 08.5 | 20.0 | 313 41.4 | 41.7 | 22 59.2 | 23.6 | 65 35.5 | 13.1 | Acrux | 173 02.9 | S63 13.4 |
| 03 | 43 00.2 | 234 08.1 .. | 18.8 | 328 42.7 .. | 41.8 | 38 02.0 .. | 23.5 | 80 38.1 .. | 13.1 | Adhara | 255 07.5 | S28 59.9 |
| 04 | 58 02.7 | 249 07.7 | 17.6 | 343 44.0 | 42.0 | 53 04.8 | 23.4 | 95 40.7 | 13.2 | Aldebaran | 290 41.7 | N16 33.3 |
| 05 | 73 05.2 | 264 07.3 | 16.4 | 358 45.3 | 42.2 | 68 07.5 | 23.2 | 110 43.3 | 13.2 | | | |
| 06 | 88 07.6 | 279 06.8 N 6 15.2 | | 13 46.6 N21 42.4 | | 83 10.3 N 0 23.1 | | 125 45.9 S16 13.3 | | Alioth | 166 15.2 | N55 50.4 |
| 07 | 103 10.1 | 294 06.4 | 14.1 | 28 47.9 | 42.5 | 98 13.0 | 23.0 | 140 48.5 | 13.3 | Alkaid | 152 53.9 | N49 12.2 |
| 08 | 118 12.6 | 309 06.0 | 12.9 | 43 49.3 | 42.7 | 113 15.8 | 22.8 | 155 51.1 | 13.3 | Alnair | 27 34.9 | S46 51.1 |
| M 09 | 133 15.0 | 324 05.6 .. | 11.7 | 58 50.6 .. | 42.9 | 128 18.6 .. | 22.7 | 170 53.7 .. | 13.4 | Alnilam | 275 39.6 | S 1 11.1 |
| O 10 | 148 17.5 | 339 05.2 | 10.5 | 73 51.9 | 43.1 | 143 21.3 | 22.6 | 185 56.3 | 13.4 | Alphard | 217 49.9 | S 8 45.2 |
| N 11 | 163 20.0 | 354 04.7 | 09.3 | 88 53.2 | 43.2 | 158 24.1 | 22.4 | 200 58.8 | 13.5 | | | |
| D 12 | 178 22.4 | 9 04.3 N 6 08.1 | | 103 54.5 N21 43.4 | | 173 26.9 N 0 22.3 | | 216 01.4 S16 13.5 | | Alphecca | 126 05.6 | N26 38.6 |
| A 13 | 193 24.9 | 24 03.9 | 06.9 | 118 55.8 | 43.6 | 188 29.6 | 22.2 | 231 04.0 | 13.5 | Alpheratz | 357 36.4 | N29 13.0 |
| Y 14 | 208 27.4 | 39 03.5 | 05.7 | 133 57.1 | 43.8 | 203 32.4 | 22.0 | 246 06.6 | 13.6 | Altair | 62 01.7 | N 8 55.8 |
| 15 | 223 29.8 | 54 03.1 .. | 04.5 | 148 58.4 .. | 43.9 | 218 35.2 .. | 21.9 | 261 09.2 .. | 13.6 | Ankaa | 353 08.6 | S42 10.9 |
| 16 | 238 32.3 | 69 02.7 | 03.3 | 163 59.7 | 44.1 | 233 37.9 | 21.8 | 276 11.8 | 13.7 | Antares | 112 18.3 | S26 28.9 |
| 17 | 253 34.7 | 84 02.2 | 02.1 | 179 01.1 | 44.3 | 248 40.7 | 21.6 | 291 14.4 | 13.7 | | | |
| 18 | 268 37.2 | 99 01.8 N 6 00.9 | | 194 02.4 N21 44.4 | | 263 43.5 N 0 21.5 | | 306 17.0 S16 13.7 | | Arcturus | 145 49.9 | N19 04.1 |
| 19 | 283 39.7 | 114 01.4 5 59.7 | | 209 03.7 | 44.6 | 278 46.2 | 21.4 | 321 19.6 | 13.8 | Atria | 107 14.4 | S69 04.3 |
| 20 | 298 42.1 | 129 01.0 | 58.5 | 224 05.0 | 44.8 | 293 49.0 | 21.2 | 336 22.2 | 13.8 | Avior | 234 15.9 | S59 34.6 |
| 21 | 313 44.6 | 144 00.6 .. | 57.3 | 239 06.3 .. | 45.0 | 308 51.8 .. | 21.1 | 351 24.8 .. | 13.9 | Bellatrix | 278 24.9 | N 6 22.3 |
| 22 | 328 47.1 | 159 00.1 | 56.1 | 254 07.6 | 45.1 | 323 54.5 | 21.0 | 6 27.4 | 13.9 | Betelgeuse | 270 54.2 | N 7 24.8 |
| 23 | 343 49.5 | 173 59.7 | 54.9 | 269 09.0 | 45.3 | 338 57.3 | 20.8 | 21 29.9 | 13.9 | | | |
| **20 00** | 358 52.0 | 188 59.3 N 5 53.7 | | 284 10.3 N21 45.5 | | 354 00.0 N 0 20.7 | | 36 32.5 S16 14.0 | | Canopus | 263 53.3 | S52 42.1 |
| 01 | 13 54.5 | 203 58.9 | 52.5 | 299 11.6 | 45.7 | 9 02.8 | 20.6 | 51 35.1 | 14.0 | Capella | 280 24.6 | N46 01.1 |
| 02 | 28 56.9 | 218 58.5 | 51.2 | 314 12.9 | 45.8 | 24 05.6 | 20.4 | 66 37.7 | 14.1 | Deneb | 49 26.8 | N45 21.9 |
| 03 | 43 59.4 | 233 58.1 .. | 50.0 | 329 14.3 .. | 46.0 | 39 08.3 .. | 20.3 | 81 40.3 .. | 14.1 | Denebola | 182 26.2 | N14 26.9 |
| 04 | 59 01.9 | 248 57.6 | 48.8 | 344 15.6 | 46.2 | 54 11.1 | 20.2 | 96 42.9 | 14.1 | Diphda | 348 48.9 | S17 51.6 |
| 05 | 74 04.3 | 263 57.2 | 47.6 | 359 16.9 | 46.3 | 69 13.9 | 20.0 | 111 45.5 | 14.2 | | | |
| 06 | 89 06.8 | 278 56.8 N 5 46.4 | | 14 18.2 N21 46.5 | | 84 16.6 N 0 19.9 | | 126 48.1 S16 14.2 | | Dubhe | 193 44.0 | N61 37.8 |
| 07 | 104 09.2 | 293 56.4 | 45.2 | 29 19.5 | 46.7 | 99 19.4 | 19.8 | 141 50.7 | 14.3 | Elnath | 278 04.2 | N28 37.5 |
| 08 | 119 11.7 | 308 56.0 | 44.0 | 44 20.9 | 46.8 | 114 22.2 | 19.7 | 156 53.3 | 14.3 | Eltanin | 90 43.1 | N51 29.4 |
| T 09 | 134 14.2 | 323 55.6 .. | 42.8 | 59 22.2 .. | 47.0 | 129 24.9 .. | 19.5 | 171 55.8 .. | 14.3 | Enif | 33 40.4 | N 9 58.8 |
| U 10 | 149 16.6 | 338 55.2 | 41.6 | 74 23.5 | 47.2 | 144 27.7 | 19.4 | 186 58.4 | 14.4 | Fomalhaut | 15 16.3 | S29 30.1 |
| E 11 | 164 19.1 | 353 54.7 | 40.4 | 89 24.9 | 47.4 | 159 30.5 | 19.3 | 202 01.0 | 14.4 | | | |
| S 12 | 179 21.6 | 8 54.3 N 5 39.2 | | 104 26.2 N21 47.5 | | 174 33.2 N 0 19.1 | | 217 03.6 S16 14.4 | | Gacrux | 171 54.3 | S57 14.3 |
| D 13 | 194 24.0 | 23 53.9 | 38.0 | 119 27.5 | 47.7 | 189 36.0 | 19.0 | 232 06.2 | 14.5 | Gienah | 175 45.9 | S17 39.9 |
| A 14 | 209 26.5 | 38 53.5 | 36.8 | 134 28.8 | 47.9 | 204 38.8 | 18.9 | 247 08.8 | 14.5 | Hadar | 148 39.3 | S60 29.0 |
| Y 15 | 224 29.0 | 53 53.1 .. | 35.6 | 149 30.2 .. | 48.0 | 219 41.5 .. | 18.7 | 262 11.4 .. | 14.6 | Hamal | 327 53.1 | N23 34.2 |
| 16 | 239 31.4 | 68 52.7 | 34.4 | 164 31.5 | 48.2 | 234 44.3 | 18.6 | 277 14.0 | 14.6 | Kaus Aust. | 83 35.0 | S34 22.5 |
| 17 | 254 33.9 | 83 52.3 | 33.2 | 179 32.8 | 48.4 | 249 47.1 | 18.5 | 292 16.5 | 14.6 | | | |
| 18 | 269 36.3 | 98 51.8 N 5 32.0 | | 194 34.2 N21 48.5 | | 264 49.8 N 0 18.3 | | 307 19.1 S16 14.7 | | Kochab | 137 20.6 | N74 04.0 |
| 19 | 284 38.8 | 113 51.4 | 30.8 | 209 35.5 | 48.7 | 279 52.6 | 18.2 | 322 21.7 | 14.7 | Markab | 13 31.5 | N15 19.7 |
| 20 | 299 41.3 | 128 51.0 | 29.5 | 224 36.8 | 48.9 | 294 55.4 | 18.1 | 337 24.3 | 14.8 | Menkar | 314 07.9 | N 4 10.8 |
| 21 | 314 43.7 | 143 50.6 .. | 28.3 | 239 38.2 .. | 49.0 | 309 58.1 .. | 17.9 | 352 26.9 .. | 14.8 | Menkent | 148 00.2 | S36 28.8 |
| 22 | 329 46.2 | 158 50.2 | 27.1 | 254 39.5 | 49.2 | 325 00.9 | 17.8 | 7 29.5 | 14.8 | Miaplacidus | 221 39.4 | S69 48.3 |
| 23 | 344 48.7 | 173 49.8 | 25.9 | 269 40.9 | 49.4 | 340 03.7 | 17.7 | 22 32.1 | 14.9 | | | |
| **21 00** | 359 51.1 | 188 49.4 N 5 24.7 | | 284 42.2 N21 49.5 | | 355 06.4 N 0 17.5 | | 37 34.7 S16 14.9 | | Mirfak | 308 30.7 | N49 56.3 |
| 01 | 14 53.6 | 203 49.0 | 23.5 | 299 43.5 | 49.7 | 10 09.2 | 17.4 | 52 37.3 | 15.0 | Nunki | 75 50.0 | S26 16.1 |
| 02 | 29 56.1 | 218 48.5 | 22.3 | 314 44.9 | 49.9 | 25 12.0 | 17.3 | 67 39.8 | 15.0 | Peacock | 53 08.4 | S56 39.9 |
| 03 | 44 58.5 | 233 48.1 .. | 21.1 | 329 46.2 .. | 50.0 | 40 14.7 .. | 17.1 | 82 42.4 .. | 15.0 | Pollux | 243 19.8 | N27 58.3 |
| 04 | 60 01.0 | 248 47.7 | 19.9 | 344 47.5 | 50.2 | 55 17.5 | 17.0 | 97 45.0 | 15.1 | Procyon | 244 53.0 | N 5 10.2 |
| 05 | 75 03.5 | 263 47.3 | 18.7 | 359 48.9 | 50.4 | 70 20.3 | 16.9 | 112 47.6 | 15.1 | | | |
| 06 | 90 05.9 | 278 46.9 N 5 17.4 | | 14 50.2 N21 50.5 | | 85 23.0 N 0 16.7 | | 127 50.2 S16 15.1 | | Rasalhague | 96 00.3 | N12 32.8 |
| W 07 | 105 08.4 | 293 46.5 | 16.2 | 29 51.6 | 50.7 | 100 25.8 | 16.6 | 142 52.8 | 15.2 | Regulus | 207 36.8 | N11 51.5 |
| E 08 | 120 10.8 | 308 46.1 | 15.0 | 44 52.9 | 50.9 | 115 28.6 | 16.5 | 157 55.4 | 15.2 | Rigel | 281 05.7 | S 8 10.3 |
| D 09 | 135 13.3 | 323 45.7 .. | 13.8 | 59 54.3 .. | 51.0 | 130 31.3 .. | 16.3 | 172 57.9 .. | 15.3 | Rigil Kent. | 139 43.4 | S60 55.8 |
| N 10 | 150 15.8 | 338 45.2 | 12.6 | 74 55.6 | 51.2 | 145 34.1 | 16.2 | 188 00.5 | 15.3 | Sabik | 102 05.0 | S15 45.1 |
| E 11 | 165 18.2 | 353 44.8 | 11.4 | 89 57.0 | 51.4 | 160 36.9 | 16.0 | 203 03.1 | 15.3 | | | |
| S 12 | 180 20.7 | 8 44.4 N 5 10.2 | | 104 58.3 N21 51.5 | | 175 39.6 N 0 15.9 | | 218 05.7 S16 15.4 | | Schedar | 349 32.7 | N56 39.7 |
| D 13 | 195 23.2 | 23 44.0 | 09.0 | 119 59.6 | 51.7 | 190 42.4 | 15.8 | 233 08.3 | 15.4 | Shaula | 96 13.0 | S37 07.3 |
| A 14 | 210 25.6 | 38 43.6 | 07.7 | 135 01.0 | 51.9 | 205 45.2 | 15.6 | 248 10.9 | 15.5 | Sirius | 258 28.0 | S16 44.6 |
| Y 15 | 225 28.1 | 53 43.2 .. | 06.5 | 150 02.3 .. | 52.0 | 220 47.9 .. | 15.5 | 263 13.5 .. | 15.5 | Spica | 158 24.6 | S11 16.6 |
| 16 | 240 30.6 | 68 42.8 | 05.3 | 165 03.7 | 52.2 | 235 50.7 | 15.4 | 278 16.0 | 15.6 | Suhail | 222 48.0 | S43 31.1 |
| 17 | 255 33.0 | 83 42.4 | 04.1 | 180 05.0 | 52.4 | 250 53.5 | 15.2 | 293 18.6 | 15.6 | | | |
| 18 | 270 35.5 | 98 42.0 N 5 02.9 | | 195 06.4 N21 52.5 | | 265 56.2 N 0 15.1 | | 308 21.2 S16 15.6 | | Vega | 80 34.4 | N38 48.5 |
| 19 | 285 38.0 | 113 41.6 | 01.7 | 210 07.8 | 52.7 | 280 59.0 | 15.0 | 323 23.8 | 15.6 | Zuben'ubi | 136 58.4 | S16 08.0 |
| 20 | 300 40.4 | 128 41.2 5 00.5 | | 225 09.1 | 52.9 | 296 01.8 | 14.8 | 338 26.4 | 15.7 | | SHA | Mer. Pass. |
| 21 | 315 42.9 | 143 40.7 4 59.2 | | 240 10.5 .. | 53.0 | 311 04.6 .. | 14.7 | 353 29.0 .. | 15.7 | Venus | 190 07.3 | h m 11 24 |
| 22 | 330 45.3 | 158 40.3 | 58.0 | 255 11.8 | 53.2 | 326 07.3 | 14.6 | 8 31.6 | 15.8 | Mars | 285 18.3 | 5 03 |
| 23 | 345 47.8 | 173 39.9 | 56.8 | 270 13.2 | 53.4 | 341 10.1 | 14.4 | 23 34.1 | 15.8 | Jupiter | 355 08.1 | 0 24 |
| Mer. Pass. | h m 0 04.5 | v −0.4 d 1.2 | | v 1.3 d 0.2 | | v 2.8 d 0.1 | | v 2.6 d 0.0 | | Saturn | 37 40.5 | 21 30 |

| UT | SUN GHA | SUN Dec | MOON GHA | v | MOON Dec | d | HP |
|---|---|---|---|---|---|---|---|
| d h | ° ′ | ° ′ | ° ′ | ′ | ° ′ | ′ | ′ |
| **19** 00 | 181 30.7 | N 1 34.3 | 258 59.4 | 10.2 | N27 18.9 | 0.3 | 54.2 |
| 01 | 196 30.9 | 33.3 | 273 28.6 | 10.1 | 27 18.6 | 0.5 | 54.2 |
| 02 | 211 31.1 | 32.4 | 287 57.7 | 10.2 | 27 18.1 | 0.5 | 54.2 |
| 03 | 226 31.3 .. | 31.4 | 302 26.9 | 10.2 | 27 17.6 | 0.7 | 54.2 |
| 04 | 241 31.5 | 30.4 | 316 56.1 | 10.2 | 27 16.9 | 0.9 | 54.2 |
| 05 | 256 31.8 | 29.5 | 331 25.3 | 10.2 | 27 16.0 | 0.9 | 54.2 |
| 06 | 271 32.0 | N 1 28.5 | 345 54.5 | 10.3 | N27 15.1 | 1.1 | 54.2 |
| 07 | 286 32.2 | 27.5 | 0 23.8 | 10.2 | 27 14.0 | 1.2 | 54.2 |
| M 08 | 301 32.4 | 26.5 | 14 53.0 | 10.3 | 27 12.8 | 1.4 | 54.2 |
| O 09 | 316 32.7 .. | 25.6 | 29 22.3 | 10.2 | 27 11.4 | 1.5 | 54.2 |
| N 10 | 331 32.9 | 24.6 | 43 51.5 | 10.3 | 27 09.9 | 1.6 | 54.2 |
| D 11 | 346 33.1 | 23.6 | 58 20.8 | 10.3 | 27 08.3 | 1.7 | 54.2 |
| A 12 | 1 33.3 | N 1 22.7 | 72 50.1 | 10.3 | N27 06.6 | 1.9 | 54.2 |
| Y 13 | 16 33.5 | 21.7 | 87 19.4 | 10.4 | 27 04.7 | 2.0 | 54.2 |
| 14 | 31 33.8 | 20.7 | 101 48.8 | 10.3 | 27 02.7 | 2.1 | 54.2 |
| 15 | 46 34.0 .. | 19.8 | 116 18.1 | 10.4 | 27 00.6 | 2.3 | 54.2 |
| 16 | 61 34.2 | 18.8 | 130 47.5 | 10.4 | 26 58.3 | 2.4 | 54.2 |
| 17 | 76 34.4 | 17.8 | 145 16.9 | 10.4 | 26 55.9 | 2.5 | 54.2 |
| 18 | 91 34.7 | N 1 16.8 | 159 46.3 | 10.4 | N26 53.4 | 2.7 | 54.2 |
| 19 | 106 34.9 | 15.9 | 174 15.7 | 10.5 | 26 50.7 | 2.7 | 54.2 |
| 20 | 121 35.1 | 14.9 | 188 45.2 | 10.5 | 26 48.0 | 2.9 | 54.2 |
| 21 | 136 35.3 .. | 13.9 | 203 14.7 | 10.5 | 26 45.1 | 3.1 | 54.2 |
| 22 | 151 35.5 | 13.0 | 217 44.2 | 10.5 | 26 42.0 | 3.1 | 54.2 |
| 23 | 166 35.8 | 12.0 | 232 13.7 | 10.6 | 26 38.9 | 3.3 | 54.2 |
| **20** 00 | 181 36.0 | N 1 11.0 | 246 43.3 | 10.6 | N26 35.6 | 3.4 | 54.2 |
| 01 | 196 36.2 | 10.1 | 261 12.9 | 10.6 | 26 32.2 | 3.6 | 54.2 |
| 02 | 211 36.4 | 09.1 | 275 42.5 | 10.6 | 26 28.6 | 3.6 | 54.2 |
| 03 | 226 36.7 .. | 08.1 | 290 12.1 | 10.7 | 26 25.0 | 3.8 | 54.2 |
| 04 | 241 36.9 | 07.1 | 304 41.8 | 10.7 | 26 21.2 | 3.9 | 54.2 |
| 05 | 256 37.1 | 06.2 | 319 11.5 | 10.7 | 26 17.3 | 4.1 | 54.2 |
| 06 | 271 37.3 | N 1 05.2 | 333 41.2 | 10.8 | N26 13.2 | 4.1 | 54.2 |
| 07 | 286 37.5 | 04.2 | 348 11.0 | 10.8 | 26 09.1 | 4.3 | 54.2 |
| T 08 | 301 37.8 | 03.3 | 2 40.8 | 10.8 | 26 04.8 | 4.4 | 54.2 |
| U 09 | 316 38.0 .. | 02.3 | 17 10.6 | 10.9 | 26 00.4 | 4.6 | 54.2 |
| E 10 | 331 38.2 | 01.3 | 31 40.5 | 10.9 | 25 55.8 | 4.6 | 54.3 |
| S 11 | 346 38.4 | 1 00.3 | 46 10.4 | 10.9 | 25 51.2 | 4.8 | 54.3 |
| D 12 | 1 38.7 | N 0 59.4 | 60 40.3 | 11.0 | N25 46.4 | 4.9 | 54.3 |
| A 13 | 16 38.9 | 58.4 | 75 10.3 | 11.0 | 25 41.5 | 5.0 | 54.3 |
| Y 14 | 31 39.1 | 57.4 | 89 40.3 | 11.0 | 25 36.5 | 5.2 | 54.3 |
| 15 | 46 39.3 .. | 56.5 | 104 10.3 | 11.1 | 25 31.3 | 5.3 | 54.3 |
| 16 | 61 39.5 | 55.5 | 118 40.4 | 11.1 | 25 26.0 | 5.3 | 54.3 |
| 17 | 76 39.8 | 54.5 | 133 10.5 | 11.1 | 25 20.7 | 5.6 | 54.3 |
| 18 | 91 40.0 | N 0 53.6 | 147 40.6 | 11.2 | N25 15.1 | 5.6 | 54.3 |
| 19 | 106 40.2 | 52.6 | 162 10.8 | 11.2 | 25 09.5 | 5.7 | 54.3 |
| 20 | 121 40.4 | 51.6 | 176 41.0 | 11.3 | 25 03.8 | 5.9 | 54.3 |
| 21 | 136 40.7 .. | 50.6 | 191 11.3 | 11.3 | 24 57.9 | 6.0 | 54.3 |
| 22 | 151 40.9 | 49.7 | 205 41.6 | 11.3 | 24 51.9 | 6.1 | 54.3 |
| 23 | 166 41.1 | 48.7 | 220 11.9 | 11.4 | 24 45.8 | 6.2 | 54.3 |
| **21** 00 | 181 41.3 | N 0 47.7 | 234 42.3 | 11.4 | N24 39.6 | 6.3 | 54.4 |
| 01 | 196 41.5 | 46.8 | 249 12.7 | 11.5 | 24 33.3 | 6.5 | 54.4 |
| 02 | 211 41.8 | 45.8 | 263 43.2 | 11.5 | 24 26.8 | 6.5 | 54.4 |
| 03 | 226 42.0 .. | 44.8 | 278 13.7 | 11.5 | 24 20.3 | 6.7 | 54.4 |
| 04 | 241 42.2 | 43.8 | 292 44.2 | 11.6 | 24 13.6 | 6.8 | 54.4 |
| 05 | 256 42.4 | 42.9 | 307 14.8 | 11.6 | 24 06.8 | 6.9 | 54.4 |
| 06 | 271 42.6 | N 0 41.9 | 321 45.4 | 11.7 | N23 59.9 | 7.0 | 54.4 |
| W 07 | 286 42.9 | 40.9 | 336 16.1 | 11.7 | 23 52.9 | 7.1 | 54.4 |
| E 08 | 301 43.1 | 39.9 | 350 46.8 | 11.8 | 23 45.8 | 7.3 | 54.4 |
| D 09 | 316 43.3 .. | 39.0 | 5 17.6 | 11.8 | 23 38.5 | 7.3 | 54.4 |
| N 10 | 331 43.5 | 38.0 | 19 48.4 | 11.8 | 23 31.2 | 7.5 | 54.5 |
| E 11 | 346 43.8 | 37.0 | 34 19.2 | 11.9 | 23 23.7 | 7.6 | 54.5 |
| S 12 | 1 44.0 | N 0 36.1 | 48 50.1 | 11.9 | N23 16.1 | 7.6 | 54.5 |
| D 13 | 16 44.2 | 35.1 | 63 21.0 | 12.0 | 23 08.5 | 7.8 | 54.5 |
| A 14 | 31 44.4 | 34.1 | 77 52.0 | 12.0 | 23 00.7 | 7.9 | 54.5 |
| Y 15 | 46 44.6 .. | 33.1 | 92 23.0 | 12.1 | 22 52.8 | 8.0 | 54.5 |
| 16 | 61 44.9 | 32.2 | 106 54.1 | 12.1 | 22 44.8 | 8.1 | 54.5 |
| 17 | 76 45.1 | 31.2 | 121 25.2 | 12.1 | 22 36.7 | 8.3 | 54.5 |
| 18 | 91 45.3 | N 0 30.2 | 135 56.3 | 12.2 | N22 28.4 | 8.3 | 54.6 |
| 19 | 106 45.5 | 29.3 | 150 27.5 | 12.3 | 22 20.1 | 8.4 | 54.6 |
| 20 | 121 45.7 | 28.3 | 164 58.8 | 12.2 | 22 11.7 | 8.5 | 54.6 |
| 21 | 136 46.0 .. | 27.3 | 179 30.0 | 12.4 | 22 03.2 | 8.7 | 54.6 |
| 22 | 151 46.2 | 26.3 | 194 01.4 | 12.4 | 21 54.5 | 8.7 | 54.6 |
| 23 | 166 46.4 | 25.4 | 208 32.8 | 12.4 | N21 45.8 | 8.9 | 54.6 |
| | SD 16.0 | d 1.0 | SD 14.8 | | 14.8 | | 14.8 |

| Lat. | Twilight Naut. | Twilight Civil | Sunrise | Moonrise 19 | Moonrise 20 | Moonrise 21 | Moonrise 22 |
|---|---|---|---|---|---|---|---|
| ° | h m | h m | h m | h m | h m | h m | h m |
| N 72 | 02 45 | 04 20 | 05 29 | ▭ | ▭ | ▭ | 22 26 |
| N 70 | 03 08 | 04 29 | 05 32 | ▭ | ▭ | ▭ | 23 52 |
| 68 | 03 25 | 04 37 | 05 34 | ▭ | ▭ | 21 26 | 24 30 |
| 66 | 03 39 | 04 44 | 05 35 | ▭ | ▭ | 22 53 | 24 57 |
| 64 | 03 50 | 04 49 | 05 37 | ▭ | 21 30 | 23 30 | 25 17 |
| 62 | 03 59 | 04 54 | 05 38 | 20 43 | 22 17 | 23 56 | 25 33 |
| 60 | 04 07 | 04 57 | 05 39 | 21 27 | 22 48 | 24 16 | 00 16 |
| N 58 | 04 13 | 05 01 | 05 40 | 21 56 | 23 11 | 24 33 | 00 33 |
| 56 | 04 19 | 05 04 | 05 41 | 22 18 | 23 29 | 24 47 | 00 47 |
| 54 | 04 24 | 05 06 | 05 42 | 22 36 | 23 45 | 24 59 | 00 59 |
| 52 | 04 29 | 05 09 | 05 43 | 22 52 | 23 58 | 25 10 | 01 10 |
| 50 | 04 32 | 05 11 | 05 43 | 23 05 | 24 10 | 00 10 | 01 19 |
| 45 | 04 40 | 05 15 | 05 44 | 23 33 | 24 34 | 00 34 | 01 39 |
| N 40 | 04 47 | 05 18 | 05 46 | 23 54 | 24 53 | 00 53 | 01 55 |
| 35 | 04 52 | 05 21 | 05 46 | 24 12 | 00 12 | 01 09 | 02 09 |
| 30 | 04 55 | 05 23 | 05 47 | 24 27 | 00 27 | 01 23 | 02 21 |
| 20 | 05 01 | 05 26 | 05 48 | 00 01 | 00 53 | 01 47 | 02 41 |
| N 10 | 05 04 | 05 28 | 05 49 | 00 24 | 01 16 | 02 07 | 02 58 |
| 0 | 05 06 | 05 30 | 05 50 | 00 46 | 01 37 | 02 26 | 03 14 |
| S 10 | 05 06 | 05 30 | 05 51 | 01 08 | 01 58 | 02 45 | 03 30 |
| 20 | 05 04 | 05 30 | 05 52 | 01 31 | 02 20 | 03 06 | 03 48 |
| 30 | 05 01 | 05 28 | 05 52 | 01 58 | 02 46 | 03 29 | 04 07 |
| 35 | 04 58 | 05 27 | 05 53 | 02 14 | 03 01 | 03 43 | 04 19 |
| 40 | 04 54 | 05 26 | 05 53 | 02 33 | 03 19 | 03 58 | 04 32 |
| 45 | 04 50 | 05 24 | 05 53 | 02 55 | 03 40 | 04 17 | 04 47 |
| S 50 | 04 44 | 05 21 | 05 54 | 03 24 | 04 07 | 04 40 | 05 06 |
| 52 | 04 41 | 05 20 | 05 54 | 03 38 | 04 20 | 04 51 | 05 15 |
| 54 | 04 37 | 05 19 | 05 54 | 03 54 | 04 35 | 05 04 | 05 25 |
| 56 | 04 33 | 05 17 | 05 54 | 04 13 | 04 52 | 05 19 | 05 36 |
| 58 | 04 29 | 05 15 | 05 54 | 04 37 | 05 14 | 05 36 | 05 49 |
| S 60 | 04 24 | 05 13 | 05 54 | 05 09 | 05 41 | 05 56 | 06 04 |

| Lat. | Sunset | Twilight Civil | Twilight Naut. | Moonset 19 | Moonset 20 | Moonset 21 | Moonset 22 |
|---|---|---|---|---|---|---|---|
| ° | h m | h m | h m | h m | h m | h m | h m |
| N 72 | 18 15 | 19 24 | 20 57 | ▭ | ▭ | ▭ | 21 31 |
| N 70 | 18 13 | 19 15 | 20 35 | ▭ | ▭ | ▭ | 20 04 |
| 68 | 18 11 | 19 07 | 20 19 | ▭ | ▭ | 20 51 | 19 25 |
| 66 | 18 10 | 19 01 | 20 05 | ▭ | ▭ | 19 24 | 18 57 |
| 64 | 18 08 | 18 56 | 19 55 | ▭ | 19 05 | 18 46 | 18 36 |
| 62 | 18 07 | 18 52 | 19 46 | 18 08 | 18 18 | 18 19 | 18 18 |
| 60 | 18 06 | 18 48 | 19 38 | 17 24 | 17 47 | 17 58 | 18 04 |
| N 58 | 18 05 | 18 45 | 19 32 | 16 55 | 17 24 | 17 41 | 17 52 |
| 56 | 18 05 | 18 42 | 19 26 | 16 33 | 17 05 | 17 26 | 17 41 |
| 54 | 18 04 | 18 39 | 19 21 | 16 14 | 16 49 | 17 14 | 17 31 |
| 52 | 18 03 | 18 37 | 19 17 | 15 58 | 16 35 | 17 02 | 17 23 |
| 50 | 18 03 | 18 35 | 19 13 | 15 45 | 16 23 | 16 52 | 17 15 |
| 45 | 18 02 | 18 31 | 19 05 | 15 17 | 15 58 | 16 32 | 16 59 |
| N 40 | 18 01 | 18 28 | 18 59 | 14 55 | 15 38 | 16 15 | 16 45 |
| 35 | 18 00 | 18 25 | 18 55 | 14 37 | 15 22 | 16 00 | 16 34 |
| 30 | 17 59 | 18 23 | 18 51 | 14 22 | 15 07 | 15 48 | 16 24 |
| 20 | 17 58 | 18 20 | 18 46 | 13 55 | 14 42 | 15 26 | 16 06 |
| N 10 | 17 57 | 18 18 | 18 43 | 13 32 | 14 21 | 15 07 | 15 51 |
| 0 | 17 57 | 18 17 | 18 41 | 13 11 | 14 01 | 14 50 | 15 37 |
| S 10 | 17 56 | 18 17 | 18 41 | 12 49 | 13 41 | 14 32 | 15 22 |
| 20 | 17 56 | 18 18 | 18 43 | 12 26 | 13 19 | 14 13 | 15 07 |
| 30 | 17 55 | 18 19 | 18 47 | 11 59 | 12 54 | 13 51 | 14 49 |
| 35 | 17 55 | 18 20 | 18 50 | 11 44 | 12 39 | 13 38 | 14 38 |
| 40 | 17 55 | 18 22 | 18 53 | 11 25 | 12 22 | 13 23 | 14 26 |
| 45 | 17 54 | 18 24 | 18 58 | 11 03 | 12 01 | 13 05 | 14 12 |
| S 50 | 17 54 | 18 27 | 19 04 | 10 34 | 11 35 | 12 43 | 13 54 |
| 52 | 17 54 | 18 28 | 19 08 | 10 20 | 11 22 | 12 32 | 13 46 |
| 54 | 17 54 | 18 29 | 19 11 | 10 04 | 11 07 | 12 20 | 13 36 |
| 56 | 17 54 | 18 31 | 19 15 | 09 45 | 10 50 | 12 06 | 13 26 |
| 58 | 17 54 | 18 33 | 19 20 | 09 21 | 10 29 | 11 49 | 13 13 |
| S 60 | 17 54 | 18 35 | 19 25 | 08 49 | 10 02 | 11 29 | 12 59 |

| Day | SUN Eqn. of Time 00h | SUN Eqn. of Time 12h | SUN Mer. Pass. | MOON Mer. Pass. Upper | MOON Mer. Pass. Lower | Age | Phase |
|---|---|---|---|---|---|---|---|
| d | m s | m s | h m | h m | h m | d % | |
| 19 | 06 02 | 06 13 | 11 54 | 06 58 | 19 24 | 23 35 | |
| 20 | 06 24 | 06 34 | 11 53 | 07 49 | 20 14 | 24 27 | |
| 21 | 06 45 | 06 55 | 11 53 | 08 38 | 21 02 | 25 19 | |

| UT (d h) | ARIES GHA | VENUS −3.9 GHA | Dec | MARS −0.5 GHA | Dec | JUPITER −2.9 GHA | Dec | SATURN +0.4 GHA | Dec | STARS Name | SHA | Dec |
|---|---|---|---|---|---|---|---|---|---|---|---|---|
| **22 00** | 0 50.3 | 188 39.5 | N 4 55.6 | 285 14.5 | N21 53.5 | 356 12.9 | N 0 14.3 | 38 36.7 | S16 15.8 | Acamar | 315 12.9 | S40 12.6 |
| 01 | 15 52.7 | 203 39.1 | 54.4 | 300 15.9 | 53.7 | 11 15.6 | 14.2 | 53 39.3 | 15.9 | Achernar | 335 21.1 | S57 07.2 |
| 02 | 30 55.2 | 218 38.7 | 53.2 | 315 17.2 | 53.8 | 26 18.4 | 14.0 | 68 41.9 | 15.9 | Acrux | 173 02.9 | S63 13.4 |
| 03 | 45 57.7 | 233 38.3 | .. 51.9 | 330 18.6 | .. 54.0 | 41 21.2 | .. 13.9 | 83 44.5 | .. 15.9 | Adhara | 255 07.4 | S28 59.9 |
| 04 | 61 00.1 | 248 37.9 | 50.7 | 345 20.0 | 54.2 | 56 23.9 | 13.8 | 98 47.1 | 16.0 | Aldebaran | 290 41.7 | N16 33.3 |
| 05 | 76 02.6 | 263 37.5 | 49.5 | 0 21.3 | 54.3 | 71 26.7 | 13.6 | 113 49.6 | 16.0 | | | |
| **06** | 91 05.1 | 278 37.1 | N 4 48.3 | 15 22.7 | N21 54.5 | 86 29.5 | N 0 13.5 | 128 52.2 | S16 16.1 | Alioth | 166 15.2 | N55 50.4 |
| 07 | 106 07.5 | 293 36.7 | 47.1 | 30 24.0 | 54.7 | 101 32.2 | 13.4 | 143 54.8 | 16.1 | Alkaid | 152 53.9 | N49 12.2 |
| T 08 | 121 10.0 | 308 36.3 | 45.9 | 45 25.4 | 54.8 | 116 35.0 | 13.2 | 158 57.4 | 16.1 | Alnair | 27 34.9 | S46 51.1 |
| H 09 | 136 12.5 | 323 35.8 | .. 44.6 | 60 26.8 | .. 55.0 | 131 37.8 | .. 13.1 | 174 00.0 | .. 16.2 | Alnilam | 275 39.6 | S 1 11.1 |
| U 10 | 151 14.9 | 338 35.4 | 43.4 | 75 28.1 | 55.1 | 146 40.5 | 13.0 | 189 02.6 | 16.2 | Alphard | 217 49.9 | S 8 45.2 |
| R 11 | 166 17.4 | 353 35.0 | 42.2 | 90 29.5 | 55.3 | 161 43.3 | 12.8 | 204 05.1 | 16.2 | | | |
| S 12 | 181 19.8 | 8 34.6 | N 4 41.0 | 105 30.9 | N21 55.5 | 176 46.1 | N 0 12.7 | 219 07.8 | S16 16.3 | Alphecca | 126 05.6 | N26 38.5 |
| D 13 | 196 22.3 | 23 34.2 | 39.8 | 120 32.2 | 55.6 | 191 48.8 | 12.6 | 234 10.3 | 16.3 | Alpheratz | 357 36.4 | N29 13.0 |
| A 14 | 211 24.8 | 38 33.8 | 38.5 | 135 33.6 | 55.8 | 206 51.6 | 12.4 | 249 12.9 | 16.3 | Altair | 62 01.7 | N 8 55.8 |
| Y 15 | 226 27.2 | 53 33.4 | .. 37.3 | 150 35.0 | .. 56.0 | 221 54.4 | .. 12.3 | 264 15.5 | .. 16.4 | Ankaa | 353 08.6 | S42 10.9 |
| 16 | 241 29.7 | 68 33.0 | 36.1 | 165 36.3 | 56.1 | 236 57.2 | 12.2 | 279 18.1 | 16.4 | Antares | 112 18.3 | S26 28.9 |
| 17 | 256 32.2 | 83 32.6 | 34.9 | 180 37.7 | 56.3 | 251 59.9 | 12.0 | 294 20.6 | 16.5 | | | |
| 18 | 271 34.6 | 98 32.2 | N 4 33.7 | 195 39.1 | N21 56.4 | 267 02.7 | N 0 11.9 | 309 23.2 | S16 16.5 | Arcturus | 145 49.9 | N19 04.1 |
| 19 | 286 37.1 | 113 31.8 | 32.4 | 210 40.4 | 56.6 | 282 05.5 | 11.8 | 324 25.8 | 16.5 | Atria | 107 14.4 | S69 04.3 |
| 20 | 301 39.6 | 128 31.4 | 31.2 | 225 41.8 | 56.8 | 297 08.2 | 11.6 | 339 28.4 | 16.6 | Avior | 234 15.9 | S59 34.6 |
| 21 | 316 42.0 | 143 31.0 | .. 30.0 | 240 43.2 | .. 56.9 | 312 11.0 | .. 11.5 | 354 31.0 | .. 16.6 | Bellatrix | 278 24.9 | N 6 22.3 |
| 22 | 331 44.5 | 158 30.6 | 28.8 | 255 44.6 | 57.1 | 327 13.8 | 11.4 | 9 33.5 | 16.6 | Betelgeuse | 270 54.1 | N 7 24.8 |
| 23 | 346 46.9 | 173 30.2 | 27.6 | 270 45.9 | 57.2 | 342 16.5 | 11.2 | 24 36.1 | 16.7 | | | |
| **23 00** | 1 49.4 | 188 29.8 | N 4 26.3 | 285 47.3 | N21 57.4 | 357 19.3 | N 0 11.1 | 39 38.7 | S16 16.7 | Canopus | 263 53.3 | S52 42.1 |
| 01 | 16 51.9 | 203 29.3 | 25.1 | 300 48.7 | 57.6 | 12 22.1 | 11.0 | 54 41.3 | 16.8 | Capella | 280 24.6 | N46 01.1 |
| 02 | 31 54.3 | 218 28.9 | 23.9 | 315 50.1 | 57.7 | 27 24.8 | 10.8 | 69 43.9 | 16.8 | Deneb | 49 26.8 | N45 21.9 |
| 03 | 46 56.8 | 233 28.5 | .. 22.7 | 330 51.4 | .. 57.9 | 42 27.6 | .. 10.7 | 84 46.4 | .. 16.8 | Denebola | 182 27.2 | N14 26.9 |
| 04 | 61 59.3 | 248 28.1 | 21.4 | 345 52.8 | 58.0 | 57 30.4 | 10.6 | 99 49.0 | 16.9 | Diphda | 348 48.9 | S17 51.6 |
| 05 | 77 01.7 | 263 27.7 | 20.2 | 0 54.2 | 58.2 | 72 33.2 | 10.4 | 114 51.6 | 16.9 | | | |
| **06** | 92 04.2 | 278 27.3 | N 4 19.0 | 15 55.6 | N21 58.4 | 87 35.9 | N 0 10.3 | 129 54.2 | S16 16.9 | Dubhe | 193 44.0 | N61 37.8 |
| 07 | 107 06.7 | 293 26.9 | 17.8 | 30 56.9 | 58.5 | 102 38.7 | 10.2 | 144 56.8 | 17.0 | Elnath | 278 04.2 | N28 37.5 |
| F 08 | 122 09.1 | 308 26.5 | 16.5 | 45 58.3 | 58.7 | 117 41.5 | 10.0 | 159 59.3 | 17.0 | Eltanin | 90 43.1 | N51 29.4 |
| R 09 | 137 11.6 | 323 26.1 | .. 15.3 | 60 59.7 | .. 58.8 | 132 44.2 | .. 09.9 | 175 01.9 | .. 17.0 | Enif | 33 40.4 | N 9 58.8 |
| I 10 | 152 14.1 | 338 25.7 | 14.1 | 76 01.1 | 59.0 | 147 47.0 | 09.8 | 190 04.5 | 17.1 | Fomalhaut | 15 16.3 | S29 30.1 |
| D 11 | 167 16.5 | 353 25.3 | 12.9 | 91 02.5 | 59.1 | 162 49.8 | 09.6 | 205 07.1 | 17.1 | | | |
| A 12 | 182 19.0 | 8 24.9 | N 4 11.6 | 106 03.9 | N21 59.3 | 177 52.5 | N 0 09.5 | 220 09.7 | S16 17.1 | Gacrux | 171 54.3 | S57 14.3 |
| Y 13 | 197 21.4 | 23 24.5 | 10.4 | 121 05.2 | 59.5 | 192 55.3 | 09.4 | 235 12.2 | 17.2 | Gienah | 175 45.9 | S17 39.9 |
| 14 | 212 23.9 | 38 24.1 | 09.2 | 136 06.6 | 59.6 | 207 58.1 | 09.2 | 250 14.8 | 17.2 | Hadar | 148 39.3 | S60 28.9 |
| 15 | 227 26.4 | 53 23.7 | .. 08.0 | 151 08.0 | .. 59.8 | 223 00.9 | .. 09.1 | 265 17.4 | .. 17.3 | Hamal | 327 53.1 | N23 34.2 |
| 16 | 242 28.8 | 68 23.3 | 06.7 | 166 09.4 | 21 59.9 | 238 03.6 | 09.0 | 280 20.0 | 17.3 | Kaus Aust. | 83 35.0 | S34 22.5 |
| 17 | 257 31.3 | 83 22.9 | 05.5 | 181 10.8 | 22 00.1 | 253 06.4 | 08.8 | 295 22.6 | 17.3 | | | |
| 18 | 272 33.8 | 98 22.5 | N 4 04.3 | 196 12.2 | N22 00.2 | 268 09.2 | N 0 08.7 | 310 25.1 | S16 17.4 | Kochab | 137 20.6 | N74 04.0 |
| 19 | 287 36.2 | 113 22.1 | 03.1 | 211 13.6 | 00.4 | 283 11.9 | 08.6 | 325 27.7 | 17.4 | Markab | 13 31.5 | N15 19.7 |
| 20 | 302 38.7 | 128 21.7 | 01.8 | 226 15.0 | 00.6 | 298 14.7 | 08.4 | 340 30.3 | 17.4 | Menkar | 314 07.9 | N 4 10.8 |
| 21 | 317 41.2 | 143 21.3 | 4 00.6 | 241 16.4 | .. 00.7 | 313 17.5 | .. 08.3 | 355 32.9 | .. 17.5 | Menkent | 148 00.2 | S36 28.8 |
| 22 | 332 43.6 | 158 20.9 | 3 59.4 | 256 17.7 | 00.9 | 328 20.2 | 08.2 | 10 35.5 | 17.5 | Miaplacidus | 221 39.3 | S69 48.3 |
| 23 | 347 46.1 | 173 20.5 | 58.2 | 271 19.1 | 01.0 | 343 23.0 | 08.0 | 25 38.0 | 17.5 | | | |
| **24 00** | 2 48.5 | 188 20.1 | N 3 56.9 | 286 20.5 | N22 01.2 | 358 25.8 | N 0 07.9 | 40 40.6 | S16 17.6 | Mirfak | 308 30.7 | N49 56.4 |
| 01 | 17 51.0 | 203 19.7 | 55.7 | 301 21.9 | 01.3 | 13 28.6 | 07.8 | 55 43.2 | 17.6 | Nunki | 75 50.0 | S26 16.1 |
| 02 | 32 53.5 | 218 19.3 | 54.5 | 316 23.3 | 01.5 | 28 31.3 | 07.6 | 70 45.8 | 17.6 | Peacock | 53 08.4 | S56 39.9 |
| 03 | 47 55.9 | 233 18.9 | .. 53.2 | 331 24.7 | .. 01.7 | 43 34.1 | .. 07.5 | 85 48.3 | .. 17.7 | Pollux | 243 19.8 | N27 58.3 |
| 04 | 62 58.4 | 248 18.5 | 52.0 | 346 26.1 | 01.8 | 58 36.9 | 07.4 | 100 50.9 | 17.7 | Procyon | 244 53.0 | N 5 10.2 |
| 05 | 78 00.9 | 263 18.1 | 50.8 | 1 27.5 | 02.0 | 73 39.6 | 07.2 | 115 53.5 | 17.7 | | | |
| **06** | 93 03.3 | 278 17.7 | N 3 49.6 | 16 28.9 | N22 02.1 | 88 42.4 | N 0 07.1 | 130 56.1 | S16 17.8 | Rasalhague | 96 00.4 | N12 32.8 |
| 07 | 108 05.8 | 293 17.3 | 48.3 | 31 30.3 | 02.3 | 103 45.2 | 07.0 | 145 58.7 | 17.8 | Regulus | 207 36.8 | N11 51.5 |
| S 08 | 123 08.3 | 308 16.9 | 47.1 | 46 31.7 | 02.4 | 118 47.9 | 06.8 | 161 01.2 | 17.9 | Rigel | 281 05.6 | S 8 10.3 |
| A 09 | 138 10.7 | 323 16.5 | .. 45.9 | 61 33.1 | .. 02.6 | 133 50.7 | .. 06.7 | 176 03.8 | .. 17.9 | Rigil Kent. | 139 43.4 | S60 55.7 |
| T 10 | 153 13.2 | 338 16.1 | 44.6 | 76 34.5 | 02.7 | 148 53.5 | 06.5 | 191 06.4 | 17.9 | Sabik | 102 05.0 | S15 45.1 |
| U 11 | 168 15.7 | 353 15.7 | 43.4 | 91 35.9 | 02.9 | 163 56.3 | 06.4 | 206 09.0 | 18.0 | | | |
| R 12 | 183 18.1 | 8 15.3 | N 3 42.2 | 106 37.3 | N22 03.1 | 178 59.0 | N 0 06.3 | 221 11.5 | S16 18.0 | Schedar | 349 32.6 | N56 39.7 |
| D 13 | 198 20.6 | 23 14.9 | 41.0 | 121 38.7 | 03.2 | 194 01.8 | 06.1 | 236 14.1 | 18.0 | Shaula | 96 13.0 | S37 07.3 |
| A 14 | 213 23.0 | 38 14.5 | 39.7 | 136 40.1 | 03.4 | 209 04.6 | 06.0 | 251 16.7 | 18.1 | Sirius | 258 28.0 | S16 44.6 |
| Y 15 | 228 25.5 | 53 14.1 | .. 38.5 | 151 41.5 | .. 03.5 | 224 07.3 | .. 05.9 | 266 19.3 | .. 18.1 | Spica | 158 24.6 | S11 16.6 |
| 16 | 243 28.0 | 68 13.7 | 37.3 | 166 42.9 | 03.7 | 239 10.1 | 05.7 | 281 21.8 | 18.1 | Suhail | 222 48.0 | S43 31.1 |
| 17 | 258 30.4 | 83 13.3 | 36.0 | 181 44.4 | 03.8 | 254 12.9 | 05.6 | 296 24.4 | 18.2 | | | |
| 18 | 273 32.9 | 98 12.9 | N 3 34.8 | 196 45.8 | N22 04.0 | 269 15.7 | N 0 05.5 | 311 27.0 | S16 18.2 | Vega | 80 34.5 | N38 48.5 |
| 19 | 288 35.4 | 113 12.5 | 33.6 | 211 47.2 | 04.1 | 284 18.4 | 05.3 | 326 29.6 | 18.2 | Zuben'ubi | 136 58.4 | S16 08.0 |
| 20 | 303 37.8 | 128 12.1 | 32.3 | 226 48.6 | 04.3 | 299 21.2 | 05.2 | 341 32.1 | 18.3 | | | |
| 21 | 318 40.3 | 143 11.7 | .. 31.1 | 241 50.0 | .. 04.4 | 314 24.0 | .. 05.1 | 356 34.7 | .. 18.3 | | SHA | Mer. Pass. |
| 22 | 333 42.8 | 158 11.3 | 29.9 | 256 51.4 | 04.6 | 329 26.7 | 04.9 | 11 37.3 | 18.3 | Venus | 186 40.3 | 11 26 |
| 23 | 348 45.2 | 173 10.9 | 28.6 | 271 52.8 | 04.7 | 344 29.5 | 04.8 | 26 39.9 | 18.4 | Mars | 283 57.9 | 4 56 |
| Mer. Pass. 23 48.8 | | v −0.4 | d 1.2 | v 1.4 | d 0.2 | v 2.8 | d 0.1 | v 2.6 | d 0.0 | Jupiter | 355 29.9 | 0 11 |
| | | | | | | | | | | Saturn | 37 49.3 | 21 18 |

### SUN and MOON

| UT (d h) | SUN GHA | SUN Dec | MOON GHA | v | Dec | d | HP |
|---|---|---|---|---|---|---|---|
| 22 00 | 181 46.6 | N 0 24.4 | 223 04.2 | 12.4 | N21 36.9 | 8.9 | 54.6 |
| 01 | 196 46.8 | 23.4 | 237 35.6 | 12.5 | 21 28.0 | 9.1 | 54.7 |
| 02 | 211 47.1 | 22.4 | 252 07.1 | 12.6 | 21 18.9 | 9.1 | 54.7 |
| 03 | 226 47.3 | .. 21.5 | 266 38.7 | 12.6 | 21 09.8 | 9.2 | 54.7 |
| 04 | 241 47.5 | 20.5 | 281 10.3 | 12.6 | 21 00.6 | 9.4 | 54.7 |
| 05 | 256 47.7 | 19.5 | 295 41.9 | 12.7 | 20 51.2 | 9.4 | 54.7 |
| 06 | 271 47.9 | N 0 18.6 | 310 13.6 | 12.7 | N20 41.8 | 9.6 | 54.7 |
| 07 | 286 48.2 | 17.6 | 324 45.3 | 12.8 | 20 32.2 | 9.6 | 54.7 |
| 08 | 301 48.4 | 16.6 | 339 17.1 | 12.8 | 20 22.6 | 9.7 | 54.8 |
| 09 | 316 48.6 | .. 15.6 | 353 48.9 | 12.9 | 20 12.9 | 9.9 | 54.8 |
| 10 | 331 48.8 | 14.7 | 8 20.8 | 12.9 | 20 03.0 | 9.9 | 54.8 |
| 11 | 346 49.0 | 13.7 | 22 52.7 | 12.9 | 19 53.1 | 10.0 | 54.8 |
| 12 | 1 49.3 | N 0 12.7 | 37 24.6 | 13.0 | N19 43.1 | 10.1 | 54.8 |
| 13 | 16 49.5 | 11.7 | 51 56.6 | 13.1 | 19 33.0 | 10.2 | 54.8 |
| 14 | 31 49.7 | 10.8 | 66 28.7 | 13.0 | 19 22.8 | 10.3 | 54.9 |
| 15 | 46 49.9 | .. 09.8 | 81 00.7 | 13.1 | 19 12.5 | 10.4 | 54.9 |
| 16 | 61 50.1 | 08.8 | 95 32.8 | 13.2 | 19 02.1 | 10.5 | 54.9 |
| 17 | 76 50.4 | 07.9 | 110 05.0 | 13.2 | 18 51.6 | 10.5 | 54.9 |
| 18 | 91 50.6 | N 0 06.9 | 124 37.2 | 13.2 | N18 41.1 | 10.7 | 54.9 |
| 19 | 106 50.8 | 05.9 | 139 09.4 | 13.3 | 18 30.4 | 10.7 | 54.9 |
| 20 | 121 51.0 | 04.9 | 153 41.7 | 13.3 | 18 19.7 | 10.8 | 55.0 |
| 21 | 136 51.2 | .. 04.0 | 168 14.0 | 13.4 | 18 08.9 | 10.9 | 55.0 |
| 22 | 151 51.5 | 03.0 | 182 46.4 | 13.4 | 17 58.0 | 11.0 | 55.0 |
| 23 | 166 51.7 | 02.0 | 197 18.8 | 13.4 | 17 47.0 | 11.1 | 55.0 |
| 23 00 | 181 51.9 | N 0 01.0 | 211 51.2 | 13.5 | N17 35.9 | 11.2 | 55.0 |
| 01 | 196 52.1 | N 00.1 | 226 23.7 | 13.5 | 17 24.7 | 11.3 | 55.1 |
| 02 | 211 52.3 | S 00.9 | 240 56.2 | 13.6 | 17 13.4 | 11.3 | 55.1 |
| 03 | 226 52.6 | .. 01.9 | 255 28.8 | 13.6 | 17 02.1 | 11.4 | 55.1 |
| 04 | 241 52.8 | 02.8 | 270 01.4 | 13.6 | 16 50.7 | 11.5 | 55.1 |
| 05 | 256 53.0 | 03.8 | 284 34.0 | 13.7 | 16 39.2 | 11.6 | 55.1 |
| 06 | 271 53.2 | S 0 04.8 | 299 06.7 | 13.7 | N16 27.6 | 11.6 | 55.2 |
| 07 | 286 53.4 | 05.8 | 313 39.4 | 13.7 | 16 16.0 | 11.8 | 55.2 |
| 08 | 301 53.7 | 06.7 | 328 12.1 | 13.8 | 16 04.2 | 11.8 | 55.2 |
| 09 | 316 53.9 | .. 07.7 | 342 44.9 | 13.8 | 15 52.4 | 11.9 | 55.2 |
| 10 | 331 54.1 | 08.7 | 357 17.7 | 13.9 | 15 40.5 | 11.9 | 55.2 |
| 11 | 346 54.3 | 09.7 | 11 50.6 | 13.8 | 15 28.6 | 12.1 | 55.3 |
| 12 | 1 54.5 | S 0 10.6 | 26 23.4 | 13.9 | N15 16.5 | 12.1 | 55.3 |
| 13 | 16 54.7 | 11.6 | 40 56.3 | 14.0 | 15 04.4 | 12.2 | 55.3 |
| 14 | 31 55.0 | 12.6 | 55 29.3 | 14.0 | 14 52.2 | 12.3 | 55.3 |
| 15 | 46 55.2 | .. 13.6 | 70 02.3 | 14.0 | 14 39.9 | 12.3 | 55.3 |
| 16 | 61 55.4 | 14.5 | 84 35.3 | 14.0 | 14 27.6 | 12.4 | 55.4 |
| 17 | 76 55.6 | 15.5 | 99 08.3 | 14.1 | 14 15.2 | 12.5 | 55.4 |
| 18 | 91 55.8 | S 0 16.5 | 113 41.4 | 14.1 | N14 02.7 | 12.5 | 55.4 |
| 19 | 106 56.1 | 17.5 | 128 14.5 | 14.1 | 13 50.2 | 12.6 | 55.4 |
| 20 | 121 56.3 | 18.4 | 142 47.6 | 14.1 | 13 37.6 | 12.7 | 55.4 |
| 21 | 136 56.5 | .. 19.4 | 157 20.7 | 14.2 | 13 24.9 | 12.8 | 55.5 |
| 22 | 151 56.7 | 20.4 | 171 53.9 | 14.2 | 13 12.1 | 12.8 | 55.5 |
| 23 | 166 56.9 | 21.3 | 186 27.1 | 14.2 | 12 59.3 | 12.9 | 55.5 |
| 24 00 | 181 57.1 | S 0 22.3 | 201 00.3 | 14.3 | N12 46.4 | 12.9 | 55.5 |
| 01 | 196 57.4 | 23.3 | 215 33.6 | 14.3 | 12 33.5 | 13.0 | 55.5 |
| 02 | 211 57.6 | 24.3 | 230 06.9 | 14.3 | 12 20.5 | 13.1 | 55.6 |
| 03 | 226 57.8 | .. 25.2 | 244 40.2 | 14.3 | 12 07.4 | 13.2 | 55.6 |
| 04 | 241 58.0 | 26.2 | 259 13.5 | 14.4 | 11 54.2 | 13.2 | 55.6 |
| 05 | 256 58.2 | 27.2 | 273 46.9 | 14.3 | 11 41.0 | 13.2 | 55.6 |
| 06 | 271 58.4 | S 0 28.2 | 288 20.2 | 14.4 | N11 27.8 | 13.3 | 55.7 |
| 07 | 286 58.7 | 29.1 | 302 53.6 | 14.5 | 11 14.5 | 13.4 | 55.7 |
| 08 | 301 58.9 | 30.1 | 317 27.1 | 14.4 | 11 01.1 | 13.4 | 55.7 |
| 09 | 316 59.1 | .. 31.1 | 332 00.5 | 14.4 | 10 47.7 | 13.5 | 55.7 |
| 10 | 331 59.3 | 32.1 | 346 33.9 | 14.5 | 10 34.2 | 13.6 | 55.7 |
| 11 | 346 59.5 | 33.0 | 1 07.4 | 14.5 | 10 20.6 | 13.6 | 55.8 |
| 12 | 1 59.8 | S 0 34.0 | 15 40.9 | 14.5 | N10 07.0 | 13.8 | 55.8 |
| 13 | 17 00.0 | 35.0 | 30 14.4 | 14.5 | 9 53.4 | 13.8 | 55.8 |
| 14 | 32 00.2 | 36.0 | 44 47.9 | 14.6 | 9 39.6 | 13.7 | 55.8 |
| 15 | 47 00.4 | .. 36.9 | 59 21.5 | 14.5 | 9 25.9 | 13.8 | 55.9 |
| 16 | 62 00.6 | 37.9 | 73 55.0 | 14.6 | 9 12.1 | 13.9 | 55.9 |
| 17 | 77 00.8 | 38.9 | 88 28.6 | 14.6 | 8 58.2 | 13.9 | 55.9 |
| 18 | 92 01.1 | S 0 39.8 | 103 02.2 | 14.5 | N 8 44.3 | 14.0 | 55.9 |
| 19 | 107 01.3 | 40.8 | 117 35.7 | 14.6 | 8 30.3 | 14.0 | 56.0 |
| 20 | 122 01.5 | 41.8 | 132 09.3 | 14.6 | 8 16.3 | 14.0 | 56.0 |
| 21 | 137 01.7 | .. 42.8 | 146 42.9 | 14.7 | 8 02.3 | 14.1 | 56.0 |
| 22 | 152 01.9 | 43.7 | 161 16.6 | 14.6 | 7 48.2 | 14.2 | 56.0 |
| 23 | 167 02.1 | 44.7 | 175 50.2 | 14.6 | N 7 34.0 | 14.2 | 56.0 |
| | SD 16.0 | d 1.0 | SD 14.9 | | 15.1 | | 15.2 |

Thursday (d 22), Friday (d 23), Saturday (d 24)

### Twilight, Sunrise and Moonrise

| Lat. | Naut. | Civil | Sunrise | Moonrise 22 | 23 | 24 | 25 |
|---|---|---|---|---|---|---|---|
| N 72 | 03 04 | 04 34 | 05 43 | 22 26 | 25 51 | 01 51 | 04 07 |
| N 70 | 03 23 | 04 42 | 05 44 | 23 52 | 26 15 | 02 15 | 04 17 |
| 68 | 03 38 | 04 48 | 05 44 | 24 30 | 00 30 | 02 32 | 04 24 |
| 66 | 03 50 | 04 53 | 05 45 | 24 57 | 00 57 | 02 46 | 04 31 |
| 64 | 04 00 | 04 58 | 05 45 | 25 17 | 01 17 | 02 58 | 04 36 |
| 62 | 04 08 | 05 02 | 05 46 | 25 33 | 01 33 | 03 07 | 04 40 |
| 60 | 04 15 | 05 05 | 05 46 | 00 16 | 01 47 | 03 16 | 04 44 |
| N 58 | 04 20 | 05 07 | 05 47 | 00 33 | 01 58 | 03 23 | 04 48 |
| 56 | 04 26 | 05 10 | 05 47 | 00 47 | 02 08 | 03 29 | 04 51 |
| 54 | 04 30 | 05 12 | 05 47 | 00 59 | 02 17 | 03 35 | 04 54 |
| 52 | 04 34 | 05 14 | 05 47 | 01 10 | 02 25 | 03 40 | 04 56 |
| 50 | 04 37 | 05 15 | 05 48 | 01 19 | 02 32 | 03 45 | 04 58 |
| 45 | 04 44 | 05 19 | 05 48 | 01 39 | 02 47 | 03 55 | 05 03 |
| N 40 | 04 50 | 05 21 | 05 48 | 01 55 | 02 59 | 04 03 | 05 07 |
| 35 | 04 54 | 05 23 | 05 49 | 02 09 | 03 09 | 04 10 | 05 11 |
| 30 | 04 57 | 05 25 | 05 49 | 02 21 | 03 18 | 04 16 | 05 14 |
| 20 | 05 01 | 05 27 | 05 49 | 02 41 | 03 34 | 04 27 | 05 19 |
| N 10 | 05 04 | 05 28 | 05 49 | 02 58 | 03 48 | 04 36 | 05 24 |
| 0 | 05 04 | 05 28 | 05 49 | 03 14 | 04 00 | 04 45 | 05 28 |
| S 10 | 05 04 | 05 28 | 05 49 | 03 30 | 04 13 | 04 54 | 05 33 |
| 20 | 05 01 | 05 27 | 05 49 | 03 48 | 04 26 | 05 03 | 05 38 |
| 30 | 04 57 | 05 25 | 05 48 | 04 07 | 04 42 | 05 13 | 05 43 |
| 35 | 04 53 | 05 23 | 05 48 | 04 19 | 04 50 | 05 19 | 05 46 |
| 40 | 04 49 | 05 21 | 05 48 | 04 32 | 05 00 | 05 26 | 05 49 |
| 45 | 04 44 | 05 10 | 05 47 | 04 47 | 05 12 | 05 34 | 05 53 |
| S 50 | 04 37 | 05 15 | 05 47 | 05 06 | 05 26 | 05 43 | 05 58 |
| 52 | 04 33 | 05 13 | 05 47 | 05 15 | 05 33 | 05 47 | 06 00 |
| 54 | 04 29 | 05 11 | 05 46 | 05 25 | 05 40 | 05 52 | 06 02 |
| 56 | 04 25 | 05 09 | 05 46 | 05 36 | 05 48 | 05 57 | 06 05 |
| 58 | 04 20 | 05 07 | 05 46 | 05 49 | 05 57 | 06 03 | 06 08 |
| S 60 | 04 14 | 05 04 | 05 45 | 06 04 | 06 08 | 06 10 | 06 11 |

### Sunset, Twilight and Moonset

| Lat. | Sunset | Civil | Naut. | Moonset 22 | 23 | 24 | 25 |
|---|---|---|---|---|---|---|---|
| N 72 | 18 00 | 19 08 | 20 36 | 21 31 | 19 41 | 18 58 | 18 25 |
| N 70 | 17 59 | 19 00 | 20 18 | 20 04 | 19 15 | 18 46 | 18 21 |
| 68 | 17 58 | 18 54 | 20 03 | 19 25 | 18 56 | 18 36 | 18 18 |
| 66 | 17 58 | 18 49 | 19 52 | 18 57 | 18 40 | 18 27 | 18 16 |
| 64 | 17 58 | 18 45 | 19 43 | 18 36 | 18 27 | 18 20 | 18 13 |
| 62 | 17 57 | 18 42 | 19 35 | 18 18 | 18 16 | 18 14 | 18 11 |
| 60 | 17 57 | 18 39 | 19 28 | 18 04 | 18 07 | 18 09 | 18 10 |
| N 58 | 17 57 | 18 36 | 19 23 | 17 52 | 17 59 | 18 04 | 18 08 |
| 56 | 17 57 | 18 34 | 19 18 | 17 41 | 17 51 | 18 00 | 18 07 |
| 54 | 17 56 | 18 32 | 19 13 | 17 31 | 17 45 | 17 56 | 18 06 |
| 52 | 17 56 | 18 30 | 19 10 | 17 23 | 17 39 | 17 52 | 18 05 |
| 50 | 17 56 | 18 28 | 19 06 | 17 15 | 17 34 | 17 49 | 18 04 |
| 45 | 17 56 | 18 25 | 18 59 | 16 59 | 17 22 | 17 42 | 18 01 |
| N 40 | 17 56 | 18 23 | 18 54 | 16 45 | 17 12 | 17 37 | 17 59 |
| 35 | 17 56 | 18 21 | 18 50 | 16 34 | 17 04 | 17 32 | 17 58 |
| 30 | 17 56 | 18 19 | 18 47 | 16 24 | 16 57 | 17 27 | 17 56 |
| 20 | 17 55 | 18 17 | 18 43 | 16 06 | 16 44 | 17 19 | 17 54 |
| N 10 | 17 55 | 18 16 | 18 41 | 15 51 | 16 33 | 17 12 | 17 51 |
| 0 | 17 56 | 18 16 | 18 40 | 15 37 | 16 22 | 17 06 | 17 49 |
| S 10 | 17 56 | 18 17 | 18 41 | 15 22 | 16 11 | 16 59 | 17 47 |
| 20 | 17 56 | 18 18 | 18 44 | 15 07 | 16 00 | 16 52 | 17 45 |
| 30 | 17 57 | 18 21 | 18 49 | 14 49 | 15 46 | 16 44 | 17 42 |
| 35 | 17 57 | 18 22 | 18 52 | 14 38 | 15 39 | 16 39 | 17 40 |
| 40 | 17 58 | 18 25 | 18 56 | 14 26 | 15 30 | 16 34 | 17 39 |
| 45 | 17 58 | 18 27 | 19 02 | 14 12 | 15 19 | 16 28 | 17 36 |
| S 50 | 17 59 | 18 31 | 19 09 | 13 54 | 15 07 | 16 20 | 17 34 |
| 52 | 17 59 | 18 33 | 19 13 | 13 46 | 15 01 | 16 17 | 17 33 |
| 54 | 17 59 | 18 35 | 19 17 | 13 36 | 14 54 | 16 13 | 17 31 |
| 56 | 18 00 | 18 37 | 19 21 | 13 26 | 14 47 | 16 08 | 17 30 |
| 58 | 18 00 | 18 40 | 19 27 | 13 13 | 14 39 | 16 04 | 17 28 |
| S 60 | 18 01 | 18 43 | 19 33 | 12 59 | 14 29 | 15 58 | 17 27 |

### SUN and MOON daily data

| Day | SUN Eqn. of Time 00h | 12h | Mer. Pass. | MOON Mer. Pass. Upper | Lower | Age | Phase |
|---|---|---|---|---|---|---|---|
| 22 | 07 06 | 07 17 | 11 53 | 09 26 | 21 49 | 26 | 12 |
| 23 | 07 27 | 07 38 | 11 52 | 10 11 | 22 33 | 27 | 6 |
| 24 | 07 48 | 07 59 | 11 52 | 10 55 | 23 17 | 28 | 2 |

| UT | ARIES GHA | VENUS −3.9 GHA | Dec | MARS −0.5 GHA | Dec | JUPITER −2.9 GHA | Dec | SATURN +0.4 GHA | Dec | STARS Name | SHA | Dec |
|---|---|---|---|---|---|---|---|---|---|---|---|---|
| d h | ° ′ | ° ′ | ° ′ | ° ′ | ° ′ | ° ′ | ° ′ | ° ′ | ° ′ | | ° ′ | ° ′ |
| 25 00 | 3 47.7 | 188 10.5 | N 3 27.4 | 286 54.2 | N22 04.9 | 359 32.3 | N 0 04.7 | 41 42.4 | S16 18.4 | Acamar | 315 12.9 | S40 12.6 |
| 01 | 18 50.1 | 203 10.1 | 26.2 | 301 55.6 | 05.0 | 14 35.1 | 04.5 | 56 45.0 | 18.4 | Achernar | 335 21.1 | S57 07.2 |
| 02 | 33 52.6 | 218 09.7 | 24.9 | 316 57.1 | 05.2 | 29 37.8 | 04.4 | 71 47.6 | 18.5 | Acrux | 173 02.9 | S63 13.4 |
| 03 | 48 55.1 | 233 09.3 .. | 23.7 | 331 58.5 .. | 05.4 | 44 40.6 .. | 04.3 | 86 50.2 .. | 18.5 | Adhara | 255 07.4 | S28 59.9 |
| 04 | 63 57.5 | 248 08.9 | 22.5 | 346 59.9 | 05.5 | 59 43.4 | 04.1 | 101 52.7 | 18.5 | Aldebaran | 290 41.7 | N16 33.3 |
| 05 | 79 00.0 | 263 08.5 | 21.2 | 2 01.3 | 05.7 | 74 46.1 | 04.0 | 116 55.3 | 18.6 | | | |
| 06 | 94 02.5 | 278 08.1 | N 3 20.0 | 17 02.7 | N22 05.8 | 89 48.9 | N 0 03.9 | 131 57.9 | S16 18.6 | Alioth | 166 15.2 | N55 50.4 |
| 07 | 109 04.9 | 293 07.7 | 18.8 | 32 04.1 | 06.0 | 104 51.7 | 03.7 | 147 00.5 | 18.6 | Alkaid | 152 54.0 | N49 12.2 |
| 08 | 124 07.4 | 308 07.3 | 17.5 | 47 05.6 | 06.1 | 119 54.4 | 03.6 | 162 03.0 | 18.7 | Alnair | 27 34.9 | S46 51.2 |
| S 09 | 139 09.9 | 323 06.9 .. | 16.3 | 62 07.0 .. | 06.3 | 134 57.2 .. | 03.5 | 177 05.6 .. | 18.7 | Alnilam | 275 39.6 | S 1 11.1 |
| U 10 | 154 12.3 | 338 06.5 | 15.1 | 77 08.4 | 06.4 | 150 00.0 | 03.3 | 192 08.2 | 18.7 | Alphard | 217 49.9 | S 8 45.2 |
| N 11 | 169 14.8 | 353 06.1 | 13.8 | 92 09.8 | 06.6 | 165 02.8 | 03.2 | 207 10.7 | 18.8 | | | |
| D 12 | 184 17.3 | 8 05.7 | N 3 12.6 | 107 11.3 | N22 06.7 | 180 05.5 | N 0 03.1 | 222 13.3 | S16 18.8 | Alphecca | 126 05.6 | N26 38.5 |
| A 13 | 199 19.7 | 23 05.3 | 11.4 | 122 12.7 | 06.9 | 195 08.3 | 02.9 | 237 15.9 | 18.8 | Alpheratz | 357 36.4 | N29 13.0 |
| Y 14 | 214 22.2 | 38 04.9 | 10.1 | 137 14.1 | 07.0 | 210 11.1 | 02.8 | 252 18.5 | 18.9 | Altair | 62 01.7 | N 8 55.8 |
| 15 | 229 24.6 | 53 04.5 .. | 08.9 | 152 15.5 .. | 07.2 | 225 13.8 .. | 02.7 | 267 21.0 .. | 18.9 | Ankaa | 353 08.6 | S42 10.9 |
| 16 | 244 27.1 | 68 04.1 | 07.7 | 167 17.0 | 07.3 | 240 16.6 | 02.5 | 282 23.6 | 18.9 | Antares | 112 18.3 | S26 28.9 |
| 17 | 259 29.6 | 83 03.7 | 06.4 | 182 18.4 | 07.5 | 255 19.4 | 02.4 | 297 26.2 | 19.0 | | | |
| 18 | 274 32.0 | 98 03.3 | N 3 05.2 | 197 19.8 | N22 07.6 | 270 22.2 | N 0 02.3 | 312 28.8 | S16 19.0 | Arcturus | 145 49.9 | N19 04.1 |
| 19 | 289 34.5 | 113 02.9 | 03.9 | 212 21.2 | 07.8 | 285 24.9 | 02.1 | 327 31.3 | 19.0 | Atria | 107 14.4 | S69 04.3 |
| 20 | 304 37.0 | 128 02.5 | 02.7 | 227 22.7 | 07.9 | 300 27.7 | 02.0 | 342 33.9 | 19.1 | Avior | 234 15.8 | S59 34.5 |
| 21 | 319 39.4 | 143 02.1 .. | 01.5 | 242 24.1 .. | 08.1 | 315 30.5 .. | 01.9 | 357 36.5 .. | 19.1 | Bellatrix | 278 24.9 | N 6 22.3 |
| 22 | 334 41.9 | 158 01.7 | 3 00.2 | 257 25.5 | 08.2 | 330 33.2 | 01.7 | 12 39.0 | 19.1 | Betelgeuse | 270 54.1 | N 7 24.8 |
| 23 | 349 44.4 | 173 01.3 | 2 59.0 | 272 27.0 | 08.4 | 345 36.0 | 01.6 | 27 41.6 | 19.2 | | | |
| 26 00 | 4 46.8 | 188 00.9 | N 2 57.8 | 287 28.4 | N22 08.5 | 0 38.8 | N 0 01.5 | 42 44.2 | S16 19.2 | Canopus | 263 53.3 | S52 42.1 |
| 01 | 19 49.3 | 203 00.5 | 56.5 | 302 29.8 | 08.7 | 15 41.6 | 01.3 | 57 46.8 | 19.2 | Capella | 280 24.6 | N46 01.1 |
| 02 | 34 51.8 | 218 00.1 | 55.3 | 317 31.3 | 08.8 | 30 44.3 | 01.2 | 72 49.3 | 19.3 | Deneb | 49 26.8 | N45 21.9 |
| 03 | 49 54.2 | 232 59.7 .. | 54.0 | 332 32.7 .. | 09.0 | 45 47.1 .. | 01.1 | 87 51.9 .. | 19.3 | Denebola | 182 27.2 | N14 26.9 |
| 04 | 64 56.7 | 247 59.3 | 52.8 | 347 34.2 | 09.1 | 60 49.9 | 00.9 | 102 54.5 | 19.3 | Diphda | 348 48.9 | S17 51.6 |
| 05 | 79 59.1 | 262 58.9 | 51.6 | 2 35.6 | 09.3 | 75 52.6 | 00.8 | 117 57.0 | 19.4 | | | |
| 06 | 95 01.6 | 277 58.5 | N 2 50.3 | 17 37.0 | N22 09.4 | 90 55.4 | N 0 00.7 | 132 59.6 | S16 19.4 | Dubhe | 193 44.0 | N61 37.8 |
| 07 | 110 04.1 | 292 58.1 | 49.1 | 32 38.5 | 09.6 | 105 58.2 | 00.5 | 148 02.2 | 19.4 | Elnath | 278 04.2 | N28 37.5 |
| 08 | 125 06.5 | 307 57.7 | 47.9 | 47 39.9 | 09.7 | 121 01.0 | 00.4 | 163 04.7 | 19.5 | Eltanin | 90 43.1 | N51 29.4 |
| M 09 | 140 09.0 | 322 57.3 .. | 46.6 | 62 41.3 .. | 09.9 | 136 03.7 .. | 00.3 | 178 07.3 .. | 19.5 | Enif | 33 40.4 | N 9 58.8 |
| O 10 | 155 11.5 | 337 56.9 | 45.4 | 77 42.8 | 10.0 | 151 06.5 | N 00.0 | 193 09.9 | 19.5 | Fomalhaut | 15 16.3 | S29 30.1 |
| N 11 | 170 13.9 | 352 56.5 | 44.1 | 92 44.2 | 10.2 | 166 09.3 | 00.0 | 208 12.5 | 19.6 | | | |
| D 12 | 185 16.4 | 7 56.1 | N 2 42.9 | 107 45.7 | N22 10.3 | 181 12.0 | S 0 00.1 | 223 15.0 | S16 19.6 | Gacrux | 171 54.4 | S57 14.3 |
| A 13 | 200 18.9 | 22 55.8 | 41.7 | 122 47.1 | 10.4 | 196 14.8 | 00.3 | 238 17.6 | 19.6 | Gienah | 175 45.9 | S17 39.9 |
| Y 14 | 215 21.3 | 37 55.4 | 40.4 | 137 48.6 | 10.6 | 211 17.6 | 00.4 | 253 20.2 | 19.7 | Hadar | 148 39.3 | S60 28.9 |
| 15 | 230 23.8 | 52 55.0 .. | 39.2 | 152 50.0 .. | 10.7 | 226 20.4 .. | 00.5 | 268 22.7 .. | 19.7 | Hamal | 327 53.0 | N23 34.2 |
| 16 | 245 26.2 | 67 54.6 | 37.9 | 167 51.5 | 10.9 | 241 23.1 | 00.7 | 283 25.3 | 19.7 | Kaus Aust. | 83 35.0 | S34 22.5 |
| 17 | 260 28.7 | 82 54.2 | 36.7 | 182 52.9 | 11.0 | 256 25.9 | 00.8 | 298 27.9 | 19.8 | | | |
| 18 | 275 31.2 | 97 53.8 | N 2 35.5 | 197 54.4 | N22 11.2 | 271 28.7 | S 0 00.9 | 313 30.4 | S16 19.8 | Kochab | 137 20.7 | N74 04.0 |
| 19 | 290 33.6 | 112 53.4 | 34.2 | 212 55.8 | 11.3 | 286 31.4 | 01.1 | 328 33.0 | 19.8 | Markab | 13 31.5 | N15 19.7 |
| 20 | 305 36.1 | 127 53.0 | 33.0 | 227 57.3 | 11.5 | 301 34.2 | 01.2 | 343 35.6 | 19.9 | Menkar | 314 07.9 | N 4 10.8 |
| 21 | 320 38.6 | 142 52.6 .. | 31.7 | 242 58.7 .. | 11.6 | 316 37.0 .. | 01.3 | 358 38.1 .. | 19.9 | Menkent | 148 00.2 | S36 28.8 |
| 22 | 335 41.0 | 157 52.2 | 30.5 | 258 00.2 | 11.8 | 331 39.8 | 01.5 | 13 40.7 | 19.9 | Miaplacidus | 221 39.3 | S69 48.3 |
| 23 | 350 43.5 | 172 51.8 | 29.3 | 273 01.6 | 11.9 | 346 42.5 | 01.6 | 28 43.3 | 20.0 | | | |
| 27 00 | 5 46.0 | 187 51.4 | N 2 28.0 | 288 03.1 | N22 12.1 | 1 45.3 | S 0 01.7 | 43 45.8 | S16 20.0 | Mirfak | 308 30.7 | N49 56.4 |
| 01 | 20 48.4 | 202 51.0 | 26.8 | 303 04.5 | 12.2 | 16 48.1 | 01.9 | 58 48.4 | 20.0 | Nunki | 75 50.1 | S26 16.1 |
| 02 | 35 50.9 | 217 50.6 | 25.5 | 318 06.0 | 12.4 | 31 50.8 | 02.0 | 73 51.0 | 20.0 | Peacock | 53 08.4 | S56 39.9 |
| 03 | 50 53.4 | 232 50.2 .. | 24.3 | 333 07.4 .. | 12.5 | 46 53.6 .. | 02.1 | 88 53.5 .. | 20.1 | Pollux | 243 19.8 | N27 58.3 |
| 04 | 65 55.8 | 247 49.8 | 23.0 | 348 08.9 | 12.6 | 61 56.4 | 02.3 | 103 56.1 | 20.1 | Procyon | 244 52.9 | N 5 10.2 |
| 05 | 80 58.3 | 262 49.4 | 21.8 | 3 10.4 | 12.8 | 76 59.2 | 02.4 | 118 58.7 | 20.1 | | | |
| 06 | 96 00.7 | 277 49.0 | N 2 20.6 | 18 11.8 | N22 12.9 | 92 01.9 | S 0 02.5 | 134 01.3 | S16 20.2 | Rasalhague | 96 00.4 | N12 32.8 |
| 07 | 111 03.2 | 292 48.6 | 19.3 | 33 13.3 | 13.1 | 107 04.7 | 02.7 | 149 03.8 | 20.2 | Regulus | 207 36.7 | N11 51.5 |
| 08 | 126 05.7 | 307 48.2 | 18.1 | 48 14.7 | 13.2 | 122 07.5 | 02.8 | 164 06.4 | 20.2 | Rigel | 281 05.6 | S 8 10.3 |
| T 09 | 141 08.1 | 322 47.9 .. | 16.8 | 63 16.2 .. | 13.4 | 137 10.2 .. | 02.9 | 179 09.0 .. | 20.3 | Rigil Kent. | 139 43.5 | S60 55.7 |
| U 10 | 156 10.6 | 337 47.5 | 15.6 | 78 17.7 | 13.5 | 152 13.0 | 03.1 | 194 11.5 | 20.3 | Sabik | 102 05.1 | S15 45.1 |
| E 11 | 171 13.1 | 352 47.1 | 14.3 | 93 19.1 | 13.7 | 167 15.8 | 03.2 | 209 14.1 | 20.3 | | | |
| S 12 | 186 15.5 | 7 46.7 | N 2 13.1 | 108 20.6 | N22 13.8 | 182 18.6 | S 0 03.3 | 224 16.6 | S16 20.4 | Schedar | 349 32.6 | N56 39.7 |
| D 13 | 201 18.0 | 22 46.3 | 11.9 | 123 22.1 | 13.9 | 197 21.3 | 03.5 | 239 19.2 | 20.4 | Shaula | 96 13.0 | S37 07.3 |
| A 14 | 216 20.5 | 37 45.9 | 10.6 | 138 23.5 | 14.1 | 212 24.1 | 03.6 | 254 21.8 | 20.4 | Sirius | 258 28.0 | S16 44.6 |
| Y 15 | 231 22.9 | 52 45.5 .. | 09.4 | 153 25.0 .. | 14.2 | 227 26.9 .. | 03.7 | 269 24.3 .. | 20.5 | Spica | 158 24.6 | S11 16.6 |
| 16 | 246 25.4 | 67 45.1 | 08.1 | 168 26.5 | 14.4 | 242 29.6 | 03.9 | 284 26.9 | 20.5 | Suhail | 222 48.0 | S43 31.1 |
| 17 | 261 27.8 | 82 44.7 | 06.9 | 183 27.9 | 14.5 | 257 32.4 | 04.0 | 299 29.5 | 20.5 | | | |
| 18 | 276 30.3 | 97 44.3 | N 2 05.6 | 198 29.4 | N22 14.7 | 272 35.2 | S 0 04.1 | 314 32.0 | S16 20.5 | Vega | 80 34.5 | N38 48.5 |
| 19 | 291 32.8 | 112 43.9 | 04.4 | 213 30.9 | 14.8 | 287 38.0 | 04.3 | 329 34.6 | 20.6 | Zuben'ubi | 136 58.4 | S16 08.0 |
| 20 | 306 35.2 | 127 43.5 | 03.2 | 228 32.3 | 15.0 | 302 40.7 | 04.4 | 344 37.2 | 20.6 | | | |
| 21 | 321 37.7 | 142 43.1 .. | 01.9 | 243 33.8 .. | 15.1 | 317 43.5 .. | 04.5 | 359 39.7 .. | 20.6 | | SHA | Mer. Pass. |
| 22 | 336 40.2 | 157 42.7 | 2 00.7 | 258 35.3 | 15.2 | 332 46.3 | 04.7 | 14 42.3 | 20.7 | | ° ′ | h m |
| 23 | 351 42.6 | 172 42.3 | N 1 59.4 | 273 36.8 | 15.4 | 347 49.0 | 04.8 | 29 44.9 | 20.7 | Venus | 183 14.1 | 11 28 |
| Mer. Pass. 23 37.0 | | v −0.4 | d 1.2 | v 1.4 | d 0.1 | v 2.8 | d 0.1 | v 2.6 | d 0.0 | Mars | 282 41.6 | 4 50 |
| | | | | | | | | | | Jupiter | 355 52.0 | 23 53 |
| | | | | | | | | | | Saturn | 37 57.4 | 21 05 |

| UT | SUN | | MOON | | | | Lat. | Twilight | | Sunrise | Moonrise | | | |
|---|---|---|---|---|---|---|---|---|---|---|---|---|---|---|
| | | | | | | | | Naut. | Civil | | 25 | 26 | 27 | 28 |
| | GHA | Dec | GHA | v | Dec | d | HP | | | | | | | |
| d h | ° ′ | ° ′ | ° ′ | ′ | ° ′ | ′ | ′ | N 72 | h m | h m | h m | h m | h m | h m | h m |
| | | | | | | | | N 72 | 03 22 | 04 48 | 05 56 | 04 07 | 06 14 | 08 25 | 10 54 |
| 25 00 | 182 02.3 | S 0 45.7 | 190 23.8 | 14.7 | N 7 19.8 | 14.2 | 56.1 | N 70 | 03 38 | 04 54 | 05 55 | 04 17 | 06 14 | 08 15 | 10 27 |
| 01 | 197 02.6 | 46.7 | 204 57.5 | 14.6 | 7 05.6 | 14.3 | 56.1 | 68 | 03 51 | 04 59 | 05 55 | 04 24 | 06 14 | 08 06 | 10 07 |
| 02 | 212 02.8 | 47.6 | 219 31.1 | 14.6 | 6 51.3 | 14.3 | 56.1 | 66 | 04 01 | 05 03 | 05 54 | 04 31 | 06 14 | 07 59 | 09 52 |
| 03 | 227 03.0 | .. 48.6 | 234 04.7 | 14.7 | 6 37.0 | 14.4 | 56.1 | 64 | 04 09 | 05 07 | 05 54 | 04 36 | 06 13 | 07 53 | 09 39 |
| 04 | 242 03.2 | 49.6 | 248 38.4 | 14.6 | 6 22.6 | 14.4 | 56.2 | 62 | 04 16 | 05 09 | 05 54 | 04 40 | 06 13 | 07 48 | 09 28 |
| 05 | 257 03.4 | 50.6 | 263 12.0 | 14.7 | 6 08.2 | 14.4 | 56.2 | 60 | 04 22 | 05 12 | 05 53 | 04 44 | 06 13 | 07 44 | 09 19 |
| 06 | 272 03.6 | S 0 51.5 | 277 45.7 | 14.7 | N 5 53.8 | 14.5 | 56.2 | N 58 | 04 27 | 05 14 | 05 53 | 04 48 | 06 13 | 07 40 | 09 11 |
| 07 | 287 03.9 | 52.5 | 292 19.4 | 14.6 | 5 39.3 | 14.5 | 56.2 | 56 | 04 32 | 05 16 | 05 53 | 04 51 | 06 13 | 07 37 | 09 04 |
| 08 | 302 04.1 | 53.5 | 306 53.0 | 14.7 | 5 24.8 | 14.5 | 56.3 | 54 | 04 36 | 05 17 | 05 53 | 04 54 | 06 13 | 07 34 | 08 58 |
| S 09 | 317 04.3 | .. 54.5 | 321 26.7 | 14.6 | 5 10.3 | 14.6 | 56.3 | 52 | 04 39 | 05 19 | 05 52 | 04 56 | 06 13 | 07 31 | 08 53 |
| U 10 | 332 04.5 | 55.4 | 336 00.3 | 14.7 | 4 55.7 | 14.6 | 56.3 | 50 | 04 42 | 05 20 | 05 52 | 04 58 | 06 13 | 07 29 | 08 48 |
| N 11 | 347 04.7 | 56.4 | 350 34.0 | 14.6 | 4 41.1 | 14.6 | 56.3 | 45 | 04 48 | 05 22 | 05 52 | 05 03 | 06 13 | 07 23 | 08 37 |
| D 12 | 2 04.9 | S 0 57.4 | 5 07.6 | 14.7 | N 4 26.5 | 14.7 | 56.3 | N 40 | 04 53 | 05 24 | 05 51 | 05 07 | 06 12 | 07 19 | 08 28 |
| A 13 | 17 05.2 | 58.4 | 19 41.3 | 14.6 | 4 11.8 | 14.7 | 56.4 | 35 | 04 56 | 05 26 | 05 51 | 05 11 | 06 12 | 07 15 | 00 20 |
| Y 14 | 32 05.4 | 0 59.3 | 34 14.9 | 14.6 | 3 57.1 | 14.8 | 56.4 | 30 | 04 59 | 05 27 | 05 50 | 05 14 | 06 12 | 07 12 | 08 14 |
| 15 | 47 05.6 | 1 00.3 | 48 48.5 | 14.6 | 3 42.3 | 14.7 | 56.4 | 20 | 05 02 | 05 28 | 05 50 | 05 19 | 06 12 | 07 06 | 08 02 |
| 16 | 62 05.8 | 01.3 | 63 22.1 | 14.6 | 3 27.6 | 14.8 | 56.4 | N 10 | 05 04 | 05 28 | 05 49 | 05 24 | 06 12 | 07 01 | 07 53 |
| 17 | 77 06.0 | 02.2 | 77 55.7 | 14.7 | 3 12.8 | 14.8 | 56.5 | 0 | 05 03 | 05 27 | 05 48 | 05 28 | 06 12 | 06 57 | 07 43 |
| 18 | 92 06.2 | S 1 03.2 | 92 29.4 | 14.5 | N 2 58.0 | 14.9 | 56.5 | S 10 | 05 02 | 05 26 | 05 47 | 05 33 | 06 12 | 06 52 | 07 34 |
| 19 | 107 06.4 | 04.2 | 107 02.9 | 14.6 | 2 43.1 | 14.8 | 56.5 | 20 | 04 58 | 05 24 | 05 46 | 05 38 | 06 12 | 06 47 | 07 25 |
| 20 | 122 06.7 | 05.2 | 121 36.5 | 14.6 | 2 28.3 | 14.9 | 56.5 | 30 | 04 53 | 05 21 | 05 45 | 05 43 | 06 12 | 06 42 | 07 14 |
| 21 | 137 06.9 | .. 06.1 | 136 10.1 | 14.5 | 2 13.4 | 14.9 | 56.6 | 35 | 04 49 | 05 19 | 05 44 | 05 46 | 06 12 | 06 39 | 07 07 |
| 22 | 152 07.1 | 07.1 | 150 43.6 | 14.6 | 1 58.5 | 14.9 | 56.6 | 40 | 04 44 | 05 16 | 05 43 | 05 49 | 06 12 | 06 35 | 07 00 |
| 23 | 167 07.3 | 08.1 | 165 17.2 | 14.5 | 1 43.6 | 15.0 | 56.6 | 45 | 04 38 | 05 12 | 05 42 | 05 53 | 06 12 | 06 31 | 06 52 |
| 26 00 | 182 07.5 | S 1 09.1 | 179 50.7 | 14.5 | N 1 28.6 | 15.0 | 56.6 | S 50 | 04 30 | 05 08 | 05 40 | 05 58 | 06 12 | 06 26 | 06 42 |
| 01 | 197 07.7 | 10.0 | 194 24.2 | 14.5 | 1 13.6 | 15.0 | 56.6 | 52 | 04 26 | 05 06 | 05 40 | 06 00 | 06 12 | 06 24 | 06 38 |
| 02 | 212 07.9 | 11.0 | 208 57.7 | 14.5 | 0 58.6 | 15.0 | 56.7 | 54 | 04 21 | 05 04 | 05 39 | 06 02 | 06 12 | 06 22 | 06 33 |
| 03 | 227 08.2 | .. 12.0 | 223 31.2 | 14.4 | 0 43.6 | 15.0 | 56.7 | 56 | 04 16 | 05 01 | 05 38 | 06 05 | 06 12 | 06 19 | 06 28 |
| 04 | 242 08.4 | 13.0 | 238 04.6 | 14.4 | 0 28.6 | 15.0 | 56.7 | 58 | 04 10 | 04 58 | 05 37 | 06 08 | 06 12 | 06 16 | 06 22 |
| 05 | 257 08.6 | 13.9 | 252 38.0 | 14.4 | N 0 13.6 | 15.0 | 56.7 | S 60 | 04 04 | 04 54 | 05 36 | 06 11 | 06 12 | 06 13 | 06 15 |

| UT | SUN | | MOON | | | | Lat. | Sunset | Twilight | | Moonset | | | |
|---|---|---|---|---|---|---|---|---|---|---|---|---|---|---|
| | | | | | | | | | Civil | Naut. | 25 | 26 | 27 | 28 |
| 06 | 272 08.8 | S 1 14.9 | 267 11.4 | 14.4 | S 0 01.4 | 15.1 | 56.8 | ° | h m | h m | h m | h m | h m | h m | h m |
| 07 | 287 09.0 | 15.9 | 281 44.8 | 14.4 | 0 16.5 | 15.1 | 56.8 | N 72 | 17 44 | 18 52 | 20 17 | 18 25 | 17 54 | 17 19 | 16 29 |
| 08 | 302 09.2 | 16.9 | 296 18.2 | 14.3 | 0 31.6 | 15.1 | 56.8 | N 70 | 17 45 | 18 46 | 20 01 | 18 21 | 17 58 | 17 32 | 16 58 |
| M 09 | 317 09.4 | .. 17.8 | 310 51.5 | 14.3 | 0 46.7 | 15.0 | 56.8 | 68 | 17 46 | 18 41 | 19 49 | 18 18 | 18 01 | 17 43 | 17 20 |
| O 10 | 332 09.7 | 18.8 | 325 24.8 | 14.3 | 1 01.7 | 15.1 | 56.8 | 66 | 17 47 | 18 37 | 19 39 | 18 16 | 18 04 | 17 52 | 17 37 |
| N 11 | 347 09.9 | 19.8 | 339 58.1 | 14.2 | 1 16.8 | 15.1 | 56.9 | 64 | 17 47 | 18 34 | 19 31 | 18 13 | 18 06 | 17 59 | 17 51 |
| D 12 | 2 10.1 | S 1 20.8 | 354 31.3 | 14.3 | S 1 31.9 | 15.1 | 56.9 | 62 | 17 48 | 18 32 | 19 24 | 18 11 | 18 09 | 18 06 | 18 03 |
| A 13 | 17 10.3 | 21.7 | 9 04.6 | 14.2 | 1 47.0 | 15.2 | 56.9 | 60 | 17 48 | 18 29 | 19 19 | 18 10 | 18 11 | 18 12 | 18 14 |
| Y 14 | 32 10.5 | 22.7 | 23 37.8 | 14.1 | 2 02.2 | 15.1 | 56.9 | N 58 | 17 48 | 18 27 | 19 14 | 18 08 | 18 12 | 18 17 | 18 23 |
| 15 | 47 10.7 | .. 23.7 | 38 10.9 | 14.1 | 2 17.3 | 15.1 | 57.0 | 56 | 17 49 | 18 26 | 19 09 | 18 07 | 18 14 | 18 21 | 18 31 |
| 16 | 62 10.9 | 24.6 | 52 44.0 | 14.1 | 2 32.4 | 15.1 | 57.0 | 54 | 17 49 | 18 24 | 19 06 | 18 06 | 18 15 | 18 25 | 18 38 |
| 17 | 77 11.1 | 25.6 | 67 17.1 | 14.1 | 2 47.5 | 15.1 | 57.0 | 52 | 17 49 | 18 23 | 19 02 | 18 05 | 18 16 | 18 29 | 18 44 |
| 18 | 92 11.4 | S 1 26.6 | 81 50.2 | 14.0 | S 3 02.6 | 15.1 | 57.0 | 50 | 17 50 | 18 22 | 18 59 | 18 04 | 18 18 | 18 32 | 18 50 |
| 19 | 107 11.6 | 27.6 | 96 23.2 | 14.0 | 3 17.7 | 15.1 | 57.1 | 45 | 17 50 | 18 19 | 18 54 | 18 01 | 18 20 | 18 40 | 19 02 |
| 20 | 122 11.8 | 28.5 | 110 56.2 | 13.9 | 3 32.8 | 15.1 | 57.1 | N 40 | 17 51 | 18 18 | 18 49 | 17 59 | 18 22 | 18 46 | 19 13 |
| 21 | 137 12.0 | .. 29.5 | 125 29.1 | 14.0 | 3 47.9 | 15.1 | 57.1 | 35 | 17 51 | 18 16 | 18 46 | 17 58 | 18 24 | 18 51 | 19 22 |
| 22 | 152 12.2 | 30.5 | 140 02.1 | 13.8 | 4 03.0 | 15.1 | 57.1 | 30 | 17 52 | 18 16 | 18 43 | 17 56 | 18 26 | 18 56 | 19 30 |
| 23 | 167 12.4 | 31.5 | 154 34.9 | 13.9 | 4 18.1 | 15.1 | 57.1 | 20 | 17 53 | 18 15 | 18 40 | 17 54 | 18 28 | 19 04 | 19 43 |
| 27 00 | 182 12.6 | S 1 32.4 | 169 07.8 | 13.7 | S 4 33.2 | 15.1 | 57.2 | N 10 | 17 54 | 18 15 | 18 39 | 17 51 | 18 31 | 19 12 | 19 55 |
| 01 | 197 12.8 | 33.4 | 183 40.5 | 13.8 | 4 48.3 | 15.1 | 57.2 | 0 | 17 55 | 18 15 | 18 39 | 17 49 | 18 33 | 19 19 | 20 07 |
| 02 | 212 13.1 | 34.4 | 198 13.3 | 13.7 | 5 03.4 | 15.1 | 57.2 | S 10 | 17 56 | 18 17 | 18 41 | 17 47 | 18 35 | 19 25 | 20 18 |
| 03 | 227 13.3 | .. 35.4 | 212 46.0 | 13.6 | 5 18.4 | 15.1 | 57.2 | 20 | 17 57 | 18 19 | 18 45 | 17 45 | 18 38 | 19 33 | 20 30 |
| 04 | 242 13.5 | 36.3 | 227 18.6 | 13.6 | 5 33.5 | 15.0 | 57.2 | 30 | 17 58 | 18 22 | 18 50 | 17 42 | 18 41 | 19 41 | 20 44 |
| 05 | 257 13.7 | 37.3 | 241 51.2 | 13.6 | 5 48.5 | 15.0 | 57.3 | 35 | 17 59 | 18 25 | 18 54 | 17 40 | 18 42 | 19 46 | 20 52 |
| 06 | 272 13.9 | S 1 38.3 | 256 23.8 | 13.5 | S 6 03.5 | 15.0 | 57.3 | 40 | 18 00 | 18 28 | 18 59 | 17 39 | 18 44 | 19 52 | 21 02 |
| 07 | 287 14.1 | 39.3 | 270 56.3 | 13.5 | 6 18.5 | 15.0 | 57.3 | 45 | 18 02 | 18 31 | 19 06 | 17 36 | 18 46 | 19 58 | 21 13 |
| T 08 | 302 14.4 | 40.2 | 285 28.8 | 13.4 | 6 33.5 | 15.0 | 57.3 | S 50 | 18 03 | 18 36 | 19 14 | 17 34 | 18 49 | 20 06 | 21 26 |
| U 09 | 317 14.5 | .. 41.2 | 300 01.2 | 13.3 | 6 48.5 | 14.9 | 57.4 | 52 | 18 04 | 18 38 | 19 18 | 17 33 | 18 50 | 20 10 | 21 32 |
| E 10 | 332 14.8 | 42.2 | 314 33.5 | 13.3 | 7 03.4 | 14.9 | 57.4 | 54 | 18 05 | 18 40 | 19 23 | 17 31 | 18 51 | 20 14 | 21 39 |
| S 11 | 347 15.0 | 43.1 | 329 05.8 | 13.3 | 7 18.3 | 14.9 | 57.4 | 56 | 18 06 | 18 43 | 19 28 | 17 30 | 18 53 | 20 18 | 21 47 |
| D 12 | 2 15.2 | S 1 44.1 | 343 38.1 | 13.2 | S 7 33.2 | 14.9 | 57.4 | 58 | 18 07 | 18 46 | 19 34 | 17 28 | 18 54 | 20 23 | 21 56 |
| A 13 | 17 15.4 | 45.1 | 358 10.3 | 13.1 | 7 48.1 | 14.8 | 57.4 | S 60 | 18 08 | 18 50 | 19 41 | 17 27 | 18 56 | 20 29 | 22 06 |
| Y 14 | 32 15.6 | 46.1 | 12 42.4 | 13.1 | 8 02.9 | 14.9 | 57.5 | | | | | | | | |
| 15 | 47 15.8 | .. 47.0 | 27 14.5 | 13.0 | 8 17.8 | 14.7 | 57.5 | | SUN | | | MOON | | | |
| 16 | 62 16.0 | 48.0 | 41 46.5 | 13.0 | 8 32.5 | 14.8 | 57.5 | | Eqn. of Time | | Mer. | Mer. Pass. | | Age | Phase |
| 17 | 77 16.2 | 49.0 | 56 18.5 | 12.9 | 8 47.3 | 14.7 | 57.5 | Day | 00ʰ | 12ʰ | Pass. | Upper | Lower | | |
| 18 | 92 16.4 | S 1 50.0 | 70 50.4 | 12.8 | S 9 02.0 | 14.7 | 57.5 | d | m s | m s | h m | h m | h m | d | % |
| 19 | 107 16.7 | 50.9 | 85 22.2 | 12.8 | 9 16.7 | 14.7 | 57.6 | 25 | 08 09 | 08 19 | 11 52 | 11 39 | 24 01 | 29 | 0 |
| 20 | 122 16.9 | 51.9 | 99 54.0 | 12.7 | 9 31.4 | 14.6 | 57.6 | 26 | 08 30 | 08 40 | 11 51 | 12 23 | 00 01 | 01 | 0 |
| 21 | 137 17.1 | .. 52.9 | 114 25.7 | 12.7 | 9 46.0 | 14.6 | 57.6 | 27 | 08 50 | 09 00 | 11 51 | 13 08 | 00 45 | 02 | 3 |
| 22 | 152 17.3 | 53.9 | 128 57.4 | 12.5 | 10 00.6 | 14.6 | 57.6 | | | | | | | | |
| 23 | 167 17.5 | 54.8 | 143 28.9 | 12.6 | S10 15.2 | 14.5 | 57.6 | | | | | | | | |
| | SD 16.0 | d 1.0 | SD 15.4 | | 15.5 | | 15.6 | | | | | | | | | |

| UT | ARIES | VENUS −3.9 | | MARS −0.6 | | JUPITER −2.9 | | SATURN +0.4 | | STARS | | |
|---|---|---|---|---|---|---|---|---|---|---|---|---|
| | GHA | GHA | Dec | GHA | Dec | GHA | Dec | GHA | Dec | Name | SHA | Dec |
| d h | ° ′ | ° ′ | ° ′ | ° ′ | ° ′ | ° ′ | ° ′ | ° ′ | ° ′ | | ° ′ | ° ′ |
| 28 00 | 6 45.1 | 187 41.9 | N 1 58.2 | 288 38.2 | N22 15.5 | 2 51.8 | S 0 04.9 | 44 47.4 | S16 20.7 | Acamar | 315 12.9 | S40 12.6 |
| 01 | 21 47.6 | 202 41.6 | 56.9 | 303 39.7 | 15.7 | 17 54.6 | 05.1 | 59 50.0 | 20.8 | Achernar | 335 21.1 | S57 07.2 |
| 02 | 36 50.0 | 217 41.2 | 55.7 | 318 41.2 | 15.8 | 32 57.4 | 05.2 | 74 52.6 | 20.8 | Acrux | 173 02.9 | S63 13.4 |
| 03 | 51 52.5 | 232 40.8 .. | 54.4 | 333 42.7 .. | 16.0 | 48 00.1 .. | 05.3 | 89 55.1 .. | 20.8 | Adhara | 255 07.4 | S28 59.9 |
| 04 | 66 55.0 | 247 40.4 | 53.2 | 348 44.2 | 16.1 | 63 02.9 | 05.5 | 104 57.7 | 20.9 | Aldebaran | 290 41.6 | N16 33.3 |
| 05 | 81 57.4 | 262 40.0 | 52.0 | 3 45.6 | 16.2 | 78 05.7 | 05.6 | 120 00.2 | 20.9 | | | |
| 06 | 96 59.9 | 277 39.6 | N 1 50.7 | 18 47.1 | N22 16.4 | 93 08.4 | S 0 05.7 | 135 02.8 | S16 20.9 | Alioth | 166 15.2 | N55 50.4 |
| W 07 | 112 02.3 | 292 39.2 | 49.5 | 33 48.6 | 16.5 | 108 11.2 | 05.9 | 150 05.4 | 20.9 | Alkaid | 152 54.9 | N49 12.2 |
| E 08 | 127 04.8 | 307 38.8 | 48.2 | 48 50.1 | 16.7 | 123 14.0 | 06.0 | 165 07.9 | 21.0 | Alnair | 27 34.9 | S46 51.2 |
| D 09 | 142 07.3 | 322 38.4 .. | 47.0 | 63 51.6 .. | 16.8 | 138 16.8 .. | 06.1 | 180 10.5 .. | 21.0 | Alnilam | 275 39.6 | S 1 11.1 |
| N 10 | 157 09.7 | 337 38.0 | 45.7 | 78 53.0 | 17.0 | 153 19.5 | 06.3 | 195 13.1 | 21.0 | Alphard | 217 49.8 | S 8 45.2 |
| E 11 | 172 12.2 | 352 37.6 | 44.5 | 93 54.5 | 17.1 | 168 22.3 | 06.4 | 210 15.6 | 21.1 | | | |
| S 12 | 187 14.7 | 7 37.2 | N 1 43.2 | 108 56.0 | N22 17.2 | 183 25.1 | S 0 06.5 | 225 18.2 | S16 21.1 | Alphecca | 126 05.6 | N26 38.5 |
| D 13 | 202 17.1 | 22 36.8 | 42.0 | 123 57.5 | 17.4 | 198 27.8 | 06.7 | 240 20.8 | 21.1 | Alpheratz | 357 36.4 | N29 13.0 |
| A 14 | 217 19.6 | 37 36.4 | 40.7 | 138 59.0 | 17.5 | 213 30.6 | 06.8 | 255 23.3 | 21.2 | Altair | 62 01.7 | N 8 55.8 |
| Y 15 | 232 22.1 | 52 36.1 .. | 39.5 | 154 00.5 .. | 17.7 | 228 33.4 .. | 06.9 | 270 25.9 .. | 21.2 | Ankaa | 353 08.6 | S42 10.9 |
| 16 | 247 24.5 | 67 35.7 | 38.2 | 169 02.0 | 17.8 | 243 36.2 | 07.1 | 285 28.4 | 21.2 | Antares | 112 18.3 | S26 28.9 |
| 17 | 262 27.0 | 82 35.3 | 37.0 | 184 03.5 | 17.9 | 258 38.9 | 07.2 | 300 31.0 | 21.2 | | | |
| 18 | 277 29.4 | 97 34.9 | N 1 35.7 | 199 05.0 | N22 18.1 | 273 41.7 | S 0 07.3 | 315 33.6 | S16 21.3 | Arcturus | 145 50.0 | N19 04.1 |
| 19 | 292 31.9 | 112 34.5 | 34.5 | 214 06.4 | 18.2 | 288 44.5 | 07.5 | 330 36.1 | 21.3 | Atria | 107 14.5 | S69 04.3 |
| 20 | 307 34.4 | 127 34.1 | 33.3 | 229 07.9 | 18.4 | 303 47.2 | 07.6 | 345 38.7 | 21.3 | Avior | 234 15.8 | S59 34.5 |
| 21 | 322 36.8 | 142 33.7 .. | 32.0 | 244 09.4 .. | 18.5 | 318 50.0 .. | 07.7 | 0 41.2 .. | 21.4 | Bellatrix | 278 24.8 | N 6 22.3 |
| 22 | 337 39.3 | 157 33.3 | 30.8 | 259 10.9 | 18.6 | 333 52.8 | 07.9 | 15 43.8 | 21.4 | Betelgeuse | 270 54.1 | N 7 24.8 |
| 23 | 352 41.8 | 172 32.9 | 29.5 | 274 12.4 | 18.8 | 348 55.6 | 08.0 | 30 46.4 | 21.4 | | | |
| 29 00 | 7 44.2 | 187 32.5 | N 1 28.3 | 289 13.9 | N22 18.9 | 3 58.3 | S 0 08.1 | 45 48.9 | S16 21.4 | Canopus | 263 53.2 | S52 42.1 |
| 01 | 22 46.7 | 202 32.1 | 27.0 | 304 15.4 | 19.1 | 19 01.1 | 08.3 | 60 51.5 | 21.5 | Capella | 280 24.6 | N46 01.1 |
| 02 | 37 49.2 | 217 31.7 | 25.8 | 319 16.9 | 19.2 | 34 03.9 | 08.4 | 75 54.0 | 21.5 | Deneb | 49 26.8 | N45 21.9 |
| 03 | 52 51.6 | 232 31.3 .. | 24.5 | 334 18.4 .. | 19.3 | 49 06.6 .. | 08.5 | 90 56.6 .. | 21.5 | Denebola | 182 27.2 | N14 26.9 |
| 04 | 67 54.1 | 247 31.0 | 23.3 | 349 19.9 | 19.5 | 64 09.4 | 08.7 | 105 59.2 | 21.6 | Diphda | 348 48.9 | S17 51.7 |
| 05 | 82 56.6 | 262 30.6 | 22.0 | 4 21.4 | 19.6 | 79 12.2 | 08.8 | 121 01.7 | 21.6 | | | |
| 06 | 97 59.0 | 277 30.2 | N 1 20.8 | 19 22.9 | N22 19.8 | 94 15.0 | S 0 08.9 | 136 04.3 | S16 21.6 | Dubhe | 193 44.0 | N61 37.7 |
| T 07 | 113 01.5 | 292 29.8 | 19.5 | 34 24.4 | 19.9 | 109 17.7 | 09.1 | 151 06.8 | 21.6 | Elnath | 278 04.2 | N28 37.5 |
| H 08 | 128 03.9 | 307 29.4 | 18.3 | 49 25.9 | 20.0 | 124 20.5 | 09.2 | 166 09.4 | 21.7 | Eltanin | 90 43.1 | N51 29.4 |
| U 09 | 143 06.4 | 322 29.0 .. | 17.0 | 64 27.4 .. | 20.2 | 139 23.3 .. | 09.3 | 181 12.0 .. | 21.7 | Enif | 33 40.4 | N 9 58.8 |
| R 10 | 158 08.9 | 337 28.6 | 15.8 | 79 28.9 | 20.3 | 154 26.0 | 09.5 | 196 14.5 | 21.7 | Fomalhaut | 15 16.3 | S29 30.1 |
| S 11 | 173 11.3 | 352 28.2 | 14.5 | 94 30.5 | 20.5 | 169 28.8 | 09.6 | 211 17.1 | 21.8 | | | |
| D 12 | 188 13.8 | 7 27.8 | N 1 13.3 | 109 32.0 | N22 20.6 | 184 31.6 | S 0 09.7 | 226 19.6 | S16 21.8 | Gacrux | 171 54.4 | S57 14.3 |
| A 13 | 203 16.3 | 22 27.4 | 12.0 | 124 33.5 | 20.7 | 199 34.3 | 09.9 | 241 22.2 | 21.8 | Gienah | 175 45.9 | S17 39.9 |
| Y 14 | 218 18.7 | 37 27.0 | 10.8 | 139 35.0 | 20.9 | 214 37.1 | 10.0 | 256 24.8 | 21.9 | Hadar | 148 39.3 | S60 28.9 |
| 15 | 233 21.2 | 52 26.6 .. | 09.5 | 154 36.5 .. | 21.0 | 229 39.9 .. | 10.1 | 271 27.3 .. | 21.9 | Hamal | 327 53.0 | N23 34.2 |
| 16 | 248 23.7 | 67 26.3 | 08.3 | 169 38.0 | 21.2 | 244 42.7 | 10.3 | 286 29.9 | 21.9 | Kaus Aust. | 83 35.0 | S34 22.5 |
| 17 | 263 26.1 | 82 25.9 | 07.0 | 184 39.5 | 21.3 | 259 45.4 | 10.4 | 301 32.4 | 21.9 | | | |
| 18 | 278 28.6 | 97 25.5 | N 1 05.8 | 199 41.0 | N22 21.4 | 274 48.2 | S 0 10.5 | 316 35.0 | S16 22.0 | Kochab | 137 20.7 | N74 03.9 |
| 19 | 293 31.1 | 112 25.1 | 04.5 | 214 42.5 | 21.6 | 289 51.0 | 10.6 | 331 37.6 | 22.0 | Markab | 13 31.5 | N15 19.7 |
| 20 | 308 33.5 | 127 24.7 | 03.3 | 229 44.1 | 21.7 | 304 53.7 | 10.8 | 346 40.1 | 22.0 | Menkar | 314 07.9 | N 4 10.8 |
| 21 | 323 36.0 | 142 24.3 .. | 02.0 | 244 45.6 .. | 21.8 | 319 56.5 .. | 10.9 | 1 42.7 .. | 22.0 | Menkent | 148 00.2 | S36 28.8 |
| 22 | 338 38.4 | 157 23.9 | 1 00.8 | 259 47.1 | 22.0 | 334 59.3 | 11.0 | 16 45.2 | 22.1 | Miaplacidus | 221 39.3 | S69 48.3 |
| 23 | 353 40.9 | 172 23.5 | 0 59.5 | 274 48.6 | 22.1 | 350 02.1 | 11.2 | 31 47.8 | 22.1 | | | |
| 30 00 | 8 43.4 | 187 23.1 | N 0 58.3 | 289 50.1 | N22 22.3 | 5 04.8 | S 0 11.3 | 46 50.3 | S16 22.1 | Mirfak | 308 30.6 | N49 56.4 |
| 01 | 23 45.8 | 202 22.7 | 57.0 | 304 51.7 | 22.4 | 20 07.6 | 11.4 | 61 52.9 | 22.2 | Nunki | 75 50.1 | S26 16.1 |
| 02 | 38 48.3 | 217 22.3 | 55.8 | 319 53.2 | 22.5 | 35 10.4 | 11.6 | 76 55.5 | 22.2 | Peacock | 53 08.4 | S56 39.9 |
| 03 | 53 50.8 | 232 22.0 .. | 54.5 | 334 54.7 .. | 22.7 | 50 13.1 .. | 11.7 | 91 58.0 .. | 22.2 | Pollux | 243 19.8 | N27 58.3 |
| 04 | 68 53.2 | 247 21.6 | 53.3 | 349 56.2 | 22.8 | 65 15.9 | 11.8 | 107 00.6 | 22.2 | Procyon | 244 52.9 | N 5 10.1 |
| 05 | 83 55.7 | 262 21.2 | 52.0 | 4 57.7 | 22.9 | 80 18.7 | 12.0 | 122 03.1 | 22.3 | | | |
| 06 | 98 58.2 | 277 20.8 | N 0 50.8 | 19 59.3 | N22 23.1 | 95 21.4 | S 0 12.1 | 137 05.7 | S16 22.3 | Rasalhague | 96 00.4 | N12 32.8 |
| 07 | 114 00.6 | 292 20.4 | 49.5 | 35 00.8 | 23.2 | 110 24.2 | 12.2 | 152 08.2 | 22.3 | Regulus | 207 36.7 | N11 51.5 |
| F 08 | 129 03.1 | 307 20.0 | 48.3 | 50 02.3 | 23.4 | 125 27.0 | 12.4 | 167 10.8 | 22.4 | Rigel | 281 05.6 | S 8 10.3 |
| R 09 | 144 05.5 | 322 19.6 .. | 47.0 | 65 03.8 .. | 23.5 | 140 29.8 .. | 12.5 | 182 13.3 .. | 22.4 | Rigil Kent. | 139 45.3 | S60 55.7 |
| I 10 | 159 08.0 | 337 19.2 | 45.8 | 80 05.4 | 23.6 | 155 32.5 | 12.6 | 197 15.9 | 22.4 | Sabik | 102 05.1 | S15 45.1 |
| D 11 | 174 10.5 | 352 18.8 | 44.5 | 95 06.9 | 23.8 | 170 35.3 | 12.8 | 212 18.5 | 22.4 | | | |
| A 12 | 189 12.9 | 7 18.4 | N 0 43.3 | 110 08.4 | N22 23.9 | 185 38.1 | S 0 12.9 | 227 21.0 | S16 22.5 | Schedar | 349 32.6 | N56 39.7 |
| Y 13 | 204 15.4 | 22 18.0 | 42.0 | 125 10.0 | 24.0 | 200 40.8 | 13.0 | 242 23.6 | 22.5 | Shaula | 96 13.0 | S37 07.3 |
| 14 | 219 17.9 | 37 17.6 | 40.8 | 140 11.5 | 24.2 | 215 43.6 | 13.2 | 257 26.1 | 22.5 | Sirius | 258 27.9 | S16 44.6 |
| 15 | 234 20.3 | 52 17.3 .. | 39.5 | 155 13.0 .. | 24.3 | 230 46.4 .. | 13.3 | 272 28.7 .. | 22.5 | Spica | 158 24.6 | S11 16.6 |
| 16 | 249 22.8 | 67 16.9 | 38.3 | 170 14.6 | 24.4 | 245 49.2 | 13.4 | 287 31.2 | 22.6 | Suhail | 222 48.0 | S43 31.1 |
| 17 | 264 25.3 | 82 16.5 | 37.0 | 185 16.1 | 24.6 | 260 51.9 | 13.6 | 302 33.8 | 22.6 | | | |
| 18 | 279 27.7 | 97 16.1 | N 0 35.8 | 200 17.6 | N22 24.7 | 275 54.7 | S 0 13.7 | 317 36.3 | S16 22.6 | Vega | 80 34.5 | N38 48.5 |
| 19 | 294 30.2 | 112 15.7 | 34.5 | 215 19.2 | 24.8 | 290 57.5 | 13.8 | 332 38.9 | 22.7 | Zuben'ubi | 136 58.4 | S16 08.0 |
| 20 | 309 32.7 | 127 15.3 | 33.3 | 230 20.7 | 25.0 | 306 00.2 | 13.9 | 347 41.4 | 22.7 | | SHA | Mer. Pass. |
| 21 | 324 35.1 | 142 14.9 .. | 32.0 | 245 22.3 .. | 25.1 | 321 03.0 .. | 14.1 | 2 44.0 .. | 22.7 | | ° ′ | h m |
| 22 | 339 37.6 | 157 14.5 | 30.8 | 260 23.8 | 25.3 | 336 05.8 | 14.2 | 17 46.6 | 22.7 | Venus | 179 48.3 | 11 30 |
| 23 | 354 40.0 | 172 14.1 | 29.5 | 275 25.3 | 25.4 | 351 08.5 | 14.3 | 32 49.1 | 22.8 | Mars | 281 29.7 | 4 43 |
| | h m | | | | | | | | | Jupiter | 356 14.1 | 23 40 |
| Mer. Pass. 23 25.2 | | v −0.4 | d 1.2 | v 1.5 | d 0.1 | v 2.8 | d 0.1 | v 2.6 | d 0.0 | Saturn | 38 04.7 | 20 53 |

### SUN and MOON

| UT | SUN GHA | SUN Dec | MOON GHA | v | MOON Dec | d | HP |
|---|---|---|---|---|---|---|---|
| **28** 00 | 182 17.7 | S 1 55.8 | 158 00.5 | 12.4 | S10 29.7 | 14.5 | 57.7 |
| 01 | 197 17.9 | 56.8 | 172 31.9 | 12.4 | 10 44.2 | 14.4 | 57.7 |
| 02 | 212 18.1 | 57.7 | 187 03.3 | 12.3 | 10 58.6 | 14.4 | 57.7 |
| 03 | 227 18.3 | .. 58.7 | 201 34.6 | 12.3 | 11 13.0 | 14.3 | 57.7 |
| 04 | 242 18.5 | 1 59.7 | 216 05.9 | 12.1 | 11 27.3 | 14.3 | 57.7 |
| 05 | 257 18.8 | 2 00.7 | 230 37.0 | 12.1 | 11 41.6 | 14.3 | 57.8 |
| 06 | 272 19.0 | S 2 01.6 | 245 08.1 | 12.0 | S11 55.9 | 14.2 | 57.8 |
| W 07 | 287 19.2 | 02.6 | 259 39.1 | 12.0 | 12 10.1 | 14.1 | 57.8 |
| E 08 | 302 19.4 | 03.6 | 274 10.1 | 11.9 | 12 24.2 | 14.1 | 57.8 |
| D 09 | 317 19.6 | .. 04.6 | 288 41.0 | 11.8 | 12 38.3 | 14.1 | 57.8 |
| N 10 | 332 19.8 | 05.5 | 303 11.8 | 11.7 | 12 52.4 | 14.0 | 57.9 |
| E 11 | 347 20.0 | 06.5 | 317 42.5 | 11.6 | 13 06.4 | 13.9 | 57.9 |
| S 12 | 2 20.2 | S 2 07.5 | 332 13.1 | 11.6 | S13 20.3 | 13.9 | 57.9 |
| D 13 | 17 20.4 | 08.4 | 346 43.7 | 11.5 | 13 34.2 | 13.8 | 57.9 |
| A 14 | 32 20.6 | 09.4 | 1 14.2 | 11.4 | 13 48.0 | 13.8 | 57.9 |
| Y 15 | 47 20.9 | .. 10.4 | 15 44.6 | 11.3 | 14 01.8 | 13.6 | 57.9 |
| 16 | 62 21.1 | 11.4 | 30 14.9 | 11.2 | 14 15.4 | 13.7 | 58.0 |
| 17 | 77 21.3 | 12.3 | 44 45.1 | 11.2 | 14 29.1 | 13.5 | 58.0 |
| 18 | 92 21.5 | S 2 13.3 | 59 15.3 | 11.0 | S14 42.6 | 13.5 | 58.0 |
| 19 | 107 21.7 | 14.3 | 73 45.3 | 11.0 | 14 56.1 | 13.5 | 58.0 |
| 20 | 122 21.9 | 15.3 | 88 15.3 | 10.9 | 15 09.6 | 13.3 | 58.0 |
| 21 | 137 22.1 | .. 16.2 | 102 45.2 | 10.8 | 15 22.9 | 13.3 | 58.1 |
| 22 | 152 22.3 | 17.2 | 117 15.0 | 10.7 | 15 36.2 | 13.2 | 58.1 |
| 23 | 167 22.5 | 18.2 | 131 44.7 | 10.7 | 15 49.4 | 13.1 | 58.1 |
| **29** 00 | 182 22.7 | S 2 19.1 | 146 14.4 | 10.5 | S16 02.5 | 13.1 | 58.1 |
| 01 | 197 22.9 | 20.1 | 160 43.9 | 10.5 | 16 15.6 | 13.0 | 58.1 |
| 02 | 212 23.1 | 21.1 | 175 13.4 | 10.3 | 16 28.6 | 12.9 | 58.1 |
| 03 | 227 23.4 | .. 22.1 | 189 42.7 | 10.3 | 16 41.5 | 12.8 | 58.2 |
| 04 | 242 23.6 | 23.0 | 204 12.0 | 10.2 | 16 54.3 | 12.7 | 58.2 |
| 05 | 257 23.8 | 24.0 | 218 41.2 | 10.1 | 17 07.0 | 12.7 | 58.2 |
| 06 | 272 24.0 | S 2 25.0 | 233 10.3 | 10.0 | S17 19.7 | 12.6 | 58.2 |
| T 07 | 287 24.2 | 26.0 | 247 39.3 | 9.9 | 17 32.3 | 12.4 | 58.2 |
| H 08 | 302 24.4 | 26.9 | 262 08.2 | 9.8 | 17 44.7 | 12.4 | 58.3 |
| U 09 | 317 24.6 | .. 27.9 | 276 37.0 | 9.7 | 17 57.1 | 12.3 | 58.3 |
| R 10 | 332 24.8 | 28.9 | 291 05.7 | 9.6 | 18 09.4 | 12.2 | 58.3 |
| S 11 | 347 25.0 | 29.8 | 305 34.3 | 9.5 | 18 21.6 | 12.2 | 58.3 |
| D 12 | 2 25.2 | S 2 30.8 | 320 02.8 | 9.5 | S18 33.8 | 12.0 | 58.3 |
| A 13 | 17 25.4 | 31.8 | 334 31.3 | 9.3 | 18 45.8 | 11.9 | 58.3 |
| Y 14 | 32 25.6 | 32.8 | 348 59.6 | 9.2 | 18 57.7 | 11.8 | 58.3 |
| 15 | 47 25.8 | .. 33.7 | 3 27.8 | 9.2 | 19 09.5 | 11.7 | 58.4 |
| 16 | 62 26.0 | 34.7 | 17 56.0 | 9.0 | 19 21.2 | 11.7 | 58.4 |
| 17 | 77 26.2 | 35.7 | 32 24.0 | 8.9 | 19 32.9 | 11.5 | 58.4 |
| 18 | 92 26.5 | S 2 36.6 | 46 51.9 | 8.9 | S19 44.4 | 11.4 | 58.4 |
| 19 | 107 26.7 | 37.6 | 61 19.8 | 8.7 | 19 55.8 | 11.3 | 58.4 |
| 20 | 122 26.9 | 38.6 | 75 47.5 | 8.7 | 20 07.1 | 11.2 | 58.4 |
| 21 | 137 27.1 | .. 39.6 | 90 15.2 | 8.5 | 20 18.3 | 11.1 | 58.4 |
| 22 | 152 27.3 | 40.5 | 104 42.7 | 8.5 | 20 29.4 | 10.9 | 58.5 |
| 23 | 167 27.5 | 41.5 | 119 10.2 | 8.3 | 20 40.3 | 10.9 | 58.5 |
| **30** 00 | 182 27.7 | S 2 42.5 | 133 37.5 | 8.3 | S20 51.2 | 10.8 | 58.5 |
| 01 | 197 27.9 | 43.4 | 148 04.8 | 8.1 | 21 02.0 | 10.6 | 58.5 |
| 02 | 212 28.1 | 44.4 | 162 31.9 | 8.1 | 21 12.6 | 10.5 | 58.5 |
| 03 | 227 28.3 | .. 45.4 | 176 59.0 | 7.9 | 21 23.1 | 10.4 | 58.5 |
| 04 | 242 28.5 | 46.4 | 191 25.9 | 7.9 | 21 33.5 | 10.3 | 58.5 |
| 05 | 257 28.7 | 47.3 | 205 52.8 | 7.7 | 21 43.8 | 10.1 | 58.6 |
| 06 | 272 28.9 | S 2 48.3 | 220 19.5 | 7.7 | S21 53.9 | 10.0 | 58.6 |
| F 07 | 287 29.1 | 49.3 | 234 46.2 | 7.5 | 22 03.9 | 9.9 | 58.6 |
| R 08 | 302 29.3 | 50.2 | 249 12.7 | 7.5 | 22 13.8 | 9.8 | 58.6 |
| I 09 | 317 29.5 | .. 51.2 | 263 39.2 | 7.4 | 22 23.6 | 9.6 | 58.6 |
| D 10 | 332 29.7 | 52.2 | 278 05.6 | 7.2 | 22 33.2 | 9.5 | 58.6 |
| A 11 | 347 29.9 | 53.2 | 292 31.8 | 7.2 | 22 42.7 | 9.4 | 58.6 |
| Y 12 | 2 30.1 | S 2 54.1 | 306 58.0 | 7.1 | S22 52.1 | 9.3 | 58.7 |
| 13 | 17 30.4 | 55.1 | 321 24.1 | 6.9 | 23 01.4 | 9.1 | 58.7 |
| 14 | 32 30.6 | 56.1 | 335 50.0 | 6.9 | 23 10.5 | 8.9 | 58.7 |
| 15 | 47 30.8 | .. 57.0 | 350 15.9 | 6.8 | 23 19.4 | 8.8 | 58.7 |
| 16 | 62 31.0 | 58.0 | 4 41.7 | 6.7 | 23 28.3 | 8.7 | 58.7 |
| 17 | 77 31.2 | 59.0 | 19 07.4 | 6.6 | 23 37.0 | 8.5 | 58.7 |
| 18 | 92 31.4 | S 2 59.9 | 33 33.0 | 6.5 | S23 45.5 | 8.4 | 58.7 |
| 19 | 107 31.6 | 3 00.9 | 47 58.5 | 6.4 | 23 53.9 | 8.3 | 58.7 |
| 20 | 122 31.8 | 01.9 | 62 23.9 | 6.3 | 24 02.2 | 8.1 | 58.8 |
| 21 | 137 32.0 | .. 02.9 | 76 49.2 | 6.2 | 24 10.3 | 8.0 | 58.8 |
| 22 | 152 32.2 | 03.8 | 91 14.4 | 6.2 | 24 18.3 | 7.8 | 58.8 |
| 23 | 167 32.4 | 04.8 | 105 39.6 | 6.0 | S24 26.1 | 7.7 | 58.8 |
| | SD 16.0 | d 1.0 | SD 15.8 | | 15.9 | | 16.0 |

### Moonrise

| Lat. | Naut. | Civil | Sunrise | Moonrise 28 | 29 | 30 | 1 |
|---|---|---|---|---|---|---|---|
| N 72 | 03 38 | 05 02 | 06 09 | 10 54 | ▬▬ | ▬▬ | ▬▬ |
| N 70 | 03 52 | 05 06 | 06 07 | 10 27 | 13 27 | ▬▬ | ▬▬ |
| 68 | 04 03 | 05 10 | 06 05 | 10 07 | 12 31 | ▬▬ | ▬▬ |
| 66 | 04 12 | 05 13 | 06 04 | 09 52 | 11 58 | 14 45 | ▬▬ |
| 64 | 04 19 | 05 15 | 06 03 | 09 39 | 11 34 | 13 44 | ▬▬ |
| 62 | 04 25 | 05 17 | 06 01 | 09 28 | 11 15 | 13 10 | 15 10 |
| 60 | 04 30 | 05 19 | 06 00 | 09 19 | 10 59 | 12 45 | 14 29 |
| N 58 | 04 34 | 05 20 | 06 00 | 09 11 | 10 47 | 12 25 | 14 01 |
| 56 | 04 38 | 05 22 | 05 59 | 09 04 | 10 35 | 12 09 | 13 40 |
| 54 | 04 41 | 05 24 | 05 58 | 08 58 | 10 26 | 11 55 | 13 22 |
| 52 | 04 44 | 05 24 | 05 57 | 08 53 | 10 17 | 11 43 | 13 07 |
| 50 | 04 47 | 05 25 | 05 57 | 08 48 | 10 09 | 11 32 | 12 53 |
| 45 | 04 52 | 05 26 | 05 55 | 08 37 | 09 53 | 11 10 | 12 27 |
| N 40 | 04 56 | 05 27 | 05 54 | 08 28 | 09 39 | 10 53 | 12 05 |
| 35 | 04 58 | 05 28 | 05 53 | 08 20 | 09 28 | 10 38 | 11 48 |
| 30 | 05 01 | 05 28 | 05 52 | 08 14 | 09 18 | 10 25 | 11 33 |
| 20 | 05 03 | 05 28 | 05 50 | 08 02 | 09 01 | 10 03 | 11 07 |
| N 10 | 05 03 | 05 28 | 05 49 | 07 53 | 08 47 | 09 44 | 10 45 |
| 0 | 05 02 | 05 26 | 05 47 | 07 43 | 08 33 | 09 27 | 10 25 |
| S 10 | 05 00 | 05 24 | 05 45 | 07 34 | 08 20 | 09 10 | 10 05 |
| 20 | 04 56 | 05 21 | 05 43 | 07 25 | 08 05 | 08 51 | 09 43 |
| 30 | 04 49 | 05 17 | 05 41 | 07 14 | 07 49 | 08 30 | 09 18 |
| 35 | 04 45 | 05 14 | 05 40 | 07 07 | 07 40 | 08 18 | 09 03 |
| 40 | 04 39 | 05 11 | 05 38 | 07 00 | 07 29 | 08 04 | 08 47 |
| 45 | 04 32 | 05 07 | 05 36 | 06 52 | 07 17 | 07 47 | 08 27 |
| S 50 | 04 23 | 05 01 | 05 34 | 06 42 | 07 02 | 07 27 | 08 01 |
| 52 | 04 18 | 04 59 | 05 33 | 06 38 | 06 55 | 07 17 | 07 49 |
| 54 | 04 13 | 04 56 | 05 31 | 06 33 | 06 47 | 07 07 | 07 35 |
| 56 | 04 08 | 04 53 | 05 30 | 06 28 | 06 39 | 06 54 | 07 19 |
| 58 | 04 01 | 04 49 | 05 29 | 06 22 | 06 29 | 06 40 | 07 00 |
| S 60 | 03 54 | 04 45 | 05 27 | 06 15 | 06 18 | 06 24 | 06 37 |

### Moonset

| Lat. | Sunset | Civil | Naut. | Moonset 28 | 29 | 30 | 1 |
|---|---|---|---|---|---|---|---|
| N 72 | 17 29 | 18 36 | 19 59 | 16 29 | ▬▬ | ▬▬ | ▬▬ |
| N 70 | 17 31 | 18 32 | 19 45 | 16 58 | 15 44 | ▬▬ | ▬▬ |
| 68 | 17 33 | 18 28 | 19 35 | 17 20 | 16 42 | ▬▬ | ▬▬ |
| 66 | 17 35 | 18 26 | 19 27 | 17 37 | 17 16 | 16 22 | ▬▬ |
| 64 | 17 36 | 18 24 | 19 20 | 17 51 | 17 41 | 17 25 | ▬▬ |
| 62 | 17 37 | 18 22 | 19 14 | 18 03 | 18 01 | 18 00 | 18 02 |
| 60 | 17 39 | 18 20 | 19 09 | 18 14 | 18 17 | 18 25 | 18 43 |
| N 58 | 17 40 | 18 19 | 19 05 | 18 23 | 18 31 | 18 46 | 19 12 |
| 56 | 17 41 | 18 18 | 19 01 | 18 31 | 18 43 | 19 02 | 19 34 |
| 54 | 17 42 | 18 17 | 18 58 | 18 38 | 18 54 | 19 17 | 19 52 |
| 52 | 17 42 | 18 16 | 18 55 | 18 44 | 19 03 | 19 29 | 20 07 |
| 50 | 17 43 | 18 15 | 18 53 | 18 50 | 19 11 | 19 40 | 20 21 |
| 45 | 17 45 | 18 14 | 18 48 | 19 02 | 19 29 | 20 04 | 20 48 |
| N 40 | 17 46 | 18 13 | 18 44 | 19 13 | 19 44 | 20 22 | 21 10 |
| 35 | 17 47 | 18 12 | 18 42 | 19 22 | 19 57 | 20 38 | 21 28 |
| 30 | 17 48 | 18 12 | 18 40 | 19 30 | 20 07 | 20 52 | 21 43 |
| 20 | 17 50 | 18 12 | 18 38 | 19 43 | 20 26 | 21 15 | 22 10 |
| N 10 | 17 52 | 18 13 | 18 37 | 19 55 | 20 43 | 21 35 | 22 33 |
| 0 | 17 54 | 18 14 | 18 38 | 20 07 | 20 58 | 21 54 | 22 54 |
| S 10 | 17 55 | 18 16 | 18 41 | 20 18 | 21 14 | 22 13 | 23 15 |
| 20 | 17 58 | 18 20 | 18 45 | 20 30 | 21 31 | 22 34 | 23 38 |
| 30 | 18 00 | 18 24 | 18 52 | 20 44 | 21 50 | 22 57 | 24 04 |
| 35 | 18 02 | 18 27 | 18 57 | 20 52 | 22 01 | 23 11 | 24 20 |
| 40 | 18 03 | 18 31 | 19 03 | 21 02 | 22 14 | 23 27 | 24 38 |
| 45 | 18 05 | 18 35 | 19 10 | 21 13 | 22 29 | 23 47 | 25 00 |
| S 50 | 18 08 | 18 40 | 19 19 | 21 26 | 22 49 | 24 11 | 00 11 |
| 52 | 18 09 | 18 43 | 19 24 | 21 32 | 22 58 | 24 23 | 00 23 |
| 54 | 18 10 | 18 46 | 19 29 | 21 39 | 23 08 | 24 36 | 00 36 |
| 56 | 18 12 | 18 49 | 19 35 | 21 47 | 23 19 | 24 52 | 00 52 |
| 58 | 18 13 | 18 53 | 19 41 | 21 56 | 23 33 | 25 10 | 01 10 |
| S 60 | 18 15 | 18 57 | 19 49 | 22 06 | 23 48 | 25 33 | 01 33 |

### SUN and MOON

| Day | Eqn. of Time 00h | 12h | Mer. Pass. | Mer. Pass. Upper | Lower | Age | Phase |
|---|---|---|---|---|---|---|---|
| d | m s | m s | h m | h m | h m | d | % |
| 28 | 09 10 | 09 20 | 11 51 | 13 55 | 01 31 | 03 | 8 |
| 29 | 09 30 | 09 40 | 11 50 | 14 46 | 02 20 | 04 | 14 |
| 30 | 09 50 | 10 00 | 11 50 | 15 40 | 03 13 | 05 | 23 |

| UT | ARIES GHA | VENUS −3.9 GHA | Dec | MARS −0.6 GHA | Dec | JUPITER −2.9 GHA | Dec | SATURN +0.4 GHA | Dec |
|---|---|---|---|---|---|---|---|---|---|
| **1** 00 | 9 42.5 | 187 13.7 | N 0 28.3 | 290 26.9 | N22 25.5 | 6 11.3 | S 0 14.5 | 47 51.7 | S16 22.8 |
| 01 | 24 45.0 | 202 13.3 | 27.0 | 305 28.4 | 25.7 | 21 14.1 | 14.6 | 62 54.2 | 22.8 |
| 02 | 39 47.4 | 217 13.0 | 25.7 | 320 30.0 | 25.8 | 36 16.8 | 14.7 | 77 56.8 | 22.8 |
| 03 | 54 49.9 | 232 12.6 .. | 24.5 | 335 31.5 .. | 25.9 | 51 19.6 .. | 14.9 | 92 59.3 .. | 22.9 |
| 04 | 69 52.4 | 247 12.2 | 23.2 | 350 33.1 | 26.1 | 66 22.4 | 15.0 | 108 01.9 | 22.9 |
| 05 | 84 54.8 | 262 11.8 | 22.0 | 5 34.6 | 26.2 | 81 25.2 | 15.1 | 123 04.4 | 22.9 |
| 06 | 99 57.3 | 277 11.4 | N 0 20.7 | 20 36.1 | N22 26.3 | 96 27.9 | S 0 15.3 | 138 07.0 | S16 22.9 |
| S 07 | 114 59.8 | 292 11.0 | 19.5 | 35 37.7 | 26.5 | 111 30.7 | 15.4 | 153 09.5 | 23.0 |
| A 08 | 130 02.2 | 307 10.6 | 18.2 | 50 39.2 | 26.6 | 126 33.5 | 15.5 | 168 12.1 | 23.0 |
| T 09 | 145 04.7 | 322 10.2 .. | 17.0 | 65 40.8 .. | 26.7 | 141 36.2 .. | 15.7 | 183 14.6 .. | 23.0 |
| U 10 | 160 07.2 | 337 09.8 | 15.7 | 80 42.3 | 26.9 | 156 39.0 | 15.8 | 198 17.2 | 23.1 |
| R 11 | 175 09.6 | 352 09.4 | 14.5 | 95 43.9 | 27.0 | 171 41.8 | 15.9 | 213 19.7 | 23.1 |
| D 12 | 190 12.1 | 7 09.0 | N 0 13.2 | 110 45.5 | N22 27.1 | 186 44.5 | S 0 16.0 | 228 22.3 | S16 23.1 |
| A 13 | 205 14.5 | 22 08.7 | 12.0 | 125 47.0 | 27.3 | 201 47.3 | 16.2 | 243 24.8 | 23.1 |
| Y 14 | 220 17.0 | 37 08.3 | 10.7 | 140 48.6 | 27.4 | 216 50.1 | 16.3 | 258 27.4 | 23.2 |
| 15 | 235 19.5 | 52 07.9 .. | 09.5 | 155 50.1 .. | 27.5 | 231 52.8 .. | 16.4 | 273 29.9 .. | 23.2 |
| 16 | 250 21.9 | 67 07.5 | 08.2 | 170 51.7 | 27.7 | 246 55.6 | 16.6 | 288 32.5 | 23.2 |
| 17 | 265 24.4 | 82 07.1 | 07.0 | 185 53.2 | 27.8 | 261 58.4 | 16.7 | 303 35.0 | 23.2 |
| 18 | 280 26.9 | 97 06.7 | N 0 05.7 | 200 54.8 | N22 27.9 | 277 01.2 | S 0 16.8 | 318 37.6 | S16 23.3 |
| 19 | 295 29.3 | 112 06.3 | 04.4 | 215 56.4 | 28.1 | 292 03.9 | 17.0 | 333 40.2 | 23.3 |
| 20 | 310 31.8 | 127 05.9 | 03.2 | 230 57.9 | 28.2 | 307 06.7 | 17.1 | 348 42.7 | 23.3 |
| 21 | 325 34.3 | 142 05.5 .. | 01.9 | 245 59.5 .. | 28.3 | 322 09.5 .. | 17.2 | 3 45.3 .. | 23.3 |
| 22 | 340 36.7 | 157 05.1 | N 00.7 | 261 01.0 | 28.5 | 337 12.2 | 17.4 | 18 47.8 | 23.4 |
| 23 | 355 39.2 | 172 04.7 | S 00.6 | 276 02.6 | 28.6 | 352 15.0 | 17.5 | 33 50.4 | 23.4 |
| **2** 00 | 10 41.7 | 187 04.4 | S 0 01.8 | 291 04.2 | N22 28.7 | 7 17.8 | S 0 17.6 | 48 52.9 | S16 23.4 |
| 01 | 25 44.1 | 202 04.0 | 03.1 | 306 05.7 | 28.9 | 22 20.5 | 17.7 | 63 55.5 | 23.4 |
| 02 | 40 46.6 | 217 03.6 | 04.3 | 321 07.3 | 29.0 | 37 23.3 | 17.9 | 78 58.0 | 23.5 |
| 03 | 55 49.0 | 232 03.2 .. | 05.6 | 336 08.9 .. | 29.1 | 52 26.1 .. | 18.0 | 94 00.5 .. | 23.5 |
| 04 | 70 51.5 | 247 02.8 | 06.8 | 351 10.4 | 29.3 | 67 28.8 | 18.1 | 109 03.1 | 23.5 |
| 05 | 85 54.0 | 262 02.4 | 08.1 | 6 12.0 | 29.4 | 82 31.6 | 18.3 | 124 05.6 | 23.5 |
| 06 | 100 56.4 | 277 02.0 | S 0 09.3 | 21 13.6 | N22 29.5 | 97 34.4 | S 0 18.4 | 139 08.2 | S16 23.6 |
| S 07 | 115 58.9 | 292 01.6 | 10.6 | 36 15.2 | 29.7 | 112 37.1 | 18.5 | 154 10.7 | 23.6 |
| U 08 | 131 01.4 | 307 01.2 | 11.9 | 51 16.7 | 29.8 | 127 39.9 | 18.7 | 169 13.3 | 23.6 |
| N 09 | 146 03.8 | 322 00.8 .. | 13.1 | 66 18.3 .. | 29.9 | 142 42.7 .. | 18.8 | 184 15.8 .. | 23.6 |
| D 10 | 161 06.3 | 337 00.4 | 14.4 | 81 19.9 | 30.0 | 157 45.5 | 18.9 | 199 18.4 | 23.7 |
| A 11 | 176 08.8 | 352 00.1 | 15.6 | 96 21.4 | 30.2 | 172 48.2 | 19.0 | 214 20.9 | 23.7 |
| Y 12 | 191 11.2 | 6 59.7 | S 0 16.9 | 111 23.0 | N22 30.3 | 187 51.0 | S 0 19.2 | 229 23.5 | S16 23.7 |
| 13 | 206 13.7 | 21 59.3 | 18.1 | 126 24.6 | 30.4 | 202 53.8 | 19.3 | 244 26.0 | 23.7 |
| 14 | 221 16.2 | 36 58.9 | 19.4 | 141 26.2 | 30.6 | 217 56.5 | 19.4 | 259 28.6 | 23.8 |
| 15 | 236 18.6 | 51 58.5 .. | 20.6 | 156 27.8 .. | 30.7 | 232 59.3 .. | 19.6 | 274 31.1 .. | 23.8 |
| 16 | 251 21.1 | 66 58.1 | 21.9 | 171 29.3 | 30.8 | 248 02.1 | 19.7 | 289 33.7 | 23.8 |
| 17 | 266 23.5 | 81 57.7 | 23.1 | 186 30.9 | 31.0 | 263 04.8 | 19.8 | 304 36.2 | 23.8 |
| 18 | 281 26.0 | 96 57.3 | S 0 24.4 | 201 32.5 | N22 31.1 | 278 07.6 | S 0 20.0 | 319 38.8 | S16 23.9 |
| 19 | 296 28.5 | 111 56.9 | 25.6 | 216 34.1 | 31.2 | 293 10.4 | 20.1 | 334 41.3 | 23.9 |
| 20 | 311 30.9 | 126 56.5 | 26.9 | 231 35.7 | 31.4 | 308 13.1 | 20.2 | 349 43.9 | 23.9 |
| 21 | 326 33.4 | 141 56.1 .. | 28.2 | 246 37.3 .. | 31.5 | 323 15.9 .. | 20.3 | 4 46.4 .. | 23.9 |
| 22 | 341 35.9 | 156 55.8 | 29.4 | 261 38.8 | 31.6 | 338 18.7 | 20.5 | 19 49.0 | 24.0 |
| 23 | 356 38.3 | 171 55.4 | 30.7 | 276 40.4 | 31.7 | 353 21.4 | 20.6 | 34 51.5 | 24.0 |
| **3** 00 | 11 40.8 | 186 55.0 | S 0 31.9 | 291 42.0 | N22 31.9 | 8 24.2 | S 0 20.7 | 49 54.0 | S16 24.0 |
| 01 | 26 43.3 | 201 54.6 | 33.2 | 306 43.6 | 32.0 | 23 27.0 | 20.9 | 64 56.6 | 24.0 |
| 02 | 41 45.7 | 216 54.2 | 34.4 | 321 45.2 | 32.1 | 38 29.7 | 21.0 | 79 59.1 | 24.1 |
| 03 | 56 48.2 | 231 53.8 .. | 35.7 | 336 46.8 .. | 32.3 | 53 32.5 .. | 21.1 | 95 01.7 .. | 24.1 |
| 04 | 71 50.6 | 246 53.4 | 36.9 | 351 48.4 | 32.4 | 68 35.3 | 21.3 | 110 04.2 | 24.1 |
| 05 | 86 53.1 | 261 53.0 | 38.2 | 6 50.0 | 32.5 | 83 38.0 | 21.4 | 125 06.8 | 24.1 |
| 06 | 101 55.6 | 276 52.6 | S 0 39.4 | 21 51.6 | N22 32.7 | 98 40.8 | S 0 21.5 | 140 09.3 | S16 24.2 |
| M 07 | 116 58.0 | 291 52.2 | 40.7 | 36 53.2 | 32.8 | 113 43.6 | 21.6 | 155 11.9 | 24.2 |
| O 08 | 132 00.5 | 306 51.8 | 42.0 | 51 54.8 | 32.9 | 128 46.3 | 21.8 | 170 14.4 | 24.2 |
| N 09 | 147 03.0 | 321 51.4 .. | 43.2 | 66 56.4 .. | 33.0 | 143 49.1 .. | 21.9 | 185 17.0 .. | 24.2 |
| D 10 | 162 05.4 | 336 51.1 | 44.5 | 81 58.0 | 33.2 | 158 51.9 | 22.0 | 200 19.5 | 24.3 |
| A 11 | 177 07.9 | 351 50.7 | 45.7 | 96 59.6 | 33.3 | 173 54.6 | 22.2 | 215 22.0 | 24.3 |
| Y 12 | 192 10.4 | 6 50.3 | S 0 47.0 | 112 01.2 | N22 33.4 | 188 57.4 | S 0 22.3 | 230 24.6 | S16 24.3 |
| 13 | 207 12.8 | 21 49.9 | 48.2 | 127 02.8 | 33.6 | 204 00.2 | 22.4 | 245 27.1 | 24.3 |
| 14 | 222 15.3 | 36 49.5 | 49.5 | 142 04.4 | 33.7 | 219 02.9 | 22.5 | 260 29.7 | 24.3 |
| 15 | 237 17.8 | 51 49.1 .. | 50.7 | 157 06.0 .. | 33.8 | 234 05.7 .. | 22.7 | 275 32.2 .. | 24.4 |
| 16 | 252 20.2 | 66 48.7 | 52.0 | 172 07.6 | 33.9 | 249 08.5 | 22.8 | 290 34.8 | 24.4 |
| 17 | 267 22.7 | 81 48.3 | 53.3 | 187 09.2 | 34.1 | 264 11.2 | 22.9 | 305 37.3 | 24.4 |
| 18 | 282 25.1 | 96 47.9 | S 0 54.5 | 202 10.8 | N22 34.2 | 279 14.0 | S 0 23.1 | 320 39.9 | S16 24.4 |
| 19 | 297 27.6 | 111 47.5 | 55.8 | 217 12.4 | 34.3 | 294 16.8 | 23.2 | 335 42.4 | 24.5 |
| 20 | 312 30.1 | 126 47.1 | 57.0 | 232 14.0 | 34.5 | 309 19.5 | 23.3 | 350 44.9 | 24.5 |
| 21 | 327 32.5 | 141 46.7 .. | 58.3 | 247 15.6 .. | 34.6 | 324 22.3 .. | 23.4 | 5 47.5 .. | 24.5 |
| 22 | 342 35.0 | 156 46.4 | 0 59.5 | 262 17.2 | 34.7 | 339 25.1 | 23.6 | 20 50.0 | 24.5 |
| 23 | 357 37.5 | 171 46.0 | S 1 00.8 | 277 18.8 | 34.8 | 354 27.8 | 23.7 | 35 52.6 | 24.6 |
| Mer.Pass. | 23 13.4 | v −0.4 | d 1.3 | v 1.6 | d 0.1 | v 2.8 | d 0.1 | v 2.5 | d 0.0 |

### STARS

| Name | SHA | Dec |
|---|---|---|
| Acamar | 315 12.9 | S40 12.6 |
| Achernar | 335 21.0 | S57 07.2 |
| Acrux | 173 02.9 | S63 13.4 |
| Adhara | 255 07.4 | S28 59.9 |
| Aldebaran | 290 41.6 | N16 33.3 |
| Alioth | 166 15.2 | N55 50.3 |
| Alkaid | 152 54.0 | N49 12.2 |
| Alnair | 27 34.9 | S46 51.2 |
| Alnilam | 275 39.6 | S 1 11.1 |
| Alphard | 217 49.8 | S 8 45.2 |
| Alphecca | 126 05.6 | N26 38.5 |
| Alpheratz | 357 36.4 | N29 13.0 |
| Altair | 62 01.7 | N 8 55.8 |
| Ankaa | 353 08.6 | S42 10.9 |
| Antares | 112 18.3 | S26 28.9 |
| Arcturus | 145 50.0 | N19 04.1 |
| Atria | 107 14.5 | S69 04.3 |
| Avior | 234 15.8 | S59 34.5 |
| Bellatrix | 278 24.8 | N 6 22.3 |
| Betelgeuse | 270 54.1 | N 7 24.8 |
| Canopus | 263 53.2 | S52 42.1 |
| Capella | 280 24.5 | N46 01.1 |
| Deneb | 49 26.9 | N45 21.9 |
| Denebola | 182 27.2 | N14 26.9 |
| Diphda | 348 48.9 | S17 51.7 |
| Dubhe | 193 43.9 | N61 37.7 |
| Elnath | 278 04.1 | N28 37.5 |
| Eltanin | 90 43.2 | N51 29.4 |
| Enif | 33 40.4 | N 9 58.9 |
| Fomalhaut | 15 16.3 | S29 30.1 |
| Gacrux | 171 54.3 | S57 14.3 |
| Gienah | 175 45.9 | S17 39.9 |
| Hadar | 148 39.3 | S60 28.9 |
| Hamal | 327 53.0 | N23 34.2 |
| Kaus Aust. | 83 35.1 | S34 22.5 |
| Kochab | 137 20.7 | N74 03.9 |
| Markab | 13 31.5 | N15 19.7 |
| Menkar | 314 07.9 | N 4 10.8 |
| Menkent | 148 00.2 | S36 28.8 |
| Miaplacidus | 221 39.2 | S69 48.2 |
| Mirfak | 308 30.6 | N49 56.4 |
| Nunki | 75 50.1 | S26 16.1 |
| Peacock | 53 08.4 | S56 39.9 |
| Pollux | 243 19.7 | N27 58.3 |
| Procyon | 244 52.9 | N 5 10.1 |
| Rasalhague | 96 00.4 | N12 32.8 |
| Regulus | 207 36.7 | N11 51.5 |
| Rigel | 281 05.6 | S 8 10.3 |
| Rigil Kent. | 139 43.5 | S60 55.7 |
| Sabik | 102 05.1 | S15 45.1 |
| Schedar | 349 32.6 | N56 39.7 |
| Shaula | 96 13.1 | S37 07.3 |
| Sirius | 258 27.9 | S16 44.6 |
| Spica | 158 24.6 | S11 16.6 |
| Suhail | 222 48.0 | S43 31.1 |
| Vega | 80 34.5 | N38 48.5 |
| Zuben'ubi | 136 58.4 | S16 08.0 |

| | SHA | Mer.Pass. |
|---|---|---|
| Venus | 176 22.7 | 11 32 |
| Mars | 280 22.5 | 4 35 |
| Jupiter | 356 36.1 | 23 26 |
| Saturn | 38 11.2 | 20 41 |

| UT | SUN | | MOON | | | | | Lat. | Twilight | | Sunrise | Moonrise | | | |
|----|-----|--|------|--|--|--|--|------|----------|--|---------|----------|--|--|--|
| | | | | | | | | | Naut. | Civil | | 1 | 2 | 3 | 4 |
| | GHA | Dec | GHA | v | Dec | d | HP | | | | | | | | |
| d h | ° ′ | ° ′ | ° ′ | ′ | ° ′ | ′ | ′ | ° | h m | h m | h m | h m | h m | h m | h m |
| 1 00 | 182 32.6 | S 3 05.8 | 120 04.6 | 6.0 | S24 33.8 | 7.5 | 58.8 | N 72 | 03 54 | 05 16 | 06 23 | ■■■ | ■■■ | ■■■ | ■■■ |
| 01 | 197 32.8 | 06.7 | 134 29.6 | 5.8 | 24 41.3 | 7.3 | 58.8 | N 70 | 04 05 | 05 18 | 06 19 | ■■■ | ■■■ | ■■■ | ■■■ |
| 02 | 212 33.0 | 07.7 | 148 54.4 | 5.8 | 24 48.6 | 7.3 | 58.8 | 68 | 04 15 | 05 21 | 06 16 | ■■■ | ■■■ | ■■■ | ■■■ |
| 03 | 227 33.2 | .. 08.7 | 163 19.2 | 5.7 | 24 55.9 | 7.0 | 58.8 | 66 | 04 22 | 05 22 | 06 14 | ■■■ | ■■■ | ■■■ | 18 09 |
| 04 | 242 33.4 | 09.6 | 177 43.9 | 5.6 | 25 02.9 | 6.9 | 58.9 | 64 | 04 28 | 05 24 | 06 11 | 15 10 | 16 55 | 17 28 | 17 31 |
| 05 | 257 33.6 | 10.6 | 192 08.5 | 5.6 | 25 09.8 | 6.7 | 58.9 | 62 | 04 33 | 05 25 | 06 09 | 14 29 | 15 55 | 16 43 | 17 04 |
| 06 | 272 33.8 | S 3 11.6 | 206 33.1 | 5.4 | S25 16.5 | 6.6 | 58.9 | 60 | 04 37 | 05 26 | 06 08 | 14 01 | 15 21 | 16 14 | 16 43 |
| 07 | 287 34.0 | 12.6 | 220 57.5 | 5.4 | 25 23.1 | 6.4 | 58.9 | N 58 | 04 41 | 05 27 | 06 06 | 13 40 | 14 57 | 15 51 | 16 25 |
| 08 | 302 34.2 | 13.5 | 235 21.9 | 5.3 | 25 29.5 | 6.3 | 58.9 | 56 | 04 44 | 05 28 | 06 05 | 13 22 | 14 37 | 15 33 | 16 11 |
| S 09 | 317 34.4 | .. 14.5 | 249 46.2 | 5.2 | 25 35.8 | 6.1 | 58.9 | 54 | 04 47 | 05 28 | 06 04 | 13 07 | 14 20 | 15 17 | 15 58 |
| A 10 | 332 34.6 | 15.5 | 264 10.4 | 5.1 | 25 41.9 | 5.9 | 58.9 | 52 | 04 49 | 05 29 | 06 02 | 12 53 | 14 06 | 15 04 | 15 46 |
| T 11 | 347 34.8 | 16.4 | 278 34.5 | 5.1 | 25 47.8 | 5.8 | 58.9 | 50 | 04 52 | 05 29 | 06 01 | 12 27 | 13 37 | 14 36 | 15 22 |
| U 12 | 2 35.0 | S 3 17.4 | 292 58.6 | 5.0 | S25 53.6 | 5.6 | 58.9 | 45 | 04 56 | 05 30 | 05 59 | 12 05 | 13 14 | 14 14 | 15 03 |
| R 13 | 17 35.2 | 18.4 | 307 22.6 | 4.9 | 25 59.2 | 5.4 | 59.0 | N 40 | 04 59 | 05 30 | 05 57 | 11 48 | 12 55 | 13 55 | 14 47 |
| D 14 | 32 35.4 | 19.3 | 321 46.5 | 4.8 | 26 04.6 | 5.3 | 59.0 | 35 | 05 01 | 05 30 | 05 55 | 11 33 | 12 39 | 13 40 | 14 33 |
| A 15 | 47 35.6 | .. 20.3 | 336 10.3 | 4.8 | 26 09.9 | 5.1 | 59.0 | 30 | 05 02 | 05 30 | 05 54 | 11 07 | 12 11 | 13 13 | 14 09 |
| Y 16 | 62 35.8 | 21.3 | 350 34.1 | 4.7 | 26 15.0 | 4.9 | 59.0 | 20 | 05 04 | 05 29 | 05 51 | 10 45 | 11 48 | 12 50 | 13 49 |
| 17 | 77 36.0 | 22.2 | 4 57.8 | 4.6 | 26 19.9 | 4.7 | 59.0 | N 10 | 05 03 | 05 28 | 05 49 | 10 25 | 11 26 | 12 28 | 13 29 |
| 18 | 92 36.2 | S 3 23.2 | 19 21.4 | 4.6 | S26 24.6 | 4.6 | 59.0 | 0 | 05 01 | 05 25 | 05 46 | 10 05 | 11 04 | 12 07 | 13 10 |
| 19 | 107 36.4 | 24.2 | 33 45.0 | 4.5 | 26 29.2 | 4.4 | 59.0 | S 10 | 04 58 | 05 22 | 05 44 | 09 43 | 10 41 | 11 44 | 12 49 |
| 20 | 122 36.6 | 25.2 | 48 08.5 | 4.5 | 26 33.6 | 4.2 | 59.0 | 20 | 04 53 | 05 19 | 05 41 | 09 18 | 10 14 | 11 17 | 12 25 |
| 21 | 137 36.8 | .. 26.1 | 62 32.0 | 4.4 | 26 37.8 | 4.1 | 59.0 | 30 | 04 45 | 05 13 | 05 37 | 09 03 | 09 58 | 11 01 | 12 11 |
| 22 | 152 37.0 | 27.1 | 76 55.4 | 4.3 | 26 41.9 | 3.8 | 59.0 | 35 | 04 40 | 05 10 | 05 35 | 08 47 | 09 40 | 10 43 | 11 54 |
| 23 | 167 37.2 | 28.1 | 91 18.7 | 4.3 | 26 45.7 | 3.7 | 59.1 | 40 | 04 34 | 05 06 | 05 33 | 08 26 | 09 17 | 10 21 | 11 33 |
| 2 00 | 182 37.4 | S 3 29.0 | 105 42.0 | 4.3 | S26 49.4 | 3.5 | 59.1 | 45 | 04 26 | 05 01 | 05 30 | 08 01 | 08 49 | 09 52 | 11 09 |
| 01 | 197 37.6 | 30.0 | 120 05.3 | 4.2 | 26 52.9 | 3.4 | 59.1 | S 50 | 04 16 | 04 55 | 05 27 | 07 49 | 08 35 | 09 38 | 10 57 |
| 02 | 212 37.8 | 31.0 | 134 28.5 | 4.1 | 26 56.3 | 3.1 | 59.1 | 52 | 04 11 | 04 52 | 05 26 | 07 35 | 08 19 | 09 22 | 10 43 |
| 03 | 227 38.0 | .. 31.9 | 148 51.6 | 4.1 | 26 59.4 | 3.0 | 59.1 | 54 | 04 05 | 04 48 | 05 24 | 07 19 | 08 00 | 09 03 | 10 27 |
| 04 | 242 38.2 | 32.9 | 163 14.7 | 4.0 | 27 02.4 | 2.8 | 59.1 | 56 | 03 59 | 04 45 | 05 22 | 07 00 | 07 37 | 08 40 | 10 08 |
| 05 | 257 38.4 | 33.9 | 177 37.7 | 4.0 | 27 05.2 | 2.6 | 59.1 | 58 | 03 52 | 04 40 | 05 20 | 06 37 | 07 07 | 00 09 | 09 44 |
| 06 | 272 38.6 | S 3 34.8 | 192 00.7 | 4.0 | S27 07.8 | 2.4 | 59.1 | S 60 | 03 43 | 04 35 | 05 18 | 06 37 | 07 07 | 00 09 | 09 44 |

| UT | SUN | | MOON | | | | | Lat. | Sunset | Twilight | | Moonset | | | |
|----|-----|--|------|--|--|--|--|------|--------|----------|--|---------|--|--|--|
| | GHA | Dec | GHA | v | Dec | d | HP | | | Civil | Naut. | 1 | 2 | 3 | 4 |
| d h | ° ′ | ° ′ | ° ′ | ′ | ° ′ | ′ | ′ | ° | h m | h m | h m | h m | h m | h m | h m |
| 07 | 287 38.8 | 35.8 | 206 23.7 | 3.9 | 27 10.2 | 2.2 | 59.1 | N 72 | 17 14 | 18 20 | 19 41 | ■■■ | ■■■ | ■■■ | ■■■ |
| 08 | 302 39.0 | 36.8 | 220 46.6 | 3.9 | 27 12.4 | 2.1 | 59.1 | N 70 | 17 18 | 18 18 | 19 30 | ■■■ | ■■■ | ■■■ | ■■■ |
| S 09 | 317 39.2 | .. 37.7 | 235 09.5 | 3.9 | 27 14.5 | 1.8 | 59.1 | 68 | 17 21 | 18 16 | 19 22 | ■■■ | ■■■ | ■■■ | ■■■ |
| U 10 | 332 39.4 | 38.7 | 249 32.4 | 3.8 | 27 16.3 | 1.7 | 59.1 | 66 | 17 24 | 18 14 | 19 14 | ■■■ | ■■■ | ■■■ | ■■■ |
| N 11 | 347 39.6 | 39.7 | 263 55.2 | 3.8 | 27 18.0 | 1.5 | 59.2 | 64 | 17 26 | 18 13 | 19 09 | ■■■ | ■■■ | ■■■ | 21 30 |
| D 12 | 2 39.8 | S 3 40.6 | 278 18.0 | 3.8 | S27 19.5 | 1.3 | 59.2 | 62 | 17 28 | 18 12 | 19 04 | 10 02 | 10 27 | 20 01 | 22 07 |
| A 13 | 17 40.0 | 41.6 | 292 40.8 | 3.8 | 27 20.8 | 1.2 | 59.2 | 60 | 17 30 | 18 11 | 19 00 | 18 43 | 19 26 | 20 48 | 22 33 |
| Y 14 | 32 40.2 | 42.6 | 307 03.6 | 3.7 | 27 22.0 | 0.9 | 59.2 | N 58 | 17 31 | 18 10 | 18 56 | 19 12 | 20 00 | 21 17 | 22 54 |
| 15 | 47 40.4 | .. 43.5 | 321 26.3 | 3.7 | 27 22.9 | 0.7 | 59.2 | 56 | 17 33 | 18 10 | 18 53 | 19 34 | 20 25 | 21 40 | 23 11 |
| 16 | 62 40.6 | 44.5 | 335 49.0 | 3.7 | 27 23.6 | 0.6 | 59.2 | 54 | 17 34 | 18 09 | 18 50 | 19 52 | 20 45 | 21 58 | 23 25 |
| 17 | 77 40.8 | 45.5 | 350 11.7 | 3.7 | 27 24.2 | 0.4 | 59.2 | 52 | 17 35 | 18 09 | 18 48 | 20 07 | 21 01 | 22 13 | 23 38 |
| 18 | 92 41.0 | S 3 46.4 | 4 34.4 | 3.6 | S27 24.6 | 0.2 | 59.2 | 50 | 17 36 | 18 09 | 18 46 | 20 21 | 21 16 | 22 27 | 23 49 |
| 19 | 107 41.2 | 47.4 | 18 57.0 | 3.7 | 27 24.8 | 0.0 | 59.2 | 45 | 17 39 | 18 08 | 18 42 | 20 48 | 21 45 | 22 54 | 24 11 |
| 20 | 122 41.4 | 48.4 | 33 19.7 | 3.6 | 27 24.8 | 0.2 | 59.2 | N 40 | 17 41 | 18 08 | 18 39 | 21 10 | 22 08 | 23 16 | 24 30 |
| 21 | 137 41.6 | .. 49.3 | 47 42.3 | 3.7 | 27 24.6 | 0.4 | 59.2 | 35 | 17 43 | 18 08 | 18 37 | 21 28 | 22 27 | 23 34 | 24 45 |
| 22 | 152 41.8 | 50.3 | 62 05.0 | 3.6 | 27 24.2 | 0.6 | 59.2 | 30 | 17 44 | 18 08 | 18 36 | 21 43 | 22 43 | 23 49 | 24 58 |
| 23 | 167 42.0 | 51.3 | 76 27.6 | 3.7 | 27 23.6 | 0.7 | 59.2 | 20 | 17 47 | 18 09 | 18 35 | 22 10 | 23 10 | 24 15 | 00 15 |
| 3 00 | 182 42.2 | S 3 52.2 | 90 50.3 | 3.6 | S27 22.9 | 1.0 | 59.2 | N 10 | 17 50 | 18 11 | 18 35 | 22 33 | 23 34 | 24 37 | 00 37 |
| 01 | 197 42.4 | 53.2 | 105 12.9 | 3.7 | 27 21.9 | 1.1 | 59.2 | 0 | 17 53 | 18 13 | 18 37 | 22 54 | 23 56 | 24 58 | 00 58 |
| 02 | 212 42.6 | 54.2 | 119 35.6 | 3.6 | 27 20.8 | 1.3 | 59.3 | S 10 | 17 55 | 18 16 | 18 41 | 23 15 | 24 18 | 00 18 | 01 18 |
| 03 | 227 42.8 | .. 55.1 | 133 58.2 | 3.7 | 27 19.5 | 1.6 | 59.3 | 20 | 17 58 | 18 20 | 18 46 | 23 38 | 24 41 | 00 41 | 01 40 |
| 04 | 242 43.0 | 56.1 | 148 20.9 | 3.7 | 27 17.9 | 1.7 | 59.3 | 30 | 18 02 | 18 26 | 18 54 | 24 04 | 00 04 | 01 08 | 02 06 |
| 05 | 257 43.2 | 57.1 | 162 43.6 | 3.7 | 27 16.2 | 1.8 | 59.3 | 35 | 18 04 | 18 29 | 18 59 | 24 20 | 00 20 | 01 24 | 02 20 |
| 06 | 272 43.4 | S 3 58.0 | 177 06.3 | 3.7 | S27 14.4 | 2.1 | 59.3 | 40 | 18 06 | 18 34 | 19 06 | 24 38 | 00 38 | 01 43 | 02 38 |
| 07 | 287 43.6 | 3 59.0 | 191 29.0 | 3.7 | 27 12.3 | 2.3 | 59.3 | 45 | 18 09 | 18 39 | 19 14 | 25 00 | 01 00 | 02 05 | 02 58 |
| 08 | 302 43.8 | 4 00.0 | 205 51.7 | 3.7 | 27 10.0 | 2.4 | 59.3 | S 50 | 18 13 | 18 45 | 19 24 | 00 11 | 01 28 | 02 34 | 03 24 |
| M 09 | 317 43.9 | .. 00.9 | 220 14.4 | 3.8 | 27 07.6 | 2.7 | 59.3 | 52 | 18 14 | 18 48 | 19 29 | 00 23 | 01 42 | 02 48 | 03 36 |
| O 10 | 332 44.1 | 01.9 | 234 37.2 | 3.8 | 27 04.9 | 2.8 | 59.3 | 54 | 18 16 | 18 52 | 19 35 | 00 36 | 01 58 | 03 04 | 03 51 |
| N 11 | 347 44.3 | 02.9 | 249 00.0 | 3.8 | 27 02.1 | 3.0 | 59.3 | 56 | 18 18 | 18 56 | 19 42 | 00 52 | 02 17 | 03 23 | 04 07 |
| D 12 | 2 44.5 | S 4 03.8 | 263 22.8 | 3.9 | S26 59.1 | 3.2 | 59.3 | 58 | 18 20 | 19 00 | 19 49 | 01 10 | 02 40 | 03 47 | 04 27 |
| A 13 | 17 44.7 | 04.8 | 277 45.7 | 3.8 | 26 55.9 | 3.4 | 59.3 | S 60 | 18 22 | 19 05 | 19 58 | 01 33 | 03 10 | 04 18 | 04 51 |
| Y 14 | 32 44.9 | 05.8 | 292 08.5 | 4.0 | 26 52.5 | 3.5 | 59.3 | | | | | | | | |
| 15 | 47 45.1 | .. 06.7 | 306 31.5 | 3.9 | 26 49.0 | 3.8 | 59.3 | | | | | | | | |
| 16 | 62 45.3 | 07.7 | 320 54.4 | 4.0 | 26 45.2 | 3.9 | 59.3 | | | | | | | | |
| 17 | 77 45.5 | 08.7 | 335 17.4 | 4.0 | 26 41.3 | 4.1 | 59.3 | | | | | | | | |
| 18 | 92 45.7 | S 4 09.6 | 349 40.4 | 4.1 | S26 37.2 | 4.3 | 59.3 | | SUN | | | MOON | | | |
| 19 | 107 45.9 | 10.6 | 4 03.5 | 4.1 | 26 32.9 | 4.5 | 59.3 | Day | Eqn. of Time | | Mer. | Mer. Pass. | | Age | Phase |
| 20 | 122 46.1 | 11.6 | 18 26.6 | 4.2 | 26 28.4 | 4.6 | 59.3 | | 00h | 12h | Pass. | Upper | Lower | | |
| 21 | 137 46.3 | .. 12.5 | 32 49.8 | 4.2 | 26 23.8 | 4.9 | 59.3 | d | m s | m s | h m | h m | h m | d % | |
| 22 | 152 46.5 | 13.5 | 47 13.0 | 4.3 | 26 18.9 | 5.0 | 59.3 | 1 | 10 10 | 10 20 | 11 50 | 16 39 | 04 09 | 06 33 | |
| 23 | 167 46.7 | 14.5 | 61 36.3 | 4.3 | S26 13.9 | 5.2 | 59.3 | 2 | 10 29 | 10 39 | 11 49 | 17 41 | 05 10 | 07 44 | |
| | SD 16.0 | d 1.0 | SD 16.1 | | 16.1 | | 16.2 | 3 | 10 48 | 10 58 | 11 49 | 18 43 | 06 12 | 08 56 | |

| UT | ARIES GHA | VENUS −3.9 GHA | VENUS Dec | MARS −0.7 GHA | MARS Dec | JUPITER −2.9 GHA | JUPITER Dec | SATURN +0.5 GHA | SATURN Dec | STARS Name | SHA | Dec |
|---|---|---|---|---|---|---|---|---|---|---|---|---|
| **4** 00 | 12 39.9 | 186 45.6 | S 1 02.0 | 292 20.4 | N22 35.0 | 9 30.6 | S 0 23.8 | 50 55.1 | S16 24.6 | Acamar | 315 12.9 | S40 12.6 |
| 01 | 27 42.4 | 201 45.2 | 03.3 | 307 22.1 | 35.1 | 24 33.4 | 24.0 | 65 57.6 | 24.6 | Achernar | 335 21.0 | S57 07.2 |
| 02 | 42 44.9 | 216 44.8 | 04.5 | 322 23.7 | 35.2 | 39 36.1 | 24.1 | 81 00.2 | 24.6 | Acrux | 173 02.9 | S63 13.3 |
| 03 | 57 47.3 | 231 44.4 .. | 05.8 | 337 25.3 .. | 35.4 | 54 38.9 .. | 24.2 | 96 02.7 .. | 24.6 | Adhara | 255 07.4 | S28 59.9 |
| 04 | 72 49.8 | 246 44.0 | 07.1 | 352 26.9 | 35.5 | 69 41.7 | 24.3 | 111 05.3 | 24.7 | Aldebaran | 290 41.6 | N16 33.3 |
| 05 | 87 52.3 | 261 43.6 | 08.3 | 7 28.5 | 35.6 | 84 44.4 | 24.5 | 126 07.8 | 24.7 | | | |
| 06 | 102 54.7 | 276 43.2 | S 1 09.6 | 22 30.1 | N22 35.7 | 99 47.2 | S 0 24.6 | 141 10.4 | S16 24.7 | Alioth | 166 15.2 | N55 50.3 |
| 07 | 117 57.2 | 291 42.8 | 10.8 | 37 31.8 | 35.9 | 114 50.0 | 24.7 | 156 12.9 | 24.7 | Alkaid | 152 54.0 | N49 12.2 |
| T 08 | 132 59.6 | 306 42.4 | 12.1 | 52 33.4 | 36.0 | 129 52.7 | 24.9 | 171 15.4 | 24.8 | Alnair | 27 34.9 | S46 51.2 |
| U 09 | 148 02.1 | 321 42.0 .. | 13.3 | 67 35.0 .. | 36.1 | 144 55.5 .. | 25.0 | 186 18.0 .. | 24.8 | Alnilam | 275 39.5 | S 1 11.1 |
| E 10 | 163 04.6 | 336 41.6 | 14.6 | 82 36.6 | 36.3 | 159 58.2 | 25.1 | 201 20.5 | 24.8 | Alphard | 217 49.8 | S 8 45.2 |
| S 11 | 178 07.0 | 351 41.2 | 15.8 | 97 38.2 | 36.4 | 175 01.0 | 25.2 | 216 23.1 | 24.8 | | | |
| D 12 | 193 09.5 | 6 40.9 | S 1 17.1 | 112 39.9 | N22 36.5 | 190 03.8 | S 0 25.4 | 231 25.6 | S16 24.9 | Alphecca | 126 05.6 | N26 38.5 |
| A 13 | 208 12.0 | 21 40.5 | 18.3 | 127 41.5 | 36.6 | 205 06.5 | 25.5 | 246 28.1 | 24.9 | Alpheratz | 357 36.4 | N29 13.0 |
| Y 14 | 223 14.4 | 36 40.1 | 19.6 | 142 43.1 | 36.8 | 220 09.3 | 25.6 | 261 30.7 | 24.9 | Altair | 62 01.7 | N 8 55.8 |
| 15 | 238 16.9 | 51 39.7 .. | 20.9 | 157 44.7 .. | 36.9 | 235 12.1 .. | 25.8 | 276 33.2 .. | 24.9 | Ankaa | 353 08.6 | S42 10.9 |
| 16 | 253 19.4 | 66 39.3 | 22.1 | 172 46.4 | 37.0 | 250 14.8 | 25.9 | 291 35.8 | 24.9 | Antares | 112 18.4 | S26 28.9 |
| 17 | 268 21.8 | 81 38.9 | 23.4 | 187 48.0 | 37.1 | 265 17.6 | 26.0 | 306 38.3 | 25.0 | | | |
| 18 | 283 24.3 | 96 38.5 | S 1 24.6 | 202 49.6 | N22 37.3 | 280 20.4 | S 0 26.1 | 321 40.8 | S16 25.0 | Arcturus | 145 50.0 | N19 04.0 |
| 19 | 298 26.8 | 111 38.1 | 25.9 | 217 51.3 | 37.4 | 295 23.1 | 26.3 | 336 43.4 | 25.0 | Atria | 107 14.5 | S69 04.3 |
| 20 | 313 29.2 | 126 37.7 | 27.1 | 232 52.9 | 37.5 | 310 25.9 | 26.4 | 351 45.9 | 25.0 | Avior | 234 15.7 | S59 34.5 |
| 21 | 328 31.7 | 141 37.3 .. | 28.4 | 247 54.5 .. | 37.6 | 325 28.7 .. | 26.5 | 6 48.5 .. | 25.1 | Bellatrix | 278 24.8 | N 6 22.3 |
| 22 | 343 34.1 | 156 36.9 | 29.6 | 262 56.2 | 37.8 | 340 31.4 | 26.7 | 21 51.0 | 25.1 | Betelgeuse | 270 54.0 | N 7 24.8 |
| 23 | 358 36.6 | 171 36.5 | 30.9 | 277 57.8 | 37.9 | 355 34.2 | 26.8 | 36 53.5 | 25.1 | | | |
| **5** 00 | 13 39.1 | 186 36.1 | S 1 32.2 | 292 59.4 | N22 38.0 | 10 37.0 | S 0 26.9 | 51 56.1 | S16 25.1 | Canopus | 263 53.2 | S52 42.1 |
| 01 | 28 41.5 | 201 35.7 | 33.4 | 308 01.1 | 38.1 | 25 39.7 | 27.0 | 66 58.6 | 25.2 | Capella | 280 24.5 | N46 01.1 |
| 02 | 43 44.0 | 216 35.4 | 34.7 | 323 02.7 | 38.3 | 40 42.5 | 27.2 | 82 01.2 | 25.2 | Deneb | 49 26.9 | N45 21.9 |
| 03 | 58 46.5 | 231 35.0 .. | 35.9 | 338 04.4 .. | 38.4 | 55 45.2 .. | 27.3 | 97 03.7 .. | 25.2 | Denebola | 182 27.2 | N14 26.9 |
| 04 | 73 48.9 | 246 34.6 | 37.2 | 353 06.0 | 38.5 | 70 48.0 | 27.4 | 112 06.2 | 25.2 | Diphda | 348 48.9 | S17 51.7 |
| 05 | 88 51.4 | 261 34.2 | 38.4 | 8 07.6 | 38.7 | 85 50.8 | 27.5 | 127 08.8 | 25.2 | | | |
| 06 | 103 53.9 | 276 33.8 | S 1 39.7 | 23 09.3 | N22 38.8 | 100 53.5 | S 0 27.7 | 142 11.3 | S16 25.2 | Dubhe | 193 43.9 | N61 37.7 |
| W 07 | 118 56.3 | 291 33.4 | 40.9 | 38 10.9 | 38.9 | 115 56.3 | 27.8 | 157 13.8 | 25.3 | Elnath | 278 04.1 | N28 37.6 |
| E 08 | 133 58.8 | 306 33.0 | 42.2 | 53 12.6 | 39.0 | 130 59.1 | 27.9 | 172 16.4 | 25.3 | Eltanin | 90 43.2 | N51 29.4 |
| D 09 | 149 01.2 | 321 32.6 .. | 43.4 | 68 14.2 .. | 39.2 | 146 01.8 .. | 28.1 | 187 18.9 .. | 25.3 | Enif | 33 40.4 | N 9 58.9 |
| N 10 | 164 03.7 | 336 32.2 | 44.7 | 83 15.9 | 39.3 | 161 04.6 | 28.2 | 202 21.4 | 25.3 | Fomalhaut | 15 16.3 | S29 30.1 |
| E 11 | 179 06.2 | 351 31.8 | 46.0 | 98 17.5 | 39.4 | 176 07.3 | 28.3 | 217 24.0 | 25.4 | | | |
| S 12 | 194 08.6 | 6 31.4 | S 1 47.2 | 113 19.2 | N22 39.5 | 191 10.1 | S 0 28.4 | 232 26.5 | S16 25.4 | Gacrux | 171 54.3 | S57 14.3 |
| D 13 | 209 11.1 | 21 31.0 | 48.5 | 128 20.8 | 39.7 | 206 12.9 | 28.6 | 247 29.1 | 25.4 | Gienah | 175 45.9 | S17 39.9 |
| A 14 | 224 13.6 | 36 30.6 | 49.7 | 143 22.5 | 39.8 | 221 15.6 | 28.7 | 262 31.6 | 25.4 | Hadar | 148 39.3 | S60 28.9 |
| Y 15 | 239 16.0 | 51 30.2 .. | 51.0 | 158 24.1 .. | 39.9 | 236 18.4 .. | 28.8 | 277 34.1 .. | 25.4 | Hamal | 327 53.0 | N23 34.2 |
| 16 | 254 18.5 | 66 29.8 | 52.2 | 173 25.8 | 40.0 | 251 21.2 | 28.9 | 292 36.7 | 25.5 | Kaus Aust. | 83 35.1 | S34 22.5 |
| 17 | 269 21.0 | 81 29.4 | 53.5 | 188 27.4 | 40.2 | 266 23.9 | 29.1 | 307 39.2 | 25.5 | | | |
| 18 | 284 23.4 | 96 29.0 | S 1 54.7 | 203 29.1 | N22 40.3 | 281 26.7 | S 0 29.2 | 322 41.7 | S16 25.5 | Kochab | 137 20.8 | N74 03.9 |
| 19 | 299 25.9 | 111 28.6 | 56.0 | 218 30.7 | 40.4 | 296 29.5 | 29.3 | 337 44.3 | 25.5 | Markab | 13 31.5 | N15 19.7 |
| 20 | 314 28.4 | 126 28.3 | 57.2 | 233 32.4 | 40.5 | 311 32.2 | 29.4 | 352 46.8 | 25.5 | Menkar | 314 07.9 | N 4 10.8 |
| 21 | 329 30.8 | 141 27.9 .. | 58.5 | 248 34.1 .. | 40.7 | 326 35.0 .. | 29.6 | 7 49.3 .. | 25.6 | Menkent | 148 00.2 | S36 28.8 |
| 22 | 344 33.3 | 156 27.5 | 1 59.8 | 263 35.7 | 40.8 | 341 37.7 | 29.7 | 22 51.9 | 25.6 | Miaplacidus | 221 39.2 | S69 48.2 |
| 23 | 359 35.7 | 171 27.1 | 2 01.0 | 278 37.4 | 40.9 | 356 40.5 | 29.8 | 37 54.4 | 25.6 | | | |
| **6** 00 | 14 38.2 | 186 26.7 | S 2 02.3 | 293 39.0 | N22 41.0 | 11 43.3 | S 0 30.0 | 52 56.9 | S16 25.6 | Mirfak | 308 30.6 | N49 56.4 |
| 01 | 29 40.7 | 201 26.3 | 03.5 | 308 40.7 | 41.1 | 26 46.0 | 30.1 | 67 59.5 | 25.6 | Nunki | 75 50.1 | S26 16.1 |
| 02 | 44 43.1 | 216 25.9 | 04.8 | 323 42.4 | 41.3 | 41 48.8 | 30.2 | 83 02.0 | 25.7 | Peacock | 53 08.5 | S56 39.9 |
| 03 | 59 45.6 | 231 25.5 .. | 06.0 | 338 44.0 .. | 41.4 | 56 51.5 .. | 30.3 | 98 04.6 .. | 25.7 | Pollux | 243 19.7 | N27 58.3 |
| 04 | 74 48.1 | 246 25.1 | 07.3 | 353 45.7 | 41.5 | 71 54.3 | 30.5 | 113 07.1 | 25.7 | Procyon | 244 52.9 | N 5 10.1 |
| 05 | 89 50.5 | 261 24.7 | 08.5 | 8 47.4 | 41.6 | 86 57.1 | 30.6 | 128 09.6 | 25.7 | | | |
| 06 | 104 53.0 | 276 24.3 | S 2 09.8 | 23 49.0 | N22 41.8 | 101 59.8 | S 0 30.7 | 143 12.2 | S16 25.7 | Rasalhague | 96 00.4 | N12 32.8 |
| T 07 | 119 55.5 | 291 23.9 | 11.0 | 38 50.7 | 41.9 | 117 02.6 | 30.8 | 158 14.7 | 25.8 | Regulus | 207 36.7 | N11 51.5 |
| H 08 | 134 57.9 | 306 23.5 | 12.3 | 53 52.4 | 42.0 | 132 05.4 | 31.0 | 173 17.2 | 25.8 | Rigel | 281 05.5 | S 8 10.3 |
| U 09 | 150 00.4 | 321 23.1 .. | 13.5 | 68 54.0 .. | 42.1 | 147 08.1 .. | 31.1 | 188 19.8 .. | 25.8 | Rigil Kent. | 139 43.5 | S60 55.7 |
| R 10 | 165 02.9 | 336 22.7 | 14.8 | 83 55.7 | 42.3 | 162 10.9 | 31.2 | 203 22.3 | 25.8 | Sabik | 102 05.1 | S15 45.1 |
| S 11 | 180 05.3 | 351 22.3 | 16.1 | 98 57.4 | 42.4 | 177 13.6 | 31.3 | 218 24.8 | 25.8 | | | |
| D 12 | 195 07.8 | 6 21.9 | S 2 17.3 | 113 59.1 | N22 42.5 | 192 16.4 | S 0 31.5 | 233 27.4 | S16 25.9 | Schedar | 349 32.6 | N56 39.7 |
| A 13 | 210 10.2 | 21 21.5 | 18.6 | 129 00.7 | 42.6 | 207 19.2 | 31.6 | 248 29.9 | 25.9 | Shaula | 96 13.1 | S37 07.3 |
| Y 14 | 225 12.7 | 36 21.1 | 19.8 | 144 02.4 | 42.8 | 222 21.9 | 31.7 | 263 32.4 | 25.9 | Sirius | 258 27.9 | S16 44.6 |
| 15 | 240 15.2 | 51 20.7 .. | 21.1 | 159 04.1 .. | 42.9 | 237 24.7 .. | 31.8 | 278 35.0 .. | 25.9 | Spica | 158 24.6 | S11 16.6 |
| 16 | 255 17.6 | 66 20.3 | 22.3 | 174 05.8 | 43.0 | 252 27.4 | 32.0 | 293 37.5 | 25.9 | Suhail | 222 47.9 | S43 31.1 |
| 17 | 270 20.1 | 81 19.9 | 23.6 | 189 07.4 | 43.1 | 267 30.2 | 32.1 | 308 40.0 | 26.0 | | | |
| 18 | 285 22.6 | 96 19.5 | S 2 24.8 | 204 09.1 | N22 43.2 | 282 33.0 | S 0 32.2 | 323 42.5 | S16 26.0 | Vega | 80 34.5 | N38 48.5 |
| 19 | 300 25.0 | 111 19.1 | 26.1 | 219 10.8 | 43.4 | 297 35.7 | 32.3 | 338 45.1 | 26.0 | Zuben'ubi | 136 58.4 | S16 08.0 |
| 20 | 315 27.5 | 126 18.7 | 27.3 | 234 12.5 | 43.5 | 312 38.5 | 32.5 | 353 47.6 | 26.0 | | SHA | Mer. Pass. |
| 21 | 330 30.0 | 141 18.3 .. | 28.6 | 249 14.2 .. | 43.6 | 327 41.2 .. | 32.6 | 8 50.1 .. | 26.0 | Venus | 172 57.1 | 11 34 |
| 22 | 345 32.4 | 156 18.0 | 29.8 | 264 15.9 | 43.7 | 342 44.0 | 32.7 | 23 52.7 | 26.1 | Mars | 279 20.4 | 4 28 |
| 23 | 0 34.9 | 171 17.6 | 31.1 | 279 17.5 | 43.9 | 357 46.8 | 32.8 | 38 55.2 | 26.1 | Jupiter | 356 57.9 | 23 13 |
| Mer. Pass. 23 01.6 | | v −0.4 | d 1.3 | v 1.6 | d 0.1 | v 2.8 | d 0.1 | v 2.5 | d 0.0 | Saturn | 38 17.0 | 20 29 |

| UT | SUN GHA | SUN Dec | MOON GHA | v | MOON Dec | d | HP |
|---|---|---|---|---|---|---|---|
| d h | ° ' | ° ' | ° ' | ' | ° ' | ' | ' |
| **4** 00 | 182 46.9 | S 4 15.4 | 75 59.6 | 4.4 | S26 08.7 | 5.3 | 59.3 |
| 01 | 197 47.1 | 16.4 | 90 23.0 | 4.4 | 26 03.4 | 5.6 | 59.4 |
| 02 | 212 47.3 | 17.3 | 104 46.4 | 4.5 | 25 57.8 | 5.7 | 59.4 |
| 03 | 227 47.4 | .. 18.3 | 119 09.9 | 4.5 | 25 52.1 | 5.9 | 59.4 |
| 04 | 242 47.6 | 19.3 | 133 33.4 | 4.6 | 25 46.2 | 6.0 | 59.4 |
| 05 | 257 47.8 | 20.2 | 147 57.0 | 4.7 | 25 40.2 | 6.3 | 59.4 |
| 06 | 272 48.0 | S 4 21.2 | 162 20.7 | 4.7 | S25 33.9 | 6.4 | 59.4 |
| 07 | 287 48.2 | 22.2 | 176 44.4 | 4.8 | 25 27.5 | 6.6 | 59.4 |
| T 08 | 302 48.4 | 23.1 | 191 08.2 | 4.9 | 25 20.9 | 6.7 | 59.4 |
| U 09 | 317 48.6 | .. 24.1 | 205 32.1 | 4.9 | 25 14.2 | 6.9 | 59.4 |
| E 10 | 332 48.8 | 25.1 | 219 56.0 | 5.0 | 25 07.3 | 7.1 | 59.4 |
| S 11 | 347 49.0 | 26.0 | 234 20.0 | 5.1 | 25 00.2 | 7.2 | 59.4 |
| D 12 | 2 49.2 | S 4 27.0 | 248 44.1 | 5.1 | S24 53.0 | 7.5 | 59.4 |
| A 13 | 17 49.4 | 27.9 | 263 08.2 | 5.3 | 24 45.5 | 7.5 | 59.4 |
| Y 14 | 32 49.6 | 28.9 | 277 32.5 | 5.3 | 24 38.0 | 7.8 | 59.4 |
| 15 | 47 49.8 | .. 29.9 | 291 56.8 | 5.3 | 24 30.2 | 7.8 | 59.4 |
| 16 | 62 49.9 | 30.8 | 306 21.1 | 5.5 | 24 22.4 | 8.1 | 59.4 |
| 17 | 77 50.1 | 31.8 | 320 45.6 | 5.5 | 24 14.3 | 8.2 | 59.4 |
| 18 | 92 50.3 | S 4 32.8 | 335 10.1 | 5.6 | S24 06.1 | 8.4 | 59.4 |
| 19 | 107 50.5 | 33.7 | 349 34.7 | 5.7 | 23 57.7 | 8.5 | 59.4 |
| 20 | 122 50.7 | 34.7 | 3 59.4 | 5.8 | 23 49.2 | 8.7 | 59.4 |
| 21 | 137 50.9 | .. 35.6 | 18 24.2 | 5.9 | 23 40.5 | 8.8 | 59.4 |
| 22 | 152 51.1 | 36.6 | 32 49.1 | 5.9 | 23 31.7 | 9.0 | 59.4 |
| 23 | 167 51.3 | 37.6 | 47 14.0 | 6.0 | 23 22.7 | 9.1 | 59.4 |
| **5** 00 | 182 51.5 | S 4 38.5 | 61 39.0 | 6.1 | S23 13.6 | 9.3 | 59.4 |
| 01 | 197 51.7 | 39.5 | 76 04.1 | 6.2 | 23 04.3 | 9.4 | 59.4 |
| 02 | 212 51.8 | 40.5 | 90 29.3 | 6.3 | 22 54.9 | 9.5 | 59.4 |
| 03 | 227 52.0 | .. 41.4 | 104 54.6 | 6.4 | 22 45.4 | 9.7 | 59.4 |
| 04 | 242 52.2 | 42.4 | 119 20.0 | 6.4 | 22 35.7 | 9.9 | 59.4 |
| 05 | 257 52.4 | 43.3 | 133 45.4 | 6.6 | 22 25.8 | 10.0 | 59.4 |
| 06 | 272 52.6 | S 4 44.3 | 148 11.0 | 6.6 | S22 15.8 | 10.1 | 59.4 |
| W 07 | 287 52.8 | 45.3 | 162 36.6 | 6.8 | 22 05.7 | 10.3 | 59.4 |
| E 08 | 302 53.0 | 46.2 | 177 02.4 | 6.8 | 21 55.4 | 10.4 | 59.4 |
| D 09 | 317 53.2 | .. 47.2 | 191 28.2 | 6.9 | 21 45.0 | 10.5 | 59.3 |
| N 10 | 332 53.4 | 48.2 | 205 54.1 | 7.0 | 21 34.5 | 10.7 | 59.3 |
| E 11 | 347 53.5 | 49.1 | 220 20.1 | 7.1 | 21 23.8 | 10.8 | 59.3 |
| S 12 | 2 53.7 | S 4 50.1 | 234 46.2 | 7.2 | S21 13.0 | 10.9 | 59.3 |
| D 13 | 17 53.9 | 51.0 | 249 12.4 | 7.2 | 21 02.1 | 11.0 | 59.3 |
| A 14 | 32 54.1 | 52.0 | 263 38.6 | 7.4 | 20 51.1 | 11.2 | 59.3 |
| Y 15 | 47 54.3 | .. 53.0 | 278 05.0 | 7.4 | 20 39.9 | 11.3 | 59.3 |
| 16 | 62 54.5 | 53.9 | 292 31.4 | 7.6 | 20 28.6 | 11.5 | 59.3 |
| 17 | 77 54.7 | 54.9 | 306 58.0 | 7.6 | 20 17.1 | 11.5 | 59.3 |
| 18 | 92 54.9 | S 4 55.8 | 321 24.6 | 7.8 | S20 05.6 | 11.7 | 59.3 |
| 19 | 107 55.1 | 56.8 | 335 51.4 | 7.8 | 19 53.9 | 11.7 | 59.3 |
| 20 | 122 55.2 | 57.8 | 350 18.2 | 7.9 | 19 42.2 | 11.9 | 59.3 |
| 21 | 137 55.4 | .. 58.7 | 4 45.1 | 8.0 | 19 30.3 | 12.1 | 59.3 |
| 22 | 152 55.6 | 4 59.7 | 19 12.1 | 8.1 | 19 18.2 | 12.1 | 59.3 |
| 23 | 167 55.8 | 5 00.6 | 33 39.2 | 8.2 | 19 06.1 | 12.2 | 59.3 |
| **6** 00 | 182 56.0 | S 5 01.6 | 48 06.4 | 8.3 | S18 53.9 | 12.4 | 59.3 |
| 01 | 197 56.2 | 02.6 | 62 33.7 | 8.3 | 18 41.5 | 12.4 | 59.3 |
| 02 | 212 56.4 | 03.5 | 77 01.0 | 8.5 | 18 29.1 | 12.6 | 59.3 |
| 03 | 227 56.5 | .. 04.5 | 91 28.5 | 8.5 | 18 16.5 | 12.6 | 59.3 |
| 04 | 242 56.7 | 05.4 | 105 56.0 | 8.7 | 18 03.9 | 12.8 | 59.3 |
| 05 | 257 56.9 | 06.4 | 120 23.7 | 8.7 | 17 51.1 | 12.9 | 59.2 |
| 06 | 272 57.1 | S 5 07.4 | 134 51.4 | 8.8 | S17 38.2 | 12.9 | 59.2 |
| 07 | 287 57.3 | 08.3 | 149 19.2 | 8.9 | 17 25.3 | 13.1 | 59.2 |
| T 08 | 302 57.5 | 09.3 | 163 47.1 | 9.0 | 17 12.2 | 13.2 | 59.2 |
| H 09 | 317 57.7 | .. 10.2 | 178 15.1 | 9.1 | 16 59.0 | 13.2 | 59.2 |
| U 10 | 332 57.8 | 11.2 | 192 43.2 | 9.2 | 16 45.8 | 13.3 | 59.2 |
| R 11 | 347 58.0 | 12.1 | 207 11.4 | 9.2 | 16 32.5 | 13.5 | 59.2 |
| S 12 | 2 58.2 | S 5 13.1 | 221 39.6 | 9.4 | S16 19.0 | 13.5 | 59.2 |
| D 13 | 17 58.4 | 14.1 | 236 08.0 | 9.4 | 16 05.5 | 13.6 | 59.2 |
| A 14 | 32 58.6 | 15.0 | 250 36.4 | 9.5 | 15 51.9 | 13.7 | 59.2 |
| Y 15 | 47 58.8 | .. 16.0 | 265 04.9 | 9.6 | 15 38.2 | 13.8 | 59.2 |
| 16 | 62 58.9 | 16.9 | 279 33.5 | 9.7 | 15 24.4 | 13.8 | 59.2 |
| 17 | 77 59.1 | 17.9 | 294 02.2 | 9.7 | 15 10.6 | 14.0 | 59.1 |
| 18 | 92 59.3 | S 5 18.8 | 308 30.9 | 9.9 | S14 56.6 | 14.0 | 59.1 |
| 19 | 107 59.5 | 19.8 | 322 59.8 | 9.9 | 14 42.6 | 14.1 | 59.1 |
| 20 | 122 59.7 | 20.8 | 337 28.7 | 10.0 | 14 28.5 | 14.2 | 59.1 |
| 21 | 137 59.9 | .. 21.7 | 351 57.7 | 10.1 | 14 14.3 | 14.2 | 59.1 |
| 22 | 153 00.0 | 22.7 | 6 26.8 | 10.2 | 14 00.1 | 14.3 | 59.1 |
| 23 | 168 00.2 | 23.6 | 20 56.0 | 10.2 | S13 45.8 | 14.4 | 59.1 |
| | SD 16.0 | d 1.0 | SD 16.2 | | 16.2 | | 16.1 |

| Lat. | Twilight Naut. | Twilight Civil | Sunrise | Moonrise 4 | 5 | 6 | 7 |
|---|---|---|---|---|---|---|---|
| ° | h m | h m | h m | h m | h m | h m | h m |
| N 72 | 04 09 | 05 29 | 06 37 | ■■ | ■■ | 19 07 | 18 14 |
| N 70 | 04 18 | 05 30 | 06 31 | ■■ | 20 08 | 18 36 | 18 00 |
| 68 | 04 26 | 05 31 | 06 27 | ■■ | 18 55 | 18 13 | 17 49 |
| 66 | 04 32 | 05 32 | 06 23 | ■■ | 18 18 | 17 55 | 17 40 |
| 64 | 04 37 | 05 33 | 06 20 | 18 09 | 17 51 | 17 41 | 17 32 |
| 62 | 04 41 | 05 33 | 06 17 | 17 31 | 17 30 | 17 28 | 17 25 |
| 60 | 04 45 | 05 33 | 06 15 | 17 04 | 17 13 | 17 17 | 17 20 |
| N 58 | 04 48 | 05 33 | 06 13 | 16 43 | 16 59 | 17 08 | 17 14 |
| 56 | 04 50 | 05 34 | 06 11 | 16 25 | 16 46 | 17 00 | 17 10 |
| 54 | 04 53 | 05 34 | 06 09 | 16 11 | 16 35 | 16 53 | 17 06 |
| 52 | 04 55 | 05 34 | 06 07 | 15 58 | 16 26 | 16 46 | 17 02 |
| 50 | 04 56 | 05 34 | 06 06 | 15 46 | 16 17 | 16 40 | 16 58 |
| 45 | 04 59 | 05 33 | 06 03 | 15 22 | 15 59 | 16 27 | 16 51 |
| N 40 | 05 02 | 05 33 | 06 00 | 15 03 | 15 43 | 16 16 | 16 45 |
| 35 | 05 03 | 05 32 | 05 58 | 14 47 | 15 31 | 16 07 | 16 39 |
| 30 | 05 04 | 05 32 | 05 56 | 14 33 | 15 19 | 15 59 | 16 34 |
| 20 | 05 04 | 05 30 | 05 52 | 14 09 | 15 00 | 15 45 | 16 26 |
| N 10 | 05 03 | 05 27 | 05 48 | 13 49 | 14 43 | 15 33 | 16 18 |
| 0 | 05 00 | 05 24 | 05 45 | 13 29 | 14 27 | 15 21 | 16 11 |
| S 10 | 04 56 | 05 21 | 05 42 | 13 10 | 14 11 | 15 09 | 16 04 |
| 20 | 04 50 | 05 16 | 05 38 | 12 49 | 13 54 | 14 57 | 15 57 |
| 30 | 04 41 | 05 10 | 05 34 | 12 25 | 13 34 | 14 42 | 15 48 |
| 35 | 04 36 | 05 06 | 05 31 | 12 11 | 13 23 | 14 34 | 15 43 |
| 40 | 04 29 | 05 01 | 05 28 | 11 54 | 13 09 | 14 24 | 15 38 |
| 45 | 04 20 | 04 55 | 05 25 | 11 34 | 12 53 | 14 13 | 15 31 |
| S 50 | 04 09 | 04 48 | 05 21 | 11 09 | 12 34 | 13 59 | 15 23 |
| 52 | 04 03 | 04 44 | 05 19 | 10 57 | 12 24 | 13 53 | 15 19 |
| 54 | 03 57 | 04 41 | 05 17 | 10 43 | 12 14 | 13 46 | 15 15 |
| 56 | 03 50 | 04 36 | 05 14 | 10 27 | 12 02 | 13 38 | 15 11 |
| 58 | 03 42 | 04 31 | 05 12 | 10 08 | 11 48 | 13 29 | 15 06 |
| S 60 | 03 32 | 04 26 | 05 09 | 09 44 | 11 32 | 13 18 | 15 00 |

| Lat. | Sunset | Twilight Civil | Twilight Naut. | Moonset 4 | 5 | 6 | 7 |
|---|---|---|---|---|---|---|---|
| ° | h m | h m | h m | h m | h m | h m | h m |
| N 72 | 16 58 | 18 05 | 19 25 | ■■ | ■■ | ■■ | 00 27 |
| N 70 | 17 04 | 18 04 | 19 16 | ■■ | 21 33 | 24 56 | 00 56 |
| 68 | 17 08 | 18 04 | 19 09 | ■■ | 22 44 | 25 17 | 01 17 |
| 66 | 17 12 | 18 03 | 19 03 | ■■ | 23 20 | 25 33 | 01 33 |
| 64 | 17 15 | 18 03 | 18 58 | 21 00 | 23 16 | 25 46 | 01 46 |
| 62 | 17 18 | 18 02 | 18 54 | 22 07 | 24 06 | 00 06 | 01 58 |
| 60 | 17 21 | 18 02 | 18 50 | 22 33 | 24 22 | 00 22 | 02 07 |
| N 58 | 17 23 | 18 02 | 18 48 | 22 54 | 24 36 | 00 36 | 02 15 |
| 56 | 17 25 | 18 02 | 18 45 | 23 11 | 24 47 | 00 47 | 02 22 |
| 54 | 17 27 | 18 02 | 18 43 | 23 25 | 24 57 | 00 57 | 02 29 |
| 52 | 17 29 | 18 02 | 18 41 | 23 38 | 25 06 | 01 06 | 02 34 |
| 50 | 17 30 | 18 02 | 18 40 | 23 49 | 25 14 | 01 14 | 02 40 |
| 45 | 17 33 | 18 03 | 18 37 | 24 11 | 00 11 | 01 31 | 02 51 |
| N 40 | 17 36 | 18 03 | 18 34 | 24 30 | 00 30 | 01 45 | 03 00 |
| 35 | 17 39 | 18 04 | 18 33 | 24 45 | 00 45 | 01 57 | 03 07 |
| 30 | 17 41 | 18 05 | 18 32 | 24 58 | 00 58 | 02 07 | 03 14 |
| 20 | 17 45 | 18 07 | 18 32 | 00 15 | 01 20 | 02 24 | 03 26 |
| N 10 | 17 48 | 18 09 | 18 34 | 00 37 | 01 39 | 02 39 | 03 35 |
| 0 | 17 52 | 18 12 | 18 37 | 00 58 | 01 57 | 02 53 | 03 45 |
| S 10 | 17 55 | 18 16 | 18 41 | 01 18 | 02 15 | 03 07 | 03 55 |
| 20 | 17 59 | 18 21 | 18 47 | 01 40 | 02 34 | 03 22 | 04 05 |
| 30 | 18 04 | 18 28 | 18 56 | 02 06 | 02 55 | 03 38 | 04 16 |
| 35 | 18 06 | 18 32 | 19 02 | 02 20 | 03 08 | 03 48 | 04 22 |
| 40 | 18 09 | 18 37 | 19 09 | 02 38 | 03 22 | 03 59 | 04 29 |
| 45 | 18 13 | 18 43 | 19 18 | 02 58 | 03 39 | 04 12 | 04 38 |
| S 50 | 18 17 | 18 50 | 19 30 | 03 24 | 04 00 | 04 27 | 04 48 |
| 52 | 18 19 | 18 54 | 19 35 | 03 36 | 04 10 | 04 34 | 04 52 |
| 54 | 18 21 | 18 58 | 19 42 | 03 51 | 04 21 | 04 42 | 04 57 |
| 56 | 18 24 | 19 02 | 19 49 | 04 07 | 04 34 | 04 51 | 05 03 |
| 58 | 18 27 | 19 07 | 19 57 | 04 27 | 04 49 | 05 01 | 05 09 |
| S 60 | 18 30 | 19 13 | 20 07 | 04 51 | 05 06 | 05 13 | 05 16 |

| Day | SUN Eqn. of Time 00h | SUN Eqn. of Time 12h | SUN Mer. Pass. | MOON Mer Pass. Upper | MOON Mer Pass. Lower | Age | Phase |
|---|---|---|---|---|---|---|---|
| d | m s | m s | h m | h m | h m | d | % |
| 4 | 11 07 | 11 16 | 11 49 | 19 43 | 07 14 | 09 | 67 |
| 5 | 11 25 | 11 35 | 11 48 | 20 40 | 08 12 | 10 | 77 |
| 6 | 11 44 | 11 52 | 11 48 | 21 33 | 09 07 | 11 | 86 |

| UT | ARIES GHA | VENUS −3.9 GHA | Dec | MARS −0.7 GHA | Dec | JUPITER −2.9 GHA | Dec | SATURN +0.5 GHA | Dec | STARS Name | SHA | Dec |
|---|---|---|---|---|---|---|---|---|---|---|---|---|
| **7** d h 00 | 15 37.3 | 186 17.2 | S 2 32.3 | 294 19.2 | N22 44.0 | 12 49.5 | S 0 33.0 | 53 57.7 | S16 26.1 | Acamar | 315 12.8 | S40 12.6 |
| 01 | 30 39.8 | 201 16.8 | 33.6 | 309 20.9 | 44.1 | 27 52.3 | 33.1 | 69 00.3 | 26.1 | Achernar | 335 21.0 | S57 07.2 |
| 02 | 45 42.3 | 216 16.4 | 34.9 | 324 22.6 | 44.2 | 42 55.0 | 33.2 | 84 02.8 | 26.1 | Acrux | 173 02.9 | S63 13.3 |
| 03 | 60 44.7 | 231 16.0 .. | 36.1 | 339 24.3 .. | 44.4 | 57 57.8 .. | 33.3 | 99 05.3 .. | 26.2 | Adhara | 255 07.3 | S28 59.9 |
| 04 | 75 47.2 | 246 15.6 | 37.4 | 354 26.0 | 44.5 | 73 00.6 | 33.5 | 114 07.9 | 26.2 | Aldebaran | 290 41.6 | N16 33.3 |
| 05 | 90 49.7 | 261 15.2 | 38.6 | 9 27.7 | 44.6 | 88 03.3 | 33.6 | 129 10.4 | 26.2 | | | |
| 06 | 105 52.1 | 276 14.8 | S 2 39.9 | 24 29.4 | N22 44.7 | 103 06.1 | S 0 33.7 | 144 12.9 | S16 26.2 | Alioth | 166 15.2 | N55 50.3 |
| F 07 | 120 54.6 | 291 14.4 | 41.1 | 39 31.1 | 44.8 | 118 08.8 | 33.8 | 159 15.4 | 26.2 | Alkaid | 152 54.0 | N49 12.2 |
| R 08 | 135 57.1 | 306 14.0 | 42.4 | 54 32.8 | 45.0 | 133 11.6 | 34.0 | 174 18.0 | 26.3 | Alnair | 27 34.9 | S46 51.2 |
| I 09 | 150 59.5 | 321 13.6 .. | 43.6 | 69 34.5 .. | 45.1 | 148 14.4 .. | 34.1 | 189 20.5 .. | 26.3 | Alnilam | 275 39.5 | S 1 11.1 |
| D 10 | 166 02.0 | 336 13.2 | 44.9 | 84 36.2 | 45.2 | 163 17.1 | 34.2 | 204 23.0 | 26.3 | Alphard | 217 49.8 | S 8 45.2 |
| A 11 | 181 04.5 | 351 12.8 | 46.1 | 99 37.9 | 45.3 | 178 19.9 | 34.3 | 219 25.6 | 26.3 | | | |
| Y 12 | 196 06.9 | 6 12.4 | S 2 47.4 | 114 39.6 | N22 45.4 | 193 22.6 | S 0 34.5 | 234 28.1 | S16 26.3 | Alphecca | 126 05.6 | N26 38.5 |
| 13 | 211 09.4 | 21 12.0 | 48.6 | 129 41.3 | 45.6 | 208 25.4 | 34.6 | 249 30.6 | 26.3 | Alpheratz | 357 36.4 | N29 13.0 |
| 14 | 226 11.8 | 36 11.6 | 49.9 | 144 43.0 | 45.7 | 223 28.2 | 34.7 | 264 33.1 | 26.4 | Altair | 62 01.7 | N 8 55.8 |
| 15 | 241 14.3 | 51 11.2 .. | 51.1 | 159 44.7 .. | 45.8 | 238 30.9 .. | 34.8 | 279 35.7 .. | 26.4 | Ankaa | 353 08.6 | S42 11.0 |
| 16 | 256 16.8 | 66 10.8 | 52.4 | 174 46.4 | 45.9 | 253 33.7 | 35.0 | 294 38.2 | 26.4 | Antares | 112 18.4 | S26 28.9 |
| 17 | 271 19.2 | 81 10.4 | 53.6 | 189 48.1 | 46.1 | 268 36.4 | 35.1 | 309 40.7 | 26.4 | | | |
| 18 | 286 21.7 | 96 10.0 | S 2 54.9 | 204 49.8 | N22 46.2 | 283 39.2 | S 0 35.2 | 324 43.3 | S16 26.4 | Arcturus | 145 50.0 | N19 04.0 |
| 19 | 301 24.2 | 111 09.6 | 56.1 | 219 51.5 | 46.3 | 298 41.9 | 35.3 | 339 45.8 | 26.5 | Atria | 107 14.6 | S69 04.3 |
| 20 | 316 26.6 | 126 09.2 | 57.4 | 234 53.2 | 46.4 | 313 44.7 | 35.5 | 354 48.3 | 26.5 | Avior | 234 15.7 | S59 34.5 |
| 21 | 331 29.1 | 141 08.8 .. | 58.6 | 249 54.9 .. | 46.5 | 328 47.5 .. | 35.6 | 9 50.8 .. | 26.5 | Bellatrix | 278 24.8 | N 6 22.3 |
| 22 | 346 31.6 | 156 08.4 | 2 59.9 | 264 56.6 | 46.7 | 343 50.2 | 35.7 | 24 53.4 | 26.5 | Betelgeuse | 270 54.0 | N 7 24.8 |
| 23 | 1 34.0 | 171 08.0 | 3 01.1 | 279 58.3 | 46.8 | 358 53.0 | 35.8 | 39 55.9 | 26.5 | | | |
| **8** 00 | 16 36.5 | 186 07.6 | S 3 02.4 | 295 00.0 | N22 46.9 | 13 55.7 | S 0 36.0 | 54 58.4 | S16 26.5 | Canopus | 263 53.1 | S52 42.1 |
| 01 | 31 39.0 | 201 07.2 | 03.7 | 310 01.8 | 47.0 | 28 58.5 | 36.1 | 70 01.0 | 26.6 | Capella | 280 24.5 | N46 01.1 |
| 02 | 46 41.4 | 216 06.8 | 04.9 | 325 03.5 | 47.1 | 44 01.2 | 36.2 | 85 03.5 | 26.6 | Deneb | 49 26.9 | N45 21.9 |
| 03 | 61 43.9 | 231 06.4 .. | 06.2 | 340 05.2 .. | 47.3 | 59 04.0 .. | 36.3 | 100 06.0 .. | 26.6 | Denebola | 182 27.2 | N14 26.9 |
| 04 | 76 46.3 | 246 06.0 | 07.4 | 355 06.9 | 47.4 | 74 06.8 | 36.5 | 115 08.5 | 26.6 | Diphda | 348 48.9 | S17 51.7 |
| 05 | 91 48.8 | 261 05.6 | 08.7 | 10 08.6 | 47.5 | 89 09.5 | 36.6 | 130 11.1 | 26.6 | | | |
| 06 | 106 51.3 | 276 05.2 | S 3 09.9 | 25 10.4 | N22 47.6 | 104 12.3 | S 0 36.7 | 145 13.6 | S16 26.7 | Dubhe | 193 43.9 | N61 37.7 |
| S 07 | 121 53.7 | 291 04.8 | 11.2 | 40 12.1 | 47.8 | 119 15.0 | 36.8 | 160 16.1 | 26.7 | Elnath | 278 04.1 | N28 37.6 |
| A 08 | 136 56.2 | 306 04.4 | 12.4 | 55 13.8 | 47.9 | 134 17.8 | 36.9 | 175 18.6 | 26.7 | Eltanin | 90 43.2 | N51 29.4 |
| T 09 | 151 58.7 | 321 04.0 .. | 13.7 | 70 15.5 .. | 48.0 | 149 20.5 .. | 37.1 | 190 21.2 .. | 26.7 | Enif | 33 40.4 | N 9 58.9 |
| U 10 | 167 01.1 | 336 03.6 | 14.9 | 85 17.2 | 48.1 | 164 23.3 | 37.2 | 205 23.7 | 26.7 | Fomalhaut | 15 16.3 | S29 30.1 |
| R 11 | 182 03.6 | 351 03.2 | 16.2 | 100 19.0 | 48.2 | 179 26.1 | 37.3 | 220 26.2 | 26.7 | | | |
| D 12 | 197 06.1 | 6 02.8 | S 3 17.4 | 115 20.7 | N22 48.4 | 194 28.8 | S 0 37.4 | 235 28.7 | S16 26.8 | Gacrux | 171 54.3 | S57 14.2 |
| A 13 | 212 08.5 | 21 02.4 | 18.7 | 130 22.4 | 48.5 | 209 31.6 | 37.6 | 250 31.3 | 26.8 | Gienah | 175 45.9 | S17 39.9 |
| Y 14 | 227 11.0 | 36 02.0 | 19.9 | 145 24.2 | 48.6 | 224 34.3 | 37.7 | 265 33.8 | 26.8 | Hadar | 148 39.3 | S60 28.9 |
| 15 | 242 13.4 | 51 01.6 .. | 21.2 | 160 25.9 .. | 48.7 | 239 37.1 .. | 37.8 | 280 36.3 .. | 26.8 | Hamal | 327 53.0 | N23 34.2 |
| 16 | 257 15.9 | 66 01.2 | 22.4 | 175 27.6 | 48.8 | 254 39.8 | 37.9 | 295 38.8 | 26.8 | Kaus Aust. | 83 35.1 | S34 22.5 |
| 17 | 272 18.4 | 81 00.8 | 23.7 | 190 29.3 | 49.0 | 269 42.6 | 38.1 | 310 41.4 | 26.8 | | | |
| 18 | 287 20.8 | 96 00.4 | S 3 24.9 | 205 31.1 | N22 49.1 | 284 45.3 | S 0 38.2 | 325 43.9 | S16 26.9 | Kochab | 137 20.8 | N74 03.9 |
| 19 | 302 23.3 | 111 00.0 | 26.2 | 220 32.8 | 49.2 | 299 48.1 | 38.3 | 340 46.4 | 26.9 | Markab | 13 31.5 | N15 19.7 |
| 20 | 317 25.8 | 125 59.6 | 27.4 | 235 34.5 | 49.3 | 314 50.9 | 38.4 | 355 48.9 | 26.9 | Menkar | 314 07.8 | N 4 10.8 |
| 21 | 332 28.2 | 140 59.2 .. | 28.7 | 250 36.3 .. | 49.4 | 329 53.6 .. | 38.5 | 10 51.5 .. | 26.9 | Menkent | 148 00.2 | S36 28.8 |
| 22 | 347 30.7 | 155 58.7 | 29.9 | 265 38.0 | 49.6 | 344 56.4 | 38.7 | 25 54.0 | 26.9 | Miaplacidus | 221 39.1 | S69 48.2 |
| 23 | 2 33.2 | 170 58.3 | 31.2 | 280 39.8 | 49.7 | 359 59.1 | 38.8 | 40 56.5 | 26.9 | | | |
| **9** 00 | 17 35.6 | 185 57.9 | S 3 32.4 | 295 41.5 | N22 49.8 | 15 01.9 | S 0 38.9 | 55 59.0 | S16 27.0 | Mirfak | 308 30.5 | N49 56.4 |
| 01 | 32 38.1 | 200 57.5 | 33.7 | 310 43.2 | 49.9 | 30 04.6 | 39.0 | 71 01.5 | 27.0 | Nunki | 75 50.1 | S26 16.1 |
| 02 | 47 40.6 | 215 57.1 | 34.9 | 325 45.0 | 50.0 | 45 07.4 | 39.2 | 86 04.1 | 27.0 | Peacock | 53 08.5 | S56 39.9 |
| 03 | 62 43.0 | 230 56.7 .. | 36.2 | 340 46.7 .. | 50.2 | 60 10.1 .. | 39.3 | 101 06.6 .. | 27.0 | Pollux | 243 19.7 | N27 58.3 |
| 04 | 77 45.5 | 245 56.3 | 37.4 | 355 48.5 | 50.3 | 75 12.9 | 39.4 | 116 09.1 | 27.0 | Procyon | 244 52.8 | N 5 10.1 |
| 05 | 92 47.9 | 260 55.9 | 38.7 | 10 50.2 | 50.4 | 90 15.6 | 39.5 | 131 11.6 | 27.0 | | | |
| 06 | 107 50.4 | 275 55.5 | S 3 39.9 | 25 52.0 | N22 50.5 | 105 18.4 | S 0 39.6 | 146 14.2 | S16 27.1 | Rasalhague | 96 00.4 | N12 32.8 |
| 07 | 122 52.9 | 290 55.1 | 41.1 | 40 53.7 | 50.6 | 120 21.2 | 39.8 | 161 16.7 | 27.1 | Regulus | 207 36.7 | N11 51.5 |
| S 08 | 137 55.3 | 305 54.7 | 42.4 | 55 55.5 | 50.7 | 135 23.9 | 39.9 | 176 19.2 | 27.1 | Rigel | 281 05.5 | S 8 10.3 |
| U 09 | 152 57.8 | 320 54.3 .. | 43.6 | 70 57.2 .. | 50.9 | 150 26.7 .. | 40.0 | 191 21.7 .. | 27.1 | Rigil Kent. | 139 43.5 | S60 55.7 |
| N 10 | 168 00.3 | 335 53.9 | 44.9 | 85 59.0 | 51.0 | 165 29.4 | 40.1 | 206 24.2 | 27.1 | Sabik | 102 05.1 | S15 45.1 |
| D 11 | 183 02.7 | 350 53.5 | 46.1 | 101 00.7 | 51.1 | 180 32.2 | 40.3 | 221 26.8 | 27.1 | | | |
| A 12 | 198 05.2 | 5 53.1 | S 3 47.4 | 116 02.5 | N22 51.2 | 195 34.9 | S 0 40.4 | 236 29.3 | S16 27.2 | Schedar | 349 32.6 | N56 39.8 |
| Y 13 | 213 07.7 | 20 52.7 | 48.6 | 131 04.2 | 51.3 | 210 37.7 | 40.5 | 251 31.8 | 27.2 | Shaula | 96 13.1 | S37 07.3 |
| 14 | 228 10.1 | 35 52.3 | 49.9 | 146 06.0 | 51.5 | 225 40.4 | 40.6 | 266 34.3 | 27.2 | Sirius | 258 27.9 | S16 44.6 |
| 15 | 243 12.6 | 50 51.9 .. | 51.1 | 161 07.7 .. | 51.6 | 240 43.2 .. | 40.7 | 281 36.8 .. | 27.2 | Spica | 158 24.6 | S11 16.6 |
| 16 | 258 15.0 | 65 51.5 | 52.4 | 176 09.5 | 51.7 | 255 45.9 | 40.9 | 296 39.4 | 27.2 | Suhail | 222 47.9 | S43 31.1 |
| 17 | 273 17.5 | 80 51.1 | 53.6 | 191 11.2 | 51.8 | 270 48.7 | 41.0 | 311 41.9 | 27.2 | | | |
| 18 | 288 20.0 | 95 50.7 | S 3 54.9 | 206 13.0 | N22 51.9 | 285 51.4 | S 0 41.1 | 326 44.4 | S16 27.2 | Vega | 80 34.5 | N38 48.5 |
| 19 | 303 22.4 | 110 50.3 | 56.1 | 221 14.8 | 52.1 | 300 54.2 | 41.2 | 341 46.9 | 27.3 | Zuben'ubi | 136 58.4 | S16 08.0 |
| 20 | 318 24.9 | 125 49.8 | 57.4 | 236 16.5 | 52.2 | 315 56.9 | 41.3 | 356 49.4 | 27.3 | | | |
| 21 | 333 27.4 | 140 49.4 .. | 58.6 | 251 18.3 .. | 52.3 | 330 59.7 .. | 41.5 | 11 52.0 .. | 27.3 | | | |
| 22 | 348 29.8 | 155 49.0 | 3 59.9 | 266 20.1 | 52.4 | 346 02.5 | 41.6 | 26 54.5 | 27.3 | | | |
| 23 | 3 32.3 | 170 48.6 | S 4 01.1 | 281 21.8 | 52.5 | 1 05.2 | 41.7 | 41 57.0 | 27.3 | | | |

|  | SHA | Mer. Pass. |
|---|---|---|
| Venus | 169 31.1 | 11 36 |
| Mars | 278 23.6 | 4 20 |
| Jupiter | 357 19.2 | 23 00 |
| Saturn | 38 21.9 | 20 17 |

| | | | | | | | | | |
|---|---|---|---|---|---|---|---|---|---|
| Mer. Pass. 22 49.8 | v −0.4 | d 1.3 | v 1.7 | d 0.1 | v 2.8 | d 0.1 | v 2.5 | d 0.0 | |

| UT | SUN GHA | SUN Dec | MOON GHA | v | Dec | d | HP |
|---|---|---|---|---|---|---|---|
| **d h** | ° ′ | ° ′ | ° ′ | ′ | ° ′ | ′ | ′ |
| **7 00** | 183 00.4 | S 5 24.6 | 35 25.2 | 10.3 | S13 31.4 | 14.5 | 59.1 |
| 01 | 198 00.6 | 25.5 | 49 54.5 | 10.4 | 13 16.9 | 14.5 | 59.1 |
| 02 | 213 00.8 | 26.5 | 64 23.9 | 10.5 | 13 02.4 | 14.6 | 59.0 |
| 03 | 228 01.0 | .. 27.5 | 78 53.4 | 10.5 | 12 47.8 | 14.6 | 59.0 |
| 04 | 243 01.1 | 28.4 | 93 22.9 | 10.7 | 12 33.2 | 14.8 | 59.0 |
| 05 | 258 01.3 | 29.4 | 107 52.6 | 10.7 | 12 18.4 | 14.7 | 59.0 |
| 06 | 273 01.5 | S 5 30.3 | 122 22.3 | 10.7 | S12 03.7 | 14.9 | 59.0 |
| 07 | 288 01.7 | 31.3 | 136 52.0 | 10.9 | 11 48.8 | 14.9 | 59.0 |
| 08 | 303 01.9 | 32.2 | 151 21.9 | 10.9 | 11 33.9 | 14.9 | 59.0 |
| 09 | 318 02.0 | .. 33.2 | 165 51.8 | 10.9 | 11 19.0 | 15.0 | 59.0 |
| 10 | 333 02.2 | 34.2 | 180 21.7 | 11.1 | 11 04.0 | 15.0 | 58.9 |
| 11 | 348 02.4 | 35.1 | 194 51.8 | 11.1 | 10 49.0 | 15.1 | 58.9 |
| 12 | 3 02.6 | S 5 36.1 | 209 21.9 | 11.2 | S10 33.9 | 15.2 | 58.9 |
| 13 | 18 02.8 | 37.0 | 223 52.1 | 11.2 | 10 18.7 | 15.2 | 58.9 |
| 14 | 33 02.9 | 38.0 | 238 22.3 | 11.3 | 10 03.5 | 15.2 | 58.9 |
| 15 | 48 03.1 | .. 38.9 | 252 52.6 | 11.4 | 9 48.3 | 15.3 | 58.9 |
| 16 | 63 03.3 | 39.9 | 267 23.0 | 11.4 | 9 33.0 | 15.3 | 58.9 |
| 17 | 78 03.5 | 40.8 | 281 53.4 | 11.5 | 9 17.7 | 15.4 | 58.8 |
| 18 | 93 03.7 | S 5 41.8 | 296 23.9 | 11.6 | S 9 02.3 | 15.4 | 58.8 |
| 19 | 108 03.8 | 42.7 | 310 54.5 | 11.6 | 8 46.9 | 15.5 | 58.8 |
| 20 | 123 04.0 | 43.7 | 325 25.1 | 11.7 | 8 31.4 | 15.5 | 58.8 |
| 21 | 138 04.2 | .. 44.7 | 339 55.8 | 11.7 | 8 16.0 | 15.6 | 58.8 |
| 22 | 153 04.4 | 45.6 | 354 26.5 | 11.8 | 8 00.4 | 15.5 | 58.8 |
| 23 | 168 04.6 | 46.6 | 8 57.3 | 11.9 | 7 44.9 | 15.6 | 58.7 |
| **8 00** | 183 04.7 | S 5 47.5 | 23 28.2 | 11.9 | S 7 29.3 | 15.6 | 58.7 |
| 01 | 198 04.9 | 48.5 | 37 59.1 | 11.9 | 7 13.7 | 15.6 | 58.7 |
| 02 | 213 05.1 | 49.4 | 52 30.0 | 12.0 | 6 58.1 | 15.7 | 58.7 |
| 03 | 228 05.3 | .. 50.4 | 67 01.0 | 12.1 | 6 42.4 | 15.7 | 58.7 |
| 04 | 243 05.4 | 51.3 | 81 32.1 | 12.1 | 6 26.7 | 15.7 | 58.7 |
| 05 | 258 05.6 | 52.3 | 96 03.2 | 12.1 | 6 11.0 | 15.7 | 58.6 |
| 06 | 273 05.8 | S 5 53.2 | 110 34.3 | 12.2 | S 5 55.3 | 15.8 | 58.6 |
| 07 | 288 06.0 | 54.2 | 125 05.5 | 12.3 | 5 39.5 | 15.8 | 58.6 |
| 08 | 303 06.2 | 55.1 | 139 36.8 | 12.2 | 5 23.7 | 15.7 | 58.6 |
| 09 | 318 06.3 | .. 56.1 | 154 08.0 | 12.4 | 5 08.0 | 15.9 | 58.6 |
| 10 | 333 06.5 | 57.0 | 168 39.4 | 12.4 | 4 52.1 | 15.8 | 58.6 |
| 11 | 348 06.7 | 58.0 | 183 10.8 | 12.4 | 4 36.3 | 15.8 | 58.5 |
| 12 | 3 06.9 | S 5 58.9 | 197 42.2 | 12.4 | S 4 20.5 | 15.9 | 58.5 |
| 13 | 18 07.0 | 5 59.9 | 212 13.6 | 12.5 | 4 04.6 | 15.8 | 58.5 |
| 14 | 33 07.2 | 6 00.9 | 226 45.1 | 12.6 | 3 48.8 | 15.9 | 58.5 |
| 15 | 48 07.4 | .. 01.8 | 241 16.7 | 12.5 | 3 32.9 | 15.8 | 58.5 |
| 16 | 63 07.6 | 02.8 | 255 48.2 | 12.7 | 3 17.1 | 15.9 | 58.4 |
| 17 | 78 07.7 | 03.7 | 270 19.9 | 12.6 | 3 01.2 | 15.9 | 58.4 |
| 18 | 93 07.9 | S 6 04.7 | 284 51.5 | 12.7 | S 2 45.3 | 15.9 | 58.4 |
| 19 | 108 08.1 | 05.6 | 299 23.2 | 12.7 | 2 29.4 | 15.9 | 58.4 |
| 20 | 123 08.3 | 06.6 | 313 54.9 | 12.8 | 2 13.5 | 15.9 | 58.4 |
| 21 | 138 08.4 | .. 07.5 | 328 26.7 | 12.7 | 1 57.6 | 15.9 | 58.3 |
| 22 | 153 08.6 | 08.5 | 342 58.4 | 12.8 | 1 41.7 | 15.8 | 58.3 |
| 23 | 168 08.8 | 09.4 | 357 30.2 | 12.9 | 1 25.9 | 15.9 | 58.3 |
| **9 00** | 183 09.0 | S 6 10.4 | 12 02.1 | 12.8 | S 1 10.0 | 15.9 | 58.3 |
| 01 | 198 09.1 | 11.3 | 26 33.9 | 12.9 | 0 54.1 | 15.9 | 58.2 |
| 02 | 213 09.3 | 12.3 | 41 05.8 | 13.0 | 0 38.2 | 15.9 | 58.2 |
| 03 | 228 09.5 | .. 13.2 | 55 37.8 | 12.9 | 0 22.4 | 15.9 | 58.2 |
| 04 | 243 09.6 | 14.2 | 70 09.7 | 13.0 | S 0 06.5 | 15.8 | 58.2 |
| 05 | 258 09.8 | 15.1 | 84 41.7 | 12.9 | N 0 09.3 | 15.8 | 58.2 |
| 06 | 273 10.0 | S 6 16.1 | 99 13.6 | 13.1 | N 0 25.1 | 15.8 | 58.1 |
| 07 | 288 10.2 | 17.0 | 113 45.7 | 13.0 | 0 40.9 | 15.8 | 58.1 |
| 08 | 303 10.3 | 18.0 | 128 17.7 | 13.0 | 0 56.7 | 15.8 | 58.1 |
| 09 | 318 10.5 | .. 18.9 | 142 49.7 | 13.1 | 1 12.5 | 15.8 | 58.1 |
| 10 | 333 10.7 | 19.9 | 157 21.8 | 13.1 | 1 28.3 | 15.7 | 58.0 |
| 11 | 348 10.9 | 20.8 | 171 53.9 | 13.1 | 1 44.0 | 15.7 | 58.0 |
| 12 | 3 11.0 | S 6 21.8 | 186 26.0 | 13.1 | N 1 59.7 | 15.7 | 58.0 |
| 13 | 18 11.2 | 22.7 | 200 58.1 | 13.1 | 2 15.4 | 15.7 | 58.0 |
| 14 | 33 11.4 | 23.7 | 215 30.2 | 13.2 | 2 31.1 | 15.7 | 58.0 |
| 15 | 48 11.5 | .. 24.6 | 230 02.4 | 13.1 | 2 46.8 | 15.6 | 57.9 |
| 16 | 63 11.7 | 25.5 | 244 34.5 | 13.2 | 3 02.4 | 15.6 | 57.9 |
| 17 | 78 11.9 | 26.5 | 259 06.7 | 13.1 | 3 18.0 | 15.6 | 57.9 |
| 18 | 93 12.1 | S 6 27.4 | 273 38.8 | 13.2 | N 3 33.6 | 15.5 | 57.9 |
| 19 | 108 12.2 | 28.4 | 288 11.0 | 13.2 | 3 49.1 | 15.5 | 57.8 |
| 20 | 123 12.4 | 29.3 | 302 43.2 | 13.2 | 4 04.6 | 15.5 | 57.8 |
| 21 | 138 12.6 | .. 30.3 | 317 15.4 | 13.2 | 4 20.1 | 15.4 | 57.8 |
| 22 | 153 12.7 | 31.2 | 331 47.6 | 13.2 | 4 35.5 | 15.3 | 57.7 |
| 23 | 168 12.9 | 32.2 | 346 19.8 | 13.2 | N 4 51.0 | 15.3 | 57.7 |
| | SD 16.0 | d 1.0 | SD 16.1 | | 15.9 | | 15.8 |

The days of the week marked in the left margin: **FRIDAY**, **SATURDAY**, **SUNDAY**.

### Twilight / Sunrise / Moonrise

| Lat. | Twilight Naut. | Twilight Civil | Sunrise | Moonrise 7 | 8 | 9 | 10 |
|---|---|---|---|---|---|---|---|
| ° | h m | h m | h m | h m | h m | h m | h m |
| N 72 | 04 23 | 05 42 | 06 50 | 18 14 | 17 37 | 17 04 | 16 29 |
| N 70 | 04 31 | 05 42 | 06 43 | 18 00 | 17 33 | 17 09 | 16 43 |
| 68 | 04 37 | 05 42 | 06 38 | 17 49 | 17 30 | 17 12 | 16 53 |
| 66 | 04 42 | 05 41 | 06 33 | 17 40 | 17 27 | 17 15 | 17 03 |
| 64 | 04 46 | 05 41 | 06 29 | 17 32 | 17 25 | 17 18 | 17 10 |
| 62 | 04 49 | 05 41 | 06 25 | 17 25 | 17 23 | 17 20 | 17 17 |
| 60 | 04 52 | 05 40 | 06 22 | 17 20 | 17 21 | 17 22 | 17 23 |
| N 58 | 04 54 | 05 40 | 06 19 | 17 14 | 17 19 | 17 23 | 17 28 |
| 56 | 04 56 | 05 40 | 06 17 | 17 10 | 17 18 | 17 25 | 17 33 |
| 54 | 04 58 | 05 39 | 06 15 | 17 06 | 17 16 | 17 26 | 17 37 |
| 52 | 05 00 | 05 39 | 06 12 | 17 02 | 17 15 | 17 28 | 17 41 |
| 50 | 05 01 | 05 38 | 06 11 | 16 58 | 17 14 | 17 29 | 17 41 |
| 45 | 05 03 | 05 37 | 06 07 | 16 51 | 17 12 | 17 32 | 17 52 |
| N 40 | 05 05 | 05 36 | 06 03 | 16 45 | 17 10 | 17 34 | 17 58 |
| 35 | 05 05 | 05 35 | 06 00 | 16 39 | 17 08 | 17 36 | 18 03 |
| 30 | 05 06 | 05 33 | 05 57 | 16 34 | 17 06 | 17 37 | 18 08 |
| 20 | 05 05 | 05 31 | 05 53 | 16 26 | 17 04 | 17 40 | 18 17 |
| N 10 | 05 03 | 05 27 | 05 48 | 16 18 | 17 01 | 17 43 | 18 24 |
| 0 | 04 59 | 05 23 | 05 44 | 16 11 | 16 59 | 17 46 | 18 31 |
| S 10 | 04 54 | 05 19 | 05 40 | 16 04 | 16 57 | 17 48 | 18 39 |
| 20 | 04 47 | 05 13 | 05 35 | 15 57 | 16 55 | 17 51 | 18 46 |
| 30 | 04 38 | 05 06 | 05 30 | 15 48 | 16 52 | 17 54 | 18 55 |
| 35 | 04 31 | 05 01 | 05 27 | 15 43 | 16 50 | 17 56 | 19 00 |
| 40 | 04 23 | 04 56 | 05 23 | 15 38 | 16 49 | 17 58 | 19 06 |
| 45 | 04 14 | 04 49 | 05 19 | 15 31 | 16 47 | 18 00 | 19 13 |
| S 50 | 04 01 | 04 41 | 05 14 | 15 23 | 16 44 | 18 03 | 19 21 |
| 52 | 03 55 | 04 37 | 05 12 | 15 19 | 16 43 | 18 05 | 19 25 |
| 54 | 03 49 | 04 33 | 05 09 | 15 15 | 16 42 | 18 06 | 19 29 |
| 56 | 03 41 | 04 28 | 05 06 | 15 11 | 16 41 | 18 08 | 19 34 |
| 58 | 03 32 | 04 23 | 05 03 | 15 06 | 16 39 | 18 10 | 19 40 |
| S 60 | 03 22 | 04 16 | 05 00 | 15 00 | 16 37 | 18 12 | 19 46 |

### Sunset / Twilight / Moonset

| Lat. | Sunset | Twilight Civil | Twilight Naut. | Moonset 7 | 8 | 9 | 10 |
|---|---|---|---|---|---|---|---|
| ° | h m | h m | h m | h m | h m | h m | h m |
| N 72 | 16 43 | 17 50 | 19 09 | 00 27 | 03 06 | 05 23 | 07 38 |
| N 70 | 16 50 | 17 51 | 19 02 | 00 56 | 03 16 | 05 23 | 07 28 |
| 68 | 16 56 | 17 51 | 18 56 | 01 17 | 03 25 | 05 23 | 07 19 |
| 66 | 17 01 | 17 52 | 18 51 | 01 33 | 03 32 | 05 23 | 07 12 |
| 64 | 17 05 | 17 52 | 18 47 | 01 46 | 03 37 | 05 23 | 07 06 |
| 62 | 17 09 | 17 53 | 18 44 | 01 58 | 03 42 | 05 23 | 07 01 |
| 60 | 17 12 | 17 53 | 18 41 | 02 07 | 03 47 | 05 23 | 06 56 |
| N 58 | 17 15 | 17 54 | 18 39 | 02 15 | 03 51 | 05 23 | 06 53 |
| 56 | 17 17 | 17 54 | 18 37 | 02 22 | 03 54 | 05 22 | 06 49 |
| 54 | 17 20 | 17 55 | 18 36 | 02 29 | 03 57 | 05 22 | 06 46 |
| 52 | 17 22 | 17 55 | 18 34 | 02 34 | 04 00 | 05 22 | 06 43 |
| 50 | 17 24 | 17 56 | 18 33 | 02 40 | 04 02 | 05 22 | 06 41 |
| 45 | 17 28 | 17 57 | 18 31 | 02 51 | 04 07 | 05 22 | 06 35 |
| N 40 | 17 31 | 17 58 | 18 30 | 03 00 | 04 12 | 05 22 | 06 31 |
| 35 | 17 35 | 18 00 | 18 29 | 03 07 | 04 16 | 05 22 | 06 27 |
| 30 | 17 37 | 18 01 | 18 29 | 03 14 | 04 19 | 05 22 | 06 23 |
| 20 | 17 42 | 18 04 | 18 30 | 03 26 | 04 25 | 05 22 | 06 17 |
| N 10 | 17 47 | 18 08 | 18 32 | 03 36 | 04 30 | 05 22 | 06 12 |
| 0 | 17 51 | 18 12 | 18 36 | 03 45 | 04 34 | 05 21 | 06 07 |
| S 10 | 17 55 | 18 16 | 18 41 | 03 55 | 04 39 | 05 21 | 06 02 |
| 20 | 18 00 | 18 22 | 18 48 | 04 05 | 04 44 | 05 21 | 05 57 |
| 30 | 18 05 | 18 30 | 18 58 | 04 16 | 04 49 | 05 21 | 05 51 |
| 35 | 18 09 | 18 34 | 19 05 | 04 22 | 04 52 | 05 20 | 05 48 |
| 40 | 18 12 | 18 40 | 19 12 | 04 29 | 04 56 | 05 20 | 05 44 |
| 45 | 18 17 | 18 47 | 19 22 | 04 38 | 05 00 | 05 20 | 05 40 |
| S 50 | 18 22 | 18 55 | 19 34 | 04 48 | 05 05 | 05 20 | 05 35 |
| 52 | 18 24 | 18 59 | 19 41 | 04 52 | 05 07 | 05 20 | 05 32 |
| 54 | 18 27 | 19 04 | 19 48 | 04 57 | 05 09 | 05 20 | 05 30 |
| 56 | 18 30 | 19 09 | 19 56 | 05 03 | 05 12 | 05 19 | 05 27 |
| 58 | 18 33 | 19 14 | 20 05 | 05 09 | 05 15 | 05 19 | 05 24 |
| S 60 | 18 37 | 19 21 | 20 16 | 05 16 | 05 18 | 05 19 | 05 20 |

| Day | SUN Eqn. of Time 00h | 12h | Mer. Pass. | MOON Mer. Pass. Upper | Lower | Age | Phase |
|---|---|---|---|---|---|---|---|
| d | m s | m s | h m | h m | h m | d | % |
| 7 | 12 01 | 12 10 | 11 48 | 22 23 | 09 58 | 12 | 93 |
| 8 | 12 19 | 12 27 | 11 48 | 23 10 | 10 47 | 13 | 98 |
| 9 | 12 35 | 12 44 | 11 47 | 23 56 | 11 33 | 14 | 100 |

| UT | ARIES | VENUS −3.9 | | MARS −0.8 | | JUPITER −2.9 | | SATURN +0.5 | | STARS | | |
|---|---|---|---|---|---|---|---|---|---|---|---|---|
| | GHA | GHA | Dec | GHA | Dec | GHA | Dec | GHA | Dec | Name | SHA | Dec |
| d h | ° ′ | ° ′ | ° ′ | ° ′ | ° ′ | ° ′ | ° ′ | ° ′ | ° ′ | | ° ′ | ° ′ |
| 10 00 | 18 34.8 | 185 48.2 | S 4 02.4 | 296 23.6 | N22 52.6 | 16 08.0 | S 0 41.8 | 56 59.5 | S16 27.3 | Acamar | 315 12.8 | S40 12.7 |
| 01 | 33 37.2 | 200 47.8 | 03.6 | 311 25.4 | 52.8 | 31 10.7 | 41.9 | 72 02.0 | 27.4 | Achernar | 335 21.0 | S57 07.2 |
| 02 | 48 39.7 | 215 47.4 | 04.8 | 326 27.1 | 52.9 | 46 13.5 | 42.1 | 87 04.6 | 27.4 | Acrux | 173 02.8 | S63 13.3 |
| 03 | 63 42.2 | 230 47.0 | .. 06.1 | 341 28.9 | .. 53.0 | 61 16.2 | .. 42.2 | 102 07.1 | .. 27.4 | Adhara | 255 07.3 | S28 59.9 |
| 04 | 78 44.6 | 245 46.6 | 07.3 | 356 30.7 | 53.1 | 76 19.0 | 42.3 | 117 09.6 | 27.4 | Aldebaran | 290 41.6 | N16 33.3 |
| 05 | 93 47.1 | 260 46.2 | 08.6 | 11 32.4 | 53.2 | 91 21.7 | 42.4 | 132 12.1 | 27.4 | | | |
| 06 | 108 49.5 | 275 45.8 | S 4 09.8 | 26 34.2 | N22 53.4 | 106 24.5 | S 0 42.6 | 147 14.6 | S16 27.4 | Alioth | 166 15.2 | N55 50.3 |
| 07 | 123 52.0 | 290 45.4 | 11.1 | 41 36.0 | 53.5 | 121 27.2 | 42.7 | 162 17.2 | 27.4 | Alkaid | 152 54.0 | N49 12.1 |
| 08 | 138 54.5 | 305 45.0 | 12.3 | 56 37.8 | 53.6 | 136 30.0 | 42.8 | 177 19.7 | 27.5 | Alnair | 27 35.0 | S46 51.2 |
| M 09 | 153 56.9 | 320 44.6 | .. 13.6 | 71 39.6 | .. 53.7 | 151 32.7 | .. 42.9 | 192 22.2 | .. 27.5 | Alnilam | 275 39.5 | S 1 11.1 |
| O 10 | 168 59.4 | 335 44.1 | 14.8 | 86 41.3 | 53.8 | 166 35.5 | 43.0 | 207 24.7 | 27.5 | Alphard | 217 49.8 | S 8 45.2 |
| N 11 | 184 01.9 | 350 43.7 | 16.1 | 101 43.1 | 53.9 | 181 38.2 | 43.2 | 222 27.2 | 27.5 | | | |
| D 12 | 199 04.3 | 5 43.3 | S 4 17.3 | 116 44.9 | N22 54.1 | 196 41.0 | S 0 43.3 | 237 29.7 | S16 27.5 | Alphecca | 126 05.6 | N26 38.5 |
| A 13 | 214 06.8 | 20 42.9 | 18.5 | 131 46.7 | 54.2 | 211 43.7 | 43.4 | 252 32.3 | 27.5 | Alpheratz | 357 36.4 | N29 13.0 |
| Y 14 | 229 09.3 | 35 42.5 | 19.8 | 146 48.5 | 54.3 | 226 46.5 | 43.5 | 267 34.8 | 27.5 | Altair | 62 01.7 | N 8 55.8 |
| 15 | 244 11.7 | 50 42.1 | .. 21.0 | 161 50.2 | .. 54.4 | 241 49.2 | .. 43.6 | 282 37.3 | .. 27.6 | Ankaa | 353 08.6 | S42 11.0 |
| 16 | 259 14.2 | 65 41.7 | 22.3 | 176 52.0 | 54.5 | 256 52.0 | 43.8 | 297 39.8 | 27.6 | Antares | 112 18.4 | S26 28.9 |
| 17 | 274 16.6 | 80 41.3 | 23.5 | 191 53.8 | 54.6 | 271 54.7 | 43.9 | 312 42.3 | 27.6 | | | |
| 18 | 289 19.1 | 95 40.9 | S 4 24.8 | 206 55.6 | N22 54.8 | 286 57.5 | S 0 44.0 | 327 44.8 | S16 27.6 | Arcturus | 145 50.0 | N19 04.0 |
| 19 | 304 21.6 | 110 40.5 | 26.0 | 221 57.4 | 54.9 | 302 00.2 | 44.1 | 342 47.4 | 27.6 | Atria | 107 14.6 | S69 04.2 |
| 20 | 319 24.0 | 125 40.1 | 27.3 | 236 59.2 | 55.0 | 317 03.0 | 44.2 | 357 49.9 | 27.6 | Avior | 234 15.7 | S59 34.5 |
| 21 | 334 26.5 | 140 39.6 | .. 28.5 | 252 01.0 | .. 55.1 | 332 05.7 | .. 44.3 | 12 52.4 | .. 27.6 | Bellatrix | 278 24.7 | N 6 22.3 |
| 22 | 349 29.0 | 155 39.2 | 29.7 | 267 02.8 | 55.2 | 347 08.5 | 44.5 | 27 54.9 | 27.7 | Betelgeuse | 270 54.0 | N 7 24.8 |
| 23 | 4 31.4 | 170 38.8 | 31.0 | 282 04.6 | 55.4 | 2 11.2 | 44.6 | 42 57.4 | 27.7 | | | |
| 11 00 | 19 33.9 | 185 38.4 | S 4 32.2 | 297 06.4 | N22 55.5 | 17 14.0 | S 0 44.7 | 57 59.9 | S16 27.7 | Canopus | 263 53.1 | S52 42.1 |
| 01 | 34 36.4 | 200 38.0 | 33.5 | 312 08.1 | 55.6 | 32 16.7 | 44.8 | 73 02.4 | 27.7 | Capella | 280 24.4 | N46 01.1 |
| 02 | 49 38.8 | 215 37.6 | 34.7 | 327 09.9 | 55.7 | 47 19.5 | 44.9 | 88 05.0 | 27.7 | Deneb | 49 26.9 | N45 21.9 |
| 03 | 64 41.3 | 230 37.2 | .. 36.0 | 342 11.7 | .. 55.8 | 62 22.2 | .. 45.1 | 103 07.5 | .. 27.7 | Denebola | 182 27.2 | N14 26.9 |
| 04 | 79 43.8 | 245 36.8 | 37.2 | 357 13.5 | 55.9 | 77 25.0 | 45.2 | 118 10.0 | 27.7 | Diphda | 348 48.9 | S17 51.7 |
| 05 | 94 46.2 | 260 36.4 | 38.4 | 12 15.3 | 56.1 | 92 27.7 | 45.3 | 133 12.5 | 27.8 | | | |
| 06 | 109 48.7 | 275 35.9 | S 4 39.7 | 27 17.1 | N22 56.2 | 107 30.5 | S 0 45.4 | 148 15.0 | S16 27.8 | Dubhe | 193 43.9 | N61 37.7 |
| 07 | 124 51.1 | 290 35.5 | 40.9 | 42 19.0 | 56.3 | 122 33.2 | 45.5 | 163 17.5 | 27.8 | Elnath | 278 04.1 | N28 37.6 |
| T 08 | 139 53.6 | 305 35.1 | 42.2 | 57 20.8 | 56.4 | 137 36.0 | 45.7 | 178 20.0 | 27.8 | Eltanin | 90 43.2 | N51 29.4 |
| U 09 | 154 56.1 | 320 34.7 | .. 43.4 | 72 22.6 | .. 56.5 | 152 38.7 | .. 45.8 | 193 22.6 | .. 27.8 | Enif | 33 40.5 | N 9 58.9 |
| E 10 | 169 58.5 | 335 34.3 | 44.7 | 87 24.4 | 56.6 | 167 41.4 | 45.9 | 208 25.1 | 27.8 | Fomalhaut | 15 16.3 | S29 30.2 |
| S 11 | 185 01.0 | 350 33.9 | 45.9 | 102 26.2 | 56.8 | 182 44.2 | 46.0 | 223 27.6 | 27.8 | | | |
| D 12 | 200 03.5 | 5 33.5 | S 4 47.1 | 117 28.0 | N22 56.9 | 197 46.9 | S 0 46.1 | 238 30.1 | S16 27.9 | Gacrux | 171 54.3 | S57 14.2 |
| A 13 | 215 05.9 | 20 33.1 | 48.4 | 132 29.8 | 57.0 | 212 49.7 | 46.2 | 253 32.6 | 27.9 | Gienah | 175 45.8 | S17 39.9 |
| Y 14 | 230 08.4 | 35 32.6 | 49.6 | 147 31.6 | 57.1 | 227 52.4 | 46.4 | 268 35.1 | 27.9 | Hadar | 148 39.3 | S60 28.9 |
| 15 | 245 10.9 | 50 32.2 | .. 50.9 | 162 33.4 | .. 57.2 | 242 55.2 | .. 46.5 | 283 37.6 | .. 27.9 | Hamal | 327 53.0 | N23 34.2 |
| 16 | 260 13.3 | 65 31.8 | 52.1 | 177 35.2 | 57.3 | 257 57.9 | 46.6 | 298 40.2 | 27.9 | Kaus Aust. | 83 35.1 | S34 22.5 |
| 17 | 275 15.8 | 80 31.4 | 53.3 | 192 37.0 | 57.5 | 273 00.7 | 46.7 | 313 42.7 | 27.9 | | | |
| 18 | 290 18.2 | 95 31.0 | S 4 54.6 | 207 38.9 | N22 57.6 | 288 03.4 | S 0 46.8 | 328 45.2 | S16 27.9 | Kochab | 137 20.8 | N74 03.9 |
| 19 | 305 20.7 | 110 30.6 | 55.8 | 222 40.7 | 57.7 | 303 06.2 | 47.0 | 343 47.7 | 27.9 | Markab | 13 31.5 | N15 19.8 |
| 20 | 320 23.2 | 125 30.2 | 57.1 | 237 42.5 | 57.8 | 318 08.9 | 47.1 | 358 50.2 | 28.0 | Menkar | 314 07.8 | N 4 10.8 |
| 21 | 335 25.6 | 140 29.7 | .. 58.3 | 252 44.3 | .. 57.9 | 333 11.7 | .. 47.2 | 13 52.7 | .. 28.0 | Menkent | 148 00.2 | S36 28.8 |
| 22 | 350 28.1 | 155 29.3 | 59.6 | 267 46.1 | 58.0 | 348 14.4 | 47.3 | 28 55.2 | 28.0 | Miaplacidus | 221 39.1 | S69 48.2 |
| 23 | 5 30.6 | 170 28.9 | 5 00.8 | 282 48.0 | 58.1 | 3 17.2 | 47.4 | 43 57.7 | 28.0 | | | |
| 12 00 | 20 33.0 | 185 28.5 | S 5 02.0 | 297 49.8 | N22 58.3 | 18 19.9 | S 0 47.5 | 59 00.2 | S16 28.0 | Mirfak | 308 30.5 | N49 56.4 |
| 01 | 35 35.5 | 200 28.1 | 03.3 | 312 51.6 | 58.4 | 33 22.6 | 47.7 | 74 02.8 | 28.0 | Nunki | 75 50.1 | S26 16.1 |
| 02 | 50 38.0 | 215 27.7 | 04.5 | 327 53.4 | 58.5 | 48 25.4 | 47.8 | 89 05.3 | 28.0 | Peacock | 53 08.5 | S56 39.9 |
| 03 | 65 40.4 | 230 27.2 | .. 05.7 | 342 55.3 | .. 58.6 | 63 28.1 | .. 47.9 | 104 07.8 | .. 28.0 | Pollux | 243 19.6 | N27 58.3 |
| 04 | 80 42.9 | 245 26.8 | 07.0 | 357 57.1 | 58.7 | 78 30.9 | 48.0 | 119 10.3 | 28.1 | Procyon | 244 52.8 | N 5 10.1 |
| 05 | 95 45.4 | 260 26.4 | 08.2 | 12 58.9 | 58.8 | 93 33.6 | 48.1 | 134 12.8 | 28.1 | | | |
| 06 | 110 47.8 | 275 26.0 | S 5 09.5 | 28 00.8 | N22 59.0 | 108 36.4 | S 0 48.2 | 149 15.3 | S16 28.1 | Rasalhague | 96 00.4 | N12 32.8 |
| W 07 | 125 50.3 | 290 25.6 | 10.7 | 43 02.6 | 59.1 | 123 39.1 | 48.4 | 164 17.8 | 28.1 | Regulus | 207 36.7 | N11 51.5 |
| E 08 | 140 52.7 | 305 25.2 | 11.9 | 58 04.4 | 59.2 | 138 41.9 | 48.5 | 179 20.3 | 28.1 | Rigel | 281 05.5 | S 8 10.4 |
| D 09 | 155 55.2 | 320 24.8 | .. 13.2 | 73 06.3 | .. 59.3 | 153 44.6 | .. 48.6 | 194 22.8 | .. 28.1 | Rigil Kent. | 139 43.5 | S60 55.7 |
| N 10 | 170 57.7 | 335 24.3 | 14.4 | 88 08.1 | 59.4 | 168 47.4 | 48.7 | 209 25.3 | 28.1 | Sabik | 102 05.1 | S15 45.1 |
| 11 | 186 00.1 | 350 23.9 | 15.7 | 103 09.9 | 59.5 | 183 50.1 | 48.8 | 224 27.9 | 28.1 | | | |
| S 12 | 201 02.6 | 5 23.5 | S 5 16.9 | 118 11.8 | N22 59.7 | 198 52.8 | S 0 48.9 | 239 30.4 | S16 28.2 | Schedar | 349 32.6 | N56 39.8 |
| D 13 | 216 05.1 | 20 23.1 | 18.1 | 133 13.6 | 59.8 | 213 55.6 | 49.1 | 254 32.9 | 28.2 | Shaula | 96 13.1 | S37 07.3 |
| A 14 | 231 07.5 | 35 22.7 | 19.4 | 148 15.4 | 22 59.9 | 228 58.3 | 49.2 | 269 35.4 | 28.2 | Sirius | 258 27.8 | S16 44.6 |
| Y 15 | 246 10.0 | 50 22.2 | .. 20.6 | 163 17.3 | 23 00.0 | 244 01.1 | .. 49.3 | 284 37.9 | .. 28.2 | Spica | 158 24.6 | S11 16.6 |
| 16 | 261 12.5 | 65 21.8 | 21.8 | 178 19.1 | 00.1 | 259 03.8 | 49.4 | 299 40.4 | 28.2 | Suhail | 222 47.9 | S43 31.1 |
| 17 | 276 14.9 | 80 21.4 | 23.1 | 193 21.0 | 00.2 | 274 06.6 | 49.5 | 314 42.9 | 28.2 | | | |
| 18 | 291 17.4 | 95 21.0 | S 5 24.3 | 208 22.8 | N23 00.3 | 289 09.3 | S 0 49.6 | 329 45.4 | S16 28.2 | Vega | 80 34.6 | N38 48.5 |
| 19 | 306 19.9 | 110 20.6 | 25.5 | 223 24.7 | 00.5 | 304 12.0 | 49.8 | 344 47.9 | 28.2 | Zuben'ubi | 136 58.4 | S16 08.0 |
| 20 | 321 22.3 | 125 20.1 | 26.8 | 238 26.5 | 00.6 | 319 14.8 | 49.9 | 359 50.4 | 28.3 | | SHA | Mer. Pass. |
| 21 | 336 24.8 | 140 19.7 | .. 28.0 | 253 28.4 | .. 00.7 | 334 17.5 | .. 50.0 | 14 52.9 | .. 28.3 | | ° ′ | h m |
| 22 | 351 27.2 | 155 19.3 | 29.3 | 268 30.2 | 00.8 | 349 20.3 | 50.1 | 29 55.4 | 28.3 | Venus | 166 04.5 | 11 38 |
| 23 | 6 29.7 | 170 18.9 | 30.5 | 283 32.1 | 00.9 | 4 23.0 | 50.2 | 44 58.0 | 28.3 | Mars | 277 32.5 | 4 11 |
| | h m | | | | | | | | | Jupiter | 357 40.1 | 22 47 |
| Mer. Pass. 22 38.0 | | v −0.4 | d 1.2 | v 1.8 | d 0.1 | v 2.7 | d 0.1 | v 2.5 | d 0.0 | Saturn | 38 26.0 | 20 05 |

| UT | SUN GHA | SUN Dec | MOON GHA | v | MOON Dec | d | HP |
|---|---|---|---|---|---|---|---|
| d h | ° ′ | ° ′ | ° ′ | ′ | ° ′ | ′ | ′ |
| **10** 00 | 183 13.1 | S 6 33.1 | 0 52.0 | 13.2 | N 5 06.3 | 15.4 | 57.7 |
| 01 | 198 13.2 | 34.1 | 15 24.2 | 13.2 | 5 21.7 | 15.3 | 57.7 |
| 02 | 213 13.4 | 35.0 | 29 56.4 | 13.2 | 5 37.0 | 15.2 | 57.7 |
| 03 | 228 13.6 .. | 36.0 | 44 28.6 | 13.3 | 5 52.2 | 15.2 | 57.6 |
| 04 | 243 13.7 | 36.9 | 59 00.9 | 13.2 | 6 07.4 | 15.2 | 57.6 |
| 05 | 258 13.9 | 37.9 | 73 33.1 | 13.2 | 6 22.6 | 15.2 | 57.6 |
| 06 | 273 14.1 | S 6 38.8 | 88 05.3 | 13.2 | N 6 37.8 | 15.1 | 57.6 |
| M 07 | 288 14.2 | 39.8 | 102 37.5 | 13.2 | 6 52.9 | 15.0 | 57.5 |
| O 08 | 303 14.4 | 40.7 | 117 09.7 | 13.2 | 7 07.9 | 15.0 | 57.5 |
| N 09 | 318 14.6 .. | 41.6 | 131 41.9 | 13.2 | 7 22.9 | 15.0 | 57.5 |
| D 10 | 333 14.7 | 42.6 | 146 14.1 | 13.2 | 7 37.9 | 14.9 | 57.4 |
| A 11 | 348 14.9 | 43.5 | 160 46.3 | 13.1 | 7 52.8 | 14.8 | 57.4 |
| Y 12 | 3 15.1 | S 6 44.5 | 175 18.4 | 13.2 | N 8 07.6 | 14.8 | 57.4 |
| 13 | 18 15.2 | 45.4 | 189 50.6 | 13.2 | 8 22.4 | 14.8 | 57.4 |
| 14 | 33 15.4 | 46.4 | 204 22.8 | 13.1 | 8 37.2 | 14.7 | 57.3 |
| 15 | 48 15.6 .. | 47.3 | 218 54.9 | 13.1 | 8 51.9 | 14.6 | 57.3 |
| 16 | 63 15.7 | 48.3 | 233 27.0 | 13.2 | 9 06.5 | 14.6 | 57.3 |
| 17 | 78 15.9 | 49.2 | 247 59.2 | 13.1 | 9 21.1 | 14.5 | 57.3 |
| 18 | 93 16.1 | S 6 50.1 | 262 31.3 | 13.1 | N 9 35.6 | 14.5 | 57.2 |
| 19 | 108 16.2 | 51.1 | 277 03.4 | 13.1 | 9 50.1 | 14.4 | 57.2 |
| 20 | 123 16.4 | 52.0 | 291 35.5 | 13.0 | 10 04.5 | 14.4 | 57.2 |
| 21 | 138 16.6 .. | 53.0 | 306 07.5 | 13.1 | 10 18.9 | 14.2 | 57.2 |
| 22 | 153 16.7 | 53.9 | 320 39.6 | 13.0 | 10 33.1 | 14.3 | 57.1 |
| 23 | 168 16.9 | 54.9 | 335 11.6 | 13.0 | 10 47.4 | 14.1 | 57.1 |
| **11** 00 | 183 17.1 | S 6 55.8 | 349 43.6 | 13.0 | N11 01.5 | 14.1 | 57.1 |
| 01 | 198 17.2 | 56.7 | 4 15.6 | 13.0 | 11 15.6 | 14.1 | 57.0 |
| 02 | 213 17.4 | 57.7 | 18 47.6 | 13.0 | 11 29.7 | 13.9 | 57.0 |
| 03 | 228 17.6 .. | 58.6 | 33 19.6 | 12.9 | 11 43.6 | 13.9 | 57.0 |
| 04 | 243 17.7 | 6 59.6 | 47 51.5 | 12.9 | 11 57.5 | 13.9 | 57.0 |
| 05 | 258 17.9 | 7 00.5 | 62 23.4 | 12.9 | 12 11.4 | 13.7 | 56.9 |
| 06 | 273 18.0 | S 7 01.5 | 76 55.3 | 12.9 | N12 25.1 | 13.7 | 56.9 |
| T 07 | 288 18.2 | 02.4 | 91 27.2 | 12.9 | 12 38.8 | 13.6 | 56.9 |
| U 08 | 303 18.4 | 03.3 | 105 59.1 | 12.8 | 12 52.4 | 13.6 | 56.8 |
| E 09 | 318 18.5 .. | 04.3 | 120 30.9 | 12.8 | 13 06.0 | 13.5 | 56.8 |
| S 10 | 333 18.7 | 05.2 | 135 02.7 | 12.8 | 13 19.5 | 13.4 | 56.8 |
| D 11 | 348 18.9 | 06.2 | 149 34.5 | 12.7 | 13 32.9 | 13.3 | 56.8 |
| A 12 | 3 19.0 | S 7 07.1 | 164 06.2 | 12.7 | N13 46.2 | 13.2 | 56.7 |
| Y 13 | 18 19.2 | 08.1 | 178 37.9 | 12.7 | 13 59.4 | 13.2 | 56.7 |
| 14 | 33 19.3 | 09.0 | 193 09.6 | 12.7 | 14 12.6 | 13.1 | 56.7 |
| 15 | 48 19.5 .. | 09.9 | 207 41.3 | 12.7 | 14 25.7 | 13.0 | 56.7 |
| 16 | 63 19.7 | 10.9 | 222 13.0 | 12.6 | 14 38.7 | 12.9 | 56.6 |
| 17 | 78 19.8 | 11.8 | 236 44.6 | 12.6 | 14 51.6 | 12.9 | 56.6 |
| 18 | 93 20.0 | S 7 12.8 | 251 16.2 | 12.5 | N15 04.5 | 12.7 | 56.6 |
| 19 | 108 20.1 | 13.7 | 265 47.7 | 12.5 | 15 17.2 | 12.7 | 56.5 |
| 20 | 123 20.3 | 14.6 | 280 19.2 | 12.5 | 15 29.9 | 12.6 | 56.5 |
| 21 | 138 20.5 .. | 15.6 | 294 50.7 | 12.5 | 15 42.5 | 12.5 | 56.5 |
| 22 | 153 20.6 | 16.5 | 309 22.2 | 12.4 | 15 55.0 | 12.4 | 56.5 |
| 23 | 168 20.8 | 17.5 | 323 53.6 | 12.4 | 16 07.4 | 12.4 | 56.4 |
| **12** 00 | 183 20.9 | S 7 18.4 | 338 25.0 | 12.4 | N16 19.8 | 12.2 | 56.4 |
| 01 | 198 21.1 | 19.3 | 352 56.4 | 12.3 | 16 32.0 | 12.2 | 56.4 |
| 02 | 213 21.3 | 20.3 | 7 27.7 | 12.3 | 16 44.2 | 12.0 | 56.4 |
| 03 | 228 21.4 .. | 21.2 | 21 59.0 | 12.3 | 16 56.2 | 12.0 | 56.3 |
| 04 | 243 21.6 | 22.1 | 36 30.3 | 12.2 | 17 08.2 | 11.9 | 56.3 |
| 05 | 258 21.7 | 23.1 | 51 01.5 | 12.2 | 17 20.1 | 11.8 | 56.3 |
| 06 | 273 21.9 | S 7 24.0 | 65 32.7 | 12.1 | N17 31.9 | 11.7 | 56.2 |
| W 07 | 288 22.0 | 25.0 | 80 03.8 | 12.2 | 17 43.6 | 11.6 | 56.2 |
| E 08 | 303 22.2 | 25.9 | 94 35.0 | 12.1 | 17 55.2 | 11.5 | 56.2 |
| D 09 | 318 22.4 .. | 26.8 | 109 06.1 | 12.0 | 18 06.7 | 11.4 | 56.2 |
| N 10 | 333 22.5 | 27.8 | 123 37.1 | 12.0 | 18 18.1 | 11.3 | 56.1 |
| E 11 | 348 22.7 | 28.7 | 138 08.1 | 12.0 | 18 29.4 | 11.2 | 56.1 |
| S 12 | 3 22.8 | S 7 29.6 | 152 39.1 | 11.9 | N18 40.6 | 11.1 | 56.1 |
| D 13 | 18 23.0 | 30.6 | 167 10.0 | 12.0 | 18 51.7 | 11.0 | 56.1 |
| A 14 | 33 23.1 | 31.5 | 181 41.0 | 11.8 | 19 02.7 | 10.9 | 56.0 |
| Y 15 | 48 23.3 .. | 32.5 | 196 11.8 | 11.9 | 19 13.6 | 10.9 | 56.0 |
| 16 | 63 23.5 | 33.4 | 210 42.7 | 11.7 | 19 24.5 | 10.7 | 56.0 |
| 17 | 78 23.6 | 34.3 | 225 13.4 | 11.8 | 19 35.2 | 10.6 | 55.9 |
| 18 | 93 23.8 | S 7 35.3 | 239 44.2 | 11.7 | N19 45.8 | 10.5 | 55.9 |
| 19 | 108 23.9 | 36.2 | 254 14.9 | 11.7 | 19 56.3 | 10.4 | 55.9 |
| 20 | 123 24.1 | 37.1 | 268 45.6 | 11.6 | 20 06.7 | 10.3 | 55.9 |
| 21 | 138 24.2 .. | 38.1 | 283 16.2 | 11.6 | 20 17.0 | 10.2 | 55.8 |
| 22 | 153 24.4 | 39.0 | 297 46.8 | 11.6 | 20 27.2 | 10.0 | 55.8 |
| 23 | 168 24.5 | 39.9 | 312 17.4 | 11.5 | N20 37.2 | 10.0 | 55.8 |
| | SD 16.0 | d 0.9 | SD 15.6 | | 15.5 | | 15.3 |

| Lat. | Twilight Naut. | Twilight Civil | Sunrise | Moonrise 10 | 11 | 12 | 13 |
|---|---|---|---|---|---|---|---|
| ° | h m | h m | h m | h m | h m | h m | h m |
| N 72 | 04 37 | 05 56 | 07 05 | 16 29 | 15 41 | □ | □ |
| N 70 | 04 43 | 05 54 | 06 56 | 16 43 | 16 09 | 15 06 | □ |
| 68 | 04 48 | 05 52 | 06 49 | 16 53 | 16 31 | 15 57 | □ |
| 66 | 04 52 | 05 51 | 06 43 | 17 03 | 16 48 | 16 29 | 15 52 |
| 64 | 04 55 | 05 50 | 06 38 | 17 10 | 17 03 | 16 53 | 16 40 |
| 62 | 04 57 | 05 48 | 06 33 | 17 17 | 17 14 | 17 12 | 17 11 |
| 60 | 04 59 | 05 47 | 06 29 | 17 23 | 17 25 | 17 28 | 17 35 |
| N 58 | 05 01 | 05 46 | 06 26 | 17 28 | 17 34 | 17 42 | 17 54 |
| 56 | 05 02 | 05 45 | 06 23 | 17 33 | 17 42 | 17 53 | 18 10 |
| 54 | 05 04 | 05 45 | 06 20 | 17 37 | 17 49 | 18 03 | 18 23 |
| 52 | 05 05 | 05 44 | 06 18 | 17 41 | 17 55 | 18 13 | 18 35 |
| 50 | 05 05 | 05 43 | 06 15 | 17 44 | 18 01 | 18 21 | 18 46 |
| 45 | 05 07 | 05 41 | 06 10 | 17 52 | 18 13 | 18 38 | 19 08 |
| N 40 | 05 08 | 05 39 | 06 06 | 17 58 | 18 24 | 18 53 | 19 26 |
| 35 | 05 08 | 05 37 | 06 02 | 18 03 | 18 33 | 19 05 | 19 41 |
| 30 | 05 07 | 05 35 | 05 59 | 18 08 | 18 41 | 19 16 | 19 54 |
| 20 | 05 06 | 05 31 | 05 54 | 18 17 | 18 54 | 19 34 | 20 17 |
| N 10 | 05 03 | 05 27 | 05 48 | 18 24 | 19 06 | 19 50 | 20 36 |
| 0 | 04 58 | 05 23 | 05 43 | 18 31 | 19 18 | 20 06 | 20 55 |
| S 10 | 04 53 | 05 17 | 05 38 | 18 39 | 19 29 | 20 21 | 21 13 |
| 20 | 04 45 | 05 11 | 05 33 | 18 46 | 19 42 | 20 38 | 21 33 |
| 30 | 04 34 | 05 02 | 05 27 | 18 55 | 19 56 | 20 57 | 21 57 |
| 35 | 04 27 | 04 57 | 05 23 | 19 00 | 20 04 | 21 08 | 22 10 |
| 40 | 04 18 | 04 51 | 05 19 | 19 06 | 20 14 | 21 21 | 22 26 |
| 45 | 04 08 | 04 44 | 05 14 | 19 13 | 20 25 | 21 36 | 22 45 |
| S 50 | 03 54 | 04 35 | 05 08 | 19 21 | 20 39 | 21 55 | 23 09 |
| 52 | 03 48 | 04 30 | 05 05 | 19 25 | 20 45 | 22 04 | 23 20 |
| 54 | 03 40 | 04 25 | 05 02 | 19 29 | 20 52 | 22 14 | 23 33 |
| 56 | 03 32 | 04 20 | 04 59 | 19 34 | 21 00 | 22 26 | 23 48 |
| 58 | 03 22 | 04 14 | 04 55 | 19 40 | 21 09 | 22 39 | 24 06 |
| S 60 | 03 10 | 04 07 | 04 51 | 19 46 | 21 20 | 22 54 | 24 28 |

| Lat. | Sunset | Twilight Civil | Twilight Naut. | Moonset 10 | 11 | 12 | 13 |
|---|---|---|---|---|---|---|---|
| ° | h m | h m | h m | h m | h m | h m | h m |
| N 72 | 16 27 | 17 36 | 18 54 | 07 38 | 10 05 | □ | □ |
| N 70 | 16 36 | 17 38 | 18 48 | 07 28 | 09 38 | 12 21 | □ |
| 68 | 16 43 | 17 39 | 18 44 | 07 19 | 09 18 | 11 32 | □ |
| 66 | 16 49 | 17 41 | 18 40 | 07 12 | 09 03 | 11 00 | 13 20 |
| 64 | 16 55 | 17 42 | 18 37 | 07 06 | 08 50 | 10 37 | 12 32 |
| 62 | 16 59 | 17 44 | 18 35 | 07 01 | 08 39 | 10 19 | 12 02 |
| 60 | 17 03 | 17 45 | 18 33 | 06 56 | 08 30 | 10 04 | 11 39 |
| N 58 | 17 06 | 17 46 | 18 31 | 06 53 | 08 22 | 09 52 | 11 21 |
| 56 | 17 10 | 17 47 | 18 30 | 06 49 | 08 15 | 09 41 | 11 05 |
| 54 | 17 12 | 17 48 | 18 29 | 06 46 | 08 09 | 09 31 | 10 52 |
| 52 | 17 15 | 17 49 | 18 28 | 06 43 | 08 03 | 09 23 | 10 41 |
| 50 | 17 17 | 17 50 | 18 27 | 06 41 | 07 58 | 09 15 | 10 31 |
| 45 | 17 22 | 17 52 | 18 26 | 06 35 | 07 48 | 08 59 | 10 09 |
| N 40 | 17 27 | 17 54 | 18 25 | 06 31 | 07 39 | 08 46 | 09 52 |
| 35 | 17 30 | 17 56 | 18 25 | 06 27 | 07 31 | 08 35 | 09 38 |
| 30 | 17 34 | 17 58 | 18 26 | 06 23 | 07 24 | 08 25 | 09 26 |
| 20 | 17 40 | 18 02 | 18 28 | 06 17 | 07 13 | 08 09 | 09 04 |
| N 10 | 17 45 | 18 06 | 18 31 | 06 12 | 07 03 | 07 54 | 08 46 |
| 0 | 17 50 | 18 11 | 18 35 | 06 07 | 06 53 | 07 41 | 08 29 |
| S 10 | 17 55 | 18 16 | 18 41 | 06 02 | 06 44 | 07 27 | 08 12 |
| 20 | 18 01 | 18 23 | 18 49 | 05 57 | 06 34 | 07 13 | 07 54 |
| 30 | 18 07 | 18 32 | 19 00 | 05 51 | 06 23 | 06 57 | 07 33 |
| 35 | 18 11 | 18 37 | 19 07 | 05 48 | 06 17 | 06 47 | 07 21 |
| 40 | 18 15 | 18 43 | 19 16 | 05 44 | 06 09 | 06 36 | 07 07 |
| 45 | 18 21 | 18 51 | 19 27 | 05 40 | 06 01 | 06 24 | 06 51 |
| S 50 | 18 27 | 19 00 | 19 41 | 05 35 | 05 51 | 06 09 | 06 31 |
| 52 | 18 30 | 19 05 | 19 47 | 05 32 | 05 46 | 06 02 | 06 21 |
| 54 | 18 33 | 19 10 | 19 55 | 05 30 | 05 41 | 05 54 | 06 11 |
| 56 | 18 36 | 19 15 | 20 04 | 05 27 | 05 35 | 05 45 | 05 59 |
| 58 | 18 40 | 19 21 | 20 14 | 05 24 | 05 29 | 05 35 | 05 45 |
| S 60 | 18 44 | 19 29 | 20 26 | 05 20 | 05 21 | 05 24 | 05 28 |

| | SUN | | MOON | | | |
|---|---|---|---|---|---|---|
| Day | Eqn. of Time 00h | 12h | Mer. Pass. | Mer. Pass. Upper | Lower | Age | Phase |
| d | m s | m s | h m | h m | h m | d | % |
| 10 | 12 52 | 13 00 | 11 47 | 24 42 | 12 19 | 15 | 100 |
| 11 | 13 08 | 13 16 | 11 47 | 00 42 | 13 06 | 16 | 97 |
| 12 | 13 23 | 13 31 | 11 46 | 01 29 | 13 53 | 17 | 92 |

| UT | ARIES GHA | VENUS −3.9 GHA | Dec | MARS −0.9 GHA | Dec | JUPITER −2.9 GHA | Dec | SATURN +0.5 GHA | Dec | STARS Name | SHA | Dec |
|---|---|---|---|---|---|---|---|---|---|---|---|---|
| **13** 00 | 21 32.2 | 185 18.5 | S 5 31.7 | 298 33.9 | N23 01.0 | 19 25.8 | S 0 50.3 | 60 00.5 | S16 28.3 | Acamar | 315 12.8 | S40 12.7 |
| 01 | 36 34.6 | 200 18.1 | 33.0 | 313 35.8 | 01.2 | 34 28.5 | 50.5 | 75 03.0 | 28.3 | Achernar | 335 21.0 | S57 07.3 |
| 02 | 51 37.1 | 215 17.6 | 34.2 | 328 37.6 | 01.3 | 49 31.2 | 50.6 | 90 05.5 | 28.3 | Acrux | 173 02.8 | S63 13.3 |
| 03 | 66 39.6 | 230 17.2 .. | 35.4 | 343 39.5 .. | 01.4 | 64 34.0 .. | 50.7 | 105 08.0 .. | 28.3 | Adhara | 255 07.3 | S28 59.9 |
| 04 | 81 42.0 | 245 16.8 | 36.7 | 358 41.3 | 01.5 | 79 36.7 | 50.8 | 120 10.5 | 28.3 | Aldebaran | 290 41.5 | N16 33.3 |
| 05 | 96 44.5 | 260 16.4 | 37.9 | 13 43.2 | 01.6 | 94 39.5 | 50.9 | 135 13.0 | 28.4 | | | |
| 06 | 111 47.0 | 275 15.9 | S 5 39.1 | 28 45.1 | N23 01.7 | 109 42.2 | S 0 51.0 | 150 15.5 | S16 28.4 | Alioth | 166 15.2 | N55 50.3 |
| T 07 | 126 49.4 | 290 15.5 | 40.4 | 43 46.9 | 01.8 | 124 44.9 | 51.1 | 165 18.0 | 28.4 | Alkaid | 152 54.0 | N49 12.1 |
| H 08 | 141 51.9 | 305 15.1 | 41.6 | 58 48.8 | 02.0 | 139 47.7 | 51.3 | 180 20.5 | 28.4 | Al Na'ir | 27 35.0 | S46 51.2 |
| U 09 | 156 54.4 | 320 14.7 .. | 42.8 | 73 50.6 .. | 02.1 | 154 50.4 .. | 51.4 | 195 23.0 .. | 28.4 | Alnilam | 275 39.5 | S 1 11.1 |
| R 10 | 171 56.8 | 335 14.3 | 44.1 | 88 52.5 | 02.2 | 169 53.2 | 51.5 | 210 25.5 | 28.4 | Alphard | 217 49.8 | S 8 45.2 |
| S 11 | 186 59.3 | 350 13.8 | 45.3 | 103 54.4 | 02.3 | 184 55.9 | 51.6 | 225 28.0 | 28.4 | | | |
| D 12 | 202 01.7 | 5 13.4 | S 5 46.5 | 118 56.2 | N23 02.4 | 199 58.7 | S 0 51.7 | 240 30.5 | S16 28.4 | Alphecca | 126 05.6 | N26 38.5 |
| A 13 | 217 04.2 | 20 13.0 | 47.8 | 133 58.1 | 02.5 | 215 01.4 | 51.8 | 255 33.0 | 28.4 | Alpheratz | 357 36.4 | N29 13.1 |
| Y 14 | 232 06.7 | 35 12.6 | 49.0 | 149 00.0 | 02.6 | 230 04.1 | 52.0 | 270 35.5 | 28.4 | Altair | 62 01.8 | N 8 55.8 |
| 15 | 247 09.1 | 50 12.1 .. | 50.2 | 164 01.9 .. | 02.8 | 245 06.9 .. | 52.1 | 285 38.0 .. | 28.5 | Ankaa | 353 08.6 | S42 11.0 |
| 16 | 262 11.6 | 65 11.7 | 51.5 | 179 03.7 | 02.9 | 260 09.6 | 52.2 | 300 40.6 | 28.5 | Antares | 112 18.4 | S26 28.9 |
| 17 | 277 14.1 | 80 11.3 | 52.7 | 194 05.6 | 03.0 | 275 12.4 | 52.3 | 315 43.1 | 28.5 | | | |
| 18 | 292 16.5 | 95 10.9 | S 5 53.9 | 209 07.5 | N23 03.1 | 290 15.1 | S 0 52.4 | 330 45.6 | S16 28.5 | Arcturus | 145 50.0 | N19 04.0 |
| 19 | 307 19.0 | 110 10.4 | 55.2 | 224 09.3 | 03.2 | 305 17.8 | 52.5 | 345 48.1 | 28.5 | Atria | 107 14.6 | S69 04.2 |
| 20 | 322 21.5 | 125 10.0 | 56.4 | 239 11.2 | 03.3 | 320 20.6 | 52.6 | 0 50.6 | 28.5 | Avior | 234 15.6 | S59 34.5 |
| 21 | 337 23.9 | 140 09.6 .. | 57.6 | 254 13.1 .. | 03.4 | 335 23.3 .. | 52.8 | 15 53.1 .. | 28.5 | Bellatrix | 278 24.7 | N 6 22.3 |
| 22 | 352 26.4 | 155 09.2 | 5 58.9 | 269 15.0 | 03.6 | 350 26.0 | 52.9 | 30 55.6 | 28.5 | Betelgeuse | 270 54.0 | N 7 24.8 |
| 23 | 7 28.8 | 170 08.7 | 6 00.1 | 284 16.9 | 03.7 | 5 28.8 | 53.0 | 45 58.1 | 28.5 | | | |
| **14** 00 | 22 31.3 | 185 08.3 | S 6 01.3 | 299 18.7 | N23 03.8 | 20 31.5 | S 0 53.1 | 61 00.6 | S16 28.6 | Canopus | 263 53.1 | S52 42.1 |
| 01 | 37 33.8 | 200 07.9 | 02.6 | 314 20.6 | 03.9 | 35 34.3 | 53.2 | 76 03.1 | 28.6 | Capella | 280 24.4 | N46 01.1 |
| 02 | 52 36.2 | 215 07.5 | 03.8 | 329 22.5 | 04.0 | 50 37.0 | 53.3 | 91 05.6 | 28.6 | Deneb | 49 26.9 | N45 21.9 |
| 03 | 67 38.7 | 230 07.0 .. | 05.0 | 344 24.4 .. | 04.1 | 65 39.7 .. | 53.4 | 106 08.1 .. | 28.6 | Denebola | 182 27.2 | N14 26.9 |
| 04 | 82 41.2 | 245 06.6 | 06.2 | 359 26.3 | 04.2 | 80 42.5 | 53.5 | 121 10.6 | 28.6 | Diphda | 348 48.9 | S17 51.7 |
| 05 | 97 43.6 | 260 06.2 | 07.5 | 14 28.2 | 04.4 | 95 45.2 | 53.7 | 136 13.1 | 28.6 | | | |
| 06 | 112 46.1 | 275 05.8 | S 6 08.7 | 29 30.1 | N23 04.5 | 110 48.0 | S 0 53.8 | 151 15.6 | S16 28.6 | Dubhe | 193 43.8 | N61 37.7 |
| 07 | 127 48.6 | 290 05.3 | 09.9 | 44 32.0 | 04.6 | 125 50.7 | 53.9 | 166 18.1 | 28.6 | Elnath | 278 04.0 | N28 37.6 |
| F 08 | 142 51.0 | 305 04.9 | 11.2 | 59 33.9 | 04.7 | 140 53.4 | 54.0 | 181 20.6 | 28.6 | Eltanin | 90 43.3 | N51 29.4 |
| R 09 | 157 53.5 | 320 04.5 .. | 12.4 | 74 35.7 .. | 04.8 | 155 56.2 .. | 54.1 | 196 23.1 .. | 28.6 | Enif | 33 40.5 | N 9 58.9 |
| I 10 | 172 56.0 | 335 04.1 | 13.6 | 89 37.6 | 04.9 | 170 58.9 | 54.2 | 211 25.6 | 28.6 | Fomalhaut | 15 16.3 | S29 30.2 |
| D 11 | 187 58.4 | 350 03.6 | 14.8 | 104 39.5 | 05.0 | 186 01.6 | 54.3 | 226 28.1 | 28.7 | | | |
| A 12 | 203 00.9 | 5 03.2 | S 6 16.1 | 119 41.4 | N23 05.2 | 201 04.4 | S 0 54.5 | 241 30.6 | S16 28.7 | Gacrux | 171 54.3 | S57 14.2 |
| Y 13 | 218 03.3 | 20 02.8 | 17.3 | 134 43.3 | 05.3 | 216 07.1 | 54.6 | 256 33.1 | 28.7 | Gienah | 175 45.8 | S17 39.9 |
| 14 | 233 05.8 | 35 02.3 | 18.5 | 149 45.2 | 05.4 | 231 09.8 | 54.7 | 271 35.6 | 28.7 | Hadar | 148 39.3 | S60 28.9 |
| 15 | 248 08.3 | 50 01.9 .. | 19.8 | 164 47.1 .. | 05.5 | 246 12.6 .. | 54.8 | 286 38.1 .. | 28.7 | Hamal | 327 53.0 | N23 34.2 |
| 16 | 263 10.7 | 65 01.5 | 21.0 | 179 49.0 | 05.6 | 261 15.3 | 54.9 | 301 40.6 | 28.7 | Kaus Aust. | 83 35.1 | S34 22.5 |
| 17 | 278 13.2 | 80 01.1 | 22.2 | 194 50.9 | 05.7 | 276 18.1 | 55.0 | 316 43.1 | 28.7 | | | |
| 18 | 293 15.7 | 95 00.6 | S 6 23.4 | 209 52.8 | N23 05.8 | 291 20.8 | S 0 55.1 | 331 45.6 | S16 28.7 | Kochab | 137 20.9 | N74 03.9 |
| 19 | 308 18.1 | 110 00.2 | 24.7 | 224 54.8 | 06.0 | 306 23.5 | 55.2 | 346 48.1 | 28.7 | Markab | 13 31.5 | N15 19.8 |
| 20 | 323 20.6 | 124 59.8 | 25.9 | 239 56.7 | 06.1 | 321 26.3 | 55.3 | 1 50.6 | 28.7 | Menkar | 314 07.8 | N 4 10.8 |
| 21 | 338 23.1 | 139 59.3 .. | 27.1 | 254 58.6 .. | 06.2 | 336 29.0 .. | 55.5 | 16 53.1 .. | 28.7 | Menkent | 148 00.2 | S36 28.8 |
| 22 | 353 25.5 | 154 58.9 | 28.3 | 270 00.5 | 06.3 | 351 31.7 | 55.6 | 31 55.6 | 28.8 | Miaplacidus | 221 39.0 | S69 48.2 |
| 23 | 8 28.0 | 169 58.5 | 29.6 | 285 02.4 | 06.4 | 6 34.5 | 55.7 | 46 58.1 | 28.8 | | | |
| **15** 00 | 23 30.5 | 184 58.0 | S 6 30.8 | 300 04.3 | N23 06.5 | 21 37.2 | S 0 55.8 | 62 00.6 | S16 28.8 | Mirfak | 308 30.5 | N49 56.4 |
| 01 | 38 32.9 | 199 57.6 | 32.0 | 315 06.2 | 06.6 | 36 39.9 | 55.9 | 77 03.1 | 28.8 | Nunki | 75 50.1 | S26 16.1 |
| 02 | 53 35.4 | 214 57.2 | 33.2 | 330 08.1 | 06.8 | 51 42.7 | 56.0 | 92 05.6 | 28.8 | Peacock | 53 08.5 | S56 39.9 |
| 03 | 68 37.8 | 229 56.7 .. | 34.5 | 345 10.1 .. | 06.9 | 66 45.4 .. | 56.1 | 107 08.1 .. | 28.8 | Pollux | 243 19.6 | N27 58.3 |
| 04 | 83 40.3 | 244 56.3 | 35.7 | 0 12.0 | 07.0 | 81 48.1 | 56.2 | 122 10.6 | 28.8 | Procyon | 244 52.8 | N 5 10.1 |
| 05 | 98 42.8 | 259 55.9 | 36.9 | 15 13.9 | 07.1 | 96 50.9 | 56.4 | 137 13.1 | 28.8 | | | |
| 06 | 113 45.2 | 274 55.5 | S 6 38.1 | 30 15.8 | N23 07.2 | 111 53.6 | S 0 56.5 | 152 15.6 | S16 28.8 | Rasalhague | 96 00.4 | N12 32.8 |
| 07 | 128 47.7 | 289 55.0 | 39.4 | 45 17.7 | 07.3 | 126 56.3 | 56.6 | 167 18.1 | 28.8 | Regulus | 207 36.6 | N11 51.5 |
| S 08 | 143 50.2 | 304 54.6 | 40.6 | 60 19.7 | 07.4 | 141 59.1 | 56.7 | 182 20.6 | 28.8 | Rigel | 281 05.5 | S 8 10.4 |
| A 09 | 158 52.6 | 319 54.2 .. | 41.8 | 75 21.6 .. | 07.5 | 157 01.8 .. | 56.8 | 197 23.1 .. | 28.9 | Rigil Kent. | 139 43.5 | S60 55.7 |
| T 10 | 173 55.1 | 334 53.7 | 43.0 | 90 23.5 | 07.7 | 172 04.5 | 56.9 | 212 25.6 | 28.9 | Sabik | 102 05.1 | S15 45.1 |
| U 11 | 188 57.6 | 349 53.3 | 44.3 | 105 25.4 | 07.8 | 187 07.3 | 57.0 | 227 28.1 | 28.9 | | | |
| R 12 | 204 00.0 | 4 52.8 | S 6 45.5 | 120 27.4 | N23 07.9 | 202 10.0 | S 0 57.1 | 242 30.6 | S16 28.9 | Schedar | 349 32.6 | N56 39.8 |
| D 13 | 219 02.5 | 19 52.4 | 46.7 | 135 29.3 | 08.0 | 217 12.7 | 57.2 | 257 33.1 | 28.9 | Shaula | 96 13.1 | S37 07.3 |
| A 14 | 234 05.0 | 34 52.0 | 47.9 | 150 31.2 | 08.1 | 232 15.5 | 57.4 | 272 35.6 | 28.9 | Sirius | 258 27.8 | S16 44.6 |
| Y 15 | 249 07.4 | 49 51.5 .. | 49.1 | 165 33.2 .. | 08.2 | 247 18.2 .. | 57.5 | 287 38.1 .. | 28.9 | Spica | 158 24.6 | S11 16.6 |
| 16 | 264 09.9 | 64 51.1 | 50.4 | 180 35.1 | 08.3 | 262 20.9 | 57.6 | 302 40.6 | 28.9 | Suhail | 222 47.9 | S43 31.1 |
| 17 | 279 12.3 | 79 50.7 | 51.6 | 195 37.0 | 08.5 | 277 23.7 | 57.7 | 317 43.1 | 28.9 | | | |
| 18 | 294 14.8 | 94 50.2 | S 6 52.8 | 210 39.0 | N23 08.6 | 292 26.4 | S 0 57.8 | 332 45.6 | S16 28.9 | Vega | 80 34.6 | N38 48.5 |
| 19 | 309 17.3 | 109 49.8 | 54.0 | 225 40.9 | 08.7 | 307 29.1 | 57.9 | 347 48.1 | 28.9 | Zuben'ubi | 136 58.4 | S16 08.0 |
| 20 | 324 19.7 | 124 49.4 | 55.3 | 240 42.8 | 08.8 | 322 31.9 | 58.0 | 2 50.5 | 28.9 | | SHA | Mer. Pass. |
| 21 | 339 22.2 | 139 48.9 .. | 56.5 | 255 44.8 .. | 08.9 | 337 34.6 .. | 58.1 | 17 53.0 .. | 28.9 | | ° ′ | h m |
| 22 | 354 24.7 | 154 48.5 | 57.7 | 270 46.7 | 09.0 | 352 37.3 | 58.2 | 32 55.5 | 29.0 | Venus | 162 37.0 | 11 40 |
| 23 | 9 27.1 | 169 48.1 | 58.9 | 285 48.7 | 09.1 | 7 40.1 | 58.3 | 47 58.0 | 29.0 | Mars | 276 47.4 | 4 02 |
| Mer. Pass. | h m 22 26.2 | v −0.4 | d 1.2 | v 1.9 | d 0.1 | v 2.7 | d 0.1 | v 2.5 | d 0.0 | Jupiter | 358 00.2 | 22 34 |
| | | | | | | | | | | Saturn | 38 29.3 | 19 53 |

| UT | SUN | | MOON | | | | | Lat. | Twilight | | Sunrise | Moonrise | | | |
|---|---|---|---|---|---|---|---|---|---|---|---|---|---|---|---|
| | | | | | | | | | Naut. | Civil | | 13 | 14 | 15 | 16 |
| | GHA | Dec | GHA | v | Dec | d | HP | | | | | | | | |
| d h | ° ′ | ° ′ | ° ′ | ′ | ° ′ | ′ | ′ | N 72 | h m | h m | h m | h m | h m | h m | h m |
| | | | | | | | | | 04 51 | 06 09 | 07 19 | ▭ | ▭ | ▭ | ▭ |
| 13 00 | 183 24.7 | S 7 40.9 | 326 47.9 | 11.5 | N20 47.2 | 9.9 | 55.8 | N 70 | 04 55 | 06 05 | 07 08 | ▭ | ▭ | ▭ | ▭ |
| 01 | 198 24.8 | 41.8 | 341 18.4 | 11.5 | 20 57.1 | 9.7 | 55.7 | 68 | 04 58 | 06 03 | 07 00 | ▭ | ▭ | ▭ | ▭ |
| 02 | 213 25.0 | 42.7 | 355 48.9 | 11.4 | 21 06.8 | 9.7 | 55.7 | 66 | 05 01 | 06 00 | 06 53 | 15 52 | ▭ | ▭ | ▭ |
| 03 | 228 25.1 | .. 43.7 | 10 19.3 | 11.4 | 21 16.5 | 9.5 | 55.7 | 64 | 05 03 | 05 58 | 06 46 | 16 40 | 16 07 | ▭ | ▭ |
| 04 | 243 25.3 | 44.6 | 24 49.7 | 11.3 | 21 26.0 | 9.5 | 55.7 | 62 | 05 05 | 05 56 | 06 41 | 17 11 | 17 13 | 17 25 | 18 16 |
| 05 | 258 25.5 | 45.6 | 39 20.0 | 11.3 | 21 35.5 | 9.3 | 55.6 | 60 | 05 06 | 05 54 | 06 37 | 17 35 | 17 48 | 18 16 | 19 08 |
| 06 | 273 25.6 | S 7 46.5 | 53 50.3 | 11.3 | N21 44.8 | 9.2 | 55.6 | N 58 | 05 07 | 05 53 | 06 33 | 17 54 | 18 14 | 18 47 | 19 39 |
| 07 | 288 25.8 | 47.4 | 68 20.6 | 11.2 | 21 54.0 | 9.1 | 55.6 | 56 | 05 08 | 05 51 | 06 29 | 18 10 | 18 34 | 19 11 | 20 03 |
| 08 | 303 25.9 | 48.4 | 82 50.8 | 11.2 | 22 03.1 | 8.9 | 55.6 | 54 | 05 09 | 05 50 | 06 26 | 18 23 | 18 51 | 19 30 | 20 22 |
| 09 | 318 26.1 | .. 49.3 | 97 21.0 | 11.1 | 22 12.0 | 8.9 | 55.5 | 52 | 05 10 | 05 49 | 06 23 | 18 35 | 19 05 | 19 46 | 20 38 |
| 10 | 333 26.2 | 50.2 | 111 51.1 | 11.2 | 22 20.9 | 8.7 | 55.5 | 50 | 05 10 | 05 47 | 06 20 | 18 46 | 19 18 | 20 00 | 20 52 |
| 11 | 348 26.4 | 51.2 | 126 21.3 | 11.0 | 22 29.6 | 8.7 | 55.5 | 45 | 05 11 | 05 45 | 06 14 | 19 08 | 19 44 | 20 28 | 21 20 |
| 12 | 3 26.5 | S 7 52.1 | 140 51.3 | 11.1 | N22 38.3 | 8.5 | 55.5 | N 40 | 05 11 | 05 42 | 06 09 | 19 26 | 20 05 | 20 51 | 21 43 |
| 13 | 18 26.7 | 53.0 | 155 21.4 | 11.0 | 22 46.8 | 8.4 | 55.4 | 35 | 05 10 | 05 39 | 06 05 | 19 41 | 20 22 | 21 09 | 22 01 |
| 14 | 33 26.8 | 54.0 | 169 51.4 | 10.9 | 22 55.2 | 8.2 | 55.4 | 30 | 05 09 | 05 37 | 06 01 | 19 54 | 20 37 | 21 25 | 22 17 |
| 15 | 48 27.0 | .. 54.9 | 184 21.3 | 11.0 | 23 03.4 | 8.2 | 55.4 | 20 | 05 07 | 05 32 | 05 54 | 20 17 | 21 03 | 21 52 | 22 44 |
| 16 | 63 27.1 | 55.8 | 198 51.3 | 10.9 | 23 11.6 | 8.0 | 55.4 | N 10 | 05 03 | 05 27 | 05 48 | 20 36 | 21 25 | 22 15 | 23 07 |
| 17 | 78 27.3 | 56.7 | 213 21.2 | 10.8 | 23 19.6 | 8.0 | 55.4 | 0 | 04 58 | 05 22 | 05 43 | 20 55 | 21 46 | 22 37 | 23 28 |
| 18 | 93 27.4 | S 7 57.7 | 227 51.0 | 10.9 | N23 27.6 | 7.8 | 55.3 | S 10 | 04 51 | 05 16 | 05 37 | 21 13 | 22 06 | 22 59 | 23 50 |
| 19 | 108 27.6 | 58.6 | 242 20.9 | 10.7 | 23 35.4 | 7.6 | 55.3 | 20 | 04 42 | 05 08 | 05 31 | 21 33 | 22 29 | 23 22 | 24 13 |
| 20 | 123 27.7 | 7 59.5 | 256 50.6 | 10.8 | 23 43.0 | 7.6 | 55.3 | 30 | 04 30 | 04 59 | 05 23 | 21 57 | 22 55 | 23 49 | 24 40 |
| 21 | 138 27.9 | 8 00.5 | 271 20.4 | 10.7 | 23 50.6 | 7.4 | 55.3 | 35 | 04 23 | 04 53 | 05 19 | 22 10 | 23 10 | 24 06 | 00 06 |
| 22 | 153 28.0 | 01.4 | 285 50.1 | 10.7 | 23 58.0 | 7.4 | 55.2 | 40 | 04 13 | 04 46 | 05 14 | 22 26 | 23 28 | 24 24 | 00 24 |
| 23 | 168 28.2 | 02.3 | 300 19.8 | 10.7 | 24 05.4 | 7.1 | 55.2 | 45 | 04 02 | 04 38 | 05 08 | 22 45 | 23 49 | 24 47 | 00 47 |
| 14 00 | 183 28.3 | S 8 03.3 | 314 49.5 | 10.6 | N24 12.5 | 7.1 | 55.2 | S 50 | 03 47 | 04 28 | 05 02 | 23 09 | 24 17 | 00 17 | 01 16 |
| 01 | 198 28.5 | 04.2 | 329 19.1 | 10.6 | 24 19.6 | 7.0 | 55.2 | 52 | 03 40 | 04 23 | 04 58 | 23 20 | 24 30 | 00 30 | 01 30 |
| 02 | 213 28.6 | 05.1 | 343 48.7 | 10.6 | 24 26.6 | 6.8 | 55.2 | 54 | 03 32 | 04 18 | 04 55 | 23 33 | 24 46 | 00 46 | 01 47 |
| 03 | 228 28.7 | .. 06.1 | 358 18.3 | 10.5 | 24 33.4 | 6.7 | 55.1 | 56 | 03 22 | 04 12 | 04 51 | 23 48 | 25 04 | 01 04 | 02 07 |
| 04 | 243 28.9 | 07.0 | 12 47.8 | 10.5 | 24 40.1 | 6.5 | 55.1 | 58 | 03 12 | 04 05 | 04 47 | 24 06 | 00 06 | 01 27 | 02 31 |
| 05 | 258 29.0 | 07.9 | 27 17.3 | 10.5 | 24 46.6 | 6.5 | 55.1 | S 60 | 02 59 | 03 57 | 04 42 | 24 28 | 00 28 | 01 56 | 03 05 |
| 06 | 273 29.2 | S 8 08.8 | 41 46.8 | 10.4 | N24 53.1 | 6.3 | 55.1 | | | | | | | | |
| 07 | 288 29.3 | 09.8 | 56 16.2 | 10.4 | 24 59.4 | 6.2 | 55.0 | Lat. | Sunset | Twilight | | Moonset | | | |
| 08 | 303 29.5 | 10.7 | 70 45.6 | 10.4 | 25 05.6 | 6.1 | 55.0 | | | Civil | Naut. | 13 | 14 | 15 | 16 |
| 09 | 318 29.6 | .. 11.6 | 85 15.0 | 10.3 | 25 11.7 | 5.9 | 55.0 | ° | h m | h m | h m | h m | h m | h m | h m |
| 10 | 333 29.8 | 12.6 | 99 44.3 | 10.4 | 25 17.6 | 5.8 | 55.0 | N 72 | 16 11 | 17 21 | 18 39 | ▭ | ▭ | ▭ | ▭ |
| 11 | 348 29.9 | 13.5 | 114 13.7 | 10.3 | 25 23.4 | 5.7 | 55.0 | N 70 | 16 22 | 17 25 | 18 35 | ▭ | ▭ | ▭ | ▭ |
| 12 | 3 30.1 | S 8 14.4 | 128 43.0 | 10.3 | N25 29.1 | 5.5 | 54.9 | 68 | 16 31 | 17 28 | 18 32 | ▭ | ▭ | ▭ | ▭ |
| 13 | 18 30.2 | 15.3 | 143 12.3 | 10.2 | 25 34.6 | 5.5 | 54.9 | 66 | 16 38 | 17 30 | 18 29 | 13 20 | ▭ | ▭ | ▭ |
| 14 | 33 30.4 | 16.3 | 157 41.5 | 10.2 | 25 40.1 | 5.3 | 54.9 | 64 | 16 44 | 17 32 | 18 27 | 12 32 | 14 50 | ▭ | ▭ |
| 15 | 48 30.5 | .. 17.2 | 172 10.7 | 10.2 | 25 45.4 | 5.1 | 54.9 | 62 | 16 50 | 17 34 | 18 26 | 12 02 | 13 45 | 15 20 | 16 16 |
| 16 | 63 30.6 | 18.1 | 186 39.9 | 10.2 | 25 50.5 | 5.1 | 54.9 | 60 | 16 54 | 17 36 | 18 24 | 11 39 | 13 10 | 14 29 | 15 25 |
| 17 | 78 30.8 | 19.1 | 201 09.1 | 10.2 | 25 55.6 | 4.9 | 54.9 | | | | | | | | |
| 18 | 93 30.9 | S 8 20.0 | 215 30.3 | 10.1 | N26 00.5 | 4.7 | 54.8 | N 58 | 16 58 | 17 38 | 18 23 | 11 21 | 12 45 | 13 58 | 14 53 |
| 19 | 108 31.1 | 20.9 | 230 07.4 | 10.1 | 26 05.2 | 4.7 | 54.8 | 56 | 17 02 | 17 40 | 18 22 | 11 05 | 12 25 | 13 35 | 14 29 |
| 20 | 123 31.2 | 21.8 | 244 36.5 | 10.1 | 26 09.9 | 4.5 | 54.8 | 54 | 17 05 | 17 41 | 18 22 | 10 52 | 12 09 | 13 16 | 14 10 |
| 21 | 138 31.4 | .. 22.8 | 259 05.6 | 10.1 | 26 14.4 | 4.4 | 54.8 | 52 | 17 08 | 17 42 | 18 21 | 10 41 | 11 54 | 13 00 | 13 54 |
| 22 | 153 31.5 | 23.7 | 273 34.7 | 10.1 | 26 18.8 | 4.2 | 54.8 | 50 | 17 11 | 17 44 | 18 21 | 10 31 | 11 42 | 12 46 | 13 40 |
| 23 | 168 31.6 | 24.6 | 288 03.8 | 10.0 | 26 23.0 | 4.1 | 54.7 | 45 | 17 17 | 17 47 | 18 21 | 10 09 | 11 16 | 12 18 | 13 11 |
| 15 00 | 183 31.8 | S 8 25.5 | 302 32.8 | 10.1 | N26 27.1 | 4.0 | 54.7 | N 40 | 17 22 | 17 49 | 18 21 | 09 52 | 10 56 | 11 56 | 12 49 |
| 01 | 198 31.9 | 26.5 | 317 01.9 | 10.0 | 26 31.1 | 3.9 | 54.7 | 35 | 17 27 | 17 52 | 18 21 | 09 38 | 10 39 | 11 37 | 12 30 |
| 02 | 213 32.1 | 27.4 | 331 30.9 | 10.0 | 26 35.0 | 3.7 | 54.7 | 30 | 17 30 | 17 55 | 18 22 | 09 26 | 10 25 | 11 21 | 12 14 |
| 03 | 228 32.2 | .. 28.3 | 345 59.9 | 10.0 | 26 38.7 | 3.6 | 54.7 | 20 | 17 37 | 17 59 | 18 25 | 09 04 | 10 00 | 10 55 | 11 47 |
| 04 | 243 32.4 | 29.2 | 0 28.9 | 9.9 | 26 42.3 | 3.4 | 54.7 | N 10 | 17 43 | 18 05 | 18 29 | 08 46 | 09 39 | 10 32 | 11 24 |
| 05 | 258 32.5 | 30.2 | 14 57.8 | 10.0 | 26 45.7 | 3.3 | 54.7 | 0 | 17 49 | 18 10 | 18 34 | 08 29 | 09 19 | 10 10 | 11 02 |
| 06 | 273 32.6 | S 8 31.1 | 29 26.8 | 9.9 | N26 49.0 | 3.2 | 54.6 | S 10 | 17 55 | 18 17 | 18 41 | 08 12 | 09 00 | 09 49 | 10 40 |
| 07 | 288 32.8 | 32.0 | 43 55.7 | 10.0 | 26 52.2 | 3.1 | 54.6 | 20 | 18 02 | 18 24 | 18 50 | 07 54 | 08 38 | 09 26 | 10 17 |
| 08 | 303 32.9 | 32.9 | 58 24.7 | 9.9 | 26 55.3 | 2.9 | 54.6 | 30 | 18 09 | 18 34 | 19 02 | 07 33 | 08 14 | 09 00 | 09 50 |
| 09 | 318 33.1 | .. 33.9 | 72 53.6 | 9.9 | 26 58.2 | 2.8 | 54.6 | 35 | 18 14 | 18 40 | 19 10 | 07 21 | 08 00 | 08 44 | 09 33 |
| 10 | 333 33.2 | 34.8 | 87 22.5 | 9.9 | 27 01.0 | 2.6 | 54.6 | 40 | 18 19 | 18 46 | 19 20 | 07 07 | 07 43 | 08 26 | 09 15 |
| 11 | 348 33.3 | 35.7 | 101 51.4 | 9.9 | 27 03.6 | 2.5 | 54.6 | 45 | 18 24 | 18 55 | 19 31 | 06 51 | 07 24 | 08 04 | 08 52 |
| 12 | 3 33.5 | S 8 36.6 | 116 20.3 | 9.9 | N27 06.1 | 2.4 | 54.5 | S 50 | 18 32 | 19 05 | 19 46 | 06 31 | 06 59 | 07 36 | 08 23 |
| 13 | 18 33.6 | 37.6 | 130 49.2 | 9.9 | 27 08.5 | 2.3 | 54.5 | 52 | 18 35 | 19 10 | 19 54 | 06 21 | 06 47 | 07 22 | 08 09 |
| 14 | 33 33.7 | 38.5 | 145 18.1 | 9.9 | 27 10.8 | 2.1 | 54.5 | 54 | 18 38 | 19 16 | 20 02 | 06 11 | 06 34 | 07 07 | 07 52 |
| 15 | 48 33.9 | .. 39.4 | 159 47.0 | 9.9 | 27 12.9 | 1.9 | 54.5 | 56 | 18 42 | 19 22 | 20 12 | 05 59 | 06 18 | 06 48 | 07 32 |
| 16 | 63 34.0 | 40.3 | 174 15.9 | 9.9 | 27 14.8 | 1.9 | 54.5 | 58 | 18 47 | 19 29 | 20 23 | 05 45 | 06 00 | 06 25 | 07 08 |
| 17 | 78 34.2 | 41.2 | 188 44.8 | 9.9 | 27 16.7 | 1.7 | 54.5 | S 60 | 18 52 | 19 37 | 20 36 | 05 28 | 05 37 | 05 56 | 06 34 |
| 18 | 93 34.3 | S 8 42.2 | 203 13.7 | 9.9 | N27 18.4 | 1.6 | 54.5 | | | SUN | | | MOON | | |
| 19 | 108 34.4 | 43.1 | 217 42.6 | 9.9 | 27 20.0 | 1.4 | 54.5 | Day | Eqn. of Time | | Mer. | Mer. Pass. | | Age | Phase |
| 20 | 123 34.6 | 44.0 | 232 11.5 | 9.9 | 27 21.4 | 1.3 | 54.5 | | 00h | 12h | Pass. | Upper | Lower | | |
| 21 | 138 34.7 | .. 44.9 | 246 40.4 | 9.9 | 27 22.7 | 1.2 | 54.4 | d | m s | m s | h m | h m | h m | d % | |
| 22 | 153 34.8 | 45.9 | 261 09.3 | 9.8 | 27 23.9 | 1.0 | 54.4 | 13 | 13 38 | 13 46 | 11 46 | 02 17 | 14 42 | 18 86 | |
| 23 | 168 35.0 | 46.8 | 275 38.1 | 10.0 | N27 24.9 | 0.9 | 54.4 | 14 | 13 53 | 14 00 | 11 46 | 03 07 | 15 32 | 19 79 | |
| | SD 16.1 | d 0.9 | SD 15.1 | | 15.0 | | 14.9 | 15 | 14 07 | 14 14 | 11 46 | 03 58 | 16 24 | 20 71 | ◗ |

| UT (d h) | ARIES GHA | VENUS −3.9 GHA | Dec | MARS −0.9 GHA | Dec | JUPITER −2.9 GHA | Dec | SATURN +0.5 GHA | Dec | STARS Name | SHA | Dec |
|---|---|---|---|---|---|---|---|---|---|---|---|---|
| 16 00 | 24 29.6 | 184 47.6 | S 7 00.1 | 300 50.6 | N23 09.2 | 22 42.8 | S 0 58.5 | 63 00.5 | S16 29.0 | Acamar | 315 12.8 | S40 12.7 |
| 01 | 39 32.1 | 199 47.2 | 01.4 | 315 52.6 | 09.4 | 37 45.5 | 58.6 | 78 03.0 | 29.0 | Achernar | 335 21.0 | S57 07.3 |
| 02 | 54 34.5 | 214 46.7 | 02.6 | 330 54.5 | 09.5 | 52 48.3 | 58.7 | 93 05.5 | 29.0 | Acrux | 173 02.8 | S63 13.3 |
| 03 | 69 37.0 | 229 46.3 .. | 03.8 | 345 56.4 .. | 09.6 | 67 51.0 .. | 58.8 | 108 08.0 .. | 29.0 | Adhara | 255 07.3 | S28 59.9 |
| 04 | 84 39.4 | 244 45.9 | 05.0 | 0 58.4 | 09.7 | 82 53.7 | 58.9 | 123 10.5 | 29.0 | Aldebaran | 290 41.5 | N16 33.3 |
| 05 | 99 41.9 | 259 45.4 | 06.2 | 16 00.3 | 09.8 | 97 56.4 | 59.0 | 138 13.0 | 29.0 | | | |
| 06 | 114 44.4 | 274 45.0 | S 7 07.4 | 31 02.3 | N23 09.9 | 112 59.2 | S 0 59.1 | 153 15.5 | S16 29.0 | Alioth | 166 15.2 | N55 50.3 |
| 07 | 129 46.8 | 289 44.6 | 08.7 | 46 04.3 | 10.0 | 128 01.9 | 59.2 | 168 18.0 | 29.0 | Alkaid | 152 54.0 | N49 12.1 |
| 08 | 144 49.3 | 304 44.1 | 09.9 | 61 06.2 | 10.2 | 143 04.6 | 59.3 | 183 20.5 | 29.0 | Alnair | 27 35.0 | S46 51.2 |
| 09 | 159 51.8 | 319 43.7 .. | 11.1 | 76 08.2 .. | 10.3 | 158 07.4 .. | 59.4 | 198 23.0 .. | 29.0 | Alnilam | 275 39.5 | S 1 11.1 |
| 10 | 174 54.2 | 334 43.2 | 12.3 | 91 10.1 | 10.4 | 173 10.1 | 59.5 | 213 25.5 | 29.0 | Alphard | 217 49.7 | S 8 45.2 |
| 11 | 189 56.7 | 349 42.8 | 13.5 | 106 12.1 | 10.5 | 188 12.8 | 59.7 | 228 28.0 | 29.0 | | | |
| 12 | 204 59.2 | 4 42.4 | S 7 14.7 | 121 14.0 | N23 10.6 | 203 15.5 | S 0 59.8 | 243 30.5 | S16 29.1 | Alphecca | 126 05.6 | N26 38.5 |
| 13 | 220 01.6 | 19 41.9 | 16.0 | 136 16.0 | 10.7 | 218 18.3 | 59.9 | 258 32.9 | 29.1 | Alpheratz | 357 36.4 | N29 13.1 |
| 14 | 235 04.1 | 34 41.5 | 17.2 | 151 18.0 | 10.8 | 233 21.0 | 1 00.0 | 273 35.4 | 29.1 | Altair | 62 01.8 | N 8 55.8 |
| 15 | 250 06.6 | 49 41.0 .. | 18.4 | 166 19.9 .. | 10.9 | 248 23.7 .. | 00.1 | 288 37.9 .. | 29.1 | Ankaa | 353 08.6 | S42 11.0 |
| 16 | 265 09.0 | 64 40.6 | 19.6 | 181 21.9 | 11.1 | 263 26.5 | 00.2 | 303 40.4 | 29.1 | Antares | 112 18.4 | S26 28.9 |
| 17 | 280 11.5 | 79 40.1 | 20.8 | 196 23.9 | 11.2 | 278 29.2 | 00.3 | 318 42.9 | 29.1 | | | |
| 18 | 295 13.9 | 94 39.7 | S 7 22.0 | 211 25.8 | N23 11.3 | 293 31.9 | S 1 00.4 | 333 45.4 | S16 29.1 | Arcturus | 145 50.0 | N19 04.0 |
| 19 | 310 16.4 | 109 39.3 | 23.3 | 226 27.8 | 11.4 | 308 34.6 | 00.5 | 348 47.9 | 29.1 | Atria | 107 14.6 | S69 04.2 |
| 20 | 325 18.9 | 124 38.8 | 24.5 | 241 29.8 | 11.5 | 323 37.4 | 00.6 | 3 50.4 | 29.1 | Avior | 234 15.6 | S59 34.5 |
| 21 | 340 21.3 | 139 38.4 .. | 25.7 | 256 31.7 .. | 11.6 | 338 40.1 .. | 00.7 | 18 52.9 .. | 29.1 | Bellatrix | 278 24.7 | N 6 22.3 |
| 22 | 355 23.8 | 154 37.9 | 26.9 | 271 33.7 | 11.7 | 353 42.8 | 00.8 | 33 55.4 | 29.1 | Betelgeuse | 270 54.0 | N 7 24.8 |
| 23 | 10 26.3 | 169 37.5 | 28.1 | 286 35.7 | 11.8 | 8 45.5 | 01.0 | 48 57.9 | 29.1 | | | |
| 17 00 | 25 28.7 | 184 37.0 | S 7 29.3 | 301 37.7 | N23 12.0 | 23 48.3 | S 1 01.1 | 64 00.4 | S16 29.1 | Canopus | 263 53.0 | S52 42.1 |
| 01 | 40 31.2 | 199 36.6 | 30.5 | 316 39.6 | 12.1 | 38 51.0 | 01.2 | 79 02.8 | 29.1 | Capella | 280 24.4 | N46 01.1 |
| 02 | 55 33.7 | 214 36.2 | 31.8 | 331 41.6 | 12.2 | 53 53.7 | 01.3 | 94 05.3 | 29.1 | Deneb | 49 27.0 | N45 21.9 |
| 03 | 70 36.1 | 229 35.7 .. | 33.0 | 346 43.6 .. | 12.3 | 68 56.5 .. | 01.4 | 109 07.8 .. | 29.1 | Denebola | 182 27.1 | N14 26.8 |
| 04 | 85 38.6 | 244 35.3 | 34.2 | 1 45.6 | 12.4 | 83 59.2 | 01.5 | 124 10.3 | 29.1 | Diphda | 348 48.8 | S17 51.7 |
| 05 | 100 41.1 | 259 34.8 | 35.4 | 16 47.6 | 12.5 | 99 01.9 | 01.6 | 139 12.8 | 29.2 | | | |
| 06 | 115 43.5 | 274 34.4 | S 7 36.6 | 31 49.5 | N23 12.6 | 114 04.6 | S 1 01.7 | 154 15.3 | S16 29.2 | Dubhe | 193 43.8 | N61 37.6 |
| 07 | 130 46.0 | 289 33.9 | 37.8 | 46 51.5 | 12.7 | 129 07.4 | 01.8 | 169 17.8 | 29.2 | Elnath | 278 04.0 | N28 37.6 |
| 08 | 145 48.4 | 304 33.5 | 39.0 | 61 53.5 | 12.9 | 144 10.1 | 01.9 | 184 20.3 | 29.2 | Eltanin | 90 43.3 | N51 29.4 |
| 09 | 160 50.9 | 319 33.0 .. | 40.2 | 76 55.5 .. | 13.0 | 159 12.8 .. | 02.0 | 199 22.8 .. | 29.2 | Enif | 33 40.5 | N 9 58.9 |
| 10 | 175 53.4 | 334 32.6 | 41.4 | 91 57.5 | 13.1 | 174 15.5 | 02.1 | 214 25.3 | 29.2 | Fomalhaut | 15 16.3 | S29 30.2 |
| 11 | 190 55.8 | 349 32.1 | 42.7 | 106 59.5 | 13.2 | 189 18.3 | 02.2 | 229 27.7 | 29.2 | | | |
| 12 | 205 58.3 | 4 31.7 | S 7 43.9 | 122 01.5 | N23 13.3 | 204 21.0 | S 1 02.3 | 244 30.2 | S16 29.2 | Gacrux | 171 54.3 | S57 14.2 |
| 13 | 221 00.8 | 19 31.2 | 45.1 | 137 03.5 | 13.4 | 219 23.7 | 02.5 | 259 32.7 | 29.2 | Gienah | 175 45.8 | S17 39.9 |
| 14 | 236 03.2 | 34 30.8 | 46.3 | 152 05.5 | 13.5 | 234 26.4 | 02.6 | 274 35.2 | 29.2 | Hadar | 148 39.3 | S60 28.9 |
| 15 | 251 05.7 | 49 30.4 .. | 47.5 | 167 07.5 .. | 13.6 | 249 29.2 .. | 02.7 | 289 37.7 .. | 29.2 | Hamal | 327 53.0 | N23 34.2 |
| 16 | 266 08.2 | 64 29.9 | 48.7 | 182 09.5 | 13.8 | 264 31.9 | 02.8 | 304 40.2 | 29.2 | Kaus Aust. | 83 35.1 | S34 22.5 |
| 17 | 281 10.6 | 79 29.5 | 49.9 | 197 11.5 | 13.9 | 279 34.6 | 02.9 | 319 42.7 | 29.2 | | | |
| 18 | 296 13.1 | 94 29.0 | S 7 51.1 | 212 13.5 | N23 14.0 | 294 37.3 | S 1 03.0 | 334 45.2 | S16 29.2 | Kochab | 137 20.9 | N74 03.8 |
| 19 | 311 15.6 | 109 28.6 | 52.3 | 227 15.5 | 14.1 | 309 40.0 | 03.1 | 349 47.6 | 29.2 | Markab | 13 31.5 | N15 19.8 |
| 20 | 326 18.0 | 124 28.1 | 53.5 | 242 17.5 | 14.2 | 324 42.8 | 03.2 | 4 50.1 | 29.2 | Menkar | 314 07.8 | N 4 10.8 |
| 21 | 341 20.5 | 139 27.7 .. | 54.7 | 257 19.5 .. | 14.3 | 339 45.5 .. | 03.3 | 19 52.6 .. | 29.2 | Menkent | 148 00.2 | S36 28.8 |
| 22 | 356 22.9 | 154 27.2 | 56.0 | 272 21.5 | 14.4 | 354 48.2 | 03.4 | 34 55.1 | 29.2 | Miaplacidus | 221 39.0 | S69 48.2 |
| 23 | 11 25.4 | 169 26.8 | 57.2 | 287 23.5 | 14.5 | 9 50.9 | 03.5 | 49 57.6 | 29.2 | | | |
| 18 00 | 26 27.9 | 184 26.3 | S 7 58.4 | 302 25.5 | N23 14.7 | 24 53.7 | S 1 03.6 | 65 00.1 | S16 29.3 | Mirfak | 308 30.5 | N49 56.4 |
| 01 | 41 30.3 | 199 25.9 | 7 59.6 | 317 27.5 | 14.8 | 39 56.4 | 03.7 | 80 02.6 | 29.3 | Nunki | 75 50.1 | S26 16.1 |
| 02 | 56 32.8 | 214 25.4 | 8 00.8 | 332 29.5 | 14.9 | 54 59.1 | 03.8 | 95 05.1 | 29.3 | Peacock | 53 08.6 | S56 39.9 |
| 03 | 71 35.3 | 229 25.0 .. | 02.0 | 347 31.5 .. | 15.0 | 70 01.8 .. | 03.9 | 110 07.5 .. | 29.3 | Pollux | 243 19.6 | N27 58.3 |
| 04 | 86 37.7 | 244 24.5 | 03.2 | 2 33.5 | 15.1 | 85 04.5 | 04.0 | 125 10.0 | 29.3 | Procyon | 244 52.8 | N 5 10.1 |
| 05 | 101 40.2 | 259 24.0 | 04.4 | 17 35.6 | 15.2 | 100 07.3 | 04.1 | 140 12.5 | 29.3 | | | |
| 06 | 116 42.7 | 274 23.6 | S 8 05.6 | 32 37.6 | N23 15.3 | 115 10.0 | S 1 04.2 | 155 15.0 | S16 29.3 | Rasalhague | 96 00.5 | N12 32.8 |
| 07 | 131 45.1 | 289 23.1 | 06.8 | 47 39.6 | 15.4 | 130 12.7 | 04.4 | 170 17.5 | 29.3 | Regulus | 207 36.6 | N11 51.5 |
| 08 | 146 47.6 | 304 22.7 | 08.0 | 62 41.6 | 15.6 | 145 15.4 | 04.5 | 185 20.0 | 29.3 | Rigel | 281 05.5 | S 8 10.4 |
| 09 | 161 50.0 | 319 22.2 .. | 09.2 | 77 43.6 .. | 15.7 | 160 18.1 .. | 04.6 | 200 22.4 .. | 29.3 | Rigil Kent. | 139 43.5 | S60 55.7 |
| 10 | 176 52.5 | 334 21.8 | 10.4 | 92 45.7 | 15.8 | 175 20.9 | 04.7 | 215 24.9 | 29.3 | Sabik | 102 05.1 | S15 45.1 |
| 11 | 191 55.0 | 349 21.3 | 11.6 | 107 47.7 | 15.9 | 190 23.6 | 04.8 | 230 27.4 | 29.3 | | | |
| 12 | 206 57.4 | 4 20.9 | S 8 12.8 | 122 49.7 | N23 16.0 | 205 26.3 | S 1 04.9 | 245 29.9 | S16 29.3 | Schedar | 349 32.6 | N56 39.8 |
| 13 | 221 59.9 | 19 20.4 | 14.0 | 137 51.7 | 16.1 | 220 29.0 | 05.0 | 260 32.4 | 29.3 | Shaula | 96 13.1 | S37 07.3 |
| 14 | 237 02.4 | 34 20.0 | 15.2 | 152 53.8 | 16.2 | 235 31.7 | 05.1 | 275 34.9 | 29.3 | Sirius | 258 27.8 | S16 44.6 |
| 15 | 252 04.8 | 49 19.5 .. | 16.4 | 167 55.8 .. | 16.3 | 250 34.5 .. | 05.2 | 290 37.4 .. | 29.3 | Spica | 158 24.6 | S11 16.6 |
| 16 | 267 07.3 | 64 19.1 | 17.6 | 182 57.8 | 16.4 | 265 37.2 | 05.3 | 305 39.8 | 29.3 | Suhail | 222 47.8 | S43 31.1 |
| 17 | 282 09.8 | 79 18.6 | 18.8 | 197 59.9 | 16.6 | 280 39.9 | 05.4 | 320 42.3 | 29.3 | | | |
| 18 | 297 12.2 | 94 18.1 | S 8 20.0 | 213 01.9 | N23 16.7 | 295 42.6 | S 1 05.5 | 335 44.8 | S16 29.3 | Vega | 80 34.6 | N38 48.5 |
| 19 | 312 14.7 | 109 17.7 | 21.2 | 228 03.9 | 16.8 | 310 45.3 | 05.6 | 350 47.3 | 29.3 | Zuben'ubi | 136 58.4 | S16 08.0 |
| 20 | 327 17.2 | 124 17.2 | 22.4 | 243 06.0 | 16.9 | 325 48.1 | 05.7 | 5 49.8 | 29.3 | | | |
| 21 | 342 19.6 | 139 16.8 .. | 23.6 | 258 08.0 .. | 17.0 | 340 50.8 .. | 05.8 | 20 52.3 .. | 29.3 | | SHA | Mer. Pass. |
| 22 | 357 22.1 | 154 16.3 | 24.8 | 273 10.0 | 17.1 | 355 53.5 | 05.9 | 35 54.7 | 29.3 | Venus | 159 08.3 | h m 11 42 |
| 23 | 12 24.5 | 169 15.9 | 26.0 | 288 12.1 | 17.2 | 10 56.2 | 06.0 | 50 57.2 | 29.3 | Mars | 276 08.9 | 3 53 |
| | | | | | | | | | | Jupiter | 358 19.5 | 22 21 |
| Mer. Pass. | h m 22 14.4 | v −0.4 | d 1.2 | v 2.0 | d 0.1 | v 2.7 | d 0.1 | v 2.5 | d 0.0 | Saturn | 38 31.6 | 19 41 |

| UT | | SUN | | MOON | | | | Lat. | Twilight | | Sunrise | Moonrise | | | |
|---|---|---|---|---|---|---|---|---|---|---|---|---|---|---|---|
| | | | | | | | | | Naut. | Civil | | 16 | 17 | 18 | 19 |
| | | GHA | Dec | GHA | v | Dec | d | HP | | | | | | | |
| d h | | ° ′ | ° ′ | ° ′ | ′ | ° ′ | ′ | ′ | ° | h m | h m | h m | h m | h m | h m | h m |
| **16** 00 | | 183 35.1 | S 8 47.7 | 290 07.1 | 9.9 | N27 25.8 | 0.8 | 54.4 | N 72 | 05 04 | 06 22 | 07 34 | ☐ | ☐ | ☐ | ☐ |
| 01 | | 198 35.3 | 48.6 | 304 36.0 | 9.9 | 27 26.6 | 0.6 | 54.4 | N 70 | 05 07 | 06 17 | 07 21 | ☐ | ☐ | ☐ | 20 21 |
| 02 | | 213 35.4 | 49.5 | 319 04.9 | 9.9 | 27 27.2 | 0.5 | 54.4 | 68 | 05 09 | 06 13 | 07 11 | ☐ | ☐ | ☐ | 21 40 |
| 03 | | 228 35.5 .. | 50.5 | 333 33.8 | 9.9 | 27 27.7 | 0.4 | 54.4 | 66 | 05 10 | 06 10 | 07 03 | ☐ | ☐ | 19 53 | 22 17 |
| 04 | | 243 35.7 | 51.4 | 348 02.7 | 10.0 | 27 28.1 | 0.2 | 54.4 | 64 | 05 12 | 06 07 | 06 55 | ☐ | 18 19 | 20 52 | 22 43 |
| 05 | | 258 35.8 | 52.3 | 2 31.7 | 9.9 | 27 28.3 | 0.1 | 54.4 | 62 | 05 13 | 06 04 | 06 49 | 18 16 | 19 46 | 21 25 | 23 03 |
| 06 | | 273 35.9 | S 8 53.2 | 17 00.6 | 10.0 | N27 28.4 | 0.0 | 54.4 | 60 | 05 13 | 06 02 | 06 44 | 19 08 | 20 23 | 21 50 | 23 20 |
| 07 | | 288 36.1 | 54.1 | 31 29.6 | 10.0 | 27 28.4 | 0.2 | 54.3 | N 58 | 05 14 | 05 59 | 06 39 | 19 39 | 20 49 | 22 09 | 23 33 |
| 08 | | 303 36.2 | 55.1 | 45 58.6 | 10.0 | 27 28.2 | 0.3 | 54.3 | 56 | 05 14 | 05 57 | 06 35 | 20 03 | 21 09 | 22 25 | 23 45 |
| S 09 | | 318 36.3 .. | 56.0 | 60 27.6 | 10.0 | 27 27.9 | 0.4 | 54.3 | 54 | 05 15 | 05 55 | 06 31 | 20 22 | 21 26 | 22 39 | 23 55 |
| U 10 | | 333 36.5 | 56.9 | 74 56.6 | 10.0 | 27 27.5 | 0.6 | 54.3 | 52 | 05 15 | 05 54 | 06 28 | 20 38 | 21 41 | 22 51 | 24 04 |
| N 11 | | 348 36.6 | 57.8 | 89 25.6 | 10.0 | 27 26.9 | 0.7 | 54.3 | 50 | 05 15 | 05 52 | 06 25 | 20 52 | 21 54 | 23 01 | 24 13 |
| D 12 | | 3 36.7 | S 8 58.7 | 103 54.6 | 10.1 | N27 26.2 | 0.8 | 54.3 | 45 | 05 14 | 05 48 | 06 18 | 21 20 | 22 20 | 23 23 | 24 30 |
| A 13 | | 18 36.9 | 8 59.6 | 118 23.7 | 10.0 | 27 25.4 | 1.0 | 54.3 | N 40 | 05 14 | 05 45 | 06 12 | 21 43 | 22 40 | 23 41 | 24 44 |
| Y 14 | | 33 37.0 | 9 00.6 | 132 52.7 | 10.1 | 27 24.4 | 1.1 | 54.3 | 35 | 05 12 | 05 42 | 06 07 | 22 01 | 22 57 | 23 56 | 24 56 |
| 15 | | 48 37.1 .. | 01.5 | 147 21.8 | 10.1 | 27 23.3 | 1.2 | 54.3 | 30 | 05 11 | 05 39 | 06 03 | 22 17 | 23 12 | 24 09 | 00 09 |
| 16 | | 63 37.3 | 02.4 | 161 50.9 | 10.1 | 27 22.1 | 1.4 | 54.3 | 20 | 05 07 | 05 33 | 05 55 | 22 44 | 23 37 | 24 30 | 00 30 |
| 17 | | 78 37.4 | 03.3 | 176 20.1 | 10.1 | 27 20.7 | 1.5 | 54.3 | N 10 | 05 03 | 05 27 | 05 49 | 23 07 | 23 58 | 24 49 | 00 49 |
| 18 | | 93 37.5 | S 9 04.2 | 190 49.2 | 10.2 | N27 19.2 | 1.6 | 54.3 | 0 | 04 57 | 05 21 | 05 42 | 23 28 | 24 18 | 00 18 | 01 07 |
| 19 | | 108 37.7 | 05.1 | 205 18.4 | 10.2 | 27 17.6 | 1.7 | 54.3 | S 10 | 04 49 | 05 14 | 05 35 | 23 50 | 24 38 | 00 38 | 01 24 |
| 20 | | 123 37.8 | 06.1 | 219 47.6 | 10.2 | 27 15.9 | 1.9 | 54.3 | 20 | 04 40 | 05 06 | 05 28 | 24 13 | 00 13 | 01 00 | 01 43 |
| 21 | | 138 37.9 .. | 07.0 | 234 16.8 | 10.3 | 27 14.0 | 2.0 | 54.3 | 30 | 04 27 | 04 55 | 05 20 | 24 40 | 00 40 | 01 25 | 02 04 |
| 22 | | 153 38.1 | 07.9 | 248 46.1 | 10.3 | 27 12.0 | 2.2 | 54.3 | 35 | 04 18 | 04 49 | 05 15 | 00 06 | 00 55 | 01 39 | 02 17 |
| 23 | | 168 38.2 | 08.8 | 263 15.4 | 10.3 | 27 09.8 | 2.3 | 54.3 | 40 | 04 08 | 04 42 | 05 10 | 00 24 | 01 14 | 01 56 | 02 31 |
| **17** 00 | | 183 38.3 | S 9 09.7 | 277 44.7 | 10.3 | N27 07.5 | 2.4 | 54.2 | 45 | 03 56 | 04 33 | 05 03 | 00 47 | 01 36 | 02 16 | 02 48 |
| 01 | | 198 38.4 | 10.6 | 292 14.0 | 10.4 | 27 05.1 | 2.5 | 54.2 | S 50 | 03 40 | 04 21 | 04 55 | 01 16 | 02 04 | 02 41 | 03 09 |
| 02 | | 213 38.6 | 11.6 | 306 43.4 | 10.4 | 27 02.6 | 2.7 | 54.2 | 52 | 03 32 | 04 16 | 04 52 | 01 30 | 02 18 | 02 53 | 03 19 |
| 03 | | 228 38.7 .. | 12.5 | 321 12.8 | 10.4 | 26 59.9 | 2.7 | 54.2 | 54 | 03 23 | 04 10 | 04 48 | 01 47 | 02 34 | 03 07 | 03 30 |
| 04 | | 243 38.8 | 13.4 | 335 42.2 | 10.4 | 26 57.2 | 3.0 | 54.2 | 56 | 03 13 | 04 04 | 04 43 | 02 07 | 02 52 | 03 23 | 03 43 |
| 05 | | 258 39.0 | 14.3 | 350 11.6 | 10.5 | 26 54.2 | 3.0 | 54.2 | 58 | 03 01 | 03 56 | 04 38 | 02 31 | 03 15 | 03 42 | 03 58 |
| 06 | | 273 39.1 | S 9 15.2 | 4 41.1 | 10.5 | N26 51.2 | 3.2 | 54.2 | S 60 | 02 47 | 03 47 | 04 33 | 03 05 | 03 46 | 04 05 | 04 15 |
| 07 | | 288 39.2 | 16.1 | 19 10.6 | 10.6 | 26 48.0 | 3.3 | 54.2 | | | | | | | | |
| 08 | | 303 39.3 | 17.0 | 33 40.2 | 10.6 | 26 44.7 | 3.4 | 54.2 | Lat. | Sunset | Twilight | | Moonset | | | |
| M 09 | | 318 39.5 .. | 18.0 | 48 09.8 | 10.6 | 26 41.3 | 3.6 | 54.2 | | | Civil | Naut. | 16 | 17 | 18 | 19 |
| O 10 | | 333 39.6 | 18.9 | 62 39.4 | 10.6 | 26 37.7 | 3.6 | 54.2 | | | | | | | | |
| N 11 | | 348 39.7 | 19.8 | 77 09.0 | 10.7 | 26 34.1 | 3.8 | 54.2 | ° | h m | h m | h m | h m | h m | h m | h m |
| D 12 | | 3 39.9 | S 9 20.7 | 91 38.7 | 10.7 | N26 30.3 | 4.0 | 54.2 | N 72 | 15 55 | 17 07 | 18 24 | ☐ | ☐ | ☐ | ☐ |
| A 13 | | 18 40.0 | 21.6 | 106 08.4 | 10.8 | 26 26.3 | 4.0 | 54.2 | N 70 | 16 08 | 17 12 | 18 22 | ☐ | ☐ | ☐ | 19 18 |
| Y 14 | | 33 40.1 | 22.5 | 120 38.2 | 10.8 | 26 22.3 | 4.2 | 54.2 | 68 | 16 18 | 17 16 | 18 20 | ☐ | ☐ | ☐ | 17 59 |
| 15 | | 48 40.2 .. | 23.4 | 135 08.0 | 10.8 | 26 18.1 | 4.3 | 54.2 | 66 | 16 27 | 17 19 | 18 19 | ☐ | ☐ | 18 07 | 17 21 |
| 16 | | 63 40.4 | 24.3 | 149 37.8 | 10.9 | 26 13.8 | 4.4 | 54.2 | 64 | 16 34 | 17 23 | 18 17 | ☐ | 17 59 | 17 07 | 16 33 |
| 17 | | 78 40.5 | 25.3 | 164 07.7 | 10.9 | 26 09.4 | 4.6 | 54.2 | 62 | 16 40 | 17 25 | 18 17 | 16 16 | 16 31 | 16 33 | 16 33 |
| 18 | | 93 40.6 | S 9 26.2 | 178 37.6 | 11.0 | N26 04.8 | 4.6 | 54.2 | 60 | 16 46 | 17 28 | 18 16 | 15 25 | 15 54 | 16 08 | 16 15 |
| 19 | | 108 40.7 | 27.1 | 193 07.6 | 11.0 | 26 00.2 | 4.8 | 54.2 | N 58 | 16 50 | 17 30 | 18 16 | 14 53 | 15 28 | 15 49 | 16 01 |
| 20 | | 123 40.9 | 28.0 | 207 37.6 | 11.0 | 25 55.4 | 4.9 | 54.2 | 56 | 16 55 | 17 32 | 18 15 | 14 29 | 15 07 | 15 32 | 15 49 |
| 21 | | 138 41.0 .. | 28.9 | 222 07.6 | 11.1 | 25 50.5 | 5.1 | 54.2 | 54 | 16 58 | 17 34 | 18 15 | 14 10 | 14 50 | 15 18 | 15 38 |
| 22 | | 153 41.1 | 29.8 | 236 37.7 | 11.1 | 25 45.4 | 5.1 | 54.3 | 52 | 17 02 | 17 36 | 18 15 | 13 54 | 14 35 | 15 05 | 15 28 |
| 23 | | 168 41.2 | 30.7 | 251 07.8 | 11.1 | 25 40.3 | 5.3 | 54.3 | 50 | 17 05 | 17 38 | 18 15 | 13 40 | 14 22 | 14 55 | 15 19 |
| **18** 00 | | 183 41.4 | S 9 31.6 | 265 37.9 | 11.2 | N25 35.0 | 5.4 | 54.3 | 45 | 17 12 | 17 42 | 18 16 | 13 11 | 13 56 | 14 32 | 15 01 |
| 01 | | 198 41.5 | 32.5 | 280 08.1 | 11.3 | 25 29.6 | 5.5 | 54.3 | N 40 | 17 17 | 17 45 | 18 16 | 12 49 | 13 34 | 14 13 | 14 46 |
| 02 | | 213 41.6 | 33.5 | 294 38.4 | 11.3 | 25 24.1 | 5.6 | 54.3 | 35 | 17 23 | 17 48 | 18 18 | 12 30 | 13 17 | 13 58 | 14 33 |
| 03 | | 228 41.7 .. | 34.4 | 309 08.7 | 11.3 | 25 18.5 | 5.7 | 54.3 | 30 | 17 27 | 17 51 | 18 19 | 12 14 | 13 02 | 13 44 | 14 22 |
| 04 | | 243 41.8 | 35.3 | 323 39.0 | 11.4 | 25 12.8 | 5.9 | 54.3 | 20 | 17 35 | 17 57 | 18 23 | 11 47 | 12 36 | 13 21 | 14 02 |
| 05 | | 258 42.0 | 36.2 | 338 09.4 | 11.4 | 25 06.9 | 6.0 | 54.3 | N 10 | 17 42 | 18 03 | 18 28 | 11 24 | 12 14 | 13 01 | 13 45 |
| 06 | | 273 42.1 | S 9 37.1 | 352 39.8 | 11.5 | N25 00.9 | 6.1 | 54.3 | 0 | 17 49 | 18 10 | 18 34 | 11 02 | 11 53 | 12 42 | 13 29 |
| 07 | | 288 42.2 | 38.0 | 7 10.3 | 11.5 | 24 54.8 | 6.2 | 54.3 | S 10 | 17 55 | 18 17 | 18 42 | 10 40 | 11 32 | 12 23 | 13 13 |
| T 08 | | 303 42.3 | 38.9 | 21 40.8 | 11.6 | 24 48.6 | 6.3 | 54.3 | 20 | 18 03 | 18 25 | 18 51 | 10 17 | 11 09 | 12 03 | 12 56 |
| U 09 | | 318 42.5 .. | 39.8 | 36 11.4 | 11.6 | 24 42.3 | 6.4 | 54.3 | 30 | 18 11 | 18 36 | 19 05 | 09 50 | 10 43 | 11 39 | 12 36 |
| E 10 | | 333 42.6 | 40.7 | 50 42.0 | 11.6 | 24 35.9 | 6.6 | 54.3 | 35 | 18 16 | 18 42 | 19 13 | 09 33 | 10 28 | 11 25 | 12 25 |
| S 11 | | 348 42.7 | 41.6 | 65 12.6 | 11.7 | 24 29.3 | 6.6 | 54.3 | 40 | 18 22 | 18 50 | 19 23 | 09 15 | 10 10 | 11 09 | 12 11 |
| D 12 | | 3 42.8 | S 9 42.5 | 79 43.3 | 11.7 | N24 22.7 | 6.8 | 54.3 | 45 | 18 28 | 18 59 | 19 36 | 08 52 | 09 48 | 10 50 | 11 55 |
| A 13 | | 18 42.9 | 43.4 | 94 14.0 | 11.8 | 24 15.9 | 6.9 | 54.3 | S 50 | 18 36 | 19 11 | 19 52 | 08 23 | 09 20 | 10 25 | 11 35 |
| Y 14 | | 33 43.1 | 44.3 | 108 44.8 | 11.9 | 24 09.0 | 7.0 | 54.3 | 52 | 18 40 | 19 16 | 20 00 | 08 09 | 09 07 | 10 14 | 11 26 |
| 15 | | 48 43.2 .. | 45.3 | 123 15.7 | 11.8 | 24 02.0 | 7.1 | 54.4 | 54 | 18 44 | 19 22 | 20 09 | 07 52 | 08 51 | 10 00 | 11 15 |
| 16 | | 63 43.3 | 46.2 | 137 46.5 | 12.0 | 23 54.9 | 7.2 | 54.4 | 56 | 18 49 | 19 29 | 20 20 | 07 32 | 08 32 | 09 44 | 11 03 |
| 17 | | 78 43.4 | 47.1 | 152 17.5 | 11.9 | 23 47.7 | 7.3 | 54.4 | 58 | 18 54 | 19 37 | 20 32 | 07 08 | 08 09 | 09 26 | 10 49 |
| 18 | | 93 43.5 | S 9 48.0 | 166 48.4 | 12.1 | N23 40.4 | 7.5 | 54.4 | S 60 | 18 59 | 19 45 | 20 46 | 06 34 | 07 39 | 09 03 | 10 32 |
| 19 | | 108 43.6 | 48.9 | 181 19.5 | 12.0 | 23 32.9 | 7.5 | 54.4 | | | | | | | | |
| 20 | | 123 43.8 | 49.8 | 195 50.5 | 12.1 | 23 25.4 | 7.7 | 54.4 | | | SUN | | | MOON | | |
| 21 | | 138 43.9 .. | 50.7 | 210 21.6 | 12.2 | 23 17.7 | 7.7 | 54.4 | Day | Eqn. of Time | | Mer. | Mer. Pass. | | Age | Phase |
| 22 | | 153 44.0 | 51.6 | 224 52.8 | 12.2 | 23 10.0 | 7.9 | 54.4 | | 00ʰ | 12ʰ | Pass. | Upper | Lower | | |
| 23 | | 168 44.1 | 52.5 | 239 24.0 | 12.3 | N23 02.1 | 7.9 | 54.4 | d | m s | m s | h m | h m | h m | d % | |
| | | | | | | | | | 16 | 14 20 | 14 27 | 11 46 | 04 50 | 17 15 | 21 62 | |
| | | SD 16.1 | d 0.9 | SD 14.8 | | 14.8 | | 14.8 | 17 | 14 33 | 14 39 | 11 45 | 05 41 | 18 06 | 22 52 | |
| | | | | | | | | | 18 | 14 45 | 14 51 | 11 45 | 06 30 | 18 55 | 23 43 | |

| UT | ARIES GHA | VENUS −3.9 GHA | Dec | MARS −1.0 GHA | Dec | JUPITER −2.9 GHA | Dec | SATURN +0.5 GHA | Dec | STARS Name | SHA | Dec |
|---|---|---|---|---|---|---|---|---|---|---|---|---|
| **19** 00 | 27 27.0 | 184 15.4 | S 8 27.2 | 303 14.1 | N23 17.3 | 25 58.9 | S 1 06.1 | 65 59.7 | S16 29.4 | Acamar | 315 12.8 | S40 12.7 |
| 01 | 42 29.5 | 199 14.9 | 28.4 | 318 16.2 | 17.5 | 41 01.6 | 06.2 | 81 02.2 | 29.4 | Achernar | 335 21.0 | S57 07.3 |
| 02 | 57 31.9 | 214 14.5 | 29.6 | 333 18.2 | 17.6 | 56 04.4 | 06.3 | 96 04.7 | 29.4 | Acrux | 173 02.8 | S63 13.3 |
| 03 | 72 34.4 | 229 14.0 .. | 30.8 | 348 20.3 .. | 17.7 | 71 07.1 .. | 06.4 | 111 07.2 .. | 29.4 | Adhara | 255 07.2 | S28 59.9 |
| 04 | 87 36.9 | 244 13.6 | 32.0 | 3 22.3 | 17.8 | 86 09.8 | 06.5 | 126 09.6 | 29.4 | Aldebaran | 290 41.5 | N16 33.3 |
| 05 | 102 39.3 | 259 13.1 | 33.2 | 18 24.3 | 17.9 | 101 12.5 | 06.6 | 141 12.1 | 29.4 | | | |
| 06 | 117 41.8 | 274 12.6 | S 8 34.4 | 33 26.4 | N23 18.0 | 116 15.2 | S 1 06.7 | 156 14.6 | S16 29.4 | Alioth | 166 15.2 | N55 50.2 |
| W 07 | 132 44.3 | 289 12.2 | 35.6 | 48 28.4 | 18.1 | 131 17.9 | 06.8 | 171 17.1 | 29.4 | Alkaid | 152 54.0 | N49 12.1 |
| E 08 | 147 46.7 | 304 11.7 | 36.8 | 63 30.5 | 18.2 | 146 20.7 | 06.9 | 186 19.6 | 29.4 | Alnair | 27 35.0 | S46 51.2 |
| D 09 | 162 49.2 | 319 11.3 .. | 38.0 | 78 32.6 .. | 18.4 | 161 23.4 .. | 07.0 | 201 22.0 .. | 29.4 | Alnilam | 275 39.4 | S 1 11.1 |
| N 10 | 177 51.7 | 334 10.8 | 39.2 | 93 34.6 | 18.5 | 176 26.1 | 07.1 | 216 24.5 | 29.4 | Alphard | 217 49.7 | S 8 45.2 |
| E 11 | 192 54.1 | 349 10.3 | 40.4 | 108 36.7 | 18.6 | 191 28.8 | 07.2 | 231 27.0 | 29.4 | | | |
| S 12 | 207 56.6 | 4 09.9 | S 8 41.6 | 123 38.7 | N23 18.7 | 206 31.5 | S 1 07.3 | 246 29.5 | S16 29.4 | Alphecca | 126 05.6 | N26 38.5 |
| D 13 | 222 59.0 | 19 09.4 | 42.8 | 138 40.8 | 18.8 | 221 34.2 | 07.4 | 261 32.0 | 29.4 | Alpheratz | 357 36.4 | N29 13.1 |
| A 14 | 238 01.5 | 34 09.0 | 44.0 | 153 42.9 | 18.9 | 236 37.0 | 07.6 | 276 34.4 | 29.4 | Altair | 62 01.8 | N 8 55.8 |
| Y 15 | 253 04.0 | 49 08.5 .. | 45.2 | 168 44.9 .. | 19.0 | 251 39.7 .. | 07.7 | 291 36.9 .. | 29.4 | Ankaa | 353 08.6 | S42 11.0 |
| 16 | 268 06.4 | 64 08.0 | 46.4 | 183 47.0 | 19.1 | 266 42.4 | 07.8 | 306 39.4 | 29.4 | Antares | 112 18.4 | S26 28.9 |
| 17 | 283 08.9 | 79 07.6 | 47.6 | 198 49.0 | 19.2 | 281 45.1 | 07.9 | 321 41.9 | 29.4 | | | |
| 18 | 298 11.4 | 94 07.1 | S 8 48.8 | 213 51.1 | N23 19.4 | 296 47.8 | S 1 08.0 | 336 44.4 | S16 29.4 | Arcturus | 145 50.0 | N19 04.0 |
| 19 | 313 13.8 | 109 06.6 | 49.9 | 228 53.2 | 19.5 | 311 50.5 | 08.1 | 351 46.8 | 29.4 | Atria | 107 14.7 | S69 04.2 |
| 20 | 328 16.3 | 124 06.2 | 51.1 | 243 55.3 | 19.6 | 326 53.2 | 08.2 | 6 49.3 | 29.4 | Avior | 234 15.6 | S59 34.5 |
| 21 | 343 18.8 | 139 05.7 .. | 52.3 | 258 57.3 .. | 19.7 | 341 56.0 .. | 08.3 | 21 51.8 .. | 29.4 | Bellatrix | 278 24.7 | N 6 22.3 |
| 22 | 358 21.2 | 154 05.2 | 53.5 | 273 59.4 | 19.8 | 356 58.7 | 08.4 | 36 54.3 | 29.4 | Betelgeuse | 270 53.9 | N 7 24.8 |
| 23 | 13 23.7 | 169 04.8 | 54.7 | 289 01.5 | 19.9 | 12 01.4 | 08.5 | 51 56.8 | 29.4 | | | |
| **20** 00 | 28 26.1 | 184 04.3 | S 8 55.9 | 304 03.5 | N23 20.0 | 27 04.1 | S 1 08.6 | 66 59.2 | S16 29.4 | Canopus | 263 53.0 | S52 42.1 |
| 01 | 43 28.6 | 199 03.8 | 57.1 | 319 05.6 | 20.1 | 42 06.8 | 08.7 | 82 01.7 | 29.4 | Capella | 280 24.3 | N46 01.1 |
| 02 | 58 31.1 | 214 03.4 | 58.3 | 334 07.7 | 20.3 | 57 09.5 | 08.8 | 97 04.2 | 29.4 | Deneb | 49 27.0 | N45 21.9 |
| 03 | 73 33.5 | 229 02.9 | 8 59.5 | 349 09.8 .. | 20.4 | 72 12.2 .. | 08.9 | 112 06.7 .. | 29.4 | Denebola | 182 27.1 | N14 26.8 |
| 04 | 88 36.0 | 244 02.4 | 9 00.7 | 4 11.9 | 20.5 | 87 14.9 | 09.0 | 127 09.1 | 29.4 | Diphda | 348 48.8 | S17 51.7 |
| 05 | 103 38.5 | 259 02.0 | 01.9 | 19 13.9 | 20.6 | 102 17.7 | 09.1 | 142 11.6 | 29.4 | | | |
| 06 | 118 40.9 | 274 01.5 | S 9 03.0 | 34 16.0 | N23 20.7 | 117 20.4 | S 1 09.2 | 157 14.1 | S16 29.4 | Dubhe | 193 43.8 | N61 37.6 |
| T 07 | 133 43.4 | 289 01.0 | 04.2 | 49 18.1 | 20.8 | 132 23.1 | 09.3 | 172 16.6 | 29.4 | Elnath | 278 04.0 | N28 37.6 |
| H 08 | 148 45.9 | 304 00.6 | 05.4 | 64 20.2 | 20.9 | 147 25.8 | 09.4 | 187 19.1 | 29.4 | Eltanin | 90 43.3 | N51 29.4 |
| U 09 | 163 48.3 | 319 00.1 .. | 06.6 | 79 22.3 .. | 21.0 | 162 28.5 .. | 09.5 | 202 21.5 .. | 29.4 | Enif | 33 40.5 | N 9 58.9 |
| R 10 | 178 50.8 | 333 59.6 | 07.8 | 94 24.4 | 21.2 | 177 31.2 | 09.6 | 217 24.0 | 29.4 | Fomalhaut | 15 16.3 | S29 30.2 |
| S 11 | 193 53.3 | 348 59.2 | 09.0 | 109 26.5 | 21.3 | 192 33.9 | 09.7 | 232 26.5 | 29.4 | | | |
| D 12 | 208 55.7 | 3 58.7 | S 9 10.2 | 124 28.6 | N23 21.4 | 207 36.6 | S 1 09.8 | 247 29.0 | S16 29.4 | Gacrux | 171 54.3 | S57 14.2 |
| A 13 | 223 58.2 | 18 58.2 | 11.4 | 139 30.7 | 21.5 | 222 39.3 | 09.9 | 262 31.4 | 29.4 | Gienah | 175 45.8 | S17 39.9 |
| Y 14 | 239 00.6 | 33 57.8 | 12.5 | 154 32.8 | 21.6 | 237 42.0 | 10.0 | 277 33.9 | 29.4 | Hadar | 148 39.3 | S60 28.8 |
| 15 | 254 03.1 | 48 57.3 .. | 13.7 | 169 34.9 .. | 21.7 | 252 44.8 .. | 10.1 | 292 36.4 .. | 29.4 | Hamal | 327 52.9 | N23 34.2 |
| 16 | 269 05.6 | 63 56.8 | 14.9 | 184 37.0 | 21.8 | 267 47.5 | 10.2 | 307 38.9 | 29.4 | Kaus Aust. | 83 35.1 | S34 22.5 |
| 17 | 284 08.0 | 78 56.3 | 16.1 | 199 39.1 | 21.9 | 282 50.2 | 10.3 | 322 41.3 | 29.4 | | | |
| 18 | 299 10.5 | 93 55.9 | S 9 17.3 | 214 41.2 | N23 22.0 | 297 52.9 | S 1 10.4 | 337 43.8 | S16 29.4 | Kochab | 137 20.9 | N74 03.8 |
| 19 | 314 13.0 | 108 55.4 | 18.5 | 229 43.3 | 22.2 | 312 55.6 | 10.5 | 352 46.3 | 29.4 | Markab | 13 31.5 | N15 19.8 |
| 20 | 329 15.4 | 123 54.9 | 19.7 | 244 45.4 | 22.3 | 327 58.3 | 10.6 | 7 48.8 | 29.4 | Menkar | 314 07.8 | N 4 10.8 |
| 21 | 344 17.9 | 138 54.4 .. | 20.8 | 259 47.5 .. | 22.4 | 343 01.0 .. | 10.7 | 22 51.2 .. | 29.4 | Menkent | 148 00.2 | S36 28.8 |
| 22 | 359 20.4 | 153 54.0 | 22.0 | 274 49.6 | 22.5 | 358 03.7 | 10.8 | 37 53.7 | 29.4 | Miaplacidus | 221 39.0 | S69 48.2 |
| 23 | 14 22.8 | 168 53.5 | 23.2 | 289 51.7 | 22.6 | 13 06.4 | 10.9 | 52 56.2 | 29.4 | | | |
| **21** 00 | 29 25.3 | 183 53.0 | S 9 24.4 | 304 53.8 | N23 22.7 | 28 09.1 | S 1 11.0 | 67 58.7 | S16 29.4 | Mirfak | 308 30.5 | N49 56.4 |
| 01 | 44 27.8 | 198 52.6 | 25.6 | 319 55.9 | 22.8 | 43 11.8 | 11.1 | 83 01.1 | 29.4 | Nunki | 75 50.2 | S26 16.1 |
| 02 | 59 30.2 | 213 52.1 | 26.8 | 334 58.0 | 22.9 | 58 14.5 | 11.1 | 98 03.6 | 29.4 | Peacock | 53 08.6 | S56 39.9 |
| 03 | 74 32.7 | 228 51.6 .. | 27.9 | 350 00.1 .. | 23.1 | 73 17.3 .. | 11.2 | 113 06.1 .. | 29.4 | Pollux | 243 19.6 | N27 58.3 |
| 04 | 89 35.1 | 243 51.1 | 29.1 | 5 02.2 | 23.2 | 88 20.0 | 11.3 | 128 08.6 | 29.4 | Procyon | 244 52.8 | N 5 10.1 |
| 05 | 104 37.6 | 258 50.7 | 30.3 | 20 04.4 | 23.3 | 103 22.7 | 11.4 | 143 11.0 | 29.4 | | | |
| 06 | 119 40.1 | 273 50.2 | S 9 31.5 | 35 06.5 | N23 23.4 | 118 25.4 | S 1 11.5 | 158 13.5 | S16 29.4 | Rasalhague | 96 00.5 | N12 32.8 |
| 07 | 134 42.5 | 288 49.7 | 32.7 | 50 08.6 | 23.5 | 133 28.1 | 11.6 | 173 16.0 | 29.4 | Regulus | 207 36.6 | N11 51.5 |
| F 08 | 149 45.0 | 303 49.2 | 33.8 | 65 10.7 | 23.6 | 148 30.8 | 11.7 | 188 18.4 | 29.5 | Rigel | 281 05.4 | S 8 10.4 |
| R 09 | 164 47.5 | 318 48.7 .. | 35.0 | 80 12.9 .. | 23.7 | 163 33.5 .. | 11.8 | 203 20.9 .. | 29.5 | Rigil Kent. | 139 43.5 | S60 55.6 |
| I 10 | 179 49.9 | 333 48.3 | 36.2 | 95 15.0 | 23.8 | 178 36.2 | 11.9 | 218 23.4 | 29.5 | Sabik | 102 05.1 | S15 45.1 |
| D 11 | 194 52.4 | 348 47.8 | 37.4 | 110 17.1 | 23.9 | 193 38.9 | 12.0 | 233 25.9 | 29.5 | | | |
| A 12 | 209 54.9 | 3 47.3 | S 9 38.6 | 125 19.2 | N23 24.1 | 208 41.6 | S 1 12.1 | 248 28.3 | S16 29.5 | Schedar | 349 32.6 | N56 39.8 |
| Y 13 | 224 57.3 | 18 46.8 | 39.7 | 140 21.4 | 24.2 | 223 44.3 | 12.2 | 263 30.8 | 29.5 | Shaula | 96 13.1 | S37 07.3 |
| 14 | 239 59.8 | 33 46.4 | 40.9 | 155 23.5 | 24.3 | 238 47.0 | 12.3 | 278 33.3 | 29.5 | Sirius | 258 27.8 | S16 44.6 |
| 15 | 255 02.2 | 48 45.9 .. | 42.1 | 170 25.6 .. | 24.4 | 253 49.7 .. | 12.4 | 293 35.7 .. | 29.5 | Spica | 158 24.6 | S11 16.6 |
| 16 | 270 04.7 | 63 45.4 | 43.3 | 185 27.8 | 24.5 | 268 52.4 | 12.5 | 308 38.2 | 29.4 | Suhail | 222 47.8 | S43 31.1 |
| 17 | 285 07.2 | 78 44.9 | 44.4 | 200 29.9 | 24.6 | 283 55.1 | 12.6 | 323 40.7 | 29.4 | | | |
| 18 | 300 09.6 | 93 44.4 | S 9 45.6 | 215 32.0 | N23 24.7 | 298 57.8 | S 1 12.7 | 338 43.2 | S16 29.5 | Vega | 80 34.6 | N38 48.5 |
| 19 | 315 12.1 | 108 44.0 | 46.8 | 230 34.2 | 24.8 | 314 00.5 | 12.8 | 353 45.6 | 29.4 | Zuben'ubi | 136 58.4 | S16 08.0 |
| 20 | 330 14.6 | 123 43.5 | 48.0 | 245 36.3 | 25.0 | 329 03.2 | 12.9 | 8 48.1 | 29.4 | | | |
| 21 | 345 17.0 | 138 43.0 .. | 49.1 | 260 38.4 .. | 25.1 | 344 05.9 .. | 13.0 | 23 50.6 .. | 29.4 | | SHA | Mer. Pass. |
| 22 | 0 19.5 | 153 42.5 | 50.3 | 275 40.6 | 25.2 | 359 08.6 | 13.1 | 38 53.0 | 29.4 | Venus | 155 38.2 | 11 44 |
| 23 | 15 22.0 | 168 42.0 | 51.5 | 290 42.7 | 25.3 | 14 11.4 | 13.2 | 53 55.5 | 29.4 | Mars | 275 37.4 | 3 43 |
| Mer. Pass. 22 02.6 | | v −0.5 | d 1.2 | v 2.1 | d 0.1 | v 2.7 | d 0.1 | v 2.5 | d 0.0 | Jupiter | 358 37.9 | 22 08 |
| | | | | | | | | | | Saturn | 38 33.1 | 19 29 |

## SUN / MOON

| UT (d h) | SUN GHA | SUN Dec | MOON GHA | v | MOON Dec | d | HP |
|---|---|---|---|---|---|---|---|
| 19 00 | 183 44.2 | S 9 53.4 | 253 55.3 | 12.3 | N22 54.2 | 8.1 | 54.4 |
| 01 | 198 44.4 | 54.3 | 268 26.6 | 12.3 | 22 46.1 | 8.2 | 54.5 |
| 02 | 213 44.5 | 55.2 | 282 57.9 | 12.4 | 22 37.9 | 8.3 | 54.5 |
| 03 | 228 44.6 | .. 56.1 | 297 29.3 | 12.5 | 22 29.6 | 8.4 | 54.5 |
| 04 | 243 44.7 | 57.0 | 312 00.8 | 12.5 | 22 21.2 | 8.5 | 54.5 |
| 05 | 258 44.8 | 57.9 | 326 32.3 | 12.5 | 22 12.7 | 8.5 | 54.5 |
| 06 | 273 44.9 | S 9 58.8 | 341 03.8 | 12.6 | N22 04.2 | 8.7 | 54.5 |
| W 07 | 288 45.0 | 9 59.7 | 355 35.4 | 12.6 | 21 55.5 | 8.8 | 54.5 |
| E 08 | 303 45.2 | 10 00.6 | 10 07.0 | 12.7 | 21 46.7 | 8.9 | 54.5 |
| D 09 | 318 45.3 | .. 01.5 | 24 38.7 | 12.7 | 21 37.8 | 9.0 | 54.6 |
| N 10 | 333 45.4 | 02.4 | 39 10.4 | 12.8 | 21 28.8 | 9.1 | 54.6 |
| E 11 | 348 45.5 | 03.3 | 53 42.2 | 12.8 | 21 19.7 | 9.2 | 54.6 |
| S 12 | 3 45.6 | S10 04.2 | 68 14.0 | 12.9 | N21 10.5 | 9.3 | 54.6 |
| D 13 | 18 45.7 | 05.1 | 82 45.9 | 12.9 | 21 01.2 | 9.4 | 54.6 |
| A 14 | 33 45.8 | 06.0 | 97 17.8 | 12.9 | 20 51.8 | 9.4 | 54.6 |
| Y 15 | 48 46.0 | .. 06.9 | 111 49.7 | 13.0 | 20 42.4 | 9.6 | 54.6 |
| 16 | 63 46.1 | 07.8 | 126 21.7 | 13.1 | 20 32.8 | 9.7 | 54.7 |
| 17 | 78 46.2 | 08.7 | 140 53.8 | 13.1 | 20 23.1 | 9.8 | 54.7 |
| 18 | 93 46.3 | S10 09.6 | 155 25.9 | 13.1 | N20 13.3 | 9.8 | 54.7 |
| 19 | 108 46.4 | 10.5 | 169 58.0 | 13.2 | 20 03.5 | 10.0 | 54.7 |
| 20 | 123 46.5 | 11.4 | 184 30.2 | 13.2 | 19 53.5 | 10.0 | 54.7 |
| 21 | 138 46.6 | .. 12.3 | 199 02.4 | 13.3 | 19 43.5 | 10.1 | 54.7 |
| 22 | 153 46.7 | 13.2 | 213 34.7 | 13.3 | 19 33.4 | 10.3 | 54.8 |
| 23 | 168 46.8 | 14.1 | 228 07.0 | 13.3 | 19 23.1 | 10.3 | 54.8 |
| 20 00 | 183 47.0 | S10 15.0 | 242 39.3 | 13.4 | N19 12.8 | 10.4 | 54.8 |
| 01 | 198 47.1 | 15.9 | 257 11.7 | 13.4 | 19 02.4 | 10.5 | 54.8 |
| 02 | 213 47.2 | 16.8 | 271 44.1 | 13.5 | 18 51.9 | 10.6 | 54.8 |
| 03 | 228 47.3 | .. 17.7 | 286 16.6 | 13.5 | 18 41.3 | 10.6 | 54.9 |
| 04 | 243 47.4 | 18.6 | 300 49.1 | 13.5 | 18 30.7 | 10.8 | 54.9 |
| 05 | 258 47.5 | 19.5 | 315 21.6 | 13.6 | 18 19.9 | 10.8 | 54.9 |
| 06 | 273 47.6 | S10 20.4 | 329 54.2 | 13.6 | N18 09.1 | 10.9 | 54.9 |
| T 07 | 288 47.7 | 21.3 | 344 26.8 | 13.7 | 17 58.2 | 11.1 | 54.9 |
| H 08 | 303 47.8 | 22.2 | 358 59.5 | 13.7 | 17 47.1 | 11.1 | 55.0 |
| U 09 | 318 47.9 | .. 23.1 | 13 32.2 | 13.7 | 17 36.0 | 11.1 | 55.0 |
| R 10 | 333 48.0 | 24.0 | 28 04.9 | 13.8 | 17 24.9 | 11.3 | 55.0 |
| S 11 | 348 48.2 | 24.9 | 42 37.7 | 13.8 | 17 13.6 | 11.3 | 55.0 |
| D 12 | 3 48.3 | S10 25.8 | 57 10.5 | 13.9 | N17 02.3 | 11.5 | 55.0 |
| A 13 | 18 48.4 | 26.7 | 71 43.4 | 13.8 | 16 50.8 | 11.5 | 55.1 |
| Y 14 | 33 48.5 | 27.6 | 86 16.2 | 14.0 | 16 39.3 | 11.5 | 55.1 |
| 15 | 48 48.6 | .. 28.5 | 100 49.2 | 13.9 | 16 27.8 | 11.7 | 55.1 |
| 16 | 63 48.7 | 29.4 | 115 22.1 | 14.0 | 16 16.1 | 11.8 | 55.1 |
| 17 | 78 48.8 | 30.3 | 129 55.1 | 14.0 | 16 04.3 | 11.8 | 55.1 |
| 18 | 93 48.9 | S10 31.2 | 144 28.1 | 14.1 | N15 52.5 | 11.9 | 55.2 |
| 19 | 108 49.0 | 32.0 | 159 01.2 | 14.0 | 15 40.6 | 11.9 | 55.2 |
| 20 | 123 49.1 | 32.9 | 173 34.2 | 14.1 | 15 28.7 | 12.1 | 55.2 |
| 21 | 138 49.2 | .. 33.8 | 188 07.3 | 14.2 | 15 16.6 | 12.1 | 55.2 |
| 22 | 153 49.3 | 34.7 | 202 40.5 | 14.1 | 15 04.5 | 12.2 | 55.3 |
| 23 | 168 49.4 | 35.6 | 217 13.6 | 14.2 | 14 52.3 | 12.3 | 55.3 |
| 21 00 | 183 49.5 | S10 36.5 | 231 46.8 | 14.3 | N14 40.0 | 12.3 | 55.3 |
| 01 | 198 49.6 | 37.4 | 246 20.1 | 14.2 | 14 27.7 | 12.4 | 55.3 |
| 02 | 213 49.7 | 38.3 | 260 53.3 | 14.3 | 14 15.3 | 12.5 | 55.3 |
| 03 | 228 49.8 | .. 39.2 | 275 26.6 | 14.3 | 14 02.8 | 12.6 | 55.4 |
| 04 | 243 49.9 | 40.1 | 289 59.9 | 14.3 | 13 50.2 | 12.6 | 55.4 |
| 05 | 258 50.0 | 41.0 | 304 33.2 | 14.4 | 13 37.6 | 12.7 | 55.4 |
| 06 | 273 50.1 | S10 41.9 | 319 06.6 | 14.3 | N13 24.9 | 12.7 | 55.4 |
| 07 | 288 50.2 | 42.7 | 333 39.9 | 14.4 | 13 12.2 | 12.9 | 55.5 |
| 08 | 303 50.3 | 43.6 | 348 13.3 | 14.4 | 12 59.3 | 12.9 | 55.5 |
| F 09 | 318 50.4 | .. 44.5 | 2 46.7 | 14.5 | 12 46.4 | 12.9 | 55.5 |
| R 10 | 333 50.5 | 45.4 | 17 20.2 | 14.4 | 12 33.5 | 13.1 | 55.5 |
| I 11 | 348 50.6 | 46.3 | 31 53.6 | 14.5 | 12 20.4 | 13.0 | 55.6 |
| D 12 | 3 50.7 | S10 47.2 | 46 27.1 | 14.5 | N12 07.4 | 13.2 | 55.6 |
| A 13 | 18 50.8 | 48.1 | 61 00.6 | 14.5 | 11 54.2 | 13.2 | 55.6 |
| Y 14 | 33 50.9 | 49.0 | 75 34.1 | 14.5 | 11 41.0 | 13.3 | 55.6 |
| 15 | 48 51.0 | .. 49.9 | 90 07.6 | 14.6 | 11 27.7 | 13.3 | 55.7 |
| 16 | 63 51.1 | 50.7 | 104 41.2 | 14.5 | 11 14.4 | 13.4 | 55.7 |
| 17 | 78 51.2 | 51.6 | 119 14.7 | 14.6 | 11 01.0 | 13.5 | 55.7 |
| 18 | 93 51.3 | S10 52.5 | 133 48.3 | 14.6 | N10 47.5 | 13.5 | 55.8 |
| 19 | 108 51.4 | 53.4 | 148 21.9 | 14.6 | 10 34.0 | 13.6 | 55.8 |
| 20 | 123 51.5 | 54.3 | 162 55.5 | 14.6 | 10 20.4 | 13.6 | 55.8 |
| 21 | 138 51.6 | .. 55.2 | 177 29.1 | 14.6 | 10 06.8 | 13.7 | 55.8 |
| 22 | 153 51.7 | 56.1 | 192 02.7 | 14.7 | 9 53.1 | 13.7 | 55.9 |
| 23 | 168 51.8 | 56.9 | 206 36.4 | 14.6 | N 9 39.4 | 13.8 | 55.9 |
| SD | 16.1 | d 0.9 | SD 14.9 | | 15.0 | | 15.1 |

## Twilight / Moonrise

| Lat. | Naut. | Civil | Sunrise | Moonrise 19 | 20 | 21 | 22 |
|---|---|---|---|---|---|---|---|
| N 72 | 05 17 | 06 35 | 07 49 | ▢ | 22 54 | 25 21 | 01 21 |
| N 70 | 05 18 | 06 29 | 07 34 | 20 21 | 23 28 | 25 36 | 01 36 |
| 68 | 05 19 | 06 24 | 07 22 | 21 40 | 23 52 | 25 47 | 01 47 |
| 66 | 05 20 | 06 19 | 07 13 | 22 17 | 24 11 | 00 11 | 01 57 |
| 64 | 05 20 | 06 15 | 07 05 | 22 43 | 24 26 | 00 26 | 02 05 |
| 62 | 05 20 | 06 12 | 06 58 | 23 03 | 24 38 | 00 38 | 02 12 |
| 60 | 05 20 | 06 09 | 06 52 | 23 20 | 24 49 | 00 49 | 02 17 |
| N 58 | 05 20 | 06 06 | 06 46 | 23 33 | 24 58 | 00 58 | 02 22 |
| 56 | 05 20 | 06 03 | 06 41 | 23 45 | 25 06 | 01 06 | 02 27 |
| 54 | 05 20 | 06 01 | 06 37 | 23 55 | 25 13 | 01 13 | 02 31 |
| 52 | 05 20 | 05 59 | 06 33 | 24 04 | 00 04 | 01 19 | 02 35 |
| 50 | 05 19 | 05 57 | 06 30 | 24 13 | 00 13 | 01 25 | 02 38 |
| 45 | 05 18 | 05 52 | 06 22 | 24 30 | 00 30 | 01 37 | 02 45 |
| N 40 | 05 17 | 05 48 | 06 16 | 24 44 | 00 44 | 01 47 | 02 51 |
| 35 | 05 15 | 05 44 | 06 10 | 24 56 | 00 56 | 01 56 | 02 56 |
| 30 | 05 13 | 05 41 | 06 05 | 00 09 | 01 06 | 02 03 | 03 01 |
| 20 | 05 08 | 05 34 | 05 56 | 00 30 | 01 24 | 02 16 | 03 09 |
| N 10 | 05 03 | 05 27 | 05 49 | 00 49 | 01 39 | 02 28 | 03 15 |
| 0 | 04 56 | 05 20 | 05 41 | 01 07 | 01 53 | 02 38 | 03 22 |
| S 10 | 04 48 | 05 13 | 05 34 | 01 24 | 02 08 | 02 48 | 03 28 |
| 20 | 04 37 | 05 04 | 05 26 | 01 43 | 02 23 | 03 00 | 03 35 |
| 30 | 04 23 | 04 52 | 05 17 | 02 04 | 02 40 | 03 12 | 03 42 |
| 35 | 04 14 | 04 45 | 05 11 | 02 17 | 02 50 | 03 19 | 03 47 |
| 40 | 04 03 | 04 37 | 05 05 | 02 31 | 03 01 | 03 28 | 03 52 |
| 45 | 03 50 | 04 27 | 04 58 | 02 48 | 03 15 | 03 37 | 03 57 |
| S 50 | 03 33 | 04 15 | 04 49 | 03 09 | 03 31 | 03 49 | 04 04 |
| 52 | 03 24 | 04 09 | 04 45 | 03 19 | 03 39 | 03 54 | 04 07 |
| 54 | 03 15 | 04 03 | 04 41 | 03 30 | 03 47 | 04 00 | 04 11 |
| 56 | 03 04 | 03 55 | 04 36 | 03 43 | 03 57 | 04 07 | 04 15 |
| 58 | 02 51 | 03 47 | 04 30 | 03 58 | 04 07 | 04 14 | 04 19 |
| S 60 | 02 35 | 03 38 | 04 24 | 04 15 | 04 20 | 04 22 | 04 23 |

## Sunset / Twilight / Moonset

| Lat. | Sunset | Civil | Naut. | Moonset 19 | 20 | 21 | 22 |
|---|---|---|---|---|---|---|---|
| N 72 | 15 39 | 16 52 | 18 11 | ▢ | 18 22 | 17 28 | 16 51 |
| N 70 | 15 54 | 16 59 | 18 10 | 19 18 | 17 46 | 17 11 | 16 44 |
| 68 | 16 06 | 17 04 | 18 09 | 17 59 | 17 20 | 16 57 | 16 38 |
| 66 | 16 16 | 17 09 | 18 08 | 17 21 | 17 00 | 16 46 | 16 33 |
| 64 | 16 24 | 17 13 | 18 08 | 16 54 | 16 44 | 16 36 | 16 29 |
| 62 | 16 31 | 17 17 | 18 08 | 16 33 | 16 31 | 16 28 | 16 25 |
| 60 | 16 37 | 17 20 | 18 08 | 16 15 | 16 19 | 16 21 | 16 22 |
| N 58 | 16 42 | 17 23 | 18 08 | 16 01 | 16 09 | 16 15 | 16 19 |
| 56 | 16 47 | 17 25 | 18 08 | 15 49 | 16 00 | 16 09 | 16 16 |
| 54 | 16 52 | 17 28 | 18 09 | 15 38 | 15 52 | 16 04 | 16 14 |
| 52 | 16 55 | 17 30 | 18 09 | 15 28 | 15 45 | 15 59 | 16 12 |
| 50 | 16 59 | 17 32 | 18 09 | 15 19 | 15 39 | 15 55 | 16 10 |
| 45 | 17 07 | 17 37 | 18 11 | 15 01 | 15 25 | 15 46 | 16 05 |
| N 40 | 17 13 | 17 41 | 18 12 | 14 46 | 15 14 | 15 39 | 16 02 |
| 35 | 17 19 | 17 45 | 18 14 | 14 33 | 15 04 | 15 32 | 15 59 |
| 30 | 17 24 | 17 48 | 18 16 | 14 22 | 14 55 | 15 26 | 15 56 |
| 20 | 17 33 | 17 55 | 18 21 | 14 02 | 14 40 | 15 16 | 15 51 |
| N 10 | 17 41 | 18 02 | 18 27 | 13 45 | 14 27 | 15 07 | 15 47 |
| 0 | 17 48 | 18 09 | 18 34 | 13 29 | 14 15 | 14 59 | 15 42 |
| S 10 | 17 56 | 18 17 | 18 42 | 13 13 | 14 02 | 14 51 | 15 38 |
| 20 | 18 04 | 18 26 | 18 53 | 12 56 | 13 49 | 14 41 | 15 34 |
| 30 | 18 13 | 18 38 | 19 07 | 12 36 | 13 34 | 14 31 | 15 29 |
| 35 | 18 19 | 18 45 | 19 16 | 12 25 | 13 25 | 14 25 | 15 26 |
| 40 | 18 25 | 18 53 | 19 27 | 12 11 | 13 14 | 14 18 | 15 22 |
| 45 | 18 32 | 19 03 | 19 41 | 11 55 | 13 02 | 14 10 | 15 18 |
| S 50 | 18 41 | 19 16 | 19 58 | 11 35 | 12 47 | 14 00 | 15 13 |
| 52 | 18 45 | 19 22 | 20 07 | 11 26 | 12 40 | 13 56 | 15 11 |
| 54 | 18 50 | 19 28 | 20 17 | 11 15 | 12 32 | 13 50 | 15 09 |
| 56 | 18 55 | 19 36 | 20 28 | 11 03 | 12 24 | 13 45 | 15 06 |
| 58 | 19 01 | 19 44 | 20 42 | 10 49 | 12 14 | 13 38 | 15 03 |
| S 60 | 19 07 | 19 54 | 20 58 | 10 32 | 12 02 | 13 31 | 15 00 |

## SUN / MOON

| Day | Eqn. of Time 00h | 12h | Mer. Pass. | Mer. Pass. Upper | Lower | Age | Phase |
|---|---|---|---|---|---|---|---|
| 19 | 14 57 | 15 02 | 11 45 | 07 18 | 19 41 | 24 | 33 |
| 20 | 15 08 | 15 13 | 11 45 | 08 04 | 20 27 | 25 | 25 |
| 21 | 15 18 | 15 23 | 11 45 | 08 49 | 21 10 | 26 | 17 |

| UT | ARIES | VENUS −3.9 | | MARS −1.0 | | JUPITER −2.9 | | SATURN +0.5 | | STARS | | |
|---|---|---|---|---|---|---|---|---|---|---|---|---|
| | GHA | GHA | Dec | GHA | Dec | GHA | Dec | GHA | Dec | Name | SHA | Dec |
| d h | ° ′ | ° ′ | ° ′ | ° ′ | ° ′ | ° ′ | ° ′ | ° ′ | ° ′ | | ° ′ | ° ′ |
| 22 00 | 30 24.4 | 183 41.6 S 9 52.7 | | 305 44.9 N23 25.4 | | 29 14.1 S 1 13.3 | | 68 58.0 S16 29.4 | | Acamar | 315 12.8 | S40 12.7 |
| 01 | 45 26.9 | 198 41.1 | 53.8 | 320 47.0 | 25.5 | 44 16.8 | 13.4 | 84 00.5 | 29.4 | Achernar | 335 21.0 | S57 07.3 |
| 02 | 60 29.4 | 213 40.6 | 55.0 | 335 49.2 | 25.6 | 59 19.5 | 13.5 | 99 02.9 | 29.4 | Acrux | 173 02.8 | S63 13.3 |
| 03 | 75 31.8 | 228 40.1 . . | 56.2 | 350 51.3 . . | 25.7 | 74 22.2 . . | 13.6 | 114 05.4 . . | 29.4 | Adhara | 255 07.2 | S28 59.9 |
| 04 | 90 34.3 | 243 39.6 | 57.4 | 5 53.5 | 25.8 | 89 24.9 | 13.7 | 129 07.9 | 29.4 | Aldebaran | 290 41.5 | N16 33.3 |
| 05 | 105 36.7 | 258 39.1 | 58.5 | 20 55.6 | 26.0 | 104 27.6 | 13.8 | 144 10.3 | 29.4 | | | |
| 06 | 120 39.2 | 273 38.6 S 9 59.7 | | 35 57.8 N23 26.1 | | 119 30.3 S 1 13.9 | | 159 12.8 S16 29.4 | | Alioth | 166 15.1 | N55 50.2 |
| 07 | 135 41.7 | 288 38.2 10 00.9 | | 50 59.9 | 26.2 | 134 33.0 | 13.9 | 174 15.3 | 29.4 | Alkaid | 152 54.0 | N49 12.1 |
| S 08 | 150 44.1 | 303 37.7 | 02.0 | 66 02.1 | 26.3 | 149 35.7 | 14.0 | 189 17.7 | 29.4 | Alnair | 27 35.0 | S46 51.2 |
| A 09 | 165 46.6 | 318 37.2 . . | 03.2 | 81 04.3 . . | 26.4 | 164 38.4 . . | 14.1 | 204 20.2 . . | 29.4 | Alnilam | 275 39.4 | S 1 11.1 |
| T 10 | 180 49.1 | 333 36.7 | 04.4 | 96 06.4 | 26.5 | 179 41.1 | 14.2 | 219 22.7 | 29.4 | Alphard | 217 49.7 | S 8 45.2 |
| U 11 | 195 51.5 | 348 36.2 | 05.5 | 111 08.6 | 26.6 | 194 43.8 | 14.3 | 234 25.1 | 29.4 | | | |
| R 12 | 210 54.0 | 3 35.7 S10 06.7 | | 126 10.7 N23 26.7 | | 209 46.5 S 1 14.4 | | 249 27.6 S16 29.4 | | Alphecca | 126 05.7 | N26 38.5 |
| D 13 | 225 56.5 | 18 35.2 | 07.9 | 141 12.9 | 26.9 | 224 49.2 | 14.5 | 264 30.1 | 29.4 | Alpheratz | 357 36.4 | N29 13.1 |
| A 14 | 240 58.9 | 33 34.8 | 09.0 | 156 15.1 | 27.0 | 239 51.9 | 14.6 | 279 32.5 | 29.4 | Altair | 62 01.8 | N 8 55.8 |
| Y 15 | 256 01.4 | 48 34.3 . . | 10.2 | 171 17.2 . . | 27.1 | 254 54.6 . . | 14.7 | 294 35.0 . . | 29.4 | Ankaa | 353 08.6 | S42 11.0 |
| 16 | 271 03.8 | 63 33.8 | 11.4 | 186 19.4 | 27.2 | 269 57.3 | 14.8 | 309 37.5 | 29.4 | Antares | 112 18.4 | S26 28.9 |
| 17 | 286 06.3 | 78 33.3 | 12.6 | 201 21.6 | 27.3 | 285 00.0 | 14.9 | 324 39.9 | 29.4 | | | |
| 18 | 301 08.8 | 93 32.8 S10 13.7 | | 216 23.8 N23 27.4 | | 300 02.7 S 1 15.0 | | 339 42.4 S16 29.4 | | Arcturus | 145 50.0 | N19 04.0 |
| 19 | 316 11.2 | 108 32.3 | 14.9 | 231 25.9 | 27.5 | 315 05.4 | 15.1 | 354 44.9 | 29.4 | Atria | 107 14.7 | S69 04.2 |
| 20 | 331 13.7 | 123 31.8 | 16.0 | 246 28.1 | 27.6 | 330 08.1 | 15.2 | 9 47.3 | 29.4 | Avior | 234 15.5 | S59 34.5 |
| 21 | 346 16.2 | 138 31.3 . . | 17.2 | 261 30.3 . . | 27.7 | 345 10.8 . . | 15.3 | 24 49.8 . . | 29.4 | Bellatrix | 278 24.7 | N 6 22.3 |
| 22 | 1 18.6 | 153 30.8 | 18.4 | 276 32.5 | 27.9 | 0 13.5 | 15.4 | 39 52.3 | 29.4 | Betelgeuse | 270 53.9 | N 7 24.8 |
| 23 | 16 21.1 | 168 30.4 | 19.5 | 291 34.6 | 28.0 | 15 16.1 | 15.5 | 54 54.7 | 29.4 | | | |
| 23 00 | 31 23.6 | 183 29.9 S10 20.7 | | 306 36.8 N23 28.1 | | 30 18.8 S 1 15.6 | | 69 57.2 S16 29.4 | | Canopus | 263 53.0 | S52 42.1 |
| 01 | 46 26.0 | 198 29.4 | 21.9 | 321 39.0 | 28.2 | 45 21.5 | 15.6 | 84 59.7 | 29.4 | Capella | 280 24.3 | N46 01.1 |
| 02 | 61 28.5 | 213 28.9 | 23.0 | 336 41.2 | 28.3 | 60 24.2 | 15.7 | 100 02.1 | 29.4 | Deneb | 49 27.0 | N45 21.9 |
| 03 | 76 31.0 | 228 28.4 . . | 24.2 | 351 43.4 . . | 28.4 | 75 26.9 . . | 15.8 | 115 04.6 . . | 29.4 | Denebola | 182 27.1 | N14 26.8 |
| 04 | 91 33.4 | 243 27.9 | 25.4 | 6 45.6 | 28.5 | 90 29.6 | 15.9 | 130 07.1 | 29.4 | Diphda | 348 48.8 | S17 51.7 |
| 05 | 106 35.9 | 258 27.4 | 26.5 | 21 47.7 | 28.6 | 105 32.3 | 16.0 | 145 09.5 | 29.4 | | | |
| 06 | 121 38.3 | 273 26.9 S10 27.7 | | 36 49.9 N23 28.8 | | 120 35.0 S 1 16.1 | | 160 12.0 S16 29.4 | | Dubhe | 193 43.8 | N61 37.6 |
| 07 | 136 40.8 | 288 26.4 | 28.9 | 51 52.1 | 28.9 | 135 37.7 | 16.2 | 175 14.5 | 29.4 | Elnath | 278 04.0 | N28 37.6 |
| 08 | 151 43.3 | 303 25.9 | 30.0 | 66 54.3 | 29.0 | 150 40.4 | 16.3 | 190 16.9 | 29.4 | Eltanin | 90 43.3 | N51 29.4 |
| S 09 | 166 45.7 | 318 25.4 . . | 31.2 | 81 56.5 . . | 29.1 | 165 43.1 . . | 16.4 | 205 19.4 . . | 29.4 | Enif | 33 40.5 | N 9 58.9 |
| U 10 | 181 48.2 | 333 24.9 | 32.3 | 96 58.7 | 29.2 | 180 45.8 | 16.5 | 220 21.9 | 29.4 | Fomalhaut | 15 16.3 | S29 30.2 |
| N 11 | 196 50.7 | 348 24.4 | 33.5 | 112 00.9 | 29.3 | 195 48.5 | 16.6 | 235 24.3 | 29.4 | | | |
| D 12 | 211 53.1 | 3 23.9 S10 34.6 | | 127 03.1 N23 29.4 | | 210 51.2 S 1 16.7 | | 250 26.8 S16 29.4 | | Gacrux | 171 54.3 | S57 14.2 |
| A 13 | 226 55.6 | 18 23.4 | 35.8 | 142 05.3 | 29.5 | 225 53.9 | 16.8 | 265 29.2 | 29.4 | Gienah | 175 45.8 | S17 39.9 |
| Y 14 | 241 58.1 | 33 22.9 | 37.0 | 157 07.5 | 29.6 | 240 56.6 | 16.8 | 280 31.7 | 29.4 | Hadar | 148 39.3 | S60 28.8 |
| 15 | 257 00.5 | 48 22.5 . . | 38.1 | 172 09.7 . . | 29.8 | 255 59.3 . . | 16.9 | 295 34.2 . . | 29.4 | Hamal | 327 52.9 | N23 34.3 |
| 16 | 272 03.0 | 63 22.0 | 39.3 | 187 11.9 | 29.9 | 271 02.0 | 17.0 | 310 36.6 | 29.4 | Kaus Aust. | 83 35.1 | S34 22.5 |
| 17 | 287 05.4 | 78 21.5 | 40.4 | 202 14.1 | 30.0 | 286 04.7 | 17.1 | 325 39.1 | 29.4 | | | |
| 18 | 302 07.9 | 93 21.0 S10 41.6 | | 217 16.3 N23 30.1 | | 301 07.4 S 1 17.2 | | 340 41.6 S16 29.4 | | Kochab | 137 20.9 | N74 03.8 |
| 19 | 317 10.4 | 108 20.5 | 42.7 | 232 18.5 | 30.2 | 316 10.0 | 17.3 | 355 44.0 | 29.4 | Markab | 13 31.5 | N15 19.8 |
| 20 | 332 12.8 | 123 20.0 | 43.9 | 247 20.8 | 30.3 | 331 12.7 | 17.4 | 10 46.5 | 29.4 | Menkar | 314 07.8 | N 4 10.8 |
| 21 | 347 15.3 | 138 19.5 . . | 45.1 | 262 23.0 . . | 30.4 | 346 15.4 . . | 17.5 | 25 48.9 . . | 29.4 | Menkent | 148 00.2 | S36 28.8 |
| 22 | 2 17.8 | 153 19.0 | 46.2 | 277 25.2 | 30.5 | 1 18.1 | 17.6 | 40 51.4 | 29.4 | Miaplacidus | 221 38.9 | S69 48.2 |
| 23 | 17 20.2 | 168 18.5 | 47.4 | 292 27.4 | 30.7 | 16 20.8 | 17.7 | 55 53.9 | 29.4 | | | |
| 24 00 | 32 22.7 | 183 18.0 S10 48.5 | | 307 29.6 N23 30.8 | | 31 23.5 S 1 17.8 | | 70 56.3 S16 29.3 | | Mirfak | 308 30.4 | N49 56.5 |
| 01 | 47 25.2 | 198 17.5 | 49.7 | 322 31.8 | 30.9 | 46 26.2 | 17.8 | 85 58.8 | 29.3 | Nunki | 75 50.2 | S26 16.1 |
| 02 | 62 27.6 | 213 17.0 | 50.8 | 337 34.1 | 31.0 | 61 28.9 | 17.9 | 101 01.2 | 29.3 | Peacock | 53 08.6 | S56 39.9 |
| 03 | 77 30.1 | 228 16.5 . . | 52.0 | 352 36.3 . . | 31.1 | 76 31.6 . . | 18.0 | 116 03.7 . . | 29.3 | Pollux | 243 19.5 | N27 58.3 |
| 04 | 92 32.6 | 243 16.0 | 53.1 | 7 38.5 | 31.2 | 91 34.3 | 18.1 | 131 06.2 | 29.3 | Procyon | 244 52.7 | N 5 10.1 |
| 05 | 107 35.0 | 258 15.5 | 54.3 | 22 40.7 | 31.3 | 106 37.0 | 18.2 | 146 08.6 | 29.3 | | | |
| 06 | 122 37.5 | 273 15.0 S10 55.4 | | 37 43.0 N23 31.4 | | 121 39.7 S 1 18.3 | | 161 11.1 S16 29.3 | | Rasalhague | 96 00.5 | N12 32.8 |
| 07 | 137 39.9 | 288 14.5 | 56.6 | 52 45.2 | 31.5 | 136 42.3 | 18.4 | 176 13.6 | 29.3 | Regulus | 207 36.6 | N11 51.5 |
| 08 | 152 42.4 | 303 13.9 | 57.7 | 67 47.4 | 31.7 | 151 45.0 | 18.5 | 191 16.0 | 29.3 | Rigel | 281 05.4 | S 8 10.4 |
| M 09 | 167 44.9 | 318 13.4 10 58.9 | | 82 49.6 . . | 31.8 | 166 47.7 . . | 18.6 | 206 18.5 . . | 29.3 | Rigil Kent. | 139 43.5 | S60 55.6 |
| O 10 | 182 47.3 | 333 12.9 11 00.0 | | 97 51.9 | 31.9 | 181 50.4 | 18.7 | 221 20.9 | 29.3 | Sabik | 102 05.1 | S15 45.1 |
| N 11 | 197 49.8 | 348 12.4 | 01.2 | 112 54.1 | 32.0 | 196 53.1 | 18.7 | 236 23.4 | 29.3 | | | |
| D 12 | 212 52.3 | 3 11.9 S11 02.3 | | 127 56.4 N23 32.1 | | 211 55.8 S 1 18.8 | | 251 25.8 S16 29.3 | | Schedar | 349 32.6 | N56 39.8 |
| A 13 | 227 54.7 | 18 11.4 | 03.5 | 142 58.6 | 32.2 | 226 58.5 | 18.9 | 266 28.3 | 29.3 | Shaula | 96 13.1 | S37 07.3 |
| Y 14 | 242 57.2 | 33 10.9 | 04.6 | 158 00.8 | 32.3 | 242 01.2 | 19.0 | 281 30.8 | 29.3 | Sirius | 258 27.7 | S16 44.6 |
| 15 | 257 59.7 | 48 10.4 . . | 05.8 | 173 03.1 . . | 32.4 | 257 03.9 . . | 19.1 | 296 33.2 . . | 29.3 | Spica | 158 24.6 | S11 16.6 |
| 16 | 273 02.1 | 63 09.9 | 06.9 | 188 05.3 | 32.6 | 272 06.5 | 19.2 | 311 35.7 | 29.3 | Suhail | 222 47.8 | S43 31.1 |
| 17 | 288 04.6 | 78 09.4 | 08.1 | 203 07.6 | 32.7 | 287 09.2 | 19.3 | 326 38.1 | 29.3 | | | |
| 18 | 303 07.1 | 93 08.9 S11 09.2 | | 218 09.8 N23 32.8 | | 302 11.9 S 1 19.4 | | 341 40.6 S16 29.3 | | Vega | 80 34.6 | N38 48.5 |
| 19 | 318 09.5 | 108 08.4 | 10.4 | 233 12.0 | 32.9 | 317 14.6 | 19.5 | 356 43.1 | 29.3 | Zuben'ubi | 136 58.4 | S16 08.0 |
| 20 | 333 12.0 | 123 07.9 | 11.5 | 248 14.3 | 33.0 | 332 17.3 | 19.5 | 11 45.5 | 29.3 | | SHA | Mer. Pass. |
| 21 | 348 14.4 | 138 07.4 . . | 12.6 | 263 16.5 . . | 33.1 | 347 20.0 . . | 19.6 | 26 48.0 . . | 29.3 | | ° ′ | h m |
| 22 | 3 16.9 | 153 06.9 | 13.8 | 278 18.8 | 33.2 | 2 22.7 | 19.7 | 41 50.4 | 29.3 | Venus | 152 06.3 | 11 46 |
| 23 | 18 19.4 | 168 06.3 | 14.9 | 293 21.0 | 33.3 | 17 25.4 | 19.8 | 56 52.9 | 29.3 | Mars | 275 13.3 | 3 33 |
| | h m | | | | | | | | | Jupiter | 358 55.3 | 21 55 |
| Mer. Pass. 21 50.8 | | v −0.5 d 1.2 | | v 2.2 d 0.1 | | v 2.7 d 0.1 | | v 2.5 d 0.0 | | Saturn | 38 33.6 | 19 17 |

| UT | SUN GHA | SUN Dec | MOON GHA | MOON v | MOON Dec | MOON d | MOON HP |
|---|---|---|---|---|---|---|---|
| d h | ° ′ | ° ′ | ° ′ | ′ | ° ′ | ′ | ′ |
| 22 00 | 183 51.9 | S10 57.8 | 221 10.0 | 14.7 | N 9 25.6 | 13.9 | 55.9 |
| 01 | 198 52.0 | 58.7 | 235 43.7 | 14.6 | 9 11.7 | 13.9 | 55.9 |
| 02 | 213 52.1 | 10 59.6 | 250 17.3 | 14.7 | 8 57.8 | 14.0 | 56.0 |
| 03 | 228 52.2 | 11 00.5 | 264 51.0 | 14.6 | 8 43.8 | 14.0 | 56.0 |
| 04 | 243 52.3 | 01.4 | 279 24.6 | 14.7 | 8 29.8 | 14.0 | 56.0 |
| 05 | 258 52.4 | 02.3 | 293 58.3 | 14.7 | 8 15.8 | 14.1 | 56.1 |
| 06 | 273 52.5 | S11 03.1 | 308 32.0 | 14.7 | N 8 01.7 | 14.2 | 56.1 |
| 07 | 288 52.6 | 04.0 | 323 05.7 | 14.6 | 7 47.5 | 14.2 | 56.1 |
| S 08 | 303 52.7 | 04.9 | 337 39.3 | 14.7 | 7 33.3 | 14.3 | 56.1 |
| A 09 | 318 52.8 | 05.8 | 352 13.0 | 14.7 | 7 19.0 | 14.3 | 56.2 |
| T 10 | 333 52.9 | 06.7 | 6 46.7 | 14.7 | 7 04.7 | 14.3 | 56.2 |
| U 11 | 348 53.0 | 07.6 | 21 20.4 | 14.6 | 6 50.4 | 14.4 | 56.2 |
| R 12 | 3 53.0 | S11 08.4 | 35 54.0 | 14.7 | N 6 36.0 | 14.4 | 56.2 |
| D 13 | 18 53.1 | 09.3 | 50 27.7 | 14.7 | 6 21.6 | 14.5 | 56.3 |
| A 14 | 33 53.2 | 10.2 | 65 01.4 | 14.6 | 6 07.1 | 14.5 | 56.3 |
| Y 15 | 48 53.3 | 11.1 | 79 35.0 | 14.7 | 5 52.6 | 14.6 | 56.3 |
| 16 | 63 53.4 | 12.0 | 94 08.7 | 14.6 | 5 38.0 | 14.6 | 56.4 |
| 17 | 78 53.5 | 12.8 | 108 42.3 | 14.6 | 5 23.4 | 14.6 | 56.4 |
| 18 | 93 53.6 | S11 13.7 | 123 15.9 | 14.7 | N 5 08.8 | 14.7 | 56.4 |
| 19 | 108 53.7 | 14.6 | 137 49.6 | 14.6 | 4 54.1 | 14.7 | 56.5 |
| 20 | 123 53.8 | 15.5 | 152 23.2 | 14.6 | 4 39.4 | 14.7 | 56.5 |
| 21 | 138 53.9 | 16.4 | 166 56.8 | 14.6 | 4 24.7 | 14.8 | 56.5 |
| 22 | 153 54.0 | 17.2 | 181 30.4 | 14.6 | 4 09.9 | 14.8 | 56.5 |
| 23 | 168 54.0 | 18.1 | 196 04.0 | 14.5 | 3 55.1 | 14.9 | 56.6 |
| 23 00 | 183 54.1 | S11 19.0 | 210 37.5 | 14.6 | N 3 40.2 | 14.9 | 56.6 |
| 01 | 198 54.2 | 19.9 | 225 11.1 | 14.5 | 3 25.3 | 14.9 | 56.6 |
| 02 | 213 54.3 | 20.8 | 239 44.6 | 14.5 | 3 10.4 | 14.9 | 56.7 |
| 03 | 228 54.4 | 21.6 | 254 18.1 | 14.5 | 2 55.5 | 15.0 | 56.7 |
| 04 | 243 54.5 | 22.5 | 268 51.6 | 14.5 | 2 40.5 | 15.0 | 56.7 |
| 05 | 258 54.6 | 23.4 | 283 25.1 | 14.4 | 2 25.5 | 15.0 | 56.7 |
| 06 | 273 54.7 | S11 24.3 | 297 58.5 | 14.4 | N 2 10.5 | 15.1 | 56.8 |
| 07 | 288 54.8 | 25.1 | 312 31.9 | 14.4 | 1 55.4 | 15.0 | 56.8 |
| 08 | 303 54.8 | 26.0 | 327 05.3 | 14.4 | 1 40.4 | 15.1 | 56.8 |
| S 09 | 318 54.9 | 26.9 | 341 38.7 | 14.4 | 1 25.3 | 15.2 | 56.9 |
| U 10 | 333 55.0 | 27.8 | 356 12.1 | 14.3 | 1 10.1 | 15.1 | 56.9 |
| N 11 | 348 55.1 | 28.6 | 10 45.4 | 14.3 | 0 55.0 | 15.2 | 56.9 |
| D 12 | 3 55.2 | S11 29.5 | 25 18.7 | 14.2 | N 0 39.8 | 15.2 | 57.0 |
| A 13 | 18 55.3 | 30.4 | 39 51.9 | 14.3 | 0 24.6 | 15.2 | 57.0 |
| Y 14 | 33 55.4 | 31.3 | 54 25.2 | 14.2 | N 0 09.4 | 15.2 | 57.0 |
| 15 | 48 55.4 | 32.1 | 68 58.4 | 14.2 | S 0 05.8 | 15.2 | 57.0 |
| 16 | 63 55.5 | 33.0 | 83 31.6 | 14.1 | 0 21.0 | 15.3 | 57.1 |
| 17 | 78 55.6 | 33.9 | 98 04.7 | 14.1 | 0 36.3 | 15.3 | 57.1 |
| 18 | 93 55.7 | S11 34.8 | 112 37.8 | 14.1 | S 0 51.6 | 15.2 | 57.1 |
| 19 | 108 55.8 | 35.6 | 127 10.9 | 14.0 | 1 06.8 | 15.3 | 57.2 |
| 20 | 123 55.9 | 36.5 | 141 43.9 | 14.0 | 1 22.1 | 15.3 | 57.2 |
| 21 | 138 55.9 | 37.4 | 156 16.9 | 14.0 | 1 37.4 | 15.4 | 57.2 |
| 22 | 153 56.0 | 38.2 | 170 49.9 | 13.9 | 1 52.8 | 15.3 | 57.3 |
| 23 | 168 56.1 | 39.1 | 185 22.8 | 13.8 | 2 08.1 | 15.3 | 57.3 |
| 24 00 | 183 56.2 | S11 40.0 | 199 55.6 | 13.9 | S 2 23.4 | 15.3 | 57.3 |
| 01 | 198 56.3 | 40.9 | 214 28.5 | 13.8 | 2 38.7 | 15.4 | 57.3 |
| 02 | 213 56.3 | 41.7 | 229 01.3 | 13.7 | 2 54.1 | 15.3 | 57.4 |
| 03 | 228 56.4 | 42.6 | 243 34.0 | 13.7 | 3 09.4 | 15.4 | 57.4 |
| 04 | 243 56.5 | 43.5 | 258 06.7 | 13.6 | 3 24.8 | 15.3 | 57.4 |
| 05 | 258 56.6 | 44.3 | 272 39.3 | 13.6 | 3 40.1 | 15.4 | 57.5 |
| 06 | 273 56.7 | S11 45.2 | 287 11.9 | 13.6 | S 3 55.5 | 15.3 | 57.5 |
| 07 | 288 56.8 | 46.1 | 301 44.5 | 13.5 | 4 10.8 | 15.3 | 57.5 |
| 08 | 303 56.8 | 46.9 | 316 17.0 | 13.5 | 4 26.1 | 15.4 | 57.5 |
| M 09 | 318 56.9 | 47.8 | 330 49.5 | 13.3 | 4 41.5 | 15.3 | 57.6 |
| O 10 | 333 57.0 | 48.7 | 345 21.8 | 13.4 | 4 56.8 | 15.3 | 57.6 |
| N 11 | 348 57.1 | 49.5 | 359 54.2 | 13.3 | 5 12.1 | 15.4 | 57.6 |
| D 12 | 3 57.1 | S11 50.4 | 14 26.5 | 13.2 | S 5 27.5 | 15.3 | 57.7 |
| A 13 | 18 57.2 | 51.3 | 28 58.7 | 13.2 | 5 42.8 | 15.3 | 57.7 |
| Y 14 | 33 57.3 | 52.2 | 43 30.9 | 13.1 | 5 58.1 | 15.2 | 57.7 |
| 15 | 48 57.4 | 53.0 | 58 03.0 | 13.1 | 6 13.3 | 15.3 | 57.7 |
| 16 | 63 57.5 | 53.9 | 72 35.1 | 12.9 | 6 28.6 | 15.3 | 57.8 |
| 17 | 78 57.5 | 54.7 | 87 07.0 | 13.0 | 6 43.9 | 15.2 | 57.8 |
| 18 | 93 57.6 | S11 55.6 | 101 39.0 | 12.8 | S 6 59.1 | 15.2 | 57.8 |
| 19 | 108 57.7 | 56.5 | 116 10.8 | 12.9 | 7 14.3 | 15.2 | 57.8 |
| 20 | 123 57.8 | 57.3 | 130 42.7 | 12.7 | 7 29.5 | 15.2 | 57.9 |
| 21 | 138 57.8 | 58.2 | 145 14.4 | 12.7 | 7 44.7 | 15.2 | 57.9 |
| 22 | 153 57.9 | 59.1 | 159 46.1 | 12.6 | 7 59.9 | 15.1 | 57.9 |
| 23 | 168 58.0 | 59.9 | 174 17.7 | 12.5 | S 8 15.0 | 15.1 | 58.0 |
| | SD 16.1 | d 0.9 | SD 15.3 | | 15.5 | | 15.7 |

| Lat. | Twilight Naut. | Twilight Civil | Sunrise | Moonrise 22 | Moonrise 23 | Moonrise 24 | Moonrise 25 |
|---|---|---|---|---|---|---|---|
| ° | h m | h m | h m | h m | h m | h m | h m |
| N 72 | 05 29 | 06 49 | 08 05 | 01 21 | 03 31 | 05 40 | 08 02 |
| N 70 | 05 29 | 06 41 | 07 48 | 01 36 | 03 35 | 05 34 | 07 43 |
| 68 | 05 29 | 06 34 | 07 34 | 01 47 | 03 38 | 05 29 | 07 28 |
| 66 | 05 29 | 06 28 | 07 23 | 01 57 | 03 40 | 05 26 | 07 17 |
| 64 | 05 28 | 06 24 | 07 14 | 02 05 | 03 43 | 05 22 | 07 07 |
| 62 | 05 28 | 06 19 | 07 06 | 02 12 | 03 44 | 05 19 | 06 59 |
| 60 | 05 27 | 06 16 | 06 59 | 02 17 | 03 46 | 05 17 | 06 52 |
| N 58 | 05 27 | 06 12 | 06 53 | 02 22 | 03 48 | 05 15 | 06 46 |
| 56 | 05 26 | 06 09 | 06 48 | 02 27 | 03 49 | 05 13 | 06 40 |
| 54 | 05 25 | 06 06 | 06 43 | 02 31 | 03 50 | 05 11 | 06 35 |
| 52 | 05 25 | 06 04 | 06 39 | 02 35 | 03 51 | 05 10 | 06 31 |
| 50 | 05 24 | 06 01 | 06 35 | 02 38 | 03 52 | 05 08 | 06 27 |
| 45 | 05 22 | 05 56 | 06 26 | 02 45 | 03 54 | 05 05 | 06 19 |
| N 40 | 05 20 | 05 51 | 06 19 | 02 51 | 03 56 | 05 03 | 06 12 |
| 35 | 05 17 | 05 47 | 06 13 | 02 56 | 03 58 | 05 00 | 06 06 |
| 30 | 05 15 | 05 43 | 06 07 | 03 01 | 03 59 | 04 58 | 06 00 |
| 20 | 05 09 | 05 35 | 05 58 | 03 09 | 04 01 | 04 55 | 05 51 |
| N 10 | 05 03 | 05 28 | 05 49 | 03 15 | 04 02 | 04 52 | 05 43 |
| 0 | 04 55 | 05 20 | 05 41 | 03 22 | 04 05 | 04 50 | 05 36 |
| S 10 | 04 46 | 05 11 | 05 33 | 03 28 | 04 07 | 04 47 | 05 29 |
| 20 | 04 35 | 05 01 | 05 24 | 03 35 | 04 09 | 04 44 | 05 21 |
| 30 | 04 20 | 04 49 | 05 14 | 03 42 | 04 12 | 04 41 | 05 12 |
| 35 | 04 10 | 04 41 | 05 08 | 03 47 | 04 13 | 04 39 | 05 07 |
| 40 | 03 59 | 04 33 | 05 01 | 03 52 | 04 14 | 04 37 | 05 02 |
| 45 | 03 44 | 04 22 | 04 53 | 03 57 | 04 16 | 04 35 | 04 55 |
| S 50 | 03 26 | 04 09 | 04 43 | 04 04 | 04 18 | 04 32 | 04 48 |
| 52 | 03 16 | 04 02 | 04 39 | 04 07 | 04 19 | 04 31 | 04 44 |
| 54 | 03 06 | 03 55 | 04 34 | 04 11 | 04 20 | 04 30 | 04 40 |
| 56 | 02 54 | 03 47 | 04 29 | 04 14 | 04 21 | 04 28 | 04 36 |
| 58 | 02 40 | 03 38 | 04 22 | 04 19 | 04 23 | 04 27 | 04 31 |
| S 60 | 02 22 | 03 28 | 04 15 | 04 23 | 04 24 | 04 25 | 04 26 |

| Lat. | Sunset | Twilight Civil | Twilight Naut. | Moonset 22 | Moonset 23 | Moonset 24 | Moonset 25 |
|---|---|---|---|---|---|---|---|
| ° | h m | h m | h m | h m | h m | h m | h m |
| N 72 | 15 22 | 16 38 | 17 57 | 16 51 | 16 20 | 15 46 | 15 04 |
| N 70 | 15 40 | 16 46 | 17 58 | 16 44 | 16 20 | 15 55 | 15 25 |
| 68 | 15 53 | 16 53 | 17 58 | 16 38 | 16 21 | 16 03 | 15 42 |
| 66 | 16 04 | 16 59 | 17 58 | 16 33 | 16 21 | 16 09 | 15 55 |
| 64 | 16 14 | 17 04 | 17 59 | 16 29 | 16 22 | 16 15 | 16 07 |
| 62 | 16 22 | 17 08 | 18 00 | 16 25 | 16 22 | 16 19 | 16 16 |
| 60 | 16 29 | 17 12 | 18 00 | 16 22 | 16 22 | 16 23 | 16 25 |
| N 58 | 16 35 | 17 15 | 18 01 | 16 19 | 16 23 | 16 27 | 16 32 |
| 56 | 16 40 | 17 18 | 18 02 | 16 16 | 16 23 | 16 30 | 16 38 |
| 54 | 16 45 | 17 21 | 18 02 | 16 14 | 16 23 | 16 33 | 16 44 |
| 52 | 16 49 | 17 24 | 18 03 | 16 12 | 16 23 | 16 36 | 16 50 |
| 50 | 16 53 | 17 26 | 18 04 | 16 10 | 16 24 | 16 38 | 16 54 |
| 45 | 17 02 | 17 32 | 18 06 | 16 05 | 16 24 | 16 43 | 17 05 |
| N 40 | 17 09 | 17 37 | 18 08 | 16 02 | 16 25 | 16 48 | 17 14 |
| 35 | 17 16 | 17 41 | 18 11 | 15 59 | 16 25 | 16 52 | 17 21 |
| 30 | 17 21 | 17 45 | 18 13 | 15 56 | 16 25 | 16 55 | 17 28 |
| 20 | 17 31 | 17 53 | 18 19 | 15 51 | 16 25 | 17 01 | 17 39 |
| N 10 | 17 39 | 18 01 | 18 26 | 15 47 | 16 26 | 17 06 | 17 50 |
| 0 | 17 48 | 18 09 | 18 33 | 15 42 | 16 26 | 17 11 | 17 59 |
| S 10 | 17 56 | 18 18 | 18 43 | 15 38 | 16 27 | 17 16 | 18 09 |
| 20 | 18 05 | 18 28 | 18 54 | 15 34 | 16 27 | 17 22 | 18 19 |
| 30 | 18 15 | 18 40 | 19 10 | 15 29 | 16 27 | 17 28 | 18 31 |
| 35 | 18 22 | 18 48 | 19 19 | 15 26 | 16 27 | 17 31 | 18 38 |
| 40 | 18 28 | 18 57 | 19 31 | 15 22 | 16 28 | 17 35 | 18 46 |
| 45 | 18 37 | 19 08 | 19 46 | 15 18 | 16 28 | 17 40 | 18 55 |
| S 50 | 18 46 | 19 21 | 20 05 | 15 13 | 16 28 | 17 45 | 19 06 |
| 52 | 18 51 | 19 28 | 20 14 | 15 11 | 16 28 | 17 48 | 19 11 |
| 54 | 18 56 | 19 35 | 20 25 | 15 09 | 16 28 | 17 51 | 19 17 |
| 56 | 19 02 | 19 43 | 20 37 | 15 06 | 16 29 | 17 54 | 19 23 |
| 58 | 19 08 | 19 52 | 20 52 | 15 03 | 16 29 | 17 57 | 19 30 |
| S 60 | 19 15 | 20 03 | 21 10 | 15 00 | 16 29 | 18 01 | 19 39 |

| Day | SUN Eqn. of Time 00h | SUN Eqn. of Time 12h | SUN Mer. Pass. | MOON Mer. Pass. Upper | MOON Mer. Pass. Lower | Age | Phase |
|---|---|---|---|---|---|---|---|
| d | m s | m s | h m | h m | h m | d % | |
| 22 | 15 27 | 15 32 | 11 44 | 09 32 | 21 54 | 27 10 | |
| 23 | 15 36 | 15 41 | 11 44 | 10 16 | 22 38 | 28 5 | |
| 24 | 15 45 | 15 48 | 11 44 | 11 00 | 23 24 | 29 1 | ● |

| UT | ARIES GHA | VENUS −3.9 GHA | Dec | MARS −1.1 GHA | Dec | JUPITER −2.8 GHA | Dec | SATURN +0.6 GHA | Dec | STARS Name | SHA | Dec |
|---|---|---|---|---|---|---|---|---|---|---|---|---|
| **25** 00 | 33 21.8 | 183 05.8 | S11 16.1 | 308 23.3 | N23 33.5 | 32 28.0 | S 1 19.9 | 71 55.3 | S16 29.2 | Acamar | 315 12.8 | S40 12.7 |
| 01 | 48 24.3 | 198 05.3 | 17.2 | 323 25.6 | 33.6 | 47 30.7 | 20.0 | 86 57.8 | 29.2 | Achernar | 335 21.0 | S57 07.3 |
| 02 | 63 26.8 | 213 04.8 | 18.4 | 338 27.8 | 33.7 | 62 33.4 | 20.1 | 102 00.3 | 29.2 | Acrux | 173 02.8 | S63 13.3 |
| 03 | 78 29.2 | 228 04.3 .. | 19.5 | 353 30.1 .. | 33.8 | 77 36.1 .. | 20.2 | 117 02.7 .. | 29.2 | Adhara | 255 07.2 | S28 59.9 |
| 04 | 93 31.7 | 243 03.8 | 20.6 | 8 32.3 | 33.9 | 92 38.8 | 20.2 | 132 05.2 | 29.2 | Aldebaran | 290 41.5 | N16 33.3 |
| 05 | 108 34.2 | 258 03.3 | 21.8 | 23 34.6 | 34.0 | 107 41.5 | 20.3 | 147 07.6 | 29.2 | | | |
| 06 | 123 36.6 | 273 02.8 | S11 22.9 | 38 36.9 | N23 34.1 | 122 44.1 | S 1 20.4 | 162 10.1 | S16 29.2 | Alioth | 166 15.1 | N55 50.2 |
| T 07 | 138 39.1 | 288 02.3 | 24.1 | 53 39.1 | 34.2 | 137 46.8 | 20.5 | 177 12.5 | 29.2 | Alkaid | 152 54.0 | N49 12.1 |
| U 08 | 153 41.5 | 303 01.7 | 25.2 | 68 41.4 | 34.3 | 152 49.5 | 20.6 | 192 15.0 | 29.2 | Alnair | 27 35.0 | S46 51.2 |
| E 09 | 168 44.0 | 318 01.2 .. | 26.3 | 83 43.7 .. | 34.5 | 167 52.2 .. | 20.7 | 207 17.5 .. | 29.2 | Alnilam | 275 39.4 | S 1 11.1 |
| S 10 | 183 46.5 | 333 00.7 | 27.5 | 98 45.9 | 34.6 | 182 54.9 | 20.8 | 222 19.9 | 29.2 | Alphard | 217 49.7 | S 8 45.2 |
| D 11 | 198 48.9 | 348 00.2 | 28.6 | 113 48.2 | 34.7 | 197 57.6 | 20.9 | 237 22.4 | 29.2 | | | |
| A 12 | 213 51.4 | 2 59.7 | S11 29.8 | 128 50.5 | N23 34.8 | 213 00.3 | S 1 20.9 | 252 24.8 | S16 29.2 | Alphecca | 126 05.7 | N26 38.5 |
| Y 13 | 228 53.9 | 17 59.2 | 30.9 | 143 52.8 | 34.9 | 228 02.9 | 21.0 | 267 27.3 | 29.2 | Alpheratz | 357 36.4 | N29 13.1 |
| 14 | 243 56.3 | 32 58.7 | 32.0 | 158 55.0 | 35.0 | 243 05.6 | 21.1 | 282 29.7 | 29.2 | Altair | 62 01.8 | N 8 55.8 |
| 15 | 258 58.8 | 47 58.1 .. | 33.2 | 173 57.3 .. | 35.1 | 258 08.3 .. | 21.2 | 297 32.2 .. | 29.2 | Ankaa | 353 08.6 | S42 11.0 |
| 16 | 274 01.3 | 62 57.6 | 34.3 | 188 59.6 | 35.2 | 273 11.0 | 21.3 | 312 34.6 | 29.2 | Antares | 112 18.4 | S26 28.9 |
| 17 | 289 03.7 | 77 57.1 | 35.4 | 204 01.9 | 35.4 | 288 13.7 | 21.4 | 327 37.1 | 29.2 | | | |
| 18 | 304 06.2 | 92 56.6 | S11 36.6 | 219 04.2 | N23 35.5 | 303 16.3 | S 1 21.5 | 342 39.5 | S16 29.2 | Arcturus | 145 50.0 | N19 04.0 |
| 19 | 319 08.7 | 107 56.1 | 37.7 | 234 06.4 | 35.6 | 318 19.0 | 21.5 | 357 42.0 | 29.1 | Atria | 107 14.7 | S69 04.2 |
| 20 | 334 11.1 | 122 55.6 | 38.8 | 249 08.7 | 35.7 | 333 21.7 | 21.6 | 12 44.5 | 29.1 | Avior | 234 15.5 | S59 34.5 |
| 21 | 349 13.6 | 137 55.0 .. | 40.0 | 264 11.0 .. | 35.8 | 348 24.4 .. | 21.7 | 27 46.9 .. | 29.1 | Bellatrix | 278 24.6 | N 6 22.3 |
| 22 | 4 16.0 | 152 54.5 | 41.1 | 279 13.3 | 35.9 | 3 27.1 | 21.8 | 42 49.4 | 29.1 | Betelgeuse | 270 53.9 | N 7 24.8 |
| 23 | 19 18.5 | 167 54.0 | 42.2 | 294 15.6 | 36.0 | 18 29.7 | 21.9 | 57 51.8 | 29.1 | | | |
| **26** 00 | 34 21.0 | 182 53.5 | S11 43.4 | 309 17.9 | N23 36.1 | 33 32.4 | S 1 22.0 | 72 54.3 | S16 29.1 | Canopus | 263 53.0 | S52 42.1 |
| 01 | 49 23.4 | 197 53.0 | 44.5 | 324 20.2 | 36.3 | 48 35.1 | 22.1 | 87 56.7 | 29.1 | Capella | 280 24.3 | N46 01.1 |
| 02 | 64 25.9 | 212 52.4 | 45.6 | 339 22.5 | 36.4 | 63 37.8 | 22.1 | 102 59.2 | 29.1 | Deneb | 49 27.0 | N45 21.9 |
| 03 | 79 28.4 | 227 51.9 .. | 46.8 | 354 24.8 .. | 36.5 | 78 40.5 .. | 22.2 | 118 01.6 .. | 29.1 | Denebola | 182 27.1 | N14 26.8 |
| 04 | 94 30.8 | 242 51.4 | 47.9 | 9 27.1 | 36.6 | 93 43.1 | 22.3 | 133 04.1 | 29.1 | Diphda | 348 48.8 | S17 51.7 |
| 05 | 109 33.3 | 257 50.9 | 49.0 | 24 29.4 | 36.7 | 108 45.8 | 22.4 | 148 06.5 | 29.1 | | | |
| 06 | 124 35.8 | 272 50.4 | S11 50.2 | 39 31.7 | N23 36.8 | 123 48.5 | S 1 22.5 | 163 09.0 | S16 29.1 | Dubhe | 193 43.7 | N61 37.6 |
| W 07 | 139 38.2 | 287 49.8 | 51.3 | 54 34.0 | 36.9 | 138 51.2 | 22.6 | 178 11.4 | 29.1 | Elnath | 278 04.0 | N28 37.6 |
| E 08 | 154 40.7 | 302 49.3 | 52.4 | 69 36.3 | 37.0 | 153 53.9 | 22.6 | 193 13.9 | 29.1 | Eltanin | 90 43.4 | N51 29.4 |
| D 09 | 169 43.1 | 317 48.8 .. | 53.5 | 84 38.6 .. | 37.2 | 168 56.5 .. | 22.7 | 208 16.3 .. | 29.1 | Enif | 33 40.5 | N 9 58.9 |
| N 10 | 184 45.6 | 332 48.3 | 54.7 | 99 40.9 | 37.3 | 183 59.2 | 22.8 | 223 18.8 | 29.1 | Fomalhaut | 15 16.3 | S29 30.2 |
| E 11 | 199 48.1 | 347 47.7 | 55.8 | 114 43.2 | 37.4 | 199 01.9 | 22.9 | 238 21.2 | 29.0 | | | |
| S 12 | 214 50.5 | 2 47.2 | S11 56.9 | 129 45.5 | N23 37.5 | 214 04.6 | S 1 23.0 | 253 23.7 | S16 29.0 | Gacrux | 171 54.2 | S57 14.2 |
| D 13 | 229 53.0 | 17 46.7 | 58.0 | 144 47.8 | 37.6 | 229 07.2 | 23.1 | 268 26.1 | 29.0 | Gienah | 175 45.8 | S17 39.9 |
| A 14 | 244 55.5 | 32 46.2 | 11 59.2 | 159 50.1 | 37.7 | 244 09.9 | 23.2 | 283 28.6 | 29.0 | Hadar | 148 39.3 | S60 28.8 |
| Y 15 | 259 57.9 | 47 45.6 | 12 00.3 | 174 52.4 .. | 37.8 | 259 12.6 .. | 23.2 | 298 31.0 .. | 29.0 | Hamal | 327 52.9 | N23 34.3 |
| 16 | 275 00.4 | 62 45.1 | 01.4 | 189 54.8 | 37.9 | 274 15.3 | 23.3 | 313 33.5 | 29.0 | Kaus Aust. | 83 35.2 | S34 22.5 |
| 17 | 290 02.9 | 77 44.6 | 02.5 | 204 57.1 | 38.1 | 289 17.9 | 23.4 | 328 35.9 | 29.0 | | | |
| 18 | 305 05.3 | 92 44.1 | S12 03.7 | 219 59.4 | N23 38.2 | 304 20.6 | S 1 23.5 | 343 38.4 | S16 29.0 | Kochab | 137 20.9 | N74 03.8 |
| 19 | 320 07.8 | 107 43.5 | 04.8 | 235 01.7 | 38.3 | 319 23.3 | 23.6 | 358 40.8 | 29.0 | Markab | 13 31.5 | N15 19.8 |
| 20 | 335 10.3 | 122 43.0 | 05.9 | 250 04.0 | 38.4 | 334 26.0 | 23.7 | 13 43.3 | 29.0 | Menkar | 314 07.8 | N 4 10.8 |
| 21 | 350 12.7 | 137 42.5 .. | 07.0 | 265 06.4 .. | 38.5 | 349 28.6 .. | 23.7 | 28 45.7 .. | 29.0 | Menkent | 148 00.2 | S36 28.7 |
| 22 | 5 15.2 | 152 42.0 | 08.1 | 280 08.7 | 38.6 | 4 31.3 | 23.8 | 43 48.2 | 29.0 | Miaplacidus | 221 38.9 | S69 48.2 |
| 23 | 20 17.6 | 167 41.4 | 09.3 | 295 11.0 | 38.7 | 19 34.0 | 23.9 | 58 50.6 | 29.0 | | | |
| **27** 00 | 35 20.1 | 182 40.9 | S12 10.4 | 310 13.4 | N23 38.8 | 34 36.7 | S 1 24.0 | 73 53.1 | S16 29.0 | Mirfak | 308 30.4 | N49 56.5 |
| 01 | 50 22.6 | 197 40.4 | 11.5 | 325 15.7 | 39.0 | 49 39.3 | 24.1 | 88 55.5 | 28.9 | Nunki | 75 50.2 | S26 16.1 |
| 02 | 65 25.0 | 212 39.8 | 12.6 | 340 18.0 | 39.1 | 64 42.0 | 24.1 | 103 58.0 | 28.9 | Peacock | 53 08.6 | S56 39.9 |
| 03 | 80 27.5 | 227 39.3 .. | 13.7 | 355 20.4 .. | 39.2 | 79 44.7 .. | 24.2 | 119 00.4 .. | 28.9 | Pollux | 243 19.5 | N27 58.2 |
| 04 | 95 30.0 | 242 38.8 | 14.9 | 10 22.7 | 39.3 | 94 47.4 | 24.3 | 134 02.9 | 28.9 | Procyon | 244 52.7 | N 5 10.1 |
| 05 | 110 32.4 | 257 38.2 | 16.0 | 25 25.0 | 39.4 | 109 50.0 | 24.4 | 149 05.3 | 28.9 | | | |
| 06 | 125 34.9 | 272 37.7 | S12 17.1 | 40 27.4 | N23 39.5 | 124 52.7 | S 1 24.5 | 164 07.8 | S16 28.9 | Rasalhague | 96 00.5 | N12 32.8 |
| T 07 | 140 37.4 | 287 37.2 | 18.2 | 55 29.7 | 39.6 | 139 55.4 | 24.6 | 179 10.2 | 28.9 | Regulus | 207 36.6 | N11 51.5 |
| H 08 | 155 39.8 | 302 36.6 | 19.3 | 70 32.1 | 39.7 | 154 58.1 | 24.6 | 194 12.7 | 28.9 | Rigel | 281 05.4 | S 8 10.4 |
| U 09 | 170 42.3 | 317 36.1 .. | 20.4 | 85 34.4 .. | 39.9 | 170 00.7 .. | 24.7 | 209 15.1 .. | 28.9 | Rigil Kent. | 139 43.5 | S60 55.6 |
| R 10 | 185 44.8 | 332 35.6 | 21.6 | 100 36.7 | 40.0 | 185 03.4 | 24.8 | 224 17.6 | 28.9 | Sabik | 102 05.2 | S15 45.1 |
| S 11 | 200 47.2 | 347 35.0 | 22.7 | 115 39.1 | 40.1 | 200 06.1 | 24.9 | 239 20.0 | 28.9 | | | |
| D 12 | 215 49.7 | 2 34.5 | S12 23.8 | 130 41.4 | N23 40.2 | 215 08.7 | S 1 25.0 | 254 22.5 | S16 28.9 | Schedar | 349 32.6 | N56 39.8 |
| A 13 | 230 52.1 | 17 34.0 | 24.9 | 145 43.8 | 40.3 | 230 11.4 | 25.0 | 269 24.9 | 28.9 | Shaula | 96 13.2 | S37 07.2 |
| Y 14 | 245 54.6 | 32 33.4 | 26.0 | 160 46.1 | 40.4 | 245 14.1 | 25.1 | 284 27.3 | 28.8 | Sirius | 258 27.7 | S16 44.6 |
| 15 | 260 57.1 | 47 32.9 .. | 27.1 | 175 48.5 .. | 40.5 | 260 16.8 .. | 25.2 | 299 29.8 .. | 28.8 | Spica | 158 24.6 | S11 16.6 |
| 16 | 275 59.5 | 62 32.4 | 28.2 | 190 50.9 | 40.6 | 275 19.4 | 25.3 | 314 32.2 | 28.8 | Suhail | 222 47.8 | S43 31.1 |
| 17 | 291 02.0 | 77 31.8 | 29.3 | 205 53.2 | 40.8 | 290 22.1 | 25.4 | 329 34.7 | 28.8 | | | |
| 18 | 306 04.5 | 92 31.3 | S12 30.5 | 220 55.6 | N23 40.9 | 305 24.8 | S 1 25.4 | 344 37.1 | S16 28.8 | Vega | 80 34.7 | N38 48.5 |
| 19 | 321 06.9 | 107 30.7 | 31.6 | 235 57.9 | 41.0 | 320 27.4 | 25.5 | 359 39.6 | 28.8 | Zuben'ubi | 136 58.4 | S16 08.0 |
| 20 | 336 09.4 | 122 30.2 | 32.7 | 251 00.3 | 41.1 | 335 30.1 | 25.6 | 14 42.0 | 28.8 | | SHA | Mer. Pass. |
| 21 | 351 11.9 | 137 29.7 .. | 33.8 | 266 02.7 .. | 41.2 | 350 32.8 .. | 25.7 | 29 44.5 .. | 28.8 | Venus | 148 32.5 | 11 49 |
| 22 | 6 14.3 | 152 29.1 | 34.9 | 281 05.0 | 41.3 | 5 35.4 | 25.8 | 44 46.9 | 28.8 | Mars | 274 56.9 | 3 22 |
| 23 | 21 16.8 | 167 28.6 | 36.0 | 296 07.4 | 41.4 | 20 38.1 | 25.8 | 59 49.4 | 28.8 | Jupiter | 359 11.5 | 21 42 |
| Mer. Pass. 21 39.0 | | v −0.5 | d 1.1 | v 2.3 | d 0.1 | v 2.7 | d 0.1 | v 2.5 | d 0.0 | Saturn | 38 33.3 | 19 05 |

| UT | SUN GHA | SUN Dec | MOON GHA | v | MOON Dec | d | HP |
|---|---|---|---|---|---|---|---|
| d h | ° ′ | ° ′ | ° ′ | ′ | ° ′ | ′ | ′ |
| 25 00 | 183 58.1 | S12 00.8 | 188 49.2 | 12.5 | S 8 30.1 | 15.1 | 58.0 |
| 01 | 198 58.1 | 01.7 | 203 20.7 | 12.4 | 8 45.2 | 15.0 | 58.0 |
| 02 | 213 58.2 | 02.5 | 217 52.1 | 12.3 | 9 00.2 | 15.1 | 58.0 |
| 03 | 228 58.3 | .. 03.4 | 232 23.4 | 12.3 | 9 15.3 | 15.0 | 58.1 |
| 04 | 243 58.4 | 04.3 | 246 54.7 | 12.1 | 9 30.3 | 14.9 | 58.1 |
| 05 | 258 58.4 | 05.1 | 261 25.8 | 12.1 | S 9 45.2 | 15.0 | 58.1 |
| 06 | 273 58.5 | S12 06.0 | | | | | |
| 07 | 288 58.6 | 06.8 | | | | | |
| T 08 | 303 58.6 | 07.7 | | A partial eclipse of | | | |
| U 09 | 318 58.7 | .. 08.6 | | the Sun occurs on this | | | |
| E 10 | 333 58.8 | 09.4 | | date. See page 5. | | | |
| S 11 | 348 58.9 | 10.3 | | | | | |
| D 12 | 3 58.9 | S12 11.1 | 3 01.9 | 11.6 | S11 28.9 | 14.7 | 58.3 |
| A 13 | 18 59.0 | 12.0 | 17 32.5 | 11.5 | 11 43.6 | 14.6 | 58.3 |
| Y 14 | 33 59.1 | 12.9 | 32 03.0 | 11.3 | 11 58.2 | 14.5 | 58.3 |
| 15 | 48 59.1 | .. 13.7 | 46 33.3 | 11.3 | 12 12.7 | 14.5 | 58.4 |
| 16 | 63 59.2 | 14.6 | 61 03.6 | 11.2 | 12 27.2 | 14.5 | 58.4 |
| 17 | 78 59.3 | 15.4 | 75 33.8 | 11.2 | 12 41.7 | 14.4 | 58.4 |
| 18 | 93 59.3 | S12 16.3 | 90 04.0 | 11.0 | S12 56.1 | 14.3 | 58.4 |
| 19 | 108 59.4 | 17.2 | 104 34.0 | 11.0 | 13 10.4 | 14.3 | 58.5 |
| 20 | 123 59.5 | 18.0 | 119 04.0 | 10.8 | 13 24.7 | 14.2 | 58.5 |
| 21 | 138 59.5 | .. 18.9 | 133 33.8 | 10.8 | 13 38.9 | 14.2 | 58.5 |
| 22 | 153 59.6 | 19.7 | 148 03.6 | 10.7 | 13 53.1 | 14.1 | 58.5 |
| 23 | 168 59.7 | 20.6 | 162 33.3 | 10.5 | 14 07.2 | 14.0 | 58.6 |
| 26 00 | 183 59.8 | S12 21.4 | 177 02.8 | 10.5 | S14 21.2 | 14.0 | 58.6 |
| 01 | 198 59.8 | 22.3 | 191 32.3 | 10.4 | 14 35.2 | 13.9 | 58.6 |
| 02 | 213 59.9 | 23.1 | 206 01.7 | 10.3 | 14 49.1 | 13.8 | 58.6 |
| 03 | 229 00.0 | .. 24.0 | 220 31.0 | 10.2 | 15 02.9 | 13.8 | 58.6 |
| 04 | 244 00.0 | 24.9 | 235 00.2 | 10.2 | 15 16.7 | 13.7 | 58.7 |
| 05 | 259 00.1 | 25.7 | 249 29.4 | 10.0 | 15 30.4 | 13.6 | 58.7 |
| 06 | 274 00.1 | S12 26.6 | 263 58.4 | 9.9 | S15 44.0 | 13.6 | 58.7 |
| W 07 | 289 00.2 | 27.4 | 278 27.3 | 9.8 | 15 57.6 | 13.4 | 58.7 |
| E 08 | 304 00.3 | 28.3 | 292 56.1 | 9.7 | 16 11.0 | 13.4 | 58.7 |
| D 09 | 319 00.3 | .. 29.1 | 307 24.8 | 9.6 | 16 24.4 | 13.3 | 58.8 |
| N 10 | 334 00.4 | 30.0 | 321 53.4 | 9.6 | 16 37.7 | 13.3 | 58.8 |
| E 11 | 349 00.5 | 30.8 | 336 22.0 | 9.4 | 16 51.0 | 13.1 | 58.8 |
| S 12 | 4 00.5 | S12 31.7 | 350 50.4 | 9.3 | S17 04.1 | 13.0 | 58.8 |
| D 13 | 19 00.6 | 32.5 | 5 18.7 | 9.2 | 17 17.1 | 13.0 | 58.8 |
| A 14 | 34 00.7 | 33.4 | 19 46.9 | 9.1 | 17 30.1 | 12.9 | 58.9 |
| Y 15 | 49 00.7 | .. 34.2 | 34 15.0 | 9.0 | 17 43.0 | 12.8 | 58.9 |
| 16 | 64 00.8 | 35.1 | 48 43.0 | 9.0 | 17 55.8 | 12.7 | 58.9 |
| 17 | 79 00.8 | 35.9 | 63 11.0 | 8.8 | 18 08.5 | 12.6 | 58.9 |
| 18 | 94 00.9 | S12 36.8 | 77 38.8 | 8.7 | S18 21.1 | 12.4 | 58.9 |
| 19 | 109 01.0 | 37.6 | 92 06.5 | 8.6 | 18 33.5 | 12.4 | 59.0 |
| 20 | 124 01.0 | 38.5 | 106 34.1 | 8.5 | 18 45.9 | 12.3 | 59.0 |
| 21 | 139 01.1 | .. 39.3 | 121 01.6 | 8.4 | 18 58.2 | 12.2 | 59.0 |
| 22 | 154 01.1 | 40.2 | 135 29.0 | 8.2 | 19 10.4 | 12.1 | 59.0 |
| 23 | 169 01.2 | 41.0 | 149 56.2 | 8.2 | 19 22.5 | 12.0 | 59.0 |
| 27 00 | 184 01.3 | S12 41.9 | 164 23.4 | 8.1 | S19 34.5 | 11.9 | 59.0 |
| 01 | 199 01.3 | 42.7 | 178 50.5 | 8.0 | 19 46.4 | 11.7 | 59.1 |
| 02 | 214 01.4 | 43.6 | 193 17.5 | 7.8 | 19 58.1 | 11.7 | 59.1 |
| 03 | 229 01.4 | .. 44.4 | 207 44.3 | 7.8 | 20 09.8 | 11.5 | 59.1 |
| 04 | 244 01.5 | 45.3 | 222 11.1 | 7.6 | 20 21.3 | 11.4 | 59.1 |
| 05 | 259 01.6 | 46.1 | 236 37.7 | 7.6 | 20 32.7 | 11.3 | 59.1 |
| 06 | 274 01.6 | S12 47.0 | 251 04.3 | 7.4 | S20 44.0 | 11.2 | 59.1 |
| T 07 | 289 01.7 | 47.8 | 265 30.7 | 7.4 | 20 55.2 | 11.1 | 59.1 |
| H 08 | 304 01.7 | 48.6 | 279 57.1 | 7.2 | 21 06.3 | 10.9 | 59.2 |
| U 09 | 319 01.8 | .. 49.5 | 294 23.3 | 7.1 | 21 17.2 | 10.8 | 59.2 |
| R 10 | 334 01.8 | 50.3 | 308 49.4 | 7.1 | 21 28.0 | 10.7 | 59.2 |
| S 11 | 349 01.9 | 51.2 | 323 15.5 | 6.9 | 21 38.7 | 10.6 | 59.2 |
| D 12 | 4 02.0 | S12 52.0 | 337 41.4 | 6.8 | S21 49.3 | 10.4 | 59.2 |
| A 13 | 19 02.0 | 52.9 | 352 07.2 | 6.7 | 21 59.7 | 10.3 | 59.2 |
| Y 14 | 34 02.1 | 53.7 | 6 32.9 | 6.6 | 22 10.0 | 10.2 | 59.2 |
| 15 | 49 02.1 | .. 54.6 | 20 58.5 | 6.6 | 22 20.2 | 10.0 | 59.3 |
| 16 | 64 02.2 | 55.4 | 35 24.1 | 6.4 | 22 30.2 | 9.9 | 59.3 |
| 17 | 79 02.2 | 56.2 | 49 49.5 | 6.3 | 22 40.1 | 9.7 | 59.3 |
| 18 | 94 02.3 | S12 57.1 | 64 14.8 | 6.2 | S22 49.8 | 9.6 | 59.3 |
| 19 | 109 02.3 | 57.9 | 78 40.0 | 6.1 | 22 59.4 | 9.5 | 59.3 |
| 20 | 124 02.4 | 58.8 | 93 05.1 | 6.0 | 23 08.9 | 9.3 | 59.3 |
| 21 | 139 02.4 | 12 59.6 | 107 30.1 | 5.9 | 23 18.2 | 9.2 | 59.3 |
| 22 | 154 02.5 | 13 00.4 | 121 55.0 | 5.8 | 23 27.4 | 9.0 | 59.3 |
| 23 | 169 02.5 | S13 01.3 | 136 19.8 | 5.8 | S23 36.4 | 8.9 | 59.3 |
| | SD 16.1 | d 0.9 | SD 15.9 | | 16.0 | | 16.1 |

| Lat. | Twilight Naut. | Twilight Civil | Sunrise | Moonrise 25 | Moonrise 26 | Moonrise 27 | Moonrise 28 |
|---|---|---|---|---|---|---|---|
| ° | h m | h m | h m | h m | h m | h m | h m |
| N 72 | 05 42 | 07 02 | 08 21 | 08 02 | 11 19 | ■■ | ■■ |
| N 70 | 05 40 | 06 52 | 08 01 | 07 43 | 10 18 | ■■ | ■■ |
| 68 | 05 39 | 06 44 | 07 46 | 07 28 | 09 44 | ■■ | ■■ |
| 66 | 05 38 | 06 38 | 07 34 | 07 17 | 09 20 | 11 48 | ■■ |
| 64 | 05 36 | 06 32 | 07 23 | 07 07 | 09 01 | 11 08 | 13 52 |
| 62 | 05 35 | 06 27 | 07 14 | 06 59 | 08 45 | 10 41 | 12 44 |
| 60 | 05 34 | 06 23 | 07 07 | 06 52 | 08 33 | 10 20 | 12 09 |
| N 58 | 05 33 | 06 19 | 07 00 | 06 46 | 08 22 | 10 02 | 11 44 |
| 56 | 05 32 | 06 15 | 06 54 | 06 40 | 08 12 | 09 48 | 11 23 |
| 54 | 05 31 | 06 12 | 06 49 | 06 35 | 08 04 | 09 36 | 11 07 |
| 52 | 05 29 | 06 09 | 06 44 | 06 31 | 07 56 | 09 25 | 10 53 |
| 50 | 05 28 | 06 06 | 06 40 | 06 27 | 07 50 | 09 15 | 10 40 |
| 45 | 05 26 | 06 00 | 06 30 | 06 19 | 07 35 | 08 55 | 10 14 |
| N 40 | 05 23 | 05 54 | 06 22 | 06 12 | 07 24 | 08 39 | 09 54 |
| 35 | 05 20 | 05 49 | 06 15 | 06 06 | 07 14 | 08 25 | 09 37 |
| 30 | 05 17 | 05 45 | 06 09 | 06 00 | 07 05 | 08 13 | 09 23 |
| 20 | 05 10 | 05 36 | 05 59 | 05 51 | 06 50 | 07 53 | 08 58 |
| N 10 | 05 03 | 05 28 | 05 49 | 05 43 | 06 38 | 07 35 | 08 37 |
| 0 | 04 55 | 05 19 | 05 41 | 05 36 | 06 26 | 07 19 | 08 17 |
| S 10 | 04 45 | 05 10 | 05 32 | 05 29 | 06 14 | 07 03 | 07 58 |
| 20 | 04 33 | 04 59 | 05 22 | 05 21 | 06 01 | 06 46 | 07 37 |
| 30 | 04 16 | 04 46 | 05 11 | 05 12 | 05 47 | 06 27 | 07 13 |
| 35 | 04 06 | 04 38 | 05 04 | 05 07 | 05 39 | 06 15 | 06 59 |
| 40 | 03 54 | 04 28 | 04 57 | 05 02 | 05 30 | 06 03 | 06 43 |
| 45 | 03 38 | 04 17 | 04 48 | 04 55 | 05 19 | 05 47 | 06 24 |
| S 50 | 03 18 | 04 02 | 04 38 | 04 48 | 05 06 | 05 29 | 06 00 |
| 52 | 03 09 | 03 56 | 04 33 | 04 44 | 05 00 | 05 20 | 05 49 |
| 54 | 02 57 | 03 48 | 04 27 | 04 40 | 04 53 | 05 11 | 05 36 |
| 56 | 02 44 | 03 39 | 04 21 | 04 36 | 04 46 | 05 00 | 05 21 |
| 58 | 02 28 | 03 29 | 04 15 | 04 31 | 04 38 | 04 47 | 05 04 |
| S 60 | 02 09 | 03 18 | 04 07 | 04 26 | 04 28 | 04 33 | 04 43 |

| Lat. | Sunset | Twilight Civil | Twilight Naut. | Moonset 25 | Moonset 26 | Moonset 27 | Moonset 28 |
|---|---|---|---|---|---|---|---|
| ° | h m | h m | h m | h m | h m | h m | h m |
| N 72 | 15 05 | 16 24 | 17 44 | 15 04 | 13 33 | ■■ | ■■ |
| N 70 | 15 25 | 16 34 | 17 46 | 15 25 | 14 35 | ■■ | ■■ |
| 68 | 15 41 | 16 42 | 17 47 | 15 42 | 15 11 | ■■ | ■■ |
| 66 | 15 53 | 16 49 | 17 49 | 15 55 | 15 37 | 15 02 | ■■ |
| 64 | 16 04 | 16 55 | 17 50 | 16 07 | 15 57 | 15 43 | 15 02 |
| 62 | 16 13 | 17 00 | 17 52 | 16 16 | 16 14 | 16 11 | 16 11 |
| 60 | 16 20 | 17 04 | 17 53 | 16 25 | 16 27 | 16 33 | 16 47 |
| N 58 | 16 27 | 17 08 | 17 54 | 16 32 | 16 39 | 16 51 | 17 13 |
| 56 | 16 33 | 17 12 | 17 55 | 16 38 | 16 50 | 17 06 | 17 33 |
| 54 | 16 39 | 17 15 | 17 56 | 16 44 | 16 59 | 17 19 | 17 50 |
| 52 | 16 43 | 17 18 | 17 58 | 16 50 | 17 07 | 17 31 | 18 05 |
| 50 | 16 48 | 17 21 | 17 59 | 16 54 | 17 15 | 17 41 | 18 18 |
| 45 | 16 57 | 17 27 | 18 02 | 17 05 | 17 30 | 18 02 | 18 44 |
| N 40 | 17 05 | 17 33 | 18 05 | 17 14 | 17 44 | 18 20 | 19 05 |
| 35 | 17 12 | 17 38 | 18 08 | 17 21 | 17 55 | 18 35 | 19 23 |
| 30 | 17 18 | 17 43 | 18 11 | 17 28 | 18 05 | 18 47 | 19 38 |
| 20 | 17 29 | 17 51 | 18 17 | 17 39 | 18 22 | 19 09 | 20 03 |
| N 10 | 17 38 | 18 00 | 18 25 | 17 50 | 18 37 | 19 29 | 20 26 |
| 0 | 17 47 | 18 09 | 18 33 | 17 59 | 18 51 | 19 46 | 20 46 |
| S 10 | 17 56 | 18 18 | 18 43 | 18 09 | 19 05 | 20 04 | 21 07 |
| 20 | 18 06 | 18 29 | 18 56 | 18 19 | 19 20 | 20 24 | 21 30 |
| 30 | 18 18 | 18 43 | 19 12 | 18 31 | 19 37 | 20 46 | 21 56 |
| 35 | 18 24 | 18 51 | 19 23 | 18 38 | 19 47 | 20 59 | 22 11 |
| 40 | 18 32 | 19 00 | 19 35 | 18 46 | 19 59 | 21 15 | 22 29 |
| 45 | 18 41 | 19 12 | 19 51 | 18 55 | 20 13 | 21 33 | 22 50 |
| S 50 | 18 51 | 19 27 | 20 11 | 19 06 | 20 30 | 21 55 | 23 17 |
| 52 | 18 56 | 19 34 | 20 21 | 19 11 | 20 38 | 22 06 | 23 31 |
| 54 | 19 02 | 19 42 | 20 33 | 19 17 | 20 47 | 22 19 | 23 46 |
| 56 | 19 08 | 19 50 | 20 46 | 19 23 | 20 57 | 22 33 | 24 04 |
| 58 | 19 15 | 20 00 | 21 02 | 19 30 | 21 09 | 22 50 | 24 26 |
| S 60 | 19 23 | 20 12 | 21 22 | 19 39 | 21 22 | 23 10 | 24 55 |

| Day | SUN Eqn. of Time 00h | SUN Eqn. of Time 12h | SUN Mer. Pass. | MOON Mer. Pass. Upper | MOON Mer. Pass. Lower | Age | Phase |
|---|---|---|---|---|---|---|---|
| d | m s | m s | h m | h m | h m | d | % |
| 25 | 15 52 | 15 56 | 11 44 | 11 47 | 24 12 | 00 | 0 |
| 26 | 15 59 | 16 02 | 11 44 | 12 38 | 00 12 | 01 | 1 |
| 27 | 16 05 | 16 08 | 11 44 | 13 33 | 01 05 | 02 | 5 |

| UT | ARIES GHA | VENUS −3.9 GHA | Dec | MARS −1.2 GHA | Dec | JUPITER −2.8 GHA | Dec | SATURN +0.6 GHA | Dec | STARS Name | SHA | Dec |
|---|---|---|---|---|---|---|---|---|---|---|---|---|
| 28 00 | 36 19.3 | 182 28.1 | S12 37.1 | 311 09.8 | N23 41.5 | 35 40.8 | S 1 25.9 | 74 51.8 | S16 28.8 | Acamar | 315 12.8 | S40 12.7 |
| 01 | 51 21.7 | 197 27.5 | 38.2 | 326 12.1 | 41.7 | 50 43.4 | 26.0 | 89 54.2 | 28.7 | Achernar | 335 21.0 | S57 07.3 |
| 02 | 66 24.2 | 212 27.0 | 39.3 | 341 14.5 | 41.8 | 65 46.1 | 26.1 | 104 56.7 | 28.7 | Acrux | 173 02.7 | S63 13.3 |
| 03 | 81 26.6 | 227 26.4 .. | 40.4 | 356 16.9 .. | 41.9 | 80 48.8 .. | 26.2 | 119 59.1 .. | 28.7 | Adhara | 255 07.2 | S28 59.9 |
| 04 | 96 29.1 | 242 25.9 | 41.5 | 11 19.2 | 42.0 | 95 51.4 | 26.2 | 135 01.6 | 28.7 | Aldebaran | 290 41.4 | N16 33.3 |
| 05 | 111 31.6 | 257 25.3 | 42.6 | 26 21.6 | 42.1 | 110 54.1 | 26.3 | 150 04.0 | 28.7 | | | |
| 06 | 126 34.0 | 272 24.8 | S12 43.7 | 41 24.0 | N23 42.2 | 125 56.8 | S 1 26.4 | 165 06.5 | S16 28.7 | Alioth | 166 15.1 | N55 50.2 |
| 07 | 141 36.5 | 287 24.3 | 44.9 | 56 26.4 | 42.3 | 140 59.4 | 26.5 | 180 08.9 | 28.7 | Alkaid | 152 54.0 | N49 12.0 |
| 08 | 156 39.0 | 302 23.7 | 46.0 | 71 28.8 | 42.4 | 156 02.1 | 26.5 | 195 11.3 | 28.7 | Alnair | 27 35.0 | S46 51.2 |
| F 09 | 171 41.4 | 317 23.2 .. | 47.1 | 86 31.1 .. | 42.6 | 171 04.8 .. | 26.6 | 210 13.8 .. | 28.7 | Alnilam | 275 39.4 | S 1 11.1 |
| R 10 | 186 43.9 | 332 22.6 | 48.2 | 101 33.5 | 42.7 | 186 07.4 | 26.7 | 225 16.2 | 28.7 | Alphard | 217 49.6 | S 8 45.2 |
| I 11 | 201 46.4 | 347 22.1 | 49.3 | 116 35.9 | 42.8 | 201 10.1 | 26.8 | 240 18.7 | 28.7 | | | |
| D 12 | 216 48.8 | 2 21.5 | S12 50.4 | 131 38.3 | N23 42.9 | 216 12.8 | S 1 26.9 | 255 21.1 | S16 28.6 | Alphecca | 126 05.7 | N26 38.4 |
| A 13 | 231 51.3 | 17 21.0 | 51.5 | 146 40.7 | 43.0 | 231 15.4 | 26.9 | 270 23.6 | 28.6 | Alpheratz | 357 36.4 | N29 13.1 |
| Y 14 | 246 53.8 | 32 20.5 | 52.6 | 161 43.1 | 43.1 | 246 18.1 | 27.0 | 285 26.0 | 28.6 | Altair | 62 01.8 | N 8 55.8 |
| 15 | 261 56.2 | 47 19.9 .. | 53.7 | 176 45.5 .. | 43.2 | 261 20.8 .. | 27.1 | 300 28.4 .. | 28.6 | Ankaa | 353 08.6 | S42 11.0 |
| 16 | 276 58.7 | 62 19.4 | 54.8 | 191 47.9 | 43.3 | 276 23.4 | 27.2 | 315 30.9 | 28.6 | Antares | 112 18.4 | S26 28.9 |
| 17 | 292 01.1 | 77 18.8 | 55.9 | 206 50.3 | 43.5 | 291 26.1 | 27.2 | 330 33.3 | 28.6 | | | |
| 18 | 307 03.6 | 92 18.3 | S12 57.0 | 221 52.6 | N23 43.6 | 306 28.7 | S 1 27.3 | 345 35.8 | S16 28.6 | Arcturus | 145 49.9 | N19 04.0 |
| 19 | 322 06.1 | 107 17.7 | 58.1 | 236 55.0 | 43.7 | 321 31.4 | 27.4 | 0 38.2 | 28.6 | Atria | 107 14.7 | S69 04.2 |
| 20 | 337 08.5 | 122 17.2 | 12 59.2 | 251 57.4 | 43.8 | 336 34.1 | 27.5 | 15 40.6 | 28.6 | Avior | 234 15.4 | S59 34.5 |
| 21 | 352 11.0 | 137 16.6 | 13 00.2 | 266 59.9 .. | 43.9 | 351 36.7 .. | 27.6 | 30 43.1 .. | 28.6 | Bellatrix | 278 24.6 | N 6 22.3 |
| 22 | 7 13.5 | 152 16.1 | 01.3 | 282 02.3 | 44.0 | 6 39.4 | 27.6 | 45 45.5 | 28.5 | Betelgeuse | 270 53.9 | N 7 24.8 |
| 23 | 22 15.9 | 167 15.5 | 02.4 | 297 04.7 | 44.1 | 21 42.1 | 27.7 | 60 48.0 | 28.5 | | | |
| 29 00 | 37 18.4 | 182 15.0 | S13 03.5 | 312 07.1 | N23 44.3 | 36 44.7 | S 1 27.8 | 75 50.4 | S16 28.5 | Canopus | 263 52.9 | S52 42.1 |
| 01 | 52 20.9 | 197 14.4 | 04.6 | 327 09.5 | 44.4 | 51 47.4 | 27.9 | 90 52.8 | 28.5 | Capella | 280 24.3 | N46 01.1 |
| 02 | 67 23.3 | 212 13.9 | 05.7 | 342 11.9 | 44.5 | 66 50.0 | 27.9 | 105 55.3 | 28.5 | Deneb | 49 27.0 | N45 21.9 |
| 03 | 82 25.8 | 227 13.3 .. | 06.8 | 357 14.3 .. | 44.6 | 81 52.7 .. | 28.0 | 120 57.7 .. | 28.5 | Denebola | 182 27.1 | N14 26.8 |
| 04 | 97 28.2 | 242 12.8 | 07.9 | 12 16.7 | 44.7 | 96 55.4 | 28.1 | 136 00.2 | 28.5 | Diphda | 348 48.8 | S17 51.7 |
| 05 | 112 30.7 | 257 12.2 | 09.0 | 27 19.1 | 44.8 | 111 58.0 | 28.2 | 151 02.6 | 28.5 | | | |
| 06 | 127 33.2 | 272 11.7 | S13 10.1 | 42 21.5 | N23 44.9 | 127 00.7 | S 1 28.2 | 166 05.0 | S16 28.5 | Dubhe | 193 43.7 | N61 37.6 |
| 07 | 142 35.6 | 287 11.1 | 11.2 | 57 24.0 | 45.0 | 142 03.3 | 28.3 | 181 07.5 | 28.5 | Elnath | 278 03.9 | N28 37.6 |
| S 08 | 157 38.1 | 302 10.5 | 12.3 | 72 26.4 | 45.2 | 157 06.0 | 28.4 | 196 09.9 | 28.4 | Eltanin | 90 43.4 | N51 29.4 |
| A 09 | 172 40.6 | 317 10.0 .. | 13.4 | 87 28.8 .. | 45.3 | 172 08.7 .. | 28.5 | 211 12.4 .. | 28.4 | Enif | 33 40.5 | N 9 58.9 |
| T 10 | 187 43.0 | 332 09.4 | 14.4 | 102 31.2 | 45.4 | 187 11.3 | 28.5 | 226 14.8 | 28.4 | Fomalhaut | 15 16.3 | S29 30.2 |
| U 11 | 202 45.5 | 347 08.9 | 15.5 | 117 33.6 | 45.5 | 202 14.0 | 28.6 | 241 17.2 | 28.4 | | | |
| R 12 | 217 48.0 | 2 08.3 | S13 16.6 | 132 36.1 | N23 45.6 | 217 16.6 | S 1 28.7 | 256 19.7 | S16 28.4 | Gacrux | 171 54.2 | S57 14.2 |
| D 13 | 232 50.4 | 17 07.8 | 17.7 | 147 38.5 | 45.7 | 232 19.3 | 28.8 | 271 22.1 | 28.4 | Gienah | 175 45.8 | S17 39.9 |
| A 14 | 247 52.9 | 32 07.2 | 18.8 | 162 40.9 | 45.8 | 247 22.0 | 28.8 | 286 24.6 | 28.4 | Hadar | 148 39.3 | S60 28.8 |
| Y 15 | 262 55.4 | 47 06.7 .. | 19.9 | 177 43.4 .. | 46.0 | 262 24.6 .. | 28.9 | 301 27.0 .. | 28.4 | Hamal | 327 52.9 | N23 34.3 |
| 16 | 277 57.8 | 62 06.1 | 21.0 | 192 45.8 | 46.1 | 277 27.3 | 29.0 | 316 29.4 | 28.4 | Kaus Aust. | 83 35.2 | S34 22.5 |
| 17 | 293 00.3 | 77 05.5 | 22.1 | 207 48.2 | 46.2 | 292 29.9 | 29.1 | 331 31.9 | 28.3 | | | |
| 18 | 308 02.7 | 92 05.0 | S13 23.1 | 222 50.7 | N23 46.3 | 307 32.6 | S 1 29.1 | 346 34.3 | S16 28.3 | Kochab | 137 21.0 | N74 03.8 |
| 19 | 323 05.2 | 107 04.4 | 24.2 | 237 53.1 | 46.4 | 322 35.2 | 29.2 | 1 36.7 | 28.3 | Markab | 13 31.5 | N15 19.8 |
| 20 | 338 07.7 | 122 03.9 | 25.3 | 252 55.5 | 46.5 | 337 37.9 | 29.3 | 16 39.2 | 28.3 | Menkar | 314 07.8 | N 4 10.8 |
| 21 | 353 10.1 | 137 03.3 .. | 26.4 | 267 58.0 .. | 46.6 | 352 40.6 .. | 29.4 | 31 41.6 .. | 28.3 | Menkent | 148 00.2 | S36 28.7 |
| 22 | 8 12.6 | 152 02.7 | 27.5 | 283 00.4 | 46.7 | 7 43.2 | 29.4 | 46 44.0 | 28.3 | Miaplacidus | 221 38.8 | S69 48.2 |
| 23 | 23 15.1 | 167 02.2 | 28.6 | 298 02.9 | 46.9 | 22 45.9 | 29.5 | 61 46.5 | 28.3 | | | |
| 30 00 | 38 17.5 | 182 01.6 | S13 29.6 | 313 05.3 | N23 47.0 | 37 48.5 | S 1 29.6 | 76 48.9 | S16 28.3 | Mirfak | 308 30.4 | N49 56.5 |
| 01 | 53 20.0 | 197 01.1 | 30.7 | 328 07.8 | 47.1 | 52 51.2 | 29.7 | 91 51.4 | 28.3 | Nunki | 75 50.2 | S26 16.1 |
| 02 | 68 22.5 | 212 00.5 | 31.8 | 343 10.2 | 47.2 | 67 53.8 | 29.7 | 106 53.8 | 28.2 | Peacock | 53 08.7 | S56 39.9 |
| 03 | 83 24.9 | 226 59.9 .. | 32.9 | 358 12.7 .. | 47.3 | 82 56.5 .. | 29.8 | 121 56.2 .. | 28.2 | Pollux | 243 19.5 | N27 58.2 |
| 04 | 98 27.4 | 241 59.4 | 34.0 | 13 15.1 | 47.4 | 97 59.1 | 29.9 | 136 58.7 | 28.2 | Procyon | 244 52.7 | N 5 10.1 |
| 05 | 113 29.9 | 256 58.8 | 35.0 | 28 17.6 | 47.5 | 113 01.8 | 29.9 | 152 01.1 | 28.2 | | | |
| 06 | 128 32.3 | 271 58.2 | S13 36.1 | 43 20.0 | N23 47.7 | 128 04.4 | S 1 30.0 | 167 03.5 | S16 28.2 | Rasalhague | 96 00.5 | N12 32.8 |
| 07 | 143 34.8 | 286 57.7 | 37.2 | 58 22.5 | 47.8 | 143 07.1 | 30.1 | 182 06.0 | 28.2 | Regulus | 207 36.5 | N11 51.5 |
| 08 | 158 37.2 | 301 57.1 | 38.3 | 73 24.9 | 47.9 | 158 09.7 | 30.2 | 197 08.4 | 28.2 | Rigel | 281 05.4 | S 8 10.4 |
| S 09 | 173 39.7 | 316 56.5 .. | 39.3 | 88 27.4 .. | 48.0 | 173 12.4 .. | 30.2 | 212 10.8 .. | 28.2 | Rigil Kent. | 139 43.5 | S60 55.6 |
| U 10 | 188 42.2 | 331 56.0 | 40.4 | 103 29.9 | 48.1 | 188 15.1 | 30.3 | 227 13.3 | 28.1 | Sabik | 102 05.2 | S15 45.1 |
| N 11 | 203 44.6 | 346 55.4 | 41.5 | 118 32.3 | 48.2 | 203 17.7 | 30.4 | 242 15.7 | 28.1 | | | |
| D 12 | 218 47.1 | 1 54.8 | S13 42.6 | 133 34.8 | N23 48.3 | 218 20.4 | S 1 30.4 | 257 18.1 | S16 28.1 | Schedar | 349 32.6 | N56 39.9 |
| A 13 | 233 49.6 | 16 54.3 | 43.6 | 148 37.3 | 48.4 | 233 23.0 | 30.5 | 272 20.6 | 28.1 | Shaula | 96 13.2 | S37 07.2 |
| Y 14 | 248 52.0 | 31 53.7 | 44.7 | 163 39.7 | 48.6 | 248 25.7 | 30.6 | 287 23.0 | 28.1 | Sirius | 258 27.7 | S16 44.6 |
| 15 | 263 54.5 | 46 53.1 .. | 45.8 | 178 42.2 .. | 48.7 | 263 28.3 .. | 30.7 | 302 25.4 .. | 28.1 | Spica | 158 24.6 | S11 16.6 |
| 16 | 278 57.0 | 61 52.6 | 46.9 | 193 44.7 | 48.8 | 278 31.0 | 30.7 | 317 27.9 | 28.1 | Suhail | 222 47.7 | S43 31.1 |
| 17 | 293 59.4 | 76 52.0 | 47.9 | 208 47.1 | 48.9 | 293 33.6 | 30.8 | 332 30.3 | 28.1 | | | |
| 18 | 309 01.9 | 91 51.4 | S13 49.0 | 223 49.6 | N23 49.0 | 308 36.3 | S 1 30.9 | 347 32.7 | S16 28.0 | Vega | 80 34.7 | N38 48.5 |
| 19 | 324 04.4 | 106 50.9 | 50.1 | 238 52.1 | 49.1 | 323 38.9 | 30.9 | 2 35.2 | 28.0 | Zuben'ubi | 136 58.4 | S16 08.0 |
| 20 | 339 06.8 | 121 50.3 | 51.1 | 253 54.6 | 49.2 | 338 41.6 | 31.0 | 17 37.6 | 28.0 | | SHA | Mer. Pass. |
| 21 | 354 09.3 | 136 49.7 .. | 52.2 | 268 57.0 .. | 49.4 | 353 44.2 .. | 31.1 | 32 40.0 .. | 28.0 | | ° ′ | h m |
| 22 | 9 11.7 | 151 49.2 | 53.3 | 283 59.5 | 49.5 | 8 46.9 | 31.2 | 47 42.5 | 28.0 | Venus | 144 56.6 | 11 51 |
| 23 | 24 14.2 | 166 48.6 | 54.3 | 299 02.0 | 49.6 | 23 49.5 | 31.2 | 62 44.9 | 28.0 | Mars | 274 48.7 | 3 11 |
| Mer. Pass. | 21 27.2 | v −0.6 | d 1.1 | v 2.4 | d 0.1 | v 2.7 | d 0.1 | v 2.4 | d 0.0 | Jupiter | 359 26.3 | 21 29 |
| | | | | | | | | | | Saturn | 38 32.0 | 18 54 |

| UT | SUN GHA | Dec | MOON GHA | v | Dec | d | HP |
|---|---|---|---|---|---|---|---|
| d h | ° ′ | ° ′ | ° ′ | ′ | ° ′ | ′ | ′ |
| 28 00 | 184 02.6 | S13 02.1 | 150 44.6 | 5.6 | S23 45.3 | 8.7 | 59.4 |
| 01 | 199 02.6 | 03.0 | 165 09.2 | 5.5 | 23 54.0 | 8.6 | 59.4 |
| 02 | 214 02.7 | 03.8 | 179 33.7 | 5.5 | 24 02.6 | 8.4 | 59.4 |
| 03 | 229 02.7 | .. 04.6 | 193 58.2 | 5.3 | 24 11.0 | 8.3 | 59.4 |
| 04 | 244 02.8 | 05.5 | 208 22.5 | 5.3 | 24 19.3 | 8.1 | 59.4 |
| 05 | 259 02.8 | 06.3 | 222 46.8 | 5.1 | 24 27.4 | 7.9 | 59.4 |
| 06 | 274 02.9 | S13 07.2 | 237 10.9 | 5.1 | S24 35.3 | 7.8 | 59.4 |
| 07 | 289 02.9 | 08.0 | 251 35.0 | 5.0 | 24 43.1 | 7.7 | 59.4 |
| F 08 | 304 03.0 | 08.8 | 265 59.0 | 4.9 | 24 50.8 | 7.4 | 59.4 |
| R 09 | 319 03.0 | .. 09.7 | 280 22.9 | 4.8 | 24 58.2 | 7.3 | 59.4 |
| I 10 | 334 03.1 | 10.5 | 294 46.7 | 4.8 | 25 05.5 | 7.2 | 59.4 |
| D 11 | 349 03.1 | 11.3 | 309 10.5 | 4.6 | 25 12.7 | 6.9 | 59.4 |
| A 12 | 4 03.2 | S13 12.2 | 323 34.1 | 4.6 | S25 19.6 | 6.8 | 59.5 |
| Y 13 | 19 03.2 | 13.0 | 337 57.7 | 4.5 | 25 26.4 | 6.7 | 59.5 |
| 14 | 34 03.3 | 13.8 | 352 21.2 | 4.4 | 25 33.1 | 6.4 | 59.5 |
| 15 | 49 03.3 | .. 14.7 | 6 44.6 | 4.4 | 25 39.5 | 6.3 | 59.5 |
| 16 | 64 03.4 | 15.5 | 21 08.0 | 4.3 | 25 45.8 | 6.1 | 59.5 |
| 17 | 79 03.4 | 16.3 | 35 31.3 | 4.2 | 25 51.9 | 6.0 | 59.5 |
| 18 | 94 03.5 | S13 17.2 | 49 54.5 | 4.1 | S25 57.9 | 5.7 | 59.5 |
| 19 | 109 03.5 | 18.0 | 64 17.6 | 4.1 | 26 03.6 | 5.6 | 59.5 |
| 20 | 124 03.6 | 18.8 | 78 40.7 | 4.0 | 26 09.2 | 5.4 | 59.5 |
| 21 | 139 03.6 | .. 19.7 | 93 03.7 | 3.9 | 26 14.6 | 5.2 | 59.5 |
| 22 | 154 03.6 | 20.5 | 107 26.6 | 3.9 | 26 19.8 | 5.1 | 59.5 |
| 23 | 169 03.7 | 21.3 | 121 49.5 | 3.8 | 26 24.9 | 4.8 | 59.5 |
| 29 00 | 184 03.7 | S13 22.2 | 136 12.3 | 3.8 | S26 29.7 | 4.7 | 59.5 |
| 01 | 199 03.8 | 23.0 | 150 35.1 | 3.7 | 26 34.4 | 4.5 | 59.5 |
| 02 | 214 03.8 | 23.8 | 164 57.8 | 3.7 | 26 38.9 | 4.3 | 59.5 |
| 03 | 229 03.9 | .. 24.7 | 179 20.5 | 3.6 | 26 43.2 | 4.2 | 59.5 |
| 04 | 244 03.9 | 25.5 | 193 43.1 | 3.6 | 26 47.4 | 3.9 | 59.5 |
| 05 | 259 03.9 | 26.3 | 208 05.7 | 3.5 | 26 51.3 | 3.8 | 59.5 |
| 06 | 274 04.0 | S13 27.1 | 222 28.2 | 3.5 | S26 55.1 | 3.5 | 59.5 |
| S 07 | 289 04.0 | 28.0 | 236 50.7 | 3.4 | 26 58.6 | 3.4 | 59.5 |
| A 08 | 304 04.1 | 28.8 | 251 13.1 | 3.4 | 27 02.0 | 3.2 | 59.5 |
| T 09 | 319 04.1 | .. 29.6 | 265 35.5 | 3.3 | 27 05.2 | 3.0 | 59.5 |
| U 10 | 334 04.2 | 30.5 | 279 57.8 | 3.4 | 27 08.2 | 2.8 | 59.5 |
| R 11 | 349 04.2 | 31.3 | 294 20.2 | 3.3 | 27 11.0 | 2.6 | 59.5 |
| D 12 | 4 04.2 | S13 32.1 | 308 42.5 | 3.2 | S27 13.6 | 2.5 | 59.5 |
| A 13 | 19 04.3 | 32.9 | 323 04.7 | 3.3 | 27 16.1 | 2.2 | 59.5 |
| Y 14 | 34 04.3 | 33.8 | 337 27.0 | 3.2 | 27 18.3 | 2.0 | 59.5 |
| 15 | 49 04.4 | .. 34.6 | 351 49.2 | 3.2 | 27 20.3 | 1.9 | 59.5 |
| 16 | 64 04.4 | 35.4 | 6 11.4 | 3.2 | 27 22.2 | 1.7 | 59.5 |
| 17 | 79 04.4 | 36.2 | 20 33.6 | 3.2 | 27 23.9 | 1.4 | 59.5 |
| 18 | 94 04.5 | S13 37.1 | 34 55.8 | 3.1 | S27 25.3 | 1.3 | 59.5 |
| 19 | 109 04.5 | 37.9 | 49 17.9 | 3.1 | 27 26.6 | 1.1 | 59.5 |
| 20 | 124 04.5 | 38.7 | 63 40.0 | 3.2 | 27 27.7 | 0.9 | 59.5 |
| 21 | 139 04.6 | .. 39.5 | 78 02.2 | 3.1 | 27 28.6 | 0.7 | 59.5 |
| 22 | 154 04.6 | 40.3 | 92 24.3 | 3.1 | 27 29.3 | 0.5 | 59.5 |
| 23 | 169 04.7 | 41.2 | 106 46.4 | 3.2 | 27 29.8 | 0.3 | 59.5 |
| 30 00 | 184 04.7 | S13 42.0 | 121 08.6 | 3.1 | S27 30.1 | 0.1 | 59.5 |
| 01 | 199 04.7 | 42.8 | 135 30.7 | 3.1 | 27 30.2 | 0.1 | 59.5 |
| 02 | 214 04.8 | 43.6 | 149 52.8 | 3.2 | 27 30.1 | 0.3 | 59.5 |
| 03 | 229 04.8 | .. 44.5 | 164 15.0 | 3.1 | 27 29.8 | 0.5 | 59.5 |
| 04 | 244 04.8 | 45.3 | 178 37.1 | 3.2 | 27 29.3 | 0.6 | 59.5 |
| 05 | 259 04.9 | 46.1 | 192 59.3 | 3.2 | 27 28.7 | 0.9 | 59.5 |
| 06 | 274 04.9 | S13 46.9 | 207 21.5 | 3.2 | S27 27.8 | 1.0 | 59.5 |
| 07 | 289 04.9 | 47.7 | 221 43.7 | 3.2 | 27 26.8 | 1.3 | 59.5 |
| S 08 | 304 05.0 | 48.6 | 236 05.9 | 3.3 | 27 25.5 | 1.4 | 59.5 |
| U 09 | 319 05.0 | .. 49.4 | 250 28.2 | 3.2 | 27 24.1 | 1.6 | 59.5 |
| N 10 | 334 05.0 | 50.2 | 264 50.4 | 3.3 | 27 22.5 | 1.8 | 59.5 |
| D 11 | 349 05.1 | 51.0 | 279 12.7 | 3.4 | 27 20.7 | 2.0 | 59.5 |
| A 12 | 4 05.1 | S13 51.8 | 293 35.1 | 3.4 | S27 18.7 | 2.2 | 59.5 |
| Y 13 | 19 05.1 | 52.6 | 307 57.5 | 3.4 | 27 16.5 | 2.4 | 59.5 |
| 14 | 34 05.2 | 53.5 | 322 19.9 | 3.4 | 27 14.1 | 2.6 | 59.5 |
| 15 | 49 05.2 | .. 54.3 | 336 42.3 | 3.5 | 27 11.5 | 2.8 | 59.5 |
| 16 | 64 05.2 | 55.1 | 351 04.8 | 3.5 | 27 08.7 | 2.9 | 59.5 |
| 17 | 79 05.3 | 55.9 | 5 27.3 | 3.6 | 27 05.8 | 3.2 | 59.5 |
| 18 | 94 05.3 | S13 56.7 | 19 49.9 | 3.6 | S27 02.6 | 3.3 | 59.5 |
| 19 | 109 05.3 | 57.5 | 34 12.5 | 3.7 | 26 59.3 | 3.5 | 59.4 |
| 20 | 124 05.3 | 58.4 | 48 35.2 | 3.7 | 26 55.8 | 3.7 | 59.4 |
| 21 | 139 05.4 | 13 59.2 | 62 57.9 | 3.8 | 26 52.1 | 3.9 | 59.4 |
| 22 | 154 05.4 | 14 00.0 | 77 20.7 | 3.8 | 26 48.2 | 4.1 | 59.4 |
| 23 | 169 05.4 | S14 00.8 | 91 43.5 | 3.9 | S26 44.1 | 4.2 | 59.4 |
| | SD 16.1 | d 0.8 | SD 16.2 | | 16.2 | | 16.2 |

### Twilight / Sunrise / Moonrise

| Lat. | Naut. | Civil | Sunrise | Moonrise 28 | 29 | 30 | 31 |
|---|---|---|---|---|---|---|---|
| ° | h m | h m | h m | h m | h m | h m | h m |
| N 72 | 05 54 | 07 15 | 08 38 | ▬ | ▬ | ▬ | ▬ |
| N 70 | 05 51 | 07 04 | 08 16 | ▬ | ▬ | ▬ | ▬ |
| 68 | 05 49 | 06 55 | 07 58 | ▬ | ▬ | ▬ | ▬ |
| 66 | 05 46 | 06 47 | 07 44 | ▬ | ▬ | ▬ | ▬ |
| 64 | 05 44 | 06 41 | 07 33 | 13 52 | ▬ | ▬ | 16 36 |
| 62 | 05 42 | 06 35 | 07 23 | 12 44 | 14 44 | 15 40 | 15 45 |
| 60 | 05 41 | 06 30 | 07 14 | 12 09 | 13 46 | 14 47 | 15 14 |
| N 58 | 05 39 | 06 25 | 07 07 | 11 44 | 13 13 | 14 15 | 14 50 |
| 56 | 05 37 | 06 21 | 07 00 | 11 23 | 12 48 | 13 51 | 14 31 |
| 54 | 05 36 | 06 17 | 06 55 | 11 07 | 12 29 | 13 32 | 14 15 |
| 52 | 05 34 | 06 14 | 06 49 | 10 53 | 12 12 | 13 15 | 14 01 |
| 50 | 05 33 | 06 11 | 06 44 | 10 40 | 11 58 | 13 01 | 13 48 |
| 45 | 05 29 | 06 04 | 06 34 | 10 14 | 11 29 | 12 32 | 13 23 |
| N 40 | 05 26 | 05 58 | 06 26 | 09 54 | 11 06 | 12 10 | 13 03 |
| 35 | 05 22 | 05 52 | 06 18 | 09 37 | 10 47 | 11 51 | 12 46 |
| 30 | 05 19 | 05 47 | 06 12 | 09 23 | 10 31 | 11 35 | 12 31 |
| 20 | 05 11 | 05 37 | 06 00 | 08 58 | 10 04 | 11 08 | 12 06 |
| N 10 | 05 03 | 05 28 | 05 50 | 08 37 | 09 41 | 10 44 | 11 44 |
| 0 | 04 54 | 05 19 | 05 40 | 08 17 | 09 19 | 10 22 | 11 24 |
| S 10 | 04 44 | 05 09 | 05 31 | 07 58 | 08 58 | 10 00 | 11 04 |
| 20 | 04 30 | 04 57 | 05 20 | 07 37 | 08 34 | 09 37 | 10 42 |
| 30 | 04 13 | 04 43 | 05 08 | 07 13 | 08 08 | 09 10 | 10 17 |
| 35 | 04 02 | 04 34 | 05 01 | 06 59 | 07 52 | 08 54 | 10 02 |
| 40 | 03 49 | 04 24 | 04 53 | 06 43 | 07 34 | 08 35 | 09 45 |
| 45 | 03 33 | 04 12 | 04 43 | 06 24 | 07 12 | 08 12 | 09 24 |
| S 50 | 03 11 | 03 56 | 04 32 | 06 00 | 06 44 | 07 43 | 08 57 |
| 52 | 03 01 | 03 49 | 04 27 | 05 49 | 06 31 | 07 29 | 00 45 |
| 54 | 02 49 | 03 41 | 04 21 | 05 36 | 06 15 | 07 13 | 08 30 |
| 56 | 02 34 | 03 31 | 04 14 | 05 21 | 05 57 | 06 53 | 08 13 |
| 58 | 02 17 | 03 21 | 04 07 | 05 04 | 05 34 | 06 29 | 07 52 |
| S 60 | 01 55 | 03 08 | 03 58 | 04 43 | 05 05 | 05 57 | 07 25 |

### Sunset / Twilight / Moonset

| Lat. | Sunset | Civil | Naut. | Moonset 28 | 29 | 30 | 31 |
|---|---|---|---|---|---|---|---|
| ° | h m | h m | h m | h m | h m | h m | h m |
| N 72 | 14 48 | 16 10 | 17 32 | ▬ | ▬ | ▬ | ▬ |
| N 70 | 15 10 | 16 22 | 17 35 | ▬ | ▬ | ▬ | ▬ |
| 68 | 15 28 | 16 31 | 17 37 | ▬ | ▬ | ▬ | ▬ |
| 66 | 15 42 | 16 39 | 17 40 | ▬ | ▬ | ▬ | ▬ |
| 64 | 15 54 | 16 46 | 17 42 | 15 02 | ▬ | ▬ | 18 52 |
| 62 | 16 04 | 16 51 | 17 44 | 16 11 | 16 21 | 17 38 | 19 41 |
| 60 | 16 12 | 16 57 | 17 46 | 16 47 | 17 20 | 18 31 | 20 12 |
| N 58 | 16 20 | 17 01 | 17 47 | 17 13 | 17 53 | 19 03 | 20 36 |
| 56 | 16 26 | 17 05 | 17 49 | 17 33 | 18 18 | 19 27 | 20 54 |
| 54 | 16 32 | 17 09 | 17 51 | 17 50 | 18 38 | 19 46 | 21 10 |
| 52 | 16 37 | 17 13 | 17 52 | 18 05 | 18 54 | 20 02 | 21 24 |
| 50 | 16 42 | 17 16 | 17 54 | 18 18 | 19 09 | 20 16 | 21 35 |
| 45 | 16 53 | 17 23 | 17 58 | 18 44 | 19 38 | 20 44 | 22 00 |
| N 40 | 17 01 | 17 29 | 18 01 | 19 05 | 20 01 | 21 07 | 22 19 |
| 35 | 17 09 | 17 35 | 18 05 | 19 23 | 20 20 | 21 25 | 22 36 |
| 30 | 17 16 | 17 40 | 18 08 | 19 38 | 20 36 | 21 41 | 22 50 |
| 20 | 17 27 | 17 50 | 18 16 | 20 03 | 21 04 | 22 08 | 23 13 |
| N 10 | 17 37 | 17 59 | 18 24 | 20 26 | 21 27 | 22 31 | 23 34 |
| 0 | 17 47 | 18 08 | 18 33 | 20 46 | 21 49 | 22 52 | 23 53 |
| S 10 | 17 57 | 18 19 | 18 44 | 21 07 | 22 11 | 23 13 | 24 11 |
| 20 | 18 08 | 18 30 | 18 57 | 21 30 | 22 35 | 23 36 | 24 31 |
| 30 | 18 20 | 18 45 | 19 15 | 21 56 | 23 02 | 24 02 | 00 02 |
| 35 | 18 27 | 18 54 | 19 26 | 22 11 | 23 18 | 24 18 | 00 18 |
| 40 | 18 35 | 19 04 | 19 39 | 22 29 | 23 37 | 24 36 | 00 36 |
| 45 | 18 45 | 19 17 | 19 56 | 22 50 | 24 00 | 00 00 | 00 57 |
| S 50 | 18 56 | 19 32 | 20 18 | 23 17 | 24 29 | 00 29 | 01 24 |
| 52 | 19 02 | 19 40 | 20 28 | 23 31 | 24 43 | 00 43 | 01 37 |
| 54 | 19 08 | 19 48 | 20 41 | 23 46 | 24 59 | 00 59 | 01 52 |
| 56 | 19 15 | 19 58 | 20 56 | 24 04 | 00 04 | 01 19 | 02 10 |
| 58 | 19 22 | 20 09 | 21 13 | 24 26 | 00 26 | 01 43 | 02 31 |
| S 60 | 19 31 | 20 22 | 21 36 | 24 55 | 00 55 | 02 15 | 02 58 |

### SUN / MOON

| Day | Eqn. of Time 00h | 12h | Mer. Pass. | Mer. Pass. Upper | Lower | Age | Phase |
|---|---|---|---|---|---|---|---|
| d | m s | m s | h m | h m | h m | d % | |
| 28 | 16 10 | 16 13 | 11 44 | 14 32 | 02 02 | 03 12 | |
| 29 | 16 15 | 16 17 | 11 44 | 15 34 | 03 03 | 04 20 | |
| 30 | 16 19 | 16 20 | 11 44 | 16 37 | 04 06 | 05 30 | |

| UT | ARIES GHA | VENUS −3.9 GHA | Dec | MARS −1·2 GHA | Dec | JUPITER −2·8 GHA | Dec | SATURN +0·6 GHA | Dec | STARS Name | SHA | Dec |
|---|---|---|---|---|---|---|---|---|---|---|---|---|
| **31 00** | 39 16.7 | 181 48.0 | S13 55.4 | 314 04.5 | N23 49.7 | 38 52.2 | S 1 31.3 | 77 47.3 | S16 28.0 | Acamar | 315 12.7 | S40 12.7 |
| 01 | 54 19.1 | 196 47.4 | 56.5 | 329 07.0 | 49.8 | 53 54.8 | 31.4 | 92 49.8 | 28.0 | Achernar | 335 21.0 | S57 07.3 |
| 02 | 69 21.6 | 211 46.9 | 57.5 | 344 09.5 | 49.9 | 68 57.5 | 31.4 | 107 52.2 | 27.9 | Acrux | 173 02.7 | S63 13.2 |
| 03 | 84 24.1 | 226 46.3 .. | 58.6 | 359 12.0 .. | 50.0 | 84 00.1 .. | 31.5 | 122 54.6 .. | 27.9 | Adhara | 255 07.1 | S28 59.9 |
| 04 | 99 26.5 | 241 45.7 | 13 59.7 | 14 14.5 | 50.1 | 99 02.7 | 31.6 | 137 57.0 | 27.9 | Aldebaran | 290 41.4 | N16 33.3 |
| 05 | 114 29.0 | 256 45.1 | 14 00.7 | 29 16.9 | 50.3 | 114 05.4 | 31.6 | 152 59.5 | 27.9 | | | |
| 06 | 129 31.5 | 271 44.6 | S14 01.8 | 44 19.4 | N23 50.4 | 129 08.0 | S 1 31.7 | 168 01.9 | S16 27.9 | Alioth | 166 15.1 | N55 50.2 |
| 07 | 144 33.9 | 286 44.0 | 02.9 | 59 21.9 | 50.5 | 144 10.7 | 31.8 | 183 04.3 | 27.9 | Alkaid | 152 53.9 | N49 12.0 |
| 08 | 159 36.4 | 301 43.4 | 03.9 | 74 24.4 | 50.6 | 159 13.3 | 31.9 | 198 06.8 | 27.9 | Alnair | 27 35.0 | S46 51.2 |
| **M** 09 | 174 38.9 | 316 42.8 .. | 05.0 | 89 26.9 .. | 50.7 | 174 16.0 .. | 31.9 | 213 09.2 .. | 27.9 | Alnilam | 275 39.4 | S 1 11.1 |
| **O** 10 | 189 41.3 | 331 42.3 | 06.0 | 104 29.4 | 50.8 | 189 18.6 | 32.0 | 228 11.6 | 27.8 | Alphard | 217 49.6 | S 8 45.2 |
| **N** 11 | 204 43.8 | 346 41.7 | 07.1 | 119 31.9 | 50.9 | 204 21.3 | 32.1 | 243 14.1 | 27.8 | | | |
| **D** 12 | 219 46.2 | 1 41.1 | S14 08.2 | 134 34.4 | N23 51.1 | 219 23.9 | S 1 32.1 | 258 16.5 | S16 27.8 | Alphecca | 126 05.7 | N26 38.4 |
| **A** 13 | 234 48.7 | 16 40.5 | 09.2 | 149 36.9 | 51.2 | 234 26.6 | 32.2 | 273 18.9 | 27.8 | Alpheratz | 357 36.4 | N29 13.1 |
| **Y** 14 | 249 51.2 | 31 39.9 | 10.3 | 164 39.5 | 51.3 | 249 29.2 | 32.3 | 288 21.3 | 27.8 | Altair | 62 01.8 | N 8 55.8 |
| 15 | 264 53.6 | 46 39.4 .. | 11.3 | 179 42.0 .. | 51.4 | 264 31.9 .. | 32.3 | 303 23.8 .. | 27.8 | Ankaa | 353 08.6 | S42 11.0 |
| 16 | 279 56.1 | 61 38.8 | 12.4 | 194 44.5 | 51.5 | 279 34.5 | 32.4 | 318 26.2 | 27.8 | Antares | 112 18.4 | S26 28.9 |
| 17 | 294 58.6 | 76 38.2 | 13.5 | 209 47.0 | 51.6 | 294 37.1 | 32.5 | 333 28.6 | 27.7 | | | |
| 18 | 310 01.0 | 91 37.6 | S14 14.5 | 224 49.5 | N23 51.7 | 309 39.8 | S 1 32.5 | 348 31.1 | S16 27.7 | Arcturus | 145 49.9 | N19 04.0 |
| 19 | 325 03.5 | 106 37.0 | 15.6 | 239 52.0 | 51.9 | 324 42.4 | 32.6 | 3 33.5 | 27.7 | Atria | 107 14.7 | S69 04.2 |
| 20 | 340 06.0 | 121 36.5 | 16.6 | 254 54.5 | 52.0 | 339 45.1 | 32.7 | 18 35.9 | 27.7 | Avior | 234 15.4 | S59 34.5 |
| 21 | 355 08.4 | 136 35.9 .. | 17.7 | 269 57.1 .. | 52.1 | 354 47.7 .. | 32.7 | 33 38.3 .. | 27.7 | Bellatrix | 278 24.6 | N 6 22.3 |
| 22 | 10 10.9 | 151 35.3 | 18.7 | 284 59.6 | 52.2 | 9 50.4 | 32.8 | 48 40.8 | 27.7 | Betelgeuse | 270 53.8 | N 7 24.8 |
| 23 | 25 13.4 | 166 34.7 | 19.8 | 300 02.1 | 52.3 | 24 53.0 | 32.9 | 63 43.2 | 27.7 | | | |
| **1 00** | 40 15.8 | 181 34.1 | S14 20.8 | 315 04.6 | N23 52.4 | 39 55.6 | S 1 32.9 | 78 45.6 | S16 27.6 | Canopus | 263 52.9 | S52 42.1 |
| 01 | 55 18.3 | 196 33.5 | 21.9 | 330 07.2 | 52.5 | 54 58.3 | 33.0 | 93 48.1 | 27.6 | Capella | 280 24.2 | N46 01.1 |
| 02 | 70 20.7 | 211 33.0 | 22.9 | 345 09.7 | 52.7 | 70 00.9 | 33.1 | 108 50.5 | 27.6 | Deneb | 49 27.1 | N45 21.9 |
| 03 | 85 23.2 | 226 32.4 .. | 24.0 | 0 12.2 .. | 52.8 | 85 03.6 .. | 33.1 | 123 52.9 .. | 27.6 | Denebola | 182 27.1 | N14 26.8 |
| 04 | 100 25.7 | 241 31.8 | 25.0 | 15 14.7 | 52.9 | 100 06.2 | 33.2 | 138 55.3 | 27.6 | Diphda | 348 48.8 | S17 51.7 |
| 05 | 115 28.1 | 256 31.2 | 26.1 | 30 17.3 | 53.0 | 115 08.8 | 33.3 | 153 57.8 | 27.6 | | | |
| 06 | 130 30.6 | 271 30.6 | S14 27.1 | 45 19.8 | N23 53.1 | 130 11.5 | S 1 33.3 | 169 00.2 | S16 27.6 | Dubhe | 193 43.7 | N61 37.6 |
| 07 | 145 33.1 | 286 30.0 | 28.2 | 60 22.3 | 53.2 | 145 14.1 | 33.4 | 184 02.6 | 27.5 | Elnath | 278 03.9 | N28 37.6 |
| 08 | 160 35.5 | 301 29.4 | 29.2 | 75 24.9 | 53.3 | 160 16.8 | 33.5 | 199 05.0 | 27.5 | Eltanin | 90 43.4 | N51 29.4 |
| **T** 09 | 175 38.0 | 316 28.9 .. | 30.3 | 90 27.4 .. | 53.4 | 175 19.4 .. | 33.5 | 214 07.5 .. | 27.5 | Enif | 33 40.5 | N 9 58.9 |
| **U** 10 | 190 40.5 | 331 28.3 | 31.3 | 105 30.0 | 53.6 | 190 22.0 | 33.6 | 229 09.9 | 27.5 | Fomalhaut | 15 16.3 | S29 30.2 |
| **E** 11 | 205 42.9 | 346 27.7 | 32.4 | 120 32.5 | 53.7 | 205 24.7 | 33.7 | 244 12.3 | 27.5 | | | |
| **S** 12 | 220 45.4 | 1 27.1 | S14 33.4 | 135 35.0 | N23 53.8 | 220 27.3 | S 1 33.7 | 259 14.7 | S16 27.5 | Gacrux | 171 54.2 | S57 14.2 |
| **D** 13 | 235 47.8 | 16 26.5 | 34.5 | 150 37.6 | 53.9 | 235 30.0 | 33.8 | 274 17.2 | 27.5 | Gienah | 175 45.7 | S17 39.9 |
| **A** 14 | 250 50.3 | 31 25.9 | 35.5 | 165 40.1 | 54.0 | 250 32.6 | 33.9 | 289 19.6 | 27.4 | Hadar | 148 39.3 | S60 28.8 |
| **Y** 15 | 265 52.8 | 46 25.3 .. | 36.5 | 180 42.7 .. | 54.1 | 265 35.2 .. | 33.9 | 304 22.0 .. | 27.4 | Hamal | 327 53.9 | N23 34.3 |
| 16 | 280 55.2 | 61 24.7 | 37.6 | 195 45.2 | 54.2 | 280 37.9 | 34.0 | 319 24.4 | 27.4 | Kaus Aust. | 83 35.2 | S34 22.5 |
| 17 | 295 57.7 | 76 24.1 | 38.6 | 210 47.8 | 54.4 | 295 40.5 | 34.1 | 334 26.9 | 27.4 | | | |
| 18 | 311 00.2 | 91 23.5 | S14 39.7 | 225 50.3 | N23 54.5 | 310 43.1 | S 1 34.1 | 349 29.3 | S16 27.4 | Kochab | 137 21.0 | N74 03.7 |
| 19 | 326 02.6 | 106 23.0 | 40.7 | 240 52.9 | 54.6 | 325 45.8 | 34.2 | 4 31.7 | 27.4 | Markab | 13 31.5 | N15 19.8 |
| 20 | 341 05.1 | 121 22.4 | 41.7 | 255 55.5 | 54.7 | 340 48.4 | 34.3 | 19 34.1 | 27.3 | Menkar | 314 07.7 | N 4 10.8 |
| 21 | 356 07.6 | 136 21.8 .. | 42.8 | 270 58.0 .. | 54.8 | 355 51.1 .. | 34.3 | 34 36.6 .. | 27.3 | Menkent | 148 00.2 | S36 28.7 |
| 22 | 11 10.0 | 151 21.2 | 43.8 | 286 00.6 | 54.9 | 10 53.7 | 34.4 | 49 39.0 | 27.3 | Miaplacidus | 221 38.7 | S69 48.2 |
| 23 | 26 12.5 | 166 20.6 | 44.9 | 301 03.1 | 55.0 | 25 56.3 | 34.5 | 64 41.4 | 27.3 | | | |
| **2 00** | 41 15.0 | 181 20.0 | S14 45.9 | 316 05.7 | N23 55.2 | 40 59.0 | S 1 34.5 | 79 43.8 | S16 27.3 | Mirfak | 308 30.4 | N49 56.5 |
| 01 | 56 17.4 | 196 19.4 | 46.9 | 331 08.3 | 55.3 | 56 01.6 | 34.6 | 94 46.3 | 27.3 | Nunki | 75 50.2 | S26 16.1 |
| 02 | 71 19.9 | 211 18.8 | 48.0 | 346 10.8 | 55.4 | 71 04.2 | 34.6 | 109 48.7 | 27.3 | Peacock | 53 08.7 | S56 39.9 |
| 03 | 86 22.3 | 226 18.2 .. | 49.0 | 1 13.4 .. | 55.5 | 86 06.9 .. | 34.7 | 124 51.1 .. | 27.2 | Pollux | 243 19.5 | N27 58.2 |
| 04 | 101 24.8 | 241 17.6 | 50.0 | 16 16.0 | 55.6 | 101 09.5 | 34.8 | 139 53.5 | 27.2 | Procyon | 244 52.7 | N 5 10.1 |
| 05 | 116 27.3 | 256 17.0 | 51.1 | 31 18.5 | 55.7 | 116 12.1 | 34.8 | 154 55.9 | 27.2 | | | |
| 06 | 131 29.7 | 271 16.4 | S14 52.1 | 46 21.1 | N23 55.8 | 131 14.8 | S 1 34.9 | 169 58.4 | S16 27.2 | Rasalhague | 96 00.5 | N12 32.7 |
| **W** 07 | 146 32.2 | 286 15.8 | 53.1 | 61 23.7 | 56.0 | 146 17.4 | 35.0 | 185 00.8 | 27.2 | Regulus | 207 36.5 | N11 51.5 |
| **E** 08 | 161 34.7 | 301 15.2 | 54.2 | 76 26.3 | 56.1 | 161 20.0 | 35.0 | 200 03.2 | 27.2 | Rigel | 281 05.4 | S 8 10.4 |
| **D** 09 | 176 37.1 | 316 14.6 .. | 55.2 | 91 28.9 .. | 56.2 | 176 22.7 .. | 35.1 | 215 05.6 .. | 27.1 | Rigil Kent. | 139 45.3 | S60 55.6 |
| **N** 10 | 191 39.6 | 331 14.0 | 56.2 | 106 31.4 | 56.3 | 191 25.3 | 35.2 | 230 08.1 | 27.1 | Sabik | 102 05.2 | S15 45.1 |
| **E** 11 | 206 42.1 | 346 13.4 | 57.3 | 121 34.0 | 56.4 | 206 27.9 | 35.2 | 245 10.5 | 27.1 | | | |
| **S** 12 | 221 44.5 | 1 12.8 | S14 58.3 | 136 36.6 | N23 56.5 | 221 30.6 | S 1 35.3 | 260 12.9 | S16 27.1 | Schedar | 349 32.6 | N56 39.9 |
| **D** 13 | 236 47.0 | 16 12.2 | 14 59.3 | 151 39.2 | 56.6 | 236 33.2 | 35.3 | 275 15.3 | 27.1 | Shaula | 96 13.2 | S37 07.2 |
| **A** 14 | 251 49.5 | 31 11.6 | 15 00.3 | 166 41.8 | 56.8 | 251 35.8 | 35.4 | 290 17.7 | 27.1 | Sirius | 258 27.7 | S16 44.6 |
| **Y** 15 | 266 51.9 | 46 11.0 .. | 01.4 | 181 44.4 .. | 56.9 | 266 38.4 .. | 35.5 | 305 20.2 .. | 27.0 | Spica | 158 24.5 | S11 16.6 |
| 16 | 281 54.4 | 61 10.4 | 02.4 | 196 47.0 | 57.0 | 281 41.1 | 35.5 | 320 22.6 | 27.0 | Suhail | 222 47.7 | S43 31.1 |
| 17 | 296 56.8 | 76 09.8 | 03.4 | 211 49.5 | 57.1 | 296 43.7 | 35.6 | 335 25.0 | 27.0 | | | |
| 18 | 311 59.3 | 91 09.2 | S15 04.5 | 226 52.1 | N23 57.2 | 311 46.3 | S 1 35.7 | 350 27.4 | S16 27.0 | Vega | 80 34.7 | N38 48.5 |
| 19 | 327 01.8 | 106 08.6 | 05.5 | 241 54.7 | 57.3 | 326 49.0 | 35.7 | 5 29.8 | 27.0 | Zuben'ubi | 136 58.4 | S16 08.0 |
| 20 | 342 04.2 | 121 08.0 | 06.5 | 256 57.3 | 57.4 | 341 51.6 | 35.8 | 20 32.3 | 27.0 | | | |
| 21 | 357 06.7 | 136 07.4 .. | 07.5 | 271 59.9 .. | 57.6 | 356 54.2 .. | 35.8 | 35 34.7 .. | 26.9 | | | |
| 22 | 12 09.2 | 151 06.8 | 08.5 | 287 02.5 | 57.7 | 11 56.9 | 35.9 | 50 37.1 | 26.9 | | | |
| 23 | 27 11.6 | 166 06.2 | 09.6 | 302 05.1 | 57.8 | 26 59.5 | 36.0 | 65 39.5 | 26.9 | | | |

| | | SHA | Mer. Pass. |
|---|---|---|---|
| | | ° ′ | h m |
| Venus | | 141 18.3 | 11 54 |
| Mars | | 274 48.8 | 2 59 |
| Jupiter | | 359 39.8 | 21 17 |
| Saturn | | 38 29.8 | 18 42 |

Mer. Pass. 21 15.5    v −0.6   d 1.0    v 2.5   d 0.1    v 2.6   d 0.1    v 2.4   d 0.0

| UT | SUN | | MOON | | | | | Lat. | Twilight | | Sunrise | Moonrise | | | |
|---|---|---|---|---|---|---|---|---|---|---|---|---|---|---|---|
| | | | | | | | | | Naut. | Civil | | 31 | 1 | 2 | 3 |
| | GHA | Dec | GHA | v | Dec | d | HP | ° | h m | h m | h m | h m | h m | h m | h m |
| d h | ° ' | ° ' | ° ' | ' | ° ' | ' | ' | N 72 | 06 06 | 07 29 | 08 56 | ▬▬ | ▬▬ | 17 51 | 16 42 |
| 31 00 | 184 05.5 | S14 01.6 | 106 06.4 | 3.9 | S26 39.9 | 4.4 | 59.4 | N 70 | 06 02 | 07 16 | 08 30 | ▬▬ | ▬▬ | 17 07 | 16 24 |
| 01 | 199 05.5 | 02.4 | 120 29.3 | 4.0 | 26 35.5 | 4.6 | 59.4 | 68 | 05 58 | 07 05 | 08 11 | ▬▬ | 17 39 | 16 37 | 16 10 |
| 02 | 214 05.5 | 03.2 | 134 52.3 | 4.1 | 26 30.9 | 4.8 | 59.4 | 66 | 05 55 | 06 57 | 07 55 | ▬▬ | 16 43 | 16 15 | 15 58 |
| 03 | 229 05.5 .. | 04.0 | 149 15.4 | 4.2 | 26 26.1 | 5.0 | 59.4 | 64 | 05 52 | 06 49 | 07 42 | 16 36 | 16 09 | 15 57 | 15 48 |
| 04 | 244 05.6 | 04.9 | 163 38.6 | 4.2 | 26 21.1 | 5.1 | 59.4 | 62 | 05 50 | 06 43 | 07 31 | 15 45 | 15 44 | 15 42 | 15 39 |
| 05 | 259 05.6 | 05.7 | 178 01.8 | 4.3 | 26 16.0 | 5.4 | 59.4 | 60 | 05 47 | 06 37 | 07 22 | 15 14 | 15 25 | 15 30 | 15 32 |
| 06 | 274 05.6 | S14 06.5 | 192 25.1 | 4.3 | S26 10.6 | 5.4 | 59.4 | N 58 | 05 45 | 06 32 | 07 14 | 14 50 | 15 08 | 15 19 | 15 25 |
| M 07 | 289 05.6 | 07.3 | 206 48.4 | 4.4 | 26 05.2 | 5.7 | 59.4 | 56 | 05 43 | 06 27 | 07 07 | 14 31 | 14 54 | 15 09 | 15 20 |
| O 08 | 304 05.7 | 08.1 | 221 11.8 | 4.5 | 25 59.5 | 5.9 | 59.4 | 54 | 05 41 | 06 23 | 07 00 | 14 15 | 14 42 | 15 01 | 15 14 |
| N 09 | 319 05.7 .. | 08.9 | 235 35.3 | 4.6 | 25 53.6 | 6.0 | 59.4 | 52 | 05 39 | 06 19 | 06 55 | 14 01 | 14 31 | 14 53 | 15 10 |
| D 10 | 334 05.7 | 09.7 | 249 58.9 | 4.7 | 25 47.6 | 6.2 | 59.3 | 50 | 05 37 | 06 16 | 06 49 | 13 48 | 14 22 | 14 46 | 15 05 |
| A 11 | 349 05.7 | 10.5 | 264 22.6 | 4.7 | 25 41.4 | 6.3 | 59.3 | 45 | 05 33 | 06 08 | 06 38 | 13 23 | 14 02 | 14 32 | 14 56 |
| Y 12 | 4 05.8 | S14 11.3 | 278 46.3 | 4.8 | S25 35.1 | 6.5 | 59.3 | N 40 | 05 29 | 06 01 | 06 29 | 13 03 | 13 45 | 14 19 | 14 48 |
| 13 | 19 05.8 | 12.1 | 293 10.1 | 4.9 | 25 28.6 | 6.7 | 59.3 | 35 | 05 25 | 05 55 | 06 21 | 12 46 | 13 31 | 14 09 | 14 41 |
| 14 | 34 05.8 | 12.9 | 307 34.0 | 5.0 | 25 21.9 | 6.9 | 59.3 | 30 | 05 21 | 05 49 | 06 14 | 12 31 | 13 19 | 14 00 | 14 35 |
| 15 | 49 05.8 .. | 13.7 | 321 58.0 | 5.1 | 25 15.0 | 7.0 | 59.3 | 20 | 05 13 | 05 39 | 06 01 | 12 06 | 12 58 | 13 44 | 14 25 |
| 16 | 64 05.9 | 14.6 | 336 22.1 | 5.2 | 25 08.0 | 7.1 | 59.3 | N 10 | 05 04 | 05 29 | 05 50 | 11 44 | 12 40 | 13 30 | 14 16 |
| 17 | 79 05.9 | 15.4 | 350 46.3 | 5.2 | 25 00.9 | 7.4 | 59.3 | 0 | 04 54 | 05 19 | 05 40 | 11 24 | 12 23 | 13 17 | 14 07 |
| 18 | 94 05.9 | S14 16.2 | 5 10.5 | 5.3 | S24 53.5 | 7.5 | 59.3 | S 10 | 04 43 | 05 08 | 05 30 | 11 04 | 12 05 | 13 04 | 13 58 |
| 19 | 109 05.9 | 17.0 | 19 34.8 | 5.5 | 24 46.0 | 7.6 | 59.3 | 20 | 04 28 | 04 55 | 05 18 | 10 42 | 11 47 | 12 50 | 13 49 |
| 20 | 124 05.9 | 17.8 | 33 59.3 | 5.5 | 24 38.4 | 7.8 | 59.3 | 30 | 04 10 | 04 40 | 05 05 | 10 17 | 11 26 | 12 33 | 13 39 |
| 21 | 139 06.0 .. | 18.6 | 48 23.8 | 5.6 | 24 30.6 | 8.0 | 59.3 | 35 | 03 59 | 04 31 | 04 58 | 10 02 | 11 13 | 12 24 | 13 32 |
| 22 | 154 06.0 | 19.4 | 62 48.4 | 5.7 | 24 22.6 | 8.1 | 59.2 | 40 | 03 45 | 04 20 | 04 49 | 09 45 | 10 59 | 12 13 | 13 25 |
| 23 | 169 06.0 | 20.2 | 77 13.1 | 5.8 | 24 14.5 | 8.3 | 59.2 | 45 | 03 27 | 04 07 | 04 39 | 09 24 | 10 41 | 12 00 | 13 17 |
| 1 00 | 184 06.0 | S14 21.0 | 91 37.9 | 5.9 | S24 06.2 | 8.4 | 59.2 | S 50 | 03 05 | 03 50 | 04 27 | 08 57 | 10 20 | 11 44 | 13 07 |
| 01 | 199 06.0 | 21.8 | 106 02.8 | 6.0 | 23 57.8 | 8.6 | 59.2 | 52 | 02 53 | 03 43 | 04 21 | 08 45 | 10 10 | 11 37 | 13 03 |
| 02 | 214 06.1 | 22.6 | 120 27.8 | 6.0 | 23 49.2 | 8.7 | 59.2 | 54 | 02 40 | 03 34 | 04 14 | 08 30 | 09 58 | 11 29 | 12 57 |
| 03 | 229 06.1 .. | 23.4 | 134 52.8 | 6.2 | 23 40.5 | 8.9 | 59.2 | 56 | 02 24 | 03 24 | 04 07 | 08 13 | 09 45 | 11 20 | 12 52 |
| 04 | 244 06.1 | 24.2 | 149 18.0 | 6.3 | 23 31.6 | 9.0 | 59.2 | 58 | 02 05 | 03 12 | 03 59 | 07 52 | 09 29 | 11 09 | 12 45 |
| 05 | 259 06.1 | 25.0 | 163 43.3 | 6.4 | 23 22.6 | 9.1 | 59.2 | S 60 | 01 40 | 02 58 | 03 50 | 07 25 | 09 11 | 10 57 | 12 38 |
| 06 | 274 06.1 | S14 25.8 | 178 08.7 | 6.4 | S23 13.5 | 9.3 | 59.2 | Lat. | Sunset | Twilight | | Moonset | | | |
| T 07 | 289 06.2 | 26.6 | 192 34.1 | 6.6 | 23 04.2 | 9.4 | 59.1 | | | Civil | Naut. | 31 | 1 | 2 | 3 |
| U 08 | 304 06.2 | 27.4 | 206 59.7 | 6.7 | 22 54.8 | 9.6 | 59.1 | | | | | | | | |
| E 09 | 319 06.2 .. | 28.2 | 221 25.4 | 6.8 | 22 45.2 | 9.7 | 59.1 | ° | h m | h m | h m | h m | h m | h m | h m |
| S 10 | 334 06.2 | 29.0 | 235 51.2 | 6.8 | 22 35.5 | 9.9 | 59.1 | N 72 | 14 29 | 15 57 | 17 19 | ▬▬ | ▬▬ | 21 33 | 24 26 |
| D 11 | 349 06.2 | 29.8 | 250 17.0 | 7.0 | 22 25.6 | 9.9 | 59.1 | N 70 | 14 56 | 16 10 | 17 24 | ▬▬ | ▬▬ | 22 15 | 24 41 |
| A 12 | 4 06.2 | S14 30.6 | 264 43.0 | 7.1 | S22 15.7 | 10.1 | 59.1 | 68 | 15 15 | 16 20 | 17 27 | ▬▬ | 19 50 | 22 43 | 24 53 |
| Y 13 | 19 06.3 | 31.4 | 279 09.1 | 7.2 | 22 05.6 | 10.3 | 59.1 | 66 | 15 31 | 16 29 | 17 31 | ▬▬ | 20 45 | 23 04 | 25 03 |
| 14 | 34 06.3 | 32.2 | 293 35.3 | 7.2 | 21 55.3 | 10.3 | 59.1 | 64 | 15 44 | 16 37 | 17 34 | 18 52 | 21 18 | 23 20 | 25 11 |
| 15 | 49 06.3 .. | 33.0 | 308 01.5 | 7.4 | 21 45.0 | 10.5 | 59.1 | 62 | 15 55 | 16 44 | 17 36 | 19 41 | 21 42 | 23 34 | 25 18 |
| 16 | 64 06.3 | 33.8 | 322 27.9 | 7.5 | 21 34.5 | 10.7 | 59.0 | 60 | 16 04 | 16 49 | 17 39 | 20 12 | 22 01 | 23 45 | 25 24 |
| 17 | 79 06.3 | 34.6 | 336 54.4 | 7.6 | 21 23.8 | 10.7 | 59.0 | | | | | | | | |
| 18 | 94 06.3 | S14 35.4 | 351 21.0 | 7.7 | S21 13.1 | 10.9 | 59.0 | N 58 | 16 12 | 16 55 | 17 41 | 20 36 | 22 16 | 23 55 | 25 30 |
| 19 | 109 06.4 | 36.2 | 5 47.7 | 7.7 | 21 02.2 | 10.9 | 59.0 | 56 | 16 20 | 16 59 | 17 43 | 20 54 | 22 29 | 24 04 | 00 04 |
| 20 | 124 06.4 | 37.0 | 20 14.4 | 7.9 | 20 51.3 | 11.1 | 59.0 | 54 | 16 26 | 17 03 | 17 45 | 21 10 | 22 41 | 24 11 | 00 11 |
| 21 | 139 06.4 .. | 37.8 | 34 41.3 | 8.0 | 20 40.2 | 11.3 | 59.0 | 52 | 16 32 | 17 07 | 17 47 | 21 24 | 22 51 | 24 18 | 00 18 |
| 22 | 154 06.4 | 38.6 | 49 08.3 | 8.1 | 20 28.9 | 11.3 | 59.0 | 50 | 16 37 | 17 11 | 17 49 | 21 35 | 23 00 | 24 24 | 00 24 |
| 23 | 169 06.4 | 39.4 | 63 35.4 | 8.2 | 20 17.6 | 11.4 | 59.0 | 45 | 16 48 | 17 19 | 17 53 | 22 00 | 23 19 | 24 37 | 00 37 |
| 2 00 | 184 06.4 | S14 40.1 | 78 02.6 | 8.3 | S20 06.2 | 11.6 | 58.9 | N 40 | 16 58 | 17 26 | 17 58 | 22 19 | 23 34 | 24 48 | 00 48 |
| 01 | 199 06.4 | 40.9 | 92 29.9 | 8.4 | 19 54.6 | 11.7 | 58.9 | 35 | 17 06 | 17 32 | 18 02 | 22 36 | 23 47 | 24 57 | 00 57 |
| 02 | 214 06.4 | 41.7 | 106 57.3 | 8.4 | 19 42.9 | 11.7 | 58.9 | 30 | 17 13 | 17 38 | 18 06 | 22 50 | 23 58 | 25 05 | 01 05 |
| 03 | 229 06.5 .. | 42.5 | 121 24.7 | 8.6 | 19 31.2 | 11.9 | 58.9 | 20 | 17 26 | 17 48 | 18 14 | 23 13 | 24 17 | 00 17 | 01 18 |
| 04 | 244 06.5 | 43.3 | 135 52.3 | 8.7 | 19 19.3 | 12.0 | 58.9 | N 10 | 17 37 | 17 58 | 18 23 | 23 34 | 24 34 | 00 34 | 01 30 |
| 05 | 259 06.5 | 44.1 | 150 20.0 | 8.8 | 19 07.3 | 12.1 | 58.9 | 0 | 17 47 | 18 08 | 18 33 | 23 53 | 24 49 | 00 49 | 01 41 |
| 06 | 274 06.5 | S14 44.9 | 164 47.8 | 8.9 | S18 55.2 | 12.2 | 58.9 | S 10 | 17 58 | 18 19 | 18 45 | 24 11 | 00 11 | 01 04 | 01 52 |
| W 07 | 289 06.5 | 45.7 | 179 15.7 | 9.0 | 18 43.0 | 12.3 | 58.9 | 20 | 18 09 | 18 32 | 18 59 | 24 31 | 00 31 | 01 20 | 02 04 |
| E 08 | 304 06.5 | 46.5 | 193 43.7 | 9.0 | 18 30.7 | 12.4 | 58.8 | 30 | 18 22 | 18 47 | 19 18 | 00 02 | 00 54 | 01 39 | 02 17 |
| D 09 | 319 06.5 .. | 47.3 | 208 11.7 | 9.2 | 18 18.3 | 12.5 | 58.8 | 35 | 18 30 | 18 57 | 19 29 | 00 18 | 01 08 | 01 49 | 02 24 |
| N 10 | 334 06.5 | 48.1 | 222 39.9 | 9.3 | 18 05.8 | 12.6 | 58.8 | 40 | 18 39 | 19 08 | 19 43 | 00 36 | 01 23 | 02 01 | 02 33 |
| E 11 | 349 06.5 | 48.8 | 237 08.2 | 9.4 | 17 53.2 | 12.6 | 58.8 | 45 | 18 49 | 19 21 | 20 01 | 00 57 | 01 41 | 02 16 | 02 43 |
| S 12 | 4 06.5 | S14 49.6 | 251 36.6 | 9.4 | S17 40.6 | 12.8 | 58.8 | S 50 | 19 02 | 19 38 | 20 24 | 01 24 | 02 04 | 02 33 | 02 54 |
| D 13 | 19 06.5 | 50.4 | 266 05.0 | 9.6 | 17 27.8 | 12.9 | 58.8 | 52 | 19 07 | 19 46 | 20 36 | 01 37 | 02 15 | 02 41 | 03 00 |
| A 14 | 34 06.5 | 51.2 | 280 33.6 | 9.6 | 17 14.9 | 12.9 | 58.8 | 54 | 19 14 | 19 55 | 20 49 | 01 52 | 02 27 | 02 50 | 03 06 |
| Y 15 | 49 06.5 .. | 52.0 | 295 02.2 | 9.8 | 17 02.0 | 13.1 | 58.8 | 56 | 19 21 | 20 05 | 21 05 | 02 10 | 02 41 | 03 00 | 03 12 |
| 16 | 64 06.6 | 52.8 | 309 31.0 | 9.8 | 16 48.9 | 13.1 | 58.7 | 58 | 19 29 | 20 17 | 21 25 | 02 31 | 02 57 | 03 11 | 03 20 |
| 17 | 79 06.6 | 53.6 | 323 59.8 | 9.9 | 16 35.8 | 13.2 | 58.7 | S 60 | 19 39 | 20 31 | 21 51 | 02 58 | 03 16 | 03 24 | 03 28 |
| 18 | 94 06.6 | S14 54.4 | 338 28.7 | 10.0 | S16 22.6 | 13.3 | 58.7 | | SUN | | | MOON | | | |
| 19 | 109 06.6 | 55.1 | 352 57.7 | 10.1 | 16 09.3 | 13.4 | 58.7 | Day | Eqn. of Time | | Mer. | Mer. Pass. | | Age | Phase |
| 20 | 124 06.6 | 55.9 | 7 26.8 | 10.2 | 15 55.9 | 13.4 | 58.7 | | 00ʰ | 12ʰ | Pass. | Upper | Lower | | |
| 21 | 139 06.6 .. | 56.7 | 21 56.0 | 10.3 | 15 42.5 | 13.5 | 58.7 | d | m s | m s | h m | h m | h m | d % | |
| 22 | 154 06.6 | 57.5 | 36 25.3 | 10.4 | 15 29.0 | 13.6 | 58.7 | 31 | 16 22 | 16 23 | 11 44 | 17 38 | 05 08 | 06 41 | ◗ |
| 23 | 169 06.6 | 58.3 | 50 54.7 | 10.4 | S15 15.4 | 13.7 | 58.6 | 1 | 16 24 | 16 25 | 11 44 | 18 36 | 06 08 | 07 53 | |
| | SD 16.1 | d 0.8 | SD 16.2 | | 16.1 | | 16.0 | 2 | 16 26 | 16 26 | 11 44 | 19 29 | 07 03 | 08 64 | |

| UT | ARIES GHA | VENUS −3.9 GHA | Dec | MARS −1.3 GHA | Dec | JUPITER −2.8 GHA | Dec | SATURN +0.6 GHA | Dec | STARS Name | SHA | Dec |
|---|---|---|---|---|---|---|---|---|---|---|---|---|
| **3** 00 | 42 14.1 | 181 05.5 | S15 10.6 | 317 07.7 | N23 57.9 | 42 02.1 | S 1 36.0 | 80 41.9 | S16 26.9 | Acamar | 315 12.7 | S40 12.8 |
| 01 | 57 16.6 | 196 04.9 | 11.6 | 332 10.3 | 58.0 | 57 04.7 | 36.1 | 95 44.4 | 26.9 | Achernar | 335 21.0 | S57 07.4 |
| 02 | 72 19.0 | 211 04.3 | 12.6 | 347 13.0 | 58.1 | 72 07.4 | 36.1 | 110 46.8 | 26.9 | Acrux | 173 02.7 | S63 13.2 |
| 03 | 87 21.5 | 226 03.7 .. | 13.6 | 2 15.6 .. | 58.2 | 87 10.0 .. | 36.2 | 125 49.2 .. | 26.8 | Adhara | 255 07.1 | S28 59.9 |
| 04 | 102 23.9 | 241 03.1 | 14.7 | 17 18.2 | 58.3 | 102 12.6 | 36.3 | 140 51.6 | 26.8 | Aldebaran | 290 41.4 | N16 33.3 |
| 05 | 117 26.4 | 256 02.5 | 15.7 | 32 20.8 | 58.5 | 117 15.2 | 36.3 | 155 54.0 | 26.8 | | | |
| 06 | 132 28.9 | 271 01.9 | S15 16.7 | 47 23.4 | N23 58.6 | 132 17.9 | S 1 36.4 | 170 56.4 | S16 26.8 | Alioth | 166 15.1 | N55 50.1 |
| 07 | 147 31.3 | 286 01.3 | 17.7 | 62 26.0 | 58.7 | 147 20.5 | 36.4 | 185 58.9 | 26.8 | Alkaid | 152 53.9 | N49 12.0 |
| 08 | 162 33.8 | 301 00.7 | 18.7 | 77 28.6 | 58.8 | 162 23.1 | 36.5 | 201 01.3 | 26.8 | Alnair | 27 35.1 | S46 51.3 |
| 09 | 177 36.3 | 316 00.1 .. | 19.7 | 92 31.2 .. | 58.9 | 177 25.8 .. | 36.6 | 216 03.7 .. | 26.7 | Alnilam | 275 39.3 | S 1 11.1 |
| 10 | 192 38.7 | 330 59.4 | 20.8 | 107 33.9 | 59.0 | 192 28.4 | 36.6 | 231 06.1 | 26.7 | Alphard | 217 49.6 | S 8 45.2 |
| 11 | 207 41.2 | 345 58.8 | 21.8 | 122 36.5 | 59.1 | 207 31.0 | 36.7 | 246 08.5 | 26.7 | | | |
| 12 | 222 43.7 | 0 58.2 | S15 22.8 | 137 39.1 | N23 59.3 | 222 33.6 | S 1 36.7 | 261 11.0 | S16 26.7 | Alphecca | 126 05.7 | N26 38.4 |
| 13 | 237 46.1 | 15 57.6 | 23.8 | 152 41.7 | 59.4 | 237 36.3 | 36.8 | 276 13.4 | 26.7 | Alpheratz | 357 36.4 | N29 13.1 |
| 14 | 252 48.6 | 30 57.0 | 24.8 | 167 44.4 | 59.5 | 252 38.9 | 36.9 | 291 15.8 | 26.7 | Altair | 62 01.8 | N 8 55.8 |
| 15 | 267 51.1 | 45 56.4 .. | 25.8 | 182 47.0 .. | 59.6 | 267 41.5 .. | 36.9 | 306 18.2 .. | 26.6 | Ankaa | 353 08.6 | S42 11.1 |
| 16 | 282 53.5 | 60 55.8 | 26.8 | 197 49.6 | 59.7 | 282 44.1 | 37.0 | 321 20.6 | 26.6 | Antares | 112 18.4 | S26 28.9 |
| 17 | 297 56.0 | 75 55.2 | 27.8 | 212 52.3 | 59.8 | 297 46.7 | 37.0 | 336 23.0 | 26.6 | | | |
| 18 | 312 58.4 | 90 54.5 | S15 28.9 | 227 54.9 | N23 59.9 | 312 49.4 | S 1 37.1 | 351 25.4 | S16 26.6 | Arcturus | 145 49.9 | N19 03.9 |
| 19 | 328 00.9 | 105 53.9 | 29.9 | 242 57.5 | 24 00.1 | 327 52.0 | 37.2 | 6 27.9 | 26.6 | Atria | 107 14.8 | S69 04.2 |
| 20 | 343 03.4 | 120 53.3 | 30.9 | 258 00.2 | 00.2 | 342 54.6 | 37.2 | 21 30.3 | 26.5 | Avior | 234 15.4 | S59 34.5 |
| 21 | 358 05.8 | 135 52.7 .. | 31.9 | 273 02.8 .. | 00.3 | 357 57.2 .. | 37.3 | 36 32.7 .. | 26.5 | Bellatrix | 278 24.6 | N 6 22.3 |
| 22 | 13 08.3 | 150 52.1 | 32.9 | 288 05.4 | 00.4 | 12 59.9 | 37.3 | 51 35.1 | 26.5 | Betelgeuse | 270 53.8 | N 7 24.8 |
| 23 | 28 10.8 | 165 51.4 | 33.9 | 303 08.1 | 00.5 | 28 02.5 | 37.4 | 66 37.5 | 26.5 | | | |
| **4** 00 | 43 13.2 | 180 50.8 | S15 34.9 | 318 10.7 | N24 00.6 | 43 05.1 | S 1 37.4 | 81 39.9 | S16 26.5 | Canopus | 263 52.9 | S52 42.1 |
| 01 | 58 15.7 | 195 50.2 | 35.9 | 333 13.4 | 00.7 | 58 07.7 | 37.5 | 96 42.4 | 26.5 | Capella | 280 24.2 | N46 01.2 |
| 02 | 73 18.2 | 210 49.6 | 36.9 | 348 16.0 | 00.9 | 73 10.3 | 37.6 | 111 44.8 | 26.4 | Deneb | 49 27.1 | N45 21.9 |
| 03 | 88 20.6 | 225 49.0 .. | 37.9 | 3 18.7 .. | 01.0 | 88 13.0 .. | 37.6 | 126 47.2 .. | 26.4 | Denebola | 182 27.0 | N14 26.8 |
| 04 | 103 23.1 | 240 48.3 | 38.9 | 18 21.3 | 01.1 | 103 15.6 | 37.7 | 141 49.6 | 26.4 | Diphda | 348 48.8 | S17 51.7 |
| 05 | 118 25.6 | 255 47.7 | 39.9 | 33 24.0 | 01.2 | 118 18.2 | 37.7 | 156 52.0 | 26.4 | | | |
| 06 | 133 28.0 | 270 47.1 | S15 40.9 | 48 26.6 | N24 01.3 | 133 20.8 | S 1 37.8 | 171 54.4 | S16 26.4 | Dubhe | 193 43.6 | N61 37.6 |
| 07 | 148 30.5 | 285 46.5 | 41.9 | 63 29.3 | 01.4 | 148 23.4 | 37.8 | 186 56.8 | 26.3 | Elnath | 278 03.9 | N28 37.6 |
| 08 | 163 32.9 | 300 45.9 | 42.9 | 78 31.9 | 01.5 | 163 26.1 | 37.9 | 201 59.3 | 26.3 | Eltanin | 90 43.4 | N51 29.3 |
| 09 | 178 35.4 | 315 45.2 .. | 43.9 | 93 34.6 .. | 01.7 | 178 28.7 .. | 38.0 | 217 01.7 .. | 26.3 | Enif | 33 40.5 | N 9 58.9 |
| 10 | 193 37.9 | 330 44.6 | 44.9 | 108 37.3 | 01.8 | 193 31.3 | 38.0 | 232 04.1 | 26.3 | Fomalhaut | 15 16.3 | S29 30.2 |
| 11 | 208 40.3 | 345 44.0 | 45.9 | 123 39.9 | 01.9 | 208 33.9 | 38.1 | 247 06.5 | 26.3 | | | |
| 12 | 223 42.8 | 0 43.4 | S15 46.9 | 138 42.6 | N24 02.0 | 223 36.5 | S 1 38.1 | 262 08.9 | S16 26.3 | Gacrux | 171 54.2 | S57 14.2 |
| 13 | 238 45.3 | 15 42.7 | 47.9 | 153 45.3 | 02.1 | 238 39.1 | 38.2 | 277 11.3 | 26.2 | Gienah | 175 45.7 | S17 39.9 |
| 14 | 253 47.7 | 30 42.1 | 48.9 | 168 47.9 | 02.2 | 253 41.8 | 38.2 | 292 13.7 | 26.2 | Hadar | 148 39.3 | S60 28.8 |
| 15 | 268 50.2 | 45 41.5 .. | 49.9 | 183 50.6 .. | 02.3 | 268 44.4 .. | 38.3 | 307 16.1 .. | 26.2 | Hamal | 327 52.9 | N23 34.3 |
| 16 | 283 52.7 | 60 40.9 | 50.9 | 198 53.3 | 02.5 | 283 47.0 | 38.3 | 322 18.6 | 26.2 | Kaus Aust. | 83 35.2 | S34 22.5 |
| 17 | 298 55.1 | 75 40.2 | 51.9 | 213 55.9 | 02.6 | 298 49.6 | 38.4 | 337 21.0 | 26.2 | | | |
| 18 | 313 57.6 | 90 39.6 | S15 52.9 | 228 58.6 | N24 02.7 | 313 52.2 | S 1 38.5 | 352 23.4 | S16 26.1 | Kochab | 137 21.0 | N74 03.7 |
| 19 | 329 00.0 | 105 39.0 | 53.9 | 244 01.3 | 02.8 | 328 54.8 | 38.5 | 7 25.8 | 26.1 | Markab | 13 31.5 | N15 19.8 |
| 20 | 344 02.5 | 120 38.3 | 54.8 | 259 04.0 | 02.9 | 343 57.5 | 38.6 | 22 28.2 | 26.1 | Menkar | 314 07.7 | N 4 10.8 |
| 21 | 359 05.0 | 135 37.7 .. | 55.8 | 274 06.6 .. | 03.0 | 359 00.1 .. | 38.6 | 37 30.6 .. | 26.1 | Menkent | 148 00.2 | S36 28.7 |
| 22 | 14 07.4 | 150 37.1 | 56.8 | 289 09.3 | 03.1 | 14 02.7 | 38.7 | 52 33.0 | 26.1 | Miaplacidus | 221 38.7 | S69 48.2 |
| 23 | 29 09.9 | 165 36.5 | 57.8 | 304 12.0 | 03.2 | 29 05.3 | 38.7 | 67 35.4 | 26.0 | | | |
| **5** 00 | 44 12.4 | 180 35.8 | S15 58.8 | 319 14.7 | N24 03.4 | 44 07.9 | S 1 38.8 | 82 37.8 | S16 26.0 | Mirfak | 308 30.4 | N49 56.5 |
| 01 | 59 14.8 | 195 35.2 | 15 59.8 | 334 17.4 | 03.5 | 59 10.5 | 38.8 | 97 40.3 | 26.0 | Nunki | 75 50.2 | S26 16.1 |
| 02 | 74 17.3 | 210 34.6 | 16 00.8 | 349 20.1 | 03.6 | 74 13.1 | 38.9 | 112 42.7 | 26.0 | Peacock | 53 08.7 | S56 39.9 |
| 03 | 89 19.8 | 225 33.9 .. | 01.8 | 4 22.8 .. | 03.7 | 89 15.8 .. | 38.9 | 127 45.1 .. | 26.0 | Pollux | 243 19.4 | N27 58.2 |
| 04 | 104 22.2 | 240 33.3 | 02.7 | 19 25.4 | 03.8 | 104 18.4 | 39.0 | 142 47.5 | 25.9 | Procyon | 244 52.6 | N 5 10.1 |
| 05 | 119 24.7 | 255 32.7 | 03.7 | 34 28.1 | 03.9 | 119 21.0 | 39.1 | 157 49.9 | 25.9 | | | |
| 06 | 134 27.2 | 270 32.0 | S16 04.7 | 49 30.8 | N24 04.0 | 134 23.6 | S 1 39.1 | 172 52.3 | S16 25.9 | Rasalhague | 96 00.5 | N12 32.7 |
| 07 | 149 29.6 | 285 31.4 | 05.7 | 64 33.5 | 04.2 | 149 26.2 | 39.2 | 187 54.7 | 25.9 | Regulus | 207 36.5 | N11 51.4 |
| 08 | 164 32.1 | 300 30.8 | 06.7 | 79 36.2 | 04.3 | 164 28.8 | 39.2 | 202 57.1 | 25.9 | Rigel | 281 05.4 | S 8 10.4 |
| 09 | 179 34.5 | 315 30.1 .. | 07.7 | 94 38.9 .. | 04.4 | 179 31.4 .. | 39.3 | 217 59.5 .. | 25.8 | Rigil Kent. | 139 43.5 | S60 55.6 |
| 10 | 194 37.0 | 330 29.5 | 08.6 | 109 41.6 | 04.5 | 194 34.0 | 39.3 | 233 01.9 | 25.8 | Sabik | 102 05.2 | S15 45.1 |
| 11 | 209 39.5 | 345 28.8 | 09.6 | 124 44.3 | 04.6 | 209 36.7 | 39.4 | 248 04.3 | 25.8 | | | |
| 12 | 224 41.9 | 0 28.2 | S16 10.6 | 139 47.0 | N24 04.7 | 224 39.3 | S 1 39.4 | 263 06.8 | S16 25.8 | Schedar | 349 32.6 | N56 39.9 |
| 13 | 239 44.4 | 15 27.6 | 11.6 | 154 49.7 | 04.8 | 239 41.9 | 39.5 | 278 09.2 | 25.8 | Shaula | 96 13.2 | S37 07.2 |
| 14 | 254 46.9 | 30 26.9 | 12.6 | 169 52.4 | 05.0 | 254 44.5 | 39.5 | 293 11.6 | 25.7 | Sirius | 258 27.7 | S16 44.6 |
| 15 | 269 49.3 | 45 26.3 .. | 13.5 | 184 55.2 .. | 05.1 | 269 47.1 .. | 39.6 | 308 14.0 .. | 25.7 | Spica | 158 24.5 | S11 16.6 |
| 16 | 284 51.8 | 60 25.7 | 14.5 | 199 57.9 | 05.2 | 284 49.7 | 39.6 | 323 16.4 | 25.7 | Suhail | 222 47.7 | S43 31.1 |
| 17 | 299 54.3 | 75 25.0 | 15.5 | 215 00.6 | 05.3 | 299 52.3 | 39.7 | 338 18.8 | 25.7 | | | |
| 18 | 314 56.7 | 90 24.4 | S16 16.5 | 230 03.3 | N24 05.4 | 314 54.9 | S 1 39.7 | 353 21.2 | S16 25.7 | Vega | 80 34.7 | N38 48.5 |
| 19 | 329 59.2 | 105 23.7 | 17.4 | 245 06.0 | 05.5 | 329 57.5 | 39.8 | 8 23.6 | 25.6 | Zuben'ubi | 136 58.4 | S16 08.0 |
| 20 | 345 01.6 | 120 23.1 | 18.4 | 260 08.7 | 05.6 | 345 00.1 | 39.8 | 23 26.0 | 25.6 | | SHA | Mer.Pass. |
| 21 | 0 04.1 | 135 22.4 .. | 19.4 | 275 11.4 .. | 05.8 | 0 02.7 .. | 39.9 | 38 28.4 .. | 25.6 | | ° ′ | h m |
| 22 | 15 06.6 | 150 21.8 | 20.4 | 290 14.2 | 05.9 | 15 05.4 | 39.9 | 53 30.8 | 25.6 | Venus | 137 37.6 | 11 57 |
| 23 | 30 09.0 | 165 21.2 | 21.3 | 305 16.9 | 06.0 | 30 08.0 | 40.0 | 68 33.2 | 25.6 | Mars | 274 57.5 | 2 47 |
| Mer. Pass. 21 03.7 | | v −0.6 | d 1.0 | v 2.7 | d 0.1 | v 2.6 | d 0.1 | v 2.4 | d 0.0 | Jupiter | 359 51.9 | 21 04 |
| | | | | | | | | | | Saturn | 38 26.7 | 18 30 |

| UT | SUN GHA | SUN Dec | MOON GHA | v | MOON Dec | d | HP |
|---|---|---|---|---|---|---|---|
| d h | ° ′ | ° ′ | ° ′ | ′ | ° ′ | ′ | ′ |
| 3 00 | 184 06.6 | S14 59.1 | 65 24.1 | 10.6 | S15 01.7 | 13.8 | 58.6 |
| 01 | 199 06.6 | 14 59.8 | 79 53.7 | 10.6 | 14 47.9 | 13.8 | 58.6 |
| 02 | 214 06.6 | 15 00.6 | 94 23.3 | 10.7 | 14 34.1 | 13.9 | 58.6 |
| 03 | 229 06.6 | .. 01.4 | 108 53.0 | 10.8 | 14 20.2 | 14.0 | 58.6 |
| 04 | 244 06.6 | 02.2 | 123 22.8 | 10.9 | 14 06.2 | 14.0 | 58.6 |
| 05 | 259 06.6 | 03.0 | 137 52.7 | 10.9 | 13 52.2 | 14.1 | 58.5 |
| 06 | 274 06.6 | S15 03.7 | 152 22.6 | 11.1 | S13 38.1 | 14.1 | 58.5 |
| 07 | 289 06.6 | 04.5 | 166 52.7 | 11.1 | 13 24.0 | 14.3 | 58.5 |
| T 08 | 304 06.6 | 05.3 | 181 22.8 | 11.2 | 13 09.7 | 14.3 | 58.5 |
| H 09 | 319 06.6 | .. 06.1 | 195 53.0 | 11.2 | 12 55.4 | 14.3 | 58.5 |
| U 10 | 334 06.6 | 06.9 | 210 23.2 | 11.4 | 12 41.1 | 14.4 | 58.5 |
| R 11 | 349 06.6 | 07.6 | 224 53.6 | 11.4 | 12 26.7 | 14.5 | 58.5 |
| S 12 | 4 06.6 | S15 08.4 | 239 24.0 | 11.5 | S12 12.2 | 14.5 | 58.4 |
| D 13 | 19 06.6 | 09.2 | 253 54.5 | 11.5 | 11 57.7 | 14.5 | 58.4 |
| A 14 | 34 06.6 | 10.0 | 268 25.0 | 11.7 | 11 43.2 | 14.6 | 58.4 |
| Y 15 | 49 06.6 | .. 10.8 | 282 55.7 | 11.7 | 11 28.6 | 14.7 | 58.4 |
| 16 | 64 06.6 | 11.5 | 297 26.4 | 11.7 | 11 13.9 | 14.7 | 58.4 |
| 17 | 79 06.6 | 12.3 | 311 57.1 | 11.9 | 10 59.2 | 14.8 | 58.4 |
| 18 | 94 06.6 | S15 13.1 | 326 28.0 | 11.9 | S10 44.4 | 14.8 | 58.3 |
| 19 | 109 06.6 | 13.9 | 340 58.9 | 11.9 | 10 29.6 | 14.8 | 58.3 |
| 20 | 124 06.6 | 14.6 | 355 29.8 | 12.1 | 10 14.8 | 14.9 | 58.3 |
| 21 | 139 06.6 | .. 15.4 | 10 00.9 | 12.1 | 9 59.9 | 15.0 | 58.3 |
| 22 | 154 06.6 | 16.2 | 24 32.0 | 12.1 | 9 44.9 | 15.0 | 58.3 |
| 23 | 169 06.6 | 17.0 | 39 03.1 | 12.2 | 9 29.9 | 15.0 | 58.3 |
| 4 00 | 184 06.6 | S15 17.7 | 53 34.3 | 12.3 | S 9 14.9 | 15.0 | 58.2 |
| 01 | 199 06.6 | 18.5 | 68 05.6 | 12.4 | 8 59.9 | 15.1 | 58.2 |
| 02 | 214 06.6 | 19.3 | 82 37.0 | 12.4 | 8 44.8 | 15.2 | 58.2 |
| 03 | 229 06.6 | .. 20.0 | 97 08.4 | 12.4 | 8 29.6 | 15.1 | 58.2 |
| 04 | 244 06.6 | 20.8 | 111 39.8 | 12.5 | 8 14.5 | 15.2 | 58.2 |
| 05 | 259 06.6 | 21.6 | 126 11.3 | 12.6 | 7 59.3 | 15.2 | 58.2 |
| 06 | 274 06.5 | S15 22.4 | 140 42.9 | 12.6 | S 7 44.1 | 15.3 | 58.1 |
| 07 | 289 06.5 | 23.1 | 155 14.5 | 12.7 | 7 28.8 | 15.3 | 58.1 |
| F 08 | 304 06.5 | 23.9 | 169 46.2 | 12.7 | 7 13.5 | 15.3 | 58.1 |
| R 09 | 319 06.5 | .. 24.7 | 184 17.9 | 12.8 | 6 58.2 | 15.3 | 58.1 |
| I 10 | 334 06.5 | 25.4 | 198 49.7 | 12.8 | 6 42.9 | 15.4 | 58.1 |
| D 11 | 349 06.5 | 26.2 | 213 21.5 | 12.8 | 6 27.5 | 15.3 | 58.1 |
| A 12 | 4 06.5 | S15 27.0 | 227 53.3 | 12.9 | S 6 12.2 | 15.4 | 58.0 |
| Y 13 | 19 06.5 | 27.7 | 242 25.2 | 13.0 | 5 56.8 | 15.4 | 58.0 |
| 14 | 34 06.5 | 28.5 | 256 57.2 | 13.0 | 5 41.4 | 15.5 | 58.0 |
| 15 | 49 06.5 | .. 29.3 | 271 29.2 | 13.0 | 5 25.9 | 15.4 | 58.0 |
| 16 | 64 06.5 | 30.0 | 286 01.2 | 13.1 | 5 10.5 | 15.5 | 58.0 |
| 17 | 79 06.4 | 30.8 | 300 33.3 | 13.1 | 4 55.0 | 15.5 | 58.0 |
| 18 | 94 06.4 | S15 31.6 | 315 05.4 | 13.2 | S 4 39.5 | 15.5 | 57.9 |
| 19 | 109 06.4 | 32.3 | 329 37.6 | 13.2 | 4 24.0 | 15.5 | 57.9 |
| 20 | 124 06.4 | 33.1 | 344 09.8 | 13.2 | 4 08.5 | 15.5 | 57.9 |
| 21 | 139 06.4 | .. 33.9 | 358 42.0 | 13.2 | 3 53.0 | 15.5 | 57.9 |
| 22 | 154 06.4 | 34.6 | 13 14.2 | 13.3 | 3 37.4 | 15.5 | 57.9 |
| 23 | 169 06.4 | 35.4 | 27 46.5 | 13.4 | 3 21.9 | 15.5 | 57.8 |
| 5 00 | 184 06.4 | S15 36.1 | 42 18.9 | 13.3 | S 3 06.4 | 15.6 | 57.8 |
| 01 | 199 06.3 | 36.9 | 56 51.2 | 13.4 | 2 50.8 | 15.6 | 57.8 |
| 02 | 214 06.3 | 37.7 | 71 23.6 | 13.5 | 2 35.2 | 15.6 | 57.8 |
| 03 | 229 06.3 | .. 38.4 | 85 56.1 | 13.4 | 2 19.7 | 15.6 | 57.8 |
| 04 | 244 06.3 | 39.2 | 100 28.5 | 13.5 | 2 04.1 | 15.5 | 57.8 |
| 05 | 259 06.3 | 39.9 | 115 01.0 | 13.5 | 1 48.6 | 15.6 | 57.7 |
| 06 | 274 06.3 | S15 40.7 | 129 33.5 | 13.5 | S 1 33.0 | 15.6 | 57.7 |
| 07 | 289 06.3 | 41.5 | 144 06.0 | 13.5 | 1 17.4 | 15.6 | 57.7 |
| S 08 | 304 06.2 | 42.2 | 158 38.5 | 13.6 | 1 01.9 | 15.6 | 57.7 |
| A 09 | 319 06.2 | .. 43.0 | 173 11.1 | 13.6 | 0 46.3 | 15.5 | 57.7 |
| T 10 | 334 06.2 | 43.7 | 187 43.7 | 13.6 | 0 30.8 | 15.6 | 57.6 |
| U 11 | 349 06.2 | 44.5 | 202 16.3 | 13.6 | S 0 15.2 | 15.5 | 57.6 |
| R 12 | 4 06.2 | S15 45.3 | 216 48.9 | 13.7 | N 0 00.3 | 15.5 | 57.6 |
| D 13 | 19 06.2 | 46.0 | 231 21.6 | 13.7 | 0 15.8 | 15.5 | 57.6 |
| A 14 | 34 06.1 | 46.8 | 245 54.3 | 13.6 | 0 31.3 | 15.5 | 57.6 |
| Y 15 | 49 06.1 | .. 47.5 | 260 26.9 | 13.7 | 0 46.8 | 15.5 | 57.5 |
| 16 | 64 06.1 | 48.3 | 274 59.6 | 13.7 | 1 02.3 | 15.5 | 57.5 |
| 17 | 79 06.1 | 49.0 | 289 32.3 | 13.7 | 1 17.8 | 15.5 | 57.5 |
| 18 | 94 06.1 | S15 49.8 | 304 05.0 | 13.8 | N 1 33.3 | 15.4 | 57.5 |
| 19 | 109 06.0 | 50.5 | 318 37.8 | 13.7 | 1 48.7 | 15.4 | 57.5 |
| 20 | 124 06.0 | 51.3 | 333 10.5 | 13.8 | 2 04.1 | 15.4 | 57.5 |
| 21 | 139 06.0 | .. 52.0 | 347 43.3 | 13.7 | 2 19.5 | 15.4 | 57.4 |
| 22 | 154 06.0 | 52.8 | 2 16.0 | 13.8 | 2 34.9 | 15.4 | 57.4 |
| 23 | 169 06.0 | 53.5 | 16 48.8 | 13.7 | N 2 50.3 | 15.3 | 57.4 |
| | SD 16.2 | d 0.8 | SD 15.9 | | 15.8 | | 15.7 |

| Lat. | Twilight Naut. | Twilight Civil | Sunrise | Moonrise 3 | 4 | 5 | 6 |
|---|---|---|---|---|---|---|---|
| ° | h m | h m | h m | h m | h m | h m | h m |
| N 72 | 06 18 | 07 43 | 09 16 | 16 42 | 16 02 | 15 30 | 14 57 |
| N 70 | 06 12 | 07 28 | 08 46 | 16 24 | 15 55 | 15 31 | 15 06 |
| 68 | 06 08 | 07 16 | 08 23 | 16 10 | 15 49 | 15 32 | 15 14 |
| 66 | 06 04 | 07 06 | 08 06 | 15 58 | 15 44 | 15 32 | 15 20 |
| 64 | 06 00 | 06 57 | 07 52 | 15 48 | 15 40 | 15 33 | 15 26 |
| 62 | 05 57 | 06 50 | 07 40 | 15 39 | 15 36 | 15 33 | 15 30 |
| 60 | 05 54 | 06 44 | 07 30 | 15 32 | 15 33 | 15 34 | 15 35 |
| N 58 | 05 51 | 06 38 | 07 21 | 15 25 | 15 30 | 15 34 | 15 38 |
| 56 | 05 49 | 06 33 | 07 13 | 15 20 | 15 28 | 15 35 | 15 42 |
| 54 | 05 46 | 06 28 | 07 06 | 15 14 | 15 25 | 15 35 | 15 45 |
| 52 | 05 44 | 06 24 | 07 00 | 15 10 | 15 23 | 15 35 | 15 48 |
| 50 | 05 42 | 06 20 | 06 54 | 15 05 | 15 21 | 15 36 | 15 50 |
| 45 | 05 37 | 06 12 | 06 42 | 14 56 | 15 17 | 15 36 | 15 56 |
| N 40 | 05 32 | 06 04 | 06 32 | 14 48 | 15 13 | 15 37 | 16 00 |
| 35 | 05 27 | 05 57 | 06 24 | 14 41 | 15 10 | 15 37 | 16 04 |
| 30 | 05 23 | 05 51 | 06 16 | 14 35 | 15 07 | 15 38 | 16 08 |
| 20 | 05 14 | 05 40 | 06 03 | 14 25 | 15 03 | 15 39 | 16 14 |
| N 10 | 05 04 | 05 29 | 05 51 | 14 16 | 14 58 | 15 39 | 16 20 |
| 0 | 04 54 | 05 19 | 05 40 | 14 07 | 14 54 | 15 40 | 16 25 |
| S 10 | 04 42 | 05 05 | 05 29 | 13 58 | 14 50 | 15 41 | 16 30 |
| 20 | 04 27 | 04 54 | 05 17 | 13 49 | 14 46 | 15 41 | 16 36 |
| 30 | 04 07 | 04 38 | 05 03 | 13 39 | 14 41 | 15 42 | 16 42 |
| 35 | 03 55 | 04 28 | 04 55 | 13 32 | 14 39 | 15 43 | 16 46 |
| 40 | 03 40 | 04 16 | 04 46 | 13 25 | 14 35 | 15 43 | 16 51 |
| 45 | 03 22 | 04 02 | 04 35 | 13 17 | 14 32 | 15 44 | 16 56 |
| S 50 | 02 58 | 03 45 | 04 21 | 13 07 | 14 27 | 15 45 | 17 02 |
| 52 | 02 46 | 03 36 | 04 15 | 13 03 | 14 25 | 15 45 | 17 05 |
| 54 | 02 31 | 03 27 | 04 08 | 12 57 | 14 23 | 15 46 | 17 08 |
| 56 | 02 14 | 03 16 | 04 01 | 12 52 | 14 20 | 15 46 | 17 11 |
| 58 | 01 53 | 03 03 | 03 52 | 12 45 | 14 18 | 15 47 | 17 15 |
| S 60 | 01 24 | 02 49 | 03 42 | 12 38 | 14 14 | 15 48 | 17 19 |

| Lat. | Sunset | Twilight Civil | Twilight Naut. | Moonset 3 | 4 | 5 | 6 |
|---|---|---|---|---|---|---|---|
| ° | h m | h m | h m | h m | h m | h m | h m |
| N 72 | 14 10 | 15 43 | 17 08 | 24 26 | 00 26 | 02 44 | 04 56 |
| N 70 | 14 40 | 15 58 | 17 13 | 24 41 | 00 41 | 02 48 | 04 50 |
| 68 | 15 03 | 16 10 | 17 18 | 24 53 | 00 53 | 02 51 | 04 45 |
| 66 | 15 20 | 16 20 | 17 22 | 25 03 | 01 03 | 02 54 | 04 41 |
| 64 | 15 34 | 16 29 | 17 26 | 25 11 | 01 11 | 02 56 | 04 37 |
| 62 | 15 46 | 16 36 | 17 29 | 25 10 | 01 18 | 02 57 | 04 34 |
| 60 | 15 57 | 16 42 | 17 32 | 25 24 | 01 24 | 02 59 | 04 31 |
| N 58 | 16 05 | 16 48 | 17 35 | 25 30 | 01 30 | 03 00 | 04 29 |
| 56 | 16 13 | 16 53 | 17 38 | 00 04 | 01 34 | 03 02 | 04 27 |
| 54 | 16 20 | 16 58 | 17 40 | 00 11 | 01 38 | 03 03 | 04 25 |
| 52 | 16 26 | 17 02 | 17 42 | 00 18 | 01 42 | 03 04 | 04 23 |
| 50 | 16 32 | 17 06 | 17 45 | 00 24 | 01 46 | 03 05 | 04 22 |
| 45 | 16 44 | 17 15 | 17 50 | 00 37 | 01 53 | 03 06 | 04 18 |
| N 40 | 16 54 | 17 23 | 17 55 | 00 48 | 01 59 | 03 08 | 04 16 |
| 35 | 17 03 | 17 29 | 17 59 | 00 57 | 02 04 | 03 09 | 04 13 |
| 30 | 17 11 | 17 36 | 18 04 | 01 05 | 02 09 | 03 11 | 04 11 |
| 20 | 17 24 | 17 47 | 18 13 | 01 18 | 02 17 | 03 13 | 04 08 |
| N 10 | 17 36 | 17 58 | 18 23 | 01 30 | 02 24 | 03 15 | 04 04 |
| 0 | 17 47 | 18 08 | 18 33 | 01 41 | 02 30 | 03 16 | 04 01 |
| S 10 | 17 58 | 18 20 | 18 46 | 01 52 | 02 36 | 03 18 | 03 58 |
| 20 | 18 10 | 18 34 | 19 01 | 02 04 | 02 43 | 03 20 | 03 55 |
| 30 | 18 25 | 18 50 | 19 20 | 02 17 | 02 50 | 03 21 | 03 52 |
| 35 | 18 33 | 19 00 | 19 33 | 02 24 | 02 55 | 03 23 | 03 49 |
| 40 | 18 42 | 19 12 | 19 48 | 02 33 | 02 59 | 03 24 | 03 47 |
| 45 | 18 53 | 19 26 | 20 06 | 02 43 | 03 05 | 03 25 | 03 44 |
| S 50 | 19 07 | 19 44 | 20 31 | 02 54 | 03 12 | 03 27 | 03 41 |
| 52 | 19 13 | 19 52 | 20 44 | 03 00 | 03 15 | 03 28 | 03 40 |
| 54 | 19 20 | 20 02 | 20 58 | 03 06 | 03 18 | 03 28 | 03 38 |
| 56 | 19 28 | 20 13 | 21 16 | 03 12 | 03 22 | 03 29 | 03 36 |
| 58 | 19 37 | 20 26 | 21 38 | 03 20 | 03 26 | 03 30 | 03 34 |
| S 60 | 19 47 | 20 41 | 22 08 | 03 28 | 03 30 | 03 31 | 03 32 |

| Day | SUN Eqn. of Time 00h | 12h | Mer. Pass. | MOON Mer. Pass. Upper | Lower | Age | Phase |
|---|---|---|---|---|---|---|---|
| d | m s | m s | h m | h m | h m | d | % |
| 3 | 16 26 | 16 26 | 11 44 | 20 19 | 07 54 | 09 | 74 |
| 4 | 16 26 | 16 26 | 11 44 | 21 05 | 08 42 | 10 | 83 |
| 5 | 16 25 | 16 25 | 11 44 | 21 51 | 09 28 | 11 | 91 |

| UT | ARIES GHA | VENUS −3.9 GHA | Dec | MARS −1.4 GHA | Dec | JUPITER −2.8 GHA | Dec | SATURN +0.6 GHA | Dec | STARS Name | SHA | Dec |
|---|---|---|---|---|---|---|---|---|---|---|---|---|
| **6 00** | 45 11.5 | 180 20.5 | S16 22.3 | 320 19.6 | N24 06.1 | 45 10.6 | S 1 40.1 | 83 35.6 | S16 25.5 | Acamar | 315 12.7 | S40 12.8 |
| 01 | 60 14.0 | 195 19.9 | 23.3 | 335 22.3 | 06.2 | 60 13.2 | 40.1 | 98 38.1 | 25.5 | Achernar | 335 21.0 | S57 07.4 |
| 02 | 75 16.4 | 210 19.2 | 24.2 | 350 25.1 | 06.3 | 75 15.8 | 40.2 | 113 40.5 | 25.5 | Acrux | 173 02.6 | S63 13.2 |
| 03 | 90 18.9 | 225 18.6 .. | 25.2 | 5 27.8 .. | 06.4 | 90 18.4 .. | 40.2 | 128 42.9 .. | 25.5 | Adhara | 255 07.1 | S28 59.9 |
| 04 | 105 21.4 | 240 17.9 | 26.2 | 20 30.5 | 06.5 | 105 21.0 | 40.3 | 143 45.3 | 25.5 | Aldebaran | 290 41.4 | N16 33.3 |
| 05 | 120 23.8 | 255 17.3 | 27.1 | 35 33.3 | 06.7 | 120 23.6 | 40.3 | 158 47.7 | 25.4 | | | |
| **S 06** | 135 26.3 | 270 16.6 | S16 28.1 | 50 36.0 | N24 06.8 | 135 26.2 | S 1 40.4 | 173 50.1 | S16 25.4 | Alioth | 166 15.1 | N55 50.1 |
| **U** 07 | 150 28.8 | 285 16.0 | 29.1 | 65 38.7 | 06.9 | 150 28.8 | 40.4 | 188 52.5 | 25.4 | Alkaid | 152 53.9 | N49 12.0 |
| **N** 08 | 165 31.2 | 300 15.4 | 30.0 | 80 41.5 | 07.0 | 165 31.4 | 40.5 | 203 54.9 | 25.4 | Alnair | 27 35.1 | S46 51.3 |
| **D** 09 | 180 33.7 | 315 14.7 .. | 31.0 | 95 44.2 .. | 07.1 | 180 34.0 .. | 40.5 | 218 57.3 .. | 25.3 | Alnilam | 275 39.3 | S 1 11.1 |
| **A** 10 | 195 36.1 | 330 14.1 | 32.0 | 110 46.9 | 07.2 | 195 36.6 | 40.6 | 233 59.7 | 25.3 | Alphard | 217 49.6 | S 8 45.2 |
| **Y** 11 | 210 38.6 | 345 13.4 | 32.9 | 125 49.7 | 07.3 | 210 39.2 | 40.6 | 249 02.1 | 25.3 | | | |
| 12 | 225 41.1 | 0 12.8 | S16 33.9 | 140 52.4 | N24 07.5 | 225 41.8 | S 1 40.7 | 264 04.5 | S16 25.3 | Alphecca | 126 05.7 | N26 38.4 |
| 13 | 240 43.5 | 15 12.1 | 34.8 | 155 55.2 | 07.6 | 240 44.4 | 40.7 | 279 06.9 | 25.2 | Alpheratz | 357 36.4 | N29 13.1 |
| 14 | 255 46.0 | 30 11.5 | 35.8 | 170 57.9 | 07.7 | 255 47.0 | 40.8 | 294 09.3 | 25.2 | Altair | 62 01.9 | N 8 55.8 |
| 15 | 270 48.5 | 45 10.8 .. | 36.8 | 186 00.7 .. | 07.8 | 270 49.6 .. | 40.8 | 309 11.7 .. | 25.2 | Ankaa | 353 08.6 | S42 11.1 |
| 16 | 285 50.9 | 60 10.2 | 37.7 | 201 03.4 | 07.9 | 285 52.2 | 40.9 | 324 14.1 | 25.2 | Antares | 112 18.4 | S26 28.9 |
| 17 | 300 53.4 | 75 09.5 | 38.7 | 216 06.2 | 08.0 | 300 54.8 | 40.9 | 339 16.5 | 25.2 | | | |
| 18 | 315 55.9 | 90 08.8 | S16 39.6 | 231 08.9 | N24 08.1 | 315 57.4 | S 1 40.9 | 354 18.9 | S16 25.2 | Arcturus | 145 49.9 | N19 03.9 |
| 19 | 330 58.3 | 105 08.2 | 40.6 | 246 11.7 | 08.2 | 331 00.0 | 41.0 | 9 21.3 | 25.1 | Atria | 107 14.8 | S69 04.1 |
| 20 | 346 00.8 | 120 07.5 | 41.5 | 261 14.4 | 08.4 | 346 02.6 | 41.0 | 24 23.7 | 25.1 | Avior | 234 15.3 | S59 34.5 |
| 21 | 1 03.3 | 135 06.9 .. | 42.5 | 276 17.2 .. | 08.5 | 1 05.2 .. | 41.1 | 39 26.1 .. | 25.1 | Bellatrix | 278 24.6 | N 6 22.3 |
| 22 | 16 05.7 | 150 06.2 | 43.5 | 291 20.0 | 08.6 | 16 07.8 | 41.1 | 54 28.5 | 25.1 | Betelgeuse | 270 53.8 | N 7 24.7 |
| 23 | 31 08.2 | 165 05.6 | 44.4 | 306 22.7 | 08.7 | 31 10.4 | 41.2 | 69 30.9 | 25.0 | | | |
| **7 00** | 46 10.6 | 180 04.9 | S16 45.4 | 321 25.5 | N24 08.8 | 46 13.0 | S 1 41.2 | 84 33.3 | S16 25.0 | Canopus | 263 52.8 | S52 42.2 |
| 01 | 61 13.1 | 195 04.3 | 46.3 | 336 28.3 | 08.9 | 61 15.6 | 41.3 | 99 35.7 | 25.0 | Capella | 280 24.2 | N46 01.2 |
| 02 | 76 15.6 | 210 03.6 | 47.3 | 351 31.0 | 09.0 | 76 18.2 | 41.3 | 114 38.2 | 25.0 | Deneb | 49 27.1 | N45 21.9 |
| 03 | 91 18.0 | 225 02.9 .. | 48.2 | 6 33.8 .. | 09.1 | 91 20.8 .. | 41.4 | 129 40.6 .. | 25.0 | Denebola | 182 27.0 | N14 26.8 |
| 04 | 106 20.5 | 240 02.3 | 49.2 | 21 36.6 | 09.3 | 106 23.4 | 41.4 | 144 43.0 | 24.9 | Diphda | 348 48.9 | S17 51.7 |
| 05 | 121 23.0 | 255 01.6 | 50.1 | 36 39.3 | 09.4 | 121 26.0 | 41.5 | 159 45.4 | 24.9 | | | |
| **M 06** | 136 25.4 | 270 01.0 | S16 51.1 | 51 42.1 | N24 09.5 | 136 28.6 | S 1 41.5 | 174 47.8 | S16 24.9 | Dubhe | 193 43.6 | N61 37.5 |
| **O** 07 | 151 27.9 | 285 00.3 | 52.0 | 66 44.9 | 09.6 | 151 31.2 | 41.6 | 189 50.2 | 24.9 | Elnath | 278 03.9 | N28 37.6 |
| **N** 08 | 166 30.4 | 299 59.7 | 53.0 | 81 47.7 | 09.7 | 166 33.8 | 41.6 | 204 52.6 | 24.8 | Eltanin | 90 43.4 | N51 29.3 |
| **D** 09 | 181 32.8 | 314 59.0 .. | 53.9 | 96 50.5 .. | 09.8 | 181 36.4 .. | 41.7 | 219 55.0 .. | 24.8 | Enif | 33 40.5 | N 9 58.9 |
| **A** 10 | 196 35.3 | 329 58.3 | 54.8 | 111 53.2 | 09.9 | 196 39.0 | 41.7 | 234 57.4 | 24.8 | Fomalhaut | 15 16.4 | S29 30.2 |
| **Y** 11 | 211 37.7 | 344 57.7 | 55.8 | 126 56.0 | 10.1 | 211 41.6 | 41.8 | 249 59.8 | 24.8 | | | |
| 12 | 226 40.2 | 359 57.0 | S16 56.7 | 141 58.8 | N24 10.2 | 226 44.2 | S 1 41.8 | 265 02.2 | S16 24.7 | Gacrux | 171 54.1 | S57 14.1 |
| 13 | 241 42.7 | 14 56.3 | 57.7 | 157 01.6 | 10.3 | 241 46.8 | 41.8 | 280 04.6 | 24.7 | Gienah | 175 45.7 | S17 39.9 |
| 14 | 256 45.1 | 29 55.7 | 58.6 | 172 04.4 | 10.4 | 256 49.4 | 41.9 | 295 07.0 | 24.7 | Hadar | 148 39.2 | S60 28.8 |
| 15 | 271 47.6 | 44 55.0 | 16 59.6 | 187 07.2 .. | 10.5 | 271 52.0 .. | 41.9 | 310 09.4 .. | 24.7 | Hamal | 327 52.9 | N23 34.3 |
| 16 | 286 50.1 | 59 54.4 | 17 00.5 | 202 10.0 | 10.6 | 286 54.6 | 42.0 | 325 11.8 | 24.7 | Kaus Aust. | 83 35.2 | S34 22.5 |
| 17 | 301 52.5 | 74 53.7 | 01.4 | 217 12.8 | 10.7 | 301 57.2 | 42.0 | 340 14.2 | 24.6 | | | |
| 18 | 316 55.0 | 89 53.0 | S17 02.4 | 232 15.5 | N24 10.8 | 316 59.8 | S 1 42.1 | 355 16.6 | S16 24.6 | Kochab | 137 21.0 | N74 03.7 |
| 19 | 331 57.5 | 104 52.4 | 03.3 | 247 18.3 | 11.0 | 332 02.4 | 42.1 | 10 19.0 | 24.6 | Markab | 13 31.6 | N15 19.8 |
| 20 | 346 59.9 | 119 51.7 | 04.3 | 262 21.1 | 11.1 | 347 05.0 | 42.2 | 25 21.4 | 24.6 | Menkar | 314 07.7 | N 4 10.8 |
| 21 | 2 02.4 | 134 51.0 .. | 05.2 | 277 23.9 .. | 11.2 | 2 07.6 .. | 42.2 | 40 23.8 .. | 24.5 | Menkent | 148 00.2 | S36 28.7 |
| 22 | 17 04.9 | 149 50.4 | 06.1 | 292 26.7 | 11.3 | 17 10.2 | 42.3 | 55 26.2 | 24.5 | Miaplacidus | 221 38.6 | S69 48.2 |
| 23 | 32 07.3 | 164 49.7 | 07.1 | 307 29.5 | 11.4 | 32 12.8 | 42.3 | 70 28.6 | 24.5 | | | |
| **8 00** | 47 09.8 | 179 49.0 | S17 08.0 | 322 32.4 | N24 11.5 | 47 15.3 | S 1 42.3 | 85 31.0 | S16 24.5 | Mirfak | 308 30.4 | N49 56.5 |
| 01 | 62 12.2 | 194 48.3 | 08.9 | 337 35.2 | 11.6 | 62 17.9 | 42.4 | 100 33.3 | 24.4 | Nunki | 75 50.2 | S26 16.1 |
| 02 | 77 14.7 | 209 47.7 | 09.9 | 352 38.0 | 11.7 | 77 20.5 | 42.4 | 115 35.7 | 24.4 | Peacock | 53 08.7 | S56 39.9 |
| 03 | 92 17.2 | 224 47.0 .. | 10.8 | 7 40.8 .. | 11.9 | 92 23.1 .. | 42.5 | 130 38.1 .. | 24.4 | Pollux | 243 19.4 | N27 58.2 |
| 04 | 107 19.6 | 239 46.3 | 11.7 | 22 43.6 | 12.0 | 107 25.7 | 42.5 | 145 40.5 | 24.4 | Procyon | 244 52.6 | N 5 10.1 |
| 05 | 122 22.1 | 254 45.7 | 12.7 | 37 46.4 | 12.1 | 122 28.3 | 42.6 | 160 42.9 | 24.4 | | | |
| **T 06** | 137 24.6 | 269 45.0 | S17 13.6 | 52 49.2 | N24 12.2 | 137 30.9 | S 1 42.6 | 175 45.3 | S16 24.3 | Rasalhague | 96 00.5 | N12 32.7 |
| **U** 07 | 152 27.0 | 284 44.3 | 14.5 | 67 52.0 | 12.3 | 152 33.5 | 42.7 | 190 47.7 | 24.3 | Regulus | 207 36.5 | N11 51.4 |
| **E** 08 | 167 29.5 | 299 43.6 | 15.4 | 82 54.9 | 12.4 | 167 36.1 | 42.7 | 205 50.1 | 24.3 | Rigel | 281 05.3 | S 8 10.4 |
| **S** 09 | 182 32.0 | 314 43.0 .. | 16.4 | 97 57.7 .. | 12.5 | 182 38.7 .. | 42.7 | 220 52.5 .. | 24.3 | Rigil Kent. | 139 43.5 | S60 55.6 |
| **D** 10 | 197 34.4 | 329 42.3 | 17.3 | 113 00.5 | 12.6 | 197 41.3 | 42.8 | 235 54.9 | 24.2 | Sabik | 102 05.2 | S15 45.1 |
| **A** 11 | 212 36.9 | 344 41.6 | 18.2 | 128 03.3 | 12.8 | 212 43.8 | 42.8 | 250 57.3 | 24.2 | | | |
| **Y** 12 | 227 39.3 | 359 41.0 | S17 19.1 | 143 06.1 | N24 12.9 | 227 46.4 | S 1 42.9 | 265 59.7 | S16 24.2 | Schedar | 349 32.6 | N56 39.9 |
| 13 | 242 41.8 | 14 40.3 | 20.1 | 158 09.0 | 13.0 | 242 49.0 | 42.9 | 281 02.1 | 24.2 | Shaula | 96 13.2 | S37 07.2 |
| 14 | 257 44.3 | 29 39.6 | 21.0 | 173 11.8 | 13.1 | 257 51.6 | 43.0 | 296 04.5 | 24.1 | Sirius | 258 27.6 | S16 44.6 |
| 15 | 272 46.7 | 44 38.9 .. | 21.9 | 188 14.6 .. | 13.2 | 272 54.2 .. | 43.0 | 311 06.9 .. | 24.1 | Spica | 158 24.5 | S11 16.6 |
| 16 | 287 49.2 | 59 38.2 | 22.8 | 203 17.5 | 13.3 | 287 56.8 | 43.0 | 326 09.3 | 24.1 | Suhail | 222 47.6 | S43 31.1 |
| 17 | 302 51.7 | 74 37.6 | 23.8 | 218 20.3 | 13.4 | 302 59.4 | 43.1 | 341 11.7 | 24.1 | | | |
| 18 | 317 54.1 | 89 36.9 | S17 24.7 | 233 23.1 | N24 13.5 | 318 02.0 | S 1 43.1 | 356 14.1 | S16 24.0 | Vega | 80 34.7 | N38 48.5 |
| 19 | 332 56.6 | 104 36.2 | 25.6 | 248 26.0 | 13.6 | 333 04.5 | 43.2 | 11 16.5 | 24.0 | Zuben'ubi | 136 58.4 | S16 08.0 |
| 20 | 347 59.1 | 119 35.5 | 26.5 | 263 28.8 | 13.8 | 348 07.1 | 43.2 | 26 18.9 | 24.0 | | SHA | Mer. Pass. |
| 21 | 3 01.5 | 134 34.9 .. | 27.4 | 278 31.6 .. | 13.9 | 3 09.7 .. | 43.2 | 41 21.3 .. | 24.0 | Venus | 133 54.3 | 12 00 |
| 22 | 18 04.0 | 149 34.2 | 28.3 | 293 34.5 | 14.0 | 18 12.3 | 43.3 | 56 23.7 | 23.9 | Mars | 275 14.9 | 2 34 |
| 23 | 33 06.5 | 164 33.5 | 29.3 | 308 37.3 | 14.1 | 33 14.9 | 43.3 | 71 26.1 | 23.9 | Jupiter | 0 02.4 | 20 52 |
| Mer. Pass. 20 51.9 | | v −0.7 | d 0.9 | v 2.8 | d 0.1 | v 2.6 | d 0.0 | v 2.4 | d 0.0 | Saturn | 38 22.7 | 18 19 |

| UT | SUN GHA | SUN Dec | MOON GHA | v | MOON Dec | d | HP |
|---|---|---|---|---|---|---|---|
| d h | ° ′ | ° ′ | ° ′ | ′ | ° ′ | ′ | ′ |
| 6 00 | 184 05.9 | S15 54.3 | 31 21.5 | 13.8 | N 3 05.6 | 15.4 | 57.4 |
| 01 | 199 05.9 | 55.0 | 45 54.3 | 13.8 | 3 21.0 | 15.3 | 57.4 |
| 02 | 214 05.9 | 55.8 | 60 27.1 | 13.7 | 3 36.3 | 15.2 | 57.3 |
| 03 | 229 05.9 .. | 56.5 | 74 59.8 | 13.8 | 3 51.5 | 15.3 | 57.3 |
| 04 | 244 05.9 | 57.3 | 89 32.6 | 13.8 | 4 06.8 | 15.2 | 57.3 |
| 05 | 259 05.8 | 58.0 | 104 05.4 | 13.8 | 4 22.0 | 15.2 | 57.3 |
| 06 | 274 05.8 | S15 58.8 | 118 38.2 | 13.7 | N 4 37.2 | 15.1 | 57.3 |
| 07 | 289 05.8 | 15 59.5 | 133 10.9 | 13.8 | 4 52.3 | 15.2 | 57.2 |
| 08 | 304 05.8 | 16 00.3 | 147 43.7 | 13.8 | 5 07.5 | 15.1 | 57.2 |
| S 09 | 319 05.7 .. | 01.0 | 162 16.5 | 13.7 | 5 22.6 | 15.0 | 57.2 |
| U 10 | 334 05.7 | 01.8 | 176 49.2 | 13.8 | 5 37.6 | 15.0 | 57.2 |
| N 11 | 349 05.7 | 02.5 | 191 22.0 | 13.7 | 5 52.6 | 15.0 | 57.2 |
| D 12 | 4 05.7 | S16 03.3 | 205 54.7 | 13.8 | N 6 07.6 | 15.0 | 57.1 |
| A 13 | 19 05.6 | 04.0 | 220 27.5 | 13.7 | 6 22.6 | 14.9 | 57.1 |
| Y 14 | 34 05.6 | 04.8 | 235 00.2 | 13.7 | 6 37.5 | 14.9 | 57.1 |
| 15 | 49 05.6 .. | 05.5 | 249 32.9 | 13.7 | 6 52.4 | 14.8 | 57.1 |
| 16 | 64 05.5 | 06.3 | 264 05.6 | 13.7 | 7 07.2 | 14.8 | 57.0 |
| 17 | 79 05.5 | 07.0 | 278 38.3 | 13.7 | 7 22.0 | 14.7 | 57.0 |
| 18 | 94 05.5 | S16 07.7 | 293 11.0 | 13.6 | N 7 36.7 | 14.8 | 57.0 |
| 19 | 109 05.5 | 08.5 | 307 43.6 | 13.7 | 7 51.5 | 14.6 | 57.0 |
| 20 | 124 05.4 | 09.2 | 322 16.3 | 13.6 | 8 06.1 | 14.6 | 57.0 |
| 21 | 139 05.4 .. | 10.0 | 336 48.9 | 13.6 | 8 20.7 | 14.6 | 56.9 |
| 22 | 154 05.4 | 10.7 | 351 21.5 | 13.7 | 8 35.3 | 14.5 | 56.9 |
| 23 | 169 05.3 | 11.4 | 5 54.2 | 13.5 | 8 49.8 | 14.5 | 56.9 |
| 7 00 | 184 05.3 | S16 12.2 | 20 26.7 | 13.6 | N 9 04.3 | 14.4 | 56.9 |
| 01 | 199 05.3 | 12.9 | 34 59.3 | 13.5 | 9 18.7 | 14.4 | 56.9 |
| 02 | 214 05.3 | 13.7 | 49 31.8 | 13.6 | 9 33.1 | 14.3 | 56.8 |
| 03 | 229 05.2 .. | 14.4 | 64 04.4 | 13.5 | 9 47.4 | 14.2 | 56.8 |
| 04 | 244 05.2 | 15.1 | 78 36.9 | 13.4 | 10 01.6 | 14.3 | 56.8 |
| 05 | 259 05.2 | 15.9 | 93 09.3 | 13.5 | 10 15.9 | 14.1 | 56.8 |
| 06 | 274 05.1 | S16 16.6 | 107 41.8 | 13.4 | N10 30.0 | 14.1 | 56.8 |
| 07 | 289 05.1 | 17.4 | 122 14.2 | 13.4 | 10 44.1 | 14.0 | 56.7 |
| 08 | 304 05.1 | 18.1 | 136 46.6 | 13.4 | 10 58.1 | 14.0 | 56.7 |
| M 09 | 319 05.0 .. | 18.8 | 151 19.0 | 13.3 | 11 12.1 | 13.9 | 56.7 |
| O 10 | 334 05.0 | 19.6 | 165 51.3 | 13.4 | 11 26.0 | 13.9 | 56.7 |
| N 11 | 349 05.0 | 20.3 | 180 23.7 | 13.3 | 11 39.9 | 13.8 | 56.6 |
| D 12 | 4 04.9 | S16 21.0 | 194 56.0 | 13.2 | N11 53.7 | 13.7 | 56.6 |
| A 13 | 19 04.9 | 21.8 | 209 28.2 | 13.3 | 12 07.4 | 13.7 | 56.6 |
| Y 14 | 34 04.9 | 22.5 | 224 00.5 | 13.2 | 12 21.1 | 13.6 | 56.6 |
| 15 | 49 04.8 | 23.2 | 238 32.7 | 13.1 | 12 34.7 | 13.5 | 56.6 |
| 16 | 64 04.8 | 24.0 | 253 04.8 | 13.2 | 12 48.2 | 13.5 | 56.5 |
| 17 | 79 04.7 | 24.7 | 267 37.0 | 13.1 | 13 01.7 | 13.4 | 56.5 |
| 18 | 94 04.7 | S16 25.4 | 282 09.1 | 13.1 | N13 15.1 | 13.3 | 56.5 |
| 19 | 109 04.7 | 26.2 | 296 41.2 | 13.0 | 13 28.4 | 13.2 | 56.5 |
| 20 | 124 04.6 | 26.9 | 311 13.2 | 13.0 | 13 41.6 | 13.2 | 56.5 |
| 21 | 139 04.6 .. | 27.6 | 325 45.2 | 13.0 | 13 54.8 | 13.1 | 56.4 |
| 22 | 154 04.6 | 28.4 | 340 17.2 | 12.9 | 14 07.9 | 13.1 | 56.4 |
| 23 | 169 04.5 | 29.1 | 354 49.1 | 12.9 | 14 21.0 | 12.9 | 56.4 |
| 8 00 | 184 04.5 | S16 29.8 | 9 21.0 | 12.9 | N14 33.9 | 12.9 | 56.4 |
| 01 | 199 04.4 | 30.5 | 23 52.9 | 12.8 | 14 46.8 | 12.8 | 56.3 |
| 02 | 214 04.4 | 31.3 | 38 24.7 | 12.8 | 14 59.6 | 12.8 | 56.3 |
| 03 | 229 04.4 .. | 32.0 | 52 56.5 | 12.8 | 15 12.4 | 12.6 | 56.3 |
| 04 | 244 04.3 | 32.7 | 67 28.3 | 12.7 | 15 25.0 | 12.6 | 56.3 |
| 05 | 259 04.3 | 33.4 | 82 00.0 | 12.7 | 15 37.6 | 12.5 | 56.3 |
| 06 | 274 04.2 | S16 34.2 | 96 31.7 | 12.6 | N15 50.1 | 12.4 | 56.2 |
| 07 | 289 04.2 | 34.9 | 111 03.3 | 12.6 | 16 02.5 | 12.3 | 56.2 |
| 08 | 304 04.2 | 35.6 | 125 34.9 | 12.6 | 16 14.8 | 12.2 | 56.2 |
| T 09 | 319 04.1 .. | 36.3 | 140 06.5 | 12.5 | 16 27.0 | 12.2 | 56.2 |
| U 10 | 334 04.1 | 37.1 | 154 38.0 | 12.4 | 16 39.2 | 12.1 | 56.1 |
| E 11 | 349 04.0 | 37.8 | 169 09.4 | 12.5 | 16 51.3 | 12.0 | 56.1 |
| S 12 | 4 04.0 | S16 38.5 | 183 40.9 | 12.4 | N17 03.3 | 11.9 | 56.1 |
| D 13 | 19 03.9 | 39.2 | 198 12.3 | 12.3 | 17 15.2 | 11.8 | 56.1 |
| A 14 | 34 03.9 | 40.0 | 212 43.6 | 12.3 | 17 27.0 | 11.7 | 56.1 |
| Y 15 | 49 03.9 .. | 40.7 | 227 14.9 | 12.3 | 17 38.7 | 11.6 | 56.0 |
| 16 | 64 03.8 | 41.4 | 241 46.2 | 12.2 | 17 50.3 | 11.5 | 56.0 |
| 17 | 79 03.8 | 42.1 | 256 17.4 | 12.1 | 18 01.8 | 11.5 | 56.0 |
| 18 | 94 03.7 | S16 42.8 | 270 48.5 | 12.2 | N18 13.3 | 11.3 | 56.0 |
| 19 | 109 03.7 | 43.6 | 285 19.7 | 12.1 | 18 24.6 | 11.3 | 56.0 |
| 20 | 124 03.6 | 44.3 | 299 50.8 | 12.0 | 18 35.9 | 11.1 | 55.9 |
| 21 | 139 03.6 .. | 45.0 | 314 21.8 | 12.0 | 18 47.0 | 11.1 | 55.9 |
| 22 | 154 03.5 | 45.7 | 328 52.8 | 11.9 | 18 58.1 | 11.0 | 55.9 |
| 23 | 169 03.5 | 46.4 | 343 23.7 | 11.9 | N19 09.1 | 10.8 | 55.9 |
| | SD 16.2 | d 0.7 | SD 15.6 | | 15.4 | | 15.3 |

| Lat. | Naut. | Civil | Sunrise | Moonrise 6 | 7 | 8 | 9 |
|---|---|---|---|---|---|---|---|
| ° | h m | h m | h m | h m | h m | h m | h m |
| N 72 | 06 29 | 07 56 | 09 37 | 14 57 | 14 16 | 13 01 | ▭ |
| N 70 | 06 23 | 07 40 | 09 01 | 15 06 | 14 37 | 13 53 | ▭ |
| 68 | 06 17 | 07 26 | 08 36 | 15 14 | 14 53 | 14 26 | 13 27 |
| 66 | 06 12 | 07 15 | 08 17 | 15 20 | 15 07 | 14 50 | 14 25 |
| 64 | 06 08 | 07 06 | 08 01 | 15 26 | 15 18 | 15 10 | 14 59 |
| 62 | 06 04 | 06 58 | 07 48 | 15 30 | 15 28 | 15 25 | 15 24 |
| 60 | 06 00 | 06 51 | 07 37 | 15 35 | 15 36 | 15 39 | 15 43 |
| N 58 | 05 57 | 06 44 | 07 28 | 15 38 | 15 43 | 15 50 | 16 00 |
| 56 | 05 54 | 06 39 | 07 20 | 15 42 | 15 50 | 16 00 | 16 14 |
| 54 | 05 51 | 06 34 | 07 12 | 15 45 | 15 56 | 16 09 | 16 26 |
| 52 | 05 49 | 06 29 | 07 05 | 15 48 | 16 01 | 16 17 | 16 37 |
| 50 | 05 46 | 06 25 | 06 59 | 15 50 | 16 06 | 16 24 | 16 46 |
| 45 | 05 40 | 06 15 | 06 46 | 15 56 | 16 16 | 16 39 | 17 07 |
| N 40 | 05 35 | 06 07 | 06 36 | 16 00 | 16 25 | 16 52 | 17 23 |
| 35 | 05 30 | 06 00 | 06 27 | 16 04 | 16 32 | 17 03 | 17 37 |
| 30 | 05 25 | 05 53 | 06 18 | 16 08 | 16 39 | 17 12 | 17 49 |
| 20 | 05 15 | 05 41 | 06 04 | 16 14 | 16 50 | 17 29 | 18 10 |
| N 10 | 05 05 | 05 30 | 05 52 | 16 20 | 17 01 | 17 43 | 18 29 |
| 0 | 04 54 | 05 19 | 05 40 | 16 25 | 17 10 | 17 57 | 18 46 |
| S 10 | 04 41 | 05 06 | 05 28 | 16 30 | 17 20 | 18 11 | 19 03 |
| 20 | 04 25 | 04 52 | 05 16 | 16 36 | 17 30 | 18 26 | 19 22 |
| 30 | 04 05 | 04 35 | 05 01 | 16 42 | 17 43 | 18 43 | 19 43 |
| 35 | 03 52 | 04 25 | 04 52 | 16 46 | 17 50 | 18 53 | 19 56 |
| 40 | 03 36 | 04 13 | 04 42 | 16 51 | 17 58 | 19 04 | 20 11 |
| 45 | 03 17 | 03 58 | 04 31 | 16 56 | 18 07 | 19 18 | 20 28 |
| S 50 | 02 51 | 03 39 | 04 17 | 17 02 | 18 18 | 19 35 | 20 50 |
| 52 | 02 38 | 03 30 | 04 10 | 17 05 | 18 24 | 19 43 | 21 00 |
| 54 | 02 23 | 03 20 | 04 03 | 17 08 | 18 29 | 19 51 | 21 12 |
| 56 | 02 04 | 03 08 | 03 54 | 17 11 | 18 36 | 20 01 | 21 26 |
| 58 | 01 40 | 02 55 | 03 45 | 17 15 | 18 43 | 20 13 | 21 42 |
| S 60 | 01 06 | 02 39 | 03 34 | 17 19 | 18 52 | 20 26 | 22 01 |

| Lat. | Sunset | Civil | Naut. | Moonset 6 | 7 | 8 | 9 |
|---|---|---|---|---|---|---|---|
| ° | h m | h m | h m | h m | h m | h m | h m |
| N 72 | 13 49 | 15 29 | 16 56 | 04 56 | 07 13 | 10 07 | ▭ |
| N 70 | 14 25 | 15 46 | 17 03 | 04 50 | 06 54 | 09 16 | ▭ |
| 68 | 14 50 | 16 00 | 17 09 | 04 45 | 06 40 | 08 44 | 11 24 |
| 66 | 15 09 | 16 11 | 17 14 | 04 41 | 06 28 | 08 21 | 10 27 |
| 64 | 15 25 | 16 21 | 17 19 | 04 37 | 06 19 | 08 03 | 09 54 |
| 62 | 15 38 | 16 29 | 17 22 | 04 34 | 06 10 | 07 49 | 09 30 |
| 60 | 15 49 | 16 36 | 17 26 | 04 31 | 06 03 | 07 36 | 09 11 |
| N 58 | 15 59 | 16 42 | 17 29 | 04 29 | 05 57 | 07 26 | 08 55 |
| 56 | 16 07 | 16 48 | 17 32 | 04 27 | 05 52 | 07 17 | 08 42 |
| 54 | 16 15 | 16 53 | 17 35 | 04 25 | 05 47 | 07 09 | 08 30 |
| 52 | 16 21 | 16 58 | 17 38 | 04 23 | 05 42 | 07 01 | 08 20 |
| 50 | 16 27 | 17 02 | 17 40 | 04 22 | 05 38 | 06 55 | 08 11 |
| 45 | 16 40 | 17 11 | 17 46 | 04 18 | 05 30 | 06 41 | 07 52 |
| N 40 | 16 51 | 17 20 | 17 52 | 04 16 | 05 23 | 06 30 | 07 36 |
| 35 | 17 00 | 17 27 | 17 57 | 04 13 | 05 17 | 06 20 | 07 23 |
| 30 | 17 09 | 17 34 | 18 02 | 04 11 | 05 11 | 06 11 | 07 12 |
| 20 | 17 23 | 17 46 | 18 12 | 04 08 | 05 02 | 05 57 | 06 53 |
| N 10 | 17 35 | 17 57 | 18 22 | 04 04 | 04 54 | 05 44 | 06 36 |
| 0 | 17 47 | 18 09 | 18 34 | 04 01 | 04 46 | 05 33 | 06 20 |
| S 10 | 17 59 | 18 21 | 18 47 | 03 58 | 04 39 | 05 21 | 06 05 |
| 20 | 18 12 | 18 35 | 19 03 | 03 55 | 04 31 | 05 08 | 05 48 |
| 30 | 18 27 | 18 53 | 19 23 | 03 52 | 04 22 | 04 54 | 05 29 |
| 35 | 18 36 | 19 03 | 19 36 | 03 49 | 04 17 | 04 46 | 05 18 |
| 40 | 18 46 | 19 15 | 19 52 | 03 47 | 04 11 | 04 37 | 05 06 |
| 45 | 18 57 | 19 30 | 20 12 | 03 44 | 04 04 | 04 26 | 04 51 |
| S 50 | 19 12 | 19 49 | 20 38 | 03 41 | 03 56 | 04 13 | 04 37 |
| 52 | 19 19 | 19 59 | 20 51 | 03 40 | 03 52 | 04 07 | 04 24 |
| 54 | 19 26 | 20 09 | 21 07 | 03 38 | 03 48 | 04 00 | 04 15 |
| 56 | 19 34 | 20 21 | 21 26 | 03 36 | 03 44 | 03 53 | 04 04 |
| 58 | 19 44 | 20 35 | 21 51 | 03 34 | 03 39 | 03 44 | 03 52 |
| S 60 | 19 55 | 20 51 | 22 28 | 03 32 | 03 33 | 03 35 | 03 35 |

| Day | SUN Eqn. of Time 00h | 12h | Mer. Pass. | MOON Mer. Pass. Upper | Lower | Age | Phase |
|---|---|---|---|---|---|---|---|
| d | m s | m s | h m | h m | h m | d | % |
| 6 | 16 24 | 16 23 | 11 44 | 22 36 | 10 13 | 12 | 96 |
| 7 | 16 21 | 16 20 | 11 44 | 23 21 | 10 58 | 13 | 99 |
| 8 | 16 18 | 16 16 | 11 44 | 24 09 | 11 45 | 14 | 100 |

| UT | ARIES GHA | VENUS −3.9 GHA | Dec | MARS −1.4 GHA | Dec | JUPITER −2.7 GHA | Dec | SATURN +0.6 GHA | Dec | STARS Name | SHA | Dec |
|---|---|---|---|---|---|---|---|---|---|---|---|---|
| d h | ° ′ | ° ′ | ° ′ | ° ′ | ° ′ | ° ′ | ° ′ | ° ′ | ° ′ | | ° ′ | ° ′ |
| 9 00 | 48 08.9 | 179 32.8 | S17 30.2 | 323 40.2 | N24 14.2 | 48 17.5 | S 1 43.4 | 86 28.5 | S16 23.9 | Acamar | 315 12.7 | S40 12.8 |
| 01 | 63 11.4 | 194 32.1 | 31.1 | 338 43.0 | 14.3 | 63 20.1 | 43.4 | 101 30.8 | 23.9 | Achernar | 335 21.0 | S57 07.4 |
| 02 | 78 13.8 | 209 31.4 | 32.0 | 353 45.9 | 14.4 | 78 22.6 | 43.5 | 116 33.2 | 23.8 | Acrux | 173 02.6 | S63 13.2 |
| 03 | 93 16.3 | 224 30.8 .. | 32.9 | 8 48.7 .. | 14.5 | 93 25.2 .. | 43.5 | 131 35.6 .. | 23.8 | Adhara | 255 07.1 | S28 59.9 |
| 04 | 108 18.8 | 239 30.1 | 33.8 | 23 51.6 | 14.7 | 108 27.8 | 43.5 | 146 38.0 | 23.8 | Aldebaran | 290 41.4 | N16 33.3 |
| 05 | 123 21.2 | 254 29.4 | 34.7 | 38 54.4 | 14.8 | 123 30.4 | 43.6 | 161 40.4 | 23.8 | | | |
| W 06 | 138 23.7 | 269 28.7 | S17 35.6 | 53 57.3 | N24 14.9 | 138 33.0 | S 1 43.6 | 176 42.8 | S16 23.7 | Alioth | 166 15.1 | N55 50.1 |
| E 07 | 153 26.2 | 284 28.0 | 36.6 | 69 00.1 | 15.0 | 153 35.6 | 43.7 | 191 45.2 | 23.7 | Alkaid | 152 53.9 | N49 12.0 |
| D 08 | 168 28.6 | 299 27.3 | 37.5 | 84 03.0 | 15.1 | 168 38.1 | 43.7 | 206 47.6 | 23.7 | Alnair | 27 35.1 | S46 51.3 |
| N 09 | 183 31.1 | 314 26.7 .. | 38.4 | 99 05.9 .. | 15.2 | 183 40.7 .. | 43.7 | 221 50.0 .. | 23.7 | Alnilam | 275 39.3 | S 1 11.1 |
| E 10 | 198 33.6 | 329 26.0 | 39.3 | 114 08.7 | 15.3 | 198 43.3 | 43.8 | 236 52.4 | 23.6 | Alphard | 217 49.6 | S 8 45.2 |
| S 11 | 213 36.0 | 344 25.3 | 40.2 | 129 11.6 | 15.4 | 213 45.9 | 43.8 | 251 54.8 | 23.6 | | | |
| D 12 | 228 38.5 | 359 24.6 | S17 41.1 | 144 14.5 | N24 15.5 | 228 48.5 | S 1 43.9 | 266 57.2 | S16 23.6 | Alphecca | 126 05.7 | N26 38.4 |
| A 13 | 243 41.0 | 14 23.9 | 42.0 | 159 17.3 | 15.7 | 243 51.1 | 43.9 | 281 59.6 | 23.6 | Alpheratz | 357 36.4 | N29 13.1 |
| Y 14 | 258 43.4 | 29 23.2 | 42.9 | 174 20.2 | 15.8 | 258 53.6 | 43.9 | 297 02.0 | 23.5 | Altair | 62 01.9 | N 8 55.8 |
| 15 | 273 45.9 | 44 22.5 .. | 43.8 | 189 23.1 .. | 15.9 | 273 56.2 .. | 44.0 | 312 04.3 .. | 23.5 | Ankaa | 353 08.6 | S42 11.1 |
| 16 | 288 48.3 | 59 21.8 | 44.7 | 204 25.9 | 16.0 | 288 58.8 | 44.0 | 327 06.7 | 23.5 | Antares | 112 18.4 | S26 28.9 |
| 17 | 303 50.8 | 74 21.1 | 45.6 | 219 28.8 | 16.1 | 304 01.4 | 44.1 | 342 09.1 | 23.5 | | | |
| 18 | 318 53.3 | 89 20.5 | S17 46.5 | 234 31.7 | N24 16.2 | 319 04.0 | S 1 44.1 | 357 11.5 | S16 23.4 | Arcturus | 145 49.9 | N19 03.9 |
| 19 | 333 55.7 | 104 19.8 | 47.4 | 249 34.6 | 16.3 | 334 06.5 | 44.1 | 12 13.9 | 23.4 | Atria | 107 14.8 | S69 04.1 |
| 20 | 348 58.2 | 119 19.1 | 48.3 | 264 37.4 | 16.4 | 349 09.1 | 44.2 | 27 16.3 | 23.4 | Avior | 234 15.3 | S59 34.6 |
| 21 | 4 00.7 | 134 18.4 .. | 49.2 | 279 40.3 .. | 16.5 | 4 11.7 .. | 44.2 | 42 18.7 .. | 23.4 | Bellatrix | 278 24.5 | N 6 22.3 |
| 22 | 19 03.1 | 149 17.7 | 50.1 | 294 43.2 | 16.7 | 19 14.3 | 44.2 | 57 21.1 | 23.3 | Betelgeuse | 270 53.8 | N 7 24.7 |
| 23 | 34 05.6 | 164 17.0 | 51.0 | 309 46.1 | 16.8 | 34 16.8 | 44.3 | 72 23.5 | 23.3 | | | |
| 10 00 | 49 08.1 | 179 16.3 | S17 51.9 | 324 49.0 | N24 16.9 | 49 19.4 | S 1 44.3 | 87 25.9 | S16 23.3 | Canopus | 263 52.8 | S52 42.2 |
| 01 | 64 10.5 | 194 15.6 | 52.8 | 339 51.9 | 17.0 | 64 22.0 | 44.4 | 102 28.3 | 23.2 | Capella | 280 24.2 | N46 01.2 |
| 02 | 79 13.0 | 209 14.9 | 53.7 | 354 54.7 | 17.1 | 79 24.6 | 44.4 | 117 30.6 | 23.2 | Deneb | 49 27.1 | N45 21.9 |
| 03 | 94 15.5 | 224 14.2 .. | 54.6 | 9 57.6 .. | 17.2 | 94 27.2 .. | 44.4 | 132 33.0 .. | 23.2 | Denebola | 182 27.0 | N14 26.8 |
| 04 | 109 17.9 | 239 13.5 | 55.5 | 25 00.5 | 17.3 | 109 29.7 | 44.5 | 147 35.4 | 23.2 | Diphda | 348 48.9 | S17 51.7 |
| 05 | 124 20.4 | 254 12.8 | 56.4 | 40 03.4 | 17.4 | 124 32.3 | 44.5 | 162 37.8 | 23.1 | | | |
| T 06 | 139 22.8 | 269 12.1 | S17 57.2 | 55 06.3 | N24 17.5 | 139 34.9 | S 1 44.5 | 177 40.2 | S16 23.1 | Dubhe | 193 43.6 | N61 37.5 |
| H 07 | 154 25.3 | 284 11.4 | 58.1 | 70 09.2 | 17.6 | 154 37.5 | 44.6 | 192 42.6 | 23.1 | Elnath | 278 03.8 | N28 37.6 |
| U 08 | 169 27.8 | 299 10.7 | 59.0 | 85 12.1 | 17.8 | 169 40.0 | 44.6 | 207 45.0 | 23.1 | Eltanin | 90 43.4 | N51 29.3 |
| R 09 | 184 30.2 | 314 10.0 | 17 59.9 | 100 15.0 .. | 17.9 | 184 42.6 .. | 44.7 | 222 47.4 .. | 23.0 | Enif | 33 40.5 | N 9 58.9 |
| S 10 | 199 32.7 | 329 09.3 | 18 00.8 | 115 17.9 | 18.0 | 199 45.2 | 44.7 | 237 49.8 | 23.0 | Fomalhaut | 15 16.4 | S29 30.2 |
| D 11 | 214 35.2 | 344 08.6 | 01.7 | 130 20.8 | 18.1 | 214 47.8 | 44.7 | 252 52.1 | 23.0 | | | |
| A 12 | 229 37.6 | 359 07.9 | S18 02.6 | 145 23.7 | N24 18.2 | 229 50.3 | S 1 44.8 | 267 54.5 | S16 23.0 | Gacrux | 171 54.1 | S57 14.1 |
| Y 13 | 244 40.1 | 14 07.2 | 03.5 | 160 26.6 | 18.3 | 244 52.9 | 44.8 | 282 56.9 | 22.9 | Gienah | 175 45.7 | S17 39.9 |
| 14 | 259 42.6 | 29 06.5 | 04.3 | 175 29.5 | 18.4 | 259 55.5 | 44.8 | 297 59.3 | 22.9 | Hadar | 148 39.2 | S60 28.8 |
| 15 | 274 45.0 | 44 05.8 .. | 05.2 | 190 32.4 .. | 18.5 | 274 58.1 .. | 44.9 | 313 01.7 .. | 22.9 | Hamal | 327 52.9 | N23 34.3 |
| 16 | 289 47.5 | 59 05.1 | 06.1 | 205 35.4 | 18.6 | 290 00.6 | 44.9 | 328 04.1 | 22.9 | Kaus Aust. | 83 35.2 | S34 22.5 |
| 17 | 304 49.9 | 74 04.4 | 07.0 | 220 38.3 | 18.7 | 305 03.2 | 44.9 | 343 06.5 | 22.8 | | | |
| 18 | 319 52.4 | 89 03.7 | S18 07.9 | 235 41.2 | N24 18.9 | 320 05.8 | S 1 45.0 | 358 08.9 | S16 22.8 | Kochab | 137 21.0 | N74 03.7 |
| 19 | 334 54.9 | 104 03.0 | 08.7 | 250 44.1 | 19.0 | 335 08.3 | 45.0 | 13 11.2 | 22.8 | Markab | 13 31.6 | N15 19.8 |
| 20 | 349 57.3 | 119 02.3 | 09.6 | 265 47.0 | 19.1 | 350 10.9 | 45.0 | 28 13.6 | 22.7 | Menkar | 314 07.7 | N 4 10.8 |
| 21 | 4 59.8 | 134 01.6 .. | 10.5 | 280 49.9 .. | 19.2 | 5 13.5 .. | 45.1 | 43 16.0 .. | 22.7 | Menkent | 148 00.2 | S36 28.7 |
| 22 | 20 02.3 | 149 00.9 | 11.4 | 295 52.9 | 19.3 | 20 16.1 | 45.1 | 58 18.4 | 22.7 | Miaplacidus | 221 38.6 | S69 48.2 |
| 23 | 35 04.7 | 164 00.2 | 12.3 | 310 55.8 | 19.4 | 35 18.6 | 45.2 | 73 20.8 | 22.7 | | | |
| 11 00 | 50 07.2 | 178 59.5 | S18 13.1 | 325 58.7 | N24 19.5 | 50 21.2 | S 1 45.2 | 88 23.2 | S16 22.6 | Mirfak | 308 30.3 | N49 56.5 |
| 01 | 65 09.7 | 193 58.8 | 14.0 | 341 01.6 | 19.6 | 65 23.8 | 45.2 | 103 25.6 | 22.6 | Nunki | 75 50.2 | S26 16.1 |
| 02 | 80 12.1 | 208 58.1 | 14.9 | 356 04.6 | 19.7 | 80 26.3 | 45.3 | 118 27.9 | 22.6 | Peacock | 53 08.7 | S56 39.9 |
| 03 | 95 14.6 | 223 57.4 .. | 15.8 | 11 07.5 .. | 19.8 | 95 28.9 .. | 45.3 | 133 30.3 .. | 22.6 | Pollux | 243 19.4 | N27 58.2 |
| 04 | 110 17.1 | 238 56.6 | 16.6 | 26 10.4 | 20.0 | 110 31.5 | 45.3 | 148 32.7 | 22.5 | Procyon | 244 52.6 | N 5 10.1 |
| 05 | 125 19.5 | 253 55.9 | 17.5 | 41 13.4 | 20.1 | 125 34.0 | 45.4 | 163 35.1 | 22.5 | | | |
| F 06 | 140 22.0 | 268 55.2 | S18 18.4 | 56 16.3 | N24 20.2 | 140 36.6 | S 1 45.4 | 178 37.5 | S16 22.5 | Rasalhague | 96 00.5 | N12 32.7 |
| R 07 | 155 24.4 | 283 54.5 | 19.2 | 71 19.2 | 20.3 | 155 39.2 | 45.4 | 193 39.9 | 22.4 | Regulus | 207 36.5 | N11 51.4 |
| I 08 | 170 26.9 | 298 53.8 | 20.1 | 86 22.2 | 20.4 | 170 41.7 | 45.5 | 208 42.2 | 22.4 | Rigel | 281 05.3 | S 8 10.4 |
| D 09 | 185 29.4 | 313 53.1 .. | 21.0 | 101 25.1 .. | 20.5 | 185 44.3 .. | 45.5 | 223 44.6 .. | 22.4 | Rigil Kent. | 139 43.5 | S60 55.6 |
| A 10 | 200 31.8 | 328 52.4 | 21.8 | 116 28.1 | 20.6 | 200 46.9 | 45.5 | 238 47.0 | 22.4 | Sabik | 102 05.2 | S15 45.1 |
| Y 11 | 215 34.3 | 343 51.7 | 22.7 | 131 31.0 | 20.7 | 215 49.4 | 45.6 | 253 49.4 | 22.3 | | | |
| 12 | 230 36.8 | 358 51.0 | S18 23.6 | 146 33.9 | N24 20.8 | 230 52.0 | S 1 45.6 | 268 51.8 | S16 22.3 | Schedar | 349 32.6 | N56 39.9 |
| 13 | 245 39.2 | 13 50.2 | 24.4 | 161 36.9 | 20.9 | 245 54.6 | 45.6 | 283 54.2 | 22.3 | Shaula | 96 13.2 | S37 07.2 |
| 14 | 260 41.7 | 28 49.5 | 25.3 | 176 39.8 | 21.0 | 260 57.1 | 45.7 | 298 56.6 | 22.2 | Sirius | 258 27.6 | S16 44.7 |
| 15 | 275 44.2 | 43 48.8 .. | 26.2 | 191 42.8 .. | 21.2 | 275 59.7 .. | 45.7 | 313 58.9 .. | 22.2 | Spica | 158 24.5 | S11 16.6 |
| 16 | 290 46.6 | 58 48.1 | 27.0 | 206 45.7 | 21.3 | 291 02.3 | 45.7 | 329 01.3 | 22.2 | Suhail | 222 47.6 | S43 31.1 |
| 17 | 305 49.1 | 73 47.4 | 27.9 | 221 48.7 | 21.4 | 306 04.8 | 45.8 | 344 03.7 | 22.2 | | | |
| 18 | 320 51.6 | 88 46.7 | S18 28.7 | 236 51.7 | N24 21.5 | 321 07.4 | S 1 45.8 | 359 06.1 | S16 22.1 | Vega | 80 34.7 | N38 48.5 |
| 19 | 335 54.0 | 103 45.9 | 29.6 | 251 54.6 | 21.6 | 336 10.0 | 45.8 | 14 08.5 | 22.1 | Zuben'ubi | 136 58.4 | S16 08.0 |
| 20 | 350 56.5 | 118 45.2 | 30.5 | 266 57.6 | 21.7 | 351 12.5 | 45.8 | 29 10.9 | 22.1 | | SHA | Mer. Pass. |
| 21 | 5 58.9 | 133 44.5 .. | 31.3 | 282 00.5 .. | 21.8 | 6 15.1 .. | 45.9 | 44 13.2 .. | 22.0 | | ° ′ | h m |
| 22 | 21 01.4 | 148 43.8 | 32.2 | 297 03.5 | 21.9 | 21 17.7 | 45.9 | 59 15.6 | 22.0 | Venus | 130 08.2 | 12 03 |
| 23 | 36 03.9 | 163 43.1 | 33.0 | 312 06.5 | 22.0 | 36 20.2 | 45.9 | 74 18.0 | 22.0 | Mars | 275 40.9 | 2 20 |
| | h m | | | | | | | | | Jupiter | 0 11.4 | 20 39 |
| Mer. Pass. 20 40.1 | v −0.7 d 0.9 | v 2.9 d 0.1 | | v 2.6 d 0.0 | | v 2.4 d 0.0 | | | | Saturn | 38 17.8 | 18 07 |

| UT | SUN GHA | SUN Dec | MOON GHA | v | MOON Dec | d | HP |
|---|---|---|---|---|---|---|---|
| **d h** | ° ′ | ° ′ | ° ′ | ′ | ° ′ | ′ | ′ |
| **9 00** | 184 03.4 | S16 47.2 | 357 54.6 | 11.9 | N19 19.9 | 10.8 | 55.8 |
| 01 | 199 03.4 | 47.9 | 12 25.5 | 11.8 | 19 30.7 | 10.7 | 55.8 |
| 02 | 214 03.3 | 48.6 | 26 56.3 | 11.8 | 19 41.4 | 10.5 | 55.8 |
| 03 | 229 03.3 | .. 49.3 | 41 27.1 | 11.7 | 19 51.9 | 10.5 | 55.8 |
| 04 | 244 03.2 | 50.0 | 55 57.8 | 11.7 | 20 02.4 | 10.4 | 55.8 |
| 05 | 259 03.2 | 50.7 | 70 28.5 | 11.6 | 20 12.8 | 10.2 | 55.7 |
| **06** | 274 03.1 | S16 51.4 | 84 59.1 | 11.6 | N20 23.0 | 10.2 | 55.7 |
| W 07 | 289 03.1 | 52.2 | 99 29.7 | 11.6 | 20 33.2 | 10.0 | 55.7 |
| E 08 | 304 03.0 | 52.9 | 114 00.3 | 11.5 | 20 43.2 | 10.0 | 55.7 |
| D 09 | 319 03.0 | .. 53.6 | 128 30.8 | 11.4 | 20 53.2 | 9.8 | 55.7 |
| N 10 | 334 02.9 | 54.3 | 143 01.2 | 11.4 | 21 03.0 | 9.7 | 55.6 |
| E 11 | 349 02.9 | 55.0 | 157 31.6 | 11.4 | 21 12.7 | 9.6 | 55.6 |
| S 12 | 4 02.8 | S16 55.7 | 172 02.0 | 11.3 | N21 22.3 | 9.5 | 55.6 |
| D 13 | 19 02.8 | 56.4 | 186 32.3 | 11.3 | 21 31.8 | 9.4 | 55.6 |
| A 14 | 34 02.7 | 57.1 | 201 02.6 | 11.2 | 21 41.2 | 9.3 | 55.6 |
| Y 15 | 49 02.7 | .. 57.8 | 215 32.8 | 11.2 | 21 50.5 | 9.2 | 55.5 |
| 16 | 64 02.6 | 58.6 | 230 03.0 | 11.1 | 21 59.7 | 9.1 | 55.5 |
| 17 | 79 02.6 | 16 59.3 | 244 33.1 | 11.1 | 22 08.8 | 8.9 | 55.5 |
| 18 | 94 02.5 | S17 00.0 | 259 03.2 | 11.1 | N22 17.7 | 8.9 | 55.5 |
| 19 | 109 02.5 | 00.7 | 273 33.3 | 11.0 | 22 26.6 | 8.7 | 55.5 |
| 20 | 124 02.4 | 01.4 | 288 03.3 | 11.0 | 22 35.3 | 8.6 | 55.4 |
| 21 | 139 02.4 | .. 02.1 | 302 33.3 | 10.9 | 22 43.9 | 8.5 | 55.4 |
| 22 | 154 02.3 | 02.8 | 317 03.2 | 10.9 | 22 52.4 | 8.4 | 55.4 |
| 23 | 169 02.2 | 03.5 | 331 33.1 | 10.8 | 23 00.8 | 8.2 | 55.4 |
| **10 00** | 184 02.2 | S17 04.2 | 346 02.9 | 10.8 | N23 09.0 | 8.1 | 55.4 |
| 01 | 199 02.1 | 04.9 | 0 32.7 | 10.8 | 23 17.1 | 8.1 | 55.3 |
| 02 | 214 02.1 | 05.6 | 15 02.5 | 10.7 | 23 25.2 | 7.9 | 55.3 |
| 03 | 229 02.0 | .. 06.3 | 29 32.2 | 10.7 | 23 33.1 | 7.7 | 55.3 |
| 04 | 244 02.0 | 07.0 | 44 01.9 | 10.6 | 23 40.8 | 7.7 | 55.3 |
| 05 | 259 01.9 | 07.7 | 58 31.5 | 10.6 | 23 48.5 | 7.5 | 55.3 |
| **06** | 274 01.8 | S17 08.4 | 73 01.1 | 10.6 | N23 56.0 | 7.4 | 55.2 |
| T 07 | 289 01.8 | 09.1 | 87 30.7 | 10.5 | 24 03.4 | 7.3 | 55.2 |
| H 08 | 304 01.7 | 09.8 | 102 00.2 | 10.5 | 24 10.7 | 7.2 | 55.2 |
| U 09 | 319 01.7 | .. 10.5 | 116 29.7 | 10.4 | 24 17.9 | 7.0 | 55.2 |
| R 10 | 334 01.6 | 11.2 | 130 59.1 | 10.5 | 24 24.9 | 7.0 | 55.2 |
| S 11 | 349 01.5 | 11.9 | 145 28.6 | 10.3 | 24 31.9 | 6.8 | 55.1 |
| D 12 | 4 01.5 | S17 12.6 | 159 57.9 | 10.4 | N24 38.7 | 6.6 | 55.1 |
| A 13 | 19 01.4 | 13.3 | 174 27.3 | 10.3 | 24 45.3 | 6.6 | 55.1 |
| Y 14 | 34 01.4 | 14.0 | 188 56.6 | 10.3 | 24 51.9 | 6.4 | 55.1 |
| 15 | 49 01.3 | .. 14.7 | 203 25.9 | 10.2 | 24 58.3 | 6.3 | 55.1 |
| 16 | 64 01.2 | 15.4 | 217 55.1 | 10.2 | 25 04.6 | 6.1 | 55.0 |
| 17 | 79 01.2 | 16.1 | 232 24.3 | 10.2 | 25 10.7 | 6.0 | 55.0 |
| 18 | 94 01.1 | S17 16.8 | 246 53.5 | 10.1 | N25 16.7 | 5.9 | 55.0 |
| 19 | 109 01.0 | 17.5 | 261 22.6 | 10.2 | 25 22.6 | 5.8 | 55.0 |
| 20 | 124 01.0 | 18.2 | 275 51.8 | 10.1 | 25 28.4 | 5.6 | 55.0 |
| 21 | 139 00.9 | .. 18.9 | 290 20.9 | 10.0 | 25 34.0 | 5.6 | 55.0 |
| 22 | 154 00.8 | 19.6 | 304 49.9 | 10.1 | 25 39.6 | 5.3 | 54.9 |
| 23 | 169 00.8 | 20.3 | 319 19.0 | 10.0 | 25 44.9 | 5.3 | 54.9 |
| **11 00** | 184 00.7 | S17 21.0 | 333 48.0 | 10.0 | N25 50.2 | 5.1 | 54.9 |
| 01 | 199 00.7 | 21.7 | 348 17.0 | 9.9 | 25 55.3 | 5.0 | 54.9 |
| 02 | 214 00.6 | 22.4 | 2 45.9 | 9.9 | 26 00.3 | 4.8 | 54.9 |
| 03 | 229 00.5 | .. 23.1 | 17 14.8 | 10.0 | 26 05.1 | 4.8 | 54.9 |
| 04 | 244 00.5 | 23.7 | 31 43.8 | 9.9 | 26 09.9 | 4.6 | 54.8 |
| 05 | 259 00.4 | 24.4 | 46 12.7 | 9.8 | 26 14.5 | 4.4 | 54.8 |
| **06** | 274 00.3 | S17 25.1 | 60 41.5 | 9.9 | N26 18.9 | 4.3 | 54.8 |
| F 07 | 289 00.2 | 25.8 | 75 10.4 | 9.8 | 26 23.2 | 4.2 | 54.8 |
| R 08 | 304 00.2 | 26.5 | 89 39.2 | 9.8 | 26 27.4 | 4.1 | 54.8 |
| I 09 | 319 00.1 | .. 27.2 | 104 08.0 | 9.8 | 26 31.5 | 3.9 | 54.8 |
| D 10 | 334 00.0 | 27.9 | 118 36.8 | 9.8 | 26 35.4 | 3.8 | 54.7 |
| A 11 | 349 00.0 | 28.6 | 133 05.6 | 9.8 | 26 39.2 | 3.6 | 54.7 |
| Y 12 | 3 59.9 | S17 29.3 | 147 34.4 | 9.7 | N26 42.8 | 3.5 | 54.7 |
| 13 | 18 59.8 | 29.9 | 162 03.1 | 9.8 | 26 46.3 | 3.4 | 54.7 |
| 14 | 33 59.8 | 30.6 | 176 31.9 | 9.7 | 26 49.7 | 3.3 | 54.7 |
| 15 | 48 59.7 | .. 31.3 | 191 00.6 | 9.7 | 26 53.0 | 3.1 | 54.7 |
| 16 | 63 59.6 | 32.0 | 205 29.3 | 9.7 | 26 56.1 | 2.9 | 54.6 |
| 17 | 78 59.5 | 32.7 | 219 58.0 | 9.7 | 26 59.0 | 2.9 | 54.6 |
| 18 | 93 59.5 | S17 33.4 | 234 26.7 | 9.7 | N27 01.9 | 2.7 | 54.6 |
| 19 | 108 59.4 | 34.0 | 248 55.4 | 9.7 | 27 04.6 | 2.5 | 54.6 |
| 20 | 123 59.3 | 34.7 | 263 24.1 | 9.7 | 27 07.1 | 2.5 | 54.6 |
| 21 | 138 59.3 | .. 35.4 | 277 52.8 | 9.7 | 27 09.6 | 2.3 | 54.6 |
| 22 | 153 59.2 | 36.1 | 292 21.5 | 9.7 | 27 11.9 | 2.1 | 54.6 |
| 23 | 168 59.1 | 36.8 | 306 50.2 | 9.7 | N27 14.0 | 2.0 | 54.5 |
| | SD 16.2 | d 0.7 | SD 15.1 | | 15.0 | | 14.9 |

| Lat. | Twilight Naut. | Twilight Civil | Sunrise | Moonrise 9 | 10 | 11 | 12 |
|---|---|---|---|---|---|---|---|
| ° | h m | h m | h m | h m | h m | h m | h m |
| N 72 | 06 41 | 08 10 | 10 02 | □ | □ | □ | □ |
| N 70 | 06 33 | 07 52 | 09 18 | □ | □ | □ | □ |
| 68 | 06 26 | 07 37 | 08 50 | 13 27 | □ | □ | □ |
| 66 | 06 20 | 07 24 | 08 28 | 14 25 | □ | □ | □ |
| 64 | 06 15 | 07 14 | 08 11 | 14 59 | 14 39 | □ | □ |
| 62 | 06 11 | 07 05 | 07 57 | 15 24 | 15 24 | 15 29 | 15 59 |
| 60 | 06 07 | 06 58 | 07 45 | 15 43 | 15 53 | 16 14 | 16 55 |
| N 58 | 06 03 | 06 51 | 07 35 | 16 00 | 16 16 | 16 43 | 17 27 |
| 56 | 06 00 | 06 45 | 07 26 | 16 14 | 16 34 | 17 05 | 17 51 |
| 54 | 05 56 | 06 39 | 07 18 | 16 26 | 16 50 | 17 24 | 18 11 |
| 52 | 05 53 | 06 34 | 07 11 | 16 37 | 17 03 | 17 39 | 18 27 |
| 50 | 05 51 | 06 29 | 07 04 | 16 46 | 17 15 | 17 53 | 18 41 |
| 45 | 05 44 | 06 19 | 06 51 | 17 07 | 17 40 | 18 21 | 19 10 |
| N 40 | 05 38 | 06 11 | 06 39 | 17 23 | 18 00 | 18 43 | 19 33 |
| 35 | 05 32 | 06 03 | 06 29 | 17 37 | 18 16 | 19 01 | 19 51 |
| 30 | 05 27 | 05 56 | 06 21 | 17 49 | 18 31 | 19 17 | 20 07 |
| 20 | 05 16 | 05 43 | 06 06 | 18 10 | 18 55 | 19 43 | 20 34 |
| N 10 | 05 06 | 05 31 | 05 53 | 18 29 | 19 16 | 20 06 | 20 58 |
| 0 | 04 54 | 05 19 | 05 40 | 18 46 | 19 36 | 20 28 | 21 20 |
| S 10 | 04 40 | 05 06 | 05 28 | 19 03 | 19 56 | 20 49 | 21 41 |
| 20 | 04 23 | 04 51 | 05 14 | 19 22 | 20 18 | 21 12 | 22 05 |
| 30 | 04 02 | 04 33 | 04 59 | 19 43 | 20 43 | 21 39 | 22 32 |
| 35 | 03 49 | 04 22 | 04 50 | 19 56 | 20 57 | 21 55 | 22 48 |
| 40 | 03 33 | 04 09 | 04 39 | 20 11 | 21 15 | 22 14 | 23 07 |
| 45 | 03 12 | 03 54 | 04 27 | 20 28 | 21 35 | 22 36 | 23 29 |
| S 50 | 02 45 | 03 34 | 04 12 | 20 50 | 22 01 | 23 05 | 23 58 |
| 52 | 02 31 | 03 24 | 04 05 | 21 00 | 22 14 | 23 19 | 24 12 |
| 54 | 02 14 | 03 14 | 03 57 | 21 12 | 22 29 | 23 36 | 24 29 |
| 56 | 01 53 | 03 01 | 03 48 | 21 26 | 22 46 | 23 55 | 24 48 |
| 58 | 01 26 | 02 47 | 03 38 | 21 42 | 23 06 | 24 19 | 00 19 |
| S 60 | 00 43 | 02 29 | 03 27 | 22 01 | 23 33 | 24 52 | 00 52 |

| Lat. | Sunset | Twilight Civil | Twilight Naut. | Moonset 9 | 10 | 11 | 12 |
|---|---|---|---|---|---|---|---|
| ° | h m | h m | h m | h m | h m | h m | h m |
| N 72 | 13 25 | 15 16 | 16 46 | □ | □ | □ | □ |
| N 70 | 14 08 | 15 35 | 16 54 | □ | □ | □ | □ |
| 68 | 14 37 | 15 50 | 17 01 | 11 24 | □ | □ | □ |
| 66 | 14 59 | 16 02 | 17 06 | 10 27 | □ | □ | □ |
| 64 | 15 16 | 16 13 | 17 12 | 09 54 | 11 58 | □ | □ |
| 62 | 15 30 | 16 22 | 17 16 | 09 30 | 11 14 | 12 55 | 14 13 |
| 60 | 15 42 | 16 29 | 17 20 | 09 11 | 10 45 | 12 11 | 13 18 |
| N 58 | 15 52 | 16 36 | 17 24 | 08 55 | 10 22 | 11 42 | 12 46 |
| 56 | 16 01 | 16 42 | 17 27 | 08 42 | 10 04 | 11 20 | 12 21 |
| 54 | 16 09 | 16 48 | 17 31 | 08 30 | 09 49 | 11 01 | 12 02 |
| 52 | 16 16 | 16 53 | 17 34 | 08 20 | 09 36 | 10 46 | 11 45 |
| 50 | 16 23 | 16 58 | 17 37 | 08 11 | 09 25 | 10 33 | 11 31 |
| 45 | 16 37 | 17 08 | 17 43 | 07 52 | 09 01 | 10 05 | 11 02 |
| N 40 | 16 48 | 17 17 | 17 49 | 07 36 | 08 42 | 09 44 | 10 40 |
| 35 | 16 58 | 17 25 | 17 55 | 07 23 | 08 26 | 09 26 | 10 21 |
| 30 | 17 07 | 17 32 | 18 00 | 07 12 | 08 12 | 09 10 | 10 05 |
| 20 | 17 22 | 17 45 | 18 11 | 06 53 | 07 49 | 08 44 | 09 38 |
| N 10 | 17 35 | 17 57 | 18 22 | 06 36 | 07 29 | 08 22 | 09 15 |
| 0 | 17 47 | 18 09 | 18 34 | 06 20 | 07 10 | 08 01 | 08 53 |
| S 10 | 18 00 | 18 22 | 18 48 | 06 05 | 06 51 | 07 40 | 08 31 |
| 20 | 18 14 | 18 37 | 19 05 | 05 48 | 06 31 | 07 18 | 08 08 |
| 30 | 18 29 | 18 55 | 19 26 | 05 29 | 06 08 | 06 52 | 07 40 |
| 35 | 18 39 | 19 06 | 19 40 | 05 18 | 05 55 | 06 37 | 07 24 |
| 40 | 18 49 | 19 19 | 19 56 | 05 06 | 05 39 | 06 19 | 07 06 |
| 45 | 19 02 | 19 35 | 20 17 | 04 51 | 05 21 | 05 58 | 06 43 |
| S 50 | 19 17 | 19 55 | 20 45 | 04 33 | 04 58 | 05 31 | 06 14 |
| 52 | 19 24 | 20 05 | 20 59 | 04 24 | 04 47 | 05 18 | 06 00 |
| 54 | 19 32 | 20 16 | 21 16 | 04 15 | 04 35 | 05 03 | 05 43 |
| 56 | 19 41 | 20 28 | 21 38 | 04 04 | 04 21 | 04 46 | 05 23 |
| 58 | 19 51 | 20 43 | 22 06 | 03 52 | 04 04 | 04 25 | 05 00 |
| S 60 | 20 03 | 21 01 | 22 54 | 03 38 | 03 45 | 03 58 | 04 27 |

| Day | SUN Eqn. of Time 00h | SUN Eqn. of Time 12h | SUN Mer. Pass. | MOON Mer. Pass. Upper | MOON Mer. Pass. Lower | Age | Phase |
|---|---|---|---|---|---|---|---|
| d | m s | m s | h m | h m | h m | d | % |
| 9 | 16 14 | 16 11 | 11 44 | 00 09 | 12 33 | 15 | 99 |
| 10 | 16 09 | 16 06 | 11 44 | 00 58 | 13 23 | 16 | 96 |
| 11 | 16 03 | 16 00 | 11 44 | 01 49 | 14 14 | 17 | 91 |

| UT (d h) | ARIES GHA | VENUS −3.9 GHA | Dec | MARS −1.5 GHA | Dec | JUPITER −2.7 GHA | Dec | SATURN +0.6 GHA | Dec | STARS Name | SHA | Dec |
|---|---|---|---|---|---|---|---|---|---|---|---|---|
| 12 00 | 51 06.3 | 178 42.4 | S18 33.9 | 327 09.4 | N24 22.1 | 51 22.8 | S 1 46.0 | 89 20.4 | S16 22.0 | Acamar | 315 12.7 | S40 12.8 |
| 01 | 66 08.8 | 193 41.6 | 34.7 | 342 12.4 | 22.2 | 66 25.3 | 46.0 | 104 22.8 | 21.9 | Achernar | 335 21.0 | S57 07.4 |
| 02 | 81 11.3 | 208 40.9 | 35.6 | 357 15.4 | 22.3 | 81 27.9 | 46.0 | 119 25.1 | 21.9 | Acrux | 173 02.6 | S63 13.2 |
| 03 | 96 13.7 | 223 40.2 .. | 36.4 | 12 18.3 .. | 22.5 | 96 30.5 .. | 46.1 | 134 27.5 .. | 21.9 | Adhara | 255 07.0 | S28 59.9 |
| 04 | 111 16.2 | 238 39.5 | 37.3 | 27 21.3 | 22.6 | 111 33.0 | 46.1 | 149 29.9 | 21.8 | Aldebaran | 290 41.4 | N16 33.3 |
| 05 | 126 18.7 | 253 38.7 | 38.1 | 42 24.3 | 22.7 | 126 35.6 | 46.1 | 164 32.3 | 21.8 | | | |
| 06 | 141 21.1 | 268 38.0 | S18 39.0 | 57 27.2 | N24 22.8 | 141 38.2 | S 1 46.2 | 179 34.7 | S16 21.8 | Alioth | 166 15.0 | N55 50.1 |
| 07 | 156 23.6 | 283 37.3 | 39.8 | 72 30.2 | 22.9 | 156 40.7 | 46.2 | 194 37.0 | 21.8 | Alkaid | 152 53.9 | N49 12.0 |
| 08 | 171 26.1 | 298 36.6 | 40.7 | 87 33.2 | 23.0 | 171 43.3 | 46.2 | 209 39.4 | 21.7 | Alnair | 27 35.1 | S46 51.3 |
| 09 | 186 28.5 | 313 35.9 .. | 41.5 | 102 36.2 .. | 23.1 | 186 45.8 .. | 46.2 | 224 41.8 .. | 21.7 | Alnilam | 275 39.3 | S 1 11.2 |
| 10 | 201 31.0 | 328 35.1 | 42.4 | 117 39.2 | 23.2 | 201 48.4 | 46.3 | 239 44.2 | 21.7 | Alphard | 217 49.5 | S 8 45.3 |
| 11 | 216 33.4 | 343 34.4 | 43.2 | 132 42.1 | 23.3 | 216 50.9 | 46.3 | 254 46.6 | 21.6 | | | |
| 12 | 231 35.9 | 358 33.7 | S18 44.1 | 147 45.1 | N24 23.4 | 231 53.5 | S 1 46.4 | 269 48.9 | S16 21.6 | Alphecca | 126 05.7 | N26 38.4 |
| 13 | 246 38.4 | 13 32.9 | 44.9 | 162 48.1 | 23.5 | 246 56.1 | 46.4 | 284 51.3 | 21.6 | Alpheratz | 357 36.4 | N29 13.1 |
| 14 | 261 40.8 | 28 32.2 | 45.8 | 177 51.1 | 23.6 | 261 58.6 | 46.4 | 299 53.7 | 21.6 | Altair | 62 01.9 | N 8 55.8 |
| 15 | 276 43.3 | 43 31.5 .. | 46.6 | 192 54.1 .. | 23.7 | 277 01.2 .. | 46.4 | 314 56.1 .. | 21.5 | Ankaa | 353 08.6 | S42 11.1 |
| 16 | 291 45.8 | 58 30.8 | 47.4 | 207 57.1 | 23.8 | 292 03.7 | 46.4 | 329 58.5 | 21.5 | Antares | 112 18.4 | S26 28.9 |
| 17 | 306 48.2 | 73 30.0 | 48.3 | 223 00.1 | 24.0 | 307 06.3 | 46.5 | 345 00.8 | 21.5 | | | |
| 18 | 321 50.7 | 88 29.3 | S18 49.1 | 238 03.1 | N24 24.1 | 322 08.9 | S 1 46.5 | 0 03.2 | S16 21.4 | Arcturus | 145 49.9 | N19 03.9 |
| 19 | 336 53.2 | 103 28.6 | 50.0 | 253 06.1 | 24.2 | 337 11.4 | 46.5 | 15 05.6 | 21.4 | Atria | 107 14.8 | S69 04.1 |
| 20 | 351 55.6 | 118 27.8 | 50.8 | 268 09.1 | 24.3 | 352 14.0 | 46.6 | 30 08.0 | 21.4 | Avior | 234 15.3 | S59 34.6 |
| 21 | 6 58.1 | 133 27.1 .. | 51.6 | 283 12.1 .. | 24.4 | 7 16.5 .. | 46.6 | 45 10.4 .. | 21.3 | Bellatrix | 278 24.5 | N 6 22.3 |
| 22 | 22 00.6 | 148 26.4 | 52.5 | 298 15.1 | 24.5 | 22 19.1 | 46.6 | 60 12.7 | 21.3 | Betelgeuse | 270 53.8 | N 7 24.7 |
| 23 | 37 03.0 | 163 25.6 | 53.3 | 313 18.1 | 24.6 | 37 21.6 | 46.6 | 75 15.1 | 21.3 | | | |
| 13 00 | 52 05.5 | 178 24.9 | S18 54.1 | 328 21.1 | N24 24.7 | 52 24.2 | S 1 46.7 | 90 17.5 | S16 21.3 | Canopus | 263 52.8 | S52 42.2 |
| 01 | 67 07.9 | 193 24.2 | 55.0 | 343 24.1 | 24.8 | 67 26.7 | 46.7 | 105 19.9 | 21.2 | Capella | 280 24.1 | N46 01.2 |
| 02 | 82 10.4 | 208 23.4 | 55.8 | 358 27.1 | 24.9 | 82 29.3 | 46.7 | 120 22.2 | 21.2 | Deneb | 49 27.1 | N45 21.9 |
| 03 | 97 12.9 | 223 22.7 .. | 56.6 | 13 30.1 .. | 25.0 | 97 31.9 .. | 46.8 | 135 24.6 .. | 21.2 | Denebola | 182 27.0 | N14 26.8 |
| 04 | 112 15.3 | 238 22.0 | 57.5 | 28 33.1 | 25.1 | 112 34.4 | 46.8 | 150 27.0 | 21.1 | Diphda | 348 48.9 | S17 51.7 |
| 05 | 127 17.8 | 253 21.2 | 58.3 | 43 36.1 | 25.2 | 127 37.0 | 46.8 | 165 29.4 | 21.1 | | | |
| 06 | 142 20.3 | 268 20.5 | S18 59.1 | 58 39.1 | N24 25.3 | 142 39.5 | S 1 46.8 | 180 31.8 | S16 21.1 | Dubhe | 193 43.5 | N61 37.5 |
| 07 | 157 22.7 | 283 19.8 | 18 59.9 | 73 42.1 | 25.4 | 157 42.1 | 46.9 | 195 34.1 | 21.0 | Elnath | 278 03.8 | N28 37.6 |
| 08 | 172 25.2 | 298 19.0 | 19 00.8 | 88 45.2 | 25.5 | 172 44.6 | 46.9 | 210 36.5 | 21.0 | Eltanin | 90 43.5 | N51 29.3 |
| 09 | 187 27.7 | 313 18.3 .. | 01.6 | 103 48.2 .. | 25.7 | 187 47.2 .. | 46.9 | 225 38.9 .. | 21.0 | Enif | 33 40.6 | N 9 58.9 |
| 10 | 202 30.1 | 328 17.6 | 02.4 | 118 51.2 | 25.8 | 202 49.7 | 46.9 | 240 41.3 | 21.0 | Fomalhaut | 15 16.4 | S29 30.2 |
| 11 | 217 32.6 | 343 16.8 | 03.2 | 133 54.2 | 25.9 | 217 52.3 | 47.0 | 255 43.6 | 20.9 | | | |
| 12 | 232 35.1 | 358 16.1 | S19 04.1 | 148 57.2 | N24 26.0 | 232 54.8 | S 1 47.0 | 270 46.0 | S16 20.9 | Gacrux | 171 54.1 | S57 14.1 |
| 13 | 247 37.5 | 13 15.3 | 04.9 | 164 00.3 | 26.1 | 247 57.4 | 47.0 | 285 48.4 | 20.9 | Gienah | 175 45.7 | S17 39.9 |
| 14 | 262 40.0 | 28 14.6 | 05.7 | 179 03.3 | 26.2 | 262 59.9 | 47.0 | 300 50.8 | 20.8 | Hadar | 148 39.2 | S60 28.8 |
| 15 | 277 42.4 | 43 13.9 .. | 06.5 | 194 06.3 .. | 26.3 | 278 02.5 .. | 47.1 | 315 53.1 .. | 20.8 | Hamal | 327 52.9 | N23 34.3 |
| 16 | 292 44.9 | 58 13.1 | 07.3 | 209 09.4 | 26.4 | 293 05.0 | 47.1 | 330 55.5 | 20.8 | Kaus Aust. | 83 35.2 | S34 22.5 |
| 17 | 307 47.4 | 73 12.4 | 08.2 | 224 12.4 | 26.5 | 308 07.6 | 47.1 | 345 57.9 | 20.7 | | | |
| 18 | 322 49.8 | 88 11.6 | S19 09.0 | 239 15.4 | N24 26.6 | 323 10.1 | S 1 47.1 | 1 00.3 | S16 20.7 | Kochab | 137 21.0 | N74 03.7 |
| 19 | 337 52.3 | 103 10.9 | 09.8 | 254 18.5 | 26.7 | 338 12.7 | 47.2 | 16 02.6 | 20.7 | Markab | 13 31.6 | N15 19.3 |
| 20 | 352 54.8 | 118 10.1 | 10.6 | 269 21.5 | 26.8 | 353 15.2 | 47.2 | 31 05.0 | 20.6 | Menkar | 314 07.7 | N 4 10.8 |
| 21 | 7 57.2 | 133 09.4 .. | 11.4 | 284 24.5 .. | 26.9 | 8 17.8 .. | 47.2 | 46 07.4 .. | 20.6 | Menkent | 148 00.1 | S36 28.7 |
| 22 | 22 59.7 | 148 08.7 | 12.2 | 299 27.6 | 27.0 | 23 20.3 | 47.2 | 61 09.8 | 20.6 | Miaplacidus | 221 38.5 | S69 48.2 |
| 23 | 38 02.2 | 163 07.9 | 13.0 | 314 30.6 | 27.1 | 38 22.9 | 47.3 | 76 12.1 | 20.5 | | | |
| 14 00 | 53 04.6 | 178 07.2 | S19 13.9 | 329 33.7 | N24 27.2 | 53 25.4 | S 1 47.3 | 91 14.5 | S16 20.5 | Mirfak | 308 30.3 | N49 56.5 |
| 01 | 68 07.1 | 193 06.4 | 14.7 | 344 36.7 | 27.3 | 68 28.0 | 47.3 | 106 16.9 | 20.5 | Nunki | 75 50.2 | S26 16.1 |
| 02 | 83 09.5 | 208 05.7 | 15.5 | 359 39.7 | 27.4 | 83 30.5 | 47.3 | 121 19.3 | 20.5 | Peacock | 53 08.8 | S56 39.9 |
| 03 | 98 12.0 | 223 04.9 .. | 16.3 | 14 42.8 .. | 27.5 | 98 33.1 .. | 47.4 | 136 21.6 .. | 20.4 | Pollux | 243 19.4 | N27 58.2 |
| 04 | 113 14.5 | 238 04.2 | 17.1 | 29 45.8 | 27.6 | 113 35.6 | 47.4 | 151 24.0 | 20.4 | Procyon | 244 52.6 | N 5 10.1 |
| 05 | 128 16.9 | 253 03.4 | 17.9 | 44 48.9 | 27.8 | 128 38.1 | 47.4 | 166 26.4 | 20.4 | | | |
| 06 | 143 19.4 | 268 02.7 | S19 18.7 | 59 51.9 | N24 27.9 | 143 40.7 | S 1 47.4 | 181 28.7 | S16 20.3 | Rasalhague | 96 00.5 | N12 32.7 |
| 07 | 158 21.9 | 283 01.9 | 19.5 | 74 55.0 | 28.0 | 158 43.2 | 47.5 | 196 31.1 | 20.3 | Regulus | 207 36.4 | N11 51.4 |
| 08 | 173 24.3 | 298 01.2 | 20.3 | 89 58.1 | 28.1 | 173 45.8 | 47.5 | 211 33.5 | 20.3 | Rigel | 281 05.3 | S 8 10.4 |
| 09 | 188 26.8 | 313 00.4 .. | 21.1 | 105 01.1 .. | 28.2 | 188 48.3 .. | 47.5 | 226 35.9 .. | 20.2 | Rigil Kent. | 139 43.5 | S60 55.6 |
| 10 | 203 29.3 | 327 59.7 | 21.9 | 120 04.2 | 28.3 | 203 50.9 | 47.5 | 241 38.2 | 20.2 | Sabik | 102 05.2 | S15 45.1 |
| 11 | 218 31.7 | 342 58.9 | 22.7 | 135 07.2 | 28.4 | 218 53.4 | 47.6 | 256 40.6 | 20.2 | | | |
| 12 | 233 34.2 | 357 58.2 | S19 23.5 | 150 10.3 | N24 28.5 | 233 56.0 | S 1 47.6 | 271 43.0 | S16 20.1 | Schedar | 349 32.6 | N56 39.9 |
| 13 | 248 36.7 | 12 57.4 | 24.3 | 165 13.4 | 28.6 | 248 58.5 | 47.6 | 286 45.3 | 20.1 | Shaula | 96 13.2 | S37 07.2 |
| 14 | 263 39.1 | 27 56.7 | 25.1 | 180 16.4 | 28.7 | 264 01.0 | 47.6 | 301 47.7 | 20.1 | Sirius | 258 27.6 | S16 44.7 |
| 15 | 278 41.6 | 42 55.9 .. | 25.9 | 195 19.5 .. | 28.8 | 279 03.6 .. | 47.6 | 316 50.1 .. | 20.0 | Spica | 158 24.5 | S11 16.6 |
| 16 | 293 44.0 | 57 55.2 | 26.7 | 210 22.6 | 28.9 | 294 06.1 | 47.7 | 331 52.5 | 20.0 | Suhail | 222 47.6 | S43 31.1 |
| 17 | 308 46.5 | 72 54.4 | 27.5 | 225 25.6 | 29.0 | 309 08.7 | 47.7 | 346 54.8 | 20.0 | | | |
| 18 | 323 49.0 | 87 53.7 | S19 28.3 | 240 28.7 | N24 29.1 | 324 11.2 | S 1 47.7 | 1 57.2 | S16 19.9 | Vega | 80 34.7 | N38 48.5 |
| 19 | 338 51.4 | 102 52.9 | 29.1 | 255 31.8 | 29.2 | 339 13.8 | 47.7 | 16 59.6 | 19.9 | Zuben'ubi | 136 58.4 | S16 08.0 |
| 20 | 353 53.9 | 117 52.1 | 29.9 | 270 34.8 | 29.3 | 354 16.3 | 47.8 | 32 01.9 | 19.9 | | | |
| 21 | 8 56.4 | 132 51.4 .. | 30.7 | 285 37.9 .. | 29.4 | 9 18.8 .. | 47.8 | 47 04.3 .. | 19.8 | | SHA | Mer. Pass. |
| 22 | 23 58.8 | 147 50.6 | 31.5 | 300 41.0 | 29.5 | 24 21.4 | 47.8 | 62 06.7 | 19.8 | Venus | 126 19.4 | 12 07 |
| 23 | 39 01.3 | 162 49.9 | 32.3 | 315 44.1 | 29.6 | 39 23.9 | 47.8 | 77 09.1 | 19.8 | Mars | 276 15.6 | 2 06 |
| Mer. Pass. | h m 20 28.3 | v −0.7 d 0.8 | | v 3.0 d 0.1 | | v 2.6 d 0.0 | | v 2.4 d 0.0 | | Jupiter | 0 18.7 | 20 27 |
| | | | | | | | | | | Saturn | 38 12.0 | 17 56 |

### SUN and MOON

| UT (d h) | SUN GHA | SUN Dec | MOON GHA | v | MOON Dec | d | HP |
|---|---|---|---|---|---|---|---|
| **12 00** | 183 59.0 | S17 37.5 | 321 18.9 | 9.6 | N27 16.0 | 1.9 | 54.5 |
| 01 | 198 59.0 | 38.1 | 335 47.5 | 9.7 | 27 17.9 | 1.8 | 54.5 |
| 02 | 213 58.9 | 38.8 | 350 16.2 | 9.7 | 27 19.7 | 1.6 | 54.5 |
| 03 | 228 58.8 | .. 39.5 | 4 44.9 | 9.7 | 27 21.3 | 1.4 | 54.5 |
| 04 | 243 58.7 | 40.2 | 19 13.6 | 9.7 | 27 22.7 | 1.4 | 54.5 |
| 05 | 258 58.7 | 40.8 | 33 42.3 | 9.6 | 27 24.1 | 1.2 | 54.5 |
| 06 | 273 58.6 | S17 41.5 | 48 10.9 | 9.7 | N27 25.3 | 1.0 | 54.5 |
| 07 | 288 58.5 | 42.2 | 62 39.6 | 9.8 | 27 26.3 | 1.0 | 54.4 |
| **S** 08 | 303 58.4 | 42.9 | 77 08.4 | 9.7 | 27 27.3 | 0.8 | 54.4 |
| **A** 09 | 318 58.3 | .. 43.6 | 91 37.1 | 9.7 | 27 28.1 | 0.6 | 54.4 |
| **T** 10 | 333 58.3 | 44.2 | 106 05.8 | 9.7 | 27 28.7 | 0.5 | 54.4 |
| **U** 11 | 348 58.2 | 44.9 | 120 34.5 | 9.8 | 27 29.2 | 0.4 | 54.4 |
| **R** 12 | 3 50.1 | S17 45.6 | 135 03.3 | 9.7 | N27 29.6 | 0.3 | 54.4 |
| **D** 13 | 18 58.0 | 46.3 | 149 32.0 | 9.8 | 27 29.9 | 0.1 | 54.4 |
| **A** 14 | 33 58.0 | 46.9 | 164 00.8 | 9.8 | 27 30.0 | 0.0 | 54.4 |
| **Y** 15 | 48 57.9 | .. 47.6 | 178 29.6 | 9.8 | 27 30.0 | 0.2 | 54.4 |
| 16 | 63 57.8 | 48.3 | 192 58.4 | 9.8 | 27 29.8 | 0.3 | 54.4 |
| 17 | 78 57.7 | 48.9 | 207 27.2 | 9.9 | 27 29.5 | 0.4 | 54.3 |
| 18 | 93 57.6 | S17 49.6 | 221 56.1 | 9.8 | N27 29.1 | 0.6 | 54.3 |
| 19 | 108 57.5 | 50.3 | 236 24.9 | 9.9 | 27 28.5 | 0.7 | 54.3 |
| 20 | 123 57.5 | 51.0 | 250 53.8 | 9.9 | 27 27.8 | 0.8 | 54.3 |
| 21 | 138 57.4 | .. 51.6 | 265 22.7 | 10.0 | 27 27.0 | 0.9 | 54.3 |
| 22 | 153 57.3 | 52.3 | 279 51.7 | 9.9 | 27 26.1 | 1.1 | 54.3 |
| 23 | 168 57.2 | 53.0 | 294 20.6 | 10.0 | 27 25.0 | 1.3 | 54.3 |
| **13 00** | 183 57.1 | S17 53.6 | 308 49.6 | 10.0 | N27 23.7 | 1.3 | 54.3 |
| 01 | 198 57.1 | 54.3 | 323 18.6 | 10.0 | 27 22.4 | 1.5 | 54.3 |
| 02 | 213 57.0 | 55.0 | 337 47.6 | 10.1 | 27 20.9 | 1.6 | 54.3 |
| 03 | 228 56.9 | .. 55.6 | 352 16.7 | 10.1 | 27 19.3 | 1.8 | 54.3 |
| 04 | 243 56.8 | 56.3 | 6 45.8 | 10.1 | 27 17.5 | 1.9 | 54.2 |
| 05 | 258 56.7 | 57.0 | 21 14.9 | 10.1 | 27 15.6 | 2.0 | 54.2 |
| 06 | 273 56.6 | S17 57.6 | 35 44.0 | 10.2 | N27 13.6 | 2.2 | 54.2 |
| 07 | 288 56.5 | 58.3 | 50 13.2 | 10.2 | 27 11.4 | 2.2 | 54.2 |
| 08 | 303 56.5 | 58.9 | 64 42.4 | 10.3 | 27 09.2 | 2.4 | 54.2 |
| **S** 09 | 318 56.4 | 17 59.6 | 79 11.7 | 10.2 | 27 06.8 | 2.6 | 54.2 |
| **U** 10 | 333 56.3 | 18 00.3 | 93 40.9 | 10.4 | 27 04.2 | 2.7 | 54.2 |
| **N** 11 | 348 56.2 | 00.9 | 108 10.3 | 10.3 | 27 01.5 | 2.8 | 54.2 |
| **D** 12 | 3 56.1 | S18 01.6 | 122 39.6 | 10.4 | N26 58.7 | 2.9 | 54.2 |
| **A** 13 | 18 56.0 | 02.3 | 137 09.0 | 10.4 | 26 55.8 | 3.0 | 54.2 |
| **Y** 14 | 33 55.9 | 02.9 | 151 38.4 | 10.5 | 26 52.8 | 3.2 | 54.2 |
| 15 | 48 55.8 | .. 03.6 | 166 07.9 | 10.5 | 26 49.6 | 3.3 | 54.2 |
| 16 | 63 55.8 | 04.2 | 180 37.4 | 10.5 | 26 46.3 | 3.4 | 54.2 |
| 17 | 78 55.7 | 04.9 | 195 06.9 | 10.6 | 26 42.9 | 3.6 | 54.2 |
| 18 | 93 55.6 | S18 05.6 | 209 36.5 | 10.6 | N26 39.3 | 3.7 | 54.2 |
| 19 | 108 55.5 | 06.2 | 224 06.1 | 10.7 | 26 35.6 | 3.8 | 54.2 |
| 20 | 123 55.4 | 06.9 | 238 35.8 | 10.7 | 26 31.8 | 3.9 | 54.2 |
| 21 | 138 55.3 | .. 07.5 | 253 05.5 | 10.8 | 26 27.9 | 4.1 | 54.2 |
| 22 | 153 55.2 | 08.2 | 267 35.3 | 10.8 | 26 23.8 | 4.2 | 54.2 |
| 23 | 168 55.1 | 08.8 | 282 05.1 | 10.8 | 26 19.6 | 4.3 | 54.2 |
| **14 00** | 183 55.0 | S18 09.5 | 296 34.9 | 10.9 | N26 15.3 | 4.4 | 54.2 |
| 01 | 198 54.9 | 10.1 | 311 04.8 | 11.0 | 26 10.9 | 4.5 | 54.2 |
| 02 | 213 54.8 | 10.8 | 325 34.8 | 10.9 | 26 06.4 | 4.7 | 54.2 |
| 03 | 228 54.7 | .. 11.4 | 340 04.7 | 11.1 | 26 01.7 | 4.8 | 54.2 |
| 04 | 243 54.7 | 12.1 | 354 34.8 | 11.0 | 25 56.9 | 4.9 | 54.2 |
| 05 | 258 54.6 | 12.8 | 9 04.8 | 11.2 | 25 52.0 | 5.0 | 54.2 |
| 06 | 273 54.5 | S18 13.4 | 23 35.0 | 11.1 | N25 47.0 | 5.2 | 54.2 |
| 07 | 288 54.4 | 14.1 | 38 05.1 | 11.3 | 25 41.8 | 5.2 | 54.2 |
| 08 | 303 54.3 | 14.7 | 52 35.4 | 11.2 | 25 36.6 | 5.4 | 54.2 |
| **M** 09 | 318 54.2 | .. 15.4 | 67 05.6 | 11.4 | 25 31.2 | 5.5 | 54.2 |
| **O** 10 | 333 54.1 | 16.0 | 81 36.0 | 11.3 | 25 25.7 | 5.6 | 54.2 |
| **N** 11 | 348 54.0 | 16.7 | 96 06.3 | 11.5 | 25 20.1 | 5.7 | 54.2 |
| **D** 12 | 3 53.9 | S18 17.3 | 110 36.8 | 11.4 | N25 14.4 | 5.9 | 54.2 |
| **A** 13 | 18 53.8 | 17.9 | 125 07.2 | 11.6 | 25 08.5 | 5.9 | 54.2 |
| **Y** 14 | 33 53.7 | 18.6 | 139 37.8 | 11.5 | 25 02.6 | 6.1 | 54.2 |
| 15 | 48 53.6 | .. 19.2 | 154 08.3 | 11.7 | 24 56.5 | 6.2 | 54.2 |
| 16 | 63 53.5 | 19.9 | 168 39.0 | 11.7 | 24 50.3 | 6.3 | 54.2 |
| 17 | 78 53.4 | 20.5 | 183 09.7 | 11.7 | 24 44.0 | 6.4 | 54.2 |
| 18 | 93 53.3 | S18 21.2 | 197 40.4 | 11.8 | N24 37.6 | 6.5 | 54.2 |
| 19 | 108 53.2 | 21.8 | 212 11.2 | 11.8 | 24 31.1 | 6.6 | 54.2 |
| 20 | 123 53.1 | 22.5 | 226 42.0 | 11.9 | 24 24.5 | 6.8 | 54.2 |
| 21 | 138 53.0 | .. 23.1 | 241 12.9 | 12.0 | 24 17.7 | 6.8 | 54.2 |
| 22 | 153 52.9 | 23.8 | 255 43.9 | 12.0 | 24 10.9 | 7.0 | 54.2 |
| 23 | 168 52.8 | 24.4 | 270 14.9 | 12.0 | N24 03.9 | 7.0 | 54.2 |
| | SD 16.2 | d 0.7 | SD 14.8 | | 14.8 | | 14.8 |

### Twilight, Sunrise and Moonrise

| Lat. | Naut. | Civil | Sunrise | Moonrise 12 | 13 | 14 | 15 |
|---|---|---|---|---|---|---|---|
| N 72 | 06 52 | 08 24 | 10 32 | □ | □ | □ | □ |
| N 70 | 06 43 | 08 03 | 09 36 | □ | □ | □ | □ |
| 68 | 06 35 | 07 47 | 09 03 | □ | □ | □ | 18 34 |
| 66 | 06 28 | 07 33 | 08 39 | □ | □ | □ | 19 36 |
| 64 | 06 22 | 07 22 | 08 21 | □ | □ | 18 13 | 20 10 |
| 62 | 06 17 | 07 13 | 08 05 | 15 59 | 17 19 | 18 56 | 20 34 |
| 60 | 06 13 | 07 04 | 07 53 | 16 55 | 18 02 | 19 25 | 20 54 |
| N 58 | 06 09 | 06 57 | 07 42 | 17 27 | 18 30 | 19 47 | 21 10 |
| 56 | 06 05 | 06 50 | 07 32 | 17 51 | 18 53 | 20 05 | 21 23 |
| 54 | 06 01 | 06 44 | 07 24 | 18 11 | 19 11 | 20 20 | 21 35 |
| 52 | 05 58 | 06 39 | 07 16 | 18 27 | 19 26 | 20 34 | 21 45 |
| 50 | 05 55 | 06 34 | 07 09 | 18 41 | 19 39 | 20 45 | 21 54 |
| 45 | 05 48 | 06 23 | 06 55 | 19 10 | 20 07 | 21 09 | 22 14 |
| N 40 | 05 41 | 06 14 | 06 43 | 19 33 | 20 28 | 21 28 | 22 29 |
| 35 | 05 35 | 06 06 | 06 32 | 19 51 | 20 46 | 21 44 | 22 43 |
| 30 | 05 29 | 05 58 | 06 23 | 20 07 | 21 01 | 21 57 | 22 54 |
| 20 | 05 18 | 05 44 | 06 08 | 20 34 | 21 27 | 22 21 | 23 14 |
| N 10 | 05 06 | 05 32 | 05 54 | 20 58 | 21 50 | 22 41 | 23 30 |
| 0 | 04 54 | 05 19 | 05 41 | 21 20 | 22 10 | 22 59 | 23 46 |
| S 10 | 04 39 | 05 05 | 05 28 | 21 41 | 22 31 | 23 18 | 24 02 |
| 20 | 04 22 | 04 50 | 05 13 | 22 05 | 22 53 | 23 38 | 24 19 |
| 30 | 04 00 | 04 31 | 04 57 | 22 32 | 23 19 | 24 01 | 00 01 |
| 35 | 03 46 | 04 20 | 04 47 | 22 48 | 23 34 | 24 14 | 00 14 |
| 40 | 03 29 | 04 06 | 04 36 | 23 07 | 23 52 | 24 30 | 00 30 |
| 45 | 03 07 | 03 50 | 04 23 | 23 29 | 24 13 | 00 13 | 00 48 |
| S 50 | 02 38 | 03 29 | 04 07 | 23 58 | 24 39 | 00 39 | 01 11 |
| 52 | 02 23 | 03 19 | 04 00 | 24 12 | 00 12 | 00 52 | 01 22 |
| 54 | 02 05 | 03 07 | 03 52 | 24 29 | 00 29 | 01 07 | 01 34 |
| 56 | 01 42 | 02 54 | 03 42 | 24 48 | 00 48 | 01 24 | 01 48 |
| 58 | 01 11 | 02 38 | 03 32 | 00 19 | 01 12 | 01 45 | 02 04 |
| S 60 | 00 04 | 02 19 | 03 19 | 00 52 | 01 45 | 02 12 | 02 24 |

### Sunset, Twilight and Moonset

| Lat. | Sunset | Civil | Naut. | Moonset 12 | 13 | 14 | 15 |
|---|---|---|---|---|---|---|---|
| N 72 | 12 55 | 15 03 | 16 35 | □ | □ | □ | □ |
| N 70 | 13 51 | 15 24 | 16 45 | □ | □ | □ | □ |
| 68 | 14 24 | 15 41 | 16 52 | □ | □ | □ | 16 48 |
| 66 | 14 48 | 15 54 | 16 59 | □ | □ | □ | 15 46 |
| 64 | 15 07 | 16 05 | 17 05 | □ | □ | 15 30 | 15 11 |
| 62 | 15 22 | 16 15 | 17 10 | 14 13 | 14 41 | 14 46 | 14 46 |
| 60 | 15 35 | 16 23 | 17 15 | 13 18 | 13 57 | 14 16 | 14 26 |
| N 58 | 15 46 | 16 31 | 17 19 | 12 46 | 13 28 | 13 54 | 14 09 |
| 56 | 15 56 | 16 37 | 17 23 | 12 21 | 13 06 | 13 35 | 13 55 |
| 54 | 16 04 | 16 43 | 17 27 | 12 02 | 12 48 | 13 20 | 13 43 |
| 52 | 16 12 | 16 49 | 17 30 | 11 45 | 12 32 | 13 07 | 13 32 |
| 50 | 16 19 | 16 54 | 17 33 | 11 31 | 12 18 | 12 55 | 13 22 |
| 45 | 16 33 | 17 05 | 17 40 | 11 02 | 11 51 | 12 30 | 13 02 |
| N 40 | 16 45 | 17 14 | 17 47 | 10 40 | 11 29 | 12 10 | 12 45 |
| 35 | 16 56 | 17 23 | 17 53 | 10 21 | 11 11 | 11 54 | 12 31 |
| 30 | 17 05 | 17 30 | 17 59 | 10 05 | 10 55 | 11 40 | 12 19 |
| 20 | 17 21 | 17 44 | 18 10 | 09 38 | 10 29 | 11 15 | 11 58 |
| N 10 | 17 35 | 17 57 | 18 22 | 09 15 | 10 06 | 10 54 | 11 39 |
| 0 | 17 48 | 18 10 | 18 35 | 08 53 | 09 44 | 10 34 | 11 22 |
| S 10 | 18 01 | 18 23 | 18 49 | 08 31 | 09 23 | 10 14 | 11 05 |
| 20 | 18 15 | 18 39 | 19 07 | 08 08 | 09 00 | 09 53 | 10 46 |
| 30 | 18 32 | 18 58 | 19 29 | 07 40 | 08 33 | 09 28 | 10 25 |
| 35 | 18 42 | 19 09 | 19 43 | 07 24 | 08 17 | 09 14 | 10 12 |
| 40 | 18 53 | 19 23 | 20 01 | 07 06 | 07 59 | 08 56 | 09 57 |
| 45 | 19 06 | 19 40 | 20 22 | 06 43 | 07 36 | 08 36 | 09 40 |
| S 50 | 19 22 | 20 01 | 20 52 | 06 14 | 07 08 | 08 10 | 09 18 |
| 52 | 19 30 | 20 11 | 21 07 | 06 00 | 06 54 | 07 57 | 09 07 |
| 54 | 19 38 | 20 23 | 21 26 | 05 43 | 06 37 | 07 43 | 08 56 |
| 56 | 19 48 | 20 36 | 21 49 | 05 24 | 06 18 | 07 26 | 08 42 |
| 58 | 19 58 | 20 52 | 22 23 | 05 00 | 05 54 | 07 05 | 08 26 |
| S 60 | 20 11 | 21 12 | //// | 04 27 | 05 21 | 06 39 | 08 07 |

### SUN and MOON

| Day | SUN Eqn. of Time 00h | 12h | Mer. Pass. | MOON Mer. Pass. Upper | Lower | Age | Phase |
|---|---|---|---|---|---|---|---|
| | m s | m s | h m | h m | h m | d | % |
| 12 | 15 56 | 15 53 | 11 44 | 02 40 | 15 06 | 18 | 85 |
| 13 | 15 49 | 15 45 | 11 44 | 03 32 | 15 57 | 19 | 77 |
| 14 | 15 40 | 15 36 | 11 44 | 04 22 | 16 47 | 20 | 69 |

| UT | ARIES | VENUS −3.9 | | MARS −1.6 | | JUPITER −2.7 | | SATURN +0.6 | | STARS | | |
|---|---|---|---|---|---|---|---|---|---|---|---|---|
| | GHA | GHA | Dec | GHA | Dec | GHA | Dec | GHA | Dec | Name | SHA | Dec |
| d h | ° ′ | ° ′ | ° ′ | ° ′ | ° ′ | ° ′ | ° ′ | ° ′ | ° ′ | | ° ′ | ° ′ |
| 15 00 | 54 03.8 | 177 49.1 | S19 33.1 | 330 47.2 | N24 29.7 | 54 26.5 | S 1 47.8 | 92 11.4 | S16 19.8 | Acamar | 315 12.7 | S40 12.8 |
| 01 | 69 06.2 | 192 48.4 | 33.9 | 345 50.2 | 29.8 | 69 29.0 | 47.9 | 107 13.8 | 19.7 | Achernar | 335 21.0 | S57 07.4 |
| 02 | 84 08.7 | 207 47.6 | 34.6 | 0 53.3 | 29.9 | 84 31.5 | 47.9 | 122 16.2 | 19.7 | Acrux | 173 02.5 | S63 13.2 |
| 03 | 99 11.2 | 222 46.8 .. | 35.4 | 15 56.4 .. | 30.0 | 99 34.1 .. | 47.9 | 137 18.5 .. | 19.7 | Adhara | 255 07.0 | S29 00.0 |
| 04 | 114 13.6 | 237 46.1 | 36.2 | 30 59.5 | 30.1 | 114 36.6 | 47.9 | 152 20.9 | 19.6 | Aldebaran | 290 41.3 | N16 33.3 |
| 05 | 129 16.1 | 252 45.3 | 37.0 | 46 02.6 | 30.2 | 129 39.1 | 47.9 | 167 23.3 | 19.6 | | | |
| 06 | 144 18.5 | 267 44.6 | S19 37.8 | 61 05.7 | N24 30.3 | 144 41.7 | S 1 48.0 | 182 25.6 | S16 19.6 | Alioth | 166 15.0 | N55 50.1 |
| 07 | 159 21.0 | 282 43.8 | 38.6 | 76 08.8 | 30.4 | 159 44.2 | 48.0 | 197 28.0 | 19.5 | Alkaid | 152 53.9 | N49 11.9 |
| 08 | 174 23.5 | 297 43.0 | 39.3 | 91 11.9 | 30.5 | 174 46.8 | 48.0 | 212 30.4 | 19.5 | Alnair | 27 35.1 | S46 51.3 |
| 09 | 189 25.9 | 312 42.3 .. | 40.1 | 106 15.0 .. | 30.6 | 189 49.3 .. | 48.0 | 227 32.7 .. | 19.5 | Alnilam | 275 39.3 | S 1 11.2 |
| 10 | 204 28.4 | 327 41.5 | 40.9 | 121 18.1 | 30.7 | 204 51.8 | 48.0 | 242 35.1 | 19.4 | Alphard | 217 49.5 | S 8 45.3 |
| 11 | 219 30.9 | 342 40.7 | 41.7 | 136 21.2 | 30.8 | 219 54.4 | 48.1 | 257 37.5 | 19.4 | | | |
| 12 | 234 33.3 | 357 40.0 | S19 42.5 | 151 24.3 | N24 30.9 | 234 56.9 | S 1 48.1 | 272 39.8 | S16 19.4 | Alphecca | 126 05.6 | N26 38.4 |
| 13 | 249 35.8 | 12 39.2 | 43.2 | 166 27.4 | 31.0 | 249 59.4 | 48.1 | 287 42.2 | 19.3 | Alpheratz | 357 36.4 | N29 13.1 |
| 14 | 264 38.3 | 27 38.4 | 44.0 | 181 30.5 | 31.1 | 265 02.0 | 48.1 | 302 44.6 | 19.3 | Altair | 62 01.9 | N 8 55.8 |
| 15 | 279 40.7 | 42 37.7 .. | 44.8 | 196 33.6 .. | 31.2 | 280 04.5 .. | 48.1 | 317 47.0 .. | 19.3 | Ankaa | 353 08.6 | S42 11.1 |
| 16 | 294 43.2 | 57 36.9 | 45.6 | 211 36.7 | 31.3 | 295 07.0 | 48.1 | 332 49.3 | 19.2 | Antares | 112 18.4 | S26 28.9 |
| 17 | 309 45.7 | 72 36.1 | 46.3 | 226 39.8 | 31.4 | 310 09.6 | 48.2 | 347 51.7 | 19.2 | | | |
| 18 | 324 48.1 | 87 35.4 | S19 47.1 | 241 42.9 | N24 31.5 | 325 12.1 | S 1 48.2 | 2 54.1 | S16 19.2 | Arcturus | 145 49.9 | N19 03.9 |
| 19 | 339 50.6 | 102 34.6 | 47.9 | 256 46.0 | 31.6 | 340 14.6 | 48.2 | 17 56.4 | 19.1 | Atria | 107 14.8 | S69 04.1 |
| 20 | 354 53.0 | 117 33.8 | 48.7 | 271 49.1 | 31.7 | 355 17.2 | 48.2 | 32 58.8 | 19.1 | Avior | 234 15.2 | S59 34.6 |
| 21 | 9 55.5 | 132 33.1 .. | 49.4 | 286 52.2 .. | 31.8 | 10 19.7 .. | 48.2 | 48 01.2 .. | 19.1 | Bellatrix | 278 24.5 | N 6 22.3 |
| 22 | 24 58.0 | 147 32.3 | 50.2 | 301 55.3 | 31.9 | 25 22.2 | 48.3 | 63 03.5 | 19.0 | Betelgeuse | 270 53.8 | N 7 24.7 |
| 23 | 40 00.4 | 162 31.5 | 51.0 | 316 58.5 | 32.0 | 40 24.8 | 48.3 | 78 05.9 | 19.0 | | | |
| 16 00 | 55 02.9 | 177 30.8 | S19 51.7 | 332 01.6 | N24 32.1 | 55 27.3 | S 1 48.3 | 93 08.2 | S16 19.0 | Canopus | 263 52.8 | S52 42.2 |
| 01 | 70 05.4 | 192 30.0 | 52.5 | 347 04.7 | 32.2 | 70 29.8 | 48.3 | 108 10.6 | 18.9 | Capella | 280 24.1 | N46 01.2 |
| 02 | 85 07.8 | 207 29.2 | 53.3 | 2 07.8 | 32.3 | 85 32.4 | 48.3 | 123 13.0 | 18.9 | Deneb | 49 27.2 | N45 21.9 |
| 03 | 100 10.3 | 222 28.4 .. | 54.0 | 17 10.9 .. | 32.4 | 100 34.9 .. | 48.3 | 138 15.3 .. | 18.9 | Denebola | 182 27.0 | N14 26.7 |
| 04 | 115 12.8 | 237 27.7 | 54.8 | 32 14.1 | 32.5 | 115 37.4 | 48.4 | 153 17.7 | 18.8 | Diphda | 348 48.9 | S17 51.7 |
| 05 | 130 15.2 | 252 26.9 | 55.6 | 47 17.2 | 32.6 | 130 40.0 | 48.4 | 168 20.1 | 18.8 | | | |
| 06 | 145 17.7 | 267 26.1 | S19 56.3 | 62 20.3 | N24 32.7 | 145 42.5 | S 1 48.4 | 183 22.4 | S16 18.8 | Dubhe | 193 43.5 | N61 37.5 |
| 07 | 160 20.1 | 282 25.3 | 57.1 | 77 23.5 | 32.8 | 160 45.0 | 48.4 | 198 24.8 | 18.7 | Elnath | 278 03.8 | N28 37.6 |
| 08 | 175 22.6 | 297 24.6 | 57.8 | 92 26.6 | 32.9 | 175 47.6 | 48.4 | 213 27.2 | 18.7 | Eltanin | 90 43.5 | N51 29.3 |
| 09 | 190 25.1 | 312 23.8 .. | 58.6 | 107 29.7 .. | 33.0 | 190 50.1 .. | 48.4 | 228 29.5 .. | 18.7 | Enif | 33 40.6 | N 9 58.9 |
| 10 | 205 27.5 | 327 23.0 | 19 59.3 | 122 32.9 | 33.1 | 205 52.6 | 48.5 | 243 31.9 | 18.6 | Fomalhaut | 15 16.4 | S29 30.2 |
| 11 | 220 30.0 | 342 22.2 | 20 00.1 | 137 36.0 | 33.2 | 220 55.1 | 48.5 | 258 34.3 | 18.6 | | | |
| 12 | 235 32.5 | 357 21.5 | S20 00.9 | 152 39.1 | N24 33.3 | 235 57.7 | S 1 48.5 | 273 36.6 | S16 18.5 | Gacrux | 171 54.1 | S57 14.1 |
| 13 | 250 34.9 | 12 20.7 | 01.6 | 167 42.3 | 33.4 | 251 00.2 | 48.5 | 288 39.0 | 18.5 | Gienah | 175 45.7 | S17 39.9 |
| 14 | 265 37.4 | 27 19.9 | 02.4 | 182 45.4 | 33.5 | 266 02.7 | 48.5 | 303 41.4 | 18.5 | Hadar | 148 39.2 | S60 28.7 |
| 15 | 280 39.9 | 42 19.1 .. | 03.1 | 197 48.5 .. | 33.6 | 281 05.2 .. | 48.5 | 318 43.7 .. | 18.4 | Hamal | 327 52.9 | N23 34.3 |
| 16 | 295 42.3 | 57 18.3 | 03.9 | 212 51.7 | 33.7 | 296 07.8 | 48.5 | 333 46.1 | 18.4 | Kaus Aust. | 83 35.2 | S34 22.5 |
| 17 | 310 44.8 | 72 17.6 | 04.6 | 227 54.8 | 33.8 | 311 10.3 | 48.6 | 348 48.4 | 18.4 | | | |
| 18 | 325 47.3 | 87 16.8 | S20 05.4 | 242 58.0 | N24 33.9 | 326 12.8 | S 1 48.6 | 3 50.8 | S16 18.3 | Kochab | 137 21.0 | N74 03.6 |
| 19 | 340 49.7 | 102 16.0 | 06.1 | 258 01.1 | 34.0 | 341 15.4 | 48.6 | 18 53.2 | 18.3 | Markab | 13 31.6 | N15 19.8 |
| 20 | 355 52.2 | 117 15.2 | 06.9 | 273 04.3 | 34.1 | 356 17.9 | 48.6 | 33 55.5 | 18.3 | Menkar | 314 07.7 | N 4 10.8 |
| 21 | 10 54.6 | 132 14.4 .. | 07.6 | 288 07.4 .. | 34.2 | 11 20.4 .. | 48.6 | 48 57.9 .. | 18.2 | Menkent | 148 00.1 | S36 28.7 |
| 22 | 25 57.1 | 147 13.7 | 08.4 | 303 10.6 | 34.3 | 26 22.9 | 48.6 | 64 00.3 | 18.2 | Miaplacidus | 221 38.5 | S69 48.2 |
| 23 | 40 59.6 | 162 12.9 | 09.1 | 318 13.7 | 34.4 | 41 25.5 | 48.7 | 79 02.6 | 18.2 | | | |
| 17 00 | 56 02.0 | 177 12.1 | S20 09.8 | 333 16.9 | N24 34.5 | 56 28.0 | S 1 48.7 | 94 05.0 | S16 18.1 | Mirfak | 308 30.3 | N49 56.5 |
| 01 | 71 04.5 | 192 11.3 | 10.6 | 348 20.0 | 34.6 | 71 30.5 | 48.7 | 109 07.3 | 18.1 | Nunki | 75 50.2 | S26 16.1 |
| 02 | 86 07.0 | 207 10.5 | 11.3 | 3 23.2 | 34.7 | 86 33.0 | 48.7 | 124 09.7 | 18.1 | Peacock | 53 08.8 | S56 39.9 |
| 03 | 101 09.4 | 222 09.7 .. | 12.1 | 18 26.4 .. | 34.8 | 101 35.5 .. | 48.7 | 139 12.1 .. | 18.0 | Pollux | 243 19.3 | N27 58.2 |
| 04 | 116 11.9 | 237 08.9 | 12.8 | 33 29.5 | 34.9 | 116 38.1 | 48.7 | 154 14.4 | 18.0 | Procyon | 244 52.5 | N 5 10.1 |
| 05 | 131 14.4 | 252 08.2 | 13.5 | 48 32.7 | 35.0 | 131 40.6 | 48.7 | 169 16.8 | 18.0 | | | |
| 06 | 146 16.8 | 267 07.4 | S20 14.3 | 63 35.8 | N24 35.1 | 146 43.1 | S 1 48.7 | 184 19.1 | S16 17.9 | Rasalhague | 96 00.5 | N12 32.7 |
| 07 | 161 19.3 | 282 06.6 | 15.0 | 78 39.0 | 35.2 | 161 45.6 | 48.8 | 199 21.5 | 17.9 | Regulus | 207 36.4 | N11 51.4 |
| 08 | 176 21.8 | 297 05.8 | 15.8 | 93 42.2 | 35.3 | 176 48.2 | 48.8 | 214 23.9 | 17.8 | Rigel | 281 05.3 | S 8 10.4 |
| 09 | 191 24.2 | 312 05.0 .. | 16.5 | 108 45.4 .. | 35.4 | 191 50.7 .. | 48.8 | 229 26.2 .. | 17.8 | Rigil Kent. | 139 43.4 | S60 55.5 |
| 10 | 206 26.7 | 327 04.2 | 17.2 | 123 48.5 | 35.5 | 206 53.2 | 48.8 | 244 28.6 | 17.8 | Sabik | 102 05.2 | S15 45.1 |
| 11 | 221 29.1 | 342 03.4 | 18.0 | 138 51.7 | 35.6 | 221 55.7 | 48.8 | 259 30.9 | 17.7 | | | |
| 12 | 236 31.6 | 357 02.6 | S20 18.7 | 153 54.9 | N24 35.7 | 236 58.2 | S 1 48.8 | 274 33.3 | S16 17.7 | Schedar | 349 32.7 | N56 39.9 |
| 13 | 251 34.1 | 12 01.9 | 19.4 | 168 58.0 | 35.8 | 252 00.8 | 48.8 | 289 35.7 | 17.7 | Shaula | 96 13.2 | S37 07.2 |
| 14 | 266 36.5 | 27 01.1 | 20.1 | 184 01.2 | 35.9 | 267 03.3 | 48.8 | 304 38.0 | 17.6 | Sirius | 258 27.6 | S16 44.7 |
| 15 | 281 39.0 | 42 00.3 .. | 20.9 | 199 04.4 .. | 35.9 | 282 05.8 .. | 48.9 | 319 40.4 .. | 17.6 | Spica | 158 24.5 | S11 16.6 |
| 16 | 296 41.5 | 56 59.5 | 21.6 | 214 07.6 | 36.0 | 297 08.3 | 48.9 | 334 42.7 | 17.6 | Suhail | 222 47.6 | S43 31.1 |
| 17 | 311 43.9 | 71 58.7 | 22.3 | 229 10.8 | 36.1 | 312 10.8 | 48.9 | 349 45.1 | 17.5 | | | |
| 18 | 326 46.4 | 86 57.9 | S20 23.1 | 244 13.9 | N24 36.2 | 327 13.4 | S 1 48.9 | 4 47.5 | S16 17.5 | Vega | 80 34.8 | N38 48.5 |
| 19 | 341 48.9 | 101 57.1 | 23.8 | 259 17.1 | 36.3 | 342 15.9 | 48.9 | 19 49.8 | 17.5 | Zuben'ubi | 136 58.4 | S16 08.0 |
| 20 | 356 51.3 | 116 56.3 | 24.5 | 274 20.3 | 36.4 | 357 18.4 | 48.9 | 34 52.2 | 17.4 | | SHA | Mer. Pass. |
| 21 | 11 53.8 | 131 55.5 .. | 25.2 | 289 23.5 .. | 36.5 | 12 20.9 .. | 48.9 | 49 54.5 .. | 17.4 | | ° ′ | h m |
| 22 | 26 56.2 | 146 54.7 | 25.9 | 304 26.7 | 36.6 | 27 23.4 | 48.9 | 64 56.9 | 17.3 | Venus | 122 27.9 | 12 11 |
| 23 | 41 58.7 | 161 53.9 | 26.7 | 319 29.9 | 36.7 | 42 25.9 | 48.9 | 79 59.3 | 17.3 | Mars | 276 58.7 | 1 52 |
| | h m | | | | | | | | | Jupiter | 0 24.4 | 20 15 |
| Mer. Pass. 20 16.5 | | v −0.8 | d 0.8 | v 3.1 | d 0.1 | v 2.5 | d 0.0 | v 2.4 | d 0.0 | Saturn | 38 05.3 | 17 45 |

## SUN and MOON

| UT | SUN GHA | SUN Dec | MOON GHA | v | MOON Dec | d | HP |
|---|---|---|---|---|---|---|---|
| d h | ° ′ | ° ′ | ° ′ | ′ | ° ′ | ′ | ′ |
| **15** 00 | 183 52.7 | S18 25.0 | 284 45.9 | 12.1 | N23 56.9 | 7.2 | 54.2 |
| 01 | 198 52.6 | 25.7 | 299 17.0 | 12.2 | 23 49.7 | 7.3 | 54.2 |
| 02 | 213 52.5 | 26.3 | 313 48.2 | 12.2 | 23 42.4 | 7.4 | 54.2 |
| 03 | 228 52.4 | .. 27.0 | 328 19.4 | 12.3 | 23 35.0 | 7.5 | 54.2 |
| 04 | 243 52.3 | 27.6 | 342 50.7 | 12.3 | 23 27.5 | 7.6 | 54.2 |
| 05 | 258 52.2 | 28.2 | 357 22.0 | 12.4 | 23 19.9 | 7.7 | 54.2 |
| 06 | 273 52.1 | S18 28.9 | 11 53.4 | 12.4 | N23 12.2 | 7.8 | 54.2 |
| 07 | 288 52.0 | 29.5 | 26 24.8 | 12.5 | 23 04.4 | 7.9 | 54.2 |
| T 08 | 303 51.9 | 30.1 | 40 56.3 | 12.5 | 22 56.5 | 8.0 | 54.2 |
| U 09 | 318 51.8 | .. 30.8 | 55 27.8 | 12.6 | 22 48.5 | 8.1 | 54.3 |
| E 10 | 333 51.7 | 31.4 | 69 59.4 | 12.7 | 22 40.4 | 8.2 | 54.3 |
| S 11 | 348 51.6 | 32.1 | 84 31.1 | 12.7 | 22 32.2 | 8.3 | 54.3 |
| D 12 | 3 51.4 | S18 32.7 | 99 02.8 | 12.7 | N22 23.9 | 8.4 | 54.3 |
| A 13 | 18 51.3 | 33.3 | 113 34.5 | 12.8 | 22 15.5 | 8.5 | 54.3 |
| Y 14 | 33 51.2 | 34.0 | 128 06.3 | 12.9 | 22 07.0 | 8.6 | 54.3 |
| 15 | 48 51.1 | .. 34.6 | 142 38.2 | 12.9 | 21 58.4 | 8.7 | 54.3 |
| 16 | 63 51.0 | 35.2 | 157 10.1 | 12.9 | 21 49.7 | 8.8 | 54.3 |
| 17 | 78 50.9 | 35.9 | 171 42.0 | 13.0 | 21 40.9 | 8.9 | 54.3 |
| 18 | 93 50.8 | S18 36.5 | 186 14.0 | 13.1 | N21 32.0 | 9.0 | 54.3 |
| 19 | 108 50.7 | 37.1 | 200 46.1 | 13.1 | 21 23.0 | 9.1 | 54.3 |
| 20 | 123 50.6 | 37.7 | 215 18.2 | 13.2 | 21 13.9 | 9.2 | 54.4 |
| 21 | 138 50.5 | .. 38.4 | 229 50.4 | 13.2 | 21 04.7 | 9.2 | 54.4 |
| 22 | 153 50.4 | 39.0 | 244 22.6 | 13.3 | 20 55.5 | 9.4 | 54.4 |
| 23 | 168 50.3 | 39.6 | 258 54.9 | 13.3 | 20 46.1 | 9.4 | 54.4 |
| **16** 00 | 183 50.2 | S18 40.3 | 273 27.2 | 13.4 | N20 36.7 | 9.6 | 54.4 |
| 01 | 198 50.0 | 40.9 | 287 59.6 | 13.4 | 20 27.1 | 9.6 | 54.4 |
| 02 | 213 49.9 | 41.5 | 302 32.0 | 13.4 | 20 17.5 | 9.7 | 54.4 |
| 03 | 228 49.8 | .. 42.1 | 317 04.4 | 13.5 | 20 07.8 | 9.9 | 54.4 |
| 04 | 243 49.7 | 42.8 | 331 36.9 | 13.6 | 19 57.9 | 9.9 | 54.4 |
| 05 | 258 49.6 | 43.4 | 346 09.5 | 13.6 | 19 48.0 | 10.0 | 54.5 |
| 06 | 273 49.5 | S18 44.0 | 0 42.1 | 13.7 | N19 38.0 | 10.0 | 54.5 |
| W 07 | 288 49.4 | 44.6 | 15 14.8 | 13.7 | 19 28.0 | 10.2 | 54.5 |
| E 08 | 303 49.3 | 45.3 | 29 47.5 | 13.7 | 19 17.8 | 10.2 | 54.5 |
| D 09 | 318 49.1 | .. 45.9 | 44 20.2 | 13.8 | 19 07.6 | 10.4 | 54.5 |
| N 10 | 333 49.0 | 46.5 | 58 53.0 | 13.9 | 18 57.2 | 10.4 | 54.5 |
| E 11 | 348 48.9 | 47.1 | 73 25.9 | 13.8 | 18 46.8 | 10.5 | 54.6 |
| S 12 | 3 48.8 | S18 47.7 | 87 58.7 | 14.0 | N18 36.3 | 10.6 | 54.6 |
| D 13 | 18 48.7 | 48.4 | 102 31.7 | 13.9 | 18 25.7 | 10.6 | 54.6 |
| A 14 | 33 48.6 | 49.0 | 117 04.6 | 14.0 | 18 15.1 | 10.8 | 54.6 |
| Y 15 | 48 48.5 | .. 49.6 | 131 37.6 | 14.1 | 18 04.3 | 10.8 | 54.6 |
| 16 | 63 48.3 | 50.2 | 146 10.7 | 14.1 | 17 53.5 | 10.9 | 54.6 |
| 17 | 78 48.2 | 50.8 | 160 43.8 | 14.1 | 17 42.6 | 11.0 | 54.7 |
| 18 | 93 48.1 | S18 51.5 | 175 16.9 | 14.2 | N17 31.6 | 11.1 | 54.7 |
| 19 | 108 48.0 | 52.1 | 189 50.1 | 14.2 | 17 20.5 | 11.1 | 54.7 |
| 20 | 123 47.9 | 52.7 | 204 23.3 | 14.3 | 17 09.4 | 11.3 | 54.7 |
| 21 | 138 47.7 | .. 53.3 | 218 56.6 | 14.3 | 16 58.1 | 11.3 | 54.7 |
| 22 | 153 47.6 | 53.9 | 233 29.9 | 14.3 | 16 46.8 | 11.3 | 54.7 |
| 23 | 168 47.5 | 54.5 | 248 03.2 | 14.4 | 16 35.5 | 11.5 | 54.8 |
| **17** 00 | 183 47.4 | S18 55.2 | 262 36.6 | 14.4 | N16 24.0 | 11.5 | 54.8 |
| 01 | 198 47.3 | 55.8 | 277 10.0 | 14.4 | 16 12.5 | 11.6 | 54.8 |
| 02 | 213 47.2 | 56.4 | 291 43.4 | 14.5 | 16 00.9 | 11.7 | 54.8 |
| 03 | 228 47.0 | .. 57.0 | 306 16.9 | 14.5 | 15 49.2 | 11.8 | 54.8 |
| 04 | 243 46.9 | 57.6 | 320 50.4 | 14.6 | 15 37.4 | 11.8 | 54.9 |
| 05 | 258 46.8 | 58.2 | 335 24.0 | 14.5 | 15 25.6 | 11.9 | 54.9 |
| 06 | 273 46.7 | S18 58.8 | 349 57.5 | 14.6 | N15 13.7 | 11.9 | 54.9 |
| T 07 | 288 46.5 | 18 59.4 | 4 31.1 | 14.7 | 15 01.8 | 12.1 | 54.9 |
| H 08 | 303 46.4 | 19 00.0 | 19 04.8 | 14.6 | 14 49.7 | 12.1 | 54.9 |
| U 09 | 318 46.3 | .. 00.7 | 33 38.4 | 14.7 | 14 37.6 | 12.1 | 55.0 |
| R 10 | 333 46.2 | 01.3 | 48 12.1 | 14.8 | 14 25.5 | 12.3 | 55.0 |
| S 11 | 348 46.1 | 01.9 | 62 45.9 | 14.7 | 14 13.2 | 12.3 | 55.0 |
| D 12 | 3 45.9 | S19 02.5 | 77 19.6 | 14.8 | N14 00.9 | 12.4 | 55.0 |
| A 13 | 18 45.8 | 03.1 | 91 53.4 | 14.8 | 13 48.5 | 12.4 | 55.1 |
| Y 14 | 33 45.7 | 03.7 | 106 27.2 | 14.8 | 13 36.1 | 12.5 | 55.1 |
| 15 | 48 45.6 | .. 04.3 | 121 01.0 | 14.9 | 13 23.6 | 12.6 | 55.1 |
| 16 | 63 45.4 | 04.9 | 135 34.9 | 14.9 | 13 11.0 | 12.6 | 55.1 |
| 17 | 78 45.3 | 05.5 | 150 08.8 | 14.9 | 12 58.4 | 12.7 | 55.2 |
| 18 | 93 45.2 | S19 06.1 | 164 42.7 | 14.9 | N12 45.7 | 12.8 | 55.2 |
| 19 | 108 45.1 | 06.7 | 179 16.6 | 14.9 | 12 32.9 | 12.8 | 55.2 |
| 20 | 123 44.9 | 07.3 | 193 50.5 | 15.0 | 12 20.1 | 12.9 | 55.2 |
| 21 | 138 44.8 | .. 07.9 | 208 24.5 | 15.0 | 12 07.2 | 12.9 | 55.3 |
| 22 | 153 44.7 | 08.5 | 222 58.5 | 15.0 | 11 54.3 | 13.1 | 55.3 |
| 23 | 168 44.5 | 09.1 | 237 32.5 | 15.0 | N11 41.2 | 13.0 | 55.3 |
| | SD 16.2 | d 0.6 | SD 14.8 | | 14.9 | | 15.0 |

## Twilight / Moonrise

| Lat. | Naut. | Civil | Sunrise | Moonrise 15 | 16 | 17 | 18 |
|---|---|---|---|---|---|---|---|
| ° | h m | h m | h m | h m | h m | h m | h m |
| N 72 | 07 03 | 08 39 | 11 28 | ▭ | 19 35 | 22 31 | 24 43 |
| N 70 | 06 52 | 08 15 | 09 56 | ▭ | 20 36 | 22 52 | 24 51 |
| 68 | 06 43 | 07 57 | 09 17 | 18 34 | 21 11 | 23 09 | 24 58 |
| 66 | 06 36 | 07 42 | 08 51 | 19 36 | 21 35 | 23 22 | 25 04 |
| 64 | 06 30 | 07 30 | 08 30 | 20 10 | 21 54 | 23 33 | 25 09 |
| 62 | 06 24 | 07 20 | 08 14 | 20 34 | 22 09 | 23 42 | 25 13 |
| 60 | 06 19 | 07 11 | 08 00 | 20 54 | 22 22 | 23 50 | 25 16 |
| N 58 | 06 14 | 07 03 | 07 49 | 21 10 | 22 33 | 23 56 | 25 20 |
| 56 | 06 10 | 06 56 | 07 38 | 21 23 | 22 43 | 24 02 | 00 02 |
| 54 | 06 06 | 06 50 | 07 29 | 21 35 | 22 51 | 24 08 | 00 08 |
| 52 | 06 02 | 06 44 | 07 21 | 21 45 | 22 59 | 24 13 | 00 13 |
| 50 | 05 59 | 06 39 | 07 14 | 21 54 | 23 06 | 24 17 | 00 17 |
| 45 | 05 51 | 06 27 | 06 59 | 22 14 | 23 20 | 24 27 | 00 27 |
| N 40 | 05 44 | 06 17 | 06 46 | 22 29 | 23 32 | 24 34 | 00 34 |
| 35 | 05 38 | 06 08 | 06 35 | 22 43 | 23 42 | 24 41 | 00 41 |
| 30 | 05 31 | 06 00 | 06 26 | 22 54 | 23 51 | 24 47 | 00 47 |
| 20 | 05 19 | 05 46 | 06 09 | 23 14 | 24 06 | 00 06 | 00 57 |
| N 10 | 05 07 | 05 33 | 05 55 | 23 30 | 24 19 | 00 19 | 01 06 |
| 0 | 04 54 | 05 19 | 05 41 | 23 46 | 24 31 | 00 31 | 01 14 |
| S 10 | 04 39 | 05 05 | 05 27 | 24 02 | 00 02 | 00 43 | 01 22 |
| 20 | 04 21 | 04 49 | 05 13 | 24 19 | 00 19 | 00 56 | 01 31 |
| 30 | 03 58 | 04 29 | 04 55 | 00 01 | 00 38 | 01 11 | 01 41 |
| 35 | 03 43 | 04 17 | 04 45 | 00 14 | 00 49 | 01 19 | 01 47 |
| 40 | 03 25 | 04 03 | 04 34 | 00 30 | 01 02 | 01 29 | 01 53 |
| 45 | 03 03 | 03 46 | 04 20 | 00 48 | 01 17 | 01 40 | 02 01 |
| S 50 | 02 32 | 03 24 | 04 03 | 01 11 | 01 35 | 01 54 | 02 10 |
| 52 | 02 16 | 03 14 | 03 56 | 01 22 | 01 43 | 02 00 | 02 14 |
| 54 | 01 57 | 03 01 | 03 47 | 01 34 | 01 53 | 02 07 | 02 18 |
| 56 | 01 31 | 02 47 | 03 37 | 01 48 | 02 04 | 02 15 | 02 23 |
| 58 | 00 53 | 02 30 | 03 25 | 02 04 | 02 16 | 02 23 | 02 29 |
| S 60 | //// | 02 10 | 03 12 | 02 24 | 02 30 | 02 33 | 02 35 |

## Sunset / Twilight / Moonset

| Lat. | Sunset | Civil | Naut. | Moonset 15 | 16 | 17 | 18 |
|---|---|---|---|---|---|---|---|
| ° | h m | h m | h m | h m | h m | h m | h m |
| N 72 | 12 00 | 14 50 | 16 25 | ▭ | 17 24 | 16 00 | 15 19 |
| N 70 | 13 33 | 15 13 | 16 36 | ▭ | 16 22 | 15 37 | 15 08 |
| 68 | 14 11 | 15 31 | 16 45 | 16 48 | 15 46 | 15 19 | 14 59 |
| 66 | 14 38 | 15 46 | 16 52 | 15 46 | 15 20 | 15 04 | 14 51 |
| 64 | 14 58 | 15 58 | 16 59 | 15 11 | 15 00 | 14 52 | 14 44 |
| 62 | 15 15 | 16 09 | 17 05 | 14 46 | 14 44 | 14 41 | 14 39 |
| 60 | 15 29 | 16 18 | 17 10 | 14 26 | 14 30 | 14 32 | 14 34 |
| N 58 | 15 40 | 16 26 | 17 14 | 14 09 | 14 18 | 14 25 | 14 29 |
| 56 | 15 50 | 16 33 | 17 19 | 13 55 | 14 08 | 14 18 | 14 25 |
| 54 | 15 59 | 16 39 | 17 23 | 13 43 | 13 59 | 14 11 | 14 22 |
| 52 | 16 08 | 16 45 | 17 26 | 13 32 | 13 51 | 14 06 | 14 18 |
| 50 | 16 15 | 16 50 | 17 30 | 13 22 | 13 43 | 14 01 | 14 15 |
| 45 | 16 30 | 17 02 | 17 38 | 13 02 | 13 28 | 13 49 | 14 09 |
| N 40 | 16 43 | 17 12 | 17 45 | 12 45 | 13 15 | 13 40 | 14 03 |
| 35 | 16 54 | 17 21 | 17 51 | 12 31 | 13 03 | 13 32 | 13 59 |
| 30 | 17 03 | 17 29 | 17 58 | 12 19 | 12 54 | 13 25 | 13 55 |
| 20 | 17 20 | 17 43 | 18 10 | 11 58 | 12 37 | 13 13 | 13 47 |
| N 10 | 17 35 | 17 57 | 18 22 | 11 39 | 12 22 | 13 02 | 13 41 |
| 0 | 17 48 | 18 10 | 18 36 | 11 22 | 12 08 | 12 52 | 13 35 |
| S 10 | 18 02 | 18 25 | 18 51 | 11 05 | 11 54 | 12 41 | 13 28 |
| 20 | 18 17 | 18 41 | 19 09 | 10 46 | 11 39 | 12 30 | 13 22 |
| 30 | 18 34 | 19 01 | 19 32 | 10 25 | 11 21 | 12 18 | 13 14 |
| 35 | 18 45 | 19 13 | 19 47 | 10 12 | 11 11 | 12 10 | 13 10 |
| 40 | 18 56 | 19 27 | 20 05 | 09 57 | 10 59 | 12 02 | 13 05 |
| 45 | 19 10 | 19 44 | 20 28 | 09 40 | 10 46 | 11 52 | 12 59 |
| S 50 | 19 27 | 20 06 | 20 59 | 09 18 | 10 28 | 11 40 | 12 52 |
| 52 | 19 35 | 20 17 | 21 15 | 09 07 | 10 20 | 11 34 | 12 48 |
| 54 | 19 44 | 20 30 | 21 35 | 08 56 | 10 11 | 11 28 | 12 45 |
| 56 | 19 54 | 20 44 | 22 02 | 08 42 | 10 01 | 11 21 | 12 41 |
| 58 | 20 06 | 21 01 | 22 42 | 08 26 | 09 50 | 11 13 | 12 36 |
| S 60 | 20 19 | 21 23 | //// | 08 07 | 09 36 | 11 04 | 12 31 |

## SUN and MOON

| Day | SUN Eqn. of Time 00ʰ | 12ʰ | Mer. Pass. | MOON Mer. Pass. Upper | Lower | Age | Phase |
|---|---|---|---|---|---|---|---|
| d | m s | m s | h m | h m | h m | d | % |
| 15 | 15 31 | 15 26 | 11 45 | 05 11 | 17 34 | 21 | 60 |
| 16 | 15 21 | 15 15 | 11 45 | 05 57 | 18 19 | 22 | 51 |
| 17 | 15 10 | 15 04 | 11 45 | 06 41 | 19 03 | 23 | 41 |

| UT | ARIES GHA | VENUS −3.9 GHA | Dec | MARS −1.6 GHA | Dec | JUPITER −2.7 GHA | Dec | SATURN +0.7 GHA | Dec | STARS Name | SHA | Dec |
|---|---|---|---|---|---|---|---|---|---|---|---|---|
| **18 00** | 57 01.2 | 176 53.1 | S20 27.4 | 334 33.1 | N24 36.8 | 57 28.5 | S 1 49.0 | 95 01.6 | S16 17.3 | Acamar | 315 12.7 | S40 12.8 |
| 01 | 72 03.6 | 191 52.3 | 28.1 | 349 36.3 | 36.9 | 72 31.0 | 49.0 | 110 04.0 | 17.2 | Achernar | 335 21.0 | S57 07.4 |
| 02 | 87 06.1 | 206 51.5 | 28.8 | 4 39.4 | 37.0 | 87 33.5 | 49.0 | 125 06.3 | 17.2 | Acrux | 173 02.5 | S63 13.2 |
| 03 | 102 08.6 | 221 50.7 | .. 29.5 | 19 42.6 | .. 37.1 | 102 36.0 | .. 49.0 | 140 08.7 | .. 17.2 | Adhara | 255 07.0 | S29 00.0 |
| 04 | 117 11.0 | 236 49.9 | 30.3 | 34 45.8 | 37.2 | 117 38.5 | 49.0 | 155 11.0 | 17.1 | Aldebaran | 290 41.3 | N16 33.3 |
| 05 | 132 13.5 | 251 49.1 | 31.0 | 49 49.0 | 37.3 | 132 41.0 | 49.0 | 170 13.4 | 17.1 | | | |
| 06 | 147 16.0 | 266 48.3 | S20 31.7 | 64 52.2 | N24 37.4 | 147 43.5 | S 1 49.0 | 185 15.8 | S16 17.1 | Alioth | 166 15.0 | N55 50.1 |
| 07 | 162 18.4 | 281 47.5 | 32.4 | 79 55.4 | 37.5 | 162 46.1 | 49.0 | 200 18.1 | 17.0 | Alkaid | 152 53.9 | N49 11.9 |
| 08 | 177 20.9 | 296 46.7 | 33.1 | 94 58.6 | 37.5 | 177 48.6 | 49.0 | 215 20.5 | 17.0 | Alnair | 27 35.1 | S46 51.3 |
| F 09 | 192 23.4 | 311 45.9 | .. 33.8 | 110 01.8 | .. 37.6 | 192 51.1 | .. 49.0 | 230 22.8 | .. 16.9 | Alnilam | 275 39.2 | S 1 11.2 |
| R 10 | 207 25.8 | 326 45.1 | 34.5 | 125 05.0 | 37.7 | 207 53.6 | 49.1 | 245 25.2 | 16.9 | Alphard | 217 49.5 | S 8 45.3 |
| I 11 | 222 28.3 | 341 44.3 | 35.2 | 140 08.3 | 37.8 | 222 56.1 | 49.1 | 260 27.5 | 16.9 | | | |
| D 12 | 237 30.7 | 356 43.5 | S20 35.9 | 155 11.5 | N24 37.9 | 237 58.6 | S 1 49.1 | 275 29.9 | S16 16.8 | Alphecca | 126 05.6 | N26 38.3 |
| A 13 | 252 33.2 | 11 42.7 | 36.7 | 170 14.7 | 38.0 | 253 01.1 | 49.1 | 290 32.2 | 16.8 | Alpheratz | 357 36.4 | N29 13.1 |
| Y 14 | 267 35.7 | 26 41.9 | 37.4 | 185 17.9 | 38.1 | 268 03.6 | 49.1 | 305 34.6 | 16.8 | Altair | 62 01.9 | N 8 55.8 |
| 15 | 282 38.1 | 41 41.1 | .. 38.1 | 200 21.1 | .. 38.2 | 283 06.2 | .. 49.1 | 320 37.0 | .. 16.7 | Ankaa | 353 08.7 | S42 11.1 |
| 16 | 297 40.6 | 56 40.3 | 38.8 | 215 24.3 | 38.3 | 298 08.7 | 49.1 | 335 39.3 | 16.7 | Antares | 112 18.4 | S26 28.9 |
| 17 | 312 43.1 | 71 39.5 | 39.5 | 230 27.5 | 38.4 | 313 11.2 | 49.1 | 350 41.7 | 16.6 | | | |
| 18 | 327 45.5 | 86 38.7 | S20 40.2 | 245 30.7 | N24 38.5 | 328 13.7 | S 1 49.1 | 5 44.0 | S16 16.6 | Arcturus | 145 49.9 | N19 03.9 |
| 19 | 342 48.0 | 101 37.9 | 40.9 | 260 34.0 | 38.6 | 343 16.2 | 49.1 | 20 46.4 | 16.6 | Atria | 107 14.8 | S69 04.1 |
| 20 | 357 50.5 | 116 37.1 | 41.6 | 275 37.2 | 38.7 | 358 18.7 | 49.1 | 35 48.7 | 16.5 | Avior | 234 15.2 | S59 34.6 |
| 21 | 12 52.9 | 131 36.3 | .. 42.3 | 290 40.4 | .. 38.7 | 13 21.2 | .. 49.1 | 50 51.1 | .. 16.5 | Bellatrix | 278 24.5 | N 6 22.3 |
| 22 | 27 55.4 | 146 35.5 | 43.0 | 305 43.6 | 38.8 | 28 23.7 | 49.1 | 65 53.4 | 16.5 | Betelgeuse | 270 53.7 | N 7 24.7 |
| 23 | 42 57.9 | 161 34.7 | 43.7 | 320 46.9 | 38.9 | 43 26.2 | 49.2 | 80 55.8 | 16.4 | | | |
| **19 00** | 58 00.3 | 176 33.9 | S20 44.4 | 335 50.1 | N24 39.0 | 58 28.7 | S 1 49.2 | 95 58.1 | S16 16.4 | Canopus | 263 52.7 | S52 42.2 |
| 01 | 73 02.8 | 191 33.0 | 45.1 | 350 53.3 | 39.1 | 73 31.3 | 49.2 | 111 00.5 | 16.4 | Capella | 280 24.1 | N46 01.2 |
| 02 | 88 05.2 | 206 32.2 | 45.7 | 5 56.5 | 39.2 | 88 33.8 | 49.2 | 126 02.9 | 16.3 | Deneb | 49 27.2 | N45 21.9 |
| 03 | 103 07.7 | 221 31.4 | .. 46.4 | 20 59.8 | .. 39.3 | 103 36.3 | .. 49.2 | 141 05.2 | .. 16.3 | Denebola | 182 26.9 | N14 26.7 |
| 04 | 118 10.2 | 236 30.6 | 47.1 | 36 03.0 | 39.4 | 118 38.8 | 49.2 | 156 07.6 | 16.2 | Diphda | 348 48.9 | S17 51.8 |
| 05 | 133 12.6 | 251 29.8 | 47.8 | 51 06.2 | 39.5 | 133 41.3 | 49.2 | 171 09.9 | 16.2 | | | |
| 06 | 148 15.1 | 266 29.0 | S20 48.5 | 66 09.5 | N24 39.6 | 148 43.8 | S 1 49.2 | 186 12.3 | S16 16.2 | Dubhe | 193 43.4 | N61 37.5 |
| 07 | 163 17.6 | 281 28.2 | 49.2 | 81 12.7 | 39.6 | 163 46.3 | 49.2 | 201 14.6 | 16.1 | Elnath | 278 03.8 | N28 37.6 |
| S 08 | 178 20.0 | 296 27.4 | 49.9 | 96 15.9 | 39.7 | 178 48.8 | 49.2 | 216 17.0 | 16.1 | Eltanin | 90 43.5 | N51 29.3 |
| A 09 | 193 22.5 | 311 26.6 | .. 50.6 | 111 19.2 | .. 39.8 | 193 51.3 | .. 49.2 | 231 19.3 | .. 16.0 | Enif | 33 40.6 | N 9 58.8 |
| T 10 | 208 25.0 | 326 25.7 | 51.3 | 126 22.4 | 39.9 | 208 53.8 | 49.2 | 246 21.7 | 16.0 | Fomalhaut | 15 16.4 | S29 30.2 |
| U 11 | 223 27.4 | 341 24.9 | 51.9 | 141 25.7 | 40.0 | 223 56.3 | 49.2 | 261 24.0 | 16.0 | | | |
| R 12 | 238 29.9 | 356 24.1 | S20 52.6 | 156 28.9 | N24 40.1 | 238 58.8 | S 1 49.2 | 276 26.4 | S16 15.9 | Gacrux | 171 54.0 | S57 14.1 |
| D 13 | 253 32.3 | 11 23.3 | 53.3 | 171 32.1 | 40.2 | 254 01.3 | 49.2 | 291 28.7 | 15.9 | Gienah | 175 45.6 | S17 39.9 |
| A 14 | 268 34.8 | 26 22.5 | 54.0 | 186 35.4 | 40.3 | 269 03.8 | 49.2 | 306 31.1 | 15.9 | Hadar | 148 39.2 | S60 28.7 |
| Y 15 | 283 37.3 | 41 21.7 | .. 54.7 | 201 38.6 | .. 40.4 | 284 06.3 | .. 49.2 | 321 33.4 | .. 15.8 | Hamal | 327 52.9 | N23 34.3 |
| 16 | 298 39.7 | 56 20.9 | 55.3 | 216 41.9 | 40.4 | 299 08.8 | 49.3 | 336 35.8 | 15.8 | Kaus Aust. | 83 35.2 | S34 22.5 |
| 17 | 313 42.2 | 71 20.0 | 56.0 | 231 45.1 | 40.5 | 314 11.3 | 49.3 | 351 38.1 | 15.7 | | | |
| 18 | 328 44.7 | 86 19.2 | S20 56.7 | 246 48.4 | N24 40.6 | 329 13.8 | S 1 49.3 | 6 40.5 | S16 15.7 | Kochab | 137 21.0 | N74 03.6 |
| 19 | 343 47.1 | 101 18.4 | 57.4 | 261 51.6 | 40.7 | 344 16.3 | 49.3 | 21 42.8 | 15.7 | Markab | 13 31.6 | N15 19.8 |
| 20 | 358 49.6 | 116 17.6 | 58.1 | 276 54.9 | 40.8 | 359 18.8 | 49.3 | 36 45.2 | 15.6 | Menkar | 314 07.7 | N 4 10.8 |
| 21 | 13 52.1 | 131 16.8 | .. 58.7 | 291 58.1 | .. 40.9 | 14 21.3 | .. 49.3 | 51 47.5 | .. 15.6 | Menkent | 148 00.1 | S36 28.7 |
| 22 | 28 54.5 | 146 15.9 | 20 59.4 | 307 01.4 | 41.0 | 29 23.8 | 49.3 | 66 49.9 | 15.5 | Miaplacidus | 221 38.4 | S69 48.2 |
| 23 | 43 57.0 | 161 15.1 | 21 00.1 | 322 04.7 | 41.1 | 44 26.3 | 49.3 | 81 52.2 | 15.5 | | | |
| **20 00** | 58 59.5 | 176 14.3 | S21 00.7 | 337 07.9 | N24 41.2 | 59 28.8 | S 1 49.3 | 96 54.6 | S16 15.5 | Mirfak | 308 30.3 | N49 56.6 |
| 01 | 74 01.9 | 191 13.5 | 01.4 | 352 11.2 | 41.2 | 74 31.3 | 49.3 | 111 56.9 | 15.4 | Nunki | 75 50.3 | S26 16.1 |
| 02 | 89 04.4 | 206 12.7 | 02.1 | 7 14.4 | 41.3 | 89 33.8 | 49.3 | 126 59.3 | 15.4 | Peacock | 53 08.8 | S56 39.9 |
| 03 | 104 06.8 | 221 11.8 | .. 02.7 | 22 17.7 | .. 41.4 | 104 36.3 | .. 49.3 | 142 01.6 | .. 15.4 | Pollux | 243 19.3 | N27 58.2 |
| 04 | 119 09.3 | 236 11.0 | 03.4 | 37 21.0 | 41.5 | 119 38.8 | 49.3 | 157 04.0 | 15.3 | Procyon | 244 52.5 | N 5 10.1 |
| 05 | 134 11.8 | 251 10.2 | 04.1 | 52 24.2 | 41.6 | 134 41.3 | 49.3 | 172 06.3 | 15.3 | | | |
| 06 | 149 14.2 | 266 09.4 | S21 04.7 | 67 27.5 | N24 41.7 | 149 43.8 | S 1 49.3 | 187 08.7 | S16 15.2 | Rasalhague | 96 00.5 | N12 32.7 |
| 07 | 164 16.7 | 281 08.5 | 05.4 | 82 30.8 | 41.8 | 164 46.3 | 49.3 | 202 11.0 | 15.2 | Regulus | 207 36.4 | N11 51.4 |
| 08 | 179 19.2 | 296 07.7 | 06.1 | 97 34.0 | 41.8 | 179 48.8 | 49.3 | 217 13.4 | 15.2 | Rigel | 281 05.3 | S 8 10.4 |
| S 09 | 194 21.6 | 311 06.9 | .. 06.7 | 112 37.3 | .. 41.9 | 194 51.3 | .. 49.3 | 232 15.7 | .. 15.1 | Rigil Kent. | 139 43.4 | S60 55.5 |
| U 10 | 209 24.1 | 326 06.1 | 07.4 | 127 40.6 | 42.0 | 209 53.8 | 49.3 | 247 18.1 | 15.1 | Sabik | 102 05.2 | S15 45.1 |
| N 11 | 224 26.6 | 341 05.2 | 08.0 | 142 43.8 | 42.1 | 224 56.3 | 49.3 | 262 20.4 | 15.0 | | | |
| D 12 | 239 29.0 | 356 04.4 | S21 08.7 | 157 47.1 | N24 42.2 | 239 58.8 | S 1 49.3 | 277 22.8 | S16 15.0 | Schedar | 349 32.7 | N56 39.9 |
| A 13 | 254 31.5 | 11 03.6 | 09.4 | 172 50.4 | 42.3 | 255 01.3 | 49.3 | 292 25.1 | 15.0 | Shaula | 96 13.2 | S37 07.2 |
| Y 14 | 269 33.9 | 26 02.8 | 10.0 | 187 53.7 | 42.4 | 270 03.8 | 49.3 | 307 27.5 | 14.9 | Sirius | 258 27.6 | S16 44.7 |
| 15 | 284 36.4 | 41 01.9 | .. 10.7 | 202 57.0 | .. 42.4 | 285 06.3 | .. 49.3 | 322 29.8 | .. 14.9 | Spica | 158 24.5 | S11 16.7 |
| 16 | 299 38.9 | 56 01.1 | 11.3 | 218 00.2 | 42.5 | 300 08.8 | 49.3 | 337 32.2 | 14.8 | Suhail | 222 47.5 | S43 31.1 |
| 17 | 314 41.3 | 71 00.3 | 12.0 | 233 03.5 | 42.6 | 315 11.3 | 49.3 | 352 34.5 | 14.8 | | | |
| 18 | 329 43.8 | 85 59.4 | S21 12.6 | 248 06.8 | N24 42.7 | 330 13.8 | S 1 49.3 | 7 36.9 | S16 14.8 | Vega | 80 34.8 | N38 48.4 |
| 19 | 344 46.3 | 100 58.6 | 13.3 | 263 10.1 | 42.8 | 345 16.3 | 49.3 | 22 39.2 | 14.7 | Zuben'ubi | 136 58.3 | S16 08.0 |
| 20 | 359 48.7 | 115 57.8 | 13.9 | 278 13.4 | 42.9 | 0 18.8 | 49.3 | 37 41.6 | 14.7 | | SHA | Mer. Pass. |
| 21 | 14 51.2 | 130 57.0 | .. 14.6 | 293 16.7 | .. 42.9 | 15 21.3 | .. 49.3 | 52 43.9 | .. 14.6 | | | h m |
| 22 | 29 53.7 | 145 56.1 | 15.2 | 308 19.9 | 43.0 | 30 23.8 | 49.3 | 67 46.2 | 14.6 | Venus | 118 33.5 | 12 14 |
| 23 | 44 56.1 | 160 55.3 | 15.9 | 323 23.2 | 43.1 | 45 26.3 | 49.3 | 82 48.6 | 14.6 | Mars | 277 49.8 | 1 36 |
| | h m | | | | | | | | | Jupiter | 0 28.4 | 20 03 |
| Mer.Pass. 20 04.7 | v −0.8  d 0.7 | | | v 3.2  d 0.1 | | v 2.5  d 0.0 | | v 2.4  d 0.0 | | Saturn | 37 57.8 | 17 33 |

## SUN and MOON

| UT (d h) | SUN GHA | SUN Dec | MOON GHA | v | Dec | d | HP |
|---|---|---|---|---|---|---|---|
| **18** 00 | 183 44.4 | S19 09.7 | 252 06.5 | 15.0 | N11 28.2 | 13.1 | 55.3 |
| 01 | 198 44.3 | 10.3 | 266 40.5 | 15.0 | 11 15.1 | 13.2 | 55.4 |
| 02 | 213 44.2 | 10.9 | 281 14.5 | 15.1 | 11 01.9 | 13.3 | 55.4 |
| 03 | 228 44.0 | .. 11.5 | 295 48.6 | 15.1 | 10 48.6 | 13.3 | 55.4 |
| 04 | 243 43.9 | 12.1 | 310 22.7 | 15.1 | 10 35.3 | 13.3 | 55.4 |
| 05 | 258 43.8 | 12.7 | 324 56.8 | 15.1 | 10 22.0 | 13.4 | 55.5 |
| 06 | 273 43.6 | S19 13.3 | 339 30.9 | 15.1 | N10 08.6 | 13.5 | 55.5 |
| **F** 07 | 288 43.5 | 13.9 | 354 05.0 | 15.1 | 9 55.1 | 13.5 | 55.5 |
| **R** 08 | 303 43.4 | 14.5 | 8 39.1 | 15.1 | 9 41.6 | 13.6 | 55.5 |
| **I** 09 | 318 43.3 | .. 15.1 | 23 13.2 | 15.1 | 9 28.0 | 13.6 | 55.6 |
| **D** 10 | 333 43.1 | 15.7 | 37 47.3 | 15.2 | 9 14.4 | 13.7 | 55.6 |
| **A** 11 | 348 43.0 | 16.3 | 52 21.5 | 15.1 | 9 00.7 | 13.7 | 55.6 |
| **Y** 12 | 3 42.9 | S19 16.9 | 66 55.6 | 15.1 | N 8 47.0 | 13.8 | 55.7 |
| 13 | 18 42.7 | 17.5 | 81 29.7 | 15.2 | 8 33.2 | 13.8 | 55.7 |
| 14 | 33 42.6 | 18.1 | 96 03.9 | 15.1 | 8 19.4 | 13.9 | 55.7 |
| 15 | 48 42.5 | .. 18.6 | 110 38.0 | 15.2 | 8 05.5 | 13.9 | 55.7 |
| 16 | 63 42.3 | 19.2 | 125 12.2 | 15.1 | 7 51.6 | 14.0 | 55.8 |
| 17 | 78 42.2 | 19.8 | 139 46.3 | 15.2 | 7 37.6 | 14.0 | 55.8 |
| 18 | 93 42.1 | S19 20.4 | 154 20.5 | 15.1 | N 7 23.6 | 14.1 | 55.8 |
| 19 | 108 41.9 | 21.0 | 168 54.6 | 15.2 | 7 09.5 | 14.1 | 55.9 |
| 20 | 123 41.8 | 21.6 | 183 28.8 | 15.1 | 6 55.4 | 14.1 | 55.9 |
| 21 | 138 41.6 | .. 22.2 | 198 02.9 | 15.1 | 6 41.3 | 14.2 | 55.9 |
| 22 | 153 41.5 | 22.8 | 212 37.0 | 15.1 | 6 27.1 | 14.2 | 56.0 |
| 23 | 168 41.4 | 23.3 | 227 11.1 | 15.2 | 6 12.9 | 14.3 | 56.0 |
| **19** 00 | 183 41.2 | S19 23.9 | 241 45.3 | 15.1 | N 5 58.6 | 14.4 | 56.0 |
| 01 | 198 41.1 | 24.5 | 256 19.4 | 15.1 | 5 44.2 | 14.3 | 56.1 |
| 02 | 213 41.0 | 25.1 | 270 53.5 | 15.0 | 5 29.9 | 14.4 | 56.1 |
| 03 | 228 40.8 | .. 25.7 | 285 27.5 | 15.1 | 5 15.5 | 14.5 | 56.1 |
| 04 | 243 40.7 | 26.3 | 300 01.6 | 15.1 | 5 01.0 | 14.4 | 56.2 |
| 05 | 258 40.5 | 26.9 | 314 35.7 | 15.0 | 4 46.6 | 14.6 | 56.2 |
| 06 | 273 40.4 | S19 27.4 | 329 09.7 | 15.0 | N 4 32.0 | 14.5 | 56.2 |
| **S** 07 | 288 40.3 | 28.0 | 343 43.7 | 15.0 | 4 17.5 | 14.6 | 56.2 |
| **A** 08 | 303 40.1 | 28.6 | 358 17.7 | 15.0 | 4 02.9 | 14.6 | 56.3 |
| **T** 09 | 318 40.0 | 29.2 | 12 51.7 | 15.0 | 3 48.3 | 14.7 | 56.3 |
| **U** 10 | 333 39.8 | 29.8 | 27 25.7 | 15.0 | 3 33.6 | 14.7 | 56.3 |
| **R** 11 | 348 39.7 | 30.3 | 41 59.7 | 14.9 | 3 18.9 | 14.7 | 56.4 |
| **D** 12 | 3 39.6 | S19 30.9 | 56 33.6 | 14.9 | N 3 04.2 | 14.7 | 56.4 |
| **A** 13 | 18 39.4 | 31.5 | 71 07.5 | 14.9 | 2 49.5 | 14.0 | 56.4 |
| **Y** 14 | 33 39.3 | 32.1 | 85 41.4 | 14.8 | 2 34.7 | 14.8 | 56.5 |
| 15 | 48 39.1 | .. 32.6 | 100 15.2 | 14.9 | 2 19.9 | 14.9 | 56.5 |
| 16 | 63 39.0 | 33.2 | 114 49.1 | 14.8 | 2 05.0 | 14.8 | 56.6 |
| 17 | 78 38.9 | 33.8 | 129 22.9 | 14.7 | 1 50.2 | 14.9 | 56.6 |
| 18 | 93 38.7 | S19 34.4 | 143 56.6 | 14.8 | N 1 35.3 | 15.0 | 56.6 |
| 19 | 108 38.6 | 34.9 | 158 30.4 | 14.7 | 1 20.3 | 14.9 | 56.7 |
| 20 | 123 38.4 | 35.5 | 173 04.1 | 14.7 | 1 05.4 | 15.0 | 56.7 |
| 21 | 138 38.3 | .. 36.1 | 187 37.8 | 14.6 | 0 50.4 | 15.0 | 56.7 |
| 22 | 153 38.1 | 36.7 | 202 11.4 | 14.6 | 0 35.4 | 15.0 | 56.8 |
| 23 | 168 38.0 | 37.2 | 216 45.0 | 14.6 | N 0 20.4 | 15.0 | 56.8 |
| **20** 00 | 183 37.8 | S19 37.8 | 231 18.6 | 14.5 | N 0 05.4 | 15.1 | 56.8 |
| 01 | 198 37.7 | 38.4 | 245 52.1 | 14.5 | S 0 09.7 | 15.1 | 56.9 |
| 02 | 213 37.5 | 38.9 | 260 25.6 | 14.5 | 0 24.8 | 15.1 | 56.9 |
| 03 | 228 37.4 | .. 39.5 | 274 59.1 | 14.4 | 0 39.9 | 15.1 | 56.9 |
| 04 | 243 37.3 | 40.1 | 289 32.5 | 14.3 | 0 55.0 | 15.1 | 57.0 |
| 05 | 258 37.1 | 40.6 | 304 05.8 | 14.4 | 1 10.1 | 15.1 | 57.0 |
| 06 | 273 37.0 | S19 41.2 | 318 39.2 | 14.2 | S 1 25.2 | 15.2 | 57.0 |
| **S** 07 | 288 36.8 | 41.8 | 333 12.4 | 14.3 | 1 40.4 | 15.2 | 57.1 |
| **U** 08 | 303 36.7 | 42.3 | 347 45.7 | 14.1 | 1 55.6 | 15.2 | 57.1 |
| **N** 09 | 318 36.5 | .. 42.9 | 2 18.9 | 14.1 | 2 10.8 | 15.1 | 57.1 |
| **D** 10 | 333 36.4 | 43.5 | 16 52.0 | 14.1 | 2 25.9 | 15.3 | 57.2 |
| **A** 11 | 348 36.2 | 44.0 | 31 25.1 | 14.0 | 2 41.1 | 15.3 | 57.2 |
| **Y** 12 | 3 36.1 | S19 44.6 | 45 58.1 | 14.0 | S 2 56.4 | 15.2 | 57.3 |
| 13 | 18 35.9 | 45.2 | 60 31.1 | 13.9 | 3 11.6 | 15.2 | 57.3 |
| 14 | 33 35.8 | 45.7 | 75 04.0 | 13.9 | 3 26.8 | 15.3 | 57.3 |
| 15 | 48 35.6 | .. 46.3 | 89 36.9 | 13.8 | 3 42.0 | 15.3 | 57.4 |
| 16 | 63 35.5 | 46.9 | 104 09.7 | 13.8 | 3 57.3 | 15.2 | 57.4 |
| 17 | 78 35.3 | 47.4 | 118 42.5 | 13.7 | 4 12.5 | 15.2 | 57.4 |
| 18 | 93 35.2 | S19 48.0 | 133 15.2 | 13.6 | S 4 27.7 | 15.3 | 57.5 |
| 19 | 108 35.0 | 48.5 | 147 47.8 | 13.6 | 4 43.0 | 15.2 | 57.5 |
| 20 | 123 34.9 | 49.1 | 162 20.4 | 13.5 | 4 58.2 | 15.2 | 57.5 |
| 21 | 138 34.7 | .. 49.7 | 176 52.9 | 13.5 | 5 13.4 | 15.3 | 57.6 |
| 22 | 153 34.5 | 50.2 | 191 25.4 | 13.3 | 5 28.7 | 15.2 | 57.6 |
| 23 | 168 34.4 | 50.8 | 205 57.7 | 13.4 | S 5 43.9 | 15.2 | 57.7 |
| | SD 16.2 | d 0.6 | SD 15.2 | | 15.4 | | 15.6 |

## Twilight, Sunrise, Moonrise

| Lat. | Twilight Naut. | Twilight Civil | Sunrise | Moonrise 18 | 19 | 20 | 21 |
|---|---|---|---|---|---|---|---|
| N 72 | 07 13 | 08 53 | ■■■ | 24 43 | 00 43 | 02 49 | 05 02 |
| N 70 | 07 02 | 08 27 | 10 18 | 24 51 | 00 51 | 02 48 | 04 50 |
| 68 | 06 52 | 08 07 | 09 32 | 24 58 | 00 58 | 02 47 | 04 41 |
| 66 | 06 44 | 07 51 | 09 02 | 25 04 | 01 04 | 02 46 | 04 33 |
| 64 | 06 37 | 07 38 | 08 40 | 25 09 | 01 09 | 02 46 | 04 27 |
| 62 | 06 30 | 07 27 | 08 22 | 25 13 | 01 13 | 02 45 | 04 21 |
| 60 | 06 25 | 07 17 | 08 08 | 25 16 | 01 16 | 02 45 | 04 17 |
| N 58 | 06 20 | 07 09 | 07 55 | 25 20 | 01 20 | 02 44 | 04 13 |
| 56 | 06 15 | 07 01 | 07 44 | 00 02 | 01 22 | 02 44 | 04 09 |
| 54 | 06 11 | 06 55 | 07 35 | 00 08 | 01 25 | 02 43 | 04 06 |
| 52 | 06 07 | 06 49 | 07 27 | 00 13 | 01 27 | 02 43 | 04 03 |
| 50 | 06 03 | 06 43 | 07 19 | 00 17 | 01 29 | 02 43 | 04 00 |
| 45 | 05 55 | 06 31 | 07 03 | 00 27 | 01 34 | 02 43 | 03 54 |
| N 40 | 05 47 | 06 20 | 06 49 | 00 34 | 01 38 | 02 42 | 03 49 |
| 35 | 05 40 | 06 11 | 06 38 | 00 40 | 01 41 | 02 42 | 03 45 |
| 30 | 05 34 | 06 03 | 06 28 | 00 47 | 01 44 | 02 41 | 03 41 |
| 20 | 05 21 | 05 48 | 06 11 | 00 57 | 01 48 | 02 41 | 03 35 |
| N 10 | 05 08 | 05 34 | 05 56 | 01 06 | 01 53 | 02 40 | 03 30 |
| 0 | 04 54 | 05 20 | 05 42 | 01 14 | 01 57 | 02 40 | 03 25 |
| S 10 | 04 39 | 05 05 | 05 27 | 01 22 | 02 01 | 02 40 | 03 20 |
| 20 | 04 20 | 04 48 | 05 12 | 01 31 | 02 05 | 02 39 | 03 15 |
| 30 | 03 56 | 04 28 | 04 54 | 01 41 | 02 10 | 02 39 | 03 09 |
| 35 | 03 41 | 04 15 | 04 44 | 01 47 | 02 13 | 02 38 | 03 05 |
| 40 | 03 22 | 04 01 | 04 32 | 01 53 | 02 16 | 02 38 | 03 01 |
| 45 | 02 59 | 03 43 | 04 17 | 02 01 | 02 19 | 02 38 | 02 57 |
| S 50 | 02 26 | 03 20 | 04 00 | 02 10 | 02 24 | 02 37 | 02 52 |
| 52 | 02 09 | 03 09 | 03 51 | 02 14 | 02 26 | 02 37 | 02 50 |
| 54 | 01 48 | 02 56 | 03 42 | 02 18 | 02 28 | 02 37 | 02 47 |
| 56 | 01 19 | 02 41 | 03 32 | 02 23 | 02 30 | 02 37 | 02 44 |
| 58 | 00 32 | 02 23 | 03 20 | 02 29 | 02 33 | 02 37 | 02 41 |
| S 60 | //// | 02 00 | 03 06 | 02 35 | 02 36 | 02 36 | 02 37 |

## Sunset, Twilight, Moonset

| Lat. | Sunset | Twilight Civil | Twilight Naut. | Moonset 18 | 19 | 20 | 21 |
|---|---|---|---|---|---|---|---|
| N 72 | ■■■ | 14 37 | 16 16 | 15 19 | 14 47 | 14 15 | 13 39 |
| N 70 | 13 12 | 15 03 | 16 28 | 15 08 | 14 44 | 14 20 | 13 53 |
| 68 | 13 58 | 15 23 | 16 38 | 14 59 | 14 41 | 14 24 | 14 05 |
| 66 | 14 28 | 15 39 | 16 46 | 14 51 | 14 39 | 14 27 | 14 14 |
| 64 | 14 50 | 15 52 | 16 53 | 14 44 | 14 37 | 14 30 | 14 22 |
| 62 | 15 08 | 16 03 | 17 00 | 14 39 | 14 36 | 14 33 | 14 30 |
| 60 | 15 22 | 16 13 | 17 05 | 14 34 | 14 34 | 14 35 | 14 36 |
| N 58 | 15 35 | 16 21 | 17 10 | 14 29 | 14 33 | 14 37 | 14 41 |
| 56 | 15 46 | 16 29 | 17 15 | 14 25 | 14 32 | 14 39 | 14 46 |
| 54 | 15 55 | 16 36 | 17 19 | 14 22 | 14 31 | 14 40 | 14 50 |
| 52 | 16 04 | 16 42 | 17 23 | 14 18 | 14 30 | 14 42 | 14 54 |
| 50 | 16 11 | 16 47 | 17 27 | 14 15 | 14 29 | 14 43 | 14 58 |
| 45 | 16 27 | 17 00 | 17 35 | 14 09 | 14 27 | 14 46 | 15 06 |
| N 40 | 16 41 | 17 10 | 17 43 | 14 03 | 14 26 | 14 48 | 15 13 |
| 35 | 16 52 | 17 19 | 17 50 | 13 59 | 14 24 | 14 50 | 15 18 |
| 30 | 17 02 | 17 28 | 17 57 | 13 55 | 14 23 | 14 52 | 15 23 |
| 20 | 17 19 | 17 43 | 18 10 | 13 47 | 14 21 | 14 55 | 15 32 |
| N 10 | 17 35 | 17 57 | 18 23 | 13 41 | 14 19 | 14 58 | 15 40 |
| 0 | 17 49 | 18 11 | 18 36 | 13 35 | 14 17 | 15 01 | 15 47 |
| S 10 | 18 03 | 18 26 | 18 52 | 13 28 | 14 15 | 15 04 | 15 55 |
| 20 | 18 19 | 18 43 | 19 11 | 13 22 | 14 13 | 15 07 | 16 02 |
| 30 | 18 37 | 19 03 | 19 35 | 13 14 | 14 11 | 15 10 | 16 11 |
| 35 | 18 48 | 19 16 | 19 50 | 13 10 | 14 10 | 15 12 | 16 17 |
| 40 | 19 00 | 19 31 | 20 09 | 13 05 | 14 08 | 15 14 | 16 23 |
| 45 | 19 14 | 19 49 | 20 33 | 12 59 | 14 07 | 15 16 | 16 30 |
| S 50 | 19 32 | 20 12 | 21 06 | 12 52 | 14 04 | 15 19 | 16 38 |
| 52 | 19 40 | 20 23 | 21 24 | 12 48 | 14 03 | 15 21 | 16 42 |
| 54 | 19 50 | 20 36 | 21 45 | 12 45 | 14 02 | 15 22 | 16 46 |
| 56 | 20 00 | 20 52 | 22 15 | 12 41 | 14 01 | 15 24 | 16 51 |
| 58 | 20 13 | 21 10 | 23 09 | 12 36 | 14 00 | 15 26 | 16 56 |
| S 60 | 20 27 | 21 34 | //// | 12 31 | 13 58 | 15 28 | 17 02 |

## SUN and MOON — daily data

| Day | SUN Eqn. of Time 00h | 12h | Mer. Pass. | MOON Mer. Pass. Upper | Lower | Age | Phase |
|---|---|---|---|---|---|---|---|
| d | m s | m s | h m | h m | h m | d | % |
| 18 | 14 58 | 14 52 | 11 45 | 07 24 | 19 46 | 24 | 32 |
| 19 | 14 45 | 14 39 | 11 45 | 08 07 | 20 29 | 25 | 23 |
| 20 | 14 32 | 14 25 | 11 46 | 08 50 | 21 13 | 26 | 14 |

| UT | ARIES | VENUS −3·9 | | MARS −1·7 | | JUPITER −2·6 | | SATURN +0·7 | | STARS | | |
|---|---|---|---|---|---|---|---|---|---|---|---|---|
| | GHA | GHA | Dec | GHA | Dec | GHA | Dec | GHA | Dec | Name | SHA | Dec |
| d h | ° ′ | ° ′ | ° ′ | ° ′ | ° ′ | ° ′ | ° ′ | ° ′ | ° ′ | | ° ′ | ° ′ |
| 21 00 | 59 58.6 | 175 54.5 | S21 16.5 | 338 26.5 | N24 43.2 | 60 28.8 | S 1 49.3 | 97 50.9 | S16 14.5 | Acamar | 315 12.7 | S40 12.8 |
| 01 | 75 01.1 | 190 53.6 | 17.2 | 353 29.8 | 43.3 | 75 31.3 | 49.3 | 112 53.3 | 14.5 | Achernar | 335 21.1 | S57 07.4 |
| 02 | 90 03.5 | 205 52.8 | 17.8 | 8 33.1 | 43.4 | 90 33.7 | 49.3 | 127 55.6 | 14.4 | Acrux | 173 02.5 | S63 13.2 |
| 03 | 105 06.0 | 220 52.0 .. | 18.5 | 23 36.4 .. | 43.4 | 105 36.2 .. | 49.3 | 142 58.0 .. | 14.4 | Adhara | 255 07.0 | S29 00.0 |
| 04 | 120 08.4 | 235 51.1 | 19.1 | 38 39.7 | 43.5 | 120 38.7 | 49.3 | 158 00.3 | 14.4 | Aldebaran | 290 41.3 | N16 33.3 |
| 05 | 135 10.9 | 250 50.3 | 19.7 | 53 43.0 | 43.6 | 135 41.2 | 49.3 | 173 02.7 | 14.3 | | | |
| 06 | 150 13.4 | 265 49.5 | S21 20.4 | 68 46.3 | N24 43.7 | 150 43.7 | S 1 49.3 | 188 05.0 | S16 14.3 | Alioth | 166 15.0 | N55 50.0 |
| 07 | 165 15.8 | 280 48.6 | 21.0 | 83 49.6 | 43.8 | 165 46.2 | 49.3 | 203 07.4 | 14.2 | Alkaid | 152 53.9 | N49 11.9 |
| 08 | 180 18.3 | 295 47.8 | 21.6 | 98 52.9 | 43.9 | 180 48.7 | 49.3 | 218 09.7 | 14.2 | Alnair | 27 35.2 | S46 51.3 |
| M 09 | 195 20.8 | 310 46.9 .. | 22.3 | 113 56.2 .. | 43.9 | 195 51.2 .. | 49.3 | 233 12.0 .. | 14.2 | Alnilam | 275 39.2 | S 1 11.2 |
| O 10 | 210 23.2 | 325 46.1 | 22.9 | 128 59.5 | 44.0 | 210 53.7 | 49.3 | 248 14.4 | 14.1 | Alphard | 217 49.5 | S 8 45.3 |
| N 11 | 225 25.7 | 340 45.3 | 23.6 | 144 02.8 | 44.1 | 225 56.2 | 49.3 | 263 16.7 | 14.1 | | | |
| D 12 | 240 28.2 | 355 44.4 | S21 24.2 | 159 06.1 | N24 44.2 | 240 58.6 | S 1 49.3 | 278 19.1 | S16 14.0 | Alphecca | 126 05.6 | N26 38.3 |
| A 13 | 255 30.6 | 10 43.6 | 24.8 | 174 09.4 | 44.3 | 256 01.1 | 49.3 | 293 21.4 | 14.0 | Alpheratz | 357 36.4 | N29 13.1 |
| Y 14 | 270 33.1 | 25 42.8 | 25.4 | 189 12.7 | 44.3 | 271 03.6 | 49.3 | 308 23.8 | 14.0 | Altair | 62 01.9 | N 8 55.8 |
| 15 | 285 35.6 | 40 41.9 .. | 26.1 | 204 16.0 .. | 44.4 | 286 06.1 .. | 49.3 | 323 26.1 .. | 13.9 | Ankaa | 353 08.7 | S42 11.1 |
| 16 | 300 38.0 | 55 41.1 | 26.7 | 219 19.4 | 44.5 | 301 08.6 | 49.3 | 338 28.5 | 13.9 | Antares | 112 18.4 | S26 28.9 |
| 17 | 315 40.5 | 70 40.2 | 27.3 | 234 22.7 | 44.6 | 316 11.1 | 49.3 | 353 30.8 | 13.8 | | | |
| 18 | 330 42.9 | 85 39.4 | S21 28.0 | 249 26.0 | N24 44.7 | 331 13.6 | S 1 49.3 | 8 33.1 | S16 13.8 | Arcturus | 145 49.9 | N19 03.9 |
| 19 | 345 45.4 | 100 38.6 | 28.6 | 264 29.3 | 44.7 | 346 16.1 | 49.3 | 23 35.5 | 13.8 | Atria | 107 14.8 | S69 04.1 |
| 20 | 0 47.9 | 115 37.7 | 29.2 | 279 32.6 | 44.8 | 1 18.5 | 49.3 | 38 37.8 | 13.7 | Avior | 234 15.2 | S59 34.6 |
| 21 | 15 50.3 | 130 36.9 .. | 29.8 | 294 35.9 .. | 44.9 | 16 21.0 .. | 49.3 | 53 40.2 .. | 13.7 | Bellatrix | 278 24.5 | N 6 22.3 |
| 22 | 30 52.8 | 145 36.0 | 30.5 | 309 39.3 | 45.0 | 31 23.5 | 49.3 | 68 42.5 | 13.6 | Betelgeuse | 270 53.7 | N 7 24.7 |
| 23 | 45 55.3 | 160 35.2 | 31.1 | 324 42.6 | 45.1 | 46 26.0 | 49.3 | 83 44.9 | 13.6 | | | |
| 22 00 | 60 57.7 | 175 34.3 | S21 31.7 | 339 45.9 | N24 45.1 | 61 28.5 | S 1 49.3 | 98 47.2 | S16 13.5 | Canopus | 263 52.7 | S52 42.2 |
| 01 | 76 00.2 | 190 33.5 | 32.3 | 354 49.2 | 45.2 | 76 31.0 | 49.3 | 113 49.5 | 13.5 | Capella | 280 24.1 | N46 01.2 |
| 02 | 91 02.7 | 205 32.6 | 32.9 | 9 52.5 | 45.3 | 91 33.5 | 49.3 | 128 51.9 | 13.5 | Deneb | 49 27.2 | N45 21.9 |
| 03 | 106 05.1 | 220 31.8 .. | 33.5 | 24 55.9 .. | 45.4 | 106 35.9 .. | 49.3 | 143 54.2 .. | 13.4 | Denebola | 182 26.9 | N14 26.7 |
| 04 | 121 07.6 | 235 31.0 | 34.2 | 39 59.2 | 45.5 | 121 38.4 | 49.3 | 158 56.6 | 13.4 | Diphda | 348 48.9 | S17 51.8 |
| 05 | 136 10.0 | 250 30.1 | 34.8 | 55 02.5 | 45.5 | 136 40.9 | 49.3 | 173 58.9 | 13.3 | | | |
| 06 | 151 12.5 | 265 29.3 | S21 35.4 | 70 05.9 | N24 45.6 | 151 43.4 | S 1 49.3 | 189 01.2 | S16 13.3 | Dubhe | 193 43.4 | N61 37.5 |
| 07 | 166 15.0 | 280 28.4 | 36.0 | 85 09.2 | 45.7 | 166 45.9 | 49.3 | 204 03.6 | 13.3 | Elnath | 278 03.8 | N28 37.6 |
| 08 | 181 17.4 | 295 27.6 | 36.6 | 100 12.5 | 45.8 | 181 48.3 | 49.2 | 219 05.9 | 13.2 | Eltanin | 90 43.5 | N51 29.3 |
| T 09 | 196 19.9 | 310 26.7 .. | 37.2 | 115 15.8 .. | 45.9 | 196 50.8 .. | 49.2 | 234 08.3 .. | 13.2 | Enif | 33 40.6 | N 9 58.8 |
| U 10 | 211 22.4 | 325 25.9 | 37.8 | 130 19.2 | 45.9 | 211 53.3 | 49.2 | 249 10.6 | 13.1 | Fomalhaut | 15 16.4 | S29 30.2 |
| E 11 | 226 24.8 | 340 25.0 | 38.4 | 145 22.5 | 46.0 | 226 55.8 | 49.2 | 264 13.0 | 13.1 | | | |
| S 12 | 241 27.3 | 355 24.2 | S21 39.0 | 160 25.9 | N24 46.1 | 241 58.3 | S 1 49.2 | 279 15.3 | S16 13.0 | Gacrux | 171 54.0 | S57 14.1 |
| D 13 | 256 29.8 | 10 23.3 | 39.7 | 175 29.2 | 46.2 | 257 00.8 | 49.2 | 294 17.6 | 13.0 | Gienah | 175 45.6 | S17 39.9 |
| A 14 | 271 32.2 | 25 22.5 | 40.3 | 190 32.5 | 46.2 | 272 03.2 | 49.2 | 309 20.0 | 13.0 | Hadar | 148 39.1 | S60 28.7 |
| Y 15 | 286 34.7 | 40 21.6 .. | 40.9 | 205 35.9 .. | 46.3 | 287 05.7 .. | 49.2 | 324 22.3 .. | 12.9 | Hamal | 327 52.9 | N23 34.3 |
| 16 | 301 37.2 | 55 20.8 | 41.5 | 220 39.2 | 46.4 | 302 08.2 | 49.2 | 339 24.7 | 12.9 | Kaus Aust. | 83 35.2 | S34 22.5 |
| 17 | 316 39.6 | 70 19.9 | 42.1 | 235 42.5 | 46.5 | 317 10.7 | 49.2 | 354 27.0 | 12.8 | | | |
| 18 | 331 42.1 | 85 19.1 | S21 42.7 | 250 45.9 | N24 46.5 | 332 13.1 | S 1 49.2 | 9 29.3 | S16 12.8 | Kochab | 137 20.9 | N74 03.6 |
| 19 | 346 44.5 | 100 18.2 | 43.3 | 265 49.2 | 46.6 | 347 15.6 | 49.2 | 24 31.7 | 12.8 | Markab | 13 31.6 | N15 19.8 |
| 20 | 1 47.0 | 115 17.4 | 43.9 | 280 52.6 | 46.7 | 2 18.1 | 49.2 | 39 34.0 | 12.7 | Menkar | 314 07.7 | N 4 10.8 |
| 21 | 16 49.5 | 130 16.5 .. | 44.5 | 295 55.9 .. | 46.8 | 17 20.6 .. | 49.2 | 54 36.3 .. | 12.7 | Menkent | 148 00.1 | S36 28.7 |
| 22 | 31 51.9 | 145 15.7 | 45.1 | 310 59.3 | 46.8 | 32 23.1 | 49.2 | 69 38.7 | 12.6 | Miaplacidus | 221 38.4 | S69 48.2 |
| 23 | 46 54.4 | 160 14.8 | 45.7 | 326 02.6 | 46.9 | 47 25.5 | 49.2 | 84 41.0 | 12.6 | | | |
| 23 00 | 61 56.9 | 175 13.9 | S21 46.2 | 341 06.0 | N24 47.0 | 62 28.0 | S 1 49.2 | 99 43.4 | S16 12.5 | Mirfak | 308 30.3 | N49 56.6 |
| 01 | 76 59.3 | 190 13.1 | 46.8 | 356 09.3 | 47.1 | 77 30.5 | 49.1 | 114 45.7 | 12.5 | Nunki | 75 50.3 | S26 16.1 |
| 02 | 92 01.8 | 205 12.2 | 47.4 | 11 12.7 | 47.1 | 92 33.0 | 49.1 | 129 48.0 | 12.5 | Peacock | 53 08.8 | S56 39.9 |
| 03 | 107 04.3 | 220 11.4 .. | 48.0 | 26 16.0 .. | 47.2 | 107 35.4 .. | 49.1 | 144 50.4 .. | 12.4 | Pollux | 243 19.3 | N27 58.2 |
| 04 | 122 06.7 | 235 10.5 | 48.6 | 41 19.4 | 47.3 | 122 37.9 | 49.1 | 159 52.7 | 12.4 | Procyon | 244 52.5 | N 5 10.1 |
| 05 | 137 09.2 | 250 09.7 | 49.2 | 56 22.7 | 47.4 | 137 40.4 | 49.1 | 174 55.1 | 12.3 | | | |
| 06 | 152 11.7 | 265 08.8 | S21 49.8 | 71 26.1 | N24 47.4 | 152 42.9 | S 1 49.1 | 189 57.4 | S16 12.3 | Rasalhague | 96 00.5 | N12 32.7 |
| W 07 | 167 14.1 | 280 07.9 | 50.4 | 86 29.5 | 47.5 | 167 45.3 | 49.1 | 204 59.7 | 12.2 | Regulus | 207 36.4 | N11 51.4 |
| E 08 | 182 16.6 | 295 07.1 | 51.0 | 101 32.8 | 47.6 | 182 47.8 | 49.1 | 220 02.1 | 12.2 | Rigel | 281 05.3 | S 8 10.4 |
| D 09 | 197 19.0 | 310 06.2 .. | 51.5 | 116 36.2 .. | 47.7 | 197 50.3 .. | 49.1 | 235 04.4 .. | 12.2 | Rigil Kent. | 139 43.4 | S60 55.5 |
| N 10 | 212 21.5 | 325 05.4 | 52.1 | 131 39.5 | 47.7 | 212 52.8 | 49.1 | 250 06.7 | 12.1 | Sabik | 102 05.2 | S15 45.1 |
| E 11 | 227 24.0 | 340 04.5 | 52.7 | 146 42.9 | 47.8 | 227 55.2 | 49.1 | 265 09.1 | 12.1 | | | |
| S 12 | 242 26.4 | 355 03.6 | S21 53.3 | 161 46.3 | N24 47.9 | 242 57.7 | S 1 49.1 | 280 11.4 | S16 12.0 | Schedar | 349 32.7 | N56 39.9 |
| D 13 | 257 28.9 | 10 02.8 | 53.9 | 176 49.6 | 47.9 | 258 00.2 | 49.0 | 295 13.7 | 12.0 | Shaula | 96 13.2 | S37 07.2 |
| A 14 | 272 31.4 | 25 01.9 | 54.4 | 191 53.0 | 48.0 | 273 02.6 | 49.0 | 310 16.1 | 11.9 | Sirius | 258 27.5 | S16 44.7 |
| Y 15 | 287 33.8 | 40 01.1 .. | 55.0 | 206 56.4 .. | 48.1 | 288 05.1 .. | 49.0 | 325 18.4 .. | 11.9 | Spica | 158 24.5 | S11 16.7 |
| 16 | 302 36.3 | 55 00.2 | 55.6 | 221 59.7 | 48.2 | 303 07.6 | 49.0 | 340 20.8 | 11.9 | Suhail | 222 47.5 | S43 31.1 |
| 17 | 317 38.8 | 69 59.3 | 56.2 | 237 03.1 | 48.2 | 318 10.1 | 49.0 | 355 23.1 | 11.8 | | | |
| 18 | 332 41.2 | 84 58.5 | S21 56.7 | 252 06.5 | N24 48.3 | 333 12.5 | S 1 49.0 | 10 25.4 | S16 11.8 | Vega | 80 34.8 | N38 48.4 |
| 19 | 347 43.7 | 99 57.6 | 57.3 | 267 09.9 | 48.4 | 348 15.0 | 49.0 | 25 27.8 | 11.7 | Zuben'ubi | 136 58.3 | S16 08.1 |
| 20 | 2 46.2 | 114 56.7 | 57.9 | 282 13.2 | 48.5 | 3 17.5 | 49.0 | 40 30.1 | 11.7 | | SHA | Mer. Pass. |
| 21 | 17 48.6 | 129 55.9 .. | 58.5 | 297 16.6 .. | 48.5 | 18 19.9 .. | 49.0 | 55 32.4 .. | 11.6 | | ° ′ | h m |
| 22 | 32 51.1 | 144 55.0 | 59.0 | 312 20.0 | 48.6 | 33 22.4 | 49.0 | 70 34.8 | 11.6 | Venus | 114 36.6 | 12 18 |
| 23 | 47 53.5 | 159 54.1 | 59.6 | 327 23.4 | 48.7 | 48 24.9 | 48.9 | 85 37.1 | 11.6 | Mars | 278 48.2 | 1 21 |
| | h m | | | | | | | | | Jupiter | 0 30.8 | 19 51 |
| Mer. Pass. 19 52.9 | | v −0.8 | d 0.6 | v 3.3 | d 0.1 | v 2.5 | d 0.0 | v 2.3 | d 0.0 | Saturn | 37 49.5 | 17 22 |

| UT | SUN | | MOON | | | | | Lat. | Twilight | | Sunrise | Moonrise | | | |
|---|---|---|---|---|---|---|---|---|---|---|---|---|---|---|---|
| | GHA | Dec | GHA | v | Dec | d | HP | | Naut. | Civil | | 21 | 22 | 23 | 24 |
| d h | ° ′ | ° ′ | ° ′ | ′ | ° ′ | ′ | ′ | ° | h m | h m | h m | h m | h m | h m | h m |
| **21** 00 | 183 34.2 | S19 51.3 | 220 30.1 | 13.2 | S 5 59.1 | 15.2 | 57.7 | N 72 | 07 23 | 09 07 | ■ | 05 02 | 07 39 | ■ | ■ |
| 01 | 198 34.1 | 51.9 | 235 02.3 | 13.2 | 6 14.3 | 15.2 | 57.7 | N 70 | 07 10 | 08 38 | 10 44 | 04 50 | 07 09 | ■ | ■ |
| 02 | 213 33.9 | 52.4 | 249 34.5 | 13.1 | 6 29.5 | 15.2 | 57.8 | 68 | 07 00 | 08 17 | 09 47 | 04 41 | 06 47 | 09 23 | ■ |
| 03 | 228 33.8 | .. 53.0 | 264 06.6 | 13.0 | 6 44.7 | 15.2 | 57.8 | 66 | 06 51 | 08 00 | 09 13 | 04 33 | 06 30 | 08 44 | ■ |
| 04 | 243 33.6 | 53.5 | 278 38.6 | 13.0 | 6 59.9 | 15.2 | 57.8 | 64 | 06 43 | 07 46 | 08 49 | 04 27 | 06 16 | 08 17 | 10 40 |
| 05 | 258 33.5 | 54.1 | 293 10.6 | 12.9 | 7 15.1 | 15.2 | 57.9 | 62 | 06 36 | 07 34 | 08 30 | 04 21 | 06 04 | 07 57 | 10 00 |
| 06 | 273 33.3 | S19 54.6 | 307 42.5 | 12.8 | S 7 30.3 | 15.1 | 57.9 | 60 | 06 30 | 07 24 | 08 15 | 04 17 | 05 55 | 07 40 | 09 32 |
| 07 | 288 33.1 | 55.2 | 322 14.3 | 12.7 | 7 45.4 | 15.1 | 57.9 | N 58 | 06 25 | 07 15 | 08 02 | 04 13 | 05 46 | 07 26 | 09 11 |
| 08 | 303 33.0 | 55.7 | 336 46.0 | 12.7 | 8 00.5 | 15.1 | 58.0 | 56 | 06 20 | 07 07 | 07 50 | 04 09 | 05 39 | 07 14 | 08 53 |
| M 09 | 318 32.8 | .. 56.3 | 351 17.7 | 12.6 | 8 15.6 | 15.1 | 58.0 | 54 | 06 15 | 07 00 | 07 40 | 04 06 | 05 32 | 07 04 | 08 38 |
| O 10 | 333 32.7 | 56.8 | 5 49.3 | 12.4 | 8 30.7 | 15.1 | 58.0 | 52 | 06 11 | 06 53 | 07 32 | 04 03 | 05 26 | 06 54 | 08 25 |
| N 11 | 348 32.5 | 57.4 | 20 20.7 | 12.5 | 8 45.8 | 15.0 | 58.1 | 50 | 06 07 | 06 47 | 07 24 | 04 00 | 05 21 | 06 46 | 08 14 |
| D 12 | 3 32.4 | S19 57.9 | 34 52.2 | 12.3 | S 9 00.8 | 15.0 | 58.1 | 45 | 05 58 | 06 34 | 07 07 | 03 54 | 05 09 | 06 29 | 07 51 |
| A 13 | 18 32.2 | 58.5 | 49 23.5 | 12.2 | 9 15.8 | 15.0 | 58.2 | N 40 | 05 50 | 06 23 | 06 53 | 03 49 | 05 00 | 06 15 | 07 32 |
| Y 14 | 33 32.0 | 59.0 | 63 54.7 | 12.2 | 9 30.8 | 15.0 | 58.2 | 35 | 05 43 | 06 14 | 06 41 | 03 45 | 04 52 | 06 03 | 07 17 |
| 15 | 48 31.9 | 19 59.6 | 78 25.9 | 12.1 | 9 45.8 | 14.9 | 58.2 | 30 | 05 36 | 06 05 | 06 31 | 03 42 | 04 45 | 05 52 | 07 03 |
| 16 | 63 31.7 | 20 00.1 | 92 57.0 | 11.9 | 10 00.7 | 14.9 | 58.3 | 20 | 05 23 | 05 49 | 06 13 | 03 35 | 04 33 | 05 35 | 06 40 |
| 17 | 78 31.6 | 00.7 | 107 27.9 | 11.9 | 10 15.6 | 14.9 | 58.3 | N 10 | 05 09 | 05 35 | 05 57 | 03 30 | 04 23 | 05 19 | 06 21 |
| 18 | 93 31.4 | S20 01.2 | 121 58.8 | 11.8 | S10 30.5 | 14.9 | 58.3 | 0 | 04 55 | 05 20 | 05 42 | 03 25 | 04 13 | 05 05 | 06 03 |
| 19 | 108 31.2 | 01.8 | 136 29.6 | 11.7 | 10 45.4 | 14.8 | 58.4 | S 10 | 04 39 | 05 05 | 05 28 | 03 20 | 04 03 | 04 51 | 05 45 |
| 20 | 123 31.1 | 02.3 | 151 00.3 | 11.7 | 11 00.2 | 14.7 | 58.4 | 20 | 04 19 | 04 48 | 05 12 | 03 15 | 03 53 | 04 36 | 05 25 |
| 21 | 138 30.9 | .. 02.9 | 165 31.0 | 11.5 | 11 14.9 | 14.8 | 58.4 | 30 | 03 55 | 04 27 | 04 53 | 03 09 | 03 42 | 04 19 | 05 03 |
| 22 | 153 30.8 | 03.4 | 180 01.5 | 11.4 | 11 29.7 | 14.7 | 58.5 | 35 | 03 39 | 04 14 | 04 42 | 03 05 | 03 35 | 04 09 | 04 50 |
| 23 | 168 30.6 | 03.9 | 194 31.9 | 11.3 | 11 44.4 | 14.6 | 58.5 | 40 | 03 20 | 03 58 | 04 30 | 03 01 | 03 27 | 03 58 | 04 36 |
| **22** 00 | 183 30.4 | S20 04.5 | 209 02.2 | 11.3 | S11 59.0 | 14.6 | 58.5 | 45 | 02 55 | 03 40 | 04 15 | 02 57 | 03 19 | 03 45 | 04 18 |
| 01 | 198 30.3 | 05.0 | 223 32.5 | 11.1 | 12 13.6 | 14.6 | 58.6 | S 50 | 02 21 | 03 16 | 03 56 | 02 52 | 03 08 | 03 29 | 03 57 |
| 02 | 213 30.1 | 05.6 | 238 02.6 | 11.0 | 12 28.2 | 14.5 | 58.6 | 52 | 02 02 | 03 04 | 03 48 | 02 50 | 03 04 | 03 22 | 03 47 |
| 03 | 228 29.9 | .. 06.1 | 252 32.6 | 11.0 | 12 42.7 | 14.5 | 58.6 | 54 | 01 39 | 02 51 | 03 38 | 02 47 | 02 58 | 03 14 | 03 35 |
| 04 | 243 29.8 | 06.6 | 267 02.6 | 10.8 | 12 57.2 | 14.4 | 58.7 | 56 | 01 07 | 02 35 | 03 27 | 02 44 | 02 53 | 03 05 | 03 22 |
| 05 | 258 29.6 | 07.2 | 281 32.4 | 10.7 | 13 11.6 | 14.3 | 58.7 | 58 | //// | 02 15 | 03 14 | 02 41 | 02 46 | 02 54 | 03 07 |
| 06 | 273 29.4 | S20 07.7 | 296 02.1 | 10.7 | S13 25.9 | 14.4 | 58.7 | S 60 | //// | 01 50 | 02 59 | 02 37 | 02 39 | 02 43 | 02 50 |

| UT | SUN | | MOON | | | | | Lat. | Sunset | Twilight | | Moonset | | | |
|---|---|---|---|---|---|---|---|---|---|---|---|---|---|---|---|
| | GHA | Dec | GHA | v | Dec | d | HP | | | Civil | Naut. | 21 | 22 | 23 | 24 |
| d h | ° ′ | ° ′ | ° ′ | ′ | ° ′ | ′ | ′ | ° | h m | h m | h m | h m | h m | h m | h m |
| 07 | 288 29.3 | S20 08.2 | 310 31.8 | 10.5 | 13 40.3 | 14.2 | 58.8 | N 72 | ■ | 14 24 | 16 08 | 13 39 | 12 43 | ■ | ■ |
| T 08 | 303 29.1 | 08.8 | 325 01.3 | 10.4 | 13 54.5 | 14.2 | 58.8 | N 70 | 12 47 | 14 53 | 16 21 | 13 53 | 13 16 | ■ | ■ |
| U 09 | 318 29.0 | .. 09.3 | 339 30.7 | 10.3 | 14 08.7 | 14.1 | 58.8 | 68 | 13 45 | 15 15 | 16 31 | 14 05 | 13 40 | 12 54 | ■ |
| E 10 | 333 28.8 | 09.8 | 354 00.0 | 10.2 | 14 22.8 | 14.1 | 58.9 | 66 | 14 18 | 15 32 | 16 40 | 14 14 | 13 59 | 13 35 | ■ |
| S 11 | 348 28.6 | 10.4 | 8 29.2 | 10.1 | 14 36.9 | 14.0 | 58.9 | 64 | 14 42 | 15 46 | 16 48 | 14 22 | 14 14 | 14 03 | 13 42 |
| D 12 | 3 28.5 | S20 10.9 | 22 58.3 | 9.9 | S14 50.9 | 14.0 | 58.9 | 62 | 15 01 | 15 58 | 16 55 | 14 30 | 14 27 | 14 24 | 14 23 |
| A 13 | 18 28.3 | 11.4 | 37 27.2 | 9.9 | 15 04.9 | 13.9 | 59.0 | 60 | 15 17 | 16 08 | 17 01 | 14 36 | 14 38 | 14 42 | 14 51 |
| Y 14 | 33 28.1 | 12.0 | 51 56.1 | 9.8 | 15 18.8 | 13.8 | 59.0 | N 58 | 15 30 | 16 17 | 17 07 | 14 41 | 14 47 | 14 57 | 15 14 |
| 15 | 48 27.9 | 12.5 | 66 24.9 | 9.6 | 15 32.6 | 13.7 | 59.0 | 56 | 15 41 | 16 25 | 17 12 | 14 46 | 14 56 | 15 10 | 15 32 |
| 16 | 63 27.8 | 13.0 | 80 53.5 | 9.5 | 15 46.3 | 13.7 | 59.1 | 54 | 15 51 | 16 32 | 17 16 | 14 50 | 15 03 | 15 21 | 15 47 |
| 17 | 78 27.6 | 13.6 | 95 22.0 | 9.5 | 16 00.0 | 13.6 | 59.1 | 52 | 16 00 | 16 39 | 17 20 | 14 54 | 15 10 | 15 31 | 16 00 |
| 18 | 93 27.4 | S20 14.1 | 109 50.5 | 9.2 | S16 13.6 | 13.5 | 59.1 | 50 | 16 08 | 16 45 | 17 24 | 14 58 | 15 16 | 15 40 | 16 12 |
| 19 | 108 27.3 | 14.6 | 124 18.7 | 9.2 | 16 27.1 | 13.5 | 59.2 | 45 | 16 25 | 16 57 | 17 34 | 15 06 | 15 29 | 15 58 | 16 36 |
| 20 | 123 27.1 | 15.2 | 138 46.9 | 9.1 | 16 40.6 | 13.3 | 59.2 | N 40 | 16 39 | 17 08 | 17 42 | 15 13 | 15 40 | 16 14 | 16 56 |
| 21 | 138 26.9 | .. 15.7 | 153 15.0 | 8.9 | 16 53.9 | 13.3 | 59.2 | 35 | 16 51 | 17 18 | 17 49 | 15 18 | 15 50 | 16 27 | 17 12 |
| 22 | 153 26.8 | 16.2 | 167 42.9 | 8.9 | 17 07.2 | 13.2 | 59.2 | 30 | 17 01 | 17 27 | 17 56 | 15 23 | 15 58 | 16 39 | 17 27 |
| 23 | 168 26.6 | 16.7 | 182 10.8 | 8.7 | 17 20.4 | 13.1 | 59.3 | 20 | 17 19 | 17 43 | 18 09 | 15 32 | 16 13 | 16 58 | 17 51 |
| **23** 00 | 183 26.4 | S20 17.3 | 196 38.5 | 8.6 | S17 33.5 | 13.0 | 59.3 | N 10 | 17 35 | 17 57 | 18 23 | 15 40 | 16 25 | 17 16 | 18 12 |
| 01 | 198 26.3 | 17.8 | 211 06.1 | 8.5 | 17 46.5 | 13.0 | 59.3 | 0 | 17 50 | 18 12 | 18 37 | 15 47 | 16 37 | 17 32 | 18 32 |
| 02 | 213 26.1 | 18.3 | 225 33.6 | 8.3 | 17 59.5 | 12.8 | 59.4 | S 10 | 18 05 | 18 27 | 18 54 | 15 55 | 16 49 | 17 48 | 18 51 |
| 03 | 228 25.9 | .. 18.8 | 240 00.9 | 8.2 | 18 12.3 | 12.7 | 59.4 | 20 | 18 21 | 18 45 | 19 13 | 16 02 | 17 02 | 18 06 | 19 13 |
| 04 | 243 25.7 | 19.4 | 254 28.1 | 8.2 | 18 25.0 | 12.7 | 59.4 | 30 | 18 40 | 19 06 | 19 38 | 16 11 | 17 17 | 18 26 | 19 37 |
| 05 | 258 25.6 | 19.9 | 268 55.3 | 7.9 | 18 37.7 | 12.5 | 59.4 | 35 | 18 51 | 19 19 | 19 54 | 16 17 | 17 25 | 18 38 | 19 52 |
| 06 | 273 25.4 | S20 20.4 | 283 22.2 | 7.9 | S18 50.2 | 12.5 | 59.5 | 40 | 19 03 | 19 34 | 20 13 | 16 23 | 17 35 | 18 51 | 20 09 |
| W 07 | 288 25.2 | 20.9 | 297 49.1 | 7.8 | 19 02.7 | 12.3 | 59.5 | 45 | 19 18 | 19 53 | 20 38 | 16 30 | 17 47 | 19 07 | 20 29 |
| E 08 | 303 25.0 | 21.4 | 312 15.9 | 7.6 | 19 15.0 | 12.3 | 59.5 | S 50 | 19 37 | 20 17 | 21 13 | 16 38 | 18 01 | 19 28 | 20 54 |
| D 09 | 318 24.9 | .. 22.0 | 326 42.5 | 7.5 | 19 27.3 | 12.1 | 59.6 | 52 | 19 45 | 20 29 | 21 32 | 16 42 | 18 07 | 19 37 | 21 07 |
| N 10 | 333 24.7 | 22.5 | 341 09.0 | 7.4 | 19 39.4 | 12.0 | 59.6 | 54 | 19 55 | 20 43 | 21 55 | 16 46 | 18 15 | 19 48 | 21 21 |
| E 11 | 348 24.5 | 23.0 | 355 35.4 | 7.2 | 19 51.4 | 11.9 | 59.6 | 56 | 20 07 | 20 59 | 22 29 | 16 51 | 18 23 | 20 00 | 21 37 |
| S 12 | 3 24.3 | S20 23.5 | 10 01.6 | 7.2 | S20 03.3 | 11.8 | 59.6 | 58 | 20 19 | 21 19 | //// | 16 56 | 18 32 | 20 14 | 21 57 |
| D 13 | 18 24.2 | 24.0 | 24 27.8 | 7.0 | 20 15.1 | 11.7 | 59.7 | S 60 | 20 35 | 21 45 | //// | 17 02 | 18 43 | 20 31 | 22 22 |

| UT | SUN | | MOON | | | | |
|---|---|---|---|---|---|---|---|
| A 14 | 33 24.0 | 24.6 | 38 53.8 | 6.9 | 20 26.8 | 11.6 | 59.7 |
| Y 15 | 48 23.8 | .. 25.1 | 53 19.7 | 6.7 | 20 38.4 | 11.4 | 59.7 |
| 16 | 63 23.6 | 25.6 | 67 45.4 | 6.7 | 20 49.8 | 11.4 | 59.7 |
| 17 | 78 23.5 | 26.1 | 82 11.1 | 6.5 | 21 01.2 | 11.2 | 59.8 |
| 18 | 93 23.3 | S20 26.6 | 96 36.6 | 6.4 | S21 12.4 | 11.0 | 59.8 |
| 19 | 108 23.1 | 27.1 | 111 02.0 | 6.3 | 21 23.4 | 11.0 | 59.8 |
| 20 | 123 22.9 | 27.6 | 125 27.3 | 6.1 | 21 34.4 | 10.8 | 59.8 |
| 21 | 138 22.8 | .. 28.1 | 139 52.4 | 6.1 | 21 45.2 | 10.7 | 59.9 |
| 22 | 153 22.6 | 28.7 | 154 17.5 | 5.9 | 21 55.9 | 10.6 | 59.9 |
| 23 | 168 22.4 | 29.2 | 168 42.4 | 5.8 | S22 06.5 | 10.4 | 59.9 |
| | SD 16.2 | d 0.5 | SD 15.8 | | 16.1 | | 16.2 |

| | SUN | | | MOON | | | |
|---|---|---|---|---|---|---|---|
| Day | Eqn. of Time | | Mer. | Mer. Pass. | | Age | Phase |
| | 00ʰ | 12ʰ | Pass. | Upper | Lower | | |
| d | m s | m s | h m | h m | h m | d | % |
| 21 | 14 17 | 14 10 | 11 46 | 09 36 | 22 00 | 27 | 8 |
| 22 | 14 02 | 13 54 | 11 46 | 10 25 | 22 51 | 28 | 3 |
| 23 | 13 46 | 13 38 | 11 46 | 11 18 | 23 47 | 29 | 0 |

| UT | ARIES | VENUS −3.9 | | MARS −1.8 | | JUPITER −2.6 | | SATURN +0.7 | | STARS | | |
|---|---|---|---|---|---|---|---|---|---|---|---|---|
| | GHA | GHA | Dec | GHA | Dec | GHA | Dec | GHA | Dec | Name | SHA | Dec |
| d h | ° ′ | ° ′ | ° ′ | ° ′ | ° ′ | ° ′ | ° ′ | ° ′ | ° ′ | | ° ′ | ° ′ |
| 24 00 | 62 56.0 | 174 53.3 | S22 00.2 | 342 26.7 | N24 48.7 | 63 27.4 | S 1 48.9 | 100 39.4 | S16 11.5 | Acamar | 315 12.7 | S40 12.8 |
| 01 | 77 58.5 | 189 52.4 | 00.7 | 357 30.1 | 48.8 | 78 29.8 | 48.9 | 115 41.8 | 11.5 | Achernar | 335 21.1 | S57 07.5 |
| 02 | 93 00.9 | 204 51.5 | 01.3 | 12 33.5 | 48.9 | 93 32.3 | 48.9 | 130 44.1 | 11.4 | Acrux | 173 02.4 | S63 13.2 |
| 03 | 108 03.4 | 219 50.7 . . | 01.9 | 27 36.9 . . | 48.9 | 108 34.8 . . | 48.9 | 145 46.4 . . | 11.4 | Adhara | 255 07.0 | S29 00.0 |
| 04 | 123 05.9 | 234 49.8 | 02.4 | 42 40.3 | 49.0 | 123 37.2 | 48.9 | 160 48.8 | 11.3 | Aldebaran | 290 41.3 | N16 33.3 |
| 05 | 138 08.3 | 249 48.9 | 03.0 | 57 43.6 | 49.1 | 138 39.7 | 48.9 | 175 51.1 | 11.3 | | | |
| 06 | 153 10.8 | 264 48.1 | S22 03.5 | 72 47.0 | N24 49.2 | 153 42.2 | S 1 48.9 | 190 53.4 | S16 11.2 | Alioth | 166 14.9 | N55 50.0 |
| 07 | 168 13.3 | 279 47.2 | 04.1 | 87 50.4 | 49.2 | 168 44.6 | 48.9 | 205 55.8 | 11.2 | Alkaid | 152 53.8 | N49 11.9 |
| T 08 | 183 15.7 | 294 46.3 | 04.7 | 102 53.8 | 49.3 | 183 47.1 | 48.8 | 220 58.1 | 11.2 | Alnair | 27 35.2 | S46 51.3 |
| H 09 | 198 18.2 | 309 45.5 . . | 05.2 | 117 57.2 . . | 49.4 | 198 49.6 . . | 48.8 | 236 00.4 . . | 11.1 | Alnilam | 275 39.2 | S 1 11.2 |
| U 10 | 213 20.6 | 324 44.6 | 05.8 | 133 00.6 | 49.4 | 213 52.0 | 48.8 | 251 02.8 | 11.1 | Alphard | 217 49.4 | S 8 45.3 |
| R 11 | 228 23.1 | 339 43.7 | 06.3 | 148 04.0 | 49.5 | 228 54.5 | 48.8 | 266 05.1 | 11.0 | | | |
| S 12 | 243 25.6 | 354 42.9 | S22 06.9 | 163 07.3 | N24 49.6 | 243 56.9 | S 1 48.8 | 281 07.4 | S16 11.0 | Alphecca | 126 05.6 | N26 38.3 |
| D 13 | 258 28.0 | 9 42.0 | 07.4 | 178 10.7 | 49.6 | 258 59.4 | 48.8 | 296 09.8 | 10.9 | Alpheratz | 357 36.4 | N29 13.1 |
| A 14 | 273 30.5 | 24 41.1 | 08.0 | 193 14.1 | 49.7 | 274 01.9 | 48.8 | 311 12.1 | 10.9 | Altair | 62 01.9 | N 8 55.8 |
| Y 15 | 288 33.0 | 39 40.2 . . | 08.5 | 208 17.5 . . | 49.8 | 289 04.3 . . | 48.8 | 326 14.4 . . | 10.8 | Ankaa | 353 08.7 | S42 11.1 |
| 16 | 303 35.4 | 54 39.4 | 09.1 | 223 20.9 | 49.8 | 304 06.8 | 48.7 | 341 16.8 | 10.8 | Antares | 112 18.4 | S26 28.9 |
| 17 | 318 37.9 | 69 38.5 | 09.6 | 238 24.3 | 49.9 | 319 09.3 | 48.7 | 356 19.1 | 10.8 | | | |
| 18 | 333 40.4 | 84 37.6 | S22 10.2 | 253 27.7 | N24 50.0 | 334 11.7 | S 1 48.7 | 11 21.4 | S16 10.7 | Arcturus | 145 49.9 | N19 03.9 |
| 19 | 348 42.8 | 99 36.7 | 10.7 | 268 31.1 | 50.0 | 349 14.2 | 48.7 | 26 23.8 | 10.7 | Atria | 107 14.8 | S69 04.1 |
| 20 | 3 45.3 | 114 35.9 | 11.3 | 283 34.5 | 50.1 | 4 16.7 | 48.7 | 41 26.1 | 10.6 | Avior | 234 15.1 | S59 34.6 |
| 21 | 18 47.8 | 129 35.0 . . | 11.8 | 298 37.9 . . | 50.2 | 19 19.1 . . | 48.7 | 56 28.4 . . | 10.6 | Bellatrix | 278 24.5 | N 6 22.3 |
| 22 | 33 50.2 | 144 34.1 | 12.4 | 313 41.3 | 50.2 | 34 21.6 | 48.7 | 71 30.8 | 10.5 | Betelgeuse | 270 53.7 | N 7 24.7 |
| 23 | 48 52.7 | 159 33.2 | 12.9 | 328 44.7 | 50.3 | 49 24.0 | 48.7 | 86 33.1 | 10.5 | | | |
| 25 00 | 63 55.1 | 174 32.4 | S22 13.4 | 343 48.1 | N24 50.4 | 64 26.5 | S 1 48.6 | 101 35.4 | S16 10.4 | Canopus | 263 52.7 | S52 42.2 |
| 01 | 78 57.6 | 189 31.5 | 14.0 | 358 51.5 | 50.4 | 79 29.0 | 48.6 | 116 37.8 | 10.4 | Capella | 280 24.0 | N46 01.2 |
| 02 | 94 00.1 | 204 30.6 | 14.5 | 13 54.9 | 50.5 | 94 31.4 | 48.6 | 131 40.1 | 10.4 | Deneb | 49 27.2 | N45 21.9 |
| 03 | 109 02.5 | 219 29.7 . . | 15.1 | 28 58.3 . . | 50.6 | 109 33.9 . . | 48.6 | 146 42.4 . . | 10.3 | Denebola | 182 26.9 | N14 26.7 |
| 04 | 124 05.0 | 234 28.9 | 15.6 | 44 01.7 | 50.6 | 124 36.3 | 48.6 | 161 44.7 | 10.3 | Diphda | 348 48.9 | S17 51.8 |
| 05 | 139 07.5 | 249 28.0 | 16.1 | 59 05.1 | 50.7 | 139 38.8 | 48.6 | 176 47.1 | 10.2 | | | |
| 06 | 154 09.9 | 264 27.1 | S22 16.7 | 74 08.5 | N24 50.7 | 154 41.3 | S 1 48.6 | 191 49.4 | S16 10.2 | Dubhe | 193 43.3 | N61 37.5 |
| 07 | 169 12.4 | 279 26.2 | 17.2 | 89 12.0 | 50.8 | 169 43.7 | 48.5 | 206 51.7 | 10.1 | Elnath | 278 03.8 | N28 37.6 |
| 08 | 184 14.9 | 294 25.3 | 17.7 | 104 15.4 | 50.9 | 184 46.2 | 48.5 | 221 54.1 | 10.1 | Eltanin | 90 43.5 | N51 29.3 |
| F 09 | 199 17.3 | 309 24.5 . . | 18.2 | 119 18.8 . . | 50.9 | 199 48.6 . . | 48.5 | 236 56.4 . . | 10.0 | Enif | 33 40.6 | N 9 58.8 |
| R 10 | 214 19.8 | 324 23.6 | 18.8 | 134 22.2 | 51.0 | 214 51.1 | 48.5 | 251 58.7 | 10.0 | Fomalhaut | 15 16.4 | S29 30.2 |
| I 11 | 229 22.3 | 339 22.7 | 19.3 | 149 25.6 | 51.1 | 229 53.5 | 48.5 | 267 01.1 | 09.9 | | | |
| D 12 | 244 24.7 | 354 21.8 | S22 19.8 | 164 29.0 | N24 51.1 | 244 56.0 | S 1 48.5 | 282 03.4 | S16 09.9 | Gacrux | 171 54.0 | S57 14.1 |
| A 13 | 259 27.2 | 9 20.9 | 20.4 | 179 32.4 | 51.2 | 259 58.5 | 48.4 | 297 05.7 | 09.9 | Gienah | 175 45.6 | S17 39.9 |
| Y 14 | 274 29.6 | 24 20.0 | 20.9 | 194 35.9 | 51.3 | 275 00.9 | 48.4 | 312 08.0 | 09.8 | Hadar | 148 39.1 | S60 28.7 |
| 15 | 289 32.1 | 39 19.2 . . | 21.4 | 209 39.3 . . | 51.3 | 290 03.4 . . | 48.4 | 327 10.4 . . | 09.8 | Hamal | 327 52.9 | N23 34.3 |
| 16 | 304 34.6 | 54 18.3 | 21.9 | 224 42.7 | 51.4 | 305 05.8 | 48.4 | 342 12.7 | 09.7 | Kaus Aust. | 83 35.2 | S34 22.5 |
| 17 | 319 37.0 | 69 17.4 | 22.4 | 239 46.1 | 51.4 | 320 08.3 | 48.4 | 357 15.0 | 09.7 | | | |
| 18 | 334 39.5 | 84 16.5 | S22 23.0 | 254 49.5 | N24 51.5 | 335 10.7 | S 1 48.4 | 12 17.4 | S16 09.6 | Kochab | 137 20.9 | N74 03.6 |
| 19 | 349 42.0 | 99 15.6 | 23.5 | 269 53.0 | 51.6 | 350 13.2 | 48.3 | 27 19.7 | 09.6 | Markab | 13 31.6 | N15 19.8 |
| 20 | 4 44.4 | 114 14.7 | 24.0 | 284 56.4 | 51.6 | 5 15.6 | 48.3 | 42 22.0 | 09.5 | Menkar | 314 07.7 | N 4 10.8 |
| 21 | 19 46.9 | 129 13.9 . . | 24.5 | 299 59.8 . . | 51.7 | 20 18.1 . . | 48.3 | 57 24.3 . . | 09.5 | Menkent | 148 00.1 | S36 28.7 |
| 22 | 34 49.4 | 144 13.0 | 25.0 | 315 03.2 | 51.7 | 35 20.5 | 48.3 | 72 26.7 | 09.4 | Miaplacidus | 221 38.3 | S69 48.2 |
| 23 | 49 51.8 | 159 12.1 | 25.5 | 330 06.6 | 51.8 | 50 23.0 | 48.3 | 87 29.0 | 09.4 | | | |
| 26 00 | 64 54.3 | 174 11.2 | S22 26.1 | 345 10.1 | N24 51.9 | 65 25.5 | S 1 48.3 | 102 31.3 | S16 09.3 | Mirfak | 308 30.3 | N49 56.6 |
| 01 | 79 56.8 | 189 10.3 | 26.6 | 0 13.5 | 51.9 | 80 27.9 | 48.2 | 117 33.6 | 09.3 | Nunki | 75 50.3 | S26 16.1 |
| 02 | 94 59.2 | 204 09.4 | 27.1 | 15 16.9 | 52.0 | 95 30.4 | 48.2 | 132 36.0 | 09.3 | Peacock | 53 08.8 | S56 39.9 |
| 03 | 110 01.7 | 219 08.5 . . | 27.6 | 30 20.4 . . | 52.1 | 110 32.8 . . | 48.2 | 147 38.3 . . | 09.2 | Pollux | 243 19.3 | N27 58.2 |
| 04 | 125 04.1 | 234 07.6 | 28.1 | 45 23.8 | 52.1 | 125 35.3 | 48.2 | 162 40.6 | 09.2 | Procyon | 244 52.5 | N 5 10.0 |
| 05 | 140 06.6 | 249 06.8 | 28.6 | 60 27.2 | 52.2 | 140 37.7 | 48.2 | 177 42.9 | 09.1 | | | |
| 06 | 155 09.1 | 264 05.9 | S22 29.1 | 75 30.6 | N24 52.2 | 155 40.2 | S 1 48.1 | 192 45.3 | S16 09.1 | Rasalhague | 96 00.5 | N12 32.7 |
| 07 | 170 11.5 | 279 05.0 | 29.6 | 90 34.1 | 52.3 | 170 42.6 | 48.1 | 207 47.6 | 09.0 | Regulus | 207 36.3 | N11 51.4 |
| S 08 | 185 14.0 | 294 04.1 | 30.1 | 105 37.5 | 52.3 | 185 45.1 | 48.1 | 222 49.9 | 09.0 | Rigel | 281 05.2 | S 8 10.5 |
| A 09 | 200 16.5 | 309 03.2 . . | 30.6 | 120 40.9 . . | 52.4 | 200 47.5 . . | 48.1 | 237 52.3 . . | 08.9 | Rigil Kent. | 139 43.4 | S60 55.5 |
| T 10 | 215 18.9 | 324 02.3 | 31.1 | 135 44.4 | 52.5 | 215 50.0 | 48.1 | 252 54.6 | 08.9 | Sabik | 102 05.2 | S15 45.1 |
| U 11 | 230 21.4 | 339 01.4 | 31.6 | 150 47.8 | 52.5 | 230 52.4 | 48.1 | 267 56.9 | 08.8 | | | |
| R 12 | 245 23.9 | 354 00.5 | S22 32.1 | 165 51.3 | N24 52.6 | 245 54.9 | S 1 48.0 | 282 59.2 | S16 08.8 | Schedar | 349 32.7 | N56 40.0 |
| D 13 | 260 26.3 | 8 59.6 | 32.6 | 180 54.7 | 52.6 | 260 57.3 | 48.0 | 298 01.6 | 08.7 | Shaula | 96 13.2 | S37 07.2 |
| A 14 | 275 28.8 | 23 58.7 | 33.1 | 195 58.1 | 52.7 | 275 59.8 | 48.0 | 313 03.9 | 08.7 | Sirius | 258 27.5 | S16 44.7 |
| Y 15 | 290 31.3 | 38 57.9 . . | 33.6 | 211 01.6 . . | 52.8 | 291 02.2 . . | 48.0 | 328 06.2 . . | 08.6 | Spica | 158 24.4 | S11 16.7 |
| 16 | 305 33.7 | 53 57.0 | 34.1 | 226 05.0 | 52.8 | 306 04.6 | 48.0 | 343 08.5 | 08.6 | Suhail | 222 47.5 | S43 31.2 |
| 17 | 320 36.2 | 68 56.1 | 34.6 | 241 08.5 | 52.9 | 321 07.1 | 47.9 | 358 10.9 | 08.6 | | | |
| 18 | 335 38.6 | 83 55.2 | S22 35.1 | 256 11.9 | N24 52.9 | 336 09.5 | S 1 47.9 | 13 13.2 | S16 08.5 | Vega | 80 34.8 | N38 48.4 |
| 19 | 350 41.1 | 98 54.3 | 35.6 | 271 15.3 | 53.0 | 351 12.0 | 47.9 | 28 15.5 | 08.5 | Zuben'ubi | 136 58.3 | S16 08.1 |
| 20 | 5 43.6 | 113 53.4 | 36.1 | 286 18.8 | 53.0 | 6 14.4 | 47.9 | 43 17.8 | 08.4 | | SHA | Mer. Pass. |
| 21 | 20 46.0 | 128 52.5 . . | 36.6 | 301 22.2 . . | 53.1 | 21 16.9 . . | 47.9 | 58 20.1 . . | 08.4 | | ° ′ | h m |
| 22 | 35 48.5 | 143 51.6 | 37.0 | 316 25.7 | 53.1 | 36 19.3 | 47.8 | 73 22.5 | 08.3 | Venus | 110 37.2 | 12 23 |
| 23 | 50 51.0 | 158 50.7 | 37.5 | 331 29.1 | 53.2 | 51 21.8 | 47.8 | 88 24.8 | 08.3 | Mars | 279 53.0 | 1 05 |
| | h m | | | | | | | | | Jupiter | 0 31.3 | 19 39 |
| Mer. Pass. 19 41.1 | | v −0.9 | d 0.5 | v 3.4 | d 0.1 | v 2.5 | d 0.0 | v 2.3 | d 0.0 | Saturn | 37 40.3 | 17 11 |

## SUN and MOON

| UT | SUN GHA | SUN Dec | MOON GHA | v | MOON Dec | d | HP |
|---|---|---|---|---|---|---|---|
| d h | ° ′ | ° ′ | ° ′ | ′ | ° ′ | ′ | ′ |
| **24** 00 | 183 22.2 | S20 29.7 | 183 07.2 | 5.7 | S22 16.9 | 10.3 | 59.9 |
| 01 | 198 22.0 | 30.2 | 197 31.9 | 5.5 | 22 27.2 | 10.1 | 59.9 |
| 02 | 213 21.9 | 30.7 | 211 56.4 | 5.5 | 22 37.3 | 10.0 | 59.9 |
| 03 | 228 21.7 | .. 31.2 | 226 20.9 | 5.3 | 22 47.3 | 9.8 | 60.0 |
| 04 | 243 21.5 | 31.7 | 240 45.2 | 5.2 | 22 57.1 | 9.7 | 60.0 |
| 05 | 258 21.3 | 32.2 | 255 09.4 | 5.1 | 23 06.8 | 9.6 | 60.0 |
| 06 | 273 21.1 | S20 32.7 | 269 33.5 | 5.0 | S23 16.4 | 9.4 | 60.0 |
| T 07 | 288 21.0 | 33.2 | 283 57.5 | 4.8 | 23 25.8 | 9.3 | 60.0 |
| H 08 | 303 20.8 | 33.7 | 298 21.3 | 4.8 | 23 35.1 | 9.1 | 60.1 |
| U 09 | 318 20.6 | .. 34.2 | 312 45.1 | 4.6 | 23 44.2 | 8.9 | 60.1 |
| R 10 | 333 20.4 | 34.7 | 327 08.7 | 4.5 | 23 53.1 | 8.8 | 60.1 |
| S 11 | 348 20.2 | 35.2 | 341 32.2 | 4.4 | 24 01.9 | 8.6 | 60.1 |
| D 12 | 3 20.0 | S20 35.7 | 355 55.6 | 4.4 | S24 10.5 | 8.5 | 60.1 |
| A 13 | 18 19.9 | 36.2 | 10 19.0 | 4.2 | 24 19.0 | 8.3 | 60.1 |
| Y 14 | 33 19.7 | 36.7 | 24 42.2 | 4.1 | 24 27.3 | 8.1 | 60.2 |
| 15 | 48 19.5 | .. 37.2 | 39 05.3 | 4.0 | 24 35.4 | 8.0 | 60.2 |
| 16 | 63 19.3 | 37.7 | 53 28.3 | 3.8 | 24 43.4 | 7.8 | 60.2 |
| 17 | 78 19.1 | 38.2 | 67 51.1 | 3.8 | 24 51.2 | 7.6 | 60.2 |
| 18 | 93 18.9 | S20 38.7 | 82 13.9 | 3.7 | S24 58.8 | 7.5 | 60.2 |
| 19 | 108 18.7 | 39.2 | 96 36.6 | 3.6 | 25 06.3 | 7.3 | 60.2 |
| 20 | 123 18.6 | 39.7 | 110 59.2 | 3.5 | 25 13.6 | 7.1 | 60.2 |
| 21 | 138 18.4 | .. 40.2 | 125 21.7 | 3.5 | 25 20.7 | 6.9 | 60.3 |
| 22 | 153 18.2 | 40.7 | 139 44.2 | 3.3 | 25 27.6 | 6.7 | 60.3 |
| 23 | 168 18.0 | 41.2 | 154 06.5 | 3.2 | 25 34.3 | 6.6 | 60.3 |
| **25** 00 | 183 17.8 | S20 41.7 | 168 28.7 | 3.2 | S25 40.9 | 6.4 | 60.3 |
| 01 | 198 17.6 | 42.2 | 182 50.9 | 3.0 | 25 47.3 | 6.2 | 60.3 |
| 02 | 213 17.4 | 42.7 | 197 12.9 | 3.0 | 25 53.5 | 6.0 | 60.3 |
| 03 | 228 17.3 | .. 43.2 | 211 34.9 | 2.9 | 25 59.5 | 5.8 | 60.3 |
| 04 | 243 17.1 | 43.7 | 225 56.8 | 2.8 | 26 05.3 | 5.7 | 60.3 |
| 05 | 258 16.9 | 44.2 | 240 18.6 | 2.8 | 26 11.0 | 5.4 | 60.3 |
| 06 | 273 16.7 | S20 44.7 | 254 40.4 | 2.7 | S26 16.4 | 5.3 | 60.4 |
| 07 | 288 16.5 | 45.2 | 269 02.1 | 2.6 | 26 21.7 | 5.1 | 60.4 |
| F 08 | 303 16.3 | 45.6 | 283 23.7 | 2.5 | 26 26.8 | 4.9 | 60.4 |
| R 09 | 318 16.1 | .. 46.1 | 297 45.2 | 2.5 | 26 31.7 | 4.6 | 60.4 |
| I 10 | 333 15.9 | 46.6 | 312 06.7 | 2.4 | 26 36.3 | 4.5 | 60.4 |
| D 11 | 348 15.7 | 47.1 | 326 28.1 | 2.4 | 26 40.8 | 4.3 | 60.4 |
| A 12 | 3 15.5 | S20 47.6 | 340 49.5 | 2.3 | S26 45.1 | 4.1 | 60.4 |
| Y 13 | 18 15.4 | 48.1 | 355 10.8 | 2.2 | 26 49.2 | 3.9 | 60.4 |
| 14 | 33 15.2 | 48.6 | 9 32.0 | 2.2 | 26 53.1 | 3.7 | 60.4 |
| 15 | 48 15.0 | .. 49.0 | 23 53.2 | 2.1 | 26 56.8 | 3.5 | 60.4 |
| 16 | 63 14.8 | 49.5 | 38 14.3 | 2.1 | 27 00.3 | 3.3 | 60.4 |
| 17 | 78 14.6 | 50.0 | 52 35.4 | 2.1 | 27 03.6 | 3.1 | 60.4 |
| 18 | 93 14.4 | S20 50.5 | 66 56.5 | 2.0 | S27 06.7 | 2.9 | 60.4 |
| 19 | 108 14.2 | 51.0 | 81 17.5 | 2.0 | 27 09.6 | 2.7 | 60.4 |
| 20 | 123 14.0 | 51.5 | 95 38.5 | 2.0 | 27 12.3 | 2.4 | 60.4 |
| 21 | 138 13.8 | .. 51.9 | 109 59.5 | 1.9 | 27 14.7 | 2.3 | 60.4 |
| 22 | 153 13.6 | 52.4 | 124 20.4 | 1.9 | 27 17.0 | 2.1 | 60.4 |
| 23 | 168 13.4 | 52.9 | 138 41.3 | 1.9 | 27 19.1 | 1.9 | 60.4 |
| **26** 00 | 183 13.2 | S20 53.4 | 153 02.2 | 1.8 | S27 21.0 | 1.6 | 60.4 |
| 01 | 198 13.0 | 53.8 | 167 23.0 | 1.8 | 27 22.6 | 1.5 | 60.4 |
| 02 | 213 12.8 | 54.3 | 181 43.8 | 1.9 | 27 24.1 | 1.2 | 60.4 |
| 03 | 228 12.6 | .. 54.8 | 196 04.7 | 1.8 | 27 25.3 | 1.1 | 60.4 |
| 04 | 243 12.4 | 55.3 | 210 25.5 | 1.8 | 27 26.4 | 0.8 | 60.4 |
| 05 | 258 12.2 | 55.7 | 224 46.3 | 1.8 | 27 27.2 | 0.6 | 60.4 |
| 06 | 273 12.1 | S20 56.2 | 239 07.1 | 1.8 | S27 27.8 | 0.5 | 60.4 |
| S 07 | 288 11.9 | 56.7 | 253 27.9 | 1.8 | 27 28.3 | 0.2 | 60.4 |
| A 08 | 303 11.7 | 57.2 | 267 48.7 | 1.8 | 27 28.5 | 0.0 | 60.4 |
| T 09 | 318 11.5 | .. 57.6 | 282 09.5 | 1.8 | 27 28.5 | 0.2 | 60.4 |
| U 10 | 333 11.3 | 58.1 | 296 30.3 | 1.8 | 27 28.3 | 0.4 | 60.4 |
| R 11 | 348 11.1 | 58.6 | 310 51.1 | 1.8 | 27 27.9 | 0.6 | 60.4 |
| D 12 | 3 10.9 | S20 59.0 | 325 11.9 | 1.9 | S27 27.3 | 0.8 | 60.4 |
| A 13 | 18 10.7 | 20 59.5 | 339 32.8 | 1.9 | 27 26.5 | 1.0 | 60.4 |
| Y 14 | 33 10.5 | 21 00.0 | 353 53.7 | 1.9 | 27 25.5 | 1.3 | 60.4 |
| 15 | 48 10.3 | .. 00.5 | 8 14.6 | 1.9 | 27 24.2 | 1.4 | 60.4 |
| 16 | 63 10.1 | 00.9 | 22 35.5 | 1.9 | 27 22.8 | 1.6 | 60.4 |
| 17 | 78 09.9 | 01.4 | 36 56.4 | 2.0 | 27 21.2 | 1.9 | 60.4 |
| 18 | 93 09.7 | S21 01.8 | 51 17.4 | 2.1 | S27 19.3 | 2.0 | 60.4 |
| 19 | 108 09.5 | 02.3 | 65 38.5 | 2.0 | 27 17.3 | 2.3 | 60.4 |
| 20 | 123 09.3 | 02.8 | 79 59.5 | 2.1 | 27 15.0 | 2.4 | 60.4 |
| 21 | 138 09.1 | .. 03.2 | 94 20.6 | 2.2 | 27 12.6 | 2.7 | 60.4 |
| 22 | 153 08.9 | 03.7 | 108 41.8 | 2.2 | 27 09.9 | 2.8 | 60.3 |
| 23 | 168 08.7 | 04.2 | 123 03.0 | 2.2 | S27 07.1 | 3.1 | 60.3 |
| SD | 16.2 | d 0.5 | SD 16.4 | | 16.5 | | 16.5 |

## Twilight, Sunrise and Moonrise

| Lat. | Naut. | Civil | Sunrise | Moonrise 24 | 25 | 26 | 27 |
|---|---|---|---|---|---|---|---|
| ° | h m | h m | h m | h m | h m | h m | h m |
| N 72 | 07 33 | 09 22 | ■ | ■ | ■ | ■ | ■ |
| N 70 | 07 19 | 08 49 | 11 31 | ■ | ■ | ■ | ■ |
| 68 | 07 07 | 08 26 | 10 02 | ■ | ■ | ■ | ■ |
| 66 | 06 58 | 08 08 | 09 25 | ■ | ■ | ■ | ■ |
| 64 | 06 49 | 07 53 | 08 59 | 10 40 | ■ | ■ | ■ |
| 62 | 06 42 | 07 40 | 08 38 | 10 00 | 12 08 | 13 41 | 13 57 |
| 60 | 06 36 | 07 30 | 08 22 | 09 32 | 11 21 | 12 41 | 13 19 |
| N 58 | 06 30 | 07 20 | 08 08 | 09 11 | 10 50 | 12 07 | 12 52 |
| 56 | 06 25 | 07 12 | 07 56 | 08 53 | 10 27 | 11 42 | 12 31 |
| 54 | 06 20 | 07 04 | 07 46 | 08 38 | 10 08 | 11 22 | 12 14 |
| 52 | 06 15 | 06 58 | 07 36 | 08 25 | 09 52 | 11 05 | 11 59 |
| 50 | 06 11 | 06 51 | 07 28 | 08 14 | 09 38 | 10 51 | 11 46 |
| 45 | 06 02 | 06 38 | 07 11 | 07 51 | 09 11 | 10 21 | 11 19 |
| N 40 | 05 53 | 06 26 | 06 56 | 07 32 | 08 49 | 09 58 | 10 57 |
| 35 | 05 45 | 06 16 | 06 44 | 07 17 | 08 30 | 09 39 | 10 40 |
| 30 | 05 38 | 06 07 | 06 33 | 07 03 | 08 15 | 09 23 | 10 24 |
| 20 | 05 24 | 05 51 | 06 15 | 06 40 | 07 48 | 08 56 | 09 58 |
| N 10 | 05 10 | 05 36 | 05 59 | 06 21 | 07 26 | 08 32 | 09 36 |
| 0 | 04 55 | 05 21 | 05 43 | 06 03 | 07 05 | 08 10 | 09 15 |
| S 10 | 04 39 | 05 05 | 05 28 | 05 45 | 06 44 | 07 48 | 08 54 |
| 20 | 04 19 | 04 47 | 05 11 | 05 25 | 06 22 | 07 24 | 08 31 |
| 30 | 03 53 | 04 26 | 04 52 | 05 03 | 05 56 | 06 57 | 08 05 |
| 35 | 03 37 | 04 12 | 04 41 | 04 50 | 05 41 | 06 41 | 07 49 |
| 40 | 03 17 | 03 56 | 04 20 | 04 36 | 05 23 | 06 22 | 07 31 |
| 45 | 02 51 | 03 37 | 04 12 | 04 18 | 05 02 | 06 00 | 07 10 |
| S 50 | 02 16 | 03 12 | 03 53 | 03 57 | 04 36 | 05 31 | 06 42 |
| 52 | 01 56 | 03 00 | 03 44 | 03 47 | 04 23 | 05 17 | 06 29 |
| 54 | 01 31 | 02 46 | 03 34 | 03 35 | 04 09 | 05 00 | 06 13 |
| 56 | 00 54 | 02 29 | 03 23 | 03 22 | 03 52 | 04 41 | 05 55 |
| 58 | //// | 02 08 | 03 09 | 03 07 | 03 31 | 04 17 | 05 32 |
| S 60 | //// | 01 41 | 02 54 | 02 50 | 03 06 | 03 45 | 05 03 |

## Sunset, Twilight and Moonset

| Lat. | Sunset | Civil | Naut. | Moonset 24 | 25 | 26 | 27 |
|---|---|---|---|---|---|---|---|
| ° | h m | h m | h m | h m | h m | h m | h m |
| N 72 | ■ | 14 11 | 16 00 | ■ | ■ | ■ | ■ |
| N 70 | 12 02 | 14 44 | 16 14 | ■ | ■ | ■ | ■ |
| 68 | 13 31 | 15 07 | 16 26 | ■ | ■ | ■ | ■ |
| 66 | 14 08 | 15 25 | 16 35 | ■ | ■ | ■ | ■ |
| 64 | 14 35 | 15 40 | 16 44 | 13 42 | ■ | ■ | ■ |
| 62 | 14 55 | 15 53 | 16 51 | 14 23 | 14 27 | 15 11 | 17 11 |
| 60 | 15 12 | 16 04 | 16 58 | 14 51 | 15 15 | 16 12 | 17 48 |
| N 58 | 15 25 | 16 13 | 17 03 | 15 14 | 15 46 | 16 45 | 18 15 |
| 56 | 15 37 | 16 22 | 17 09 | 15 32 | 16 09 | 17 10 | 18 35 |
| 54 | 15 48 | 16 29 | 17 14 | 15 47 | 16 28 | 17 30 | 18 52 |
| 52 | 15 57 | 16 36 | 17 18 | 16 00 | 16 44 | 17 47 | 19 07 |
| 50 | 16 05 | 16 42 | 17 22 | 16 12 | 16 58 | 18 01 | 19 20 |
| 45 | 16 23 | 16 56 | 17 32 | 16 36 | 17 27 | 18 31 | 19 46 |
| N 40 | 16 37 | 17 07 | 17 40 | 16 56 | 17 49 | 18 53 | 20 07 |
| 35 | 16 50 | 17 17 | 17 48 | 17 12 | 18 08 | 19 12 | 20 24 |
| 30 | 17 00 | 17 26 | 17 56 | 17 27 | 18 24 | 19 28 | 20 38 |
| 20 | 17 19 | 17 43 | 18 10 | 17 51 | 18 51 | 19 56 | 21 03 |
| N 10 | 17 35 | 17 58 | 18 24 | 18 12 | 19 14 | 20 19 | 21 25 |
| 0 | 17 51 | 18 13 | 18 38 | 18 32 | 19 36 | 20 41 | 21 45 |
| S 10 | 18 06 | 18 29 | 18 55 | 18 51 | 19 57 | 21 03 | 22 04 |
| 20 | 18 23 | 18 47 | 19 15 | 19 13 | 20 21 | 21 26 | 22 26 |
| 30 | 18 42 | 19 09 | 19 41 | 19 37 | 20 48 | 21 53 | 22 50 |
| 35 | 18 53 | 19 22 | 19 57 | 19 52 | 21 04 | 22 09 | 23 04 |
| 40 | 19 07 | 19 38 | 20 17 | 20 09 | 21 22 | 22 27 | 23 20 |
| 45 | 19 22 | 19 58 | 20 43 | 20 29 | 21 45 | 22 49 | 23 40 |
| S 50 | 19 41 | 20 23 | 21 20 | 20 54 | 22 14 | 23 17 | 24 04 |
| 52 | 19 50 | 20 35 | 21 40 | 21 07 | 22 28 | 23 31 | 24 16 |
| 54 | 20 01 | 20 50 | 22 06 | 21 21 | 22 44 | 23 47 | 24 29 |
| 56 | 20 12 | 21 07 | 22 45 | 21 37 | 23 03 | 24 06 | 00 06 |
| 58 | 20 26 | 21 28 | //// | 21 57 | 23 27 | 24 28 | 00 28 |
| S 60 | 20 42 | 21 56 | //// | 22 22 | 23 59 | 24 58 | 00 58 |

## SUN and MOON

| Day | Eqn. of Time 00ʰ | Eqn. of Time 12ʰ | Mer. Pass. | Mer. Pass. Upper | Mer. Pass. Lower | Age | Phase |
|---|---|---|---|---|---|---|---|
| d | m s | m s | h m | h m | h m | d | % |
| 24 | 13 29 | 13 21 | 11 47 | 12 17 | 24 48 | 01 | 0 |
| 25 | 13 12 | 13 03 | 11 47 | 13 20 | 00 48 | 02 | 3 |
| 26 | 12 53 | 12 44 | 11 47 | 14 26 | 01 53 | 03 | 9 |

| UT | ARIES GHA | VENUS −3.9 GHA | Dec | MARS −1.8 GHA | Dec | JUPITER −2.6 GHA | Dec | SATURN +0.7 GHA | Dec | Name | SHA | Dec |
|---|---|---|---|---|---|---|---|---|---|---|---|---|
| **27 00** | 65 53.4 | 173 49.8 | S22 38.0 | 346 32.6 | N24 53.3 | 66 24.2 | S 1 47.8 | 103 27.1 | S16 08.2 | Acamar | 315 12.7 | S40 12.9 |
| 01 | 80 55.9 | 188 48.9 | 38.5 | 1 36.0 | 53.3 | 81 26.7 | 47.8 | 118 29.4 | 08.2 | Achernar | 335 21.1 | S57 07.5 |
| 02 | 95 58.4 | 203 48.0 | 39.0 | 16 39.5 | 53.4 | 96 29.1 | 47.7 | 133 31.8 | 08.1 | Acrux | 173 02.4 | S63 13.2 |
| 03 | 111 00.8 | 218 47.1 | .. 39.5 | 31 42.9 | .. 53.4 | 111 31.5 | .. 47.7 | 148 34.1 | .. 08.1 | Adhara | 255 06.9 | S29 00.0 |
| 04 | 126 03.3 | 233 46.2 | 39.9 | 46 46.4 | 53.5 | 126 34.0 | 47.7 | 163 36.4 | 08.0 | Aldebaran | 290 41.3 | N16 33.3 |
| 05 | 141 05.8 | 248 45.3 | 40.4 | 61 49.8 | 53.5 | 141 36.4 | 47.7 | 178 38.7 | 08.0 | | | |
| 06 | 156 08.2 | 263 44.4 | S22 40.9 | 76 53.3 | N24 53.6 | 156 38.9 | S 1 47.7 | 193 41.1 | S16 07.9 | Alioth | 166 14.9 | N55 50.0 |
| 07 | 171 10.7 | 278 43.5 | 41.4 | 91 56.7 | 53.6 | 171 41.3 | 47.6 | 208 43.4 | 07.9 | Alkaid | 152 53.8 | N49 11.9 |
| S 08 | 186 13.1 | 293 42.6 | 41.9 | 107 00.2 | 53.7 | 186 43.8 | 47.6 | 223 45.7 | 07.8 | Alnair | 27 35.2 | S46 51.3 |
| U 09 | 201 15.6 | 308 41.7 | .. 42.3 | 122 03.6 | .. 53.7 | 201 46.2 | .. 47.6 | 238 48.0 | .. 07.8 | Alnilam | 275 39.2 | S 1 11.2 |
| N 10 | 216 18.1 | 323 40.8 | 42.8 | 137 07.1 | 53.8 | 216 48.6 | 47.6 | 253 50.3 | 07.7 | Alphard | 217 49.4 | S 8 45.3 |
| D 11 | 231 20.5 | 338 39.9 | 43.3 | 152 10.5 | 53.9 | 231 51.1 | 47.5 | 268 52.7 | 07.7 | | | |
| A 12 | 246 23.0 | 353 39.0 | S22 43.7 | 167 14.0 | N24 53.9 | 246 53.5 | S 1 47.5 | 283 55.0 | S16 07.7 | Alphecca | 126 05.6 | N26 38.3 |
| Y 13 | 261 25.5 | 8 38.1 | 44.2 | 182 17.5 | 54.0 | 261 56.0 | 47.5 | 298 57.3 | 07.6 | Alpheratz | 357 36.4 | N29 13.1 |
| 14 | 276 27.9 | 23 37.2 | 44.7 | 197 20.9 | 54.0 | 276 58.4 | 47.5 | 313 59.6 | 07.6 | Altair | 62 01.9 | N 8 55.8 |
| 15 | 291 30.4 | 38 36.3 | .. 45.2 | 212 24.4 | .. 54.1 | 292 00.8 | .. 47.5 | 329 02.0 | .. 07.5 | Ankaa | 353 08.7 | S42 11.1 |
| 16 | 306 32.9 | 53 35.4 | 45.6 | 227 27.8 | 54.1 | 307 03.3 | 47.4 | 344 04.3 | 07.5 | Antares | 112 18.4 | S26 28.9 |
| 17 | 321 35.3 | 68 34.5 | 46.1 | 242 31.3 | 54.2 | 322 05.7 | 47.4 | 359 06.6 | 07.4 | | | |
| 18 | 336 37.8 | 83 33.6 | S22 46.6 | 257 34.8 | N24 54.2 | 337 08.2 | S 1 47.4 | 14 08.9 | S16 07.4 | Arcturus | 145 49.8 | N19 03.8 |
| 19 | 351 40.3 | 98 32.7 | 47.0 | 272 38.2 | 54.3 | 352 10.6 | 47.4 | 29 11.2 | 07.3 | Atria | 107 14.8 | S69 04.1 |
| 20 | 6 42.7 | 113 31.8 | 47.5 | 287 41.7 | 54.3 | 7 13.0 | 47.3 | 44 13.6 | 07.3 | Avior | 234 15.1 | S59 34.6 |
| 21 | 21 45.2 | 128 30.9 | .. 47.9 | 302 45.1 | .. 54.4 | 22 15.5 | .. 47.3 | 59 15.9 | .. 07.2 | Bellatrix | 278 24.4 | N 6 22.3 |
| 22 | 36 47.6 | 143 30.0 | 48.4 | 317 48.6 | 54.4 | 37 17.9 | 47.3 | 74 18.2 | 07.2 | Betelgeuse | 270 53.7 | N 7 24.7 |
| 23 | 51 50.1 | 158 29.1 | 48.9 | 332 52.1 | 54.5 | 52 20.4 | 47.3 | 89 20.5 | 07.1 | | | |
| **28 00** | 66 52.6 | 173 28.2 | S22 49.3 | 347 55.5 | N24 54.5 | 67 22.8 | S 1 47.2 | 104 22.8 | S16 07.1 | Canopus | 263 52.7 | S52 42.3 |
| 01 | 81 55.0 | 188 27.3 | 49.8 | 2 59.0 | 54.6 | 82 25.2 | 47.2 | 119 25.2 | 07.0 | Capella | 280 24.0 | N46 01.2 |
| 02 | 96 57.5 | 203 26.4 | 50.2 | 18 02.5 | 54.6 | 97 27.7 | 47.2 | 134 27.5 | 07.0 | Deneb | 49 27.2 | N45 21.9 |
| 03 | 112 00.0 | 218 25.5 | .. 50.7 | 33 05.9 | .. 54.7 | 112 30.1 | .. 47.2 | 149 29.8 | .. 06.9 | Denebola | 182 26.9 | N14 26.7 |
| 04 | 127 02.4 | 233 24.5 | 51.1 | 48 09.4 | 54.7 | 127 32.5 | 47.1 | 164 32.1 | 06.9 | Diphda | 348 48.9 | S17 51.8 |
| 05 | 142 04.9 | 248 23.6 | 51.6 | 63 12.9 | 54.8 | 142 35.0 | 47.1 | 179 34.4 | 06.8 | | | |
| 06 | 157 07.4 | 263 22.7 | S22 52.0 | 78 16.4 | N24 54.8 | 157 37.4 | S 1 47.1 | 194 36.7 | S16 06.8 | Dubhe | 193 43.3 | N61 37.5 |
| 07 | 172 09.8 | 278 21.8 | 52.5 | 93 19.8 | 54.9 | 172 39.8 | 47.1 | 209 39.1 | 06.7 | Elnath | 278 03.7 | N28 37.6 |
| M 08 | 187 12.3 | 293 20.9 | 52.9 | 108 23.3 | 54.9 | 187 42.3 | 47.0 | 224 41.4 | 06.7 | Eltanin | 90 43.5 | N51 29.2 |
| O 09 | 202 14.8 | 308 20.0 | .. 53.4 | 123 26.8 | .. 55.0 | 202 44.7 | .. 47.0 | 239 43.7 | .. 06.6 | Enif | 33 40.6 | N 9 58.8 |
| N 10 | 217 17.2 | 323 19.1 | 53.8 | 138 30.2 | 55.0 | 217 47.1 | 47.0 | 254 46.0 | 06.6 | Fomalhaut | 15 16.4 | S29 30.2 |
| D 11 | 232 19.7 | 338 18.2 | 54.3 | 153 33.7 | 55.1 | 232 49.6 | 47.0 | 269 48.3 | 06.5 | | | |
| A 12 | 247 22.1 | 353 17.3 | S22 54.7 | 168 37.2 | N24 55.1 | 247 52.0 | S 1 46.9 | 284 50.7 | S16 06.5 | Gacrux | 171 53.9 | S57 14.1 |
| Y 13 | 262 24.6 | 8 16.4 | 55.1 | 183 40.7 | 55.2 | 262 54.4 | 46.9 | 299 53.0 | 06.4 | Gienah | 175 45.6 | S17 39.9 |
| 14 | 277 27.1 | 23 15.5 | 55.6 | 198 44.1 | 55.2 | 277 56.9 | 46.9 | 314 55.3 | 06.4 | Hadar | 148 39.1 | S60 28.7 |
| 15 | 292 29.5 | 38 14.5 | .. 56.0 | 213 47.6 | .. 55.2 | 292 59.3 | .. 46.9 | 329 57.6 | .. 06.3 | Hamal | 327 52.9 | N23 34.3 |
| 16 | 307 32.0 | 53 13.6 | 56.5 | 228 51.1 | 55.3 | 308 01.7 | 46.8 | 344 59.9 | 06.3 | Kaus Aust. | 83 35.2 | S34 22.5 |
| 17 | 322 34.5 | 68 12.7 | 56.9 | 243 54.6 | 55.3 | 323 04.2 | 46.8 | 0 02.2 | 06.2 | | | |
| 18 | 337 36.9 | 83 11.8 | S22 57.3 | 258 58.1 | N24 55.4 | 338 06.6 | S 1 46.8 | 15 04.6 | S16 06.2 | Kochab | 137 20.9 | N74 03.6 |
| 19 | 352 39.4 | 98 10.9 | 57.8 | 274 01.5 | 55.4 | 353 09.0 | 46.7 | 30 06.9 | 06.1 | Markab | 13 31.6 | N15 19.8 |
| 20 | 7 41.9 | 113 10.0 | 58.2 | 289 05.0 | 55.5 | 8 11.5 | 46.7 | 45 09.2 | 06.1 | Menkar | 314 07.7 | N 4 10.8 |
| 21 | 22 44.3 | 128 09.1 | .. 58.6 | 304 08.5 | .. 55.5 | 23 13.9 | .. 46.7 | 60 11.5 | .. 06.0 | Menkent | 148 00.0 | S36 28.7 |
| 22 | 37 46.8 | 143 08.2 | 59.1 | 319 12.0 | 55.6 | 38 16.3 | 46.7 | 75 13.8 | 06.0 | Miaplacidus | 221 38.3 | S69 48.3 |
| 23 | 52 49.2 | 158 07.2 | 59.5 | 334 15.5 | 55.6 | 53 18.7 | 46.6 | 90 16.1 | 05.9 | | | |
| **29 00** | 67 51.7 | 173 06.3 | S22 59.9 | 349 18.9 | N24 55.7 | 68 21.2 | S 1 46.6 | 105 18.5 | S16 05.9 | Mirfak | 308 30.3 | N49 56.6 |
| 01 | 82 54.2 | 188 05.4 | 23 00.3 | 4 22.4 | 55.7 | 83 23.6 | 46.6 | 120 20.8 | 05.8 | Nunki | 75 50.3 | S26 16.1 |
| 02 | 97 56.6 | 203 04.5 | 00.8 | 19 25.9 | 55.7 | 98 26.0 | 46.5 | 135 23.1 | 05.8 | Peacock | 53 08.8 | S56 39.9 |
| 03 | 112 59.1 | 218 03.6 | .. 01.2 | 34 29.4 | .. 55.8 | 113 28.5 | .. 46.5 | 150 25.4 | .. 05.7 | Pollux | 243 19.2 | N27 58.2 |
| 04 | 128 01.6 | 233 02.7 | 01.6 | 49 32.9 | 55.8 | 128 30.9 | 46.5 | 165 27.7 | 05.7 | Procyon | 244 52.5 | N 5 10.0 |
| 05 | 143 04.0 | 248 01.8 | 02.0 | 64 36.4 | 55.9 | 143 33.3 | 46.5 | 180 30.0 | 05.6 | | | |
| 06 | 158 06.5 | 263 00.8 | S23 02.5 | 79 39.8 | N24 55.9 | 158 35.7 | S 1 46.4 | 195 32.4 | S16 05.6 | Rasalhague | 96 00.5 | N12 32.7 |
| 07 | 173 09.0 | 277 59.9 | 02.9 | 94 43.3 | 56.0 | 173 38.2 | 46.4 | 210 34.7 | 05.5 | Regulus | 207 36.3 | N11 51.4 |
| T 08 | 188 11.4 | 292 59.0 | 03.3 | 109 46.8 | 56.0 | 188 40.6 | 46.4 | 225 37.0 | 05.5 | Rigel | 281 05.2 | S 8 10.5 |
| U 09 | 203 13.9 | 307 58.1 | .. 03.7 | 124 50.3 | .. 56.0 | 203 43.0 | .. 46.3 | 240 39.3 | .. 05.4 | Rigil Kent. | 139 43.3 | S60 55.5 |
| E 10 | 218 16.4 | 322 57.2 | 04.1 | 139 53.8 | 56.1 | 218 45.4 | 46.3 | 255 41.6 | 05.4 | Sabik | 102 05.2 | S15 45.1 |
| S 11 | 233 18.8 | 337 56.3 | 04.6 | 154 57.3 | 56.1 | 233 47.9 | 46.3 | 270 43.9 | 05.3 | | | |
| D 12 | 248 21.3 | 352 55.3 | S23 05.0 | 170 00.8 | N24 56.2 | 248 50.3 | S 1 46.3 | 285 46.2 | S16 05.3 | Schedar | 349 32.7 | N56 40.0 |
| A 13 | 263 23.7 | 7 54.4 | 05.4 | 185 04.3 | 56.2 | 263 52.7 | 46.2 | 300 48.6 | 05.2 | Shaula | 96 13.2 | S37 07.2 |
| Y 14 | 278 26.2 | 22 53.5 | 05.8 | 200 07.8 | 56.3 | 278 55.1 | 46.2 | 315 50.9 | 05.2 | Sirius | 258 27.5 | S16 44.7 |
| 15 | 293 28.7 | 37 52.6 | .. 06.2 | 215 11.3 | .. 56.3 | 293 57.6 | .. 46.2 | 330 53.2 | .. 05.1 | Spica | 158 24.4 | S11 16.7 |
| 16 | 308 31.1 | 52 51.7 | 06.6 | 230 14.7 | 56.3 | 309 00.0 | 46.1 | 345 55.5 | 05.1 | Suhail | 222 47.4 | S43 31.2 |
| 17 | 323 33.6 | 67 50.7 | 07.0 | 245 18.2 | 56.4 | 324 02.4 | 46.1 | 0 57.8 | 05.0 | | | |
| 18 | 338 36.1 | 82 49.8 | S23 07.4 | 260 21.7 | N24 56.4 | 339 04.8 | S 1 46.1 | 16 00.1 | S16 05.0 | Vega | 80 34.8 | N38 48.4 |
| 19 | 353 38.5 | 97 48.9 | 07.8 | 275 25.2 | 56.5 | 354 07.3 | 46.0 | 31 02.4 | 04.9 | Zuben'ubi | 136 58.3 | S16 08.1 |
| 20 | 8 41.0 | 112 48.0 | 08.2 | 290 28.7 | 56.5 | 9 09.7 | 46.0 | 46 04.8 | 04.9 | | SHA | Mer. Pass. |
| 21 | 23 43.5 | 127 47.1 | .. 08.6 | 305 32.2 | .. 56.5 | 24 12.1 | .. 46.0 | 61 07.1 | .. 04.8 | | | h m |
| 22 | 38 45.9 | 142 46.1 | 09.0 | 320 35.7 | 56.6 | 39 14.5 | 45.9 | 76 09.4 | 04.8 | Venus | 106 35.6 | 12 27 |
| 23 | 53 48.4 | 157 45.2 | 09.4 | 335 39.2 | 56.6 | 54 16.9 | 45.9 | 91 11.7 | 04.7 | Mars | 281 03.0 | 0 48 |
| | h m | | | | | | | | | Jupiter | 0 30.2 | 19 27 |
| Mer. Pass. 19 29.3 | v −0.9 d 0.4 | | v 3.5 d 0.0 | | v 2.4 d 0.0 | | v 2.3 d 0.0 | | | Saturn | 37 30.3 | 17 00 |

| UT | SUN GHA | SUN Dec | MOON GHA | v | MOON Dec | d | HP |
|---|---|---|---|---|---|---|---|
| **27 00** | 183 08.5 | S21 04.6 | 137 24.2 | 2.3 | S27 04.0 | 3.2 | 60.3 |
| 01 | 198 08.3 | 05.1 | 151 45.5 | 2.4 | 27 00.8 | 3.5 | 60.3 |
| 02 | 213 08.0 | 05.5 | 166 06.9 | 2.4 | 26 57.3 | 3.6 | 60.3 |
| 03 | 228 07.8 .. | 06.0 | 180 28.3 | 2.5 | 26 53.7 | 3.9 | 60.3 |
| 04 | 243 07.6 | 06.5 | 194 49.8 | 2.6 | 26 49.8 | 4.0 | 60.3 |
| 05 | 258 07.4 | 06.9 | 209 11.4 | 2.6 | 26 45.8 | 4.2 | 60.3 |
| 06 | 273 07.2 | S21 07.4 | 223 33.0 | 2.7 | S26 41.6 | 4.4 | 60.3 |
| 07 | 288 07.0 | 07.8 | 237 54.7 | 2.7 | 26 37.2 | 4.7 | 60.3 |
| 08 | 303 06.8 | 08.3 | 252 16.4 | 2.9 | 26 32.5 | 4.8 | 60.3 |
| **S** 09 | 318 06.6 .. | 08.7 | 266 38.3 | 2.9 | 26 27.7 | 4.9 | 60.2 |
| **U** 10 | 333 06.4 | 09.2 | 281 00.2 | 3.0 | 26 22.8 | 5.2 | 60.2 |
| **N** 11 | 348 06.2 | 09.7 | 295 22.2 | 3.0 | 26 17.6 | 5.4 | 60.2 |
| **D** 12 | 3 06.0 | S21 10.1 | 309 44.2 | 3.2 | S26 12.2 | 5.5 | 60.2 |
| **A** 13 | 18 05.8 | 10.6 | 324 06.4 | 3.2 | 26 06.7 | 5.0 | 60.2 |
| **Y** 14 | 33 05.6 | 11.0 | 338 28.6 | 3.4 | 26 00.9 | 5.9 | 60.2 |
| 15 | 48 05.4 .. | 11.5 | 352 51.0 | 3.4 | 25 55.0 | 6.1 | 60.2 |
| 16 | 63 05.2 | 11.9 | 7 13.4 | 3.5 | 25 48.9 | 6.3 | 60.1 |
| 17 | 78 05.0 | 12.4 | 21 35.9 | 3.6 | 25 42.6 | 6.4 | 60.1 |
| 18 | 93 04.8 | S21 12.8 | 35 58.5 | 3.7 | S25 36.2 | 6.7 | 60.1 |
| 19 | 108 04.6 | 13.3 | 50 21.2 | 3.8 | 25 29.5 | 6.7 | 60.1 |
| 20 | 123 04.3 | 13.7 | 64 44.0 | 3.9 | 25 22.7 | 6.9 | 60.1 |
| 21 | 138 04.1 .. | 14.2 | 79 06.9 | 4.0 | 25 15.8 | 7.2 | 60.1 |
| 22 | 153 03.9 | 14.6 | 93 29.9 | 4.1 | 25 08.6 | 7.3 | 60.1 |
| 23 | 168 03.7 | 15.0 | 107 53.0 | 4.1 | 25 01.3 | 7.5 | 60.0 |
| **28 00** | 183 03.5 | S21 15.5 | 122 16.1 | 4.4 | S24 53.8 | 7.7 | 60.0 |
| 01 | 198 03.3 | 15.9 | 136 39.5 | 4.4 | 24 46.1 | 7.8 | 60.0 |
| 02 | 213 03.1 | 16.4 | 151 02.9 | 4.5 | 24 38.3 | 8.0 | 60.0 |
| 03 | 228 02.9 .. | 16.8 | 165 26.4 | 4.6 | 24 30.3 | 8.1 | 60.0 |
| 04 | 243 02.7 | 17.3 | 179 50.0 | 4.7 | 24 22.2 | 8.3 | 60.0 |
| 05 | 258 02.5 | 17.7 | 194 13.7 | 4.9 | 24 13.9 | 8.5 | 59.9 |
| 06 | 273 02.2 | S21 18.1 | 208 37.6 | 4.9 | S24 05.4 | 8.6 | 59.9 |
| 07 | 288 02.0 | 18.6 | 223 01.5 | 5.1 | 23 56.8 | 8.7 | 59.9 |
| 08 | 303 01.8 | 19.0 | 237 25.6 | 5.2 | 23 48.1 | 9.0 | 59.9 |
| **M** 09 | 318 01.6 .. | 19.5 | 251 49.8 | 5.3 | 23 39.1 | 9.0 | 59.9 |
| **O** 10 | 333 01.4 | 19.9 | 266 14.1 | 5.4 | 23 30.1 | 9.2 | 59.8 |
| **N** 11 | 348 01.2 | 20.3 | 280 38.5 | 5.5 | 23 20.9 | 9.4 | 59.8 |
| **D** 12 | 3 01.0 | S21 20.8 | 295 03.0 | 5.6 | S23 11.5 | 9.5 | 59.8 |
| **A** 13 | 18 00.8 | 21.2 | 309 27.6 | 5.8 | 23 02.0 | 9.7 | 59.8 |
| **Y** 14 | 33 00.5 | 21.6 | 323 52.4 | 5.9 | 22 52.3 | 9.8 | 59.8 |
| 15 | 48 00.3 .. | 22.1 | 338 17.3 | 6.0 | 22 42.5 | 9.9 | 59.7 |
| 16 | 63 00.1 | 22.5 | 352 43.3 | 6.1 | 22 32.6 | 10.1 | 59.7 |
| 17 | 77 59.9 | 22.9 | 7 07.4 | 6.2 | 22 22.5 | 10.2 | 59.7 |
| 18 | 92 59.7 | S21 23.4 | 21 32.6 | 6.4 | S22 12.3 | 10.3 | 59.7 |
| 19 | 107 59.5 | 23.8 | 35 58.0 | 6.4 | 22 02.0 | 10.5 | 59.7 |
| 20 | 122 59.2 | 24.2 | 50 23.4 | 6.6 | 21 51.5 | 10.6 | 59.6 |
| 21 | 137 59.0 .. | 24.7 | 64 49.0 | 6.7 | 21 40.9 | 10.7 | 59.6 |
| 22 | 152 58.8 | 25.1 | 79 14.7 | 6.8 | 21 30.2 | 10.8 | 59.6 |
| 23 | 167 58.6 | 25.5 | 93 40.5 | 7.0 | 21 19.4 | 11.0 | 59.6 |
| **29 00** | 182 58.4 | S21 26.0 | 108 06.5 | 7.0 | S21 08.4 | 11.1 | 59.6 |
| 01 | 197 58.2 | 26.4 | 122 32.5 | 7.2 | 20 57.3 | 11.2 | 59.5 |
| 02 | 212 57.9 | 26.8 | 136 58.7 | 7.3 | 20 46.1 | 11.3 | 59.5 |
| 03 | 227 57.7 .. | 27.2 | 151 25.0 | 7.4 | 20 34.8 | 11.5 | 59.5 |
| 04 | 242 57.5 | 27.7 | 165 51.4 | 7.6 | 20 23.3 | 11.5 | 59.5 |
| 05 | 257 57.3 | 28.1 | 180 18.0 | 7.6 | 20 11.8 | 11.7 | 59.4 |
| 06 | 272 57.1 | S21 28.5 | 194 44.6 | 7.8 | S20 00.1 | 11.8 | 59.4 |
| 07 | 287 56.9 | 28.9 | 209 11.4 | 7.9 | 19 48.3 | 11.9 | 59.4 |
| 08 | 302 56.6 | 29.3 | 223 38.3 | 8.0 | 19 36.4 | 12.0 | 59.4 |
| **T** 09 | 317 56.4 .. | 29.8 | 238 05.3 | 8.1 | 19 24.4 | 12.1 | 59.4 |
| **U** 10 | 332 56.2 | 30.2 | 252 32.4 | 8.3 | 19 12.3 | 12.2 | 59.3 |
| **E** 11 | 347 56.0 | 30.6 | 266 59.7 | 8.3 | 19 00.1 | 12.3 | 59.3 |
| **S** 12 | 2 55.8 | S21 31.0 | 281 27.0 | 8.5 | S18 47.8 | 12.4 | 59.3 |
| **D** 13 | 17 55.5 | 31.4 | 295 54.5 | 8.6 | 18 35.4 | 12.5 | 59.3 |
| **A** 14 | 32 55.3 | 31.9 | 310 22.1 | 8.7 | 18 22.9 | 12.6 | 59.2 |
| **Y** 15 | 47 55.1 .. | 32.3 | 324 49.8 | 8.8 | 18 10.3 | 12.7 | 59.2 |
| 16 | 62 54.9 | 32.7 | 339 17.6 | 8.9 | 17 57.6 | 12.8 | 59.2 |
| 17 | 77 54.7 | 33.1 | 353 45.5 | 9.0 | 17 44.8 | 12.8 | 59.2 |
| 18 | 92 54.4 | S21 33.5 | 8 13.5 | 9.2 | S17 32.0 | 13.0 | 59.1 |
| 19 | 107 54.2 | 33.9 | 22 41.7 | 9.2 | 17 19.0 | 13.0 | 59.1 |
| 20 | 122 54.0 | 34.4 | 37 09.9 | 9.4 | 17 06.0 | 13.2 | 59.1 |
| 21 | 137 53.8 .. | 34.8 | 51 38.3 | 9.5 | 16 52.8 | 13.2 | 59.1 |
| 22 | 152 53.5 | 35.2 | 66 06.8 | 9.5 | 16 39.6 | 13.3 | 59.0 |
| 23 | 167 53.3 | 35.6 | 80 35.3 | 9.7 | S16 26.3 | 13.3 | 59.0 |
| | SD 16.2 | d 0.4 | SD 16.4 | | 16.3 | | 16.2 |

| Lat. | Twilight Naut. | Twilight Civil | Sunrise | Moonrise 27 | 28 | 29 | 30 |
|---|---|---|---|---|---|---|---|
| ° | h m | h m | h m | h m | h m | h m | h m |
| N 72 | 07 42 | 09 36 | ■ | ■ | ■ | 17 00 | 15 09 |
| N 70 | 07 27 | 09 00 | ■ | ■ | ■ | 15 40 | 14 46 |
| 68 | 07 15 | 08 35 | 10 19 | ■ | ■ | 15 01 | 14 29 |
| 66 | 07 04 | 08 16 | 09 36 | ■ | 15 12 | 14 33 | 14 14 |
| 64 | 06 55 | 08 00 | 09 07 | ■ | 14 27 | 14 12 | 14 03 |
| 62 | 06 48 | 07 47 | 08 46 | 13 57 | 13 57 | 13 55 | 13 52 |
| 60 | 06 41 | 07 35 | 08 28 | 13 19 | 13 34 | 13 41 | 13 44 |
| N 58 | 06 35 | 07 25 | 08 14 | 12 52 | 13 16 | 13 28 | 13 36 |
| 56 | 06 29 | 07 17 | 08 02 | 12 31 | 13 00 | 13 18 | 13 29 |
| 54 | 06 24 | 07 09 | 07 51 | 12 14 | 12 47 | 13 08 | 13 23 |
| 52 | 06 19 | 07 02 | 07 41 | 11 59 | 12 35 | 13 00 | 13 17 |
| 50 | 06 15 | 06 55 | 07 32 | 11 46 | 12 24 | 12 52 | 13 12 |
| 45 | 06 05 | 06 41 | 07 14 | 11 19 | 12 02 | 12 35 | 13 01 |
| N 40 | 05 56 | 06 30 | 06 59 | 10 57 | 11 45 | 12 22 | 12 52 |
| 35 | 05 48 | 06 19 | 06 47 | 10 40 | 11 30 | 12 10 | 12 45 |
| 30 | 05 40 | 06 10 | 06 36 | 10 24 | 11 17 | 12 00 | 12 38 |
| 20 | 05 26 | 05 53 | 06 17 | 09 58 | 10 54 | 11 43 | 12 26 |
| N 10 | 05 12 | 05 37 | 06 00 | 09 36 | 10 35 | 11 28 | 12 15 |
| 0 | 04 56 | 05 22 | 05 44 | 09 15 | 10 16 | 11 13 | 12 05 |
| S 10 | 04 39 | 05 06 | 05 28 | 08 54 | 09 58 | 10 59 | 11 55 |
| 20 | 04 19 | 04 47 | 05 11 | 08 31 | 09 38 | 10 43 | 11 44 |
| 30 | 03 52 | 04 25 | 04 52 | 08 05 | 09 16 | 10 25 | 11 32 |
| 35 | 03 36 | 04 11 | 04 40 | 07 49 | 09 02 | 10 15 | 11 25 |
| 40 | 03 15 | 03 55 | 04 27 | 07 31 | 08 47 | 10 03 | 11 17 |
| 45 | 02 48 | 03 35 | 04 11 | 07 10 | 08 28 | 09 49 | 11 07 |
| S 50 | 02 11 | 03 09 | 03 51 | 06 42 | 08 05 | 09 31 | 10 55 |
| 52 | 01 50 | 02 56 | 03 41 | 06 29 | 07 54 | 09 23 | 10 50 |
| 54 | 01 23 | 02 41 | 03 31 | 06 13 | 07 41 | 09 14 | 10 44 |
| 56 | 00 38 | 02 24 | 03 19 | 05 55 | 07 27 | 09 03 | 10 37 |
| 58 | //// | 02 01 | 03 05 | 05 32 | 07 09 | 08 51 | 10 30 |
| S 60 | //// | 01 32 | 02 48 | 05 03 | 06 48 | 08 37 | 10 21 |

| Lat. | Sunset | Twilight Civil | Twilight Naut. | Moonset 27 | 28 | 29 | 30 |
|---|---|---|---|---|---|---|---|
| ° | h m | h m | h m | h m | h m | h m | h m |
| N 72 | ■ | 13 59 | 15 53 | ■ | ■ | 18 16 | 21 53 |
| N 70 | ■ | 14 35 | 16 08 | ■ | ■ | 19 34 | 22 14 |
| 68 | 13 17 | 15 00 | 16 20 | ■ | ■ | 20 11 | 22 29 |
| 66 | 13 50 | 15 20 | 16 31 | ■ | 18 04 | 20 38 | 22 42 |
| 64 | 14 28 | 15 36 | 16 40 | ■ | 18 57 | 20 57 | 22 52 |
| 62 | 14 49 | 15 49 | 16 48 | 17 11 | 19 17 | 21 14 | 23 01 |
| 60 | 15 07 | 16 00 | 16 54 | 17 48 | 19 39 | 21 27 | 23 08 |
| N 58 | 15 21 | 16 10 | 17 01 | 18 15 | 19 57 | 21 38 | 23 15 |
| 56 | 15 34 | 16 19 | 17 06 | 18 35 | 20 12 | 21 48 | 23 20 |
| 54 | 15 45 | 16 27 | 17 11 | 18 52 | 20 24 | 21 57 | 23 26 |
| 52 | 15 54 | 16 34 | 17 16 | 19 07 | 20 36 | 22 05 | 23 30 |
| 50 | 16 03 | 16 40 | 17 21 | 19 20 | 20 46 | 22 12 | 23 34 |
| 45 | 16 21 | 16 54 | 17 31 | 19 46 | 21 06 | 22 26 | 23 43 |
| N 40 | 16 36 | 17 06 | 17 39 | 20 07 | 21 23 | 22 38 | 23 51 |
| 35 | 16 49 | 17 16 | 17 48 | 20 24 | 21 37 | 22 49 | 23 57 |
| 30 | 17 00 | 17 26 | 17 55 | 20 38 | 21 49 | 22 58 | 24 03 |
| 20 | 17 19 | 17 43 | 18 10 | 21 03 | 22 10 | 23 13 | 24 12 |
| N 10 | 17 36 | 17 58 | 18 24 | 21 25 | 22 28 | 23 26 | 24 21 |
| 0 | 17 52 | 18 14 | 18 40 | 21 45 | 22 44 | 23 38 | 24 28 |
| S 10 | 18 08 | 18 30 | 18 57 | 22 04 | 23 00 | 23 51 | 24 36 |
| 20 | 18 25 | 18 49 | 19 17 | 22 26 | 23 18 | 24 03 | 00 03 |
| 30 | 18 45 | 19 11 | 19 44 | 22 50 | 23 38 | 24 18 | 00 18 |
| 35 | 18 56 | 19 25 | 20 01 | 23 04 | 23 49 | 24 27 | 00 27 |
| 40 | 19 10 | 19 42 | 20 21 | 23 20 | 24 02 | 00 02 | 00 36 |
| 45 | 19 26 | 20 02 | 20 48 | 23 40 | 24 18 | 00 18 | 00 47 |
| S 50 | 19 46 | 20 28 | 21 26 | 24 04 | 00 04 | 00 37 | 01 01 |
| 52 | 19 55 | 20 41 | 21 48 | 24 16 | 00 16 | 00 46 | 01 07 |
| 54 | 20 06 | 20 56 | 22 16 | 24 29 | 00 29 | 00 56 | 01 14 |
| 56 | 20 18 | 21 14 | 23 04 | 00 06 | 00 44 | 01 07 | 01 21 |
| 58 | 20 32 | 21 36 | //// | 00 28 | 01 02 | 01 20 | 01 30 |
| S 60 | 20 49 | 22 07 | //// | 00 58 | 01 23 | 01 34 | 01 40 |

| Day | SUN Eqn. of Time 00ʰ | 12ʰ | Mer. Pass. | MOON Mer. Pass. Upper | Lower | Age | Phase |
|---|---|---|---|---|---|---|---|
| d | m s | m s | h m | h m | h m | d | % |
| 27 | 12 34 | 12 24 | 11 48 | 15 30 | 02 58 | 04 | 17 |
| 28 | 12 14 | 12 04 | 11 48 | 16 30 | 04 01 | 05 | 27 |
| 29 | 11 54 | 11 43 | 11 48 | 17 26 | 04 59 | 06 | 38 |

# 2022 NOV. 30, DEC. 1, 2 (WED., THURS., FRI.)

| UT | ARIES | VENUS −3.9 | | MARS −1.9 | | JUPITER −2.6 | | SATURN +0.7 | | STARS | | |
|---|---|---|---|---|---|---|---|---|---|---|---|---|
| | GHA | GHA | Dec | GHA | Dec | GHA | Dec | GHA | Dec | Name | SHA | Dec |
| d h | ° ′ | ° ′ | ° ′ | ° ′ | ° ′ | ° ′ | ° ′ | ° ′ | ° ′ | | ° ′ | ° ′ |
| 30 00 | 68 50.9 | 172 44.3 | S23 09.8 | 350 42.7 | N24 56.7 | 69 19.4 | S 1 45.9 | 106 14.0 | S16 04.7 | Acamar | 315 12.7 | S40 12.9 |
| 01 | 83 53.3 | 187 43.4 | 10.2 | 5 46.2 | 56.7 | 84 21.8 | 45.9 | 121 16.3 | 04.6 | Achernar | 335 21.1 | S57 07.5 |
| 02 | 98 55.8 | 202 42.4 | 10.6 | 20 49.7 | 56.7 | 99 24.2 | 45.8 | 136 18.6 | 04.6 | Acrux | 173 02.3 | S63 13.2 |
| 03 | 113 58.2 | 217 41.5 .. | 11.0 | 35 53.2 .. | 56.8 | 114 26.6 .. | 45.8 | 151 20.9 .. | 04.5 | Adhara | 255 06.9 | S29 00.0 |
| 04 | 129 00.7 | 232 40.6 | 11.4 | 50 56.7 | 56.8 | 129 29.0 | 45.8 | 166 23.3 | 04.5 | Aldebaran | 290 41.3 | N16 33.3 |
| 05 | 144 03.2 | 247 39.7 | 11.8 | 66 00.2 | 56.8 | 144 31.5 | 45.7 | 181 25.6 | 04.4 | | | |
| 06 | 159 05.6 | 262 38.7 | S23 12.2 | 81 03.7 | N24 56.9 | 159 33.9 | S 1 45.7 | 196 27.9 | S16 04.4 | Alioth | 166 14.9 | N55 50.0 |
| W 07 | 174 08.1 | 277 37.8 | 12.6 | 96 07.2 | 56.9 | 174 36.3 | 45.7 | 211 30.2 | 04.3 | Alkaid | 152 53.8 | N49 11.8 |
| E 08 | 189 10.6 | 292 36.9 | 13.0 | 111 10.7 | 57.0 | 189 38.7 | 45.6 | 226 32.5 | 04.3 | Alnair | 27 35.2 | S46 51.3 |
| D 09 | 204 13.0 | 307 36.0 .. | 13.4 | 126 14.2 .. | 57.0 | 204 41.1 .. | 45.6 | 241 34.8 .. | 04.2 | Alnilam | 275 39.2 | S 1 11.2 |
| N 10 | 219 15.5 | 322 35.0 | 13.8 | 141 17.7 | 57.0 | 219 43.5 | 45.6 | 256 37.1 | 04.2 | Alphard | 217 49.4 | S 8 45.3 |
| E 11 | 234 18.0 | 337 34.1 | 14.2 | 156 21.2 | 57.1 | 234 46.0 | 45.5 | 271 39.4 | 04.1 | | | |
| S 12 | 249 20.4 | 352 33.2 | S23 14.5 | 171 24.7 | N24 57.1 | 249 48.4 | S 1 45.5 | 286 41.7 | S16 04.1 | Alphecca | 126 05.6 | N26 38.3 |
| D 13 | 264 22.9 | 7 32.3 | 14.9 | 186 28.2 | 57.1 | 264 50.8 | 45.5 | 301 44.1 | 04.0 | Alpheratz | 357 36.4 | N29 13.1 |
| A 14 | 279 25.4 | 22 31.3 | 15.3 | 201 31.7 | 57.2 | 279 53.2 | 45.4 | 316 46.4 | 04.0 | Altair | 62 01.9 | N 8 55.8 |
| Y 15 | 294 27.8 | 37 30.4 .. | 15.7 | 216 35.2 .. | 57.2 | 294 55.6 .. | 45.4 | 331 48.7 .. | 03.9 | Ankaa | 353 08.7 | S42 11.1 |
| 16 | 309 30.3 | 52 29.5 | 16.1 | 231 38.7 | 57.2 | 309 58.0 | 45.3 | 346 51.0 | 03.9 | Antares | 112 18.4 | S26 28.9 |
| 17 | 324 32.7 | 67 28.6 | 16.4 | 246 42.2 | 57.3 | 325 00.5 | 45.3 | 1 53.3 | 03.8 | | | |
| 18 | 339 35.2 | 82 27.6 | S23 16.8 | 261 45.7 | N24 57.3 | 340 02.9 | S 1 45.3 | 16 55.6 | S16 03.8 | Arcturus | 145 49.8 | N19 03.8 |
| 19 | 354 37.7 | 97 26.7 | 17.2 | 276 49.3 | 57.3 | 355 05.3 | 45.3 | 31 57.9 | 03.7 | Atria | 107 14.8 | S69 04.1 |
| 20 | 9 40.1 | 112 25.8 | 17.6 | 291 52.8 | 57.4 | 10 07.7 | 45.2 | 47 00.2 | 03.7 | Avior | 234 15.1 | S59 34.6 |
| 21 | 24 42.6 | 127 24.8 .. | 18.0 | 306 56.3 .. | 57.4 | 25 10.1 .. | 45.2 | 62 02.5 .. | 03.6 | Bellatrix | 278 24.4 | N 6 22.3 |
| 22 | 39 45.1 | 142 23.9 | 18.3 | 321 59.8 | 57.4 | 40 12.5 | 45.2 | 77 04.8 | 03.6 | Betelgeuse | 270 53.7 | N 7 24.7 |
| 23 | 54 47.5 | 157 23.0 | 18.7 | 337 03.3 | 57.5 | 55 14.9 | 45.1 | 92 07.2 | 03.5 | | | |
| 1 00 | 69 50.0 | 172 22.1 | S23 19.1 | 352 06.8 | N24 57.5 | 70 17.4 | S 1 45.1 | 107 09.5 | S16 03.5 | Canopus | 263 52.7 | S52 42.3 |
| 01 | 84 52.5 | 187 21.1 | 19.4 | 7 10.3 | 57.5 | 85 19.8 | 45.1 | 122 11.8 | 03.4 | Capella | 280 24.0 | N46 01.2 |
| 02 | 99 54.9 | 202 20.2 | 19.8 | 22 13.8 | 57.6 | 100 22.2 | 45.0 | 137 14.1 | 03.4 | Deneb | 49 27.2 | N45 21.9 |
| 03 | 114 57.4 | 217 19.3 .. | 20.2 | 37 17.3 .. | 57.6 | 115 24.6 .. | 45.0 | 152 16.4 .. | 03.3 | Denebola | 182 26.9 | N14 26.7 |
| 04 | 129 59.8 | 232 18.3 | 20.5 | 52 20.8 | 57.6 | 130 27.0 | 44.9 | 167 18.7 | 03.2 | Diphda | 348 48.9 | S17 51.8 |
| 05 | 145 02.3 | 247 17.4 | 20.9 | 67 24.3 | 57.7 | 145 29.4 | 44.9 | 182 21.0 | 03.2 | | | |
| 06 | 160 04.8 | 262 16.5 | S23 21.3 | 82 27.9 | N24 57.7 | 160 31.8 | S 1 44.9 | 197 23.3 | S16 03.1 | Dubhe | 193 43.2 | N61 37.4 |
| 07 | 175 07.2 | 277 15.5 | 21.6 | 97 31.4 | 57.7 | 175 34.2 | 44.8 | 212 25.6 | 03.1 | Elnath | 278 03.7 | N28 37.6 |
| T 08 | 190 09.7 | 292 14.6 | 22.0 | 112 34.9 | 57.8 | 190 36.7 | 44.8 | 227 27.9 | 03.0 | Eltanin | 90 43.5 | N51 29.2 |
| H 09 | 205 12.2 | 307 13.7 .. | 22.3 | 127 38.4 .. | 57.8 | 205 39.1 .. | 44.8 | 242 30.2 .. | 03.0 | Enif | 33 40.6 | N 9 58.8 |
| U 10 | 220 14.6 | 322 12.7 | 22.7 | 142 41.9 | 57.8 | 220 41.5 | 44.7 | 257 32.5 | 02.9 | Fomalhaut | 15 16.4 | S29 30.3 |
| R 11 | 235 17.1 | 337 11.8 | 23.1 | 157 45.4 | 57.9 | 235 43.9 | 44.7 | 272 34.9 | 02.9 | | | |
| S 12 | 250 19.6 | 352 10.9 | S23 23.4 | 172 48.9 | N24 57.9 | 250 46.3 | S 1 44.7 | 287 37.2 | S16 02.8 | Gacrux | 171 53.9 | S57 14.1 |
| D 13 | 265 22.0 | 7 09.9 | 23.8 | 187 52.5 | 57.9 | 265 48.7 | 44.6 | 302 39.5 | 02.8 | Gienah | 175 45.5 | S17 39.9 |
| A 14 | 280 24.5 | 22 09.0 | 24.1 | 202 56.0 | 58.0 | 280 51.1 | 44.6 | 317 41.8 | 02.7 | Hadar | 148 39.0 | S60 28.7 |
| Y 15 | 295 27.0 | 37 08.1 .. | 24.5 | 217 59.5 .. | 58.0 | 295 53.5 .. | 44.5 | 332 44.1 .. | 02.7 | Hamal | 327 52.9 | N23 34.3 |
| 16 | 310 29.4 | 52 07.1 | 24.8 | 233 03.0 | 58.0 | 310 55.9 | 44.5 | 347 46.4 | 02.6 | Kaus Aust. | 83 35.2 | S34 22.5 |
| 17 | 325 31.9 | 67 06.2 | 25.2 | 248 06.5 | 58.0 | 325 58.3 | 44.5 | 2 48.7 | 02.6 | | | |
| 18 | 340 34.3 | 82 05.3 | S23 25.5 | 263 10.0 | N24 58.1 | 341 00.7 | S 1 44.4 | 17 51.0 | S16 02.5 | Kochab | 137 20.9 | N74 03.5 |
| 19 | 355 36.8 | 97 04.3 | 25.9 | 278 13.6 | 58.1 | 356 03.1 | 44.4 | 32 53.3 | 02.5 | Markab | 13 31.6 | N15 19.8 |
| 20 | 10 39.3 | 112 03.4 | 26.2 | 293 17.1 | 58.1 | 11 05.5 | 44.4 | 47 55.6 | 02.4 | Menkar | 314 07.7 | N 4 10.8 |
| 21 | 25 41.7 | 127 02.5 .. | 26.6 | 308 20.6 .. | 58.2 | 26 08.0 .. | 44.3 | 62 57.9 .. | 02.4 | Menkent | 148 00.0 | S36 28.7 |
| 22 | 40 44.2 | 142 01.5 | 26.9 | 323 24.1 | 58.2 | 41 10.4 | 44.3 | 78 00.2 | 02.3 | Miaplacidus | 221 38.2 | S69 48.3 |
| 23 | 55 46.7 | 157 00.6 | 27.2 | 338 27.6 | 58.2 | 56 12.8 | 44.2 | 93 02.5 | 02.2 | | | |
| 2 00 | 70 49.1 | 171 59.6 | S23 27.6 | 353 31.1 | N24 58.2 | 71 15.2 | S 1 44.2 | 108 04.8 | S16 02.2 | Mirfak | 308 30.3 | N49 56.6 |
| 01 | 85 51.6 | 186 58.7 | 27.9 | 8 34.7 | 58.3 | 86 17.6 | 44.2 | 123 07.1 | 02.1 | Nunki | 75 50.3 | S26 16.1 |
| 02 | 100 54.1 | 201 57.8 | 28.3 | 23 38.2 | 58.3 | 101 20.0 | 44.1 | 138 09.4 | 02.1 | Peacock | 53 08.9 | S56 39.9 |
| 03 | 115 56.5 | 216 56.8 .. | 28.6 | 38 41.7 .. | 58.3 | 116 22.4 .. | 44.1 | 153 11.8 .. | 02.0 | Pollux | 243 19.2 | N27 58.2 |
| 04 | 130 59.0 | 231 55.9 | 28.9 | 53 45.2 | 58.3 | 131 24.8 | 44.1 | 168 14.1 | 02.0 | Procyon | 244 52.4 | N 5 10.0 |
| 05 | 146 01.5 | 246 55.0 | 29.3 | 68 48.7 | 58.4 | 146 27.2 | 44.0 | 183 16.4 | 01.9 | | | |
| 06 | 161 03.9 | 261 54.0 | S23 29.6 | 83 52.3 | N24 58.4 | 161 29.6 | S 1 44.0 | 198 18.7 | S16 01.9 | Rasalhague | 96 00.5 | N12 32.7 |
| 07 | 176 06.4 | 276 53.1 | 29.9 | 98 55.8 | 58.4 | 176 32.0 | 43.9 | 213 21.0 | 01.8 | Regulus | 207 36.3 | N11 51.4 |
| 08 | 191 08.8 | 291 52.2 | 30.3 | 113 59.3 | 58.5 | 191 34.4 | 43.9 | 228 23.3 | 01.8 | Rigel | 281 05.2 | S 8 10.5 |
| F 09 | 206 11.3 | 306 51.2 .. | 30.6 | 129 02.8 .. | 58.5 | 206 36.8 .. | 43.9 | 243 25.6 .. | 01.7 | Rigil Kent. | 139 43.3 | S60 55.5 |
| R 10 | 221 13.8 | 321 50.3 | 30.9 | 144 06.4 | 58.5 | 221 39.2 | 43.8 | 258 27.9 | 01.7 | Sabik | 102 05.2 | S15 45.1 |
| I 11 | 236 16.2 | 336 49.3 | 31.3 | 159 09.9 | 58.5 | 236 41.6 | 43.8 | 273 30.2 | 01.6 | | | |
| D 12 | 251 18.7 | 351 48.4 | S23 31.6 | 174 13.4 | N24 58.6 | 251 44.0 | S 1 43.7 | 288 32.5 | S16 01.6 | Schedar | 349 32.7 | N56 40.0 |
| A 13 | 266 21.2 | 6 47.4 | 31.9 | 189 16.9 | 58.6 | 266 46.4 | 43.7 | 303 34.8 | 01.5 | Shaula | 96 13.2 | S37 07.2 |
| Y 14 | 281 23.6 | 21 46.5 | 32.2 | 204 20.4 | 58.6 | 281 48.8 | 43.7 | 318 37.1 | 01.4 | Sirius | 258 27.5 | S16 44.7 |
| 15 | 296 26.1 | 36 45.6 .. | 32.6 | 219 24.0 .. | 58.6 | 296 51.2 .. | 43.6 | 333 39.4 .. | 01.4 | Spica | 158 24.4 | S11 16.7 |
| 16 | 311 28.6 | 51 44.6 | 32.9 | 234 27.5 | 58.6 | 311 53.6 | 43.6 | 348 41.7 | 01.3 | Suhail | 222 47.4 | S43 31.2 |
| 17 | 326 31.0 | 66 43.7 | 33.2 | 249 31.0 | 58.7 | 326 56.0 | 43.5 | 3 44.0 | 01.3 | | | |
| 18 | 341 33.5 | 81 42.7 | S23 33.5 | 264 34.5 | N24 58.7 | 341 58.4 | S 1 43.5 | 18 46.3 | S16 01.2 | Vega | 80 34.8 | N38 48.4 |
| 19 | 356 35.9 | 96 41.8 | 33.8 | 279 38.1 | 58.7 | 357 00.8 | 43.5 | 33 48.6 | 01.2 | Zuben'ubi | 136 58.3 | S16 08.1 |
| 20 | 11 38.4 | 111 40.9 | 34.1 | 294 41.6 | 58.7 | 12 03.2 | 43.4 | 48 50.9 | 01.1 | | SHA | Mer. Pass. |
| 21 | 26 40.9 | 126 39.9 .. | 34.5 | 309 45.1 .. | 58.8 | 27 05.6 .. | 43.4 | 63 53.2 .. | 01.1 | | ° ′ | h m |
| 22 | 41 43.3 | 141 39.0 | 34.8 | 324 48.6 | 58.8 | 42 08.0 | 43.3 | 78 55.5 | 01.0 | Venus | 102 32.1 | 12 31 |
| 23 | 56 45.8 | 156 38.0 | 35.1 | 339 52.2 | 58.8 | 57 10.4 | 43.3 | 93 57.8 | 01.0 | Mars | 282 16.8 | 0 31 |
| | h m | | | | | | | | | Jupiter | 0 27.4 | 19 16 |
| Mer. Pass. 19 17.5 | | v −0.9 | d 0.4 | v 3.5 | d 0.0 | v 2.4 | d 0.0 | v 2.3 | d 0.1 | Saturn | 37 19.5 | 16 49 |

| UT | SUN GHA | Dec | MOON GHA | v | Dec | d | HP |
|---|---|---|---|---|---|---|---|
| d h | ° ′ | ° ′ | ° ′ | ′ | ° ′ | ′ | ′ |
| 30 00 | 182 53.1 | S21 36.0 | 95 04.0 | 9.8 | S16 13.0 | 13.5 | 59.0 |
| 01 | 197 52.9 | 36.4 | 109 32.8 | 9.9 | 15 59.5 | 13.5 | 59.0 |
| 02 | 212 52.6 | 36.8 | 124 01.7 | 10.0 | 15 46.0 | 13.6 | 58.9 |
| 03 | 227 52.4 | .. 37.2 | 138 30.7 | 10.1 | 15 32.4 | 13.7 | 58.9 |
| 04 | 242 52.2 | 37.6 | 152 59.8 | 10.2 | 15 18.7 | 13.7 | 58.9 |
| 05 | 257 52.0 | 38.0 | 167 29.0 | 10.3 | 15 05.0 | 13.8 | 58.9 |
| 06 | 272 51.7 | S21 38.5 | 181 58.3 | 10.4 | S14 51.2 | 13.9 | 58.8 |
| W 07 | 287 51.5 | 38.9 | 196 27.7 | 10.5 | 14 37.3 | 13.9 | 58.8 |
| E 08 | 302 51.3 | 39.3 | 210 57.2 | 10.6 | 14 23.4 | 14.1 | 58.8 |
| D 09 | 317 51.1 | .. 39.7 | 225 26.8 | 10.7 | 14 09.3 | 14.0 | 58.8 |
| N 10 | 332 50.8 | 40.1 | 239 56.5 | 10.8 | 13 55.3 | 14.1 | 58.7 |
| E 11 | 347 50.6 | 40.5 | 254 26.3 | 10.8 | 13 41.2 | 14.2 | 58.7 |
| S 12 | 2 50.4 | S21 40.9 | 268 56.1 | 11.0 | S13 27.0 | 14.3 | 58.7 |
| D 13 | 17 50.2 | 41.3 | 283 26.1 | 11.1 | 13 12.7 | 14.3 | 58.7 |
| A 14 | 32 49.9 | 41.7 | 297 56.2 | 11.1 | 12 58.4 | 14.3 | 58.6 |
| Y 15 | 47 49.7 | .. 42.1 | 312 26.3 | 11.3 | 12 44.1 | 14.4 | 58.6 |
| 16 | 62 49.5 | 42.5 | 326 56.6 | 11.3 | 12 29.7 | 14.5 | 58.6 |
| 17 | 77 49.2 | 42.9 | 341 26.9 | 11.4 | 12 15.2 | 14.5 | 58.6 |
| 18 | 92 49.0 | S21 43.3 | 355 57.3 | 11.5 | S12 00.7 | 14.6 | 58.5 |
| 19 | 107 48.8 | 43.7 | 10 27.8 | 11.6 | 11 46.1 | 14.6 | 58.5 |
| 20 | 122 48.6 | 44.1 | 24 58.4 | 11.7 | 11 31.5 | 14.6 | 58.5 |
| 21 | 137 48.3 | .. 44.5 | 39 29.1 | 11.7 | 11 16.9 | 14.7 | 58.5 |
| 22 | 152 48.1 | 44.9 | 53 59.8 | 11.8 | 11 02.2 | 14.7 | 58.4 |
| 23 | 167 47.9 | 45.3 | 68 30.6 | 11.9 | 10 47.5 | 14.8 | 58.4 |
| 1 00 | 182 47.6 | S21 45.6 | 83 01.5 | 12.0 | S10 32.7 | 14.8 | 58.4 |
| 01 | 197 47.4 | 46.0 | 97 32.5 | 12.1 | 10 17.9 | 14.9 | 58.4 |
| 02 | 212 47.2 | 46.4 | 112 03.6 | 12.1 | 10 03.0 | 14.9 | 58.3 |
| 03 | 227 46.9 | .. 46.8 | 126 34.7 | 12.2 | 9 48.1 | 14.9 | 58.3 |
| 04 | 242 46.7 | 47.2 | 141 05.9 | 12.3 | 9 33.2 | 15.0 | 58.3 |
| 05 | 257 46.5 | 47.6 | 155 37.2 | 12.4 | 9 18.2 | 14.9 | 58.3 |
| 06 | 272 46.3 | S21 48.0 | 170 08.6 | 12.4 | S 9 03.3 | 15.1 | 58.2 |
| T 07 | 287 46.0 | 48.4 | 184 40.0 | 12.5 | 8 48.2 | 15.0 | 58.2 |
| H 08 | 302 45.8 | 48.8 | 199 11.5 | 12.6 | 8 33.2 | 15.1 | 58.2 |
| U 09 | 317 45.6 | .. 49.2 | 213 43.1 | 12.6 | 8 18.1 | 15.1 | 58.2 |
| R 10 | 332 45.3 | 49.5 | 228 14.7 | 12.7 | 8 03.0 | 15.1 | 58.1 |
| S 11 | 347 45.1 | 49.9 | 242 46.4 | 12.7 | 7 47.9 | 15.2 | 58.1 |
| D 12 | 2 44.9 | S21 50.3 | 257 18.1 | 12.8 | S 7 32.7 | 15.2 | 58.1 |
| A 13 | 17 44.6 | 50.7 | 271 49.9 | 12.9 | 7 17.5 | 15.2 | 58.1 |
| Y 14 | 32 44.4 | 51.1 | 286 21.8 | 12.9 | 7 02.3 | 15.2 | 58.0 |
| 15 | 47 44.2 | .. 51.5 | 300 53.7 | 13.0 | 6 47.1 | 15.2 | 58.0 |
| 16 | 62 43.9 | 51.8 | 315 25.7 | 13.1 | 6 31.9 | 15.3 | 58.0 |
| 17 | 77 43.7 | 52.2 | 329 57.8 | 13.1 | 6 16.6 | 15.2 | 58.0 |
| 18 | 92 43.4 | S21 52.6 | 344 29.9 | 13.1 | S 6 01.4 | 15.3 | 57.9 |
| 19 | 107 43.2 | 53.0 | 359 02.0 | 13.2 | 5 46.1 | 15.3 | 57.9 |
| 20 | 122 43.0 | 53.4 | 13 34.2 | 13.3 | 5 30.8 | 15.3 | 57.9 |
| 21 | 137 42.7 | .. 53.7 | 28 06.5 | 13.3 | 5 15.5 | 15.4 | 57.9 |
| 22 | 152 42.5 | 54.1 | 42 38.8 | 13.4 | 5 00.1 | 15.3 | 57.8 |
| 23 | 167 42.3 | 54.5 | 57 11.2 | 13.4 | 4 44.8 | 15.3 | 57.8 |
| 2 00 | 182 42.0 | S21 54.9 | 71 43.6 | 13.4 | S 4 29.5 | 15.4 | 57.8 |
| 01 | 197 41.8 | 55.2 | 86 16.0 | 13.5 | 4 14.1 | 15.4 | 57.8 |
| 02 | 212 41.6 | 55.6 | 100 48.5 | 13.5 | 3 58.7 | 15.3 | 57.7 |
| 03 | 227 41.3 | .. 56.0 | 115 21.0 | 13.6 | 3 43.4 | 15.4 | 57.7 |
| 04 | 242 41.1 | 56.4 | 129 53.6 | 13.6 | 3 28.0 | 15.4 | 57.7 |
| 05 | 257 40.8 | 56.7 | 144 26.2 | 13.7 | 3 12.6 | 15.3 | 57.7 |
| 06 | 272 40.6 | S21 57.1 | 158 58.9 | 13.7 | S 2 57.3 | 15.4 | 57.6 |
| 07 | 287 40.4 | 57.5 | 173 31.6 | 13.7 | 2 41.9 | 15.4 | 57.6 |
| 08 | 302 40.1 | 57.9 | 188 04.3 | 13.8 | 2 26.5 | 15.4 | 57.6 |
| F 09 | 317 39.9 | .. 58.2 | 202 37.1 | 13.8 | 2 11.1 | 15.3 | 57.6 |
| R 10 | 332 39.6 | 58.6 | 217 09.9 | 13.8 | 1 55.8 | 15.4 | 57.5 |
| I 11 | 347 39.4 | 59.0 | 231 42.7 | 13.9 | 1 40.4 | 15.4 | 57.5 |
| D 12 | 2 39.2 | S21 59.3 | 246 15.6 | 13.9 | S 1 25.0 | 15.3 | 57.5 |
| A 13 | 17 38.9 | 21 59.7 | 260 48.5 | 13.9 | 1 09.7 | 15.4 | 57.5 |
| Y 14 | 32 38.7 | 22 00.1 | 275 21.4 | 13.9 | 0 54.3 | 15.3 | 57.4 |
| 15 | 47 38.4 | .. 00.4 | 289 54.3 | 14.0 | 0 39.0 | 15.3 | 57.4 |
| 16 | 62 38.2 | 00.8 | 304 27.3 | 14.0 | 0 23.7 | 15.4 | 57.4 |
| 17 | 77 38.0 | 01.2 | 319 00.3 | 14.0 | S 0 08.3 | 15.3 | 57.4 |
| 18 | 92 37.7 | S22 01.5 | 333 33.3 | 14.1 | N 0 07.0 | 15.3 | 57.3 |
| 19 | 107 37.5 | 01.9 | 348 06.4 | 14.1 | 0 22.3 | 15.2 | 57.3 |
| 20 | 122 37.2 | 02.2 | 2 39.5 | 14.0 | 0 37.5 | 15.3 | 57.3 |
| 21 | 137 37.0 | .. 02.6 | 17 12.5 | 14.1 | 0 52.8 | 15.3 | 57.3 |
| 22 | 152 36.8 | 03.0 | 31 45.6 | 14.2 | 1 08.1 | 15.2 | 57.2 |
| 23 | 167 36.5 | 03.3 | 46 18.8 | 14.1 | N 1 23.3 | 15.2 | 57.2 |
| | SD 16.2 | d 0.4 | SD 16.0 | | 15.8 | | 15.7 |

| Lat. | Twilight Naut. | Civil | Sunrise | Moonrise 30 | 1 | 2 | 3 |
|---|---|---|---|---|---|---|---|
| ° | h m | h m | h m | h m | h m | h m | h m |
| N 72 | 07 51 | 09 50 | ▬▬ | 15 09 | 14 25 | 13 52 | 13 20 |
| N 70 | 07 35 | 09 11 | ▬▬ | 14 46 | 14 15 | 13 50 | 13 26 |
| 68 | 07 21 | 08 44 | 10 36 | 14 29 | 14 07 | 13 49 | 13 32 |
| 66 | 07 10 | 08 23 | 09 47 | 14 14 | 14 00 | 13 48 | 13 36 |
| 64 | 07 01 | 08 06 | 09 16 | 14 03 | 13 55 | 13 47 | 13 40 |
| 62 | 06 53 | 07 52 | 08 53 | 13 52 | 13 50 | 13 47 | 13 44 |
| 60 | 06 46 | 07 41 | 08 35 | 13 44 | 13 45 | 13 46 | 13 47 |
| N 58 | 06 39 | 07 30 | 08 20 | 13 36 | 13 41 | 13 45 | 13 49 |
| 56 | 06 33 | 07 21 | 08 07 | 13 29 | 13 38 | 13 45 | 13 52 |
| 54 | 06 28 | 07 13 | 07 55 | 13 23 | 13 34 | 13 44 | 13 54 |
| 52 | 06 23 | 07 06 | 07 45 | 13 17 | 13 32 | 13 44 | 13 56 |
| 50 | 06 18 | 06 59 | 07 37 | 13 12 | 13 29 | 13 44 | 13 58 |
| 45 | 06 08 | 06 45 | 07 18 | 13 01 | 13 23 | 13 43 | 14 02 |
| N 40 | 05 59 | 06 32 | 07 02 | 12 52 | 13 18 | 13 42 | 14 05 |
| 35 | 05 50 | 06 21 | 06 49 | 12 45 | 13 14 | 13 41 | 14 08 |
| 30 | 05 43 | 06 12 | 06 38 | 12 38 | 13 10 | 13 41 | 14 10 |
| 20 | 05 28 | 05 55 | 06 19 | 12 26 | 13 04 | 13 40 | 14 15 |
| N 10 | 05 13 | 05 39 | 06 01 | 12 15 | 12 58 | 13 39 | 14 19 |
| 0 | 04 57 | 05 23 | 05 45 | 12 05 | 12 53 | 13 38 | 14 23 |
| S 10 | 04 40 | 05 06 | 05 29 | 11 55 | 12 48 | 13 38 | 14 27 |
| 20 | 04 19 | 04 47 | 05 12 | 11 44 | 12 42 | 13 37 | 14 31 |
| 30 | 03 52 | 04 24 | 04 51 | 11 32 | 12 35 | 13 36 | 14 35 |
| 35 | 03 35 | 04 10 | 04 39 | 11 25 | 12 32 | 13 36 | 14 38 |
| 40 | 03 13 | 03 54 | 04 25 | 11 17 | 12 27 | 13 35 | 14 41 |
| 45 | 02 46 | 03 33 | 04 09 | 11 07 | 12 22 | 13 34 | 14 45 |
| S 50 | 02 07 | 03 06 | 03 49 | 10 55 | 12 16 | 13 34 | 14 49 |
| 52 | 01 45 | 02 53 | 03 39 | 10 50 | 12 13 | 13 33 | 14 51 |
| 54 | 01 15 | 02 37 | 03 28 | 10 44 | 12 10 | 13 33 | 14 54 |
| 56 | 00 17 | 02 19 | 03 15 | 10 37 | 12 07 | 13 33 | 14 56 |
| 58 | //// | 01 55 | 03 01 | 10 30 | 12 03 | 13 32 | 14 59 |
| S 60 | //// | 01 23 | 02 44 | 10 21 | 11 59 | 13 32 | 15 02 |

| Lat. | Sunset | Twilight Civil | Naut. | Moonset 30 | 1 | 2 | 3 |
|---|---|---|---|---|---|---|---|
| ° | h m | h m | h m | h m | h m | h m | h m |
| N 72 | ▬▬ | 13 47 | 15 46 | 21 53 | 24 17 | 00 17 | 02 27 |
| N 70 | ▬▬ | 14 27 | 16 03 | 22 14 | 24 23 | 00 23 | 02 24 |
| 68 | 13 02 | 14 54 | 16 16 | 22 29 | 24 29 | 00 29 | 02 22 |
| 66 | 13 51 | 15 15 | 16 27 | 22 42 | 24 33 | 00 33 | 02 20 |
| 64 | 14 22 | 15 31 | 16 36 | 22 52 | 24 37 | 00 37 | 02 18 |
| 62 | 14 44 | 15 45 | 16 45 | 23 01 | 24 41 | 00 41 | 02 16 |
| 60 | 15 03 | 15 57 | 16 52 | 23 08 | 24 43 | 00 43 | 02 15 |
| N 58 | 15 18 | 16 07 | 16 58 | 23 15 | 24 46 | 00 46 | 02 14 |
| 56 | 15 31 | 16 16 | 17 04 | 23 20 | 24 48 | 00 48 | 02 13 |
| 54 | 15 42 | 16 24 | 17 10 | 23 26 | 24 50 | 00 50 | 02 12 |
| 52 | 15 52 | 16 32 | 17 15 | 23 30 | 24 52 | 00 52 | 02 11 |
| 50 | 16 01 | 16 39 | 17 19 | 23 34 | 24 54 | 00 54 | 02 10 |
| 45 | 16 20 | 16 53 | 17 30 | 23 43 | 24 57 | 00 57 | 02 08 |
| N 40 | 16 35 | 17 05 | 17 39 | 23 51 | 25 00 | 01 00 | 02 07 |
| 35 | 16 48 | 17 16 | 17 47 | 23 57 | 25 02 | 01 02 | 02 06 |
| 30 | 17 00 | 17 26 | 17 55 | 24 03 | 00 03 | 01 05 | 02 05 |
| 20 | 17 19 | 17 43 | 18 10 | 24 12 | 00 12 | 01 08 | 02 03 |
| N 10 | 17 37 | 17 59 | 18 25 | 24 21 | 00 21 | 01 12 | 02 01 |
| 0 | 17 53 | 18 15 | 18 41 | 24 28 | 00 28 | 01 15 | 02 00 |
| S 10 | 18 09 | 18 32 | 18 59 | 24 36 | 00 36 | 01 18 | 01 58 |
| 20 | 18 27 | 18 51 | 19 20 | 00 03 | 00 44 | 01 21 | 01 56 |
| 30 | 18 47 | 19 14 | 19 47 | 00 18 | 00 53 | 01 25 | 01 54 |
| 35 | 18 59 | 19 28 | 20 04 | 00 27 | 00 58 | 01 27 | 01 53 |
| 40 | 19 13 | 19 45 | 20 25 | 00 36 | 01 04 | 01 29 | 01 52 |
| 45 | 19 29 | 20 06 | 20 53 | 00 47 | 01 11 | 01 32 | 01 51 |
| S 50 | 19 50 | 20 33 | 21 33 | 01 01 | 01 19 | 01 35 | 01 49 |
| 52 | 20 00 | 20 46 | 21 55 | 01 07 | 01 23 | 01 36 | 01 48 |
| 54 | 20 11 | 21 02 | 22 26 | 01 14 | 01 27 | 01 38 | 01 47 |
| 56 | 20 24 | 21 21 | 23 32 | 01 21 | 01 31 | 01 39 | 01 46 |
| 58 | 20 38 | 21 45 | //// | 01 30 | 01 36 | 01 41 | 01 45 |
| S 60 | 20 56 | 22 18 | //// | 01 40 | 01 42 | 01 43 | 01 44 |

| | SUN | | | MOON | | | |
|---|---|---|---|---|---|---|---|
| Day | Eqn. of Time 00ʰ | 12ʰ | Mer. Pass. | Mer. Pass. Upper | Lower | Age | Phase |
| d | m s | m s | h m | h m | h m | d | % |
| 30 | 11 33 | 11 22 | 11 49 | 18 17 | 05 52 | 07 | 49 | |
| 1 | 11 11 | 11 00 | 11 49 | 19 04 | 06 41 | 08 | 60 | |
| 2 | 10 49 | 10 37 | 11 49 | 19 49 | 07 27 | 09 | 70 | |

| UT | ARIES GHA | VENUS −3.9 GHA | VENUS Dec | MARS −1.9 GHA | MARS Dec | JUPITER −2.5 GHA | JUPITER Dec | SATURN +0.7 GHA | SATURN Dec | STARS Name | SHA | Dec |
|---|---|---|---|---|---|---|---|---|---|---|---|---|
| **3 00** | 71 48.3 | 171 37.1 | S23 35.4 | 354 55.7 | N24 58.8 | 72 12.8 | S 1 43.2 | 109 00.1 | S16 00.9 | Acamar | 315 12.7 | S40 12.9 |
| 01 | 86 50.7 | 186 36.1 | 35.7 | 9 59.2 | 58.9 | 87 15.2 | 43.2 | 124 02.4 | 00.9 | Achernar | 335 21.1 | S57 07.5 |
| 02 | 101 53.2 | 201 35.2 | 36.0 | 25 02.8 | 58.9 | 102 17.6 | 43.2 | 139 04.7 | 00.8 | Acrux | 173 02.3 | S63 13.2 |
| 03 | 116 55.7 | 216 34.2 .. | 36.3 | 40 06.3 .. | 58.9 | 117 20.0 .. | 43.1 | 154 07.0 .. | 00.7 | Adhara | 255 06.9 | S29 00.0 |
| 04 | 131 58.1 | 231 33.3 | 36.6 | 55 09.8 | 58.9 | 132 22.4 | 43.1 | 169 09.3 | 00.7 | Aldebaran | 290 41.3 | N16 33.3 |
| 05 | 147 00.6 | 246 32.4 | 36.9 | 70 13.3 | 58.9 | 147 24.8 | 43.0 | 184 11.6 | 00.6 | | | |
| **S** 06 | 162 03.1 | 261 31.4 | S23 37.2 | 85 16.9 | N24 59.0 | 162 27.2 | S 1 43.0 | 199 13.9 | S16 00.6 | Alioth | 166 14.8 | N55 50.0 |
| **A** 07 | 177 05.5 | 276 30.5 | 37.5 | 100 20.4 | 59.0 | 177 29.6 | 42.9 | 214 16.2 | 00.5 | Alkaid | 152 53.8 | N49 11.8 |
| **T** 08 | 192 08.0 | 291 29.5 | 37.8 | 115 23.9 | 59.0 | 192 32.0 | 42.9 | 229 18.5 | 00.5 | Alnair | 27 35.2 | S46 51.3 |
| **U** 09 | 207 10.4 | 306 28.6 .. | 38.1 | 130 27.4 .. | 59.0 | 207 34.4 .. | 42.9 | 244 20.8 .. | 00.4 | Alnilam | 275 39.2 | S 1 11.2 |
| **R** 10 | 222 12.9 | 321 27.6 | 38.4 | 145 31.0 | 59.0 | 222 36.7 | 42.8 | 259 23.1 | 00.4 | Alphard | 217 49.4 | S 8 45.3 |
| **D** 11 | 237 15.4 | 336 26.7 | 38.7 | 160 34.5 | 59.1 | 237 39.1 | 42.8 | 274 25.4 | 00.3 | | | |
| **A** 12 | 252 17.8 | 351 25.7 | S23 39.0 | 175 38.0 | N24 59.1 | 252 41.5 | S 1 42.7 | 289 27.7 | S16 00.2 | Alphecca | 126 05.6 | N26 38.3 |
| **Y** 13 | 267 20.3 | 6 24.8 | 39.3 | 190 41.6 | 59.1 | 267 43.9 | 42.7 | 304 30.0 | 00.2 | Alpheratz | 357 36.5 | N29 13.1 |
| 14 | 282 22.8 | 21 23.8 | 39.6 | 205 45.1 | 59.1 | 282 46.3 | 42.6 | 319 32.3 | 00.1 | Altair | 62 01.9 | N 8 55.8 |
| 15 | 297 25.2 | 36 22.9 .. | 39.9 | 220 48.6 .. | 59.1 | 297 48.7 .. | 42.6 | 334 34.6 .. | 00.1 | Ankaa | 353 08.7 | S42 11.1 |
| 16 | 312 27.7 | 51 21.9 | 40.2 | 235 52.2 | 59.1 | 312 51.1 | 42.6 | 349 36.9 | 00.0 | Antares | 112 18.4 | S26 28.9 |
| 17 | 327 30.2 | 66 21.0 | 40.5 | 250 55.7 | 59.2 | 327 53.5 | 42.5 | 4 39.2 | 16 00.0 | | | |
| 18 | 342 32.6 | 81 20.0 | S23 40.8 | 265 59.2 | N24 59.2 | 342 55.9 | S 1 42.5 | 19 41.5 | S15 59.9 | Arcturus | 145 49.8 | N19 03.8 |
| 19 | 357 35.1 | 96 19.1 | 41.1 | 281 02.7 | 59.2 | 357 58.3 | 42.4 | 34 43.8 | 59.9 | Atria | 107 14.8 | S69 04.0 |
| 20 | 12 37.5 | 111 18.2 | 41.4 | 296 06.3 | 59.2 | 13 00.7 | 42.4 | 49 46.1 | 59.8 | Avior | 234 15.0 | S59 34.6 |
| 21 | 27 40.0 | 126 17.2 .. | 41.6 | 311 09.8 .. | 59.2 | 28 03.1 .. | 42.3 | 64 48.4 .. | 59.8 | Bellatrix | 278 24.4 | N 6 22.2 |
| 22 | 42 42.5 | 141 16.3 | 41.9 | 326 13.3 | 59.2 | 43 05.5 | 42.3 | 79 50.7 | 59.7 | Betelgeuse | 270 53.7 | N 7 24.7 |
| 23 | 57 44.9 | 156 15.3 | 42.2 | 341 16.9 | 59.3 | 58 07.8 | 42.2 | 94 53.0 | 59.6 | | | |
| **4 00** | 72 47.4 | 171 14.4 | S23 42.5 | 356 20.4 | N24 59.3 | 73 10.2 | S 1 42.2 | 109 55.3 | S15 59.6 | Canopus | 263 52.7 | S52 42.3 |
| 01 | 87 49.9 | 186 13.4 | 42.8 | 11 23.9 | 59.3 | 88 12.6 | 42.2 | 124 57.6 | 59.5 | Capella | 280 24.0 | N46 01.2 |
| 02 | 102 52.3 | 201 12.5 | 43.0 | 26 27.5 | 59.3 | 103 15.0 | 42.1 | 139 59.9 | 59.5 | Deneb | 49 27.3 | N45 21.9 |
| 03 | 117 54.8 | 216 11.5 .. | 43.3 | 41 31.0 .. | 59.3 | 118 17.4 .. | 42.1 | 155 02.2 .. | 59.4 | Denebola | 182 26.8 | N14 26.7 |
| 04 | 132 57.3 | 231 10.6 | 43.6 | 56 34.5 | 59.4 | 133 19.8 | 42.0 | 170 04.5 | 59.4 | Diphda | 348 48.9 | S17 51.8 |
| 05 | 147 59.7 | 246 09.6 | 43.9 | 71 38.1 | 59.4 | 148 22.2 | 42.0 | 185 06.8 | 59.3 | | | |
| **S** 06 | 163 02.2 | 261 08.7 | S23 44.2 | 86 41.6 | N24 59.4 | 163 24.6 | S 1 41.9 | 200 09.1 | S15 59.3 | Dubhe | 193 43.2 | N61 37.4 |
| **U** 07 | 178 04.7 | 276 07.7 | 44.4 | 101 45.1 | 59.4 | 178 26.9 | 41.9 | 215 11.4 | 59.2 | Elnath | 278 03.7 | N28 37.6 |
| **N** 08 | 193 07.1 | 291 06.7 | 44.7 | 116 48.7 | 59.4 | 193 29.3 | 41.8 | 230 13.7 | 59.1 | Eltanin | 90 43.5 | N51 29.2 |
| **D** 09 | 208 09.6 | 306 05.8 .. | 45.0 | 131 52.2 .. | 59.4 | 208 31.7 .. | 41.8 | 245 16.0 .. | 59.1 | Enif | 33 40.6 | N 9 58.8 |
| **A** 10 | 223 12.0 | 321 04.8 | 45.2 | 146 55.7 | 59.4 | 223 34.1 | 41.7 | 260 18.3 | 59.0 | Fomalhaut | 15 16.5 | S29 30.3 |
| **Y** 11 | 238 14.5 | 336 03.9 | 45.5 | 161 59.3 | 59.4 | 238 36.5 | 41.7 | 275 20.6 | 59.0 | | | |
| 12 | 253 17.0 | 351 02.9 | S23 45.8 | 177 02.8 | N24 59.5 | 253 38.9 | S 1 41.7 | 290 22.9 | S15 58.9 | Gacrux | 171 53.9 | S57 14.1 |
| 13 | 268 19.4 | 6 02.0 | 46.0 | 192 06.3 | 59.5 | 268 41.3 | 41.6 | 305 25.2 | 58.9 | Gienah | 175 45.5 | S17 39.9 |
| 14 | 283 21.9 | 21 01.0 | 46.3 | 207 09.9 | 59.5 | 283 43.6 | 41.6 | 320 27.5 | 58.8 | Hadar | 148 39.9 | S60 28.7 |
| 15 | 298 24.4 | 36 00.1 .. | 46.6 | 222 13.4 .. | 59.5 | 298 46.0 .. | 41.5 | 335 29.8 .. | 58.8 | Hamal | 327 52.9 | N23 34.3 |
| 16 | 313 26.8 | 50 59.1 | 46.8 | 237 16.9 | 59.5 | 313 48.4 | 41.5 | 350 32.1 | 58.7 | Kaus Aust. | 83 35.2 | S34 22.4 |
| 17 | 328 29.3 | 65 58.2 | 47.1 | 252 20.5 | 59.5 | 328 50.8 | 41.4 | 5 34.4 | 58.6 | | | |
| 18 | 343 31.8 | 80 57.2 | S23 47.3 | 267 24.0 | N24 59.5 | 343 53.2 | S 1 41.4 | 20 36.7 | S15 58.6 | Kochab | 137 20.9 | N74 03.5 |
| 19 | 358 34.2 | 95 56.3 | 47.6 | 282 27.5 | 59.5 | 358 55.6 | 41.3 | 35 39.0 | 58.5 | Markab | 13 31.6 | N15 19.8 |
| 20 | 13 36.7 | 110 55.3 | 47.9 | 297 31.1 | 59.5 | 13 58.0 | 41.3 | 50 41.3 | 58.5 | Menkar | 314 07.7 | N 4 10.8 |
| 21 | 28 39.2 | 125 54.4 .. | 48.1 | 312 34.6 .. | 59.6 | 29 00.3 .. | 41.2 | 65 43.6 .. | 58.4 | Menkent | 148 00.0 | S36 28.7 |
| 22 | 43 41.6 | 140 53.4 | 48.4 | 327 38.1 | 59.6 | 44 02.7 | 41.2 | 80 45.9 | 58.4 | Miaplacidus | 221 38.2 | S69 48.3 |
| 23 | 58 44.1 | 155 52.5 | 48.6 | 342 41.7 | 59.6 | 59 05.1 | 41.1 | 95 48.2 | 58.3 | | | |
| **5 00** | 73 46.5 | 170 51.5 | S23 48.9 | 357 45.2 | N24 59.6 | 74 07.5 | S 1 41.1 | 110 50.5 | S15 58.2 | Mirfak | 308 30.3 | N49 56.6 |
| 01 | 88 49.0 | 185 50.5 | 49.1 | 12 48.7 | 59.6 | 89 09.9 | 41.0 | 125 52.8 | 58.2 | Nunki | 75 50.3 | S26 16.1 |
| 02 | 103 51.5 | 200 49.6 | 49.4 | 27 52.3 | 59.6 | 104 12.2 | 41.0 | 140 55.1 | 58.1 | Peacock | 53 08.9 | S56 39.9 |
| 03 | 118 53.9 | 215 48.6 .. | 49.6 | 42 55.8 .. | 59.6 | 119 14.6 .. | 40.9 | 155 57.3 .. | 58.1 | Pollux | 243 19.2 | N27 58.2 |
| 04 | 133 56.4 | 230 47.7 | 49.9 | 57 59.3 | 59.6 | 134 17.0 | 40.9 | 170 59.6 | 58.0 | Procyon | 244 52.4 | N 5 10.0 |
| 05 | 148 58.9 | 245 46.7 | 50.1 | 73 02.9 | 59.6 | 149 19.4 | 40.8 | 186 01.9 | 58.0 | | | |
| **M** 06 | 164 01.3 | 260 45.8 | S23 50.3 | 88 06.4 | N24 59.6 | 164 21.8 | S 1 40.8 | 201 04.2 | S15 57.9 | Rasalhague | 96 00.5 | N12 32.7 |
| **O** 07 | 179 03.8 | 275 44.8 | 50.6 | 103 09.9 | 59.7 | 179 24.1 | 40.7 | 216 06.5 | 57.9 | Regulus | 207 36.2 | N11 51.4 |
| **N** 08 | 194 06.3 | 290 43.8 | 50.8 | 118 13.5 | 59.7 | 194 26.5 | 40.7 | 231 08.8 | 57.8 | Rigel | 281 05.2 | S 8 10.5 |
| **D** 09 | 209 08.7 | 305 42.9 .. | 51.1 | 133 17.0 .. | 59.7 | 209 28.9 .. | 40.6 | 246 11.1 .. | 57.7 | Rigil Kent. | 139 43.3 | S60 55.5 |
| **A** 10 | 224 11.2 | 320 41.9 | 51.3 | 148 20.5 | 59.7 | 224 31.3 | 40.6 | 261 13.4 | 57.7 | Sabik | 102 05.2 | S15 45.1 |
| **Y** 11 | 239 13.6 | 335 41.0 | 51.5 | 163 24.1 | 59.7 | 239 33.7 | 40.5 | 276 15.7 | 57.6 | | | |
| 12 | 254 16.1 | 350 40.0 | S23 51.8 | 178 27.6 | N24 59.7 | 254 36.0 | S 1 40.5 | 291 18.0 | S15 57.6 | Schedar | 349 32.8 | N56 40.0 |
| 13 | 269 18.6 | 5 39.1 | 52.0 | 193 31.2 | 59.7 | 269 38.4 | 40.4 | 306 20.3 | 57.5 | Shaula | 96 13.2 | S37 07.2 |
| 14 | 284 21.0 | 20 38.1 | 52.2 | 208 34.7 | 59.7 | 284 40.8 | 40.4 | 321 22.6 | 57.5 | Sirius | 258 27.5 | S16 44.7 |
| 15 | 299 23.5 | 35 37.1 .. | 52.5 | 223 38.2 .. | 59.7 | 299 43.2 .. | 40.3 | 336 24.9 .. | 57.4 | Spica | 158 24.4 | S11 16.7 |
| 16 | 314 26.0 | 50 36.2 | 52.7 | 238 41.8 | 59.7 | 314 45.5 | 40.3 | 351 27.2 | 57.3 | Suhail | 222 47.4 | S43 31.2 |
| 17 | 329 28.4 | 65 35.2 | 52.9 | 253 45.3 | 59.7 | 329 47.9 | 40.2 | 6 29.5 | 57.3 | | | |
| 18 | 344 30.9 | 80 34.3 | S23 53.2 | 268 48.8 | N24 59.7 | 344 50.3 | S 1 40.2 | 21 31.8 | S15 57.2 | Vega | 80 34.8 | N38 48.4 |
| 19 | 359 33.4 | 95 33.3 | 53.4 | 283 52.4 | 59.7 | 359 52.7 | 40.1 | 36 34.0 | 57.2 | Zuben'ubi | 136 58.3 | S16 08.1 |
| 20 | 14 35.8 | 110 32.4 | 53.6 | 298 55.9 | 59.7 | 14 55.0 | 40.1 | 51 36.3 | 57.1 | | SHA | Mer. Pass. |
| 21 | 29 38.3 | 125 31.4 .. | 53.8 | 313 59.4 .. | 59.8 | 29 57.4 .. | 40.0 | 66 38.6 .. | 57.1 | Venus | 98 26.9 | 12 36 |
| 22 | 44 40.8 | 140 30.4 | 54.1 | 329 03.0 | 59.8 | 44 59.8 | 40.0 | 81 40.9 | 57.0 | Mars | 283 33.0 | 0 15 |
| 23 | 59 43.2 | 155 29.5 | 54.3 | 344 06.5 | 59.8 | 60 02.2 | 39.9 | 96 43.2 | 56.9 | Jupiter | 0 22.8 | 19 04 |
| Mer. Pass. 19 05.7 | | v −1.0 d 0.3 | | v 3.5 d 0.0 | | v 2.4 d 0.0 | | v 2.3 d 0.1 | | Saturn | 37 07.9 | 16 38 |

| UT | SUN GHA | SUN Dec | MOON GHA | v | MOON Dec | d | HP |
|---|---|---|---|---|---|---|---|
| d h | ° ' | ° ' | ° ' | ' | ° ' | ' | ' |
| **3** 00 | 182 36.3 | S22 03.7 | 60 51.9 | 14.2 | N 1 38.5 | 15.2 | 57.2 |
| 01 | 197 36.0 | 04.0 | 75 25.1 | 14.1 | 1 53.7 | 15.2 | 57.2 |
| 02 | 212 35.8 | 04.4 | 89 58.2 | 14.2 | 2 08.9 | 15.2 | 57.2 |
| 03 | 227 35.5 | .. 04.7 | 104 31.4 | 14.2 | 2 24.1 | 15.1 | 57.1 |
| 04 | 242 35.3 | 05.1 | 119 04.6 | 14.2 | 2 39.2 | 15.1 | 57.1 |
| 05 | 257 35.1 | 05.5 | 133 37.8 | 14.2 | 2 54.3 | 15.1 | 57.1 |
| S 06 | 272 34.8 | S22 05.8 | 148 11.0 | 14.2 | N 3 09.4 | 15.1 | 57.1 |
| A 07 | 287 34.6 | 06.2 | 162 44.2 | 14.2 | 3 24.5 | 15.0 | 57.0 |
| T 08 | 302 34.3 | 06.5 | 177 17.4 | 14.3 | 3 39.5 | 15.0 | 57.0 |
| U 09 | 317 34.1 | .. 06.9 | 191 50.7 | 14.2 | 3 54.5 | 15.0 | 57.0 |
| R 10 | 332 33.8 | 07.2 | 206 23.9 | 14.2 | 4 09.5 | 15.0 | 57.0 |
| D 11 | 347 33.6 | 07.6 | 220 57.1 | 14.3 | 4 24.5 | 14.9 | 56.9 |
| A 12 | 2 33.3 | S22 07.9 | 235 30.4 | 14.2 | N 4 39.4 | 14.9 | 56.9 |
| Y 13 | 17 33.1 | 08.3 | 250 03.6 | 14.3 | 4 54.3 | 14.9 | 56.9 |
| 14 | 32 32.8 | 08.6 | 264 36.9 | 14.2 | 5 09.2 | 14.8 | 56.9 |
| 15 | 47 32.6 | .. 09.0 | 279 10.1 | 14.2 | 5 24.0 | 14.8 | 56.9 |
| 16 | 62 32.3 | 09.3 | 293 43.3 | 14.2 | 5 38.8 | 14.7 | 56.8 |
| 17 | 77 32.1 | 09.7 | 308 16.5 | 14.3 | 5 53.5 | 14.8 | 56.8 |
| 18 | 92 31.9 | S22 10.0 | 322 49.8 | 14.2 | N 6 08.3 | 14.6 | 56.8 |
| 19 | 107 31.6 | 10.3 | 337 23.0 | 14.2 | 6 22.9 | 14.7 | 56.8 |
| 20 | 122 31.4 | 10.7 | 351 56.2 | 14.2 | 6 37.6 | 14.6 | 56.7 |
| 21 | 137 31.1 | .. 11.0 | 6 29.4 | 14.2 | 6 52.2 | 14.6 | 56.7 |
| 22 | 152 30.9 | 11.4 | 21 02.6 | 14.2 | 7 06.8 | 14.5 | 56.7 |
| 23 | 167 30.6 | 11.7 | 35 35.8 | 14.1 | 7 21.3 | 14.5 | 56.7 |
| **4** 00 | 182 30.4 | S22 12.1 | 50 08.9 | 14.2 | N 7 35.8 | 14.4 | 56.6 |
| 01 | 197 30.1 | 12.4 | 64 42.1 | 14.2 | 7 50.2 | 14.4 | 56.6 |
| 02 | 212 29.9 | 12.8 | 79 15.3 | 14.1 | 8 04.6 | 14.4 | 56.6 |
| 03 | 227 29.6 | .. 13.1 | 93 48.4 | 14.1 | 8 19.0 | 14.3 | 56.6 |
| 04 | 242 29.4 | 13.4 | 108 21.5 | 14.1 | 8 33.3 | 14.3 | 56.6 |
| 05 | 257 29.1 | 13.7 | 122 54.6 | 14.1 | 8 47.6 | 14.2 | 56.5 |
| 06 | 272 28.9 | S22 14.1 | 137 27.7 | 14.0 | N 9 01.8 | 14.1 | 56.5 |
| 07 | 287 28.6 | 14.4 | 152 00.7 | 14.1 | 9 15.9 | 14.1 | 56.5 |
| S 08 | 302 28.4 | 14.7 | 166 33.8 | 14.0 | 9 30.0 | 14.1 | 56.5 |
| U 09 | 317 28.1 | .. 15.1 | 181 06.8 | 14.0 | 9 44.1 | 14.0 | 56.5 |
| N 10 | 332 27.9 | 15.4 | 195 39.8 | 14.0 | 9 58.1 | 14.0 | 56.4 |
| D 11 | 347 27.6 | 15.7 | 210 12.8 | 13.9 | 10 12.1 | 13.9 | 56.4 |
| A 12 | 2 27.4 | S22 16.1 | 224 45.7 | 14.0 | N10 26.0 | 13.8 | 56.4 |
| Y 13 | 17 27.1 | 16.4 | 239 18.7 | 13.9 | 10 39.8 | 13.8 | 56.4 |
| 14 | 32 26.8 | 16.7 | 253 51.6 | 13.9 | 10 53.6 | 13.8 | 56.3 |
| 15 | 47 26.6 | .. 17.1 | 268 24.5 | 13.8 | 11 07.4 | 13.7 | 56.3 |
| 16 | 62 26.3 | 17.4 | 282 57.3 | 13.8 | 11 21.1 | 13.6 | 56.3 |
| 17 | 77 26.1 | 17.7 | 297 30.1 | 13.8 | 11 34.7 | 13.5 | 56.3 |
| 18 | 92 25.8 | S22 18.1 | 312 02.9 | 13.8 | N11 48.2 | 13.6 | 56.3 |
| 19 | 107 25.6 | 18.4 | 326 35.7 | 13.8 | 12 01.8 | 13.4 | 56.2 |
| 20 | 122 25.3 | 18.7 | 341 08.5 | 13.7 | 12 15.2 | 13.4 | 56.2 |
| 21 | 137 25.1 | .. 19.0 | 355 41.2 | 13.6 | 12 28.6 | 13.3 | 56.2 |
| 22 | 152 24.8 | 19.4 | 10 13.8 | 13.7 | 12 41.9 | 13.2 | 56.2 |
| 23 | 167 24.6 | 19.7 | 24 46.5 | 13.6 | 12 55.1 | 13.2 | 56.2 |
| **5** 00 | 182 24.3 | S22 20.0 | 39 19.1 | 13.6 | N13 08.3 | 13.1 | 56.1 |
| 01 | 197 24.1 | 20.3 | 53 51.7 | 13.5 | 13 21.4 | 13.1 | 56.1 |
| 02 | 212 23.8 | 20.6 | 68 24.2 | 13.5 | 13 34.5 | 13.0 | 56.1 |
| 03 | 227 23.5 | .. 21.0 | 82 56.7 | 13.5 | 13 47.5 | 12.9 | 56.1 |
| 04 | 242 23.3 | 21.3 | 97 29.2 | 13.4 | 14 00.4 | 12.8 | 56.1 |
| 05 | 257 23.0 | 21.6 | 112 01.6 | 13.4 | 14 13.2 | 12.8 | 56.0 |
| 06 | 272 22.8 | S22 21.9 | 126 34.0 | 13.4 | N14 26.0 | 12.7 | 56.0 |
| 07 | 287 22.5 | 22.2 | 141 06.4 | 13.3 | 14 38.7 | 12.7 | 56.0 |
| 08 | 302 22.3 | 22.6 | 155 38.7 | 13.3 | 14 51.4 | 12.5 | 56.0 |
| M 09 | 317 22.0 | .. 22.9 | 170 11.0 | 13.2 | 15 03.9 | 12.5 | 56.0 |
| O 10 | 332 21.7 | 23.2 | 184 43.2 | 13.2 | 15 16.4 | 12.4 | 55.9 |
| N 11 | 347 21.5 | 23.5 | 199 15.4 | 13.2 | 15 28.8 | 12.3 | 55.9 |
| D 12 | 2 21.2 | S22 23.8 | 213 47.6 | 13.1 | N15 41.1 | 12.3 | 55.9 |
| A 13 | 17 21.0 | 24.1 | 228 19.7 | 13.0 | 15 53.4 | 12.2 | 55.9 |
| Y 14 | 32 20.7 | 24.4 | 242 51.7 | 13.1 | 16 05.6 | 12.1 | 55.9 |
| 15 | 47 20.5 | .. 24.7 | 257 23.8 | 13.0 | 16 17.7 | 12.0 | 55.8 |
| 16 | 62 20.2 | 25.1 | 271 55.8 | 12.9 | 16 29.7 | 11.9 | 55.8 |
| 17 | 77 19.9 | 25.4 | 286 27.7 | 12.9 | 16 41.6 | 11.9 | 55.8 |
| 18 | 92 19.7 | S22 25.7 | 300 59.6 | 12.9 | N16 53.5 | 11.7 | 55.8 |
| 19 | 107 19.4 | 26.0 | 315 31.5 | 12.8 | 17 05.2 | 11.7 | 55.8 |
| 20 | 122 19.2 | 26.3 | 330 03.3 | 12.7 | 17 16.9 | 11.6 | 55.7 |
| 21 | 137 18.9 | .. 26.6 | 344 35.0 | 12.7 | 17 28.5 | 11.5 | 55.7 |
| 22 | 152 18.6 | 26.9 | 359 06.7 | 12.7 | 17 40.0 | 11.4 | 55.7 |
| 23 | 167 18.4 | 27.2 | 13 38.4 | 12.6 | N17 51.4 | 11.4 | 55.7 |
| | SD 16.3 | d 0.3 | SD 15.5 | | 15.4 | | 15.2 |

| Lat. | Twilight Naut. | Twilight Civil | Sunrise | Moonrise 3 | 4 | 5 | 6 |
|---|---|---|---|---|---|---|---|
| ° | h m | h m | h m | h m | h m | h m | h m |
| N 72 | 07 59 | 10 04 | ■ | 13 20 | 12 43 | 11 49 | ▢ |
| N 70 | 07 41 | 09 20 | ■ | 13 26 | 13 00 | 12 24 | 10 52 |
| 68 | 07 28 | 08 51 | 10 55 | 13 32 | 13 13 | 12 49 | 12 10 |
| 66 | 07 16 | 08 30 | 09 57 | 13 36 | 13 24 | 13 09 | 12 49 |
| 64 | 07 06 | 08 12 | 09 24 | 13 40 | 13 33 | 13 25 | 13 15 |
| 62 | 06 58 | 07 58 | 09 00 | 13 44 | 13 41 | 13 38 | 13 34 |
| 60 | 06 50 | 07 46 | 08 41 | 13 47 | 13 48 | 13 50 | 13 54 |
| N 58 | 06 43 | 07 35 | 08 25 | 13 49 | 13 54 | 14 00 | 14 08 |
| 56 | 06 37 | 07 25 | 08 11 | 13 52 | 13 59 | 14 08 | 14 20 |
| 54 | 06 32 | 07 17 | 08 00 | 13 54 | 14 04 | 14 16 | 14 31 |
| 52 | 06 27 | 07 10 | 07 50 | 13 56 | 14 08 | 14 23 | 14 41 |
| 50 | 06 22 | 07 03 | 07 40 | 13 58 | 14 12 | 14 29 | 14 50 |
| 45 | 06 11 | 06 48 | 07 21 | 14 02 | 14 21 | 14 43 | 15 08 |
| N 40 | 06 01 | 06 35 | 07 05 | 14 05 | 14 28 | 14 54 | 15 23 |
| 35 | 05 53 | 06 24 | 06 52 | 14 08 | 14 35 | 15 04 | 15 36 |
| 30 | 05 45 | 06 14 | 06 40 | 14 10 | 14 40 | 15 12 | 15 47 |
| 20 | 05 29 | 05 57 | 06 20 | 14 15 | 14 50 | 15 27 | 16 07 |
| N 10 | 05 14 | 05 40 | 06 03 | 14 19 | 14 59 | 15 40 | 16 24 |
| 0 | 04 58 | 05 24 | 05 46 | 14 23 | 15 07 | 15 53 | 16 40 |
| S 10 | 04 40 | 05 07 | 05 30 | 14 27 | 15 15 | 16 05 | 16 56 |
| 20 | 04 19 | 04 48 | 05 12 | 14 31 | 15 24 | 16 18 | 17 13 |
| 30 | 03 51 | 04 24 | 04 51 | 14 35 | 15 34 | 16 34 | 17 33 |
| 35 | 03 34 | 04 10 | 04 39 | 14 38 | 15 40 | 16 42 | 17 45 |
| 40 | 03 12 | 03 53 | 04 25 | 14 41 | 15 47 | 16 53 | 17 58 |
| 45 | 02 44 | 03 32 | 04 08 | 14 45 | 15 55 | 17 05 | 18 14 |
| S 50 | 02 03 | 03 04 | 03 47 | 14 49 | 16 05 | 17 20 | 18 34 |
| 52 | 01 40 | 02 50 | 03 37 | 14 51 | 16 09 | 17 27 | 18 44 |
| 54 | 01 07 | 02 34 | 03 26 | 14 54 | 16 14 | 17 34 | 18 55 |
| 56 | //// | 02 15 | 03 13 | 14 56 | 16 19 | 17 43 | 19 07 |
| 58 | //// | 01 50 | 02 58 | 14 59 | 16 26 | 17 53 | 19 21 |
| S 60 | //// | 01 14 | 02 39 | 15 02 | 16 33 | 18 04 | 19 38 |

| Lat. | Sunset | Twilight Civil | Twilight Naut. | Moonset 3 | 4 | 5 | 6 |
|---|---|---|---|---|---|---|---|
| ° | h m | h m | h m | h m | h m | h m | h m |
| N 72 | ■ | 13 36 | 15 41 | 02 27 | 04 38 | 07 08 | ▢ |
| N 70 | ■ | 14 19 | 15 58 | 02 24 | 04 25 | 06 35 | 09 45 |
| 68 | 12 45 | 14 48 | 16 12 | 02 22 | 04 14 | 06 11 | 08 28 |
| 66 | 13 43 | 15 10 | 16 24 | 02 20 | 04 05 | 05 53 | 07 51 |
| 64 | 14 16 | 15 28 | 16 34 | 02 18 | 03 57 | 05 38 | 07 25 |
| 62 | 14 40 | 15 42 | 16 42 | 02 16 | 03 51 | 05 26 | 07 05 |
| 60 | 14 59 | 15 54 | 16 50 | 02 15 | 03 45 | 05 16 | 06 48 |
| N 58 | 15 15 | 16 05 | 16 57 | 02 14 | 03 40 | 05 07 | 06 35 |
| 56 | 15 29 | 16 14 | 17 03 | 02 13 | 03 36 | 04 59 | 06 23 |
| 54 | 15 40 | 16 23 | 17 08 | 02 12 | 03 32 | 04 52 | 06 13 |
| 52 | 15 50 | 16 30 | 17 13 | 02 11 | 03 29 | 04 46 | 06 04 |
| 50 | 16 00 | 16 37 | 17 18 | 02 10 | 03 25 | 04 40 | 05 56 |
| 45 | 16 19 | 16 52 | 17 29 | 02 08 | 03 19 | 04 28 | 05 38 |
| N 40 | 16 35 | 17 05 | 17 39 | 02 07 | 03 13 | 04 19 | 05 24 |
| 35 | 16 48 | 17 16 | 17 47 | 02 06 | 03 08 | 04 10 | 05 12 |
| 30 | 17 00 | 17 26 | 17 55 | 02 05 | 03 04 | 04 03 | 05 02 |
| 20 | 17 20 | 17 44 | 18 11 | 02 03 | 02 56 | 03 50 | 04 45 |
| N 10 | 17 37 | 18 00 | 18 26 | 02 01 | 02 50 | 03 39 | 04 29 |
| 0 | 17 54 | 18 16 | 18 42 | 02 00 | 02 44 | 03 29 | 04 15 |
| S 10 | 18 11 | 18 33 | 19 00 | 01 58 | 02 38 | 03 18 | 04 01 |
| 20 | 18 29 | 18 53 | 19 22 | 01 56 | 02 31 | 03 07 | 03 46 |
| 30 | 18 49 | 19 16 | 19 49 | 01 54 | 02 24 | 02 55 | 03 28 |
| 35 | 19 02 | 19 31 | 20 07 | 01 53 | 02 20 | 02 48 | 03 18 |
| 40 | 19 16 | 19 48 | 20 29 | 01 52 | 02 15 | 02 40 | 03 07 |
| 45 | 19 33 | 20 09 | 20 57 | 01 51 | 02 10 | 02 30 | 02 54 |
| S 50 | 19 54 | 20 37 | 21 38 | 01 49 | 02 03 | 02 19 | 02 37 |
| 52 | 20 04 | 20 51 | 22 02 | 01 48 | 02 00 | 02 14 | 02 30 |
| 54 | 20 15 | 21 07 | 22 36 | 01 47 | 01 57 | 02 08 | 02 21 |
| 56 | 20 28 | 21 27 | //// | 01 46 | 01 53 | 02 02 | 02 12 |
| 58 | 20 44 | 21 52 | //// | 01 45 | 01 49 | 01 54 | 02 01 |
| S 60 | 21 02 | 22 29 | //// | 01 44 | 01 45 | 01 46 | 01 49 |

| Day | SUN Eqn. of Time 00h | SUN Eqn. of Time 12h | SUN Mer. Pass. | MOON Mer. Pass. Upper | MOON Mer. Pass. Lower | Age | Phase |
|---|---|---|---|---|---|---|---|
| d | m s | m s | h m | h m | h m | d | % |
| 3 | 10 26 | 10 14 | 11 50 | 20 33 | 08 11 | 10 | 79 |
| 4 | 10 02 | 09 50 | 11 50 | 21 18 | 08 55 | 11 | 87 |
| 5 | 09 38 | 09 25 | 11 51 | 22 04 | 09 41 | 12 | 93 |

| UT | ARIES GHA | VENUS −3.9 GHA | Dec | MARS −1.9 GHA | Dec | JUPITER −2.5 GHA | Dec | SATURN +0.7 GHA | Dec | Star Name | SHA | Dec |
|---|---|---|---|---|---|---|---|---|---|---|---|---|
| **6 00** | 74 45.7 | 170 28.5 | S23 54.5 | 359 10.0 | N24 59.8 | 75 04.5 | S 1 39.9 | 111 45.5 | S15 56.9 | Acamar | 315 12.7 | S40 12.9 |
| 01 | 89 48.1 | 185 27.6 | 54.7 | 14 13.6 | 59.8 | 90 06.9 | 39.8 | 126 47.8 | 56.8 | Achernar | 335 21.1 | S57 07.5 |
| 02 | 104 50.6 | 200 26.6 | 54.9 | 29 17.1 | 59.8 | 105 09.3 | 39.8 | 141 50.1 | 56.8 | Acrux | 173 02.3 | S63 13.2 |
| 03 | 119 53.1 | 215 25.6 .. | 55.2 | 44 20.6 .. | 59.8 | 120 11.7 .. | 39.7 | 156 52.4 .. | 56.7 | Adhara | 255 06.9 | S29 00.0 |
| 04 | 134 55.5 | 230 24.7 | 55.4 | 59 24.2 | 59.8 | 135 14.0 | 39.7 | 171 54.7 | 56.6 | Aldebaran | 290 41.3 | N16 33.3 |
| 05 | 149 58.0 | 245 23.7 | 55.6 | 74 27.7 | 59.8 | 150 16.4 | 39.6 | 186 57.0 | 56.6 | | | |
| **T 06** | 165 00.5 | 260 22.8 | S23 55.8 | 89 31.2 | N24 59.8 | 165 18.8 | S 1 39.6 | 201 59.3 | S15 56.5 | Alioth | 166 14.8 | N55 50.0 |
| **U** 07 | 180 02.9 | 275 21.8 | 56.0 | 104 34.8 | 59.8 | 180 21.2 | 39.5 | 217 01.5 | 56.5 | Alkaid | 152 53.7 | N49 11.8 |
| **E** 08 | 195 05.4 | 290 20.8 | 56.2 | 119 38.3 | 59.8 | 195 23.5 | 39.5 | 232 03.8 | 56.4 | Alnair | 27 35.2 | S46 51.3 |
| **S** 09 | 210 07.9 | 305 19.9 .. | 56.4 | 134 41.8 .. | 59.8 | 210 25.9 .. | 39.4 | 247 06.1 .. | 56.4 | Alnilam | 275 39.2 | S 1 11.2 |
| **D** 10 | 225 10.3 | 320 18.9 | 56.6 | 149 45.4 | 59.8 | 225 28.3 | 39.3 | 262 08.4 | 56.3 | Alphard | 217 49.3 | S 8 45.3 |
| **A** 11 | 240 12.8 | 335 17.9 | 56.8 | 164 48.9 | 59.8 | 240 30.6 | 39.3 | 277 10.7 | 56.2 | | | |
| **Y** 12 | 255 15.3 | 350 17.0 | S23 57.1 | 179 52.4 | N24 59.8 | 255 33.0 | S 1 39.2 | 292 13.0 | S15 56.2 | Alphecca | 126 05.6 | N26 38.3 |
| 13 | 270 17.7 | 5 16.0 | 57.3 | 194 56.0 | 59.8 | 270 35.4 | 39.2 | 307 15.3 | 56.1 | Alpheratz | 357 36.5 | N29 13.1 |
| 14 | 285 20.2 | 20 15.1 | 57.5 | 209 59.5 | 59.8 | 285 37.7 | 39.1 | 322 17.6 | 56.1 | Altair | 62 01.9 | N 8 55.8 |
| 15 | 300 22.6 | 35 14.1 .. | 57.7 | 225 03.1 .. | 59.8 | 300 40.1 .. | 39.1 | 337 19.9 .. | 56.0 | Ankaa | 353 08.7 | S42 11.1 |
| 16 | 315 25.1 | 50 13.1 | 57.9 | 240 06.6 | 59.8 | 315 42.5 | 39.0 | 352 22.2 | 56.0 | Antares | 112 18.4 | S26 28.9 |
| 17 | 330 27.6 | 65 12.2 | 58.1 | 255 10.1 | 59.8 | 330 44.9 | 39.0 | 7 24.5 | 55.9 | | | |
| 18 | 345 30.0 | 80 11.2 | S23 58.3 | 270 13.7 | N24 59.8 | 345 47.2 | S 1 38.9 | 22 26.7 | S15 55.8 | Arcturus | 145 49.8 | N19 03.8 |
| 19 | 0 32.5 | 95 10.2 | 58.5 | 285 17.2 | 59.8 | 0 49.6 | 38.9 | 37 29.0 | 55.8 | Atria | 107 14.7 | S69 04.0 |
| 20 | 15 35.0 | 110 09.3 | 58.7 | 300 20.7 | 59.8 | 15 52.0 | 38.8 | 52 31.3 | 55.7 | Avior | 234 15.0 | S59 34.7 |
| 21 | 30 37.4 | 125 08.3 .. | 58.8 | 315 24.3 .. | 59.8 | 30 54.3 .. | 38.8 | 67 33.6 .. | 55.7 | Bellatrix | 278 24.4 | N 6 22.2 |
| 22 | 45 39.9 | 140 07.4 | 59.0 | 330 27.8 | 59.8 | 45 56.7 | 38.7 | 82 35.9 | 55.6 | Betelgeuse | 270 53.6 | N 7 24.7 |
| 23 | 60 42.4 | 155 06.4 | 59.2 | 345 31.3 | 59.8 | 60 59.1 | 38.6 | 97 38.2 | 55.5 | | | |
| **7 00** | 75 44.8 | 170 05.4 | S23 59.4 | 0 34.9 | N24 59.8 | 76 01.4 | S 1 38.6 | 112 40.5 | S15 55.5 | Canopus | 263 52.6 | S52 42.3 |
| 01 | 90 47.3 | 185 04.5 | 59.6 | 15 38.4 | 59.8 | 91 03.8 | 38.5 | 127 42.8 | 55.4 | Capella | 280 24.0 | N46 01.2 |
| 02 | 105 49.8 | 200 03.5 | 23 59.8 | 30 41.9 | 59.8 | 106 06.2 | 38.5 | 142 45.1 | 55.4 | Deneb | 49 27.3 | N45 21.9 |
| 03 | 120 52.2 | 215 02.5 | 24 00.0 | 45 45.4 .. | 59.8 | 121 08.5 .. | 38.4 | 157 47.3 .. | 55.3 | Denebola | 182 26.8 | N14 26.7 |
| 04 | 135 54.7 | 230 01.6 | 00.2 | 60 49.0 | 59.8 | 136 10.9 | 38.4 | 172 49.6 | 55.3 | Diphda | 348 48.9 | S17 51.8 |
| 05 | 150 57.1 | 245 00.6 | 00.3 | 75 52.5 | 59.8 | 151 13.3 | 38.3 | 187 51.9 | 55.2 | | | |
| **W 06** | 165 59.6 | 259 59.6 | S24 00.5 | 90 56.0 | N24 59.8 | 166 15.6 | S 1 38.3 | 202 54.2 | S15 55.1 | Dubhe | 193 43.2 | N61 37.4 |
| **E** 07 | 181 02.1 | 274 58.7 | 00.7 | 105 59.6 | 59.8 | 181 18.0 | 38.2 | 217 56.5 | 55.1 | Elnath | 278 03.7 | N28 37.6 |
| **D** 08 | 196 04.5 | 289 57.7 | 00.9 | 121 03.1 | 59.8 | 196 20.3 | 38.1 | 232 58.8 | 55.0 | Eltanin | 90 43.5 | N51 29.2 |
| **N** 09 | 211 07.0 | 304 56.7 .. | 01.1 | 136 06.6 .. | 59.8 | 211 22.7 .. | 38.1 | 248 01.1 .. | 55.0 | Enif | 33 40.6 | N 9 58.8 |
| **E** 10 | 226 09.5 | 319 55.8 | 01.2 | 151 10.2 | 59.8 | 226 25.1 | 38.0 | 263 03.4 | 54.9 | Fomalhaut | 15 16.5 | S29 30.3 |
| **S** 11 | 241 11.9 | 334 54.8 | 01.4 | 166 13.7 | 59.8 | 241 27.4 | 38.0 | 278 05.6 | 54.8 | | | |
| **D** 12 | 256 14.4 | 349 53.8 | S24 01.6 | 181 17.2 | N24 59.8 | 256 29.8 | S 1 37.9 | 293 07.9 | S15 54.8 | Gacrux | 171 53.8 | S57 14.1 |
| **A** 13 | 271 16.9 | 4 52.9 | 01.8 | 196 20.8 | 59.8 | 271 32.2 | 37.9 | 308 10.2 | 54.7 | Gienah | 175 45.5 | S17 39.9 |
| **Y** 14 | 286 19.3 | 19 51.9 | 01.9 | 211 24.3 | 59.8 | 286 34.5 | 37.8 | 323 12.5 | 54.7 | Hadar | 148 39.0 | S60 28.7 |
| 15 | 301 21.8 | 34 50.9 .. | 02.1 | 226 27.8 .. | 59.8 | 301 36.9 .. | 37.7 | 338 14.8 .. | 54.6 | Hamal | 327 52.9 | N23 34.3 |
| 16 | 316 24.3 | 49 50.0 | 02.3 | 241 31.4 | 59.8 | 316 39.2 | 37.7 | 353 17.1 | 54.6 | Kaus Aust. | 83 35.2 | S34 22.4 |
| 17 | 331 26.7 | 64 49.0 | 02.5 | 256 34.9 | 59.8 | 331 41.6 | 37.6 | 8 19.4 | 54.5 | | | |
| 18 | 346 29.2 | 79 48.0 | S24 02.6 | 271 38.4 | N24 59.8 | 346 44.0 | S 1 37.6 | 23 21.7 | S15 54.4 | Kochab | 137 20.8 | N74 03.5 |
| 19 | 1 31.6 | 94 47.1 | 02.8 | 286 41.9 | 59.7 | 1 46.3 | 37.5 | 38 23.9 | 54.4 | Markab | 13 31.6 | N15 19.8 |
| 20 | 16 34.1 | 109 46.1 | 03.0 | 301 45.5 | 59.7 | 16 48.7 | 37.5 | 53 26.2 | 54.3 | Menkar | 314 07.7 | N 4 10.8 |
| 21 | 31 36.6 | 124 45.1 .. | 03.1 | 316 49.0 .. | 59.7 | 31 51.0 .. | 37.4 | 68 28.5 .. | 54.2 | Menkent | 148 00.0 | S36 28.7 |
| 22 | 46 39.0 | 139 44.2 | 03.3 | 331 52.5 | 59.7 | 46 53.4 | 37.3 | 83 30.8 | 54.2 | Miaplacidus | 221 38.1 | S69 48.3 |
| 23 | 61 41.5 | 154 43.2 | 03.4 | 346 56.1 | 59.7 | 61 55.8 | 37.3 | 98 33.1 | 54.1 | | | |
| **8 00** | 76 44.0 | 169 42.2 | S24 03.6 | 1 59.6 | N24 59.7 | 76 58.1 | S 1 37.2 | 113 35.4 | S15 54.1 | Mirfak | 308 30.3 | N49 56.6 |
| 01 | 91 46.4 | 184 41.3 | 03.8 | 17 03.1 | 59.7 | 92 00.5 | 37.2 | 128 37.7 | 54.0 | Nunki | 75 50.3 | S26 16.1 |
| 02 | 106 48.9 | 199 40.3 | 03.9 | 32 06.7 | 59.7 | 107 02.8 | 37.1 | 143 39.9 | 53.9 | Peacock | 53 08.9 | S56 39.9 |
| 03 | 121 51.4 | 214 39.3 .. | 04.1 | 47 10.2 .. | 59.7 | 122 05.2 .. | 37.1 | 158 42.2 .. | 53.9 | Pollux | 243 19.2 | N27 58.2 |
| 04 | 136 53.8 | 229 38.4 | 04.2 | 62 13.7 | 59.7 | 137 07.6 | 37.0 | 173 44.5 | 53.8 | Procyon | 244 52.4 | N 5 10.0 |
| 05 | 151 56.3 | 244 37.4 | 04.4 | 77 17.2 | 59.7 | 152 09.9 | 36.9 | 188 46.8 | 53.8 | | | |
| **T 06** | 166 58.7 | 259 36.4 | S24 04.5 | 92 20.8 | N24 59.7 | 167 12.3 | S 1 36.9 | 203 49.1 | S15 53.7 | Rasalhague | 96 00.5 | N12 32.6 |
| **H** 07 | 182 01.2 | 274 35.5 | 04.7 | 107 24.3 | 59.7 | 182 14.6 | 36.8 | 218 51.4 | 53.6 | Regulus | 207 36.2 | N11 51.3 |
| **U** 08 | 197 03.7 | 289 34.5 | 04.8 | 122 27.8 | 59.7 | 197 17.0 | 36.8 | 233 53.6 | 53.6 | Rigel | 281 05.2 | S 8 10.5 |
| **R** 09 | 212 06.1 | 304 33.5 .. | 05.0 | 137 31.3 .. | 59.6 | 212 19.3 .. | 36.7 | 248 55.9 .. | 53.5 | Rigil Kent. | 139 43.3 | S60 55.5 |
| **S** 10 | 227 08.6 | 319 32.6 | 05.1 | 152 34.9 | 59.6 | 227 21.7 | 36.6 | 263 58.2 | 53.5 | Sabik | 102 05.1 | S15 45.1 |
| **D** 11 | 242 11.1 | 334 31.6 | 05.3 | 167 38.4 | 59.6 | 242 24.0 | 36.6 | 279 00.5 | 53.4 | | | |
| **A** 12 | 257 13.5 | 349 30.6 | S24 05.4 | 182 41.9 | N24 59.6 | 257 26.4 | S 1 36.5 | 294 02.8 | S15 53.3 | Schedar | 349 32.8 | N56 40.0 |
| **Y** 13 | 272 16.0 | 4 29.7 | 05.6 | 197 45.4 | 59.6 | 272 28.8 | 36.5 | 309 05.1 | 53.3 | Shaula | 96 13.2 | S37 07.2 |
| 14 | 287 18.5 | 19 28.7 | 05.7 | 212 49.0 | 59.6 | 287 31.1 | 36.4 | 324 07.3 | 53.2 | Sirius | 258 27.5 | S16 44.8 |
| 15 | 302 20.9 | 34 27.7 .. | 05.8 | 227 52.5 .. | 59.6 | 302 33.5 .. | 36.3 | 339 09.6 .. | 53.2 | Spica | 158 24.3 | S11 16.7 |
| 16 | 317 23.4 | 49 26.7 | 06.0 | 242 56.0 | 59.6 | 317 35.8 | 36.3 | 354 11.9 | 53.1 | Suhail | 222 47.4 | S43 31.2 |
| 17 | 332 25.9 | 64 25.8 | 06.1 | 257 59.5 | 59.6 | 332 38.2 | 36.2 | 9 14.2 | 53.0 | | | |
| 18 | 347 28.3 | 79 24.8 | S24 06.2 | 273 03.1 | N24 59.6 | 347 40.5 | S 1 36.2 | 24 16.5 | S15 53.0 | Vega | 80 34.8 | N38 48.4 |
| 19 | 2 30.8 | 94 23.8 | 06.4 | 288 06.6 | 59.6 | 2 42.9 | 36.1 | 39 18.8 | 52.9 | Zuben'ubi | 136 58.3 | S16 08.1 |
| 20 | 17 33.2 | 109 22.9 | 06.5 | 303 10.1 | 59.5 | 17 45.2 | 36.0 | 54 21.0 | 52.9 | | SHA | Mer. Pass. |
| 21 | 32 35.7 | 124 21.9 .. | 06.6 | 318 13.6 .. | 59.5 | 32 47.6 .. | 36.0 | 69 23.3 .. | 52.8 | Venus | 94 20.6 | 12 40 |
| 22 | 47 38.2 | 139 20.9 | 06.8 | 333 17.2 | 59.5 | 47 49.9 | 35.9 | 84 25.6 | 52.7 | Mars | 284 50.0 | 23 52 |
| 23 | 62 40.6 | 154 20.0 | 06.9 | 348 20.7 | 59.5 | 62 52.3 | 35.8 | 99 27.9 | 52.7 | Jupiter | 0 16.6 | 18 53 |
| Mer. Pass. 18 53.9 | | v −1.0   d 0.2 | | v 3.5   d 0.0 | | v 2.4   d 0.1 | | v 2.3   d 0.1 | | Saturn | 36 55.7 | 16 27 |

### SUN and MOON

| UT | SUN GHA | SUN Dec | MOON GHA | v | MOON Dec | d | HP |
|---|---|---|---|---|---|---|---|
| d h | ° ′ | ° ′ | ° ′ | ′ | ° ′ | ′ | ′ |
| **6** 00 | 182 18.1 | S22 27.5 | 28 10.0 | 12.6 | N18 02.8 | 11.2 | 55.7 |
| 01 | 197 17.9 | 27.8 | 42 41.6 | 12.5 | 18 14.0 | 11.2 | 55.6 |
| 02 | 212 17.6 | 28.1 | 57 13.1 | 12.5 | 18 25.2 | 11.0 | 55.6 |
| 03 | 227 17.3 .. | 28.4 | 71 44.6 | 12.4 | 18 36.2 | 11.0 | 55.6 |
| 04 | 242 17.1 | 28.7 | 86 16.0 | 12.4 | 18 47.2 | 10.9 | 55.6 |
| 05 | 257 16.8 | 29.0 | 100 47.4 | 12.3 | 18 58.1 | 10.8 | 55.6 |
| 06 | 272 16.6 | S22 29.3 | 115 18.7 | 12.3 | N19 08.9 | 10.7 | 55.5 |
| 07 | 287 16.3 | 29.6 | 129 50.0 | 12.3 | 19 19.6 | 10.6 | 55.5 |
| T 08 | 302 16.0 | 29.9 | 144 21.3 | 12.2 | 19 30.2 | 10.5 | 55.5 |
| U 09 | 317 15.8 .. | 30.2 | 158 52.5 | 12.1 | 19 40.7 | 10.4 | 55.5 |
| E 10 | 332 15.5 | 30.5 | 173 23.6 | 12.1 | 19 51.1 | 10.3 | 55.5 |
| S 11 | 347 15.2 | 30.8 | 187 54.7 | 12.0 | 20 01.4 | 10.2 | 55.5 |
| D 12 | 2 15.0 | S22 31.1 | 202 25.7 | 12.0 | N20 11.6 | 10.1 | 55.4 |
| A 13 | 17 14.7 | 31.4 | 216 56.7 | 11.9 | 20 21.7 | 10.1 | 55.4 |
| Y 14 | 32 14.4 | 31.7 | 231 27.6 | 11.9 | 20 31.8 | 9.9 | 55.4 |
| 15 | 47 14.2 .. | 32.0 | 245 58.5 | 11.9 | 20 41.7 | 9.8 | 55.4 |
| 16 | 62 13.9 | 32.3 | 260 29.4 | 11.8 | 20 51.5 | 9.7 | 55.4 |
| 17 | 77 13.7 | 32.6 | 275 00.2 | 11.7 | 21 01.2 | 9.6 | 55.4 |
| 18 | 92 13.4 | S22 32.9 | 289 30.9 | 11.7 | N21 10.8 | 9.5 | 55.3 |
| 19 | 107 13.1 | 33.1 | 304 01.6 | 11.6 | 21 20.3 | 9.4 | 55.3 |
| 20 | 122 12.9 | 33.4 | 318 32.2 | 11.6 | 21 29.7 | 9.3 | 55.3 |
| 21 | 137 12.6 .. | 33.7 | 333 02.8 | 11.5 | 21 39.0 | 9.1 | 55.3 |
| 22 | 152 12.3 | 34.0 | 347 33.3 | 11.5 | 21 48.1 | 9.1 | 55.3 |
| 23 | 167 12.1 | 34.3 | 2 03.8 | 11.5 | 21 57.2 | 9.0 | 55.2 |
| **7** 00 | 182 11.8 | S22 34.6 | 16 34.3 | 11.4 | N22 06.2 | 8.8 | 55.2 |
| 01 | 197 11.5 | 34.9 | 31 04.7 | 11.3 | 22 15.0 | 8.8 | 55.2 |
| 02 | 212 11.3 | 35.2 | 45 35.0 | 11.3 | 22 23.8 | 8.6 | 55.2 |
| 03 | 227 11.0 .. | 35.4 | 60 05.3 | 11.2 | 22 32.4 | 8.5 | 55.2 |
| 04 | 242 10.7 | 35.7 | 74 35.5 | 11.2 | 22 40.9 | 8.4 | 55.2 |
| 05 | 257 10.5 | 36.0 | 89 05.7 | 11.2 | 22 49.3 | 8.3 | 55.1 |
| 06 | 272 10.2 | S22 36.3 | 103 35.9 | 11.1 | N22 57.6 | 8.2 | 55.1 |
| W 07 | 287 09.9 | 36.6 | 118 06.0 | 11.0 | 23 05.8 | 8.1 | 55.1 |
| E 08 | 302 09.7 | 36.8 | 132 36.0 | 11.1 | 23 13.9 | 7.9 | 55.1 |
| D 09 | 317 09.4 .. | 37.1 | 147 06.1 | 10.9 | 23 21.8 | 7.9 | 55.1 |
| N 10 | 332 09.1 | 37.4 | 161 36.0 | 10.9 | 23 29.7 | 7.7 | 55.1 |
| E 11 | 347 08.9 | 37.7 | 176 05.9 | 10.9 | 23 37.4 | 7.6 | 55.0 |
| S 12 | 2 08.6 | S22 38.0 | 190 35.8 | 10.8 | N23 45.0 | 7.4 | 55.0 |
| D 13 | 17 08.3 | 38.2 | 205 05.6 | 10.8 | 23 52.4 | 7.4 | 55.0 |
| A 14 | 32 08.1 | 38.5 | 219 35.4 | 10.8 | 23 59.8 | 7.2 | 55.0 |
| Y 15 | 47 07.8 .. | 38.8 | 234 05.2 | 10.7 | 24 07.0 | 7.2 | 55.0 |
| 16 | 62 07.5 | 39.1 | 248 34.9 | 10.6 | 24 14.2 | 7.0 | 55.0 |
| 17 | 77 07.2 | 39.3 | 263 04.5 | 10.6 | 24 21.2 | 6.8 | 55.0 |
| 18 | 92 07.0 | S22 39.6 | 277 34.1 | 10.6 | N24 28.0 | 6.8 | 54.9 |
| 19 | 107 06.7 | 39.9 | 292 03.7 | 10.5 | 24 34.8 | 6.6 | 54.9 |
| 20 | 122 06.4 | 40.1 | 306 33.2 | 10.5 | 24 41.4 | 6.5 | 54.9 |
| 21 | 137 06.2 .. | 40.4 | 321 02.7 | 10.5 | 24 47.9 | 6.4 | 54.9 |
| 22 | 152 05.9 | 40.7 | 335 32.2 | 10.4 | 24 54.3 | 6.3 | 54.9 |
| 23 | 167 05.6 | 41.0 | 350 01.6 | 10.3 | 25 00.6 | 6.1 | 54.9 |
| **8** 00 | 182 05.4 | S22 41.2 | 4 30.9 | 10.4 | N25 06.7 | 6.0 | 54.8 |
| 01 | 197 05.1 | 41.5 | 19 00.3 | 10.3 | 25 12.7 | 5.9 | 54.8 |
| 02 | 212 04.8 | 41.8 | 33 29.6 | 10.2 | 25 18.6 | 5.7 | 54.8 |
| 03 | 227 04.5 .. | 42.0 | 47 58.8 | 10.3 | 25 24.3 | 5.7 | 54.8 |
| 04 | 242 04.3 | 42.3 | 62 28.1 | 10.2 | 25 30.0 | 5.5 | 54.8 |
| 05 | 257 04.0 | 42.5 | 76 57.3 | 10.1 | 25 35.5 | 5.3 | 54.8 |
| 06 | 272 03.7 | S22 42.8 | 91 26.4 | 10.2 | N25 40.8 | 5.3 | 54.8 |
| 07 | 287 03.5 | 43.1 | 105 55.6 | 10.1 | 25 46.1 | 5.1 | 54.7 |
| T 08 | 302 03.2 | 43.3 | 120 24.7 | 10.0 | 25 51.2 | 4.9 | 54.7 |
| H 09 | 317 02.9 .. | 43.6 | 134 53.7 | 10.1 | 25 56.1 | 4.9 | 54.7 |
| U 10 | 332 02.6 | 43.9 | 149 22.8 | 10.0 | 26 01.0 | 4.7 | 54.7 |
| R 11 | 347 02.4 | 44.1 | 163 51.8 | 10.0 | 26 05.7 | 4.6 | 54.7 |
| S 12 | 2 02.1 | S22 44.4 | 178 20.8 | 9.9 | N26 10.3 | 4.5 | 54.7 |
| D 13 | 17 01.8 | 44.6 | 192 49.7 | 10.0 | 26 14.8 | 4.3 | 54.7 |
| A 14 | 32 01.5 | 44.9 | 207 18.7 | 9.9 | 26 19.1 | 4.2 | 54.6 |
| Y 15 | 47 01.3 .. | 45.1 | 221 47.6 | 9.9 | 26 23.3 | 4.0 | 54.6 |
| 16 | 62 01.0 | 45.4 | 236 16.5 | 9.8 | 26 27.3 | 3.9 | 54.6 |
| 17 | 77 00.7 | 45.7 | 250 45.3 | 9.9 | 26 31.2 | 3.8 | 54.6 |
| 18 | 92 00.4 | S22 45.9 | 265 14.2 | 9.8 | N26 35.0 | 3.7 | 54.6 |
| 19 | 107 00.2 | 46.2 | 279 43.0 | 9.8 | 26 38.7 | 3.5 | 54.6 |
| 20 | 121 59.9 | 46.4 | 294 11.8 | 9.8 | 26 42.2 | 3.4 | 54.5 |
| 21 | 136 59.6 .. | 46.7 | 308 40.6 | 9.8 | 26 45.6 | 3.3 | 54.5 |
| 22 | 151 59.3 | 46.9 | 323 09.4 | 9.7 | 26 48.9 | 3.1 | 54.5 |
| 23 | 166 59.1 | 47.2 | 337 38.1 | 9.8 | N26 52.0 | 3.0 | 54.5 |
| | SD 16.3 | d 0.3 | SD 15.1 | | 15.0 | | 14.9 |

### Twilight, Sunrise and Moonrise

| Lat. | Naut. | Civil | Sunrise | Moonrise 6 | 7 | 8 | 9 |
|---|---|---|---|---|---|---|---|
| ° | h m | h m | h m | h m | h m | h m | h m |
| N 72 | 08 06 | 10 17 | ■■■■ | □ | □ | □ | □ |
| N 70 | 07 48 | 09 29 | ■■■■ | 10 52 | □ | □ | □ |
| 68 | 07 33 | 08 59 | 11 18 | 12 10 | □ | □ | □ |
| 66 | 07 21 | 08 36 | 10 07 | 12 49 | 11 59 | □ | □ |
| 64 | 07 11 | 08 18 | 09 31 | 13 15 | 13 01 | □ | □ |
| 62 | 07 02 | 08 03 | 09 06 | 13 36 | 13 36 | 13 39 | 13 57 |
| 60 | 06 54 | 07 50 | 08 46 | 13 54 | 14 01 | 14 17 | 14 49 |
| N 58 | 06 47 | 07 39 | 08 30 | 14 08 | 14 21 | 14 44 | 15 21 |
| 56 | 06 41 | 07 29 | 08 16 | 14 20 | 14 38 | 15 05 | 15 45 |
| 54 | 06 35 | 07 21 | 08 04 | 14 31 | 14 52 | 15 22 | 16 04 |
| 52 | 06 30 | 07 13 | 07 53 | 14 41 | 15 05 | 15 37 | 16 20 |
| 50 | 06 25 | 07 06 | 07 44 | 14 50 | 15 16 | 15 50 | 16 34 |
| 45 | 06 14 | 06 51 | 07 24 | 15 08 | 15 39 | 16 17 | 17 03 |
| N 40 | 06 04 | 06 38 | 07 08 | 15 23 | 15 57 | 16 38 | 17 25 |
| 35 | 05 55 | 06 27 | 06 55 | 15 36 | 16 13 | 16 56 | 17 44 |
| 30 | 05 47 | 06 16 | 06 43 | 15 47 | 16 27 | 17 11 | 18 00 |
| 20 | 05 31 | 05 58 | 06 22 | 16 07 | 16 50 | 17 37 | 18 27 |
| N 10 | 05 16 | 05 42 | 06 04 | 16 24 | 17 10 | 17 59 | 18 50 |
| 0 | 04 59 | 05 25 | 05 48 | 16 40 | 17 29 | 18 20 | 19 12 |
| S 10 | 04 41 | 05 08 | 05 31 | 16 56 | 17 48 | 18 41 | 19 34 |
| 20 | 04 19 | 04 48 | 05 13 | 17 13 | 18 09 | 19 04 | 19 57 |
| 30 | 03 51 | 04 24 | 04 51 | 17 33 | 18 32 | 19 30 | 20 24 |
| 35 | 03 33 | 04 10 | 04 39 | 17 45 | 18 46 | 19 46 | 20 40 |
| 40 | 03 11 | 03 52 | 04 24 | 17 58 | 19 03 | 20 04 | 20 59 |
| 45 | 02 42 | 03 31 | 04 07 | 18 14 | 19 22 | 20 26 | 21 22 |
| S 50 | 02 00 | 03 02 | 03 46 | 18 34 | 19 47 | 20 54 | 21 51 |
| 52 | 01 36 | 02 48 | 03 36 | 18 44 | 19 59 | 21 07 | 22 05 |
| 54 | 01 00 | 02 32 | 03 24 | 18 55 | 20 12 | 21 23 | 22 22 |
| 56 | //// | 02 11 | 03 11 | 19 07 | 20 28 | 21 42 | 22 41 |
| 58 | //// | 01 45 | 02 55 | 19 21 | 20 47 | 22 05 | 23 06 |
| S 60 | //// | 01 06 | 02 36 | 19 38 | 21 11 | 22 35 | 23 39 |

### Sunset, Twilight and Moonset

| Lat. | Sunset | Civil | Naut. | Moonset 6 | 7 | 8 | 9 |
|---|---|---|---|---|---|---|---|
| ° | h m | h m | h m | h m | h m | h m | h m |
| N 72 | ■■■■ | 13 25 | 15 37 | □ | □ | □ | □ |
| N 70 | ■■■■ | 14 13 | 15 55 | 09 45 | □ | □ | □ |
| 68 | 12 24 | 14 44 | 16 09 | 08 28 | □ | □ | □ |
| 66 | 13 36 | 15 07 | 16 21 | 07 51 | 10 22 | □ | □ |
| 64 | 14 11 | 15 25 | 16 32 | 07 25 | 09 20 | □ | □ |
| 62 | 14 37 | 15 40 | 16 40 | 07 05 | 08 46 | 10 29 | 11 59 |
| 60 | 14 57 | 15 52 | 16 48 | 06 48 | 08 22 | 09 51 | 11 07 |
| N 58 | 15 13 | 16 03 | 16 55 | 06 35 | 08 02 | 09 25 | 10 35 |
| 56 | 15 27 | 16 13 | 17 02 | 06 23 | 07 46 | 09 04 | 10 11 |
| 54 | 15 39 | 16 22 | 17 07 | 06 13 | 07 32 | 08 47 | 09 52 |
| 52 | 15 49 | 16 29 | 17 13 | 06 04 | 07 20 | 08 32 | 09 36 |
| 50 | 15 59 | 16 37 | 17 18 | 05 56 | 07 09 | 08 20 | 09 22 |
| 45 | 16 18 | 16 52 | 17 29 | 05 38 | 06 47 | 07 53 | 08 53 |
| N 40 | 16 35 | 17 05 | 17 39 | 05 24 | 06 30 | 07 33 | 08 31 |
| 35 | 16 48 | 17 16 | 17 48 | 05 12 | 06 15 | 07 15 | 08 13 |
| 30 | 17 00 | 17 26 | 17 56 | 05 02 | 06 02 | 07 01 | 07 57 |
| 20 | 17 20 | 17 44 | 18 12 | 04 45 | 05 40 | 06 35 | 07 30 |
| N 10 | 17 38 | 18 01 | 18 27 | 04 29 | 05 21 | 06 14 | 07 07 |
| 0 | 17 55 | 18 18 | 18 44 | 04 15 | 05 03 | 05 54 | 06 45 |
| S 10 | 18 12 | 18 35 | 19 02 | 04 01 | 04 46 | 05 33 | 06 24 |
| 20 | 18 30 | 18 55 | 19 24 | 03 46 | 04 27 | 05 12 | 06 01 |
| 30 | 18 52 | 19 19 | 19 52 | 03 28 | 04 05 | 04 47 | 05 34 |
| 35 | 19 04 | 19 34 | 20 10 | 03 18 | 03 53 | 04 32 | 05 18 |
| 40 | 19 19 | 19 51 | 20 32 | 03 07 | 03 38 | 04 16 | 04 59 |
| 45 | 19 36 | 20 13 | 21 01 | 02 54 | 03 21 | 03 55 | 04 37 |
| S 50 | 19 58 | 20 41 | 21 44 | 02 37 | 03 00 | 03 30 | 04 09 |
| 52 | 20 08 | 20 55 | 22 09 | 02 30 | 02 50 | 03 18 | 03 55 |
| 54 | 20 20 | 21 12 | 22 45 | 02 21 | 02 39 | 03 04 | 03 39 |
| 56 | 20 33 | 21 33 | //// | 02 12 | 02 26 | 02 48 | 03 20 |
| 58 | 20 49 | 21 59 | //// | 02 01 | 02 12 | 02 28 | 02 57 |
| S 60 | 21 08 | 22 39 | //// | 01 49 | 01 54 | 02 05 | 02 27 |

### SUN and MOON

| Day | Eqn. of Time 00h | 12h | Mer. Pass. | Mer. Pass. Upper | Lower | Age | Phase |
|---|---|---|---|---|---|---|---|
| d | m s | m s | h m | h m | h m | d % | |
| 6 | 09 13 | 09 00 | 11 51 | 22 51 | 10 27 | 13 97 | |
| 7 | 08 48 | 08 35 | 11 51 | 23 41 | 11 16 | 14 100 | ◯ |
| 8 | 08 22 | 08 09 | 11 52 | 24 33 | 12 07 | 15 100 | |

| UT | ARIES | VENUS −3·9 | | MARS −1·9 | | JUPITER −2·5 | | SATURN +0·7 | | STARS | | |
|---|---|---|---|---|---|---|---|---|---|---|---|---|
| | GHA | GHA | Dec | GHA | Dec | GHA | Dec | GHA | Dec | Name | SHA | Dec |
| d h | ° ′ | ° ′ | ° ′ | ° ′ | ° ′ | ° ′ | ° ′ | ° ′ | ° ′ | | ° ′ | ° ′ |
| 9 00 | 77 43.1 | 169 19.0 | S24 07.0 | 3 24.2 | N24 59.5 | 77 54.6 | S 1 35.8 | 114 30.2 | S15 52.6 | Acamar | 315 12.7 | S40 12.9 |
| 01 | 92 45.6 | 184 18.0 | 07.2 | 18 27.7 | 59.5 | 92 57.0 | 35.7 | 129 32.5 | 52.6 | Achernar | 335 21.1 | S57 07.5 |
| 02 | 107 48.0 | 199 17.0 | 07.3 | 33 31.3 | 59.5 | 107 59.3 | 35.7 | 144 34.7 | 52.5 | Acrux | 173 02.2 | S63 13.2 |
| 03 | 122 50.5 | 214 16.1 | . . 07.4 | 48 34.8 | . . 59.5 | 123 01.7 | . . 35.6 | 159 37.0 | . . 52.4 | Adhara | 255 06.9 | S29 00.1 |
| 04 | 137 53.0 | 229 15.1 | 07.5 | 63 38.3 | 59.4 | 138 04.0 | 35.5 | 174 39.3 | 52.4 | Aldebaran | 290 41.3 | N16 33.3 |
| 05 | 152 55.4 | 244 14.1 | 07.7 | 78 41.8 | 59.4 | 153 06.4 | 35.5 | 189 41.6 | 52.3 | | | |
| 06 | 167 57.9 | 259 13.2 | S24 07.8 | 93 45.3 | N24 59.4 | 168 08.7 | S 1 35.4 | 204 43.9 | S15 52.3 | Alioth | 166 14.8 | N55 49.9 |
| 07 | 183 00.4 | 274 12.2 | 07.9 | 108 48.9 | 59.4 | 183 11.1 | 35.3 | 219 46.1 | 52.2 | Alkaid | 152 53.7 | N49 11.8 |
| 08 | 198 02.8 | 289 11.2 | 08.0 | 123 52.4 | 59.4 | 198 13.4 | 35.3 | 234 48.4 | 52.1 | Alnair | 27 35.3 | S46 51.3 |
| F 09 | 213 05.3 | 304 10.2 | . . 08.1 | 138 55.9 | . . 59.4 | 213 15.8 | . . 35.2 | 249 50.7 | . . 52.1 | Alnilam | 275 39.2 | S 1 11.2 |
| R 10 | 228 07.7 | 319 09.3 | 08.2 | 153 59.4 | 59.4 | 228 18.1 | 35.2 | 264 53.0 | 52.0 | Alphard | 217 49.3 | S 8 45.3 |
| I 11 | 243 10.2 | 334 08.3 | 08.4 | 169 02.9 | 59.4 | 243 20.5 | 35.1 | 279 55.3 | 51.9 | | | |
| D 12 | 258 12.7 | 349 07.3 | S24 08.5 | 184 06.5 | N24 59.3 | 258 22.8 | S 1 35.0 | 294 57.6 | S15 51.9 | Alphecca | 126 05.6 | N26 38.2 |
| A 13 | 273 15.1 | 4 06.4 | 08.6 | 199 10.0 | 59.3 | 273 25.2 | 35.0 | 309 59.8 | 51.8 | Alpheratz | 357 36.5 | N29 13.1 |
| Y 14 | 288 17.6 | 19 05.4 | 08.7 | 214 13.5 | 59.3 | 288 27.5 | 34.9 | 325 02.1 | 51.8 | Altair | 62 01.9 | N 8 55.8 |
| 15 | 303 20.1 | 34 04.4 | . . 08.8 | 229 17.0 | . . 59.3 | 303 29.9 | . . 34.8 | 340 04.4 | . . 51.7 | Ankaa | 353 08.7 | S42 11.2 |
| 16 | 318 22.5 | 49 03.4 | 08.9 | 244 20.5 | 59.3 | 318 32.2 | 34.8 | 355 06.7 | 51.6 | Antares | 112 18.3 | S26 28.9 |
| 17 | 333 25.0 | 64 02.5 | 09.0 | 259 24.0 | 59.3 | 333 34.6 | 34.7 | 10 09.0 | 51.6 | | | |
| 18 | 348 27.5 | 79 01.5 | S24 09.1 | 274 27.6 | N24 59.3 | 348 36.9 | S 1 34.7 | 25 11.2 | S15 51.5 | Arcturus | 145 49.8 | N19 03.8 |
| 19 | 3 29.9 | 94 00.5 | 09.2 | 289 31.1 | 59.2 | 3 39.3 | 34.6 | 40 13.5 | 51.5 | Atria | 107 14.7 | S69 04.0 |
| 20 | 18 32.4 | 108 59.6 | 09.3 | 304 34.6 | 59.2 | 18 41.6 | 34.5 | 55 15.8 | 51.4 | Avior | 234 15.0 | S59 34.7 |
| 21 | 33 34.9 | 123 58.6 | . . 09.4 | 319 38.1 | . . 59.2 | 33 43.9 | . . 34.5 | 70 18.1 | . . 51.3 | Bellatrix | 278 24.4 | N 6 22.2 |
| 22 | 48 37.3 | 138 57.6 | 09.5 | 334 41.6 | 59.2 | 48 46.3 | 34.4 | 85 20.4 | 51.3 | Betelgeuse | 270 53.6 | N 7 24.7 |
| 23 | 63 39.8 | 153 56.6 | 09.6 | 349 45.1 | 59.2 | 63 48.6 | 34.3 | 100 22.6 | 51.2 | | | |
| 10 00 | 78 42.2 | 168 55.7 | S24 09.7 | 4 48.6 | N24 59.2 | 78 51.0 | S 1 34.3 | 115 24.9 | S15 51.1 | Canopus | 263 52.6 | S52 42.3 |
| 01 | 93 44.7 | 183 54.7 | 09.8 | 19 52.2 | 59.1 | 93 53.3 | 34.2 | 130 27.2 | 51.1 | Capella | 280 24.0 | N46 01.2 |
| 02 | 108 47.2 | 198 53.7 | 09.9 | 34 55.7 | 59.1 | 108 55.7 | 34.1 | 145 29.5 | 51.0 | Deneb | 49 27.3 | N45 21.9 |
| 03 | 123 49.6 | 213 52.7 | . . 10.0 | 49 59.2 | . . 59.1 | 123 58.0 | . . 34.1 | 160 31.7 | . . 51.0 | Denebola | 182 26.8 | N14 26.6 |
| 04 | 138 52.1 | 228 51.8 | 10.1 | 65 02.7 | 59.1 | 139 00.3 | 34.0 | 175 34.0 | 50.9 | Diphda | 348 48.9 | S17 51.8 |
| 05 | 153 54.6 | 243 50.8 | 10.2 | 80 06.2 | 59.1 | 154 02.7 | 33.9 | 190 36.3 | 50.8 | | | |
| 06 | 168 57.0 | 258 49.8 | S24 10.3 | 95 09.7 | N24 59.0 | 169 05.0 | S 1 33.9 | 205 38.6 | S15 50.8 | Dubhe | 193 43.1 | N61 37.4 |
| 07 | 183 59.5 | 273 48.8 | 10.4 | 110 13.2 | 59.0 | 184 07.4 | 33.8 | 220 40.9 | 50.7 | Elnath | 278 03.7 | N28 37.6 |
| S 08 | 199 02.0 | 288 47.9 | 10.5 | 125 16.7 | 59.0 | 199 09.7 | 33.7 | 235 43.1 | 50.6 | Eltanin | 90 43.5 | N51 29.2 |
| A 09 | 214 04.4 | 303 46.9 | . . 10.5 | 140 20.2 | . . 59.0 | 214 12.1 | . . 33.7 | 250 45.4 | . . 50.6 | Enif | 33 40.6 | N 9 58.8 |
| T 10 | 229 06.9 | 318 45.9 | 10.6 | 155 23.8 | 59.0 | 229 14.4 | 33.6 | 265 47.7 | 50.5 | Fomalhaut | 15 16.5 | S29 30.3 |
| U 11 | 244 09.4 | 333 45.0 | 10.7 | 170 27.3 | 59.0 | 244 16.7 | 33.5 | 280 50.0 | 50.5 | | | |
| R 12 | 259 11.8 | 348 44.0 | S24 10.8 | 185 30.8 | N24 58.9 | 259 19.1 | S 1 33.5 | 295 52.3 | S15 50.4 | Gacrux | 171 53.8 | S57 14.1 |
| D 13 | 274 14.3 | 3 43.0 | 10.9 | 200 34.3 | 58.9 | 274 21.4 | 33.4 | 310 54.5 | 50.3 | Gienah | 175 45.5 | S17 40.0 |
| A 14 | 289 16.7 | 18 42.0 | 11.0 | 215 37.8 | 58.9 | 289 23.8 | 33.3 | 325 56.8 | 50.3 | Hadar | 148 38.9 | S60 28.7 |
| Y 15 | 304 19.2 | 33 41.1 | . . 11.0 | 230 41.3 | . . 58.9 | 304 26.1 | . . 33.3 | 340 59.1 | . . 50.2 | Hamal | 327 52.9 | N23 34.3 |
| 16 | 319 21.7 | 48 40.1 | 11.1 | 245 44.8 | 58.9 | 319 28.4 | 33.2 | 356 01.4 | 50.2 | Kaus Aust. | 83 35.2 | S34 22.4 |
| 17 | 334 24.1 | 63 39.1 | 11.2 | 260 48.3 | 58.8 | 334 30.8 | 33.1 | 11 03.6 | 50.1 | | | |
| 18 | 349 26.6 | 78 38.1 | S24 11.3 | 275 51.8 | N24 58.8 | 349 33.1 | S 1 33.1 | 26 05.9 | S15 50.0 | Kochab | 137 20.8 | N74 03.5 |
| 19 | 4 29.1 | 93 37.2 | 11.3 | 290 55.3 | 58.8 | 4 35.4 | 33.0 | 41 08.2 | 50.0 | Markab | 13 31.6 | N15 19.8 |
| 20 | 19 31.5 | 108 36.2 | 11.4 | 305 58.8 | 58.8 | 19 37.8 | 32.9 | 56 10.5 | 49.9 | Menkar | 314 07.7 | N 4 10.8 |
| 21 | 34 34.0 | 123 35.2 | . . 11.5 | 321 02.3 | . . 58.8 | 34 40.1 | . . 32.9 | 71 12.7 | . . 49.8 | Menkent | 148 00.0 | S36 28.7 |
| 22 | 49 36.5 | 138 34.2 | 11.5 | 336 05.8 | 58.7 | 49 42.5 | 32.8 | 86 15.0 | 49.8 | Miaplacidus | 221 38.1 | S69 48.3 |
| 23 | 64 38.9 | 153 33.3 | 11.6 | 351 09.3 | 58.7 | 64 44.8 | 32.7 | 101 17.3 | 49.7 | | | |
| 11 00 | 79 41.4 | 168 32.3 | S24 11.7 | 6 12.8 | N24 58.7 | 79 47.1 | S 1 32.7 | 116 19.6 | S15 49.6 | Mirfak | 308 30.3 | N49 56.6 |
| 01 | 94 43.9 | 183 31.3 | 11.7 | 21 16.3 | 58.7 | 94 49.5 | 32.6 | 131 21.8 | 49.6 | Nunki | 75 50.3 | S26 16.1 |
| 02 | 109 46.3 | 198 30.3 | 11.8 | 36 19.8 | 58.6 | 109 51.8 | 32.5 | 146 24.1 | 49.5 | Peacock | 53 08.9 | S56 39.9 |
| 03 | 124 48.8 | 213 29.4 | . . 11.9 | 51 23.3 | . . 58.6 | 124 54.1 | . . 32.5 | 161 26.4 | . . 49.5 | Pollux | 243 19.1 | N27 58.2 |
| 04 | 139 51.2 | 228 28.4 | 11.9 | 66 26.8 | 58.6 | 139 56.5 | 32.4 | 176 28.7 | 49.4 | Procyon | 244 52.4 | N 5 10.0 |
| 05 | 154 53.7 | 243 27.4 | 12.0 | 81 30.3 | 58.6 | 154 58.8 | 32.3 | 191 31.0 | 49.3 | | | |
| 06 | 169 56.2 | 258 26.4 | S24 12.1 | 96 33.8 | N24 58.6 | 170 01.1 | S 1 32.3 | 206 33.2 | S15 49.3 | Rasalhague | 96 00.5 | N12 32.6 |
| 07 | 184 58.6 | 273 25.5 | 12.1 | 111 37.3 | 58.5 | 185 03.5 | 32.2 | 221 35.5 | 49.2 | Regulus | 207 36.2 | N11 51.3 |
| 08 | 200 01.1 | 288 24.5 | 12.2 | 126 40.8 | 58.5 | 200 05.8 | 32.1 | 236 37.8 | 49.1 | Rigel | 281 05.2 | S 8 10.5 |
| S 09 | 215 03.6 | 303 23.5 | . . 12.2 | 141 44.3 | . . 58.5 | 215 08.1 | . . 32.1 | 251 40.1 | . . 49.1 | Rigil Kent. | 139 43.2 | S60 55.5 |
| U 10 | 230 06.0 | 318 22.5 | 12.3 | 156 47.8 | 58.5 | 230 10.5 | 32.0 | 266 42.3 | 49.0 | Sabik | 102 05.1 | S15 45.1 |
| N 11 | 245 08.5 | 333 21.6 | 12.3 | 171 51.3 | 58.4 | 245 12.8 | 31.9 | 281 44.6 | 49.0 | | | |
| D 12 | 260 11.0 | 348 20.6 | S24 12.4 | 186 54.8 | N24 58.4 | 260 15.1 | S 1 31.8 | 296 46.9 | S15 48.9 | Schedar | 349 32.8 | N56 40.0 |
| A 13 | 275 13.4 | 3 19.6 | 12.4 | 201 58.3 | 58.4 | 275 17.5 | 31.8 | 311 49.1 | 48.8 | Shaula | 96 13.2 | S37 07.2 |
| Y 14 | 290 15.9 | 18 18.6 | 12.5 | 217 01.8 | 58.4 | 290 19.8 | 31.7 | 326 51.4 | 48.8 | Sirius | 258 27.4 | S16 44.8 |
| 15 | 305 18.3 | 33 17.7 | . . 12.5 | 232 05.3 | . . 58.3 | 305 22.1 | . . 31.6 | 341 53.7 | . . 48.7 | Spica | 158 24.3 | S11 16.7 |
| 16 | 320 20.8 | 48 16.7 | 12.6 | 247 08.8 | 58.3 | 320 24.5 | 31.6 | 356 56.0 | 48.6 | Suhail | 222 47.3 | S43 31.2 |
| 17 | 335 23.3 | 63 15.7 | 12.6 | 262 12.3 | 58.3 | 335 26.8 | 31.5 | 11 58.2 | 48.6 | | | |
| 18 | 350 25.7 | 78 14.7 | S24 12.7 | 277 15.8 | N24 58.3 | 350 29.1 | S 1 31.4 | 27 00.5 | S15 48.5 | Vega | 80 34.8 | N38 48.4 |
| 19 | 5 28.2 | 93 13.8 | 12.7 | 292 19.3 | 58.2 | 5 31.5 | 31.4 | 42 02.8 | 48.4 | Zuben'ubi | 136 58.2 | S16 08.1 |
| 20 | 20 30.7 | 108 12.8 | 12.7 | 307 22.8 | 58.2 | 20 33.8 | 31.3 | 57 05.1 | 48.4 | | SHA | Mer. Pass. |
| 21 | 35 33.1 | 123 11.8 | . . 12.8 | 322 26.3 | . . 58.2 | 35 36.1 | . . 31.2 | 72 07.3 | . . 48.3 | | ° ′ | h m |
| 22 | 50 35.6 | 138 10.8 | 12.8 | 337 29.8 | 58.2 | 50 38.4 | 31.1 | 87 09.6 | 48.3 | Venus | 90 13.4 | 12 45 |
| 23 | 65 38.1 | 153 09.9 | 12.9 | 352 33.3 | 58.1 | 65 40.8 | 31.1 | 102 11.9 | 48.2 | Mars | 286 06.4 | 23 35 |
| | h m | | | | | | | | | Jupiter | 0 08.7 | 18 42 |
| Mer. Pass. 18 42.1 | | v −1.0 | d 0.1 | v 3.5 | d 0.0 | v 2.3 | d 0.1 | v 2.3 | d 0.1 | Saturn | 36 42.7 | 16 16 |

| UT | SUN GHA | SUN Dec | MOON GHA | v | MOON Dec | d | HP |
|---|---|---|---|---|---|---|---|
| d h | ° ′ | ° ′ | ° ′ | ′ | ° ′ | ′ | ′ |
| 9 00 | 181 58.8 | S22 47.4 | 352 06.9 | 9.7 | N26 55.0 | 2.8 | 54.5 |
| 01 | 196 58.5 | 47.7 | 6 35.6 | 9.7 | 26 57.8 | 2.7 | 54.5 |
| 02 | 211 58.2 | 47.9 | 21 04.3 | 9.8 | 27 00.5 | 2.6 | 54.5 |
| 03 | 226 58.0 | .. 48.2 | 35 33.1 | 9.7 | 27 03.1 | 2.4 | 54.5 |
| 04 | 241 57.7 | 48.4 | 50 01.8 | 9.6 | 27 05.5 | 2.3 | 54.5 |
| 05 | 256 57.4 | 48.6 | 64 30.4 | 9.7 | 27 07.8 | 2.2 | 54.5 |
| 06 | 271 57.1 | S22 48.9 | 78 59.1 | 9.7 | N27 10.0 | 2.0 | 54.4 |
| 07 | 286 56.9 | 49.1 | 93 27.8 | 9.7 | 27 12.0 | 1.9 | 54.4 |
| 08 | 301 56.6 | 49.4 | 107 56.5 | 9.7 | 27 13.9 | 1.8 | 54.4 |
| 09 | 316 56.3 | .. 49.6 | 122 25.2 | 9.6 | 27 15.7 | 1.6 | 54.4 |
| 10 | 331 56.0 | 49.9 | 136 53.8 | 9.7 | 27 17.3 | 1.5 | 54.4 |
| 11 | 346 55.7 | 50.1 | 151 22.5 | 9.7 | 27 18.8 | 1.4 | 54.4 |
| 12 | 1 55.5 | S22 50.3 | 165 51.2 | 9.6 | N27 20.2 | 1.2 | 54.4 |
| 13 | 16 55.2 | 50.6 | 180 19.8 | 9.7 | 27 21.4 | 1.1 | 54.4 |
| 14 | 31 54.9 | 50.8 | 194 48.5 | 9.7 | 27 22.5 | 0.9 | 54.4 |
| 15 | 46 54.6 | .. 51.1 | 209 17.2 | 9.7 | 27 23.4 | 0.8 | 54.3 |
| 16 | 61 54.3 | 51.3 | 223 45.9 | 9.7 | 27 24.2 | 0.7 | 54.3 |
| 17 | 76 54.1 | 51.5 | 238 14.6 | 9.7 | 27 24.9 | 0.5 | 54.3 |
| 18 | 91 53.8 | S22 51.8 | 252 43.3 | 9.7 | N27 25.4 | 0.4 | 54.3 |
| 19 | 106 53.5 | 52.0 | 267 12.0 | 9.7 | 27 25.8 | 0.3 | 54.3 |
| 20 | 121 53.2 | 52.2 | 281 40.7 | 9.7 | 27 26.1 | 0.1 | 54.3 |
| 21 | 136 52.9 | .. 52.5 | 296 09.4 | 9.8 | 27 26.2 | 0.0 | 54.3 |
| 22 | 151 52.7 | 52.7 | 310 38.2 | 9.8 | 27 26.2 | 0.1 | 54.3 |
| 23 | 166 52.4 | 52.9 | 325 07.0 | 9.7 | 27 26.1 | 0.3 | 54.3 |
| 10 00 | 181 52.1 | S22 53.2 | 339 35.7 | 9.8 | N27 25.8 | 0.4 | 54.3 |
| 01 | 196 51.8 | 53.4 | 354 04.5 | 9.8 | 27 25.4 | 0.6 | 54.3 |
| 02 | 211 51.5 | 53.6 | 8 33.3 | 9.9 | 27 24.8 | 0.7 | 54.2 |
| 03 | 226 51.3 | .. 53.8 | 23 02.2 | 9.8 | 27 24.1 | 0.8 | 54.2 |
| 04 | 241 51.0 | 54.1 | 37 31.0 | 9.9 | 27 23.3 | 0.9 | 54.2 |
| 05 | 256 50.7 | 54.3 | 51 59.9 | 9.9 | 27 22.4 | 1.1 | 54.2 |
| 06 | 271 50.4 | S22 54.5 | 66 28.8 | 9.9 | N27 21.3 | 1.2 | 54.2 |
| 07 | 286 50.1 | 54.7 | 80 57.7 | 9.9 | 27 20.1 | 1.4 | 54.2 |
| 08 | 301 49.9 | 55.0 | 95 26.6 | 10.0 | 27 18.7 | 1.5 | 54.2 |
| 09 | 316 49.6 | .. 55.2 | 109 55.6 | 10.0 | 27 17.2 | 1.6 | 54.2 |
| 10 | 331 49.3 | 55.4 | 124 24.6 | 10.0 | 27 15.6 | 1.8 | 54.2 |
| 11 | 346 49.0 | 55.6 | 138 53.6 | 10.1 | 27 13.8 | 1.8 | 54.2 |
| 12 | 1 48.7 | S22 55.9 | 153 22.7 | 10.1 | N27 12.0 | 2.1 | 54.2 |
| 13 | 16 48.4 | 56.1 | 167 51.8 | 10.1 | 27 09.9 | 2.1 | 54.2 |
| 14 | 31 48.2 | 56.3 | 182 20.9 | 10.2 | 27 07.0 | 2.3 | 54.1 |
| 15 | 46 47.9 | .. 56.5 | 196 50.1 | 10.1 | 27 04.7 | 2.4 | 54.1 |
| 16 | 61 47.6 | 56.7 | 211 19.2 | 10.3 | 27 02.3 | 2.5 | 54.1 |
| 17 | 76 47.3 | 57.0 | 225 48.5 | 10.2 | 27 00.6 | 2.7 | 54.1 |
| 18 | 91 47.0 | S22 57.2 | 240 17.7 | 10.3 | N26 57.9 | 2.8 | 54.1 |
| 19 | 106 46.7 | 57.4 | 254 47.0 | 10.3 | 26 55.1 | 2.9 | 54.1 |
| 20 | 121 46.5 | 57.6 | 269 16.3 | 10.4 | 26 52.2 | 3.0 | 54.1 |
| 21 | 136 46.2 | .. 57.8 | 283 45.7 | 10.4 | 26 49.2 | 3.2 | 54.1 |
| 22 | 151 45.9 | 58.0 | 298 15.1 | 10.5 | 26 46.0 | 3.3 | 54.1 |
| 23 | 166 45.6 | 58.2 | 312 44.6 | 10.5 | 26 42.7 | 3.5 | 54.1 |
| 11 00 | 181 45.3 | S22 58.5 | 327 14.1 | 10.5 | N26 39.2 | 3.5 | 54.1 |
| 01 | 196 45.0 | 58.7 | 341 43.6 | 10.6 | 26 35.7 | 3.7 | 54.1 |
| 02 | 211 44.8 | 58.9 | 356 13.2 | 10.6 | 26 32.0 | 3.8 | 54.1 |
| 03 | 226 44.5 | .. 59.1 | 10 42.8 | 10.7 | 26 28.2 | 3.9 | 54.1 |
| 04 | 241 44.2 | 59.3 | 25 12.5 | 10.7 | 26 24.3 | 4.1 | 54.1 |
| 05 | 256 43.9 | 59.5 | 39 42.2 | 10.7 | 26 20.2 | 4.2 | 54.1 |
| 06 | 271 43.6 | S22 59.7 | 54 11.9 | 10.8 | N26 16.0 | 4.3 | 54.1 |
| 07 | 286 43.3 | 22 59.9 | 68 41.7 | 10.9 | 26 11.7 | 4.4 | 54.1 |
| 08 | 301 43.0 | 23 00.1 | 83 11.6 | 10.9 | 26 07.3 | 4.5 | 54.1 |
| 09 | 316 42.8 | .. 00.3 | 97 41.5 | 11.0 | 26 02.8 | 4.7 | 54.1 |
| 10 | 331 42.5 | 00.5 | 112 11.5 | 11.0 | 25 58.1 | 4.8 | 54.0 |
| 11 | 346 42.2 | 00.7 | 126 41.5 | 11.0 | 25 53.3 | 4.9 | 54.0 |
| 12 | 1 41.9 | S23 00.9 | 141 11.5 | 11.1 | N25 48.4 | 5.0 | 54.0 |
| 13 | 16 41.6 | 01.1 | 155 41.6 | 11.2 | 25 43.4 | 5.2 | 54.0 |
| 14 | 31 41.3 | 01.3 | 170 11.8 | 11.2 | 25 38.2 | 5.2 | 54.0 |
| 15 | 46 41.0 | .. 01.5 | 184 42.0 | 11.2 | 25 33.0 | 5.4 | 54.0 |
| 16 | 61 40.7 | 01.7 | 199 12.2 | 11.4 | 25 27.6 | 5.5 | 54.0 |
| 17 | 76 40.5 | 01.9 | 213 42.6 | 11.3 | 25 22.1 | 5.6 | 54.0 |
| 18 | 91 40.2 | S23 02.1 | 228 12.9 | 11.5 | N25 16.5 | 5.7 | 54.0 |
| 19 | 106 39.9 | 02.3 | 242 43.4 | 11.4 | 25 10.8 | 5.9 | 54.0 |
| 20 | 121 39.6 | 02.5 | 257 13.8 | 11.6 | 25 04.9 | 5.9 | 54.0 |
| 21 | 136 39.3 | .. 02.7 | 271 44.4 | 11.6 | 24 59.0 | 6.1 | 54.0 |
| 22 | 151 39.0 | 02.9 | 286 15.0 | 11.6 | 24 52.9 | 6.1 | 54.0 |
| 23 | 166 38.7 | 03.1 | 300 45.6 | 11.7 | N24 46.8 | 6.3 | 54.0 |
| | SD 16.3 | d 0.2 | SD 14.8 | | 14.8 | | 14.7 |

Friday = 9, Saturday = 10, Sunday = 11

| Lat. | Twilight Naut. | Twilight Civil | Sunrise | Moonrise 9 | 10 | 11 | 12 |
|---|---|---|---|---|---|---|---|
| ° | h m | h m | h m | h m | h m | h m | h m |
| N 72 | 08 12 | 10 29 | ■ | ☐ | ☐ | ☐ | ☐ |
| N 70 | 07 53 | 09 37 | ■ | ☐ | ☐ | ☐ | ☐ |
| 68 | 07 38 | 09 05 | ■ | ☐ | ☐ | ☐ | ☐ |
| 66 | 07 26 | 08 41 | 10 15 | ☐ | ☐ | ☐ | 16 56 |
| 64 | 07 15 | 08 22 | 09 38 | ☐ | ☐ | 15 35 | 17 41 |
| 62 | 07 06 | 08 07 | 09 11 | 13 57 | 14 59 | 16 33 | 18 11 |
| 60 | 06 58 | 07 54 | 08 51 | 14 49 | 15 47 | 17 06 | 18 33 |
| N 58 | 06 51 | 07 43 | 08 34 | 15 21 | 16 18 | 17 30 | 18 51 |
| 56 | 06 44 | 07 33 | 08 20 | 15 45 | 16 41 | 17 50 | 19 06 |
| 54 | 06 38 | 07 24 | 08 08 | 16 04 | 16 59 | 18 06 | 19 19 |
| 52 | 06 33 | 07 16 | 07 57 | 16 20 | 17 15 | 18 20 | 19 30 |
| 50 | 06 28 | 07 09 | 07 47 | 16 34 | 17 29 | 18 32 | 19 40 |
| 45 | 06 16 | 06 53 | 07 27 | 17 03 | 17 57 | 18 57 | 20 01 |
| N 40 | 06 06 | 06 40 | 07 11 | 17 25 | 18 19 | 19 17 | 20 10 |
| 35 | 05 57 | 06 29 | 06 57 | 17 44 | 18 37 | 19 34 | 20 32 |
| 30 | 05 49 | 06 19 | 06 45 | 18 00 | 18 53 | 19 48 | 20 45 |
| 20 | 05 33 | 06 00 | 06 24 | 18 27 | 19 19 | 20 13 | 21 06 |
| N 10 | 05 17 | 05 43 | 06 06 | 18 50 | 19 42 | 20 34 | 21 24 |
| 0 | 05 00 | 05 27 | 05 49 | 19 12 | 20 03 | 20 53 | 21 41 |
| S 10 | 04 42 | 05 09 | 05 32 | 19 34 | 20 25 | 21 13 | 21 57 |
| 20 | 04 20 | 04 49 | 05 13 | 19 57 | 20 47 | 21 34 | 22 15 |
| 30 | 03 51 | 04 25 | 04 52 | 20 24 | 21 14 | 21 58 | 22 36 |
| 35 | 03 33 | 04 10 | 04 39 | 20 40 | 21 29 | 22 12 | 22 48 |
| 40 | 03 12 | 03 52 | 04 24 | 20 59 | 21 47 | 22 28 | 23 02 |
| 45 | 02 41 | 03 30 | 04 07 | 21 22 | 22 09 | 22 47 | 23 18 |
| S 50 | 01 58 | 03 01 | 03 45 | 21 51 | 22 37 | 23 11 | 23 38 |
| 52 | 01 32 | 02 47 | 03 35 | 22 05 | 22 50 | 23 23 | 23 47 |
| 54 | 00 53 | 02 30 | 03 23 | 22 22 | 23 05 | 23 36 | 23 58 |
| 56 | //// | 02 09 | 03 09 | 22 41 | 23 24 | 23 51 | 24 10 |
| 58 | //// | 01 41 | 02 53 | 23 06 | 23 46 | 24 09 | 00 09 |
| S 60 | //// | 00 59 | 02 34 | 23 39 | 24 14 | 00 14 | 00 31 |

| Lat. | Sunset | Twilight Civil | Twilight Naut. | Moonset 9 | 10 | 11 | 12 |
|---|---|---|---|---|---|---|---|
| ° | h m | h m | h m | h m | h m | h m | h m |
| N 72 | ■ | 13 16 | 15 33 | ☐ | ☐ | ☐ | ☐ |
| N 70 | ■ | 14 08 | 15 52 | ☐ | ☐ | ☐ | ☐ |
| 68 | ■ | 14 40 | 16 07 | ☐ | ☐ | ☐ | ☐ |
| 66 | 13 30 | 15 04 | 16 20 | ☐ | ☐ | ☐ | 14 13 |
| 64 | 14 08 | 15 23 | 16 30 | ☐ | ☐ | 13 54 | 13 27 |
| 62 | 14 34 | 15 38 | 16 39 | 11 59 | 12 44 | 12 55 | 12 57 |
| 60 | 14 55 | 15 51 | 16 47 | 11 07 | 11 56 | 12 22 | 12 34 |
| N 58 | 15 11 | 16 02 | 16 55 | 10 35 | 11 26 | 11 57 | 12 15 |
| 56 | 15 26 | 16 12 | 17 01 | 10 11 | 11 02 | 11 37 | 12 00 |
| 54 | 15 38 | 16 21 | 17 07 | 09 52 | 10 43 | 11 20 | 11 46 |
| 52 | 15 49 | 16 29 | 17 12 | 09 36 | 10 27 | 11 06 | 11 35 |
| 50 | 15 58 | 16 36 | 17 18 | 09 22 | 10 14 | 10 54 | 11 24 |
| 45 | 16 18 | 16 52 | 17 29 | 08 53 | 09 45 | 10 28 | 11 02 |
| N 40 | 16 35 | 17 05 | 17 39 | 08 31 | 09 23 | 10 07 | 10 44 |
| 35 | 16 48 | 17 16 | 17 48 | 08 13 | 09 05 | 09 50 | 10 29 |
| 30 | 17 01 | 17 27 | 17 57 | 07 57 | 08 49 | 09 35 | 10 16 |
| 20 | 17 21 | 17 45 | 18 13 | 07 30 | 08 22 | 09 10 | 09 54 |
| N 10 | 17 38 | 18 02 | 18 28 | 07 07 | 07 59 | 08 48 | 09 35 |
| 0 | 17 56 | 18 19 | 18 45 | 06 45 | 07 37 | 08 28 | 09 16 |
| S 10 | 18 14 | 18 37 | 19 04 | 06 24 | 07 15 | 08 07 | 08 58 |
| 20 | 18 32 | 18 57 | 19 26 | 06 01 | 06 52 | 07 45 | 08 38 |
| 30 | 18 52 | 19 21 | 19 54 | 05 34 | 06 25 | 07 19 | 08 16 |
| 35 | 19 07 | 19 36 | 20 13 | 05 18 | 06 09 | 07 04 | 08 02 |
| 40 | 19 21 | 19 54 | 20 35 | 04 59 | 05 50 | 06 47 | 07 47 |
| 45 | 19 39 | 20 16 | 21 05 | 04 37 | 05 28 | 06 25 | 07 28 |
| S 50 | 20 01 | 20 45 | 21 49 | 04 09 | 04 59 | 05 58 | 07 05 |
| 52 | 20 11 | 20 59 | 22 15 | 03 55 | 04 45 | 05 45 | 06 53 |
| 54 | 20 23 | 21 17 | 22 54 | 03 39 | 04 28 | 05 30 | 06 40 |
| 56 | 20 37 | 21 38 | //// | 03 20 | 04 08 | 05 12 | 06 26 |
| 58 | 20 53 | 22 06 | //// | 02 57 | 03 44 | 04 50 | 06 08 |
| S 60 | 21 13 | 22 49 | //// | 02 27 | 03 11 | 04 22 | 05 47 |

| Day | SUN Eqn. of Time 00ʰ | SUN Eqn. of Time 12ʰ | SUN Mer. Pass. | MOON Mer. Pass. Upper | MOON Mer. Pass. Lower | Age | Phase |
|---|---|---|---|---|---|---|---|
| d | m s | m s | h m | h m | h m | d | % |
| 9 | 07 56 | 07 42 | 11 52 | 00 33 | 12 59 | 16 | 98 |
| 10 | 07 29 | 07 15 | 11 53 | 01 25 | 13 50 | 17 | 95 |
| 11 | 07 02 | 06 48 | 11 53 | 02 16 | 14 41 | 18 | 90 |

| UT | ARIES GHA | VENUS −3.9 GHA | Dec | MARS −1.8 GHA | Dec | JUPITER −2.5 GHA | Dec | SATURN +0.7 GHA | Dec |
|---|---|---|---|---|---|---|---|---|---|
| **12 00** | 80 40.5 | 168 08.9 | S24 12.9 | 7 36.8 | N24 58.1 | 80 43.1 | S 1 31.0 | 117 14.2 | S15 48.1 |
| 01 | 95 43.0 | 183 07.9 | 12.9 | 22 40.2 | 58.1 | 95 45.4 | 30.9 | 132 16.4 | 48.1 |
| 02 | 110 45.5 | 198 06.9 | 13.0 | 37 43.7 | 58.1 | 110 47.8 | 30.9 | 147 18.7 | 48.0 |
| 03 | 125 47.9 | 213 06.0 .. | 13.0 | 52 47.2 .. | 58.0 | 125 50.1 .. | 30.8 | 162 21.0 .. | 47.9 |
| 04 | 140 50.4 | 228 05.0 | 13.0 | 67 50.7 | 58.0 | 140 52.4 | 30.7 | 177 23.2 | 47.9 |
| 05 | 155 52.8 | 243 04.0 | 13.0 | 82 54.2 | 58.0 | 155 54.7 | 30.6 | 192 25.5 | 47.8 |
| M 06 | 170 55.3 | 258 03.0 | S24 13.1 | 97 57.7 | N24 58.0 | 170 57.1 | S 1 30.6 | 207 27.8 | S15 47.7 |
| O 07 | 185 57.8 | 273 02.1 | 13.1 | 113 01.2 | 57.9 | 185 59.4 | 30.5 | 222 30.1 | 47.7 |
| N 08 | 201 00.2 | 288 01.1 | 13.1 | 128 04.7 | 57.9 | 201 01.7 | 30.4 | 237 32.3 | 47.6 |
| D 09 | 216 02.7 | 303 00.1 .. | 13.1 | 143 08.1 .. | 57.9 | 216 04.0 .. | 30.3 | 252 34.6 .. | 47.6 |
| A 10 | 231 05.2 | 317 59.1 | 13.2 | 158 11.6 | 57.8 | 231 06.4 | 30.3 | 267 36.9 | 47.5 |
| Y 11 | 246 07.6 | 332 58.2 | 13.2 | 173 15.1 | 57.8 | 246 08.7 | 30.2 | 282 39.2 | 47.4 |
| 12 | 261 10.1 | 347 57.2 | S24 13.2 | 188 18.6 | N24 57.8 | 261 11.0 | S 1 30.1 | 297 41.4 | S15 47.4 |
| 13 | 276 12.6 | 2 56.2 | 13.2 | 203 22.1 | 57.8 | 276 13.3 | 30.1 | 312 43.7 | 47.3 |
| 14 | 291 15.0 | 17 55.2 | 13.2 | 218 25.6 | 57.7 | 291 15.7 | 30.0 | 327 46.0 | 47.2 |
| 15 | 306 17.5 | 32 54.3 .. | 13.3 | 233 29.0 .. | 57.7 | 306 18.0 .. | 29.9 | 342 48.2 .. | 47.2 |
| 16 | 321 20.0 | 47 53.3 | 13.3 | 248 32.5 | 57.7 | 321 20.3 | 29.8 | 357 50.5 | 47.1 |
| 17 | 336 22.4 | 62 52.3 | 13.3 | 263 36.0 | 57.6 | 336 22.6 | 29.8 | 12 52.8 | 47.0 |
| 18 | 351 24.9 | 77 51.3 | S24 13.3 | 278 39.5 | N24 57.6 | 351 25.0 | S 1 29.7 | 27 55.0 | S15 47.0 |
| 19 | 6 27.3 | 92 50.4 | 13.3 | 293 42.9 | 57.6 | 6 27.3 | 29.6 | 42 57.3 | 46.9 |
| 20 | 21 29.8 | 107 49.4 | 13.3 | 308 46.4 | 57.6 | 21 29.6 | 29.5 | 57 59.6 | 46.8 |
| 21 | 36 32.3 | 122 48.4 .. | 13.3 | 323 49.9 .. | 57.5 | 36 31.9 .. | 29.5 | 73 01.9 .. | 46.8 |
| 22 | 51 34.7 | 137 47.4 | 13.3 | 338 53.4 | 57.5 | 51 34.3 | 29.4 | 88 04.1 | 46.7 |
| 23 | 66 37.2 | 152 46.5 | 13.3 | 353 56.9 | 57.5 | 66 36.6 | 29.3 | 103 06.4 | 46.6 |
| **13 00** | 81 39.7 | 167 45.5 | S24 13.3 | 9 00.3 | N24 57.4 | 81 38.9 | S 1 29.2 | 118 08.7 | S15 46.6 |
| 01 | 96 42.1 | 182 44.5 | 13.3 | 24 03.8 | 57.4 | 96 41.2 | 29.2 | 133 10.9 | 46.5 |
| 02 | 111 44.6 | 197 43.5 | 13.3 | 39 07.3 | 57.4 | 111 43.5 | 29.1 | 148 13.2 | 46.5 |
| 03 | 126 47.1 | 212 42.6 .. | 13.3 | 54 10.7 .. | 57.3 | 126 45.9 .. | 29.0 | 163 15.5 .. | 46.4 |
| 04 | 141 49.5 | 227 41.6 | 13.3 | 69 14.2 | 57.3 | 141 48.2 | 28.9 | 178 17.7 | 46.3 |
| 05 | 156 52.0 | 242 40.6 | 13.3 | 84 17.7 | 57.3 | 156 50.5 | 28.9 | 193 20.0 | 46.3 |
| T 06 | 171 54.5 | 257 39.6 | S24 13.3 | 99 21.2 | N24 57.2 | 171 52.8 | S 1 28.8 | 208 22.3 | S15 46.2 |
| U 07 | 186 56.9 | 272 38.7 | 13.3 | 114 24.6 | 57.2 | 186 55.1 | 28.7 | 223 24.6 | 46.1 |
| E 08 | 201 59.4 | 287 37.7 | 13.3 | 129 28.1 | 57.2 | 201 57.5 | 28.6 | 238 26.8 | 46.1 |
| S 09 | 217 01.8 | 302 36.7 .. | 13.3 | 144 31.6 .. | 57.2 | 216 59.8 .. | 28.6 | 253 29.1 .. | 46.0 |
| D 10 | 232 04.3 | 317 35.7 | 13.3 | 159 35.0 | 57.1 | 232 02.1 | 28.5 | 268 31.4 | 45.9 |
| A 11 | 247 06.8 | 332 34.8 | 13.3 | 174 38.5 | 57.1 | 247 04.4 | 28.4 | 283 33.6 | 45.9 |
| Y 12 | 262 09.2 | 347 33.8 | S24 13.3 | 189 42.0 | N24 57.1 | 262 06.7 | S 1 28.3 | 298 35.9 | S15 45.8 |
| 13 | 277 11.7 | 2 32.8 | 13.3 | 204 45.4 | 57.0 | 277 09.1 | 28.3 | 313 38.2 | 45.7 |
| 14 | 292 14.2 | 17 31.8 | 13.3 | 219 48.9 | 57.0 | 292 11.4 | 28.2 | 328 40.4 | 45.7 |
| 15 | 307 16.6 | 32 30.8 .. | 13.2 | 234 52.4 .. | 57.0 | 307 13.7 .. | 28.1 | 343 42.7 .. | 45.6 |
| 16 | 322 19.1 | 47 29.9 | 13.2 | 249 55.8 | 56.9 | 322 16.0 | 28.0 | 358 45.0 | 45.5 |
| 17 | 337 21.6 | 62 28.9 | 13.2 | 264 59.3 | 56.9 | 337 18.3 | 28.0 | 13 47.2 | 45.5 |
| 18 | 352 24.0 | 77 27.9 | S24 13.2 | 280 02.8 | N24 56.9 | 352 20.6 | S 1 27.9 | 28 49.5 | S15 45.4 |
| 19 | 7 26.5 | 92 26.9 | 13.2 | 295 06.2 | 56.8 | 7 22.9 | 27.8 | 43 51.8 | 45.3 |
| 20 | 22 29.0 | 107 26.0 | 13.2 | 310 09.7 | 56.8 | 22 25.3 | 27.7 | 58 54.0 | 45.3 |
| 21 | 37 31.4 | 122 25.0 .. | 13.1 | 325 13.1 .. | 56.8 | 37 27.6 .. | 27.7 | 73 56.3 .. | 45.2 |
| 22 | 52 33.9 | 137 24.0 | 13.1 | 340 16.6 | 56.7 | 52 29.9 | 27.6 | 88 58.6 | 45.1 |
| 23 | 67 36.3 | 152 23.0 | 13.0 | 355 20.1 | 56.7 | 67 32.2 | 27.5 | 104 00.8 | 45.1 |
| **14 00** | 82 38.8 | 167 22.1 | S24 13.0 | 10 23.5 | N24 56.7 | 82 34.5 | S 1 27.4 | 119 03.1 | S15 45.0 |
| 01 | 97 41.3 | 182 21.1 | 13.0 | 25 27.0 | 56.6 | 97 36.8 | 27.3 | 134 05.4 | 44.9 |
| 02 | 112 43.7 | 197 20.1 .. | 13.0 | 40 30.4 | 56.6 | 112 39.1 | 27.3 | 149 07.6 | 44.9 |
| 03 | 127 46.2 | 212 19.1 .. | 13.0 | 55 33.9 .. | 56.5 | 127 41.5 .. | 27.2 | 164 09.9 .. | 44.8 |
| 04 | 142 48.7 | 227 18.2 | 12.9 | 70 37.3 | 56.5 | 142 43.8 | 27.1 | 179 12.2 | 44.7 |
| 05 | 157 51.1 | 242 17.2 | 12.9 | 85 40.8 | 56.5 | 157 46.1 | 27.0 | 194 14.4 | 44.7 |
| W 06 | 172 53.6 | 257 16.2 | S24 12.9 | 100 44.2 | N24 56.4 | 172 48.4 | S 1 27.0 | 209 16.7 | S15 44.6 |
| E 07 | 187 56.1 | 272 15.2 | 12.8 | 115 47.7 | 56.4 | 187 50.7 | 26.9 | 224 19.0 | 44.6 |
| D 08 | 202 58.5 | 287 14.3 | 12.8 | 130 51.2 | 56.4 | 202 53.0 | 26.8 | 239 21.2 | 44.5 |
| N 09 | 218 01.0 | 302 13.3 .. | 12.7 | 145 54.6 .. | 56.3 | 217 55.3 .. | 26.7 | 254 23.5 .. | 44.4 |
| E 10 | 233 03.4 | 317 12.3 | 12.7 | 160 58.1 | 56.3 | 232 57.6 | 26.6 | 269 25.8 | 44.4 |
| S 11 | 248 05.9 | 332 11.3 | 12.7 | 176 01.5 | 56.3 | 248 00.0 | 26.6 | 284 28.0 | 44.3 |
| D 12 | 263 08.4 | 347 10.4 | S24 12.6 | 191 04.9 | N24 56.2 | 263 02.3 | S 1 26.5 | 299 30.3 | S15 44.2 |
| A 13 | 278 10.8 | 2 09.4 | 12.6 | 206 08.4 | 56.2 | 278 04.6 | 26.4 | 314 32.6 | 44.2 |
| Y 14 | 293 13.3 | 17 08.4 | 12.5 | 221 11.8 | 56.2 | 293 06.9 | 26.3 | 329 34.8 | 44.1 |
| 15 | 308 15.8 | 32 07.4 .. | 12.5 | 236 15.3 .. | 56.1 | 308 09.2 .. | 26.2 | 344 37.1 .. | 44.0 |
| 16 | 323 18.2 | 47 06.5 | 12.4 | 251 18.7 | 56.1 | 323 11.5 | 26.2 | 359 39.4 | 44.0 |
| 17 | 338 20.7 | 62 05.5 | 12.4 | 266 22.2 | 56.0 | 338 13.8 | 26.1 | 14 41.6 | 43.9 |
| 18 | 353 23.2 | 77 04.5 | S24 12.3 | 281 25.6 | N24 56.0 | 353 16.1 | S 1 26.0 | 29 43.9 | S15 43.8 |
| 19 | 8 25.6 | 92 03.5 | 12.3 | 296 29.1 | 56.0 | 8 18.4 | 25.9 | 44 46.2 | 43.8 |
| 20 | 23 28.1 | 107 02.6 | 12.2 | 311 32.5 | 55.9 | 23 20.7 | 25.8 | 59 48.4 | 43.7 |
| 21 | 38 30.6 | 122 01.6 .. | 12.2 | 326 35.9 .. | 55.9 | 38 23.0 .. | 25.8 | 74 50.7 .. | 43.6 |
| 22 | 53 33.0 | 137 00.6 | 12.1 | 341 39.4 | 55.9 | 53 25.4 | 25.7 | 89 52.9 | 43.6 |
| 23 | 68 35.5 | 151 59.7 | 12.1 | 356 42.8 | 55.8 | 68 27.7 | 25.6 | 104 55.2 | 43.5 |
| Mer. Pass. | h m 18 30.3 | v −1.0 | d 0.0 | v 3.5 | d 0.0 | v 2.3 | d 0.1 | v 2.3 | d 0.1 |

### STARS

| Name | SHA | Dec |
|---|---|---|
| Acamar | 315 12.7 | S40 12.9 |
| Achernar | 335 21.2 | S57 07.5 |
| Acrux | 173 02.2 | S63 13.2 |
| Adhara | 255 06.9 | S29 00.1 |
| Aldebaran | 290 41.3 | N16 33.3 |
| Alioth | 166 14.7 | N55 49.9 |
| Alkaid | 152 53.7 | N49 11.8 |
| Alnair | 27 35.3 | S46 51.3 |
| Alnilam | 275 39.1 | S 1 11.2 |
| Alphard | 217 49.3 | S 8 45.4 |
| Alphecca | 126 05.5 | N26 38.2 |
| Alpheratz | 357 36.5 | N29 13.1 |
| Altair | 62 01.9 | N 8 55.7 |
| Ankaa | 353 08.7 | S42 11.2 |
| Antares | 112 18.3 | S26 28.9 |
| Arcturus | 145 49.7 | N19 03.8 |
| Atria | 107 14.7 | S69 04.0 |
| Avior | 234 14.9 | S59 34.7 |
| Bellatrix | 278 24.4 | N 6 22.2 |
| Betelgeuse | 270 53.6 | N 7 24.7 |
| Canopus | 263 52.6 | S52 42.3 |
| Capella | 280 23.9 | N46 01.2 |
| Deneb | 49 27.3 | N45 21.9 |
| Denebola | 182 26.7 | N14 26.6 |
| Diphda | 348 48.9 | S17 51.8 |
| Dubhe | 193 43.1 | N61 37.4 |
| Elnath | 278 03.7 | N28 37.6 |
| Eltanin | 90 43.5 | N51 29.2 |
| Enif | 33 40.6 | N 9 58.8 |
| Fomalhaut | 15 16.5 | S29 30.3 |
| Gacrux | 171 53.7 | S57 14.1 |
| Gienah | 175 45.4 | S17 40.0 |
| Hadar | 148 38.9 | S60 28.7 |
| Hamal | 327 52.9 | N23 34.3 |
| Kaus Aust. | 83 35.2 | S34 22.4 |
| Kochab | 137 20.8 | N74 03.5 |
| Markab | 13 31.6 | N15 19.8 |
| Menkar | 314 07.7 | N 4 10.8 |
| Menkent | 147 59.9 | S36 28.7 |
| Miaplacidus | 221 38.1 | S69 48.3 |
| Mirfak | 308 30.3 | N49 56.6 |
| Nunki | 75 50.3 | S26 16.1 |
| Peacock | 53 08.9 | S56 39.9 |
| Pollux | 243 19.1 | N27 58.2 |
| Procyon | 244 52.4 | N 5 10.0 |
| Rasalhague | 96 00.5 | N12 32.6 |
| Regulus | 207 36.2 | N11 51.3 |
| Rigel | 281 05.2 | S 8 10.5 |
| Rigil Kent. | 139 43.2 | S60 55.5 |
| Sabik | 102 05.1 | S15 45.1 |
| Schedar | 349 32.8 | N56 40.0 |
| Shaula | 96 13.1 | S37 07.2 |
| Sirius | 258 27.4 | S16 44.8 |
| Spica | 158 24.3 | S11 16.7 |
| Suhail | 222 47.3 | S43 31.2 |
| Vega | 80 34.8 | N38 48.3 |
| Zuben'ubi | 136 58.2 | S16 08.1 |

| | SHA | Mer. Pass. |
|---|---|---|
| | ° ′ | h m |
| Venus | 86 05.8 | 12 50 |
| Mars | 287 20.7 | 23 19 |
| Jupiter | 359 59.2 | 18 31 |
| Saturn | 36 29.0 | 16 05 |

| UT | SUN | | MOON | | | | | Lat. | Twilight | | Sunrise | Moonrise | | | |
|---|---|---|---|---|---|---|---|---|---|---|---|---|---|---|---|
| | GHA | Dec | GHA | v | Dec | d | HP | | Naut. | Civil | | 12 | 13 | 14 | 15 |
| d h | ° ′ | ° ′ | ° ′ | ′ | ° ′ | ′ | ′ | ° N 72 | h m 08 17 | h m 10 40 | h m ▬▬ | h m ▭ | h m ▭ | h m | h m 19 46 | h m 22 02 |
| 12 00 | 181 38.4 | S23 03.3 | 315 16.3 | 11.8 | N24 40.5 | 6.4 | 54.0 | N 70 | 07 58 | 09 44 | ▬▬ | ▭ | ▭ | 17 43 | 20 15 | 22 15 |
| 01 | 196 38.1 | 03.5 | 329 47.1 | 11.8 | 24 34.1 | 6.5 | 54.0 | 68 | 07 42 | 09 10 | ▬▬ | ▭ | 18 33 | 20 36 | 22 26 |
| 02 | 211 37.9 | 03.7 | 344 17.9 | 11.9 | 24 27.6 | 6.7 | 54.0 | 66 | 07 29 | 08 46 | 10 23 | 16 56 | 19 05 | 20 53 | 22 34 |
| 03 | 226 37.6 | . . 03.9 | 358 48.8 | 11.9 | 24 20.9 | 6.7 | 54.0 | 64 | 07 19 | 08 27 | 09 43 | 17 41 | 19 28 | 21 07 | 22 41 |
| 04 | 241 37.3 | 04.1 | 13 19.7 | 12.0 | 24 14.2 | 6.8 | 54.0 | 62 | 07 09 | 08 11 | 09 16 | 18 11 | 19 46 | 21 18 | 22 47 |
| 05 | 256 37.0 | 04.2 | 27 50.7 | 12.0 | 24 07.4 | 7.0 | 54.0 | 60 | 07 01 | 07 58 | 08 55 | 18 33 | 20 01 | 21 28 | 22 52 |
| 06 | 271 36.7 | S23 04.4 | 42 21.7 | 12.2 | N24 00.4 | 7.0 | 54.0 | N 58 | 06 54 | 07 46 | 08 38 | 18 51 | 20 14 | 21 36 | 22 57 |
| 07 | 286 36.4 | 04.6 | 56 52.9 | 12.1 | 23 53.4 | 7.2 | 54.0 | 56 | 06 47 | 07 36 | 08 23 | 19 06 | 20 25 | 21 43 | 23 01 |
| M 08 | 301 36.1 | 04.8 | 71 24.0 | 12.2 | 23 46.2 | 7.2 | 54.0 | 54 | 06 41 | 07 27 | 08 11 | 19 19 | 20 34 | 21 50 | 23 05 |
| O 09 | 316 35.8 | . . 05.0 | 85 55.2 | 12.3 | 23 39.0 | 7.4 | 54.0 | 52 | 06 35 | 07 19 | 08 00 | 19 30 | 20 43 | 21 56 | 23 08 |
| N 10 | 331 35.5 | 05.2 | 100 26.5 | 12.4 | 23 31.6 | 7.4 | 54.0 | 50 | 06 30 | 07 12 | 07 50 | 19 40 | 20 51 | 22 01 | 23 11 |
| D 11 | 346 35.2 | 05.4 | 114 57.9 | 12.4 | 23 24.2 | 7.6 | 54.0 | 45 | 06 19 | 06 56 | 07 30 | 20 01 | 21 07 | 22 12 | 23 18 |
| A 12 | 1 35.0 | S23 05.5 | 129 29.3 | 12.4 | N23 16.6 | 7.7 | 54.0 | N 40 | 06 09 | 06 43 | 07 13 | 20 18 | 21 20 | 22 22 | 23 23 |
| Y 13 | 16 34.7 | 05.7 | 144 00.7 | 12.6 | 23 08.9 | 7.7 | 54.0 | 35 | 05 59 | 06 31 | 06 59 | 20 32 | 21 31 | 22 29 | 23 28 |
| 14 | 31 34.4 | 05.9 | 158 32.3 | 12.5 | 23 01.2 | 7.9 | 54.0 | 30 | 05 51 | 06 21 | 06 47 | 20 45 | 21 41 | 22 36 | 23 32 |
| 15 | 46 34.1 | . . 06.1 | 173 03.8 | 12.7 | 22 53.3 | 8.0 | 54.0 | 20 | 05 34 | 06 02 | 06 26 | 21 06 | 21 58 | 22 49 | 23 39 |
| 16 | 61 33.8 | 06.3 | 187 35.5 | 12.7 | 22 45.3 | 8.1 | 54.1 | N 10 | 05 19 | 05 45 | 06 08 | 21 24 | 22 12 | 22 59 | 23 45 |
| 17 | 76 33.5 | 06.4 | 202 07.2 | 12.7 | 22 37.2 | 8.1 | 54.1 | 0 | 05 02 | 05 28 | 05 50 | 21 41 | 22 26 | 23 09 | 23 51 |
| 18 | 91 33.2 | S23 06.6 | 216 38.9 | 12.8 | N22 29.1 | 8.3 | 54.1 | S 10 | 04 43 | 05 10 | 05 33 | 21 57 | 22 39 | 23 19 | 23 56 |
| 19 | 106 32.9 | 06.8 | 231 10.7 | 12.9 | 22 20.8 | 8.4 | 54.1 | 20 | 04 21 | 04 50 | 05 14 | 22 15 | 22 54 | 23 29 | 24 02 |
| 20 | 121 32.6 | 07.0 | 245 42.6 | 13.0 | 22 12.4 | 8.4 | 54.1 | 30 | 03 52 | 04 25 | 04 53 | 22 36 | 23 10 | 23 41 | 24 09 |
| 21 | 136 32.3 | . . 07.2 | 260 14.6 | 12.9 | 22 04.0 | 8.6 | 54.1 | 35 | 03 33 | 04 10 | 04 40 | 22 48 | 23 19 | 23 47 | 24 13 |
| 22 | 151 32.0 | 07.3 | 274 46.5 | 13.1 | 21 55.4 | 8.6 | 54.1 | 40 | 03 11 | 03 52 | 04 25 | 23 02 | 23 30 | 23 55 | 24 18 |
| 23 | 166 31.7 | 07.5 | 289 18.6 | 13.1 | 21 46.8 | 8.8 | 54.1 | 45 | 02 41 | 03 30 | 04 07 | 23 18 | 23 43 | 24 04 | 00 04 |
| 13 00 | 181 31.5 | S23 07.7 | 303 50.7 | 13.2 | N21 38.0 | 8.8 | 54.1 | S 50 | 01 56 | 03 01 | 03 45 | 23 38 | 23 58 | 24 15 | 00 15 |
| 01 | 196 31.2 | 07.9 | 318 22.9 | 13.2 | 21 29.2 | 8.9 | 54.1 | 52 | 01 30 | 02 46 | 03 34 | 23 47 | 24 05 | 00 05 | 00 20 |
| 02 | 211 30.9 | 08.0 | 332 55.1 | 13.3 | 21 20.3 | 9.0 | 54.1 | 54 | 00 48 | 02 28 | 03 22 | 23 58 | 24 13 | 00 13 | 00 25 |
| 03 | 226 30.6 | . . 08.2 | 347 27.4 | 13.3 | 21 11.3 | 9.1 | 54.1 | 56 | //// | 02 07 | 03 08 | 24 10 | 00 10 | 00 22 | 00 31 |
| 04 | 241 30.3 | 08.4 | 1 59.7 | 13.4 | 21 02.2 | 9.2 | 54.1 | 58 | //// | 01 38 | 02 52 | 00 09 | 00 23 | 00 32 | 00 38 |
| 05 | 256 30.0 | 08.5 | 16 32.1 | 13.5 | 20 53.0 | 9.3 | 54.1 | S 60 | //// | 00 53 | 02 32 | 00 31 | 00 39 | 00 43 | 00 45 |
| 06 | 271 29.7 | S23 08.7 | 31 04.6 | 13.5 | N20 43.7 | 9.4 | 54.1 | | | | | | | | |
| 07 | 286 29.4 | 08.9 | 45 37.1 | 13.5 | 20 34.3 | 9.5 | 54.1 | Lat. | Sunset | Twilight | | Moonset | | | |
| T 08 | 301 29.1 | 09.0 | 60 09.6 | 13.7 | 20 24.8 | 9.5 | 54.1 | | | Civil | Naut. | 12 | 13 | 14 | 15 |
| U 09 | 316 28.8 | . . 09.2 | 74 42.3 | 13.6 | 20 15.3 | 9.7 | 54.2 | ° | h m | h m | h m | h m | h m | h m | h m |
| E 10 | 331 28.5 | 09.4 | 89 14.9 | 13.8 | 20 05.6 | 9.7 | 54.2 | N 72 | ▬▬ | 13 08 | 15 31 | ▭ | ▭ | 14 33 | 13 45 |
| S 11 | 346 28.2 | 09.5 | 103 47.7 | 13.7 | 19 55.9 | 9.8 | 54.2 | N 70 | ▬▬ | 14 04 | 15 50 | ▭ | 15 03 | 14 02 | 13 30 |
| D 12 | 1 27.9 | S23 09.7 | 118 20.4 | 13.9 | N19 46.1 | 9.9 | 54.2 | 68 | ▬▬ | 14 38 | 16 06 | ▭ | 14 11 | 13 39 | 13 17 |
| A 13 | 16 27.6 | 09.9 | 132 53.3 | 13.9 | 19 36.2 | 9.9 | 54.2 | 66 | 13 25 | 15 02 | 16 19 | 14 13 | 13 39 | 13 21 | 13 07 |
| Y 14 | 31 27.3 | 10.0 | 147 26.2 | 13.9 | 19 26.3 | 10.1 | 54.2 | 64 | 14 05 | 15 21 | 16 29 | 13 27 | 13 15 | 13 06 | 12 58 |
| 15 | 46 27.0 | . . 10.2 | 161 59.1 | 14.0 | 19 16.2 | 10.1 | 54.2 | 62 | 14 32 | 15 37 | 16 39 | 12 57 | 12 56 | 12 53 | 12 51 |
| 16 | 61 26.8 | 10.3 | 176 32.1 | 14.1 | 19 06.1 | 10.3 | 54.2 | 60 | 14 53 | 15 50 | 16 47 | 12 34 | 12 40 | 12 43 | 12 44 |
| 17 | 76 26.5 | 10.5 | 191 05.2 | 14.1 | 18 55.8 | 10.3 | 54.2 | N 58 | 15 10 | 16 02 | 16 54 | 12 15 | 12 26 | 12 34 | 12 39 |
| 18 | 91 26.2 | S23 10.7 | 205 38.3 | 14.1 | N18 45.5 | 10.3 | 54.2 | 56 | 15 25 | 16 12 | 17 01 | 12 00 | 12 13 | 12 25 | 12 33 |
| 19 | 106 25.9 | 10.8 | 220 11.4 | 14.2 | 18 35.2 | 10.5 | 54.2 | 54 | 15 37 | 16 21 | 17 07 | 11 46 | 12 05 | 12 18 | 12 29 |
| 20 | 121 25.6 | 11.0 | 234 44.6 | 14.3 | 18 24.7 | 10.5 | 54.3 | 52 | 15 48 | 16 29 | 17 13 | 11 35 | 11 55 | 12 12 | 12 25 |
| 21 | 136 25.3 | . . 11.1 | 249 17.9 | 14.3 | 18 14.2 | 10.6 | 54.3 | 50 | 15 58 | 16 36 | 17 18 | 11 24 | 11 47 | 12 06 | 12 21 |
| 22 | 151 25.0 | 11.3 | 263 51.2 | 14.3 | 18 03.6 | 10.7 | 54.3 | 45 | 16 18 | 16 52 | 17 29 | 11 02 | 11 30 | 11 53 | 12 13 |
| 23 | 166 24.7 | 11.5 | 278 24.5 | 14.4 | 17 52.9 | 10.8 | 54.3 | N 40 | 16 35 | 17 06 | 17 40 | 10 44 | 11 15 | 11 42 | 12 06 |
| 14 00 | 181 24.4 | S23 11.6 | 292 57.9 | 14.5 | N17 42.1 | 10.8 | 54.3 | 35 | 16 49 | 17 17 | 17 49 | 10 29 | 11 03 | 11 33 | 12 00 |
| 01 | 196 24.1 | 11.8 | 307 31.4 | 14.5 | 17 31.3 | 11.0 | 54.3 | 30 | 17 01 | 17 28 | 17 57 | 10 16 | 10 53 | 11 25 | 11 54 |
| 02 | 211 23.8 | 11.9 | 322 04.9 | 14.5 | 17 20.3 | 10.9 | 54.3 | 20 | 17 22 | 17 46 | 18 14 | 09 54 | 10 34 | 11 11 | 11 45 |
| 03 | 226 23.5 | . . 12.1 | 336 38.4 | 14.6 | 17 09.4 | 11.1 | 54.3 | N 10 | 17 41 | 18 03 | 18 30 | 09 35 | 10 18 | 10 58 | 11 37 |
| 04 | 241 23.2 | 12.2 | 351 12.0 | 14.6 | 16 58.3 | 11.1 | 54.4 | 0 | 17 58 | 18 20 | 18 47 | 09 16 | 10 03 | 10 47 | 11 29 |
| 05 | 256 22.9 | 12.4 | 5 45.6 | 14.7 | 16 47.2 | 11.2 | 54.4 | S 10 | 18 15 | 18 38 | 19 05 | 08 58 | 09 47 | 10 35 | 11 21 |
| 06 | 271 22.6 | S23 12.5 | 20 19.3 | 14.7 | N16 36.0 | 11.3 | 54.4 | 20 | 18 34 | 18 59 | 19 28 | 08 38 | 09 31 | 10 22 | 11 13 |
| W 07 | 286 22.3 | 12.7 | 34 53.0 | 14.8 | 16 24.7 | 11.4 | 54.4 | 30 | 18 56 | 19 23 | 19 57 | 08 16 | 09 12 | 10 08 | 11 03 |
| E 08 | 301 22.0 | 12.8 | 49 26.8 | 14.8 | 16 13.3 | 11.4 | 54.4 | 35 | 19 09 | 19 38 | 20 15 | 08 02 | 09 01 | 09 59 | 10 58 |
| D 09 | 316 21.7 | . . 13.0 | 64 00.6 | 14.8 | 16 01.9 | 11.5 | 54.4 | 40 | 19 24 | 19 56 | 20 38 | 07 47 | 08 48 | 09 50 | 10 51 |
| N 10 | 331 21.4 | 13.1 | 78 34.4 | 14.9 | 15 50.4 | 11.5 | 54.4 | 45 | 19 41 | 20 19 | 21 08 | 07 28 | 08 33 | 09 38 | 10 44 |
| E 11 | 346 21.1 | 13.3 | 93 08.3 | 15.0 | 15 38.9 | 11.6 | 54.4 | S 50 | 20 04 | 20 48 | 21 53 | 07 05 | 08 14 | 09 24 | 10 35 |
| S 12 | 1 20.8 | S23 13.4 | 107 42.3 | 14.9 | N15 27.3 | 11.7 | 54.5 | 52 | 20 14 | 21 03 | 22 20 | 06 53 | 08 05 | 09 18 | 10 30 |
| D 13 | 16 20.5 | 13.5 | 122 16.2 | 15.0 | 15 15.6 | 11.8 | 54.5 | 54 | 20 27 | 21 20 | 23 02 | 06 40 | 07 55 | 09 11 | 10 26 |
| A 14 | 31 20.2 | 13.7 | 136 50.2 | 15.1 | 15 03.8 | 11.8 | 54.5 | 56 | 20 40 | 21 42 | //// | 06 26 | 07 44 | 09 02 | 10 21 |
| Y 15 | 46 19.9 | . . 13.8 | 151 24.3 | 15.0 | 14 52.0 | 11.9 | 54.5 | 58 | 20 57 | 22 11 | //// | 06 08 | 07 31 | 08 53 | 10 15 |
| 16 | 61 19.6 | 14.0 | 165 58.3 | 15.2 | 14 40.1 | 11.9 | 54.5 | S 60 | 21 17 | 22 58 | //// | 05 47 | 07 15 | 08 43 | 10 08 |
| 17 | 76 19.3 | 14.1 | 180 32.5 | 15.1 | 14 28.2 | 12.0 | 54.5 | | | | | | | | |
| 18 | 91 19.0 | S23 14.3 | 195 06.6 | 15.2 | N14 16.2 | 12.1 | 54.6 | | | SUN | | | MOON | | |
| 19 | 106 18.7 | 14.4 | 209 40.8 | 15.2 | 14 04.1 | 12.2 | 54.6 | Day | Eqn. of Time | | Mer. | Mer. Pass. | | Age | Phase |
| 20 | 121 18.4 | 14.5 | 224 15.0 | 15.3 | 13 51.9 | 12.1 | 54.6 | | 00ʰ | 12ʰ | Pass. | Upper | Lower | | |
| 21 | 136 18.1 | . . 14.7 | 238 49.3 | 15.2 | 13 39.8 | 12.3 | 54.6 | d | m s | m s | h m | h m | h m | d % | |
| 22 | 151 17.8 | 14.8 | 253 23.5 | 15.4 | 13 27.5 | 12.3 | 54.6 | 12 | 06 34 | 06 20 | 11 54 | 03 05 | 15 29 | 19 84 | ◑ |
| 23 | 166 17.5 | 14.9 | 267 57.9 | 15.3 | N13 15.2 | 12.4 | 54.7 | 13 | 06 06 | 05 52 | 11 54 | 03 52 | 16 14 | 20 76 | |
| | SD 16.3 | d 0.2 | SD 14.7 | | 14.8 | | 14.8 | 14 | 05 38 | 05 24 | 11 55 | 04 36 | 16 58 | 21 68 | |

| UT | ARIES GHA | VENUS −3.9 GHA | VENUS Dec | MARS −1.7 GHA | MARS Dec | JUPITER −2.5 GHA | JUPITER Dec | SATURN +0.7 GHA | SATURN Dec | STARS Name | SHA | Dec |
|---|---|---|---|---|---|---|---|---|---|---|---|---|
| **15 00** | 83 37.9 | 166 58.7 | S24 12.0 | 11 46.3 | N24 55.8 | 83 30.0 | S 1 25.5 | 119 57.5 | S15 43.4 | Acamar | 315 12.7 | S40 12.9 |
| 01 | 98 40.4 | 181 57.7 | 11.9 | 26 49.7 | 55.7 | 98 32.3 | 25.4 | 134 59.7 | 43.4 | Achernar | 335 21.2 | S57 07.5 |
| 02 | 113 42.9 | 196 56.7 | 11.9 | 41 53.1 | 55.7 | 113 34.6 | 25.4 | 150 02.0 | 43.3 | Acrux | 173 02.1 | S63 13.2 |
| 03 | 128 45.3 | 211 55.8 .. | 11.8 | 56 56.6 .. | 55.7 | 128 36.9 .. | 25.3 | 165 04.3 .. | 43.2 | Adhara | 255 06.8 | S29 00.1 |
| 04 | 143 47.8 | 226 54.8 | 11.8 | 72 00.0 | 55.6 | 143 39.2 | 25.2 | 180 06.5 | 43.2 | Aldebaran | 290 41.2 | N16 33.3 |
| 05 | 158 50.3 | 241 53.8 | 11.7 | 87 03.4 | 55.6 | 158 41.5 | 25.1 | 195 08.8 | 43.1 | | | |
| 06 | 173 52.7 | 256 52.8 | S24 11.6 | 102 06.9 | N24 55.5 | 173 43.8 | S 1 25.0 | 210 11.1 | S15 43.0 | Alioth | 166 14.7 | N55 49.9 |
| 07 | 188 55.2 | 271 51.9 | 11.6 | 117 10.3 | 55.5 | 188 46.1 | 25.0 | 225 13.3 | 43.0 | Alkaid | 152 53.7 | N49 11.8 |
| T 08 | 203 57.7 | 286 50.9 | 11.5 | 132 13.7 | 55.5 | 203 48.4 | 24.9 | 240 15.6 | 42.9 | Alnair | 27 35.3 | S46 51.3 |
| H 09 | 219 00.1 | 301 49.9 .. | 11.4 | 147 17.2 .. | 55.4 | 218 50.7 .. | 24.8 | 255 17.8 .. | 42.8 | Alnilam | 275 39.1 | S 1 11.2 |
| U 10 | 234 02.6 | 316 48.9 | 11.4 | 162 20.6 | 55.4 | 233 53.0 | 24.7 | 270 20.1 | 42.7 | Alphard | 217 49.3 | S 8 45.4 |
| R 11 | 249 05.1 | 331 48.0 | 11.3 | 177 24.0 | 55.3 | 248 55.3 | 24.6 | 285 22.4 | 42.7 | | | |
| S 12 | 264 07.5 | 346 47.0 | S24 11.2 | 192 27.5 | N24 55.3 | 263 57.6 | S 1 24.5 | 300 24.6 | S15 42.6 | Alphecca | 126 05.5 | N26 38.2 |
| D 13 | 279 10.0 | 1 46.0 | 11.1 | 207 30.9 | 55.3 | 278 59.9 | 24.5 | 315 26.9 | 42.5 | Alpheratz | 357 36.5 | N29 13.1 |
| A 14 | 294 12.4 | 16 45.0 | 11.1 | 222 34.3 | 55.2 | 294 02.2 | 24.4 | 330 29.2 | 42.5 | Altair | 62 01.9 | N 8 55.7 |
| Y 15 | 309 14.9 | 31 44.1 .. | 11.0 | 237 37.7 .. | 55.2 | 309 04.5 .. | 24.3 | 345 31.4 .. | 42.4 | Ankaa | 353 08.8 | S42 11.2 |
| 16 | 324 17.4 | 46 43.1 | 10.9 | 252 41.2 | 55.1 | 324 06.8 | 24.2 | 0 33.7 | 42.3 | Antares | 112 18.3 | S26 28.9 |
| 17 | 339 19.8 | 61 42.1 | 10.8 | 267 44.6 | 55.1 | 339 09.1 | 24.1 | 15 35.9 | 42.3 | | | |
| 18 | 354 22.3 | 76 41.2 | S24 10.7 | 282 48.0 | N24 55.1 | 354 11.4 | S 1 24.1 | 30 38.2 | S15 42.2 | Arcturus | 145 49.7 | N19 03.8 |
| 19 | 9 24.8 | 91 40.2 | 10.7 | 297 51.4 | 55.0 | 9 13.7 | 24.0 | 45 40.5 | 42.1 | Atria | 107 14.7 | S69 04.0 |
| 20 | 24 27.2 | 106 39.2 | 10.6 | 312 54.9 | 55.0 | 24 16.0 | 23.9 | 60 42.7 | 42.1 | Avior | 234 14.9 | S59 34.7 |
| 21 | 39 29.7 | 121 38.2 .. | 10.5 | 327 58.3 .. | 54.9 | 39 18.3 .. | 23.8 | 75 45.0 .. | 42.0 | Bellatrix | 278 24.4 | N 6 22.2 |
| 22 | 54 32.2 | 136 37.3 | 10.4 | 343 01.7 | 54.9 | 54 20.6 | 23.7 | 90 47.2 | 41.9 | Betelgeuse | 270 53.6 | N 7 24.7 |
| 23 | 69 34.6 | 151 36.3 | 10.3 | 358 05.1 | 54.9 | 69 22.9 | 23.6 | 105 49.5 | 41.9 | | | |
| **16 00** | 84 37.1 | 166 35.3 | S24 10.2 | 13 08.5 | N24 54.8 | 84 25.2 | S 1 23.6 | 120 51.8 | S15 41.8 | Canopus | 263 52.6 | S52 42.4 |
| 01 | 99 39.5 | 181 34.3 | 10.1 | 28 12.0 | 54.8 | 99 27.5 | 23.5 | 135 54.0 | 41.7 | Capella | 280 23.9 | N46 01.3 |
| 02 | 114 42.0 | 196 33.4 | 10.0 | 43 15.4 | 54.7 | 114 29.8 | 23.4 | 150 56.3 | 41.7 | Deneb | 49 27.3 | N45 21.8 |
| 03 | 129 44.5 | 211 32.4 .. | 09.9 | 58 18.8 .. | 54.7 | 129 32.1 .. | 23.3 | 165 58.6 .. | 41.6 | Denebola | 182 26.7 | N14 26.6 |
| 04 | 144 46.9 | 226 31.4 | 09.8 | 73 22.2 | 54.6 | 144 34.4 | 23.2 | 181 00.8 | 41.5 | Diphda | 348 48.9 | S17 51.8 |
| 05 | 159 49.4 | 241 30.5 | 09.7 | 88 25.6 | 54.6 | 159 36.7 | 23.1 | 196 03.1 | 41.5 | | | |
| 06 | 174 51.9 | 256 29.5 | S24 09.7 | 103 29.0 | N24 54.6 | 174 39.0 | S 1 23.0 | 211 05.3 | S15 41.4 | Dubhe | 193 43.0 | N61 37.4 |
| 07 | 189 54.3 | 271 28.5 | 09.6 | 118 32.4 | 54.5 | 189 41.3 | 23.0 | 226 07.6 | 41.3 | Elnath | 278 03.7 | N28 37.6 |
| F 08 | 204 56.8 | 286 27.5 | 09.5 | 133 35.8 | 54.5 | 204 43.6 | 22.9 | 241 09.9 | 41.3 | Eltanin | 90 43.5 | N51 29.1 |
| R 09 | 219 59.3 | 301 26.6 .. | 09.4 | 148 39.3 .. | 54.4 | 219 45.9 .. | 22.8 | 256 12.1 .. | 41.2 | Enif | 33 40.7 | N 9 58.8 |
| I 10 | 235 01.7 | 316 25.6 | 09.3 | 163 42.7 | 54.4 | 234 48.2 | 22.7 | 271 14.4 | 41.1 | Fomalhaut | 15 16.5 | S29 30.3 |
| D 11 | 250 04.2 | 331 24.6 | 09.1 | 178 46.1 | 54.3 | 249 50.5 | 22.6 | 286 16.6 | 41.1 | | | |
| A 12 | 265 06.7 | 346 23.7 | S24 09.0 | 193 49.5 | N24 54.3 | 264 52.8 | S 1 22.5 | 301 18.9 | S15 41.0 | Gacrux | 171 53.7 | S57 14.1 |
| Y 13 | 280 09.1 | 1 22.7 | 08.9 | 208 52.9 | 54.3 | 279 55.1 | 22.5 | 316 21.1 | 40.9 | Gienah | 175 45.4 | S17 40.0 |
| 14 | 295 11.6 | 16 21.7 | 08.8 | 223 56.3 | 54.2 | 294 57.4 | 22.4 | 331 23.4 | 40.8 | Hadar | 148 38.9 | S60 28.7 |
| 15 | 310 14.0 | 31 20.7 .. | 08.7 | 238 59.7 .. | 54.2 | 309 59.7 .. | 22.3 | 346 25.7 .. | 40.8 | Hamal | 327 52.9 | N23 34.3 |
| 16 | 325 16.5 | 46 19.8 | 08.6 | 254 03.1 | 54.1 | 325 02.0 | 22.2 | 1 27.9 | 40.7 | Kaus Aust. | 83 35.2 | S34 22.4 |
| 17 | 340 19.0 | 61 18.8 | 08.5 | 269 06.5 | 54.1 | 340 04.3 | 22.1 | 16 30.2 | 40.6 | | | |
| 18 | 355 21.4 | 76 17.8 | S24 08.4 | 284 09.9 | N24 54.0 | 355 06.6 | S 1 22.0 | 31 32.4 | S15 40.6 | Kochab | 137 20.7 | N74 03.5 |
| 19 | 10 23.9 | 91 16.9 | 08.3 | 299 13.3 | 54.0 | 10 08.9 | 21.9 | 46 34.7 | 40.5 | Markab | 13 31.7 | N15 19.8 |
| 20 | 25 26.4 | 106 15.9 | 08.2 | 314 16.7 | 54.0 | 25 11.2 | 21.9 | 61 37.0 | 40.4 | Menkar | 314 07.7 | N 4 10.8 |
| 21 | 40 28.8 | 121 14.9 .. | 08.0 | 329 20.1 .. | 53.9 | 40 13.5 .. | 21.8 | 76 39.2 .. | 40.4 | Menkent | 147 59.9 | S36 28.7 |
| 22 | 55 31.3 | 136 13.9 | 07.9 | 344 23.5 | 53.9 | 55 15.8 | 21.7 | 91 41.5 | 40.3 | Miaplacidus | 221 38.0 | S69 48.3 |
| 23 | 70 33.8 | 151 13.0 | 07.8 | 359 26.9 | 53.8 | 70 18.0 | 21.6 | 106 43.7 | 40.2 | | | |
| **17 00** | 85 36.2 | 166 12.0 | S24 07.7 | 14 30.3 | N24 53.8 | 85 20.3 | S 1 21.5 | 121 46.0 | S15 40.2 | Mirfak | 308 30.3 | N49 56.6 |
| 01 | 100 38.7 | 181 11.0 | 07.6 | 29 33.7 | 53.7 | 100 22.6 | 21.4 | 136 48.3 | 40.1 | Nunki | 75 50.3 | S26 16.1 |
| 02 | 115 41.2 | 196 10.1 | 07.4 | 44 37.1 | 53.7 | 115 24.9 | 21.3 | 151 50.5 | 40.0 | Peacock | 53 08.9 | S56 39.9 |
| 03 | 130 43.6 | 211 09.1 .. | 07.3 | 59 40.5 .. | 53.6 | 130 27.2 .. | 21.2 | 166 52.8 .. | 40.0 | Pollux | 243 19.1 | N27 58.2 |
| 04 | 145 46.1 | 226 08.1 | 07.2 | 74 43.9 | 53.6 | 145 29.5 | 21.2 | 181 55.0 | 39.9 | Procyon | 244 52.3 | N 5 10.0 |
| 05 | 160 48.5 | 241 07.2 | 07.1 | 89 47.2 | 53.6 | 160 31.8 | 21.1 | 196 57.3 | 39.8 | | | |
| 06 | 175 51.0 | 256 06.2 | S24 06.9 | 104 50.6 | N24 53.5 | 175 34.1 | S 1 21.0 | 211 59.5 | S15 39.7 | Rasalhague | 96 00.5 | N12 32.6 |
| 07 | 190 53.5 | 271 05.2 | 06.8 | 119 54.0 | 53.5 | 190 36.4 | 20.9 | 227 01.8 | 39.7 | Regulus | 207 36.1 | N11 51.3 |
| S 08 | 205 55.9 | 286 04.3 | 06.7 | 134 57.4 | 53.4 | 205 38.7 | 20.8 | 242 04.1 | 39.6 | Rigel | 281 05.2 | S 8 10.5 |
| A 09 | 220 58.4 | 301 03.3 .. | 06.5 | 150 00.8 .. | 53.4 | 220 41.0 .. | 20.7 | 257 06.3 .. | 39.5 | Rigil Kent. | 139 43.2 | S60 55.5 |
| T 10 | 236 00.9 | 316 02.3 | 06.4 | 165 04.2 | 53.3 | 235 43.2 | 20.6 | 272 08.6 | 39.5 | Sabik | 102 05.1 | S15 45.1 |
| U 11 | 251 03.3 | 331 01.3 | 06.3 | 180 07.6 | 53.3 | 250 45.5 | 20.5 | 287 10.8 | 39.4 | | | |
| R 12 | 266 05.8 | 346 00.4 | S24 06.1 | 195 10.9 | N24 53.2 | 265 47.8 | S 1 20.5 | 302 13.1 | S15 39.3 | Schedar | 349 32.8 | N56 40.0 |
| D 13 | 281 08.3 | 0 59.4 | 06.0 | 210 14.3 | 53.2 | 280 50.1 | 20.4 | 317 15.3 | 39.3 | Shaula | 96 13.1 | S37 07.2 |
| A 14 | 296 10.7 | 15 58.4 | 05.9 | 225 17.7 | 53.1 | 295 52.4 | 20.3 | 332 17.6 | 39.2 | Sirius | 258 27.4 | S16 44.8 |
| Y 15 | 311 13.2 | 30 57.5 .. | 05.7 | 240 21.1 .. | 53.1 | 310 54.7 .. | 20.2 | 347 19.8 .. | 39.1 | Spica | 158 24.3 | S11 16.7 |
| 16 | 326 15.6 | 45 56.5 | 05.6 | 255 24.5 | 53.0 | 325 57.0 | 20.1 | 2 22.1 | 39.1 | Suhail | 222 47.3 | S43 31.2 |
| 17 | 341 18.1 | 60 55.5 | 05.4 | 270 27.8 | 53.0 | 340 59.3 | 20.0 | 17 24.4 | 39.0 | | | |
| 18 | 356 20.6 | 75 54.6 | S24 05.3 | 285 31.2 | N24 53.0 | 356 01.5 | S 1 19.9 | 32 26.6 | S15 38.9 | Vega | 80 34.8 | N38 48.3 |
| 19 | 11 23.0 | 90 53.6 | 05.1 | 300 34.6 | 52.9 | 11 03.8 | 19.8 | 47 28.9 | 38.8 | Zuben'ubi | 136 58.2 | S16 08.1 |
| 20 | 26 25.5 | 105 52.6 | 05.0 | 315 38.0 | 52.9 | 26 06.1 | 19.7 | 62 31.1 | 38.8 | | SHA | Mer. Pass. |
| 21 | 41 28.0 | 120 51.7 .. | 04.8 | 330 41.3 .. | 52.8 | 41 08.4 .. | 19.7 | 77 33.4 .. | 38.7 | Venus | 81 58.2 | 12 54 |
| 22 | 56 30.4 | 135 50.7 | 04.7 | 345 44.7 | 52.8 | 56 10.7 | 19.6 | 92 35.6 | 38.6 | Mars | 288 31.5 | 23 02 |
| 23 | 71 32.9 | 150 49.7 | 04.5 | 0 48.1 | 52.7 | 71 13.0 | 19.5 | 107 37.9 | 38.6 | Jupiter | 359 48.2 | 18 20 |
| Mer. Pass. | 18 18.5 | v −1.0 d 0.1 | | v 3.4 d 0.0 | | v 2.3 d 0.1 | | v 2.3 d 0.1 | | Saturn | 36 14.7 | 15 54 |

## SUN and MOON

| UT | SUN GHA | SUN Dec | MOON GHA | v | MOON Dec | d | HP |
|---|---|---|---|---|---|---|---|
| **15** 00 | 181 17.2 | S23 15.1 | 282 32.2 | 15.4 | N13 02.8 | 12.4 | 54.7 |
| 01 | 196 16.9 | 15.2 | 297 06.6 | 15.4 | 12 50.4 | 12.5 | 54.7 |
| 02 | 211 16.6 | 15.3 | 311 41.0 | 15.4 | 12 37.9 | 12.6 | 54.7 |
| 03 | 226 16.3 .. | 15.5 | 326 15.4 | 15.5 | 12 25.3 | 12.6 | 54.7 |
| 04 | 241 16.0 | 15.6 | 340 49.9 | 15.4 | 12 12.7 | 12.6 | 54.7 |
| 05 | 256 15.7 | 15.7 | 355 24.3 | 15.5 | 12 00.1 | 12.8 | 54.8 |
| **T** 06 | 271 15.4 | S23 15.9 | 9 58.8 | 15.6 | N11 47.3 | 12.7 | 54.8 |
| **H** 07 | 286 15.1 | 16.0 | 24 33.4 | 15.5 | 11 34.6 | 12.9 | 54.8 |
| **U** 08 | 301 14.8 | 16.1 | 39 07.9 | 15.6 | 11 21.7 | 12.8 | 54.8 |
| **R** 09 | 316 14.5 .. | 16.3 | 53 42.5 | 15.6 | 11 08.9 | 13.0 | 54.9 |
| **S** 10 | 331 14.2 | 16.4 | 68 17.1 | 15.6 | 10 55.9 | 13.0 | 54.9 |
| **D** 11 | 346 13.9 | 16.5 | 82 51.7 | 15.6 | 10 42.9 | 13.0 | 54.9 |
| **A** 12 | 1 13.6 | S23 16.6 | 97 26.3 | 15.7 | N10 29.9 | 13.1 | 54.9 |
| **Y** 13 | 16 13.3 | 16.8 | 112 01.0 | 15.6 | 10 16.8 | 13.1 | 54.9 |
| 14 | 31 13.0 | 16.9 | 126 35.6 | 15.7 | 10 03.7 | 13.2 | 55.0 |
| 15 | 46 12.7 .. | 17.0 | 141 10.3 | 15.7 | 9 50.5 | 13.2 | 55.0 |
| 16 | 61 12.4 | 17.1 | 155 45.0 | 15.7 | 9 37.3 | 13.3 | 55.0 |
| 17 | 76 12.1 | 17.2 | 170 19.7 | 15.7 | 9 24.0 | 13.3 | 55.0 |
| 18 | 91 11.8 | S23 17.3 | 184 54.4 | 15.7 | N 9 10.7 | 13.4 | 55.1 |
| 19 | 106 11.5 | 17.5 | 199 29.1 | 15.8 | 8 57.3 | 13.4 | 55.1 |
| 20 | 121 11.2 | 17.6 | 214 03.9 | 15.7 | 8 43.9 | 13.5 | 55.1 |
| 21 | 136 10.9 .. | 17.7 | 228 38.6 | 15.8 | 8 30.4 | 13.5 | 55.1 |
| 22 | 151 10.6 | 17.8 | 243 13.4 | 15.8 | 8 16.9 | 13.6 | 55.2 |
| 23 | 166 10.3 | 18.0 | 257 48.2 | 15.7 | 8 03.3 | 13.6 | 55.2 |
| **16** 00 | 181 10.0 | S23 18.1 | 272 22.9 | 15.0 | N 7 49.7 | 13.6 | 55.2 |
| 01 | 196 09.7 | 18.2 | 286 57.7 | 15.8 | 7 36.1 | 13.7 | 55.2 |
| 02 | 211 09.4 | 18.3 | 301 32.5 | 15.8 | 7 22.4 | 13.7 | 55.3 |
| 03 | 226 09.1 .. | 18.4 | 316 07.3 | 15.7 | 7 08.7 | 13.8 | 55.3 |
| 04 | 241 08.8 | 18.5 | 330 42.0 | 15.8 | 6 54.9 | 13.8 | 55.3 |
| 05 | 256 08.5 | 18.6 | 345 16.8 | 15.8 | 6 41.1 | 13.8 | 55.3 |
| 06 | 271 08.2 | S23 18.8 | 359 51.6 | 15.8 | N 6 27.3 | 13.9 | 55.4 |
| **F** 07 | 286 07.9 | 18.9 | 14 26.4 | 15.8 | 6 13.4 | 13.9 | 55.4 |
| **R** 08 | 301 07.6 | 19.0 | 29 01.2 | 15.7 | 5 59.5 | 14.0 | 55.4 |
| **I** 09 | 316 07.3 .. | 19.1 | 43 35.9 | 15.8 | 5 45.5 | 14.0 | 55.4 |
| **D** 10 | 331 07.0 | 19.2 | 58 10.7 | 15.8 | 5 31.5 | 14.0 | 55.5 |
| **A** 11 | 346 06.7 | 19.3 | 72 45.5 | 15.7 | 5 17.5 | 14.1 | 55.5 |
| **Y** 12 | 1 06.4 | S23 19.4 | 87 20.2 | 15.8 | N 5 03.4 | 14.1 | 55.5 |
| 13 | 16 06.1 | 19.5 | 101 55.0 | 15.7 | 4 49.3 | 14.1 | 55.6 |
| 14 | 31 05.8 | 19.6 | 116 29.7 | 15.7 | 4 35.2 | 14.2 | 55.6 |
| 15 | 46 05.5 .. | 19.7 | 131 04.4 | 15.7 | 4 21.0 | 14.2 | 55.6 |
| 16 | 61 05.2 | 19.8 | 145 39.1 | 15.7 | 4 06.8 | 14.2 | 55.6 |
| 17 | 76 04.9 | 19.9 | 160 13.8 | 15.7 | 3 52.6 | 14.2 | 55.7 |
| 18 | 91 04.6 | S23 20.0 | 174 48.5 | 15.7 | N 3 38.4 | 14.3 | 55.7 |
| 19 | 106 04.3 | 20.1 | 189 23.2 | 15.6 | 3 24.1 | 14.4 | 55.7 |
| 20 | 121 04.0 | 20.2 | 203 57.8 | 15.7 | 3 09.7 | 14.3 | 55.8 |
| 21 | 136 03.7 .. | 20.3 | 218 32.5 | 15.6 | 2 55.4 | 14.4 | 55.8 |
| 22 | 151 03.3 | 20.4 | 233 07.1 | 15.6 | 2 41.0 | 14.4 | 55.8 |
| 23 | 166 03.0 | 20.5 | 247 41.7 | 15.5 | 2 26.6 | 14.4 | 55.9 |
| **17** 00 | 181 02.7 | S23 20.6 | 262 16.2 | 15.6 | N 2 12.2 | 14.5 | 55.9 |
| 01 | 196 02.4 | 20.7 | 276 50.8 | 15.5 | 1 57.7 | 14.4 | 55.9 |
| 02 | 211 02.1 | 20.8 | 291 25.3 | 15.5 | 1 43.3 | 14.5 | 56.0 |
| 03 | 226 01.8 .. | 20.9 | 305 59.8 | 15.5 | 1 28.8 | 14.6 | 56.0 |
| 04 | 241 01.5 | 21.0 | 320 34.3 | 15.4 | 1 14.2 | 14.5 | 56.0 |
| 05 | 256 01.2 | 21.1 | 335 08.7 | 15.4 | 0 59.7 | 14.6 | 56.1 |
| 06 | 271 00.9 | S23 21.2 | 349 43.1 | 15.4 | N 0 45.1 | 14.6 | 56.1 |
| **S** 07 | 286 00.6 | 21.3 | 4 17.5 | 15.3 | 0 30.5 | 14.6 | 56.1 |
| **A** 08 | 301 00.3 | 21.4 | 18 51.8 | 15.3 | N 0 15.9 | 14.6 | 56.2 |
| **T** 09 | 316 00.0 .. | 21.4 | 33 26.1 | 15.3 | N 0 01.3 | 14.7 | 56.2 |
| **U** 10 | 330 59.7 | 21.5 | 48 00.4 | 15.3 | S 0 13.4 | 14.6 | 56.2 |
| **R** 11 | 345 59.4 | 21.6 | 62 34.7 | 15.2 | 0 28.0 | 14.7 | 56.3 |
| **D** 12 | 0 59.1 | S23 21.7 | 77 08.9 | 15.1 | S 0 42.7 | 14.7 | 56.3 |
| **A** 13 | 15 58.8 | 21.8 | 91 43.0 | 15.1 | 0 57.4 | 14.7 | 56.3 |
| **Y** 14 | 30 58.5 | 21.9 | 106 17.1 | 15.1 | 1 12.1 | 14.7 | 56.4 |
| 15 | 45 58.2 .. | 22.0 | 120 51.2 | 15.1 | 1 26.8 | 14.8 | 56.4 |
| 16 | 60 57.9 | 22.1 | 135 25.3 | 15.0 | 1 41.6 | 14.7 | 56.4 |
| 17 | 75 57.5 | 22.1 | 149 59.3 | 14.9 | 1 56.3 | 14.8 | 56.5 |
| 18 | 90 57.2 | S23 22.2 | 164 33.2 | 14.9 | S 2 11.1 | 14.8 | 56.5 |
| 19 | 105 56.9 | 22.3 | 179 07.1 | 14.9 | 2 25.9 | 14.7 | 56.5 |
| 20 | 120 56.6 | 22.4 | 193 41.0 | 14.8 | 2 40.6 | 14.8 | 56.6 |
| 21 | 135 56.3 .. | 22.5 | 208 14.8 | 14.7 | 2 55.4 | 14.8 | 56.6 |
| 22 | 150 56.0 | 22.5 | 222 48.5 | 14.7 | 3 10.2 | 14.8 | 56.7 |
| 23 | 165 55.7 | 22.6 | 237 22.2 | 14.7 | S 3 25.0 | 14.8 | 56.7 |
| | SD 16.3   d 0.1 | | SD 15.0 | | 15.1 | | 15.3 |

## Twilight, Sunrise, Moonrise

| Lat. | Naut. | Civil | Sunrise | Moonrise 15 | 16 | 17 | 18 |
|---|---|---|---|---|---|---|---|
| N 72 | 08 21 | 10 49 | ■■ | 22 02 | 24 06 | 00 06 | 02 10 |
| N 70 | 08 01 | 09 49 | ■■ | 22 15 | 24 09 | 00 09 | 02 04 |
| 68 | 07 46 | 09 14 | ■■ | 22 26 | 24 11 | 00 11 | 01 58 |
| 66 | 07 33 | 08 49 | 10 29 | 22 34 | 24 13 | 00 13 | 01 54 |
| 64 | 07 22 | 08 30 | 09 47 | 22 41 | 24 15 | 00 15 | 01 51 |
| 62 | 07 12 | 08 14 | 09 19 | 22 47 | 24 16 | 00 16 | 01 48 |
| 60 | 07 04 | 08 01 | 08 58 | 22 52 | 24 18 | 00 18 | 01 45 |
| N 58 | 06 56 | 07 49 | 08 41 | 22 57 | 24 19 | 00 19 | 01 42 |
| 56 | 06 50 | 07 39 | 08 26 | 23 01 | 24 20 | 00 20 | 01 40 |
| 54 | 06 43 | 07 30 | 08 13 | 23 05 | 24 21 | 00 21 | 01 38 |
| 52 | 06 38 | 07 22 | 08 02 | 23 08 | 24 21 | 00 21 | 01 37 |
| 50 | 06 33 | 07 14 | 07 53 | 23 11 | 24 22 | 00 22 | 01 35 |
| 45 | 06 21 | 06 58 | 07 32 | 23 18 | 24 24 | 00 24 | 01 32 |
| N 40 | 06 11 | 06 45 | 07 15 | 23 23 | 24 25 | 00 25 | 01 29 |
| 35 | 06 01 | 06 33 | 07 01 | 23 28 | 24 26 | 00 26 | 01 27 |
| 30 | 05 53 | 06 22 | 06 49 | 23 32 | 24 27 | 00 27 | 01 25 |
| 20 | 05 36 | 06 04 | 06 28 | 23 39 | 24 29 | 00 29 | 01 21 |
| N 10 | 05 20 | 05 46 | 06 09 | 23 45 | 24 31 | 00 31 | 01 18 |
| 0 | 05 03 | 05 29 | 05 52 | 23 51 | 24 32 | 00 32 | 01 15 |
| S 10 | 04 44 | 05 11 | 05 34 | 23 56 | 24 34 | 00 34 | 01 12 |
| 20 | 04 22 | 04 51 | 05 15 | 24 02 | 00 02 | 00 35 | 01 09 |
| 30 | 03 53 | 04 26 | 04 53 | 24 09 | 00 09 | 00 37 | 01 06 |
| 35 | 03 34 | 04 11 | 04 41 | 24 13 | 00 13 | 00 38 | 01 04 |
| 40 | 03 11 | 03 53 | 04 26 | 24 10 | 00 18 | 00 39 | 01 02 |
| 45 | 02 41 | 03 30 | 04 08 | 00 04 | 00 23 | 00 41 | 00 59 |
| S 50 | 01 56 | 03 01 | 03 45 | 00 15 | 00 29 | 00 43 | 00 56 |
| 52 | 01 28 | 02 46 | 03 34 | 00 20 | 00 32 | 00 43 | 00 55 |
| 54 | 00 44 | 02 28 | 03 22 | 00 25 | 00 35 | 00 44 | 00 53 |
| 56 | //// | 02 06 | 03 08 | 00 31 | 00 38 | 00 45 | 00 52 |
| 58 | //// | 01 37 | 02 51 | 00 38 | 00 42 | 00 46 | 00 50 |
| S 60 | //// | 00 48 | 02 31 | 00 45 | 00 46 | 00 47 | 00 48 |

## Sunset, Twilight, Moonset

| Lat. | Sunset | Civil | Naut. | Moonset 15 | 16 | 17 | 18 |
|---|---|---|---|---|---|---|---|
| N 72 | ■■ | 13 02 | 15 30 | 13 45 | 13 11 | 12 40 | 12 08 |
| N 70 | ■■ | 14 02 | 15 50 | 13 30 | 13 05 | 12 42 | 12 17 |
| 68 | ■■ | 14 37 | 16 05 | 13 17 | 12 59 | 12 43 | 12 25 |
| 66 | 13 22 | 15 01 | 16 18 | 13 07 | 12 55 | 12 44 | 12 32 |
| 64 | 14 04 | 15 21 | 16 29 | 12 58 | 12 51 | 12 44 | 12 37 |
| 62 | 14 32 | 15 37 | 16 39 | 12 51 | 12 48 | 12 45 | 12 42 |
| 60 | 14 53 | 15 50 | 16 47 | 12 44 | 12 45 | 12 46 | 12 46 |
| N 58 | 15 10 | 16 02 | 16 55 | 12 39 | 12 43 | 12 46 | 12 50 |
| 56 | 15 25 | 16 12 | 17 01 | 12 33 | 12 40 | 12 47 | 12 53 |
| 54 | 15 38 | 16 21 | 17 08 | 12 29 | 12 38 | 12 47 | 12 56 |
| 52 | 15 49 | 16 29 | 17 13 | 12 25 | 12 36 | 12 47 | 12 59 |
| 50 | 15 58 | 16 37 | 17 18 | 12 21 | 12 35 | 12 48 | 13 02 |
| 45 | 16 19 | 16 53 | 17 30 | 12 13 | 12 31 | 12 49 | 13 07 |
| N 40 | 16 36 | 17 06 | 17 40 | 12 06 | 12 28 | 12 49 | 13 12 |
| 35 | 16 50 | 17 18 | 17 50 | 12 00 | 12 25 | 12 50 | 13 16 |
| 30 | 17 02 | 17 29 | 17 59 | 11 54 | 12 22 | 12 50 | 13 19 |
| 20 | 17 23 | 17 47 | 18 15 | 11 45 | 12 18 | 12 51 | 13 25 |
| N 10 | 17 42 | 18 05 | 18 31 | 11 37 | 12 14 | 12 52 | 13 31 |
| 0 | 17 59 | 18 22 | 18 48 | 11 29 | 12 11 | 12 52 | 13 36 |
| S 10 | 18 17 | 18 40 | 19 07 | 11 21 | 12 07 | 12 53 | 13 41 |
| 20 | 18 36 | 19 00 | 19 30 | 11 13 | 12 03 | 12 54 | 13 47 |
| 30 | 18 58 | 19 25 | 19 59 | 11 03 | 11 58 | 12 55 | 13 53 |
| 35 | 19 11 | 19 40 | 20 17 | 10 58 | 11 56 | 12 55 | 13 57 |
| 40 | 19 26 | 19 59 | 20 40 | 10 51 | 11 53 | 12 56 | 14 01 |
| 45 | 19 44 | 20 21 | 21 11 | 10 44 | 11 49 | 12 56 | 14 06 |
| S 50 | 20 06 | 20 51 | 21 56 | 10 35 | 11 45 | 12 57 | 14 11 |
| 52 | 20 17 | 21 06 | 22 24 | 10 30 | 11 43 | 12 57 | 14 14 |
| 54 | 20 29 | 21 24 | 23 09 | 10 26 | 11 41 | 12 57 | 14 17 |
| 56 | 20 43 | 21 45 | //// | 10 21 | 11 39 | 12 58 | 14 20 |
| 58 | 21 00 | 22 15 | //// | 10 15 | 11 36 | 12 58 | 14 24 |
| S 60 | 21 20 | 23 05 | //// | 10 08 | 11 33 | 12 59 | 14 28 |

## SUN and MOON data

| Day | SUN Eqn. of Time 00h | 12h | Mer. Pass. | MOON Mer. Pass. Upper | Lower | Age | Phase |
|---|---|---|---|---|---|---|---|
| 15 | 05 10 | 04 55 | 11 55 | 05 19 | 17 40 | 22 | 59 % |
| 16 | 04 41 | 04 26 | 11 56 | 06 01 | 18 21 | 23 | 49 |
| 17 | 04 12 | 03 57 | 11 56 | 06 42 | 19 04 | 24 | 39 |

| UT | ARIES GHA | VENUS −3.9 GHA | Dec | MARS −1.6 GHA | Dec | JUPITER −2.4 GHA | Dec | SATURN +0.8 GHA | Dec | STARS Name | SHA | Dec |
|---|---|---|---|---|---|---|---|---|---|---|---|---|
| **18 00** | 86 35.4 | 165 48.8 | S24 04.4 | 15 51.5 | N24 52.7 | 86 15.3 | S 1 19.4 | 122 40.2 | S15 38.5 | Acamar | 315 12.8 | S40 12.9 |
| 01 | 101 37.8 | 180 47.8 | 04.2 | 30 54.8 | 52.6 | 101 17.5 | 19.3 | 137 42.4 | 38.4 | Achernar | 335 21.2 | S57 07.5 |
| 02 | 116 40.3 | 195 46.8 | 04.1 | 45 58.2 | 52.6 | 116 19.8 | 19.2 | 152 44.7 | 38.4 | Acrux | 173 02.1 | S63 13.2 |
| 03 | 131 42.8 | 210 45.9 .. | 03.9 | 61 01.6 .. | 52.5 | 131 22.1 .. | 19.1 | 167 46.9 .. | 38.3 | Adhara | 255 06.8 | S29 00.1 |
| 04 | 146 45.2 | 225 44.9 | 03.8 | 76 04.9 | 52.5 | 146 24.4 | 19.0 | 182 49.2 | 38.2 | Aldebaran | 290 41.2 | N16 33.3 |
| 05 | 161 47.7 | 240 43.9 | 03.6 | 91 08.3 | 52.4 | 161 26.7 | 18.9 | 197 51.4 | 38.1 | | | |
| **S 06** | 176 50.1 | 255 43.0 | S24 03.5 | 106 11.7 | N24 52.4 | 176 29.0 | S 1 18.8 | 212 53.7 | S15 38.1 | Alioth | 166 14.7 | N55 49.9 |
| **U 07** | 191 52.6 | 270 42.0 | 03.3 | 121 15.0 | 52.3 | 191 31.2 | 18.8 | 227 55.9 | 38.0 | Alkaid | 152 53.6 | N49 11.7 |
| **N 08** | 206 55.1 | 285 41.0 | 03.1 | 136 18.4 | 52.3 | 206 33.5 | 18.7 | 242 58.2 | 37.9 | Alnair | 27 35.3 | S46 51.3 |
| **D 09** | 221 57.5 | 300 40.1 .. | 03.0 | 151 21.7 .. | 52.2 | 221 35.8 .. | 18.6 | 258 00.4 .. | 37.9 | Alnilam | 275 39.1 | S 1 11.2 |
| **A 10** | 237 00.0 | 315 39.1 | 02.8 | 166 25.1 | 52.2 | 236 38.1 | 18.5 | 273 02.7 | 37.8 | Alphard | 217 49.2 | S 8 45.4 |
| **Y 11** | 252 02.5 | 330 38.1 | 02.6 | 181 28.5 | 52.1 | 251 40.4 | 18.4 | 288 04.9 | 37.7 | | | |
| 12 | 267 04.9 | 345 37.2 | S24 02.5 | 196 31.8 | N24 52.1 | 266 42.7 | S 1 18.3 | 303 07.2 | S15 37.7 | Alphecca | 126 05.5 | N26 38.2 |
| 13 | 282 07.4 | 0 36.2 | 02.3 | 211 35.2 | 52.0 | 281 44.9 | 18.2 | 318 09.5 | 37.6 | Alpheratz | 357 36.5 | N29 13.1 |
| 14 | 297 09.9 | 15 35.2 | 02.1 | 226 38.5 | 52.0 | 296 47.2 | 18.1 | 333 11.7 | 37.5 | Altair | 62 01.9 | N 8 55.7 |
| 15 | 312 12.3 | 30 34.3 .. | 02.0 | 241 41.9 .. | 52.0 | 311 49.5 .. | 18.0 | 348 14.0 .. | 37.4 | Ankaa | 353 08.8 | S42 11.2 |
| 16 | 327 14.8 | 45 33.3 | 01.8 | 256 45.2 | 51.9 | 326 51.8 | 17.9 | 3 16.2 | 37.4 | Antares | 112 18.3 | S26 28.9 |
| 17 | 342 17.2 | 60 32.4 | 01.6 | 271 48.6 | 51.9 | 341 54.1 | 17.8 | 18 18.5 | 37.3 | | | |
| 18 | 357 19.7 | 75 31.4 | S24 01.4 | 286 51.9 | N24 51.8 | 356 56.3 | S 1 17.7 | 33 20.7 | S15 37.2 | Arcturus | 145 49.7 | N19 03.7 |
| 19 | 12 22.2 | 90 30.4 | 01.3 | 301 55.3 | 51.8 | 11 58.6 | 17.7 | 48 23.0 | 37.2 | Atria | 107 14.6 | S69 04.0 |
| 20 | 27 24.6 | 105 29.5 | 01.1 | 316 58.6 | 51.7 | 27 00.9 | 17.6 | 63 25.2 | 37.1 | Avior | 234 14.9 | S59 34.7 |
| 21 | 42 27.1 | 120 28.5 .. | 00.9 | 332 02.0 .. | 51.7 | 42 03.2 .. | 17.5 | 78 27.5 .. | 37.0 | Bellatrix | 278 24.4 | N 6 22.2 |
| 22 | 57 29.6 | 135 27.5 | 00.7 | 347 05.3 | 51.6 | 57 05.5 | 17.4 | 93 29.7 | 37.0 | Betelgeuse | 270 53.6 | N 7 24.7 |
| 23 | 72 32.0 | 150 26.6 | 00.5 | 2 08.7 | 51.6 | 72 07.7 | 17.3 | 108 32.0 | 36.9 | | | |
| **19 00** | 87 34.5 | 165 25.6 | S24 00.4 | 17 12.0 | N24 51.5 | 87 10.0 | S 1 17.2 | 123 34.2 | S15 36.8 | Canopus | 263 52.6 | S52 42.4 |
| 01 | 102 37.0 | 180 24.6 | 00.2 | 32 15.4 | 51.5 | 102 12.3 | 17.1 | 138 36.5 | 36.7 | Capella | 280 23.9 | N46 01.3 |
| 02 | 117 39.4 | 195 23.7 | 24 00.0 | 47 18.7 | 51.4 | 117 14.6 | 17.0 | 153 38.7 | 36.7 | Deneb | 49 27.3 | N45 21.8 |
| 03 | 132 41.9 | 210 22.7 | 23 59.8 | 62 22.1 .. | 51.4 | 132 16.8 .. | 16.9 | 168 41.0 .. | 36.6 | Denebola | 182 26.7 | N14 26.6 |
| 04 | 147 44.4 | 225 21.8 | 59.6 | 77 25.4 | 51.3 | 147 19.1 | 16.8 | 183 43.2 | 36.5 | Diphda | 348 48.9 | S17 51.8 |
| 05 | 162 46.8 | 240 20.8 | 59.4 | 92 28.7 | 51.3 | 162 21.4 | 16.7 | 198 45.5 | 36.5 | | | |
| **M 06** | 177 49.3 | 255 19.8 | S23 59.2 | 107 32.1 | N24 51.2 | 177 23.7 | S 1 16.6 | 213 47.8 | S15 36.4 | Dubhe | 193 43.0 | N61 37.4 |
| **O 07** | 192 51.7 | 270 18.9 | 59.0 | 122 35.4 | 51.2 | 192 26.0 | 16.5 | 228 50.0 | 36.3 | Elnath | 278 03.6 | N28 37.6 |
| **N 08** | 207 54.2 | 285 17.9 | 58.9 | 137 38.7 | 51.1 | 207 28.2 | 16.4 | 243 52.3 | 36.2 | Eltanin | 90 43.5 | N51 29.1 |
| **D 09** | 222 56.7 | 300 16.9 .. | 58.7 | 152 42.1 .. | 51.1 | 222 30.5 .. | 16.4 | 258 54.5 .. | 36.2 | Enif | 33 40.7 | N 9 58.8 |
| **A 10** | 237 59.1 | 315 16.0 | 58.5 | 167 45.4 | 51.0 | 237 32.8 | 16.3 | 273 56.8 | 36.1 | Fomalhaut | 15 16.5 | S29 30.3 |
| **Y 11** | 253 01.6 | 330 15.0 | 58.3 | 182 48.7 | 51.0 | 252 35.1 | 16.2 | 288 59.0 | 36.0 | | | |
| 12 | 268 04.1 | 345 14.1 | S23 58.1 | 197 52.1 | N24 50.9 | 267 37.3 | S 1 16.1 | 304 01.3 | S15 36.0 | Gacrux | 171 53.7 | S57 14.1 |
| 13 | 283 06.5 | 0 13.1 | 57.9 | 212 55.4 | 50.9 | 282 39.6 | 16.0 | 319 03.5 | 35.9 | Gienah | 175 45.4 | S17 40.0 |
| 14 | 298 09.0 | 15 12.1 | 57.7 | 227 58.7 | 50.8 | 297 41.9 | 15.9 | 334 05.8 | 35.8 | Hadar | 148 38.8 | S60 28.7 |
| 15 | 313 11.5 | 30 11.2 .. | 57.5 | 243 02.1 .. | 50.8 | 312 44.2 .. | 15.8 | 349 08.0 .. | 35.7 | Hamal | 327 52.9 | N23 34.3 |
| 16 | 328 13.9 | 45 10.2 | 57.3 | 258 05.4 | 50.7 | 327 46.4 | 15.7 | 4 10.3 | 35.7 | Kaus Aust. | 83 35.2 | S34 22.4 |
| 17 | 343 16.4 | 60 09.3 | 57.1 | 273 08.7 | 50.7 | 342 48.7 | 15.6 | 19 12.5 | 35.6 | | | |
| 18 | 358 18.9 | 75 08.3 | S23 56.9 | 288 12.0 | N24 50.6 | 357 51.0 | S 1 15.5 | 34 14.8 | S15 35.5 | Kochab | 137 20.7 | N74 03.4 |
| 19 | 13 21.3 | 90 07.3 | 56.6 | 303 15.4 | 50.5 | 12 53.2 | 15.4 | 49 17.0 | 35.5 | Markab | 13 31.7 | N15 19.7 |
| 20 | 28 23.8 | 105 06.4 | 56.4 | 318 18.7 | 50.5 | 27 55.5 | 15.3 | 64 19.3 | 35.4 | Menkar | 314 07.7 | N 4 10.8 |
| 21 | 43 26.2 | 120 05.4 .. | 56.2 | 333 22.0 .. | 50.4 | 42 57.8 .. | 15.2 | 79 21.5 .. | 35.3 | Menkent | 147 59.9 | S36 28.7 |
| 22 | 58 28.7 | 135 04.5 | 56.0 | 348 25.3 | 50.4 | 58 00.1 | 15.1 | 94 23.8 | 35.2 | Miaplacidus | 221 38.0 | S69 48.3 |
| 23 | 73 31.2 | 150 03.5 | 55.8 | 3 28.6 | 50.3 | 73 02.3 | 15.0 | 109 26.0 | 35.2 | | | |
| **20 00** | 88 33.6 | 165 02.5 | S23 55.6 | 18 31.9 | N24 50.3 | 88 04.6 | S 1 14.9 | 124 28.3 | S15 35.1 | Mirfak | 308 30.3 | N49 56.7 |
| 01 | 103 36.1 | 180 01.6 | 55.4 | 33 35.3 | 50.2 | 103 06.9 | 14.8 | 139 30.5 | 35.0 | Nunki | 75 50.3 | S26 16.1 |
| 02 | 118 38.6 | 195 00.6 | 55.2 | 48 38.6 | 50.2 | 118 09.1 | 14.7 | 154 32.8 | 35.0 | Peacock | 53 08.9 | S56 39.9 |
| 03 | 133 41.0 | 209 59.7 .. | 54.9 | 63 41.9 .. | 50.1 | 133 11.4 .. | 14.6 | 169 35.0 .. | 34.9 | Pollux | 243 19.1 | N27 58.2 |
| 04 | 148 43.5 | 224 58.7 | 54.7 | 78 45.2 | 50.1 | 148 13.7 | 14.5 | 184 37.3 | 34.8 | Procyon | 244 52.3 | N 5 10.0 |
| 05 | 163 46.0 | 239 57.8 | 54.5 | 93 48.5 | 50.0 | 163 16.0 | 14.4 | 199 39.5 | 34.7 | | | |
| **T 06** | 178 48.4 | 254 56.8 | S23 54.3 | 108 51.8 | N24 50.0 | 178 18.2 | S 1 14.3 | 214 41.8 | S15 34.7 | Rasalhague | 96 00.5 | N12 32.6 |
| **U 07** | 193 50.9 | 269 55.8 | 54.1 | 123 55.1 | 49.9 | 193 20.5 | 14.3 | 229 44.0 | 34.6 | Regulus | 207 36.1 | N11 51.3 |
| **E 08** | 208 53.4 | 284 54.9 | 53.8 | 138 58.4 | 49.9 | 208 22.8 | 14.2 | 244 46.3 | 34.5 | Rigel | 281 05.2 | S 8 10.5 |
| **S 09** | 223 55.8 | 299 53.9 .. | 53.6 | 154 01.7 .. | 49.8 | 223 25.0 .. | 14.1 | 259 48.5 .. | 34.4 | Rigil Kent. | 139 43.1 | S60 55.5 |
| **D 10** | 238 58.3 | 314 53.0 | 53.4 | 169 05.0 | 49.8 | 238 27.3 | 14.0 | 274 50.8 | 34.4 | Sabik | 102 05.1 | S15 45.2 |
| **A 11** | 254 00.7 | 329 52.0 | 53.2 | 184 08.3 | 49.7 | 253 29.6 | 13.9 | 289 53.0 | 34.3 | | | |
| **Y 12** | 269 03.2 | 344 51.1 | S23 52.9 | 199 11.7 | N24 49.7 | 268 31.8 | S 1 13.8 | 304 55.2 | S15 34.2 | Schedar | 349 32.8 | N56 40.0 |
| 13 | 284 05.7 | 359 50.1 | 52.7 | 214 15.0 | 49.6 | 283 34.1 | 13.7 | 319 57.5 | 34.2 | Shaula | 96 13.1 | S37 07.2 |
| 14 | 299 08.1 | 14 49.1 | 52.5 | 229 18.3 | 49.6 | 298 36.4 | 13.6 | 334 59.7 | 34.1 | Sirius | 258 27.4 | S16 44.8 |
| 15 | 314 10.6 | 29 48.2 .. | 52.2 | 244 21.5 .. | 49.5 | 313 38.6 .. | 13.5 | 350 02.0 .. | 34.0 | Spica | 158 24.3 | S11 16.7 |
| 16 | 329 13.1 | 44 47.2 | 52.0 | 259 24.8 | 49.5 | 328 40.9 | 13.4 | 5 04.2 | 33.9 | Suhail | 222 47.3 | S43 31.3 |
| 17 | 344 15.5 | 59 46.3 | 51.8 | 274 28.1 | 49.4 | 343 43.2 | 13.3 | 20 06.5 | 33.9 | | | |
| 18 | 359 18.0 | 74 45.3 | S23 51.5 | 289 31.4 | N24 49.4 | 358 45.4 | S 1 13.2 | 35 08.7 | S15 33.8 | Vega | 80 34.8 | N38 48.3 |
| 19 | 14 20.5 | 89 44.4 | 51.3 | 304 34.7 | 49.3 | 13 47.7 | 13.1 | 50 11.0 | 33.7 | Zuben'ubi | 136 58.2 | S16 08.1 |
| 20 | 29 22.9 | 104 43.4 | 51.0 | 319 38.0 | 49.3 | 28 50.0 | 13.0 | 65 13.2 | 33.7 | | | |
| 21 | 44 25.4 | 119 42.5 .. | 50.8 | 334 41.3 .. | 49.2 | 43 52.2 .. | 12.9 | 80 15.5 .. | 33.6 | | | |
| 22 | 59 27.8 | 134 41.5 | 50.6 | 349 44.6 | 49.1 | 58 54.5 | 12.8 | 95 17.7 | 33.5 | | | |
| 23 | 74 30.3 | 149 40.6 | 50.3 | 4 47.9 | 49.1 | 73 56.8 | 12.7 | 110 20.0 | 33.4 | | | |

| | SHA | Mer. Pass. |
|---|---|---|
| | ° ′ | h m |
| Venus | 77 51.1 | 12 59 |
| Mars | 289 37.5 | 22 46 |
| Jupiter | 359 35.5 | 18 09 |
| Saturn | 35 59.7 | 15 43 |

Mer. Pass. 18 06.7 | v −1.0 d 0.2 | v 3.3 d 0.1 | v 2.3 d 0.1 | v 2.3 d 0.1

| UT | SUN GHA | SUN Dec | MOON GHA | v | MOON Dec | d | HP |
|---|---|---|---|---|---|---|---|
| d h | ° ′ | ° ′ | ° ′ | ′ | ° ′ | ′ | ′ |
| **18 00** | 180 55.4 | S23 22.7 | 251 55.9 | 14.6 | S 3 39.8 | 14.8 | 56.7 |
| 01 | 195 55.1 | 22.8 | 266 29.5 | 14.5 | 3 54.6 | 14.9 | 56.8 |
| 02 | 210 54.8 | 22.8 | 281 03.0 | 14.5 | 4 09.5 | 14.8 | 56.8 |
| 03 | 225 54.5 | .. 22.9 | 295 36.5 | 14.4 | 4 24.3 | 14.8 | 56.8 |
| 04 | 240 54.2 | 23.0 | 310 09.9 | 14.3 | 4 39.1 | 14.8 | 56.9 |
| 05 | 255 53.9 | 23.1 | 324 43.2 | 14.3 | 4 53.9 | 14.9 | 56.9 |
| 06 | 270 53.6 | S23 23.1 | 339 16.5 | 14.3 | S 5 08.8 | 14.8 | 57.0 |
| 07 | 285 53.3 | 23.2 | 353 49.8 | 14.1 | 5 23.6 | 14.8 | 57.0 |
| **S** 08 | 300 52.9 | 23.3 | 8 22.9 | 14.1 | 5 38.4 | 14.8 | 57.0 |
| **U** 09 | 315 52.6 | .. 23.3 | 22 56.0 | 14.1 | 5 53.2 | 14.8 | 57.1 |
| **N** 10 | 330 52.3 | 23.4 | 37 29.1 | 13.9 | 6 08.0 | 14.8 | 57.1 |
| **D** 11 | 345 52.0 | 23.5 | 52 02.0 | 13.9 | 6 22.8 | 14.8 | 57.1 |
| **A** 12 | 0 51.7 | S23 23.5 | 66 34.9 | 13.9 | S 6 37.6 | 14.8 | 57.2 |
| **Y** 13 | 15 51.4 | 23.6 | 81 07.8 | 13.7 | 6 52.4 | 14.8 | 57.2 |
| 14 | 30 51.1 | 23.7 | 95 40.5 | 13.7 | 7 07.2 | 14.7 | 57.3 |
| 15 | 45 50.8 | .. 23.7 | 110 13.2 | 13.6 | 7 21.9 | 14.8 | 57.3 |
| 16 | 60 50.5 | 23.8 | 124 45.8 | 13.5 | 7 36.7 | 14.7 | 57.3 |
| 17 | 75 50.2 | 23.9 | 139 18.3 | 13.4 | 7 51.4 | 14.8 | 57.4 |
| 18 | 90 49.9 | S23 23.9 | 153 50.7 | 13.4 | S 8 06.2 | 14.7 | 57.4 |
| 19 | 105 49.6 | 24.0 | 168 23.1 | 13.3 | 8 20.9 | 14.7 | 57.5 |
| 20 | 120 49.2 | 24.1 | 182 55.4 | 13.2 | 8 35.6 | 14.6 | 57.5 |
| 21 | 135 48.9 | .. 24.1 | 197 27.6 | 13.1 | 8 50.2 | 14.7 | 57.5 |
| 22 | 150 48.6 | 24.2 | 211 59.7 | 13.0 | 9 04.9 | 14.6 | 57.6 |
| 23 | 165 48.3 | 24.2 | 226 31.7 | 13.0 | 9 19.5 | 14.7 | 57.6 |
| **19 00** | 180 48.0 | S23 24.3 | 241 03.7 | 12.9 | S 9 34.2 | 14.6 | 57.7 |
| 01 | 195 47.7 | 24.3 | 255 35.5 | 12.8 | 9 48.8 | 14.5 | 57.7 |
| 02 | 210 47.4 | 24.4 | 270 07.3 | 12.6 | 10 03.3 | 14.6 | 57.7 |
| 03 | 225 47.1 | .. 24.5 | 284 38.9 | 12.6 | 10 17.9 | 14.5 | 57.8 |
| 04 | 240 46.8 | 24.5 | 299 10.5 | 12.5 | 10 32.4 | 14.5 | 57.8 |
| 05 | 255 46.5 | 24.6 | 313 42.0 | 12.4 | 10 46.9 | 14.4 | 57.9 |
| 06 | 270 46.2 | S23 24.6 | 328 13.4 | 12.3 | S11 01.3 | 14.4 | 57.9 |
| 07 | 285 45.9 | 24.7 | 342 44.7 | 12.2 | 11 15.7 | 14.4 | 57.9 |
| **M** 08 | 300 45.5 | 24.7 | 357 15.9 | 12.1 | 11 30.1 | 14.4 | 58.0 |
| **O** 09 | 315 45.2 | .. 24.8 | 11 47.0 | 12.0 | 11 44.5 | 14.3 | 58.0 |
| **N** 10 | 330 44.9 | 24.8 | 26 18.0 | 11.9 | 11 58.8 | 14.3 | 58.1 |
| **D** 11 | 345 44.6 | 24.9 | 40 48.9 | 11.7 | 12 13.1 | 14.2 | 58.1 |
| **A** 12 | 0 44.3 | S23 24.9 | 55 19.6 | 11.7 | S12 27.3 | 14.2 | 58.1 |
| **Y** 13 | 15 44.0 | 25.0 | 69 50.3 | 11.6 | 12 41.5 | 14.2 | 58.2 |
| 14 | 30 43.7 | 25.0 | 84 20.9 | 11.5 | 12 55.7 | 14.1 | 58.2 |
| 15 | 45 43.4 | .. 25.1 | 98 51.4 | 11.3 | 13 09.8 | 14.1 | 58.3 |
| 16 | 60 43.1 | 25.1 | 113 21.7 | 11.3 | 13 23.9 | 14.0 | 58.3 |
| 17 | 75 42.8 | 25.1 | 127 52.0 | 11.1 | 13 37.9 | 13.9 | 58.3 |
| 18 | 90 42.5 | S23 25.2 | 142 22.1 | 11.0 | S13 51.8 | 14.0 | 58.4 |
| 19 | 105 42.1 | 25.2 | 156 52.1 | 11.0 | 14 05.8 | 13.8 | 58.4 |
| 20 | 120 41.8 | 25.3 | 171 22.1 | 10.8 | 14 19.6 | 13.8 | 58.5 |
| 21 | 135 41.5 | .. 25.3 | 185 51.9 | 10.6 | 14 33.4 | 13.8 | 58.5 |
| 22 | 150 41.2 | 25.4 | 200 21.5 | 10.6 | 14 47.2 | 13.7 | 58.5 |
| 23 | 165 40.9 | 25.4 | 214 51.1 | 10.5 | 15 00.9 | 13.6 | 58.6 |
| **20 00** | 180 40.6 | S23 25.4 | 229 20.6 | 10.3 | S15 14.5 | 13.6 | 58.6 |
| 01 | 195 40.3 | 25.5 | 243 49.9 | 10.2 | 15 28.1 | 13.6 | 58.7 |
| 02 | 210 40.0 | 25.5 | 258 19.1 | 10.1 | 15 41.6 | 13.5 | 58.7 |
| 03 | 225 39.7 | .. 25.5 | 272 48.2 | 9.9 | 15 55.1 | 13.4 | 58.7 |
| 04 | 240 39.4 | 25.6 | 287 17.1 | 9.9 | 16 08.5 | 13.3 | 58.8 |
| 05 | 255 39.0 | 25.6 | 301 46.0 | 9.7 | 16 21.8 | 13.2 | 58.8 |
| 06 | 270 38.7 | S23 25.6 | 316 14.7 | 9.6 | S16 35.0 | 13.2 | 58.9 |
| 07 | 285 38.4 | 25.7 | 330 43.3 | 9.5 | 16 48.2 | 13.1 | 58.9 |
| **T** 08 | 300 38.1 | 25.7 | 345 11.8 | 9.3 | 17 01.3 | 13.0 | 58.9 |
| **U** 09 | 315 37.8 | .. 25.7 | 359 40.1 | 9.2 | 17 14.3 | 13.0 | 59.0 |
| **E** 10 | 330 37.5 | 25.8 | 14 08.3 | 9.1 | 17 27.3 | 12.8 | 59.0 |
| **S** 11 | 345 37.2 | 25.8 | 28 36.4 | 8.9 | 17 40.1 | 12.8 | 59.1 |
| **D** 12 | 0 36.9 | S23 25.8 | 43 04.3 | 8.8 | S17 52.9 | 12.7 | 59.1 |
| **A** 13 | 15 36.6 | 25.8 | 57 32.1 | 8.7 | 18 05.6 | 12.6 | 59.1 |
| **Y** 14 | 30 36.2 | 25.9 | 71 59.8 | 8.6 | 18 18.2 | 12.5 | 59.2 |
| 15 | 45 35.9 | .. 25.9 | 86 27.4 | 8.4 | 18 30.7 | 12.5 | 59.2 |
| 16 | 60 35.6 | 25.9 | 100 54.8 | 8.3 | 18 43.2 | 12.3 | 59.3 |
| 17 | 75 35.3 | 25.9 | 115 22.1 | 8.1 | 18 55.5 | 12.3 | 59.3 |
| 18 | 90 35.0 | S23 26.0 | 129 49.2 | 8.1 | S19 07.8 | 12.1 | 59.3 |
| 19 | 105 34.7 | 26.0 | 144 16.3 | 7.8 | 19 19.9 | 12.1 | 59.4 |
| 20 | 120 34.4 | 26.0 | 158 43.1 | 7.8 | 19 32.0 | 11.9 | 59.4 |
| 21 | 135 34.1 | .. 26.0 | 173 09.9 | 7.6 | 19 43.9 | 11.9 | 59.4 |
| 22 | 150 33.8 | 26.1 | 187 36.5 | 7.5 | 19 55.8 | 11.7 | 59.5 |
| 23 | 165 33.4 | 26.1 | 202 03.0 | 7.3 | S20 07.5 | 11.6 | 59.5 |
| | SD 16.3 | d 0.0 | SD 15.6 | | 15.8 | | 16.1 |

### Twilight / Sunrise / Moonrise

| Lat. | Naut. | Civil | Sunrise | 18 | 19 | 20 | 21 |
|---|---|---|---|---|---|---|---|
| ° | h m | h m | h m | h m | h m | h m | h m |
| N 72 | 08 24 | 10 55 | ■ | 02 10 | 04 28 | 07 44 | ■ |
| N 70 | 08 04 | 09 53 | ■ | 02 04 | 04 09 | 06 43 | ■ |
| 68 | 07 48 | 09 18 | ■ | 01 58 | 03 54 | 06 08 | ■ |
| 66 | 07 35 | 08 52 | 10 33 | 01 54 | 03 42 | 05 44 | 08 14 |
| 64 | 07 24 | 08 33 | 09 51 | 01 51 | 03 32 | 05 25 | 07 33 |
| 62 | 07 14 | 08 16 | 09 22 | 01 48 | 03 24 | 05 09 | 07 05 |
| 60 | 07 06 | 08 03 | 09 01 | 01 45 | 03 17 | 04 56 | 06 44 |
| N 58 | 06 58 | 07 51 | 08 43 | 01 42 | 03 11 | 04 45 | 06 27 |
| 56 | 06 52 | 07 41 | 08 28 | 01 40 | 03 05 | 04 36 | 06 12 |
| 54 | 06 46 | 07 32 | 08 16 | 01 38 | 03 00 | 04 28 | 06 00 |
| 52 | 06 40 | 07 24 | 08 05 | 01 37 | 02 56 | 04 20 | 05 49 |
| 50 | 06 35 | 07 16 | 07 55 | 01 35 | 02 52 | 04 13 | 05 39 |
| 45 | 06 23 | 07 00 | 07 34 | 01 32 | 02 43 | 03 59 | 05 19 |
| N 40 | 06 12 | 06 46 | 07 17 | 01 29 | 02 36 | 03 47 | 05 03 |
| 35 | 06 03 | 06 35 | 07 03 | 01 27 | 02 30 | 03 37 | 04 49 |
| 30 | 05 54 | 06 24 | 06 51 | 01 25 | 02 25 | 03 29 | 04 37 |
| 20 | 05 38 | 06 05 | 06 29 | 01 21 | 02 15 | 03 14 | 04 17 |
| N 10 | 05 22 | 05 48 | 06 11 | 01 18 | 02 07 | 03 01 | 03 59 |
| 0 | 05 05 | 05 31 | 05 53 | 01 15 | 02 00 | 02 49 | 03 43 |
| S 10 | 04 46 | 05 13 | 05 36 | 01 12 | 01 53 | 02 37 | 03 27 |
| 20 | 04 23 | 04 52 | 05 17 | 01 09 | 01 45 | 02 25 | 03 10 |
| 30 | 03 54 | 04 27 | 04 55 | 01 06 | 01 36 | 02 10 | 02 50 |
| 35 | 03 35 | 04 12 | 04 42 | 01 04 | 01 31 | 02 02 | 02 39 |
| 40 | 03 12 | 03 54 | 04 27 | 01 02 | 01 25 | 01 53 | 02 26 |
| 45 | 02 41 | 03 31 | 04 09 | 00 59 | 01 19 | 01 42 | 02 11 |
| S 50 | 01 56 | 03 01 | 03 46 | 00 56 | 01 11 | 01 29 | 01 53 |
| 52 | 01 28 | 02 46 | 03 35 | 00 55 | 01 07 | 01 23 | 01 44 |
| 54 | 00 44 | 02 28 | 03 23 | 00 53 | 01 04 | 01 16 | 01 34 |
| 56 | //// | 02 06 | 03 09 | 00 52 | 00 59 | 01 09 | 01 23 |
| 58 | //// | 01 36 | 02 52 | 00 50 | 00 54 | 01 01 | 01 11 |
| S 60 | //// | 00 45 | 02 31 | 00 48 | 00 49 | 00 51 | 00 56 |

### Sunset / Twilight / Moonset

| Lat. | Sunset | Civil | Naut. | 18 | 19 | 20 | 21 |
|---|---|---|---|---|---|---|---|
| ° | h m | h m | h m | h m | h m | h m | h m |
| N 72 | ■ | 12 59 | 15 30 | 12 08 | 11 26 | 09 54 | ■ |
| N 70 | ■ | 14 01 | 15 50 | 12 17 | 11 47 | 10 58 | ■ |
| 68 | ■ | 14 36 | 16 06 | 12 25 | 12 04 | 11 34 | ■ |
| 66 | 13 21 | 15 02 | 16 19 | 12 32 | 12 18 | 12 00 | 11 25 |
| 64 | 14 03 | 15 21 | 16 30 | 12 37 | 12 29 | 12 20 | 12 06 |
| 62 | 14 32 | 15 38 | 16 40 | 12 42 | 12 39 | 12 37 | 12 35 |
| 60 | 14 53 | 15 51 | 16 48 | 12 46 | 12 48 | 12 50 | 12 57 |
| N 58 | 15 11 | 16 03 | 16 56 | 12 50 | 12 55 | 13 02 | 13 15 |
| 56 | 15 26 | 16 13 | 17 02 | 12 53 | 13 02 | 13 13 | 13 30 |
| 54 | 15 38 | 16 22 | 17 08 | 12 56 | 13 07 | 13 22 | 13 43 |
| 52 | 15 49 | 16 30 | 17 14 | 12 59 | 13 13 | 13 30 | 13 55 |
| 50 | 15 59 | 16 38 | 17 19 | 13 02 | 13 18 | 13 38 | 14 05 |
| 45 | 16 20 | 16 54 | 17 31 | 13 07 | 13 28 | 13 54 | 14 26 |
| N 40 | 16 37 | 17 08 | 17 42 | 13 12 | 13 37 | 14 07 | 14 44 |
| 35 | 16 51 | 17 19 | 17 51 | 13 16 | 13 45 | 14 18 | 14 59 |
| 30 | 17 04 | 17 30 | 18 00 | 13 19 | 13 51 | 14 28 | 15 12 |
| 20 | 17 25 | 17 49 | 18 16 | 13 25 | 14 03 | 14 45 | 15 34 |
| N 10 | 17 43 | 18 06 | 18 33 | 13 31 | 14 13 | 15 00 | 15 53 |
| 0 | 18 01 | 18 23 | 18 50 | 13 36 | 14 23 | 15 14 | 16 11 |
| S 10 | 18 18 | 18 41 | 19 09 | 13 41 | 14 32 | 15 28 | 16 29 |
| 20 | 18 37 | 19 02 | 19 31 | 13 47 | 14 43 | 15 43 | 16 48 |
| 30 | 18 59 | 19 27 | 20 00 | 13 53 | 14 55 | 16 01 | 17 11 |
| 35 | 19 12 | 19 42 | 20 19 | 13 57 | 15 02 | 16 11 | 17 24 |
| 40 | 19 28 | 20 00 | 20 42 | 14 01 | 15 10 | 16 23 | 17 39 |
| 45 | 19 46 | 20 23 | 21 13 | 14 06 | 15 19 | 16 37 | 17 58 |
| S 50 | 20 08 | 20 53 | 21 59 | 14 11 | 15 30 | 16 54 | 18 20 |
| 52 | 20 19 | 21 08 | 22 26 | 14 14 | 15 35 | 17 02 | 18 31 |
| 54 | 20 31 | 21 26 | 23 13 | 14 17 | 15 41 | 17 11 | 18 44 |
| 56 | 20 46 | 21 48 | //// | 14 20 | 15 47 | 17 21 | 18 58 |
| 58 | 21 02 | 22 18 | //// | 14 24 | 15 55 | 17 32 | 19 15 |
| S 60 | 21 23 | 23 09 | //// | 14 28 | 16 03 | 17 46 | 19 36 |

### SUN / MOON

| Day | Eqn. of Time 00h | Eqn. of Time 12h | Mer. Pass. | Mer. Pass. Upper | Mer. Pass. Lower | Age | Phase |
|---|---|---|---|---|---|---|---|
| d | m s | m s | h m | h m | h m | d | % |
| 18 | 03 42 | 03 27 | 11 57 | 07 25 | 19 48 | 25 | 29 |
| 19 | 03 13 | 02 58 | 11 57 | 08 11 | 20 36 | 26 | 20 |
| 20 | 02 43 | 02 28 | 11 58 | 09 01 | 21 28 | 27 | 12 |

| UT | ARIES GHA | VENUS −3.9 GHA | Dec | MARS −1.5 GHA | Dec | JUPITER −2.4 GHA | Dec | SATURN +0.8 GHA | Dec | STARS Name | SHA | Dec |
|---|---|---|---|---|---|---|---|---|---|---|---|---|
| **21** 00 | 89 32.8 | 164 39.6 | S23 50.1 | 19 51.2 | N24 49.0 | 88 59.0 | S 1 12.6 | 125 22.2 | S15 33.4 | Acamar | 315 12.8 | S40 13.0 |
| 01 | 104 35.2 | 179 38.6 | 49.8 | 34 54.5 | 49.0 | 104 01.3 | 12.5 | 140 24.5 | 33.3 | Achernar | 335 21.2 | S57 07.5 |
| 02 | 119 37.7 | 194 37.7 | 49.6 | 49 57.8 | 48.9 | 119 03.5 | 12.4 | 155 26.7 | 33.2 | Acrux | 173 02.0 | S63 13.2 |
| 03 | 134 40.2 | 209 36.7 | .. 49.3 | 65 01.0 | .. 48.9 | 134 05.8 | .. 12.3 | 170 29.0 | .. 33.1 | Adhara | 255 06.8 | S29 00.1 |
| 04 | 149 42.6 | 224 35.8 | 49.1 | 80 04.3 | 48.8 | 149 08.1 | 12.2 | 185 31.2 | 33.1 | Aldebaran | 290 41.2 | N16 33.3 |
| 05 | 164 45.1 | 239 34.8 | 48.8 | 95 07.6 | 48.8 | 164 10.3 | 12.1 | 200 33.5 | 33.0 | | | |
| 06 | 179 47.6 | 254 33.9 | S23 48.6 | 110 10.9 | N24 48.7 | 179 12.6 | S 1 12.0 | 215 35.7 | S15 32.9 | Alioth | 166 14.6 | N55 49.9 |
| W 07 | 194 50.0 | 269 32.9 | 48.3 | 125 14.2 | 48.7 | 194 14.9 | 11.9 | 230 37.9 | 32.9 | Alkaid | 152 53.6 | N49 11.7 |
| E 08 | 209 52.5 | 284 32.0 | 48.1 | 140 17.4 | 48.6 | 209 17.1 | 11.8 | 245 40.2 | 32.8 | Alnair | 27 35.3 | S46 51.3 |
| D 09 | 224 55.0 | 299 31.0 | .. 47.8 | 155 20.7 | .. 48.6 | 224 19.4 | .. 11.7 | 260 42.4 | .. 32.7 | Alnilam | 275 39.1 | S 1 11.2 |
| N 10 | 239 57.4 | 314 30.1 | 47.6 | 170 24.0 | 48.5 | 239 21.6 | 11.6 | 275 44.7 | 32.6 | Alphard | 217 49.2 | S 8 45.4 |
| E 11 | 254 59.9 | 329 29.1 | 47.3 | 185 27.3 | 48.5 | 254 23.9 | 11.5 | 290 46.9 | 32.6 | | | |
| S 12 | 270 02.3 | 344 28.2 | S23 47.0 | 200 30.5 | N24 48.4 | 269 26.2 | S 1 11.4 | 305 49.2 | S15 32.5 | Alphecca | 126 05.5 | N26 38.2 |
| D 13 | 285 04.8 | 359 27.2 | 46.8 | 215 33.8 | 48.3 | 284 28.4 | 11.3 | 320 51.4 | 32.4 | Alpheratz | 357 36.5 | N29 13.1 |
| A 14 | 300 07.3 | 14 26.3 | 46.5 | 230 37.1 | 48.3 | 299 30.7 | 11.2 | 335 53.7 | 32.3 | Altair | 62 01.9 | N 8 55.7 |
| Y 15 | 315 09.7 | 29 25.3 | .. 46.3 | 245 40.3 | .. 48.2 | 314 32.9 | .. 11.1 | 350 55.9 | .. 32.3 | Ankaa | 353 08.8 | S42 11.2 |
| 16 | 330 12.2 | 44 24.4 | 46.0 | 260 43.6 | 48.2 | 329 35.2 | 11.0 | 5 58.2 | 32.2 | Antares | 112 18.3 | S26 28.9 |
| 17 | 345 14.7 | 59 23.4 | 45.7 | 275 46.9 | 48.1 | 344 37.5 | 10.9 | 21 00.4 | 32.1 | | | |
| 18 | 0 17.1 | 74 22.5 | S23 45.5 | 290 50.1 | N24 48.1 | 359 39.7 | S 1 10.8 | 36 02.6 | S15 32.0 | Arcturus | 145 49.7 | N19 03.7 |
| 19 | 15 19.6 | 89 21.5 | 45.2 | 305 53.4 | 48.0 | 14 42.0 | 10.7 | 51 04.9 | 32.0 | Atria | 107 14.6 | S69 04.0 |
| 20 | 30 22.1 | 104 20.6 | 44.9 | 320 56.7 | 48.0 | 29 44.2 | 10.6 | 66 07.1 | 31.9 | Avior | 234 14.9 | S59 34.7 |
| 21 | 45 24.5 | 119 19.6 | .. 44.7 | 335 59.9 | .. 47.9 | 44 46.5 | .. 10.5 | 81 09.4 | .. 31.8 | Bellatrix | 278 24.4 | N 6 22.2 |
| 22 | 60 27.0 | 134 18.7 | 44.4 | 351 03.2 | 47.9 | 59 48.8 | 10.4 | 96 11.6 | 31.8 | Betelgeuse | 270 53.6 | N 7 24.7 |
| 23 | 75 29.5 | 149 17.7 | 44.1 | 6 06.4 | 47.8 | 74 51.0 | 10.3 | 111 13.9 | 31.7 | | | |
| **22** 00 | 90 31.9 | 164 16.8 | S23 43.8 | 21 09.7 | N24 47.8 | 89 53.3 | S 1 10.2 | 126 16.1 | S15 31.6 | Canopus | 263 52.6 | S52 42.4 |
| 01 | 105 34.4 | 179 15.8 | 43.6 | 36 13.0 | 47.7 | 104 55.5 | 10.1 | 141 18.4 | 31.5 | Capella | 280 23.9 | N46 01.3 |
| 02 | 120 36.8 | 194 14.9 | 43.3 | 51 16.2 | 47.6 | 119 57.8 | 10.0 | 156 20.6 | 31.5 | Deneb | 49 27.3 | N45 21.8 |
| 03 | 135 39.3 | 209 13.9 | .. 43.0 | 66 19.5 | .. 47.6 | 135 00.0 | .. 09.9 | 171 22.8 | .. 31.4 | Denebola | 182 26.7 | N14 26.6 |
| 04 | 150 41.8 | 224 13.0 | 42.7 | 81 22.7 | 47.5 | 150 02.3 | 09.8 | 186 25.1 | 31.3 | Diphda | 348 48.9 | S17 51.8 |
| 05 | 165 44.2 | 239 12.1 | 42.4 | 96 26.0 | 47.5 | 165 04.5 | 09.7 | 201 27.3 | 31.2 | | | |
| 06 | 180 46.7 | 254 11.1 | S23 42.2 | 111 29.2 | N24 47.4 | 180 06.8 | S 1 09.6 | 216 29.6 | S15 31.2 | Dubhe | 193 42.9 | N61 37.4 |
| T 07 | 195 49.2 | 269 10.2 | 41.9 | 126 32.5 | 47.4 | 195 09.1 | 09.5 | 231 31.8 | 31.1 | Elnath | 278 03.6 | N28 37.6 |
| H 08 | 210 51.6 | 284 09.2 | 41.6 | 141 35.7 | 47.3 | 210 11.3 | 09.4 | 246 34.1 | 31.0 | Eltanin | 90 43.5 | N51 29.1 |
| U 09 | 225 54.1 | 299 08.3 | .. 41.3 | 156 38.9 | .. 47.3 | 225 13.6 | .. 09.3 | 261 36.3 | .. 30.9 | Enif | 33 40.7 | N 9 58.8 |
| R 10 | 240 56.6 | 314 07.3 | 41.0 | 171 42.2 | 47.2 | 240 15.8 | 09.2 | 276 38.5 | 30.9 | Fomalhaut | 15 16.5 | S29 30.3 |
| S 11 | 255 59.0 | 329 06.4 | 40.7 | 186 45.4 | 47.2 | 255 18.1 | 09.1 | 291 40.8 | 30.8 | | | |
| D 12 | 271 01.5 | 344 05.4 | S23 40.4 | 201 48.7 | N24 47.1 | 270 20.3 | S 1 09.0 | 306 43.0 | S15 30.7 | Gacrux | 171 53.6 | S57 14.1 |
| A 13 | 286 04.0 | 359 04.5 | 40.1 | 216 51.9 | 47.1 | 285 22.6 | 08.8 | 321 45.3 | 30.6 | Gienah | 175 45.4 | S17 40.0 |
| Y 14 | 301 06.4 | 14 03.5 | 39.9 | 231 55.2 | 47.0 | 300 24.8 | 08.7 | 336 47.5 | 30.6 | Hadar | 148 38.8 | S60 28.7 |
| 15 | 316 08.9 | 29 02.6 | .. 39.6 | 246 58.4 | .. 46.9 | 315 27.1 | .. 08.6 | 351 49.8 | .. 30.5 | Hamal | 327 52.9 | N23 34.3 |
| 16 | 331 11.3 | 44 01.7 | 39.3 | 262 01.6 | 46.9 | 330 29.3 | 08.5 | 6 52.0 | 30.4 | Kaus Aust. | 83 35.2 | S34 22.4 |
| 17 | 346 13.8 | 59 00.7 | 39.0 | 277 04.9 | 46.8 | 345 31.6 | 08.4 | 21 54.2 | 30.3 | | | |
| 18 | 1 16.3 | 73 59.8 | S23 38.7 | 292 08.1 | N24 46.8 | 0 33.8 | S 1 08.3 | 36 56.5 | S15 30.3 | Kochab | 137 20.6 | N74 03.4 |
| 19 | 16 18.7 | 88 58.8 | 38.4 | 307 11.3 | 46.7 | 15 36.1 | 08.2 | 51 58.7 | 30.2 | Markab | 13 31.7 | N15 19.7 |
| 20 | 31 21.2 | 103 57.9 | 38.1 | 322 14.6 | 46.7 | 30 38.3 | 08.1 | 67 01.0 | 30.1 | Menkar | 314 07.7 | N 4 10.8 |
| 21 | 46 23.7 | 118 56.9 | .. 37.8 | 337 17.8 | .. 46.6 | 45 40.6 | .. 08.0 | 82 03.2 | .. 30.1 | Menkent | 147 59.9 | S36 28.7 |
| 22 | 61 26.1 | 133 56.0 | 37.5 | 352 21.0 | 46.6 | 60 42.9 | 07.9 | 97 05.5 | 30.0 | Miaplacidus | 221 37.9 | S69 48.4 |
| 23 | 76 28.6 | 148 55.1 | 37.2 | 7 24.2 | 46.5 | 75 45.1 | 07.8 | 112 07.7 | 29.9 | | | |
| **23** 00 | 91 31.1 | 163 54.1 | S23 36.9 | 22 27.5 | N24 46.5 | 90 47.4 | S 1 07.7 | 127 09.9 | S15 29.8 | Mirfak | 308 30.3 | N49 56.7 |
| 01 | 106 33.5 | 178 53.2 | 36.5 | 37 30.7 | 46.4 | 105 49.6 | 07.6 | 142 12.2 | 29.8 | Nunki | 75 50.2 | S26 16.1 |
| 02 | 121 36.0 | 193 52.2 | 36.2 | 52 33.9 | 46.3 | 120 51.9 | 07.5 | 157 14.4 | 29.7 | Peacock | 53 08.9 | S56 39.9 |
| 03 | 136 38.5 | 208 51.3 | .. 35.9 | 67 37.1 | .. 46.3 | 135 54.1 | .. 07.4 | 172 16.7 | .. 29.6 | Pollux | 243 19.0 | N27 58.2 |
| 04 | 151 40.9 | 223 50.4 | 35.6 | 82 40.3 | 46.2 | 150 56.3 | 07.3 | 187 18.9 | 29.5 | Procyon | 244 52.3 | N 5 10.0 |
| 05 | 166 43.4 | 238 49.4 | 35.3 | 97 43.6 | 46.2 | 165 58.6 | 07.2 | 202 21.1 | 29.5 | | | |
| 06 | 181 45.8 | 253 48.5 | S23 35.0 | 112 46.8 | N24 46.1 | 181 00.8 | S 1 07.1 | 217 23.4 | S15 29.4 | Rasalhague | 96 00.5 | N12 32.6 |
| 07 | 196 48.3 | 268 47.5 | 34.7 | 127 50.0 | 46.1 | 196 03.1 | 07.0 | 232 25.6 | 29.3 | Regulus | 207 36.1 | N11 51.3 |
| F 08 | 211 50.8 | 283 46.6 | 34.4 | 142 53.2 | 46.0 | 211 05.3 | 06.9 | 247 27.9 | 29.2 | Rigel | 281 05.2 | S 8 10.5 |
| R 09 | 226 53.2 | 298 45.7 | .. 34.1 | 157 56.4 | .. 46.0 | 226 07.6 | .. 06.8 | 262 30.1 | .. 29.2 | Rigil Kent. | 139 43.1 | S60 55.5 |
| I 10 | 241 55.7 | 313 44.7 | 33.7 | 172 59.6 | 45.9 | 241 09.8 | 06.6 | 277 32.3 | 29.1 | Sabik | 102 05.1 | S15 45.2 |
| D 11 | 256 58.2 | 328 43.8 | 33.4 | 188 02.8 | 45.9 | 256 12.1 | 06.5 | 292 34.6 | 29.0 | | | |
| A 12 | 272 00.6 | 343 42.8 | S23 33.1 | 203 06.1 | N24 45.8 | 271 14.3 | S 1 06.4 | 307 36.8 | S15 28.9 | Schedar | 349 32.9 | N56 40.0 |
| Y 13 | 287 03.1 | 358 41.9 | 32.8 | 218 09.3 | 45.7 | 286 16.6 | 06.3 | 322 39.1 | 28.9 | Shaula | 96 13.1 | S37 07.2 |
| 14 | 302 05.6 | 13 41.0 | 32.5 | 233 12.5 | 45.7 | 301 18.8 | 06.2 | 337 41.3 | 28.8 | Sirius | 258 27.4 | S16 44.8 |
| 15 | 317 08.0 | 28 40.0 | .. 32.1 | 248 15.7 | .. 45.6 | 316 21.1 | .. 06.1 | 352 43.5 | .. 28.7 | Spica | 158 24.2 | S11 16.7 |
| 16 | 332 10.5 | 43 39.1 | 31.8 | 263 18.9 | 45.6 | 331 23.3 | 06.0 | 7 45.8 | 28.6 | Suhail | 222 47.2 | S43 31.3 |
| 17 | 347 13.0 | 58 38.2 | 31.5 | 278 22.1 | 45.5 | 346 25.6 | 05.9 | 22 48.0 | 28.6 | | | |
| 18 | 2 15.4 | 73 37.2 | S23 31.1 | 293 25.3 | N24 45.5 | 1 27.8 | S 1 05.8 | 37 50.3 | S15 28.5 | Vega | 80 34.8 | N38 48.3 |
| 19 | 17 17.9 | 88 36.3 | 30.8 | 308 28.5 | 45.4 | 16 30.1 | 05.7 | 52 52.5 | 28.4 | Zuben'ubi | 136 58.1 | S16 08.1 |
| 20 | 32 20.3 | 103 35.3 | 30.5 | 323 31.7 | 45.4 | 31 32.3 | 05.6 | 67 54.7 | 28.3 | | SHA | Mer. Pass. |
| 21 | 47 22.8 | 118 34.4 | .. 30.2 | 338 34.9 | .. 45.3 | 46 34.5 | .. 05.5 | 82 57.0 | .. 28.3 | | | |
| 22 | 62 25.3 | 133 33.5 | 29.8 | 353 38.1 | 45.2 | 61 36.8 | 05.4 | 97 59.2 | 28.2 | Venus | 73 44.9 | 13 04 |
| 23 | 77 27.7 | 148 32.5 | 29.5 | 8 41.3 | 45.2 | 76 39.0 | 05.3 | 113 01.5 | 28.1 | Mars | 290 37.8 | 22 30 |
| Mer. Pass. 17 54.9 | | v −0.9 | d 0.3 | v 3.2 | d 0.1 | v 2.3 | d 0.1 | v 2.2 | d 0.1 | Jupiter | 359 21.3 | 17 58 |
| | | | | | | | | | | Saturn | 35 44.2 | 15 33 |

| UT | SUN GHA | SUN Dec | MOON GHA | v | MOON Dec | d | HP |
|---|---|---|---|---|---|---|---|
| d h | ° ′ | ° ′ | ° ′ | ′ | ° ′ | ′ | ′ |
| **21** 00 | 180 33.1 | S23 26.1 | 216 29.3 | 7.2 | S20 19.1 | 11.6 | 59.6 |
| 01 | 195 32.8 | 26.1 | 230 55.5 | 7.1 | 20 30.7 | 11.4 | 59.6 |
| 02 | 210 32.5 | 26.1 | 245 21.6 | 6.9 | 20 42.1 | 11.3 | 59.6 |
| 03 | 225 32.2 | .. 26.1 | 259 47.5 | 6.8 | 20 53.4 | 11.2 | 59.7 |
| 04 | 240 31.9 | 26.2 | 274 13.3 | 6.6 | 21 04.6 | 11.0 | 59.7 |
| 05 | 255 31.6 | 26.2 | 288 38.9 | 6.5 | 21 15.6 | 11.0 | 59.7 |
| 06 | 270 31.3 | S23 26.2 | 303 04.4 | 6.4 | S21 26.6 | 10.8 | 59.8 |
| W 07 | 285 31.0 | 26.2 | 317 29.8 | 6.3 | 21 37.4 | 10.7 | 59.8 |
| E 08 | 300 30.6 | 26.2 | 331 55.1 | 6.1 | 21 48.1 | 10.6 | 59.8 |
| D 09 | 315 30.3 | .. 26.2 | 346 20.2 | 5.9 | 21 58.7 | 10.4 | 59.9 |
| N 10 | 330 30.0 | 26.2 | 0 45.1 | 5.8 | 22 09.1 | 10.3 | 59.9 |
| E 11 | 345 29.7 | 26.2 | 15 09.9 | 5.7 | 22 19.4 | 10.2 | 59.9 |
| S 12 | 0 29.4 | S23 26.2 | 29 34.6 | 5.6 | S22 29.6 | 10.0 | 60.0 |
| D 13 | 15 29.1 | 26.3 | 43 59.2 | 5.4 | 22 39.6 | 9.9 | 60.0 |
| A 14 | 30 28.8 | 26.3 | 58 23.6 | 5.3 | 22 49.5 | 9.8 | 60.0 |
| Y 15 | 45 28.5 | .. 26.3 | 72 47.9 | 5.1 | 22 59.3 | 9.6 | 60.1 |
| 16 | 60 28.2 | 26.3 | 87 12.0 | 5.0 | 23 08.9 | 9.5 | 60.1 |
| 17 | 75 27.8 | 26.3 | 101 36.0 | 4.9 | 23 18.4 | 9.3 | 60.1 |
| 18 | 90 27.5 | S23 26.3 | 115 59.9 | 4.7 | S23 27.7 | 9.2 | 60.2 |
| 19 | 105 27.2 | 26.3 | 130 23.6 | 4.6 | 23 36.9 | 9.0 | 60.2 |
| 20 | 120 26.9 | 26.3 | 144 47.2 | 4.5 | 23 45.9 | 8.9 | 60.2 |
| 21 | 135 26.6 | .. 26.3 | 159 10.7 | 4.4 | 23 54.8 | 8.7 | 60.3 |
| 22 | 150 26.3 | 26.3 | 173 34.1 | 4.2 | 24 03.5 | 8.6 | 60.3 |
| 23 | 165 26.0 | 26.3 | 187 57.3 | 4.1 | 24 12.1 | 8.4 | 60.3 |
| **22** 00 | 180 25.7 | S23 26.3 | 202 20.4 | 4.0 | S24 20.5 | 8.2 | 60.3 |
| 01 | 195 25.4 | 26.3 | 216 43.4 | 3.8 | 24 28.7 | 8.1 | 60.4 |
| 02 | 210 25.0 | 26.3 | 231 06.2 | 3.7 | 24 36.8 | 7.9 | 60.4 |
| 03 | 225 24.7 | .. 26.3 | 245 28.9 | 3.6 | 24 44.7 | 7.8 | 60.4 |
| 04 | 240 24.4 | 26.3 | 259 51.5 | 3.5 | 24 52.5 | 7.5 | 60.5 |
| 05 | 255 24.1 | 26.3 | 274 14.0 | 3.4 | 25 00.0 | 7.4 | 60.5 |
| 06 | 270 23.8 | S23 26.3 | 288 36.4 | 3.2 | S25 07.4 | 7.3 | 60.5 |
| T 07 | 285 23.5 | 26.3 | 302 58.6 | 3.1 | 25 14.7 | 7.0 | 60.5 |
| H 08 | 300 23.2 | 26.2 | 317 20.7 | 3.1 | 25 21.7 | 6.9 | 60.6 |
| U 09 | 315 22.9 | .. 26.2 | 331 42.8 | 2.9 | 25 28.6 | 6.7 | 60.6 |
| R 10 | 330 22.5 | 26.2 | 346 04.7 | 2.8 | 25 35.3 | 6.5 | 60.6 |
| S 11 | 345 22.2 | 26.2 | 0 26.5 | 2.6 | 25 41.8 | 6.3 | 60.6 |
| D 12 | 0 21.9 | S23 26.2 | 14 48.1 | 2.6 | S25 48.1 | 6.2 | 60.7 |
| A 13 | 15 21.6 | 26.2 | 29 09.7 | 2.5 | 25 54.3 | 5.9 | 60.7 |
| Y 14 | 30 21.3 | 26.2 | 43 31.2 | 2.4 | 26 00.2 | 5.8 | 60.7 |
| 15 | 45 21.0 | .. 26.2 | 57 52.6 | 2.3 | 26 06.0 | 5.6 | 60.7 |
| 16 | 60 20.7 | 26.2 | 72 13.9 | 2.2 | 26 11.6 | 5.4 | 60.7 |
| 17 | 75 20.4 | 26.1 | 86 35.1 | 2.0 | 26 17.0 | 5.1 | 60.8 |
| 18 | 90 20.1 | S23 26.1 | 100 56.1 | 2.0 | S26 22.1 | 5.0 | 60.8 |
| 19 | 105 19.7 | 26.1 | 115 17.1 | 2.0 | 26 27.1 | 4.8 | 60.8 |
| 20 | 120 19.4 | 26.1 | 129 38.1 | 1.8 | 26 31.9 | 4.6 | 60.8 |
| 21 | 135 19.1 | .. 26.1 | 143 58.9 | 1.7 | 26 36.5 | 4.4 | 60.9 |
| 22 | 150 18.8 | 26.1 | 158 19.6 | 1.7 | 26 40.9 | 4.2 | 60.9 |
| 23 | 165 18.5 | 26.0 | 172 40.3 | 1.6 | 26 45.1 | 4.0 | 60.9 |
| **23** 00 | 180 18.2 | S23 26.0 | 187 00.9 | 1.5 | S26 49.1 | 3.8 | 60.9 |
| 01 | 195 17.9 | 26.0 | 201 21.4 | 1.5 | 26 52.9 | 3.6 | 60.9 |
| 02 | 210 17.6 | 26.0 | 215 41.9 | 1.4 | 26 56.5 | 3.4 | 60.9 |
| 03 | 225 17.2 | .. 25.9 | 230 02.3 | 1.3 | 26 59.9 | 3.2 | 61.0 |
| 04 | 240 16.9 | 25.9 | 244 22.6 | 1.2 | 27 03.1 | 2.9 | 61.0 |
| 05 | 255 16.6 | 25.9 | 258 42.8 | 1.2 | 27 06.0 | 2.8 | 61.0 |
| 06 | 270 16.3 | S23 25.9 | 273 03.0 | 1.2 | S27 08.8 | 2.5 | 61.0 |
| F 07 | 285 16.0 | 25.8 | 287 23.2 | 1.1 | 27 11.3 | 2.4 | 61.0 |
| R 08 | 300 15.7 | 25.8 | 301 43.3 | 1.0 | 27 13.7 | 2.1 | 61.0 |
| I 09 | 315 15.4 | .. 25.8 | 316 03.3 | 1.0 | 27 15.8 | 1.9 | 61.0 |
| D 10 | 330 15.1 | 25.8 | 330 23.3 | 1.0 | 27 17.7 | 1.7 | 61.1 |
| A 11 | 345 14.8 | 25.7 | 344 43.3 | 0.9 | 27 19.4 | 1.5 | 61.1 |
| Y 12 | 0 14.4 | S23 25.7 | 359 03.2 | 0.9 | S27 20.9 | 1.3 | 61.1 |
| 13 | 15 14.1 | 25.7 | 13 23.1 | 0.9 | 27 22.2 | 1.0 | 61.1 |
| 14 | 30 13.8 | 25.6 | 27 43.0 | 0.8 | 27 23.2 | 0.9 | 61.1 |
| 15 | 45 13.5 | .. 25.6 | 42 02.8 | 0.8 | 27 24.1 | 0.6 | 61.1 |
| 16 | 60 13.2 | 25.6 | 56 22.6 | 0.8 | 27 24.7 | 0.4 | 61.1 |
| 17 | 75 12.9 | 25.5 | 70 42.4 | 0.8 | 27 25.1 | 0.2 | 61.1 |
| 18 | 90 12.6 | S23 25.5 | 85 02.2 | 0.8 | S27 25.3 | 0.1 | 61.1 |
| 19 | 105 12.3 | 25.5 | 99 22.0 | 0.7 | 27 25.2 | 0.2 | 61.2 |
| 20 | 120 11.9 | 25.4 | 113 41.7 | 0.8 | 27 25.0 | 0.5 | 61.2 |
| 21 | 135 11.6 | .. 25.4 | 128 01.5 | 0.7 | 27 24.5 | 0.7 | 61.2 |
| 22 | 150 11.3 | 25.3 | 142 21.2 | 0.8 | 27 23.8 | 0.9 | 61.2 |
| 23 | 165 11.0 | 25.3 | 156 41.0 | 0.7 | S27 22.9 | 1.1 | 61.2 |
| SD | 16.3 | d 0.0 | SD 16.3 | | 16.5 | | 16.6 |

| Lat. | Twilight Naut. | Twilight Civil | Sunrise | Moonrise 21 | 22 | 23 | 24 |
|---|---|---|---|---|---|---|---|
| ° | h m | h m | h m | h m | h m | h m | h m |
| N 72 | 08 26 | 10 58 | ▬ | ▬ | ▬ | ▬ | ▬ |
| N 70 | 08 06 | 09 55 | ▬ | ▬ | ▬ | ▬ | ▬ |
| 68 | 07 50 | 09 19 | ▬ | ▬ | ▬ | ▬ | ▬ |
| 66 | 07 37 | 08 54 | 10 35 | 08 14 | ▬ | ▬ | ▬ |
| 64 | 07 26 | 08 34 | 09 52 | 07 33 | 10 27 | ▬ | ▬ |
| 62 | 07 16 | 08 18 | 09 24 | 07 05 | 09 12 | 11 15 | 12 03 |
| 60 | 07 08 | 08 05 | 09 02 | 06 44 | 08 37 | 10 16 | 11 15 |
| N 58 | 07 00 | 07 53 | 08 45 | 06 27 | 08 11 | 09 43 | 10 45 |
| 56 | 06 53 | 07 43 | 08 30 | 06 12 | 07 51 | 09 18 | 10 22 |
| 54 | 06 47 | 07 33 | 08 17 | 06 00 | 07 34 | 08 58 | 10 03 |
| 52 | 06 41 | 07 25 | 08 06 | 05 49 | 07 19 | 08 42 | 09 47 |
| 50 | 06 36 | 07 18 | 07 56 | 05 39 | 07 07 | 08 27 | 09 33 |
| 45 | 06 24 | 07 02 | 07 36 | 05 19 | 06 41 | 07 58 | 09 04 |
| N 40 | 06 14 | 06 48 | 07 19 | 05 03 | 06 20 | 07 35 | 08 42 |
| 35 | 06 05 | 06 36 | 07 04 | 04 49 | 06 03 | 07 17 | 08 23 |
| 30 | 05 56 | 06 26 | 06 52 | 04 37 | 05 49 | 07 00 | 08 07 |
| 20 | 05 39 | 06 07 | 06 31 | 04 17 | 05 24 | 06 33 | 07 40 |
| N 10 | 05 23 | 05 49 | 06 12 | 03 59 | 05 03 | 06 10 | 07 17 |
| 0 | 05 06 | 05 32 | 05 55 | 03 43 | 04 43 | 05 48 | 06 55 |
| S 10 | 04 47 | 05 14 | 05 37 | 03 27 | 04 24 | 05 26 | 06 34 |
| 20 | 04 24 | 04 54 | 05 18 | 03 10 | 04 03 | 05 03 | 06 10 |
| 30 | 03 55 | 04 29 | 04 56 | 02 50 | 03 39 | 04 36 | 05 43 |
| 35 | 03 36 | 04 13 | 04 43 | 02 39 | 03 25 | 04 21 | 05 27 |
| 40 | 03 13 | 03 55 | 04 28 | 02 26 | 03 08 | 04 02 | 05 09 |
| 45 | 02 43 | 03 32 | 04 10 | 02 11 | 02 49 | 03 40 | 04 46 |
| S 50 | 01 57 | 03 03 | 03 47 | 01 53 | 02 25 | 03 12 | 04 18 |
| 52 | 01 29 | 02 47 | 03 36 | 01 44 | 02 14 | 02 59 | 04 04 |
| 54 | 00 42 | 02 29 | 03 24 | 01 34 | 02 01 | 02 43 | 03 47 |
| 56 | //// | 02 07 | 03 10 | 01 23 | 01 46 | 02 25 | 03 28 |
| 58 | //// | 01 37 | 02 53 | 01 11 | 01 28 | 02 02 | 03 04 |
| S 60 | //// | 00 46 | 02 32 | 00 56 | 01 07 | 01 33 | 02 33 |

| Lat. | Sunset | Twilight Civil | Twilight Naut. | Moonset 21 | 22 | 23 | 24 |
|---|---|---|---|---|---|---|---|
| ° | h m | h m | h m | h m | h m | h m | h m |
| N 72 | ▬ | 12 59 | 15 31 | ▬ | ▬ | ▬ | ▬ |
| N 70 | ▬ | 14 02 | 15 51 | ▬ | ▬ | ▬ | ▬ |
| 68 | ▬ | 14 38 | 16 07 | ▬ | ▬ | ▬ | ▬ |
| 66 | 13 22 | 15 03 | 16 20 | 11 25 | ▬ | ▬ | ▬ |
| 64 | 14 05 | 15 23 | 16 31 | 12 06 | 11 20 | ▬ | ▬ |
| 62 | 14 33 | 15 39 | 16 41 | 12 35 | 12 35 | 12 51 | 14 25 |
| 60 | 14 55 | 15 52 | 16 49 | 12 57 | 13 12 | 13 50 | 15 12 |
| N 58 | 15 12 | 16 04 | 16 57 | 13 15 | 13 38 | 14 23 | 15 42 |
| 56 | 15 27 | 16 14 | 17 04 | 13 30 | 13 59 | 14 48 | 16 05 |
| 54 | 15 40 | 16 24 | 17 10 | 13 43 | 14 16 | 15 08 | 16 24 |
| 52 | 15 51 | 16 32 | 17 16 | 13 55 | 14 31 | 15 25 | 16 40 |
| 50 | 16 01 | 16 39 | 17 21 | 14 05 | 14 44 | 15 39 | 16 54 |
| 45 | 16 22 | 16 55 | 17 33 | 14 26 | 15 10 | 16 09 | 17 21 |
| N 40 | 16 38 | 17 09 | 17 43 | 14 44 | 15 31 | 16 32 | 17 43 |
| 35 | 16 53 | 17 21 | 17 52 | 14 59 | 15 49 | 16 51 | 18 01 |
| 30 | 17 05 | 17 31 | 18 01 | 15 12 | 16 04 | 17 07 | 18 17 |
| 20 | 17 26 | 17 50 | 18 18 | 15 34 | 16 30 | 17 34 | 18 43 |
| N 10 | 17 45 | 18 08 | 18 34 | 15 53 | 16 53 | 17 58 | 19 06 |
| 0 | 18 02 | 18 25 | 18 51 | 16 11 | 17 13 | 18 20 | 19 27 |
| S 10 | 18 20 | 18 43 | 19 10 | 16 29 | 17 34 | 18 42 | 19 48 |
| 20 | 18 39 | 19 03 | 19 33 | 16 48 | 17 57 | 19 05 | 20 10 |
| 30 | 19 01 | 19 28 | 20 02 | 17 11 | 18 23 | 19 33 | 20 36 |
| 35 | 19 14 | 19 44 | 20 21 | 17 24 | 18 38 | 19 49 | 20 51 |
| 40 | 19 29 | 20 02 | 20 44 | 17 39 | 18 56 | 20 08 | 21 08 |
| 45 | 19 47 | 20 25 | 21 14 | 17 58 | 19 18 | 20 30 | 21 29 |
| S 50 | 20 10 | 20 54 | 22 00 | 18 20 | 19 45 | 20 59 | 21 55 |
| 52 | 20 21 | 21 10 | 22 28 | 18 31 | 19 59 | 21 13 | 22 08 |
| 54 | 20 33 | 21 28 | 23 15 | 18 44 | 20 14 | 21 29 | 22 22 |
| 56 | 20 47 | 21 50 | //// | 18 58 | 20 32 | 21 49 | 22 39 |
| 58 | 21 04 | 22 20 | //// | 19 15 | 20 54 | 22 13 | 22 59 |
| S 60 | 21 25 | 23 11 | //// | 19 36 | 21 23 | 22 44 | 23 24 |

| Day | SUN Eqn. of Time 00h | 12h | Mer. Pass. | MOON Mer. Pass. Upper | Lower | Age | Phase |
|---|---|---|---|---|---|---|---|
| d | m s | m s | h m | h m | h m | d | % |
| 21 | 02 13 | 01 58 | 11 58 | 09 57 | 22 27 | 28 | 5 |
| 22 | 01 43 | 01 28 | 11 59 | 10 58 | 23 31 | 29 | 1 |
| 23 | 01 13 | 00 58 | 11 59 | 12 04 | 24 38 | 00 | 0 ● |

| UT | ARIES GHA | VENUS −3.9 GHA | Dec | MARS −1.4 GHA | Dec | JUPITER −2.4 GHA | Dec | SATURN +0.8 GHA | Dec | STARS Name | SHA | Dec |
|---|---|---|---|---|---|---|---|---|---|---|---|---|
| **24** 00 | 92 30.2 | 163 31.6 | S23 29.2 | 23 44.4 | N24 45.1 | 91 41.3 | S 1 05.2 | 128 03.7 | S15 28.0 | Acamar | 315 12.8 | S40 13.0 |
| 01 | 107 32.7 | 178 30.7 | 28.8 | 38 47.6 | 45.1 | 106 43.5 | 05.0 | 143 05.9 | 28.0 | Achernar | 335 21.2 | S57 07.5 |
| 02 | 122 35.1 | 193 29.7 | 28.5 | 53 50.8 | 45.0 | 121 45.8 | 04.9 | 158 08.2 | 27.9 | Acrux | 173 02.0 | S63 13.2 |
| 03 | 137 37.6 | 208 28.8 .. | 28.1 | 68 54.0 .. | 45.0 | 136 48.0 .. | 04.8 | 173 10.4 .. | 27.8 | Adhara | 255 06.8 | S29 00.1 |
| 04 | 152 40.1 | 223 27.9 | 27.8 | 83 57.2 | 44.9 | 151 50.2 | 04.7 | 188 12.7 | 27.7 | Aldebaran | 290 41.2 | N16 33.3 |
| 05 | 167 42.5 | 238 26.9 | 27.5 | 99 00.4 | 44.9 | 166 52.5 | 04.6 | 203 14.9 | 27.6 | | | |
| 06 | 182 45.0 | 253 26.0 | S23 27.1 | 114 03.6 | N24 44.8 | 181 54.7 | S 1 04.5 | 218 17.1 | S15 27.6 | Alioth | 166 14.6 | N55 49.9 |
| 07 | 197 47.5 | 268 25.1 | 26.8 | 129 06.7 | 44.8 | 196 57.0 | 04.4 | 233 19.4 | 27.5 | Alkaid | 152 53.6 | N49 11.7 |
| S 08 | 212 49.9 | 283 24.1 | 26.4 | 144 09.9 | 44.7 | 211 59.2 | 04.3 | 248 21.6 | 27.4 | Alnair | 27 35.3 | S46 51.3 |
| A 09 | 227 52.4 | 298 23.2 .. | 26.1 | 159 13.1 .. | 44.6 | 227 01.4 .. | 04.2 | 263 23.8 .. | 27.3 | Alnilam | 275 39.1 | S 1 11.3 |
| T 10 | 242 54.8 | 313 22.3 | 25.7 | 174 16.3 | 44.6 | 242 03.7 | 04.1 | 278 26.1 | 27.3 | Alphard | 217 49.2 | S 8 45.4 |
| U 11 | 257 57.3 | 328 21.3 | 25.4 | 189 19.5 | 44.5 | 257 05.9 | 04.0 | 293 28.3 | 27.2 | | | |
| R 12 | 272 59.8 | 343 20.4 | S23 25.0 | 204 22.6 | N24 44.5 | 272 08.2 | S 1 03.9 | 308 30.6 | S15 27.1 | Alphecca | 126 05.5 | N26 38.2 |
| D 13 | 288 02.2 | 358 19.5 | 24.7 | 219 25.8 | 44.4 | 287 10.4 | 03.7 | 323 32.8 | 27.0 | Alpheratz | 357 36.5 | N29 13.1 |
| A 14 | 303 04.7 | 13 18.6 | 24.3 | 234 29.0 | 44.4 | 302 12.7 | 03.6 | 338 35.0 | 27.0 | Altair | 62 01.9 | N 8 55.7 |
| Y 15 | 318 07.2 | 28 17.6 .. | 24.0 | 249 32.2 .. | 44.3 | 317 14.9 .. | 03.5 | 353 37.3 .. | 26.9 | Ankaa | 353 08.8 | S42 11.2 |
| 16 | 333 09.6 | 43 16.7 | 23.6 | 264 35.3 | 44.3 | 332 17.1 | 03.4 | 8 39.5 | 26.8 | Antares | 112 18.3 | S26 28.9 |
| 17 | 348 12.1 | 58 15.8 | 23.3 | 279 38.5 | 44.2 | 347 19.4 | 03.3 | 23 41.7 | 26.7 | | | |
| 18 | 3 14.6 | 73 14.8 | S23 22.9 | 294 41.7 | N24 44.2 | 2 21.6 | S 1 03.2 | 38 44.0 | S15 26.7 | Arcturus | 145 49.7 | N19 03.7 |
| 19 | 18 17.0 | 88 13.9 | 22.5 | 309 44.8 | 44.1 | 17 23.8 | 03.1 | 53 46.2 | 26.6 | Atria | 107 14.6 | S69 04.0 |
| 20 | 33 19.5 | 103 13.0 | 22.2 | 324 48.0 | 44.0 | 32 26.1 | 03.0 | 68 48.5 | 26.5 | Avior | 234 14.8 | S59 34.8 |
| 21 | 48 22.0 | 118 12.1 .. | 21.8 | 339 51.1 .. | 44.0 | 47 28.3 .. | 02.9 | 83 50.7 .. | 26.4 | Bellatrix | 278 24.4 | N 6 22.2 |
| 22 | 63 24.4 | 133 11.1 | 21.5 | 354 54.3 | 43.9 | 62 30.6 | 02.8 | 98 52.9 | 26.4 | Betelgeuse | 270 53.6 | N 7 24.7 |
| 23 | 78 26.9 | 148 10.2 | 21.1 | 9 57.5 | 43.9 | 77 32.8 | 02.6 | 113 55.2 | 26.3 | | | |
| **25** 00 | 93 29.3 | 163 09.3 | S23 20.7 | 25 00.6 | N24 43.8 | 92 35.0 | S 1 02.5 | 128 57.4 | S15 26.2 | Canopus | 263 52.6 | S52 42.4 |
| 01 | 108 31.8 | 178 08.3 | 20.4 | 40 03.8 | 43.8 | 107 37.3 | 02.4 | 143 59.6 | 26.1 | Capella | 280 23.9 | N46 01.3 |
| 02 | 123 34.3 | 193 07.4 | 20.0 | 55 06.9 | 43.7 | 122 39.5 | 02.3 | 159 01.9 | 26.1 | Deneb | 49 27.3 | N45 21.8 |
| 03 | 138 36.7 | 208 06.5 .. | 19.6 | 70 10.1 .. | 43.7 | 137 41.7 .. | 02.2 | 174 04.1 .. | 26.0 | Denebola | 182 26.6 | N14 26.6 |
| 04 | 153 39.2 | 223 05.6 | 19.3 | 85 13.2 | 43.6 | 152 44.0 | 02.1 | 189 06.3 | 25.9 | Diphda | 348 48.9 | S17 51.8 |
| 05 | 168 41.7 | 238 04.6 | 18.9 | 100 16.4 | 43.6 | 167 46.2 | 02.0 | 204 08.6 | 25.8 | | | |
| 06 | 183 44.1 | 253 03.7 | S23 18.5 | 115 19.5 | N24 43.5 | 182 48.4 | S 1 01.9 | 219 10.8 | S15 25.7 | Dubhe | 193 42.9 | N61 37.4 |
| 07 | 198 46.6 | 268 02.8 | 18.1 | 130 22.7 | 43.4 | 197 50.7 | 01.8 | 234 13.1 | 25.7 | Elnath | 278 03.6 | N28 37.6 |
| 08 | 213 49.1 | 283 01.9 | 17.8 | 145 25.8 | 43.4 | 212 52.9 | 01.7 | 249 15.3 | 25.6 | Eltanin | 90 43.5 | N51 29.1 |
| S 09 | 228 51.5 | 298 00.9 .. | 17.4 | 160 29.0 .. | 43.3 | 227 55.1 .. | 01.5 | 264 17.5 .. | 25.5 | Enif | 33 40.7 | N 9 58.8 |
| U 10 | 243 54.0 | 313 00.0 | 17.0 | 175 32.1 | 43.3 | 242 57.4 | 01.4 | 279 19.8 | 25.4 | Fomalhaut | 15 16.5 | S29 30.3 |
| N 11 | 258 56.5 | 327 59.1 | 16.6 | 190 35.3 | 43.2 | 257 59.6 | 01.3 | 294 22.0 | 25.4 | | | |
| D 12 | 273 58.9 | 342 58.2 | S23 16.3 | 205 38.4 | N24 43.2 | 273 01.8 | S 1 01.2 | 309 24.2 | S15 25.3 | Gacrux | 171 53.6 | S57 14.2 |
| A 13 | 289 01.4 | 357 57.3 | 15.9 | 220 41.5 | 43.1 | 288 04.1 | 01.1 | 324 26.5 | 25.2 | Gienah | 175 45.3 | S17 40.0 |
| Y 14 | 304 03.8 | 12 56.3 | 15.5 | 235 44.7 | 43.1 | 303 06.3 | 01.0 | 339 28.7 | 25.1 | Hadar | 148 38.7 | S60 28.7 |
| 15 | 319 06.3 | 27 55.4 .. | 15.1 | 250 47.8 .. | 43.0 | 318 08.5 .. | 00.9 | 354 30.9 .. | 25.1 | Hamal | 327 52.9 | N23 34.3 |
| 16 | 334 08.8 | 42 54.5 | 14.7 | 265 51.0 | 43.0 | 333 10.8 | 00.8 | 9 33.2 | 25.0 | Kaus Aust. | 83 35.2 | S34 22.4 |
| 17 | 349 11.2 | 57 53.6 | 14.3 | 280 54.1 | 42.9 | 348 13.0 | 00.6 | 24 35.4 | 24.9 | | | |
| 18 | 4 13.7 | 72 52.6 | S23 14.0 | 295 57.2 | N24 42.8 | 3 15.2 | S 1 00.5 | 39 37.6 | S15 24.8 | Kochab | 137 20.6 | N74 03.4 |
| 19 | 19 16.2 | 87 51.7 | 13.6 | 311 00.3 | 42.8 | 18 17.5 | 00.4 | 54 39.9 | 24.7 | Markab | 13 31.7 | N15 19.7 |
| 20 | 34 18.6 | 102 50.8 | 13.2 | 326 03.5 | 42.7 | 33 19.7 | 00.3 | 69 42.1 | 24.7 | Menkar | 314 07.7 | N 4 10.7 |
| 21 | 49 21.1 | 117 49.9 .. | 12.8 | 341 06.6 .. | 42.7 | 48 21.9 .. | 00.2 | 84 44.3 .. | 24.6 | Menkent | 147 59.8 | S36 28.7 |
| 22 | 64 23.6 | 132 49.0 | 12.4 | 356 09.7 | 42.6 | 63 24.2 | 00.1 | 99 46.6 | 24.5 | Miaplacidus | 221 37.9 | S69 48.4 |
| 23 | 79 26.0 | 147 48.1 | 12.0 | 11 12.9 | 42.6 | 78 26.4 | 1 00.0 | 114 48.8 | 24.4 | | | |
| **26** 00 | 94 28.5 | 162 47.1 | S23 11.6 | 26 16.0 | N24 42.5 | 93 28.6 | S 0 59.9 | 129 51.0 | S15 24.4 | Mirfak | 308 30.3 | N49 56.7 |
| 01 | 109 31.0 | 177 46.2 | 11.2 | 41 19.1 | 42.5 | 108 30.9 | 59.7 | 144 53.3 | 24.3 | Nunki | 75 50.2 | S26 16.1 |
| 02 | 124 33.4 | 192 45.3 | 10.8 | 56 22.2 | 42.4 | 123 33.1 | 59.6 | 159 55.5 | 24.2 | Peacock | 53 08.9 | S56 39.8 |
| 03 | 139 35.9 | 207 44.4 .. | 10.4 | 71 25.3 .. | 42.4 | 138 35.3 .. | 59.5 | 174 57.7 .. | 24.1 | Pollux | 243 19.0 | N27 58.2 |
| 04 | 154 38.3 | 222 43.5 | 10.0 | 86 28.5 | 42.3 | 153 37.5 | 59.4 | 190 00.0 | 24.1 | Procyon | 244 52.3 | N 5 10.0 |
| 05 | 169 40.8 | 237 42.5 | 09.6 | 101 31.6 | 42.2 | 168 39.8 | 59.3 | 205 02.2 | 24.0 | | | |
| 06 | 184 43.3 | 252 41.6 | S23 09.2 | 116 34.7 | N24 42.2 | 183 42.0 | S 0 59.2 | 220 04.4 | S15 23.9 | Rasalhague | 96 00.5 | N12 32.6 |
| 07 | 199 45.7 | 267 40.7 | 08.8 | 131 37.8 | 42.1 | 198 44.2 | 59.1 | 235 06.7 | 23.8 | Regulus | 207 36.1 | N11 51.3 |
| 08 | 214 48.2 | 282 39.8 | 08.4 | 146 40.9 | 42.1 | 213 46.5 | 58.9 | 250 08.9 | 23.7 | Rigel | 281 05.2 | S 8 10.5 |
| M 09 | 229 50.7 | 297 38.9 .. | 08.0 | 161 44.0 .. | 42.0 | 228 48.7 .. | 58.8 | 265 11.1 .. | 23.7 | Rigil Kent. | 139 43.0 | S60 55.5 |
| O 10 | 244 53.1 | 312 38.0 | 07.6 | 176 47.1 | 42.0 | 243 50.9 | 58.7 | 280 13.4 | 23.6 | Sabik | 102 05.1 | S15 45.2 |
| N 11 | 259 55.6 | 327 37.1 | 07.2 | 191 50.2 | 41.9 | 258 53.1 | 58.6 | 295 15.6 | 23.5 | | | |
| D 12 | 274 58.1 | 342 36.1 | S23 06.8 | 206 53.3 | N24 41.9 | 273 55.4 | S 0 58.5 | 310 17.8 | S15 23.4 | Schedar | 349 32.9 | N56 40.0 |
| A 13 | 290 00.5 | 357 35.2 | 06.4 | 221 56.4 | 41.8 | 288 57.6 | 58.4 | 325 20.1 | 23.4 | Shaula | 96 13.1 | S37 07.2 |
| Y 14 | 305 03.0 | 12 34.3 | 05.9 | 236 59.5 | 41.8 | 303 59.8 | 58.3 | 340 22.3 | 23.3 | Sirius | 258 27.4 | S16 44.8 |
| 15 | 320 05.4 | 27 33.4 .. | 05.5 | 252 02.6 .. | 41.7 | 319 02.0 .. | 58.1 | 355 24.5 .. | 23.2 | Spica | 158 24.2 | S11 16.8 |
| 16 | 335 07.9 | 42 32.5 | 05.1 | 267 05.7 | 41.7 | 334 04.3 | 58.0 | 10 26.8 | 23.1 | Suhail | 222 47.2 | S43 31.3 |
| 17 | 350 10.4 | 57 31.6 | 04.7 | 282 08.8 | 41.6 | 349 06.5 | 57.9 | 25 29.0 | 23.0 | | | |
| 18 | 5 12.8 | 72 30.7 | S23 04.3 | 297 11.9 | N24 41.6 | 4 08.7 | S 0 57.8 | 40 31.2 | S15 23.0 | Vega | 80 34.8 | N38 48.3 |
| 19 | 20 15.3 | 87 29.7 | 03.9 | 312 15.0 | 41.5 | 19 10.9 | 57.7 | 55 33.5 | 22.9 | Zuben'ubi | 136 58.1 | S16 08.1 |
| 20 | 35 17.8 | 102 28.8 | 03.4 | 327 18.1 | 41.4 | 34 13.2 | 57.6 | 70 35.7 | 22.8 | | SHA | Mer. Pass. |
| 21 | 50 20.2 | 117 27.9 .. | 03.0 | 342 21.2 .. | 41.4 | 49 15.4 .. | 57.4 | 85 37.9 .. | 22.7 | Venus | 69 39.9 | 13 08 |
| 22 | 65 22.7 | 132 27.0 | 02.6 | 357 24.3 | 41.3 | 64 17.6 | 57.3 | 100 40.2 | 22.7 | Mars | 291 31.3 | 22 15 |
| 23 | 80 25.2 | 147 26.1 | 02.2 | 12 27.4 | 41.3 | 79 19.8 | 57.2 | 115 42.4 | 22.6 | Jupiter | 359 05.7 | 17 47 |
| Mer. Pass. 17 43.1 | | v −0.9 | d 0.4 | v 3.1 | d 0.1 | v 2.2 | d 0.1 | v 2.2 | d 0.1 | Saturn | 35 28.1 | 15 22 |

| UT | SUN | | MOON | | | | | Lat. | Twilight | | Sunrise | Moonrise | | | |
|---|---|---|---|---|---|---|---|---|---|---|---|---|---|---|---|
| | | | | | | | | | Naut. | Civil | | 24 | 25 | 26 | 27 |
| | GHA | Dec | GHA | v | Dec | d | HP | ° | h m | h m | h m | h m | h m | h m | h m |
| d h | ° ' | ° ' | ° ' | ' | ° ' | ' | ' | N 72 | 08 27 | 10 57 | ■ | ■ | ■ | ■ | 13 41 |
| 24 00 | 180 10.7 | S23 25.3 | 171 00.7 | 0.8 | S27 21.8 | 1.3 | 61.2 | N 70 | 08 07 | 09 55 | ■ | ■ | ■ | ■ | 13 11 |
| 01 | 195 10.4 | 25.2 | 185 20.5 | 0.8 | 27 20.5 | 1.6 | 61.2 | 68 | 07 51 | 09 20 | ■ | ■ | ■ | 14 47 | 13 11 |
| 02 | 210 10.1 | 25.2 | 199 40.3 | 0.8 | 27 18.9 | 1.7 | 61.2 | 66 | 07 38 | 08 55 | 10 35 | ■ | ■ | 13 32 | 12 49 |
| 03 | 225 09.8 ·· | 25.1 | 214 00.1 | 0.8 | 27 17.2 | 2.0 | 61.2 | 64 | 07 27 | 08 35 | 09 53 | ■ | 12 47 | 12 54 | 12 31 |
| 04 | 240 09.5 | 25.1 | 228 19.9 | 0.9 | 27 15.2 | 2.2 | 61.2 | 62 | 07 17 | 08 19 | 09 25 | 12 03 | 12 07 | 12 27 | 12 16 |
| 05 | 255 09.1 | 25.0 | 242 39.8 | 0.9 | 27 13.0 | 2.4 | 61.2 | 60 | 07 09 | 08 06 | 09 03 | 11 15 | 11 40 | 12 06 | 12 04 |
| 06 | 270 08.8 | S23 25.0 | 256 59.7 | 0.9 | S27 10.6 | 2.6 | 61.2 | N 58 | 07 01 | 07 54 | 08 46 | 10 45 | 11 18 | 11 49 | 11 54 |
| 07 | 285 08.5 | 25.0 | 271 19.6 | 0.9 | 27 08.0 | 2.9 | 61.2 | 56 | 06 55 | 07 44 | 08 31 | 10 22 | 11 00 | 11 35 | 11 44 |
| S 08 | 300 08.2 | 24.9 | 285 39.5 | 1.0 | 27 05.1 | 3.0 | 61.2 | 54 | 06 48 | 07 35 | 08 19 | 10 03 | 10 45 | 11 22 | 11 36 |
| A 09 | 315 07.9 ·· | 24.9 | 299 59.5 | 1.0 | 27 02.1 | 3.3 | 61.2 | 52 | 06 43 | 07 26 | 08 07 | 09 47 | 10 32 | 11 11 | 11 29 |
| T 10 | 330 07.6 | 24.8 | 314 19.5 | 1.1 | 26 58.8 | 3.5 | 61.2 | 50 | 06 37 | 07 19 | 07 58 | 09 33 | 10 20 | 11 02 | 11 23 |
| U 11 | 345 07.3 | 24.8 | 328 39.6 | 1.1 | 26 55.3 | 3.7 | 61.2 | 45 | 06 26 | 07 03 | 07 37 | 09 04 | 09 56 | 10 53 | 11 17 |
| R 12 | 0 07.0 | S23 24.7 | 342 59.7 | 1.2 | S26 51.6 | 3.9 | 61.2 | N 40 | 06 15 | 06 49 | 07 20 | 08 42 | 09 36 | 10 34 | 11 04 |
| D 13 | 15 06.6 | 24.7 | 357 19.9 | 1.2 | 26 47.7 | 4.1 | 61.2 | 35 | 06 06 | 06 38 | 07 06 | 08 23 | 09 20 | 10 19 | 10 53 |
| A 14 | 30 06.3 | 24.6 | 11 40.1 | 1.3 | 26 43.6 | 4.3 | 61.2 | 30 | 05 57 | 06 27 | 06 53 | 08 07 | 09 06 | 10 06 | 10 44 |
| Y 15 | 45 06.0 ·· | 24.6 | 26 00.4 | 1.3 | 26 39.3 | 4.5 | 61.2 | 20 | 05 41 | 06 08 | 06 32 | 07 40 | 08 42 | 09 55 | 10 36 |
| 16 | 60 05.7 | 24.5 | 40 20.7 | 1.4 | 26 34.8 | 4.8 | 61.2 | N 10 | 05 25 | 05 51 | 06 14 | 07 17 | 08 21 | 09 35 | 10 22 |
| 17 | 75 05.4 | 24.4 | 54 41.1 | 1.5 | 26 30.0 | 4.9 | 61.2 | 0 | 05 08 | 05 34 | 05 56 | 06 55 | 08 01 | 09 18 | 10 10 |
| 18 | 90 05.1 | S23 24.4 | 69 01.6 | 1.5 | S26 25.1 | 5.1 | 61.2 | S 10 | 04 49 | 05 16 | 05 39 | 06 34 | 07 41 | 09 02 | 09 58 |
| 19 | 105 04.8 | 24.3 | 83 22.1 | 1.6 | 26 20.0 | 5.4 | 61.2 | 20 | 04 26 | 04 55 | 05 20 | 06 10 | 07 20 | 08 46 | 09 47 |
| 20 | 120 04.5 | 24.3 | 97 42.7 | 1.7 | 26 14.6 | 5.5 | 61.2 | 30 | 03 57 | 04 30 | 04 58 | 05 43 | 06 56 | 08 29 | 09 34 |
| 21 | 135 04.2 ·· | 24.2 | 112 03.4 | 1.8 | 26 09.1 | 5.8 | 61.2 | 35 | 03 38 | 04 15 | 04 45 | 05 27 | 06 41 | 08 09 | 09 20 |
| 22 | 150 03.8 | 24.2 | 126 24.2 | 1.9 | 26 03.3 | 5.9 | 61.2 | 40 | 03 15 | 03 57 | 04 30 | 05 09 | 06 25 | 07 57 | 09 12 |
| 23 | 165 03.5 | 24.1 | 140 45.1 | 1.9 | 25 57.4 | 6.1 | 61.1 | 45 | 02 44 | 03 34 | 04 12 | 04 46 | 06 04 | 07 44 | 09 02 |
| 25 00 | 180 03.2 | S23 24.0 | 155 06.0 | 2.0 | S25 51.3 | 6.3 | 61.1 | S 50 | 01 59 | 03 04 | 03 49 | 04 18 | 05 39 | 07 28 | 08 51 |
| 01 | 195 02.9 | 24.0 | 169 27.0 | 2.1 | 25 45.0 | 6.6 | 61.1 | 52 | 01 31 | 02 49 | 03 38 | 04 04 | 05 27 | 07 08 | 08 37 |
| 02 | 210 02.6 | 23.9 | 183 48.1 | 2.2 | 25 38.4 | 6.6 | 61.1 | 54 | 00 45 | 02 31 | 03 26 | 03 47 | 05 13 | 06 59 | 08 31 |
| 03 | 225 02.3 ·· | 23.9 | 198 09.3 | 2.3 | 25 31.7 | 6.9 | 61.1 | 56 | //// | 02 09 | 03 12 | 03 28 | 04 56 | 06 48 | 08 24 |
| 04 | 240 02.0 | 23.8 | 212 30.6 | 2.4 | 25 24.8 | 7.1 | 61.1 | 58 | //// | 01 39 | 02 55 | 03 04 | 04 37 | 06 36 | 08 16 |
| 05 | 255 01.7 | 23.7 | 226 52.0 | 2.5 | 25 17.7 | 7.3 | 61.1 | S 60 | //// | 00 49 | 02 34 | 02 33 | 04 12 | 06 22 | 08 07 |

| Lat. | Sunset | Twilight | | Moonset | | | | |
|---|---|---|---|---|---|---|---|---|
| | | Civil | Naut. | 24 | 25 | 26 | 27 | |
| ° | h m | h m | h m | h m | h m | h m | h m | |
| 25 06 | 270 01.4 | S23 23.7 | 241 13.5 | 2.6 | S25 10.4 | 7.4 | 61.1 |
| 07 | 285 01.0 | 23.6 | 255 35.1 | 2.7 | 25 03.0 | 7.7 | 61.1 |

| Lat. | Sunset | Twilight | | Moonset | | | | |
|---|---|---|---|---|---|---|---|---|
| | | Civil | Naut. | 24 | 25 | 26 | 27 | |
| ° | h m | h m | h m | h m | h m | h m | h m | |
| N 72 | ■ | 13 03 | 15 33 | ■ | ■ | ■ | 19 08 | |
| N 70 | ■ | 14 05 | 15 53 | ■ | ■ | 16 07 | 19 36 | |
| 68 | ■ | 14 40 | 16 09 | ■ | ■ | 17 20 | 19 56 | |
| 66 | 13 25 | 15 05 | 16 22 | ■ | ■ | 17 56 | 20 13 | |
| 64 | 14 07 | 15 26 | 16 33 | ■ | 15 57 | 18 22 | 20 26 | |
| 62 | 14 35 | 15 41 | 16 43 | 14 25 | 16 36 | 18 42 | 20 36 | |
| 60 | 14 57 | 15 54 | 16 51 | 15 12 | 17 04 | 18 58 | 20 46 | |
| N 58 | 15 14 | 16 06 | 16 59 | 15 42 | 17 25 | 19 12 | 20 54 | |
| 56 | 15 29 | 16 16 | 17 06 | 16 05 | 17 42 | 19 23 | 21 01 | |
| 54 | 15 42 | 16 25 | 17 12 | 16 24 | 17 57 | 19 33 | 21 07 | |
| 52 | 15 53 | 16 34 | 17 17 | 16 40 | 18 09 | 19 42 | 21 13 | |
| 50 | 16 03 | 16 41 | 17 23 | 16 54 | 18 20 | 19 51 | 21 18 | |
| 45 | 16 23 | 16 57 | 17 34 | 17 21 | 18 44 | 20 08 | 21 29 | |

| 25 08 | 300 00.7 | 23.5 | 269 56.8 | 2.8 | 24 55.3 | 7.8 | 61.1 |
| S 09 | 315 00.4 ·· | 23.5 | 284 18.6 | 2.9 | 24 47.5 | 8.0 | 61.0 |
| U 10 | 330 00.1 | 23.4 | 298 40.5 | 3.1 | 24 39.5 | 8.2 | 61.0 |
| N 11 | 344 59.8 | 23.3 | 313 02.6 | 3.1 | 24 31.3 | 8.3 | 61.0 |
| D 12 | 359 59.5 | S23 23.3 | 327 24.7 | 3.2 | S24 23.0 | 8.6 | 61.0 |
| A 13 | 14 59.2 | 23.2 | 341 46.9 | 3.4 | 24 14.4 | 8.7 | 61.0 |
| Y 14 | 29 58.9 | 23.1 | 356 09.3 | 3.4 | 24 05.7 | 8.8 | 61.0 |
| 15 | 44 58.6 ·· | 23.0 | 10 31.7 | 3.6 | 23 56.9 | 9.1 | 61.0 |
| 16 | 59 58.3 | 23.0 | 24 54.3 | 3.7 | 23 47.8 | 9.2 | 60.9 |
| 17 | 74 57.9 | 22.9 | 39 17.0 | 3.8 | 23 38.6 | 9.3 | 60.9 |
| 18 | 89 57.6 | S23 22.8 | 53 39.8 | 4.0 | S23 29.3 | 9.6 | 60.9 |
| 19 | 104 57.3 | 22.7 | 68 02.8 | 4.0 | 23 19.7 | 9.7 | 60.9 |
| 20 | 119 57.0 | 22.7 | 82 25.8 | 4.2 | 23 10.0 | 9.8 | 60.9 |
| 21 | 134 56.7 ·· | 22.6 | 96 49.0 | 4.3 | 23 00.2 | 10.0 | 60.8 |
| 22 | 149 56.4 | 22.5 | 111 12.3 | 4.4 | 22 50.2 | 10.1 | 60.8 |
| 23 | 164 56.1 | 22.4 | 125 35.7 | 4.6 | 22 40.1 | 10.3 | 60.8 |

| Lat. | Sunset | Twilight | | Moonset | | | | |
|---|---|---|---|---|---|---|---|---|
| | | Civil | Naut. | 24 | 25 | 26 | 27 | |
| ° | h m | h m | h m | h m | h m | h m | h m | |
| N 40 | 16 40 | 17 11 | 17 45 | 17 43 | 19 02 | 20 21 | 21 38 | |
| 35 | 16 54 | 17 22 | 17 54 | 18 01 | 19 17 | 20 33 | 21 45 | |
| 30 | 17 07 | 17 33 | 18 03 | 18 17 | 19 31 | 20 43 | 21 52 | |
| 20 | 17 28 | 17 52 | 18 19 | 18 43 | 19 53 | 21 01 | 22 04 | |
| N 10 | 17 46 | 18 09 | 18 36 | 19 06 | 20 13 | 21 16 | 22 14 | |
| 0 | 18 04 | 18 26 | 18 53 | 19 27 | 20 31 | 21 30 | 22 23 | |
| S 10 | 18 21 | 18 44 | 19 12 | 19 48 | 20 49 | 21 43 | 22 32 | |
| 20 | 18 40 | 19 05 | 19 34 | 20 10 | 21 08 | 21 58 | 22 42 | |
| 30 | 19 02 | 19 30 | 20 03 | 20 36 | 21 30 | 22 15 | 22 53 | |
| 35 | 19 15 | 19 45 | 20 22 | 20 51 | 21 42 | 22 24 | 22 59 | |
| 40 | 19 30 | 20 03 | 20 45 | 21 08 | 21 57 | 22 35 | 23 06 | |
| 45 | 19 48 | 20 26 | 21 15 | 21 29 | 22 14 | 22 48 | 23 14 | |

| 26 00 | 179 55.8 | S23 22.3 | 139 59.3 | 4.7 | S22 29.8 | 10.5 | 60.8 |
| 01 | 194 55.5 | 22.3 | 154 23.0 | 4.8 | 22 19.3 | 10.5 | 60.8 |
| 02 | 209 55.1 | 22.2 | 168 46.8 | 4.9 | 22 08.7 | 10.7 | 60.7 |
| 03 | 224 54.8 ·· | 22.1 | 183 10.7 | 5.1 | 21 58.0 | 10.9 | 60.7 |
| 04 | 239 54.5 | 22.0 | 197 34.8 | 5.2 | 21 47.1 | 11.0 | 60.7 |
| 05 | 254 54.2 | 21.9 | 211 59.0 | 5.3 | 21 36.1 | 11.2 | 60.7 |
| 06 | 269 53.9 | S23 21.9 | 226 23.3 | 5.4 | S21 24.9 | 11.3 | 60.7 |
| 07 | 284 53.6 | 21.8 | 240 47.7 | 5.6 | 21 13.6 | 11.4 | 60.6 |
| 08 | 299 53.3 | 21.7 | 255 12.3 | 5.7 | 21 02.2 | 11.5 | 60.6 |
| M 09 | 314 53.0 ·· | 21.6 | 269 37.0 | 5.8 | 20 50.7 | 11.7 | 60.6 |
| O 10 | 329 52.7 | 21.5 | 284 01.8 | 6.0 | 20 39.0 | 11.8 | 60.6 |
| N 11 | 344 52.4 | 21.4 | 298 26.8 | 6.1 | 20 27.2 | 11.9 | 60.5 |
| D 12 | 359 52.1 | S23 21.3 | 312 51.9 | 6.2 | S20 15.3 | 12.1 | 60.5 |
| A 13 | 14 51.7 | 21.2 | 327 17.1 | 6.4 | 20 03.2 | 12.1 | 60.5 |
| Y 14 | 29 51.4 | 21.1 | 341 42.5 | 6.4 | 19 51.1 | 12.3 | 60.5 |
| 15 | 44 51.1 ·· | 21.1 | 356 07.9 | 6.6 | 19 38.8 | 12.4 | 60.4 |
| 16 | 59 50.8 | 21.0 | 10 33.5 | 6.8 | 19 26.4 | 12.6 | 60.4 |
| 17 | 74 50.5 | 20.9 | 24 59.3 | 6.8 | 19 13.9 | 12.7 | 60.4 |
| 18 | 89 50.2 | S23 20.8 | 39 25.1 | 7.0 | S19 01.2 | 12.7 | 60.4 |
| 19 | 104 49.9 | 20.7 | 53 51.1 | 7.2 | 18 48.5 | 12.8 | 60.3 |
| 20 | 119 49.6 | 20.6 | 68 17.3 | 7.2 | 18 35.7 | 13.0 | 60.3 |
| 21 | 134 49.3 ·· | 20.5 | 82 43.5 | 7.4 | 18 22.7 | 13.0 | 60.3 |
| 22 | 149 49.0 | 20.4 | 97 09.9 | 7.5 | 18 09.7 | 13.1 | 60.3 |
| 23 | 164 48.7 | 20.3 | 111 36.4 | 7.6 | S17 56.6 | 13.3 | 60.2 |

| | SUN | | | MOON | | | |
|---|---|---|---|---|---|---|---|
| Day | Eqn. of Time | | Mer. | Mer. Pass. | | Age | Phase |
| | 00ʰ | 12ʰ | Pass. | Upper | Lower | | |
| d | m s | m s | h m | h m | h m | d | % |
| 24 | 00 43 | 00 28 | 12 00 | 13 11 | 00 38 | 01 | 2 |
| 25 | 00 14 | 00 01 | 12 00 | 14 16 | 01 44 | 02 | 7 |
| 26 | 00 16 | 00 31 | 12 01 | 15 16 | 02 47 | 03 | 14 |

| SD 16.3 | d 0.1 | SD 16.7 | 16.6 | 16.5 |

| UT | ARIES GHA | VENUS −3.9 GHA | Dec | MARS −1.3 GHA | Dec | JUPITER −2.4 GHA | Dec | SATURN +0.8 GHA | Dec | STARS Name | SHA | Dec |
|---|---|---|---|---|---|---|---|---|---|---|---|---|
| 27 00 | 95 27.6 | 162 25.2 | S23 01.8 | 27 30.5 | N24 41.2 | 94 22.1 | S 0 57.1 | 130 44.6 | S15 22.5 | Acamar | 315 12.8 | S40 13.0 |
| 01 | 110 30.1 | 177 24.3 | 01.3 | 42 33.6 | 41.2 | 109 24.3 | 57.0 | 145 46.9 | 22.4 | Achernar | 335 21.3 | S57 07.5 |
| 02 | 125 32.6 | 192 23.4 | 00.9 | 57 36.6 | 41.1 | 124 26.5 | 56.9 | 160 49.1 | 22.3 | Acrux | 173 01.9 | S63 13.2 |
| 03 | 140 35.0 | 207 22.5 .. | 00.5 | 72 39.7 .. | 41.1 | 139 28.7 .. | 56.8 | 175 51.3 .. | 22.3 | Adhara | 255 06.8 | S29 00.1 |
| 04 | 155 37.5 | 222 21.6 | 23 00.1 | 87 42.8 | 41.0 | 154 31.0 | 56.6 | 190 53.6 | 22.2 | Aldebaran | 290 41.2 | N16 33.3 |
| 05 | 170 39.9 | 237 20.7 | 22 59.6 | 102 45.9 | 41.0 | 169 33.2 | 56.5 | 205 55.8 | 22.1 | | | |
| 06 | 185 42.4 | 252 19.7 | S22 59.2 | 117 49.0 | N24 40.9 | 184 35.4 | S 0 56.4 | 220 58.0 | S15 22.0 | Alioth | 166 14.5 | N55 49.9 |
| 07 | 200 44.9 | 267 18.8 | 58.8 | 132 52.0 | 40.9 | 199 37.6 | 56.3 | 236 00.2 | 22.0 | Alkaid | 152 53.5 | N49 11.7 |
| 08 | 215 47.3 | 282 17.9 | 58.3 | 147 55.1 | 40.8 | 214 39.8 | 56.2 | 251 02.5 | 21.9 | Alnair | 27 35.3 | S46 51.3 |
| T 09 | 230 49.8 | 297 17.0 .. | 57.9 | 162 58.2 .. | 40.8 | 229 42.1 .. | 56.1 | 266 04.7 .. | 21.8 | Alnilam | 275 39.1 | S 1 11.3 |
| U 10 | 245 52.3 | 312 16.1 | 57.5 | 178 01.3 | 40.7 | 244 44.3 | 55.9 | 281 06.9 | 21.7 | Alphard | 217 49.2 | S 8 45.4 |
| E 11 | 260 54.7 | 327 15.2 | 57.0 | 193 04.3 | 40.6 | 259 46.5 | 55.8 | 296 09.2 | 21.6 | | | |
| S 12 | 275 57.2 | 342 14.3 | S22 56.6 | 208 07.4 | N24 40.6 | 274 48.7 | S 0 55.7 | 311 11.4 | S15 21.6 | Alphecca | 126 05.5 | N26 38.1 |
| D 13 | 290 59.7 | 357 13.4 | 56.1 | 223 10.5 | 40.5 | 289 50.9 | 55.6 | 326 13.6 | 21.5 | Alpheratz | 357 36.5 | N29 13.1 |
| A 14 | 306 02.1 | 12 12.5 | 55.7 | 238 13.5 | 40.5 | 304 53.2 | 55.5 | 341 15.9 | 21.4 | Altair | 62 01.9 | N 8 55.7 |
| Y 15 | 321 04.6 | 27 11.6 .. | 55.3 | 253 16.6 .. | 40.4 | 319 55.4 .. | 55.3 | 356 18.1 .. | 21.3 | Ankaa | 353 08.8 | S42 11.2 |
| 16 | 336 07.1 | 42 10.7 | 54.8 | 268 19.7 | 40.4 | 334 57.6 | 55.2 | 11 20.3 | 21.2 | Antares | 112 18.2 | S26 28.9 |
| 17 | 351 09.5 | 57 09.8 | 54.4 | 283 22.7 | 40.3 | 349 59.8 | 55.1 | 26 22.5 | 21.2 | | | |
| 18 | 6 12.0 | 72 08.9 | S22 53.9 | 298 25.8 | N24 40.3 | 5 02.0 | S 0 55.0 | 41 24.8 | S15 21.1 | Arcturus | 145 49.6 | N19 03.7 |
| 19 | 21 14.4 | 87 08.0 | 53.5 | 313 28.8 | 40.2 | 20 04.3 | 54.9 | 56 27.0 | 21.0 | Atria | 107 14.5 | S69 03.9 |
| 20 | 36 16.9 | 102 07.1 | 53.0 | 328 31.9 | 40.2 | 35 06.5 | 54.8 | 71 29.2 | 20.9 | Avior | 234 14.8 | S59 34.8 |
| 21 | 51 19.4 | 117 06.2 .. | 52.6 | 343 35.0 .. | 40.1 | 50 08.7 .. | 54.6 | 86 31.5 .. | 20.9 | Bellatrix | 278 24.3 | N 6 22.2 |
| 22 | 66 21.8 | 132 05.3 | 52.1 | 358 38.0 | 40.1 | 65 10.9 | 54.5 | 101 33.7 | 20.8 | Betelgeuse | 270 53.6 | N 7 24.7 |
| 23 | 81 24.3 | 147 04.4 | 51.7 | 13 41.1 | 40.0 | 80 13.1 | 54.4 | 116 35.9 | 20.7 | | | |
| 28 00 | 96 26.8 | 162 03.5 | S22 51.2 | 28 44.1 | N24 40.0 | 95 15.3 | S 0 54.3 | 131 38.2 | S15 20.6 | Canopus | 263 52.6 | S52 42.4 |
| 01 | 111 29.2 | 177 02.6 | 50.8 | 43 47.2 | 39.9 | 110 17.6 | 54.2 | 146 40.4 | 20.5 | Capella | 280 23.9 | N46 01.3 |
| 02 | 126 31.7 | 192 01.7 | 50.3 | 58 50.2 | 39.9 | 125 19.8 | 54.0 | 161 42.6 | 20.5 | Deneb | 49 27.3 | N45 21.8 |
| 03 | 141 34.2 | 207 00.8 .. | 49.9 | 73 53.2 .. | 39.8 | 140 22.0 .. | 53.9 | 176 44.8 .. | 20.4 | Denebola | 182 26.6 | N14 26.6 |
| 04 | 156 36.6 | 221 59.9 | 49.4 | 88 56.3 | 39.8 | 155 24.2 | 53.8 | 191 47.1 | 20.3 | Diphda | 348 49.0 | S17 51.8 |
| 05 | 171 39.1 | 236 59.0 | 48.9 | 103 59.3 | 39.7 | 170 26.4 | 53.7 | 206 49.3 | 20.2 | | | |
| 06 | 186 41.5 | 251 58.1 | S22 48.5 | 119 02.4 | N24 39.7 | 185 28.6 | S 0 53.6 | 221 51.5 | S15 20.1 | Dubhe | 193 42.8 | N61 37.4 |
| W 07 | 201 44.0 | 266 57.2 | 48.0 | 134 05.4 | 39.6 | 200 30.9 | 53.5 | 236 53.8 | 20.1 | Elnath | 278 03.6 | N28 37.6 |
| E 08 | 216 46.5 | 281 56.3 | 47.6 | 149 08.5 | 39.6 | 215 33.1 | 53.3 | 251 56.0 | 20.0 | Eltanin | 90 43.5 | N51 29.1 |
| D 09 | 231 48.9 | 296 55.4 .. | 47.1 | 164 11.5 .. | 39.5 | 230 35.3 .. | 53.2 | 266 58.2 .. | 19.9 | Enif | 33 40.7 | N 9 58.8 |
| N 10 | 246 51.4 | 311 54.5 | 46.6 | 179 14.5 | 39.4 | 245 37.5 | 53.1 | 282 00.4 | 19.8 | Fomalhaut | 15 16.5 | S29 30.3 |
| E 11 | 261 53.9 | 326 53.6 | 46.2 | 194 17.6 | 39.4 | 260 39.7 | 53.0 | 297 02.7 | 19.7 | | | |
| S 12 | 276 56.3 | 341 52.7 | S22 45.7 | 209 20.6 | N24 39.3 | 275 41.9 | S 0 52.9 | 312 04.9 | S15 19.7 | Gacrux | 171 53.5 | S57 14.2 |
| D 13 | 291 58.8 | 356 51.8 | 45.2 | 224 23.6 | 39.3 | 290 44.1 | 52.7 | 327 07.1 | 19.6 | Gienah | 175 45.3 | S17 40.0 |
| A 14 | 307 01.3 | 11 50.9 | 44.8 | 239 26.7 | 39.2 | 305 46.4 | 52.6 | 342 09.4 | 19.5 | Hadar | 148 38.7 | S60 28.7 |
| Y 15 | 322 03.7 | 26 50.0 .. | 44.3 | 254 29.7 .. | 39.2 | 320 48.6 .. | 52.5 | 357 11.6 .. | 19.4 | Hamal | 327 52.9 | N23 34.3 |
| 16 | 337 06.2 | 41 49.1 | 43.8 | 269 32.7 | 39.1 | 335 50.8 | 52.4 | 12 13.8 | 19.4 | Kaus Aust. | 83 35.2 | S34 22.4 |
| 17 | 352 08.7 | 56 48.2 | 43.3 | 284 35.7 | 39.1 | 350 53.0 | 52.2 | 27 16.0 | 19.3 | | | |
| 18 | 7 11.1 | 71 47.3 | S22 42.9 | 299 38.8 | N24 39.0 | 5 55.2 | S 0 52.1 | 42 18.3 | S15 19.2 | Kochab | 137 20.5 | N74 03.4 |
| 19 | 22 13.6 | 86 46.4 | 42.4 | 314 41.8 | 39.0 | 20 57.4 | 52.0 | 57 20.5 | 19.1 | Markab | 13 31.7 | N15 19.7 |
| 20 | 37 16.0 | 101 45.6 | 41.9 | 329 44.8 | 38.9 | 35 59.6 | 51.9 | 72 22.7 | 19.0 | Menkar | 314 07.7 | N 4 10.7 |
| 21 | 52 18.5 | 116 44.7 .. | 41.4 | 344 47.8 .. | 38.9 | 51 01.8 .. | 51.8 | 87 24.9 .. | 19.0 | Menkent | 147 59.8 | S36 28.7 |
| 22 | 67 21.0 | 131 43.8 | 40.9 | 359 50.8 | 38.8 | 66 04.1 | 51.6 | 102 27.2 | 18.9 | Miaplacidus | 221 37.9 | S69 48.4 |
| 23 | 82 23.4 | 146 42.9 | 40.5 | 14 53.8 | 38.8 | 81 06.3 | 51.5 | 117 29.4 | 18.8 | | | |
| 29 00 | 97 25.9 | 161 42.0 | S22 40.0 | 29 56.9 | N24 38.7 | 96 08.5 | S 0 51.4 | 132 31.6 | S15 18.7 | Mirfak | 308 30.3 | N49 56.7 |
| 01 | 112 28.4 | 176 41.1 | 39.5 | 44 59.9 | 38.7 | 111 10.7 | 51.3 | 147 33.9 | 18.6 | Nunki | 75 50.2 | S26 16.1 |
| 02 | 127 30.8 | 191 40.2 | 39.0 | 60 02.9 | 38.6 | 126 12.9 | 51.2 | 162 36.1 | 18.6 | Peacock | 53 08.9 | S56 39.8 |
| 03 | 142 33.3 | 206 39.3 .. | 38.5 | 75 05.9 .. | 38.6 | 141 15.1 .. | 51.0 | 177 38.3 .. | 18.5 | Pollux | 243 19.0 | N27 58.2 |
| 04 | 157 35.8 | 221 38.4 | 38.0 | 90 08.9 | 38.5 | 156 17.3 | 50.9 | 192 40.5 | 18.4 | Procyon | 244 52.3 | N 5 10.0 |
| 05 | 172 38.2 | 236 37.5 | 37.6 | 105 11.9 | 38.5 | 171 19.5 | 50.8 | 207 42.8 | 18.3 | | | |
| 06 | 187 40.7 | 251 36.7 | S22 37.1 | 120 14.9 | N24 38.4 | 186 21.7 | S 0 50.7 | 222 45.0 | S15 18.2 | Rasalhague | 96 00.5 | N12 32.6 |
| 07 | 202 43.2 | 266 35.8 | 36.6 | 135 17.9 | 38.4 | 201 23.9 | 50.6 | 237 47.2 | 18.2 | Regulus | 207 36.0 | N11 51.3 |
| T 08 | 217 45.6 | 281 34.9 | 36.1 | 150 20.9 | 38.3 | 216 26.1 | 50.4 | 252 49.4 | 18.1 | Rigel | 281 05.2 | S 8 10.5 |
| H 09 | 232 48.1 | 296 34.0 .. | 35.6 | 165 23.9 .. | 38.3 | 231 28.4 .. | 50.3 | 267 51.7 .. | 18.0 | Rigil Kent. | 139 43.0 | S60 55.5 |
| U 10 | 247 50.5 | 311 33.1 | 35.1 | 180 26.9 | 38.2 | 246 30.6 | 50.2 | 282 53.9 | 17.9 | Sabik | 102 05.1 | S15 45.2 |
| R 11 | 262 53.0 | 326 32.2 | 34.6 | 195 29.9 | 38.2 | 261 32.8 | 50.1 | 297 56.1 | 17.8 | | | |
| S 12 | 277 55.5 | 341 31.3 | S22 34.1 | 210 32.9 | N24 38.1 | 276 35.0 | S 0 49.9 | 312 58.3 | S15 17.8 | Schedar | 349 32.9 | N56 40.0 |
| D 13 | 292 57.9 | 356 30.5 | 33.6 | 225 35.9 | 38.1 | 291 37.2 | 49.8 | 328 00.6 | 17.7 | Shaula | 96 13.1 | S37 07.2 |
| A 14 | 308 00.4 | 11 29.6 | 33.1 | 240 38.9 | 38.0 | 306 39.4 | 49.7 | 343 02.8 | 17.6 | Sirius | 258 27.4 | S16 44.8 |
| Y 15 | 323 02.9 | 26 28.7 .. | 32.6 | 255 41.9 .. | 38.0 | 321 41.6 .. | 49.6 | 358 05.0 .. | 17.5 | Spica | 158 24.2 | S11 16.8 |
| 16 | 338 05.3 | 41 27.8 | 32.1 | 270 44.9 | 37.9 | 336 43.8 | 49.4 | 13 07.2 | 17.4 | Suhail | 222 47.2 | S43 31.3 |
| 17 | 353 07.8 | 56 26.9 | 31.6 | 285 47.9 | 37.9 | 351 46.0 | 49.3 | 28 09.5 | 17.4 | | | |
| 18 | 8 10.3 | 71 26.0 | S22 31.1 | 300 50.8 | N24 37.8 | 6 48.2 | S 0 49.2 | 43 11.7 | S15 17.3 | Vega | 80 34.8 | N38 48.3 |
| 19 | 23 12.7 | 86 25.2 | 30.6 | 315 53.8 | 37.8 | 21 50.4 | 49.1 | 58 13.9 | 17.2 | Zuben'ubi | 136 58.1 | S16 08.1 |
| 20 | 38 15.2 | 101 24.3 | 30.1 | 330 56.8 | 37.7 | 36 52.6 | 49.0 | 73 16.1 | 17.1 | | SHA | Mer. Pass. |
| 21 | 53 17.6 | 116 23.4 .. | 29.6 | 345 59.8 .. | 37.7 | 51 54.8 .. | 48.8 | 88 18.4 .. | 17.0 | | ° ′ | h m |
| 22 | 68 20.1 | 131 22.5 | 29.1 | 1 02.8 | 37.6 | 66 57.0 | 48.7 | 103 20.6 | 17.0 | Venus | 65 36.7 | 13 13 |
| 23 | 83 22.6 | 146 21.6 | 28.6 | 16 05.7 | 37.6 | 81 59.2 | 48.6 | 118 22.8 | 16.9 | Mars | 292 17.3 | 22 01 |
| | h m | | | | | | | | | Jupiter | 358 48.6 | 17 36 |
| Mer. Pass. 17 31.3 | v −0.9 | d 0.5 | v 3.0 | d 0.1 | v 2.2 | d 0.1 | v 2.2 | d 0.1 | Saturn | 35 11.4 | 15 11 |

| UT | SUN | | MOON | | | | | Lat. | Twilight | | Sunrise | Moonrise | | | |
|---|---|---|---|---|---|---|---|---|---|---|---|---|---|---|---|
| | | | | | | | | | Naut. | Civil | | 27 | 28 | 29 | 30 |
| | GHA | Dec | GHA | v | Dec | d | HP | ° | h m | h m | h m | h m | h m | h m | h m |
| d h | ° ' | ° ' | ° ' | ' | ° ' | ' | ' | N 72 | 08 26 | 10 53 | ■■■ | 13 41 | 12 48 | 12 12 | 11 40 |
| 27 00 | 179 48.3 | S23 20.2 | 126 03.0 | 7.8 | S17 43.3 | 13.3 | 60.2 | N 70 | 08 07 | 09 54 | ■■■ | 13 11 | 12 35 | 12 08 | 11 44 |
| 01 | 194 48.0 | 20.1 | 140 29.8 | 7.8 | 17 30.0 | 13.4 | 60.2 | 68 | 07 51 | 09 20 | ■■■ | 12 49 | 12 24 | 12 05 | 11 48 |
| 02 | 209 47.7 | 20.0 | 154 56.6 | 8.0 | 17 16.6 | 13.5 | 60.1 | 66 | 07 38 | 08 55 | 10 33 | 12 31 | 12 16 | 12 03 | 11 51 |
| 03 | 224 47.4 | .. 19.9 | 169 23.6 | 8.2 | 17 03.1 | 13.6 | 60.1 | 64 | 07 27 | 08 35 | 09 52 | 12 16 | 12 08 | 12 01 | 11 53 |
| 04 | 239 47.1 | 19.8 | 183 50.8 | 8.2 | 16 49.5 | 13.7 | 60.1 | 62 | 07 18 | 08 19 | 09 25 | 12 04 | 12 01 | 11 59 | 11 56 |
| 05 | 254 46.8 | 19.7 | 198 18.0 | 8.4 | 16 35.8 | 13.8 | 60.1 | 60 | 07 09 | 08 06 | 09 03 | 11 54 | 11 56 | 11 57 | 11 58 |
| 06 | 269 46.5 | S23 19.6 | 212 45.4 | 8.5 | S16 22.0 | 13.8 | 60.0 | N 58 | 07 02 | 07 55 | 08 46 | 11 44 | 11 51 | 11 55 | 11 59 |
| 07 | 284 46.2 | 19.5 | 227 12.9 | 8.6 | 16 08.2 | 14.0 | 60.0 | 56 | 06 55 | 07 44 | 08 32 | 11 36 | 11 46 | 11 54 | 12 01 |
| T 08 | 299 45.9 | 19.4 | 241 40.5 | 8.7 | 15 54.2 | 14.0 | 60.0 | 54 | 06 49 | 07 35 | 08 19 | 11 29 | 11 42 | 11 53 | 12 02 |
| U 09 | 314 45.6 | .. 19.3 | 256 08.2 | 8.8 | 15 40.2 | 14.0 | 59.9 | 52 | 06 44 | 07 27 | 08 08 | 11 23 | 11 38 | 11 52 | 12 04 |
| E 10 | 329 45.3 | 19.2 | 270 36.0 | 9.0 | 15 26.2 | 14.2 | 59.9 | 50 | 06 38 | 07 20 | 07 58 | 11 17 | 11 35 | 11 50 | 12 05 |
| S 11 | 344 45.0 | 19.0 | 285 04.0 | 9.1 | 15 12.0 | 14.2 | 59.9 | 45 | 06 27 | 07 04 | 07 38 | 11 04 | 11 28 | 11 48 | 12 07 |
| D 12 | 359 44.6 | S23 18.9 | 299 32.1 | 9.2 | S14 57.8 | 14.3 | 59.8 | N 40 | 06 16 | 06 50 | 07 21 | 10 53 | 11 21 | 11 46 | 12 10 |
| A 13 | 14 44.3 | 18.8 | 314 00.3 | 9.3 | 14 43.5 | 14.4 | 59.8 | 35 | 06 07 | 06 39 | 07 07 | 10 44 | 11 16 | 11 45 | 12 12 |
| Y 14 | 29 44.0 | 18.7 | 328 28.6 | 9.4 | 14 29.1 | 14.4 | 59.8 | 30 | 05 58 | 06 28 | 06 55 | 10 36 | 11 11 | 11 43 | 12 13 |
| 15 | 44 43.7 | .. 18.6 | 342 57.0 | 9.5 | 14 14.7 | 14.5 | 59.7 | 20 | 05 42 | 06 10 | 06 34 | 10 22 | 11 03 | 11 41 | 12 16 |
| 16 | 59 43.4 | 18.5 | 357 25.5 | 9.7 | 14 00.2 | 14.6 | 59.7 | N 10 | 05 26 | 05 52 | 06 15 | 10 10 | 10 56 | 11 38 | 12 19 |
| 17 | 74 43.1 | 18.4 | 11 54.2 | 9.7 | 13 45.6 | 14.6 | 59.7 | 0 | 05 09 | 05 35 | 05 58 | 09 58 | 10 49 | 11 36 | 12 22 |
| 18 | 89 42.8 | S23 18.3 | 26 22.9 | 9.9 | S13 31.0 | 14.7 | 59.6 | S 10 | 04 50 | 05 17 | 05 40 | 09 47 | 10 42 | 11 34 | 12 24 |
| 19 | 104 42.5 | 18.1 | 40 51.8 | 9.9 | 13 16.3 | 14.7 | 59.6 | 20 | 04 28 | 04 57 | 05 21 | 09 34 | 10 35 | 11 32 | 12 27 |
| 20 | 119 42.2 | 18.0 | 55 20.7 | 10.1 | 13 01.6 | 14.8 | 59.6 | 30 | 03 59 | 04 32 | 04 59 | 09 20 | 10 27 | 11 30 | 12 30 |
| 21 | 134 41.9 | .. 17.9 | 69 49.8 | 10.2 | 12 46.8 | 14.8 | 59.5 | 35 | 03 40 | 04 17 | 04 47 | 09 12 | 10 22 | 11 28 | 12 32 |
| 22 | 149 41.6 | 17.8 | 84 19.0 | 10.2 | 12 32.0 | 14.9 | 59.5 | 40 | 03 17 | 03 59 | 04 32 | 09 02 | 10 16 | 11 26 | 12 34 |
| 23 | 164 41.3 | 17.7 | 98 48.2 | 10.4 | 12 17.1 | 15.0 | 59.5 | 45 | 02 47 | 03 36 | 04 14 | 08 51 | 10 10 | 11 25 | 12 37 |
| 28 00 | 179 41.0 | S23 17.6 | 113 17.6 | 10.5 | S12 02.1 | 14.9 | 59.4 | S 50 | 02 02 | 03 07 | 03 51 | 08 37 | 10 02 | 11 22 | 12 39 |
| 01 | 194 40.7 | 17.4 | 127 47.1 | 10.6 | 11 47.2 | 15.1 | 59.4 | 52 | 01 34 | 02 52 | 03 40 | 08 31 | 09 58 | 11 21 | 12 41 |
| 02 | 209 40.3 | 17.3 | 142 16.7 | 10.7 | 11 32.1 | 15.1 | 59.4 | 54 | 00 50 | 02 34 | 03 28 | 08 24 | 09 54 | 11 20 | 12 42 |
| 03 | 224 40.0 | .. 17.2 | 156 46.4 | 10.7 | 11 17.0 | 15.1 | 59.3 | 56 | //// | 02 12 | 03 14 | 08 16 | 09 50 | 11 19 | 12 44 |
| 04 | 239 39.7 | 17.1 | 171 16.1 | 10.9 | 11 01.9 | 15.1 | 59.3 | 58 | //// | 01 43 | 02 58 | 08 07 | 09 45 | 11 17 | 12 46 |
| 05 | 254 39.4 | 17.0 | 185 46.0 | 11.0 | 10 46.8 | 15.2 | 59.3 | S 60 | //// | 00 54 | 02 37 | 07 56 | 09 39 | 11 16 | 12 48 |
| 06 | 269 39.1 | S23 16.8 | 200 16.0 | 11.0 | S10 31.6 | 15.3 | 59.2 | | | | | | | | |
| W 07 | 284 38.8 | 16.7 | 214 46.0 | 11.2 | 10 16.3 | 15.2 | 59.2 | Lat. | Sunset | Twilight | | Moonset | | | |
| E 08 | 299 38.5 | 16.6 | 229 16.2 | 11.2 | 10 01.1 | 15.3 | 59.2 | | | Civil | Naut. | 27 | 28 | 29 | 30 |
| D 09 | 314 38.2 | .. 16.5 | 243 46.4 | 11.3 | 9 45.8 | 15.4 | 59.1 | | | | | | | | |
| N 10 | 329 37.9 | 16.3 | 258 16.7 | 11.4 | 9 30.4 | 15.3 | 59.1 | ° | h m | h m | h m | h m | h m | h m | h m |
| E 11 | 344 37.6 | 16.2 | 272 47.1 | 11.5 | 9 15.1 | 15.4 | 59.1 | N 72 | ■■■ | 13 11 | 15 37 | 19 08 | 21 46 | 24 01 | 00 01 |
| S 12 | 359 37.3 | S23 16.1 | 287 17.6 | 11.6 | S 8 59.7 | 15.4 | 59.0 | N 70 | ■■■ | 14 09 | 15 56 | 19 36 | 21 56 | 24 01 | 00 01 |
| D 13 | 14 37.0 | 15.9 | 301 48.2 | 11.7 | 8 44.3 | 15.5 | 59.0 | 68 | ■■■ | 14 44 | 16 12 | 19 56 | 22 04 | 24 01 | 00 01 |
| A 14 | 29 36.7 | 15.8 | 316 18.9 | 11.7 | 8 28.8 | 15.4 | 59.0 | 66 | 13 30 | 15 08 | 16 25 | 20 13 | 22 11 | 24 01 | 00 01 |
| Y 15 | 44 36.4 | .. 15.7 | 330 49.6 | 11.9 | 8 13.4 | 15.5 | 58.9 | 64 | 14 11 | 15 28 | 16 36 | 20 26 | 22 17 | 24 00 | 00 00 |
| 16 | 59 36.1 | 15.5 | 345 20.5 | 11.9 | 7 57.9 | 15.5 | 58.9 | 62 | 14 38 | 15 44 | 16 45 | 20 36 | 22 22 | 24 00 | 00 00 |
| 17 | 74 35.8 | 15.4 | 359 51.4 | 12.0 | 7 42.4 | 15.6 | 58.9 | 60 | 15 00 | 15 57 | 16 54 | 20 46 | 22 26 | 24 00 | 00 00 |
| 18 | 89 35.5 | S23 15.3 | 14 22.4 | 12.0 | S 7 26.8 | 15.5 | 58.8 | N 58 | 15 17 | 16 09 | 17 01 | 20 54 | 22 29 | 24 00 | 00 00 |
| 19 | 104 35.1 | 15.1 | 28 53.4 | 12.2 | 7 11.3 | 15.6 | 58.8 | 56 | 15 32 | 16 19 | 17 08 | 21 01 | 22 33 | 24 00 | 00 00 |
| 20 | 119 34.8 | 15.0 | 43 24.6 | 12.2 | 6 55.7 | 15.6 | 58.8 | 54 | 15 44 | 16 28 | 17 14 | 21 07 | 22 36 | 24 00 | 00 00 |
| 21 | 134 34.5 | .. 14.9 | 57 55.8 | 12.2 | 6 40.1 | 15.6 | 58.7 | 52 | 15 55 | 16 36 | 17 20 | 21 13 | 22 38 | 24 00 | 00 00 |
| 22 | 149 34.2 | 14.7 | 72 27.0 | 12.4 | 6 24.5 | 15.6 | 58.7 | 50 | 16 05 | 16 43 | 17 25 | 21 18 | 22 41 | 23 59 | 25 16 |
| 23 | 164 33.9 | 14.6 | 86 58.4 | 12.4 | 6 08.9 | 15.6 | 58.7 | 45 | 16 25 | 16 59 | 17 36 | 21 29 | 22 46 | 23 59 | 25 10 |
| 29 00 | 179 33.6 | S23 14.5 | 101 29.8 | 12.5 | S 5 53.3 | 15.6 | 58.6 | N 40 | 16 42 | 17 13 | 17 47 | 21 38 | 22 50 | 23 59 | 25 06 |
| 01 | 194 33.3 | 14.3 | 116 01.3 | 12.5 | 5 37.7 | 15.6 | 58.6 | 35 | 16 56 | 17 24 | 17 56 | 21 45 | 22 54 | 23 59 | 25 02 |
| 02 | 209 33.0 | 14.2 | 130 32.8 | 12.7 | 5 22.1 | 15.7 | 58.5 | 30 | 17 08 | 17 35 | 18 05 | 21 52 | 22 57 | 23 59 | 24 59 |
| 03 | 224 32.7 | .. 14.0 | 145 04.5 | 12.6 | 5 06.4 | 15.6 | 58.5 | 20 | 17 30 | 17 54 | 18 21 | 22 04 | 23 03 | 23 59 | 24 53 |
| 04 | 239 32.4 | 13.9 | 159 36.1 | 12.8 | 4 50.8 | 15.7 | 58.5 | N 10 | 17 48 | 18 11 | 18 37 | 22 14 | 23 07 | 23 58 | 24 48 |
| 05 | 254 32.1 | 13.8 | 174 07.9 | 12.8 | 4 35.1 | 15.6 | 58.4 | 0 | 18 05 | 18 28 | 18 54 | 22 23 | 23 12 | 23 58 | 24 43 |
| 06 | 269 31.8 | S23 13.6 | 188 39.7 | 12.8 | S 4 19.5 | 15.7 | 58.4 | S 10 | 18 23 | 18 46 | 19 13 | 22 32 | 23 16 | 23 58 | 24 38 |
| 07 | 284 31.5 | 13.5 | 203 11.5 | 13.0 | 4 03.8 | 15.6 | 58.4 | 20 | 18 42 | 19 06 | 19 34 | 22 42 | 23 21 | 23 57 | 24 33 |
| T 08 | 299 31.2 | 13.3 | 217 43.5 | 12.9 | 3 48.2 | 15.7 | 58.3 | 30 | 19 03 | 19 31 | 20 04 | 22 53 | 23 26 | 23 57 | 24 27 |
| H 09 | 314 30.9 | .. 13.2 | 232 15.4 | 13.1 | 3 32.5 | 15.7 | 58.3 | 35 | 19 16 | 19 46 | 20 23 | 22 59 | 23 29 | 23 57 | 24 24 |
| U 10 | 329 30.6 | 13.0 | 246 47.5 | 13.0 | 3 16.9 | 15.7 | 58.3 | 40 | 19 31 | 20 04 | 20 46 | 23 06 | 23 33 | 23 57 | 24 20 |
| R 11 | 344 30.3 | 12.9 | 261 19.5 | 13.2 | 3 01.2 | 15.6 | 58.2 | 45 | 19 49 | 20 26 | 21 16 | 23 14 | 23 37 | 23 56 | 24 16 |
| S 12 | 359 30.0 | S23 12.7 | 275 51.7 | 13.2 | S 2 45.6 | 15.7 | 58.2 | S 50 | 20 11 | 20 56 | 22 01 | 23 24 | 23 41 | 23 56 | 24 11 |
| D 13 | 14 29.7 | 12.6 | 290 23.9 | 13.2 | 2 29.9 | 15.6 | 58.2 | 52 | 20 22 | 21 11 | 22 28 | 23 29 | 23 43 | 23 56 | 24 08 |
| A 14 | 29 29.4 | 12.4 | 304 56.1 | 13.3 | 2 14.3 | 15.6 | 58.1 | 54 | 20 34 | 21 29 | 23 12 | 23 34 | 23 46 | 23 56 | 24 05 |
| Y 15 | 44 29.1 | .. 12.3 | 319 28.4 | 13.3 | 1 58.7 | 15.6 | 58.1 | 56 | 20 48 | 21 50 | //// | 23 39 | 23 48 | 23 56 | 24 03 |
| 16 | 59 28.8 | 12.1 | 334 00.7 | 13.4 | 1 43.1 | 15.6 | 58.1 | 58 | 21 05 | 22 19 | //// | 23 45 | 23 51 | 23 55 | 24 00 |
| 17 | 74 28.5 | 12.0 | 348 33.1 | 13.4 | 1 27.5 | 15.6 | 58.0 | S 60 | 21 25 | 23 07 | //// | 23 52 | 23 54 | 23 55 | 23 56 |
| 18 | 89 28.2 | S23 11.8 | 3 05.5 | 13.4 | S 1 11.9 | 15.6 | 58.0 | | | | | | | | |
| 19 | 104 27.9 | 11.7 | 17 37.9 | 13.5 | 0 56.3 | 15.5 | 58.0 | | | SUN | | | MOON | | |
| 20 | 119 27.6 | 11.5 | 32 10.4 | 13.6 | 0 40.8 | 15.7 | 57.9 | Day | Eqn. of Time | | Mer. | Mer. Pass. | | Age | Phase |
| 21 | 134 27.3 | .. 11.4 | 46 43.0 | 13.5 | 0 25.2 | 15.5 | 57.9 | | 00ʰ | 12ʰ | Pass. | Upper | Lower | | |
| 22 | 149 27.0 | 11.2 | 61 15.5 | 13.6 | S 0 09.7 | 15.5 | 57.9 | d | m s | m s | h m | h m | h m | d % | |
| 23 | 164 26.6 | 11.1 | 75 48.1 | 13.7 | N 0 05.8 | 15.5 | 57.8 | 27 | 00 46 | 01 01 | 12 01 | 16 11 | 03 44 | 04 23 | |
| | | | | | | | | 28 | 01 16 | 01 30 | 12 02 | 17 01 | 04 36 | 05 33 | |
| | SD 16.3 | d 0.1 | SD 16.3 | | 16.1 | | 15.9 | 29 | 01 45 | 01 59 | 12 02 | 17 47 | 05 24 | 06 44 | |

| UT | ARIES GHA | VENUS −3.9 GHA | Dec | MARS −1.2 GHA | Dec | JUPITER −2.4 GHA | Dec | SATURN +0.8 GHA | Dec | STARS Name | SHA | Dec |
|---|---|---|---|---|---|---|---|---|---|---|---|---|
| d h | ° ′ | ° ′ | ° ′ | ° ′ | ° ′ | ° ′ | ° ′ | ° ′ | ° ′ | | ° ′ | ° ′ |
| 30 00 | 98 25.0 | 161 20.7 | S22 28.1 | 31 08.7 | N24 37.5 | 97 01.4 | S 0 48.5 | 133 25.0 | S15 16.8 | Acamar | 315 12.8 | S40 13.0 |
| 01 | 113 27.5 | 176 19.9 | 27.6 | 46 11.7 | 37.5 | 112 03.6 | 48.3 | 148 27.3 | 16.7 | Achernar | 335 21.3 | S57 07.5 |
| 02 | 128 30.0 | 191 19.0 | 27.0 | 61 14.7 | 37.4 | 127 05.9 | 48.2 | 163 29.5 | 16.6 | Acrux | 173 01.9 | S63 13.2 |
| 03 | 143 32.4 | 206 18.1 . . | 26.5 | 76 17.6 . . | 37.4 | 142 08.1 . . | 48.1 | 178 31.7 . . | 16.6 | Adhara | 255 06.8 | S29 00.2 |
| 04 | 158 34.9 | 221 17.2 | 26.0 | 91 20.6 | 37.3 | 157 10.3 | 48.0 | 193 33.9 | 16.5 | Aldebaran | 290 41.2 | N16 33.3 |
| 05 | 173 37.4 | 236 16.4 | 25.5 | 106 23.6 | 37.3 | 172 12.5 | 47.8 | 208 36.2 | 16.4 | | | |
| 06 | 188 39.8 | 251 15.5 | S22 25.0 | 121 26.5 | N24 37.3 | 187 14.7 | S 0 47.7 | 223 38.4 | S15 16.3 | Alioth | 166 14.5 | N55 49.9 |
| 07 | 203 42.3 | 266 14.6 | 24.5 | 136 29.5 | 37.2 | 202 16.9 | 47.6 | 238 40.6 | 16.2 | Alkaid | 152 53.5 | N49 11.7 |
| 08 | 218 44.8 | 281 13.7 | 23.9 | 151 32.5 | 37.2 | 217 19.1 | 47.5 | 253 42.8 | 16.1 | Alnair | 27 35.3 | S46 51.2 |
| F 09 | 233 47.2 | 296 12.8 . . | 23.4 | 166 35.4 . . | 37.1 | 232 21.3 . . | 47.3 | 268 45.1 . . | 16.1 | Alnilam | 275 39.1 | S 1 11.3 |
| R 10 | 248 49.7 | 311 12.0 | 22.9 | 181 38.4 | 37.1 | 247 23.5 | 47.2 | 283 47.3 | 16.0 | Alphard | 217 49.2 | S 8 45.4 |
| I 11 | 263 52.1 | 326 11.1 | 22.4 | 196 41.4 | 37.0 | 262 25.7 | 47.1 | 298 49.5 | 15.9 | | | |
| D 12 | 278 54.6 | 341 10.2 | S22 21.9 | 211 44.3 | N24 37.0 | 277 27.9 | S 0 47.0 | 313 51.7 | S15 15.8 | Alphecca | 126 05.4 | N26 38.1 |
| A 13 | 293 57.1 | 356 09.3 | 21.3 | 226 47.3 | 36.9 | 292 30.1 | 46.8 | 328 54.0 | 15.7 | Alpheratz | 357 36.5 | N29 13.1 |
| Y 14 | 308 59.5 | 11 08.5 | 20.8 | 241 50.2 | 36.9 | 307 32.3 | 46.7 | 343 56.2 | 15.7 | Altair | 62 01.9 | N 8 55.7 |
| 15 | 324 02.0 | 26 07.6 . . | 20.3 | 256 53.2 . . | 36.8 | 322 34.5 . . | 46.6 | 358 58.4 . . | 15.6 | Ankaa | 353 08.8 | S42 11.2 |
| 16 | 339 04.5 | 41 06.7 | 19.7 | 271 56.1 | 36.8 | 337 36.7 | 46.5 | 14 00.6 | 15.5 | Antares | 112 18.2 | S26 28.9 |
| 17 | 354 06.9 | 56 05.9 | 19.2 | 286 59.1 | 36.7 | 352 38.9 | 46.3 | 29 02.8 | 15.4 | | | |
| 18 | 9 09.4 | 71 05.0 | S22 18.7 | 302 02.0 | N24 36.7 | 7 41.1 | S 0 46.2 | 44 05.1 | S15 15.3 | Arcturus | 145 49.6 | N19 03.7 |
| 19 | 24 11.9 | 86 04.1 | 18.2 | 317 05.0 | 36.6 | 22 43.3 | 46.1 | 59 07.3 | 15.3 | Atria | 107 14.5 | S69 03.9 |
| 20 | 39 14.3 | 101 03.2 | 17.6 | 332 07.9 | 36.6 | 37 45.5 | 46.0 | 74 09.5 | 15.2 | Avior | 234 14.8 | S59 34.8 |
| 21 | 54 16.8 | 116 02.4 . . | 17.1 | 347 10.9 . . | 36.5 | 52 47.7 . . | 45.8 | 89 11.7 . . | 15.1 | Bellatrix | 278 24.3 | N 6 22.2 |
| 22 | 69 19.3 | 131 01.5 | 16.6 | 2 13.8 | 36.5 | 67 49.9 | 45.7 | 104 14.0 | 15.0 | Betelgeuse | 270 53.6 | N 7 24.7 |
| 23 | 84 21.7 | 146 00.6 | 16.0 | 17 16.7 | 36.4 | 82 52.1 | 45.6 | 119 16.2 | 14.9 | | | |
| 31 00 | 99 24.2 | 160 59.8 | S22 15.5 | 32 19.7 | N24 36.4 | 97 54.3 | S 0 45.4 | 134 18.4 | S15 14.9 | Canopus | 263 52.6 | S52 42.5 |
| 01 | 114 26.6 | 175 58.9 | 14.9 | 47 22.6 | 36.3 | 112 56.5 | 45.3 | 149 20.6 | 14.8 | Capella | 280 23.9 | N46 01.3 |
| 02 | 129 29.1 | 190 58.0 | 14.4 | 62 25.6 | 36.3 | 127 58.7 | 45.2 | 164 22.8 | 14.7 | Deneb | 49 27.4 | N45 21.8 |
| 03 | 144 31.6 | 205 57.2 . . | 13.9 | 77 28.5 . . | 36.3 | 143 00.9 . . | 45.1 | 179 25.1 . . | 14.6 | Denebola | 182 26.6 | N14 26.6 |
| 04 | 159 34.0 | 220 56.3 | 13.3 | 92 31.4 | 36.2 | 158 03.1 | 44.9 | 194 27.3 | 14.5 | Diphda | 348 49.0 | S17 51.8 |
| 05 | 174 36.5 | 235 55.4 | 12.8 | 107 34.4 | 36.2 | 173 05.3 | 44.8 | 209 29.5 | 14.4 | | | |
| 06 | 189 39.0 | 250 54.6 | S22 12.2 | 122 37.3 | N24 36.1 | 188 07.4 | S 0 44.7 | 224 31.7 | S15 14.4 | Dubhe | 193 42.8 | N61 37.4 |
| 07 | 204 41.4 | 265 53.7 | 11.7 | 137 40.2 | 36.1 | 203 09.6 | 44.6 | 239 34.0 | 14.3 | Elnath | 278 03.6 | N28 37.6 |
| S 08 | 219 43.9 | 280 52.8 | 11.1 | 152 43.1 | 36.0 | 218 11.8 | 44.4 | 254 36.2 | 14.2 | Eltanin | 90 43.5 | N51 29.1 |
| A 09 | 234 46.4 | 295 52.0 . . | 10.6 | 167 46.1 . . | 36.0 | 233 14.0 . . | 44.3 | 269 38.4 . . | 14.1 | Enif | 33 40.7 | N 9 58.8 |
| T 10 | 249 48.8 | 310 51.1 | 10.0 | 182 49.0 | 35.9 | 248 16.2 | 44.2 | 284 40.6 | 14.0 | Fomalhaut | 15 16.5 | S29 30.3 |
| U 11 | 264 51.3 | 325 50.2 | 09.5 | 197 51.9 | 35.9 | 263 18.4 | 44.0 | 299 42.8 | 14.0 | | | |
| R 12 | 279 53.7 | 340 49.4 | S22 08.9 | 212 54.8 | N24 35.8 | 278 20.6 | S 0 43.9 | 314 45.1 | S15 13.9 | Gacrux | 171 53.5 | S57 14.2 |
| D 13 | 294 56.2 | 355 48.5 . . | 08.4 | 227 57.7 | 35.8 | 293 22.8 | 43.8 | 329 47.3 | 13.8 | Gienah | 175 45.3 | S17 40.0 |
| A 14 | 309 58.7 | 10 47.6 | 07.8 | 243 00.7 | 35.7 | 308 25.0 | 43.7 | 344 49.5 | 13.7 | Hadar | 148 38.6 | S60 28.7 |
| Y 15 | 325 01.1 | 25 46.8 . . | 07.3 | 258 03.6 . . | 35.7 | 323 27.2 . . | 43.5 | 359 51.7 . . | 13.6 | Hamal | 327 52.9 | N23 34.3 |
| 16 | 340 03.6 | 40 45.9 | 06.7 | 273 06.5 | 35.7 | 338 29.4 | 43.4 | 14 53.9 | 13.5 | Kaus Aust. | 83 35.2 | S34 22.4 |
| 17 | 355 06.1 | 55 45.1 | 06.2 | 288 09.4 | 35.6 | 353 31.6 | 43.3 | 29 56.2 | 13.5 | | | |
| 18 | 10 08.5 | 70 44.2 | S22 05.6 | 303 12.3 | N24 35.6 | 8 33.8 | S 0 43.1 | 44 58.4 | S15 13.4 | Kochab | 137 20.5 | N74 03.4 |
| 19 | 25 11.0 | 85 43.3 | 05.0 | 318 15.2 | 35.5 | 23 36.0 | 43.0 | 60 00.6 | 13.3 | Markab | 13 31.7 | N15 19.7 |
| 20 | 40 13.5 | 100 42.5 | 04.5 | 333 18.1 | 35.5 | 38 38.2 | 42.9 | 75 02.8 | 13.2 | Menkar | 314 07.7 | N 4 10.7 |
| 21 | 55 15.9 | 115 41.6 . . | 03.9 | 348 21.0 . . | 35.4 | 53 40.4 . . | 42.8 | 90 05.1 . . | 13.1 | Menkent | 147 59.8 | S36 28.7 |
| 22 | 70 18.4 | 130 40.8 | 03.3 | 3 23.9 | 35.4 | 68 42.6 | 42.6 | 105 07.3 | 13.1 | Miaplacidus | 221 37.8 | S69 48.4 |
| 23 | 85 20.9 | 145 39.9 | 02.8 | 18 26.8 | 35.3 | 83 44.7 | 42.5 | 120 09.5 | 13.0 | | | |
| 1 00 | 100 23.3 | 160 39.0 | S22 02.2 | 33 29.7 | N24 35.3 | 98 46.9 | S 0 42.4 | 135 11.7 | S15 12.9 | Mirfak | 308 30.3 | N49 56.7 |
| 01 | 115 25.8 | 175 38.2 | 01.6 | 48 32.6 | 35.3 | 113 49.1 | 42.2 | 150 13.9 | 12.8 | Nunki | 75 50.2 | S26 16.1 |
| 02 | 130 28.2 | 190 37.3 | 01.1 | 63 35.5 | 35.2 | 128 51.3 | 42.1 | 165 16.2 | 12.7 | Peacock | 53 08.9 | S56 39.8 |
| 03 | 145 30.7 | 205 36.5 | 22 00.5 | 78 38.4 . . | 35.2 | 143 53.5 . . | 42.0 | 180 18.4 . . | 12.6 | Pollux | 243 19.0 | N27 58.2 |
| 04 | 160 33.2 | 220 35.6 | 21 59.9 | 93 41.3 | 35.1 | 158 55.7 | 41.9 | 195 20.6 | 12.6 | Procyon | 244 52.3 | N 5 10.0 |
| 05 | 175 35.6 | 235 34.8 | 59.4 | 108 44.2 | 35.1 | 173 57.9 | 41.7 | 210 22.8 | 12.5 | | | |
| 06 | 190 38.1 | 250 33.9 | S21 58.8 | 123 47.1 | N24 35.0 | 189 00.1 | S 0 41.6 | 225 25.0 | S15 12.4 | Rasalhague | 96 00.4 | N12 32.6 |
| 07 | 205 40.6 | 265 33.0 | 58.2 | 138 50.0 | 35.0 | 204 02.3 | 41.5 | 240 27.3 | 12.3 | Regulus | 207 36.0 | N11 51.3 |
| 08 | 220 43.0 | 280 32.2 | 57.6 | 153 52.9 | 34.9 | 219 04.5 | 41.3 | 255 29.5 | 12.2 | Rigel | 281 05.2 | S 8 10.5 |
| S 09 | 235 45.5 | 295 31.3 . . | 57.1 | 168 55.8 . . | 34.9 | 234 06.7 . . | 41.2 | 270 31.7 . . | 12.1 | Rigil Kent. | 139 43.0 | S60 55.5 |
| U 10 | 250 48.0 | 310 30.5 | 56.5 | 183 58.7 | 34.9 | 249 08.8 | 41.1 | 285 33.9 | 12.1 | Sabik | 102 05.0 | S15 45.2 |
| N 11 | 265 50.4 | 325 29.6 | 55.9 | 199 01.6 | 34.8 | 264 11.0 | 40.9 | 300 36.1 | 12.0 | | | |
| D 12 | 280 52.9 | 340 28.8 | S21 55.3 | 214 04.4 | N24 34.8 | 279 13.2 | S 0 40.8 | 315 38.3 | S15 11.9 | Schedar | 349 32.9 | N56 40.0 |
| A 13 | 295 55.4 | 355 27.9 | 54.8 | 229 07.3 | 34.7 | 294 15.4 | 40.7 | 330 40.6 | 11.8 | Shaula | 96 13.1 | S37 07.2 |
| Y 14 | 310 57.8 | 10 27.1 | 54.2 | 244 10.2 | 34.7 | 309 17.6 | 40.6 | 345 42.8 | 11.7 | Sirius | 258 27.4 | S16 44.9 |
| 15 | 326 00.3 | 25 26.2 . . | 53.6 | 259 13.1 . . | 34.6 | 324 19.8 . . | 40.4 | 0 45.0 . . | 11.7 | Spica | 158 24.1 | S11 16.8 |
| 16 | 341 02.7 | 40 25.4 | 53.0 | 274 16.0 | 34.6 | 339 22.0 | 40.3 | 15 47.2 | 11.6 | Suhail | 222 47.2 | S43 31.3 |
| 17 | 356 05.2 | 55 24.5 | 52.4 | 289 18.8 | 34.6 | 354 24.2 | 40.2 | 30 49.4 | 11.5 | | | |
| 18 | 11 07.7 | 70 23.7 | S21 51.8 | 304 21.7 | N24 34.5 | 9 26.3 | S 0 40.0 | 45 51.7 | S15 11.4 | Vega | 80 34.8 | N38 48.2 |
| 19 | 26 10.1 | 85 22.8 | 51.3 | 319 24.6 | 34.5 | 24 28.5 | 39.9 | 60 53.9 | 11.3 | Zuben'ubi | 136 58.1 | S16 08.1 |
| 20 | 41 12.6 | 100 22.0 | 50.7 | 334 27.4 | 34.4 | 39 30.7 | 39.8 | 75 56.1 | 11.2 | | SHA | Mer. Pass. |
| 21 | 56 15.1 | 115 21.1 . . | 50.1 | 349 30.3 . . | 34.4 | 54 32.9 . . | 39.6 | 90 58.3 . . | 11.2 | | ° ′ | h m |
| 22 | 71 17.5 | 130 20.3 | 49.5 | 4 33.2 | 34.3 | 69 35.1 | 39.5 | 106 00.5 | 11.1 | Venus | 61 35.6 | 13 17 |
| 23 | 86 20.0 | 145 19.4 | 48.9 | 19 36.0 | 34.3 | 84 37.3 | 39.4 | 121 02.8 | 11.0 | Mars | 292 55.5 | 21 46 |
| Mer. Pass. | h m 17 19.5 | v −0.9 | d 0.6 | v 2.9 | d 0.0 | v 2.2 | d 0.1 | v 2.2 | d 0.1 | Jupiter | 358 30.1 | 17 26 |
| | | | | | | | | | | Saturn | 34 54.2 | 15 01 |

| UT | SUN GHA | SUN Dec | MOON GHA | v | MOON Dec | d | HP |
|---|---|---|---|---|---|---|---|
| d h | ° ′ | ° ′ | ° ′ | ′ | ° ′ | ′ | ′ |
| **30** 00 | 179 26.3 | S23 10.9 | 90 20.8 | 13.6 | N 0 21.3 | 15.5 | 57.8 |
| 01 | 194 26.0 | 10.7 | 104 53.4 | 13.8 | 0 36.8 | 15.4 | 57.7 |
| 02 | 209 25.7 | 10.6 | 119 26.2 | 13.7 | 0 52.2 | 15.5 | 57.7 |
| 03 | 224 25.4 | .. 10.4 | 133 58.9 | 13.8 | 1 07.7 | 15.4 | 57.7 |
| 04 | 239 25.1 | 10.3 | 148 31.7 | 13.8 | 1 23.1 | 15.3 | 57.6 |
| 05 | 254 24.8 | 10.1 | 163 04.5 | 13.8 | 1 38.4 | 15.4 | 57.6 |
| 06 | 269 24.5 | S23 09.9 | 177 37.3 | 13.8 | N 1 53.8 | 15.3 | 57.6 |
| 07 | 284 24.2 | 09.8 | 192 10.1 | 13.9 | 2 09.1 | 15.3 | 57.5 |
| F  08 | 299 23.9 | 09.6 | 206 43.0 | 13.9 | 2 24.4 | 15.3 | 57.5 |
| R  09 | 314 23.6 | .. 09.4 | 221 15.9 | 13.9 | 2 39.7 | 15.2 | 57.5 |
| I  10 | 329 23.3 | 09.3 | 235 48.8 | 13.9 | 2 54.9 | 15.3 | 57.4 |
| D  11 | 344 23.0 | 09.1 | 250 21.7 | 14.0 | 3 10.2 | 15.1 | 57.4 |
| A  12 | 359 22.7 | S23 08.9 | 264 54.7 | 14.0 | N 3 25.3 | 15.2 | 57.4 |
| Y  13 | 14 22.4 | 08.8 | 279 27.7 | 14.0 | 3 40.5 | 15.1 | 57.3 |
| 14 | 29 22.1 | 08.6 | 294 00.7 | 14.0 | 3 55.6 | 15.1 | 57.3 |
| 15 | 44 21.8 | .. 08.4 | 308 33.7 | 14.0 | 4 10.7 | 15.0 | 57.3 |
| 16 | 59 21.5 | 08.3 | 323 06.7 | 14.0 | 4 25.7 | 15.1 | 57.3 |
| 17 | 74 21.2 | 08.1 | 337 39.7 | 14.1 | 4 40.8 | 14.9 | 57.2 |
| 18 | 89 20.9 | S23 07.9 | 352 12.8 | 14.0 | N 4 55.7 | 15.0 | 57.2 |
| 19 | 104 20.6 | 07.8 | 6 45.8 | 14.1 | 5 10.7 | 14.9 | 57.2 |
| 20 | 119 20.3 | 07.6 | 21 18.9 | 14.1 | 5 25.6 | 14.8 | 57.1 |
| 21 | 134 20.0 | .. 07.4 | 35 52.0 | 14.0 | 5 40.4 | 14.8 | 57.1 |
| 22 | 149 19.7 | 07.2 | 50 25.0 | 14.1 | 5 55.2 | 14.8 | 57.1 |
| 23 | 164 19.4 | 07.1 | 64 58.1 | 14.1 | 6 10.0 | 14.7 | 57.0 |
| **31** 00 | 179 19.1 | S23 06.9 | 79 31.2 | 14.1 | N 6 24.7 | 14.7 | 57.0 |
| 01 | 194 18.8 | 06.7 | 94 04.3 | 14.1 | 6 39.4 | 14.7 | 57.0 |
| 02 | 209 18.5 | 06.5 | 108 37.4 | 14.1 | 6 54.1 | 14.6 | 56.9 |
| 03 | 224 18.2 | .. 06.3 | 123 10.5 | 14.1 | 7 08.7 | 14.5 | 56.9 |
| 04 | 239 17.9 | 06.2 | 137 43.6 | 14.1 | 7 23.2 | 14.5 | 56.9 |
| 05 | 254 17.6 | 06.0 | 152 16.7 | 14.0 | 7 37.7 | 14.5 | 56.8 |
| 06 | 269 17.3 | S23 05.8 | 166 49.7 | 14.1 | N 7 52.2 | 14.4 | 56.8 |
| S  07 | 284 17.0 | 05.6 | 181 22.8 | 14.1 | 8 06.6 | 14.4 | 56.8 |
| A  08 | 299 16.7 | 05.4 | 195 55.9 | 14.1 | 8 21.0 | 14.3 | 56.8 |
| T  09 | 314 16.4 | .. 05.2 | 210 29.0 | 14.0 | 8 35.3 | 14.2 | 56.7 |
| U  10 | 329 16.1 | 05.1 | 225 02.0 | 14.1 | 8 49.5 | 14.2 | 56.7 |
| R  11 | 344 15.8 | 04.9 | 239 35.1 | 14.0 | 9 03.7 | 14.2 | 56.7 |
| D  12 | 359 15.6 | S23 04.7 | 254 08.1 | 14.1 | N 9 17.9 | 14.1 | 56.6 |
| A  13 | 14 15.3 | 04.5 | 268 41.2 | 14.0 | 9 32.0 | 14.0 | 56.6 |
| Y  14 | 29 15.0 | 04.3 | 283 14.2 | 14.0 | 9 46.0 | 14.0 | 56.6 |
| 15 | 44 14.7 | .. 04.1 | 297 47.2 | 14.0 | 10 00.0 | 13.9 | 56.5 |
| 16 | 59 14.4 | 03.9 | 312 20.2 | 14.0 | 10 13.9 | 13.9 | 56.5 |
| 17 | 74 14.1 | 03.7 | 326 53.2 | 14.0 | 10 27.8 | 13.8 | 56.5 |
| 18 | 89 13.8 | S23 03.5 | 341 26.2 | 13.9 | N10 41.6 | 13.8 | 56.5 |
| 19 | 104 13.5 | 03.4 | 355 59.1 | 13.9 | 10 55.4 | 13.7 | 56.4 |
| 20 | 119 13.2 | 03.2 | 10 32.0 | 14.0 | 11 09.1 | 13.6 | 56.4 |
| 21 | 134 12.9 | .. 03.0 | 25 05.0 | 13.9 | 11 22.7 | 13.6 | 56.4 |
| 22 | 149 12.6 | 02.8 | 39 37.9 | 13.8 | 11 36.3 | 13.5 | 56.3 |
| 23 | 164 12.3 | 02.6 | 54 10.7 | 13.9 | 11 49.8 | 13.4 | 56.3 |
| **1** 00 | 179 12.0 | S23 02.4 | 68 43.6 | 13.8 | N12 03.2 | 13.4 | 56.3 |
| 01 | 194 11.7 | 02.2 | 83 16.4 | 13.8 | 12 16.6 | 13.3 | 56.3 |
| 02 | 209 11.4 | 02.0 | 97 49.2 | 13.8 | 12 29.9 | 13.3 | 56.2 |
| 03 | 224 11.1 | .. 01.8 | 112 22.0 | 13.8 | 12 43.2 | 13.1 | 56.2 |
| 04 | 239 10.8 | 01.6 | 126 54.8 | 13.7 | 12 56.3 | 13.2 | 56.2 |
| 05 | 254 10.5 | 01.4 | 141 27.5 | 13.7 | 13 09.5 | 13.0 | 56.2 |
| 06 | 269 10.2 | S23 01.2 | 156 00.2 | 13.7 | N13 22.5 | 13.0 | 56.1 |
| 07 | 284 09.9 | 01.0 | 170 32.9 | 13.6 | 13 35.5 | 12.9 | 56.1 |
| S  08 | 299 09.6 | 00.8 | 185 05.5 | 13.6 | 13 48.4 | 12.8 | 56.1 |
| U  09 | 314 09.3 | .. 00.6 | 199 38.1 | 13.6 | 14 01.2 | 12.8 | 56.0 |
| N  10 | 329 09.0 | 00.4 | 214 10.7 | 13.6 | 14 14.0 | 12.7 | 56.0 |
| 11 | 344 08.7 | 00.2 | 228 43.3 | 13.5 | 14 26.7 | 12.6 | 56.0 |
| D  12 | 359 08.4 | S23 00.0 | 243 15.8 | 13.5 | N14 39.3 | 12.5 | 56.0 |
| A  13 | 14 08.2 | 22 59.8 | 257 48.3 | 13.5 | 14 51.8 | 12.5 | 55.9 |
| Y  14 | 29 07.9 | 59.6 | 272 20.8 | 13.4 | 15 04.3 | 12.4 | 55.9 |
| 15 | 44 07.6 | .. 59.3 | 286 53.2 | 13.4 | 15 16.7 | 12.3 | 55.9 |
| 16 | 59 07.3 | 59.1 | 301 25.6 | 13.4 | 15 29.0 | 12.2 | 55.9 |
| 17 | 74 07.0 | 58.9 | 315 58.0 | 13.3 | 15 41.2 | 12.1 | 55.8 |
| 18 | 89 06.7 | S22 58.7 | 330 30.3 | 13.3 | N15 53.3 | 12.1 | 55.8 |
| 19 | 104 06.4 | 58.5 | 345 02.6 | 13.2 | 16 05.4 | 12.0 | 55.8 |
| 20 | 119 06.1 | 58.3 | 359 34.8 | 13.2 | 16 17.4 | 11.9 | 55.8 |
| 21 | 134 05.8 | .. 58.1 | 14 07.0 | 13.2 | 16 29.3 | 11.9 | 55.8 |
| 22 | 149 05.5 | 57.9 | 28 39.2 | 13.1 | 16 41.2 | 11.7 | 55.7 |
| 23 | 164 05.2 | 57.6 | 43 11.3 | 13.1 | N16 52.9 | 11.7 | 55.7 |
| | SD 16.3 | d 0.2 | SD 15.6 | | 15.4 | | 15.3 |

### Twilight / Sunrise / Moonrise

| Lat. | Naut. | Civil | Sunrise | Moonrise 30 | 31 | 1 | 2 |
|---|---|---|---|---|---|---|---|
| ° | h m | h m | h m | h m | h m | h m | h m |
| N 72 | 08 25 | 10 46 | ■■■ | 11 40 | 11 06 | 10 20 | □ |
| N 70 | 08 06 | 09 51 | ■■■ | 11 44 | 11 19 | 10 47 | 09 50 |
| 68 | 07 50 | 09 18 | ■■■ | 11 48 | 11 30 | 11 08 | 10 36 |
| 66 | 07 38 | 08 54 | 10 30 | 11 51 | 11 39 | 11 25 | 11 07 |
| 64 | 07 27 | 08 35 | 09 51 | 11 53 | 11 46 | 11 39 | 11 30 |
| 62 | 07 18 | 08 19 | 09 24 | 11 56 | 11 53 | 11 50 | 11 48 |
| 60 | 07 09 | 08 06 | 09 03 | 11 58 | 11 59 | 12 00 | 12 03 |
| N 58 | 07 02 | 07 54 | 08 46 | 11 59 | 12 04 | 12 09 | 12 16 |
| 56 | 06 56 | 07 44 | 08 31 | 12 01 | 12 08 | 12 17 | 12 28 |
| 54 | 06 50 | 07 36 | 08 19 | 12 02 | 12 12 | 12 24 | 12 38 |
| 52 | 06 44 | 07 28 | 08 08 | 12 04 | 12 16 | 12 30 | 12 47 |
| 50 | 06 39 | 07 20 | 07 59 | 12 05 | 12 19 | 12 35 | 12 55 |
| 45 | 06 27 | 07 04 | 07 38 | 12 07 | 12 27 | 12 48 | 13 12 |
| N 40 | 06 17 | 06 51 | 07 22 | 12 10 | 12 33 | 12 58 | 13 26 |
| 35 | 06 08 | 06 40 | 07 08 | 12 12 | 12 38 | 13 07 | 13 38 |
| 30 | 05 59 | 06 29 | 06 56 | 12 13 | 12 43 | 13 14 | 13 48 |
| 20 | 05 43 | 06 11 | 06 35 | 12 16 | 12 52 | 13 28 | 14 06 |
| N 10 | 05 27 | 05 54 | 06 16 | 12 19 | 12 59 | 13 40 | 14 22 |
| 0 | 05 11 | 05 37 | 05 59 | 12 22 | 13 06 | 13 51 | 14 37 |
| S 10 | 04 52 | 05 19 | 05 42 | 12 24 | 13 13 | 14 02 | 14 52 |
| 20 | 04 30 | 04 59 | 05 23 | 12 27 | 13 21 | 14 14 | 15 08 |
| 30 | 04 01 | 04 34 | 05 01 | 12 30 | 13 29 | 14 28 | 15 27 |
| 35 | 03 42 | 04 19 | 04 49 | 12 32 | 13 34 | 14 36 | 15 38 |
| 40 | 03 20 | 04 01 | 04 34 | 12 34 | 13 40 | 14 45 | 15 51 |
| 45 | 02 50 | 03 39 | 04 16 | 12 37 | 13 47 | 14 56 | 16 05 |
| S 50 | 02 05 | 03 10 | 03 54 | 12 39 | 13 55 | 15 10 | 16 24 |
| 52 | 01 39 | 02 55 | 03 43 | 12 41 | 13 59 | 15 16 | 16 33 |
| 54 | 00 57 | 02 37 | 03 31 | 12 42 | 14 03 | 15 23 | 16 42 |
| 56 | //// | 02 16 | 03 17 | 12 44 | 14 08 | 15 31 | 16 54 |
| 58 | //// | 01 47 | 03 01 | 12 46 | 14 13 | 15 39 | 17 06 |
| S 60 | //// | 01 02 | 02 41 | 12 48 | 14 19 | 15 49 | 17 22 |

### Sunset / Twilight / Moonset

| Lat. | Sunset | Civil | Naut. | Moonset 30 | 31 | 1 | 2 |
|---|---|---|---|---|---|---|---|
| ° | h m | h m | h m | h m | h m | h m | h m |
| N 72 | ■■■ | 13 20 | 15 41 | 00 01 | 02 12 | 04 33 | □ |
| N 70 | ■■■ | 14 15 | 16 01 | 00 01 | 02 02 | 04 08 | 06 41 |
| 68 | ■■■ | 14 48 | 16 16 | 00 01 | 01 53 | 03 49 | 05 56 |
| 66 | 13 37 | 15 13 | 16 29 | 00 01 | 01 46 | 03 33 | 05 27 |
| 64 | 14 16 | 15 32 | 16 39 | 00 00 | 01 41 | 03 21 | 05 05 |
| 62 | 14 43 | 15 47 | 16 49 | 00 00 | 01 36 | 03 11 | 04 47 |
| 60 | 15 03 | 16 00 | 16 57 | 00 00 | 01 31 | 03 02 | 04 33 |
| N 58 | 15 20 | 16 12 | 17 04 | 00 00 | 01 27 | 02 54 | 04 21 |
| 56 | 15 35 | 16 22 | 17 11 | 00 00 | 01 24 | 02 47 | 04 10 |
| 54 | 15 47 | 16 31 | 17 17 | 00 00 | 01 21 | 02 41 | 04 01 |
| 52 | 15 58 | 16 39 | 17 22 | 00 00 | 01 18 | 02 36 | 03 53 |
| 50 | 16 08 | 16 46 | 17 27 | 25 16 | 01 16 | 02 31 | 03 45 |
| 45 | 16 28 | 17 02 | 17 39 | 25 10 | 01 10 | 02 20 | 03 30 |
| N 40 | 16 44 | 17 15 | 17 49 | 25 06 | 01 06 | 02 11 | 03 17 |
| 35 | 16 58 | 17 26 | 17 58 | 25 02 | 01 02 | 02 04 | 03 06 |
| 30 | 17 10 | 17 37 | 18 07 | 24 59 | 00 59 | 01 57 | 02 56 |
| 20 | 17 31 | 17 55 | 18 23 | 24 53 | 00 53 | 01 46 | 02 40 |
| N 10 | 17 50 | 18 12 | 18 39 | 24 48 | 00 48 | 01 39 | 02 26 |
| 0 | 18 07 | 18 29 | 18 55 | 24 43 | 00 43 | 01 27 | 02 13 |
| S 10 | 18 24 | 18 47 | 19 14 | 24 38 | 00 38 | 01 18 | 02 00 |
| 20 | 18 43 | 19 07 | 19 36 | 24 33 | 00 33 | 01 08 | 01 46 |
| 30 | 19 04 | 19 32 | 20 05 | 24 27 | 00 27 | 00 57 | 01 30 |
| 35 | 19 17 | 19 47 | 20 23 | 24 24 | 00 24 | 00 51 | 01 21 |
| 40 | 19 32 | 20 05 | 20 46 | 24 20 | 00 20 | 00 44 | 01 10 |
| 45 | 19 50 | 20 27 | 21 16 | 24 16 | 00 16 | 00 36 | 00 58 |
| S 50 | 20 12 | 20 56 | 22 00 | 24 10 | 00 10 | 00 26 | 00 43 |
| 52 | 20 22 | 21 10 | 22 26 | 24 08 | 00 08 | 00 21 | 00 36 |
| 54 | 20 34 | 21 28 | 23 07 | 24 05 | 00 05 | 00 16 | 00 28 |
| 56 | 20 48 | 21 49 | //// | 24 03 | 00 03 | 00 10 | 00 20 |
| 58 | 21 04 | 22 17 | //// | 24 00 | 00 00 | 00 10 | 00 10 |
| S 60 | 21 24 | 23 01 | //// | 23 56 | 23 57 | 23 59 | 24 04 |

### SUN / MOON

| Day | Eqn. of Time 00ʰ | Eqn. of Time 12ʰ | Mer. Pass. | Mer. Pass. Upper | Mer. Pass. Lower | Age | Phase |
|---|---|---|---|---|---|---|---|
| d | m s | m s | h m | h m | h m | d | % |
| 30 | 02 14 | 02 28 | 12 02 | 18 32 | 06 10 | 07 | 55 |
| 31 | 02 43 | 02 57 | 12 03 | 19 17 | 06 54 | 08 | 65 |
| 1 | 03 11 | 03 26 | 12 03 | 20 02 | 07 39 | 09 | 74 |

# EXPLANATION

## PRINCIPLE AND ARRANGEMENT

1. *Object.* The object of this Almanac is to provide, in a convenient form, the data required for the practice of astronomical navigation at sea.

2. *Principle.* The main contents of the Almanac consist of data from which the *Greenwich Hour Angle* (GHA) and the *Declination* (Dec) of all the bodies used for navigation can be obtained for any instant of *Universal Time* (UT, specifically UT1, or previously Greenwich Mean Time (GMT)).

The *Local Hour Angle* (LHA) can then be obtained by means of the formula:

$$LHA = GHA \; \begin{matrix} - \text{ west} \\ + \text{ east} \end{matrix} \; \text{longitude}$$

The remaining data consist of: times of rising and setting of the Sun and Moon, and times of twilight; miscellaneous calendarial and planning data and auxiliary tables, including a list of Standard Times; corrections to be applied to observed altitude.

For the Sun, Moon, and planets, the GHA and Dec are tabulated directly for each hour of UT throughout the year. For the stars, the *Sidereal Hour Angle* (SHA) is given, and the GHA is obtained from:

$$GHA \; Star = GHA \; Aries + SHA \; Star$$

The SHA and Dec of the stars change slowly and may be regarded as constant over periods of several days. GHA Aries, or the Greenwich Hour Angle of the first point of Aries (the Vernal Equinox), is tabulated for each hour. Permanent tables give the appropriate increments and corrections to the tabulated hourly values of GHA and Dec for the minutes and seconds of UT.

The six-volume series of *Sight Reduction Tables for Marine Navigation* (published in U.S.A. as Pub. No. 229) has been designed for the solution of the navigational triangle and is intended for use with *The Nautical Almanac*.

Two alternative procedures for sight reduction are described on pages 277–318. The first requires the use of programmable calculators or computers, while the second uses a set of concise tables that is given on pages 286–317.

The tabular accuracy is $0\!'\!.1$ throughout. The time argument on the daily pages of this Almanac is UT1 denoted throughout by UT. This scale may differ from the broadcast time signals (UTC) by an amount which, if ignored, will introduce an error of up to $0\!'\!.2$ in longitude determined from astronomical observations. The difference arises because the time argument depends on the variable rate of rotation of the Earth while the broadcast time signals are based on an atomic time-scale. Step adjustments of exactly one second are made to the time signals as required (normally at $24^h$ on December 31 and June 30) so that the difference between the time signals and UT, as used in this Almanac, may not exceed $0\!^s\!.9$. Those who require to reduce observations to a precision of better than $1^s$ must therefore obtain the correction (DUT1) to the time signals from coding in the signal, or from other sources; the required time is given by UT1=UTC+DUT1 to a precision of $0\!^s\!.1$. Alternatively, the longitude, when determined from astronomical observations, may be corrected by the corresponding amount shown in the following table:

| Correction to time signals | Correction to longitude |
|---|---|
| $-0\!^s\!.9$ to $-0\!^s\!.7$ | $0\!'\!.2$ to east |
| $-0\!^s\!.6$ to $-0\!^s\!.3$ | $0\!'\!.1$ to east |
| $-0\!^s\!.2$ to $+0\!^s\!.2$ | no correction |
| $+0\!^s\!.3$ to $+0\!^s\!.6$ | $0\!'\!.1$ to west |
| $+0\!^s\!.7$ to $+0\!^s\!.9$ | $0\!'\!.2$ to west |

3. *Lay-out.*   The ephemeral data for three days are presented on an opening of two pages: the left-hand page contains the data for the planets and stars; the right-hand page contains the data for the Sun and Moon, together with times of twilight, sunrise, sunset, moonrise and moonset.

The remaining contents are arranged as follows: for ease of reference the altitude-correction tables are given on pages A2, A3, A4, xxxiv and xxxv; calendar, Moon's phases, eclipses, and planet notes (i.e. data of general interest) precede the main tabulations. The Explanation is followed by information on standard times, star charts and list of star positions, sight reduction procedures and concise sight reduction tables, polar phenomena information and graphs, tables of increments and corrections and other auxiliary tables that are frequently used.

## MAIN DATA

4. *Daily pages.*   The daily pages give the GHA of Aries, the GHA and Dec of the Sun, Moon, and the four navigational planets, for each hour of UT. For the Moon, values of $v$ and $d$ are also tabulated for each hour to facilitate the correction of GHA and Dec to intermediate times; $v$ and $d$ for the Sun and planets change so slowly that they are given, at the foot of the appropriate columns, once only on the page; $v$ is zero for Aries and negligible for the Sun, and is omitted. The SHA and Dec of the 57 selected stars, arranged in alphabetical order of proper name, are also given.

5. *Stars.*   The SHA and Dec of 173 stars, including the 57 selected stars, are tabulated for each month on pages 268–273; no interpolation is required and the data can be used in precisely the same way as those for the selected stars on the daily pages. The stars are arranged in order of SHA.

The list of 173 includes all stars down to magnitude 3·0, together with a few fainter ones to fill the larger gaps. The 57 selected stars have been chosen from amongst these on account of brightness and distribution in the sky; they will suffice for the majority of observations.

The 57 selected stars are known by their proper names, but they are also numbered in descending order of SHA. In the list of 173 stars, the constellation names are always given on the left hand page; on the facing page proper names are given where well-known names exist. Numbers for the selected stars are given in both columns.

An index to the selected stars, containing lists in both alphabetical and numerical order, is given on page xxxiii and is also reprinted on the bookmark.

6. *Increments and corrections.*   The tables printed on tinted paper (pages ii–xxxi) at the back of the Almanac provide the increments and corrections for minutes and seconds to be applied to the hourly values of GHA and Dec. They consist of sixty tables, one for each minute, separated into two parts: increments to GHA for Sun and planets, Aries, and Moon for every minute and second; and, for each minute, corrections to be applied to GHA and Dec corresponding to the values of $v$ and $d$ given on the daily pages.

The increments are based on the following adopted hourly rates of increase of the GHA: Sun and planets, 15° precisely; Aries, 15° 02ʹ46; Moon, 14° 19ʹ0. The values of $v$ on the daily pages are the excesses of the actual hourly motions over the adopted values; they are generally positive, except for Venus. The tabulated hourly values of the Sun's GHA have been adjusted to reduce to a minimum the error caused by treating $v$ as negligible. The values of $d$ on the daily pages are the hourly differences of the Dec. For the Moon, the true values of $v$ and $d$ are given for each hour; otherwise mean values are given for the three days on the page.

7. *Method of entry.*   The UT of an observation is expressed as a day and hour, followed by a number of minutes and seconds. The tabular values of GHA and Dec, and, where necessary, the corresponding values of $v$ and $d$, are taken directly from the daily pages for the day and hour of UT; this hour is always *before* the time of observation. SHA and Dec of the selected stars are also taken from the daily pages.

The table of Increments and Corrections for the minute of UT is then selected. For the GHA, the increment for minutes and seconds is taken from the appropriate column opposite the seconds of UT; the $v$-correction is taken from the second part of the same table opposite the value of $v$ as given on the daily pages. Both increment and $v$-correction are to be added to the GHA, except for Venus when $v$ is prefixed by a minus sign and the $v$-correction is to be subtracted. For the Dec there is no increment, but a $d$-correction is applied in the same way as the $v$-correction; $d$ is given without sign on the daily pages and the sign of the correction is to be supplied by inspection of the Dec column. In many cases the correction may be applied mentally.

8. *Examples.* (a) Sun and Moon. Required the GHA and Dec of the Sun and Moon on 2022 February 7 at $15^h$ $47^m$ $13^s$ UT.

| | SUN | | | MOON | | | |
|---|---|---|---|---|---|---|---|
| | GHA | Dec | d | GHA | v | Dec | d |
| | ° ′ | ° ′ | ′ | ° ′ | ′ | ° ′ | ′ |
| Daily page, February 7ᵈ 15ʰ | 41 28·5 | S 15 11·2 | 0·8 | 326 15·1 | 14·6 | N 12 39·1 | 12·1 |
| Increments for 47ᵐ 13ˢ | 11 48·3 | | | 11 16·0 | | | |
| v or d corrections for 47ᵐ | | −0·6 | | | +11·6 | +9·6 | |
| Sum for February 7ᵈ 15ʰ 47ᵐ 13ˢ | 53 16·8 | S 15 10·6 | | 337 42·7 | | N 12 48·7 | |

(b) Planets. Required the LHA and Dec of (i) Venus on 2022 February 7 at $11^h$ $14^m$ $29^s$ UT in longitude W 86° 18′; (ii) Jupiter on 2022 February 7 at $7^h$ $37^m$ $34^s$ UT in longitude E 165° 24′.

| | VENUS | | | | JUPITER | | | |
|---|---|---|---|---|---|---|---|---|
| | GHA | v | Dec | d | GHA | v | Dec | d |
| | ° ′ | ′ | ° ′ | ′ | ° ′ | ′ | ° ′ | ′ |
| Daily page, Feb. 7ᵈ | (11ʰ) 19 25·7 | 1·6 | S 16 29·4 | 0·1 | (7ʰ) 261 43·2 | 1·9 | S 9 13·0 | 0·2 |
| Increments (planets) | (14ᵐ 29ˢ) 3 37·3 | | | | (37ᵐ 34ˢ) 9 23·5 | | | |
| v or d corrections | (14ᵐ) +0·4 | | +0·0 | | (37ᵐ) +1·2 | | −0·1 | |
| Sum = GHA and Dec. | 23 03·4 | | S 16 29·4 | | 271 07·9 | | S 9 12·9 | |
| Longitude | (west) − 86 18·0 | | | | (east) +165 24·0 | | | |
| Multiples of 360° | +360 | | | | −360 | | | |
| LHA planet | 296 45·4 | | | | 76 31·9 | | | |

(c) Stars. Required the GHA and Dec of (i) *Aldebaran* on 2022 February 7 at $20^h$ $20^m$ $22^s$ UT; (ii) *Vega* on 2022 February 7 at $7^h$ $30^m$ $27^s$ UT.

| | Aldebaran | | Vega | |
|---|---|---|---|---|
| | GHA | Dec | GHA | Dec |
| | ° ′ | ° ′ | ° ′ | ° ′ |
| Daily page (SHA and Dec) | 290 42·2 | N 16 33.2 | 80 35·2 | N 38 48.0 |
| Daily page (GHA Aries) | (20ʰ) 77 55·0 | | (7ʰ) 242 23·0 | |
| Increments (Aries) | (20ᵐ 22ˢ) 5 06·3 | | (30ᵐ 27ˢ) 7 38·0 | |
| Sum = GHA star | 373 43·5 | | 330 36·2 | |
| Multiples of 360° | −360 | | | |
| GHA star | 13 43·5 | | 330 36·2 | |

9. *Polaris (Pole Star) tables.* The tables on pages 274–276 provide means by which the latitude can be deduced from an observed altitude of *Polaris*, and they also give its azimuth; their use is explained and illustrated on those pages. They are based on the following formula:

$$\text{Latitude} - H_O = -p \cos h + \tfrac{1}{2} p \sin p \sin^2 h \, \tan(\text{latitude})$$

where

$H_O$ = Apparent altitude (corrected for refraction)

$p$ = polar distance of *Polaris* = 90° − Dec

$h$ = local hour angle of *Polaris* = LHA Aries + SHA

$a_0$, which is a function of LHA Aries only, is the value of both terms of the above formula calculated for mean values of the SHA (314° 59′) and Dec (N 89° 21′·5) of *Polaris*, for a mean latitude of 50°, and adjusted by the addition of a constant (58′·8).

$a_1$, which is a function of LHA Aries and latitude, is the excess of the value of the second term over its mean value for latitude 50°, increased by a constant (0ʹ6) to make it always positive. $a_2$, which is a function of LHA Aries and date, is the correction to the first term for the variation of *Polaris* from its adopted mean position; it is increased by a constant (0ʹ6) to make it positive. The sum of the added constants is 1°, so that:

$$\text{Latitude} = \text{Apparent altitude (corrected for refraction)} - 1° + a_0 + a_1 + a_2$$

### RISING AND SETTING PHENOMENA

10. *General.* On the right-hand daily pages are given the times of sunrise and sunset, of the beginning and end of civil and nautical twilights, and of moonrise and moonset for a range of latitudes from N 72° to S 60°. These times, which are given to the nearest minute, are strictly the UT of the phenomena on the Greenwich meridian; they are given for every day for moonrise and moonset, but only for the middle day of the three on each page for the solar phenomena.

They are approximately the Local Mean Times (LMT) of the corresponding phenomena on other meridians; they can be formally interpolated if desired. The UT of a phenomenon is obtained from the LMT by:

$$\text{UT} = \text{LMT} \genfrac{}{}{0pt}{}{+\ \text{west}}{-\ \text{east}} \text{ longitude}$$

in which the longitude must first be converted to time by the table on page i or otherwise. Interpolation for latitude can be done mentally or with the aid of Table I on page xxxii.

The following symbols are used to indicate the conditions under which, in high latitudes, some of the phenomena do not occur:

☐ Sun or Moon remains continuously above the horizon;

■ Sun or Moon remains continuously below the horizon;

//// twilight lasts all night.

*Basis of the tabulations.* At sunrise and sunset 16ʹ is allowed for semi-diameter and 34ʹ for horizontal refraction, so that at the times given the Sun's upper limb is on the visible horizon; all times refer to phenomena as seen from sea level with a clear horizon.

At the times given for the beginning and end of twilight, the Sun's zenith distance is 96° for civil, and 102° for nautical twilight. The degree of illumination at the times given for civil twilight (in good conditions and in the absence of other illumination) is such that the brightest stars are visible and the horizon is clearly defined. At the times given for nautical twilight, the horizon is in general not visible, and it is too dark for observation with a marine sextant.

Times corresponding to other depressions of the Sun may be obtained by interpolation or, for depressions of more than 12°, less reliably, by extrapolation; times so obtained will be subject to considerable uncertainty near extreme conditions.

At moonrise and moonset, allowance is made for semi-diameter, parallax, and refraction (34ʹ), so that at the times given the Moon's upper limb is on the visible horizon as seen from sea level.

*Polar phenomena.* Information and graphs concerning the rising and setting of the Sun and Moon and the duration of civil twilight for high latitudes are given on pages 320–325.

11. *Sunrise, sunset, twilight.* The tabulated times may be regarded, without serious error, as the LMT of the phenomena on any of the three days on the page and in any longitude. Precise times may normally be obtained by interpolating the tabular values for latitude and to the correct day and longitude, the latter being expressed as a fraction of a day by dividing it by 360°, positive for west and negative for east longitudes. In the extreme conditions near ☐, ■ or //// interpolation may not be possible in one direction, but accurate times are of little value in these circumstances.

*Examples.* Required the UT of (a) the beginning of morning twilights and sunrise on 2022 January 13 for latitude S 48° 55ʹ, longitude E 75° 18ʹ; (b) sunset and the end of evening twilights on 2022 January 15 for latitude N 67° 10ʹ, longitude W 168° 05ʹ.

| | (a) | Twilight Nautical | Civil | Sunrise | (b) | Sunset | Twilight Civil | Nautical |
|---|---|---|---|---|---|---|---|---|
| From p. 19 | | d h m | d h m | d h m | | d h m | d h m | d h m |
| LMT for Lat | S 45° | 13 03 09 | 13 03 56 | 13 04 32 | N 66° | 15 14 23 | 15 15 43 | 15 16 54 |
| Corr. to (p. xxxii, Table I) | S 48° 55′ | −27 | −20 | −16 | N 67° 10′ | −22 | −12 | −6 |
| Long (p. i) | E 75° 18′ | −5 01 | −5 01 | −5 01 | W 168° 05′ | +11 12 | +11 12 | +11 12 |
| UT | | 12 21 41 | 12 22 35 | 12 23 15 | | 16 01 13 | 16 02 43 | 16 04 00 |

The LMT are strictly for January 14 (middle date on page) and 0° longitude; for more precise times it is necessary to interpolate, but rounding errors may accumulate to about $2^m$.

(a) to January $13^d - 75°/360° = $ Jan. $12^d{\cdot}8$, i.e. $\frac{1}{3}(1{\cdot}2) = 0{\cdot}4$ backwards towards the data for the same latitude interpolated similarly from page 17; the corrections are $-3^m$ to nautical twilight, $-2^m$ to civil twilight and $-2^m$ to sunrise.

(b) to January $15^d + 168°/360° = $ Jan. $15^d{\cdot}5$, i.e. $\frac{1}{3}(1{\cdot}5) = 0{\cdot}5$ forwards towards the data for the same latitude interpolated similarly from page 21; the corrections are $+7^m$ to sunset, $+4^m$ to civil twilight, and $+3^m$ to nautical twilight.

12. *Moonrise, moonset.* Precise times of moonrise and moonset are rarely needed; a glance at the tables will generally give sufficient indication of whether the Moon is available for observation and of the hours of rising and setting. If needed, precise times may be obtained as follows. Interpolate for latitude, using Table I on page xxxii, on the day wanted and also on the preceding day in east longitudes or the following day in west longitudes; take the difference between these times and interpolate for longitude by applying to the time for the day wanted the correction from Table II on page xxxii, so that the resulting time is between the two times used. In extreme conditions near □ or ■ interpolation for latitude or longitude may be possible only in one direction; accurate times are of little value in these circumstances.

To facilitate this interpolation, the times of moonrise and moonset are given for four days on each page; where no phenomenon occurs during a particular day (as happens once a month) the time of the phenomenon on the following day, increased by $24^h$, is given; extra care must be taken when interpolating between two values, when one of those values exceeds $24^h$. In practice it suffices to use the daily difference between the times for the nearest tabular latitude, and generally, to enter Table II with the nearest tabular arguments as in the examples below.

*Examples.* Required the UT of moonrise and moonset in latitude S 47° 10′, longitudes E 124° 00′ and W 78° 31′ on 2022 January 9.

| | Longitude E 124° 00′ Moonrise | Moonset | Longitude W 78° 31′ Moonrise | Moonset |
|---|---|---|---|---|
| | d h m | d h m | d h m | d h m |
| LMT for Lat. S 45° | 9 12 02 | 9 23 46 | 9 12 02 | 9 23 46 |
| Lat correction (p. xxxii, Table I) | +02 | −02 | +02 | −02 |
| Long correction (p. xxxii, Table II) | −23 | −07 | +16 | +04 |
| Correct LMT | 9 11 41 | 9 23 37 | 9 12 20 | 9 23 48 |
| Longitude (p. i) | −8 16 | −8 16 | +5 14 | +5 14 |
| UT | 9 03 25 | 9 15 21 | 9 17 34 | 10 05 02 |

## ALTITUDE CORRECTION TABLES

13. *General.* In general, two corrections are given for application to altitudes observed with a marine sextant; additional corrections are required for Venus and Mars and also for very low altitudes.

Tables of the correction for dip of the horizon, due to height of eye above sea level, are given on pages A2 and xxxiv. Strictly this correction should be applied first and subtracted from the sextant altitude to give apparent altitude, which is the correct argument for the other tables.

Separate tables are given of the second correction for the Sun, for stars and planets (on pages A2 and A3), and for the Moon (on pages xxxiv and xxxv). For the Sun, values are given for both lower and upper limbs, for two periods of the year. The star tables are used for the planets, but additional corrections for parallax (page A2) are required for Venus and Mars. The Moon tables are in two parts: the main correction is a function of apparent altitude only and is tabulated for the lower limb (30′ must be subtracted to obtain the correction for the upper limb); the other, which is given for both lower and upper limbs, depends also on the horizontal parallax, which has to be taken from the daily pages.

An additional correction, given on page A4, is required for the change in the refraction, due to variations of pressure and temperature from the adopted standard conditions; it may generally be ignored for altitudes greater than 10°, except possibly in extreme conditions. The correction tables for the Sun, stars, and planets are in two parts; only those for altitudes greater than 10° are reprinted on the bookmark.

14. *Critical tables.* Some of the altitude correction tables are arranged as critical tables. In these, an interval of apparent altitude (or height of eye) corresponds to a single value of the correction; no interpolation is required. At a "critical" entry the upper of the two possible values of the correction is to be taken. For example, in the table of dip, a correction of −4′1 corresponds to all values of the height of eye from 5·3 to 5·5 metres (17·5 to 18·3 feet) inclusive.

15. *Examples.* The following examples illustrate the use of the altitude correction tables; the sextant altitudes given are assumed to be taken on 2022 March 12 with a marine sextant at height 5·4 metres (18 feet), temperature −3°C and pressure 982 mb, the Moon sights being taken at about $10^h$ UT.

| | SUN lower limb | SUN upper limb | MOON lower limb | MOON upper limb | VENUS | *Polaris* |
|---|---|---|---|---|---|---|
| | ° ′ | ° ′ | ° ′ | ° ′ | ° ′ | ° ′ |
| Sextant altitude | 21 19·7 | 3 20·2 | 33 27·6 | 26 06·7 | 4 32·6 | 49 36·5 |
| Dip, height 5·4 metres (18 feet) | −4·1 | −4·1 | −4·1 | −4·1 | −4·1 | −4·1 |
| Main correction | +13·8 | −29·6 | +57·4 | +60·5 | −10·8 | −0·8 |
| −30′ for upper limb (Moon) | — | — | — | −30·0 | — | — |
| L, U correction for Moon | — | — | +1·3 | +1·6 | — | — |
| Additional correction for Venus | — | — | — | — | +0·2 | — |
| Additional refraction correction | −0·1 | −0·6 | −0·1 | −0·1 | −0·5 | 0·0 |
| Corrected sextant altitude | 21 29·3 | 2 45·9 | 34 22·1 | 26 34·6 | 4 17·4 | 49 31·6 |

The main corrections have been taken out with apparent altitude (sextant altitude corrected for index error and dip) as argument, interpolating where possible. These refinements are rarely necessary.

16. *Composition of the Corrections.* The table for the dip of the sea horizon is based on the formula:

Correction for dip = $-1'76\sqrt{\text{(height of eye in metres)}} = -0'97\sqrt{\text{(height of eye in feet)}}$

The correction table for the Sun includes the effects of semi-diameter, parallax and mean refraction.

The correction tables for the stars and planets allow for the effect of mean refraction.

The phase correction for Venus has been incorporated in the tabulations for GHA and Dec, and no correction for phase is required. The additional corrections for Venus and Mars allow for parallax. Alternatively, the correction for parallax may be calculated from $p \cos H$, where $p$ is the parallax and $H$ is the altitude. In 2022 the values for $p$ are:

| | Jan. 1 | Jan. 6 | Jan. 10 | Jan. 29 | Feb. 13 | Mar. 8 | Apr. 28 | Dec. 31 |
|---|---|---|---|---|---|---|---|---|
| Venus | 0′5 | 0′6 | 0′5 | 0′4 | 0′3 | 0′2 | 0′1 | |

| | Jan. 1 | Aug. 28 | Nov. 9 | Dec. 21 | Dec. 31 |
|---|---|---|---|---|---|
| Mars | 0′1 | 0′2 | 0′3 | 0′2 | |

The correction table for the Moon includes the effect of semi-diameter, parallax, augmentation and mean refraction.

Mean refraction is calculated for a temperature of 10°C (50°F), a pressure of 1010 mb (29·83 inches), humidity of 80% and wavelength 0·50169 $\mu$m.

17. *Bubble sextant observations.* When observing with a bubble sextant, no correction is necessary for dip, semi-diameter, or augmentation. The altitude corrections for the stars and planets on page A2 and on the bookmark should be used for the Sun as well as for the stars and planets; for the Moon, it is easiest to take the mean of the corrections for lower and upper limbs and subtract 15′ from the altitude; the correction for dip must not be applied.

## AUXILIARY AND PLANNING DATA

18. *Sun and Moon.* On the daily pages are given: hourly values of the horizontal parallax of the Moon; the semi-diameters and the times of meridian passage of both Sun and Moon over the Greenwich meridian; the equation of time; the age of the Moon, the percent (%) illuminated and a symbol indicating the phase. The times of the phases of the Moon are given in UT on page 4. For the Moon, the semi-diameters for each of the three days are given at the foot of the column; for the Sun a single value is sufficient. Table II on page xxxii may be used for interpolating the time of the Moon's meridian passage for longitude. The equation of time is given daily at $00^h$ and $12^h$ UT. The sign is *positive* for unshaded values and *negative* for shaded values. To obtain apparent time add the equation of time to mean time when the sign is *positive*. Subtract the equation of time from mean time when the sign is *negative*. At $12^h$ UT, when the sign is *positive*, meridian passage of the Sun occurs *before* $12^h$ UT, otherwise it occurs *after* $12^h$ UT.

19. *Planets.* The magnitudes of the planets are given immediately following their names in the headings on the daily pages; also given, for the middle day of the three on the page, are their SHA at $00^h$ UT and their times of meridian passage.

The planet notes and diagram on pages 8 and 9 provide descriptive information as to the suitability of the planets for observation during the year, and of their positions and movements.

20. *Stars.* The time of meridian passage of the first point of Aries over the Greenwich meridian is given on the daily pages, for the middle day of the three on the page, to $0^m1$. The interval between successive meridian passages is $23^h 56^m1$ ($24^h$ less $3^m9$), so that times for intermediate days and other meridians can readily be derived. If a precise time is required, it may be obtained by finding the UT at which LHA Aries is zero.

The meridian passage of a star occurs when its LHA is zero, that is when LHA Aries + SHA = 360°. An approximate time can be obtained from the planet diagram on page 9.

The star charts on pages 266 and 267 are intended to assist identification. They show the relative positions of the stars in the sky as seen from the Earth and include all 173 stars used in the Almanac, together with a few others to complete the main constellation configurations. The local meridian at any time may be located on the chart by means of its SHA which is 360° − LHA Aries, or west longitude − GHA Aries.

21. *Star globe.* To set a star globe on which is printed a scale of LHA Aries, first set the globe for latitude and then rotate about the polar axis until the scale under the edge of the meridian circle reads LHA Aries.

To mark the positions of the Sun, Moon, and planets on the star globe, take the difference GHA Aries − GHA body and use this along the LHA Aries scale, in conjunction with the declination, to plot the position. GHA Aries − GHA body is most conveniently found by taking the difference when the GHA of the body is small (less than 15°), which happens once a day.

22. *Calendar.* On page 4 are given lists of ecclesiastical festivals, and of the principal anniversaries and holidays in the United Kingdom and the United States of America. The calendar on page 5 includes the day of the year as well as the day of the week.

Brief particulars are given, at the foot of page 5, of the solar and lunar eclipses occurring during the year; the times given are in UT. The principal features of the more important solar eclipses are shown on the maps on pages 6 and 7.

23. *Standard times.* The lists on pages 262–265 give the standard times used in most countries. In general no attempt is made to give details of the beginning and end of summer time, since they are liable to frequent changes at short notice. For the latest information consult Admiralty List of Radio Signals Volume 2 (NP 282) corrected by Section VI of the weekly edition of Admiralty Notices to Mariners.

The Date or Calendar Line is an arbitrary line, on either side of which the date differs by one day; when crossing this line on a westerly course, the date must be advanced one day; when crossing it on an easterly course, the date must be put back one day. The line is a modification of the line of the 180th meridian, and is drawn so as to include, as far as possible, islands of any one group, etc., on the same side of the line. It may be traced by starting at the South Pole and joining up to the following positions:

| Lat | S 51·0 | S 45·0 | S 15·0 | S 5·0 | N 48·0 | N 53·0 | N 65·5 |
|-----|--------|--------|--------|-------|--------|--------|--------|
| Long | 180·0 | W 172·5 | W 172·5 | 180·0 | 180·0 | E 170·0 | W 169·0 |

thence through the middle of the Diomede Islands to Lat N 68°0, Long W 169°0, passing east of Ostrov Vrangelya (Wrangel Island) to Lat N 75°0, Long 180°0, and thence to the North Pole.

## ACCURACY

24. *Main data.* The quantities tabulated in this Almanac are generally correct to the nearest $0''1$; the exception is the Sun's GHA which is deliberately adjusted by up to $0''15$ to reduce the error due to ignoring the $v$-correction. The GHA and Dec at intermediate times cannot be obtained to this precision, since at least two quantities must be added; moreover, the $v$- and $d$-corrections are based on mean values of $v$ and $d$ and are taken from tables for the whole minute only. The largest error that can occur in the GHA or Dec of any body other than the Sun or Moon is less than $0''2$; it may reach $0''25$ for the GHA of the Sun and $0''3$ for that of the Moon.

In practice, it may be expected that only one third of the values of GHA and Dec taken out will have errors larger than $0''05$ and less than one tenth will have errors larger than $0''1$.

25. *Altitude corrections.* The errors in the altitude corrections are nominally of the same order as those in GHA and Dec, as they result from the addition of several quantities each correctly rounded off to $0''1$. But the actual values of the dip and of the refraction at low altitudes may, in extreme atmospheric conditions, differ considerably from the mean values used in the tables.

## USE OF THIS ALMANAC IN 2023

This Almanac may be used for the Sun and stars in 2023 in the following manner.

For the Sun, take out the GHA and Dec for the same date but for a time $5^h\ 48^m\ 00^s$ *earlier* than the UT of observation; add 87° 00′ to the GHA so obtained. The error, mainly due to planetary perturbations of the Earth, is unlikely to exceed $0''4$.

For the stars, calculate the GHA and Dec for the same date and the same time, but *subtract* $15''1$ from the GHA so found. The error due to incomplete correction for precession and nutation is unlikely to exceed $0''4$. If preferred, the same result can be obtained by using a time $5^h\ 48^m\ 00^s$ earlier than the UT of observation (as for the Sun) and adding 86° 59′2 to the GHA (or adding 87° as for the Sun and subtracting $0''8$, for precession, from the SHA of the star).

The Almanac cannot be so used for the Moon or planets.

## LIST I — PLACES FAST ON UTC (mainly those EAST OF GREENWICH)

The times given ⎱ *added* to UTC to give Standard Time
below should be ⎰ *subtracted* from Standard Time to give UTC.

| | h | m | | h | m |
|---|---|---|---|---|---|
| Admiralty Islands ... ... ... ... | 10 | | Denmark*† ... ... ... ... ... | 01 | |
| Afghanistan ... ... ... ... ... | 04 | 30 | Djibouti ... ... ... ... ... ... | 03 | |
| Albania* ... ... ... ... ... | 01 | | Egypt, Arab Republic of ... ... ... | 02 | |
| Algeria ... ... ... ... ... | 01 | | Equatorial Guinea, Republic of ... ... | 01 | |
| Amirante Islands ... ... ... ... | 04 | | Bioko ... ... ... ... ... ... | 01 | |
| Andaman Islands ... ... ... ... | 05 | 30 | Eritrea ... ... ... ... ... ... | 03 | |
| Angola ... ... ... ... ... | 01 | | Estonia*† ... ... ... ... ... | 02 | |
| Armenia ... ... ... ... ... | 04 | | Eswatini ... ... ... ... ... | 02 | |
| Australia | | | Ethiopia ... ... ... ... ... | 03 | |
| Australian Capital Territory* ... ... | 10 | | Fiji* ... ... ... ... ... | 12 | |
| New South Wales*¹ ... ... ... ... | 10 | | Finland*† ... ... ... ... ... | 02 | |
| Northern Territory ... ... ... | 09 | 30 | France*† ... ... ... ... ... | 01 | |
| Queensland ... ... ... ... | 10 | | | | |
| South Australia* ... ... ... | 09 | 30 | Gabon ... ... ... ... ... | 01 | |
| Tasmania* ... ... ... ... | 10 | | Georgia ... ... ... ... ... | 04 | |
| Victoria* ... ... ... ... ... | 10 | | Germany*† ... ... ... ... ... | 01 | |
| Western Australia ... ... ... | 08 | | Gibraltar* ... ... ... ... ... | 01 | |
| Whitsunday Islands ... ... ... | 10 | | Greece*† ... ... ... ... ... | 02 | |
| Austria*† ... ... ... ... | 01 | | Guam ... ... ... ... ... | 10 | |
| Azerbaijan ... ... ... ... ... | 04 | | Hong Kong ... ... ... ... ... | 08 | |
| Bahrain ... ... ... ... ... | 03 | | Hungary*† ... ... ... ... ... | 01 | |
| Balearic Islands*† ... ... ... | 01 | | India ... ... ... ... ... ... ... | 05 | 30 |
| Bangladesh ... ... ... ... | 06 | | Indonesia, Republic of | | |
| Belarus ... ... ... ... ... | 03 | | Bangka, Billiton, Java, West and | | |
| Belgium*† ... ... ... ... | 01 | | Central Kalimantan, Madura, Sumatra | 07 | |
| Benin ... ... ... ... ... | 01 | | Bali, Flores, South, North and East | | |
| Bosnia and Herzegovina* ... ... | 01 | | Kalimantan, Lombok, Sulawesi, | | |
| Botswana, Republic of ... ... ... | 02 | | Sumba, Sumbawa, West Timor ... | 08 | |
| Brunei ... ... ... ... ... | 08 | | Aru, Irian Jaya, Kai, Moluccas | | |
| Bulgaria*† ... ... ... ... | 02 | | Tanimbar ... ... ... ... | 09 | |
| Burma (Myanmar) ... ... ... | 06 | 30 | Iran* ... ... ... ... ... ... | 03 | 30 |
| Burundi ... ... ... ... ... | 02 | | Iraq ... ... ... ... ... ... | 03 | |
| | | | Israel* ... ... ... ... ... ... | 02 | |
| Cambodia ... ... ... ... | 07 | | Italy*† ... ... ... ... ... ... | 01 | |
| Cameroon Republic ... ... ... | 01 | | Jan Mayen Island* ... ... ... ... | 01 | |
| Caroline Islands² ... ... ... ... | 10 | | Japan ... ... ... ... ... ... | 09 | |
| Central African Republic ... ... | 01 | | Jordan* ... ... ... ... ... ... | 02 | |
| Chad ... ... ... ... ... ... | 01 | | | | |
| Chagos Archipelago & Diego Garcia | 06 | | Kazakhstan | | |
| Chatham Islands* ... ... ... ... | 12 | 45 | Western: Aktau, Uralsk, Atyrau ... | 05 | |
| China, People's Republic of ... ... | 08 | | Eastern & Central: Astana ... ... | 06 | |
| Christmas Island, Indian Ocean ... | 07 | | Kenya ... ... ... ... ... ... | 03 | |
| Cocos (Keeling) Islands ... ... ... | 06 | 30 | Kerguelen Islands ... ... ... ... | 05 | |
| Comoro Islands (Comoros) ... ... | 03 | | Kiribati Republic | | |
| Congo, Democratic Republic | | | Gilbert Islands ... ... ... ... | 12 | |
| West: Kinshasa, Equateur ... ... | 01 | | Phoenix Islands³ ... ... ... | 13 | |
| East: Orientale, Kasai, Kivu, Shaba | 02 | | Line Islands³ ... ... ... ... | 14 | |
| Congo Republic ... ... ... ... | 01 | | Korea, North ... ... ... ... | 09 | |
| Corsica*† ... ... ... ... ... | 01 | | Korea, South ... ... ... ... | 09 | |
| Crete*† ... ... ... ... ... | 02 | | Kuwait ... ... ... ... ... | 03 | |
| Croatia*† ... ... ... ... ... | 01 | | Kyrgyzstan ... ... ... ... | 06 | |
| Cyprus†: Ercan*, Larnaca* ... ... | 02 | | Laccadive Islands ... ... ... ... | 05 | 30 |
| Czech Republic*† ... ... ... | 01 | | Laos ... ... ... ... ... ... | 07 | |

---

\* Daylight-saving time may be kept in these places.  † For Summer time dates see List II footnotes.
¹ Except Broken Hill Area* which keeps 09ʰ 30ᵐ.
² Except Pohnpei, Pingelap and Kosrae which keep 11ʰ and Palau which keeps 09ʰ.
³ The Line and Phoenix Is. not part of the Kiribati Republic may keep other time zones.

## LIST I — (*continued*)

| | h | m | | h | m |
|---|---|---|---|---|---|
| Latvia*† ... ... ... ... ... ... | 02 | | Norilsk, Krasnoyarsk, Dikson, | | |
| Lebanon* ... ... ... ... ... ... | 02 | | Novosibirsk, Tomsk ... ... ... | 07 | |
| Lesotho ... ... ... ... ... ... ... | 02 | | Irkutsk, Bratsk, Ulan-Ude ... ... | 08 | |
| Libya ... ... ... ... ... ... ... | 02 | | Tiksi, Yakutsk, Chita ... ... ... | 09 | |
| Liechtenstein* ... ... ... ... ... | 01 | | Vladivostok, Khabarovsk, Okhotsk | 10 | |
| Lithuania*† ... ... ... ... ... ... | 02 | | Severo-Kurilsk, Magadan, | | |
| Lord Howe Island* ... ... ... | 10 | 30 | Sakhalin Island ... ... ... ... | 11 | |
| Luxembourg*† ... ... ... ... ... | 01 | | Petropavlovsk-K., Anadyr ... ... | 12 | |
| Macau ... ... ... ... ... ... ... | 08 | | Rwanda ... ... ... ... ... ... ... | 02 | |
| Macedonia*, former Yugoslav Republic | 01 | | Ryukyu Islands ... ... ... ... ... | 09 | |
| Madagascar, Democratic Republic of | 03 | | | | |
| Malawi ... ... ... ... ... ... ... | 02 | | Samoa* ... ... ... ... ... ... ... | 13 | |
| Malaysia, Malaya, Sabah, Sarawak ... | 08 | | Santa Cruz Islands ... ... ... ... | 11 | |
| Maldives, Republic of The ... ... ... | 05 | | Sardinia*† ... ... ... ... ... ... | 01 | |
| Malta*† ... ... ... ... ... ... ... | 01 | | Saudi Arabia ... ... ... ... ... | 03 | |
| Mariana Islands ... ... ... ... ... | 10 | | Schouten Islands ... ... ... ... | 09 | |
| Marshall Islands ... ... ... ... ... | 12 | | Serbia* ... ... ... ... ... ... ... | 01 | |
| Mauritius ... ... ... ... ... ... | 04 | | Seychelles ... ... ... ... ... ... | 04 | |
| Moldova* ... ... ... ... ... ... | 02 | | Sicily*† ... ... ... ... ... ... ... | 01 | |
| Monaco* ... ... ... ... ... ... | 01 | | Singapore ... ... ... ... ... ... | 08 | |
| Mongolia ... ... ... ... ... ... | 08 | | Slovakia*† ... ... ... ... ... ... | 01 | |
| Montenegro* ... ... ... ... ... | 01 | | Slovenia*† ... ... ... ... ... ... | 01 | |
| Morocco ... ... ... ... ... ... | 01 | | Socotra ... ... ... ... ... ... ... | 03 | |
| Mozambique ... ... ... ... ... ... | 02 | | Solomon Islands ... ... ... ... | 11 | |
| Namibia ... ... ... ... ... ... | 02 | | Somalia Republic ... ... ... ... | 03 | |
| Nauru ... ... ... ... ... ... ... | 12 | | South Africa, Republic of ... ... | 02 | |
| Nepal ... ... ... ... ... ... ... | 05 | 45 | South Sudan ... ... ... ... ... ... | 03 | |
| Netherlands, The*† ... ... ... ... | 01 | | Spain*† ... ... ... ... ... ... ... | 01 | |
| New Caledonia ... ... ... ... ... | 11 | | Spanish Possessions in North Africa* | 01 | |
| New Zealand* ... ... ... ... ... | 12 | | Spitsbergen (Svalbard)* ... ... ... | 01 | |
| Nicobar Islands ... ... ... ... ... | 05 | 30 | Sri Lanka ... ... ... ... ... ... | 05 | 30 |
| Niger ... ... ... ... ... ... ... | 01 | | Sudan, Republic of ... ... ... | 02 | |
| Nigeria, Republic of ... ... ... | 01 | | Sweden*† ... ... ... ... ... ... | 01 | |
| Norfolk Island* ... ... ... ... ... | 11 | | Switzerland* ... ... ... ... ... | 01 | |
| Norway* ... ... ... ... ... ... | 01 | | Syria (Syrian Arab Republic)* ... ... | 02 | |
| Novaya Zemlya ... ... ... ... ... | 03 | | | | |
| Okinawa ... ... ... ... ... ... | 09 | | Taiwan ... ... ... ... ... ... ... | 08 | |
| Oman ... ... ... ... ... ... ... | 04 | | Tajikistan ... ... ... ... ... ... | 05 | |
| | | | Tanzania ... ... ... ... ... ... | 03 | |
| Pagalu (Annobon Islands) ... ... ... | 01 | | Thailand ... ... ... ... ... ... | 07 | |
| Pakistan ... ... ... ... ... ... ... | 05 | | Timor-Leste ... ... ... ... ... ... | 09 | |
| Palau Islands ... ... ... ... ... | 09 | | Tonga ... ... ... ... ... ... ... | 13 | |
| Papua New Guinea[4] ... ... ... ... | 10 | | Tunisia ... ... ... ... ... ... ... | 01 | |
| Pescadores Islands ... ... ... ... | 08 | | Turkey ... ... ... ... ... ... ... | 03 | |
| Philippine Republic ... ... ... ... | 08 | | Turkmenistan ... ... ... ... ... | 05 | |
| Poland*† ... ... ... ... ... ... | 01 | | Tuvalu ... ... ... ... ... ... ... | 12 | |
| Qatar ... ... ... ... ... ... ... | 03 | | Uganda ... ... ... ... ... ... ... | 03 | |
| Reunion ... ... ... ... ... ... | 04 | | Ukraine* ... ... ... ... ... ... | 02 | |
| Romania*† ... ... ... ... ... ... | 02 | | United Arab Emirates ... ... ... | 04 | |
| Russia[5] | | | Uzbekistan ... ... ... ... ... ... | 05 | |
| Kaliningrad ... ... ... ... ... | 02 | | | | |
| Moscow, St. Petersburg, Arkhangelsk | 03 | | Vanuatu, Republic of ... ... ... ... | 11 | |
| Samara, Astrakhan, Saratov, ... ... | | | Vietnam, Socialist Republic of ... ... | 07 | |
| Volgograd ... ... ... ... ... | 04 | | | | |
| Ekaterinburg, Ufa, Perm, Novyy Port | 05 | | Yemen ... ... ... ... ... ... ... | 03 | |
| Omsk ... ... ... ... ... ... ... | 06 | | Zambia, Republic of ... ... ... ... | 02 | |
| | | | Zimbabwe ... ... ... ... ... ... | 02 | |

\* Daylight-saving time may be kept in these places.  † For Summer time dates see List II footnotes.
[4] Excluding the Autonomous Region of Bougainville which keeps 11ʰ.
[5] The boundaries between the zones are irregular; listed are chief towns in each zone.

## LIST II — PLACES NORMALLY KEEPING UTC

| | | | | |
|---|---|---|---|---|
| Ascension Island | Ghana | Irish Republic*† | Portugal*† | Togo Republic |
| Burkina-Faso | Great Britain† | Ivory Coast | Principe | Tristan da Cunha |
| Canary Islands*† | Guinea-Bissau | Liberia | St. Helena | |
| Channel Islands† | Guinea Republic | Madeira*† | São Tomé | |
| Faeroes*, The | Iceland | Mali | Senegal | |
| Gambia, The | Ireland, Northern† | Mauritania | Sierra Leone | |

\* Daylight-saving time may be kept in these places.

† Summer time (daylight-saving time), one hour in advance of UTC, will be kept from 2022 March $27^d$ $01^h$ to October $30^d$ $01^h$ UTC (Ninth Summer Time Directive of the European Union). Ratification by member countries has not been verified.

## LIST III — PLACES SLOW ON UTC (WEST OF GREENWICH)

The times given ⎫ *subtracted* from UTC to give Standard Time
below should be ⎰ *added* to Standard Time to give UTC.

| | h | m | | | h | m |
|---|---|---|---|---|---|---|
| American Samoa ... ... ... ... ... | 11 | | Canada (*continued*) | | | |
| Argentina ... ... ... ... ... ... | 03 | |   Prince Edward Island* ... ... ... | 04 | |
| Austral (Tubuai) Islands[1] ... ... ... | 10 | |   Quebec, east of long. W. 63° ... ... | 04 | |
| Azores*† ... ... ... ... ... | 01 | |         west of long. W. 63°* ... | 05 | |
| | | |   Saskatchewan ... ... ... ... ... | 06 | |
| Bahamas* ... ... ... ... ... | 05 | |   Yukon ... ... ... ... ... ... | 07 | |
| Barbados ... ... ... ... ... | 04 | | Cape Verde Islands ... ... ... | 01 | |
| Belize ... ... ... ... ... ... | 06 | | Cayman Islands ... ... ... ... | 05 | |
| Bermuda* ... ... ... ... ... | 04 | | Chile | | |
| Bolivia ... ... ... ... ... ... | 04 | |   General* ... ... ... ... ... ... | 04 | |
| Brazil | | |   Magallanes and Chilean Antarctic ... | 03 | |
|   Fernando de Noronha I., Trindade I., | | | Colombia ... ... ... ... ... ... | 05 | |
|     Oceanic Is. ... ... ... ... | 02 | | Cook Islands ... ... ... ... | 10 | |
|   N and NE coastal states, Tocantins, | | | Costa Rica ... ... ... ... ... | 06 | |
|     Minas Gerais, Goiás, Brasilia, | | | Cuba* ... ... ... ... ... ... | 05 | |
|     S and E coastal states ... ... ... | 03 | | Curaçao Island ... ... ... ... | 04 | |
|   Amazonas[2], Mato Grosso do Sul, | | | | | |
|     Mato Grosso, Rondônia, Roraima | 04 | | Dominican Republic ... ... ... | 04 | |
|   Acre ... ... ... ... ... ... | 05 | | | | |
| British Antarctic Territory[3,4] ... ... | 03 | | Easter Island (I. de Pascua)* ... ... | 06 | |
| | | | Ecuador ... ... ... ... ... ... | 05 | |
| Canada[4]‡ | | | El Salvador ... ... ... ... ... | 06 | |
|   Alberta* ... ... ... ... ... ... | 07 | | | | |
|   British Columbia*[4] ... ... ... ... | 08 | | Falkland Islands ... ... ... ... | 03 | |
|   Labrador* ... ... ... ... ... | 04 | | Fernando de Noronha Island ... ... | 02 | |
|   Manitoba* ... ... ... ... ... | 06 | | French Guiana ... ... ... ... | 03 | |
|   New Brunswick* ... ... ... ... | 04 | | | | |
|   Newfoundland* ... ... ... ... | 03 | 30 | Galápagos Islands ... ... ... ... | 06 | |
|   Nunavut* | | | Greenland | | |
|     east of long. W. 85° ... ... ... ... | 05 | |   Danmarkshavn, Mesters Vig ... ... | 00 | |
|     long. W. 85° to W. 102° ... ... ... | 06 | |   General* ... ... ... ... ... ... | 03 | |
|     west of long. W. 102° ... ... ... | 07 | |   Scoresby Sound* ... ... ... ... | 01 | |
|   Northwest Territories* ... ... ... | 07 | |   Thule*, Pituffik* ... ... ... ... | 04 | |
|   Nova Scotia* ... ... ... ... ... | 04 | | Grenada ... ... ... ... ... ... | 04 | |
|   Ontario, east of long. W. 90°* ... ... | 05 | | Guadeloupe ... ... ... ... ... | 04 | |
|   Ontario, west of long. W. 90°* ... | 06 | | Guatemala ... ... ... ... ... | 06 | |
| | | | Guyana, Republic of ... ... ... ... | 04 | |

\* Daylight-saving time may be kept in these places.      ‡ Dates for DST are given at the end of List III.

[1] This is the legal standard time, but local mean time is generally used.

[2] Except the cities of Eirunepe, Benjamin Constant and Tabatinga which keep $05^h$.

[3] Stations may use UTC.

[4] Some areas may keep another time zone.

LIST III — (*continued*)

| | h | m | | h | m |
|---|---|---|---|---|---|
| Haiti* ... ... ... ... ... ... | 05 | | United States of America‡(*continued*) | | |
| Honduras ... ... ... ... ... | 06 | |   Idaho, southern part ... ... ... ... | 07 | |
| | | |      northern part ... ... ... ... | 08 | |
| Jamaica ... ... ... ... ... ... ... | 05 | |   Illinois ... ... ... ... ... ... ... | 06 | |
| Johnston Island ... ... ... ... ... | 10 | |   Indiana⁶ ... ... ... ... ... ... | 05 | |
| Juan Fernandez Islands* ... ... ... | 04 | |   Iowa ... ... ... ... ... ... ... | 06 | |
| | | |   Kansas⁶ ... ... ... ... ... ... | 06 | |
| Leeward Islands ... ... ... ... ... | 04 | |   Kentucky, eastern part ... ... | 05 | |
| | | |      western part ... ... | 06 | |
| Marquesas Islands ... ... ... ... | 09 | 30 |   Louisiana ... ... ... ... ... | 06 | |
| Martinique ... ... ... ... ... ... | 04 | |   Maine ... ... ... ... ... | 05 | |
| Mexico | | |   Maryland ... ... ... ... | 05 | |
|   General* ... ... ... ... ... ... | 06 | |   Massachusetts ... ... ... ... | 05 | |
|   Quintana Roo ... ... ... ... ... | 05 | |   Michigan⁶ ... ... ... ... ... | 05 | |
|   Baja California Sur*, Chihuahua* | | |   Minnesota ... ... ... ... ... | 06 | |
|   Nayarit*, Sinaloa* and Sonara ... | 07 | |   Mississippi ... ... ... ... ... | 06 | |
|   Baja California Norte* ... ... ... | 08 | |   Missouri ... ... ... ... ... | 06 | |
| Midway Islands ... ... ... ... ... | 11 | |   Montana ... ... ... ... ... | 07 | |
| | | |   Nebraska, eastern part ... ... | 06 | |
| Nicaragua ... ... ... ... ... ... | 06 | |      western part ... ... | 07 | |
| Niue ... ... ... ... ... ... ... | 11 | |   Nevada ... ... ... ... ... | 08 | |
| | | |   New Hampshire ... ... ... | 05 | |
| Panama, Republic of ... ... ... ... | 05 | |   New Jersey ... ... ... ... ... | 05 | |
| Paraguay* ... ... ... ... ... ... | 04 | |   New Mexico ... ... ... ... | 07 | |
| Peru ... ... ... ... ... ... ... | 05 | |   New York ... ... ... ... ... | 05 | |
| Pitcairn Island ... ... ... ... ... | 08 | |   North Carolina ... ... ... ... | 05 | |
| Puerto Rico ... ... ... ... ... ... | 04 | |   North Dakota, eastern part ... ... | 06 | |
| | | |      western part ... ... | 07 | |
| St. Pierre and Miquelon* ... ... ... | 03 | |   Ohio ... ... ... ... ... ... | 05 | |
| Society Islands ... ... ... ... ... | 10 | |   Oklahoma ... ... ... ... ... | 06 | |
| South Georgia ... ... ... ... ... | 02 | |   Oregon⁶ ... ... ... ... ... | 08 | |
| Suriname ... ... ... ... ... ... | 03 | |   Pennsylvania ... ... ... ... | 05 | |
| | | |   Rhode Island ... ... ... ... | 05 | |
| Trindade Island, South Atlantic ... | 02 | |   South Carolina ... ... ... ... | 05 | |
| Trinidad and Tobago ... ... ... ... | 04 | |   South Dakota, eastern part ... ... | 06 | |
| Tuamotu Archipelago ... ... ... ... | 10 | |      western part ... ... | 07 | |
| Tubuai (Austral) Islands ... ... ... | 10 | |   Tennessee, eastern part ... ... | 05 | |
| Turks and Caicos Islands* ... ... ... | 05 | |      western part ... ... | 06 | |
| | | |   Texas⁶ ... ... ... ... ... ... | 06 | |
| United States of America‡ | | |   Utah ... ... ... ... ... ... | 07 | |
|   Alabama ... ... ... ... ... ... | 06 | |   Vermont ... ... ... ... ... | 05 | |
|   Alaska ... ... ... ... ... ... ... | 09 | |   Virginia ... ... ... ... ... | 05 | |
|   Aleutian Islands, east of W. 169° 30′ | 09 | |   Washington D.C. ... ... ... | 05 | |
|   Aleutian Islands, west of W. 169° 30′ | 10 | |   Washington ... ... ... ... | 08 | |
|   Arizona⁵ ... ... ... ... ... ... | 07 | |   West Virginia ... ... ... ... | 05 | |
|   Arkansas ... ... ... ... ... ... | 06 | |   Wisconsin ... ... ... ... ... | 06 | |
|   California ... ... ... ... ... ... | 08 | |   Wyoming ... ... ... ... ... | 07 | |
|   Colorado ... ... ... ... ... ... | 07 | | Uruguay ... ... ... ... ... | 03 | |
|   Connecticut ... ... ... ... ... | 05 | | | | |
|   Delaware ... ... ... ... ... ... | 05 | | Venezuela ... ... ... ... ... | 04 | |
|   District of Columbia ... ... ... | 05 | | Virgin Islands ... ... ... ... ... | 04 | |
|   Florida⁶ ... ... ... ... ... ... | 05 | | | | |
|   Georgia ... ... ... ... ... ... | 05 | | Windward Islands ... ... ... ... | 04 | |
|   Hawaii⁵ ... ... ... ... ... ... | 10 | | | | |

\* Daylight-saving time may be kept in these places.

‡ Daylight-saving (Summer) time, one hour fast on the time given, is kept during 2022 from March 13 (second Sunday) to November 6 (first Sunday), changing at 02$^h$ 00$^m$ local clock time.

⁵ Exempt from keeping daylight-saving time, except for a portion of Arizona.

⁶ A small portion of the state is in another time zone.

## NORTHERN STARS

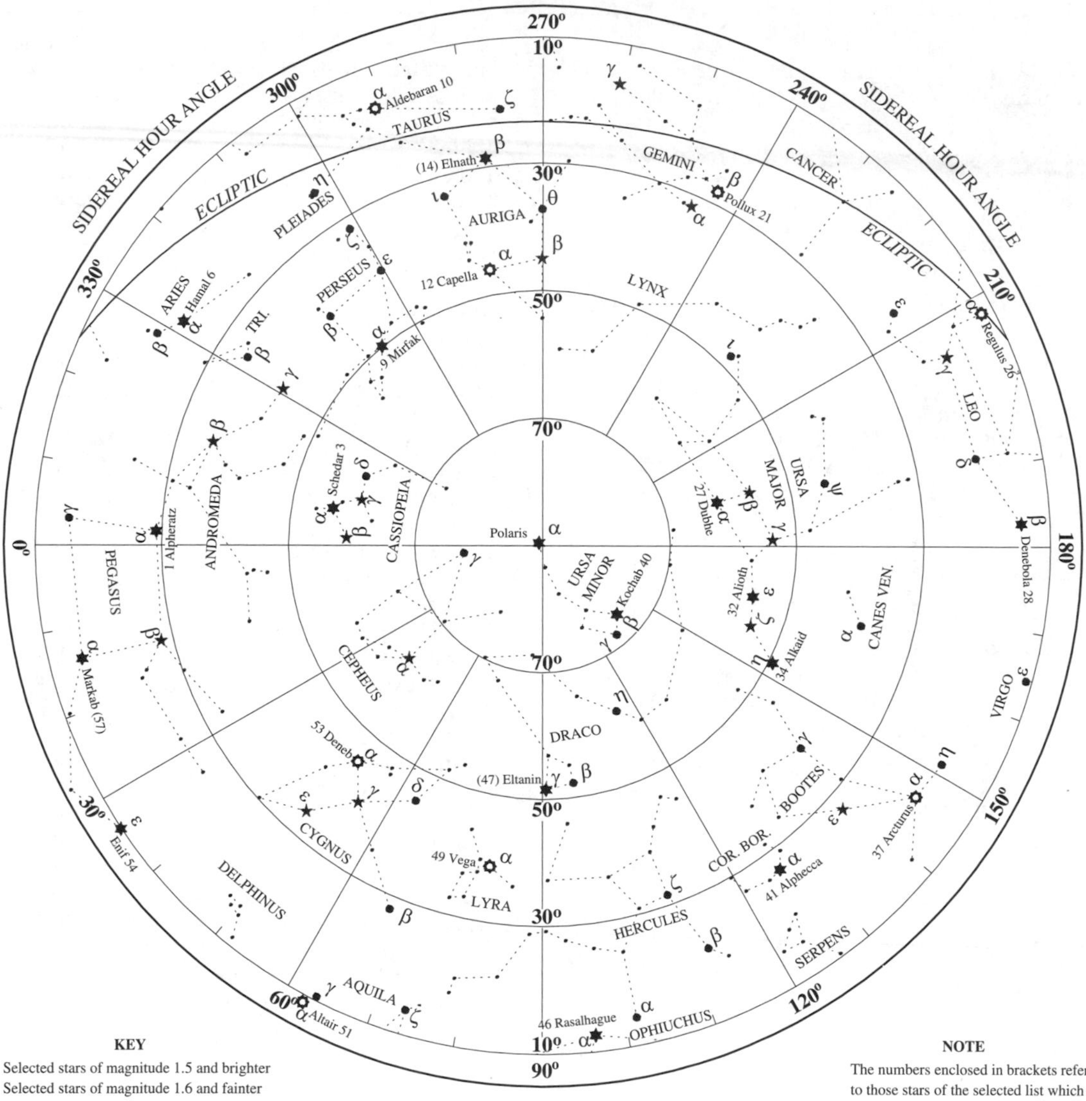

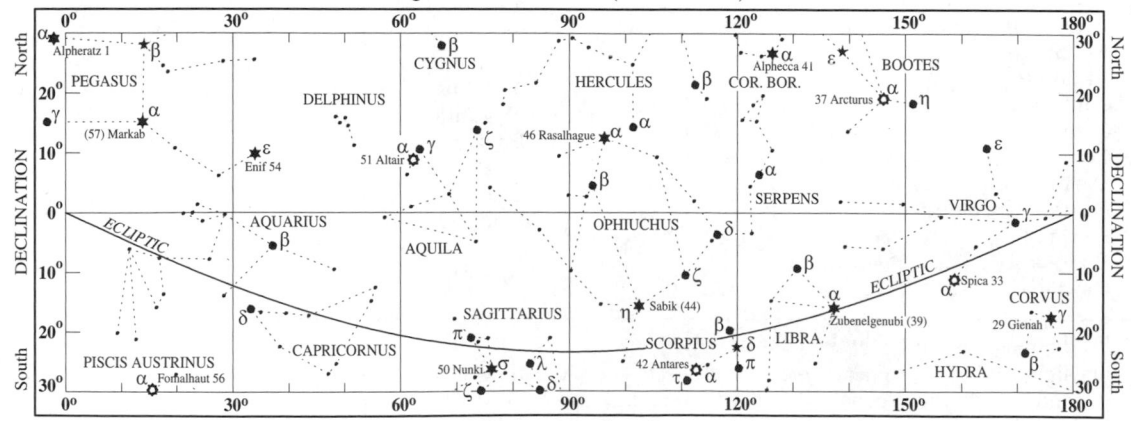

**EQUATORIAL STARS (SHA 0° to 180°)**

## SOUTHERN STARS

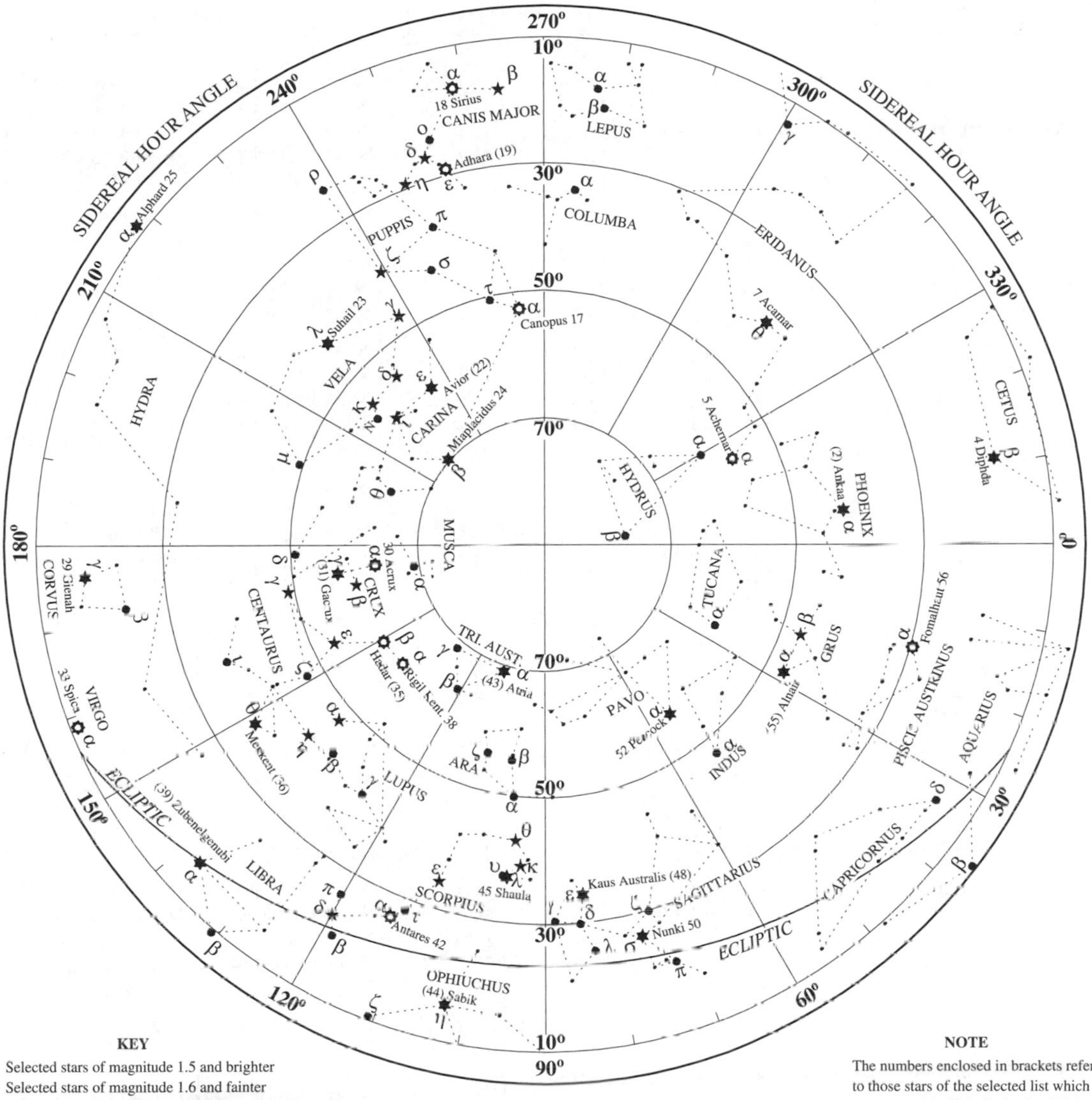

**KEY**

- ✿ Selected stars of magnitude 1.5 and brighter
- ★ Selected stars of magnitude 1.6 and fainter
- ★ Other tabulated stars of magnitude 2.5 and brighter
- ● Other tabulated stars of magnitude 2.6 and fainter
- · Untabulated stars

**NOTE**

The numbers enclosed in brackets refer to those stars of the selected list which are not used in Sight Reduction Tables A.P. 3270, N.P. 303.

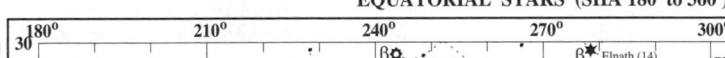

## EQUATORIAL STARS (SHA 180° to 360°)

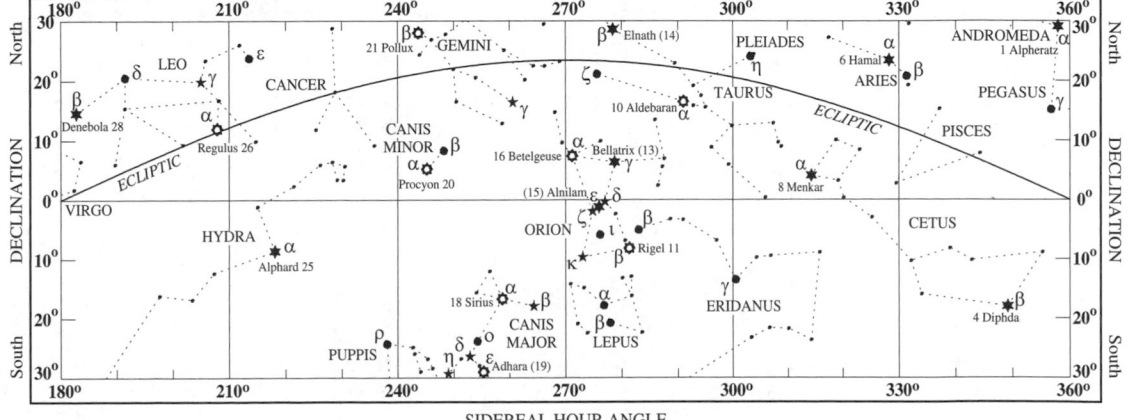

SIDEREAL HOUR ANGLE

| Mag. | Name and Number | | ° | SHA JAN. | FEB. | MAR. | APR. | MAY | JUNE | | ° | Dec. JAN. | FEB. | MAR. | APR. | MAY | JUNE |
|---|---|---|---|---|---|---|---|---|---|---|---|---|---|---|---|---|---|
| 3·2 | γ Cephei | | 4 | 57·2 | 57·7 | 57·9 | 57·7 | 57·1 | 56·2 | N | 77 | 45·5 | 45·4 | 45·3 | 45·1 | 45·0 | 45·0 |
| 2·5 | α Pegasi | 57 | 13 | 32·5 | 32·6 | 32·5 | 32·4 | 32·2 | 32·0 | N | 15 | 19·4 | 19·3 | 19·3 | 19·2 | 19·3 | 19·4 |
| 2·4 | β Pegasi | | 13 | 47·8 | 47·8 | 47·8 | 47·7 | 47·5 | 47·2 | N | 28 | 12·1 | 12·1 | 12·0 | 11·9 | 11·9 | 12·0 |
| 1·2 | α Piscis Aust. | 56 | 15 | 17·5 | 17·5 | 17·4 | 17·3 | 17·1 | 16·8 | S | 29 | 30·6 | 30·5 | 30·5 | 30·3 | 30·2 | 30·1 |
| 2·1 | β Gruis | | 19 | 00·9 | 00·9 | 00·8 | 00·7 | 00·4 | 00·1 | S | 46 | 46·5 | 46·4 | 46·2 | 46·1 | 46·0 | 45·9 |
| 2·9 | α Tucanæ | | 24 | 60·8 | 60·8 | 60·7 | 60·4 | 60·0 | 59·6 | S | 60 | 09·3 | 09·1 | 09·0 | 08·8 | 08·7 | 08·7 |
| 1·7 | α Gruis | 55 | 27 | 36·4 | 36·4 | 36·3 | 36·1 | 35·8 | 35·4 | S | 46 | 51·5 | 51·4 | 51·3 | 51·2 | 51·0 | 51·0 |
| 2·9 | δ Capricorni | | 32 | 56·7 | 56·6 | 56·5 | 56·4 | 56·1 | 55·9 | S | 16 | 01·8 | 01·8 | 01·8 | 01·7 | 01·6 | 01·5 |
| 2·4 | ε Pegasi | 54 | 33 | 41·5 | 41·4 | 41·4 | 41·2 | 41·0 | 40·7 | N | 9 | 58·5 | 58·4 | 58·4 | 58·4 | 58·4 | 58·5 |
| 2·9 | β Aquarii | | 36 | 49·7 | 49·7 | 49·6 | 49·4 | 49·2 | 48·9 | S | 5 | 28·6 | 28·6 | 28·6 | 28·6 | 28·5 | 28·4 |
| 2·4 | α Cephei | | 40 | 14·3 | 14·3 | 14·2 | 13·9 | 13·5 | 13·1 | N | 62 | 40·8 | 40·6 | 40·5 | 40·4 | 40·4 | 40·5 |
| 2·5 | ε Cygni | | 48 | 14·0 | 14·0 | 13·8 | 13·6 | 13·4 | 13·1 | N | 34 | 03·1 | 03·0 | 02·9 | 02·9 | 02·9 | 03·1 |
| 1·3 | α Cygni | 53 | 49 | 27·9 | 27·8 | 27·7 | 27·4 | 27·2 | 26·9 | N | 45 | 21·5 | 21·4 | 21·3 | 21·2 | 21·3 | 21·4 |
| 3·1 | α Indi | | 50 | 14·1 | 14·0 | 13·8 | 13·5 | 13·2 | 12·8 | S | 47 | 13·0 | 12·9 | 12·8 | 12·7 | 12·7 | 12·6 |
| 1·9 | α Pavonis | 52 | 53 | 10·2 | 10·0 | 09·8 | 09·4 | 09·0 | 08·6 | S | 56 | 40·0 | 39·8 | 39·7 | 39·6 | 39·6 | 39·6 |
| 2·2 | γ Cygni | | 54 | 15·3 | 15·2 | 15·1 | 14·8 | 14·6 | 14·3 | N | 40 | 19·6 | 19·4 | 19·3 | 19·3 | 19·4 | 19·5 |
| 0·8 | α Aquilæ | 51 | 62 | 02·7 | 02·6 | 02·4 | 02·2 | 02·0 | 01·7 | N | 8 | 55·5 | 55·4 | 55·4 | 55·4 | 55·5 | 55·6 |
| 2·7 | γ Aquilæ | | 63 | 10·9 | 10·8 | 10·7 | 10·4 | 10·2 | 10·0 | N | 10 | 39·9 | 39·9 | 39·8 | 39·8 | 39·9 | 40·0 |
| 2·9 | δ Cygni | | 63 | 35·7 | 35·6 | 35·4 | 35·1 | 34·8 | 34·6 | N | 45 | 11·0 | 10·8 | 10·7 | 10·7 | 10·8 | 10·9 |
| 3·1 | β Cygni | | 67 | 06·4 | 06·3 | 06·1 | 05·9 | 05·6 | 05·4 | N | 28 | 00·3 | 00·2 | 00·1 | 00·1 | 00·2 | 00·3 |
| 2·9 | π Sagittarii | | 72 | 14·5 | 14·3 | 14·1 | 13·9 | 13·6 | 13·4 | S | 20 | 59·3 | 59·3 | 59·3 | 59·3 | 59·3 | 59·2 |
| 3·0 | ζ Aquilæ | | 73 | 24·2 | 24·1 | 23·9 | 23·6 | 23·4 | 23·2 | N | 13 | 53·7 | 53·6 | 53·6 | 53·6 | 53·6 | 53·7 |
| 2·6 | ζ Sagittarii | | 73 | 60·5 | 60·3 | 60·0 | 59·8 | 59·5 | 59·3 | S | 29 | 50·9 | 50·9 | 50·9 | 50·8 | 50·8 | 50·8 |
| 2·0 | σ Sagittarii | 50 | 75 | 51·2 | 51·0 | 50·8 | 50·5 | 50·3 | 50·0 | S | 26 | 16·2 | 16·2 | 16·1 | 16·1 | 16·1 | 16·1 |
| 0·0 | α Lyræ | 49 | 80 | 35·3 | 35·1 | 34·9 | 34·6 | 34·4 | 34·2 | N | 38 | 48·1 | 48·0 | 47·9 | 47·9 | 48·0 | 48·2 |
| 2·8 | λ Sagittarii | | 82 | 40·7 | 40·5 | 40·2 | 40·0 | 39·7 | 39·5 | S | 25 | 24·5 | 24·5 | 24·5 | 24·5 | 24·5 | 24·5 |
| 1·9 | ε Sagittarii | 48 | 83 | 36·2 | 35·9 | 35·7 | 35·4 | 35·1 | 34·9 | S | 34 | 22·4 | 22·4 | 22·4 | 22·4 | 22·4 | 22·4 |
| 2·7 | δ Sagittarii | | 84 | 24·6 | 24·4 | 24·1 | 23·8 | 23·6 | 23·4 | S | 29 | 49·1 | 49·1 | 49·1 | 49·1 | 49·1 | 49·1 |
| 3·0 | γ Sagittarii | | 88 | 12·3 | 12·0 | 11·8 | 11·5 | 11·3 | 11·1 | S | 30 | 25·4 | 25·4 | 25·4 | 25·4 | 25·4 | 25·4 |
| 2·2 | γ Draconis | 47 | 90 | 43·8 | 43·6 | 43·3 | 43·0 | 42·8 | 42·6 | N | 51 | 29·0 | 28·9 | 28·8 | 28·8 | 28·9 | 29·1 |
| 2·8 | β Ophiuchi | | 93 | 52·1 | 51·9 | 51·7 | 51·4 | 51·3 | 51·1 | N | 4 | 33·4 | 33·4 | 33·3 | 33·3 | 33·4 | 33·5 |
| 2·4 | κ Scorpii | | 93 | 60·5 | 60·2 | 59·9 | 59·6 | 59·4 | 59·2 | S | 39 | 02·4 | 02·3 | 02·3 | 02·4 | 02·4 | 02·4 |
| 1·9 | θ Scorpii | | 95 | 17·1 | 16·9 | 16·6 | 16·3 | 16·0 | 15·8 | S | 43 | 00·6 | 00·5 | 00·5 | 00·6 | 00·6 | 00·7 |
| 2·1 | α Ophiuchi | 46 | 96 | 01·1 | 00·9 | 00·7 | 00·5 | 00·3 | 00·2 | N | 12 | 32·6 | 32·5 | 32·4 | 32·5 | 32·5 | 32·6 |
| 1·6 | λ Scorpii | 45 | 96 | 14·1 | 13·8 | 13·5 | 13·2 | 13·0 | 12·8 | S | 37 | 07·1 | 07·1 | 07·1 | 07·1 | 07·1 | 07·2 |
| 3·0 | α Aræ | | 96 | 37·6 | 37·3 | 36·9 | 36·6 | 36·3 | 36·1 | S | 49 | 53·4 | 53·4 | 53·4 | 53·4 | 53·5 | 53·6 |
| 2·7 | υ Scorpii | | 96 | 56·7 | 56·4 | 56·2 | 55·9 | 55·6 | 55·5 | S | 37 | 18·7 | 18·7 | 18·7 | 18·7 | 18·7 | 18·8 |
| 2·8 | β Draconis | | 97 | 16·6 | 16·3 | 16·0 | 15·7 | 15·5 | 15·4 | N | 52 | 16·9 | 16·8 | 16·7 | 16·8 | 16·9 | 17·1 |
| 2·8 | β Aræ | | 98 | 13·8 | 13·5 | 13·1 | 12·7 | 12·4 | 12·2 | S | 55 | 32·8 | 32·8 | 32·8 | 32·8 | 32·9 | 33·0 |
| Var.‡ | α Herculis | | 101 | 05·7 | 05·5 | 05·2 | 05·0 | 04·9 | 04·7 | N | 14 | 21·8 | 21·7 | 21·7 | 21·7 | 21·8 | 21·9 |
| 2·4 | η Ophiuchi | 44 | 102 | 05·9 | 05·6 | 05·4 | 05·2 | 05·0 | 04·9 | S | 15 | 45·1 | 45·1 | 45·2 | 45·2 | 45·2 | 45·1 |
| 3·1 | ζ Aræ | | 104 | 54·1 | 53·7 | 53·3 | 53·0 | 52·7 | 52·5 | S | 56 | 01·2 | 01·2 | 01·2 | 01·3 | 01·4 | 01·5 |
| 2·3 | ε Scorpii | | 107 | 06·7 | 06·4 | 06·1 | 05·9 | 05·7 | 05·6 | S | 34 | 19·8 | 19·9 | 19·9 | 19·9 | 20·0 | 20·0 |
| 1·9 | α Triang. Aust. | 43 | 107 | 16·0 | 15·4 | 14·8 | 14·3 | 13·9 | 13·6 | S | 69 | 03·8 | 03·7 | 03·7 | 03·8 | 03·9 | 04·1 |
| 2·8 | ζ Herculis | | 109 | 28·7 | 28·4 | 28·2 | 28·0 | 27·8 | 27·8 | N | 31 | 33·6 | 33·5 | 33·5 | 33·5 | 33·6 | 33·8 |
| 2·6 | ζ Ophiuchi | | 110 | 24·9 | 24·6 | 24·4 | 24·2 | 24·0 | 23·9 | S | 10 | 36·7 | 36·7 | 36·8 | 36·8 | 36·8 | 36·7 |
| 2·8 | τ Scorpii | | 110 | 41·7 | 41·4 | 41·2 | 40·9 | 40·8 | 40·6 | S | 28 | 15·6 | 15·6 | 15·6 | 15·7 | 15·7 | 15·7 |
| 2·8 | β Herculis | | 112 | 12·9 | 12·7 | 12·4 | 12·2 | 12·1 | 12·0 | N | 21 | 26·4 | 26·3 | 26·3 | 26·3 | 26·4 | 26·5 |
| 1·0 | α Scorpii | 42 | 112 | 19·1 | 18·8 | 18·6 | 18·4 | 18·2 | 18·1 | S | 26 | 28·7 | 28·8 | 28·8 | 28·8 | 28·9 | 28·9 |
| 2·7 | η Draconis | | 113 | 56·1 | 55·7 | 55·3 | 55·0 | 54·8 | 54·8 | N | 61 | 27·6 | 27·5 | 27·5 | 27·6 | 27·7 | 27·9 |
| 2·7 | δ Ophiuchi | | 116 | 07·9 | 07·7 | 07·4 | 07·2 | 07·1 | 07·0 | S | 3 | 45·0 | 45·1 | 45·2 | 45·2 | 45·1 | 45·1 |
| 2·6 | β Scorpii | | 118 | 19·6 | 19·4 | 19·2 | 19·0 | 18·8 | 18·7 | S | 19 | 51·8 | 51·9 | 51·9 | 52·0 | 52·0 | 52·0 |
| 2·3 | δ Scorpii | | 119 | 35·9 | 35·5 | 35·2 | 35·0 | 35·0 | 34·9 | S | 22 | 40·9 | 41·0 | 41·1 | 41·1 | 41·1 | 41·1 |
| 2·9 | π Scorpii | | 119 | 57·7 | 57·4 | 57·1 | 56·9 | 56·8 | 56·7 | S | 26 | 10·5 | 10·6 | 10·6 | 10·7 | 10·7 | 10·7 |
| 2·8 | β Trianguli Aust. | | 120 | 44·3 | 43·8 | 43·4 | 43·0 | 42·7 | 42·6 | S | 63 | 29·6 | 29·6 | 29·6 | 29·8 | 29·9 | 30·0 |
| 2·6 | α Serpentis | | 123 | 40·1 | 39·8 | 39·6 | 39·4 | 39·3 | 39·3 | N | 6 | 21·4 | 21·3 | 21·2 | 21·2 | 21·3 | 21·4 |
| 2·8 | γ Lupi | | 125 | 51·3 | 51·0 | 50·7 | 50·5 | 50·3 | 50·3 | S | 41 | 14·2 | 14·2 | 14·3 | 14·4 | 14·5 | 14·6 |
| 2·2 | α Coronæ Bor. | 41 | 126 | 06·0 | 05·8 | 05·5 | 05·4 | 05·3 | 05·2 | N | 26 | 38·3 | 38·2 | 38·2 | 38·3 | 38·4 | 38·5 |

‡ 2·9 — 3·6

| Mag. | Name and Number | | SHA | | | | | | | Declination | | | | | | |
|---|---|---|---|---|---|---|---|---|---|---|---|---|---|---|---|---|
| | | | | JULY | AUG. | SEPT. | OCT. | NOV. | DEC. | | JULY | AUG. | SEPT. | OCT. | NOV. | DEC. |
| | | | ° | ′ | ′ | ′ | ′ | ′ | ′ | ° | ′ | ′ | ′ | ′ | ′ | ′ |
| 3·2 | *Errai* | | 4 | 55·5 | 54·9 | 54·7 | 54·8 | 55·3 | 55·9 | N 77 | 45·1 | 45·3 | 45·5 | 45·7 | 45·8 | 45·9 |
| 2·5 | *Markab* | 57 | 13 | 31·7 | 31·6 | 31·5 | 31·5 | 31·6 | 31·7 | N 15 | 19·5 | 19·6 | 19·7 | 19·8 | 19·8 | 19·8 |
| 2·4 | *Scheat* | | 13 | 47·0 | 46·8 | 46·7 | 46·7 | 46·8 | 46·9 | N 28 | 12·1 | 12·3 | 12·4 | 12·5 | 12·5 | 12·5 |
| 1·2 | *Fomalhaut* | 56 | 15 | 16·5 | 16·4 | 16·3 | 16·3 | 16·4 | 16·5 | S 29 | 30·1 | 30·1 | 30·1 | 30·2 | 30·2 | 30·3 |
| 2·1 | *Tiaki* | | 18 | 59·8 | 59·5 | 59·5 | 59·5 | 59·6 | 59·8 | S 46 | 45·8 | 45·9 | 46·0 | 46·1 | 46·2 | 46·2 |
| 2·9 | α *Tucanæ* | | 24 | 59·2 | 59·0 | 58·9 | 59·0 | 59·2 | 59·5 | S 60 | 08·7 | 08·7 | 08·9 | 09·0 | 09·0 | 09·0 |
| 1·7 | *Alnair* | 55 | 27 | 35·1 | 34·9 | 34·9 | 35·0 | 35·1 | 35·3 | S 46 | 51·0 | 51·0 | 51·1 | 51·2 | 51·3 | 51·3 |
| 2·9 | *Deneb Algedi* | | 32 | 55·7 | 55·5 | 55·5 | 55·6 | 55·7 | 55·8 | S 16 | 01·5 | 01·4 | 01·4 | 01·5 | 01·5 | 01·5 |
| 2·4 | *Enif* | 54 | 33 | 40·5 | 40·4 | 40·4 | 40·5 | 40·6 | 40·6 | N 9 | 58·7 | 58·8 | 58·8 | 58·9 | 58·9 | 58·8 |
| 2·9 | *Sadalsuud* | | 36 | 48·7 | 48·6 | 48·6 | 48·7 | 48·8 | 48·9 | S 5 | 28·3 | 28·3 | 28·2 | 28·2 | 28·3 | 28·3 |
| 2·4 | *Alderamin* | | 40 | 12·8 | 12·8 | 12·9 | 13·1 | 13·5 | 13·8 | N 62 | 40·7 | 40·8 | 41·0 | 41·1 | 41·2 | 41·1 |
| 2·5 | *Aljanah* | | 48 | 12·9 | 12·9 | 12·9 | 13·1 | 13·2 | 13·3 | N 34 | 03·2 | 03·3 | 03·5 | 03·5 | 03·5 | 03·5 |
| 1·3 | *Deneb* | 53 | 49 | 26·7 | 26·7 | 26·8 | 26·9 | 27·1 | 27·3 | N 45 | 21·5 | 21·7 | 21·8 | 21·9 | 21·9 | 21·9 |
| 3·1 | α *Indi* | | 50 | 12·6 | 12·5 | 12·5 | 12·7 | 12·8 | 12·9 | S 47 | 12·7 | 12·8 | 12·8 | 12·9 | 12·9 | 12·9 |
| 1·9 | *Peacock* | 52 | 53 | 08·4 | 08·3 | 08·3 | 08·5 | 08·8 | 08·9 | S 56 | 39·7 | 39·8 | 39·9 | 39·9 | 39·9 | 39·9 |
| 2·2 | *Sadr* | | 54 | 14·2 | 14·2 | 14·3 | 14·4 | 14·6 | 14·7 | N 40 | 19·7 | 19·8 | 19·9 | 20·0 | 20·0 | 19·9 |
| 0·8 | *Altair* | 51 | 62 | 01·6 | 01·6 | 01·6 | 01·8 | 01·9 | 01·9 | N 8 | 55·7 | 55·8 | 55·8 | 55·8 | 55·8 | 55·7 |
| 2·7 | γ *Aquilæ* | | 63 | 09·9 | 09·8 | 09·9 | 10·0 | 10·2 | 10·2 | N 10 | 40·1 | 40·2 | 40·2 | 40·3 | 40·2 | 40·2 |
| 2·9 | *Fawaris* | | 63 | 34·5 | 34·5 | 34·7 | 34·9 | 35·1 | 35·2 | N 45 | 11·1 | 11·3 | 11·4 | 11·4 | 11·4 | 11·3 |
| 3·1 | *Albireo* | | 67 | 05·3 | 05·3 | 05·4 | 05·6 | 05·7 | 05·8 | N 28 | 00·4 | 00·5 | 00·6 | 00·6 | 00·6 | 00·5 |
| 2·9 | *Albuldah* | | 72 | 13·3 | 13·3 | 13·4 | 13·5 | 13·6 | 13·6 | S 20 | 59·2 | 59·2 | 59·2 | 59·3 | 59·3 | 59·3 |
| 3·0 | ζ *Aquilæ* | | 73 | 23·1 | 23·1 | 23·2 | 23·4 | 23·5 | 23·5 | N 13 | 53·9 | 53·9 | 54·0 | 54·0 | 54·0 | 53·9 |
| 2·6 | *Ascella* | | 73 | 59·2 | 59·2 | 59·3 | 59·4 | 59·5 | 59·5 | S 29 | 50·8 | 50·9 | 50·9 | 50·9 | 50·9 | 50·9 |
| 2·0 | *Nunki* | 50 | 75 | 49·9 | 49·9 | 50·0 | 50·1 | 50·2 | 50·3 | S 26 | 16·1 | 16·1 | 16·1 | 16·1 | 16·1 | 16·1 |
| 0·0 | *Vega* | 49 | 80 | 34·2 | 34·2 | 34·4 | 34·6 | 34·7 | 34·8 | N 38 | 48·3 | 48·5 | 48·5 | 48·5 | 48·5 | 48·3 |
| 2·8 | *Kaus Borealis* | | 82 | 39·4 | 39·5 | 39·6 | 39·7 | 39·8 | 39·8 | S 25 | 24·5 | 24·5 | 24·6 | 24·6 | 24·6 | 24·6 |
| 1·9 | *Kaus Australis* | 48 | 83 | 34·8 | 34·8 | 35·0 | 35·1 | 35·2 | 35·2 | S 34 | 22·4 | 22·5 | 22·5 | 22·5 | 22·5 | 22·4 |
| 2·7 | *Kaus Media* | | 84 | 23·3 | 23·3 | 23·4 | 23·6 | 23·7 | 23·7 | S 29 | 49·1 | 49·1 | 49·1 | 49·1 | 49·1 | 49·1 |
| 3·0 | *Alnasl* | | 88 | 11·0 | 11·0 | 11·2 | 11·3 | 11·4 | 11·4 | S 30 | 25·4 | 25·4 | 25·5 | 25·5 | 25·4 | 25·4 |
| 2·2 | *Eltanin* | 47 | 90 | 42·6 | 42·8 | 43·0 | 43·3 | 43·5 | 43·5 | N 51 | 29·3 | 29·4 | 29·4 | 29·4 | 29·3 | 29·1 |
| 2·8 | *Cebalrai* | | 93 | 51·1 | 51·1 | 51·2 | 51·4 | 51·4 | 51·4 | N 4 | 33·5 | 33·6 | 33·6 | 33·6 | 33·6 | 33·5 |
| 2·4 | κ *Scorpii* | | 93 | 59·1 | 59·2 | 59·3 | 59·5 | 59·6 | 59·5 | S 39 | 02·5 | 02·5 | 02·6 | 02·6 | 02·5 | 02·5 |
| 1·9 | *Sargas* | | 95 | 15·8 | 15·8 | 16·0 | 16·1 | 16·2 | 16·2 | S 43 | 00·7 | 00·8 | 00·8 | 00·8 | 00·7 | 00·7 |
| 2·1 | *Rasalhague* | 46 | 96 | 00·1 | 00·2 | 00·3 | 00·4 | 00·5 | 00·5 | N 12 | 32·7 | 32·8 | 32·8 | 32·8 | 32·7 | 32·6 |
| 1·6 | *Shaula* | 45 | 96 | 12·8 | 12·8 | 13·0 | 13·1 | 13·2 | 13·1 | S 37 | 07·2 | 07·3 | 07·3 | 07·3 | 07·2 | 07·2 |
| 3·0 | α *Aræ* | | 96 | 36·0 | 36·1 | 36·3 | 36·5 | 36·6 | 36·5 | S 49 | 53·7 | 53·7 | 53·8 | 53·7 | 53·7 | 53·6 |
| 2·7 | *Lesath* | | 96 | 55·4 | 55·5 | 55·6 | 55·8 | 55·8 | 55·8 | S 37 | 18·8 | 18·9 | 18·9 | 18·9 | 18·8 | 18·8 |
| 2·8 | *Rastaban* | | 97 | 15·4 | 15·6 | 15·9 | 16·1 | 16·3 | 16·3 | N 52 | 17·2 | 17·3 | 17·3 | 17·3 | 17·2 | 17·0 |
| 2·8 | β *Aræ* | | 98 | 12·1 | 12·2 | 12·5 | 12·7 | 12·8 | 12·7 | S 55 | 33·1 | 33·2 | 33·2 | 33·2 | 33·1 | 33·0 |
| Var.‡ | *Rasalgethi* | | 101 | 04·7 | 04·8 | 04·9 | 05·0 | 05·1 | 05·1 | N 14 | 22·0 | 22·0 | 22·1 | 22·0 | 22·0 | 21·9 |
| 2·4 | *Sabik* | 44 | 102 | 04·8 | 04·9 | 05·0 | 05·1 | 05·2 | 05·1 | S 15 | 45·1 | 45·1 | 45·1 | 45·1 | 45·1 | 45·1 |
| 3·1 | ζ *Aræ* | | 104 | 52·5 | 52·6 | 52·8 | 53·0 | 53·1 | 53·0 | S 56 | 01·6 | 01·7 | 01·7 | 01·6 | 01·5 | 01·5 |
| 2·3 | *Larawag* | | 107 | 05·5 | 05·6 | 05·8 | 05·9 | 05·9 | 05·8 | S 34 | 20·1 | 20·1 | 20·1 | 20·1 | 20·0 | 20·0 |
| 1·9 | *Atria* | 43 | 107 | 13·7 | 13·9 | 14·3 | 14·6 | 14·8 | 14·7 | S 69 | 04·2 | 04·3 | 04·3 | 04·2 | 04·1 | 04·0 |
| 2·8 | ζ *Herculis* | | 109 | 27·8 | 27·9 | 28·0 | 28·2 | 28·3 | 28·2 | N 31 | 33·9 | 33·9 | 33·9 | 33·9 | 33·8 | 33·6 |
| 2·6 | ζ *Ophiuchi* | | 110 | 23·9 | 24·0 | 24·1 | 24·2 | 24·2 | 24·2 | S 10 | 36·7 | 36·7 | 36·7 | 36·7 | 36·7 | 36·7 |
| 2·8 | *Paikauhale* | | 110 | 40·6 | 40·7 | 40·8 | 40·9 | 41·0 | 40·9 | S 28 | 15·8 | 15·8 | 15·8 | 15·8 | 15·7 | 15·7 |
| 2·8 | *Kornephoros* | | 112 | 12·0 | 12·1 | 12·3 | 12·4 | 12·4 | 12·4 | N 21 | 26·6 | 26·6 | 26·6 | 26·6 | 26·5 | 26·4 |
| 1·0 | *Antares* | 42 | 112 | 18·1 | 18·1 | 18·3 | 18·4 | 18·4 | 18·3 | S 26 | 28·9 | 28·9 | 28·9 | 28·9 | 28·9 | 28·9 |
| 2·7 | *Athebyne* | | 113 | 55·0 | 55·2 | 55·6 | 55·9 | 56·1 | 56·1 | N 61 | 28·0 | 28·1 | 28·0 | 28·0 | 27·8 | 27·6 |
| 2·7 | *Yed Prior* | | 116 | 07·0 | 07·1 | 07·2 | 07·3 | 07·3 | 07·2 | S 3 | 45·1 | 45·0 | 45·0 | 45·0 | 45·1 | 45·1 |
| 2·6 | *Acrab* | | 118 | 18·7 | 18·8 | 18·9 | 19·0 | 19·0 | 18·9 | S 19 | 52·0 | 52·0 | 52·0 | 52·0 | 52·0 | 52·0 |
| 2·3 | *Dschubba* | | 119 | 34·9 | 35·0 | 35·2 | 35·3 | 35·3 | 35·1 | S 22 | 41·1 | 41·1 | 41·1 | 41·1 | 41·1 | 41·1 |
| 2·9 | *Fang* | | 119 | 56·7 | 56·8 | 56·9 | 57·0 | 57·0 | 56·9 | S 26 | 10·7 | 10·7 | 10·7 | 10·7 | 10·7 | 10·7 |
| 2·8 | β *Trianguli Aust.* | | 120 | 42·7 | 43·0 | 43·3 | 43·5 | 43·5 | 43·3 | S 63 | 30·1 | 30·2 | 30·2 | 30·1 | 30·0 | 29·9 |
| 2·6 | *Unukalhai* | | 123 | 39·3 | 39·4 | 39·5 | 39·6 | 39·6 | 39·5 | N 6 | 21·4 | 21·4 | 21·4 | 21·4 | 21·3 | 21·2 |
| 2·8 | γ *Lupi* | | 125 | 50·3 | 50·4 | 50·6 | 50·7 | 50·7 | 50·5 | S 41 | 14·6 | 14·6 | 14·6 | 14·5 | 14·5 | 14·4 |
| 2·2 | *Alphecca* | 41 | 126 | 05·3 | 05·4 | 05·5 | 05·6 | 05·6 | 05·5 | N 26 | 38·5 | 38·6 | 38·6 | 38·5 | 38·4 | 38·2 |

‡ 2·9 — 3·6

| Mag. | | Name and Number | | SHA | JAN. | FEB. | MAR. | APR. | MAY | JUNE | Declination | | JAN. | FEB. | MAR. | APR. | MAY | JUNE |
|---|---|---|---|---|---|---|---|---|---|---|---|---|---|---|---|---|---|---|
| | | | | ° | ′ | ′ | ′ | ′ | ′ | ′ | | ° | ′ | ′ | ′ | ′ | ′ | ′ |
| 2·9 | γ | Trianguli Aust. | | 129 | 45·9 | 45·4 | 44·8 | 44·4 | 44·2 | 44·2 | S 68 | | 45·3 | 45·3 | 45·4 | 45·5 | 45·7 | 45·8 |
| 3·1 | γ | Ursæ Minoris | | 129 | 49·7 | 49·1 | 48·6 | 48·2 | 48·1 | 48·3 | N 71 | | 45·0 | 45·0 | 45·0 | 45·1 | 45·3 | 45·4 |
| 2·6 | β | Libræ | | 130 | 27·4 | 27·2 | 27·0 | 26·8 | 26·7 | 26·7 | S 9 | | 27·8 | 27·9 | 27·9 | 27·9 | 27·9 | 27·9 |
| 2·7 | β | Lupi | | 134 | 60·7 | 60·4 | 60·1 | 59·9 | 59·8 | 59·8 | S 43 | | 13·1 | 13·2 | 13·2 | 13·4 | 13·4 | 13·5 |
| 2·8 | α | Libræ | 39 | 136 | 58·8 | 58·6 | 58·4 | 58·2 | 58·1 | 58·1 | S 16 | | 07·9 | 08·0 | 08·0 | 08·1 | 08·1 | 08·1 |
| 2·1 | β | Ursæ Minoris | 40 | 137 | 20·3 | 19·6 | 19·1 | 18·7 | 18·6 | 18·9 | N 74 | | 03·6 | 03·6 | 03·6 | 03·7 | 03·9 | 04·0 |
| 2·4 | ε | Bootis | | 138 | 31·0 | 30·8 | 30·6 | 30·4 | 30·4 | 30·4 | N 26 | | 58·8 | 58·7 | 58·7 | 58·8 | 58·9 | 59·0 |
| 2·3 | α | Lupi | | 139 | 09·4 | 09·1 | 08·8 | 08·6 | 08·5 | 08·5 | S 47 | | 28·7 | 28·7 | 28·8 | 29·0 | 29·1 | 29·2 |
| −0·3 | α | Centauri | 38 | 139 | 43·8 | 43·4 | 43·0 | 42·8 | 42·7 | 42·7 | S 60 | | 55·2 | 55·3 | 55·4 | 55·5 | 55·7 | 55·8 |
| 2·3 | η | Centauri | | 140 | 46·7 | 46·4 | 46·1 | 46·0 | 45·9 | 45·9 | S 42 | | 15·0 | 15·1 | 15·2 | 15·3 | 15·4 | 15·5 |
| 3·0 | γ | Bootis | | 141 | 45·8 | 45·5 | 45·3 | 45·1 | 45·1 | 45·1 | N 38 | | 12·5 | 12·5 | 12·5 | 12·6 | 12·7 | 12·8 |
| 0·0 | α | Bootis | 37 | 145 | 50·2 | 50·0 | 49·8 | 49·7 | 49·6 | 49·6 | N 19 | | 04·0 | 03·9 | 03·9 | 03·9 | 04·0 | 04·1 |
| 2·1 | θ | Centauri | 36 | 147 | 60·5 | 60·3 | 60·0 | 59·9 | 59·9 | 59·9 | S 36 | | 28·4 | 28·5 | 28·7 | 28·8 | 28·8 | 28·9 |
| 0·6 | β | Centauri | 35 | 148 | 39·5 | 39·1 | 38·8 | 38·6 | 38·5 | 38·6 | S 60 | | 28·4 | 28·5 | 28·6 | 28·8 | 28·9 | 29·0 |
| 2·6 | ζ | Centauri | | 150 | 46·5 | 46·2 | 45·9 | 45·8 | 45·7 | 45·8 | S 47 | | 23·5 | 23·6 | 23·7 | 23·9 | 24·0 | 24·1 |
| 2·7 | η | Bootis | | 151 | 04·2 | 03·9 | 03·8 | 03·7 | 03·6 | 03·7 | N 18 | | 17·2 | 17·1 | 17·1 | 17·1 | 17·2 | 17·3 |
| 1·9 | η | Ursæ Majoris | 34 | 152 | 54·0 | 53·7 | 53·5 | 53·3 | 53·3 | 53·4 | N 49 | | 12·0 | 11·9 | 12·0 | 12·1 | 12·2 | 12·4 |
| 2·3 | ε | Centauri | | 154 | 40·9 | 40·5 | 40·3 | 40·2 | 40·1 | 40·2 | S 53 | | 34·4 | 34·5 | 34·6 | 34·8 | 34·9 | 35·0 |
| 1·0 | α | Virginis | 33 | 158 | 24·9 | 24·6 | 24·5 | 24·4 | 24·4 | 24·4 | S 11 | | 16·5 | 16·6 | 16·6 | 16·7 | 16·7 | 16·7 |
| 2·3 | ζ | Ursæ Majoris | | 158 | 47·9 | 47·6 | 47·3 | 47·2 | 47·2 | 47·4 | N 54 | | 48·4 | 48·4 | 48·4 | 48·6 | 48·7 | 48·8 |
| 2·8 | ι | Centauri | | 159 | 32·6 | 32·3 | 32·2 | 32·1 | 32·1 | 32·1 | S 36 | | 49·5 | 49·6 | 49·7 | 49·8 | 49·9 | 49·9 |
| 2·8 | ε | Virginis | | 164 | 11·0 | 10·8 | 10·7 | 10·6 | 10·6 | 10·6 | N 10 | | 50·4 | 50·3 | 50·3 | 50·3 | 50·4 | 50·4 |
| 2·9 | α | Canum Venat. | | 165 | 44·2 | 44·0 | 43·8 | 43·7 | 43·8 | 43·9 | N 38 | | 11·8 | 11·8 | 11·8 | 11·9 | 12·0 | 12·1 |
| 1·8 | ε | Ursæ Majoris | 32 | 166 | 15·1 | 14·7 | 14·5 | 14·4 | 14·5 | 14·7 | N 55 | | 50·2 | 50·2 | 50·3 | 50·4 | 50·5 | 50·6 |
| 1·3 | β | Crucis | | 167 | 44·9 | 44·5 | 44·3 | 44·2 | 44·3 | 44·4 | S 59 | | 48·2 | 48·3 | 48·5 | 48·7 | 48·8 | 48·9 |
| 2·9 | γ | Virginis | | 169 | 18·5 | 18·3 | 18·1 | 18·1 | 18·1 | 18·1 | S 1 | | 34·2 | 34·3 | 34·3 | 34·3 | 34·3 | 34·3 |
| 2·2 | γ | Centauri | | 169 | 19·1 | 18·8 | 18·6 | 18·5 | 18·6 | 18·7 | S 49 | | 04·5 | 04·7 | 04·8 | 05·0 | 05·1 | 05·1 |
| 2·7 | α | Muscæ | | 170 | 22·4 | 21·9 | 21·7 | 21·6 | 21·7 | 22·0 | S 69 | | 15·0 | 15·2 | 15·3 | 15·5 | 15·7 | 15·8 |
| 2·7 | β | Corvi | | 171 | 06·9 | 06·7 | 06·6 | 06·5 | 06·5 | 06·6 | S 23 | | 30·9 | 31·1 | 31·2 | 31·3 | 31·3 | 31·3 |
| 1·6 | γ | Crucis | 31 | 171 | 54·1 | 53·8 | 53·6 | 53·6 | 53·7 | 53·8 | S 57 | | 13·9 | 14·0 | 14·2 | 14·3 | 14·5 | 14·5 |
| 1·3 | α | Crucis | 30 | 173 | 02·5 | 02·1 | 01·9 | 01·9 | 02·0 | 02·2 | S 63 | | 12·9 | 13·1 | 13·2 | 13·4 | 13·5 | 13·6 |
| 2·6 | γ | Corvi | 29 | 175 | 46·0 | 45·8 | 45·6 | 45·6 | 45·7 | 45·7 | S 17 | | 39·7 | 39·8 | 39·9 | 40·0 | 40·0 | 40·0 |
| 2·6 | δ | Centauri | | 177 | 37·5 | 37·2 | 37·1 | 37·1 | 37·1 | 37·3 | S 50 | | 50·4 | 50·6 | 50·7 | 50·9 | 51·0 | 51·0 |
| 2·4 | γ | Ursæ Majoris | | 181 | 15·2 | 14·9 | 14·7 | 14·7 | 14·8 | 15·0 | N 53 | | 34·1 | 34·2 | 34·3 | 34·4 | 34·5 | 34·5 |
| 2·1 | β | Leonis | 28 | 182 | 27·3 | 27·1 | 27·0 | 27·0 | 27·0 | 27·1 | N 14 | | 26·9 | 26·8 | 26·8 | 26·9 | 26·9 | 27·0 |
| 2·6 | δ | Leonis | | 191 | 10·8 | 10·6 | 10·5 | 10·6 | 10·6 | 10·7 | N 20 | | 24·1 | 24·1 | 24·1 | 24·1 | 24·2 | 24·2 |
| 3·0 | ψ | Ursæ Majoris | | 192 | 16·5 | 16·2 | 16·1 | 16·2 | 16·3 | 16·4 | N 44 | | 22·6 | 22·6 | 22·7 | 22·8 | 22·9 | 22·9 |
| 1·8 | α | Ursæ Majoris | 27 | 193 | 43·7 | 43·3 | 43·2 | 43·3 | 43·5 | 43·8 | N 61 | | 37·7 | 37·8 | 37·9 | 38·1 | 38·1 | 38·2 |
| 2·4 | β | Ursæ Majoris | | 194 | 12·4 | 12·1 | 12·0 | 12·1 | 12·3 | 12·5 | N 56 | | 15·7 | 15·7 | 15·8 | 16·0 | 16·1 | 16·1 |
| 2·7 | μ | Velorum | | 198 | 04·1 | 03·9 | 03·9 | 04·0 | 04·1 | 04·3 | S 49 | | 32·0 | 32·1 | 32·3 | 32·4 | 32·5 | 32·5 |
| 2·8 | θ | Carinæ | | 199 | 03·5 | 03·3 | 03·3 | 03·5 | 03·7 | 04·0 | S 64 | | 30·3 | 30·5 | 30·7 | 30·8 | 30·9 | 30·9 |
| 2·3 | γ | Leonis | | 204 | 42·2 | 42·0 | 42·0 | 42·0 | 42·1 | 42·2 | N 19 | | 43·7 | 43·7 | 43·7 | 43·8 | 43·8 | 43·8 |
| 1·4 | α | Leonis | 26 | 207 | 36·8 | 36·6 | 36·6 | 36·7 | 36·8 | 36·8 | N 11 | | 51·5 | 51·5 | 51·5 | 51·5 | 51·5 | 51·6 |
| 3·0 | ε | Leonis | | 213 | 13·4 | 13·3 | 13·3 | 13·4 | 13·5 | 13·5 | N 23 | | 40·3 | 40·3 | 40·3 | 40·4 | 40·4 | 40·4 |
| 3·1 | N | Velorum | | 217 | 01·3 | 01·2 | 01·3 | 01·5 | 01·7 | 02·0 | S 57 | | 07·7 | 07·9 | 08·1 | 08·2 | 08·2 | 08·2 |
| 2·0 | α | Hydræ | 25 | 217 | 49·9 | 49·8 | 49·8 | 49·8 | 50·0 | 50·0 | S 8 | | 45·2 | 45·3 | 45·4 | 45·4 | 45·4 | 45·4 |
| 2·5 | κ | Velorum | | 219 | 17·7 | 17·6 | 17·7 | 17·9 | 18·2 | 18·4 | S 55 | | 06·1 | 06·3 | 06·5 | 06·6 | 06·6 | 06·5 |
| 2·2 | ι | Carinæ | | 220 | 34·4 | 34·3 | 34·5 | 34·7 | 35·0 | 35·2 | S 59 | | 21·9 | 22·1 | 22·2 | 22·3 | 22·4 | 22·3 |
| 1·7 | β | Carinæ | 24 | 221 | 37·8 | 37·8 | 38·0 | 38·4 | 38·8 | 39·2 | S 69 | | 48·3 | 48·5 | 48·6 | 48·7 | 48·8 | 48·7 |
| 2·2 | λ | Velorum | 23 | 222 | 47·7 | 47·6 | 47·7 | 47·8 | 48·0 | 48·1 | S 43 | | 31·2 | 31·3 | 31·5 | 31·6 | 31·6 | 31·5 |
| 3·1 | ι | Ursæ Majoris | | 224 | 49·2 | 49·0 | 49·1 | 49·2 | 49·4 | 49·5 | N 47 | | 57·2 | 57·3 | 57·4 | 57·4 | 57·5 | 57·4 |
| 2·0 | δ | Velorum | | 228 | 39·9 | 39·9 | 40·0 | 40·3 | 40·5 | 40·7 | S 54 | | 47·3 | 47·4 | 47·6 | 47·7 | 47·7 | 47·6 |
| 1·9 | ε | Carinæ | 22 | 234 | 15·0 | 15·1 | 15·2 | 15·5 | 15·8 | 16·1 | S 59 | | 34·7 | 34·9 | 35·0 | 35·1 | 35·1 | 35·0 |
| 1·8 | γ | Velorum | | 237 | 26·5 | 26·5 | 26·6 | 26·8 | 27·0 | 27·2 | S 47 | | 24·0 | 24·2 | 24·3 | 24·4 | 24·3 | 24·3 |
| 2·8 | ρ | Puppis | | 237 | 52·6 | 52·5 | 52·6 | 52·8 | 52·9 | 53·0 | S 24 | | 22·1 | 22·2 | 22·3 | 22·3 | 22·3 | 22·2 |
| 2·3 | ζ | Puppis | | 238 | 54·3 | 54·3 | 54·5 | 54·6 | 54·8 | 54·9 | S 40 | | 03·9 | 04·0 | 04·1 | 04·2 | 04·2 | 04·1 |
| 1·1 | β | Geminorum | 21 | 243 | 19·9 | 19·9 | 20·0 | 20·1 | 20·2 | 20·2 | N 27 | | 58·3 | 58·3 | 58·4 | 58·4 | 58·4 | 58·4 |
| 0·4 | α | Canis Minoris | 20 | 244 | 53·1 | 53·0 | 53·1 | 53·2 | 53·3 | 53·4 | N 5 | | 10·1 | 10·0 | 10·0 | 10·0 | 10·0 | 10·1 |

| Mag. | | Name and Number | | | SHA JULY | AUG. | SEPT. | OCT. | NOV. | DEC. | Declination | JULY | AUG. | SEPT. | OCT. | NOV. | DEC. |
|---|---|---|---|---|---|---|---|---|---|---|---|---|---|---|---|---|---|
| | | | | ° | ′ | ′ | ′ | ′ | ′ | ′ | ° | ′ | ′ | ′ | ′ | ′ | ′ |
| 2·9 | γ | Trianguli Aust. | | 129 | 44·3 | 44·7 | 45·0 | 45·3 | 45·3 | 45·0 | S 68 | 45·9 | 45·9 | 45·9 | 45·8 | 45·7 | 45·6 |
| 3·1 | | Pherkad | | 129 | 48·6 | 49·1 | 49·7 | 50·0 | 50·2 | 50·1 | N 71 | 45·5 | 45·5 | 45·4 | 45·3 | 45·1 | 44·9 |
| 2·6 | | Zubeneschamali | | 130 | 26·7 | 26·8 | 26·9 | 27·0 | 26·9 | 26·8 | S 9 | 27·9 | 27·9 | 27·9 | 27·9 | 27·9 | 28·0 |
| 2·7 | β | Lupi | | 134 | 59·8 | 60·0 | 60·1 | 60·2 | 60·2 | 60·0 | S 43 | 13·6 | 13·6 | 13·5 | 13·5 | 13·4 | 13·4 |
| 2·8 | | Zubenelgenubi | 39 | 136 | 58·1 | 58·2 | 58·4 | 58·4 | 58·4 | 58·2 | S 16 | 08·1 | 08·1 | 08·0 | 08·0 | 08·0 | 08·1 |
| 2·1 | | Kochab | 40 | 137 | 19·4 | 19·9 | 20·5 | 20·9 | 21·0 | 20·7 | N 74 | 04·1 | 04·1 | 04·0 | 03·9 | 03·7 | 03·5 |
| 2·4 | | Izar | | 138 | 30·4 | 30·6 | 30·7 | 30·8 | 30·7 | 30·6 | N 26 | 59·0 | 59·1 | 59·0 | 58·9 | 58·8 | 58·6 |
| 2·3 | α | Lupi | | 139 | 08·6 | 08·7 | 08·9 | 09·0 | 08·9 | 08·7 | S 47 | 29·2 | 29·2 | 29·1 | 29·1 | 29·0 | 28·9 |
| −0·3 | | Rigil Kent. | 38 | 139 | 42·9 | 43·1 | 43·4 | 43·5 | 43·4 | 43·2 | S 60 | 55·8 | 55·8 | 55·8 | 55·7 | 55·6 | 55·5 |
| 2·3 | η | Centauri | | 140 | 45·9 | 46·1 | 46·2 | 46·3 | 46·2 | 46·0 | S 42 | 15·5 | 15·5 | 15·4 | 15·4 | 15·3 | 15·3 |
| 3·0 | | Seginus | | 141 | 45·2 | 45·3 | 45·5 | 45·6 | 45·5 | 45·4 | N 38 | 12·9 | 12·9 | 12·8 | 12·7 | 12·5 | 12·4 |
| 0·0 | | Arcturus | 37 | 145 | 49·7 | 49·8 | 49·9 | 50·0 | 49·9 | 49·7 | N 19 | 04·1 | 04·1 | 04·1 | 04·0 | 03·9 | 03·8 |
| 2·1 | | Menkent | 36 | 147 | 59·9 | 60·1 | 60·2 | 60·2 | 60·1 | 59·9 | S 36 | 28·9 | 28·9 | 28·8 | 28·8 | 28·7 | 28·7 |
| 0·6 | | Hadar | 35 | 148 | 38·8 | 39·0 | 39·2 | 39·3 | 39·2 | 38·9 | S 60 | 29·1 | 29·1 | 29·0 | 28·9 | 28·8 | 28·7 |
| 2·6 | ζ | Centauri | | 150 | 45·9 | 46·0 | 46·2 | 46·2 | 46·1 | 45·9 | S 47 | 24·1 | 24·1 | 24·0 | 23·9 | 23·8 | 23·8 |
| 2·7 | | Muphrid | | 151 | 03·7 | 03·8 | 03·9 | 03·9 | 03·9 | 03·7 | N 18 | 17·3 | 17·3 | 17·3 | 17·2 | 17·1 | 16·9 |
| 1·9 | | Alkaid | 34 | 152 | 53·6 | 53·8 | 53·9 | 54·0 | 53·9 | 53·7 | N 49 | 12·4 | 12·4 | 12·3 | 12·1 | 11·9 | 11·8 |
| 2·3 | ε | Centauri | | 154 | 40·3 | 40·5 | 40·7 | 40·7 | 40·6 | 40·3 | S 53 | 35·0 | 35·0 | 34·9 | 34·8 | 34·7 | 34·7 |
| 1·0 | | Spica | 33 | 158 | 24·4 | 24·5 | 24·6 | 24·6 | 24·5 | 24·3 | S 11 | 16·7 | 16·6 | 16·6 | 16·6 | 16·6 | 16·7 |
| 2·3 | | Mizar | | 158 | 47·6 | 47·8 | 47·9 | 48·0 | 47·8 | 47·6 | N 54 | 48·8 | 48·8 | 48·7 | 48·5 | 48·3 | 48·1 |
| 2·8 | ι | Centauri | | 159 | 32·2 | 32·3 | 32·4 | 32·4 | 32·3 | 32·0 | S 36 | 49·9 | 49·9 | 49·8 | 49·8 | 49·7 | 49·7 |
| 2·8 | | Vindemiatrix | | 164 | 10·7 | 10·8 | 10·8 | 10·8 | 10·7 | 10·5 | N 10 | 50·5 | 50·5 | 50·5 | 50·4 | 50·3 | 50·2 |
| 2·9 | | Cor Caroli | | 165 | 44·0 | 44·1 | 44·2 | 44·1 | 44·0 | 43·8 | N 38 | 12·1 | 12·1 | 12·0 | 11·9 | 11·7 | 11·5 |
| 1·8 | | Alioth | 32 | 166 | 14·9 | 15·1 | 15·2 | 15·2 | 15·0 | 14·7 | N 55 | 50·6 | 50·6 | 50·4 | 50·3 | 50·1 | 49·9 |
| 1·3 | | Mimosa | | 167 | 44·7 | 44·9 | 45·0 | 45·0 | 44·8 | 44·4 | S 59 | 48·9 | 48·8 | 48·7 | 48·6 | 48·5 | 48·5 |
| 2·9 | | Porrima | | 169 | 18·2 | 18·3 | 18·3 | 18·3 | 18·1 | 17·9 | S 1 | 34·3 | 34·3 | 34·2 | 34·3 | 34·3 | 34·4 |
| 2·2 | | Muhlifain | | 169 | 18·8 | 19·0 | 19·1 | 19·0 | 18·9 | 18·6 | S 49 | 05·1 | 05·1 | 05·0 | 04·9 | 04·8 | 04·8 |
| 2·7 | α | Muscæ | | 170 | 22·3 | 22·7 | 22·9 | 22·9 | 22·6 | 22·1 | S 69 | 15·8 | 15·7 | 15·6 | 15·5 | 15·5 | 15·3 |
| 2·7 | | Kraz | | 171 | 06·7 | 06·8 | 06·8 | 06·8 | 06·6 | 06·4 | S 23 | 31·3 | 31·2 | 31·2 | 31·1 | 31·1 | 31·2 |
| 1·6 | | Gacrux | 31 | 171 | 54·0 | 54·2 | 54·3 | 54·3 | 54·1 | 53·7 | S 57 | 14·5 | 14·5 | 14·3 | 14·2 | 14·1 | 14·1 |
| 1·3 | | Acrux | 30 | 173 | 02·5 | 02·7 | 02·9 | 02·8 | 02·6 | 02·1 | S 63 | 13·6 | 13·6 | 13·4 | 13·3 | 13·2 | 13·2 |
| 2·6 | | Gienah | 29 | 175 | 45·8 | 45·9 | 45·9 | 45·8 | 45·7 | 45·4 | S 17 | 40·0 | 39·9 | 39·9 | 39·9 | 39·9 | 40·0 |
| 2·6 | δ | Centauri | | 177 | 37·4 | 37·6 | 37·7 | 37·6 | 37·4 | 37·0 | S 50 | 51·0 | 50·9 | 50·8 | 50·7 | 50·6 | 50·7 |
| 2·4 | | Phecda | | 181 | 15·2 | 15·3 | 15·3 | 15·2 | 15·0 | 14·7 | N 53 | 34·5 | 34·4 | 34·3 | 34·1 | 34·0 | 33·8 |
| 2·1 | | Denebola | 28 | 182 | 27·2 | 27·2 | 27·2 | 27·2 | 27·0 | 26·7 | N 14 | 27·0 | 27·0 | 26·9 | 26·9 | 26·7 | 26·6 |
| 2·6 | | Zosma | | 191 | 10·8 | 10·8 | 10·8 | 10·7 | 10·5 | 10·2 | N 20 | 24·2 | 24·2 | 24·2 | 24·1 | 24·0 | 23·8 |
| 3·0 | ψ | Ursæ Majoris | | 192 | 16·5 | 16·6 | 16·6 | 16·4 | 16·2 | 15·9 | N 44 | 22·9 | 22·8 | 22·7 | 22·5 | 22·4 | 22·3 |
| 1·8 | | Dubhe | 27 | 193 | 44·0 | 44·1 | 44·0 | 43·8 | 43·5 | 43·0 | N 61 | 38·1 | 38·0 | 37·8 | 37·7 | 37·5 | 37·4 |
| 2·4 | | Merak | | 194 | 12·6 | 12·7 | 12·7 | 12·5 | 12·2 | 11·8 | N 56 | 16·0 | 15·9 | 15·8 | 15·6 | 15·5 | 15·4 |
| 2·7 | μ | Velorum | | 198 | 04·4 | 04·5 | 04·5 | 04·3 | 04·1 | 03·7 | S 49 | 32·4 | 32·3 | 32·2 | 32·1 | 32·1 | 32·1 |
| 2·8 | θ | Carinæ | | 199 | 04·3 | 04·5 | 04·5 | 04·3 | 03·9 | 03·4 | S 64 | 30·9 | 30·7 | 30·6 | 30·5 | 30·4 | 30·5 |
| 2·3 | | Algieba | | 204 | 42·2 | 42·2 | 42·2 | 42·0 | 41·8 | 41·5 | N 19 | 43·8 | 43·8 | 43·8 | 43·7 | 43·6 | 43·5 |
| 1·4 | | Regulus | 26 | 207 | 36·9 | 36·9 | 36·8 | 36·6 | 36·4 | 36·2 | N 11 | 51·6 | 51·6 | 51·6 | 51·5 | 51·4 | 51·3 |
| 3·0 | ε | Leonis | | 213 | 13·6 | 13·5 | 13·4 | 13·3 | 13·0 | 12·7 | N 23 | 40·4 | 40·4 | 40·3 | 40·2 | 40·1 | 40·1 |
| 3·1 | N | Velorum | | 217 | 02·1 | 02·2 | 02·1 | 01·8 | 01·5 | 01·1 | S 57 | 08·1 | 07·9 | 07·8 | 07·7 | 07·7 | 07·8 |
| 2·0 | | Alphard | 25 | 217 | 50·0 | 50·0 | 49·9 | 49·7 | 49·5 | 49·3 | S 8 | 45·3 | 45·2 | 45·2 | 45·2 | 45·3 | 45·4 |
| 2·5 | | Markeb | | 219 | 18·5 | 18·6 | 18·4 | 18·2 | 17·8 | 17·5 | S 55 | 06·4 | 06·3 | 06·2 | 06·1 | 06·1 | 06·2 |
| 2·2 | | Aspidiske | | 220 | 35·4 | 35·4 | 35·3 | 35·0 | 34·6 | 34·3 | S 59 | 22·2 | 22·1 | 21·9 | 21·8 | 21·8 | 21·9 |
| 1·7 | | Miaplacidus | 24 | 221 | 39·5 | 39·6 | 39·4 | 39·0 | 38·5 | 38·0 | S 69 | 48·6 | 48·5 | 48·3 | 48·2 | 48·2 | 48·3 |
| 2·2 | | Suhail | 23 | 222 | 48·2 | 48·2 | 48·1 | 47·9 | 47·6 | 47·3 | S 43 | 31·4 | 31·3 | 31·1 | 31·1 | 31·1 | 31·2 |
| 3·1 | | Talitha | | 224 | 49·5 | 49·4 | 49·3 | 49·0 | 48·6 | 48·3 | N 47 | 57·4 | 57·3 | 57·2 | 57·1 | 57·0 | 56·9 |
| 2·0 | | Alsephina | | 228 | 40·8 | 40·8 | 40·7 | 40·4 | 40·0 | 39·7 | S 54 | 47·5 | 47·3 | 47·2 | 47·1 | 47·2 | 47·3 |
| 1·9 | | Avior | 22 | 234 | 16·2 | 16·1 | 15·9 | 15·6 | 15·2 | 14·9 | S 59 | 34·9 | 34·7 | 34·6 | 34·5 | 34·6 | 34·7 |
| 1·8 | γ | Velorum | | 237 | 27·2 | 27·2 | 27·0 | 26·7 | 26·4 | 26·2 | S 47 | 24·1 | 24·0 | 23·9 | 23·8 | 23·9 | 24·0 |
| 2·8 | | Tureis | | 237 | 53·0 | 52·9 | 52·7 | 52·5 | 52·3 | 52·0 | S 24 | 22·1 | 22·0 | 21·9 | 21·9 | 22·0 | 22·1 |
| 2·3 | | Naos | | 238 | 54·9 | 54·9 | 54·7 | 54·5 | 54·2 | 53·9 | S 40 | 03·9 | 03·8 | 03·7 | 03·7 | 03·7 | 03·9 |
| 1·1 | | Pollux | 21 | 243 | 20·2 | 20·1 | 19·9 | 19·6 | 19·3 | 19·1 | N 27 | 58·4 | 58·3 | 58·3 | 58·3 | 58·2 | 58·2 |
| 0·4 | | Procyon | 20 | 244 | 53·3 | 53·2 | 53·0 | 52·8 | 52·6 | 52·3 | N 5 | 10·1 | 10·1 | 10·2 | 10·1 | 10·1 | 10·0 |

| Mag. | Name and Number | | SHA | | | | | | Declination | | | | | | |
|---|---|---|---|---|---|---|---|---|---|---|---|---|---|---|---|
| | | | JAN. | FEB. | MAR. | APR. | MAY | JUNE | | JAN. | FEB. | MAR. | APR. | MAY | JUNE |
| | | ° | ′ | ′ | ′ | ′ | ′ | ′ | ° | ′ | ′ | ′ | ′ | ′ | ′ |
| 1·6 | α Geminorum | 245 | 59·8 | 59·8 | 59·9 | 60·0 | 60·1 | 60·2 | N 31 | 50·3 | 50·4 | 50·4 | 50·4 | 50·4 | 50·4 |
| 3·3 | σ Puppis | 247 | 30·7 | 30·8 | 30·9 | 31·1 | 31·3 | 31·4 | S 43 | 20·8 | 20·9 | 21·0 | 21·0 | 21·0 | 20·9 |
| 2·9 | β Canis Minoris | 247 | 54·7 | 54·7 | 54·7 | 54·9 | 55·0 | 55·0 | N 8 | 14·6 | 14·6 | 14·6 | 14·6 | 14·6 | 14·7 |
| 2·4 | η Canis Majoris | 248 | 45·3 | 45·3 | 45·4 | 45·6 | 45·7 | 45·8 | S 29 | 20·8 | 20·9 | 21·0 | 21·0 | 21·0 | 20·9 |
| 2·7 | π Puppis | 250 | 30·9 | 30·9 | 31·1 | 31·3 | 31·4 | 31·5 | S 37 | 08·2 | 08·4 | 08·5 | 08·5 | 08·4 | 08·3 |
| 1·8 | δ Canis Majoris | 252 | 40·5 | 40·5 | 40·6 | 40·8 | 40·9 | 40·9 | S 26 | 25·7 | 25·9 | 25·9 | 25·9 | 25·9 | 25·8 |
| 3·0 | o Canis Majoris | 254 | 00·6 | 00·7 | 00·8 | 00·9 | 01·0 | 01·1 | S 23 | 52·0 | 52·1 | 52·1 | 52·1 | 52·1 | 52·0 |
| 1·5 | ε Canis Majoris 19 | 255 | 07·4 | 07·4 | 07·6 | 07·7 | 07·9 | 07·9 | S 29 | 00·2 | 00·3 | 00·4 | 00·4 | 00·3 | 00·2 |
| 2·9 | τ Puppis | 257 | 22·3 | 22·4 | 22·6 | 22·9 | 23·1 | 23·2 | S 50 | 38·5 | 38·6 | 38·7 | 38·7 | 38·6 | 38·5 |
| −1·5 | α Canis Majoris 18 | 258 | 28·0 | 28·1 | 28·2 | 28·3 | 28·4 | 28·5 | S 16 | 44·9 | 44·9 | 45·0 | 45·0 | 44·9 | 44·8 |
| 1·9 | γ Geminorum | 260 | 15·1 | 15·1 | 15·2 | 15·4 | 15·5 | 15·5 | N 16 | 22·8 | 22·8 | 22·8 | 22·8 | 22·8 | 22·8 |
| −0·7 | α Carinæ 17 | 263 | 52·9 | 53·1 | 53·3 | 53·6 | 53·8 | 53·9 | S 52 | 42·5 | 42·7 | 42·7 | 42·7 | 42·6 | 42·5 |
| 2·0 | β Canis Majoris | 264 | 04·8 | 04·8 | 04·9 | 05·1 | 05·2 | 05·2 | S 17 | 58·1 | 58·2 | 58·2 | 58·2 | 58·2 | 58·1 |
| 2·6 | θ Aurigæ | 269 | 41·5 | 41·6 | 41·7 | 41·8 | 41·9 | 41·9 | N 37 | 12·8 | 12·9 | 12·9 | 12·9 | 12·9 | 12·8 |
| 1·9 | β Aurigæ | 269 | 42·7 | 42·7 | 42·9 | 43·1 | 43·2 | 43·1 | N 44 | 57·0 | 57·0 | 57·1 | 57·0 | 57·0 | 56·9 |
| Var.‡ | α Orionis 16 | 270 | 54·4 | 54·5 | 54·6 | 54·7 | 54·8 | 54·7 | N 7 | 24·6 | 24·6 | 24·6 | 24·6 | 24·6 | 24·6 |
| 2·1 | κ Orionis | 272 | 47·8 | 47·9 | 48·0 | 48·1 | 48·2 | 48·2 | S 9 | 39·8 | 39·9 | 39·9 | 39·9 | 39·8 | 39·7 |
| 1·9 | ζ Orionis | 274 | 31·8 | 31·9 | 32·0 | 32·1 | 32·2 | 32·1 | S 1 | 56·0 | 56·0 | 56·0 | 56·0 | 55·9 | 55·9 |
| 2·6 | α Columbæ | 274 | 53·1 | 53·2 | 53·3 | 53·5 | 53·6 | 53·6 | S 34 | 03·9 | 04·0 | 04·0 | 04·0 | 03·9 | 03·7 |
| 3·0 | ζ Tauri | 275 | 15·5 | 15·5 | 15·6 | 15·8 | 15·8 | 15·8 | N 21 | 09·3 | 09·3 | 09·3 | 09·3 | 09·3 | 09·3 |
| 1·7 | ε Orionis 15 | 275 | 39·9 | 40·0 | 40·1 | 40·2 | 40·3 | 40·2 | S 1 | 11·4 | 11·4 | 11·4 | 11·4 | 11·4 | 11·3 |
| 2·8 | ι Orionis | 275 | 52·2 | 52·3 | 52·4 | 52·5 | 52·6 | 52·5 | S 5 | 53·8 | 53·9 | 53·9 | 53·9 | 53·8 | 53·7 |
| 2·6 | α Leporis | 276 | 34·3 | 34·4 | 34·5 | 34·7 | 34·7 | 34·7 | S 17 | 48·5 | 48·6 | 48·6 | 48·6 | 48·5 | 48·4 |
| 2·2 | δ Orionis | 276 | 42·9 | 43·0 | 43·1 | 43·2 | 43·3 | 43·2 | S 0 | 17·1 | 17·1 | 17·1 | 17·1 | 17·1 | 17·0 |
| 2·8 | β Leporis | 277 | 42·0 | 42·1 | 42·2 | 42·4 | 42·4 | 42·4 | S 20 | 44·7 | 44·7 | 44·7 | 44·7 | 44·6 | 44·5 |
| 1·7 | β Tauri 14 | 278 | 04·6 | 04·7 | 04·8 | 04·9 | 05·0 | 04·9 | N 28 | 37·5 | 37·6 | 37·6 | 37·6 | 37·5 | 37·5 |
| 1·6 | γ Orionis 13 | 278 | 25·2 | 25·3 | 25·4 | 25·5 | 25·6 | 25·5 | N 6 | 22·1 | 22·1 | 22·1 | 22·1 | 22·1 | 22·1 |
| 0·1 | α Aurigæ 12 | 280 | 25·1 | 25·2 | 25·3 | 25·5 | 25·6 | 25·5 | N 46 | 01·2 | 01·3 | 01·3 | 01·3 | 01·2 | 01·1 |
| 0·1 | β Orionis 11 | 281 | 05·9 | 06·0 | 06·1 | 06·3 | 06·3 | 06·3 | S 8 | 10·7 | 10·7 | 10·8 | 10·7 | 10·7 | 10·6 |
| 2·8 | β Eridani | 282 | 45·9 | 46·0 | 46·1 | 46·2 | 46·3 | 46·2 | S 5 | 03·6 | 03·6 | 03·6 | 03·6 | 03·6 | 03·5 |
| 2·7 | ι Aurigæ | 285 | 23·5 | 23·5 | 23·7 | 23·8 | 23·9 | 23·8 | N 33 | 12·0 | 12·1 | 12·1 | 12·1 | 12·0 | 12·0 |
| 0·9 | α Tauri 10 | 290 | 42·2 | 42·2 | 42·4 | 42·5 | 42·5 | 42·4 | N 16 | 33·2 | 33·2 | 33·1 | 33·1 | 33·1 | 33·2 |
| 2·9 | ε Persei | 300 | 09·9 | 10·1 | 10·2 | 10·3 | 10·3 | 10·2 | N 40 | 04·5 | 04·5 | 04·5 | 04·4 | 04·4 | 04·3 |
| 3·0 | γ Eridani | 300 | 14·1 | 14·2 | 14·3 | 14·4 | 14·4 | 14·3 | S 13 | 26·9 | 27·0 | 27·0 | 26·9 | 26·8 | 26·7 |
| 2·9 | ζ Persei | 301 | 07·2 | 07·3 | 07·4 | 07·5 | 07·5 | 07·4 | N 31 | 57·0 | 57·0 | 56·9 | 56·9 | 56·9 | 56·8 |
| 2·9 | η Tauri | 302 | 48·1 | 48·2 | 48·3 | 48·4 | 48·4 | 48·2 | N 24 | 10·4 | 10·4 | 10·4 | 10·3 | 10·3 | 10·3 |
| 1·8 | α Persei 9 | 308 | 31·5 | 31·6 | 31·8 | 31·9 | 31·9 | 31·7 | N 49 | 56·5 | 56·5 | 56·4 | 56·4 | 56·3 | 56·2 |
| Var.§ | β Persei | 312 | 35·9 | 36·1 | 36·2 | 36·3 | 36·3 | 36·1 | N 41 | 02·5 | 02·5 | 02·5 | 02·4 | 02·3 | 02·3 |
| 2·5 | α Ceti 8 | 314 | 08·6 | 08·7 | 08·8 | 08·8 | 08·8 | 08·6 | N 4 | 10·4 | 10·4 | 10·4 | 10·4 | 10·5 | 10·6 |
| 2·0 | α Ursæ Minoris | 314 | 59·3 | 72·6 | 84·9 | 92·4 | 91·6 | 83·6 | N 89 | 21·7 | 21·7 | 21·6 | 21·5 | 21·4 | 21·3 |
| 3·2 | θ Eridani 7 | 315 | 13·5 | 13·7 | 13·8 | 13·9 | 13·9 | 13·8 | S 40 | 13·3 | 13·3 | 13·3 | 13·1 | 13·0 | 12·8 |
| 3·0 | β Trianguli | 327 | 17·3 | 17·4 | 17·5 | 17·5 | 17·5 | 17·2 | N 35 | 05·5 | 05·5 | 05·5 | 05·4 | 05·3 | 05·4 |
| 2·0 | α Arietis 6 | 327 | 53·9 | 54·0 | 54·1 | 54·1 | 54·0 | 53·8 | N 23 | 34·0 | 34·0 | 33·9 | 33·9 | 33·9 | 33·9 |
| 2·3 | γ Andromedæ | 328 | 41·3 | 41·5 | 41·6 | 41·6 | 41·5 | 41·3 | N 42 | 26·2 | 26·2 | 26·1 | 26·0 | 26·0 | 26·0 |
| 2·9 | α Hydri | 330 | 08·0 | 08·3 | 08·5 | 08·6 | 08·5 | 08·2 | S 61 | 28·2 | 28·1 | 28·0 | 27·8 | 27·6 | 27·5 |
| 2·6 | β Arietis | 331 | 02·3 | 02·4 | 02·5 | 02·5 | 02·4 | 02·2 | N 20 | 54·9 | 54·9 | 54·8 | 54·8 | 54·8 | 54·9 |
| 0·5 | α Eridani 5 | 335 | 22·1 | 22·3 | 22·4 | 22·5 | 22·4 | 22·1 | S 57 | 07·9 | 07·8 | 07·7 | 07·6 | 07·4 | 07·2 |
| 2·7 | δ Cassiopeiæ | 338 | 11·2 | 11·5 | 11·7 | 11·7 | 11·5 | 11·1 | N 60 | 21·2 | 21·1 | 21·0 | 20·9 | 20·8 | 20·8 |
| 2·1 | β Andromedæ | 342 | 15·7 | 15·8 | 15·9 | 15·9 | 15·8 | 15·5 | N 35 | 44·3 | 44·2 | 44·2 | 44·1 | 44·1 | 44·1 |
| Var.‖ | γ Cassiopeiæ | 345 | 29·6 | 29·9 | 30·0 | 30·0 | 29·8 | 29·4 | N 60 | 50·3 | 50·3 | 50·2 | 50·0 | 49·9 | 49·9 |
| 2·0 | β Ceti 4 | 348 | 49·8 | 49·9 | 49·9 | 49·9 | 49·8 | 49·5 | S 17 | 52·2 | 52·2 | 52·1 | 52·0 | 51·9 | 51·8 |
| 2·2 | α Cassiopeiæ 3 | 349 | 33·9 | 34·1 | 34·2 | 34·2 | 33·9 | 33·6 | N 56 | 39·6 | 39·6 | 39·5 | 39·3 | 39·3 | 39·3 |
| 2·4 | α Phœnicis 2 | 353 | 09·7 | 09·8 | 09·9 | 09·8 | 09·6 | 09·4 | S 42 | 11·5 | 11·5 | 11·4 | 11·2 | 11·1 | 10·9 |
| 2·8 | β Hydri | 353 | 17·1 | 17·6 | 17·8 | 17·7 | 17·3 | 16·6 | S 77 | 08·2 | 08·1 | 07·9 | 07·7 | 07·6 | 07·4 |
| 2·8 | γ Pegasi | 356 | 24·7 | 24·8 | 24·8 | 24·8 | 24·6 | 24·4 | N 15 | 18·3 | 18·3 | 18·2 | 18·2 | 18·2 | 18·3 |
| 2·3 | β Cassiopeiæ | 357 | 25·1 | 25·3 | 25·3 | 25·3 | 25·0 | 24·6 | N 59 | 16·4 | 16·3 | 16·2 | 16·1 | 16·0 | 16·0 |
| 2·1 | α Andromedæ 1 | 357 | 37·4 | 37·5 | 37·5 | 37·4 | 37·3 | 37·0 | N 29 | 12·7 | 12·7 | 12·6 | 12·5 | 12·5 | 12·6 |

‡ 0·1 — 1·2   § 2·1 — 3·4   ‖ Irregular variable; 2020 mag. 2·2

| Mag. | Name and Number | | SHA | | | | | | | Declination | | | | | |
|---|---|---|---|---|---|---|---|---|---|---|---|---|---|---|---|
| | | | JULY | AUG. | SEPT. | OCT. | NOV. | DEC. | | JULY | AUG. | SEPT. | OCT. | NOV. | DEC. |
| | | ° | ′ | ′ | ′ | ′ | ′ | ′ | ° | ′ | ′ | ′ | ′ | ′ | ′ |
| 1·6 | Castor | 245 | 60·1 | 60·0 | 59·8 | 59·5 | 59·2 | 59·0 | N 31 | 50·4 | 50·3 | 50·3 | 50·2 | 50·2 | 50·2 |
| 3·3 | σ Puppis | 247 | 31·4 | 31·3 | 31·1 | 30·8 | 30·6 | 30·3 | S 43 | 20·7 | 20·6 | 20·5 | 20·5 | 20·5 | 20·7 |
| 2·9 | Gomeisa | 247 | 54·9 | 54·8 | 54·6 | 54·4 | 54·2 | 54·0 | N 8 | 14·7 | 14·7 | 14·7 | 14·7 | 14·7 | 14·6 |
| 2·4 | Aludra | 248 | 45·7 | 45·6 | 45·4 | 45·4 | 45·2 | 44·8 | S 29 | 20·7 | 20·6 | 20·5 | 20·5 | 20·6 | 20·7 |
| 2·7 | π Puppis | 250 | 31·5 | 31·4 | 31·2 | 30·9 | 30·7 | 30·4 | S 37 | 08·2 | 08·0 | 08·0 | 07·9 | 08·0 | 08·2 |
| 1·8 | Wezen | 252 | 40·9 | 40·8 | 40·6 | 40·4 | 40·1 | 39·9 | S 26 | 25·7 | 25·5 | 25·5 | 25·5 | 25·5 | 25·7 |
| 3·0 | o Canis Majoris | 254 | 01·0 | 00·9 | 00·7 | 00·5 | 00·2 | 00·1 | S 23 | 51·9 | 51·8 | 51·7 | 51·7 | 51·8 | 51·9 |
| 1·5 | Adhara 19 | 255 | 07·8 | 07·7 | 07·5 | 07·3 | 07·0 | 06·9 | S 28 | 60·1 | 59·9 | 59·9 | 59·9 | 59·9 | 60·1 |
| 2·9 | τ Puppis | 257 | 23·2 | 23·0 | 22·8 | 22·5 | 22·2 | 22·0 | S 50 | 38·4 | 38·2 | 38·1 | 38·1 | 38·2 | 38·3 |
| −1·5 | Sirius 18 | 258 | 28·4 | 28·2 | 28·0 | 27·8 | 27·6 | 27·4 | S 16 | 44·7 | 44·6 | 44·6 | 44·6 | 44·7 | 44·8 |
| 1·9 | Alhena | 260 | 15·4 | 15·2 | 15·0 | 14·7 | 14·5 | 14·3 | N 16 | 22·8 | 22·8 | 22·8 | 22·8 | 22·8 | 22·8 |
| −0·7 | Canopus 17 | 263 | 53·8 | 53·7 | 53·4 | 53·1 | 52·8 | 52·6 | S 52 | 42·3 | 42·2 | 42·1 | 42·1 | 42·2 | 42·4 |
| 2·0 | Mirzam | 264 | 05·1 | 04·9 | 04·7 | 04·5 | 04·3 | 04·1 | S 17 | 57·9 | 57·8 | 57·8 | 57·8 | 57·9 | 58·0 |
| 2·6 | Mahasim | 269 | 41·8 | 41·5 | 41·3 | 41·0 | 40·7 | 40·5 | N 37 | 12·8 | 12·8 | 12·7 | 12·8 | 12·8 | 12·8 |
| 1·9 | Menkalinan | 269 | 43·0 | 42·7 | 42·4 | 42·1 | 41·8 | 41·6 | N 44 | 56·9 | 56·8 | 56·8 | 56·8 | 56·9 | 56·9 |
| Var.‡ | Betelgeuse 16 | 270 | 54·6 | 54·4 | 54·2 | 54·0 | 53·8 | 53·6 | N 7 | 24·7 | 24·7 | 24·8 | 24·8 | 24·7 | 24·7 |
| 2·1 | Saiph | 272 | 48·1 | 47·9 | 47·7 | 47·5 | 47·3 | 47·1 | S 9 | 39·6 | 39·5 | 39·5 | 39·5 | 39·6 | 39·7 |
| 1·9 | Alnitak | 274 | 32·0 | 31·8 | 31·6 | 31·4 | 31·2 | 31·1 | S 1 | 55·8 | 55·7 | 55·7 | 55·7 | 55·7 | 55·8 |
| 2·6 | Phact | 274 | 53·5 | 53·3 | 53·1 | 52·8 | 52·6 | 52·5 | S 34 | 03·6 | 03·5 | 03·4 | 03·4 | 03·5 | 03·7 |
| 3·0 | Tianguan | 275 | 15·6 | 15·4 | 15·2 | 14·9 | 14·7 | 14·6 | N 21 | 09·3 | 09·4 | 09·4 | 09·4 | 09·4 | 09·4 |
| 1·7 | Alnilam 15 | 275 | 40·1 | 39·9 | 39·7 | 39·5 | 39·3 | 39·1 | S 1 | 11·2 | 11·1 | 11·1 | 11·1 | 11·2 | 11·2 |
| 2·8 | Hatysa | 275 | 52·4 | 52·2 | 52·0 | 51·8 | 51·6 | 51·5 | S 5 | 53·7 | 53·6 | 53·5 | 53·5 | 53·6 | 53·7 |
| 2·6 | Arneb | 276 | 34·6 | 34·4 | 34·2 | 34·0 | 33·8 | 33·6 | S 17 | 48·3 | 48·2 | 48·1 | 48·1 | 48·2 | 48·3 |
| 2·2 | Mintaka | 276 | 43·1 | 42·9 | 42·7 | 42·5 | 42·3 | 42·1 | S 0 | 16·9 | 16·8 | 16·8 | 16·8 | 16·9 | 16·9 |
| 2·8 | Nihal | 277 | 42·3 | 42·1 | 41·9 | 41·6 | 41·4 | 41·3 | S 20 | 44·4 | 44·3 | 44·2 | 44·2 | 44·3 | 44·4 |
| 1·7 | Elnath 14 | 278 | 04·8 | 04·6 | 04·3 | 04·0 | 03·8 | 03·7 | N 28 | 37·5 | 37·5 | 37·5 | 37·6 | 37·6 | 37·6 |
| 1·6 | Bellatrix 13 | 278 | 25·4 | 25·2 | 24·9 | 24·7 | 24·5 | 24·4 | N 6 | 22·2 | 22·3 | 22·3 | 22·3 | 22·3 | 22·2 |
| 0·1 | Capella 12 | 280 | 25·3 | 25·0 | 24·7 | 24·4 | 24·1 | 23·9 | N 46 | 01·1 | 01·1 | 01·1 | 01·1 | 01·2 | 01·3 |
| 0·1 | Rigel 11 | 281 | 06·1 | 05·9 | 05·7 | 05·5 | 05·3 | 05·2 | S 8 | 10·5 | 10·4 | 10·3 | 10·4 | 10·4 | 10·5 |
| 2·8 | Cursa | 282 | 46·1 | 45·9 | 45·6 | 45·4 | 45·2 | 45·1 | S 5 | 03·4 | 03·3 | 03·3 | 03·3 | 03·3 | 03·4 |
| 2·7 | Hassaleh | 285 | 23·6 | 23·3 | 23·1 | 22·8 | 22·6 | 22·5 | N 33 | 12·0 | 12·0 | 12·0 | 12·1 | 12·1 | 12·1 |
| 0·9 | Aldebaran 10 | 290 | 42·2 | 42·0 | 41·8 | 41·5 | 41·4 | 41·3 | N 16 | 33·2 | 33·3 | 33·3 | 33·3 | 33·3 | 33·3 |
| 2·9 | ε Persei | 300 | 10·0 | 09·7 | 09·4 | 09·1 | 08·9 | 08·8 | N 40 | 04·3 | 04·4 | 04·4 | 04·5 | 04·6 | 04·6 |
| 3·0 | Zaurak | 300 | 14·1 | 13·9 | 13·7 | 13·5 | 13·4 | 13·3 | S 13 | 26·6 | 26·5 | 26·5 | 26·5 | 26·6 | 26·6 |
| 2·9 | ζ Persei | 301 | 07·2 | 06·9 | 06·6 | 06·4 | 06·2 | 06·2 | N 31 | 56·9 | 56·9 | 57·0 | 57·0 | 57·1 | 57·1 |
| 2·9 | Alcyone | 302 | 48·0 | 47·8 | 47·5 | 47·3 | 47·2 | 47·1 | N 24 | 10·4 | 10·4 | 10·5 | 10·5 | 10·6 | 10·6 |
| 1·8 | Mirfak 9 | 308 | 31·4 | 31·1 | 30·8 | 30·5 | 30·3 | 30·3 | N 49 | 56·2 | 56·2 | 56·3 | 56·4 | 56·5 | 56·6 |
| Var.§ | Algol | 312 | 35·8 | 35·5 | 35·2 | 35·0 | 34·9 | 34·8 | N 41 | 02·3 | 02·4 | 02·5 | 02·5 | 02·6 | 02·7 |
| 2·5 | Menkar 8 | 314 | 08·4 | 08·2 | 08·0 | 07·8 | 07·7 | 07·7 | N 4 | 10·7 | 10·7 | 10·8 | 10·8 | 10·8 | 10·8 |
| 2·0 | Polaris | 314 | 70·5 | 55·0 | 40·5 | 29·6 | 24·6 | 27·9 | N 89 | 21·2 | 21·2 | 21·3 | 21·5 | 21·6 | 21·8 |
| 3·2 | Acamar 7 | 315 | 13·5 | 13·2 | 13·0 | 12·8 | 12·7 | 12·7 | S 40 | 12·7 | 12·6 | 12·6 | 12·7 | 12·8 | 12·9 |
| 3·0 | β Trianguli | 327 | 17·0 | 16·7 | 16·5 | 16·3 | 16·2 | 16·2 | N 35 | 05·4 | 05·5 | 05·6 | 05·7 | 05·8 | 05·8 |
| 2·0 | Hamal 6 | 327 | 53·6 | 53·3 | 53·1 | 53·0 | 52·9 | 52·9 | N 23 | 34·0 | 34·1 | 34·2 | 34·2 | 34·3 | 34·3 |
| 2·3 | Almach | 328 | 41·0 | 40·7 | 40·4 | 40·3 | 40·2 | 40·2 | N 42 | 26·0 | 26·1 | 26·2 | 26·3 | 26·4 | 26·5 |
| 2·9 | α Hydri | 330 | 07·9 | 07·5 | 07·1 | 07·0 | 07·0 | 07·1 | S 61 | 27·4 | 27·3 | 27·4 | 27·5 | 27·7 | 27·8 |
| 2·6 | Sheratan | 331 | 01·9 | 01·7 | 01·5 | 01·4 | 01·3 | 01·3 | N 20 | 54·9 | 55·0 | 55·1 | 55·2 | 55·2 | 55·3 |
| 0·5 | Achernar 5 | 335 | 21·8 | 21·4 | 21·1 | 21·0 | 21·0 | 21·2 | S 57 | 07·1 | 07·1 | 07·1 | 07·3 | 07·4 | 07·5 |
| 2·7 | Ruchbah | 338 | 10·7 | 10·4 | 10·1 | 09·9 | 09·9 | 10·0 | N 60 | 20·8 | 20·9 | 21·0 | 21·2 | 21·4 | 21·5 |
| 2·1 | Mirach | 342 | 15·2 | 15·0 | 14·8 | 14·7 | 14·7 | 14·7 | N 35 | 44·2 | 44·3 | 44·4 | 44·5 | 44·6 | 44·7 |
| Var.‖ | γ Cassiopeiæ | 345 | 29·0 | 28·6 | 28·4 | 28·3 | 28·3 | 28·4 | N 60 | 50·0 | 50·1 | 50·3 | 50·4 | 50·6 | 50·7 |
| 2·0 | Diphda 4 | 348 | 49·3 | 49·1 | 48·9 | 48·8 | 48·9 | 48·9 | S 17 | 51·7 | 51·6 | 51·6 | 51·7 | 51·7 | 51·8 |
| 2·2 | Schedar 3 | 349 | 33·2 | 32·9 | 32·7 | 32·6 | 32·7 | 32·8 | N 56 | 39·3 | 39·5 | 39·6 | 39·8 | 39·9 | 40·0 |
| 2·4 | Ankaa 2 | 353 | 09·1 | 08·8 | 08·6 | 08·6 | 08·6 | 08·8 | S 42 | 10·8 | 10·8 | 10·9 | 11·0 | 11·1 | 11·2 |
| 2·8 | β Hydri | 353 | 15·8 | 15·0 | 14·6 | 14·5 | 14·9 | 15·5 | S 77 | 07·4 | 07·4 | 07·6 | 07·7 | 07·8 | 07·9 |
| 2·8 | Algenib | 356 | 24·1 | 23·9 | 23·8 | 23·7 | 23·8 | 23·8 | N 15 | 18·4 | 18·5 | 18·6 | 18·7 | 18·7 | 18·7 |
| 2·3 | Caph | 357 | 24·2 | 23·9 | 23·7 | 23·7 | 23·8 | 24·0 | N 59 | 16·1 | 16·3 | 16·4 | 16·6 | 16·7 | 16·8 |
| 2·1 | Alpheratz 1 | 357 | 36·7 | 36·5 | 36·4 | 36·4 | 36·4 | 36·5 | N 29 | 12·7 | 12·8 | 13·0 | 13·1 | 13·1 | 13·1 |

‡ 0·1 — 1·2    § 2·1 — 3·4    ‖ Irregular variable; 2020 mag. 2·2

# POLARIS (POLE STAR) TABLES, 2022
### FOR DETERMINING LATITUDE FROM SEXTANT ALTITUDE AND FOR AZIMUTH

| LHA ARIES | 0° – 9° | 10° – 19° | 20° – 29° | 30° – 39° | 40° – 49° | 50° – 59° | 60° – 69° | 70° – 79° | 80° – 89° | 90° – 99° | 100° – 109° | 110° – 119° |
|---|---|---|---|---|---|---|---|---|---|---|---|---|
| | $a_0$ | $a_0$ | $a_0$ | $a_0$ | $a_0$ | $a_0$ | $a_0$ | $a_0$ | $a_0$ | $a_0$ | $a_0$ | $a_0$ |
| ° | ° ′ | ° ′ | ° ′ | ° ′ | ° ′ | ° ′ | ° ′ | ° ′ | ° ′ | ° ′ | ° ′ | ° ′ |
| 0 | 0 31·7 | 0 27·4 | 0 24·0 | 0 21·6 | 0 20·4 | 0 20·4 | 0 21·6 | 0 23·9 | 0 27·3 | 0 31·7 | 0 36·9 | 0 42·7 |
| 1 | 31·2 | 27·0 | 23·7 | 21·5 | 20·4 | 20·5 | 21·8 | 24·2 | 27·7 | 32·2 | 37·4 | 43·3 |
| 2 | 30·8 | 26·6 | 23·4 | 21·3 | 20·4 | 20·6 | 22·0 | 24·5 | 28·1 | 32·7 | 38·0 | 44·0 |
| 3 | 30·3 | 26·2 | 23·1 | 21·2 | 20·3 | 20·7 | 22·2 | 24·9 | 28·6 | 33·2 | 38·6 | 44·6 |
| 4 | 29·9 | 25·9 | 22·9 | 21·0 | 20·3 | 20·8 | 22·4 | 25·2 | 29·0 | 33·7 | 39·2 | 45·2 |
| 5 | 0 29·4 | 0 25·5 | 0 22·7 | 0 20·9 | 0 20·3 | 0 20·9 | 0 22·6 | 0 25·5 | 0 29·4 | 0 34·2 | 0 39·7 | 0 45·8 |
| 6 | 29·0 | 25·2 | 22·4 | 20·8 | 20·3 | 21·0 | 22·9 | 25·9 | 29·8 | 34·7 | 40·3 | 46·5 |
| 7 | 28·6 | 24·9 | 22·2 | 20·7 | 20·3 | 21·2 | 23·1 | 26·2 | 30·3 | 35·2 | 40·9 | 47·1 |
| 8 | 28·2 | 24·6 | 22·0 | 20·6 | 20·4 | 21·3 | 23·4 | 26·6 | 30·8 | 35·8 | 41·5 | 47·8 |
| 9 | 27·7 | 24·3 | 21·8 | 20·5 | 20·4 | 21·5 | 23·7 | 27·0 | 31·2 | 36·3 | 42·1 | 48·4 |
| 10 | 0 27·4 | 0 24·0 | 0 21·6 | 0 20·4 | 0 20·4 | 0 21·6 | 0 23·9 | 0 27·3 | 0 31·7 | 0 36·9 | 0 42·7 | 0 49·1 |

| Lat. | $a_1$ | $a_1$ | $a_1$ | $a_1$ | $a_1$ | $a_1$ | $a_1$ | $a_1$ | $a_1$ | $a_1$ | $a_1$ | $a_1$ |
|---|---|---|---|---|---|---|---|---|---|---|---|---|
| ° | ′ | ′ | ′ | ′ | ′ | ′ | ′ | ′ | ′ | ′ | ′ | ′ |
| 0 | 0·5 | 0·5 | 0·6 | 0·6 | 0·6 | 0·6 | 0·6 | 0·5 | 0·5 | 0·4 | 0·4 | 0·4 |
| 10 | ·5 | ·5 | ·6 | ·6 | ·6 | ·6 | ·6 | ·5 | ·5 | ·5 | ·4 | ·4 |
| 20 | ·5 | ·6 | ·6 | ·6 | ·6 | ·6 | ·6 | ·6 | ·5 | ·5 | ·5 | ·4 |
| 30 | ·5 | ·6 | ·6 | ·6 | ·6 | ·6 | ·6 | ·6 | ·5 | ·5 | ·5 | ·5 |
| 40 | 0·6 | 0·6 | 0·6 | 0·6 | 0·6 | 0·6 | 0·6 | 0·6 | 0·6 | 0·6 | 0·5 | 0·5 |
| 45 | ·6 | ·6 | ·6 | ·6 | ·6 | ·6 | ·6 | ·6 | ·6 | ·6 | ·6 | ·6 |
| 50 | ·6 | ·6 | ·6 | ·6 | ·6 | ·6 | ·6 | ·6 | ·6 | ·6 | ·6 | ·6 |
| 55 | ·6 | ·6 | ·6 | ·6 | ·6 | ·6 | ·6 | ·6 | ·6 | ·6 | ·6 | ·6 |
| 60 | ·6 | ·6 | ·6 | ·6 | ·6 | ·6 | ·6 | ·6 | ·6 | ·7 | ·7 | ·7 |
| 62 | 0·7 | 0·6 | 0·6 | 0·6 | 0·6 | 0·6 | 0·6 | 0·6 | 0·7 | 0·7 | 0·7 | 0·7 |
| 64 | ·7 | ·6 | ·6 | ·6 | ·6 | ·6 | ·6 | ·6 | ·7 | ·7 | ·7 | ·8 |
| 66 | ·7 | ·7 | ·6 | ·6 | ·6 | ·6 | ·6 | ·7 | ·7 | ·7 | ·8 | ·8 |
| 68 | 0·7 | 0·7 | 0·6 | 0·6 | 0·6 | 0·6 | 0·6 | 0·7 | 0·7 | 0·8 | 0·8 | 0·8 |

| Month | $a_2$ | $a_2$ | $a_2$ | $a_2$ | $a_2$ | $a_2$ | $a_2$ | $a_2$ | $a_2$ | $a_2$ | $a_2$ | $a_2$ |
|---|---|---|---|---|---|---|---|---|---|---|---|---|
| | ′ | ′ | ′ | ′ | ′ | ′ | ′ | ′ | ′ | ′ | ′ | ′ |
| Jan. | 0·7 | 0·7 | 0·8 | 0·8 | 0·8 | 0·8 | 0·8 | 0·7 | 0·7 | 0·7 | 0·7 | 0·7 |
| Feb. | ·7 | ·7 | ·7 | ·8 | ·8 | ·8 | ·8 | ·8 | ·9 | ·8 | ·8 | ·8 |
| Mar. | ·5 | ·6 | ·6 | ·7 | ·7 | ·8 | ·8 | ·9 | ·9 | ·9 | ·9 | 0·9 |
| Apr. | 0·4 | 0·4 | 0·5 | 0·6 | 0·6 | 0·7 | 0·7 | 0·8 | 0·9 | 0·9 | 0·9 | 1·0 |
| May | ·3 | ·3 | ·4 | ·4 | ·5 | ·5 | ·6 | ·7 | ·7 | ·8 | ·9 | 0·9 |
| June | ·2 | ·2 | ·3 | ·3 | ·4 | ·4 | ·5 | ·5 | ·6 | ·7 | ·7 | ·8 |
| July | 0·3 | 0·3 | 0·3 | 0·3 | 0·3 | 0·3 | 0·4 | 0·4 | 0·5 | 0·5 | 0·6 | 0·6 |
| Aug. | ·4 | ·4 | ·4 | ·3 | ·3 | ·3 | ·3 | ·3 | ·4 | ·4 | ·4 | ·5 |
| Sept. | ·6 | ·5 | ·5 | ·5 | ·4 | ·4 | ·4 | ·3 | ·3 | ·3 | ·3 | ·3 |
| Oct. | 0·8 | 0·7 | 0·7 | 0·6 | 0·6 | 0·5 | 0·5 | 0·4 | 0·4 | 0·3 | 0·3 | 0·3 |
| Nov. | 1·0 | 0·9 | 0·9 | 0·8 | ·7 | ·7 | ·6 | ·5 | ·5 | ·4 | ·3 | ·3 |
| Dec. | 1·1 | 1·1 | 1·0 | 1·0 | 0·9 | 0·9 | 0·8 | 0·7 | 0·6 | 0·5 | 0·5 | 0·4 |

| Lat. | AZIMUTH | | | | | | | | | | | |
|---|---|---|---|---|---|---|---|---|---|---|---|---|
| ° | ° | ° | ° | ° | ° | ° | ° | ° | ° | ° | ° | ° |
| 0 | 0·4 | 0·3 | 0·2 | 0·1 | 0·0 | 359·9 | 359·8 | 359·7 | 359·6 | 359·5 | 359·4 | 359·4 |
| 20 | 0·4 | 0·3 | 0·2 | 0·1 | 0·0 | 359·9 | 359·8 | 359·7 | 359·6 | 359·5 | 359·4 | 359·4 |
| 40 | 0·5 | 0·4 | 0·3 | 0·1 | 0·0 | 359·9 | 359·7 | 359·6 | 359·5 | 359·4 | 359·3 | 359·2 |
| 50 | 0·6 | 0·5 | 0·3 | 0·2 | 0·0 | 359·8 | 359·7 | 359·5 | 359·4 | 359·2 | 359·1 | 359·1 |
| 55 | 0·7 | 0·6 | 0·4 | 0·2 | 0·0 | 359·8 | 359·6 | 359·4 | 359·3 | 359·1 | 359·0 | 358·9 |
| 60 | 0·8 | 0·7 | 0·4 | 0·2 | 0·0 | 359·8 | 359·6 | 359·3 | 359·2 | 359·0 | 358·9 | 358·8 |
| 65 | 1·0 | 0·8 | 0·5 | 0·3 | 0·0 | 359·7 | 359·5 | 359·2 | 359·0 | 358·8 | 358·7 | 358·6 |

Latitude = Apparent altitude (corrected for refraction) $-1° + a_0 + a_1 + a_2$

The table is entered with LHA Aries to determine the column to be used; each column refers to a range of 10°. $a_0$ is taken, with mental interpolation, from the upper table with the units of LHA Aries in degrees as argument; $a_1$, $a_2$ are taken, without interpolation, from the second and third tables with arguments latitude and month respectively. $a_0$, $a_1$, $a_2$, are always positive. The final table gives the azimuth of *Polaris*.

# POLARIS (POLE STAR) TABLES, 2022
## FOR DETERMINING LATITUDE FROM SEXTANT ALTITUDE AND FOR AZIMUTH

| LHA ARIES | 120° – 129° | 130° – 139° | 140° – 149° | 150° – 159° | 160° – 169° | 170° – 179° | 180° – 189° | 190° – 199° | 200° – 209° | 210° – 219° | 220° – 229° | 230° – 239° |
|---|---|---|---|---|---|---|---|---|---|---|---|---|
| ° | $a_0$ | $a_0$ | $a_0$ | $a_0$ | $a_0$ | $a_0$ | $a_0$ | $a_0$ | $a_0$ | $a_0$ | $a_0$ | $a_0$ |
| | ° ′ | ° ′ | ° ′ | ° ′ | ° ′ | ° ′ | ° ′ | ° ′ | ° ′ | ° ′ | ° ′ | ° ′ |
| 0 | 0 49·1 | 0 55·7 | 1 02·4 | 1 09·0 | 1 15·3 | 1 21·0 | 1 26·1 | 1 30·4 | 1 33·7 | 1 36·0 | 1 37·2 | 1 37·2 |
| 1 | 49·7 | 56·4 | 03·1 | 09·6 | 15·9 | 21·6 | 26·6 | 30·8 | 34·0 | 36·2 | 37·2 | 37·1 |
| 2 | 50·4 | 57·0 | 03·7 | 10·3 | 16·5 | 22·1 | 27·1 | 31·2 | 34·3 | 36·3 | 37·2 | 37·0 |
| 3 | 51·0 | 57·7 | 04·4 | 10·9 | 17·1 | 22·7 | 27·5 | 31·5 | 34·5 | 36·5 | 37·3 | 36·9 |
| 4 | 51·7 | 58·4 | 05·1 | 11·6 | 17·7 | 23·2 | 28·0 | 31·9 | 34·8 | 36·6 | 37·3 | 36·8 |
| 5 | 0 52·4 | 0 59·0 | 1 05·7 | 1 12·2 | 1 18·2 | 1 23·7 | 1 28·4 | 1 32·2 | 1 35·0 | 1 36·7 | 1 37·3 | 1 36·7 |
| 6 | 53·0 | 0 59·7 | 06·4 | 12·8 | 18·8 | 24·2 | 28·8 | 32·5 | 35·2 | 36·8 | 37·3 | 36·6 |
| 7 | 53·7 | 1 00·4 | 07·0 | 13·4 | 19·4 | 24·7 | 29·2 | 32·8 | 35·4 | 36·9 | 37·3 | 36·5 |
| 8 | 54·4 | 01·1 | 07·7 | 14·1 | 19·9 | 25·2 | 29·6 | 33·2 | 35·6 | 37·0 | 37·2 | 36·3 |
| 9 | 55·0 | 01·7 | 08·3 | 14·7 | 20·5 | 25·7 | 30·0 | 33·4 | 35·8 | 37·1 | 37·2 | 36·2 |
| 10 | 0 55·7 | 1 02·4 | 1 09·0 | 1 15·3 | 1 21·0 | 1 26·1 | 1 30·4 | 1 33·7 | 1 36·0 | 1 37·2 | 1 37·2 | 1 36·0 |

| Lat. | $a_1$ | $a_1$ | $a_1$ | $a_1$ | $a_1$ | $a_1$ | $a_1$ | $a_1$ | $a_1$ | $a_1$ | $a_1$ | $a_1$ |
|---|---|---|---|---|---|---|---|---|---|---|---|---|
| ° | ′ | ′ | ′ | ′ | ′ | ′ | ′ | ′ | ′ | ′ | ′ | ′ |
| 0 | 0·4 | 0·3 | 0·4 | 0·4 | 0·4 | 0·4 | 0·5 | 0·5 | 0·6 | 0·6 | 0·6 | 0·6 |
| 10 | ·4 | ·4 | ·4 | ·4 | ·4 | ·5 | ·5 | ·5 | ·6 | ·6 | ·6 | ·6 |
| 20 | ·4 | ·4 | ·4 | ·4 | ·5 | ·5 | ·5 | ·6 | ·6 | ·6 | ·6 | ·6 |
| 30 | ·5 | ·5 | ·5 | ·5 | ·5 | ·5 | ·5 | ·6 | ·6 | ·6 | ·6 | ·6 |
| 40 | 0·5 | 0·5 | 0·5 | 0·5 | 0·5 | 0·6 | 0·6 | 0·6 | 0·6 | 0·6 | 0·6 | 0·6 |
| 45 | ·6 | ·6 | ·6 | ·6 | ·6 | ·6 | ·6 | ·6 | ·6 | ·6 | ·6 | ·6 |
| 50 | ·6 | ·6 | ·6 | ·6 | ·6 | ·6 | ·6 | ·6 | ·6 | ·6 | ·6 | ·6 |
| 55 | ·6 | ·7 | 6 | ·6 | ·6 | ·6 | ·6 | ·6 | ·6 | ·6 | ·6 | ·6 |
| 60 | ·7 | ·7 | ·7 | ·7 | ·7 | ·7 | ·6 | ·6 | ·6 | ·6 | ·6 | ·6 |
| 62 | 0·7 | 0·7 | 0·7 | 0·7 | 0·7 | 0·7 | 0·7 | 0·6 | 0·6 | 0·6 | 0·6 | 0·6 |
| 64 | ·8 | ·8 | ·8 | ·8 | ·7 | ·7 | ·7 | ·6 | ·6 | ·6 | ·6 | ·6 |
| 66 | ·8 | ·8 | ·8 | ·8 | ·8 | ·7 | ·7 | ·7 | ·6 | ·6 | ·6 | ·6 |
| 68 | 0·9 | 0·9 | 0·9 | 0·8 | 0·8 | 0·8 | 0·7 | 0·7 | 0·6 | 0·6 | 0·6 | 0·6 |

| Month | $a_2$ | $a_2$ | $a_2$ | $a_2$ | $a_2$ | $a_2$ | $a_2$ | $a_2$ | $a_2$ | $a_2$ | $a_2$ | $a_2$ |
|---|---|---|---|---|---|---|---|---|---|---|---|---|
| | ′ | ′ | ′ | ′ | ′ | ′ | ′ | ′ | ′ | ′ | ′ | ′ |
| Jan. | 0·6 | 0·6 | 0·6 | 0·5 | 0·5 | 0·5 | 0·5 | 0·5 | 0·4 | 0·4 | 0·4 | 0·4 |
| Feb. | ·8 | ·8 | ·7 | ·7 | ·6 | ·6 | ·5 | ·5 | ·5 | ·4 | ·4 | ·4 |
| Mar. | 0·9 | 0·9 | 0·9 | ·8 | ·8 | ·7 | ·7 | ·6 | ·6 | ·5 | ·5 | ·4 |
| Apr. | 1·0 | 1·0 | 1·0 | 0·9 | 0·9 | 0·9 | 0·8 | 0·8 | 0·7 | 0·6 | 0·6 | 0·5 |
| May | 0·9 | 1·0 | 1·0 | 1·0 | 1·0 | 1·0 | 0·9 | 0·9 | ·8 | ·8 | ·7 | ·7 |
| June | ·8 | 0·9 | 0·9 | 0·9 | 1·0 | 1·0 | 1·0 | 1·0 | ·9 | ·9 | ·8 | ·8 |
| July | 0·7 | 0·7 | 0·8 | 0·8 | 0·9 | 0·9 | 0·9 | 0·9 | 0·9 | 0·9 | 0·9 | 0·9 |
| Aug. | ·5 | ·6 | ·6 | ·7 | ·7 | ·7 | ·8 | ·8 | ·8 | ·9 | ·9 | ·9 |
| Sept. | ·4 | ·4 | ·4 | ·5 | ·5 | ·6 | ·6 | ·7 | ·7 | ·7 | ·8 | ·8 |
| Oct. | 0·3 | 0·3 | 0·3 | 0·3 | 0·3 | 0·4 | 0·4 | 0·5 | 0·5 | 0·6 | 0·6 | 0·7 |
| Nov. | ·2 | ·2 | ·2 | ·2 | ·2 | ·2 | ·2 | ·3 | ·3 | ·4 | ·5 | ·5 |
| Dec. | 0·3 | 0·3 | 0·2 | 0·2 | 0·1 | 0·1 | 0·1 | 0·1 | 0·2 | 0·2 | 0·3 | 0·3 |

| Lat. | AZIMUTH | | | | | | | | | | | |
|---|---|---|---|---|---|---|---|---|---|---|---|---|
| ° | ° | ° | ° | ° | ° | ° | ° | ° | ° | ° | ° | ° |
| 0 | 359·4 | 359·4 | 359·4 | 359·4 | 359·4 | 359·5 | 359·6 | 359·7 | 359·8 | 359·9 | 0·0 | 0·1 |
| 20 | 359·3 | 359·3 | 359·3 | 359·4 | 359·4 | 359·5 | 359·6 | 359·7 | 359·8 | 359·9 | 0·0 | 0·1 |
| 40 | 359·2 | 359·2 | 359·2 | 359·2 | 359·3 | 359·4 | 359·5 | 359·6 | 359·7 | 359·9 | 0·0 | 0·1 |
| 50 | 359·0 | 359·0 | 359·0 | 359·1 | 359·1 | 359·2 | 359·4 | 359·5 | 359·7 | 359·8 | 0·0 | 0·2 |
| 55 | 358·9 | 358·9 | 358·9 | 359·0 | 359·0 | 359·2 | 359·3 | 359·4 | 359·6 | 359·8 | 0·0 | 0·2 |
| 60 | 358·7 | 358·7 | 358·7 | 358·8 | 358·9 | 359·0 | 359·2 | 359·4 | 359·6 | 359·8 | 0·0 | 0·2 |
| 65 | 358·5 | 358·5 | 358·5 | 358·6 | 358·7 | 358·9 | 359·0 | 359·3 | 359·5 | 359·7 | 0·0 | 0·3 |

### ILLUSTRATION

On 2022 April 21 at 23ʰ 18ᵐ 56ˢ UT in longitude W 37° 14′, the apparent altitude (corrected for refraction), $H_O$, of Polaris was 49° 31′·6

| From the daily pages: | ° | ′ |
|---|---|---|
| GHA Aries (23ʰ) | 194 | 59·5 |
| Increment (18ᵐ 56ˢ) | 4 | 44·8 |
| Longitude (west) | −37 | 14 |
| LHA Aries | 162 | 30 |

| | ° | ′ |
|---|---|---|
| $H_O$ | 49 | 31·6 |
| $a_0$ (argument 162° 30′) | 1 | 16·8 |
| $a_1$ (Lat 50° approx.) | | 0·6 |
| $a_2$ (April) | | 0·9 |
| Sum − 1° = Lat = | 49 | 49·9 |

# POLARIS (POLE STAR) TABLES, 2022
### FOR DETERMINING LATITUDE FROM SEXTANT ALTITUDE AND FOR AZIMUTH

| LHA ARIES | 240°–249° | 250°–259° | 260°–269° | 270°–279° | 280°–289° | 290°–299° | 300°–309° | 310°–319° | 320°–329° | 330°–339° | 340°–349° | 350°–359° |
|---|---|---|---|---|---|---|---|---|---|---|---|---|
| ° | $a_0$ | $a_0$ | $a_0$ | $a_0$ | $a_0$ | $a_0$ | $a_0$ | $a_0$ | $a_0$ | $a_0$ | $a_0$ | $a_0$ |
| 0 | I 36·0 | I 33·7 | I 30·4 | I 26·2 | I 21·1 | I 15·3 | I 09·0 | I 02·4 | 0 55·7 | 0 49·1 | 0 42·8 | 0 36·9 |
| 1 | 35·8 | 33·5 | 30·0 | 25·7 | 20·5 | 14·7 | 08·4 | 01·8 | 55·0 | 48·4 | 42·1 | 36·3 |
| 2 | 35·6 | 33·2 | 29·6 | 25·2 | 20·0 | 14·1 | 07·7 | 01·1 | 54·4 | 47·8 | 41·5 | 35·8 |
| 3 | 35·4 | 32·9 | 29·2 | 24·7 | 19·4 | 13·5 | 07·1 | I 00·4 | 53·7 | 47·1 | 40·9 | 35·3 |
| 4 | 35·2 | 32·5 | 28·8 | 24·2 | 18·8 | 12·8 | 06·4 | 0 59·7 | 53·0 | 46·5 | 40·3 | 34·7 |
| 5 | I 35·0 | I 32·2 | I 28·4 | I 23·7 | I 18·3 | I 12·2 | I 05·7 | 0 59·1 | 0 52·4 | 0 45·9 | 0 39·8 | 0 34·2 |
| 6 | 34·8 | 31·9 | 28·0 | 23·2 | 17·7 | 11·6 | 05·1 | 58·4 | 51·7 | 45·2 | 39·2 | 33·7 |
| 7 | 34·5 | 31·5 | 27·5 | 22·7 | 17·1 | 10·9 | 04·4 | 57·7 | 51·1 | 44·6 | 38·6 | 33·2 |
| 8 | 34·3 | 31·2 | 27·1 | 22·1 | 16·5 | 10·3 | 03·8 | 57·1 | 50·4 | 44·0 | 38·0 | 32·7 |
| 9 | 34·0 | 30·8 | 26·6 | 21·6 | 15·9 | 09·7 | 03·1 | 56·4 | 49·7 | 43·4 | 37·5 | 32·2 |
| 10 | I 33·7 | I 30·4 | I 26·2 | I 21·1 | I 15·3 | I 09·0 | I 02·4 | 0 55·7 | 0 49·1 | 0 42·8 | 0 36·9 | 0 31·7 |

| Lat. | $a_1$ | $a_1$ | $a_1$ | $a_1$ | $a_1$ | $a_1$ | $a_1$ | $a_1$ | $a_1$ | $a_1$ | $a_1$ | $a_1$ |
|---|---|---|---|---|---|---|---|---|---|---|---|---|
| ° | ′ | ′ | ′ | ′ | ′ | ′ | ′ | ′ | ′ | ′ | ′ | ′ |
| 0 | 0·6 | 0·5 | 0·5 | 0·4 | 0·4 | 0·4 | 0·4 | 0·3 | 0·4 | 0·4 | 0·4 | 0·4 |
| 10 | ·6 | ·5 | ·5 | ·5 | ·4 | ·4 | ·4 | ·4 | ·4 | ·4 | ·4 | ·5 |
| 20 | ·6 | ·6 | ·5 | ·5 | ·5 | ·4 | ·4 | ·4 | ·4 | ·4 | ·5 | ·5 |
| 30 | ·6 | ·6 | ·5 | ·5 | ·5 | ·5 | ·5 | ·5 | ·5 | ·5 | ·5 | ·5 |
| 40 | 0·6 | 0·6 | 0·6 | 0·6 | 0·5 | 0·5 | 0·5 | 0·5 | 0·5 | 0·5 | 0·5 | 0·6 |
| 45 | ·6 | ·6 | ·6 | ·6 | ·6 | ·6 | ·6 | ·6 | ·6 | ·6 | ·6 | ·6 |
| 50 | ·6 | ·6 | ·6 | ·6 | ·6 | ·6 | ·6 | ·6 | ·6 | ·6 | ·6 | ·6 |
| 55 | ·6 | ·6 | ·6 | ·6 | ·6 | ·6 | ·6 | ·7 | ·6 | ·6 | ·6 | ·6 |
| 60 | ·6 | ·6 | ·6 | ·7 | ·7 | ·7 | ·7 | ·7 | ·7 | ·7 | ·7 | ·7 |
| 62 | 0·6 | 0·6 | 0·7 | 0·7 | 0·7 | 0·7 | 0·7 | 0·7 | 0·7 | 0·7 | 0·7 | 0·7 |
| 64 | ·6 | ·6 | ·7 | ·7 | ·7 | ·8 | ·8 | ·8 | ·8 | ·8 | ·7 | ·7 |
| 66 | ·6 | ·7 | ·7 | ·7 | ·8 | ·8 | ·8 | ·8 | ·8 | ·8 | ·8 | ·7 |
| 68 | 0·6 | 0·7 | 0·7 | 0·8 | 0·8 | 0·8 | 0·9 | 0·9 | 0·9 | 0·8 | 0·8 | 0·8 |

| Month | $a_2$ | $a_2$ | $a_2$ | $a_2$ | $a_2$ | $a_2$ | $a_2$ | $a_2$ | $a_2$ | $a_2$ | $a_2$ | $a_2$ |
|---|---|---|---|---|---|---|---|---|---|---|---|---|
| | ′ | ′ | ′ | ′ | ′ | ′ | ′ | ′ | ′ | ′ | ′ | ′ |
| Jan. | 0·4 | 0·5 | 0·5 | 0·5 | 0·5 | 0·5 | 0·6 | 0·6 | 0·6 | 0·7 | 0·7 | 0·7 |
| Feb. | ·4 | ·4 | ·3 | ·4 | ·4 | ·4 | ·4 | ·4 | ·5 | ·5 | ·6 | ·6 |
| Mar. | ·4 | ·3 | ·3 | ·3 | ·3 | ·3 | ·3 | ·3 | ·3 | ·4 | ·4 | ·5 |
| Apr. | 0·5 | 0·4 | 0·3 | 0·3 | 0·3 | 0·2 | 0·2 | 0·2 | 0·2 | 0·3 | 0·3 | 0·3 |
| May | ·6 | ·5 | ·5 | ·4 | ·3 | ·3 | ·3 | ·2 | ·2 | ·2 | ·2 | ·2 |
| June | ·7 | ·7 | ·6 | ·5 | ·5 | ·4 | ·4 | ·3 | ·3 | ·3 | ·2 | ·2 |
| July | 0·8 | 0·8 | 0·7 | 0·7 | 0·6 | 0·6 | 0·5 | 0·5 | 0·4 | 0·4 | 0·3 | 0·3 |
| Aug. | ·9 | ·9 | ·8 | ·8 | ·8 | ·7 | ·7 | ·6 | ·6 | ·5 | ·5 | ·5 |
| Sept. | ·8 | ·9 | ·9 | ·9 | ·9 | ·9 | ·8 | ·8 | ·8 | ·7 | ·7 | ·6 |
| Oct. | 0·7 | 0·8 | 0·8 | 0·9 | 0·9 | 0·9 | 0·9 | 0·9 | 0·9 | 0·9 | 0·9 | 0·8 |
| Nov. | ·6 | ·7 | ·7 | ·8 | ·9 | ·9 | I·0 | I·0 | I·0 | I·0 | I·0 | I·0 |
| Dec. | 0·4 | 0·5 | 0·6 | 0·7 | 0·7 | 0·8 | 0·9 | 0·9 | I·0 | I·0 | I·1 | I·1 |

| Lat. | AZIMUTH | | | | | | | | | | | |
|---|---|---|---|---|---|---|---|---|---|---|---|---|
| ° | ° | ° | ° | ° | ° | ° | ° | ° | ° | ° | ° | ° |
| 0 | 0·2 | 0·3 | 0·4 | 0·5 | 0·6 | 0·6 | 0·6 | 0·6 | 0·6 | 0·6 | 0·6 | 0·5 |
| 20 | 0·2 | 0·3 | 0·4 | 0·5 | 0·6 | 0·6 | 0·7 | 0·7 | 0·7 | 0·6 | 0·6 | 0·5 |
| 40 | 0·3 | 0·4 | 0·5 | 0·6 | 0·7 | 0·8 | 0·8 | 0·8 | 0·8 | 0·8 | 0·7 | 0·6 |
| 50 | 0·3 | 0·5 | 0·6 | 0·8 | 0·9 | 0·9 | I·0 | I·0 | I·0 | 0·9 | 0·9 | 0·8 |
| 55 | 0·4 | 0·6 | 0·7 | 0·8 | I·0 | I·0 | I·1 | I·1 | I·1 | I·1 | I·0 | 0·9 |
| 60 | 0·4 | 0·6 | 0·8 | I·0 | I·1 | I·2 | I·3 | I·3 | I·3 | I·2 | I·1 | I·0 |
| 65 | 0·5 | 0·7 | I·0 | I·1 | I·3 | I·4 | I·5 | I·5 | I·5 | I·4 | I·3 | I·2 |

Latitude = Apparent altitude (corrected for refraction) $-1° + a_0 + a_1 + a_2$

The table is entered with LHA Aries to determine the column to be used; each column refers to a range of 10°. $a_0$ is taken, with mental interpolation, from the upper table with the units of LHA Aries in degrees as argument; $a_1$, $a_2$ are taken, without interpolation, from the second and third tables with arguments latitude and month respectively. $a_0$, $a_1$, $a_2$, are always positive. The final table gives the azimuth of *Polaris*.

# SIGHT REDUCTION PROCEDURES

## METHODS AND FORMULAE FOR DIRECT COMPUTATION

1. *Introduction.* In this section, formulae and methods are provided for *calculating* position at sea from observed altitudes taken with a marine sextant using a computer or programmable calculator.

The method uses analogous concepts and similar terminology as that used in *manual* methods of astro-navigation, where position is found by plotting position lines from their intercept and azimuth on a marine chart.

The algorithms are presented in standard algebra suitable for translating into the programming language of the user's computer. The basic ephemeris data may be taken directly from the main tabular pages of a current version of *The Nautical Almanac*. Formulae are given for calculating altitude and azimuth from the *GHA* and *Dec* of a body, and the estimated position of the observer. Formulae are also given for reducing sextant observations to observed altitudes by applying the corrections for dip, refraction, parallax and semi-diameter.

The intercept and azimuth obtained from each observation determine a position line, and the observer should lie on or close to each position line. The method of least squares is used to calculate the fix by finding the position where the sum of the squares of the distances from the position lines is a minimum. The use of least squares has other advantages. For example, it is possible to improve the estimated position at the time of fix by repeating the calculation. It is also possible to include more observations in the solution and to reject doubtful ones.

2. *Notation.*

$GHA$ = Greenwich hour angle. The range of *GHA* is from $0°$ to $360°$ starting at $0°$ on the Greenwich meridian increasing to the west, back to $360°$ on the Greenwich meridian.

$SHA$ = sidereal hour angle. The range is $0°$ to $360°$.

$Dec$ = declination. The sign convention for declination is north is positive, south is negative. The range is from $-90°$ at the south celestial pole to $+90°$ at the north celestial pole.

$Long$ = longitude. The sign convention is east is positive, west is negative. The range is $-180°$ to $+180°$.

$Lat$ = latitude. The sign convention is north is positive, south is negative. The range is from $-90°$ to $+90°$.

$LHA$ = $GHA + Long$ = local hour angle. The *LHA* increases to the west from $0°$ on the local meridian to $360°$.

$H_c$ = calculated altitude. Above the horizon is positive, below the horizon is negative. The range is from $-90°$ in the nadir to $+90°$ in the zenith.

$H_s$ = sextant altitude.

$H$ = apparent altitude = sextant altitude corrected for instrumental error and dip.

$H_o$ = observed altitude = apparent altitude corrected for refraction and, in appropriate cases, corrected for parallax and semi-diameter.

$Z$ = $Z_n$ = true azimuth. $Z$ is measured from true north through east, south, west and back to north. The range is from $0°$ to $360°$.

$I$ = sextant index error.

$D$ = dip of horizon.

$R$ = atmospheric refraction.

$HP$ = horizontal parallax of the Sun, Moon, Venus or Mars.
$PA$ = parallax in altitude of the Sun, Moon, Venus or Mars.
$SD$ = semi-diameter of the Sun or Moon.
$p$ = intercept = $H_O - H_C$. Towards is positive, away is negative.
$T$ = course or track, measured as for azimuth from the north.
$V$ = speed in knots.

3. *Entering Basic Data.* When quantities such as *GHA* are entered, which in *The Nautical Almanac* are given in degrees and minutes, convert them to degrees and decimals of a degree by dividing the minutes by 60 and adding to the degrees; for example, if $GHA = 123°\ 45'\!.6$, enter the two numbers 123 and 45·6 into the memory and set $GHA = 123 + 45·6/60 = 123°\!.7600$. Although four decimal places of a degree are shown in the examples, it is assumed that full precision is maintained in the calculations.

When using a computer or programmable calculator, write a subroutine to convert degrees and minutes to degrees and decimals. Scientific calculators usually have a special key for this purpose. For quantities like *Dec* which require a minus sign for southern declination, change the sign from plus to minus after the value has been converted to degrees and decimals, e.g. $Dec = S\,0°\ 12'\!.3 = S\,0°\!.2050 = -0°\!.2050$. Other quantities which require conversion are semi-diameter, horizontal parallax, longitude and latitude.

4. *Interpolation of GHA and Dec* The *GHA* and *Dec* of the Sun, Moon and planets are interpolated to the time of observation by direct calculation as follows: If the universal time is $a^h\ b^m\ c^s$, form the interpolation factor $x = b/60 + c/3600$. Enter the tabular value $GHA_0$ for the preceding hour ($a$) and the tabular value $GHA_1$ for the following hour ($a + 1$) then the interpolated value *GHA* is given by

$$GHA = GHA_0 + x(GHA_1 - GHA_0)$$

If the *GHA* passes through 360° between tabular values, add 360° to $GHA_1$ before interpolation. If the interpolated value exceeds 360°, subtract 360° from *GHA*.

Similarly for declination, enter the tabular value $Dec_0$ for the preceding hour ($a$) and the tabular value $Dec_1$ for the following hour ($a + 1$), then the interpolated value *Dec* is given by
$$Dec = Dec_0 + x(Dec_1 - Dec_0)$$

5. *Example.* (a) Find the *GHA* and *Dec* of the Sun on 2022 February 7 at $11^h\ 47^m\ 13^s$ UT.

The interpolation factor $x = 47/60 + 13/3600 = 0^h\!.7869$

page 35    $11^h\ GHA_0 = 341°\ 28'\!.6 = 341°\!.4767$

$12^h\ GHA_1 = 356°\ 28'\!.6 = 356°\!.4767$

$11^h\!.7869\ GHA = 341·4767 + 0·7869(356·4767 - 341·4767) = 353°\!.2808$

$11^h\ Dec_0 = S\,15°\ 14'\!.3 = -15°\!.2383$

$12^h\ Dec_1 = S\,15°\ 13'\!.5 = -15°\!.2250$

$11^h\!.7869\ Dec = -15·2383 + 0·7869(-15·2250 + 15·2383) = -15°\!.2278$

*GHA* Aries is interpolated in the same way as *GHA* of a body. For a star the *SHA* and *Dec* are taken from the tabular page and do not require interpolation, then

$$GHA = GHA\ \text{Aries} + SHA$$

where *GHA* Aries is interpolated to the time of observation.

(b) Find the *GHA* and *Dec* of *Vega* on 2022 February 7 at $14^h\ 47^m\ 13^s$ UT.

The interpolation factor $x = 0^h\!.7869$ as in the previous example

$$\text{page 34} \qquad 14^h\ GHA\ \text{Aries}_0 = 347°\ 40'\!.2 = 347°\!.6700$$
$$15^h\ GHA\ \text{Aries}_1 = 2°\ 42'\!.7 = 362°\!.7117 \quad (360° \text{ added})$$
$$14^h\!.7869\ GHA\ \text{Aries} = 347\!\cdot\!6700 + 0\!\cdot\!7869(362\!\cdot\!7117 - 347\!\cdot\!6700) = 359°\!.5070$$
$$SHA = 80°\ 35'\!.2 = 80°\!.5867$$
$$GHA = GHA\ \text{Aries} + SHA = 80°\!.0936 \quad (\text{multiple of } 360° \text{ removed})$$
$$Dec = \text{N } 38°\ 48'\!.0 = +38°\!.8000$$

6. *The calculated altitude and azimuth.* The calculated altitude $H_C$ and true azimuth $Z$ are determined from the *GHA* and *Dec* interpolated to the time of observation and from the *Long* and *Lat* estimated at the time of observation as follows:

*Step* 1.  Calculate the local hour angle

$$LHA = GHA + Long$$

Add or subtract multiples of $360°$ to set *LHA* in the range $0°$ to $360°$.

*Step* 2.  Calculate $S$, $C$ and the altitude $H_C$ from

$$S = \sin Dec$$
$$C = \cos Dec \cos LHA$$
$$H_C = \sin^{-1}(S \sin Lat + C \cos Lat)$$

where $\sin^{-1}$ is the inverse function of sine.

*Step* 3.  Calculate $X$ and $A$ from

$$X = (S \cos Lat - C \sin Lat)/\cos H_C$$
$$\text{If } X > +1 \quad \text{set} \quad X = +1$$
$$\text{If } X < -1 \quad \text{set} \quad X = -1$$
$$A = \cos^{-1} X$$

where $\cos^{-1}$ is the inverse function of cosine.

*Step* 4.  Determine the azimuth $Z$

$$\text{If } LHA > 180° \quad \text{then} \quad Z = A$$
$$\text{Otherwise} \quad Z = 360° - A$$

7. *Example.*  Find the calculated altitude $H_C$ and azimuth $Z$ when

$$GHA = 53° \quad Dec = \text{S } 15° \quad Lat = \text{N } 32° \quad Long = \text{W } 16°$$

For the calculation

$$GHA = 53°\!.0000 \quad Dec = -15°\!.0000 \quad Lat = +32°\!.0000 \quad Long = -16°\!.0000$$

*Step* 1. $\qquad\qquad LHA = 53\!\cdot\!0000 - 16\!\cdot\!0000 = 37\!\cdot\!0000$
*Step* 2. $\qquad\qquad\quad S = -0\!\cdot\!2588$
$$C = +0\!\cdot\!9659 \times 0\!\cdot\!7986 = 0\!\cdot\!7714$$
$$\sin H_C = -0\!\cdot\!2588 \times 0\!\cdot\!5299 + 0\!\cdot\!7714 \times 0\!\cdot\!8480 = 0\!\cdot\!5171$$
$$H_C = 31°\!.1346$$

*Step* 3.                   $X = (-0.2588 \times 0.8480 - 0.7714 \times 0.5299)/0.8560 = -0.7340$

$A = 137°2239$

*Step* 4.      Since      $LHA \leq 180°$   then   $Z = 360° - A = 222°7761$

8. *Reduction from sextant altitude to observed altitude.*    The sextant altitude $H_S$ is corrected for both dip and index error to produce the apparent altitude. The observed altitude $H_O$ is calculated by applying a correction for refraction. For the Sun, Moon, Venus and Mars a correction for parallax is also applied to $H$, and for the Sun and Moon a further correction for semi-diameter is required. The corrections are calculated as follows:

*Step* 1.   Calculate dip

$$D = 0°0293\sqrt{h}$$

where $h$ is the height of eye above the horizon in metres.

*Step* 2.   Calculate apparent altitude

$$H = H_S + I - D$$

where $I$ is the sextant index error.

*Step* 3.   Calculate refraction $(R)$ at a standard temperature of $10°$ Celsius (C) and pressure of 1010 millibars (mb)

$$R_0 = 0°0167/\tan(H + 7.32/(H + 4.32))$$

If the temperature $T°\,C$ and pressure $P$ mb are known calculate the refraction from

$$R = fR_0 \qquad \text{where} \qquad f = 0.28P/(T + 273)$$

otherwise set     $R = R_0$

*Step* 4.   Calculate the parallax in altitude $(PA)$ from the horizontal parallax $(HP)$ and the apparent altitude $(H)$ for the Sun, Moon, Venus and Mars as follows:

$$PA = HP\cos H$$

For the Sun $HP = 0°0024$. This correction is very small and could be ignored.

For the Moon $HP$ is taken for the nearest hour from the main tabular page and converted to degrees.

For Venus and Mars the $HP$ is taken from the critical table at the bottom of page 259 and converted to degrees.

For the navigational stars and the remaining planets, Jupiter and Saturn, set $PA = 0$.

If an error of $0'2$ is significant the expression for the parallax in altitude for the Moon should include a small correction $OB$ for the oblateness of the Earth as follows:

$$PA = HP\cos H + OB$$

where    $OB = -0°0032\sin^2 Lat \cos H + 0°0032\sin(2Lat)\cos Z \sin H$

At mid-latitudes and for altitudes of the Moon below $60°$ a simple approximation to $OB$ is

$$OB = -0°0017\cos H$$

*Step* 5.   Calculate the semi-diameter for the Sun and Moon as follows:

Sun: *SD* is taken from the main tabular page and converted to degrees.

Moon: $SD = 0°2724HP$ where *HP* is taken for the nearest hour from the main tabular page and converted to degrees.

*Step* 6.   Calculate the observed altitude

$$H_O = H - R + PA \pm SD$$

where the plus sign is used if the lower limb of the Sun or Moon was observed and the minus sign if the upper limb was observed.

9. *Example.*   The following example illustrates how to use a calculator to reduce the sextant altitude ($H_S$) to observed altitude ($H_O$); the sextant altitudes given are assumed to be taken on 2022 March 12 with a marine sextant, zero index error, at height 5·4 m, temperature $-3°$ C and pressure 982 mb, the Moon sights are assumed to be taken at $10^h$ UT.

| Body limb | Sun lower | Sun upper | Moon lower | Moon upper | Venus — | *Polaris* — |
|---|---|---|---|---|---|---|
| Sextant altitude: $H_S$ | 21·3283 | 3·3367 | 33·4600 | 26·1117 | 4·5433 | 49·6083 |
| Step 1. Dip: $D = 0·0293\sqrt{h}$ | 0·0681 | 0·0681 | 0·0681 | 0·0681 | 0·0681 | 0 0681 |
| Step 2. Apparent altitude: $H = H_S + I - D$ | 21·2602 | 3·2686 | 33·3919 | 26·0436 | 4·4752 | 49·5402 |
| Step 3. Refraction: $R_0$ | 0·0423 | 0·2256 | 0·0251 | 0·0338 | 0·1798 | 0·0142 |
| $f$ | 1·0184 | 1·0184 | 1·0184 | 1·0184 | 1·0184 | 1·0184 |
| $R = fR_0$ | 0·0431 | 0·2298 | 0·0256 | 0·0344 | 0·1831 | 0·0144 |
| Step 4. Parallax: | | | (54′4) | (54′4) | (0′2) | |
| *HP* | 0·0024 | 0·0024 | 0·9067 | 0·9067 | 0·0033 | — |
| Parallax in altitude: $PA = HP \cos H$ | 0·0022 | 0·0024 | 0·7570 | 0·8146 | 0·0033 | — |
| Step 5. Semi-diameter: Sun : $SD = 16·1/60$ | 0·2683 | 0·2683 | — | — | — | — |
| Moon : $SD = 0·2724HP$ | — | — | 0·2470 | 0·2470 | — | — |
| Step 6. Observed altitude: $H_O = H - R + PA \pm SD$ | 21·4877 | 2·7729 | 34·3703 | 26·5768 | 4·2955 | 49·5258 |

Note that for the Moon the correction for the oblateness of the Earth of about $-0°0017\cos H$, which equals $-0°0014$ for the lower limb and $-0°0015$ for the upper limb, has been ignored in the above calculation.

10. *Position from intercept and azimuth using a chart.*   An estimate is made of the position at the adopted time of fix. The position at the time of observation is then calculated by dead reckoning from the time of fix. For example, if the course (track) *T* and the speed *V* (in knots) of the observer are constant, then *Long* and *Lat* at the time of observation are calculated from

$$Long = L_F + t\,(V/60)\sin T / \cos B_F$$
$$Lat = B_F + t\,(V/60)\cos T$$

where $L_F$ and $B_F$ are the estimated longitude and latitude at the time of fix and $t$ is the time interval in hours from the time of fix to the time of observation, $t$ is positive if the time of observation is after the time of fix and negative if it was before.

The position line of an observation is plotted on a chart using the intercept

$$p = H_O - H_C$$

and azimuth $Z$ with origin at the calculated position (*Long*, *Lat*) at the time of observation, where $H_C$ and $Z$ are calculated using the method in section 6, page 279. Starting from this calculated position a line is drawn on the chart along the direction of the azimuth to the body. Convert $p$ to nautical miles by multiplying by 60. The position line is drawn at right angles to the azimuth line, distance $p$ from (*Long*, *Lat*) towards the body if $p$ is positive and distance $p$ away from the body if $p$ is negative. Provided there are no gross errors, the navigator should be somewhere on or near the position line at the time of observation. Two or more position lines are required to determine a fix.

11. *Position from intercept and azimuth by calculation.* The position of the fix may be calculated from two or more sextant observations as follows.

If $p_1$, $Z_1$, are the intercept and azimuth of the first observation, $p_2$, $Z_2$, of the second observation and so on, form the summations

$$A = \cos^2 Z_1 + \cos^2 Z_2 + \cdots$$
$$B = \cos Z_1 \sin Z_1 + \cos Z_2 \sin Z_2 + \cdots$$
$$C = \sin^2 Z_1 + \sin^2 Z_2 + \cdots$$
$$D = p_1 \cos Z_1 + p_2 \cos Z_2 + \cdots$$
$$E = p_1 \sin Z_1 + p_2 \sin Z_2 + \cdots$$

where the number of terms in each summation is equal to the number of observations.

With $G = A\,C - B^2$, an improved estimate of the position at the time of fix $(L_I, B_I)$ is given by

$$L_I = L_F + (A\,E - B\,D)/(G\cos B_F), \qquad B_I = B_F + (C\,D - B\,E)/G$$

Calculate the distance $d$ between the initial estimated position $(L_F, B_F)$ at the time of fix and the improved estimated position $(L_I, B_I)$ in nautical miles from

$$d = 60\sqrt{((L_I - L_F)^2 \cos^2 B_F + (B_I - B_F)^2)}$$

If $d$ exceeds about 20 nautical miles set $L_F = L_I$, $B_F = B_I$ and repeat the calculation until $d$, the distance between the position at the previous estimate and the improved estimate, is less than about 20 nautical miles.

12. *Example of direct computation.* Using the method described above, calculate the position of a ship on 2022 July 4 at $21^h\ 00^m\ 00^s$ UT from the marine sextant observations of the three stars *Regulus* (No. 26) at $20^h\ 39^m\ 23^s$ UT, *Antares* (No. 42) at $20^h\ 45^m\ 47^s$ UT and *Kochab* (No. 40) at $21^h\ 10^m\ 34^s$ UT, where the observed altitudes of the three stars corrected for the effects of refraction, dip and instrumental error, are $27°\!.0772$, $25°\!.9361$ and $47°\!.5563$ respectively. The ship was travelling at a constant speed of 20 knots on a course of $325°$ during the period of observation, and the position of the ship at the time of fix $21^h\ 00^m\ 00^s$ UT is only known to the nearest whole degree W $15°$, N $32°$.

Intermediate values for the first iteration are shown in the table. *GHA* Aries was interpolated from the nearest tabular values on page 132. For the first iteration set $L_F = -15°0000$, $B_F = +32°0000$ at the time of fix at $21^h\ 00^m\ 00^s$ UT.

### First Iteration

| Body | Regulus | Antares | Kochab |
|---|---|---|---|
| No. | 26 | 42 | 40 |
| time of observation | $20^h\ 39^m\ 23^s$ | $20^h\ 45^m\ 47^s$ | $21^h\ 10^m\ 34^s$ |
| $H_O$ | 27·0772 | 25·9361 | 47·5563 |
| interpolation factor | 0·6564 | 0·7631 | 0·1761 |
| *GHA* Aries | 232·6798 | 234·2843 | 240·4973 |
| *SHA* (page 132) | 207·6150 | 112·3017 | 137·3200 |
| *GHA* | 80·2948 | 346·5860 | 17·8173 |
| *Dec* (page 132) | +11·8600 | −26·4817 | +74·0683 |
| $t$ | −0·3436 | −0·2369 | +0·1761 |
| *Long* | −14·9225 | −14·9466 | −15·0397 |
| *Lat* | +31·9062 | +31·9353 | +32·0481 |
| $Z$ | 267·3563 | 151·8630 | 358·8619 |
| $H_C$ | 27·0541 | 25·6303 | 47·9564 |
| $p$ | +0·0231 | +0·3058 | −0·4001 |

$$A = 1·7793 \quad B = -0·3896 \quad C = 1·2207 \quad D = -0·6707 \quad E = 0·1291 \quad G = 2·0202$$
$$(A\,E - B\,D)/(G\cos B_F) = 0·0185, \qquad (C\,D - B\,E)/G = 0·3804$$

An improved estimate of the position at the time of fix is

$$L_I = L_F - 0·0185 = -15·0185 \quad \text{and} \quad B_I = B_F - 0·3804 = +31·6196$$

Since the distance between the previous estimated position and the improved estimate is $d = 22·8$ nautical miles, set $L_F = -15·0185$, and $B_F = +31·6196$ and repeat the calculation. The table shows the intermediate values of the calculation for the second iteration. In each iteration the quantities $H_O$, *GHA*, *Dec* and $t$ do not change.

### Second Iteration

| Body | Regulus | Antares | Kochab |
|---|---|---|---|
| No. | 26 | 42 | 40 |
| *Long* | −14·9413 | −14·9653 | −15·0580 |
| *Lat* | +31·5258 | +31·5549 | +31·6677 |
| $Z$ | 267·5403 | 151·7596 | 358·8776 |
| $H_C$ | 27·0870 | 25·9581 | 47·5763 |
| $p$ | −0·0098 | −0·0220 | −0·0201 |

$$A = 1·7776 \quad B = -0·3936 \quad C = 1·2224 \quad D = -0·0003 \quad E = -0·0002 \quad G = 2·0181$$
$$(A\,E - B\,D)/(G\cos B_F) = -0·0003, \qquad (C\,D - B\,E)/G = -0·0002$$

An improved estimate of the position at the time of fix is

$$L_I = L_F - 0·0003 = -15·0188 \quad \text{and} \quad B_I = B_F - 0·0002 = +31·6194$$

The distance between the previous estimated position and the improved estimated position, $d = 0·02$ nautical miles, is so small that a third iteration would produce a negligible improvement to the estimate of the position.

### USE OF CONCISE SIGHT REDUCTION TABLES

1. *Introduction.*    The concise sight reduction tables given on pages 286 to 317 are intended for use when neither more extensive tables nor electronic computing aids are available. These "NAO sight reduction tables" provide for the reduction of the local hour angle and declination of a celestial object to azimuth and altitude, referred to an assumed position on the Earth, for use in the intercept method of celestial navigation which is now standard practice.

2. *Form of tables.*    Entries in the reduction table are at a fixed interval of one degree for all latitudes and hour angles. A compact arrangement results from division of the navigational triangle into two right spherical triangles, so that the table has to be entered twice. Assumed latitude and local hour angle are the arguments for the first entry. The reduction table responds with the intermediate arguments $A$, $B$, and $Z_1$, where $A$ is used as one of the arguments for the second entry to the table, $B$ has to be incremented by the declination to produce the quantity $F$, and $Z_1$ is a component of the azimuth angle. The reduction table is then reentered with $A$ and $F$ and yields $H$, $P$, and $Z_2$ where $H$ is the altitude, $P$ is the complement of the parallactic angle, and $Z_2$ is the second component of the azimuth angle. It is usually necessary to adjust the tabular altitude for the fractional parts of the intermediate entering arguments to derive computed altitude, and an auxiliary table is provided for the purpose. Rules governing signs of the quantities which must be added or subtracted are given in the instructions and summarized on each tabular page. Azimuth angle is the sum of two components and is converted to true azimuth by familiar rules, repeated at the bottom of the tabular pages.

Tabular altitude and intermediate quantities are given to the nearest minute of arc, although errors of $2'$ in computed altitude may accrue during adjustment for the minutes parts of entering arguments. Components of azimuth angle are stated to $0°\!.1$; for derived true azimuth, only whole degrees are warranted. Since objects near the zenith are difficult to observe with a marine sextant, they should be avoided; altitudes greater than about $80°$ are not suited to reduction by this method.

In many circumstances, the accuracy provided by these tables is sufficient. However, to maintain the full accuracy $(0'\!.1)$ of the ephemeral data in the almanac throughout their reduction to altitude and azimuth, more extensive tables or a calculator should be used.

3. *Use of Tables.*

*Step* 1.    Determine the Greenwich hour angle $(GHA)$ and Declination $(Dec)$ of the body from the almanac. Select an assumed latitude $(Lat)$ of integral degrees nearest to the estimated latitude. Choose an assumed longitude nearest to the estimated longitude such that the local hour angle

$$LHA = GHA \; {{- \text{ west}} \atop {+ \text{ east}}} \; \text{longitude}$$

has integral degrees.

*Step* 2.    Enter the reduction table with *Lat* and *LHA* as arguments. Record the quantities $A$, $B$ and $Z_1$. Apply the rules for the sign of $B$ and $Z_1$: $B$ is minus if $90° < LHA < 270°$: $Z_1$ has the same sign as $B$. Set $A° =$ nearest whole degree of $A$ and $A' =$ minutes part of $A$. This step may be repeated for all reductions before leaving the latitude opening of the table.

*Step* 3.    Record the declination *Dec*. Apply the rules for the sign of *Dec*: *Dec* is minus if the name of *Dec* (*i.e.* N or S) is contrary to latitude. Add $B$ and *Dec* algebraically to produce $F$. If $F$ is negative, the object is below the horizon (in sight reduction, this can occur when the objects are close to the horizon). Regard $F$ as positive until step 7. Set $F° =$ nearest whole degree of $F$ and $F' =$ minutes part of $F$.

*Step* 4.    Enter the reduction table a second time with $A°$ and $F°$ as arguments and record $H$, $P$, and $Z_2$. Set $P° = $ nearest whole degree of $P$ and $Z_2° = $ nearest whole degree of $Z_2$.

*Step* 5.    Enter the auxiliary table with $F'$ and $P°$ as arguments to obtain $corr_1$ to $H$ for $F'$. Apply the rule for the sign of $corr_1$: $corr_1$ is minus if $F < 90°$ and $F' > 29'$ or if $F > 90°$ and $F' < 30'$, otherwise $corr_1$ is plus.

*Step* 6.    Enter the auxiliary table with $A'$ and $Z_2°$ as arguments to obtain $corr_2$ to $H$ for $A'$. Apply the rule for the sign of $corr_2$: $corr_2$ is minus if $A' < 30'$, otherwise $corr_2$ is plus.

*Step* 7.    Calculate the computed altitude $H_C$ as the sum of $H$, $corr_1$ and $corr_2$. Apply the rule for the sign of $H_C$: $H_C$ is minus if $F$ is negative.

*Step* 8.    Apply the rule for the sign of $Z_2$: $Z_2$ is minus if $F > 90°$. If $F$ is negative, replace $Z_2$ by $180° - Z_2$. Set the azimuth angle $Z$ equal to the algebraic sum of $Z_1$ and $Z_2$ and ignore the resulting sign. Obtain the true azimuth $Z_n$ from the rules

$$\text{For N latitude, if } \quad LHA > 180° \quad Z_n = Z$$
$$\text{if } \quad LHA < 180° \quad Z_n = 360° - Z$$

$$\text{For S latitude, if } \quad LHA > 180° \quad Z_n = 180° - Z$$
$$\text{if } \quad LHA < 180° \quad Z_n = 180° + Z$$

Observed altitude $H_O$ is compared with $H_C$ to obtain the altitude difference, which, with $Z_n$, is used to plot the position line.

4. *Example.*    (a) Required the altitude and azimuth of *Schedar* on 2022 February 4 at UT $06^h$ $33^m$ from the estimated position N 53°, E 5°.

1. Assumed latitude         $Lat = $   53° N
    From the almanac         $GHA = $ 222° 14'
    Assumed longitude                4° 46' E
    Local hour angle         $LHA = $ 227

2. Reduction table, 1st entry
    $(Lat, LHA) = (53, 227)$      $A = $   26   07    $A° = 26, A' = 7$
                               $B = -27$   12    $Z_1 = -49\cdot4,$       $90° < LHA < 270°$
3. From the almanac        $Dec = +56$   40                 *Lat* and *Dec* same
    Sum $= B + Dec$         $F = +29$   28    $F° = 29, F' = 28$

4. Reduction table, 2nd entry
    $(A°, F°) = (26, 29)$         $H = $   25   50    $P° = 61$
                                           $Z_2 = 76\cdot3, Z_2° = 76$

5. Auxiliary table, 1st entry
    $(F', P°) = (28, 61)$         $corr_1 = $     $+24$               $F < 90°, F' < 29'$
    Sum                                26   14
6. Auxiliary table, 2nd entry
    $(A', Z_2°) = (7, 76)$         $corr_2 = $      $-2$                    $A' < 30'$
7. Sum $= $ computed altitude    $H_C = +26°$   12'                $F > 0°$

8. Azimuth,   first component   $Z_1 = -49\cdot4$              same sign as $B$
             second component   $Z_2 = +76\cdot3$           $F < 90°, F > 0°$
    Sum $= $ azimuth angle     $Z = $   26·9

    True azimuth                  $Z_n = $   027°              N *Lat, LHA* $> 180°$

*continued on page* 318

SIGHT REDUCTION TABLE

B: (−) for 90° < LHA < 270°  
Dec: (−) for Lat. contrary name

Z₁: same sign as B  
Z₂: (−) for F > 90°

| LHA/F | 0° A/H | 0° B/P | 0° Z₁/Z₂ | 1° A/H | 1° B/P | 1° Z₁/Z₂ | 2° A/H | 2° B/P | 2° Z₁/Z₂ | 3° A/H | 3° B/P | 3° Z₁/Z₂ | 4° A/H | 4° B/P | 4° Z₁/Z₂ | 5° A/H | 5° B/P | 5° Z₁/Z₂ | LHA | Lat./A |
|---|---|---|---|---|---|---|---|---|---|---|---|---|---|---|---|---|---|---|---|---|
| 0 180 | 0 00 | 90 00 | 90·0 | 0 00 | 89 00 | 90·0 | 0 00 | 88 00 | 90·0 | 0 00 | 87 00 | 90·0 | 0 00 | 86 00 | 90·0 | 0 00 | 85 00 | 90·0 | 180 | 360 |
| 1 179 | 1 00 | 90 00 | 90·0 | 1 00 | 89 00 | 90·0 | 1 00 | 88 00 | 90·0 | 1 00 | 87 00 | 89·9 | 1 00 | 86 00 | 89·9 | 1 00 | 85 00 | 89·9 | 181 | 359 |
| 2 178 | 2 00 | 90 00 | 90·0 | 2 00 | 89 00 | 90·0 | 2 00 | 88 00 | 89·9 | 2 00 | 87 00 | 89·9 | 2 00 | 86 00 | 89·9 | 2 00 | 85 00 | 89·8 | 182 | 358 |
| 3 177 | 3 00 | 90 00 | 90·0 | 3 00 | 89 00 | 89·9 | 3 00 | 88 00 | 89·9 | 3 00 | 87 00 | 89·8 | 3 00 | 86 00 | 89·8 | 2 59 | 85 00 | 89·7 | 183 | 357 |
| 4 176 | 4 00 | 90 00 | 90·0 | 4 00 | 89 00 | 89·9 | 4 00 | 88 00 | 89·9 | 4 00 | 87 00 | 89·8 | 3 59 | 85 59 | 89·7 | 3 59 | 84 59 | 89·7 | 184 | 356 |
| 5 175 | 5 00 | 90 00 | 90·0 | 5 00 | 89 00 | 89·9 | 5 00 | 88 00 | 89·8 | 5 00 | 86 59 | 89·7 | 4 59 | 85 59 | 89·7 | 4 59 | 84 59 | 89·6 | 185 | 355 |
| 6 174 | 6 00 | 90 00 | 90·0 | 6 00 | 89 00 | 89·9 | 6 00 | 87 59 | 89·8 | 6 00 | 86 59 | 89·7 | 5 59 | 85 59 | 89·6 | 5 59 | 84 58 | 89·5 | 186 | 354 |
| 7 173 | 7 00 | 90 00 | 90·0 | 7 00 | 89 00 | 89·9 | 7 00 | 87 59 | 89·8 | 7 00 | 86 59 | 89·6 | 6 59 | 85 59 | 89·5 | 6 58 | 84 58 | 89·4 | 187 | 353 |
| 8 172 | 8 00 | 90 00 | 90·0 | 8 00 | 88 59 | 89·9 | 8 00 | 87 59 | 89·7 | 8 00 | 86 58 | 89·6 | 7 59 | 85 58 | 89·4 | 7 58 | 84 57 | 89·3 | 188 | 352 |
| 9 171 | 9 00 | 90 00 | 90·0 | 9 00 | 88 59 | 89·8 | 9 00 | 87 59 | 89·7 | 8 59 | 86 58 | 89·5 | 8 59 | 85 57 | 89·4 | 8 58 | 84 56 | 89·2 | 189 | 351 |
| 10 170 | 10 00 | 90 00 | 90·0 | 10 00 | 88 59 | 89·8 | 10 00 | 87 59 | 89·6 | 9 59 | 86 58 | 89·5 | 9 59 | 85 57 | 89·3 | 9 58 | 84 55 | 89·1 | 190 | 350 |
| 11 169 | 11 00 | 90 00 | 90·0 | 11 00 | 88 59 | 89·8 | 11 00 | 87 58 | 89·6 | 10 59 | 86 57 | 89·4 | 10 58 | 85 56 | 89·2 | 10 57 | 84 54 | 89·0 | 191 | 349 |
| 12 168 | 12 00 | 90 00 | 90·0 | 12 00 | 88 59 | 89·8 | 12 00 | 87 57 | 89·6 | 11 59 | 86 56 | 89·4 | 11 58 | 85 55 | 89·2 | 11 57 | 84 53 | 88·9 | 192 | 348 |
| 13 167 | 13 00 | 90 00 | 90·0 | 13 00 | 88 58 | 89·8 | 13 00 | 87 57 | 89·5 | 12 59 | 86 55 | 89·3 | 12 58 | 85 54 | 89·1 | 12 57 | 84 52 | 88·8 | 193 | 347 |
| 14 166 | 14 00 | 90 00 | 90·0 | 14 00 | 88 58 | 89·8 | 13 59 | 87 56 | 89·5 | 13 59 | 86 55 | 89·3 | 13 58 | 85 53 | 89·0 | 13 57 | 84 51 | 88·8 | 194 | 346 |
| 15 165 | 15 00 | 90 00 | 90·0 | 15 00 | 88 58 | 89·7 | 14 59 | 87 56 | 89·5 | 14 59 | 86 54 | 89·2 | 14 58 | 85 52 | 88·9 | 14 56 | 84 49 | 88·7 | 195 | 345 |
| 16 164 | 16 00 | 90 00 | 90·0 | 16 00 | 88 58 | 89·7 | 15 59 | 87 55 | 89·4 | 15 59 | 86 53 | 89·1 | 15 58 | 85 51 | 88·9 | 15 56 | 84 48 | 88·6 | 196 | 344 |
| 17 163 | 17 00 | 90 00 | 90·0 | 17 00 | 88 57 | 89·7 | 16 59 | 87 55 | 89·4 | 16 59 | 86 52 | 89·1 | 16 57 | 85 49 | 88·8 | 16 56 | 84 46 | 88·5 | 197 | 343 |
| 18 162 | 18 00 | 90 00 | 90·0 | 18 00 | 88 57 | 89·7 | 17 59 | 87 54 | 89·4 | 17 58 | 86 51 | 89·0 | 17 57 | 85 48 | 88·7 | 17 56 | 84 45 | 88·4 | 198 | 342 |
| 19 161 | 19 00 | 90 00 | 90·0 | 19 00 | 88 57 | 89·7 | 18 59 | 87 53 | 89·3 | 18 58 | 86 50 | 89·0 | 18 57 | 85 46 | 88·6 | 18 55 | 84 43 | 88·3 | 199 | 341 |
| 20 160 | 20 00 | 90 00 | 90·0 | 20 00 | 88 56 | 89·6 | 19 59 | 87 52 | 89·3 | 19 58 | 86 48 | 88·9 | 19 57 | 85 45 | 88·5 | 19 55 | 84 41 | 88·2 | 200 | 340 |
| 21 159 | 21 00 | 90 00 | 90·0 | 21 00 | 88 56 | 89·6 | 20 59 | 87 51 | 89·2 | 20 58 | 86 47 | 88·9 | 20 57 | 85 43 | 88·5 | 20 55 | 84 39 | 88·1 | 201 | 339 |
| 22 158 | 22 00 | 90 00 | 90·0 | 22 00 | 88 55 | 89·6 | 21 59 | 87 51 | 89·2 | 21 58 | 86 46 | 88·8 | 21 57 | 85 41 | 88·4 | 21 55 | 84 37 | 88·0 | 202 | 338 |
| 23 157 | 23 00 | 90 00 | 90·0 | 23 00 | 88 55 | 89·6 | 22 59 | 87 50 | 89·2 | 22 58 | 86 44 | 88·7 | 22 56 | 85 39 | 88·3 | 22 54 | 84 34 | 87·9 | 203 | 337 |
| 24 156 | 24 00 | 90 00 | 90·0 | 24 00 | 88 54 | 89·5 | 23 59 | 87 49 | 89·1 | 23 58 | 86 43 | 88·7 | 23 56 | 85 37 | 88·2 | 23 54 | 84 32 | 87·8 | 204 | 336 |
| 25 155 | 25 00 | 90 00 | 90·0 | 25 00 | 88 54 | 89·5 | 24 59 | 87 48 | 89·1 | 24 58 | 86 41 | 88·6 | 24 56 | 85 35 | 88·1 | 24 54 | 84 29 | 87·7 | 205 | 335 |
| 26 154 | 26 00 | 90 00 | 90·0 | 26 00 | 88 53 | 89·5 | 25 59 | 87 47 | 89·0 | 25 58 | 86 40 | 88·5 | 25 56 | 85 33 | 88·1 | 25 54 | 84 26 | 87·6 | 206 | 334 |
| 27 153 | 27 00 | 90 00 | 90·0 | 27 00 | 88 53 | 89·5 | 26 59 | 87 45 | 89·0 | 26 57 | 86 38 | 88·5 | 26 56 | 85 31 | 88·0 | 26 53 | 84 24 | 87·5 | 207 | 333 |
| 28 152 | 28 00 | 90 00 | 90·0 | 28 00 | 88 52 | 89·5 | 27 59 | 87 44 | 89·0 | 27 57 | 86 36 | 88·4 | 27 56 | 85 28 | 87·9 | 27 53 | 84 20 | 87·3 | 208 | 332 |
| 29 151 | 29 00 | 90 00 | 90·0 | 29 00 | 88 51 | 89·4 | 28 59 | 87 43 | 88·9 | 28 57 | 86 34 | 88·3 | 28 55 | 85 26 | 87·8 | 28 53 | 84 17 | 87·2 | 209 | 331 |
| 30 150 | 30 00 | 90 00 | 90·0 | 30 00 | 88 51 | 89·4 | 29 59 | 87 41 | 88·9 | 29 57 | 86 32 | 88·3 | 29 55 | 85 23 | 87·7 | 29 52 | 84 14 | 87·1 | 210 | 330 |
| 31 149 | 31 00 | 90 00 | 90·0 | 31 00 | 88 50 | 89·4 | 30 59 | 87 40 | 88·8 | 30 57 | 86 30 | 88·2 | 30 55 | 85 20 | 87·6 | 30 52 | 84 10 | 87·0 | 211 | 329 |
| 32 148 | 32 00 | 90 00 | 90·0 | 32 00 | 88 49 | 89·4 | 31 59 | 87 39 | 88·8 | 31 57 | 86 28 | 88·1 | 31 55 | 85 17 | 87·5 | 31 52 | 84 07 | 86·9 | 212 | 328 |
| 33 147 | 33 00 | 90 00 | 90·0 | 33 00 | 88 48 | 89·4 | 32 59 | 87 37 | 88·7 | 32 57 | 86 25 | 88·1 | 32 55 | 85 14 | 87·4 | 32 51 | 84 03 | 86·8 | 213 | 327 |
| 34 146 | 34 00 | 90 00 | 90·0 | 34 00 | 88 48 | 89·3 | 33 59 | 87 35 | 88·7 | 33 57 | 86 23 | 88·0 | 33 54 | 85 11 | 87·3 | 33 51 | 83 59 | 86·6 | 214 | 326 |
| 35 145 | 35 00 | 90 00 | 90·0 | 35 00 | 88 47 | 89·3 | 34 59 | 87 34 | 88·6 | 34 57 | 86 20 | 87·9 | 34 54 | 85 07 | 87·2 | 34 51 | 83 54 | 86·5 | 215 | 325 |
| 36 144 | 36 00 | 90 00 | 90·0 | 36 00 | 88 46 | 89·3 | 35 58 | 87 32 | 88·6 | 35 57 | 86 18 | 87·8 | 35 54 | 85 04 | 87·1 | 35 51 | 83 50 | 86·4 | 216 | 324 |
| 37 143 | 37 00 | 90 00 | 90·0 | 37 00 | 88 45 | 89·2 | 36 58 | 87 30 | 88·5 | 36 56 | 86 15 | 87·7 | 36 54 | 85 00 | 87·0 | 36 50 | 83 45 | 86·2 | 217 | 323 |
| 38 142 | 38 00 | 90 00 | 90·0 | 38 00 | 88 44 | 89·2 | 37 58 | 87 28 | 88·5 | 37 56 | 86 12 | 87·7 | 37 53 | 84 56 | 86·9 | 37 50 | 83 40 | 86·1 | 218 | 322 |
| 39 141 | 39 00 | 90 00 | 90·0 | 39 00 | 88 43 | 89·2 | 38 58 | 87 26 | 88·4 | 38 56 | 86 09 | 87·6 | 38 53 | 84 52 | 86·8 | 38 49 | 83 35 | 86·0 | 219 | 321 |
| 40 140 | 40 00 | 90 00 | 90·0 | 40 00 | 88 42 | 89·2 | 39 58 | 87 23 | 88·4 | 39 56 | 86 05 | 87·5 | 39 53 | 84 47 | 86·7 | 39 49 | 83 29 | 85·8 | 220 | 320 |
| 41 139 | 41 00 | 90 00 | 90·0 | 41 00 | 88 41 | 89·1 | 40 58 | 87 21 | 88·3 | 40 56 | 86 02 | 87·4 | 40 53 | 84 42 | 86·5 | 40 49 | 83 23 | 85·7 | 221 | 319 |
| 42 138 | 42 00 | 90 00 | 90·0 | 42 00 | 88 39 | 89·1 | 41 58 | 87 19 | 88·2 | 41 56 | 85 58 | 87·3 | 41 52 | 84 37 | 86·4 | 41 48 | 83 17 | 85·5 | 222 | 318 |
| 43 137 | 43 00 | 90 00 | 90·0 | 43 00 | 88 38 | 89·1 | 42 58 | 87 16 | 88·1 | 42 56 | 85 54 | 87·2 | 42 52 | 84 32 | 86·3 | 42 48 | 83 11 | 85·4 | 223 | 317 |
| 44 136 | 44 00 | 90 00 | 90·0 | 43 59 | 88 37 | 89·0 | 43 58 | 87 13 | 88·1 | 43 55 | 85 50 | 87·1 | 43 52 | 84 27 | 86·1 | 43 47 | 83 04 | 85·2 | 224 | 316 |
| 45 135 | 45 00 | 90 00 | 90·0 | 44 59 | 88 35 | 89·0 | 44 58 | 87 10 | 88·0 | 44 55 | 85 46 | 87·0 | 44 52 | 84 21 | 86·0 | 44 47 | 82 57 | 85·0 | 225 | 315 |

| Lat./A | | 0° | | | 1° | | | 2° | | | 3° | | | 4° | | | 5° | | | Lat./A | |
| LHA | F | A/H | B/P | Z₁/Z₂ | A/H | B/P | Z₁/Z₂ | A/H | B/P | Z₁/Z₂ | A/H | B/P | Z₁/Z₂ | A/H | B/P | Z₁/Z₂ | A/H | B/P | Z₁/Z₂ | LHA | |
|---|---|---|---|---|---|---|---|---|---|---|---|---|---|---|---|---|---|---|---|---|---|
| 45 | 135 | 45 00 | 90 00 | 90.0 | 44 59 | 88 35 | 89.0 | 44 58 | 87 10 | 88.0 | 44 55 | 85 46 | 87.0 | 44 52 | 84 21 | 86.0 | 44 47 | 82 57 | 85.0 | 225 | 315 |
| 46 | 134 | 46 00 | 90 00 | 90.0 | 45 59 | 88 34 | 89.0 | 45 58 | 87 07 | 87.9 | 45 55 | 85 41 | 86.9 | 45 51 | 84 15 | 85.9 | 45 46 | 82 49 | 84.8 | 226 | 314 |
| 47 | 133 | 47 00 | 90 00 | 90.0 | 46 59 | 88 32 | 88.9 | 46 58 | 87 04 | 87.9 | 46 55 | 85 36 | 86.8 | 46 51 | 84 09 | 85.7 | 46 46 | 82 41 | 84.7 | 227 | 313 |
| 48 | 132 | 48 00 | 90 00 | 90.0 | 47 59 | 88 30 | 88.9 | 47 58 | 87 01 | 87.8 | 47 55 | 85 31 | 86.7 | 47 51 | 84 02 | 85.6 | 47 46 | 82 33 | 84.5 | 228 | 312 |
| 49 | 131 | 49 00 | 90 00 | 90.0 | 48 59 | 88 29 | 88.8 | 48 58 | 86 57 | 87.8 | 48 55 | 85 26 | 86.7 | 48 50 | 83 55 | 85.4 | 48 45 | 82 24 | 84.3 | 229 | 311 |
| 50 | 130 | 50 00 | 90 00 | 90.0 | 49 59 | 88 27 | 88.8 | 49 58 | 86 53 | 87.6 | 49 54 | 85 20 | 86.6 | 49 50 | 83 47 | 85.2 | 49 44 | 82 15 | 84.1 | 230 | 310 |
| 51 | 129 | 51 00 | 90 00 | 90.0 | 50 59 | 88 25 | 88.8 | 50 57 | 86 49 | 87.5 | 50 54 | 85 14 | 86.3 | 50 50 | 83 40 | 85.1 | 50 44 | 82 05 | 83.9 | 231 | 309 |
| 52 | 128 | 52 00 | 90 00 | 90.0 | 51 59 | 88 23 | 88.7 | 51 57 | 86 45 | 87.4 | 51 54 | 85 08 | 86.2 | 51 49 | 83 31 | 84.9 | 51 43 | 81 55 | 83.6 | 232 | 308 |
| 53 | 127 | 53 00 | 90 00 | 90.0 | 52 59 | 88 20 | 88.7 | 52 57 | 86 41 | 87.3 | 52 54 | 85 01 | 86.0 | 52 49 | 83 22 | 84.7 | 52 43 | 81 44 | 83.4 | 233 | 307 |
| 54 | 126 | 54 00 | 90 00 | 90.0 | 53 59 | 88 18 | 88.6 | 53 57 | 86 36 | 87.2 | 53 54 | 84 54 | 85.9 | 53 49 | 83 13 | 84.5 | 53 42 | 81 32 | 83.2 | 234 | 306 |
| 55 | 125 | 55 00 | 90 00 | 90.0 | 54 59 | 88 15 | 88.6 | 54 57 | 86 31 | 87.1 | 54 53 | 84 47 | 85.7 | 54 48 | 83 03 | 84.3 | 54 41 | 81 20 | 82.9 | 235 | 305 |
| 56 | 124 | 56 00 | 90 00 | 90.0 | 55 59 | 88 13 | 88.5 | 55 57 | 86 26 | 87.0 | 55 53 | 84 39 | 85.6 | 55 48 | 82 52 | 84.1 | 55 41 | 81 06 | 82.6 | 236 | 304 |
| 57 | 123 | 57 00 | 90 00 | 90.0 | 56 59 | 88 10 | 88.5 | 56 57 | 86 20 | 86.9 | 56 53 | 84 30 | 85.4 | 56 47 | 82 41 | 83.9 | 56 40 | 80 52 | 82.4 | 237 | 303 |
| 58 | 122 | 58 00 | 90 00 | 90.0 | 57 59 | 88 07 | 88.4 | 57 57 | 86 14 | 86.8 | 57 52 | 84 21 | 85.2 | 57 47 | 82 29 | 83.6 | 57 39 | 80 38 | 82.1 | 238 | 302 |
| 59 | 121 | 59 00 | 90 00 | 90.0 | 58 59 | 88 04 | 88.3 | 58 57 | 86 07 | 86.7 | 58 52 | 84 11 | 85.0 | 58 46 | 82 16 | 83.4 | 58 38 | 80 22 | 81.7 | 239 | 301 |
| 60 | 120 | 60 00 | 90 00 | 90.0 | 59 59 | 88 00 | 88.3 | 59 56 | 86 00 | 86.5 | 59 52 | 84 01 | 84.8 | 59 46 | 82 02 | 83.1 | 59 37 | 80 05 | 81.4 | 240 | 300 |
| 61 | 119 | 61 00 | 90 00 | 90.0 | 60 59 | 87 56 | 88.2 | 60 56 | 85 53 | 86.4 | 60 52 | 83 50 | 84.6 | 60 45 | 81 48 | 82.8 | 60 37 | 79 46 | 81.1 | 241 | 299 |
| 62 | 118 | 62 00 | 90 00 | 90.0 | 61 59 | 87 52 | 88.1 | 61 56 | 85 45 | 86.2 | 61 51 | 83 38 | 84.4 | 61 44 | 81 32 | 82.5 | 61 36 | 79 27 | 80.7 | 242 | 298 |
| 63 | 117 | 63 00 | 90 00 | 90.0 | 62 59 | 87 48 | 88.0 | 62 56 | 85 36 | 86.1 | 62 51 | 83 25 | 84.1 | 62 44 | 81 15 | 82.2 | 62 35 | 79 06 | 80.3 | 243 | 297 |
| 64 | 116 | 64 00 | 90 00 | 90.0 | 63 59 | 87 43 | 88.0 | 63 56 | 85 27 | 85.9 | 63 50 | 83 11 | 83.9 | 63 43 | 80 56 | 81.9 | 63 33 | 78 43 | 79.9 | 244 | 296 |
| 65 | 115 | 65 00 | 90 00 | 90.0 | 64 59 | 87 38 | 87.9 | 64 56 | 85 18 | 85.7 | 64 50 | 82 56 | 83.6 | 64 42 | 80 36 | 81.5 | 64 32 | 78 18 | 79.4 | 245 | 295 |
| 66 | 114 | 66 00 | 90 00 | 90.0 | 65 59 | 87 33 | 87.8 | 65 55 | 85 06 | 85.5 | 65 49 | 82 39 | 83.3 | 65 41 | 80 15 | 81.1 | 65 31 | 77 52 | 78.9 | 246 | 294 |
| 67 | 113 | 67 00 | 90 00 | 90.0 | 66 59 | 87 27 | 87.6 | 66 55 | 84 54 | 85.3 | 66 49 | 82 22 | 83.0 | 66 40 | 79 51 | 80.7 | 66 29 | 77 23 | 78.4 | 247 | 293 |
| 68 | 112 | 68 00 | 90 00 | 90.0 | 67 59 | 87 20 | 87.5 | 67 55 | 84 40 | 85.1 | 67 48 | 82 02 | 82.6 | 67 39 | 79 26 | 80.2 | 67 28 | 76 51 | 77.8 | 248 | 292 |
| 69 | 111 | 69 00 | 90 00 | 90.0 | 68 59 | 87 13 | 87.4 | 68 55 | 84 26 | 84.8 | 68 48 | 81 41 | 82.2 | 68 38 | 78 58 | 79.7 | 68 26 | 76 17 | 77.2 | 249 | 291 |
| 70 | 110 | 70 00 | 90 00 | 90.0 | 69 59 | 87 05 | 87.3 | 69 54 | 84 11 | 84.5 | 69 47 | 81 17 | 81.8 | 69 37 | 78 27 | 79.2 | 69 25 | 75 39 | 76.5 | 250 | 290 |
| 71 | 109 | 71 00 | 90 00 | 90.0 | 70 58 | 86 56 | 87.1 | 70 54 | 83 53 | 84.2 | 70 46 | 80 51 | 81.4 | 70 36 | 77 53 | 78.5 | 70 23 | 74 58 | 75.8 | 251 | 289 |
| 72 | 108 | 72 00 | 90 00 | 90.0 | 71 58 | 86 46 | 86.9 | 71 54 | 83 33 | 83.9 | 71 46 | 80 22 | 80.8 | 71 35 | 77 15 | 77.9 | 71 20 | 74 12 | 75.0 | 252 | 288 |
| 73 | 107 | 73 00 | 90 00 | 90.0 | 72 58 | 86 35 | 86.7 | 72 53 | 83 11 | 83.5 | 72 45 | 79 50 | 80.3 | 72 33 | 76 33 | 77.1 | 72 18 | 73 20 | 74.1 | 253 | 287 |
| 74 | 106 | 74 00 | 90 00 | 90.0 | 73 58 | 86 23 | 86.5 | 73 53 | 82 47 | 83.1 | 73 44 | 79 14 | 79.7 | 73 31 | 75 46 | 76.3 | 73 15 | 72 23 | 73.1 | 254 | 286 |
| 75 | 105 | 75 00 | 90 00 | 90.0 | 74 58 | 86 09 | 86.3 | 74 52 | 82 19 | 82.6 | 74 43 | 78 33 | 78.9 | 74 29 | 74 53 | 75.4 | 74 12 | 71 19 | 72.0 | 255 | 285 |
| 76 | 104 | 76 00 | 90 00 | 90.0 | 75 58 | 85 52 | 86.0 | 75 52 | 81 47 | 82.0 | 75 41 | 77 47 | 78.1 | 75 27 | 73 53 | 74.4 | 75 09 | 70 07 | 70.7 | 256 | 284 |
| 77 | 103 | 77 00 | 90 00 | 90.0 | 76 58 | 85 34 | 85.7 | 76 51 | 81 11 | 81.4 | 76 40 | 76 53 | 77.2 | 76 25 | 72 44 | 73.2 | 76 05 | 68 45 | 69.3 | 257 | 283 |
| 78 | 102 | 78 00 | 90 00 | 90.0 | 77 58 | 85 12 | 85.3 | 77 50 | 80 28 | 80.7 | 77 38 | 75 51 | 76.2 | 77 22 | 71 25 | 71.8 | 77 01 | 67 11 | 67.7 | 258 | 282 |
| 79 | 101 | 79 00 | 90 00 | 90.0 | 78 57 | 84 46 | 84.9 | 78 49 | 79 38 | 79.8 | 78 36 | 74 39 | 74.9 | 78 18 | 69 51 | 70.3 | 77 56 | 65 22 | 65.8 | 259 | 281 |
| 80 | 100 | 80 00 | 90 00 | 90.0 | 79 57 | 84 16 | 84.3 | 79 48 | 78 38 | 78.8 | 79 34 | 73 12 | 73.5 | 79 14 | 68 04 | 68.4 | 78 50 | 63 16 | 63.7 | 260 | 280 |
| 81 | 99 | 81 00 | 90 00 | 90.0 | 80 57 | 83 38 | 83.7 | 80 47 | 77 25 | 77.6 | 80 31 | 71 29 | 71.7 | 80 09 | 65 55 | 66.2 | 79 43 | 60 47 | 61.2 | 261 | 279 |
| 82 | 98 | 82 00 | 90 00 | 90.0 | 81 56 | 82 51 | 82.9 | 81 45 | 75 55 | 76.1 | 81 28 | 69 22 | 69.6 | 81 04 | 63 19 | 63.6 | 80 34 | 57 51 | 58.2 | 262 | 278 |
| 83 | 97 | 83 00 | 90 00 | 90.0 | 82 56 | 81 51 | 81.9 | 82 43 | 74 01 | 74.1 | 82 23 | 66 44 | 66.9 | 81 57 | 60 09 | 60.4 | 81 24 | 54 20 | 54.6 | 263 | 277 |
| 84 | 96 | 84 00 | 90 00 | 90.0 | 83 55 | 80 31 | 80.6 | 83 41 | 71 32 | 71.6 | 83 18 | 63 22 | 63.5 | 82 48 | 56 13 | 56.4 | 82 12 | 50 04 | 50.3 | 264 | 276 |
| 85 | 95 | 85 00 | 90 00 | 90.0 | 84 54 | 78 40 | 78.7 | 84 37 | 68 10 | 68.3 | 84 10 | 58 59 | 59.1 | 83 36 | 51 16 | 51.4 | 82 56 | 44 53 | 45.1 | 265 | 275 |
| 86 | 94 | 86 00 | 90 00 | 90.0 | 85 53 | 75 57 | 76.0 | 85 32 | 63 24 | 63.5 | 85 00 | 53 05 | 53.2 | 84 21 | 44 56 | 45.1 | 83 36 | 38 34 | 38.7 | 266 | 274 |
| 87 | 93 | 87 00 | 90 00 | 90.0 | 86 50 | 71 33 | 71.6 | 86 24 | 56 17 | 56.3 | 85 45 | 44 58 | 45.0 | 85 00 | 36 49 | 36.9 | 84 10 | 30 53 | 31.0 | 267 | 273 |
| 88 | 92 | 88 00 | 90 00 | 90.0 | 87 46 | 63 26 | 63.4 | 87 10 | 44 59 | 45.0 | 86 24 | 33 40 | 33.7 | 85 32 | 26 31 | 26.6 | 84 37 | 21 45 | 21.8 | 268 | 272 |
| 89 | 91 | 89 00 | 90 00 | 90.0 | 88 35 | 45 00 | 45.0 | 87 46 | 26 33 | 26.6 | 86 50 | 18 25 | 18.4 | 85 53 | 14 01 | 14.0 | 84 54 | 11 17 | 11.3 | 269 | 271 |
| 90 | 90 | 90 00 | 0 00 | 0.0 | 89 00 | 0 00 | 0.0 | 88 00 | 0 00 | 0.0 | 87 00 | 0 00 | 0.0 | 86 00 | 0 00 | 0.0 | 85 00 | 0 00 | 0.0 | 270 | 270 |

N. Lat: for LHA > 180° ... $Z_n = Z$
for LHA < 180° ... $Z_n = 360° - Z$

S. Lat: for LHA > 180° ... $Z_n = 180° - Z$
for LHA < 180° ... $Z_n = 180° + Z$

# LATITUDE / A: 6° – 11°

## SIGHT REDUCTION TABLE

B: (−) for 90° < LHA < 270°
Dec:(−) for Lat. contrary name

Z₁: same sign as B
Z₂: (−) for F > 90°

| LHA/F | A | 6° A/H | 6° B/P | 6° $Z_1/Z_2$ | 7° A/H | 7° B/P | 7° $Z_1/Z_2$ | 8° A/H | 8° B/P | 8° $Z_1/Z_2$ | 9° A/H | 9° B/P | 9° $Z_1/Z_2$ | 10° A/H | 10° B/P | 10° $Z_1/Z_2$ | 11° A/H | 11° B/P | 11° $Z_1/Z_2$ | LHA |
|---|---|---|---|---|---|---|---|---|---|---|---|---|---|---|---|---|---|---|---|---|
| 0 | 180 | 0 00 | 84 00 | 90·0 | 0 00 | 83 00 | 90·0 | 0 00 | 82 00 | 90·0 | 0 00 | 81 00 | 90·0 | 0 00 | 80 00 | 90·0 | 0 00 | 79 00 | 90·0 | 180 |
| 1 | 179 | 1 00 | 84 00 | 89·9 | 1 00 | 83 00 | 89·9 | 0 59 | 82 00 | 89·9 | 0 59 | 81 00 | 89·8 | 0 59 | 80 00 | 89·8 | 0 59 | 79 00 | 89·8 | 181 |
| 2 | 178 | 1 59 | 84 00 | 89·8 | 1 59 | 83 00 | 89·8 | 1 59 | 82 00 | 89·7 | 1 59 | 81 00 | 89·7 | 1 58 | 80 00 | 89·7 | 1 58 | 79 00 | 89·6 | 182 |
| 3 | 177 | 2 59 | 83 59 | 89·7 | 2 59 | 82 59 | 89·6 | 2 58 | 81 59 | 89·6 | 2 58 | 80 59 | 89·5 | 2 57 | 79 59 | 89·5 | 2 57 | 78 59 | 89·4 | 183 |
| 4 | 176 | 3 59 | 83 59 | 89·6 | 3 58 | 82 59 | 89·5 | 3 58 | 81 59 | 89·4 | 3 57 | 80 59 | 89·4 | 3 56 | 79 59 | 89·3 | 3 56 | 78 58 | 89·2 | 184 |
| 5 | 175 | 4 58 | 83 59 | 89·5 | 4 58 | 82 58 | 89·4 | 4 57 | 81 58 | 89·3 | 4 56 | 80 58 | 89·2 | 4 55 | 79 58 | 89·1 | 4 54 | 78 58 | 89·0 | 185 |
| 6 | 174 | 5 58 | 83 58 | 89·4 | 5 57 | 82 58 | 89·3 | 5 56 | 81 57 | 89·2 | 5 56 | 80 57 | 89·1 | 5 55 | 79 57 | 89·0 | 5 53 | 78 56 | 88·9 | 186 |
| 7 | 173 | 6 58 | 83 57 | 89·3 | 6 57 | 82 57 | 89·1 | 6 56 | 81 56 | 89·0 | 6 55 | 80 56 | 88·9 | 6 54 | 79 56 | 88·8 | 6 52 | 78 55 | 88·7 | 187 |
| 8 | 172 | 7 57 | 83 56 | 89·2 | 7 56 | 82 56 | 89·0 | 7 55 | 81 55 | 88·9 | 7 54 | 80 55 | 88·7 | 7 53 | 79 54 | 88·6 | 7 51 | 78 54 | 88·5 | 188 |
| 9 | 171 | 8 57 | 83 56 | 89·1 | 8 56 | 82 55 | 88·9 | 8 55 | 81 54 | 88·7 | 8 53 | 80 53 | 88·6 | 8 52 | 79 53 | 88·4 | 8 50 | 78 52 | 88·3 | 189 |
| 10 | 170 | 9 57 | 83 54 | 88·9 | 9 55 | 82 54 | 88·8 | 9 54 | 81 53 | 88·6 | 9 53 | 80 52 | 88·4 | 9 51 | 79 51 | 88·2 | 9 49 | 78 50 | 88·1 | 190 |
| 11 | 169 | 10 56 | 83 53 | 88·8 | 10 55 | 82 52 | 88·6 | 10 53 | 81 51 | 88·5 | 10 52 | 80 50 | 88·3 | 10 50 | 79 49 | 88·1 | 10 48 | 78 48 | 87·9 | 191 |
| 12 | 168 | 11 56 | 83 52 | 88·7 | 11 55 | 82 51 | 88·5 | 11 53 | 81 49 | 88·3 | 11 51 | 80 48 | 88·1 | 11 49 | 79 47 | 87·9 | 11 47 | 78 46 | 87·7 | 192 |
| 13 | 167 | 12 56 | 83 51 | 88·6 | 12 54 | 82 49 | 88·4 | 12 52 | 81 48 | 88·2 | 12 50 | 80 46 | 87·9 | 12 48 | 79 45 | 87·7 | 12 45 | 78 43 | 87·5 | 193 |
| 14 | 166 | 13 55 | 83 49 | 88·5 | 13 54 | 82 47 | 88·3 | 13 52 | 81 46 | 88·0 | 13 49 | 80 44 | 87·8 | 13 47 | 79 42 | 87·5 | 13 44 | 78 40 | 87·3 | 194 |
| 15 | 165 | 14 55 | 83 47 | 88·4 | 14 53 | 82 45 | 88·1 | 14 51 | 81 43 | 87·9 | 14 49 | 80 41 | 87·6 | 14 46 | 79 39 | 87·3 | 14 43 | 78 37 | 87·1 | 195 |
| 16 | 164 | 15 55 | 83 46 | 88·3 | 15 53 | 82 43 | 88·0 | 15 50 | 81 41 | 87·7 | 15 48 | 80 39 | 87·4 | 15 45 | 79 36 | 87·1 | 15 42 | 78 34 | 86·9 | 196 |
| 17 | 163 | 16 54 | 83 44 | 88·2 | 16 52 | 82 41 | 87·9 | 16 50 | 81 38 | 87·6 | 16 47 | 80 36 | 87·3 | 16 44 | 79 33 | 87·0 | 16 41 | 78 31 | 86·7 | 197 |
| 18 | 162 | 17 54 | 83 42 | 88·1 | 17 52 | 82 39 | 87·7 | 17 49 | 81 36 | 87·4 | 17 46 | 80 33 | 87·1 | 17 43 | 79 30 | 86·8 | 17 39 | 78 27 | 86·5 | 198 |
| 19 | 161 | 18 54 | 83 39 | 87·9 | 18 51 | 82 36 | 87·6 | 18 48 | 81 33 | 87·3 | 18 45 | 80 29 | 86·9 | 18 42 | 79 26 | 86·6 | 18 38 | 78 23 | 86·2 | 199 |
| 20 | 160 | 19 53 | 83 37 | 87·8 | 19 51 | 82 33 | 87·5 | 19 48 | 81 30 | 87·1 | 19 45 | 80 26 | 86·7 | 19 41 | 79 22 | 86·4 | 19 37 | 78 19 | 86·0 | 200 |
| 21 | 159 | 20 53 | 83 35 | 87·7 | 20 50 | 82 30 | 87·3 | 20 47 | 81 26 | 86·9 | 20 44 | 80 22 | 86·6 | 20 40 | 79 18 | 86·2 | 20 36 | 78 14 | 85·8 | 201 |
| 22 | 158 | 21 52 | 83 32 | 87·6 | 21 50 | 82 27 | 87·2 | 21 46 | 81 23 | 86·8 | 21 43 | 80 18 | 86·4 | 21 39 | 79 14 | 86·0 | 21 35 | 78 10 | 85·6 | 202 |
| 23 | 157 | 22 52 | 83 29 | 87·5 | 22 49 | 82 24 | 87·0 | 22 46 | 81 19 | 86·6 | 22 42 | 80 14 | 86·2 | 22 38 | 79 09 | 85·8 | 22 33 | 78 05 | 85·4 | 203 |
| 24 | 156 | 23 52 | 83 26 | 87·3 | 23 49 | 82 21 | 86·9 | 23 45 | 81 15 | 86·5 | 23 41 | 80 10 | 86·0 | 23 37 | 79 05 | 85·6 | 23 32 | 77 59 | 85·1 | 204 |
| 25 | 155 | 24 51 | 83 23 | 87·2 | 24 48 | 82 17 | 86·7 | 24 44 | 81 11 | 86·3 | 24 40 | 80 05 | 85·8 | 24 36 | 78 59 | 85·4 | 24 31 | 77 54 | 84·9 | 205 |
| 26 | 154 | 25 51 | 83 20 | 87·1 | 25 48 | 82 13 | 86·6 | 25 44 | 81 07 | 86·1 | 25 39 | 80 00 | 85·6 | 25 35 | 78 54 | 85·2 | 25 29 | 77 48 | 84·7 | 206 |
| 27 | 153 | 26 50 | 83 16 | 87·0 | 26 47 | 82 09 | 86·4 | 26 43 | 81 02 | 85·9 | 26 38 | 79 55 | 85·4 | 26 33 | 78 48 | 84·9 | 26 28 | 77 42 | 84·4 | 207 |
| 28 | 152 | 27 50 | 83 13 | 86·8 | 27 46 | 82 05 | 86·3 | 27 42 | 80 57 | 85·8 | 27 38 | 79 50 | 85·2 | 27 32 | 78 42 | 84·7 | 27 27 | 77 35 | 84·2 | 208 |
| 29 | 151 | 28 50 | 83 09 | 86·7 | 28 46 | 82 01 | 86·1 | 28 41 | 80 52 | 85·6 | 28 37 | 79 44 | 85·0 | 28 31 | 78 36 | 84·5 | 28 25 | 77 28 | 84·0 | 209 |
| 30 | 150 | 29 49 | 83 05 | 86·5 | 29 45 | 81 56 | 86·0 | 29 41 | 80 47 | 85·4 | 29 36 | 79 38 | 84·8 | 29 30 | 78 29 | 84·3 | 29 24 | 77 21 | 83·7 | 210 |
| 31 | 149 | 30 49 | 83 01 | 86·4 | 30 45 | 81 51 | 85·8 | 30 40 | 80 41 | 85·2 | 30 35 | 79 32 | 84·6 | 30 29 | 78 23 | 84·0 | 30 22 | 77 13 | 83·5 | 211 |
| 32 | 148 | 31 48 | 82 56 | 86·3 | 31 44 | 81 46 | 85·6 | 31 39 | 80 35 | 85·0 | 31 34 | 79 25 | 84·4 | 31 27 | 78 15 | 83·8 | 31 21 | 77 05 | 83·2 | 212 |
| 33 | 147 | 32 48 | 82 51 | 86·1 | 32 43 | 81 40 | 85·5 | 32 38 | 80 29 | 84·8 | 32 33 | 79 18 | 84·2 | 32 26 | 78 08 | 83·6 | 32 19 | 76 57 | 82·9 | 213 |
| 34 | 146 | 33 47 | 82 46 | 86·0 | 33 43 | 81 35 | 85·3 | 33 37 | 80 23 | 84·6 | 33 32 | 79 11 | 84·0 | 33 25 | 78 00 | 83·3 | 33 18 | 76 48 | 82·7 | 214 |
| 35 | 145 | 34 47 | 82 41 | 85·8 | 34 42 | 81 29 | 85·1 | 34 37 | 80 16 | 84·4 | 34 30 | 79 03 | 83·7 | 34 24 | 77 51 | 83·1 | 34 16 | 76 39 | 82·4 | 215 |
| 36 | 144 | 35 46 | 82 36 | 85·7 | 35 41 | 81 22 | 84·9 | 35 36 | 80 09 | 84·2 | 35 29 | 78 55 | 83·5 | 35 22 | 77 42 | 82·8 | 35 14 | 76 29 | 82·1 | 216 |
| 37 | 143 | 36 46 | 82 30 | 85·5 | 36 41 | 81 16 | 84·8 | 36 35 | 80 01 | 84·0 | 36 28 | 78 47 | 83·3 | 36 21 | 77 33 | 82·5 | 36 13 | 76 19 | 81·8 | 217 |
| 38 | 142 | 37 45 | 82 24 | 85·3 | 37 40 | 81 09 | 84·6 | 37 34 | 79 53 | 83·8 | 37 27 | 78 38 | 83·0 | 37 19 | 77 23 | 82·3 | 37 11 | 76 09 | 81·5 | 218 |
| 39 | 141 | 38 45 | 82 18 | 85·2 | 38 39 | 81 01 | 84·4 | 38 33 | 79 45 | 83·6 | 38 26 | 78 29 | 82·8 | 38 18 | 77 13 | 82·0 | 38 09 | 75 57 | 81·2 | 219 |
| 40 | 140 | 39 44 | 82 11 | 85·0 | 39 39 | 80 54 | 84·2 | 39 32 | 79 36 | 83·3 | 39 25 | 78 19 | 82·5 | 39 16 | 77 02 | 81·7 | 39 07 | 75 46 | 80·9 | 220 |
| 41 | 139 | 40 44 | 82 04 | 84·8 | 40 38 | 80 46 | 84·0 | 40 31 | 79 27 | 83·1 | 40 23 | 78 09 | 82·3 | 40 15 | 76 51 | 81·4 | 40 05 | 75 33 | 80·6 | 221 |
| 42 | 138 | 41 43 | 81 57 | 84·6 | 41 37 | 80 37 | 83·7 | 41 30 | 79 17 | 82·9 | 41 22 | 77 58 | 82·0 | 41 13 | 76 39 | 81·1 | 41 04 | 75 21 | 80·3 | 222 |
| 43 | 137 | 42 42 | 81 49 | 84·4 | 42 36 | 80 28 | 83·5 | 42 29 | 79 07 | 82·6 | 42 21 | 77 47 | 81·7 | 42 12 | 76 27 | 80·8 | 42 02 | 75 07 | 79·9 | 223 |
| 44 | 136 | 43 42 | 81 41 | 84·2 | 43 35 | 80 19 | 83·3 | 43 28 | 78 57 | 82·3 | 43 19 | 77 35 | 81·4 | 43 10 | 76 14 | 80·5 | 43 00 | 74 53 | 79·6 | 224 |
| 45 | 135 | 44 41 | 81 33 | 84·0 | 44 34 | 80 09 | 83·1 | 44 27 | 78 46 | 82·1 | 44 18 | 77 22 | 81·1 | 44 08 | 76 00 | 80·1 | 43 57 | 74 38 | 79·2 | 225 |

Lat. / A

| Lat. / A | LHA/F | 6° A/H | 6° B/P | 6° Z₁/Z₂ | 7° A/H | 7° B/P | 7° Z₁/Z₂ | 8° A/H | 8° B/P | 8° Z₁/Z₂ | 9° A/H | 9° B/P | 9° Z₁/Z₂ | 10° A/H | 10° B/P | 10° Z₁/Z₂ | 11° A/H | 11° B/P | 11° Z₁/Z₂ | Lat. / A | LHA |
|---|---|---|---|---|---|---|---|---|---|---|---|---|---|---|---|---|---|---|---|---|---|
| 45 | 135 | 44 41 | 81 33 | 84.0 | 44 34 | 80 09 | 83.1 | 44 27 | 78 46 | 82.1 | 44 18 | 77 22 | 81.1 | 44 08 | 76 00 | 80.1 | 43 57 | 74 38 | 79.2 | | 225 |
| 46 | 134 | 45 41 | 81 21 | 83.8 | 45 34 | 79 59 | 82.8 | 45 26 | 78 34 | 81.8 | 45 16 | 77 09 | 80.8 | 45 06 | 75 45 | 79.8 | 44 55 | 74 22 | 78.8 | | 226 |
| 47 | 133 | 46 40 | 81 14 | 83.6 | 46 33 | 79 48 | 82.6 | 46 24 | 78 21 | 81.5 | 46 15 | 76 56 | 80.5 | 46 04 | 75 30 | 79.5 | 45 53 | 74 05 | 78.4 | | 227 |
| 48 | 132 | 47 39 | 81 04 | 83.4 | 47 32 | 79 36 | 82.3 | 47 23 | 78 08 | 81.2 | 47 13 | 76 41 | 80.1 | 47 03 | 75 14 | 79.1 | 46 51 | 73 48 | 78.0 | | 228 |
| 49 | 131 | 48 38 | 80 54 | 83.1 | 48 31 | 79 24 | 82.0 | 48 22 | 77 55 | 80.9 | 48 12 | 76 26 | 79.8 | 48 01 | 74 57 | 78.7 | 47 48 | 73 30 | 77.6 | | 229 |
| 50 | 130 | 49 38 | 80 43 | 82.9 | 49 30 | 79 11 | 81.7 | 49 20 | 77 40 | 80.6 | 49 10 | 76 09 | 79.4 | 48 58 | 74 40 | 78.3 | 48 46 | 73 10 | 77.2 | | 230 |
| 51 | 129 | 50 37 | 80 31 | 82.6 | 50 29 | 78 58 | 81.4 | 50 19 | 77 25 | 80.2 | 50 08 | 75 52 | 79.1 | 49 55 | 74 21 | 77.9 | 49 43 | 72 50 | 76.7 | | 231 |
| 52 | 128 | 51 36 | 80 19 | 82.4 | 51 27 | 78 43 | 81.1 | 51 18 | 77 08 | 79.9 | 51 06 | 75 34 | 78.7 | 50 54 | 74 01 | 77.5 | 50 40 | 72 29 | 76.3 | | 232 |
| 53 | 127 | 52 35 | 80 06 | 82.1 | 52 26 | 78 28 | 80.8 | 52 16 | 76 51 | 79.5 | 52 04 | 75 15 | 78.3 | 51 52 | 73 40 | 77.0 | 51 37 | 72 06 | 75.8 | | 233 |
| 54 | 126 | 53 34 | 79 52 | 81.8 | 53 25 | 78 12 | 80.5 | 53 14 | 76 33 | 79.2 | 53 02 | 74 55 | 77.9 | 52 49 | 73 18 | 76.6 | 52 35 | 71 42 | 75.3 | | 234 |
| 55 | 125 | 54 33 | 79 37 | 81.5 | 54 24 | 77 55 | 80.1 | 54 13 | 76 14 | 78.8 | 54 00 | 74 34 | 77.4 | 53 47 | 72 55 | 76.1 | 53 31 | 71 17 | 74.8 | | 235 |
| 56 | 124 | 55 32 | 79 21 | 81.2 | 55 22 | 77 37 | 79.8 | 55 11 | 75 54 | 78.3 | 54 58 | 74 11 | 76.9 | 54 44 | 72 30 | 75.6 | 54 28 | 70 50 | 74.2 | | 236 |
| 57 | 123 | 56 31 | 79 05 | 80.9 | 56 21 | 77 18 | 79.4 | 56 09 | 75 32 | 77.9 | 55 56 | 73 47 | 76.5 | 55 41 | 72 04 | 75.0 | 55 25 | 70 22 | 73.6 | | 237 |
| 58 | 122 | 57 30 | 78 47 | 80.5 | 57 19 | 76 57 | 79.0 | 57 07 | 75 09 | 77.4 | 56 53 | 73 22 | 75.9 | 56 38 | 71 36 | 74.5 | 56 21 | 69 51 | 73.0 | | 238 |
| 59 | 121 | 58 29 | 78 28 | 80.1 | 58 18 | 76 35 | 78.5 | 58 05 | 74 44 | 77.0 | 57 51 | 72 54 | 75.4 | 57 35 | 71 06 | 73.9 | 57 17 | 69 19 | 72.4 | | 239 |
| 60 | 120 | 59 28 | 78 08 | 79.7 | 59 16 | 76 12 | 78.1 | 59 03 | 74 18 | 76.4 | 58 48 | 72 25 | 74.8 | 58 32 | 70 34 | 73.3 | 58 13 | 68 45 | 71.7 | | 240 |
| 61 | 119 | 60 26 | 77 46 | 79.3 | 60 14 | 75 47 | 77.6 | 60 01 | 73 50 | 75.9 | 59 45 | 71 54 | 74.2 | 59 28 | 70 01 | 72.6 | 59 09 | 68 09 | 71.0 | | 241 |
| 62 | 118 | 61 25 | 77 23 | 78.9 | 61 12 | 75 21 | 77.1 | 60 58 | 73 20 | 75.3 | 60 42 | 71 21 | 73.6 | 60 24 | 69 25 | 71.9 | 60 05 | 67 31 | 70.3 | | 242 |
| 63 | 117 | 62 23 | 76 58 | 78.4 | 62 10 | 74 52 | 76.5 | 61 56 | 72 48 | 74.7 | 61 39 | 70 46 | 72.9 | 61 20 | 68 46 | 71.2 | 61 00 | 66 49 | 69.5 | | 243 |
| 64 | 116 | 63 22 | 76 31 | 77.9 | 63 08 | 74 21 | 76.0 | 62 53 | 72 13 | 74.1 | 62 35 | 70 08 | 72.2 | 62 16 | 68 05 | 70.4 | 61 55 | 66 05 | 68.6 | | 244 |
| 65 | 115 | 64 20 | 76 02 | 77.4 | 64 06 | 73 48 | 75.4 | 63 50 | 71 36 | 73.4 | 63 32 | 69 27 | 71.5 | 63 12 | 67 21 | 69.6 | 62 50 | 65 18 | 67.7 | | 245 |
| 66 | 114 | 65 18 | 75 31 | 76.8 | 65 03 | 73 12 | 74.7 | 64 47 | 70 56 | 72.6 | 64 28 | 68 43 | 70.6 | 64 07 | 66 34 | 68.7 | 63 44 | 64 27 | 66.8 | | 246 |
| 67 | 113 | 66 16 | 74 57 | 76.2 | 66 01 | 72 33 | 74.0 | 65 43 | 70 13 | 71.8 | 65 23 | 67 56 | 69.8 | 65 02 | 65 43 | 67.8 | 64 38 | 63 33 | 65.8 | | 247 |
| 68 | 112 | 67 14 | 74 20 | 75.5 | 66 58 | 71 51 | 73.2 | 66 40 | 69 26 | 71.0 | 66 19 | 67 05 | 68.8 | 65 56 | 64 48 | 66.7 | 65 32 | 62 35 | 64.7 | | 248 |
| 69 | 111 | 68 12 | 73 39 | 74.8 | 67 55 | 71 05 | 72.4 | 67 36 | 68 35 | 70.1 | 67 14 | 66 09 | 67.8 | 66 50 | 63 48 | 65.7 | 66 25 | 61 31 | 63.6 | | 249 |
| 70 | 110 | 69 09 | 72 55 | 74.0 | 68 51 | 70 15 | 71.5 | 68 31 | 67 40 | 69.1 | 68 09 | 65 09 | 66.7 | 67 44 | 62 44 | 64.5 | 67 17 | 60 23 | 62.3 | | 250 |
| 71 | 109 | 70 07 | 72 06 | 73.1 | 69 48 | 69 20 | 70.5 | 69 27 | 66 33 | 68.0 | 69 03 | 64 03 | 65.6 | 68 37 | 61 34 | 63.2 | 68 09 | 59 10 | 61.0 | | 251 |
| 72 | 108 | 71 03 | 71 13 | 72.2 | 70 44 | 68 20 | 69.4 | 70 21 | 65 33 | 66.8 | 69 57 | 62 52 | 64.3 | 69 29 | 60 17 | 61.9 | 69 00 | 57 50 | 59.6 | | 252 |
| 73 | 107 | 72 00 | 70 14 | 71.1 | 71 39 | 67 13 | 68.3 | 71 16 | 64 20 | 65.5 | 70 50 | 61 33 | 62.9 | 70 21 | 58 54 | 60.4 | 69 50 | 56 23 | 58.0 | | 253 |
| 74 | 106 | 72 56 | 69 08 | 70.0 | 72 34 | 65 59 | 67.0 | 72 09 | 62 59 | 64.1 | 71 42 | 60 07 | 61.4 | 71 12 | 57 24 | 58.8 | 70 40 | 54 49 | 56.4 | | 254 |
| 75 | 105 | 73 52 | 67 54 | 68.7 | 73 29 | 64 37 | 65.5 | 73 03 | 61 30 | 62.6 | 72 34 | 58 32 | 59.7 | 72 02 | 55 44 | 57.1 | 71 28 | 53 06 | 54.5 | | 255 |
| 76 | 104 | 74 48 | 66 31 | 67.3 | 74 23 | 63 05 | 64.0 | 73 55 | 59 51 | 60.8 | 73 24 | 56 47 | 57.9 | 72 51 | 53 55 | 55.1 | 72 16 | 51 13 | 52.6 | | 256 |
| 77 | 103 | 75 42 | 64 57 | 65.6 | 75 16 | 61 22 | 62.2 | 74 46 | 58 00 | 58.9 | 74 14 | 54 51 | 55.9 | 73 39 | 51 55 | 53.1 | 73 02 | 49 10 | 50.4 | | 257 |
| 78 | 102 | 76 36 | 63 11 | 63.7 | 76 08 | 59 26 | 60.2 | 75 37 | 55 57 | 56.8 | 75 02 | 52 42 | 53.6 | 74 26 | 49 42 | 50.8 | 73 47 | 46 56 | 48.1 | | 258 |
| 79 | 101 | 77 29 | 61 09 | 61.7 | 76 59 | 57 16 | 57.9 | 76 26 | 53 38 | 54.4 | 75 49 | 50 18 | 51.2 | 75 11 | 47 16 | 48.2 | 74 30 | 44 28 | 45.5 | | 259 |
| 80 | 100 | 78 21 | 58 49 | 59.3 | 77 49 | 54 44 | 55.3 | 77 13 | 51 01 | 51.7 | 76 35 | 47 38 | 48.4 | 75 54 | 44 34 | 45.4 | 75 11 | 41 47 | 42.7 | | 260 |
| 81 | 99 | 79 12 | 56 06 | 56.6 | 78 37 | 51 52 | 52.4 | 77 59 | 48 04 | 48.7 | 77 18 | 44 39 | 45.4 | 76 35 | 41 35 | 42.4 | 75 49 | 38 50 | 39.7 | | 261 |
| 82 | 98 | 80 01 | 52 56 | 53.4 | 79 23 | 48 35 | 49.1 | 78 42 | 44 43 | 45.3 | 77 59 | 41 18 | 41.9 | 77 13 | 38 17 | 39.0 | 76 26 | 35 36 | 36.4 | | 262 |
| 83 | 97 | 80 47 | 49 13 | 49.6 | 80 07 | 44 47 | 45.2 | 79 23 | 40 56 | 41.4 | 78 37 | 37 35 | 38.1 | 77 49 | 34 39 | 35.3 | 76 59 | 32 05 | 32.8 | | 263 |
| 84 | 96 | 81 31 | 44 51 | 45.2 | 80 47 | 40 24 | 40.8 | 80 01 | 36 38 | 37.1 | 79 12 | 33 25 | 33.9 | 78 21 | 30 40 | 31.2 | 77 29 | 28 16 | 28.8 | | 264 |
| 85 | 95 | 82 12 | 39 40 | 39.9 | 81 24 | 35 22 | 35.7 | 80 34 | 31 48 | 32.2 | 79 43 | 28 56 | 29.2 | 78 50 | 26 18 | 26.7 | 77 56 | 24 09 | 24.6 | | 265 |
| 86 | 94 | 82 48 | 33 34 | 33.8 | 81 57 | 29 36 | 29.8 | 81 04 | 26 24 | 26.7 | 80 09 | 23 46 | 24.1 | 79 14 | 21 35 | 21.9 | 78 18 | 19 44 | 20.1 | | 266 |
| 87 | 93 | 83 18 | 26 28 | 26.6 | 82 23 | 23 05 | 23.3 | 81 28 | 20 25 | 20.6 | 80 31 | 18 17 | 18.5 | 79 34 | 16 32 | 16.8 | 78 36 | 15 04 | 15.4 | | 267 |
| 88 | 92 | 83 41 | 18 22 | 18.5 | 82 43 | 15 52 | 16.0 | 81 45 | 13 57 | 14.1 | 80 47 | 12 25 | 12.6 | 79 48 | 11 12 | 11.4 | 78 49 | 10 11 | 10.4 | | 268 |
| 89 | 91 | 83 55 | 9 26 | 9.5 | 82 56 | 8 05 | 8.2 | 81 56 | 7 05 | 7.1 | 80 57 | 6 17 | 6.4 | 79 57 | 5 39 | 5.7 | 78 57 | 5 08 | 5.2 | | 269 |
| 90 | 90 | 84 00 | 0 00 | 0.0 | 83 00 | 0 00 | 0.0 | 82 00 | 0 00 | 0.0 | 81 00 | 0 00 | 0.0 | 80 00 | 0 00 | 0.0 | 79 00 | 0 00 | 0.0 | | 270 |

N. Lat: for LHA > 180° ... Zn = Z
for LHA < 180° ... Zn = 360° − Z

S. Lat: for LHA > 180° ... Zn = 180° − Z
for LHA < 180° ... Zn = 180° + Z

**SIGHT REDUCTION TABLE**

B: (−) for 90° < LHA < 270°
Dec:(−) for Lat. contrary name

Z₁: same sign as B
Z₂: (−) for F > 90°

| Lat. / A | | 12° | | | 13° | | | 14° | | | 15° | | | 16° | | | 17° | | | Lat. / A | |
|---|---|---|---|---|---|---|---|---|---|---|---|---|---|---|---|---|---|---|---|---|---|
| LHA/F | A | A/H | B/P | $Z_1/Z_2$ | A/H | B/P | $Z_1/Z_2$ | A/H | B/P | $Z_1/Z_2$ | A/H | B/P | $Z_1/Z_2$ | A/H | B/P | $Z_1/Z_2$ | A/H | B/P | $Z_1/Z_2$ | A | LHA |
| 0 | 180 | 0 00 | 78 00 | 90·0 | 0 00 | 77 00 | 90·0 | 0 00 | 76 00 | 90·0 | 0 00 | 75 00 | 90·0 | 0 00 | 74 00 | 90·0 | 0 00 | 73 00 | 90·0 | 180 | 360 |
| 1 | 179 | 0 59 | 78 00 | 89·8 | 0 58 | 77 00 | 89·8 | 0 58 | 76 00 | 89·8 | 0 58 | 75 00 | 89·7 | 0 58 | 74 00 | 89·7 | 0 57 | 73 00 | 89·7 | 181 | 359 |
| 2 | 178 | 1 57 | 78 00 | 89·6 | 1 57 | 77 00 | 89·5 | 1 56 | 76 00 | 89·5 | 1 56 | 74 59 | 89·5 | 1 55 | 73 59 | 89·4 | 1 55 | 72 59 | 89·4 | 182 | 358 |
| 3 | 177 | 2 56 | 77 59 | 89·4 | 2 55 | 76 58 | 89·3 | 2 55 | 75 59 | 89·3 | 2 54 | 74 59 | 89·2 | 2 53 | 73 59 | 89·2 | 2 52 | 72 59 | 89·1 | 183 | 357 |
| 4 | 176 | 3 55 | 77 58 | 89·2 | 3 54 | 76 58 | 89·1 | 3 53 | 75 58 | 89·0 | 3 52 | 74 58 | 89·0 | 3 51 | 73 58 | 88·9 | 3 49 | 72 58 | 88·9 | 184 | 356 |
| 5 | 175 | 4 53 | 77 57 | 89·0 | 4 52 | 76 57 | 88·9 | 4 51 | 75 57 | 88·8 | 4 50 | 74 57 | 88·7 | 4 48 | 73 57 | 88·6 | 4 47 | 72 56 | 88·5 | 185 | 355 |
| 6 | 174 | 5 52 | 77 56 | 88·7 | 5 51 | 76 56 | 88·6 | 5 49 | 75 56 | 88·5 | 5 48 | 74 55 | 88·4 | 5 46 | 73 55 | 88·3 | 5 44 | 72 55 | 88·2 | 186 | 354 |
| 7 | 173 | 6 51 | 77 55 | 88·5 | 6 49 | 76 54 | 88·4 | 6 47 | 75 54 | 88·3 | 6 46 | 74 54 | 88·2 | 6 44 | 73 53 | 88·1 | 6 42 | 72 53 | 87·9 | 187 | 353 |
| 8 | 172 | 7 49 | 77 53 | 88·3 | 7 48 | 76 53 | 88·2 | 7 46 | 75 52 | 88·1 | 7 44 | 74 52 | 87·9 | 7 41 | 73 51 | 87·8 | 7 39 | 72 51 | 87·6 | 188 | 352 |
| 9 | 171 | 8 48 | 77 51 | 88·1 | 8 46 | 76 51 | 88·0 | 8 44 | 75 50 | 87·8 | 8 41 | 74 49 | 87·7 | 8 39 | 73 49 | 87·5 | 8 36 | 72 48 | 87·3 | 189 | 351 |
| 10 | 170 | 9 47 | 77 49 | 87·9 | 9 44 | 76 48 | 87·7 | 9 42 | 75 48 | 87·6 | 9 39 | 74 47 | 87·4 | 9 37 | 73 46 | 87·2 | 9 34 | 72 45 | 87·0 | 190 | 350 |
| 11 | 169 | 10 45 | 77 47 | 87·7 | 10 43 | 76 46 | 87·5 | 10 40 | 75 45 | 87·3 | 10 37 | 74 44 | 87·1 | 10 34 | 73 43 | 86·9 | 10 31 | 72 42 | 86·7 | 191 | 349 |
| 12 | 168 | 11 44 | 77 44 | 87·5 | 11 41 | 76 43 | 87·3 | 11 38 | 75 42 | 87·1 | 11 35 | 74 41 | 86·9 | 11 32 | 73 40 | 86·6 | 11 28 | 72 39 | 86·4 | 192 | 348 |
| 13 | 167 | 12 43 | 77 42 | 87·3 | 12 40 | 76 40 | 87·0 | 12 36 | 75 39 | 86·8 | 12 33 | 74 37 | 86·6 | 12 29 | 73 36 | 86·4 | 12 25 | 72 35 | 86·1 | 193 | 347 |
| 14 | 166 | 13 41 | 77 39 | 87·0 | 13 38 | 76 37 | 86·8 | 13 35 | 75 35 | 86·6 | 13 31 | 74 34 | 86·3 | 13 27 | 73 32 | 86·1 | 13 23 | 72 31 | 85·8 | 194 | 346 |
| 15 | 165 | 14 40 | 77 35 | 86·8 | 14 36 | 76 33 | 86·6 | 14 33 | 75 32 | 86·3 | 14 29 | 74 30 | 86·0 | 14 24 | 73 28 | 85·8 | 14 20 | 72 26 | 85·5 | 195 | 345 |
| 16 | 164 | 15 38 | 77 32 | 86·6 | 15 35 | 76 30 | 86·3 | 15 31 | 75 28 | 86·0 | 15 26 | 74 25 | 85·8 | 15 22 | 73 23 | 85·5 | 15 17 | 72 21 | 85·2 | 196 | 344 |
| 17 | 163 | 16 37 | 77 28 | 86·4 | 16 33 | 76 26 | 86·1 | 16 29 | 75 23 | 85·8 | 16 24 | 74 21 | 85·5 | 16 19 | 73 19 | 85·2 | 16 14 | 72 16 | 84·9 | 197 | 343 |
| 18 | 162 | 17 36 | 77 24 | 86·1 | 17 31 | 76 21 | 85·8 | 17 27 | 75 19 | 85·5 | 17 22 | 74 16 | 85·2 | 17 17 | 73 13 | 84·9 | 17 11 | 72 11 | 84·6 | 198 | 342 |
| 19 | 161 | 18 34 | 77 20 | 85·9 | 18 30 | 76 17 | 85·6 | 18 25 | 75 14 | 85·2 | 18 20 | 74 11 | 84·9 | 18 14 | 73 08 | 84·6 | 18 08 | 72 05 | 84·3 | 199 | 341 |
| 20 | 160 | 19 33 | 77 15 | 85·7 | 19 28 | 76 12 | 85·3 | 19 23 | 75 08 | 85·0 | 19 17 | 74 05 | 84·6 | 19 12 | 73 02 | 84·3 | 19 05 | 71 59 | 83·9 | 200 | 340 |
| 21 | 159 | 20 31 | 77 10 | 85·4 | 20 26 | 76 07 | 85·1 | 20 21 | 75 03 | 84·7 | 20 15 | 73 59 | 84·3 | 20 09 | 72 56 | 84·0 | 20 03 | 71 52 | 83·6 | 201 | 339 |
| 22 | 158 | 21 30 | 77 05 | 85·2 | 21 24 | 76 01 | 84·8 | 21 19 | 74 57 | 84·4 | 21 13 | 73 53 | 84·0 | 21 06 | 72 49 | 83·6 | 21 00 | 71 45 | 83·3 | 202 | 338 |
| 23 | 157 | 22 28 | 77 00 | 85·0 | 22 23 | 75 55 | 84·5 | 22 17 | 74 51 | 84·1 | 22 10 | 73 46 | 83·7 | 22 04 | 72 42 | 83·3 | 21 56 | 71 38 | 82·9 | 203 | 337 |
| 24 | 156 | 23 27 | 76 54 | 84·7 | 23 21 | 75 49 | 84·3 | 23 15 | 74 44 | 83·9 | 23 08 | 73 39 | 83·4 | 23 01 | 72 34 | 83·0 | 22 53 | 71 30 | 82·6 | 204 | 336 |
| 25 | 155 | 24 25 | 76 48 | 84·5 | 24 19 | 75 43 | 84·0 | 24 13 | 74 37 | 83·6 | 24 06 | 73 32 | 83·1 | 23 58 | 72 27 | 82·7 | 23 50 | 71 22 | 82·2 | 205 | 335 |
| 26 | 154 | 25 23 | 76 42 | 84·2 | 25 17 | 75 36 | 83·7 | 25 10 | 74 30 | 83·3 | 25 03 | 73 24 | 82·8 | 24 55 | 72 18 | 82·3 | 24 47 | 71 13 | 81·9 | 206 | 334 |
| 27 | 153 | 26 22 | 76 35 | 84·0 | 26 15 | 75 28 | 83·5 | 26 08 | 74 22 | 83·0 | 26 01 | 73 16 | 82·5 | 25 52 | 72 10 | 82·0 | 25 44 | 71 04 | 81·5 | 207 | 333 |
| 28 | 152 | 27 20 | 76 28 | 83·7 | 27 13 | 75 21 | 83·2 | 27 06 | 74 14 | 82·7 | 26 58 | 73 07 | 82·2 | 26 50 | 72 00 | 81·7 | 26 41 | 70 54 | 81·2 | 208 | 332 |
| 29 | 151 | 28 18 | 76 20 | 83·4 | 28 11 | 75 13 | 82·9 | 28 04 | 74 05 | 82·4 | 27 55 | 72 58 | 81·8 | 27 47 | 71 51 | 81·3 | 27 37 | 70 44 | 80·8 | 209 | 331 |
| 30 | 150 | 29 17 | 76 13 | 83·2 | 29 09 | 75 04 | 82·6 | 29 01 | 73 56 | 82·0 | 28 53 | 72 48 | 81·5 | 28 44 | 71 41 | 81·0 | 28 34 | 70 33 | 80·4 | 210 | 330 |
| 31 | 149 | 30 15 | 76 04 | 82·9 | 30 07 | 74 56 | 82·3 | 29 59 | 73 47 | 81·7 | 29 50 | 72 38 | 81·2 | 29 41 | 71 30 | 80·6 | 29 30 | 70 22 | 80·0 | 211 | 329 |
| 32 | 148 | 31 13 | 75 56 | 82·6 | 31 05 | 74 46 | 82·0 | 30 57 | 73 37 | 81·4 | 30 47 | 72 28 | 80·8 | 30 37 | 71 19 | 80·2 | 30 27 | 70 11 | 79·6 | 212 | 328 |
| 33 | 147 | 32 11 | 75 47 | 82·3 | 32 03 | 74 37 | 81·7 | 31 54 | 73 27 | 81·0 | 31 44 | 72 17 | 80·5 | 31 34 | 71 07 | 79·9 | 31 23 | 69 58 | 79·2 | 213 | 327 |
| 34 | 146 | 33 10 | 75 37 | 82·0 | 33 01 | 74 26 | 81·4 | 32 52 | 73 16 | 80·7 | 32 42 | 72 05 | 80·1 | 32 31 | 70 55 | 79·5 | 32 20 | 69 45 | 78·8 | 214 | 326 |
| 35 | 145 | 34 08 | 75 27 | 81·7 | 33 59 | 74 16 | 81·0 | 33 49 | 73 04 | 80·4 | 33 39 | 71 53 | 79·7 | 33 28 | 70 42 | 79·1 | 33 16 | 69 32 | 78·4 | 215 | 325 |
| 36 | 144 | 35 06 | 75 17 | 81·4 | 34 56 | 74 04 | 80·7 | 34 46 | 72 52 | 80·0 | 34 36 | 71 40 | 79·4 | 34 24 | 70 29 | 78·7 | 34 12 | 69 18 | 78·0 | 216 | 324 |
| 37 | 143 | 36 04 | 75 06 | 81·1 | 35 54 | 73 53 | 80·4 | 35 44 | 72 40 | 79·7 | 35 33 | 71 27 | 79·0 | 35 21 | 70 15 | 78·3 | 35 08 | 69 03 | 77·6 | 217 | 323 |
| 38 | 142 | 37 02 | 74 54 | 80·8 | 36 52 | 73 40 | 80·0 | 36 41 | 72 27 | 79·3 | 36 29 | 71 13 | 78·6 | 36 17 | 70 00 | 77·8 | 36 04 | 68 48 | 77·1 | 218 | 322 |
| 39 | 141 | 38 00 | 74 42 | 80·4 | 37 49 | 73 27 | 79·7 | 37 38 | 72 13 | 78·9 | 37 26 | 70 59 | 78·2 | 37 13 | 69 45 | 77·4 | 37 00 | 68 32 | 76·7 | 219 | 321 |
| 40 | 140 | 38 57 | 74 30 | 80·1 | 38 47 | 73 14 | 79·3 | 38 35 | 71 58 | 78·5 | 38 23 | 70 43 | 77·7 | 38 10 | 69 29 | 77·0 | 37 56 | 68 15 | 76·2 | 220 | 320 |
| 41 | 139 | 39 55 | 74 16 | 79·8 | 39 44 | 72 59 | 78·9 | 39 32 | 71 43 | 78·1 | 39 19 | 70 27 | 77·3 | 39 06 | 69 12 | 76·5 | 38 51 | 67 57 | 75·7 | 221 | 319 |
| 42 | 138 | 40 53 | 74 02 | 79·4 | 40 41 | 72 45 | 78·5 | 40 29 | 71 27 | 77·7 | 40 16 | 70 10 | 76·9 | 40 02 | 68 54 | 76·1 | 39 47 | 67 38 | 75·3 | 222 | 318 |
| 43 | 137 | 41 51 | 73 48 | 79·0 | 41 39 | 72 29 | 78·2 | 41 26 | 71 11 | 77·3 | 41 12 | 69 53 | 76·4 | 40 58 | 68 35 | 75·6 | 40 42 | 67 19 | 74·7 | 223 | 317 |
| 44 | 136 | 42 48 | 73 32 | 78·6 | 42 36 | 72 12 | 77·7 | 42 23 | 70 53 | 76·9 | 42 09 | 69 34 | 76·0 | 41 54 | 68 16 | 75·1 | 41 38 | 66 58 | 74·2 | 224 | 316 |
| 45 | 135 | 43 46 | 73 16 | 78·3 | 43 33 | 71 55 | 77·3 | 43 19 | 70 35 | 76·4 | 43 05 | 69 15 | 75·5 | 42 49 | 67 56 | 74·6 | 42 33 | 66 37 | 73·7 | 225 | 315 |

| Lat./A LHA | F | 12° A/H | 12° B/P | 12° $Z_1/Z_2$ | 13° A/H | 13° B/P | 13° $Z_1/Z_2$ | 14° A/H | 14° B/P | 14° $Z_1/Z_2$ | 15° A/H | 15° B/P | 15° $Z_1/Z_2$ | 16° A/H | 16° B/P | 16° $Z_1/Z_2$ | 17° A/H | 17° B/P | 17° $Z_1/Z_2$ | Lat./A LHA | LHA |
|---|---|---|---|---|---|---|---|---|---|---|---|---|---|---|---|---|---|---|---|---|---|
| 45 | 135 | 43 46 | 73 16 | 78·3 | 43 33 | 71 55 | 77·3 | 43 19 | 70 35 | 76·4 | 43 05 | 69 15 | 75·5 | 42 49 | 67 56 | 74·6 | 42 33 | 66 37 | 73·7 | 225 | 315 |
| 46 | 134 | 44 43 | 72 59 | 77·8 | 44 30 | 71 37 | 76·9 | 44 16 | 70 15 | 75·9 | 44 01 | 68 54 | 75·0 | 43 45 | 67 34 | 74·1 | 43 28 | 66 15 | 73·2 | 226 | 314 |
| 47 | 133 | 45 40 | 72 41 | 77·4 | 45 27 | 71 18 | 76·4 | 45 12 | 69 55 | 75·5 | 44 57 | 68 33 | 74·5 | 44 40 | 67 12 | 73·5 | 44 23 | 65 51 | 72·6 | 227 | 313 |
| 48 | 132 | 46 38 | 72 23 | 77·0 | 46 24 | 70 58 | 76·0 | 46 09 | 69 34 | 75·0 | 45 53 | 68 11 | 74·0 | 45 35 | 66 48 | 73·0 | 45 17 | 65 27 | 72·0 | 228 | 312 |
| 49 | 131 | 47 35 | 72 03 | 76·5 | 47 20 | 70 37 | 75·5 | 47 05 | 69 11 | 74·4 | 46 48 | 67 47 | 73·4 | 46 30 | 66 23 | 72·4 | 46 12 | 65 01 | 71·4 | 229 | 311 |
| 50 | 130 | 48 32 | 71 42 | 76·1 | 48 17 | 70 15 | 75·0 | 48 01 | 68 48 | 73·9 | 47 44 | 67 22 | 72·9 | 47 25 | 65 58 | 71·8 | 47 06 | 64 34 | 70·8 | 230 | 310 |
| 51 | 129 | 49 29 | 71 20 | 75·6 | 49 13 | 69 51 | 74·5 | 48 57 | 68 23 | 73·4 | 48 39 | 66 56 | 72·3 | 48 20 | 65 30 | 71·2 | 48 00 | 64 05 | 70·1 | 231 | 309 |
| 52 | 128 | 50 25 | 70 57 | 75·1 | 50 09 | 69 27 | 73·9 | 49 52 | 67 57 | 72·8 | 49 34 | 66 29 | 71·7 | 49 15 | 65 02 | 70·6 | 48 54 | 63 35 | 69·5 | 232 | 308 |
| 53 | 127 | 51 22 | 70 33 | 74·6 | 51 06 | 69 01 | 73·4 | 50 48 | 67 30 | 72·2 | 50 29 | 66 00 | 71·0 | 50 09 | 64 31 | 69·9 | 49 48 | 63 04 | 68·8 | 233 | 307 |
| 54 | 126 | 52 19 | 70 07 | 74·0 | 52 02 | 68 33 | 72·8 | 51 43 | 67 01 | 71·6 | 51 24 | 65 30 | 70·4 | 51 03 | 64 00 | 69·2 | 50 41 | 62 31 | 68·1 | 234 | 306 |
| 55 | 125 | 53 15 | 69 40 | 73·5 | 52 58 | 68 04 | 72·2 | 52 38 | 66 30 | 70·9 | 52 18 | 64 58 | 69·7 | 51 57 | 63 26 | 68·5 | 51 34 | 61 56 | 67·3 | 235 | 305 |
| 56 | 124 | 54 11 | 69 11 | 72·9 | 53 53 | 67 34 | 71·6 | 53 33 | 65 58 | 70·3 | 53 12 | 64 24 | 69·0 | 52 50 | 62 51 | 67·8 | 52 27 | 61 20 | 66·6 | 236 | 304 |
| 57 | 123 | 55 07 | 68 41 | 72·2 | 54 48 | 67 02 | 70·9 | 54 28 | 65 24 | 69·6 | 54 06 | 63 48 | 68·3 | 53 43 | 62 14 | 67·0 | 53 19 | 60 42 | 65·8 | 237 | 303 |
| 58 | 122 | 56 03 | 68 09 | 71·6 | 55 43 | 66 28 | 70·2 | 55 22 | 64 48 | 68·8 | 55 00 | 63 11 | 67·5 | 54 36 | 61 35 | 66·2 | 54 12 | 60 01 | 64·9 | 238 | 302 |
| 59 | 121 | 56 59 | 67 34 | 70·9 | 56 38 | 65 51 | 69·5 | 56 16 | 64 10 | 68·1 | 55 53 | 62 31 | 66·7 | 55 29 | 60 54 | 65·4 | 55 03 | 59 18 | 64·1 | 239 | 301 |
| 60 | 120 | 57 54 | 66 58 | 70·2 | 57 33 | 65 13 | 68·7 | 57 10 | 63 30 | 67·3 | 56 46 | 61 49 | 65·9 | 56 21 | 60 10 | 64·5 | 55 55 | 58 33 | 63·1 | 240 | 300 |
| 61 | 119 | 58 49 | 66 20 | 69·4 | 58 29 | 64 32 | 67·9 | 58 04 | 62 47 | 66·4 | 57 39 | 61 04 | 65·0 | 57 13 | 59 24 | 63·6 | 56 46 | 57 46 | 62·2 | 241 | 299 |
| 62 | 118 | 59 44 | 65 38 | 68·6 | 59 21 | 63 49 | 67·1 | 58 57 | 62 02 | 65·5 | 58 31 | 60 17 | 64·0 | 58 05 | 58 35 | 62·6 | 57 36 | 56 56 | 61·2 | 242 | 298 |
| 63 | 117 | 60 38 | 64 55 | 67·8 | 60 15 | 63 03 | 66·2 | 59 50 | 61 13 | 64·6 | 59 23 | 59 27 | 63·1 | 58 55 | 57 43 | 61·6 | 58 26 | 56 03 | 60·2 | 243 | 297 |
| 64 | 116 | 61 32 | 64 08 | 66·9 | 61 08 | 62 14 | 65·2 | 60 42 | 60 22 | 63·6 | 60 15 | 58 34 | 62·0 | 59 46 | 56 49 | 60·5 | 59 16 | 55 06 | 59·1 | 244 | 296 |
| 65 | 115 | 62 26 | 63 18 | 66·0 | 62 01 | 61 21 | 64·2 | 61 34 | 59 28 | 62·6 | 61 06 | 57 37 | 61·0 | 60 36 | 55 51 | 59·4 | 60 05 | 54 07 | 57·9 | 245 | 295 |
| 66 | 114 | 63 20 | 62 25 | 65·0 | 62 53 | 60 25 | 63·2 | 62 26 | 58 30 | 61·5 | 61 56 | 56 37 | 59·8 | 61 25 | 54 49 | 58·2 | 60 53 | 53 04 | 56·7 | 246 | 294 |
| 67 | 113 | 64 13 | 61 27 | 63·9 | 63 45 | 59 25 | 62·1 | 63 16 | 57 27 | 60·3 | 62 46 | 55 34 | 58·6 | 62 14 | 53 44 | 57·0 | 61 41 | 51 57 | 55·4 | 247 | 293 |
| 68 | 112 | 65 05 | 60 26 | 62·8 | 64 37 | 58 21 | 60·9 | 64 07 | 56 21 | 59·1 | 63 35 | 54 25 | 57·4 | 63 02 | 52 34 | 55·7 | 62 27 | 50 47 | 54·1 | 248 | 292 |
| 69 | 111 | 65 57 | 59 20 | 61·6 | 65 27 | 57 13 | 59·6 | 64 56 | 55 10 | 57·8 | 64 23 | 53 13 | 56·0 | 63 49 | 51 20 | 54·3 | 63 14 | 49 32 | 52·7 | 249 | 291 |
| 70 | 110 | 66 48 | 58 08 | 60·3 | 66 18 | 55 59 | 58·3 | 65 45 | 53 55 | 56·4 | 65 11 | 51 55 | 54·6 | 64 36 | 50 02 | 52·9 | 63 59 | 48 12 | 51·2 | 250 | 290 |
| 71 | 109 | 67 39 | 56 52 | 59·0 | 67 07 | 54 40 | 56·8 | 66 33 | 52 35 | 54·9 | 65 58 | 50 33 | 53·1 | 65 21 | 48 38 | 51·3 | 64 43 | 46 48 | 49·7 | 251 | 289 |
| 72 | 108 | 68 29 | 55 29 | 57·4 | 67 55 | 53 14 | 55·3 | 67 20 | 51 06 | 53·3 | 66 44 | 49 04 | 51·5 | 66 06 | 47 08 | 49·7 | 65 26 | 45 18 | 48·0 | 252 | 288 |
| 73 | 107 | 69 18 | 53 59 | 55·8 | 68 43 | 51 42 | 53·7 | 68 07 | 49 33 | 51·6 | 67 29 | 47 30 | 49·8 | 66 49 | 45 33 | 48·0 | 66 08 | 43 43 | 46·3 | 253 | 287 |
| 74 | 106 | 70 06 | 52 22 | 54·1 | 69 30 | 50 03 | 51·9 | 68 52 | 47 52 | 49·8 | 68 12 | 45 49 | 47·9 | 67 31 | 43 52 | 46·1 | 66 49 | 42 02 | 44·4 | 254 | 286 |
| 75 | 105 | 70 53 | 50 36 | 52·2 | 70 15 | 48 16 | 50·0 | 69 36 | 46 04 | 47·9 | 68 55 | 44 00 | 46·0 | 68 12 | 42 04 | 44·2 | 67 29 | 40 15 | 42·5 | 255 | 285 |
| 76 | 104 | 71 38 | 48 42 | 50·2 | 70 59 | 46 20 | 47·9 | 70 18 | 44 08 | 45·9 | 69 36 | 42 05 | 43·9 | 68 52 | 40 00 | 42·1 | 68 07 | 38 21 | 40·5 | 256 | 284 |
| 77 | 103 | 72 23 | 46 37 | 48·0 | 71 42 | 44 15 | 45·7 | 70 59 | 42 03 | 43·7 | 70 15 | 40 01 | 41·7 | 69 30 | 38 07 | 39·9 | 68 43 | 36 21 | 38·3 | 257 | 283 |
| 78 | 102 | 73 06 | 44 22 | 45·6 | 72 23 | 42 00 | 43·4 | 71 38 | 39 49 | 41·3 | 70 53 | 37 49 | 39·4 | 70 06 | 35 57 | 37·6 | 69 18 | 34 13 | 36·0 | 258 | 282 |
| 79 | 101 | 73 47 | 41 55 | 43·1 | 73 02 | 39 34 | 40·8 | 72 15 | 37 26 | 38·8 | 71 28 | 35 27 | 36·9 | 70 41 | 33 31 | 35·2 | 69 50 | 31 57 | 33·6 | 259 | 281 |
| 80 | 100 | 74 26 | 39 15 | 40·3 | 73 39 | 36 57 | 38·1 | 72 51 | 34 51 | 36·1 | 72 02 | 32 57 | 34·3 | 71 12 | 31 12 | 32·6 | 70 21 | 29 36 | 31·1 | 260 | 280 |
| 81 | 99 | 75 02 | 36 21 | 37·3 | 74 14 | 34 07 | 35·1 | 73 24 | 32 06 | 33·2 | 72 34 | 30 17 | 31·5 | 71 42 | 28 37 | 29·9 | 70 50 | 27 06 | 28·4 | 261 | 279 |
| 82 | 98 | 75 37 | 33 13 | 34·1 | 74 46 | 31 05 | 32·0 | 73 55 | 29 10 | 30·2 | 73 03 | 27 27 | 28·5 | 72 09 | 25 53 | 27·0 | 71 16 | 24 29 | 25·7 | 262 | 278 |
| 83 | 97 | 76 08 | 29 50 | 30·6 | 75 16 | 27 50 | 28·6 | 74 23 | 26 03 | 26·9 | 73 29 | 24 27 | 25·4 | 72 34 | 23 02 | 24·0 | 71 39 | 21 44 | 22·8 | 263 | 277 |
| 84 | 96 | 76 36 | 26 11 | 26·8 | 75 42 | 24 21 | 25·0 | 74 48 | 22 45 | 23·5 | 73 52 | 21 19 | 22·1 | 72 56 | 20 05 | 20·9 | 72 00 | 18 53 | 19·8 | 264 | 276 |
| 85 | 95 | 77 01 | 22 18 | 22·8 | 76 05 | 20 41 | 21·3 | 75 09 | 19 15 | 19·9 | 74 12 | 18 01 | 18·7 | 73 15 | 16 54 | 17·6 | 72 18 | 15 51 | 16·7 | 265 | 275 |
| 86 | 94 | 77 22 | 18 10 | 18·6 | 76 25 | 16 49 | 17·3 | 75 27 | 15 33 | 16·1 | 74 29 | 14 36 | 15·1 | 73 31 | 13 40 | 14·2 | 72 33 | 12 51 | 13·5 | 266 | 274 |
| 87 | 93 | 77 38 | 13 50 | 14·1 | 76 40 | 12 46 | 13·1 | 75 41 | 11 51 | 12·2 | 74 43 | 11 03 | 11·4 | 73 44 | 10 21 | 10·8 | 72 45 | 9 43 | 10·2 | 267 | 273 |
| 88 | 92 | 77 50 | 9 19 | 9·5 | 76 51 | 8 36 | 8·8 | 75 52 | 7 53 | 8·2 | 74 52 | 7 25 | 7·7 | 73 53 | 6 56 | 7·2 | 72 53 | 6 31 | 6·8 | 268 | 272 |
| 89 | 91 | 77 58 | 4 42 | 4·8 | 76 58 | 4 19 | 4·4 | 75 58 | 4 00 | 4·1 | 74 58 | 3 44 | 3·9 | 73 58 | 3 29 | 3·6 | 72 58 | 3 16 | 3·4 | 269 | 271 |
| 90 | 90 | 78 00 | 0 00 | 0·0 | 77 00 | 0 00 | 0·0 | 76 00 | 0 00 | 0·0 | 75 00 | 0 00 | 0·0 | 74 00 | 0 00 | 0·0 | 73 00 | 0 00 | 0·0 | 270 | 270 |

N. Lat.: for LHA > 180° ... $Z_n = Z$
for LHA < 180° ... $Z_n = 360° − Z$

S. Lat.: for LHA > 180° ... $Z_n = 180° − Z$
for LHA < 180° ... $Z_n = 180° + Z$

## SIGHT REDUCTION TABLE

B: (−) for 90° < LHA < 270°
Dec:(−) for Lat. contrary name

Z₁: same sign as B
Z₂: (−) for F > 90°

| LHA/F | 18° A/H | 18° B/P | 18° Z₁/Z₂ | 19° A/H | 19° B/P | 19° Z₁/Z₂ | 20° A/H | 20° B/P | 20° Z₁/Z₂ | 21° A/H | 21° B/P | 21° Z₁/Z₂ | 22° A/H | 22° B/P | 22° Z₁/Z₂ | 23° A/H | 23° B/P | 23° Z₁/Z₂ | Lat./A | LHA |
|---|---|---|---|---|---|---|---|---|---|---|---|---|---|---|---|---|---|---|---|---|
| 0 / 180 | 0 00 | 72 00 | 90·0 | 0 00 | 71 00 | 90·0 | 0 00 | 70 00 | 90·0 | 0 00 | 69 00 | 90·0 | 0 00 | 68 00 | 90·0 | 0 00 | 67 00 | 90·0 | 180 | 360 |
| 1 / 179 | 0 57 | 72 00 | 89·7 | 0 57 | 71 00 | 89·7 | 0 56 | 70 00 | 89·7 | 0 56 | 69 00 | 89·6 | 0 56 | 68 00 | 89·6 | 0 55 | 67 00 | 89·6 | 181 | 359 |
| 2 / 178 | 1 54 | 71 59 | 89·4 | 1 53 | 70 59 | 89·3 | 1 53 | 69 59 | 89·3 | 1 52 | 68 59 | 89·3 | 1 51 | 67 59 | 89·3 | 1 50 | 66 59 | 89·2 | 182 | 358 |
| 3 / 177 | 2 51 | 71 59 | 89·1 | 2 50 | 70 59 | 89·0 | 2 49 | 69 59 | 89·0 | 2 48 | 68 58 | 89·0 | 2 47 | 67 58 | 88·9 | 2 46 | 66 58 | 88·8 | 183 | 357 |
| 4 / 176 | 3 48 | 71 58 | 88·8 | 3 47 | 70 57 | 88·7 | 3 46 | 69 57 | 88·6 | 3 44 | 68 57 | 88·6 | 3 42 | 67 57 | 88·5 | 3 41 | 66 57 | 88·4 | 184 | 356 |
| 5 / 175 | 4 45 | 71 56 | 88·5 | 4 44 | 70 56 | 88·4 | 4 42 | 69 56 | 88·3 | 4 40 | 68 56 | 88·2 | 4 38 | 67 55 | 88·1 | 4 36 | 66 55 | 88·0 | 185 | 355 |
| 6 / 174 | 5 42 | 71 54 | 88·1 | 5 40 | 70 54 | 88·0 | 5 38 | 69 54 | 87·9 | 5 36 | 68 54 | 87·8 | 5 34 | 67 53 | 87·7 | 5 31 | 66 53 | 87·6 | 186 | 354 |
| 7 / 173 | 6 39 | 71 52 | 87·8 | 6 37 | 70 52 | 87·7 | 6 35 | 69 52 | 87·6 | 6 32 | 68 51 | 87·5 | 6 29 | 67 51 | 87·4 | 6 26 | 66 51 | 87·3 | 187 | 353 |
| 8 / 172 | 7 36 | 71 50 | 87·5 | 7 34 | 70 50 | 87·3 | 7 31 | 69 49 | 87·2 | 7 28 | 68 49 | 87·1 | 7 25 | 67 48 | 87·0 | 7 22 | 66 48 | 86·9 | 188 | 352 |
| 9 / 171 | 8 33 | 71 47 | 87·2 | 8 30 | 70 47 | 87·0 | 8 27 | 69 46 | 86·9 | 8 24 | 68 46 | 86·8 | 8 20 | 67 45 | 86·6 | 8 17 | 66 45 | 86·5 | 189 | 351 |
| 10 / 170 | 9 30 | 71 44 | 86·9 | 9 27 | 70 44 | 86·7 | 9 23 | 69 43 | 86·5 | 9 20 | 68 42 | 86·4 | 9 16 | 67 42 | 86·2 | 9 12 | 66 41 | 86·1 | 190 | 350 |
| 11 / 169 | 10 27 | 71 41 | 86·6 | 10 24 | 70 40 | 86·4 | 10 20 | 69 39 | 86·2 | 10 16 | 68 39 | 86·0 | 10 11 | 67 38 | 85·8 | 10 07 | 66 37 | 85·7 | 191 | 349 |
| 12 / 168 | 11 24 | 71 37 | 86·2 | 11 20 | 70 36 | 86·0 | 11 16 | 69 35 | 85·8 | 11 12 | 68 34 | 85·6 | 11 07 | 67 33 | 85·4 | 11 02 | 66 32 | 85·3 | 192 | 348 |
| 13 / 167 | 12 21 | 71 33 | 85·9 | 12 17 | 70 32 | 85·7 | 12 12 | 69 31 | 85·5 | 12 07 | 68 30 | 85·3 | 12 02 | 67 29 | 85·1 | 11 57 | 66 28 | 84·8 | 193 | 347 |
| 14 / 166 | 13 18 | 71 29 | 85·6 | 13 13 | 70 28 | 85·4 | 13 08 | 69 26 | 85·1 | 13 03 | 68 25 | 84·9 | 12 58 | 67 24 | 84·7 | 12 52 | 66 22 | 84·4 | 194 | 346 |
| 15 / 165 | 14 15 | 71 24 | 85·3 | 14 10 | 70 23 | 85·0 | 14 05 | 69 21 | 84·8 | 13 59 | 68 20 | 84·5 | 13 53 | 67 18 | 84·3 | 13 47 | 66 17 | 84·0 | 195 | 345 |
| 16 / 164 | 15 12 | 71 19 | 84·9 | 15 06 | 70 18 | 84·7 | 15 01 | 69 16 | 84·4 | 14 55 | 68 14 | 84·1 | 14 48 | 67 12 | 83·9 | 14 42 | 66 10 | 83·6 | 196 | 344 |
| 17 / 163 | 16 09 | 71 14 | 84·6 | 16 03 | 70 12 | 84·3 | 15 57 | 69 10 | 84·0 | 15 50 | 68 08 | 83·7 | 15 44 | 67 06 | 83·5 | 15 37 | 66 04 | 83·2 | 197 | 343 |
| 18 / 162 | 17 05 | 71 08 | 84·3 | 16 59 | 70 06 | 84·0 | 16 53 | 69 03 | 83·7 | 16 46 | 68 01 | 83·4 | 16 39 | 66 59 | 83·1 | 16 32 | 65 57 | 82·8 | 198 | 342 |
| 19 / 161 | 18 02 | 71 02 | 83·9 | 17 56 | 69 59 | 83·6 | 17 49 | 68 57 | 83·3 | 17 42 | 67 54 | 83·0 | 17 34 | 66 52 | 82·7 | 17 26 | 65 49 | 82·3 | 199 | 341 |
| 20 / 160 | 18 59 | 70 56 | 83·6 | 18 52 | 69 53 | 83·2 | 18 45 | 68 50 | 82·9 | 18 37 | 67 47 | 82·6 | 18 29 | 66 44 | 82·2 | 18 21 | 65 41 | 81·9 | 200 | 340 |
| 21 / 159 | 19 56 | 70 49 | 83·2 | 19 48 | 69 45 | 82·9 | 19 41 | 68 42 | 82·5 | 19 33 | 67 39 | 82·2 | 19 24 | 66 36 | 81·8 | 19 16 | 65 33 | 81·5 | 201 | 339 |
| 22 / 158 | 20 52 | 70 41 | 82·9 | 20 45 | 69 38 | 82·5 | 20 37 | 68 34 | 82·1 | 20 28 | 67 31 | 81·8 | 20 20 | 66 27 | 81·4 | 20 10 | 65 24 | 81·0 | 202 | 338 |
| 23 / 157 | 21 49 | 70 33 | 82·5 | 21 41 | 69 29 | 82·1 | 21 32 | 68 26 | 81·7 | 21 24 | 67 22 | 81·4 | 21 14 | 66 18 | 81·0 | 21 05 | 65 15 | 80·6 | 203 | 337 |
| 24 / 156 | 22 45 | 70 25 | 82·2 | 22 37 | 69 21 | 81·8 | 22 28 | 68 17 | 81·3 | 22 19 | 67 12 | 80·9 | 22 09 | 66 09 | 80·5 | 21 59 | 65 05 | 80·1 | 204 | 336 |
| 25 / 155 | 23 42 | 70 17 | 81·8 | 23 33 | 69 12 | 81·4 | 23 24 | 68 07 | 80·9 | 23 14 | 67 03 | 80·5 | 23 04 | 65 58 | 80·1 | 22 54 | 64 54 | 79·7 | 205 | 335 |
| 26 / 154 | 24 38 | 70 07 | 81·4 | 24 29 | 69 02 | 81·0 | 24 20 | 67 57 | 80·5 | 24 09 | 66 52 | 80·1 | 23 59 | 65 48 | 79·6 | 23 48 | 64 43 | 79·2 | 206 | 334 |
| 27 / 153 | 25 35 | 69 58 | 81·1 | 25 25 | 68 53 | 80·6 | 25 15 | 67 47 | 80·1 | 25 05 | 66 42 | 79·7 | 24 54 | 65 36 | 79·2 | 24 42 | 64 32 | 78·7 | 207 | 333 |
| 28 / 152 | 26 31 | 69 48 | 80·7 | 26 21 | 68 42 | 80·2 | 26 11 | 67 36 | 79·7 | 26 00 | 66 30 | 79·2 | 25 48 | 65 25 | 78·7 | 25 36 | 64 19 | 78·3 | 208 | 332 |
| 29 / 151 | 27 27 | 69 37 | 80·3 | 27 17 | 68 31 | 79·8 | 27 06 | 67 24 | 79·3 | 26 55 | 66 18 | 78·8 | 26 43 | 65 12 | 78·3 | 26 30 | 64 07 | 77·8 | 209 | 331 |
| 30 / 150 | 28 24 | 69 26 | 79·9 | 28 13 | 68 19 | 79·4 | 28 01 | 67 12 | 78·8 | 27 50 | 66 06 | 78·3 | 27 37 | 64 59 | 77·8 | 27 24 | 63 53 | 77·3 | 210 | 330 |
| 31 / 149 | 29 20 | 69 14 | 79·5 | 29 09 | 68 07 | 78·9 | 28 57 | 67 00 | 78·4 | 28 44 | 65 53 | 77·8 | 28 31 | 64 46 | 77·3 | 28 18 | 63 39 | 76·8 | 211 | 329 |
| 32 / 148 | 30 16 | 69 02 | 79·1 | 30 04 | 67 54 | 78·5 | 29 52 | 66 46 | 77·9 | 29 39 | 65 39 | 77·4 | 29 26 | 64 32 | 76·8 | 29 12 | 63 25 | 76·3 | 212 | 328 |
| 33 / 147 | 31 12 | 68 49 | 78·7 | 31 00 | 67 41 | 78·1 | 30 47 | 66 32 | 77·5 | 30 34 | 65 24 | 76·9 | 30 20 | 64 17 | 76·3 | 30 05 | 63 09 | 75·8 | 213 | 327 |
| 34 / 146 | 32 08 | 68 36 | 78·2 | 31 55 | 67 27 | 77·6 | 31 42 | 66 18 | 77·0 | 31 28 | 65 09 | 76·4 | 31 14 | 64 01 | 75·8 | 30 59 | 62 53 | 75·2 | 214 | 326 |
| 35 / 145 | 33 04 | 68 22 | 77·8 | 32 51 | 67 12 | 77·2 | 32 37 | 66 03 | 76·5 | 32 23 | 64 54 | 75·9 | 32 08 | 63 45 | 75·3 | 31 52 | 62 36 | 74·7 | 215 | 325 |
| 36 / 144 | 33 59 | 68 07 | 77·3 | 33 46 | 66 57 | 76·7 | 33 32 | 65 47 | 76·0 | 33 17 | 64 37 | 75·4 | 33 01 | 63 28 | 74·8 | 32 45 | 62 19 | 74·2 | 216 | 324 |
| 37 / 143 | 34 55 | 67 52 | 76·9 | 34 41 | 66 41 | 76·2 | 34 26 | 65 30 | 75·5 | 34 11 | 64 20 | 74·9 | 33 55 | 63 10 | 74·2 | 33 38 | 62 01 | 73·6 | 217 | 323 |
| 38 / 142 | 35 50 | 67 36 | 76·4 | 35 36 | 66 24 | 75·7 | 35 21 | 65 13 | 75·0 | 35 05 | 64 02 | 74·4 | 34 48 | 62 52 | 73·7 | 34 31 | 61 41 | 73·0 | 218 | 322 |
| 39 / 141 | 36 46 | 67 19 | 76·0 | 36 31 | 66 06 | 75·2 | 36 15 | 64 54 | 74·5 | 35 59 | 63 43 | 73·8 | 35 42 | 62 32 | 73·1 | 35 24 | 61 21 | 72·4 | 219 | 321 |
| 40 / 140 | 37 41 | 67 01 | 75·5 | 37 26 | 65 48 | 74·7 | 37 10 | 64 35 | 74·0 | 36 53 | 63 23 | 73·3 | 36 35 | 62 12 | 72·6 | 36 17 | 61 01 | 71·8 | 220 | 320 |
| 41 / 139 | 38 36 | 66 42 | 75·0 | 38 20 | 65 29 | 74·2 | 38 04 | 64 15 | 73·4 | 37 46 | 63 02 | 72·7 | 37 28 | 61 50 | 72·0 | 37 09 | 60 39 | 71·2 | 221 | 319 |
| 42 / 138 | 39 31 | 66 23 | 74·5 | 39 15 | 65 08 | 73·7 | 38 58 | 63 54 | 72·9 | 38 40 | 62 41 | 72·1 | 38 21 | 61 28 | 71·4 | 38 01 | 60 16 | 70·6 | 222 | 318 |
| 43 / 137 | 40 26 | 66 03 | 74·0 | 40 09 | 64 47 | 73·1 | 39 51 | 63 33 | 72·3 | 39 33 | 62 18 | 71·5 | 39 13 | 61 05 | 70·7 | 38 53 | 59 52 | 70·0 | 223 | 317 |
| 44 / 136 | 41 21 | 65 42 | 73·4 | 41 03 | 64 25 | 72·5 | 40 45 | 63 10 | 71·7 | 40 26 | 61 55 | 70·9 | 40 06 | 60 41 | 70·1 | 39 45 | 59 27 | 69·3 | 224 | 316 |
| 45 / 135 | 42 16 | 65 19 | 72·8 | 41 57 | 64 02 | 72·0 | 41 38 | 62 46 | 71·1 | 41 19 | 61 30 | 70·3 | 40 58 | 60 15 | 69·5 | 40 37 | 59 01 | 68·7 | 225 | 315 |

| Lat./A LHA/F | 18° A/H | 18° B/P | 18° Z₁/Z₂ | 19° A/H | 19° B/P | 19° Z₁/Z₂ | 20° A/H | 20° B/P | 20° Z₁/Z₂ | 21° A/H | 21° B/P | 21° Z₁/Z₂ | 22° A/H | 22° B/P | 22° Z₁/Z₂ | 23° A/H | 23° B/P | 23° Z₁/Z₂ | Lat./A LHA |
|---|---|---|---|---|---|---|---|---|---|---|---|---|---|---|---|---|---|---|---|
| 45 / 135 | 42 16 | 65 19 | 72.8 | 41 57 | 64 02 | 72.0 | 41 38 | 62 46 | 71.1 | 41 19 | 61 30 | 70.3 | 40 58 | 60 15 | 69.5 | 40 37 | 59 01 | 68.7 | 225 / 315 |
| 46 / 134 | 43 10 | 64 56 | 72.3 | 42 51 | 63 38 | 71.4 | 42 32 | 62 21 | 70.5 | 42 11 | 61 05 | 69.6 | 41 50 | 59 49 | 68.8 | 41 28 | 58 34 | 68.0 | 226 / 314 |
| 47 / 133 | 44 04 | 64 32 | 71.7 | 43 45 | 63 13 | 70.8 | 43 25 | 61 55 | 69.9 | 43 04 | 60 38 | 69.0 | 42 42 | 59 21 | 68.1 | 42 19 | 58 06 | 67.3 | 227 / 313 |
| 48 / 132 | 44 58 | 64 06 | 71.1 | 44 38 | 62 46 | 70.1 | 44 18 | 61 27 | 69.2 | 43 56 | 60 09 | 68.3 | 43 33 | 58 53 | 67.4 | 43 10 | 57 37 | 66.5 | 228 / 312 |
| 49 / 131 | 45 52 | 63 39 | 70.4 | 45 32 | 62 18 | 69.5 | 45 10 | 60 59 | 68.5 | 44 48 | 59 40 | 67.6 | 44 24 | 58 22 | 66.7 | 44 00 | 57 06 | 65.8 | 229 / 311 |
| 50 / 130 | 46 46 | 63 11 | 69.8 | 46 25 | 61 49 | 68.8 | 46 03 | 60 29 | 67.8 | 45 39 | 59 09 | 66.9 | 45 15 | 57 51 | 65.9 | 44 50 | 56 34 | 65.0 | 230 / 310 |
| 51 / 129 | 47 39 | 62 42 | 69.1 | 47 17 | 61 19 | 68.1 | 46 55 | 59 57 | 67.1 | 46 31 | 58 37 | 66.1 | 46 06 | 57 18 | 65.2 | 45 40 | 56 00 | 64.2 | 231 / 309 |
| 52 / 128 | 48 33 | 62 11 | 68.4 | 48 10 | 60 47 | 67.4 | 47 46 | 59 25 | 66.4 | 47 22 | 58 03 | 65.4 | 46 56 | 56 44 | 64.4 | 46 30 | 55 25 | 63.4 | 232 / 308 |
| 53 / 127 | 49 25 | 61 38 | 67.7 | 49 02 | 60 13 | 66.6 | 48 38 | 58 50 | 65.6 | 48 13 | 57 28 | 64.6 | 47 46 | 56 07 | 63.6 | 47 19 | 54 48 | 62.6 | 233 / 307 |
| 54 / 126 | 50 18 | 61 04 | 67.0 | 49 54 | 59 38 | 65.9 | 49 29 | 58 14 | 64.8 | 49 03 | 56 51 | 63.7 | 48 36 | 55 30 | 62.7 | 48 08 | 54 10 | 61.7 | 234 / 306 |
| 55 / 125 | 51 10 | 60 28 | 66.2 | 50 46 | 59 01 | 65.1 | 50 20 | 57 37 | 64.0 | 49 53 | 56 12 | 62.9 | 49 26 | 54 51 | 61.9 | 48 56 | 53 30 | 60.8 | 235 / 305 |
| 56 / 124 | 52 03 | 59 50 | 65.4 | 51 37 | 58 23 | 64.2 | 51 10 | 56 56 | 63.1 | 50 43 | 55 32 | 62.0 | 50 14 | 54 09 | 61.0 | 49 44 | 52 48 | 59.9 | 236 / 304 |
| 57 / 123 | 52 54 | 59 11 | 64.6 | 52 28 | 57 42 | 63.4 | 52 00 | 56 15 | 62.2 | 51 32 | 54 49 | 61.1 | 51 02 | 53 26 | 60.0 | 50 32 | 52 04 | 59.0 | 237 / 303 |
| 58 / 122 | 53 46 | 58 29 | 63.7 | 53 18 | 56 59 | 62.5 | 52 50 | 55 31 | 61.3 | 52 21 | 54 05 | 60.2 | 51 50 | 52 41 | 59.1 | 51 19 | 51 18 | 58.0 | 238 / 302 |
| 59 / 121 | 54 37 | 57 45 | 62.8 | 54 08 | 56 14 | 61.5 | 53 39 | 54 45 | 60.4 | 53 09 | 53 18 | 59.2 | 52 38 | 51 53 | 58.1 | 52 06 | 50 30 | 57.0 | 239 / 301 |
| 60 / 120 | 55 27 | 57 00 | 61.8 | 54 58 | 55 27 | 60.6 | 54 28 | 53 57 | 59.4 | 53 57 | 52 29 | 58.2 | 53 25 | 51 04 | 57.0 | 52 52 | 49 40 | 55.9 | 240 / 300 |
| 61 / 119 | 56 17 | 56 10 | 60.9 | 55 47 | 54 37 | 59.6 | 55 16 | 53 06 | 58.3 | 54 44 | 51 38 | 57.1 | 54 11 | 50 12 | 55.9 | 53 37 | 48 48 | 54.8 | 241 / 299 |
| 62 / 118 | 57 07 | 55 19 | 59.8 | 56 36 | 53 45 | 58.5 | 56 04 | 52 13 | 57.2 | 55 31 | 50 44 | 56.0 | 54 57 | 49 17 | 54.8 | 54 22 | 47 53 | 53.7 | 242 / 298 |
| 63 / 117 | 57 56 | 54 25 | 58.8 | 57 24 | 52 49 | 57.4 | 56 51 | 51 17 | 56.1 | 56 17 | 49 47 | 54.9 | 55 42 | 48 20 | 53.7 | 55 06 | 46 55 | 52.5 | 243 / 297 |
| 64 / 116 | 58 44 | 53 27 | 57.6 | 58 12 | 51 51 | 56.3 | 57 38 | 50 18 | 55.0 | 57 03 | 48 48 | 53.7 | 56 27 | 47 20 | 52.5 | 55 50 | 45 55 | 51.3 | 244 / 296 |
| 65 / 115 | 59 32 | 52 27 | 56.5 | 58 58 | 50 50 | 55.1 | 58 24 | 49 16 | 53.7 | 57 47 | 47 45 | 52.5 | 57 10 | 46 11 | 51.2 | 56 32 | 44 52 | 50.0 | 245 / 295 |
| 66 / 114 | 60 19 | 51 23 | 55.2 | 59 45 | 49 45 | 53.8 | 59 09 | 48 11 | 52.5 | 58 32 | 46 39 | 51.2 | 57 53 | 45 11 | 49.9 | 57 14 | 43 47 | 48.7 | 246 / 294 |
| 67 / 113 | 61 06 | 50 15 | 53.9 | 60 30 | 48 37 | 52.5 | 59 53 | 47 02 | 51.1 | 59 15 | 45 30 | 49.8 | 58 36 | 44 02 | 48.6 | 57 55 | 42 38 | 47.4 | 247 / 293 |
| 68 / 112 | 61 52 | 49 04 | 52.6 | 61 15 | 47 25 | 51.1 | 60 36 | 45 50 | 49.8 | 59 57 | 44 18 | 48.4 | 59 17 | 42 50 | 47.2 | 58 36 | 41 26 | 46.0 | 248 / 292 |
| 69 / 111 | 62 37 | 47 48 | 51.2 | 61 58 | 46 09 | 49.7 | 61 19 | 44 33 | 48.3 | 60 39 | 43 02 | 47.0 | 59 57 | 41 34 | 45.7 | 59 15 | 40 10 | 44.5 | 249 / 291 |
| 70 / 110 | 63 21 | 46 28 | 49.7 | 62 41 | 44 48 | 48.2 | 62 01 | 43 13 | 46.8 | 61 19 | 41 42 | 45.4 | 60 36 | 40 15 | 44.2 | 59 53 | 38 52 | 43.0 | 250 / 290 |
| 71 / 109 | 64 04 | 45 03 | 48.1 | 63 23 | 43 24 | 46.6 | 62 41 | 41 49 | 45.2 | 61 58 | 40 18 | 43.9 | 61 15 | 38 52 | 42.6 | 60 30 | 37 29 | 41.4 | 251 / 289 |
| 72 / 108 | 64 45 | 43 34 | 46.4 | 64 04 | 41 54 | 44.9 | 63 21 | 40 20 | 43.5 | 62 37 | 38 50 | 42.2 | 61 52 | 37 25 | 40.9 | 61 06 | 36 03 | 39.7 | 252 / 288 |
| 73 / 107 | 65 26 | 41 59 | 44.7 | 64 43 | 40 20 | 43.2 | 63 59 | 38 46 | 41.8 | 63 14 | 37 18 | 40.5 | 62 27 | 35 53 | 39.2 | 61 41 | 34 34 | 38.0 | 253 / 287 |
| 74 / 106 | 66 06 | 40 19 | 42.9 | 65 21 | 38 41 | 41.4 | 64 36 | 37 08 | 40.0 | 63 49 | 35 41 | 38.7 | 63 02 | 34 18 | 37.4 | 62 14 | 33 00 | 36.3 | 254 / 286 |
| 75 / 105 | 66 44 | 38 32 | 40.9 | 65 58 | 36 56 | 39.5 | 65 11 | 35 25 | 38.1 | 64 23 | 33 59 | 36.8 | 63 35 | 32 39 | 35.6 | 62 46 | 31 22 | 34.4 | 255 / 285 |
| 76 / 104 | 67 20 | 36 40 | 38.9 | 66 33 | 35 05 | 37.4 | 65 45 | 33 37 | 36.1 | 64 56 | 32 13 | 34.8 | 64 07 | 30 56 | 33.6 | 63 16 | 29 41 | 32.5 | 256 / 284 |
| 77 / 103 | 67 55 | 34 42 | 36.8 | 67 07 | 33 09 | 35.3 | 66 18 | 31 43 | 34.0 | 65 27 | 30 22 | 32.8 | 64 37 | 29 06 | 31.6 | 63 45 | 27 55 | 30.6 | 257 / 283 |
| 78 / 102 | 68 29 | 32 37 | 34.5 | 67 39 | 31 07 | 33.1 | 66 48 | 29 44 | 31.9 | 65 57 | 28 26 | 30.7 | 65 05 | 27 14 | 29.6 | 64 13 | 26 06 | 28.5 | 258 / 282 |
| 79 / 101 | 69 00 | 30 25 | 32.2 | 68 09 | 29 00 | 30.8 | 67 17 | 27 40 | 29.6 | 66 25 | 26 26 | 28.5 | 65 32 | 25 18 | 27.4 | 64 38 | 24 12 | 26.4 | 259 / 281 |
| 80 / 100 | 69 29 | 28 07 | 29.7 | 68 37 | 26 46 | 28.4 | 67 44 | 25 30 | 27.3 | 66 50 | 24 20 | 26.2 | 65 56 | 23 15 | 25.2 | 65 02 | 22 15 | 24.3 | 260 / 280 |
| 81 / 99 | 69 57 | 25 43 | 27.1 | 69 03 | 24 26 | 25.9 | 68 09 | 23 15 | 24.8 | 67 14 | 22 10 | 23.8 | 66 19 | 21 10 | 22.9 | 65 23 | 20 14 | 22.1 | 261 / 279 |
| 82 / 98 | 70 21 | 23 11 | 24.5 | 69 27 | 22 00 | 23.3 | 68 31 | 20 56 | 22.3 | 67 36 | 19 56 | 21.4 | 66 40 | 19 00 | 20.6 | 65 43 | 18 09 | 19.8 | 262 / 278 |
| 83 / 97 | 70 44 | 20 34 | 21.7 | 69 48 | 19 29 | 20.7 | 68 51 | 18 31 | 19.7 | 67 55 | 17 37 | 18.9 | 66 58 | 16 47 | 18.1 | 66 01 | 16 01 | 17.4 | 263 / 277 |
| 84 / 96 | 71 03 | 17 50 | 18.8 | 70 07 | 16 53 | 17.9 | 69 09 | 16 01 | 17.1 | 68 12 | 15 14 | 16.3 | 67 14 | 14 30 | 15.7 | 66 16 | 13 50 | 15.1 | 264 / 276 |
| 85 / 95 | 71 21 | 15 01 | 15.8 | 70 23 | 14 12 | 15.0 | 69 25 | 13 28 | 14.3 | 68 26 | 12 48 | 13.7 | 67 29 | 12 10 | 13.1 | 66 29 | 11 36 | 12.6 | 265 / 275 |
| 86 / 94 | 71 35 | 12 07 | 12.8 | 70 36 | 11 27 | 12.1 | 69 37 | 10 51 | 11.6 | 68 38 | 10 18 | 11.0 | 67 39 | 9 48 | 10.6 | 66 40 | 9 20 | 10.1 | 266 / 274 |
| 87 / 93 | 71 46 | 9 09 | 9.6 | 70 46 | 8 39 | 9.1 | 69 47 | 8 11 | 8.7 | 68 48 | 7 46 | 8.3 | 67 48 | 7 23 | 8.0 | 66 49 | 7 02 | 7.6 | 267 / 273 |
| 88 / 92 | 71 54 | 6 08 | 6.4 | 70 54 | 5 47 | 6.1 | 69 54 | 5 29 | 5.8 | 68 55 | 5 12 | 5.6 | 67 55 | 4 56 | 5.3 | 66 55 | 4 42 | 5.1 | 268 / 272 |
| 89 / 91 | 71 58 | 3 04 | 3.2 | 70 58 | 2 54 | 3.1 | 69 59 | 2 45 | 2.9 | 68 59 | 2 36 | 2.8 | 67 59 | 2 28 | 2.7 | 66 59 | 2 21 | 2.6 | 269 / 271 |
| 90 / 90 | 72 00 | 0 00 | 0.0 | 71 00 | 0 00 | 0.0 | 70 00 | 0 00 | 0.0 | 69 00 | 0 00 | 0.0 | 68 00 | 0 00 | 0.0 | 67 00 | 0 00 | 0.0 | 270 / 270 |

N. Lat: for LHA > 180° ... $Z_n = Z$
for LHA < 180° ... $Z_n = 360° − Z$

S. Lat.: for LHA > 180° ... $Z_n = 180° − Z$
for LHA < 180° ... $Z_n = 180° + Z$

SIGHT REDUCTION TABLE

B: (−) for 90° < LHA < 270°  
Dec:(−) for Lat. contrary name

Z₁: same sign as B  
Z₂: (−) for F > 90°

| LHA | F | 24° A/H | 24° B/P | 24° Z₁/Z₂ | 25° A/H | 25° B/P | 25° Z₁/Z₂ | 26° A/H | 26° B/P | 26° Z₁/Z₂ | 27° A/H | 27° B/P | 27° Z₁/Z₂ | 28° A/H | 28° B/P | 28° Z₁/Z₂ | 29° A/H | 29° B/P | 29° Z₁/Z₂ | LHA | LHA |
|---|---|---|---|---|---|---|---|---|---|---|---|---|---|---|---|---|---|---|---|---|---|
| 0 | 180 | 0 00 | 66 00 | 90·0 | 0 00 | 65 00 | 90·0 | 0 00 | 64 00 | 90·0 | 0 00 | 63 00 | 90·0 | 0 00 | 62 00 | 90·0 | 0 00 | 61 00 | 90·0 | 180 | 360 |
| 1 | 179 | 0 55 | 66 00 | 89·6 | 0 54 | 65 00 | 89·6 | 0 54 | 64 00 | 89·6 | 0 53 | 63 00 | 89·5 | 0 53 | 62 00 | 89·5 | 0 52 | 61 00 | 89·5 | 181 | 359 |
| 2 | 178 | 1 50 | 65 59 | 89·2 | 1 49 | 64 59 | 89·2 | 1 48 | 63 59 | 89·1 | 1 47 | 62 59 | 89·1 | 1 46 | 61 59 | 89·1 | 1 45 | 60 59 | 89·0 | 182 | 358 |
| 3 | 177 | 2 44 | 65 58 | 88·8 | 2 43 | 64 58 | 88·7 | 2 42 | 63 58 | 88·7 | 2 40 | 62 58 | 88·6 | 2 39 | 61 58 | 88·6 | 2 37 | 60 58 | 88·5 | 183 | 357 |
| 4 | 176 | 3 39 | 65 57 | 88·4 | 3 37 | 64 57 | 88·3 | 3 36 | 63 57 | 88·2 | 3 34 | 62 57 | 88·2 | 3 32 | 61 57 | 88·1 | 3 30 | 60 56 | 88·1 | 184 | 356 |
| 5 | 175 | 4 34 | 65 55 | 88·0 | 4 32 | 64 55 | 87·9 | 4 30 | 63 55 | 87·8 | 4 27 | 62 55 | 87·7 | 4 25 | 61 55 | 87·6 | 4 22 | 60 54 | 87·6 | 185 | 355 |
| 6 | 174 | 5 29 | 65 53 | 87·6 | 5 26 | 64 53 | 87·5 | 5 23 | 63 53 | 87·4 | 5 21 | 62 52 | 87·3 | 5 18 | 61 52 | 87·2 | 5 15 | 60 52 | 87·1 | 186 | 354 |
| 7 | 173 | 6 24 | 65 50 | 87·1 | 6 20 | 64 50 | 87·0 | 6 17 | 63 50 | 86·9 | 6 14 | 62 50 | 86·8 | 6 11 | 61 50 | 86·7 | 6 07 | 60 49 | 86·6 | 187 | 353 |
| 8 | 172 | 7 18 | 65 47 | 86·7 | 7 15 | 64 47 | 86·6 | 7 11 | 63 47 | 86·5 | 7 07 | 62 46 | 86·3 | 7 04 | 61 46 | 86·2 | 6 59 | 60 46 | 86·1 | 188 | 352 |
| 9 | 171 | 8 13 | 65 44 | 86·3 | 8 09 | 64 44 | 86·2 | 8 05 | 63 43 | 86·0 | 8 01 | 62 43 | 85·9 | 7 56 | 61 42 | 85·7 | 7 52 | 60 42 | 85·6 | 189 | 351 |
| 10 | 170 | 9 08 | 65 40 | 85·9 | 9 03 | 64 40 | 85·7 | 8 59 | 63 39 | 85·6 | 8 54 | 62 39 | 85·4 | 8 49 | 61 38 | 85·3 | 8 44 | 60 38 | 85·1 | 190 | 350 |
| 11 | 169 | 10 02 | 65 36 | 85·5 | 9 57 | 64 35 | 85·3 | 9 52 | 63 35 | 85·1 | 9 47 | 62 34 | 85·0 | 9 42 | 61 33 | 84·8 | 9 36 | 60 33 | 84·6 | 191 | 349 |
| 12 | 168 | 10 57 | 65 32 | 85·1 | 10 52 | 64 31 | 84·9 | 10 46 | 63 30 | 84·7 | 10 41 | 62 29 | 84·5 | 10 35 | 61 28 | 84·3 | 10 29 | 60 28 | 84·1 | 192 | 348 |
| 13 | 167 | 11 52 | 65 27 | 84·6 | 11 46 | 64 26 | 84·4 | 11 40 | 63 25 | 84·2 | 11 34 | 62 24 | 84·0 | 11 27 | 61 23 | 83·8 | 11 21 | 60 22 | 83·6 | 193 | 347 |
| 14 | 166 | 12 46 | 65 21 | 84·2 | 12 40 | 64 20 | 84·0 | 12 34 | 63 19 | 83·8 | 12 27 | 62 18 | 83·5 | 12 20 | 61 17 | 83·3 | 12 13 | 60 16 | 83·1 | 194 | 346 |
| 15 | 165 | 13 41 | 65 15 | 83·8 | 13 34 | 64 14 | 83·5 | 13 27 | 63 13 | 83·3 | 13 20 | 62 11 | 83·1 | 13 13 | 61 10 | 82·8 | 13 05 | 60 09 | 82·6 | 195 | 345 |
| 16 | 164 | 14 35 | 65 09 | 83·3 | 14 28 | 64 07 | 83·1 | 14 21 | 63 06 | 82·8 | 14 13 | 62 04 | 82·6 | 14 05 | 61 03 | 82·3 | 13 57 | 60 02 | 82·1 | 196 | 344 |
| 17 | 163 | 15 29 | 65 02 | 82·9 | 15 22 | 64 00 | 82·6 | 15 14 | 62 59 | 82·4 | 15 06 | 61 57 | 82·1 | 14 58 | 60 56 | 81·8 | 14 49 | 59 54 | 81·6 | 197 | 343 |
| 18 | 162 | 16 24 | 64 55 | 82·5 | 16 16 | 63 53 | 82·2 | 16 08 | 62 51 | 81·9 | 15 59 | 61 49 | 81·6 | 15 50 | 60 47 | 81·3 | 15 41 | 59 46 | 81·0 | 198 | 342 |
| 19 | 161 | 17 18 | 64 47 | 82·0 | 17 10 | 63 45 | 81·7 | 17 01 | 62 43 | 81·4 | 16 52 | 61 41 | 81·1 | 16 42 | 60 39 | 80·8 | 16 33 | 59 37 | 80·5 | 199 | 341 |
| 20 | 160 | 18 12 | 64 39 | 81·6 | 18 03 | 63 36 | 81·3 | 17 54 | 62 34 | 80·9 | 17 45 | 61 32 | 80·6 | 17 35 | 60 30 | 80·3 | 17 24 | 59 28 | 80·0 | 200 | 340 |
| 21 | 159 | 19 07 | 64 30 | 81·1 | 18 57 | 63 28 | 80·8 | 18 47 | 62 25 | 80·4 | 18 37 | 61 23 | 80·1 | 18 27 | 60 20 | 79·8 | 18 16 | 59 18 | 79·5 | 201 | 339 |
| 22 | 158 | 20 01 | 64 21 | 80·7 | 19 51 | 63 18 | 80·3 | 19 41 | 62 15 | 80·0 | 19 30 | 61 13 | 79·6 | 19 19 | 60 10 | 79·3 | 19 08 | 59 08 | 78·9 | 202 | 338 |
| 23 | 157 | 20 55 | 64 11 | 80·2 | 20 44 | 63 08 | 79·8 | 20 34 | 62 05 | 79·5 | 20 22 | 61 02 | 79·1 | 20 11 | 59 59 | 78·7 | 19 59 | 58 57 | 78·4 | 203 | 337 |
| 24 | 156 | 21 49 | 64 01 | 79·7 | 21 38 | 62 58 | 79·3 | 21 27 | 61 54 | 79·0 | 21 15 | 60 51 | 78·6 | 21 03 | 59 48 | 78·2 | 20 50 | 58 45 | 77·8 | 204 | 336 |
| 25 | 155 | 22 43 | 63 50 | 79·3 | 22 31 | 62 46 | 78·9 | 22 19 | 61 43 | 78·4 | 22 07 | 60 39 | 78·0 | 21 55 | 59 36 | 77·7 | 21 42 | 58 33 | 77·3 | 205 | 335 |
| 26 | 154 | 23 36 | 63 39 | 78·8 | 23 25 | 62 35 | 78·4 | 23 12 | 61 31 | 77·9 | 22 59 | 60 27 | 77·5 | 22 46 | 59 24 | 77·1 | 22 33 | 58 20 | 76·7 | 206 | 334 |
| 27 | 153 | 24 30 | 63 27 | 78·3 | 24 18 | 62 22 | 77·9 | 24 05 | 61 18 | 77·4 | 23 52 | 60 14 | 77·0 | 23 38 | 59 10 | 76·5 | 23 24 | 58 07 | 76·1 | 207 | 333 |
| 28 | 152 | 25 24 | 63 14 | 77·8 | 25 11 | 62 10 | 77·3 | 24 57 | 61 05 | 76·9 | 24 44 | 60 01 | 76·4 | 24 29 | 58 57 | 76·0 | 24 15 | 57 53 | 75·5 | 208 | 332 |
| 29 | 151 | 26 17 | 63 01 | 77·3 | 26 04 | 61 56 | 76·8 | 25 50 | 60 51 | 76·3 | 25 36 | 59 47 | 75·9 | 25 21 | 58 42 | 75·4 | 25 05 | 57 38 | 75·0 | 209 | 331 |
| 30 | 150 | 27 11 | 62 48 | 76·8 | 26 57 | 61 42 | 76·3 | 26 42 | 60 37 | 75·8 | 26 27 | 59 32 | 75·3 | 26 12 | 58 27 | 74·8 | 25 56 | 57 23 | 74·4 | 210 | 330 |
| 31 | 149 | 28 04 | 62 33 | 76·3 | 27 50 | 61 27 | 75·8 | 27 35 | 60 22 | 75·2 | 27 19 | 59 16 | 74·7 | 27 03 | 58 11 | 74·2 | 26 46 | 57 07 | 73·8 | 211 | 329 |
| 32 | 148 | 28 57 | 62 18 | 75·7 | 28 42 | 61 12 | 75·2 | 28 27 | 60 06 | 74·7 | 28 10 | 59 00 | 74·2 | 27 54 | 57 55 | 73·7 | 27 37 | 56 50 | 73·1 | 212 | 328 |
| 33 | 147 | 29 50 | 62 02 | 75·2 | 29 35 | 60 56 | 74·7 | 29 19 | 59 49 | 74·1 | 29 02 | 58 43 | 73·6 | 28 45 | 57 38 | 73·0 | 28 27 | 56 32 | 72·5 | 213 | 327 |
| 34 | 146 | 30 43 | 61 46 | 74·7 | 30 27 | 60 39 | 74·1 | 30 10 | 59 32 | 73·5 | 29 53 | 58 26 | 73·0 | 29 35 | 57 20 | 72·4 | 29 17 | 56 14 | 71·9 | 214 | 326 |
| 35 | 145 | 31 36 | 61 28 | 74·1 | 31 19 | 60 21 | 73·5 | 31 02 | 59 14 | 72·9 | 30 44 | 58 07 | 72·4 | 30 26 | 57 01 | 71·8 | 30 07 | 55 55 | 71·2 | 215 | 325 |
| 36 | 144 | 32 29 | 61 10 | 73·5 | 32 11 | 60 02 | 72·9 | 31 53 | 58 55 | 72·3 | 31 35 | 57 48 | 71·7 | 31 16 | 56 41 | 71·2 | 30 56 | 55 35 | 70·6 | 216 | 324 |
| 37 | 143 | 33 21 | 60 52 | 73·0 | 33 03 | 59 43 | 72·3 | 32 45 | 58 35 | 71·7 | 32 26 | 57 28 | 71·1 | 32 06 | 56 21 | 70·5 | 31 46 | 55 14 | 69·9 | 217 | 323 |
| 38 | 142 | 34 13 | 60 32 | 72·4 | 33 55 | 59 23 | 71·7 | 33 36 | 58 15 | 71·1 | 33 16 | 57 07 | 70·5 | 32 56 | 56 00 | 69·9 | 32 35 | 54 53 | 69·3 | 218 | 322 |
| 39 | 141 | 35 06 | 60 11 | 71·8 | 34 47 | 59 02 | 71·1 | 34 27 | 57 53 | 70·5 | 34 06 | 56 45 | 69·8 | 33 45 | 55 37 | 69·2 | 33 24 | 54 30 | 68·6 | 219 | 321 |
| 40 | 140 | 35 58 | 59 50 | 71·2 | 35 38 | 58 40 | 70·5 | 35 17 | 57 31 | 69·8 | 34 56 | 56 22 | 69·1 | 34 35 | 55 14 | 68·5 | 34 12 | 54 07 | 67·9 | 220 | 320 |
| 41 | 139 | 36 49 | 59 28 | 70·5 | 36 29 | 58 17 | 69·8 | 36 08 | 57 08 | 69·1 | 35 46 | 55 59 | 68·5 | 35 24 | 54 50 | 67·8 | 35 01 | 53 42 | 67·1 | 221 | 319 |
| 42 | 138 | 37 41 | 59 04 | 69·9 | 37 20 | 57 54 | 69·2 | 36 58 | 56 43 | 68·5 | 36 36 | 55 34 | 67·8 | 36 13 | 54 25 | 67·1 | 35 49 | 53 17 | 66·4 | 222 | 318 |
| 43 | 137 | 38 32 | 58 40 | 69·2 | 38 11 | 57 29 | 68·5 | 37 48 | 56 18 | 67·8 | 37 25 | 55 08 | 67·1 | 37 02 | 53 59 | 66·4 | 36 37 | 52 50 | 65·7 | 223 | 317 |
| 44 | 136 | 39 23 | 58 15 | 68·6 | 39 01 | 57 03 | 67·8 | 38 38 | 55 52 | 67·1 | 38 14 | 54 41 | 66·3 | 37 50 | 53 32 | 65·6 | 37 25 | 52 23 | 64·9 | 224 | 316 |
| 45 | 135 | 40 14 | 57 48 | 67·9 | 39 51 | 56 36 | 67·1 | 39 28 | 55 24 | 66·3 | 39 03 | 54 13 | 65·6 | 38 38 | 53 04 | 64·9 | 38 12 | 51 54 | 64·1 | 225 | 315 |

| Lat./A | LHA/F | 24° A/H | 24° B/P | 24° $Z_1/Z_2$ | 25° A/H | 25° B/P | 25° $Z_1/Z_2$ | 26° A/H | 26° B/P | 26° $Z_1/Z_2$ | 27° A/H | 27° B/P | 27° $Z_1/Z_2$ | 28° A/H | 28° B/P | 28° $Z_1/Z_2$ | 29° A/H | 29° B/P | 29° $Z_1/Z_2$ | Lat./A | LHA |
|---|---|---|---|---|---|---|---|---|---|---|---|---|---|---|---|---|---|---|---|---|---|
| 135 | 45 | 40 14 | 57 48 | 67·9 | 39 51 | 56 36 | 67·1 | 39 28 | 55 24 | 66·3 | 39 03 | 54 13 | 65·6 | 38 38 | 53 04 | 64·9 | 38 12 | 51 54 | 64·1 | 225 | 315 |
| 134 | 46 | 41 05 | 57 21 | 67·2 | 40 44 | 56 08 | 66·4 | 40 17 | 54 56 | 65·6 | 39 52 | 53 44 | 64·8 | 39 26 | 52 34 | 64·1 | 38 59 | 51 25 | 63·3 | 226 | 314 |
| 133 | 47 | 41 55 | 56 52 | 66·4 | 41 31 | 55 38 | 65·6 | 41 06 | 54 26 | 64·8 | 40 40 | 53 14 | 64·0 | 40 13 | 52 04 | 63·3 | 39 46 | 50 54 | 62·5 | 227 | 313 |
| 132 | 48 | 42 45 | 56 22 | 65·7 | 42 20 | 55 08 | 64·9 | 41 54 | 53 55 | 64·0 | 41 28 | 52 43 | 63·2 | 41 00 | 51 32 | 62·5 | 40 32 | 50 22 | 61·7 | 228 | 312 |
| 131 | 49 | 43 35 | 55 50 | 64·9 | 43 09 | 54 36 | 64·1 | 42 43 | 53 22 | 63·2 | 42 15 | 52 10 | 62·4 | 41 47 | 50 59 | 61·6 | 41 18 | 49 48 | 60·9 | 229 | 311 |
| 130 | 50 | 44 25 | 55 17 | 64·1 | 43 58 | 54 02 | 63·3 | 43 31 | 52 49 | 62·4 | 43 03 | 51 36 | 61·6 | 42 34 | 50 24 | 60·8 | 42 04 | 49 14 | 60·0 | 230 | 310 |
| 129 | 51 | 45 14 | 54 43 | 63·3 | 44 47 | 53 28 | 62·4 | 44 18 | 52 13 | 61·6 | 43 49 | 51 00 | 60·7 | 43 20 | 49 48 | 59·9 | 42 49 | 48 38 | 59·1 | 231 | 309 |
| 128 | 52 | 46 03 | 54 08 | 62·5 | 45 35 | 52 52 | 61·6 | 45 06 | 51 37 | 60·7 | 44 36 | 50 23 | 59·8 | 44 05 | 49 11 | 59·0 | 43 34 | 48 00 | 58·2 | 232 | 308 |
| 127 | 53 | 46 51 | 53 30 | 61·6 | 46 22 | 52 14 | 60·7 | 45 52 | 50 59 | 59·8 | 45 22 | 49 45 | 58·9 | 44 51 | 48 32 | 58·1 | 44 18 | 47 21 | 57·2 | 233 | 307 |
| 126 | 54 | 47 39 | 52 51 | 60·8 | 47 09 | 51 34 | 59·8 | 46 39 | 50 19 | 58·9 | 46 07 | 49 05 | 58·0 | 45 35 | 47 52 | 57·1 | 45 02 | 46 41 | 56·3 | 234 | 306 |
| 125 | 55 | 48 27 | 52 11 | 59·8 | 47 56 | 50 53 | 58·9 | 47 25 | 49 37 | 58·0 | 46 52 | 48 23 | 57·1 | 46 19 | 47 10 | 56·2 | 45 46 | 45 59 | 55·3 | 235 | 305 |
| 124 | 56 | 49 14 | 51 28 | 58·9 | 48 43 | 50 11 | 57·9 | 48 10 | 48 54 | 57·0 | 47 37 | 47 40 | 56·1 | 47 03 | 46 27 | 55·2 | 46 29 | 45 15 | 54·3 | 236 | 304 |
| 123 | 57 | 50 01 | 50 44 | 57·9 | 49 28 | 49 26 | 56·9 | 48 55 | 48 09 | 56·0 | 48 21 | 46 54 | 55·0 | 47 46 | 45 41 | 54·1 | 47 11 | 44 30 | 53·3 | 237 | 303 |
| 122 | 58 | 50 47 | 49 58 | 56·9 | 50 14 | 48 39 | 55·9 | 49 40 | 47 22 | 54·9 | 49 05 | 46 07 | 54·0 | 48 29 | 44 54 | 53·1 | 47 53 | 43 43 | 52·2 | 238 | 302 |
| 121 | 59 | 51 33 | 49 09 | 55·9 | 50 58 | 47 51 | 54·9 | 50 23 | 46 34 | 53·9 | 49 47 | 45 18 | 52·9 | 49 11 | 44 05 | 52·0 | 48 34 | 42 54 | 51·1 | 239 | 301 |
| 120 | 60 | 52 18 | 48 19 | 54·8 | 51 43 | 47 00 | 53·8 | 51 07 | 45 43 | 52·8 | 50 30 | 44 28 | 51·8 | 49 52 | 43 15 | 50·9 | 49 14 | 42 03 | 50·0 | 240 | 300 |
| 119 | 61 | 53 02 | 47 26 | 53·7 | 52 26 | 46 07 | 52·7 | 51 49 | 44 50 | 51·7 | 51 11 | 43 35 | 50·7 | 50 32 | 42 22 | 49·7 | 49 54 | 41 10 | 48·8 | 241 | 299 |
| 118 | 62 | 53 46 | 46 31 | 52·6 | 53 09 | 45 12 | 51·5 | 52 31 | 43 54 | 50·5 | 51 52 | 42 39 | 49·5 | 51 12 | 41 27 | 48·6 | 50 33 | 40 16 | 47·6 | 242 | 298 |
| 117 | 63 | 54 29 | 45 33 | 51·4 | 53 51 | 44 14 | 50·3 | 53 13 | 42 57 | 49·3 | 52 33 | 41 42 | 48·3 | 51 52 | 40 30 | 47·3 | 51 12 | 39 19 | 46·4 | 243 | 297 |
| 116 | 64 | 55 12 | 44 33 | 50·2 | 54 33 | 43 14 | 49·1 | 53 53 | 41 57 | 48·1 | 53 11 | 40 42 | 47·1 | 52 30 | 39 30 | 46·1 | 51 49 | 38 20 | 45·2 | 244 | 296 |
| 115 | 65 | 55 53 | 43 30 | 48·9 | 55 13 | 42 14 | 47·8 | 54 33 | 40 55 | 46·8 | 53 50 | 39 40 | 45·8 | 53 08 | 38 29 | 44·8 | 52 26 | 37 19 | 43·9 | 245 | 295 |
| 114 | 66 | 56 34 | 42 25 | 47·6 | 55 53 | 41 06 | 46·5 | 55 12 | 39 50 | 45·4 | 54 29 | 38 36 | 44·4 | 53 45 | 37 25 | 43·5 | 53 02 | 36 16 | 42·6 | 246 | 294 |
| 113 | 67 | 57 14 | 41 16 | 46·2 | 56 32 | 39 58 | 45·1 | 55 50 | 38 42 | 44·1 | 55 06 | 37 29 | 43·1 | 54 21 | 36 19 | 42·1 | 53 37 | 35 11 | 41·2 | 247 | 293 |
| 112 | 68 | 57 53 | 40 05 | 44·8 | 57 10 | 38 47 | 43·7 | 56 27 | 37 32 | 42·7 | 55 42 | 36 19 | 41·7 | 54 56 | 35 10 | 40·7 | 54 11 | 34 03 | 39·8 | 248 | 292 |
| 111 | 69 | 58 32 | 38 50 | 43·3 | 57 47 | 37 33 | 42·2 | 57 03 | 36 18 | 41·2 | 56 17 | 35 07 | 40·2 | 55 30 | 33 59 | 39·3 | 54 44 | 32 53 | 38·4 | 249 | 291 |
| 110 | 70 | 59 09 | 37 32 | 41·8 | 58 24 | 36 16 | 40·7 | 57 38 | 35 02 | 39·7 | 56 51 | 33 52 | 38·7 | 56 03 | 32 46 | 37·8 | 55 16 | 31 41 | 36·9 | 250 | 290 |
| 109 | 71 | 59 45 | 36 11 | 40·2 | 58 58 | 34 55 | 39·2 | 58 12 | 33 43 | 38·1 | 57 24 | 32 35 | 37·2 | 56 35 | 31 30 | 36·3 | 55 47 | 30 26 | 35·4 | 251 | 289 |
| 108 | 72 | 60 19 | 34 46 | 38·6 | 59 32 | 33 32 | 37·6 | 58 44 | 32 21 | 36·5 | 57 55 | 31 14 | 35·6 | 57 06 | 30 10 | 34·7 | 56 17 | 29 08 | 33·8 | 252 | 288 |
| 107 | 73 | 60 53 | 33 18 | 36·9 | 60 05 | 32 05 | 35·9 | 59 16 | 30 56 | 34·9 | 58 26 | 29 51 | 34·0 | 57 36 | 28 49 | 33·1 | 56 46 | 27 49 | 32·2 | 253 | 287 |
| 106 | 74 | 61 25 | 31 46 | 35·2 | 60 36 | 30 35 | 34·2 | 59 46 | 29 28 | 33·2 | 58 55 | 28 25 | 32·3 | 58 04 | 27 25 | 31·4 | 57 13 | 26 26 | 30·6 | 254 | 286 |
| 105 | 75 | 61 56 | 30 10 | 33·4 | 61 06 | 29 02 | 32·4 | 60 15 | 27 57 | 31·4 | 59 23 | 26 56 | 30·5 | 58 31 | 25 58 | 29·7 | 57 39 | 25 02 | 28·9 | 255 | 285 |
| 104 | 76 | 62 26 | 28 31 | 31·5 | 61 34 | 27 25 | 30·5 | 60 42 | 26 23 | 29·6 | 59 50 | 25 24 | 28·8 | 58 57 | 24 29 | 28·0 | 58 04 | 23 35 | 27·2 | 256 | 284 |
| 103 | 77 | 62 53 | 26 48 | 29·6 | 62 01 | 25 45 | 28·6 | 61 08 | 24 46 | 27·8 | 60 15 | 23 49 | 27·0 | 59 21 | 22 56 | 26·2 | 58 27 | 22 05 | 25·5 | 257 | 283 |
| 102 | 78 | 63 20 | 25 02 | 27·6 | 62 26 | 24 02 | 26·7 | 61 32 | 23 05 | 25·9 | 60 38 | 22 12 | 25·1 | 59 43 | 21 22 | 24·4 | 58 49 | 20 34 | 23·7 | 258 | 282 |
| 101 | 79 | 63 44 | 23 12 | 25·5 | 62 50 | 22 15 | 24·7 | 61 55 | 21 22 | 23·9 | 61 00 | 20 32 | 23·2 | 60 04 | 19 45 | 22·5 | 59 09 | 19 00 | 21·8 | 259 | 281 |
| 100 | 80 | 64 07 | 21 18 | 23·4 | 63 12 | 20 25 | 22·6 | 62 16 | 19 36 | 21·9 | 61 20 | 18 49 | 21·2 | 60 24 | 18 06 | 20·6 | 59 28 | 17 24 | 20·0 | 260 | 280 |
| 99 | 81 | 64 28 | 19 22 | 21·3 | 63 32 | 18 33 | 20·5 | 62 35 | 17 47 | 19·9 | 61 39 | 17 04 | 19·2 | 60 42 | 16 24 | 18·6 | 59 45 | 15 46 | 18·1 | 261 | 279 |
| 98 | 82 | 64 47 | 17 22 | 19·1 | 63 50 | 16 37 | 18·4 | 62 53 | 15 56 | 17·8 | 61 56 | 15 17 | 17·2 | 60 58 | 14 41 | 16·7 | 60 01 | 14 06 | 16·2 | 262 | 278 |
| 97 | 83 | 65 03 | 15 18 | 16·8 | 64 06 | 14 39 | 16·2 | 63 08 | 14 02 | 15·6 | 62 10 | 13 27 | 15·1 | 61 12 | 12 55 | 14·7 | 60 14 | 12 24 | 14·2 | 263 | 277 |
| 96 | 84 | 65 18 | 13 13 | 14·5 | 64 20 | 12 38 | 14·0 | 63 22 | 12 06 | 13·5 | 62 23 | 11 36 | 13·0 | 61 25 | 11 08 | 12·6 | 60 26 | 10 41 | 12·2 | 264 | 276 |
| 95 | 85 | 65 31 | 11 05 | 12·1 | 64 32 | 10 35 | 11·7 | 63 33 | 10 08 | 11·3 | 62 35 | 9 42 | 10·9 | 61 36 | 9 19 | 10·6 | 60 37 | 8 56 | 10·2 | 265 | 275 |
| 94 | 86 | 65 41 | 8 54 | 9·8 | 64 42 | 8 30 | 9·4 | 63 43 | 8 08 | 9·1 | 62 44 | 7 48 | 8·8 | 61 44 | 7 28 | 8·5 | 60 45 | 7 10 | 8·2 | 266 | 274 |
| 93 | 87 | 65 49 | 6 42 | 7·3 | 64 50 | 6 24 | 7·1 | 63 50 | 6 07 | 6·8 | 62 51 | 5 52 | 6·6 | 61 51 | 5 37 | 6·4 | 60 52 | 5 24 | 6·2 | 267 | 273 |
| 92 | 88 | 65 55 | 4 29 | 4·9 | 64 56 | 4 17 | 4·7 | 63 56 | 4 06 | 4·6 | 62 56 | 3 55 | 4·4 | 61 56 | 3 45 | 4·3 | 60 56 | 3 36 | 4·1 | 268 | 272 |
| 91 | 89 | 65 59 | 2 15 | 2·5 | 64 59 | 2 09 | 2·4 | 63 59 | 2 03 | 2·3 | 62 59 | 1 58 | 2·2 | 61 59 | 1 53 | 2·1 | 60 59 | 1 48 | 2·1 | 269 | 271 |
| 90 | 90 | 66 00 | 0 00 | 0·0 | 65 00 | 0 00 | 0·0 | 64 00 | 0 00 | 0·0 | 63 00 | 0 00 | 0·0 | 62 00 | 0 00 | 0·0 | 61 00 | 0 00 | 0·0 | 270 | 270 |

N. Lat.: for LHA $> 180°$ … $Z_n = Z$
for LHA $< 180°$ … $Z_n = 360° - Z$

S. Lat.: for LHA $> 180°$ … $Z_n = 180° - Z$
for LHA $< 180°$ … $Z_n = 180° + Z$

SIGHT REDUCTION TABLE

B: (−) for 90° < LHA < 270°
Dec:(−) for Lat. contrary name

Z₁: same sign as B
Z₂: (−) for F > 90°

| LHA/F | 30° A/H | 30° B/P | 30° Z₁/Z₂ | 31° A/H | 31° B/P | 31° Z₁/Z₂ | 32° A/H | 32° B/P | 32° Z₁/Z₂ | 33° A/H | 33° B/P | 33° Z₁/Z₂ | 34° A/H | 34° B/P | 34° Z₁/Z₂ | 35° A/H | 35° B/P | 35° Z₁/Z₂ | Lat./A LHA |
|---|---|---|---|---|---|---|---|---|---|---|---|---|---|---|---|---|---|---|---|
| 0 / 180 | 0 00 | 60 00 | 90·0 | 0 00 | 59 00 | 90·0 | 0 00 | 58 00 | 90·0 | 0 00 | 57 00 | 90·0 | 0 00 | 56 00 | 90·0 | 0 00 | 55 00 | 90·0 | 180 / 360 |
| 1 / 179 | 0 52 | 60 00 | 89·5 | 0 51 | 59 00 | 89·5 | 0 51 | 58 00 | 89·5 | 0 50 | 57 00 | 89·5 | 0 50 | 56 00 | 89·4 | 0 49 | 55 00 | 89·4 | 181 / 359 |
| 2 / 178 | 1 44 | 59 59 | 89·0 | 1 43 | 58 59 | 89·0 | 1 42 | 57 59 | 88·9 | 1 41 | 56 59 | 88·9 | 1 39 | 55 59 | 88·9 | 1 38 | 54 58 | 88·9 | 182 / 358 |
| 3 / 177 | 2 36 | 59 58 | 88·5 | 2 34 | 58 58 | 88·5 | 2 33 | 57 58 | 88·4 | 2 31 | 56 58 | 88·4 | 2 29 | 55 58 | 88·3 | 2 27 | 54 58 | 88·3 | 183 / 357 |
| 4 / 176 | 3 28 | 59 56 | 88·0 | 3 26 | 58 56 | 87·9 | 3 23 | 57 56 | 87·9 | 3 21 | 56 56 | 87·8 | 3 19 | 55 56 | 87·8 | 3 17 | 54 56 | 87·7 | 184 / 356 |
| 5 / 175 | 4 20 | 59 54 | 87·5 | 4 17 | 58 54 | 87·4 | 4 14 | 57 54 | 87·3 | 4 12 | 56 54 | 87·3 | 4 09 | 55 54 | 87·2 | 4 06 | 54 54 | 87·1 | 185 / 355 |
| 6 / 174 | 5 12 | 59 52 | 87·0 | 5 08 | 58 52 | 86·9 | 5 05 | 57 52 | 86·8 | 5 02 | 56 51 | 86·7 | 4 58 | 55 51 | 86·6 | 4 55 | 54 51 | 86·6 | 186 / 354 |
| 7 / 173 | 6 04 | 59 49 | 86·5 | 6 00 | 58 49 | 86·4 | 5 56 | 57 48 | 86·3 | 5 52 | 56 48 | 86·2 | 5 48 | 55 48 | 86·1 | 5 44 | 54 48 | 86·0 | 187 / 353 |
| 8 / 172 | 6 55 | 59 45 | 86·0 | 6 51 | 58 45 | 85·9 | 6 47 | 57 45 | 85·7 | 6 42 | 56 45 | 85·6 | 6 38 | 55 44 | 85·5 | 6 33 | 54 44 | 85·4 | 188 / 352 |
| 9 / 171 | 7 47 | 59 42 | 85·5 | 7 42 | 58 41 | 85·3 | 7 37 | 57 41 | 85·2 | 7 32 | 56 40 | 85·1 | 7 27 | 55 40 | 84·9 | 7 22 | 54 40 | 84·8 | 189 / 351 |
| 10 / 170 | 8 39 | 59 37 | 85·0 | 8 34 | 58 37 | 84·8 | 8 28 | 57 36 | 84·7 | 8 22 | 56 36 | 84·5 | 8 17 | 55 36 | 84·4 | 8 11 | 54 35 | 84·2 | 190 / 350 |
| 11 / 169 | 9 31 | 59 32 | 84·4 | 9 25 | 58 32 | 84·3 | 9 19 | 57 31 | 84·1 | 9 13 | 56 31 | 84·0 | 9 06 | 55 30 | 83·8 | 9 00 | 54 30 | 83·6 | 191 / 349 |
| 12 / 168 | 10 22 | 59 27 | 83·9 | 10 16 | 58 26 | 83·8 | 10 09 | 57 26 | 83·6 | 10 03 | 56 25 | 83·4 | 9 56 | 55 25 | 83·2 | 9 48 | 54 24 | 83·0 | 192 / 348 |
| 13 / 167 | 11 14 | 59 21 | 83·4 | 11 07 | 58 20 | 83·2 | 11 00 | 57 20 | 83·0 | 10 52 | 56 19 | 82·8 | 10 45 | 55 18 | 82·6 | 10 37 | 54 18 | 82·5 | 193 / 347 |
| 14 / 166 | 12 06 | 59 15 | 82·9 | 11 58 | 58 14 | 82·7 | 11 50 | 57 13 | 82·5 | 11 42 | 56 12 | 82·3 | 11 34 | 55 12 | 82·1 | 11 26 | 54 11 | 81·9 | 194 / 346 |
| 15 / 165 | 12 57 | 59 08 | 82·4 | 12 49 | 58 07 | 82·1 | 12 41 | 57 06 | 81·9 | 12 32 | 56 05 | 81·7 | 12 23 | 55 04 | 81·5 | 12 14 | 54 04 | 81·3 | 195 / 345 |
| 16 / 164 | 13 49 | 59 01 | 81·8 | 13 40 | 58 00 | 81·6 | 13 31 | 56 58 | 81·4 | 13 22 | 55 57 | 81·1 | 13 13 | 54 57 | 80·9 | 13 03 | 53 56 | 80·7 | 196 / 344 |
| 17 / 163 | 14 40 | 58 53 | 81·3 | 14 31 | 57 51 | 81·1 | 14 21 | 56 50 | 80·8 | 14 12 | 55 49 | 80·5 | 14 02 | 54 48 | 80·3 | 13 51 | 53 47 | 80·1 | 197 / 343 |
| 18 / 162 | 15 31 | 58 44 | 80·8 | 15 22 | 57 43 | 80·5 | 15 12 | 56 42 | 80·2 | 15 01 | 55 40 | 80·0 | 14 51 | 54 39 | 79·7 | 14 40 | 53 38 | 79·4 | 198 / 342 |
| 19 / 161 | 16 23 | 58 35 | 80·2 | 16 12 | 57 34 | 79·9 | 16 02 | 56 32 | 79·7 | 15 51 | 55 31 | 79·4 | 15 40 | 54 30 | 79·1 | 15 28 | 53 29 | 78·8 | 199 / 341 |
| 20 / 160 | 17 14 | 58 26 | 79·7 | 17 03 | 57 24 | 79·4 | 16 52 | 56 23 | 79·1 | 16 40 | 55 21 | 78·8 | 16 28 | 54 20 | 78·5 | 16 16 | 53 19 | 78·2 | 200 / 340 |
| 21 / 159 | 18 05 | 58 16 | 79·1 | 17 53 | 57 14 | 78·8 | 17 42 | 56 12 | 78·5 | 17 29 | 55 11 | 78·2 | 17 17 | 54 09 | 77·9 | 17 04 | 53 08 | 77·6 | 201 / 339 |
| 22 / 158 | 18 56 | 58 05 | 78·6 | 18 44 | 57 03 | 78·2 | 18 31 | 56 01 | 77·9 | 18 19 | 55 00 | 77·6 | 18 06 | 53 58 | 77·3 | 17 52 | 52 56 | 77·0 | 202 / 338 |
| 23 / 157 | 19 47 | 57 54 | 78·0 | 19 34 | 56 52 | 77·7 | 19 21 | 55 50 | 77·3 | 19 08 | 54 48 | 77·0 | 18 54 | 53 46 | 76·6 | 18 40 | 52 44 | 76·3 | 203 / 337 |
| 24 / 156 | 20 37 | 57 42 | 77·4 | 20 24 | 56 40 | 77·1 | 20 11 | 55 38 | 76·7 | 19 57 | 54 36 | 76·4 | 19 42 | 53 34 | 76·0 | 19 28 | 52 32 | 75·7 | 204 / 336 |
| 25 / 155 | 21 28 | 57 30 | 76·9 | 21 14 | 56 27 | 76·5 | 21 00 | 55 25 | 76·1 | 20 46 | 54 23 | 75·7 | 20 31 | 53 21 | 75·4 | 20 15 | 52 19 | 75·0 | 205 / 335 |
| 26 / 154 | 22 19 | 57 17 | 76·3 | 22 04 | 56 14 | 75·9 | 21 49 | 55 12 | 75·5 | 21 34 | 54 09 | 75·1 | 21 19 | 53 07 | 74·7 | 21 03 | 52 05 | 74·4 | 206 / 334 |
| 27 / 153 | 23 09 | 57 03 | 75·7 | 22 54 | 56 00 | 75·3 | 22 39 | 54 57 | 74·9 | 22 23 | 53 55 | 74·5 | 22 07 | 52 52 | 74·1 | 21 50 | 51 50 | 73·7 | 207 / 333 |
| 28 / 152 | 23 59 | 56 49 | 75·1 | 23 44 | 55 46 | 74·7 | 23 28 | 54 43 | 74·3 | 23 11 | 53 40 | 73·8 | 22 54 | 52 37 | 73·4 | 22 37 | 51 35 | 73·0 | 208 / 332 |
| 29 / 151 | 24 50 | 56 34 | 74·5 | 24 33 | 55 31 | 74·1 | 24 17 | 54 27 | 73·6 | 23 59 | 53 24 | 73·2 | 23 42 | 52 22 | 72·8 | 23 24 | 51 19 | 72·4 | 209 / 331 |
| 30 / 150 | 25 40 | 56 19 | 73·9 | 25 23 | 55 15 | 73·4 | 25 05 | 54 11 | 73·0 | 24 48 | 53 08 | 72·5 | 24 29 | 52 05 | 72·1 | 24 11 | 51 03 | 71·7 | 210 / 330 |
| 31 / 149 | 26 29 | 56 02 | 73·3 | 26 12 | 54 58 | 72·8 | 25 54 | 53 54 | 72·3 | 25 35 | 52 51 | 71·9 | 25 17 | 51 48 | 71·4 | 24 57 | 50 45 | 71·0 | 211 / 329 |
| 32 / 148 | 27 19 | 55 45 | 72·6 | 27 01 | 54 41 | 72·2 | 26 42 | 53 37 | 71·7 | 26 23 | 52 33 | 71·2 | 26 04 | 51 31 | 70·7 | 25 44 | 50 27 | 70·3 | 212 / 328 |
| 33 / 147 | 28 09 | 55 27 | 72·0 | 27 50 | 54 23 | 71·5 | 27 31 | 53 19 | 71·0 | 27 11 | 52 15 | 70·5 | 26 50 | 51 12 | 70·0 | 26 30 | 50 08 | 69·6 | 213 / 327 |
| 34 / 146 | 28 58 | 55 09 | 71·4 | 28 38 | 54 04 | 70·8 | 28 19 | 53 00 | 70·3 | 27 58 | 51 56 | 69·8 | 27 37 | 50 52 | 69·3 | 27 16 | 49 49 | 68·8 | 214 / 326 |
| 35 / 145 | 29 47 | 54 49 | 70·7 | 29 27 | 53 44 | 70·2 | 29 06 | 52 40 | 69·6 | 28 45 | 51 36 | 69·1 | 28 24 | 50 32 | 68·6 | 28 01 | 49 29 | 68·1 | 215 / 325 |
| 36 / 144 | 30 36 | 54 29 | 70·0 | 30 15 | 53 24 | 69·5 | 29 54 | 52 19 | 68·9 | 29 32 | 51 15 | 68·4 | 29 10 | 50 11 | 67·9 | 28 47 | 49 07 | 67·4 | 216 / 324 |
| 37 / 143 | 31 25 | 54 08 | 69·4 | 31 03 | 53 03 | 68·8 | 30 41 | 51 58 | 68·2 | 30 19 | 50 53 | 67·7 | 29 56 | 49 49 | 67·2 | 29 32 | 48 45 | 66·6 | 217 / 323 |
| 38 / 142 | 32 13 | 53 46 | 68·7 | 31 51 | 52 40 | 68·1 | 31 28 | 51 35 | 67·5 | 31 05 | 50 30 | 66·9 | 30 41 | 49 26 | 66·4 | 30 17 | 48 23 | 65·9 | 218 / 322 |
| 39 / 141 | 33 02 | 53 23 | 68·0 | 32 39 | 52 17 | 67·4 | 32 15 | 51 12 | 66·8 | 31 51 | 50 07 | 66·2 | 31 27 | 49 03 | 65·6 | 31 02 | 47 59 | 65·1 | 219 / 321 |
| 40 / 140 | 33 50 | 53 00 | 67·2 | 33 26 | 51 53 | 66·6 | 33 02 | 50 48 | 66·0 | 32 37 | 49 43 | 65·4 | 32 12 | 48 38 | 64·9 | 31 46 | 47 34 | 64·3 | 220 / 320 |
| 41 / 139 | 34 37 | 52 35 | 66·5 | 34 13 | 51 29 | 65·9 | 33 48 | 50 23 | 65·3 | 33 23 | 49 17 | 64·7 | 32 57 | 48 13 | 64·1 | 32 30 | 47 09 | 63·5 | 221 / 319 |
| 42 / 138 | 35 25 | 52 09 | 65·8 | 35 00 | 51 03 | 65·1 | 34 34 | 49 56 | 64·5 | 34 08 | 48 51 | 63·9 | 33 42 | 47 46 | 63·3 | 33 14 | 46 42 | 62·7 | 222 / 318 |
| 43 / 137 | 36 12 | 51 43 | 65·0 | 35 46 | 50 36 | 64·3 | 35 20 | 49 29 | 63·7 | 34 53 | 48 24 | 63·1 | 34 26 | 47 19 | 62·5 | 33 58 | 46 15 | 61·9 | 223 / 317 |
| 44 / 136 | 36 59 | 51 15 | 64·2 | 36 33 | 50 08 | 63·6 | 36 06 | 49 01 | 62·9 | 35 38 | 47 55 | 62·3 | 35 10 | 46 51 | 61·6 | 34 41 | 45 46 | 61·0 | 224 / 316 |
| 45 / 135 | 37 46 | 50 46 | 63·4 | 37 19 | 49 39 | 62·7 | 36 51 | 48 32 | 62·1 | 36 22 | 47 26 | 61·4 | 35 53 | 46 21 | 60·8 | 35 24 | 45 17 | 60·2 | 225 / 315 |

| Lat./A | LHA/F | 30° A/H | 30° B/P | 30° Z₁/Z₂ | 31° A/H | 31° B/P | 31° Z₁/Z₂ | 32° A/H | 32° B/P | 32° Z₁/Z₂ | 33° A/H | 33° B/P | 33° Z₁/Z₂ | 34° A/H | 34° B/P | 34° Z₁/Z₂ | 35° A/H | 35° B/P | 35° Z₁/Z₂ | Lat./A | LHA |
|---|---|---|---|---|---|---|---|---|---|---|---|---|---|---|---|---|---|---|---|---|---|
| 135 | 45 | 37 46 | 50 46 | 63·4 | 37 19 | 49 39 | 62·7 | 36 51 | 48 32 | 62·1 | 36 22 | 47 26 | 61·4 | 35 53 | 46 21 | 60·8 | 35 24 | 45 17 | 60·2 | 315 | 225 |
| 134 | 46 | 38 32 | 50 16 | 62·6 | 38 04 | 49 08 | 61·9 | 37 36 | 48 02 | 61·2 | 37 06 | 46 56 | 60·6 | 36 37 | 45 51 | 59·9 | 36 06 | 44 46 | 59·3 | 314 | 226 |
| 133 | 47 | 39 18 | 49 45 | 61·8 | 38 49 | 48 37 | 61·1 | 38 20 | 47 30 | 60·4 | 37 50 | 46 24 | 59·7 | 37 19 | 45 19 | 59·1 | 36 48 | 44 15 | 58·4 | 313 | 227 |
| 132 | 48 | 40 04 | 49 13 | 61·0 | 39 34 | 48 05 | 60·2 | 39 04 | 46 58 | 59·5 | 38 33 | 45 51 | 58·8 | 38 02 | 44 46 | 58·2 | 37 30 | 43 42 | 57·5 | 312 | 228 |
| 131 | 49 | 40 49 | 48 39 | 60·1 | 40 19 | 47 31 | 59·4 | 39 48 | 46 24 | 58·6 | 39 16 | 45 18 | 58·0 | 38 44 | 44 12 | 57·2 | 38 11 | 43 08 | 56·6 | 311 | 229 |
| 130 | 50 | 41 34 | 48 04 | 59·2 | 41 03 | 46 56 | 58·5 | 40 31 | 45 49 | 57·7 | 39 59 | 44 42 | 57·0 | 39 26 | 43 37 | 56·3 | 38 52 | 42 33 | 55·6 | 310 | 230 |
| 129 | 51 | 42 18 | 47 28 | 58·3 | 41 46 | 46 20 | 57·5 | 41 14 | 45 12 | 56·8 | 40 41 | 44 06 | 56·1 | 40 07 | 43 01 | 55·4 | 39 32 | 41 57 | 54·7 | 309 | 231 |
| 128 | 52 | 43 02 | 46 50 | 57·4 | 42 29 | 45 42 | 56·6 | 41 56 | 44 34 | 55·9 | 41 22 | 43 28 | 55·1 | 40 47 | 42 23 | 54·4 | 40 12 | 41 19 | 53·7 | 308 | 232 |
| 127 | 53 | 43 46 | 46 11 | 56·4 | 43 12 | 45 03 | 55·6 | 42 38 | 43 55 | 54·9 | 42 03 | 42 49 | 54·1 | 41 28 | 41 44 | 53·4 | 40 52 | 40 41 | 52·7 | 307 | 233 |
| 126 | 54 | 44 29 | 45 31 | 55·5 | 43 54 | 44 22 | 54·7 | 43 19 | 43 15 | 53·9 | 42 44 | 42 09 | 53·1 | 42 08 | 41 04 | 52·4 | 41 30 | 40 01 | 51·7 | 306 | 234 |
| 125 | 55 | 45 11 | 44 49 | 54·5 | 44 36 | 43 40 | 53·7 | 44 00 | 42 33 | 52·9 | 43 24 | 41 27 | 52·1 | 42 46 | 40 23 | 51·4 | 42 09 | 39 19 | 50·7 | 305 | 235 |
| 124 | 56 | 45 53 | 44 05 | 53·5 | 45 17 | 42 57 | 52·6 | 44 40 | 41 50 | 51·8 | 44 03 | 40 44 | 51·1 | 43 25 | 39 40 | 50·3 | 42 46 | 38 37 | 49·6 | 304 | 236 |
| 123 | 57 | 46 35 | 43 20 | 52·4 | 45 58 | 42 11 | 51·6 | 45 20 | 41 05 | 50·8 | 44 42 | 39 59 | 50·0 | 44 03 | 38 55 | 49·3 | 43 24 | 37 53 | 48·5 | 303 | 237 |
| 122 | 58 | 47 16 | 42 33 | 51·3 | 46 38 | 41 25 | 50·5 | 45 59 | 40 18 | 49·7 | 45 20 | 39 13 | 48·9 | 44 40 | 38 09 | 48·2 | 44 00 | 37 07 | 47·5 | 302 | 238 |
| 121 | 59 | 47 56 | 41 44 | 50·2 | 47 17 | 40 36 | 49·4 | 46 38 | 39 30 | 48·6 | 45 58 | 38 25 | 47·8 | 45 17 | 37 21 | 47·1 | 44 36 | 36 20 | 46·3 | 301 | 239 |
| 120 | 60 | 48 35 | 40 54 | 49·1 | 47 56 | 39 46 | 48·3 | 47 16 | 38 40 | 47·5 | 46 35 | 37 36 | 46·7 | 45 53 | 36 33 | 45·9 | 45 11 | 35 32 | 45·2 | 300 | 240 |
| 119 | 61 | 49 14 | 40 01 | 47·9 | 48 34 | 38 54 | 47·1 | 47 53 | 37 48 | 46·3 | 47 11 | 36 45 | 45·5 | 46 29 | 35 42 | 44·7 | 45 46 | 34 42 | 44·0 | 299 | 241 |
| 118 | 62 | 49 53 | 39 07 | 46·8 | 49 11 | 38 00 | 45·9 | 48 29 | 36 55 | 45·1 | 47 46 | 35 52 | 44·3 | 47 03 | 34 50 | 43·6 | 46 19 | 33 50 | 42·8 | 298 | 242 |
| 117 | 63 | 50 30 | 38 11 | 45·5 | 49 48 | 37 04 | 44·7 | 49 05 | 36 00 | 43·9 | 48 21 | 34 57 | 43·1 | 47 37 | 33 57 | 42·3 | 46 53 | 32 57 | 41·6 | 297 | 243 |
| 116 | 64 | 51 07 | 37 13 | 44·3 | 50 23 | 36 07 | 43·4 | 49 40 | 35 03 | 42·6 | 48 55 | 34 01 | 41·8 | 48 10 | 33 01 | 41·1 | 47 25 | 32 03 | 40·4 | 296 | 244 |
| 115 | 65 | 51 43 | 36 12 | 43·0 | 50 58 | 35 07 | 42·2 | 50 14 | 34 04 | 41·3 | 49 28 | 33 03 | 40·6 | 48 43 | 32 04 | 39·8 | 47 56 | 31 07 | 39·1 | 295 | 245 |
| 114 | 66 | 52 18 | 35 10 | 41·7 | 51 33 | 34 06 | 40·8 | 50 47 | 33 04 | 40·0 | 50 01 | 32 04 | 39·3 | 49 14 | 31 05 | 38·5 | 48 27 | 30 09 | 37·8 | 294 | 246 |
| 113 | 67 | 52 52 | 34 05 | 40·3 | 52 06 | 33 02 | 39·5 | 51 19 | 32 01 | 38·7 | 50 32 | 31 02 | 37·9 | 49 44 | 30 05 | 37·2 | 48 56 | 29 10 | 36·5 | 293 | 247 |
| 112 | 68 | 53 25 | 32 59 | 38·9 | 52 38 | 31 56 | 38·1 | 51 50 | 30 57 | 37·3 | 51 02 | 29 59 | 36·6 | 50 14 | 29 03 | 35·8 | 49 25 | 28 09 | 35·2 | 292 | 248 |
| 111 | 69 | 53 57 | 31 50 | 37·5 | 53 09 | 30 49 | 36·7 | 52 21 | 29 50 | 35·9 | 51 32 | 28 53 | 35·2 | 50 43 | 27 59 | 34·5 | 49 53 | 27 06 | 33·8 | 291 | 249 |
| 110 | 70 | 54 28 | 30 39 | 36·1 | 53 39 | 29 39 | 35·2 | 52 50 | 28 42 | 34·5 | 52 00 | 27 46 | 33·8 | 51 10 | 26 53 | 33·1 | 50 20 | 26 02 | 32·4 | 290 | 250 |
| 109 | 71 | 54 58 | 29 25 | 34·6 | 54 08 | 28 27 | 33·8 | 53 18 | 27 31 | 33·0 | 52 28 | 26 38 | 32·3 | 51 37 | 25 46 | 31·6 | 50 46 | 24 56 | 31·0 | 289 | 251 |
| 108 | 72 | 55 27 | 28 09 | 33·0 | 54 37 | 27 13 | 32·2 | 53 46 | 26 19 | 31·5 | 52 54 | 25 27 | 30·8 | 52 03 | 24 37 | 30·2 | 51 10 | 23 49 | 29·5 | 288 | 252 |
| 107 | 73 | 55 55 | 26 51 | 31·4 | 55 03 | 25 57 | 30·7 | 54 12 | 25 04 | 30·0 | 53 19 | 24 14 | 29·3 | 52 27 | 23 26 | 28·7 | 51 34 | 22 42 | 28·1 | 287 | 253 |
| 106 | 74 | 56 21 | 25 31 | 29·8 | 55 29 | 24 39 | 29·1 | 54 36 | 23 48 | 28·4 | 53 43 | 23 00 | 27·8 | 52 50 | 22 14 | 27·1 | 51 57 | 21 29 | 26·6 | 286 | 254 |
| 105 | 75 | 56 46 | 24 09 | 28·2 | 55 53 | 23 18 | 27·5 | 55 00 | 22 30 | 26·8 | 54 06 | 21 44 | 26·2 | 53 12 | 21 00 | 25·6 | 52 18 | 20 17 | 25·0 | 285 | 255 |
| 104 | 76 | 57 10 | 22 44 | 26·5 | 56 16 | 21 56 | 25·8 | 55 22 | 21 10 | 25·2 | 54 28 | 20 26 | 24·6 | 53 33 | 19 44 | 24·1 | 52 38 | 19 04 | 23·5 | 284 | 256 |
| 103 | 77 | 57 33 | 21 17 | 24·8 | 56 38 | 20 31 | 24·1 | 55 43 | 19 48 | 23·5 | 54 48 | 19 06 | 23·0 | 53 53 | 18 27 | 22·5 | 52 57 | 17 49 | 21·9 | 283 | 257 |
| 102 | 78 | 57 54 | 19 48 | 23·0 | 56 59 | 19 05 | 22·4 | 56 03 | 18 24 | 21·9 | 55 07 | 17 45 | 21·3 | 54 11 | 17 08 | 20·8 | 53 15 | 16 32 | 20·3 | 282 | 258 |
| 101 | 79 | 58 13 | 18 17 | 21·2 | 57 17 | 17 37 | 20·7 | 56 23 | 16 59 | 20·1 | 55 25 | 16 22 | 19·6 | 54 28 | 15 48 | 19·2 | 53 31 | 15 15 | 18·7 | 281 | 259 |
| 100 | 80 | 58 32 | 16 44 | 19·4 | 57 35 | 16 07 | 18·9 | 56 38 | 15 32 | 18·4 | 55 41 | 14 58 | 17·9 | 54 44 | 14 26 | 17·5 | 53 47 | 13 56 | 17·1 | 280 | 260 |
| 99 | 81 | 58 48 | 15 10 | 17·6 | 57 51 | 14 36 | 17·1 | 56 53 | 14 03 | 16·6 | 55 56 | 13 33 | 16·2 | 54 58 | 13 03 | 15·8 | 54 00 | 12 36 | 15·4 | 279 | 261 |
| 98 | 82 | 59 03 | 13 33 | 15·7 | 58 05 | 13 02 | 15·3 | 57 07 | 12 33 | 14·9 | 56 09 | 12 06 | 14·5 | 55 11 | 11 40 | 14·1 | 54 13 | 11 14 | 13·8 | 278 | 262 |
| 97 | 83 | 59 16 | 11 55 | 13·8 | 58 18 | 11 28 | 13·4 | 57 19 | 11 02 | 13·0 | 56 21 | 10 38 | 12·7 | 55 24 | 10 14 | 12·4 | 54 24 | 9 52 | 12·1 | 277 | 263 |
| 96 | 84 | 59 28 | 10 16 | 11·9 | 58 29 | 9 52 | 11·5 | 57 30 | 9 30 | 11·2 | 56 31 | 9 09 | 10·9 | 55 33 | 8 49 | 10·6 | 54 33 | 8 29 | 10·4 | 276 | 264 |
| 95 | 85 | 59 37 | 8 35 | 9·9 | 58 38 | 8 15 | 9·6 | 57 39 | 7 56 | 9·4 | 56 40 | 7 39 | 9·1 | 55 41 | 7 22 | 8·9 | 54 41 | 7 06 | 8·7 | 275 | 265 |
| 94 | 86 | 59 46 | 6 53 | 8·0 | 58 46 | 6 37 | 7·7 | 57 47 | 6 22 | 7·5 | 56 47 | 6 08 | 7·3 | 55 48 | 5 54 | 7·1 | 54 48 | 5 41 | 7·0 | 274 | 266 |
| 93 | 87 | 59 52 | 5 11 | 6·0 | 58 52 | 4 59 | 5·8 | 57 52 | 4 47 | 5·6 | 56 53 | 4 36 | 5·5 | 55 53 | 4 26 | 5·4 | 54 53 | 4 16 | 5·2 | 273 | 267 |
| 92 | 88 | 59 56 | 3 28 | 4·0 | 58 57 | 3 19 | 3·9 | 57 57 | 3 12 | 3·8 | 56 57 | 3 05 | 3·7 | 55 57 | 2 58 | 3·6 | 54 57 | 2 51 | 3·5 | 272 | 268 |
| 91 | 89 | 59 59 | 1 44 | 2·0 | 58 59 | 1 40 | 1·9 | 57 59 | 1 36 | 1·9 | 56 59 | 1 32 | 1·8 | 55 59 | 1 29 | 1·8 | 54 59 | 1 26 | 1·7 | 271 | 269 |
| 90 | 90 | 60 00 | 0 00 | 0·0 | 59 00 | 0 00 | 0·0 | 58 00 | 0 00 | 0·0 | 57 00 | 0 00 | 0·0 | 56 00 | 0 00 | 0·0 | 55 00 | 0 00 | 0·0 | 270 | 270 |

N. Lat.: for LHA > 180° .... Zₙ = Z
for LHA < 180° .... Zₙ = 360° − Z

S. Lat.: for LHA > 180° .... Zₙ = 180° − Z
for LHA < 180° .... Zₙ = 180° + Z

**SIGHT REDUCTION TABLE**

B: (−) for 90° < LHA < 270°  
Dec:(−) for Lat. contrary name

Z₁: same sign as B  
Z₂: (−) for F > 90°

| LHA/F | F | 36° A/H | 36° B/P | 36° Z₁/Z₂ | 37° A/H | 37° B/P | 37° Z₁/Z₂ | 38° A/H | 38° B/P | 38° Z₁/Z₂ | 39° A/H | 39° B/P | 39° Z₁/Z₂ | 40° A/H | 40° B/P | 40° Z₁/Z₂ | 41° A/H | 41° B/P | 41° Z₁/Z₂ | Lat./A | LHA |
|---|---|---|---|---|---|---|---|---|---|---|---|---|---|---|---|---|---|---|---|---|---|
| 0 | 180 | 0 00 | 54 00 | 90.0 | 0 00 | 53 00 | 90.0 | 0 00 | 52 00 | 90.0 | 0 00 | 51 00 | 90.0 | 0 00 | 50 00 | 90.0 | 0 00 | 49 00 | 90.0 | 180 | 360 |
| 1 | 179 | 0 49 | 54 00 | 89.4 | 0 48 | 53 00 | 89.4 | 0 47 | 52 00 | 89.4 | 0 47 | 51 00 | 89.4 | 0 46 | 50 00 | 89.4 | 0 45 | 49 00 | 89.3 | 181 | 359 |
| 2 | 178 | 1 37 | 53 59 | 88.8 | 1 36 | 52 59 | 88.8 | 1 35 | 51 59 | 88.8 | 1 33 | 50 59 | 88.7 | 1 32 | 49 59 | 88.7 | 1 31 | 48 59 | 88.7 | 182 | 358 |
| 3 | 177 | 2 26 | 53 58 | 88.2 | 2 24 | 52 58 | 88.2 | 2 22 | 51 58 | 88.2 | 2 20 | 50 58 | 88.1 | 2 18 | 49 58 | 88.1 | 2 16 | 48 58 | 88.0 | 183 | 357 |
| 4 | 176 | 3 14 | 53 56 | 87.6 | 3 12 | 52 56 | 87.6 | 3 09 | 51 56 | 87.5 | 3 06 | 50 56 | 87.5 | 3 04 | 49 56 | 87.4 | 3 01 | 48 56 | 87.4 | 184 | 356 |
| 5 | 175 | 4 03 | 53 54 | 87.1 | 3 59 | 52 54 | 87.0 | 3 56 | 51 54 | 86.9 | 3 53 | 50 54 | 86.8 | 3 50 | 49 54 | 86.8 | 3 46 | 48 54 | 86.7 | 185 | 355 |
| 6 | 174 | 4 51 | 53 51 | 86.5 | 4 47 | 52 51 | 86.4 | 4 43 | 51 51 | 86.3 | 4 40 | 50 51 | 86.2 | 4 36 | 49 51 | 86.1 | 4 31 | 48 51 | 86.1 | 186 | 354 |
| 7 | 173 | 5 39 | 53 48 | 85.9 | 5 35 | 52 48 | 85.8 | 5 31 | 51 48 | 85.7 | 5 26 | 50 47 | 85.6 | 5 21 | 49 47 | 85.5 | 5 17 | 48 47 | 85.4 | 187 | 353 |
| 8 | 172 | 6 28 | 53 44 | 85.3 | 6 23 | 52 44 | 85.2 | 6 18 | 51 44 | 85.1 | 6 13 | 50 44 | 84.9 | 6 07 | 49 43 | 84.8 | 6 02 | 48 43 | 84.7 | 188 | 352 |
| 9 | 171 | 7 16 | 53 40 | 84.7 | 7 11 | 52 39 | 84.6 | 7 05 | 51 39 | 84.4 | 6 59 | 50 39 | 84.3 | 6 53 | 49 39 | 84.2 | 6 47 | 48 39 | 84.1 | 189 | 351 |
| 10 | 170 | 8 05 | 53 35 | 84.1 | 7 58 | 52 35 | 83.9 | 7 52 | 51 34 | 83.8 | 7 45 | 50 34 | 83.7 | 7 39 | 49 34 | 83.5 | 7 32 | 48 34 | 83.4 | 190 | 350 |
| 11 | 169 | 8 53 | 53 30 | 83.5 | 8 46 | 52 29 | 83.3 | 8 39 | 51 29 | 83.2 | 8 32 | 50 29 | 83.0 | 8 24 | 49 29 | 82.9 | 8 17 | 48 28 | 82.7 | 191 | 349 |
| 12 | 168 | 9 41 | 53 24 | 82.9 | 9 33 | 52 23 | 82.7 | 9 26 | 51 23 | 82.5 | 9 18 | 50 23 | 82.4 | 9 10 | 49 23 | 82.2 | 9 02 | 48 22 | 82.1 | 192 | 348 |
| 13 | 167 | 10 29 | 53 17 | 82.3 | 10 21 | 52 17 | 82.1 | 10 13 | 51 17 | 81.9 | 10 04 | 50 16 | 81.7 | 9 55 | 49 16 | 81.6 | 9 46 | 48 16 | 81.4 | 193 | 347 |
| 14 | 166 | 11 17 | 53 10 | 81.7 | 11 08 | 52 10 | 81.5 | 10 59 | 51 10 | 81.3 | 10 50 | 50 09 | 81.1 | 10 41 | 49 09 | 80.9 | 10 31 | 48 09 | 80.7 | 194 | 346 |
| 15 | 165 | 12 05 | 53 03 | 81.0 | 11 56 | 52 02 | 80.8 | 11 46 | 51 02 | 80.6 | 11 36 | 50 02 | 80.4 | 11 26 | 49 01 | 80.2 | 11 16 | 48 01 | 80.0 | 195 | 345 |
| 16 | 164 | 12 53 | 52 55 | 80.4 | 12 43 | 51 54 | 80.2 | 12 33 | 50 54 | 80.0 | 12 22 | 49 53 | 79.8 | 12 11 | 48 53 | 79.6 | 12 00 | 47 53 | 79.3 | 196 | 344 |
| 17 | 163 | 13 41 | 52 46 | 79.8 | 13 30 | 51 46 | 79.6 | 13 19 | 50 45 | 79.3 | 13 08 | 49 45 | 79.1 | 12 57 | 48 44 | 78.9 | 12 45 | 47 44 | 78.7 | 197 | 343 |
| 18 | 162 | 14 29 | 52 37 | 79.2 | 14 17 | 51 37 | 78.9 | 14 06 | 50 36 | 78.7 | 13 54 | 49 35 | 78.4 | 13 42 | 48 35 | 78.2 | 13 29 | 47 34 | 78.0 | 198 | 342 |
| 19 | 161 | 15 16 | 52 28 | 78.6 | 15 04 | 51 27 | 78.3 | 14 52 | 50 26 | 78.0 | 14 39 | 49 25 | 77.8 | 14 27 | 48 25 | 77.5 | 14 13 | 47 24 | 77.3 | 199 | 341 |
| 20 | 160 | 16 04 | 52 17 | 77.9 | 15 51 | 51 16 | 77.6 | 15 38 | 50 16 | 77.4 | 15 25 | 49 15 | 77.1 | 15 11 | 48 14 | 76.8 | 14 58 | 47 14 | 76.6 | 200 | 340 |
| 21 | 159 | 16 51 | 52 07 | 77.3 | 16 38 | 51 05 | 77.0 | 16 24 | 50 05 | 76.7 | 16 10 | 49 04 | 76.4 | 15 56 | 48 03 | 76.1 | 15 42 | 47 03 | 75.9 | 201 | 339 |
| 22 | 158 | 17 39 | 51 55 | 76.6 | 17 24 | 50 54 | 76.3 | 17 10 | 49 53 | 76.0 | 16 56 | 48 52 | 75.7 | 16 41 | 47 51 | 75.4 | 16 25 | 46 51 | 75.2 | 202 | 338 |
| 23 | 157 | 18 26 | 51 43 | 76.0 | 18 11 | 50 42 | 75.7 | 17 56 | 49 41 | 75.4 | 17 41 | 48 40 | 75.0 | 17 25 | 47 39 | 74.7 | 17 09 | 46 38 | 74.4 | 203 | 337 |
| 24 | 156 | 19 13 | 51 30 | 75.3 | 18 57 | 50 29 | 75.0 | 18 42 | 49 28 | 74.7 | 18 26 | 48 27 | 74.3 | 18 09 | 47 26 | 74.0 | 17 53 | 46 25 | 73.7 | 204 | 336 |
| 25 | 155 | 20 00 | 51 17 | 74.7 | 19 44 | 50 15 | 74.3 | 19 27 | 49 14 | 74.0 | 19 10 | 48 13 | 73.6 | 18 53 | 47 12 | 73.3 | 18 36 | 46 12 | 73.0 | 205 | 335 |
| 26 | 154 | 20 46 | 51 03 | 74.0 | 20 30 | 50 01 | 73.6 | 20 13 | 49 00 | 73.3 | 19 55 | 47 59 | 72.9 | 19 37 | 46 59 | 72.6 | 19 19 | 45 57 | 72.3 | 206 | 334 |
| 27 | 153 | 21 33 | 50 48 | 73.3 | 21 15 | 49 47 | 73.0 | 20 58 | 48 45 | 72.6 | 20 40 | 47 44 | 72.2 | 20 21 | 46 43 | 71.9 | 20 02 | 45 42 | 71.5 | 207 | 333 |
| 28 | 152 | 22 19 | 50 33 | 72.6 | 22 01 | 49 31 | 72.3 | 21 43 | 48 30 | 71.9 | 21 24 | 47 28 | 71.5 | 21 05 | 46 28 | 71.1 | 20 45 | 45 27 | 70.8 | 208 | 332 |
| 29 | 151 | 23 06 | 50 17 | 72.0 | 22 47 | 49 15 | 71.6 | 22 28 | 48 14 | 71.2 | 22 08 | 47 12 | 70.8 | 21 48 | 46 11 | 70.4 | 21 28 | 45 11 | 70.0 | 209 | 331 |
| 30 | 150 | 23 52 | 50 00 | 71.3 | 23 32 | 48 58 | 70.8 | 23 12 | 47 57 | 70.4 | 22 52 | 46 55 | 70.0 | 22 31 | 45 54 | 69.6 | 22 10 | 44 54 | 69.3 | 210 | 330 |
| 31 | 149 | 24 37 | 49 43 | 70.5 | 24 17 | 48 41 | 70.1 | 23 57 | 47 39 | 69.7 | 23 36 | 46 38 | 69.3 | 23 14 | 45 36 | 68.9 | 22 52 | 44 36 | 68.5 | 211 | 329 |
| 32 | 148 | 25 23 | 49 25 | 69.8 | 25 02 | 48 23 | 69.4 | 24 41 | 47 21 | 69.0 | 24 19 | 46 19 | 68.5 | 23 57 | 45 18 | 68.1 | 23 34 | 44 17 | 67.7 | 212 | 328 |
| 33 | 147 | 26 09 | 49 06 | 69.1 | 25 47 | 48 04 | 68.7 | 25 25 | 47 02 | 68.2 | 25 02 | 46 00 | 67.8 | 24 40 | 44 59 | 67.3 | 24 16 | 43 58 | 66.9 | 213 | 327 |
| 34 | 146 | 26 54 | 48 46 | 68.4 | 26 32 | 47 44 | 67.9 | 26 09 | 46 42 | 67.4 | 25 45 | 45 40 | 67.0 | 25 22 | 44 39 | 66.6 | 24 58 | 43 39 | 66.1 | 214 | 326 |
| 35 | 145 | 27 39 | 48 26 | 67.6 | 27 16 | 47 24 | 67.1 | 26 52 | 46 21 | 66.7 | 26 28 | 45 20 | 66.2 | 26 04 | 44 19 | 65.8 | 25 39 | 43 18 | 65.3 | 215 | 325 |
| 36 | 144 | 28 24 | 48 04 | 66.9 | 28 00 | 47 02 | 66.4 | 27 36 | 46 00 | 65.9 | 27 11 | 44 58 | 65.4 | 26 46 | 43 57 | 65.0 | 26 20 | 42 57 | 64.5 | 216 | 324 |
| 37 | 143 | 29 08 | 47 42 | 66.1 | 28 44 | 46 40 | 65.6 | 28 19 | 45 38 | 65.1 | 27 53 | 44 36 | 64.6 | 27 27 | 43 35 | 64.2 | 27 01 | 42 34 | 63.7 | 217 | 323 |
| 38 | 142 | 29 52 | 47 19 | 65.3 | 29 27 | 46 17 | 64.8 | 29 01 | 45 15 | 64.3 | 28 35 | 44 13 | 63.8 | 28 08 | 43 12 | 63.3 | 27 41 | 42 12 | 62.9 | 218 | 322 |
| 39 | 141 | 30 36 | 46 56 | 64.5 | 30 10 | 45 53 | 64.0 | 29 44 | 44 51 | 63.5 | 29 17 | 43 49 | 63.0 | 28 49 | 42 48 | 62.5 | 28 21 | 41 48 | 62.0 | 219 | 321 |
| 40 | 140 | 31 20 | 46 31 | 63.7 | 30 53 | 45 28 | 63.2 | 30 26 | 44 26 | 62.7 | 29 58 | 43 25 | 62.2 | 29 30 | 42 25 | 61.7 | 29 01 | 41 23 | 61.2 | 220 | 320 |
| 41 | 139 | 32 03 | 46 05 | 62.9 | 31 36 | 45 03 | 62.4 | 31 08 | 44 01 | 61.8 | 30 39 | 42 59 | 61.3 | 30 10 | 41 58 | 60.8 | 29 41 | 40 58 | 60.3 | 221 | 319 |
| 42 | 138 | 32 46 | 45 39 | 62.1 | 32 18 | 44 36 | 61.5 | 31 49 | 43 34 | 61.0 | 31 20 | 42 33 | 60.5 | 30 50 | 41 32 | 59.9 | 30 20 | 40 32 | 59.4 | 222 | 318 |
| 43 | 137 | 33 29 | 45 11 | 61.3 | 33 00 | 44 09 | 60.7 | 32 30 | 43 07 | 60.1 | 32 00 | 42 05 | 59.6 | 31 30 | 41 05 | 59.1 | 30 59 | 40 04 | 58.5 | 223 | 317 |
| 44 | 136 | 34 12 | 44 43 | 60.4 | 33 42 | 43 40 | 59.8 | 33 11 | 42 38 | 59.3 | 32 40 | 41 37 | 58.7 | 32 09 | 40 36 | 58.2 | 31 37 | 39 36 | 57.6 | 224 | 316 |
| 45 | 135 | 34 54 | 44 13 | 59.6 | 34 23 | 43 11 | 59.0 | 33 52 | 42 09 | 58.4 | 33 20 | 41 08 | 57.8 | 32 48 | 40 07 | 57.3 | 32 15 | 39 08 | 56.7 | 225 | 315 |

| Lat. / A | | 36° | | | 37° | | | 38° | | | 39° | | | 40° | | | 41° | | | Lat. / A | |
|---|---|---|---|---|---|---|---|---|---|---|---|---|---|---|---|---|---|---|---|---|---|
| LHA/F | F | A/H | B/P | $Z_1/Z_2$ | A/H | B/P | $Z_1/Z_2$ | A/H | B/P | $Z_1/Z_2$ | A/H | B/P | $Z_1/Z_2$ | A/H | B/P | $Z_1/Z_2$ | A/H | B/P | $Z_1/Z_2$ | A | LHA |
| 45 | 135 | 34 54 | 44 13 | 59.6 | 34 23 | 43 11 | 59.0 | 33 52 | 42 09 | 58.4 | 33 20 | 41 08 | 57.8 | 32 48 | 40 07 | 57.3 | 32 15 | 39 08 | 56.7 | 315 | 225 |
| 46 | 134 | 35 35 | 43 43 | 58.7 | 35 04 | 42 40 | 58.1 | 34 32 | 41 38 | 57.5 | 33 59 | 40 37 | 56.9 | 33 26 | 39 37 | 56.4 | 32 53 | 38 38 | 55.8 | 314 | 226 |
| 47 | 133 | 36 17 | 43 11 | 57.8 | 35 44 | 42 09 | 57.2 | 35 12 | 41 07 | 56.6 | 34 38 | 40 06 | 56.0 | 34 04 | 39 06 | 55.4 | 33 30 | 38 07 | 54.9 | 313 | 227 |
| 48 | 132 | 36 57 | 42 39 | 56.9 | 36 24 | 41 36 | 56.2 | 35 51 | 40 35 | 55.6 | 35 17 | 39 34 | 55.1 | 34 42 | 38 34 | 54.5 | 34 07 | 37 35 | 53.9 | 312 | 228 |
| 49 | 131 | 37 38 | 42 05 | 55.9 | 37 04 | 41 03 | 55.3 | 36 30 | 40 01 | 54.7 | 35 55 | 39 01 | 54.1 | 35 19 | 38 01 | 53.5 | 34 43 | 37 03 | 53.0 | 311 | 229 |
| 50 | 130 | 38 18 | 41 30 | 55.0 | 37 43 | 40 28 | 54.4 | 37 08 | 39 27 | 53.7 | 36 32 | 38 27 | 53.1 | 35 56 | 37 27 | 52.5 | 35 19 | 36 29 | 52.0 | 310 | 230 |
| 51 | 129 | 38 57 | 40 54 | 54.0 | 38 22 | 39 52 | 53.4 | 37 46 | 38 51 | 52.8 | 37 09 | 37 51 | 52.1 | 36 32 | 36 52 | 51.6 | 35 55 | 35 54 | 51.0 | 309 | 231 |
| 52 | 128 | 39 36 | 40 17 | 53.0 | 39 00 | 39 15 | 52.4 | 38 23 | 38 14 | 51.8 | 37 46 | 37 15 | 51.1 | 37 08 | 36 16 | 50.6 | 36 30 | 35 18 | 50.0 | 308 | 232 |
| 53 | 127 | 40 15 | 39 38 | 52.0 | 39 38 | 38 37 | 51.4 | 39 00 | 37 36 | 50.8 | 38 22 | 36 37 | 50.1 | 37 43 | 35 39 | 49.5 | 37 04 | 34 42 | 49.0 | 307 | 233 |
| 54 | 126 | 40 53 | 38 58 | 51.0 | 40 15 | 37 57 | 50.4 | 39 36 | 36 57 | 49.7 | 38 57 | 35 58 | 49.1 | 38 18 | 35 01 | 48.5 | 37 38 | 34 04 | 47.9 | 306 | 234 |
| 55 | 125 | 41 30 | 38 17 | 50.0 | 40 52 | 37 17 | 49.4 | 40 12 | 36 17 | 48.7 | 39 32 | 35 19 | 48.1 | 38 52 | 34 21 | 47.4 | 38 11 | 33 25 | 46.9 | 305 | 235 |
| 56 | 124 | 42 07 | 37 35 | 48.9 | 41 28 | 36 35 | 48.3 | 40 47 | 35 36 | 47.6 | 40 07 | 34 38 | 47.0 | 39 26 | 33 41 | 46.4 | 38 44 | 32 45 | 45.8 | 304 | 236 |
| 57 | 123 | 42 44 | 36 51 | 47.9 | 42 03 | 35 51 | 47.2 | 41 22 | 34 53 | 46.5 | 40 41 | 33 55 | 45.9 | 39 59 | 32 59 | 45.3 | 39 16 | 32 04 | 44.7 | 303 | 237 |
| 58 | 122 | 43 19 | 36 06 | 46.8 | 42 38 | 35 07 | 46.1 | 41 56 | 34 09 | 45.4 | 41 14 | 33 12 | 44.8 | 40 31 | 32 16 | 44.2 | 39 48 | 31 22 | 43.6 | 302 | 238 |
| 59 | 121 | 43 54 | 35 20 | 45.6 | 43 12 | 34 21 | 45.0 | 42 29 | 33 24 | 44.3 | 41 46 | 32 27 | 43.7 | 41 03 | 31 32 | 43.1 | 40 19 | 30 39 | 42.5 | 301 | 239 |
| 60 | 120 | 44 29 | 34 32 | 44.5 | 43 46 | 33 34 | 43.8 | 43 02 | 32 38 | 43.2 | 42 18 | 31 42 | 42.5 | 41 34 | 30 47 | 41.9 | 40 49 | 29 55 | 41.3 | 300 | 240 |
| 61 | 119 | 45 02 | 33 43 | 43.3 | 44 18 | 32 45 | 42.6 | 43 34 | 31 49 | 42.0 | 42 49 | 30 55 | 41.4 | 42 04 | 30 01 | 40.8 | 41 18 | 29 09 | 40.2 | 299 | 241 |
| 62 | 118 | 45 35 | 32 52 | 42.1 | 44 51 | 31 55 | 41.5 | 44 05 | 31 00 | 40.8 | 43 20 | 30 06 | 40.2 | 42 34 | 29 14 | 39.6 | 41 47 | 28 22 | 39.0 | 298 | 242 |
| 63 | 117 | 46 07 | 32 00 | 40.9 | 45 22 | 31 04 | 40.3 | 44 36 | 30 10 | 39.6 | 43 49 | 29 17 | 39.0 | 43 03 | 28 25 | 38.4 | 42 15 | 27 35 | 37.8 | 297 | 243 |
| 64 | 116 | 46 39 | 31 06 | 39.7 | 45 52 | 30 11 | 39.0 | 45 06 | 29 18 | 38.4 | 44 18 | 28 26 | 37.8 | 43 31 | 27 35 | 37.2 | 42 43 | 26 46 | 36.6 | 296 | 244 |
| 65 | 115 | 47 09 | 30 11 | 38.4 | 46 22 | 29 17 | 37.8 | 45 35 | 28 25 | 37.1 | 44 47 | 27 34 | 36.5 | 43 58 | 26 44 | 36.0 | 43 09 | 25 56 | 35.4 | 295 | 245 |
| 66 | 114 | 47 39 | 29 14 | 37.1 | 46 51 | 28 21 | 36.5 | 46 03 | 27 30 | 35.9 | 45 14 | 26 40 | 35.3 | 44 25 | 25 52 | 34.7 | 43 35 | 25 04 | 34.2 | 294 | 246 |
| 67 | 113 | 48 08 | 28 16 | 35.8 | 47 19 | 27 24 | 35.2 | 46 30 | 26 34 | 34.6 | 45 40 | 25 45 | 34.0 | 44 50 | 24 58 | 33.4 | 44 00 | 24 12 | 32.9 | 293 | 247 |
| 68 | 112 | 48 36 | 27 17 | 34.5 | 47 46 | 26 26 | 33.9 | 46 56 | 25 37 | 33.3 | 46 06 | 24 50 | 32.7 | 45 15 | 24 03 | 32.2 | 44 24 | 23 19 | 31.6 | 292 | 248 |
| 69 | 111 | 49 03 | 26 15 | 33.1 | 48 13 | 25 26 | 32.5 | 47 22 | 24 38 | 31.9 | 46 31 | 23 52 | 31.4 | 45 39 | 23 08 | 30.8 | 44 48 | 22 24 | 30.3 | 291 | 249 |
| 70 | 110 | 49 29 | 25 13 | 31.8 | 48 38 | 24 25 | 31.2 | 47 46 | 23 39 | 30.6 | 46 55 | 22 54 | 30.0 | 46 03 | 22 12 | 29.5 | 45 10 | 21 29 | 29.0 | 290 | 250 |
| 71 | 109 | 49 54 | 24 08 | 30.4 | 49 02 | 23 22 | 29.8 | 48 10 | 22 37 | 29.2 | 47 17 | 21 54 | 28.7 | 46 25 | 21 12 | 28.2 | 45 32 | 20 32 | 27.7 | 289 | 251 |
| 72 | 108 | 50 18 | 23 02 | 28.9 | 49 25 | 22 18 | 28.4 | 48 33 | 21 35 | 27.8 | 47 39 | 20 53 | 27.3 | 46 46 | 20 13 | 26.8 | 45 52 | 19 34 | 26.3 | 288 | 252 |
| 73 | 107 | 50 41 | 21 55 | 27.5 | 49 48 | 21 12 | 26.9 | 48 54 | 20 31 | 26.4 | 48 00 | 19 51 | 25.9 | 47 06 | 19 13 | 25.4 | 46 12 | 18 35 | 25.0 | 287 | 253 |
| 74 | 106 | 51 03 | 20 47 | 26.0 | 50 09 | 20 06 | 25.5 | 49 15 | 19 26 | 25.0 | 48 20 | 18 48 | 24.5 | 47 25 | 18 11 | 24.0 | 46 30 | 17 36 | 23.6 | 286 | 254 |
| 75 | 105 | 51 24 | 19 36 | 24.5 | 50 29 | 18 57 | 24.0 | 49 34 | 18 20 | 23.5 | 48 39 | 17 43 | 23.1 | 47 44 | 17 09 | 22.6 | 46 48 | 16 35 | 22.2 | 285 | 255 |
| 76 | 104 | 51 43 | 18 25 | 23.0 | 50 48 | 17 48 | 22.5 | 49 52 | 17 12 | 22.0 | 48 57 | 16 38 | 21.6 | 48 01 | 16 05 | 21.2 | 47 05 | 15 33 | 20.8 | 284 | 256 |
| 77 | 103 | 52 02 | 17 12 | 21.4 | 51 06 | 16 37 | 21.0 | 50 09 | 16 04 | 20.6 | 49 13 | 15 31 | 20.1 | 48 17 | 15 00 | 19.8 | 47 20 | 14 31 | 19.4 | 283 | 257 |
| 78 | 102 | 52 19 | 15 58 | 19.9 | 51 22 | 15 25 | 19.5 | 50 25 | 14 54 | 19.0 | 49 29 | 14 24 | 18.7 | 48 32 | 13 55 | 18.3 | 47 35 | 13 27 | 18.0 | 282 | 258 |
| 79 | 101 | 52 35 | 14 43 | 18.3 | 51 37 | 14 13 | 17.9 | 50 40 | 13 43 | 17.5 | 49 43 | 13 16 | 17.2 | 48 46 | 12 49 | 16.8 | 47 48 | 12 23 | 16.5 | 281 | 259 |
| 80 | 100 | 52 49 | 13 27 | 16.7 | 51 52 | 12 59 | 16.3 | 50 54 | 12 32 | 16.0 | 49 56 | 12 06 | 15.7 | 48 58 | 11 42 | 15.3 | 48 01 | 11 18 | 15.0 | 280 | 260 |
| 81 | 99 | 53 02 | 12 09 | 15.1 | 52 04 | 11 44 | 14.7 | 51 06 | 11 19 | 14.4 | 50 08 | 10 56 | 14.1 | 49 10 | 10 34 | 13.8 | 48 12 | 10 12 | 13.6 | 279 | 261 |
| 82 | 98 | 53 14 | 10 51 | 13.4 | 52 16 | 10 28 | 13.1 | 51 18 | 10 06 | 12.9 | 50 19 | 9 45 | 12.6 | 49 20 | 9 25 | 12.3 | 48 22 | 9 06 | 12.1 | 278 | 262 |
| 83 | 97 | 53 25 | 9 31 | 11.8 | 52 26 | 9 11 | 11.5 | 51 28 | 8 52 | 11.3 | 50 29 | 8 34 | 11.0 | 49 30 | 8 16 | 10.8 | 48 31 | 7 59 | 10.6 | 277 | 263 |
| 84 | 96 | 53 34 | 8 11 | 10.1 | 52 35 | 7 54 | 9.9 | 51 36 | 7 37 | 9.7 | 50 37 | 7 21 | 9.5 | 49 38 | 7 06 | 9.3 | 48 38 | 6 51 | 9.1 | 276 | 264 |
| 85 | 95 | 53 42 | 6 50 | 8.5 | 52 43 | 6 36 | 8.3 | 51 44 | 6 22 | 8.1 | 50 44 | 6 09 | 7.9 | 49 44 | 5 56 | 7.8 | 48 45 | 5 44 | 7.6 | 275 | 265 |
| 86 | 94 | 53 49 | 5 29 | 6.8 | 52 49 | 5 17 | 6.6 | 51 50 | 5 06 | 6.5 | 50 50 | 4 55 | 6.3 | 49 50 | 4 45 | 6.2 | 48 50 | 4 35 | 6.1 | 274 | 266 |
| 87 | 93 | 53 54 | 4 07 | 5.1 | 52 54 | 3 58 | 5.0 | 51 54 | 3 50 | 4.9 | 50 54 | 3 42 | 4.8 | 49 54 | 3 34 | 4.7 | 48 55 | 3 27 | 4.6 | 273 | 267 |
| 88 | 92 | 53 57 | 2 45 | 3.4 | 52 57 | 2 39 | 3.3 | 51 57 | 2 33 | 3.2 | 50 57 | 2 28 | 3.2 | 49 58 | 2 23 | 3.1 | 48 58 | 2 18 | 3.0 | 272 | 268 |
| 89 | 91 | 53 59 | 1 23 | 1.7 | 52 59 | 1 20 | 1.7 | 51 59 | 1 17 | 1.6 | 50 59 | 1 14 | 1.6 | 49 59 | 1 11 | 1.6 | 48 59 | 1 09 | 1.5 | 271 | 269 |
| 90 | 90 | 54 00 | 0 00 | 0.0 | 53 00 | 0 00 | 0.0 | 52 00 | 0 00 | 0.0 | 51 00 | 0 00 | 0.0 | 50 00 | 0 00 | 0.0 | 49 00 | 0 00 | 0.0 | 270 | 270 |

N. Lat.: for LHA > 180° ... $Z_n = Z$
for LHA < 180° ... $Z_n = 360° - Z$

S. Lat.: for LHA > 180° ... $Z_n = 180° - Z$
for LHA < 180° ... $Z_n = 180° + Z$

**B:** (−) for 90° < LHA < 270°  
**Dec:**(−) for Lat. contrary name

**Z₁:** same sign as B  
**Z₂:** (−) for F > 90°

## SIGHT REDUCTION TABLE

| Lat./A LHA/F | 42° A/H | 42° B/P | 42° Z₁/Z₂ | 43° A/H | 43° B/P | 43° Z₁/Z₂ | 44° A/H | 44° B/P | 44° Z₁/Z₂ | 45° A/H | 45° B/P | 45° Z₁/Z₂ | 46° A/H | 46° B/P | 46° Z₁/Z₂ | 47° A/H | 47° B/P | 47° Z₁/Z₂ | Lat./A LHA | LHA |
|---|---|---|---|---|---|---|---|---|---|---|---|---|---|---|---|---|---|---|---|---|
| 0 | 0 00 | 48 00 | 90·0 | 0 00 | 47 00 | 90·0 | 0 00 | 46 00 | 90·0 | 0 00 | 45 00 | 90·0 | 0 00 | 44 00 | 90·0 | 0 00 | 43 00 | 90·0 | 180 | 360 |
| 1 | 0 45 | 48 00 | 89·3 | 0 44 | 47 00 | 89·3 | 0 43 | 46 00 | 89·3 | 0 42 | 45 00 | 89·3 | 0 42 | 44 00 | 89·3 | 0 41 | 43 00 | 89·3 | 181 | 359 |
| 2 | 1 29 | 47 59 | 88·7 | 1 28 | 46 59 | 88·6 | 1 26 | 45 59 | 88·6 | 1 25 | 44 59 | 88·6 | 1 23 | 43 59 | 88·6 | 1 22 | 42 59 | 88·5 | 182 | 358 |
| 3 | 2 14 | 47 58 | 88·0 | 2 12 | 46 58 | 88·0 | 2 09 | 45 58 | 87·9 | 2 07 | 44 58 | 87·9 | 2 05 | 43 58 | 87·8 | 2 03 | 42 58 | 87·8 | 183 | 357 |
| 4 | 2 58 | 47 56 | 87·3 | 2 55 | 46 56 | 87·3 | 2 53 | 45 56 | 87·2 | 2 50 | 44 56 | 87·2 | 2 47 | 43 56 | 87·1 | 2 44 | 42 56 | 87·1 | 184 | 356 |
| 5 | 3 43 | 47 53 | 86·6 | 3 39 | 46 53 | 86·6 | 3 36 | 45 53 | 86·5 | 3 32 | 44 53 | 86·5 | 3 28 | 43 53 | 86·4 | 3 24 | 42 53 | 86·3 | 185 | 355 |
| 6 | 4 27 | 47 51 | 86·0 | 4 23 | 46 51 | 85·9 | 4 19 | 45 51 | 85·8 | 4 14 | 44 51 | 85·7 | 4 10 | 43 51 | 85·7 | 4 05 | 42 51 | 85·6 | 186 | 354 |
| 7 | 5 12 | 47 47 | 85·3 | 5 07 | 46 47 | 85·2 | 5 02 | 45 47 | 85·1 | 4 57 | 44 47 | 85·0 | 4 51 | 43 47 | 85·0 | 4 46 | 42 47 | 84·9 | 187 | 353 |
| 8 | 5 56 | 47 43 | 84·6 | 5 51 | 46 43 | 84·5 | 5 45 | 45 43 | 84·4 | 5 39 | 44 43 | 84·3 | 5 33 | 43 43 | 84·2 | 5 27 | 42 43 | 84·1 | 188 | 352 |
| 9 | 6 41 | 47 39 | 84·0 | 6 34 | 46 39 | 83·8 | 6 28 | 45 39 | 83·7 | 6 21 | 44 39 | 83·6 | 6 14 | 43 39 | 83·5 | 6 07 | 42 39 | 83·4 | 189 | 351 |
| 10 | 7 25 | 47 34 | 83·3 | 7 18 | 46 34 | 83·1 | 7 11 | 45 34 | 83·0 | 7 03 | 44 34 | 82·9 | 6 56 | 43 34 | 82·8 | 6 48 | 42 34 | 82·7 | 190 | 350 |
| 11 | 8 09 | 47 28 | 82·6 | 8 01 | 46 28 | 82·4 | 7 53 | 45 28 | 82·3 | 7 45 | 44 28 | 82·2 | 7 37 | 43 28 | 82·0 | 7 29 | 42 28 | 81·9 | 191 | 349 |
| 12 | 8 53 | 47 22 | 81·9 | 8 45 | 46 22 | 81·8 | 8 36 | 45 22 | 81·6 | 8 27 | 44 22 | 81·5 | 8 18 | 43 22 | 81·3 | 8 09 | 42 22 | 81·2 | 192 | 348 |
| 13 | 9 37 | 47 16 | 81·2 | 9 28 | 46 15 | 81·1 | 9 19 | 45 15 | 80·9 | 9 09 | 44 15 | 80·7 | 8 59 | 43 15 | 80·6 | 8 49 | 42 16 | 80·4 | 193 | 347 |
| 14 | 10 21 | 47 08 | 80·5 | 10 11 | 46 08 | 80·3 | 10 01 | 45 08 | 80·2 | 9 51 | 44 08 | 80·0 | 9 40 | 43 08 | 79·8 | 9 30 | 42 08 | 79·7 | 194 | 346 |
| 15 | 11 05 | 47 01 | 79·8 | 10 55 | 46 00 | 79·6 | 10 44 | 45 00 | 79·5 | 10 33 | 44 00 | 79·3 | 10 21 | 43 00 | 79·1 | 10 10 | 42 01 | 78·9 | 195 | 345 |
| 16 | 11 49 | 46 52 | 79·1 | 11 38 | 45 52 | 78·9 | 11 26 | 44 52 | 78·7 | 11 14 | 43 52 | 78·5 | 11 02 | 42 52 | 78·3 | 10 50 | 41 52 | 78·2 | 196 | 344 |
| 17 | 12 33 | 46 43 | 78·4 | 12 21 | 45 43 | 78·2 | 12 08 | 44 44 | 78·0 | 11 56 | 43 43 | 77·8 | 11 43 | 42 43 | 77·6 | 11 30 | 41 44 | 77·4 | 197 | 343 |
| 18 | 13 17 | 46 34 | 77·7 | 13 04 | 45 34 | 77·5 | 12 51 | 44 34 | 77·3 | 12 37 | 43 34 | 77·1 | 12 24 | 42 34 | 76·8 | 12 10 | 41 34 | 76·6 | 198 | 342 |
| 19 | 14 00 | 46 24 | 77·0 | 13 46 | 45 24 | 76·8 | 13 33 | 44 24 | 76·5 | 13 19 | 43 24 | 76·3 | 13 04 | 42 24 | 76·1 | 12 50 | 41 24 | 75·9 | 199 | 341 |
| 20 | 14 43 | 46 13 | 76·3 | 14 29 | 45 13 | 76·1 | 14 15 | 44 13 | 75·8 | 14 00 | 43 13 | 75·6 | 13 45 | 42 13 | 75·3 | 13 29 | 41 14 | 75·1 | 200 | 340 |
| 21 | 15 27 | 46 02 | 75·6 | 15 12 | 45 02 | 75·3 | 14 56 | 44 02 | 75·1 | 14 41 | 43 02 | 74·8 | 14 25 | 42 02 | 74·6 | 14 09 | 41 03 | 74·3 | 201 | 339 |
| 22 | 16 10 | 45 50 | 74·9 | 15 54 | 44 50 | 74·6 | 15 38 | 43 50 | 74·3 | 15 22 | 42 50 | 74·1 | 15 05 | 41 50 | 73·8 | 14 48 | 40 51 | 73·5 | 202 | 338 |
| 23 | 16 53 | 45 38 | 74·1 | 16 36 | 44 38 | 73·9 | 16 19 | 43 38 | 73·6 | 16 02 | 42 38 | 73·3 | 15 45 | 41 38 | 73·0 | 15 27 | 40 39 | 72·8 | 203 | 337 |
| 24 | 17 36 | 45 25 | 73·4 | 17 18 | 44 25 | 73·1 | 17 01 | 43 25 | 72·8 | 16 43 | 42 25 | 72·5 | 16 25 | 41 25 | 72·2 | 16 06 | 40 26 | 72·0 | 204 | 336 |
| 25 | 18 18 | 45 11 | 72·7 | 18 00 | 44 11 | 72·4 | 17 42 | 43 11 | 72·1 | 17 23 | 42 11 | 71·8 | 17 04 | 41 12 | 71·5 | 16 45 | 40 12 | 71·2 | 205 | 335 |
| 26 | 19 01 | 44 57 | 71·9 | 18 42 | 43 57 | 71·6 | 18 23 | 42 57 | 71·3 | 18 03 | 41 57 | 71·0 | 17 44 | 40 57 | 70·7 | 17 24 | 39 58 | 70·4 | 206 | 334 |
| 27 | 19 43 | 44 42 | 71·2 | 19 24 | 43 42 | 70·8 | 19 04 | 42 42 | 70·5 | 18 43 | 41 42 | 70·2 | 18 23 | 40 43 | 69·9 | 18 02 | 39 43 | 69·6 | 207 | 333 |
| 28 | 20 25 | 44 26 | 70·4 | 20 05 | 43 26 | 70·1 | 19 44 | 42 26 | 69·7 | 19 23 | 41 27 | 69·4 | 19 02 | 40 27 | 69·1 | 18 40 | 39 28 | 68·8 | 208 | 332 |
| 29 | 21 07 | 44 10 | 69·6 | 20 46 | 43 10 | 69·3 | 20 25 | 42 10 | 68·9 | 20 03 | 41 10 | 68·6 | 19 41 | 40 11 | 68·3 | 19 18 | 39 12 | 67·9 | 209 | 331 |
| 30 | 21 49 | 43 53 | 68·9 | 21 27 | 42 53 | 68·5 | 21 05 | 41 53 | 68·1 | 20 42 | 40 54 | 67·8 | 20 19 | 39 54 | 67·4 | 19 56 | 38 55 | 67·1 | 210 | 330 |
| 31 | 22 30 | 43 35 | 68·1 | 22 08 | 42 35 | 67·7 | 21 45 | 41 36 | 67·3 | 21 21 | 40 36 | 67·0 | 20 58 | 39 37 | 66·6 | 20 34 | 38 38 | 66·3 | 211 | 329 |
| 32 | 23 11 | 43 17 | 67·3 | 22 48 | 42 17 | 66·9 | 22 24 | 41 17 | 66·5 | 22 00 | 40 18 | 66·2 | 21 36 | 39 19 | 65·8 | 21 11 | 38 20 | 65·4 | 212 | 328 |
| 33 | 23 53 | 42 58 | 66·5 | 23 28 | 41 58 | 66·1 | 23 04 | 40 58 | 65·7 | 22 39 | 39 59 | 65·3 | 22 14 | 39 00 | 65·0 | 21 48 | 38 02 | 64·6 | 213 | 327 |
| 34 | 24 33 | 42 38 | 65·7 | 24 08 | 41 38 | 65·3 | 23 43 | 40 39 | 64·9 | 23 17 | 39 40 | 64·5 | 22 51 | 38 41 | 64·1 | 22 25 | 37 42 | 63·7 | 214 | 326 |
| 35 | 25 14 | 42 18 | 64·9 | 24 48 | 41 18 | 64·5 | 24 22 | 40 18 | 64·1 | 23 56 | 39 19 | 63·7 | 23 29 | 38 21 | 63·3 | 23 02 | 37 23 | 62·9 | 215 | 325 |
| 36 | 25 54 | 41 56 | 64·1 | 25 28 | 40 57 | 63·6 | 25 01 | 39 57 | 63·2 | 24 34 | 38 58 | 62·8 | 24 06 | 38 00 | 62·4 | 23 38 | 37 02 | 62·0 | 216 | 324 |
| 37 | 26 34 | 41 34 | 63·2 | 26 07 | 40 35 | 62·8 | 25 39 | 39 35 | 62·4 | 25 11 | 38 37 | 61·9 | 24 43 | 37 38 | 61·5 | 24 14 | 36 41 | 61·1 | 217 | 323 |
| 38 | 27 14 | 41 11 | 62·4 | 26 46 | 40 12 | 61·9 | 26 17 | 39 13 | 61·5 | 25 48 | 38 14 | 61·1 | 25 19 | 37 16 | 60·7 | 24 50 | 36 16 | 60·3 | 218 | 322 |
| 39 | 27 53 | 40 48 | 61·5 | 27 24 | 39 48 | 61·1 | 26 55 | 38 50 | 60·6 | 26 25 | 37 51 | 60·2 | 25 55 | 36 53 | 59·8 | 25 25 | 35 56 | 59·4 | 219 | 321 |
| 40 | 28 32 | 40 23 | 60·7 | 28 02 | 39 24 | 60·2 | 27 32 | 38 25 | 59·8 | 27 02 | 37 27 | 59·3 | 26 31 | 36 30 | 58·9 | 26 00 | 35 32 | 58·5 | 220 | 320 |
| 41 | 29 11 | 39 58 | 59·8 | 28 40 | 38 59 | 59·3 | 28 10 | 38 01 | 58·9 | 27 38 | 37 03 | 58·4 | 27 07 | 36 05 | 58·0 | 26 35 | 35 08 | 57·6 | 221 | 319 |
| 42 | 29 49 | 39 32 | 58·9 | 29 18 | 38 33 | 58·4 | 28 46 | 37 35 | 58·0 | 28 14 | 36 37 | 57·5 | 27 42 | 35 40 | 57·1 | 27 09 | 34 43 | 56·6 | 222 | 318 |
| 43 | 30 27 | 39 05 | 58·0 | 29 55 | 38 06 | 57·5 | 29 23 | 37 09 | 57·1 | 28 50 | 36 11 | 56·6 | 28 17 | 35 14 | 56·1 | 27 43 | 34 18 | 55·7 | 223 | 317 |
| 44 | 31 05 | 38 37 | 57·1 | 30 32 | 37 39 | 56·6 | 29 59 | 36 41 | 56·1 | 29 25 | 35 44 | 55·7 | 28 51 | 34 47 | 55·2 | 28 17 | 33 51 | 54·8 | 224 | 316 |
| 45 | 31 42 | 38 09 | 56·2 | 31 08 | 37 10 | 55·7 | 30 34 | 36 13 | 55·2 | 30 00 | 35 16 | 54·7 | 29 25 | 34 20 | 54·3 | 28 50 | 33 24 | 53·8 | 225 | 315 |

Top reference (Lat. / A → LHA 225–270, latitudes 47°, 46°, 45°); bottom reference (Lat. / A, LHA/F 45–90, latitudes 42°, 43°, 44°). Sub‑columns for each latitude: A/H, B/P, $Z_1/Z_2$.

| LHA/F | 42° A/H | 42° B/P | 42° $Z_1/Z_2$ | 43° A/H | 43° B/P | 43° $Z_1/Z_2$ | 44° A/H | 44° B/P | 44° $Z_1/Z_2$ | 45° A/H | 45° B/P | 45° $Z_1/Z_2$ | 46° A/H | 46° B/P | 46° $Z_1/Z_2$ | 47° A/H | 47° B/P | 47° $Z_1/Z_2$ | LHA |
|---|---|---|---|---|---|---|---|---|---|---|---|---|---|---|---|---|---|---|---|
| 45 | 31 42 | 38 09 | 56·2 | 31 08 | 37 10 | 55·7 | 30 34 | 36 13 | 55·2 | 30 00 | 35 16 | 54·7 | 29 25 | 34 20 | 54·3 | 28 50 | 33 24 | 53·8 | 225 |
| 46 | 32 19 | 37 39 | 55·3 | 31 45 | 36 41 | 54·8 | 31 10 | 35 44 | 54·3 | 30 34 | 34 47 | 53·8 | 29 59 | 33 51 | 53·3 | 29 23 | 32 56 | 52·9 | 226 |
| 47 | 32 55 | 37 08 | 54·3 | 32 20 | 36 11 | 53·8 | 31 45 | 35 14 | 53·3 | 31 08 | 34 18 | 52·8 | 30 32 | 33 22 | 52·4 | 29 55 | 32 27 | 51·9 | 227 |
| 48 | 33 31 | 36 37 | 53·4 | 32 55 | 35 40 | 52·9 | 32 19 | 34 43 | 52·3 | 31 42 | 33 47 | 51·9 | 31 05 | 32 52 | 51·4 | 30 27 | 31 58 | 50·9 | 228 |
| 49 | 34 07 | 36 05 | 52·4 | 33 30 | 35 08 | 51·9 | 32 53 | 34 11 | 51·4 | 32 15 | 33 16 | 50·9 | 31 37 | 32 21 | 50·4 | 30 59 | 31 27 | 49·9 | 229 |
| 50 | 34 42 | 35 31 | 51·4 | 34 04 | 34 35 | 50·9 | 33 26 | 33 39 | 50·4 | 32 48 | 32 44 | 49·9 | 32 09 | 31 50 | 49·4 | 31 30 | 30 56 | 48·9 | 230 |
| 51 | 35 17 | 34 57 | 50·4 | 34 38 | 34 01 | 49·9 | 33 59 | 33 05 | 49·4 | 33 20 | 32 11 | 48·9 | 32 40 | 31 17 | 48·4 | 32 00 | 30 24 | 47·9 | 231 |
| 52 | 35 51 | 34 22 | 49·4 | 35 12 | 33 26 | 48·9 | 34 32 | 32 31 | 48·4 | 33 52 | 31 37 | 47·9 | 33 11 | 30 44 | 47·4 | 32 30 | 29 52 | 46·9 | 232 |
| 53 | 36 24 | 33 45 | 48·4 | 35 44 | 32 50 | 47·9 | 35 04 | 31 56 | 47·3 | 34 23 | 31 02 | 46·8 | 33 42 | 30 10 | 46·3 | 33 00 | 29 18 | 45·9 | 233 |
| 54 | 36 57 | 33 08 | 47·4 | 36 17 | 32 13 | 46·8 | 35 35 | 31 20 | 46·3 | 34 54 | 30 27 | 45·8 | 34 12 | 29 35 | 45·3 | 33 29 | 28 44 | 44·8 | 234 |
| 55 | 37 30 | 32 30 | 46·3 | 36 48 | 31 36 | 45·8 | 36 06 | 30 43 | 45·2 | 35 24 | 29 50 | 44·7 | 34 41 | 28 59 | 44·2 | 33 58 | 28 08 | 43·8 | 235 |
| 56 | 38 02 | 31 51 | 45·2 | 37 19 | 30 57 | 44·7 | 36 37 | 30 04 | 44·2 | 35 53 | 29 13 | 43·6 | 35 10 | 28 22 | 43·2 | 34 26 | 27 32 | 42·7 | 236 |
| 57 | 38 33 | 31 10 | 44·1 | 37 50 | 30 17 | 43·6 | 37 06 | 29 25 | 43·1 | 36 22 | 28 34 | 42·6 | 35 38 | 27 45 | 42·1 | 34 53 | 26 56 | 41·6 | 237 |
| 58 | 39 04 | 30 29 | 43·0 | 38 20 | 29 36 | 42·5 | 37 36 | 28 45 | 42·0 | 36 51 | 27 55 | 41·5 | 36 06 | 27 06 | 41·0 | 35 20 | 26 18 | 40·5 | 238 |
| 59 | 39 34 | 29 46 | 41·9 | 38 50 | 28 55 | 41·4 | 38 04 | 28 04 | 40·9 | 37 19 | 27 15 | 40·4 | 36 33 | 26 27 | 39·9 | 35 46 | 25 39 | 39·4 | 239 |
| 60 | 40 04 | 29 03 | 40·8 | 39 18 | 28 12 | 40·2 | 38 32 | 27 22 | 39·7 | 37 46 | 26 34 | 39·2 | 37 00 | 25 46 | 38·8 | 36 12 | 25 00 | 38·3 | 240 |
| 61 | 40 32 | 28 18 | 39·6 | 39 46 | 27 28 | 39·1 | 38 59 | 26 39 | 38·6 | 38 12 | 25 52 | 38·1 | 37 25 | 25 05 | 37·6 | 36 37 | 24 20 | 37·2 | 241 |
| 62 | 41 00 | 27 32 | 38·5 | 40 13 | 26 43 | 37·9 | 39 26 | 25 56 | 37·4 | 38 38 | 25 09 | 36·9 | 37 50 | 24 23 | 36·5 | 37 02 | 23 39 | 36·0 | 242 |
| 63 | 41 28 | 26 45 | 37·3 | 40 40 | 25 58 | 36·8 | 39 52 | 25 11 | 36·3 | 39 03 | 24 25 | 35·8 | 38 14 | 23 40 | 35·3 | 37 25 | 22 57 | 34·9 | 243 |
| 64 | 41 54 | 25 58 | 36·1 | 41 06 | 25 11 | 35·6 | 40 17 | 24 25 | 35·1 | 39 28 | 23 40 | 34·6 | 38 38 | 22 57 | 34·1 | 37 48 | 22 14 | 33·7 | 244 |
| 65 | 42 20 | 25 09 | 34·9 | 41 31 | 24 23 | 34·4 | 40 41 | 23 38 | 33·9 | 39 51 | 22 55 | 33·4 | 39 01 | 22 12 | 33·0 | 38 11 | 21 31 | 32·5 | 245 |
| 66 | 42 45 | 24 19 | 33·6 | 41 55 | 23 34 | 33·1 | 41 05 | 22 50 | 32·7 | 40 14 | 22 08 | 32·2 | 39 23 | 21 27 | 31·8 | 38 32 | 20 46 | 31·3 | 246 |
| 67 | 43 10 | 23 28 | 32·4 | 42 19 | 22 44 | 31·9 | 41 28 | 22 02 | 31·4 | 40 37 | 21 21 | 31·0 | 39 45 | 20 40 | 30·5 | 38 53 | 20 01 | 30·1 | 247 |
| 68 | 43 33 | 22 35 | 31·1 | 42 42 | 21 53 | 30·6 | 41 50 | 21 12 | 30·2 | 40 58 | 20 32 | 29·7 | 40 06 | 19 53 | 29·3 | 39 13 | 19 15 | 28·9 | 248 |
| 69 | 43 56 | 21 42 | 29·8 | 43 04 | 21 01 | 29·4 | 42 11 | 20 22 | 28·9 | 41 19 | 19 43 | 28·5 | 40 26 | 19 05 | 28·1 | 39 33 | 18 29 | 27·7 | 249 |
| 70 | 44 18 | 20 48 | 28·5 | 43 25 | 20 08 | 28·1 | 42 32 | 19 30 | 27·7 | 41 38 | 18 53 | 27·2 | 40 45 | 18 17 | 26·8 | 39 51 | 17 41 | 26·5 | 250 |
| 71 | 44 38 | 19 53 | 27·2 | 43 45 | 19 15 | 26·8 | 42 51 | 18 38 | 26·4 | 41 57 | 18 02 | 26·0 | 41 03 | 17 27 | 25·6 | 40 09 | 16 53 | 25·2 | 251 |
| 72 | 44 58 | 18 57 | 25·9 | 44 04 | 18 20 | 25·5 | 43 10 | 17 45 | 25·1 | 42 16 | 17 10 | 24·7 | 41 21 | 16 37 | 24·3 | 40 26 | 16 05 | 24·0 | 252 |
| 73 | 45 17 | 17 59 | 24·6 | 44 23 | 17 24 | 24·1 | 43 28 | 16 51 | 23·8 | 42 33 | 16 18 | 23·4 | 41 38 | 15 46 | 23·0 | 40 42 | 15 15 | 22·7 | 253 |
| 74 | 45 35 | 17 01 | 23·2 | 44 40 | 16 28 | 22·8 | 43 45 | 15 56 | 22·4 | 42 49 | 15 25 | 22·1 | 41 54 | 14 54 | 21·7 | 40 58 | 14 25 | 21·4 | 254 |
| 75 | 45 53 | 16 02 | 21·8 | 44 57 | 15 31 | 21·4 | 44 01 | 15 00 | 21·1 | 43 05 | 14 31 | 20·8 | 42 09 | 14 02 | 20·4 | 41 12 | 13 34 | 20·1 | 255 |
| 76 | 46 09 | 15 02 | 20·4 | 45 12 | 14 33 | 20·1 | 44 16 | 14 04 | 19·7 | 43 19 | 13 36 | 19·4 | 42 23 | 13 09 | 19·1 | 41 26 | 12 43 | 18·8 | 256 |
| 77 | 46 24 | 14 00 | 19·0 | 45 27 | 13 34 | 18·7 | 44 30 | 13 07 | 18·4 | 43 33 | 12 41 | 18·1 | 42 36 | 12 15 | 17·8 | 41 39 | 11 51 | 17·5 | 257 |
| 78 | 46 38 | 13 00 | 17·6 | 45 40 | 12 34 | 17·3 | 44 43 | 12 09 | 17·0 | 43 46 | 11 45 | 16·7 | 42 48 | 11 20 | 16·5 | 41 51 | 10 58 | 16·2 | 258 |
| 79 | 46 51 | 11 58 | 16·2 | 45 53 | 11 34 | 15·9 | 44 55 | 11 11 | 15·6 | 43 57 | 10 48 | 15·4 | 43 00 | 10 26 | 15·1 | 42 02 | 10 05 | 14·9 | 259 |
| 80 | 47 03 | 10 55 | 14·8 | 46 04 | 10 33 | 14·5 | 45 06 | 10 12 | 14·2 | 44 08 | 9 51 | 14·0 | 43 10 | 9 31 | 13·8 | 42 12 | 9 12 | 13·6 | 260 |
| 81 | 47 13 | 9 51 | 13·3 | 46 15 | 9 31 | 13·1 | 45 16 | 9 12 | 12·8 | 44 18 | 8 53 | 12·6 | 43 19 | 8 35 | 12·4 | 42 21 | 8 18 | 12·2 | 261 |
| 82 | 47 23 | 8 47 | 11·9 | 46 24 | 8 29 | 11·6 | 45 25 | 8 12 | 11·4 | 44 27 | 7 55 | 11·2 | 43 28 | 7 39 | 11·1 | 42 29 | 7 24 | 10·9 | 262 |
| 83 | 47 32 | 7 42 | 10·4 | 46 33 | 7 27 | 10·2 | 45 34 | 7 12 | 10·0 | 44 34 | 6 57 | 9·9 | 43 35 | 6 43 | 9·7 | 42 36 | 6 29 | 9·5 | 263 |
| 84 | 47 39 | 6 37 | 8·9 | 46 40 | 6 24 | 8·8 | 45 41 | 6 08 | 8·6 | 44 41 | 5 58 | 8·5 | 43 42 | 5 46 | 8·3 | 42 42 | 5 34 | 8·2 | 264 |
| 85 | 47 46 | 5 32 | 7·4 | 46 46 | 5 20 | 7·3 | 45 46 | 5 08 | 7·2 | 44 47 | 4 59 | 7·1 | 43 47 | 4 49 | 6·9 | 42 48 | 4 39 | 6·8 | 265 |
| 86 | 47 51 | 4 26 | 6·0 | 46 51 | 4 17 | 5·9 | 45 51 | 4 08 | 5·7 | 44 52 | 3 59 | 5·6 | 43 52 | 3 51 | 5·6 | 42 52 | 3 43 | 5·5 | 266 |
| 87 | 47 55 | 3 20 | 4·5 | 46 55 | 3 13 | 4·4 | 45 55 | 3 06 | 4·3 | 44 55 | 3 00 | 4·2 | 43 55 | 2 54 | 4·2 | 42 56 | 2 48 | 4·1 | 267 |
| 88 | 47 58 | 2 13 | 3·0 | 46 58 | 2 09 | 2·9 | 45 58 | 2 04 | 2·9 | 44 58 | 2 00 | 2·8 | 43 58 | 1 56 | 2·8 | 42 58 | 1 52 | 2·7 | 268 |
| 89 | 47 59 | 1 07 | 1·5 | 46 59 | 1 04 | 1·5 | 45 59 | 1 02 | 1·4 | 44 59 | 1 00 | 1·4 | 43 59 | 0 58 | 1·4 | 42 59 | 0 56 | 1·4 | 269 |
| 90 | 48 00 | 0 00 | 0·0 | 47 00 | 0 00 | 0·0 | 46 00 | 0 00 | 0·0 | 45 00 | 0 00 | 0·0 | 44 00 | 0 00 | 0·0 | 43 00 | 0 00 | 0·0 | 270 |

S. Lat.: for LHA > 180° ... $Z_n = 180° - Z$
for LHA < 180° ... $Z_n = 180° + Z$

N. Lat.: for LHA > 180° ... $Z_n = Z$
for LHA < 180° ... $Z_n = 360° - Z$

## SIGHT REDUCTION TABLE

B: (−) for 90° < LHA < 270°
Dec:(−) for Lat. contrary name

Z₁: same sign as B
Z₂: (−) for F > 90°

| Lat./A LHA/F | F | 48° A/H | 48° B/P | 48° Z₁/Z₂ | 49° A/H | 49° B/P | 49° Z₁/Z₂ | 50° A/H | 50° B/P | 50° Z₁/Z₂ | 51° A/H | 51° B/P | 51° Z₁/Z₂ | 52° A/H | 52° B/P | 52° Z₁/Z₂ | 53° A/H | 53° B/P | 53° Z₁/Z₂ | Lat./A LHA | LHA |
|---|---|---|---|---|---|---|---|---|---|---|---|---|---|---|---|---|---|---|---|---|---|
| 0 | 180 | 0 00 | 42 00 | 90.0 | 0 00 | 41 00 | 90.0 | 0 00 | 40 00 | 90.0 | 0 00 | 39 00 | 90.0 | 0 00 | 38 00 | 90.0 | 0 00 | 37 00 | 90.0 | 180 | 360 |
| 1 | 179 | 0 40 | 42 00 | 89.3 | 0 39 | 41 00 | 89.2 | 0 39 | 40 00 | 89.2 | 0 38 | 39 00 | 89.2 | 0 37 | 38 00 | 89.2 | 0 36 | 37 00 | 89.2 | 181 | 359 |
| 2 | 178 | 1 20 | 41 59 | 88.5 | 1 19 | 40 59 | 88.5 | 1 17 | 39 59 | 88.5 | 1 16 | 38 59 | 88.4 | 1 14 | 37 58 | 88.4 | 1 12 | 36 58 | 88.4 | 182 | 358 |
| 3 | 177 | 2 00 | 41 58 | 87.7 | 1 58 | 40 58 | 87.7 | 1 56 | 39 58 | 87.7 | 1 53 | 38 58 | 87.7 | 1 51 | 37 58 | 87.6 | 1 48 | 36 58 | 87.6 | 183 | 357 |
| 4 | 176 | 2 41 | 41 56 | 87.0 | 2 37 | 40 56 | 87.0 | 2 34 | 39 56 | 86.9 | 2 31 | 38 56 | 86.9 | 2 28 | 37 56 | 86.8 | 2 24 | 36 56 | 86.8 | 184 | 356 |
| 5 | 175 | 3 21 | 41 53 | 86.3 | 3 17 | 40 54 | 86.2 | 3 13 | 39 54 | 86.2 | 3 09 | 38 54 | 86.1 | 3 05 | 37 54 | 86.1 | 3 00 | 36 54 | 86.0 | 185 | 355 |
| 6 | 174 | 4 01 | 41 51 | 85.5 | 3 56 | 40 51 | 85.5 | 3 51 | 39 51 | 85.4 | 3 46 | 38 51 | 85.3 | 3 41 | 37 51 | 85.3 | 3 36 | 36 51 | 85.2 | 186 | 354 |
| 7 | 173 | 4 41 | 41 47 | 84.8 | 4 35 | 40 47 | 84.7 | 4 30 | 39 47 | 84.6 | 4 24 | 38 47 | 84.5 | 4 18 | 37 48 | 84.5 | 4 12 | 36 48 | 84.4 | 187 | 353 |
| 8 | 172 | 5 21 | 41 43 | 84.0 | 5 14 | 40 43 | 84.0 | 5 08 | 39 43 | 83.9 | 5 01 | 38 44 | 83.8 | 4 55 | 37 44 | 83.7 | 4 48 | 36 44 | 83.6 | 188 | 352 |
| 9 | 171 | 6 01 | 41 39 | 83.3 | 5 53 | 40 39 | 83.2 | 5 46 | 39 39 | 83.1 | 5 39 | 38 39 | 83.0 | 5 32 | 37 39 | 82.9 | 5 24 | 36 40 | 82.8 | 189 | 351 |
| 10 | 170 | 6 40 | 41 34 | 82.5 | 6 32 | 40 34 | 82.4 | 6 25 | 39 34 | 82.3 | 6 16 | 38 34 | 82.2 | 6 08 | 37 35 | 82.1 | 6 00 | 36 35 | 82.0 | 190 | 350 |
| 11 | 169 | 7 20 | 41 28 | 81.8 | 7 11 | 40 28 | 81.7 | 7 03 | 39 29 | 81.5 | 6 54 | 38 29 | 81.4 | 6 45 | 37 29 | 81.3 | 6 36 | 36 29 | 81.2 | 191 | 349 |
| 12 | 168 | 8 00 | 41 22 | 81.0 | 7 50 | 40 22 | 80.9 | 7 41 | 39 23 | 80.8 | 7 31 | 38 23 | 80.6 | 7 21 | 37 23 | 80.5 | 7 11 | 36 24 | 80.4 | 192 | 348 |
| 13 | 167 | 8 39 | 41 16 | 80.3 | 8 29 | 40 16 | 80.1 | 8 19 | 39 16 | 80.0 | 8 08 | 38 16 | 79.8 | 7 58 | 37 17 | 79.7 | 7 47 | 36 17 | 79.6 | 193 | 347 |
| 14 | 166 | 9 19 | 41 09 | 79.5 | 9 08 | 40 09 | 79.3 | 8 57 | 39 09 | 79.2 | 8 45 | 38 09 | 79.0 | 8 34 | 37 10 | 78.9 | 8 22 | 36 10 | 78.7 | 194 | 346 |
| 15 | 165 | 9 58 | 41 01 | 78.7 | 9 47 | 40 01 | 78.6 | 9 35 | 39 02 | 78.4 | 9 22 | 38 02 | 78.2 | 9 10 | 37 02 | 78.1 | 8 58 | 36 03 | 77.9 | 195 | 345 |
| 16 | 164 | 10 38 | 40 53 | 78.0 | 10 25 | 39 53 | 77.8 | 10 12 | 38 53 | 77.6 | 9 59 | 37 54 | 77.4 | 9 46 | 36 54 | 77.3 | 9 33 | 35 55 | 77.1 | 196 | 344 |
| 17 | 163 | 11 17 | 40 44 | 77.2 | 11 04 | 39 44 | 77.0 | 10 50 | 38 45 | 76.8 | 10 36 | 37 45 | 76.6 | 10 22 | 36 46 | 76.5 | 10 08 | 35 47 | 76.3 | 197 | 343 |
| 18 | 162 | 11 56 | 40 34 | 76.4 | 11 42 | 39 35 | 76.2 | 11 27 | 38 35 | 76.0 | 11 13 | 37 36 | 75.8 | 10 58 | 36 37 | 75.6 | 10 43 | 35 38 | 75.5 | 198 | 342 |
| 19 | 161 | 12 35 | 40 25 | 75.6 | 12 20 | 39 25 | 75.4 | 12 05 | 38 26 | 75.2 | 11 49 | 37 26 | 75.0 | 11 34 | 36 27 | 74.8 | 11 18 | 35 28 | 74.6 | 199 | 341 |
| 20 | 160 | 13 14 | 40 14 | 74.9 | 12 58 | 39 15 | 74.6 | 12 42 | 38 15 | 74.4 | 12 26 | 37 16 | 74.2 | 12 09 | 36 17 | 74.0 | 11 53 | 35 18 | 73.8 | 200 | 340 |
| 21 | 159 | 13 52 | 40 03 | 74.1 | 13 36 | 39 04 | 73.8 | 13 19 | 38 04 | 73.6 | 13 02 | 37 05 | 73.4 | 12 45 | 36 06 | 73.2 | 12 27 | 35 08 | 73.0 | 201 | 339 |
| 22 | 158 | 14 31 | 39 51 | 73.3 | 14 14 | 38 52 | 73.0 | 13 56 | 37 53 | 72.8 | 13 38 | 36 54 | 72.6 | 13 20 | 35 55 | 72.3 | 13 02 | 34 56 | 72.1 | 202 | 338 |
| 23 | 157 | 15 09 | 39 39 | 72.5 | 14 51 | 38 40 | 72.2 | 14 33 | 37 41 | 72.0 | 14 14 | 36 42 | 71.7 | 13 55 | 35 43 | 71.5 | 13 36 | 34 45 | 71.3 | 203 | 337 |
| 24 | 156 | 15 48 | 39 26 | 71.7 | 15 29 | 38 27 | 71.4 | 15 09 | 37 28 | 71.2 | 14 50 | 36 30 | 70.9 | 14 30 | 35 31 | 70.7 | 14 10 | 34 33 | 70.4 | 204 | 336 |
| 25 | 155 | 16 26 | 39 13 | 70.9 | 16 06 | 38 14 | 70.6 | 15 46 | 37 15 | 70.3 | 15 25 | 36 17 | 70.1 | 15 05 | 35 18 | 69.8 | 14 44 | 34 20 | 69.6 | 205 | 335 |
| 26 | 154 | 17 03 | 38 59 | 70.1 | 16 43 | 38 00 | 69.8 | 16 22 | 37 01 | 69.5 | 16 01 | 36 03 | 69.2 | 15 39 | 35 05 | 69.0 | 15 18 | 34 07 | 68.7 | 206 | 334 |
| 27 | 153 | 17 41 | 38 44 | 69.3 | 17 20 | 37 46 | 69.0 | 16 58 | 36 47 | 68.7 | 16 36 | 35 49 | 68.4 | 16 14 | 34 51 | 68.1 | 15 51 | 33 53 | 67.9 | 207 | 333 |
| 28 | 152 | 18 19 | 38 29 | 68.4 | 17 56 | 37 30 | 68.1 | 17 34 | 36 32 | 67.8 | 17 11 | 35 34 | 67.5 | 16 48 | 34 36 | 67.3 | 16 25 | 33 38 | 67.0 | 208 | 332 |
| 29 | 151 | 18 56 | 38 13 | 67.6 | 18 33 | 37 15 | 67.3 | 18 09 | 36 16 | 67.0 | 17 46 | 35 18 | 66.7 | 17 22 | 34 21 | 66.4 | 16 58 | 33 23 | 66.1 | 209 | 331 |
| 30 | 150 | 19 33 | 37 57 | 66.8 | 19 09 | 36 58 | 66.5 | 18 45 | 36 00 | 66.1 | 18 20 | 35 03 | 65.8 | 17 56 | 34 05 | 65.5 | 17 31 | 33 08 | 65.2 | 210 | 330 |
| 31 | 149 | 20 10 | 37 40 | 65.9 | 19 45 | 36 41 | 65.6 | 19 20 | 35 44 | 65.3 | 18 55 | 34 46 | 65.0 | 18 29 | 33 49 | 64.7 | 18 03 | 32 52 | 64.4 | 211 | 329 |
| 32 | 148 | 20 46 | 37 22 | 65.1 | 20 21 | 36 24 | 64.8 | 19 55 | 35 26 | 64.4 | 19 29 | 34 29 | 64.1 | 19 02 | 33 32 | 63.8 | 18 36 | 32 35 | 63.5 | 212 | 328 |
| 33 | 147 | 21 22 | 37 03 | 64.2 | 20 56 | 36 06 | 63.9 | 20 30 | 35 08 | 63.6 | 20 03 | 34 11 | 63.2 | 19 35 | 33 14 | 62.9 | 19 08 | 32 18 | 62.6 | 213 | 327 |
| 34 | 146 | 21 58 | 36 44 | 63.4 | 21 31 | 35 47 | 63.0 | 21 04 | 34 49 | 62.7 | 20 36 | 33 53 | 62.3 | 20 08 | 32 56 | 62.0 | 19 40 | 32 00 | 61.7 | 214 | 326 |
| 35 | 145 | 22 34 | 36 25 | 62.5 | 22 06 | 35 27 | 62.1 | 21 38 | 34 30 | 61.8 | 21 10 | 33 33 | 61.4 | 20 41 | 32 37 | 61.1 | 20 12 | 31 41 | 60.8 | 215 | 325 |
| 36 | 144 | 23 10 | 36 04 | 61.6 | 22 41 | 35 07 | 61.3 | 22 12 | 34 10 | 60.9 | 21 43 | 33 14 | 60.5 | 21 13 | 32 18 | 60.2 | 20 43 | 31 22 | 59.9 | 216 | 324 |
| 37 | 143 | 23 45 | 35 43 | 60.8 | 23 15 | 34 46 | 60.4 | 22 45 | 33 50 | 60.0 | 22 15 | 32 53 | 59.6 | 21 45 | 31 58 | 59.3 | 21 14 | 31 02 | 59.0 | 217 | 323 |
| 38 | 142 | 24 20 | 35 21 | 60.0 | 23 49 | 34 24 | 59.5 | 23 19 | 33 28 | 59.1 | 22 48 | 32 33 | 58.7 | 22 16 | 31 38 | 58.4 | 21 45 | 30 42 | 58.0 | 218 | 322 |
| 39 | 141 | 24 54 | 34 59 | 59.0 | 24 23 | 34 02 | 58.6 | 23 52 | 33 07 | 58.2 | 23 20 | 32 11 | 57.8 | 22 48 | 31 16 | 57.5 | 22 15 | 30 21 | 57.1 | 219 | 321 |
| 40 | 140 | 25 28 | 34 36 | 58.1 | 24 57 | 33 40 | 57.7 | 24 24 | 32 44 | 57.3 | 23 52 | 31 49 | 56.9 | 23 19 | 30 54 | 56.5 | 22 45 | 30 00 | 56.2 | 220 | 320 |
| 41 | 139 | 26 02 | 34 12 | 57.1 | 25 30 | 33 16 | 56.7 | 24 57 | 32 21 | 56.3 | 24 23 | 31 26 | 56.0 | 23 49 | 30 32 | 55.6 | 23 15 | 29 38 | 55.2 | 221 | 319 |
| 42 | 138 | 26 36 | 33 47 | 56.2 | 26 02 | 32 52 | 55.8 | 25 28 | 31 57 | 55.4 | 24 54 | 31 02 | 55.0 | 24 20 | 30 08 | 54.6 | 23 45 | 29 15 | 54.3 | 222 | 318 |
| 43 | 137 | 27 09 | 33 22 | 55.3 | 26 35 | 32 27 | 54.9 | 26 00 | 31 32 | 54.5 | 25 25 | 30 38 | 54.1 | 24 50 | 29 45 | 53.7 | 24 14 | 28 52 | 53.3 | 223 | 317 |
| 44 | 136 | 27 42 | 32 56 | 54.3 | 27 07 | 32 01 | 53.9 | 26 31 | 31 07 | 53.5 | 25 55 | 30 13 | 53.1 | 25 19 | 29 20 | 52.7 | 24 43 | 28 28 | 52.4 | 224 | 316 |
| 45 | 135 | 28 14 | 32 29 | 53.4 | 27 38 | 31 35 | 53.0 | 27 02 | 30 41 | 52.5 | 26 25 | 29 48 | 52.1 | 25 48 | 28 55 | 51.8 | 25 11 | 28 03 | 51.4 | 225 | 315 |

| Lat. / A | | 48° | | | 49° | | | 50° | | | 51° | | | 52° | | | 53° | | | Lat. / A | |
|---|---|---|---|---|---|---|---|---|---|---|---|---|---|---|---|---|---|---|---|---|---|
| LHA/F | | A/H | B/P | Z₁/Z₂ | A/H | B/P | Z₁/Z₂ | A/H | B/P | Z₁/Z₂ | A/H | B/P | Z₁/Z₂ | A/H | B/P | Z₁/Z₂ | A/H | B/P | Z₁/Z₂ | | LHA |
| 135 | 45 | 28 14 | 32 29 | 53·4 | 27 38 | 31 35 | 53·4 | 27 02 | 30 41 | 53·0 | 26 25 | 29 48 | 52·5 | 25 48 | 28 55 | 51·8 | 25 11 | 28 03 | 51·4 | 315 | 225 |
| 134 | 46 | 28 46 | 32 01 | 52·4 | 28 10 | 31 08 | 52·4 | 27 32 | 30 14 | 52·0 | 26 55 | 29 22 | 51·6 | 26 17 | 28 29 | 50·8 | 25 39 | 27 38 | 50·4 | 314 | 226 |
| 133 | 47 | 29 18 | 31 33 | 51·4 | 28 40 | 30 40 | 51·4 | 28 02 | 29 47 | 51·0 | 27 24 | 28 55 | 50·6 | 26 46 | 28 03 | 49·8 | 26 07 | 27 12 | 49·4 | 313 | 227 |
| 132 | 48 | 29 49 | 31 04 | 50·5 | 29 11 | 30 11 | 50·5 | 28 32 | 29 19 | 50·0 | 27 53 | 28 27 | 49·6 | 27 14 | 27 36 | 48·8 | 26 34 | 26 46 | 48·4 | 312 | 228 |
| 131 | 49 | 30 20 | 30 34 | 49·5 | 29 41 | 29 42 | 49·5 | 29 01 | 28 50 | 49·0 | 28 21 | 27 59 | 48·6 | 27 41 | 27 08 | 47·8 | 27 01 | 26 18 | 47·4 | 311 | 229 |
| 130 | 50 | 30 50 | 30 04 | 48·5 | 30 10 | 29 12 | 48·5 | 29 30 | 28 20 | 48·0 | 28 49 | 27 30 | 47·6 | 28 08 | 26 40 | 46·8 | 27 27 | 25 51 | 46·4 | 310 | 230 |
| 129 | 51 | 31 20 | 29 32 | 47·5 | 30 39 | 28 41 | 47·5 | 29 58 | 27 50 | 47·0 | 29 17 | 27 00 | 46·6 | 28 35 | 26 11 | 45·8 | 27 53 | 25 22 | 45·4 | 309 | 231 |
| 128 | 52 | 31 49 | 29 00 | 46·4 | 31 08 | 28 09 | 46·4 | 30 26 | 27 19 | 46·0 | 29 44 | 26 30 | 45·6 | 29 01 | 25 41 | 44·8 | 28 19 | 24 53 | 44·4 | 308 | 232 |
| 127 | 53 | 32 18 | 28 27 | 45·4 | 31 36 | 27 37 | 45·4 | 30 53 | 26 48 | 45·0 | 30 10 | 25 59 | 44·5 | 29 27 | 25 11 | 43·7 | 28 44 | 24 24 | 43·3 | 307 | 233 |
| 126 | 54 | 32 46 | 27 53 | 44·4 | 32 03 | 27 04 | 43·9 | 31 20 | 26 15 | 43·9 | 30 36 | 25 27 | 43·5 | 29 52 | 24 40 | 42·7 | 29 08 | 23 53 | 42·3 | 306 | 234 |
| 125 | 55 | 33 14 | 27 19 | 43·3 | 32 30 | 26 30 | 42·9 | 31 46 | 25 42 | 42·9 | 31 02 | 24 55 | 42·4 | 30 17 | 24 08 | 41·6 | 29 32 | 23 23 | 41·2 | 305 | 235 |
| 124 | 56 | 33 42 | 26 44 | 42·2 | 32 57 | 25 55 | 41·8 | 32 12 | 25 08 | 41·4 | 31 27 | 24 22 | 41·4 | 30 41 | 23 36 | 40·6 | 29 56 | 22 51 | 40·2 | 304 | 236 |
| 123 | 57 | 34 08 | 26 07 | 41·1 | 33 23 | 25 20 | 40·7 | 32 37 | 24 34 | 40·3 | 31 51 | 23 48 | 39·9 | 31 05 | 23 03 | 39·5 | 30 19 | 22 19 | 39·1 | 303 | 237 |
| 122 | 58 | 34 34 | 25 30 | 40·1 | 33 48 | 24 44 | 39·6 | 33 02 | 23 58 | 39·2 | 32 15 | 23 14 | 38·8 | 31 28 | 22 29 | 38·4 | 30 41 | 21 46 | 38·0 | 302 | 238 |
| 121 | 59 | 35 00 | 24 53 | 39·0 | 34 13 | 24 07 | 38·5 | 33 26 | 23 22 | 38·1 | 32 39 | 22 38 | 37·7 | 31 51 | 21 55 | 37·3 | 31 03 | 21 13 | 37·0 | 301 | 239 |
| 120 | 60 | 35 25 | 24 14 | 37·8 | 34 37 | 23 30 | 37·4 | 33 50 | 22 46 | 37·0 | 33 02 | 22 03 | 36·6 | 32 13 | 21 21 | 36·2 | 31 25 | 20 39 | 35·9 | 300 | 240 |
| 119 | 61 | 35 49 | 23 35 | 36·7 | 35 01 | 22 51 | 36·3 | 34 12 | 22 08 | 35·9 | 33 24 | 21 26 | 35·5 | 32 35 | 20 45 | 35·1 | 31 46 | 20 04 | 34·8 | 299 | 241 |
| 118 | 62 | 36 13 | 22 55 | 35·6 | 35 24 | 22 12 | 35·2 | 34 35 | 21 30 | 34·8 | 33 45 | 20 49 | 34·4 | 32 56 | 20 09 | 34·0 | 32 06 | 19 29 | 33·7 | 298 | 242 |
| 117 | 63 | 36 36 | 22 14 | 34·4 | 35 46 | 21 32 | 34·0 | 34 56 | 20 51 | 33·6 | 34 06 | 20 11 | 33·3 | 33 16 | 19 32 | 32·9 | 32 26 | 18 53 | 32·5 | 297 | 243 |
| 116 | 64 | 36 58 | 21 32 | 33·3 | 36 08 | 20 52 | 32·9 | 35 17 | 20 12 | 32·5 | 34 27 | 19 33 | 32·1 | 33 36 | 18 54 | 31·8 | 32 45 | 18 17 | 31·4 | 296 | 244 |
| 115 | 65 | 37 20 | 20 50 | 32·1 | 36 29 | 20 10 | 31·7 | 35 38 | 19 32 | 31·3 | 34 47 | 18 54 | 31·0 | 33 55 | 18 16 | 30·6 | 33 03 | 17 40 | 30·3 | 295 | 245 |
| 114 | 66 | 37 41 | 20 07 | 30·9 | 36 49 | 19 28 | 30·5 | 35 58 | 18 51 | 30·2 | 35 06 | 18 14 | 29·8 | 34 13 | 17 38 | 29·5 | 33 21 | 17 02 | 29·1 | 294 | 246 |
| 113 | 67 | 38 01 | 19 23 | 29·7 | 37 09 | 18 46 | 29·4 | 36 17 | 18 09 | 29·0 | 35 24 | 17 33 | 28·6 | 34 31 | 16 59 | 28·3 | 33 38 | 16 24 | 28·0 | 293 | 247 |
| 112 | 68 | 38 21 | 18 38 | 28·5 | 37 28 | 18 02 | 28·2 | 36 35 | 17 27 | 27·8 | 35 42 | 16 53 | 27·5 | 34 48 | 16 19 | 27·1 | 33 55 | 15 46 | 26·8 | 292 | 248 |
| 111 | 69 | 38 40 | 17 53 | 27·3 | 37 46 | 17 18 | 27·0 | 36 53 | 16 44 | 26·6 | 35 59 | 16 11 | 26·3 | 35 05 | 15 38 | 26·0 | 34 11 | 15 07 | 25·7 | 291 | 249 |
| 110 | 70 | 38 58 | 17 07 | 26·1 | 38 04 | 16 33 | 25·7 | 37 10 | 16 01 | 25·4 | 36 15 | 15 29 | 25·0 | 35 21 | 14 58 | 24·8 | 34 26 | 14 27 | 24·5 | 290 | 250 |
| 109 | 71 | 39 15 | 16 20 | 24·9 | 38 20 | 15 48 | 24·5 | 37 26 | 15 17 | 24·2 | 36 31 | 14 46 | 23·8 | 35 36 | 14 16 | 23·6 | 34 41 | 13 47 | 23·3 | 289 | 251 |
| 108 | 72 | 39 31 | 15 33 | 23·6 | 38 36 | 15 02 | 23·3 | 37 41 | 14 32 | 23·0 | 36 46 | 14 03 | 22·6 | 35 50 | 13 34 | 22·4 | 34 55 | 13 07 | 22·1 | 288 | 252 |
| 107 | 73 | 39 47 | 14 45 | 22·4 | 38 51 | 14 16 | 22·1 | 37 56 | 13 47 | 21·8 | 37 00 | 13 19 | 21·4 | 36 04 | 12 52 | 21·2 | 35 08 | 12 25 | 20·9 | 287 | 253 |
| 106 | 74 | 40 02 | 13 56 | 21·1 | 39 06 | 13 28 | 20·8 | 38 10 | 13 01 | 20·5 | 37 13 | 12 35 | 20·2 | 36 17 | 12 09 | 20·0 | 35 21 | 11 44 | 19·8 | 286 | 254 |
| 105 | 75 | 40 16 | 13 07 | 19·8 | 39 20 | 12 41 | 19·5 | 38 23 | 12 15 | 19·3 | 37 26 | 11 50 | 19·0 | 36 29 | 11 26 | 18·8 | 35 33 | 11 02 | 18·5 | 285 | 255 |
| 104 | 76 | 40 29 | 12 17 | 18·5 | 39 32 | 11 53 | 18·3 | 38 35 | 11 28 | 18·0 | 37 38 | 11 05 | 17·8 | 36 41 | 10 42 | 17·6 | 35 44 | 10 20 | 17·3 | 284 | 256 |
| 103 | 77 | 40 41 | 11 27 | 17·3 | 39 44 | 11 04 | 17·0 | 38 47 | 10 41 | 16·8 | 37 49 | 10 19 | 16·5 | 36 52 | 9 58 | 16·3 | 35 54 | 9 37 | 16·1 | 283 | 257 |
| 102 | 78 | 40 53 | 10 36 | 16·0 | 39 55 | 10 15 | 15·7 | 38 57 | 9 54 | 15·5 | 38 00 | 9 33 | 15·3 | 37 02 | 9 14 | 15·1 | 36 04 | 8 54 | 14·9 | 282 | 258 |
| 101 | 79 | 41 04 | 9 45 | 14·7 | 40 05 | 9 25 | 14·4 | 39 07 | 9 06 | 14·2 | 38 09 | 8 47 | 14·0 | 37 11 | 8 29 | 13·9 | 36 13 | 8 11 | 13·7 | 281 | 259 |
| 100 | 80 | 41 13 | 8 53 | 13·3 | 40 15 | 8 35 | 13·2 | 39 16 | 8 17 | 13·0 | 38 18 | 8 00 | 12·8 | 37 19 | 7 44 | 12·6 | 36 21 | 7 27 | 12·5 | 280 | 260 |
| 99 | 81 | 41 22 | 8 01 | 12·0 | 40 23 | 7 45 | 11·9 | 39 25 | 7 29 | 11·7 | 38 26 | 7 13 | 11·5 | 37 27 | 6 58 | 11·4 | 36 28 | 6 43 | 11·2 | 279 | 261 |
| 98 | 82 | 41 30 | 7 09 | 10·7 | 40 31 | 6 54 | 10·5 | 39 32 | 6 40 | 10·4 | 38 33 | 6 26 | 10·3 | 37 34 | 6 12 | 10·1 | 36 35 | 5 59 | 10·0 | 278 | 262 |
| 97 | 83 | 41 37 | 6 16 | 9·4 | 40 38 | 6 03 | 9·2 | 39 39 | 5 50 | 9·1 | 38 39 | 5 38 | 9·0 | 37 40 | 5 26 | 8·9 | 36 41 | 5 15 | 8·7 | 277 | 263 |
| 96 | 84 | 41 43 | 5 23 | 8·1 | 40 44 | 5 12 | 7·9 | 39 44 | 5 01 | 7·8 | 38 45 | 4 50 | 7·7 | 37 45 | 4 40 | 7·6 | 36 46 | 4 30 | 7·5 | 276 | 264 |
| 95 | 85 | 41 48 | 4 29 | 6·7 | 40 49 | 4 20 | 6·6 | 39 49 | 4 11 | 6·5 | 38 49 | 4 02 | 6·4 | 37 50 | 3 54 | 6·3 | 36 50 | 3 45 | 6·3 | 275 | 265 |
| 94 | 86 | 41 52 | 3 36 | 5·4 | 40 53 | 3 28 | 5·3 | 39 53 | 3 21 | 5·2 | 38 53 | 3 14 | 5·1 | 37 53 | 3 07 | 5·1 | 36 54 | 3 01 | 5·0 | 274 | 266 |
| 93 | 87 | 41 56 | 2 42 | 4·0 | 40 56 | 2 36 | 4·0 | 39 56 | 2 31 | 3·9 | 38 56 | 2 26 | 3·9 | 37 56 | 2 20 | 3·8 | 36 56 | 2 16 | 3·8 | 273 | 267 |
| 92 | 88 | 41 58 | 1 48 | 2·7 | 40 58 | 1 44 | 2·6 | 39 58 | 1 41 | 2·6 | 38 58 | 1 37 | 2·6 | 37 58 | 1 34 | 2·5 | 36 58 | 1 30 | 2·5 | 272 | 268 |
| 91 | 89 | 42 00 | 0 54 | 1·3 | 41 00 | 0 52 | 1·3 | 40 00 | 0 50 | 1·3 | 39 00 | 0 49 | 1·3 | 38 00 | 0 47 | 1·3 | 37 00 | 0 45 | 1·3 | 271 | 269 |
| 90 | 90 | 42 00 | 0 00 | 0·0 | 41 00 | 0 00 | 0·0 | 40 00 | 0 00 | 0·0 | 39 00 | 0 00 | 0·0 | 38 00 | 0 00 | 0·0 | 37 00 | 0 00 | 0·0 | 270 | 270 |

N. Lat.: for LHA > 180° ... Zₙ = Z  
for LHA < 180° ... Zₙ = 360° − Z

S. Lat.: for LHA > 180° ... Zₙ = 180° − Z  
for LHA < 180° ... Zₙ = 180° + Z

B: (−) for 90° < LHA < 270°  
Dec:(−) for Lat. contrary name

Z₁: same sign as B  
Z₂: (−) for F > 90°

## SIGHT REDUCTION TABLE

| LHA/F | | 54° A/H | 54° B/P | 54° Z₁/Z₂ | 55° A/H | 55° B/P | 55° Z₁/Z₂ | 56° A/H | 56° B/P | 56° Z₁/Z₂ | 57° A/H | 57° B/P | 57° Z₁/Z₂ | 58° A/H | 58° B/P | 58° Z₁/Z₂ | 59° A/H | 59° B/P | 59° Z₁/Z₂ | LHA | |
|---|---|---|---|---|---|---|---|---|---|---|---|---|---|---|---|---|---|---|---|---|---|
| 0 | 180 | 0 00 | 36 00 | 90·0 | 0 00 | 35 00 | 90·0 | 0 00 | 34 00 | 90·0 | 0 00 | 33 00 | 90·0 | 0 00 | 32 00 | 90·0 | 0 00 | 31 00 | 90·0 | 180 | 360 |
| 1 | 179 | 0 35 | 36 00 | 89·2 | 0 34 | 35 00 | 89·2 | 0 34 | 34 00 | 89·2 | 0 33 | 33 00 | 89·2 | 0 32 | 32 00 | 89·2 | 0 31 | 31 00 | 89·1 | 181 | 359 |
| 2 | 178 | 1 11 | 35 59 | 88·4 | 1 09 | 34 59 | 88·4 | 1 07 | 33 59 | 88·3 | 1 05 | 32 59 | 88·3 | 1 04 | 31 59 | 88·3 | 1 02 | 30 59 | 88·3 | 182 | 358 |
| 3 | 177 | 1 46 | 35 58 | 87·6 | 1 43 | 34 58 | 87·5 | 1 41 | 33 58 | 87·5 | 1 38 | 32 58 | 87·5 | 1 35 | 31 58 | 87·5 | 1 33 | 30 58 | 87·4 | 183 | 357 |
| 4 | 176 | 2 21 | 35 56 | 86·8 | 2 18 | 34 56 | 86·7 | 2 14 | 33 56 | 86·7 | 2 11 | 32 56 | 86·6 | 2 07 | 31 56 | 86·6 | 2 04 | 30 56 | 86·6 | 184 | 356 |
| 5 | 175 | 2 56 | 35 54 | 86·0 | 2 52 | 34 54 | 85·9 | 2 48 | 33 54 | 85·9 | 2 43 | 32 54 | 85·8 | 2 39 | 31 54 | 85·8 | 2 34 | 30 54 | 85·7 | 185 | 355 |
| 6 | 174 | 3 31 | 35 51 | 85·1 | 3 26 | 34 51 | 85·1 | 3 21 | 33 51 | 85·0 | 3 16 | 32 51 | 85·0 | 3 11 | 31 52 | 84·9 | 3 05 | 30 52 | 84·9 | 186 | 354 |
| 7 | 173 | 4 06 | 35 48 | 84·3 | 4 00 | 34 48 | 84·3 | 3 54 | 33 48 | 84·2 | 3 48 | 32 48 | 84·1 | 3 42 | 31 48 | 84·1 | 3 36 | 30 49 | 84·0 | 187 | 353 |
| 8 | 172 | 4 42 | 35 44 | 83·5 | 4 35 | 34 44 | 83·4 | 4 28 | 33 44 | 83·4 | 4 21 | 32 45 | 83·3 | 4 14 | 31 45 | 83·2 | 4 07 | 30 45 | 83·1 | 188 | 352 |
| 9 | 171 | 5 17 | 35 40 | 82·7 | 5 09 | 34 40 | 82·6 | 5 01 | 33 40 | 82·5 | 4 53 | 32 41 | 82·4 | 4 45 | 31 41 | 82·3 | 4 37 | 30 41 | 82·3 | 189 | 351 |
| 10 | 170 | 5 51 | 35 35 | 81·9 | 5 43 | 34 35 | 81·8 | 5 34 | 33 36 | 81·7 | 5 26 | 32 36 | 81·6 | 5 17 | 31 36 | 81·5 | 5 08 | 30 37 | 81·4 | 190 | 350 |
| 11 | 169 | 6 26 | 35 30 | 81·1 | 6 17 | 34 30 | 81·0 | 6 08 | 33 31 | 80·8 | 5 58 | 32 31 | 80·7 | 5 48 | 31 31 | 80·6 | 5 38 | 30 32 | 80·5 | 191 | 349 |
| 12 | 168 | 7 01 | 35 24 | 80·2 | 6 51 | 34 24 | 80·1 | 6 41 | 33 25 | 80·0 | 6 30 | 32 25 | 79·9 | 6 20 | 31 26 | 79·8 | 6 09 | 30 27 | 79·7 | 192 | 348 |
| 13 | 167 | 7 36 | 35 18 | 79·4 | 7 25 | 34 18 | 79·3 | 7 14 | 33 19 | 79·2 | 7 02 | 32 19 | 79·0 | 6 51 | 31 20 | 78·9 | 6 39 | 30 21 | 78·8 | 193 | 347 |
| 14 | 166 | 8 11 | 35 11 | 78·6 | 7 59 | 34 12 | 78·5 | 7 46 | 33 12 | 78·3 | 7 34 | 32 13 | 78·2 | 7 22 | 31 14 | 78·1 | 7 09 | 30 15 | 77·9 | 194 | 346 |
| 15 | 165 | 8 45 | 35 04 | 77·8 | 8 32 | 34 04 | 77·6 | 8 19 | 33 05 | 77·5 | 8 06 | 32 06 | 77·3 | 7 53 | 31 07 | 77·2 | 7 40 | 30 08 | 77·1 | 195 | 345 |
| 16 | 164 | 9 19 | 34 56 | 76·9 | 9 06 | 33 57 | 76·8 | 8 52 | 32 58 | 76·6 | 8 38 | 31 58 | 76·5 | 8 24 | 31 00 | 76·3 | 8 10 | 30 01 | 76·2 | 196 | 344 |
| 17 | 163 | 9 54 | 34 47 | 76·1 | 9 39 | 33 48 | 75·9 | 9 25 | 32 49 | 75·8 | 9 10 | 31 50 | 75·6 | 8 55 | 30 52 | 75·5 | 8 40 | 29 53 | 75·3 | 197 | 343 |
| 18 | 162 | 10 28 | 34 39 | 75·3 | 10 13 | 33 40 | 75·1 | 9 57 | 32 41 | 74·9 | 9 41 | 31 42 | 74·8 | 9 25 | 30 43 | 74·6 | 9 09 | 29 45 | 74·4 | 198 | 342 |
| 19 | 161 | 11 02 | 34 29 | 74·4 | 10 46 | 33 30 | 74·2 | 10 29 | 32 32 | 74·1 | 10 13 | 31 33 | 73·9 | 9 56 | 30 35 | 73·7 | 9 39 | 29 36 | 73·6 | 199 | 341 |
| 20 | 160 | 11 36 | 34 19 | 73·6 | 11 19 | 33 21 | 73·4 | 11 02 | 32 22 | 73·2 | 10 44 | 31 24 | 73·0 | 10 27 | 30 25 | 72·8 | 10 09 | 29 27 | 72·7 | 200 | 340 |
| 21 | 159 | 12 10 | 34 09 | 72·7 | 11 52 | 33 10 | 72·5 | 11 34 | 32 12 | 72·3 | 11 15 | 31 14 | 72·2 | 10 57 | 30 15 | 72·0 | 10 38 | 29 17 | 71·8 | 201 | 339 |
| 22 | 158 | 12 43 | 33 58 | 71·9 | 12 24 | 33 00 | 71·7 | 12 06 | 32 01 | 71·5 | 11 46 | 31 03 | 71·3 | 11 27 | 30 05 | 71·1 | 11 07 | 29 07 | 70·9 | 202 | 338 |
| 23 | 157 | 13 17 | 33 46 | 71·0 | 12 57 | 32 48 | 70·8 | 12 37 | 31 50 | 70·6 | 12 17 | 30 52 | 70·4 | 11 57 | 29 54 | 70·2 | 11 37 | 28 57 | 70·0 | 203 | 337 |
| 24 | 156 | 13 50 | 33 34 | 70·2 | 13 29 | 32 36 | 70·0 | 13 09 | 31 38 | 69·7 | 12 48 | 30 41 | 69·5 | 12 27 | 29 43 | 69·3 | 12 06 | 28 46 | 69·1 | 204 | 336 |
| 25 | 155 | 14 23 | 33 22 | 69·3 | 14 02 | 32 24 | 69·1 | 13 40 | 31 26 | 68·9 | 13 18 | 30 29 | 68·6 | 12 56 | 29 31 | 68·4 | 12 34 | 28 34 | 68·2 | 205 | 335 |
| 26 | 154 | 14 56 | 33 09 | 68·5 | 14 34 | 32 11 | 68·2 | 14 11 | 31 14 | 68·0 | 13 49 | 30 16 | 67·7 | 13 26 | 29 19 | 67·5 | 13 03 | 28 22 | 67·3 | 206 | 334 |
| 27 | 153 | 15 29 | 32 55 | 67·6 | 15 06 | 31 58 | 67·3 | 14 42 | 31 00 | 67·1 | 14 19 | 30 03 | 66·9 | 13 55 | 29 06 | 66·6 | 13 31 | 28 10 | 66·4 | 207 | 333 |
| 28 | 152 | 16 01 | 32 41 | 66·7 | 15 37 | 31 44 | 66·5 | 15 13 | 30 47 | 66·2 | 14 49 | 29 50 | 66·0 | 14 24 | 28 53 | 65·7 | 14 00 | 27 57 | 65·5 | 208 | 332 |
| 29 | 151 | 16 33 | 32 26 | 65·8 | 16 09 | 31 29 | 65·6 | 15 44 | 30 32 | 65·3 | 15 19 | 29 36 | 65·1 | 14 53 | 28 39 | 64·8 | 14 28 | 27 43 | 64·6 | 209 | 331 |
| 30 | 150 | 17 05 | 32 11 | 65·0 | 16 40 | 31 14 | 64·7 | 16 14 | 30 17 | 64·4 | 15 48 | 29 21 | 64·2 | 15 22 | 28 25 | 63·9 | 14 55 | 27 29 | 63·7 | 210 | 330 |
| 31 | 149 | 17 37 | 31 55 | 64·1 | 17 11 | 30 58 | 63·8 | 16 44 | 30 02 | 63·5 | 16 17 | 29 06 | 63·3 | 15 50 | 28 10 | 63·0 | 15 23 | 27 15 | 62·7 | 211 | 329 |
| 32 | 148 | 18 09 | 31 38 | 63·2 | 17 42 | 30 42 | 62·9 | 17 14 | 29 46 | 62·6 | 16 47 | 28 51 | 62·3 | 16 19 | 27 55 | 62·1 | 15 50 | 27 00 | 61·8 | 212 | 328 |
| 33 | 147 | 18 40 | 31 21 | 62·3 | 18 12 | 30 25 | 62·0 | 17 44 | 29 30 | 61·7 | 17 15 | 28 34 | 61·4 | 16 47 | 27 39 | 61·2 | 16 17 | 26 45 | 60·9 | 213 | 327 |
| 34 | 146 | 19 11 | 31 04 | 61·4 | 18 42 | 30 08 | 61·1 | 18 13 | 29 13 | 60·8 | 17 44 | 28 18 | 60·5 | 17 14 | 27 23 | 60·2 | 16 44 | 26 29 | 60·0 | 214 | 326 |
| 35 | 145 | 19 42 | 30 46 | 60·5 | 19 12 | 29 50 | 60·2 | 18 42 | 28 55 | 59·9 | 18 12 | 28 01 | 59·6 | 17 42 | 27 06 | 59·3 | 17 11 | 26 12 | 59·0 | 215 | 325 |
| 36 | 144 | 20 13 | 30 27 | 59·6 | 19 42 | 29 32 | 59·2 | 19 11 | 28 37 | 58·9 | 18 40 | 27 43 | 58·7 | 18 09 | 26 49 | 58·4 | 17 37 | 25 55 | 58·1 | 216 | 324 |
| 37 | 143 | 20 43 | 30 07 | 58·6 | 20 12 | 29 13 | 58·3 | 19 40 | 28 19 | 58·0 | 19 08 | 27 25 | 57·7 | 18 36 | 26 31 | 57·4 | 18 03 | 25 38 | 57·1 | 217 | 323 |
| 38 | 142 | 21 13 | 29 48 | 57·7 | 20 41 | 28 53 | 57·4 | 20 08 | 27 59 | 57·1 | 19 35 | 27 06 | 56·8 | 19 02 | 26 13 | 56·5 | 18 29 | 25 20 | 56·2 | 218 | 322 |
| 39 | 141 | 21 43 | 29 27 | 56·8 | 21 10 | 28 33 | 56·4 | 20 36 | 27 40 | 56·1 | 20 03 | 26 47 | 55·8 | 19 29 | 25 54 | 55·5 | 18 55 | 25 02 | 55·2 | 219 | 321 |
| 40 | 140 | 22 12 | 29 06 | 55·8 | 21 38 | 28 13 | 55·5 | 21 04 | 27 20 | 55·2 | 20 30 | 26 27 | 54·9 | 19 55 | 25 35 | 54·6 | 19 20 | 24 43 | 54·3 | 220 | 320 |
| 41 | 139 | 22 41 | 28 44 | 54·9 | 22 06 | 27 51 | 54·5 | 21 31 | 26 59 | 54·2 | 20 56 | 26 07 | 53·9 | 20 21 | 25 15 | 53·6 | 19 45 | 24 24 | 53·3 | 221 | 319 |
| 42 | 138 | 23 10 | 28 22 | 53·9 | 22 34 | 27 29 | 53·6 | 21 58 | 26 37 | 53·3 | 21 22 | 25 46 | 52·9 | 20 46 | 24 55 | 52·6 | 20 10 | 24 04 | 52·3 | 222 | 318 |
| 43 | 137 | 23 38 | 27 59 | 53·0 | 23 02 | 27 07 | 52·6 | 22 25 | 26 15 | 52·3 | 21 48 | 25 24 | 52·0 | 21 11 | 24 34 | 51·7 | 20 34 | 23 43 | 51·4 | 223 | 317 |
| 44 | 136 | 24 06 | 27 36 | 52·0 | 23 29 | 26 44 | 51·7 | 22 51 | 25 53 | 51·3 | 22 14 | 25 02 | 51·0 | 21 36 | 24 12 | 50·7 | 20 58 | 23 23 | 50·4 | 224 | 316 |
| 45 | 135 | 24 34 | 27 11 | 51·0 | 23 56 | 26 20 | 50·7 | 23 17 | 25 30 | 50·3 | 22 39 | 24 40 | 50·0 | 22 00 | 23 50 | 49·7 | 21 21 | 23 01 | 49·4 | 225 | 315 |

S. Lat: for LHA > 180° .... $Z_n = 180° − Z$
for LHA < 180° .... $Z_n = 180° + Z$

| Lat./A LHA | | 59° A/H | 59° B/P | 59° Z₁/Z₂ | 58° A/H | 58° B/P | 58° Z₁/Z₂ | 57° A/H | 57° B/P | 57° Z₁/Z₂ | 56° A/H | 56° B/P | 56° Z₁/Z₂ | 55° A/H | 55° B/P | 55° Z₁/Z₂ | 54° A/H | 54° B/P | 54° Z₁/Z₂ | Lat./A LHA/F |
|---|---|---|---|---|---|---|---|---|---|---|---|---|---|---|---|---|---|---|---|---|
| 225 315 | | 21 21 | 23 01 | 49.4 | 22 00 | 23 50 | 49.7 | 22 39 | 24 40 | 50.0 | 23 17 | 25 30 | 50.3 | 23 56 | 26 20 | 50.7 | 24 34 | 27 11 | 51.0 | 45 135 |
| 226 314 | | 21 45 | 22 39 | 48.4 | 22 24 | 23 28 | 48.7 | 23 04 | 24 17 | 49.0 | 23 43 | 25 06 | 49.4 | 24 22 | 25 56 | 49.7 | 25 01 | 26 47 | 50.0 | 46 134 |
| 227 313 | | 22 08 | 22 17 | 47.4 | 22 48 | 23 05 | 47.7 | 23 28 | 23 53 | 48.0 | 24 08 | 24 42 | 48.4 | 24 48 | 25 32 | 48.7 | 25 28 | 26 22 | 49.1 | 47 133 |
| 228 312 | | 22 30 | 21 54 | 46.4 | 23 11 | 22 41 | 46.7 | 23 53 | 23 29 | 47.0 | 24 33 | 24 17 | 47.4 | 25 14 | 25 06 | 47.7 | 25 54 | 25 56 | 48.1 | 48 132 |
| 229 311 | | 22 52 | 21 31 | 45.4 | 23 34 | 22 17 | 45.7 | 24 16 | 23 05 | 46.0 | 24 58 | 23 52 | 46.4 | 25 39 | 24 40 | 46.7 | 26 20 | 25 29 | 47.1 | 49 131 |
| 230 310 | | 23 14 | 21 07 | 44.4 | 23 57 | 21 53 | 44.7 | 24 40 | 22 39 | 45.0 | 25 22 | 23 25 | 45.3 | 26 04 | 24 14 | 45.7 | 26 46 | 25 02 | 46.0 | 50 130 |
| 231 309 | | 23 36 | 20 43 | 43.4 | 24 19 | 21 28 | 43.7 | 25 02 | 22 14 | 44.0 | 25 45 | 23 00 | 44.3 | 26 28 | 23 47 | 44.7 | 27 11 | 24 34 | 45.0 | 51 129 |
| 232 308 | | 23 57 | 20 18 | 42.3 | 24 41 | 21 03 | 42.7 | 25 25 | 21 48 | 43.0 | 26 09 | 22 33 | 43.3 | 26 52 | 23 19 | 43.6 | 27 36 | 24 06 | 44.0 | 52 128 |
| 233 307 | | 24 17 | 19 53 | 41.3 | 25 02 | 20 37 | 41.6 | 25 47 | 21 21 | 41.9 | 26 32 | 22 06 | 42.3 | 27 16 | 22 51 | 42.6 | 28 00 | 23 37 | 43.0 | 53 127 |
| 234 306 | | 24 37 | 19 27 | 40.3 | 25 23 | 20 10 | 40.6 | 26 09 | 20 54 | 40.9 | 26 54 | 21 38 | 41.2 | 27 39 | 22 22 | 41.6 | 28 24 | 23 07 | 41.9 | 54 126 |
| 235 305 | | 24 57 | 19 01 | 39.2 | 25 44 | 19 43 | 39.5 | 26 30 | 20 26 | 39.9 | 27 16 | 21 09 | 40.2 | 28 01 | 21 53 | 40.5 | 28 47 | 22 37 | 40.9 | 55 125 |
| 236 304 | | 25 17 | 18 34 | 38.2 | 26 04 | 19 16 | 38.5 | 26 50 | 19 57 | 38.8 | 27 37 | 20 40 | 39.1 | 28 24 | 21 23 | 39.5 | 29 10 | 22 07 | 39.8 | 56 124 |
| 237 303 | | 25 35 | 18 07 | 37.1 | 26 23 | 18 48 | 37.4 | 27 11 | 19 29 | 37.8 | 27 58 | 20 10 | 38.1 | 28 45 | 20 52 | 38.4 | 29 32 | 21 35 | 38.8 | 57 123 |
| 238 302 | | 25 54 | 17 40 | 36.1 | 26 42 | 18 19 | 36.4 | 27 31 | 18 59 | 36.7 | 28 19 | 19 40 | 37.0 | 29 06 | 20 21 | 37.3 | 29 54 | 21 03 | 37.7 | 58 122 |
| 239 301 | | 26 12 | 17 12 | 35.0 | 27 01 | 17 50 | 35.3 | 27 50 | 18 30 | 35.6 | 28 38 | 19 09 | 35.9 | 29 27 | 19 50 | 36.3 | 30 15 | 20 31 | 36.6 | 59 121 |
| 240 300 | | 26 29 | 16 44 | 34.0 | 27 19 | 17 21 | 34.2 | 28 09 | 18 00 | 34.5 | 28 58 | 18 38 | 34.9 | 29 47 | 19 18 | 35.2 | 30 36 | 19 58 | 35.5 | 60 120 |
| 241 299 | | 26 46 | 16 14 | 32.9 | 27 37 | 16 51 | 33.2 | 28 27 | 17 29 | 33.5 | 29 17 | 18 06 | 33.8 | 30 07 | 18 45 | 34.1 | 30 56 | 19 24 | 34.4 | 61 119 |
| 242 298 | | 27 03 | 15 45 | 31.8 | 27 54 | 16 21 | 32.1 | 28 45 | 16 57 | 32.4 | 29 35 | 17 34 | 32.7 | 30 26 | 18 12 | 33.0 | 31 16 | 18 50 | 33.3 | 62 118 |
| 243 297 | | 27 19 | 15 15 | 30.7 | 28 10 | 15 50 | 31.0 | 29 02 | 16 26 | 31.3 | 29 53 | 17 02 | 31.6 | 30 44 | 17 38 | 31.9 | 31 35 | 18 15 | 32.2 | 63 117 |
| 244 296 | | 27 35 | 14 45 | 29.6 | 28 27 | 15 19 | 29.9 | 29 19 | 15 53 | 30.2 | 30 10 | 16 28 | 30.5 | 31 02 | 17 04 | 30.8 | 31 53 | 17 40 | 31.1 | 64 116 |
| 245 295 | | 27 50 | 14 15 | 28.5 | 28 42 | 14 48 | 28.8 | 29 35 | 15 21 | 29.1 | 30 27 | 15 55 | 29.4 | 31 19 | 16 29 | 29.7 | 32 11 | 17 04 | 30.0 | 65 115 |
| 246 294 | | 28 04 | 13 44 | 27.4 | 28 57 | 14 16 | 27.7 | 29 50 | 14 48 | 28.0 | 30 43 | 15 20 | 28.2 | 31 36 | 15 54 | 28.5 | 32 29 | 16 28 | 28.8 | 66 114 |
| 247 293 | | 28 18 | 13 13 | 26.3 | 29 12 | 13 43 | 26.6 | 30 05 | 14 14 | 26.8 | 30 59 | 14 46 | 27.1 | 31 52 | 15 18 | 27.4 | 32 45 | 15 51 | 27.7 | 67 113 |
| 248 292 | | 28 31 | 12 41 | 25.2 | 29 26 | 13 10 | 25.5 | 30 20 | 13 40 | 25.7 | 31 14 | 14 11 | 26.0 | 32 08 | 14 42 | 26.3 | 33 01 | 15 14 | 26.5 | 68 112 |
| 249 291 | | 28 44 | 12 09 | 24.1 | 29 39 | 12 37 | 24.4 | 30 34 | 13 06 | 24.6 | 31 28 | 13 35 | 24.8 | 32 23 | 14 05 | 25.1 | 33 17 | 14 36 | 25.4 | 69 111 |
| 250 290 | | 28 57 | 11 37 | 23.0 | 29 52 | 12 04 | 23.2 | 30 47 | 12 31 | 23.5 | 31 42 | 12 59 | 23.7 | 32 37 | 13 28 | 24.0 | 33 32 | 13 57 | 24.2 | 70 110 |
| 251 289 | | 29 09 | 11 04 | 21.9 | 30 05 | 11 30 | 22.1 | 31 00 | 11 56 | 22.3 | 31 55 | 12 23 | 22.6 | 32 51 | 12 51 | 22.8 | 33 46 | 13 18 | 23.1 | 71 109 |
| 252 288 | | 29 20 | 10 31 | 20.8 | 30 16 | 10 56 | 21.0 | 31 12 | 11 21 | 21.2 | 32 08 | 11 46 | 21.4 | 33 04 | 12 13 | 21.6 | 33 59 | 12 39 | 21.9 | 72 108 |
| 253 287 | | 29 30 | 9 58 | 19.6 | 30 27 | 10 21 | 19.8 | 31 23 | 10 45 | 20.0 | 32 20 | 11 09 | 20.2 | 33 16 | 11 34 | 20.5 | 34 12 | 12 00 | 20.7 | 73 107 |
| 254 286 | | 29 41 | 9 24 | 18.5 | 30 37 | 9 46 | 18.7 | 31 34 | 10 09 | 18.9 | 32 31 | 10 32 | 19.1 | 33 28 | 10 55 | 19.3 | 34 24 | 11 19 | 19.5 | 74 106 |
| 255 285 | | 29 50 | 8 50 | 17.4 | 30 47 | 9 11 | 17.5 | 31 44 | 9 32 | 17.7 | 32 42 | 9 54 | 17.9 | 33 39 | 10 16 | 18.1 | 34 36 | 10 39 | 18.3 | 75 105 |
| 256 284 | | 29 59 | 8 16 | 16.2 | 30 57 | 8 36 | 16.4 | 31 54 | 8 56 | 16.6 | 32 52 | 9 16 | 16.7 | 33 49 | 9 37 | 16.9 | 34 46 | 9 58 | 17.1 | 76 104 |
| 257 283 | | 30 07 | 7 42 | 15.1 | 31 05 | 8 00 | 15.2 | 32 03 | 8 19 | 15.4 | 33 01 | 8 38 | 15.6 | 33 59 | 8 57 | 15.7 | 34 56 | 9 17 | 15.9 | 77 103 |
| 258 282 | | 30 15 | 7 07 | 13.9 | 31 13 | 7 24 | 14.1 | 32 11 | 7 41 | 14.2 | 33 10 | 7 59 | 14.4 | 34 08 | 8 17 | 14.5 | 35 06 | 8 35 | 14.7 | 78 102 |
| 259 281 | | 30 22 | 6 32 | 12.8 | 31 21 | 6 48 | 12.9 | 32 19 | 7 04 | 13.0 | 33 18 | 7 20 | 13.2 | 34 16 | 7 37 | 13.3 | 35 14 | 7 54 | 13.5 | 79 101 |
| 260 280 | | 30 29 | 5 57 | 11.6 | 31 27 | 6 12 | 11.7 | 32 26 | 6 26 | 11.9 | 33 25 | 6 41 | 12.0 | 34 24 | 6 56 | 12.1 | 35 22 | 7 11 | 12.3 | 80 100 |
| 261 279 | | 30 35 | 5 22 | 10.5 | 31 34 | 5 35 | 10.6 | 32 33 | 5 48 | 10.7 | 33 32 | 6 01 | 10.8 | 34 30 | 6 15 | 10.9 | 35 29 | 6 29 | 11.1 | 81 99 |
| 262 278 | | 30 40 | 4 47 | 9.3 | 31 39 | 4 58 | 9.4 | 32 38 | 5 10 | 9.5 | 33 37 | 5 22 | 9.6 | 34 37 | 5 34 | 9.7 | 35 36 | 5 46 | 9.9 | 82 98 |
| 263 277 | | 30 45 | 4 11 | 8.2 | 31 44 | 4 21 | 8.2 | 32 43 | 4 32 | 8.3 | 33 43 | 4 42 | 8.4 | 34 42 | 4 53 | 8.5 | 35 41 | 5 04 | 8.6 | 83 97 |
| 264 276 | | 30 49 | 3 36 | 7.0 | 31 48 | 3 44 | 7.1 | 32 48 | 3 53 | 7.1 | 33 47 | 4 02 | 7.2 | 34 47 | 4 11 | 7.3 | 35 46 | 4 21 | 7.4 | 84 96 |
| 265 275 | | 30 52 | 3 00 | 5.8 | 31 52 | 3 07 | 5.9 | 32 52 | 3 14 | 6.0 | 33 51 | 3 22 | 6.0 | 34 51 | 3 30 | 6.1 | 35 51 | 3 37 | 6.2 | 85 95 |
| 266 274 | | 30 55 | 2 24 | 4.7 | 31 55 | 2 30 | 4.7 | 32 55 | 2 36 | 4.8 | 33 54 | 2 42 | 4.8 | 34 54 | 2 48 | 4.9 | 35 55 | 2 54 | 4.9 | 86 94 |
| 267 273 | | 30 57 | 1 48 | 3.5 | 31 57 | 1 52 | 3.5 | 32 57 | 1 57 | 3.6 | 33 57 | 2 01 | 3.6 | 34 57 | 2 06 | 3.7 | 35 57 | 2 11 | 3.7 | 87 93 |
| 268 272 | | 30 59 | 1 12 | 2.3 | 31 59 | 1 15 | 2.4 | 32 59 | 1 18 | 2.4 | 33 59 | 1 21 | 2.4 | 34 59 | 1 24 | 2.5 | 35 58 | 1 27 | 2.5 | 88 92 |
| 269 271 | | 31 00 | 0 36 | 1.2 | 32 00 | 0 37 | 1.2 | 33 00 | 0 39 | 1.2 | 34 00 | 0 40 | 1.2 | 35 00 | 0 42 | 1.2 | 36 00 | 0 44 | 1.2 | 89 91 |
| 270 270 | | 31 00 | 0 00 | 0.0 | 32 00 | 0 00 | 0.0 | 33 00 | 0 00 | 0.0 | 34 00 | 0 00 | 0.0 | 35 00 | 0 00 | 0.0 | 36 00 | 0 00 | 0.0 | 90 90 |

N. Lat: for LHA > 180° .... $Z_n = Z$
for LHA < 180° .... $Z_n = 360° − Z$

SIGHT REDUCTION TABLE

B: (−) for 90° < LHA < 270°
Dec: (−) for Lat. contrary name

Z₁: same sign as B
Z₂: (−) for F > 90°

| LHA/F | 60° A/H | 60° B/P | 60° Z₁/Z₂ | 61° A/H | 61° B/P | 61° Z₁/Z₂ | 62° A/H | 62° B/P | 62° Z₁/Z₂ | 63° A/H | 63° B/P | 63° Z₁/Z₂ | 64° A/H | 64° B/P | 64° Z₁/Z₂ | 65° A/H | 65° B/P | 65° Z₁/Z₂ | LHA |
|---|---|---|---|---|---|---|---|---|---|---|---|---|---|---|---|---|---|---|---|
| 0 | 0 00 | 30 00 | 90·0 | 0 00 | 29 00 | 90·0 | 0 00 | 28 00 | 90·0 | 0 00 | 27 00 | 90·0 | 0 00 | 26 00 | 90·0 | 0 00 | 25 00 | 90·0 | 180 |
| 1 | 0 30 | 30 00 | 89·1 | 0 29 | 29 00 | 89·1 | 0 28 | 28 00 | 89·1 | 0 27 | 27 00 | 89·1 | 0 26 | 26 00 | 89·1 | 0 25 | 25 00 | 89·1 | 181 |
| 2 | 1 00 | 29 59 | 88·3 | 0 58 | 28 59 | 88·3 | 0 56 | 27 59 | 88·2 | 0 54 | 26 59 | 88·2 | 0 53 | 25 59 | 88·2 | 0 51 | 24 59 | 88·2 | 182 |
| 3 | 1 30 | 29 58 | 87·4 | 1 27 | 28 58 | 87·4 | 1 24 | 27 58 | 87·4 | 1 22 | 26 58 | 87·3 | 1 19 | 25 58 | 87·3 | 1 16 | 24 58 | 87·3 | 183 |
| 4 | 2 00 | 29 56 | 86·5 | 1 56 | 28 56 | 86·5 | 1 53 | 27 57 | 86·5 | 1 49 | 26 57 | 86·5 | 1 45 | 25 57 | 86·4 | 1 41 | 24 57 | 86·4 | 184 |
| 5 | 2 30 | 29 54 | 85·7 | 2 25 | 28 54 | 85·6 | 2 21 | 27 55 | 85·6 | 2 16 | 26 55 | 85·5 | 2 11 | 25 55 | 85·5 | 2 07 | 24 55 | 85·5 | 185 |
| 6 | 3 00 | 29 52 | 84·8 | 2 54 | 28 52 | 84·7 | 2 49 | 27 52 | 84·7 | 2 43 | 26 52 | 84·6 | 2 38 | 25 53 | 84·6 | 2 32 | 24 53 | 84·6 | 186 |
| 7 | 3 30 | 29 49 | 83·9 | 3 23 | 28 49 | 83·9 | 3 17 | 27 49 | 83·8 | 3 10 | 26 50 | 83·8 | 3 04 | 25 50 | 83·7 | 2 57 | 24 50 | 83·7 | 187 |
| 8 | 3 59 | 29 45 | 83·1 | 3 52 | 28 46 | 83·0 | 3 45 | 27 46 | 82·9 | 3 37 | 26 46 | 82·9 | 3 30 | 25 47 | 82·8 | 3 22 | 24 47 | 82·7 | 188 |
| 9 | 4 29 | 29 42 | 82·2 | 4 21 | 28 42 | 82·1 | 4 13 | 27 42 | 82·0 | 4 04 | 26 43 | 82·0 | 3 56 | 25 43 | 81·9 | 3 47 | 24 44 | 81·8 | 189 |
| 10 | 4 59 | 29 37 | 81·3 | 4 50 | 28 38 | 81·2 | 4 41 | 27 38 | 81·2 | 4 31 | 26 39 | 81·1 | 4 22 | 25 39 | 81·0 | 4 13 | 24 40 | 80·9 | 190 |
| 11 | 5 28 | 29 33 | 80·4 | 5 18 | 28 33 | 80·4 | 5 08 | 27 34 | 80·3 | 4 58 | 26 34 | 80·2 | 4 48 | 25 35 | 80·1 | 4 38 | 24 36 | 80·0 | 191 |
| 12 | 5 58 | 29 27 | 79·6 | 5 47 | 28 28 | 79·5 | 5 36 | 27 29 | 79·4 | 5 25 | 26 29 | 79·3 | 5 14 | 25 30 | 79·2 | 5 02 | 24 31 | 79·1 | 192 |
| 13 | 6 27 | 29 22 | 78·7 | 6 16 | 28 22 | 78·6 | 6 04 | 27 23 | 78·5 | 5 52 | 26 24 | 78·4 | 5 40 | 25 25 | 78·3 | 5 27 | 24 26 | 78·2 | 193 |
| 14 | 6 57 | 29 15 | 77·8 | 6 44 | 28 16 | 77·7 | 6 31 | 27 17 | 77·6 | 6 18 | 26 18 | 77·5 | 6 05 | 25 20 | 77·4 | 5 52 | 24 21 | 77·3 | 194 |
| 15 | 7 26 | 29 09 | 76·9 | 7 13 | 28 10 | 76·8 | 6 59 | 27 11 | 76·7 | 6 45 | 26 12 | 76·6 | 6 31 | 25 14 | 76·5 | 6 17 | 24 15 | 76·4 | 195 |
| 16 | 7 55 | 29 02 | 76·1 | 7 41 | 28 03 | 75·9 | 7 26 | 27 04 | 75·8 | 7 11 | 26 06 | 75·7 | 6 56 | 25 07 | 75·5 | 6 41 | 24 09 | 75·4 | 196 |
| 17 | 8 24 | 28 54 | 75·2 | 8 09 | 27 56 | 75·0 | 7 53 | 26 57 | 74·9 | 7 38 | 25 59 | 74·8 | 7 22 | 25 00 | 74·6 | 7 06 | 24 02 | 74·5 | 197 |
| 18 | 8 53 | 28 46 | 74·3 | 8 37 | 27 48 | 74·1 | 8 20 | 26 50 | 74·0 | 8 04 | 25 51 | 73·9 | 7 47 | 24 53 | 73·7 | 7 30 | 23 55 | 73·6 | 198 |
| 19 | 9 22 | 28 38 | 73·4 | 9 05 | 27 40 | 73·2 | 8 48 | 26 41 | 73·1 | 8 30 | 25 43 | 72·9 | 8 12 | 24 45 | 72·8 | 7 55 | 23 48 | 72·7 | 199 |
| 20 | 9 51 | 28 29 | 72·5 | 9 33 | 27 31 | 72·3 | 9 14 | 26 33 | 72·2 | 8 56 | 25 35 | 72·0 | 8 37 | 24 37 | 71·9 | 8 19 | 23 40 | 71·7 | 200 |
| 21 | 10 19 | 28 19 | 71·6 | 10 00 | 27 21 | 71·4 | 9 41 | 26 24 | 71·3 | 9 22 | 25 26 | 71·1 | 9 02 | 24 29 | 71·0 | 8 43 | 23 32 | 70·8 | 201 |
| 22 | 10 48 | 28 10 | 70·7 | 10 28 | 27 12 | 70·5 | 10 08 | 26 15 | 70·4 | 9 48 | 25 17 | 70·2 | 9 27 | 24 20 | 70·0 | 9 07 | 23 23 | 69·9 | 202 |
| 23 | 11 16 | 27 59 | 69·8 | 10 55 | 27 02 | 69·6 | 10 34 | 26 05 | 69·5 | 10 13 | 25 08 | 69·3 | 9 52 | 24 11 | 69·1 | 9 30 | 23 14 | 69·0 | 203 |
| 24 | 11 44 | 27 49 | 68·9 | 11 22 | 26 51 | 68·7 | 11 00 | 25 54 | 68·5 | 10 38 | 24 58 | 68·4 | 10 16 | 24 01 | 68·2 | 9 54 | 23 04 | 68·0 | 204 |
| 25 | 12 12 | 27 37 | 68·0 | 11 49 | 26 40 | 67·8 | 11 27 | 25 44 | 67·6 | 11 04 | 24 47 | 67·6 | 10 41 | 23 51 | 67·3 | 10 17 | 22 55 | 67·1 | 205 |
| 26 | 12 40 | 27 26 | 67·1 | 12 16 | 26 29 | 66·9 | 11 53 | 25 33 | 66·7 | 11 29 | 24 36 | 66·5 | 11 05 | 23 40 | 66·3 | 10 41 | 22 44 | 66·2 | 206 |
| 27 | 13 07 | 27 13 | 66·2 | 12 43 | 26 17 | 66·0 | 12 18 | 25 21 | 65·8 | 11 54 | 24 25 | 65·6 | 11 29 | 23 29 | 65·4 | 11 04 | 22 34 | 65·2 | 207 |
| 28 | 13 35 | 27 01 | 65·3 | 13 09 | 26 05 | 65·1 | 12 44 | 25 09 | 64·9 | 12 18 | 24 13 | 64·7 | 11 53 | 23 18 | 64·5 | 11 27 | 22 23 | 64·3 | 208 |
| 29 | 14 02 | 26 48 | 64·4 | 13 36 | 25 52 | 64·1 | 13 09 | 24 56 | 63·9 | 12 43 | 24 01 | 63·7 | 12 16 | 23 06 | 63·5 | 11 49 | 22 11 | 63·3 | 209 |
| 30 | 14 29 | 26 34 | 63·4 | 14 02 | 25 39 | 63·2 | 13 35 | 24 43 | 63·0 | 13 07 | 23 49 | 62·8 | 12 40 | 22 54 | 62·6 | 12 12 | 21 59 | 62·4 | 210 |
| 31 | 14 55 | 26 20 | 62·5 | 14 28 | 25 25 | 62·3 | 14 00 | 24 30 | 62·1 | 13 31 | 23 36 | 61·8 | 13 03 | 22 41 | 61·6 | 12 34 | 21 47 | 61·4 | 211 |
| 32 | 15 22 | 26 05 | 61·6 | 14 53 | 25 11 | 61·3 | 14 24 | 24 16 | 61·1 | 13 55 | 23 22 | 60·9 | 13 26 | 22 28 | 60·7 | 12 56 | 21 35 | 60·5 | 212 |
| 33 | 15 48 | 25 50 | 60·6 | 15 19 | 24 56 | 60·4 | 14 49 | 24 02 | 60·2 | 14 19 | 23 08 | 59·9 | 13 49 | 22 15 | 59·7 | 13 18 | 21 22 | 59·5 | 213 |
| 34 | 16 14 | 25 35 | 59·7 | 15 44 | 24 41 | 59·5 | 15 13 | 23 47 | 59·2 | 14 42 | 22 54 | 59·0 | 14 11 | 22 01 | 58·8 | 13 40 | 21 08 | 58·6 | 214 |
| 35 | 16 40 | 25 19 | 58·8 | 16 09 | 24 25 | 58·5 | 15 37 | 23 32 | 58·3 | 15 06 | 22 39 | 58·0 | 14 34 | 21 47 | 57·8 | 14 02 | 20 54 | 57·6 | 215 |
| 36 | 17 05 | 25 02 | 57·8 | 16 33 | 24 09 | 57·6 | 16 01 | 23 17 | 57·3 | 15 29 | 22 24 | 57·1 | 14 56 | 21 32 | 56·9 | 14 23 | 20 40 | 56·6 | 216 |
| 37 | 17 31 | 24 45 | 56·9 | 16 58 | 23 53 | 56·6 | 16 25 | 23 00 | 56·4 | 15 51 | 22 09 | 56·1 | 15 18 | 21 17 | 55·9 | 14 44 | 20 26 | 55·7 | 217 |
| 38 | 17 56 | 24 28 | 55·9 | 17 22 | 23 36 | 55·7 | 16 48 | 22 44 | 55·4 | 16 14 | 21 53 | 55·2 | 15 39 | 21 01 | 54·9 | 15 05 | 20 11 | 54·7 | 218 |
| 39 | 18 20 | 24 10 | 55·0 | 17 46 | 23 18 | 54·7 | 17 11 | 22 27 | 54·4 | 16 36 | 21 36 | 54·2 | 16 01 | 20 46 | 54·0 | 15 25 | 19 55 | 53·7 | 219 |
| 40 | 18 45 | 23 52 | 54·0 | 18 09 | 23 00 | 53·7 | 17 34 | 22 10 | 53·5 | 16 58 | 21 19 | 53·2 | 16 22 | 20 29 | 53·0 | 15 46 | 19 39 | 52·7 | 220 |
| 41 | 19 09 | 23 33 | 53·0 | 18 33 | 22 42 | 52·8 | 17 56 | 21 52 | 52·5 | 17 20 | 21 02 | 52·2 | 16 43 | 20 13 | 52·0 | 16 06 | 19 23 | 51·8 | 221 |
| 42 | 19 33 | 23 13 | 52·1 | 18 56 | 22 23 | 51·8 | 18 19 | 21 34 | 51·5 | 17 41 | 20 44 | 51·3 | 17 03 | 19 55 | 51·0 | 16 26 | 19 07 | 50·8 | 222 |
| 43 | 19 56 | 22 54 | 51·1 | 19 18 | 22 04 | 50·8 | 18 40 | 21 15 | 50·5 | 18 02 | 20 26 | 50·3 | 17 24 | 19 38 | 50·0 | 16 45 | 18 50 | 49·8 | 223 |
| 44 | 20 19 | 22 33 | 50·1 | 19 41 | 21 44 | 49·8 | 19 02 | 20 56 | 49·5 | 18 23 | 20 08 | 49·3 | 17 44 | 19 20 | 49·0 | 17 04 | 18 33 | 48·8 | 224 |
| 45 | 20 42 | 22 12 | 49·1 | 20 03 | 21 24 | 48·8 | 19 23 | 20 36 | 48·5 | 18 43 | 19 49 | 48·3 | 18 03 | 19 02 | 48·1 | 17 23 | 18 15 | 47·8 | 225 |

| Lat./A LHA/F | | 60° A/H | 60° B/P | 60° Z₁/Z₂ | 61° A/H | 61° B/P | 61° Z₁/Z₂ | 62° A/H | 62° B/P | 62° Z₁/Z₂ | 63° A/H | 63° B/P | 63° Z₁/Z₂ | 64° A/H | 64° B/P | 64° Z₁/Z₂ | 65° A/H | 65° B/P | 65° Z₁/Z₂ | Lat./A LHA | |
|---|---|---|---|---|---|---|---|---|---|---|---|---|---|---|---|---|---|---|---|---|---|
| 135 | 45 | 20 42 | 22 12 | 49·1 | 20 03 | 21 24 | 48·8 | 19 23 | 20 36 | 48·6 | 18 43 | 19 49 | 48·3 | 18 03 | 19 02 | 48·1 | 17 23 | 18 15 | 47·8 | 225 | 315 |
| 134 | 46 | 21 05 | 21 51 | 48·1 | 20 25 | 21 04 | 47·8 | 19 44 | 20 16 | 47·6 | 19 04 | 19 29 | 47·3 | 18 23 | 18 43 | 47·1 | 17 42 | 17 57 | 46·8 | 226 | 314 |
| 133 | 47 | 21 27 | 21 30 | 47·1 | 20 46 | 20 43 | 46·8 | 20 05 | 19 56 | 46·6 | 19 24 | 19 10 | 46·3 | 18 42 | 18 24 | 46·1 | 18 00 | 17 39 | 45·8 | 227 | 313 |
| 132 | 48 | 21 49 | 21 07 | 46·1 | 21 07 | 20 20 | 45·8 | 20 25 | 19 35 | 45·6 | 19 43 | 18 50 | 45·3 | 19 01 | 18 04 | 45·1 | 18 18 | 17 20 | 44·8 | 228 | 312 |
| 131 | 49 | 22 10 | 20 45 | 45·1 | 21 28 | 19 59 | 44·8 | 20 45 | 19 14 | 44·6 | 20 02 | 18 29 | 44·3 | 19 19 | 17 45 | 44·0 | 18 36 | 17 01 | 43·8 | 229 | 311 |
| 130 | 50 | 22 31 | 20 22 | 44·1 | 21 48 | 19 37 | 43·8 | 21 05 | 18 52 | 43·5 | 20 21 | 18 08 | 43·3 | 19 37 | 17 24 | 43·0 | 18 53 | 16 41 | 42·8 | 230 | 310 |
| 129 | 51 | 22 52 | 19 58 | 43·1 | 22 08 | 19 14 | 42·8 | 21 24 | 18 30 | 42·5 | 20 40 | 17 47 | 42·3 | 19 55 | 17 04 | 42·0 | 19 10 | 16 21 | 41·8 | 231 | 309 |
| 128 | 52 | 23 12 | 19 34 | 42·1 | 22 28 | 18 51 | 41·8 | 21 43 | 18 08 | 41·5 | 20 58 | 17 25 | 41·2 | 20 13 | 16 43 | 41·0 | 19 27 | 16 01 | 40·8 | 232 | 308 |
| 127 | 53 | 23 32 | 19 10 | 41·0 | 22 47 | 18 27 | 40·7 | 22 01 | 17 45 | 40·5 | 21 15 | 17 03 | 40·2 | 20 30 | 16 21 | 40·0 | 19 44 | 15 41 | 39·7 | 233 | 307 |
| 126 | 54 | 23 52 | 18 45 | 40·0 | 23 06 | 18 03 | 39·7 | 22 19 | 17 21 | 39·4 | 21 33 | 16 40 | 39·2 | 20 46 | 16 00 | 39·0 | 20 00 | 15 20 | 38·7 | 234 | 306 |
| 125 | 55 | 24 11 | 18 19 | 39·0 | 23 24 | 17 38 | 38·7 | 22 37 | 16 58 | 38·4 | 21 50 | 16 17 | 38·2 | 21 03 | 15 38 | 38·0 | 20 15 | 14 58 | 37·7 | 235 | 305 |
| 124 | 56 | 24 29 | 17 54 | 37·9 | 23 42 | 17 13 | 37·6 | 22 54 | 16 34 | 37·4 | 22 07 | 15 54 | 37·1 | 21 19 | 15 15 | 36·9 | 20 31 | 14 37 | 36·7 | 236 | 304 |
| 123 | 57 | 24 48 | 17 27 | 36·9 | 23 59 | 16 48 | 36·6 | 23 11 | 16 09 | 36·3 | 22 23 | 15 31 | 36·1 | 21 34 | 14 53 | 35·8 | 20 46 | 14 15 | 35·6 | 237 | 303 |
| 122 | 58 | 25 05 | 17 01 | 35·8 | 24 17 | 16 22 | 35·5 | 23 28 | 15 44 | 35·3 | 22 39 | 15 07 | 35·0 | 21 49 | 14 29 | 34·8 | 21 00 | 13 53 | 34·6 | 238 | 302 |
| 121 | 59 | 25 23 | 16 34 | 34·8 | 24 33 | 15 56 | 34·5 | 23 44 | 15 19 | 34·2 | 22 54 | 14 42 | 34·0 | 22 04 | 14 06 | 33·8 | 21 14 | 13 30 | 33·5 | 239 | 301 |
| 120 | 60 | 25 40 | 16 06 | 33·7 | 24 50 | 15 29 | 33·4 | 23 59 | 14 53 | 33·2 | 23 09 | 14 18 | 32·9 | 22 19 | 13 42 | 32·7 | 21 28 | 13 07 | 32·5 | 240 | 300 |
| 119 | 61 | 25 56 | 15 38 | 32·6 | 25 05 | 15 03 | 32·4 | 24 15 | 14 27 | 32·1 | 23 24 | 13 53 | 31·9 | 22 33 | 13 18 | 31·7 | 21 42 | 12 44 | 31·5 | 241 | 299 |
| 118 | 62 | 26 12 | 15 10 | 31·5 | 25 21 | 14 35 | 31·3 | 24 29 | 14 01 | 31·1 | 23 38 | 13 27 | 30·8 | 22 46 | 12 54 | 30·6 | 21 55 | 12 21 | 30·4 | 242 | 298 |
| 117 | 63 | 26 27 | 14 41 | 30·5 | 25 36 | 14 08 | 30·2 | 24 44 | 13 34 | 30·0 | 23 52 | 13 01 | 29·8 | 22 59 | 12 29 | 29·5 | 22 07 | 11 57 | 29·3 | 243 | 297 |
| 116 | 64 | 26 42 | 14 12 | 29·4 | 25 50 | 13 39 | 29·1 | 24 57 | 13 07 | 28·9 | 24 05 | 12 35 | 28·7 | 23 12 | 12 04 | 28·5 | 22 19 | 11 33 | 28·3 | 244 | 296 |
| 115 | 65 | 26 57 | 13 43 | 28·3 | 26 04 | 13 11 | 28·1 | 25 11 | 12 40 | 27·8 | 24 18 | 12 09 | 27·6 | 23 25 | 11 39 | 27·4 | 22 31 | 11 09 | 27·2 | 245 | 295 |
| 114 | 66 | 27 11 | 13 13 | 27·2 | 26 17 | 12 42 | 27·0 | 25 24 | 12 12 | 26·8 | 24 30 | 11 43 | 26·6 | 23 36 | 11 13 | 26·4 | 22 43 | 10 44 | 26·2 | 246 | 294 |
| 113 | 67 | 27 24 | 12 43 | 26·1 | 26 30 | 12 13 | 25·9 | 25 36 | 11 44 | 25·7 | 24 42 | 11 16 | 25·5 | 23 48 | 10 47 | 25·3 | 22 54 | 10 20 | 25·1 | 247 | 293 |
| 112 | 68 | 27 37 | 12 12 | 25·0 | 26 43 | 11 44 | 24·8 | 25 48 | 11 16 | 24·6 | 24 54 | 10 48 | 24·4 | 23 59 | 10 21 | 24·2 | 23 04 | 9 55 | 24·0 | 248 | 292 |
| 111 | 69 | 27 50 | 11 41 | 23·9 | 26 55 | 11 14 | 23·7 | 26 00 | 10 47 | 23·5 | 25 05 | 10 21 | 23·3 | 24 09 | 9 55 | 23·1 | 23 14 | 9 29 | 23·0 | 249 | 291 |
| 110 | 70 | 28 01 | 11 10 | 22·8 | 27 06 | 10 44 | 22·6 | 26 11 | 10 18 | 22·4 | 25 15 | 9 53 | 22·2 | 24 20 | 9 28 | 22·0 | 23 24 | 9 04 | 21·9 | 250 | 290 |
| 109 | 71 | 28 13 | 10 39 | 21·7 | 27 17 | 10 14 | 21·5 | 26 21 | 9 49 | 21·3 | 25 25 | 9 25 | 21·1 | 24 29 | 9 01 | 21·0 | 23 33 | 8 38 | 20·8 | 251 | 289 |
| 108 | 72 | 28 24 | 10 07 | 20·6 | 27 27 | 9 43 | 20·4 | 26 31 | 9 20 | 20·2 | 25 35 | 8 57 | 20·0 | 24 38 | 8 34 | 19·9 | 23 42 | 8 12 | 19·7 | 252 | 288 |
| 107 | 73 | 28 34 | 9 35 | 19·4 | 27 37 | 9 12 | 19·3 | 26 41 | 8 50 | 19·1 | 25 44 | 8 28 | 18·9 | 24 47 | 8 07 | 18·8 | 23 50 | 7 46 | 18·6 | 253 | 287 |
| 106 | 74 | 28 44 | 9 03 | 18·3 | 27 47 | 8 41 | 18·2 | 26 50 | 8 20 | 18·0 | 25 52 | 8 00 | 17·8 | 24 55 | 7 39 | 17·7 | 23 58 | 7 19 | 17·6 | 254 | 286 |
| 105 | 75 | 28 53 | 8 30 | 17·2 | 27 55 | 8 10 | 17·0 | 26 58 | 7 50 | 16·9 | 26 01 | 7 31 | 16·7 | 25 03 | 7 12 | 16·6 | 24 06 | 6 53 | 16·5 | 255 | 285 |
| 104 | 76 | 29 01 | 7 57 | 16·1 | 28 04 | 7 38 | 15·9 | 27 06 | 7 20 | 15·8 | 26 08 | 7 02 | 15·6 | 25 10 | 6 44 | 15·5 | 24 13 | 6 26 | 15·4 | 256 | 284 |
| 103 | 77 | 29 09 | 7 24 | 14·9 | 28 11 | 7 06 | 14·8 | 27 13 | 6 49 | 14·7 | 26 15 | 6 32 | 14·5 | 25 17 | 6 16 | 14·4 | 24 19 | 5 59 | 14·3 | 257 | 283 |
| 102 | 78 | 29 17 | 6 51 | 13·8 | 28 18 | 6 34 | 13·7 | 27 20 | 6 18 | 13·5 | 26 22 | 6 03 | 13·4 | 25 23 | 5 47 | 13·3 | 24 25 | 5 32 | 13·2 | 258 | 282 |
| 101 | 79 | 29 24 | 6 17 | 12·7 | 28 25 | 6 02 | 12·5 | 27 27 | 5 48 | 12·4 | 26 28 | 5 33 | 12·3 | 25 29 | 5 19 | 12·2 | 24 31 | 5 05 | 12·1 | 259 | 281 |
| 100 | 80 | 29 30 | 5 44 | 11·5 | 28 31 | 5 30 | 11·4 | 27 32 | 5 17 | 11·3 | 26 33 | 5 03 | 11·2 | 25 35 | 4 50 | 11·1 | 24 36 | 4 38 | 11·0 | 260 | 280 |
| 99 | 81 | 29 36 | 5 10 | 10·4 | 28 37 | 4 57 | 10·3 | 27 38 | 4 45 | 10·2 | 26 38 | 4 33 | 10·1 | 25 39 | 4 22 | 10·0 | 24 40 | 4 10 | 9·9 | 261 | 279 |
| 98 | 82 | 29 41 | 4 36 | 9·2 | 28 41 | 4 25 | 9·1 | 27 42 | 4 14 | 9·0 | 26 43 | 4 03 | 9·0 | 25 44 | 3 53 | 8·9 | 24 44 | 3 43 | 8·8 | 262 | 278 |
| 97 | 83 | 29 45 | 4 01 | 8·1 | 28 46 | 3 52 | 8·0 | 27 46 | 3 42 | 7·9 | 26 47 | 3 33 | 7·8 | 25 48 | 3 24 | 7·8 | 24 48 | 3 15 | 7·7 | 263 | 277 |
| 96 | 84 | 29 49 | 3 27 | 6·9 | 28 50 | 3 19 | 6·9 | 27 50 | 3 11 | 6·8 | 26 50 | 3 03 | 6·7 | 25 51 | 2 55 | 6·7 | 24 51 | 2 47 | 6·6 | 264 | 276 |
| 95 | 85 | 29 52 | 2 53 | 5·8 | 28 53 | 2 46 | 5·7 | 27 53 | 2 39 | 5·7 | 26 53 | 2 33 | 5·6 | 25 54 | 2 26 | 5·6 | 24 54 | 2 20 | 5·5 | 265 | 275 |
| 94 | 86 | 29 55 | 2 18 | 4·6 | 28 55 | 2 13 | 4·6 | 27 56 | 2 07 | 4·5 | 26 56 | 2 02 | 4·5 | 25 56 | 1 57 | 4·4 | 24 56 | 1 52 | 4·4 | 266 | 274 |
| 93 | 87 | 29 57 | 1 44 | 3·5 | 28 57 | 1 40 | 3·4 | 27 57 | 1 36 | 3·4 | 26 58 | 1 32 | 3·4 | 25 58 | 1 28 | 3·3 | 24 58 | 1 24 | 3·3 | 267 | 273 |
| 92 | 88 | 29 59 | 1 09 | 2·3 | 28 59 | 1 06 | 2·3 | 27 59 | 1 04 | 2·3 | 26 59 | 1 01 | 2·2 | 25 59 | 0 59 | 2·2 | 24 59 | 0 56 | 2·2 | 268 | 272 |
| 91 | 89 | 30 00 | 0 35 | 1·2 | 29 00 | 0 33 | 1·1 | 28 00 | 0 32 | 1·1 | 27 00 | 0 31 | 1·1 | 26 00 | 0 29 | 1·1 | 25 00 | 0 28 | 1·1 | 269 | 271 |
| 90 | 90 | 30 00 | 0 00 | 0·0 | 29 00 | 0 00 | 0·0 | 28 00 | 0 00 | 0·0 | 27 00 | 0 00 | 0·0 | 26 00 | 0 00 | 0·0 | 25 00 | 0 00 | 0·0 | 270 | 270 |

N. Lat.: for LHA > 180° ... Zn = Z; for LHA < 180° ... Zn = 360° − Z

S. Lat.: for LHA > 180° ... Zn = 180° − Z; for LHA < 180° ... Zn = 180° + Z

SIGHT REDUCTION TABLE

B: (−) for 90° < LHA < 270°
Dec:(−) for Lat. contrary name

Z₁: same sign as B
Z₂: (−) for F > 90°

| Lat./A LHA/F | F | 66° A/H | 66° B/P | 66° Z₁/Z₂ | 67° A/H | 67° B/P | 67° Z₁/Z₂ | 68° A/H | 68° B/P | 68° Z₁/Z₂ | 69° A/H | 69° B/P | 69° Z₁/Z₂ | 70° A/H | 70° B/P | 70° Z₁/Z₂ | 71° A/H | 71° B/P | 71° Z₁/Z₂ | Lat./A LHA |
|---|---|---|---|---|---|---|---|---|---|---|---|---|---|---|---|---|---|---|---|---|
| 0 | 180 | 0 00 | 24 00 | 90.0 | 0 00 | 23 00 | 90.0 | 0 00 | 22 00 | 90.0 | 0 00 | 21 00 | 90.0 | 0 00 | 20 00 | 90.0 | 0 00 | 19 00 | 90.0 | 180 |
| 1 | 179 | 0 24 | 24 00 | 89.1 | 0 23 | 23 00 | 89.1 | 0 22 | 22 00 | 89.1 | 0 22 | 21 00 | 89.1 | 0 21 | 20 00 | 89.1 | 0 20 | 19 00 | 89.1 | 181 |
| 2 | 178 | 0 49 | 23 59 | 88.2 | 0 47 | 22 59 | 88.2 | 0 45 | 21 59 | 88.1 | 0 43 | 20 59 | 88.1 | 0 41 | 19 59 | 88.1 | 0 39 | 18 59 | 88.1 | 182 |
| 3 | 177 | 1 13 | 23 58 | 87.3 | 1 10 | 22 58 | 87.2 | 1 07 | 21 58 | 87.2 | 1 04 | 20 58 | 87.2 | 1 02 | 19 58 | 87.2 | 0 59 | 18 59 | 87.2 | 183 |
| 4 | 176 | 1 38 | 23 57 | 86.3 | 1 34 | 22 57 | 86.3 | 1 30 | 21 57 | 86.3 | 1 26 | 20 57 | 86.3 | 1 22 | 19 57 | 86.2 | 1 18 | 18 57 | 86.2 | 184 |
| 5 | 175 | 2 02 | 23 55 | 85.4 | 1 57 | 22 55 | 85.4 | 1 52 | 21 55 | 85.4 | 1 47 | 20 56 | 85.4 | 1 42 | 19 56 | 85.3 | 1 38 | 18 56 | 85.3 | 185 |
| 6 | 174 | 2 26 | 23 53 | 84.5 | 2 20 | 22 53 | 84.5 | 2 15 | 21 53 | 84.4 | 2 09 | 20 54 | 84.4 | 2 03 | 19 54 | 84.4 | 1 57 | 18 54 | 84.3 | 186 |
| 7 | 173 | 2 50 | 23 50 | 83.6 | 2 44 | 22 51 | 83.6 | 2 37 | 21 51 | 83.5 | 2 30 | 20 51 | 83.5 | 2 23 | 19 52 | 83.4 | 2 16 | 18 52 | 83.4 | 187 |
| 8 | 172 | 3 15 | 23 48 | 82.7 | 3 07 | 22 48 | 82.6 | 2 59 | 21 48 | 82.6 | 2 52 | 20 49 | 82.5 | 2 44 | 19 49 | 82.5 | 2 36 | 18 50 | 82.4 | 188 |
| 9 | 171 | 3 39 | 23 44 | 81.8 | 3 30 | 22 45 | 81.7 | 3 22 | 21 45 | 81.6 | 3 13 | 20 46 | 81.6 | 3 04 | 19 46 | 81.5 | 2 55 | 18 47 | 81.5 | 189 |
| 10 | 170 | 4 03 | 23 41 | 80.8 | 3 53 | 22 41 | 80.8 | 3 44 | 21 42 | 80.7 | 3 34 | 20 42 | 80.7 | 3 24 | 19 42 | 80.6 | 3 14 | 18 44 | 80.5 | 190 |
| 11 | 169 | 4 27 | 23 36 | 79.9 | 4 17 | 22 37 | 79.9 | 4 06 | 21 38 | 79.8 | 3 55 | 20 39 | 79.7 | 3 45 | 19 40 | 79.6 | 3 34 | 18 41 | 79.6 | 191 |
| 12 | 168 | 4 51 | 23 32 | 79.0 | 4 40 | 22 33 | 78.9 | 4 28 | 21 34 | 78.9 | 4 16 | 20 35 | 78.8 | 4 05 | 19 36 | 78.7 | 3 53 | 18 37 | 78.6 | 192 |
| 13 | 167 | 5 15 | 23 27 | 78.1 | 5 03 | 22 28 | 78.0 | 4 50 | 21 29 | 77.9 | 4 37 | 20 30 | 77.8 | 4 25 | 19 32 | 77.8 | 4 12 | 18 33 | 77.7 | 193 |
| 14 | 166 | 5 39 | 23 22 | 77.2 | 5 25 | 22 23 | 77.1 | 5 12 | 21 24 | 77.0 | 4 58 | 20 26 | 76.9 | 4 45 | 19 27 | 76.8 | 4 31 | 18 28 | 76.7 | 194 |
| 15 | 165 | 6 03 | 23 16 | 76.2 | 5 48 | 22 18 | 76.1 | 5 34 | 21 19 | 76.0 | 5 19 | 20 21 | 76.0 | 5 05 | 19 22 | 75.9 | 4 50 | 18 24 | 75.8 | 195 |
| 16 | 164 | 6 26 | 23 10 | 75.3 | 6 11 | 22 12 | 75.2 | 5 56 | 21 13 | 75.1 | 5 40 | 20 15 | 75.1 | 5 25 | 19 17 | 74.9 | 5 09 | 18 19 | 74.8 | 196 |
| 17 | 163 | 6 50 | 23 04 | 74.4 | 6 34 | 22 06 | 74.3 | 6 17 | 21 08 | 74.2 | 6 01 | 20 09 | 74.1 | 5 44 | 19 11 | 74.0 | 5 28 | 18 14 | 73.9 | 197 |
| 18 | 162 | 7 13 | 22 57 | 73.5 | 6 56 | 21 59 | 73.3 | 6 39 | 21 01 | 73.2 | 6 21 | 20 03 | 73.1 | 6 04 | 19 06 | 73.0 | 5 46 | 18 08 | 72.9 | 198 |
| 19 | 161 | 7 37 | 22 50 | 72.5 | 7 19 | 21 52 | 72.4 | 7 00 | 20 54 | 72.3 | 6 42 | 19 57 | 72.2 | 6 24 | 18 59 | 72.1 | 6 05 | 18 02 | 72.0 | 199 |
| 20 | 160 | 8 00 | 22 42 | 71.6 | 7 41 | 21 45 | 71.5 | 7 22 | 20 47 | 71.4 | 7 02 | 19 50 | 71.2 | 6 43 | 18 53 | 71.1 | 6 24 | 17 56 | 71.0 | 200 |
| 21 | 159 | 8 23 | 22 34 | 70.7 | 8 03 | 21 37 | 70.5 | 7 43 | 20 40 | 70.4 | 7 23 | 19 43 | 70.3 | 7 02 | 18 46 | 70.2 | 6 42 | 17 49 | 70.1 | 201 |
| 22 | 158 | 8 46 | 22 26 | 69.7 | 8 25 | 21 29 | 69.6 | 8 04 | 20 32 | 69.5 | 7 43 | 19 35 | 69.3 | 7 22 | 18 39 | 69.2 | 7 00 | 17 42 | 69.1 | 202 |
| 23 | 157 | 9 09 | 22 17 | 68.8 | 8 47 | 21 21 | 68.7 | 8 25 | 20 24 | 68.5 | 8 03 | 19 28 | 68.4 | 7 41 | 18 31 | 68.3 | 7 19 | 17 35 | 68.1 | 203 |
| 24 | 156 | 9 31 | 22 08 | 67.9 | 9 09 | 21 12 | 67.7 | 8 46 | 20 16 | 67.6 | 8 23 | 19 19 | 67.4 | 8 00 | 18 24 | 67.3 | 7 37 | 17 28 | 67.2 | 204 |
| 25 | 155 | 9 54 | 21 58 | 66.9 | 9 30 | 21 03 | 66.8 | 9 07 | 20 07 | 66.6 | 8 43 | 19 11 | 66.5 | 8 19 | 18 15 | 66.3 | 7 55 | 17 20 | 66.2 | 205 |
| 26 | 154 | 10 16 | 21 49 | 66.0 | 9 52 | 20 53 | 65.8 | 9 27 | 19 57 | 65.7 | 9 02 | 19 02 | 65.5 | 8 37 | 18 07 | 65.4 | 8 12 | 17 12 | 65.2 | 206 |
| 27 | 153 | 10 38 | 21 38 | 65.0 | 10 13 | 20 43 | 64.9 | 9 48 | 19 48 | 64.7 | 9 22 | 18 53 | 64.5 | 8 56 | 17 58 | 64.4 | 8 30 | 17 03 | 64.3 | 207 |
| 28 | 152 | 11 00 | 21 28 | 64.1 | 10 34 | 20 33 | 63.9 | 10 08 | 19 38 | 63.8 | 9 41 | 18 43 | 63.6 | 9 14 | 17 49 | 63.5 | 8 48 | 16 55 | 63.3 | 208 |
| 29 | 151 | 11 22 | 21 17 | 63.1 | 10 55 | 20 22 | 63.0 | 10 28 | 19 28 | 62.8 | 10 00 | 18 34 | 62.6 | 9 33 | 17 39 | 62.5 | 9 05 | 16 46 | 62.3 | 209 |
| 30 | 150 | 11 44 | 21 05 | 62.2 | 11 16 | 20 11 | 62.0 | 10 48 | 19 17 | 61.8 | 10 19 | 18 23 | 61.7 | 9 51 | 17 30 | 61.5 | 9 22 | 16 36 | 61.4 | 210 |
| 31 | 149 | 12 06 | 20 53 | 61.2 | 11 37 | 20 00 | 61.1 | 11 07 | 19 06 | 60.9 | 10 38 | 18 13 | 60.7 | 10 09 | 17 20 | 60.5 | 9 39 | 16 27 | 60.4 | 211 |
| 32 | 148 | 12 27 | 20 41 | 60.3 | 11 57 | 19 48 | 60.1 | 11 27 | 18 55 | 59.9 | 10 57 | 18 02 | 59.7 | 10 27 | 17 09 | 59.6 | 9 56 | 16 17 | 59.4 | 212 |
| 33 | 147 | 12 48 | 20 29 | 59.3 | 12 17 | 19 36 | 59.1 | 11 46 | 18 43 | 58.9 | 11 15 | 17 51 | 58.8 | 10 44 | 16 58 | 58.6 | 10 13 | 16 06 | 58.4 | 213 |
| 34 | 146 | 13 09 | 20 16 | 58.4 | 12 37 | 19 23 | 58.2 | 12 06 | 18 31 | 58.0 | 11 34 | 17 39 | 57.8 | 11 02 | 16 47 | 57.6 | 10 29 | 15 56 | 57.5 | 214 |
| 35 | 145 | 13 29 | 20 02 | 57.4 | 12 57 | 19 10 | 57.2 | 12 24 | 18 19 | 57.0 | 11 52 | 17 27 | 56.8 | 11 19 | 16 36 | 56.7 | 10 46 | 15 45 | 56.5 | 215 |
| 36 | 144 | 13 50 | 19 49 | 56.4 | 13 17 | 18 57 | 56.2 | 12 43 | 18 06 | 56.0 | 12 10 | 17 15 | 55.9 | 11 36 | 16 24 | 55.7 | 11 02 | 15 34 | 55.5 | 216 |
| 37 | 143 | 14 10 | 19 34 | 55.5 | 13 36 | 18 44 | 55.3 | 13 02 | 17 53 | 55.1 | 12 27 | 17 03 | 54.9 | 11 53 | 16 12 | 54.7 | 11 18 | 15 23 | 54.5 | 217 |
| 38 | 142 | 14 30 | 19 20 | 54.5 | 13 55 | 18 30 | 54.3 | 13 20 | 17 40 | 54.1 | 12 45 | 16 50 | 53.9 | 12 10 | 16 00 | 53.7 | 11 34 | 15 11 | 53.5 | 218 |
| 39 | 141 | 14 50 | 19 05 | 53.5 | 14 14 | 18 16 | 53.3 | 13 38 | 17 26 | 53.1 | 13 02 | 16 37 | 52.9 | 12 26 | 15 48 | 52.7 | 11 49 | 14 59 | 52.6 | 219 |
| 40 | 140 | 15 09 | 18 50 | 52.5 | 14 33 | 18 01 | 52.3 | 13 56 | 17 12 | 52.1 | 13 19 | 16 23 | 51.9 | 12 42 | 15 35 | 51.7 | 12 05 | 14 47 | 51.6 | 220 |
| 41 | 139 | 15 29 | 18 34 | 51.5 | 14 51 | 17 46 | 51.3 | 14 14 | 16 57 | 51.1 | 13 36 | 16 09 | 50.9 | 12 58 | 15 22 | 50.8 | 12 20 | 14 34 | 50.6 | 221 |
| 42 | 138 | 15 48 | 18 18 | 50.6 | 15 09 | 17 30 | 50.3 | 14 31 | 16 43 | 50.1 | 13 52 | 15 55 | 49.9 | 13 14 | 15 08 | 49.8 | 12 35 | 14 21 | 49.6 | 222 |
| 43 | 137 | 16 06 | 18 02 | 49.6 | 15 27 | 17 15 | 49.4 | 14 48 | 16 28 | 49.2 | 14 09 | 15 41 | 49.0 | 13 29 | 14 54 | 48.8 | 12 50 | 14 08 | 48.6 | 223 |
| 44 | 136 | 16 25 | 17 46 | 48.6 | 15 45 | 16 59 | 48.4 | 15 05 | 16 12 | 48.2 | 14 25 | 15 26 | 48.0 | 13 45 | 14 40 | 47.8 | 13 04 | 13 55 | 47.6 | 224 |
| 45 | 135 | 16 43 | 17 29 | 47.6 | 16 02 | 16 42 | 47.4 | 15 22 | 15 57 | 47.2 | 14 41 | 15 11 | 47.0 | 14 00 | 14 26 | 46.8 | 13 19 | 13 41 | 46.6 | 225 |

Z₁: same sign as B
Z₂: (−) for F > 90°

| Lat. / A | 66° | | | 67° | | | 68° | | | 69° | | | 70° | | | 71° | | | Lat. / A |
|---|---|---|---|---|---|---|---|---|---|---|---|---|---|---|---|---|---|---|---|
| LHA/F | A/H | B/P | Z₁/Z₂ | A/H | B/P | Z₁/Z₂ | A/H | B/P | Z₁/Z₂ | A/H | B/P | Z₁/Z₂ | A/H | B/P | Z₁/Z₂ | A/H | B/P | Z₁/Z₂ | LHA |
| 45 / 135 | 16 43 | 17 29 | 47·6 | 16 02 | 16 42 | 47·4 | 15 22 | 15 57 | 47·2 | 14 41 | 15 11 | 47·0 | 14 00 | 14 26 | 46·8 | 13 19 | 13 41 | 46·6 | 225 / 315 |
| 46 / 134 | 17 01 | 17 11 | 46·6 | 16 19 | 16 26 | 46·4 | 15 38 | 15 41 | 46·2 | 14 56 | 14 56 | 46·0 | 14 15 | 14 11 | 45·8 | 13 33 | 13 27 | 45·6 | 226 / 314 |
| 47 / 133 | 17 18 | 16 53 | 45·6 | 16 36 | 16 09 | 45·4 | 15 54 | 15 24 | 45·2 | 15 12 | 14 40 | 45·0 | 14 29 | 13 56 | 44·8 | 13 46 | 13 13 | 44·6 | 227 / 313 |
| 48 / 132 | 17 36 | 16 35 | 44·6 | 16 53 | 15 51 | 44·4 | 16 10 | 15 08 | 44·2 | 15 27 | 14 24 | 44·0 | 14 43 | 13 41 | 43·8 | 14 00 | 12 58 | 43·6 | 228 / 312 |
| 49 / 131 | 17 53 | 16 17 | 43·6 | 17 09 | 15 34 | 43·4 | 16 25 | 14 51 | 43·2 | 15 42 | 14 08 | 43·0 | 14 58 | 13 26 | 42·8 | 14 13 | 12 44 | 42·6 | 229 / 311 |
| 50 / 130 | 18 09 | 15 58 | 42·6 | 17 25 | 15 16 | 42·4 | 16 41 | 14 33 | 42·1 | 15 56 | 13 52 | 41·9 | 15 11 | 13 10 | 41·8 | 14 27 | 12 29 | 41·6 | 230 / 310 |
| 51 / 129 | 18 26 | 15 39 | 41·6 | 17 41 | 14 57 | 41·3 | 16 56 | 14 16 | 41·1 | 16 10 | 13 35 | 40·9 | 15 25 | 12 54 | 40·8 | 14 39 | 12 14 | 40·6 | 231 / 309 |
| 52 / 128 | 18 42 | 15 20 | 40·5 | 17 56 | 14 39 | 40·3 | 17 10 | 13 58 | 40·1 | 16 24 | 13 18 | 39·9 | 15 38 | 12 38 | 39·7 | 14 52 | 11 58 | 39·6 | 232 / 308 |
| 53 / 127 | 18 57 | 15 00 | 39·5 | 18 11 | 14 20 | 39·3 | 17 24 | 13 40 | 39·1 | 16 38 | 13 00 | 38·9 | 15 51 | 12 21 | 38·7 | 15 04 | 11 42 | 38·6 | 233 / 307 |
| 54 / 126 | 19 13 | 14 40 | 38·5 | 18 26 | 14 01 | 38·3 | 17 39 | 13 22 | 38·1 | 16 51 | 12 43 | 37·9 | 16 04 | 12 05 | 37·7 | 15 16 | 11 26 | 37·5 | 234 / 306 |
| 55 / 125 | 19 28 | 14 20 | 37·5 | 18 40 | 13 41 | 37·3 | 17 53 | 13 03 | 37·1 | 17 04 | 12 25 | 36·9 | 16 16 | 11 48 | 36·7 | 15 28 | 11 10 | 36·5 | 235 / 305 |
| 56 / 124 | 19 42 | 13 59 | 36·4 | 18 54 | 13 21 | 36·2 | 18 06 | 12 44 | 36·0 | 17 17 | 12 07 | 35·8 | 16 28 | 11 30 | 35·7 | 15 40 | 10 54 | 35·5 | 236 / 304 |
| 57 / 123 | 19 57 | 13 38 | 35·4 | 19 08 | 13 01 | 35·2 | 18 19 | 12 25 | 35·0 | 17 29 | 11 49 | 34·8 | 16 40 | 11 13 | 34·6 | 15 51 | 10 37 | 34·5 | 237 / 303 |
| 58 / 122 | 20 11 | 13 17 | 34·4 | 19 21 | 12 41 | 34·2 | 18 31 | 12 05 | 34·0 | 17 42 | 11 30 | 33·8 | 16 52 | 10 55 | 33·6 | 16 02 | 10 20 | 33·5 | 238 / 302 |
| 59 / 121 | 20 24 | 12 55 | 33·3 | 19 34 | 12 20 | 33·1 | 18 44 | 11 45 | 32·9 | 17 53 | 11 11 | 32·8 | 17 03 | 10 37 | 32·6 | 16 12 | 10 03 | 32·4 | 239 / 301 |
| 60 / 120 | 20 37 | 12 33 | 32·3 | 19 47 | 11 59 | 32·1 | 18 56 | 11 25 | 31·9 | 18 05 | 10 52 | 31·7 | 17 14 | 10 19 | 31·6 | 16 23 | 9 46 | 31·4 | 240 / 300 |
| 61 / 119 | 20 50 | 12 11 | 31·2 | 19 59 | 11 38 | 31·1 | 19 08 | 11 05 | 30·9 | 18 16 | 10 33 | 30·7 | 17 24 | 10 00 | 30·5 | 16 33 | 9 29 | 30·4 | 241 / 299 |
| 62 / 118 | 21 03 | 11 48 | 30·2 | 20 11 | 11 16 | 30·0 | 19 19 | 10 44 | 29·8 | 18 27 | 10 13 | 29·7 | 17 35 | 9 42 | 29·5 | 16 42 | 9 11 | 29·4 | 242 / 298 |
| 63 / 117 | 21 15 | 11 26 | 29·2 | 20 22 | 10 54 | 29·0 | 19 30 | 10 24 | 28·8 | 18 37 | 9 53 | 28·6 | 17 45 | 9 23 | 28·5 | 16 52 | 8 53 | 28·3 | 243 / 297 |
| 64 / 116 | 21 27 | 11 03 | 28·1 | 20 34 | 10 32 | 27·9 | 19 41 | 10 03 | 27·7 | 18 47 | 9 33 | 27·6 | 17 54 | 9 04 | 27·4 | 17 01 | 8 35 | 27·3 | 244 / 296 |
| 65 / 115 | 21 38 | 10 39 | 27·0 | 20 44 | 10 10 | 26·9 | 19 51 | 9 41 | 26·7 | 18 57 | 9 13 | 26·5 | 18 04 | 8 45 | 26·4 | 17 10 | 8 17 | 26·3 | 245 / 295 |
| 66 / 114 | 21 49 | 10 16 | 26·0 | 20 55 | 9 48 | 25·8 | 20 01 | 9 20 | 25·7 | 19 07 | 8 52 | 25·5 | 18 12 | 8 26 | 25·4 | 17 18 | 7 58 | 25·2 | 246 / 294 |
| 67 / 113 | 21 59 | 9 52 | 24·9 | 21 05 | 9 25 | 24·8 | 20 10 | 8 58 | 24·6 | 19 16 | 8 32 | 24·5 | 18 21 | 8 06 | 24·3 | 17 26 | 7 40 | 24·2 | 247 / 293 |
| 68 / 112 | 22 09 | 9 28 | 23·9 | 21 14 | 9 02 | 23·7 | 20 19 | 8 36 | 23·5 | 19 24 | 8 11 | 23·4 | 18 29 | 7 46 | 23·3 | 17 34 | 7 21 | 23·1 | 248 / 292 |
| 69 / 111 | 22 19 | 9 04 | 22·8 | 21 24 | 8 39 | 22·6 | 20 28 | 8 14 | 22·5 | 19 33 | 7 50 | 22·4 | 18 37 | 7 26 | 22·2 | 17 42 | 7 02 | 22·1 | 249 / 291 |
| 70 / 110 | 22 28 | 8 39 | 21·7 | 21 32 | 8 16 | 21·6 | 20 37 | 7 52 | 21·4 | 19 41 | 7 29 | 21·3 | 18 45 | 7 06 | 21·2 | 17 49 | 6 43 | 21·1 | 250 / 290 |
| 71 / 109 | 22 37 | 8 15 | 20·7 | 21 41 | 7 52 | 20·5 | 20 45 | 7 30 | 20·4 | 19 48 | 7 07 | 20·3 | 18 52 | 6 45 | 20·1 | 17 56 | 6 23 | 20·0 | 251 / 289 |
| 72 / 108 | 22 45 | 7 50 | 19·6 | 21 49 | 7 28 | 19·4 | 20 52 | 7 07 | 19·3 | 19 56 | 6 46 | 19·2 | 18 59 | 6 25 | 19·1 | 18 02 | 6 04 | 19·0 | 252 / 288 |
| 73 / 107 | 22 53 | 7 25 | 18·5 | 21 56 | 7 04 | 18·4 | 21 00 | 6 44 | 18·2 | 20 03 | 6 24 | 18·1 | 19 05 | 6 04 | 18·0 | 18 08 | 5 45 | 17·9 | 253 / 287 |
| 74 / 106 | 23 01 | 7 00 | 17·4 | 22 04 | 6 40 | 17·3 | 21 06 | 6 21 | 17·2 | 20 09 | 6 02 | 17·1 | 19 12 | 5 44 | 17·0 | 18 14 | 5 25 | 16·9 | 254 / 286 |
| 75 / 105 | 23 08 | 6 34 | 16·3 | 22 10 | 6 16 | 16·2 | 21 13 | 5 58 | 16·1 | 20 15 | 5 40 | 16·0 | 19 17 | 5 23 | 15·9 | 18 20 | 5 06 | 15·8 | 255 / 285 |
| 76 / 104 | 23 15 | 6 09 | 15·3 | 22 17 | 5 52 | 15·1 | 21 17 | 5 35 | 15·0 | 20 21 | 5 18 | 15·0 | 19 23 | 5 02 | 14·8 | 18 25 | 4 46 | 14·8 | 256 / 284 |
| 77 / 103 | 23 21 | 5 43 | 14·2 | 22 23 | 5 27 | 14·1 | 21 24 | 5 12 | 14·0 | 20 26 | 4 56 | 13·9 | 19 28 | 4 41 | 13·8 | 18 30 | 4 26 | 13·7 | 257 / 283 |
| 78 / 102 | 23 27 | 5 17 | 13·1 | 22 28 | 5 03 | 13·0 | 21 30 | 4 48 | 12·9 | 20 31 | 4 34 | 12·8 | 19 33 | 4 20 | 12·7 | 18 34 | 4 06 | 12·7 | 258 / 282 |
| 79 / 101 | 23 32 | 4 51 | 12·0 | 22 33 | 4 38 | 11·9 | 21 35 | 4 24 | 11·8 | 20 36 | 4 11 | 11·8 | 19 37 | 3 58 | 11·7 | 18 38 | 3 46 | 11·6 | 259 / 281 |
| 80 / 100 | 23 37 | 4 25 | 10·9 | 22 38 | 4 13 | 10·8 | 21 39 | 4 01 | 10·8 | 20 40 | 3 49 | 10·7 | 19 41 | 3 37 | 10·6 | 18 42 | 3 25 | 10·6 | 260 / 280 |
| 81 / 99 | 23 41 | 3 59 | 9·8 | 22 42 | 3 48 | 9·8 | 21 43 | 3 37 | 9·7 | 20 44 | 3 26 | 9·6 | 19 45 | 3 16 | 9·6 | 18 45 | 3 05 | 9·5 | 261 / 279 |
| 82 / 98 | 23 45 | 3 33 | 8·7 | 22 46 | 3 23 | 8·7 | 21 46 | 3 13 | 8·6 | 20 47 | 3 03 | 8·6 | 19 48 | 2 54 | 8·5 | 18 48 | 2 45 | 8·5 | 262 / 278 |
| 83 / 97 | 23 49 | 3 06 | 7·7 | 22 49 | 2 58 | 7·6 | 21 50 | 2 49 | 7·5 | 20 50 | 2 41 | 7·5 | 19 51 | 2 32 | 7·4 | 18 51 | 2 24 | 7·4 | 263 / 277 |
| 84 / 96 | 23 52 | 2 40 | 6·6 | 22 52 | 2 32 | 6·5 | 21 52 | 2 25 | 6·5 | 20 53 | 2 18 | 6·4 | 19 53 | 2 11 | 6·4 | 18 54 | 2 04 | 6·3 | 264 / 276 |
| 85 / 95 | 23 54 | 2 13 | 5·5 | 22 54 | 2 07 | 5·4 | 21 55 | 2 01 | 5·4 | 20 55 | 1 55 | 5·4 | 19 55 | 1 49 | 5·3 | 18 55 | 1 43 | 5·3 | 265 / 275 |
| 86 / 94 | 23 56 | 1 47 | 4·4 | 22 56 | 1 42 | 4·3 | 21 57 | 1 37 | 4·3 | 20 57 | 1 32 | 4·3 | 19 57 | 1 27 | 4·2 | 18 57 | 1 23 | 4·2 | 266 / 274 |
| 87 / 93 | 23 58 | 1 20 | 3·3 | 22 58 | 1 16 | 3·3 | 21 58 | 1 13 | 3·2 | 20 58 | 1 09 | 3·2 | 19 58 | 1 05 | 3·2 | 18 58 | 1 02 | 3·2 | 267 / 273 |
| 88 / 92 | 23 59 | 0 53 | 2·2 | 22 59 | 0 51 | 2·2 | 21 59 | 0 48 | 2·2 | 20 59 | 0 46 | 2·1 | 19 59 | 0 44 | 2·1 | 18 59 | 0 41 | 2·1 | 268 / 272 |
| 89 / 91 | 24 00 | 0 27 | 1·1 | 23 00 | 0 25 | 1·1 | 22 00 | 0 24 | 1·1 | 21 00 | 0 23 | 1·1 | 20 00 | 0 22 | 1·1 | 19 00 | 0 21 | 1·1 | 269 / 271 |
| 90 / 90 | 24 00 | 0 00 | 0·0 | 23 00 | 0 00 | 0·0 | 22 00 | 0 00 | 0·0 | 21 00 | 0 00 | 0·0 | 20 00 | 0 00 | 0·0 | 19 00 | 0 00 | 0·0 | 270 / 270 |

N. Lat.: for LHA > 180° ... $Z_n = Z$ / for LHA < 180° ... $Z_n = 360° - Z$

S. Lat.: for LHA > 180° ... $Z_n = 180° - Z$ / for LHA < 180° ... $Z_n = 180° + Z$

## SIGHT REDUCTION TABLE

B: (−) for 90° < LHA < 270°
Dec: (−) for Lat. contrary name

Z₁: same sign as B
Z₂: (−) for F > 90°

Left index — Lat. / A — LHA/F · A  |  Right index — Lat. / A — LHA/A · A

| LHA/F · A | 72° A/H | 72° B/P | 72° Z₁/Z₂ | 73° A/H | 73° B/P | 73° Z₁/Z₂ | 74° A/H | 74° B/P | 74° Z₁/Z₂ | 75° A/H | 75° B/P | 75° Z₁/Z₂ | 76° A/H | 76° B/P | 76° Z₁/Z₂ | 77° A/H | 77° B/P | 77° Z₁/Z₂ | LHA/A · A |
|---|---|---|---|---|---|---|---|---|---|---|---|---|---|---|---|---|---|---|---|
| 0 · 180 | 0 00 | 18 00 | 90.0 | 0 00 | 17 00 | 90.0 | 0 00 | 16 00 | 90.0 | 0 00 | 15 00 | 90.0 | 0 00 | 14 00 | 90.0 | 0 00 | 13 00 | 90.0 | 180 · 360 |
| 1 · 179 | 0 19 | 18 00 | 89.0 | 0 18 | 17 00 | 89.0 | 0 17 | 16 00 | 89.0 | 0 16 | 15 00 | 89.0 | 0 15 | 14 00 | 89.0 | 0 13 | 13 00 | 89.0 | 181 · 359 |
| 2 · 178 | 0 37 | 17 59 | 88.1 | 0 35 | 16 59 | 88.1 | 0 33 | 15 59 | 88.1 | 0 31 | 14 59 | 88.1 | 0 29 | 14 00 | 88.1 | 0 27 | 13 00 | 88.1 | 182 · 358 |
| 3 · 177 | 0 56 | 17 59 | 87.1 | 0 53 | 16 59 | 87.1 | 0 50 | 15 59 | 87.1 | 0 47 | 14 59 | 87.1 | 0 44 | 13 59 | 87.1 | 0 40 | 12 59 | 87.1 | 183 · 357 |
| 4 · 176 | 1 14 | 17 58 | 86.2 | 1 10 | 16 58 | 86.2 | 1 06 | 15 58 | 86.2 | 1 02 | 14 58 | 86.1 | 0 58 | 13 58 | 86.1 | 0 54 | 12 58 | 86.1 | 184 · 356 |
| 5 · 175 | 1 33 | 17 56 | 85.2 | 1 28 | 16 56 | 85.2 | 1 23 | 15 57 | 85.2 | 1 18 | 14 57 | 85.2 | 1 12 | 13 57 | 85.1 | 1 07 | 12 57 | 85.1 | 185 · 355 |
| 6 · 174 | 1 51 | 17 54 | 84.3 | 1 45 | 16 55 | 84.3 | 1 39 | 15 55 | 84.2 | 1 33 | 14 55 | 84.2 | 1 27 | 13 56 | 84.2 | 1 21 | 12 56 | 84.2 | 186 · 354 |
| 7 · 173 | 2 09 | 17 52 | 83.3 | 2 03 | 16 53 | 83.3 | 1 56 | 15 53 | 83.3 | 1 48 | 14 54 | 83.2 | 1 41 | 13 54 | 83.2 | 1 34 | 12 54 | 83.2 | 187 · 353 |
| 8 · 172 | 2 28 | 17 50 | 82.3 | 2 20 | 16 51 | 82.3 | 2 12 | 15 51 | 82.3 | 2 04 | 14 52 | 82.3 | 1 56 | 13 52 | 82.2 | 1 48 | 12 53 | 82.2 | 188 · 352 |
| 9 · 171 | 2 46 | 17 48 | 81.4 | 2 37 | 16 48 | 81.4 | 2 28 | 15 49 | 81.3 | 2 19 | 14 49 | 81.3 | 2 10 | 13 50 | 81.2 | 2 01 | 12 51 | 81.2 | 189 · 351 |
| 10 · 170 | 3 05 | 17 45 | 80.5 | 2 55 | 16 45 | 80.4 | 2 45 | 15 46 | 80.4 | 2 35 | 14 47 | 80.3 | 2 24 | 13 48 | 80.3 | 2 14 | 12 49 | 80.3 | 190 · 350 |
| 11 · 169 | 3 23 | 17 41 | 79.5 | 3 12 | 16 42 | 79.5 | 3 01 | 15 43 | 79.4 | 2 50 | 14 44 | 79.4 | 2 39 | 13 45 | 79.3 | 2 28 | 12 46 | 79.3 | 191 · 349 |
| 12 · 168 | 3 41 | 17 38 | 78.6 | 3 29 | 16 39 | 78.5 | 3 17 | 15 40 | 78.5 | 3 05 | 14 41 | 78.4 | 2 53 | 13 42 | 78.3 | 2 41 | 12 44 | 78.3 | 192 · 348 |
| 13 · 167 | 3 59 | 17 34 | 77.6 | 3 46 | 16 35 | 77.5 | 3 33 | 15 37 | 77.5 | 3 20 | 14 38 | 77.4 | 3 07 | 13 39 | 77.3 | 2 54 | 12 41 | 77.4 | 193 · 347 |
| 14 · 166 | 4 17 | 17 30 | 76.7 | 4 03 | 16 31 | 76.6 | 3 49 | 15 33 | 76.5 | 3 35 | 14 34 | 76.5 | 3 21 | 13 36 | 76.3 | 3 07 | 12 38 | 76.4 | 194 · 346 |
| 15 · 165 | 4 35 | 17 25 | 75.7 | 4 20 | 16 27 | 75.6 | 4 05 | 15 29 | 75.6 | 3 50 | 14 31 | 75.5 | 3 35 | 13 32 | 75.4 | 3 20 | 12 34 | 75.4 | 195 · 345 |
| 16 · 164 | 4 53 | 17 21 | 74.7 | 4 37 | 16 23 | 74.7 | 4 21 | 15 25 | 74.6 | 4 05 | 14 27 | 74.5 | 3 49 | 13 29 | 74.4 | 3 33 | 12 31 | 74.4 | 196 · 344 |
| 17 · 163 | 5 11 | 17 16 | 73.8 | 4 54 | 16 18 | 73.7 | 4 37 | 15 20 | 73.6 | 4 20 | 14 22 | 73.5 | 4 03 | 13 25 | 73.4 | 3 46 | 12 27 | 73.5 | 197 · 343 |
| 18 · 162 | 5 29 | 17 10 | 72.8 | 5 11 | 16 13 | 72.7 | 4 53 | 15 15 | 72.7 | 4 35 | 14 18 | 72.6 | 4 17 | 13 20 | 72.4 | 3 59 | 12 23 | 72.5 | 198 · 342 |
| 19 · 161 | 5 46 | 17 05 | 71.9 | 5 28 | 16 07 | 71.8 | 5 09 | 15 10 | 71.7 | 4 50 | 14 13 | 71.6 | 4 31 | 13 16 | 71.5 | 4 12 | 12 19 | 71.5 | 199 · 341 |
| 20 · 160 | 6 04 | 16 59 | 70.9 | 5 44 | 16 02 | 70.8 | 5 25 | 15 05 | 70.7 | 5 05 | 14 08 | 70.6 | 4 45 | 13 11 | 70.5 | 4 25 | 12 14 | 70.5 | 200 · 340 |
| 21 · 159 | 6 21 | 16 52 | 69.9 | 6 01 | 15 56 | 69.8 | 5 40 | 14 59 | 69.7 | 5 19 | 14 03 | 69.7 | 4 58 | 13 06 | 69.5 | 4 37 | 12 10 | 69.5 | 201 · 339 |
| 22 · 158 | 6 39 | 16 46 | 69.0 | 6 17 | 15 50 | 68.9 | 5 56 | 14 53 | 68.8 | 5 34 | 13 57 | 68.7 | 5 12 | 13 01 | 68.5 | 4 50 | 12 05 | 68.5 | 202 · 338 |
| 23 · 157 | 6 56 | 16 39 | 68.0 | 6 34 | 15 43 | 67.9 | 6 11 | 14 47 | 67.8 | 5 48 | 13 51 | 67.7 | 5 25 | 12 56 | 67.5 | 5 03 | 12 00 | 67.5 | 203 · 337 |
| 24 · 156 | 7 13 | 16 32 | 67.1 | 6 50 | 15 36 | 66.9 | 6 26 | 14 41 | 66.8 | 6 03 | 13 45 | 66.7 | 5 39 | 12 50 | 66.5 | 5 15 | 11 55 | 66.5 | 204 · 336 |
| 25 · 155 | 7 30 | 16 25 | 66.1 | 7 06 | 15 29 | 66.0 | 6 41 | 14 34 | 65.9 | 6 17 | 13 39 | 65.8 | 5 52 | 12 44 | 65.6 | 5 27 | 11 49 | 65.6 | 205 · 335 |
| 26 · 154 | 7 47 | 16 17 | 65.1 | 7 22 | 15 22 | 65.0 | 6 56 | 14 27 | 64.9 | 6 31 | 13 32 | 64.8 | 6 05 | 12 38 | 64.6 | 5 40 | 11 43 | 64.6 | 206 · 334 |
| 27 · 153 | 8 04 | 16 09 | 64.1 | 7 38 | 15 14 | 64.0 | 7 11 | 14 20 | 63.9 | 6 45 | 13 26 | 63.8 | 6 18 | 12 32 | 63.6 | 5 52 | 11 37 | 63.6 | 207 · 333 |
| 28 · 152 | 8 20 | 16 00 | 63.2 | 7 53 | 15 06 | 63.0 | 7 26 | 14 12 | 62.9 | 6 59 | 13 19 | 62.8 | 6 31 | 12 25 | 62.6 | 6 04 | 11 31 | 62.6 | 208 · 332 |
| 29 · 151 | 8 37 | 15 52 | 62.2 | 8 09 | 14 58 | 62.1 | 7 41 | 14 05 | 61.9 | 7 13 | 13 11 | 61.8 | 6 44 | 12 18 | 61.6 | 6 16 | 11 25 | 61.6 | 209 · 331 |
| 30 · 150 | 8 53 | 15 43 | 61.2 | 8 24 | 14 50 | 61.1 | 7 55 | 13 57 | 61.0 | 7 26 | 13 04 | 60.9 | 6 57 | 12 11 | 60.6 | 6 27 | 11 18 | 60.7 | 210 · 330 |
| 31 · 149 | 9 09 | 15 34 | 60.3 | 8 40 | 14 41 | 60.1 | 8 10 | 13 49 | 60.0 | 7 40 | 12 56 | 59.9 | 7 09 | 12 04 | 59.7 | 6 39 | 11 12 | 59.8 | 211 · 329 |
| 32 · 148 | 9 25 | 15 24 | 59.3 | 8 55 | 14 32 | 59.1 | 8 24 | 13 40 | 59.0 | 7 53 | 12 48 | 58.9 | 7 22 | 11 56 | 58.7 | 6 51 | 11 05 | 58.8 | 212 · 328 |
| 33 · 147 | 9 41 | 15 15 | 58.3 | 9 10 | 14 23 | 58.2 | 8 38 | 13 31 | 58.0 | 8 06 | 12 40 | 57.9 | 7 34 | 11 49 | 57.7 | 7 02 | 10 57 | 57.8 | 213 · 327 |
| 34 · 146 | 9 57 | 15 05 | 57.3 | 9 25 | 14 13 | 57.2 | 8 52 | 13 22 | 57.0 | 8 19 | 12 31 | 56.9 | 7 46 | 11 41 | 56.7 | 7 14 | 10 50 | 56.8 | 214 · 326 |
| 35 · 145 | 10 13 | 14 54 | 56.3 | 9 39 | 14 04 | 56.2 | 9 06 | 13 13 | 56.1 | 8 32 | 12 23 | 55.9 | 7 59 | 11 33 | 55.7 | 7 25 | 10 43 | 55.9 | 215 · 325 |
| 36 · 144 | 10 28 | 14 44 | 55.4 | 9 54 | 13 54 | 55.2 | 9 19 | 13 04 | 55.1 | 8 45 | 12 14 | 54.9 | 8 11 | 11 24 | 54.7 | 7 36 | 10 35 | 54.8 | 216 · 324 |
| 37 · 143 | 10 43 | 14 33 | 54.4 | 10 08 | 13 43 | 54.2 | 9 33 | 12 54 | 54.1 | 8 58 | 12 05 | 53.9 | 8 22 | 11 16 | 53.7 | 7 47 | 10 27 | 53.8 | 217 · 323 |
| 38 · 142 | 10 58 | 14 22 | 53.4 | 10 22 | 13 33 | 53.2 | 9 46 | 12 44 | 53.1 | 9 10 | 11 55 | 53.0 | 8 34 | 11 07 | 52.7 | 7 58 | 10 19 | 52.8 | 218 · 322 |
| 39 · 141 | 11 13 | 14 10 | 52.4 | 10 36 | 13 22 | 52.2 | 9 59 | 12 34 | 52.1 | 9 22 | 11 46 | 52.0 | 8 45 | 10 58 | 51.7 | 8 08 | 10 10 | 51.8 | 219 · 321 |
| 40 · 140 | 11 27 | 13 59 | 51.4 | 10 50 | 13 11 | 51.3 | 10 12 | 12 23 | 51.1 | 9 35 | 11 36 | 51.0 | 8 57 | 10 49 | 50.7 | 8 19 | 10 02 | 50.8 | 220 · 320 |
| 41 · 139 | 11 42 | 13 47 | 50.4 | 11 04 | 13 00 | 50.3 | 10 25 | 12 13 | 50.1 | 9 47 | 11 26 | 50.0 | 9 08 | 10 39 | 49.7 | 8 29 | 9 53 | 49.9 | 221 · 319 |
| 42 · 138 | 11 56 | 13 34 | 49.4 | 11 17 | 12 48 | 49.3 | 10 38 | 12 02 | 49.1 | 9 58 | 11 16 | 49.0 | 9 19 | 10 30 | 48.7 | 8 39 | 9 44 | 48.9 | 222 · 318 |
| 43 · 137 | 12 10 | 13 22 | 48.4 | 11 30 | 12 36 | 48.3 | 10 50 | 11 51 | 48.1 | 10 10 | 11 05 | 48.0 | 9 30 | 10 20 | 47.7 | 8 49 | 9 35 | 47.9 | 223 · 317 |
| 44 · 136 | 12 24 | 13 09 | 47.4 | 11 43 | 12 24 | 47.3 | 11 02 | 11 39 | 47.1 | 10 21 | 10 55 | 47.0 | 9 40 | 10 10 | 46.7 | 8 59 | 9 26 | 46.9 | 224 · 316 |
| 45 · 135 | 12 37 | 12 56 | 46.4 | 11 56 | 12 12 | 46.3 | 11 14 | 11 28 | 46.1 | 10 33 | 10 44 | 46.0 | 9 51 | 10 00 | 45.7 | 9 09 | 9 16 | 45.9 | 225 · 315 |

| Lat./A | | 72° | | | 73° | | | 74° | | | 75° | | | 76° | | | 77° | | | Lat./A | |
|---|---|---|---|---|---|---|---|---|---|---|---|---|---|---|---|---|---|---|---|---|---|
| A | LHA/F | A/H | B/P | $Z_1/Z_2$ | A/H | B/P | $Z_1/Z_2$ | A/H | B/P | $Z_1/Z_2$ | A/H | B/P | $Z_1/Z_2$ | A/H | B/P | $Z_1/Z_2$ | A/H | B/P | $Z_1/Z_2$ | LHA | A |
| 135 | 45 | 12 37 | 12 56 | 46·4 | 11 56 | 12 12 | 46·3 | 11 14 | 11 28 | 46·1 | 10 33 | 10 44 | 46·0 | 9 51 | 10 00 | 45·9 | 9 09 | 9 16 | 45·7 | 225 | 315 |
| 134 | 46 | 12 51 | 12 43 | 45·4 | 12 08 | 11 59 | 45·3 | 11 26 | 11 16 | 45·1 | 10 44 | 10 33 | 45·0 | 10 01 | 9 50 | 44·9 | 9 19 | 9 07 | 44·7 | 226 | 314 |
| 133 | 47 | 13 04 | 12 30 | 44·4 | 12 21 | 11 47 | 44·3 | 11 38 | 11 04 | 44·1 | 10 55 | 10 21 | 44·0 | 10 11 | 9 39 | 43·9 | 9 28 | 8 57 | 43·7 | 227 | 313 |
| 132 | 48 | 13 17 | 12 16 | 43·4 | 12 33 | 11 34 | 43·3 | 11 49 | 10 52 | 43·1 | 11 05 | 10 10 | 43·0 | 10 21 | 9 28 | 42·9 | 9 37 | 8 47 | 42·7 | 228 | 312 |
| 131 | 49 | 13 29 | 12 02 | 42·4 | 12 45 | 11 21 | 42·3 | 12 00 | 10 39 | 42·1 | 11 15 | 9 58 | 42·0 | 10 31 | 9 17 | 41·9 | 9 46 | 8 37 | 41·7 | 229 | 311 |
| 130 | 50 | 13 42 | 11 48 | 41·4 | 12 57 | 11 07 | 41·3 | 12 11 | 10 27 | 41·1 | 11 25 | 9 46 | 41·0 | 10 41 | 9 06 | 40·9 | 9 55 | 8 26 | 40·7 | 230 | 310 |
| 129 | 51 | 13 54 | 11 33 | 40·4 | 13 08 | 10 53 | 40·3 | 12 22 | 10 14 | 40·1 | 11 35 | 9 34 | 40·0 | 10 50 | 8 55 | 39·8 | 10 04 | 8 16 | 39·7 | 231 | 309 |
| 128 | 52 | 14 06 | 11 19 | 39·4 | 13 19 | 10 40 | 39·2 | 12 33 | 10 01 | 39·1 | 11 46 | 9 22 | 39·0 | 10 59 | 8 44 | 38·8 | 10 13 | 8 05 | 38·7 | 232 | 308 |
| 127 | 53 | 14 17 | 11 04 | 38·4 | 13 30 | 10 26 | 38·2 | 12 43 | 9 47 | 38·1 | 11 56 | 9 10 | 38·0 | 11 08 | 8 32 | 37·8 | 10 21 | 7 55 | 37·7 | 233 | 307 |
| 126 | 54 | 14 29 | 10 49 | 37·4 | 13 41 | 10 11 | 37·2 | 12 53 | 9 34 | 37·1 | 12 05 | 8 57 | 36·9 | 11 17 | 8 20 | 36·8 | 10 29 | 7 44 | 36·7 | 234 | 306 |
| 125 | 55 | 14 40 | 10 33 | 36·4 | 13 51 | 9 57 | 36·2 | 13 03 | 9 20 | 36·1 | 12 14 | 8 44 | 35·9 | 11 26 | 8 08 | 35·8 | 10 37 | 7 33 | 35·7 | 235 | 305 |
| 124 | 56 | 14 51 | 10 18 | 35·3 | 14 02 | 9 42 | 35·2 | 13 13 | 9 07 | 35·1 | 12 24 | 8 31 | 34·9 | 11 34 | 7 56 | 34·8 | 10 45 | 7 21 | 34·7 | 236 | 304 |
| 123 | 57 | 15 01 | 10 02 | 34·3 | 14 12 | 9 27 | 34·2 | 13 22 | 8 53 | 34·0 | 12 32 | 8 18 | 33·9 | 11 42 | 7 44 | 33·8 | 10 52 | 7 10 | 33·7 | 237 | 303 |
| 122 | 58 | 15 12 | 9 46 | 33·3 | 14 21 | 9 12 | 33·2 | 13 31 | 8 39 | 33·0 | 12 41 | 8 05 | 32·9 | 11 50 | 7 32 | 32·8 | 11 00 | 6 58 | 32·7 | 238 | 302 |
| 121 | 59 | 15 22 | 9 30 | 32·3 | 14 31 | 8 57 | 32·1 | 13 40 | 8 24 | 32·0 | 12 49 | 7 51 | 31·9 | 11 58 | 7 19 | 31·8 | 11 07 | 6 47 | 31·7 | 239 | 301 |
| 120 | 60 | 15 31 | 9 14 | 31·3 | 14 40 | 8 41 | 31·1 | 13 49 | 8 10 | 31·0 | 12 58 | 7 38 | 30·9 | 12 06 | 7 06 | 30·8 | 11 14 | 6 35 | 30·6 | 240 | 300 |
| 119 | 61 | 15 41 | 8 57 | 30·2 | 14 49 | 8 26 | 30·1 | 13 57 | 7 55 | 30·0 | 13 05 | 7 24 | 29·8 | 12 13 | 6 54 | 29·7 | 11 21 | 6 23 | 29·6 | 241 | 299 |
| 118 | 62 | 15 50 | 8 40 | 29·2 | 14 58 | 8 10 | 29·1 | 14 05 | 7 40 | 28·9 | 13 13 | 7 10 | 28·8 | 12 20 | 6 41 | 28·7 | 11 27 | 6 11 | 28·6 | 242 | 298 |
| 117 | 63 | 15 59 | 8 23 | 28·2 | 15 06 | 7 54 | 28·0 | 14 13 | 7 25 | 27·9 | 13 20 | 6 56 | 27·8 | 12 27 | 6 27 | 27·7 | 11 34 | 5 59 | 27·6 | 243 | 297 |
| 116 | 64 | 16 08 | 8 06 | 27·1 | 15 14 | 7 38 | 27·0 | 14 21 | 7 10 | 26·9 | 13 28 | 6 42 | 26·9 | 12 34 | 6 14 | 26·7 | 11 40 | 5 47 | 26·6 | 244 | 296 |
| 115 | 65 | 16 16 | 7 49 | 26·1 | 15 22 | 7 22 | 26·0 | 14 28 | 6 55 | 25·9 | 13 34 | 6 28 | 25·8 | 12 40 | 6 01 | 25·7 | 11 46 | 5 34 | 25·6 | 245 | 295 |
| 114 | 66 | 16 24 | 7 32 | 25·1 | 15 29 | 7 05 | 25·0 | 14 35 | 6 39 | 24·9 | 13 41 | 6 13 | 24·7 | 12 46 | 5 47 | 24·6 | 11 52 | 5 22 | 24·6 | 246 | 294 |
| 113 | 67 | 16 32 | 7 14 | 24·1 | 15 37 | 6 49 | 23·9 | 14 42 | 6 24 | 23·8 | 13 47 | 5 59 | 23·7 | 12 52 | 5 34 | 23·6 | 11 57 | 5 09 | 23·5 | 247 | 293 |
| 112 | 68 | 16 39 | 6 56 | 23·0 | 15 44 | 6 32 | 22·9 | 14 48 | 6 08 | 22·8 | 13 53 | 5 44 | 22·7 | 12 58 | 5 20 | 22·6 | 12 02 | 4 57 | 22·5 | 248 | 292 |
| 111 | 69 | 16 46 | 6 38 | 22·0 | 15 50 | 6 15 | 21·9 | 14 55 | 5 52 | 21·8 | 13 59 | 5 29 | 21·7 | 13 03 | 5 06 | 21·6 | 12 07 | 4 44 | 21·5 | 249 | 291 |
| 110 | 70 | 16 53 | 6 20 | 20·9 | 15 57 | 5 58 | 20·8 | 15 01 | 5 36 | 20·7 | 14 05 | 5 14 | 20·6 | 13 08 | 4 52 | 20·6 | 12 12 | 4 31 | 20·5 | 250 | 290 |
| 109 | 71 | 16 59 | 6 02 | 19·9 | 16 03 | 5 41 | 19·8 | 15 06 | 5 20 | 19·7 | 14 10 | 4 59 | 19·6 | 13 13 | 4 38 | 19·5 | 12 17 | 4 18 | 19·5 | 251 | 289 |
| 108 | 72 | 17 05 | 5 44 | 18·9 | 16 09 | 5 24 | 18·8 | 15 12 | 5 04 | 18·7 | 14 15 | 4 44 | 18·6 | 13 18 | 4 24 | 18·5 | 12 21 | 4 05 | 18·4 | 252 | 288 |
| 107 | 73 | 17 11 | 5 26 | 17·8 | 16 14 | 5 06 | 17·7 | 15 17 | 4 48 | 17·6 | 14 20 | 4 29 | 17·6 | 13 23 | 4 10 | 17·5 | 12 25 | 3 52 | 17·4 | 253 | 287 |
| 106 | 74 | 17 17 | 5 07 | 16·8 | 16 19 | 4 49 | 16·7 | 15 22 | 4 31 | 16·6 | 14 25 | 4 13 | 16·5 | 13 27 | 3 56 | 16·5 | 12 29 | 3 38 | 16·4 | 254 | 286 |
| 105 | 75 | 17 22 | 4 48 | 15·7 | 16 24 | 4 31 | 15·7 | 15 26 | 4 15 | 15·6 | 14 29 | 3 58 | 15·5 | 13 31 | 3 42 | 15·4 | 12 33 | 3 25 | 15·4 | 255 | 285 |
| 104 | 76 | 17 27 | 4 30 | 14·7 | 16 29 | 4 14 | 14·6 | 15 31 | 3 58 | 14·5 | 14 33 | 3 43 | 14·5 | 13 35 | 3 27 | 14·4 | 12 36 | 3 12 | 14·4 | 256 | 284 |
| 103 | 77 | 17 31 | 4 11 | 13·6 | 16 33 | 3 56 | 13·6 | 15 35 | 3 41 | 13·5 | 14 37 | 3 27 | 13·4 | 13 38 | 3 13 | 13·4 | 12 40 | 2 58 | 13·3 | 257 | 283 |
| 102 | 78 | 17 36 | 3 52 | 12·6 | 16 37 | 3 38 | 12·5 | 15 38 | 3 25 | 12·5 | 14 40 | 3 11 | 12·4 | 13 41 | 2 58 | 12·4 | 12 43 | 2 45 | 12·3 | 258 | 282 |
| 101 | 79 | 17 39 | 3 33 | 11·6 | 16 41 | 3 20 | 11·5 | 15 42 | 3 08 | 11·4 | 14 43 | 2 56 | 11·4 | 13 44 | 2 43 | 11·3 | 12 45 | 2 31 | 11·3 | 259 | 281 |
| 100 | 80 | 17 43 | 3 14 | 10·5 | 16 44 | 3 02 | 10·4 | 15 45 | 2 51 | 10·4 | 14 46 | 2 40 | 10·3 | 13 47 | 2 29 | 10·3 | 12 48 | 2 18 | 10·3 | 260 | 280 |
| 99 | 81 | 17 46 | 2 55 | 9·5 | 16 47 | 2 44 | 9·4 | 15 48 | 2 34 | 9·4 | 14 49 | 2 24 | 9·3 | 13 49 | 2 14 | 9·3 | 12 50 | 2 04 | 9·2 | 261 | 279 |
| 98 | 82 | 17 49 | 2 35 | 8·4 | 16 50 | 2 26 | 8·4 | 15 50 | 2 17 | 8·3 | 14 51 | 2 08 | 8·3 | 13 52 | 1 59 | 8·2 | 12 52 | 1 50 | 8·2 | 262 | 278 |
| 97 | 83 | 17 52 | 2 16 | 7·4 | 16 52 | 2 08 | 7·3 | 15 53 | 2 00 | 7·3 | 14 54 | 1 52 | 7·2 | 13 54 | 1 44 | 7·2 | 12 54 | 1 37 | 7·2 | 263 | 277 |
| 96 | 84 | 17 54 | 1 57 | 6·3 | 16 54 | 1 50 | 6·3 | 15 55 | 1 43 | 6·2 | 14 55 | 1 36 | 6·2 | 13 55 | 1 30 | 6·2 | 12 56 | 1 23 | 6·2 | 264 | 276 |
| 95 | 85 | 17 56 | 1 37 | 5·3 | 16 56 | 1 32 | 5·2 | 15 56 | 1 26 | 5·2 | 14 57 | 1 20 | 5·2 | 13 57 | 1 15 | 5·2 | 12 57 | 1 09 | 5·1 | 265 | 275 |
| 94 | 86 | 17 57 | 1 18 | 4·2 | 16 57 | 1 13 | 4·2 | 15 58 | 1 09 | 4·2 | 14 58 | 1 04 | 4·1 | 13 58 | 1 00 | 4·1 | 12 58 | 0 55 | 4·1 | 266 | 274 |
| 93 | 87 | 17 58 | 0 58 | 3·2 | 16 59 | 0 55 | 3·1 | 15 59 | 0 52 | 3·1 | 14 59 | 0 48 | 3·1 | 13 59 | 0 45 | 3·1 | 12 59 | 0 42 | 3·1 | 267 | 273 |
| 92 | 88 | 17 59 | 0 39 | 2·1 | 16 59 | 0 37 | 2·1 | 15 59 | 0 34 | 2·1 | 14 59 | 0 32 | 2·1 | 13 59 | 0 30 | 2·1 | 13 00 | 0 28 | 2·1 | 268 | 272 |
| 91 | 89 | 18 00 | 0 19 | 1·1 | 17 00 | 0 18 | 1·0 | 16 00 | 0 17 | 1·0 | 15 00 | 0 16 | 1·0 | 14 00 | 0 15 | 1·0 | 13 00 | 0 14 | 1·0 | 269 | 271 |
| 90 | 90 | 18 00 | 0 00 | 0·0 | 17 00 | 0 00 | 0·0 | 16 00 | 0 00 | 0·0 | 15 00 | 0 00 | 0·0 | 14 00 | 0 00 | 0·0 | 13 00 | 0 00 | 0·0 | 270 | 270 |

N. Lat: for LHA > 180° .... $Z_n = Z$ ; for LHA < 180° .... $Z_n = 360° - Z$

S. Lat.: for LHA > 180° .... $Z_n = 180° - Z$ ; for LHA < 180° .... $Z_n = 180° + Z$

SIGHT REDUCTION TABLE

B: (−) for 90° < LHA < 270°  
Dec:(−) for Lat. contrary name

Z₁: same sign as B  
Z₂: (−) for F > 90°

| Lat./A LHA/F | F | 78° A/H | 78° B/P | 78° Z₁/Z₂ | 79° A/H | 79° B/P | 79° Z₁/Z₂ | 80° A/H | 80° B/P | 80° Z₁/Z₂ | 81° A/H | 81° B/P | 81° Z₁/Z₂ | 82° A/H | 82° B/P | 82° Z₁/Z₂ | 83° A/H | 83° B/P | 83° Z₁/Z₂ | Lat./A LHA | LHA |
|---|---|---|---|---|---|---|---|---|---|---|---|---|---|---|---|---|---|---|---|---|---|
| 0 | 180 | 0 00 | 12 00 | 90·0 | 0 00 | 11 00 | 90·0 | 0 00 | 10 00 | 90·0 | 0 00 | 9 00 | 90·0 | 0 00 | 8 00 | 90·0 | 0 00 | 7 00 | 90·0 | 180 | 360 |
| 1 | 179 | 0 12 | 12 00 | 89·0 | 0 11 | 11 00 | 89·0 | 0 10 | 10 00 | 89·0 | 0 09 | 9 00 | 89·0 | 0 08 | 8 00 | 89·0 | 0 07 | 7 00 | 89·0 | 181 | 359 |
| 2 | 178 | 0 25 | 12 00 | 88·0 | 0 23 | 11 00 | 88·0 | 0 21 | 10 00 | 88·0 | 0 19 | 9 00 | 88·0 | 0 17 | 8 00 | 88·0 | 0 15 | 7 00 | 88·0 | 182 | 358 |
| 3 | 177 | 0 37 | 11 59 | 87·1 | 0 34 | 10 59 | 87·1 | 0 31 | 9 59 | 87·0 | 0 28 | 8 59 | 87·0 | 0 25 | 7 59 | 87·0 | 0 22 | 6 59 | 87·0 | 183 | 357 |
| 4 | 176 | 0 50 | 11 58 | 86·1 | 0 46 | 10 58 | 86·1 | 0 42 | 9 59 | 86·1 | 0 38 | 8 59 | 86·0 | 0 33 | 7 59 | 86·0 | 0 29 | 6 59 | 86·0 | 184 | 356 |
| 5 | 175 | 1 02 | 11 57 | 85·1 | 0 57 | 10 58 | 85·1 | 0 52 | 9 58 | 85·1 | 0 47 | 8 58 | 85·1 | 0 42 | 7 58 | 85·0 | 0 37 | 6 58 | 85·0 | 185 | 355 |
| 6 | 174 | 1 15 | 11 56 | 84·1 | 1 09 | 10 56 | 84·1 | 1 02 | 9 57 | 84·1 | 0 56 | 8 57 | 84·1 | 0 50 | 7 57 | 84·1 | 0 44 | 6 58 | 84·0 | 186 | 354 |
| 7 | 173 | 1 27 | 11 55 | 83·2 | 1 20 | 10 55 | 83·1 | 1 13 | 9 56 | 83·1 | 1 06 | 8 56 | 83·1 | 0 58 | 7 56 | 83·1 | 0 51 | 6 57 | 83·1 | 187 | 353 |
| 8 | 172 | 1 39 | 11 53 | 82·2 | 1 31 | 10 54 | 82·1 | 1 23 | 9 54 | 82·1 | 1 15 | 8 55 | 82·1 | 1 07 | 7 55 | 82·1 | 0 58 | 6 56 | 82·1 | 188 | 352 |
| 9 | 171 | 1 52 | 11 51 | 81·2 | 1 43 | 10 52 | 81·2 | 1 33 | 9 53 | 81·1 | 1 24 | 8 53 | 81·1 | 1 15 | 7 54 | 81·1 | 1 06 | 6 55 | 81·1 | 189 | 351 |
| 10 | 170 | 2 04 | 11 49 | 80·2 | 1 54 | 10 50 | 80·2 | 1 44 | 9 51 | 80·2 | 1 33 | 8 52 | 80·1 | 1 23 | 7 53 | 80·1 | 1 13 | 6 54 | 80·1 | 190 | 350 |
| 11 | 169 | 2 16 | 11 47 | 79·2 | 2 05 | 10 48 | 79·2 | 1 54 | 9 49 | 79·2 | 1 43 | 8 50 | 79·1 | 1 31 | 7 51 | 79·1 | 1 20 | 6 52 | 79·1 | 191 | 349 |
| 12 | 168 | 2 29 | 11 45 | 78·3 | 2 16 | 10 46 | 78·2 | 2 04 | 9 47 | 78·2 | 1 52 | 8 48 | 78·1 | 1 39 | 7 50 | 78·1 | 1 27 | 6 51 | 78·1 | 192 | 348 |
| 13 | 167 | 2 41 | 11 42 | 77·3 | 2 28 | 10 43 | 77·2 | 2 14 | 9 45 | 77·2 | 2 01 | 8 46 | 77·2 | 1 48 | 7 48 | 77·1 | 1 34 | 6 49 | 77·1 | 193 | 347 |
| 14 | 166 | 2 53 | 11 39 | 76·3 | 2 39 | 10 41 | 76·2 | 2 24 | 9 43 | 76·2 | 2 10 | 8 44 | 76·2 | 1 56 | 7 46 | 76·1 | 1 41 | 6 48 | 76·1 | 194 | 346 |
| 15 | 165 | 3 05 | 11 36 | 75·3 | 2 50 | 10 38 | 75·3 | 2 35 | 9 40 | 75·2 | 2 19 | 8 42 | 75·2 | 2 04 | 7 44 | 75·2 | 1 48 | 6 46 | 75·1 | 195 | 345 |
| 16 | 164 | 3 17 | 11 33 | 74·3 | 3 01 | 10 35 | 74·3 | 2 45 | 9 38 | 74·2 | 2 28 | 8 39 | 74·2 | 2 12 | 7 42 | 74·2 | 1 56 | 6 44 | 74·1 | 196 | 344 |
| 17 | 163 | 3 29 | 11 29 | 73·4 | 3 12 | 10 32 | 73·3 | 2 55 | 9 34 | 73·3 | 2 37 | 8 37 | 73·2 | 2 20 | 7 39 | 73·2 | 2 03 | 6 42 | 73·1 | 197 | 343 |
| 18 | 162 | 3 41 | 11 26 | 72·4 | 3 23 | 10 28 | 72·3 | 3 05 | 9 31 | 72·3 | 2 46 | 8 34 | 72·2 | 2 28 | 7 37 | 72·2 | 2 09 | 6 40 | 72·1 | 198 | 342 |
| 19 | 161 | 3 53 | 11 22 | 71·4 | 3 34 | 10 25 | 71·3 | 3 14 | 9 28 | 71·3 | 2 55 | 8 31 | 71·2 | 2 36 | 7 34 | 71·2 | 2 16 | 6 37 | 71·1 | 199 | 341 |
| 20 | 160 | 4 05 | 11 18 | 70·4 | 3 45 | 10 21 | 70·3 | 3 24 | 9 24 | 70·3 | 3 04 | 8 28 | 70·2 | 2 44 | 7 31 | 70·2 | 2 23 | 6 35 | 70·1 | 200 | 340 |
| 21 | 159 | 4 16 | 11 13 | 69·4 | 3 55 | 10 17 | 69·4 | 3 34 | 9 21 | 69·3 | 3 13 | 8 25 | 69·2 | 2 52 | 7 28 | 69·2 | 2 30 | 6 32 | 69·1 | 201 | 339 |
| 22 | 158 | 4 28 | 11 09 | 68·4 | 4 06 | 10 13 | 68·4 | 3 44 | 9 17 | 68·3 | 3 22 | 8 21 | 68·2 | 2 59 | 7 25 | 68·2 | 2 37 | 6 30 | 68·1 | 202 | 338 |
| 23 | 157 | 4 40 | 11 04 | 67·5 | 4 17 | 10 09 | 67·4 | 3 53 | 9 13 | 67·3 | 3 30 | 8 18 | 67·3 | 3 07 | 7 22 | 67·2 | 2 44 | 6 27 | 67·2 | 203 | 337 |
| 24 | 156 | 4 51 | 10 59 | 66·5 | 4 27 | 10 04 | 66·4 | 4 03 | 9 09 | 66·3 | 3 39 | 8 14 | 66·3 | 3 15 | 7 19 | 66·2 | 2 50 | 6 24 | 66·2 | 204 | 336 |
| 25 | 155 | 5 02 | 10 54 | 65·5 | 4 38 | 9 59 | 65·4 | 4 13 | 9 05 | 65·3 | 3 47 | 8 10 | 65·3 | 3 22 | 7 16 | 65·2 | 2 57 | 6 21 | 65·2 | 205 | 335 |
| 26 | 154 | 5 14 | 10 49 | 64·5 | 4 48 | 9 55 | 64·4 | 4 22 | 9 00 | 64·4 | 3 56 | 8 06 | 64·3 | 3 30 | 7 12 | 64·2 | 3 04 | 6 18 | 64·2 | 206 | 334 |
| 27 | 153 | 5 25 | 10 43 | 63·5 | 4 58 | 9 50 | 63·4 | 4 31 | 8 56 | 63·4 | 4 04 | 8 02 | 63·3 | 3 37 | 7 08 | 63·2 | 3 10 | 6 15 | 63·2 | 207 | 333 |
| 28 | 152 | 5 36 | 10 38 | 62·5 | 5 08 | 9 44 | 62·4 | 4 41 | 8 51 | 62·4 | 4 13 | 7 58 | 62·3 | 3 45 | 7 04 | 62·2 | 3 17 | 6 11 | 62·2 | 208 | 332 |
| 29 | 151 | 5 47 | 10 32 | 61·5 | 5 18 | 9 39 | 61·4 | 4 50 | 8 46 | 61·4 | 4 21 | 7 53 | 61·3 | 3 52 | 7 00 | 61·2 | 3 23 | 6 08 | 61·2 | 209 | 331 |
| 30 | 150 | 5 58 | 10 26 | 60·5 | 5 28 | 9 33 | 60·5 | 4 59 | 8 41 | 60·4 | 4 29 | 7 49 | 60·3 | 3 59 | 6 56 | 60·2 | 3 30 | 6 04 | 60·2 | 210 | 330 |
| 31 | 149 | 6 09 | 10 20 | 59·6 | 5 38 | 9 28 | 59·5 | 5 08 | 8 36 | 59·4 | 4 37 | 7 44 | 59·3 | 4 07 | 6 52 | 59·2 | 3 36 | 6 00 | 59·2 | 211 | 329 |
| 32 | 148 | 6 20 | 10 13 | 58·6 | 5 48 | 9 22 | 58·5 | 5 17 | 8 30 | 58·4 | 4 45 | 7 39 | 58·3 | 4 14 | 6 48 | 58·3 | 3 42 | 5 57 | 58·2 | 212 | 328 |
| 33 | 147 | 6 30 | 10 06 | 57·6 | 5 58 | 9 16 | 57·5 | 5 26 | 8 25 | 57·4 | 4 53 | 7 34 | 57·3 | 4 21 | 6 43 | 57·3 | 3 48 | 5 53 | 57·2 | 213 | 327 |
| 34 | 146 | 6 41 | 10 00 | 56·6 | 6 08 | 9 09 | 56·5 | 5 34 | 8 19 | 56·4 | 5 01 | 7 29 | 56·3 | 4 28 | 6 39 | 56·3 | 3 54 | 5 49 | 56·2 | 214 | 326 |
| 35 | 145 | 6 51 | 9 53 | 55·6 | 6 17 | 9 03 | 55·5 | 5 43 | 8 13 | 55·5 | 5 09 | 7 24 | 55·3 | 4 35 | 6 34 | 55·3 | 4 00 | 5 45 | 55·2 | 215 | 325 |
| 36 | 144 | 7 01 | 9 45 | 54·6 | 6 26 | 8 56 | 54·6 | 5 51 | 8 07 | 54·4 | 5 17 | 7 18 | 54·3 | 4 42 | 6 29 | 54·3 | 4 06 | 5 40 | 54·2 | 216 | 324 |
| 37 | 143 | 7 11 | 9 38 | 53·6 | 6 36 | 8 49 | 53·6 | 6 00 | 8 01 | 53·4 | 5 24 | 7 13 | 53·3 | 4 48 | 6 24 | 53·3 | 4 12 | 5 36 | 53·2 | 217 | 323 |
| 38 | 142 | 7 21 | 9 31 | 52·6 | 6 45 | 8 43 | 52·6 | 6 08 | 7 55 | 52·4 | 5 32 | 7 07 | 52·3 | 4 55 | 6 19 | 52·3 | 4 18 | 5 32 | 52·2 | 218 | 322 |
| 39 | 141 | 7 31 | 9 23 | 51·6 | 6 54 | 8 35 | 51·6 | 6 16 | 7 48 | 51·4 | 5 39 | 7 01 | 51·3 | 5 01 | 6 14 | 51·3 | 4 24 | 5 27 | 51·2 | 219 | 321 |
| 40 | 140 | 7 41 | 9 15 | 50·6 | 7 03 | 8 28 | 50·6 | 6 25 | 7 42 | 50·4 | 5 46 | 6 55 | 50·3 | 5 08 | 6 09 | 50·3 | 4 30 | 5 22 | 50·2 | 220 | 320 |
| 41 | 139 | 7 50 | 9 07 | 49·6 | 7 11 | 8 21 | 49·6 | 6 32 | 7 35 | 49·4 | 5 53 | 6 49 | 49·4 | 5 14 | 6 03 | 49·3 | 4 35 | 5 18 | 49·2 | 221 | 319 |
| 42 | 138 | 8 00 | 8 59 | 48·6 | 7 20 | 8 13 | 48·6 | 6 40 | 7 28 | 48·4 | 6 01 | 6 43 | 48·4 | 5 21 | 5 58 | 48·3 | 4 41 | 5 13 | 48·2 | 222 | 318 |
| 43 | 137 | 8 09 | 8 50 | 47·6 | 7 29 | 8 05 | 47·6 | 6 48 | 7 21 | 47·4 | 6 07 | 6 36 | 47·4 | 5 27 | 5 52 | 47·3 | 4 46 | 5 08 | 47·2 | 223 | 317 |
| 44 | 136 | 8 18 | 8 42 | 46·6 | 7 37 | 7 58 | 46·6 | 6 56 | 7 14 | 46·4 | 6 14 | 6 30 | 46·4 | 5 33 | 5 46 | 46·3 | 4 51 | 5 03 | 46·2 | 224 | 316 |
| 45 | 135 | 8 27 | 8 33 | 45·6 | 7 45 | 7 50 | 45·6 | 7 03 | 7 06 | 45·4 | 6 21 | 6 23 | 45·4 | 5 39 | 5 41 | 45·3 | 4 57 | 4 58 | 45·2 | 225 | 315 |

| Lat./A | LHA | 83° Z₁/Z₂ | 83° B/P | 83° A/H | 82° Z₁/Z₂ | 82° B/P | 82° A/H | 81° Z₁/Z₂ | 81° B/P | 81° A/H | 80° A/H | 80° B/P | 80° Z₁/Z₂ | 79° A/H | 79° B/P | 79° Z₁/Z₂ | 78° A/H | 78° B/P | 78° Z₁/Z₂ | Lat./A LHA/F | |
|---|---|---|---|---|---|---|---|---|---|---|---|---|---|---|---|---|---|---|---|---|---|
| 315 | 225 | 45.2 | 4 58 | 4 57 | 45.3 | 5 41 | 5 39 | 45.4 | 6 23 | 6 21 | 7 03 | 7 06 | 45.4 | 7 45 | 7 50 | 45.5 | 8 27 | 8 33 | 45.6 | 135 | 45 |
| 314 | 226 | 44.2 | 4 53 | 5 02 | 44.3 | 5 35 | 5 45 | 44.4 | 6 17 | 6 28 | 7 11 | 6 59 | 44.4 | 7 53 | 7 41 | 44.5 | 8 36 | 8 24 | 44.6 | 134 | 46 |
| 313 | 227 | 43.2 | 4 47 | 5 07 | 43.3 | 5 28 | 5 51 | 43.4 | 6 10 | 6 34 | 7 18 | 6 51 | 43.4 | 8 01 | 7 33 | 43.5 | 8 45 | 8 15 | 43.6 | 133 | 47 |
| 312 | 228 | 42.2 | 4 42 | 5 12 | 42.3 | 5 22 | 5 56 | 42.4 | 6 03 | 6 41 | 7 25 | 6 44 | 42.4 | 8 09 | 7 25 | 42.5 | 8 53 | 8 06 | 42.6 | 132 | 48 |
| 311 | 229 | 41.2 | 4 36 | 5 17 | 41.3 | 5 16 | 6 02 | 41.4 | 5 56 | 6 47 | 7 32 | 6 36 | 41.4 | 8 17 | 7 16 | 41.5 | 9 02 | 7 56 | 41.6 | 131 | 49 |
| 310 | 230 | 40.2 | 4 31 | 5 21 | 40.3 | 5 10 | 6 07 | 40.3 | 5 49 | 6 53 | 7 39 | 6 28 | 40.4 | 8 24 | 7 07 | 40.5 | 9 10 | 7 47 | 40.6 | 130 | 50 |
| 309 | 231 | 39.2 | 4 25 | 5 26 | 39.3 | 5 03 | 6 13 | 39.3 | 5 42 | 6 59 | 7 45 | 6 20 | 39.4 | 8 32 | 6 58 | 39.5 | 9 18 | 7 37 | 39.6 | 129 | 51 |
| 308 | 232 | 38.2 | 4 19 | 5 31 | 38.3 | 4 57 | 6 18 | 38.3 | 5 34 | 7 05 | 7 52 | 6 12 | 38.4 | 8 39 | 6 49 | 38.5 | 9 26 | 7 27 | 38.6 | 128 | 52 |
| 307 | 233 | 37.2 | 4 14 | 5 35 | 37.3 | 4 50 | 6 23 | 37.3 | 5 27 | 7 11 | 7 58 | 6 03 | 37.4 | 8 46 | 6 40 | 37.5 | 9 33 | 7 17 | 37.6 | 127 | 53 |
| 306 | 234 | 36.2 | 4 08 | 5 39 | 36.3 | 4 43 | 6 28 | 36.3 | 5 19 | 7 16 | 8 05 | 5 55 | 36.4 | 8 53 | 6 31 | 36.5 | 9 41 | 7 07 | 36.6 | 126 | 54 |
| 305 | 235 | 35.2 | 4 02 | 5 44 | 35.3 | 4 37 | 6 33 | 35.3 | 5 11 | 7 22 | 8 11 | 5 47 | 35.4 | 9 00 | 6 22 | 35.5 | 9 48 | 6 57 | 35.6 | 125 | 55 |
| 304 | 236 | 34.2 | 3 56 | 5 48 | 34.3 | 4 30 | 6 38 | 34.3 | 5 04 | 7 27 | 8 17 | 5 38 | 34.4 | 9 06 | 6 12 | 34.5 | 9 56 | 6 47 | 34.6 | 124 | 56 |
| 303 | 237 | 33.2 | 3 50 | 5 52 | 33.3 | 4 23 | 6 42 | 33.3 | 4 56 | 7 32 | 8 22 | 5 29 | 33.4 | 9 13 | 6 03 | 33.5 | 10 03 | 6 36 | 33.6 | 123 | 57 |
| 302 | 238 | 32.2 | 3 43 | 5 56 | 32.3 | 4 16 | 6 47 | 32.3 | 4 48 | 7 37 | 8 28 | 5 20 | 32.4 | 9 19 | 5 53 | 32.5 | 10 09 | 6 26 | 32.6 | 122 | 58 |
| 301 | 239 | 31.2 | 3 37 | 6 00 | 31.2 | 4 08 | 6 51 | 31.3 | 4 40 | 7 42 | 8 34 | 5 11 | 31.4 | 9 25 | 5 43 | 31.5 | 10 16 | 6 15 | 31.6 | 121 | 59 |
| 300 | 240 | 30.2 | 3 31 | 6 04 | 30.2 | 4 01 | 6 55 | 30.3 | 4 32 | 7 47 | 8 39 | 5 02 | 30.4 | 9 31 | 5 33 | 30.5 | 10 22 | 6 04 | 30.6 | 120 | 60 |
| 299 | 241 | 29.2 | 3 24 | 6 07 | 29.2 | 3 54 | 6 59 | 29.3 | 4 23 | 7 52 | 8 44 | 4 53 | 29.4 | 9 36 | 5 23 | 29.5 | 10 29 | 5 53 | 29.5 | 119 | 61 |
| 298 | 242 | 28.2 | 3 18 | 6 11 | 28.2 | 3 46 | 7 04 | 28.3 | 4 15 | 7 56 | 8 49 | 4 44 | 28.4 | 9 42 | 5 13 | 28.4 | 10 35 | 5 42 | 28.5 | 118 | 62 |
| 297 | 243 | 27.2 | 3 11 | 6 14 | 27.2 | 3 39 | 7 07 | 27.3 | 4 07 | 8 01 | 8 54 | 4 35 | 27.4 | 9 47 | 5 03 | 27.4 | 10 41 | 5 31 | 27.5 | 117 | 63 |
| 296 | 244 | 26.2 | 3 05 | 6 17 | 26.2 | 3 32 | 7 11 | 26.3 | 3 58 | 8 05 | 8 59 | 4 25 | 26.3 | 9 52 | 4 52 | 26.4 | 10 46 | 5 19 | 26.5 | 116 | 64 |
| 295 | 245 | 25.2 | 2 58 | 6 20 | 25.2 | 3 24 | 7 15 | 25.3 | 3 50 | 8 09 | 9 03 | 4 16 | 25.3 | 9 57 | 4 42 | 25.4 | 10 52 | 5 08 | 25.5 | 115 | 65 |
| 294 | 246 | 24.2 | 2 52 | 6 24 | 24.2 | 3 16 | 7 18 | 24.3 | 3 41 | 8 13 | 9 08 | 4 06 | 24.3 | 10 02 | 4 31 | 24.4 | 10 57 | 4 56 | 24.5 | 114 | 66 |
| 293 | 247 | 23.2 | 2 45 | 6 26 | 23.2 | 3 09 | 7 22 | 23.3 | 3 32 | 8 17 | 9 12 | 3 56 | 23.3 | 10 07 | 4 21 | 23.4 | 11 02 | 4 45 | 23.5 | 113 | 67 |
| 292 | 248 | 22.1 | 2 38 | 6 29 | 22.2 | 3 01 | 7 25 | 22.2 | 3 24 | 8 20 | 9 16 | 3 47 | 22.3 | 10 11 | 4 10 | 22.4 | 11 07 | 4 33 | 22.4 | 112 | 68 |
| 291 | 249 | 21.1 | 2 31 | 6 32 | 21.2 | 2 53 | 7 28 | 21.2 | 3 15 | 8 24 | 9 20 | 3 37 | 21.3 | 10 16 | 3 59 | 21.4 | 11 12 | 4 21 | 21.4 | 111 | 69 |
| 290 | 250 | 20.1 | 2 24 | 6 35 | 20.2 | 2 45 | 7 31 | 20.2 | 3 06 | 8 27 | 9 23 | 3 27 | 20.3 | 10 20 | 3 48 | 20.4 | 11 16 | 4 09 | 20.4 | 110 | 70 |
| 289 | 251 | 19.1 | 2 17 | 6 37 | 19.2 | 2 37 | 7 34 | 19.2 | 2 57 | 8 30 | 9 27 | 3 17 | 19.3 | 10 24 | 3 37 | 19.3 | 11 20 | 3 58 | 19.4 | 109 | 71 |
| 288 | 252 | 18.1 | 2 10 | 6 39 | 18.2 | 2 29 | 7 36 | 18.2 | 2 48 | 8 33 | 9 30 | 3 07 | 18.3 | 10 27 | 3 26 | 18.3 | 11 24 | 3 45 | 18.4 | 108 | 72 |
| 287 | 253 | 17.1 | 2 03 | 6 42 | 17.2 | 2 21 | 7 39 | 17.2 | 2 39 | 8 36 | 9 34 | 2 57 | 17.2 | 10 31 | 3 15 | 17.3 | 11 28 | 3 33 | 17.4 | 107 | 73 |
| 286 | 254 | 16.1 | 1 56 | 6 44 | 16.1 | 2 13 | 7 41 | 16.2 | 2 30 | 8 39 | 9 37 | 2 47 | 16.2 | 10 34 | 3 04 | 16.3 | 11 32 | 3 21 | 16.3 | 106 | 74 |
| 285 | 255 | 15.1 | 1 49 | 6 46 | 15.1 | 2 05 | 7 44 | 15.2 | 2 21 | 8 41 | 9 39 | 2 37 | 15.2 | 10 37 | 2 53 | 15.3 | 11 35 | 3 09 | 15.3 | 105 | 75 |
| 284 | 256 | 14.1 | 1 42 | 6 47 | 14.1 | 1 57 | 7 46 | 14.2 | 2 12 | 8 44 | 9 42 | 2 27 | 14.2 | 10 40 | 2 42 | 14.3 | 11 38 | 2 57 | 14.3 | 104 | 76 |
| 283 | 257 | 13.1 | 1 35 | 6 49 | 13.1 | 1 49 | 7 48 | 13.2 | 2 02 | 8 46 | 9 44 | 2 16 | 13.2 | 10 43 | 2 30 | 13.2 | 11 41 | 2 44 | 13.3 | 103 | 77 |
| 282 | 258 | 12.1 | 1 28 | 6 51 | 12.1 | 1 40 | 7 49 | 12.1 | 1 53 | 8 48 | 9 47 | 2 06 | 12.2 | 10 45 | 2 19 | 12.2 | 11 44 | 2 32 | 12.3 | 102 | 78 |
| 281 | 259 | 11.1 | 1 21 | 6 52 | 11.1 | 1 32 | 7 51 | 11.1 | 1 44 | 8 50 | 9 49 | 1 56 | 11.2 | 10 48 | 2 07 | 11.2 | 11 47 | 2 19 | 11.2 | 101 | 79 |
| 280 | 260 | 10.1 | 1 13 | 6 54 | 10.1 | 1 24 | 7 53 | 10.1 | 1 35 | 8 52 | 9 51 | 1 45 | 10.2 | 10 50 | 1 56 | 10.2 | 11 49 | 2 07 | 10.2 | 100 | 80 |
| 279 | 261 | 9.1 | 1 06 | 6 55 | 9.1 | 1 16 | 7 54 | 9.1 | 1 25 | 8 53 | 9 53 | 1 35 | 9.1 | 10 52 | 1 45 | 9.2 | 11 51 | 1 54 | 9.2 | 99 | 81 |
| 278 | 262 | 8.1 | 0 59 | 6 56 | 8.1 | 1 07 | 7 55 | 8.1 | 1 16 | 8 55 | 9 54 | 1 24 | 8.1 | 10 53 | 1 33 | 8.1 | 11 53 | 1 42 | 8.2 | 98 | 82 |
| 277 | 263 | 7.1 | 0 51 | 6 57 | 7.1 | 0 59 | 7 56 | 7.1 | 1 06 | 8 56 | 9 55 | 1 14 | 7.1 | 10 55 | 1 21 | 7.1 | 11 55 | 1 29 | 7.2 | 97 | 83 |
| 276 | 264 | 6.0 | 0 44 | 6 58 | 6.1 | 0 50 | 7 57 | 6.1 | 0 57 | 8 57 | 9 57 | 1 03 | 6.1 | 10 56 | 1 10 | 6.1 | 11 56 | 1 16 | 6.1 | 96 | 84 |
| 275 | 265 | 5.0 | 0 37 | 6 58 | 5.0 | 0 42 | 7 58 | 5.1 | 0 47 | 8 58 | 9 58 | 0 53 | 5.1 | 10 57 | 0 58 | 5.1 | 11 57 | 1 04 | 5.1 | 95 | 85 |
| 274 | 266 | 4.0 | 0 29 | 6 59 | 4.0 | 0 34 | 7 59 | 4.0 | 0 38 | 8 59 | 9 59 | 0 42 | 4.1 | 10 58 | 0 47 | 4.1 | 11 58 | 0 51 | 4.1 | 94 | 86 |
| 273 | 267 | 3.0 | 0 22 | 6 59 | 3.0 | 0 25 | 7 59 | 3.0 | 0 28 | 8 59 | 9 59 | 0 32 | 3.0 | 10 59 | 0 35 | 3.1 | 11 59 | 0 38 | 3.1 | 93 | 87 |
| 272 | 268 | 2.0 | 0 15 | 7 00 | 2.0 | 0 17 | 8 00 | 2.0 | 0 19 | 9 00 | 10 00 | 0 21 | 2.0 | 11 00 | 0 23 | 2.0 | 12 00 | 0 26 | 2.0 | 92 | 88 |
| 271 | 269 | 1.0 | 0 07 | 7 00 | 1.0 | 0 08 | 8 00 | 1.0 | 0 10 | 9 00 | 10 00 | 0 11 | 1.0 | 11 00 | 0 12 | 1.0 | 12 00 | 0 13 | 1.0 | 91 | 89 |
| 270 | 270 | 0.0 | 0 00 | 7 00 | 0.0 | 0 00 | 8 00 | 0.0 | 0 00 | 9 00 | 10 00 | 0 00 | 0.0 | 11 00 | 0 00 | 0.0 | 12 00 | 0 00 | 0.0 | 90 | 90 |

N. Lat: for LHA > 180° ... Zₙ = Z
for LHA < 180° ... Zₙ = 360° − Z

S. Lat.: for LHA > 180° ... Zₙ = 180° − Z
for LHA < 180° ... Zₙ = 180° + Z

SIGHT REDUCTION TABLE

B: (−) for 90° < LHA < 270°
Dec:(−) for Lat. contrary name

Z1: same sign as B
Z2: (−) for F > 90°

| LHA/F | F | 84° A/H | 84° B/P | 84° Z1/Z2 | 85° A/H | 85° B/P | 85° Z1/Z2 | 86° A/H | 86° B/P | 86° Z1/Z2 | 87° A/H | 87° B/P | 87° Z1/Z2 | 88° A/H | 88° B/P | 88° Z1/Z2 | 89° A/H | 89° B/P | 89° Z1/Z2 | LHA | A |
|---|---|---|---|---|---|---|---|---|---|---|---|---|---|---|---|---|---|---|---|---|---|
| 0 | 180 | 0 00 | 6 00 | 90·0 | 0 00 | 5 00 | 90·0 | 0 00 | 4 00 | 90·0 | 0 00 | 3 00 | 90·0 | 0 00 | 2 00 | 90·0 | 0 00 | 1 00 | 90·0 | 180 | 360 |
| 1 | 179 | 0 06 | 6 00 | 89·0 | 0 05 | 5 00 | 89·0 | 0 04 | 4 00 | 89·0 | 0 03 | 3 00 | 89·0 | 0 02 | 2 00 | 89·0 | 0 01 | 1 00 | 89·0 | 181 | 359 |
| 2 | 178 | 0 13 | 6 00 | 88·0 | 0 10 | 5 00 | 88·0 | 0 08 | 4 00 | 88·0 | 0 06 | 3 00 | 88·0 | 0 04 | 2 00 | 88·0 | 0 02 | 1 00 | 88·0 | 182 | 358 |
| 3 | 177 | 0 19 | 6 00 | 87·0 | 0 16 | 5 00 | 87·0 | 0 13 | 4 00 | 87·0 | 0 09 | 3 00 | 87·0 | 0 06 | 2 00 | 87·0 | 0 03 | 1 00 | 87·0 | 183 | 357 |
| 4 | 176 | 0 25 | 5 59 | 86·0 | 0 21 | 4 59 | 86·0 | 0 17 | 3 59 | 86·0 | 0 13 | 2 59 | 86·0 | 0 08 | 2 00 | 86·0 | 0 04 | 1 00 | 86·0 | 184 | 356 |
| 5 | 175 | 0 31 | 5 59 | 85·0 | 0 26 | 4 59 | 85·0 | 0 21 | 3 59 | 85·0 | 0 16 | 2 59 | 85·0 | 0 10 | 2 00 | 85·0 | 0 05 | 1 00 | 85·0 | 185 | 355 |
| 6 | 174 | 0 38 | 5 58 | 84·0 | 0 31 | 4 58 | 84·0 | 0 25 | 3 58 | 84·0 | 0 19 | 2 59 | 84·0 | 0 13 | 1 59 | 84·0 | 0 06 | 1 00 | 84·0 | 186 | 354 |
| 7 | 173 | 0 44 | 5 57 | 83·0 | 0 37 | 4 58 | 83·0 | 0 29 | 3 58 | 83·0 | 0 22 | 2 59 | 83·0 | 0 15 | 1 59 | 83·0 | 0 07 | 1 00 | 83·0 | 187 | 353 |
| 8 | 172 | 0 50 | 5 57 | 82·0 | 0 42 | 4 57 | 82·0 | 0 33 | 3 58 | 82·0 | 0 25 | 2 58 | 82·0 | 0 17 | 1 59 | 82·0 | 0 08 | 0 59 | 82·0 | 188 | 352 |
| 9 | 171 | 0 56 | 5 56 | 81·0 | 0 47 | 4 56 | 81·0 | 0 38 | 3 57 | 81·0 | 0 28 | 2 58 | 81·0 | 0 19 | 1 59 | 81·0 | 0 09 | 0 59 | 81·0 | 189 | 351 |
| 10 | 170 | 1 02 | 5 55 | 80·1 | 0 52 | 4 55 | 80·1 | 0 42 | 3 56 | 80·0 | 0 31 | 2 57 | 80·0 | 0 21 | 1 58 | 80·0 | 0 10 | 0 59 | 80·0 | 190 | 350 |
| 11 | 169 | 1 09 | 5 53 | 79·1 | 0 57 | 4 55 | 79·1 | 0 46 | 3 56 | 79·0 | 0 34 | 2 57 | 79·0 | 0 23 | 1 58 | 79·0 | 0 11 | 0 59 | 79·0 | 191 | 349 |
| 12 | 168 | 1 15 | 5 52 | 78·1 | 1 02 | 4 53 | 78·1 | 0 50 | 3 55 | 78·0 | 0 37 | 2 56 | 78·0 | 0 25 | 1 57 | 78·0 | 0 12 | 0 59 | 78·0 | 192 | 348 |
| 13 | 167 | 1 21 | 5 51 | 77·1 | 1 07 | 4 52 | 77·0 | 0 54 | 3 54 | 77·0 | 0 40 | 2 55 | 77·0 | 0 27 | 1 57 | 77·0 | 0 13 | 0 58 | 77·0 | 193 | 347 |
| 14 | 166 | 1 27 | 5 49 | 76·1 | 1 12 | 4 51 | 76·1 | 0 58 | 3 53 | 76·1 | 0 44 | 2 55 | 76·0 | 0 29 | 1 56 | 76·0 | 0 15 | 0 58 | 76·0 | 194 | 346 |
| 15 | 165 | 1 33 | 5 48 | 75·1 | 1 18 | 4 50 | 75·1 | 1 02 | 3 52 | 75·1 | 0 47 | 2 54 | 75·0 | 0 31 | 1 56 | 75·0 | 0 16 | 0 58 | 75·0 | 195 | 345 |
| 16 | 164 | 1 39 | 5 46 | 74·1 | 1 23 | 4 48 | 74·1 | 1 06 | 3 51 | 74·1 | 0 50 | 2 53 | 74·0 | 0 33 | 1 55 | 74·0 | 0 17 | 0 58 | 74·0 | 196 | 344 |
| 17 | 163 | 1 45 | 5 44 | 73·1 | 1 28 | 4 47 | 73·1 | 1 10 | 3 50 | 73·1 | 0 53 | 2 52 | 73·0 | 0 35 | 1 55 | 73·0 | 0 18 | 0 57 | 73·0 | 197 | 343 |
| 18 | 162 | 1 51 | 5 42 | 72·1 | 1 33 | 4 45 | 72·1 | 1 14 | 3 48 | 72·1 | 0 56 | 2 51 | 72·0 | 0 37 | 1 54 | 72·0 | 0 19 | 0 57 | 72·0 | 198 | 342 |
| 19 | 161 | 1 57 | 5 41 | 71·1 | 1 38 | 4 44 | 71·1 | 1 18 | 3 47 | 71·1 | 0 59 | 2 50 | 71·0 | 0 39 | 1 53 | 71·0 | 0 20 | 0 57 | 71·0 | 199 | 341 |
| 20 | 160 | 2 03 | 5 38 | 70·1 | 1 42 | 4 42 | 70·1 | 1 22 | 3 46 | 70·1 | 1 02 | 2 49 | 70·0 | 0 41 | 1 53 | 70·0 | 0 21 | 0 56 | 70·0 | 200 | 340 |
| 21 | 159 | 2 09 | 5 36 | 69·1 | 1 47 | 4 40 | 69·1 | 1 26 | 3 44 | 69·1 | 1 04 | 2 48 | 69·0 | 0 43 | 1 52 | 69·0 | 0 22 | 0 56 | 69·0 | 201 | 339 |
| 22 | 158 | 2 15 | 5 34 | 68·1 | 1 52 | 4 38 | 68·1 | 1 30 | 3 43 | 68·1 | 1 07 | 2 47 | 68·0 | 0 45 | 1 51 | 68·0 | 0 22 | 0 56 | 68·0 | 202 | 338 |
| 23 | 157 | 2 20 | 5 32 | 67·1 | 1 57 | 4 36 | 67·1 | 1 34 | 3 41 | 67·1 | 1 10 | 2 46 | 67·0 | 0 47 | 1 50 | 67·0 | 0 23 | 0 55 | 67·0 | 203 | 337 |
| 24 | 156 | 2 26 | 5 29 | 66·1 | 2 02 | 4 34 | 66·1 | 1 38 | 3 39 | 66·1 | 1 13 | 2 44 | 66·0 | 0 49 | 1 50 | 66·0 | 0 24 | 0 55 | 66·0 | 204 | 336 |
| 25 | 155 | 2 32 | 5 26 | 65·1 | 2 07 | 4 32 | 65·1 | 1 41 | 3 38 | 65·1 | 1 16 | 2 43 | 65·0 | 0 51 | 1 49 | 65·0 | 0 25 | 0 54 | 65·0 | 205 | 335 |
| 26 | 154 | 2 38 | 5 24 | 64·1 | 2 11 | 4 30 | 64·1 | 1 45 | 3 36 | 64·1 | 1 19 | 2 42 | 64·0 | 0 53 | 1 48 | 64·0 | 0 26 | 0 54 | 64·0 | 206 | 334 |
| 27 | 153 | 2 43 | 5 21 | 63·1 | 2 16 | 4 27 | 63·1 | 1 49 | 3 34 | 63·1 | 1 22 | 2 40 | 63·0 | 0 54 | 1 47 | 63·0 | 0 27 | 0 53 | 63·0 | 207 | 333 |
| 28 | 152 | 2 49 | 5 18 | 62·1 | 2 21 | 4 25 | 62·1 | 1 53 | 3 32 | 62·1 | 1 24 | 2 39 | 62·0 | 0 56 | 1 46 | 62·0 | 0 28 | 0 53 | 62·0 | 208 | 332 |
| 29 | 151 | 2 54 | 5 15 | 61·1 | 2 25 | 4 23 | 61·1 | 1 56 | 3 30 | 61·1 | 1 27 | 2 37 | 61·0 | 0 58 | 1 45 | 61·0 | 0 29 | 0 52 | 61·0 | 209 | 331 |
| 30 | 150 | 3 00 | 5 12 | 60·1 | 2 30 | 4 20 | 60·1 | 2 00 | 3 28 | 60·1 | 1 30 | 2 36 | 60·0 | 1 00 | 1 44 | 60·0 | 0 30 | 0 52 | 60·0 | 210 | 330 |
| 31 | 149 | 3 05 | 5 09 | 59·1 | 2 34 | 4 17 | 59·1 | 2 04 | 3 26 | 59·1 | 1 33 | 2 34 | 59·0 | 1 02 | 1 43 | 59·0 | 0 31 | 0 51 | 59·0 | 211 | 329 |
| 32 | 148 | 3 11 | 5 06 | 58·1 | 2 39 | 4 15 | 58·1 | 2 07 | 3 24 | 58·1 | 1 35 | 2 33 | 58·0 | 1 04 | 1 42 | 58·0 | 0 32 | 0 51 | 58·0 | 212 | 328 |
| 33 | 147 | 3 16 | 5 02 | 57·1 | 2 43 | 4 12 | 57·1 | 2 11 | 3 21 | 57·1 | 1 38 | 2 31 | 57·0 | 1 05 | 1 41 | 57·0 | 0 33 | 0 50 | 57·0 | 213 | 327 |
| 34 | 146 | 3 21 | 4 59 | 56·1 | 2 48 | 4 09 | 56·1 | 2 14 | 3 19 | 56·1 | 1 41 | 2 29 | 56·0 | 1 07 | 1 39 | 56·0 | 0 34 | 0 49 | 56·0 | 214 | 326 |
| 35 | 145 | 3 26 | 4 55 | 55·1 | 2 52 | 4 06 | 55·1 | 2 18 | 3 17 | 55·1 | 1 43 | 2 27 | 55·0 | 1 09 | 1 38 | 55·0 | 0 34 | 0 49 | 55·0 | 215 | 325 |
| 36 | 144 | 3 31 | 4 52 | 54·1 | 2 56 | 4 03 | 54·1 | 2 21 | 3 14 | 54·1 | 1 46 | 2 26 | 54·0 | 1 11 | 1 37 | 54·0 | 0 35 | 0 49 | 54·0 | 216 | 324 |
| 37 | 143 | 3 36 | 4 48 | 53·2 | 3 00 | 4 00 | 53·1 | 2 24 | 3 12 | 53·1 | 1 48 | 2 24 | 53·0 | 1 12 | 1 36 | 53·0 | 0 36 | 0 48 | 53·0 | 217 | 323 |
| 38 | 142 | 3 41 | 4 44 | 52·2 | 3 05 | 3 57 | 52·1 | 2 28 | 3 09 | 52·1 | 1 51 | 2 22 | 52·0 | 1 14 | 1 35 | 52·0 | 0 37 | 0 47 | 52·0 | 218 | 322 |
| 39 | 141 | 3 46 | 4 40 | 51·2 | 3 09 | 3 53 | 51·2 | 2 31 | 3 07 | 51·1 | 1 53 | 2 20 | 51·0 | 1 16 | 1 33 | 51·0 | 0 38 | 0 47 | 51·0 | 219 | 321 |
| 40 | 140 | 3 51 | 4 36 | 50·2 | 3 13 | 3 50 | 50·2 | 2 34 | 3 04 | 50·1 | 1 56 | 2 18 | 50·0 | 1 17 | 1 32 | 50·0 | 0 39 | 0 46 | 50·0 | 220 | 320 |
| 41 | 139 | 3 56 | 4 32 | 49·2 | 3 17 | 3 47 | 49·2 | 2 37 | 3 01 | 49·1 | 1 58 | 2 16 | 49·0 | 1 19 | 1 31 | 49·0 | 0 39 | 0 45 | 49·0 | 221 | 319 |
| 42 | 138 | 4 01 | 4 28 | 48·2 | 3 21 | 3 43 | 48·2 | 2 41 | 2 58 | 48·1 | 2 00 | 2 14 | 48·0 | 1 20 | 1 29 | 48·0 | 0 40 | 0 45 | 48·0 | 222 | 318 |
| 43 | 137 | 4 05 | 4 24 | 47·2 | 3 24 | 3 40 | 47·2 | 2 44 | 2 56 | 47·1 | 2 03 | 2 12 | 47·0 | 1 22 | 1 28 | 47·0 | 0 41 | 0 44 | 47·0 | 223 | 317 |
| 44 | 136 | 4 10 | 4 19 | 46·2 | 3 28 | 3 36 | 46·2 | 2 47 | 2 53 | 46·1 | 2 05 | 2 10 | 46·0 | 1 23 | 1 26 | 46·0 | 0 42 | 0 43 | 46·0 | 224 | 316 |
| 45 | 135 | 4 14 | 4 15 | 45·2 | 3 32 | 3 32 | 45·1 | 2 50 | 2 50 | 45·1 | 2 07 | 2 07 | 45·0 | 1 25 | 1 25 | 45·0 | 0 42 | 0 42 | 45·0 | 225 | 315 |

| Lat./A | | 84° | | | 85° | | | 86° | | | 87° | | | 88° | | | 89° | | | Lat./A |
|---|---|---|---|---|---|---|---|---|---|---|---|---|---|---|---|---|---|---|---|---|
| LHA/F | | A/H | B/P | Z₁/Z₂ | A/H | B/P | Z₁/Z₂ | A/H | B/P | Z₁/Z₂ | A/H | B/P | Z₁/Z₂ | A/H | B/P | Z₁/Z₂ | A/H | B/P | Z₁/Z₂ | LHA |
| 45 | 135 | 4 14 | 4 15 | 45.2 | 3 32 | 3 32 | 45.1 | 2 50 | 2 50 | 45.1 | 2 07 | 2 07 | 45.0 | 1 25 | 1 25 | 45.0 | 0 42 | 0 42 | 45.0 | 225 |
| 46 | 134 | 4 19 | 4 11 | 44.2 | 3 36 | 3 29 | 44.1 | 2 53 | 2 47 | 44.1 | 2 09 | 2 05 | 44.0 | 1 26 | 1 23 | 44.0 | 0 43 | 0 42 | 44.0 | 226 |
| 47 | 133 | 4 23 | 4 06 | 43.2 | 3 39 | 3 25 | 43.1 | 2 55 | 2 44 | 43.1 | 2 12 | 2 03 | 43.0 | 1 28 | 1 22 | 43.0 | 0 44 | 0 41 | 43.0 | 227 |
| 48 | 132 | 4 27 | 4 01 | 42.2 | 3 43 | 3 21 | 42.1 | 2 58 | 2 41 | 42.1 | 2 14 | 2 01 | 42.0 | 1 29 | 1 20 | 42.0 | 0 45 | 0 40 | 42.0 | 228 |
| 49 | 131 | 4 31 | 3 57 | 41.2 | 3 46 | 3 17 | 41.1 | 3 01 | 2 38 | 41.1 | 2 15 | 1 58 | 41.0 | 1 31 | 1 19 | 41.0 | 0 45 | 0 39 | 41.0 | 229 |
| 50 | 130 | 4 36 | 3 52 | 40.2 | 3 50 | 3 13 | 40.1 | 3 04 | 2 34 | 40.1 | 2 18 | 1 56 | 40.0 | 1 32 | 1 17 | 40.0 | 0 46 | 0 39 | 40.0 | 230 |
| 51 | 129 | 4 40 | 3 47 | 39.2 | 3 53 | 3 09 | 39.1 | 3 06 | 2 31 | 39.1 | 2 20 | 1 53 | 39.0 | 1 33 | 1 16 | 39.0 | 0 47 | 0 38 | 39.0 | 231 |
| 52 | 128 | 4 43 | 3 42 | 38.2 | 3 56 | 3 05 | 38.1 | 3 09 | 2 28 | 38.1 | 2 22 | 1 51 | 38.0 | 1 35 | 1 14 | 38.0 | 0 47 | 0 37 | 38.0 | 232 |
| 53 | 127 | 4 47 | 3 37 | 37.2 | 3 59 | 3 01 | 37.1 | 3 12 | 2 25 | 37.1 | 2 24 | 1 48 | 37.0 | 1 36 | 1 12 | 37.0 | 0 48 | 0 36 | 37.0 | 233 |
| 54 | 126 | 4 51 | 3 32 | 36.1 | 4 03 | 2 57 | 36.1 | 3 14 | 2 21 | 36.1 | 2 26 | 1 46 | 36.0 | 1 37 | 1 11 | 36.0 | 0 49 | 0 35 | 36.0 | 234 |
| 55 | 125 | 4 55 | 3 27 | 35.1 | 4 06 | 2 52 | 35.1 | 3 17 | 2 18 | 35.1 | 2 27 | 1 43 | 35.0 | 1 38 | 1 09 | 35.0 | 0 49 | 0 34 | 35.0 | 235 |
| 56 | 124 | 4 58 | 3 22 | 34.1 | 4 09 | 2 48 | 34.1 | 3 19 | 2 14 | 34.1 | 2 29 | 1 41 | 34.0 | 1 39 | 1 07 | 34.0 | 0 50 | 0 34 | 34.0 | 236 |
| 57 | 123 | 5 02 | 3 17 | 33.1 | 4 12 | 2 44 | 33.1 | 3 21 | 2 11 | 33.1 | 2 31 | 1 38 | 33.0 | 1 41 | 1 05 | 33.0 | 0 50 | 0 33 | 33.0 | 237 |
| 58 | 122 | 5 05 | 3 11 | 32.1 | 4 14 | 2 39 | 32.1 | 3 23 | 2 07 | 32.1 | 2 33 | 1 35 | 32.0 | 1 42 | 1 04 | 32.0 | 0 51 | 0 32 | 32.0 | 238 |
| 59 | 121 | 5 08 | 3 06 | 31.1 | 4 17 | 2 35 | 31.1 | 3 26 | 2 04 | 31.1 | 2 34 | 1 33 | 31.0 | 1 43 | 1 02 | 31.0 | 0 51 | 0 31 | 31.0 | 239 |
| 60 | 120 | 5 12 | 3 00 | 30.1 | 4 20 | 2 30 | 30.1 | 3 28 | 2 00 | 30.1 | 2 36 | 1 30 | 30.0 | 1 44 | 1 00 | 30.0 | 0 52 | 0 30 | 30.0 | 240 |
| 61 | 119 | 5 15 | 2 55 | 29.1 | 4 22 | 2 26 | 29.1 | 3 30 | 1 56 | 29.0 | 2 37 | 1 27 | 29.0 | 1 45 | 0 58 | 29.0 | 0 52 | 0 29 | 29.0 | 241 |
| 62 | 118 | 5 18 | 2 49 | 28.1 | 4 25 | 2 21 | 28.1 | 3 32 | 1 53 | 28.1 | 2 39 | 1 25 | 28.0 | 1 46 | 0 56 | 28.0 | 0 53 | 0 28 | 28.0 | 242 |
| 63 | 117 | 5 21 | 2 44 | 27.1 | 4 27 | 2 16 | 27.1 | 3 34 | 1 49 | 27.1 | 2 40 | 1 22 | 27.0 | 1 47 | 0 54 | 27.0 | 0 53 | 0 27 | 27.0 | 243 |
| 64 | 116 | 5 23 | 2 38 | 26.1 | 4 30 | 2 12 | 26.1 | 3 36 | 1 45 | 26.1 | 2 42 | 1 19 | 26.0 | 1 48 | 0 53 | 26.0 | 0 54 | 0 26 | 26.0 | 244 |
| 65 | 115 | 5 26 | 2 33 | 25.1 | 4 32 | 2 07 | 25.1 | 3 37 | 1 42 | 25.1 | 2 43 | 1 16 | 25.0 | 1 49 | 0 51 | 25.0 | 0 54 | 0 25 | 25.0 | 245 |
| 66 | 114 | 5 29 | 2 27 | 24.1 | 4 34 | 2 02 | 24.1 | 3 39 | 1 38 | 24.1 | 2 44 | 1 13 | 24.0 | 1 50 | 0 49 | 24.0 | 0 55 | 0 24 | 24.0 | 246 |
| 67 | 113 | 5 31 | 2 21 | 23.1 | 4 36 | 1 57 | 23.1 | 3 41 | 1 34 | 23.1 | 2 46 | 1 10 | 23.0 | 1 50 | 0 47 | 23.0 | 0 55 | 0 23 | 23.0 | 247 |
| 68 | 112 | 5 34 | 2 15 | 22.1 | 4 38 | 1 53 | 22.1 | 3 42 | 1 30 | 22.1 | 2 47 | 1 07 | 22.0 | 1 51 | 0 45 | 22.0 | 0 56 | 0 22 | 22.0 | 248 |
| 69 | 111 | 5 36 | 2 09 | 21.1 | 4 40 | 1 48 | 21.1 | 3 44 | 1 26 | 21.1 | 2 48 | 1 05 | 21.0 | 1 52 | 0 43 | 21.0 | 0 56 | 0 22 | 21.0 | 249 |
| 70 | 110 | 5 38 | 2 04 | 20.1 | 4 42 | 1 43 | 20.1 | 3 46 | 1 22 | 20.1 | 2 49 | 1 02 | 20.0 | 1 52 | 0 41 | 20.0 | 0 56 | 0 21 | 20.0 | 250 |
| 71 | 109 | 5 40 | 1 58 | 19.1 | 4 44 | 1 38 | 19.1 | 3 47 | 1 18 | 19.0 | 2 50 | 0 59 | 19.0 | 1 53 | 0 39 | 19.0 | 0 57 | 0 20 | 19.0 | 251 |
| 72 | 108 | 5 42 | 1 52 | 18.1 | 4 45 | 1 33 | 18.1 | 3 48 | 1 14 | 18.1 | 2 51 | 0 56 | 18.0 | 1 54 | 0 37 | 18.0 | 0 57 | 0 19 | 18.0 | 252 |
| 73 | 107 | 5 44 | 1 46 | 17.1 | 4 47 | 1 28 | 17.1 | 3 49 | 1 10 | 17.1 | 2 52 | 0 53 | 17.0 | 1 55 | 0 35 | 17.0 | 0 57 | 0 18 | 17.0 | 253 |
| 74 | 106 | 5 46 | 1 40 | 16.1 | 4 48 | 1 23 | 16.1 | 3 51 | 1 06 | 16.0 | 2 53 | 0 50 | 16.0 | 1 55 | 0 33 | 16.0 | 0 58 | 0 17 | 16.0 | 254 |
| 75 | 105 | 5 48 | 1 33 | 15.1 | 4 50 | 1 18 | 15.1 | 3 52 | 1 02 | 15.1 | 2 54 | 0 47 | 15.0 | 1 56 | 0 31 | 15.0 | 0 58 | 0 16 | 15.0 | 255 |
| 76 | 104 | 5 49 | 1 27 | 14.1 | 4 51 | 1 13 | 14.1 | 3 53 | 0 58 | 14.0 | 2 55 | 0 44 | 14.0 | 1 56 | 0 29 | 14.0 | 0 58 | 0 15 | 14.0 | 256 |
| 77 | 103 | 5 51 | 1 21 | 13.1 | 4 52 | 1 08 | 13.0 | 3 54 | 0 54 | 13.0 | 2 55 | 0 41 | 13.0 | 1 57 | 0 27 | 13.0 | 0 58 | 0 13 | 13.0 | 257 |
| 78 | 102 | 5 52 | 1 15 | 12.1 | 4 53 | 1 03 | 12.0 | 3 55 | 0 50 | 12.0 | 2 56 | 0 37 | 12.0 | 1 57 | 0 25 | 12.0 | 0 59 | 0 12 | 12.0 | 258 |
| 79 | 101 | 5 53 | 1 09 | 11.1 | 4 54 | 0 57 | 11.0 | 3 56 | 0 46 | 11.0 | 2 57 | 0 34 | 11.0 | 1 58 | 0 23 | 11.0 | 0 59 | 0 11 | 11.0 | 259 |
| 80 | 100 | 5 55 | 1 03 | 10.1 | 4 55 | 0 52 | 10.0 | 3 56 | 0 42 | 10.0 | 2 57 | 0 31 | 10.0 | 1 58 | 0 21 | 10.0 | 0 59 | 0 10 | 10.0 | 260 |
| 81 | 99 | 5 56 | 0 57 | 9.0 | 4 56 | 0 47 | 9.0 | 3 57 | 0 38 | 9.0 | 2 58 | 0 28 | 9.0 | 1 59 | 0 19 | 9.0 | 0 59 | 0 09 | 9.0 | 261 |
| 82 | 98 | 5 56 | 0 50 | 8.0 | 4 57 | 0 42 | 8.0 | 3 58 | 0 33 | 8.0 | 2 58 | 0 25 | 8.0 | 1 59 | 0 17 | 8.0 | 0 59 | 0 08 | 8.0 | 262 |
| 83 | 97 | 5 57 | 0 44 | 7.0 | 4 58 | 0 37 | 7.0 | 3 58 | 0 29 | 7.0 | 2 59 | 0 22 | 7.0 | 1 59 | 0 15 | 7.0 | 1 00 | 0 07 | 7.0 | 263 |
| 84 | 96 | 5 58 | 0 38 | 6.0 | 4 58 | 0 31 | 6.0 | 3 59 | 0 25 | 6.0 | 2 59 | 0 19 | 6.0 | 1 59 | 0 13 | 6.0 | 1 00 | 0 06 | 6.0 | 264 |
| 85 | 95 | 5 58 | 0 31 | 5.0 | 4 58 | 0 26 | 5.0 | 3 59 | 0 21 | 5.0 | 2 59 | 0 16 | 5.0 | 2 00 | 0 10 | 5.0 | 1 00 | 0 05 | 5.0 | 265 |
| 86 | 94 | 5 59 | 0 25 | 4.0 | 4 59 | 0 21 | 4.0 | 3 59 | 0 17 | 4.0 | 3 00 | 0 13 | 4.0 | 2 00 | 0 08 | 4.0 | 1 00 | 0 04 | 4.0 | 266 |
| 87 | 93 | 6 00 | 0 19 | 3.0 | 5 00 | 0 16 | 3.0 | 4 00 | 0 13 | 3.0 | 3 00 | 0 09 | 3.0 | 2 00 | 0 06 | 3.0 | 1 00 | 0 03 | 3.0 | 267 |
| 88 | 92 | 6 00 | 0 13 | 2.0 | 5 00 | 0 10 | 2.0 | 4 00 | 0 08 | 2.0 | 3 00 | 0 06 | 2.0 | 2 00 | 0 04 | 2.0 | 1 00 | 0 02 | 2.0 | 268 |
| 89 | 91 | 6 00 | 0 06 | 1.0 | 5 00 | 0 05 | 1.0 | 4 00 | 0 04 | 1.0 | 3 00 | 0 03 | 1.0 | 2 00 | 0 02 | 1.0 | 1 00 | 0 01 | 1.0 | 269 |
| 90 | 90 | 6 00 | 0 00 | 0.0 | 5 00 | 0 00 | 0.0 | 4 00 | 0 00 | 0.0 | 3 00 | 0 00 | 0.0 | 2 00 | 0 00 | 0.0 | 1 00 | 0 00 | 0.0 | 270 |

N. Lat: for LHA > 180° … Zₙ = Z
for LHA < 180° … Zₙ = 360° − Z

S. Lat: for LHA > 180° … Zₙ = 180° − Z
for LHA < 180° … Zₙ = 180° + Z

**AUXILIARY TABLE**

Sign for $corr_2$ for A'. → − A'. ← + A'.

Sign of $corr_1$ for F'. *Reverse sign if F > 90°.*

| Z₂ | □/30 | 29/31 | 28/32 | 27/33 | 26/34 | 25/35 | 24/36 | 23/37 | 22/38 | 21/39 | 20/40 | 19/41 | 18/42 | 17/43 | 16/44 | 15/45 | 14/46 | 13/47 | 12/48 | 11/49 | 10/50 | 9/51 | 8/52 | 7/53 | 6/54 | 5/55 | 4/56 | 3/57 | 2/58 | 1/59 | P° |
|---|---|---|---|---|---|---|---|---|---|---|---|---|---|---|---|---|---|---|---|---|---|---|---|---|---|---|---|---|---|---|---|
| 89 | ~ | ~ | ~ | ~ | ~ | ~ | ~ | ~ | ~ | ~ | ~ | ~ | ~ | ~ | ~ | ~ | ~ | ~ | ~ | ~ | ~ | ~ | ~ | ~ | ~ | ~ | ~ | ~ | ~ | ~ | 1 |
| 88 | 1 | 1 | 0 | 0 | 0 | 0 | 0 | 0 | 0 | 0 | 0 | 0 | 0 | 0 | 0 | 0 | 0 | 0 | 0 | 0 | 0 | 0 | 0 | 0 | 0 | 0 | 0 | 0 | 0 | 0 | 2 |
| 87 | 1 | 1 | 1 | 1 | 1 | 1 | 1 | 1 | 1 | 1 | 1 | 1 | 1 | 1 | 1 | 1 | 0 | 0 | 0 | 0 | 0 | 0 | 0 | 0 | 0 | 0 | 0 | 0 | 0 | 0 | 3 |
| 86 | 2 | 2 | 1 | 1 | 1 | 1 | 1 | 1 | 1 | 1 | 1 | 1 | 1 | 1 | 1 | 1 | 1 | 1 | 1 | 1 | 1 | 0 | 0 | 0 | 0 | 0 | 0 | 0 | 0 | 0 | 4 |
| 85 | 2 | 2 | 2 | 2 | 2 | 2 | 2 | 2 | 2 | 2 | 2 | 2 | 2 | 1 | 1 | 1 | 1 | 1 | 1 | 1 | 1 | 1 | 1 | 0 | 0 | 0 | 0 | 0 | 0 | 0 | 5 |
| 84 | 3 | 3 | 2 | 2 | 2 | 2 | 2 | 2 | 2 | 2 | 2 | 2 | 2 | 2 | 2 | 2 | 1 | 1 | 1 | 1 | 1 | 1 | 1 | 1 | 1 | 1 | 0 | 0 | 0 | 0 | 6 |
| 83 | 3 | 3 | 3 | 3 | 3 | 3 | 3 | 2 | 2 | 2 | 2 | 2 | 2 | 2 | 2 | 2 | 2 | 1 | 1 | 1 | 1 | 1 | 1 | 1 | 1 | 1 | 0 | 0 | 0 | 0 | 7 |
| 82 | 4 | 4 | 3 | 3 | 3 | 3 | 3 | 3 | 3 | 3 | 2 | 2 | 2 | 2 | 2 | 2 | 2 | 2 | 1 | 1 | 2 | 1 | 1 | 1 | 1 | 1 | 1 | 0 | 0 | 0 | 8 |
| 81 | 4 | 4 | 4 | 4 | 4 | 4 | 3 | 3 | 3 | 3 | 3 | 3 | 3 | 2 | 3 | 2 | 2 | 2 | 2 | 2 | 2 | 1 | 1 | 1 | 1 | 1 | 1 | 0 | 0 | 0 | 9 |
| 80 | 5 | 5 | 4 | 4 | 4 | 4 | 4 | 4 | 3 | 3 | 3 | 3 | 3 | 3 | 3 | 3 | 2 | 2 | 2 | 2 | 2 | 2 | 1 | 1 | 1 | 1 | 1 | 1 | 0 | 0 | 10 |
| 79 | 5 | 5 | 5 | 5 | 5 | 4 | 4 | 4 | 4 | 4 | 4 | 3 | 3 | 3 | 3 | 3 | 3 | 2 | 2 | 2 | 2 | 2 | 2 | 1 | 1 | 1 | 1 | 1 | 0 | 0 | 11 |
| 78 | 6 | 6 | 5 | 5 | 5 | 5 | 5 | 5 | 5 | 4 | 4 | 4 | 4 | 4 | 3 | 3 | 3 | 3 | 2 | 2 | 2 | 2 | 2 | 2 | 1 | 1 | 1 | 1 | 0 | 0 | 12 |
| 77 | 6 | 6 | 6 | 6 | 6 | 5 | 5 | 5 | 5 | 4 | 4 | 4 | 4 | 4 | 4 | 3 | 3 | 3 | 2 | 2 | 3 | 2 | 2 | 2 | 2 | 1 | 1 | 1 | 0 | 0 | 13 |
| 76 | 7 | 7 | 7 | 6 | 6 | 6 | 5 | 6 | 5 | 5 | 5 | 4 | 4 | 4 | 4 | 4 | 3 | 3 | 3 | 3 | 3 | 2 | 2 | 2 | 2 | 2 | 1 | 1 | 0 | 0 | 14 |
| 75 | 7 | 7 | 7 | 7 | 7 | 6 | 6 | 6 | 6 | 5 | 5 | 5 | 5 | 4 | 4 | 4 | 4 | 3 | 3 | 3 | 3 | 2 | 2 | 2 | 2 | 2 | 1 | 1 | 1 | 0 | 15 |
| 74 | 8 | 8 | 7 | 7 | 7 | 6 | 6 | 6 | 6 | 6 | 6 | 5 | 5 | 5 | 4 | 4 | 4 | 4 | 3 | 3 | 3 | 3 | 2 | 2 | 2 | 2 | 1 | 1 | 1 | 0 | 16 |
| 73 | 8 | 8 | 7 | 8 | 8 | 7 | 7 | 7 | 6 | 6 | 6 | 6 | 5 | 5 | 5 | 4 | 4 | 4 | 3 | 3 | 3 | 3 | 3 | 2 | 2 | 2 | 2 | 1 | 1 | 0 | 17 |
| 72 | 9 | 8 | 8 | 8 | 8 | 7 | 7 | 7 | 7 | 6 | 6 | 6 | 6 | 5 | 5 | 5 | 4 | 4 | 4 | 4 | 4 | 3 | 3 | 2 | 2 | 2 | 2 | 1 | 1 | 0 | 18 |
| 71 | 9 | 9 | 8 | 9 | 8 | 8 | 7 | 7 | 7 | 7 | 7 | 6 | 6 | 6 | 5 | 5 | 5 | 4 | 4 | 4 | 4 | 3 | 3 | 3 | 2 | 2 | 2 | 1 | 1 | 0 | 19 |
| 70 | 10 | 9 | 9 | 9 | 9 | 8 | 8 | 8 | 8 | 7 | 7 | 6 | 6 | 6 | 5 | 5 | 5 | 4 | 4 | 4 | 4 | 3 | 3 | 3 | 2 | 2 | 2 | 1 | 1 | 0 | 20 |
| 69 | 10 | 10 | 9 | 9 | 9 | 9 | 8 | 8 | 8 | 8 | 7 | 7 | 6 | 6 | 6 | 6 | 5 | 5 | 4 | 4 | 4 | 3 | 3 | 3 | 3 | 2 | 2 | 1 | 1 | 1 | 21 |
| 68 | 11 | 10 | 10 | 10 | 9 | 9 | 9 | 9 | 8 | 8 | 8 | 7 | 7 | 6 | 6 | 6 | 5 | 5 | 4 | 4 | 4 | 3 | 3 | 3 | 3 | 2 | 2 | 1 | 1 | 1 | 22 |
| 67 | 11 | 11 | 10 | 10 | 10 | 9 | 9 | 9 | 9 | 8 | 8 | 7 | 7 | 7 | 6 | 6 | 6 | 5 | 5 | 4 | 4 | 4 | 3 | 3 | 3 | 2 | 2 | 1 | 1 | 1 | 23 |
| 66 | 12 | 11 | 11 | 11 | 10 | 10 | 9 | 9 | 9 | 9 | 8 | 8 | 7 | 7 | 7 | 6 | 6 | 5 | 5 | 5 | 4 | 4 | 4 | 3 | 3 | 3 | 2 | 1 | 1 | 1 | 24 |
| 65 | 12 | 12 | 11 | 11 | 11 | 10 | 10 | 10 | 9 | 9 | 9 | 8 | 8 | 7 | 7 | 6 | 6 | 5 | 5 | 5 | 4 | 4 | 4 | 3 | 3 | 3 | 2 | 1 | 1 | 1 | 25 |
| 64 | 13 | 12 | 12 | 11 | 11 | 11 | 10 | 10 | 10 | 9 | 9 | 8 | 8 | 7 | 7 | 7 | 6 | 6 | 5 | 5 | 5 | 4 | 4 | 3 | 3 | 3 | 2 | 1 | 1 | 1 | 26 |
| 63 | 13 | 13 | 12 | 12 | 11 | 11 | 11 | 10 | 10 | 10 | 9 | 9 | 8 | 8 | 7 | 7 | 6 | 6 | 6 | 5 | 5 | 4 | 4 | 4 | 3 | 3 | 2 | 1 | 1 | 1 | 27 |
| 62 | 14 | 13 | 13 | 12 | 12 | 12 | 11 | 11 | 10 | 10 | 10 | 9 | 8 | 8 | 8 | 7 | 7 | 6 | 6 | 5 | 5 | 4 | 4 | 4 | 3 | 3 | 2 | 1 | 1 | 1 | 28 |
| 61 | 14 | 14 | 13 | 13 | 12 | 12 | 11 | 11 | 11 | 10 | 10 | 9 | 9 | 8 | 8 | 7 | 7 | 6 | 6 | 5 | 5 | 5 | 4 | 4 | 3 | 3 | 2 | 1 | 1 | 1 | 29 |
| 60 | 15 | 14 | 14 | 13 | 13 | 12 | 12 | 11 | 11 | 10 | 10 | 9 | 9 | 8 | 8 | 8 | 7 | 6 | 6 | 6 | 5 | 5 | 4 | 4 | 3 | 3 | 2 | 1 | 1 | 1 | 30 |
| 59 | 15 | 15 | 15 | 14 | 14 | 13 | 12 | 12 | 12 | 11 | 11 | 10 | 9 | 9 | 8 | 8 | 7 | 7 | 6 | 6 | 5 | 5 | 4 | 4 | 4 | 3 | 3 | 2 | 1 | 1 | 31 |
| 58 | 16 | 15 | 15 | 14 | 14 | 13 | 13 | 12 | 12 | 11 | 11 | 10 | 10 | 9 | 9 | 8 | 8 | 7 | 7 | 6 | 5 | 5 | 4 | 4 | 4 | 3 | 3 | 2 | 1 | 1 | 32 |
| 57 | 16 | 16 | 15 | 15 | 15 | 14 | 13 | 13 | 12 | 11 | 11 | 10 | 10 | 9 | 9 | 8 | 8 | 7 | 7 | 6 | 6 | 5 | 5 | 4 | 4 | 3 | 3 | 2 | 1 | 1 | 33 |
| 56 | 17 | 16 | 16 | 15 | 15 | 14 | 14 | 13 | 12 | 12 | 11 | 11 | 10 | 10 | 9 | 9 | 8 | 7 | 7 | 6 | 6 | 5 | 5 | 4 | 4 | 3 | 3 | 2 | 1 | 1 | 34 |
| 55 | 17 | 17 | 16 | 15 | 15 | 14 | 14 | 13 | 13 | 12 | 12 | 11 | 10 | 10 | 9 | 9 | 8 | 7 | 7 | 6 | 6 | 5 | 5 | 4 | 4 | 3 | 3 | 2 | 1 | 1 | 35 |
| 54 | 18 | 17 | 16 | 16 | 15 | 15 | 14 | 14 | 13 | 12 | 12 | 11 | 11 | 10 | 9 | 9 | 8 | 8 | 7 | 6 | 6 | 5 | 5 | 4 | 4 | 3 | 3 | 2 | 1 | 1 | 36 |
| 53 | 18 | 17 | 17 | 16 | 16 | 15 | 14 | 14 | 13 | 13 | 12 | 12 | 11 | 11 | 10 | 9 | 8 | 8 | 7 | 7 | 6 | 5 | 5 | 4 | 4 | 3 | 3 | 2 | 1 | 1 | 37 |
| 52 | 18 | 18 | 17 | 17 | 16 | 15 | 15 | 14 | 14 | 13 | 13 | 12 | 11 | 11 | 10 | 9 | 9 | 8 | 8 | 7 | 6 | 5 | 5 | 4 | 4 | 3 | 3 | 2 | 1 | 1 | 38 |
| 51 | 19 | 18 | 18 | 17 | 16 | 16 | 15 | 14 | 14 | 13 | 13 | 12 | 11 | 11 | 10 | 9 | 9 | 8 | 8 | 7 | 6 | 6 | 5 | 4 | 4 | 3 | 3 | 2 | 1 | 1 | 39 |
| 50 | 19 | 19 | 18 | 17 | 17 | 16 | 15 | 15 | 14 | 13 | 13 | 12 | 12 | 11 | 10 | 10 | 9 | 8 | 8 | 7 | 6 | 6 | 5 | 4 | 4 | 3 | 3 | 2 | 1 | 1 | 40 |

F': + / −

For $Z_2 < 10°$, use $10°$

| $Z_2°$ | $P°$ | □ / 30 | 29 / 31 | 28 / 32 | 27 / 33 | 26 / 34 | 25 / 35 | 24 / 36 | 23 / 37 | 22 / 38 | 21 / 39 | 20 / 40 | 19 / 41 | 18 / 42 | 17 / 43 | 16 / 44 | 15 / 45 | 14 / 46 | 13 / 47 | 12 / 48 | 11 / 49 | 10 / 50 | 9 / 51 | 8 / 52 | 7 / 53 | 6 / 54 | 5 / 55 | 4 / 56 | 3 / 57 | 2 / 58 | 1 / 59 |
|---|---|---|---|---|---|---|---|---|---|---|---|---|---|---|---|---|---|---|---|---|---|---|---|---|---|---|---|---|---|---|---|
| 49 | 41 | 20 | 19 | 18 | 18 | 17 | 16 | 16 | 15 | 14 | 14 | 13 | 12 | 12 | 11 | 10 | 10 | 9 | 9 | 8 | 7 | 7 | 6 | 5 | 5 | 4 | 3 | 3 | 2 | 1 | 1 |
| 48 | 42 | 20 | 19 | 19 | 18 | 17 | 17 | 16 | 15 | 15 | 14 | 13 | 13 | 12 | 11 | 11 | 10 | 9 | 9 | 8 | 7 | 7 | 6 | 5 | 5 | 4 | 3 | 3 | 2 | 1 | 1 |
| 47 | 43 | 20 | 20 | 19 | 18 | 18 | 17 | 16 | 16 | 15 | 14 | 14 | 13 | 12 | 12 | 11 | 10 | 10 | 9 | 8 | 8 | 7 | 6 | 5 | 5 | 4 | 3 | 3 | 2 | 1 | 1 |
| 46 | 44 | 21 | 20 | 19 | 19 | 18 | 17 | 17 | 16 | 15 | 15 | 14 | 13 | 12 | 12 | 11 | 10 | 10 | 9 | 8 | 8 | 7 | 6 | 6 | 5 | 4 | 3 | 3 | 2 | 1 | 1 |
| 45 | 45 | 21 | 21 | 20 | 19 | 18 | 18 | 17 | 16 | 16 | 15 | 14 | 13 | 13 | 12 | 11 | 11 | 10 | 9 | 8 | 8 | 7 | 6 | 6 | 5 | 4 | 4 | 3 | 2 | 1 | 1 |
| 44 | 46 | 22 | 21 | 20 | 19 | 19 | 18 | 17 | 17 | 16 | 15 | 14 | 14 | 13 | 12 | 12 | 11 | 10 | 10 | 9 | 8 | 7 | 6 | 6 | 5 | 4 | 4 | 3 | 2 | 1 | 1 |
| 43 | 47 | 22 | 21 | 20 | 19 | 19 | 18 | 18 | 17 | 16 | 15 | 15 | 14 | 13 | 13 | 12 | 11 | 10 | 10 | 9 | 8 | 7 | 7 | 6 | 5 | 4 | 4 | 3 | 2 | 1 | 1 |
| 42 | 48 | 22 | 22 | 21 | 20 | 19 | 19 | 18 | 17 | 16 | 16 | 15 | 14 | 13 | 13 | 12 | 11 | 11 | 10 | 9 | 8 | 7 | 7 | 6 | 5 | 4 | 4 | 3 | 2 | 2 | 1 |
| 41 | 49 | 23 | 22 | 21 | 20 | 20 | 19 | 18 | 17 | 17 | 16 | 15 | 14 | 14 | 13 | 12 | 12 | 11 | 10 | 9 | 8 | 8 | 7 | 6 | 5 | 5 | 4 | 3 | 2 | 2 | 1 |
| 40 | 50 | 23 | 22 | 21 | 21 | 20 | 19 | 18 | 18 | 17 | 16 | 15 | 15 | 14 | 13 | 12 | 12 | 11 | 10 | 9 | 8 | 8 | 7 | 6 | 5 | 5 | 5 | 3 | 2 | 2 | 1 |
| 39 | 51 | 23 | 23 | 22 | 21 | 20 | 19 | 19 | 18 | 17 | 16 | 16 | 15 | 14 | 13 | 12 | 12 | 11 | 10 | 9 | 9 | 8 | 7 | 6 | 5 | 5 | 4 | 3 | 2 | 2 | 1 |
| 38 | 52 | 24 | 23 | 22 | 21 | 20 | 20 | 19 | 18 | 17 | 17 | 16 | 15 | 14 | 14 | 13 | 12 | 11 | 10 | 9 | 9 | 8 | 7 | 6 | 6 | 5 | 4 | 3 | 2 | 2 | 1 |
| 37 | 53 | 24 | 23 | 22 | 22 | 21 | 20 | 19 | 18 | 18 | 17 | 16 | 15 | 15 | 14 | 13 | 13 | 11 | 11 | 9 | 9 | 8 | 7 | 6 | 6 | 5 | 4 | 3 | 3 | 2 | 1 |
| 36 | 54 | 24 | 23 | 23 | 22 | 21 | 20 | 19 | 18 | 18 | 17 | 16 | 15 | 15 | 14 | 13 | 13 | 11 | 11 | 10 | 9 | 8 | 7 | 6 | 6 | 5 | 4 | 3 | 3 | 2 | 1 |
| 35 | 55 | 25 | 24 | 23 | 22 | 21 | 20 | 20 | 19 | 18 | 17 | 16 | 16 | 15 | 14 | 13 | 13 | 12 | 11 | 10 | 9 | 8 | 7 | 7 | 6 | 5 | 4 | 3 | 3 | 2 | 1 |
| 34 | 56 | 25 | 24 | 23 | 22 | 22 | 21 | 20 | 19 | 18 | 17 | 17 | 16 | 15 | 14 | 13 | 13 | 12 | 11 | 10 | 9 | 8 | 7 | 7 | 6 | 5 | 4 | 3 | 3 | 2 | 1 |
| 33 | 57 | 25 | 24 | 23 | 23 | 22 | 21 | 20 | 20 | 18 | 18 | 17 | 16 | 15 | 14 | 13 | 13 | 12 | 11 | 10 | 9 | 8 | 8 | 7 | 6 | 5 | 4 | 4 | 3 | 2 | 1 |
| 32 | 58 | 25 | 25 | 24 | 23 | 22 | 21 | 21 | 20 | 19 | 18 | 17 | 16 | 15 | 15 | 13 | 13 | 12 | 11 | 10 | 9 | 8 | 8 | 7 | 6 | 5 | 4 | 4 | 3 | 2 | 1 |
| 31 | 59 | 26 | 25 | 24 | 23 | 22 | 21 | 21 | 20 | 19 | 18 | 17 | 16 | 15 | 15 | 14 | 13 | 12 | 11 | 10 | 9 | 8 | 8 | 7 | 6 | 5 | 4 | 4 | 3 | 2 | 1 |
| 30 | 60 | 26 | 25 | 24 | 23 | 23 | 22 | 21 | 20 | 19 | 18 | 17 | 16 | 16 | 15 | 14 | 14 | 13 | 11 | 10 | 10 | 8 | 8 | 7 | 6 | 5 | 5 | 4 | 3 | 2 | 1 |
| 29 | 61 | 26 | 26 | 24 | 24 | 23 | 22 | 21 | 20 | 19 | 18 | 17 | 17 | 16 | 15 | 13 | 13 | 12 | 11 | 10 | 10 | 9 | 8 | 7 | 6 | 5 | 5 | 4 | 3 | 2 | 1 |
| 28 | 62 | 26 | 26 | 25 | 24 | 23 | 22 | 21 | 20 | 19 | 19 | 18 | 17 | 16 | 15 | 13 | 13 | 12 | 12 | 10 | 10 | 9 | 8 | 7 | 6 | 6 | 5 | 4 | 3 | 2 | 1 |
| 27 | 63 | 27 | 26 | 25 | 24 | 23 | 22 | 21 | 21 | 20 | 19 | 18 | 17 | 16 | 15 | 14 | 14 | 13 | 12 | 11 | 10 | 9 | 8 | 7 | 6 | 6 | 5 | 4 | 3 | 2 | 1 |
| 26 | 64 | 27 | 26 | 25 | 24 | 24 | 23 | 22 | 21 | 20 | 19 | 18 | 17 | 16 | 15 | 15 | 14 | 13 | 12 | 11 | 10 | 9 | 8 | 7 | 6 | 6 | 5 | 4 | 3 | 2 | 1 |
| 25 | 65 | 27 | 27 | 25 | 24 | 24 | 23 | 22 | 21 | 20 | 19 | 18 | 17 | 16 | 15 | 15 | 14 | 13 | 12 | 11 | 10 | 9 | 8 | 7 | 6 | 6 | 5 | 4 | 3 | 2 | 1 |
| 24 | 66 | 27 | 27 | 26 | 25 | 24 | 23 | 22 | 21 | 20 | 19 | 18 | 17 | 16 | 16 | 15 | 14 | 13 | 12 | 11 | 10 | 9 | 8 | 7 | 6 | 6 | 5 | 4 | 3 | 2 | 1 |
| 23 | 67 | 28 | 27 | 26 | 25 | 24 | 23 | 22 | 21 | 20 | 19 | 19 | 18 | 17 | 16 | 15 | 14 | 13 | 12 | 11 | 10 | 9 | 8 | 7 | 6 | 6 | 5 | 4 | 3 | 2 | 1 |
| 22 | 68 | 28 | 27 | 26 | 25 | 24 | 23 | 22 | 21 | 21 | 19 | 19 | 18 | 17 | 16 | 15 | 14 | 13 | 12 | 11 | 10 | 9 | 8 | 7 | 6 | 6 | 5 | 4 | 3 | 2 | 1 |
| 21 | 69 | 28 | 28 | 26 | 25 | 24 | 23 | 22 | 21 | 21 | 20 | 19 | 18 | 17 | 16 | 15 | 14 | 13 | 12 | 11 | 10 | 9 | 8 | 7 | 6 | 6 | 5 | 4 | 3 | 2 | 1 |
| 20 | 70 | 28 | 28 | 26 | 25 | 24 | 23 | 23 | 22 | 21 | 20 | 19 | 18 | 17 | 16 | 15 | 14 | 13 | 12 | 11 | 10 | 9 | 8 | 8 | 7 | 6 | 5 | 4 | 3 | 2 | 1 |
| 19 | 71 | 28 | 28 | 26 | 26 | 25 | 24 | 23 | 22 | 21 | 20 | 19 | 18 | 17 | 16 | 15 | 14 | 13 | 13 | 11 | 10 | 10 | 9 | 7 | 7 | 6 | 5 | 4 | 3 | 2 | 1 |
| 18 | 72 | 29 | 28 | 27 | 26 | 25 | 24 | 23 | 22 | 21 | 20 | 19 | 18 | 18 | 16 | 15 | 14 | 13 | 13 | 11 | 11 | 10 | 9 | 8 | 7 | 6 | 5 | 4 | 3 | 2 | 1 |
| 17 | 73 | 29 | 28 | 27 | 26 | 25 | 24 | 23 | 22 | 21 | 20 | 19 | 18 | 18 | 16 | 15 | 14 | 13 | 13 | 11 | 11 | 10 | 9 | 8 | 7 | 6 | 5 | 4 | 3 | 2 | 1 |
| 16 | 74 | 29 | 28 | 27 | 26 | 25 | 24 | 23 | 22 | 21 | 20 | 19 | 18 | 18 | 16 | 15 | 14 | 13 | 13 | 11 | 11 | 10 | 9 | 8 | 7 | 6 | 5 | 4 | 3 | 2 | 1 |
| 15 | 75 | 29 | 28 | 27 | 26 | 25 | 24 | 23 | 22 | 21 | 20 | 19 | 18 | 18 | 16 | 15 | 14 | 13 | 13 | 12 | 11 | 10 | 9 | 8 | 7 | 6 | 5 | 4 | 3 | 2 | 1 |
| 14 | 76 | 29 | 28 | 27 | 26 | 25 | 24 | 23 | 22 | 21 | 20 | 19 | 18 | 17 | 16 | 16 | 15 | 14 | 13 | 12 | 11 | 10 | 9 | 8 | 7 | 6 | 5 | 4 | 3 | 2 | 1 |
| 13 | 77 | 29 | 28 | 27 | 26 | 25 | 24 | 23 | 22 | 21 | 21 | 19 | 19 | 18 | 17 | 16 | 15 | 14 | 13 | 12 | 11 | 10 | 9 | 8 | 7 | 6 | 5 | 4 | 3 | 2 | 1 |
| 12 | 78 | 29 | 28 | 27 | 26 | 25 | 25 | 23 | 22 | 22 | 21 | 20 | 19 | 18 | 17 | 16 | 15 | 14 | 13 | 12 | 11 | 10 | 9 | 8 | 7 | 6 | 5 | 4 | 3 | 2 | 1 |
| 11 | 79 | 30 | 29 | 27 | 27 | 26 | 25 | 24 | 23 | 22 | 21 | 20 | 19 | 18 | 17 | 16 | 15 | 14 | 13 | 12 | 11 | 10 | 9 | 8 | 7 | 6 | 5 | 4 | 3 | 2 | 1 |
| 10 | 80 | 30 | 29 | 28 | 27 | 26 | 25 | 24 | 23 | 22 | 21 | 20 | 19 | 18 | 17 | 16 | 15 | 14 | 13 | 12 | 11 | 10 | 9 | 8 | 7 | 6 | 5 | 4 | 3 | 2 | 1 |

Left axis: $-/+$ $A'$ (with $Z_2°$); bottom axis: $F'$ $+/-$ (with $P°$)

For $P > 80°$, use $80°$

### USE OF CONCISE SIGHT REDUCTION TABLES (continued)

4. *Example.* (b) Required the altitude and azimuth of *Vega* on 2022 July 29 at UT $04^h$ $49^m$ from the estimated position S 15°, W 152°.

1. Assumed latitude            $Lat =$   15° S
   From the almanac         $GHA =$   99°  39′
   Assumed longitude           151°  39′ W
   Local hour angle          $LHA =$   308

2. Reduction table, 1st entry
   $(Lat, LHA) = (15, 308)$      $A =$    49   34    $A° = 50, A' = 34$
                                  $B =$ +66   29    $Z_1 = +71{\cdot}7,$                 $LHA > 270°$

3. From the almanac         $Dec =$ −38   48                 *Lat* and *Dec* contrary
   Sum $= B + Dec$        $F =$ +27   41    $F° = 28, F' = 41$

4. Reduction table, 2nd entry
   $(A°, F°) = (50, 28)$        $H =$    17   34    $P° = 37$
                                            $Z_2 = 67{\cdot}8, Z_2° = 68$

5. Auxiliary table, 1st entry
   $(F', P°) = (41, 37)$       $corr_1 =$      −11           $F < 90°, \ F' > 29'$
   Sum                                   17   23

6. Auxiliary table, 2nd entry
   $(A', Z_2°) = (34, 68)$      $corr_2 =$      +10              $A' > 30'$

7. Sum = computed altitude    $H_C = +17°$   33′              $F > 0°$

8. Azimuth,   first component    $Z_1 = +71{\cdot}7$           same sign as $B$
             second component    $Z_2 = +67{\cdot}8$          $F < 90°, \ F > 0°$
   Sum = azimuth angle       $Z =$   139·5

   True azimuth                  $Z_n =$   040°            S *Lat*, $LHA > 180°$

5. *Form for use with the Concise Sight Reduction Tables.* The form on the following page lays out the procedure explained on pages 284-285. Each step is shown, with notes and rules to ensure accuracy, rather than speed, throughout the calculation. The form is mainly intended for the calculation of star positions. It therefore includes the formation of the Greenwich hour of Aries (*GHA* Aries), and thus the Greenwich hour angle of the star (*GHA*) from its tabular sidereal hour angle (*SHA*). These calculations, included in step 1 of the form, can easily be replaced by the interpolation of *GHA* and *Dec* for the Sun, Moon or planets.

The form may be freely copied; however, acknowledgement of the source is requested.

| Date & UT of observation | | Body | Estimated Latitude & Longitude |
|---|---|---|---|
| h     m     s | | | °     ′     °     ′ |

| Step | Calculate Altitude & Azimuth | Summary of Rules & Notes |
|---|---|---|
| Assumed latitude | $Lat =$ ° | Nearest estimated latitude, integral number of degrees. |
| Assumed longitude | $Long =$ ° ′ | Choose $Long$ so that $LHA$ has integral number of degrees. |
| **1.** From the almanac: | $Dec =$ ° ′ | Record the $Dec$ for use in Step 3. |
| $GHA$ Aries $^h$ | $=$ ° ! | Needed if using $SHA$. Tabular value. |
| Increment $^m$ $^s$ | $=$ ° ! | for minutes and seconds of time. |
| $SHA$ | $SHA =$ ° ! | |
| $GHA = GHA\ Aries + SHA$ | $GHA =$ ° ′ | Remove multiples of 360°. |
| Assumed longitude | $Long =$ ° ′ | West longitudes are negative. |
| $LHA = GHA + Long$ | $LHA =$ ° | Remove multiples of 360°. |
| **2.** Reduction table, $1^{st}$ entry $(Lat, LHA) = ($ °, °$)$ record $A$, $B$ and $Z_1$. | $A =$ ° ′  $A° -$ ° | nearest whole degree of $A$. |
| | $A' =$ ′ | minutes part of $A$. |
| | $B =$ ° ′ | $B$ is minus if $90° < LHA < 270°$. |
| | $Z_1 =$ ° | $Z_1$ has the same sign as $B$. |
| **3.** From step 1 | $Dec =$ ° ′ | $Dec$ is minus if contrary to $Lat$. |
| $F = B + Dec$ | $F =$ ° ′ | Regard $F$ as positive until step 7. |
| | $F° =$ ° | nearest whole degree of $F$. |
| | $F' =$ ′ | minutes part of $F$. |
| **4.** Reduction table, $2^{nd}$ entry $(A°, F°) = ($ °, °$)$ record $H$, $P$ and $Z_2$. | $H -$ ° ′  $P° =$ ° | nearest whole degree of $P$. |
| | $Z_2 =$ ° | |
| **5.** Auxiliary table, $1^{st}$ entry $(F', P°) = ($ ′, °$)$ record $corr_1$ | $corr_1 =$ ′ | $corr_1$ is minus if $F < 90°$ & $F' > 29'$, or if $F > 90°$ & $F' < 30'$. |
| **6.** Auxiliary table, $2^{nd}$ entry $(A', Z_2°) = ($ ′, °$)$ record $corr_2$ | $corr_2 =$ ′ | $Z_2°$ nearest whole degree of $Z_2$. $corr_2$ is minus if $A' < 30'$. |
| **7.** Calculated altitude $=$ $H_c = H + corr_1 + corr_2$ | $H_c =$ ° ′ | $H_c$ is minus if $F$ is negative, and object is below the horizon. |
| **8.** Azimuth, $1^{st}$ component | $Z_1 =$ ° | $Z_1$ has the same sign as $B$. |
| $2^{nd}$ component | $Z_2 =$ ° | $Z_2$ is minus if $F > 90°$. If $F$ is negative, $Z_2 = 180° - Z_2$ |
| $Z = Z_1 + Z_2$ | $Z =$ ° | Ignore the sign of $Z$. |
| | | N $Lat$: If $LHA > 180°$, $Z_n = Z$, or if $LHA < 180°$, $Z_n = 360° - Z$, |
| | | S $Lat$: If $LHA > 180°$, $Z_n = 180° - Z$, or if $LHA < 180°$, $Z_n = 180° + Z$. |
| True azimuth | $Z_n =$ ° | |

For use with *The Nautical Almanac's* Concise Sight Reduction Tables pages 284-318.

# POLAR PHENOMENA

## EXPLANATION

1. *Introduction.* The graphs on pages 322-325 give data concerning the rising and setting of the Sun and Moon and the duration of civil twilight for high latitudes. Graphs are given instead of tables for high latitudes because they give a clearer picture of the phenomena and of the attainable accuracy in any given case. In the regions of the graph that are difficult to read accurately, the phenomenon itself is generally uncertain.

2. *Semiduration of sunlight.* The graphs for the semiduration of sunlight (page 322) give for latitudes north of N 65° the number of hours from sunrise to meridian passage or from meridian passage to sunset. There is continuous daylight in an area marked "Sun above horizon", and no direct sunlight in an area marked "Sun below horizon". The figures near the top indicate, for several convenient dates, the local mean times of meridian passage; with the aid of the intermediate dots the LMT on any given day may be obtained to the nearest minute. The LMT of sunrise may be found by subtracting the semiduration from the time of meridian passage, and the time of sunset by adding. The equation of time is given by subtracting the time of meridian passage from noon.

*Examples.* (a) Estimate the time of sunrise and sunset on 2022 March 10 at latitude N 77°. The semiduration of sunlight (page 322) is about $5^h 00^m$. The time of meridian passage is $12^h 10^m$, and hence the LMT of sunrise is $07^h 10^m$, and of sunset $17^h 10^m$. (b) Estimate the dates, for the first half of 2022, when the Sun is continuously below and above the horizon at latitude N 80°. The semiduration of sunlight graph (page 322) indicates the Sun is continuously below the horizon until about February 21, and is continuously above the horizon after April 14.

3. *Duration of civil twilight.* The graphs for the duration of twilight (page 322) give the interval from the beginning of morning civil twilight (Sun 6° below the horizon) to the time of sunrise or from the time of sunset to the end of evening civil twilight. In a region marked "No twilight or sunlight", the Sun is continuously below the horizon by more than 6°. In a region marked "Continuous twilight or sunlight", the Sun never goes lower than 6° below the horizon.

Adjacent to a region marked "No twilight or sunlight" is a region in which the Sun is continuously below the horizon, but so near to the horizon during a portion of the day that there is twilight. This area is the shaded region. The value given by the graph in this shaded region is the interval from the beginning of morning twilight to meridian passage of the Sun, or from meridian passage to the end of evening twilight, the total duration of twilight being twice the value given by the graph. The border between this shaded region and the remainder of the graph indicates that the Sun only just rises at meridian passage at the date and latitude shown. The remainder of the graph gives the total duration of civil twilight.

*Examples.* (a) Estimate the time of the beginning of morning civil twilight at latitude N 77° on 2022 March 10. The duration of twilight (page 322) is about $1^h 35^m$. Applying this to the time of sunrise, $07^h 10^m$, found in the preceding example, the beginning of morning civil twilight is $05^h 35^m$ LMT. (b) Estimate, for the first half of 2022, the limiting dates of civil twilight and sunlight at latitude N 80°. The graphs (page 322) indicate there is no sunlight or twilight till about February 5, there is twilight but no sunlight from February 5 until February 21, sunlight and twilight till March 31, continuous twilight or sunlight till April 14, and then continuous sunlight. (c) Estimate the time of the beginning and end of civil twilight on 2022 February 14 at latitude N 80°. The graph (page 322) indicates there is no direct sunlight at this date and latitude, but three hours of twilight before and after meridian passage occurring at $12^h 14^m$. Thus civil twilight begins at about $09^h 14^m$ and ends at about $15^h 14^m$ LMT.

4. *Semiduration of moonlight*  The graphs, for each month, for the semiduration of moonlight give for the Moon the same data as the graphs for the semiduration of sunlight give for the Sun. The scale near the top gives the LMT of meridian passage. In addition, the phase symbols are placed on the graphs to show the day on which each phase occurs. Since the times of meridian passage and the semiduration change more rapidly from day to day for the Moon than for the Sun, special care will be required in reading the graphs accurately.

For most purposes, in these high latitudes, a rough idea of the time of moonrise or moonset is all that is required, and this may be obtained by a glance at the graph.

*Example*. Estimate the moon phase and the time of moonrise and moonset on 2022 January 25 at latitude N 73°. The phase is found from pages 323-325 to be near last quarter, and the Moon crosses the meridian at $06^h$ LMT. The semiduration of moonlight taken for the time of meridian passage is 4 hours, giving moonrise at $02^h$ LMT on January 25 and moonset at $10^h$ on January 25.

If greater accuracy is required, it is necessary to read the graph for the UT of each phenomenon at the desired meridian. The dates indicated on the graph are for $00^h$ UT, and intermediate values of the UT may be located by estimation.

*Example*. Required to improve the results obtained in the preceding example, assuming the observer to be in longitude W 90° ($6^h$) west.

The values found previously were:

|  |  |  | d | h |  |  |  | d | h |  |
|---|---|---|---|---|---|---|---|---|---|---|
| Time of meridian passage | 2022 | Jan. | 25 | 06 | LMT | = | Jan. | 25 | 12 | UT |
| Semiduration of moonlight |  |  |  | 4 |  |  |  |  |  |  |
| Time of moonrise |  | Jan. | 25 | 02 | LMT | = | Jan. | 25 | 08 | UT |
| Time of moonset |  | Jan. | 25 | 10 | LMT | = | Jan. | 25 | 16 | UT |

Returning to the graphs (pages 323-325) with these three values of the UT, the following results are obtained:

|  |  |  | d | h | m |  |  |  | d | h | m |  |
|---|---|---|---|---|---|---|---|---|---|---|---|---|
| Time of meridian passage | 2022 | Jan. | 25 | 06 | 10 | LMT | = | Jan. | 25 | 12 | 10 | UT |
| Semiduration for moonrise |  |  |  | 03 | 50 |  |  |  |  |  |  |  |
| Time of moonrise |  | Jan. | 25 | 02 | 20 | LMT | = | Jan. | 25 | 08 | 20 | UT |
| Semiduration for moonset |  |  |  | 03 | 20 |  |  |  |  |  |  |  |
| Time of moonset |  | Jan. | 25 | 09 | 30 | LMT | = | Jan. | 25 | 15 | 30 | UT |

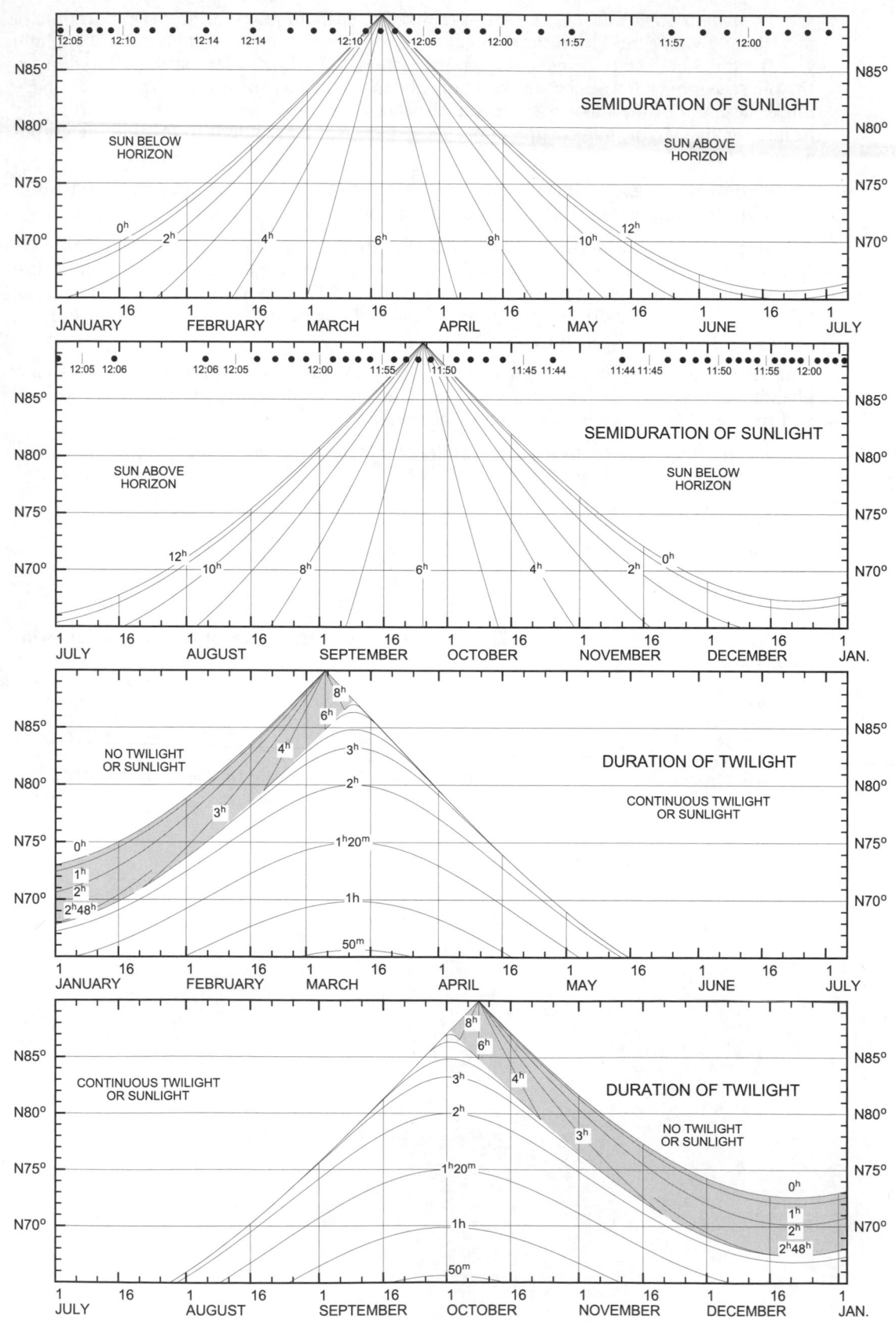

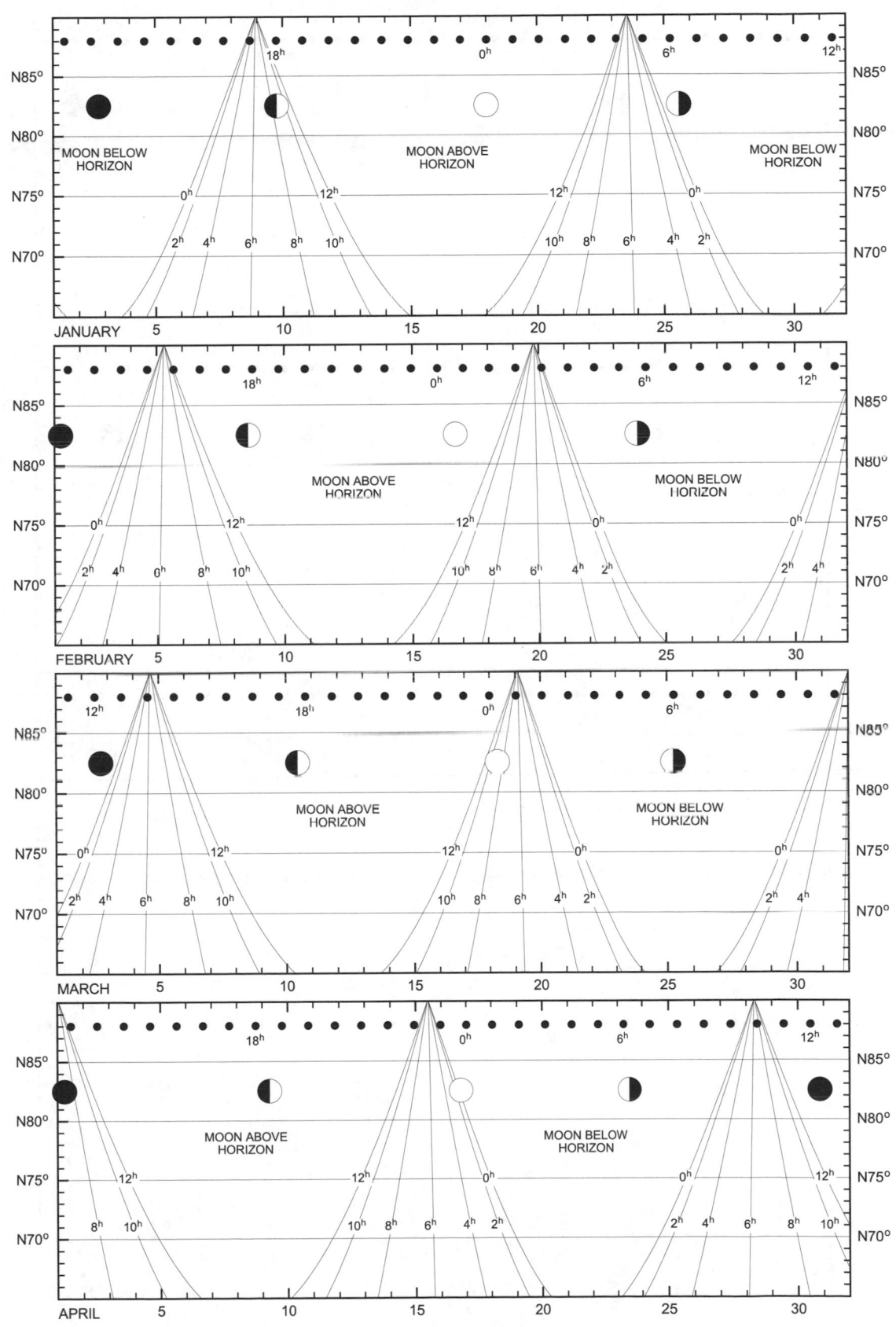

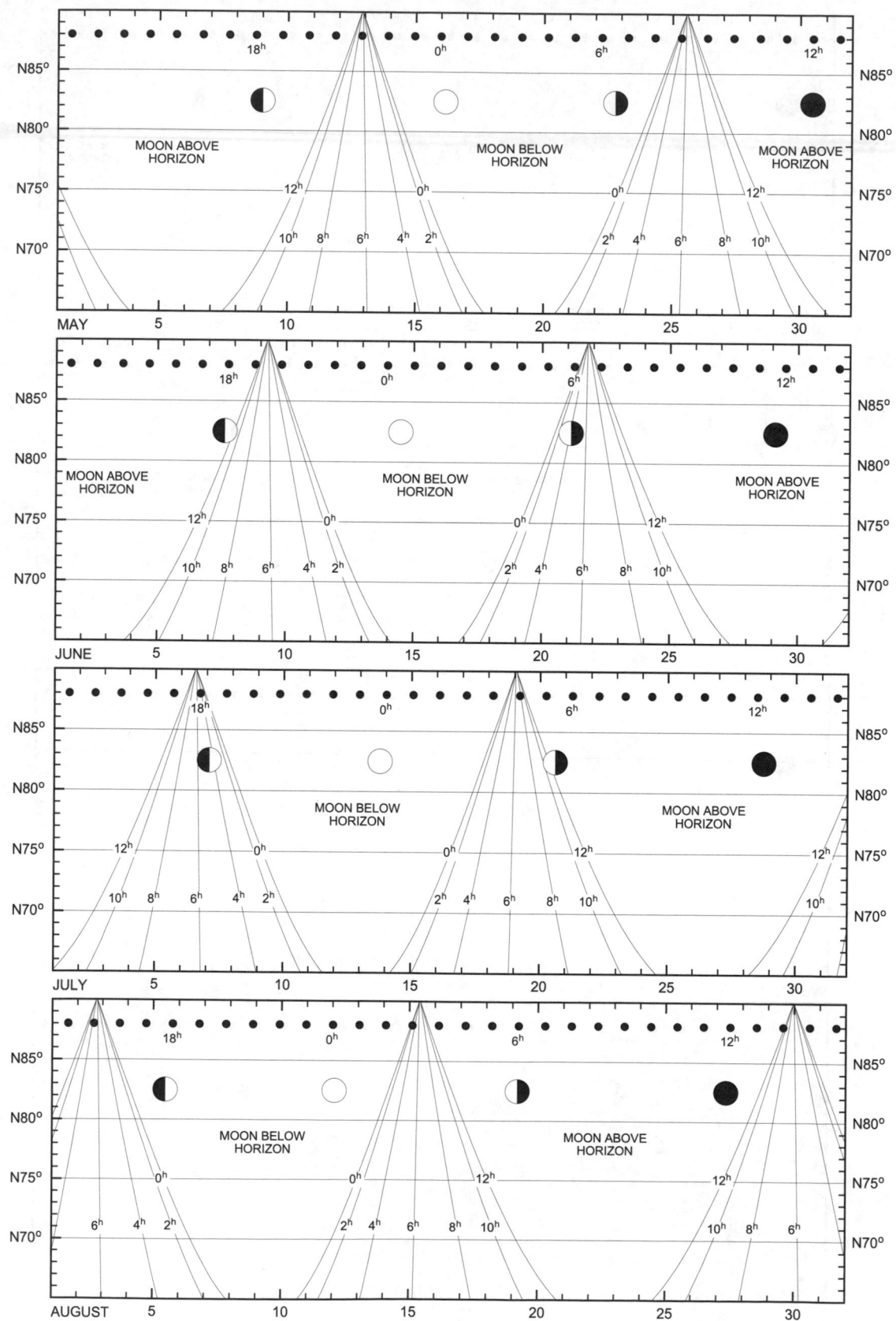

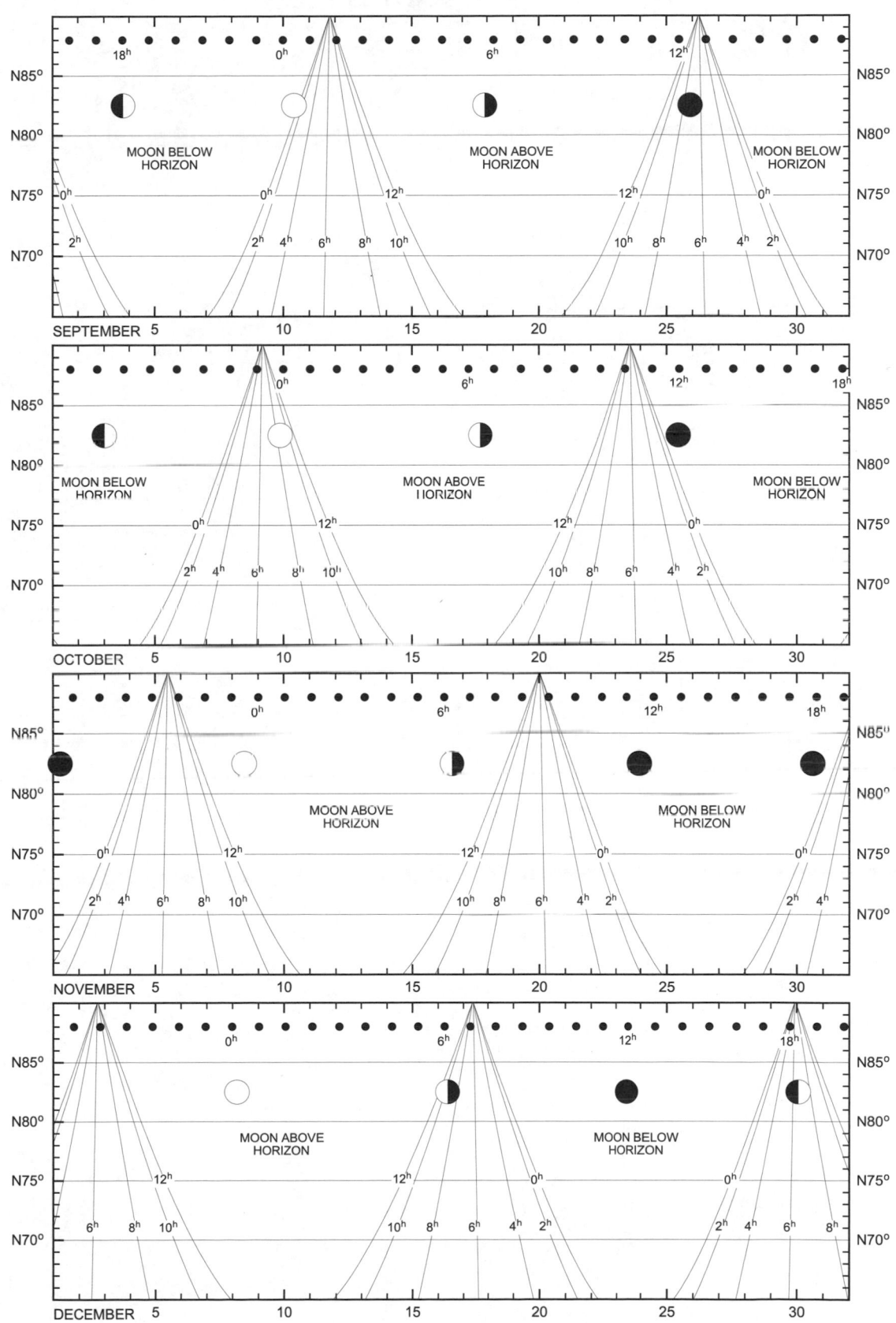

# NOTES

# CONVERSION OF ARC TO TIME

| 0°–59° | h m | 60°–119° | h m | 120°–179° | h m | 180°–239° | h m | 240°–299° | h m | 300°–359° | h m | ′ | 0′.00 m s | 0′.25 m s | 0′.50 m s | 0′.75 m s |
|---|---|---|---|---|---|---|---|---|---|---|---|---|---|---|---|---|
| 0 | 0 00 | 60 | 4 00 | 120 | 8 00 | 180 | 12 00 | 240 | 16 00 | 300 | 20 00 | 0 | 0 00 | 0 01 | 0 02 | 0 03 |
| 1 | 0 04 | 61 | 4 04 | 121 | 8 04 | 181 | 12 04 | 241 | 16 04 | 301 | 20 04 | 1 | 0 04 | 0 05 | 0 06 | 0 07 |
| 2 | 0 08 | 62 | 4 08 | 122 | 8 08 | 182 | 12 08 | 242 | 16 08 | 302 | 20 08 | 2 | 0 08 | 0 09 | 0 10 | 0 11 |
| 3 | 0 12 | 63 | 4 12 | 123 | 8 12 | 183 | 12 12 | 243 | 16 12 | 303 | 20 12 | 3 | 0 12 | 0 13 | 0 14 | 0 15 |
| 4 | 0 16 | 64 | 4 16 | 124 | 8 16 | 184 | 12 16 | 244 | 16 16 | 304 | 20 16 | 4 | 0 16 | 0 17 | 0 18 | 0 19 |
| 5 | 0 20 | 65 | 4 20 | 125 | 8 20 | 185 | 12 20 | 245 | 16 20 | 305 | 20 20 | 5 | 0 20 | 0 21 | 0 22 | 0 23 |
| 6 | 0 24 | 66 | 4 24 | 126 | 8 24 | 186 | 12 24 | 246 | 16 24 | 306 | 20 24 | 6 | 0 24 | 0 25 | 0 26 | 0 27 |
| 7 | 0 28 | 67 | 4 28 | 127 | 8 28 | 187 | 12 28 | 247 | 16 28 | 307 | 20 28 | 7 | 0 28 | 0 29 | 0 30 | 0 31 |
| 8 | 0 32 | 68 | 4 32 | 128 | 8 32 | 188 | 12 32 | 248 | 16 32 | 308 | 20 32 | 8 | 0 32 | 0 33 | 0 34 | 0 35 |
| 9 | 0 36 | 69 | 4 36 | 129 | 8 36 | 189 | 12 36 | 249 | 16 36 | 309 | 20 36 | 9 | 0 36 | 0 37 | 0 38 | 0 39 |
| 10 | 0 40 | 70 | 4 40 | 130 | 8 40 | 190 | 12 40 | 250 | 16 40 | 310 | 20 40 | 10 | 0 40 | 0 41 | 0 42 | 0 43 |
| 11 | 0 44 | 71 | 4 44 | 131 | 8 44 | 191 | 12 44 | 251 | 16 44 | 311 | 20 44 | 11 | 0 44 | 0 45 | 0 46 | 0 47 |
| 12 | 0 48 | 72 | 4 48 | 132 | 8 48 | 192 | 12 48 | 252 | 16 48 | 312 | 20 48 | 12 | 0 48 | 0 49 | 0 50 | 0 51 |
| 13 | 0 52 | 73 | 4 52 | 133 | 8 52 | 193 | 12 52 | 253 | 16 52 | 313 | 20 52 | 13 | 0 52 | 0 53 | 0 54 | 0 55 |
| 14 | 0 56 | 74 | 4 56 | 134 | 8 56 | 194 | 12 56 | 254 | 16 56 | 314 | 20 56 | 14 | 0 56 | 0 57 | 0 58 | 0 59 |
| 15 | 1 00 | 75 | 5 00 | 135 | 9 00 | 195 | 13 00 | 255 | 17 00 | 315 | 21 00 | 15 | 1 00 | 1 01 | 1 02 | 1 03 |
| 16 | 1 04 | 76 | 5 04 | 136 | 9 04 | 196 | 13 04 | 256 | 17 04 | 316 | 21 04 | 16 | 1 04 | 1 05 | 1 06 | 1 07 |
| 17 | 1 08 | 77 | 5 08 | 137 | 9 08 | 197 | 13 08 | 257 | 17 08 | 317 | 21 08 | 17 | 1 08 | 1 09 | 1 10 | 1 11 |
| 18 | 1 12 | 78 | 5 12 | 138 | 9 12 | 198 | 13 12 | 258 | 17 12 | 318 | 21 12 | 18 | 1 12 | 1 13 | 1 14 | 1 15 |
| 19 | 1 16 | 79 | 5 16 | 139 | 9 16 | 199 | 13 16 | 259 | 17 16 | 319 | 21 16 | 19 | 1 16 | 1 17 | 1 18 | 1 19 |
| 20 | 1 20 | 80 | 5 20 | 140 | 9 20 | 200 | 13 20 | 260 | 17 20 | 320 | 21 20 | 20 | 1 20 | 1 21 | 1 22 | 1 23 |
| 21 | 1 24 | 81 | 5 24 | 141 | 9 24 | 201 | 13 24 | 261 | 17 24 | 321 | 21 24 | 21 | 1 24 | 1 25 | 1 26 | 1 27 |
| 22 | 1 28 | 82 | 5 28 | 142 | 9 28 | 202 | 13 28 | 262 | 17 28 | 322 | 21 28 | 22 | 1 28 | 1 29 | 1 30 | 1 31 |
| 23 | 1 32 | 83 | 5 32 | 143 | 9 32 | 203 | 13 32 | 263 | 17 32 | 323 | 21 32 | 23 | 1 32 | 1 33 | 1 34 | 1 35 |
| 24 | 1 36 | 84 | 5 36 | 144 | 9 36 | 204 | 13 36 | 264 | 17 36 | 324 | 21 36 | 24 | 1 36 | 1 37 | 1 38 | 1 39 |
| 25 | 1 40 | 85 | 5 40 | 145 | 9 40 | 205 | 13 40 | 265 | 17 40 | 325 | 21 40 | 25 | 1 40 | 1 41 | 1 42 | 1 43 |
| 26 | 1 44 | 86 | 5 44 | 146 | 9 44 | 206 | 13 44 | 266 | 17 44 | 326 | 21 44 | 26 | 1 44 | 1 45 | 1 46 | 1 47 |
| 27 | 1 48 | 87 | 5 48 | 147 | 9 48 | 207 | 13 48 | 267 | 17 48 | 327 | 21 48 | 27 | 1 48 | 1 49 | 1 50 | 1 51 |
| 28 | 1 52 | 88 | 5 52 | 148 | 9 52 | 208 | 13 52 | 268 | 17 52 | 328 | 21 52 | 28 | 1 52 | 1 53 | 1 54 | 1 55 |
| 29 | 1 56 | 89 | 5 56 | 149 | 9 56 | 209 | 13 56 | 269 | 17 56 | 329 | 21 56 | 29 | 1 56 | 1 57 | 1 58 | 1 59 |
| 30 | 2 00 | 90 | 6 00 | 150 | 10 00 | 210 | 14 00 | 270 | 18 00 | 330 | 22 00 | 30 | 2 00 | 2 01 | 2 02 | 2 03 |
| 31 | 2 04 | 91 | 6 04 | 151 | 10 04 | 211 | 14 04 | 271 | 18 04 | 331 | 22 04 | 31 | 2 04 | 2 05 | 2 06 | 2 07 |
| 32 | 2 08 | 92 | 6 08 | 152 | 10 08 | 212 | 14 08 | 272 | 18 08 | 332 | 22 08 | 32 | 2 08 | 2 09 | 2 10 | 2 11 |
| 33 | 2 12 | 93 | 6 12 | 153 | 10 12 | 213 | 14 12 | 273 | 18 12 | 333 | 22 12 | 33 | 2 12 | 2 13 | 2 14 | 2 15 |
| 34 | 2 16 | 94 | 6 16 | 154 | 10 16 | 214 | 14 16 | 274 | 18 16 | 334 | 22 16 | 34 | 2 16 | 2 17 | 2 18 | 2 19 |
| 35 | 2 20 | 95 | 6 20 | 155 | 10 20 | 215 | 14 20 | 275 | 18 20 | 335 | 22 20 | 35 | 2 20 | 2 21 | 2 22 | 2 23 |
| 36 | 2 24 | 96 | 6 24 | 156 | 10 24 | 216 | 14 24 | 276 | 18 24 | 336 | 22 24 | 36 | 2 24 | 2 25 | 2 26 | 2 27 |
| 37 | 2 28 | 97 | 6 28 | 157 | 10 28 | 217 | 14 28 | 277 | 18 28 | 337 | 22 28 | 37 | 2 28 | 2 29 | 2 30 | 2 31 |
| 38 | 2 32 | 98 | 6 32 | 158 | 10 32 | 218 | 14 32 | 278 | 18 32 | 338 | 22 32 | 38 | 2 32 | 2 33 | 2 34 | 2 35 |
| 39 | 2 36 | 99 | 6 36 | 159 | 10 36 | 219 | 14 36 | 279 | 18 36 | 339 | 22 36 | 39 | 2 36 | 2 37 | 2 38 | 2 39 |
| 40 | 2 40 | 100 | 6 40 | 160 | 10 40 | 220 | 14 40 | 280 | 18 40 | 340 | 22 40 | 40 | 2 40 | 2 41 | 2 42 | 2 43 |
| 41 | 2 44 | 101 | 6 44 | 161 | 10 44 | 221 | 14 44 | 281 | 18 44 | 341 | 22 44 | 41 | 2 44 | 2 45 | 2 46 | 2 47 |
| 42 | 2 48 | 102 | 6 48 | 162 | 10 48 | 222 | 14 48 | 282 | 18 48 | 342 | 22 48 | 42 | 2 48 | 2 49 | 2 50 | 2 51 |
| 43 | 2 52 | 103 | 6 52 | 163 | 10 52 | 223 | 14 52 | 283 | 18 52 | 343 | 22 52 | 43 | 2 52 | 2 53 | 2 54 | 2 55 |
| 44 | 2 56 | 104 | 6 56 | 164 | 10 56 | 224 | 14 56 | 284 | 18 56 | 344 | 22 56 | 44 | 2 56 | 2 57 | 2 58 | 2 59 |
| 45 | 3 00 | 105 | 7 00 | 165 | 11 00 | 225 | 15 00 | 285 | 19 00 | 345 | 23 00 | 45 | 3 00 | 3 01 | 3 02 | 3 03 |
| 46 | 3 04 | 106 | 7 04 | 166 | 11 04 | 226 | 15 04 | 286 | 19 04 | 346 | 23 04 | 46 | 3 04 | 3 05 | 3 06 | 3 07 |
| 47 | 3 08 | 107 | 7 08 | 167 | 11 08 | 227 | 15 08 | 287 | 19 08 | 347 | 23 08 | 47 | 3 08 | 3 09 | 3 10 | 3 11 |
| 48 | 3 12 | 108 | 7 12 | 168 | 11 12 | 228 | 15 12 | 288 | 19 12 | 348 | 23 12 | 48 | 3 12 | 3 13 | 3 14 | 3 15 |
| 49 | 3 16 | 109 | 7 16 | 169 | 11 16 | 229 | 15 16 | 289 | 19 16 | 349 | 23 16 | 49 | 3 16 | 3 17 | 3 18 | 3 19 |
| 50 | 3 20 | 110 | 7 20 | 170 | 11 20 | 230 | 15 20 | 290 | 19 20 | 350 | 23 20 | 50 | 3 20 | 3 21 | 3 22 | 3 23 |
| 51 | 3 24 | 111 | 7 24 | 171 | 11 24 | 231 | 15 24 | 291 | 19 24 | 351 | 23 24 | 51 | 3 24 | 3 25 | 3 26 | 3 27 |
| 52 | 3 28 | 112 | 7 28 | 172 | 11 28 | 232 | 15 28 | 292 | 19 28 | 352 | 23 28 | 52 | 3 28 | 3 29 | 3 30 | 3 31 |
| 53 | 3 32 | 113 | 7 32 | 173 | 11 32 | 233 | 15 32 | 293 | 19 32 | 353 | 23 32 | 53 | 3 32 | 3 33 | 3 34 | 3 35 |
| 54 | 3 36 | 114 | 7 36 | 174 | 11 36 | 234 | 15 36 | 294 | 19 36 | 354 | 23 36 | 54 | 3 36 | 3 37 | 3 38 | 3 39 |
| 55 | 3 40 | 115 | 7 40 | 175 | 11 40 | 235 | 15 40 | 295 | 19 40 | 355 | 23 40 | 55 | 3 40 | 3 41 | 3 42 | 3 43 |
| 56 | 3 44 | 116 | 7 44 | 176 | 11 44 | 236 | 15 44 | 296 | 19 44 | 356 | 23 44 | 56 | 3 44 | 3 45 | 3 46 | 3 47 |
| 57 | 3 48 | 117 | 7 48 | 177 | 11 48 | 237 | 15 48 | 297 | 19 48 | 357 | 23 48 | 57 | 3 48 | 3 49 | 3 50 | 3 51 |
| 58 | 3 52 | 118 | 7 52 | 178 | 11 52 | 238 | 15 52 | 298 | 19 52 | 358 | 23 52 | 58 | 3 52 | 3 53 | 3 54 | 3 55 |
| 59 | 3 56 | 119 | 7 56 | 179 | 11 56 | 239 | 15 56 | 299 | 19 56 | 359 | 23 56 | 59 | 3 56 | 3 57 | 3 58 | 3 59 |

The above table is for converting expressions in arc to their equivalent in time; its main use in this Almanac is for the conversion of longitude for application to LMT (*added* if *west*, *subtracted* if *east*) to give UT or vice versa, particularly in the case of sunrise, sunset, etc.

INCREMENTS AND CORRECTIONS

| m 0 | SUN PLANETS | ARIES | MOON | v or d Corrⁿ | v or d Corrⁿ | v or d Corrⁿ | m 1 | SUN PLANETS | ARIES | MOON | v or d Corrⁿ | v or d Corrⁿ | v or d Corrⁿ |
|---|---|---|---|---|---|---|---|---|---|---|---|---|---|
| s | ° ′ | ° ′ | ° ′ | ′ ′ | ′ ′ | ′ ′ | s | ° ′ | ° ′ | ° ′ | ′ ′ | ′ ′ | ′ ′ |
| 00 | 0 00·0 | 0 00·0 | 0 00·0 | 0·0 0·0 | 6·0 0·1 | 12·0 0·1 | 00 | 0 15·0 | 0 15·0 | 0 14·3 | 0·0 0·0 | 6·0 0·2 | 12·0 0·3 |
| 01 | 0 00·3 | 0 00·3 | 0 00·2 | 0·1 0·0 | 6·1 0·1 | 12·1 0·1 | 01 | 0 15·3 | 0 15·3 | 0 14·6 | 0·1 0·0 | 6·1 0·2 | 12·1 0·3 |
| 02 | 0 00·5 | 0 00·5 | 0 00·5 | 0·2 0·0 | 6·2 0·1 | 12·2 0·1 | 02 | 0 15·5 | 0 15·5 | 0 14·8 | 0·2 0·0 | 6·2 0·2 | 12·2 0·3 |
| 03 | 0 00·8 | 0 00·8 | 0 00·7 | 0·3 0·0 | 6·3 0·1 | 12·3 0·1 | 03 | 0 15·8 | 0 15·8 | 0 15·0 | 0·3 0·0 | 6·3 0·2 | 12·3 0·3 |
| 04 | 0 01·0 | 0 01·0 | 0 01·0 | 0·4 0·0 | 6·4 0·1 | 12·4 0·1 | 04 | 0 16·0 | 0 16·0 | 0 15·3 | 0·4 0·0 | 6·4 0·2 | 12·4 0·3 |
| 05 | 0 01·3 | 0 01·3 | 0 01·2 | 0·5 0·0 | 6·5 0·1 | 12·5 0·1 | 05 | 0 16·3 | 0 16·3 | 0 15·5 | 0·5 0·0 | 6·5 0·2 | 12·5 0·3 |
| 06 | 0 01·5 | 0 01·5 | 0 01·4 | 0·6 0·0 | 6·6 0·1 | 12·6 0·1 | 06 | 0 16·5 | 0 16·5 | 0 15·7 | 0·6 0·0 | 6·6 0·2 | 12·6 0·3 |
| 07 | 0 01·8 | 0 01·8 | 0 01·7 | 0·7 0·0 | 6·7 0·1 | 12·7 0·1 | 07 | 0 16·8 | 0 16·8 | 0 16·0 | 0·7 0·0 | 6·7 0·2 | 12·7 0·3 |
| 08 | 0 02·0 | 0 02·0 | 0 01·9 | 0·8 0·0 | 6·8 0·1 | 12·8 0·1 | 08 | 0 17·0 | 0 17·0 | 0 16·2 | 0·8 0·0 | 6·8 0·2 | 12·8 0·3 |
| 09 | 0 02·3 | 0 02·3 | 0 02·1 | 0·9 0·0 | 6·9 0·1 | 12·9 0·1 | 09 | 0 17·3 | 0 17·3 | 0 16·5 | 0·9 0·0 | 6·9 0·2 | 12·9 0·3 |
| 10 | 0 02·5 | 0 02·5 | 0 02·4 | 1·0 0·0 | 7·0 0·1 | 13·0 0·1 | 10 | 0 17·5 | 0 17·5 | 0 16·7 | 1·0 0·0 | 7·0 0·2 | 13·0 0·3 |
| 11 | 0 02·8 | 0 02·8 | 0 02·6 | 1·1 0·0 | 7·1 0·1 | 13·1 0·1 | 11 | 0 17·8 | 0 17·8 | 0 16·9 | 1·1 0·0 | 7·1 0·2 | 13·1 0·3 |
| 12 | 0 03·0 | 0 03·0 | 0 02·9 | 1·2 0·0 | 7·2 0·1 | 13·2 0·1 | 12 | 0 18·0 | 0 18·0 | 0 17·2 | 1·2 0·0 | 7·2 0·2 | 13·2 0·3 |
| 13 | 0 03·3 | 0 03·3 | 0 03·1 | 1·3 0·0 | 7·3 0·1 | 13·3 0·1 | 13 | 0 18·3 | 0 18·3 | 0 17·4 | 1·3 0·0 | 7·3 0·2 | 13·3 0·3 |
| 14 | 0 03·5 | 0 03·5 | 0 03·3 | 1·4 0·0 | 7·4 0·1 | 13·4 0·1 | 14 | 0 18·5 | 0 18·6 | 0 17·7 | 1·4 0·0 | 7·4 0·2 | 13·4 0·3 |
| 15 | 0 03·8 | 0 03·8 | 0 03·6 | 1·5 0·0 | 7·5 0·1 | 13·5 0·1 | 15 | 0 18·8 | 0 18·8 | 0 17·9 | 1·5 0·0 | 7·5 0·2 | 13·5 0·3 |
| 16 | 0 04·0 | 0 04·0 | 0 03·8 | 1·6 0·0 | 7·6 0·1 | 13·6 0·1 | 16 | 0 19·0 | 0 19·1 | 0 18·1 | 1·6 0·0 | 7·6 0·2 | 13·6 0·3 |
| 17 | 0 04·3 | 0 04·3 | 0 04·1 | 1·7 0·0 | 7·7 0·1 | 13·7 0·1 | 17 | 0 19·3 | 0 19·3 | 0 18·4 | 1·7 0·0 | 7·7 0·2 | 13·7 0·3 |
| 18 | 0 04·5 | 0 04·5 | 0 04·3 | 1·8 0·0 | 7·8 0·1 | 13·8 0·1 | 18 | 0 19·5 | 0 19·6 | 0 18·6 | 1·8 0·0 | 7·8 0·2 | 13·8 0·3 |
| 19 | 0 04·8 | 0 04·8 | 0 04·5 | 1·9 0·0 | 7·9 0·1 | 13·9 0·1 | 19 | 0 19·8 | 0 19·8 | 0 18·9 | 1·9 0·0 | 7·9 0·2 | 13·9 0·3 |
| 20 | 0 05·0 | 0 05·0 | 0 04·8 | 2·0 0·0 | 8·0 0·1 | 14·0 0·1 | 20 | 0 20·0 | 0 20·1 | 0 19·1 | 2·0 0·1 | 8·0 0·2 | 14·0 0·4 |
| 21 | 0 05·3 | 0 05·3 | 0 05·0 | 2·1 0·0 | 8·1 0·1 | 14·1 0·1 | 21 | 0 20·3 | 0 20·3 | 0 19·3 | 2·1 0·1 | 8·1 0·2 | 14·1 0·4 |
| 22 | 0 05·5 | 0 05·5 | 0 05·2 | 2·2 0·0 | 8·2 0·1 | 14·2 0·1 | 22 | 0 20·5 | 0 20·6 | 0 19·6 | 2·2 0·1 | 8·2 0·2 | 14·2 0·4 |
| 23 | 0 05·8 | 0 05·8 | 0 05·5 | 2·3 0·0 | 8·3 0·1 | 14·3 0·1 | 23 | 0 20·8 | 0 20·8 | 0 19·8 | 2·3 0·1 | 8·3 0·2 | 14·3 0·4 |
| 24 | 0 06·0 | 0 06·0 | 0 05·7 | 2·4 0·0 | 8·4 0·1 | 14·4 0·1 | 24 | 0 21·0 | 0 21·1 | 0 20·0 | 2·4 0·1 | 8·4 0·2 | 14·4 0·4 |
| 25 | 0 06·3 | 0 06·3 | 0 06·0 | 2·5 0·0 | 8·5 0·1 | 14·5 0·1 | 25 | 0 21·3 | 0 21·3 | 0 20·3 | 2·5 0·1 | 8·5 0·2 | 14·5 0·4 |
| 26 | 0 06·5 | 0 06·5 | 0 06·2 | 2·6 0·0 | 8·6 0·1 | 14·6 0·1 | 26 | 0 21·5 | 0 21·6 | 0 20·5 | 2·6 0·1 | 8·6 0·2 | 14·6 0·4 |
| 27 | 0 06·8 | 0 06·8 | 0 06·4 | 2·7 0·0 | 8·7 0·1 | 14·7 0·1 | 27 | 0 21·8 | 0 21·8 | 0 20·8 | 2·7 0·1 | 8·7 0·2 | 14·7 0·4 |
| 28 | 0 07·0 | 0 07·0 | 0 06·7 | 2·8 0·0 | 8·8 0·1 | 14·8 0·1 | 28 | 0 22·0 | 0 22·1 | 0 21·0 | 2·8 0·1 | 8·8 0·2 | 14·8 0·4 |
| 29 | 0 07·3 | 0 07·3 | 0 06·9 | 2·9 0·0 | 8·9 0·1 | 14·9 0·1 | 29 | 0 22·3 | 0 22·3 | 0 21·2 | 2·9 0·1 | 8·9 0·2 | 14·9 0·4 |
| 30 | 0 07·5 | 0 07·5 | 0 07·2 | 3·0 0·0 | 9·0 0·1 | 15·0 0·1 | 30 | 0 22·5 | 0 22·6 | 0 21·5 | 3·0 0·1 | 9·0 0·2 | 15·0 0·4 |
| 31 | 0 07·8 | 0 07·8 | 0 07·4 | 3·1 0·0 | 9·1 0·1 | 15·1 0·1 | 31 | 0 22·8 | 0 22·8 | 0 21·7 | 3·1 0·1 | 9·1 0·2 | 15·1 0·4 |
| 32 | 0 08·0 | 0 08·0 | 0 07·6 | 3·2 0·0 | 9·2 0·1 | 15·2 0·1 | 32 | 0 23·0 | 0 23·1 | 0 22·0 | 3·2 0·1 | 9·2 0·2 | 15·2 0·4 |
| 33 | 0 08·3 | 0 08·3 | 0 07·9 | 3·3 0·0 | 9·3 0·1 | 15·3 0·1 | 33 | 0 23·3 | 0 23·3 | 0 22·2 | 3·3 0·1 | 9·3 0·2 | 15·3 0·4 |
| 34 | 0 08·5 | 0 08·5 | 0 08·1 | 3·4 0·0 | 9·4 0·1 | 15·4 0·1 | 34 | 0 23·5 | 0 23·6 | 0 22·4 | 3·4 0·1 | 9·4 0·2 | 15·4 0·4 |
| 35 | 0 08·8 | 0 08·8 | 0 08·4 | 3·5 0·0 | 9·5 0·1 | 15·5 0·1 | 35 | 0 23·8 | 0 23·8 | 0 22·7 | 3·5 0·1 | 9·5 0·2 | 15·5 0·4 |
| 36 | 0 09·0 | 0 09·0 | 0 08·6 | 3·6 0·0 | 9·6 0·1 | 15·6 0·1 | 36 | 0 24·0 | 0 24·1 | 0 22·9 | 3·6 0·1 | 9·6 0·2 | 15·6 0·4 |
| 37 | 0 09·3 | 0 09·3 | 0 08·8 | 3·7 0·0 | 9·7 0·1 | 15·7 0·1 | 37 | 0 24·3 | 0 24·3 | 0 23·1 | 3·7 0·1 | 9·7 0·2 | 15·7 0·4 |
| 38 | 0 09·5 | 0 09·5 | 0 09·1 | 3·8 0·0 | 9·8 0·1 | 15·8 0·1 | 38 | 0 24·5 | 0 24·6 | 0 23·4 | 3·8 0·1 | 9·8 0·2 | 15·8 0·4 |
| 39 | 0 09·8 | 0 09·8 | 0 09·3 | 3·9 0·0 | 9·9 0·1 | 15·9 0·1 | 39 | 0 24·8 | 0 24·8 | 0 23·6 | 3·9 0·1 | 9·9 0·2 | 15·9 0·4 |
| 40 | 0 10·0 | 0 10·0 | 0 09·5 | 4·0 0·0 | 10·0 0·1 | 16·0 0·1 | 40 | 0 25·0 | 0 25·1 | 0 23·9 | 4·0 0·1 | 10·0 0·3 | 16·0 0·4 |
| 41 | 0 10·3 | 0 10·3 | 0 09·8 | 4·1 0·0 | 10·1 0·1 | 16·1 0·1 | 41 | 0 25·3 | 0 25·3 | 0 24·1 | 4·1 0·1 | 10·1 0·3 | 16·1 0·4 |
| 42 | 0 10·5 | 0 10·5 | 0 10·0 | 4·2 0·0 | 10·2 0·1 | 16·2 0·1 | 42 | 0 25·5 | 0 25·6 | 0 24·3 | 4·2 0·1 | 10·2 0·3 | 16·2 0·4 |
| 43 | 0 10·8 | 0 10·8 | 0 10·3 | 4·3 0·0 | 10·3 0·1 | 16·3 0·1 | 43 | 0 25·8 | 0 25·8 | 0 24·6 | 4·3 0·1 | 10·3 0·3 | 16·3 0·4 |
| 44 | 0 11·0 | 0 11·0 | 0 10·5 | 4·4 0·0 | 10·4 0·1 | 16·4 0·1 | 44 | 0 26·0 | 0 26·1 | 0 24·8 | 4·4 0·1 | 10·4 0·3 | 16·4 0·4 |
| 45 | 0 11·3 | 0 11·3 | 0 10·7 | 4·5 0·0 | 10·5 0·1 | 16·5 0·1 | 45 | 0 26·3 | 0 26·3 | 0 25·1 | 4·5 0·1 | 10·5 0·3 | 16·5 0·4 |
| 46 | 0 11·5 | 0 11·5 | 0 11·0 | 4·6 0·0 | 10·6 0·1 | 16·6 0·1 | 46 | 0 26·5 | 0 26·6 | 0 25·3 | 4·6 0·1 | 10·6 0·3 | 16·6 0·4 |
| 47 | 0 11·8 | 0 11·8 | 0 11·2 | 4·7 0·0 | 10·7 0·1 | 16·7 0·1 | 47 | 0 26·8 | 0 26·8 | 0 25·5 | 4·7 0·1 | 10·7 0·3 | 16·7 0·4 |
| 48 | 0 12·0 | 0 12·0 | 0 11·5 | 4·8 0·0 | 10·8 0·1 | 16·8 0·1 | 48 | 0 27·0 | 0 27·1 | 0 25·8 | 4·8 0·1 | 10·8 0·3 | 16·8 0·4 |
| 49 | 0 12·3 | 0 12·3 | 0 11·7 | 4·9 0·0 | 10·9 0·1 | 16·9 0·1 | 49 | 0 27·3 | 0 27·3 | 0 26·0 | 4·9 0·1 | 10·9 0·3 | 16·9 0·4 |
| 50 | 0 12·5 | 0 12·5 | 0 11·9 | 5·0 0·0 | 11·0 0·1 | 17·0 0·1 | 50 | 0 27·5 | 0 27·6 | 0 26·2 | 5·0 0·1 | 11·0 0·3 | 17·0 0·4 |
| 51 | 0 12·8 | 0 12·8 | 0 12·2 | 5·1 0·0 | 11·1 0·1 | 17·1 0·1 | 51 | 0 27·8 | 0 27·8 | 0 26·5 | 5·1 0·1 | 11·1 0·3 | 17·1 0·4 |
| 52 | 0 13·0 | 0 13·0 | 0 12·4 | 5·2 0·0 | 11·2 0·1 | 17·2 0·1 | 52 | 0 28·0 | 0 28·1 | 0 26·7 | 5·2 0·1 | 11·2 0·3 | 17·2 0·4 |
| 53 | 0 13·3 | 0 13·3 | 0 12·6 | 5·3 0·0 | 11·3 0·1 | 17·3 0·1 | 53 | 0 28·3 | 0 28·3 | 0 27·0 | 5·3 0·1 | 11·3 0·3 | 17·3 0·4 |
| 54 | 0 13·5 | 0 13·5 | 0 12·9 | 5·4 0·0 | 11·4 0·1 | 17·4 0·1 | 54 | 0 28·5 | 0 28·6 | 0 27·2 | 5·4 0·1 | 11·4 0·3 | 17·4 0·4 |
| 55 | 0 13·8 | 0 13·8 | 0 13·1 | 5·5 0·0 | 11·5 0·1 | 17·5 0·1 | 55 | 0 28·8 | 0 28·8 | 0 27·4 | 5·5 0·1 | 11·5 0·3 | 17·5 0·4 |
| 56 | 0 14·0 | 0 14·0 | 0 13·4 | 5·6 0·0 | 11·6 0·1 | 17·6 0·1 | 56 | 0 29·0 | 0 29·1 | 0 27·7 | 5·6 0·1 | 11·6 0·3 | 17·6 0·4 |
| 57 | 0 14·3 | 0 14·3 | 0 13·6 | 5·7 0·0 | 11·7 0·1 | 17·7 0·1 | 57 | 0 29·3 | 0 29·3 | 0 27·9 | 5·7 0·1 | 11·7 0·3 | 17·7 0·4 |
| 58 | 0 14·5 | 0 14·5 | 0 13·8 | 5·8 0·0 | 11·8 0·1 | 17·8 0·1 | 58 | 0 29·5 | 0 29·6 | 0 28·2 | 5·8 0·1 | 11·8 0·3 | 17·8 0·4 |
| 59 | 0 14·8 | 0 14·8 | 0 14·1 | 5·9 0·0 | 11·9 0·1 | 17·9 0·1 | 59 | 0 29·8 | 0 29·8 | 0 28·4 | 5·9 0·1 | 11·9 0·3 | 17·9 0·4 |
| 60 | 0 15·0 | 0 15·0 | 0 14·3 | 6·0 0·1 | 12·0 0·1 | 18·0 0·2 | 60 | 0 30·0 | 0 30·1 | 0 28·6 | 6·0 0·2 | 12·0 0·3 | 18·0 0·5 |

| m<br>2 | SUN<br>PLANETS | ARIES | MOON | v<br>or Corr<sup>n</sup><br>d | v<br>or Corr<sup>n</sup><br>d | v<br>or Corr<sup>n</sup><br>d | m<br>3 | SUN<br>PLANETS | ARIES | MOON | v<br>or Corr<sup>n</sup><br>d | v<br>or Corr<sup>n</sup><br>d | v<br>or Corr<sup>n</sup><br>d |
|---|---|---|---|---|---|---|---|---|---|---|---|---|---|
| s | ° ′ | ° ′ | ° ′ | ′ ′ | ′ ′ | ′ ′ | s | ° ′ | ° ′ | ° ′ | ′ ′ | ′ ′ | ′ ′ |
| 00 | 0 30·0 | 0 30·1 | 0 28·6 | 0·0 0·0 | 6·0 0·3 | 12·0 0·5 | 00 | 0 45·0 | 0 45·1 | 0 43·0 | 0·0 0·0 | 6·0 0·4 | 12·0 0·7 |
| 01 | 0 30·3 | 0 30·3 | 0 28·9 | 0·1 0·0 | 6·1 0·3 | 12·1 0·5 | 01 | 0 45·3 | 0 45·4 | 0 43·2 | 0·1 0·0 | 6·1 0·4 | 12·1 0·7 |
| 02 | 0 30·5 | 0 30·6 | 0 29·1 | 0·2 0·0 | 6·2 0·3 | 12·2 0·5 | 02 | 0 45·5 | 0 45·6 | 0 43·4 | 0·2 0·0 | 6·2 0·4 | 12·2 0·7 |
| 03 | 0 30·8 | 0 30·8 | 0 29·3 | 0·3 0·0 | 6·3 0·3 | 12·3 0·5 | 03 | 0 45·8 | 0 45·9 | 0 43·7 | 0·3 0·0 | 6·3 0·4 | 12·3 0·7 |
| 04 | 0 31·0 | 0 31·1 | 0 29·6 | 0·4 0·0 | 6·4 0·3 | 12·4 0·5 | 04 | 0 46·0 | 0 46·1 | 0 43·9 | 0·4 0·0 | 6·4 0·4 | 12·4 0·7 |
| 05 | 0 31·3 | 0 31·3 | 0 29·8 | 0·5 0·0 | 6·5 0·3 | 12·5 0·5 | 05 | 0 46·3 | 0 46·4 | 0 44·1 | 0·5 0·0 | 6·5 0·4 | 12·5 0·7 |
| 06 | 0 31·5 | 0 31·6 | 0 30·1 | 0·6 0·0 | 6·6 0·3 | 12·6 0·5 | 06 | 0 46·5 | 0 46·6 | 0 44·4 | 0·6 0·0 | 6·6 0·4 | 12·6 0·7 |
| 07 | 0 31·8 | 0 31·8 | 0 30·3 | 0·7 0·0 | 6·7 0·3 | 12·7 0·5 | 07 | 0 46·8 | 0 46·9 | 0 44·6 | 0·7 0·0 | 6·7 0·4 | 12·7 0·7 |
| 08 | 0 32·0 | 0 32·1 | 0 30·5 | 0·8 0·0 | 6·8 0·3 | 12·8 0·5 | 08 | 0 47·0 | 0 47·1 | 0 44·9 | 0·8 0·0 | 6·8 0·4 | 12·8 0·7 |
| 09 | 0 32·3 | 0 32·3 | 0 30·8 | 0·9 0·0 | 6·9 0·3 | 12·9 0·5 | 09 | 0 47·3 | 0 47·4 | 0 45·1 | 0·9 0·1 | 6·9 0·4 | 12·9 0·8 |
| 10 | 0 32·5 | 0 32·6 | 0 31·0 | 1·0 0·0 | 7·0 0·3 | 13·0 0·5 | 10 | 0 47·5 | 0 47·6 | 0 45·3 | 1·0 0·1 | 7·0 0·4 | 13·0 0·8 |
| 11 | 0 32·8 | 0 32·8 | 0 31·3 | 1·1 0·0 | 7·1 0·3 | 13·1 0·5 | 11 | 0 47·8 | 0 47·9 | 0 45·6 | 1·1 0·1 | 7·1 0·4 | 13·1 0·8 |
| 12 | 0 33·0 | 0 33·1 | 0 31·5 | 1·2 0·1 | 7·2 0·3 | 13·2 0·6 | 12 | 0 48·0 | 0 48·1 | 0 45·8 | 1·2 0·1 | 7·2 0·4 | 13·2 0·8 |
| 13 | 0 33·3 | 0 33·3 | 0 31·7 | 1·3 0·1 | 7·3 0·3 | 13·3 0·6 | 13 | 0 48·3 | 0 48·4 | 0 46·1 | 1·3 0·1 | 7·3 0·4 | 13·3 0·8 |
| 14 | 0 33·5 | 0 33·6 | 0 32·0 | 1·4 0·1 | 7·4 0·3 | 13·4 0·6 | 14 | 0 48·5 | 0 48·6 | 0 46·3 | 1·4 0·1 | 7·4 0·4 | 13·4 0·8 |
| 15 | 0 33·8 | 0 33·8 | 0 32·2 | 1·5 0·1 | 7·5 0·3 | 13·5 0·6 | 15 | 0 48·8 | 0 48·9 | 0 46·5 | 1·5 0·1 | 7·5 0·4 | 13·5 0·8 |
| 16 | 0 34·0 | 0 34·1 | 0 32·5 | 1·6 0·1 | 7·6 0·3 | 13·6 0·6 | 16 | 0 49·0 | 0 49·1 | 0 46·8 | 1·6 0·1 | 7·6 0·4 | 13·6 0·8 |
| 17 | 0 34·3 | 0 34·3 | 0 32·7 | 1·7 0·1 | 7·7 0·3 | 13·7 0·6 | 17 | 0 49·3 | 0 49·4 | 0 47·0 | 1·7 0·1 | 7·7 0·4 | 13·7 0·8 |
| 18 | 0 34·5 | 0 34·6 | 0 32·9 | 1·8 0·1 | 7·8 0·3 | 13·8 0·6 | 18 | 0 49·5 | 0 49·6 | 0 47·2 | 1·8 0·1 | 7·8 0·5 | 13·8 0·8 |
| 19 | 0 34·8 | 0 34·8 | 0 33·2 | 1·9 0·1 | 7·9 0·3 | 13·9 0·6 | 19 | 0 49·8 | 0 49·9 | 0 47·5 | 1·9 0·1 | 7·9 0·5 | 13·9 0·8 |
| 20 | 0 35·0 | 0 35·1 | 0 33·4 | 2·0 0·1 | 8·0 0·3 | 14·0 0·6 | 20 | 0 50·0 | 0 50·1 | 0 47·7 | 2·0 0·1 | 8·0 0·5 | 14·0 0·8 |
| 21 | 0 35·3 | 0 35·3 | 0 33·6 | 2·1 0·1 | 8·1 0·3 | 14·1 0·6 | 21 | 0 50·3 | 0 50·4 | 0 48·0 | 2·1 0·1 | 8·1 0·5 | 14·1 0·8 |
| 22 | 0 35·5 | 0 35·6 | 0 33·9 | 2·2 0·1 | 8·2 0·3 | 14·2 0·6 | 22 | 0 50·5 | 0 50·6 | 0 48·2 | 2·2 0·1 | 8·2 0·5 | 14·2 0·8 |
| 23 | 0 35·8 | 0 35·8 | 0 34·1 | 2·3 0·1 | 8·3 0·3 | 14·3 0·6 | 23 | 0 50·8 | 0 50·9 | 0 48·4 | 2·3 0·1 | 8·3 0·5 | 14·3 0·8 |
| 24 | 0 36·0 | 0 36·1 | 0 34·4 | 2·4 0·1 | 8·4 0·4 | 14·4 0·6 | 24 | 0 51·0 | 0 51·1 | 0 48·7 | 2·4 0·1 | 8·4 0·5 | 14·4 0·8 |
| 25 | 0 36·3 | 0 36·3 | 0 34·6 | 2·5 0·1 | 8·5 0·4 | 14·5 0·6 | 25 | 0 51·3 | 0 51·4 | 0 48·9 | 2·5 0·1 | 8·5 0·5 | 14·5 0·8 |
| 26 | 0 36·5 | 0 36·6 | 0 34·8 | 2·6 0·1 | 8·6 0·4 | 14·6 0·6 | 26 | 0 51·5 | 0 51·6 | 0 49·2 | 2·6 0·2 | 8·6 0·5 | 14·6 0·9 |
| 27 | 0 36·8 | 0 36·9 | 0 35·1 | 2·7 0·1 | 8·7 0·4 | 14·7 0·6 | 27 | 0 51·8 | 0 51·9 | 0 49·4 | 2·7 0·2 | 8·7 0·5 | 14·7 0·9 |
| 28 | 0 37·0 | 0 37·1 | 0 35·3 | 2·8 0·1 | 8·8 0·4 | 14·8 0·6 | 28 | 0 52·0 | 0 52·1 | 0 49·6 | 2·8 0·2 | 8·8 0·5 | 14·8 0·9 |
| 29 | 0 37·3 | 0 37·4 | 0 35·6 | 2·9 0·1 | 8·9 0·4 | 14·9 0·6 | 29 | 0 52·3 | 0 52·4 | 0 49·9 | 2·9 0·2 | 8·9 0·5 | 14·9 0·9 |
| 30 | 0 37·5 | 0 37·6 | 0 35·8 | 3·0 0·1 | 9·0 0·4 | 15·0 0·6 | 30 | 0 52·5 | 0 52·6 | 0 50·1 | 3·0 0·2 | 9·0 0·5 | 15·0 0·9 |
| 31 | 0 37·8 | 0 37·9 | 0 36·0 | 3·1 0·1 | 9·1 0·4 | 15·1 0·6 | 31 | 0 52·8 | 0 52·9 | 0 50·3 | 3·1 0·2 | 9·1 0·5 | 15·1 0·9 |
| 32 | 0 38·0 | 0 38·1 | 0 36·3 | 3·2 0·1 | 9·2 0·4 | 15·2 0·6 | 32 | 0 53·0 | 0 53·1 | 0 50·6 | 3·2 0·2 | 9·2 0·5 | 15·2 0·9 |
| 33 | 0 38·3 | 0 38·4 | 0 36·5 | 3·3 0·1 | 9·3 0·4 | 15·3 0·6 | 33 | 0 53·3 | 0 53·4 | 0 50·8 | 3·3 0·2 | 9·3 0·5 | 15·3 0·9 |
| 34 | 0 38·5 | 0 38·6 | 0 36·7 | 3·4 0·1 | 9·4 0·4 | 15·4 0·6 | 34 | 0 53·5 | 0 53·6 | 0 51·1 | 3·4 0·2 | 9·4 0·5 | 15·4 0·9 |
| 35 | 0 38·8 | 0 38·9 | 0 37·0 | 3·5 0·1 | 9·5 0·4 | 15·5 0·6 | 35 | 0 53·8 | 0 53·9 | 0 51·3 | 3·5 0·2 | 9·5 0·6 | 15·5 0·9 |
| 36 | 0 39·0 | 0 39·1 | 0 37·2 | 3·6 0·2 | 9·6 0·4 | 15·6 0·7 | 36 | 0 54·0 | 0 54·1 | 0 51·5 | 3·6 0·2 | 9·6 0·6 | 15·6 0·9 |
| 37 | 0 39·3 | 0 39·4 | 0 37·5 | 3·7 0·2 | 9·7 0·4 | 15·7 0·7 | 37 | 0 54·3 | 0 54·4 | 0 51·8 | 3·7 0·2 | 9·7 0·6 | 15·7 0·9 |
| 38 | 0 39·5 | 0 39·6 | 0 37·7 | 3·8 0·2 | 9·8 0·4 | 15·8 0·7 | 38 | 0 54·5 | 0 54·6 | 0 52·0 | 3·8 0·2 | 9·8 0·6 | 15·8 0·9 |
| 39 | 0 39·8 | 0 39·9 | 0 37·9 | 3·9 0·2 | 9·9 0·4 | 15·9 0·7 | 39 | 0 54·8 | 0 54·9 | 0 52·3 | 3·9 0·2 | 9·9 0·6 | 15·9 0·9 |
| 40 | 0 40·0 | 0 40·1 | 0 38·2 | 4·0 0·2 | 10·0 0·4 | 16·0 0·7 | 40 | 0 55·0 | 0 55·2 | 0 52·5 | 4·0 0·2 | 10·0 0·6 | 16·0 0·9 |
| 41 | 0 40·3 | 0 40·4 | 0 38·4 | 4·1 0·2 | 10·1 0·4 | 16·1 0·7 | 41 | 0 55·3 | 0 55·4 | 0 52·7 | 4·1 0·2 | 10·1 0·6 | 16·1 0·9 |
| 42 | 0 40·5 | 0 40·6 | 0 38·7 | 4·2 0·2 | 10·2 0·4 | 16·2 0·7 | 42 | 0 55·5 | 0 55·7 | 0 53·0 | 4·2 0·2 | 10·2 0·6 | 16·2 0·9 |
| 43 | 0 40·8 | 0 40·9 | 0 38·9 | 4·3 0·2 | 10·3 0·4 | 16·3 0·7 | 43 | 0 55·8 | 0 55·9 | 0 53·2 | 4·3 0·3 | 10·3 0·6 | 16·3 1·0 |
| 44 | 0 41·0 | 0 41·1 | 0 39·1 | 4·4 0·2 | 10·4 0·4 | 16·4 0·7 | 44 | 0 56·0 | 0 56·2 | 0 53·4 | 4·4 0·3 | 10·4 0·6 | 16·4 1·0 |
| 45 | 0 41·3 | 0 41·4 | 0 39·4 | 4·5 0·2 | 10·5 0·4 | 16·5 0·7 | 45 | 0 56·3 | 0 56·4 | 0 53·7 | 4·5 0·3 | 10·5 0·6 | 16·5 1·0 |
| 46 | 0 41·5 | 0 41·6 | 0 39·6 | 4·6 0·2 | 10·6 0·4 | 16·6 0·7 | 46 | 0 56·5 | 0 56·7 | 0 53·9 | 4·6 0·3 | 10·6 0·6 | 16·6 1·0 |
| 47 | 0 41·8 | 0 41·9 | 0 39·8 | 4·7 0·2 | 10·7 0·4 | 16·7 0·7 | 47 | 0 56·8 | 0 56·9 | 0 54·2 | 4·7 0·3 | 10·7 0·6 | 16·7 1·0 |
| 48 | 0 42·0 | 0 42·1 | 0 40·1 | 4·8 0·2 | 10·8 0·5 | 16·8 0·7 | 48 | 0 57·0 | 0 57·2 | 0 54·4 | 4·8 0·3 | 10·8 0·6 | 16·8 1·0 |
| 49 | 0 42·3 | 0 42·4 | 0 40·3 | 4·9 0·2 | 10·9 0·5 | 16·9 0·7 | 49 | 0 57·3 | 0 57·4 | 0 54·6 | 4·9 0·3 | 10·9 0·6 | 16·9 1·0 |
| 50 | 0 42·5 | 0 42·6 | 0 40·6 | 5·0 0·2 | 11·0 0·5 | 17·0 0·7 | 50 | 0 57·5 | 0 57·7 | 0 54·9 | 5·0 0·3 | 11·0 0·6 | 17·0 1·0 |
| 51 | 0 42·8 | 0 42·9 | 0 40·8 | 5·1 0·2 | 11·1 0·5 | 17·1 0·7 | 51 | 0 57·8 | 0 57·9 | 0 55·1 | 5·1 0·3 | 11·1 0·6 | 17·1 1·0 |
| 52 | 0 43·0 | 0 43·1 | 0 41·0 | 5·2 0·2 | 11·2 0·5 | 17·2 0·7 | 52 | 0 58·0 | 0 58·2 | 0 55·4 | 5·2 0·3 | 11·2 0·7 | 17·2 1·0 |
| 53 | 0 43·3 | 0 43·4 | 0 41·3 | 5·3 0·2 | 11·3 0·5 | 17·3 0·7 | 53 | 0 58·3 | 0 58·4 | 0 55·6 | 5·3 0·3 | 11·3 0·7 | 17·3 1·0 |
| 54 | 0 43·5 | 0 43·6 | 0 41·5 | 5·4 0·2 | 11·4 0·5 | 17·4 0·7 | 54 | 0 58·5 | 0 58·7 | 0 55·8 | 5·4 0·3 | 11·4 0·7 | 17·4 1·0 |
| 55 | 0 43·8 | 0 43·9 | 0 41·8 | 5·5 0·2 | 11·5 0·5 | 17·5 0·7 | 55 | 0 58·8 | 0 58·9 | 0 56·1 | 5·5 0·3 | 11·5 0·7 | 17·5 1·0 |
| 56 | 0 44·0 | 0 44·1 | 0 42·0 | 5·6 0·2 | 11·6 0·5 | 17·6 0·7 | 56 | 0 59·0 | 0 59·2 | 0 56·3 | 5·6 0·3 | 11·6 0·7 | 17·6 1·0 |
| 57 | 0 44·3 | 0 44·4 | 0 42·2 | 5·7 0·2 | 11·7 0·5 | 17·7 0·7 | 57 | 0 59·3 | 0 59·4 | 0 56·6 | 5·7 0·3 | 11·7 0·7 | 17·7 1·0 |
| 58 | 0 44·5 | 0 44·6 | 0 42·5 | 5·8 0·2 | 11·8 0·5 | 17·8 0·7 | 58 | 0 59·5 | 0 59·7 | 0 56·8 | 5·8 0·3 | 11·8 0·7 | 17·8 1·0 |
| 59 | 0 44·8 | 0 44·9 | 0 42·7 | 5·9 0·2 | 11·9 0·5 | 17·9 0·7 | 59 | 0 59·8 | 0 59·9 | 0 57·0 | 5·9 0·3 | 11·9 0·7 | 17·9 1·0 |
| 60 | 0 45·0 | 0 45·1 | 0 43·0 | 6·0 0·3 | 12·0 0·5 | 18·0 0·8 | 60 | 1 00·0 | 1 00·2 | 0 57·3 | 6·0 0·4 | 12·0 0·7 | 18·0 1·1 |

| m 4 | SUN PLANETS | ARIES | MOON | v or d Corrⁿ | | v or d Corrⁿ | | v or d Corrⁿ | | m 5 | SUN PLANETS | ARIES | MOON | v or d Corrⁿ | | v or d Corrⁿ | | v or d Corrⁿ | |
|---|---|---|---|---|---|---|---|---|---|---|---|---|---|---|---|---|---|---|---|
| s | ° ′ | ° ′ | ° ′ | ′ | ′ | ′ | ′ | ′ | ′ | s | ° ′ | ° ′ | ° ′ | ′ | ′ | ′ | ′ | ′ | ′ |
| 00 | 1 00·0 | 1 00·2 | 0 57·3 | 0·0 | 0·0 | 6·0 | 0·5 | 12·0 | 0·9 | 00 | 1 15·0 | 1 15·2 | 1 11·6 | 0·0 | 0·0 | 6·0 | 0·6 | 12·0 | 1·1 |
| 01 | 1 00·3 | 1 00·4 | 0 57·5 | 0·1 | 0·0 | 6·1 | 0·5 | 12·1 | 0·9 | 01 | 1 15·3 | 1 15·5 | 1 11·8 | 0·1 | 0·0 | 6·1 | 0·6 | 12·1 | 1·1 |
| 02 | 1 00·5 | 1 00·7 | 0 57·7 | 0·2 | 0·0 | 6·2 | 0·5 | 12·2 | 0·9 | 02 | 1 15·5 | 1 15·7 | 1 12·1 | 0·2 | 0·0 | 6·2 | 0·6 | 12·2 | 1·1 |
| 03 | 1 00·8 | 1 00·9 | 0 58·0 | 0·3 | 0·0 | 6·3 | 0·5 | 12·3 | 0·9 | 03 | 1 15·8 | 1 16·0 | 1 12·3 | 0·3 | 0·0 | 6·3 | 0·6 | 12·3 | 1·1 |
| 04 | 1 01·0 | 1 01·2 | 0 58·2 | 0·4 | 0·0 | 6·4 | 0·5 | 12·4 | 0·9 | 04 | 1 16·0 | 1 16·2 | 1 12·5 | 0·4 | 0·0 | 6·4 | 0·6 | 12·4 | 1·1 |
| 05 | 1 01·3 | 1 01·4 | 0 58·5 | 0·5 | 0·0 | 6·5 | 0·5 | 12·5 | 0·9 | 05 | 1 16·3 | 1 16·5 | 1 12·8 | 0·5 | 0·0 | 6·5 | 0·6 | 12·5 | 1·1 |
| 06 | 1 01·5 | 1 01·7 | 0 58·7 | 0·6 | 0·0 | 6·6 | 0·5 | 12·6 | 0·9 | 06 | 1 16·5 | 1 16·7 | 1 13·0 | 0·6 | 0·1 | 6·6 | 0·6 | 12·6 | 1·2 |
| 07 | 1 01·8 | 1 01·9 | 0 58·9 | 0·7 | 0·1 | 6·7 | 0·5 | 12·7 | 1·0 | 07 | 1 16·8 | 1 17·0 | 1 13·3 | 0·7 | 0·1 | 6·7 | 0·6 | 12·7 | 1·2 |
| 08 | 1 02·0 | 1 02·2 | 0 59·2 | 0·8 | 0·1 | 6·8 | 0·5 | 12·8 | 1·0 | 08 | 1 17·0 | 1 17·2 | 1 13·5 | 0·8 | 0·1 | 6·8 | 0·6 | 12·8 | 1·2 |
| 09 | 1 02·3 | 1 02·4 | 0 59·4 | 0·9 | 0·1 | 6·9 | 0·5 | 12·9 | 1·0 | 09 | 1 17·3 | 1 17·5 | 1 13·7 | 0·9 | 0·1 | 6·9 | 0·6 | 12·9 | 1·2 |
| 10 | 1 02·5 | 1 02·7 | 0 59·7 | 1·0 | 0·1 | 7·0 | 0·5 | 13·0 | 1·0 | 10 | 1 17·5 | 1 17·7 | 1 14·0 | 1·0 | 0·1 | 7·0 | 0·6 | 13·0 | 1·2 |
| 11 | 1 02·8 | 1 02·9 | 0 59·9 | 1·1 | 0·1 | 7·1 | 0·5 | 13·1 | 1·0 | 11 | 1 17·8 | 1 18·0 | 1 14·2 | 1·1 | 0·1 | 7·1 | 0·7 | 13·1 | 1·2 |
| 12 | 1 03·0 | 1 03·2 | 1 00·1 | 1·2 | 0·1 | 7·2 | 0·5 | 13·2 | 1·0 | 12 | 1 18·0 | 1 18·2 | 1 14·4 | 1·2 | 0·1 | 7·2 | 0·7 | 13·2 | 1·2 |
| 13 | 1 03·3 | 1 03·4 | 1 00·4 | 1·3 | 0·1 | 7·3 | 0·5 | 13·3 | 1·0 | 13 | 1 18·3 | 1 18·5 | 1 14·7 | 1·3 | 0·1 | 7·3 | 0·7 | 13·3 | 1·2 |
| 14 | 1 03·5 | 1 03·7 | 1 00·6 | 1·4 | 0·1 | 7·4 | 0·6 | 13·4 | 1·0 | 14 | 1 18·5 | 1 18·7 | 1 14·9 | 1·4 | 0·1 | 7·4 | 0·7 | 13·4 | 1·2 |
| 15 | 1 03·8 | 1 03·9 | 1 00·8 | 1·5 | 0·1 | 7·5 | 0·6 | 13·5 | 1·0 | 15 | 1 18·8 | 1 19·0 | 1 15·2 | 1·5 | 0·1 | 7·5 | 0·7 | 13·5 | 1·2 |
| 16 | 1 04·0 | 1 04·2 | 1 01·1 | 1·6 | 0·1 | 7·6 | 0·6 | 13·6 | 1·0 | 16 | 1 19·0 | 1 19·2 | 1 15·4 | 1·6 | 0·1 | 7·6 | 0·7 | 13·6 | 1·2 |
| 17 | 1 04·3 | 1 04·4 | 1 01·3 | 1·7 | 0·1 | 7·7 | 0·6 | 13·7 | 1·0 | 17 | 1 19·3 | 1 19·5 | 1 15·6 | 1·7 | 0·2 | 7·7 | 0·7 | 13·7 | 1·3 |
| 18 | 1 04·5 | 1 04·7 | 1 01·6 | 1·8 | 0·1 | 7·8 | 0·6 | 13·8 | 1·0 | 18 | 1 19·5 | 1 19·7 | 1 15·9 | 1·8 | 0·2 | 7·8 | 0·7 | 13·8 | 1·3 |
| 19 | 1 04·8 | 1 04·9 | 1 01·8 | 1·9 | 0·1 | 7·9 | 0·6 | 13·9 | 1·0 | 19 | 1 19·8 | 1 20·0 | 1 16·1 | 1·9 | 0·2 | 7·9 | 0·7 | 13·9 | 1·3 |
| 20 | 1 05·0 | 1 05·2 | 1 02·0 | 2·0 | 0·2 | 8·0 | 0·6 | 14·0 | 1·1 | 20 | 1 20·0 | 1 20·2 | 1 16·4 | 2·0 | 0·2 | 8·0 | 0·7 | 14·0 | 1·3 |
| 21 | 1 05·3 | 1 05·4 | 1 02·3 | 2·1 | 0·2 | 8·1 | 0·6 | 14·1 | 1·1 | 21 | 1 20·3 | 1 20·5 | 1 16·6 | 2·1 | 0·2 | 8·1 | 0·7 | 14·1 | 1·3 |
| 22 | 1 05·5 | 1 05·7 | 1 02·5 | 2·2 | 0·2 | 8·2 | 0·6 | 14·2 | 1·1 | 22 | 1 20·5 | 1 20·7 | 1 16·8 | 2·2 | 0·2 | 8·2 | 0·8 | 14·2 | 1·3 |
| 23 | 1 05·8 | 1 05·9 | 1 02·8 | 2·3 | 0·2 | 8·3 | 0·6 | 14·3 | 1·1 | 23 | 1 20·8 | 1 21·0 | 1 17·1 | 2·3 | 0·2 | 8·3 | 0·8 | 14·3 | 1·3 |
| 24 | 1 06·0 | 1 06·2 | 1 03·0 | 2·4 | 0·2 | 8·4 | 0·6 | 14·4 | 1·1 | 24 | 1 21·0 | 1 21·2 | 1 17·3 | 2·4 | 0·2 | 8·4 | 0·8 | 14·4 | 1·3 |
| 25 | 1 06·3 | 1 06·4 | 1 03·2 | 2·5 | 0·2 | 8·5 | 0·6 | 14·5 | 1·1 | 25 | 1 21·3 | 1 21·5 | 1 17·5 | 2·5 | 0·2 | 8·5 | 0·8 | 14·5 | 1·3 |
| 26 | 1 06·5 | 1 06·7 | 1 03·5 | 2·6 | 0·2 | 8·6 | 0·6 | 14·6 | 1·1 | 26 | 1 21·5 | 1 21·7 | 1 17·8 | 2·6 | 0·2 | 8·6 | 0·8 | 14·6 | 1·3 |
| 27 | 1 06·8 | 1 06·9 | 1 03·7 | 2·7 | 0·2 | 8·7 | 0·7 | 14·7 | 1·1 | 27 | 1 21·8 | 1 22·0 | 1 18·0 | 2·7 | 0·2 | 8·7 | 0·8 | 14·7 | 1·3 |
| 28 | 1 07·0 | 1 07·2 | 1 03·9 | 2·8 | 0·2 | 8·8 | 0·7 | 14·8 | 1·1 | 28 | 1 22·0 | 1 22·2 | 1 18·3 | 2·8 | 0·3 | 8·8 | 0·8 | 14·8 | 1·4 |
| 29 | 1 07·3 | 1 07·4 | 1 04·2 | 2·9 | 0·2 | 8·9 | 0·7 | 14·9 | 1·1 | 29 | 1 22·3 | 1 22·5 | 1 18·5 | 2·9 | 0·3 | 8·9 | 0·8 | 14·9 | 1·4 |
| 30 | 1 07·5 | 1 07·7 | 1 04·4 | 3·0 | 0·2 | 9·0 | 0·7 | 15·0 | 1·1 | 30 | 1 22·5 | 1 22·7 | 1 18·7 | 3·0 | 0·3 | 9·0 | 0·8 | 15·0 | 1·4 |
| 31 | 1 07·8 | 1 07·9 | 1 04·7 | 3·1 | 0·2 | 9·1 | 0·7 | 15·1 | 1·1 | 31 | 1 22·8 | 1 23·0 | 1 19·0 | 3·1 | 0·3 | 9·1 | 0·8 | 15·1 | 1·4 |
| 32 | 1 08·0 | 1 08·2 | 1 04·9 | 3·2 | 0·2 | 9·2 | 0·7 | 15·2 | 1·1 | 32 | 1 23·0 | 1 23·2 | 1 19·2 | 3·2 | 0·3 | 9·2 | 0·8 | 15·2 | 1·4 |
| 33 | 1 08·3 | 1 08·4 | 1 05·1 | 3·3 | 0·2 | 9·3 | 0·7 | 15·3 | 1·1 | 33 | 1 23·3 | 1 23·5 | 1 19·5 | 3·3 | 0·3 | 9·3 | 0·9 | 15·3 | 1·4 |
| 34 | 1 08·5 | 1 08·7 | 1 05·4 | 3·4 | 0·3 | 9·4 | 0·7 | 15·4 | 1·2 | 34 | 1 23·5 | 1 23·7 | 1 19·7 | 3·4 | 0·3 | 9·4 | 0·9 | 15·4 | 1·4 |
| 35 | 1 08·8 | 1 08·9 | 1 05·6 | 3·5 | 0·3 | 9·5 | 0·7 | 15·5 | 1·2 | 35 | 1 23·8 | 1 24·0 | 1 19·9 | 3·5 | 0·3 | 9·5 | 0·9 | 15·5 | 1·4 |
| 36 | 1 09·0 | 1 09·2 | 1 05·9 | 3·6 | 0·3 | 9·6 | 0·7 | 15·6 | 1·2 | 36 | 1 24·0 | 1 24·2 | 1 20·2 | 3·6 | 0·3 | 9·6 | 0·9 | 15·6 | 1·4 |
| 37 | 1 09·3 | 1 09·4 | 1 06·1 | 3·7 | 0·3 | 9·7 | 0·7 | 15·7 | 1·2 | 37 | 1 24·3 | 1 24·5 | 1 20·4 | 3·7 | 0·3 | 9·7 | 0·9 | 15·7 | 1·4 |
| 38 | 1 09·5 | 1 09·7 | 1 06·3 | 3·8 | 0·3 | 9·8 | 0·7 | 15·8 | 1·2 | 38 | 1 24·5 | 1 24·7 | 1 20·7 | 3·8 | 0·3 | 9·8 | 0·9 | 15·8 | 1·4 |
| 39 | 1 09·8 | 1 09·9 | 1 06·6 | 3·9 | 0·3 | 9·9 | 0·7 | 15·9 | 1·2 | 39 | 1 24·8 | 1 25·0 | 1 20·9 | 3·9 | 0·4 | 9·9 | 0·9 | 15·9 | 1·5 |
| 40 | 1 10·0 | 1 10·2 | 1 06·8 | 4·0 | 0·3 | 10·0 | 0·8 | 16·0 | 1·2 | 40 | 1 25·0 | 1 25·2 | 1 21·1 | 4·0 | 0·4 | 10·0 | 0·9 | 16·0 | 1·5 |
| 41 | 1 10·3 | 1 10·4 | 1 07·0 | 4·1 | 0·3 | 10·1 | 0·8 | 16·1 | 1·2 | 41 | 1 25·3 | 1 25·5 | 1 21·4 | 4·1 | 0·4 | 10·1 | 0·9 | 16·1 | 1·5 |
| 42 | 1 10·5 | 1 10·7 | 1 07·3 | 4·2 | 0·3 | 10·2 | 0·8 | 16·2 | 1·2 | 42 | 1 25·5 | 1 25·7 | 1 21·6 | 4·2 | 0·4 | 10·2 | 0·9 | 16·2 | 1·5 |
| 43 | 1 10·8 | 1 10·9 | 1 07·5 | 4·3 | 0·3 | 10·3 | 0·8 | 16·3 | 1·2 | 43 | 1 25·8 | 1 26·0 | 1 21·8 | 4·3 | 0·4 | 10·3 | 0·9 | 16·3 | 1·5 |
| 44 | 1 11·0 | 1 11·2 | 1 07·8 | 4·4 | 0·3 | 10·4 | 0·8 | 16·4 | 1·2 | 44 | 1 26·0 | 1 26·2 | 1 22·1 | 4·4 | 0·4 | 10·4 | 1·0 | 16·4 | 1·5 |
| 45 | 1 11·3 | 1 11·4 | 1 08·0 | 4·5 | 0·3 | 10·5 | 0·8 | 16·5 | 1·2 | 45 | 1 26·3 | 1 26·5 | 1 22·3 | 4·5 | 0·4 | 10·5 | 1·0 | 16·5 | 1·5 |
| 46 | 1 11·5 | 1 11·7 | 1 08·2 | 4·6 | 0·3 | 10·6 | 0·8 | 16·6 | 1·2 | 46 | 1 26·5 | 1 26·7 | 1 22·6 | 4·6 | 0·4 | 10·6 | 1·0 | 16·6 | 1·5 |
| 47 | 1 11·8 | 1 11·9 | 1 08·5 | 4·7 | 0·4 | 10·7 | 0·8 | 16·7 | 1·3 | 47 | 1 26·8 | 1 27·0 | 1 22·8 | 4·7 | 0·4 | 10·7 | 1·0 | 16·7 | 1·5 |
| 48 | 1 12·0 | 1 12·2 | 1 08·7 | 4·8 | 0·4 | 10·8 | 0·8 | 16·8 | 1·3 | 48 | 1 27·0 | 1 27·2 | 1 23·0 | 4·8 | 0·4 | 10·8 | 1·0 | 16·8 | 1·5 |
| 49 | 1 12·3 | 1 12·4 | 1 09·0 | 4·9 | 0·4 | 10·9 | 0·8 | 16·9 | 1·3 | 49 | 1 27·3 | 1 27·5 | 1 23·3 | 4·9 | 0·4 | 10·9 | 1·0 | 16·9 | 1·5 |
| 50 | 1 12·5 | 1 12·7 | 1 09·2 | 5·0 | 0·4 | 11·0 | 0·8 | 17·0 | 1·3 | 50 | 1 27·5 | 1 27·7 | 1 23·5 | 5·0 | 0·5 | 11·0 | 1·0 | 17·0 | 1·6 |
| 51 | 1 12·8 | 1 12·9 | 1 09·4 | 5·1 | 0·4 | 11·1 | 0·8 | 17·1 | 1·3 | 51 | 1 27·8 | 1 28·0 | 1 23·8 | 5·1 | 0·5 | 11·1 | 1·0 | 17·1 | 1·6 |
| 52 | 1 13·0 | 1 13·2 | 1 09·7 | 5·2 | 0·4 | 11·2 | 0·8 | 17·2 | 1·3 | 52 | 1 28·0 | 1 28·2 | 1 24·0 | 5·2 | 0·5 | 11·2 | 1·0 | 17·2 | 1·6 |
| 53 | 1 13·3 | 1 13·5 | 1 09·9 | 5·3 | 0·4 | 11·3 | 0·8 | 17·3 | 1·3 | 53 | 1 28·3 | 1 28·5 | 1 24·2 | 5·3 | 0·5 | 11·3 | 1·0 | 17·3 | 1·6 |
| 54 | 1 13·5 | 1 13·7 | 1 10·2 | 5·4 | 0·4 | 11·4 | 0·9 | 17·4 | 1·3 | 54 | 1 28·5 | 1 28·7 | 1 24·5 | 5·4 | 0·5 | 11·4 | 1·0 | 17·4 | 1·6 |
| 55 | 1 13·8 | 1 14·0 | 1 10·4 | 5·5 | 0·4 | 11·5 | 0·9 | 17·5 | 1·3 | 55 | 1 28·8 | 1 29·0 | 1 24·7 | 5·5 | 0·5 | 11·5 | 1·1 | 17·5 | 1·6 |
| 56 | 1 14·0 | 1 14·2 | 1 10·6 | 5·6 | 0·4 | 11·6 | 0·9 | 17·6 | 1·3 | 56 | 1 29·0 | 1 29·2 | 1 24·9 | 5·6 | 0·5 | 11·6 | 1·1 | 17·6 | 1·6 |
| 57 | 1 14·3 | 1 14·5 | 1 10·9 | 5·7 | 0·4 | 11·7 | 0·9 | 17·7 | 1·3 | 57 | 1 29·3 | 1 29·5 | 1 25·2 | 5·7 | 0·5 | 11·7 | 1·1 | 17·7 | 1·6 |
| 58 | 1 14·5 | 1 14·7 | 1 11·1 | 5·8 | 0·4 | 11·8 | 0·9 | 17·8 | 1·3 | 58 | 1 29·5 | 1 29·7 | 1 25·4 | 5·8 | 0·5 | 11·8 | 1·1 | 17·8 | 1·6 |
| 59 | 1 14·8 | 1 15·0 | 1 11·3 | 5·9 | 0·4 | 11·9 | 0·9 | 17·9 | 1·3 | 59 | 1 29·8 | 1 30·0 | 1 25·7 | 5·9 | 0·5 | 11·9 | 1·1 | 17·9 | 1·6 |
| 60 | 1 15·0 | 1 15·2 | 1 11·6 | 6·0 | 0·5 | 12·0 | 0·9 | 18·0 | 1·4 | 60 | 1 30·0 | 1 30·2 | 1 25·9 | 6·0 | 0·6 | 12·0 | 1·1 | 18·0 | 1·7 |

| m 6 | SUN PLANETS | ARIES | MOON | v or Corrⁿ d | | v or Corrⁿ d | | v or Corrⁿ d | | m 7 | SUN PLANETS | ARIES | MOON | v or Corrⁿ d | | v or Corrⁿ d | | v or Corrⁿ d | |
|---|---|---|---|---|---|---|---|---|---|---|---|---|---|---|---|---|---|---|---|
| s | ° ′ | ° ′ | ° ′ | ′ | ′ | ′ | ′ | ′ | ′ | s | ° ′ | ° ′ | ° ′ | ′ | ′ | ′ | ′ | ′ | ′ |
| 00 | 1 30·0 | 1 30·2 | 1 25·9 | 0·0 | 0·0 | 6·0 | 0·7 | 12·0 | 1·3 | 00 | 1 45·0 | 1 45·3 | 1 40·2 | 0·0 | 0·0 | 6·0 | 0·8 | 12·0 | 1·5 |
| 01 | 1 30·3 | 1 30·5 | 1 26·1 | 0·1 | 0·0 | 6·1 | 0·7 | 12·1 | 1·3 | 01 | 1 45·3 | 1 45·5 | 1 40·5 | 0·1 | 0·0 | 6·1 | 0·8 | 12·1 | 1·5 |
| 02 | 1 30·5 | 1 30·7 | 1 26·4 | 0·2 | 0·0 | 6·2 | 0·7 | 12·2 | 1·3 | 02 | 1 45·5 | 1 45·8 | 1 40·7 | 0·2 | 0·0 | 6·2 | 0·8 | 12·2 | 1·5 |
| 03 | 1 30·8 | 1 31·0 | 1 26·6 | 0·3 | 0·0 | 6·3 | 0·7 | 12·3 | 1·3 | 03 | 1 45·8 | 1 46·0 | 1 40·9 | 0·3 | 0·0 | 6·3 | 0·8 | 12·3 | 1·5 |
| 04 | 1 31·0 | 1 31·2 | 1 26·9 | 0·4 | 0·0 | 6·4 | 0·7 | 12·4 | 1·3 | 04 | 1 46·0 | 1 46·3 | 1 41·2 | 0·4 | 0·1 | 6·4 | 0·8 | 12·4 | 1·6 |
| 05 | 1 31·3 | 1 31·5 | 1 27·1 | 0·5 | 0·1 | 6·5 | 0·7 | 12·5 | 1·4 | 05 | 1 46·3 | 1 46·5 | 1 41·4 | 0·5 | 0·1 | 6·5 | 0·8 | 12·5 | 1·6 |
| 06 | 1 31·5 | 1 31·8 | 1 27·3 | 0·6 | 0·1 | 6·6 | 0·7 | 12·6 | 1·4 | 06 | 1 46·5 | 1 46·8 | 1 41·6 | 0·6 | 0·1 | 6·6 | 0·8 | 12·6 | 1·6 |
| 07 | 1 31·8 | 1 32·0 | 1 27·6 | 0·7 | 0·1 | 6·7 | 0·7 | 12·7 | 1·4 | 07 | 1 46·8 | 1 47·0 | 1 41·9 | 0·7 | 0·1 | 6·7 | 0·8 | 12·7 | 1·6 |
| 08 | 1 32·0 | 1 32·3 | 1 27·8 | 0·8 | 0·1 | 6·8 | 0·7 | 12·8 | 1·4 | 08 | 1 47·0 | 1 47·3 | 1 42·1 | 0·8 | 0·1 | 6·8 | 0·9 | 12·8 | 1·6 |
| 09 | 1 32·3 | 1 32·5 | 1 28·0 | 0·9 | 0·1 | 6·9 | 0·7 | 12·9 | 1·4 | 09 | 1 47·3 | 1 47·5 | 1 42·4 | 0·9 | 0·1 | 6·9 | 0·9 | 12·9 | 1·6 |
| 10 | 1 32·5 | 1 32·8 | 1 28·3 | 1·0 | 0·1 | 7·0 | 0·8 | 13·0 | 1·4 | 10 | 1 47·5 | 1 47·8 | 1 42·6 | 1·0 | 0·1 | 7·0 | 0·9 | 13·0 | 1·6 |
| 11 | 1 32·8 | 1 33·0 | 1 28·5 | 1·1 | 0·1 | 7·1 | 0·8 | 13·1 | 1·4 | 11 | 1 47·8 | 1 48·0 | 1 42·8 | 1·1 | 0·1 | 7·1 | 0·9 | 13·1 | 1·6 |
| 12 | 1 33·0 | 1 33·3 | 1 28·8 | 1·2 | 0·1 | 7·2 | 0·8 | 13·2 | 1·4 | 12 | 1 48·0 | 1 48·3 | 1 43·1 | 1·2 | 0·2 | 7·2 | 0·9 | 13·2 | 1·7 |
| 13 | 1 33·3 | 1 33·5 | 1 29·0 | 1·3 | 0·1 | 7·3 | 0·8 | 13·3 | 1·4 | 13 | 1 48·3 | 1 48·5 | 1 43·3 | 1·3 | 0·2 | 7·3 | 0·9 | 13·3 | 1·7 |
| 14 | 1 33·5 | 1 33·8 | 1 29·2 | 1·4 | 0·2 | 7·4 | 0·8 | 13·4 | 1·5 | 14 | 1 48·5 | 1 48·8 | 1 43·6 | 1·4 | 0·2 | 7·4 | 0·9 | 13·4 | 1·7 |
| 15 | 1 33·8 | 1 34·0 | 1 29·5 | 1·5 | 0·2 | 7·5 | 0·8 | 13·5 | 1·5 | 15 | 1 48·8 | 1 49·0 | 1 43·8 | 1·5 | 0·2 | 7·5 | 0·9 | 13·5 | 1·7 |
| 16 | 1 34·0 | 1 34·3 | 1 29·7 | 1·6 | 0·2 | 7·6 | 0·8 | 13·6 | 1·5 | 16 | 1 49·0 | 1 49·3 | 1 44·0 | 1·6 | 0·2 | 7·6 | 1·0 | 13·6 | 1·7 |
| 17 | 1 34·3 | 1 34·5 | 1 30·0 | 1·7 | 0·2 | 7·7 | 0·8 | 13·7 | 1·5 | 17 | 1 49·3 | 1 49·5 | 1 44·3 | 1·7 | 0·2 | 7·7 | 1·0 | 13·7 | 1·7 |
| 18 | 1 34·5 | 1 34·8 | 1 30·2 | 1·8 | 0·2 | 7·8 | 0·8 | 13·8 | 1·5 | 18 | 1 49·5 | 1 49·8 | 1 44·5 | 1·8 | 0·2 | 7·8 | 1·0 | 13·8 | 1·7 |
| 19 | 1 34·8 | 1 35·0 | 1 30·4 | 1·9 | 0·2 | 7·9 | 0·9 | 13·9 | 1·5 | 19 | 1 49·8 | 1 50·1 | 1 44·8 | 1·9 | 0·2 | 7·9 | 1·0 | 13·9 | 1·7 |
| 20 | 1 35·0 | 1 35·3 | 1 30·7 | 2·0 | 0·2 | 8·0 | 0·9 | 14·0 | 1·5 | 20 | 1 50·0 | 1 50·3 | 1 45·0 | 2·0 | 0·3 | 8·0 | 1·0 | 14·0 | 1·8 |
| 21 | 1 35·3 | 1 35·5 | 1 30·9 | 2·1 | 0·2 | 8·1 | 0·9 | 14·1 | 1·5 | 21 | 1 50·3 | 1 50·6 | 1 45·2 | 2·1 | 0·3 | 8·1 | 1·0 | 14·1 | 1·8 |
| 22 | 1 35·5 | 1 35·8 | 1 31·1 | 2·2 | 0·2 | 8·2 | 0·9 | 14·2 | 1·5 | 22 | 1 50·5 | 1 50·8 | 1 45·5 | 2·2 | 0·3 | 8·2 | 1·0 | 14·2 | 1·8 |
| 23 | 1 35·8 | 1 36·0 | 1 31·4 | 2·3 | 0·2 | 8·3 | 0·9 | 14·3 | 1·5 | 23 | 1 50·8 | 1 51·1 | 1 45·7 | 2·3 | 0·3 | 8·3 | 1·0 | 14·3 | 1·8 |
| 24 | 1 36·0 | 1 36·3 | 1 31·6 | 2·4 | 0·3 | 8·4 | 0·9 | 14·4 | 1·6 | 24 | 1 51·0 | 1 51·3 | 1 45·9 | 2·4 | 0·3 | 8·4 | 1·1 | 14·4 | 1·8 |
| 25 | 1 36·3 | 1 36·5 | 1 31·9 | 2·5 | 0·3 | 8·5 | 0·9 | 14·5 | 1·6 | 25 | 1 51·3 | 1 51·6 | 1 46·2 | 2·5 | 0·3 | 8·5 | 1·1 | 14·5 | 1·8 |
| 26 | 1 36·5 | 1 36·8 | 1 32·1 | 2·6 | 0·3 | 8·6 | 0·9 | 14·6 | 1·6 | 26 | 1 51·5 | 1 51·8 | 1 46·4 | 2·6 | 0·3 | 8·6 | 1·1 | 14·6 | 1·8 |
| 27 | 1 36·8 | 1 37·0 | 1 32·3 | 2·7 | 0·3 | 8·7 | 0·9 | 14·7 | 1·6 | 27 | 1 51·8 | 1 52·1 | 1 46·7 | 2·7 | 0·3 | 8·7 | 1·1 | 14·7 | 1·8 |
| 28 | 1 37·0 | 1 37·3 | 1 32·6 | 2·8 | 0·3 | 8·8 | 1·0 | 14·8 | 1·6 | 28 | 1 52·0 | 1 52·3 | 1 46·9 | 2·8 | 0·4 | 8·8 | 1·1 | 14·8 | 1·9 |
| 29 | 1 37·3 | 1 37·5 | 1 32·8 | 2·9 | 0·3 | 8·9 | 1·0 | 14·9 | 1·6 | 29 | 1 52·3 | 1 52·6 | 1 47·1 | 2·9 | 0·4 | 8·9 | 1·1 | 14·9 | 1·9 |
| 30 | 1 37·5 | 1 37·8 | 1 33·1 | 3·0 | 0·3 | 9·0 | 1·0 | 15·0 | 1·6 | 30 | 1 52·5 | 1 52·8 | 1 47·4 | 3·0 | 0·4 | 9·0 | 1·1 | 15·0 | 1·9 |
| 31 | 1 37·8 | 1 38·0 | 1 33·3 | 3·1 | 0·3 | 9·1 | 1·0 | 15·1 | 1·6 | 31 | 1 52·8 | 1 53·1 | 1 47·6 | 3·1 | 0·4 | 9·1 | 1·1 | 15·1 | 1·9 |
| 32 | 1 38·0 | 1 38·3 | 1 33·5 | 3·2 | 0·3 | 9·2 | 1·0 | 15·2 | 1·6 | 32 | 1 53·0 | 1 53·3 | 1 47·9 | 3·2 | 0·4 | 9·2 | 1·2 | 15·2 | 1·9 |
| 33 | 1 38·3 | 1 38·5 | 1 33·8 | 3·3 | 0·4 | 9·3 | 1·0 | 15·3 | 1·7 | 33 | 1 53·3 | 1 53·6 | 1 48·1 | 3·3 | 0·4 | 9·3 | 1·2 | 15·3 | 1·9 |
| 34 | 1 38·5 | 1 38·8 | 1 34·0 | 3·4 | 0·4 | 9·4 | 1·0 | 15·4 | 1·7 | 34 | 1 53·5 | 1 53·8 | 1 48·3 | 3·4 | 0·4 | 9·4 | 1·2 | 15·4 | 1·9 |
| 35 | 1 38·8 | 1 39·0 | 1 34·3 | 3·5 | 0·4 | 9·5 | 1·0 | 15·5 | 1·7 | 35 | 1 53·8 | 1 54·1 | 1 48·6 | 3·5 | 0·4 | 9·5 | 1·2 | 15·5 | 1·9 |
| 36 | 1 39·0 | 1 39·3 | 1 34·5 | 3·6 | 0·4 | 9·6 | 1·0 | 15·6 | 1·7 | 36 | 1 54·0 | 1 54·3 | 1 48·8 | 3·6 | 0·5 | 9·6 | 1·2 | 15·6 | 2·0 |
| 37 | 1 39·3 | 1 39·5 | 1 34·7 | 3·7 | 0·4 | 9·7 | 1·1 | 15·7 | 1·7 | 37 | 1 54·3 | 1 54·6 | 1 49·0 | 3·7 | 0·5 | 9·7 | 1·2 | 15·7 | 2·0 |
| 38 | 1 39·5 | 1 39·8 | 1 35·0 | 3·8 | 0·4 | 9·8 | 1·1 | 15·8 | 1·7 | 38 | 1 54·5 | 1 54·8 | 1 49·3 | 3·8 | 0·5 | 9·8 | 1·2 | 15·8 | 2·0 |
| 39 | 1 39·8 | 1 40·0 | 1 35·2 | 3·9 | 0·4 | 9·9 | 1·1 | 15·9 | 1·7 | 39 | 1 54·8 | 1 55·1 | 1 49·5 | 3·9 | 0·5 | 9·9 | 1·2 | 15·9 | 2·0 |
| 40 | 1 40·0 | 1 40·3 | 1 35·4 | 4·0 | 0·4 | 10·0 | 1·1 | 16·0 | 1·7 | 40 | 1 55·0 | 1 55·3 | 1 49·8 | 4·0 | 0·5 | 10·0 | 1·3 | 16·0 | 2·0 |
| 41 | 1 40·3 | 1 40·5 | 1 35·7 | 4·1 | 0·4 | 10·1 | 1·1 | 16·1 | 1·7 | 41 | 1 55·3 | 1 55·6 | 1 50·0 | 4·1 | 0·5 | 10·1 | 1·3 | 16·1 | 2·0 |
| 42 | 1 40·5 | 1 40·8 | 1 35·9 | 4·2 | 0·5 | 10·2 | 1·1 | 16·2 | 1·8 | 42 | 1 55·5 | 1 55·8 | 1 50·2 | 4·2 | 0·5 | 10·2 | 1·3 | 16·2 | 2·0 |
| 43 | 1 40·8 | 1 41·0 | 1 36·2 | 4·3 | 0·5 | 10·3 | 1·1 | 16·3 | 1·8 | 43 | 1 55·8 | 1 56·1 | 1 50·5 | 4·3 | 0·5 | 10·3 | 1·3 | 16·3 | 2·0 |
| 44 | 1 41·0 | 1 41·3 | 1 36·4 | 4·4 | 0·5 | 10·4 | 1·1 | 16·4 | 1·8 | 44 | 1 56·0 | 1 56·3 | 1 50·7 | 4·4 | 0·6 | 10·4 | 1·3 | 16·4 | 2·1 |
| 45 | 1 41·3 | 1 41·5 | 1 36·6 | 4·5 | 0·5 | 10·5 | 1·1 | 16·5 | 1·8 | 45 | 1 56·3 | 1 56·6 | 1 51·0 | 4·5 | 0·6 | 10·5 | 1·3 | 16·5 | 2·1 |
| 46 | 1 41·5 | 1 41·8 | 1 36·9 | 4·6 | 0·5 | 10·6 | 1·1 | 16·6 | 1·8 | 46 | 1 56·5 | 1 56·8 | 1 51·2 | 4·6 | 0·6 | 10·6 | 1·3 | 16·6 | 2·1 |
| 47 | 1 41·8 | 1 42·0 | 1 37·1 | 4·7 | 0·5 | 10·7 | 1·2 | 16·7 | 1·8 | 47 | 1 56·8 | 1 57·1 | 1 51·4 | 4·7 | 0·6 | 10·7 | 1·3 | 16·7 | 2·1 |
| 48 | 1 42·0 | 1 42·3 | 1 37·4 | 4·8 | 0·5 | 10·8 | 1·2 | 16·8 | 1·8 | 48 | 1 57·0 | 1 57·3 | 1 51·7 | 4·8 | 0·6 | 10·8 | 1·4 | 16·8 | 2·1 |
| 49 | 1 42·3 | 1 42·5 | 1 37·6 | 4·9 | 0·5 | 10·9 | 1·2 | 16·9 | 1·8 | 49 | 1 57·3 | 1 57·6 | 1 51·9 | 4·9 | 0·6 | 10·9 | 1·4 | 16·9 | 2·1 |
| 50 | 1 42·5 | 1 42·8 | 1 37·8 | 5·0 | 0·5 | 11·0 | 1·2 | 17·0 | 1·8 | 50 | 1 57·5 | 1 57·8 | 1 52·1 | 5·0 | 0·6 | 11·0 | 1·4 | 17·0 | 2·1 |
| 51 | 1 42·8 | 1 43·0 | 1 38·1 | 5·1 | 0·6 | 11·1 | 1·2 | 17·1 | 1·9 | 51 | 1 57·8 | 1 58·1 | 1 52·4 | 5·1 | 0·6 | 11·1 | 1·4 | 17·1 | 2·1 |
| 52 | 1 43·0 | 1 43·3 | 1 38·3 | 5·2 | 0·6 | 11·2 | 1·2 | 17·2 | 1·9 | 52 | 1 58·0 | 1 58·3 | 1 52·6 | 5·2 | 0·7 | 11·2 | 1·4 | 17·2 | 2·2 |
| 53 | 1 43·3 | 1 43·5 | 1 38·5 | 5·3 | 0·6 | 11·3 | 1·2 | 17·3 | 1·9 | 53 | 1 58·3 | 1 58·6 | 1 52·9 | 5·3 | 0·7 | 11·3 | 1·4 | 17·3 | 2·2 |
| 54 | 1 43·5 | 1 43·8 | 1 38·8 | 5·4 | 0·6 | 11·4 | 1·2 | 17·4 | 1·9 | 54 | 1 58·5 | 1 58·8 | 1 53·1 | 5·4 | 0·7 | 11·4 | 1·4 | 17·4 | 2·2 |
| 55 | 1 43·8 | 1 44·0 | 1 39·0 | 5·5 | 0·6 | 11·5 | 1·2 | 17·5 | 1·9 | 55 | 1 58·8 | 1 59·1 | 1 53·3 | 5·5 | 0·7 | 11·5 | 1·4 | 17·5 | 2·2 |
| 56 | 1 44·0 | 1 44·3 | 1 39·3 | 5·6 | 0·6 | 11·6 | 1·3 | 17·6 | 1·9 | 56 | 1 59·0 | 1 59·3 | 1 53·6 | 5·6 | 0·7 | 11·6 | 1·5 | 17·6 | 2·2 |
| 57 | 1 44·3 | 1 44·5 | 1 39·5 | 5·7 | 0·6 | 11·7 | 1·3 | 17·7 | 1·9 | 57 | 1 59·3 | 1 59·6 | 1 53·8 | 5·7 | 0·7 | 11·7 | 1·5 | 17·7 | 2·2 |
| 58 | 1 44·5 | 1 44·8 | 1 39·7 | 5·8 | 0·6 | 11·8 | 1·3 | 17·8 | 1·9 | 58 | 1 59·5 | 1 59·8 | 1 54·1 | 5·8 | 0·7 | 11·8 | 1·5 | 17·8 | 2·2 |
| 59 | 1 44·8 | 1 45·0 | 1 40·0 | 5·9 | 0·6 | 11·9 | 1·3 | 17·9 | 1·9 | 59 | 1 59·8 | 2 00·1 | 1 54·3 | 5·9 | 0·7 | 11·9 | 1·5 | 17·9 | 2·2 |
| 60 | 1 45·0 | 1 45·3 | 1 40·2 | 6·0 | 0·7 | 12·0 | 1·3 | 18·0 | 2·0 | 60 | 2 00·0 | 2 00·3 | 1 54·5 | 6·0 | 0·8 | 12·0 | 1·5 | 18·0 | 2·3 |

## 8ᵐ

| 8 ᵐ / s | SUN PLANETS | ARIES | MOON | v or d | Corrⁿ | v or d | Corrⁿ | v or d | Corrⁿ |
|---|---|---|---|---|---|---|---|---|---|
| | ° ′ | ° ′ | ° ′ | ′ | ′ | ′ | ′ | ′ | ′ |
| 00 | 2 00·0 | 2 00·3 | 1 54·5 | 0·0 | 0·0 | 6·0 | 0·9 | 12·0 | 1·7 |
| 01 | 2 00·3 | 2 00·6 | 1 54·8 | 0·1 | 0·0 | 6·1 | 0·9 | 12·1 | 1·7 |
| 02 | 2 00·5 | 2 00·8 | 1 55·0 | 0·2 | 0·0 | 6·2 | 0·9 | 12·2 | 1·7 |
| 03 | 2 00·8 | 2 01·1 | 1 55·2 | 0·3 | 0·0 | 6·3 | 0·9 | 12·3 | 1·7 |
| 04 | 2 01·0 | 2 01·3 | 1 55·5 | 0·4 | 0·1 | 6·4 | 0·9 | 12·4 | 1·8 |
| 05 | 2 01·3 | 2 01·6 | 1 55·7 | 0·5 | 0·1 | 6·5 | 0·9 | 12·5 | 1·8 |
| 06 | 2 01·5 | 2 01·8 | 1 56·0 | 0·6 | 0·1 | 6·6 | 0·9 | 12·6 | 1·8 |
| 07 | 2 01·8 | 2 02·1 | 1 56·2 | 0·7 | 0·1 | 6·7 | 0·9 | 12·7 | 1·8 |
| 08 | 2 02·0 | 2 02·3 | 1 56·4 | 0·8 | 0·1 | 6·8 | 1·0 | 12·8 | 1·8 |
| 09 | 2 02·3 | 2 02·6 | 1 56·7 | 0·9 | 0·1 | 6·9 | 1·0 | 12·9 | 1·8 |
| 10 | 2 02·5 | 2 02·8 | 1 56·9 | 1·0 | 0·1 | 7·0 | 1·0 | 13·0 | 1·8 |
| 11 | 2 02·8 | 2 03·1 | 1 57·2 | 1·1 | 0·2 | 7·1 | 1·0 | 13·1 | 1·9 |
| 12 | 2 03·0 | 2 03·3 | 1 57·4 | 1·2 | 0·2 | 7·2 | 1·0 | 13·2 | 1·9 |
| 13 | 2 03·3 | 2 03·6 | 1 57·6 | 1·3 | 0·2 | 7·3 | 1·0 | 13·3 | 1·9 |
| 14 | 2 03·5 | 2 03·8 | 1 57·9 | 1·4 | 0·2 | 7·4 | 1·0 | 13·4 | 1·9 |
| 15 | 2 03·8 | 2 04·1 | 1 58·1 | 1·5 | 0·2 | 7·5 | 1·1 | 13·5 | 1·9 |
| 16 | 2 04·0 | 2 04·3 | 1 58·4 | 1·6 | 0·2 | 7·6 | 1·1 | 13·6 | 1·9 |
| 17 | 2 04·3 | 2 04·6 | 1 58·6 | 1·7 | 0·2 | 7·7 | 1·1 | 13·7 | 1·9 |
| 18 | 2 04·5 | 2 04·8 | 1 58·8 | 1·8 | 0·3 | 7·8 | 1·1 | 13·8 | 2·0 |
| 19 | 2 04·8 | 2 05·1 | 1 59·1 | 1·9 | 0·3 | 7·9 | 1·1 | 13·9 | 2·0 |
| 20 | 2 05·0 | 2 05·3 | 1 59·3 | 2·0 | 0·3 | 8·0 | 1·1 | 14·0 | 2·0 |
| 21 | 2 05·3 | 2 05·6 | 1 59·5 | 2·1 | 0·3 | 8·1 | 1·1 | 14·1 | 2·0 |
| 22 | 2 05·5 | 2 05·8 | 1 59·8 | 2·2 | 0·3 | 8·2 | 1·2 | 14·2 | 2·0 |
| 23 | 2 05·8 | 2 06·1 | 2 00·0 | 2·3 | 0·3 | 8·3 | 1·2 | 14·3 | 2·0 |
| 24 | 2 06·0 | 2 06·3 | 2 00·3 | 2·4 | 0·3 | 8·4 | 1·2 | 14·4 | 2·0 |
| 25 | 2 06·3 | 2 06·6 | 2 00·5 | 2·5 | 0·4 | 8·5 | 1·2 | 14·5 | 2·1 |
| 26 | 2 06·5 | 2 06·8 | 2 00·7 | 2·6 | 0·4 | 8·6 | 1·2 | 14·6 | 2·1 |
| 27 | 2 06·8 | 2 07·1 | 2 01·0 | 2·7 | 0·4 | 8·7 | 1·2 | 14·7 | 2·1 |
| 28 | 2 07·0 | 2 07·3 | 2 01·2 | 2·8 | 0·4 | 8·8 | 1·2 | 14·8 | 2·1 |
| 29 | 2 07·3 | 2 07·6 | 2 01·5 | 2·9 | 0·4 | 8·9 | 1·3 | 14·9 | 2·1 |
| 30 | 2 07·5 | 2 07·8 | 2 01·7 | 3·0 | 0·4 | 9·0 | 1·3 | 15·0 | 2·1 |
| 31 | 2 07·8 | 2 08·1 | 2 01·9 | 3·1 | 0·4 | 9·1 | 1·3 | 15·1 | 2·1 |
| 32 | 2 08·0 | 2 08·4 | 2 02·2 | 3·2 | 0·5 | 9·2 | 1·3 | 15·2 | 2·2 |
| 33 | 2 08·3 | 2 08·6 | 2 02·4 | 3·3 | 0·5 | 9·3 | 1·3 | 15·3 | 2·2 |
| 34 | 2 08·5 | 2 08·9 | 2 02·6 | 3·4 | 0·5 | 9·4 | 1·3 | 15·4 | 2·2 |
| 35 | 2 08·8 | 2 09·1 | 2 02·9 | 3·5 | 0·5 | 9·5 | 1·3 | 15·5 | 2·2 |
| 36 | 2 09·0 | 2 09·4 | 2 03·1 | 3·6 | 0·5 | 9·6 | 1·4 | 15·6 | 2·2 |
| 37 | 2 09·3 | 2 09·6 | 2 03·4 | 3·7 | 0·5 | 9·7 | 1·4 | 15·7 | 2·2 |
| 38 | 2 09·5 | 2 09·9 | 2 03·6 | 3·8 | 0·5 | 9·8 | 1·4 | 15·8 | 2·2 |
| 39 | 2 09·8 | 2 10·1 | 2 03·8 | 3·9 | 0·6 | 9·9 | 1·4 | 15·9 | 2·3 |
| 40 | 2 10·0 | 2 10·4 | 2 04·1 | 4·0 | 0·6 | 10·0 | 1·4 | 16·0 | 2·3 |
| 41 | 2 10·3 | 2 10·6 | 2 04·3 | 4·1 | 0·6 | 10·1 | 1·4 | 16·1 | 2·3 |
| 42 | 2 10·5 | 2 10·9 | 2 04·6 | 4·2 | 0·6 | 10·2 | 1·4 | 16·2 | 2·3 |
| 43 | 2 10·8 | 2 11·1 | 2 04·8 | 4·3 | 0·6 | 10·3 | 1·5 | 16·3 | 2·3 |
| 44 | 2 11·0 | 2 11·4 | 2 05·0 | 4·4 | 0·6 | 10·4 | 1·5 | 16·4 | 2·3 |
| 45 | 2 11·3 | 2 11·6 | 2 05·3 | 4·5 | 0·6 | 10·5 | 1·5 | 16·5 | 2·3 |
| 46 | 2 11·5 | 2 11·9 | 2 05·5 | 4·6 | 0·7 | 10·6 | 1·5 | 16·6 | 2·4 |
| 47 | 2 11·8 | 2 12·1 | 2 05·7 | 4·7 | 0·7 | 10·7 | 1·5 | 16·7 | 2·4 |
| 48 | 2 12·0 | 2 12·4 | 2 06·0 | 4·8 | 0·7 | 10·8 | 1·5 | 16·8 | 2·4 |
| 49 | 2 12·3 | 2 12·6 | 2 06·2 | 4·9 | 0·7 | 10·9 | 1·5 | 16·9 | 2·4 |
| 50 | 2 12·5 | 2 12·9 | 2 06·5 | 5·0 | 0·7 | 11·0 | 1·6 | 17·0 | 2·4 |
| 51 | 2 12·8 | 2 13·1 | 2 06·7 | 5·1 | 0·7 | 11·1 | 1·6 | 17·1 | 2·4 |
| 52 | 2 13·0 | 2 13·4 | 2 06·9 | 5·2 | 0·7 | 11·2 | 1·6 | 17·2 | 2·4 |
| 53 | 2 13·3 | 2 13·6 | 2 07·2 | 5·3 | 0·8 | 11·3 | 1·6 | 17·3 | 2·5 |
| 54 | 2 13·5 | 2 13·9 | 2 07·4 | 5·4 | 0·8 | 11·4 | 1·6 | 17·4 | 2·5 |
| 55 | 2 13·8 | 2 14·1 | 2 07·7 | 5·5 | 0·8 | 11·5 | 1·6 | 17·5 | 2·5 |
| 56 | 2 14·0 | 2 14·4 | 2 07·9 | 5·6 | 0·8 | 11·6 | 1·6 | 17·6 | 2·5 |
| 57 | 2 14·3 | 2 14·6 | 2 08·1 | 5·7 | 0·8 | 11·7 | 1·7 | 17·7 | 2·5 |
| 58 | 2 14·5 | 2 14·9 | 2 08·4 | 5·8 | 0·8 | 11·8 | 1·7 | 17·8 | 2·5 |
| 59 | 2 14·8 | 2 15·1 | 2 08·6 | 5·9 | 0·8 | 11·9 | 1·7 | 17·9 | 2·5 |
| 60 | 2 15·0 | 2 15·4 | 2 08·9 | 6·0 | 0·9 | 12·0 | 1·7 | 18·0 | 2·6 |

## 9ᵐ

| 9 ᵐ / s | SUN PLANETS | ARIES | MOON | v or d | Corrⁿ | v or d | Corrⁿ | v or d | Corrⁿ |
|---|---|---|---|---|---|---|---|---|---|
| | ° ′ | ° ′ | ° ′ | ′ | ′ | ′ | ′ | ′ | ′ |
| 00 | 2 15·0 | 2 15·4 | 2 08·9 | 0·0 | 0·0 | 6·0 | 1·0 | 12·0 | 1·9 |
| 01 | 2 15·3 | 2 15·6 | 2 09·1 | 0·1 | 0·0 | 6·1 | 1·0 | 12·1 | 1·9 |
| 02 | 2 15·5 | 2 15·9 | 2 09·3 | 0·2 | 0·0 | 6·2 | 1·0 | 12·2 | 1·9 |
| 03 | 2 15·8 | 2 16·1 | 2 09·6 | 0·3 | 0·0 | 6·3 | 1·0 | 12·3 | 1·9 |
| 04 | 2 16·0 | 2 16·4 | 2 09·8 | 0·4 | 0·1 | 6·4 | 1·0 | 12·4 | 2·0 |
| 05 | 2 16·3 | 2 16·6 | 2 10·0 | 0·5 | 0·1 | 6·5 | 1·0 | 12·5 | 2·0 |
| 06 | 2 16·5 | 2 16·9 | 2 10·3 | 0·6 | 0·1 | 6·6 | 1·0 | 12·6 | 2·0 |
| 07 | 2 16·8 | 2 17·1 | 2 10·5 | 0·7 | 0·1 | 6·7 | 1·1 | 12·7 | 2·0 |
| 08 | 2 17·0 | 2 17·4 | 2 10·8 | 0·8 | 0·1 | 6·8 | 1·1 | 12·8 | 2·0 |
| 09 | 2 17·3 | 2 17·6 | 2 11·0 | 0·9 | 0·1 | 6·9 | 1·1 | 12·9 | 2·0 |
| 10 | 2 17·5 | 2 17·9 | 2 11·2 | 1·0 | 0·2 | 7·0 | 1·1 | 13·0 | 2·1 |
| 11 | 2 17·8 | 2 18·1 | 2 11·5 | 1·1 | 0·2 | 7·1 | 1·1 | 13·1 | 2·1 |
| 12 | 2 18·0 | 2 18·4 | 2 11·7 | 1·2 | 0·2 | 7·2 | 1·1 | 13·2 | 2·1 |
| 13 | 2 18·3 | 2 18·6 | 2 12·0 | 1·3 | 0·2 | 7·3 | 1·2 | 13·3 | 2·1 |
| 14 | 2 18·5 | 2 18·9 | 2 12·2 | 1·4 | 0·2 | 7·4 | 1·2 | 13·4 | 2·1 |
| 15 | 2 18·8 | 2 19·1 | 2 12·4 | 1·5 | 0·2 | 7·5 | 1·2 | 13·5 | 2·1 |
| 16 | 2 19·0 | 2 19·4 | 2 12·7 | 1·6 | 0·3 | 7·6 | 1·2 | 13·6 | 2·2 |
| 17 | 2 19·3 | 2 19·6 | 2 12·9 | 1·7 | 0·3 | 7·7 | 1·2 | 13·7 | 2·2 |
| 18 | 2 19·5 | 2 19·9 | 2 13·1 | 1·8 | 0·3 | 7·8 | 1·2 | 13·8 | 2·2 |
| 19 | 2 19·8 | 2 20·1 | 2 13·4 | 1·9 | 0·3 | 7·9 | 1·3 | 13·9 | 2·2 |
| 20 | 2 20·0 | 2 20·4 | 2 13·6 | 2·0 | 0·3 | 8·0 | 1·3 | 14·0 | 2·2 |
| 21 | 2 20·3 | 2 20·6 | 2 13·9 | 2·1 | 0·3 | 8·1 | 1·3 | 14·1 | 2·2 |
| 22 | 2 20·5 | 2 20·9 | 2 14·1 | 2·2 | 0·3 | 8·2 | 1·3 | 14·2 | 2·2 |
| 23 | 2 20·8 | 2 21·1 | 2 14·3 | 2·3 | 0·4 | 8·3 | 1·3 | 14·3 | 2·3 |
| 24 | 2 21·0 | 2 21·4 | 2 14·6 | 2·4 | 0·4 | 8·4 | 1·3 | 14·4 | 2·3 |
| 25 | 2 21·3 | 2 21·6 | 2 14·8 | 2·5 | 0·4 | 8·5 | 1·3 | 14·5 | 2·3 |
| 26 | 2 21·5 | 2 21·9 | 2 15·1 | 2·6 | 0·4 | 8·6 | 1·4 | 14·6 | 2·3 |
| 27 | 2 21·8 | 2 22·1 | 2 15·3 | 2·7 | 0·4 | 8·7 | 1·4 | 14·7 | 2·3 |
| 28 | 2 22·0 | 2 22·4 | 2 15·5 | 2·8 | 0·4 | 8·8 | 1·4 | 14·8 | 2·3 |
| 29 | 2 22·3 | 2 22·6 | 2 15·8 | 2·9 | 0·5 | 8·9 | 1·4 | 14·9 | 2·4 |
| 30 | 2 22·5 | 2 22·9 | 2 16·0 | 3·0 | 0·5 | 9·0 | 1·4 | 15·0 | 2·4 |
| 31 | 2 22·8 | 2 23·1 | 2 16·2 | 3·1 | 0·5 | 9·1 | 1·4 | 15·1 | 2·4 |
| 32 | 2 23·0 | 2 23·4 | 2 16·5 | 3·2 | 0·5 | 9·2 | 1·5 | 15·2 | 2·4 |
| 33 | 2 23·3 | 2 23·6 | 2 16·7 | 3·3 | 0·5 | 9·3 | 1·5 | 15·3 | 2·4 |
| 34 | 2 23·5 | 2 23·9 | 2 17·0 | 3·4 | 0·5 | 9·4 | 1·5 | 15·4 | 2·4 |
| 35 | 2 23·8 | 2 24·1 | 2 17·2 | 3·5 | 0·6 | 9·5 | 1·5 | 15·5 | 2·5 |
| 36 | 2 24·0 | 2 24·4 | 2 17·4 | 3·6 | 0·6 | 9·6 | 1·5 | 15·6 | 2·5 |
| 37 | 2 24·3 | 2 24·6 | 2 17·7 | 3·7 | 0·6 | 9·7 | 1·5 | 15·7 | 2·5 |
| 38 | 2 24·5 | 2 24·9 | 2 17·9 | 3·8 | 0·6 | 9·8 | 1·6 | 15·8 | 2·5 |
| 39 | 2 24·8 | 2 25·1 | 2 18·2 | 3·9 | 0·6 | 9·9 | 1·6 | 15·9 | 2·5 |
| 40 | 2 25·0 | 2 25·4 | 2 18·4 | 4·0 | 0·6 | 10·0 | 1·6 | 16·0 | 2·5 |
| 41 | 2 25·3 | 2 25·6 | 2 18·6 | 4·1 | 0·6 | 10·1 | 1·6 | 16·1 | 2·5 |
| 42 | 2 25·5 | 2 25·9 | 2 18·9 | 4·2 | 0·7 | 10·2 | 1·6 | 16·2 | 2·6 |
| 43 | 2 25·8 | 2 26·1 | 2 19·1 | 4·3 | 0·7 | 10·3 | 1·6 | 16·3 | 2·6 |
| 44 | 2 26·0 | 2 26·4 | 2 19·3 | 4·4 | 0·7 | 10·4 | 1·6 | 16·4 | 2·6 |
| 45 | 2 26·3 | 2 26·7 | 2 19·6 | 4·5 | 0·7 | 10·5 | 1·7 | 16·5 | 2·6 |
| 46 | 2 26·5 | 2 26·9 | 2 19·8 | 4·6 | 0·7 | 10·6 | 1·7 | 16·6 | 2·6 |
| 47 | 2 26·8 | 2 27·2 | 2 20·1 | 4·7 | 0·7 | 10·7 | 1·7 | 16·7 | 2·6 |
| 48 | 2 27·0 | 2 27·4 | 2 20·3 | 4·8 | 0·8 | 10·8 | 1·7 | 16·8 | 2·7 |
| 49 | 2 27·3 | 2 27·7 | 2 20·5 | 4·9 | 0·8 | 10·9 | 1·7 | 16·9 | 2·7 |
| 50 | 2 27·5 | 2 27·9 | 2 20·8 | 5·0 | 0·8 | 11·0 | 1·7 | 17·0 | 2·7 |
| 51 | 2 27·8 | 2 28·2 | 2 21·0 | 5·1 | 0·8 | 11·1 | 1·8 | 17·1 | 2·7 |
| 52 | 2 28·0 | 2 28·4 | 2 21·3 | 5·2 | 0·8 | 11·2 | 1·8 | 17·2 | 2·7 |
| 53 | 2 28·3 | 2 28·7 | 2 21·5 | 5·3 | 0·8 | 11·3 | 1·8 | 17·3 | 2·7 |
| 54 | 2 28·5 | 2 28·9 | 2 21·7 | 5·4 | 0·9 | 11·4 | 1·8 | 17·4 | 2·8 |
| 55 | 2 28·8 | 2 29·2 | 2 22·0 | 5·5 | 0·9 | 11·5 | 1·8 | 17·5 | 2·8 |
| 56 | 2 29·0 | 2 29·4 | 2 22·2 | 5·6 | 0·9 | 11·6 | 1·8 | 17·6 | 2·8 |
| 57 | 2 29·3 | 2 29·7 | 2 22·5 | 5·7 | 0·9 | 11·7 | 1·9 | 17·7 | 2·8 |
| 58 | 2 29·5 | 2 29·9 | 2 22·7 | 5·8 | 0·9 | 11·8 | 1·9 | 17·8 | 2·8 |
| 59 | 2 29·8 | 2 30·2 | 2 22·9 | 5·9 | 0·9 | 11·9 | 1·9 | 17·9 | 2·8 |
| 60 | 2 30·0 | 2 30·4 | 2 23·2 | 6·0 | 1·0 | 12·0 | 1·9 | 18·0 | 2·9 |

| 10ᵐ (s) | SUN PLANETS | ARIES | MOON | v or Corrⁿ d | v or Corrⁿ d | v or Corrⁿ d |
|---|---|---|---|---|---|---|
| | ° ′ | ° ′ | ° ′ | ′ ′ | ′ ′ | ′ ′ |
| 00 | 2 30·0 | 2 30·4 | 2 23·2 | 0·0 0·0 | 6·0 1·1 | 12·0 2·1 |
| 01 | 2 30·3 | 2 30·7 | 2 23·4 | 0·1 0·0 | 6·1 1·1 | 12·1 2·1 |
| 02 | 2 30·5 | 2 30·9 | 2 23·6 | 0·2 0·0 | 6·2 1·1 | 12·2 2·1 |
| 03 | 2 30·8 | 2 31·2 | 2 23·9 | 0·3 0·1 | 6·3 1·1 | 12·3 2·2 |
| 04 | 2 31·0 | 2 31·4 | 2 24·1 | 0·4 0·1 | 6·4 1·1 | 12·4 2·2 |
| 05 | 2 31·3 | 2 31·7 | 2 24·4 | 0·5 0·1 | 6·5 1·1 | 12·5 2·2 |
| 06 | 2 31·5 | 2 31·9 | 2 24·6 | 0·6 0·1 | 6·6 1·2 | 12·6 2·2 |
| 07 | 2 31·8 | 2 32·2 | 2 24·8 | 0·7 0·1 | 6·7 1·2 | 12·7 2·2 |
| 08 | 2 32·0 | 2 32·4 | 2 25·1 | 0·8 0·1 | 6·8 1·2 | 12·8 2·2 |
| 09 | 2 32·3 | 2 32·7 | 2 25·3 | 0·9 0·2 | 6·9 1·2 | 12·9 2·3 |
| 10 | 2 32·5 | 2 32·9 | 2 25·6 | 1·0 0·2 | 7·0 1·2 | 13·0 2·3 |
| 11 | 2 32·8 | 2 33·2 | 2 25·8 | 1·1 0·2 | 7·1 1·2 | 13·1 2·3 |
| 12 | 2 33·0 | 2 33·4 | 2 26·0 | 1·2 0·2 | 7·2 1·3 | 13·2 2·3 |
| 13 | 2 33·3 | 2 33·7 | 2 26·3 | 1·3 0·2 | 7·3 1·3 | 13·3 2·3 |
| 14 | 2 33·5 | 2 33·9 | 2 26·5 | 1·4 0·2 | 7·4 1·3 | 13·4 2·3 |
| 15 | 2 33·8 | 2 34·2 | 2 26·7 | 1·5 0·3 | 7·5 1·3 | 13·5 2·4 |
| 16 | 2 34·0 | 2 34·4 | 2 27·0 | 1·6 0·3 | 7·6 1·3 | 13·6 2·4 |
| 17 | 2 34·3 | 2 34·7 | 2 27·2 | 1·7 0·3 | 7·7 1·3 | 13·7 2·4 |
| 18 | 2 34·5 | 2 34·9 | 2 27·5 | 1·8 0·3 | 7·8 1·4 | 13·8 2·4 |
| 19 | 2 34·8 | 2 35·2 | 2 27·7 | 1·9 0·3 | 7·9 1·4 | 13·9 2·4 |
| 20 | 2 35·0 | 2 35·4 | 2 27·9 | 2·0 0·4 | 8·0 1·4 | 14·0 2·5 |
| 21 | 2 35·3 | 2 35·7 | 2 28·2 | 2·1 0·4 | 8·1 1·4 | 14·1 2·5 |
| 22 | 2 35·5 | 2 35·9 | 2 28·4 | 2·2 0·4 | 8·2 1·4 | 14·2 2·5 |
| 23 | 2 35·8 | 2 36·2 | 2 28·7 | 2·3 0·4 | 8·3 1·5 | 14·3 2·5 |
| 24 | 2 36·0 | 2 36·4 | 2 28·9 | 2·4 0·4 | 8·4 1·5 | 14·4 2·5 |
| 25 | 2 36·3 | 2 36·7 | 2 29·1 | 2·5 0·4 | 8·5 1·5 | 14·5 2·5 |
| 26 | 2 36·5 | 2 36·9 | 2 29·4 | 2·6 0·5 | 8·6 1·5 | 14·6 2·6 |
| 27 | 2 36·8 | 2 37·2 | 2 29·6 | 2·7 0·5 | 8·7 1·5 | 14·7 2·6 |
| 28 | 2 37·0 | 2 37·4 | 2 29·8 | 2·8 0·5 | 8·8 1·5 | 14·8 2·6 |
| 29 | 2 37·3 | 2 37·7 | 2 30·1 | 2·9 0·5 | 8·9 1·6 | 14·9 2·6 |
| 30 | 2 37·5 | 2 37·9 | 2 30·3 | 3·0 0·5 | 9·0 1·6 | 15·0 2·6 |
| 31 | 2 37·8 | 2 38·2 | 2 30·6 | 3·1 0·5 | 9·1 1·6 | 15·1 2·6 |
| 32 | 2 38·0 | 2 38·4 | 2 30·8 | 3·2 0·6 | 9·2 1·6 | 15·2 2·7 |
| 33 | 2 38·3 | 2 38·7 | 2 31·0 | 3·3 0·6 | 9·3 1·6 | 15·3 2·7 |
| 34 | 2 38·5 | 2 38·9 | 2 31·3 | 3·4 0·6 | 9·4 1·6 | 15·4 2·7 |
| 35 | 2 38·8 | 2 39·2 | 2 31·5 | 3·5 0·6 | 9·5 1·7 | 15·5 2·7 |
| 36 | 2 39·0 | 2 39·4 | 2 31·8 | 3·6 0·6 | 9·6 1·7 | 15·6 2·7 |
| 37 | 2 39·3 | 2 39·7 | 2 32·0 | 3·7 0·6 | 9·7 1·7 | 15·7 2·7 |
| 38 | 2 39·5 | 2 39·9 | 2 32·2 | 3·8 0·7 | 9·8 1·7 | 15·8 2·8 |
| 39 | 2 39·8 | 2 40·2 | 2 32·5 | 3·9 0·7 | 9·9 1·7 | 15·9 2·8 |
| 40 | 2 40·0 | 2 40·4 | 2 32·7 | 4·0 0·7 | 10·0 1·8 | 16·0 2·8 |
| 41 | 2 40·3 | 2 40·7 | 2 32·9 | 4·1 0·7 | 10·1 1·8 | 16·1 2·8 |
| 42 | 2 40·5 | 2 40·9 | 2 33·2 | 4·2 0·7 | 10·2 1·8 | 16·2 2·8 |
| 43 | 2 40·8 | 2 41·2 | 2 33·4 | 4·3 0·8 | 10·3 1·8 | 16·3 2·9 |
| 44 | 2 41·0 | 2 41·4 | 2 33·7 | 4·4 0·8 | 10·4 1·8 | 16·4 2·9 |
| 45 | 2 41·3 | 2 41·7 | 2 33·9 | 4·5 0·8 | 10·5 1·8 | 16·5 2·9 |
| 46 | 2 41·5 | 2 41·9 | 2 34·1 | 4·6 0·8 | 10·6 1·9 | 16·6 2·9 |
| 47 | 2 41·8 | 2 42·2 | 2 34·4 | 4·7 0·8 | 10·7 1·9 | 16·7 2·9 |
| 48 | 2 42·0 | 2 42·4 | 2 34·6 | 4·8 0·8 | 10·8 1·9 | 16·8 2·9 |
| 49 | 2 42·3 | 2 42·7 | 2 34·9 | 4·9 0·9 | 10·9 1·9 | 16·9 3·0 |
| 50 | 2 42·5 | 2 42·9 | 2 35·1 | 5·0 0·9 | 11·0 1·9 | 17·0 3·0 |
| 51 | 2 42·8 | 2 43·2 | 2 35·3 | 5·1 0·9 | 11·1 1·9 | 17·1 3·0 |
| 52 | 2 43·0 | 2 43·4 | 2 35·6 | 5·2 0·9 | 11·2 2·0 | 17·2 3·0 |
| 53 | 2 43·3 | 2 43·7 | 2 35·8 | 5·3 0·9 | 11·3 2·0 | 17·3 3·0 |
| 54 | 2 43·5 | 2 43·9 | 2 36·1 | 5·4 0·9 | 11·4 2·0 | 17·4 3·0 |
| 55 | 2 43·8 | 2 44·2 | 2 36·3 | 5·5 1·0 | 11·5 2·0 | 17·5 3·1 |
| 56 | 2 44·0 | 2 44·4 | 2 36·5 | 5·6 1·0 | 11·6 2·0 | 17·6 3·1 |
| 57 | 2 44·3 | 2 44·7 | 2 36·8 | 5·7 1·0 | 11·7 2·0 | 17·7 3·1 |
| 58 | 2 44·5 | 2 45·0 | 2 37·0 | 5·8 1·0 | 11·8 2·1 | 17·8 3·1 |
| 59 | 2 44·8 | 2 45·2 | 2 37·2 | 5·9 1·0 | 11·9 2·1 | 17·9 3·1 |
| 60 | 2 45·0 | 2 45·5 | 2 37·5 | 6·0 1·1 | 12·0 2·1 | 18·0 3·2 |

| 11ᵐ (s) | SUN PLANETS | ARIES | MOON | v or Corrⁿ d | v or Corrⁿ d | v or Corrⁿ d |
|---|---|---|---|---|---|---|
| | ° ′ | ° ′ | ° ′ | ′ ′ | ′ ′ | ′ ′ |
| 00 | 2 45·0 | 2 45·5 | 2 37·5 | 0·0 0·0 | 6·0 1·2 | 12·0 2·3 |
| 01 | 2 45·3 | 2 45·7 | 2 37·7 | 0·1 0·0 | 6·1 1·2 | 12·1 2·3 |
| 02 | 2 45·5 | 2 46·0 | 2 38·0 | 0·2 0·0 | 6·2 1·2 | 12·2 2·3 |
| 03 | 2 45·8 | 2 46·2 | 2 38·2 | 0·3 0·1 | 6·3 1·2 | 12·3 2·4 |
| 04 | 2 46·0 | 2 46·5 | 2 38·4 | 0·4 0·1 | 6·4 1·2 | 12·4 2·4 |
| 05 | 2 46·3 | 2 46·7 | 2 38·7 | 0·5 0·1 | 6·5 1·2 | 12·5 2·4 |
| 06 | 2 46·5 | 2 47·0 | 2 38·9 | 0·6 0·1 | 6·6 1·3 | 12·6 2·4 |
| 07 | 2 46·8 | 2 47·2 | 2 39·2 | 0·7 0·1 | 6·7 1·3 | 12·7 2·4 |
| 08 | 2 47·0 | 2 47·5 | 2 39·4 | 0·8 0·2 | 6·8 1·3 | 12·8 2·5 |
| 09 | 2 47·3 | 2 47·7 | 2 39·6 | 0·9 0·2 | 6·9 1·3 | 12·9 2·5 |
| 10 | 2 47·5 | 2 48·0 | 2 39·9 | 1·0 0·2 | 7·0 1·3 | 13·0 2·5 |
| 11 | 2 47·8 | 2 48·2 | 2 40·1 | 1·1 0·2 | 7·1 1·4 | 13·1 2·5 |
| 12 | 2 48·0 | 2 48·5 | 2 40·3 | 1·2 0·2 | 7·2 1·4 | 13·2 2·5 |
| 13 | 2 48·3 | 2 48·7 | 2 40·6 | 1·3 0·2 | 7·3 1·4 | 13·3 2·6 |
| 14 | 2 48·5 | 2 49·0 | 2 40·8 | 1·4 0·3 | 7·4 1·4 | 13·4 2·6 |
| 15 | 2 48·8 | 2 49·2 | 2 41·1 | 1·5 0·3 | 7·5 1·4 | 13·5 2·6 |
| 16 | 2 49·0 | 2 49·5 | 2 41·3 | 1·6 0·3 | 7·6 1·5 | 13·6 2·6 |
| 17 | 2 49·3 | 2 49·7 | 2 41·5 | 1·7 0·3 | 7·7 1·5 | 13·7 2·6 |
| 18 | 2 49·5 | 2 50·0 | 2 41·8 | 1·8 0·3 | 7·8 1·5 | 13·8 2·6 |
| 19 | 2 49·8 | 2 50·2 | 2 42·0 | 1·9 0·4 | 7·9 1·5 | 13·9 2·7 |
| 20 | 2 50·0 | 2 50·5 | 2 42·3 | 2·0 0·4 | 8·0 1·5 | 14·0 2·7 |
| 21 | 2 50·3 | 2 50·7 | 2 42·5 | 2·1 0·4 | 8·1 1·6 | 14·1 2·7 |
| 22 | 2 50·5 | 2 51·0 | 2 42·7 | 2·2 0·4 | 8·2 1·6 | 14·2 2·7 |
| 23 | 2 50·8 | 2 51·2 | 2 43·0 | 2·3 0·4 | 8·3 1·6 | 14·3 2·7 |
| 24 | 2 51·0 | 2 51·5 | 2 43·2 | 2·4 0·5 | 8·4 1·6 | 14·4 2·8 |
| 25 | 2 51·3 | 2 51·7 | 2 43·4 | 2·5 0·5 | 8·5 1·6 | 14·5 2·8 |
| 26 | 2 51·5 | 2 52·0 | 2 43·7 | 2·6 0·5 | 8·6 1·6 | 14·6 2·8 |
| 27 | 2 51·8 | 2 52·2 | 2 43·9 | 2·7 0·5 | 8·7 1·7 | 14·7 2·8 |
| 28 | 2 52·0 | 2 52·5 | 2 44·2 | 2·8 0·5 | 8·8 1·7 | 14·8 2·8 |
| 29 | 2 52·3 | 2 52·7 | 2 44·4 | 2·9 0·6 | 8·9 1·7 | 14·9 2·9 |
| 30 | 2 52·5 | 2 53·0 | 2 44·6 | 3·0 0·6 | 9·0 1·7 | 15·0 2·9 |
| 31 | 2 52·8 | 2 53·2 | 2 44·9 | 3·1 0·6 | 9·1 1·7 | 15·1 2·9 |
| 32 | 2 53·0 | 2 53·5 | 2 45·1 | 3·2 0·6 | 9·2 1·8 | 15·2 2·9 |
| 33 | 2 53·3 | 2 53·7 | 2 45·4 | 3·3 0·6 | 9·3 1·8 | 15·3 2·9 |
| 34 | 2 53·5 | 2 54·0 | 2 45·6 | 3·4 0·7 | 9·4 1·8 | 15·4 3·0 |
| 35 | 2 53·8 | 2 54·2 | 2 45·8 | 3·5 0·7 | 9·5 1·8 | 15·5 3·0 |
| 36 | 2 54·0 | 2 54·5 | 2 46·1 | 3·6 0·7 | 9·6 1·8 | 15·6 3·0 |
| 37 | 2 54·3 | 2 54·7 | 2 46·3 | 3·7 0·7 | 9·7 1·9 | 15·7 3·0 |
| 38 | 2 54·5 | 2 55·0 | 2 46·6 | 3·8 0·7 | 9·8 1·9 | 15·8 3·0 |
| 39 | 2 54·8 | 2 55·2 | 2 46·8 | 3·9 0·7 | 9·9 1·9 | 15·9 3·0 |
| 40 | 2 55·0 | 2 55·5 | 2 47·0 | 4·0 0·8 | 10·0 1·9 | 16·0 3·1 |
| 41 | 2 55·3 | 2 55·7 | 2 47·3 | 4·1 0·8 | 10·1 1·9 | 16·1 3·1 |
| 42 | 2 55·5 | 2 56·0 | 2 47·5 | 4·2 0·8 | 10·2 2·0 | 16·2 3·1 |
| 43 | 2 55·8 | 2 56·2 | 2 47·7 | 4·3 0·8 | 10·3 2·0 | 16·3 3·1 |
| 44 | 2 56·0 | 2 56·5 | 2 48·0 | 4·4 0·8 | 10·4 2·0 | 16·4 3·1 |
| 45 | 2 56·3 | 2 56·7 | 2 48·2 | 4·5 0·9 | 10·5 2·0 | 16·5 3·2 |
| 46 | 2 56·5 | 2 57·0 | 2 48·5 | 4·6 0·9 | 10·6 2·0 | 16·6 3·2 |
| 47 | 2 56·8 | 2 57·2 | 2 48·7 | 4·7 0·9 | 10·7 2·1 | 16·7 3·2 |
| 48 | 2 57·0 | 2 57·5 | 2 48·9 | 4·8 0·9 | 10·8 2·1 | 16·8 3·2 |
| 49 | 2 57·3 | 2 57·7 | 2 49·2 | 4·9 0·9 | 10·9 2·1 | 16·9 3·2 |
| 50 | 2 57·5 | 2 58·0 | 2 49·4 | 5·0 1·0 | 11·0 2·1 | 17·0 3·3 |
| 51 | 2 57·8 | 2 58·2 | 2 49·7 | 5·1 1·0 | 11·1 2·1 | 17·1 3·3 |
| 52 | 2 58·0 | 2 58·5 | 2 49·9 | 5·2 1·0 | 11·2 2·1 | 17·2 3·3 |
| 53 | 2 58·3 | 2 58·7 | 2 50·1 | 5·3 1·0 | 11·3 2·2 | 17·3 3·3 |
| 54 | 2 58·5 | 2 59·0 | 2 50·4 | 5·4 1·0 | 11·4 2·2 | 17·4 3·3 |
| 55 | 2 58·8 | 2 59·2 | 2 50·6 | 5·5 1·1 | 11·5 2·2 | 17·5 3·4 |
| 56 | 2 59·0 | 2 59·5 | 2 50·8 | 5·6 1·1 | 11·6 2·2 | 17·6 3·4 |
| 57 | 2 59·3 | 2 59·7 | 2 51·1 | 5·7 1·1 | 11·7 2·2 | 17·7 3·4 |
| 58 | 2 59·5 | 3 00·0 | 2 51·3 | 5·8 1·1 | 11·8 2·3 | 17·8 3·4 |
| 59 | 2 59·8 | 3 00·2 | 2 51·6 | 5·9 1·1 | 11·9 2·3 | 17·9 3·4 |
| 60 | 3 00·0 | 3 00·5 | 2 51·8 | 6·0 1·2 | 12·0 2·3 | 18·0 3·5 |

| 12ᵐ s | SUN PLANETS ° ' | ARIES ° ' | MOON ° ' | v or Corrⁿ d ' ' | v or Corrⁿ d ' ' | v or Corrⁿ d ' ' | 13ᵐ s | SUN PLANETS ° ' | ARIES ° ' | MOON ° ' | v or Corrⁿ d ' ' | v or Corrⁿ d ' ' | v or Corrⁿ d ' ' |
|---|---|---|---|---|---|---|---|---|---|---|---|---|---|
| 00 | 3 00·0 | 3 00·5 | 2 51·8 | 0·0 0·0 | 6·0 1·3 | 12·0 2·5 | 00 | 3 15·0 | 3 15·5 | 3 06·1 | 0·0 0·0 | 6·0 1·4 | 12·0 2·7 |
| 01 | 3 00·3 | 3 00·7 | 2 52·0 | 0·1 0·0 | 6·1 1·3 | 12·1 2·5 | 01 | 3 15·3 | 3 15·8 | 3 06·4 | 0·1 0·0 | 6·1 1·4 | 12·1 2·7 |
| 02 | 3 00·5 | 3 01·0 | 2 52·3 | 0·2 0·0 | 6·2 1·3 | 12·2 2·5 | 02 | 3 15·5 | 3 16·0 | 3 06·6 | 0·2 0·0 | 6·2 1·4 | 12·2 2·7 |
| 03 | 3 00·8 | 3 01·2 | 2 52·5 | 0·3 0·1 | 6·3 1·3 | 12·3 2·6 | 03 | 3 15·8 | 3 16·3 | 3 06·8 | 0·3 0·1 | 6·3 1·4 | 12·3 2·8 |
| 04 | 3 01·0 | 3 01·5 | 2 52·8 | 0·4 0·1 | 6·4 1·3 | 12·4 2·6 | 04 | 3 16·0 | 3 16·5 | 3 07·1 | 0·4 0·1 | 6·4 1·4 | 12·4 2·8 |
| 05 | 3 01·3 | 3 01·7 | 2 53·0 | 0·5 0·1 | 6·5 1·4 | 12·5 2·6 | 05 | 3 16·3 | 3 16·8 | 3 07·3 | 0·5 0·1 | 6·5 1·5 | 12·5 2·8 |
| 06 | 3 01·5 | 3 02·0 | 2 53·2 | 0·6 0·1 | 6·6 1·4 | 12·6 2·6 | 06 | 3 16·5 | 3 17·0 | 3 07·5 | 0·6 0·1 | 6·6 1·5 | 12·6 2·8 |
| 07 | 3 01·8 | 3 02·2 | 2 53·5 | 0·7 0·1 | 6·7 1·4 | 12·7 2·6 | 07 | 3 16·8 | 3 17·3 | 3 07·8 | 0·7 0·2 | 6·7 1·5 | 12·7 2·9 |
| 08 | 3 02·0 | 3 02·5 | 2 53·7 | 0·8 0·2 | 6·8 1·4 | 12·8 2·7 | 08 | 3 17·0 | 3 17·5 | 3 08·0 | 0·8 0·2 | 6·8 1·5 | 12·8 2·9 |
| 09 | 3 02·3 | 3 02·7 | 2 53·9 | 0·9 0·2 | 6·9 1·4 | 12·9 2·7 | 09 | 3 17·3 | 3 17·8 | 3 08·3 | 0·9 0·2 | 6·9 1·6 | 12·9 2·9 |
| 10 | 3 02·5 | 3 03·0 | 2 54·2 | 1·0 0·2 | 7·0 1·5 | 13·0 2·7 | 10 | 3 17·5 | 3 18·0 | 3 08·5 | 1·0 0·2 | 7·0 1·6 | 13·0 2·9 |
| 11 | 3 02·8 | 3 03·3 | 2 54·4 | 1·1 0·2 | 7·1 1·5 | 13·1 2·7 | 11 | 3 17·8 | 3 18·3 | 3 08·7 | 1·1 0·2 | 7·1 1·6 | 13·1 2·9 |
| 12 | 3 03·0 | 3 03·5 | 2 54·7 | 1·2 0·3 | 7·2 1·5 | 13·2 2·8 | 12 | 3 18·0 | 3 18·5 | 3 09·0 | 1·2 0·3 | 7·2 1·6 | 13·2 3·0 |
| 13 | 3 03·3 | 3 03·8 | 2 54·9 | 1·3 0·3 | 7·3 1·5 | 13·3 2·8 | 13 | 3 18·3 | 3 18·8 | 3 09·2 | 1·3 0·3 | 7·3 1·6 | 13·3 3·0 |
| 14 | 3 03·5 | 3 04·0 | 2 55·1 | 1·4 0·3 | 7·4 1·5 | 13·4 2·8 | 14 | 3 18·5 | 3 19·0 | 3 09·5 | 1·4 0·3 | 7·4 1·7 | 13·4 3·0 |
| 15 | 3 03·8 | 3 04·3 | 2 55·4 | 1·5 0·3 | 7·5 1·6 | 13·5 2·8 | 15 | 3 18·8 | 3 19·3 | 3 09·7 | 1·5 0·3 | 7·5 1·7 | 13·5 3·0 |
| 16 | 3 04·0 | 3 04·5 | 2 55·6 | 1·6 0·3 | 7·6 1·6 | 13·6 2·8 | 16 | 3 19·0 | 3 19·5 | 3 09·9 | 1·6 0·4 | 7·6 1·7 | 13·6 3·1 |
| 17 | 3 04·3 | 3 04·8 | 2 55·9 | 1·7 0·4 | 7·7 1·6 | 13·7 2·9 | 17 | 3 19·3 | 3 19·8 | 3 10·2 | 1·7 0·4 | 7·7 1·7 | 13·7 3·1 |
| 18 | 3 04·5 | 3 05·0 | 2 56·1 | 1·8 0·4 | 7·8 1·6 | 13·8 2·9 | 18 | 3 19·5 | 3 20·0 | 3 10·4 | 1·8 0·4 | 7·8 1·8 | 13·8 3·1 |
| 19 | 3 04·8 | 3 05·3 | 2 56·3 | 1·9 0·4 | 7·9 1·6 | 13·9 2·9 | 19 | 3 19·8 | 3 20·3 | 3 10·7 | 1·9 0·4 | 7·9 1·8 | 13·9 3·1 |
| 20 | 3 05·0 | 3 05·5 | 2 56·6 | 2·0 0·4 | 8·0 1·7 | 14·0 2·9 | 20 | 3 20·0 | 3 20·5 | 3 10·9 | 2·0 0·5 | 8·0 1·8 | 14·0 3·2 |
| 21 | 3 05·3 | 3 05·8 | 2 56·8 | 2·1 0·4 | 8·1 1·7 | 14·1 2·9 | 21 | 3 20·3 | 3 20·8 | 3 11·1 | 2·1 0·5 | 8·1 1·8 | 14·1 3·2 |
| 22 | 3 05·5 | 3 06·0 | 2 57·0 | 2·2 0·5 | 8·2 1·7 | 14·2 3·0 | 22 | 3 20·5 | 3 21·0 | 3 11·4 | 2·2 0·5 | 8·2 1·8 | 14·2 3·2 |
| 23 | 3 05·8 | 3 06·3 | 2 57·3 | 2·3 0·5 | 8·3 1·7 | 14·3 3·0 | 23 | 3 20·8 | 3 21·3 | 3 11·6 | 2·3 0·5 | 8·3 1·9 | 14·3 3·2 |
| 24 | 3 06·0 | 3 06·5 | 2 57·5 | 2·4 0·5 | 8·4 1·8 | 14·4 3·0 | 24 | 3 21·0 | 3 21·6 | 3 11·8 | 2·4 0·5 | 8·4 1·9 | 14·4 3·2 |
| 25 | 3 06·3 | 3 06·8 | 2 57·8 | 2·5 0·5 | 8·5 1·8 | 14·5 3·0 | 25 | 3 21·3 | 3 21·8 | 3 12·1 | 2·5 0·6 | 8·5 1·9 | 14·5 3·3 |
| 26 | 3 06·5 | 3 07·0 | 2 58·0 | 2·6 0·5 | 8·6 1·8 | 14·6 3·0 | 26 | 3 21·5 | 3 22·1 | 3 12·3 | 2·6 0·6 | 8·6 1·9 | 14·6 3·3 |
| 27 | 3 06·8 | 3 07·3 | 2 58·2 | 2·7 0·6 | 8·7 1·8 | 14·7 3·1 | 27 | 3 21·8 | 3 22·3 | 3 12·6 | 2·7 0·6 | 8·7 2·0 | 14·7 3·3 |
| 28 | 3 07·0 | 3 07·5 | 2 58·5 | 2·8 0·6 | 8·8 1·8 | 14·8 3·1 | 28 | 3 22·0 | 3 22·6 | 3 12·8 | 2·8 0·6 | 8·8 2·0 | 14·8 3·3 |
| 29 | 3 07·3 | 3 07·8 | 2 58·7 | 2·9 0·6 | 8·9 1·9 | 14·9 3·1 | 29 | 3 22·3 | 3 22·8 | 3 13·0 | 2·9 0·7 | 8·9 2·0 | 14·9 3·4 |
| 30 | 3 07·5 | 3 08·0 | 2 59·0 | 3·0 0·6 | 9·0 1·9 | 15·0 3·1 | 30 | 3 22·5 | 3 23·1 | 3 13·3 | 3·0 0·7 | 9·0 2·0 | 15·0 3·4 |
| 31 | 3 07·8 | 3 08·3 | 2 59·2 | 3·1 0·6 | 9·1 1·9 | 15·1 3·1 | 31 | 3 22·8 | 3 23·3 | 3 13·5 | 3·1 0·7 | 9·1 2·0 | 15·1 3·4 |
| 32 | 3 08·0 | 3 08·5 | 2 59·4 | 3·2 0·7 | 9·2 1·9 | 15·2 3·2 | 32 | 3 23·0 | 3 23·6 | 3 13·8 | 3·2 0·7 | 9·2 2·1 | 15·2 3·4 |
| 33 | 3 08·3 | 3 08·8 | 2 59·7 | 3·3 0·7 | 9·3 1·9 | 15·3 3·2 | 33 | 3 23·3 | 3 23·8 | 3 14·0 | 3·3 0·7 | 9·3 2·1 | 15·3 3·4 |
| 34 | 3 08·5 | 3 09·0 | 2 59·9 | 3·4 0·7 | 9·4 2·0 | 15·4 3·2 | 34 | 3 23·5 | 3 24·1 | 3 14·2 | 3·4 0·8 | 9·4 2·1 | 15·4 3·5 |
| 35 | 3 08·8 | 3 09·3 | 3 00·2 | 3·5 0·7 | 9·5 2·0 | 15·5 3·2 | 35 | 3 23·8 | 3 24·3 | 3 14·5 | 3·5 0·8 | 9·5 2·1 | 15·5 3·5 |
| 36 | 3 09·0 | 3 09·5 | 3 00·4 | 3·6 0·8 | 9·6 2·0 | 15·6 3·3 | 36 | 3 24·0 | 3 24·6 | 3 14·7 | 3·6 0·8 | 9·6 2·2 | 15·6 3·5 |
| 37 | 3 09·3 | 3 09·8 | 3 00·6 | 3·7 0·8 | 9·7 2·0 | 15·7 3·3 | 37 | 3 24·3 | 3 24·8 | 3 14·9 | 3·7 0·8 | 9·7 2·2 | 15·7 3·5 |
| 38 | 3 09·5 | 3 10·0 | 3 00·9 | 3·8 0·8 | 9·8 2·0 | 15·8 3·3 | 38 | 3 24·5 | 3 25·1 | 3 15·2 | 3·8 0·9 | 9·8 2·2 | 15·8 3·6 |
| 39 | 3 09·8 | 3 10·3 | 3 01·1 | 3·9 0·8 | 9·9 2·1 | 15·9 3·3 | 39 | 3 24·8 | 3 25·3 | 3 15·4 | 3·9 0·9 | 9·9 2·2 | 15·9 3·6 |
| 40 | 3 10·0 | 3 10·5 | 3 01·3 | 4·0 0·8 | 10·0 2·1 | 16·0 3·3 | 40 | 3 25·0 | 3 25·6 | 3 15·7 | 4·0 0·9 | 10·0 2·3 | 16·0 3·6 |
| 41 | 3 10·3 | 3 10·8 | 3 01·6 | 4·1 0·9 | 10·1 2·1 | 16·1 3·4 | 41 | 3 25·3 | 3 25·8 | 3 15·9 | 4·1 0·9 | 10·1 2·3 | 16·1 3·6 |
| 42 | 3 10·5 | 3 11·0 | 3 01·8 | 4·2 0·9 | 10·2 2·1 | 16·2 3·4 | 42 | 3 25·5 | 3 26·1 | 3 16·1 | 4·2 0·9 | 10·2 2·3 | 16·2 3·6 |
| 43 | 3 10·8 | 3 11·3 | 3 02·1 | 4·3 0·9 | 10·3 2·1 | 16·3 3·4 | 43 | 3 25·8 | 3 26·3 | 3 16·4 | 4·3 1·0 | 10·3 2·3 | 16·3 3·7 |
| 44 | 3 11·0 | 3 11·5 | 3 02·3 | 4·4 0·9 | 10·4 2·2 | 16·4 3·4 | 44 | 3 26·0 | 3 26·6 | 3 16·6 | 4·4 1·0 | 10·4 2·3 | 16·4 3·7 |
| 45 | 3 11·3 | 3 11·8 | 3 02·5 | 4·5 0·9 | 10·5 2·2 | 16·5 3·4 | 45 | 3 26·3 | 3 26·8 | 3 16·9 | 4·5 1·0 | 10·5 2·4 | 16·5 3·7 |
| 46 | 3 11·5 | 3 12·0 | 3 02·8 | 4·6 1·0 | 10·6 2·2 | 16·6 3·5 | 46 | 3 26·5 | 3 27·1 | 3 17·1 | 4·6 1·0 | 10·6 2·4 | 16·6 3·7 |
| 47 | 3 11·8 | 3 12·3 | 3 03·0 | 4·7 1·0 | 10·7 2·2 | 16·7 3·5 | 47 | 3 26·8 | 3 27·3 | 3 17·3 | 4·7 1·1 | 10·7 2·4 | 16·7 3·8 |
| 48 | 3 12·0 | 3 12·5 | 3 03·3 | 4·8 1·0 | 10·8 2·3 | 16·8 3·5 | 48 | 3 27·0 | 3 27·6 | 3 17·6 | 4·8 1·1 | 10·8 2·4 | 16·8 3·8 |
| 49 | 3 12·3 | 3 12·8 | 3 03·5 | 4·9 1·0 | 10·9 2·3 | 16·9 3·5 | 49 | 3 27·3 | 3 27·8 | 3 17·8 | 4·9 1·1 | 10·9 2·5 | 16·9 3·8 |
| 50 | 3 12·5 | 3 13·0 | 3 03·7 | 5·0 1·0 | 11·0 2·3 | 17·0 3·5 | 50 | 3 27·5 | 3 28·1 | 3 18·0 | 5·0 1·1 | 11·0 2·5 | 17·0 3·8 |
| 51 | 3 12·8 | 3 13·3 | 3 04·0 | 5·1 1·1 | 11·1 2·3 | 17·1 3·6 | 51 | 3 27·8 | 3 28·3 | 3 18·3 | 5·1 1·1 | 11·1 2·5 | 17·1 3·8 |
| 52 | 3 13·0 | 3 13·5 | 3 04·2 | 5·2 1·1 | 11·2 2·3 | 17·2 3·6 | 52 | 3 28·0 | 3 28·6 | 3 18·5 | 5·2 1·2 | 11·2 2·5 | 17·2 3·9 |
| 53 | 3 13·3 | 3 13·8 | 3 04·4 | 5·3 1·1 | 11·3 2·4 | 17·3 3·6 | 53 | 3 28·3 | 3 28·8 | 3 18·8 | 5·3 1·2 | 11·3 2·5 | 17·3 3·9 |
| 54 | 3 13·5 | 3 14·0 | 3 04·7 | 5·4 1·1 | 11·4 2·4 | 17·4 3·6 | 54 | 3 28·5 | 3 29·1 | 3 19·0 | 5·4 1·2 | 11·4 2·6 | 17·4 3·9 |
| 55 | 3 13·8 | 3 14·3 | 3 04·9 | 5·5 1·1 | 11·5 2·4 | 17·5 3·6 | 55 | 3 28·8 | 3 29·3 | 3 19·2 | 5·5 1·2 | 11·5 2·6 | 17·5 3·9 |
| 56 | 3 14·0 | 3 14·5 | 3 05·2 | 5·6 1·2 | 11·6 2·4 | 17·6 3·7 | 56 | 3 29·0 | 3 29·6 | 3 19·5 | 5·6 1·3 | 11·6 2·6 | 17·6 4·0 |
| 57 | 3 14·3 | 3 14·8 | 3 05·4 | 5·7 1·2 | 11·7 2·4 | 17·7 3·7 | 57 | 3 29·3 | 3 29·8 | 3 19·7 | 5·7 1·3 | 11·7 2·6 | 17·7 4·0 |
| 58 | 3 14·5 | 3 15·0 | 3 05·6 | 5·8 1·2 | 11·8 2·5 | 17·8 3·7 | 58 | 3 29·5 | 3 30·1 | 3 20·0 | 5·8 1·3 | 11·8 2·7 | 17·8 4·0 |
| 59 | 3 14·8 | 3 15·3 | 3 05·9 | 5·9 1·2 | 11·9 2·5 | 17·9 3·7 | 59 | 3 29·8 | 3 30·3 | 3 20·2 | 5·9 1·3 | 11·9 2·7 | 17·9 4·0 |
| 60 | 3 15·0 | 3 15·5 | 3 06·1 | 6·0 1·3 | 12·0 2·5 | 18·0 3·8 | 60 | 3 30·0 | 3 30·6 | 3 20·4 | 6·0 1·4 | 12·0 2·7 | 18·0 4·1 |

## 14$^m$

| 14 s | SUN PLANETS ° ′ | ARIES ° ′ | MOON ° ′ | $v$ or $d$ | Corrⁿ | $v$ or $d$ | Corrⁿ | $v$ or $d$ | Corrⁿ |
|---|---|---|---|---|---|---|---|---|---|
| 00 | 3 30·0 | 3 30·6 | 3 20·4 | 0·0 | 0·0 | 6·0 | 1·5 | 12·0 | 2·9 |
| 01 | 3 30·3 | 3 30·8 | 3 20·7 | 0·1 | 0·0 | 6·1 | 1·5 | 12·1 | 2·9 |
| 02 | 3 30·5 | 3 31·1 | 3 20·9 | 0·2 | 0·0 | 6·2 | 1·5 | 12·2 | 2·9 |
| 03 | 3 30·8 | 3 31·3 | 3 21·1 | 0·3 | 0·1 | 6·3 | 1·5 | 12·3 | 3·0 |
| 04 | 3 31·0 | 3 31·6 | 3 21·4 | 0·4 | 0·1 | 6·4 | 1·5 | 12·4 | 3·0 |
| 05 | 3 31·3 | 3 31·8 | 3 21·6 | 0·5 | 0·1 | 6·5 | 1·6 | 12·5 | 3·0 |
| 06 | 3 31·5 | 3 32·1 | 3 21·9 | 0·6 | 0·1 | 6·6 | 1·6 | 12·6 | 3·0 |
| 07 | 3 31·8 | 3 32·3 | 3 22·1 | 0·7 | 0·2 | 6·7 | 1·6 | 12·7 | 3·1 |
| 08 | 3 32·0 | 3 32·6 | 3 22·3 | 0·8 | 0·2 | 6·8 | 1·6 | 12·8 | 3·1 |
| 09 | 3 32·3 | 3 32·8 | 3 22·6 | 0·9 | 0·2 | 6·9 | 1·7 | 12·9 | 3·1 |
| 10 | 3 32·5 | 3 33·1 | 3 22·8 | 1·0 | 0·2 | 7·0 | 1·7 | 13·0 | 3·1 |
| 11 | 3 32·8 | 3 33·3 | 3 23·1 | 1·1 | 0·3 | 7·1 | 1·7 | 13·1 | 3·2 |
| 12 | 3 33·0 | 3 33·6 | 3 23·3 | 1·2 | 0·3 | 7·2 | 1·7 | 13·2 | 3·2 |
| 13 | 3 33·3 | 3 33·8 | 3 23·5 | 1·3 | 0·3 | 7·3 | 1·8 | 13·3 | 3·2 |
| 14 | 3 33·5 | 3 34·1 | 3 23·8 | 1·4 | 0·3 | 7·4 | 1·8 | 13·4 | 3·2 |
| 15 | 3 33·8 | 3 34·3 | 3 24·0 | 1·5 | 0·4 | 7·5 | 1·8 | 13·5 | 3·3 |
| 16 | 3 34·0 | 3 34·6 | 3 24·3 | 1·6 | 0·4 | 7·6 | 1·8 | 13·6 | 3·3 |
| 17 | 3 34·3 | 3 34·8 | 3 24·5 | 1·7 | 0·4 | 7·7 | 1·9 | 13·7 | 3·3 |
| 18 | 3 34·5 | 3 35·1 | 3 24·7 | 1·8 | 0·4 | 7·8 | 1·9 | 13·8 | 3·3 |
| 19 | 3 34·8 | 3 35·3 | 3 25·0 | 1·9 | 0·5 | 7·9 | 1·9 | 13·9 | 3·4 |
| 20 | 3 35·0 | 3 35·6 | 3 25·2 | 2·0 | 0·5 | 8·0 | 1·9 | 14·0 | 3·4 |
| 21 | 3 35·3 | 3 35·8 | 3 25·4 | 2·1 | 0·5 | 8·1 | 2·0 | 14·1 | 3·4 |
| 22 | 3 35·5 | 3 36·1 | 3 25·7 | 2·2 | 0·5 | 8·2 | 2·0 | 14·2 | 3·4 |
| 23 | 3 35·8 | 3 36·3 | 3 25·9 | 2·3 | 0·6 | 8·3 | 2·0 | 14·3 | 3·5 |
| 24 | 3 36·0 | 3 36·6 | 3 26·2 | 2·4 | 0·6 | 8·4 | 2·0 | 14·4 | 3·5 |
| 25 | 3 36·3 | 3 36·8 | 3 26·4 | 2·5 | 0·6 | 8·5 | 2·1 | 14·5 | 3·5 |
| 26 | 3 36·5 | 3 37·1 | 3 26·6 | 2·6 | 0·6 | 8·6 | 2·1 | 14·6 | 3·5 |
| 27 | 3 36·8 | 3 37·3 | 3 26·9 | 2·7 | 0·7 | 8·7 | 2·1 | 14·7 | 3·6 |
| 28 | 3 37·0 | 3 37·6 | 3 27·1 | 2·8 | 0·7 | 8·8 | 2·1 | 14·8 | 3·6 |
| 29 | 3 37·3 | 3 37·8 | 3 27·4 | 2·9 | 0·7 | 8·9 | 2·2 | 14·9 | 3·6 |
| 30 | 3 37·5 | 3 38·1 | 3 27·6 | 3·0 | 0·7 | 9·0 | 2·2 | 15·0 | 3·6 |
| 31 | 3 37·8 | 3 38·3 | 3 27·8 | 3·1 | 0·7 | 9·1 | 2·2 | 15·1 | 3·6 |
| 32 | 3 38·0 | 3 38·6 | 3 28·1 | 3·2 | 0·8 | 9·2 | 2·2 | 15·2 | 3·7 |
| 33 | 3 38·3 | 3 38·8 | 3 28·3 | 3·3 | 0·8 | 9·3 | 2·2 | 15·3 | 3·7 |
| 34 | 3 38·5 | 3 39·1 | 3 28·5 | 3·4 | 0·8 | 9·4 | 2·3 | 15·4 | 3·7 |
| 35 | 3 38·8 | 3 39·3 | 3 28·8 | 3·5 | 0·8 | 9·5 | 2·3 | 15·5 | 3·7 |
| 36 | 3 39·0 | 3 39·6 | 3 29·0 | 3·6 | 0·9 | 9·6 | 2·3 | 15·6 | 3·8 |
| 37 | 3 39·3 | 3 39·9 | 3 29·3 | 3·7 | 0·9 | 9·7 | 2·3 | 15·7 | 3·8 |
| 38 | 3 39·5 | 3 40·1 | 3 29·5 | 3·8 | 0·9 | 9·8 | 2·4 | 15·8 | 3·8 |
| 39 | 3 39·8 | 3 40·4 | 3 29·7 | 3·9 | 0·9 | 9·9 | 2·4 | 15·9 | 3·8 |
| 40 | 3 40·0 | 3 40·6 | 3 30·0 | 4·0 | 1·0 | 10·0 | 2·4 | 16·0 | 3·9 |
| 41 | 3 40·3 | 3 40·9 | 3 30·2 | 4·1 | 1·0 | 10·1 | 2·4 | 16·1 | 3·9 |
| 42 | 3 40·5 | 3 41·1 | 3 30·5 | 4·2 | 1·0 | 10·2 | 2·5 | 16·2 | 3·9 |
| 43 | 3 40·8 | 3 41·4 | 3 30·7 | 4·3 | 1·0 | 10·3 | 2·5 | 16·3 | 3·9 |
| 44 | 3 41·0 | 3 41·6 | 3 30·9 | 4·4 | 1·1 | 10·4 | 2·5 | 16·4 | 4·0 |
| 45 | 3 41·3 | 3 41·9 | 3 31·2 | 4·5 | 1·1 | 10·5 | 2·5 | 16·5 | 4·0 |
| 46 | 3 41·5 | 3 42·1 | 3 31·4 | 4·6 | 1·1 | 10·6 | 2·6 | 16·6 | 4·0 |
| 47 | 3 41·8 | 3 42·4 | 3 31·6 | 4·7 | 1·1 | 10·7 | 2·6 | 16·7 | 4·0 |
| 48 | 3 42·0 | 3 42·6 | 3 31·9 | 4·8 | 1·2 | 10·8 | 2·6 | 16·8 | 4·1 |
| 49 | 3 42·3 | 3 42·9 | 3 32·1 | 4·9 | 1·2 | 10·9 | 2·6 | 16·9 | 4·1 |
| 50 | 3 42·5 | 3 43·1 | 3 32·4 | 5·0 | 1·2 | 11·0 | 2·7 | 17·0 | 4·1 |
| 51 | 3 42·8 | 3 43·4 | 3 32·6 | 5·1 | 1·2 | 11·1 | 2·7 | 17·1 | 4·1 |
| 52 | 3 43·0 | 3 43·6 | 3 32·8 | 5·2 | 1·3 | 11·2 | 2·7 | 17·2 | 4·2 |
| 53 | 3 43·3 | 3 43·9 | 3 33·1 | 5·3 | 1·3 | 11·3 | 2·7 | 17·3 | 4·2 |
| 54 | 3 43·5 | 3 44·1 | 3 33·3 | 5·4 | 1·3 | 11·4 | 2·8 | 17·4 | 4·2 |
| 55 | 3 43·8 | 3 44·4 | 3 33·6 | 5·5 | 1·3 | 11·5 | 2·8 | 17·5 | 4·2 |
| 56 | 3 44·0 | 3 44·6 | 3 33·8 | 5·6 | 1·4 | 11·6 | 2·8 | 17·6 | 4·3 |
| 57 | 3 44·3 | 3 44·9 | 3 34·0 | 5·7 | 1·4 | 11·7 | 2·8 | 17·7 | 4·3 |
| 58 | 3 44·5 | 3 45·1 | 3 34·3 | 5·8 | 1·4 | 11·8 | 2·9 | 17·8 | 4·3 |
| 59 | 3 44·8 | 3 45·4 | 3 34·5 | 5·9 | 1·4 | 11·9 | 2·9 | 17·9 | 4·3 |
| 60 | 3 45·0 | 3 45·6 | 3 34·8 | 6·0 | 1·5 | 12·0 | 2·9 | 18·0 | 4·4 |

## 15$^m$

| 15 s | SUN PLANETS ° ′ | ARIES ° ′ | MOON ° ′ | $v$ or $d$ | Corrⁿ | $v$ or $d$ | Corrⁿ | $v$ or $d$ | Corrⁿ |
|---|---|---|---|---|---|---|---|---|---|
| 00 | 3 45·0 | 3 45·6 | 3 34·8 | 0·0 | 0·0 | 6·0 | 1·6 | 12·0 | 3·1 |
| 01 | 3 45·3 | 3 45·9 | 3 35·0 | 0·1 | 0·0 | 6·1 | 1·6 | 12·1 | 3·1 |
| 02 | 3 45·5 | 3 46·1 | 3 35·2 | 0·2 | 0·1 | 6·2 | 1·6 | 12·2 | 3·2 |
| 03 | 3 45·8 | 3 46·4 | 3 35·5 | 0·3 | 0·1 | 6·3 | 1·6 | 12·3 | 3·2 |
| 04 | 3 46·0 | 3 46·6 | 3 35·7 | 0·4 | 0·1 | 6·4 | 1·7 | 12·4 | 3·2 |
| 05 | 3 46·3 | 3 46·9 | 3 35·9 | 0·5 | 0·1 | 6·5 | 1·7 | 12·5 | 3·2 |
| 06 | 3 46·5 | 3 47·1 | 3 36·2 | 0·6 | 0·2 | 6·6 | 1·7 | 12·6 | 3·3 |
| 07 | 3 46·8 | 3 47·4 | 3 36·4 | 0·7 | 0·2 | 6·7 | 1·7 | 12·7 | 3·3 |
| 08 | 3 47·0 | 3 47·6 | 3 36·7 | 0·8 | 0·2 | 6·8 | 1·8 | 12·8 | 3·3 |
| 09 | 3 47·3 | 3 47·9 | 3 36·9 | 0·9 | 0·2 | 6·9 | 1·8 | 12·9 | 3·3 |
| 10 | 3 47·5 | 3 48·1 | 3 37·1 | 1·0 | 0·3 | 7·0 | 1·8 | 13·0 | 3·4 |
| 11 | 3 47·8 | 3 48·4 | 3 37·4 | 1·1 | 0·3 | 7·1 | 1·8 | 13·1 | 3·4 |
| 12 | 3 48·0 | 3 48·6 | 3 37·6 | 1·2 | 0·3 | 7·2 | 1·9 | 13·2 | 3·4 |
| 13 | 3 48·3 | 3 48·9 | 3 37·9 | 1·3 | 0·3 | 7·3 | 1·9 | 13·3 | 3·4 |
| 14 | 3 48·5 | 3 49·1 | 3 38·1 | 1·4 | 0·4 | 7·4 | 1·9 | 13·4 | 3·5 |
| 15 | 3 48·8 | 3 49·4 | 3 38·3 | 1·5 | 0·4 | 7·5 | 1·9 | 13·5 | 3·5 |
| 16 | 3 49·0 | 3 49·6 | 3 38·6 | 1·6 | 0·4 | 7·6 | 2·0 | 13·6 | 3·5 |
| 17 | 3 49·3 | 3 49·9 | 3 38·8 | 1·7 | 0·4 | 7·7 | 2·0 | 13·7 | 3·5 |
| 18 | 3 49·5 | 3 50·1 | 3 39·0 | 1·8 | 0·5 | 7·8 | 2·0 | 13·8 | 3·6 |
| 19 | 3 49·8 | 3 50·4 | 3 39·3 | 1·9 | 0·5 | 7·9 | 2·0 | 13·9 | 3·6 |
| 20 | 3 50·0 | 3 50·6 | 3 39·5 | 2·0 | 0·5 | 8·0 | 2·1 | 14·0 | 3·6 |
| 21 | 3 50·3 | 3 50·9 | 3 39·8 | 2·1 | 0·5 | 8·1 | 2·1 | 14·1 | 3·6 |
| 22 | 3 50·5 | 3 51·1 | 3 40·0 | 2·2 | 0·6 | 8·2 | 2·1 | 14·2 | 3·7 |
| 23 | 3 50·8 | 3 51·4 | 3 40·2 | 2·3 | 0·6 | 8·3 | 2·1 | 14·3 | 3·7 |
| 24 | 3 51·0 | 3 51·6 | 3 40·5 | 2·4 | 0·6 | 8·4 | 2·2 | 14·4 | 3·7 |
| 25 | 3 51·3 | 3 51·9 | 3 40·7 | 2·5 | 0·6 | 8·5 | 2·2 | 14·5 | 3·7 |
| 26 | 3 51·5 | 3 52·1 | 3 41·0 | 2·6 | 0·7 | 8·6 | 2·2 | 14·6 | 3·8 |
| 27 | 3 51·8 | 3 52·4 | 3 41·2 | 2·7 | 0·7 | 8·7 | 2·2 | 14·7 | 3·8 |
| 28 | 3 52·0 | 3 52·6 | 3 41·4 | 2·8 | 0·7 | 8·8 | 2·3 | 14·8 | 3·8 |
| 29 | 3 52·3 | 3 52·9 | 3 41·7 | 2·9 | 0·7 | 8·9 | 2·3 | 14·9 | 3·8 |
| 30 | 3 52·5 | 3 53·1 | 3 41·9 | 3·0 | 0·8 | 9·0 | 2·3 | 15·0 | 3·9 |
| 31 | 3 52·8 | 3 53·4 | 3 42·1 | 3·1 | 0·8 | 9·1 | 2·4 | 15·1 | 3·9 |
| 32 | 3 53·0 | 3 53·6 | 3 42·4 | 3·2 | 0·8 | 9·2 | 2·4 | 15·2 | 3·9 |
| 33 | 3 53·3 | 3 53·9 | 3 42·6 | 3·3 | 0·9 | 9·3 | 2·4 | 15·3 | 4·0 |
| 34 | 3 53·5 | 3 54·1 | 3 42·9 | 3·4 | 0·9 | 9·4 | 2·4 | 15·4 | 4·0 |
| 35 | 3 53·8 | 3 54·4 | 3 43·1 | 3·5 | 0·9 | 9·5 | 2·5 | 15·5 | 4·0 |
| 36 | 3 54·0 | 3 54·6 | 3 43·3 | 3·6 | 0·9 | 9·6 | 2·5 | 15·6 | 4·0 |
| 37 | 3 54·3 | 3 54·9 | 3 43·6 | 3·7 | 1·0 | 9·7 | 2·5 | 15·7 | 4·1 |
| 38 | 3 54·5 | 3 55·1 | 3 43·8 | 3·8 | 1·0 | 9·8 | 2·5 | 15·8 | 4·1 |
| 39 | 3 54·8 | 3 55·4 | 3 44·1 | 3·9 | 1·0 | 9·9 | 2·6 | 15·9 | 4·1 |
| 40 | 3 55·0 | 3 55·6 | 3 44·3 | 4·0 | 1·0 | 10·0 | 2·6 | 16·0 | 4·1 |
| 41 | 3 55·3 | 3 55·9 | 3 44·5 | 4·1 | 1·1 | 10·1 | 2·6 | 16·1 | 4·2 |
| 42 | 3 55·5 | 3 56·1 | 3 44·8 | 4·2 | 1·1 | 10·2 | 2·6 | 16·2 | 4·2 |
| 43 | 3 55·8 | 3 56·4 | 3 45·0 | 4·3 | 1·1 | 10·3 | 2·7 | 16·3 | 4·2 |
| 44 | 3 56·0 | 3 56·6 | 3 45·2 | 4·4 | 1·1 | 10·4 | 2·7 | 16·4 | 4·2 |
| 45 | 3 56·3 | 3 56·9 | 3 45·5 | 4·5 | 1·2 | 10·5 | 2·7 | 16·5 | 4·3 |
| 46 | 3 56·5 | 3 57·1 | 3 45·7 | 4·6 | 1·2 | 10·6 | 2·7 | 16·6 | 4·3 |
| 47 | 3 56·8 | 3 57·4 | 3 46·0 | 4·7 | 1·2 | 10·7 | 2·8 | 16·7 | 4·3 |
| 48 | 3 57·0 | 3 57·6 | 3 46·2 | 4·8 | 1·2 | 10·8 | 2·8 | 16·8 | 4·3 |
| 49 | 3 57·3 | 3 57·9 | 3 46·4 | 4·9 | 1·3 | 10·9 | 2·8 | 16·9 | 4·4 |
| 50 | 3 57·5 | 3 58·2 | 3 46·7 | 5·0 | 1·3 | 11·0 | 2·8 | 17·0 | 4·4 |
| 51 | 3 57·8 | 3 58·4 | 3 46·9 | 5·1 | 1·3 | 11·1 | 2·9 | 17·1 | 4·4 |
| 52 | 3 58·0 | 3 58·7 | 3 47·2 | 5·2 | 1·3 | 11·2 | 2·9 | 17·2 | 4·4 |
| 53 | 3 58·3 | 3 58·9 | 3 47·4 | 5·3 | 1·4 | 11·3 | 2·9 | 17·3 | 4·5 |
| 54 | 3 58·5 | 3 59·2 | 3 47·6 | 5·4 | 1·4 | 11·4 | 2·9 | 17·4 | 4·5 |
| 55 | 3 58·8 | 3 59·4 | 3 47·9 | 5·5 | 1·4 | 11·5 | 3·0 | 17·5 | 4·5 |
| 56 | 3 59·0 | 3 59·7 | 3 48·1 | 5·6 | 1·4 | 11·6 | 3·0 | 17·6 | 4·5 |
| 57 | 3 59·3 | 3 59·9 | 3 48·4 | 5·7 | 1·5 | 11·7 | 3·0 | 17·7 | 4·6 |
| 58 | 3 59·5 | 4 00·2 | 3 48·6 | 5·8 | 1·5 | 11·8 | 3·0 | 17·8 | 4·6 |
| 59 | 3 59·8 | 4 00·4 | 3 48·8 | 5·9 | 1·5 | 11·9 | 3·1 | 17·9 | 4·6 |
| 60 | 4 00·0 | 4 00·7 | 3 49·1 | 6·0 | 1·6 | 12·0 | 3·1 | 18·0 | 4·7 |

| 16<sup>m</sup> | SUN PLANETS | ARIES | MOON | v or Corrⁿ d | | v or Corrⁿ d | | v or Corrⁿ d | |
|---|---|---|---|---|---|---|---|---|---|
| s | ° ′ | ° ′ | ° ′ | ′ | ′ | ′ | ′ | ′ | ′ |
| 00 | 4 00·0 | 4 00·7 | 3 49·1 | 0·0 | 0·0 | 6·0 | 1·7 | 12·0 | 3·3 |
| 01 | 4 00·3 | 4 00·9 | 3 49·3 | 0·1 | 0·0 | 6·1 | 1·7 | 12·1 | 3·3 |
| 02 | 4 00·5 | 4 01·2 | 3 49·5 | 0·2 | 0·1 | 6·2 | 1·7 | 12·2 | 3·4 |
| 03 | 4 00·8 | 4 01·4 | 3 49·8 | 0·3 | 0·1 | 6·3 | 1·7 | 12·3 | 3·4 |
| 04 | 4 01·0 | 4 01·7 | 3 50·0 | 0·4 | 0·1 | 6·4 | 1·8 | 12·4 | 3·4 |
| 05 | 4 01·3 | 4 01·9 | 3 50·3 | 0·5 | 0·1 | 6·5 | 1·8 | 12·5 | 3·4 |
| 06 | 4 01·5 | 4 02·2 | 3 50·5 | 0·6 | 0·2 | 6·6 | 1·8 | 12·6 | 3·5 |
| 07 | 4 01·8 | 4 02·4 | 3 50·7 | 0·7 | 0·2 | 6·7 | 1·8 | 12·7 | 3·5 |
| 08 | 4 02·0 | 4 02·7 | 3 51·0 | 0·8 | 0·2 | 6·8 | 1·9 | 12·8 | 3·5 |
| 09 | 4 02·3 | 4 02·9 | 3 51·2 | 0·9 | 0·2 | 6·9 | 1·9 | 12·9 | 3·5 |
| 10 | 4 02·5 | 4 03·2 | 3 51·5 | 1·0 | 0·3 | 7·0 | 1·9 | 13·0 | 3·6 |
| 11 | 4 02·8 | 4 03·4 | 3 51·7 | 1·1 | 0·3 | 7·1 | 2·0 | 13·1 | 3·6 |
| 12 | 4 03·0 | 4 03·7 | 3 51·9 | 1·2 | 0·3 | 7·2 | 2·0 | 13·2 | 3·6 |
| 13 | 4 03·3 | 4 03·9 | 3 52·2 | 1·3 | 0·4 | 7·3 | 2·0 | 13·3 | 3·7 |
| 14 | 4 03·5 | 4 04·2 | 3 52·4 | 1·4 | 0·4 | 7·4 | 2·0 | 13·4 | 3·7 |
| 15 | 4 03·8 | 4 04·4 | 3 52·6 | 1·5 | 0·4 | 7·5 | 2·1 | 13·5 | 3·7 |
| 16 | 4 04·0 | 4 04·7 | 3 52·9 | 1·6 | 0·4 | 7·6 | 2·1 | 13·6 | 3·7 |
| 17 | 4 04·3 | 4 04·9 | 3 53·1 | 1·7 | 0·5 | 7·7 | 2·1 | 13·7 | 3·8 |
| 18 | 4 04·5 | 4 05·2 | 3 53·4 | 1·8 | 0·5 | 7·8 | 2·1 | 13·8 | 3·8 |
| 19 | 4 04·8 | 4 05·4 | 3 53·6 | 1·9 | 0·5 | 7·9 | 2·2 | 13·9 | 3·8 |
| 20 | 4 05·0 | 4 05·7 | 3 53·8 | 2·0 | 0·6 | 8·0 | 2·2 | 14·0 | 3·9 |
| 21 | 4 05·3 | 4 05·9 | 3 54·1 | 2·1 | 0·6 | 8·1 | 2·2 | 14·1 | 3·9 |
| 22 | 4 05·5 | 4 06·2 | 3 54·3 | 2·2 | 0·6 | 8·2 | 2·3 | 14·2 | 3·9 |
| 23 | 4 05·8 | 4 06·4 | 3 54·6 | 2·3 | 0·6 | 8·3 | 2·3 | 14·3 | 3·9 |
| 24 | 4 06·0 | 4 06·7 | 3 54·8 | 2·4 | 0·7 | 8·4 | 2·3 | 14·4 | 4·0 |
| 25 | 4 06·3 | 4 06·9 | 3 55·0 | 2·5 | 0·7 | 8·5 | 2·3 | 14·5 | 4·0 |
| 26 | 4 06·5 | 4 07·2 | 3 55·3 | 2·6 | 0·7 | 8·6 | 2·4 | 14·6 | 4·0 |
| 27 | 4 06·8 | 4 07·4 | 3 55·5 | 2·7 | 0·7 | 8·7 | 2·4 | 14·7 | 4·0 |
| 28 | 4 07·0 | 4 07·7 | 3 55·7 | 2·8 | 0·8 | 8·8 | 2·4 | 14·8 | 4·1 |
| 29 | 4 07·3 | 4 07·9 | 3 56·0 | 2·9 | 0·8 | 8·9 | 2·4 | 14·9 | 4·1 |
| 30 | 4 07·5 | 4 08·2 | 3 56·2 | 3·0 | 0·8 | 9·0 | 2·5 | 15·0 | 4·1 |
| 31 | 4 07·8 | 4 08·4 | 3 56·5 | 3·1 | 0·9 | 9·1 | 2·5 | 15·1 | 4·2 |
| 32 | 4 08·0 | 4 08·7 | 3 56·7 | 3·2 | 0·9 | 9·2 | 2·5 | 15·2 | 4·2 |
| 33 | 4 08·3 | 4 08·9 | 3 56·9 | 3·3 | 0·9 | 9·3 | 2·6 | 15·3 | 4·2 |
| 34 | 4 08·5 | 4 09·2 | 3 57·2 | 3·4 | 0·9 | 9·4 | 2·6 | 15·4 | 4·2 |
| 35 | 4 08·8 | 4 09·4 | 3 57·4 | 3·5 | 1·0 | 9·5 | 2·6 | 15·5 | 4·3 |
| 36 | 4 09·0 | 4 09·7 | 3 57·7 | 3·6 | 1·0 | 9·6 | 2·6 | 15·6 | 4·3 |
| 37 | 4 09·3 | 4 09·9 | 3 57·9 | 3·7 | 1·0 | 9·7 | 2·7 | 15·7 | 4·3 |
| 38 | 4 09·5 | 4 10·2 | 3 58·1 | 3·8 | 1·0 | 9·8 | 2·7 | 15·8 | 4·3 |
| 39 | 4 09·8 | 4 10·4 | 3 58·4 | 3·9 | 1·1 | 9·9 | 2·7 | 15·9 | 4·4 |
| 40 | 4 10·0 | 4 10·7 | 3 58·6 | 4·0 | 1·1 | 10·0 | 2·8 | 16·0 | 4·4 |
| 41 | 4 10·3 | 4 10·9 | 3 58·8 | 4·1 | 1·1 | 10·1 | 2·8 | 16·1 | 4·4 |
| 42 | 4 10·5 | 4 11·2 | 3 59·1 | 4·2 | 1·2 | 10·2 | 2·8 | 16·2 | 4·5 |
| 43 | 4 10·8 | 4 11·4 | 3 59·3 | 4·3 | 1·2 | 10·3 | 2·8 | 16·3 | 4·5 |
| 44 | 4 11·0 | 4 11·7 | 3 59·6 | 4·4 | 1·2 | 10·4 | 2·9 | 16·4 | 4·5 |
| 45 | 4 11·3 | 4 11·9 | 3 59·8 | 4·5 | 1·2 | 10·5 | 2·9 | 16·5 | 4·5 |
| 46 | 4 11·5 | 4 12·2 | 4 00·0 | 4·6 | 1·3 | 10·6 | 2·9 | 16·6 | 4·6 |
| 47 | 4 11·8 | 4 12·4 | 4 00·3 | 4·7 | 1·3 | 10·7 | 2·9 | 16·7 | 4·6 |
| 48 | 4 12·0 | 4 12·7 | 4 00·5 | 4·8 | 1·3 | 10·8 | 3·0 | 16·8 | 4·6 |
| 49 | 4 12·3 | 4 12·9 | 4 00·8 | 4·9 | 1·3 | 10·9 | 3·0 | 16·9 | 4·6 |
| 50 | 4 12·5 | 4 13·2 | 4 01·0 | 5·0 | 1·4 | 11·0 | 3·0 | 17·0 | 4·7 |
| 51 | 4 12·8 | 4 13·4 | 4 01·2 | 5·1 | 1·4 | 11·1 | 3·1 | 17·1 | 4·7 |
| 52 | 4 13·0 | 4 13·7 | 4 01·5 | 5·2 | 1·4 | 11·2 | 3·1 | 17·2 | 4·7 |
| 53 | 4 13·3 | 4 13·9 | 4 01·7 | 5·3 | 1·5 | 11·3 | 3·1 | 17·3 | 4·8 |
| 54 | 4 13·5 | 4 14·2 | 4 02·0 | 5·4 | 1·5 | 11·4 | 3·1 | 17·4 | 4·8 |
| 55 | 4 13·8 | 4 14·4 | 4 02·2 | 5·5 | 1·5 | 11·5 | 3·2 | 17·5 | 4·8 |
| 56 | 4 14·0 | 4 14·7 | 4 02·4 | 5·6 | 1·5 | 11·6 | 3·2 | 17·6 | 4·8 |
| 57 | 4 14·3 | 4 14·9 | 4 02·7 | 5·7 | 1·6 | 11·7 | 3·2 | 17·7 | 4·9 |
| 58 | 4 14·5 | 4 15·2 | 4 02·9 | 5·8 | 1·6 | 11·8 | 3·2 | 17·8 | 4·9 |
| 59 | 4 14·8 | 4 15·4 | 4 03·1 | 5·9 | 1·6 | 11·9 | 3·3 | 17·9 | 4·9 |
| 60 | 4 15·0 | 4 15·7 | 4 03·4 | 6·0 | 1·7 | 12·0 | 3·3 | 18·0 | 5·0 |

| 17<sup>m</sup> | SUN PLANETS | ARIES | MOON | v or Corrⁿ d | | v or Corrⁿ d | | v or Corrⁿ d | |
|---|---|---|---|---|---|---|---|---|---|
| s | ° ′ | ° ′ | ° ′ | ′ | ′ | ′ | ′ | ′ | ′ |
| 00 | 4 15·0 | 4 15·7 | 4 03·4 | 0·0 | 0·0 | 6·0 | 1·8 | 12·0 | 3·5 |
| 01 | 4 15·3 | 4 15·9 | 4 03·6 | 0·1 | 0·0 | 6·1 | 1·8 | 12·1 | 3·5 |
| 02 | 4 15·5 | 4 16·2 | 4 03·9 | 0·2 | 0·1 | 6·2 | 1·8 | 12·2 | 3·6 |
| 03 | 4 15·8 | 4 16·5 | 4 04·1 | 0·3 | 0·1 | 6·3 | 1·8 | 12·3 | 3·6 |
| 04 | 4 16·0 | 4 16·7 | 4 04·3 | 0·4 | 0·1 | 6·4 | 1·9 | 12·4 | 3·6 |
| 05 | 4 16·3 | 4 17·0 | 4 04·6 | 0·5 | 0·1 | 6·5 | 1·9 | 12·5 | 3·6 |
| 06 | 4 16·5 | 4 17·2 | 4 04·8 | 0·6 | 0·2 | 6·6 | 1·9 | 12·6 | 3·7 |
| 07 | 4 16·8 | 4 17·5 | 4 05·1 | 0·7 | 0·2 | 6·7 | 2·0 | 12·7 | 3·7 |
| 08 | 4 17·0 | 4 17·7 | 4 05·3 | 0·8 | 0·2 | 6·8 | 2·0 | 12·8 | 3·7 |
| 09 | 4 17·3 | 4 18·0 | 4 05·5 | 0·9 | 0·3 | 6·9 | 2·0 | 12·9 | 3·8 |
| 10 | 4 17·5 | 4 18·2 | 4 05·8 | 1·0 | 0·3 | 7·0 | 2·0 | 13·0 | 3·8 |
| 11 | 4 17·8 | 4 18·5 | 4 06·0 | 1·1 | 0·3 | 7·1 | 2·1 | 13·1 | 3·8 |
| 12 | 4 18·0 | 4 18·7 | 4 06·2 | 1·2 | 0·4 | 7·2 | 2·1 | 13·2 | 3·9 |
| 13 | 4 18·3 | 4 19·0 | 4 06·5 | 1·3 | 0·4 | 7·3 | 2·1 | 13·3 | 3·9 |
| 14 | 4 18·5 | 4 19·2 | 4 06·7 | 1·4 | 0·4 | 7·4 | 2·2 | 13·4 | 3·9 |
| 15 | 4 18·8 | 4 19·5 | 4 07·0 | 1·5 | 0·4 | 7·5 | 2·2 | 13·5 | 3·9 |
| 16 | 4 19·0 | 4 19·7 | 4 07·2 | 1·6 | 0·5 | 7·6 | 2·2 | 13·6 | 4·0 |
| 17 | 4 19·3 | 4 20·0 | 4 07·4 | 1·7 | 0·5 | 7·7 | 2·2 | 13·7 | 4·0 |
| 18 | 4 19·5 | 4 20·2 | 4 07·7 | 1·8 | 0·5 | 7·8 | 2·3 | 13·8 | 4·0 |
| 19 | 4 19·8 | 4 20·5 | 4 07·9 | 1·9 | 0·6 | 7·9 | 2·3 | 13·9 | 4·1 |
| 20 | 4 20·0 | 4 20·7 | 4 08·2 | 2·0 | 0·6 | 8·0 | 2·3 | 14·0 | 4·1 |
| 21 | 4 20·3 | 4 21·0 | 4 08·4 | 2·1 | 0·6 | 8·1 | 2·4 | 14·1 | 4·1 |
| 22 | 4 20·5 | 4 21·2 | 4 08·6 | 2·2 | 0·6 | 8·2 | 2·4 | 14·2 | 4·1 |
| 23 | 4 20·8 | 4 21·5 | 4 08·9 | 2·3 | 0·7 | 8·3 | 2·4 | 14·3 | 4·2 |
| 24 | 4 21·0 | 4 21·7 | 4 09·1 | 2·4 | 0·7 | 8·4 | 2·5 | 14·4 | 4·2 |
| 25 | 4 21·3 | 4 22·0 | 4 09·3 | 2·5 | 0·7 | 8·5 | 2·5 | 14·5 | 4·2 |
| 26 | 4 21·5 | 4 22·2 | 4 09·6 | 2·6 | 0·8 | 8·6 | 2·5 | 14·6 | 4·3 |
| 27 | 4 21·8 | 4 22·5 | 4 09·8 | 2·7 | 0·8 | 8·7 | 2·5 | 14·7 | 4·3 |
| 28 | 4 22·0 | 4 22·7 | 4 10·1 | 2·8 | 0·8 | 8·8 | 2·6 | 14·8 | 4·3 |
| 29 | 4 22·3 | 4 23·0 | 4 10·3 | 2·9 | 0·8 | 8·9 | 2·6 | 14·9 | 4·3 |
| 30 | 4 22·5 | 4 23·2 | 4 10·5 | 3·0 | 0·9 | 9·0 | 2·6 | 15·0 | 4·4 |
| 31 | 4 22·8 | 4 23·5 | 4 10·8 | 3·1 | 0·9 | 9·1 | 2·7 | 15·1 | 4·4 |
| 32 | 4 23·0 | 4 23·7 | 4 11·0 | 3·2 | 0·9 | 9·2 | 2·7 | 15·2 | 4·4 |
| 33 | 4 23·3 | 4 24·0 | 4 11·3 | 3·3 | 1·0 | 9·3 | 2·7 | 15·3 | 4·5 |
| 34 | 4 23·5 | 4 24·2 | 4 11·5 | 3·4 | 1·0 | 9·4 | 2·7 | 15·4 | 4·5 |
| 35 | 4 23·8 | 4 24·5 | 4 11·7 | 3·5 | 1·0 | 9·5 | 2·8 | 15·5 | 4·5 |
| 36 | 4 24·0 | 4 24·7 | 4 12·0 | 3·6 | 1·1 | 9·6 | 2·8 | 15·6 | 4·6 |
| 37 | 4 24·3 | 4 25·0 | 4 12·2 | 3·7 | 1·1 | 9·7 | 2·8 | 15·7 | 4·6 |
| 38 | 4 24·5 | 4 25·2 | 4 12·5 | 3·8 | 1·1 | 9·8 | 2·9 | 15·8 | 4·6 |
| 39 | 4 24·8 | 4 25·5 | 4 12·7 | 3·9 | 1·1 | 9·9 | 2·9 | 15·9 | 4·6 |
| 40 | 4 25·0 | 4 25·7 | 4 12·9 | 4·0 | 1·2 | 10·0 | 2·9 | 16·0 | 4·7 |
| 41 | 4 25·3 | 4 26·0 | 4 13·2 | 4·1 | 1·2 | 10·1 | 2·9 | 16·1 | 4·7 |
| 42 | 4 25·5 | 4 26·2 | 4 13·4 | 4·2 | 1·2 | 10·2 | 3·0 | 16·2 | 4·7 |
| 43 | 4 25·8 | 4 26·5 | 4 13·6 | 4·3 | 1·3 | 10·3 | 3·0 | 16·3 | 4·8 |
| 44 | 4 26·0 | 4 26·7 | 4 13·9 | 4·4 | 1·3 | 10·4 | 3·0 | 16·4 | 4·8 |
| 45 | 4 26·3 | 4 27·0 | 4 14·1 | 4·5 | 1·3 | 10·5 | 3·1 | 16·5 | 4·8 |
| 46 | 4 26·5 | 4 27·2 | 4 14·4 | 4·6 | 1·3 | 10·6 | 3·1 | 16·6 | 4·8 |
| 47 | 4 26·8 | 4 27·5 | 4 14·6 | 4·7 | 1·4 | 10·7 | 3·1 | 16·7 | 4·9 |
| 48 | 4 27·0 | 4 27·7 | 4 14·8 | 4·8 | 1·4 | 10·8 | 3·2 | 16·8 | 4·9 |
| 49 | 4 27·3 | 4 28·0 | 4 15·1 | 4·9 | 1·4 | 10·9 | 3·2 | 16·9 | 4·9 |
| 50 | 4 27·5 | 4 28·2 | 4 15·3 | 5·0 | 1·5 | 11·0 | 3·2 | 17·0 | 5·0 |
| 51 | 4 27·8 | 4 28·5 | 4 15·6 | 5·1 | 1·5 | 11·1 | 3·2 | 17·1 | 5·0 |
| 52 | 4 28·0 | 4 28·7 | 4 15·8 | 5·2 | 1·5 | 11·2 | 3·3 | 17·2 | 5·0 |
| 53 | 4 28·3 | 4 29·0 | 4 16·0 | 5·3 | 1·5 | 11·3 | 3·3 | 17·3 | 5·0 |
| 54 | 4 28·5 | 4 29·2 | 4 16·3 | 5·4 | 1·6 | 11·4 | 3·3 | 17·4 | 5·1 |
| 55 | 4 28·8 | 4 29·5 | 4 16·5 | 5·5 | 1·6 | 11·5 | 3·4 | 17·5 | 5·1 |
| 56 | 4 29·0 | 4 29·7 | 4 16·7 | 5·6 | 1·6 | 11·6 | 3·4 | 17·6 | 5·1 |
| 57 | 4 29·3 | 4 30·0 | 4 17·0 | 5·7 | 1·7 | 11·7 | 3·4 | 17·7 | 5·2 |
| 58 | 4 29·5 | 4 30·2 | 4 17·2 | 5·8 | 1·7 | 11·8 | 3·4 | 17·8 | 5·2 |
| 59 | 4 29·8 | 4 30·5 | 4 17·5 | 5·9 | 1·7 | 11·9 | 3·5 | 17·9 | 5·2 |
| 60 | 4 30·0 | 4 30·7 | 4 17·7 | 6·0 | 1·8 | 12·0 | 3·5 | 18·0 | 5·3 |

| 18 | SUN PLANETS | ARIES | MOON | v or d Corrⁿ | | v or d Corrⁿ | | v or d Corrⁿ | | 19 | SUN PLANETS | ARIES | MOON | v or d Corrⁿ | | v or d Corrⁿ | | v or d Corrⁿ | |
|---|---|---|---|---|---|---|---|---|---|---|---|---|---|---|---|---|---|---|---|
| s | ° ′ | ° ′ | ° ′ | ′ | ′ | ′ | ′ | ′ | ′ | s | ° ′ | ° ′ | ° ′ | ′ | ′ | ′ | ′ | ′ | ′ |
| 00 | 4 30·0 | 4 30·7 | 4 17·7 | 0·0 | 0·0 | 6·0 | 1·9 | 12·0 | 3·7 | 00 | 4 45·0 | 4 45·8 | 4 32·0 | 0·0 | 0·0 | 6·0 | 2·0 | 12·0 | 3·9 |
| 01 | 4 30·3 | 4 31·0 | 4 17·9 | 0·1 | 0·0 | 6·1 | 1·9 | 12·1 | 3·7 | 01 | 4 45·3 | 4 46·0 | 4 32·3 | 0·1 | 0·0 | 6·1 | 2·0 | 12·1 | 3·9 |
| 02 | 4 30·5 | 4 31·2 | 4 18·2 | 0·2 | 0·1 | 6·2 | 1·9 | 12·2 | 3·8 | 02 | 4 45·5 | 4 46·3 | 4 32·5 | 0·2 | 0·1 | 6·2 | 2·0 | 12·2 | 4·0 |
| 03 | 4 30·8 | 4 31·5 | 4 18·4 | 0·3 | 0·1 | 6·3 | 1·9 | 12·3 | 3·8 | 03 | 4 45·8 | 4 46·5 | 4 32·7 | 0·3 | 0·1 | 6·3 | 2·0 | 12·3 | 4·0 |
| 04 | 4 31·0 | 4 31·7 | 4 18·7 | 0·4 | 0·1 | 6·4 | 2·0 | 12·4 | 3·8 | 04 | 4 46·0 | 4 46·8 | 4 33·0 | 0·4 | 0·1 | 6·4 | 2·1 | 12·4 | 4·0 |
| 05 | 4 31·3 | 4 32·0 | 4 18·9 | 0·5 | 0·2 | 6·5 | 2·0 | 12·5 | 3·9 | 05 | 4 46·3 | 4 47·0 | 4 33·2 | 0·5 | 0·2 | 6·5 | 2·1 | 12·5 | 4·1 |
| 06 | 4 31·5 | 4 32·2 | 4 19·1 | 0·6 | 0·2 | 6·6 | 2·0 | 12·6 | 3·9 | 06 | 4 46·5 | 4 47·3 | 4 33·4 | 0·6 | 0·2 | 6·6 | 2·1 | 12·6 | 4·1 |
| 07 | 4 31·8 | 4 32·5 | 4 19·4 | 0·7 | 0·2 | 6·7 | 2·1 | 12·7 | 3·9 | 07 | 4 46·8 | 4 47·5 | 4 33·7 | 0·7 | 0·2 | 6·7 | 2·2 | 12·7 | 4·1 |
| 08 | 4 32·0 | 4 32·7 | 4 19·6 | 0·8 | 0·2 | 6·8 | 2·1 | 12·8 | 3·9 | 08 | 4 47·0 | 4 47·8 | 4 33·9 | 0·8 | 0·3 | 6·8 | 2·2 | 12·8 | 4·2 |
| 09 | 4 32·3 | 4 33·0 | 4 19·8 | 0·9 | 0·3 | 6·9 | 2·1 | 12·9 | 4·0 | 09 | 4 47·3 | 4 48·0 | 4 34·2 | 0·9 | 0·3 | 6·9 | 2·2 | 12·9 | 4·2 |
| 10 | 4 32·5 | 4 33·2 | 4 20·1 | 1·0 | 0·3 | 7·0 | 2·2 | 13·0 | 4·0 | 10 | 4 47·5 | 4 48·3 | 4 34·4 | 1·0 | 0·3 | 7·0 | 2·3 | 13·0 | 4·2 |
| 11 | 4 32·8 | 4 33·5 | 4 20·3 | 1·1 | 0·3 | 7·1 | 2·2 | 13·1 | 4·0 | 11 | 4 47·8 | 4 48·5 | 4 34·6 | 1·1 | 0·4 | 7·1 | 2·3 | 13·1 | 4·3 |
| 12 | 4 33·0 | 4 33·7 | 4 20·6 | 1·2 | 0·4 | 7·2 | 2·2 | 13·2 | 4·1 | 12 | 4 48·0 | 4 48·8 | 4 34·9 | 1·2 | 0·4 | 7·2 | 2·3 | 13·2 | 4·3 |
| 13 | 4 33·3 | 4 34·0 | 4 20·8 | 1·3 | 0·4 | 7·3 | 2·3 | 13·3 | 4·1 | 13 | 4 48·3 | 4 49·0 | 4 35·1 | 1·3 | 0·4 | 7·3 | 2·4 | 13·3 | 4·3 |
| 14 | 4 33·5 | 4 34·2 | 4 21·0 | 1·4 | 0·4 | 7·4 | 2·3 | 13·4 | 4·1 | 14 | 4 48·5 | 4 49·3 | 4 35·4 | 1·4 | 0·5 | 7·4 | 2·4 | 13·4 | 4·4 |
| 15 | 4 33·8 | 4 34·5 | 4 21·3 | 1·5 | 0·5 | 7·5 | 2·3 | 13·5 | 4·2 | 15 | 4 48·8 | 4 49·5 | 4 35·6 | 1·5 | 0·5 | 7·5 | 2·4 | 13·5 | 4·4 |
| 16 | 4 34·0 | 4 34·8 | 4 21·5 | 1·6 | 0·5 | 7·6 | 2·3 | 13·6 | 4·2 | 16 | 4 49·0 | 4 49·8 | 4 35·8 | 1·6 | 0·5 | 7·6 | 2·5 | 13·6 | 4·4 |
| 17 | 4 34·3 | 4 35·0 | 4 21·8 | 1·7 | 0·5 | 7·7 | 2·4 | 13·7 | 4·2 | 17 | 4 49·3 | 4 50·0 | 4 36·1 | 1·7 | 0·6 | 7·7 | 2·5 | 13·7 | 4·5 |
| 18 | 4 34·5 | 4 35·3 | 4 22·0 | 1·8 | 0·6 | 7·8 | 2·4 | 13·8 | 4·3 | 18 | 4 49·5 | 4 50·3 | 4 36·3 | 1·8 | 0·6 | 7·8 | 2·5 | 13·8 | 4·5 |
| 19 | 4 34·8 | 4 35·5 | 4 22·2 | 1·9 | 0·6 | 7·9 | 2·4 | 13·9 | 4·3 | 19 | 4 49·8 | 4 50·5 | 4 36·6 | 1·9 | 0·6 | 7·9 | 2·6 | 13·9 | 4·5 |
| 20 | 4 35·0 | 4 35·8 | 4 22·5 | 2·0 | 0·6 | 8·0 | 2·5 | 14·0 | 4·3 | 20 | 4 50·0 | 4 50·8 | 4 36·8 | 2·0 | 0·7 | 8·0 | 2·6 | 14·0 | 4·6 |
| 21 | 4 35·3 | 4 36·0 | 4 22·7 | 2·1 | 0·6 | 8·1 | 2·5 | 14·1 | 4·3 | 21 | 4 50·3 | 4 51·0 | 4 37·0 | 2·1 | 0·7 | 8·1 | 2·6 | 14·1 | 4·6 |
| 22 | 4 35·5 | 4 36·3 | 4 22·9 | 2·2 | 0·7 | 8·2 | 2·5 | 14·2 | 4·4 | 22 | 4 50·5 | 4 51·3 | 4 37·3 | 2·2 | 0·7 | 8·2 | 2·7 | 14·2 | 4·6 |
| 23 | 4 35·8 | 4 36·5 | 4 23·2 | 2·3 | 0·7 | 8·3 | 2·6 | 14·3 | 4·4 | 23 | 4 50·8 | 4 51·5 | 4 37·5 | 2·3 | 0·7 | 8·3 | 2·7 | 14·3 | 4·6 |
| 24 | 4 36·0 | 4 36·8 | 4 23·4 | 2·4 | 0·7 | 8·4 | 2·6 | 14·4 | 4·4 | 24 | 4 51·0 | 4 51·8 | 4 37·7 | 2·4 | 0·8 | 8·4 | 2·7 | 14·4 | 4·7 |
| 25 | 4 36·3 | 4 37·0 | 4 23·7 | 2·5 | 0·8 | 8·5 | 2·6 | 14·5 | 4·5 | 25 | 4 51·3 | 4 52·0 | 4 38·0 | 2·5 | 0·8 | 8·5 | 2·8 | 14·5 | 4·7 |
| 26 | 4 36·5 | 4 37·3 | 4 23·9 | 2·6 | 0·8 | 8·6 | 2·7 | 14·6 | 4·5 | 26 | 4 51·5 | 4 52·3 | 4 38·2 | 2·6 | 0·8 | 8·6 | 2·8 | 14·6 | 4·7 |
| 27 | 4 36·8 | 4 37·5 | 4 24·1 | 2·7 | 0·8 | 8·7 | 2·7 | 14·7 | 4·5 | 27 | 4 51·8 | 4 52·5 | 4 38·5 | 2·7 | 0·9 | 8·7 | 2·8 | 14·7 | 4·8 |
| 28 | 4 37·0 | 4 37·8 | 4 24·4 | 2·8 | 0·9 | 8·8 | 2·7 | 14·8 | 4·6 | 28 | 4 52·0 | 4 52·8 | 4 38·7 | 2·8 | 0·9 | 8·8 | 2·9 | 14·8 | 4·8 |
| 29 | 4 37·3 | 4 38·0 | 4 24·6 | 2·9 | 0·9 | 8·9 | 2·7 | 14·9 | 4·6 | 29 | 4 52·3 | 4 53·1 | 4 38·9 | 2·9 | 0·9 | 8·9 | 2·9 | 14·9 | 4·8 |
| 30 | 4 37·5 | 4 38·3 | 4 24·9 | 3·0 | 0·9 | 9·0 | 2·8 | 15·0 | 4·6 | 30 | 4 52·5 | 4 53·3 | 4 39·2 | 3·0 | 1·0 | 9·0 | 2·9 | 15·0 | 4·9 |
| 31 | 4 37·8 | 4 38·5 | 4 25·1 | 3·1 | 1·0 | 9·1 | 2·8 | 15·1 | 4·7 | 31 | 4 52·8 | 4 53·6 | 4 39·4 | 3·1 | 1·0 | 9·1 | 3·0 | 15·1 | 4·9 |
| 32 | 4 38·0 | 4 38·8 | 4 25·3 | 3·2 | 1·0 | 9·2 | 2·8 | 15·2 | 4·7 | 32 | 4 53·0 | 4 53·8 | 4 39·7 | 3·2 | 1·0 | 9·2 | 3·0 | 15·2 | 4·9 |
| 33 | 4 38·3 | 4 39·0 | 4 25·6 | 3·3 | 1·0 | 9·3 | 2·9 | 15·3 | 4·7 | 33 | 4 53·3 | 4 54·1 | 4 39·9 | 3·3 | 1·1 | 9·3 | 3·0 | 15·3 | 5·0 |
| 34 | 4 38·5 | 4 39·3 | 4 25·8 | 3·4 | 1·0 | 9·4 | 2·9 | 15·4 | 4·7 | 34 | 4 53·5 | 4 54·3 | 4 40·1 | 3·4 | 1·1 | 9·4 | 3·1 | 15·4 | 5·0 |
| 35 | 4 38·8 | 4 39·5 | 4 26·1 | 3·5 | 1·1 | 9·5 | 2·9 | 15·5 | 4·8 | 35 | 4 53·8 | 4 54·6 | 4 40·4 | 3·5 | 1·1 | 9·5 | 3·1 | 15·5 | 5·0 |
| 36 | 4 39·0 | 4 39·8 | 4 26·3 | 3·6 | 1·1 | 9·6 | 3·0 | 15·6 | 4·8 | 36 | 4 54·0 | 4 54·8 | 4 40·6 | 3·6 | 1·2 | 9·6 | 3·1 | 15·6 | 5·1 |
| 37 | 4 39·3 | 4 40·0 | 4 26·5 | 3·7 | 1·1 | 9·7 | 3·0 | 15·7 | 4·8 | 37 | 4 54·3 | 4 55·1 | 4 40·8 | 3·7 | 1·2 | 9·7 | 3·2 | 15·7 | 5·1 |
| 38 | 4 39·5 | 4 40·3 | 4 26·8 | 3·8 | 1·2 | 9·8 | 3·0 | 15·8 | 4·9 | 38 | 4 54·5 | 4 55·3 | 4 41·1 | 3·8 | 1·2 | 9·8 | 3·2 | 15·8 | 5·1 |
| 39 | 4 39·8 | 4 40·5 | 4 27·0 | 3·9 | 1·2 | 9·9 | 3·1 | 15·9 | 4·9 | 39 | 4 54·8 | 4 55·6 | 4 41·3 | 3·9 | 1·3 | 9·9 | 3·2 | 15·9 | 5·2 |
| 40 | 4 40·0 | 4 40·8 | 4 27·2 | 4·0 | 1·2 | 10·0 | 3·1 | 16·0 | 4·9 | 40 | 4 55·0 | 4 55·8 | 4 41·6 | 4·0 | 1·3 | 10·0 | 3·3 | 16·0 | 5·2 |
| 41 | 4 40·3 | 4 41·0 | 4 27·5 | 4·1 | 1·3 | 10·1 | 3·1 | 16·1 | 5·0 | 41 | 4 55·3 | 4 56·1 | 4 41·8 | 4·1 | 1·3 | 10·1 | 3·3 | 16·1 | 5·2 |
| 42 | 4 40·5 | 4 41·3 | 4 27·7 | 4·2 | 1·3 | 10·2 | 3·1 | 16·2 | 5·0 | 42 | 4 55·5 | 4 56·3 | 4 42·0 | 4·2 | 1·4 | 10·2 | 3·3 | 16·2 | 5·3 |
| 43 | 4 40·8 | 4 41·5 | 4 28·0 | 4·3 | 1·3 | 10·3 | 3·2 | 16·3 | 5·0 | 43 | 4 55·8 | 4 56·6 | 4 42·3 | 4·3 | 1·4 | 10·3 | 3·3 | 16·3 | 5·3 |
| 44 | 4 41·0 | 4 41·8 | 4 28·2 | 4·4 | 1·4 | 10·4 | 3·2 | 16·4 | 5·1 | 44 | 4 56·0 | 4 56·8 | 4 42·5 | 4·4 | 1·4 | 10·4 | 3·4 | 16·4 | 5·3 |
| 45 | 4 41·3 | 4 42·0 | 4 28·4 | 4·5 | 1·4 | 10·5 | 3·2 | 16·5 | 5·1 | 45 | 4 56·3 | 4 57·1 | 4 42·8 | 4·5 | 1·5 | 10·5 | 3·4 | 16·5 | 5·4 |
| 46 | 4 41·5 | 4 42·3 | 4 28·7 | 4·6 | 1·4 | 10·6 | 3·3 | 16·6 | 5·1 | 46 | 4 56·5 | 4 57·3 | 4 43·0 | 4·6 | 1·5 | 10·6 | 3·4 | 16·6 | 5·4 |
| 47 | 4 41·8 | 4 42·5 | 4 28·9 | 4·7 | 1·4 | 10·7 | 3·3 | 16·7 | 5·1 | 47 | 4 56·8 | 4 57·6 | 4 43·2 | 4·7 | 1·5 | 10·7 | 3·5 | 16·7 | 5·4 |
| 48 | 4 42·0 | 4 42·8 | 4 29·2 | 4·8 | 1·5 | 10·8 | 3·3 | 16·8 | 5·2 | 48 | 4 57·0 | 4 57·8 | 4 43·5 | 4·8 | 1·6 | 10·8 | 3·5 | 16·8 | 5·5 |
| 49 | 4 42·3 | 4 43·0 | 4 29·4 | 4·9 | 1·5 | 10·9 | 3·4 | 16·9 | 5·2 | 49 | 4 57·3 | 4 58·1 | 4 43·7 | 4·9 | 1·6 | 10·9 | 3·5 | 16·9 | 5·5 |
| 50 | 4 42·5 | 4 43·3 | 4 29·6 | 5·0 | 1·5 | 11·0 | 3·4 | 17·0 | 5·2 | 50 | 4 57·5 | 4 58·3 | 4 43·9 | 5·0 | 1·6 | 11·0 | 3·6 | 17·0 | 5·6 |
| 51 | 4 42·8 | 4 43·5 | 4 29·9 | 5·1 | 1·6 | 11·1 | 3·4 | 17·1 | 5·3 | 51 | 4 57·8 | 4 58·6 | 4 44·2 | 5·1 | 1·7 | 11·1 | 3·6 | 17·1 | 5·6 |
| 52 | 4 43·0 | 4 43·8 | 4 30·1 | 5·2 | 1·6 | 11·2 | 3·5 | 17·2 | 5·3 | 52 | 4 58·0 | 4 58·8 | 4 44·4 | 5·2 | 1·7 | 11·2 | 3·6 | 17·2 | 5·6 |
| 53 | 4 43·3 | 4 44·0 | 4 30·3 | 5·3 | 1·6 | 11·3 | 3·5 | 17·3 | 5·3 | 53 | 4 58·3 | 4 59·1 | 4 44·7 | 5·3 | 1·7 | 11·3 | 3·7 | 17·3 | 5·6 |
| 54 | 4 43·5 | 4 44·3 | 4 30·6 | 5·4 | 1·7 | 11·4 | 3·5 | 17·4 | 5·4 | 54 | 4 58·5 | 4 59·3 | 4 44·9 | 5·4 | 1·8 | 11·4 | 3·7 | 17·4 | 5·7 |
| 55 | 4 43·8 | 4 44·5 | 4 30·8 | 5·5 | 1·7 | 11·5 | 3·5 | 17·5 | 5·4 | 55 | 4 58·8 | 4 59·6 | 4 45·1 | 5·5 | 1·8 | 11·5 | 3·7 | 17·5 | 5·7 |
| 56 | 4 44·0 | 4 44·8 | 4 31·1 | 5·6 | 1·7 | 11·6 | 3·6 | 17·6 | 5·4 | 56 | 4 59·0 | 4 59·8 | 4 45·4 | 5·6 | 1·8 | 11·6 | 3·8 | 17·6 | 5·7 |
| 57 | 4 44·3 | 4 45·0 | 4 31·3 | 5·7 | 1·8 | 11·7 | 3·6 | 17·7 | 5·5 | 57 | 4 59·3 | 5 00·1 | 4 45·6 | 5·7 | 1·9 | 11·7 | 3·8 | 17·7 | 5·8 |
| 58 | 4 44·5 | 4 45·3 | 4 31·5 | 5·8 | 1·8 | 11·8 | 3·6 | 17·8 | 5·5 | 58 | 4 59·5 | 5 00·3 | 4 45·9 | 5·8 | 1·9 | 11·8 | 3·8 | 17·8 | 5·8 |
| 59 | 4 44·8 | 4 45·5 | 4 31·8 | 5·9 | 1·8 | 11·9 | 3·7 | 17·9 | 5·5 | 59 | 4 59·8 | 5 00·6 | 4 46·1 | 5·9 | 1·9 | 11·9 | 3·9 | 17·9 | 5·8 |
| 60 | 4 45·0 | 4 45·8 | 4 32·0 | 6·0 | 1·9 | 12·0 | 3·7 | 18·0 | 5·6 | 60 | 5 00·0 | 5 00·8 | 4 46·3 | 6·0 | 2·0 | 12·0 | 3·9 | 18·0 | 5·9 |

xi

## 20ᵐ

| 20ᵐ s | SUN PLANETS | ARIES | MOON | v or d | Corrⁿ | v or d | Corrⁿ | v or d | Corrⁿ |
|---|---|---|---|---|---|---|---|---|---|
| 00 | 5 00·0 | 5 00·8 | 4 46·3 | 0·0 | 0·0 | 6·0 | 2·1 | 12·0 | 4·1 |
| 01 | 5 00·3 | 5 01·1 | 4 46·6 | 0·1 | 0·0 | 6·1 | 2·1 | 12·1 | 4·1 |
| 02 | 5 00·5 | 5 01·3 | 4 46·8 | 0·2 | 0·1 | 6·2 | 2·1 | 12·2 | 4·2 |
| 03 | 5 00·8 | 5 01·6 | 4 47·0 | 0·3 | 0·1 | 6·3 | 2·2 | 12·3 | 4·2 |
| 04 | 5 01·0 | 5 01·8 | 4 47·3 | 0·4 | 0·1 | 6·4 | 2·2 | 12·4 | 4·2 |
| 05 | 5 01·3 | 5 02·1 | 4 47·5 | 0·5 | 0·2 | 6·5 | 2·2 | 12·5 | 4·3 |
| 06 | 5 01·5 | 5 02·3 | 4 47·8 | 0·6 | 0·2 | 6·6 | 2·3 | 12·6 | 4·3 |
| 07 | 5 01·8 | 5 02·6 | 4 48·0 | 0·7 | 0·2 | 6·7 | 2·3 | 12·7 | 4·3 |
| 08 | 5 02·0 | 5 02·8 | 4 48·2 | 0·8 | 0·3 | 6·8 | 2·3 | 12·8 | 4·4 |
| 09 | 5 02·3 | 5 03·1 | 4 48·5 | 0·9 | 0·3 | 6·9 | 2·4 | 12·9 | 4·4 |
| 10 | 5 02·5 | 5 03·3 | 4 48·7 | 1·0 | 0·3 | 7·0 | 2·4 | 13·0 | 4·4 |
| 11 | 5 02·8 | 5 03·6 | 4 49·0 | 1·1 | 0·4 | 7·1 | 2·4 | 13·1 | 4·5 |
| 12 | 5 03·0 | 5 03·8 | 4 49·2 | 1·2 | 0·4 | 7·2 | 2·5 | 13·2 | 4·5 |
| 13 | 5 03·3 | 5 04·1 | 4 49·4 | 1·3 | 0·4 | 7·3 | 2·5 | 13·3 | 4·5 |
| 14 | 5 03·5 | 5 04·3 | 4 49·7 | 1·4 | 0·5 | 7·4 | 2·5 | 13·4 | 4·6 |
| 15 | 5 03·8 | 5 04·6 | 4 49·9 | 1·5 | 0·5 | 7·5 | 2·6 | 13·5 | 4·6 |
| 16 | 5 04·0 | 5 04·8 | 4 50·2 | 1·6 | 0·5 | 7·6 | 2·6 | 13·6 | 4·6 |
| 17 | 5 04·3 | 5 05·1 | 4 50·4 | 1·7 | 0·6 | 7·7 | 2·6 | 13·7 | 4·7 |
| 18 | 5 04·5 | 5 05·3 | 4 50·6 | 1·8 | 0·6 | 7·8 | 2·7 | 13·8 | 4·7 |
| 19 | 5 04·8 | 5 05·6 | 4 50·9 | 1·9 | 0·6 | 7·9 | 2·7 | 13·9 | 4·7 |
| 20 | 5 05·0 | 5 05·8 | 4 51·1 | 2·0 | 0·7 | 8·0 | 2·7 | 14·0 | 4·8 |
| 21 | 5 05·3 | 5 06·1 | 4 51·3 | 2·1 | 0·7 | 8·1 | 2·8 | 14·1 | 4·8 |
| 22 | 5 05·5 | 5 06·3 | 4 51·6 | 2·2 | 0·8 | 8·2 | 2·8 | 14·2 | 4·9 |
| 23 | 5 05·8 | 5 06·6 | 4 51·8 | 2·3 | 0·8 | 8·3 | 2·8 | 14·3 | 4·9 |
| 24 | 5 06·0 | 5 06·8 | 4 52·1 | 2·4 | 0·8 | 8·4 | 2·9 | 14·4 | 4·9 |
| 25 | 5 06·3 | 5 07·1 | 4 52·3 | 2·5 | 0·9 | 8·5 | 2·9 | 14·5 | 5·0 |
| 26 | 5 06·5 | 5 07·3 | 4 52·5 | 2·6 | 0·9 | 8·6 | 2·9 | 14·6 | 5·0 |
| 27 | 5 06·8 | 5 07·6 | 4 52·8 | 2·7 | 0·9 | 8·7 | 3·0 | 14·7 | 5·0 |
| 28 | 5 07·0 | 5 07·8 | 4 53·0 | 2·8 | 1·0 | 8·8 | 3·0 | 14·8 | 5·1 |
| 29 | 5 07·3 | 5 08·1 | 4 53·3 | 2·9 | 1·0 | 8·9 | 3·0 | 14·9 | 5·1 |
| 30 | 5 07·5 | 5 08·3 | 4 53·5 | 3·0 | 1·0 | 9·0 | 3·1 | 15·0 | 5·1 |
| 31 | 5 07·8 | 5 08·6 | 4 53·7 | 3·1 | 1·1 | 9·1 | 3·1 | 15·1 | 5·2 |
| 32 | 5 08·0 | 5 08·8 | 4 54·0 | 3·2 | 1·1 | 9·2 | 3·1 | 15·2 | 5·2 |
| 33 | 5 08·3 | 5 09·1 | 4 54·2 | 3·3 | 1·1 | 9·3 | 3·2 | 15·3 | 5·2 |
| 34 | 5 08·5 | 5 09·3 | 4 54·4 | 3·4 | 1·2 | 9·4 | 3·2 | 15·4 | 5·3 |
| 35 | 5 08·8 | 5 09·6 | 4 54·7 | 3·5 | 1·2 | 9·5 | 3·2 | 15·5 | 5·3 |
| 36 | 5 09·0 | 5 09·8 | 4 54·9 | 3·6 | 1·2 | 9·6 | 3·3 | 15·6 | 5·3 |
| 37 | 5 09·3 | 5 10·1 | 4 55·2 | 3·7 | 1·3 | 9·7 | 3·3 | 15·7 | 5·4 |
| 38 | 5 09·5 | 5 10·3 | 4 55·4 | 3·8 | 1·3 | 9·8 | 3·3 | 15·8 | 5·4 |
| 39 | 5 09·8 | 5 10·6 | 4 55·6 | 3·9 | 1·3 | 9·9 | 3·4 | 15·9 | 5·4 |
| 40 | 5 10·0 | 5 10·8 | 4 55·9 | 4·0 | 1·4 | 10·0 | 3·4 | 16·0 | 5·5 |
| 41 | 5 10·3 | 5 11·1 | 4 56·1 | 4·1 | 1·4 | 10·1 | 3·5 | 16·1 | 5·5 |
| 42 | 5 10·5 | 5 11·4 | 4 56·4 | 4·2 | 1·4 | 10·2 | 3·5 | 16·2 | 5·5 |
| 43 | 5 10·8 | 5 11·6 | 4 56·6 | 4·3 | 1·5 | 10·3 | 3·5 | 16·3 | 5·6 |
| 44 | 5 11·0 | 5 11·9 | 4 56·8 | 4·4 | 1·5 | 10·4 | 3·6 | 16·4 | 5·6 |
| 45 | 5 11·3 | 5 12·1 | 4 57·1 | 4·5 | 1·5 | 10·5 | 3·6 | 16·5 | 5·6 |
| 46 | 5 11·5 | 5 12·4 | 4 57·3 | 4·6 | 1·6 | 10·6 | 3·6 | 16·6 | 5·7 |
| 47 | 5 11·8 | 5 12·6 | 4 57·5 | 4·7 | 1·6 | 10·7 | 3·7 | 16·7 | 5·7 |
| 48 | 5 12·0 | 5 12·9 | 4 57·8 | 4·8 | 1·6 | 10·8 | 3·7 | 16·8 | 5·7 |
| 49 | 5 12·3 | 5 13·1 | 4 58·0 | 4·9 | 1·7 | 10·9 | 3·7 | 16·9 | 5·8 |
| 50 | 5 12·5 | 5 13·4 | 4 58·3 | 5·0 | 1·7 | 11·0 | 3·8 | 17·0 | 5·8 |
| 51 | 5 12·8 | 5 13·6 | 4 58·5 | 5·1 | 1·7 | 11·1 | 3·8 | 17·1 | 5·8 |
| 52 | 5 13·0 | 5 13·9 | 4 58·7 | 5·2 | 1·8 | 11·2 | 3·8 | 17·2 | 5·9 |
| 53 | 5 13·3 | 5 14·1 | 4 59·0 | 5·3 | 1·8 | 11·3 | 3·9 | 17·3 | 5·9 |
| 54 | 5 13·5 | 5 14·4 | 4 59·2 | 5·4 | 1·8 | 11·4 | 3·9 | 17·4 | 5·9 |
| 55 | 5 13·8 | 5 14·6 | 4 59·5 | 5·5 | 1·9 | 11·5 | 3·9 | 17·5 | 6·0 |
| 56 | 5 14·0 | 5 14·9 | 4 59·7 | 5·6 | 1·9 | 11·6 | 4·0 | 17·6 | 6·0 |
| 57 | 5 14·3 | 5 15·1 | 4 59·9 | 5·7 | 1·9 | 11·7 | 4·0 | 17·7 | 6·0 |
| 58 | 5 14·5 | 5 15·4 | 5 00·2 | 5·8 | 2·0 | 11·8 | 4·0 | 17·8 | 6·1 |
| 59 | 5 14·8 | 5 15·6 | 5 00·4 | 5·9 | 2·0 | 11·9 | 4·1 | 17·9 | 6·1 |
| 60 | 5 15·0 | 5 15·9 | 5 00·7 | 6·0 | 2·1 | 12·0 | 4·1 | 18·0 | 6·2 |

## 21ᵐ

| 21ᵐ s | SUN PLANETS | ARIES | MOON | v or d | Corrⁿ | v or d | Corrⁿ | v or d | Corrⁿ |
|---|---|---|---|---|---|---|---|---|---|
| 00 | 5 15·0 | 5 15·9 | 5 00·7 | 0·0 | 0·0 | 6·0 | 2·2 | 12·0 | 4·3 |
| 01 | 5 15·3 | 5 16·1 | 5 00·9 | 0·1 | 0·0 | 6·1 | 2·2 | 12·1 | 4·3 |
| 02 | 5 15·5 | 5 16·4 | 5 01·1 | 0·2 | 0·1 | 6·2 | 2·2 | 12·2 | 4·4 |
| 03 | 5 15·8 | 5 16·6 | 5 01·4 | 0·3 | 0·1 | 6·3 | 2·3 | 12·3 | 4·4 |
| 04 | 5 16·0 | 5 16·9 | 5 01·6 | 0·4 | 0·1 | 6·4 | 2·3 | 12·4 | 4·4 |
| 05 | 5 16·3 | 5 17·1 | 5 01·8 | 0·5 | 0·2 | 6·5 | 2·3 | 12·5 | 4·5 |
| 06 | 5 16·5 | 5 17·4 | 5 02·1 | 0·6 | 0·2 | 6·6 | 2·4 | 12·6 | 4·5 |
| 07 | 5 16·8 | 5 17·6 | 5 02·3 | 0·7 | 0·3 | 6·7 | 2·4 | 12·7 | 4·6 |
| 08 | 5 17·0 | 5 17·9 | 5 02·6 | 0·8 | 0·3 | 6·8 | 2·4 | 12·8 | 4·6 |
| 09 | 5 17·3 | 5 18·1 | 5 02·8 | 0·9 | 0·3 | 6·9 | 2·5 | 12·9 | 4·6 |
| 10 | 5 17·5 | 5 18·4 | 5 03·0 | 1·0 | 0·4 | 7·0 | 2·5 | 13·0 | 4·7 |
| 11 | 5 17·8 | 5 18·6 | 5 03·3 | 1·1 | 0·4 | 7·1 | 2·5 | 13·1 | 4·7 |
| 12 | 5 18·0 | 5 18·9 | 5 03·5 | 1·2 | 0·4 | 7·2 | 2·6 | 13·2 | 4·7 |
| 13 | 5 18·3 | 5 19·1 | 5 03·8 | 1·3 | 0·5 | 7·3 | 2·6 | 13·3 | 4·8 |
| 14 | 5 18·5 | 5 19·4 | 5 04·0 | 1·4 | 0·5 | 7·4 | 2·7 | 13·4 | 4·8 |
| 15 | 5 18·8 | 5 19·6 | 5 04·2 | 1·5 | 0·5 | 7·5 | 2·7 | 13·5 | 4·8 |
| 16 | 5 19·0 | 5 19·9 | 5 04·5 | 1·6 | 0·6 | 7·6 | 2·7 | 13·6 | 4·9 |
| 17 | 5 19·3 | 5 20·1 | 5 04·7 | 1·7 | 0·6 | 7·7 | 2·8 | 13·7 | 4·9 |
| 18 | 5 19·5 | 5 20·4 | 5 04·9 | 1·8 | 0·6 | 7·8 | 2·8 | 13·8 | 4·9 |
| 19 | 5 19·8 | 5 20·6 | 5 05·2 | 1·9 | 0·7 | 7·9 | 2·8 | 13·9 | 5·0 |
| 20 | 5 20·0 | 5 20·9 | 5 05·4 | 2·0 | 0·7 | 8·0 | 2·9 | 14·0 | 5·0 |
| 21 | 5 20·3 | 5 21·1 | 5 05·7 | 2·1 | 0·8 | 8·1 | 2·9 | 14·1 | 5·1 |
| 22 | 5 20·5 | 5 21·4 | 5 05·9 | 2·2 | 0·8 | 8·2 | 2·9 | 14·2 | 5·1 |
| 23 | 5 20·8 | 5 21·6 | 5 06·1 | 2·3 | 0·8 | 8·3 | 3·0 | 14·3 | 5·1 |
| 24 | 5 21·0 | 5 21·9 | 5 06·4 | 2·4 | 0·9 | 8·4 | 3·0 | 14·4 | 5·2 |
| 25 | 5 21·3 | 5 22·1 | 5 06·6 | 2·5 | 0·9 | 8·5 | 3·0 | 14·5 | 5·2 |
| 26 | 5 21·5 | 5 22·4 | 5 06·9 | 2·6 | 0·9 | 8·6 | 3·1 | 14·6 | 5·2 |
| 27 | 5 21·8 | 5 22·6 | 5 07·1 | 2·7 | 1·0 | 8·7 | 3·1 | 14·7 | 5·3 |
| 28 | 5 22·0 | 5 22·9 | 5 07·3 | 2·8 | 1·0 | 8·8 | 3·2 | 14·8 | 5·3 |
| 29 | 5 22·3 | 5 23·1 | 5 07·6 | 2·9 | 1·0 | 8·9 | 3·2 | 14·9 | 5·3 |
| 30 | 5 22·5 | 5 23·4 | 5 07·8 | 3·0 | 1·1 | 9·0 | 3·2 | 15·0 | 5·4 |
| 31 | 5 22·8 | 5 23·6 | 5 08·0 | 3·1 | 1·1 | 9·1 | 3·3 | 15·1 | 5·4 |
| 32 | 5 23·0 | 5 23·9 | 5 08·3 | 3·2 | 1·1 | 9·2 | 3·3 | 15·2 | 5·4 |
| 33 | 5 23·3 | 5 24·1 | 5 08·5 | 3·3 | 1·2 | 9·3 | 3·3 | 15·3 | 5·5 |
| 34 | 5 23·5 | 5 24·4 | 5 08·8 | 3·4 | 1·2 | 9·4 | 3·4 | 15·4 | 5·5 |
| 35 | 5 23·8 | 5 24·6 | 5 09·0 | 3·5 | 1·3 | 9·5 | 3·4 | 15·5 | 5·6 |
| 36 | 5 24·0 | 5 24·9 | 5 09·2 | 3·6 | 1·3 | 9·6 | 3·4 | 15·6 | 5·6 |
| 37 | 5 24·3 | 5 25·1 | 5 09·5 | 3·7 | 1·3 | 9·7 | 3·5 | 15·7 | 5·6 |
| 38 | 5 24·5 | 5 25·4 | 5 09·7 | 3·8 | 1·4 | 9·8 | 3·5 | 15·8 | 5·7 |
| 39 | 5 24·8 | 5 25·6 | 5 10·0 | 3·9 | 1·4 | 9·9 | 3·5 | 15·9 | 5·7 |
| 40 | 5 25·0 | 5 25·9 | 5 10·2 | 4·0 | 1·4 | 10·0 | 3·6 | 16·0 | 5·7 |
| 41 | 5 25·3 | 5 26·1 | 5 10·4 | 4·1 | 1·5 | 10·1 | 3·6 | 16·1 | 5·8 |
| 42 | 5 25·5 | 5 26·4 | 5 10·7 | 4·2 | 1·5 | 10·2 | 3·7 | 16·2 | 5·8 |
| 43 | 5 25·8 | 5 26·6 | 5 10·9 | 4·3 | 1·5 | 10·3 | 3·7 | 16·3 | 5·8 |
| 44 | 5 26·0 | 5 26·9 | 5 11·1 | 4·4 | 1·6 | 10·4 | 3·7 | 16·4 | 5·9 |
| 45 | 5 26·3 | 5 27·1 | 5 11·4 | 4·5 | 1·6 | 10·5 | 3·8 | 16·5 | 5·9 |
| 46 | 5 26·5 | 5 27·4 | 5 11·6 | 4·6 | 1·6 | 10·6 | 3·8 | 16·6 | 5·9 |
| 47 | 5 26·8 | 5 27·6 | 5 11·9 | 4·7 | 1·7 | 10·7 | 3·8 | 16·7 | 6·0 |
| 48 | 5 27·0 | 5 27·9 | 5 12·1 | 4·8 | 1·7 | 10·8 | 3·9 | 16·8 | 6·0 |
| 49 | 5 27·3 | 5 28·1 | 5 12·3 | 4·9 | 1·8 | 10·9 | 3·9 | 16·9 | 6·1 |
| 50 | 5 27·5 | 5 28·4 | 5 12·6 | 5·0 | 1·8 | 11·0 | 3·9 | 17·0 | 6·1 |
| 51 | 5 27·8 | 5 28·6 | 5 12·8 | 5·1 | 1·8 | 11·1 | 4·0 | 17·1 | 6·1 |
| 52 | 5 28·0 | 5 28·9 | 5 13·1 | 5·2 | 1·9 | 11·2 | 4·0 | 17·2 | 6·2 |
| 53 | 5 28·3 | 5 29·1 | 5 13·3 | 5·3 | 1·9 | 11·3 | 4·0 | 17·3 | 6·2 |
| 54 | 5 28·5 | 5 29·4 | 5 13·5 | 5·4 | 1·9 | 11·4 | 4·1 | 17·4 | 6·2 |
| 55 | 5 28·8 | 5 29·7 | 5 13·8 | 5·5 | 2·0 | 11·5 | 4·1 | 17·5 | 6·3 |
| 56 | 5 29·0 | 5 29·9 | 5 14·0 | 5·6 | 2·0 | 11·6 | 4·2 | 17·6 | 6·3 |
| 57 | 5 29·3 | 5 30·2 | 5 14·3 | 5·7 | 2·0 | 11·7 | 4·2 | 17·7 | 6·3 |
| 58 | 5 29·5 | 5 30·4 | 5 14·5 | 5·8 | 2·1 | 11·8 | 4·2 | 17·8 | 6·4 |
| 59 | 5 29·8 | 5 30·7 | 5 14·7 | 5·9 | 2·1 | 11·9 | 4·3 | 17·9 | 6·4 |
| 60 | 5 30·0 | 5 30·9 | 5 15·0 | 6·0 | 2·2 | 12·0 | 4·3 | 18·0 | 6·5 |

| 22 s | SUN PLANETS | ARIES | MOON | v or Corrn d | v or Corrn d | v or Corrn d |
|---|---|---|---|---|---|---|
| 00 | 5 30·0 | 5 30·9 | 5 15·0 | 0·0 0·0 | 6·0 2·3 | 12·0 4·5 |
| 01 | 5 30·3 | 5 31·2 | 5 15·2 | 0·1 0·0 | 6·1 2·3 | 12·1 4·5 |
| 02 | 5 30·5 | 5 31·4 | 5 15·4 | 0·2 0·1 | 6·2 2·3 | 12·2 4·6 |
| 03 | 5 30·8 | 5 31·7 | 5 15·7 | 0·3 0·1 | 6·3 2·4 | 12·3 4·6 |
| 04 | 5 31·0 | 5 31·9 | 5 15·9 | 0·4 0·2 | 6·4 2·4 | 12·4 4·7 |
| 05 | 5 31·3 | 5 32·2 | 5 16·2 | 0·5 0·2 | 6·5 2·4 | 12·5 4·7 |
| 06 | 5 31·5 | 5 32·4 | 5 16·4 | 0·6 0·2 | 6·6 2·5 | 12·6 4·7 |
| 07 | 5 31·8 | 5 32·7 | 5 16·6 | 0·7 0·3 | 6·7 2·5 | 12·7 4·8 |
| 08 | 5 32·0 | 5 32·9 | 5 16·9 | 0·8 0·3 | 6·8 2·6 | 12·8 4·8 |
| 09 | 5 32·3 | 5 33·2 | 5 17·1 | 0·9 0·3 | 6·9 2·6 | 12·9 4·8 |
| 10 | 5 32·5 | 5 33·4 | 5 17·4 | 1·0 0·4 | 7·0 2·6 | 13·0 4·9 |
| 11 | 5 32·8 | 5 33·7 | 5 17·6 | 1·1 0·4 | 7·1 2·7 | 13·1 4·9 |
| 12 | 5 33·0 | 5 33·9 | 5 17·8 | 1·2 0·5 | 7·2 2·7 | 13·2 5·0 |
| 13 | 5 33·3 | 5 34·2 | 5 18·1 | 1·3 0·5 | 7·3 2·7 | 13·3 5·0 |
| 14 | 5 33·5 | 5 34·4 | 5 18·3 | 1·4 0·5 | 7·4 2·8 | 13·4 5·0 |
| 15 | 5 33·8 | 5 34·7 | 5 18·5 | 1·5 0·6 | 7·5 2·8 | 13·5 5·1 |
| 16 | 5 34·0 | 5 34·9 | 5 18·8 | 1·6 0·6 | 7·6 2·9 | 13·6 5·1 |
| 17 | 5 34·3 | 5 35·2 | 5 19·0 | 1·7 0·6 | 7·7 2·9 | 13·7 5·1 |
| 18 | 5 34·5 | 5 35·4 | 5 19·3 | 1·8 0·7 | 7·8 2·9 | 13·8 5·2 |
| 19 | 5 34·8 | 5 35·7 | 5 19·5 | 1·9 0·7 | 7·9 3·0 | 13·9 5·2 |
| 20 | 5 35·0 | 5 35·9 | 5 19·7 | 2·0 0·8 | 8·0 3·0 | 14·0 5·3 |
| 21 | 5 35·3 | 5 36·2 | 5 20·0 | 2·1 0·8 | 8·1 3·0 | 14·1 5·3 |
| 22 | 5 35·5 | 5 36·4 | 5 20·2 | 2·2 0·8 | 8·2 3·1 | 14·2 5·3 |
| 23 | 5 35·8 | 5 36·7 | 5 20·5 | 2·3 0·9 | 8·3 3·1 | 14·3 5·4 |
| 24 | 5 36·0 | 5 36·9 | 5 20·7 | 2·4 0·9 | 8·4 3·2 | 14·4 5·4 |
| 25 | 5 36·3 | 5 37·2 | 5 20·9 | 2·5 0·9 | 8·5 3·2 | 14·5 5·4 |
| 26 | 5 36·5 | 5 37·4 | 5 21·2 | 2·6 1·0 | 8·6 3·2 | 14·6 5·5 |
| 27 | 5 36·8 | 5 37·7 | 5 21·4 | 2·7 1·0 | 8·7 3·3 | 14·7 5·5 |
| 28 | 5 37·0 | 5 37·9 | 5 21·6 | 2·8 1·0 | 8·8 3·3 | 14·8 5·6 |
| 29 | 5 37·3 | 5 38·2 | 5 21·9 | 2·9 1·1 | 8·9 3·3 | 14·9 5·6 |
| 30 | 5 37·5 | 5 38·4 | 5 22·1 | 3·0 1·1 | 9·0 3·4 | 15·0 5·6 |
| 31 | 5 37·8 | 5 38·7 | 5 22·4 | 3·1 1·2 | 9·1 3·4 | 15·1 5·7 |
| 32 | 5 38·0 | 5 38·9 | 5 22·6 | 3·2 1·2 | 9·2 3·5 | 15·2 5·7 |
| 33 | 5 38·3 | 5 39·2 | 5 22·8 | 3·3 1·2 | 9·3 3·5 | 15·3 5·7 |
| 34 | 5 38·5 | 5 39·4 | 5 23·1 | 3·4 1·3 | 9·4 3·5 | 15·4 5·8 |
| 35 | 5 38·8 | 5 39·7 | 5 23·3 | 3·5 1·3 | 9·5 3·6 | 15·5 5·8 |
| 36 | 5 39·0 | 5 39·9 | 5 23·6 | 3·6 1·4 | 9·6 3·6 | 15·6 5·9 |
| 37 | 5 39·3 | 5 40·2 | 5 23·8 | 3·7 1·4 | 9·7 3·6 | 15·7 5·9 |
| 38 | 5 39·5 | 5 40·4 | 5 24·0 | 3·8 1·4 | 9·8 3·7 | 15·8 5·9 |
| 39 | 5 39·8 | 5 40·7 | 5 24·3 | 3·9 1·5 | 9·9 3·7 | 15·9 6·0 |
| 40 | 5 40·0 | 5 40·9 | 5 24·5 | 4·0 1·5 | 10·0 3·8 | 16·0 6·0 |
| 41 | 5 40·3 | 5 41·2 | 5 24·7 | 4·1 1·5 | 10·1 3·8 | 16·1 6·0 |
| 42 | 5 40·5 | 5 41·4 | 5 25·0 | 4·2 1·6 | 10·2 3·8 | 16·2 6·1 |
| 43 | 5 40·8 | 5 41·7 | 5 25·2 | 4·3 1·6 | 10·3 3·9 | 16·3 6·1 |
| 44 | 5 41·0 | 5 41·9 | 5 25·5 | 4·4 1·7 | 10·4 3·9 | 16·4 6·1 |
| 45 | 5 41·3 | 5 42·2 | 5 25·7 | 4·5 1·7 | 10·5 3·9 | 16·5 6·2 |
| 46 | 5 41·5 | 5 42·4 | 5 25·9 | 4·6 1·7 | 10·6 4·0 | 16·6 6·2 |
| 47 | 5 41·8 | 5 42·7 | 5 26·2 | 4·7 1·8 | 10·7 4·0 | 16·7 6·3 |
| 48 | 5 42·0 | 5 42·9 | 5 26·4 | 4·8 1·8 | 10·8 4·1 | 16·8 6·3 |
| 49 | 5 42·3 | 5 43·2 | 5 26·7 | 4·9 1·8 | 10·9 4·1 | 16·9 6·3 |
| 50 | 5 42·5 | 5 43·4 | 5 26·9 | 5·0 1·9 | 11·0 4·1 | 17·0 6·4 |
| 51 | 5 42·8 | 5 43·7 | 5 27·1 | 5·1 1·9 | 11·1 4·2 | 17·1 6·4 |
| 52 | 5 43·0 | 5 43·9 | 5 27·4 | 5·2 2·0 | 11·2 4·2 | 17·2 6·5 |
| 53 | 5 43·3 | 5 44·2 | 5 27·6 | 5·3 2·0 | 11·3 4·2 | 17·3 6·5 |
| 54 | 5 43·5 | 5 44·4 | 5 27·9 | 5·4 2·0 | 11·4 4·3 | 17·4 6·5 |
| 55 | 5 43·8 | 5 44·7 | 5 28·1 | 5·5 2·1 | 11·5 4·3 | 17·5 6·6 |
| 56 | 5 44·0 | 5 44·9 | 5 28·3 | 5·6 2·1 | 11·6 4·4 | 17·6 6·6 |
| 57 | 5 44·3 | 5 45·2 | 5 28·6 | 5·7 2·1 | 11·7 4·4 | 17·7 6·6 |
| 58 | 5 44·5 | 5 45·4 | 5 28·8 | 5·8 2·2 | 11·8 4·4 | 17·8 6·7 |
| 59 | 5 44·8 | 5 45·7 | 5 29·0 | 5·9 2·2 | 11·9 4·5 | 17·9 6·7 |
| 60 | 5 45·0 | 5 45·9 | 5 29·3 | 6·0 2·3 | 12·0 4·5 | 18·0 6·8 |

| 23 s | SUN PLANETS | ARIES | MOON | v or Corrn d | v or Corrn d | v or Corrn d |
|---|---|---|---|---|---|---|
| 00 | 5 45·0 | 5 45·9 | 5 29·3 | 0·0 0·0 | 6·0 2·4 | 12·0 4·7 |
| 01 | 5 45·3 | 5 46·2 | 5 29·5 | 0·1 0·0 | 6·1 2·4 | 12·1 4·7 |
| 02 | 5 45·5 | 5 46·4 | 5 29·8 | 0·2 0·1 | 6·2 2·4 | 12·2 4·8 |
| 03 | 5 45·8 | 5 46·7 | 5 30·0 | 0·3 0·1 | 6·3 2·5 | 12·3 4·8 |
| 04 | 5 46·0 | 5 46·9 | 5 30·2 | 0·4 0·2 | 6·4 2·5 | 12·4 4·9 |
| 05 | 5 46·3 | 5 47·2 | 5 30·5 | 0·5 0·2 | 6·5 2·5 | 12·5 4·9 |
| 06 | 5 46·5 | 5 47·4 | 5 30·7 | 0·6 0·2 | 6·6 2·6 | 12·6 4·9 |
| 07 | 5 46·8 | 5 47·7 | 5 31·0 | 0·7 0·3 | 6·7 2·6 | 12·7 5·0 |
| 08 | 5 47·0 | 5 48·0 | 5 31·2 | 0·8 0·3 | 6·8 2·7 | 12·8 5·0 |
| 09 | 5 47·3 | 5 48·2 | 5 31·4 | 0·9 0·4 | 6·9 2·7 | 12·9 5·1 |
| 10 | 5 47·5 | 5 48·5 | 5 31·7 | 1·0 0·4 | 7·0 2·7 | 13·0 5·1 |
| 11 | 5 47·8 | 5 48·7 | 5 31·9 | 1·1 0·4 | 7·1 2·8 | 13·1 5·1 |
| 12 | 5 48·0 | 5 49·0 | 5 32·1 | 1·2 0·5 | 7·2 2·8 | 13·2 5·2 |
| 13 | 5 48·3 | 5 49·2 | 5 32·4 | 1·3 0·5 | 7·3 2·9 | 13·3 5·2 |
| 14 | 5 48·5 | 5 49·5 | 5 32·6 | 1·4 0·5 | 7·4 2·9 | 13·4 5·2 |
| 15 | 5 48·8 | 5 49·7 | 5 32·9 | 1·5 0·6 | 7·5 2·9 | 13·5 5·3 |
| 16 | 5 49·0 | 5 50·0 | 5 33·1 | 1·6 0·6 | 7·6 3·0 | 13·6 5·3 |
| 17 | 5 49·3 | 5 50·2 | 5 33·3 | 1·7 0·7 | 7·7 3·0 | 13·7 5·4 |
| 18 | 5 49·5 | 5 50·5 | 5 33·6 | 1·8 0·7 | 7·8 3·1 | 13·8 5·4 |
| 19 | 5 49·8 | 5 50·7 | 5 33·8 | 1·9 0·7 | 7·9 3·1 | 13·9 5·4 |
| 20 | 5 50·0 | 5 51·0 | 5 34·1 | 2·0 0·8 | 8·0 3·1 | 14·0 5·5 |
| 21 | 5 50·3 | 5 51·2 | 5 34·3 | 2·1 0·8 | 8·1 3·2 | 14·1 5·5 |
| 22 | 5 50·5 | 5 51·5 | 5 34·5 | 2·2 0·9 | 8·2 3·2 | 14·2 5·6 |
| 23 | 5 50·8 | 5 51·7 | 5 34·8 | 2·3 0·9 | 8·3 3·3 | 14·3 5·6 |
| 24 | 5 51·0 | 5 52·0 | 5 35·0 | 2·4 0·9 | 8·4 3·3 | 14·4 5·6 |
| 25 | 5 51·3 | 5 52·2 | 5 35·2 | 2·5 1·0 | 8·5 3·3 | 14·5 5·7 |
| 26 | 5 51·5 | 5 52·5 | 5 35·5 | 2·6 1·0 | 8·6 3·4 | 14·6 5·7 |
| 27 | 5 51·8 | 5 52·7 | 5 35·7 | 2·7 1·1 | 8·7 3·4 | 14·7 5·8 |
| 28 | 5 52·0 | 5 53·0 | 5 36·0 | 2·8 1·1 | 8·8 3·4 | 14·8 5·8 |
| 29 | 5 52·3 | 5 53·2 | 5 36·2 | 2·9 1·1 | 8·9 3·5 | 14·9 5·8 |
| 30 | 5 52·5 | 5 53·5 | 5 36·4 | 3·0 1·2 | 9·0 3·5 | 15·0 5·9 |
| 31 | 5 52·8 | 5 53·7 | 5 36·7 | 3·1 1·2 | 9·1 3·6 | 15·1 5·9 |
| 32 | 5 53·0 | 5 54·0 | 5 36·9 | 3·2 1·3 | 9·2 3·6 | 15·2 6·0 |
| 33 | 5 53·3 | 5 54·2 | 5 37·2 | 3·3 1·3 | 9·3 3·6 | 15·3 6·0 |
| 34 | 5 53·5 | 5 54·5 | 5 37·4 | 3·4 1·3 | 9·4 3·7 | 15·4 6·0 |
| 35 | 5 53·8 | 5 54·7 | 5 37·6 | 3·5 1·4 | 9·5 3·7 | 15·5 6·1 |
| 36 | 5 54·0 | 5 55·0 | 5 37·9 | 3·6 1·4 | 9·6 3·8 | 15·6 6·1 |
| 37 | 5 54·3 | 5 55·2 | 5 38·1 | 3·7 1·4 | 9·7 3·8 | 15·7 6·1 |
| 38 | 5 54·5 | 5 55·5 | 5 38·4 | 3·8 1·5 | 9·8 3·8 | 15·8 6·2 |
| 39 | 5 54·8 | 5 55·7 | 5 38·6 | 3·9 1·5 | 9·9 3·9 | 15·9 6·2 |
| 40 | 5 55·0 | 5 56·0 | 5 38·8 | 4·0 1·6 | 10·0 3·9 | 16·0 6·3 |
| 41 | 5 55·3 | 5 56·2 | 5 39·1 | 4·1 1·6 | 10·1 4·0 | 16·1 6·3 |
| 42 | 5 55·5 | 5 56·5 | 5 39·3 | 4·2 1·6 | 10·2 4·0 | 16·2 6·3 |
| 43 | 5 55·8 | 5 56·7 | 5 39·5 | 4·3 1·7 | 10·3 4·0 | 16·3 6·4 |
| 44 | 5 56·0 | 5 57·0 | 5 39·8 | 4·4 1·7 | 10·4 4·1 | 16·4 6·4 |
| 45 | 5 56·3 | 5 57·2 | 5 40·0 | 4·5 1·8 | 10·5 4·1 | 16·5 6·5 |
| 46 | 5 56·5 | 5 57·5 | 5 40·3 | 4·6 1·8 | 10·6 4·2 | 16·6 6·5 |
| 47 | 5 56·8 | 5 57·7 | 5 40·5 | 4·7 1·8 | 10·7 4·2 | 16·7 6·5 |
| 48 | 5 57·0 | 5 58·0 | 5 40·7 | 4·8 1·9 | 10·8 4·2 | 16·8 6·6 |
| 49 | 5 57·3 | 5 58·2 | 5 41·0 | 4·9 1·9 | 10·9 4·3 | 16·9 6·6 |
| 50 | 5 57·5 | 5 58·5 | 5 41·2 | 5·0 2·0 | 11·0 4·3 | 17·0 6·7 |
| 51 | 5 57·8 | 5 58·7 | 5 41·5 | 5·1 2·0 | 11·1 4·3 | 17·1 6·7 |
| 52 | 5 58·0 | 5 59·0 | 5 41·7 | 5·2 2·0 | 11·2 4·4 | 17·2 6·7 |
| 53 | 5 58·3 | 5 59·2 | 5 41·9 | 5·3 2·1 | 11·3 4·4 | 17·3 6·8 |
| 54 | 5 58·5 | 5 59·5 | 5 42·2 | 5·4 2·1 | 11·4 4·5 | 17·4 6·8 |
| 55 | 5 58·8 | 5 59·7 | 5 42·4 | 5·5 2·2 | 11·5 4·5 | 17·5 6·9 |
| 56 | 5 59·0 | 6 00·0 | 5 42·6 | 5·6 2·2 | 11·6 4·5 | 17·6 6·9 |
| 57 | 5 59·3 | 6 00·2 | 5 42·9 | 5·7 2·2 | 11·7 4·6 | 17·7 6·9 |
| 58 | 5 59·5 | 6 00·5 | 5 43·1 | 5·8 2·3 | 11·8 4·6 | 17·8 7·0 |
| 59 | 5 59·8 | 6 00·7 | 5 43·4 | 5·9 2·3 | 11·9 4·7 | 17·9 7·0 |
| 60 | 6 00·0 | 6 01·0 | 5 43·6 | 6·0 2·4 | 12·0 4·7 | 18·0 7·1 |

| m 24 | SUN PLANETS | ARIES | MOON | v or Corrⁿ d | | v or Corrⁿ d | | v or Corrⁿ d | | m 25 | SUN PLANETS | ARIES | MOON | v or Corrⁿ d | | v or Corrⁿ d | | v or Corrⁿ d | |
|---|---|---|---|---|---|---|---|---|---|---|---|---|---|---|---|---|---|---|---|
| s | ° ′ | ° ′ | ° ′ | ′ | ′ | ′ | ′ | ′ | ′ | s | ° ′ | ° ′ | ° ′ | ′ | ′ | ′ | ′ | ′ | ′ |
| 00 | 6 00·0 | 6 01·0 | 5 43·6 | 0·0 | 0·0 | 6·0 | 2·5 | 12·0 | 4·9 | 00 | 6 15·0 | 6 16·0 | 5 57·9 | 0·0 | 0·0 | 6·0 | 2·6 | 12·0 | 5·1 |
| 01 | 6 00·3 | 6 01·2 | 5 43·8 | 0·1 | 0·0 | 6·1 | 2·5 | 12·1 | 4·9 | 01 | 6 15·3 | 6 16·3 | 5 58·2 | 0·1 | 0·0 | 6·1 | 2·6 | 12·1 | 5·1 |
| 02 | 6 00·5 | 6 01·5 | 5 44·1 | 0·2 | 0·1 | 6·2 | 2·5 | 12·2 | 5·0 | 02 | 6 15·5 | 6 16·5 | 5 58·4 | 0·2 | 0·1 | 6·2 | 2·6 | 12·2 | 5·2 |
| 03 | 6 00·8 | 6 01·7 | 5 44·3 | 0·3 | 0·1 | 6·3 | 2·6 | 12·3 | 5·0 | 03 | 6 15·8 | 6 16·8 | 5 58·6 | 0·3 | 0·1 | 6·3 | 2·7 | 12·3 | 5·2 |
| 04 | 6 01·0 | 6 02·0 | 5 44·6 | 0·4 | 0·2 | 6·4 | 2·6 | 12·4 | 5·1 | 04 | 6 16·0 | 6 17·0 | 5 58·9 | 0·4 | 0·2 | 6·4 | 2·7 | 12·4 | 5·3 |
| 05 | 6 01·3 | 6 02·2 | 5 44·8 | 0·5 | 0·2 | 6·5 | 2·7 | 12·5 | 5·1 | 05 | 6 16·3 | 6 17·3 | 5 59·1 | 0·5 | 0·2 | 6·5 | 2·8 | 12·5 | 5·3 |
| 06 | 6 01·5 | 6 02·5 | 5 45·0 | 0·6 | 0·2 | 6·6 | 2·7 | 12·6 | 5·1 | 06 | 6 16·5 | 6 17·5 | 5 59·3 | 0·6 | 0·3 | 6·6 | 2·8 | 12·6 | 5·4 |
| 07 | 6 01·8 | 6 02·7 | 5 45·3 | 0·7 | 0·3 | 6·7 | 2·7 | 12·7 | 5·2 | 07 | 6 16·8 | 6 17·8 | 5 59·6 | 0·7 | 0·3 | 6·7 | 2·8 | 12·7 | 5·4 |
| 08 | 6 02·0 | 6 03·0 | 5 45·5 | 0·8 | 0·3 | 6·8 | 2·8 | 12·8 | 5·2 | 08 | 6 17·0 | 6 18·0 | 5 59·8 | 0·8 | 0·3 | 6·8 | 2·9 | 12·8 | 5·4 |
| 09 | 6 02·3 | 6 03·2 | 5 45·7 | 0·9 | 0·4 | 6·9 | 2·8 | 12·9 | 5·3 | 09 | 6 17·3 | 6 18·3 | 6 00·1 | 0·9 | 0·4 | 6·9 | 2·9 | 12·9 | 5·5 |
| 10 | 6 02·5 | 6 03·5 | 5 46·0 | 1·0 | 0·4 | 7·0 | 2·9 | 13·0 | 5·3 | 10 | 6 17·5 | 6 18·5 | 6 00·3 | 1·0 | 0·4 | 7·0 | 3·0 | 13·0 | 5·5 |
| 11 | 6 02·8 | 6 03·7 | 5 46·2 | 1·1 | 0·4 | 7·1 | 2·9 | 13·1 | 5·3 | 11 | 6 17·8 | 6 18·8 | 6 00·5 | 1·1 | 0·5 | 7·1 | 3·0 | 13·1 | 5·6 |
| 12 | 6 03·0 | 6 04·0 | 5 46·5 | 1·2 | 0·5 | 7·2 | 2·9 | 13·2 | 5·4 | 12 | 6 18·0 | 6 19·0 | 6 00·8 | 1·2 | 0·5 | 7·2 | 3·1 | 13·2 | 5·6 |
| 13 | 6 03·3 | 6 04·2 | 5 46·7 | 1·3 | 0·5 | 7·3 | 3·0 | 13·3 | 5·4 | 13 | 6 18·3 | 6 19·3 | 6 01·0 | 1·3 | 0·6 | 7·3 | 3·1 | 13·3 | 5·7 |
| 14 | 6 03·5 | 6 04·5 | 5 46·9 | 1·4 | 0·6 | 7·4 | 3·0 | 13·4 | 5·5 | 14 | 6 18·5 | 6 19·5 | 6 01·3 | 1·4 | 0·6 | 7·4 | 3·1 | 13·4 | 5·7 |
| 15 | 6 03·8 | 6 04·7 | 5 47·2 | 1·5 | 0·6 | 7·5 | 3·1 | 13·5 | 5·5 | 15 | 6 18·8 | 6 19·8 | 6 01·5 | 1·5 | 0·6 | 7·5 | 3·2 | 13·5 | 5·7 |
| 16 | 6 04·0 | 6 05·0 | 5 47·4 | 1·6 | 0·7 | 7·6 | 3·1 | 13·6 | 5·6 | 16 | 6 19·0 | 6 20·0 | 6 01·7 | 1·6 | 0·7 | 7·6 | 3·2 | 13·6 | 5·8 |
| 17 | 6 04·3 | 6 05·2 | 5 47·7 | 1·7 | 0·7 | 7·7 | 3·1 | 13·7 | 5·6 | 17 | 6 19·3 | 6 20·3 | 6 02·0 | 1·7 | 0·7 | 7·7 | 3·3 | 13·7 | 5·8 |
| 18 | 6 04·5 | 6 05·5 | 5 47·9 | 1·8 | 0·7 | 7·8 | 3·2 | 13·8 | 5·6 | 18 | 6 19·5 | 6 20·5 | 6 02·2 | 1·8 | 0·8 | 7·8 | 3·3 | 13·8 | 5·9 |
| 19 | 6 04·8 | 6 05·7 | 5 48·1 | 1·9 | 0·8 | 7·9 | 3·2 | 13·9 | 5·7 | 19 | 6 19·8 | 6 20·8 | 6 02·5 | 1·9 | 0·8 | 7·9 | 3·4 | 13·9 | 5·9 |
| 20 | 6 05·0 | 6 06·0 | 5 48·4 | 2·0 | 0·8 | 8·0 | 3·3 | 14·0 | 5·7 | 20 | 6 20·0 | 6 21·0 | 6 02·7 | 2·0 | 0·9 | 8·0 | 3·4 | 14·0 | 6·0 |
| 21 | 6 05·3 | 6 06·3 | 5 48·6 | 2·1 | 0·9 | 8·1 | 3·3 | 14·1 | 5·8 | 21 | 6 20·3 | 6 21·3 | 6 02·9 | 2·1 | 0·9 | 8·1 | 3·4 | 14·1 | 6·0 |
| 22 | 6 05·5 | 6 06·5 | 5 48·8 | 2·2 | 0·9 | 8·2 | 3·3 | 14·2 | 5·8 | 22 | 6 20·5 | 6 21·5 | 6 03·2 | 2·2 | 0·9 | 8·2 | 3·5 | 14·2 | 6·0 |
| 23 | 6 05·8 | 6 06·8 | 5 49·1 | 2·3 | 0·9 | 8·3 | 3·4 | 14·3 | 5·8 | 23 | 6 20·8 | 6 21·8 | 6 03·4 | 2·3 | 1·0 | 8·3 | 3·5 | 14·3 | 6·1 |
| 24 | 6 06·0 | 6 07·0 | 5 49·3 | 2·4 | 1·0 | 8·4 | 3·4 | 14·4 | 5·9 | 24 | 6 21·0 | 6 22·0 | 6 03·6 | 2·4 | 1·0 | 8·4 | 3·6 | 14·4 | 6·1 |
| 25 | 6 06·3 | 6 07·3 | 5 49·6 | 2·5 | 1·0 | 8·5 | 3·5 | 14·5 | 5·9 | 25 | 6 21·3 | 6 22·3 | 6 03·9 | 2·5 | 1·1 | 8·5 | 3·6 | 14·5 | 6·2 |
| 26 | 6 06·5 | 6 07·5 | 5 49·8 | 2·6 | 1·1 | 8·6 | 3·5 | 14·6 | 6·0 | 26 | 6 21·5 | 6 22·5 | 6 04·1 | 2·6 | 1·1 | 8·6 | 3·7 | 14·6 | 6·2 |
| 27 | 6 06·8 | 6 07·8 | 5 50·0 | 2·7 | 1·1 | 8·7 | 3·6 | 14·7 | 6·0 | 27 | 6 21·8 | 6 22·8 | 6 04·4 | 2·7 | 1·1 | 8·7 | 3·7 | 14·7 | 6·3 |
| 28 | 6 07·0 | 6 08·0 | 5 50·3 | 2·8 | 1·1 | 8·8 | 3·6 | 14·8 | 6·0 | 28 | 6 22·0 | 6 23·0 | 6 04·6 | 2·8 | 1·2 | 8·8 | 3·7 | 14·8 | 6·3 |
| 29 | 6 07·3 | 6 08·3 | 5 50·5 | 2·9 | 1·2 | 8·9 | 3·6 | 14·9 | 6·1 | 29 | 6 22·3 | 6 23·3 | 6 04·8 | 2·9 | 1·2 | 8·9 | 3·8 | 14·9 | 6·3 |
| 30 | 6 07·5 | 6 08·5 | 5 50·8 | 3·0 | 1·2 | 9·0 | 3·7 | 15·0 | 6·1 | 30 | 6 22·5 | 6 23·5 | 6 05·1 | 3·0 | 1·3 | 9·0 | 3·8 | 15·0 | 6·4 |
| 31 | 6 07·8 | 6 08·8 | 5 51·0 | 3·1 | 1·3 | 9·1 | 3·7 | 15·1 | 6·2 | 31 | 6 22·8 | 6 23·8 | 6 05·3 | 3·1 | 1·3 | 9·1 | 3·9 | 15·1 | 6·4 |
| 32 | 6 08·0 | 6 09·0 | 5 51·2 | 3·2 | 1·3 | 9·2 | 3·8 | 15·2 | 6·2 | 32 | 6 23·0 | 6 24·0 | 6 05·6 | 3·2 | 1·4 | 9·2 | 3·9 | 15·2 | 6·5 |
| 33 | 6 08·3 | 6 09·3 | 5 51·5 | 3·3 | 1·3 | 9·3 | 3·8 | 15·3 | 6·2 | 33 | 6 23·3 | 6 24·3 | 6 05·8 | 3·3 | 1·4 | 9·3 | 4·0 | 15·3 | 6·5 |
| 34 | 6 08·5 | 6 09·5 | 5 51·7 | 3·4 | 1·4 | 9·4 | 3·8 | 15·4 | 6·3 | 34 | 6 23·5 | 6 24·5 | 6 06·0 | 3·4 | 1·4 | 9·4 | 4·0 | 15·4 | 6·5 |
| 35 | 6 08·8 | 6 09·8 | 5 52·0 | 3·5 | 1·4 | 9·5 | 3·9 | 15·5 | 6·3 | 35 | 6 23·8 | 6 24·8 | 6 06·3 | 3·5 | 1·5 | 9·5 | 4·0 | 15·5 | 6·6 |
| 36 | 6 09·0 | 6 10·0 | 5 52·2 | 3·6 | 1·5 | 9·6 | 3·9 | 15·6 | 6·4 | 36 | 6 24·0 | 6 25·1 | 6 06·5 | 3·6 | 1·5 | 9·6 | 4·1 | 15·6 | 6·6 |
| 37 | 6 09·3 | 6 10·3 | 5 52·4 | 3·7 | 1·5 | 9·7 | 4·0 | 15·7 | 6·4 | 37 | 6 24·3 | 6 25·3 | 6 06·7 | 3·7 | 1·6 | 9·7 | 4·1 | 15·7 | 6·7 |
| 38 | 6 09·5 | 6 10·5 | 5 52·7 | 3·8 | 1·6 | 9·8 | 4·0 | 15·8 | 6·5 | 38 | 6 24·5 | 6 25·6 | 6 07·0 | 3·8 | 1·6 | 9·8 | 4·2 | 15·8 | 6·7 |
| 39 | 6 09·8 | 6 10·8 | 5 52·9 | 3·9 | 1·6 | 9·9 | 4·0 | 15·9 | 6·5 | 39 | 6 24·8 | 6 25·8 | 6 07·2 | 3·9 | 1·7 | 9·9 | 4·2 | 15·9 | 6·8 |
| 40 | 6 10·0 | 6 11·0 | 5 53·1 | 4·0 | 1·6 | 10·0 | 4·1 | 16·0 | 6·5 | 40 | 6 25·0 | 6 26·1 | 6 07·5 | 4·0 | 1·7 | 10·0 | 4·3 | 16·0 | 6·8 |
| 41 | 6 10·3 | 6 11·3 | 5 53·4 | 4·1 | 1·7 | 10·1 | 4·1 | 16·1 | 6·6 | 41 | 6 25·3 | 6 26·3 | 6 07·7 | 4·1 | 1·7 | 10·1 | 4·3 | 16·1 | 6·8 |
| 42 | 6 10·5 | 6 11·5 | 5 53·6 | 4·2 | 1·7 | 10·2 | 4·2 | 16·2 | 6·6 | 42 | 6 25·5 | 6 26·6 | 6 07·9 | 4·2 | 1·8 | 10·2 | 4·3 | 16·2 | 6·9 |
| 43 | 6 10·8 | 6 11·8 | 5 53·9 | 4·3 | 1·8 | 10·3 | 4·2 | 16·3 | 6·7 | 43 | 6 25·8 | 6 26·8 | 6 08·2 | 4·3 | 1·8 | 10·3 | 4·4 | 16·3 | 6·9 |
| 44 | 6 11·0 | 6 12·0 | 5 54·1 | 4·4 | 1·8 | 10·4 | 4·2 | 16·4 | 6·7 | 44 | 6 26·0 | 6 27·1 | 6 08·4 | 4·4 | 1·9 | 10·4 | 4·4 | 16·4 | 7·0 |
| 45 | 6 11·3 | 6 12·3 | 5 54·3 | 4·5 | 1·8 | 10·5 | 4·3 | 16·5 | 6·7 | 45 | 6 26·3 | 6 27·3 | 6 08·7 | 4·5 | 1·9 | 10·5 | 4·5 | 16·5 | 7·0 |
| 46 | 6 11·5 | 6 12·5 | 5 54·6 | 4·6 | 1·9 | 10·6 | 4·3 | 16·6 | 6·8 | 46 | 6 26·5 | 6 27·6 | 6 08·9 | 4·6 | 2·0 | 10·6 | 4·5 | 16·6 | 7·1 |
| 47 | 6 11·8 | 6 12·8 | 5 54·8 | 4·7 | 1·9 | 10·7 | 4·4 | 16·7 | 6·8 | 47 | 6 26·8 | 6 27·8 | 6 09·1 | 4·7 | 2·0 | 10·7 | 4·5 | 16·7 | 7·1 |
| 48 | 6 12·0 | 6 13·0 | 5 55·1 | 4·8 | 2·0 | 10·8 | 4·4 | 16·8 | 6·9 | 48 | 6 27·0 | 6 28·1 | 6 09·4 | 4·8 | 2·0 | 10·8 | 4·6 | 16·8 | 7·1 |
| 49 | 6 12·3 | 6 13·3 | 5 55·3 | 4·9 | 2·0 | 10·9 | 4·5 | 16·9 | 6·9 | 49 | 6 27·3 | 6 28·3 | 6 09·6 | 4·9 | 2·1 | 10·9 | 4·6 | 16·9 | 7·2 |
| 50 | 6 12·5 | 6 13·5 | 5 55·5 | 5·0 | 2·0 | 11·0 | 4·5 | 17·0 | 6·9 | 50 | 6 27·5 | 6 28·6 | 6 09·8 | 5·0 | 2·1 | 11·0 | 4·7 | 17·0 | 7·2 |
| 51 | 6 12·8 | 6 13·8 | 5 55·8 | 5·1 | 2·1 | 11·1 | 4·5 | 17·1 | 7·0 | 51 | 6 27·8 | 6 28·8 | 6 10·1 | 5·1 | 2·2 | 11·1 | 4·7 | 17·1 | 7·3 |
| 52 | 6 13·0 | 6 14·0 | 5 56·0 | 5·2 | 2·1 | 11·2 | 4·6 | 17·2 | 7·0 | 52 | 6 28·0 | 6 29·1 | 6 10·3 | 5·2 | 2·2 | 11·2 | 4·8 | 17·2 | 7·3 |
| 53 | 6 13·3 | 6 14·3 | 5 56·2 | 5·3 | 2·2 | 11·3 | 4·6 | 17·3 | 7·1 | 53 | 6 28·3 | 6 29·3 | 6 10·6 | 5·3 | 2·3 | 11·3 | 4·8 | 17·3 | 7·3 |
| 54 | 6 13·5 | 6 14·5 | 5 56·5 | 5·4 | 2·2 | 11·4 | 4·7 | 17·4 | 7·1 | 54 | 6 28·5 | 6 29·6 | 6 10·8 | 5·4 | 2·3 | 11·4 | 4·8 | 17·4 | 7·4 |
| 55 | 6 13·8 | 6 14·8 | 5 56·7 | 5·5 | 2·2 | 11·5 | 4·7 | 17·5 | 7·1 | 55 | 6 28·8 | 6 29·8 | 6 11·0 | 5·5 | 2·3 | 11·5 | 4·9 | 17·5 | 7·4 |
| 56 | 6 14·0 | 6 15·0 | 5 57·0 | 5·6 | 2·3 | 11·6 | 4·7 | 17·6 | 7·2 | 56 | 6 29·0 | 6 30·1 | 6 11·3 | 5·6 | 2·4 | 11·6 | 4·9 | 17·6 | 7·5 |
| 57 | 6 14·3 | 6 15·3 | 5 57·2 | 5·7 | 2·3 | 11·7 | 4·8 | 17·7 | 7·2 | 57 | 6 29·3 | 6 30·3 | 6 11·5 | 5·7 | 2·4 | 11·7 | 5·0 | 17·7 | 7·5 |
| 58 | 6 14·5 | 6 15·5 | 5 57·4 | 5·8 | 2·4 | 11·8 | 4·8 | 17·8 | 7·3 | 58 | 6 29·5 | 6 30·6 | 6 11·8 | 5·8 | 2·5 | 11·8 | 5·0 | 17·8 | 7·6 |
| 59 | 6 14·8 | 6 15·8 | 5 57·7 | 5·9 | 2·4 | 11·9 | 4·9 | 17·9 | 7·3 | 59 | 6 29·8 | 6 30·8 | 6 12·0 | 5·9 | 2·5 | 11·9 | 5·1 | 17·9 | 7·6 |
| 60 | 6 15·0 | 6 16·0 | 5 57·9 | 6·0 | 2·5 | 12·0 | 4·9 | 18·0 | 7·4 | 60 | 6 30·0 | 6 31·1 | 6 12·2 | 6·0 | 2·6 | 12·0 | 5·1 | 18·0 | 7·7 |

## 26ᵐ

| 26 (m) s | SUN PLANETS ° ' | ARIES ° ' | MOON ° ' | v or Corrn d ' ' | v or Corrn d ' ' | v or Corrn d ' ' |
|---|---|---|---|---|---|---|
| 00 | 6 30·0 | 6 31·1 | 6 12·2 | 0·0 0·0 | 6·0 2·7 | 12·0 5·3 |
| 01 | 6 30·3 | 6 31·3 | 6 12·5 | 0·1 0·0 | 6·1 2·7 | 12·1 5·3 |
| 02 | 6 30·5 | 6 31·6 | 6 12·7 | 0·2 0·1 | 6·2 2·7 | 12·2 5·4 |
| 03 | 6 30·8 | 6 31·8 | 6 12·9 | 0·3 0·1 | 6·3 2·8 | 12·3 5·4 |
| 04 | 6 31·0 | 6 32·1 | 6 13·2 | 0·4 0·2 | 6·4 2·8 | 12·4 5·5 |
| 05 | 6 31·3 | 6 32·3 | 6 13·4 | 0·5 0·2 | 6·5 2·9 | 12·5 5·5 |
| 06 | 6 31·5 | 6 32·6 | 6 13·7 | 0·6 0·3 | 6·6 2·9 | 12·6 5·6 |
| 07 | 6 31·8 | 6 32·8 | 6 13·9 | 0·7 0·3 | 6·7 3·0 | 12·7 5·6 |
| 08 | 6 32·0 | 6 33·1 | 6 14·1 | 0·8 0·4 | 6·8 3·0 | 12·8 5·7 |
| 09 | 6 32·3 | 6 33·3 | 6 14·4 | 0·9 0·4 | 6·9 3·0 | 12·9 5·7 |
| 10 | 6 32·5 | 6 33·6 | 6 14·6 | 1·0 0·4 | 7·0 3·1 | 13·0 5·7 |
| 11 | 6 32·8 | 6 33·8 | 6 14·9 | 1·1 0·5 | 7·1 3·1 | 13·1 5·8 |
| 12 | 6 33·0 | 6 34·1 | 6 15·1 | 1·2 0·5 | 7·2 3·2 | 13·2 5·8 |
| 13 | 6 33·3 | 6 34·3 | 6 15·3 | 1·3 0·6 | 7·3 3·2 | 13·3 5·9 |
| 14 | 6 33·5 | 6 34·6 | 6 15·6 | 1·4 0·6 | 7·4 3·3 | 13·4 5·9 |
| 15 | 6 33·8 | 6 34·8 | 6 15·8 | 1·5 0·7 | 7·5 3·3 | 13·5 6·0 |
| 16 | 6 34·0 | 6 35·1 | 6 16·1 | 1·6 0·7 | 7·6 3·4 | 13·6 6·0 |
| 17 | 6 34·3 | 6 35·3 | 6 16·3 | 1·7 0·8 | 7·7 3·4 | 13·7 6·1 |
| 18 | 6 34·5 | 6 35·6 | 6 16·5 | 1·8 0·8 | 7·8 3·4 | 13·8 6·1 |
| 19 | 6 34·8 | 6 35·8 | 6 16·8 | 1·9 0·8 | 7·9 3·5 | 13·9 6·1 |
| 20 | 6 35·0 | 6 36·1 | 6 17·0 | 2·0 0·9 | 8·0 3·5 | 14·0 6·2 |
| 21 | 6 35·3 | 6 36·3 | 6 17·2 | 2·1 0·9 | 8·1 3·6 | 14·1 6·2 |
| 22 | 6 35·5 | 6 36·6 | 6 17·5 | 2·2 1·0 | 8·2 3·6 | 14·2 6·3 |
| 23 | 6 35·8 | 6 36·8 | 6 17·7 | 2·3 1·0 | 8·3 3·7 | 14·3 6·3 |
| 24 | 6 36·0 | 6 37·1 | 6 18·0 | 2·4 1·1 | 8·4 3·7 | 14·4 6·4 |
| 25 | 6 36·3 | 6 37·3 | 6 18·2 | 2·5 1·1 | 8·5 3·8 | 14·5 6·4 |
| 26 | 6 36·5 | 6 37·6 | 6 18·4 | 2·6 1·1 | 8·6 3·8 | 14·6 6·4 |
| 27 | 6 36·8 | 6 37·8 | 6 18·7 | 2·7 1·2 | 8·7 3·8 | 14·7 6·5 |
| 28 | 6 37·0 | 6 38·1 | 6 18·9 | 2·8 1·2 | 8·8 3·9 | 14·8 6·5 |
| 29 | 6 37·3 | 6 38·3 | 6 19·2 | 2·9 1·3 | 8·9 3·9 | 14·9 6·6 |
| 30 | 6 37·5 | 6 38·6 | 6 19·4 | 3·0 1·3 | 9·0 4·0 | 15·0 6·6 |
| 31 | 6 37·8 | 6 38·8 | 6 19·6 | 3·1 1·4 | 9·1 4·0 | 15·1 6·7 |
| 32 | 6 38·0 | 6 39·1 | 6 19·9 | 3·2 1·4 | 9·2 4·1 | 15·2 6·7 |
| 33 | 6 38·3 | 6 39·3 | 6 20·1 | 3·3 1·5 | 9·3 4·1 | 15·3 6·8 |
| 34 | 6 38·5 | 6 39·6 | 6 20·3 | 3·4 1·5 | 9·4 4·1 | 15·4 6·8 |
| 35 | 6 38·8 | 6 39·8 | 6 20·6 | 3·5 1·5 | 9·5 4·2 | 15·5 6·8 |
| 36 | 6 39·0 | 6 40·1 | 6 20·8 | 3·6 1·6 | 9·6 4·2 | 15·6 6·9 |
| 37 | 6 39·3 | 6 40·3 | 6 21·1 | 3·7 1·6 | 9·7 4·3 | 15·7 6·9 |
| 38 | 6 39·5 | 6 40·6 | 6 21·3 | 3·8 1·7 | 9·8 4·3 | 15·8 7·0 |
| 39 | 6 39·8 | 6 40·8 | 6 21·5 | 3·9 1·7 | 9·9 4·4 | 15·9 7·0 |
| 40 | 6 40·0 | 6 41·1 | 6 21·8 | 4·0 1·8 | 10·0 4·4 | 16·0 7·1 |
| 41 | 6 40·3 | 6 41·3 | 6 22·0 | 4·1 1·8 | 10·1 4·5 | 16·1 7·1 |
| 42 | 6 40·5 | 6 41·6 | 6 22·3 | 4·2 1·9 | 10·2 4·5 | 16·2 7·2 |
| 43 | 6 40·8 | 6 41·8 | 6 22·5 | 4·3 1·9 | 10·3 4·5 | 16·3 7·2 |
| 44 | 6 41·0 | 6 42·1 | 6 22·7 | 4·4 1·9 | 10·4 4·6 | 16·4 7·2 |
| 45 | 6 41·3 | 6 42·3 | 6 23·0 | 4·5 2·0 | 10·5 4·6 | 16·5 7·3 |
| 46 | 6 41·5 | 6 42·6 | 6 23·2 | 4·6 2·0 | 10·6 4·7 | 16·6 7·3 |
| 47 | 6 41·8 | 6 42·8 | 6 23·4 | 4·7 2·1 | 10·7 4·7 | 16·7 7·4 |
| 48 | 6 42·0 | 6 43·1 | 6 23·7 | 4·8 2·1 | 10·8 4·8 | 16·8 7·4 |
| 49 | 6 42·3 | 6 43·4 | 6 23·9 | 4·9 2·2 | 10·9 4·8 | 16·9 7·5 |
| 50 | 6 42·5 | 6 43·6 | 6 24·2 | 5·0 2·2 | 11·0 4·9 | 17·0 7·5 |
| 51 | 6 42·8 | 6 43·9 | 6 24·4 | 5·1 2·3 | 11·1 4·9 | 17·1 7·6 |
| 52 | 6 43·0 | 6 44·1 | 6 24·6 | 5·2 2·3 | 11·2 4·9 | 17·2 7·6 |
| 53 | 6 43·3 | 6 44·4 | 6 24·9 | 5·3 2·3 | 11·3 5·0 | 17·3 7·6 |
| 54 | 6 43·5 | 6 44·6 | 6 25·1 | 5·4 2·4 | 11·4 5·0 | 17·4 7·7 |
| 55 | 6 43·8 | 6 44·9 | 6 25·4 | 5·5 2·4 | 11·5 5·1 | 17·5 7·7 |
| 56 | 6 44·0 | 6 45·1 | 6 25·6 | 5·6 2·5 | 11·6 5·1 | 17·6 7·8 |
| 57 | 6 44·3 | 6 45·4 | 6 25·8 | 5·7 2·5 | 11·7 5·2 | 17·7 7·8 |
| 58 | 6 44·5 | 6 45·6 | 6 26·1 | 5·8 2·6 | 11·8 5·2 | 17·8 7·9 |
| 59 | 6 44·8 | 6 45·9 | 6 26·3 | 5·9 2·6 | 11·9 5·3 | 17·9 7·9 |
| 60 | 6 45·0 | 6 46·1 | 6 26·6 | 6·0 2·7 | 12·0 5·3 | 18·0 8·0 |

## 27ᵐ

| 27 (m) s | SUN PLANETS ° ' | ARIES ° ' | MOON ° ' | v or Corrn d ' ' | v or Corrn d ' ' | v or Corrn d ' ' |
|---|---|---|---|---|---|---|
| 00 | 6 45·0 | 6 46·1 | 6 26·6 | 0·0 0·0 | 6·0 2·8 | 12·0 5·5 |
| 01 | 6 45·3 | 6 46·4 | 6 26·8 | 0·1 0·0 | 6·1 2·8 | 12·1 5·5 |
| 02 | 6 45·5 | 6 46·6 | 6 27·0 | 0·2 0·1 | 6·2 2·8 | 12·2 5·6 |
| 03 | 6 45·8 | 6 46·9 | 6 27·3 | 0·3 0·1 | 6·3 2·9 | 12·3 5·6 |
| 04 | 6 46·0 | 6 47·1 | 6 27·5 | 0·4 0·2 | 6·4 2·9 | 12·4 5·7 |
| 05 | 6 46·3 | 6 47·4 | 6 27·7 | 0·5 0·2 | 6·5 3·0 | 12·5 5·7 |
| 06 | 6 46·5 | 6 47·6 | 6 28·0 | 0·6 0·3 | 6·6 3·0 | 12·6 5·8 |
| 07 | 6 46·8 | 6 47·9 | 6 28·2 | 0·7 0·3 | 6·7 3·1 | 12·7 5·8 |
| 08 | 6 47·0 | 6 48·1 | 6 28·5 | 0·8 0·4 | 6·8 3·1 | 12·8 5·9 |
| 09 | 6 47·3 | 6 48·4 | 6 28·7 | 0·9 0·4 | 6·9 3·2 | 12·9 5·9 |
| 10 | 6 47·5 | 6 48·6 | 6 28·9 | 1·0 0·5 | 7·0 3·2 | 13·0 6·0 |
| 11 | 6 47·8 | 6 48·9 | 6 29·2 | 1·1 0·5 | 7·1 3·3 | 13·1 6·0 |
| 12 | 6 48·0 | 6 49·1 | 6 29·4 | 1·2 0·6 | 7·2 3·3 | 13·2 6·1 |
| 13 | 6 48·3 | 6 49·4 | 6 29·7 | 1·3 0·6 | 7·3 3·3 | 13·3 6·1 |
| 14 | 6 48·5 | 6 49·6 | 6 29·9 | 1·4 0·6 | 7·4 3·4 | 13·4 6·1 |
| 15 | 6 48·8 | 6 49·9 | 6 30·1 | 1·5 0·7 | 7·5 3·4 | 13·5 6·2 |
| 16 | 6 49·0 | 6 50·1 | 6 30·4 | 1·6 0·7 | 7·6 3·5 | 13·6 6·2 |
| 17 | 6 49·3 | 6 50·4 | 6 30·6 | 1·7 0·8 | 7·7 3·5 | 13·7 6·3 |
| 18 | 6 49·5 | 6 50·6 | 6 30·8 | 1·8 0·8 | 7·8 3·6 | 13·8 6·3 |
| 19 | 6 49·8 | 6 50·9 | 6 31·1 | 1·9 0·9 | 7·9 3·6 | 13·9 6·4 |
| 20 | 6 50·0 | 6 51·1 | 6 31·3 | 2·0 0·9 | 8·0 3·7 | 14·0 6·4 |
| 21 | 6 50·3 | 6 51·4 | 6 31·6 | 2·1 1·0 | 8·1 3·7 | 14·1 6·5 |
| 22 | 6 50·5 | 6 51·6 | 6 31·8 | 2·2 1·0 | 8·2 3·8 | 14·2 6·5 |
| 23 | 6 50·8 | 6 51·9 | 6 32·0 | 2·3 1·1 | 8·3 3·8 | 14·3 6·6 |
| 24 | 6 51·0 | 6 52·1 | 6 32·3 | 2·4 1·1 | 8·4 3·9 | 14·4 6·6 |
| 25 | 6 51·3 | 6 52·4 | 6 32·5 | 2·5 1·1 | 8·5 3·9 | 14·5 6·6 |
| 26 | 6 51·5 | 6 52·6 | 6 32·8 | 2·6 1·2 | 8·6 3·9 | 14·6 6·7 |
| 27 | 6 51·8 | 6 52·9 | 6 33·0 | 2·7 1·2 | 8·7 4·0 | 14·7 6·7 |
| 28 | 6 52·0 | 6 53·1 | 6 33·2 | 2·8 1·3 | 8·8 4·0 | 14·8 6·8 |
| 29 | 6 52·3 | 6 53·4 | 6 33·5 | 2·9 1·3 | 8·9 4·1 | 14·9 6·8 |
| 30 | 6 52·5 | 6 53·6 | 6 33·7 | 3·0 1·4 | 9·0 4·1 | 15·0 6·9 |
| 31 | 6 52·8 | 6 53·9 | 6 33·9 | 3·1 1·4 | 9·1 4·2 | 15·1 6·9 |
| 32 | 6 53·0 | 6 54·1 | 6 34·2 | 3·2 1·5 | 9·2 4·2 | 15·2 7·0 |
| 33 | 6 53·3 | 6 54·4 | 6 34·4 | 3·3 1·5 | 9·3 4·3 | 15·3 7·0 |
| 34 | 6 53·5 | 6 54·6 | 6 34·7 | 3·4 1·6 | 9·4 4·3 | 15·4 7·1 |
| 35 | 6 53·8 | 6 54·9 | 6 34·9 | 3·5 1·6 | 9·5 4·4 | 15·5 7·1 |
| 36 | 6 54·0 | 6 55·1 | 6 35·1 | 3·6 1·7 | 9·6 4·4 | 15·6 7·2 |
| 37 | 6 54·3 | 6 55·4 | 6 35·4 | 3·7 1·7 | 9·7 4·4 | 15·7 7·2 |
| 38 | 6 54·5 | 6 55·6 | 6 35·6 | 3·8 1·7 | 9·8 4·5 | 15·8 7·2 |
| 39 | 6 54·8 | 6 55·9 | 6 35·9 | 3·9 1·8 | 9·9 4·5 | 15·9 7·3 |
| 40 | 6 55·0 | 6 56·1 | 6 36·1 | 4·0 1·8 | 10·0 4·6 | 16·0 7·3 |
| 41 | 6 55·3 | 6 56·4 | 6 36·3 | 4·1 1·9 | 10·1 4·6 | 16·1 7·4 |
| 42 | 6 55·5 | 6 56·6 | 6 36·6 | 4·2 1·9 | 10·2 4·7 | 16·2 7·4 |
| 43 | 6 55·8 | 6 56·9 | 6 36·8 | 4·3 2·0 | 10·3 4·7 | 16·3 7·5 |
| 44 | 6 56·0 | 6 57·1 | 6 37·0 | 4·4 2·0 | 10·4 4·8 | 16·4 7·5 |
| 45 | 6 56·3 | 6 57·4 | 6 37·3 | 4·5 2·1 | 10·5 4·8 | 16·5 7·6 |
| 46 | 6 56·5 | 6 57·6 | 6 37·5 | 4·6 2·1 | 10·6 4·9 | 16·6 7·6 |
| 47 | 6 56·8 | 6 57·9 | 6 37·8 | 4·7 2·2 | 10·7 4·9 | 16·7 7·7 |
| 48 | 6 57·0 | 6 58·1 | 6 38·0 | 4·8 2·2 | 10·8 5·0 | 16·8 7·7 |
| 49 | 6 57·3 | 6 58·4 | 6 38·2 | 4·9 2·2 | 10·9 5·0 | 16·9 7·7 |
| 50 | 6 57·5 | 6 58·6 | 6 38·5 | 5·0 2·3 | 11·0 5·0 | 17·0 7·8 |
| 51 | 6 57·8 | 6 58·9 | 6 38·7 | 5·1 2·3 | 11·1 5·1 | 17·1 7·8 |
| 52 | 6 58·0 | 6 59·1 | 6 39·0 | 5·2 2·4 | 11·2 5·1 | 17·2 7·9 |
| 53 | 6 58·3 | 6 59·4 | 6 39·2 | 5·3 2·4 | 11·3 5·2 | 17·3 7·9 |
| 54 | 6 58·5 | 6 59·6 | 6 39·4 | 5·4 2·5 | 11·4 5·2 | 17·4 8·0 |
| 55 | 6 58·8 | 6 59·9 | 6 39·7 | 5·5 2·5 | 11·5 5·3 | 17·5 8·0 |
| 56 | 6 59·0 | 7 00·1 | 6 39·9 | 5·6 2·6 | 11·6 5·3 | 17·6 8·1 |
| 57 | 6 59·3 | 7 00·4 | 6 40·2 | 5·7 2·6 | 11·7 5·4 | 17·7 8·1 |
| 58 | 6 59·5 | 7 00·6 | 6 40·4 | 5·8 2·7 | 11·8 5·4 | 17·8 8·2 |
| 59 | 6 59·8 | 7 00·9 | 6 40·6 | 5·9 2·7 | 11·9 5·5 | 17·9 8·2 |
| 60 | 7 00·0 | 7 01·1 | 6 40·9 | 6·0 2·8 | 12·0 5·5 | 18·0 8·3 |

| m 28 s | SUN PLANETS ° ′ | ARIES ° ′ | MOON ° ′ | v or d ′ | Corrⁿ ′ | v or d ′ | Corrⁿ ′ | v or d ′ | Corrⁿ ′ |
|---|---|---|---|---|---|---|---|---|---|
| 00 | 7 00·0 | 7 01·1 | 6 40·9 | 0·0 | 0·0 | 6·0 | 2·9 | 12·0 | 5·7 |
| 01 | 7 00·3 | 7 01·4 | 6 41·1 | 0·1 | 0·0 | 6·1 | 2·9 | 12·1 | 5·7 |
| 02 | 7 00·5 | 7 01·7 | 6 41·3 | 0·2 | 0·1 | 6·2 | 2·9 | 12·2 | 5·8 |
| 03 | 7 00·8 | 7 01·9 | 6 41·6 | 0·3 | 0·1 | 6·3 | 3·0 | 12·3 | 5·8 |
| 04 | 7 01·0 | 7 02·2 | 6 41·8 | 0·4 | 0·2 | 6·4 | 3·0 | 12·4 | 5·9 |
| 05 | 7 01·3 | 7 02·4 | 6 42·1 | 0·5 | 0·2 | 6·5 | 3·1 | 12·5 | 5·9 |
| 06 | 7 01·5 | 7 02·7 | 6 42·3 | 0·6 | 0·3 | 6·6 | 3·1 | 12·6 | 6·0 |
| 07 | 7 01·8 | 7 02·9 | 6 42·5 | 0·7 | 0·3 | 6·7 | 3·2 | 12·7 | 6·0 |
| 08 | 7 02·0 | 7 03·2 | 6 42·8 | 0·8 | 0·4 | 6·8 | 3·2 | 12·8 | 6·1 |
| 09 | 7 02·3 | 7 03·4 | 6 43·0 | 0·9 | 0·4 | 6·9 | 3·3 | 12·9 | 6·1 |
| 10 | 7 02·5 | 7 03·7 | 6 43·3 | 1·0 | 0·5 | 7·0 | 3·3 | 13·0 | 6·2 |
| 11 | 7 02·8 | 7 03·9 | 6 43·5 | 1·1 | 0·5 | 7·1 | 3·4 | 13·1 | 6·2 |
| 12 | 7 03·0 | 7 04·2 | 6 43·7 | 1·2 | 0·6 | 7·2 | 3·4 | 13·2 | 6·3 |
| 13 | 7 03·3 | 7 04·4 | 6 44·0 | 1·3 | 0·6 | 7·3 | 3·5 | 13·3 | 6·3 |
| 14 | 7 03·5 | 7 04·7 | 6 44·2 | 1·4 | 0·7 | 7·4 | 3·5 | 13·4 | 6·4 |
| 15 | 7 03·8 | 7 04·9 | 6 44·4 | 1·5 | 0·7 | 7·5 | 3·6 | 13·5 | 6·4 |
| 16 | 7 04·0 | 7 05·2 | 6 44·7 | 1·6 | 0·8 | 7·6 | 3·6 | 13·6 | 6·5 |
| 17 | 7 04·3 | 7 05·4 | 6 44·9 | 1·7 | 0·8 | 7·7 | 3·7 | 13·7 | 6·5 |
| 18 | 7 04·5 | 7 05·7 | 6 45·2 | 1·8 | 0·9 | 7·8 | 3·7 | 13·8 | 6·6 |
| 19 | 7 04·8 | 7 05·9 | 6 45·4 | 1·9 | 0·9 | 7·9 | 3·8 | 13·9 | 6·6 |
| 20 | 7 05·0 | 7 06·2 | 6 45·6 | 2·0 | 1·0 | 8·0 | 3·8 | 14·0 | 6·7 |
| 21 | 7 05·3 | 7 06·4 | 6 45·9 | 2·1 | 1·0 | 8·1 | 3·8 | 14·1 | 6·7 |
| 22 | 7 05·5 | 7 06·7 | 6 46·1 | 2·2 | 1·0 | 8·2 | 3·9 | 14·2 | 6·7 |
| 23 | 7 05·8 | 7 06·9 | 6 46·4 | 2·3 | 1·1 | 8·3 | 3·9 | 14·3 | 6·8 |
| 24 | 7 06·0 | 7 07·2 | 6 46·6 | 2·4 | 1·1 | 8·4 | 4·0 | 14·4 | 6·8 |
| 25 | 7 06·3 | 7 07·4 | 6 46·8 | 2·5 | 1·2 | 8·5 | 4·0 | 14·5 | 6·9 |
| 26 | 7 06·5 | 7 07·7 | 6 47·1 | 2·6 | 1·2 | 8·6 | 4·1 | 14·6 | 6·9 |
| 27 | 7 06·8 | 7 07·9 | 6 47·3 | 2·7 | 1·3 | 8·7 | 4·1 | 14·7 | 7·0 |
| 28 | 7 07·0 | 7 08·2 | 6 47·5 | 2·8 | 1·3 | 8·8 | 4·2 | 14·8 | 7·0 |
| 29 | 7 07·3 | 7 08·4 | 6 47·8 | 2·9 | 1·4 | 8·9 | 4·2 | 14·9 | 7·1 |
| 30 | 7 07·5 | 7 08·7 | 6 48·0 | 3·0 | 1·4 | 9·0 | 4·3 | 15·0 | 7·1 |
| 31 | 7 07·8 | 7 08·9 | 6 48·3 | 3·1 | 1·5 | 9·1 | 4·3 | 15·1 | 7·2 |
| 32 | 7 08·0 | 7 09·2 | 6 48·5 | 3·2 | 1·5 | 9·2 | 4·4 | 15·2 | 7·2 |
| 33 | 7 08·3 | 7 09·4 | 6 48·7 | 3·3 | 1·6 | 9·3 | 4·4 | 15·3 | 7·3 |
| 34 | 7 08·5 | 7 09·7 | 6 49·0 | 3·4 | 1·6 | 9·4 | 4·5 | 15·4 | 7·3 |
| 35 | 7 08·8 | 7 09·9 | 6 49·2 | 3·5 | 1·7 | 9·5 | 4·5 | 15·5 | 7·4 |
| 36 | 7 09·0 | 7 10·2 | 6 49·5 | 3·6 | 1·7 | 9·6 | 4·6 | 15·6 | 7·4 |
| 37 | 7 09·3 | 7 10·4 | 6 49·7 | 3·7 | 1·8 | 9·7 | 4·6 | 15·7 | 7·5 |
| 38 | 7 09·5 | 7 10·7 | 6 49·9 | 3·8 | 1·8 | 9·8 | 4·7 | 15·8 | 7·5 |
| 39 | 7 09·8 | 7 10·9 | 6 50·2 | 3·9 | 1·9 | 9·9 | 4·7 | 15·9 | 7·6 |
| 40 | 7 10·0 | 7 11·2 | 6 50·4 | 4·0 | 1·9 | 10·0 | 4·8 | 16·0 | 7·6 |
| 41 | 7 10·3 | 7 11·4 | 6 50·6 | 4·1 | 1·9 | 10·1 | 4·8 | 16·1 | 7·6 |
| 42 | 7 10·5 | 7 11·7 | 6 50·9 | 4·2 | 2·0 | 10·2 | 4·8 | 16·2 | 7·7 |
| 43 | 7 10·8 | 7 11·9 | 6 51·1 | 4·3 | 2·0 | 10·3 | 4·9 | 16·3 | 7·7 |
| 44 | 7 11·0 | 7 12·2 | 6 51·4 | 4·4 | 2·1 | 10·4 | 4·9 | 16·4 | 7·8 |
| 45 | 7 11·3 | 7 12·4 | 6 51·6 | 4·5 | 2·1 | 10·5 | 5·0 | 16·5 | 7·8 |
| 46 | 7 11·5 | 7 12·7 | 6 51·8 | 4·6 | 2·2 | 10·6 | 5·0 | 16·6 | 7·9 |
| 47 | 7 11·8 | 7 12·9 | 6 52·1 | 4·7 | 2·2 | 10·7 | 5·1 | 16·7 | 7·9 |
| 48 | 7 12·0 | 7 13·2 | 6 52·3 | 4·8 | 2·3 | 10·8 | 5·1 | 16·8 | 8·0 |
| 49 | 7 12·3 | 7 13·4 | 6 52·6 | 4·9 | 2·3 | 10·9 | 5·2 | 16·9 | 8·0 |
| 50 | 7 12·5 | 7 13·7 | 6 52·8 | 5·0 | 2·4 | 11·0 | 5·2 | 17·0 | 8·1 |
| 51 | 7 12·8 | 7 13·9 | 6 53·0 | 5·1 | 2·4 | 11·1 | 5·3 | 17·1 | 8·1 |
| 52 | 7 13·0 | 7 14·2 | 6 53·3 | 5·2 | 2·5 | 11·2 | 5·3 | 17·2 | 8·2 |
| 53 | 7 13·3 | 7 14·4 | 6 53·5 | 5·3 | 2·5 | 11·3 | 5·4 | 17·3 | 8·2 |
| 54 | 7 13·5 | 7 14·7 | 6 53·8 | 5·4 | 2·6 | 11·4 | 5·4 | 17·4 | 8·3 |
| 55 | 7 13·8 | 7 14·9 | 6 54·0 | 5·5 | 2·6 | 11·5 | 5·5 | 17·5 | 8·3 |
| 56 | 7 14·0 | 7 15·2 | 6 54·2 | 5·6 | 2·7 | 11·6 | 5·5 | 17·6 | 8·4 |
| 57 | 7 14·3 | 7 15·4 | 6 54·5 | 5·7 | 2·7 | 11·7 | 5·6 | 17·7 | 8·4 |
| 58 | 7 14·5 | 7 15·7 | 6 54·7 | 5·8 | 2·8 | 11·8 | 5·6 | 17·8 | 8·5 |
| 59 | 7 14·8 | 7 15·9 | 6 54·9 | 5·9 | 2·8 | 11·9 | 5·7 | 17·9 | 8·5 |
| 60 | 7 15·0 | 7 16·2 | 6 55·2 | 6·0 | 2·9 | 12·0 | 5·7 | 18·0 | 8·6 |

| m 29 s | SUN PLANETS ° ′ | ARIES ° ′ | MOON ° ′ | v or d ′ | Corrⁿ ′ | v or d ′ | Corrⁿ ′ | v or d ′ | Corrⁿ ′ |
|---|---|---|---|---|---|---|---|---|---|
| 00 | 7 15·0 | 7 16·2 | 6 55·2 | 0·0 | 0·0 | 6·0 | 3·0 | 12·0 | 5·9 |
| 01 | 7 15·3 | 7 16·4 | 6 55·4 | 0·1 | 0·0 | 6·1 | 3·0 | 12·1 | 5·9 |
| 02 | 7 15·5 | 7 16·7 | 6 55·7 | 0·2 | 0·1 | 6·2 | 3·0 | 12·2 | 6·0 |
| 03 | 7 15·8 | 7 16·9 | 6 55·9 | 0·3 | 0·1 | 6·3 | 3·1 | 12·3 | 6·0 |
| 04 | 7 16·0 | 7 17·2 | 6 56·1 | 0·4 | 0·2 | 6·4 | 3·1 | 12·4 | 6·1 |
| 05 | 7 16·3 | 7 17·4 | 6 56·4 | 0·5 | 0·2 | 6·5 | 3·2 | 12·5 | 6·1 |
| 06 | 7 16·5 | 7 17·7 | 6 56·6 | 0·6 | 0·3 | 6·6 | 3·2 | 12·6 | 6·2 |
| 07 | 7 16·8 | 7 17·9 | 6 56·9 | 0·7 | 0·3 | 6·7 | 3·3 | 12·7 | 6·2 |
| 08 | 7 17·0 | 7 18·2 | 6 57·1 | 0·8 | 0·4 | 6·8 | 3·3 | 12·8 | 6·3 |
| 09 | 7 17·3 | 7 18·4 | 6 57·3 | 0·9 | 0·4 | 6·9 | 3·4 | 12·9 | 6·3 |
| 10 | 7 17·5 | 7 18·7 | 6 57·6 | 1·0 | 0·5 | 7·0 | 3·4 | 13·0 | 6·4 |
| 11 | 7 17·8 | 7 18·9 | 6 57·8 | 1·1 | 0·5 | 7·1 | 3·5 | 13·1 | 6·4 |
| 12 | 7 18·0 | 7 19·2 | 6 58·0 | 1·2 | 0·6 | 7·2 | 3·5 | 13·2 | 6·5 |
| 13 | 7 18·3 | 7 19·4 | 6 58·3 | 1·3 | 0·6 | 7·3 | 3·6 | 13·3 | 6·5 |
| 14 | 7 18·5 | 7 19·7 | 6 58·5 | 1·4 | 0·7 | 7·4 | 3·6 | 13·4 | 6·6 |
| 15 | 7 18·8 | 7 20·0 | 6 58·8 | 1·5 | 0·7 | 7·5 | 3·7 | 13·5 | 6·6 |
| 16 | 7 19·0 | 7 20·2 | 6 59·0 | 1·6 | 0·8 | 7·6 | 3·7 | 13·6 | 6·7 |
| 17 | 7 19·3 | 7 20·5 | 6 59·2 | 1·7 | 0·8 | 7·7 | 3·8 | 13·7 | 6·7 |
| 18 | 7 19·5 | 7 20·7 | 6 59·5 | 1·8 | 0·9 | 7·8 | 3·8 | 13·8 | 6·8 |
| 19 | 7 19·8 | 7 21·0 | 6 59·7 | 1·9 | 0·9 | 7·9 | 3·9 | 13·9 | 6·8 |
| 20 | 7 20·0 | 7 21·2 | 7 00·0 | 2·0 | 1·0 | 8·0 | 3·9 | 14·0 | 6·9 |
| 21 | 7 20·3 | 7 21·5 | 7 00·2 | 2·1 | 1·0 | 8·1 | 4·0 | 14·1 | 6·9 |
| 22 | 7 20·5 | 7 21·7 | 7 00·4 | 2·2 | 1·1 | 8·2 | 4·0 | 14·2 | 7·0 |
| 23 | 7 20·8 | 7 22·0 | 7 00·7 | 2·3 | 1·1 | 8·3 | 4·1 | 14·3 | 7·0 |
| 24 | 7 21·0 | 7 22·2 | 7 00·9 | 2·4 | 1·2 | 8·4 | 4·1 | 14·4 | 7·1 |
| 25 | 7 21·3 | 7 22·5 | 7 01·1 | 2·5 | 1·2 | 8·5 | 4·2 | 14·5 | 7·1 |
| 26 | 7 21·5 | 7 22·7 | 7 01·4 | 2·6 | 1·3 | 8·6 | 4·2 | 14·6 | 7·2 |
| 27 | 7 21·8 | 7 23·0 | 7 01·6 | 2·7 | 1·3 | 8·7 | 4·3 | 14·7 | 7·2 |
| 28 | 7 22·0 | 7 23·2 | 7 01·9 | 2·8 | 1·4 | 8·8 | 4·3 | 14·8 | 7·3 |
| 29 | 7 22·3 | 7 23·5 | 7 02·1 | 2·9 | 1·4 | 8·9 | 4·4 | 14·9 | 7·3 |
| 30 | 7 22·5 | 7 23·7 | 7 02·3 | 3·0 | 1·5 | 9·0 | 4·4 | 15·0 | 7·4 |
| 31 | 7 22·8 | 7 24·0 | 7 02·6 | 3·1 | 1·5 | 9·1 | 4·5 | 15·1 | 7·4 |
| 32 | 7 23·0 | 7 24·2 | 7 02·8 | 3·2 | 1·6 | 9·2 | 4·5 | 15·2 | 7·5 |
| 33 | 7 23·3 | 7 24·5 | 7 03·1 | 3·3 | 1·6 | 9·3 | 4·6 | 15·3 | 7·5 |
| 34 | 7 23·5 | 7 24·7 | 7 03·3 | 3·4 | 1·7 | 9·4 | 4·6 | 15·4 | 7·6 |
| 35 | 7 23·8 | 7 25·0 | 7 03·5 | 3·5 | 1·7 | 9·5 | 4·7 | 15·5 | 7·6 |
| 36 | 7 24·0 | 7 25·2 | 7 03·8 | 3·6 | 1·8 | 9·6 | 4·7 | 15·6 | 7·7 |
| 37 | 7 24·3 | 7 25·5 | 7 04·0 | 3·7 | 1·8 | 9·7 | 4·8 | 15·7 | 7·7 |
| 38 | 7 24·5 | 7 25·7 | 7 04·3 | 3·8 | 1·9 | 9·8 | 4·8 | 15·8 | 7·8 |
| 39 | 7 24·8 | 7 26·0 | 7 04·5 | 3·9 | 1·9 | 9·9 | 4·9 | 15·9 | 7·8 |
| 40 | 7 25·0 | 7 26·2 | 7 04·7 | 4·0 | 2·0 | 10·0 | 4·9 | 16·0 | 7·9 |
| 41 | 7 25·3 | 7 26·5 | 7 05·0 | 4·1 | 2·0 | 10·1 | 5·0 | 16·1 | 7·9 |
| 42 | 7 25·5 | 7 26·7 | 7 05·2 | 4·2 | 2·1 | 10·2 | 5·0 | 16·2 | 8·0 |
| 43 | 7 25·8 | 7 27·0 | 7 05·4 | 4·3 | 2·1 | 10·3 | 5·1 | 16·3 | 8·0 |
| 44 | 7 26·0 | 7 27·2 | 7 05·7 | 4·4 | 2·2 | 10·4 | 5·1 | 16·4 | 8·1 |
| 45 | 7 26·3 | 7 27·5 | 7 05·9 | 4·5 | 2·2 | 10·5 | 5·2 | 16·5 | 8·1 |
| 46 | 7 26·5 | 7 27·7 | 7 06·2 | 4·6 | 2·3 | 10·6 | 5·2 | 16·6 | 8·2 |
| 47 | 7 26·8 | 7 28·0 | 7 06·4 | 4·7 | 2·3 | 10·7 | 5·3 | 16·7 | 8·2 |
| 48 | 7 27·0 | 7 28·2 | 7 06·6 | 4·8 | 2·4 | 10·8 | 5·3 | 16·8 | 8·3 |
| 49 | 7 27·3 | 7 28·5 | 7 06·9 | 4·9 | 2·4 | 10·9 | 5·4 | 16·9 | 8·3 |
| 50 | 7 27·5 | 7 28·7 | 7 07·1 | 5·0 | 2·5 | 11·0 | 5·4 | 17·0 | 8·4 |
| 51 | 7 27·8 | 7 29·0 | 7 07·4 | 5·1 | 2·5 | 11·1 | 5·5 | 17·1 | 8·4 |
| 52 | 7 28·0 | 7 29·2 | 7 07·6 | 5·2 | 2·6 | 11·2 | 5·5 | 17·2 | 8·5 |
| 53 | 7 28·3 | 7 29·5 | 7 07·8 | 5·3 | 2·6 | 11·3 | 5·6 | 17·3 | 8·5 |
| 54 | 7 28·5 | 7 29·7 | 7 08·1 | 5·4 | 2·7 | 11·4 | 5·6 | 17·4 | 8·6 |
| 55 | 7 28·8 | 7 30·0 | 7 08·3 | 5·5 | 2·7 | 11·5 | 5·7 | 17·5 | 8·6 |
| 56 | 7 29·0 | 7 30·2 | 7 08·5 | 5·6 | 2·8 | 11·6 | 5·7 | 17·6 | 8·7 |
| 57 | 7 29·3 | 7 30·5 | 7 08·8 | 5·7 | 2·8 | 11·7 | 5·8 | 17·7 | 8·7 |
| 58 | 7 29·5 | 7 30·7 | 7 09·0 | 5·8 | 2·9 | 11·8 | 5·8 | 17·8 | 8·8 |
| 59 | 7 29·8 | 7 31·0 | 7 09·3 | 5·9 | 2·9 | 11·9 | 5·9 | 17·9 | 8·8 |
| 60 | 7 30·0 | 7 31·2 | 7 09·5 | 6·0 | 3·0 | 12·0 | 5·9 | 18·0 | 8·9 |

## 30ᵐ

| 30 s | SUN PLANETS | ARIES | MOON | v or Corrⁿ d | | v or Corrⁿ d | | v or Corrⁿ d | |
|---|---|---|---|---|---|---|---|---|---|
| 00 | 7 30·0 | 7 31·2 | 7 09·5 | 0·0 | 0·0 | 6·0 | 3·1 | 12·0 | 6·1 |
| 01 | 7 30·3 | 7 31·5 | 7 09·7 | 0·1 | 0·1 | 6·1 | 3·1 | 12·1 | 6·2 |
| 02 | 7 30·5 | 7 31·7 | 7 10·0 | 0·2 | 0·1 | 6·2 | 3·2 | 12·2 | 6·2 |
| 03 | 7 30·8 | 7 32·0 | 7 10·2 | 0·3 | 0·2 | 6·3 | 3·2 | 12·3 | 6·3 |
| 04 | 7 31·0 | 7 32·2 | 7 10·5 | 0·4 | 0·2 | 6·4 | 3·3 | 12·4 | 6·3 |
| 05 | 7 31·3 | 7 32·5 | 7 10·7 | 0·5 | 0·3 | 6·5 | 3·3 | 12·5 | 6·4 |
| 06 | 7 31·5 | 7 32·7 | 7 10·9 | 0·6 | 0·3 | 6·6 | 3·4 | 12·6 | 6·4 |
| 07 | 7 31·8 | 7 33·0 | 7 11·2 | 0·7 | 0·4 | 6·7 | 3·4 | 12·7 | 6·5 |
| 08 | 7 32·0 | 7 33·2 | 7 11·4 | 0·8 | 0·4 | 6·8 | 3·5 | 12·8 | 6·5 |
| 09 | 7 32·3 | 7 33·5 | 7 11·6 | 0·9 | 0·5 | 6·9 | 3·5 | 12·9 | 6·6 |
| 10 | 7 32·5 | 7 33·7 | 7 11·9 | 1·0 | 0·5 | 7·0 | 3·6 | 13·0 | 6·6 |
| 11 | 7 32·8 | 7 34·0 | 7 12·1 | 1·1 | 0·6 | 7·1 | 3·6 | 13·1 | 6·7 |
| 12 | 7 33·0 | 7 34·2 | 7 12·4 | 1·2 | 0·6 | 7·2 | 3·7 | 13·2 | 6·7 |
| 13 | 7 33·3 | 7 34·5 | 7 12·6 | 1·3 | 0·7 | 7·3 | 3·7 | 13·3 | 6·8 |
| 14 | 7 33·5 | 7 34·7 | 7 12·8 | 1·4 | 0·7 | 7·4 | 3·8 | 13·4 | 6·8 |
| 15 | 7 33·8 | 7 35·0 | 7 13·1 | 1·5 | 0·8 | 7·5 | 3·8 | 13·5 | 6·9 |
| 16 | 7 34·0 | 7 35·2 | 7 13·3 | 1·6 | 0·8 | 7·6 | 3·9 | 13·6 | 6·9 |
| 17 | 7 34·3 | 7 35·5 | 7 13·6 | 1·7 | 0·9 | 7·7 | 3·9 | 13·7 | 7·0 |
| 18 | 7 34·5 | 7 35·7 | 7 13·8 | 1·8 | 0·9 | 7·8 | 4·0 | 13·8 | 7·0 |
| 19 | 7 34·8 | 7 36·0 | 7 14·0 | 1·9 | 1·0 | 7·9 | 4·0 | 13·9 | 7·1 |
| 20 | 7 35·0 | 7 36·2 | 7 14·3 | 2·0 | 1·0 | 8·0 | 4·1 | 14·0 | 7·1 |
| 21 | 7 35·3 | 7 36·5 | 7 14·5 | 2·1 | 1·1 | 8·1 | 4·1 | 14·1 | 7·2 |
| 22 | 7 35·5 | 7 36·7 | 7 14·7 | 2·2 | 1·1 | 8·2 | 4·2 | 14·2 | 7·2 |
| 23 | 7 35·8 | 7 37·0 | 7 15·0 | 2·3 | 1·2 | 8·3 | 4·2 | 14·3 | 7·3 |
| 24 | 7 36·0 | 7 37·2 | 7 15·2 | 2·4 | 1·2 | 8·4 | 4·3 | 14·4 | 7·3 |
| 25 | 7 36·3 | 7 37·5 | 7 15·5 | 2·5 | 1·3 | 8·5 | 4·3 | 14·5 | 7·4 |
| 26 | 7 36·5 | 7 37·7 | 7 15·7 | 2·6 | 1·3 | 8·6 | 4·4 | 14·6 | 7·4 |
| 27 | 7 36·8 | 7 38·0 | 7 15·9 | 2·7 | 1·4 | 8·7 | 4·4 | 14·7 | 7·5 |
| 28 | 7 37·0 | 7 38·3 | 7 16·2 | 2·8 | 1·4 | 8·8 | 4·5 | 14·8 | 7·5 |
| 29 | 7 37·3 | 7 38·5 | 7 16·4 | 2·9 | 1·5 | 8·9 | 4·5 | 14·9 | 7·6 |
| 30 | 7 37·5 | 7 38·8 | 7 16·7 | 3·0 | 1·5 | 9·0 | 4·6 | 15·0 | 7·6 |
| 31 | 7 37·8 | 7 39·0 | 7 16·9 | 3·1 | 1·6 | 9·1 | 4·6 | 15·1 | 7·7 |
| 32 | 7 38·0 | 7 39·3 | 7 17·1 | 3·2 | 1·6 | 9·2 | 4·7 | 15·2 | 7·7 |
| 33 | 7 38·3 | 7 39·5 | 7 17·4 | 3·3 | 1·7 | 9·3 | 4·7 | 15·3 | 7·8 |
| 34 | 7 38·5 | 7 39·8 | 7 17·6 | 3·4 | 1·7 | 9·4 | 4·8 | 15·4 | 7·8 |
| 35 | 7 38·8 | 7 40·0 | 7 17·9 | 3·5 | 1·8 | 9·5 | 4·8 | 15·5 | 7·9 |
| 36 | 7 39·0 | 7 40·3 | 7 18·1 | 3·6 | 1·8 | 9·6 | 4·9 | 15·6 | 7·9 |
| 37 | 7 39·3 | 7 40·5 | 7 18·3 | 3·7 | 1·9 | 9·7 | 4·9 | 15·7 | 8·0 |
| 38 | 7 39·5 | 7 40·8 | 7 18·6 | 3·8 | 1·9 | 9·8 | 5·0 | 15·8 | 8·0 |
| 39 | 7 39·8 | 7 41·0 | 7 18·8 | 3·9 | 2·0 | 9·9 | 5·0 | 15·9 | 8·1 |
| 40 | 7 40·0 | 7 41·3 | 7 19·0 | 4·0 | 2·0 | 10·0 | 5·1 | 16·0 | 8·1 |
| 41 | 7 40·3 | 7 41·5 | 7 19·3 | 4·1 | 2·1 | 10·1 | 5·1 | 16·1 | 8·2 |
| 42 | 7 40·5 | 7 41·8 | 7 19·5 | 4·2 | 2·1 | 10·2 | 5·2 | 16·2 | 8·2 |
| 43 | 7 40·8 | 7 42·0 | 7 19·8 | 4·3 | 2·2 | 10·3 | 5·2 | 16·3 | 8·3 |
| 44 | 7 41·0 | 7 42·3 | 7 20·0 | 4·4 | 2·2 | 10·4 | 5·3 | 16·4 | 8·3 |
| 45 | 7 41·3 | 7 42·5 | 7 20·2 | 4·5 | 2·3 | 10·5 | 5·3 | 16·5 | 8·4 |
| 46 | 7 41·5 | 7 42·8 | 7 20·5 | 4·6 | 2·3 | 10·6 | 5·4 | 16·6 | 8·4 |
| 47 | 7 41·8 | 7 43·0 | 7 20·7 | 4·7 | 2·4 | 10·7 | 5·4 | 16·7 | 8·5 |
| 48 | 7 42·0 | 7 43·3 | 7 21·0 | 4·8 | 2·4 | 10·8 | 5·5 | 16·8 | 8·5 |
| 49 | 7 42·3 | 7 43·5 | 7 21·2 | 4·9 | 2·5 | 10·9 | 5·5 | 16·9 | 8·6 |
| 50 | 7 42·5 | 7 43·8 | 7 21·4 | 5·0 | 2·5 | 11·0 | 5·6 | 17·0 | 8·6 |
| 51 | 7 42·8 | 7 44·0 | 7 21·7 | 5·1 | 2·6 | 11·1 | 5·6 | 17·1 | 8·7 |
| 52 | 7 43·0 | 7 44·3 | 7 21·9 | 5·2 | 2·6 | 11·2 | 5·7 | 17·2 | 8·7 |
| 53 | 7 43·3 | 7 44·5 | 7 22·1 | 5·3 | 2·7 | 11·3 | 5·7 | 17·3 | 8·8 |
| 54 | 7 43·5 | 7 44·8 | 7 22·4 | 5·4 | 2·8 | 11·4 | 5·8 | 17·4 | 8·8 |
| 55 | 7 43·8 | 7 45·0 | 7 22·6 | 5·5 | 2·8 | 11·5 | 5·8 | 17·5 | 8·9 |
| 56 | 7 44·0 | 7 45·3 | 7 22·9 | 5·6 | 2·8 | 11·6 | 5·9 | 17·6 | 8·9 |
| 57 | 7 44·3 | 7 45·5 | 7 23·1 | 5·7 | 2·9 | 11·7 | 5·9 | 17·7 | 9·0 |
| 58 | 7 44·5 | 7 45·8 | 7 23·3 | 5·8 | 2·9 | 11·8 | 6·0 | 17·8 | 9·0 |
| 59 | 7 44·8 | 7 46·0 | 7 23·6 | 5·9 | 3·0 | 11·9 | 6·0 | 17·9 | 9·1 |
| 60 | 7 45·0 | 7 46·3 | 7 23·8 | 6·0 | 3·1 | 12·0 | 6·1 | 18·0 | 9·2 |

## 31ᵐ

| 31 s | SUN PLANETS | ARIES | MOON | v or Corrⁿ d | | v or Corrⁿ d | | v or Corrⁿ d | |
|---|---|---|---|---|---|---|---|---|---|
| 00 | 7 45·0 | 7 46·3 | 7 23·8 | 0·0 | 0·0 | 6·0 | 3·2 | 12·0 | 6·3 |
| 01 | 7 45·3 | 7 46·5 | 7 24·1 | 0·1 | 0·1 | 6·1 | 3·2 | 12·1 | 6·4 |
| 02 | 7 45·5 | 7 46·8 | 7 24·3 | 0·2 | 0·1 | 6·2 | 3·3 | 12·2 | 6·4 |
| 03 | 7 45·8 | 7 47·0 | 7 24·5 | 0·3 | 0·2 | 6·3 | 3·3 | 12·3 | 6·5 |
| 04 | 7 46·0 | 7 47·3 | 7 24·8 | 0·4 | 0·2 | 6·4 | 3·4 | 12·4 | 6·5 |
| 05 | 7 46·3 | 7 47·5 | 7 25·0 | 0·5 | 0·3 | 6·5 | 3·4 | 12·5 | 6·6 |
| 06 | 7 46·5 | 7 47·8 | 7 25·2 | 0·6 | 0·3 | 6·6 | 3·5 | 12·6 | 6·6 |
| 07 | 7 46·8 | 7 48·0 | 7 25·5 | 0·7 | 0·4 | 6·7 | 3·5 | 12·7 | 6·7 |
| 08 | 7 47·0 | 7 48·3 | 7 25·7 | 0·8 | 0·4 | 6·8 | 3·6 | 12·8 | 6·7 |
| 09 | 7 47·3 | 7 48·5 | 7 26·0 | 0·9 | 0·5 | 6·9 | 3·6 | 12·9 | 6·8 |
| 10 | 7 47·5 | 7 48·8 | 7 26·2 | 1·0 | 0·5 | 7·0 | 3·7 | 13·0 | 6·8 |
| 11 | 7 47·8 | 7 49·0 | 7 26·4 | 1·1 | 0·6 | 7·1 | 3·7 | 13·1 | 6·9 |
| 12 | 7 48·0 | 7 49·3 | 7 26·7 | 1·2 | 0·6 | 7·2 | 3·8 | 13·2 | 6·9 |
| 13 | 7 48·3 | 7 49·5 | 7 26·9 | 1·3 | 0·7 | 7·3 | 3·8 | 13·3 | 7·0 |
| 14 | 7 48·5 | 7 49·8 | 7 27·2 | 1·4 | 0·7 | 7·4 | 3·9 | 13·4 | 7·0 |
| 15 | 7 48·8 | 7 50·0 | 7 27·4 | 1·5 | 0·8 | 7·5 | 3·9 | 13·5 | 7·1 |
| 16 | 7 49·0 | 7 50·3 | 7 27·6 | 1·6 | 0·8 | 7·6 | 4·0 | 13·6 | 7·1 |
| 17 | 7 49·3 | 7 50·5 | 7 27·9 | 1·7 | 0·9 | 7·7 | 4·0 | 13·7 | 7·2 |
| 18 | 7 49·5 | 7 50·8 | 7 28·1 | 1·8 | 0·9 | 7·8 | 4·1 | 13·8 | 7·2 |
| 19 | 7 49·8 | 7 51·0 | 7 28·4 | 1·9 | 1·0 | 7·9 | 4·1 | 13·9 | 7·3 |
| 20 | 7 50·0 | 7 51·3 | 7 28·6 | 2·0 | 1·1 | 8·0 | 4·2 | 14·0 | 7·4 |
| 21 | 7 50·3 | 7 51·5 | 7 28·8 | 2·1 | 1·1 | 8·1 | 4·3 | 14·1 | 7·4 |
| 22 | 7 50·5 | 7 51·8 | 7 29·1 | 2·2 | 1·2 | 8·2 | 4·3 | 14·2 | 7·5 |
| 23 | 7 50·8 | 7 52·0 | 7 29·3 | 2·3 | 1·2 | 8·3 | 4·4 | 14·3 | 7·5 |
| 24 | 7 51·0 | 7 52·3 | 7 29·5 | 2·4 | 1·3 | 8·4 | 4·4 | 14·4 | 7·6 |
| 25 | 7 51·3 | 7 52·5 | 7 29·8 | 2·5 | 1·3 | 8·5 | 4·5 | 14·5 | 7·6 |
| 26 | 7 51·5 | 7 52·8 | 7 30·0 | 2·6 | 1·4 | 8·6 | 4·5 | 14·6 | 7·7 |
| 27 | 7 51·8 | 7 53·0 | 7 30·3 | 2·7 | 1·4 | 8·7 | 4·6 | 14·7 | 7·7 |
| 28 | 7 52·0 | 7 53·3 | 7 30·5 | 2·8 | 1·5 | 8·8 | 4·6 | 14·8 | 7·8 |
| 29 | 7 52·3 | 7 53·5 | 7 30·7 | 2·9 | 1·5 | 8·9 | 4·7 | 14·9 | 7·8 |
| 30 | 7 52·5 | 7 53·8 | 7 31·0 | 3·0 | 1·6 | 9·0 | 4·7 | 15·0 | 7·9 |
| 31 | 7 52·8 | 7 54·0 | 7 31·2 | 3·1 | 1·6 | 9·1 | 4·8 | 15·1 | 7·9 |
| 32 | 7 53·0 | 7 54·3 | 7 31·5 | 3·2 | 1·7 | 9·2 | 4·8 | 15·2 | 8·0 |
| 33 | 7 53·3 | 7 54·5 | 7 31·7 | 3·3 | 1·7 | 9·3 | 4·9 | 15·3 | 8·0 |
| 34 | 7 53·5 | 7 54·8 | 7 31·9 | 3·4 | 1·8 | 9·4 | 4·9 | 15·4 | 8·1 |
| 35 | 7 53·8 | 7 55·0 | 7 32·2 | 3·5 | 1·8 | 9·5 | 5·0 | 15·5 | 8·1 |
| 36 | 7 54·0 | 7 55·3 | 7 32·4 | 3·6 | 1·9 | 9·6 | 5·0 | 15·6 | 8·2 |
| 37 | 7 54·3 | 7 55·5 | 7 32·6 | 3·7 | 1·9 | 9·7 | 5·1 | 15·7 | 8·2 |
| 38 | 7 54·5 | 7 55·8 | 7 32·9 | 3·8 | 2·0 | 9·8 | 5·1 | 15·8 | 8·3 |
| 39 | 7 54·8 | 7 56·0 | 7 33·1 | 3·9 | 2·0 | 9·9 | 5·2 | 15·9 | 8·3 |
| 40 | 7 55·0 | 7 56·3 | 7 33·4 | 4·0 | 2·1 | 10·0 | 5·3 | 16·0 | 8·4 |
| 41 | 7 55·3 | 7 56·6 | 7 33·6 | 4·1 | 2·2 | 10·1 | 5·3 | 16·1 | 8·5 |
| 42 | 7 55·5 | 7 56·8 | 7 33·8 | 4·2 | 2·2 | 10·2 | 5·4 | 16·2 | 8·5 |
| 43 | 7 55·8 | 7 57·1 | 7 34·1 | 4·3 | 2·3 | 10·3 | 5·4 | 16·3 | 8·6 |
| 44 | 7 56·0 | 7 57·3 | 7 34·3 | 4·4 | 2·3 | 10·4 | 5·5 | 16·4 | 8·6 |
| 45 | 7 56·3 | 7 57·6 | 7 34·6 | 4·5 | 2·4 | 10·5 | 5·5 | 16·5 | 8·7 |
| 46 | 7 56·5 | 7 57·8 | 7 34·8 | 4·6 | 2·4 | 10·6 | 5·6 | 16·6 | 8·7 |
| 47 | 7 56·8 | 7 58·1 | 7 35·0 | 4·7 | 2·5 | 10·7 | 5·6 | 16·7 | 8·8 |
| 48 | 7 57·0 | 7 58·3 | 7 35·3 | 4·8 | 2·5 | 10·8 | 5·7 | 16·8 | 8·8 |
| 49 | 7 57·3 | 7 58·6 | 7 35·5 | 4·9 | 2·6 | 10·9 | 5·7 | 16·9 | 8·9 |
| 50 | 7 57·5 | 7 58·8 | 7 35·7 | 5·0 | 2·6 | 11·0 | 5·8 | 17·0 | 8·9 |
| 51 | 7 57·8 | 7 59·1 | 7 36·0 | 5·1 | 2·7 | 11·1 | 5·8 | 17·1 | 9·0 |
| 52 | 7 58·0 | 7 59·3 | 7 36·2 | 5·2 | 2·7 | 11·2 | 5·9 | 17·2 | 9·0 |
| 53 | 7 58·3 | 7 59·6 | 7 36·5 | 5·3 | 2·8 | 11·3 | 5·9 | 17·3 | 9·1 |
| 54 | 7 58·5 | 7 59·8 | 7 36·7 | 5·4 | 2·8 | 11·4 | 6·0 | 17·4 | 9·1 |
| 55 | 7 58·8 | 8 00·1 | 7 36·9 | 5·5 | 2·9 | 11·5 | 6·0 | 17·5 | 9·2 |
| 56 | 7 59·0 | 8 00·3 | 7 37·2 | 5·6 | 2·9 | 11·6 | 6·1 | 17·6 | 9·2 |
| 57 | 7 59·3 | 8 00·6 | 7 37·4 | 5·7 | 3·0 | 11·7 | 6·1 | 17·7 | 9·3 |
| 58 | 7 59·5 | 8 00·8 | 7 37·7 | 5·8 | 3·0 | 11·8 | 6·2 | 17·8 | 9·3 |
| 59 | 7 59·8 | 8 01·1 | 7 37·9 | 5·9 | 3·1 | 11·9 | 6·2 | 17·9 | 9·4 |
| 60 | 8 00·0 | 8 01·3 | 7 38·1 | 6·0 | 3·2 | 12·0 | 6·3 | 18·0 | 9·5 |

## 32ᵐ

| 32 s | SUN PLANETS | ARIES | MOON | v or d | Corrⁿ | v or d | Corrⁿ | v or d | Corrⁿ |
|---|---|---|---|---|---|---|---|---|---|
| 00 | 8 00·0 | 8 01·3 | 7 38·1 | 0·0 | 0·0 | 6·0 | 3·3 | 12·0 | 6·5 |
| 01 | 8 00·3 | 8 01·6 | 7 38·4 | 0·1 | 0·1 | 6·1 | 3·3 | 12·1 | 6·6 |
| 02 | 8 00·5 | 8 01·8 | 7 38·6 | 0·2 | 0·1 | 6·2 | 3·4 | 12·2 | 6·6 |
| 03 | 8 00·8 | 8 02·1 | 7 38·8 | 0·3 | 0·2 | 6·3 | 3·4 | 12·3 | 6·7 |
| 04 | 8 01·0 | 8 02·3 | 7 39·1 | 0·4 | 0·2 | 6·4 | 3·5 | 12·4 | 6·7 |
| 05 | 8 01·3 | 8 02·6 | 7 39·3 | 0·5 | 0·3 | 6·5 | 3·5 | 12·5 | 6·8 |
| 06 | 8 01·5 | 8 02·8 | 7 39·6 | 0·6 | 0·3 | 6·6 | 3·6 | 12·6 | 6·8 |
| 07 | 8 01·8 | 8 03·1 | 7 39·8 | 0·7 | 0·4 | 6·7 | 3·6 | 12·7 | 6·9 |
| 08 | 8 02·0 | 8 03·3 | 7 40·0 | 0·8 | 0·4 | 6·8 | 3·7 | 12·8 | 6·9 |
| 09 | 8 02·3 | 8 03·6 | 7 40·3 | 0·9 | 0·5 | 6·9 | 3·7 | 12·9 | 7·0 |
| 10 | 8 02·5 | 8 03·8 | 7 40·5 | 1·0 | 0·5 | 7·0 | 3·8 | 13·0 | 7·0 |
| 11 | 8 02·8 | 8 04·1 | 7 40·8 | 1·1 | 0·6 | 7·1 | 3·8 | 13·1 | 7·1 |
| 12 | 8 03·0 | 8 04·3 | 7 41·0 | 1·2 | 0·7 | 7·2 | 3·9 | 13·2 | 7·2 |
| 13 | 8 03·3 | 8 04·6 | 7 41·2 | 1·3 | 0·7 | 7·3 | 4·0 | 13·3 | 7·2 |
| 14 | 8 03·5 | 8 04·8 | 7 41·5 | 1·4 | 0·8 | 7·4 | 4·0 | 13·4 | 7·3 |
| 15 | 8 03·8 | 8 05·1 | 7 41·7 | 1·5 | 0·8 | 7·5 | 4·1 | 13·5 | 7·3 |
| 16 | 8 04·0 | 8 05·3 | 7 42·0 | 1·6 | 0·9 | 7·6 | 4·1 | 13·6 | 7·4 |
| 17 | 8 04·3 | 8 05·6 | 7 42·2 | 1·7 | 0·9 | 7·7 | 4·2 | 13·7 | 7·4 |
| 18 | 8 04·5 | 8 05·8 | 7 42·4 | 1·8 | 1·0 | 7·8 | 4·2 | 13·8 | 7·5 |
| 19 | 8 04·8 | 8 06·1 | 7 42·7 | 1·9 | 1·0 | 7·9 | 4·3 | 13·9 | 7·5 |
| 20 | 8 05·0 | 8 06·3 | 7 42·9 | 2·0 | 1·1 | 8·0 | 4·3 | 14·0 | 7·6 |
| 21 | 8 05·3 | 8 06·6 | 7 43·1 | 2·1 | 1·1 | 8·1 | 4·4 | 14·1 | 7·6 |
| 22 | 8 05·5 | 8 06·8 | 7 43·4 | 2·2 | 1·2 | 8·2 | 4·4 | 14·2 | 7·7 |
| 23 | 8 05·8 | 8 07·1 | 7 43·6 | 2·3 | 1·2 | 8·3 | 4·5 | 14·3 | 7·7 |
| 24 | 8 06·0 | 8 07·3 | 7 43·9 | 2·4 | 1·3 | 8·4 | 4·6 | 14·4 | 7·8 |
| 25 | 8 06·3 | 8 07·6 | 7 44·1 | 2·5 | 1·4 | 8·5 | 4·6 | 14·5 | 7·9 |
| 26 | 8 06·5 | 8 07·8 | 7 44·3 | 2·6 | 1·4 | 8·6 | 4·7 | 14·6 | 7·9 |
| 27 | 8 06·8 | 8 08·1 | 7 44·6 | 2·7 | 1·5 | 8·7 | 4·7 | 14·7 | 8·0 |
| 28 | 8 07·0 | 8 08·3 | 7 44·8 | 2·8 | 1·5 | 8·8 | 4·8 | 14·8 | 8·0 |
| 29 | 8 07·3 | 8 08·6 | 7 45·1 | 2·9 | 1·6 | 8·9 | 4·8 | 14·9 | 8·1 |
| 30 | 8 07·5 | 8 08·8 | 7 45·3 | 3·0 | 1·6 | 9·0 | 4·9 | 15·0 | 8·1 |
| 31 | 8 07·8 | 8 09·1 | 7 45·5 | 3·1 | 1·7 | 9·1 | 4·9 | 15·1 | 8·2 |
| 32 | 8 08·0 | 8 09·3 | 7 45·8 | 3·2 | 1·7 | 9·2 | 5·0 | 15·2 | 8·2 |
| 33 | 8 08·3 | 8 09·6 | 7 46·0 | 3·3 | 1·8 | 9·3 | 5·0 | 15·3 | 8·3 |
| 34 | 8 08·5 | 8 09·8 | 7 46·2 | 3·4 | 1·8 | 9·4 | 5·1 | 15·4 | 8·3 |
| 35 | 8 08·8 | 8 10·1 | 7 46·5 | 3·5 | 1·9 | 9·5 | 5·1 | 15·5 | 8·4 |
| 36 | 8 09·0 | 8 10·3 | 7 46·7 | 3·6 | 2·0 | 9·6 | 5·2 | 15·6 | 8·5 |
| 37 | 8 09·3 | 8 10·6 | 7 47·0 | 3·7 | 2·0 | 9·7 | 5·3 | 15·7 | 8·5 |
| 38 | 8 09·5 | 8 10·8 | 7 47·2 | 3·8 | 2·1 | 9·8 | 5·3 | 15·8 | 8·6 |
| 39 | 8 09·8 | 8 11·1 | 7 47·4 | 3·9 | 2·1 | 9·9 | 5·4 | 15·9 | 8·6 |
| 40 | 8 10·0 | 8 11·3 | 7 47·7 | 4·0 | 2·2 | 10·0 | 5·4 | 16·0 | 8·7 |
| 41 | 8 10·3 | 8 11·6 | 7 47·9 | 4·1 | 2·2 | 10·1 | 5·5 | 16·1 | 8·7 |
| 42 | 8 10·5 | 8 11·8 | 7 48·2 | 4·2 | 2·3 | 10·2 | 5·5 | 16·2 | 8·8 |
| 43 | 8 10·8 | 8 12·1 | 7 48·4 | 4·3 | 2·3 | 10·3 | 5·6 | 16·3 | 8·8 |
| 44 | 8 11·0 | 8 12·3 | 7 48·6 | 4·4 | 2·4 | 10·4 | 5·6 | 16·4 | 8·9 |
| 45 | 8 11·3 | 8 12·6 | 7 48·9 | 4·5 | 2·4 | 10·5 | 5·7 | 16·5 | 8·9 |
| 46 | 8 11·5 | 8 12·8 | 7 49·1 | 4·6 | 2·5 | 10·6 | 5·7 | 16·6 | 9·0 |
| 47 | 8 11·8 | 8 13·1 | 7 49·3 | 4·7 | 2·5 | 10·7 | 5·8 | 16·7 | 9·0 |
| 48 | 8 12·0 | 8 13·3 | 7 49·6 | 4·8 | 2·6 | 10·8 | 5·9 | 16·8 | 9·1 |
| 49 | 8 12·3 | 8 13·6 | 7 49·8 | 4·9 | 2·7 | 10·9 | 5·9 | 16·9 | 9·2 |
| 50 | 8 12·5 | 8 13·8 | 7 50·1 | 5·0 | 2·7 | 11·0 | 6·0 | 17·0 | 9·2 |
| 51 | 8 12·8 | 8 14·1 | 7 50·3 | 5·1 | 2·8 | 11·1 | 6·0 | 17·1 | 9·3 |
| 52 | 8 13·0 | 8 14·3 | 7 50·5 | 5·2 | 2·8 | 11·2 | 6·1 | 17·2 | 9·3 |
| 53 | 8 13·3 | 8 14·6 | 7 50·8 | 5·3 | 2·9 | 11·3 | 6·1 | 17·3 | 9·4 |
| 54 | 8 13·5 | 8 14·9 | 7 51·0 | 5·4 | 2·9 | 11·4 | 6·2 | 17·4 | 9·4 |
| 55 | 8 13·8 | 8 15·1 | 7 51·3 | 5·5 | 3·0 | 11·5 | 6·2 | 17·5 | 9·5 |
| 56 | 8 14·0 | 8 15·4 | 7 51·5 | 5·6 | 3·0 | 11·6 | 6·3 | 17·6 | 9·5 |
| 57 | 8 14·3 | 8 15·6 | 7 51·7 | 5·7 | 3·1 | 11·7 | 6·3 | 17·7 | 9·6 |
| 58 | 8 14·5 | 8 15·9 | 7 52·0 | 5·8 | 3·1 | 11·8 | 6·4 | 17·8 | 9·6 |
| 59 | 8 14·8 | 8 16·1 | 7 52·2 | 5·9 | 3·2 | 11·9 | 6·4 | 17·9 | 9·7 |
| 60 | 8 15·0 | 8 16·4 | 7 52·5 | 6·0 | 3·3 | 12·0 | 6·5 | 18·0 | 9·8 |

## 33ᵐ

| 33 s | SUN PLANETS | ARIES | MOON | v or d | Corrⁿ | v or d | Corrⁿ | v or d | Corrⁿ |
|---|---|---|---|---|---|---|---|---|---|
| 00 | 8 15·0 | 8 16·4 | 7 52·5 | 0·0 | 0·0 | 6·0 | 3·4 | 12·0 | 6·7 |
| 01 | 8 15·3 | 8 16·6 | 7 52·7 | 0·1 | 0·1 | 6·1 | 3·4 | 12·1 | 6·8 |
| 02 | 8 15·5 | 8 16·9 | 7 52·9 | 0·2 | 0·1 | 6·2 | 3·5 | 12·2 | 6·8 |
| 03 | 8 15·8 | 8 17·1 | 7 53·2 | 0·3 | 0·2 | 6·3 | 3·5 | 12·3 | 6·9 |
| 04 | 8 16·0 | 8 17·4 | 7 53·4 | 0·4 | 0·2 | 6·4 | 3·6 | 12·4 | 6·9 |
| 05 | 8 16·3 | 8 17·6 | 7 53·6 | 0·5 | 0·3 | 6·5 | 3·6 | 12·5 | 7·0 |
| 06 | 8 16·5 | 8 17·9 | 7 53·9 | 0·6 | 0·3 | 6·6 | 3·7 | 12·6 | 7·0 |
| 07 | 8 16·8 | 8 18·1 | 7 54·1 | 0·7 | 0·4 | 6·7 | 3·7 | 12·7 | 7·1 |
| 08 | 8 17·0 | 8 18·4 | 7 54·4 | 0·8 | 0·4 | 6·8 | 3·8 | 12·8 | 7·1 |
| 09 | 8 17·3 | 8 18·6 | 7 54·6 | 0·9 | 0·5 | 6·9 | 3·9 | 12·9 | 7·2 |
| 10 | 8 17·5 | 8 18·9 | 7 54·8 | 1·0 | 0·6 | 7·0 | 3·9 | 13·0 | 7·3 |
| 11 | 8 17·8 | 8 19·1 | 7 55·1 | 1·1 | 0·6 | 7·1 | 4·0 | 13·1 | 7·3 |
| 12 | 8 18·0 | 8 19·4 | 7 55·3 | 1·2 | 0·7 | 7·2 | 4·0 | 13·2 | 7·4 |
| 13 | 8 18·3 | 8 19·6 | 7 55·6 | 1·3 | 0·7 | 7·3 | 4·1 | 13·3 | 7·4 |
| 14 | 8 18·5 | 8 19·9 | 7 55·8 | 1·4 | 0·8 | 7·4 | 4·1 | 13·4 | 7·5 |
| 15 | 8 18·8 | 8 20·1 | 7 56·0 | 1·5 | 0·8 | 7·5 | 4·2 | 13·5 | 7·5 |
| 16 | 8 19·0 | 8 20·4 | 7 56·3 | 1·6 | 0·9 | 7·6 | 4·2 | 13·6 | 7·6 |
| 17 | 8 19·3 | 8 20·6 | 7 56·5 | 1·7 | 0·9 | 7·7 | 4·3 | 13·7 | 7·6 |
| 18 | 8 19·5 | 8 20·9 | 7 56·7 | 1·8 | 1·0 | 7·8 | 4·4 | 13·8 | 7·7 |
| 19 | 8 19·8 | 8 21·1 | 7 57·0 | 1·9 | 1·1 | 7·9 | 4·4 | 13·9 | 7·8 |
| 20 | 8 20·0 | 8 21·4 | 7 57·2 | 2·0 | 1·1 | 8·0 | 4·5 | 14·0 | 7·8 |
| 21 | 8 20·3 | 8 21·6 | 7 57·5 | 2·1 | 1·2 | 8·1 | 4·5 | 14·1 | 7·9 |
| 22 | 8 20·5 | 8 21·9 | 7 57·7 | 2·2 | 1·2 | 8·2 | 4·6 | 14·2 | 7·9 |
| 23 | 8 20·8 | 8 22·1 | 7 57·9 | 2·3 | 1·3 | 8·3 | 4·6 | 14·3 | 8·0 |
| 24 | 8 21·0 | 8 22·4 | 7 58·2 | 2·4 | 1·3 | 8·4 | 4·7 | 14·4 | 8·0 |
| 25 | 8 21·3 | 8 22·6 | 7 58·4 | 2·5 | 1·4 | 8·5 | 4·7 | 14·5 | 8·1 |
| 26 | 8 21·5 | 8 22·9 | 7 58·7 | 2·6 | 1·5 | 8·6 | 4·8 | 14·6 | 8·2 |
| 27 | 8 21·8 | 8 23·1 | 7 58·9 | 2·7 | 1·5 | 8·7 | 4·9 | 14·7 | 8·2 |
| 28 | 8 22·0 | 8 23·4 | 7 59·1 | 2·8 | 1·6 | 8·8 | 4·9 | 14·8 | 8·3 |
| 29 | 8 22·3 | 8 23·6 | 7 59·4 | 2·9 | 1·6 | 8·9 | 5·0 | 14·9 | 8·3 |
| 30 | 8 22·5 | 8 23·9 | 7 59·6 | 3·0 | 1·7 | 9·0 | 5·0 | 15·0 | 8·4 |
| 31 | 8 22·8 | 8 24·1 | 7 59·8 | 3·1 | 1·7 | 9·1 | 5·1 | 15·1 | 8·4 |
| 32 | 8 23·0 | 8 24·4 | 8 00·1 | 3·2 | 1·8 | 9·2 | 5·1 | 15·2 | 8·5 |
| 33 | 8 23·3 | 8 24·6 | 8 00·3 | 3·3 | 1·8 | 9·3 | 5·2 | 15·3 | 8·5 |
| 34 | 8 23·5 | 8 24·9 | 8 00·6 | 3·4 | 1·9 | 9·4 | 5·2 | 15·4 | 8·6 |
| 35 | 8 23·8 | 8 25·1 | 8 00·8 | 3·5 | 2·0 | 9·5 | 5·3 | 15·5 | 8·7 |
| 36 | 8 24·0 | 8 25·4 | 8 01·0 | 3·6 | 2·0 | 9·6 | 5·4 | 15·6 | 8·7 |
| 37 | 8 24·3 | 8 25·6 | 8 01·3 | 3·7 | 2·1 | 9·7 | 5·4 | 15·7 | 8·8 |
| 38 | 8 24·5 | 8 25·9 | 8 01·5 | 3·8 | 2·1 | 9·8 | 5·5 | 15·8 | 8·8 |
| 39 | 8 24·8 | 8 26·1 | 8 01·8 | 3·9 | 2·2 | 9·9 | 5·5 | 15·9 | 8·9 |
| 40 | 8 25·0 | 8 26·4 | 8 02·0 | 4·0 | 2·2 | 10·0 | 5·6 | 16·0 | 8·9 |
| 41 | 8 25·3 | 8 26·6 | 8 02·2 | 4·1 | 2·3 | 10·1 | 5·6 | 16·1 | 9·0 |
| 42 | 8 25·5 | 8 26·9 | 8 02·5 | 4·2 | 2·3 | 10·2 | 5·7 | 16·2 | 9·0 |
| 43 | 8 25·8 | 8 27·1 | 8 02·7 | 4·3 | 2·4 | 10·3 | 5·8 | 16·3 | 9·1 |
| 44 | 8 26·0 | 8 27·4 | 8 02·9 | 4·4 | 2·5 | 10·4 | 5·8 | 16·4 | 9·2 |
| 45 | 8 26·3 | 8 27·6 | 8 03·2 | 4·5 | 2·5 | 10·5 | 5·9 | 16·5 | 9·2 |
| 46 | 8 26·5 | 8 27·9 | 8 03·4 | 4·6 | 2·6 | 10·6 | 5·9 | 16·6 | 9·3 |
| 47 | 8 26·8 | 8 28·1 | 8 03·7 | 4·7 | 2·6 | 10·7 | 6·0 | 16·7 | 9·3 |
| 48 | 8 27·0 | 8 28·4 | 8 03·9 | 4·8 | 2·7 | 10·8 | 6·0 | 16·8 | 9·4 |
| 49 | 8 27·3 | 8 28·6 | 8 04·1 | 4·9 | 2·7 | 10·9 | 6·1 | 16·9 | 9·4 |
| 50 | 8 27·5 | 8 28·9 | 8 04·4 | 5·0 | 2·8 | 11·0 | 6·1 | 17·0 | 9·5 |
| 51 | 8 27·8 | 8 29·1 | 8 04·6 | 5·1 | 2·8 | 11·1 | 6·2 | 17·1 | 9·5 |
| 52 | 8 28·0 | 8 29·4 | 8 04·9 | 5·2 | 2·9 | 11·2 | 6·3 | 17·2 | 9·6 |
| 53 | 8 28·3 | 8 29·6 | 8 05·1 | 5·3 | 3·0 | 11·3 | 6·3 | 17·3 | 9·7 |
| 54 | 8 28·5 | 8 29·9 | 8 05·3 | 5·4 | 3·0 | 11·4 | 6·4 | 17·4 | 9·7 |
| 55 | 8 28·8 | 8 30·1 | 8 05·6 | 5·5 | 3·1 | 11·5 | 6·4 | 17·5 | 9·8 |
| 56 | 8 29·0 | 8 30·4 | 8 05·8 | 5·6 | 3·1 | 11·6 | 6·5 | 17·6 | 9·8 |
| 57 | 8 29·3 | 8 30·6 | 8 06·1 | 5·7 | 3·2 | 11·7 | 6·5 | 17·7 | 9·9 |
| 58 | 8 29·5 | 8 30·9 | 8 06·3 | 5·8 | 3·2 | 11·8 | 6·6 | 17·8 | 9·9 |
| 59 | 8 29·8 | 8 31·1 | 8 06·5 | 5·9 | 3·3 | 11·9 | 6·6 | 17·9 | 10·0 |
| 60 | 8 30·0 | 8 31·4 | 8 06·8 | 6·0 | 3·4 | 12·0 | 6·7 | 18·0 | 10·1 |

## 34ᵐ

| 34 m | SUN PLANETS | ARIES | MOON | v or d Corr[n] | | v or d Corr[n] | | v or d Corr[n] | |
|---|---|---|---|---|---|---|---|---|---|
| s | ° ′ | ° ′ | ° ′ | ′ | ′ | ′ | ′ | ′ | ′ |
| 00 | 8 30·0 | 8 31·4 | 8 06·8 | 0·0 | 0·0 | 6·0 | 3·5 | 12·0 | 6·9 |
| 01 | 8 30·3 | 8 31·6 | 8 07·0 | 0·1 | 0·1 | 6·1 | 3·5 | 12·1 | 7·0 |
| 02 | 8 30·5 | 8 31·9 | 8 07·2 | 0·2 | 0·1 | 6·2 | 3·6 | 12·2 | 7·0 |
| 03 | 8 30·8 | 8 32·1 | 8 07·5 | 0·3 | 0·2 | 6·3 | 3·6 | 12·3 | 7·1 |
| 04 | 8 31·0 | 8 32·4 | 8 07·7 | 0·4 | 0·2 | 6·4 | 3·7 | 12·4 | 7·1 |
| 05 | 8 31·3 | 8 32·6 | 8 08·0 | 0·5 | 0·3 | 6·5 | 3·7 | 12·5 | 7·2 |
| 06 | 8 31·5 | 8 32·9 | 8 08·2 | 0·6 | 0·3 | 6·6 | 3·8 | 12·6 | 7·2 |
| 07 | 8 31·8 | 8 33·2 | 8 08·4 | 0·7 | 0·4 | 6·7 | 3·9 | 12·7 | 7·3 |
| 08 | 8 32·0 | 8 33·4 | 8 08·7 | 0·8 | 0·5 | 6·8 | 3·9 | 12·8 | 7·4 |
| 09 | 8 32·3 | 8 33·7 | 8 08·9 | 0·9 | 0·5 | 6·9 | 4·0 | 12·9 | 7·4 |
| 10 | 8 32·5 | 8 33·9 | 8 09·2 | 1·0 | 0·6 | 7·0 | 4·0 | 13·0 | 7·5 |
| 11 | 8 32·8 | 8 34·2 | 8 09·4 | 1·1 | 0·6 | 7·1 | 4·1 | 13·1 | 7·5 |
| 12 | 8 33·0 | 8 34·4 | 8 09·6 | 1·2 | 0·7 | 7·2 | 4·1 | 13·2 | 7·6 |
| 13 | 8 33·3 | 8 34·7 | 8 09·9 | 1·3 | 0·7 | 7·3 | 4·2 | 13·3 | 7·6 |
| 14 | 8 33·5 | 8 34·9 | 8 10·1 | 1·4 | 0·8 | 7·4 | 4·3 | 13·4 | 7·7 |
| 15 | 8 33·8 | 8 35·2 | 8 10·3 | 1·5 | 0·9 | 7·5 | 4·3 | 13·5 | 7·8 |
| 16 | 8 34·0 | 8 35·4 | 8 10·6 | 1·6 | 0·9 | 7·6 | 4·4 | 13·6 | 7·8 |
| 17 | 8 34·3 | 8 35·7 | 8 10·8 | 1·7 | 1·0 | 7·7 | 4·4 | 13·7 | 7·9 |
| 18 | 8 34·5 | 8 35·9 | 8 11·1 | 1·8 | 1·0 | 7·8 | 4·5 | 13·8 | 7·9 |
| 19 | 8 34·8 | 8 36·2 | 8 11·3 | 1·9 | 1·1 | 7·9 | 4·5 | 13·9 | 8·0 |
| 20 | 8 35·0 | 8 36·4 | 8 11·5 | 2·0 | 1·2 | 8·0 | 4·6 | 14·0 | 8·1 |
| 21 | 8 35·3 | 8 36·7 | 8 11·8 | 2·1 | 1·2 | 8·1 | 4·7 | 14·1 | 8·1 |
| 22 | 8 35·5 | 8 36·9 | 8 12·0 | 2·2 | 1·3 | 8·2 | 4·7 | 14·2 | 8·2 |
| 23 | 8 35·8 | 8 37·2 | 8 12·3 | 2·3 | 1·3 | 8·3 | 4·8 | 14·3 | 8·2 |
| 24 | 8 36·0 | 8 37·4 | 8 12·5 | 2·4 | 1·4 | 8·4 | 4·8 | 14·4 | 8·3 |
| 25 | 8 36·3 | 8 37·7 | 8 12·7 | 2·5 | 1·4 | 8·5 | 4·9 | 14·5 | 8·3 |
| 26 | 8 36·5 | 8 37·9 | 8 13·0 | 2·6 | 1·5 | 8·6 | 4·9 | 14·6 | 8·4 |
| 27 | 8 36·8 | 8 38·2 | 8 13·2 | 2·7 | 1·6 | 8·7 | 5·0 | 14·7 | 8·5 |
| 28 | 8 37·0 | 8 38·4 | 8 13·4 | 2·8 | 1·6 | 8·8 | 5·1 | 14·8 | 8·5 |
| 29 | 8 37·3 | 8 38·7 | 8 13·7 | 2·9 | 1·7 | 8·9 | 5·1 | 14·9 | 8·6 |
| 30 | 8 37·5 | 8 38·9 | 8 13·9 | 3·0 | 1·7 | 9·0 | 5·2 | 15·0 | 8·6 |
| 31 | 8 37·8 | 8 39·2 | 8 14·2 | 3·1 | 1·8 | 9·1 | 5·2 | 15·1 | 8·7 |
| 32 | 8 38·0 | 8 39·4 | 8 14·4 | 3·2 | 1·8 | 9·2 | 5·3 | 15·2 | 8·7 |
| 33 | 8 38·3 | 8 39·7 | 8 14·6 | 3·3 | 1·9 | 9·3 | 5·3 | 15·3 | 8·8 |
| 34 | 8 38·5 | 8 39·9 | 8 14·9 | 3·4 | 2·0 | 9·4 | 5·4 | 15·4 | 8·9 |
| 35 | 8 38·8 | 8 40·2 | 8 15·1 | 3·5 | 2·0 | 9·5 | 5·5 | 15·5 | 8·9 |
| 36 | 8 39·0 | 8 40·4 | 8 15·4 | 3·6 | 2·1 | 9·6 | 5·5 | 15·6 | 9·0 |
| 37 | 8 39·3 | 8 40·7 | 8 15·6 | 3·7 | 2·1 | 9·7 | 5·6 | 15·7 | 9·0 |
| 38 | 8 39·5 | 8 40·9 | 8 15·8 | 3·8 | 2·2 | 9·8 | 5·6 | 15·8 | 9·1 |
| 39 | 8 39·8 | 8 41·2 | 8 16·1 | 3·9 | 2·2 | 9·9 | 5·7 | 15·9 | 9·1 |
| 40 | 8 40·0 | 8 41·4 | 8 16·3 | 4·0 | 2·3 | 10·0 | 5·8 | 16·0 | 9·2 |
| 41 | 8 40·3 | 8 41·7 | 8 16·5 | 4·1 | 2·4 | 10·1 | 5·8 | 16·1 | 9·3 |
| 42 | 8 40·5 | 8 41·9 | 8 16·8 | 4·2 | 2·4 | 10·2 | 5·9 | 16·2 | 9·3 |
| 43 | 8 40·8 | 8 42·2 | 8 17·0 | 4·3 | 2·5 | 10·3 | 5·9 | 16·3 | 9·4 |
| 44 | 8 41·0 | 8 42·4 | 8 17·3 | 4·4 | 2·5 | 10·4 | 6·0 | 16·4 | 9·4 |
| 45 | 8 41·3 | 8 42·7 | 8 17·5 | 4·5 | 2·6 | 10·5 | 6·0 | 16·5 | 9·5 |
| 46 | 8 41·5 | 8 42·9 | 8 17·7 | 4·6 | 2·6 | 10·6 | 6·1 | 16·6 | 9·5 |
| 47 | 8 41·8 | 8 43·2 | 8 18·0 | 4·7 | 2·7 | 10·7 | 6·2 | 16·7 | 9·6 |
| 48 | 8 42·0 | 8 43·4 | 8 18·2 | 4·8 | 2·8 | 10·8 | 6·2 | 16·8 | 9·7 |
| 49 | 8 42·3 | 8 43·7 | 8 18·5 | 4·9 | 2·8 | 10·9 | 6·3 | 16·9 | 9·7 |
| 50 | 8 42·5 | 8 43·9 | 8 18·7 | 5·0 | 2·9 | 11·0 | 6·3 | 17·0 | 9·8 |
| 51 | 8 42·8 | 8 44·2 | 8 18·9 | 5·1 | 2·9 | 11·1 | 6·4 | 17·1 | 9·8 |
| 52 | 8 43·0 | 8 44·4 | 8 19·2 | 5·2 | 3·0 | 11·2 | 6·4 | 17·2 | 9·9 |
| 53 | 8 43·3 | 8 44·7 | 8 19·4 | 5·3 | 3·0 | 11·3 | 6·5 | 17·3 | 9·9 |
| 54 | 8 43·5 | 8 44·9 | 8 19·7 | 5·4 | 3·1 | 11·4 | 6·6 | 17·4 | 10·0 |
| 55 | 8 43·8 | 8 45·2 | 8 19·9 | 5·5 | 3·2 | 11·5 | 6·6 | 17·5 | 10·1 |
| 56 | 8 44·0 | 8 45·4 | 8 20·1 | 5·6 | 3·2 | 11·6 | 6·7 | 17·6 | 10·1 |
| 57 | 8 44·3 | 8 45·7 | 8 20·4 | 5·7 | 3·3 | 11·7 | 6·7 | 17·7 | 10·2 |
| 58 | 8 44·5 | 8 45·9 | 8 20·6 | 5·8 | 3·3 | 11·8 | 6·8 | 17·8 | 10·2 |
| 59 | 8 44·8 | 8 46·2 | 8 20·8 | 5·9 | 3·4 | 11·9 | 6·8 | 17·9 | 10·3 |
| 60 | 8 45·0 | 8 46·4 | 8 21·1 | 6·0 | 3·5 | 12·0 | 6·9 | 18·0 | 10·4 |

## 35ᵐ

| 35 m | SUN PLANETS | ARIES | MOON | v or d Corr[n] | | v or d Corr[n] | | v or d Corr[n] | |
|---|---|---|---|---|---|---|---|---|---|
| s | ° ′ | ° ′ | ° ′ | ′ | ′ | ′ | ′ | ′ | ′ |
| 00 | 8 45·0 | 8 46·4 | 8 21·1 | 0·0 | 0·0 | 6·0 | 3·6 | 12·0 | 7·1 |
| 01 | 8 45·3 | 8 46·7 | 8 21·3 | 0·1 | 0·1 | 6·1 | 3·6 | 12·1 | 7·2 |
| 02 | 8 45·5 | 8 46·9 | 8 21·6 | 0·2 | 0·1 | 6·2 | 3·7 | 12·2 | 7·2 |
| 03 | 8 45·8 | 8 47·2 | 8 21·8 | 0·3 | 0·2 | 6·3 | 3·7 | 12·3 | 7·3 |
| 04 | 8 46·0 | 8 47·4 | 8 22·0 | 0·4 | 0·2 | 6·4 | 3·8 | 12·4 | 7·3 |
| 05 | 8 46·3 | 8 47·7 | 8 22·3 | 0·5 | 0·3 | 6·5 | 3·8 | 12·5 | 7·4 |
| 06 | 8 46·5 | 8 47·9 | 8 22·5 | 0·6 | 0·4 | 6·6 | 3·9 | 12·6 | 7·5 |
| 07 | 8 46·8 | 8 48·2 | 8 22·8 | 0·7 | 0·4 | 6·7 | 4·0 | 12·7 | 7·5 |
| 08 | 8 47·0 | 8 48·4 | 8 23·0 | 0·8 | 0·5 | 6·8 | 4·0 | 12·8 | 7·6 |
| 09 | 8 47·3 | 8 48·7 | 8 23·2 | 0·9 | 0·5 | 6·9 | 4·1 | 12·9 | 7·6 |
| 10 | 8 47·5 | 8 48·9 | 8 23·5 | 1·0 | 0·6 | 7·0 | 4·1 | 13·0 | 7·7 |
| 11 | 8 47·8 | 8 49·2 | 8 23·7 | 1·1 | 0·7 | 7·1 | 4·2 | 13·1 | 7·8 |
| 12 | 8 48·0 | 8 49·4 | 8 23·9 | 1·2 | 0·7 | 7·2 | 4·3 | 13·2 | 7·8 |
| 13 | 8 48·3 | 8 49·7 | 8 24·2 | 1·3 | 0·8 | 7·3 | 4·3 | 13·3 | 7·9 |
| 14 | 8 48·5 | 8 49·9 | 8 24·4 | 1·4 | 0·8 | 7·4 | 4·4 | 13·4 | 7·9 |
| 15 | 8 48·8 | 8 50·2 | 8 24·7 | 1·5 | 0·9 | 7·5 | 4·4 | 13·5 | 8·0 |
| 16 | 8 49·0 | 8 50·4 | 8 24·9 | 1·6 | 0·9 | 7·6 | 4·5 | 13·6 | 8·0 |
| 17 | 8 49·3 | 8 50·7 | 8 25·1 | 1·7 | 1·0 | 7·7 | 4·6 | 13·7 | 8·1 |
| 18 | 8 49·5 | 8 50·9 | 8 25·4 | 1·8 | 1·1 | 7·8 | 4·6 | 13·8 | 8·2 |
| 19 | 8 49·8 | 8 51·2 | 8 25·6 | 1·9 | 1·1 | 7·9 | 4·7 | 13·9 | 8·2 |
| 20 | 8 50·0 | 8 51·5 | 8 25·9 | 2·0 | 1·2 | 8·0 | 4·7 | 14·0 | 8·3 |
| 21 | 8 50·3 | 8 51·7 | 8 26·1 | 2·1 | 1·2 | 8·1 | 4·8 | 14·1 | 8·3 |
| 22 | 8 50·5 | 8 52·0 | 8 26·3 | 2·2 | 1·3 | 8·2 | 4·9 | 14·2 | 8·4 |
| 23 | 8 50·8 | 8 52·2 | 8 26·6 | 2·3 | 1·4 | 8·3 | 4·9 | 14·3 | 8·5 |
| 24 | 8 51·0 | 8 52·5 | 8 26·8 | 2·4 | 1·4 | 8·4 | 5·0 | 14·4 | 8·5 |
| 25 | 8 51·3 | 8 52·7 | 8 27·0 | 2·5 | 1·5 | 8·5 | 5·0 | 14·5 | 8·6 |
| 26 | 8 51·5 | 8 53·0 | 8 27·3 | 2·6 | 1·5 | 8·6 | 5·1 | 14·6 | 8·6 |
| 27 | 8 51·8 | 8 53·2 | 8 27·5 | 2·7 | 1·6 | 8·7 | 5·1 | 14·7 | 8·7 |
| 28 | 8 52·0 | 8 53·5 | 8 27·8 | 2·8 | 1·7 | 8·8 | 5·2 | 14·8 | 8·8 |
| 29 | 8 52·3 | 8 53·7 | 8 28·0 | 2·9 | 1·7 | 8·9 | 5·3 | 14·9 | 8·8 |
| 30 | 8 52·5 | 8 54·0 | 8 28·2 | 3·0 | 1·8 | 9·0 | 5·3 | 15·0 | 8·9 |
| 31 | 8 52·8 | 8 54·2 | 8 28·5 | 3·1 | 1·8 | 9·1 | 5·4 | 15·1 | 8·9 |
| 32 | 8 53·0 | 8 54·5 | 8 28·7 | 3·2 | 1·9 | 9·2 | 5·4 | 15·2 | 9·0 |
| 33 | 8 53·3 | 8 54·7 | 8 29·0 | 3·3 | 2·0 | 9·3 | 5·5 | 15·3 | 9·1 |
| 34 | 8 53·5 | 8 55·0 | 8 29·2 | 3·4 | 2·0 | 9·4 | 5·6 | 15·4 | 9·1 |
| 35 | 8 53·8 | 8 55·2 | 8 29·4 | 3·5 | 2·1 | 9·5 | 5·6 | 15·5 | 9·2 |
| 36 | 8 54·0 | 8 55·5 | 8 29·7 | 3·6 | 2·1 | 9·6 | 5·7 | 15·6 | 9·2 |
| 37 | 8 54·3 | 8 55·7 | 8 29·9 | 3·7 | 2·2 | 9·7 | 5·7 | 15·7 | 9·3 |
| 38 | 8 54·5 | 8 56·0 | 8 30·2 | 3·8 | 2·2 | 9·8 | 5·8 | 15·8 | 9·3 |
| 39 | 8 54·8 | 8 56·2 | 8 30·4 | 3·9 | 2·3 | 9·9 | 5·9 | 15·9 | 9·4 |
| 40 | 8 55·0 | 8 56·5 | 8 30·6 | 4·0 | 2·4 | 10·0 | 5·9 | 16·0 | 9·5 |
| 41 | 8 55·3 | 8 56·7 | 8 30·9 | 4·1 | 2·4 | 10·1 | 6·0 | 16·1 | 9·5 |
| 42 | 8 55·5 | 8 57·0 | 8 31·1 | 4·2 | 2·5 | 10·2 | 6·0 | 16·2 | 9·6 |
| 43 | 8 55·8 | 8 57·2 | 8 31·3 | 4·3 | 2·5 | 10·3 | 6·1 | 16·3 | 9·6 |
| 44 | 8 56·0 | 8 57·5 | 8 31·6 | 4·4 | 2·6 | 10·4 | 6·2 | 16·4 | 9·7 |
| 45 | 8 56·3 | 8 57·7 | 8 31·8 | 4·5 | 2·7 | 10·5 | 6·2 | 16·5 | 9·8 |
| 46 | 8 56·5 | 8 58·0 | 8 32·1 | 4·6 | 2·7 | 10·6 | 6·3 | 16·6 | 9·8 |
| 47 | 8 56·8 | 8 58·2 | 8 32·3 | 4·7 | 2·8 | 10·7 | 6·3 | 16·7 | 9·9 |
| 48 | 8 57·0 | 8 58·5 | 8 32·5 | 4·8 | 2·8 | 10·8 | 6·4 | 16·8 | 9·9 |
| 49 | 8 57·3 | 8 58·7 | 8 32·8 | 4·9 | 2·9 | 10·9 | 6·4 | 16·9 | 10·0 |
| 50 | 8 57·5 | 8 59·0 | 8 33·0 | 5·0 | 3·0 | 11·0 | 6·5 | 17·0 | 10·1 |
| 51 | 8 57·8 | 8 59·2 | 8 33·3 | 5·1 | 3·0 | 11·1 | 6·6 | 17·1 | 10·1 |
| 52 | 8 58·0 | 8 59·5 | 8 33·5 | 5·2 | 3·1 | 11·2 | 6·6 | 17·2 | 10·2 |
| 53 | 8 58·3 | 8 59·7 | 8 33·7 | 5·3 | 3·1 | 11·3 | 6·7 | 17·3 | 10·2 |
| 54 | 8 58·5 | 9 00·0 | 8 34·0 | 5·4 | 3·2 | 11·4 | 6·7 | 17·4 | 10·3 |
| 55 | 8 58·8 | 9 00·2 | 8 34·2 | 5·5 | 3·3 | 11·5 | 6·8 | 17·5 | 10·4 |
| 56 | 8 59·0 | 9 00·5 | 8 34·4 | 5·6 | 3·3 | 11·6 | 6·9 | 17·6 | 10·4 |
| 57 | 8 59·3 | 9 00·7 | 8 34·7 | 5·7 | 3·4 | 11·7 | 6·9 | 17·7 | 10·5 |
| 58 | 8 59·5 | 9 01·0 | 8 34·9 | 5·8 | 3·4 | 11·8 | 7·0 | 17·8 | 10·5 |
| 59 | 8 59·8 | 9 01·2 | 8 35·2 | 5·9 | 3·5 | 11·9 | 7·0 | 17·9 | 10·6 |
| 60 | 9 00·0 | 9 01·5 | 8 35·4 | 6·0 | 3·6 | 12·0 | 7·1 | 18·0 | 10·7 |

## 36ᵐ

| 36 s | SUN PLANETS ° ′ | ARIES ° ′ | MOON ° ′ | v or d ′ | Corrⁿ ′ | v or d ′ | Corrⁿ ′ | v or d ′ | Corrⁿ ′ |
|---|---|---|---|---|---|---|---|---|---|
| 00 | 9 00·0 | 9 01·5 | 8 35·4 | 0·0 | 0·0 | 6·0 | 3·7 | 12·0 | 7·3 |
| 01 | 9 00·3 | 9 01·7 | 8 35·6 | 0·1 | 0·1 | 6·1 | 3·7 | 12·1 | 7·4 |
| 02 | 9 00·5 | 9 02·0 | 8 35·9 | 0·2 | 0·1 | 6·2 | 3·8 | 12·2 | 7·4 |
| 03 | 9 00·8 | 9 02·2 | 8 36·1 | 0·3 | 0·2 | 6·3 | 3·8 | 12·3 | 7·5 |
| 04 | 9 01·0 | 9 02·5 | 8 36·4 | 0·4 | 0·2 | 6·4 | 3·9 | 12·4 | 7·5 |
| 05 | 9 01·3 | 9 02·7 | 8 36·6 | 0·5 | 0·3 | 6·5 | 4·0 | 12·5 | 7·6 |
| 06 | 9 01·5 | 9 03·0 | 8 36·8 | 0·6 | 0·4 | 6·6 | 4·0 | 12·6 | 7·7 |
| 07 | 9 01·8 | 9 03·2 | 8 37·1 | 0·7 | 0·4 | 6·7 | 4·1 | 12·7 | 7·7 |
| 08 | 9 02·0 | 9 03·5 | 8 37·3 | 0·8 | 0·5 | 6·8 | 4·1 | 12·8 | 7·8 |
| 09 | 9 02·3 | 9 03·7 | 8 37·5 | 0·9 | 0·5 | 6·9 | 4·2 | 12·9 | 7·8 |
| 10 | 9 02·5 | 9 04·0 | 8 37·8 | 1·0 | 0·6 | 7·0 | 4·3 | 13·0 | 7·9 |
| 11 | 9 02·8 | 9 04·2 | 8 38·0 | 1·1 | 0·7 | 7·1 | 4·3 | 13·1 | 8·0 |
| 12 | 9 03·0 | 9 04·5 | 8 38·3 | 1·2 | 0·7 | 7·2 | 4·4 | 13·2 | 8·0 |
| 13 | 9 03·3 | 9 04·7 | 8 38·5 | 1·3 | 0·8 | 7·3 | 4·4 | 13·3 | 8·1 |
| 14 | 9 03·5 | 9 05·0 | 8 38·7 | 1·4 | 0·9 | 7·4 | 4·5 | 13·4 | 8·2 |
| 15 | 9 03·8 | 9 05·2 | 8 39·0 | 1·5 | 0·9 | 7·5 | 4·6 | 13·5 | 8·2 |
| 16 | 9 04·0 | 9 05·5 | 8 39·2 | 1·6 | 1·0 | 7·6 | 4·6 | 13·6 | 8·3 |
| 17 | 9 04·3 | 9 05·7 | 8 39·5 | 1·7 | 1·0 | 7·7 | 4·7 | 13·7 | 8·3 |
| 18 | 9 04·5 | 9 06·0 | 8 39·7 | 1·8 | 1·1 | 7·8 | 4·7 | 13·8 | 8·4 |
| 19 | 9 04·8 | 9 06·2 | 8 39·9 | 1·9 | 1·2 | 7·9 | 4·8 | 13·9 | 8·5 |
| 20 | 9 05·0 | 9 06·5 | 8 40·2 | 2·0 | 1·2 | 8·0 | 4·9 | 14·0 | 8·5 |
| 21 | 9 05·3 | 9 06·7 | 8 40·4 | 2·1 | 1·3 | 8·1 | 4·9 | 14·1 | 8·6 |
| 22 | 9 05·5 | 9 07·0 | 8 40·6 | 2·2 | 1·3 | 8·2 | 5·0 | 14·2 | 8·6 |
| 23 | 9 05·8 | 9 07·2 | 8 40·9 | 2·3 | 1·4 | 8·3 | 5·0 | 14·3 | 8·7 |
| 24 | 9 06·0 | 9 07·5 | 8 41·1 | 2·4 | 1·5 | 8·4 | 5·1 | 14·4 | 8·8 |
| 25 | 9 06·3 | 9 07·7 | 8 41·4 | 2·5 | 1·5 | 8·5 | 5·2 | 14·5 | 8·8 |
| 26 | 9 06·5 | 9 08·0 | 8 41·6 | 2·6 | 1·6 | 8·6 | 5·2 | 14·6 | 8·9 |
| 27 | 9 06·8 | 9 08·2 | 8 41·8 | 2·7 | 1·6 | 8·7 | 5·3 | 14·7 | 8·9 |
| 28 | 9 07·0 | 9 08·5 | 8 42·1 | 2·8 | 1·7 | 8·8 | 5·4 | 14·8 | 9·0 |
| 29 | 9 07·3 | 9 08·7 | 8 42·3 | 2·9 | 1·8 | 8·9 | 5·4 | 14·9 | 9·1 |
| 30 | 9 07·5 | 9 09·0 | 8 42·6 | 3·0 | 1·8 | 9·0 | 5·5 | 15·0 | 9·1 |
| 31 | 9 07·8 | 9 09·2 | 8 42·8 | 3·1 | 1·9 | 9·1 | 5·5 | 15·1 | 9·2 |
| 32 | 9 08·0 | 9 09·5 | 8 43·0 | 3·2 | 1·9 | 9·2 | 5·6 | 15·2 | 9·2 |
| 33 | 9 08·3 | 9 09·8 | 8 43·3 | 3·3 | 2·0 | 9·3 | 5·7 | 15·3 | 9·3 |
| 34 | 9 08·5 | 9 10·0 | 8 43·5 | 3·4 | 2·1 | 9·4 | 5·7 | 15·4 | 9·4 |
| 35 | 9 08·8 | 9 10·3 | 8 43·8 | 3·5 | 2·1 | 9·5 | 5·8 | 15·5 | 9·4 |
| 36 | 9 09·0 | 9 10·5 | 8 44·0 | 3·6 | 2·2 | 9·6 | 5·8 | 15·6 | 9·5 |
| 37 | 9 09·3 | 9 10·8 | 8 44·2 | 3·7 | 2·3 | 9·7 | 5·9 | 15·7 | 9·6 |
| 38 | 9 09·5 | 9 11·0 | 8 44·5 | 3·8 | 2·3 | 9·8 | 6·0 | 15·8 | 9·6 |
| 39 | 9 09·8 | 9 11·3 | 8 44·7 | 3·9 | 2·4 | 9·9 | 6·0 | 15·9 | 9·7 |
| 40 | 9 10·0 | 9 11·5 | 8 44·9 | 4·0 | 2·4 | 10·0 | 6·1 | 16·0 | 9·7 |
| 41 | 9 10·3 | 9 11·8 | 8 45·2 | 4·1 | 2·5 | 10·1 | 6·1 | 16·1 | 9·8 |
| 42 | 9 10·5 | 9 12·0 | 8 45·4 | 4·2 | 2·6 | 10·2 | 6·2 | 16·2 | 9·9 |
| 43 | 9 10·8 | 9 12·3 | 8 45·7 | 4·3 | 2·6 | 10·3 | 6·3 | 16·3 | 9·9 |
| 44 | 9 11·0 | 9 12·5 | 8 45·9 | 4·4 | 2·7 | 10·4 | 6·3 | 16·4 | 10·0 |
| 45 | 9 11·3 | 9 12·8 | 8 46·1 | 4·5 | 2·7 | 10·5 | 6·4 | 16·5 | 10·0 |
| 46 | 9 11·5 | 9 13·0 | 8 46·4 | 4·6 | 2·8 | 10·6 | 6·4 | 16·6 | 10·1 |
| 47 | 9 11·8 | 9 13·3 | 8 46·6 | 4·7 | 2·9 | 10·7 | 6·5 | 16·7 | 10·2 |
| 48 | 9 12·0 | 9 13·5 | 8 46·9 | 4·8 | 2·9 | 10·8 | 6·6 | 16·8 | 10·2 |
| 49 | 9 12·3 | 9 13·8 | 8 47·1 | 4·9 | 3·0 | 10·9 | 6·6 | 16·9 | 10·3 |
| 50 | 9 12·5 | 9 14·0 | 8 47·3 | 5·0 | 3·0 | 11·0 | 6·7 | 17·0 | 10·3 |
| 51 | 9 12·8 | 9 14·3 | 8 47·6 | 5·1 | 3·1 | 11·1 | 6·8 | 17·1 | 10·4 |
| 52 | 9 13·0 | 9 14·5 | 8 47·8 | 5·2 | 3·2 | 11·2 | 6·8 | 17·2 | 10·5 |
| 53 | 9 13·3 | 9 14·8 | 8 48·0 | 5·3 | 3·2 | 11·3 | 6·9 | 17·3 | 10·5 |
| 54 | 9 13·5 | 9 15·0 | 8 48·3 | 5·4 | 3·3 | 11·4 | 6·9 | 17·4 | 10·6 |
| 55 | 9 13·8 | 9 15·3 | 8 48·5 | 5·5 | 3·3 | 11·5 | 7·0 | 17·5 | 10·6 |
| 56 | 9 14·0 | 9 15·5 | 8 48·8 | 5·6 | 3·4 | 11·6 | 7·1 | 17·6 | 10·7 |
| 57 | 9 14·3 | 9 15·8 | 8 49·0 | 5·7 | 3·5 | 11·7 | 7·1 | 17·7 | 10·8 |
| 58 | 9 14·5 | 9 16·0 | 8 49·2 | 5·8 | 3·5 | 11·8 | 7·2 | 17·8 | 10·8 |
| 59 | 9 14·8 | 9 16·3 | 8 49·5 | 5·9 | 3·6 | 11·9 | 7·2 | 17·9 | 10·9 |
| 60 | 9 15·0 | 9 16·5 | 8 49·7 | 6·0 | 3·7 | 12·0 | 7·3 | 18·0 | 11·0 |

## 37ᵐ

| 37 s | SUN PLANETS ° ′ | ARIES ° ′ | MOON ° ′ | v or d ′ | Corrⁿ ′ | v or d ′ | Corrⁿ ′ | v or d ′ | Corrⁿ ′ |
|---|---|---|---|---|---|---|---|---|---|
| 00 | 9 15·0 | 9 16·5 | 8 49·7 | 0·0 | 0·0 | 6·0 | 3·8 | 12·0 | 7·5 |
| 01 | 9 15·3 | 9 16·8 | 8 50·0 | 0·1 | 0·1 | 6·1 | 3·8 | 12·1 | 7·6 |
| 02 | 9 15·5 | 9 17·0 | 8 50·2 | 0·2 | 0·1 | 6·2 | 3·9 | 12·2 | 7·6 |
| 03 | 9 15·8 | 9 17·3 | 8 50·4 | 0·3 | 0·2 | 6·3 | 3·9 | 12·3 | 7·7 |
| 04 | 9 16·0 | 9 17·5 | 8 50·7 | 0·4 | 0·3 | 6·4 | 4·0 | 12·4 | 7·8 |
| 05 | 9 16·3 | 9 17·8 | 8 50·9 | 0·5 | 0·3 | 6·5 | 4·1 | 12·5 | 7·8 |
| 06 | 9 16·5 | 9 18·0 | 8 51·1 | 0·6 | 0·4 | 6·6 | 4·1 | 12·6 | 7·9 |
| 07 | 9 16·8 | 9 18·3 | 8 51·4 | 0·7 | 0·4 | 6·7 | 4·2 | 12·7 | 7·9 |
| 08 | 9 17·0 | 9 18·5 | 8 51·6 | 0·8 | 0·5 | 6·8 | 4·3 | 12·8 | 8·0 |
| 09 | 9 17·3 | 9 18·8 | 8 51·9 | 0·9 | 0·6 | 6·9 | 4·3 | 12·9 | 8·1 |
| 10 | 9 17·5 | 9 19·0 | 8 52·1 | 1·0 | 0·6 | 7·0 | 4·4 | 13·0 | 8·1 |
| 11 | 9 17·8 | 9 19·3 | 8 52·3 | 1·1 | 0·7 | 7·1 | 4·4 | 13·1 | 8·2 |
| 12 | 9 18·0 | 9 19·5 | 8 52·6 | 1·2 | 0·8 | 7·2 | 4·5 | 13·2 | 8·3 |
| 13 | 9 18·3 | 9 19·8 | 8 52·8 | 1·3 | 0·8 | 7·3 | 4·6 | 13·3 | 8·3 |
| 14 | 9 18·5 | 9 20·0 | 8 53·1 | 1·4 | 0·9 | 7·4 | 4·6 | 13·4 | 8·4 |
| 15 | 9 18·8 | 9 20·3 | 8 53·3 | 1·5 | 0·9 | 7·5 | 4·7 | 13·5 | 8·4 |
| 16 | 9 19·0 | 9 20·5 | 8 53·5 | 1·6 | 1·0 | 7·6 | 4·8 | 13·6 | 8·5 |
| 17 | 9 19·3 | 9 20·8 | 8 53·8 | 1·7 | 1·1 | 7·7 | 4·8 | 13·7 | 8·6 |
| 18 | 9 19·5 | 9 21·0 | 8 54·0 | 1·8 | 1·1 | 7·8 | 4·9 | 13·8 | 8·6 |
| 19 | 9 19·8 | 9 21·3 | 8 54·3 | 1·9 | 1·2 | 7·9 | 4·9 | 13·9 | 8·7 |
| 20 | 9 20·0 | 9 21·5 | 8 54·5 | 2·0 | 1·3 | 8·0 | 5·0 | 14·0 | 8·8 |
| 21 | 9 20·3 | 9 21·8 | 8 54·7 | 2·1 | 1·3 | 8·1 | 5·1 | 14·1 | 8·8 |
| 22 | 9 20·5 | 9 22·0 | 8 55·0 | 2·2 | 1·4 | 8·2 | 5·1 | 14·2 | 8·9 |
| 23 | 9 20·8 | 9 22·3 | 8 55·2 | 2·3 | 1·4 | 8·3 | 5·2 | 14·3 | 8·9 |
| 24 | 9 21·0 | 9 22·5 | 8 55·4 | 2·4 | 1·5 | 8·4 | 5·3 | 14·4 | 9·0 |
| 25 | 9 21·3 | 9 22·8 | 8 55·7 | 2·5 | 1·6 | 8·5 | 5·3 | 14·5 | 9·1 |
| 26 | 9 21·5 | 9 23·0 | 8 55·9 | 2·6 | 1·6 | 8·6 | 5·4 | 14·6 | 9·1 |
| 27 | 9 21·8 | 9 23·3 | 8 56·2 | 2·7 | 1·7 | 8·7 | 5·4 | 14·7 | 9·2 |
| 28 | 9 22·0 | 9 23·5 | 8 56·4 | 2·8 | 1·8 | 8·8 | 5·5 | 14·8 | 9·3 |
| 29 | 9 22·3 | 9 23·8 | 8 56·6 | 2·9 | 1·8 | 8·9 | 5·6 | 14·9 | 9·3 |
| 30 | 9 22·5 | 9 24·0 | 8 56·9 | 3·0 | 1·9 | 9·0 | 5·6 | 15·0 | 9·4 |
| 31 | 9 22·8 | 9 24·3 | 8 57·1 | 3·1 | 1·9 | 9·1 | 5·7 | 15·1 | 9·4 |
| 32 | 9 23·0 | 9 24·5 | 8 57·4 | 3·2 | 2·0 | 9·2 | 5·8 | 15·2 | 9·5 |
| 33 | 9 23·3 | 9 24·8 | 8 57·6 | 3·3 | 2·1 | 9·3 | 5·8 | 15·3 | 9·6 |
| 34 | 9 23·5 | 9 25·0 | 8 57·8 | 3·4 | 2·1 | 9·4 | 5·9 | 15·4 | 9·6 |
| 35 | 9 23·8 | 9 25·3 | 8 58·1 | 3·5 | 2·2 | 9·5 | 5·9 | 15·5 | 9·7 |
| 36 | 9 24·0 | 9 25·5 | 8 58·3 | 3·6 | 2·3 | 9·6 | 6·0 | 15·6 | 9·8 |
| 37 | 9 24·3 | 9 25·8 | 8 58·5 | 3·7 | 2·3 | 9·7 | 6·1 | 15·7 | 9·8 |
| 38 | 9 24·5 | 9 26·0 | 8 58·8 | 3·8 | 2·4 | 9·8 | 6·1 | 15·8 | 9·9 |
| 39 | 9 24·8 | 9 26·3 | 8 59·0 | 3·9 | 2·4 | 9·9 | 6·2 | 15·9 | 9·9 |
| 40 | 9 25·0 | 9 26·5 | 8 59·3 | 4·0 | 2·5 | 10·0 | 6·3 | 16·0 | 10·0 |
| 41 | 9 25·3 | 9 26·8 | 8 59·5 | 4·1 | 2·6 | 10·1 | 6·3 | 16·1 | 10·1 |
| 42 | 9 25·5 | 9 27·0 | 8 59·7 | 4·2 | 2·6 | 10·2 | 6·4 | 16·2 | 10·1 |
| 43 | 9 25·8 | 9 27·3 | 9 00·0 | 4·3 | 2·7 | 10·3 | 6·4 | 16·3 | 10·2 |
| 44 | 9 26·0 | 9 27·5 | 9 00·2 | 4·4 | 2·8 | 10·4 | 6·5 | 16·4 | 10·3 |
| 45 | 9 26·3 | 9 27·8 | 9 00·5 | 4·5 | 2·8 | 10·5 | 6·6 | 16·5 | 10·3 |
| 46 | 9 26·5 | 9 28·1 | 9 00·7 | 4·6 | 2·9 | 10·6 | 6·6 | 16·6 | 10·4 |
| 47 | 9 26·8 | 9 28·3 | 9 00·9 | 4·7 | 2·9 | 10·7 | 6·7 | 16·7 | 10·4 |
| 48 | 9 27·0 | 9 28·6 | 9 01·2 | 4·8 | 3·0 | 10·8 | 6·8 | 16·8 | 10·5 |
| 49 | 9 27·3 | 9 28·8 | 9 01·4 | 4·9 | 3·1 | 10·9 | 6·8 | 16·9 | 10·6 |
| 50 | 9 27·5 | 9 29·1 | 9 01·6 | 5·0 | 3·1 | 11·0 | 6·9 | 17·0 | 10·6 |
| 51 | 9 27·8 | 9 29·3 | 9 01·9 | 5·1 | 3·2 | 11·1 | 6·9 | 17·1 | 10·7 |
| 52 | 9 28·0 | 9 29·6 | 9 02·1 | 5·2 | 3·3 | 11·2 | 7·0 | 17·2 | 10·7 |
| 53 | 9 28·3 | 9 29·8 | 9 02·4 | 5·3 | 3·3 | 11·3 | 7·1 | 17·3 | 10·8 |
| 54 | 9 28·5 | 9 30·1 | 9 02·6 | 5·4 | 3·4 | 11·4 | 7·1 | 17·4 | 10·9 |
| 55 | 9 28·8 | 9 30·3 | 9 02·8 | 5·5 | 3·4 | 11·5 | 7·2 | 17·5 | 10·9 |
| 56 | 9 29·0 | 9 30·6 | 9 03·1 | 5·6 | 3·5 | 11·6 | 7·3 | 17·6 | 11·0 |
| 57 | 9 29·3 | 9 30·8 | 9 03·3 | 5·7 | 3·6 | 11·7 | 7·3 | 17·7 | 11·1 |
| 58 | 9 29·5 | 9 31·1 | 9 03·6 | 5·8 | 3·6 | 11·8 | 7·4 | 17·8 | 11·1 |
| 59 | 9 29·8 | 9 31·3 | 9 03·8 | 5·9 | 3·7 | 11·9 | 7·4 | 17·9 | 11·2 |
| 60 | 9 30·0 | 9 31·6 | 9 04·0 | 6·0 | 3·8 | 12·0 | 7·5 | 18·0 | 11·3 |

| 38 | SUN PLANETS | ARIES | MOON | v or Corr^n d | | v or Corr^n d | | v or Corr^n d | | 39 | SUN PLANETS | ARIES | MOON | v or Corr^n d | | v or Corr^n d | | v or Corr^n d | |
|---|---|---|---|---|---|---|---|---|---|---|---|---|---|---|---|---|---|---|---|
| s | ° ′ | ° ′ | ° ′ | ′ | ′ | ′ | ′ | ′ | ′ | s | ° ′ | ° ′ | ° ′ | ′ | ′ | ′ | ′ | ′ | ′ |
| 00 | 9 30·0 | 9 31·6 | 9 04·0 | 0·0 | 0·0 | 6·0 | 3·9 | 12·0 | 7·7 | 00 | 9 45·0 | 9 46·6 | 9 18·4 | 0·0 | 0·0 | 6·0 | 4·0 | 12·0 | 7·9 |
| 01 | 9 30·3 | 9 31·8 | 9 04·3 | 0·1 | 0·1 | 6·1 | 3·9 | 12·1 | 7·8 | 01 | 9 45·3 | 9 46·9 | 9 18·6 | 0·1 | 0·1 | 6·1 | 4·0 | 12·1 | 8·0 |
| 02 | 9 30·5 | 9 32·1 | 9 04·5 | 0·2 | 0·1 | 6·2 | 4·0 | 12·2 | 7·8 | 02 | 9 45·5 | 9 47·1 | 9 18·8 | 0·2 | 0·1 | 6·2 | 4·1 | 12·2 | 8·0 |
| 03 | 9 30·8 | 9 32·3 | 9 04·7 | 0·3 | 0·2 | 6·3 | 4·0 | 12·3 | 7·9 | 03 | 9 45·8 | 9 47·4 | 9 19·1 | 0·3 | 0·2 | 6·3 | 4·1 | 12·3 | 8·1 |
| 04 | 9 31·0 | 9 32·6 | 9 05·0 | 0·4 | 0·3 | 6·4 | 4·1 | 12·4 | 8·0 | 04 | 9 46·0 | 9 47·6 | 9 19·3 | 0·4 | 0·3 | 6·4 | 4·2 | 12·4 | 8·2 |
| 05 | 9 31·3 | 9 32·8 | 9 05·2 | 0·5 | 0·3 | 6·5 | 4·2 | 12·5 | 8·0 | 05 | 9 46·3 | 9 47·9 | 9 19·5 | 0·5 | 0·3 | 6·5 | 4·3 | 12·5 | 8·2 |
| 06 | 9 31·5 | 9 33·1 | 9 05·5 | 0·6 | 0·4 | 6·6 | 4·2 | 12·6 | 8·1 | 06 | 9 46·5 | 9 48·1 | 9 19·8 | 0·6 | 0·4 | 6·6 | 4·3 | 12·6 | 8·3 |
| 07 | 9 31·8 | 9 33·3 | 9 05·7 | 0·7 | 0·4 | 6·7 | 4·3 | 12·7 | 8·1 | 07 | 9 46·8 | 9 48·4 | 9 20·0 | 0·7 | 0·5 | 6·7 | 4·4 | 12·7 | 8·4 |
| 08 | 9 32·0 | 9 33·6 | 9 05·9 | 0·8 | 0·5 | 6·8 | 4·4 | 12·8 | 8·2 | 08 | 9 47·0 | 9 48·6 | 9 20·3 | 0·8 | 0·5 | 6·8 | 4·5 | 12·8 | 8·4 |
| 09 | 9 32·3 | 9 33·8 | 9 06·2 | 0·9 | 0·6 | 6·9 | 4·4 | 12·9 | 8·3 | 09 | 9 47·3 | 9 48·9 | 9 20·5 | 0·9 | 0·6 | 6·9 | 4·5 | 12·9 | 8·5 |
| 10 | 9 32·5 | 9 34·1 | 9 06·4 | 1·0 | 0·6 | 7·0 | 4·5 | 13·0 | 8·3 | 10 | 9 47·5 | 9 49·1 | 9 20·7 | 1·0 | 0·7 | 7·0 | 4·6 | 13·0 | 8·6 |
| 11 | 9 32·8 | 9 34·3 | 9 06·7 | 1·1 | 0·7 | 7·1 | 4·6 | 13·1 | 8·4 | 11 | 9 47·8 | 9 49·4 | 9 21·0 | 1·1 | 0·7 | 7·1 | 4·7 | 13·1 | 8·6 |
| 12 | 9 33·0 | 9 34·6 | 9 06·9 | 1·2 | 0·8 | 7·2 | 4·6 | 13·2 | 8·5 | 12 | 9 48·0 | 9 49·6 | 9 21·2 | 1·2 | 0·8 | 7·2 | 4·7 | 13·2 | 8·7 |
| 13 | 9 33·3 | 9 34·8 | 9 07·1 | 1·3 | 0·8 | 7·3 | 4·7 | 13·3 | 8·5 | 13 | 9 48·3 | 9 49·9 | 9 21·5 | 1·3 | 0·9 | 7·3 | 4·8 | 13·3 | 8·8 |
| 14 | 9 33·5 | 9 35·1 | 9 07·4 | 1·4 | 0·9 | 7·4 | 4·7 | 13·4 | 8·6 | 14 | 9 48·5 | 9 50·1 | 9 21·7 | 1·4 | 0·9 | 7·4 | 4·9 | 13·4 | 8·8 |
| 15 | 9 33·8 | 9 35·3 | 9 07·6 | 1·5 | 1·0 | 7·5 | 4·8 | 13·5 | 8·7 | 15 | 9 48·8 | 9 50·4 | 9 21·9 | 1·5 | 1·0 | 7·5 | 4·9 | 13·5 | 8·9 |
| 16 | 9 34·0 | 9 35·6 | 9 07·9 | 1·6 | 1·0 | 7·6 | 4·9 | 13·6 | 8·7 | 16 | 9 49·0 | 9 50·6 | 9 22·2 | 1·6 | 1·1 | 7·6 | 5·0 | 13·6 | 9·0 |
| 17 | 9 34·3 | 9 35·8 | 9 08·1 | 1·7 | 1·1 | 7·7 | 4·9 | 13·7 | 8·8 | 17 | 9 49·3 | 9 50·9 | 9 22·4 | 1·7 | 1·1 | 7·7 | 5·1 | 13·7 | 9·0 |
| 18 | 9 34·5 | 9 36·1 | 9 08·3 | 1·8 | 1·2 | 7·8 | 5·0 | 13·8 | 8·9 | 18 | 9 49·5 | 9 51·1 | 9 22·6 | 1·8 | 1·2 | 7·8 | 5·1 | 13·8 | 9·1 |
| 19 | 9 34·8 | 9 36·3 | 9 08·6 | 1·9 | 1·2 | 7·9 | 5·1 | 13·9 | 8·9 | 19 | 9 49·8 | 9 51·4 | 9 22·9 | 1·9 | 1·3 | 7·9 | 5·2 | 13·9 | 9·2 |
| 20 | 9 35·0 | 9 36·6 | 9 08·8 | 2·0 | 1·3 | 8·0 | 5·1 | 14·0 | 9·0 | 20 | 9 50·0 | 9 51·6 | 9 23·1 | 2·0 | 1·3 | 8·0 | 5·3 | 14·0 | 9·2 |
| 21 | 9 35·3 | 9 36·8 | 9 09·0 | 2·1 | 1·3 | 8·1 | 5·2 | 14·1 | 9·0 | 21 | 9 50·3 | 9 51·9 | 9 23·4 | 2·1 | 1·4 | 8·1 | 5·3 | 14·1 | 9·3 |
| 22 | 9 35·5 | 9 37·1 | 9 09·3 | 2·2 | 1·4 | 8·2 | 5·3 | 14·2 | 9·1 | 22 | 9 50·5 | 9 52·1 | 9 23·6 | 2·2 | 1·4 | 8·2 | 5·4 | 14·2 | 9·3 |
| 23 | 9 35·8 | 9 37·3 | 9 09·5 | 2·3 | 1·5 | 8·3 | 5·3 | 14·3 | 9·2 | 23 | 9 50·8 | 9 52·4 | 9 23·8 | 2·3 | 1·5 | 8·3 | 5·5 | 14·3 | 9·4 |
| 24 | 9 36·0 | 9 37·6 | 9 09·8 | 2·4 | 1·5 | 8·4 | 5·4 | 14·4 | 9·2 | 24 | 9 51·0 | 9 52·6 | 9 24·1 | 2·4 | 1·6 | 8·4 | 5·5 | 14·4 | 9·5 |
| 25 | 9 36·3 | 9 37·8 | 9 10·0 | 2·5 | 1·6 | 8·5 | 5·5 | 14·5 | 9·3 | 25 | 9 51·3 | 9 52·9 | 9 24·3 | 2·5 | 1·6 | 8·5 | 5·6 | 14·5 | 9·5 |
| 26 | 9 36·5 | 9 38·1 | 9 10·2 | 2·6 | 1·7 | 8·6 | 5·5 | 14·6 | 9·4 | 26 | 9 51·5 | 9 53·1 | 9 24·6 | 2·6 | 1·7 | 8·6 | 5·7 | 14·6 | 9·6 |
| 27 | 9 36·8 | 9 38·3 | 9 10·5 | 2·7 | 1·7 | 8·7 | 5·6 | 14·7 | 9·4 | 27 | 9 51·8 | 9 53·4 | 9 24·8 | 2·7 | 1·8 | 8·7 | 5·7 | 14·7 | 9·7 |
| 28 | 9 37·0 | 9 38·6 | 9 10·7 | 2·8 | 1·8 | 8·8 | 5·6 | 14·8 | 9·5 | 28 | 9 52·0 | 9 53·6 | 9 25·0 | 2·8 | 1·8 | 8·8 | 5·8 | 14·8 | 9·7 |
| 29 | 9 37·3 | 9 38·8 | 9 11·0 | 2·9 | 1·9 | 8·9 | 5·7 | 14·9 | 9·6 | 29 | 9 52·3 | 9 53·9 | 9 25·3 | 2·9 | 1·9 | 8·9 | 5·9 | 14·9 | 9·8 |
| 30 | 9 37·5 | 9 39·1 | 9 11·2 | 3·0 | 1·9 | 9·0 | 5·8 | 15·0 | 9·6 | 30 | 9 52·5 | 9 54·1 | 9 25·5 | 3·0 | 2·0 | 9·0 | 5·9 | 15·0 | 9·9 |
| 31 | 9 37·8 | 9 39·3 | 9 11·4 | 3·1 | 2·0 | 9·1 | 5·8 | 15·1 | 9·7 | 31 | 9 52·8 | 9 54·4 | 9 25·7 | 3·1 | 2·0 | 9·1 | 6·0 | 15·1 | 9·9 |
| 32 | 9 38·0 | 9 39·6 | 9 11·7 | 3·2 | 2·1 | 9·2 | 5·9 | 15·2 | 9·8 | 32 | 9 53·0 | 9 54·6 | 9 26·0 | 3·2 | 2·1 | 9·2 | 6·1 | 15·2 | 10·0 |
| 33 | 9 38·3 | 9 39·8 | 9 11·9 | 3·3 | 2·1 | 9·3 | 6·0 | 15·3 | 9·8 | 33 | 9 53·3 | 9 54·9 | 9 26·2 | 3·3 | 2·2 | 9·3 | 6·1 | 15·3 | 10·1 |
| 34 | 9 38·5 | 9 40·1 | 9 12·1 | 3·4 | 2·2 | 9·4 | 6·0 | 15·4 | 9·9 | 34 | 9 53·5 | 9 55·1 | 9 26·5 | 3·4 | 2·2 | 9·4 | 6·2 | 15·4 | 10·1 |
| 35 | 9 38·8 | 9 40·3 | 9 12·4 | 3·5 | 2·2 | 9·5 | 6·1 | 15·5 | 9·9 | 35 | 9 53·8 | 9 55·4 | 9 26·7 | 3·5 | 2·3 | 9·5 | 6·3 | 15·5 | 10·2 |
| 36 | 9 39·0 | 9 40·6 | 9 12·6 | 3·6 | 2·3 | 9·6 | 6·2 | 15·6 | 10·0 | 36 | 9 54·0 | 9 55·6 | 9 26·9 | 3·6 | 2·4 | 9·6 | 6·3 | 15·6 | 10·3 |
| 37 | 9 39·3 | 9 40·8 | 9 12·9 | 3·7 | 2·4 | 9·7 | 6·2 | 15·7 | 10·1 | 37 | 9 54·3 | 9 55·9 | 9 27·2 | 3·7 | 2·4 | 9·7 | 6·4 | 15·7 | 10·3 |
| 38 | 9 39·5 | 9 41·1 | 9 13·1 | 3·8 | 2·4 | 9·8 | 6·3 | 15·8 | 10·1 | 38 | 9 54·5 | 9 56·1 | 9 27·4 | 3·8 | 2·5 | 9·8 | 6·5 | 15·8 | 10·4 |
| 39 | 9 39·8 | 9 41·3 | 9 13·3 | 3·9 | 2·5 | 9·9 | 6·4 | 15·9 | 10·2 | 39 | 9 54·8 | 9 56·4 | 9 27·7 | 3·9 | 2·6 | 9·9 | 6·5 | 15·9 | 10·5 |
| 40 | 9 40·0 | 9 41·6 | 9 13·6 | 4·0 | 2·6 | 10·0 | 6·4 | 16·0 | 10·3 | 40 | 9 55·0 | 9 56·6 | 9 27·9 | 4·0 | 2·6 | 10·0 | 6·6 | 16·0 | 10·5 |
| 41 | 9 40·3 | 9 41·8 | 9 13·8 | 4·1 | 2·6 | 10·1 | 6·5 | 16·1 | 10·3 | 41 | 9 55·3 | 9 56·9 | 9 28·1 | 4·1 | 2·7 | 10·1 | 6·6 | 16·1 | 10·6 |
| 42 | 9 40·5 | 9 42·1 | 9 14·1 | 4·2 | 2·7 | 10·2 | 6·5 | 16·2 | 10·4 | 42 | 9 55·5 | 9 57·1 | 9 28·4 | 4·2 | 2·8 | 10·2 | 6·7 | 16·2 | 10·7 |
| 43 | 9 40·8 | 9 42·3 | 9 14·3 | 4·3 | 2·8 | 10·3 | 6·6 | 16·3 | 10·5 | 43 | 9 55·8 | 9 57·4 | 9 28·6 | 4·3 | 2·8 | 10·3 | 6·8 | 16·3 | 10·7 |
| 44 | 9 41·0 | 9 42·6 | 9 14·5 | 4·4 | 2·8 | 10·4 | 6·7 | 16·4 | 10·5 | 44 | 9 56·0 | 9 57·6 | 9 28·8 | 4·4 | 2·9 | 10·4 | 6·8 | 16·4 | 10·8 |
| 45 | 9 41·3 | 9 42·8 | 9 14·8 | 4·5 | 2·9 | 10·5 | 6·7 | 16·5 | 10·6 | 45 | 9 56·3 | 9 57·9 | 9 29·1 | 4·5 | 3·0 | 10·5 | 6·9 | 16·5 | 10·9 |
| 46 | 9 41·5 | 9 43·1 | 9 15·0 | 4·6 | 3·0 | 10·6 | 6·8 | 16·6 | 10·7 | 46 | 9 56·5 | 9 58·1 | 9 29·3 | 4·6 | 3·0 | 10·6 | 7·0 | 16·6 | 10·9 |
| 47 | 9 41·8 | 9 43·3 | 9 15·2 | 4·7 | 3·0 | 10·7 | 6·9 | 16·7 | 10·7 | 47 | 9 56·8 | 9 58·4 | 9 29·6 | 4·7 | 3·1 | 10·7 | 7·0 | 16·7 | 11·0 |
| 48 | 9 42·0 | 9 43·6 | 9 15·5 | 4·8 | 3·1 | 10·8 | 6·9 | 16·8 | 10·8 | 48 | 9 57·0 | 9 58·6 | 9 29·8 | 4·8 | 3·2 | 10·8 | 7·1 | 16·8 | 11·1 |
| 49 | 9 42·3 | 9 43·8 | 9 15·7 | 4·9 | 3·1 | 10·9 | 7·0 | 16·9 | 10·8 | 49 | 9 57·3 | 9 58·9 | 9 30·0 | 4·9 | 3·2 | 10·9 | 7·2 | 16·9 | 11·1 |
| 50 | 9 42·5 | 9 44·1 | 9 16·0 | 5·0 | 3·2 | 11·0 | 7·1 | 17·0 | 10·9 | 50 | 9 57·5 | 9 59·1 | 9 30·3 | 5·0 | 3·3 | 11·0 | 7·2 | 17·0 | 11·2 |
| 51 | 9 42·8 | 9 44·3 | 9 16·2 | 5·1 | 3·3 | 11·1 | 7·1 | 17·1 | 11·0 | 51 | 9 57·8 | 9 59·4 | 9 30·5 | 5·1 | 3·4 | 11·1 | 7·3 | 17·1 | 11·3 |
| 52 | 9 43·0 | 9 44·6 | 9 16·4 | 5·2 | 3·3 | 11·2 | 7·2 | 17·2 | 11·0 | 52 | 9 58·0 | 9 59·6 | 9 30·8 | 5·2 | 3·4 | 11·2 | 7·4 | 17·2 | 11·3 |
| 53 | 9 43·3 | 9 44·8 | 9 16·7 | 5·3 | 3·4 | 11·3 | 7·3 | 17·3 | 11·1 | 53 | 9 58·3 | 9 59·9 | 9 31·0 | 5·3 | 3·5 | 11·3 | 7·4 | 17·3 | 11·4 |
| 54 | 9 43·5 | 9 45·1 | 9 16·9 | 5·4 | 3·5 | 11·4 | 7·3 | 17·4 | 11·2 | 54 | 9 58·5 | 10 00·1 | 9 31·2 | 5·4 | 3·6 | 11·4 | 7·5 | 17·4 | 11·5 |
| 55 | 9 43·8 | 9 45·3 | 9 17·2 | 5·5 | 3·5 | 11·5 | 7·4 | 17·5 | 11·2 | 55 | 9 58·8 | 10 00·4 | 9 31·5 | 5·5 | 3·6 | 11·5 | 7·6 | 17·5 | 11·5 |
| 56 | 9 44·0 | 9 45·6 | 9 17·4 | 5·6 | 3·6 | 11·6 | 7·5 | 17·6 | 11·3 | 56 | 9 59·0 | 10 00·6 | 9 31·7 | 5·6 | 3·7 | 11·6 | 7·6 | 17·6 | 11·6 |
| 57 | 9 44·3 | 9 45·8 | 9 17·6 | 5·7 | 3·7 | 11·7 | 7·5 | 17·7 | 11·4 | 57 | 9 59·3 | 10 00·9 | 9 32·0 | 5·7 | 3·8 | 11·7 | 7·7 | 17·7 | 11·7 |
| 58 | 9 44·5 | 9 46·1 | 9 17·9 | 5·8 | 3·7 | 11·8 | 7·6 | 17·8 | 11·4 | 58 | 9 59·5 | 10 01·1 | 9 32·2 | 5·8 | 3·8 | 11·8 | 7·8 | 17·8 | 11·7 |
| 59 | 9 44·8 | 9 46·4 | 9 18·1 | 5·9 | 3·8 | 11·9 | 7·6 | 17·9 | 11·5 | 59 | 9 59·8 | 10 01·4 | 9 32·4 | 5·9 | 3·9 | 11·9 | 7·8 | 17·9 | 11·8 |
| 60 | 9 45·0 | 9 46·6 | 9 18·4 | 6·0 | 3·9 | 12·0 | 7·7 | 18·0 | 11·6 | 60 | 10 00·0 | 10 01·6 | 9 32·7 | 6·0 | 4·0 | 12·0 | 7·9 | 18·0 | 11·9 |

## 40^m

| 40 | SUN PLANETS | ARIES | MOON | v or d | Corr^n | v or d | Corr^n | v or d | Corr^n |
|---|---|---|---|---|---|---|---|---|---|
| s | ° ′ | ° ′ | ° ′ | ′ | ′ | ′ | ′ | ′ | ′ |
| 00 | 10 00·0 | 10 01·6 | 9 32·7 | 0·0 | 0·0 | 6·0 | 4·1 | 12·0 | 8·1 |
| 01 | 10 00·3 | 10 01·9 | 9 32·9 | 0·1 | 0·1 | 6·1 | 4·1 | 12·1 | 8·2 |
| 02 | 10 00·5 | 10 02·1 | 9 33·1 | 0·2 | 0·1 | 6·2 | 4·2 | 12·2 | 8·2 |
| 03 | 10 00·8 | 10 02·4 | 9 33·4 | 0·3 | 0·2 | 6·3 | 4·3 | 12·3 | 8·3 |
| 04 | 10 01·0 | 10 02·6 | 9 33·6 | 0·4 | 0·3 | 6·4 | 4·3 | 12·4 | 8·4 |
| 05 | 10 01·3 | 10 02·9 | 9 33·9 | 0·5 | 0·3 | 6·5 | 4·4 | 12·5 | 8·4 |
| 06 | 10 01·5 | 10 03·1 | 9 34·1 | 0·6 | 0·4 | 6·6 | 4·5 | 12·6 | 8·5 |
| 07 | 10 01·8 | 10 03·4 | 9 34·3 | 0·7 | 0·5 | 6·7 | 4·5 | 12·7 | 8·6 |
| 08 | 10 02·0 | 10 03·6 | 9 34·6 | 0·8 | 0·5 | 6·8 | 4·6 | 12·8 | 8·6 |
| 09 | 10 02·3 | 10 03·9 | 9 34·8 | 0·9 | 0·6 | 6·9 | 4·7 | 12·9 | 8·7 |
| 10 | 10 02·5 | 10 04·1 | 9 35·1 | 1·0 | 0·7 | 7·0 | 4·7 | 13·0 | 8·8 |
| 11 | 10 02·8 | 10 04·4 | 9 35·3 | 1·1 | 0·7 | 7·1 | 4·8 | 13·1 | 8·8 |
| 12 | 10 03·0 | 10 04·7 | 9 35·5 | 1·2 | 0·8 | 7·2 | 4·9 | 13·2 | 8·9 |
| 13 | 10 03·3 | 10 04·9 | 9 35·8 | 1·3 | 0·9 | 7·3 | 4·9 | 13·3 | 9·0 |
| 14 | 10 03·5 | 10 05·2 | 9 36·0 | 1·4 | 0·9 | 7·4 | 5·0 | 13·4 | 9·0 |
| 15 | 10 03·8 | 10 05·4 | 9 36·2 | 1·5 | 1·0 | 7·5 | 5·1 | 13·5 | 9·1 |
| 16 | 10 04·0 | 10 05·7 | 9 36·5 | 1·6 | 1·1 | 7·6 | 5·1 | 13·6 | 9·2 |
| 17 | 10 04·3 | 10 05·9 | 9 36·7 | 1·7 | 1·1 | 7·7 | 5·2 | 13·7 | 9·2 |
| 18 | 10 04·5 | 10 06·2 | 9 37·0 | 1·8 | 1·2 | 7·8 | 5·3 | 13·8 | 9·3 |
| 19 | 10 04·8 | 10 06·4 | 9 37·2 | 1·9 | 1·3 | 7·9 | 5·3 | 13·9 | 9·4 |
| 20 | 10 05·0 | 10 06·7 | 9 37·4 | 2·0 | 1·4 | 8·0 | 5·4 | 14·0 | 9·5 |
| 21 | 10 05·3 | 10 06·9 | 9 37·7 | 2·1 | 1·4 | 8·1 | 5·5 | 14·1 | 9·5 |
| 22 | 10 05·5 | 10 07·2 | 9 37·9 | 2·2 | 1·5 | 8·2 | 5·5 | 14·2 | 9·6 |
| 23 | 10 05·8 | 10 07·4 | 9 38·2 | 2·3 | 1·6 | 8·3 | 5·6 | 14·3 | 9·7 |
| 24 | 10 06·0 | 10 07·7 | 9 38·4 | 2·4 | 1·6 | 8·4 | 5·7 | 14·4 | 9·7 |
| 25 | 10 06·3 | 10 07·9 | 9 38·6 | 2·5 | 1·7 | 8·5 | 5·7 | 14·5 | 9·8 |
| 26 | 10 06·5 | 10 08·2 | 9 38·9 | 2·6 | 1·8 | 8·6 | 5·8 | 14·6 | 9·9 |
| 27 | 10 06·8 | 10 08·4 | 9 39·1 | 2·7 | 1·8 | 8·7 | 5·9 | 14·7 | 9·9 |
| 28 | 10 07·0 | 10 08·7 | 9 39·3 | 2·8 | 1·9 | 8·8 | 5·9 | 14·8 | 10·0 |
| 29 | 10 07·3 | 10 08·9 | 9 39·6 | 2·9 | 2·0 | 8·9 | 6·0 | 14·9 | 10·1 |
| 30 | 10 07·5 | 10 09·2 | 9 39·8 | 3·0 | 2·0 | 9·0 | 6·1 | 15·0 | 10·1 |
| 31 | 10 07·8 | 10 09·4 | 9 40·1 | 3·1 | 2·1 | 9·1 | 6·1 | 15·1 | 10·2 |
| 32 | 10 08·0 | 10 09·7 | 9 40·3 | 3·2 | 2·2 | 9·2 | 6·2 | 15·2 | 10·3 |
| 33 | 10 08·3 | 10 09·9 | 9 40·5 | 3·3 | 2·2 | 9·3 | 6·3 | 15·3 | 10·3 |
| 34 | 10 08·5 | 10 10·2 | 9 40·8 | 3·4 | 2·3 | 9·4 | 6·3 | 15·4 | 10·4 |
| 35 | 10 08·8 | 10 10·4 | 9 41·0 | 3·5 | 2·4 | 9·5 | 6·4 | 15·5 | 10·5 |
| 36 | 10 09·0 | 10 10·7 | 9 41·3 | 3·6 | 2·4 | 9·6 | 6·5 | 15·6 | 10·5 |
| 37 | 10 09·3 | 10 10·9 | 9 41·5 | 3·7 | 2·5 | 9·7 | 6·5 | 15·7 | 10·6 |
| 38 | 10 09·5 | 10 11·2 | 9 41·7 | 3·8 | 2·6 | 9·8 | 6·6 | 15·8 | 10·7 |
| 39 | 10 09·8 | 10 11·4 | 9 42·0 | 3·9 | 2·6 | 9·9 | 6·7 | 15·9 | 10·7 |
| 40 | 10 10·0 | 10 11·7 | 9 42·2 | 4·0 | 2·7 | 10·0 | 6·8 | 16·0 | 10·8 |
| 41 | 10 10·3 | 10 11·9 | 9 42·4 | 4·1 | 2·8 | 10·1 | 6·8 | 16·1 | 10·9 |
| 42 | 10 10·5 | 10 12·2 | 9 42·7 | 4·2 | 2·8 | 10·2 | 6·9 | 16·2 | 10·9 |
| 43 | 10 10·8 | 10 12·4 | 9 42·9 | 4·3 | 2·9 | 10·3 | 7·0 | 16·3 | 11·0 |
| 44 | 10 11·0 | 10 12·7 | 9 43·2 | 4·4 | 3·0 | 10·4 | 7·0 | 16·4 | 11·1 |
| 45 | 10 11·3 | 10 12·9 | 9 43·4 | 4·5 | 3·0 | 10·5 | 7·1 | 16·5 | 11·1 |
| 46 | 10 11·5 | 10 13·2 | 9 43·6 | 4·6 | 3·1 | 10·6 | 7·2 | 16·6 | 11·2 |
| 47 | 10 11·8 | 10 13·4 | 9 43·9 | 4·7 | 3·2 | 10·7 | 7·2 | 16·7 | 11·3 |
| 48 | 10 12·0 | 10 13·7 | 9 44·1 | 4·8 | 3·2 | 10·8 | 7·3 | 16·8 | 11·3 |
| 49 | 10 12·3 | 10 13·9 | 9 44·4 | 4·9 | 3·3 | 10·9 | 7·4 | 16·9 | 11·4 |
| 50 | 10 12·5 | 10 14·2 | 9 44·6 | 5·0 | 3·4 | 11·0 | 7·4 | 17·0 | 11·5 |
| 51 | 10 12·8 | 10 14·4 | 9 44·8 | 5·1 | 3·4 | 11·1 | 7·5 | 17·1 | 11·5 |
| 52 | 10 13·0 | 10 14·7 | 9 45·1 | 5·2 | 3·5 | 11·2 | 7·6 | 17·2 | 11·6 |
| 53 | 10 13·3 | 10 14·9 | 9 45·3 | 5·3 | 3·6 | 11·3 | 7·6 | 17·3 | 11·7 |
| 54 | 10 13·5 | 10 15·2 | 9 45·6 | 5·4 | 3·6 | 11·4 | 7·7 | 17·4 | 11·7 |
| 55 | 10 13·8 | 10 15·4 | 9 45·8 | 5·5 | 3·7 | 11·5 | 7·8 | 17·5 | 11·8 |
| 56 | 10 14·0 | 10 15·7 | 9 46·0 | 5·6 | 3·8 | 11·6 | 7·8 | 17·6 | 11·9 |
| 57 | 10 14·3 | 10 15·9 | 9 46·3 | 5·7 | 3·8 | 11·7 | 7·9 | 17·7 | 11·9 |
| 58 | 10 14·5 | 10 16·2 | 9 46·5 | 5·8 | 3·9 | 11·8 | 8·0 | 17·8 | 12·0 |
| 59 | 10 14·8 | 10 16·4 | 9 46·7 | 5·9 | 4·0 | 11·9 | 8·0 | 17·9 | 12·1 |
| 60 | 10 15·0 | 10 16·7 | 9 47·0 | 6·0 | 4·1 | 12·0 | 8·1 | 18·0 | 12·2 |

## 41^m

| 41 | SUN PLANETS | ARIES | MOON | v or d | Corr^n | v or d | Corr^n | v or d | Corr^n |
|---|---|---|---|---|---|---|---|---|---|
| s | ° ′ | ° ′ | ° ′ | ′ | ′ | ′ | ′ | ′ | ′ |
| 00 | 10 15·0 | 10 16·7 | 9 47·0 | 0·0 | 0·0 | 6·0 | 4·2 | 12·0 | 8·3 |
| 01 | 10 15·3 | 10 16·9 | 9 47·2 | 0·1 | 0·1 | 6·1 | 4·2 | 12·1 | 8·4 |
| 02 | 10 15·5 | 10 17·2 | 9 47·5 | 0·2 | 0·1 | 6·2 | 4·3 | 12·2 | 8·4 |
| 03 | 10 15·8 | 10 17·4 | 9 47·7 | 0·3 | 0·2 | 6·3 | 4·4 | 12·3 | 8·5 |
| 04 | 10 16·0 | 10 17·7 | 9 47·9 | 0·4 | 0·3 | 6·4 | 4·4 | 12·4 | 8·6 |
| 05 | 10 16·3 | 10 17·9 | 9 48·2 | 0·5 | 0·3 | 6·5 | 4·5 | 12·5 | 8·6 |
| 06 | 10 16·5 | 10 18·2 | 9 48·4 | 0·6 | 0·4 | 6·6 | 4·6 | 12·6 | 8·7 |
| 07 | 10 16·8 | 10 18·4 | 9 48·7 | 0·7 | 0·5 | 6·7 | 4·6 | 12·7 | 8·8 |
| 08 | 10 17·0 | 10 18·7 | 9 48·9 | 0·8 | 0·6 | 6·8 | 4·7 | 12·8 | 8·9 |
| 09 | 10 17·3 | 10 18·9 | 9 49·1 | 0·9 | 0·6 | 6·9 | 4·8 | 12·9 | 8·9 |
| 10 | 10 17·5 | 10 19·2 | 9 49·4 | 1·0 | 0·7 | 7·0 | 4·8 | 13·0 | 9·0 |
| 11 | 10 17·8 | 10 19·4 | 9 49·6 | 1·1 | 0·8 | 7·1 | 4·9 | 13·1 | 9·1 |
| 12 | 10 18·0 | 10 19·7 | 9 49·8 | 1·2 | 0·8 | 7·2 | 5·0 | 13·2 | 9·1 |
| 13 | 10 18·3 | 10 19·9 | 9 50·1 | 1·3 | 0·9 | 7·3 | 5·0 | 13·3 | 9·2 |
| 14 | 10 18·5 | 10 20·2 | 9 50·3 | 1·4 | 1·0 | 7·4 | 5·1 | 13·4 | 9·3 |
| 15 | 10 18·8 | 10 20·4 | 9 50·6 | 1·5 | 1·0 | 7·5 | 5·2 | 13·5 | 9·3 |
| 16 | 10 19·0 | 10 20·7 | 9 50·8 | 1·6 | 1·1 | 7·6 | 5·3 | 13·6 | 9·4 |
| 17 | 10 19·3 | 10 20·9 | 9 51·0 | 1·7 | 1·2 | 7·7 | 5·3 | 13·7 | 9·5 |
| 18 | 10 19·5 | 10 21·2 | 9 51·3 | 1·8 | 1·2 | 7·8 | 5·4 | 13·8 | 9·5 |
| 19 | 10 19·8 | 10 21·4 | 9 51·5 | 1·9 | 1·3 | 7·9 | 5·5 | 13·9 | 9·6 |
| 20 | 10 20·0 | 10 21·7 | 9 51·8 | 2·0 | 1·4 | 8·0 | 5·5 | 14·0 | 9·7 |
| 21 | 10 20·3 | 10 21·9 | 9 52·0 | 2·1 | 1·5 | 8·1 | 5·6 | 14·1 | 9·8 |
| 22 | 10 20·5 | 10 22·2 | 9 52·2 | 2·2 | 1·5 | 8·2 | 5·7 | 14·2 | 9·8 |
| 23 | 10 20·8 | 10 22·4 | 9 52·5 | 2·3 | 1·6 | 8·3 | 5·7 | 14·3 | 9·9 |
| 24 | 10 21·0 | 10 22·7 | 9 52·7 | 2·4 | 1·7 | 8·4 | 5·8 | 14·4 | 10·0 |
| 25 | 10 21·3 | 10 23·0 | 9 52·9 | 2·5 | 1·7 | 8·5 | 5·9 | 14·5 | 10·0 |
| 26 | 10 21·5 | 10 23·2 | 9 53·2 | 2·6 | 1·8 | 8·6 | 5·9 | 14·6 | 10·1 |
| 27 | 10 21·8 | 10 23·5 | 9 53·4 | 2·7 | 1·9 | 8·7 | 6·0 | 14·7 | 10·2 |
| 28 | 10 22·0 | 10 23·7 | 9 53·7 | 2·8 | 1·9 | 8·8 | 6·1 | 14·8 | 10·2 |
| 29 | 10 22·3 | 10 24·0 | 9 53·9 | 2·9 | 2·0 | 8·9 | 6·2 | 14·9 | 10·3 |
| 30 | 10 22·5 | 10 24·2 | 9 54·1 | 3·0 | 2·1 | 9·0 | 6·2 | 15·0 | 10·4 |
| 31 | 10 22·8 | 10 24·5 | 9 54·4 | 3·1 | 2·1 | 9·1 | 6·3 | 15·1 | 10·4 |
| 32 | 10 23·0 | 10 24·7 | 9 54·6 | 3·2 | 2·2 | 9·2 | 6·4 | 15·2 | 10·5 |
| 33 | 10 23·3 | 10 25·0 | 9 54·9 | 3·3 | 2·3 | 9·3 | 6·4 | 15·3 | 10·6 |
| 34 | 10 23·5 | 10 25·2 | 9 55·1 | 3·4 | 2·4 | 9·4 | 6·5 | 15·4 | 10·7 |
| 35 | 10 23·8 | 10 25·5 | 9 55·3 | 3·5 | 2·4 | 9·5 | 6·6 | 15·5 | 10·7 |
| 36 | 10 24·0 | 10 25·7 | 9 55·6 | 3·6 | 2·5 | 9·6 | 6·6 | 15·6 | 10·8 |
| 37 | 10 24·3 | 10 26·0 | 9 55·8 | 3·7 | 2·6 | 9·7 | 6·7 | 15·7 | 10·9 |
| 38 | 10 24·5 | 10 26·2 | 9 56·1 | 3·8 | 2·6 | 9·8 | 6·8 | 15·8 | 10·9 |
| 39 | 10 24·8 | 10 26·5 | 9 56·3 | 3·9 | 2·7 | 9·9 | 6·8 | 15·9 | 11·0 |
| 40 | 10 25·0 | 10 26·7 | 9 56·5 | 4·0 | 2·8 | 10·0 | 6·9 | 16·0 | 11·1 |
| 41 | 10 25·3 | 10 27·0 | 9 56·8 | 4·1 | 2·8 | 10·1 | 7·0 | 16·1 | 11·1 |
| 42 | 10 25·5 | 10 27·2 | 9 57·0 | 4·2 | 2·9 | 10·2 | 7·1 | 16·2 | 11·2 |
| 43 | 10 25·8 | 10 27·5 | 9 57·2 | 4·3 | 3·0 | 10·3 | 7·1 | 16·3 | 11·3 |
| 44 | 10 26·0 | 10 27·7 | 9 57·5 | 4·4 | 3·0 | 10·4 | 7·2 | 16·4 | 11·3 |
| 45 | 10 26·3 | 10 28·0 | 9 57·7 | 4·5 | 3·1 | 10·5 | 7·3 | 16·5 | 11·4 |
| 46 | 10 26·5 | 10 28·2 | 9 58·0 | 4·6 | 3·2 | 10·6 | 7·3 | 16·6 | 11·5 |
| 47 | 10 26·8 | 10 28·5 | 9 58·2 | 4·7 | 3·3 | 10·7 | 7·4 | 16·7 | 11·6 |
| 48 | 10 27·0 | 10 28·7 | 9 58·4 | 4·8 | 3·3 | 10·8 | 7·5 | 16·8 | 11·6 |
| 49 | 10 27·3 | 10 29·0 | 9 58·7 | 4·9 | 3·4 | 10·9 | 7·5 | 16·9 | 11·7 |
| 50 | 10 27·5 | 10 29·2 | 9 58·9 | 5·0 | 3·5 | 11·0 | 7·6 | 17·0 | 11·8 |
| 51 | 10 27·8 | 10 29·5 | 9 59·2 | 5·1 | 3·5 | 11·1 | 7·7 | 17·1 | 11·8 |
| 52 | 10 28·0 | 10 29·7 | 9 59·4 | 5·2 | 3·6 | 11·2 | 7·7 | 17·2 | 11·9 |
| 53 | 10 28·3 | 10 30·0 | 9 59·6 | 5·3 | 3·7 | 11·3 | 7·8 | 17·3 | 12·0 |
| 54 | 10 28·5 | 10 30·2 | 9 59·9 | 5·4 | 3·7 | 11·4 | 7·9 | 17·4 | 12·0 |
| 55 | 10 28·8 | 10 30·5 | 10 00·1 | 5·5 | 3·8 | 11·5 | 8·0 | 17·5 | 12·1 |
| 56 | 10 29·0 | 10 30·7 | 10 00·3 | 5·6 | 3·9 | 11·6 | 8·0 | 17·6 | 12·2 |
| 57 | 10 29·3 | 10 31·0 | 10 00·6 | 5·7 | 3·9 | 11·7 | 8·1 | 17·7 | 12·2 |
| 58 | 10 29·5 | 10 31·2 | 10 00·8 | 5·8 | 4·0 | 11·8 | 8·2 | 17·8 | 12·3 |
| 59 | 10 29·8 | 10 31·5 | 10 01·1 | 5·9 | 4·1 | 11·9 | 8·2 | 17·9 | 12·4 |
| 60 | 10 30·0 | 10 31·7 | 10 01·3 | 6·0 | 4·2 | 12·0 | 8·3 | 18·0 | 12·5 |

| 42<sup>m</sup> | SUN PLANETS | ARIES | MOON | v or d Corrⁿ | v or d Corrⁿ | v or d Corrⁿ | 43<sup>m</sup> | SUN PLANETS | ARIES | MOON | v or d Corrⁿ | v or d Corrⁿ | v or d Corrⁿ |
|---|---|---|---|---|---|---|---|---|---|---|---|---|---|
| s | ° ′ | ° ′ | ° ′ | ′ ′ | ′ ′ | ′ ′ | s | ° ′ | ° ′ | ° ′ | ′ ′ | ′ ′ | ′ ′ |
| 00 | 10 30·0 | 10 31·7 | 10 01·3 | 0·0 0·0 | 6·0 4·3 | 12·0 8·5 | 00 | 10 45·0 | 10 46·8 | 10 15·6 | 0·0 0·0 | 6·0 4·4 | 12·0 8·7 |
| 01 | 10 30·3 | 10 32·0 | 10 01·5 | 0·1 0·1 | 6·1 4·3 | 12·1 8·6 | 01 | 10 45·3 | 10 47·0 | 10 15·9 | 0·1 0·1 | 6·1 4·4 | 12·1 8·8 |
| 02 | 10 30·5 | 10 32·2 | 10 01·8 | 0·2 0·1 | 6·2 4·4 | 12·2 8·6 | 02 | 10 45·5 | 10 47·3 | 10 16·1 | 0·2 0·1 | 6·2 4·5 | 12·2 8·8 |
| 03 | 10 30·8 | 10 32·5 | 10 02·0 | 0·3 0·2 | 6·3 4·5 | 12·3 8·7 | 03 | 10 45·8 | 10 47·5 | 10 16·3 | 0·3 0·2 | 6·3 4·6 | 12·3 8·9 |
| 04 | 10 31·0 | 10 32·7 | 10 02·3 | 0·4 0·3 | 6·4 4·5 | 12·4 8·8 | 04 | 10 46·0 | 10 47·8 | 10 16·6 | 0·4 0·3 | 6·4 4·6 | 12·4 9·0 |
| 05 | 10 31·3 | 10 33·0 | 10 02·5 | 0·5 0·4 | 6·5 4·6 | 12·5 8·9 | 05 | 10 46·3 | 10 48·0 | 10 16·8 | 0·5 0·4 | 6·5 4·7 | 12·5 9·1 |
| 06 | 10 31·5 | 10 33·2 | 10 02·7 | 0·6 0·4 | 6·6 4·7 | 12·6 8·9 | 06 | 10 46·5 | 10 48·3 | 10 17·0 | 0·6 0·4 | 6·6 4·8 | 12·6 9·1 |
| 07 | 10 31·8 | 10 33·5 | 10 03·0 | 0·7 0·5 | 6·7 4·7 | 12·7 9·0 | 07 | 10 46·8 | 10 48·5 | 10 17·3 | 0·7 0·5 | 6·7 4·9 | 12·7 9·2 |
| 08 | 10 32·0 | 10 33·7 | 10 03·2 | 0·8 0·6 | 6·8 4·8 | 12·8 9·1 | 08 | 10 47·0 | 10 48·8 | 10 17·5 | 0·8 0·6 | 6·8 4·9 | 12·8 9·3 |
| 09 | 10 32·3 | 10 34·0 | 10 03·4 | 0·9 0·6 | 6·9 4·9 | 12·9 9·1 | 09 | 10 47·3 | 10 49·0 | 10 17·8 | 0·9 0·7 | 6·9 5·0 | 12·9 9·4 |
| 10 | 10 32·5 | 10 34·2 | 10 03·7 | 1·0 0·7 | 7·0 5·0 | 13·0 9·2 | 10 | 10 47·5 | 10 49·3 | 10 18·0 | 1·0 0·7 | 7·0 5·1 | 13·0 9·4 |
| 11 | 10 32·8 | 10 34·5 | 10 03·9 | 1·1 0·8 | 7·1 5·0 | 13·1 9·3 | 11 | 10 47·8 | 10 49·5 | 10 18·2 | 1·1 0·8 | 7·1 5·1 | 13·1 9·5 |
| 12 | 10 33·0 | 10 34·7 | 10 04·2 | 1·2 0·9 | 7·2 5·1 | 13·2 9·4 | 12 | 10 48·0 | 10 49·8 | 10 18·5 | 1·2 0·9 | 7·2 5·2 | 13·2 9·6 |
| 13 | 10 33·3 | 10 35·0 | 10 04·4 | 1·3 0·9 | 7·3 5·2 | 13·3 9·4 | 13 | 10 48·3 | 10 50·0 | 10 18·7 | 1·3 0·9 | 7·3 5·3 | 13·3 9·6 |
| 14 | 10 33·5 | 10 35·2 | 10 04·6 | 1·4 1·0 | 7·4 5·2 | 13·4 9·5 | 14 | 10 48·5 | 10 50·3 | 10 19·0 | 1·4 1·0 | 7·4 5·4 | 13·4 9·7 |
| 15 | 10 33·8 | 10 35·5 | 10 04·9 | 1·5 1·1 | 7·5 5·3 | 13·5 9·6 | 15 | 10 48·8 | 10 50·5 | 10 19·2 | 1·5 1·1 | 7·5 5·4 | 13·5 9·8 |
| 16 | 10 34·0 | 10 35·7 | 10 05·1 | 1·6 1·1 | 7·6 5·4 | 13·6 9·6 | 16 | 10 49·0 | 10 50·8 | 10 19·4 | 1·6 1·2 | 7·6 5·5 | 13·6 9·9 |
| 17 | 10 34·3 | 10 36·0 | 10 05·4 | 1·7 1·2 | 7·7 5·5 | 13·7 9·7 | 17 | 10 49·3 | 10 51·0 | 10 19·7 | 1·7 1·2 | 7·7 5·6 | 13·7 9·9 |
| 18 | 10 34·5 | 10 36·2 | 10 05·6 | 1·8 1·3 | 7·8 5·5 | 13·8 9·8 | 18 | 10 49·5 | 10 51·3 | 10 19·9 | 1·8 1·3 | 7·8 5·7 | 13·8 10·0 |
| 19 | 10 34·8 | 10 36·5 | 10 05·8 | 1·9 1·3 | 7·9 5·6 | 13·9 9·8 | 19 | 10 49·8 | 10 51·5 | 10 20·2 | 1·9 1·4 | 7·9 5·7 | 13·9 10·1 |
| 20 | 10 35·0 | 10 36·7 | 10 06·1 | 2·0 1·4 | 8·0 5·7 | 14·0 9·9 | 20 | 10 50·0 | 10 51·8 | 10 20·4 | 2·0 1·5 | 8·0 5·8 | 14·0 10·2 |
| 21 | 10 35·3 | 10 37·0 | 10 06·3 | 2·1 1·5 | 8·1 5·7 | 14·1 10·0 | 21 | 10 50·3 | 10 52·0 | 10 20·6 | 2·1 1·5 | 8·1 5·9 | 14·1 10·2 |
| 22 | 10 35·5 | 10 37·2 | 10 06·5 | 2·2 1·6 | 8·2 5·8 | 14·2 10·1 | 22 | 10 50·5 | 10 52·3 | 10 20·9 | 2·2 1·6 | 8·2 5·9 | 14·2 10·3 |
| 23 | 10 35·8 | 10 37·5 | 10 06·8 | 2·3 1·6 | 8·3 5·9 | 14·3 10·1 | 23 | 10 50·8 | 10 52·5 | 10 21·1 | 2·3 1·7 | 8·3 6·0 | 14·3 10·4 |
| 24 | 10 36·0 | 10 37·7 | 10 07·0 | 2·4 1·7 | 8·4 6·0 | 14·4 10·2 | 24 | 10 51·0 | 10 52·8 | 10 21·3 | 2·4 1·7 | 8·4 6·1 | 14·4 10·4 |
| 25 | 10 36·3 | 10 38·0 | 10 07·3 | 2·5 1·8 | 8·5 6·0 | 14·5 10·3 | 25 | 10 51·3 | 10 53·0 | 10 21·6 | 2·5 1·8 | 8·5 6·2 | 14·5 10·5 |
| 26 | 10 36·5 | 10 38·2 | 10 07·5 | 2·6 1·8 | 8·6 6·1 | 14·6 10·3 | 26 | 10 51·5 | 10 53·3 | 10 21·8 | 2·6 1·9 | 8·6 6·2 | 14·6 10·6 |
| 27 | 10 36·8 | 10 38·5 | 10 07·7 | 2·7 1·9 | 8·7 6·2 | 14·7 10·4 | 27 | 10 51·8 | 10 53·5 | 10 22·1 | 2·7 2·0 | 8·7 6·3 | 14·7 10·7 |
| 28 | 10 37·0 | 10 38·7 | 10 08·0 | 2·8 2·0 | 8·8 6·2 | 14·8 10·5 | 28 | 10 52·0 | 10 53·8 | 10 22·3 | 2·8 2·0 | 8·8 6·4 | 14·8 10·7 |
| 29 | 10 37·3 | 10 39·0 | 10 08·2 | 2·9 2·1 | 8·9 6·3 | 14·9 10·6 | 29 | 10 52·3 | 10 54·0 | 10 22·5 | 2·9 2·1 | 8·9 6·5 | 14·9 10·8 |
| 30 | 10 37·5 | 10 39·2 | 10 08·5 | 3·0 2·1 | 9·0 6·4 | 15·0 10·6 | 30 | 10 52·5 | 10 54·3 | 10 22·8 | 3·0 2·2 | 9·0 6·5 | 15·0 10·9 |
| 31 | 10 37·8 | 10 39·5 | 10 08·7 | 3·1 2·2 | 9·1 6·4 | 15·1 10·7 | 31 | 10 52·8 | 10 54·5 | 10 23·0 | 3·1 2·2 | 9·1 6·6 | 15·1 10·9 |
| 32 | 10 38·0 | 10 39·7 | 10 08·9 | 3·2 2·3 | 9·2 6·5 | 15·2 10·8 | 32 | 10 53·0 | 10 54·8 | 10 23·3 | 3·2 2·3 | 9·2 6·7 | 15·2 11·0 |
| 33 | 10 38·3 | 10 40·0 | 10 09·2 | 3·3 2·3 | 9·3 6·6 | 15·3 10·8 | 33 | 10 53·3 | 10 55·0 | 10 23·5 | 3·3 2·4 | 9·3 6·7 | 15·3 11·1 |
| 34 | 10 38·5 | 10 40·2 | 10 09·4 | 3·4 2·4 | 9·4 6·7 | 15·4 10·9 | 34 | 10 53·5 | 10 55·3 | 10 23·7 | 3·4 2·5 | 9·4 6·8 | 15·4 11·2 |
| 35 | 10 38·8 | 10 40·5 | 10 09·7 | 3·5 2·5 | 9·5 6·7 | 15·5 11·0 | 35 | 10 53·8 | 10 55·5 | 10 24·0 | 3·5 2·5 | 9·5 6·9 | 15·5 11·2 |
| 36 | 10 39·0 | 10 40·7 | 10 09·9 | 3·6 2·6 | 9·6 6·8 | 15·6 11·1 | 36 | 10 54·0 | 10 55·8 | 10 24·2 | 3·6 2·6 | 9·6 7·0 | 15·6 11·3 |
| 37 | 10 39·3 | 10 41·0 | 10 10·1 | 3·7 2·6 | 9·7 6·9 | 15·7 11·1 | 37 | 10 54·3 | 10 56·0 | 10 24·4 | 3·7 2·7 | 9·7 7·0 | 15·7 11·4 |
| 38 | 10 39·5 | 10 41·3 | 10 10·4 | 3·8 2·7 | 9·8 6·9 | 15·8 11·2 | 38 | 10 54·5 | 10 56·3 | 10 24·7 | 3·8 2·8 | 9·8 7·1 | 15·8 11·5 |
| 39 | 10 39·8 | 10 41·5 | 10 10·6 | 3·9 2·8 | 9·9 7·0 | 15·9 11·3 | 39 | 10 54·8 | 10 56·5 | 10 24·9 | 3·9 2·8 | 9·9 7·2 | 15·9 11·5 |
| 40 | 10 40·0 | 10 41·8 | 10 10·8 | 4·0 2·8 | 10·0 7·1 | 16·0 11·3 | 40 | 10 55·0 | 10 56·8 | 10 25·2 | 4·0 2·9 | 10·0 7·3 | 16·0 11·6 |
| 41 | 10 40·3 | 10 42·0 | 10 11·1 | 4·1 2·9 | 10·1 7·2 | 16·1 11·4 | 41 | 10 55·3 | 10 57·0 | 10 25·4 | 4·1 3·0 | 10·1 7·3 | 16·1 11·7 |
| 42 | 10 40·5 | 10 42·3 | 10 11·3 | 4·2 3·0 | 10·2 7·2 | 16·2 11·5 | 42 | 10 55·5 | 10 57·3 | 10 25·6 | 4·2 3·0 | 10·2 7·4 | 16·2 11·7 |
| 43 | 10 40·8 | 10 42·5 | 10 11·6 | 4·3 3·0 | 10·3 7·3 | 16·3 11·5 | 43 | 10 55·8 | 10 57·5 | 10 25·9 | 4·3 3·1 | 10·3 7·5 | 16·3 11·8 |
| 44 | 10 41·0 | 10 42·8 | 10 11·8 | 4·4 3·1 | 10·4 7·4 | 16·4 11·6 | 44 | 10 56·0 | 10 57·8 | 10 26·1 | 4·4 3·2 | 10·4 7·5 | 16·4 11·9 |
| 45 | 10 41·3 | 10 43·0 | 10 12·0 | 4·5 3·2 | 10·5 7·4 | 16·5 11·7 | 45 | 10 56·3 | 10 58·0 | 10 26·4 | 4·5 3·3 | 10·5 7·6 | 16·5 12·0 |
| 46 | 10 41·5 | 10 43·3 | 10 12·3 | 4·6 3·3 | 10·6 7·5 | 16·6 11·8 | 46 | 10 56·5 | 10 58·3 | 10 26·6 | 4·6 3·3 | 10·6 7·7 | 16·6 12·0 |
| 47 | 10 41·8 | 10 43·5 | 10 12·5 | 4·7 3·3 | 10·7 7·6 | 16·7 11·8 | 47 | 10 56·8 | 10 58·5 | 10 26·8 | 4·7 3·4 | 10·7 7·8 | 16·7 12·1 |
| 48 | 10 42·0 | 10 43·8 | 10 12·8 | 4·8 3·4 | 10·8 7·7 | 16·8 11·9 | 48 | 10 57·0 | 10 58·8 | 10 27·1 | 4·8 3·5 | 10·8 7·8 | 16·8 12·2 |
| 49 | 10 42·3 | 10 44·0 | 10 13·0 | 4·9 3·5 | 10·9 7·7 | 16·9 12·0 | 49 | 10 57·3 | 10 59·0 | 10 27·3 | 4·9 3·6 | 10·9 7·9 | 16·9 12·3 |
| 50 | 10 42·5 | 10 44·3 | 10 13·2 | 5·0 3·5 | 11·0 7·8 | 17·0 12·0 | 50 | 10 57·5 | 10 59·3 | 10 27·5 | 5·0 3·6 | 11·0 8·0 | 17·0 12·3 |
| 51 | 10 42·8 | 10 44·5 | 10 13·5 | 5·1 3·6 | 11·1 7·9 | 17·1 12·1 | 51 | 10 57·8 | 10 59·5 | 10 27·8 | 5·1 3·7 | 11·1 8·0 | 17·1 12·4 |
| 52 | 10 43·0 | 10 44·8 | 10 13·7 | 5·2 3·7 | 11·2 7·9 | 17·2 12·2 | 52 | 10 58·0 | 10 59·8 | 10 28·0 | 5·2 3·8 | 11·2 8·1 | 17·2 12·5 |
| 53 | 10 43·3 | 10 45·0 | 10 13·9 | 5·3 3·8 | 11·3 8·0 | 17·3 12·3 | 53 | 10 58·3 | 11 00·1 | 10 28·3 | 5·3 3·8 | 11·3 8·2 | 17·3 12·5 |
| 54 | 10 43·5 | 10 45·3 | 10 14·2 | 5·4 3·8 | 11·4 8·1 | 17·4 12·3 | 54 | 10 58·5 | 11 00·3 | 10 28·5 | 5·4 3·9 | 11·4 8·3 | 17·4 12·6 |
| 55 | 10 43·8 | 10 45·5 | 10 14·4 | 5·5 3·9 | 11·5 8·1 | 17·5 12·4 | 55 | 10 58·8 | 11 00·6 | 10 28·7 | 5·5 4·0 | 11·5 8·3 | 17·5 12·7 |
| 56 | 10 44·0 | 10 45·8 | 10 14·7 | 5·6 4·0 | 11·6 8·2 | 17·6 12·5 | 56 | 10 59·0 | 11 00·8 | 10 29·0 | 5·6 4·1 | 11·6 8·4 | 17·6 12·8 |
| 57 | 10 44·3 | 10 46·0 | 10 14·9 | 5·7 4·0 | 11·7 8·3 | 17·7 12·5 | 57 | 10 59·3 | 11 01·1 | 10 29·2 | 5·7 4·1 | 11·7 8·5 | 17·7 12·8 |
| 58 | 10 44·5 | 10 46·3 | 10 15·1 | 5·8 4·1 | 11·8 8·4 | 17·8 12·6 | 58 | 10 59·5 | 11 01·3 | 10 29·5 | 5·8 4·2 | 11·8 8·6 | 17·8 12·9 |
| 59 | 10 44·8 | 10 46·5 | 10 15·4 | 5·9 4·2 | 11·9 8·4 | 17·9 12·7 | 59 | 10 59·8 | 11 01·6 | 10 29·7 | 5·9 4·3 | 11·9 8·6 | 17·9 13·0 |
| 60 | 10 45·0 | 10 46·8 | 10 15·6 | 6·0 4·3 | 12·0 8·5 | 18·0 12·8 | 60 | 11 00·0 | 11 01·8 | 10 29·9 | 6·0 4·4 | 12·0 8·7 | 18·0 13·1 |

## 44ᵐ

| s | SUN PLANETS | ARIES | MOON | v or d | Corrn | v or d | Corrn | v or d | Corrn |
|---|---|---|---|---|---|---|---|---|---|
| 00 | 11 00·0 | 11 01·8 | 10 29·9 | 0·0 | 0·0 | 6·0 | 4·5 | 12·0 | 8·9 |
| 01 | 11 00·3 | 11 02·1 | 10 30·2 | 0·1 | 0·1 | 6·1 | 4·5 | 12·1 | 9·0 |
| 02 | 11 00·5 | 11 02·3 | 10 30·4 | 0·2 | 0·1 | 6·2 | 4·6 | 12·2 | 9·0 |
| 03 | 11 00·8 | 11 02·6 | 10 30·6 | 0·3 | 0·2 | 6·3 | 4·7 | 12·3 | 9·1 |
| 04 | 11 01·0 | 11 02·8 | 10 30·9 | 0·4 | 0·3 | 6·4 | 4·7 | 12·4 | 9·2 |
| 05 | 11 01·3 | 11 03·1 | 10 31·1 | 0·5 | 0·4 | 6·5 | 4·8 | 12·5 | 9·3 |
| 06 | 11 01·5 | 11 03·3 | 10 31·4 | 0·6 | 0·4 | 6·6 | 4·9 | 12·6 | 9·3 |
| 07 | 11 01·8 | 11 03·6 | 10 31·6 | 0·7 | 0·5 | 6·7 | 5·0 | 12·7 | 9·4 |
| 08 | 11 02·0 | 11 03·8 | 10 31·8 | 0·8 | 0·6 | 6·8 | 5·0 | 12·8 | 9·5 |
| 09 | 11 02·3 | 11 04·1 | 10 32·1 | 0·9 | 0·7 | 6·9 | 5·1 | 12·9 | 9·6 |
| 10 | 11 02·5 | 11 04·3 | 10 32·3 | 1·0 | 0·7 | 7·0 | 5·2 | 13·0 | 9·6 |
| 11 | 11 02·8 | 11 04·6 | 10 32·6 | 1·1 | 0·8 | 7·1 | 5·3 | 13·1 | 9·7 |
| 12 | 11 03·0 | 11 04·8 | 10 32·8 | 1·2 | 0·9 | 7·2 | 5·3 | 13·2 | 9·8 |
| 13 | 11 03·3 | 11 05·1 | 10 33·0 | 1·3 | 1·0 | 7·3 | 5·4 | 13·3 | 9·9 |
| 14 | 11 03·5 | 11 05·3 | 10 33·3 | 1·4 | 1·0 | 7·4 | 5·5 | 13·4 | 9·9 |
| 15 | 11 03·8 | 11 05·6 | 10 33·5 | 1·5 | 1·1 | 7·5 | 5·6 | 13·5 | 10·0 |
| 16 | 11 04·0 | 11 05·8 | 10 33·8 | 1·6 | 1·2 | 7·6 | 5·6 | 13·6 | 10·1 |
| 17 | 11 04·3 | 11 06·1 | 10 34·0 | 1·7 | 1·3 | 7·7 | 5·7 | 13·7 | 10·2 |
| 18 | 11 04·5 | 11 06·3 | 10 34·2 | 1·8 | 1·3 | 7·8 | 5·8 | 13·8 | 10·2 |
| 19 | 11 04·8 | 11 06·6 | 10 34·5 | 1·9 | 1·4 | 7·9 | 5·9 | 13·9 | 10·3 |
| 20 | 11 05·0 | 11 06·8 | 10 34·7 | 2·0 | 1·5 | 8·0 | 5·9 | 14·0 | 10·4 |
| 21 | 11 05·3 | 11 07·1 | 10 34·9 | 2·1 | 1·6 | 8·1 | 6·0 | 14·1 | 10·5 |
| 22 | 11 05·5 | 11 07·3 | 10 35·2 | 2·2 | 1·6 | 8·2 | 6·1 | 14·2 | 10·5 |
| 23 | 11 05·8 | 11 07·6 | 10 35·4 | 2·3 | 1·7 | 8·3 | 6·2 | 14·3 | 10·6 |
| 24 | 11 06·0 | 11 07·8 | 10 35·7 | 2·4 | 1·8 | 8·4 | 6·2 | 14·4 | 10·7 |
| 25 | 11 06·3 | 11 08·1 | 10 35·9 | 2·5 | 1·9 | 8·5 | 6·3 | 14·5 | 10·8 |
| 26 | 11 06·5 | 11 08·3 | 10 36·1 | 2·6 | 1·9 | 8·6 | 6·4 | 14·6 | 10·8 |
| 27 | 11 06·8 | 11 08·6 | 10 36·4 | 2·7 | 2·0 | 8·7 | 6·5 | 14·7 | 10·9 |
| 28 | 11 07·0 | 11 08·8 | 10 36·6 | 2·8 | 2·1 | 8·8 | 6·5 | 14·8 | 11·0 |
| 29 | 11 07·3 | 11 09·1 | 10 36·9 | 2·9 | 2·2 | 8·9 | 6·6 | 14·9 | 11·1 |
| 30 | 11 07·5 | 11 09·3 | 10 37·1 | 3·0 | 2·2 | 9·0 | 6·7 | 15·0 | 11·1 |
| 31 | 11 07·8 | 11 09·6 | 10 37·3 | 3·1 | 2·3 | 9·1 | 6·7 | 15·1 | 11·2 |
| 32 | 11 08·0 | 11 09·8 | 10 37·6 | 3·2 | 2·4 | 9·2 | 6·8 | 15·2 | 11·3 |
| 33 | 11 08·3 | 11 10·1 | 10 37·8 | 3·3 | 2·4 | 9·3 | 6·9 | 15·3 | 11·3 |
| 34 | 11 08·5 | 11 10·3 | 10 38·0 | 3·4 | 2·5 | 9·4 | 7·0 | 15·4 | 11·4 |
| 35 | 11 08·8 | 11 10·6 | 10 38·3 | 3·5 | 2·6 | 9·5 | 7·0 | 15·5 | 11·5 |
| 36 | 11 09·0 | 11 10·8 | 10 38·5 | 3·6 | 2·7 | 9·6 | 7·1 | 15·6 | 11·6 |
| 37 | 11 09·3 | 11 11·1 | 10 38·8 | 3·7 | 2·7 | 9·7 | 7·2 | 15·7 | 11·6 |
| 38 | 11 09·5 | 11 11·3 | 10 39·0 | 3·8 | 2·8 | 9·8 | 7·3 | 15·8 | 11·7 |
| 39 | 11 09·8 | 11 11·6 | 10 39·2 | 3·9 | 2·9 | 9·9 | 7·3 | 15·9 | 11·8 |
| 40 | 11 10·0 | 11 11·8 | 10 39·5 | 4·0 | 3·0 | 10·0 | 7·4 | 16·0 | 11·9 |
| 41 | 11 10·3 | 11 12·1 | 10 39·7 | 4·1 | 3·0 | 10·1 | 7·5 | 16·1 | 11·9 |
| 42 | 11 10·5 | 11 12·3 | 10 40·0 | 4·2 | 3·1 | 10·2 | 7·6 | 16·2 | 12·0 |
| 43 | 11 10·8 | 11 12·6 | 10 40·2 | 4·3 | 3·2 | 10·3 | 7·6 | 16·3 | 12·1 |
| 44 | 11 11·0 | 11 12·8 | 10 40·4 | 4·4 | 3·3 | 10·4 | 7·7 | 16·4 | 12·2 |
| 45 | 11 11·3 | 11 13·1 | 10 40·7 | 4·5 | 3·3 | 10·5 | 7·8 | 16·5 | 12·2 |
| 46 | 11 11·5 | 11 13·3 | 10 40·9 | 4·6 | 3·4 | 10·6 | 7·9 | 16·6 | 12·3 |
| 47 | 11 11·8 | 11 13·6 | 10 41·1 | 4·7 | 3·5 | 10·7 | 7·9 | 16·7 | 12·4 |
| 48 | 11 12·0 | 11 13·8 | 10 41·4 | 4·8 | 3·6 | 10·8 | 8·0 | 16·8 | 12·5 |
| 49 | 11 12·3 | 11 14·1 | 10 41·6 | 4·9 | 3·6 | 10·9 | 8·1 | 16·9 | 12·5 |
| 50 | 11 12·5 | 11 14·3 | 10 41·9 | 5·0 | 3·7 | 11·0 | 8·2 | 17·0 | 12·6 |
| 51 | 11 12·8 | 11 14·6 | 10 42·1 | 5·1 | 3·8 | 11·1 | 8·2 | 17·1 | 12·7 |
| 52 | 11 13·0 | 11 14·8 | 10 42·3 | 5·2 | 3·9 | 11·2 | 8·3 | 17·2 | 12·8 |
| 53 | 11 13·3 | 11 15·1 | 10 42·6 | 5·3 | 3·9 | 11·3 | 8·4 | 17·3 | 12·8 |
| 54 | 11 13·5 | 11 15·3 | 10 42·8 | 5·4 | 4·0 | 11·4 | 8·5 | 17·4 | 12·9 |
| 55 | 11 13·8 | 11 15·6 | 10 43·1 | 5·5 | 4·1 | 11·5 | 8·5 | 17·5 | 13·0 |
| 56 | 11 14·0 | 11 15·8 | 10 43·3 | 5·6 | 4·1 | 11·6 | 8·6 | 17·6 | 13·1 |
| 57 | 11 14·3 | 11 16·1 | 10 43·5 | 5·7 | 4·2 | 11·7 | 8·7 | 17·7 | 13·1 |
| 58 | 11 14·5 | 11 16·3 | 10 43·8 | 5·8 | 4·3 | 11·8 | 8·8 | 17·8 | 13·2 |
| 59 | 11 14·8 | 11 16·6 | 10 44·0 | 5·9 | 4·4 | 11·9 | 8·8 | 17·9 | 13·3 |
| 60 | 11 15·0 | 11 16·8 | 10 44·3 | 6·0 | 4·5 | 12·0 | 8·9 | 18·0 | 13·4 |

## 45ᵐ

| s | SUN PLANETS | ARIES | MOON | v or d | Corrn | v or d | Corrn | v or d | Corrn |
|---|---|---|---|---|---|---|---|---|---|
| 00 | 11 15·0 | 11 16·8 | 10 44·3 | 0·0 | 0·0 | 6·0 | 4·6 | 12·0 | 9·1 |
| 01 | 11 15·3 | 11 17·1 | 10 44·5 | 0·1 | 0·1 | 6·1 | 4·6 | 12·1 | 9·2 |
| 02 | 11 15·5 | 11 17·3 | 10 44·7 | 0·2 | 0·2 | 6·2 | 4·7 | 12·2 | 9·3 |
| 03 | 11 15·8 | 11 17·6 | 10 45·0 | 0·3 | 0·2 | 6·3 | 4·8 | 12·3 | 9·3 |
| 04 | 11 16·0 | 11 17·9 | 10 45·2 | 0·4 | 0·3 | 6·4 | 4·9 | 12·4 | 9·4 |
| 05 | 11 16·3 | 11 18·1 | 10 45·5 | 0·5 | 0·4 | 6·5 | 4·9 | 12·5 | 9·5 |
| 06 | 11 16·5 | 11 18·4 | 10 45·7 | 0·6 | 0·5 | 6·6 | 5·0 | 12·6 | 9·6 |
| 07 | 11 16·8 | 11 18·6 | 10 45·9 | 0·7 | 0·5 | 6·7 | 5·1 | 12·7 | 9·6 |
| 08 | 11 17·0 | 11 18·9 | 10 46·2 | 0·8 | 0·6 | 6·8 | 5·2 | 12·8 | 9·7 |
| 09 | 11 17·3 | 11 19·1 | 10 46·4 | 0·9 | 0·7 | 6·9 | 5·2 | 12·9 | 9·8 |
| 10 | 11 17·5 | 11 19·4 | 10 46·6 | 1·0 | 0·8 | 7·0 | 5·3 | 13·0 | 9·9 |
| 11 | 11 17·8 | 11 19·6 | 10 46·9 | 1·1 | 0·8 | 7·1 | 5·4 | 13·1 | 9·9 |
| 12 | 11 18·0 | 11 19·9 | 10 47·1 | 1·2 | 0·9 | 7·2 | 5·5 | 13·2 | 10·0 |
| 13 | 11 18·3 | 11 20·1 | 10 47·4 | 1·3 | 1·0 | 7·3 | 5·5 | 13·3 | 10·1 |
| 14 | 11 18·5 | 11 20·4 | 10 47·6 | 1·4 | 1·1 | 7·4 | 5·6 | 13·4 | 10·2 |
| 15 | 11 18·8 | 11 20·6 | 10 47·8 | 1·5 | 1·1 | 7·5 | 5·7 | 13·5 | 10·2 |
| 16 | 11 19·0 | 11 20·9 | 10 48·1 | 1·6 | 1·2 | 7·6 | 5·8 | 13·6 | 10·3 |
| 17 | 11 19·3 | 11 21·1 | 10 48·3 | 1·7 | 1·3 | 7·7 | 5·8 | 13·7 | 10·4 |
| 18 | 11 19·5 | 11 21·4 | 10 48·5 | 1·8 | 1·4 | 7·8 | 5·9 | 13·8 | 10·5 |
| 19 | 11 19·8 | 11 21·6 | 10 48·8 | 1·9 | 1·4 | 7·9 | 6·0 | 13·9 | 10·5 |
| 20 | 11 20·0 | 11 21·9 | 10 49·0 | 2·0 | 1·5 | 8·0 | 6·1 | 14·0 | 10·6 |
| 21 | 11 20·3 | 11 22·1 | 10 49·3 | 2·1 | 1·6 | 8·1 | 6·1 | 14·1 | 10·7 |
| 22 | 11 20·5 | 11 22·4 | 10 49·5 | 2·2 | 1·7 | 8·2 | 6·2 | 14·2 | 10·8 |
| 23 | 11 20·8 | 11 22·6 | 10 49·7 | 2·3 | 1·7 | 8·3 | 6·3 | 14·3 | 10·8 |
| 24 | 11 21·0 | 11 22·9 | 10 50·0 | 2·4 | 1·8 | 8·4 | 6·4 | 14·4 | 10·9 |
| 25 | 11 21·3 | 11 23·1 | 10 50·2 | 2·5 | 1·9 | 8·5 | 6·4 | 14·5 | 11·0 |
| 26 | 11 21·5 | 11 23·4 | 10 50·5 | 2·6 | 2·0 | 8·6 | 6·5 | 14·6 | 11·1 |
| 27 | 11 21·8 | 11 23·6 | 10 50·7 | 2·7 | 2·0 | 8·7 | 6·6 | 14·7 | 11·1 |
| 28 | 11 22·0 | 11 23·9 | 10 50·9 | 2·8 | 2·1 | 8·8 | 6·7 | 14·8 | 11·2 |
| 29 | 11 22·3 | 11 24·1 | 10 51·2 | 2·9 | 2·2 | 8·9 | 6·7 | 14·9 | 11·3 |
| 30 | 11 22·5 | 11 24·4 | 10 51·4 | 3·0 | 2·3 | 9·0 | 6·8 | 15·0 | 11·4 |
| 31 | 11 22·8 | 11 24·6 | 10 51·6 | 3·1 | 2·4 | 9·1 | 6·9 | 15·1 | 11·5 |
| 32 | 11 23·0 | 11 24·9 | 10 51·9 | 3·2 | 2·4 | 9·2 | 7·0 | 15·2 | 11·5 |
| 33 | 11 23·3 | 11 25·1 | 10 52·1 | 3·3 | 2·5 | 9·3 | 7·1 | 15·3 | 11·6 |
| 34 | 11 23·5 | 11 25·4 | 10 52·4 | 3·4 | 2·6 | 9·4 | 7·1 | 15·4 | 11·7 |
| 35 | 11 23·8 | 11 25·6 | 10 52·6 | 3·5 | 2·7 | 9·5 | 7·2 | 15·5 | 11·8 |
| 36 | 11 24·0 | 11 25·9 | 10 52·8 | 3·6 | 2·7 | 9·6 | 7·3 | 15·6 | 11·8 |
| 37 | 11 24·3 | 11 26·1 | 10 53·1 | 3·7 | 2·8 | 9·7 | 7·4 | 15·7 | 11·9 |
| 38 | 11 24·5 | 11 26·4 | 10 53·3 | 3·8 | 2·9 | 9·8 | 7·4 | 15·8 | 12·0 |
| 39 | 11 24·8 | 11 26·6 | 10 53·6 | 3·9 | 3·0 | 9·9 | 7·5 | 15·9 | 12·1 |
| 40 | 11 25·0 | 11 26·9 | 10 53·8 | 4·0 | 3·0 | 10·0 | 7·6 | 16·0 | 12·1 |
| 41 | 11 25·3 | 11 27·1 | 10 54·0 | 4·1 | 3·1 | 10·1 | 7·7 | 16·1 | 12·2 |
| 42 | 11 25·5 | 11 27·4 | 10 54·3 | 4·2 | 3·2 | 10·2 | 7·7 | 16·2 | 12·3 |
| 43 | 11 25·8 | 11 27·6 | 10 54·5 | 4·3 | 3·3 | 10·3 | 7·8 | 16·3 | 12·4 |
| 44 | 11 26·0 | 11 27·9 | 10 54·7 | 4·4 | 3·3 | 10·4 | 7·9 | 16·4 | 12·4 |
| 45 | 11 26·3 | 11 28·1 | 10 55·0 | 4·5 | 3·4 | 10·5 | 8·0 | 16·5 | 12·5 |
| 46 | 11 26·5 | 11 28·4 | 10 55·2 | 4·6 | 3·5 | 10·6 | 8·0 | 16·6 | 12·6 |
| 47 | 11 26·8 | 11 28·6 | 10 55·5 | 4·7 | 3·6 | 10·7 | 8·1 | 16·7 | 12·7 |
| 48 | 11 27·0 | 11 28·9 | 10 55·7 | 4·8 | 3·6 | 10·8 | 8·2 | 16·8 | 12·7 |
| 49 | 11 27·3 | 11 29·1 | 10 55·9 | 4·9 | 3·7 | 10·9 | 8·3 | 16·9 | 12·8 |
| 50 | 11 27·5 | 11 29·4 | 10 56·2 | 5·0 | 3·8 | 11·0 | 8·3 | 17·0 | 12·9 |
| 51 | 11 27·8 | 11 29·6 | 10 56·4 | 5·1 | 3·9 | 11·1 | 8·4 | 17·1 | 13·0 |
| 52 | 11 28·0 | 11 29·9 | 10 56·7 | 5·2 | 3·9 | 11·2 | 8·5 | 17·2 | 13·0 |
| 53 | 11 28·3 | 11 30·1 | 10 56·9 | 5·3 | 4·0 | 11·3 | 8·6 | 17·3 | 13·1 |
| 54 | 11 28·5 | 11 30·4 | 10 57·1 | 5·4 | 4·1 | 11·4 | 8·6 | 17·4 | 13·2 |
| 55 | 11 28·8 | 11 30·6 | 10 57·4 | 5·5 | 4·2 | 11·5 | 8·7 | 17·5 | 13·3 |
| 56 | 11 29·0 | 11 30·9 | 10 57·6 | 5·6 | 4·2 | 11·6 | 8·8 | 17·6 | 13·3 |
| 57 | 11 29·3 | 11 31·1 | 10 57·9 | 5·7 | 4·3 | 11·7 | 8·8 | 17·7 | 13·4 |
| 58 | 11 29·5 | 11 31·4 | 10 58·1 | 5·8 | 4·4 | 11·8 | 8·9 | 17·8 | 13·5 |
| 59 | 11 29·8 | 11 31·6 | 10 58·3 | 5·9 | 4·5 | 11·9 | 9·0 | 17·9 | 13·6 |
| 60 | 11 30·0 | 11 31·9 | 10 58·6 | 6·0 | 4·6 | 12·0 | 9·1 | 18·0 | 13·7 |

## 46ᵐ

| 46ᵐ s | SUN PLANETS ° ′ | ARIES ° ′ | MOON ° ′ | v or d ′ | Corrⁿ ′ | v or d ′ | Corrⁿ ′ | v or d ′ | Corrⁿ ′ |
|---|---|---|---|---|---|---|---|---|---|
| 00 | 11 30·0 | 11 31·9 | 10 58·6 | 0·0 | 0·0 | 6·0 | 4·7 | 12·0 | 9·3 |
| 01 | 11 30·3 | 11 32·1 | 10 58·8 | 0·1 | 0·1 | 6·1 | 4·7 | 12·1 | 9·4 |
| 02 | 11 30·5 | 11 32·4 | 10 59·0 | 0·2 | 0·2 | 6·2 | 4·8 | 12·2 | 9·5 |
| 03 | 11 30·8 | 11 32·6 | 10 59·3 | 0·3 | 0·2 | 6·3 | 4·9 | 12·3 | 9·5 |
| 04 | 11 31·0 | 11 32·9 | 10 59·5 | 0·4 | 0·3 | 6·4 | 5·0 | 12·4 | 9·6 |
| 05 | 11 31·3 | 11 33·1 | 10 59·8 | 0·5 | 0·4 | 6·5 | 5·0 | 12·5 | 9·7 |
| 06 | 11 31·5 | 11 33·4 | 11 00·0 | 0·6 | 0·5 | 6·6 | 5·1 | 12·6 | 9·8 |
| 07 | 11 31·8 | 11 33·6 | 11 00·2 | 0·7 | 0·5 | 6·7 | 5·2 | 12·7 | 9·8 |
| 08 | 11 32·0 | 11 33·9 | 11 00·5 | 0·8 | 0·6 | 6·8 | 5·3 | 12·8 | 9·9 |
| 09 | 11 32·3 | 11 34·1 | 11 00·7 | 0·9 | 0·7 | 6·9 | 5·3 | 12·9 | 10·0 |
| 10 | 11 32·5 | 11 34·4 | 11 01·0 | 1·0 | 0·8 | 7·0 | 5·4 | 13·0 | 10·1 |
| 11 | 11 32·8 | 11 34·6 | 11 01·2 | 1·1 | 0·9 | 7·1 | 5·5 | 13·1 | 10·2 |
| 12 | 11 33·0 | 11 34·9 | 11 01·4 | 1·2 | 0·9 | 7·2 | 5·6 | 13·2 | 10·2 |
| 13 | 11 33·3 | 11 35·1 | 11 01·7 | 1·3 | 1·0 | 7·3 | 5·7 | 13·3 | 10·3 |
| 14 | 11 33·5 | 11 35·4 | 11 01·9 | 1·4 | 1·1 | 7·4 | 5·7 | 13·4 | 10·4 |
| 15 | 11 33·8 | 11 35·6 | 11 02·1 | 1·5 | 1·2 | 7·5 | 5·8 | 13·5 | 10·5 |
| 16 | 11 34·0 | 11 35·9 | 11 02·4 | 1·6 | 1·2 | 7·6 | 5·9 | 13·6 | 10·5 |
| 17 | 11 34·3 | 11 36·2 | 11 02·6 | 1·7 | 1·3 | 7·7 | 6·0 | 13·7 | 10·6 |
| 18 | 11 34·5 | 11 36·4 | 11 02·9 | 1·8 | 1·4 | 7·8 | 6·0 | 13·8 | 10·7 |
| 19 | 11 34·8 | 11 36·7 | 11 03·1 | 1·9 | 1·5 | 7·9 | 6·1 | 13·9 | 10·8 |
| 20 | 11 35·0 | 11 36·9 | 11 03·3 | 2·0 | 1·6 | 8·0 | 6·2 | 14·0 | 10·9 |
| 21 | 11 35·3 | 11 37·2 | 11 03·6 | 2·1 | 1·6 | 8·1 | 6·3 | 14·1 | 10·9 |
| 22 | 11 35·5 | 11 37·4 | 11 03·8 | 2·2 | 1·7 | 8·2 | 6·4 | 14·2 | 11·0 |
| 23 | 11 35·8 | 11 37·7 | 11 04·1 | 2·3 | 1·8 | 8·3 | 6·4 | 14·3 | 11·1 |
| 24 | 11 36·0 | 11 37·9 | 11 04·3 | 2·4 | 1·9 | 8·4 | 6·5 | 14·4 | 11·2 |
| 25 | 11 36·3 | 11 38·2 | 11 04·5 | 2·5 | 1·9 | 8·5 | 6·6 | 14·5 | 11·2 |
| 26 | 11 36·5 | 11 38·4 | 11 04·8 | 2·6 | 2·0 | 8·6 | 6·7 | 14·6 | 11·3 |
| 27 | 11 36·8 | 11 38·7 | 11 05·0 | 2·7 | 2·1 | 8·7 | 6·7 | 14·7 | 11·4 |
| 28 | 11 37·0 | 11 38·9 | 11 05·2 | 2·8 | 2·2 | 8·8 | 6·8 | 14·8 | 11·5 |
| 29 | 11 37·3 | 11 39·2 | 11 05·5 | 2·9 | 2·2 | 8·9 | 6·9 | 14·9 | 11·5 |
| 30 | 11 37·5 | 11 39·4 | 11 05·7 | 3·0 | 2·3 | 9·0 | 7·0 | 15·0 | 11·6 |
| 31 | 11 37·8 | 11 39·7 | 11 06·0 | 3·1 | 2·4 | 9·1 | 7·1 | 15·1 | 11·7 |
| 32 | 11 38·0 | 11 39·9 | 11 06·2 | 3·2 | 2·5 | 9·2 | 7·1 | 15·2 | 11·8 |
| 33 | 11 38·3 | 11 40·2 | 11 06·4 | 3·3 | 2·6 | 9·3 | 7·2 | 15·3 | 11·9 |
| 34 | 11 38·5 | 11 40·4 | 11 06·7 | 3·4 | 2·6 | 9·4 | 7·3 | 15·4 | 11·9 |
| 35 | 11 38·8 | 11 40·7 | 11 06·9 | 3·5 | 2·7 | 9·5 | 7·4 | 15·5 | 12·0 |
| 36 | 11 39·0 | 11 40·9 | 11 07·2 | 3·6 | 2·8 | 9·6 | 7·4 | 15·6 | 12·1 |
| 37 | 11 39·3 | 11 41·2 | 11 07·4 | 3·7 | 2·9 | 9·7 | 7·5 | 15·7 | 12·2 |
| 38 | 11 39·5 | 11 41·4 | 11 07·6 | 3·8 | 2·9 | 9·8 | 7·6 | 15·8 | 12·2 |
| 39 | 11 39·8 | 11 41·7 | 11 07·9 | 3·9 | 3·0 | 9·9 | 7·7 | 15·9 | 12·3 |
| 40 | 11 40·0 | 11 41·9 | 11 08·1 | 4·0 | 3·1 | 10·0 | 7·8 | 16·0 | 12·4 |
| 41 | 11 40·3 | 11 42·2 | 11 08·3 | 4·1 | 3·2 | 10·1 | 7·8 | 16·1 | 12·5 |
| 42 | 11 40·5 | 11 42·4 | 11 08·6 | 4·2 | 3·3 | 10·2 | 7·9 | 16·2 | 12·6 |
| 43 | 11 40·8 | 11 42·7 | 11 08·8 | 4·3 | 3·3 | 10·3 | 8·0 | 16·3 | 12·6 |
| 44 | 11 41·0 | 11 42·9 | 11 09·1 | 4·4 | 3·4 | 10·4 | 8·1 | 16·4 | 12·7 |
| 45 | 11 41·3 | 11 43·2 | 11 09·3 | 4·5 | 3·5 | 10·5 | 8·1 | 16·5 | 12·8 |
| 46 | 11 41·5 | 11 43·4 | 11 09·5 | 4·6 | 3·6 | 10·6 | 8·2 | 16·6 | 12·9 |
| 47 | 11 41·8 | 11 43·7 | 11 09·8 | 4·7 | 3·6 | 10·7 | 8·3 | 16·7 | 12·9 |
| 48 | 11 42·0 | 11 43·9 | 11 10·0 | 4·8 | 3·7 | 10·8 | 8·4 | 16·8 | 13·0 |
| 49 | 11 42·3 | 11 44·2 | 11 10·3 | 4·9 | 3·8 | 10·9 | 8·4 | 16·9 | 13·1 |
| 50 | 11 42·5 | 11 44·4 | 11 10·5 | 5·0 | 3·9 | 11·0 | 8·5 | 17·0 | 13·2 |
| 51 | 11 42·8 | 11 44·7 | 11 10·7 | 5·1 | 4·0 | 11·1 | 8·6 | 17·1 | 13·3 |
| 52 | 11 43·0 | 11 44·9 | 11 11·0 | 5·2 | 4·0 | 11·2 | 8·7 | 17·2 | 13·3 |
| 53 | 11 43·3 | 11 45·2 | 11 11·2 | 5·3 | 4·1 | 11·3 | 8·8 | 17·3 | 13·4 |
| 54 | 11 43·5 | 11 45·4 | 11 11·5 | 5·4 | 4·2 | 11·4 | 8·8 | 17·4 | 13·5 |
| 55 | 11 43·8 | 11 45·7 | 11 11·7 | 5·5 | 4·3 | 11·5 | 8·9 | 17·5 | 13·6 |
| 56 | 11 44·0 | 11 45·9 | 11 11·9 | 5·6 | 4·3 | 11·6 | 9·0 | 17·6 | 13·6 |
| 57 | 11 44·3 | 11 46·2 | 11 12·2 | 5·7 | 4·4 | 11·7 | 9·1 | 17·7 | 13·7 |
| 58 | 11 44·5 | 11 46·4 | 11 12·4 | 5·8 | 4·5 | 11·8 | 9·1 | 17·8 | 13·8 |
| 59 | 11 44·8 | 11 46·7 | 11 12·6 | 5·9 | 4·6 | 11·9 | 9·2 | 17·9 | 13·9 |
| 60 | 11 45·0 | 11 46·9 | 11 12·9 | 6·0 | 4·7 | 12·0 | 9·3 | 18·0 | 14·0 |

## 47ᵐ

| 47ᵐ s | SUN PLANETS ° ′ | ARIES ° ′ | MOON ° ′ | v or d ′ | Corrⁿ ′ | v or d ′ | Corrⁿ ′ | v or d ′ | Corrⁿ ′ |
|---|---|---|---|---|---|---|---|---|---|
| 00 | 11 45·0 | 11 46·9 | 11 12·9 | 0·0 | 0·0 | 6·0 | 4·8 | 12·0 | 9·5 |
| 01 | 11 45·3 | 11 47·2 | 11 13·1 | 0·1 | 0·1 | 6·1 | 4·8 | 12·1 | 9·6 |
| 02 | 11 45·5 | 11 47·4 | 11 13·4 | 0·2 | 0·2 | 6·2 | 4·9 | 12·2 | 9·7 |
| 03 | 11 45·8 | 11 47·7 | 11 13·6 | 0·3 | 0·2 | 6·3 | 5·0 | 12·3 | 9·7 |
| 04 | 11 46·0 | 11 47·9 | 11 13·8 | 0·4 | 0·3 | 6·4 | 5·1 | 12·4 | 9·8 |
| 05 | 11 46·3 | 11 48·2 | 11 14·1 | 0·5 | 0·4 | 6·5 | 5·1 | 12·5 | 9·9 |
| 06 | 11 46·5 | 11 48·4 | 11 14·3 | 0·6 | 0·5 | 6·6 | 5·2 | 12·6 | 10·0 |
| 07 | 11 46·8 | 11 48·7 | 11 14·6 | 0·7 | 0·6 | 6·7 | 5·3 | 12·7 | 10·1 |
| 08 | 11 47·0 | 11 48·9 | 11 14·8 | 0·8 | 0·6 | 6·8 | 5·4 | 12·8 | 10·1 |
| 09 | 11 47·3 | 11 49·2 | 11 15·0 | 0·9 | 0·7 | 6·9 | 5·5 | 12·9 | 10·2 |
| 10 | 11 47·5 | 11 49·4 | 11 15·3 | 1·0 | 0·8 | 7·0 | 5·5 | 13·0 | 10·3 |
| 11 | 11 47·8 | 11 49·7 | 11 15·5 | 1·1 | 0·9 | 7·1 | 5·6 | 13·1 | 10·4 |
| 12 | 11 48·0 | 11 49·9 | 11 15·7 | 1·2 | 1·0 | 7·2 | 5·7 | 13·2 | 10·5 |
| 13 | 11 48·3 | 11 50·2 | 11 16·0 | 1·3 | 1·0 | 7·3 | 5·8 | 13·3 | 10·5 |
| 14 | 11 48·5 | 11 50·4 | 11 16·2 | 1·4 | 1·1 | 7·4 | 5·9 | 13·4 | 10·6 |
| 15 | 11 48·8 | 11 50·7 | 11 16·5 | 1·5 | 1·2 | 7·5 | 5·9 | 13·5 | 10·7 |
| 16 | 11 49·0 | 11 50·9 | 11 16·7 | 1·6 | 1·3 | 7·6 | 6·0 | 13·6 | 10·8 |
| 17 | 11 49·3 | 11 51·2 | 11 16·9 | 1·7 | 1·3 | 7·7 | 6·1 | 13·7 | 10·8 |
| 18 | 11 49·5 | 11 51·4 | 11 17·2 | 1·8 | 1·4 | 7·8 | 6·2 | 13·8 | 10·9 |
| 19 | 11 49·8 | 11 51·7 | 11 17·4 | 1·9 | 1·5 | 7·9 | 6·3 | 13·9 | 11·0 |
| 20 | 11 50·0 | 11 51·9 | 11 17·7 | 2·0 | 1·6 | 8·0 | 6·3 | 14·0 | 11·1 |
| 21 | 11 50·3 | 11 52·2 | 11 17·9 | 2·1 | 1·7 | 8·1 | 6·4 | 14·1 | 11·2 |
| 22 | 11 50·5 | 11 52·4 | 11 18·1 | 2·2 | 1·7 | 8·2 | 6·5 | 14·2 | 11·2 |
| 23 | 11 50·8 | 11 52·7 | 11 18·4 | 2·3 | 1·8 | 8·3 | 6·6 | 14·3 | 11·3 |
| 24 | 11 51·0 | 11 52·9 | 11 18·6 | 2·4 | 1·9 | 8·4 | 6·7 | 14·4 | 11·4 |
| 25 | 11 51·3 | 11 53·2 | 11 18·8 | 2·5 | 2·0 | 8·5 | 6·7 | 14·5 | 11·5 |
| 26 | 11 51·5 | 11 53·4 | 11 19·1 | 2·6 | 2·1 | 8·6 | 6·8 | 14·6 | 11·6 |
| 27 | 11 51·8 | 11 53·7 | 11 19·3 | 2·7 | 2·1 | 8·7 | 6·9 | 14·7 | 11·6 |
| 28 | 11 52·0 | 11 53·9 | 11 19·6 | 2·8 | 2·2 | 8·8 | 7·0 | 14·8 | 11·7 |
| 29 | 11 52·3 | 11 54·2 | 11 19·8 | 2·9 | 2·3 | 8·9 | 7·0 | 14·9 | 11·8 |
| 30 | 11 52·5 | 11 54·5 | 11 20·0 | 3·0 | 2·4 | 9·0 | 7·1 | 15·0 | 11·9 |
| 31 | 11 52·8 | 11 54·7 | 11 20·3 | 3·1 | 2·5 | 9·1 | 7·2 | 15·1 | 12·0 |
| 32 | 11 53·0 | 11 55·0 | 11 20·5 | 3·2 | 2·5 | 9·2 | 7·3 | 15·2 | 12·0 |
| 33 | 11 53·3 | 11 55·2 | 11 20·8 | 3·3 | 2·6 | 9·3 | 7·4 | 15·3 | 12·1 |
| 34 | 11 53·5 | 11 55·5 | 11 21·0 | 3·4 | 2·7 | 9·4 | 7·4 | 15·4 | 12·2 |
| 35 | 11 53·8 | 11 55·7 | 11 21·2 | 3·5 | 2·8 | 9·5 | 7·5 | 15·5 | 12·3 |
| 36 | 11 54·0 | 11 56·0 | 11 21·5 | 3·6 | 2·9 | 9·6 | 7·6 | 15·6 | 12·4 |
| 37 | 11 54·3 | 11 56·2 | 11 21·7 | 3·7 | 2·9 | 9·7 | 7·7 | 15·7 | 12·4 |
| 38 | 11 54·5 | 11 56·5 | 11 22·0 | 3·8 | 3·0 | 9·8 | 7·8 | 15·8 | 12·5 |
| 39 | 11 54·8 | 11 56·7 | 11 22·2 | 3·9 | 3·1 | 9·9 | 7·8 | 15·9 | 12·6 |
| 40 | 11 55·0 | 11 57·0 | 11 22·4 | 4·0 | 3·2 | 10·0 | 7·9 | 16·0 | 12·7 |
| 41 | 11 55·3 | 11 57·2 | 11 22·7 | 4·1 | 3·2 | 10·1 | 8·0 | 16·1 | 12·7 |
| 42 | 11 55·5 | 11 57·5 | 11 22·9 | 4·2 | 3·3 | 10·2 | 8·1 | 16·2 | 12·8 |
| 43 | 11 55·8 | 11 57·7 | 11 23·1 | 4·3 | 3·4 | 10·3 | 8·2 | 16·3 | 12·9 |
| 44 | 11 56·0 | 11 58·0 | 11 23·4 | 4·4 | 3·5 | 10·4 | 8·2 | 16·4 | 13·0 |
| 45 | 11 56·3 | 11 58·2 | 11 23·6 | 4·5 | 3·6 | 10·5 | 8·3 | 16·5 | 13·1 |
| 46 | 11 56·5 | 11 58·5 | 11 23·9 | 4·6 | 3·6 | 10·6 | 8·4 | 16·6 | 13·1 |
| 47 | 11 56·8 | 11 58·7 | 11 24·1 | 4·7 | 3·7 | 10·7 | 8·5 | 16·7 | 13·2 |
| 48 | 11 57·0 | 11 59·0 | 11 24·3 | 4·8 | 3·8 | 10·8 | 8·6 | 16·8 | 13·3 |
| 49 | 11 57·3 | 11 59·2 | 11 24·6 | 4·9 | 3·9 | 10·9 | 8·6 | 16·9 | 13·4 |
| 50 | 11 57·5 | 11 59·5 | 11 24·8 | 5·0 | 4·0 | 11·0 | 8·7 | 17·0 | 13·5 |
| 51 | 11 57·8 | 11 59·7 | 11 25·1 | 5·1 | 4·0 | 11·1 | 8·8 | 17·1 | 13·5 |
| 52 | 11 58·0 | 12 00·0 | 11 25·3 | 5·2 | 4·1 | 11·2 | 8·9 | 17·2 | 13·6 |
| 53 | 11 58·3 | 12 00·2 | 11 25·5 | 5·3 | 4·2 | 11·3 | 8·9 | 17·3 | 13·7 |
| 54 | 11 58·5 | 12 00·5 | 11 25·8 | 5·4 | 4·3 | 11·4 | 9·0 | 17·4 | 13·8 |
| 55 | 11 58·8 | 12 00·7 | 11 26·0 | 5·5 | 4·4 | 11·5 | 9·1 | 17·5 | 13·9 |
| 56 | 11 59·0 | 12 01·0 | 11 26·2 | 5·6 | 4·4 | 11·6 | 9·2 | 17·6 | 13·9 |
| 57 | 11 59·3 | 12 01·2 | 11 26·5 | 5·7 | 4·5 | 11·7 | 9·3 | 17·7 | 14·0 |
| 58 | 11 59·5 | 12 01·5 | 11 26·7 | 5·8 | 4·6 | 11·8 | 9·3 | 17·8 | 14·1 |
| 59 | 11 59·8 | 12 01·7 | 11 27·0 | 5·9 | 4·7 | 11·9 | 9·4 | 17·9 | 14·2 |
| 60 | 12 00·0 | 12 02·0 | 11 27·2 | 6·0 | 4·8 | 12·0 | 9·5 | 18·0 | 14·3 |

## 48ᵐ

| s | SUN PLANETS | ARIES | MOON | v or d / Corrⁿ | v or d / Corrⁿ | v or d / Corrⁿ |
|---|---|---|---|---|---|---|
| | ° ′ | ° ′ | ° ′ | ′ ′ | ′ ′ | ′ ′ |
| 00 | 12 00·0 | 12 02·0 | 11 27·2 | 0·0 0·0 | 6·0 4·9 | 12·0 9·7 |
| 01 | 12 00·3 | 12 02·2 | 11 27·4 | 0·1 0·1 | 6·1 4·9 | 12·1 9·8 |
| 02 | 12 00·5 | 12 02·5 | 11 27·7 | 0·2 0·2 | 6·2 5·0 | 12·2 9·9 |
| 03 | 12 00·8 | 12 02·7 | 11 27·9 | 0·3 0·2 | 6·3 5·1 | 12·3 9·9 |
| 04 | 12 01·0 | 12 03·0 | 11 28·2 | 0·4 0·3 | 6·4 5·2 | 12·4 10·0 |
| 05 | 12 01·3 | 12 03·2 | 11 28·4 | 0·5 0·4 | 6·5 5·3 | 12·5 10·1 |
| 06 | 12 01·5 | 12 03·5 | 11 28·6 | 0·6 0·5 | 6·6 5·3 | 12·6 10·2 |
| 07 | 12 01·8 | 12 03·7 | 11 28·9 | 0·7 0·6 | 6·7 5·4 | 12·7 10·3 |
| 08 | 12 02·0 | 12 04·0 | 11 29·1 | 0·8 0·6 | 6·8 5·5 | 12·8 10·3 |
| 09 | 12 02·3 | 12 04·2 | 11 29·3 | 0·9 0·7 | 6·9 5·6 | 12·9 10·4 |
| 10 | 12 02·5 | 12 04·5 | 11 29·6 | 1·0 0·8 | 7·0 5·7 | 13·0 10·5 |
| 11 | 12 02·8 | 12 04·7 | 11 29·8 | 1·1 0·9 | 7·1 5·7 | 13·1 10·6 |
| 12 | 12 03·0 | 12 05·0 | 11 30·1 | 1·2 1·0 | 7·2 5·8 | 13·2 10·7 |
| 13 | 12 03·3 | 12 05·2 | 11 30·3 | 1·3 1·1 | 7·3 5·9 | 13·3 11·0 |
| 14 | 12 03·5 | 12 05·5 | 11 30·5 | 1·4 1·1 | 7·4 6·0 | 13·4 10·8 |
| 15 | 12 03·8 | 12 05·7 | 11 30·8 | 1·5 1·2 | 7·5 6·1 | 13·5 10·9 |
| 16 | 12 04·0 | 12 06·0 | 11 31·0 | 1·6 1·3 | 7·6 6·1 | 13·6 11·0 |
| 17 | 12 04·3 | 12 06·2 | 11 31·3 | 1·7 1·4 | 7·7 6·2 | 13·7 11·1 |
| 18 | 12 04·5 | 12 06·5 | 11 31·5 | 1·8 1·5 | 7·8 6·3 | 13·8 11·2 |
| 19 | 12 04·8 | 12 06·7 | 11 31·7 | 1·9 1·5 | 7·9 6·4 | 13·9 11·2 |
| 20 | 12 05·0 | 12 07·0 | 11 32·0 | 2·0 1·6 | 8·0 6·5 | 14·0 11·3 |
| 21 | 12 05·3 | 12 07·2 | 11 32·2 | 2·1 1·7 | 8·1 6·5 | 14·1 11·4 |
| 22 | 12 05·5 | 12 07·5 | 11 32·4 | 2·2 1·8 | 8·2 6·6 | 14·2 11·5 |
| 23 | 12 05·8 | 12 07·7 | 11 32·7 | 2·3 1·9 | 8·3 6·7 | 14·3 11·6 |
| 24 | 12 06·0 | 12 08·0 | 11 32·9 | 2·4 1·9 | 8·4 6·8 | 14·4 11·6 |
| 25 | 12 06·3 | 12 08·2 | 11 33·2 | 2·5 2·0 | 8·5 6·9 | 14·5 11·7 |
| 26 | 12 06·5 | 12 08·5 | 11 33·4 | 2·6 2·1 | 8·6 7·0 | 14·6 11·8 |
| 27 | 12 06·8 | 12 08·7 | 11 33·6 | 2·7 2·2 | 8·7 7·0 | 14·7 11·9 |
| 28 | 12 07·0 | 12 09·0 | 11 33·9 | 2·8 2·3 | 8·8 7·1 | 14·8 12·0 |
| 29 | 12 07·3 | 12 09·2 | 11 34·1 | 2·9 2·3 | 8·9 7·2 | 14·9 12·0 |
| 30 | 12 07·5 | 12 09·5 | 11 34·4 | 3·0 2·4 | 9·0 7·3 | 15·0 12·1 |
| 31 | 12 07·8 | 12 09·7 | 11 34·6 | 3·1 2·5 | 9·1 7·4 | 15·1 12·2 |
| 32 | 12 08·0 | 12 10·0 | 11 34·8 | 3·2 2·6 | 9·2 7·4 | 15·2 12·3 |
| 33 | 12 08·3 | 12 10·2 | 11 35·1 | 3·3 2·7 | 9·3 7·5 | 15·3 12·4 |
| 34 | 12 08·5 | 12 10·5 | 11 35·3 | 3·4 2·7 | 9·4 7·6 | 15·4 12·4 |
| 35 | 12 08·8 | 12 10·7 | 11 35·6 | 3·5 2·8 | 9·5 7·7 | 15·5 12·5 |
| 36 | 12 09·0 | 12 11·0 | 11 35·8 | 3·6 2·9 | 9·6 7·8 | 15·6 12·9 |
| 37 | 12 09·3 | 12 11·2 | 11 36·0 | 3·7 3·0 | 9·7 7·8 | 15·7 12·7 |
| 38 | 12 09·5 | 12 11·5 | 11 36·3 | 3·8 3·1 | 9·8 7·9 | 15·8 12·8 |
| 39 | 12 09·8 | 12 11·7 | 11 36·5 | 3·9 3·2 | 9·9 8·0 | 15·9 12·9 |
| 40 | 12 10·0 | 12 12·0 | 11 36·7 | 4·0 3·2 | 10·0 8·1 | 16·0 12·9 |
| 41 | 12 10·3 | 12 12·2 | 11 37·0 | 4·1 3·3 | 10·1 8·2 | 16·1 13·0 |
| 42 | 12 10·5 | 12 12·5 | 11 37·2 | 4·2 3·4 | 10·2 8·2 | 16·2 13·1 |
| 43 | 12 10·8 | 12 12·8 | 11 37·5 | 4·3 3·5 | 10·3 8·3 | 16·3 13·2 |
| 44 | 12 11·0 | 12 13·0 | 11 37·7 | 4·4 3·6 | 10·4 8·4 | 16·4 13·3 |
| 45 | 12 11·3 | 12 13·3 | 11 37·9 | 4·5 3·6 | 10·5 8·5 | 16·5 13·3 |
| 46 | 12 11·5 | 12 13·5 | 11 38·2 | 4·6 3·7 | 10·6 8·6 | 16·6 13·4 |
| 47 | 12 11·8 | 12 13·8 | 11 38·4 | 4·7 3·8 | 10·7 8·6 | 16·7 13·5 |
| 48 | 12 12·0 | 12 14·0 | 11 38·7 | 4·8 3·9 | 10·8 8·7 | 16·8 13·6 |
| 49 | 12 12·3 | 12 14·3 | 11 38·9 | 4·9 4·0 | 10·9 8·8 | 16·9 13·7 |
| 50 | 12 12·5 | 12 14·5 | 11 39·1 | 5·0 4·0 | 11·0 8·9 | 17·0 13·7 |
| 51 | 12 12·8 | 12 14·8 | 11 39·4 | 5·1 4·1 | 11·1 9·0 | 17·1 13·8 |
| 52 | 12 13·0 | 12 15·0 | 11 39·6 | 5·2 4·2 | 11·2 9·1 | 17·2 13·9 |
| 53 | 12 13·3 | 12 15·3 | 11 39·8 | 5·3 4·3 | 11·3 9·1 | 17·3 14·0 |
| 54 | 12 13·5 | 12 15·5 | 11 40·1 | 5·4 4·4 | 11·4 9·2 | 17·4 14·1 |
| 55 | 12 13·8 | 12 15·8 | 11 40·3 | 5·5 4·4 | 11·5 9·3 | 17·5 14·1 |
| 56 | 12 14·0 | 12 16·0 | 11 40·6 | 5·6 4·5 | 11·6 9·4 | 17·6 14·2 |
| 57 | 12 14·3 | 12 16·3 | 11 40·8 | 5·7 4·6 | 11·7 9·5 | 17·7 14·3 |
| 58 | 12 14·5 | 12 16·5 | 11 41·0 | 5·8 4·7 | 11·8 9·5 | 17·8 14·4 |
| 59 | 12 14·8 | 12 16·8 | 11 41·3 | 5·9 4·8 | 11·9 9·6 | 17·9 14·5 |
| 60 | 12 15·0 | 12 17·0 | 11 41·5 | 6·0 4·9 | 12·0 9·7 | 18·0 14·6 |

## 49ᵐ

| s | SUN PLANETS | ARIES | MOON | v or d / Corrⁿ | v or d / Corrⁿ | v or d / Corrⁿ |
|---|---|---|---|---|---|---|
| | ° ′ | ° ′ | ° ′ | ′ ′ | ′ ′ | ′ ′ |
| 00 | 12 15·0 | 12 17·0 | 11 41·5 | 0·0 0·0 | 6·0 5·0 | 12·0 9·9 |
| 01 | 12 15·3 | 12 17·3 | 11 41·8 | 0·1 0·1 | 6·1 5·0 | 12·1 10·0 |
| 02 | 12 15·5 | 12 17·5 | 11 42·0 | 0·2 0·2 | 6·2 5·1 | 12·2 10·1 |
| 03 | 12 15·8 | 12 17·8 | 11 42·2 | 0·3 0·2 | 6·3 5·2 | 12·3 10·1 |
| 04 | 12 16·0 | 12 18·0 | 11 42·5 | 0·4 0·3 | 6·4 5·3 | 12·4 10·2 |
| 05 | 12 16·3 | 12 18·3 | 11 42·7 | 0·5 0·4 | 6·5 5·4 | 12·5 10·3 |
| 06 | 12 16·5 | 12 18·5 | 11 42·9 | 0·6 0·5 | 6·6 5·4 | 12·6 10·4 |
| 07 | 12 16·8 | 12 18·8 | 11 43·2 | 0·7 0·6 | 6·7 5·5 | 12·7 10·5 |
| 08 | 12 17·0 | 12 19·0 | 11 43·4 | 0·8 0·7 | 6·8 5·6 | 12·8 10·6 |
| 09 | 12 17·3 | 12 19·3 | 11 43·7 | 0·9 0·7 | 6·9 5·7 | 12·9 10·6 |
| 10 | 12 17·5 | 12 19·5 | 11 43·9 | 1·0 0·8 | 7·0 5·8 | 13·0 10·7 |
| 11 | 12 17·8 | 12 19·8 | 11 44·1 | 1·1 0·9 | 7·1 5·9 | 13·1 10·8 |
| 12 | 12 18·0 | 12 20·0 | 11 44·4 | 1·2 1·0 | 7·2 5·9 | 13·2 10·9 |
| 13 | 12 18·3 | 12 20·3 | 11 44·6 | 1·3 1·1 | 7·3 6·0 | 13·3 11·0 |
| 14 | 12 18·5 | 12 20·5 | 11 44·9 | 1·4 1·2 | 7·4 6·1 | 13·4 11·1 |
| 15 | 12 18·8 | 12 20·8 | 11 45·1 | 1·5 1·2 | 7·5 6·2 | 13·5 11·1 |
| 16 | 12 19·0 | 12 21·0 | 11 45·3 | 1·6 1·3 | 7·6 6·3 | 13·6 11·2 |
| 17 | 12 19·3 | 12 21·3 | 11 45·6 | 1·7 1·4 | 7·7 6·4 | 13·7 11·3 |
| 18 | 12 19·5 | 12 21·5 | 11 45·8 | 1·8 1·5 | 7·8 6·4 | 13·8 11·4 |
| 19 | 12 19·8 | 12 21·8 | 11 46·1 | 1·9 1·6 | 7·9 6·5 | 13·9 11·5 |
| 20 | 12 20·0 | 12 22·0 | 11 46·3 | 2·0 1·7 | 8·0 6·6 | 14·0 11·6 |
| 21 | 12 20·3 | 12 22·3 | 11 46·5 | 2·1 1·7 | 8·1 6·7 | 14·1 11·6 |
| 22 | 12 20·5 | 12 22·5 | 11 46·8 | 2·2 1·8 | 8·2 6·8 | 14·2 11·7 |
| 23 | 12 20·8 | 12 22·8 | 11 47·0 | 2·3 1·9 | 8·3 6·8 | 14·3 11·8 |
| 24 | 12 21·0 | 12 23·0 | 11 47·2 | 2·4 2·0 | 8·4 6·9 | 14·4 11·9 |
| 25 | 12 21·3 | 12 23·3 | 11 47·5 | 2·5 2·1 | 8·5 7·0 | 14·5 12·0 |
| 26 | 12 21·5 | 12 23·5 | 11 47·7 | 2·6 2·1 | 8·6 7·1 | 14·6 12·0 |
| 27 | 12 21·8 | 12 23·8 | 11 48·0 | 2·7 2·2 | 8·7 7·2 | 14·7 12·1 |
| 28 | 12 22·0 | 12 24·0 | 11 48·2 | 2·8 2·3 | 8·8 7·3 | 14·8 12·2 |
| 29 | 12 22·3 | 12 24·3 | 11 48·4 | 2·9 2·4 | 8·9 7·3 | 14·9 12·3 |
| 30 | 12 22·5 | 12 24·5 | 11 48·7 | 3·0 2·5 | 9·0 7·4 | 15·0 12·4 |
| 31 | 12 22·8 | 12 24·8 | 11 48·9 | 3·1 2·6 | 9·1 7·5 | 15·1 12·5 |
| 32 | 12 23·0 | 12 25·0 | 11 49·2 | 3·2 2·6 | 9·2 7·6 | 15·2 12·5 |
| 33 | 12 23·3 | 12 25·3 | 11 49·4 | 3·3 2·7 | 9·3 7·7 | 15·3 12·6 |
| 34 | 12 23·5 | 12 25·5 | 11 49·6 | 3·4 2·8 | 9·4 7·8 | 15·4 12·7 |
| 35 | 12 23·8 | 12 25·8 | 11 49·9 | 3·5 2·9 | 9·5 7·8 | 15·5 12·8 |
| 36 | 12 24·0 | 12 26·0 | 11 50·1 | 3·6 3·0 | 9·6 7·9 | 15·6 12·9 |
| 37 | 12 24·3 | 12 26·3 | 11 50·3 | 3·7 3·1 | 9·7 8·0 | 15·7 13·0 |
| 38 | 12 24·5 | 12 26·5 | 11 50·6 | 3·8 3·1 | 9·8 8·1 | 15·8 13·0 |
| 39 | 12 24·8 | 12 26·8 | 11 50·8 | 3·9 3·2 | 9·9 8·2 | 15·9 13·1 |
| 40 | 12 25·0 | 12 27·0 | 11 51·1 | 4·0 3·3 | 10·0 8·3 | 16·0 13·2 |
| 41 | 12 25·3 | 12 27·3 | 11 51·3 | 4·1 3·4 | 10·1 8·3 | 16·1 13·3 |
| 42 | 12 25·5 | 12 27·5 | 11 51·5 | 4·2 3·5 | 10·2 8·4 | 16·2 13·4 |
| 43 | 12 25·8 | 12 27·8 | 11 51·8 | 4·3 3·5 | 10·3 8·5 | 16·3 13·4 |
| 44 | 12 26·0 | 12 28·0 | 11 52·0 | 4·4 3·6 | 10·4 8·6 | 16·4 13·5 |
| 45 | 12 26·3 | 12 28·3 | 11 52·3 | 4·5 3·7 | 10·5 8·7 | 16·5 13·6 |
| 46 | 12 26·5 | 12 28·5 | 11 52·5 | 4·6 3·8 | 10·6 8·7 | 16·6 13·7 |
| 47 | 12 26·8 | 12 28·8 | 11 52·7 | 4·7 3·9 | 10·7 8·8 | 16·7 13·8 |
| 48 | 12 27·0 | 12 29·0 | 11 53·0 | 4·8 4·0 | 10·8 8·9 | 16·8 13·9 |
| 49 | 12 27·3 | 12 29·3 | 11 53·2 | 4·9 4·0 | 10·9 9·0 | 16·9 13·9 |
| 50 | 12 27·5 | 12 29·5 | 11 53·4 | 5·0 4·1 | 11·0 9·1 | 17·0 14·0 |
| 51 | 12 27·8 | 12 29·8 | 11 53·7 | 5·1 4·2 | 11·1 9·2 | 17·1 14·1 |
| 52 | 12 28·0 | 12 30·0 | 11 53·9 | 5·2 4·3 | 11·2 9·2 | 17·2 14·2 |
| 53 | 12 28·3 | 12 30·3 | 11 54·2 | 5·3 4·4 | 11·3 9·3 | 17·3 14·3 |
| 54 | 12 28·5 | 12 30·5 | 11 54·4 | 5·4 4·5 | 11·4 9·4 | 17·4 14·4 |
| 55 | 12 28·8 | 12 30·8 | 11 54·6 | 5·5 4·5 | 11·5 9·5 | 17·5 14·4 |
| 56 | 12 29·0 | 12 31·1 | 11 54·9 | 5·6 4·6 | 11·6 9·6 | 17·6 14·5 |
| 57 | 12 29·3 | 12 31·3 | 11 55·1 | 5·7 4·7 | 11·7 9·7 | 17·7 14·6 |
| 58 | 12 29·5 | 12 31·6 | 11 55·4 | 5·8 4·8 | 11·8 9·7 | 17·8 14·7 |
| 59 | 12 29·8 | 12 31·8 | 11 55·6 | 5·9 4·9 | 11·9 9·8 | 17·9 14·8 |
| 60 | 12 30·0 | 12 32·1 | 11 55·8 | 6·0 5·0 | 12·0 9·9 | 18·0 14·9 |

| 50ᵐ | SUN PLANETS | ARIES | MOON | v or Corrⁿ d | v or Corrⁿ d | v or Corrⁿ d | 51ᵐ | SUN PLANETS | ARIES | MOON | v or Corrⁿ d | v or Corrⁿ d | v or Corrⁿ d |
|---|---|---|---|---|---|---|---|---|---|---|---|---|---|
| s | ° ′ | ° ′ | ° ′ | ′ ′ | ′ ′ | ′ ′ | s | ° ′ | ° ′ | ° ′ | ′ ′ | ′ ′ | ′ ′ |
| 00 | 12 30·0 | 12 32·1 | 11 55·8 | 0·0 0·0 | 6·0 5·1 | 12·0 10·1 | 00 | 12 45·0 | 12 47·1 | 12 10·2 | 0·0 0·0 | 6·0 5·2 | 12·0 10·3 |
| 01 | 12 30·3 | 12 32·3 | 11 56·1 | 0·1 0·1 | 6·1 5·1 | 12·1 10·2 | 01 | 12 45·3 | 12 47·3 | 12 10·4 | 0·1 0·1 | 6·1 5·2 | 12·1 10·4 |
| 02 | 12 30·5 | 12 32·6 | 11 56·3 | 0·2 0·2 | 6·2 5·2 | 12·2 10·3 | 02 | 12 45·5 | 12 47·6 | 12 10·6 | 0·2 0·2 | 6·2 5·3 | 12·2 10·5 |
| 03 | 12 30·8 | 12 32·8 | 11 56·5 | 0·3 0·3 | 6·3 5·3 | 12·3 10·4 | 03 | 12 45·8 | 12 47·8 | 12 10·9 | 0·3 0·3 | 6·3 5·4 | 12·3 10·6 |
| 04 | 12 31·0 | 12 33·1 | 11 56·8 | 0·4 0·3 | 6·4 5·4 | 12·4 10·4 | 04 | 12 46·0 | 12 48·1 | 12 11·1 | 0·4 0·3 | 6·4 5·5 | 12·4 10·6 |
| 05 | 12 31·3 | 12 33·3 | 11 57·0 | 0·5 0·4 | 6·5 5·5 | 12·5 10·5 | 05 | 12 46·3 | 12 48·3 | 12 11·3 | 0·5 0·4 | 6·5 5·6 | 12·5 10·7 |
| 06 | 12 31·5 | 12 33·6 | 11 57·3 | 0·6 0·5 | 6·6 5·6 | 12·6 10·6 | 06 | 12 46·5 | 12 48·6 | 12 11·6 | 0·6 0·5 | 6·6 5·7 | 12·6 10·8 |
| 07 | 12 31·8 | 12 33·8 | 11 57·5 | 0·7 0·6 | 6·7 5·6 | 12·7 10·7 | 07 | 12 46·8 | 12 48·8 | 12 11·8 | 0·7 0·6 | 6·7 5·8 | 12·7 10·9 |
| 08 | 12 32·0 | 12 34·1 | 11 57·7 | 0·8 0·7 | 6·8 5·7 | 12·8 10·8 | 08 | 12 47·0 | 12 49·1 | 12 12·1 | 0·8 0·7 | 6·8 5·8 | 12·8 11·0 |
| 09 | 12 32·3 | 12 34·3 | 11 58·0 | 0·9 0·8 | 6·9 5·8 | 12·9 10·9 | 09 | 12 47·3 | 12 49·4 | 12 12·3 | 0·9 0·8 | 6·9 5·9 | 12·9 11·1 |
| 10 | 12 32·5 | 12 34·6 | 11 58·2 | 1·0 0·8 | 7·0 5·9 | 13·0 10·9 | 10 | 12 47·5 | 12 49·6 | 12 12·5 | 1·0 0·9 | 7·0 6·0 | 13·0 11·2 |
| 11 | 12 32·8 | 12 34·8 | 11 58·5 | 1·1 0·9 | 7·1 6·0 | 13·1 11·0 | 11 | 12 47·8 | 12 49·9 | 12 12·8 | 1·1 0·9 | 7·1 6·1 | 13·1 11·2 |
| 12 | 12 33·0 | 12 35·1 | 11 58·7 | 1·2 1·0 | 7·2 6·1 | 13·2 11·1 | 12 | 12 48·0 | 12 50·1 | 12 13·0 | 1·2 1·0 | 7·2 6·2 | 13·2 11·3 |
| 13 | 12 33·3 | 12 35·3 | 11 58·9 | 1·3 1·1 | 7·3 6·1 | 13·3 11·2 | 13 | 12 48·3 | 12 50·4 | 12 13·3 | 1·3 1·1 | 7·3 6·3 | 13·3 11·4 |
| 14 | 12 33·5 | 12 35·6 | 11 59·2 | 1·4 1·2 | 7·4 6·2 | 13·4 11·3 | 14 | 12 48·5 | 12 50·6 | 12 13·5 | 1·4 1·2 | 7·4 6·4 | 13·4 11·5 |
| 15 | 12 33·8 | 12 35·8 | 11 59·4 | 1·5 1·3 | 7·5 6·3 | 13·5 11·4 | 15 | 12 48·8 | 12 50·9 | 12 13·7 | 1·5 1·3 | 7·5 6·4 | 13·5 11·6 |
| 16 | 12 34·0 | 12 36·1 | 11 59·7 | 1·6 1·3 | 7·6 6·4 | 13·6 11·4 | 16 | 12 49·0 | 12 51·1 | 12 14·0 | 1·6 1·4 | 7·6 6·5 | 13·6 11·7 |
| 17 | 12 34·3 | 12 36·3 | 11 59·9 | 1·7 1·4 | 7·7 6·5 | 13·7 11·5 | 17 | 12 49·3 | 12 51·4 | 12 14·2 | 1·7 1·5 | 7·7 6·6 | 13·7 11·8 |
| 18 | 12 34·5 | 12 36·6 | 12 00·1 | 1·8 1·5 | 7·8 6·6 | 13·8 11·6 | 18 | 12 49·5 | 12 51·6 | 12 14·4 | 1·8 1·5 | 7·8 6·7 | 13·8 11·8 |
| 19 | 12 34·8 | 12 36·8 | 12 00·4 | 1·9 1·6 | 7·9 6·6 | 13·9 11·7 | 19 | 12 49·8 | 12 51·9 | 12 14·7 | 1·9 1·6 | 7·9 6·8 | 13·9 11·9 |
| 20 | 12 35·0 | 12 37·1 | 12 00·6 | 2·0 1·7 | 8·0 6·7 | 14·0 11·8 | 20 | 12 50·0 | 12 52·1 | 12 14·9 | 2·0 1·7 | 8·0 6·9 | 14·0 12·0 |
| 21 | 12 35·3 | 12 37·3 | 12 00·8 | 2·1 1·8 | 8·1 6·8 | 14·1 11·9 | 21 | 12 50·3 | 12 52·4 | 12 15·2 | 2·1 1·8 | 8·1 7·0 | 14·1 12·1 |
| 22 | 12 35·5 | 12 37·6 | 12 01·1 | 2·2 1·9 | 8·2 6·9 | 14·2 12·0 | 22 | 12 50·5 | 12 52·6 | 12 15·4 | 2·2 1·9 | 8·2 7·0 | 14·2 12·2 |
| 23 | 12 35·8 | 12 37·8 | 12 01·3 | 2·3 1·9 | 8·3 7·0 | 14·3 12·0 | 23 | 12 50·8 | 12 52·9 | 12 15·6 | 2·3 2·0 | 8·3 7·1 | 14·3 12·3 |
| 24 | 12 36·0 | 12 38·1 | 12 01·6 | 2·4 2·0 | 8·4 7·1 | 14·4 12·1 | 24 | 12 51·0 | 12 53·1 | 12 15·9 | 2·4 2·1 | 8·4 7·2 | 14·4 12·4 |
| 25 | 12 36·3 | 12 38·3 | 12 01·8 | 2·5 2·1 | 8·5 7·2 | 14·5 12·2 | 25 | 12 51·3 | 12 53·4 | 12 16·1 | 2·5 2·1 | 8·5 7·3 | 14·5 12·4 |
| 26 | 12 36·5 | 12 38·6 | 12 02·0 | 2·6 2·2 | 8·6 7·2 | 14·6 12·3 | 26 | 12 51·5 | 12 53·6 | 12 16·4 | 2·6 2·2 | 8·6 7·4 | 14·6 12·5 |
| 27 | 12 36·8 | 12 38·8 | 12 02·3 | 2·7 2·3 | 8·7 7·3 | 14·7 12·4 | 27 | 12 51·8 | 12 53·9 | 12 16·6 | 2·7 2·3 | 8·7 7·5 | 14·7 12·6 |
| 28 | 12 37·0 | 12 39·1 | 12 02·5 | 2·8 2·4 | 8·8 7·4 | 14·8 12·5 | 28 | 12 52·0 | 12 54·1 | 12 16·8 | 2·8 2·4 | 8·8 7·6 | 14·8 12·7 |
| 29 | 12 37·3 | 12 39·3 | 12 02·8 | 2·9 2·4 | 8·9 7·5 | 14·9 12·5 | 29 | 12 52·3 | 12 54·4 | 12 17·1 | 2·9 2·5 | 8·9 7·6 | 14·9 12·8 |
| 30 | 12 37·5 | 12 39·6 | 12 03·0 | 3·0 2·5 | 9·0 7·6 | 15·0 12·6 | 30 | 12 52·5 | 12 54·6 | 12 17·3 | 3·0 2·6 | 9·0 7·7 | 15·0 12·9 |
| 31 | 12 37·8 | 12 39·8 | 12 03·2 | 3·1 2·6 | 9·1 7·7 | 15·1 12·7 | 31 | 12 52·8 | 12 54·9 | 12 17·5 | 3·1 2·7 | 9·1 7·8 | 15·1 13·0 |
| 32 | 12 38·0 | 12 40·1 | 12 03·5 | 3·2 2·7 | 9·2 7·7 | 15·2 12·8 | 32 | 12 53·0 | 12 55·1 | 12 17·8 | 3·2 2·7 | 9·2 7·9 | 15·2 13·0 |
| 33 | 12 38·3 | 12 40·3 | 12 03·7 | 3·3 2·8 | 9·3 7·8 | 15·3 12·9 | 33 | 12 53·3 | 12 55·4 | 12 18·0 | 3·3 2·8 | 9·3 8·0 | 15·3 13·1 |
| 34 | 12 38·5 | 12 40·6 | 12 03·9 | 3·4 2·9 | 9·4 7·9 | 15·4 13·0 | 34 | 12 53·5 | 12 55·6 | 12 18·3 | 3·4 2·9 | 9·4 8·1 | 15·4 13·2 |
| 35 | 12 38·8 | 12 40·8 | 12 04·2 | 3·5 2·9 | 9·5 8·0 | 15·5 13·0 | 35 | 12 53·8 | 12 55·9 | 12 18·5 | 3·5 3·0 | 9·5 8·2 | 15·5 13·3 |
| 36 | 12 39·0 | 12 41·1 | 12 04·4 | 3·6 3·0 | 9·6 8·1 | 15·6 13·1 | 36 | 12 54·0 | 12 56·1 | 12 18·7 | 3·6 3·1 | 9·6 8·2 | 15·6 13·4 |
| 37 | 12 39·3 | 12 41·3 | 12 04·7 | 3·7 3·1 | 9·7 8·2 | 15·7 13·2 | 37 | 12 54·3 | 12 56·4 | 12 19·0 | 3·7 3·2 | 9·7 8·3 | 15·7 13·5 |
| 38 | 12 39·5 | 12 41·6 | 12 04·9 | 3·8 3·2 | 9·8 8·2 | 15·8 13·3 | 38 | 12 54·5 | 12 56·6 | 12 19·2 | 3·8 3·3 | 9·8 8·4 | 15·8 13·6 |
| 39 | 12 39·8 | 12 41·8 | 12 05·1 | 3·9 3·3 | 9·9 8·3 | 15·9 13·4 | 39 | 12 54·8 | 12 56·9 | 12 19·5 | 3·9 3·3 | 9·9 8·5 | 15·9 13·6 |
| 40 | 12 40·0 | 12 42·1 | 12 05·4 | 4·0 3·4 | 10·0 8·4 | 16·0 13·5 | 40 | 12 55·0 | 12 57·1 | 12 19·7 | 4·0 3·4 | 10·0 8·6 | 16·0 13·7 |
| 41 | 12 40·3 | 12 42·3 | 12 05·6 | 4·1 3·5 | 10·1 8·5 | 16·1 13·6 | 41 | 12 55·3 | 12 57·4 | 12 19·9 | 4·1 3·5 | 10·1 8·7 | 16·1 13·8 |
| 42 | 12 40·5 | 12 42·6 | 12 05·9 | 4·2 3·5 | 10·2 8·6 | 16·2 13·6 | 42 | 12 55·5 | 12 57·6 | 12 20·2 | 4·2 3·6 | 10·2 8·8 | 16·2 13·9 |
| 43 | 12 40·8 | 12 42·8 | 12 06·1 | 4·3 3·6 | 10·3 8·7 | 16·3 13·7 | 43 | 12 55·8 | 12 57·9 | 12 20·4 | 4·3 3·7 | 10·3 8·8 | 16·3 14·0 |
| 44 | 12 41·0 | 12 43·1 | 12 06·3 | 4·4 3·7 | 10·4 8·8 | 16·4 13·8 | 44 | 12 56·0 | 12 58·1 | 12 20·6 | 4·4 3·8 | 10·4 8·9 | 16·4 14·1 |
| 45 | 12 41·3 | 12 43·3 | 12 06·6 | 4·5 3·8 | 10·5 8·8 | 16·5 13·9 | 45 | 12 56·3 | 12 58·4 | 12 20·9 | 4·5 3·9 | 10·5 9·0 | 16·5 14·2 |
| 46 | 12 41·5 | 12 43·6 | 12 06·8 | 4·6 3·9 | 10·6 8·9 | 16·6 14·0 | 46 | 12 56·5 | 12 58·6 | 12 21·1 | 4·6 3·9 | 10·6 9·1 | 16·6 14·2 |
| 47 | 12 41·8 | 12 43·8 | 12 07·0 | 4·7 4·0 | 10·7 9·0 | 16·7 14·1 | 47 | 12 56·8 | 12 58·9 | 12 21·4 | 4·7 4·0 | 10·7 9·2 | 16·7 14·3 |
| 48 | 12 42·0 | 12 44·1 | 12 07·3 | 4·8 4·0 | 10·8 9·1 | 16·8 14·1 | 48 | 12 57·0 | 12 59·1 | 12 21·6 | 4·8 4·1 | 10·8 9·3 | 16·8 14·4 |
| 49 | 12 42·3 | 12 44·3 | 12 07·5 | 4·9 4·1 | 10·9 9·2 | 16·9 14·2 | 49 | 12 57·3 | 12 59·4 | 12 21·8 | 4·9 4·2 | 10·9 9·4 | 16·9 14·5 |
| 50 | 12 42·5 | 12 44·6 | 12 07·8 | 5·0 4·2 | 11·0 9·3 | 17·0 14·3 | 50 | 12 57·5 | 12 59·6 | 12 22·1 | 5·0 4·3 | 11·0 9·4 | 17·0 14·6 |
| 51 | 12 42·8 | 12 44·8 | 12 08·0 | 5·1 4·3 | 11·1 9·3 | 17·1 14·4 | 51 | 12 57·8 | 12 59·9 | 12 22·3 | 5·1 4·4 | 11·1 9·5 | 17·1 14·7 |
| 52 | 12 43·0 | 12 45·1 | 12 08·2 | 5·2 4·4 | 11·2 9·4 | 17·2 14·5 | 52 | 12 58·0 | 13 00·1 | 12 22·6 | 5·2 4·5 | 11·2 9·6 | 17·2 14·8 |
| 53 | 12 43·3 | 12 45·3 | 12 08·5 | 5·3 4·5 | 11·3 9·5 | 17·3 14·6 | 53 | 12 58·3 | 13 00·4 | 12 22·8 | 5·3 4·5 | 11·3 9·7 | 17·3 14·8 |
| 54 | 12 43·5 | 12 45·6 | 12 08·7 | 5·4 4·5 | 11·4 9·6 | 17·4 14·6 | 54 | 12 58·5 | 13 00·6 | 12 23·0 | 5·4 4·6 | 11·4 9·8 | 17·4 14·9 |
| 55 | 12 43·8 | 12 45·8 | 12 09·0 | 5·5 4·6 | 11·5 9·7 | 17·5 14·7 | 55 | 12 58·8 | 13 00·9 | 12 23·3 | 5·5 4·7 | 11·5 9·9 | 17·5 15·0 |
| 56 | 12 44·0 | 12 46·1 | 12 09·2 | 5·6 4·7 | 11·6 9·8 | 17·6 14·8 | 56 | 12 59·0 | 13 01·1 | 12 23·5 | 5·6 4·8 | 11·6 10·0 | 17·6 15·1 |
| 57 | 12 44·3 | 12 46·3 | 12 09·4 | 5·7 4·8 | 11·7 9·8 | 17·7 14·9 | 57 | 12 59·3 | 13 01·4 | 12 23·8 | 5·7 4·9 | 11·7 10·0 | 17·7 15·2 |
| 58 | 12 44·5 | 12 46·6 | 12 09·7 | 5·8 4·9 | 11·8 9·9 | 17·8 15·0 | 58 | 12 59·5 | 13 01·6 | 12 24·0 | 5·8 5·0 | 11·8 10·1 | 17·8 15·3 |
| 59 | 12 44·8 | 12 46·8 | 12 09·9 | 5·9 5·0 | 11·9 10·0 | 17·9 15·1 | 59 | 12 59·8 | 13 01·9 | 12 24·2 | 5·9 5·1 | 11·9 10·2 | 17·9 15·4 |
| 60 | 12 45·0 | 12 47·1 | 12 10·2 | 6·0 5·1 | 12·0 10·1 | 18·0 15·2 | 60 | 13 00·0 | 13 02·1 | 12 24·5 | 6·0 5·2 | 12·0 10·3 | 18·0 15·5 |

## 52ᵐ

| s | SUN PLANETS | ARIES | MOON | v or d / Corrⁿ | v or d / Corrⁿ | v or d / Corrⁿ |
|---|---|---|---|---|---|---|
| 00 | 13 00·0 | 13 02·1 | 12 24·5 | 0·0 0·0 | 6·0 5·3 | 12·0 10·5 |
| 01 | 13 00·3 | 13 02·4 | 12 24·7 | 0·1 0·1 | 6·1 5·3 | 12·1 10·6 |
| 02 | 13 00·5 | 13 02·6 | 12 24·9 | 0·2 0·2 | 6·2 5·4 | 12·2 10·7 |
| 03 | 13 00·8 | 13 02·9 | 12 25·2 | 0·3 0·3 | 6·3 5·5 | 12·3 10·8 |
| 04 | 13 01·0 | 13 03·1 | 12 25·4 | 0·4 0·4 | 6·4 5·6 | 12·4 10·9 |
| 05 | 13 01·3 | 13 03·4 | 12 25·7 | 0·5 0·4 | 6·5 5·7 | 12·5 10·9 |
| 06 | 13 01·5 | 13 03·6 | 12 25·9 | 0·6 0·5 | 6·6 5·8 | 12·6 11·0 |
| 07 | 13 01·8 | 13 03·9 | 12 26·1 | 0·7 0·6 | 6·7 5·9 | 12·7 11·1 |
| 08 | 13 02·0 | 13 04·1 | 12 26·4 | 0·8 0·7 | 6·8 6·0 | 12·8 11·2 |
| 09 | 13 02·3 | 13 04·4 | 12 26·6 | 0·9 0·8 | 6·9 6·0 | 12·9 11·3 |
| 10 | 13 02·5 | 13 04·6 | 12 26·9 | 1·0 0·9 | 7·0 6·1 | 13·0 11·4 |
| 11 | 13 02·8 | 13 04·9 | 12 27·1 | 1·1 1·0 | 7·1 6·2 | 13·1 11·5 |
| 12 | 13 03·0 | 13 05·1 | 12 27·3 | 1·2 1·1 | 7·2 6·3 | 13·2 11·6 |
| 13 | 13 03·3 | 13 05·4 | 12 27·6 | 1·3 1·1 | 7·3 6·4 | 13·3 11·6 |
| 14 | 13 03·5 | 13 05·6 | 12 27·8 | 1·4 1·2 | 7·4 6·5 | 13·4 11·7 |
| 15 | 13 03·8 | 13 05·9 | 12 28·0 | 1·5 1·3 | 7·5 6·6 | 13·5 11·8 |
| 16 | 13 04·0 | 13 06·1 | 12 28·3 | 1·6 1·4 | 7·6 6·7 | 13·6 11·9 |
| 17 | 13 04·3 | 13 06·4 | 12 28·5 | 1·7 1·5 | 7·7 6·7 | 13·7 12·0 |
| 18 | 13 04·5 | 13 06·6 | 12 28·8 | 1·8 1·6 | 7·8 6·8 | 13·8 12·1 |
| 19 | 13 04·8 | 13 06·9 | 12 29·0 | 1·9 1·7 | 7·9 6·9 | 13·9 12·2 |
| 20 | 13 05·0 | 13 07·1 | 12 29·2 | 2·0 1·8 | 8·0 7·0 | 14·0 12·3 |
| 21 | 13 05·3 | 13 07·4 | 12 29·5 | 2·1 1·8 | 8·1 7·1 | 14·1 12·3 |
| 22 | 13 05·5 | 13 07·7 | 12 29·7 | 2·2 1·9 | 8·2 7·2 | 14·2 12·4 |
| 23 | 13 05·8 | 13 07·9 | 12 30·0 | 2·3 2·0 | 8·3 7·3 | 14·3 12·5 |
| 24 | 13 06·0 | 13 08·2 | 12 30·2 | 2·4 2·1 | 8·4 7·4 | 14·4 12·6 |
| 25 | 13 06·3 | 13 08·4 | 12 30·4 | 2·5 2·2 | 8·5 7·4 | 14·5 12·7 |
| 26 | 13 06·5 | 13 08·7 | 12 30·7 | 2·6 2·3 | 8·6 7·5 | 14·6 12·8 |
| 27 | 13 06·8 | 13 08·9 | 12 30·9 | 2·7 2·4 | 8·7 7·6 | 14·7 12·9 |
| 28 | 13 07·0 | 13 09·2 | 12 31·1 | 2·8 2·5 | 8·8 7·7 | 14·8 13·0 |
| 29 | 13 07·3 | 13 09·4 | 12 31·4 | 2·9 2·5 | 8·9 7·8 | 14·9 13·0 |
| 30 | 13 07·5 | 13 09·7 | 12 31·6 | 3·0 2·6 | 9·0 7·9 | 15·0 13·1 |
| 31 | 13 07·8 | 13 09·9 | 12 31·9 | 3·1 2·7 | 9·1 8·0 | 15·1 13·2 |
| 32 | 13 08·0 | 13 10·2 | 12 32·1 | 3·2 2·8 | 9·2 8·0 | 15·2 13·3 |
| 33 | 13 08·3 | 13 10·4 | 12 32·3 | 3·3 2·9 | 9·3 8·1 | 15·3 13·4 |
| 34 | 13 08·5 | 13 10·7 | 12 32·6 | 3·4 3·0 | 9·4 8·2 | 15·4 13·5 |
| 35 | 13 08·8 | 13 10·9 | 12 32·8 | 3·5 3·1 | 9·5 8·3 | 15·5 13·6 |
| 36 | 13 09·0 | 13 11·2 | 12 33·1 | 3·6 3·2 | 9·6 8·4 | 15·6 13·7 |
| 37 | 13 09·3 | 13 11·4 | 12 33·3 | 3·7 3·2 | 9·7 8·5 | 15·7 13·7 |
| 38 | 13 09·5 | 13 11·7 | 12 33·5 | 3·8 3·3 | 9·8 8·6 | 15·8 13·8 |
| 39 | 13 09·8 | 13 11·9 | 12 33·8 | 3·9 3·4 | 9·9 8·7 | 15·9 13·9 |
| 40 | 13 10·0 | 13 12·2 | 12 34·0 | 4·0 3·5 | 10·0 8·8 | 16·0 14·0 |
| 41 | 13 10·3 | 13 12·4 | 12 34·2 | 4·1 3·6 | 10·1 8·8 | 16·1 14·1 |
| 42 | 13 10·5 | 13 12·7 | 12 34·5 | 4·2 3·7 | 10·2 8·9 | 16·2 14·2 |
| 43 | 13 10·8 | 13 12·9 | 12 34·7 | 4·3 3·8 | 10·3 9·0 | 16·3 14·3 |
| 44 | 13 11·0 | 13 13·2 | 12 35·0 | 4·4 3·9 | 10·4 9·1 | 16·4 14·3 |
| 45 | 13 11·3 | 13 13·4 | 12 35·2 | 4·5 3·9 | 10·5 9·2 | 16·5 14·4 |
| 46 | 13 11·5 | 13 13·7 | 12 35·4 | 4·6 4·0 | 10·6 9·3 | 16·6 14·5 |
| 47 | 13 11·8 | 13 13·9 | 12 35·7 | 4·7 4·1 | 10·7 9·4 | 16·7 14·6 |
| 48 | 13 12·0 | 13 14·2 | 12 35·9 | 4·8 4·2 | 10·8 9·5 | 16·8 14·7 |
| 49 | 13 12·3 | 13 14·4 | 12 36·2 | 4·9 4·3 | 10·9 9·5 | 16·9 14·8 |
| 50 | 13 12·5 | 13 14·7 | 12 36·4 | 5·0 4·4 | 11·0 9·6 | 17·0 14·9 |
| 51 | 13 12·8 | 13 14·9 | 12 36·6 | 5·1 4·5 | 11·1 9·7 | 17·1 15·0 |
| 52 | 13 13·0 | 13 15·2 | 12 36·9 | 5·2 4·6 | 11·2 9·8 | 17·2 15·1 |
| 53 | 13 13·3 | 13 15·4 | 12 37·1 | 5·3 4·6 | 11·3 9·9 | 17·3 15·1 |
| 54 | 13 13·5 | 13 15·7 | 12 37·4 | 5·4 4·7 | 11·4 10·0 | 17·4 15·2 |
| 55 | 13 13·8 | 13 15·9 | 12 37·6 | 5·5 4·8 | 11·5 10·1 | 17·5 15·3 |
| 56 | 13 14·0 | 13 16·2 | 12 37·9 | 5·6 4·9 | 11·6 10·2 | 17·6 15·4 |
| 57 | 13 14·3 | 13 16·4 | 12 38·1 | 5·7 5·0 | 11·7 10·2 | 17·7 15·5 |
| 58 | 13 14·5 | 13 16·7 | 12 38·3 | 5·8 5·1 | 11·8 10·3 | 17·8 15·6 |
| 59 | 13 14·8 | 13 16·9 | 12 38·5 | 5·9 5·2 | 11·9 10·4 | 17·9 15·7 |
| 60 | 13 15·0 | 13 17·2 | 12 38·8 | 6·0 5·3 | 12·0 10·5 | 18·0 15·8 |

## 53ᵐ

| s | SUN PLANETS | ARIES | MOON | v or d / Corrⁿ | v or d / Corrⁿ | v or d / Corrⁿ |
|---|---|---|---|---|---|---|
| 00 | 13 15·0 | 13 17·2 | 12 38·8 | 0·0 0·0 | 6·0 5·4 | 12·0 10·7 |
| 01 | 13 15·3 | 13 17·4 | 12 39·0 | 0·1 0·1 | 6·1 5·4 | 12·1 10·8 |
| 02 | 13 15·5 | 13 17·7 | 12 39·3 | 0·2 0·2 | 6·2 5·5 | 12·2 10·9 |
| 03 | 13 15·8 | 13 17·9 | 12 39·5 | 0·3 0·3 | 6·3 5·6 | 12·3 11·0 |
| 04 | 13 16·0 | 13 18·2 | 12 39·7 | 0·4 0·4 | 6·4 5·7 | 12·4 11·1 |
| 05 | 13 16·3 | 13 18·4 | 12 40·0 | 0·5 0·4 | 6·5 5·8 | 12·5 11·1 |
| 06 | 13 16·5 | 13 18·7 | 12 40·2 | 0·6 0·5 | 6·6 5·9 | 12·6 11·2 |
| 07 | 13 16·8 | 13 18·9 | 12 40·5 | 0·7 0·6 | 6·7 6·0 | 12·7 11·3 |
| 08 | 13 17·0 | 13 19·2 | 12 40·7 | 0·8 0·7 | 6·8 6·1 | 12·8 11·4 |
| 09 | 13 17·3 | 13 19·4 | 12 40·9 | 0·9 0·8 | 6·9 6·2 | 12·9 11·5 |
| 10 | 13 17·5 | 13 19·7 | 12 41·2 | 1·0 0·9 | 7·0 6·2 | 13·0 11·6 |
| 11 | 13 17·8 | 13 19·9 | 12 41·4 | 1·1 1·0 | 7·1 6·3 | 13·1 11·7 |
| 12 | 13 18·0 | 13 20·2 | 12 41·6 | 1·2 1·1 | 7·2 6·4 | 13·2 11·8 |
| 13 | 13 18·3 | 13 20·4 | 12 41·9 | 1·3 1·2 | 7·3 6·5 | 13·3 11·9 |
| 14 | 13 18·5 | 13 20·7 | 12 42·1 | 1·4 1·2 | 7·4 6·6 | 13·4 11·9 |
| 15 | 13 18·8 | 13 20·9 | 12 42·4 | 1·5 1·3 | 7·5 6·7 | 13·5 12·0 |
| 16 | 13 19·0 | 13 21·2 | 12 42·6 | 1·6 1·4 | 7·6 6·8 | 13·6 12·1 |
| 17 | 13 19·3 | 13 21·4 | 12 42·8 | 1·7 1·5 | 7·7 6·9 | 13·7 12·2 |
| 18 | 13 19·5 | 13 21·7 | 12 43·1 | 1·8 1·6 | 7·8 7·0 | 13·8 12·3 |
| 19 | 13 19·8 | 13 21·9 | 12 43·3 | 1·9 1·7 | 7·9 7·0 | 13·9 12·4 |
| 20 | 13 20·0 | 13 22·2 | 12 43·6 | 2·0 1·8 | 8·0 7·1 | 14·0 12·5 |
| 21 | 13 20·3 | 13 22·4 | 12 43·8 | 2·1 1·9 | 8·1 7·2 | 14·1 12·6 |
| 22 | 13 20·5 | 13 22·7 | 12 44·0 | 2·2 2·0 | 8·2 7·3 | 14·2 12·7 |
| 23 | 13 20·8 | 13 22·9 | 12 44·3 | 2·3 2·1 | 8·3 7·4 | 14·3 12·8 |
| 24 | 13 21·0 | 13 23·2 | 12 44·5 | 2·4 2·1 | 8·4 7·5 | 14·4 12·8 |
| 25 | 13 21·3 | 13 23·4 | 12 44·7 | 2·5 2·2 | 8·5 7·6 | 14·5 12·9 |
| 26 | 13 21·5 | 13 23·7 | 12 45·0 | 2·6 2·3 | 8·6 7·7 | 14·6 13·0 |
| 27 | 13 21·8 | 13 23·9 | 12 45·2 | 2·7 2·4 | 8·7 7·8 | 14·7 13·1 |
| 28 | 13 22·0 | 13 24·2 | 12 45·5 | 2·8 2·5 | 8·8 7·8 | 14·8 13·2 |
| 29 | 13 22·3 | 13 24·4 | 12 45·7 | 2·9 2·6 | 8·9 7·9 | 14·9 13·3 |
| 30 | 13 22·5 | 13 24·7 | 12 45·9 | 3·0 2·7 | 9·0 8·0 | 15·0 13·4 |
| 31 | 13 22·8 | 13 24·9 | 12 46·2 | 3·1 2·8 | 9·1 8·1 | 15·1 13·5 |
| 32 | 13 23·0 | 13 25·2 | 12 46·4 | 3·2 2·9 | 9·2 8·2 | 15·2 13·6 |
| 33 | 13 23·3 | 13 25·4 | 12 46·7 | 3·3 2·9 | 9·3 8·3 | 15·3 13·6 |
| 34 | 13 23·5 | 13 25·7 | 12 46·9 | 3·4 3·0 | 9·4 8·4 | 15·4 13·7 |
| 35 | 13 23·8 | 13 26·0 | 12 47·1 | 3·5 3·1 | 9·5 8·5 | 15·5 13·8 |
| 36 | 13 24·0 | 13 26·2 | 12 47·4 | 3·6 3·2 | 9·6 8·6 | 15·6 13·9 |
| 37 | 13 24·3 | 13 26·5 | 12 47·6 | 3·7 3·3 | 9·7 8·6 | 15·7 14·0 |
| 38 | 13 24·5 | 13 26·7 | 12 47·9 | 3·8 3·4 | 9·8 8·7 | 15·8 14·1 |
| 39 | 13 24·8 | 13 27·0 | 12 48·1 | 3·9 3·5 | 9·9 8·8 | 15·9 14·2 |
| 40 | 13 25·0 | 13 27·2 | 12 48·3 | 4·0 3·6 | 10·0 8·9 | 16·0 14·3 |
| 41 | 13 25·3 | 13 27·5 | 12 48·6 | 4·1 3·7 | 10·1 9·0 | 16·1 14·4 |
| 42 | 13 25·5 | 13 27·7 | 12 48·8 | 4·2 3·7 | 10·2 9·1 | 16·2 14·4 |
| 43 | 13 25·8 | 13 28·0 | 12 49·0 | 4·3 3·8 | 10·3 9·2 | 16·3 14·5 |
| 44 | 13 26·0 | 13 28·2 | 12 49·3 | 4·4 3·9 | 10·4 9·3 | 16·4 14·6 |
| 45 | 13 26·3 | 13 28·5 | 12 49·5 | 4·5 4·0 | 10·5 9·4 | 16·5 14·7 |
| 46 | 13 26·5 | 13 28·7 | 12 49·8 | 4·6 4·1 | 10·6 9·5 | 16·6 14·8 |
| 47 | 13 26·8 | 13 29·0 | 12 50·0 | 4·7 4·2 | 10·7 9·5 | 16·7 14·9 |
| 48 | 13 27·0 | 13 29·2 | 12 50·2 | 4·8 4·3 | 10·8 9·6 | 16·8 15·0 |
| 49 | 13 27·3 | 13 29·5 | 12 50·5 | 4·9 4·4 | 10·9 9·7 | 16·9 15·1 |
| 50 | 13 27·5 | 13 29·7 | 12 50·7 | 5·0 4·5 | 11·0 9·8 | 17·0 15·2 |
| 51 | 13 27·8 | 13 30·0 | 12 51·0 | 5·1 4·5 | 11·1 9·9 | 17·1 15·2 |
| 52 | 13 28·0 | 13 30·2 | 12 51·2 | 5·2 4·6 | 11·2 10·0 | 17·2 15·3 |
| 53 | 13 28·3 | 13 30·5 | 12 51·4 | 5·3 4·7 | 11·3 10·1 | 17·3 15·4 |
| 54 | 13 28·5 | 13 30·7 | 12 51·7 | 5·4 4·8 | 11·4 10·2 | 17·4 15·5 |
| 55 | 13 28·8 | 13 31·0 | 12 51·9 | 5·5 4·9 | 11·5 10·3 | 17·5 15·6 |
| 56 | 13 29·0 | 13 31·2 | 12 52·1 | 5·6 5·0 | 11·6 10·3 | 17·6 15·7 |
| 57 | 13 29·3 | 13 31·5 | 12 52·4 | 5·7 5·1 | 11·7 10·4 | 17·7 15·8 |
| 58 | 13 29·5 | 13 31·7 | 12 52·6 | 5·8 5·2 | 11·8 10·5 | 17·8 15·9 |
| 59 | 13 29·8 | 13 32·0 | 12 52·9 | 5·9 5·3 | 11·9 10·6 | 17·9 16·0 |
| 60 | 13 30·0 | 13 32·2 | 12 53·1 | 6·0 5·4 | 12·0 10·7 | 18·0 16·1 |

| 54^m (s) | SUN PLANETS (° ′) | ARIES (° ′) | MOON (° ′) | v or d / Corrn | | v or d / Corrn | | v or d / Corrn | |
|---|---|---|---|---|---|---|---|---|---|
| 00 | 13 30.0 | 13 32.2 | 12 53.1 | 0.0 | 0.0 | 6.0 | 5.5 | 12.0 | 10.9 |
| 01 | 13 30.3 | 13 32.5 | 12 53.3 | 0.1 | 0.1 | 6.1 | 5.5 | 12.1 | 11.0 |
| 02 | 13 30.5 | 13 32.7 | 12 53.6 | 0.2 | 0.2 | 6.2 | 5.6 | 12.2 | 11.1 |
| 03 | 13 30.8 | 13 33.0 | 12 53.8 | 0.3 | 0.3 | 6.3 | 5.7 | 12.3 | 11.2 |
| 04 | 13 31.0 | 13 33.2 | 12 54.1 | 0.4 | 0.4 | 6.4 | 5.8 | 12.4 | 11.3 |
| 05 | 13 31.3 | 13 33.5 | 12 54.3 | 0.5 | 0.5 | 6.5 | 5.9 | 12.5 | 11.4 |
| 06 | 13 31.5 | 13 33.7 | 12 54.5 | 0.6 | 0.5 | 6.6 | 6.0 | 12.6 | 11.4 |
| 07 | 13 31.8 | 13 34.0 | 12 54.8 | 0.7 | 0.6 | 6.7 | 6.1 | 12.7 | 11.5 |
| 08 | 13 32.0 | 13 34.2 | 12 55.0 | 0.8 | 0.7 | 6.8 | 6.2 | 12.8 | 11.6 |
| 09 | 13 32.3 | 13 34.5 | 12 55.2 | 0.9 | 0.8 | 6.9 | 6.3 | 12.9 | 11.7 |
| 10 | 13 32.5 | 13 34.7 | 12 55.5 | 1.0 | 0.9 | 7.0 | 6.4 | 13.0 | 11.8 |
| 11 | 13 32.8 | 13 35.0 | 12 55.7 | 1.1 | 1.0 | 7.1 | 6.4 | 13.1 | 11.9 |
| 12 | 13 33.0 | 13 35.2 | 12 56.0 | 1.2 | 1.1 | 7.2 | 6.5 | 13.2 | 12.0 |
| 13 | 13 33.3 | 13 35.5 | 12 56.2 | 1.3 | 1.2 | 7.3 | 6.6 | 13.3 | 12.1 |
| 14 | 13 33.5 | 13 35.7 | 12 56.4 | 1.4 | 1.3 | 7.4 | 6.7 | 13.4 | 12.2 |
| 15 | 13 33.8 | 13 36.0 | 12 56.7 | 1.5 | 1.4 | 7.5 | 6.8 | 13.5 | 12.3 |
| 16 | 13 34.0 | 13 36.2 | 12 56.9 | 1.6 | 1.5 | 7.6 | 6.9 | 13.6 | 12.4 |
| 17 | 13 34.3 | 13 36.5 | 12 57.2 | 1.7 | 1.5 | 7.7 | 7.0 | 13.7 | 12.4 |
| 18 | 13 34.5 | 13 36.7 | 12 57.4 | 1.8 | 1.6 | 7.8 | 7.1 | 13.8 | 12.5 |
| 19 | 13 34.8 | 13 37.0 | 12 57.6 | 1.9 | 1.7 | 7.9 | 7.2 | 13.9 | 12.6 |
| 20 | 13 35.0 | 13 37.2 | 12 57.9 | 2.0 | 1.8 | 8.0 | 7.3 | 14.0 | 12.7 |
| 21 | 13 35.3 | 13 37.5 | 12 58.1 | 2.1 | 1.9 | 8.1 | 7.4 | 14.1 | 12.8 |
| 22 | 13 35.5 | 13 37.7 | 12 58.3 | 2.2 | 2.0 | 8.2 | 7.4 | 14.2 | 12.9 |
| 23 | 13 35.8 | 13 38.0 | 12 58.6 | 2.3 | 2.1 | 8.3 | 7.5 | 14.3 | 13.0 |
| 24 | 13 36.0 | 13 38.2 | 12 58.8 | 2.4 | 2.2 | 8.4 | 7.6 | 14.4 | 13.1 |
| 25 | 13 36.3 | 13 38.5 | 12 59.1 | 2.5 | 2.3 | 8.5 | 7.7 | 14.5 | 13.2 |
| 26 | 13 36.5 | 13 38.7 | 12 59.3 | 2.6 | 2.4 | 8.6 | 7.8 | 14.6 | 13.3 |
| 27 | 13 36.8 | 13 39.0 | 12 59.5 | 2.7 | 2.5 | 8.7 | 7.9 | 14.7 | 13.4 |
| 28 | 13 37.0 | 13 39.2 | 12 59.8 | 2.8 | 2.5 | 8.8 | 8.0 | 14.8 | 13.4 |
| 29 | 13 37.3 | 13 39.5 | 13 00.0 | 2.9 | 2.6 | 8.9 | 8.1 | 14.9 | 13.5 |
| 30 | 13 37.5 | 13 39.7 | 13 00.3 | 3.0 | 2.7 | 9.0 | 8.2 | 15.0 | 13.6 |
| 31 | 13 37.8 | 13 40.0 | 13 00.5 | 3.1 | 2.8 | 9.1 | 8.3 | 15.1 | 13.7 |
| 32 | 13 38.0 | 13 40.2 | 13 00.7 | 3.2 | 2.9 | 9.2 | 8.4 | 15.2 | 13.8 |
| 33 | 13 38.3 | 13 40.5 | 13 01.0 | 3.3 | 3.0 | 9.3 | 8.4 | 15.3 | 13.9 |
| 34 | 13 38.5 | 13 40.7 | 13 01.2 | 3.4 | 3.1 | 9.4 | 8.5 | 15.4 | 14.0 |
| 35 | 13 38.8 | 13 41.0 | 13 01.5 | 3.5 | 3.2 | 9.5 | 8.6 | 15.5 | 14.1 |
| 36 | 13 39.0 | 13 41.2 | 13 01.7 | 3.6 | 3.3 | 9.6 | 8.7 | 15.6 | 14.2 |
| 37 | 13 39.3 | 13 41.5 | 13 01.9 | 3.7 | 3.4 | 9.7 | 8.8 | 15.7 | 14.3 |
| 38 | 13 39.5 | 13 41.7 | 13 02.2 | 3.8 | 3.5 | 9.8 | 8.9 | 15.8 | 14.4 |
| 39 | 13 39.8 | 13 42.0 | 13 02.4 | 3.9 | 3.5 | 9.9 | 9.0 | 15.9 | 14.4 |
| 40 | 13 40.0 | 13 42.2 | 13 02.6 | 4.0 | 3.6 | 10.0 | 9.1 | 16.0 | 14.5 |
| 41 | 13 40.3 | 13 42.5 | 13 02.9 | 4.1 | 3.7 | 10.1 | 9.2 | 16.1 | 14.6 |
| 42 | 13 40.5 | 13 42.7 | 13 03.1 | 4.2 | 3.8 | 10.2 | 9.3 | 16.2 | 14.7 |
| 43 | 13 40.8 | 13 43.0 | 13 03.4 | 4.3 | 3.9 | 10.3 | 9.4 | 16.3 | 14.8 |
| 44 | 13 41.0 | 13 43.2 | 13 03.6 | 4.4 | 4.0 | 10.4 | 9.4 | 16.4 | 14.9 |
| 45 | 13 41.3 | 13 43.5 | 13 03.8 | 4.5 | 4.1 | 10.5 | 9.5 | 16.5 | 15.0 |
| 46 | 13 41.5 | 13 43.7 | 13 04.1 | 4.6 | 4.2 | 10.6 | 9.6 | 16.6 | 15.1 |
| 47 | 13 41.8 | 13 44.0 | 13 04.3 | 4.7 | 4.3 | 10.7 | 9.7 | 16.7 | 15.2 |
| 48 | 13 42.0 | 13 44.3 | 13 04.6 | 4.8 | 4.4 | 10.8 | 9.8 | 16.8 | 15.3 |
| 49 | 13 42.3 | 13 44.5 | 13 04.8 | 4.9 | 4.5 | 10.9 | 9.9 | 16.9 | 15.4 |
| 50 | 13 42.5 | 13 44.8 | 13 05.0 | 5.0 | 4.5 | 11.0 | 10.0 | 17.0 | 15.4 |
| 51 | 13 42.8 | 13 45.0 | 13 05.3 | 5.1 | 4.6 | 11.1 | 10.1 | 17.1 | 15.5 |
| 52 | 13 43.0 | 13 45.3 | 13 05.5 | 5.2 | 4.7 | 11.2 | 10.2 | 17.2 | 15.6 |
| 53 | 13 43.3 | 13 45.5 | 13 05.7 | 5.3 | 4.8 | 11.3 | 10.3 | 17.3 | 15.7 |
| 54 | 13 43.5 | 13 45.8 | 13 06.0 | 5.4 | 4.9 | 11.4 | 10.4 | 17.4 | 15.8 |
| 55 | 13 43.8 | 13 46.0 | 13 06.2 | 5.5 | 5.0 | 11.5 | 10.4 | 17.5 | 15.9 |
| 56 | 13 44.0 | 13 46.3 | 13 06.4 | 5.6 | 5.1 | 11.6 | 10.5 | 17.6 | 16.0 |
| 57 | 13 44.3 | 13 46.5 | 13 06.7 | 5.7 | 5.2 | 11.7 | 10.6 | 17.7 | 16.1 |
| 58 | 13 44.5 | 13 46.8 | 13 06.9 | 5.8 | 5.3 | 11.8 | 10.7 | 17.8 | 16.2 |
| 59 | 13 44.8 | 13 47.0 | 13 07.2 | 5.9 | 5.4 | 11.9 | 10.8 | 17.9 | 16.3 |
| 60 | 13 45.0 | 13 47.3 | 13 07.4 | 6.0 | 5.5 | 12.0 | 10.9 | 18.0 | 16.4 |

| 55^m (s) | SUN PLANETS (° ′) | ARIES (° ′) | MOON (° ′) | v or d / Corrn | | v or d / Corrn | | v or d / Corrn | |
|---|---|---|---|---|---|---|---|---|---|
| 00 | 13 45.0 | 13 47.3 | 13 07.4 | 0.0 | 0.0 | 6.0 | 5.6 | 12.0 | 11.1 |
| 01 | 13 45.3 | 13 47.5 | 13 07.7 | 0.1 | 0.1 | 6.1 | 5.6 | 12.1 | 11.2 |
| 02 | 13 45.5 | 13 47.8 | 13 07.9 | 0.2 | 0.2 | 6.2 | 5.7 | 12.2 | 11.3 |
| 03 | 13 45.8 | 13 48.0 | 13 08.1 | 0.3 | 0.3 | 6.3 | 5.8 | 12.3 | 11.4 |
| 04 | 13 46.0 | 13 48.3 | 13 08.4 | 0.4 | 0.4 | 6.4 | 5.9 | 12.4 | 11.5 |
| 05 | 13 46.3 | 13 48.5 | 13 08.6 | 0.5 | 0.5 | 6.5 | 6.0 | 12.5 | 11.6 |
| 06 | 13 46.5 | 13 48.8 | 13 08.8 | 0.6 | 0.6 | 6.6 | 6.1 | 12.6 | 11.7 |
| 07 | 13 46.8 | 13 49.0 | 13 09.1 | 0.7 | 0.6 | 6.7 | 6.2 | 12.7 | 11.7 |
| 08 | 13 47.0 | 13 49.3 | 13 09.3 | 0.8 | 0.7 | 6.8 | 6.3 | 12.8 | 11.8 |
| 09 | 13 47.3 | 13 49.5 | 13 09.6 | 0.9 | 0.8 | 6.9 | 6.4 | 12.9 | 11.9 |
| 10 | 13 47.5 | 13 49.8 | 13 09.8 | 1.0 | 0.9 | 7.0 | 6.5 | 13.0 | 12.0 |
| 11 | 13 47.8 | 13 50.0 | 13 10.0 | 1.1 | 1.0 | 7.1 | 6.6 | 13.1 | 12.1 |
| 12 | 13 48.0 | 13 50.3 | 13 10.3 | 1.2 | 1.1 | 7.2 | 6.7 | 13.2 | 12.2 |
| 13 | 13 48.3 | 13 50.5 | 13 10.5 | 1.3 | 1.2 | 7.3 | 6.8 | 13.3 | 12.3 |
| 14 | 13 48.5 | 13 50.8 | 13 10.8 | 1.4 | 1.3 | 7.4 | 6.8 | 13.4 | 12.4 |
| 15 | 13 48.8 | 13 51.0 | 13 11.0 | 1.5 | 1.4 | 7.5 | 6.9 | 13.5 | 12.5 |
| 16 | 13 49.0 | 13 51.3 | 13 11.2 | 1.6 | 1.5 | 7.6 | 7.0 | 13.6 | 12.6 |
| 17 | 13 49.3 | 13 51.5 | 13 11.5 | 1.7 | 1.6 | 7.7 | 7.1 | 13.7 | 12.7 |
| 18 | 13 49.5 | 13 51.8 | 13 11.7 | 1.8 | 1.7 | 7.8 | 7.2 | 13.8 | 12.8 |
| 19 | 13 49.8 | 13 52.0 | 13 12.0 | 1.9 | 1.8 | 7.9 | 7.3 | 13.9 | 12.9 |
| 20 | 13 50.0 | 13 52.3 | 13 12.2 | 2.0 | 1.9 | 8.0 | 7.4 | 14.0 | 13.0 |
| 21 | 13 50.3 | 13 52.5 | 13 12.4 | 2.1 | 1.9 | 8.1 | 7.5 | 14.1 | 13.0 |
| 22 | 13 50.5 | 13 52.8 | 13 12.7 | 2.2 | 2.0 | 8.2 | 7.6 | 14.2 | 13.1 |
| 23 | 13 50.8 | 13 53.0 | 13 12.9 | 2.3 | 2.1 | 8.3 | 7.7 | 14.3 | 13.2 |
| 24 | 13 51.0 | 13 53.3 | 13 13.1 | 2.4 | 2.2 | 8.4 | 7.8 | 14.4 | 13.3 |
| 25 | 13 51.3 | 13 53.5 | 13 13.4 | 2.5 | 2.3 | 8.5 | 7.9 | 14.5 | 13.4 |
| 26 | 13 51.5 | 13 53.8 | 13 13.6 | 2.6 | 2.4 | 8.6 | 8.0 | 14.6 | 13.5 |
| 27 | 13 51.8 | 13 54.0 | 13 13.9 | 2.7 | 2.5 | 8.7 | 8.0 | 14.7 | 13.6 |
| 28 | 13 52.0 | 13 54.3 | 13 14.1 | 2.8 | 2.6 | 8.8 | 8.1 | 14.8 | 13.7 |
| 29 | 13 52.3 | 13 54.5 | 13 14.3 | 2.9 | 2.7 | 8.9 | 8.2 | 14.9 | 13.8 |
| 30 | 13 52.5 | 13 54.8 | 13 14.6 | 3.0 | 2.8 | 9.0 | 8.3 | 15.0 | 13.9 |
| 31 | 13 52.8 | 13 55.0 | 13 14.8 | 3.1 | 2.9 | 9.1 | 8.4 | 15.1 | 14.0 |
| 32 | 13 53.0 | 13 55.3 | 13 15.1 | 3.2 | 3.0 | 9.2 | 8.5 | 15.2 | 14.1 |
| 33 | 13 53.3 | 13 55.5 | 13 15.3 | 3.3 | 3.1 | 9.3 | 8.6 | 15.3 | 14.2 |
| 34 | 13 53.5 | 13 55.8 | 13 15.5 | 3.4 | 3.1 | 9.4 | 8.7 | 15.4 | 14.2 |
| 35 | 13 53.8 | 13 56.0 | 13 15.8 | 3.5 | 3.2 | 9.5 | 8.8 | 15.5 | 14.3 |
| 36 | 13 54.0 | 13 56.3 | 13 16.0 | 3.6 | 3.3 | 9.6 | 8.9 | 15.6 | 14.4 |
| 37 | 13 54.3 | 13 56.5 | 13 16.2 | 3.7 | 3.4 | 9.7 | 9.0 | 15.7 | 14.5 |
| 38 | 13 54.5 | 13 56.8 | 13 16.5 | 3.8 | 3.5 | 9.8 | 9.1 | 15.8 | 14.6 |
| 39 | 13 54.8 | 13 57.0 | 13 16.7 | 3.9 | 3.6 | 9.9 | 9.2 | 15.9 | 14.7 |
| 40 | 13 55.0 | 13 57.3 | 13 17.0 | 4.0 | 3.7 | 10.0 | 9.3 | 16.0 | 14.8 |
| 41 | 13 55.3 | 13 57.5 | 13 17.2 | 4.1 | 3.8 | 10.1 | 9.3 | 16.1 | 14.9 |
| 42 | 13 55.5 | 13 57.8 | 13 17.4 | 4.2 | 3.9 | 10.2 | 9.4 | 16.2 | 15.0 |
| 43 | 13 55.8 | 13 58.0 | 13 17.7 | 4.3 | 4.0 | 10.3 | 9.5 | 16.3 | 15.1 |
| 44 | 13 56.0 | 13 58.3 | 13 17.9 | 4.4 | 4.1 | 10.4 | 9.6 | 16.4 | 15.2 |
| 45 | 13 56.3 | 13 58.5 | 13 18.2 | 4.5 | 4.2 | 10.5 | 9.7 | 16.5 | 15.3 |
| 46 | 13 56.5 | 13 58.8 | 13 18.4 | 4.6 | 4.3 | 10.6 | 9.8 | 16.6 | 15.4 |
| 47 | 13 56.8 | 13 59.0 | 13 18.6 | 4.7 | 4.3 | 10.7 | 9.9 | 16.7 | 15.4 |
| 48 | 13 57.0 | 13 59.3 | 13 18.9 | 4.8 | 4.4 | 10.8 | 10.0 | 16.8 | 15.5 |
| 49 | 13 57.3 | 13 59.5 | 13 19.1 | 4.9 | 4.5 | 10.9 | 10.1 | 16.9 | 15.6 |
| 50 | 13 57.5 | 13 59.8 | 13 19.3 | 5.0 | 4.6 | 11.0 | 10.2 | 17.0 | 15.7 |
| 51 | 13 57.8 | 14 00.0 | 13 19.6 | 5.1 | 4.7 | 11.1 | 10.3 | 17.1 | 15.8 |
| 52 | 13 58.0 | 14 00.3 | 13 19.8 | 5.2 | 4.8 | 11.2 | 10.4 | 17.2 | 15.9 |
| 53 | 13 58.3 | 14 00.5 | 13 20.1 | 5.3 | 4.9 | 11.3 | 10.5 | 17.3 | 16.0 |
| 54 | 13 58.5 | 14 00.8 | 13 20.3 | 5.4 | 5.0 | 11.4 | 10.5 | 17.4 | 16.1 |
| 55 | 13 58.8 | 14 01.0 | 13 20.5 | 5.5 | 5.1 | 11.5 | 10.6 | 17.5 | 16.2 |
| 56 | 13 59.0 | 14 01.3 | 13 20.8 | 5.6 | 5.2 | 11.6 | 10.7 | 17.6 | 16.3 |
| 57 | 13 59.3 | 14 01.5 | 13 21.0 | 5.7 | 5.3 | 11.7 | 10.8 | 17.7 | 16.4 |
| 58 | 13 59.5 | 14 01.8 | 13 21.3 | 5.8 | 5.4 | 11.8 | 10.9 | 17.8 | 16.5 |
| 59 | 13 59.8 | 14 02.0 | 13 21.5 | 5.9 | 5.5 | 11.9 | 11.0 | 17.9 | 16.6 |
| 60 | 14 00.0 | 14 02.3 | 13 21.7 | 6.0 | 5.6 | 12.0 | 11.1 | 18.0 | 16.7 |

| 56ᵐ | SUN PLANETS | ARIES | MOON | $v$ or $d$ | Corrⁿ | $v$ or $d$ | Corrⁿ | $v$ or $d$ | Corrⁿ | 57ᵐ | SUN PLANETS | ARIES | MOON | $v$ or $d$ | Corrⁿ | $v$ or $d$ | Corrⁿ | $v$ or $d$ | Corrⁿ |
|---|---|---|---|---|---|---|---|---|---|---|---|---|---|---|---|---|---|---|---|
| s | ° ′ | ° ′ | ° ′ | ′ | ′ | ′ | ′ | ′ | ′ | s | ° ′ | ° ′ | ° ′ | ′ | ′ | ′ | ′ | ′ | ′ |
| 00 | 14 00·0 | 14 02·3 | 13 21·7 | 0·0 | 0·0 | 6·0 | 5·7 | 12·0 | 11·3 | 00 | 14 15·0 | 14 17·3 | 13 36·1 | 0·0 | 0·0 | 6·0 | 5·8 | 12·0 | 11·5 |
| 01 | 14 00·3 | 14 02·6 | 13 22·0 | 0·1 | 0·1 | 6·1 | 5·7 | 12·1 | 11·4 | 01 | 14 15·3 | 14 17·6 | 13 36·3 | 0·1 | 0·1 | 6·1 | 5·8 | 12·1 | 11·6 |
| 02 | 14 00·5 | 14 02·8 | 13 22·2 | 0·2 | 0·2 | 6·2 | 5·8 | 12·2 | 11·5 | 02 | 14 15·5 | 14 17·8 | 13 36·5 | 0·2 | 0·2 | 6·2 | 5·9 | 12·2 | 11·7 |
| 03 | 14 00·8 | 14 03·1 | 13 22·4 | 0·3 | 0·3 | 6·3 | 5·9 | 12·3 | 11·6 | 03 | 14 15·8 | 14 18·1 | 13 36·8 | 0·3 | 0·3 | 6·3 | 6·0 | 12·3 | 11·8 |
| 04 | 14 01·0 | 14 03·3 | 13 22·7 | 0·4 | 0·4 | 6·4 | 6·0 | 12·4 | 11·7 | 04 | 14 16·0 | 14 18·3 | 13 37·0 | 0·4 | 0·4 | 6·4 | 6·1 | 12·4 | 11·9 |
| 05 | 14 01·3 | 14 03·6 | 13 22·9 | 0·5 | 0·5 | 6·5 | 6·1 | 12·5 | 11·8 | 05 | 14 16·3 | 14 18·6 | 13 37·2 | 0·5 | 0·5 | 6·5 | 6·2 | 12·5 | 12·0 |
| 06 | 14 01·5 | 14 03·8 | 13 23·2 | 0·6 | 0·6 | 6·6 | 6·2 | 12·6 | 11·9 | 06 | 14 16·5 | 14 18·8 | 13 37·5 | 0·6 | 0·6 | 6·6 | 6·3 | 12·6 | 12·1 |
| 07 | 14 01·8 | 14 04·1 | 13 23·4 | 0·7 | 0·7 | 6·7 | 6·3 | 12·7 | 12·0 | 07 | 14 16·8 | 14 19·1 | 13 37·7 | 0·7 | 0·7 | 6·7 | 6·4 | 12·7 | 12·2 |
| 08 | 14 02·0 | 14 04·3 | 13 23·6 | 0·8 | 0·8 | 6·8 | 6·4 | 12·8 | 12·1 | 08 | 14 17·0 | 14 19·3 | 13 38·0 | 0·8 | 0·8 | 6·8 | 6·5 | 12·8 | 12·3 |
| 09 | 14 02·3 | 14 04·6 | 13 23·9 | 0·9 | 0·9 | 6·9 | 6·5 | 12·9 | 12·1 | 09 | 14 17·3 | 14 19·6 | 13 38·2 | 0·9 | 0·9 | 6·9 | 6·6 | 12·9 | 12·4 |
| 10 | 14 02·5 | 14 04·8 | 13 24·1 | 1·0 | 0·9 | 7·0 | 6·6 | 13·0 | 12·2 | 10 | 14 17·5 | 14 19·8 | 13 38·4 | 1·0 | 1·0 | 7·0 | 6·7 | 13·0 | 12·5 |
| 11 | 14 02·8 | 14 05·1 | 13 24·4 | 1·1 | 1·0 | 7·1 | 6·7 | 13·1 | 12·3 | 11 | 14 17·8 | 14 20·1 | 13 38·7 | 1·1 | 1·1 | 7·1 | 6·8 | 13·1 | 12·6 |
| 12 | 14 03·0 | 14 05·3 | 13 24·6 | 1·2 | 1·1 | 7·2 | 6·8 | 13·2 | 12·4 | 12 | 14 18·0 | 14 20·3 | 13 38·9 | 1·2 | 1·2 | 7·2 | 6·9 | 13·2 | 12·7 |
| 13 | 14 03·3 | 14 05·6 | 13 24·8 | 1·3 | 1·2 | 7·3 | 6·9 | 13·3 | 12·5 | 13 | 14 18·3 | 14 20·6 | 13 39·2 | 1·3 | 1·2 | 7·3 | 7·0 | 13·3 | 12·7 |
| 14 | 14 03·5 | 14 05·8 | 13 25·1 | 1·4 | 1·3 | 7·4 | 7·0 | 13·4 | 12·6 | 14 | 14 18·5 | 14 20·9 | 13 39·4 | 1·4 | 1·3 | 7·4 | 7·1 | 13·4 | 12·8 |
| 15 | 14 03·8 | 14 06·1 | 13 25·3 | 1·5 | 1·4 | 7·5 | 7·1 | 13·5 | 12·7 | 15 | 14 18·8 | 14 21·1 | 13 39·6 | 1·5 | 1·4 | 7·5 | 7·2 | 13·5 | 12·9 |
| 16 | 14 04·0 | 14 06·3 | 13 25·6 | 1·6 | 1·5 | 7·6 | 7·2 | 13·6 | 12·8 | 16 | 14 19·0 | 14 21·4 | 13 39·9 | 1·6 | 1·5 | 7·6 | 7·3 | 13·6 | 13·0 |
| 17 | 14 04·3 | 14 06·6 | 13 25·8 | 1·7 | 1·6 | 7·7 | 7·3 | 13·7 | 12·9 | 17 | 14 19·3 | 14 21·6 | 13 40·1 | 1·7 | 1·6 | 7·7 | 7·4 | 13·7 | 13·1 |
| 18 | 14 04·5 | 14 06·8 | 13 26·0 | 1·8 | 1·7 | 7·8 | 7·3 | 13·8 | 13·0 | 18 | 14 19·5 | 14 21·9 | 13 40·3 | 1·8 | 1·7 | 7·8 | 7·5 | 13·8 | 13·2 |
| 19 | 14 04·8 | 14 07·1 | 13 26·3 | 1·9 | 1·8 | 7·9 | 7·4 | 13·9 | 13·1 | 19 | 14 19·8 | 14 22·1 | 13 40·6 | 1·9 | 1·8 | 7·9 | 7·6 | 13·9 | 13·3 |
| 20 | 14 05·0 | 14 07·3 | 13 26·5 | 2·0 | 1·9 | 8·0 | 7·5 | 14·0 | 13·2 | 20 | 14 20·0 | 14 22·4 | 13 40·8 | 2·0 | 1·9 | 8·0 | 7·7 | 14·0 | 13·4 |
| 21 | 14 05·3 | 14 07·6 | 13 26·7 | 2·1 | 2·0 | 8·1 | 7·6 | 14·1 | 13·3 | 21 | 14 20·3 | 14 22·6 | 13 41·1 | 2·1 | 2·0 | 8·1 | 7·8 | 14·1 | 13·5 |
| 22 | 14 05·5 | 14 07·8 | 13 27·0 | 2·2 | 2·1 | 8·2 | 7·7 | 14·2 | 13·4 | 22 | 14 20·5 | 14 22·9 | 13 41·3 | 2·2 | 2·1 | 8·2 | 7·9 | 14·2 | 13·6 |
| 23 | 14 05·8 | 14 08·1 | 13 27·2 | 2·3 | 2·2 | 8·3 | 7·8 | 14·3 | 13·5 | 23 | 14 20·8 | 14 23·1 | 13 41·5 | 2·3 | 2·2 | 8·3 | 8·0 | 14·3 | 13·7 |
| 24 | 14 06·0 | 14 08·3 | 13 27·5 | 2·4 | 2·3 | 8·4 | 7·9 | 14·4 | 13·6 | 24 | 14 21·0 | 14 23·4 | 13 41·8 | 2·4 | 2·3 | 8·4 | 8·1 | 14·4 | 13·8 |
| 25 | 14 06·3 | 14 08·6 | 13 27·7 | 2·5 | 2·4 | 8·5 | 8·0 | 14·5 | 13·7 | 25 | 14 21·3 | 14 23·6 | 13 42·0 | 2·5 | 2·4 | 8·5 | 8·1 | 14·5 | 13·9 |
| 26 | 14 06·5 | 14 08·8 | 13 27·9 | 2·6 | 2·4 | 8·6 | 8·1 | 14·6 | 13·7 | 26 | 14 21·5 | 14 23·9 | 13 42·3 | 2·6 | 2·5 | 8·6 | 8·2 | 14·6 | 14·0 |
| 27 | 14 06·8 | 14 09·1 | 13 28·2 | 2·7 | 2·5 | 8·7 | 8·2 | 14·7 | 13·8 | 27 | 14 21·8 | 14 24·1 | 13 42·5 | 2·7 | 2·6 | 8·7 | 8·3 | 14·7 | 14·1 |
| 28 | 14 07·0 | 14 09·3 | 13 28·4 | 2·8 | 2·6 | 8·8 | 8·3 | 14·8 | 13·9 | 28 | 14 22·0 | 14 24·4 | 13 42·7 | 2·8 | 2·7 | 8·8 | 8·4 | 14·8 | 14·2 |
| 29 | 14 07·3 | 14 09·6 | 13 28·7 | 2·9 | 2·7 | 8·9 | 8·4 | 14·9 | 14·0 | 29 | 14 22·3 | 14 24·6 | 13 43·0 | 2·9 | 2·8 | 8·9 | 8·5 | 14·9 | 14·3 |
| 30 | 14 07·5 | 14 09·8 | 13 28·9 | 3·0 | 2·8 | 9·0 | 8·5 | 15·0 | 14·1 | 30 | 14 22·5 | 14 24·9 | 13 43·2 | 3·0 | 2·9 | 9·0 | 8·6 | 15·0 | 14·4 |
| 31 | 14 07·8 | 14 10·1 | 13 29·1 | 3·1 | 2·9 | 9·1 | 8·6 | 15·1 | 14·2 | 31 | 14 22·8 | 14 25·1 | 13 43·4 | 3·1 | 3·0 | 9·1 | 8·7 | 15·1 | 14·5 |
| 32 | 14 08·0 | 14 10·3 | 13 29·4 | 3·2 | 3·0 | 9·2 | 8·7 | 15·2 | 14·3 | 32 | 14 23·0 | 14 25·4 | 13 43·7 | 3·2 | 3·1 | 9·2 | 8·8 | 15·2 | 14·6 |
| 33 | 14 08·3 | 14 10·6 | 13 29·6 | 3·3 | 3·1 | 9·3 | 8·8 | 15·3 | 14·4 | 33 | 14 23·3 | 14 25·6 | 13 43·9 | 3·3 | 3·2 | 9·3 | 8·9 | 15·3 | 14·7 |
| 34 | 14 08·5 | 14 10·8 | 13 29·8 | 3·4 | 3·2 | 9·4 | 8·9 | 15·4 | 14·5 | 34 | 14 23·5 | 14 25·9 | 13 44·2 | 3·4 | 3·3 | 9·4 | 9·0 | 15·4 | 14·8 |
| 35 | 14 08·8 | 14 11·1 | 13 30·1 | 3·5 | 3·3 | 9·5 | 8·9 | 15·5 | 14·6 | 35 | 14 23·8 | 14 26·1 | 13 44·4 | 3·5 | 3·4 | 9·5 | 9·1 | 15·5 | 14·9 |
| 36 | 14 09·0 | 14 11·3 | 13 30·3 | 3·6 | 3·4 | 9·6 | 9·0 | 15·6 | 14·7 | 36 | 14 24·0 | 14 26·4 | 13 44·6 | 3·6 | 3·5 | 9·6 | 9·2 | 15·6 | 15·0 |
| 37 | 14 09·3 | 14 11·6 | 13 30·6 | 3·7 | 3·5 | 9·7 | 9·1 | 15·7 | 14·8 | 37 | 14 24·3 | 14 26·6 | 13 44·9 | 3·7 | 3·5 | 9·7 | 9·3 | 15·7 | 15·0 |
| 38 | 14 09·5 | 14 11·8 | 13 30·8 | 3·8 | 3·6 | 9·8 | 9·2 | 15·8 | 14·9 | 38 | 14 24·5 | 14 26·9 | 13 45·1 | 3·8 | 3·6 | 9·8 | 9·4 | 15·8 | 15·1 |
| 39 | 14 09·8 | 14 12·1 | 13 31·0 | 3·9 | 3·7 | 9·9 | 9·3 | 15·9 | 15·0 | 39 | 14 24·8 | 14 27·1 | 13 45·4 | 3·9 | 3·7 | 9·9 | 9·5 | 15·9 | 15·2 |
| 40 | 14 10·0 | 14 12·3 | 13 31·3 | 4·0 | 3·8 | 10·0 | 9·4 | 16·0 | 15·1 | 40 | 14 25·0 | 14 27·4 | 13 45·6 | 4·0 | 3·8 | 10·0 | 9·6 | 16·0 | 15·3 |
| 41 | 14 10·3 | 14 12·6 | 13 31·5 | 4·1 | 3·9 | 10·1 | 9·5 | 16·1 | 15·2 | 41 | 14 25·3 | 14 27·6 | 13 45·8 | 4·1 | 3·9 | 10·1 | 9·7 | 16·1 | 15·4 |
| 42 | 14 10·5 | 14 12·8 | 13 31·8 | 4·2 | 4·0 | 10·2 | 9·6 | 16·2 | 15·3 | 42 | 14 25·5 | 14 27·9 | 13 46·1 | 4·2 | 4·0 | 10·2 | 9·8 | 16·2 | 15·5 |
| 43 | 14 10·8 | 14 13·1 | 13 32·0 | 4·3 | 4·0 | 10·3 | 9·7 | 16·3 | 15·3 | 43 | 14 25·8 | 14 28·1 | 13 46·3 | 4·3 | 4·1 | 10·3 | 9·9 | 16·3 | 15·6 |
| 44 | 14 11·0 | 14 13·3 | 13 32·2 | 4·4 | 4·1 | 10·4 | 9·8 | 16·4 | 15·4 | 44 | 14 26·0 | 14 28·4 | 13 46·5 | 4·4 | 4·2 | 10·4 | 10·0 | 16·4 | 15·7 |
| 45 | 14 11·3 | 14 13·6 | 13 32·5 | 4·5 | 4·2 | 10·5 | 9·9 | 16·5 | 15·5 | 45 | 14 26·3 | 14 28·6 | 13 46·8 | 4·5 | 4·3 | 10·5 | 10·1 | 16·5 | 15·8 |
| 46 | 14 11·5 | 14 13·8 | 13 32·7 | 4·6 | 4·3 | 10·6 | 10·0 | 16·6 | 15·6 | 46 | 14 26·5 | 14 28·9 | 13 47·0 | 4·6 | 4·4 | 10·6 | 10·2 | 16·6 | 15·9 |
| 47 | 14 11·8 | 14 14·1 | 13 32·9 | 4·7 | 4·4 | 10·7 | 10·1 | 16·7 | 15·7 | 47 | 14 26·8 | 14 29·1 | 13 47·3 | 4·7 | 4·5 | 10·7 | 10·3 | 16·7 | 16·0 |
| 48 | 14 12·0 | 14 14·3 | 13 33·2 | 4·8 | 4·5 | 10·8 | 10·2 | 16·8 | 15·8 | 48 | 14 27·0 | 14 29·4 | 13 47·5 | 4·8 | 4·6 | 10·8 | 10·4 | 16·8 | 16·1 |
| 49 | 14 12·3 | 14 14·6 | 13 33·4 | 4·9 | 4·6 | 10·9 | 10·3 | 16·9 | 15·9 | 49 | 14 27·3 | 14 29·6 | 13 47·7 | 4·9 | 4·7 | 10·9 | 10·4 | 16·9 | 16·2 |
| 50 | 14 12·5 | 14 14·8 | 13 33·7 | 5·0 | 4·7 | 11·0 | 10·4 | 17·0 | 16·0 | 50 | 14 27·5 | 14 29·9 | 13 48·0 | 5·0 | 4·8 | 11·0 | 10·5 | 17·0 | 16·3 |
| 51 | 14 12·8 | 14 15·1 | 13 33·9 | 5·1 | 4·8 | 11·1 | 10·5 | 17·1 | 16·1 | 51 | 14 27·8 | 14 30·1 | 13 48·2 | 5·1 | 4·9 | 11·1 | 10·6 | 17·1 | 16·4 |
| 52 | 14 13·0 | 14 15·3 | 13 34·1 | 5·2 | 4·9 | 11·2 | 10·5 | 17·2 | 16·2 | 52 | 14 28·0 | 14 30·4 | 13 48·5 | 5·2 | 5·0 | 11·2 | 10·7 | 17·2 | 16·5 |
| 53 | 14 13·3 | 14 15·6 | 13 34·4 | 5·3 | 5·0 | 11·3 | 10·6 | 17·3 | 16·3 | 53 | 14 28·3 | 14 30·6 | 13 48·7 | 5·3 | 5·1 | 11·3 | 10·8 | 17·3 | 16·6 |
| 54 | 14 13·5 | 14 15·8 | 13 34·6 | 5·4 | 5·1 | 11·4 | 10·7 | 17·4 | 16·4 | 54 | 14 28·5 | 14 30·9 | 13 48·9 | 5·4 | 5·2 | 11·4 | 10·9 | 17·4 | 16·7 |
| 55 | 14 13·8 | 14 16·1 | 13 34·9 | 5·5 | 5·2 | 11·5 | 10·8 | 17·5 | 16·5 | 55 | 14 28·8 | 14 31·1 | 13 49·2 | 5·5 | 5·3 | 11·5 | 11·0 | 17·5 | 16·8 |
| 56 | 14 14·0 | 14 16·3 | 13 35·1 | 5·6 | 5·3 | 11·6 | 10·9 | 17·6 | 16·6 | 56 | 14 29·0 | 14 31·4 | 13 49·4 | 5·6 | 5·4 | 11·6 | 11·1 | 17·6 | 16·9 |
| 57 | 14 14·3 | 14 16·6 | 13 35·3 | 5·7 | 5·4 | 11·7 | 11·0 | 17·7 | 16·7 | 57 | 14 29·3 | 14 31·6 | 13 49·7 | 5·7 | 5·5 | 11·7 | 11·2 | 17·7 | 17·0 |
| 58 | 14 14·5 | 14 16·8 | 13 35·6 | 5·8 | 5·5 | 11·8 | 11·1 | 17·8 | 16·8 | 58 | 14 29·5 | 14 31·9 | 13 49·9 | 5·8 | 5·6 | 11·8 | 11·3 | 17·8 | 17·1 |
| 59 | 14 14·8 | 14 17·1 | 13 35·8 | 5·9 | 5·6 | 11·9 | 11·2 | 17·9 | 16·9 | 59 | 14 29·8 | 14 32·1 | 13 50·1 | 5·9 | 5·7 | 11·9 | 11·4 | 17·9 | 17·2 |
| 60 | 14 15·0 | 14 17·3 | 13 36·1 | 6·0 | 5·7 | 12·0 | 11·3 | 18·0 | 17·0 | 60 | 14 30·0 | 14 32·4 | 13 50·4 | 6·0 | 5·8 | 12·0 | 11·5 | 18·0 | 17·3 |

xxx

| 58 | SUN PLANETS | ARIES | MOON | $v$ or $d$ | Corrⁿ | $v$ or $d$ | Corrⁿ | $v$ or $d$ | Corrⁿ |
|---|---|---|---|---|---|---|---|---|---|
| s | ° ′ | ° ′ | ° ′ | ′ | ′ | ′ | ′ | ′ | ′ |
| 00 | 14 30.0 | 14 32.4 | 13 50.4 | 0.0 | 0.0 | 6.0 | 5.9 | 12.0 | 11.7 |
| 01 | 14 30.3 | 14 32.6 | 13 50.6 | 0.1 | 0.1 | 6.1 | 5.9 | 12.1 | 11.8 |
| 02 | 14 30.5 | 14 32.9 | 13 50.8 | 0.2 | 0.2 | 6.2 | 6.0 | 12.2 | 11.9 |
| 03 | 14 30.8 | 14 33.1 | 13 51.1 | 0.3 | 0.3 | 6.3 | 6.1 | 12.3 | 12.0 |
| 04 | 14 31.0 | 14 33.4 | 13 51.3 | 0.4 | 0.4 | 6.4 | 6.2 | 12.4 | 12.1 |
| 05 | 14 31.3 | 14 33.6 | 13 51.6 | 0.5 | 0.5 | 6.5 | 6.3 | 12.5 | 12.2 |
| 06 | 14 31.5 | 14 33.9 | 13 51.8 | 0.6 | 0.6 | 6.6 | 6.4 | 12.6 | 12.3 |
| 07 | 14 31.8 | 14 34.1 | 13 52.0 | 0.7 | 0.7 | 6.7 | 6.5 | 12.7 | 12.4 |
| 08 | 14 32.0 | 14 34.4 | 13 52.3 | 0.8 | 0.8 | 6.8 | 6.6 | 12.8 | 12.5 |
| 09 | 14 32.3 | 14 34.6 | 13 52.5 | 0.9 | 0.9 | 6.9 | 6.7 | 12.9 | 12.6 |
| 10 | 14 32.5 | 14 34.9 | 13 52.8 | 1.0 | 1.0 | 7.0 | 6.8 | 13.0 | 12.7 |
| 11 | 14 32.8 | 14 35.1 | 13 53.0 | 1.1 | 1.1 | 7.1 | 6.9 | 13.1 | 12.8 |
| 12 | 14 33.0 | 14 35.4 | 13 53.2 | 1.2 | 1.2 | 7.2 | 7.0 | 13.2 | 12.9 |
| 13 | 14 33.3 | 14 35.6 | 13 53.5 | 1.3 | 1.3 | 7.3 | 7.1 | 13.3 | 13.0 |
| 14 | 14 33.5 | 14 35.9 | 13 53.7 | 1.4 | 1.4 | 7.4 | 7.2 | 13.4 | 13.1 |
| 15 | 14 33.8 | 14 36.1 | 13 53.9 | 1.5 | 1.5 | 7.5 | 7.3 | 13.5 | 13.2 |
| 16 | 14 34.0 | 14 36.4 | 13 54.2 | 1.6 | 1.6 | 7.6 | 7.4 | 13.6 | 13.3 |
| 17 | 14 34.3 | 14 36.6 | 13 54.4 | 1.7 | 1.7 | 7.7 | 7.5 | 13.7 | 13.4 |
| 18 | 14 34.5 | 14 36.9 | 13 54.7 | 1.8 | 1.8 | 7.8 | 7.6 | 13.8 | 13.5 |
| 19 | 14 34.8 | 14 37.1 | 13 54.9 | 1.9 | 1.9 | 7.9 | 7.7 | 13.9 | 13.6 |
| 20 | 14 35.0 | 14 37.4 | 13 55.1 | 2.0 | 2.0 | 8.0 | 7.8 | 14.0 | 13.7 |
| 21 | 14 35.3 | 14 37.6 | 13 55.4 | 2.1 | 2.0 | 8.1 | 7.9 | 14.1 | 13.7 |
| 22 | 14 35.5 | 14 37.9 | 13 55.6 | 2.2 | 2.1 | 8.2 | 8.0 | 14.2 | 13.8 |
| 23 | 14 35.8 | 14 38.1 | 13 55.9 | 2.3 | 2.2 | 8.3 | 8.1 | 14.3 | 13.9 |
| 24 | 14 36.0 | 14 38.4 | 13 56.1 | 2.4 | 2.3 | 8.4 | 8.2 | 14.4 | 14.0 |
| 25 | 14 36.3 | 14 38.6 | 13 56.3 | 2.5 | 2.4 | 8.5 | 8.3 | 14.5 | 14.1 |
| 26 | 14 36.5 | 14 38.9 | 13 56.6 | 2.6 | 2.5 | 8.6 | 8.4 | 14.6 | 14.2 |
| 27 | 14 36.8 | 14 39.2 | 13 56.8 | 2.7 | 2.6 | 8.7 | 8.5 | 14.7 | 14.3 |
| 28 | 14 37.0 | 14 39.4 | 13 57.0 | 2.8 | 2.7 | 8.8 | 8.6 | 14.8 | 14.4 |
| 29 | 14 37.3 | 14 39.7 | 13 57.3 | 2.9 | 2.8 | 8.9 | 8.7 | 14.9 | 14.5 |
| 30 | 14 37.5 | 14 39.9 | 13 57.5 | 3.0 | 2.9 | 9.0 | 8.8 | 15.0 | 14.6 |
| 31 | 14 37.8 | 14 40.2 | 13 57.8 | 3.1 | 3.0 | 9.1 | 8.9 | 15.1 | 14.7 |
| 32 | 14 38.0 | 14 40.4 | 13 58.0 | 3.2 | 3.1 | 9.2 | 9.0 | 15.2 | 14.8 |
| 33 | 14 38.3 | 14 40.7 | 13 58.2 | 3.3 | 3.2 | 9.3 | 9.1 | 15.3 | 14.9 |
| 34 | 14 38.5 | 14 40.9 | 13 58.5 | 3.4 | 3.3 | 9.4 | 9.2 | 15.4 | 15.0 |
| 35 | 14 38.8 | 14 41.2 | 13 58.7 | 3.5 | 3.4 | 9.5 | 9.3 | 15.5 | 15.1 |
| 36 | 14 39.0 | 14 41.4 | 13 59.0 | 3.6 | 3.5 | 9.6 | 9.4 | 15.6 | 15.2 |
| 37 | 14 39.3 | 14 41.7 | 13 59.2 | 3.7 | 3.6 | 9.7 | 9.5 | 15.7 | 15.3 |
| 38 | 14 39.5 | 14 41.9 | 13 59.4 | 3.8 | 3.7 | 9.8 | 9.6 | 15.8 | 15.4 |
| 39 | 14 39.8 | 14 42.2 | 13 59.7 | 3.9 | 3.8 | 9.9 | 9.7 | 15.9 | 15.5 |
| 40 | 14 40.0 | 14 42.4 | 13 59.9 | 4.0 | 3.9 | 10.0 | 9.8 | 16.0 | 15.6 |
| 41 | 14 40.3 | 14 42.7 | 14 00.1 | 4.1 | 4.0 | 10.1 | 9.8 | 16.1 | 15.7 |
| 42 | 14 40.5 | 14 42.9 | 14 00.4 | 4.2 | 4.1 | 10.2 | 9.9 | 16.2 | 15.8 |
| 43 | 14 40.8 | 14 43.2 | 14 00.6 | 4.3 | 4.2 | 10.3 | 10.0 | 16.3 | 15.9 |
| 44 | 14 41.0 | 14 43.4 | 14 00.9 | 4.4 | 4.3 | 10.4 | 10.1 | 16.4 | 16.0 |
| 45 | 14 41.3 | 14 43.7 | 14 01.1 | 4.5 | 4.4 | 10.5 | 10.2 | 16.5 | 16.1 |
| 46 | 14 41.5 | 14 43.9 | 14 01.3 | 4.6 | 4.5 | 10.6 | 10.3 | 16.6 | 16.2 |
| 47 | 14 41.8 | 14 44.2 | 14 01.6 | 4.7 | 4.6 | 10.7 | 10.4 | 16.7 | 16.3 |
| 48 | 14 42.0 | 14 44.4 | 14 01.8 | 4.8 | 4.7 | 10.8 | 10.5 | 16.8 | 16.4 |
| 49 | 14 42.3 | 14 44.7 | 14 02.1 | 4.9 | 4.8 | 10.9 | 10.6 | 16.9 | 16.5 |
| 50 | 14 42.5 | 14 44.9 | 14 02.3 | 5.0 | 4.9 | 11.0 | 10.7 | 17.0 | 16.6 |
| 51 | 14 42.8 | 14 45.2 | 14 02.5 | 5.1 | 5.0 | 11.1 | 10.8 | 17.1 | 16.7 |
| 52 | 14 43.0 | 14 45.4 | 14 02.8 | 5.2 | 5.1 | 11.2 | 10.9 | 17.2 | 16.8 |
| 53 | 14 43.3 | 14 45.7 | 14 03.0 | 5.3 | 5.2 | 11.3 | 11.0 | 17.3 | 16.9 |
| 54 | 14 43.5 | 14 45.9 | 14 03.3 | 5.4 | 5.3 | 11.4 | 11.1 | 17.4 | 17.0 |
| 55 | 14 43.8 | 14 46.2 | 14 03.5 | 5.5 | 5.4 | 11.5 | 11.2 | 17.5 | 17.1 |
| 56 | 14 44.0 | 14 46.4 | 14 03.7 | 5.6 | 5.5 | 11.6 | 11.3 | 17.6 | 17.2 |
| 57 | 14 44.3 | 14 46.7 | 14 04.0 | 5.7 | 5.6 | 11.7 | 11.4 | 17.7 | 17.3 |
| 58 | 14 44.5 | 14 46.9 | 14 04.2 | 5.8 | 5.7 | 11.8 | 11.5 | 17.8 | 17.4 |
| 59 | 14 44.8 | 14 47.2 | 14 04.4 | 5.9 | 5.8 | 11.9 | 11.6 | 17.9 | 17.5 |
| 60 | 14 45.0 | 14 47.4 | 14 04.7 | 6.0 | 5.9 | 12.0 | 11.7 | 18.0 | 17.6 |

| 59 | SUN PLANETS | ARIES | MOON | $v$ or $d$ | Corrⁿ | $v$ or $d$ | Corrⁿ | $v$ or $d$ | Corrⁿ |
|---|---|---|---|---|---|---|---|---|---|
| s | ° ′ | ° ′ | ° ′ | ′ | ′ | ′ | ′ | ′ | ′ |
| 00 | 14 45.0 | 14 47.4 | 14 04.7 | 0.0 | 0.0 | 6.0 | 6.0 | 12.0 | 11.9 |
| 01 | 14 45.3 | 14 47.7 | 14 04.9 | 0.1 | 0.1 | 6.1 | 6.0 | 12.1 | 12.0 |
| 02 | 14 45.5 | 14 47.9 | 14 05.2 | 0.2 | 0.2 | 6.2 | 6.1 | 12.2 | 12.1 |
| 03 | 14 45.8 | 14 48.2 | 14 05.4 | 0.3 | 0.3 | 6.3 | 6.2 | 12.3 | 12.2 |
| 04 | 14 46.0 | 14 48.4 | 14 05.6 | 0.4 | 0.4 | 6.4 | 6.3 | 12.4 | 12.3 |
| 05 | 14 46.3 | 14 48.7 | 14 05.9 | 0.5 | 0.5 | 6.5 | 6.4 | 12.5 | 12.4 |
| 06 | 14 46.5 | 14 48.9 | 14 06.1 | 0.6 | 0.6 | 6.6 | 6.5 | 12.6 | 12.5 |
| 07 | 14 46.8 | 14 49.2 | 14 06.4 | 0.7 | 0.7 | 6.7 | 6.6 | 12.7 | 12.6 |
| 08 | 14 47.0 | 14 49.4 | 14 06.6 | 0.8 | 0.8 | 6.8 | 6.7 | 12.8 | 12.7 |
| 09 | 14 47.3 | 14 49.7 | 14 06.8 | 0.9 | 0.9 | 6.9 | 6.8 | 12.9 | 12.8 |
| 10 | 14 47.5 | 14 49.9 | 14 07.1 | 1.0 | 1.0 | 7.0 | 6.9 | 13.0 | 12.9 |
| 11 | 14 47.8 | 14 50.2 | 14 07.3 | 1.1 | 1.1 | 7.1 | 7.0 | 13.1 | 13.0 |
| 12 | 14 48.0 | 14 50.4 | 14 07.5 | 1.2 | 1.2 | 7.2 | 7.1 | 13.2 | 13.1 |
| 13 | 14 48.3 | 14 50.7 | 14 07.8 | 1.3 | 1.3 | 7.3 | 7.2 | 13.3 | 13.2 |
| 14 | 14 48.5 | 14 50.9 | 14 08.0 | 1.4 | 1.4 | 7.4 | 7.3 | 13.4 | 13.3 |
| 15 | 14 48.8 | 14 51.2 | 14 08.3 | 1.5 | 1.5 | 7.5 | 7.4 | 13.5 | 13.4 |
| 16 | 14 49.0 | 14 51.4 | 14 08.5 | 1.6 | 1.6 | 7.6 | 7.5 | 13.6 | 13.5 |
| 17 | 14 49.3 | 14 51.7 | 14 08.7 | 1.7 | 1.7 | 7.7 | 7.6 | 13.7 | 13.6 |
| 18 | 14 49.5 | 14 51.9 | 14 09.0 | 1.8 | 1.8 | 7.8 | 7.7 | 13.8 | 13.7 |
| 19 | 14 49.8 | 14 52.2 | 14 09.2 | 1.9 | 1.9 | 7.9 | 7.8 | 13.9 | 13.8 |
| 20 | 14 50.0 | 14 52.4 | 14 09.5 | 2.0 | 2.0 | 8.0 | 7.9 | 14.0 | 13.9 |
| 21 | 14 50.3 | 14 52.7 | 14 09.7 | 2.1 | 2.1 | 8.1 | 8.0 | 14.1 | 14.0 |
| 22 | 14 50.5 | 14 52.9 | 14 09.9 | 2.2 | 2.2 | 8.2 | 8.1 | 14.2 | 14.1 |
| 23 | 14 50.8 | 14 53.2 | 14 10.2 | 2.3 | 2.3 | 8.3 | 8.2 | 14.3 | 14.2 |
| 24 | 14 51.0 | 14 53.4 | 14 10.4 | 2.4 | 2.4 | 8.4 | 8.3 | 14.4 | 14.3 |
| 25 | 14 51.3 | 14 53.7 | 14 10.6 | 2.5 | 2.5 | 8.5 | 8.4 | 14.5 | 14.4 |
| 26 | 14 51.5 | 14 53.9 | 14 10.9 | 2.6 | 2.6 | 8.6 | 8.5 | 14.6 | 14.5 |
| 27 | 14 51.8 | 14 54.2 | 14 11.1 | 2.7 | 2.7 | 8.7 | 8.6 | 14.7 | 14.6 |
| 28 | 14 52.0 | 14 54.4 | 14 11.4 | 2.8 | 2.8 | 8.8 | 8.7 | 14.8 | 14.7 |
| 29 | 14 52.3 | 14 54.7 | 14 11.6 | 2.9 | 2.9 | 8.9 | 8.8 | 14.9 | 14.8 |
| 30 | 14 52.5 | 14 54.9 | 14 11.8 | 3.0 | 3.0 | 9.0 | 8.9 | 15.0 | 14.9 |
| 31 | 14 52.8 | 14 55.2 | 14 12.1 | 3.1 | 3.1 | 9.1 | 9.0 | 15.1 | 15.0 |
| 32 | 14 53.0 | 14 55.4 | 14 12.3 | 3.2 | 3.2 | 9.2 | 9.1 | 15.2 | 15.1 |
| 33 | 14 53.3 | 14 55.7 | 14 12.6 | 3.3 | 3.3 | 9.3 | 9.2 | 15.3 | 15.2 |
| 34 | 14 53.5 | 14 55.9 | 14 12.8 | 3.4 | 3.4 | 9.4 | 9.3 | 15.4 | 15.3 |
| 35 | 14 53.8 | 14 56.2 | 14 13.0 | 3.5 | 3.5 | 9.5 | 9.4 | 15.5 | 15.4 |
| 36 | 14 54.0 | 14 56.4 | 14 13.3 | 3.6 | 3.6 | 9.6 | 9.5 | 15.6 | 15.5 |
| 37 | 14 54.3 | 14 56.7 | 14 13.5 | 3.7 | 3.7 | 9.7 | 9.6 | 15.7 | 15.6 |
| 38 | 14 54.5 | 14 56.9 | 14 13.8 | 3.8 | 3.8 | 9.8 | 9.7 | 15.8 | 15.7 |
| 39 | 14 54.8 | 14 57.2 | 14 14.0 | 3.9 | 3.9 | 9.9 | 9.8 | 15.9 | 15.8 |
| 40 | 14 55.0 | 14 57.5 | 14 14.2 | 4.0 | 4.0 | 10.0 | 9.9 | 16.0 | 15.9 |
| 41 | 14 55.3 | 14 57.7 | 14 14.5 | 4.1 | 4.1 | 10.1 | 10.0 | 16.1 | 16.0 |
| 42 | 14 55.5 | 14 58.0 | 14 14.7 | 4.2 | 4.2 | 10.2 | 10.1 | 16.2 | 16.1 |
| 43 | 14 55.8 | 14 58.2 | 14 14.9 | 4.3 | 4.3 | 10.3 | 10.2 | 16.3 | 16.2 |
| 44 | 14 56.0 | 14 58.5 | 14 15.2 | 4.4 | 4.4 | 10.4 | 10.3 | 16.4 | 16.3 |
| 45 | 14 56.3 | 14 58.7 | 14 15.4 | 4.5 | 4.5 | 10.5 | 10.4 | 16.5 | 16.4 |
| 46 | 14 56.5 | 14 59.0 | 14 15.7 | 4.6 | 4.6 | 10.6 | 10.5 | 16.6 | 16.5 |
| 47 | 14 56.8 | 14 59.2 | 14 15.9 | 4.7 | 4.7 | 10.7 | 10.6 | 16.7 | 16.6 |
| 48 | 14 57.0 | 14 59.5 | 14 16.1 | 4.8 | 4.8 | 10.8 | 10.7 | 16.8 | 16.7 |
| 49 | 14 57.3 | 14 59.7 | 14 16.4 | 4.9 | 4.9 | 10.9 | 10.8 | 16.9 | 16.8 |
| 50 | 14 57.5 | 15 00.0 | 14 16.6 | 5.0 | 5.0 | 11.0 | 10.9 | 17.0 | 16.9 |
| 51 | 14 57.8 | 15 00.2 | 14 16.9 | 5.1 | 5.1 | 11.1 | 11.0 | 17.1 | 17.0 |
| 52 | 14 58.0 | 15 00.5 | 14 17.1 | 5.2 | 5.2 | 11.2 | 11.1 | 17.2 | 17.1 |
| 53 | 14 58.3 | 15 00.7 | 14 17.3 | 5.3 | 5.3 | 11.3 | 11.2 | 17.3 | 17.2 |
| 54 | 14 58.5 | 15 01.0 | 14 17.6 | 5.4 | 5.4 | 11.4 | 11.3 | 17.4 | 17.3 |
| 55 | 14 58.8 | 15 01.2 | 14 17.8 | 5.5 | 5.5 | 11.5 | 11.4 | 17.5 | 17.4 |
| 56 | 14 59.0 | 15 01.5 | 14 18.0 | 5.6 | 5.6 | 11.6 | 11.5 | 17.6 | 17.5 |
| 57 | 14 59.3 | 15 01.7 | 14 18.3 | 5.7 | 5.7 | 11.7 | 11.6 | 17.7 | 17.6 |
| 58 | 14 59.5 | 15 02.0 | 14 18.5 | 5.8 | 5.8 | 11.8 | 11.7 | 17.8 | 17.7 |
| 59 | 14 59.8 | 15 02.2 | 14 18.8 | 5.9 | 5.9 | 11.9 | 11.8 | 17.9 | 17.8 |
| 60 | 15 00.0 | 15 02.5 | 14 19.0 | 6.0 | 6.0 | 12.0 | 11.9 | 18.0 | 17.9 |

# TABLES FOR INTERPOLATING SUNRISE, MOONRISE, ETC.

## TABLE I—FOR LATITUDE

| Tabular Interval | | | Difference between the times for consecutive latitudes | | | | | | | | | | | | | | | | |
|---|---|---|---|---|---|---|---|---|---|---|---|---|---|---|---|---|---|---|---|
| 10° | 5° | 2° | 5m | 10m | 15m | 20m | 25m | 30m | 35m | 40m | 45m | 50m | 55m | 60m | 1h05m | 1h10m | 1h15m | 1h20m |
| ° ′<br>0 30 | ° ′<br>0 15 | ° ′<br>0 06 | 0 | 0 | 1 | 1 | 1 | 1 | 1 | 2 | 2 | 2 | 2 | 2 | h m<br>0 02 | h m<br>0 02 | h m<br>0 02 | h m<br>0 02 |
| 1 00 | 0 30 | 0 12 | 0 | 1 | 1 | 2 | 2 | 3 | 3 | 3 | 4 | 4 | 4 | 5 | 05 | 05 | 05 | 05 |
| 1 30 | 0 45 | 0 18 | 1 | 1 | 2 | 3 | 3 | 4 | 4 | 5 | 5 | 6 | 7 | 7 | 07 | 07 | 07 | 07 |
| 2 00 | 1 00 | 0 24 | 1 | 2 | 3 | 4 | 5 | 5 | 6 | 7 | 7 | 8 | 9 | 10 | 10 | 10 | 10 | 10 |
| 2 30 | 1 15 | 0 30 | 1 | 2 | 4 | 5 | 6 | 7 | 8 | 9 | 9 | 10 | 11 | 12 | 12 | 13 | 13 | 13 |
| 3 00 | 1 30 | 0 36 | 1 | 3 | 4 | 6 | 7 | 8 | 9 | 10 | 11 | 12 | 13 | 14 | 0 15 | 0 15 | 0 16 | 0 16 |
| 3 30 | 1 45 | 0 42 | 2 | 3 | 5 | 7 | 8 | 10 | 11 | 12 | 13 | 14 | 16 | 17 | 18 | 18 | 19 | 19 |
| 4 00 | 2 00 | 0 48 | 2 | 4 | 6 | 8 | 9 | 11 | 13 | 14 | 15 | 16 | 18 | 19 | 20 | 21 | 22 | 22 |
| 4 30 | 2 15 | 0 54 | 2 | 4 | 7 | 9 | 11 | 13 | 15 | 16 | 18 | 19 | 21 | 22 | 23 | 24 | 25 | 26 |
| 5 00 | 2 30 | 1 00 | 2 | 5 | 7 | 10 | 12 | 14 | 16 | 18 | 20 | 22 | 23 | 25 | 26 | 27 | 28 | 29 |
| 5 30 | 2 45 | 1 06 | 3 | 5 | 8 | 11 | 13 | 16 | 18 | 20 | 22 | 24 | 26 | 28 | 0 29 | 0 30 | 0 31 | 0 32 |
| 6 00 | 3 00 | 1 12 | 3 | 6 | 9 | 12 | 14 | 17 | 20 | 22 | 24 | 26 | 29 | 31 | 32 | 33 | 34 | 36 |
| 6 30 | 3 15 | 1 18 | 3 | 6 | 10 | 13 | 16 | 19 | 22 | 24 | 26 | 29 | 31 | 34 | 36 | 37 | 38 | 40 |
| 7 00 | 3 30 | 1 24 | 3 | 7 | 10 | 14 | 17 | 20 | 23 | 26 | 29 | 31 | 34 | 37 | 39 | 41 | 42 | 44 |
| 7 30 | 3 45 | 1 30 | 4 | 7 | 11 | 15 | 18 | 22 | 25 | 28 | 31 | 34 | 37 | 40 | 43 | 44 | 46 | 48 |
| 8 00 | 4 00 | 1 36 | 4 | 8 | 12 | 16 | 20 | 23 | 27 | 30 | 34 | 37 | 41 | 44 | 0 47 | 0 48 | 0 51 | 0 53 |
| 8 30 | 4 15 | 1 42 | 4 | 8 | 13 | 17 | 21 | 25 | 29 | 33 | 36 | 40 | 44 | 48 | 0 51 | 0 53 | 0 56 | 0 58 |
| 9 00 | 4 30 | 1 48 | 4 | 9 | 13 | 18 | 22 | 27 | 31 | 35 | 39 | 43 | 47 | 52 | 0 55 | 0 58 | 1 01 | 1 04 |
| 9 30 | 4 45 | 1 54 | 5 | 9 | 14 | 19 | 24 | 28 | 33 | 38 | 42 | 47 | 51 | 56 | 1 00 | 1 04 | 1 08 | 1 12 |
| 10 00 | 5 00 | 2 00 | 5 | 10 | 15 | 20 | 25 | 30 | 35 | 40 | 45 | 50 | 55 | 60 | 1 05 | 1 10 | 1 15 | 1 20 |

Table I is for interpolating the LMT of sunrise, twilight, moonrise, etc., for latitude. It is to be entered, in the appropriate column on the left, with the difference between true latitude and the nearest tabular latitude which is *less* than the true latitude; and with the argument at the top which is the nearest value of the difference between the times for the tabular latitude and the next higher one; the correction so obtained is applied to the time for the tabular latitude; the sign of the correction can be seen by inspection. It is to be noted that the interpolation is not linear, so that when using this table it is essential to take out the tabular phenomenon for the latitude *less* than the true latitude.

## TABLE II—FOR LONGITUDE

| Long.<br>East<br>or<br>West | Difference between the times for given date and preceding date (for east longitude) or for given date and following date (for west longitude) | | | | | | | | | | | | | | | | | | |
|---|---|---|---|---|---|---|---|---|---|---|---|---|---|---|---|---|---|---|---|
| | 10m | 20m | 30m | 40m | 50m | 60m | 1h+<br>10m | 20m | 30m | 1h+<br>40m | 50m | 60m | 2h10m | 2h20m | 2h30m | 2h40m | 2h50m | 3h00m |
| ° | m | m | m | m | m | m | m | m | m | m | m | m | h m | h m | h m | h m | h m | h m |
| 0 | 0 | 0 | 0 | 0 | 0 | 0 | 0 | 0 | 0 | 0 | 0 | 0 | 0 00 | 0 00 | 0 00 | 0 00 | 0 00 | 0 00 |
| 10 | 0 | 1 | 1 | 1 | 1 | 2 | 2 | 2 | 2 | 3 | 3 | 3 | 04 | 04 | 04 | 04 | 05 | 05 |
| 20 | 1 | 1 | 2 | 2 | 3 | 3 | 4 | 4 | 5 | 6 | 6 | 7 | 07 | 08 | 08 | 09 | 09 | 10 |
| 30 | 1 | 2 | 2 | 3 | 4 | 5 | 6 | 7 | 7 | 8 | 9 | 10 | 11 | 12 | 12 | 13 | 14 | 15 |
| 40 | 1 | 2 | 3 | 4 | 6 | 7 | 8 | 9 | 10 | 11 | 12 | 13 | 14 | 16 | 17 | 18 | 19 | 20 |
| 50 | 1 | 3 | 4 | 6 | 7 | 8 | 10 | 11 | 12 | 14 | 15 | 17 | 0 18 | 0 19 | 0 21 | 0 22 | 0 24 | 0 25 |
| 60 | 2 | 3 | 5 | 7 | 8 | 10 | 12 | 13 | 15 | 17 | 18 | 20 | 22 | 23 | 25 | 27 | 28 | 30 |
| 70 | 2 | 4 | 6 | 8 | 10 | 12 | 14 | 16 | 17 | 19 | 21 | 23 | 25 | 27 | 29 | 31 | 33 | 35 |
| 80 | 2 | 4 | 7 | 9 | 11 | 13 | 16 | 18 | 20 | 22 | 24 | 27 | 29 | 31 | 33 | 36 | 38 | 40 |
| 90 | 2 | 5 | 7 | 10 | 12 | 15 | 17 | 20 | 22 | 25 | 27 | 30 | 32 | 35 | 37 | 40 | 42 | 45 |
| 100 | 3 | 6 | 8 | 11 | 14 | 17 | 19 | 22 | 25 | 28 | 31 | 33 | 0 36 | 0 39 | 0 42 | 0 44 | 0 47 | 0 50 |
| 110 | 3 | 6 | 9 | 12 | 15 | 18 | 21 | 24 | 27 | 31 | 34 | 37 | 40 | 43 | 46 | 49 | 0 52 | 0 55 |
| 120 | 3 | 7 | 10 | 13 | 17 | 20 | 23 | 27 | 30 | 33 | 37 | 40 | 43 | 47 | 50 | 53 | 0 57 | 1 00 |
| 130 | 4 | 7 | 11 | 14 | 18 | 22 | 25 | 29 | 32 | 36 | 40 | 43 | 47 | 51 | 54 | 0 58 | 1 01 | 1 05 |
| 140 | 4 | 8 | 12 | 16 | 19 | 23 | 27 | 31 | 35 | 39 | 43 | 47 | 51 | 54 | 0 58 | 1 02 | 1 06 | 1 10 |
| 150 | 4 | 8 | 13 | 17 | 21 | 25 | 29 | 33 | 38 | 42 | 46 | 50 | 0 54 | 0 58 | 1 03 | 1 07 | 1 11 | 1 15 |
| 160 | 4 | 9 | 13 | 18 | 22 | 27 | 31 | 36 | 40 | 44 | 49 | 53 | 0 58 | 1 02 | 1 07 | 1 11 | 1 16 | 1 20 |
| 170 | 5 | 9 | 14 | 19 | 24 | 28 | 33 | 38 | 42 | 47 | 52 | 57 | 1 01 | 1 06 | 1 11 | 1 16 | 1 20 | 1 25 |
| 180 | 5 | 10 | 15 | 20 | 25 | 30 | 35 | 40 | 45 | 50 | 55 | 60 | 1 05 | 1 10 | 1 15 | 1 20 | 1 25 | 1 30 |

Table II is for interpolating the LMT of moonrise, moonset and the Moon's meridian passage for longitude. It is entered with longitude and with the difference between the times for the given date and for the preceding date (in east longitudes) or following date (in west longitudes). The correction is normally *added* for west longitudes and *subtracted* for east longitudes, but if, as occasionally happens, the times become earlier each day instead of later, the signs of the corrections must be reversed.

# INDEX TO SELECTED STARS, 2022

| Name | No | Mag | SHA | Dec | | No | Name | Mag | SHA | Dec |
|---|---|---|---|---|---|---|---|---|---|---|
| | | | | ° | | | | | ° | ° |
| Acamar | 7 | 3·2 | 315 | S 40 | | 1 | Alpheratz | 2·1 | 358 | N 29 |
| Achernar | 5 | 0·5 | 335 | S 57 | | 2 | Ankaa | 2·4 | 353 | S 42 |
| Acrux | 30 | 1·3 | 173 | S 63 | | 3 | Schedar | 2·2 | 350 | N 57 |
| Adhara | 19 | 1·5 | 255 | S 29 | | 4 | Diphda | 2·0 | 349 | S 18 |
| Aldebaran | 10 | 0·9 | 291 | N 17 | | 5 | Achernar | 0·5 | 335 | S 57 |
| Alioth | 32 | 1·8 | 166 | N 56 | | 6 | Hamal | 2·0 | 328 | N 24 |
| Alkaid | 34 | 1·9 | 153 | N 49 | | 7 | Acamar | 3·2 | 315 | S 40 |
| Alnair | 55 | 1·7 | 28 | S 47 | | 8 | Menkar | 2·5 | 314 | N 4 |
| Alnilam | 15 | 1·7 | 276 | S 1 | | 9 | Mirfak | 1·8 | 309 | N 50 |
| Alphard | 25 | 2·0 | 218 | S 9 | | 10 | Aldebaran | 0·9 | 291 | N 17 |
| Alphecca | 41 | 2·2 | 126 | N 27 | | 11 | Rigel | 0·1 | 281 | S 8 |
| Alpheratz | 1 | 2·1 | 358 | N 29 | | 12 | Capella | 0·1 | 280 | N 46 |
| Altair | 51 | 0·8 | 62 | N 9 | | 13 | Bellatrix | 1·6 | 278 | N 6 |
| Ankaa | 2 | 2·4 | 353 | S 42 | | 14 | Elnath | 1·7 | 278 | N 29 |
| Antares | 42 | 1·0 | 112 | S 26 | | 15 | Alnilam | 1·7 | 276 | S 1 |
| Arcturus | 37 | 0·0 | 146 | N 19 | | 16 | Betelgeuse | Var.* | 271 | N 7 |
| Atria | 43 | 1·9 | 107 | S 69 | | 17 | Canopus | −0·7 | 264 | S 53 |
| Avior | 22 | 1·9 | 234 | S 60 | | 18 | Sirius | −1·5 | 258 | S 17 |
| Bellatrix | 13 | 1·6 | 278 | N 6 | | 19 | Adhara | 1·5 | 255 | S 29 |
| Betelgeuse | 16 | Var.* | 271 | N 7 | | 20 | Procyon | 0·4 | 245 | N 5 |
| Canopus | 17 | −0·7 | 264 | S 53 | | 21 | Pollux | 1·1 | 243 | N 28 |
| Capella | 12 | 0·1 | 280 | N 46 | | 22 | Avior | 1·9 | 234 | S 60 |
| Deneb | 53 | 1·3 | 49 | N 45 | | 23 | Suhail | 2·2 | 223 | S 44 |
| Denebola | 28 | 2·1 | 182 | N 14 | | 24 | Miaplacidus | 1·7 | 222 | S 70 |
| Diphda | 4 | 2·0 | 349 | S 18 | | 25 | Alphard | 2·0 | 218 | S 9 |
| Dubhe | 27 | 1·8 | 194 | N 62 | | 26 | Regulus | 1·4 | 208 | N 12 |
| Elnath | 14 | 1·7 | 278 | N 29 | | 27 | Dubhe | 1·8 | 194 | N 62 |
| Eltanin | 47 | 2·2 | 91 | N 51 | | 28 | Denebola | 2·1 | 182 | N 14 |
| Enif | 54 | 2·4 | 34 | N 10 | | 29 | Gienah | 2·6 | 176 | S 18 |
| Fomalhaut | 56 | 1·2 | 15 | S 30 | | 30 | Acrux | 1·3 | 173 | S 63 |
| Gacrux | 31 | 1·6 | 172 | S 57 | | 31 | Gacrux | 1·6 | 172 | S 57 |
| Gienah | 29 | 2·6 | 176 | S 18 | | 32 | Alioth | 1·8 | 166 | N 56 |
| Hadar | 35 | 0·6 | 149 | S 60 | | 33 | Spica | 1·0 | 158 | S 11 |
| Hamal | 6 | 2·0 | 328 | N 24 | | 34 | Alkaid | 1·9 | 153 | N 49 |
| Kaus Australis | 48 | 1·9 | 84 | S 34 | | 35 | Hadar | 0·6 | 149 | S 60 |
| Kochab | 40 | 2·1 | 137 | N 74 | | 36 | Menkent | 2·1 | 148 | S 36 |
| Markab | 57 | 2·5 | 14 | N 15 | | 37 | Arcturus | 0·0 | 146 | N 19 |
| Menkar | 8 | 2·5 | 314 | N 4 | | 38 | Rigil Kentaurus | −0·3 | 140 | S 61 |
| Menkent | 36 | 2·1 | 148 | S 36 | | 39 | Zubenelgenubi | 2·8 | 137 | S 16 |
| Miaplacidus | 24 | 1·7 | 222 | S 70 | | 40 | Kochab | 2·1 | 137 | N 74 |
| Mirfak | 9 | 1·8 | 309 | N 50 | | 41 | Alphecca | 2·2 | 126 | N 27 |
| Nunki | 50 | 2·0 | 76 | S 26 | | 42 | Antares | 1·0 | 112 | S 26 |
| Peacock | 52 | 1·9 | 53 | S 57 | | 43 | Atria | 1·9 | 107 | S 69 |
| Pollux | 21 | 1·1 | 243 | N 28 | | 44 | Sabik | 2·4 | 102 | S 16 |
| Procyon | 20 | 0·4 | 245 | N 5 | | 45 | Shaula | 1·6 | 96 | S 37 |
| Rasalhague | 46 | 2·1 | 96 | N 13 | | 46 | Rasalhague | 2·1 | 96 | N 13 |
| Regulus | 26 | 1·4 | 208 | N 12 | | 47 | Eltanin | 2·2 | 91 | N 51 |
| Rigel | 11 | 0·1 | 281 | S 8 | | 48 | Kaus Australis | 1·9 | 84 | S 34 |
| Rigil Kentaurus | 38 | −0·3 | 140 | S 61 | | 49 | Vega | 0·0 | 81 | N 39 |
| Sabik | 44 | 2·4 | 102 | S 16 | | 50 | Nunki | 2·0 | 76 | S 26 |
| Schedar | 3 | 2·2 | 350 | N 57 | | 51 | Altair | 0·8 | 62 | N 9 |
| Shaula | 45 | 1·6 | 96 | S 37 | | 52 | Peacock | 1·9 | 53 | S 57 |
| Sirius | 18 | −1·5 | 258 | S 17 | | 53 | Deneb | 1·3 | 49 | N 45 |
| Spica | 33 | 1·0 | 158 | S 11 | | 54 | Enif | 2·4 | 34 | N 10 |
| Suhail | 23 | 2·2 | 223 | S 44 | | 55 | Alnair | 1·7 | 28 | S 47 |
| Vega | 49 | 0·0 | 81 | N 39 | | 56 | Fomalhaut | 1·2 | 15 | S 30 |
| Zubenelgenubi | 39 | 2·8 | 137 | S 16 | | 57 | Markab | 2·5 | 14 | N 15 |

*0·1 — 1·2          xxxiii

# ALTITUDE CORRECTION TABLES 0°–35°— MOON

| App. Alt. | 0°–4° Corrn | 5°–9° Corrn | 10°–14° Corrn | 15°–19° Corrn | 20°–24° Corrn | 25°–29° Corrn | 30°–34° Corrn | App. Alt. |
|---|---|---|---|---|---|---|---|---|
| ′ | ° | ° | ° | ° | ° | ° | ° | ′ |
| 00 | 0 34·5 | 5 58·2 | 10 62·1 | 15 62·8 | 20 62·2 | 25 60·8 | 30 58·9 | 00 |
| 10 | 36·5 | 58·5 | 62·2 | 62·8 | 62·2 | 60·8 | 58·8 | 10 |
| 20 | 38·3 | 58·7 | 62·2 | 62·8 | 62·1 | 60·7 | 58·8 | 20 |
| 30 | 40·0 | 58·9 | 62·3 | 62·8 | 62·1 | 60·7 | 58·7 | 30 |
| 40 | 41·5 | 59·1 | 62·3 | 62·8 | 62·0 | 60·6 | 58·6 | 40 |
| 50 | 42·9 | 59·3 | 62·4 | 62·7 | 62·0 | 60·6 | 58·5 | 50 |
| 00 | 1 44·2 | 6 59·5 | 11 62·4 | 16 62·7 | 21 62·0 | 26 60·5 | 31 58·5 | 00 |
| 10 | 45·4 | 59·7 | 62·4 | 62·7 | 61·9 | 60·4 | 58·4 | 10 |
| 20 | 46·5 | 59·9 | 62·5 | 62·7 | 61·9 | 60·4 | 58·3 | 20 |
| 30 | 47·5 | 60·0 | 62·5 | 62·7 | 61·9 | 60·3 | 58·2 | 30 |
| 40 | 48·4 | 60·2 | 62·5 | 62·7 | 61·8 | 60·3 | 58·2 | 40 |
| 50 | 49·3 | 60·3 | 62·6 | 62·7 | 61·8 | 60·2 | 58·1 | 50 |
| 00 | 2 50·1 | 7 60·5 | 12 62·6 | 17 62·7 | 22 61·7 | 27 60·1 | 32 58·0 | 00 |
| 10 | 50·8 | 60·6 | 62·6 | 62·6 | 61·7 | 60·1 | 57·9 | 10 |
| 20 | 51·5 | 60·7 | 62·6 | 62·6 | 61·6 | 60·0 | 57·9 | 20 |
| 30 | 52·2 | 60·9 | 62·7 | 62·6 | 61·6 | 59·9 | 57·8 | 30 |
| 40 | 52·8 | 61·0 | 62·7 | 62·6 | 61·6 | 59·9 | 57·7 | 40 |
| 50 | 53·4 | 61·1 | 62·7 | 62·6 | 61·5 | 59·8 | 57·6 | 50 |
| 00 | 3 53·9 | 8 61·2 | 13 62·7 | 18 62·5 | 23 61·5 | 28 59·7 | 33 57·5 | 00 |
| 10 | 54·4 | 61·3 | 62·7 | 62·5 | 61·4 | 59·7 | 57·4 | 10 |
| 20 | 54·9 | 61·4 | 62·7 | 62·5 | 61·4 | 59·6 | 57·4 | 20 |
| 30 | 55·3 | 61·5 | 62·8 | 62·5 | 61·3 | 59·5 | 57·3 | 30 |
| 40 | 55·7 | 61·6 | 62·8 | 62·4 | 61·3 | 59·5 | 57·2 | 40 |
| 50 | 56·1 | 61·6 | 62·8 | 62·4 | 61·2 | 59·4 | 57·1 | 50 |
| 00 | 4 56·4 | 9 61·7 | 14 62·8 | 19 62·4 | 24 61·2 | 29 59·3 | 34 57·0 | 00 |
| 10 | 56·8 | 61·8 | 62·8 | 62·4 | 61·1 | 59·3 | 56·9 | 10 |
| 20 | 57·1 | 61·9 | 62·8 | 62·3 | 61·1 | 59·2 | 56·9 | 20 |
| 30 | 57·4 | 61·9 | 62·8 | 62·3 | 61·0 | 59·1 | 56·8 | 30 |
| 40 | 57·7 | 62·0 | 62·8 | 62·3 | 61·0 | 59·1 | 56·7 | 40 |
| 50 | 58·0 | 62·1 | 62·8 | 62·2 | 60·9 | 59·0 | 56·6 | 50 |

| HP | L U | L U | L U | L U | L U | L U | L U | HP |
|---|---|---|---|---|---|---|---|---|
| ′ | ′ ′ | ′ ′ | ′ ′ | ′ ′ | ′ ′ | ′ ′ | ′ ′ | ′ |
| 54·0 | 0·3 0·9 | 0·3 0·9 | 0·4 1·0 | 0·5 1·1 | 0·6 1·2 | 0·7 1·3 | 0·9 1·5 | 54·0 |
| 54·3 | 0·7 1·1 | 0·7 1·2 | 0·8 1·2 | 0·8 1·3 | 0·9 1·4 | 1·1 1·5 | 1·2 1·7 | 54·3 |
| 54·6 | 1·1 1·4 | 1·1 1·4 | 1·1 1·4 | 1·2 1·5 | 1·3 1·6 | 1·4 1·7 | 1·5 1·8 | 54·6 |
| 54·9 | 1·4 1·6 | 1·5 1·6 | 1·5 1·6 | 1·6 1·7 | 1·6 1·8 | 1·8 1·9 | 1·9 2·0 | 54·9 |
| 55·2 | 1·8 1·8 | 1·8 1·8 | 1·9 1·8 | 1·9 1·9 | 2·0 2·0 | 2·1 2·1 | 2·2 2·2 | 55·2 |
| 55·5 | 2·2 2·0 | 2·2 2·0 | 2·3 2·1 | 2·3 2·1 | 2·4 2·2 | 2·4 2·3 | 2·5 2·4 | 55·5 |
| 55·8 | 2·6 2·2 | 2·6 2·2 | 2·6 2·3 | 2·7 2·3 | 2·7 2·4 | 2·8 2·4 | 2·9 2·5 | 55·8 |
| 56·1 | 3·0 2·4 | 3·0 2·5 | 3·0 2·5 | 3·0 2·5 | 3·1 2·6 | 3·1 2·6 | 3·2 2·7 | 56·1 |
| 56·4 | 3·3 2·7 | 3·4 2·7 | 3·4 2·7 | 3·4 2·7 | 3·4 2·8 | 3·5 2·8 | 3·5 2·9 | 56·4 |
| 56·7 | 3·7 2·9 | 3·7 2·9 | 3·8 2·9 | 3·8 2·9 | 3·8 3·0 | 3·8 3·0 | 3·9 3·0 | 56·7 |
| 57·0 | 4·1 3·1 | 4·1 3·1 | 4·1 3·1 | 4·1 3·1 | 4·2 3·2 | 4·2 3·2 | 4·2 3·2 | 57·0 |
| 57·3 | 4·5 3·3 | 4·5 3·3 | 4·5 3·3 | 4·5 3·3 | 4·5 3·3 | 4·5 3·4 | 4·6 3·4 | 57·3 |
| 57·6 | 4·9 3·5 | 4·9 3·5 | 4·9 3·5 | 4·9 3·5 | 4·9 3·5 | 4·9 3·5 | 4·9 3·6 | 57·6 |
| 57·9 | 5·3 3·8 | 5·3 3·8 | 5·2 3·8 | 5·2 3·7 | 5·2 3·7 | 5·2 3·7 | 5·2 3·7 | 57·9 |
| 58·2 | 5·6 4·0 | 5·6 4·0 | 5·6 4·0 | 5·6 4·0 | 5·6 3·9 | 5·6 3·9 | 5·6 3·9 | 58·2 |
| 58·5 | 6·0 4·2 | 6·0 4·2 | 6·0 4·2 | 6·0 4·2 | 6·0 4·1 | 5·9 4·1 | 5·9 4·1 | 58·5 |
| 58·8 | 6·4 4·4 | 6·4 4·4 | 6·4 4·4 | 6·3 4·4 | 6·3 4·3 | 6·3 4·3 | 6·2 4·2 | 58·8 |
| 59·1 | 6·8 4·6 | 6·8 4·6 | 6·7 4·6 | 6·7 4·6 | 6·7 4·5 | 6·6 4·5 | 6·6 4·4 | 59·1 |
| 59·4 | 7·2 4·8 | 7·1 4·8 | 7·1 4·8 | 7·1 4·8 | 7·0 4·7 | 7·0 4·7 | 6·9 4·6 | 59·4 |
| 59·7 | 7·5 5·1 | 7·5 5·0 | 7·5 5·0 | 7·5 5·0 | 7·4 4·9 | 7·3 4·8 | 7·2 4·8 | 59·7 |
| 60·0 | 7·9 5·3 | 7·9 5·3 | 7·9 5·2 | 7·8 5·2 | 7·8 5·1 | 7·7 5·0 | 7·6 4·9 | 60·0 |
| 60·3 | 8·3 5·5 | 8·3 5·5 | 8·2 5·4 | 8·2 5·4 | 8·1 5·3 | 8·0 5·2 | 7·9 5·1 | 60·3 |
| 60·6 | 8·7 5·7 | 8·7 5·7 | 8·6 5·7 | 8·6 5·6 | 8·5 5·5 | 8·4 5·4 | 8·2 5·3 | 60·6 |
| 60·9 | 9·1 5·9 | 9·0 5·9 | 9·0 5·9 | 8·9 5·8 | 8·8 5·7 | 8·7 5·6 | 8·6 5·4 | 60·9 |
| 61·2 | 9·5 6·2 | 9·4 6·1 | 9·4 6·1 | 9·3 6·0 | 9·2 5·9 | 9·1 5·8 | 8·9 5·6 | 61·2 |
| 61·5 | 9·8 6·4 | 9·8 6·3 | 9·7 6·3 | 9·7 6·2 | 9·5 6·1 | 9·4 5·9 | 9·2 5·8 | 61·5 |

| DIP | | | | | | |
|---|---|---|---|---|---|---|
| Ht. of Eye | Corrn | Ht. of Eye | Ht. of Eye | Corrn | Ht. of Eye | |
| m | | ft. | m | | ft. | |
| 2·4 | −2·8 | 8·0 | 9·5 | −5·5 | 31·5 | |
| 2·6 | −2·9 | 8·6 | 9·9 | −5·6 | 32·7 | |
| 2·8 | −3·0 | 9·2 | 10·3 | −5·7 | 33·9 | |
| 3·0 | −3·1 | 9·8 | 10·6 | −5·8 | 35·1 | |
| 3·2 | −3·2 | 10·5 | 11·0 | −5·9 | 36·3 | |
| 3·4 | −3·3 | 11·2 | 11·4 | −6·0 | 37·6 | |
| 3·6 | −3·4 | 11·9 | 11·8 | −6·1 | 38·9 | |
| 3·8 | −3·5 | 12·6 | 12·2 | −6·2 | 40·1 | |
| 4·0 | −3·6 | 13·3 | 12·6 | −6·3 | 41·5 | |
| 4·3 | −3·7 | 14·1 | 13·0 | −6·4 | 42·8 | |
| 4·5 | −3·8 | 14·9 | 13·4 | −6·5 | 44·2 | |
| 4·7 | −3·9 | 15·7 | 13·8 | −6·6 | 45·5 | |
| 5·0 | −4·0 | 16·5 | 14·2 | −6·7 | 46·9 | |
| 5·2 | −4·1 | 17·4 | 14·7 | −6·8 | 48·4 | |
| 5·5 | −4·2 | 18·3 | 15·1 | −6·9 | 49·8 | |
| 5·8 | −4·3 | 19·1 | 15·5 | −7·0 | 51·3 | |
| 6·1 | −4·4 | 20·1 | 16·0 | −7·1 | 52·8 | |
| 6·3 | −4·5 | 21·0 | 16·5 | −7·2 | 54·3 | |
| 6·6 | −4·6 | 22·0 | 16·9 | −7·3 | 55·8 | |
| 6·9 | −4·7 | 22·9 | 17·4 | −7·4 | 57·4 | |
| 7·2 | −4·8 | 23·9 | 17·9 | −7·5 | 58·9 | |
| 7·5 | −4·9 | 24·9 | 18·4 | −7·6 | 60·5 | |
| 7·9 | −5·0 | 26·0 | 18·8 | −7·7 | 62·1 | |
| 8·2 | −5·1 | 27·1 | 19·3 | −7·8 | 63·8 | |
| 8·5 | −5·2 | 28·1 | 19·8 | −7·9 | 65·4 | |
| 8·8 | −5·3 | 29·2 | 20·4 | −8·0 | 67·1 | |
| 9·2 | −5·4 | 30·4 | 20·9 | −8·1 | 68·8 | |
| 9·5 | | 31·5 | 21·4 | | 70·5 | |

## MOON CORRECTION TABLE

The correction is in two parts; the first correction is taken from the upper part of the table with argument apparent altitude, and the second from the lower part, with argument HP, in the same column as that from which the first correction was taken. Separate corrections are given in the lower part for lower (L) and upper(U) limbs. All corrections are to be **added** to apparent altitude, *but 30′ is to be subtracted from the altitude of the upper limb.*

For corrections for pressure and temperature see page A4.

For bubble sextant observations ignore dip, take the mean of upper and lower limb corrections and subtract 15′ from the altitude.

App. Alt. = Apparent altitude = Sextant altitude corrected for index error and dip.

# ALTITUDE CORRECTION TABLES 35°–90°— MOON

| App. Alt. | 35°–39° Corrⁿ | 40°–44° Corrⁿ | 45°–49° Corrⁿ | 50°–54° Corrⁿ | 55°–59° Corrⁿ | 60°–64° Corrⁿ | 65°–69° Corrⁿ | 70°–74° Corrⁿ | 75°–79° Corrⁿ | 80°–84° Corrⁿ | 85°–89° Corrⁿ | App. Alt. |
|---|---|---|---|---|---|---|---|---|---|---|---|---|
| 00 | 35 56·5 | 40 53·7 | 45 50·5 | 50 46·9 | 55 43·1 | 60 38·9 | 65 34·6 | 70 30·0 | 75 25·3 | 80 20·5 | 85 15·6 | 00 |
| 10 | 56·4 | 53·6 | 50·4 | 46·8 | 42·9 | 38·8 | 34·4 | 29·9 | 25·2 | 20·4 | 15·5 | 10 |
| 20 | 56·3 | 53·5 | 50·2 | 46·7 | 42·8 | 38·7 | 34·3 | 29·7 | 25·0 | 20·2 | 15·3 | 20 |
| 30 | 56·2 | 53·4 | 50·1 | 46·5 | 42·7 | 38·5 | 34·1 | 29·6 | 24·9 | 20·0 | 15·1 | 30 |
| 40 | 56·2 | 53·3 | 50·0 | 46·4 | 42·5 | 38·4 | 34·0 | 29·4 | 24·7 | 19·9 | 15·0 | 40 |
| 50 | 56·1 | 53·2 | 49·9 | 46·3 | 42·4 | 38·2 | 33·8 | 29·3 | 24·5 | 19·7 | 14·8 | 50 |
| 00 | 36 56·0 | 41 53·1 | 46 49·8 | 51 46·2 | 56 42·3 | 61 38·1 | 66 33·7 | 71 29·1 | 76 24·4 | 81 19·6 | 86 14·6 | 00 |
| 10 | 55·9 | 53·0 | 49·7 | 46·0 | 42·1 | 37·9 | 33·5 | 29·0 | 24·2 | 19·4 | 14·5 | 10 |
| 20 | 55·8 | 52·9 | 49·5 | 45·9 | 42·0 | 37·8 | 33·4 | 28·8 | 24·1 | 19·2 | 14·3 | 20 |
| 30 | 55·7 | 52·8 | 49·4 | 45·8 | 41·9 | 37·7 | 33·2 | 28·7 | 23·9 | 19·1 | 14·2 | 30 |
| 40 | 55·6 | 52·6 | 49·3 | 45·7 | 41·7 | 37·5 | 33·1 | 28·5 | 23·8 | 18·9 | 14·0 | 40 |
| 50 | 55·5 | 52·5 | 49·2 | 45·5 | 41·6 | 37·4 | 32·9 | 28·3 | 23·6 | 18·7 | 13·8 | 50 |
| 00 | 37 55·4 | 42 52·4 | 47 49·1 | 52 45·4 | 57 41·4 | 62 37·2 | 67 32·8 | 72 28·2 | 77 23·4 | 82 18·6 | 87 13·7 | 00 |
| 10 | 55·3 | 52·3 | 49·0 | 45·3 | 41·3 | 37·1 | 32·6 | 28·0 | 23·3 | 18·4 | 13·5 | 10 |
| 20 | 55·2 | 52·2 | 48·8 | 45·2 | 41·2 | 36·9 | 32·5 | 27·9 | 23·1 | 18·2 | 13·3 | 20 |
| 30 | 55·1 | 52·1 | 48·7 | 45·0 | 41·0 | 36·8 | 32·3 | 27·7 | 22·9 | 18·1 | 13·2 | 30 |
| 40 | 55·0 | 52·0 | 48·6 | 44·9 | 40·9 | 36·6 | 32·2 | 27·6 | 22·8 | 17·9 | 13·0 | 40 |
| 50 | 55·0 | 51·9 | 48·5 | 44·8 | 40·8 | 36·5 | 32·0 | 27·4 | 22·6 | 17·8 | 12·8 | 50 |
| 00 | 38 54·9 | 43 51·8 | 48 48·4 | 53 44·6 | 58 40·6 | 63 36·4 | 68 31·9 | 73 27·2 | 78 22·5 | 83 17·6 | 88 12·7 | 00 |
| 10 | 54·8 | 51·7 | 48·3 | 44·5 | 40·5 | 36·2 | 31·7 | 27·1 | 22·3 | 17·4 | 12·5 | 10 |
| 20 | 54·7 | 51·6 | 48·1 | 44·4 | 40·3 | 36·1 | 31·6 | 26·9 | 22·1 | 17·3 | 12·3 | 20 |
| 30 | 54·6 | 51·5 | 48·0 | 44·2 | 40·2 | 35·9 | 31·4 | 26·8 | 22·0 | 17·1 | 12·2 | 30 |
| 40 | 54·5 | 51·4 | 47·9 | 44·1 | 40·1 | 35·8 | 31·3 | 26·6 | 21·8 | 16·9 | 12·0 | 40 |
| 50 | 54·4 | 51·2 | 47·8 | 44·0 | 39·9 | 35·6 | 31·1 | 26·5 | 21·7 | 16·8 | 11·8 | 50 |
| 00 | 39 54·3 | 44 51·1 | 49 47·7 | 54 43·9 | 59 39·8 | 64 35·5 | 69 31·0 | 74 26·3 | 79 21·5 | 84 16·6 | 89 11·7 | 00 |
| 10 | 54·2 | 51·0 | 47·5 | 43·7 | 39·6 | 35·3 | 30·8 | 26·1 | 21·3 | 16·4 | 11·5 | 10 |
| 20 | 54·1 | 50·9 | 47·4 | 43·6 | 39·5 | 35·2 | 30·7 | 26·0 | 21·2 | 16·3 | 11·4 | 20 |
| 30 | 54·0 | 50·8 | 47·3 | 43·5 | 39·4 | 35·0 | 30·5 | 25·8 | 21·0 | 16·1 | 11·2 | 30 |
| 40 | 53·9 | 50·7 | 47·2 | 43·3 | 39·2 | 34·9 | 30·4 | 25·7 | 20·9 | 16·0 | 11·0 | 40 |
| 50 | 53·8 | 50·6 | 47·0 | 43·2 | 39·1 | 34·7 | 30·2 | 25·5 | 20·7 | 15·8 | 10·9 | 50 |

| HP | L U | L U | L U | L U | L U | L U | L U | L U | L U | L U | L U | HP |
|---|---|---|---|---|---|---|---|---|---|---|---|---|
| 54·0 | 1·1 1·7 | 1·3 1·9 | 1·5 2·1 | 1·7 2·4 | 2·0 2·6 | 2·3 2·9 | 2·6 3·2 | 2·9 3·5 | 3·2 3·8 | 3·5 4·1 | 3·8 4·5 | 54·0 |
| 54·3 | 1·4 1·8 | 1·6 2·0 | 1·8 2·2 | 2·0 2·5 | 2·2 2·7 | 2·5 3·0 | 2·8 3·2 | 3·1 3·5 | 3·3 3·8 | 3·6 4·1 | 3·9 4·4 | 54·3 |
| 54·6 | 1·7 2·0 | 1·9 2·2 | 2·1 2·4 | 2·3 2·6 | 2·5 2·8 | 2·7 3·0 | 3·0 3·3 | 3·2 3·5 | 3·5 3·8 | 3·8 4·0 | 4·0 4·3 | 54·6 |
| 54·9 | 2·0 2·2 | 2·2 2·3 | 2·3 2·5 | 2·5 2·7 | 2·7 2·9 | 2·9 3·1 | 3·2 3·3 | 3·4 3·5 | 3·6 3·8 | 3·9 4·0 | 4·1 4·3 | 54·9 |
| 55·2 | 2·3 2·3 | 2·5 2·4 | 2·6 2·6 | 2·8 2·8 | 3·0 2·9 | 3·2 3·1 | 3·4 3·3 | 3·6 3·5 | 3·8 3·7 | 4·0 4·0 | 4·2 4·2 | 55·2 |
| 55·5 | 2·7 2·5 | 2·8 2·6 | 2·9 2·7 | 3·1 2·9 | 3·2 3·0 | 3·4 3·2 | 3·6 3·4 | 3·7 3·5 | 3·9 3·7 | 4·1 3·9 | 4·3 4·1 | 55·5 |
| 55·8 | 3·0 2·6 | 3·1 2·7 | 3·2 2·8 | 3·3 3·0 | 3·5 3·1 | 3·6 3·3 | 3·8 3·4 | 3·9 3·6 | 4·1 3·7 | 4·2 3·9 | 4·4 4·0 | 55·8 |
| 56·1 | 3·3 2·8 | 3·4 2·9 | 3·5 3·0 | 3·6 3·1 | 3·7 3·2 | 3·8 3·3 | 4·0 3·4 | 4·1 3·6 | 4·2 3·7 | 4·4 3·8 | 4·5 4·0 | 56·1 |
| 56·4 | 3·6 2·9 | 3·7 3·0 | 3·8 3·1 | 3·9 3·2 | 3·9 3·3 | 4·0 3·4 | 4·1 3·5 | 4·3 3·6 | 4·4 3·7 | 4·5 3·8 | 4·6 3·9 | 56·4 |
| 56·7 | 3·9 3·1 | 4·0 3·1 | 4·1 3·2 | 4·1 3·3 | 4·2 3·3 | 4·3 3·4 | 4·3 3·5 | 4·4 3·6 | 4·5 3·7 | 4·6 3·8 | 4·7 3·8 | 56·7 |
| 57·0 | 4·3 3·2 | 4·3 3·3 | 4·3 3·3 | 4·4 3·4 | 4·4 3·4 | 4·5 3·5 | 4·5 3·5 | 4·6 3·6 | 4·7 3·6 | 4·7 3·7 | 4·8 3·8 | 57·0 |
| 57·3 | 4·6 3·4 | 4·6 3·4 | 4·6 3·4 | 4·6 3·5 | 4·7 3·5 | 4·7 3·5 | 4·7 3·6 | 4·8 3·6 | 4·8 3·6 | 4·8 3·7 | 4·9 3·7 | 57·3 |
| 57·6 | 4·9 3·6 | 4·9 3·6 | 4·9 3·6 | 4·9 3·6 | 4·9 3·6 | 4·9 3·6 | 4·9 3·6 | 4·9 3·6 | 5·0 3·6 | 5·0 3·6 | 5·0 3·6 | 57·6 |
| 57·9 | 5·2 3·7 | 5·2 3·7 | 5·2 3·7 | 5·2 3·7 | 5·2 3·7 | 5·1 3·6 | 5·1 3·6 | 5·1 3·6 | 5·1 3·6 | 5·1 3·6 | 5·1 3·6 | 57·9 |
| 58·2 | 5·5 3·9 | 5·5 3·8 | 5·5 3·8 | 5·4 3·8 | 5·4 3·7 | 5·4 3·7 | 5·3 3·7 | 5·3 3·6 | 5·2 3·6 | 5·2 3·5 | 5·2 3·5 | 58·2 |
| 58·5 | 5·9 4·0 | 5·8 4·0 | 5·8 3·9 | 5·7 3·9 | 5·6 3·8 | 5·6 3·8 | 5·5 3·7 | 5·5 3·6 | 5·4 3·6 | 5·3 3·5 | 5·3 3·4 | 58·5 |
| 58·8 | 6·2 4·2 | 6·1 4·1 | 6·0 4·1 | 6·0 4·0 | 5·9 3·9 | 5·8 3·8 | 5·7 3·7 | 5·6 3·6 | 5·5 3·5 | 5·4 3·5 | 5·3 3·4 | 58·8 |
| 59·1 | 6·5 4·3 | 6·4 4·3 | 6·3 4·2 | 6·2 4·1 | 6·1 4·0 | 6·0 3·9 | 5·9 3·8 | 5·8 3·6 | 5·7 3·5 | 5·6 3·4 | 5·4 3·3 | 59·1 |
| 59·4 | 6·8 4·5 | 6·7 4·4 | 6·6 4·3 | 6·5 4·2 | 6·4 4·1 | 6·2 3·9 | 6·1 3·8 | 6·0 3·7 | 5·8 3·5 | 5·7 3·4 | 5·5 3·2 | 59·4 |
| 59·7 | 7·1 4·7 | 7·0 4·5 | 6·9 4·4 | 6·8 4·3 | 6·6 4·1 | 6·5 4·0 | 6·3 3·8 | 6·1 3·7 | 6·0 3·5 | 5·8 3·3 | 5·6 3·2 | 59·7 |
| 60·0 | 7·5 4·8 | 7·3 4·7 | 7·2 4·5 | 7·0 4·4 | 6·9 4·2 | 6·7 4·0 | 6·5 3·9 | 6·3 3·7 | 6·1 3·5 | 5·9 3·3 | 5·7 3·1 | 60·0 |
| 60·3 | 7·8 5·0 | 7·6 4·8 | 7·5 4·7 | 7·3 4·5 | 7·1 4·3 | 6·9 4·1 | 6·7 3·9 | 6·5 3·7 | 6·3 3·5 | 6·0 3·2 | 5·8 3·0 | 60·3 |
| 60·6 | 8·1 5·1 | 7·9 5·0 | 7·7 4·8 | 7·6 4·6 | 7·3 4·4 | 7·1 4·2 | 6·9 3·9 | 6·7 3·7 | 6·4 3·4 | 6·2 3·2 | 5·9 2·9 | 60·6 |
| 60·9 | 8·4 5·3 | 8·2 5·1 | 8·0 4·9 | 7·8 4·7 | 7·6 4·5 | 7·3 4·2 | 7·1 4·0 | 6·8 3·7 | 6·6 3·4 | 6·3 3·2 | 6·0 2·9 | 60·9 |
| 61·2 | 8·7 5·4 | 8·5 5·2 | 8·3 5·0 | 8·1 4·8 | 7·8 4·5 | 7·6 4·3 | 7·3 4·0 | 7·0 3·7 | 6·7 3·4 | 6·4 3·1 | 6·1 2·8 | 61·2 |
| 61·5 | 9·1 5·6 | 8·8 5·4 | 8·6 5·1 | 8·3 4·9 | 8·1 4·6 | 7·8 4·3 | 7·5 4·0 | 7·2 3·7 | 6·9 3·4 | 6·5 3·1 | 6·2 2·7 | 61·5 |

xxxv

# LIST OF CONTENTS

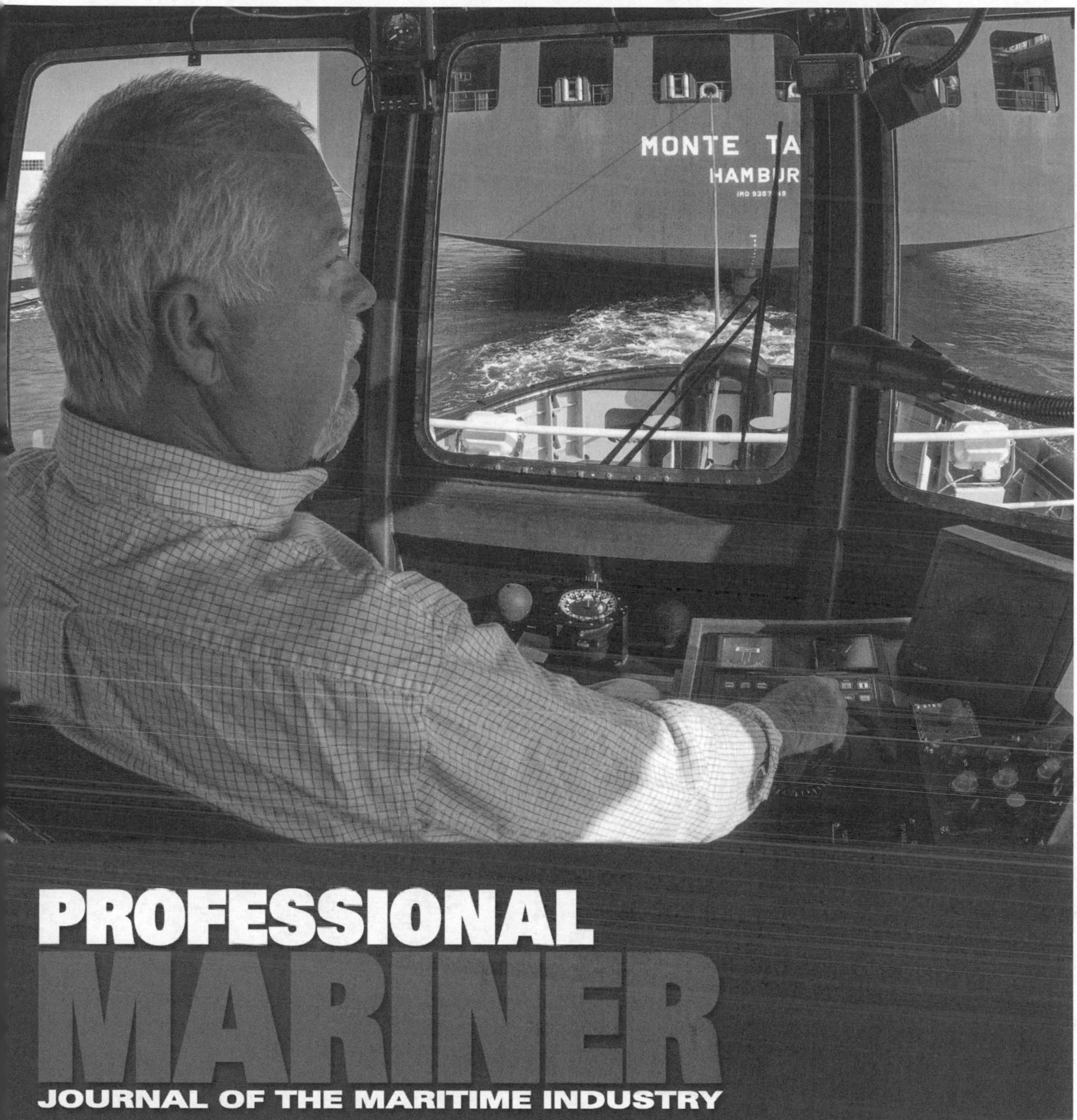

Captain

Deck Hand

Qualified Assessor

Engineer

# Gain the professional maritime training you need for the level of success you want to achieve.

MPT is the most complete full-service private maritime school in the country. Our training programs are internationally acclaimed and are utilized by government agencies, global maritime businesses and individual crew members. Our campuses boast over 61,000 sq ft of classrooms, deck and engineering training labs, student service facilities and several off-site training facilites. Whether it's captaining a vessel, safeguarding marine environments, designing advanced ocean engineering structures, crewing a luxury megayacht or keeping the world's goods moving; MPT can provide the training you need.

**EST. 1983**

**MPT**
MARITIME PROFESSIONAL TRAINING
Fort Lauderdale, Florida

**USCG | MCA | RYA | PYA | NI | MARSHALL ISLANDS**

YACHTING | MERCHANT | COMMERCIAL | PASSENGER VESSEL

*Sea The World*

To get started, call or email us today! info@mptusa.com

954.525.1014 | 1915 South Andrews Avenue, Fort Lauderdale, FL 33316 | mptusa.com

**_Islamorada_**

NAVIGATIONAL SUPPLIES & SERVICE I TELS: (507)228-4348 / 228-6069

**Business Office: Bldg 808 Balboa Road, (former Canal Zone), Republic of Panama**

**Business Hours: 0800 - 1700 hours (Local) or 1300 - 2200 hours (UTC). Fax: 507-228-1234**

Islamorada is the appointed Admiralty chart agent in the Republic of Panama, and the largest nautical bookstore in Latin America. Located in Balboa, and on the Panama Canal, Islamorada is ideally positioned to provide products and services to ships in transit through the Isthmus, as well as to other countries throughout the region.

| Digital Charts | Paper Charts | Nautical Publications | Maritime Software | Instruments | Flags & Pennants | IMO Signs |

## Nautical Books

Navigation, Seamanship

Towing & Salvage

Ship Design & Naval Architecture

Yachting & Leisure

Marine Engineering

Cargo Work

Log Books

Maritime Business, Maritime Law

## Publications

Almanacs & Sight Reduction Tables

ITU - Call Signs, Ship Stations,
Coastal Stations, MMS

Shipping Guides - Atlas, Guide to Port Entry

IMO - Solas, Marpol, STCW95
(Wide Range of Stock)

## Plotting Instrument

Binoculars & Magnifying Glasses

Sextants

Weather Instruments

Clocks & Chronometers

Global Positioning Systems (GPS)

Iridium Satellite Telephones

## Brands

C. Plath

B. Cooke & Sons

Blundell Harley

ACR

Admiralty

Oceangrafix

Maui Jim

Reactor Watches

Davis Instruments

and more.

## Software For:

Electronic Chart Viewers and ECDIS
Software/Hardware

Interactive Diesel Engine Training

Tide Tables & Tidal Current Tables

Electronic Charts

Port Guides

Vessel Traffic Services

Superyacht operations

Fleet Tracking

Nautical Surveys

Because of our strategic location, we
are able to provide fast delivery of
charts and other important products to
ships calling on ports throughout Latin
America and the Caribbean Basin.

# Nautical Charts

**NOAA**
**Print on**
**Demand**
**Charts**

## Order online at paracay.com
### or call (707) 822-9063

**NGA**
**Print on**
**Demand**
**Charts**

## NOAA BookletCharts™
### A reduced-scale nautical chart for small boaters

Made to help recreational boaters locate themselves on the water. It has been reduced in scale for convenience, but otherwise contains all the information of the full-scale nautical chart. The bar scales have also been reduced, and are accurate when used to measure distances in these BookletCharts™.

- Professionally printed and staple-bound
- High quality, durable paper
- Includes Notices to Mariners
- Printed on-demand with the latest data from NOAA
- Handy 8.5" x 11" size

## Full-Scale NOAA Charts
### Always current. Always printed on-demand

- Charts ship rolled in a sturdy cardboard tube
- Choose Traditional paper or Waterproof material

## Small-Format NOAA Charts
### Scaled down versions of the full-sized charts

- Handy for small craft and recreational use
- Choose Traditional paper or Waterproof material

## NOAA Booklet & Folio Charts

Multi-page charts that cover rivers and other waterways that are too extensive to fit onto one full-scale chart.

- 12 x 18" Booklets are spiral-bound
- 36 x 12" Folios are staple bound

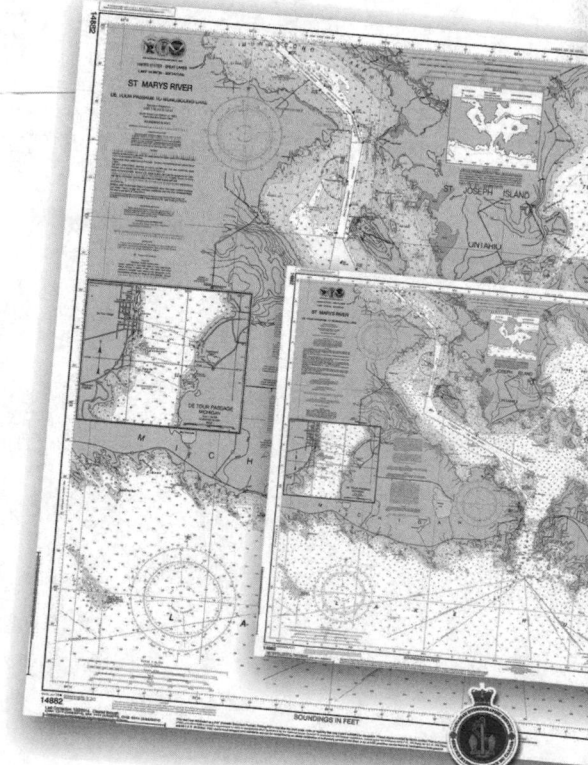

**Canadian**
**Hydrographic**
**Super Dealer**

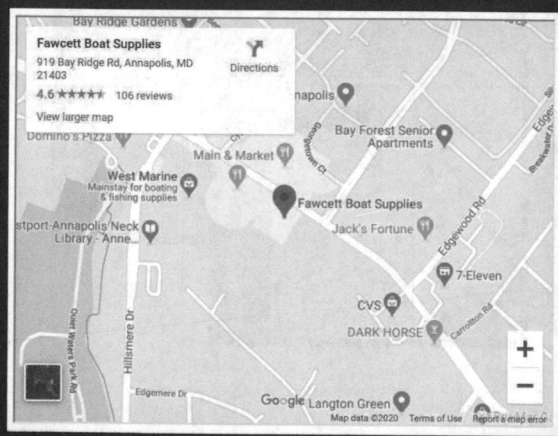

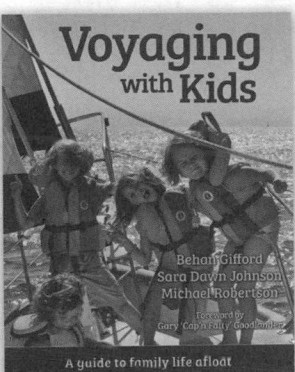

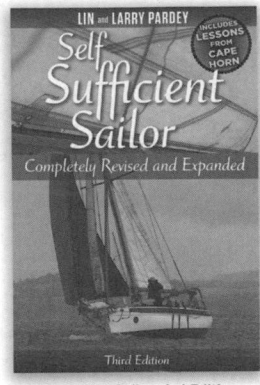
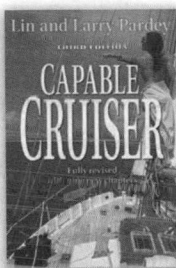

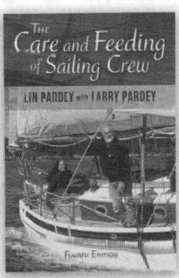
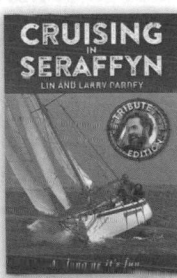

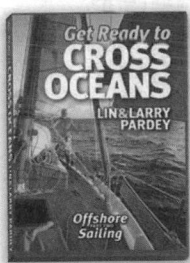
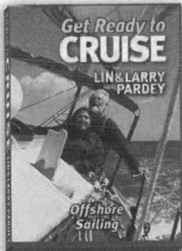

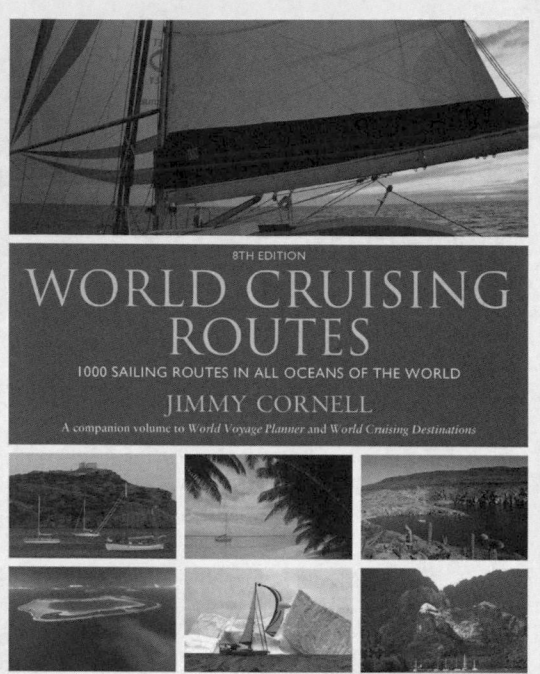

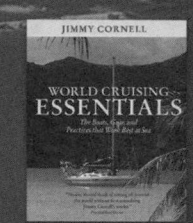

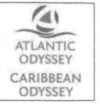

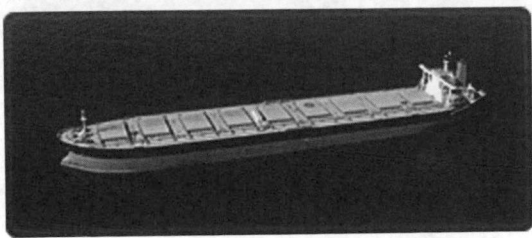

# CHARTWATCH BY EW LINER
## UKHO VERIFIED BACK-OF-BRIDGE SOFTWARE
## The Ideal Replacement for Admiralty Gateway

- ChartWatch has been developed with one main objective: to provide Mariners with an **effective yet user friendly application** for the maintenance of ENCs and Paper Chart outfits on-board vessels.
- The ChartWatch software facilitates efficient inventory management including ordering and updating through three main modules:
  **PAPER CHART MODULE | DIGITAL MODULE | DIGITAL CATALOGUE**
- The Digital and Paper Modules allow for easy maintenance of both digital and paper chart holdings of vessels ensuring navigational safety and compliance.
- ChartWatch works on vessels with fleet broadband as well as on vessels with restricted email connectivity.

### Digital Catalogue
- A comprehensive, multi-functional digital catalogue
- View, browse and select for purchase of all Admiralty digital products
- Automated port-to-port routing
- Highlights the existing on-board Admiralty digital product holdings
- Request & receive automated quotations in real time with our B2B application

### Digital Module
- Maintain & update ENCs
- Download base data for AVCS & AIO, reducing the need to send AVCS DVDs on-board
- All base ENC & AIO data is backed up on-board reducing weekly data size and resulting in significant air time costs savings
- Generate complete base and updates for ENCs & AIO if ECDIS is corrupted
- Integrated Admiralty e-NP reader

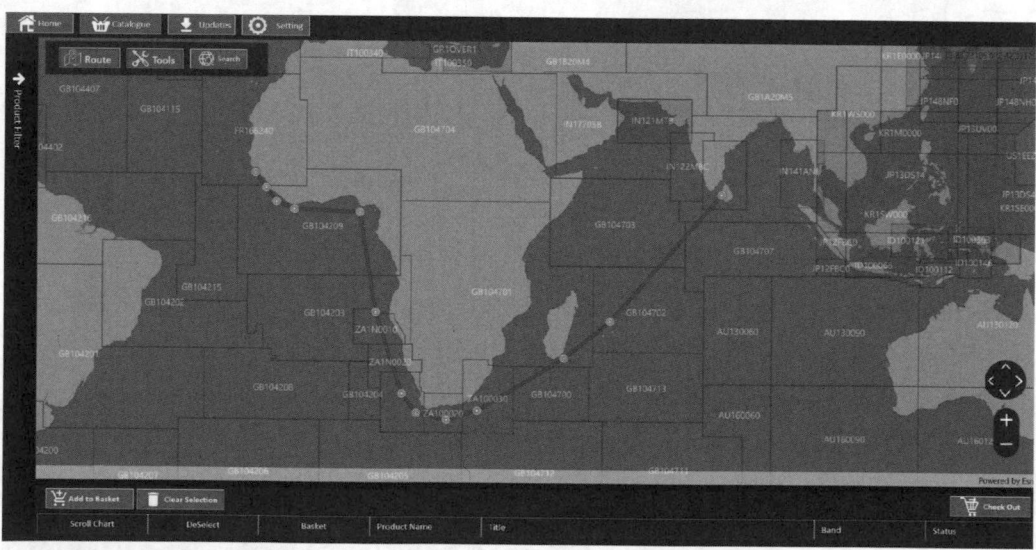

### Paper Chart Module
- Vessel can maintain & update its own inventory
- Check updated status of inventory
- Download weekly corrections complete with Tracings
- Download weekly publication corrections
- Maintain an up-to-date Chart Correction Log
- Request and download historical chart corrections

### Support
- Video tutorials for set-up, installation and training mariners. This saves time & eliminates the need to review detailed user guides.
- Further training through video conferencing or a suitable location.
- 24/7 technical support through email or remote access using Team Viewer or similar

## E.W.LINER
**Contact digitalsales@ewliner.com for a free 3-month trial**
Subscribe to the full version Chartwatch on a quarterly or annual basis

# WE'VE ALWAYS BEEN THANKFUL FOR LUCKY STARS.

Through calm and choppy waters, count on The Binnacle for all your navigational needs.
As an authorized print-on-demand chart dealer, we can print and ship NOAA
and Canadian nautical charts to wherever your lucky stars lead you.
Find us onshore and online at **binnacle.com**.

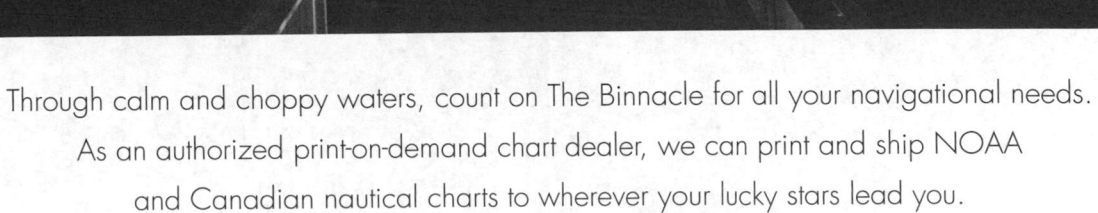

**binnacle.com**
a part of *The* BINNACLE

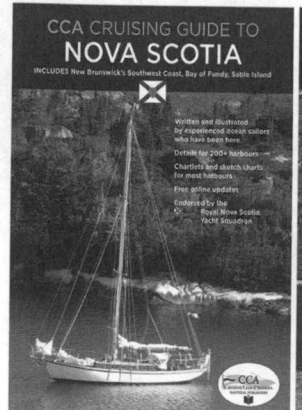